Encyclopedia of Computer Science

THIRD EDITION

Encyclopedia of Computer Science

THIRD EDITION

Editors:

Anthony Ralston

Edwin D. Reilly

Managing Editor:

Caryl Ann Dahlin

VNR **VAN NOSTRAND REINHOLD**
New York

Copyright © 1993 by Van Nostrand Reinhold

Library of Congress Catalog Card Number 92-14553
ISBN 0–442–27679–6

All rights reserved. Certain portions of this work ©1983, 1976 by
Van Nostrand Reinhold. No part of this work covered the copyright
hereon may be reproduced or used in any form or by any means—graphic,
electronic, or mechanical, including photocopying, recording, taping,
or information storage and retrieval systems—without written permission of the publisher.

Printed in the United States of America

Van Nostrand Reinhold
115 Fifth Avenue
New York, New York 10003

Chapman and Hall
2-6 Boundary Row
London SE1 8HN, England

Thomas Nelson Australia
102 Dodds Street
South Melbourne 3205
Victoria, Australia

Nelson Canada
1120 Birchmount Road
Scarborough, Ontario M1K 5G4, Canada

16 15 14 13 12 11 10 9 8 7 6 5 4 3 2 1

Library of Congress Cataloging-in-Publication Data

Encyclopedia of computer science / Anthony Ralston, Edwin D. Reilly,
    editors ; Caryl Ann Dahlin, managing editor.
        p.   cm.
    Includes bibliographical references and index.
    ISBN 0-442-27679-6
    1. Computer science—Encyclopedias.   2. Information science-
-Encyclopedias.   I. Ralston, Anthony.   II. Reilly, Edwin D.
QA76.15.E48   1992
004′ .03—dc20   92-14553
                                                              CIP

CONTENTS

EDITORIAL BOARD

Malcolm P. Atkinson
University of Glasgow

Peter J. Denning
George Mason University

Aaron Finerman
University of Michigan

Bernard A. Galler
University of Michigan

Martin Campbell-Kelly
University of Warwick

Laurence Press
California State University at Dominguez Hills

Jean E. Sammet
Programming Languages Consultant

Eric A. Weiss (Chair)
Consultant

Ian H. Witten
University of Calgary

CONTRIBUTORS

(Numbers after each name indicate the pages at which contributions by each author begin.)

W. John Hutchins, University of East Anglia, UK 733

H. V. Jagadish, AT&T Bell Laboratories 348

Everett L. Johnson, Wichita State University 341

Charles V. Jones, Ball State University 749, 1034

Phillippe Jorrand, Universitè de Grenoble 1479

David K. Kahaner, National Bureau of Standards 946

Alain Kaloyeros, SUNY at Albany 687

Laveen N. Kanal, University of Maryland 1041

Arthur I. Karshmer 572

Kenneth M. Kempner, National Institutes of Health 694

Brian W. Kernighan, AT&T Bell Laboratories 151

Robin H. Kerr 121

Helene G. Kershner, SUNY at Buffalo 311

William King, Florida Atlantic University 21

Peter T. Kirstein, University College, London 116, 351, 381

Graham Knight, University College, London 693

Kenneth E. Knight, University of Texas at Austin 588

Donald E. Knuth, Stanford University 869, 1353

Jill C. Knuth 869, 1353

Elliot B. Koffman, Temple University 493

Robert R. Korfhage, University of Pittsburgh 27, 135, 1065

Robert Kowalski, Imperial College of Science and Technology, UK 778

H. Kung, Carnegie-Mellon University 1345

Andrew Laine, University of Florida 929

Stephen Lam, SUNY at Buffalo 993

J. Paul Landauer, Scientific Analysis Tools 626

Steven P. Landry, University of Southwestern Louisiana 416

Charles L. Lawson, California Institute of Technology 740

Norman E. Layer, IBM Corp. 638

Edward Lazowska, University of Washigton 980

Burton M. Leavenworth, Consultant 934

Ruth Leavitt, University of Maryland Baltimore County 257

Olivier Lecarme, Universitè de Nice, France 206

John A. N. Lee, Virginia Polytechnic Institute and State University 80, 206, 580, 581, 645, 727, 768, 1030, 1087, 1105, 1125, 1158, 1315, 1342

Nancy Leveson, University of California, Irvine 509

Paul Levinson, The New School for Social Research 144

Brian Lewis, Sun Microsystems 367

Peter Linnington, University of Kent, UK 392, 964

Andrew Lisowski, Library of Congress 750

Joyce Currie Little, Towson State University 1058

C. L. Liu, University of Illinois at Urbana-Champaign 190

Keith R. London 478

Ralph L. London, University of California at Irvine 1111

William F. Luebbert, Computer Literacy Institute 612

John MacKrell, CIMdata, Inc. 222

Jennifer Marill, Library of Congress 750

George Marsaglia, Florida State University 899, 1145

Dorothy Marsh, Cornell University 322

Joanne Martin, IBM Corporation 123

Johannes J. Martin, University of New Orleans 541

G. Swami Mathad, IBM Corporation 687

Francis P. Mathur, California State Polytechnic University 604, 811, 1157

Richard Matick, IBM Corporation 153

David W. Matula, Southern Methodist University 1072, 1200, 1201

Stephen B. Maurer, Swarthmore College 29

David May, Inmos Ltd. 1389

Michael M. Maynard, Sperry Corporation 491, 767, 1405

John McCarthy, Stanford University 1154

E. J. McCluskey, Stanford University 775, 1332

Jeffrey McConnell, Canisius College 294, 696

Daniel D. McCracken, City College, City University of New York 114, 535, 898

William McKeeman, Digital Equipment Corporation 207

John M. McKinney, University of Cincinnati 1141

Barbara E. McMullen, McMullen & McMullen, Inc. 1053

John McMullen, McMullen & McMullen, Inc. 1053

John C. McPherson, IBM Corporation 917, 1427

Jon Meads, Jon Meads & Associates 303

Chester L. Meek, City of Grande Prairie, Canada 205, 342, 711, 715, 809, 811, 1401

Robert B. Mehnert, National Library of Medicine 847

Norman Meyrowitz, GO Corporation 1355

Jerald Mikesell, Sierra Vista Public Schools, Arizona 162

Leslie Jill Miller, Xerox Corporation 1173

Russ Miller, SUNY at Buffalo 1015, 1025

Richard G. Mills, Consultant 116

Jack Minker, University of Maryland 424

Benjamin Mittman, Northwestern University 1077

Cleve B. Moler, ARDENT Corporation 828

Michael K. Molloy, Hewlett-Packard 1062

Graham Morris 167, 434, 467

Jack Moshman, Moshman Associates, Inc. 1066

Richard R. Muntz, UCLA 1043

Miles J. Murdocca, Rutgers University 1000

Jean E. Musinski, Comshare, Inc. 30

Richard E. Nance, Virginia Polytechnic Institute and State University 989

Thomas Narten, SUNY at Albany 554, 1343, 1407, 1442

Jiri Necas 717, 1009, 1031

Anne Neirynck, Cornell University 30

Monroe M. Newborn, McGill University 269

Allen Newell, Carnegie-Mellon University 1201, 1336

Toshio Nisimura, Tukuba National University 502

Jerre D. Noe, University of Washington 602

Susan H. Nycum, Gaston Snow and Ely Bartlett 747

Richard Oehler, IBM Corporation 1165

T. William Olle, Consultant 413, 669

Holger Opderbeck, Netrix Corporation 387

E. L. Ortiz, Imperial College of Science and Technology, UK 1384

Enrique I. Oviedo, Arvin-Calspan Advanced Tecnology Center 1479

David A. Padua, University of Illinois at Urbana-Champaign 1317

Victor Ya. Pan, Herbert. H. Lehman College 1479

Donn B. Parker, SRI International 281

Yale Patt, University of Michigan 284, 492

Azaria Paz, Technion, Israel 1074, 1076

Trevor Pearcey, Caulfield Institute of Technology, Australia 168

Charls Pearson, Consultant 665

Leslie E. Perreault, Stanford University 615, 835

Linda Hutz Pesante, Carnegie-Mellon University 1222

George Peters, McDonnell Douglas Corporation 216

James L. Peterson, IBM Corporation 1062, 1266

Charles P. Pfleeger, Trusted Information Systems 403

John R. Pierce, Stanford University 671, 1196

Milton Pine, Royal Melbourne Institute of Technology 168

Martin Piszczalski, The Yankee Group 306

Seymour V. Pollack, Washington University in St. Louis 174, 347, 351, 423, 426, 535, 1091, 1280, 1385, 1390

Vaughn R. Pratt, Stanford University 789

Laurence Press, California State University at Dominguez Hills 165, 642, 1415

Jan Prokop, Levolor Corporation 179

Michael J. Quinn, Oregon State University 1011, 1028

Joseph Raben, Consultant 623

Andrew Radics, Telephoto Communications 874

Masoud Radparvar, Hypress, Inc. 1329

Anthony Ralston, SUNY at Buffalo 76, 80, 124, 173, 210, 402, 470, 532, 580, 942, 993, 1087, 1105, 1170, 1199, 1202

C. V. Ramamoorthy, University of California, Berkeley 1242

Ramaswamy Ramesh, SUNY at Buffalo 820

Brian Randell, University of Newcastle upon Tyne, UK 440

William J. Rapaport, SUNY at Buffalo 185

Sukumar Rathnam, The University of Texas at Austin 588

Ann Redelfs, Cornell University 1327

H. K. Reghbati, Consultant 396

Keith Reid-Green, Educational Testing Service 287

Edwin D. Reilly, SUNY at Albany (Emeritus) 9, 92, 114, 163, 406, 419, 425, 467, 469, 486, 489, 517, 540, 557, 590, 699, 717, 792, 868, 900, 900, 934, 964, 1071, 1072, 1154, 1175, 1249, 1308, 1388, 1390, 1406, 1436

Edward M. Reingold, University of Illinois at Urbana-Champaign 190, 1185

David A. Rennels, UCLA 547

John R. Rice, Purdue University 826

Frederic N. Ris, IBM Corporation 709

Robert Rittenhouse, Florida Atlantic University 507, 593

Ronald L. Rivest, Massachusetts Institute of Technology 369

Eric Roberts, Stanford University 335

David Rodgers, Mathematical Reviews 1069

Stephen J. Rogowski, SUNY at Albany 131, 146, 517, 557, 595, 1427

Saul Rosen, 14, 72, 120, 580, 651, 868, 965, 1214, 1232, 1330

Daniel J. Rosenkrantz, SUNY at Albany 938

Robert F. Rosin, Enhanced Service Providers, Inc. 1425

Mark Rotenberg, Computer Professionals for Social Responsibility 652

Paul Roth, Consultant 1204

Arthur I. Rubin 43

Nelson Russell, Integral 1386

Harry J. Saal, Network General Corporation 907

Arto K. Salomaa, University of Turku, Finland 1160

Gerard Salton, Cornell University 370, 660

Roy M. Salzman, Arthur D. Little, Inc. 109

Jean E. Sammet, Consultant 934, 1077, 1118, 1121, 1224, 1471

Dietmar Saupe, Universität Bremen, Germany 566

Michael Scanlan, Oregon State University 176

Jacob T. Schwartz, New York University 1195

Thomas Scott, Western Illinois University 81

Adel S. Sedra, University of Toronto 100, 375, 699, 700, 1068

Stuart C. Shapiro, SUNY at Buffalo 87

Mary Shaw, Carnegie-Mellon University 1, 10

Mildred L. G. Shaw, University of Calgary 225

Ben Shneiderman, University of Maryland 411, 429, 532, 552, 619, 632

Bruce Shriver, Consultant 416

David Shuey, McDonnell Douglas Corporation 216

Herbert A. Simon, Carnegie-Mellon University 659, 1336

Steven Skiena, SUNY at Stony Brook 214

James R. Slagel, University of Minnesota 756, 1372

Vladimir Slamecka, Georgia Institute of Technology 665

Alvy Ray Smith, Pixar Corporation 166

Kenneth C. Smith, University of Toronto 100, 131, 375, 699, 700, 1068, 1340

Kirk Snyder, New York University 1195

John S. Sobolewski, University of New Mexico 121, 196, 376, 486, 549, 595, 892, 901, 920, 921, 924, 1068, 1347

Ellen Spertus, Massachusetts Institute of Technology 1436

James C. Spohrer, Apple Computer, Inc. 535, 1007, 1134

Sargur N. Srihari, SUNY at Buffalo 993, 1034

Vason P. Srini, Dataflow Systems 416, 418

Richard Stearns, SUNY at Albany 938

Theodor D. Sterling, Simon Fraser University 347, 1091, 1280, 1390

Elizabeth Luebbert Stoll 819

Thomas Strothotte, Freie Universität, Berlin 1479

P. A. Subramanyam, AT&T Bell Laboratories 608

Andrew S. Tanenbaum, Vrije Universiteit, Amsterdam 184, 1135

Robert W. Taylor, Digital Equipment Corporation 142, 672, 789, 963

Daniel Teichroew, University of Michigan 666

David Temkin, Brown University 1355

Harold Thimbleby, University of Stirling, Scotland 761

Walter Tichy, University of Karlsruhe, Germany 898, 910, 966, 1197, 1216

Will Tracz, IBM Corporation 1244

Joseph F. Traub, Columbia University 212, 655

Mohan Trivedi, University of Tennessee 645

Henry S. Tropp, Humboldt State University 25, 134, 491, 614, 833, 1284, 1424, 1429

Murray Turoff, New Jersey Institute of Technology 280

Geoffrey Tweedale, University of Sheffield, UK 718, 817, 1432

Andries van Dam, Brown University 715

Patricia B. Van Verth, Canisius College 1234

Mary O. Vargo, Teradata Corporation 412

G. Michael Vose, Peterborough Technology Group 738

Eugene L. Wachspress, University of Tennessee 555

Jerrold L. Wagener, Amoco Production Research 361, 589

Samuel S. Wagstaff, Jr., Purdue University 543, 941

William M. Waite, University of Colorado, Boulder 1223

Deborah K. Walters, SUNY at Buffalo 330

Ronald Waxman, University of Virginia 597

Peter Wegner, Brown University 406, 725, 959, 1064, 1106, 1115, 1272, 1390, 1419

Fred W. Weingarten, Computing Research Association 315

David M. Weiss, Software Productivity Consortium 511, 657

Eric Weiss, Editor and Writer 762, 834, 1395

Barry D. Wessler, GTE Telenet Communications Corporation 1007

Andrew B. Whinston, University of Texas at Austin 588

Richard P. Wildes, David Sarnoff Research Center 1167

Maurice V. Wilkes, Olivetti Research 113, 432, 443, 503, 610, 1403

James H. Wilkinson 526, 828, 1394

Michael Williams, University of Calgary 145, 148, 157, 913

Erich R. Willner, Citibank, N. A. 116

Theodore C. Willoughby, Indiana University Northwest 1342

Robin J. Wilson, The Open University, UK 1274

Jeanette Wing, Carnegie-Mellon University 564, 1107

Franz Winkler, Johannes Kepler Universität, Austria 227

David S. Wise, Indiana University 573

Ian H. Witten, University of Calgary 329, 1240, 1411

Matthew Witten, University of Texas at Austin 125

Larry D. Wittie, SUNY at Stony Brook 874

Amy D. Wohl, Wohl Associates 507, 1437

Matthew R. Wordeman, IBM Corporation 849

David B. Wortman, University of Toronto 133, 178

Boris Yamrom, General Electric 1479

David M. Young, University of Texas at Austin 1032

Marshall C. Yovits, Indiana University—Purdue University at Indianapolis 653

Heinz Zemanek, IBM Corporation, Austria 1444

Karl L. Zinn, University of Michigan 104, 261, 263, 311, 923

Stanley Zionts, SUNY at Buffalo 820

Albert L. Zobrist, The RAND Corporation 290

Jeffery I. Zucker, McMaster University, Canada 1115

PREFACE TO THE THIRD EDITION

Nine years have elapsed since the publication of the second edition of the *Encyclopedia* (which had followed the first edition by seven years). In computer science and technology nine years is still a long time. The pace in computing may not be as breakneck as it once was, but it is still more rapid than in any other scientific or technical discipline. Therefore, this "snapshot"—for a snapshot is all that an encyclopedia can be—is markedly different from the one published in 1983.

How different?

The second edition of this encyclopedia contained 550 articles from 301 contributors (compared to, respectively, 470 and 210 in the first edition). This edition has

- 605 articles from 370 contributors of which
- 174 are new articles
- 70 are rewritten articles on subjects covered in the second edition
- 18 are second edition articles that have been extensively modified and brought up to date.

In addition, almost all the other articles from the second edition have undergone at least minor modifications. Many articles have been retitled to conform to current usage. Also, 108 articles from the second edition have been merged into other articles or deleted, generally because their subject matter is obsolete and not of historical importance.

The six appendices from the second edition have all been updated. (One—Appendix 2—has been substantially streamlined.) Also, one new appendix has been added—a Timeline of Significant Computing Milestones, which we think readers will find informative and suitably irreverent. The overall result is a third edition in which over 40% of the material was either not contained in the second edition or has been significantly modified from the second edition.

Last—and probably not least—the title has been changed from *Encyclopedia of Computer Science and Engineering* to *Encyclopedia of Computer Science*, as it was for the first edition. The reason could be—but is not—because we are implementing an algorithm to name odd-numbered editions *Encyclopedia of Computer Science* and even-numbered editions *Encyclopedia of Computer Science and Engineering*. It also could be—but is not—because the "engineering" aspects of computing have been deemphasized in this edition. Quite the contrary. Rather, it is due to some arcane marketing considerations, which are no doubt of even less interest to our readers than they are to us.

Anthony Ralston
June 1992   *Edwin D. Reilly*

NOTE: The editors and publisher would appreciate comments from readers on how future editions of this encyclopedia could be improved. What additional subjects should be covered? Did you find any errors of fact or typographical errors? (The entire Encyclopedia was typeset using PostScript, so we hope to achieve a declining number of errors—typographical ones anyhow—in future editions. (All correspondence should be sent to Editors, *Encyclopedia of Computer Science*, Van Nostrand Reinhold, 115 Fifth Avenue, New York, NY 10003.

EDITORS' FOREWORD

The most important purpose of an encyclopedia in a particular disciplinary area is to be a basic reference work for non-specialists who need elaboration of subjects in which they are not expert. The implication of "basic" is that an encyclopedia, while it should attempt to be comprehensive in *breadth* of coverage, cannot be comprehensive in the *depth* with which it treats most topics. An encyclopedia should, however (and this one does), direct the reader to information at the next level of depth through cross-references to other articles and bibliographic references.

What constitutes breadth of coverage is always a difficult question, and it is especially so for computer science and technology. As a new discipline that has evolved over the past four decades, and that is still changing rather rapidly, its boundaries are blurred. This is complicated further because there is no general agreement among computer scientists or technologists about whether certain areas are or are not part of computer science and technology.

The choice of specific subject matter for this encyclopedia has necessarily been a personal one by the editors, modulated by the editorial board, and by the practical problems of finding authors to write particular articles. Our hope is that, while inevitably there will be quibbles about the inclusion of certain topics, little or nothing of major importance has been omitted.

Articles in this encyclopedia normally contain definitions of the article titles, but even the shortest articles also contain explanatory information to broaden and deepen the reader's understanding. Long articles contain historical and survey information in order to integrate the subject matter and put it into perspective. Overall, the encyclopedia is a basic reference to computer science and technology, as well as a broad picture of the discipline, its history, and its direction.

Organization The organization of this volume is on an alphabetic basis according to the first word of each article title. Titles have been chosen in such a way that the first word is the one most likely to be selected by the reader searching for a given topic. In addition, main cross-references have been provided when more than one word in a title might reasonably be referenced. These cross-references are also used to refer to important subjects that are included in longer, more general articles rather than as separate articles.

Four additional aids to the reader have been provided. The first such aid is the CLASSIFICATION OF ARTICLES, which follows this foreword. This classification is intended to guide the reader to clusters of related articles. It may also be useful in helping readers to follow a self-study regime.

The second such aid is the CROSS-REFERENCE list at the beginning of each article, which lists titles of related articles.

The APPENDICES at the back of the book constitute the third aid. These include lists of abbreviations, acronyms, special notation, programming languages, academic departments of computer science and engineering, and research journals in computer science and technology, as well as some useful numerical tables and a five language glossary of important computer terms.

The fourth aid is the INDEX. In a dictionary or glossary, all terms appear as entries, but in an encyclopedia only the most important terms are used as article titles or even main cross-references. Without an index, the location of much important information would be left to the ingenuity of the reader. In fact, the index contains all terms that should appear in a *dictionary* of computer science. In addition, it contains entries that would not normally appear in a dictionary, such as references to subcategories.

The encyclopedia user who searches among the article titles unsuccessfully will find the index invaluable in locating specific information. In addition, the index will often provide pointers to unfamiliar terms.

Anthony Ralston
Edwin D. Reilly

CLASSIFICATION OF ARTICLES

This classification of articles embodies a taxonomy that should be helpful to the reader in grasping the scope of material contained in this volume. Articles are classified under nine categories:

1. Hardware
2. Computer Systems
3. Information and Data
4. Software
5. Mathematics of Computing
6. Theory of Computing
7. Methodologies
8. Applications
9. Computing Milieux

Each Encyclopedia article appears at least once in this classification. Some titles appear more than once in order to avoid the clutter of cross-references. Most classification headings are themselves article titles, in which case each is followed by a page reference. Headings preceded by an asterisk (*), however, are not actual titles but rather were invented to provide coherence to the classification.

1. *HARDWARE

*TYPES OF COMPUTERS

2. COMPUTER SYSTEMS 323

*ACCESS-BASED SYSTEMS

3. INFORMATION AND DATA 653

4. SOFTWARE 1214

5. *MATHEMATICS OF COMPUTING

6. *THEORY OF COMPUTATION

7. *METHODOLOGIES

8. *APPLICATIONS

9. *COMPUTING MILIEUX

ABSTRACT DATA TYPE

For articles on related subjects *see* ADA; CLASS; DATA STRUCTURES; DATA TYPE; ENCAPSULATION; INFORMATION HIDING; OBJECT-ORIENTED PROGRAMMING; PROGRAM VERIFICATION; and STRUCTURED PROGRAMMING.

A major issue for software development and maintenance is managing the complexity of the software system. Over the years, programming methodologies and languages have developed in response to new ideas about how to cope with this complexity. A dominant theme in the growth of methodologies and languages is the development of tools for dealing with abstractions. An *abstraction* is a simplified description, or *specification*, of a system that focuses on some essential structure or behavior of a real-world or conceptual object. A *good* abstraction is one in which information that is significant to the client (i.e. the user) is emphasized while details that are immaterial, at least for the moment, are suppressed. We use the principles of *information hiding* (*q.v.*) to encapsulate these details. During the late 1970s, most research activity in abstraction techniques was focused on the language and specification issues raised by these considerations; much of the work is identified with the concept of *abstract data types*.

An *abstract data type* is a programming language facility for organizing programs into modules using criteria that are based on the data structures of the program. The specification of the module should provide all information required for using the type, including the allowable values of the data and the effects of the operations. However, details about the implementation, such as data representations and algorithms for implementing the operations, are hidden within the module. This separation of specification from implementation is a key idea of abstract data types.

Each module that defines an abstract data type may include both data declarations and subroutine definitions. The criteria for organizing the modules emphasize protecting the data structures from arbitrary manipulation—malicious or accidental—by other parts of the program. Languages that support abstract data types include scope rules that guarantee this locality by hiding the names of local data from all parts of the program outside the module that defines the abstract data type. The objective of organizing a program using abstract data types is to expedite program development and to simplify maintenance by imposing a certain kind of predictable and useful structure on the program.

Like structured programming (*q.v.*), the methodology of abstract data types emphasizes locality of related collections of information. In the case of abstract data types, attention is focused on data rather than on control, and the strategy is to form modules consisting of a data structure and its associated operations. The objective is to treat these modules in the same way as ordinary types, such as integers and reals, are treated; this requires support for declarations, infix operators, specification of parameters to subroutines, etc. The resulting abstract data type effectively extends the set of types available to a program. It explains the properties of a new group of variables by specifying the values that one of these variables may have, and it explains the operations that will be permitted on the variables of the new type by giving the effects the operations have on the values of the variables.

In designing a data type abstraction, we first specify the functional properties of a data structure and its operations, then we implement them in terms of existing language constructs (and other data types) and show that the specification is accurate. When we subsequently use the abstraction, we deal with the new type solely in terms of its specification. This philosophy has been developed in several programming languages, including Ada (*q.v.*), Alphard, C++, CLU, Concurrent Pascal, Euclid, Gypsy, Mesa, Modula (*q.v.*), and Simula. In these languages, the module-definition construct for abstract data types associates a specification with the implementation of a module and hides all information that is not explicitly included in the specification. This specification does not

TRADEMARKED ITEMS MENTIONED IN ENCYCLOPEDIA ARTICLES

Item	Trademarked by	Article in Which Mentioned
AIX	IBM	IBM System 360/370/390
ESA/390, ES/9000, System 390, System 360, System 370	IBM	IBM System 360/370/390 and various others
InfoWindow	IBM	Videodisc
Intel 386, Intel 386SL	Intel Corporation	Microcomputer Chip
Lego	LEGO Systems, Inc.	Logo
Microcom Networking Protocol	Microcom	Modem
OSCAR	Hecht-Nielsen Neurocomputers	Optical Character Readers
PR/SM	IBM	IBM System 360/370/390
Quick Medical Reference	Camdat Corporation	Medical Applications
Scout View	General Electric	Tomography, Computerized
Ultrix	Digital Equipment	Digital Equipment Corporation VAX Series
Unix	AT&T Bell Laboratories	Unix Operating System, C, and various others
VAX	Digital Equipment	Digital Equipment Corporation VAX Series and various others
VAXELN	Digital Equipment	Digital Equipment Corporation VAX Series
VMS	Digital Equipment	Digital Equipment Corporation VAX Series
X Window System	M.I.T.	Computer Graphics: Standards
Zip+4	U.S. Postal Service	Optical Character Readers

tual memory associated with a process consists of 16 segments, and a segment consists of 256 pages, each of which has 4,096 bytes. The relatively small size of the virtual memory loses some of the advantages associated with virtual memory systems, but it probably has the advantage of making memory addressing more manageable. In the standard 370, the 24-bit address field* contains a 4-bit segment number, an 8-bit page number, and a 12-bit byte address within the page.

segment   page   displacement
no.   no.

The operating system maintains a 16- (or 32-) word segment table for each process that contains the pointers to the page table for each segment. The page table contains the physical address of each page that is present in main memory. These tables are automatically searched when a memory reference is made. Thus (Fig. 4), if page 6 of segment 4 is in main memory starting at physical byte location 15000 (hexadecimal), a reference to address location 406289 would cause the dynamic address translation hardware to search the segment table for segment 4 and retrieve the address of the page table for segment 4. It would search the page table for page 6 and retrieve absolute address 15. It would thus translate the segment/page address 406 into the physical address 15. (Actually 15000, but the three trailing zeros are understood.) The absolute address reference is thus 15289, and the operand is retrieved from that address.

Systems of this type usually have a small associative memory in which the most recent translations are stored (Fig. 4). Thus, the first reference to page 6 of segment 4 would proceed as discussed above, but the fact that 406 translates into 15 would be retained in the small associative memory. Then, so long as page 6 of segment 4 is one of the most recently referenced pages, its translation will be in the associative registers, and the relatively slow address translation process does not have to be repeated.

Burroughs Computers   In the Burroughs B5000 series and its successors, a job is represented in memory by a program reference table (PRT). Along with some data and other information, the PRT contains *descriptors*— pointers to data segments and to program segments. A descriptor for a data segment (an array) contains the address of the beginning of the array and the length of the array. Any reference to the array is automatically checked, and an interrupt occurs if it is attempting to reference beyond the array bounds.

In these systems, one bit of each data word is reserved as a marker bit that marks the word as a datum or as a descriptor. This has been generalized on some *tagged*

---

*An optional hardware modification on the 360/67 provided for the use of a 32-bit address field that made it possible to use a 12-bit segment system and thus address 4,096 segments. Several software systems, including TSS (Time Shared System) 360, took advantage of this extended addressing capability.

memory systems by allocating several bits of each data word to provide information about the data type and format along with each individual word or item of data.

These Burroughs systems were virtual memory systems based on the use of relatively small segments that are not broken into pages. A segment is moved as a unit between central memory and backing drum or disk storage. The operating system is a multiprogramming system. Each active job has some of its segments in core memory and the rest on the drum. Each segment descriptor in the program reference table has a *presence bit* which indicates whether or not that segment is present in central memory. Any attempt to refer to a segment that is not in central memory causes an interrupt to the supervisor, requesting that that segment be loaded. The supervisor can load the segment into any available contiguous area of memory that is large enough to hold it. If necessary, it can move out other segments. When the segment has been loaded, its new starting address in central memory is placed in its descriptor, and the program that referred to the segment can be restarted.

SAUL ROSEN

References

1971. Bell, C. G. and Newell, A. *Computer Structures: Readings and Examples*. New York: McGraw-Hill.
1972. Organick, Elliott I. *The Multics Systems—An Examination of Its Structure*. Cambridge: M.I.T. Press.

ADMINISTRATIVE APPLICATIONS

For articles on related subjects *see* BANKING APPLICATIONS; DATA PROCESSING; ELECTRONIC FUNDS TRANSFER SYSTEMS; ELECTRONIC OFFICE; INFORMATION PROCESSING; INFORMATION SYSTEMS; MANAGEMENT INFORMATION SYSTEM; NETWORKS, COMPUTER; and TELEPROCESSING SYSTEMS.

Introduction   In the early years of electronic computing, applications were classified simply as either "scientific" or "business." The essence of the distinction was that scientific applications involved substantial arithmetic operations on rather small volumes of data, whereas business applications involved modest arithmetic operations on substantial amounts of data. Internal computer speed (CPU instruction cycle time and memory access time) was the crucial variable in scientific computing applications, while input and output speed and versatility (punched card input/output [i/o], printed output, magnetic tape i/o, disk i/o, etc.) were the crucial variables in business data processing. The two types of applications were called "CPU-intensive" (sometimes "CPU-bound") or "input/output-intensive" ("i/o-bound"). Matrix inversion was "typical" of scientific applications, and insurance company premium transactions processing was "typical" of business applications. With the passage of time and with the pervasive evolution of computer applications, the original two-category distinction no longer sufficed.

First, government transactions processing grew no less rapidly than did business transactions processing, as government agencies, like the Social Security Administration, established pioneering large-scale government administrative applications that were strikingly similar to business applications. This led to the recognition that the term "administrative" applications was a more descriptive term than "business" applications, since both the private and public sectors "administer," while only the private sector does "business" in the commercial sense of the word.

Second, these simple classifications fell to the wayside with the establishment of other significant varieties of computer applications, such as process control, information retrieval, voice and message switching, and advanced technical applications such as computer-aided design (CAD-*q.v.*) and computer-aided instruction (CAI-*q.v.*).

Today, administrative applications are widely considered to be those that involve the use of computers for processing information in support of the operational, logistical, and functional activities performed by all organizations, and may be classified in a number of different ways. One is by organization type, e.g. banking, insurance, manufacturing, and government (which may be further subdivided into many different categories, such as defense, education, revenue, health services, etc.), among others. Another is by type of function (e.g. accounting, budgeting, payroll, student registration, and many others).

This article describes the evolution and growth of administrative applications, the organization of data processing activity, and the increasingly complex administrative processing environment of the 1990s.

The Evolution of Administrative and Business Applications
Interestingly, the four stages of the evolution of commercially viable computing systems closely correspond to each of the last four decades. While the earliest computers were developed during World War II for specific defense applications—some of the first computers were used to calculate artillery firing coordinates—these systems did not become commercially marketable for a number of reasons: they were special-purpose, designed for military applications; they were extremely large, occupying huge warehouses; they consumed enormous amounts of electricity, generated immense amounts of heat, required tons of chilled air, and broke down every few hours. No organization but the government could afford to own and operate one.

The first commercial systems were installed in the 1950s and ran such "business" applications as accounting, billing, payroll, and inventory control. This was a logical first step in the application of computers to solve business-related problems, for several reasons:

- These activities were well understood and reasonably well documented, which facilitated their computerization.
- These applications were well suited to the one-at-a-time sequential processing of data typically performed by the early computers.

- In many cases, these applications were already being performed on punched card tabulating equipment, which allowed them to be converted easily to the earliest punched card and magnetic tape–based computers.
- Computerization of these functions was readily justified by clerical staff reductions and by savings realized through replacement of outmoded and more expensive punched-card equipment.

These early computer systems processed data in batches, that is, they executed one program at a time and handled transactions (say, an accounting entry, such as payment of a bill) one at a time from a predefined sequence of transactions (such as all payments in a batch presorted by account number). They required considerable amounts of manual intervention and the applications they performed were limited in scope. The computers of the 1950s also tended to be physically large, internally slow, and somewhat unreliable in terms of system availability. They were vacuum-tube based, and it is clear that their price-performance ratio limited both the numbers and kinds of applications that were run on them.

The next major advance in systems came in the early 1960s, with the invention of the transistor and its implementation in the next generation of computers. These systems were smaller, faster, and more reliable. They still ran applications one at a time, but their speed encouraged development of more administrative applications. During the 1960s, virtually all large organizations computerized most of their primary "business" functions.

In the 1970s, the arrival of the integrated circuit drove the implementation of fast and reliable computer systems. Advances in operating system technology precipitated the rapid spread of multiuser systems, and data communications systems enabled more and more applications to be accessed from remote locations by employees working at CRT terminals. The applications began to provide information that resulted in a wide range of benefits, from significantly improved customer service to tighter management control over widely dispersed operations and functions.

In the 1980s, the microcomputer brought low-cost computer power to virtually anyone who wished to use it. Office automation eased the administrative workload in even the smallest offices. User-friendly word processing (*q.v.*), spreadsheets (*q.v.*), databases, and similar applications made it cost-justifiable to computerize.

The Challenges of the 1990s
In the decade of the 1990s, several trends are evident:

- Administrative applications will continue to evolve into tools for the strategic use of an organization's information assets to create a competitive advantage for the organization.
- Advances in electronic technology will continue to improve the cost-performance of computer systems; they will continue to shrink in size and increase in power.

- These high-performance systems will allow the integration of digital audio and video into previously text-only systems.
- Advances in communication technology will place more and more information at the fingertips of the average worker, as systems are tied into local, national, and international networks.
- Commuting costs will increase as telecomputing costs decrease, so that, by the end of the century, many employees will work at home.

Increasing emphasis will be placed on a number of critical issues:

- The hiring of technically competent staff, and their continued technical training.
- Adoption of standards for software, hardware, operating systems, telecommunication systems, and the like; non-standard applications and interfaces have historically ended up costing users millions, if not billions, of dollars to resolve.
- The security of information, from the point of its creation or gathering through its transmission and storage on permanent or semipermanent media, will become increasingly important, as access to systems becomes pervasive.
- The importance of these and other issues, and the value of information as an organizational asset will cause many organizations to develop strategic plans for management of their information resources.
- Competition for a portion of the high technology market will continue to increase. The Japanese use automated factories to produce one-of-a-kind custom cars built to order, and they plan 10 years into the future. Other countries will have to do the same, or lose their competitive advantage in world markets.

The Applications Development Environment

Administrative applications systems extend over a broadly based clientele, ranging from municipal governments to private corporations to public and state institutions supporting their day-to-day as well as decision-support operations. As the machine and data center centralized environments of the 1970s and 1980s evolved into cooperative and client/server environments, new computing architectures increasingly support the user by the provision of information-centered requirements. The applications evolution has followed the expanding hardware capabilities of the computer with its four major physical components; the central processing unit, main storage, auxiliary storage, and input/output devices.

Administrative applications (software) are written by technical staff identified as "programmers," "programmer analysts," and "software engineers," to name a few titles. Even though most software development projects are moving perceptibly closer to the end user, a majority of software projects are still developed in organizational departments known as data centers. These centers may be called data processing offices, management information systems offices, electronic data processing offices, etc., and they are responsible for a number of functions:

- Providing good quality service to all customers.
- Providing liaison activities to customer offices.
- Keeping current with state of the art systems and emerging standards.
- Planning, scheduling, and managing resources for operational economy and adequate service levels to customers.
- Providing separate development and operating responsibilities to increase auditing controls and to ensure formal procedures for purchasing, developing, and changing administrative software systems.
- Providing separate data processing functions and responsibilities so that security systems can be developed to maintain proper controls over the data, particularly for restricting direct control over assets, disbursement of funds, issuance of inventory, etc.

Some specific functional areas generally associated with administrative processing are:

- The support of one or more major development projects, for example, bridge construction, aircraft design, software development of new products, or nuclear reactor research.
- The support of operational activities, such as airline/hotel reservations, manufacturing control, demand deposit accounting, and electronic transfer of banking funds.
- The support of management systems, like financial management, payroll, personnel, budgeting, cost control, college admission, or registration.
- The provision of a computer utility serving authorized users.

The efficiency impacts of computer software in administrative applications are primarily visible as reductions in transaction processing costs that can reflect reductions in clerical costs, inventory costs, and measures of economy, such as office automation and desktop publishing (q.v.). Further effectiveness lies in uses of the growing body of management science, econometrics, and other advanced methodologies of informational analysis. Some administrative analytical applications are valuable at the lowest physical level in organizations, as in the daily scheduling of refinery output with the help of linear programming models.

Traditional Organization of Data Processing Activity

The organization of applications processing activities varies from organization to organization; however, there are several required areas of support:

- Systems development—This activity is usually divided into two parts: systems analysis, and design and applications programming. The basic organizational unit is project driven, either developing, installing, or modifying systems.
- Operations—Major divisions within operational functions are production support and hardware/peripheral operations. All of the planning, scheduling, control, job setup, and logistical work is done in an organization distinct from the actual "machine room floor." In production support is the scheduling and coordination unit. This group monitors production job streams, adjusts problems, and serves as a customer contact point. A second unit, job control, manages individual jobs as they flow through the systems. Controls are established, a job log is maintained, inputs are reviewed and edited, and outputs are reviewed and prepared for customer distribution.
- Library and services—This unit maintains the tape and disk library and provides support services (such as supplies inventory) to the operations group.
- Computer operations—Within this group are all computer console operations and online peripheral equipment.
- Technical support—The division of duties within the technical support group will vary within the data processing environment. Typical functions associated here can be standards, database administration, user assistance, and training.
- Management—The director/manager of data processing performs long- and short-range planning, establishes and administers project management systems, monitors resource utilization, maintains financial management systems and is responsible for personnel and budget, and manages hardware and software upgrades/acquisitions. Network communications and contingency planning are frequently a part of this person's management responsibilities.

The Administrative Applications Environment of the 1990s

"Cooperative processing" and "client/server" environments will service work group domains by using traditional mainframes as "warehouses" for data and switching points for communication (see FILE SERVER). They will also provide security and manage data access and throughput for systems of interlocking databases. This will lead to a high level of diverse database integration, enhanced system integrity, and, ultimately, a cost-effective array of hardware options, applications software, and data processing personnel.

Even though personal computers have experienced an incremental growth of power as measureed in millions of instructions per second (MIPS), they will not be viable alternatives to mainframe hardware for jobs that require robust security, task interleaving with other data processing jobs, and high rates of transaction processing. Few data centers have been able to realize the optimal organizational structures required to properly and successfully support distributed processing across microcomputer-based LAN structures (see LOCAL AREA NETWORK).

New mainframe machine families offer dramatic new features and functions with the promise of even more advanced features over the next several years. As administrative commercial applications begin to require general purpose processor speeds reaching into the 300–500 MIPS ranges within the next few years, advances in processor design will include the implementation of improved instructions that control processing within the computer. The 24-hours-per-day, seven-days-per-week applications processing schedule that is standard operating procedure in most large organizations will continue. This demanding environment will lead to distributed data center complexes that will be collections of geographically diverse data centers coupled by wideband, wide area communication capabilities.

In order to manage and control applications processing, mainframe-based expert systems (q.v.) will be widely used. Expert systems may replace the humans who are now required to make the thousands of decisions needed to run data processing complexes on a daily basis. Emphasis upon portability and integration of multi-vendor hardware and software systems will become key in the use of these expert systems. Peripherals, particularly those supporting storage devices—traditional rotating disks and optical disks—will be heavily used, as will image processing (q.v.) and microfiche replacement.

Administrative software applications will continue to drive the need for faster processing. Application developers will use new languages and tools that dramatically reduce the time required to develop new applications. Some of these will reside in the fourth generation language (4GL) environment, and some will occur in the computer-aided software engineering (CASE) environment (q.v.). Software will be forward and reverse engineered and software design recovery will become a common analysis activity within data centers. Most of these systems will be required to deal with Cobol code, estimated currently at approximately 100 billion lines. Migration to CASE and 4GL will be difficult because of this extensive coding—much of which has no applications documentation and exists only as machine code.

The trend toward computer literacy will continue into the 1990s and beyond. This will create highly pressured environments within data centers that will need to comply with tightly defined thresholds of reliability, availability and serviceability. Data center professionals will experience changing roles with client offices and will find their expertise being used at higher levels within the organization.

References

1985. Licker, Paul S. *The Art of Managing Software Development People.* New York: John Wiley & Sons. (How to manage highly creative and technically-oriented staff.)

1985. Tapscott, Henderson, and Greenberg of Trigon Systems Group, Inc. *Planning for Integrated Office Systems: A Strategic Approach.* Homewood, IL: Dow Jones-Irwin. (Planning for integrated office systems, and the strategic value of information.)

1987. Perry, William E. *The Information Center.* Englewood Cliffs, NJ: Prentice-Hall, Inc. (Mandate for change in the methods of processing information.)

1987. Schweitzer, James A. *Computers, Business, and Security: The New Role for Security.* Boston: Butterworth Publishers. (The management and protection of information as the most critical business asset.)

1987. Vella, Carolyn M., and McGonagle, John J., Jr. *Competitive Intelligence in the Computer Age.* New York: Quorum Books. (Explores the concept of locating publicly available information and converting it to useful strategic advantage over competitors.)

1990. Penrod, James I., Dolence, Michael G., and Douglas, Judith V. *The Chief Information Officer in Higher Education.* Boulder, CO: CAUSE, The Association for the Management of Information Technology in Higher Education. (Description of the role and organizational placement of the CIO.)

1991. Primozic, Kenneth, Primozic, Edward, and Leben, Joe. *Strategic Choices: Supremacy, Survival, or Sayonara.* New York: McGraw-Hill, Inc. (Description of the process of formulating strategic plans for achieving competitive advantage.)

WILLIAM R. KING AND MARY ELLEN HANLEY

AFCET. *See* ASSOCIATION FRANÇAISE POUR LA CYBERNETIQUE, ECONOMIQUE ET TECHNIQUE.

AFIPS. *See* AMERICAN FEDERATION OF INFORMATION PROCESSING SOCIETIES.

AIKEN, HOWARD

For articles on related subjects *see* DIGITAL COMPUTERS: HISTORY: EARLY; HOPPER, GRACE MURRAY; MARK I; and WATSON, THOMAS J., SR.

Howard Hathaway Aiken was born 8 March 1900, in Hoboken N.J., and died 14 March 1973, in St. Louis, Missouri. He grew up in Indianapolis, Indiana, where he attended Arsenal Technical High School while working 12 hours a night at the Indianapolis Light and Heat Company. Upon graduation he went to work for the Madison (Wisconsin) Gas Company, a position that allowed him to go to the University of Wisconsin. He received his B.A. degree in 1923 and was immediately promoted to chief engineer at Madison Gas.

In 1935 he returned to school, first at the University of Chicago and then at Harvard. His doctoral thesis at Harvard, resulting in a Ph.D. in 1939, was on the theory of space charge conduction. The research required laborious calculations of nonlinear differential equations. This experience led him to investigate the possibility of performing these types of calculations with machine assistance. His thoughts on this subject led him in 1937 to circulate a memo entitled, "Proposed Automatic Calculating Machine" (reprinted in *Spectrum,* August 1964, pp. 62–69).

Harvard was not the most likely environment to get support for this type of research. Fortunately, Harvard

FIG. 1. Howard Aiken

professors Ted Brown (Business) and Harlow Shapley (Astronomy) were impressed with his work, and both knew of the interest of Thomas Watson Sr. in projects of this nature. With their encouragement, and the knowledge that IBM had the necessary technology, Aiken approached Watson. A contract was signed in 1939 whereby IBM would build the Automatic Sequence Controlled Calculator (Harvard Mark I). The machine was running in 1944, and Aiken and Grace Hopper described it in a paper in *Electrical Engineering* (Vol. 65, 1946, pp. 384–391, 449–454, 522–528).

The Mark I was followed by the Mark II (a relay machine built for the Naval Proving Ground at Dahlgren, VA and completed in 1946), the Mark III (an electronic machine, also for Dahlgren, completed in 1950), and the Mark IV (an electronic machine built for and delivered to the Air Force in 1952). With the completion of Mark IV, Aiken got out of the business of building computers.

It is difficult to evaluate precisely the impact of Aiken's series of machines and the Harvard Computation Laboratory, which he founded. Fortunately, the documents are available to anyone interested. One need only look at the log books of the computation lab for this period to see the worldwide range of people who visited the laboratory. Another source of Aiken's work is the many publications in the "Annals of the Harvard Computation Laboratory" series. The Harvard catalog also provides clear evidence of the existence of courses in "computer science" a decade before the emergence of this program at most universities.

In 1947 and again in 1949 Aiken organized symposia on large-scale digital devices at Harvard. Programs from both meetings strongly reflect his hand and his philosophy at that time. Perhaps his most profound impact was in the environment he created at Harvard, which enabled the University to become a vital training ground for many people who are outstanding in the field today. A perusal of those who did their doctoral dissertations under his direction is an excellent example of this impact.

Aiken retired from Harvard in 1961 and moved to Fort Lauderdale, Florida, where he formed Aiken Industries. He also joined the faculty of the University of Miami as Distinguished Professor of Information Technology. In this latter position, he helped the University develop a computer science program and design a computing center.

His honors are too numerous to mention in detail. They include honorary degrees (University of Wisconsin, Wayne State University, and Technische Hochschule, Darmstadt), prizes (Rochlitz Prize, Edison Medal of IEEE, the John Price Award of the Franklin Institute) as well as medals from both the United States (Air Force and Navy for distinguished service) and foreign governments (Sweden, Belgium, France, and Spain).

Howard Aiken felt that he had to be continuously involved in challenging endeavors in order to stay alive both physically and intellectually. His career is a document of that creed. Some of his detractors accused him of living in the past, but nothing could be further from the truth. He was a man of rare vision, whose insights have had a profound effect on the entire computing profession.

References

1973. Oettinger. Anthony G. "Howard Aiken," *Communications of the ACM*, **16**. 298-299, May.

1984. Williams, M.R. "Howard Aiken and the Harvard Computation Laboratory," *Annals of the History of Computing*, 6(2), 157–159.

1984. Hurd, C.C. "Aiken Observed," *Annals of the History of Computing*, 6(2), 160–162.

1988. Cohen, I.B. "Babbage and Aiken," *Annals of the History of Computing*, 10(3), 171–194.

HENRY S. TROPP

ALGEBRA, BOOLEAN. *See* BOOLEAN ALGEBRA.

ALGEBRA, COMPUTER. *See* COMPUTER ALGEBRA.

ALGOL 60. *See* PROCEDURE-ORIENTED LANGUAGES.

ALGOL 68

For articles on related subjects *see* BLOCK STRUCTURE; EXTENSIBLE LANGUAGE; PROCEDURE-ORIENTED LANGUAGES; and PROGRAMMING LANGUAGES.

Algol 68 is a language designed by a working group (WG 2.1) of the International Federation for Information Processing (IFIP) in order to provide a general-purpose programming language that would be suitable for commu-

nicating algorithms, executing them efficiently on different computers, and teaching computer science. Even though Algol 68 is a successor of Algol 60, it is a completely new language, different from Algol 60 in many essential aspects. Its design reflects the 1968 understanding of a number of fundamental concepts of programming languages and computer science.

Algol 68 has great expressive power and yet a very elegant and interesting basic structure. It features five primitive types (called "modes") of values; **bool** (boolean), **char** (character), **int** (integer), **real** and **format**; and five rules for constructing new modes from the ones already defined. So, for example, values of mode [] **real** are one-dimensional arrays or *multiple values* of reals. Values of mode **struct** ([]**char** *name*, **bool** *sex*, **int** *age*) are personal records or *structured values*. Values of mode **union** (**real**, **int**) are either reals or integers, but no value of this mode can be both of mode **real** and **int**. *References* are values that refer (point) to other values. For example, values of mode **ref** [] **char** are references to one-dimensional arrays of characters. Values of mode **proc** (**int, real**) **bool** are *routines* (i.e. procedures) that take two arguments of respective modes **int** and **real** and return a value of mode **bool**.

Since references and routines are values, they can be manipulated like any other values. In particular, they can be passed as parameters in procedure calls. Because of this it is possible to achieve the effects of three types of procedure calls found in other programming languages: call by value, call by name, and call by reference. So, for example, values of mode **proc** (**ref** [] **char, int**) **int** are routines with the first formal parameter called by reference.

Different sorts of declarations (for example, array declarations and switch declarations) found in other programming languages are captured in the *identity declaration* of Algol 68. This concept is also the basis of the parameter-passing mechanism; it allows construction of an infinite number of new modes from the already defined ones and permits declaration of arithmetic and logical operators and their priorities.

The identity declaration and the concept of a reference clarify the distinction between a variable and a constant. An identity declaration in a program defines the value possessed by the identifier that appears in the declaration. This value may be a reference to another value, in which case the identifier is declared as a variable. An example of an initialized (i.e. one that includes assignment) declaration of that sort is **real** $x := 3.14$, which gives rise to the following scheme.

identifier $x \rightarrow$ reference to a real vaule $\rightarrow$ 3.14

The effect of a standard assignment statement is achieved by making the reference possessed by the identifier refer to the value specified in the statement. This is not possible if the value possessed by an identifier is not a reference, i.e. if this intermediate link is not present. In that case the identity declaration establishes the identifier as a constant, which can be changed only by redeclaring it. An example of a declaration that establishes *pi* as a constant 3.14 is **real** *pi* = *3.14*, which gives rise to the following scheme.

ALGORITHM **27**

identifier *pi* → 3.14

This careful distinction permits, in particular, the definition of constant and variable procedures. For example, the declaration **proc** $f = ($**real** x, **real** $y)$ **real**: $(x + y)/2 - sqrt(x \times y)$ establishes f as a constant, as opposed to **proc** $f := ($**real** x, **real** $y)$ **real**: $(x + y)/2 - sqrt(x \times y)$, which defines a variable procedure. In the latter case we can, at another point in the program, assign some other value of mode **proc (real, real) real** to f; for example, we can write $f := ($**real** x, **real** $y)$ **real**: $(x + y)/2$.

A number of standard statements are available in Algol 68: assignment, e.g. $x := (a + b)/2$; repetitive, e.g. (**for** i **from** 2 **to** n **do** $f := f \times$ i; **go to**, e.g. **go to** *loop*; conditional, e.g. **if** $x \geq y$ **then go to** *label* **else go to** *end* **fi**, etc. In addition to the conventional serial statement execution, it is possible to specify parallel or *collateral* execution. In the latter case, execution of statements is merged in time in a way to be specified by the implementation. Parallel programming facilities in Algol 68 include elementary means of control or synchronization of collateral execution. These are language-defined values called *semaphores*.

The Algol 60 concept of a *block* appears in a more general form in Algol 68 as a *range*. An example of a range is a sequence of declarations and statements placed between generalized parentheses. Examples of pairs of these parentheses are **begin** and **end, if** and **then, then** and **else, else** and **fi**, etc. References possessed by the identifiers declared in a range may be local to that range. Since the hardware representation of a reference is a memory location, storage is allocated dynamically to local variables; i.e. storage for local variables of a range is deallocated when leaving that range. In addition to these stack-controlled values, Algol 68 also has values whose lifetime does not fit into the last-in-first-out principle of a stack. Values of this sort are stored in a randomly organized memory region called the *heap*.

While Pascal, which was also designed as a successor of Algol 60, has been widely accepted and heavily used, Algol 68 has not been. Pascal is a much smaller and simpler language. Algol 68 is more complex and the generality that it offers is not always necessary nor of the right kind. Because of that, Algol 68 is more difficult to learn. This is partly due to unusual terminology that has not been widely accepted. The defining document of Algol 68 is much more elaborate and precise but also much more difficult to understand in comparison with the shorter and less formal Pascal report. This in particular applies to the two-level context sensitive grammar used in the Algol 68 report in comparison with the usual BNF (*q.v.*) syntax used for Pascal. Finally, it is much more difficult to implement full Algol 68 than Pascal, for which there are well-known, widely used, and efficient implementation techniques.

References

1969. van Wijngaarden, A. *et al.* "Report on the Algorithmic Language ALGOL 68." *Numerische Mathematik,* **14.**
1971. Branguart, P., Lewi, J., Sintzoff, M., and Wodor, P.L. "The Composition of Semantics in Algol 68," *Communications of the ACM* **14,** No. 11.
1971. Lindsey, C.H. and van der Meulen, S.G. *Informal Introduction to Algol 68.* Amsterdam: North-Holland.
1975. van Wijngaarden, A., Mailloux, B.J., Peck, J.E.L., Koster, C.H.A., Sintzoff, M., Lindsey, C.H., Meertens, L.G.L.T., and Fisher, R.G. "Revised Report on the Algorithmic Language Algol 68," *Acta Informatica* **5**: 1-3. Springer-Verlag: Berlin, Heidelberg, New York.
1976. Tanenbaum, A.S. "A Tutorial on Algol 68," *Computing Surveys* **8,** No. 2.
1978. Tanenbaum, A.S. "A Comparison of Pascal and Algol 68," *Computer Journal* **21,** No. 4.

SUAD ALAGIC

ALGORITHM

For articles on related subjects *see* ALGORITHMS, ANALYSIS OF; ALGORITHMS, CLASSIFICATION OF; ALGORITHMS, THEORY OF; ERROR ANALYSIS; PROGRAM VERIFICATION; SCHEDULING ALGORITHM; and TURING MACHINE.

In discussing problem solving, we presuppose both a problem and a device to be used in solving the problem. The problem may be mathematical or non-mathematical in nature, simple or complex. The basic requirements for a well-posed problem are that (1) the known information is clearly specified; (2) we can determine when the problem has been solved; and (3) the problem does not change during its attempted solution. The second requirement does not mean that the solution to the problem is known *a priori*, but only that we know when the solution has been attained. For example, in some numerical problems we obtain repeated approximations to the answer, terminating the solution process when two successive approximations are "sufficiently close" together. We can specify in the problem statement the exact meaning of "sufficiently close" without knowing the exact answer. The device to be used for problem solution may be human or machine, or a combination of the two.

Definition   Given both the problem and the device, an *algorithm* is the precise characterization of a method of solving the problem, presented in a language comprehensible to the device. In particular, an algorithm is characterized by these properties:

1. Application of the algorithm to a particular input set or problem description results in a finite sequence of actions.
2. The sequence of actions has a unique initial action.
3. Each action in the sequence has a unique successor.
4. The sequence terminates with either a solution to the problem, or a statement that the problem is unsolvable for that set of data.

We illustrate these concepts with an example: "Find the square root of the real number x." As it is stated, this problem is algorithmically either trivial or unsolvable, owing to the irrationality of most square roots. If we accept "$\sqrt{2}$" as the square root of 2, for example, the solution is trivial: The answer is the square root sign ($\sqrt{}$) concatenated with the input. In Snobol, the entire algorithm is

```
OUTPUT = '√ ' INPUT
END
```

However, if we want a decimal expression, then the square root of 2 can never be calculated exactly . Hence, the requirement of a finite number of actions is violated.

A modified statement of the problem is more suited to our purposes. "Find the positive square root, to four decimal places, of the real number x." This statement has three useful properties:

1. It explicitly names the *positive* square root as the desired one, whereas the earlier statement left that quality ambiguous.
2. It eliminates the string "$\sqrt{x}$" as a problem solution.
3. By stating "four decimal places" (or any other fixed number of places), it provides a test for termination.

A conceivable but questionable method of solution is:

1. Choose a number y and compute y^2.
2. If $|y^2 - x| < 5 \times 10^{-5}$, the solution is y; if not, return to step (1).

This method fails to be an algorithm, since no procedure is specified for choosing either the initial value y or subsequent values. Moreover, even if there is a solution, there is no guarantee that this method will find it.

Now consider another method:

1. Let $y = 1$.
2. Compute y^2.
3. If $|y^2 - x| < 5 \times 10^{-5}$, the solution is y, HALT; if not, go to step 4.
4. Replace y by $((x/y) + y)/2$; go to step 2.

This procedure is a special case of a general technique known as the Newton-Raphson technique, a method that has the precise definition of each step required of an algorithm. Moreover, whenever applied to a non-negative real number x, the method will produce the proper solution in a finite number of steps. However, whenever applied to a negative number, the method will endlessly recompute y without recognizing the futility of the task. This is typical of a class of methods called *semi-algorithms*: They will halt in a finite number of steps if the problem posed has a solution, but will not necessarily halt if there is no solution.

To transform the given method into an algorithm, two things must be done:

1. Add a step, (0); if $x < 0$, there is no solution; HALT; and
2. Rewrite the given method in a language suitable for the proposed device. (For English-speaking people, the given language is satisfactory; for a computer, a programming language must be used. For example, the following algorithm in Pascal is suitable for computers that support that language.)

```
program SquareRoot (input, output);
var X, Y, Z: real;
begin
    write ('Find the square root of ');
    readln (X);
    IF X >= 0 then
        begin
            Y := 1;
            Z := Y * Y;
            while abs (X − Z) >= 0.00005 do
                begin
                    Y := ((X / Y) + Y) / 2;
                    Z := Y * Y
                end;
            writeln ('The square root of ', X:7:5, 'is ', Y:7:5, '.')
        end
            else
            writeln ('There is no real square root for ',
            X:8:5, '.')
end.
```

When we run this program it requests input data and then responds with the square root of the input, or a message that there is no real square root. With successive runs with the input 3, 107, 1, 0, −4, and 3.14159, the results will be

```
Find the square root of 3
The square root of 3.00000 is 1.73205.
Find the square root of 107
The square root of 107.00000 is 10.34408.
Find the square root of 1
The square root of 1.00000 is 1.00000.
Find the square root of 0
The square root of 0.00000 is 0.00391.
Find the square root of −4
There is no real square root for −4.00000.
Find the square root of 3.14159
The square root of 3.14159 is 1.77245.
```

Significance of Algorithms While the concept of an algorithm is useful in crystallizing the informal notation of a "method of solution" for a problem, it has a much deeper significance. Whereas it was at one time assumed that any properly stated mathematical problem was solvable, mathematicians in the 1920s began to question this, asking what precisely it meant to say that we could "solve a problem" or "compute a function." Several important areas of mathematics have resulted from attempts to answer these questions, including the theory of Turing machines and the theory of algorithms. All the concepts proposed proved to be equivalent: Any problem that is solvable according to one concept is solvable according to all other concepts. Thus, while the algorithm, properly formalized, may not be the only way to solve problems, it appears to be essentially the only way that the human intellect in its present stage of development can comprehend.

Quality Judgments on Algorithms Any computer program is at least a semi-algorithm, and any program that always halts is an algorithm. (Of course, it may not solve the problem for which the programmer intended it.) Given a solvable problem, there are many algorithms (programs) to solve it, not all of equal quality. The primary practical criteria by which the quality of an algorithm is judged are time and memory requirements, accuracy of solution, and generality. To cite an extreme example, since a properly defined game of chess has only a finite number of possible moves, there exists an algorithm to determine the "perfect" chess game. Simply examine all possible move sequences, in some specified order. Unfortunately, the time required to execute any algorithm based on this idea is measured in billions of years, even at today's computer speeds. The memory requirements for such an algorithm are similarly overbearing.

On a more practical plane, several numerical methods for solving problems fail to yield satisfactory algorithms because the rate of convergence is so slow that thousands or millions of iterations may be needed to determine the answer. For other numerical methods, rounding or truncation errors may accumulate so rapidly that they destroy the answer.

There is often a trade-off in time and memory requirements that must be settled pragmatically. The simplest case of this arises in the computation and repeated use of a complicated function. If the computation of each function value is sufficiently complex, then in repeated usage much time may be saved by precomputing a table of values and using table lookup techniques (*see* SEARCHING). However, such a table may require sufficient additional memory space that this becomes a critical factor. Thus, one may have to sacrifice some speed to stay within available memory bounds.

The accuracy of an algorithm is a characteristic often more closely related to time than to memory requirements. For example, the square root algorithm previously presented is not very accurate. Changing the test constant from 0.00005 to 0.00000000005 will produce 0.00000381 as the square root of zero at the cost of more iterations through the loop of the algorithm. No additional memory is required, and the additional iterations require only a small fraction of a second. Further improvement may be obtained from the corresponding algorithm in double-precision at a cost of both run time and additional memory space. In each case the basic algorithmic concept is unchanged.

Altering the basic algorithmic concept may provide an improved algorithm to accomplish a given task. For example, three multiplications and two additions are required to evaluate the quadratic expression $ax^2 + bx + c$ in the order $((ax^2) + (bx)) + c$. Changing the concept of the evaluation algorithm to $(((ax) + b) x) + c$ eliminates one multiplication, resulting in a more efficient process. This will improve the speed of solution of the problem, and probably also improve the accuracy of the result.

The remaining important characteristic of an algorithm is its generality. While there are occasions when an algorithm is needed to solve a single isolated problem, more often algorithms are designed to handle a range of input data. Generality, like accuracy, is often attained at the cost of speed and memory requirements. A general polynomial root finder is more costly in both time and storage than an algorithm for extracting the roots of a quadratic equation. But the increased generality may justify the cost. This is a pragmatic decision. In another example, an information retrieval (*q.v.*) system based on a free vocabulary is generally more expensive to design and operate than one based on a fixed or coded vocabulary. But the difference in utility may far outweigh the additional cost burden.

Questions of the minimal time and storage requirements posed by a given class of problems, and of the time and storage requirements of any proposed algorithm, have become increasingly important as we attempt to solve larger and more complex problems. In recent years, much of the work in algorithm theory has been focused on these questions of algorithmic complexity (*see also* COMPUTATIONAL COMPLEXITY).

References

1983. Aho, Alfred V., Hopcroft, John E., and Ullman, Jeffrey D. *Data Structures and Algorithms*. Reading, MA: Addison-Wesley.
1984. Gonnet, G.H. *Handbook of Algorithms and Data Structures*. Reading, MA: Addison-Wesley.
1987. Korfhage, Robert R. and Gibbs, Norman E. *Principles of Data Structures and Algorithms with Pascal*. Dubuque, IA: Wm. C. Brown Publishers.
1988. Sedgewick, Robert. *Algorithms* (2nd Ed.). Reading, MA: Addison-Wesley.

ROBERT R. KORFHAGE

ALGORITHM, PARALLEL. *See* PARALLEL PROCESSING: ALGORITHMS.

ALGORITHMICS

For articles on related subjects *see* ALGORITHM; ALGORITHMS, ANALYSIS OF; ALGORITHMS, THEORY OF; COMPUTATIONAL COMPLEXITY; LOOP INVARIANT; and PROGRAM VERIFICATION.

Algorithmics is the systematic study of algorithms—how to devise them, describe them, validate them, and compare their relative merits. As the study of algorithms, algorithmics might be deemed a synonym for computer science. In practice, however, the term is used primarily by mathematicians and mathematics educators, and it connotes an approach to *mathematics* where the study of the calculations by which answers are obtained is an important as determining that answers exist. This is quite different from the approach to mathematics during most of the 20th century. At the school level, there has been much *doing* of algorithms, but in a rote way. At the university level, the emphasis has been on the existence and structure of mathematical objects. But now, with computers, such large and complicated problems are tackled that it is natural to be more systematic about the methodology for computing answers. Thus, algorithmics means not only being explicit about the use of algorithms to do mathematics (for instance, by using *algorithmic language* (i.e. pseudocode) to describe solution methods), but it also means regarding algorithms themselves as worthy objects of mathematical study.

Algorithmics is usually divided into three parts: design, verification, and analysis. Design is the process of creating algorithms and the study of good creation approaches (for instance, reducing to smaller cases and top-down planning). Verification is proving algorithms correct; the primary technique is mathematical induction, often expressed in terms of loop invariants (*q.v.*). Analysis is the determination of the efficiency of an algorithm (how long it takes to run as a function of input size, or how much memory is required) and, when more than one algorithm is known to solve a problem, a comparison of their relative efficiencies (*see* ALGORITHMS, ANALYSIS OF). Better yet, but usually quite difficult, is to determine or at least bound the optimal efficiency for any method that solves the problem at hand. Determining the optimum over all algorithms for a problem is called determining the *computational complexity* (*q.v.*) of the problem.

Here is a simple example. Consider the problem of evaluating a polynomial $p(x) = a_n x^n + \cdots + a_1 x + a_0$. From a classical mathematics standpoint, there isn't any "problem" here; of course the polynomial has a value. But what if n is *very* large and/or we must compute $p(x)$ for many values of x? (These situations can arise in coding theory or in approximating functions with polynomials.) Then it's worthwhile to devise competing evaluation methods and compare them.

For instance, if the standard representation above is evaluated directly, it takes n multiplications to compute $a_n x^n$, $n - 1$ to compute $a_{n-1} x^{n-1}$, etc., for a total of $n(n + 1)/2$ multiplications and n additions. If powers of x are not recomputed, then the number of multiplications is $2n - 1$. This saving can be accomplished by computing $a_n x^n$ first, but saving the intermediate powers $x^2, x^3, \ldots$ obtained along the way and recalling them when lower-order terms like $a_{n-1} x^{n-1}$ are computed. However, even these memory requirements can be avoided if terms are computed from the low end, as shown in the pseudocode below.

Further savings are obtained if $p(x)$ is rewritten in nested form,

$$p(x) = x(\cdots x(a_n x + a_{n-1}) \cdots) + a_0$$

Then only n multiplications and n additions are needed. This method is perhaps best understood if we write it and the preceding, more standard approach in algorithmic language.

Standard Algorithm
    $Poly \leftarrow a_0 + a_1 * x$
    $Power \leftarrow x$
    for $k = 2$ **to** n
        $Power \leftarrow Power * x$
        $Poly \leftarrow Poly + a_k * Power$
    endfor
    Output *Poly*

Nested Algorithm
    $Poly \leftarrow a_n$
    for $i = 1$ **to** n
        $Poly \leftarrow Poly * x + a_{n-i}$
    endfor
    Output *Poly*

Perhaps the least evident part of the discussion above is the claim that the nested algorithm is valid. This claim follows from checking that the following is a loop invariant: At the end of the ith pass through the loop, $Poly = \sum_{j=0}^{i} a_{n-j} x^{i-j}$. Upon termination, $i = n$, so it follows from this invariant that $Poly = p(x)$ at the end.

Devising these algorithms, validating them, and analyzing their efficiency illustrate the main parts of algorithmics. In fact, it can be shown that the nested method is an optimal algorithm in a strong sense. (Nested evaluation itself is quite old; Newton used it, though it usually goes under the name Horner's Method. Proofs of its optimality are much more recent.) More to the point here, the idea that evaluating polynomials is indeed a problem gets at the heart of algorithmics. When one looks for algorithmic issues in mathematics, both in elementary and advanced material, many new avenues for exploration are opened.

References

1977. Engel, Arthur. "Elementarmathematik von algorithmischen Standpunkt," Stuttgart: Ernst Klett Verlag, translated as "Elementary Mathematics from an algorithmic standpoint" by F.R. Watson, Staffordshire, U.K.: KMEP, Univ Keele.

1985. Maurer, Stephen. "The algorithmic way of life is best," *College Math J*, **16** (January) 2–18 (Forum piece and reply to responses).

1992. Maurer, Stephen. "What are algorithms? What is algorithmics?" In *The Influence of Computer Science and Informatics on Mathematics and Its Teaching*, 2nd Ed. Paris: UNESCO.

STEPHEN B. MAURER

ALGORITHMS, ANALYSIS OF

For articles on related subjects *see* ALGORITHM; ALGORITHMICS; ALGORITHMS, DESIGN AND CLASSIFICATION OF; ALGORITHMS, THEORY OF; COMBINATORICS; COMPUTATIONAL COMPLEXITY; GRAPH THEORY; NP-COMPLETE PROBLEMS; SEARCHING; and SORTING.

The analysis of algorithms can be partitioned into two areas: algorithm complexity and problem complexity. The former is concerned with consideration of a specific algorithm for a problem and the analysis of its behavior with respect to the amount of memory space, time, or other resource used. The latter is concerned with the class of all algorithms for a particular problem and the determination of its minimum requirements with respect to space and time or other resources. Such analyses are second in importance only to the determination of the correctness of an algorithm. They provide the means to choose intelligently and improve algorithms.

One might suspect that, as the speed of computers increases, the effects of the efficiency of the algorithms used decrease. Actually, just the opposite is true. The reason is that the asymptotic behavior of the algorithm becomes more important, as we will now illustrate.

With each problem, we associate an integer that we call the size of the problem. For example, the size of a matrix inversion problem is the dimension of the matrix, the size of a graph problem is the number of edges, and so forth. The growth rate of the execution time of the algorithm is determined as a function of the size of the problem. The limiting behavior of the growth rate is called the asymptotic growth rate. For example, the asymptotic behavior of the function $17 + 5n + 2n^2$ is $2n^2$, since, for sufficiently large n, $2n^2$ approximates $17 + 5n + 2n^2$ to arbitrary accuracy. For $n > 100$, the lower-order terms account for less than 3%.

In performing a hand computation, the size of the problem is usually small, and consequently the asymptotic growth rate is unimportant. On such small problems, most algorithms perform reasonably well. However, on a high-speed computer, the problem size normally encountered is large and the asymptotic growth rate becomes important. Given two algorithms with growth rates n^2 and 2^n, for problems up to size 6, the difference in execution times is never more than a factor of 2. However, with a computer, a problem of size 100 might be encountered. In this case, the n^2 algorithm is easily executed, whereas the 2^n algorithm would require centuries to compute. This example illustrates why so much effort is devoted to the analysis of algorithms.

Algorithm Complexity

Space and Time. Economy of space and time are the most important aspects of algorithm complexity. Since both are limited, it is advisable to determine how much space and time an algorithm requires. An algorithm that requires relatively little memory space for execution may have a greater running time than another algorithm that requires more space, while both algorithms may provide a solution to the same problem. Thus, there is frequently a trade-off between space and time.

As an example of a space-time trade-off, consider an algorithm that requires the storage of an undirected graph. (An undirected graph is a set V of n vertices, $V = (v_1, v_2, ..., v_n)$, and a set E of edges, where an edge is an unordered pair of vertices.) The algorithm stores the graph as an $n \times n$ *connection* (or *adjacency*) matrix A, where

$$a_{ij} = \begin{cases} 1 & \text{if } (v_i, v_j) \text{ is an edge in } E \\ 0 & \text{otherwise.} \end{cases}$$

This requires n^2 bits of memory, regardless of the number of edges.

Assume that the algorithm is used only for planar graphs. (A planar graph is an undirected graph that can be drawn on a plane surface so that no edges intersect.) Let G be a planar graph with p vertices. Then G can be represented in the computer by a linked list of n vertices, where the data structure for each vertex v_i is a linked list of all vertices adjacent to v_i. Since each edge (v_i, v_j) of G is stored twice (v_j is on the list of vertices adjacent to v_i, and v_i is on the list of vertices adjacent to v_j), the memory required to store the list representation of G is proportional to the number of edges. For planar graphs it can be shown that the number of edges is bounded by $3n$-6, where n is the number of vertices. Thus, the memory required is bounded by $C \times n$, where C is a constant, rather than the n^2 that was required for the connection matrix representation. If the algorithm is required to determine if vertex v_i is connected to vertex v_j, then a trade-off between space and time occurs, since only one operation is needed with the connection matrix representation, whereas the list representation requires searching the entire list of vertices adjacent to v_i to see if v_j is on the list.

Frequency Analysis. A *frequency analysis* of an algorithm reveals the number of times certain parts of the algorithm are executed. Such an analysis indicates which parts of the algorithm consume large quantities of time and hence where efforts should be directed toward improving the algorithm. For example, the following Pascal-like function calculates

$$\sum_{i=1}^{N+1} a_i x^{i-1}$$

```
(1)   function sum (a:array [1..N+1] of real;
          x:real): real;
(2)   var
(3)       i,j: integer;
(4)       power_of_x: real;
(5)       term: array [1..N+1] of real;
(6)   begin
(7)       for i:= 1 to N do begin
(8)           power_of_x:= 1.0;                          N
(9)           for j:= 1 to i do
(10)              power_of_x:=
                      power_of_x * x;            N(N-1)/2
(11)          term[i]:= a[i+1] * power_of_x             N
(12)      end;
(13)      sum:= a[1];                                   1
(14)      for i:= 1 to N do
(15)          sum:= sum + term[i]                       N
(16)  end;
```

The function is poorly written and just about every statement can be changed to decrease the amount of time required. To the right of each assignment statement is the number of times it is executed. As N increases, the function spends proportionately more and more time executing the statement inside the loop on j than it does for the statements on lines 8, 11, 13, and 15. Thus, it is really futile to try to improve the function by decreasing the time spent executing the latter statements without first decreasing the time spent executing the innermost statement on line 10. The function can be improved by using Horner's rule for polynomial evaluation. Again, the number of times each assignment statement is executed is given at its right.

```
(1)    function sum (a:array [1..N+1] of real;
          x:real): real;
(2)    begin
(3)        sum:= a[N+1];                              1
(4)        for i:= N downto 1 do
(5)            sum:= sum*x + a[i]                      N
(6)    end;
```

Execution Time To determine the actual execution time of an algorithm in seconds requires a knowledge of the operation times for each instruction of the computer on which the algorithm is to be executed and how the compiler generates code. In order to avoid becoming involved in the specific details of operation of a particular computer, it is customary to find upper and lower bounds c_1 and c_2, such that the execution time of every instruction is between c_1 and c_2. Then the execution time of an algorithm can be estimated from a count of the number of operations that are executed. This frees the analysis of the algorithm from peculiarities of individual computers.

Frequently, the time required by an algorithm is data dependent. In this case, one of two types of analyses is possible. The first is called the "worst case analysis," in which that set of data of given size requiring the most work is determined and the behavior of the algorithm is analyzed for that specific set of data. The other alternative is to assume a probability distribution for the possible input data and compute the distribution of the execution time as a function of the input distribution. Usually, this computation is so difficult that only the expected or average execution time as a function of size is computed. This is called the "average case analysis."

Problem Complexity In problem complexity we are concerned with analyzing a problem rather than an algorithm. The analysis provides us with lower bounds on the amount of time and space required for a solution to the problem, independent of the algorithm used. The lower bounds may be either "worst case" or "average case" bounds. These lower bounds can serve as an indication of how well an algorithm fits the problem and whether it can be improved. For example, such an analysis shows that any algorithm that evaluates an arbitrary n-degree polynomial represented by its coefficients requires at least n multiplications and n additions. Thus, Horner's rule cannot be improved upon.

On the other hand, an analysis of matrix multiplication gives a lower bound of order n^2 operations for multiplying two matrices of dimension n. The usual matrix multiplication algorithm has an asymptotic growth rate of order n^3. Thus there is substantial interest in trying either to find a better lower bound or to improve on the current matrix multiplication algorithms. At the current state of knowledge, the fastest algorithm has an asymptotic growth rate of order $n^{2.376}$, and thus there is a large gap between the best known lower bound and the performance of the best known algorithm.

In problem analysis, it is often important to consider the frequency of occurrence of a specific operation. The reason is that reducing the number of occurrences of a specific operation can lead to a recursive algorithm with a lower asymptotic growth rate. Consider multiplying two n-digit numbers, where n is a power of 2. The usual algorithm learned in elementary school requires on the order of n^2 operations. A recursive method of multiplying two n-digit numbers x and y is to write $x = a10^{n/2} + c$ and $y = b10^{n/2} + d$, where a, b, c, and d are $n/2$-digit numbers. Compute ab, cd, and $ad + bc$. Then

$$xy = ab10^a + (ad + bc)10^{a/2} + cd$$

The problem of computing xy is reduced to the problem of computing ab, cd, and $ad + bc$, which are computed by the three multiplications ab, cd, and $(a + c)(b + d)$. The formula $ad + bc$ is obtained by $(a + c)(b + d) - ab - cd$. Let $T(n)$ be the time to compute the product of two n-digit numbers. Then $T(n) \simeq 3\,T(n/2) + kn$, where the $3T(n/2)$ is the time to compute the three multiplications, k is a nonnegative constant, and kn is the time to compute the necessary sums. Successively applying the formula above to each product, we obtain

$$T(n) \simeq kn(1 + (3/2) + (3/2)^2 + \ldots + (3/2)^{\log_2 n}$$
$$\simeq 3kn^{\log_2 3} \simeq 3kn^{1.58}$$

The asymptotic growth rate is of order $n^{1.58}$ rather than the n^2 of the more elementary method. The important observation is that, in computing ab, cd, and $ad + bc$, the number of multiplications was reduced from four to three at the expense of increasing the number of additions from one to four. The reason for doing this is that the exponent in the asymptotic growth rate is affected by the number of multiplications, whereas the number of additions affects only the constant.

A major difficulty with problem analysis is that it is concerned with the class of all algorithms for a given problem. One can no longer postulate a computer with a given structure and operation set. Instead, one must envision an abstract computer that is sufficiently general to encompass any physically implementable algorithm. The difficulties involved are of such magnitude that one is forced to obtain bounds for certain limited classes of programs. For example, sorting n integers can be shown to require $n \log n$ operations if restricted to the class of algorithms that sorts by binary (two at a time) comparisons. This follows from the simple information-theoretic argument that there are $n!$ possible permutations of n items, and each comparison can at best divide the set of possible permutations by a factor of 2. Since the asymptotic growth rate of $\log(n!)$ is $n \log n$, it takes at least $n \log n$ comparisons to determine uniquely the actual permutation. Of course, if one sorts by some method other than by comparisons (radix sort, for example), then the bound is no longer valid.

A typical assumption for a class of programs might be that the computation uses only the arithmetic operations of addition, subtraction, multiplication, and division. When this is done, it is necessary to specify the underlying algebraic structure. For example, the complexity of computing an algebraic expression may depend on whether the underlying structure is the rational, real, or complex number system.

One of the most powerful techniques for establishing results of this nature is due to Winograd, who showed that any algorithm for computing the product of an arbitrary vector X times a matrix A requires a number of multiplications at least as great as the number of independent columns of A. It immediately follows from this result that Horner's rule evaluates arbitrary n-degree polynomials with the minimum number of multiplications. Let $X = (x^n, x^{n-1}, ..., x, 1)$ and let $A = (a_{n+1}, a_n, ..., a_1)^T$. Then

$$XA = \sum_{i=1}^{n+1} a_i x^{i-1}.$$

X has n nondependent columns, which implies that n multiplications are required. The result requires that the algorithm evaluate any polynomial, given its coefficients. Specific polynomials can often be evaluated with fewer multiplications. Similarly, if the polynomial is specified by parameters other than its coefficients, a saving in the number of multiplications is possible.

The one facet of problem complexity that is most intriguing is the lack of nontrivial lower bounds for various problems. Almost all known lower bounds are either linear in the size of the problem or have been obtained by restricting the classes of algorithms. The notable exceptions are lower bounds obtained by the diagonalization techniques of recursive function theory. One of the major goals of computer scientists working in the analysis of algorithms is to close the gaps in our knowledge of problem complexity.

References

1968, 1969, 1973. Knuth, D.E. *The Art of Computer Programming* 1, 2, 3. Reading, MA: Addison-Wesley.

1974. Aho, Alfred V., Hopcroft, John E., and Ullman, Jeffrey D. *The Design and Analysis of Computer Algorithms*. Reading, MA: Addison-Wesley.

1976. Wirth, Niklaus, *Algorithms + Data Structures = Programs*. Englewood Cliffs, NJ: Prentice Hall.

JOHN E. HOPCROFT, JEAN E. MUSINSKI, AND ANNE NEIRYNCK

ALGORITHMS, DESIGN AND CLASSIFICATION OF

For articles on related subjects *see* ALGORITHM; ALGORITHMICS; ALGORITHMS, ANALYSIS OF; ALGORITHMS, THEORY OF; COMBINATORICS; COMPUTATIONAL COMPLEXITY; GRAPH THEORY; SEARCHING; and SORTING.

Introduction   Algorithms are a central field of computer science. A great deal of emphasis has been placed on the analysis of algorithms, determining the time and space required for an algorithm during execution. An equally important topic is the design and classification of algorithms.

The design of algorithms attempts to answer the question: "How does one devise an algorithm in the first place?" When faced with a problem for which an algorithm is needed, one might first ask if an algorithm for this problem even exists. (see ALGORITHMS, THEORY OF and UNDECIDABLE PROBLEMS). Although it is very difficult to determine that no algorithm exists for a particular problem, it is usually the case that at least one does—the challenge is to find it. Once an algorithm is found, one can then analyze its time and space efficiency. But that leads to the question of whether another, faster algorithm for this problem exists. So, algorithm design is a subject as important as algorithm analysis.

The study of algorithm design techniques has two important payoffs. First, it leads to an organized way to devise new algorithms. Algorithm design techniques give guidance and direction on how to create a new algorithm. Though there are literally thousands of algorithms, there are very few design techniques. Second, the study of these techniques helps us to categorize or organize the algorithms we know and in that way to understand them better.

The remainder of this article discusses a basic set of design strategies. Each section describes the strategy in general terms and gives one concrete example. It concludes with some well-known algorithms that are specific cases of the design technique.

Divide-and-Conquer   The divide-and-conquer strategy suggests that a problem should be split into subproblems, which are somehow solved, and then the solutions are combined into a solution for the original problem. Usually, the subproblems are solved in the same way—by splitting, solving, and combining—and this can often be done recursively. It is generally advisable to split the problems into roughly equal size subproblems.

An ideal example of divide-and-conquer is *mergesort*, a method for sorting. The method proceeds as follows: divide the set into two approximately equal size sets. Then sort each set individually. Next, take the resulting sorted subsets and merge them to produce a single sorted set for the entire data. The algorithm is recursive so that, to sort one-half of the data, the data is divided into two roughly equal parts, sorted, and then merged. A recursive version of this algorithm written in Pascal is shown in Fig. 1.

Procedure *mergesort* is written to sort the consecutive elements in the array x from index *low* to *high*. The procedure is started with *low* = 1 and *high* = n. If, for some invocation of *mergesort, low* $>=$ *high*, the procedure ends without doing anything. Otherwise, the index of a middle element is computed and assigned to *mid*. This determines two subsets, which are sorted using recursive calls

```
procedure mergesort (var x: afile; low, high: integer);
{the consecutive elements (x[low],..., x[high]) are
sorted.}
var mid: integer;
begin
    if low < high then
        begin
            mid := (low + high) div 2;
            mergesort (x,low,mid); {apply algorithm recursively}
            mergesort (x,mid+1,high); {apply algorithm
                                        recursively}
            merge (x,low,high); {merge the two results}
        end
end; {mergesort}
```

FIG. 1   A Pascal version of Mergesort.

to *mergesort*. We assume that the *merge* procedure is smart enough to merge the two ordered sequences *x[low],...x[mid]* and *x[mid+ 1],...,x[high]* into a single ordered sequence stored in *x[low],...x[high]*.

Additional examples of divide-and-conquer algorithms are quicksort and Strassen's matrix multiplication algorithm (*see* STRUCTURED PROGRAMMING for an implementation of quicksort).

Greedy Method Given a set of inputs and some criteria for determining when a solution is both feasible and optimal, the greedy method suggests an algorithm that works in stages. At each stage, a decision is made regarding whether an input combination is feasible and better or worse than the previous solution. At the end of the final stage, the best solution is obtained. Though greedy algorithms don't always produce the best result, they do work in some cases. Moreover, they are often helpful in deriving approximation algorithms when the optimal algorithm takes intolerably long.

The greedy strategy leads to a simple sorting algorithm that works this way: look at the remaining elements to be sorted, select the smallest, and place it at the end of the list of already sorted elements. This is called *selection sort*, and its computing time on *n* elements is $O(n^2)$.

As an example of how the greedy method can be used to create an approximation algorithm, suppose you have *m* machines, all identical, and you have a set of *n* jobs that need to be carried out on the machines, $n > m$. The times for the *n* jobs vary. You want to schedule the jobs on the machines so as to complete all of the jobs in the shortest time possible. For example, suppose you have three machines and seven jobs with times 13, 13, 13, 14, 14, 15, and 15 hours. One sample schedule would be to place job 1 on machine 1, job 2 on machine 2, and job 3 on machine 3. All three machines will be available after 13 hours, so then we can assign job 4 to machine 1, job 5 to machine 2, and job 6 to machine 3. Finally, job 7 is placed on machine 1. The finish time for this schedule, the time the last job finishes, is 42 hours.

A superior assignment is to place jobs 7 and 5 on machine 1, jobs 6 and 4 on machine 2, and jobs 1, 2, and 3 on machine 3. For this assignment of jobs to machines, the finish time is 39 hours.

The best known algorithm that always finds the optimal (shortest time) assignment of jobs to processors for arbitrary *m, n*, and job times takes exponential time. For most reasonable size problems, that makes the exact solution infeasible. Therefore, an algorithm that produces a reasonably good approximation quickly is desirable. The greedy method provides such a strategy. It suggests that we consider only one job at a time, assigning it to the next processor that becomes free. We add something a little extra, namely that the jobs should first be placed in decreasing (or non-increasing) order. For our example above, that places job 7 on machine 1, job 6 on machine 2, and job 5 on machine 3 at time zero. In 14 hours we can place job 4 on machine 3, and then job 3 on machine 1 and job 2 on machine 2. Finally, job 1 is placed on machine 1. The total time to process all jobs is 41 hours. Ron Graham has shown that this approximation algorithm, using the greedy heuristic, will always produce an answer that is within four-thirds of the optimal result. Thus, the greedy method gives an algorithm whose time is the time required to sort *n* elements and whose answer is thus guaranteed never to get too bad.

Further examples of successful greedy algorithms are optimal storage on tapes, Huffman codes, minimal spanning trees, and finding a shortest path in a graph (*see* GRAPH THEORY).

Dynamic Programming Dynamic programming arises when the only algorithm we can think of is enumerating all possible configurations of the given data and testing each one to see if it is a solution. An essential idea is to keep a table that contains all previously computed configurations and their results. If the total number of configurations is large, the dynamic programming algorithm will require substantial time and space. However, if there are only a small number of distinct configurations, dynamic programming avoids recomputing the solution to these problems over and over.

To determine if there are only a small number of distinct configurations, one needs to detect when the so-called *principle of optimality* holds. This principle asserts that every decision that contributes to the final solution must be optimal with respect to the initial state. When this principle holds, dynamic programming drastically reduces the amount of computation by avoiding the enumeration of some decision sequences that cannot possibly be optimal.

As a simple example, consider computing the *n*-th Fibonacci number, F_n, where $F_n = F_{n-1} + F_{n-2}$, and $F_0 = F_1 = 1$. The first few elements of this famous sequence are 1, 1, 2, 3, 5, 8, 13, 21, 34,...The obvious recursive algorithm for computing F_n suffers from the fact that many values of F_i are computed over and over again. The total time for this recursive version is exponential. However, if we follow the dynamic programming strategy and create a table that contains all values of F_i as they are computed, a linear time algorithm results.

Some examples of dynamic programming algorithms are optimal binary search trees, optimal matrix arrangements, and the all pairs shortest path problem.

Basic Traversal and Search Often, complex objects are stored in a computer using a specific data structure (*q.v.*). The data structure consists of nodes that contain fields. These fields may contain either data or pointers to other nodes. Thus, a particular instance of some object may include many nodes, all connected in an intricate pattern. Some typical examples of objects would be lists, trees, binary trees, and graphs.

Often, one wants to devise an algorithm that computes a function of the data object. The traversal-and-search strategy for developing such an algorithm is to move along the data structure from node to node and collect information. After all nodes have been reached, the final answer should be known.

One simple example is the evaluation of an expression (*q.v.*) stored in a tree. For simplicity, we shall consider a binary tree. Fig. 2 shows such a tree, with its

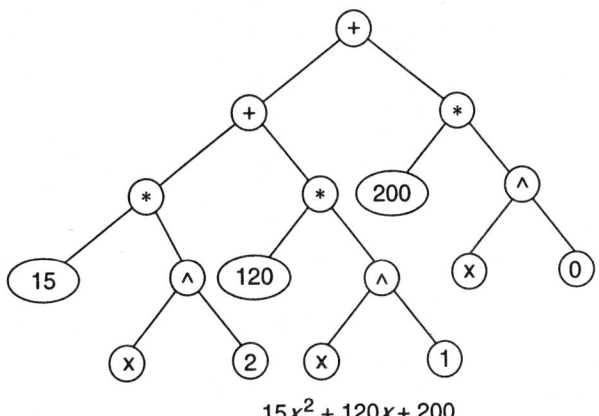

$$15x^2 + 120x + 200$$

FIG. 2 A binary tree containing an arithmetic expression.

contents being the expression shown at the bottom of the figure. In Fig. 3 you see the definition of a binary tree node and a Pascal version of an algorithm that traverses a binary tree in such a way that all children of a node are examined before the node itself. When the program has processed a node's children, it uses the *evalop* procedure to evaluate the operator on its arguments. When the field contains a variable, such as *x*, *evalop* simply stores its value in the *data* field.

Some well-known examples of traversal-and-search algorithms are preorder, postorder, and inorder traversal of binary trees, evaluation of postfix expressions, breadth-first and depth-first traversal of graphs, code optimization, "and/or" graphs of artificial intelligence (*q.v.*), and finding connected and biconnected components of a graph.

Backtracking Backtracking is an appropriate algorithm design strategy when the desired solution is expressible in the form $(x_1,...,x_n)$, where the x_i are chosen from some finite set S_i. Often, the problem calls for finding one vector that maximizes, minimizes, or satisfies some criterion function. Sometimes it seeks all such vectors. If the size of S_i is m_i, there are $m = m_1 \cdots m_n$ n-tuples that are

possible candidates. The brute force approach would generate all of these n-tuples and evaluate each one. The idea of backtracking is to build up the vector one component at a time, using modified functions to test whether the vector being formed has any chance of success. Backtracking becomes most efficient when the modified functions are able to eliminate large sets of possible vectors.

A classic combinatorial problem is to place 8 queens on an 8 × 8 chessboard so that no two "attack" that is, so that no two of them are on the same row, column, or diagonal. Assume that the rows and columns of the chessboard, as well as the eight queens, are numbered 1 to 8. We see that each queen will be on a separate row, so we can represent a solution to this problem by a vector, $(x_1,..., x_8)$, where x_i is the column on which queen i is placed. There are $8^8 = 16,777,218$ tuples, so if an algorithm attempts to enumerate all of these and requires 1/10 of a second to generate each one, the algorithm will require over 19 days to get its answer.

The backtracking solution makes use of two important facts that help to prune the number of vectors it must consider. No two x_i's can be the same (all queens in different columns). This reduces the number of tuples to $8! = 40,320$. No two x_i's can be on the same diagonal. The backtracking algorithm will proceed by generating a tuple so that, if $(x_1,...,x_i)$ has already been picked, x_{i+1} is chosen so that $(x_1,...,x_{i+1})$ represents a chessboard configuration in which no two queens are attacking.

Fig. 4 shows a chessboard on which queens have been placed in columns 1 to 5. But with the configuration shown, no queen can be placed in column 6. So we *backtrack* to column 5 and move the queen down column 5 looking for another "safe" square. However, none exists so we backtrack again to column 4 and move the queen in this column down to row 7, which is also safe. Then we try again to put a queen in column 5, etc. Eventually, we find a solution: (1,1), (5,2), (8,3), (6,4), (3,5), (7,6), (2,7), (4,8). This is one of 92 solutions, 12 of which are really distinct, (i.e. not related to each other by some type of symmetry). All 92 solutions could be found by continuing

```
type btpointer = ^btnode; { btpointer points to btnode}
     btnode = record { a record with 3 fields}
         leftchild : btpointer;
         data : char;
         rightchild : btpointer
     end;


procedure postorder (cnode:btpointer);
{this recursive procedure visits a binary tree in postorder}
begin
    if cnode <> nil then
        begin
            postorder(cnode^. leftchild);
            postorder(cnode^. rightchild);
            evalop(cnode^. data) { take the operator and
                                       apply it}

        end
end; { postorder}
```

FIG. 3 Pascal program for postorder traversal of a binary tree.

FIG. 4 Backtracking in the 8-queens problem.

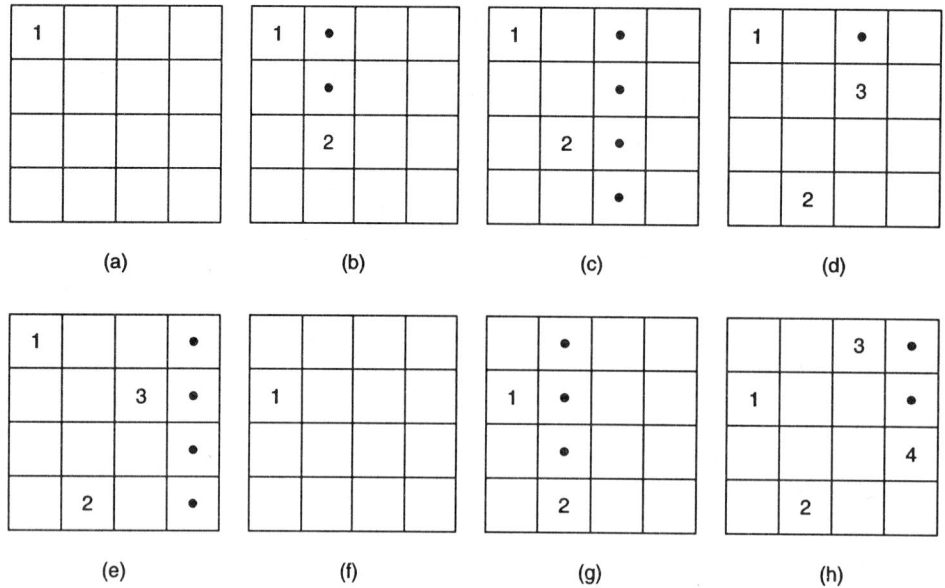

FIG. 5 Arriving at one solution to the 4-queens problem. The dots represent unsuccessful attempts to place a queen. Backtracking occurs after displays (c) and (e).

as above by backtracking to column 7 after each solution is found. Fig. 5 shows the entire backtracking process when we try to place 4 queens on a 4 × 4 board.

Backtracking algorithms have been very successful for games such as checkers and chess. Backtracking is also very valuable for solving various combinatorial optimization problems such as the knapsack and traveling salesman problems (*see* NP-COMPLETE PROBLEMS).

Other Algorithm Design Techniques

Some other design techniques which we can describe only briefly are:

- Branch-and-bound: This design strategy is similar to backtracking in that it attempts to find one or more vectors that satisfy some criteria. It differs in the way that elements of a possible solution are generated and explored. Instead of generating a solution vector element by element, all possible candidates for the next entry are produced and stored in a set. Elements in this set are said to be "alive." One is chosen for expansion, and functions are used to prune the set of candidate elements.

    To see more concretely the difference between backtracking and branch-and-bound, consider again the 4-queens problem. The backtracking algorithm assumed that the first queen is placed on location [1,1] of the chessboard. It then computes a single placement for the second queen. In branch-and-bound, all possible queens in column 1, namely those occupying rows 1, 2, 3, and 4, are produced. These are kept in a list and one is removed (say the queen at position [1,1]). Now all possibilities for the second queen are generated, namely the queens in column 2, rows 1, 2, 3, and 4. The queen in column 2, row 1 is considered and rejected according to the "non-attacking" criteria. In branch-and-bound parlance, this is termed the bounding function. Eventu-

ally, all solutions will be produced. With effective bounding functions, branch-and-bound can be quite efficient.

- Transformation of domain: Sometimes it is easier to transform the data for a problem into another domain, solve the problem in the new domain, and then transform the solution back to the original domain.

    One example is the way a digital computer does arithmetic. Though it accepts and displays numbers using decimal notation, it translates all numbers into binary notation before doing arithmetic on them. It is easier for a computer to work with binary numbers than with decimal numbers.

    Other examples of domain transformation include the Fast Fourier transform (*q.v.*), the Schwartz-Christoffel transformation of complex variable theory, and algebraic operations such as polynomial arithmetic, greatest common divisor calculations, and factorization.

- Preconditioning: If we have an algorithm that we know will be executed many times, sometimes we can improve its speed by precomputing a set of values. As these values are available during execution, the algorithm can work faster.

    Suppose we have a binary tree and we are given a pair of nodes, *i* and *j*. We want to answer the question: is *i* an ancestor of *j*? We could use the algorithm given earlier to traverse the tree and, if *i* is a subtree of *j*, then it must be an ancestor. However, the time for this algorithm is linear in the number of nodes in the tree. Though preconditioning gives us the idea that precomputing some values will give us a faster algorithm, the challenge is to determine what precomputed values would be useful. The idea is to first traverse the tree in preorder and then in postorder, assigning consecutive integers to the nodes as one goes. (In preorder, an integer is assigned the first time a node is reached.) Then i is an ancestor of j if and only if the *preorder(i) <= preorder (j) and postorder(i) >= postorder(j)*. Therefore, if we are given any i, j pair of nodes, only two comparisons are needed to answer the question of ancestry.

Other examples of successful use of preconditioning are repeated evaluation of a polynomial and searching for a pattern within a string (*see* STRING PROCESSING).

References

1966. Nemhauser, G. *Introduction to Dynamic Programming.* New York: John Wiley and Sons.

1976. Lawler, E. L. *Combinatorial Optimization: Networks and Matroids.* New York: Holt, Rinehart, and Winston.

1978. Horowitz, E. and Sahni, S. *Fundamentals of Computer Algorithms.* New York: Computer Science Press, division of W. H. Freeman.

1978. Sahni, S. and Horowitz E. "Combinatorial Problems: Reducibility and Approximation." *Operations Research,* **26,** 4, 718–759.

1984. Bentley, J. "Programming Pearls: Algorithm Design Techniques." *Communications ACM,* **27,** 9, 865–871.

1988. Brassard, G. and Bratley, P. *Algorithmics Theory and Practice.* Englewood Cliffs, NJ: Prentice-Hall.

ELLIS HOROWITZ

ALGORITHMS, THEORY OF

For articles on related subjects *see* ALGORITHM; ALGORITHMICS; ALGORITHMS, ANALYSIS OF; COMPUTATIONAL COMPLEXITY; FORMAL LANGUAGES; NP-COMPLETE PROBLEMS; and TURING MACHINE.

The meaning of the word *algorithm* is somewhat vague. In order to have a *theory of algorithms*, we need a mathematically precise definition of algorithm. Many authors have tried to capture the essence of the intuitive notion of an algorithm. We give four examples.

Hermes (1965). "An algorithm is a general procedure such that for any appropriate question the answer can be obtained by the use of a simple computation according to a specified method....[A] general procedure [is] a process the execution of which is clearly specified to the smallest details."

Minsky (1967). "...an effective procedure is a set of rules which tells us, from moment to moment, precisely how to behave."

Rogers (1967). "...an algorithm is a clerical (i.e. deterministic, bookkeeping) procedure which can be applied to any of a certain class of symbolic *inputs* and which will eventually yield, for each such input, a corresponding symbolic *output*."

Hopcroft and Ullman (1979). "A *procedure* is a finite sequence of instructions that can be mechanically carried out, such as a computer program....A procedure which always terminates is called an *algorithm*."

Note that what Hermes calls "a general procedure" is what Minsky calls an "effective procedure" is what Hopcroft and Ullman call a "procedure." Other terms are also used in the literature, and some authors use the word "algorithm" to denote any procedure whatsoever. In the remainder of this article, the Hopcroft and Ullman terminology will be used.

The notion of a procedure cannot be divorced from the environment in which it operates. What may be a procedure in certain situations may not be considered a procedure in other situations. For example, the instructions of a computer program are not usually understood by most people. Alternatively, the description of a chess game that appears in a newspaper is a perfectly clear algorithm for a chess player who wants to reproduce the game, but it is quite meaningless to people who do not play chess. Thus, when we talk about a procedure as a finite sequence of instructions, we assume that whoever is supposed to carry out those instructions, be it human or machine, understands them in the same way as whoever gave those instructions.

Another sense in which the environment influences the notions of procedure and algorithm is indicated by the following examples. If the instruction requires us to take the integral part of the square root of a number, such an instruction can be carried out if we are dealing with positive integers only, but it cannot always be carried out if we are dealing with both positive and negative integers. Thus, the same set of instructions may or may not be a procedure, depending on the subset of integers for which it is intended. Alternatively, we can easily give a procedure that, given an integer x, keeps subtracting 1 until 0 is reached and then stops. Such a procedure will be an algorithm if we intend to use it for positive integers only, but it will not be an algorithm if we also intend to apply it to negative integers.

The recognition of whether or not a sequence of instructions is a procedure or an algorithm is a subjective affair. No precise theory can be built on the vague definitions given above. In trying to build a precise theory, one must examine the situations in which the notion of algorithm is used. In the theory of computation, one is mainly concerned with algorithms that are used either for computing functions or for deciding predicates.

A *function f* with domain D and range R is a definite correspondence by which there is associated with each element x of the domain D (referred to as the "argument") a single element $f(x)$ of the range R (called the "value"). The function f is said to be *computable* (in the intuitive sense) if there exists an algorithm that, for any given x in D, provides us with the value $f(x)$. An example of a computable function is one that associates, with any pair of positive integers, their greatest common divisor. It is computable by the well-known Euclidean algorithm (Knuth 1973).

A *predicate P* with domain D is a property of the elements of D that each particular element of D either has or does not have. If x in D has the property P, we say that $P(x)$ is true; otherwise, we say that $P(x)$ is false. The predicate P is said to be *decidable* (in the intuitive sense) if there exists an algorithm that, for any given x in D, provides us with a definite answer to the question of whether or not $P(x)$ is true. An example of a decidable predicate over the set of integers greater than 1 is the predicate that determines whether a number is or is not *prime*. An algorithm for implementing this predicate is described by Hopcroft and Ullman (1979).

The computability of functions and the decidability of predicates are very closely related notions because we can associate with each predicate P a function f with range $\{0,1\}$ such that, for all x in the common domain D of P and f, $f(x) = 0$ if $P(x)$ is true and $f(x) = 1$ if $P(x)$ is false. Clearly, P is decidable if and only if f is computable. For this reason we will hereafter restrict our attention to the computability of functions.

A further restriction customary in the theory of algorithms is to consider only functions whose domain and range are both the set of non-negative integers. This is reasonable, since, in those situations where the notion of a procedure makes any sense at all, it is usually possible to *represent* elements of the domain and the range by non-negative integers. For example, if the domain comprises pairs of non-negative integers, as in the case with an arithmetic function of two arguments, we can represent the pair (a,b) by the number 2^a3^b in an effective one-to-one fashion. If the domain comprises strings of symbols over an alphabet of 15 letters, we can consider the letters to be non-zero hexadecimal digits, and assign that non-negative integer to a string that is denoted by the string in the hexadecimal notation. The device of representing elements of a set D by non-negative integers is referred to as *arithmetization* or *Gödel numbering*, after the logician Kurt Gödel, who used it to prove the undecidability of certain predicates about formal logic. From now on we will be exclusively concerned with functions whose domain and range are subsets of the set of non-negative integers.

In order to show that a certain function is computable, it is sufficient to give an algorithm that computes it. But, without a precise definition of an algorithm, all such demonstrations are open to question. The situation is even more uncertain if we want to show that a given function is uncomputable, i.e. that no algorithm whatsoever computes it. In order to avoid such uncertainty, we need a mathematically precise definition of a computable function. One possible way of making the concept precise is to define an appropriate type of machine, and then define a function to be computable if and only if it can be computed by such a machine. This has indeed been done. The machine usually used for this purpose is the *Turing machine (q.v.)*. This simple device has a tape and a read-write head, together with a control that may be in one of finitely many states. The tape is used to represent numbers. A function f is called computable if there exists a Turing machine that, given a tape representing an argument x, eventually halts with the tape representing the value $f(x)$. Since a precise definition of a Turing machine can be given, the notion of a computable function has become a precise mathematical notion.

The question arises whether or not it is indeed the case that a function is computable in the intuitive sense if and only if it is computable by a Turing machine. The claim that this is true is usually referred to as *Church's*

thesis (sometimes as *Turing's thesis*). Such a claim can never by "proved," since one of the two notions whose equivalence is claimed is mathematically imprecise. However, there are many convincing arguments in support of Church's thesis, and an overwhelming majority of workers in the theory of algorithms accept its validity. One of the strongest arguments in support of Church's thesis is the fact that all of the many diverse attempts at precisely defining the concept of computable function have ended up with defining exactly the same set of functions as can be computed by a Turing machine.

Given a precise definition of a computable function, it is now possible to show for particular functions whether they are or are not computable. We will give two examples.

Example 1. Consider the following problem. Give an algorithm that, for any Turing machine, decides whether or not the machine eventually stops if it is started on an empty tape. This problem is called the "blank-tape halting problem." The required algorithm would be considered a *solution* of the problem. A proof that there is no such algorithm would be said to show the (effective) *unsolvability* of the problem.

The blank-tape halting problem is in fact unsolvable. This is proved by rephrasing it as a problem about the computability of a function, as follows: Turing machines can be Gödel-numbered in an effective manner; i.e. there exists an algorithm that for any Turing machine will give its Gödel number. Furthermore, this can be done in such a way that every non-negative integer is the Gödel number of some Turing machine. Let f be the function defined as follows.

$$f(n) = \begin{cases} 0 & \text{if } n \text{ is the Gödel number of a Turing} \\ & \text{machine that eventually stops if} \\ & \text{started on the blank tape;} \\ 1 & \text{otherwise.} \end{cases}$$

It is easy to see that f is computable if and only if the blank-tape halting problem is solvable. The unsolvability of the blank-tape halting problem is proved by showing that the assumption that f is computable leads to a contradiction.

Example 2. Our second example indicates that there are unsolvable problems in classical mathematics. The following problem is known as "Hilbert's tenth problem" (after the German mathematician David Hilbert, 1862–1943):

Given a diophantine equation [an equation of the form $E = 0$, where E is a polynomial with integer coefficients; e.g. $xy^2 - 2x^2 + 3 = 0$] with any number of variables, give a procedure with which it is possible to decide after a finite number of operations whether or not the equation has a solution in integers.

Although this problem was stated by Hilbert in 1900 (long before there was such a thing as a theory of algorithms), only recently did the Russian mathematician I. Matiajasevitch show it to be unsolvable.

That there are clearly defined problems, like the two given above, that cannot be solved by any computer-like device is probably the most striking aspect of the theory of algorithms. A whole superstructure has been built on such results, and there are methods to find out not only whether something is uncomputable, but also how badly it is uncomputable (see Rogers, 1967).

A typical question that one may ask is the following: Suppose we had a device that, for any given Turing machine, told us whether or not the Turing machine will eventually stop on the blank tape. Can we write an "algorithm" that makes use of this device and solves Hilbert's tenth problem? It has been known for some time that such an "algorithm" exists. In this sense, Hilbert's tenth problem is *reducible* to the blank-tape halting problem. It is the proof that the reverse is also true, which gave us the unsolvability of Hilbert's tenth problem. Two problems that are both reducible to the other are said to be *equivalent*. Most of the theory of algorithms has, until recently, concerned itself with questions of the reducibility and equivalence of various unsolvable problems.

In recent years, much of the activity in the theory of algorithms has been concerned with computable functions, decidable predicates, and solvable problems. Questions about the nature of the algorithms, the type of devices that can be used for the computation, and about the difficulty or complexity of the computation have been investigated and are discussed in other articles.

References

1965. Hermes, H. *Enumerability, Decidability, Computability.* Berlin, Germany: Springer-Verlag.

1967. Minsky, M. *Computation: Finite and Infinite Machines.* Englewood Cliffs, NJ: Prentice-Hall.

1967. Rogers, H. *Theory of Recursive Functions and Effective Computability.* New York: McGraw-Hill.

1973. Knuth, D.E. "The Art of Computer Programming; Fundamental Algorithms," 2nd Ed. Reading, MA: Addison-Wesley.

1979. Hopcroft, J.E. and Ullman, J.D. *Introduction to Automata, Languages, and Computation.* Reading, MA: Addison-Wesley.

GABOR T. HERMAN

ALLOCATION, STORAGE. *See* STORAGE ALLOCATION.

ALU. *See* ARITHMETIC-LOGIC UNIT.

AMERICAN ASSOCIATION FOR ARTIFICIAL INTELLIGENCE (AAAI)

For articles on related subjects *see* ARTIFICIAL INTELLIGENCE; EXPERT SYSTEMS; KNOWLEDGE REPRESENTATION; NATURAL LANGUAGE PROCESSING; and ROBOTICS.

Purpose   The American Association for Artificial Intelligence is a scientific society devoted to the study of the theory, knowledge, and mechanisms that underlie intelligent thought and action, and how these can be embedded in computational systems. Founded in 1979 to serve the American Artificial Intelligence (AI) community, by 1991 it had about 13,000 members from all over the world. As a technical society, it is concerned not only with basic research in AI, but with AI applications that increase understanding of the science, and with the integration of AI technology into broader social and computational contexts.

History   Artificial intelligence is a term invented by John McCarthy in 1956 in connection with a conference concerned with computational mechanisms that could lead to intelligent behavior. What those mechanisms are and how to explore the science behind such mechanisms has been evolving since that time. Early in the 1960s, a special interest group on artificial intelligence (SIGART) was founded as part of the ACM and sessions on AI were made part of the ACM national conference. In 1969, the first International Joint Conference on artificial intelligence (IJCAI) was held in Washington, D.C. IJCAI conferences were held in 1971, 1973, and 1975, alternately in North America and overseas. Then in 1977 an organization was formed and incorporated to run further biennial conferences, with a North American venue to be expected every four years.

In 1979, a group of Americans headed by Raj Reddy (general chair of the 1979 IJCAI conference) recognized that the American AI community needed more frequent conferences in the United States each year to report the increasing research in the field. The American Association for Artificial Intelligence was incorporated in 1980, and had its first annual conference that year. The following have served (or will serve) as president of the society:

Allen Newell 1979–80
Edward Feigenbaum 1980–81
Marvin Minsky 1981–82
Nils Nilsson 1982–83
John McCarthy 1983–84
Woodrow Bledsoe 1984–85
Patrick Winston 1985–87
Raj Reddy 1987–89
Daniel Bobrow 1989–1991
Patrick Hayes 1991–1993
Barbara Grosz 1993–1995

Organizational Structure   The AAAI has steadfastly maintained minimal organizational structure. It is run by a council consisting of the president, past president, president elect, and 12 councillors elected at large. It has only one class of membership, with a special lower fee for students. A small number of members are honored by being elected AAAI Fellows each year, with the total number of fellows staying below 2% of the membership. There are currently 97 fellows. Special interest subgroups in medicine, manufacturing, law, and business are supported by specialized mailings.

The administration of the organization has been maintained by a small professional staff. Lou Robinson served as executive director for the first three conferences, and was succeeded by Claudia Mazzetti who held the post for nine years. Carol Hamilton has been managing the office since 1991. Communications can be sent to: AAAI, 445 Burgess Drive, Menlo Park Ca. 94025-3496 USA, Phone: 415-328-3123, FAX: 415-321-4457, Email: aaai-office@aaai.org.

Technical Program: The technical program is run by volunteers within the organization. The major activity of the society is the annual scientific meeting, which has been attended in recent years by 4,000 to 5,000 people. In years in which IJCAI is in North America, AAAI and IJCAI jointly sponsor the meeting. The conference topics include automated reasoning, cognitive modeling, education, enabling technology, knowledge representation, machine learning, mathematical foundations, natural language, robotics, perception and signal understanding, planning and scheduling, reasoning about physical systems, and intelligent user interfaces. This National Conference on Artificial Intelligence also features industrial exhibits, an extensive tutorial program, and a series of specialized workshops. Co-located with the National Conference is a conference on Innovative Applications in Artificial Intelligence. The AAAI also runs Spring and Fall Symposia on leading edge topics, with small groups of 40 to 60 people, and sponsors other small workshops in specialized areas throughout the year.

AAAI publishes the quarterly *AI Magazine*, and provides members with reduced-price access to qualified technical journals, such as *Artificial Intelligence* and *Machine Learning*. Books resulting from conferences, symposia, and workshops sponsored by AAAI are published by AAAI Press, a co-publishing effort with M.I.T. Press.

DANIEL G. BOBROW

AMERICAN FEDERATION OF INFORMATION PROCESSING SOCIETIES (AFIPS)

For articles on related terms *see* AMERICAN SOCIETY FOR IFORMATION SCIENCE; ASSOCIATION FOR COMPUTING MACHINERY; INTERNATIONAL FEDERATION FOR INFORMATION PROCESSING; INSTITUTE OF ELECTRICAL AND ELECTRONIC ENGINEERS—COMPUTER SOCIETY; SOCIETY FOR INDUSTRIAL AND APPLIED MATHEMATICS; and INTERNATIONAL SOCIETY FOR TECHNOLOGY IN EDUCATION.

Objectives The American Federation of Information Processing Societies (AFIPS) was composed of 11 major national professional societies whose members were engaged in all facets of the design, application, and management of information processing systems. Dedicated to non-profit scientific and educational purposes, the Federation acted on behalf of its approximately 240,000 constituents, to work for the benefit of the profession in those areas that did not compete with programs of the member societies and in which working as a Federation was effective because of the larger number of professionals represented.

On 13 October 1990 the AFIPS Board of Directors adopted a set of resolutions which resulted in the dissolution of AFIPS on 31 December 1990. Following this dissolution, the two most significant societies in AFIPS, ACM and the IEEE Computer Society, engaged in discussions on how to handle the continuing obligations of AFIPS, particularly the U.S. representation in IFIP (*q.v.*). In 1991, these two societies formed a new joint committee FOCUS (Federation on Computing in the United States) with the purposes of representing U.S. computing interests in IFIP as well as fostering cooperation among the two societies and others that may join FOCUS in the future.

AFIPS's primary objectives were to:

- Promote cooperation, educational programs, and information exchange in the field of information processing among educational and scientific societies, the U.S. Congress and various U.S. government agencies, and the public at large.
- Provide leadership in the organization and conduct of educational and scientific information processing activities.
- Develop and promote integrity and competence in the information processing professions.
- Serve as the official U.S. representative to the International Federation of Information Processing (IFIP).

Activities AFIPS was chartered in 1961 for the purpose of providing a structure in which professional societies with a primary interest in information processing could join forces for their mutual benefit. Its membership grew to 11 organizations, representing a wide gamut of professional activities in the computing field. The Federation carried out programs to promote the integrity and effectiveness of the profession. These activities included sponsoring major computer conferences and seminars, publishing books and periodicals on current and historical developments in the field, working with entities of the U.S. government to provide accurate and timely information on computer-related activities, and acting as the official U.S. representative to IFIP.

How Established AFIPS was organized as an unincorporated society on 10 May 1961. It was the outgrowth of the National Joint Computer Committee, which had been established ten years earlier to sponsor the Joint Computer Conferences. The AFIPS founding societies were the American Institute of Electrical Engineers and the Institute of Radio Engineers (which later merged into the Institute of Electrical and Electronic Engineers), and the Association for Computing Machinery.

The presidents who held office at AFIPS were:

Morton M. Astrahan, 1956–1958
Harry H. Goode, 1959–1960
Morris Rubinoff, 1960–1961
Willis Ware, 1961–1962
J. D. Madden, 1963
Edwin L. Harder, 1964–1965
Bruce Gilchrist, 1966–1967

Paul Armer, 1968
Richard I. Tanaka, 1969–1970
Keith W. Uncapher, 1971
Walter L. Anderson, 1972
George Glaser, 1973–1975
Anthony Ralston, 1975–1976
Theodore J. Williams, 1976–1978
Albert S. Hoagland, 1978–1980
J. Ralph Leatherman, 1980–1981
Sylvia Charp 1982–1983
Stephen S. Yau 1984–1985
Jack Moshman 1986
Eddie Ashmore 1987
Howard Funk 1988–1990

Organizational Structure   There were two classes of AFIPS participation: member societies, which had a principal interest in computers and information processing, and affiliated societies, which, although not principally concerned with computers and information processing, did have a major interest in this field. Each of the societies published a professional journal and held an educational conference. The total membership of the 11 constituent societies exceeded 240,000.

In 1989, the 11 constituent societies of AFIPS were:

The Association for Computing Machinery, Inc. (ACM)
The IEEE Computer Society
Data Processing Management Association (DPMA)
Society for Computer Simulation (SCS)
The American Society for Information Science (ASIS)
Association for Computational Linguistics (ACL)
Society for Information Display (SID)
American Statistical Association (ASA)
Society for Industrial and Applied Mathematics (SIAM)
Instrument Society of America (ISA)
Int'l. Society for Technology in Education (ISTE)

The Federation was managed by its Board of Directors. Each member society had one to three directors, depending on size. The President was the principal officer of the Federation and the Executive Director was the senior paid officer. Other AFIPS officers included a vice-president, secretary, and treasurer. Meetings of the Board of Directors were usually held twice a year to elect member and associate member societies, to act on constitutional amendments, and to conduct other pertinent business.

ISAAC L. AUERBACH

AMERICAN SOCIETY FOR INFORMATION SCIENCE (ASIS)

For an article on a related subject *see* AMERICAN FEDERATION OF INFORMATION PROCESSING SOCIETIES.

Purpose   The American Society for Information Science is a not-for-profit professional association organized for scientific, literary, and educational purposes, and dedicated to the creation, organization, dissemination, and application of knowledge concerning information and its transfer, with particular emphasis on the applications of modern technologies in these areas.

An auxiliary purpose of the Society is to provide its members with a variety of channels of communication within and outside the profession, including meetings and publications, and with a service organization to help them in their professional development and advancement.

How Established   ASIS was founded on 13 March 1937, as the American Documentation Institute (ADI) when Watson Davis, director of Science Service (which was operated out of the National Academy) and one of the first Americans to become interested in documentation as a separate field of endeavor, invited approximately 35 documentalist colleagues to meet with him at the National Academy of Sciences. ADI was made up of individuals nominated by and representing affiliated scientific and professional societies, foundations, and government agencies, of which there were 68 in 1937. In 1952, the bylaws were amended to admit individual as well as institutional members. By vote of the membership on 1 January 1968, the name was changed to American Society for Information Science, to indicate its concern with all aspects of the information-transfer process.

The following individuals have held the office of president.

Watson Davis, 1937-1943
Keyes D. Metcalf, 1944
Waldo G. Leland, 1945
Watson Davis, 1946
Waldo G. Leland, 1947
Vernon D. Tate, 1948-1949
Luther H. Evans, 1950-1952
E. Eugene Miller, 1953
Milton O. Lee, 1954
Scott Adams, 1955
Joseph Hilsenrath, 1956
James W. Perry, 1957
Herman H. Henkle, 1958
Karl F. Heumann, 1959
Cloyd Dake Gull, 1960
Gerald J. Sophar, 1961
Claire K. Schultz, 1962
Robert M. Hayes, 1963
Hans Peter Luhn, 1964
Laurence B. Heilprin, 1964-1965
Harold Borko, 1966
Bernard M. Fry, 1967
Robert S. Taylor, 1968
Joseph Becker, 1969
Charles P. Bourne, 1970
Pauline Atherton, 1971
Robert J. Kyle, 1972
John Sherrod, 1973
Herbert S. White, 1974
Dale Baker, 1975

Melvin S. Day, 1976
Margaret Fischer, 1977
Audrey Grosch, 1978
James Cretsos, 1979
Herbert Landau, 1980
Mary Berger, 1981
Ruth L. Tighe, 1982
Charles H. Davis, 1982-83
Donald W. King, 1984
Bonnie C. Carroll, 1985
Julie A. C. Virgo, 1986
Thomas H. Hogan, 1987
Martha E. Williams, 1988
W. David Penniman, 1989
Toni Carbo Bearman, 1990
Tefko Saracevic, 1991
Ann Prentice, 1992

Organizational Structure   The ASIS Council, the governing body of the Society, is composed of 15 individuals: 13 hold office by election; the other two are ex officio.

The Council meets four times a year, in January, April, July, and during the Annual Meeting in the last quarter of the year. ASIS membership now totals nearly 4,000 individuals (including about 500 students) and more than 50 institutions.

ASIS has chartered 21 Special Interest Groups (SIGs) that provide those members with similar professional specialites the opportunity to exchange ideas and information about current and specialized developments. Special Interest Groups include the following areas.

Arts and Humanities (AH)
Automated Language Processing (ALP)
Behavioral and Social Sciences (BSS)
Biological and Chemical Information Systems (BC)
Classification Research (CR)
Computerized Retrieval Services (CRS)
Education for Information Science (ED)
Foundations of Information Science (FIS)
Human-Computer Interaction (HCI)
Information Analysis and Evaluation (IAE)
Information Generation and Publishing (PUB)
International Information Issues (III)
Law and Information Technology (LAW)
Library Automation and Networks (LAN)
Management (MGT)
Medical Information Systems (MED)
Numeric Data Bases (NDB)
Office Information Systems (OIS)
Personal Computers (PC)
Storage and Retrieval Technology (SRT)
Technology, Information,and Society (TIS)

The headquarters of ASIS are located at 1424 16th Street, N.W., Suite 404, Washington, DC 20036

Technical program   The technical and professional activities of ASIS extend from the work of the Special Interest Groups and the 27 regional chapters and 27 stu-dent chapters to such activities on the national scale as operating a placement service and conducting Annual and Mid-Year Conferences.

Annual awards are presented for the Best Information Sciences Book, the Best Publication by an ASIS chapter or Special Interest Group, the Best Paper Published in the *Journal of the American Society for Information Science,* the Outstanding Information Sciences Movie, the Best ASIS Student Member Paper, and the Award of Merit, which is presented to a member of the profession who is deemed to have made a noteworthy contribution to the field of information science. Recipients of the Award of Merit are:

Hans Peter Luhn (posthumously), 1964
Charles P. Bourne, 1965
Mortimer Taube (posthumously), 1966
Robert A. Fairthorne, 1967
Carlos A. Cuadra, 1968
Cyril W. Cleverdon, 1970
Jerrold Orne, 1971
Phyllis Richmond, 1972
Jesse Shera, 1973
Manfred Kochen, 1974
Eugene Garfield, 1975
Lawrence Heilprin, 1976
Allen Kent, 1977
Calvin Mooers, 1978
Frederick G. Kilgour, 1979
Claire K. Shultz, 1980
Herbert S. White, 1981
Andrew A. Aines, 1982
Dale B. Baker, 1983
Joseph Becker and Martha Williams, 1984
Robert Lee Chartrand, 1985
Bernard M. Fry, 1986
Donald W. King, 1987
F. Wilfrid Lancaster, 1988
Gerard Salton, 1989
Pauline Atherton Cochrane, 1990
Roger K. Summit, 1991

ASIS Publications include the following:

Journal of the American Society for Information Science (JASIS)
Bulletin of the American Society for Information Science
Annual Review of Information Science and Technology (ARIST)
Proceedings of the ASIS Annual Meetings
ASIS Handbook and Directory

ISAAC L. AUERBACH

AMERICAN STANDARD CODE FOR INFORMATION INTERCHANGE. *See* ASCII.

ANALOG COMPUTER

For articles on related subjects see ANALOG-TO-DIGITAL AND DIGITAL-TO-ANALOG CONVERTERS; CONTROL APPLICATIONS; DIFFERENTIAL ANALYZER; DIGITAL COMPUTERS; HYBRID COMPUTERS; NUMERICAL ANALYSIS; and SIMULATION.

Background The history of the analog computer goes back to antiquity, when tax maps were first reported as being used for assessments and surveying. However, this article is confined to the analog computer as it evolved in the period from World War II to the present time. (For those interested in the history of the analog computer from antiquity to World War II, the reader is referred to an excellent article by J. Roedel, 1955.)

Between World Wars I and II, much work was done in developing the mechanical *differential analyzer*, a close relative of the modern analog computer. Simultaneous equation solvers and harmonic analyzers of many types appeared in the 1920s and 1930s. Special computers in the form of network analyzers for the simulation of power networks appeared around 1925. The network analyzer is a passive analog element. A scale model of the particular network to be studied is made with resistors, capacitors, and inductors. The early network analyzers could be used only to investigate steady-state problems, i.e. voltage drops along lines, possible current flow in lines, etc. The more recent network analyzers can be used to investigate transient conditions during faults or switching on networks. These may be considered true general-purpose computers.

George H. Philbrick worked on an all-electronic analog computer in the mid-1930s and is credited by many to have first used feedback amplifier theory to develop the operational amplifier (see Holst, 1971). He envisioned the analog computer as an electronic model of the system to be studied. Independently of and shortly after Philbrick's first work, the Bell Telephone Laboratories developed the M-9 Gun Director under the impetus of the then impending World War II. The M-9 computer was a union of electronic analog computation and the mechanical differential analyzer. The first published work seems to have been handbooks accompanying the M-9 Director.

Following World War II, J. B. Russell of Columbia University brought the electronic circuitry used in the M-9 Gun Director to the attention of J. Ragazzini and others. Basing their work on the operational amplifier used in the M-9 Gun Director, Ragazzini, Randall, and Russell (1947) built an all-electronic d-c analog computer.

Immediately thereafter, several companies designed and developed analog computers for their own use and for sale to others. In 1948, Reeves Instrument Co., under a Navy contract, built the forerunner of the first commercially available analog computer.

Many companies have entered and left the analog computing field since its birth in 1948. By 1992 almost all purely analog computers had been replaced by *hybrid computers* or purely digital systems.

Types of Analog Computers Fig. 1 shows the classification system used to characterize analog computers. The two main branches of analog computers are direct (special-purpose) and indirect (general-purpose) computers, as shown in the figure.

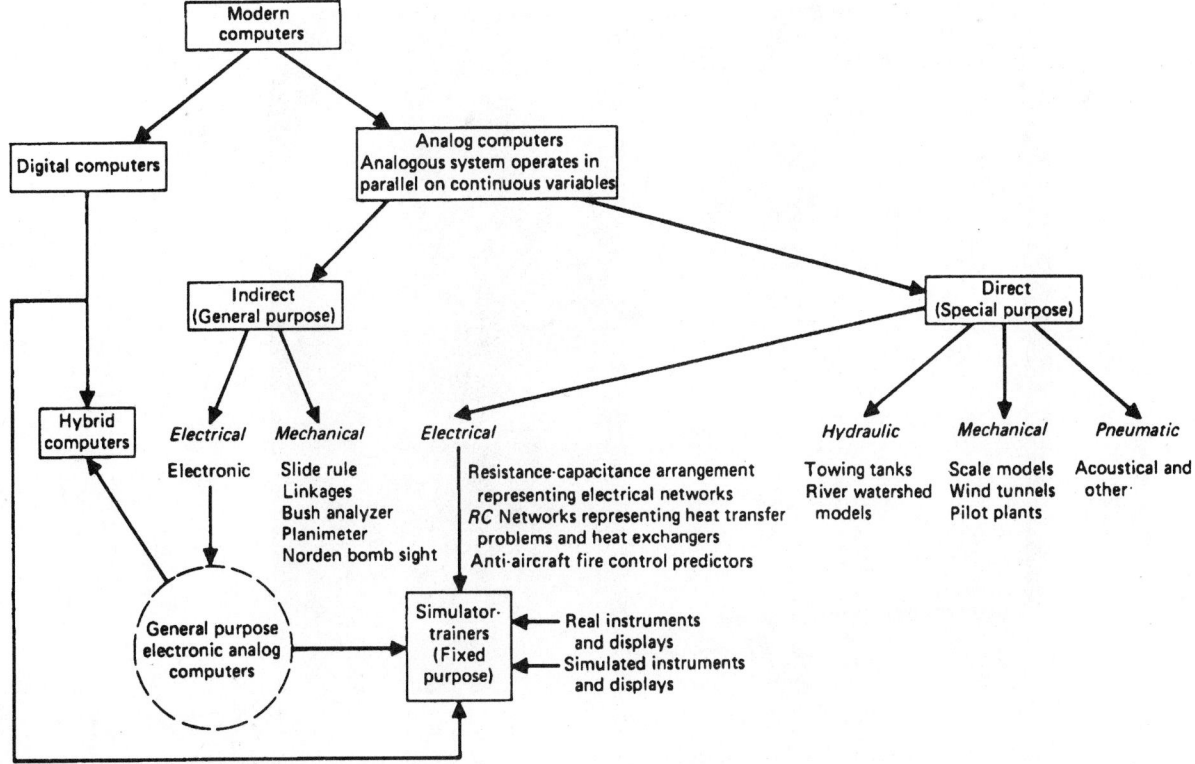

FIG. 1. Types of analog computers.

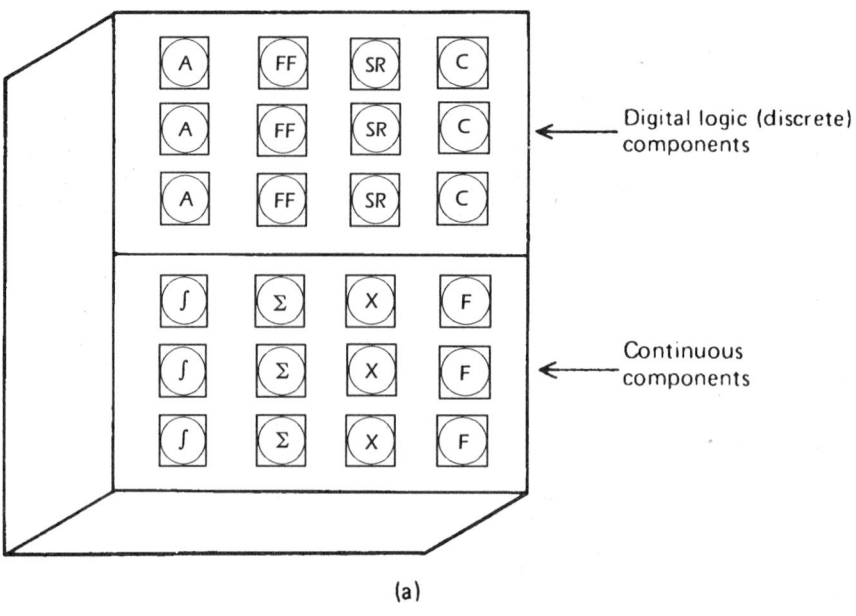

(a)

(b)

FIG. 2. Analog computers (a) Analog computer with continuous and discrete components organized in parallel fashion. (b) One of the last purely analog computing systems, EAI Model 2000. (Courtesy Electronic Associates, Inc., W. Long Branch, NJ.)

Direct Analog Computer Direct analog computers are used in the solution of so-called field problems, e.g. conductive and convective heat transfer, fluid flow, and structures. The equations for these types of problems are partial differential equations (q.v.). A *thermal analyzer* is an example of a direct analog computer that can be used in the solution of parabolic and elliptic type equations such as

$$\frac{\partial^2 \phi}{\partial x^2} = k \frac{\partial \phi}{\partial t}, \quad \frac{\partial^2 \phi}{\partial x^2} = 0$$

This type of computer has resistors and capacitors (and units that compute the fourth power of x for radiation studies). For the hyperbolic equation $\partial^2 \phi / \partial x^2 = k(\partial^2 \phi / \partial t^2)$, which describes structures, vibrating membranes, beams, etc., one might use a similar computer that has resistors, capacitors, inductors, and transformers. Both types are relatively special-purpose computers, and are usually referred to in the analog field as *passive analog computers*.

The programming techniques of the direct analog computer and its associated problems are a subject in themselves and will not be dealt with here, except to remark that the fundamental mathematical theory of programming these partial differential equations involves finite-difference techniques.

Indirect Analog Computer The electronic differential analyzer, hereafter referred to as the *analog computer*, is best suited for the solution of systems of ordinary differential equations. In mathematical terms the analog computer gives particular solutions to systems of linear or non-linear differential equations of many variables.

Combined Direct and Indirect Analogs One area of study in which the analog computer is particularly useful is the so-called real-time simulation problem. In such a problem, there is a requirement that the solution proceed exactly in step with real time because a person and/or equipment may be part of the overall computing loop. Such simulations allow realistic hardware testing as well as training and evaluation of complex human-machine systems. In these instances, there is a combination of the direct analog (a human is the direct analog of itself, and hardware is its own best direct analog) and the indirect analog (the general-purpose analog computer).

This combination of computers is also called *fixed purpose* when the computing system is designed to be dedicated to real-time simulation. This is the largest and most rapidly growing application of analog computing. These systems are known as *simulator-trainers*, and are widely used in such fields as aircraft/spacecraft pilot training, naval ship operator training, nuclear reactor operator training, power plant operator training, and process plant operator training.

The Modern Analog Computer The modern analog computer consists of a large number of individual components, organized in such a manner that the inputs and outputs of these may be interconnected by a program-

mer-user. Fig. 2(a) shows a schematic representation of a computer as seen by a programmer. The main continuous components are *integrators*, represented in the figure by the symbol $\int$; *summers*, represented by Σ; *multiplier/dividers*, represented by $\times$; and *arbitrary function generators*, represented by F. The modern analog computer also contains a number of discrete components such as "and" gates, represented in the figure by A; flip-flops, FF; shift registers, SR; and counters, C.

The inputs and outputs of all elements are brought to a central patch bay into which removable patch boards (or problem boards, prepatch panels) and outputs of these may be inserted. In turn, the patch boards are patched or plugged by the programmer, using patch cords (or plugs). These cords and plugs, when inserted, essentially specify the interconnections of the analog components to solve a particular problem. (See Korn, 1972.) A photograph of a recent medium-scale analog computer is shown in Fig. 2(b).

Voltage Range. Large-scale, general-purpose analog computers once used a voltage range of ±100 volts. However, the advent of the integrated circuit operational amplifier (op amp) has led to the development of many low-cost 10-volt systems, particularly for simulator-trainers. These systems now far outnumber the ±100-volt systems.

The high-voltage range has the advantage of good signal-to-noise ratio and relative insensitivity to small offsets and biases that are caused by components such as diodes (in multipliers). The low-voltage range has the advantages of generally greater bandwidth (higher frequency response), lower power requirements, and lower cost.

Accuracy. The accuracy of an analog computer is usually specified by its component accuracies. The linear components in high-quality computers have errors of less than 0.01% of value or full scale, as appropriate. For example, a resistor may have an error of 0.01% of its value, but a multiplier has a fixed minimum error, which is usually stated as a percent of its full-scale output. In the latter case the error changes with the output of the multiplier. The nonlinear components may have errors of 0.02% of full scale. Lower quality computers may have component errors as much as ten times larger than those given above.

The overall accuracy of an analog solution depends not only on the quality (accuracy) of the analog components used, but also on the manner in which they are used (the program), as well as on the method of formulating the problem (analysis). If best practices are used throughout the programming process, the overall error of analog solutions to large problems is on the order of 0.1–0.5% for the best quality computers. Since most analog solution outputs consist of recordings on X—Y plotters or strip-chart time-history recorders, the analog solution accuracy is of the same order as the accuracy of the usual output recording devices. The analog computer, however, is well matched for the job it is intended to perform, since it is used almost exclusively for the solution of engineering and scientific problems or in simulator-trainers, in which much of the input data is empirically determined, generally to less accuracy than the analog computer solutions thereto. For a detailed discussion of error analysis of analog programs, see Hausner (1971).

Capacity. Modern self-contained analog computers may have any capacity, from the very smallest sold today (such as ten amplifiers and ten potentiometers) to the largest capacities currently being sold as single units, which have a capacity generally measured as 250–300 amplifiers, 200–300 potentiometers, 60 multipliers, 20–40 function generators, and significant quantities of digital logic devices, such as comparators, flip-flops, "and" gates, "one-shots," shift registers, and counters. If a larger capacity than that available in a single unit is required in a single problem, then two or more units may be connected together to form a single, large, analog computing system. Analog computing systems containing more than 1,000 amplifiers have been successfully assembled.

A common use of analog computers occurs as a major portion of a *hybrid computer*. Hybrid computation generally enlarges the equivalent capacity of the analog part of the system by a factor of about 2. This is due to the mix of high-frequency and low-frequency parts of a problem. If a hybrid computer problem were put on an all-analog machine, it would usually require at least twice as much analog equipment as that required in the hybrid solution.

Basic Concepts

The Operational Amplifier

General

The operational amplifier is the basic component in the analog computer. It can be used in a "summing mode" to perform the operations of inversion, summation, and multiplication by a constant. It can also be used in an "integrating mode" to integrate a voltage or the sum of a number of voltages. The change from one mode of operation to another is determined by the feedback element around the amplifier.

The Fundamental Relationship

To understand the basic operations performed by the amplifier, consider the block diagram in Fig. 3. Associated with the high-gain amplifier are the input and feedback networks, having impedances of Z_i and Z_f, respectively. Now let the voltages at the input, the output, and the amplifier grid be V_i, V_0, and E, respectively. Using Kirchoff's and Ohm's laws, we may write

$$\frac{V_0 - E}{Z_f} + \frac{V_i - E}{Z_i} = i_s \tag{1}$$

where i_s is the grid current. By definition

$$\frac{V_0}{E} = -A \tag{2}$$

where $-A$ is the amplifier gain, and A is usually greater than 10^4.

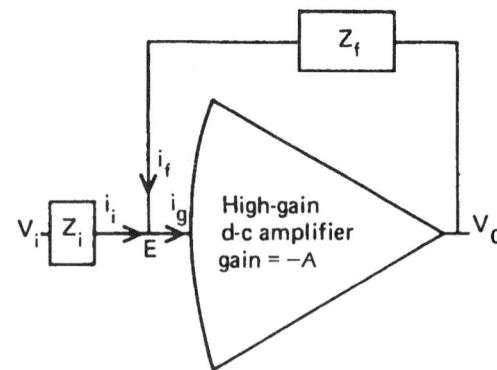

FIG. 3.   Block diagram of an operational amplifier.

A further property of the high-gain amplifier is that the current i_s is at least a factor of 10^4 smaller than i_i, so that i_s can be set equal to zero; consequently, E is a voltage that is much smaller (by at least a factor of 10^4) than either V_i or V_0 so that $E \simeq 0$. Then

$$\frac{V_0}{V_i} = -\frac{Z_f}{Z_i} \tag{3}$$

This is the fundamental relationship in analog computation. The output voltage will not be affected by the internal characteristics of the amplifier; it will be governed by, and its accuracy will be dependent upon, the accuracy of the input and feedback elements.

Inversion   When both Z_i and Z_f are resistors, the amplifier output will be a constant times the input voltage. If both are equal, the constant is unity and we have an inverter, as shown in Fig. 4.

To represent an inverter on computer circuit diagrams, the symbol shown in Fig. 5 is used. Fig. 5 is the "shorthand notation" for Fig. 4. Note that the number 1 at the input to the amplifier signifies a gain of 1. The change in sign is inherent with the amplifier.

Summation   If several input resistors are connected to a summing junction SJ at the grid of an amplifier and voltages are applied to them, as shown in Fig. 6, then

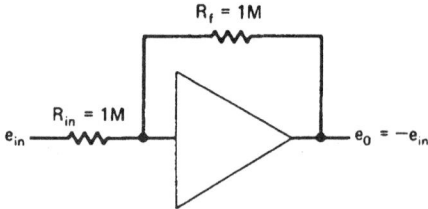

FIG. 4.   The inverting amplifier (M = megohm).

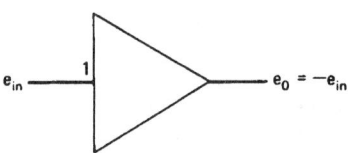

FIG. 5.   The symbol for the inverting amplifier.

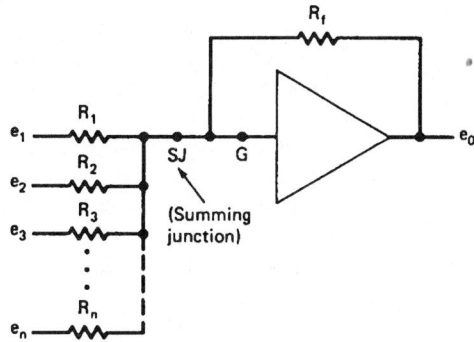

FIG. 6. The summing amplifier.

(owing to the fact that the grid voltage of the amplifier is effectively at zero potential) no single input will interfere with any other input, and their effects on the output will be independent of one another. It is easily derived, then, that

$$e_o = -\left(\frac{R_f}{R_1}e_1 + \frac{R_f}{R_2}e_2 + \frac{R_f}{R_3}e_3 + \dots + \frac{R_f}{R_n}e_n\right) \quad (4)$$

The resulting output is therefore minus the sum of the input voltages, each multiplied by a constant depending upon the ratio of the resistors involved.

From experience it was found that the most convenient values for the input resistors are 1M (1 megohm) and 0.1M for 100-volt computers. The resistors are correspondingly smaller on lower voltage computers. A typical summming amplifier with three 1 M and three 0.1 M resistors is shown in Fig. 7. These give gains of 1 and 10, as shown on the symbol for the summing amplifier in Fig. 8.

Integration with Respect to Time Integration of an input voltage is obtained if a capacitor is substituted as the feedback component (Fig. 9).

Since the grid current i_g is zero, the current i through the input resistor R must pass through the feedback capacitor C, and will produce a potential difference between the output and grid of the amplifier. Thus, in Fig. 9,

$$i = \frac{e_i}{R} \quad (5)$$

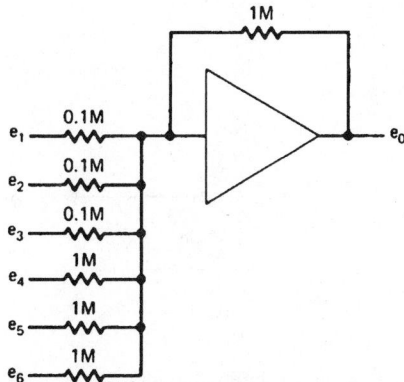

FIG. 7. Example of a summing amplifier.

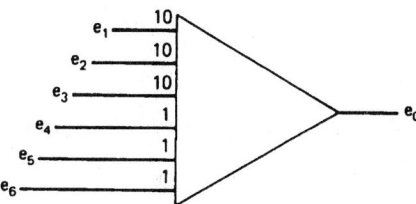

FIG. 8. Symbol for the summing amplifier.

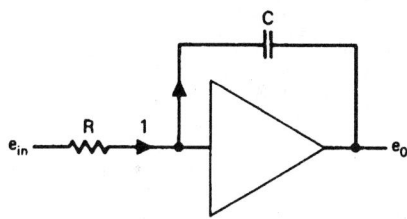

FIG. 9. Operational amplifier with capacitor feedback and resistor input.

and

$$e_0 = \frac{q}{C} = -\int_0^t \frac{1}{C}i\,dt, \quad (6)$$

where q = charge on the capacitor and C = capacitance, usually expressed in microfarads (uf). Thus,

$$e_0 = -\frac{1}{RC}\int_0^t e_i\,dt. \quad (7)$$

Alternatively, using operational notation for the impedances,

$$\frac{e_0}{e_i} = -\frac{Z_f}{Z_t} = -\frac{1}{RCp}$$

where $p = d/dt$. Therefore,

$$e_0 = -\frac{1}{RC}\int_0^t e_i\,dt.$$

Note that the proportionality factor RC is actually a time constant that, if we make $R = 1M$ and $C = 1\mu f$ (i.e. a time constant of 1 sec), will produce an integration rate of 1 volt/sec when e_i is equal to 1 volt.

Modern analog computers are equipped with integrators that have a variety of selectable time constants. The range of time constants normally encountered is from 10 sec (for very slow real-time solutions) to 100 µs (for very fast iterative and/or repetitive solutions).

Several inputs may be connected to produce the integral of the sum of a number of voltages. Figs. 10 and 11 show a typical integrating amplifier and its equivalent symbol. There is also an input terminal for inserting independent initial conditions on each integrator.

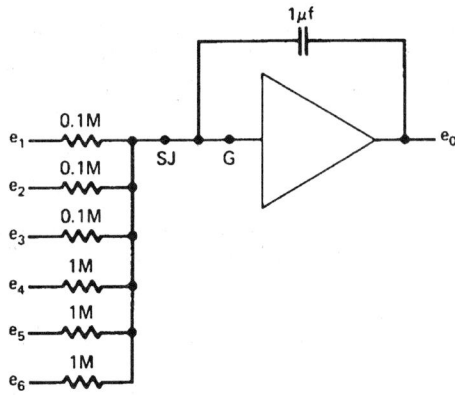

FIG. 10.   A typical integrating amplifier.

Control Modes

Ordinary Modes

Reset   This mode produces a solution at $t = 0$. All derivative terms are disconnected from the grids of the integrating amplifiers, and initial condition networks are connected by control relays or electronic gates. (For a description of IC circuitry, see Korn and Korn, 1972.)

Operate   This mode produces the time-variant solution. Derivative terms are connected to integrator grids, initial condition networks are disconnected, and capacitors associated with integrators are connected to the grids of integrator amplifiers.

Hold   This mode provides a stationary solution at $t = T$ (HOLD may be selected manually by operator or selected by a computer for a previously defined value of t). Derivative terms and initial condition networks are disconnected from the integrators, capacitors remaining associated with integrators.

Repetitive Operation

In this mode all integrators are switched or cycled automatically from reset-to-operate to reset-to-operate, etc.

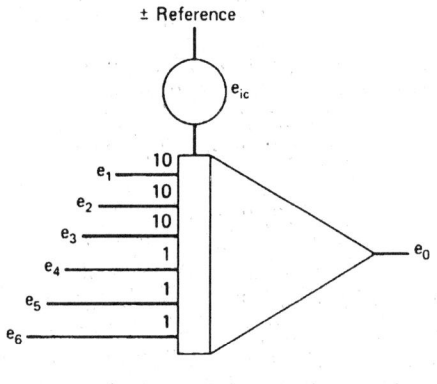

$$e_0 = \mp e_{ic} - \int_0^t (10e_1 + 10e_2 + 10e_3 + e_4 + e_5 + e_6)dt$$

FIG. 11.   The symbol for the integrating amplifier of Fig. 10, including the initial condition.

This mode is usually associated with high solution speeds, of the order of milliseconds in duration, and with the solution displayed on an oscilloscope. When such is the case, the user will obtain the impression that a solution is obtained "instantaneously." However, it is not necessary that high solution speeds be associated with repetitive operations. All that is required is the automatic cycling of the computer between the reset and operate modes for predetermined lengths of time.

Iterative Operation

This mode may appear to be similar to the repetitive mode, but it differs from it in several respects. In iterative operation, there are usually at least two, sometimes more, speeds of operation. For example, one portion of the computer may be operating at a high speed while another portion is operating at low speed. This simply requires the ability to control the integrations, either individually or in groups. The concept of "iteration" enters when the result of one speed of computation is allowed to affect the progress and/or solution of the other speed(s). This "feedback," or iterative, concept is often used in optimization, adaptive control, prediction, the solution of certain types of partial differential equations, and boundary value problems.

Multiplication by a Constant

Potentiometers

Multiplication by a positive constant less than unity can be achieved with a potentiometer. The most common "pots" on 100-volt computers are ten-turn, 30,000-ohm, linear, wire-wound potentiometers with one end connected to ground, as shown diagrammatically in Fig. 12. They can be used either in conjunction with the reference to obtain a fixed accurate voltage less than the reference or in conjunction with a signal voltage to multiply that voltage by any constant less than unity. For example, if $+100$ volts is applied to the high end of the pot, as shown in Fig. 12, the output at the wiper will be k times 100 volts, where $k = R_1/R_T$ (neglecting the effect of external loading).

The Potentiometer Symbol   Two forms of potentiometer or, as it is sometimes called, attenuator, are shown in Fig. 13; both electric circuits and analog programming symbols are shown.

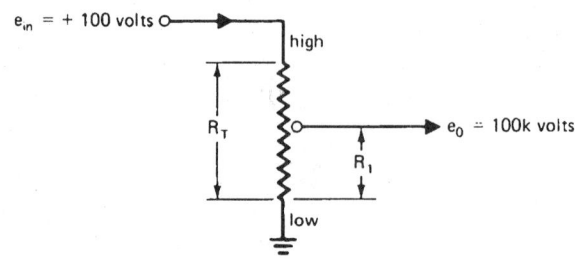

FIG. 12.   Schematic of a potentiometer shown with $+100$ volts connected to the input side to give an output at the wiper of $+100\,k$ volts, where $k = R_1/R_T$.

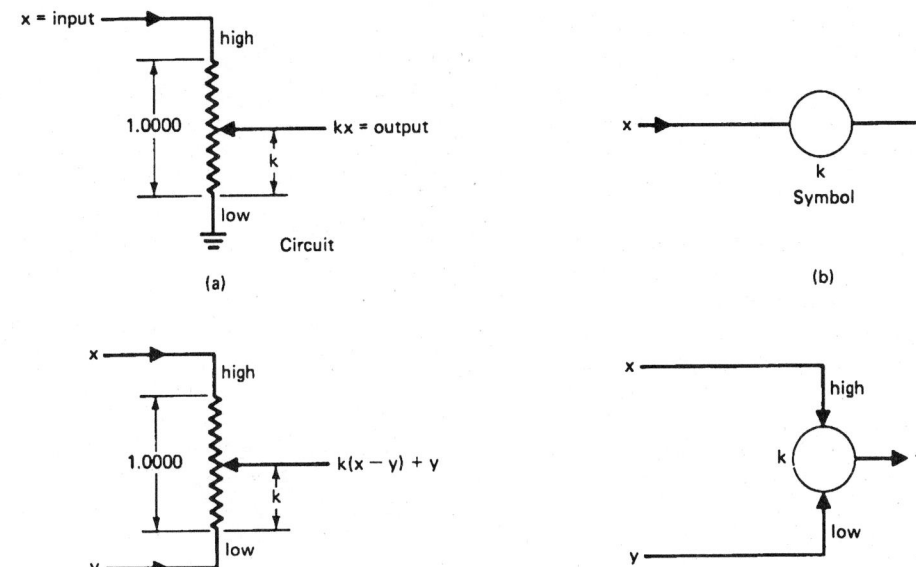

FIG. 13. Here, (b) is the symbolic representation of the attentuator shown schematically in (a); (d) is the symbol used to represent the ungrounded attentuator shown schematically in (c).

Pot-Set Mode In order to set pots to their proper values under true load conditions, a special control mode called *pot set* is supplied in most analog computers. In this mode, the SJ (input resistors) are disconnected from the grid of the operating amplifier (see Figs. 6 and 10), and the SJ are grounded. Under these conditions, there will be no inputs to the amplifiers that could cause an amplifier overload while a pot is being set, for in order to set a pot a reference must be applied to its input terminal. Note that the load seen by the pot is the same as under normal operation, for in normal operation the grid voltage E is so small that it can be considered to be the same as if it were at ground potential, the potential at which the summing junction is held during *pot set*.

Digital Coefficient Attenuators (DCA)

This component is a hybridized version of a potentiometer that permits very rapid setting of coefficient values, under digital computer control, in less than 10 μs. This unit is also known as a digital-to-analog multiplier (DAM) in some versions.

AMPLIFIER AND POTENTIOMETER CIRCUITS

Addition, Subtraction, and Sign Inversion

Amplifiers Only

Circuits are shown in Fig. 14.

Arbitrary Gains (using pots), Including Multiplication and Division by a Constant

Circuits providing these functions are shown in Fig. 15.

Rule for High-Gain Amplifiers with Feedback

High gain with feedback is expressed as

Σ input voltages multiplied by gains = 0

This rule is true because of the high gain ($>10^4$) of the amplifier. Assume for the moment that there is a small net voltage at the grid (even 1 mv). The high-gain amplifier would amplify this small voltage to more than full scale of the amplifier output, which would cause the amplifier to saturate. However, in order to prevent this saturation, there must be a compensating or balancing negative feedback from the high-gain amplifier to its own input, so that for some output of the high-gain amplifier there will be an exact balance or "null" at the input, thus leading to the rule given above. This rule is illustrated in Fig. 15, where, by invoking the rule above, we have

$$ax + 10by + \frac{e_0}{K} = 0 \tag{8}$$

so that $e_o = -K(ax + 10by)$, as indicated in Fig. 15.

Integration Circuits Several types of integration circuits are shown in Fig. 16.

Application to Linear Differential Equations
While the analog computer is most useful in solving complex, nonlinear differential equations, it is instructive to consider a linear differential equation example to learn how it is programmed.

The Bootstrap Method. Consider a mechanical system with a sinusoidal forcing function

$$F(t) = y(t) = A \sin \omega t, \tag{9}$$

where $F(t)$ is acting on a body of mass m, which is restrained by a spring of stiffness k, and a "velocity type" damper with damping constant c. This system is shown in Fig. 17.

If x is the displacement of the body from its equilib-

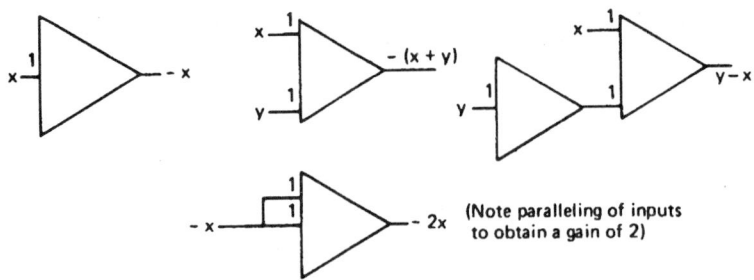

FIG. 14.

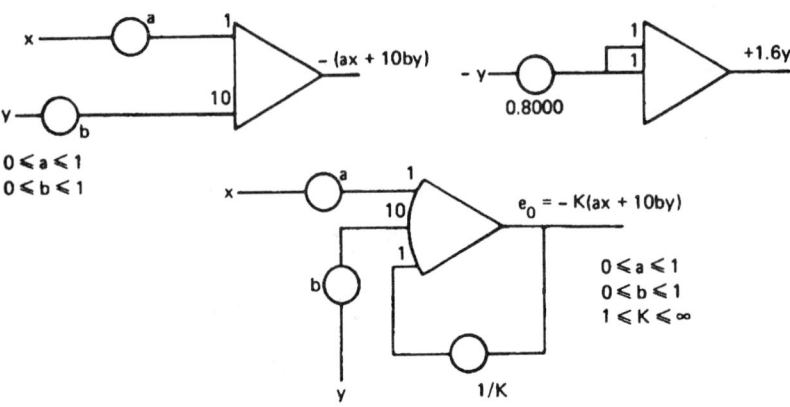

FIG. 15.

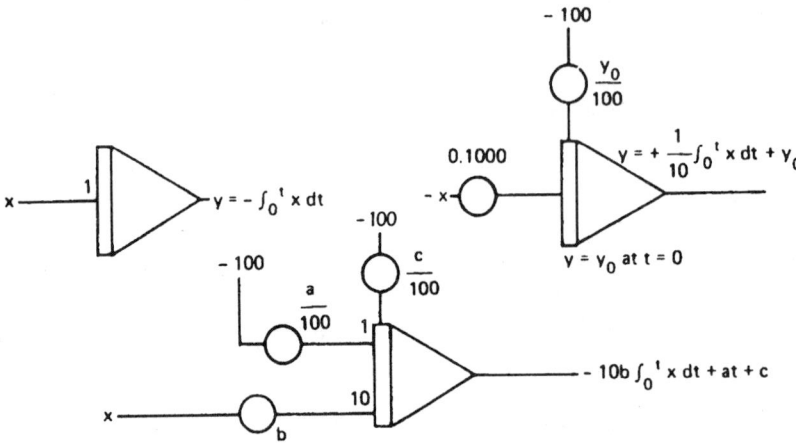

FIG. 16. Integration circuits.

rium position, the forces acting upon the body may be written as follows:

External force = $F(t) = y$,
Spring force = $-kx$,
Damping force = $-c$(velocity) = $-c(dx/dt)$.

The equations to be solved are

$$m\frac{d^2x}{dt^2} + c\frac{dx}{dt} + kx = y(t) \tag{10}$$

and

$$\frac{d^2y}{dt^2} + \omega^2 y = 0 \tag{11}$$

The solution to Eq. 11 is the desired sinusoid.

The bootstrap method assumes that the terms for generating the highest-order derivatives of each variable are available. To execute the bootstrap method, the equations are rewritten in the form

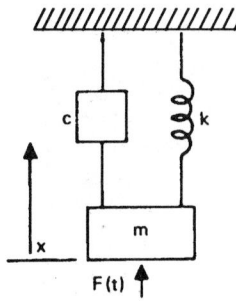

FIG. 17.

$$\ddot{x} = -\frac{c}{m}\dot{x} - \frac{k}{m}x + \frac{y}{m} \qquad (12)$$

$$\frac{\ddot{y}}{\omega^2} = -y \qquad (13)$$

where

$$\ddot{x} = \frac{d^2x}{dt^2};\ \ddot{y} = \frac{d^2y}{dt^2};\ \dot{x} = \frac{dx}{dt},\ \text{etc.}$$

The symbolic analog computer diagram for Eqs. 12 and 13 is shown in Fig. 18.

Using the necessary summers, integrators, inverters, and pots, the inputs to the derivatives are generated and the diagram of Fig. 18 becomes that of Fig. 19.

The initial condition for $-y/\omega$ is obtained from

$$-\frac{1}{\omega}\frac{d}{dt}(A\sin\omega t)\ \text{at}\ t = 0 \qquad (14)$$

An alternative method is to sum the acceleration terms for $\ddot{x}$ directly into the $\dot{x}$ integrator. This saves one summing amplifier, as shown in Fig. 20. The y circuit remains the same, since no saving of amplifiers would occur in that circuit.

NONLINEAR OPERATIONS

Multiplication and Division of Variables

The Quarter Square Multiplier

Consisting of a number of diode-resistor networks, coupled with op amps, this device can produce high-accuracy products of two variables, at frequencies up to 1 Khz. Its fundamental operation is derived from the relation.

$$\frac{1}{4}(X + Y)^2 - \frac{1}{4}(X - Y)^2 = XY. \qquad (15)$$

For example, quarter-square multiplication could be mechanized, as shown in Fig. 21. The boxes marked FG are function generators (described in the next section), which here have the property of producing the square of the input variable.

General-purpose analog computers have quarter-square multipliers with fixed squaring networks that can be used for either one product or two squares. Here we adopt the convention that the multiplier has all the necessary hardware and therefore can be regarded as a "black box." The symbol for multipliers is shown in Fig. 22.

The Transconductance Multiplier

Consisting basically of a number of transistor-resistor networks, this device can produce the best high-frequency-accuracy product available today. Manufactured in high volume, using integrated circuit and laser trimming techniques, it is also the lowest cost multiplier available (see Sheingold, 1978).

Squaring

Squaring is accomplished by connecting the same variable to both inputs of a multiplier, as shown in Fig. 23.

Division and Square Root by Use of Implicit Arithmetic

A nonlinear component may be used in the feedback loop around high-gain amplifiers to perform the inverse of the operation that the component performs in the forward loop configuration. The most frequent use of this technique is in division and square root circuits with multipliers.

Square Root   Refer to Fig. 24. Let

$$\varepsilon = X - Z^2 \qquad (16)$$

and assume that, for a high-gain amplifier, the output is related to the input grid voltage

$$Z = A\varepsilon \qquad (17)$$

where $A > 10^8$. Eliminating ε,

$$X - Z^2 = \frac{Z}{A} \approx 0. \qquad (18)$$

Therefore,

$$Z = X^{1/2} \qquad (19)$$

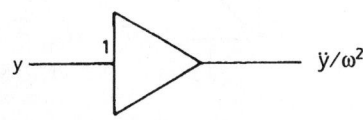

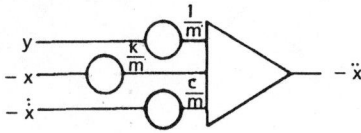

FIG. 18.

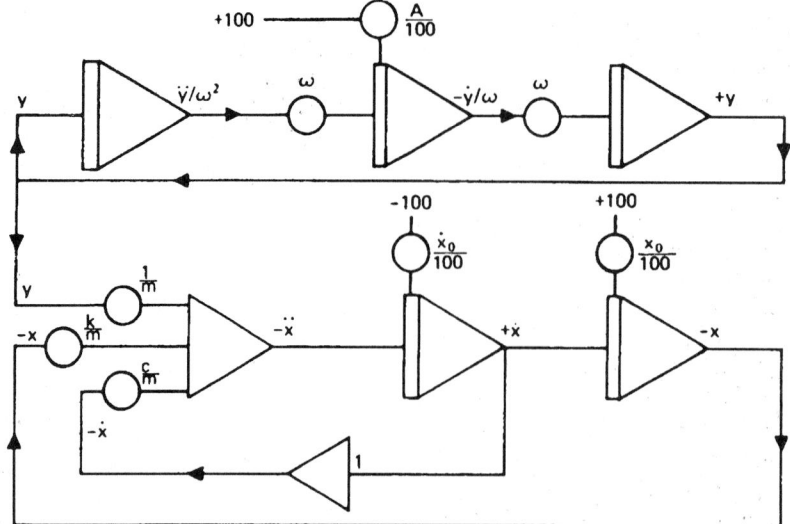

FIG. 19.

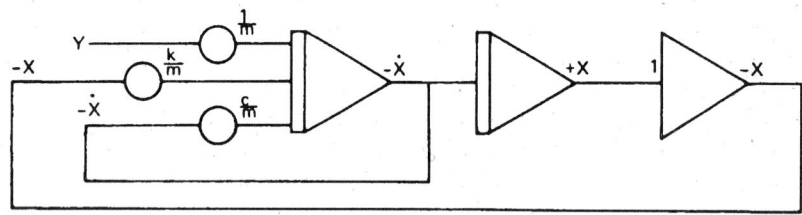

FIG. 20.

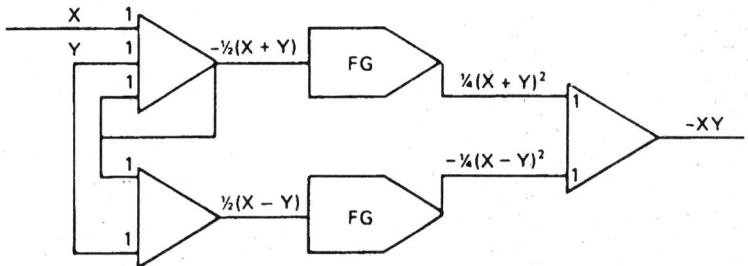

FIG. 21.   Quarter-square multiplication.

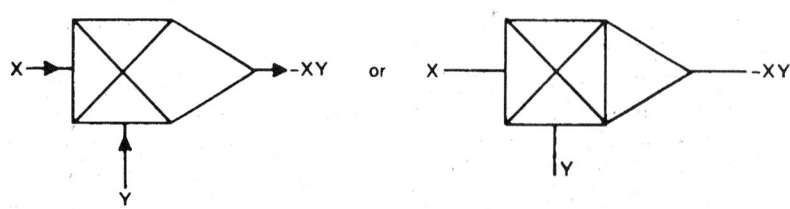

FIG. 22.   Multiplier symbol (note the sign inversion).

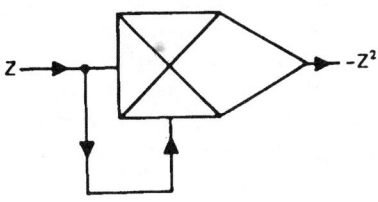

FIG. 23. Squaring circuit.

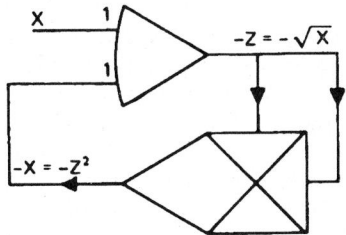

FIG. 24. Square root circuit (X >0).

For stability, the feedback loop must have an odd number of inversions of the signal so that the sum of the currents through the input resistors to the amplifier grid is equal to zero (ε). It is this rule that allows the determination of the sign of the output, which would otherwise be indeterminate.

Note that a squaring device has the property of acting as a sign changer for only one sign of the input variable. In analog multipliers there is usually a built-in sign inversion, as described previously under "Amplifier and Potentiometer Circuits," so that analog squarers act as sign inverters for positive inputs only. Consequently, in the square root circuit the squarer counts for zero inversions, since when Z is negative the output $-Z^2$ is also negative. The one inversion in the circuit is the high-gain amplifier producing $-Z = -(X)^{1/2}$.

Note also that the circuit is stable only for $X > 0$. For values of $X < 0$, an additional inverter must be placed in the feedback loop, and the output of the high-gain amplifier becomes $+Z = (-X)^{1/2}$.

Since modern analog computers have provision for automatically converting a multiplier to a square root circuit, a convenient symbol to use is shown in Fig. 25.

Division Circuit Similarly, for division (Fig. 26), let

$$\varepsilon = Y - XZ, \quad Z = A\varepsilon$$
$$y - XZ = Z/A \simeq 0, \quad Z = Y/X.$$

Note that X must be positive but that Y can be of either sign. Also note that the negative of X must be brought to

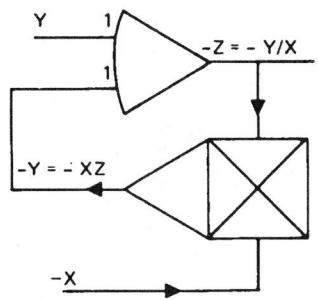

FIG. 26. Division circuit (X >0).

the multiplier terminal in order to satisfy the stability rule described above for the square root circuit.

Since some analog computers have provision for automatically converting a multiplier to a divider, a convenient symbol to use is shown in Fig. 27.

Special Multiplier Hookups

Some multipliers have provisions for obtaining special sign-sensitive squares and square roots, which are important in fluid flow phenomena. As an example, take the case of the flow of fluid through an orifice, which is proportional to the square root of the pressure drop across the orifice. If the reverse flow is to take place, it is necessary to implement the equation

$$Q = \text{sign}(\Delta P) (\Delta P)^{1/2} \qquad (20)$$

Similarly, drag forces acting on bodies moving through fluids are generally proportional to the square of the relative velocity between body and fluid, and are opposite in sign to the direction of motion. It is necessary to implement the equation

$$C_{\text{drag}} = -\text{sign}(V) \cdot V^2. \qquad (21)$$

By a simple patch change on modern analog computers, the two operations exemplified by Eqs. 20 and 21 are directly implemented without requiring any special logic-switching operations. Since these are direct analog outputs, convenient symbols may be used, as shown in Fig. 28. Note that the two special multiplier hookups in Fig. 28 apply only to squaring and extracting square roots.

Function Generators There are two types of function generators commonly in use today, diode function generators (DFG), and digitally controlled function generators (DCFG). These are used to insert, or input, arbitrary func-

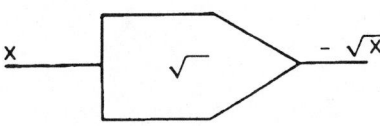

FIG. 25. Symbol for square root circuit.

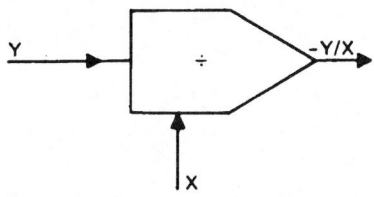

FIG. 27. Symbol for divider.

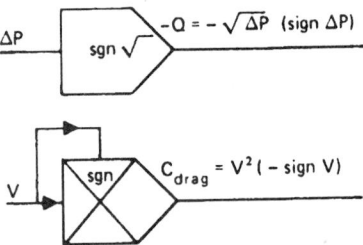

FIG. 28. Other convenient nonlinear programming symbols.

tions of one variable, using a piecewise linear approximation on from 10 to 20 arbitrarily spaced points in the independent variable.

The Diode Function Generator

This component, which has been available since 1955, accomplishes the FG operation by the circuitry shown in Fig. 29, using the techniques discussed in the next section, "Simulation of Discontinuities."

By modifying the dead-space circuit (refer to the later discussion "Simulation of Discontinuities"), thus making both signs of the input and reference voltages available, one can choose "breakpoints and slopes" at will, as shown in Fig. 30.

The circuit works as follows: If X is positive, the lower diode is biased beyond cutoff (rendered non-conducting = open circuit) so that only the upper diode circuit can contribute. In the region $0 \leq X \leq$ b.p. (where b.p. is the breakpoint setting of the upper b.p. pot), the upper diode is also biased beyond cutoff so that there is no input to the Y amplifier (both input diodes are on open circuit).

This is also shown in the characteristic graph of Y versus X in Fig. 30(b); i.e. there is no output Y between zero and the breakpoint. Now, when X is positive and greater than the upper breakpoint, the output of the upper b.p. pot will be positive, increasing linearly with X from a zero value when X is at the breakpoint value; see Fig. 13(d). The slope of the output characteristic will be determined by the slope pot. Note that the input to the Y amplifier is positive, thus creating the negative output Y as shown on the characteristic graph. In a similar manner, it can be shown that, when X is negative, the upper diode is always biased beyond cutoff, and that the lower diode will also be cut off for $-$b.p. $\leq X \leq 0$, where b.p. is the breakpoint setting of the lower b.p. pot. At this point the analysis of the lower circuit is identical to the upper circuit since $- X$, the input to the lower circuit, is now a positive voltage.

To obtain positive output values Y [in the upper two quadrants of Fig. 30(b)], it is only necessary to reverse the polarity of the diode connection while at the same time changing the polarity of the reference voltage on the corresponding breakpoint pot.

By combining the two circuits in Figs. 29-30, we have a circuit that produces an output function $Y(X)$. i.e. a superposition of the two functions. A coefficient pot from the negative reference voltage is added so that $Y_0 \neq 0$ (see Fig. 31). By extension of this technique, straight-line segment approximations are obtained for a wide variety of arbitrary functions. The symbol for an arbitrary function generator of one variable is shown in Fig. 32.

The Digitally Controlled Function Generator

The digitally controlled function generator (DCFG) is a hybrid computing device, now supplied as a fully self-con-

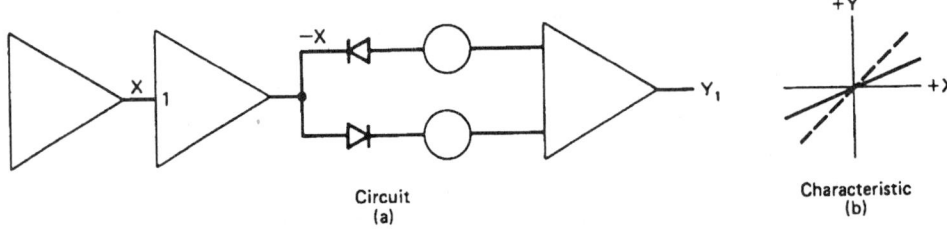

FIG. 29. Diode circuit for output slope change at origin.

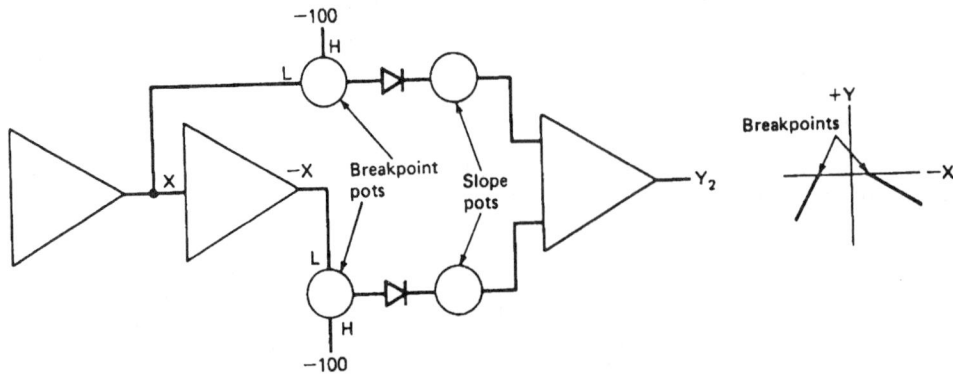

FIG. 30. Diode circuit for output slope changes away from the origin (see Fig. 13(d) for three-terminal pot).

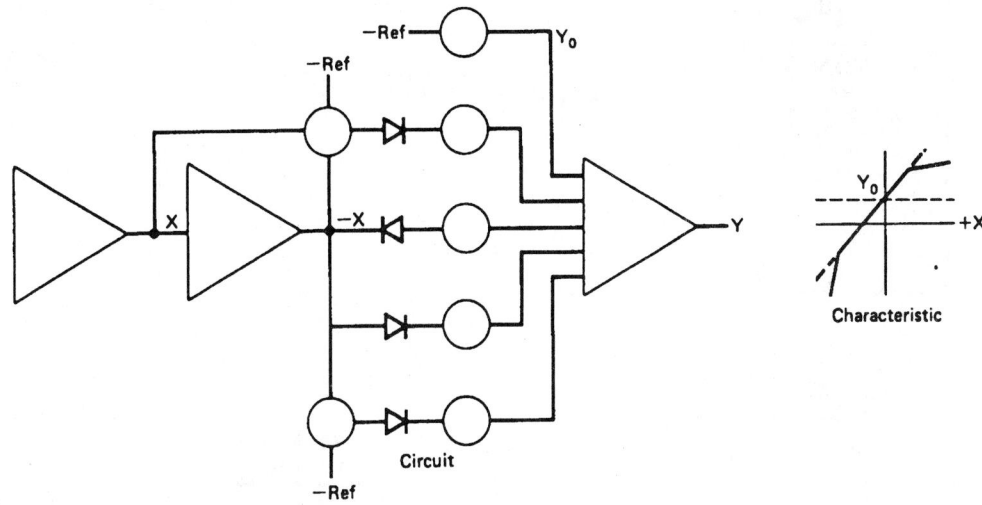

FIG. 31. Complete DFG circuits, including bias pot Y_0.

tained unit in existing analog computers. It consists of a small, high-speed core memory (to contain the function data points) and multiplying digital-to-analog converters, organized as shown in Fig. 33.

The function $f(x)$, to be generated, is computed by a linear interpolation between function values $f(x_i)$ and $f(x_{i+1})$, where x_i is a general "breakpoint" value. The number of breakpoints is typically 20, and they can be unequally spaced.

If x is the independent (input) variable, then

$$\Delta x = \frac{x - x_i}{x_{i+1} - x_i} \qquad (22)$$

is the normalized value of x in the interval $[x_i, x_{i+1}]$. The equation used to generate $f(x)$ is then

$$f(x) = \Delta x\, f(x_{i+1}) + (1 - \Delta x)f(x_i). \qquad (23)$$

In Fig. 33, the independent variable $-x$ (at the lower left) is summed with a digital-to-analog converter (DAC) containing x_i, and is divided by a multiplying DAC (MDAC) containing $x_{i+1} - x_i$. The output of this circuit is Δx, defined in Eq. 22. The output Δx is subtracted from the reference, forming $1 - \Delta x$, and both Δx and $1 - \Delta x$ are fed to the MDAC (at top of figure) containing $f(x_{i+1})$ and $f(x_i)$, respectively, thus forming the output $f(x)$.

The control and logic for changing the digital data in the DAC and MDAC are shown in the lower right of Fig. 33. Here, Δx enters two comparators (see later section, "The Analog Comparator"), one sensing when Δx is less than zero, the other sensing when Δx is greater than the refer-

ence. Both logic outputs are connected to priority interrupt lines in the processor containing the digital data $f(x_i)$ and x_i, $i = 1$ to n.

One comparator triggers a downdate of the index i and the other triggers an update of the index i. Whenever a trigger occurs, the appropriate values of x_i, $x_{i+1} - x_i$, $f(x_i)$, and $f(x_{x+1})$ are transferred within a few memory-cycle times to the appropriate DAC and DMAC, thus allowing the circuit generating $f(x)$ to be correct in all intervals $x_{i+1} - x_i$.

Special Function Generators (Fixed-Function Generators)

Certain functions such as exponentials, sines and cosines, squares, and cubes recur so often in engineering and scientific studies that it has been found useful to build fixed-function generators for these operations.

Exponential Log Generator Perhaps the most flexible method for generating an exponential is to use a fixed-function generator from which any exponential can be generated. The symbol for such a device is shown in Fig. 34. Using this device, it is possible to generate any exponential by employing the logarithm generator in the feedback of a high-gain amplifier, thus obtaining the inverse operation (or antilog). (This is analogous to using a multiplier in the feedback of a high-gain amplifier to obtain division).

For example, to generate the exponential Ae^{cx}, where A and c are constants and x is a variable, let $y = Ae^{cx}$. Then

$$\log_e y = \log_e A + cx. \qquad (24)$$

The circuit for forming the $\log_e y$ from Eq. 24 is shown in Fig. 34(b). Inserting this sum into a high-gain amplifier, which has a $\log_e$ generator in its feedback path, will take the antilog of the input, thus producing the desired output y.

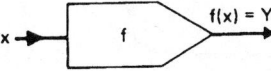

FIG. 32. Function generator symbol.

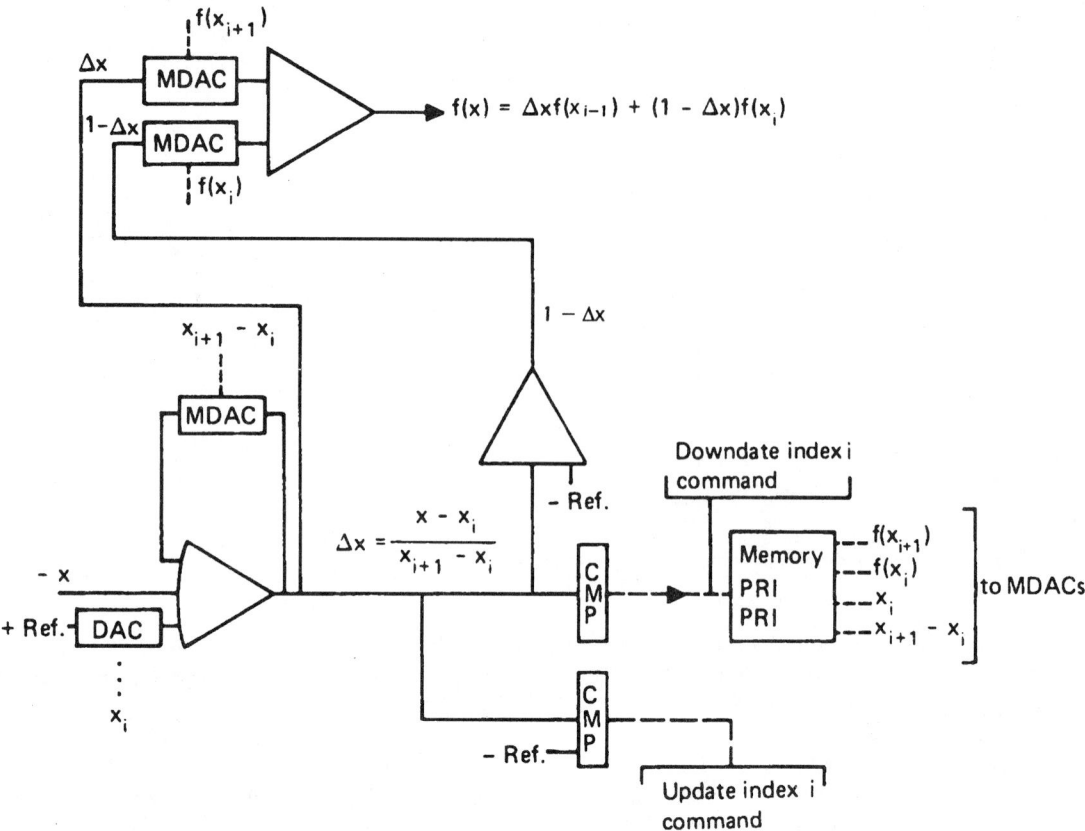

FIG. 33. Digitally controlled function generator.

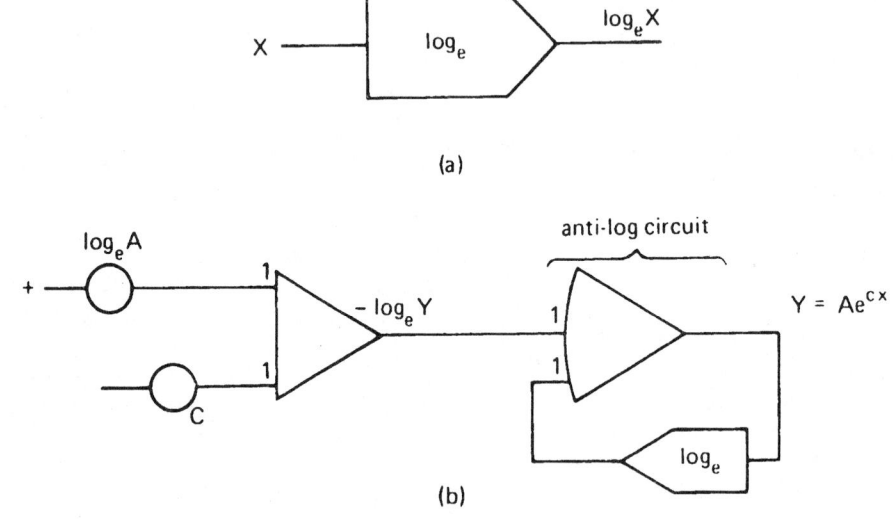

(a)

(b)

FIG. 34. Fixed function generator for generating the natural logarithm of a variable. (a) Symbol. (b) Circuit.

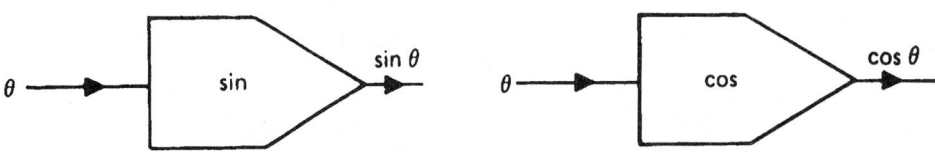

FIG. 35. The sin/cos generators.

The DCFG can easily generate the fixed function just described by loading the appropriate function table in its memory. As the cost of the DCFG comes down, it will replace the diode function generator because of its ease of set-up, convenience in storing function tables for later use, and flexibility of use for math functions or arbitrary (empirical) functions.

The Resolver (Sine-Cosine Generator) A resolver is actually a combination of computing elements, including provisions for generating $\sin \theta$ and $\cos \theta$, given θ as an input, and also allowing for the multiplication of both $\sin \theta$ and $\cos \theta$ by any other variable V, thereby generating $V \sin \theta$ and $V \cos \theta$. This device is an outgrowth of servomultiplying technology, wherein it was a relatively simple matter to change a linear pot to a sine or cosine pot (padded-pot technique) and (by applying $\pm V$ to the endpoints of the padded pot) to obtain $V \sin \theta$ and $V \cos \theta$. Modern computers, however, usually have a fixed (electronic) function generator or a DCFG to generate either the sine or the cosine function. This is shown symbolically in Fig. 35.

It is, of course, still possible to combine the preceding operation with electronic multipliers to obtain $V \sin \theta$ and $V \cos \theta$. If one merely has a sine or cosine generator, then it is termed a "sinusoid" generator to include both functions (since it requires only a single patching change to obtain either function). If the sinusoid generators are intimately packaged with the multipliers to allow direct generation of $V \sin \theta$ and $V \cos \theta$, given V and θ as inputs, then the package is called a "resolver."

$\dot{\theta}$ ***Rate Resolver*** A rate resolver allows the insertion of $\dot{\theta}$, instead of θ, into a resolver input terminal,

and $\sin \theta$ and $\cos \theta$ will be automatically produced. This is simply accomplished by inclusion of an integrator within the resolver package, which will integrate $\dot{\theta}$ and produce θ.

Continuous Rate Resolver The normal allowed range of input to the sinusoid generator (SG) is ± 180 deg. If θ should go larger than this—as, for example, in continuous rolling and/or tumbling—then a switch is incorporated on the rate input, which changes the sign of the θ input to the resolver integrator whenever $|\theta_i|$ reaches 180 deg. At the same time, the sign of $\sin \theta$ is changed. This follows from the relations

$$\theta = n\,(360°) \pm \theta_i, \quad |\theta_i| < 180°,$$
$$\sin \theta = \pm \sin \theta_i, \quad \cos \theta = \cos \theta_i,$$
$$\text{Input to SG} = \theta_i,$$

where $n = \pm 0, 1, 2$, etc.

The $\pm$ signs depend upon whether n is odd or even and whether θ is increasing or decreasing. A time history of θ and θ_i for increasing θ is shown in Fig. 36.

In particular, if $n = 1$ and $\theta = 360° - \theta_i$ and $\sin \theta = -\sin \theta_i$, then a sign change must occur at the output of the sine generator for odd n. Similarly, when $\theta = 360° - \theta_i$, then $\cos \theta = \cos \theta_i$, which is correct for all n. The circuit is shown in Fig. 37.

Polar Resolution The object here is, given the x and y components of a vector (or a complex variable), to find R, the magnitude of the vector, and θ, the angle that the vector makes with the X-axis. This is accomplished by forming the error equation $\varepsilon = x \sin \theta - y \cos \theta$, which, as can be seen from the geometry of the

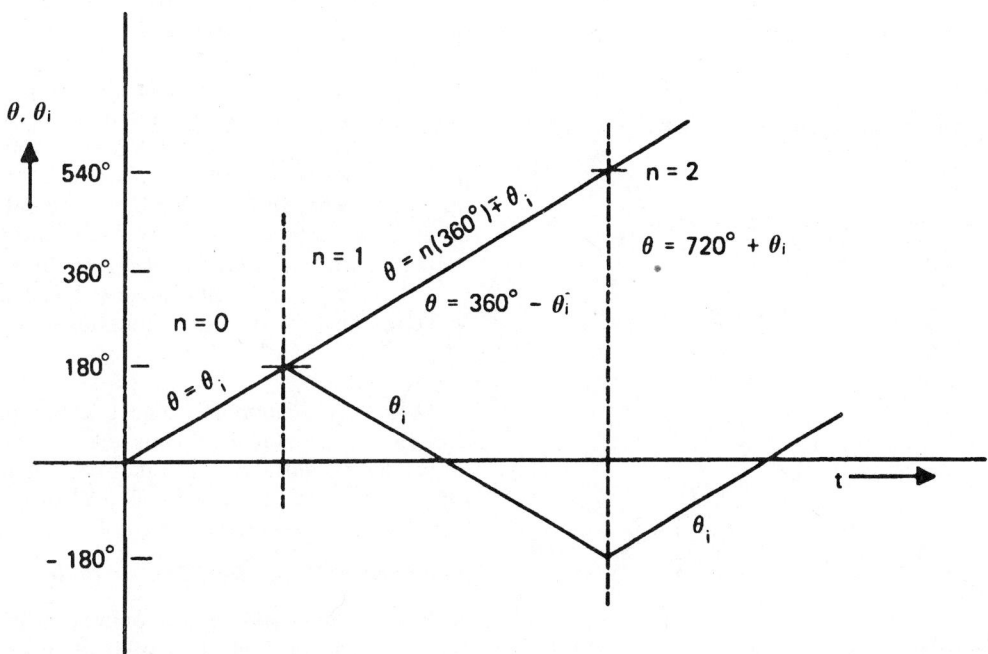

FIG. 36. Time history showing θ and θ_i with switching occurring at $\theta = 180°$ and $\theta = 540°$.

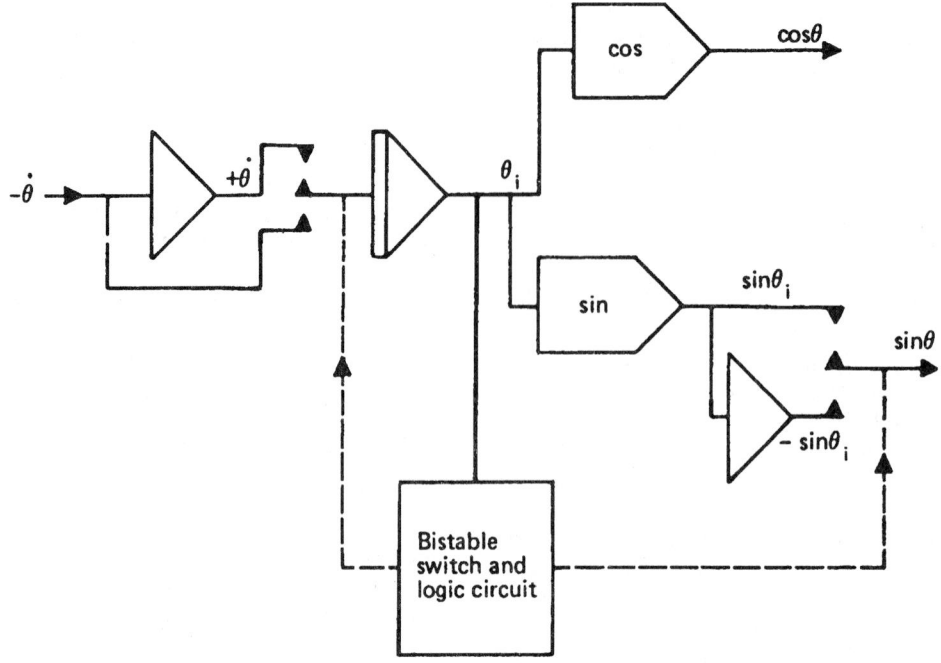

FIG. 37. Rate resolver and continuous resolver (multipliers not shown).

relationships among x, y, and θ, as shown in Fig. 38, is zero only when θ is the correct angle. In these circumstances—i.e. when an implicit algebraic relationship must be satisfied by a dependent variable θ—given the independent variables x and y, a mathematical method exists, called the "method of steepest descent" (see Hausner, 1971), which defines a stable formula for the generation of the time derivative of the dependent variable as follows:

$$\frac{d\theta}{dt} = -k\varepsilon\frac{\partial\varepsilon}{\partial\theta} \, , \qquad (25)$$

where ε is as defined above and k is an arbitrary constant. From the definition of ε we derive

$$\frac{\partial\varepsilon}{\partial\theta} = x\cos\theta + y\sin\theta . \qquad (26)$$

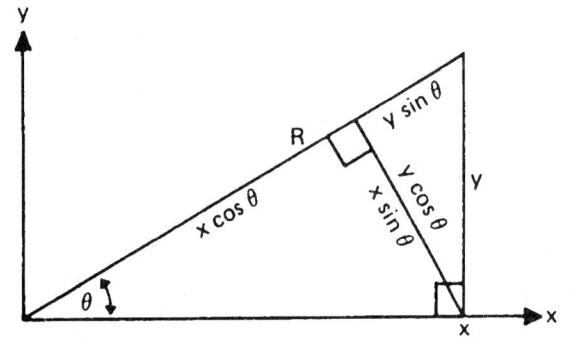

FIG. 38. Polar resolution geometry.

From the geometry of Fig. 38, we see that $x\cos\theta + y\sin\theta = R$, so that $\partial\varepsilon/\partial\theta = R$. Substituting the last expression into the original equation for $d\theta/dt$, we obtain $d\theta/dt = -k\varepsilon R$. The circuit for obtaining R and θ from x and y is shown in Fig. 39.

Polar Resolution Circuit For fastest response in this circuit, k should be made as large as loop stability will permit. This is usually a value between 1,000 and 10,000. Such large gains are obtained by using small capacitors for the integrator feedback (0.01μf or smaller).

Both the ordinary resolver and the polar resolution circuit can be readily replaced by a multivariable function generator (MVFG) (see Rubin, 1976), a new hybrid computing component that is similar in construction and operation to the DCFG. It combines several DCFG's, plus other analog components, to allow the automatic generation of an arbitrary function of 2, 3, or, by a recent extension, 4 variables, at analog speeds. The symbols for the MVFG application to resolver functions are shown in Fig. 40.

X^3 *and* X^4 *Generators* These are similar in operation to the previously discussed special generators, differing only in the output function. The programming symbols are shown in Fig. 41. The X^4 generator is particularly useful in heat radiation studies.

Functions of More Than One Variable

In the past, most analog programmers resorted to some mathematical juggling or simplification of functions in order to be able to use multivariable functions in an analog computer. For example, a function $f(x,y)$, may

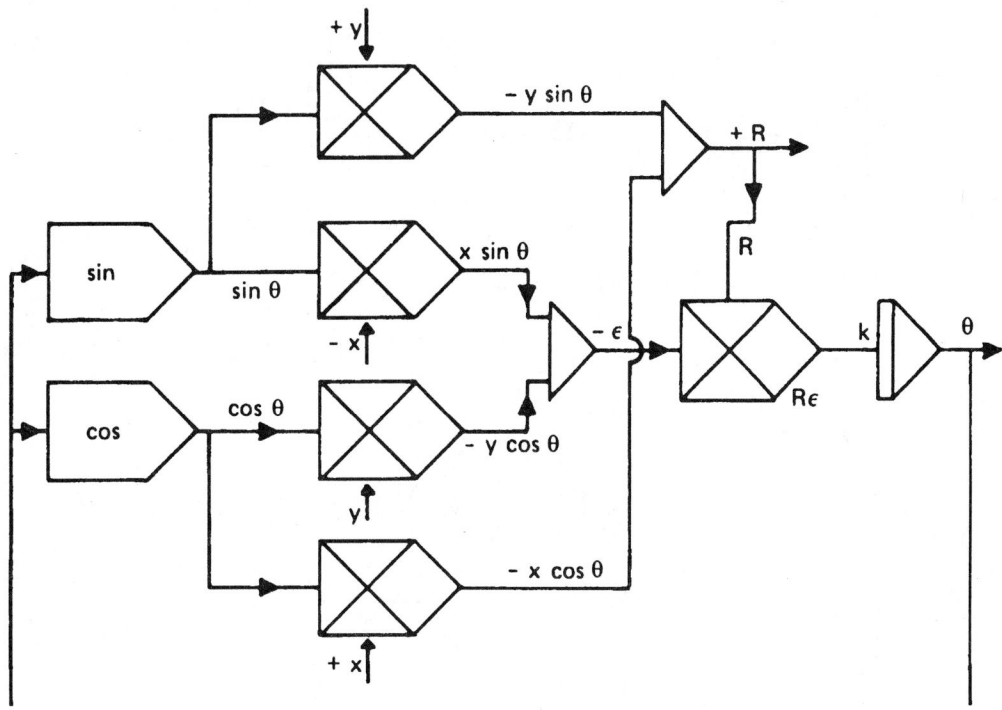

FIG. 39.   Polar resolution circuit.

sometimes be expressed as the sum or product of two functions of one variable, such as

$$f_1(x,y) = g_1(x) + h_1(y)$$

or

$$f_2(x,y) = g_2(x)h_2(y) + \text{similar terms}$$

More details on purely analog techniques for multivariable function generation may be found in Hausner (1971), and Korn and Korn (1972). There now exists a hybrid component for handling the generation of functions of up to four variables. This is an extension of the DCFG, and is described by Rubin (1976).

Simulation of Discontinuities   Discontinuities (such as limit stops, rate limits, dead zones, sudden changes of gain, and opening or closing of circuits) are programmed on the analog computer by means of diodes and/or electronic gates. A diode may be regarded as a voltage-sensi-

tive on-off switch. As a first approximation we consider the circuit to be closed (conducting), if the anode is positive with respect to the cathode, and open (non-conducting) if the anode is negative with respect to the cathode. A simple circuit for introducing a discontinuity at the origin is shown in Fig. 42.

In the circuit shown in Fig. 42, $-X$ is connected to the cathode of the diode and the anode is connected to a pot. When $-X$ is negative, the cathode of the diode is negative with respect to the anode, so the diode conducts and produces a positive output through the inversion of the Y-amplifier. When $-X$ is positive, the diode is rendered in the non-conducting state, and $Y = 0$. The circuit characteristic is shown to the right of the circuit diagram. This circuit is also called a nonnegative limiter (i.e. Y is constrained to positive values only). By reversing the diode, one can make a nonpositive limiter. The circuit in Fig. 42 can be considered to have a breakpoint at zero (a discontinuity in the derivative of the output occurs when $X = 0$). The discontinuity in the output can be made to occur at any arbitrary value of X, as in the "dead-space" circuit shown in Fig. 43; see Fig. 13(d). Notice that the discontinuity occurs at other than $X = 0$.

For more details on the use of diode circuits to represent a variety of discontinuities, and for special time function generation, such as sine wave, triangular wave, and square wave generation, see Hausner, 1971.

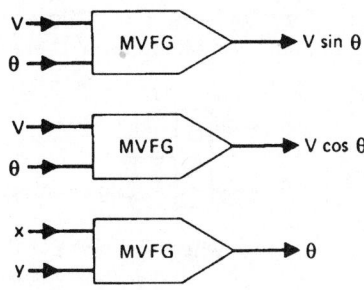

FIG. 40.   Resolver functions using MVFG.

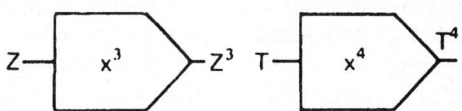

FIG. 41.   Programming symbols for X^3 and X^4 units.

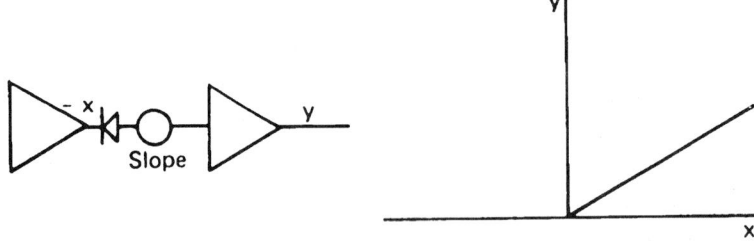

FIG. 42. Origin discontinuity circuit.

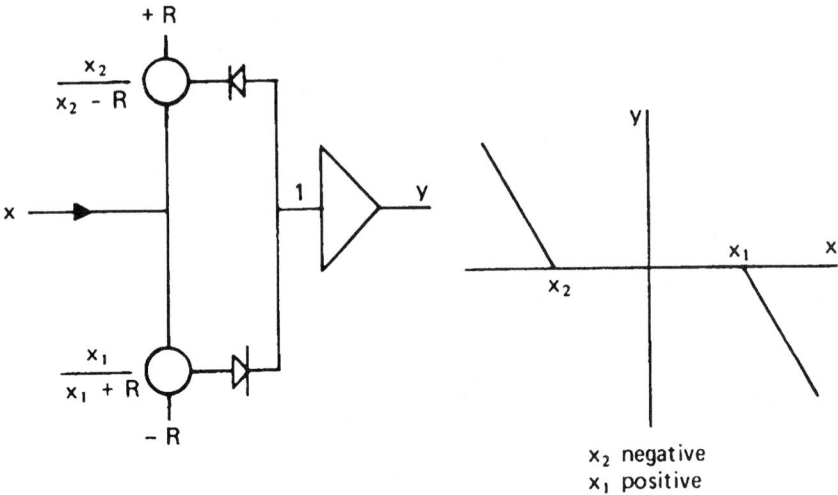

x_2 negative
x_1 positive

FIG. 43. Dead-space circuit.

Digital Logic Operations

The Analog Comparator The analog comparator has been a fundamental component of the analog computer from its inception. In the past it was intimately associated with a relay such that the comparator output drove the relay arm to one of two sets of contacts. Actually, the analog comparator is a true hybrid device, since it accepts analog inputs (usually two) and produces a digital logic level output (either a binary "1" or a binary "0"). The symbol is shown in Fig. 44.

If one of the two analog inputs is a constant voltage (as, for example, a reference voltage multiplied by a constant coefficient), then the output of the comparator shows when the other variable is greater than or less than the particular constant value.

The output of the comparator can be used to control the analog computer, to drive electronic gates, or, as inputs to other digital logic components, to sense lines, control lines, interrupt lines, or priority interrupt lines of digital computers.

General-Purpose Digital Logic Modules It may seem strange to include a section on true general-purpose digital logic components with material on analog computers, but analog programmers have always made use of digital logic in the normal course of obtaining a solution to a problem.

Many years ago, general-purpose digital logic modules were not available, so the manufacturers of analog equipment did not supply such modules. The programmer, however, by using comparators, relays, diodes, limiters, and amplifiers, was usually able to simulate digital logic. This "logic" was asynchronous, and operated in parallel, so that outputs of all logic components were available to the programmer at all times. At present, analog manufacturers include a good supply of digital logic modules as part of the normal computing complement of the analog computer. These modules are patched one to another, just as analog components are, and operate in parallel and simultaneously, as analog components do. In view of the last statement, one may consider such logic modules to be discrete analog components.

The most common types of logic modules used with analog computers are flip-flops, "and" gates, "or" gates, "one shots" (or "pulsers," or "time delays," or "monostables"), and combinations of these elements to

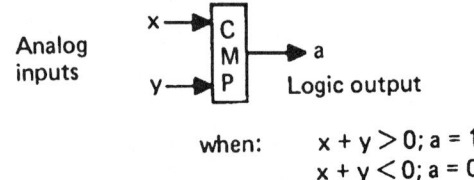

Analog inputs

x →

y →

CMP

→ a Logic output

when: $x + y > 0; a = 1$
$x + y < 0; a = 0$

FIG. 44. Analog comparator symbol.

produce "exclusive or" circuits (or "modulo 2 adder," or "ring sum"), up-and-down counters, and shift registers. For details of the use of logic modules in programming analog computers, see Bennett (1974).

Output Equipment The classical analog hard-copy output is a multi-channel voltage-time recorder. The usual recorders associated with modern analog computers are eight channels wide, write rectangularly, and have adjustable voltage scales and chart speeds. As many variable outputs as desired may be recorded simultaneously, provided one has a sufficient number of recorders. The results produced are called *time histories*. The accuracy is good to about 0.25% of the voltage range at which one is recording, and the bandwidth is about 100 Hz.

For wider bandwidth recording, an optical recorder (oscillograph) or some form of magnetic tape recorder must be used.

To obtain $X - Y$ graphs (for example, pressure vs. flow), where any variable Y is plotted as a function of any other variable X (as distinct from plotting X and Y as functions of time), a storage oscilloscope is typically used. A hard-copy attachment is available for permanent recording of the oscilloscope output.

The classical instrument for observing static or slowly changing analog computer variables is the digital voltmeter (DVM). In the most modern analog computers, the DVM is incorporated into a sophisticated digital display terminal that displays the address and state, as well as the value of the variable. These terminals may also act as line printers, displaying lists of analog variable addresses and values in digital form. The terminal may also incorporate the storage oscilloscope function with hard-copy output, thus allowing all necessary I/O functions to be performed at a single terminal.

PROGRAMMING

Amplitude Scaling Differential and/or algebraic equations, in order to be mechanized in the analog computer, must first be converted to voltage equations. A scale factor, or volts per physical unit ratio, must be chosen for all the dependent variables. Scale factors are chosen from estimated ranges of the problem variables. These estimates are usually "educated guesses," derived from the engineer's personal experience. If the first estimates prove to be poor, scale factors can be changed at the computer.

Having determined the amplitude scale factors, the problem variables in the mathematical equations are replaced by the voltages or machine units representing them, and adjustments are made to the coefficients throughout the equations in order to maintain equality. The equations are thus changed into voltage or machine unit equations from which a computer circuit diagram can be drawn.

Time Scaling With the all-electronic, high-speed analog computers available today, extremely high solution speeds (as short as several milliseconds) as well as very slow solutions (lasting several hours) can be obtained with the same computer. The choice of the solution time is largely dependent on factors external to the computer, such as the method of recording or displaying the solution, the need for tying into real hardware (hence the necessity of operating in "real time"), or the desire to display results to a "human in the loop," etc. A time-scale change is defined by the equation $T = \beta t$, where T is machine time, t is original problem time, and β is the time scale factor and has the units of machine time/original problem time.

In order to slow down a problem (i.e. to cause machine time to be larger than original problem time), β is made greater than unity; to speed up a problem (i.e. to cause machine time to be smaller than original problem time), β is made less than unity.

An objective of time scaling is to change computer time with respect to original problem time, but without causing a change in the original equations, without giving rise to new definitions of derivatives, and without changing any amplitude scaling. For details on how to program an analog computer, see Bennett (1974).

Mathematical Applications Since the analog computer can solve nonlinear ordinary differential equations, it is typically used in engineering design and real-time simulation. The analog computer can also be used effectively to solve a variety of other mathematical equations and to do analog data analysis. For example, algebraic equations, both linear and nonlinear, are readily solvable. Problems in complex variables are likewise amenable to solution by the analog computer (see Hausner, 1971), but such problems are not of major importance to analog computation. Partial differential equations (PDE), on the other hand, are of importance in the analog field.

References

1947. Ragazzini, J., Randall, R. H., and Russell, F. A. "Analysis of Problems in Dynamics by Electronic Circuits," *Proc IRE* **35**:444-452.

1955. Roedel, J. In Paynter, H. M. (Ed.), *Palimpsest on the Electric Analog Art.* George H. Philbrick Researches, pp. 27-47.

1963 to date. *Simulation*, published by Society for Computer Simulation, LaJolla, CA. (Describes current analog, digital, and hybrid computer work.)

1971. Hausner, A. *Analog and Hybrid Computer Programming.* Englewood Cliffs, NJ: Prentice-Hall.

1971. Holst, P. A. "A Note of History," *Simulation* **17**, *3*: 131-135, September.

1972. Korn, G. A. and Korn, T. M. *Electronic Analog and Hybrid Computers*, 2nd Edition. New York: McGraw-Hill.

1974. Bennett, A. W. *Introduction to Computer Simulation.* New York: West Publishing.

1976. Rubin, A. I. "Multi-Variable Function Generator," *Simulation* **27**, *1*:1-12 July.

1978. Sheingold, D. H. "Multiplier Application Guide." Published by Analog Devices, Norwood, MA.

1988. Franco, Sergio. *Design with Operational Amplifiers and Analog Integrated Circuits.* New York: McGraw-Hill.

1989. Frederiksen, T. M. *Intuitive Analog Electronics.* New York: McGraw-Hill.

ARTHUR I. RUBIN

ANALOG-TO-DIGITAL AND DIGITAL-TO-ANALOG CONVERTERS

For articles on related subjects *see* ANALOG COMPUTERS; DATA COMMUNICATIONS; and HYBRID COMPUTERS.

Whenever it is necessary to communicate between analog and digital systems, analog-to-digital (A-D) and/or digital-to-analog (D-A) converters are required. These converters form basic links between the world of "real" phenomena, where the variables are generally continuous analog quantities, and the "engineer designed" world of digital information processing and data communications, where the variables are discrete quantities.

The number of applications and types of converters available has grown significantly in recent years. This has resulted from increased recognition of the capabilities of digital, as opposed to analog, signal processing and data transmission. The importance of these capabilities is application-dependent; however, in general, the advantages of digital processing and transmission lie in the increased accuracy, noise immunity, processing flexibility, and storage facilities afforded by the digital format. This increasing use of digital processing of analog signals has been aided by the rapid development of sophisticated, yet inexpensive microcomputer systems and by the ability to now integrate both analog and digital functions on single VLSI (Very Large Scale Integration) chips.

Some Applications   A simple classification of application areas where A-D and D-A converters are used is given below.

Digital Control Systems   Fig. 1 is a block diagram illustration of a digital control system. Variables originate within the plant or system. They are sensed by an analog sensor, digitized by an A-D converter, and then transmitted to a digital processor. If the processor merely manipulates and stores this information, the system is a simple data acquisition system. If, on the basis of the input information, control signals determined by the processor are returned to the plant, then a digital control system is present. A variation on this system requiring fewer converters can be designed if the signal frequencies and number of sensors and controllers are not excessive (Fig. 2).

Communications and Entertainment Systems   The advantages of digital data transmission have resulted in extensive use of converters as parts of telemetering,

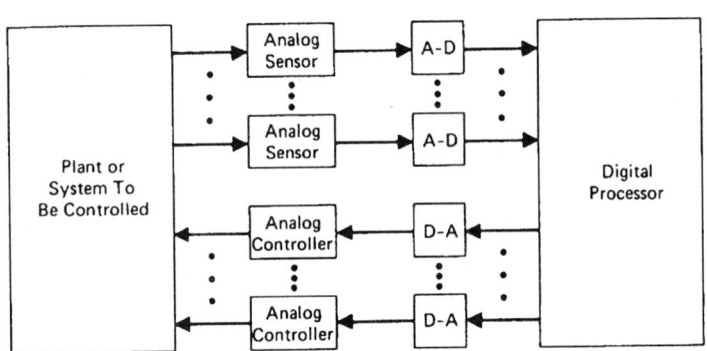

FIG. 1.   Digital control system.

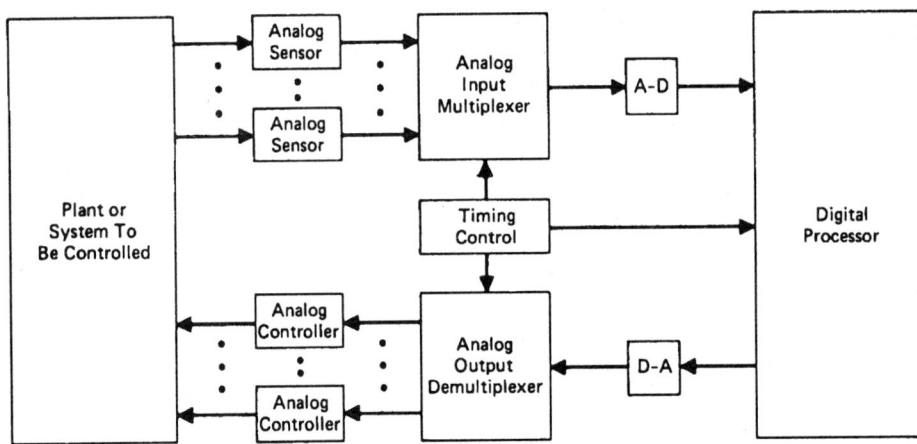

FIG. 2.   Digital control system with multiplexers.

voice communications, and entertainment systems. In telemetering systems, analog signals originating in remote locations are first converted into digital signals and then transmitted to the central station. Remote weather and defense-related monitoring systems fall in this category of applications.

Voice communications systems are also increasingly oriented toward digital signal processing. In this situation, analog voice signals are digitized with A-D converters and subsequently transmitted over time-shared channels, with many conversations being "simultaneously" carried over the same channel. Such systems can be designed to be flexible and handle both speech and data at the same time, while making nearly optimum use of the systems' bandwidth capabilities.

In the entertainment industry, digital recording and playback systems of audio signals are now commonplace. Compact disc (CD) and digital audio tape systems make extensive use of A-D and D-A converters. (*See* ENTERTAINMENT INDUSTRY, COMPUTERS IN THE)

Test, Measurement, and Monitoring   Many applications of A-D converters can be found in test and measurement equipment. Digital voltmeters, for example, are now commonplace, and the inclusion of digital readouts alongside analog displays on oscilloscopes has gained widespread acceptance. More complex measurement and monitoring applications, such as on-line real-time patient monitoring, also have converters as key system elements.

The Basic Relationship

Analog variables such as position, temperature, pressure, and process rate are typically first converted during measurement into analog voltages and currents. Conversely, to control the analog variables, analog voltages and currents are usually supplied to the inputs of a controlling transducer. Rather than deal with the basic analog variable (e.g. temperature), it is therefore convenient to deal with the voltages or currents available at the output, or produced for the input, of the transducer. The analog variable considered here is thus a pure voltage or current, and questions concerning transducer operation, signal amplification, and signal conditioning are omitted. (Material on these important practical matters can be obtained from the references.)

Digital information is generally represented by the presence or absence of a fixed voltage or current level. Each unit of information or "bit" thus has two states, referred to as the *one* and *zero* states. On a single input line, information can be represented serially by periodically changing the voltage level or state of the line. A set of parallel lines or a grouping of serial bits can be used to represent a digital word, where the meaning of this word depends on the number or symbol assigned to each possible combination of bits. This is referred to as the *code*. Different types of codes are used with A-D and D-A converters (e.g. offset binary, one's complement, two's complement). However, for simplicity, this article considers only the *unipolar* or *natural binary* code. Table 1 presents this code for a 3-bit word. In general, each word may have n bits, with the bit at left, the most significant bit (MSB),

TABLE 1.   Three-Bit Natural Binary Code

Decimal Value	Binary Value	BIT 1 MSB	BIT 2	BIT 3 LSB
0	0.000	0	0	0
$\frac{1}{8}$	0.001	0	0	1
$\frac{2}{8}$	0.010	0	1	0
$\frac{3}{8}$	0.011	0	1	1
$\frac{4}{8}$	0.100	1	0	0
$\frac{5}{8}$	0.101	1	0	1
$\frac{6}{8}$	0.110	1	1	0
$\frac{7}{8}$	0.111	1	1	1

having a weight of 2^{-1}, the bit at right, the least significant bit (LSB), having a weight of 2^{-n}, and the ith bit ($1 \le i \le n$) having a weight of 2^{-i}.

The basic conversion relationship for a three-bit binary code is given in Fig. 3(a) and (b). Any three-bit digital sequence entering into the D-A converter results in producing one of eight distinct voltage outputs, as seen in Fig. 3(a). Similarly, any voltage input into the A-D converter results in producing a distinct three-bit output code. The *ideal resolution* of these converters is equal to the value of the LSB or 2^{-n} for an n-bit converter. For A-D converters, associated with this resolution is an inherent quantization error, which reflects an uncertainty in the results of A-D conversion due to quantification of the analog signal. For the system above, transitions occur in the middle of each voltage range, thus minimizing the quantification error to an optimum $\pm 1/2$ LSB. Other errors, such as noise and various nonlinearities, may increase this above $\pm 1/2$ LSB in real systems.

In both D-A and A-D converters, there is a wide variety of techniques and manufacturers. The references provide a host of details and alternatives not considered in this review.

D-A Converters

Fig. 4 shows a block diagram for a D-A converter. The typical D-A converter contains switches and a resistor network. The switches are controlled by the digital input code and establish connections within the network needed to obtain the proper analog voltage.

Fig. 5(a) shows a simple 3-bit plus sign D-A converter. The dashed lines indicate that the switch is controlled by the associated digital bit input. The switches themselves are generally integrated circuits that ideally would have no resistance when closed and infinite resistance when open. For the 0100-input switch configuration shown, the output voltage V_0 is easily seen to be $V_R/2$. Similarly, the nth bit present can be shown to produce an output voltage increment equal to $2^{-n}V_R$; hence, the resulting output voltage is proportional to the binary input. A sign bit is present that controls a voltage reference switch. With certain codes, its absence indicates a positive digital input and results in switching in the positive reference voltage $+V_R$. Its presence indicates a negative input, and the negative reference voltage $+V_R$ is applied to the network.

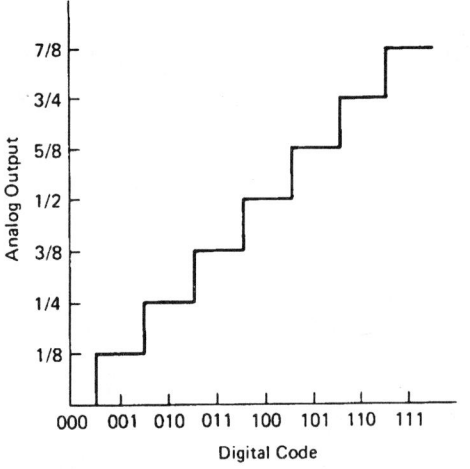

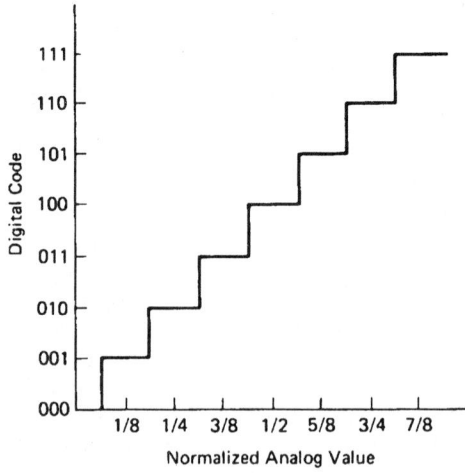

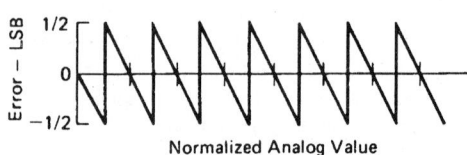

| (a) | (b) |
| Transfer Function of a D-A Converter | Transfer Function of a A-D Converter |

FIG. 3. The basic ideal relationships.

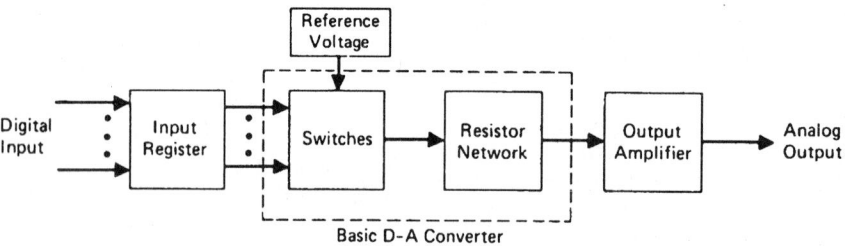

FIG. 4. D-A Converter and Accessories.

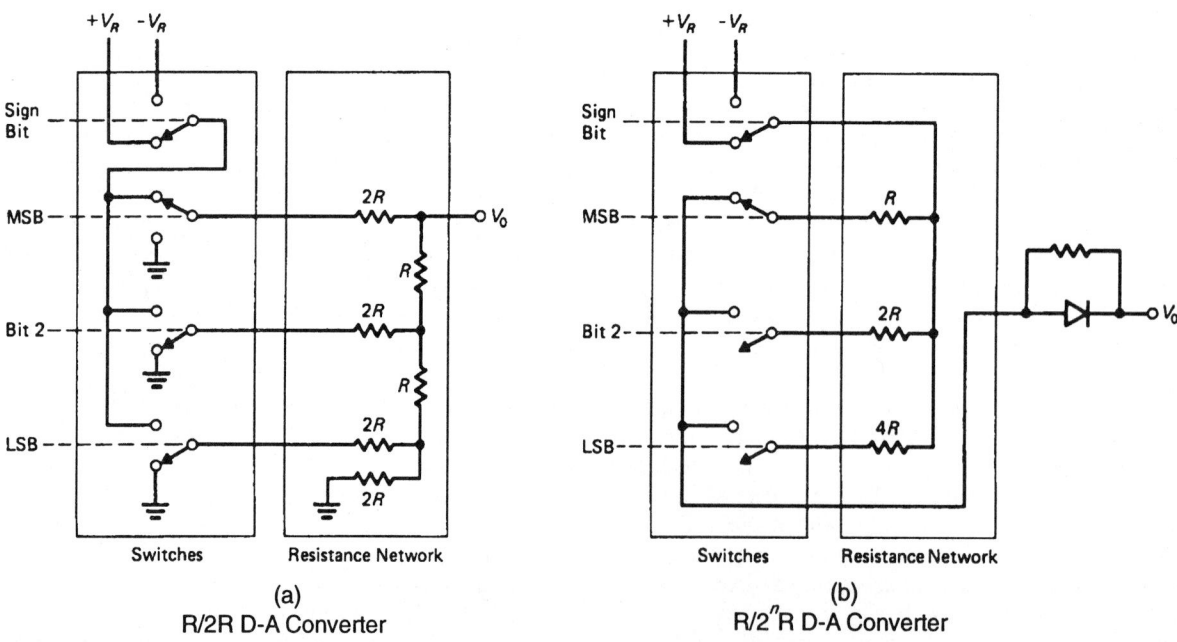

FIG. 5.

64

Another simple D-A converter based on summing currents is shown in Fig. 5(b). This has the advantage of requiring only one resistor per bit; however, a large range of resistance values is necessary, making it impractical for monolithic and hybrid circuit manufacturing techniques.

A-D Converters A simple form of A-D converter is shown in Fig. 6. A conversion begins after the reset signal clears the counter. The counter now receives clock pulses and is incremented with each pulse. The counter output is a digital word representing a voltage level. This word, received by the D-A converter, results in an analog signal, which is compared with the incoming analog signal. When the comparator signal becomes positive, the counter at that point holds the correct digital representation of the analog signal. An "output ready" signal indicates that this has occurred.

The method, though simple, requires a relatively long time for a complete A-D conversion due to the counting process. This time increases by a factor of two for each additional bit and makes the method unsuitable for certain applications. A modification to the above technique, which speeds up the converter, calls for the incrementing counter to be replaced with an "up-down" counter. Here, once a comparison has been made, the counter is designed to increment or decrement on each clock pulse, depending on the output of the comparator. The counter thus follows the analog signal and the full counting process is not necessary on each conversion if large changes in the analog input do not occur.

With the "Successive-Approximation" converter, the counter box is assumed to contain a register and control logic. The converter operates by successively considering each bit position in the register and setting that bit to a one or a zero on the basis of the comparator output. The MSB is first set to a one with all other bit positions set to zero. This word then enters the D-A converter and the D-A output is compared with the analog input. If the result indicates the analog input is larger, then the one in the MSB is kept; otherwise, it is set to zero. The remaining bit positions are considered successively in the same manner and a decision is made on each bit position. After the LSB is considered, the results of conversion are found in the register. Unlike the counting method, the conversion time with this method is constant for every possible analog input, and this approach is often used in high-speed converter design.

A somewhat lower-speed but high-accuracy A-D con-

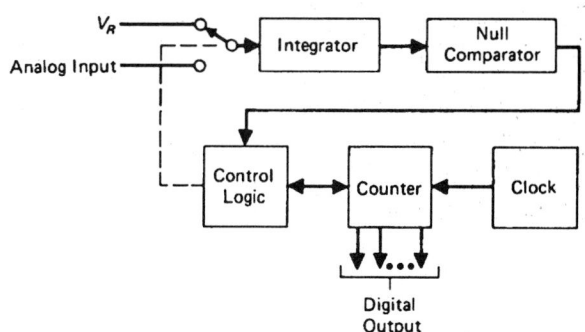

FIG. 7. Dual slope integrating A-D converter.

verter is the "Integrating" converter. A "dual slope" version is shown in Fig. 7. The converter operates by first integrating the unknown analog input voltage for a fixed period of time. During this time period, a voltage proportional to the input builds up on the integrating capacitor. After resetting the counter to zero, a fixed reference voltage of opposite polarity is now applied to the integrator and the counter is started. When the null comparator recognizes that the integrator output has reached zero, the control logic is notified and the counter is stopped. The output count is proportional to the ratio of the input voltage and referenced voltage. Since the reference voltage is known, the count is therefore a binary representation of the analog input. Triple and quad slope architectures that greatly increase the conversion speed at the cost of added complexity are also possible.

A more recent design that is gaining widespread acceptance in those applications requiring high dynamic range, accuracy, and superior noise properties (e.g. digital audio) is the Sigma-Delta A-D converter (Fig. 8). The high gain negative feedback loop provides for sampling of the analog input at a rate substantially higher then the bandwidth of interest. The loop comparator output is fed into a digital filter that, by weighting successive bits appropriately, creates the desired output (Boser and Wooley, 1988). The design exploits technology developments that permit effective integration of analog and digital functions on the same VLSI chip.

For higher-speed A-D conversion, all—or nearly all—parallel methods are available. The simplest method uses an analog comparator for each quantization (Fig. 9). Each comparator (C) represents a voltage level, and these levels are coded into the appropriate three-bit codes with an encoding network. Though conversion effectively re-

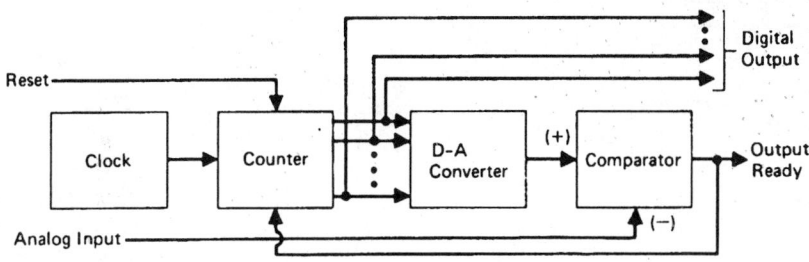

FIG. 6. Counter A-D converter.

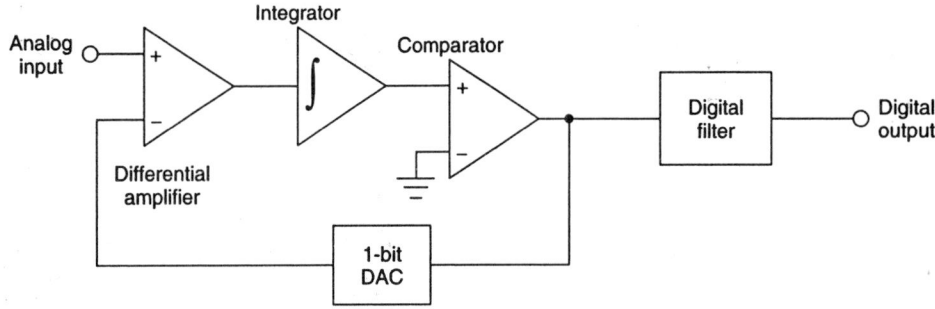

FIG. 8 1st-Order Sigma-Delta A-D Converter.

quires only a single step, the cost increases rapidly with the number of bits n, since the number of comparators needed is $2^n - 1$.

Specification of Converters A host of measures are used in specifying converter performance. These are discussed in detail in a number of the references. The user should be cautious in evaluating manufacturer specifications and be clear on the meaning of the various terms used.

The application for which the converter is intended should be well understood, since this will determine which of the multitude of converters available offer the best price performance trade-offs. In addition to accuracy and speed requirements, questions regarding logic levels and codes, scale factors, reference voltages, impedance levels, power levels, temperature stability, and noise environment must be considered. These latter questions are not considered here and the reader should consult the references for detailed information.

A number of measures are normally used in specifying converter accuracy and speed. These measures in part isolate and indicate the various sources of error. With D-A converters, *accuracy* or *absolute accuracy* refers to the deviation of actual analog output from the output predicted by the ideal transfer function. Though this may vary over the range of the unit, specifications are normally given in terms of a single number representing the maximum error over the range. This may be stated as ± a percentage of full scale or ± a fraction of LSB. *Relative*

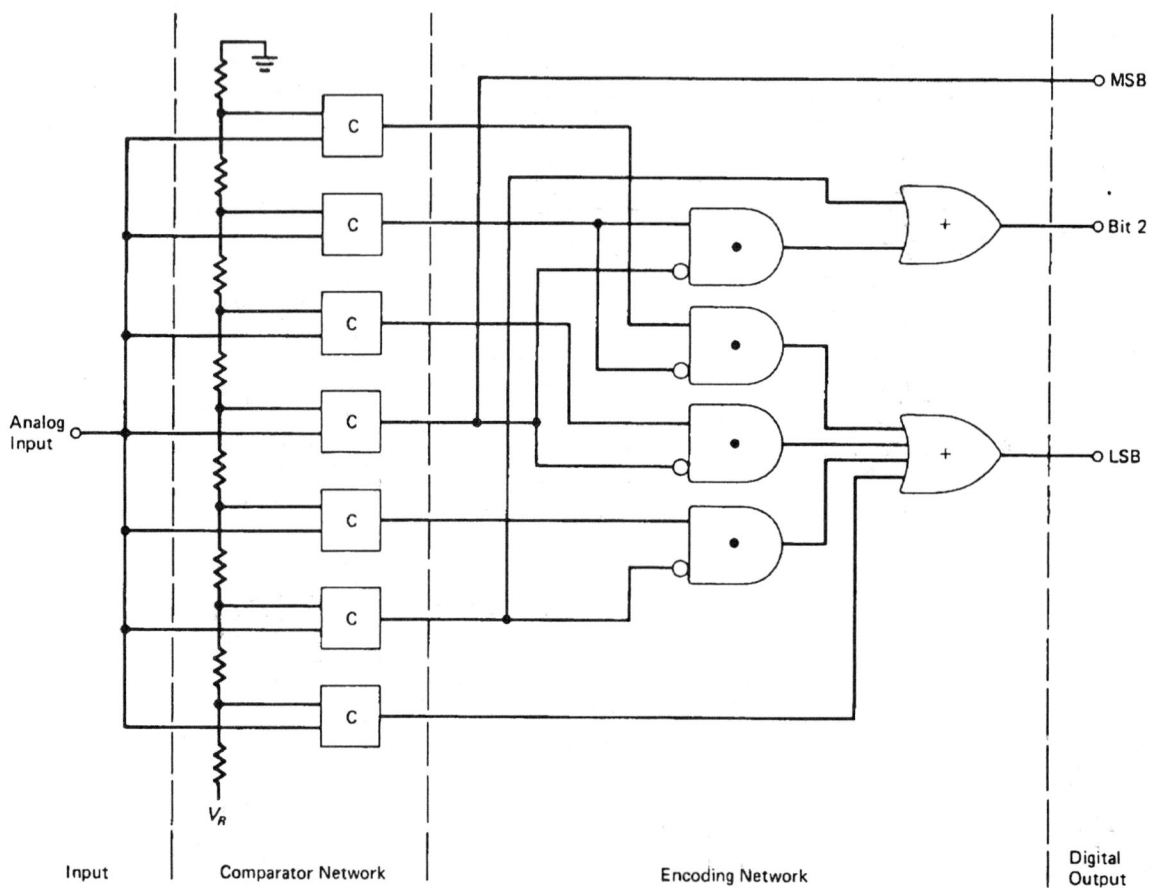

FIG. 9. Three-bit parallel A-D converter.

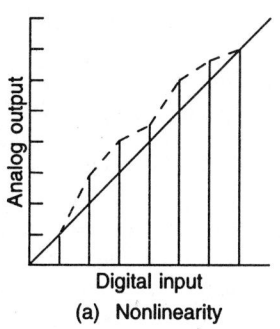

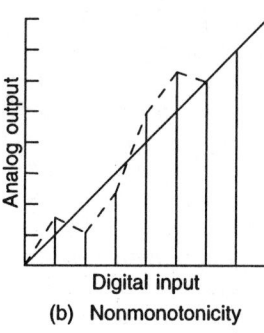

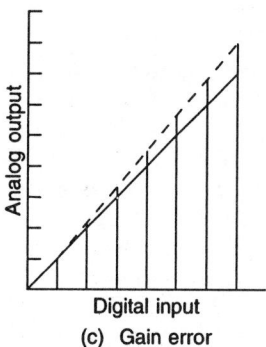

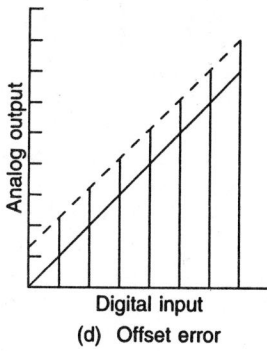

(a) Nonlinearity   (b) Nonmonotonicity   (c) Gain error   (d) Offset error

FIG. 10.   D/A errors (Sheingold, 1986).

accuracy measures the largest deviation of the analog output from a straight line drawn through the end points of a converter's transfer function.

Several common error types that contribute to a loss of accuracy are illustrated in Fig. 10(a), (b), (c), and (d). Fig. 10(a) shows *nonlinearity* in the conversion transfer function. The nonlinearity is, however, *monotonic*, since increasing digital values produce increasing analog values. Fig. 10(b) shows a *nonmonotonic* nonlinearity. Such a nonlinearity could yield the same analog value for two different digital input codes, a result that might cause oscillations to occur in certain control applications (*q.v.*). Figs. 10(c) and 10(d) illustrate *gain* and *offset* errors, which respectively change the slope and zero crossing of the transfer function. The difference between the dotted line in the figures and the solid 45° angle line is the error associated with each digital input code.

Dynamic characteristics of D-A converters are normally specified in terms of a *settling time*. This is the time between arrival of the digital code and settling of the analog output to within certain specified limits of accuracy. The shorter the settling time, the higher the conversion rate. For a high-speed converter, the full scale maximum settling time specification might read 100 μsec to settle within ±1/2 LSB.

For A-D converters, accuracy refers to the deviation of the analog level represented by the digital output from the actual analog input. As with D-A converters, this is normally stated as either a percentage of full scale or a fraction of the LSB. The relative accuracy of an A-D converter measures the largest deviation of the converter's transfer function from a straight line drawn through its endpoints and is also expressed as a percentage of full scale or a fraction of the LSB. Errors here may be divided into two parts. The first, *quantization error*, was discussed earlier in this article. This results in an inherent error of ±1/2 LSB, which can be reduced only by increasing the number of bits. All other errors are equipment errors, and error types directly corresponding to those found in D-A converters may be present. Offset, gain (scale factor) and nonlinearity errors have analogous definitions. The error corresponding to nonmonotonic nonlinearity is termed the *differential linearity error* and may result in entire digital outputs being missed.

The dynamic characteristics of A-D converters are normally specified in terms of the total conversion time. This is the time necessary for a complete measurement, its inverse being the *conversion rate* of the converter. A high-speed video 10-bit converter, for example, might have a conversion time of 500 μsec and a relative accuracy of ±1/2 LSB.

Conclusion   A-D and D-A converters are finding increasing use as the scope of digital processing and communications widens. There is every indication that this trend will continue and be augmented by further gains in performance and decreases in converter cost. This will result in large part from the growing use of monolithic and VLSI (Very Large Scale Integration) circuit technologies. A proliferation of new products can be expected with increasing emphasis placed on ease of interfacing these products with microprocessors and standard communications systems and buses.

References

1970. Schmid, H. *Electronic Analog/Digital Conversions.* New York: Van Nostrand Reinhold.

1976. Hnatek, E. R. *A User's Handbook of D/A and A/D Converters.* New York: Wiley.

1978. Gordon, B. M. "Linear Electronic Analog/Digital Conversion Architectures, Their Origins, Parameters, Limitations, and Application," *IEEE Trans. on Ckts, and Sys.,* **CAS-25** (July).

1978. Kurth, C. F. (Ed.) "Special Issue on Analog/Digital Conversion," *IEEE Trans. on Ckts. and Sys.* **CAS-25** (July).

1979. Zuch, E. L. (Ed.). *Data Acquisition and Conversion Handbook.* Mansfield, MA: Datel.

1986. Sheingold, D. H. (Ed.). *Analog-Digital Conversion Handbook.* Englewood Cliffs, NJ: Prentice Hall.

1988. Boser, B. E. and Wooley, B. A. "The Design of Sigma-Delta Modulation Analog-to-Digital Converters." *IEEE Journal of Solid State Ckts.,* **23**, 6.

MARK A. FRANKLIN

ANALYSIS OF ALGORITHMS.   *See* ALGORITHMS, ANALYSIS OF.

ANALYST.   *See* SYSTEMS ANALYST.

ANALYTICAL ENGINE

For articles on related subjects *see* BABBAGE, CHARLES; DIFFERENCE ENGINE; and DIGITAL COMPUTERS: HISTORY: ORIGINS.

The analytical engine, designed by Charles Babbage between 1833 and 1846, anticipated many features of electronic computing devices invented in the 1940s and 1950s. Although mechanical in all its operations, the analytical engine could carry out calculations of arbitrary complexity under the control of punched cards. Conditional branching was possible, and Babbage had prepared test programs that included elaborate calculations based on nested loop structures. In a beautiful anticipation of twentieth century thinking, Babbage showed that, given sufficient time, any finite calculation could be carried out by the analytical engine.

Babbage commenced work on the design of the analytical engine in 1833 after the collapse of the project to build his difference engine (*q.v.*). Babbage had realized that the second difference of the sine function is proportional to the sine itself. If the difference engine could be rearranged so that the tabulated value of the sine could be "fed back" to become the second difference, the sine could be calculated directly without an intermediate polynomial approximation. This image of the engine "eating its own tail" led Babbage to place the number stores of the difference engine around a set of central gear wheels that served as a "data bus" to transmit numbers from one store, or "register," to another.

Unfortunately, it requires a multiplication to form the second difference of the sine function. Babbage realized that this multiplication could be implemented as a sequence of shift and addition operations. This would be excessively slow, however, if the addition used the ripple-carry of the difference engine. Babbage's *anticipating carry*, a mechanical equivalent of carry-lookahead, greatly speeded multiplication. But its complexity led Babbage to separate the analytical engine into two distinct parts—the *store*, in which numbers are normally kept, and the *mill*, to which they are brought for calculations.

Division needs little more calculating apparatus than multiplication, but its control is more complex, as division is inherently a trial-and-error process. To control the analytical engine, Babbage developed *barrels*, similar in principle to a music box, in which each row of pins puts into gear those parts of the calculating mechanism that must act during one cycle of the drive shaft. Multiplication and division each require many cycles, and the barrels step backwards and forwards from one row of pins to another to control the various stages of each operation. Some pins on the barrel control this movement, which may be conditional upon an intermediate calculational result. In effect, the barrel is a microprogram (*q.v.*) store, and complex operations are implemented by microprograms represented by rows of pins on the barrel.

Babbage envisioned that the overall calculation performed by the analytical engine would be specified by a further barrel that initiated sequences of operations by the barrel just described, that is, a hierarchical organization of control. But in June 1836, Babbage borrowed from the Jacquard pattern-weaving loom the idea of a sequence of punched cards to provide a more flexible alternative to this "user program" barrel.

By late 1837, Babbage had developed all of the essential ideas for a flexible programmed calculating machine. Subsequent work on the analytical engine was more technical in nature. Babbage repeatedly re-examined all of the basic elements to see if they could be simplified or speeded up, conflicting tasks at which he proved remarkably imaginative and productive. Much work was applied to the "architecture" of the analytical engine—the functional arrangement of the component mechanisms and the all-important microprograms for multiplication, division, and other operations.

Some of the microprograms are remarkably sophisticated. Signed addition, for example, is "pipelined" so that several additions are in progress simultaneously. Each stage of the pipeline is controlled by its own barrel. These step independently through their own microprograms while co-operating to maximize the flow of operands through the pipeline. It would be an impressive piece of technical design even today.

In contrast, Babbage's user-level programs are a disappointment. Most were prepared in the early years of Babbage's work on the analytical engine, and almost all are elementary. They are well described in the notes by Ada Lovelace, where the idea of nested loops is developed in painful detail. On the strength of these notes, Ada Lovelace has been considered the "world's first programmer," but the accolade is unwarranted. The notes were written at Babbage's direction, as he had earlier directed papers by Lardner and Menabrea, and the example programs were prepared by Babbage, mostly many years before. In later years, Babbage's interest in user-level programs was almost non-existent. However, his reputation as a "programmer" rests secure in the very sophisticated microprograms of the barrels.

Disenchanted by the attempt to build the difference engine, Babbage did not attempt to build the analytical engine at this time, but treated the design as merely an intellectual pursuit. In the mid-1850s, however, Babbage returned to the analytical engine and simplified it so that it might be built within his own means. Although this period showed remarkable technological innovation, and a test piece using diecast components was nearing completion at the time of his death in 1871, the brilliance of the earlier years was missing.

References

1987 Bromley, A.G. "The Evolution of Babbage's Calculating Engines," *Annals of the History of Computing*, **9**, 113–138.
1990 Bromley, A.G. "Difference and Analytical Engines," in Aspray, W. (ed), *Computing Before Computers*, Ames, IA: Iowa State University Press.

ALLAN G. BROMLEY

ANIMATION. *See* COMPUTER ANIMATION.

APL. *See* FUNCTIONAL PROGRAMMING; and PROCEDURE-ORIENTED LANGUAGES.

APPLE COMPUTER, INC.

For articles on related subjects *see* DIGITAL COMPUTERS: HISTORY: IBM-PC AND PC-COMPATIBLES; and PERSONAL COMPUTING.

Apple's Beginnings Fourteen years after it was founded, Apple is a major power in personal computing worldwide, setting the pace for ease-of-use and graphical interfaces. The company was born out of a desire by two spirited innovators, Steve Wozniak and Steve Jobs, who wanted to bring computing power to ordinary people.

With the microprocessor, the semiconductor industry had provided the compact, inexpensive electronic brain needed to build a personal-sized computer. But it was individual computer enthusiasts, not the established mainframe and minicomputer companies, who took the next steps. Fascinated with the computers they designed and programmed by day, many young engineers longed to have their own computers on which to work and play at night. They avidly read the handful of available hobbyist magazines, formed clubs, and swapped ideas.

Stephen G. Wozniak was a regular attendee of the Homebrew Computer Club that began meeting in 1975 in Menlo Park, California, at the northern edge of what was already called Silicon Valley. Wozniak had become enthralled with computers in high school and had dropped out of the engineering program at the University of California, Berkeley, to work for Hewlett-Packard, a manufacturer of calculators and minicomputers. It was at a Homebrew meeting that Wozniak heard about the first personal computers—the Altair, the IMSAI 8080, and others—that were being offered as mail-order kits.

By mid-1976, Wozniak, 26, had written a Basic programming language interpreter for a new microprocessor from MOS Technology, the 6502, and designed a computer to run it. Wozniak proudly passed out photocopies of his

FIG. 1. Apple co-founders Steve Wozniak, left, and Steve Jobs with the original motherboard of the Apple I. (Courtesy of Apple Computer, Inc.)

design to Homebrew friends and helped them build their own machines from the plans.

Steven P. Jobs, age 21 in 1976, shared Wozniak's passion for computers. The two had collaborated on several electronics projects, including creating the video game Breakout for Atari, Inc., where Jobs worked. Convinced of the marketability of Wozniak's design, Jobs persuaded his friend to sell the Apple I kits to other hobbyists.

They sold Jobs's Volkswagen van and Wozniak's programmable calculator to raise enough money to get started. Jobs then landed an order for 50 Apple I computers from one of the first computer retail stores in the country, and, on the strength of that order, the two young men secured credit at an electronic parts house. In the garage of Jobs's parents' home in Cupertino, California, Apple Computer went into business.

"I had wanted a computer my whole life—that was the big thing in my life," Wozniak remembers. "All of a sudden I realized that microprocessors were cheap enough to let me build one myself. Steve [Jobs] went a little further. Steve saw it as a product that you could actually deliver and sell, and someone else could use."

Like all early personal computers, the Apple I was designed for experts who could put it together and write their own programs. But Jobs had a vision for Apple Computer that went far beyond the hobbyist market. He sought advice on realizing his goals from successful industry figures such as Nolan Bushnell, founder of Atari; Don Valentine, a venture capitalist; Regis McKenna, who owned a rising Silicon Valley advertising and public relations agency; and A. C. "Mike" Markkula, who at age 33 had retired from a lucrative marketing career at Intel.

Wozniak began designing a second computer that would be technically far superior to the Apple I, incorporating a keyboard, power supply, the ability to generate color graphics, and the Basic programming language. Convinced that this product—the Apple II—would spark demand for personal computers beyond the hobbyist market, Mike Markkula wrote a business plan for the young company and then invested in it. He officially joined Apple when it incorporated in January 1977, and has since served in various executive positions, including president. Apple blossomed during that first year. The firm moved out of its garage into leased quarters in Cupertino, California. It introduced the Apple II to rave reviews at the first West Coast Computer Faire. Markkula signed up dealers across the country to sell the Apple II. Regis McKenna's agency helped establish an immediate presence for Apple with an eye-catching rainbow logo, ads placed in national consumer publications, and a public relations campaign that leveraged Apple's "American dream" beginnings. An infusion of $3 million in venture capital gave Apple an enormous advantage over many of its struggling competitors. Apple finished its first fiscal year with $774,000 in sales and a $42,000 profit.

An Industry Grows Up During the next four years, the personal computer industry exploded into the consciousness of everyday life—in the U.S. and abroad. Large, well-established manufacturers of mainframe computers, office systems, and telecommunications products, such as IBM, Digital Equipment Corp., Zenith, and AT&T, recognized the opportunity for personal computers and entered the market with zeal. By the end of 1982, more than 100 companies were manufacturing PCs, including Atari, Commodore, Tandy, and a host of start-ups seeking to emulate the success of the big firms.

The boom was kindled by an avalanche of software programs that turned computers into special-purpose tools: for typing and rearranging text, analyzing financial data, sorting and filing information, and thousands of other uses never imagined by the computers' creators.

Apple contributed key products that catalyzed the development of software for the Apple II, including the Disk II floppy disk drive and disk operating system, and several programming languages and aids. As a result, landmark programs, including VisiCalc, Personal Filing System, and other business-oriented applications, were developed first for the Apple II. The benefit of these software packages cannot be underestimated: Of the 130,000 Apple II computers sold by September 1980, an estimated 25,000 were purchased specifically for their ability to run VisiCalc.

Apple also secured early dominance in the closely linked education and consumer markets by continually improving its Apple II line with the Apple II Plus in 1979, the Apple IIe in 1983, and the Apple IIc in 1984. Beginning in 1979, Apple awarded hundreds of thousands of dollars in grants to schools and individuals for the development of educational software. The large software library that ensued is a key reason that more than 60 percent of computers used in U. S. primary and secondary schools are Apple computers.

A huge infrastructure of retail dealers sprung up to deliver personal computer products to buyers. By the end of 1982, Apple had more than 3,000 authorized retail dealers worldwide.

Even with enormous competition, Apple revenues continued to grow at unprecedented rates, reaching $583.1 million for fiscal 1982, the company's fifth year of operation. The company's initial public stock offering—in December 1980—was one of the largest in Wall Street's history, raising approximately $100 million. In 1983, Apple entered the Fortune 500 and gained additional Wall Street renown by recruiting Pepsi-Cola Co. president John Sculley as its new chief executive.

However, Apple was not immune to difficulties. Driven by the prospect of IBM and other deep-pocketed firms entering the personal computer industry, Apple raced to produce a third computer designed especially for business users. It began shipping the ill-fated Apple III in late 1980 before the system could be fully tested and without some promised features. The Apple III never recovered from its stumbling start and eventually was discontinued.

IBM's personal computer, introduced in August 1981, stirred up frenzy in the industry, as software and accessory developers rushed to create products compatible with it. Development for the Apple II and Apple III, though still strong, dwindled by comparison. Awareness of personal computers grew and was symbolized by Time magazine's naming the computer as its 1982 "Man of the Year," and scores of companies were vying for market share.

Into this environment, Apple, in early 1983, launched its fourth computer, the Lisa, a radical change for Apple and the entire personal computer industry, because of its "user-friendly" graphical user interface (GUI), much of it based on technology first created by computer scientists at the Xerox Palo Alto Research Center (PARC) in California. Jobs and others at Apple were convinced that complex and cryptic software was confining the use of personal computers to people who were willing to become experts—just as the earliest microcomputer kits had been useful only to hobbyists. Apple invested $100 million during two years to develop software based on a user-friendly graphical interface. Unlike computers that used unfamiliar language and logic, the Lisa system opted for software that was, for the average user, simple and easy to understand.

The news media gave the Lisa a rapturous reception, as did Wall Street. Apple stock, which had traded as low as $10 in 1982, rose to $63 a share. But the Lisa's noisy debut had masked grave difficulties. The computer was slow, and users couldn't swap information among programs. There was no network capability. Lisa failed in the marketplace, but it did become the kernel of what was to become Apple's successful personal computer, the Macintosh. The Macintosh user interface, introduced in January 1984, included icons, windows, pull-down menus, and the mouse pointing device and set new standards for ease of use for the personal computer industry. Later, the coupling of the Macintosh and the Apple LaserWriter printer became the catalyst for a new application for personal computers—desktop publishing (q.v.).

In 1983, a major shakeout in the personal computer industry began, first affecting the companies selling low-priced machines to consumers. Companies that made strategic blunders or that lacked sufficient distribution or brand-awareness for their products disappeared. Many independent computer dealers, faced with eroding margins, either consolidated into large chains or quit the business.

The year 1985 was an extremely difficult one for Apple. Founder Steve Wozniak resigned from the company that February to start a new video electronics business, feeling that Apple was becoming too corporate. Macintosh and Apple II sales fell dramatically. Apple eliminated 1,200 jobs, sharply cut operating costs, and closed three factories. The company sustained its first quarterly loss.

The biggest blow—especially psychologically—came in September 1985 when the innovative founder Steve Jobs quit Apple, forced out by John Sculley, whom he had hired only two years before. The painful chasm between Jobs and Sculley, once close business partners, demoralized many Apple employees and had many in the industry wondering if the innovative spark that Jobs had ignited would be snuffed out by marketeer Sculley.

However, sales did start to pick up in 1986 as some businesses bought Macintoshes, spurred by introduction of the faster and more powerful Macintosh Plus, dozens of software and accessory products from Apple and third-party developers, and the new desktop publishing applications. Apple also continued to advance the technology of its original product line with a new computer, the Apple IIGS, and enhancements for older products.

Meanwhile, claiming innovation at Apple was dead, Jobs launched a rival company, NeXT, Inc., to make

FIG. 2. The popular Apple IIGS computer—the last of the Apple II line—which launched Apple computer 14 years ago. (Courtesy of Apple Computer, Inc.)

high-powered workstations for universities and businesses.

From 1987 through 1991, Apple continued to introduce new versions of the Macintosh that made it faster, more powerful, and more able to network with computers based on the MS/DOS operating system. While Apple remained dominant in the education market, by 1991 its share of the business market was just slightly more than 10 percent, with low-priced clones proving to be extremely tough competition. It was that intense price competition that spurred Apple to seek an alliance with IBM in 1991 in an attempt to insure that Apple's technology could communicate with other, more dominant computers in the business market.

After years of pursuing a strategy of high gross margins, Apple realized it would remain a niche player, especially in the business market, unless it lowered its prices and expanded its market share. Reaching this decision came at a heavy cost. Employees endured several company reorganizations, executive management hiring, and firings that included the dramatic exit of technology visionary Jean-Louis Gassee, president of Apple Products, who in many respects had years before stepped into the void left by Jobs as the company's technological leader.

FIG. 3. The Macintosh Plus—one of the earliest Macintosh computers. (Courtesy of Apple Computer, Inc.)

Gassee quite Apple in March 1990 when he and Sculley failed to agree on product development direction. Sculley took over direct supervision of Apple's research and development efforts. Michael Spindler, previous head of Apple France, was chosen as Apple's chief operating officer and later was also given the title of president of the company.

In October 1990, Apple instituted an aggressive strategy to gain share in all segments of the market with the introduction of lower-priced Macintosh systems—The Macintosh Classic, the Macintosh LC, and the Macintosh IIsi and lower-priced laser printers. As a result, Apple's market share began to increase despite an overall industry downturn. The downturn, which continued into 1991, and overspending inside Apple led to the company's second massive layoff in a decade when 1,200 persons lost their jobs, reducing Apple's worldwide employee base to about 13,000 people.

In May 1991, Apple began delivery of System 7, a new version of its proprietary operating system intended to make the system even easier to use and more powerful. Apple views System 7 as an answer to Microsoft's Windows 3.1 for the IBM-PC and compatibles.

The Alliance In October 1991, Apple Computer reached an agreement that startled and confused customers and employees alike because it paired the upstart Cupertino, California–based company with one of its arch rivals, International Business Machines, Corp. (IBM), in an alliance called Taligent to create new technologies that both companies tout as being crucial to their futures.

The agreement consists of five distinct technology initiatives. Three expand the companies' current technologies. Two focus on the creation of new technologies that both companies expect to be foundations for what they term "the second decade of personal computing."

Both companies vowed to remain tough competitors in the marketplace despite belief that alliance was necessary for long-term survival and to insure that innovation in the personal computer arena continues. Market analysts view the teaming of the two biggest makers of personal computers as a direct assault on software maker Microsoft Corporation, which during the past decade has grown increasingly powerful in the world of the IBM-PC and compatibles.

Rivals IBM and Apple agreed to more closely integrate Apple's Macintosh technology into IBM networks. They also agreed to create, with the help of Motorola, Inc., a new family of Reduced Instruction Set Computing (RISC) (*q.v.*) microprocessors optimized for personal computers and entry-level workstations (*q.v.*). Derived from IBM's single-chip implementation of its POWER RISC architecture, the proposed PowerPC chips are scheduled to be made by Motorola and IBM for both Apple Macintosh and IBM computers by 1994.

The two companies also signed licensing agreements for a new open-systems environment they called "PowerOpen," derived from AIX, IBM's industry-standard version of Unix, the Macintosh interface, and the POWER architecture. The companies claim that the environment—not available until 1994—will enable a computer system to run both Macintosh and AIX applications on RISC-based hardware from both companies.

John Sculley, Apple's chairman and chief executive officer, announced at the same time that by the end of the 1990s all Apple products will be based on RISC architecture (*q.v.*).

The two new technologies that these competitors agreed to jointly develop are multimedia technologies that enable computers to seamlessly integrate text, sound, video, and graphics and a new operating system based totally on object-oriented programming (OOP-*q.v.*) technology. Both companies say they will use the new operating system in future products—Apple in future Macintosh computers and IBM in OS/2 and AIX technology. Part of the deal included a cross-licensing of patent and visual displays, including a limited license to the Macintosh visual displays.

Apple's top-of-the-line machine is the Macintosh Quadra 900 (a tower design), and the desktop Quadra 700. Both run at twice the speed of Apple's previous top-of-the-line computer, the Macintosh FX, by virtue of being powered by the 25MHz 68040 Motorola microprocessor. The 68040 contains more than 1.2 million transistors, so key features can be incorporated directly onto the chip, including 8K of fast cache memory (*q.v.*), a floating point co-processor and a memory management unit. According to benchmark studies by Ingram Laboratories, the Quadras run faster than 80386- and 80486-based personal computers.

The Quadra line features built-in high-performance ethernet and LocalTalk and a new input/output subsystem based on ASIC—Application-Specific Integrated Circuit—that allows the Quadra computers to access peripherals and networks twice as fast as earlier Macintosh computers.

Two years after introducing the "luggable" 15-pound Macintosh Portable, Apple in October 1991 finally caught up with the rest of the portable makers by introducing three notebook-size computers (*see* LAPTOP COMPUTER). The Macintosh PowerBook line includes PowerBook 100 (co-designed and manufactured by Japanese power-

FIG. 5. Apple's latest product—Macintosh PowerBook notebook computers. (Courtesy of Apple Computer, Inc.)

house, Sony Corp.), PowerBook 140, and PowerBook 170, all of which weigh 5 pounds and include an integrated trackball and palm rest, full-size keyboard, full page-width screen, Apple's System 7 operating system, AppleTalk Remote Access software, an SCSI port for peripherals connection and a sound-output port and speaker. Each PowerBook includes at least 2 megabytes of memory expandable to 8 megabytes and a 20-megabyte or 40-megabyte internal hard disk. They differ in power, ranging from the PowerBook 100, based on the Motorola 16 MHz 68000 microprocessor, up to the PowerBook 170, featuring the 25 MHz 68030 microprocessor and 68882 math co-processor combination—computing power equivalent to Apple's Macintosh IIci.

By the end of fiscal 1991, Apple reported net sales of $6.3 billion, a 14-percent increase over fiscal 1990. Apple started fiscal 1992 (in October 1991) by announcing more CPU products than in any previous year in its history. Apple appears to have survived the personal computer industry's second major downturn and positioned itself with new products and new alliances to capture higher market share during the personal computer industry's second decade.

MARY A. C. FALLON

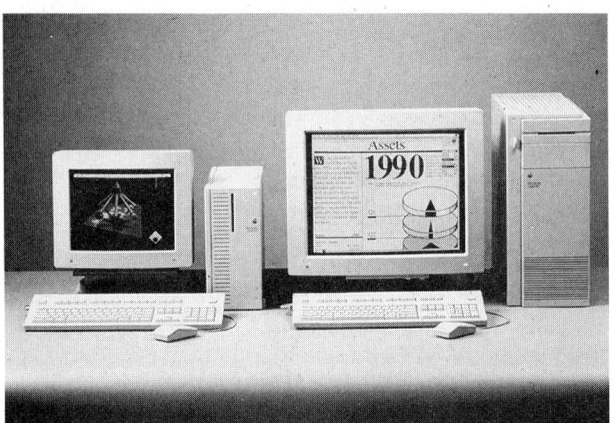

FIG. 4. Apple's newest high-performance computer, Macintosh Quadra 700 desktop computer and Macintosh Quadra 900 tower computer with security key. (Courtesy of Apple Computer, Inc.)

APPLICATIONS PROGRAMMING

For articles on related subjects *see* PROGRAMMING LANGUAGES; and SYSTEMS PROGRAMMING.

Applications programs are programs written to solve specific problems, to produce specific reports, to update specific files. The term is used in contradistinction to *systems programming* which deals with the development of the software tools that the applications programmer uses. The programming languages that are used most often in applications programming are Fortran and Ada (*q.v.*) for scientific applications and Cobol for data processing applications. Special Report Program Generator (RPG) languages are used on small data processing computers, and languages like Basic, Pascal, and APL are used extensively in time-sharing systems.

The ultimate aim of all software is to make it possible for the applications programmer to perform well and to write programs that produce results and make effective and efficient use of the computing system. Applications programs make use of subroutine libraries and special packages such as sort-merge systems and data access and data management systems. Most well-designed operating systems provide the applications programmer with special tools for analyzing and debugging programs.

There are very large applications systems such as airline reservations systems and on-line banking and merchandising systems in which many considerations of systems programming and of applications programming are intermixed.

SAUL ROSEN

APPLICATIVE PROGRAMMING. *See* FUNCTIONAL PROGRAMMING.

APPROXIMATION THEORY

For articles on related subjects *see* CHEBYSHEV APPROXIMATION; LEAST SQUARES APPROXIMATION; NUMERICAL ANALYSIS; and SPLINE.

Approximation theory concerns the following problem: Given a function $f(x)$ defined for x in a prescribed set X, a family of functions G, and a metric $d(f,g)$ (a mathematical prescription for measuring the distance between two functions), determine a function $g(x)$ in G that is "close" to $f(x)$ for x in X. For computer applications, $f(x)$ is typically a continuous function of one real variable, X is a real interval, G is a family of polynomials or of rational functions (ratios of polynomials), or of piecewise polynomials (splines - *q.v.*), and the metric is either a least squares metric

$$d_2(f,g,w) = \int_X [\, f(x) - g(x)]^2 \, w(x) \, dx,$$

or the Chebyshev metric

$$d_\infty(f,g,w) = \max_x |[f(x) - g(x)]\, w(x)|$$

where $w(x)$ is a weight function. For the Chebyshev metric, the weight is usually either $w(x) = 1$ or $w(x) = 1/f(x)$, where $f(x)$ is assumed not to vanish for x in X. This latter weighting is most useful when $f(x)$ varies considerably in magnitude across the interval X. Basic theorems examine the existence, uniqueness, and characterization of $g(x)$, sometimes in very abstract settings. In this article we will concentrate on polynomials as the most important approximating family, and on the Chebyshev metric, which is more important than the least squares metric in the

generation of approximations to functions to be used on a computer.

Let $f(x)$ be defined and continuous over a finite real interval X. The theoretical justification for using the Chebyshev metric [with $w(x) = 1$] is the Weierstrass approximation theorem, which asserts the existence of real polynomials that are arbitrarily close to $f(x)$ over the entire interval X. These polynomials are often obtained by appropriately truncating an infinite power series expansion of the function,

$$f(x) = \sum_{k=0}^{\infty} a_k x^k,$$

provided the series converges to $f(x)$ over X, i.e. provided that for any fixed value of x in X and any $\varepsilon > 0$, there is an integer N such that all partial sums

$$s_n(x) = \sum_{k=0}^{n} a_k x^k \qquad n > N$$

differ from $f(x)$ by less than ε. Such expansions are unique whenever they exist.

Some of the more important methods for generating series expansions are based upon the analytic properties of the function. Let $f(x)$ be continuous and have continuous derivatives of all orders at some point x_0 in X. Then the *Taylor series* expansion of $f(x)$ about x_0 is given by

$$f(x) = \sum_{k=0}^{\infty} a_k (x - x_0)^k$$

$$a_k = f^{(k)}(x_0)/k! = \frac{1}{k!} \frac{d^k f(x)}{dx^k}\bigg|_{x=x_0}$$

Since this expansion is based upon a detailed knowledge of the function of x_0, the Taylor polynomials $g_n(x)$ of degree n, obtained by truncating the series, approximate $f(x)$ well for small $|x - x_0|$, but the error $f(x) - g_n(x)$ typically grows monotonically in magnitude with increas-

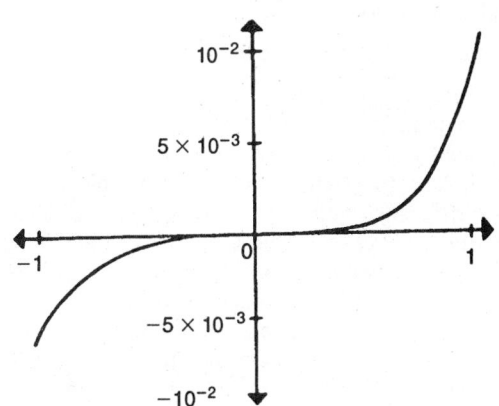

FIG. 1. Error $e^x - g_4(x) = 1 + x + (x2/2!) + (x3/3!) + (x4/4!)$ for approximation over $[-1,1]$ by fourth-degree Taylor polynomial.

ing $|x - x_0|$. Frequently $\max_x |f(x) - g_n(x)|$ occurs at one of the boundaries of X. For example, Fig. 1 shows the error associated with the fourth-degree Taylor polynomial approximation of e^x over $[-1,1]$, where the Taylor series is

$$e^x = 1 + x + \frac{x^2}{2} + \frac{x^3}{6} + \frac{x^4}{24} + \cdots + \frac{x^n}{n!} + \cdots .$$

A function $f(x)$ has a *pole* of finite integer order n at x_0 whenever the Taylor series for $(x - x_0)^m f(x)$ exists for $m = n$, but fails to exist for smaller integer values of m. The *Laurent series* is then given by $(x - x_0)^{-n}$ times the Taylor series for $(x - x_0)^n f(x)$. As an example, the Laurent series for $\csc(x)$, which has an isolated pole of order 1 at $x = 0$, is

$$\csc(x) = \frac{1}{x} + \frac{x}{6} + \frac{7x^3}{360} + \frac{31x^5}{15,120} + \cdots ,$$

which converges for $|x| < \pi$. When the function has an isolated pole of infinite order, the Laurent series takes the form

$$f(x) = \sum_{k=-\infty}^{\infty} a_k x^k ,$$

where the derivation of the coefficients a_k generally involves methods from the theory of functions of a complex variable. The expansion

$$\arctan(x) = \frac{\pi}{2} - \frac{1}{x} + \frac{1}{3x^3} - \frac{1}{5x^5} + \cdots ,$$

valid for $|x| > 1$, is of this type. Truncation of Laurent series leads to rational approximations for $f(x)$.

If the interval X is semi-infinite, $X = [b,\infty)$, $b > 0$, a divergent *asymptotic expansion* of $f(x)$,

$$f(x) \sim \sum_{k=0}^{\infty} a_k x^{-k} ,$$

may yield useful rational approximations to $f(x)$ even though it does not converge to $f(x)$ for any finite value of x. Let $s_n(x) = \sum_{k=0}^{n} a_k x^{-k}$ be the partial sum of the asymptotic series. Then, for any fixed value of x, there is an n which minimizes the error $|f(x) - s_n(x)|$. For fixed n, and x sufficiently large, the error can be made as small as desired. Thus, for particular $\varepsilon > 0$, it is usually possible to choose first an n and then an X (i.e. a,b) so that $s_n(x)$ approximates $f(x)$ to within ε over X in the Chebyshev metric. The derivation of an asymptotic series is often a difficult task involving advanced mathematical tools. As with power series, the expansions are unique.

If the Taylor series expansion for $f(x)$ exists, then the *Padé table* for $f(x)$ is the array of rational approximations

$$R_{mn}(x) = \frac{p_0 + p_1 x + \cdots + p_m x^m}{1 + q_1 x 1 \cdots + q_n x^n} ,$$

characterized by the property that the power series expansion of $R_{mn}(x)$ is identical to the Taylor series expansion through terms in x^{m+n}. The entries $R_{m0}(x)$ are the Taylor polynomials, and the entries $R_{00}(x), R_{01}(x) R_{11}(x),\ldots$ along and just above the main diagonal are the successive convergents of a Stieltjes continued fraction, or *S-fraction*, expansion of $f(x)$:

$$f(x) = \cfrac{a_0}{1 - \cfrac{a_1 x}{1 - a_2 x}}$$

Padé approximants $R_{mn}(x)$ are often better approximations to $f(x)$ than are the Taylor polynomials of degree $m + n$. All elements of the Padé table agree with $f(x)$ exactly at the point of expansion, but $f(x) - R_{mn}(x)$ tends to grow as x moves away from that point. As an example, the S-fraction expansion of e^x is

$$e^x = \cfrac{1}{1 - \cfrac{x}{1 + \cfrac{x/2}{1 - \cfrac{x/6}{1 + x/6}}}}$$

The corresponding Padé approximation $R_{22}(x)$ is obtained by truncating the S-fraction to just the terms given above, and is

$$R_{22}(x) = \frac{12 + 6x + x^2}{12 - 6x + x^2} .$$

Fig. 2 shows the error $e^x - R_{22}(x)$ over the interval $[-1,1]$. Note that the maximum error is less than half of that associated with the fourth-degree Taylor polynomial.

By sacrificing accuracy in the neighborhood of the point of expansion, it is possible to distribute the error over the interval of approximation and to obtain better approximations to $f(x)$ over X in the sense of the Chebyshev metric. The rational Chebyshev, or *minimax*, approximation to $f(x)$ of degree (m,n) is that rational

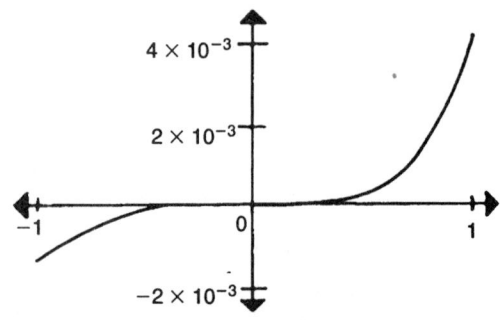

FIG. 2. Error $e^x - R_{22}(x)$ for approximation over $[-1,1]$ by Padé element.

function $R^*_{mn}(x)$, which minimizes $d(f, R_{mn}, w)$. Basic theorems assert that such an $R^*_{mn}(x)$ exists, is unique, and is characterized by the error $[f(x) - R^*_{mn}(x)]w(x)$ achieving its maximum magnitude with alternating sign a prescribed number of times as x moves across the interval X. The determination of $R^*_{mn}(x)$ is not easy, but the characterization theorem leads to algorithms, such as the Remes algorithm, for computing approximations close to $R^*_{mn}(x)$.

The Chebyshev polynomials

$$T_n(x) = 2^{1-n} \cos(n \cos^{-1} x), \quad -1 \le x \le 1,$$

are instrumental in the generation of near-minimax polynomial approximations. If $f(x)$ is continuous and sufficiently smooth, then

$$f(x) = \frac{1}{2} a_0 T_0(x) + \sum_{k=1}^{\infty} a_k T_k(x), \quad -1 \le x \le 1,$$

where

$$a_k = \frac{2}{\pi} \int_{-1}^{1} \frac{f(x) T_k(x)}{(1 - x^2)^{1/2}} \, dx,$$

is the *Chebyshev polynomial expansion* of $f(x)$. (This is related to the *Fourier series* for $f(x)$ by the change of variable $w = \cos^{-1} x$. The partial sums of this expansion are the best polynomial approximations to $f(x)$ for the metric $d_2[f, g, 1/(1 - x^2)^{1/2}]$ and are very close to the minmax polynomial approximation to $f(x)$ in most cases. As an example, the coefficients in the Chebyshev series expansion for e^x are $a_k = 2I_k(1)$, where the I_k are modified Bessel functions. Truncation of this series after five terms leads to the approximation

$$g(x) = 1.000045 + 0.997308x + 0.499197x^2$$
$$+ 0.177347x^3 + 0.043794x^4$$

for the interval $[-1,1]$. The maximum error associated with this approximation is only about one-twentieth of that associated with the fourth-degree Taylor polynomial (see Fig. 3).

Legendre, Jacobi, Hermite, Laguerre, and Gegenbauer polynomials are other important families of polynomials similarly associated with particular choices of weights and intervals in least squares approximation. Since power series expansions are unique, the expansion of $f(x)$ in polynomials from any of these families can be formally obtained by replacing each x^k in the power series by its exact representation in polynomials of the family and then collecting terms. This "rearrangement" of the power series may alter the convergence of the series so that the new series converges for a larger (or smaller) interval than the original series.

Lanczos' telescoping, or economizing, process is similar to this rearrangement process. Starting from a truncated power series, such as a Taylor polynomial, over the interval $[-1,1]$, the degree of the polynomial is lowered by successively replacing the highest-order term x^n by the polynomial

$$P_{n-1}(x) = x^n - 2^{1-n} T_n(x),$$

which is the minimax approximation to x^n by a polynomial of degree less than n. The approximation error introduced at each step tends to distribute the cumulative error over the interval of approximation so that the polynomials in the resulting sequence tend to be better approximations to $f(x)$ than the corresponding truncations of the original power series, but they are not as good as those obtained by truncating the Chebyshev polynomial expansion. For example, the approximation

$$g(x) = 1 + 0.997396x + 0.5x^2 + 0.177083x^3 + 0.041667x^4$$

to e^x is obtained by truncating the Taylor series after six terms and replacing x^5 by $P_4(x) = (20x^3 - 5x)/16$. The corresponding maximum error over $[-1,1]$ is more than four times that of the corresponding truncated Chebyshev series, but only one-fifth that of the fourth-degree Taylor polynomial (see Fig. 4).

An extensive theory of approximation exists for functions of a complex variable and for multivariate functions (functions of two or more real variables). The theory relies heavily upon convergent or asymptotic power series and continued fraction expansions. The Taylor and

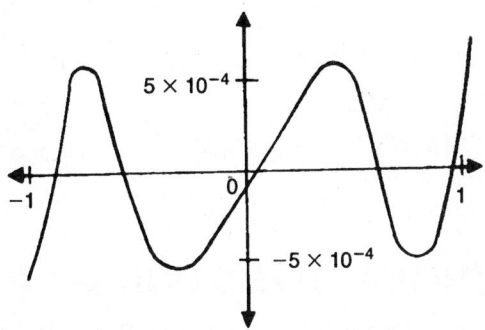

FIG. 3. Error $e^x - \sum_{k=0}^{4} a_k T_k(x)$ for approximation over $[-1,1]$ by truncated Chebyshev series.

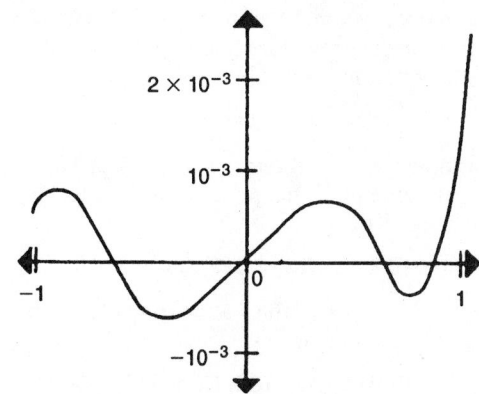

FIG. 4. Error $e^x - g(x)$ for approximation over $[-1,1]$ by fifth-degree Taylor polynomial telescoped to fourth degree.

Laurent series and the Padé table extend to the complex case directly. While the theory of minimax approximation generalizes to these functions, the generalizations are not very useful (e.g. uniqueness is lost in the multivariate case) and reliable algorithms for generating the approximations do not exist. Except for certain elementary functions, direct approximations to complex or multivariate functions are not often used in computer applications. Instead, indirect evaluation methods based upon recurrence relations, differential equations, etc., are used.

References

1967. Meinardus, G. *Approximation of Functions: Theory and Numerical Methods*, translated by L. Schumaker, New York: Springer-Verlag.

1968. Fike, C. T. *Computer Evaluation of Mathematical Functions.* Englewood Cliffs, NJ: Prentice-Hall.

1970. Cheney, E. W. *Introduction to Approximation Theory*, New York: McGraw-Hill.

WILLIAM J. CODY

ARCHITECTURE, COMPUTER. *See*
COMPUTER ARCHITECTURE.

ARGUMENT

For articles on related subjects *see* DATA TYPE; GLOBAL AND LOCAL VARIABLES; MACROINSTRUCTION; OPERAND; PROCEDURE; and SUBPROGRAM.

In strict analogy to mathematics, where an argument of a function is the value of a variable used to evaluate the function, an *argument* in computing is a value supplied to a procedure, a function, or a macroinstruction which is required in order to evaluate the procedure, function, or macro. Another term sometimes used instead of argument is *parameter*.

Two different kinds of arguments need to be distinguished: *dummy* or *formal* arguments, and *actual* or *calling* arguments. A dummy argument is an argument used in the definition of a procedure, function, or macro; an actual argument is that which is substituted when the procedure, function, or macro is invoked. For example, Fig. 1 displays a Pascal procedure to compute the solution of a quadratic equation.

$$ax^2 + bx + c = 0$$

The variables a, b, c, *mode*, $x1$, and $x2$ in Fig. 1 are all dummy arguments. If this procedure were to be used to compute the roots of

$$10.7X^2 + (R1 + 6.23)X + S*S = 0 \qquad (1)$$

where R1 and S are variables appearing elsewhere in the program, the statement

QUAD (y, z, j, 10.7, R1 + 6.23, S*S)

might be given. Each argument in this statement is an actual argument, i.e. the argument that will be associated with the dummy argument in the subroutine definition. Thus, when QUAD is executed in response to the call above:

- The values used for a, b, and c will be, respectively, 10.7, R1 + 6.23, and S*S, with the latter two being evaluated using the current calling program values for R1 and S.
- The variable i in the calling program will be set equal to the value of *mode* in the procedure.
- The main program variables y and z will contain the results of the solution of Eq. (1) after execution of Quad.

The dummy arguments that are preceded by **var** in Fig. 1 — y, z, and j — are call-by-reference arguments in that only the storage locations but not the values of the calling arguments are transferred to the procedure. In this way, the values given to $x1$, $x2$, and *mode* in the procedure are returned directly to the calling program. On the other hand, a, b, and c are call-by-value arguments in that their values are transmitted to the procedure, since there is no need to send new values of these arguments back to the calling program.

Formal arguments are always required to be identifiers, but, as the example above indicates, actual arguments may be identifiers or numbers or arithmetic expressions. Most languages allow great generality in the form of the actual arguments, although there may be requirements that the calling arguments have the same *type* as the formal arguments (i.e. a real calling argument if the formal argument denotes a real variable).

Subprogram arguments may also be classified as *input* or *output* arguments, with the former denoting arguments provided to the subprogram and the latter the arguments that convey results back to the main program. In the example given in Fig. 1, a, b, and c are input arguments and *mode*, $x1$, and $x2$ are output arguments. Sometimes an argument may be both an input and output argument; for example, when a procedure to compute the next prime number receives as input the variable P denoting the current prime number and returns the value of the next prime number to P. Sometimes the arguments of a subprogram may be *implicit*; i.e. they are not stated explicitly in the statement heading the subprogram. This happens, for example, when a procedure in a subblock uses variables global to that block.

ANTHONY RALSTON

ARITHMETIC.   *See* INTERVAL ARITHMETIC; and SIGNIFICANCE ARITHMETIC.

ARITHMETIC-LOGIC UNIT (ALU)

For articles on related subjects *see* ADDER; ARITHMETIC, COMPUTER; BOOLEAN ALGEBRA; BUS; CENTRAL PROCESSING UNIT; CODES; INSTRUCTION SET; NUMBERS AND NUMBER SYSTEMS; OPERAND; REGISTER; and SHIFTING.

```
procedure QUAD (var x1,x2: real; var mode: integer; a,b,c: real);
        var disc: real;    { discriminant }
        begin
{ Check for leading coefficient = 0 }
        if a = 0 then        { Both a and b = 0? }
            if b = 0 then
                mode := 0    {to indicate no root possible}
                else
                begin
                    x1 := −c/b;
                    mode := 1    {to indicate a single real root}
                end
            else
{ a ≠ 0 so there are two roots }
            disc := b * b −4.0 * a * c;
            if disc < 0 then
{ Complex roots (real part x1, imaginary part x2) }
                begin
                    x1 := −b/(2.0 * a);
                    x2 := sqtr(−disc)/(2.0 * a);
                    mode := 2    {to indicate complex roots}
                end
                else
{ Real roots - compute so as to avoid taking difference }
{      of two nearly equal quantities; x1 is root of}
{      larger magnitude}
                begin
                    if b < 0 then
                        x1 := −b + sqrt(disc)
                        else
                        x1 := −b − sqrt(disc);
                    if x1 = 0 then x2 := 0
                        else x2 := c/(x1 * a);
                    mode := 3    {to indicate two real roots}
                end
        end;
```

FIG. 1

The *arithmetic-logic unit* (ALU) is that functional part of the digital computer that carries out arithmetic and logic operations on machine words that represent operands. It is usually considered to be a part of the central processing unit (CPU - *q.v.*). In some computer systems, separate units exist for arithmetic operations (the arithmetic unit, AU) and for logic operations (the logic unit, LU).

Many computers contain more than one AU. For example, a separate Index AU is frequently employed to perform additions or subtraction operations on address parts of instructions for the purpose of indexing, boundary tests for memory protection, etc. Large computer systems employ separate AUs for different classes of algorithms; for example, the IBM System 360, Model 91 contained a fixed-point AU and a floating-point AU. Multiprocessor systems contain several identical ALUs; for example, the ILLIAC IV contained 64 identical ALUs with associated memory modules.

A complete discussion of an ALU must describe its three fundamental attributes:

1. Operands and results;
2. Functional organization; and
3. Algorithms.

Operands and Results   Two kinds of ALU organizations can be distinguished with respect to the length of machine words. In machines with *fixed word length*, all words consist of the same number of bits. In machines with *variable word length*, one byte (or sometimes just one bit) is the shortest machine word. Longer machine words consist of some integral number of bytes.

The operands and results of the ALU are machine words of two kinds: *arithmetic words*, which represent numerical values in digital form, and *logic words*, which represent arbitrary sets of digitally encoded symbols.

Arithmetic words consist of strings of digits. Conventional radix r number representations allow r values for one digit: $0, 1,..., r - 1$. Practical design considerations have limited the choice of radices to the values 2, 4, 8, 10, and 16. The value of every digit is represented by a set of bits. Radices 2, 4, 8, and 16 employ binary numbers having lengths of 1, 2, 3, and 4 bits, respectively, to represent the values of one digit. Radix-10 digit values are usually represented by four or five bits. Most commonly used are the four-bit BCD (binary-coded decimal) and excess-3 encodings and the five-bit biquinary encoding (*see* CODES).

Two methods have been employed to represent negative numbers. In the sign-and-magnitude form, a separate *sign bit* is attached to the string of digits to represent the + and − signs. (Usually, 0 represents the + sign, and 1 represents the − sign.) In the true-and-complement form, the negative value $-x$ is represented as the complement (*q.v.*) with respect to A of the value x; i.e.

$$-x \text{ is represented by } A - x$$

The value of A used in ALUs is either $A = r^{n+1}$ or $A = r^{n+1} - 1$, when x is represented by n digits in the sign-and-magnitude form. An illustration for radix 10 and radix 2 and $n = 4$ is given below.

Sign and Magnitude	$A = 10^5 - 1$ (9s complement)	$A = 10^5$ (10s complement)
+4902	04902	04902
−4902	95097	95098
	$A = 2^5 - 1$ (1s complement)	$A = 2^5$ (2s complement)
+1010	01010	01010
−1010	10101	10110

The use of complements to represent negative values makes it possible to replace the subtraction algorithm in an ALU by a complementation followed by an addition modulo A.

Other important properties of operands and results are (Avižienis, 1972):

1. Location of the radix point.
2. Use of multiple-precision representations.
3. Use of floating-point forms.
4. Explicit designation of the number of significant digits in a representation.

5. Encoding in error-detecting (or error-correcting) codes.

The use of non-conventional number representations in computers as a means to increase the speed of arithmetic has been proposed. Extensive studies have been made of *residue* number systems (Svoboda, 1962) and of *signed-digit* number systems (Avižienis and Tung, 1970); however, they have not reached practical application in ALU design.

Logic words that serve as operands represent alphanumeric information and are subject only to logic algorithms that are applied to individual bits of the operands. These algorithms are (1) negation for one operand, and (2) the 16 two-variable logic operations for corresponding bits of two operands.

Functional Organization and Algorithms of an ALU

An ALU consists of three types of functional parts: storage registers, operations circuits, and sequencing circuits, as shown in Fig. 1. The inputs and outputs of the ALU are connected to other functional units of the computer, such as the main memory, the program execution control unit, and input/output devices. A *bus* (*q.v.*) is most frequently used as the means of connection. In some cases the ALU may be connected to two or more buses within the computer system.

The input information received by the ALU consists of operands, operation codes, and format codes. The operands are machine words that represent numeric or alphanumeric information in the form of a string of binary digits (bits). The operation code identifies one operation from the set of available arithmetic and logic operations, and also designates the location (within local storage) of the operands and of the results. The designation of operands is omitted in ALUs with limited local storage; for example, an ADD operation code in a single-accumulator ALU always means the addition of the incoming operand to the operand in the accumulator register and storage of the sum in the accumulator. The format code is used when the ALU can operate on more than one type of operand; for example, the ADD operation can be specified either for fixed-point or for floating-point operands. Often, the operation code and the format code are represented by a single set of bits.

The output information delivered by the ALU consists of results, *condition codes*, and *singularity codes*. The results are machine words generated by the specified

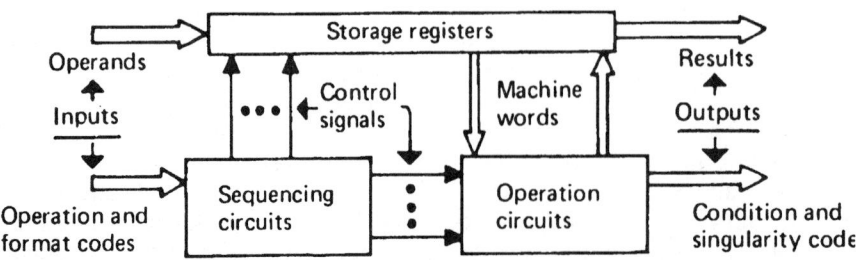

FIG. 1. Functions of an ALU.

operations and stored in the local storage registers. The condition codes are bits or sets of bits that identify specific conditions associated with a result, such as that the value of the result is positive, negative, zero; that the result consists of all zeros, all ones, etc. The singularity codes indicate that the specified operation does not yield a representable result. Examples of singularities are *overflow*, i.e. the value of the result exceeds the allowed range; attempted division by zero, excessive loss of precision in floating-point operations, error caused by a logic fault, etc. Singularity codes usually set a flip-flop in the machine status word.

Internally, the ALU is composed of storage registers, logic circuits that perform arithmetic and logic algorithms, and logic circuits that control the sequence of gating operations within the ALU. The diagram of a simple ALU is shown in Fig. 2. The ALU contains three registers: the operand register, OPR; the accumulator register, ACC; and the multiplier-quotient register, MQR. Each register contains one machine word, i.e. for a machine word length of n bits, the register consists of n flip-flops.

The gating of words into the ALU registers and from the registers into the operation circuits or out of the ALU is controlled by the sequencing logic (SL), which applies a sequence of gate-enabling signals to the gates G_i of Fig. 2. Each sequence corresponds to one of the algorithms provided within the ALU. The sequencing logic is implemented either in "hard wired" form, using counters and decoding circuits, or by means of a micro-programmed control unit. The sequence of gating signals is initiated by the receipt of the operation and format codes in the ALU.

The operation circuits consist of the adder (AD), the shifter (SH), and the logic operator circuits (LO). The adder forms the sum of the numbers in OPR and ACC and returns it to the ACC. When the length of the sum exceeds the standard word length, the overflow detection (OD) circuit issues an overflow singularity code, and the excess digit of the sum is placed into an overflow digit position (AOD), which is located at the left end of the ACC. Subtraction is usually implemented as complementation of the subtrahend in OPR, followed by its addition to the minuend in ACC. A subtractor may be used instead of an adder in Fig. 2; in this case, subtraction is carried out directly, and addition is implemented as the complementation of the addend in OPR, followed by its subtraction from the augend in ACC.

The SH circuits perform left-shift and right-shift operations on the words in ACC and MQR. A single-shift operation displaces every digit in the register to the adjacent position on the left or on the right. Shifts are specified either for one register or for both registers simultaneously, with the rightmost position of ACC adjoining the leftmost position of MQR. There are three classes of shifts:

1. *Circular shifts* (*rotations*). The rightmost and the leftmost positions of a register are treated as adjacent during the shift.
2. *Logical shifts*. Digits are discarded from end positions and zeros are inserted; e.g. during a single

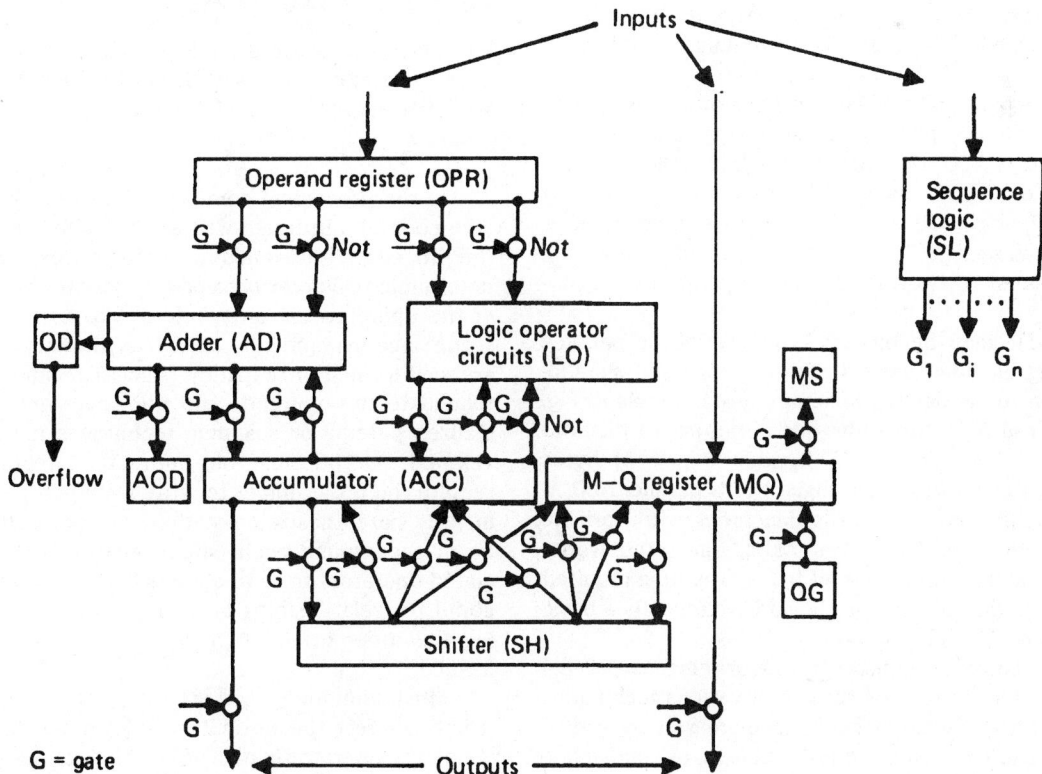

FIG. 2. Organization of an ALU.

right shift, the rightmost digit is lost and the leftmost position is filled in with zero.

3. *Arithmetic shifts.* The purpose of an arithmetic shift is to multiply (left) or to divide (right) the operand by the radix *r*. For negative numbers, the sign bit must be treated with special care (*see* SHIFTING).

The shifter is frequently designed as an integral part of the ACC and MQ registers; they are then called *shift registers*.

Multiplication and division operations are carried out as a sequence of additions or subtractions and arithmetic shifts. The MQ register serves as the third register for these operations. In multiplication, the multiplicand x is placed into the OPR register and the multiplier y into the MQ register of Fig. 2, while ACC is cleared to zero. The least significant digit y_0 of the multiplier is sensed by the multiplier sensing (MS) circuit, and x is added y_0 times to the contents of ACC. Then, ACC and MQ registers are arithmetically shifted one position to the right, and the next multiplier digit, y_1, is sensed by the MS circuit. After all n digits of y have been sensed, the double-length product xy is located in ACC and MQ registers. A roundoff operation is needed to reduce the product to single-word length.

To perform division, the dividend is placed into the ACC. If the dividend is of double length, the MQ register receives its less significant half. The divisor is placed into the OP register, and division is carried out as a sequence of trial subtractions and left arithmetic shifts. Quotient digits are generated one at a time in the quotient generation (QG) circuit and inserted at the right end of the MQ register after each shift, beginning with the most significant quotient digit, q_{n-1}. After n steps, the quotient is located in the MQ register and the remainder in the ACC register.

The logic operator LO circuits perform the specified logic operation on pairs of bits in corresponding storage positions a_i of ACC and x_i of OPR. The bits of the result are returned to ACC. The usual set of operations includes NOT (one bit: $\bar{a}_i$ or $\bar{x}_i$), AND $(a_i \wedge x_i)$, OR $(a_i \vee x_i)$, EXCLUSIVE-OR $(a_i \oplus x_i)$, EQUIVALENCE $(a_i \equiv x_i)$, NAND $(\bar{a}_i \vee \bar{x}_i)$ and NOR $(\bar{a}_i \wedge \bar{x}_i)$; sometimes all 16 two-variable logic operations are provided.

An ALU may be bit-serial, byte-serial, or parallel, depending on how many digits are processed simultaneously in the adder (or logic operator) circuits of Fig. 2. In a serial ALU, the adder adds one pair of digits at once; in a byte-serial ALU, it adds a pair of bytes (consisting of two or more digits); in a parallel ALU, it adds two full machine words. Machines with variable word length have byte-serial ALUs, since the words consist of a varying number of bytes. The time required to complete one addition in the adder circuits is a basic time unit of ALU operation.

The speed of execution of the algorithms in a parallel ALU may be increased by the use of various techniques (Garner, 1965). Addition speed is increased by use of *carry-completion sensing, carry-lookahead,* or *conditional-sum adders.* Multiplication is accelerated by multiplier recoding and by the use of multiple-operand carry-save

adders. Division employs redundant quotient recoding techniques with approximate estimates, or quadratic convergence, which uses fast multiplication to generate the quotient (Anderson et al., 1967). The technique of *pipelining* has also been employed to increase the effective throughput of an ALU (Anderson *et al.*, 1967).

The use of more storage registers within the ALU increases the speed of computing by reducing the number of memory accesses. Therefore, 8, 16, or more ALU registers are often used instead of the three registers shown in Fig. 2; each register may perform the function of ACC, OPR, MQ, or index register (*q.v.*) and hence qualify as *general registers* (*q.v.*). In some architectures, several ALU registers may be used to hold a *stack* (*q.v.*) of ALU operands and results.

References

1962. Svoboda, A. "The Numerical System of Residual Classes," in *Digital Information Processors.* New York: Wiley Interscience, 543-574.

1965. Garner, H.L. "Number Systems and Arithmetic," in Alt, F. L. (Ed.), *Advances in Computers* **6**: 131-194. New York: Academic Press.

1970. Avižienis A. and Tung, C. "A Universal Arithmetic Building Element (ABE) and Design Method for Arithmetic Processors," *IEEE Trans. Comput.* **C-19**, 8: 733-745 (August).

1979. Hwang, Kai. *Computer Arithmetic: Principles, Architecture and Design.* New York: Wiley.

ALGIRDAS AVIŽIENIS

ARITHMETIC SCAN

For articles on related subjects *see* COMPILER CONSTRUCTION; EXPRESSION; GRAMMARS; LANGUAGE PROCESSORS; OPERATOR PRECEDENCE; POLISH NOTATION; and WELL-FORMED FORMULA.

In the process of compilation into machine executable code of a program written in a high-level language, the procedure for examining arithmetic expressions and determining *operator precedence*, the order of execution of the operators, is often referred to as the *arithmetic scan*. Since syntactically correct arithmetic expressions are well formed in that they possess regular properties related to the operands and the operators, many specialized parsing or scanning techniques have been developed. One possible, but impractical, technique is to require the programmer to write arithmetic expressions in fully parenthesized notation (i.e. parentheses must be placed around each pair of operands and its associated operator) so as to obviate the need for knowledge about the relationships between operators in determining the order in which the operations are to be performed.

Most commonly used are transformational systems, which convert the normal infix form (i.e. the form in which the operator is placed between its operands) to a Polish form, in which there exists no parentheses and the order of execution of the operators is specified by their positioning. Such a system is needed because of the difficulty of associating operands with operators in infix notation. As an example, consider the expression

$$(A * X + B)/(C * X - D) \qquad (1)$$

which, because of the usual precedence relations among arithmetic operators, is to be interpreted in fully parenthesized notation, as

$$(((A*X) + B)/ ((C*X) - D)) \qquad (2)$$

By use of a classical algorithm, which scans across the string in expression (1) from left to right just once, this string can be converted to the Polish postfix string

$$AX*B + CX*D -/ \qquad (3)$$

which, without a need for parentheses or precedence relations, has uniquely the interpretation of expression (2). With one more single scan across the string, it can be compiled into machine code.

The arithmetic scan described above is a special case of a general syntactic analyzer that uses precedence relationships (*see also* COMPILER CONSTRUCTION).

J. A. N. LEE AND ANTHONY RALSTON

ARITHMETIC, COMPUTER

For articles on related subjects *see* COMPLEMENT; INTERVAL ARITHMETIC; NUMBERS AND NUMBER SYSTEMS; PRECISION; ROUNDOFF ERROR; SIGNIFICANCE ARITHMETIC; and SIGNIFICANT DIGIT.

The earliest electronic computers were developed in the 1940s to provide arithmetic engines capable of solving a variety of problems, many of them military. Computers, as general symbol manipulators, now solve other intriguing problems, but numerical calculations are still of vital importance in computer applications. How computers store numbers and perform arithmetic and how computer arithmetic differs from ordinary hand computation are topics that should be understood by anyone who uses computers.

Computer Storage of Numbers   A memory *cell* is the smallest unit of addressable computer memory. Word-oriented computers typically use large cell sizes, such as 60 or 64 bits. Byte, or character, addressable computers address memory in small units called *bytes*. (In this article, a byte is assumed to be an 8-bit cell. In the hexadecimal number system, a byte is stored as two hexadecimal digits, or *hexits*.) In word-oriented computers, a number is stored in one word, while in byte-oriented computers, a number is stored in multiple bytes (2, 4, 8, 10, and 16 bytes have been commonly used). "Single-precision" numbers typically occupy 32 bits of storage, and "double-precision" numbers occupy 64 bits.

A given number may be stored in one of two formats: *fixed-point* or *floating-point*. Fig. 1 illustrates the storage of two numbers, 0.15625 and 57.8125, as fixed-point numbers in a 32-bit format. Throughout this article, numbers in the text will be decimal numbers and those illustrated will be binary. For convenience, only positive numbers will be used in examples. Storage of negative numbers can be either in absolute value and sign form or in complement form (*see* COMPLEMENT).

Two points are worth noting about the numbers in Fig. 1:

1. The left-hand bit (S or bit 0) represents the sign of the number; 0 is used for positive numbers and 1 for negative numbers.
2. The normal binary point (i.e. the "decimal" or radix point) is assumed to be at the left end of the number, just to the right of the sign bit. The programmer, however, may choose a different or *implicit binary point*, so long as computation is done consistently with respect to the chosen

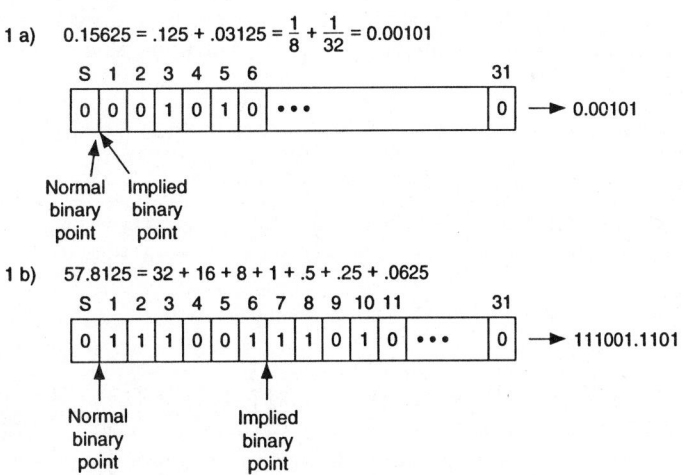

FIG. 1.   Fixed-point numbers.

alternative position. A computer calculating with fixed-point numbers assumes that the binary point is always in the same, fixed location—hence the name "fixed point." In this article and in some computers, this assumption is as shown in Fig. 1, but some computers assume the binary point to be at the right end of the number. When the latter is done, all bit patterns normally represent whole numbers, or *integers*. Integer arithmetic is discussed later.

Hardware for storing and manipulating numbers in fixed-point form was the only kind available in early computers. The arithmetic of fixed-point numbers created several major problems:

1. How could numbers with magnitudes of 1 or greater be handled? Such numbers can be stored as fixed-point numbers, but when using these numbers in computations, programmers must be careful to keep track of the implicit location of the radix point.

2. More significant problems occur when two numbers have implicit radix points in different positions. How could these be added, subtracted, multiplied, and divided? Fig. 1(b) uses an implied radix point to show how 57.8125 could be stored. As an example of these two problems, consider adding the numbers in Fig. 1(a) and Fig. 1(b). Before bit-by-bit addition can be done, one of the numbers must be shifted relative to the other.

The term *scaling* is used for the twin activities of shifting the numbers and choosing the location of the implicit binary point. Numbers are usually scaled before they are stored or used in computations. Scaling is difficult and tedious for all but the simplest calculations. Scaling problems led to the introduction of floating-point hardware capabilities, which are now used for the vast majority of numerical computations on computers.

Numbers stored in "floating-point" format closely resemble "scientific notation." A number in scientific notation is represented. $f * R^E$, where f is a fraction in the range $0 <= f < 1$, R is the radix (usually 10), and E is the signed integral power (exponent) of the radix. Thus, the number 57.8125 in Fig. 1(b) would be represented as $.578125 * 10^2$, where .578125 is the fraction, 10 is the radix, and 2 is the exponent. Using floating-point terminology, the fraction .578125 is called the *mantissa*. The term *floating-point* is used because the radix point is not fixed, but can move, or "float," depending on the value of the exponent. Floating-point implementations provide solutions to the two scaling problems and also facilitate computations with a larger range of numbers than can be handled effectively with fixed-point systems.

To store a single-precision floating-point number in a byte-addressable memory, separate portions of the four bytes must be assigned to the sign bit, the exponent, and the fraction. A floating-point format for N bits is labeled (X, Y) where 1) $X + Y + 1 = N$, 2) X bits are allocated to the exponent, and 3) Y bits are allocated to the mantissa. For any fixed number of bits N, increasing X increases the range of representable numbers but decreases the precision, while decreasing X produces a finer precision but less numeric range. Fig. 2 displays 32-bit binary floating-point formats for 0.15625 and 57.8125. Fig. 2(a) shows 0.15625 in (7,24) format, and Fig. 2(b) shows 57.8125 in (8,23) format.

The following two comments pertain to Fig. 2.

1. As with fixed-point numbers, the binary point of the mantissa is assumed to be in the same place, usually at the left end, but some implementations position the binary point at the right end. The sign bit (S or bit 0) always represents the sign of the mantissa.

2. Special techniques are needed to represent exponents, which may be zero, positive, or negative. One technique is to let bit 1 denote the sign of the exponent, but, more commonly, "biased" exponents are used. The format in Fig. 2(a) uses "bias-64" to represent any signed exponent -64 to $+63$ by producing unsigned numbers 0 to $2^7 - 1 = 127$. Thus 1000000 represents the exponent 0, 1000001 represents 1, 0111111 represents -1, and so forth. Fig. 2(b) uses "bias-128" and can represent any signed exponent from -128 to $+127$. For floating-point hardware to work correctly, the computer system's arithmetic unit must be able to interpret the biased exponents

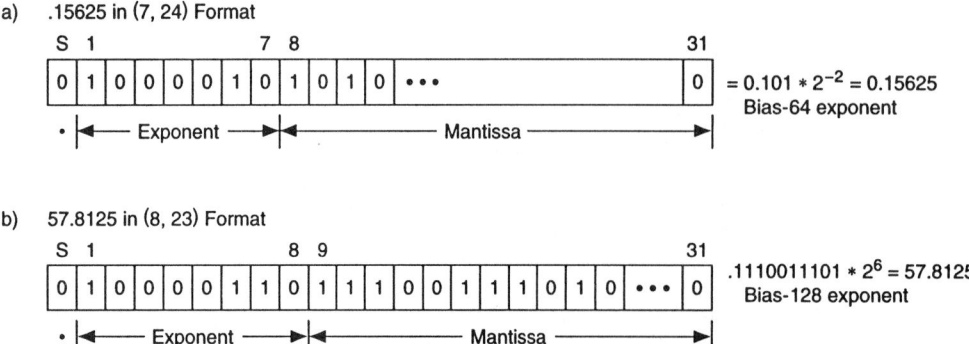

FIG. 2. Floating-point numbers.

correctly. A biased exponent is called a *characteristic*. The advantage of using biased exponents placed to the left of the floating-point word is that a sequence of such numbers can be sorted as if they were integers. (On most computers, integer comparisons are significantly faster than floating-point comparisons.)

Floating-point mantissas are usually stored in a "normalized" form, which requires the most significant digit to be non-zero. Systems using binary formats often "imply" the most significant bit (since it is always 1), but do not store it, while systems using hexadecimal cannot imply a non-zero most significant hexit, as it could be any of 1, 2,...,F. The apparent 24-bit precision of the mantissa on the IBM 360 and its successors degenerates to just 21 bits—the equivalent of six decimal digits—whenever a mantissa begins with hexadecimal 1 (binary 0001). In contrast, the apparent 23-bit precision of the mantissae on the DEC VAX actually provides 24-bit precision (about 7 decimal digits) through appendage to the implied leading 1 bit.

Most computers automatically create normalized numbers as the result of floating-point arithmetic operations and, in so doing, retain the maximum number of significant bits. Some computer systems allow the programmer to choose whether the result should be normalized. Advocates of leaving floating-point results unnormalized claim it gives better accuracy in retained results (see Fig. 10 for an example).

Double precision floating-point numbers typically are stored in 64-bits; common formats include (7,56), (8,55), and (11,52). "Extended" implementations include the 80-bit (15,64) and the 128-bit (15,112) formats.

Fixed-Point Arithmetic

Fixed-point arithmetic is done essentially like ordinary binary arithmetic, except for the restriction that negative numbers are generally stored in some complement form. However, some aspects of fixed-point arithmetic need to be considered explicitly. In the following examples, we assume that fixed-point numbers are binary fractions of magnitude less than 1 and that the binary point is at the left.

Fixed-point addition and subtraction are subject to the exceptional condition known as *overflow*. Since not only the two addends but also the result in addition and subtraction must be less than 1 in magnitude, a result greater than 1 will not be correctly handled. To be precise,

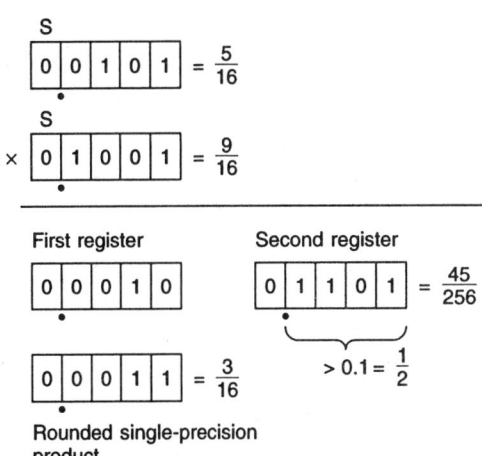

FIG. 4. Fixed-point multiplication.

when adding positive numbers *overflow occurs when bit-1 has a carry-out*, as is shown in Fig 3. In some computers, this carry-out bit is discarded, while in others it replaces the sign bit, resulting in an artificial negative number. In any case, the result is incorrect, and most hardware sets an overflow bit, which allows a programmer to test for overflow by using a *Branch-On-Overflow* instruction.

Overflow cannot occur in fixed-point multiplication, since the product of two factors less than 1 in magnitude cannot equal 1. But multiplying two n-bit numbers produces a 2n-bit product, which cannot be accommodated in an n-bit register. Normally, the least significant n-bits are placed in a second register. Fig. 4 shows such a multiplication, assuming a word length of 5 bits. Assembly language programmers can retain the bits in the second register, but normally only the rounded results are kept, as shown in Fig. 4.

Fixed-point division can result in overflow if the dividend has magnitude greater than the divisor. A fixed-point divide overflow causes an exceptional condition (different from fixed-point addition overflow) that is usually testable by programmers.

The dividend in fixed-point division is usually double-length (or precision) and occupies two paired registers. The single-precision quotient is commonly placed in one register and the remainder in another, as illustrated in Fig. 5.

Integer Calculations

In modern computers, the great majority of fixed-point calculations are performed

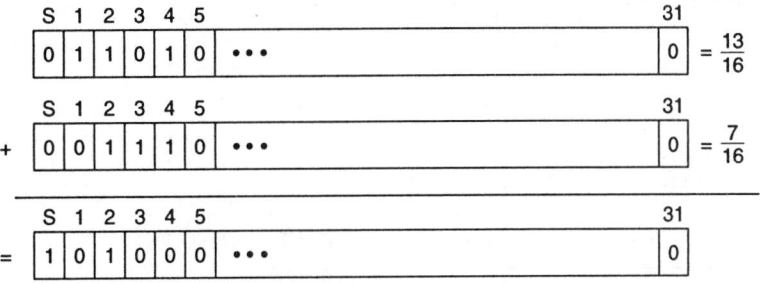

FIG. 3. Overflow in fixed-point addition.

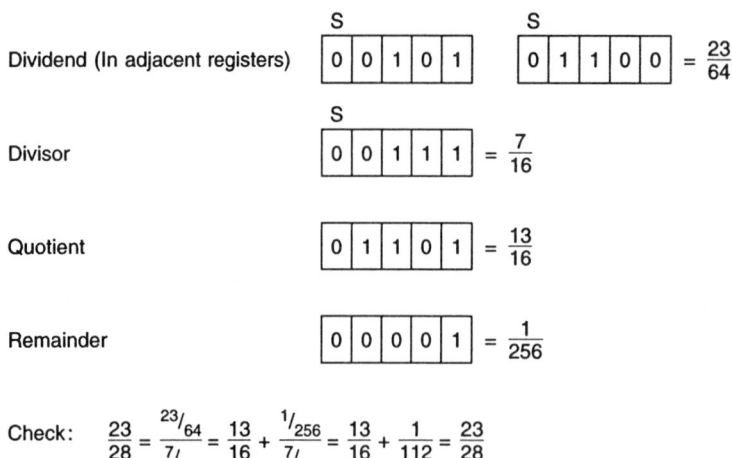

FIG. 5.   Fixed-point division.

with procedural languages using integer quantities. The fixed-point format used to represent negative integers is usually 1's or 2's complement, with the latter now being more common. Fig. 6 shows the integer representation of 32,767 in a 16-bit format.

Appropriate adjustments must be made to handle the "overflow" problem that occurs when a sum or product is larger than the specified number of bits allowed for integers. Some languages handle overflow by wrapping the overflow around without indicating an error. For example, using Turbo Pascal's 16-bit integers, the maximum expressible integer is 32,767, and overflows wrap around the value $2^{16} = 65,536$ (thus $32767 + 2 = -32767$ and $1024 * 33 = -31744$).

Integer division in Fortran, Pascal, PL/1, etc., causes remainders to be dropped. Fig. 7 illustrates what happens in our hypothetical four-bit plus-sign computer in the evaluation of the Fortran statement "K = 14/5." Because the remainder is discarded, K evaluates to 2. Procedural language programmers using Fortran, Pascal, etc., should be aware of such special handling, as the language processor normally performs the necessary manipulations.

Floating-Point Arithmetic To add or subtract two floating-point numbers, the exponents must be the same. If the rightmost mantissa digit of a floating-point number is 0, shifting the mantissa one digit to the right and increasing the exponent by one produces an equivalent floating-point number. The following algorithm for floating-point addition uses this shifting technique. Suppose A and B are to be added, producing C as a result. Let the exponent and fractional parts be denoted by E_a, E_b, and E_c and F_a, F_b, and F_c, respectively.

STEP 1. Set E_c = the larger of E_a and E_b (Assume in what follows that $E_a > = E_b$.)
STEP 2. Align the exponents. Shift F_b to the right $E_a - E_b$ places (which causes F_a and F_b to have the same exponent, but may cause a loss of precision).
STEP 3. Add the mantissas. Set $F_c = F_a + F_b$.
STEP 4. Normalize. Shift F_c to make its most significant bit 1, and adjust E_c accordingly.

This four-step algorithm is illustrated in Fig. 8, assuming a hypothetical computer with a binary (5,10) floating-point format using bias-16 exponents.

In proceeding through the four steps, several points are noteworthy:

1. Step 3 of Fig. 8(b) results in overflow. No error results because the "overflow" bit is always retained and shifted right in Step 4. The calculation in Fig. 8(a) has no overflow, and normalization is not necessary in Step 4.
2. The computed result is accurate in Fig. 8(b), but the computed result in Fig. 8(a) is 57.9375, while the theoretical result is 57.96875. The error is caused when F_b has to be right-shifted eight places, resulting in a loss of 1 bit of precision.
3. Many computers have instructions that allow programmers to choose unnormalized floating-point operations. Thus, Step 4 in our algorithm

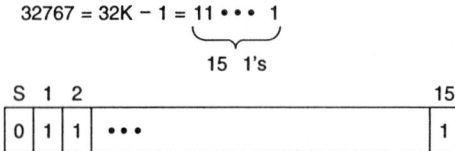

FIG. 6.   Representation of 32767 in 16-bit integer format.

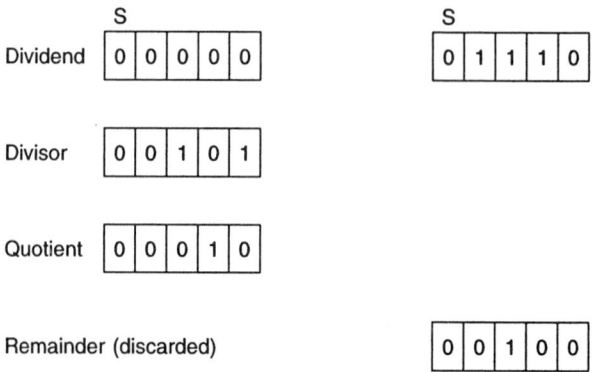

FIG. 7.   Integer division in Fortran

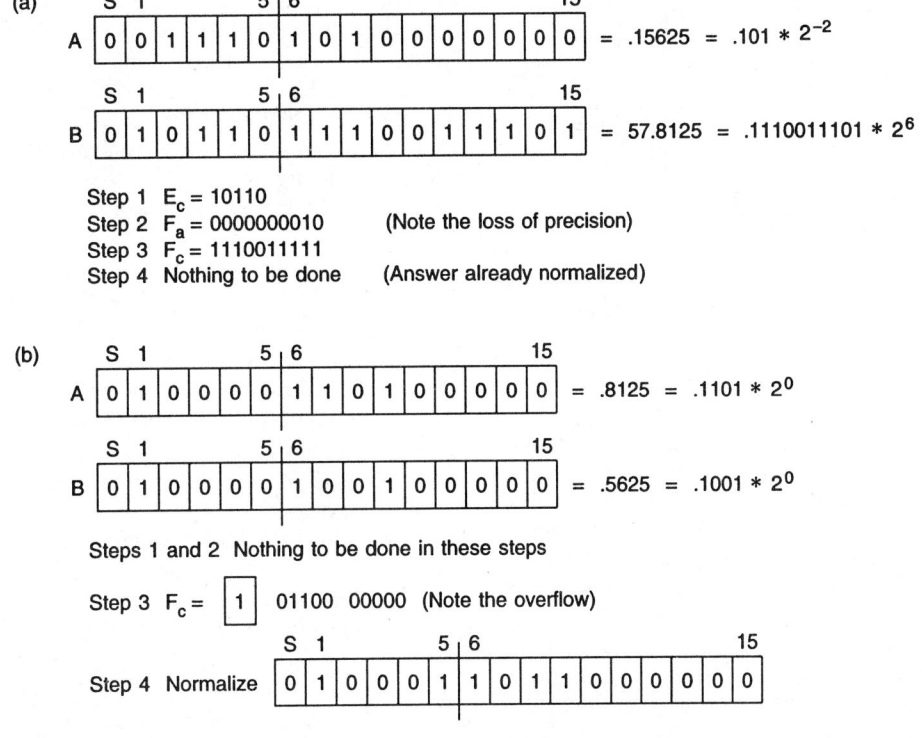

FIG. 8. Floating-point addition.

can be avoided in the unnormalized instructions. Procedural language processors always use normalized instructions. Thus, unnormalized instructions are normally available only to assembly language programmers.

4. Floating-point subtraction, or addition of numbers with differing signs, may result in a normalization that requires a left shift of F_c. In some computing systems, the bits shifted right in Step 2 will be retained, and these will now be shifted left to avoid the loss of precision that would be caused if zeros were inserted on the right. Some computers also retain *guard bit(s)* that can be shifted left during normalization.

Overflow can occur in any operation where the magnitude of the result exceeds the floating-point capacity. No matter how many bits are allotted to floating-point operations, examples illustrating overflows can easily be constructed. Fig. 9 shows an example of an addition causing an overflow in our hypothetical (5,10) system. Such an overflow can be handled in three different ways: making the overflowed result the largest possible number, setting an indicator the programmer can test, or, finally, aborting the program with an appropriate error message.

Underflow results from an attempt to produce a non-zero result smaller in magnitude than the smallest possible positive floating-point number. The usual method of handling underflow is to generate a zero result, but sometimes an underflow indicator is also set, which the programmer can test. Fig. 9 shows an example of underflow.

Floating-point multiplication and division techniques do not require exponent alignment. Instead, the appropri-

ate operation is performed on the mantissas, the result rounded, the exponents added (for multiplication) or subtracted (for division), and then the result normalized, if necessary. Examples are shown in Fig. 10.

Overflow

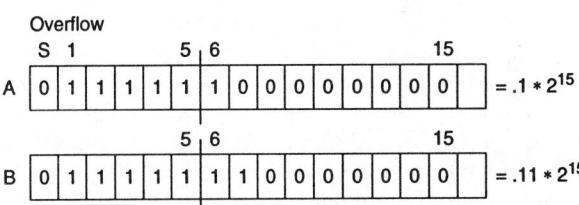

The correct sum A + B is $1.01 * 2^{16}$, which when normalized, is $.101 * 2^{16}$, and the exponent of +16 cannot be accommodated.

Underflow

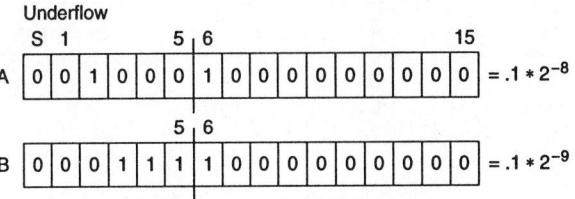

The correct product AB is $.01 * 2^{-17}$, which cannot be accomodated as a normalized number, but could be stored as

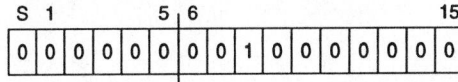

FIG. 9. Floating-point overflow and underflow.

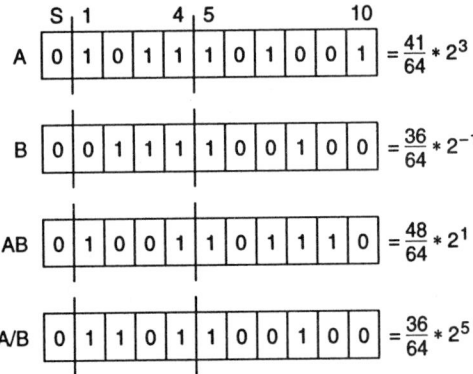

FIG. 10. Floating-point multiplication and division.

Floating-Point Standards

Modern computers normally provide some hardware support (either machine instructions or math co-processors) for floating-point arithmetic. At least 20 different floating-point formats have been implemented, and different computer systems often produce different calculated results from identical floating-point inputs.

In 1978, the Institute of Electrical and Electronics Engineers (IEEE) established a committee to develop a floating-point standard. Early work was spearheaded by W. Kahan, J. Coonan, and H. Stone (1979). Draft 8.0 was circulated (Cody, 1981), and the 754 Standard, with only minor changes from Draft 8.0, was published in 1985. The standard describes various conditions, including: Rounding Options, Invalid Operations, Overflow, Division by Zero, Underflow, and Inexact Result. It introduced extremal numbers called Infinities, DeNormal Numbers, and NANs (not a number); reserved bit patterns for these cases; and discussed how these conditions could be handled effectively. The standard is not without controversy, and a good summary of its detractors' arguments is found in Waser and Flynn (1982).

Computing machines from IBM, Digital Equipment Corporation (DEC), and other makers had floating-point hardware implementations before 1980 and thus do not conform to the IEEE standard. The standard has benefited newer designers, as math co-processors from Intel, Motorola, SUN, MIPS, and others now conform to the standard. The IBM/370, DEC VAX (*q.v.*), and IEEE floating-point formats are given in Table 1.

The IBM, Digital, and IEEE formats include "extended" capabilities of 128, 128, and 80 bits, respectively, but these are not shown or discussed here. Some comments, relating to the "single-precision" formats presented in Fig. 11, are as follows.

1. The IBM format uses 7-bit hexadecimal "bias-64" exponents and 6-hexit (24-bit) mantissas, thus increasing the exponent range over the binary formats. Shifting for alignment and normalization occurs 4 bits at a time, which often causes different computed results from those generated using binary formats.

2. The VAX and IEEE formats use 8-bit binary biased exponents. Digital uses "bias-128" exponents, while the IEEE specification, in order to reserve both the exponents $0...0$ and $1...1$ for exceptional conditions, uses "bias-127" exponents.

3. The IBM "*true zero*" consists of "a 0 sign, a $0...0$ exponent, and a $0...0$ mantissa" (a whole word of 0s). The *VAX zero* is "a 0 sign, an exponent of $0...0$, and any mantissa." The IEEE bias-127 format represents *zero* as "any sign, an exponent of $0...0$, and a mantissa of $0...0$." The IEEE thus has two zeros, while the VAX has 2^{23} different zeros. Special rules were needed in the latter two cases because, otherwise, the implicit 1 bit would imply that "all 0 bits" represents a tiny number but not literally zero.

4. The IEEE defines "denormalized" numbers (*denormals*) as "any sign, an exponent of $0...0$, and a non-zero mantissa"; an "infinity" as "any sign, an exponent of $1...1$, and a mantissa of $0...0$"; and "Not a Number" or "NAN" as "any sign, an exponent of $1...1$, and a non-zero mantissa."

5. The combination of the implied leading digit, the implied binary point, and all the fraction bits is called the "significand." The range of signif-

TABLE 1. Floating-Point Formats

Bits in:	IBM/370		DEC VAX			IEEE	
	S	D	S	D	H	S	D
Total bits	32	64	32	64	64	32	64
Mantissa	6 HX	14 HX	23 B	55 B	52 B	23 B	52 B
Exponent bits	7	7	8	8	11	8	11
Exponent bias	64	64	128	128	128	127	127
Radix	16	16	2	2	2	2	2
Hidden '1'	No	No	Yes	Yes	Yes	Yes	Yes
Maximum number	16^{63} 10^{76}	16^{63} 10^{76}	2^{127} 10^{38}	2^{127} 10^{38}	2^{1023} 10^{308}	2^{127} 10^{38}	2^{1023} 10^{308}
Minimum number	16^{-64} 10^{-77}	16^{-64} 10^{-77}	2^{-127} 10^{-38}	2^{-127} 10^{-38}	2^{-1023} 10^{-308}	2^{-126} 10^{-38}	2^{-1022} 10^{-308}
Precision	16^{-6} 10^{-7}	16^{-14} 10^{-17}	2^{-24} 10^{-7}	2^{-56} 10^{-17}	2^{-53} 10^{-16}	2^{-24} 10^{-7}	2^{-53} 10^{-16}

Notes: S = Single Precision, D = Double Precision, H = Second VAX 64-bit Form, HX = Hexadecimal Digits

The Fortran Program   The GWBASIC Program

```
    X = 78931.15      10   X = 78931.15
    DO 20 I = 1,3      20   FOR I = 1 TO 3
    X = X + 0.01       30     X = X + 0.01
    PRINT *,X          40     PRINT X
20 CONTINUE            50   NEXT I
    STOP               60   END
    END
```

The Results

IBM Fortran	VAX/VMX Fortran	IBM PC GWBASIC
78931.12	78931.16	78931.16
78931.12	78931.16	78931.16
78931.12	78931.17	78931.18

FIG. 11. Different Floating-Point Results.

icands, SN, for the three formats is: *IBM* 1/16 = 0.0625 < = SN < 1; *VAX* 1/2 = 0.5 < = SN < 1; and *IEEE* 1.0 < = SN < 2. The latter two bounds reflect a difference in treatment of the implicit 1 bit: in the IEEE format, a mantissa *f* represents 1. *f*, whereas on the VAX, *f* represents .1 *f*,—i.e. 1/2 (1. *f*). This difference, plus the difference in bias, means that any given VAX floating-point bit pattern would have four times the value if interpreted under IEEE rules.

Fig. 11 contains a short program that uses the 32-bit, single-precision formats and that illustrates the output differences in computed numbers on different machines.

Computer Arithmetic and Real Arithmetic

Four common arithmetic laws that apply to real numbers a, b, and c are:

1. Closure:
   Addition: $a + b$ is a real number.
   Multiplication: $a * b$ is a real number.
2. Associative laws:
   Addition: $a + (b + c) = (a + b) + c$.
   Multiplication: $a * (b * c) = (a * b) * c$.
3. Distributive law:
   $a * (b + c) = a*b + a*c$.
4. Cancellation Property:
   $a + b = a + c$ implies $b = c$.

For real numbers, these laws depend on two facts:
1. There are infinitely many reals.
2. Between any two reals is another real.

Because of the finiteness of floating-point numbers, the shifting required in additions, and underflow/overflow handling, *none of these laws is valid for all floating-point number combinations*. The failure of these laws for floating-point numbers is sometimes easily overcome, but, often, computed results differ dramatically from what is expected. A comprehensive treatment of floating-point numbers and their anomalies is found in Sterbenz (1974).

Despite the IEEE Standard, finding better implementations of "real number" arithmetic on computers remains an active research area. The 32-bit Symmetric Level Index (SLI) method (Clenshaw *et al.*, 1989) significantly increases both the range and precision of expressible numbers and better handles closure and underflow/overflow problems. In the early 1990s, SLI arithmetic is in a position similar to the 1950s floating-point/fixed-point scenario; SLI has obvious advantages over floating-point, but is approximately 10 times slower, and thus has seldom been implemented.

References

1974. Sterbenz, P.H. *Floating Point Computation*. Englewood Cliffs, NJ: Prentice Hall.
1979. Coonen, J., Kahan, W., Palmer, J., Pittman, T., and Stevenson, D. "A Proposed Standard for Floating-Point Arithmetic," *ACM SIGNUM Newsletter*, Oct.
1981. Cody, W.J. "Analysis of Proposals for the Floating-Point Standard," *IEEE Computer*, March.
1982. Waser, S., and Flynn, M. *Introduction to Arithmetic for Digital Systems Designers*. New York: Holt, Reinhart, and Winston.
1985. *Binary Floating-Point Arithmetic*, IEEE Standard 754, IEEE.
1989. Clenshaw, C., Olver, F., and Turner, P. "Level-Index Arithmetic: An Introductory Survey," in *Numerical Analysis and Parallel Processing*, LNM 1397. New York: Springer-Verlag.
1989. Levy, H.M., and Eckhouse, R.H., Jr. *Computer Programming and Architecture, The VAX*, 2nd Edition. Bedford, MA: Digital Press.
1991. Goldberg, David. "What Every Computer Scientist Should Know About Floating-Point Arithmetic," *ACM Computing Surveys*, **23**, 1 (March), pp. 5–48.
1991. Swartzlander, Earl E. Jr. *Computer Arithmetic*, Vols. I and II. Los Alamitos, CA: IEEE Computer Society Press.

THOMAS J. SCOTT

ARPA NETWORK. *See* NETWORKS, COMPUTER.

ART, COMPUTER. *See* COMPUTER ART.

ARTIFICIAL INTELLIGENCE

For articles on related subjects *see* COGNITIVE SCIENCE; COMPUTER CHESS; COMPUTER GAMES; COMPUTER MUSIC; COMPUTER VISION; EXPERT SYSTEMS; KNOWLEDGE REPRESENTATION; NATURAL LANGUAGE PROCESSING; PATTERN RECOGNITION; ROBOTICS; SPEECH RECOGNITION AND SYNTHESIS; and THEOREM PROVING.

Introduction Artificial intelligence[1] (AI) is a field of computer science and engineering concerned with the computational understanding of what is commonly called intelligent behavior, and with the creation of artifacts that

---

[1] This article is a revised version of Shapiro, S. C. "Artificial Intelligence," in S. C. Shapiro, Ed. *Encyclopedia of Artificial Intelligence, Second Edition*. New York: John Wiley & Sons, 1991.

exhibit such behavior. This definition may be examined more closely by considering the field from three points of view: computational psychology, computational philosophy, and advanced computer science.

Computational Psychology The goal of computational psychology is to understand human intelligent behavior by creating computer programs that behave in the same way people do. For this goal it is important that the algorithm expressed by the program be the same algorithm that people actually use, and that the data structures used by the program be the same data structures used by the human mind. The program should do quickly what people do quickly, should do more slowly what people have difficulty doing, and should even tend to make mistakes where people tend to make mistakes. If the program were put into the same experimental situations that humans are subjected to, the program's results should be within the range of human variability.

Computational Philosophy The goal of computational philosophy is to form a computational understanding of human-level intelligent behavior, without being restricted to the algorithms and data structures that the human mind actually does (or conceivably might) use. By "computational understanding" is meant a model that is expressed as a procedure that is at least implementable (if not actually implemented) on a computer. By "human-level intelligent behavior" is meant behavior that, when engaged in by people, is commonly taken as being part of human intelligent cognitive behavior. It is acceptable, though not required that the implemented model perform some tasks better than any person would. Bearing in mind Church's Thesis (*see* CHURCH, ALONZO), this goal might be reworded as asking the question, "Is intelligence a computable function?"

In the AI areas of computer vision (*q.v.*) and robotics (*q.v.*), computational philosophy is replaced by computational natural philosophy (science). For example, computer vision researchers are interested in the computational optics question of how the information contained in light waves reflected from an object can be used to reconstruct the object. Notice that this is a different question from the computational psychology question of how the human visual system uses light waves falling on the retina to identify objects in the world.

Advanced Computer Science The goal of advanced computer science is to push outwards the frontier of what we know how to program on computers, especially in the direction of tasks that, although we don't know how to program them, people can perform. This goal led to one of the oldest definitions of AI: the attempt to program computers to do what, until recently, only people could do. Although this expresses the idea of pushing out the frontier, it is also perpetually self-defeating in that, as soon as a task is conquered, it no longer falls within the domain of AI. Thus, AI is left with only its failures; its successes become other areas of computer science. The most famous example is the area of symbolic calculus (*see* COMPUTER ALGEBRA). When James Slagle wrote the SAINT

program, it was the first program in history that could solve symbolic integration problems at the level of freshman calculus students, and was considered an AI project. Now that there are multiple systems on the market that can do much more than what SAINT did, these systems are not considered to be the results of AI research.

Heuristic Programming Computational psychology, computational philosophy, and advanced computer science are subareas of AI divided by their goals. AI researchers wander among two or all three of these areas throughout their career, and may even have a mixture of these goals at the same time.

Another way of distinguishing AI as a field is by noting the AI researcher's interest in *heuristics* (*q.v.*), rather than in *algorithms* (*q.v.*). Here I am taking a wide interpretation of a *heuristic* as any problem-solving procedure that fails to be an algorithm or that has not been shown to be an algorithm, for any reason. An interesting view of the tasks that AI researchers consider to be their own may be gained by considering those ways in which a procedure (*q.v.*) may fail to qualify as an algorithm.

By common definition, an algorithm for a general problem P is an unambiguous procedure that, for every particular instance of P, terminates and produces the correct answer. The most common reasons that a heuristic H fails to be an algorithm are that it doesn't terminate for some instances of P, it has not been proved correct for all instances of P because of some problem with H, or it has not been proved correct for all instances of P because P is not well-defined. Common examples of heuristic AI programs that don't terminate for all instances of the problem that they have been designed for include searching (*q.v.*) and theorem proving (*q.v.*) programs. Any search procedure will run forever if given an infinite search space that contains no solution state. Gödel's Incompleteness Theorem states that there are formal theories that contain true but unprovable propositions. In actual practice, AI programs for these problems stop after some prespecified time, space, or work bound has been reached. They can then report only that they were unable to find a solution even though—in any given case—a little more work *might* have produced an answer. An example of an AI heuristic that has not been proved correct is any static evaluation function used in a program for playing computer chess (*q.v.*). The static evaluation function returns an estimate of the value of some state of the board. To be correct, it would return $+\infty$ if the state were a sure win for the side to move, $-\infty$ if it were a sure win for the opponent, and 0 if it were a forced draw. Moreover, for any state it is theoretically possible to find the correct answer algorithmically by doing a full minimax search of the game tree rooted in the state being examined. Such a full search is infeasible for most states, however, because of the size of the game tree. Nonetheless, static evaluation functions are still useful, even without being proved correct.

An example of a heuristic AI program that has not been proved correct because the problem for which it has been designed is not well-defined is any natural language–understanding program or natural language interface. Since no one has any well-defined criteria for whether a person understands a given language, there cannot be any well-defined criteria for programs either.

Early History Although the dream of creating intelligent artifacts has existed for many centuries, the field of artificial intelligence is considered to have had its birth at a conference held at Dartmouth College in the summer of 1956. The conference was organized by Marvin Minsky and John McCarthy, and McCarthy coined the name "artificial intelligence" for the proposal to obtain funding for the conference. Among the attendees were Herbert Simon (*q.v.*) and Allen Newell, who had already implemented the Logic Theorist program at the Rand Corporation. These four people are considered the fathers of AI. Minsky and McCarthy founded the AI Laboratory at M.I.T.; Simon and Newell founded the AI laboratory at Carnegie-Mellon University. McCarthy later moved from M.I.T. to Stanford University, where he founded the AI laboratory there. These three universities, along with Edinburgh University, whose Department of Machine Intelligence was founded by Donald Michie, have remained the premier research universities in the field. The name artificial intelligence remained controversial for some years, even among people doing research in the area, but it eventually was accepted.

The first AI text was *Computers and Thought,* edited by Edward Feigenbaum and Julian Feldman, and published by McGraw-Hill in 1963. This is a collection of 21 papers, some of them short versions of Ph.D. dissertations, by early AI researchers. Most of the papers in this collection are still considered classics of AI, but of particular note is a reprint of Alan M. Turing's 1950 paper in which the Turing Test was introduced (*see* TURING, ALAN).

Regular AI conferences began in the mid to late 1960s. The Machine Intelligence Workshops series began in 1965 in Edinburgh. A conference at Case Western University in Spring, 1968 drew many of the U. S. AI researchers of the time, and the first biennial International Joint Conference on Artificial Intelligence was held in Washington, D. C. in May, 1969. *Artificial Intelligence,* still the premier journal of AI research, began publication in 1970.

For a more complete history of AI, see McCorduck, 1979.

Neighboring Disciplines Artificial intelligence is generally considered to be a subfield of computer science, though there are some computer scientists who have only recently and grudgingly accepted this view. There are several disciplines outside computer science, however, that strongly impact AI and that, in turn, AI strongly impacts.

Cognitive psychology is the subfield of psychology that uses experimental methods to study human cognitive behavior. The goal of AI called computational psychology earlier is obviously closely related to cognitive psychology, differing mainly in the use of computational models rather than experiments on human subjects. However, most AI researchers pay some attention to the results of cognitive psychology, and cognitive psychologists tend to pay attention to AI as suggesting possible cognitive procedures that they might look for in humans.

Cognitive science (*q.v.*) is an interdisciplinary field that studies human cognitive behavior under the hypothesis that cognition is (or can usefully be modeled as) computation. AI and cognitive science overlap in that there are researchers in each field that would not consider themselves to be in the other. AI researchers whose primary goal is what was called advanced computer science earlier in this article generally do not consider themselves to be doing cognitive science. Cognitive science contains not only AI researchers, but also cognitive psychologists, linguists, philosophers, anthropologists, and others, all using the methodology of their own disciplines on a common problem—that of understanding human cognitive behavior.

Computational linguistics researchers use computers, or at least the computational paradigm, to study and/or to process human languages. Like cognitive science, computational linguistics overlaps AI. It includes those areas of AI called natural language understanding, natural language generation, speech recognition and synthesis (*q.v.*), and machine translation (*q.v.*), but also non-AI areas, such as the use of statistical methods to find index keywords useful for retrieving a document.

AI-Complete Tasks There are many subtopics in the field of AI—subtopics that vary from the consideration of a very particular, technical problem, to broad areas of research. Several of these broad areas can be considered *AI-complete,* in the sense that solving the problem of the area is equivalent to solving the entire AI problem—producing a generally intelligent computer program. Researchers in one of these areas may see themselves as attacking the entire AI problem from a particular direction. The following sections discuss some of the AI-complete areas and, where appropriate, point to other articles relevant to those areas.

Natural Language The AI subarea of natural language is essentially the overlap of AI and computational linguistics (see above). The goal is to form a computational understanding of how people learn and use their native languages, and to produce a computer program that can use a human language at the same level of competence as a native human speaker. Virtually all human knowledge has been (or could be) encoded in human languages. Moreover, research in natural language understanding has shown that encyclopedic knowledge is required to understand natural language. Therefore, a complete natural language system will also be a complete intelligent system.

Problem Solving and Search Problem solving is the area of AI that is concerned with finding or constructing the solution to a problem. That sounds like a very general area, and it is. The distinctive characteristic of the area is probably its approach of seeing tasks as problems to be solved and of seeing problems as spaces of potential solutions that must be searched to find the true one or the best one. Thus, the AI area of search is very much connected to problem solving. Since any area investigated by AI researchers may be seen as consisting of problems to be solved, all of AI may be seen as involving problem solving and search.

Knowledge Representation and Reasoning Knowledge representation (*q.v.*) is the area of AI concerned with the formal symbolic languages used to represent the knowledge (data) used by intelligent systems, and the data structures (*q.v.*) used to implement those formal languages. However, one cannot study static representation formalisms and know anything about how useful they are. Instead, one must study how they are helpful for their intended use. In most cases, they use explicitly stored knowledge to produce additional explicit knowledge. This is what reasoning is. Together, knowledge representation and reasoning can be seen to be both necessary and sufficient for producing general intelligence, another AI-complete area. Although they are bound up with each other, knowledge representation and reasoning can be teased apart, according to whether the particular study is more about the representation language/data structure or about the active process of drawing conclusions.

Learning Learning is often cited as the criterial characteristic of intelligence, and it has always seemed like the easy way to produce intelligent systems: Why build an intelligent system when we could just build a learning system and send it to school? Learning includes all styles of learning, from rote learning to the design and analysis of experiments. It also includes all subject areas, which is why it is AI-complete.

Vision Vision, or image understanding, has to do with interpreting visual images that fall on the human retina or the camera lens (*see* COMPUTER VISION). The actual scene being viewed could be two-dimensional, such as a printed page of text, or three-dimensional, such as the world about us. If we take "interpreting" broadly enough, it is clear that general intelligence may be needed to do the interpretation and that correct interpretation implies general intelligence, so this is another AI-complete area.

Robotics The area of robotics (*q.v.*) is concerned with artifacts that can move about in the actual physical world and/or that can manipulate other objects in the world. Intelligent robots must be able to accommodate to new circumstances, and to do this they need to be able to solve problems and to learn. Thus, intelligent robotics is also an AI-complete area.

Applications Throughout the existence of the field, AI research has produced spinoffs into other areas of computer science. Lately, however, programming techniques developed by AI researchers have found application to many programming problems. This has largely come about through the subarea of AI known as expert systems (*q.v.*). Whether or not any particular program should be considered intelligent or an expert according to the common use of those words is largely irrelevant to the workers in and the observers of the expert systems area. From their point of view, they have tools and a methodology that are more useful for solving their problems than

traditional programming tools and methodologies. From the point of view of AI as a whole, probably the best thing about this development is that after many years of being criticized as following an impossible dream by inappropriate and inadequate means, AI has been recognized by the general public as having applications to everyday problems.

References

1950. Turing, A.M. "Computing Machinery and Intelligence." *Mind,* **59** (October), 433–460.

1963. Feigenbaum, E. A. and Feldman, J., Eds. *Computers and Thought.* New York: McGraw-Hill.

1979. McCorduck, P. *Machines Who Think.* San Francisco: W. H. Freeman and Company.

1981. Barr, A. and Feigenbaum, E. A., Eds. *The Handbook of Artificial Intelligence,* Vol. I. Los Altos, CA: William Kaufmann, Inc.

1982. Barr, A. and Feigenbaum, E. A., Eds. *The Handbook of Artificial Intelligence,* Vol. II. Los Altos, CA: William Kaufmann, Inc.

1982. Cohen, P. R. and Feigenbaum, E. A., Eds. *The Handbook of Artificial Intelligence,* Vol. III. Los Altos, CA: William Kaufmann, Inc.

1984. Winston, Patrick A. *Artificial Intelligence.* Reading, MA: Addison-Wesley.

1985. Charniak, E. and McDermott, D. *Introduction to Artificial Intelligence.* Reading, MA: Addison-Wesley.

1989. Barr, A., Cohen, P. R., and Feigenbaum, E. A., Eds. *The Handbook of Artificial Intelligence,* Vol. IV. Reading, MA: Addison-Wesley.

1990. Schalkoff, Robert. *Artificial Intelligence: An Engineering Approach.* New York: McGraw-Hill.

1991. Shapiro, S.C., Ed. *Encyclopedia of Artificial Intelligence,* 2nd Edition. New York: John Wiley & Sons.

STUART C. SHAPIRO

ASCII

For articles on related subjects *see* BINARY-CODED DECIMAL; CODES; and EBCDIC.

The American Standard Code for Information Interchange (ASCII) is a seven-bit code also known as the USA Standard Code for information interchange (USASCII).

Because eight-bit bytes are common on computers, ASCII is commonly embedded in an eight-bit field in which the high order (leftmost) bit is either used as a parity bit or is set to zero. An 8-bit version of ASCII using the latter option is shown as Exhibit 1. The leftmost four bits (or first hexadecimal digit) of the eight-bit code are shown as column heads across the top and the rightmost four bits

Character	Code	
	Binary	Hexadecimal
4	00110100	34
Y	01011001	59
c	01100011	63
=	00111101	3D

Bit positions 4,3,2,1	Second Hexadecimal	0000	0001	0010	0011	0100	0101	0110	0111
		0	1	2	3	4	5	6	7
0000	0	NUL	DLE	SP	0	@	P	`	p
0001	1	SOH	DC1	!	1	A	Q	a	q
0010	2	STX	DC2	"	2	B	R	b	r
0011	3	ETX	DC3	#	3	C	S	c	s
0100	4	EOT	DC4	$	4	D	T	d	t
0101	5	ENQ	NAK	%	5	E	U	e	u
0110	6	ACK	SYN	&	6	F	V	f	v
0111	7	BEL	ETB	'	7	G	W	g	w
1000	8	BS	CAN	(	8	H	X	h	x
1001	9	HT	EM	)	9	I	Y	i	y
1010	A	LF	SUB	*	:	J	Z	j	z
1011	B	VT	ESC	+	;	K	[	k	{
1100	C	FF	FS	,	<	L	\	l	¦
1101	D	CR	GS	—	=	M	]	m	}
1110	E	SO	RS	.	>	N	^	n	~
1111	F	SI	US	/	?	O	—	o	DEL

EXHIBIT 1

ASCII code values. (For explanation of symbols, see next page.)

First Hexadecimal Digit · Bit positions 8,7,6,5

Control Character Representations

NUL	Null	DLE	Data Link Escape (CC)
SOH	Start of heading (CC)	DC1	Device Control 1
STX	Start of Text (CC)	DC2	Device Control 2
ETX	End of Text (CC)	DC3	Device Control 3
EOT	End of Transmission (CC)	DC4	Device Control 4
ENQ	Enquiry (CC)	NAK	Negative Acknowledge (CC)
ACK	Acknowledge (CC)	SYN	Synchronous Idle (CC)
BEL	Bell	ETB	End of Transmission Block (CC)
BS	Backspace (FE)	CAN	Cancel
HT	Horizontal Tabulation (FE)	EM	End of Medium
LF	Line Feed (FE)	SUB	Substitute
VT	Vertical Tabulation (FE)	ESC	Escape
FF	Form Feed (FE)	FS	File Separator (IS)
CR	Carriage Return (FE)	GS	Group Separator (IS)
SO	Shift Out	RS	Record Separator (IS)
SI	Shift In	US	Unit Separator (IS)
		DEL	Delete
(CC)	Communication Control		
(FE)	Format Effector		
(IS)	Information Separator		

<table>
<tr><td colspan="4" align="center">EXHIBIT 1 (Continued)
Special Graphic Characters</td></tr>
</table>

SP	Space	<	Less Than
!	Exclamation Point	=	Equals
"	Quotation Marks	>	Greater Than
#	Number Sign	?	Question Mark
$	Dollar Sign	@	Commercial At Sign
%	Percent	[	Opening Bracket
&	Ampersand	\	Reverse Slant
'	Apostrophe	]	Closing Bracket
(	Opening Parenthesis	^	Circumflex
)	Closing Parenthesis	—	Underline
*	Asterisk	`	Grave Accent
+	Plus	{	Opening Brace
,	Comma	¦	Vertical Line (This graphic is sometimes stylized to distinguish it from the unbroken Logical OR, which is not an ASCII character.)
–	Hyphen (Minus)		
.	Period (Decimal Point)		
/	Slant	}	Closing Brace
:	Colon	~	Tilde
;	Semicolon		

(or second hexadecimal digit) are listed on the side. Thus, for example, we have

The meanings of the control characters and special graphic characters are shown below the illustration.

IVAN FLORES

ASIS. *See* AMERICAN SOCIETY FOR INFORMATION SCIENCE.

ASSEMBLER

For articles on related subjects *see* ADDRESSING; BASE REGISTER; CALLING SEQUENCE; CROSS ASSEMBLERS AND COMPILERS; GENERAL REGISTER; INDEX REGISTER; INDIRECT ADDRESS; INSTRUCTION SET; LANGUAGE PROCESSORS; LINKER; LOADER; MACHINE AND ASSEMBLY LANGUAGE PROGRAMMING; MACROINSTRUCTION; NO-OP; OPERAND; and PROGRAM COUNTER.

An *assembler* is a program that facilitates the preparation of programs at the machine language level by taking symbolic representations of individual (instruction or data) words and converting them into a form (binary or byte) suitable for input to a linker or loader. It permits the use of mnemonic operation codes, allows symbolic names to be assigned to memory locations, provides facilities for address calculations in terms of such symbolic names, and (usually) enables the user to introduce numerical and character constants in various forms. Assemblers are used for systems programming when the need to access all the facilities of the "raw" machine precludes the use of a high-level language. If the micro is too small to support an assembler, a *cross-assembler* is used, an assembler that runs on one (usually larger) machine producing *object code* for another (usually smaller) machine.

Although the term "assembly subroutine" was used as long ago as 1951 for a routine that assembled a master routine and a number of subroutines into a single program (Wilkes, Wheeler, and Gill, 1951), this function is now typically called *linking*. The current established connotation of the term "assembler" probably derives from its function of assembling the internal binary form of the program from symbolic definitions.

History Although the use of a symbolic representation of machine language programs now seems obviously desirable, this was not always so. Right from the start there was a dichotomy of view between the Cambridge group (EDSAC), which advocated a measure of symbolic programming, and the Manchester group (MARK I), which believed that the programmer should write the program in a form as close as possible to the internal form (Wilkes, 1956).

The EDSAC had a rudimentary assembler called Initial Orders, which allowed the user to write machine instructions consisting of a single alphabet letter operation code, a decimal address, and a terminating letter, which caused one of 12 constants preset by the programmer to be added to the address at assembly time. (The Initial Orders were implemented in a form of read-only memory (q.v.) consisting of a wired telephone uniselector.)

Probably the first assembler in the sense used in this article was SOAP (Symbolic Optimizer and Assembly Program) on the IBM 650 computer in the mid-1950s. However, the symbolic assembly features of SOAP were not its main feature (the 650 was a decimal computer anyway, which removed some of the difficulties of direct machine language coding). The 650 had a magnetic drum memory and an instruction code in which each instruction specified the address of its successor. For maximum efficiency, instructions had to be placed on the drum in positions such that the execution of each instruction overlapped as far as possible the time for the drum to rotate to the next instruction position, thus minimizing the latency (*q.v.*) waiting for instructions. Such minimum-access coding involved a very difficult optimizing process, and it was this that SOAP achieved.

The most significant event in the history of assemblers was the Symbolic Assembly Program (SAP) for the IBM 704. The original SAP assembler (UASAP) was written by programmers at United Aircraft Corporation and was distributed by the SHARE organization. SAP set the external form of an assembly language that was to be a model for all its successors and which persists almost unchanged to the present day. On later versions of the 700 series computers, SAP was replaced by FAP (Fortran Assembly Program).

Facilities A typical machine instruction consists of an operation code, an address, and one or more register fields. The address may refer to a data area or to another instruction (e.g. the destination of a transfer of control). A SAP-like assembler provides a fixed set of mnemonic operation codes and an open-ended set of programmer-defined symbols for use in address parts. Such address symbols may be defined explicitly or implicitly by attaching them as labels to particular instructions or data words. Although a symbol stands for an address, the assembler cannot convert label symbols directly into addresses, since the address in storage into which a particular instruction will be loaded is not known at assembly time. (It is finally determined only when a number of routines are combined to form a complete program.) The difficulty is resolved by recording as the value of the label symbol the displacement of the instruction in question from the beginning of the code for the subroutine, and marking it in the assembler output as a relative or relocatable value, to be adjusted later by the linker or loader.

Thus, SAP introduced the basic structure of a symbolic instruction as being made up of three fields:

1. *Location* (possibly blank). A symbol placed here takes as its value the address of the memory cell in which the corresponding instruction or data word will be stored: Thus it serves as a label by which it can be referenced by other instructions.
2. *Operation code.* The symbol here is one of a fixed repertoire of operation-code symbols.
3. *Operand.* This field is usually made up of a number of subfields, reflecting the address/register structure of the computer. The subfields may be simple integer constants or may be expressions made up of symbols (representing addresses), constants, and simple arithmetic operations (usually plus and minus). Alternatively, a literal operand may be supplied: The assembler will store this and substitute the appropriate address in the instruction.

The following fragment of SAP coding illustrates this structure.

```
        TRA    ALPHA
        LOC    16385
ALPHA   CLA    BETA
        STO    DELTA
SYMB    FAD    = 3.14159
        SXO    SYMB-2,4
        STO    SYMB
```

Each instruction in this example is made up of three fields: location (label), operation code, and address. The operation codes are nmemonic, e.g. TRA = transfer control, CLA = clear accumulator, FAD = floating add, etc. The address fields show the various possible constructions. In the first line the address is a symbol ALPHA, as yet undefined. (It appears as a label on a later instruction.) In line 2 the address is explicit, and in lines 3 and 4 symbols (presumably defined elsewhere in the program of which this fragment forms a part) are used. Line 5 illustrates the use of a literal operand: the "equals" indicates that the 3.14159 following is the actual value to be loaded by the FAD, not the address of the operand. The next line illustrates a more complex address: It is a two-field form in which the first component is a storage address and the second component identifies an index register to be used; in this example the storage address is specified as an expression.

The following excerpt of OS/370 assembler code for the IBM System/370 computers, whose purpose is to sum 13 numbers, shows how little things have changed.

```
        L     3, = F'0'    CLEAR REGISTER
        L     5, = F'0'    USING LITERAL
        LH    4, = H'14'   LOAD REGISTER
        B     BCNT         ENTER LOOP
BNTER   AH    5,STZ(3)     INDEX STZ BY REG 3
        AH    3, = H'2'    INCREMENT INDEX
BCNT    BCT   4,BNTER      BRANCH ON COUNT

        ST    5,BSUM
STZ     DC    H'15,225,1,52,10,48,76,42,88,26,
              14,4,32'
BSUM    DC    F'0'
```

The three-field format is still used, though the mnemonics have changed. With the exception of the branch (B) order, which has a label as its address, the address field is made up of a register designator and a second field, which in these examples is either a symbolic store address or a literal. (For certain instructions it might be another register designator.)

Literals are introduced by "equals," but now include a type code (F = full word, H = half word). Indexing (modification) is illustrated in the line starting BNTER, and finally there are specifications of a number of constants introduced by the DC (Define Constants) pseudo-operation. The comments on the right are part of the programmer's documentation of the program.

Assembler Directives *Assembler directives* serve two purposes. One is to provide information to control the assembly process; the other is to provide a way of defining data words in a program. Assembler directives are often called *pseudo-operations* (a terminology introduced by SAP) since they are commonly designated by special codes in the operation field. A SAP-like pseudo operation is

symbol BSS *integer constant*

which sets the symbol equal to the location counter, and then advances the location counter by the amount designated by the constant. The effect is thus to reserve a block of memory and label it for future reference. Another typical pseudo-operation is

symbol SET *expression*

which assigns an explicit value to a symbol. Other uses of directives to control the assembly include setting the origin, marking entry points, and defining external symbols.

We have seen an example of a data-generating pseudo-operation in the fragment of 370 coding given above. Here the pseudo-operation DC (define constants) is followed by a list of constants, each with a type code. A simpler facility provided in some assemblers requires all the constants to be of the same type; e.g. the pseudo-operation DEC introduces a list of decimal constants in the address field.

Listings An assembler usually provides a variety of information about the program that it has assembled. Besides details of any obvious errors such as incorrect syntax or multiple definition of symbols, the following may be provided.

1. Listing of symbolic instructions side by side with generated binary or binary-symbolic code.
2. Table of symbols defined in a routine, with or without their values.

3. Table of symbols used in a routine.
4. Cross-reference table: for each symbol defined, its name, value, and a list of all the instructions that reference it.

The form of the listing is generally controlled by one or more pseudo-operations; for example:

```
LIST FULL
LIST NONE
LIST SYMBOLS
etc.
```

Other common pseudo-operations are EJECT, which causes a page feed on the printer at the point in the listing where it occurs, and SPACE *n*, which causes a spacing of *n* blank lines in the listing. The listing corresponding to the program fragment for the IBM System/370 (given in the section "Facilities") is shown in Fig. 1.

Quite different symbolic instructions can nonetheless generate the same sequence of object code bytes. Consider this excerpt from a DEC VAX assembler listing.

Successive Hex Bytes	Address	Line #	Source code
81 72 64 65	10E1	12	.BYTE 101,100,114,129
81 72 64 65	10E5	13	.BYTE 101,100,114,−127
8172 6465	10E9	14	.WORD 25701,33138
8172 6465	10ED	15	.WORD 25701,−32398
81726465	10F1	16	.LONG 2171757669
81726465	10F5	17	.LONG −2123209627
81 72 64 65	10F9	18	.ASCII /edr/<129>
81726465	10FD	19	.FLOAT 4.2336319e+21
81 72 64 65	1101	20	MULD3 (r4),−(r2),(r1)+

LOC	OBJECT CODE	ADDR1	ADDR2	ST#	NAME	OP	OPERANDS	
.								
.								
.								
00000C	5830 2030		00038	8		L	3, = F'0'	CLEAR REGISTER
000010	5850 2030		00038	9		L	5, = F'0'	USING LITERAL
000014	4840 2034		00030	10		LH	4, = H'14'	LOAD REGISTER
000018	47F0 2010		00024	11		B	BCNT	ENTER LOOP
00001C	4A53 2038		00040	12	BNTER	AH	5,STZ(3)	INDEX STZ BY REG 3
000020	4A30 2036		0003B	13		AH	3, = H'2'	INCREMENT INDEX
000024	4640 2014		0001C	14	BCNT	BCT	4,BNTER	BRANCH ON COUNT
000028	5050 2054		0005C	15		ST	5,BSUM	STORE SUM
				16	*			
000040	000F00E100010034 ⎫			17	STZ	DC	H'15,225,1,52,10,48,76,42,88,26,14,4,32'	
000048	000A00300046002A ⎪ (Hexadecimal equivalents							
000050	0058001A000E0004 ⎬ of 13 numbers)							
000058	0020 ⎭							
00005A	0000 ←(Filler needed to align next instruction properly)							
00005C	00000000			18	BSUM	DC	F'0'	

FIG. 1. Example of Listing from System/370 assembler. The LOC column shows the address of each instruction relative to the beginning of the program. The OBJECT CODE columns show the contents of the instructions as they will appear in memory. The ADDR1 (not used in this example) and ADDR2 columns give the effective addresses of the operands. Thus, assuming general register 2 holds the value 8, 2030 has the effective value 8 + 30 = 38. The ST# column is a sequential line number for the programmer's convenience. Note that columns to left of ST# are all given in hexadecimal.

This listing shows that the assembly language programmer submitted eight different directives and one symbolic instruction to the assembler, yet the assembler generated exactly the same 4 bytes of object code for each of the nine lines of source code. The sequence of source code instructions has no practical significance other than to demonstrate the single most important concept of stored-program computation: the *context-dependency of stored information*. By this is meant that there is no intrinsic meaning to any arbitrary object-code byte sequence; one must be told how the sequence will be used before it can be ascertained whether the bytes will be executed as an instruction or interpreted as data and, if the latter, the type of data intended.

Macro Assemblers An important attribute of an assembler is the ability to define and use *macros (macroinstructions - q.v.).* It often happens that a certain pattern of instructions occurs in several places in a program with only minor variations. This is particularly the case if there is a common operation that requires several machine orders for its execution; for example, the calling sequence for a call of another routine. Thus, to call the SAP routine SUB with parameters A and B, it might be necessary to write

```
LDX 4,*
TFR SUB
NOP A
NOP B
```

The first instruction loads into register 4 the address of itself; i.e. its location in storage. From this the subroutine can compute the return address to resume operation of the main program after the calling sequence. The parameters A and B are assumed to be addresses, and have been placed as the address parts of two no-operation [i.e. null] instructions (*see* NO-OP). Evidently, it would be convenient for the programmer to be able to write

```
CALL SUB,A,B
```

and have the system generate the four line *calling sequence* given above. The advantages of this approach are threefold. The programmer writes less; the program is more readable: and if at some future stage the calling sequence is changed, a change at one place in the program will insure that all CALLS are changed without the need to alter each one individually.

A macro assembler allows the programmer to define macroinstructions as sequences of ordinary instructions, and provides a means of inserting variable information in the generated sequences.

Macros can be used to generate built-in data sequences, as well as executable instruction sequences. The following DEC VAX assembler macro generalizes construction of any table whose values can be formed by applying a formula supplied by the user of the macro:

```
.MACRO table n, first, last, fofn
    n = first      ; initialize symbol n
```

```
    .repeat last-first+1; argument is
                        ;repeat count
    .long fofn; creates a longword
                        ;integer
    n=n+1              ;redefine
                        ;symbol n
  .endr
.ENDM table
```

Arguments *first* and *last* specify the first and last values to be used for whatever actual argument is used in place of *n*, and *fofn* ("*f* of *n*") is a formula that involves *n*. To generate 20 odd numbers, the user could then write

```
odds: table k,0,19,2*k+1
```

Similarly, to generate a *table* of cubes from 5 cubed through 15 cubed inclusive, the user could write

```
cubes: table j,5,15,j*j*j
```

Such invocations of macro *table* must, of course, be strategically placed in the source code such that flow-of-control never reaches the labels *odds* or *cubes* (or any place interior to the generated tables).

Conditional Assembly A feature of many assemblers is the ability to assemble selectively pieces of program. This is particularly useful in package programs that have to provide a large number of options. In its simplest form this facility is provided by a pseudo-instruction that controls the assembly of the immediately following instruction, but usually a more elaborate facility of assembly-time jumps and labels is provided. Typically, assembly-time labels (or sequence symbols) are preceded by a period and appear in the label field. However, they are ignored by the assembler except in the context of pseudo-instructions typically named AGO and AIF. (The mnemonics are derived from "assembler GOTO" and "assembler IF") Let .ss be a sequence symbol; then

```
AGO    .SS
```

causes assembly to be continued from the line in which the symbol .ss appears in the label field (usually, this must be a forward jump), and

```
AIF (symbol-1 relation symbol-2) .SS
```

causes assembly to be continued from the line labeled .ss if the condition is true; otherwise, assembly continues with the next line of code, as usual.

Conditional assembly is an especially powerful tool when used in conjunction with macro definition. Consider this DEC VAX macro, which places the average of operands *a* and *b* in *result*:

```
.MACRO average a, b, result
    addl a,b,result   ;result <- a+b
    ashl #-1,result,result ; result <-
                        ;(a+b)/2
.ENDM average
```

(The second instruction generated shifts the tentative result right one place (i.e. *shift left* −1 places) as a fast way of dividing by 2.) Now, in response to the user who calls the macro via

```
average low, high, mean
```

the macro will be expanded (replaced in-place by) the two instructions

```
add1 low, high, mean ; mean <- low + high
ashl #-1, mean, never ; mean <- (low+high)/2
```

(Amusingly, even the formal arguments used in the comments are replaced by their actual argument counterparts, and the expanded comments happen to be correct!)
But now consider the invocation

```
average R0, R0, ans
```

Macro expansion will still generate two instructions, even though the only one needed would be:

```
movl R0, ans ; ans <- R0
```

(i.e. the average of two identical items is a copy of either). No astute programmer would use the macro in lieu of the move instruction, but a preprocessor (*q.v.*) or a compiler might. The solution is to use conditional assembly to generate one instruction, whenever the first two operands are *symbolically* identical, and two otherwise:

```
.MACRO average a,b,result
    .if IDENTICAL a,b
        movl a, result
    .if_false
        add1 a,b,result
        ashl #-1,result,result
    .endc ; end conditional clause
.ENDM average
```

It must be emphasized that the "condition" tested by conditional assembly must be one testable at assembly time, not execution time. In the earlier invocation

```
average low, high, mean
```

it might happen that the run-time *values* of symbols *low* and *high* are the same, but, since their names were not the same at assembly time, there is no way to avoid generation of the inefficient two-instruction sequence.

The Working of the Assembler

The "classic" assembler takes a routine (or subprogram) and converts it into binary symbolic form for subsequent processing by a linker. The conversion is accomplished in two passes (i.e. the source program is scanned twice). The basic strategy is very simple. The *first pass* through the source program collects all the symbol definitions into a symbol table, and the *second pass* converts the program to binary symbolic form, using the definitions collected in the first pass.

During the second pass, the assembler will have to recognize three sorts of quantities: absolute quantities, relocatable quantities, and references to externally defined symbols. In the simplest case, all relocatable quantities are expressed relative to an origin at the beginning of the routine. The assembler therefore has to categorize the symbols as it builds up the symbol table, and then check for illegal combinations in expressions. (For example, it is meaningless to add two relocatable symbols, though their difference may be a respectable absolute quantity.) The exact form of the output from the assembler depends on the linker. Typically, the assembler might produce the following output.

Header	Name of routine,
RLB	Relocatable binary section: Consists of binary symbolic code and relocation information,
Definition table	Definitions of global symbols defined in the routine (i.e. symbols that will be referenced in other routines).
Use table	Details of use of global and COMMON symbols in the routine (i.e. symbols used here but defined elsewhere).

The *definition table* carries information about symbols defined in this routine which are to have a global meaning. Since these may be absolute or relative, the table must carry this information as well as the value. In the case of a relative symbol the value is relative to the beginning of the routine.

The *use table* is more complex, since it records all occurrences of global symbols within the routine. Its exact form will depend on the facilities provided by the assembler—in particular the circumstances in which global symbols can be used.

If multiple location counters are used, an extra block must be output giving the amount of space used by the routine relative to each location counter. Each relocatable item will carry with it an indication of the relevant location counter.

Meta Assemblers

Assemblers for different machines have much in common. They organize symbol tables, evaluate expressions, and generate binary words from a number of symbolic fields. The idea of a meta assembler is to provide a system with these general capabilities, together with a means of describing (in machine-independent form) the assembly rules for a particular machine. The meta assembler accepts this description and then functions apparently as a normal assembler.

The idea of a meta assembler originated with Ferguson (1966). The idea had been utilized in the Utmost assembler for the Univac III, Sleuth II for the Univac 1107/8, and in Metasymbol for the SDS 900 series. An important feature of these systems (which is usually glossed over in their descriptions) is that the syntax of the input to a meta assembler is fixed. The semantics (meaning) of the symbolic information can be defined by the user, but the user cannot change the syntax. Thus, although it is possible in using a meta assembler to write an assembler for most machines, it is not possible to mimic an existing assembler whose syntax will almost certainly be different than that of the meta assembler. (This is one of the many differences between a meta assembler and a *compiler- compiler - q.v.*).

The essentially new features of a meta assembler are (1) the provision of assembly-time procedures and functions, and (2) a mechanism whereby the programmer can define binary output formats and cause such binary output to be generated.

Superficially, the input to a meta assembler looks like input to any assembler; each line has three fields—label, operation, and operand. The label is optional: If there is a symbol in this field, it is assigned a value equal to the current location-counter value. The operation may be the name of a built-in system operation, in which case it is no different from a pseudo-operation in a conventional assembler. If the operation is not the name of a built-in operation, it is assumed to be the name of a programmer-defined procedure, which will be obeyed, taking the operand field as an argument. This procedure may have the effect of generating some code, or may just perform housekeeping operations such as entering items in a table. It should be particularly noted that the procedure is obeyed during assembly. It is in many ways comparable to a macro, but instead of textual substitution we obey a piece of program written in *meta*-assembly language. This may itself contain calls to other procedures.

The operand field contains an expression, or group of expressions, made up of symbols and/or constants. These expressions are evaluated by the system in the same way that a normal assembler evaluates its address field. Unlike a normal assembler, the expressions may contain calls to user-defined functions.

Included in the built-in procedures are GEN and GENB, which output the values of the operand set as a sequence of words or bytes, respectively, and FORM, which allows the user to define a named template for binary output. Thus,

```
INSTR FORM 6, 3, 15
```

defines (for a 24-bit word machine) a template made up of 3 fields consisting of 6, 3, and 15 bits, and attaches the name INSTR to this template. FORM is a built-in operation. Suppose that subsequent to the definition of INSTR, we write

```
INSTR LDA, 7, ALPHA + 1
```

(Here INSTR is in the operation field, and the operand field is a set of three expressions.) This will cause the three elements of the operand set to be evaluated, truncated, and concatenated to form a 24-bit binary output word. (Note that this technique would allow the operation code of an instruction to be written as an expression!)

The meta assembler does not have any conventional built-in operations for machine instructions. The code emitted for what seems to be an assembly-language instruction is actually determined by a procedure having the name of the desired machine instruction. In this way, and using procedures to produce the required effect for pseudo-instructions, a "conventional" assembler image can be built up.

"High-Level" Assemblers An assembly language program is necessarily written at a fine level of detail, with each instruction representing a single primitive operation. An unfortunate effect of working at this level of detail is that assembly language programs are rarely as perspicuous as programs written in a high-level language can be.

Recently there has been a development in the direction of *high-level* or *Algol-like* assembly languages that attempt to combine fine control over machine registers and storage with a structure that reflects the overall structure of the program; for example, repetition loops, conditional statements, and functions and procedures. The facilities provided in such a language must correspond fairly closely to the actual hardware. For example, we cannot include anything that depends on dynamic storage allocation if the underlying hardware does not provide such facilities. (Put another way, the compiler for an Algol-like assembly language cannot assume the existence of a "run-time system." Every source statement except a procedure call must compile into open code.) The precise facilities provided in a system will depend on the particular machine, but will typically include the following.

1. Symbolic names (identifiers) with associated types. The types will correspond to the storage units manipulated by the machine instructions; for example, on the Digital Equipment Corporation VAX Series, they would include byte, word, and longword.
2. Reserved identifiers for machine registers. A synonym facility may also be provided to associate other names with registers.
3. Block structure, giving scopes to identifiers.
4. Conditional and compound statements.
5. One-dimensional arrays, but not multidimensional arrays (these cannot be accessed by simple indexing on most machines).
6. Procedures and functions (with parameters passed as addresses in general-purpose registers or in a *stack - q.v.*).
7. Simple expressions (but nothing involving temporary storage; all operators are of equal precedence, and evaluation is by a simple left-to-right scan).
8. Provision for including basic assembly language (e.g. for input operations).

The first high-level assembler was the PL/360 system described by Wirth (1968) in a classic paper. As its name implies, it was designed for the IBM System 360 machines. An interesting development in this area is that the only assembler provided by the manufacturers of the GEC

4000 series machines is a high-level assembler (called BABBAGE).

References

1951. Wilkes, M. V., Wheeler, D. J., and Gill, S. *The Preparation of Programs for an Electronic Digital Computer*. Cambridge, MA: Addison-Wesley.

1956. Wilkes, M. V. *Automatic Digital Computers*. London: Methuen & Co.

1965. Graham, Marvin Lowell and Ingerman, Peter Zilahy. "An Assembly Language for Reprogramming," *Communications of the ACM* **8**, 769-773.

1966. Ferguson, D. E. "The Evolution of the Meta-Assembly Program," *Communications of the ACM* **9**: 190.

1968. Wirth, N. "PL/360, A Programming Language for the 360 Computers," *Journal of the ACM* **15**: 37.

1968. Feldman, Jerome and Gries, David. "Translator Writing Systems," *Communications of the ACM* **11**, 77-113 (see Section C and references therein).

1978. Barron, D. W. *Assemblers and Loaders*, 3rd Ed. New York: American-Elsevier.

1991. Federighi, F. D., and Reilly, E. D. *VAX Assembly Language*. New York: Macmillan.

DAVID W. BARRON AND EDWIN D. REILLY

ASSOCIATION FOR COMPUTING MACHINERY (ACM)

For articles on related subjects *see* AMERICAN FEDERATION OF INFORMATION PROCESSING SOCIETIES and TURING AWARD WINNERS.

Purpose The Association for Computing Machinery (ACM) is one of the two large scientific, educational, and technical societies of the computing community. (The IEEE—CS (*q.v.*) is the other.) Founded in 1947, the Association is dedicated to the development of information processing as a discipline, and to the responsible use of computers in an increasing diversity of applications.

Quoting its constitution, the purposes of the Association are: (1) To advance the sciences and arts of information processing, including but not restricted to the study, design, development, construction, and application of modern machinery, computing techniques and appropriate languages for general information processing, storage, retrieval and processing of data of all kinds and the automatic control and simulation of processes. (2) To promote the free interchange of information about the sciences and arts of information processing, both among specialists and among the public, in the best scientific and professional tradition. (3) To develop and maintain the integrity and competence of individuals engaged in the practices of the sciences and arts of information processing.

How Established ACM was founded at Columbia University on 15 September 1947, as the Eastern Association for Computing Machinery. A constitution and bylaws were adopted in September 1949. ACM was incorporated in Delaware in December 1954. The following have held the office of ACM president:

J. H. Curtiss, 1947
John W. Mauchly, 1948–1950
Franz L. Alt, 1950–1952
Samuel B. Williams, 1952–1954
Alston S. Householder, 1954–1956
John W. Carr III, 1956–1958
Richard W. Hamming, 1958–1960
Harry D. Huskey, 1960–1962
Alan J. Perlis, 1962–1964
George E. Forsythe, 1964–1966
Anthony Oettinger, 1966–1968
Bernard A. Galler, 1968–1970
Walter M. Carlson, 1970–1972
Anthony Ralston, 1972–1974
Jean E. Sammet, 1974–1976
Herbert R. J. Grosch, 1976–1978
Daniel D. McCracken, 1978–1980
Peter J. Denning, 1980–1982
David H. Brandin, 1982–1984
Adele Goldberg, 1984–1986
Paul W. Abrahams, 1986–1988
Bryan S. Kocher 1988–1990
John R. White 1990–1992

Organizational Structure The Association is organized into 4 regions, 3 covering the United States and Canada, and one international region. Each region is represented in the Council of the ACM (the elected governing body) by a regional representative. With an additional four members-at-large and the ex officio members (president, past-president, vice-president, secretary, treasurer, chair of the Publications Board, and SIG Board Chair), the full Council comprises 15 members.

Each region has local chapters and student chapters. Presently there are approximately 100 local chapters and 450 student chapters.

The four classes of ACM membership and their qualifications are:

Member—must subscribe to the purposes of the Association and have attained professional stature by demonstrating intellectual competence and ethical conduct in the arts and sciences of information processing.

Associate—must subscribe to the purposes of the Association, but need not be eligible for Member status.

Student—full-time registrant at an accredited educational institution.

Institutional—institutions that subscribe to the purposes of the Association.

Total membership is about 70,000. The headquarters of ACM are at 1515 Broadway, New York, NY 10036.

Technical Program The major organizational units of ACM devoted to technical activities of its members are the Special Interest Groups (SIGs). The SIGs operate as semiautonomous bodies within ACM for the advancement of activities in the following subject areas: Ada; APL; Applied Computing; Automata and Computability Theory; Architecture of Computer Systems; Artificial Intelligence; Business Information Technology; Biomedical Computing; Computers and the Physically Handicapped; Computers and Society; Data Communications; Computer Personnel Research; Computer Science Education; Computer Uses in Education; Design Automation; Documentation; Forth Programming Language; Computer Graphics; Hypertext, Hypermedia; Information Retrieval; Measurement and Evaluation; Microprogramming; Management of Data; Numerical Mathematics; Office Information Systems; Operating Systems; Programming Languages; Security, Audit and Control; Symbolic and Algebraic Manipulation; Simulation; Small and Personal Computing Systems and Applications; Software Engineering; and University and College Computing Services.

The ACM Lectureship Series was instituted in 1961 to enrich chapter activities by providing acknowledged specialists in various aspects of computing and its application as speakers.

In 1966, ACM established the Turing Award (*q.v.*), honoring computing pioneer Alan M. Turing (*q.v.*), and given annually to an individual selected for contributions of a technical nature made to the computing community. The award carries an honorarium of $25,000. The recipients to date have been: Alan J. Perlis, Maurice V. Wilkes, Richard W. Hamming, Marvin Minsky, J. H. Wilkinson, John McCarthy, Edsger W. Dijkstra, Charles W. Bachman, Donald E. Knuth, Allen Newell and Herbert A. Simon (jointly), Michael O. Rabin and Dana Scott (jointly), John Backus, Robert Floyd, Kenneth E. Iverson, C. A. R. Hoare, Edgar F. Codd, Stephen A. Cook, Ken Thompson and Dennis M. Ritchie (jointly), Nicklaus Wirth, John Hopcroft, Robert Tarjan, John Cocke, Ivan Sutherland, and Robin Milner.

The ACM Distinguished Service Award was instituted in 1970. Its recipients have been Franz Alt, J. Donald Madden, George E. Forsythe, William Atchison, Saul Gorn, John W. Carr III, Richard J. Canning, Thomas B. Steel, Jr., Eric A. Weiss, Carl Hammer, Bernard A. Galler, Aaron Finerman, Anthony Ralston, Grace Murray Hopper, Saul Rosen, Clair Maple, Frederick P. Brooks, Jr., Thomas A. DeFanti, and Gerald Engel. A Software Systems Award was established in 1982. In 1971, in conjunction with the twenty-fifth anniversary of the invention of the modern digital computer, ACM established the Grace Murray Hopper Award, to be given annually to the outstanding young computer professional of the year as nominated by ACM. To qualify, candidates must have been 30 years or younger at the time the qualifying contribution was made. The first award was to Donald E. Knuth.

The ACM publishes twelve major periodicals: *Journal of the Association for Computing Machinery* (established in 1954, published quarterly) is devoted to technical papers of lasting value reporting on research and advances in the computing sciences. *Communications of the ACM* (1958, monthly) publishes technical papers and timely articles on topics of interest to the computing profession. *Computing Reviews* (1960, monthly) comprehensively covers the literature on computing and its applications. *Computing Surveys* (1969, quarterly) presents comprehensive survey coverage of the state of the art in the various areas of computer science and business data processing. *Transactions on Mathematical Software* (1975, quarterly) publishes theoretical and applied articles on mathematical software as well as algorithms for computers. *Transactions on Database Systems* (1976, quarterly) publishes original papers on the theory and applications of all aspects of database systems and related subjects. *Transactions on Programming Languages and Systems* (1979, quarterly) contains original work on the development and use of programming languages, methods, and systems. *Transactions on Graphics* (1982, quarterly) contains papers on all aspects of computer graphics. *Transactions on Information Systems* (1983, quarterly) offers new concepts in office automation for practical applications. *Transactions on Computer Systems* (1983, quarterly) reports original work in the design, implementation, and use of computer systems. *Transactions on Modeling and Computer Simulation* (1991, quarterly) publishes papers on modeling and all forms of computer simulation. *Transactions on Software Engineering and Methodology* (1992, quarterly) contains papers on all aspects of the design, analysis, implementation and evaluation of software systems. ACM also publishes *Collected Algorithms of the ACM*, the annual *Guide to Computing Literature*, and other special editions under the auspices of the ACM Press.

ACM sponsors the annual Computer Science Conference, which is devoted mainly to brief reports of current research. In addition, the Special Interest Groups and other subunits sponsor numerous technical symposia and meetings, primarily in North America, but also in various other parts of the world.

ISAAC. L. AUERBACH

ASSOCIATION FRANÇAISE POUR LA CYBERNETIQUE ECONOMIQUE ET TECHNIQUE (AFCET)

For an article on a related subject *see* INTERNATIONAL FEDERATION OF INFORMATION PROCESSING.

AFCET, a non-profit association, is dedicated to pursuing and contributing to the development of the main disciplines determining the progress of computer science, and the decision, organization, and systems sciences.

AFCET is a meeting place for specialists anxious to participate and keep up with scientific and technical development. By publishing specialized journals, bulletins, and monographs, as well as by organizing local, national, and international events, AFCET ensures the diffusion of information among its members.

How Established The AFCET was established in 1969 as a result of the amalgamation of: AFIRO (Association Française d'Informatique et de Recherche Operationnelle), AFRA (Association Française de Regulation et d'Automatisme), and AFIC (Association Française d'Instrumentation et de Controle). The merger was due to the relation between measurement and instrumentation as well as the relation of operational research to automation and data processing. The presidents of AFCET since 1969 have been

R. Mercier, 1969
J. Csech, 1970–1971
F. Genuys, 1972–1973
L. Guileysse, 1974–1975
B. Roy, 1976–1977
J. Carteron, 1978–1979
A. Danzin, 1980–1981
J. P. de Blasis 1982–1983
R. Moreau 1984–1986
B. Paulré 1987–1989
B. Robinet 1990–1991
G. Roucairol 1991–

AFCET Members Members of AFCET (about 5,000) come from all representative backgrounds: research, industry and trade, public and private sectors, universities and schools. They find in the association means of maintaining and developing relations with their French and foreign peers, diffusion media for their studies and works, and logistical support for the organization of meetings and scientific and technical events.

AFCET Meetings AFCET organizes around 30 events per year: conferences, workshops, forums and several schools, gathering 2,000 to 3,000 participants. There are about 100 working groups.

AFCET Publications AFCET publishes seven scientific journals:

- *APII: Automatic Control Production Systems.*
- *MAN: Mathematical Modeling and Numerical Analysis.*
- *MBD: Models and Data Base.*
- *RIS: International Journal of Systematics.*
- *RO: Operations Research.*
- *Theoretical Informatics and Applications.*
- *TSI: Technology and Science of Informatics.*

The AFCET journal that is dedicated to all its members is *AFCET Interfaces.* There are also several collections of monographs published by Bordas-Dunod, as well as preprints of the AFCET conferences.

AFCET International Connections As the official representative of France within EURO, IAPR, IFAC, IFIP, IFORS, IMACS, IMEKO, and WOGSC, AFCET is the natural interface with its foreign homologues. Moreover, AFCET has reciprocal agreements with societies such as ACM, IEEE, organizations from other European countries, and members of the European Cooperation in Informatics. AFCET is the privileged spokesperson of the authorities and bodies of general interest when they need an impartial professional opinion.

ISAAC L. AUERBACH

ASSOCIATIVE MEMORY

For articles on related subjects *see* ADDRESSING; CACHE MEMORY; MEMORY: MAIN; and VIRTUAL MEMORY

Data in an *associative memory* or *content-addressable memory* is not accessed by address as in conventional memory. Rather than being identified by the name of its location, it is identified from properties of its own value. To retrieve a word from associative store, a search key (or descriptor) must be presented that represents particular values of all or some of the bits of the word. This key is compared in parallel with the corresponding lock or tag bits of all stored words, and all words matching this key are signaled to be available. If the key is *loose*, with few attributes, it will access many words. The memory might indicate the number of such words and would in any case normally provide each of these in turn for examination. The order in which they are presented is usually related to their order in physical storage and tells nothing of their value. Once available, each word can be used or, if not wanted, flagged (by a change of a single search bit) so that succeeding words can be retrieved.

Associative search can be fairly complex if the search key has few elements and the association is loose. A limiting case is that in which at most one occurrence of a search key match exists. This occurs in the use of associative stores between levels in a memory hierarchy where the associative store is a scratch pad denoting the existence of a copy of a record in the next higher-level store. Such is also the use of associative storage in cache memory management.

Various attempts have been made to build associative processors in which the main memory is partially or completely associative (Lewin, 1972). In this case each memory word, in addition to match or equality logic on each bit, has other facilities such as "greater than" detection.

Fig. 1 illustrates the logical structure of an associative store, showing the possibility of ("don't care") search inputs whose value results in a positive match independent of the bit stored in the associative memory. In practice, such a store will normally be implemented using integrated circuit technology. In addition to the associative search mechanism, the memory is usually equipped with conventional read/write facilities (not shown in Fig. 1).

A flip-flop is shown as the basic storage element and is shaded to indicate its current state. An equivalence circuit (denoted by =) is used to make the comparison with the search key. An additional OR circuit (denoted by +) per bit allows the use of a "don't care" search condition. The output from each bit is combined in an AND, represented by the horizontal line on the figure. A match output is 1 if and only if the stored data and key data bits match everywhere that "don't care" inputs are zero. Fig. 1 shows a match between a stored value of (1,0,0) and a search key of (1,0,X), where X indicates the "don't care" condition.

One important application of associative storage is in paged memory management. In such systems, of which Atlas (*q.v.*) was an early example, a relatively small, fast, main store is used in conjunction with a slow, large bulk or backup store. Each memory is divided into blocks or

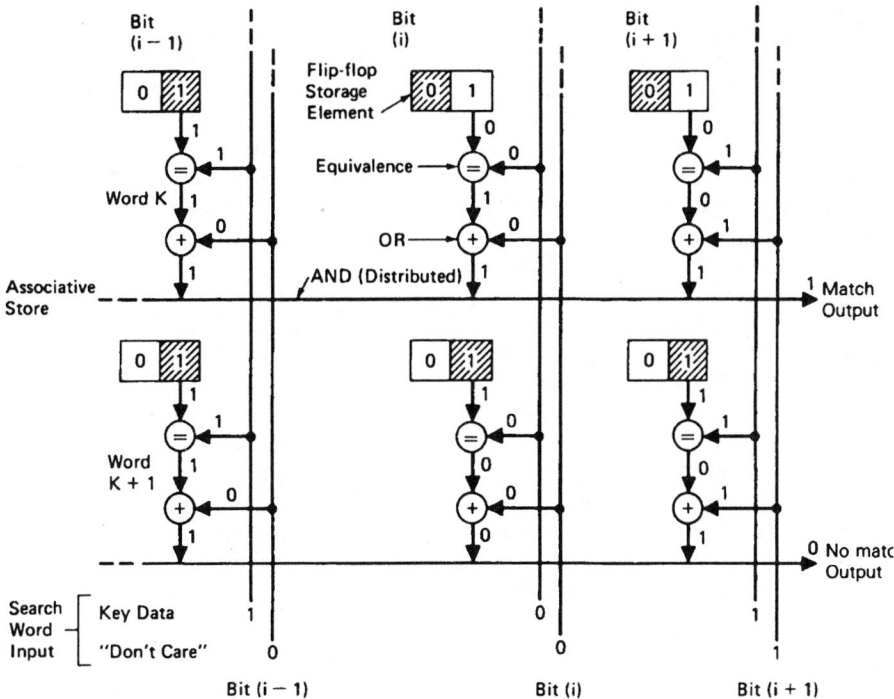

FIG. 1. Schematic of an associative store of two words of three bits each being accessed by match on two bits and by "don't care" on one.

pages whose size may vary typically from 64 to 1,024 words. The small main memory will hold a small number of these, say 8 to 32, while the bulk store may have a capacity of thousands of pages. Data is transferred between main and backup store in page-size quantities. When the central processor requires a new word of information, high-order bits of its address are checked against appropriate bits of an associative page-address store in order to ascertain the existence in main memory of the word sought. If the page is already present, the associative store provides additional bits, giving its location in main store. If not present, related central processing unit (CPU) activity is halted while the page-memory access mechanism establishes a main store page location whose contents are returned to backup storage, after which this area of main store is refilled with the required new page.

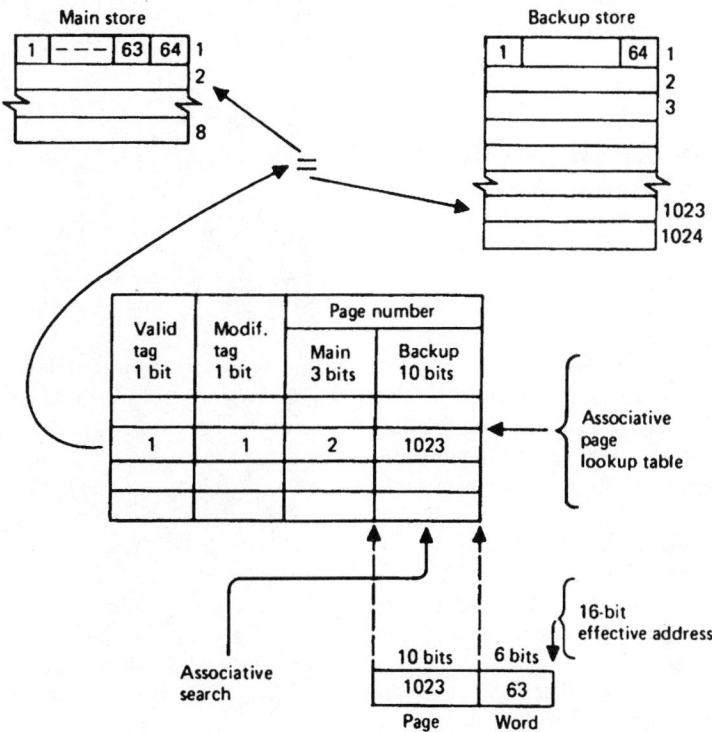

FIG. 2. A paging organization using an associative lookup table.

A paging organization using associative page lookup is shown in Fig. 2. In this example a backup store of 1,024 pages of 64 words each is illustrated. The main store has a capacity of 8 pages of 64 words. An associative page lookup table of 4 words of 15 bits each is used to maintain order. In use, the upper 10 bits or page address of the effective address (1023) from the CPU is compared associatively with 10-bit page numbers in the associative store. If a match occurs, 5 bits are provided (3,1,1), giving the page location in main store (2 = 010) as well as two data integrity tags (1, 1). The valid tag indicates that the data in main store is a valid copy of that in backup store (i.e. that the backup store data has not been modified since the page was read into main store). The modified tag indicates that the data in main store has been modified by the CPU and is therefore not the same as in backup storage.

The result in the preceding example is that the word sought, number 63 from page 1023, is present at page 2, word 63 of the main store, that it is valid, and may differ from its image in backup store. Had the desired page not been in main store, one page of main store would have been selected for replacement, ideally one whose valid tag was zero, indicating it to be no longer needed. If all valid tags were 1, a page would be selected for replacement whose recent use is low (as established, for example, by automatic decrementing, at fixed time intervals, of a use counter associated with each page in the associative page-lookup table). This page, if its modified tag is 1, is stored in backup store and then replaced in main storage by the newly required page. The lookup table is modified accordingly to reflect a new backup page number for the corresponding main store page with validity tag 1, and modified tag 0.

Reference

1972. Lewin, D. *Theory and Design of Digital Computers.* Camden, NJ: Thomas Nelson, Chapters 6 and 9.

KENNETH C. SMITH AND ADEL S. SEDRA

ASYNCHRONOUS OPERATION. *See*
SYNCHRONOUS/ASYNCHRONOUS OPERATION.

ATANASOFF, JOHN V.

For an article on a related subject, *see* ABC COMPUTER.

John V. Atanasoff is now widely recognized as the inventor of the world's first electronic computer, the digital Atanasoff-Berry Computer, or ABC (*q.v.*), so named to acknowledge the contribution of his graduate assistant, Clifford E. Berry.

Because the special-purpose ABC led directly to the general-purpose ENIAC (*q.v.*) and on to the EDVAC (*q.v.*) and other first generation stored-program computers, Atanasoff is also widely recognized as the initiator of the modern computer revolution.

Atanasoff (b. Hamilton, NY, 4 October 1903) received his B.S. in electrical engineering from Florida State University in 1925, his M.S. in mathematics from Iowa State College in 1926, and his Ph.D. in experimental physics from the University of Wisconsin in 1930. He taught mathematics and physics at Iowa State until 1942, when he left for war research at the Naval Ordnance Laboratory in Washington, D.C.

Atanasoff did not return to teaching or to computers when he left government service in 1952, but devoted the balance of his career to business enterprises, including the founding of two engineering companies, Ordnance Engineering Corporation and Cybernetics, Inc. Although unsuccessful in patenting the ABC, he obtained over 20 other patents.

Atanasoff's greatest achievement, of course, was his invention of the electronic computer. He had conceived its basic plan at Iowa State during the 1937–38 academic year, worked out the critical details the next year, and, with Berry's help, built a working model of the central computing apparatus in the fall of 1939. He and Berry then proceeded with the computer itself, completing construction in the spring of 1942.

Atanasoff designed this computer to solve unprecedentedly large systems of simultaneous linear equations, which he saw as applicable to a wide variety of problems in physics, engineering, and applied mathematics. For this purpose, he devised an original variant of the traditional Gaussian elimination method.

The ABC featured binary arithmetic, rotating drum memories, capacitor memory elements, continuous regeneration of those elements from a separate arithmetic

FIG. 1. John Vincent Atanasoff.

unit, electronic (vacuum-tube) switching and logical switching adders, base conversion, punched-card input-output systems, automatic sequential controls, modular units, and parallel operations.

Atanasoff's priority over John W. Mauchly (*q.v.*) and J. Presper Eckert (*q.v.*), whose ENIAC had been unveiled as the first electronic computer in 1946, was not established until 1973, when Federal District Judge Earl R. Larson ruled in the now famous Honeywell vs. Sperry-Rand suit. In his unappealed decision, Larson found that "Eckert and Mauchly did not themselves first invent the automatic electronic digital computer, but instead derived that subject matter from one Dr. John Vincent Atanasoff."

Mauchly's contacts with Atanasoff included a five-day visit to Iowa in 1941, during which he was allowed to examine both the machine and a detailed written description of it.

Atanasoff received several awards in the 1940s for his contributions as chief of the Naval Ordnance Lab's acoustics division, including the U.S. Navy Distinguished Service Award. In recent years he has received many honorary degrees and other citations for his invention of the electronic computer.

References

1988. Burks, A.R. and Burks, A.W. *The First Electronic Computer: The Atanasoff Story*. Ann Arbor, MI: University of Michigan Press.

1988. Mollenhoff, Clark R. *Atanasoff: Forgotten Father of the Computer*. Ames, Iowa: Iowa State University Press.

1988. Mackintosh, Allan R. "Dr. Atanasoff's Computer," *Scientific American*, **259**, 2: 90–96.

ARTHUR W. BURKS AND ALICE R. BURKS

ATANASOFF-BERRY COMPUTER

For an article on a related subjects *see* ATANASOFF, JOHN V.

The Atanasoff-Berry Computer, or ABC, named for its inventor, John V. Atanasoff (*q.v.*), and his graduate assistant, Clifford E. Berry, was arguably the world's first electronic computer. Atanasoff conceived the basic plan of the ABC during the 1937–38 academic year at Iowa State, where he was a professor of both physics and mathematics.

He spent the next year working out the details of its central computing apparatus: vacuum-tube add-subtract mechanisms, rotating drum memory, and vacuum-tube regeneration mechanisms to refresh the memory's capacitor elements. He and Berry completed a successful model of that central apparatus by December 1939, and the computer itself by May 1942.

The digital (binary) ABC was designed to solve systems of up to 29 simultaneous linear equations (see Fig. 1). Based on an original variant of Gaussian elimination, it used repeated additions and subtractions, sign-sensing, shifting, and automatic sequential controls for the main step of eliminating a designated variable from a pair of equations.

FIG. 1.   The ABC computer.

The binary digits of such a pair of equations were represented as high or low charges on capacitors housed in two drums on a common axle. As the drums rotated, their signals were transmitted in parallel to the separate arithmetic unit, where 30 add-subtract mechanisms, together with an associated carry-borrow drum, performed the appropriate additions or subtractions and sent the results back to the memory drum from which a coefficient was being eliminated. Meanwhile, 30 restore-shift mechanisms refreshed the addends or subtrahends and sent those back to the other memory drum, shifting them if necessary for the next rotation.

Computing in the binary system required base-conversion in and out. The successive elimination of variables from such long equations also required a great many intermediate binary input-output steps, for which Atanasoff devised an electrical arcing method of punching and reading cards.

In the end, an error of extremely small frequency in this latter system spoiled results for sets of more than five equations, a difficulty that Atanasoff and Berry were unable to resolve before they left Iowa for war research positions in 1942. The capacitor memory and the vacuum-tube arithmetic unit worked exactly as intended, however, and established the feasibility of electronic computing, as well as many of its principles, for all time.

The electronic switching principles of the ABC were used throughout the ENIAC (*q.v.*), and its principles of both regenerative storage and logical switching adders were also used in the ensuing EDVAC (*q.v.*). Later computers have used all of these principles, plus those of mechanically rotated memories and capacitor memory elements.

Reference

1987. Mackintosh, Allan R. "The First Electronic Computer," *Physics Today*, **40**, 3: 25–32.

1988. Burks, A.R. and Burks, A.W. *The First Electronic Computer: The Atanasoff Story*. Ann Arbor, MI: University of Michigan Press.

1988. Mackintosh, Allan R. "Dr. Atanasoff's Computer," *Scientific American*, **259**, 2: 90–96.

ARTHUR W. BURKS AND ALICE R. BURKS

ATLAS

For articles on related subject *see* DIGITAL COMPUTERS: EARLY; KILBURN, THOMAS; and MANCHESTER UNIVERSITY COMPUTERS.

The *Atlas* computer was the third in a series of early computers designed in the United Kingdom by a team under Thomas M. Kilburn in the Department of Electrical Engineering, University of Manchester, in association with Ferranti Ltd. (later ICT Ltd. and then ICL Ltd.). Previous systems were the Ferranti Mark I and Ferranti Mark II (Mercury).

Design of Atlas began in 1958, and ultimately three systems, known as Atlas 1, were constructed and installed at the University of Manchester (1962), University of London (1963), and the Atlas Laboratory, Chilton (1963). All were operated until the early 1970s, with the Chilton machine being the last to be switched off in March 1973.

In many respects, Atlas led the way in design of an integrated computer system, combining many novel hardware features with an advanced software operating system. Among the new concepts that Atlas successfully introduced were multiprogramming (*q.v.*), one-level store, and paging. It was the first major system designed for multiprogramming and was provided with a composite memory consisting of ferrite cores and magnetic drums linked by program to provide the user with a one-level memory (*q.v.*). This was achieved by a paging system in which page switching was controlled by a simple learning program, or swapping algorithm. There was also a wire-mesh/ferrite rod (hairbrush) memory of 8,000 words to hold the supervisor. The standard word length was 48 bits, equivalent to one single-address instruction with two modifiers and allowing for up to 2^{20} addresses. 128 index registers (*q.v.*) were provided. Instructions were normally executed at an average rate of 0.5 ms, about a hundred times faster than the Mercury computer.

The magnetic tape system used 1-inch tapes, although standard 0.5-inch tapes could also be used. Magnetic disks were not standard, but were fitted later to the Manchester and Chilton machines. Multiple I/O *channels* (*q.v.*) provided for both paper-tape and punched-card peripherals as well as line printers.

Other features of the supervisor program, which was produced by a small team under D. J. Howarth (1961–1962), were the facilities for scheduling and streaming of jobs, automatic control of peripherals, detailed job accounting, and a sophisticated level of operator control. It was normal, with some discretion in selecting the job mix, to obtain 60–80% effective use of the CPU.

A modified version of Atlas, known as Atlas 2, was produced with increased core memory and no magnetic drums (thereby dispensing with paging), the prototype being the Titan computer at the University of Cambridge, which was taken out of service at the end of 1973. Two others in this series were installed: one at the Atomic Weapons Research Establishment, Aldermaston, and one at the Computer-Aided Design Centre, Cambridge.

Although technical and economic reasons, partly due to advances in component manufacture, prevented the Atlas computers from achieving commercial success, they represent an important landmark in the development of advanced computer systems.

References

1961–1962. Howarth, D. J., Payne, R. B., and Summer, F. H. "The Manchester University Atlas Operating System; Part II, Users' Description," *Computer J.* **4**: 226–229.

1961–1962. Kilburn, T., Howarth, D. J., Payne, R. B., and Summer, F. H. "The Manchester University Atlas Operating System; Part I, Internal Organisation," *Computer J.* **4**: 222–225.

1962. Howarth, D. J., Jones, P. D., and Wyld, M. T. "The Atlas Scheduling System," *Computer J.* **5**: 238–244.

1962. Kilburn, T. D., Edwards, B. G., Lanigan, M. J., and Summer, F. H. "One-Level Storage System," *IRE Trans.*, **EC-11**, 2: 223–235.

RICHARD A. BUCKINGHAM

AUTHORING LANGUAGES AND SYSTEMS

For articles on related subjects *see* COMPUTER-ASSISTED INSTRUCTION; COMPUTER-ASSISTED LEARNING AND TEACHING; COMPUTER-MANAGED INSTRUCTION; and PROGRAMMING LANGUAGES.

Considerable attention has been given to providing a convenient programming language for the use of authors of computer-based learning materials. However, obtaining a single, ideal language is a fiction; different uses require different capabilities that are not conveniently provided within a single language and its associated processor.

The specific programming language used by an author is not so significant for effective computer-based instruction as are two other factors. With what notation does the author describe for personal use and others the substance and procedures of the computer-based instruction? By what means are these ideas and notes reliably transcribed into an executing computer program?

One concept of authoring languages and systems is represented in Fig. 1. The designer of material assembles information and opinion about what is needed, working with students and others who should know of the problems and resources (steps 1 through 3). The designer may work with a language or notation devised especially for the topic and objectives (step 4), delegating to the machine or technical assistants the determination of minor details (step 5). Separation of the content of instruction from the description of program logic makes curriculum development less costly.

After a program is executing, the originator should receive complete and useful information about the performance and reaction of students (steps 9 through 11). Many developers continue to test and revise instruction-related computer programs to maintain their usefulness.

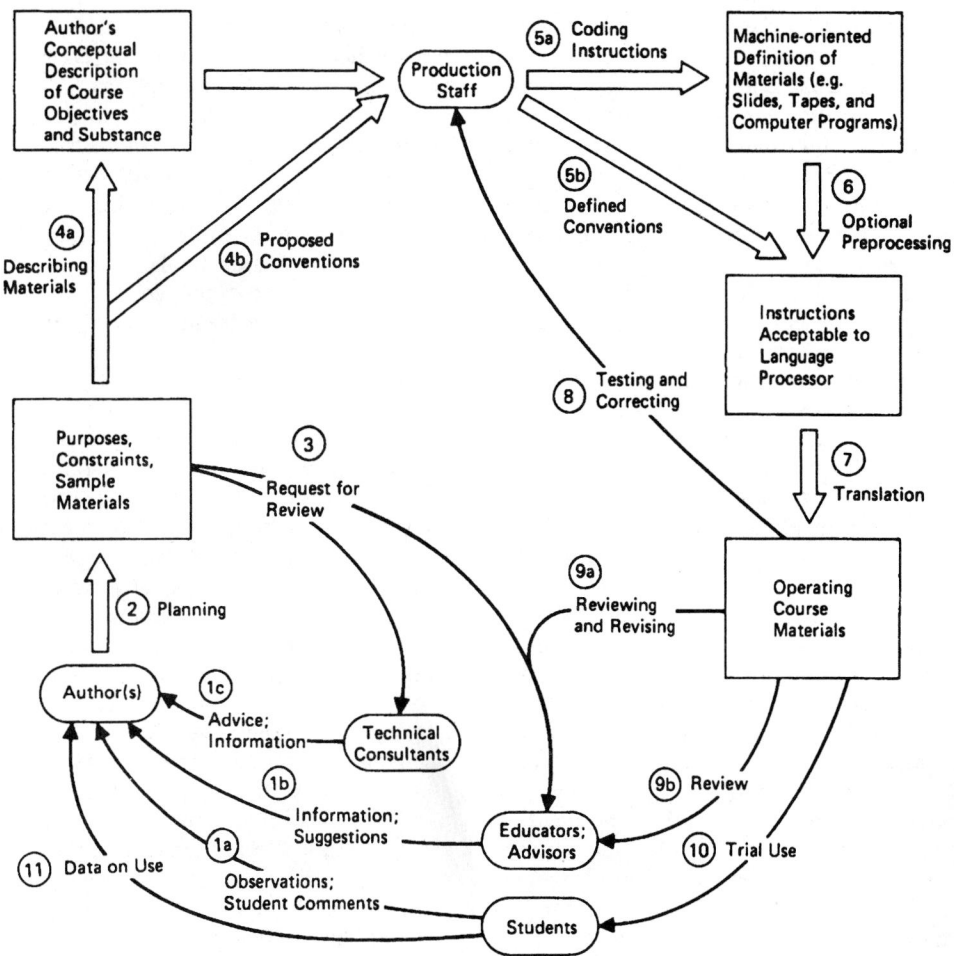

FIG. 1. One representation of authoring activity.

Over 100 different languages and dialects have been put to use specifically for programming instructional use of computers. Most may be characterized by one or two of the following approaches and uses: successive frames (computerization of programmed instruction); description of interactive case histories; description of instructional procedures; specification of data generation and simulated laboratories; retrieval of information and control of media; problem solving and programming. Information about these and many other languages can be obtained from secondary sources (Barker, 1987).

A language is efficient when it is used for the specific purpose for which it was designed to be convenient. The great diversity of instructional uses of computers requires a variety of languages.

References

1987. Barker, Philip. *Author Languages for CAL.* London: Macmillan.

1991. Venezky, Richard L. and Osin, Luis. *The Intelligent Design of Computer-Assisted Instruction.* New York: Longman.

KARL L. ZINN

AUTOMATA. *See also* CELLULAR AUTOMATA; and PROBABILISTIC AUTOMATA.

AUTOMATA THEORY

For articles on related subjects *see* ALGORITHM; CELLULAR AUTOMATA; FORMAL LANGUAGES; NEURAL NETWORKS; PERCEPTRON; PROBABILISTIC AUTOMATA; SEQUENTIAL MACHINE; and TURING MACHINE.

Introduction and Definitions *Automata theory* is a mathematical discipline concerned with the invention and study of mathematically abstract, idealized machines called *automata.* These automata are usually abstractions of information processing devices, such as computers, rather than of devices that move about, such as robots, mechanical toys or automobiles.

This article gives a short and informal survey of the major classes of automata that automata theorists have heretofore seen fit to study, and indicates the primary respective motivations (from the point of view of computer science) for the study of these classes of automata.

For the most part, the automata discussed here process strings of symbols from some finite alphabet of symbols. Let A be any alphabet (finite set of symbols). For example, A might be { $a,b,c,...,z$} or {0,1}. We write A^* to mean the set of *all* finite strings of symbols chosen from A. If A is { $a,b,c,...,z$}, then A^* contains strings representing English words, such as "cat" and "mouse," along with nonsense strings such as "czzxyh". If A is {0,1}, then A^* contains the strings representing the non-negative integers in binary notation (0,1,10,11,100,...) and also these same strings but with extra zeros on the left (e.g. 00010).

Automata generally perform one (or both) of two symbol-processing tasks. They compute partial functions from X^* to Y^* for some finite alphabets X and Y, or they *recognize* languages over some alphabet X.

A *partial function f* from X^* to Y^* is a correspondence between some subset D of X^* and the set Y^* that associates with each element of D^* a unique element in Y^*. D is called the *domain* of f, that is, $D = \{x \varepsilon X^* \mid f(x)$ is defined}. If $f(x)$ is not defined, it is *desirable* that automaton α on input x eventually halt and print some sort of "error message." However, this is not always possible—there are computable partial functions f, all of whose automata α fail to halt at all on some input x outside the domain of f. For example, let $X = Y = \{0,1\}$ and let D be the elements x of X^* such that x begins with 1 or consists of a single 0. If f associates with x the string in Y^* that denotes the binary number representing two times the binary number represented by x, then f is a partial function from X^* to Y^*.

We say roughly that an automaton α *computes* a partial function f from X^* to Y^* when, if α is given any input x in X^* such that $f(x)$ is defined, α eventually produces an output $y \varepsilon Y^*$ such that $f(x) = y$. and, otherwise, α produces no output.

Automata usually receive their inputs on a linear or one-dimensional tape which they are capable of reading one symbol at a time. The manner in which they read symbols on an input tape (left to right, back and forth, with or without changing symbols, etc.) depends on the particular class of automata under consideration. Automata for computing partial functions produce their output on a tape (perhaps the input tape, perhaps a different tape) in a manner also prescribed by the particular class of automata under consideration.

There are also automata whose storage structures more closely resemble *registers*, such as found in a typical pocket calculator, than linear tapes.

A *language* over an alphabet X is just a subset of X^*. For example, if $X = \{ a,b,c,...,z\}$, then { $a,aa,aaa,...$} and $\{x \varepsilon X^* \mid x$ is a word in the English language} are both languages over X.

We say that an automaton α *recognizes* a language L over X when α reads an input $x \epsilon X^*$ on its input tape in the manner of automata of its type; then, if $x \epsilon L$, α eventually performs some particular act of recognition. Examples of such acts of recognition are (1) halting, (2) entering a special internal state called a *final*, or *accepting*, state, or (3) emptying a designated storage tape, for instance a *pushdown store*. If $x \notin L$, then α, on input x never

performs such an act of recognition. Exactly what constitutes an act of recognition depends on the particular class of automata under consideration.

It is presumably clear why it is of interest to computer scientists to study automata that compute (partial) functions, since computer science is the computation business. Among the interesting questions to ask are whether some function is or is not computable by some representative of a particular class of automata and, if it is computable, how efficiently (with respect to some mathematically precise measure of efficiency) can it be so computed.

We motivate the study of automata that recognize languages by some examples. Let X be the set of allowable symbols for some programming language P. Include in X the necessary punctuation symbols and the blank symbol. Let $L = \{x \varepsilon X^* \mid x$ is a valid program of P}. In the process of compiling from P into some other language, it is useful to (among other things) *recognize* the valid programs of P as being valid. Automata theory gives some insight into the sort of computing ability that may be required to recognize valid programs. For example, *pushdown automata* (to be defined below) are capable of recognizing the valid syntactic classes of all Algol-like languages. Generally, there are many results of the form: The languages recognized by a particular class of automata are exactly those formal languages generated by a particular class of grammars.

Automatic *theorem proving* (*q.v.*), a sub-area of artificial intelligence (*q.v.*), is also concerned with language recognition. The language to be recognized is the set of propositions derivable from some set of axioms. Automatic theorem proving has been applied to discover new mathematical theorems, to question-answering systems, and to robotics (*q.v.*).

Types of Automata Most (but not all) types of automata are special cases of the Turing machine (see Fig. 1). Turing machines may be operated either to recognize languages or to compute partial functions. Very roughly, a Turing machine is a finite-state deterministic device with read and/or write heads (which read and/or

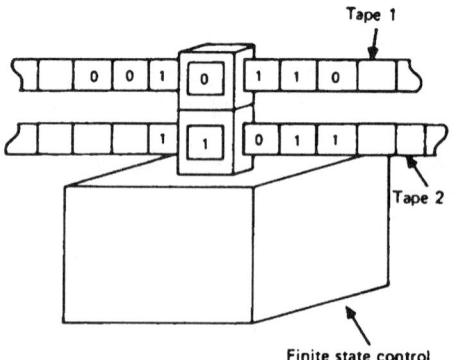

FIG. 1. A two-tape Turing machine. Each tape is scanned by a single read/write head. Tape 1 contains the string of nonblank symbols 0010110, with the underlined 0 currently being read. Tape 2 contains 11011, with the underlined 1 being currently read. If the tapes can move only in one direction, the same diagram would depict a two-tape finite automaton.

write one symbol at a time) attached to one or more tapes. *Finite state* means that the number of distinguishable internal configurations of the device is finite, and "deterministic" means that the next state of the device and its subsequent action (writing or motion) on the tapes is completely determined by its current state and the symbols it is currently reading on its tapes.

Turing machines were first introduced independently by Turing and Post in 1936 to give a precise mathematical definition of *effective procedure*. There is considerable evidence that the partial functions computed by (languages recognized by) Turing machines are exactly those computed (recognized) by informal effective procedures or algorithms. Any computation or recognition problem for which there is a known informal algorithm can be handled by a Turing machine. Turing machines with many (in general, *n*-dimensional) tapes and read/write heads can compute and recognize *no more* than can Turing machines with a single one-dimensional tape and single read/write head, although they may compute and recognize more efficiently.

Attempts to define effective procedures in terms of automata more closely resembling modern electronic stored-program digital computers have led to the *unlimited register machines* of Shepherdson and Sturgis and to the *random-access stored-program* machines of Elgot and Robinson. These machines can be shown to compute the same partial functions (recognize the same languages) computed by Turing machines.

Turing machines model the most general sort of computation processes, in part by virtue of their ability to move about freely on their tapes without fear of running out of tape. In general no a priori bound can be set on the amount of tape a Turing machine computation will require. Some Turing machine computations may require more tape than is available in the universe! This, in part, motivates our consideration of the next class of automata, finite automata. We will limit our discussion to finite automata considered as recognizers of languages, and

will leave their application as input/output devices to the article on SEQUENTIAL MACHINES.

A *finite automaton* is a deterministic finite-state device equipped with a read (only) head attached to a single input tape. A special subset of the finite set of states of a finite automaton is designated as the set of *final*, or *recognition*, states. A finite automaton α processes a string of symbols thus: α begins in a special initial, or start, state and automatically reads the symbols of x (on its tape) from left to right, changing its states in a manner depending only on its previous state and the symbol just read. If, after the last (rightmost) symbol of x is read, α goes into a final state, α recognizes x; otherwise, α does not recognize x. Let $A = \{0,1\}$. It is possible, for example, to design a finite automaton α such that α recognizes $L = \{x \varepsilon A^* \mid x$ ends in two consecutive 1s and does not contain two consecutive 0s$\}$. See Fig. 2. On the other hand, it can be shown that *no* finite automaton can recognize $L' = \{ x \varepsilon A^* \mid x$ consists of a consecutive string of *n*-squared 1s, for some positive integer $n\}$. As might be expected, however, a Turing machine can be designated to recognize L'.

In Fig. 2 the circles represent the different states of α, and the number inside each circle is a name for the state that circle represents. Hence, 0 is the start state of α and 4 is its only final state. An arrow (labeled with an alphabet symbol) from one state to another means that if α is in the first state while scanning the alphabet symbol that labels the arrow, then it goes next into the second state. For example, if α is in state 1 scanning a 0, it goes next into state 2; whereas, if it is in state 1 scanning a 1, it goes next into state 3. If α is given the input string 010111, beginning in state 0, the successive states into which it is thereafter driven are (in order) 1,3,1,3,4,4. Since 4 is a final state, α_0 (correctly) recognizes the input string 010111. If α_0 is given 10011, beginning in state 0, the successive states into which it is thereafter driven are (in order) 3,1,2,2,2. Since 2 is *not* a final state, α_0 (correctly) fails to recognize 10011.

A *nondeterministic finite automaton* is a device just like a finite automaton except that the next state is not completely determined by the current state and symbol read. Instead, a set of next *possible* states is so determined. A nondeterministic finite automaton α may be thought of as processing a string of symbols x, just like an ordinary finite automaton, except that it has to be run over again several times so that each of the different possible state-change behaviors is eventually realized. One should imagine there being a separate, deterministic control device C which runs α and completely determines α's *actual* state-change behavior each time it is run. There are but finitely many different possible state-change behaviors for α processing x, and C simply systematically runs α first one way, then another, then another, etc., until all possibilities have been exhausted.

A nondeterministic finite automaton α *recognizes* x just in case at least one of the possible ways of running α on input x results in getting α into a final state after the last symbol of x has been read (see Fig. 3).

In Fig. 3, α_1 is nondeterministic because (for example, from state 0, if it is scanning a) it can go into either state 0 or state 1 next. From state 1, if it is scanning b, it "jams," since the set of next possible

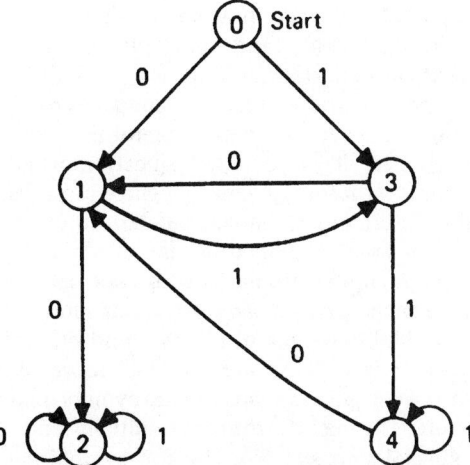

FIG. 2.   The state diagram of a finite-state automaton for recognizing $\{x \varepsilon \{0,1\}^* \mid x$ ends in two consecutive 1s and does not contain two consecutive 0s$\}$.

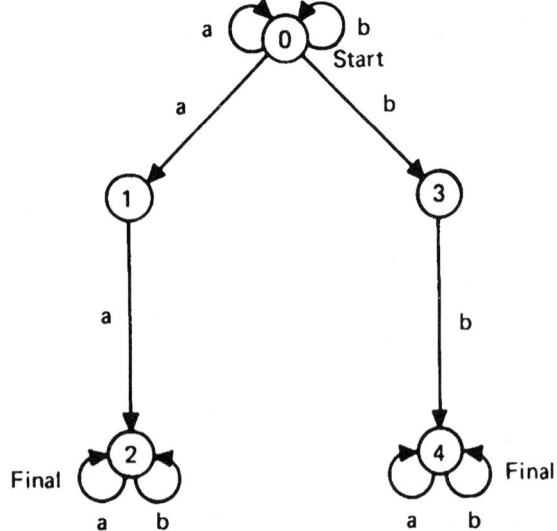

FIG. 3. The state diagram of a nondeterministic finite-state automaton α_1 for recognizing $\{x \; \varepsilon \; \{a,b\}^* | \; x$ contains two consecutive a's or two consecutive b's (or both)$\}$.

states is empty. If α_1 is given the input string *abababba*, beginning in state 0, one possible succession of states is (in order) 0,0,0,0,0,0,0,1. Here, 1 is not one of the final states, so this way of running α_1 does not lead to recognition. Another possible succession of states is (in order) 0,0,0,1, jam. Another is 1, jam. However, 0,0,0,0,0,3,4,4 is still another possible succession of states. Since 4 *is* a final state, α_1 (correctly) recognizes *abababba*. It is easy to check that, α_1 is given *babababab*, beginning in state 0, then *none* of the possible ways of running α_1 leads to a final state; hence, α_1 (correctly) does *not* recognize *babababab*.

Interestingly (and perhaps unexpectedly), it can be shown that nondeterministic finite automata recognize exactly the same class of languages as ordinary finite automata. Turing machine recognizers that operate nondeterministically can also be defined, but they cannot recognize more languages than can ordinary Turing machines. For nondeterministic Turing machine recognizers, as well as for some of the other nondeterministic devices to be discussed below, some of the different possible ways to process a given string x may take infinitely many steps. For such devices it is convenient to imagine the separate, deterministic control device C as operating in a parallel mode.

The point of nondeterminism is that it is often conceptually easier to program or design machines that operate nondeterministically. In fact, there are theoretical results to the effect that, for many types of automata, nondeterministic machines are significantly more compact than the corresponding deterministic ones. Furthermore, many practically important recognition tasks can be solved by easy-to-design nondeterministic Turing machines that run in time bounded by a polynomial in the size of their input strings. A famous open question in computer science asks if these tasks can be done at all in polynomial time by deterministic Turing machines (see NP-COMPLETE PROBLEMS).

In addition to ordinary and nondeterministic automata, a variety of automata called *probabilistic* automata have been studied. A probability of occurrence is assigned to each of the possible next states in a probabilistic automaton.

In 1943, McCulloch and Pitts introduced nets of formalized neurons and showed (in essence) that such neural nets could realize the state-change behavior of any finite automaton. These nets were composed of synchronized elements, each capable of realizing some boolean function such as *and, or,* or *not.* It has been suggested that von Neumann had these networks in mind when he established his logical design for digital computers. In 1948, von Neumann added to the computational and logical questions of automata theory by introducing new questions pertaining to construction and self-replication of automata. The iterated arrays of interconnected finite automata which he introduced have also been used to study pattern processing for patterns of symbols, including (but not restricted to) one-dimensional strings of symbols.

Automata theory, especially finite automata theory, impinges on both mathematical systems theory and modern algebra. In mathematical systems theory, one is interested in the problem of which, (if any) input sequences will drive an automaton to some desired internal state. In modern algebra one can study the relations between semigroups and automata. For example, certain decomposition theorems in group theory give information about decomposition of automata into particularly simple component automata.

A *linear-bounded automaton* is a (possibly nondeterministic), one-tape Turing machine whose read/write head is restricted to move only on the section of tape initially containing the input. Special end markers are placed on each side of an input string to prevent the tape head from leaving this restricted section of tape. A form of deterministic linear-bounded automata was first studied by Myhill in an attempt to find models of computation more realistic than the completely general Turing machines, but less restricted than the finite automata. Later it was shown that linear-bounded automata recognize all (and only) the *context-sensitive* languages, an important and natural class of languages which is more restricted than the languages recognizable by Turing machines, but more general than the *context-free* languages. It is an open question whether the linear-bounded automata can recognize more languages than the deterministic linear-bounded automata.

A *pushdown* automaton is a (possibly nondeterministic) finite automaton with a special sort of auxiliary tape called a *pushdown store.* A pushdown store is a tape quite like the stack of plates found on a spring in cafeterias. It is a "Last In-First Out" store. A special read/write head always scans the top symbol on the pushdown store. The pushdown store is initially loaded with a single special *start* symbol. The top symbol can be replaced by any finite string of symbols (stack of plates), including the empty string of symbols. Replacing the top symbol by the empty string has the effect of completely removing the top symbol and setting the read/write head to scan the next symbol down. The read (only) head on the input tape reads one symbol at a time from left to right, just as in a finite automaton, except that it is allowed (if desired) to stop scanning the input tape momentarily while only the pushdown store is operated.

Pushdown automata recognize a string x by one of two conventions. Either x is recognized by the device as it gets into one of its final states or by the pushdown store as it empties just after the rightmost symbol of x is read. The class of languages recognized by emptying the pushdown store is the same as that recognized by final states. Let $A = \{0,1\}$. For $x \in A^*$, let x^R be x written backwards. For example, 001110^R is 011100. A string x is a *palindrome* if x and x^R are the same; for instance, 0 and 1001 are palindromes. The language L = $\{x \in A^* \mid x$ is a palindrome$\}$ is recognizable by a suitable nondeterministic pushdown automaton; however, L is *not* recognizable by any finite automaton or even by any deterministic pushdown automaton. Pushdown automata recognize all (and only) the context-free (or equivalently, Algol-like) languages.

Many variations on a slight generalization of pushdown automata have been studied. A *stack automaton* is just like a pushdown automaton except that the read (only) head of the input tape is allowed to move both ways (but not off the section of tape containing the input) and the read/write head on the pushdown store is allowed to scan the entire pushdown list in a *read only* mode. The class of languages recognized by stack automata is intermediate between context-sensitive and Turing-machine recognizable.

Many other types of automata that have been and could be studied employ some other sort of limited data structure for their auxiliary storage or receive inputs in some form other than a string of symbols. For example, *tree* automata process inputs in the form of trees, usually trees associated with parsing expressions in context-free languages.

It should be remarked at the conclusion of this survey that automata theory is a growing, open-ended mathematical discipline. It readily admits of extensions of existing concepts and the introduction of totally new ideas. The motivations to make such extensions are esthetic on the one hand, and the need or desire to model some existing or proposed computational phenomenon on the other.

References

1966. Von Neumann, J. *Theory of Self-Reproducing Automata* (edited and completed by A. W. Burks). Urbana: University of Illinois Press.
1967. Minsky, M. *Computation: Finite and Infinite Machines.* Englewood Cliffs, NJ: Prentice-Hall.
1969. Hopcroft, J. E. and Ullman, J. D. *Formal Languages and Their Relation to Automata.* Reading, MA: Addison-Wesley.
1979. Hopcroft, J. E. and Ullman, J. D. *Introduction to Automata Theory, Languages, and the Theory of Computation.* Reading, MA: Addison-Wesley.
1981. Lewis H. and Papadimitriou, C. *Elements of the Theory of Computation.* Englewood Cliffs, NJ: Prentice-Hall.
1983. Davis, M. and Weyuker, E. *Computability, Complexity, and Languages: Fundamentals of Theoretical Computer Science.* New York: Academic Press.
1988. Minksy, M. and Papert, S. *Perceptrons* (expanded edition). Cambridge, MA: M.I.T. Press.

JOHN CASE

AUTOMATION

For articles on related subjects *see* COMPUTER-AIDED DESIGN/COMPUTER-AIDED MANUFACTURING; COMPUTER-AIDED ENGINEERING; COMPUTER GRAPHICS; CONTROL APPLICATIONS; ELECTRONIC OFFICE; FINITE-ELEMENT METHOD; LIBRARY AUTOMATION; ROBOTICS; and WORKSTATION.

Automation involves use of a technique to make a system or process more self-acting and self-regulating and hence less dependent on human intervention. Most recently, the word has come to be associated with the use of computers to attain these functions. Thus, we tend to use the word "computerization" as a synonym for automation and to think in terms of the application of computers not only for the handling of information associated with a process, but also for the actual control and actuation of mechanisms that facilitate or completely accomplish that process with minimal human guidance.

It is this minimization of the human element that sometimes gives automation a negative overtone. People fear the image of factories, offices, wars—indeed, even whole societies—"run by computers." Those involved with development of advanced automation techniques, however, usually assert that computers will always remain merely machines or tools for use by human beings, who always control their ultimate use. In this article, we discuss the application of computers to the automation of the most directly productive of human activities—the planning, design, engineering, production, and testing of manufactured products. It is this usage of the term *automation* that is most common.

CAD/CAE/CAM Computer-Aided Design/Engineering/ Manufacturing (CAD/CAE/CAM) activities encompass those that involve *the direct application of specialized computer hardware or software to product and manufacturing engineering and manufacturing operations.* Excluded from this definition is the application of general-purpose computers to research, analytic, and other technical problem-solving situations.

Further, CAD/CAE/CAM is distinguished from administrative data processing applications relating to manufacturing or engineering by emphasizing the engineering or technical computing orientation of the work over the file-handling and record-processing orientation of the more conventional EDP universe. Normally excluded, for example, are manufacturing data processing applications such as production control, inventory control, labor distribution, and cost accounting.

To clarify this definition, listed below are a number of engineering functions and related specific examples of CAD/CAE/CAM systems.

Function	Examples
Design layout	Computer-aided drafting, printed circuit board layout.
Design analysis	Computer optimization, finite element analysis, piping interference checking.
Manufacturing engineering	Group technology, tool design, process planning.
Facilities engineering	Plant architecture and layout, equipment optimization.
Fabrication automation	Numerically controlled tools, process control systems.
Assembly automation	Robotics, computer-controlled transfer lines.
Materials handling	Stacker cranes, driverless tractor systems, automated storage and retrieval systems.
Industrial engineering	Shop floor data collection, labor standards calculations.
Quality assurance	Coordinate measuring machines, automated circuit test equipment.

Engineering computing and manufacturing computing each may be subdivided as follows:

1. Engineering computing
   a. Design and analysis functions
   b. Engineer productivity enhancement functions (word processing, E-mail, spreadsheets, database management, etc.)
   c. Computer-based test cell or laboratory data-gathering and control functions
   d. Engineering administration and information management functions
2. Manufacturing computing
   a. Manufacturing operations functions (manufacturing engineering fabrication, assembly, inspection, etc.)
   b. Manufacturing control functions (scheduling, resource requirements planning, inventory control, etc.)

These broader classes of functions more accurately describe the total set of activities amenable to automation within the engineering/manufacturing environment. Because of the potential organizational conflicts arising from the merging of engineering, manufacturing, and data processing responsibilities, however, they are frequently considered *too* broad and pervasive in their impact, hence the more narrowly defined term "CAD/CAE/CAM" is normally used.

Automation Concepts Engineering and manufacturing have been fertile fields for improvement through the application of computer technology. Design engineers, faced with problems requiring long iterative solutions and extensive data, have relied on computers to speed up solutions and analyze problems that could not have been solved before. Manufacturing engineers have used numerically controlled equipment to control machine tools, such as lathes and complex milling machines, in production of parts that heretofore required the advanced skills of machinists and toolmakers and were subject to annoying and expensive variations. Process manufacturing technology has benefited by minimizing the need for human surveillance and reaction in order to keep manufacturing processes within design tolerances and to correct for the inherent perturbations that occur. The use of data collection and accelerated data processing techniques in manufacturing have enabled tighter management control of the manufacturing enterprise and more rapid response to changes that inadvertently occur or may be required. Even plant design and facility layout have been optimized through computerized simulations and a variety of design aids. Virtually every segment of the production process, from product design and manufacturing, through sales, warehousing and distribution, has been touched by computer technology and rendered more efficient by its implementation.

Within each of the broad categories of design engineering, manufacturing engineering, and management systems, there is a trend toward a growing interrelationship of systems. Programs and systems within these categories often have common elements within their databases; may be related by similar input data and output data; or the output of one system may serve as a portion of the input to another. The diminishing cost of computer power, the proliferation of software, and the widespread introduction of affordable mini- and microcomputers has increased the number of sites within an organization for beneficial application of computers and data processing techniques. Thus, the pressure for an overall "architecture" of the computer systems within an organization has been increasing. The needs for commonality of language, compatibility of databases, and accessibility of information from "foreign" databases all become imperative.

Not only is an overall architecture required for the efficient automation of design engineering, manufacturing operations, and business management segments, but integration transcends the traditional boundaries within an industrial organization. For example, recent advances in the automation of the design phase of activity have enabled entire design layouts to be accomplished at a computer terminal, eliminating traditional distinctions between conceptual designers, detail designers, and draftsmen. The boundaries are becoming indistinct between management information systems (MIS) and the engineering/manufacturing operations units that are employing computers for their functions, often creating organizational conflicts.

Interactive graphic displays allow the designer to produce a "drawing" on a cathode ray tube (CRT) and store the design information in memory. Devices are available that can produce a quick hard copy of the displayed graphics and/or electromechanical pen and ink plotters can be used to produce accurate high-quality, full-scale layout. The development of a profusion of database management software permits the storage and convenient access to information about standard components and subassemblies, in addition to the analytical and computation capability generally required in an engineering design. This approach, wherein an engineer/designer interacts with a computer using graphical input devices, various output systems, database information, and analytic computations, is the basis for *computer-aided design* (CAD).

In manufacturing, similar automation of data and control processes has occurred. Beyond the numerical control of individual machine tools and direct computer control of processes, there has been an explosion of available software that manipulates data on tool availability, materials requirements, flow of parts being manufactured, work-in-process inventory, finished goods inventory, etc. Different parts with similar geometric features and manufacturing characteristics have been classified and can be scheduled in manufacturing by software based on this categorization (group technology). The active control of processes and the timely collection and dissemination of production data have narrowed the response time required for the entire manufacturing operation to make decisions and cure production problems. The active involvement of the computer in the manufacturing processes and the control of production is the basis for *computer-aided manufacturing* (CAM).

Along with the consolidation of computer programs and systems within each of the design engineering, manufacturing, and management segments of an enterprise, integration is now occurring among these segments. Just as common database information is required internal to the various stages of manufacturing operation, there is a strong commonality in the data required by design, manufacturing, and management. For example, a bill of materials (or parts list), which is created in the design engineering phase of the production sequence, must be accessible to the manufacturing and management segments as well. The geometric, dimensional and configurational data for a part that is created during the design stage is the essential information required by the programmer preparing the numerical control tapes that control the machine tools of the manufacturing operation.

The pressure to communicate and integrate has always been present, but, historically, communication relied upon the active transfer of information by drawings, memoranda, or word of mouth. Now, integration is fostered by the efficient data storage and retrieval mechanisms made available by computer technology. The avenue that has now been opened is the passive communication of any bit of information required by a particular segment as soon as it becomes available. Accessibility to a bill of materials can be as easy for management as for design engineering. Corrections to bills of materials suggested by manufacturing (or purchasing) can be immediately acted upon by design engineering, and everyone in the organization has access to the updated information once the correction has been entered. The sharp line of demarcation between the design and manufacturing functions becomes diffuse and will gradually disappear. Computer-aided design and engineering can no longer be separated from computer-aided manufacturing; they are one and the same. Hence, the acronyms, CAD/CAM and CAD/CAE/CAM.

Historical Background Both CAD and CAM were born at about the same time—the early 1950s. The earliest electronic digital computers, developed in the mid- to late 1940s, were primarily used for scientific and mathematical applications—calculations of trajectories, weather forecasting, and the like. By the early 1950s, commercial versions of the early laboratory models—Univac Is, IBM 701s and 702s, etc.—were emerging and finding their way into a few highly sophisticated business and engineering organizations such as G.E., G.M., Boeing, and other aerospace and automotive firms. By the late 1950s to the early 1960s, interactive graphical display devices were appearing and Ivan Sutherland was doing his pioneering work at M.I.T.'s Lincoln Laboratory on the Sketchpad system—the forerunner of modern CAD graphics systems. Unsuccessful attempts were made to commercialize this system (by CDC) and others like it (by IBM); throughout the 1960s and into the mid-1970s, development work was performed primarily by the large engineering computing users—General Motors (with their famous DAC-1 system, which provided a foundation for much future work), Lockheed, McDonnell Aircraft, Douglas, Pratt & Whitney, Caterpillar, etc.

The basic specialized hardware devices associated with CAD—interactive graphics terminals, digitizers, light pens, and plotters—became quite well developed by the mid-1960s and have not really changed significantly since (though their cost performance in function is much better). The major changes that *have* taken place during the last 20–25 years have occurred in the areas of software and microcomputer development. Software for managing large amounts of complex and interrelated data (database management systems), for allowing communication of data and programs among computers and remote terminals (distributed processing systems), for representing the physical geometry of a part in terms that can be manipulated by a computer (geometric modeling systems), and for analyzing the effects of various external forces on complex parts (finite element analysis packages and the like) all matured significantly and were packaged in ways that made them easy and much more economical to use. Minicomputer (*q.v.*) technology also made marked advances during this period, permitting economical, dedicated systems with considerable power to be placed at the disposal of designers and draftsmen, and, with the more recent advent of the microcomputer, permitting specialized hardware devices to have intelligence built into them to perform many functions locally that previously required the attention of a large, centralized computer.

Thus, beginning in the mid-1970s, a type of product became popular that incorporated many of the specialized hardware devices, software elements, and minicomputer capabilities referred to. These are known by various names, but are most often called "turnkey CAD systems." About 2,500–3,000 of these systems were installed by 1980. Each such system is normally comprised of 4–5 workstations, on the average, each with a graphical visual display and often a supplementary alphanumeric display, a graphical digitizing or input device, and a keyboard. Also, each system typically includes a large, high-quality plotter; smaller, more rapid but lower-quality hard copy devices; a more precise digitizer; and various forms of data storage; as well as, of course, the controlling microcomputer and its software. Other offerings of packaged software or services have helped to make CAD more feasible for the user who prefers to use a mainframe computer with interactive graphics terminals.

CAM began with the advent of numerically-controlled (NC) machine tools, pioneered at M.I.T. under Air Force sponsorship in the early 1950s. These early devices merely proved that it was possible to control the movements of metal-cutting milling machines by an electronic control mechanism actuated by punched tape. The real challenge was to create the punched tape quickly and accurately, based on the geometry and physical characteristics of the part. The Air Force also helped solve that problem by sponsoring the initial development of the APT language at M.I.T. and Illinois Institute of Technology Research Institute in the late 1950s and early 1960s. This programming language allows a "part programmer" (a new occupation in the manufacturing engineering field) to describe the necessary cutting motions in an English-like notation, which is then translated into a standardized "cutter location file." That file, in turn, is processed by a special "post-processor" that produces explicit punched tape instructions for a particular machine.

This development made widespread use of NC tools possible, and they began to proliferate throughout industry in the 1960s and 1970s—most rapidly in Europe and Japan but also in the U.S. By the early 1970s (with the introduction of mini- and microcomputer technology), new control techniques were developed. Direct numerical control (DNC) and computerized numerical control (CNC) systems are being more widely accepted. These systems integrate computers directly into the machine controller to permit operator interaction or to allow more of the machine functions to be controlled in real time. Also, parts programming in the "blind" batch-processing APT mode is gradually being replaced by direct creation of the cutter file by creating a geometric model of the part using a graphical CAD system (integration of CAD and CAM to yield CAD/CAM).

In the 1980s, robot technology matured to the point where there is now a worldwide market of about $2 billion per year, projected to grow at about 8% per annum through the 1990s to about $4 billion by 2000. Robots now perform all sorts of "pick and place" operations—welding, dipping, spray painting, and assembly. General purpose automated machining and assembly systems are also evolving for efficient production of small batches of products using techniques akin to mass production assembly lines, except that they are more readily reprogrammed. Many forms of automated materials handling devices and systems are finding acceptance—from computerized stacker cranes and conveyor systems to driverless tractors. Factory floor management systems saw limited use in aerospace companies in the 1950s and 1960s, but gained respectability and widespread usage in the 1970s and 1980s with development of materials requirements planning systems (MRP). Even computer-controlled testing devices, such as coordinate measuring machines and electronic test equipment, have entered the manufacturing automation field.

Now, with the proliferation of such hardware and software components and the realization that both engineering and manufacturing are highly information-inten-

sive activities, considerable interest is being shown in the integration of all these elements. The term *computer-integrated manufacturing* (CIM-*q.v.*) is now in vogue, and many present and projected developments are taking place in that context. We project that the decade of the 1990s will see a "fourth generation" of CAD/CAM systems with common databases, much more intelligent interpretation of data as real objects rather than merely lines and surfaces, and transparent interfaces among these previously disparate subsystems.

Special Impact of Automation There is legitimate concern that automation represents a threat, not only to employment through the replacement of human workers by machines, but also to human control over increasingly more comprehensive computerized control systems. The employment threat is easily addressed by pointing out the paradox that, because of our steadily and dangerously decreasing labor productivity growth rate, more manual labor, not less, is being required to produce manufactured goods in our automated society. Also, the phenomenal growth of the computer industry during the 1980s, and its associated employment opportunities, suggests that increased automation will also provide new job opportunities for people to design, program, produce, sell, support, maintain, apply, and operate these devices and systems. Finally, the growth of automation is being spurred by critical shortages of certain classes of labor—draftsmen, skilled machinists, manufacturing engineers, etc.—so for some considerable time, automation can hardly be considered a threat to these occupations.

Over the longer term, however, there is no question but that the ultimate forms of automation—"workerless factories"—such as those that a few companies have already achieved and many others are still striving for, will have a profound effect on our society. Kurt Vonnegut's early prophetic book, *Player Piano*, depicting a futuristic society and the moral degradation that occurs when humans are almost totally replaced by machinery and electronics, suggests the kinds of problems that may occur—boredom, lethargy, class conflict, etc. While this extreme is unlikely, its potentiality suggests that the leaders of industrializing societies would do well to monitor trends and attempt to find alternative ways of maintaining human dignity in the face of inexorable automation.

References

1952. Vonnegut, K., Jr. *Player Piano*. New York: Avon.
1973. Harrington, J., Jr. *Computer-Integrated Manufacturing*. New York: Industrial Press.

ROY M. SALZMAN

AUTOMATON. *See* AUTOMATA THEORY.

AUXILIARY MEMORY. *See* MEMORY: AUXILIARY.

AVL TREE. *See* TREE.

B-TREE. *See* TREE.

BABBAGE, CHARLES

For articles on related subjects *see* ANALYTICAL ENGINE; DIFFERENCE ENGINE; DIGITAL COMPUTERS: HISTORY; and LOVELACE, COUNTESS OF.

Charles Babbage was born in London on 26 December 1791. He was educated privately and went up to Cambridge in 1810. At that time, Cambridge education was strongly oriented toward mathematics and there was intense competition for high honors in the Mathematical Tripos. Babbage, however, soon discovered that Newton's ideas still dominated the Cambridge curriculum, whereas he had been exposed to, and was much drawn toward, the type of mathematics then receiving attention on the Continent. He did not, therefore, compete for honors. Nevertheless, he acquired a high mathematical reputation that increased with the years, so much so that in 1828 he was appointed Lucasian Professor, a position that Newton himself had held many years before. The stipend in Babbage's time was only £80 to £90 per annum. He did not reside in Cambridge nor lecture there, though he performed some of the other duties of the Professorship, such as examining for the Smith's Prize.

It was while still a student that Babbage began to work on the difference engine, a device intended to mechanize the production of the final values in a mathematical table from the widely spaced pivotal values that are first computed. It would also produce a stereotype mold, ready for the printer, thus eliminating one source of error. Babbage's own attempt at implementing the difference engine failed, in spite of financial support from the British government. The soundness of his ideas was, however, demonstrated by the fact that an independent implementation by Georg and Edvard Scheutz, who had read of Babbage's ideas, was successful.

In a long life, Babbage turned his attention to many subjects, including mathematics, railroads, lighthouses, cryptography, economics, the ophthalmoscope, politics, and public controversies of various kinds. But the dominating interest of his life was calculating machinery, and his claim to fame is through his work on the analytical engine, which was to have been an automatically sequenced, general-purpose calculating machine. Here he was profoundly original. He published some of his ideas and others have come down to us in his manuscript notebooks. The real breakthrough came in 1834 and the years immediately following, but Babbage continued to work on the subject for the remainder of his life.

Babbage's thoughts on the analytical engine were entirely in mechanical terms, with no suggestion, even in later years, that electricity might be called in aid. The

FIG. 1. Charles Babbage. *Courtesy of New York Public Library.*

analytical engine was to be decimal, although Babbage considered other scales of notation. Numbers were to be stored on wheels, with ten distinguishable positions, and transferred by a system of racks to a central *mill*, or processor, where all arithmetic would be performed. He had in mind a storage capacity for a thousand numbers of 50 decimal digits. He studied exhaustively a wide variety of schemes for performing the four operations of arithmetic, and he invented the idea of anticipatory carry, which is much faster than carrying successively from one stage to another. He also knew about hoarding carry, by which a whole series of additions could be performed with one carrying operation at the end.

The sequencing of the analytical engine was to have been fully automatic, but not, of course, on what we would now call the stored-program principle (*q.v.*). Punched cards of the type used in a Jacquard loom were to be adopted both for sequencing and for the input of numbers. Babbage proposed to have two sets of sequencing cards, one for controlling the mill and one for controlling the store; these would be separately stepped and would not necessarily move together.

Babbage never arrived at the idea of instructions containing both an operation part and an address part, nor at the formal concept of a program that we have today. Lady Lovelace, the daughter of Lord Byron, in notes to a translation that she made of a paper describing some of Babbage's ideas, published by Ménabréa in French in 1842, gives what at first sight appears to be a program along modern lines for computing Bernoulli numbers. This gives the arithmetic operations in detail, but does not contain anything corresponding to the conditional jump instructions in a modern program; after the main loop there is simply the sentence: "Here follows a repetition of operations 13 to 23."

Babbage's notebooks show him struggling with various ideas for handling the repetition of parts of a calculation, and although he sketched out many schemes that would have worked satisfactorily, one feels that he never arrived at one that entirely pleased him. For subsequencing within an operation, he proposed to use drums with fixed studs, on the barrel-organ principle. It is odd that in his published writings there is no hint of the range and originality of his thoughts on the important matter of sequencing. Lady Lovelace has left us in her debt for the translation and notes referred to above, but there has been a tendency to exaggerate both her mathematical ability and her importance in the Babbage saga.

Although he had workmen in his employ until the end of his life, Babbage failed to implement the analytical engine. We must conclude, as did some of his contemporaries, that he was temperamentally incapable of carrying a project through. Unfortunately, this time, there was no Sheutz to take up his ideas, and it may well be that the ultimate development of automatic calculating machinery was delayed by the aura of failure that surrounded Babbage's work. His detailed design studies lay buried in his unpublished notebooks and were forgotten. Of his genius, however, no one who has studied his work will have any doubt.

Babbage died in London on 18 October 1871. His youngest son, Henry, who had spent most of his life in various military and civil appointments in India, did what he could to carry on his father's work, and published a collection of papers relating to it. The eldest son, Herschel, migrated in 1851 to South Australia, where he became a prominent member of the colony.

References

1889. Babbage, H. P. (Ed.). *Babbage's Calculating Engines*. London. This book has now been reprinted as vol. 2 of the Babbage Institute reprint series, I. Tomash (Ed.), Cambridge, MA: MIT Press, 1984.

1961. Morrison, P., and Morrison, E. (Eds.). *Charles Babbage and his Calculating Engines*. New York: Dover.

1968. Babbage, C. *Passages from the Life of a Philosopher*. London, 1864; facsimile edition, London: Dawson's.

1971. Wilkes, M. V. "Babbage as a Computer Pioneer," Report of the Babbage Memorial Meeting, British Computer Society. Reprinted in *Historica Mathematica* **4**:415 (1977).

1975. Wilkes, M. V. "How Babbage's Dream Came True," *Nature* **257**:641.

1982. Hyman, A. *Charles Babbage*. Princeton, NJ: Princeton University Press.

1989. Campbell-Kelly, M., (Ed.). *The Works of Charles Babbage*. 11 volumes. London: Pickering and Chatto.

1990. Wilkes, M.V. "Herschel, Peacock, Babbage, and the Development of the Cambridge Curriculum, Notes and Records of the Royal Society, **44**, 205.

MAURICE V. WILKES

BACKTRACKING. *See* ALGORITHMS, DESIGN AND CLASSIFICATION OF.

BACKUS-NAUR FORM (BNF)

For articles on related subjects *see* GRAMMARS; METACHARACTER; METALANGUAGE; PROCEDURE-ORIENTED LANGUAGES; PROGRAMMING LINGUISTICS; SYNTAX, SEMANTICS, AND PRAGMATICS; and VIENNA DEFINITION LANGUAGE.

Backus-Naur Form, named after John W. Backus of the United States and Peter Naur of Denmark, and usually written BNF, is the best-known example of a *metalanguage* (*q.v.*), i.e. one that syntactically describes a programming language. Using BNF it is possible to specify which sequences of symbols constitute a syntactically valid program in a given language. (The question of *semantics*—i.e. what such valid strings of symbols mean—must be specified separately.) A discussion of the basic concepts of BNF follows.

A *metalinguistic variable* (or *metavariable*), also called a *syntactic unit*, is one whose values are strings of symbols chosen from among the symbols permitted in the given language. In BNF, metalinguistic variables are enclosed in brackets, ⟨ ⟩, for clarity and to distinguish them from symbols in the language itself, which are called terminal symbols or just *terminals*. The symbol ::= is used to indicate metalinguistic equivalence; a vertical bar (|) is used to indicate that a choice is to be made among the items so indicated; and concatenation (linking together in a series) is indicated simply by juxtaposing the elements to be concatenated.

For an example, here is how the definition of an Algol integer is built up: First, we have a definition of what a digit is, according to the usual meaning:

⟨digit⟩ :: = 0 | 1 | 2 | 3 | 4 | 5 | 6 | 7 | 8 | 9.

Next we have a statement that an unsigned integer consists either of a single digit or an unsigned integer followed by another digit:

⟨unsigned integer ⟩:: = ⟨digit⟩ |
⟨unsigned integer⟩⟨digit⟩

This definition may be applied *recursively* to build up unsigned integers of any length whatever. Since there must be a limit on the number of digits in any actual computer implementation, this would have to be stated separately in conjunction with each particular implementation or, as in some extensions to BNF, by an addition to the definition of *unsigned integer* (e.g. placing [10] above :: = could indicate a limit of 10 digits). Finally, the definition of an integer is completed by noting that it may be preceded by a plus sign, a minus sign, or neither:

⟨integer⟩ :: = ⟨unsigned integer⟩ |
+ ⟨unsigned integer⟩ |− ⟨unsigned integer⟩.

For a second example, suppose that the metalinguistic variables ⟨unsigned number⟩, ⟨variable⟩, ⟨function designator⟩, and ⟨boolean expression⟩ have all been defined earlier, with usual meanings, and that the vertical arrow stands for exponentiation. Here, then, is the complete sequence of definitions that culminates with the definition of an Algol ⟨arithmetic expression⟩:

⟨adding operator⟩ :: = + | −
⟨multiplying operator⟩ :: = × | / | ÷
⟨primary⟩ :: = ⟨unsigned number⟩ | ⟨variable⟩ |
⟨function designator⟩ | (⟨arithmetic expression⟩)
⟨factor⟩ :: = ⟨primary⟩ | ⟨factor⟩ ↑ ⟨primary⟩
⟨term⟩ :: = ⟨factor⟩ | ⟨term⟩⟨multiplying operator⟩⟨factor⟩
⟨simple arithmetic expression⟩ :: = ⟨term⟩ | ⟨adding
operator⟩⟨term⟩ | ⟨simple arithmetic
expression⟩⟨adding operator⟩⟨term⟩
⟨if clause⟩ :: = **if** ⟨boolean expression⟩ **then** ⟨arithmetic
expression⟩ :: = ⟨simple arithmetic expression⟩ |
⟨if clause⟩⟨simple arithmetic expression⟩ |
else ⟨arithmetic expression⟩

It is no error that the third definition contains ⟨arithmetic expression⟩, enclosed in parentheses, even though

it is ⟨arithmetic expression⟩ that we are trying to define. This is another example of a recursive definition, and simply says in this case that one choice for a ⟨primary⟩ is just any ⟨arithmetic expression⟩ enclosed in parentheses.

The words **if, then,** and **else,** since they are not enclosed in the metalinguistic brackets, stand for themselves; they are, like the character set, basic elements of the Algol language that are not further defined.

An extended version of BNF (EBNF) is used in the *Pascal User Manual and Report* (Jensen and Wirth 1985) and in the definition of Modula-2 (Wirth 1985). An EBNF specification of the syntax of a programming language consists of a collection of rules (*productions*), collectively called a *grammar*, that describe the formation of sentences in the language. Each production consists of a nonterminal symbol and an EBNF expression separated by an equal sign and terminated by a period. The nonterminal symbol is a *meta-identifier* (a syntactic constant denoted by an English word), and the EBNF expression is its definition. An EBNF expression is composed of zero or more terminal symbols, nonterminals, and metasymbols, summarized as follows:

Metasymbol	Meaning
=	is defined to be
|	alternatively
.	end of production
[X]	0 or 1 instance of X
{X}	0 or more instances of X
(X | Y)	a grouping: either X or Y
"XYX"	the terminal symbol XYZ
Metaldentifier	the nonterminal symbol *Metaldentifier*

The superficial difference between BNF and EBNF is that, in the former, nonterminals need to be delimited (by angle brackets) and terminals are allowed to stand for themselves, whereas, in EBNF, terminals must be delimited (by quotation marks) and nonterminals are allowed to stand for themselves. The more profound difference is that the bracket and brace notation of EBNF allows a simpler presentation of definitions that must be expressed recursively in BNF. Consider, for example, these contrasting definitions of a Pascal ⟨identifier⟩:

BNF: ⟨identifier⟩:: = ⟨letter⟩ | ⟨identifier⟩⟨letter⟩ |
⟨identifier⟩⟨digit ⟩
meaning: An identifier is either a single letter or else
something that is already a valid identifier followed
by either a letter or a digit.
EBNF: *Identifier = Letter { Letter | Digit }.*

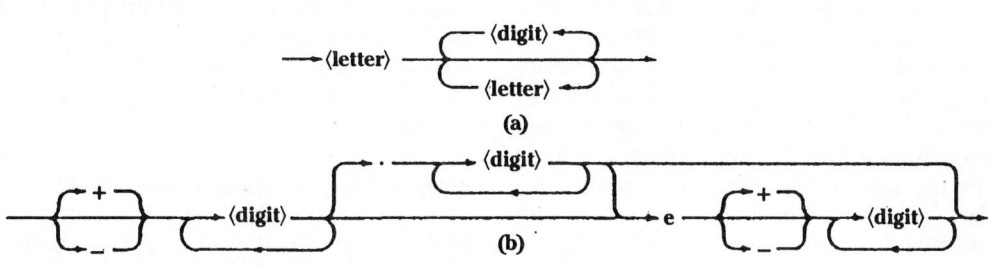

FIG. 1. (a) ⟨identifier⟩ (b) ⟨signed real ⟩.

meaning: An identifier is a single letter followed by any number of letters or digits.

The information conveyed through an EBNF production can be displayed pictorially through use of *syntax diagrams* (*railroad diagrams*), a technique popularized by the Pascal report of Jensen and Wirth (1985). The syntax diagram for a Pascal identifier is shown in Fig. 1a.

The term "railroad diagram" stems from comparison of the directed line segments to tracks along which a train can proceed on any physically realizable path. Since the train cannot avoid passing through ⟨letter⟩, an identifier consists of at least a single letter. Thereafter, the train may pass straight through to the right, indicating that a single letter is a sufficiently complete definition of an ⟨identifier⟩, or else it may traverse either the top or bottom circuits any number of times in arbitrary order (before finally using the main track to end the definition).

A more complex syntax diagram, one that defines a ⟨signed real⟩ number in Pascal, is shown in Fig. 1b.

The diagram can be used to show that such character strings as 5.7, −19.0, +3.9, −7.36e-3, and 123e4 are valid signed real numbers but that −7., .2, and 123.e4 are not.

BNF (or EBNF or syntax diagrams) can be used to describe any context-free language (*see* GRAMMARS), and hence, since most programming languages are context-free, most programming languages. There are competitive notations, however, such as the Vienna Definition Language (*q.v.*), used to describe PL/I, and the notation typically used to describe Cobol which is closer to EBNF than to BNF.

References

1985. Jensen, K., Wirth, N., Mickel, A. B., and Miner, J. F. *Pascal User Manual and Report, 3rd ed.: ISO Pascal Standard.* New York: Springer-Verlag.

1985. Wirth, N. *Programming in Modula-2, Third Corrected Edition.* New York: Springer-Verlag.

DANIEL D. MCCRACKEN and EDWIN D. REILLY

BANDWIDTH

For articles on related subjects *see* COMMUNICATIONS AND COMPUTERS; and DATA COMMUNICATIONS.

The *bandwidth* of an analog communication network is a measure of the range of frequencies it can transmit at or near maximum power levels. As an example, consider a normal telephone system, which is an analog communication network normally designed to carry voice traffic in the frequency range 300–3,400 Hz. Thus, the equipment in the telephone exchange collects incoming data from the sound spectrum and arranges to attenuate sharply the signals outside that part of the spectrum. But even within that range, there is further attenuation as the signals propagate through the telephone network, since the power of signals passing through the telephone transmission system is reduced. A typical measurement on the U. S. telephone network

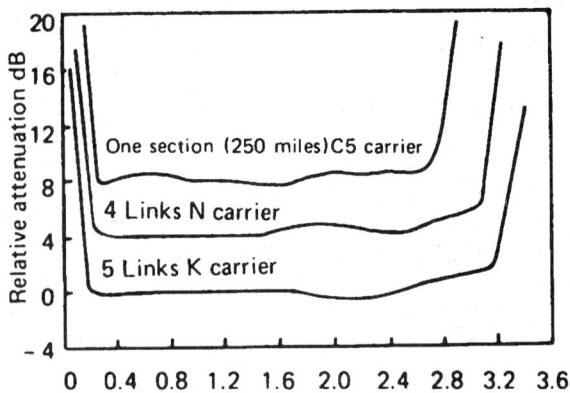

FIG. 1. Attenuation for frequency division multiplexing (FDM) systems. (reproduced from *Communication-Networks for Computers* by D. W. Davies and D. L. A. Barber. New York: Wiley, 1973, Fig. 2.16.)

of attenuation is shown in Fig. 1, which indicates that somewhere below 300 Hz and above 3–4 KHz, the attenuation rises very rapidly. The range of frequencies in which the power level stays at above one-half its peak value (the so-called 3 *db* points) is the *nominal bandwidth* of the circuit. This is typically 3 KHz in a switched telephone line.

PETER T. KIRSTEIN

BANKING APPLICATIONS

For articles on related subjects *see* ADMINISTRATIVE APPLICATIONS; DATA COMMUNICATIONS; DATABASE MANAGEMENT SYSTEMS; DISTRIBUTED SYSTEMS; ELECTRONIC FUNDS TRANSFER SYSTEMS; and TRANSACTION-BASED SYSTEMS.

Overview Since World War II, radical changes have occurred in the global economic and business environments within which banking applications of information technology must operate. The systems approach and the systems that have responded to these changes are unique to the banking industry, and the chronology of their evolution may be divided into four distinct periods.

Mid-1950s to Early 1960s This was an era of experimentation. Computer technology and the users' grasp of how to exploit it were extremely immature. Few, if any, well-developed and stable generic banking applications existed. In two notable instances, technology was seriously misunderstood and misapplied: the industry giants, Bank of America and Citibank, working, respectively, with General Electric and ITT, attempted but later abandoned the development of a special-purpose "banking computer" and a pre-magnetic-ink check-handling machine.

Early 1960s to 1970 The basic dependency of banking upon information technology became well established. With the introduction of magnetic-ink-encoded checks and the equipment to handle them, essentially all but the smallest banks became totally dependent upon automated "item" (check) processing. There was now no turning back, as volumes quickly grew to levels above those at which manual processing was feasible.

Also during this time, the traditional back-office batch-processing applications—not unique to banks—of payroll, general ledger, and other related applications became established as productivity enhancers.

From 1970 to 1980 This tumultuous decade was marked by rapid and radical change. Initially using batch-processing techniques, but later fully on line, the period was characterized by a move of banking applications out of the back office and toward the customer. Another thread of evolution was the globalization, through telecommunications, of the larger institutions' information-technology bases. Early probes by banking into the "service bureau" business, based upon the sale at incremental prices of idle raw processing capacity, ultimately went nowhere and cost a few of the more aggressive institutions dearly.

The first glimmer of recognition of banking as an "information business"—a giant step beyond a mere dependency upon the technology—began to dawn. The early "delivery-vehicle" systems began to emerge. In consumer banking these took the form of networked on-line *automated teller machines* (ATMs); in corporate banking, as on-line cash-management terminals in the corporate treasurer's office.

In the early to mid-1970s, the powerful expansion of U.S.-based banks' presence in global markets paved the way for globalization of the entire banking-application infrastructure. Telecommunications networks began to appear, overlaid upon the business "networks" represented by globally deployed offices and staff. The major institutions developed proprietary networks, while commonly accessible and industry-specific networks—public Telex and SWIFT on the international scene, others within the U.S.—met this need for the rest.

The first "common" branch-support systems, intended to serve all banking offices with essentially a single centrally developed and supported common suite of applications software, began to appear. This development was closely linked with the parallel emergence of global networks.

It was during this decade that the use of minicomputers in banking reached its peak. The first breaks from the traditions of highly centralized, mainframe-dependent computing appeared early in the period. This early form of "distributed processing" rapidly became widespread and served as the foundation for the even more radical moves that were to follow.

By 1980, the traditional primary banking business of interest-differential commercial lending had supplied the billions in earnings that were needed to fund the development of the next generation of banking businesses and were declining. The consumer market segments had begun their move toward primacy.

From 1980 to 1990 The early microcomputers of the late 1970s, with their Basic programming language, CP/M operating system, and VisiCalc spreadsheet (*q.v.*) capabilities, had drawn the attention of non-systems managers. They offered the possibility of escaping from the three-year backlogs and hyper-inflated costs of systems work of that era. In a few advanced institutions, they had even begun to make inroads into actual banking applications. It was the IBM PC announcement of 1981, however, that signalled the start of the current era of banking applications.

As the 1990s began, banks were bludgeoned by real estate, third world, and thrift institution credit problems. Despite the resistance of traditionalists, the commercial and industrial lending businesses and their related systems infrastructures continued to yield ground to the consumer-based businesses that have begun to dominate this decade.

Information is now the basic product of the banking industry (money, after all, is today only a special case of information), and networks are its delivery/distribution systems.[1] The older, more traditional banking applications will survive for decades to come, but the future of the industry lies in the information-based consumer service businesses.

TRADITIONAL COMPUTERIZED BANKING APPLICATIONS

Bank Liability Applications

Checking Accounts

Bank customers make deposits in cash or checks in their accounts in one or several currencies. In exchange for the use of the funds, the bank provides check collection and checking account services and renders periodic statements. All these processes heavily involve computers.

---

[1]The international transfer of value was for centuries accomplished by the physical movement of cash, specie, and bullion. With the advent of international telegraphy, it was increasingly done by "book entry"—entries over a network of reciprocal accounts maintained by major international banks on each others' books. An appropriately authenticated telegraphic message served as the "check" that drew on such an account. By 1970, the volume of such "wire transfers" and the related commercial bills, letters of credit, and other commercial instruments represented a major source of paper-processing workload for the large banks offering these capabilities.

During the 1970s, computers began to originate and receive authenticated funds-transfer messages directly. Major special-purpose telecommunications networks emerged. They were both proprietary networks, owned by particular banks, and common-user networks, accessible to any bank. SWIFT was and is the principal international common-user funds-transfer network; others exist at the country level.

By 1980, the role of physical money in international trade and commerce had, for practical purposes, vanished entirely. "Money" is an entry on banking books and records, which are themselves bits and bytes in electronic media. "Money movement" is a flow of data through an electronic or optical channel, where it is indistinguishable from digitized voice, image, or whatever. Money has indeed become a special case of information.

Savings Accounts

These are similar to checking accounts, but include the payment of interest and special conditions for withdrawal of funds.

Time Deposits

These are deposits for fixed periods of time, bearing negotiated interest.

Bank Asset Applications

Personal Loans

The bank makes loans to individual customers using a portion of its deposits. Computers are involved in executing the loan contracts, controlling payments, and determining the accruals for cost of deposits, earnings of interest/dividend, and taxes due.

Business Loans

Similar to personal loans, business loans also have an enormous variety of disbursement and repayment options in one or multiple currencies.

Fee-Based Services

Electronic Funds Transfer (EFT - q.v.)

This is the principal payment process among corporations. A customer gives the bank instructions to move funds from the corporation's own checking account to a payee checking account at the same or at another bank. All parties involved require advice of such transactions. Timely execution and correctly recording the date of the transfers is critical, and different currencies may be required. Computers and computer communications are the essential elements in such transfers.

Letters of Credit

A letter of credit is a financial service: banks guarantee that their customers will have funds when a payment becomes due.

Custodian Services

This is a banking service in which records are maintained for several categories of customers in return for service fees. The most frequent examples of these applications are investment accounts, securities funds, pension funds, and stock transfer registry.

Credit Cards

In this financial service, fees are collected from businesses and interest is received from cardholders. This high item volume could not be handled without computers.

Reports

Accounting

The content of reports results from government regulations and from banking traditions. The information in this application defines the financial condition of the bank. It is essential that the nature and situation of all bank assets and liabilities be represented accurately.

Management Reports

Also strongly affected by regulatory reporting requirements, these applications provide information on expenses and revenues, to evaluate the effectiveness of managers and for planning the development of customer relationships.

DOMINANT BANKING TECHNOLOGIES

Paper Continuing into the 1990s, paper as a medium for information transmission and storage stubbornly refuses to go away. In many jurisdictions, paper documents are the sole legally acceptable manifestation of a transaction and hence will continue to be indispensable. Paper continues as a primary medium for communication between bank and customer, but it is no longer the sole medium.

Item processing, primarily check processing, is still done largely as it has been since the late 1950s' introduction of magnetic-ink-encoded checks, and this early technology will continue to be important. The entrenched U.S. consumer expectation that the physical check will be returned—a practice either never established or long abandoned in most other countries—continues to impose large, technologically unnecessary costs on the banking system and its customers. The technologies of image capture and document processing have begun to show promise of providing an escape from this impasse.

Various stumbling blocks continue to delay elimination of the handwritten signature or equivalent, with its implication of the continuing need for a paper document as a transaction authenticator or token of authority. None of the impediments is technological; they are almost purely legal and traditional in nature. Perfectly adequate electronic authenticators are in hand, but, being not uniformly legally acceptable, they are rarely used in other than intra-bank applications. Until the legal and attitudinal roadblocks can be cleared away, paper will continue to be important even where adequate substitute electronic technologies are well in hand.

Computer Systems Systems of all sizes, from very small to very large, are used in computerized banking applications. The most successful systems combine the processing of all banking transactions with the accounting and regulatory information reporting.

In the early 1960s, computerized banking applications were oriented toward high-volume paper processing through such techniques as MICR. Following the announcements of the third-generation computers in the later 1960s, several new approaches emerged. These were based upon computers such as the IBM 360/40, GE 400, Burroughs B5000, RCA Spectra 70, Univac 1100, and CDC 1604. Banking applications were savings accounts, on-line tellers (checking), overdraft accounts (loans), automated customer balance information, etc. Even though the data capture and validation and data inquiry were done on-line, the transactions were stored in the computer files for end-of-day batch processing.

This approach represented a compromise between satisfying immediate customer needs and maintaining secure controls. An example of the architecture of an on-line system with batch processing is shown in Fig.1.

The minicomputer "revolution" became an important part of banking applications in the mid-1970s. Minis provided the technology for computerized banking applications at the scale of a single department. For example, a single minicomputer was dedicated to handling the letters of credit department of all the loans for one class of business customers. Although computer hardware costs actually went up, the net effect was to produce sufficient savings elsewhere to reduce the overall cost.

The microcomputer explosion of the 1980s has amplified and extended this effect, but with an important difference. In banks, as elsewhere, the "front-office" practitioners of the primary business—banking—have wrested the management of information technology from the technologists and turned its power to their own business-motivated ends. The depth and breadth of technology awareness among formerly technologically helpless traditional bankers has expanded rapidly. This development has taken place in parallel with the proliferation of microcomputers and the availability of commercial software packages that have enabled bankers to exploit this suddenly accessible processing power.

Banking leaders now recognize the strategic primacy of the information technologies. Banking is an information business, and decisions about the technology are strategic decisions about the business. Policy-level managers now make these decisions in the most forward-looking institutions. This critical shift at once disenfranchises the traditional MIS or systems managers and empowers the business managers of the 1990s to be far more functionally effective in meeting customer needs at lower cost.

Networks For many decades, banks and customers have communicated using message services. "Advices" were delivered worldwide, by teleprinter, normally within one business day, and a paper record was produced. During the 1960s and 1970s, banking applications' use of wire services increased to a point that justified establishing special funds-transfer networks.

As the decade of the 1990s opened, the total value of the funds moving over these networks had reached well into the trillions of dollars daily, and these flows have become the lifeblood of the global economic system. Disruption of these new electronic lines of communication would bring a nation's commerce to its knees within hours.

Network technology has in many respects surpassed computer technology in importance to banking applications. The globalization of business and the near elimination of the so-called "information float," with the resulting expectations by customers of essentially instantaneous responsiveness from their banks, have had a mutually reinforcing effect. Networks have evolved from, in the early 1970s, a handful of low-speed telegraph lines between the head office and distant branches to, in the 1990s, networks and multi-megabit-per-second digital trunk lines. The effect has been the smooth facilitation, across continents as easily as across town, of the interconnections among bankers, bank customers, and the information resources required by both.

An increasing variety of message and data transmission options has begun to be used. Recent years have seen very rapid growth, particularly as circuits began to facilitate direct interaction between banking applications and bank customers acting through terminals of various types. Of a less revolutionary character is the role played by telecommunications in applications that call for interconnections among internal bank computers, as shown in Fig.2.

The "live" interaction of customer-bank communication terminals (CBCTs) in supermarkets and other retail outlets with bank applications and bank databases delivers vastly improved levels of customer service, while reducing operating costs and providing control of noncredit risks. It appears that their direct service delivery via computer/communications systems will continue to drive the growth and development of computerized banking applications in the 1990s.

A needed collateral development is the technology of encryption. However strong or weak the Bureau of Standards' Digital Encryption Standard (DES) algorithm may be (see CRYPTOGRAPHY, COMPUTERS IN), it is accepted as an industry standard, thus making possible the development of compatible encryptors that are off-the-shelf items, like modems. As a result, certain of the problems of customer data privacy protection are, in effect, swept from the board, releasing resources to work on the multitude of remaining problems.

Databases Optimum information management could be approached if it were possible to collect all the information from all of a bank's internal applications into logically centralized but widely accessible files, as shown in Fig.3. This facilitates management of asset and liability aggregates and precise reporting of the bank's condition. Data-related activity, protection of customer privacy, file updating, and investigations would be greatly facilitated by a full database capability, but, at least for large banks, such a capability still eludes full realization. No database management system adequate for such a large-scale file is presently practical.

The banking applications developed from the mid-1970s and continuing into the 1990s depend on database concepts. The principal difficulties are in the administration of thousands of information definitions, in establishing and maintaining the necessary structural relationships among data elements, and in coping with the current inefficiency and complexity of available database software. This indicates that the database management function is clearly the key to future computerized banking applications.

RICHARD G. MILLS AND ERICH R. WILLNER

BAR CODE. See UNIVERSAL PRODUCT CODE.

BASE REGISTER

For articles on related subjects *see* ADDRESSING; IBM 360-370-390 SERIES; INDEX REGISTER; and REGISTER.

A *base register* is used in addressing a computer memory. In a computer that uses base registers, the effective address (i.e. the address field of the instruction, possibly modified by indexing and indirect addressing) is a relative address. The actual memory address used is determined by adding this relative address to the contents of one or more base registers.

The Control Data Cyber series is an example of a computer system that uses a single base register. Every program is written as if it were meant to run in a single memory area starting at location 0. The program may in fact be loaded starting at any memory location. When the program is run, the operating system places the address of the first word of the program in the base register. The content of the base register is automatically added to every memory reference address, and thus every relative address is converted into an absolute address. This feature is useful in multiprogramming systems (*q.v.*), since it permits programs to be loaded wherever space exists, and permits programs to be moved in memory or to be removed from memory and then resumed in a different area of memory. Such base registers are thus often called *relocation registers*.

Some computers have several base registers. A relative address must then contain a field that indicates which register is selected, and the contents of that register are added to the relative address to form the absolute address. In such a machine, a program may be constructed in parts or segments that can be independently loaded into available areas of memory. The Univac 1110 is an example of a machine with two base registers. The Multics machine (Honeywell 68/80) is an example of a machine with multiple base registers.

The term *base register* is sometimes used more or less interchangeably with the term *index register*. Thus, the IBM 360, 370 and 390 have 16 general registers, each of which provides a 24-bit base address to which the 12-bit address field (displacement) in an instruction is added to produce the effective address. These registers can be, and usually are, loaded and stored by the programs that use them. It is conceptually better to think of them as index registers and to limit the use of the term "base register" to system registers that are not accessible to the programs whose addresses they modify.

SAUL ROSEN

BASIC. *See* PROCEDURE-ORIENTED LANGUAGES.

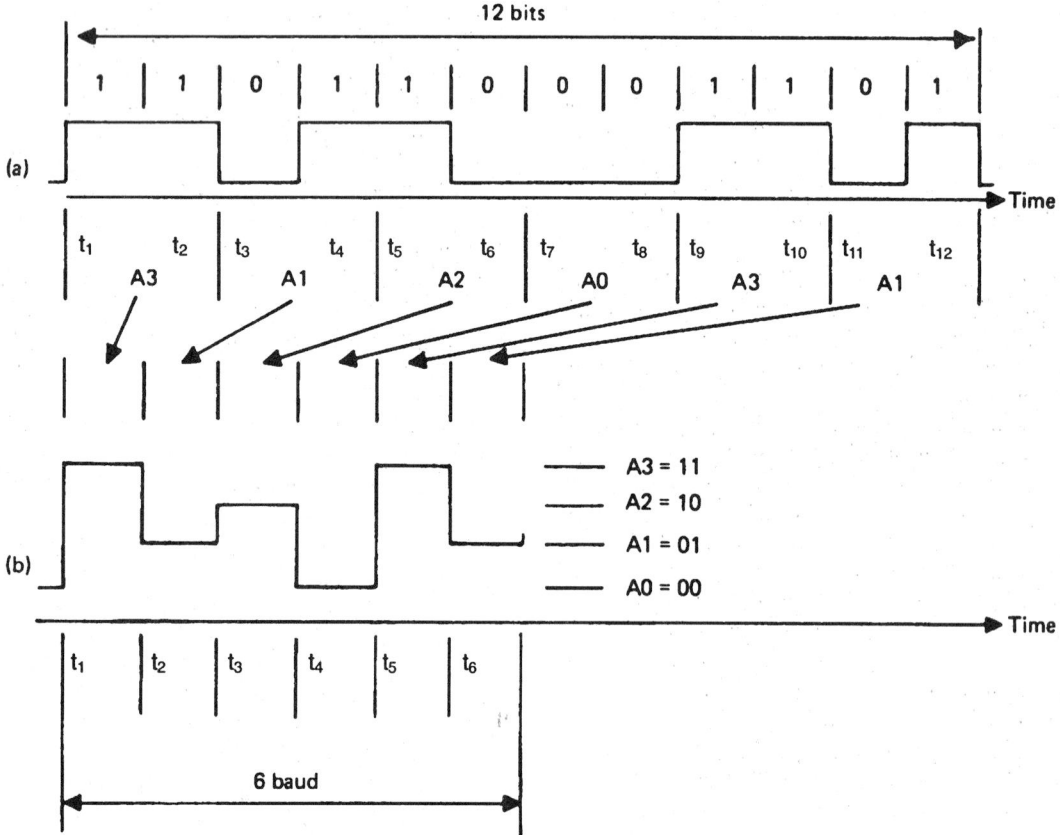

FIG. 1. Relationship between baud and bits per second. Each combination of two bits is encoded as one of four possible amplitudes; hence, for this particular case, one baud is equal to two bits per second.

BAUD

For articles on related subjects *see* BAUDOT CODE; and CHANNEL.

A *baud* is a unit of signaling speed and refers to the number of times the state (or condition) of a data communication line changes per second. It is the reciprocal of the length (in seconds) of the shortest element in the signaling code. Historically, it is a contraction of the surname of the Frenchman J. M. E. Baudot, whose five-bit code was adopted by the French telegraph system in 1877. By contrast, a bit is the smallest unit of information in a binary system. The baud rate is therefore equal to the bit rate only if each signal element represents one bit of information.

The relationship between bauds and bits per second is illustrated in Fig. 1, where amplitude is used as a coding method. In this particular case, there are four line conditions, one for each of the four combinations of two bits. Each line change signal element is therefore represented by two bits and, if we can have one line change in 1 ms, the baud rate is 1,000, whereas the bit rate is actually 2,000 bits per second. Similarly, if the signals are coded into eight possible states, one line condition could represent three bits and one baud would then equal three bits per second, etc.

Unfortunately, in much of today's literature, the terms "baud" and "bits per second" are used synonymously. This is correct in cases where pure two-state signaling is used, as in Fig. 1(a), but is incorrect in general. For this reason, the term "baud" is gradually being replaced by "bits per second," since the latter is independent of the coding method and truly represents the information rate.

JOHN S. SOBOLEWSKI

BAUDOT CODE

For articles on related subjects *see* BAUD; CODES; and ERROR–CORRECTING CODE.

The *Baudot code*, also known as the International Telegraph Code No. 1, is named after its inventor, J. M. E. Baudot (1845–1903). It was invented about 1880, and by the 1950s it had become one of the standards for international telegraph communication.

Baudot is a fixed character-length code in which each character is represented by five binary digits. The five-digit character length allows only 32 (= 2^5) unique combinations, not enough to represent the 26 letters of the alphabet, the 10 digits, and the punctuation characters needed for telegraph messages. This problem is solved by defining two unique shift-control characters, and interpreting all subsequent characters in terms of the last shift-control character received. The shift-control characters are called "letter shift" and "figure shift." This arrangement is very similar to that of a shift-lock key on a terminal, i.e. once the shift lock has been depressed, all subsequent characters are typed in the same shift.

Using the technique of two unique shift characters, a five-bit code can then represent 62 (= $2^6 - 2$) characters. However, in the Baudot code, the total number of characters is less than this because other control characters such as "line feed" and "carriage return" are given representations.

The Baudot code does not have the capability of detecting errors because all combinations of the five bits are valid characters within the code. During transmission, therefore, a character can be transformed into another character by the loss or gain of one or more bits. Particularly harmful is an error in a shift-control character because all characters after the transformed shift-control character up to the next shift-control character would be interpreted in the wrong shift. For example, in the message PAY 810 DOLLARS, if the "figure shift" character between the PAY and the 810 were transformed into, say, a J (i.e. 00010 to 10010), then the message would be received as PAYJBAD DOLLARS (see Table 1 for letter-shift, figure-shift equivalents). In order to alleviate this problem, telegraph systems frequently retransmit at the end of the message all figures that occur in the message.

TABLE 1. Baudot Code Characters

Letters		Figures
A	10000	1
B	00110	8
C	10110	9
D	11110	Ø
E	01000	2
F	01110	NA
G	01010	7
H	11010	+
I	01100	NA
J	10010	6
K	10011	(
L	11011	=
M	01011	)
N	01111	NA
O	11100	5
P	11111	%
Q	10111	/
R	00111	–
S	00101	.
T	10101	NA
U	10100	4
V	11101	'
W	01101	?
X	01001	,
Y	00100	3
Z	11001	:
LS	00001	LS
FS	00010	FS
CR	11000	CR
LF	10001	LF
ER	00011	ER
NA	00000	NA

Symbols: LS = Letter Shift, FS = Figure Shift, CR = Carriage Return, LF = Line Feed, ER = Error, NA = Not Assigned, Space = LS or FS.

The five-level code most used today is the International Telegraph Code No. 2 (Murray code), invented about 20 years after the Baudot code. In computer manufacturers' literature, there is some confusion concerning the use of the term "baudot code." It is sometimes used to apply to all five-level codes and is frequently applied to International Telegraph Code No. 2.

GEORGE D. DETLEFSEN AND ROBIN H. KERR

BCD. *See* BINARY-CODED DECIMAL.

BCS. *See* BRITISH COMPUTER SOCIETY.

BELL LABS RELAY COMPUTERS

For articles or related subjects *see* DIGITAL COMPUTERS: HISTORY: EARLY; and ENIAC.

Between 1939 and 1951, Bell Telephone Laboratories (Bell Labs) built a total of seven digital computing machines of ever-greater sophistication. Each used electromechanical relays and switching equipment for its basic computing elements. The last computers of this series were as functionally powerful as the electronic computers being built elsewhere at that time, but their use of relay switching meant that they would always remain an order of magnitude slower in arithmetic speeds. The inspiration for the initial machines came from George Stibitz, a mathematician at Bell Labs, with the engineering design due at first to Sam Williams and later E.G. Andrews.

The Model I contained about 400 relays and performed the operations of complex arithmetic on 8-digit decimal numbers. Numbers were internally coded in excess-three binary-coded decimal (Stibitz-code). The machine was accessed through a modified teletype terminal (Fig. 1). At Bell Labs, three such terminals allowed multiple (but not simultaneous) access. That the terminals need not be physically near the processor was dramatically demonstrated at a 1940 meeting of the American Mathematical Society in Hanover, New Hampshire, where a terminal was connected to the computer back at the Labs in New York City. Such remote access to digital equipment would not occur again for ten years.

The Model II, completed in 1943, contained about 440 relays and was optimized for work relating to the development of the M-9 gun director during the war. It used paper tape for input, output, and for simple sequences of operations related to interpolation of functions. Its memory capacity was seven decimal numbers of from two to five digits in length.

The Models III and IV were somewhat more powerful, containing about 1,400 relays each and having a memory capacity of ten numbers. They were installed in 1944 at Fort Bliss, Texas, and in 1945 at the Naval Research Laboratory in Washington, DC. Like the Model II, these computers were optimized for fire-control problems, although their programmability meant they could be (and were) reprogrammed to solve many other problems once the war ended.

The Model V was the most ambitious of all the Bell Labs machines, and ranks with the "Giant Brains" of the era, such as the ENIAC or Harvard Mark I (*q.v.*). Two copies were built in 1946–47, and were installed at the NACA at Langley Field, Virginia, and the Ballistic Research Laboratory at Aberdeen, Maryland. Each machine contained over 9,000 relays, a memory capacity of 30 numbers, and hard-wired floating-point arithmetic unusual for the time.

Decimal numbers were encoded as groups of two and five relays, somewhat like the beads on a Chinese abacus. This *bi-quinary code* allowed for elaborate error checking, which ensured that the machine would stop and alert an operator before ever delivering a wrong answer. Relay computers, unlike their electronic counterparts, had to have error detecting circuits because a relay can fail intermittently, usually when a piece of dust interferes with a few contact cycles before being dislodged. Such intermittent errors would have been almost impossible to detect without some sort of internal redundancy. By contrast, vacuum tubes failed catastrophically, with a resulting computer failure obvious to its operators.

A Model V could be configured so that several problems could be coded, each on a different paper tape, all of

FIG. 1: Operator H. L. Marvin seated at one of three consoles for the Bell Labs Complex Number Computer, 1940. (Photo: AT&T Bell Laboratories)

them ready to go. If an error was detected during the run of one problem, the machine would automatically switch over to another tape and begin solving another problem, using different parts of the processor and memory. This early and rudimentary form of *multiprogramming* (*q.v.*) allowed the machine to be run unattended through the night with the assurance that in the morning most, if not all, the computing work would have been done. That, plus the floating-point arithmetic, helped compensate for the machine's inherently slow speed of about one multiplication per second as compared to the ENIAC's 360 multiplications per second.

The final machine in the series, the Model VI, was built and installed at the Labs for internal use in 1949. It was essentially a simplified version of the Model V, without the multiple independent processors. Apparently it was felt that the complexity of the Model V was not worth it. The Model VI did have an ability to execute short sequences of arithmetic with single commands punched on the tape, a concept new at the time and one rediscovered and named later as "macro" commands. It interpreted these commands through ingenious electromagnetic circuits that, in effect, "microprogrammed" the machine. It is not historically misleading to use that term, since those features were seen and noticed by Maurice Wilkes (*q.v.*), who later developed that concept for stored program electronic computers.

None of the Bell machines used the stored program principle, although the Models V and VI had full conditional branching capabilities. But that made the solving of complex, iterative problems a somewhat baroque exercise involving loops of tape, multiple tape drives, partitioned processors, and other mechanical tricks. Thus, the Model V went about as far as one could with not only relay technology, but with external, paper tape programming.

The Bell Labs computers were powerful, reliable, and balanced machines. They often outperformed their vacuum-tube contemporaries in solving problems for which slower speed was not decisive. But once the von Neumann-inspired notions of computer architecture became known and accepted, that advantage was lost, as designers elsewhere learned to build electronic computers with none of the architectural drawbacks suffered by machines like the ENIAC. Thus, the Bell Labs machines represent an evolutionary dead end, although their contribution to the mainstream history of digital computing was profound.

References

1951. Andrews, E. G. "A Review of the Bell Laboratories' Digital Computer Developments," in *Review of Electronic Digital Computers*. Joint AIEE-IRE Computer Conference, 10–12 December, Philadelphia (New York: AIEE, 1952), 101–105.

PAUL E. CERUZZI

BENCHMARKS

For articles on related subjects *see* PERFORMANCE MEASUREMENT AND EVALUATION; and PERFORMANCE OF COMPUTERS.

The term *benchmarking* is drawn from its use in surveying, where it represents a mark on a stationary object whose position and elevation have been measured. The mark, once made, is used subsequently as a reference point in tidal observations and surveys. Analogously, benchmarking of computer systems is intended to measure new systems relative to a reference point on current systems. In particular, the benchmarks are standardized computer programs for which there is a history of measurement data (typically timings) for executions of the programs with specifically defined input and reproducible output.

A number of benchmarks have evolved for both scientific and commercial processors. Among the most well-known for scientific computing are the Livermore Fortran Kernels (McMahon 1986), the Los Alamos Benchmarks, the NAS Kernels, and the LINPACK tests (1989). Recently, due to a growing concern in the supercomputing community that existing benchmarks are too simplistic to fully represent scientific computing, attempts have been made to define new standards. These efforts include the Perfect Club, which is based at the University of Illinois, and the System Performance Evaluation Cooperative (SPEC), which is a vendor-sponsored benchmarking project. Each of these collections represents aspects of scientific computation and therefore provides some information about the computational speed of the systems being tested.

The founding members of SPEC were Apollo, Hewlett-Packard, MIPS, and Sun. Joining the consortium later were AT&T, Bull, CDC, Compaq, Data General, DEC, Dupont, Fujitsu, IBM, Intel, Intergraph, Motorola, NCR, Siemens Nixdorf, Silicon Graphics, Solbourne, Stardent, and Unisys. The first set of 10 SPEC benchmarks comprising 150,000 lines of source code was released in October 1989 and is distributed only under a licensing agreement. A performance index called the SPECmark is defined as the geometric mean of the relative performance of the ten separate programs in the SPEC suite.

The first program designed especially for benchmarking was the Whetstone benchmark published in 1976 by H. J. Curnow and B. A. Wichmann of the National Physical Laboratory (NPL) in Great Britain. The benchmark, originally published in Algol 60 but now more often used in its Fortran or Pascal version, is named for the Whetstone Algol compiler in use at the NPL in the mid-1970s. The Whetstone benchmark gives heavy weight to floating point operations and continues to be of value in testing the effectiveness of various *floating-point coprocessors* that may be optionally added to currently popular microprocessors. There are now so many different versions of the Whetstone benchmark that comparison of results obtained with one version vs. another is quite difficult.

The Dhrystone benchmark, named in whimsical contradistinction to Whetstone, was published by R. P. Weicker in 1984. Originally written in a Pascal subset of Ada (*q.v.*), the benchmark is now used principally in its C (*q.v.*) version. The Dhrystone benchmark places no emphasis on floating-point operations, but instead contains a mix of statements typical of nonnumeric and systems programming (*q.v.*) environments. Relative to scientific and engineering computations, such programs typically contain fewer loops, simpler computations involving just integer and logical data types, and more conditional statements and procedure calls. Dhyrstone is widely distributed via Usenet, the Unix (*q.v.*) network.

The Stanford Small Program Benchmark Set was developed concurrently with the first RISC architecture (*q.v.*) systems at Stanford and the University of California at Berkeley. The set consists of ten small programs chosen as candidates likely to illustrate the differences in performance between RISC and CISC processors: eight integer-oriented programs—Permutations, Towers of Hanoi, Eight Queens, Integer Matrix Multiplication, Puzzle, Quicksort, Bubblesort, and Treesort (*see* SORTING)—and two floating-point programs—Floating Point Matrix Multiplication and Fast Fourier Transform (*q.v.*).

One of the most popular benchmarks used on personal computers, though not necessarily a good one, is a Pascal version of the algorithm known as the Sieve of Eratosthenes. It computes all prime numbers up to some limit—usually 8,192—by eliminating (sieving out) the composite numbers from an original list of all integers less than the limit. The benchmark has been widely used, or perhaps misused, to tout the alleged superiority of one compiler over another with respect to either rate of compilation, speed of execution of object programs, size of object programs, or all three.

In contrast to other benchmarks, which measure the time taken to do a fixed task, the SLALOM benchmark measures the amount of work that can be performed in a fixed time. The rationale is that this will allow comparison over a broader range of machines. The benchmark consists of a radiosity problem together with I/O and matrix setup routines. The problem solved is similar to that of the LINPACK benchmark.

The performance of computers (*q.v.*), a complicated issue, is a function of many interrelated quantities. These quantities include the application, algorithm, size of the problem, the choices of high-level language and implementation, the level of human effort used to optimize the problem and the compiler's ability to optimize, as well as the operating system, architecture, and hardware characteristics of the system under test. Thus, the results presented for benchmark suites should not be viewed as measures of total system performance, but rather as reference points for further evaluations.

Benchmarks are typically used as one of many data points by algorithm designers seeking the optimal coding style for a given system, by system developers seeking to match machine characteristics to the requirements defined by their target workloads and represented to them through the benchmarks, and by individuals and groups seeking to procure the appropriate computing system for a given installation.

Benchmarking methods (ways to use and abuse benchmarks) are discussed in more detail in Dongarra *et al.* (1987). An overview of common benchmarks is given by Weicker (1990).

References

1986. McMahon, Frank H. The Livermore Fortran Kernals: A Computer Test of Numerical Performance Range, Lawrence Livermore National Laboratory Report UCRL-53745 (October).

1987. Dongarra, J., Martin, J., and Worlton, J. "Evaluating Computers and Their Performance: Perspectives, Pitfalls, and Paths," *IEEE Spectrum*, **24** (June).

1989. Performance of Various Computers Using Standard Linear Equations Software in a Fortran Environment, Argonne National Laboratory Report MCS-TM-23 (June).

1990. Weicker, R. P. "An Overview of Common Benchmarks," *IEEE Computer*, **23**, **12** (December) 65–75.

JACK DONGARRA and JOANNE MARTIN

BINARY ARITHMETIC. *See* NUMBERS AND NUMBER SYSTEMS.

BINARY-CODED DECIMAL (BCD)

For article on related subjects *see* ASCII; CODES; and EBCDIC.

Codes that use binary digits to represent decimal digits are required to enable decimal information to be stored by the binary (two-state) devices that are the elements of which all computers are constructed. Many such codes have been constructed for various purposes, but the most common and natural one is called binary-coded decimal (BCD). In BCD, each decimal digit is represented by its four-bit binary equivalent, as shown in Table 1.

Four bits are required, since, with three, only eight different combinations can be represented. Since there are 16 possible combinations of four bits, six (1010, 1011, 1100, 1101, 1110, and 1111) are not used in BCD. BCD is called a *weighted code,* because, reading left to right in Table 1, the four bits in each BCD combination correspond to weights of 8, 4, 2, and 1. Thus, for example, 0110 has its two 1s weighted by 4 and 2, respectively, and corresponds to a decimal 6.

ANTHONY RALSTON

TABLE 1. BCD.

Digit	BCD Combination
0	0000
1	0001
2	0010
3	0011
4	0100
5	0101
6	0110
7	0111
8	1000
9	1001

BINARY SEARCH. *See* SEARCHING.

BINARY TREE. *See* TREE.

BINDING

For articles on related subjects *see* ASSEMBLER; COMPILER CONSTRUCTION; LANGUAGE PROCESSORS; and MACHINE AND ASSEMBLY LANGUAGE PROGRAMMING.

Binding means translating an expression in a program into a form immediately interpretable by the machine on which the program is to run; *binding time* is the moment at which this translation is completed. Thus, an expression is completely bound when translated into absolute machine representation (*see* "Definition of ML" in MACHINE AND ASSEMBLY LANGUAGE PROGRAMMING) at a fixed location in a storage device. When the context so indicates, however, binding can refer to an intermediate point in this process, and binding time can mean the point at which a translator has gone as far in binding the expression as it can. For example, a compiler may, as a matter of course, leave the binding of some class of expressions to be completed by a linking loader (*q.v.*), or even, defer binding of some to run time. Similarly, a translator may partly bind a file specification by transforming it into a file descriptor block that needs further interpretation by an input/output (I/O) package or operating system before it can be used for actual I/O procedures.

In general, early binding means more efficient processing of a source program, but at some cost in flexibility and potentially useful information. The information sacrificed might have allowed the use of arrays whose dimensions could vary at run time, or the issuing of more informative error messages, or the ability to compile object programs for various configurations of the target machine or operating system. The rate at which binding is to take place, therefore, is an important design consideration in all kinds of language-processing software. Broadly speaking, the history of software development is the history of ever-later binding time, with user convenience and program adaptability given increasingly more emphasis, and processing speed obtained through use of faster hardware and by relegation of optimization to special versions of the compiler that are used only when the source program concerned is thought to be debugged and stable.

This postponement of binding in the compilation of programs is analogous to the postponement of detailed decisions in the top-down design of programs; in both cases, the principle is that all options should be kept open until the last possible moment. But in addition to sharing this general principle (one that applies well beyond the designing and compiling of programs, in fact), each of the activities mentioned has its own peculiar reason for late binding. In the compiling process, binding involves the loss of information (e.g. the mnemonic name of a program variable) that can be helpful, even essential, in dealing with bugs or other problems requiring program modification. In the design process, earlier-than-necessary binding clutters the designer's vision with unnecessary detail (e.g. the mnemonic name of a program variable), distracting the designer from essentials.

Some translators have attempted to put the question of binding time, to some degree, in the user's hands. One, at least (Strachey, 1968), has for experimental purposes gone all the way, letting the user specify for each expression the time at which it is to be bound.

References

1968. Strachey, C. "A General Purpose Macro Generator," *The Computer Journal*, **8**: 225–241.
1968. Wegner, P. *Programming Languages, Information Structures and Machine Organization*. New York: McGraw-Hill.

MARK HALPERN

BIOCOMPUTING

For articles on related subjects *see* HOSPITAL INFORMATION SYSTEMS; IMAGE PROCESSING; MEDICAL APPLICATIONS; MEDICAL IMAGING; MEDLARS/MEDLINE; NEURAL NETWORKS; SCIENTIFIC APPLICATIONS; and TOMOGRAPHY, COMPUTERIZED.

Modeling Living Systems Beginning in the late 1800s, mathematicians began to realize that biology and ecology were sources of intriguing mathematical problems. The very complexity that made life difficult for experimental biologists intrigued the mathematicians and led to the formation of the field of *mathematical biology*. More recently, as computers became more cost effective, simulation modeling became more widely used for incorporating the necessary biological complexity into the original, often simplified, mathematical models.

Experimentalists used to feel that the theoretical analyses were deficient in a variety of areas. The models were too simple to be useful in clinical and/or practical biological application. They lacked crucial biological and medical realism. Mathematical modelers balked at the demands for increased levels of biological complexity. The addition of the required biological reality often led to significant alterations in the mathematical models, making them intractable to formal mathematical analysis.

With the advent of the new computer technologies, biological reality is finally within the grasp of the biomodeler. Mathematical complexity is no longer a serious issue, as computation speeds are now sufficient to enable large modeling computations to be performed. Large memory is now routinely available. Also, high speed, efficient, optimized numerical algorithms are constantly being developed.

Visualization Visualization is a method of computing. It transforms the symbolic/numeric into the geometric, thereby enabling researchers to observe their simulations and computations. The life sciences are, by their very nature, visual/tactile sciences. They are visual in two ways: (1) directly, in that they handle data from images (X-ray, molecular modeling, computational chemistry), and (2) indirectly, in that they handle complex data and transform it to a visual representation (mathematical and computer models, enzymic reaction simulations, physiological process models, image reconstruction, medical diagnostics). In a sense, the computer becomes the laboratory. And, as a consequence, what was once done *in* the tube is now being done *on* the tube.

Imaging Perhaps the most obvious use of computers for visualization is the handling of patient image data and/or the construction/reconstruction of medical image data for the purposes of clinical diagnosis and analysis. In the area of imaging, we recognize the following three major problem classes: (1) simple rebuilding of two-dimensional image (graphics) data into a useful and useable two-dimensional image on a screen, (2) reconstruction of three-dimensional images from two-dimensional scans, and (3) visualization of an image in a real time, interactive mode. Given a 3-D image of the pelvis, for example, can we manipulate it, in real time, for the purposes of clinical examination? As an outgrowth of attempts to address these three areas from the computer science perspective, clinical medicine/clinical diagnosis has become more powerful. Nowhere has this been better demonstrated than in the areas of non-invasive medicine and image reconstruction; CAT, PET, and NMR scanners now inhabit most hospital complexes of any reasonable size. A further extension of this area of investigation may be found in the surgical planning systems at the Mayo Clinic and at the Mallinckrodt Institute (Washington University at St. Louis). With these systems, physicians are now able to simulate a surgical procedure before it is performed, thereby minimizing potential hazard to the patient and increasing surgical accuracy. Experimental science benefits as well. These same methods, when applied to experimental biology, allow us to begin to understand the biological and physiological functions of various organs and organ systems. For example, brain mapping studies have allowed us to investigate the cognitive function, as well as the physiological behavior of the brain (see Figs. 1-3, color insert page CP-1).

As an outgrowth of such analyses, interesting questions arise in the area of visualization of multiple datasets of different types. For example, how can one effectively visualize the combined CAT, PET, NMR, and simulation data for a particular patient so that it is possible to visualize the bone, muscle, and metabolic data at the same time?

Computational Genetics The analysis of genetic structure raises numerous interesting questions. One of the more important is the issue of the evolution of the structure and complexity of the human genome. As experimental molecular biology sequences more and more of the genes in various species, we have a greater database that can be used to study evolutionary biology (see later section on the matrix of biological knowledge). Evolutionary biology questions are intensely scalar processes involving complex tree search problems. Computational tree search algorithms, implemented on parallel computers and on networks of smaller workstations, can assist scientists in evaluating genetic evolutionary trees and thus help them to understand the evolution of these genomic structures. In addition, these same algorithms can be used to study the related problem of the origin of the species. Linkage analysis, a complex mathematical analysis involving tree search algorithms, is used to locate and to map gene structures for the purposes of understanding inherited disorders.

At the gene sequencing level, mathematical and computational algorithms are used to align gene sequences, match gene sequences, reconstruct gene sequences from sequence fragments, and construct theoretical three-dimensional structures based upon those sequences. These hypothesized structures are subsequently compared to the experimental data so that binding and transcription predictions can be made and analyzed for new insights into the biological dynamics of the gene. Harris et al. (Abbott-Northwestern Hospital) have developed a hypothesis for a simple code for site-specific recognition at the genetic level (see Fig. 4, color insert page CP-1). Their work, based upon information derived from genetic sequence comparisons, X-ray crystallography data, and point mutation studies is intensely computer oriented at a number of levels. Their predictions were substantiated by supercomputer simulations of the DNA-protein binding predicted by their model.

Computational Cell Biology The dynamics of cell populations is of great interest to both biologists and clinicians. Understanding the cell cycle would have impact upon our understanding of how to control better the development of various forms of cancer. From a therapeutic perspective, a mathematical model or enhanced simulation of cellular processes could be used to test treatment protocols and regimens before they were actually implemented upon the patient (see Fig. 5, color insert page CP-1). Early work in this area was performed by Morrison, Aroesty, and Lincoln, at the RAND Corporation. These investigators developed a sophisticated mathematical model/computer simulation of cancer growth and treatment using ara-c, an extremely toxic chemotherapeutic agent. More recently, mathematical models of cell growth have been studied by Webb (Vanderbilt University), Tucker and Zimmerman (M.D. Anderson Cancer Center), Witten (ETA Systems), Tyson (Virginia State), and others. These models have attempted to examine cell growth from a variety of perspectives. More recently, Witten and, subsequently, Zimmerman have proposed that these models should be augmented with an additional variable called a *particle or property* variable. This *particle* may or may not be linked to flow through the cell cycle. These models lead to a class of generalized nonlinear stochastic hyperbolic partial differential equations in three variables. The numerical issues arising in the study of these equations present highly complex as well as computer-intensive problems.

Computational Physiology Human physiology attempts to explain the physical and chemical factors that are responsible for the origin, development, and progression of human life. Human beings are complex machines built from equally complex systems (immune system, digestive system, nervous system, etc.). These systems contain multiple parts or organs (each, itself, a complex hierarchy of systems and subsystems). Realistic models of these systems can lead to deeper understanding of the basic biology of these interacting bodily systems. And, as the models become more sophisticated, they can lead to a deeper understanding of the important synergism between the systems.

Reproductive Biology The ovaries are the repository of the female reproductive component, the follicles. Of the approximately 500,000 follicles present in the two ovaries at birth, only about 375 of these follicles will eventually develop into ova (eggs). Worldwide, it has been demonstrated that there are increasing levels of infertility in both sexes. This is particularly true in the United States and in Poland, but it is not at all clear what is causing such an increase to occur. As a consequence, it is important that the dynamics of the reproductive cycle be studied in detail. Such models might give insight into how the environment and/or other factors might play into the level of infertility displayed in a particular country or population. In addition, such models can be used to study the dynamics of aging in the mammalian reproductive system.

Mathematical models of the development of an egg have been made by Lacker (Courant Institute for Mathematical Sciences), Gosden et al. (England), and Witten (ETA Systems). These models represent various increasing levels of complexity in the mathematical modeling process. The basic premise of all of these models is that the follicle undergoes a series of stages or steps in its growth. These stages and the transitions between them are modeled by differential equations. This class of compartmental or Markov models can generate systems of equations that can be extremely large and range from fairly simple to fairly complex in structure. The model system of Witten, for example, involves the solution of anywhere from 50,000 to over 200,000 nonlinear differential equations describing a probability distribution for a given number of eggs in each stage (compartment) of development. The model is clearly computationally intensive in that it involves the solution of a large number of nonlinear differential equations.

Mathematical models of swimming tails (sperm without heads) have been studied by Fauci (Tulane University). This model is numerically intensive as it involves the solution of a swimming object in a viscous fluid, a problem in computational fluid dynamics.

Cardiac Dynamics The cardiovascular system is fundamental to the life support of the human. Central to this system is the four-chambered muscle called the heart. Arthur Winfree of the University of Arizona is involved in the mathematical modeling and computer simulation of nonlinear waves in excitable media, such as heart muscle. Winfree has been studying circulating, vortex-like excitation (re-entrant tachycardia) in the heart as it is related to the onset of fibrillation (sudden loss of the rhythmic movement that allows the heart to pump blood). Within the context of his theory and simulations, Winfree has

been able to show that normal healthy heart muscle is an excitable medium. Further, he has been able to show that two- and three-dimensional vortices arise in excitable media such as heart muscle and that they do so in ways that are predicted by his theory.

At the University of Calgary, Wayne Giles heads a research team that is investigating the electrical energy of the heart and how it affects the organ's natural rhythm. He is particularly interested in how such a model could be used to study the interaction of cardiac function and cardiac drugs. Dr. Peter Backx and Dr. H. terKeurs of the University of Calgary and Dr. S. Goldman of the University of Guelph have studied the property of propagated after-contractions in cardiac preparations. Their mathematical model, involving up to 40,000 coupled ordinary differential equations, is numerically integrated to study the dynamics of calcium-mediated contractile waves in cardiac preparations.

Charles Peskin of the Courant Institute for Mathematical Sciences is involved in cardiac modeling from a different perspective. He has been performing two- and now three-dimensional modeling of the heart, including valves and ventricles, and is now adding atria and other vessels. This working model beats and moves the blood through the chambers of the heart. The model is a complex one involving a coupled system of equations modeling the wall, the blood, and the valve motion. The purpose of the Peskin research project is to develop a model that will allow for the design of artifical valves and their subsequent testing, and to study the effect of heart function on valve design.

The Peskin model may also be used to examine the timing between the atrial and ventricular contraction, a clinically important facet of cardiac function, since sophisticated pacemakers can now separately pace the chambers. Finally, Peskin points out that such a model can be used to study heart disease and its effect on cardiac dynamics. He was able to use his model to show that weakened capillary muscles lead to valve prolapse.

The Nervous System The nervous system (along with the endocrine system) provides the control functions for the human body. The nervous system is responsible for rapid activities of the body, such as muscular contraction, rapidly changing visceral events, and even the rates of secretion of some of the endocrine glands. It is a unique system in that it can control and perform a vast complex of actions. The human brain is estimated to contain approximately 10^{12} neurons. Many of these neurons are connected to 10,000 other neurons. Thus, in many ways, the brain is itself a sophisticated supercomputer.

At the single neuron level, Steve Young and Mark Ellisman of the Laboratory for Neurocytology at UC San Diego are using a supercomputer to reconstruct single neurons. The neurons are frozen, sliced into sections $0.25\text{--}5.0\mu$ thick, and photographed through a high voltage electron microscope. The computer is then used to reconstruct the slices and, subsequently, to view them on a graphics workstation. Ultimately, such techniques can be integrated with advanced simulation modeling, to allow the scientist to investigate and simulate tissue activities and structure/function relationships. As these techniques are refined, one can envision methods for viewing Alzheimer's disease at the single cell level.

T. R. Chay of the University of Pittsburgh has been studying the dynamics of excitable cells. In particular, he and his group have been trying to understand the behavior of channel gating in patch clamp data. Through mathematical modeling and computer simulation, T. D. Lagerlund of the Mayo Clinic has been examining the effects of axial diffusion on oxygen delivery in the peripheral nerves. It is known that victims of diabetes often suffer changes in their system of blood vessels, changes that reduce the supply of oxygen and nutrients to the tissue and subsequently damage the kidneys, retinas, and nerves. The work of Lagerlund has been to examine the mechanism of tissue damage in diabetes and how nutrients reach the cells. His work has been primarily concerned with diffusion of various nutrient and other substances through nerve tissue. A deeper understanding of these mechanisms could well lead to a deeper understanding of and a subsequent treatment for a variety of nerve diseases caused by diabetes and other related conditions.

At a higher level of neural organization is the brain itself. Lagerlund, in addition to his kidney work, has developed computer models for modeling various features of the electroencephalogram or EEG as recorded by scalp electrodes. Their model has been an attempt to understand the mechanisms that are responsible for the generation of rhythmic fluctuations in potential.

Computing the Kidney Body fluids are extremely important to the basic physiology of the human being. The renal system, of which the kidneys are a part, is intimately tied to the dynamics of the body fluids. The kidneys excrete most of the end-products of bodily metabolism, and they control the concentrations of most of the constituents of the bodily fluids. Loss of kidney function can lead to death. Don Marsh of the University of Southern California School of Medicine is leading a group of investigators in large scale mathematical modeling and simulation of the kidney. He and his group have looked at two problems: (1) the concentrating mechanism of the inner medulla of the kidney, and (2) the oscillation in tubular pressure initiated by the kidney's nonlinear control mechanism. The concentrating mechanism was modeled using a 3-D model of the kidney structure. It included longitudinal symmetry, tubules, and blood vessels. The group was able to demonstrate that the longitudinal symmetry played no part in the concentrating mechanism of the kidney. In their study of the oscillation in tubular pressure, Marsh's group is using a sophisticated system of partial differential equation models to describe the physiological control of the kidney tubular pressure. They have been able to show the existence of what appears to be a *chaotic attractor* in the system and that there is a period-doubling bifurcation in the development of hypertension.

Modeling the Dynamics of the Body Mathematical computer models of limb motion are of importance in a number of areas, from robotics (*q.v.*) to biomechanics. Karl Newell of the University of Illinois Urbana-Champaign simulates limb movements using spring-mass models. Such models are currently used as a metaphor for the neuromuscular organization of limb motion.

At the cellular level, Cy Frank and Raj Rangayyan of the University of Calgary are examining ligament injuries and methods of treatment. Collagen fibrils, the basic building block of normal healthy ligament, are in nearly parallel arrangement when the ligament is healthy. In injured tissue, the arrangement is highly random. These investigators have been able to demonstrate that the randomness of the distribution depends upon the nature of the injury sustained and the stage of healing. As the tissues heal, the collagen fibrils realign in a process called collagen remodeling. Using the supercomputer for sophisticated and intense image processing, these investigators are attempting to interpret the realignment stages and to use such knowledge to treat more accurately trauma to the limbs.

Patient-Based Physiological Simulation Patient-based physiological modeling has come of age. More and more computer systems are engaged in taking patient image data and reconstructing it so that a physician can view, in three dimensions, a patient's X-ray, CAT, PET, NMR, or other clinical image data. Computerized surgery systems are currently in place at the Washington University of St. Louis Mallinckrodt Institute and at the Mayo Clinic. Facial reconstruction and surgical simulation are now a practical reality.

Such workstation-based and mainframe-based systems allow one to dream of a new class of ultra-largescale patient-based physiological simulations that could be performed with a high-performance computing engine. At the VA Medical Center in Minneapolis, T.K. Johnson and R.L. Vessella are developing a patient-based simulation of radioactive decay in the organs of the body. Such a problem is computer intensive in that it requires the mapping of the three-dimensional spatial distribution of radiolabeled compounds. In addition, the difficulty of the problem is enhanced by the fact that the radiation may travel a distance before it interacts with matter, and the irregular shapes of the organs do not lend themselves to simple dose-distance relationships.

Project DaVinci at the University of Illinois is attempting to build a 3-D simulation of the human body. Researchers at International BioComputing Technologies are looking at the problem of ultra-largescale simulation of cellular systems and the interaction between aging cellular systems and cancerous ones. The increased graying of the U.S. population and the increased evidence of age-related cancer indicates that there will be increased health care costs to be born by the health care system. Understanding of the dynamics of such a complex biological system will allow us to understand better how to treat cancer in an individual of advanced years.

Project Human Beyond the complexity of such ultra-largescale simulations and models is the no longer unreasonable goal of an ultra-largescale simulation of a human being. Such a simulation would rely upon the patient's image data, non-invasive measurements of physiological functions, and assorted clinical tests. One can begin to hypothesize scenarios in which the effects of chemotherapy can be simulated before actual therapy is performed. Radical and new drug treatments can be simulated and results examined and evaluated, based upon an integrated model and patient system. Eventually, one can envision the possibility of actually testing newly designed drugs in computer-based large-scale simulations. Project Human is slowly becoming a practical reality.

Computational Population Biology

The study of populations, particularly human populations, is called *demography*. Demographic models generally involve hyperbolic partial differential equations or their approximations. The canonical system is the McKendrick/Von Foerster system given by

$$
\begin{cases}
\dfrac{\partial n(t,a)}{\partial t} + \dfrac{\partial n(t,a)}{\partial a} = -\mu(t, a, ...)n(t, a) \\[2ex]
n(t, 0) = \displaystyle\int_0^\infty \lambda(t, a, ...)n(t, a)da \\[2ex]
n(0, a) = n_0(a)
\end{cases}
$$

where $n(t,a)$ is the number (or density) of individuals of age a at time t, $\mu(t, a, ...)$ is the per capita mortality rate, $\lambda(t, a, ...)$ is the per capita birth rate, and $n_0(a)$ is a given initial population distribution. Should we choose to discretize a into a discrete age-class structure, we obtain a system of ordinary differential equations that approximate the original partial differential equation system. The study of such models is of great interest for a number of reasons. In particular, given the increasing cost of health care and the associated increase of the aged component of the population, it is of great importance to understand the dynamics of the human population in an effort to hold down the cost of health care. In addition, models of this type arise in the study of toxicological effects of the environment upon a population (ecotoxicology). For example, how does PCB exposure (at the molecular level—computational molecular biology) affect the dynamics of the liver (at the organ level—computational physiology)? And how is this result seen at the population level (the demographic level—computational population biology)?

Mathematical modeling of diseases, particularly of such diseases as AIDS and Lyme disease, requires the use of computational methods. The models are routinely complex, often stochastic in nature, and quite frequently intractable to analytic solution. Models of this class have been studied by Hyman et al. at Los Alamos National Laboratories and Levin et al. at Cornell University.

Epidemiology and biostatistics involve the study of population dynamics and characteristics from a probabilistic perspective. Clinical trials often generate large data sets. Statistical analysis of these data sets is often intense, due to the sample size and the complexity of the interactions. In addition, there are often issues of multicenter trials and the more recent problems arising in metastatistical analysis, the integration of originally disjoint data sets for the purposes of statistical analysis. In general, this class of problem is both computer dependent and computer intensive.

Computational Chemistry

The field of computational chemistry is readily divided into the following three major topic areas: (1) *biophysical properties*, such as crystallographic reconstruction and molecular visualization, (2) *molecular biochemistry* which encompasses such areas as structure/function studies, enzyme/substrate studies (reaction studies, pathway analysis), and protein dynamics and their properties, and (3) *pharmacokinetics/pharmacodynamics*, which encompasses such areas as interactive molecular modeling, drug design/drug interactions (cancer chemotherapy, orphan drugs), binding studies (binding site properties), structure/function relationships as applied to drug effectiveness, and cell receptor structures. All of these areas involve intensive numeric computation and subsequent real time graphics for the visualization of the final molecular/chemical structures. The computations are so intensive that a number of specialized high speed superworkstations dedicated to real time rapid visualization of chemistry/pharmacology-oriented problems are currently being marketed. Neural nets (Wilcox at Minnesota Supercomputing Center, Liebman at Amoco Technology Corporation) are being used to identify similar protein structures based upon recognition of pattern representations for the three-dimensional structure of proteins. This work is so computationally intensive, particularly in the early learning stages, that it is performed on a vector supercomputer.

Agricultural/Veterinary Applications

The same issues that arise in human populations—the spread of disease, environmental impact analysis, and epidemiology—also arise in animal and insect populations. One can investigate, through simulation modeling, such issues as crop yield, milk yield, nutritional demands, and more complex problems, such as the interaction between genotype and environment as it relates to dairy herd location. Other investigators have looked at breeding scheme problems in an effort to study the effects of genetic changes and genetic drift, with the goal of maximizing milk yield in a dairy herd or meat yield in a swine population. Finally, other investigators have been examining the question of how competing plants interact in an environment containing limited resources. These models and simulations have been extended to include pest management methods. Similar models exist for fisheries and for forestry management.

Computational Dentistry

What can be done with visualizing the bones and muscles in the torso can also be done with the jaw and the facial muscles. Many dental schools are collaborating with mechanical and biomedical engineers for the purpose of finite element (*q.v.*) modeling of the jaw (Michael Day at the University of Louisville). The resultant models are then applied to examining the problems of orthodonture and of computer-automated patient-based, dental prosthetics design.

One of the greatest dental health care costs is that associated with TMJ (Temporal Mandibular Joint syndrome). ETA Systems, in collaboration with the School of Dentistry at the University of Texas Health Science Center San Antonio, is developing a neuromuscular joint model, in an effort to study TMJ syndrome. The model involves not only the use of sophisticated mathematical equations to describe the dynamics of the bones and muscles of the jaw, but also patient-based data as input for describing these same structures. Thus, the models will be based upon real patient data, rather than hypothesized and/or idealized dental structures. Such models require use of a supercomputer, not only as a computation engine for model simulation, but also as an image processing system to facilitate the handling of patient-based image data (CAT, NMR, PET, etc.).

Second only to the problem of TMJ syndrome is that of periodontal disease. This complex interplay between the bacterial ecology of the patient's mouth and the basic physiology of the patient is not very well understood. In a newly initiated project between the University of Texas Health Science Center, the University-Industrial Consortium, and International BioComputing Technologies, an ultra–largescale simulation of the mouth and its bacterial environment is being developed. The purpose is to develop a method for better understanding how periodontal disease occurs, what factors may influence progression of the disease, and how it can be better treated.

The Matrix of Biological Knowledge Current understanding of biology involves complex relationships rooted in enormous amounts of data obtained from numerous experiments and observations and gleaned from diverse disciplines. As a consequence of these harsh realities, few scientists are capable of staying abreast of the ever increasing knowledge base, let alone searching that database for new and/or unsuspected biological phenomena. Yet hidden within the complete database of published biological experiments—*the matrix of biological knowledge*—lies the potential for developing a new and powerful tool for the investigation of biological principles. Many databases of biological information already exist. Perhaps the best known of these is GenBank, the database of all known gene sequences. This project is, in some sense, an outgrowth of the Human Genome Project, a worldwide effort to sequence the entire human genome. The Human Genome Project will require massive computer support in such areas as numerical computation, searching algorithms, and database design. As these databases increase in size and complexity, it becomes increasingly important that effective and efficient user interfaces be developed. One can envision user interfaces incorporating knowledge engineering, advanced graphics and mathematical capabilities, and simulation engines. The future of biocomputing is one of great excitement.

References

1971. Guyton, A.C. *Textbook of Medical Physiology.* Philadelphia: W.B. Saunders Company.
1983. Witten, M. (Ed.) *Advances in Hyperbolic Partial Differential Equations.* New York: Pergamon Press.
1987. Witten, M. (Ed.) *Advances In Mathematics and Computers in Medicine—1.* New York: Pergamon Press.
1987. Winfree, A.T., *When Time Breaks Down.* Princeton, NJ: Princeton University Press.
1987. Lagerlund, T.D. and Low, P.A. "A Mathematical Simulation of Oxygen Delivery in Rat Peripheral Nerve," *Microvascular Research,* **34**: 211.
1987. Morowitz, H. and Smith, T. *Report of The Matrix of Biological Knowledge Workshop.* Santa Fe Institute, New Mexico.
1988. Weiss, R., "High-Tech Tooth Repair," *Science News,* **134**: 376–379.
1988. Robb, R. "At Mayo, Healers Digitally Peer into the Human Machine," *Computer Graphics Today,* December: **8**.
1989. Witten, M. (Ed.) *Advances in Mathematics and Computers in Medicine—2.* New York: Pergamon Press.
1989. Peskin, C.S. and McQueen, D.M. "A Three Dimensional Computational Method for Blood Flow in The Heart: Immersed Elastic Fibers in a Viscous Incompressible Fluid," *J. Comput. Phys.,* **81**, *2*, 372–405.
1989. Spitzer, V.M. and Whitlock, D.G. "A 3-D Database of Human Anatomy," *Advanced Imaging,* March: 48–49.
1989. Witten, M., "Modeling the Aging-Cancer Interface: Some Thoughts on a Complex Biological Dynamics," *Journal of Gerontology,* **44**, *6*, 72–80.

MATTHEW WITTEN

BIOS

For articles on related subjects *see* IBM-PC AND PC-COMPATIBLES; INPUT-OUTPUT CONTROL SYSTEM; KERNEL; and LOGIN FILE.

The *basic input output system* (BIOS) of the disk operating system (DOS) for a typical microcomputer is the portion of the operating system (*q.v.*) that provides an interface between the DOS kernel and the underlying hardware. The kernel is the portion of DOS closest to the application software. It is responsible for process control, memory management, file management, and peripheral support. The kernel passes commands from the application software to the BIOS for translation into hardware-specific requests.

The BIOS consists of two parts. The firmware (*q.v.*) portion is encoded in PROM chips that cannot be erased by the user. This portion is essentially a table of interrupts (*q.v.*) and some executable code for servicing the interrupt requests. A changeable and extensible portion of the BIOS sits in files, usually hidden, on the boot disk (*see* BOOT AND REBOOT). On IBM PCs and compatibles, these files are named IO.SYS or IBMBIO.COM.

The BIOS is responsible for system checking at start-up time. It is also the module that translates commands to specific peripherals and devices into a language that the hardware can handle. The original IBM BIOS for the PC also contained part of the Basic language, but this is no longer common.

To avoid copyright infringement, manufacturers of IBM-compatible micros emulate the functions of the IBM BIOS without copying the actual code. The relative ease with which this can be done was a major factor in the rise of so many vendors capable of producing low-cost microcomputers that are 100% compatible with the IBM-PC. As long as software operates through the BIOS and only through the BIOS, compatibility can be assured.

The BIOS, however, does not support all of the hardware's capabilities. Hardware designers cannot conceive all the uses that software might want to make of new devices. The BIOS is also quite slow at many tasks, especially video graphics. Many software authors choose to bypass the BIOS and program the hardware directly. This leads to increased performance, but there is then a danger that the program will not work on all machines, especially ones whose plug-in boards and other devices are slightly out of standard.

Devices that were not available when BIOS code was originally burned into PROM can be accommodated by DEVICE commands in CONFIG.SYS files, commands that access the extensible portion of the BIOS that resides on disk (*see* LOGIN FILE).

STEPHEN J. ROGOWSKI

BIT SLICING

For articles on related subjects *see* ARITHMETIC-LOGIC UNIT; and INTEGRATED CIRCUITRY.

Bit slicing refers to the technique of constructing an m-bit arithmetic-logic unit (ALU) by interconnecting a set of identical n-bit ($n \leq m$) LSI chips called *bit slices*. Bit slice chips—typically, one, two, or four bits wide—contain all of the circuits necessary to perform a large number of ALU functions, including arithmetic, logic, register storage, and even I/O, for their segment of a processor word. Then, for example, four four-bit slices may be combined to form the CPU of a 16-bit computer.

While the interconnection of functional components within each integrated circuit (IC) may be rigidly predefined, it is usual to include a degree of flexibility under the control of peripheral pin connections on which signals are established by an external microprogrammed controller (see Fig. 1). Such signals are usually connected in parallel to the corresponding peripheral pins of each slice. Accordingly, the complexity of the controller is to a degree independent of the length m of the ALU formed. Thus, the bit slice approach is most cost-effective for long word-length computer designs.

However, the major advantage of bit slicing is to provide a rational basis for packaging very high-speed, high-performance circuits in a reasonable number of IC chips, each with limitations on die area, pin count, and

power dissipation. As a result of this approach, high-speed, high-power bipolar circuit technology can be used. For example, the Schottky TTL AMD 2900 series four-bit chip set operates with a 100-ns microcycle, while the ECL M10800 four-bit family performs typical micro-operations in tens of nanoseconds.

The same motives for bit slicing extend as well to memory construction. Thus, a semiconductor memory system is normally sliced vertically, each m bit word being resident in several n bit ($n \leq m$) slices.

References

1978. Hamacher, V. C., Vranesic, Z. G., and Zaky, S. G. *Computer Organization.* New York: McGraw-Hill.

KENNETH C. SMITH

BLOCK AND BLOCKING FACTOR

For articles on related subjects *see* FILE; MEMORY: AUXILIARY; OPEN AND CLOSE A FILE; and RECORD.

The term *block* is synonymous with *physical record:* A sequence of words or characters written contiguously by a computer on an external storage medium. Typically, one block is written each time a WRITE command is executed by an I/O channel (or equivalent I/O facility). Analogously, one block is read from an external medium each time that a READ command is executed by the channel.

The idea of a *block* is distinguished from that of a *logical record* as follows: A block is defined by the physical characteristics and constraints of the external storage medium, whereas a logical record is defined by a particular data structure in a processing program. Logical records (often shortened to "records," although this term is also loosely used for "blocks") are aggregates of data, such as bits, numbers, and character strings which are naturally and conveniently transmitted at one time from the main storage of a computer to an external medium. One type of data aggregate is a *master record*, comprising all attributes associated with a member of some population.

Blocks typically contain several logical records when written onto magnetic media such as drums, tape drives, and disk drives. The size of a block is chosen to take into account the software characteristics of a system (e.g. buffer size) and the hardware characteristics of the external medium (so as to avoid too much starting or stopping when reading or writing tape). In the case of fixed-length blocks, the standard format is as shown in Fig. 1. For fixed-length logical records, the number of records per block is called the *blocking factor*. For many computers (e.g. current IBM models), variable-length logical records are formatted into blocks, as shown in Fig. 2. Fig. 3 shows how large variable length logical records can be built up from smaller fixed-size blocks to obtain the *spanned record* format.

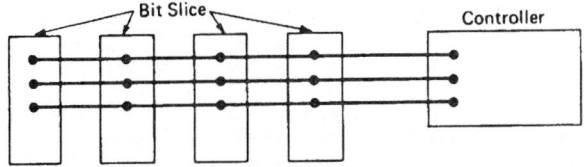

FIG. 1.   Conceptual view of a (16-bit) ALU consisting of four (four-bit) slices operated in parallel by a (shared) controller. Only three of the many control lines are shown.

DAVID N. FREEMAN

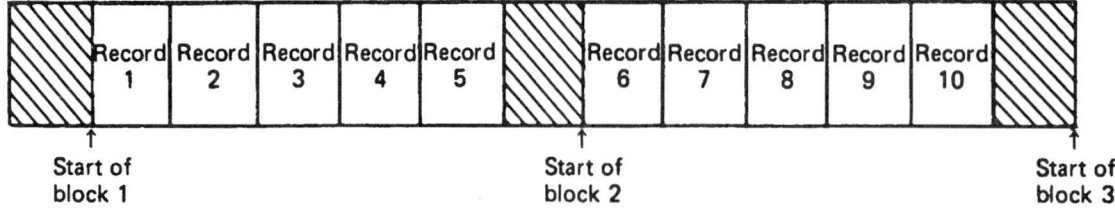

FIG. 1. Fixed-length blocks: blocking factor = 5; all records have same length; block length = 5 × (record length).

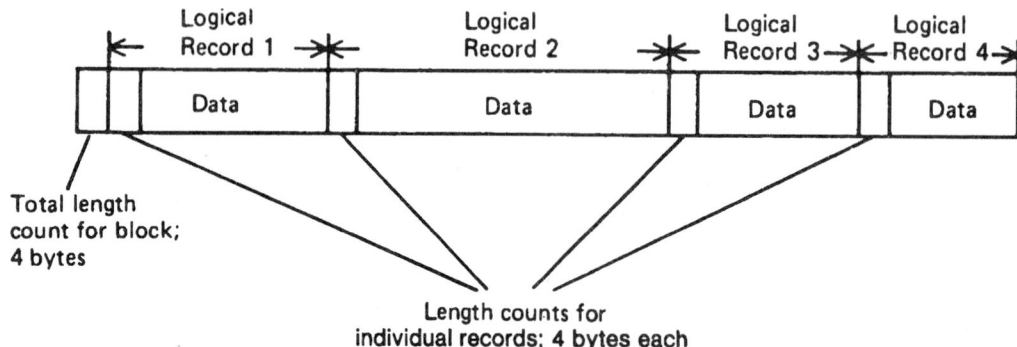

FIG. 2. Variable-block lengths (no logical record larger than one physical block): blocking factor, variable; block length = 4 + [(length of record-1) + 4] + [(length of record-2) + 4] +...

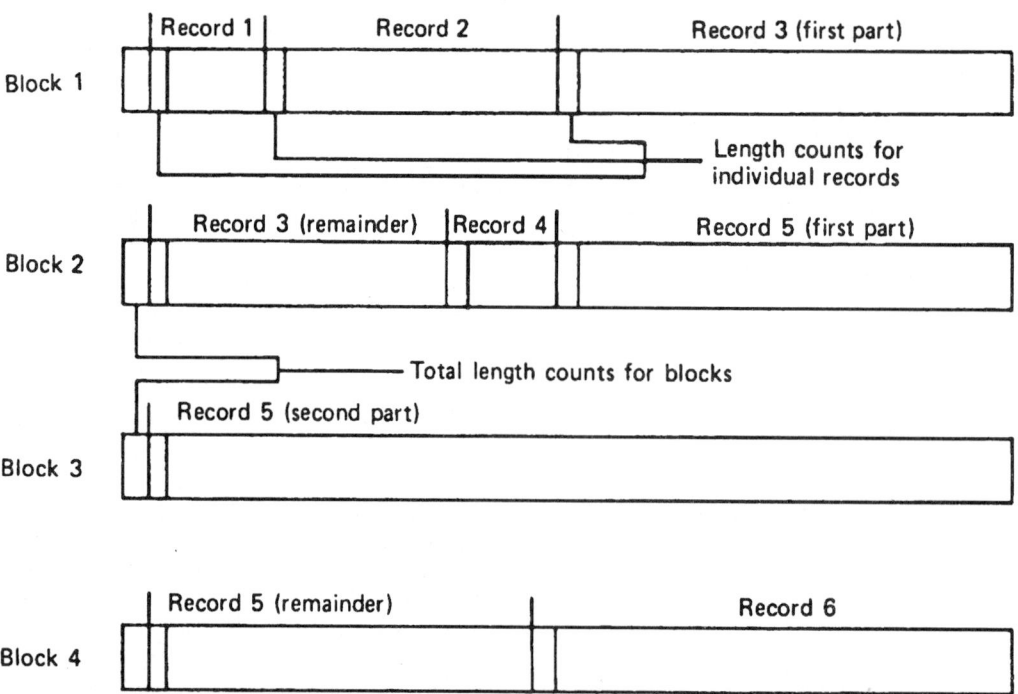

FIG 3. Variable-length records (which may be larger than fixed-length physical blocks).

BLOCK STRUCTURE

For articles on related subjects *see* ACTIVATION RECORD; CLASS; CONTROL STRUCTURE; PROCEDURE; PROCEDURE-ORIENTED LANGUAGES; PROGRAMMING LANGUAGES; and STRUCTURED PROGRAMMING.

Block structure is a programming language concept that allows related declarations and statements to be grouped together. When used judiciously, it can help transform a large, unwieldy program into a disciplined, well-structured, easy-to-understand program.

Because of the important function it performs, block structure (first introduced in Algol 60) is found in one form or another in many procedural languages developed after 1960.

A Programmer's View of Block Structure

From the programmer's point of view, block structure performs two major functions:

1. It allows a sequence of executable statements to be grouped into a single *compound statement*.
2. It provides explicit control over the allocation of storage to variables and over the programmer's ability to refer to variables.

The first function means that we can create and use a compound statement anywhere that the programming language allows a single statement to be used (e.g. in either branch of an **if-then-else** statement). This allows us to think of a sequence of statements as a single entity and thus simplify the process of program construction. Since a block may contain other blocks as components, block structure can be used to decompose a large program into an orderly nest of blocks. This is perhaps the most important use of block structure from the programmer's point of view, since it allows programs to be constructed in a hierarchical fashion which often results in increased program clarity and elegance.

Control over storage allocation and visibility of variables implies two things. First there is the ability to control dynamically the allocation and freeing of storage during program execution. The storage for variables declared within a block is allocated when the block is entered during program execution. Unless explicitly inhibited, this storage is freed automatically when the block is exited. Second, each block introduces a new *scope* (i.e. a domain of definition of variables). Variables declared within a block (i.e. local to the block) may be used only within that block (and any contained block). Thus, variables declared within a block can have no effect on the program outside of the block. This provides a degree of data security, since a programmer can use a block to "hide" variables (*information hiding - q.v.*) and thereby make them inaccessible outside of this block.

In order to appreciate the importance of block structure, let us consider the Algol 60 code segment in Fig. 1.

In the program in Fig. 1, the first block is used to declare the global variables *sumx, sumxx, x*, and *y*. The

```
begin
   comment first block - main program;
   integer sumx, sumxx;
   integer array x[1:100];
   real array y[1:50];
   ...
   begin
      comment second block;
      integer p,y;
      integer array xx[1:100];
      sumx := sumxx := 0;
      for p := 1 step 1 until 100 do
         begin
            comment third block;
            sumx := sumx + x[p];
            xx[p] := x[p] * x[p];
            sumxx := sumxx + xx[p]
         end;
      for p := 1 step 1 until 100 do
         x[p] := xx[p] ÷ sumxx
   end
end;
```

FIG. 1. An Algol program exhibiting block structure.

second block is used to introduce the new variables *p, y*, and *xx*. Storage for these variables will exist only while execution is in the block. The third block is used to group three assignment statements so that they behave as one statement in the body of the first **for** loop.

Using Block Structure in Programs The material in this section has been adopted from Wegner (1971).

Declarations In most block-structured programming languages, a block has the form:

```
begin
   <block head>
   <block body>
end
```

A <block head> consists of a (possibly empty) list of variable, procedure, and function declarations. A <block body> consists of a list of executable statements. The rules of Algol 60 state that all identifiers (e.g. names of variables) used within a block have to be declared in its block head or in the block head of some enclosing block. Identifiers can be used only within the block in which they are declared (including any contained blocks). This block is their *scope* and they are said to be *local* to it.

In addition to scalar variables, arrays may also be declared in the block head. In Algol 60, the expressions defining the lower and upper bounds for arrays are recalculated each time the block is activated. Thus, the bounds for a given array variable can be different for different activations of the same block.

Scope Rules A block body is a sequence of executable statements and a block is itself an executable statement.

Therefore, blocks may be nested to any depth. This has several consequences:

1. Although an identifier may be used only once as the name of an object in a block, the same identifier may be used to name different objects in different blocks. A good programmer will use this facility sparingly (e.g. for utility variables like i, j, k used as counters and loop indices). Widespread re-use of identifiers can make a program difficult to understand.

2. If the same identifier is used to name objects in several nested blocks, the programming language's *scope rule* is used to disambiguate references to the identifier. The *Algol 60 scope rule* (used in most procedural languages) starts at the point where the identifier is used and searches block heads starting with the block containing the use of the identifier and working outward toward the main program block until a declaration of the identifier is found. Note that with this rule the redeclaration of an identifier in an inner block will make the object named by the same identifier in an outer block inaccessible. For example, in Fig 1., the declaration of an integer variable y in the second block makes the real array y declared in the main program inaccessible in the second block (and in all contained blocks).

3. Whenever a block is entered during program execution, fresh storage is allocated for all the variables declared in the block head. This storage, known as the *activation record* of the block, defines a particular instance of the block in time. When execution leaves the block, the storage occupied by the activation record is freed. In most procedural languages, the allocation and freeing of activation records follows a strict last-in-first-out discipline. This implies that a stack mechanism is ideally suited for the storage of activation records. This also facilitates the implementation of recursive procedures (*see* RECURSION).

Fig. 2 illustrates these points. The identifier b is used to name variables in both the first and second blocks. In the block that is the body of the procedure P, the variable x declared in the first block is inaccessible because the identifier x was also used to name a formal parameter of P; the variable c declared in the first block is inaccessible in the body of P because another variable named c is declared there. In the assignment statement in the body of P, the identifier c refers to the variable c declared in P, the identifier x refers to a formal parameter of P, and the identifier b refers to the variable b declared in the first block.

Two Examples   Algol 60 and Pascal illustrate two approaches to providing block structure in a high-level pro-

```
begin
    comment first block;
    real c, b, x;
    procedure P(x,y);
        real x, y;
        begin
            comment body of P;
            real c;
            ...
            b := x + c;
            ...
        end P;
        begin
            comment second block;
            real b, d;
            ...
            P(d,b);
            ...
        end
end;
```

FIG. 2.   Block structure example.

gramming language. In Algol 60, a block may be used anywhere that a statement can be used. Any block can contain declarations and thus introduce new variables. In Pascal, declarations may appear as a prefix to a block that is the body of a *function* or *procedure*. No other blocks may contain declarations and therefore such blocks can be used only to group statements to form a *compound statement*.

References

1964. Randell, B. and Russell, L. S. *Algol 60 Implementation*. New York: Academic Press.
1967. Eckman, T. and Froberg, C. E. *Introduction to Algol 60*. London: Oxford University Press. (This book contains the complete text of the revised Algol 60 report, as well as a good discussion of the control and data structures of Algol 60.)
1971. Wegner, P. "Structured Model Building in Computer Science." Department of Applied Mathematics, Brown University, Providence, RI.
1975. Pratt, T. W. *Programming Languages: Design and Implementation*. Englewood Cliffs, NJ: Prentice-Hall.

DAVID B. WORTMAN

BNF.   *See* BACKUS-NAUR FORM.

BOOLE, GEORGE

For an article on a related subject *see* BOOLEAN ALGEBRA.

George Boole (b. Lincoln, England, 1815; d. Cork, Ireland, 1864) was one of those rarities in an era of increasing specialization: the self-taught man who followed his own path to the penetration of territory untouched by his contemporaries. Due to the family's sparse financial resources, Boole's formal education was limited to elementary school and a short stint in a commercial school. Beyond this he was almost totally self-educated.

Boole's first scientific publication was an address on Newton to mark the presentation of a bust of Newton to the Mechanics Institution in Lincoln. In 1840 he wrote his first paper for the *Cambridge Mathematical Journal*. In 1849, despite his lack of formal training, he was appointed to a professorship of mathematics in the newly established Queen's College, Cork, Ireland.

During his career he published approximately fifty scientific papers, two textbooks (on differential equations, 1859; and finite differences, 1860), and his two famous volumes on mathematical logic (*see* References). In 1844, the Royal Society awarded him a medal for his papers on differential operators, and, in 1857, they elected him a Fellow. He was married in 1855 to Mary Everest, a niece of Sir George Everest, after whom Mount Everest was named.

Although Boole made significant contributions in a number of areas of mathematics, his immortality stems from his two works that gave decisive impetus to the need to express logical concepts in mathematical form: "The Mathematical Analysis of Logic, Being an Essay Towards a Calculus of Deductive Reasoning" (1847) and "An Investigation of the Laws of Thought, on Which are Founded the Mathematical Theories of Logic and Probability" (1854). Through these works he truly became the founder of modern symbolic logic. He reduced logic to a propositional calculus, now often called *boolean algebra*, which was extremely simple and perhaps too strongly based upon classical logic.

Under the influence of his work, a school of symbolic logic evolved which made a determined effort to unify logic and mathematics. As is usual, the impact of this effort was not realized until the latter part of the nineteenth century. Although DeMorgan and Jevons expounded on his work during Boole's lifetime, it remained for Frege, Peano, and C. S. Peirce to relight the torch that finally led to the "Principia Mathematica" (1910–1913) of Russell and Whitehead.

Boole's discovery that the symbolism of algebra could be used in logic has had wide impact in the twentieth century. Today, boolean algebra is important not only in logic but also in the theory of probability, the theory of lattices, the geometry of sets, and information theory (*q.v.*). It has also led to the design of electronic computers through the interpretation of boolean combinations of sets as switching circuits. For example, the logical sum of two sets corresponds to a circuit with two switches in parallel and the logical product corresponds to a pair of switches in series.

References

1916. MacFarlane, Alexander. *Lectures on Ten British Mathematicians of the Nineteenth Century*, pp. 50–63. New York: John Wiley & Sons.
1937. Bell, E.T. *Men of Mathematics*. New York: Simon & Schuster.
1970. Broadbent, T. A. A., "George Boole," in *Dictionary of Scientific Biography* II:293-298. New York: Scribners. (This is an outstanding biography with an excellent bibliography of both primary and secondary sources.)
1982. Smith, G.C. *The Boole-DeMorgan Correspondence* Oxford, England: Clarendon Press.

HENRY S. TROPP

BOOLEAN ALGEBRA

For articles on related subjects *see* ARITHMETIC, COMPUTER; BOOLE, GEORGE; DISCRETE MATHEMATICS; LOGIC DESIGN; and LOGIC PROGRAMMING.

The concept of a *boolean algebra* was first proposed by the English mathematician George Boole in 1847. Since that time, Boole's original conception has been extensively developed and refined by algebraists and logicians. The relationships among boolean algebra, set algebra, logic, and binary arithmetic have given boolean algebras a central role in the development of electronic digital computers.

Set Algebras The most intuitive development of boolean algebras arises from the concept of a *set algebra*. Let $S = \{a,b,c\}$ and $T = \{a,b,c,d,e\}$ be two sets consisting of three and five elements, respectively. We say that S is a *subset* of T, since every element of S (namely, a, b, and c) belongs to T. Since T has five elements, there are 2^5 subsets of T, for we may choose any individual element to be included or omitted from a subset. Note that these 32 subsets include T itself and the empty set, which contains no elements at all. If T contains all elements of concern, it is called the *universal set*. Given a subset of T, such as S, we may define the *complement* of S with respect to a universal set T to consist of precisely those elements of T that are not included in the given subset. Thus, S as above defined has as its complement (with respect to T) $\overline{S} = \{d, e\}$. The *union* of any two sets (subsets of a given set) consists of those elements that are in one or the other or in both given sets; the *intersection* of two sets consists of those elements that are in both given sets. We use the symbol $\cup$ to denote the union, and $\cap$ to denote the intersection of two sets. For example, if $B = \{b, d, e\}$, then $B \cup S = \{a, b, c, d, e\}$, and $B \cap S = \{b\}$.

While other set operations may be defined, the operations of complementation, union, and intersection are of primary interest. A boolean algebra is a finite or infinite set of elements together with three operations—negation, addition, and multiplication—that correspond to the set operations of complementation, union, and intersection, respectively. Among the elements of a boolean algebra are two distinguished elements: 0, corresponding to the empty set; and 1, corresponding to the universal set. For any given element a of a boolean algebra, there is a unique complement a' with the property that $a 1 a' = 1$ and $aa' = 0$. Boolean addition and multiplication are associative and commutative, as are ordinary addition and multiplication, but otherwise have somewhat different properties. The principal properties are given in Table 1, where a, b, and c are any elements of a boolean algebra.

Since a finite set of n elements has exactly 2^n subsets, and it can be shown that the finite boolean algebras are precisely the finite set algebras, each finite boolean algebra consists of exactly 2^n elements for some integer n. For example, the set algebra for the set T defined above corresponds to a boolean algebra of 32 elements. Tables 2 and 3 define the boolean operations for boolean algebras of two and four elements, respectively.

While it is possible to use a different symbol to denote each element of a boolean algebra, it is often more useful to represent the 2^n elements of a finite boolean algebra by binary vectors having n components. With such a representation the operations of the boolean algebra are accomplished componentwise by considering each component as an independent two-element boolean algebra. This corresponds to representing subsets of a finite set by binary vectors. For example, since the set T has five elements, we may represent its subsets by five-component binary vectors, each component denoting an element of the set T. A numeral 1 in the ith component of the vector denotes the inclusion of the ith element of that particular subset; a 0 denotes its exclusion. Thus, the subset $S = \{a,b,c\}$ has the binary vector representation $\{1,1,1,0,0\}$. The set operations become boolean operations on the components of the vectors. This representation of sets, and the correspondence to boolean or logical operations, is very useful in information retrieval (*q.v.*). Because of it, sets of document and query characteristics may be easily and rapidly matched.

TABLE 1

Distributivity:	$a(b + c) 5 ab + ac$
	$a + (bc)=(a + b)(a + c)$
Idempotency:	$a + a = a$
	$aa = a$
Absorption laws:	$a + ab = a$
	$a(a + b) = a$
DeMorgan's laws:	$(a + b)' = a'\,b'$
	$(ab)' = a' + b'$

TABLE 2. Two elements

$a + b$	0 1	$a \cdot b$	0 1	a	a'
0	0 1	0	0 0	0	1
1	1 1	1	0 1	1	0

TABLE 3. Four elements.

$a + b$	0	p	p'	1	$a \cdot b$	0	p	p'	1	a	a'
0	0	p	p'	1	0	0	0	0	0	0	1
p	p	p	1	1	p	0	p	0	p	p	p'
p'	p'	1	p'	1	p'	0	0	p	p'	p'	p
1	1	1	1	1	1	0	p	p'	1	1	0

Propositional Calculus

In information retrieval work, and in identifying boolean algebras as set algebras, we find that various logical connectives, such as "and," "or," and "not," recur frequently. Thus, it is not surprising to find that the two-element boolean algebra can be identified with elementary logic or propositional calculus. A *proposition* is a statement that can be said to be either true or false. We will denote propositions by letters such as p, q, and r.

The connectives or operators "and" and "or" combine two such propositions into a new one. If we consider two propositions, p and q, each may, independently of the other, assume the value true (T) or false (F). Hence, together, the ordered pair $\langle p, q \rangle$ may assume $2 \cdot 2 = 4$ combinations of truth values: $\langle T,T \rangle, \langle T,F \rangle, \langle F,T \rangle$, and $\langle F,F \rangle$. If o denotes a binary operator, then p o q may assume either (T) or (F) independently for each of these four T-F combinations. Thus, we can define $2^4 = 16$ distinct binary logical operators, as shown in Table 4. Of the 16 binary logical operators that can be defined, 5 are commonly used and are more than sufficient to define the remaining operators.

The "negation" or "not" operation, $\sim p$, is defined to form a proposition that is true precisely when the proposition p is false, and false whenever p is true. If we equate the truth values "true" and "false" with the boolean values 1 and 0, respectively, then we find that negation corresponds to boolean complementation. That is, $\sim p$ replaces the value "true" with "false," and vice versa, just as p' replaces the value "1" with "0," and vice versa. (In Table 4, column 13 is $\sim p$ and column 11 is $\sim q$).

The logical "conjunction" or "and," $p \wedge q$, forms a proposition that is true precisely when both p and q are true, and is false otherwise. This corresponds to the boolean operation of multiplication, with the boolean expression pq having the value 1 if and only if both p and q have the value 1. (See Table 4, column 8.)

In ordinary usage the word "or" has two distinct meanings, referred to as the "inclusive or" and the "exclusive or." In the inclusive sense, the statement "p or q" is true if p or q or both are true; in the exclusive sense, the same statement is true if either p or q, but not both, is true. The logical "disjunction" or "or," $p \vee q$, is defined to be the inclusive "or." That is, $p \vee q$ is true precisely when at least one of the statements p and q is true. Thus, this operation corresponds to boolean addition as we have defined it. (See Table 4, column 2.)

The exclusive "or," $p \not\equiv q$, is commonly called *inequivalence*, since it defines a proposition that is true precisely when p and q have opposite or inequivalent truth values. This corresponds to any of several more

TABLE 4

p	q	1	2	3	4	5	6	7	8	9	10	11	12	13	14	15	16
T	T	T	T	T	T	T	T	T	T	F	F	F	F	F	F	F	F
T	F	T	T	T	T	F	F	F	F	T	T	T	T	F	F	F	F
F	T	T	T	F	F	T	T	F	F	T	T	F	F	T	T	F	F
F	F	T	F	T	F	T	F	T	F	T	F	T	F	T	F	T	F

complex boolean operations such as $pq' + p'q$, and $(p + q)(pq)'$. (See Table 4, column 10.)

The remaining conventional logical operator is the *conditional* or *implication*, $p \supset q$, corresponding to the statement "if p then q." The conditional proposition $p \supset q$ takes the value "false" if p is true and q is false, and takes the value "true" otherwise. Thus, it corresponds to the boolean operation $p' + q$. Note that if p is false, then $p \supset q$ is true, regardless of the value of q. This corresponds to the statement that one can prove anything (q, whether true or false) from a false hypothesis (p). (See Table 4, column 5.)

While the logical operators that we have defined suffice to define all logical operators, it is only necessary to use two of the above operators, namely, negation, and one of the operators conjunction, disjunction, or conditional. However, of importance to computer design is the fact that we can define all logical operators in terms of one basic operator, either the "nand" or the "nor" operator. These are the negation of the conjunction and disjunction operators, respectively. That is, the "nand" operator defines a statement, $p \mid q$, which has the value "false" precisely when both p and q are true, and the value "true" otherwise. The "nor" operator defines a statement, $p \downarrow q$, which has the value "true" precisely when both p and q are false, and the value "false" otherwise. (See Table 4, columns 9 and 15.)

Truth Tables A *truth table* gives the truth values of a logical expression for each combination of the truth values of its variables. Thus, for a logical expression in n variables, the truth table contains 2^n lines, one for each combination of truth values of its variables. Since the truth value of an expression is determined from the truth values of various subexpressions, the truth table may be given in an extended form, which explicitly lists all subexpressions, a standard form in which the subexpressions are not separately listed and a condensed form in which the lines of the table are compressed by indicating the truth value of certain critical subexpressions. Tables 5 through 7 illustrate these three forms of truth table for the logical expression

$$(p \equiv q) \supset \sim (((p \lor \sim r) \land (\sim p \lor q)) \supset r).$$

In each of these three tables the truth values for the given expression are in the boxed column. In the con-

densed form, Table 7, each line of the table may represent one or more lines of the uncondensed table. For example, the first line of Table 7 represents the two lines TFT and TFF of the uncondensed table. In this particular example, the line FTF is represented three times, namely, in lines 2, 3, and 4 of Table 7. Also in the condensed table, the dashes represent values that are immaterial and hence do not need to be calculated. For example, in the first line of Table 7, since $p \equiv q$ is false we know that the entire expression has the value "true," regardless of the value of the remaining portion of the expression.

The truth table for an unknown logical function can be used to generate an expression for that function. The expression thus generated is called a *disjunctive normal form* or, in boolean algebra, a *sum of products form*. The development of this expression is illustrated in Table 8. For each line of the table wherein the unknown function has the value "true," an expression is formed by taking the conjunction of all variables that are true in that line and the negations of all variables that are false in that line. The expression for the function f is then the disjunction of all expressions formed for the single lines. In Table 8, f is given in this form, and in the corresponding boolean algebra form, as well as in a shorter form developed by direct inspection of the function values. (Equivalence, $\equiv$, is defined by column 7 of Table 4.)

The development of the disjunctive normal form shows that the logical operators conjunction, disjunction, and negation are sufficient to develop an expression for any logical function. Furthermore, we may use DeMorgan's laws to transform conjunctions to disjunctions, or vice versa. Thus, as we previously asserted, any logical function can be developed from the operators negation and either conjunction or disjunction. Table 9 shows the development of the five common logical operators in terms of these two minimal combinations of operators. In turn, Table 10 shows the development of negation, conjunction, and disjunction in terms of both the "nand" and the "nor" operators, thus indicating that every logical operator can be defined in terms of either one of these latter two operators.

Duality There is a symmetry in the operations of addition and multiplication with a boolean algebra, which is captured in the Principle of Duality:

If a given statement holds in a boolean algebra, then

TABLE 5

p q r	(1) $p \equiv q$	(2) $p \lor \sim r$	(3) $\sim p \lor q$	(4) (2)$\land$(3)	(5) (4)$\supset r$	(6) $\sim$(5)	Expression (1)$\supset$(6)
T T T	T	T	T	T	T	F	F
T T F	T	T	T	T	F	T	T
T F T	F	T	F	F	T	F	T
T F F	F	T	F	F	T	F	T
F T T	F	F	T	F	T	F	T
F T F	F	T	T	T	F	T	T
F F T	T	F	T	F	T	F	F
F F F	T	T	T	T	F	T	T

TABLE 6

p	q	r	(p≡q)	⊃	~	(((p∨~r)∧(~p∨q))⊃r)			
T	T	T	T	F	F	T	T	T	T
T	T	F	T	T	T	T	T	T	F
T	F	T	F	T	F	T	F	F	T
T	F	F	F	T	F	T	F	F	T
F	T	T	F	T	F	F	F	T	T
F	T	F	F	T	T	T	T	T	F
F	F	T	T	F	F	F	F	T	T
F	F	F	T	T	T	T	T	T	F

TABLE 7

p	q	r	(p≡q)	⊃	~	(((p∨~r)∧(~p∨q))⊃r)			
T	F	–	F	T	–	–	–	–	–
F	T	–	F	T	–	–	–	–	–
F	–	F	–	T	T	T	T	T	F
–	T	F	–	T	T	T	T	T	F
T	T	T	T	F	F	–	–	–	T
F	F	T	T	F	F	–	–	–	T

TABLE 8

p	q	r	f(p,q,r)	Generated expression
T	T	T	F	–
T	T	F	T	p∧q∧~r
T	F	T	T	p∧~q∧r
T	F	F	F	–
F	T	T	T	~p∧q∧r
F	T	F	F	–
F	F	T	F	–
F	F	F	T	~p∧~q∧~r

$$f(p,q,r) = (p\wedge q\wedge\sim r)\vee(p\wedge\sim q\wedge r)\vee(\sim p\wedge q\wedge r)\wedge(\sim p\wedge\sim q\wedge\sim r)$$
$$f(p,q,r) = pqr' + pq'r + p'qr + p'q'r'$$
$$f(p,q,r) = p\equiv(q\not\equiv r)$$

TABLE 9

	∧,~	∨,~
~p	~p	~p
p∧q	p∧q	~(~p∨~q)
p∨q	~(~p∧~q)	p∨q
p⊃q	~(p∧~q)	~p∨q
p≡q	~(~(p∧q)∧~(~p∧q))	~(p∨q)∨~(~p∨~q)

TABLE 10

	|	↓
~p	p|p	p↓p
p∧q	(p|q)|(p|q)	(p↓p)↓(q↓q)
p∨q	(p|p)|(q|q)	(p↓q)↓(p↓q)

so does the formula obtained by interchanging addition and multiplication, and the elements 0 and 1 throughout the given formula.

The properties of commutativity and associativity, together with those shown in Table 1, are all examples of the Principle of Duality. The value of this principle lies in the fact that if one formula can be established, the second follows immediately. A separate proof of the second formula is not necessary, although in fact, the steps in such a proof would be the duals of the steps in the proof of the first formula. Here are other dual pairs of statements:

$$a + 1 = 1 \qquad\qquad a0 = 0$$
$$0' = 1 \qquad\qquad 1' = 0$$
$$a + a' = 1 \qquad\qquad aa' = 0$$
$$a + (a'b) = a + b \qquad a(a' + b) = ab$$

Computer Arithmetic The identification of the logical constants T and F with the boolean constants 1 and 0, respectively, leads to the development of the arithmetic properties of the computer in terms of its logical or boolean operators. In binary arithmetic, the multiplication of bits is exactly the same as boolean multiplication: The product of two bits is 1 if and only if both bits are 1. However, the addition of two bits is quite different from boolean addition. This is apparent, since in boolean arithmetic $1 + 1 = 1$, while in binary arithmetic $1 + 1 = 10$.

We also observe that in binary arithmetic the sum bit is 1 if and only if one, but not both, summands have the value 1, while the carry bit is 1 if and only if both summands have the value 1. Thus, we can compute the sum bit by using the logical inequivalence (exclusive or) operation, and the carry bit by using the logical conjunction or boolean multiplication operation. Finally, we observe that, since the negative of an integer is normally represented in the computer by a complementary bit pattern (1's-complement), arithmetic negation can be accomplished by logical negation, or boolean complementation, with slight modification if 2's-complement arithmetic is used.

Logical Design Logical (or logic) design of a computer is the development of computer circuitry to perform the desired functions for the particular machine. It is necessary that the circuitry be accurate and reliable, and desirable that it be relatively simple so that it is inexpensive and easy to maintain. While logical design must include consideration of timing problems and the various electromechanical attachments to the computer, the heart of the problem resides in the development of logical circuitry to perform the desired functions.

Of the various devices designed to systematize study of this logic, the Venn diagram and Karnaugh map are particularly simple and highly effective for functions of 2, 3, 4, or 5 variables. However, the use of these devices becomes increasingly difficult as the number of variables increases beyond five. The classical Venn diagram consists of a rectangle representing the universe, containing a circle or other simple closed curve for each variable represented. The interpretation is that within the circle

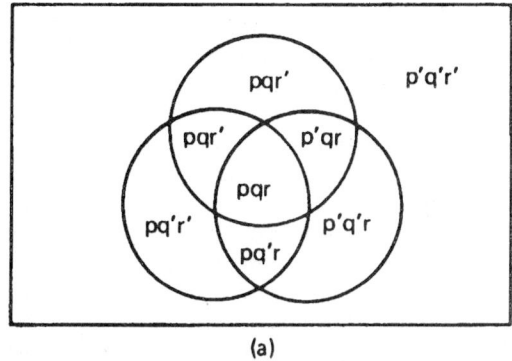 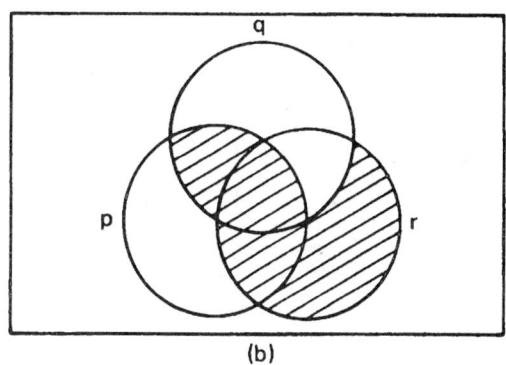

FIG. 1. Venn diagram

the given variable has the value 1, while outside it has the value 0. These circles are arranged in such a way as to include all possible combination of 1s and 0s for the variables. The Venn diagram for a 3-variable problem is given in Fig. 1, with the various regions labeled in Fig. 1(a) and certain regions shaded to represent the boolean function $pq + pr + p'r$ in Fig. 1(b). In this form the Venn diagram is relatively ineffective for logical analysis. The varying shapes of the regions cause some difficulty in visualizing possible combinations of these regions, particularly if four or more variables are involved.

The Karnaugh map is a practical modification of the Venn diagram, with each region of the diagram represented by a square within a larger rectangle. The Karnaugh maps for 2-, 3-, and 4-variable problems are given in Fig. 2. The region represented by each square is determined by the product of the letters on the edges of the rectangle. For example, the square marked A in the 4-variable rectangle represents the region $pq'rs$. To represent a boolean function, say $pq + pr + q'r$, on a Karnaugh map, first expand each term of the functions to include all variables present:

$$pq + pr + q'r$$
$$= pq \cdot 1 + p \cdot 1 \cdot r + 1 \cdot q'r$$
$$= pq(r + r') + p(q + q')r + (p + p')q'r$$
$$= pqr + pqr' + pqr + pq'r + pq'r + p'q'r$$
$$= pqr + pqr' + pq'r + p'q'r.$$

Then mark each square corresponding to a term in the expanded expression.

Thus, the boolean function $pq + pr + q'r$ is represented by the squares marked "1" in Fig. 3, while 0s fill those squares not included in the representation. Note that $pq + q'r$ is also represented by the same four marked squares, and hence is equivalent to the given function. It is also possible to label a square d, denoting "don't care," if the value of that square is irrelevant to the particular function being represented.

Minimization of Boolean Functions In the interest of economy it is often desirable to use the simplest possible expression for a boolean function in the design of computer circuitry. For example, since the expression $pq + pr + q'r$ is equivalent to the expression $pq + q'r$ in the sense that these expressions have the same value for given argument values, the former expression should be replaced by the latter whenever it occurs in a given circuit design. The determination of the simplest expression equivalent to a given one is known as *minimization*. Minimization is understood to be with respect to a given function form, such as the sum of products form, since a change in permissible operators often permits one to find an expression that is simpler yet. Karnaugh maps and a variety of algebraic or geometrical algorithms have been used to accomplish boolean function minimization.

When computers were constructed from discrete individual logic components, minimization of the number of components or "gates" was a significant task. However, with the development of integrated circuit technology and the shift to Very Large Scale Integration (VLSI), the importance of the individual logic gate in the overall cost of the

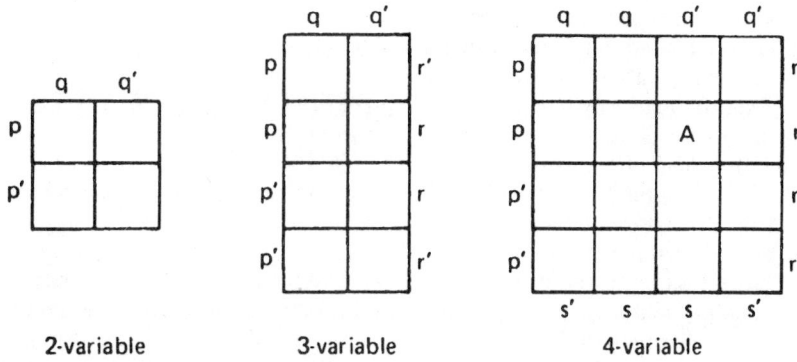

2-variable   3-variable   4-variable

FIG. 2. Karnaugh maps

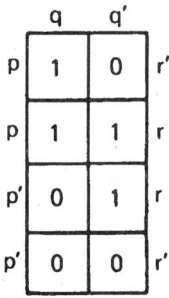

FIG. 3. Karnaugh map for pq + pr + q'r

computer diminished. In VLSI technology, each computer chip may contain hundreds or thousands of logic gates. Hence, the focus of minimization efforts shifted away from individual gates toward the problem of finding the best combination of logic gates to fit on a chip to perform a given set of functions. That is, the question is less "What is the minimal number of gates to perform this function?" and more "What is the minimum number of gates to perform the given set of functions?" The concepts of minimization are still relevant, but the designer may be willing to trade a less efficient computation of one function for a more efficient computation of the entire set of functions.

References

1983. Mott, Joe L., Kandel, Abraham, and Baker, Theodore P. *Discrete Mathematics for Computer Scientists.* Reston, VA: Reston Publishing Co.

1984. Korfhage, Robert R. *Discrete Computational Structures, Second Edition.* New York: Academic Press.

1985. Doerr, Alan and Levasseur, Kenneth, *Applied Discrete Structures for Computer Science.* Chicago: Science Research Associates.

ROBERT R. KORFHAGE

BOOT AND REBOOT

For articles on related subjects *see* BIOS; and LOGIN FILE.

To *bootstrap*—or, more commonly, to just *boot*—is to accomplish a task by means of a procedure that gives its user the first move free. The term was first used in a computing context to describe the process whereby a programmed loader, whose job it is to get other pieces of software into a machine, is itself loaded. This task, which at first glance seems to threaten infinite regression, was made possible by a very simple loader wired into the hardware; this was just adequate enough to load the programmed loader, which then loaded everything else.

From this beginning, "bootstrapping" has become a generic term for the use of any procedure that requires its user to do no more than some initial part of what would seem *a priori* to be the entire task, with the procedure itself then doing the rest, such as a staircase that magically becomes an escalator after climbing the first step or two. Such a procedure achieves its result with so little user effort that superficial estimates might lead one to

expect that it seems unnatural, a prodigy, like lifting oneself by one's own bootstraps.

The term has been applied, for example, to the programming of a complete translator for some language L by means of an already-implemented translator for a small part of L. Such bootstrapping is possible when the part of L already implemented is adequate—not necessarily good—for writing a translator. When it has this property, it can be used for the programming of a complete language L translator. The resulting program is run through the subset-translator, to yield a running translator of the whole language, bootstrapped into existence by means of the already running fragment.

The most common current use of the term is to denote the act of bringing a microcomputer to an operational state (i.e. a state in which it accepts user commands) from either an unpowered state or a powered but unresponsive state. Booting a PC from an unpowered state—a *cold boot*—is initiated simply by switching the PC on; it is normally done to start a work session, and usually includes a Power-On Self-Test (POST) that checks the memory circuitry.

Rebooting from a powered state—a *warm boot*—is usually initiated by pressing some combination of keys (such as Ctrl-Alt-Del on an IBM PC) or hitting what on the Macintosh is called a "programmer's switch." It does not include the POST, and is normally done only to recover from a condition in which user commands are not responded to. In some severe non-operational conditions (e.g. a "frozen" keyboard), the only recourse the user has is to initiate a cold boot by switching the machine off and then on again.

The boot process (built into the machine's BIOS (*q.v.*), or Basic Input-Output System), however initiated, then proceeds to load the system files needed to bring the computer's operating system or user interface (*q.v.*) into a state of readiness.

MARK HALPERN

BRANCH. *See* MACHINE AND ASSEMBLY LANGUAGE PROGRAMMING.

BREAKPOINT. *See* DEBUGGING.

BRITISH COMPUTER SOCIETY (BCS)

For an article on a related subject *see* INTERNATIONAL FEDERATION FOR INFORMATION PROCESSING.

The British Computer Society is the chartered body in the U.K. for all information technology professionals. Formed in 1957, it now has nearly 34,000 members. The Society is concerned with the development of computing and its effective application and, under its Royal Charter granted in 1984, now has responsibilities for education and training, for public awareness, and for standards, quality, and professionalism. The Society advises Parliament and the government, and its agencies. It examines and pronounces on topical issues, such as computer misuse, safety-critical systems, software certification, intellectual property rights, and the impact of information technology on society; it advises the Banking and Building Society Ombudsmen on the use and misuse of plastic cards; it inspects university and polytechnic courses in computer science and information technology; it conducts its own examinations; it is closely connected with numerous computer associations overseas, such as the ACM and the IEEE-CS, and now increasingly with associations in Europe to pave the way for the Single European Market of 1992; it is the U.K. member of the International Federation for Information Processing; and it organizes an ambitious Professional Development Scheme, which aims not only to regulate and monitor the training of young professionals but also to keep established practitioners up to date. In addition, the Society's 50 specialist groups and its 8 technical and 6 professional committees have remained in the forefront of technical and professional innovation, and its 42 branches have ensured that its influence is felt throughout Britain (and now, increasingly, overseas).

Organization The Society is governed by a council consisting of a President (currently Stephen Matheson) a Deputy President (currently Dr. Roger Johnson), four Vice-Presidents (one each for Technical, Professional, Branches, and External Relations), an Honorary Treasurer, and 39 Ordinary Members. Executive power is held by the Chief Executive, J.R. Brookes MA FBCS, and four full-time Directors. The 65 paid staff working in Mansfield Street are organized into four divisions: Administration, Professional, Services, and Technical. A trading subsidiary, the British Informatics Society Limited (BISL), has publications and conference departments. A high proportion of the staff was relocated to Swindon, Wiltshire in 1990, but a small headquarters is maintained in London.

The following have held the office of BCS President:

Prof. M. V. Wilkes FRS, 1957–1960
Dr. F. Yates CBE FRS, 1960–1961
D. W. Hooper, 1961–1962
R. L. Michaelson, 1962–1963
Sir Edward Playfair KCMG, 1963–1965
Sir Maurice Banks, 1965–1966
The Earl Mountbatten of Burma KG PC OM, 1966–1967
Dr. S. Gill, 1967–1968
B. Z. de Ferranti, 1968–1969
The Earl of Halsbury FRS, 1969–1970
A. d'Agapeyeff OBE, 1970–1971
Prof. A. S. Douglas CBE, 1971–1972
G. J. Morris, 1972–1973
R. L. Barrington, 1973–1974
E. L. Willey, 1974–1975
C. P. Marks, 1975–1976
G. A. Fisher, 1976–1977
Prof. P. A. Samet, 1977–1978

Prof. F. H. Sumner, 1978–1979
J. L. Bogod, 1979–1980
F. J. Hooper, 1980–1981
P. D. Hall OBE, 1981–1982
HRH The Duke of Kent, KG GCMG GCVO ADC, 1982–1983
D. Firnberg, 1983–1984
Dr. E. S. Page, 1984–1985
R. A. McLaughlin, 1985–1986
Sir John Fairclough, 1986–1987
E. P. Morris TD, 1987–1988
B. W. Oakley CBE, 1988–1989
V. S. Shirley OBE, 1989–1990
A. Rousell, 1990–1991
S. Matheson, 1991–1992

The Society has played and is sustaining an important part in encouraging the spread of computer knowledge through its Schools Committee, which consists of people from education administration, the teaching profession, and industry, and the Group for Computer Education, also affiliated with the Society.

The Society plays a major role in setting and maintaining standards, at many levels of competence, by its representation on the advisory committees of national examining and educational bodies.

The work of the Society's members, individually or as government representatives, in international organizations concerned with education, places it at the international center of computer education circles.

The Society Examination The Society's examination, set in two parts, is designed to assess the candidate's understanding of the underlying principles of the discipline, ability to reason and to evaluate information, and capacity for application of his or her knowledge to the solution of both practical and theoretical problems.

The part I examination, set at the level of the Higher National Diploma, requires candidates to take two compulsory papers covering the general knowledge that all computer professionals should have, together with two papers from a number of widely defined areas of more specialized computer knowledge (computer technology, programming, data processing, analysis and design of systems, computational methods, and analog and hybrid computing). The part II examination, set at the level of a university honors degree, requires candidates to take two papers in one area and one paper in a second, less specialized, area than those defined for part I. The detailed syllabus is available from the Society's Examination Department.

Publications In addition to the publications mentioned, the Society has two other major publications. *The Computer Journal* is published every two months. It contains articles and papers on scientific, business, and commercial subjects related to computers, together with reviews of the most important books and other publications in the field. *The Computer Bulletin* is published ten times a year and contains articles of a more general, tutorial nature than those in the *Journal*. The weekly periodicals "Computing" and "Computer Weekly" both contain a "BCS News Page." It carries reports of branches and specialist groups, as well as advance notice of the Society's activities. Copies are sent to those BCS members who fit the publishers' criteria for free distribution.

There are many other publications of a more specialized nature, including the *Software Engineering Journal*, which is published jointly with the IEE.

Membership   The different types of membership are as follows:

Fellow—Fellowship is by election from the Member grade. The minimum requirements are that Fellows must be over 30 and have 8 years experience in computing, 5 in a responsible position.

Member—Applicants must be over 24 and have passed BCS parts I and II plus 4 years experience in computing *or* an honors degree with between 5 years and 10 years experience *or* 10 years experience. Applicants should be supported by two Members or Fellows.

Associate Member—Applicants must be over 22 and have BCS Part I plus 3 years experience *or* an honors degree and between 3 and 5 years experience or ordinary degree plus 5 years experience *or* 7 years experience. Support by at least two fellow computer practitioners is required.

Affiliate—Minimum age 18. For those, usually professionals in other disciplines, who wish to keep up to date with developments in computing.

Student—Minimum age 18. For those following a course recognized for admission to professional membership, after minimum experience requirement.

Education   The responsibility for the Society's educational activities lies with a full-time Education Department. Education liaison officers appointed by each branch play a valuable role in communication between the Society and educational establishments throughout the country. Information is also provided on career prospects in the computer field, including presentations to schools and colleges.

The Professional Board has six committees: Professional Advisory, Membership, Education and Training, Data Protection, Intellectual Property, and Data Security. There are eight Technical Committees: Software Engineering, Value-Added Data Services, Health Informatics, Future Impact of Information Technology, Safety-Critical Systems, Informations Systems Management, Human Systems Interaction, and Graphics, Design, and Manufacture. In addition, the Society has two major projects: "IT for Disabled People" and "Women in IT." The specialist groups are as follows:

Advanced Programming
Auditing by Computer
British APL Association
Business Information Systems
Computer Aided Design/Computer Aided Engineering
CASE
Computer Arts Society
Computer Conservation
Computer Security
Computer Graphics and Display
Cybernetic Machines
Data Communications
Data Management
Data Protection
Developing Countries
Disabled
Distributed Systems
Document Imaging
Electronic Publishing
Expert Systems
Formal Aspects of Computer Science
Fortran
Fourth Generation Languages
Geographical Information Systems
Hardware
Human Computer Interaction
Information Retrieval
Law
Local Government
Mathematical Programming
Medical (three separate groups—London, Northern, Scotland)
Modula-2
Natural Language Translation
Nursing
Object Oriented Programming
Office Automation
Parallel Processing
Payroll
Performance Engineering
Primary Health Care
Process Control
Robotics
Safety-Related Computer Systems
Software Quality Management
Technology of Software Protection

TIM HACKWORTH

BUFFER

For articles on related subjects *see* CACHE MEMORY; and INPUT-OUTPUT CONTROL SYSTEM.

A *buffer* is an area of storage that temporarily holds data that will be subsequently delivered to a processor or input/output (I/O) transducer. Buffers exist as an integral part of many transducers; e.g. bits arriving serially over a telephone line are collected in a buffer before the appropriate teleprinter character is activated. Similarly, the bits representing a given keyboard stroke remain in a buffer while being serialized for transmission. Since the buffer is an integral part of the transducer, it is usually dedicated to the transducer and not shared with any other device.

Buffers are also used in conjunction with a computer's input/output control system (IOCS) to hold the data that is the object of various I/O commands. In this case, the buffer is usually a portion of main storage and is often dynamically allocated and freed by software. In either case, a buffer exists in order to accommodate the different rates at which data is produced or consumed by the processor or transducers involved.

In a typical situation, a processor will be capable of producing data several orders of magnitude faster than a transducer (e.g. a printer) can accept it. In order to make most efficient use of the processor, the data will be placed in a buffer and its location made known to the transducer. The transducer then proceeds to empty the buffer while the processor is freed for other work.

Various buffering techniques have evolved in IOCS. These techniques can be analyzed according to the policy used for (1) receiving data from the producer and (2) delivering data to the consumer.

When receiving data, two techniques are common: (1) a pool of buffers and (2) circular buffering. With the buffer-pooling technique, a number of buffers are available to the IOCS. Usually, each buffer is large enough to hold the single physical record that is being transferred. When a record is produced, a buffer is taken from the pool and used to hold the data. Data is then consumed on a first-in, first-out basis, and when all data has been transmitted, the buffer is returned to the pool.

Circular buffering, in contrast, typically uses a single buffer, usually one that is larger than a single physical record and which is managed as a queue. The basic strategy is to give the appearance that the buffer is organized in a circle, with data "wrapping around" as shown in Fig. 1. This appearance of circular organization is accomplished by using two pointers, IN and OUT, associated with the buffer; the starting and ending addresses of the buffer (START and END) are also known. Initially, START=IN=OUT. Data received from the producer fills the buffer, starting from START and incrementing the pointer IN. The consumer takes data from the buffer, incrementing the pointer OUT (and taking care not to go past IN–1). When the last word

of the buffer has been filled (IN=END), then IN is reset to START and subsequent data will wrap around to the start of the buffer.

Similarly, when OUT reaches END, it is reset to START and also wraps around. Clearly, the following restrictions hold:

1. If IN > OUT, then OUT must not become greater than IN−1.
2. If OUT > IN, then IN must not become greater than OUT−1.

If either of these two conditions is violated, then either the consumer is trying to access data that has not been produced, *or* the producer is attempting to overwrite data that has not yet been consumed.

As random access memory (RAM) has become less expensive, designers have increased average buffer size. This usually helps I/O response and throughput (*q.v.*) by exploiting local referencing patterns and achieving a cache effect in the I/O system. Mainframe systems of the 1990s use very large, "extended" RAM memories to optimize this effect to the greatest extent possible.

ROBERT W. TAYLOR

BUG

For articles on related subjects *see* DEBUGGING; GLITCH; and SOFTWARE TESTING.

A *bug* is an error in either the syntax or the logic of a computer program or circuit. Because the story has been retold so often by well-meaning people, many believe that the term originated when a moth was removed ("debugged") from an errant Mark I (*q.v.*) relay circuit in the early 1940s. Though this may very well have happened, the term *bug* was used in exactly its current context by Thomas Edison in an 1878 letter to Theodore Puskas.

Most syntactical bugs can be detected during the translation from the symbolic languages that programmers use into the (binary) language that is eventually executed. For example, the proper symbolic code for

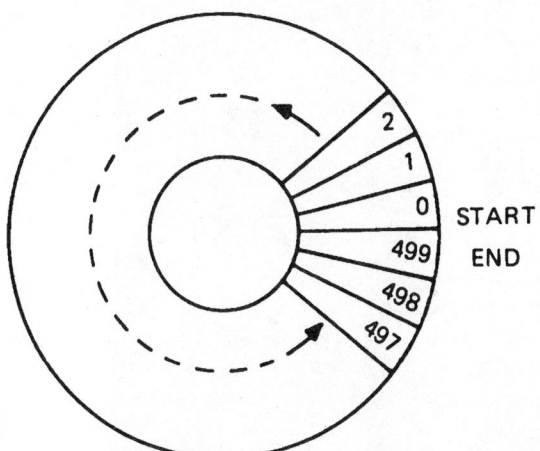
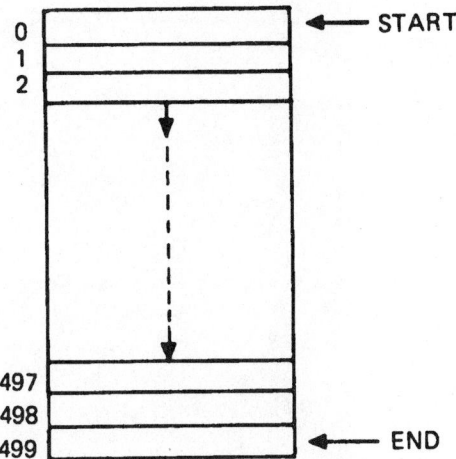

FIG. 1.   Circular buffer organization shown logically (left) and as it actually appears in memory (right).

addition on some machines is ADA ("add to accumulator"). If the programmer mistakenly writes ADD, this bug will be detected, an error message will be printed, and execution of the program will be halted, since the attempted operation code is illegal.

A bug is also created, and a more serious one, if the programmer writes the legal code SBA ("subtract from accumulator") when ADA was intended. This is a logical bug, and no coding system can catch such an error.

Properly speaking, the elimination of the first type of bug is the process of debugging, whereas the detection and elimination of the second type is the process of software testing. Program bugs can be so extremely subtle that they may resist great efforts to eliminate them. It is commonly accepted that all very large computer programs (such as compilers) have bugs remaining in them. The number of possible paths through a large computer program is enormous, and it is physically impossible to explore all of them. The single path containing a bug may not be followed in actual production runs for a long time (if ever) after the program has been certified as correct by its author or others.

FRED GRUENBERGER

BULLETIN BOARD

For articles on related subjects *see* COMPUTER CONFERENCING; DATA COMMUNICATIONS; ELECTRONIC MAIL; GROUPWARE; NETWORKS, COMPUTER; and VIDEOTEX.

An electronic *bulletin board* is a medium for posting and discussing announcements and messages of interest to a community of on-line users. Implementation and maintenance of a bulletin board requires three types of equipment: a personal computer or means of generating text and graphic material to be posted for viewing; a modem connected to a phone line, which allows transmission of computer-generated text and data to and from the bulletin board; and a central computer on which this data can be stored, organized, and made available for transmission to readers. Participants must also have word processing (*q.v.*) and telecommunications software for their personal computers.

The first bulletin boards began in the 1960s, with the U.S. Defense Department's ARPA network of interconnected mainframe computers. This system required participants to have direct links to a mainframe, usually from a military installation or other official office.

The spread of low-cost personal computers and efficient modems (*q.v.*) in the 1970s engendered the development of numerous bulletin boards or "on-line systems" that were fully accessible to the public. By the end of the 1980s, hundreds of thousands of people accessed thousands of bulletin boards around the U.S. at all times of day from their homes and places of business. These numbers are larger by a factor of at least 5 on the international scale.

Bulletin boards now differ greatly in quality of data available, cost to the user, and services rendered to the user. The most common kinds of bulletin boards are usually free to access, and support discussions on a variety of topics, ranging from politics to the latest computer software and hardware (see Fig. 1). Some of these bulletin boards specialize in specific areas, such as news, science fiction, computer games, stock quotations, or sports. Friendships, business undertakings, and romantic involvements are some of the many human relationships that regularly develop on bulletin board systems. Although many bulletin boards have facilities for "real-time" communication or "chats," most communication takes place through asynchronous exchange of messages. These messages may contain sophisticated graphics and programs in binary code, but the common denominator

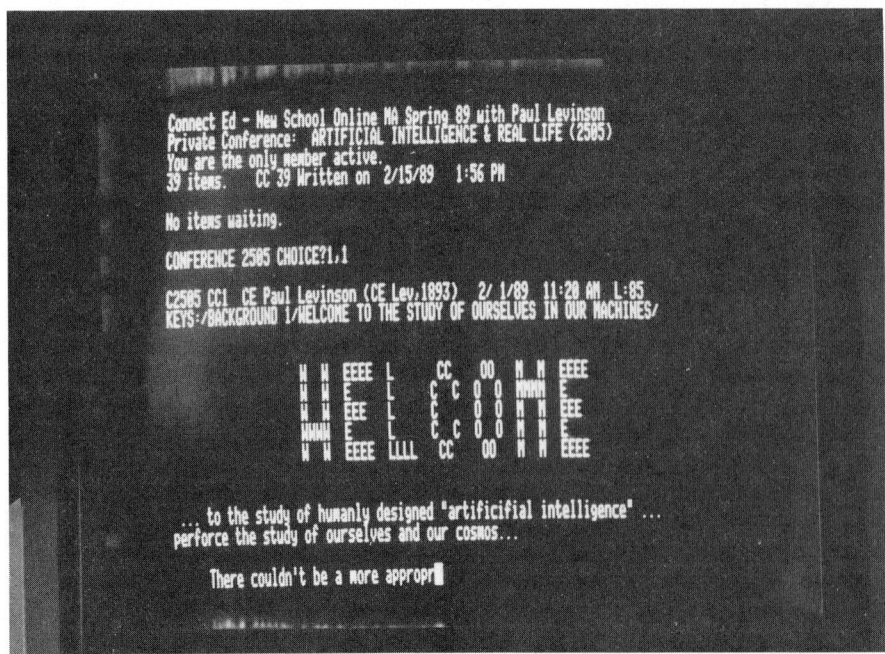

FIG. 1 The first frame of a private conference bulletin board.

of most bulletin board systems is text-only or "ASCII (*q.v.*) mode."

Bulletin boards are closely related to electronic mail (e-mail) systems, but in the latter, a correspondent typically addresses a message to a particular named recipient or selected group of recipients. The users of a bulletin board service post messages for all users to see, and browse through selected categories of messages posted by others.

Commercial on-line systems charge their customers hourly and monthly rates, and offer in-depth databases and hundreds of topics for discussion. CompuServe, an H & R Block Company, claims the largest number of users, at nearly half a million, and offers such services as electronic banking via computer, on-line encyclopedias, and numerous databases, such as Books-in-Print, medical and legal information, ability to reserve airline flights, and numerous discussions of professional and personal interest. Other well-known on-line systems are The Source, Delphi, Genie, and Prodigy. Unlike local, noncommercial bulletin boards that usually serve a city or small limited geographical area, large commercial online systems are accessible via a local phone call from most places in the nation and sometimes the world. Such long distance connections can be expensive, and require the services of a "data packet" or telecommunication network, such as GTE's Telenet, McDonnell-Douglas' Tymenet, or CompuServe's own CPN service.

One of the newer services of bulletin boards is on-line education. Since 1985, Connected Education has been offering courses for masters level credit granted by The New School for Social Research on the Electronic Information Exchange System. Students from 30 states in the U.S. and more than a dozen nations around the world attend two-month classes entirely via personal computer and modem, without ever leaving their homes or places of business. Courses take place on a special bulletin board called an "electronic campus," where faculty and students enter and read lecture and discussion messages, pursue research, access papers in an on-line library, and engage in social conversation at times of their own choosing. Such education, like all on-line services, is especially valuable to people who for reasons of physical handicap, geographic isolation, or pressure of business are unable to attend conventional classrooms.

The Internet and Bitnet systems connect mainframes in universities all around the world, and are used not only by students but by scholars and scientists. The initial investigation of claims of cold fusion in 1989 was facilitated by exchanges among scientists on these networks. Discussions on such issues as global warming and international crisis management continue on these systems.

Use of bulletin boards for such serious activities has raised issues of intellectual property and authors' rights not fully addressed by current copyright laws. The ease and speed of dissemination of electronic text makes it very difficult to control by traditional means. Computer viruses (*q.v.*) that destroy or impair computer systems are another problem resulting from uncontrolled exchange of data and programs. Mass dissemination of destructive or mischievous programs introduced by computer hackers (*q.v.*) compromised national computer systems several times in the 1980s.

Corporations and business operations, especially those with activities dispersed internationally or around the nation, make extensive use of bulletin boards, computer conferencing and electronic mail. Companies such as IBM, Digital Equipment Corporation, AT&T, Proctor and Gamble, and most major oil companies use private bulletin boards accessible to tens of thousands of executives and employees.

France is the most saturated on-line nation at present, with more than 90% of its population connected to its Minitel network. Third world nations are beginning to link into worldwide databases, encouraged by organizations such as the Agricultural Cooperative Development International group, which in 1988 began an ambitious project of "networking" third world farmers and agricultural workers via computer. The Soviet Union and citizens of the U.S. have developed a growing series of bulletin board discussions via the San Francisco–Moscow Teleport and computer conferencing on the Notepad system to help coordinate relief efforts after the 1988 earthquake in Armenia.

Current statistics show 25–30 million personal computers in the U.S., with 25% of these outfitted with modems. As these figures grow, bulletin boards will become an increasingly important part of our social and professional lives.

References

1988. Banks, Michael A. *The Modem Reference*. New York: Simon & Schuster.
1990. Glossbrenner, Alfred. *The Complete Handbook of Personal Computer Communications*, 3rd Ed. New York: St. Martin's Press.

PAUL LEVINSON

BURROUGHS, WILLIAM S.

For an article on a related subject *see* CALCULATING MACHINES.

Williams Seward Burroughs was born on 28 January 1855 in Auburn, N.Y. and died 5 September 1898 in Citronelle, Alabama. He is immortalized in the name of the Burroughs firm, but, unlike some of the other early manufacturers of mechanical calculators, his firm did not adopt that name until after Burroughs himself had died. It was through his early experience as a junior bank clerk that he developed an appreciation for the types of calculations that were required in a business environment. In 1881 he moved to St. Louis and worked in his father's shop, making models for castings, which gave him the background knowledge required for his mechanical inventions.

Inspired by other mechanical calculators, particularly the key-driven comptometers invented by Dorr E. Felt, Burroughs set about inventing one that would not only add, but also print a list of the numbers entered and

FIG. 1. William Seward Burroughs (courtesy UNISYS Corporate Archives).

the final total on a tape. An early model, capable of printing only the final total, was not a commercial success, and his financial backers withdrew their support. Burroughs continued on his own, eventually producing 50 copies of one model—all of which had to be recalled because Burroughs himself was the only one who could make them operate in a consistently reliable way.

In 1886 the American Arithmometer Company was formed by Burroughs and three associates. The company manufactured and marketed an improved calculating machine that could list both the individual entries and the totals. The earlier mechanical problems had been overcome by the introduction of a shock absorbing dash pot that cushioned the action of the activating lever on the mechanism. Upon payment of $475.00, the first customers received their machine in December 1892. By 18 January 1908, the firm, by then known as the Burroughs Adding Machine Company, could boast that it had supplied a total of 63,574 machines of 58 different types.

References

1914. Horsburgh, E. M. *Handbook of the Napier Tercentenary Celebration of Modern Instruments and Methods of Calculation*. Edinburgh: The Royal Society of Edinburgh (reprinted by MIT Press and Tomash Publishers, 1982).

1921. Turck, J. A. V. *Origin of Modern Calculating Machines*. Chicago: The Western Society of Engineers.

MICHAEL R. WILLIAMS

BUS

For articles on related subjects *see* DIGITAL COMPUTERS: HISTORY: PERSONAL COMPUTERS; IBM-PC AND PC-COMPATIBLES; OPEN ARCHITECTURE; PERSONAL COMPUTING; and SYNCHRONOUS/ASYNCHRONOUS OPERATION.

Introduction A *bus* is an electronic pathway in a digital computer that provides a communication path for data to flow between the central processing unit (CPU - *q.v.*) and its memory and between and among the CPU and the various peripheral devices connected to the computer. A bus contains one wire for each bit needed to specify the address of a device or location in memory, plus additional wires that distinguish among the various data transfer operations to be performed. A bus can transmit data in either direction between any two components of the computing system. Without a bus, a computer would need separate wires for all possible connections between components, clearly an intolerable situation.

On a microcomputer, the bus is usually called an *expansion bus* because its design determines the degree to which the minimum configuration of the system can be expanded with regard to memory, processing speed, graphics capability, and peripheral support. The expansion bus is the collection of wires, paths, connectors, and controllers responsible for distributing the data and instructions from the microprocessor to the peripheral expansion cards. *Slots* connected to the bus provide places to plug those cards in, and the bus then provides a mechanism for communicating with them. The remainder of this article discusses three generations of expansion buses used with IBM-compatible PCs and, briefly, the expansion bus used with Macintosh computers.

When microcomputers were first introduced during the 1970s, there were no standard mechanisms for expanding a computer's capabilities. Every manufacturer had a different scheme, and some manufacturers hadn't even standardized across different models in a single product line.

S-100 Bus When Altair introduced its 8080 computer, it came with an expansion bus with a published specification that used common parts and connectors. This *open architecture* soon became a standard. One hundred pins were provided for various signals on what became known as the S-100 bus. This meant that new video cards, more memory, and serial and parallel ports could be added to the computer as needed. They could even be purchased from someone other than Altair. The add-on board business was born, and more than 100 companies manufactured S-100 products. The S-100 bus was even capable of 16-bit addressing, but it had some shortcomings. It was subject to interference and crosstalk, it did not perform reliably with high-frequency signals, and there were ambiguities in the standard that led some manufacturers to define specific pins in multiple ways.

ISA Bus Just as groups of interested parties were meeting in 1981 to improve the S-100 bus, IBM announced its new personal computer, the IBM-PC. The machine was a success due in no small part to its open architecture and the flexibility of its expansion bus, whose design details were placed in the public domain. The new IBM bus came to be known as the Industry Standard Architecture (ISA) bus. In some ways it was inferior to the S-100 bus. It used strictly an 8-bit architecture with parity protection and had only 62 pins consisting of 3 grounds, 5 voltage supply lines, 20 address lines, 8 data lines, 10 lines devoted to interrupts, and a variety of special-purpose signal lines. The ISA bus was processor-specific and its edge-triggered interrupts meant that each expansion card could have only one interrupt (*q.v.*). An entire industry flourished in the shadow of IBM making products that could be placed in the expansion slots of IBM-PCs and a plethora of compatible machines.

ISA AT Bus By 1984, microcomputing was a multi-billion dollar industry. Users were demanding more power and performance than an 8-bit bus could deliver. IBM announced its new Advanced Technology (AT) machine, built around the 16-bit Intel 80286 chip, which could be run as fast as 12 MHz. An additional connector was added next to the 8-bit ISA connector, which allowed additional address and control signals while maintaining downward compatibility with ISA expansion boards. A *wait state* (*q.v.*) generator was added to allow the microprocessor to keep up with bus components that might be too slow. AT address lines were unlatched, allowing 16-bit cards to determine, as early in the bus cycle as possible, whether signals were intended for them. Information could be transferred at up to 2 megabytes per second on this bus, but its rating of 8 MHz frequency ultimately proved to be too slow. Processor speeds for the 80286 began to outrun the bus.

Micro-Channel Architecture (MCA) At the peak of popularity of the IBM AT-compatible computers, most were not actually made by IBM. A serious erosion of market share as well as a desire to enhance bus performance soon led IBM down a different path. In April 1987 IBM announced a new computer line, the Personal System/2 (PS/2), designed to recapture market share lost to the clone makers. It featured a new expansion bus based on a concept called Micro-Channel Architecture (MCA), which IBM intended to license, not give away. The MCA increased data throughput to 20 MBytes per second, more than ten times the speed of the AT ISA bus. The PS/2 was still an open architecture machine in some sense, but emulation would no longer be cost-free to the clone makers.

MCA expansion cards were smaller than those used with the ISA bus and were designed to take advantage of assembly advances using surface-mount components. It was a full 32-bit bus. Every fourth pin was a ground, markedly reducing interference and allowing much faster cycle times. Expansion cards could now communicate directly with the Video Graphics Array (VGA) card. Expansion cards could now be configured by the microprocessor: No microswitches specific to the hardware had to be set. Interrupts were level-sensitive and remained ac-tive during the entire cycle, making it easier to address multiple cards with the same interrupt.

Most significantly, expansion cards could now have their own processors and memory. No longer was the main processor the sole repository of computing power. Cards could now be more powerful and intelligent, freeing the main CPU for additional tasks. The primary disadvantage of the MCA was that it was not downward compatible with the old ISA cards.

Extended Industry Standard Architecture (EISA) Not surprisingly, clone makers were reluctant to give up their market position and even more reluctant to pay IBM royalties on every card and machine made. They saw a need to expand the ISA bus, but not at their own expense. A group of computer manufacturers banded together and formed the Gang of Nine: Wyse, AST, Tandy, Compaq, Hewlett-Packard, Zenith, Olivetti, NEC, and Epson. They agreed to develop a joint standard, publish it, and stick to it.

Through use of a clever connector scheme, EISA remained compatible with the old ISA boards. EISA was a 32-bit standard, even faster than the MCA, with a maximum transfer rate of 33 MBytes per second. The expansion cards were almost twice as large, allowing for more components. The parts could also be stock; surface-mounted components were not required. The power rating of the EISA boards were 45 watts. At +5 volts, the MCA card can draw only 1.6 amps, while an EISA card can draw 4.5 amps. Bus mastering and no-switch configuration were also part of the EISA standard. The EISA bus is synchronous and can perform transfers in long rapid-fire bursts. Only the 80386 and 80486 chips can use EISA. Interrupts are no longer edge-triggered and can be shared.

The EISA standard is producing high-performance cards for all microcomputer applications. New disk controllers reduce hard disk access times below the 1 millisecond threshold. On-board intelligence and memory hold the promise of extremely fast response, increased performance, and widely enhanced video resolutions.

NU-Bus Apple Computer (*q.v.*) also came to recognize the benefits of an open, published, expandable architecture when it introduced its NU-Bus. Until the introduction of this bus in the late 1980s, the Macintosh had been a closed machine. This was widely cited, along with higher cost, as the reason for Apple's inability to match the market share of IBM compatibles.

The 32-bit NU-Bus was introduced with the Mac II. It operates on a 10 MHz synchronous clock, providing access to all main logic board resources through six Euro-DIN connectors. This has led to many enhancements for the Mac that might not otherwise have evolved.

Reference

1989. Glass, L. B. "Inside EISA," *Byte*, **14**, 12, 417–425.

STEPHEN J. ROGOWSKI

BUSH, VANNEVAR

For an article on a related subject *see* DIFFERENTIAL AN-ALYZER.

Vannevar Bush, the son of a clergyman, was born in Massachusetts on 11 March 1890. He attended Tufts University in the years before World War I and earned both a B.S. and M.S. degree. He then continued on for a doctorate, which was conferred upon him in 1916 simultaneously by both Harvard and M.I.T. While a graduate student, he worked for General Electric and the U.S. Navy, and taught mathematics at Tufts. In 1919 he joined the teaching staff of M.I.T., obtaining a full professorship in 1923 and becoming Vice President and Dean of the Engineering School in 1932. He remained with M.I.T. until 1938, when he was elected President of the Carnegie Institution in Washington, a position he held until retiring from active public life in 1955.

During his formative years, Bush showed an interest in mechanical construction, and invented or improved upon several instruments. The most famous of these (invented during his college days) was an automatic surveying machine, resembling a child's scooter, that he constructed from two bicycle wheels with an instrument box mounted between them. It could be pushed over a trail and would automatically create a profile of the terrain over which it had traversed.

His inventive insight was immensely useful to him in later life. Coupled with a zest for hard work, it aided him in the creation of several analog computers, the most noteworthy of which were his network analyzer and differential analyzer.

Bush's first major calculating machine project resulted from his efforts to solve some very difficult differential equations describing the behavior of a power line network. After several months of effort attempting to find an analytical solution to the equations, he came to the conclusion that it would be more economical to spend his time in the design and construction of special analog machines to solve the problem by simulating the system.

The machines for which he is most famous are his mechanical differential analyzer and the more sophisticated electrical version, known as the second Rockefeller Differential Analyzer, or RDA2. These machines used mechanical integrators to perform the key step in the solution of differential equations, the results being registered as a rotation of an output shaft. The element that then allowed these to be combined into a total solution was a "torque amplifier," which enabled the values to be added and subtracted by feeding them into various gear combinations. The RDA2 replaced these rotating shafts and gears by electrically driven systems, but retained the mechanical analog integrators. Several different examples of the mechanical differential analyzer were constructed just prior to World War II, and these became the central instruments in such work as the calculation of ballistic trajectories for artillery firing tables.

Another one of his projects resulted from his realization that it is not sufficient to have some information, you must also be able to access it in a timely way. Together

FIG. 1. Vannevar Bush. (Courtesy of the M. I. T. Museum.)

with John H. Howard of M.I.T., he developed a device known as the Rapid Selector, which was designed to facilitate information retrieval (*q.v.*). A special binary code was created to label specific items of information. This code, when recorded on the edge of a microfilm, could be scanned quickly by photoelectric scanners and the required items retrieved much faster than if one had to read the entire film.

The work with information retrieval technology led Bush to imagine a machine that he called "memex"—essentially an extension of the personal memory and knowledge base of any one individual. It was an attempt to describe a device that would emulate a mind in its associative linking of items of information and their retrieval (*see* HYPERTEXT). Although the memex could never have been constructed during Bush's lifetime, it formed a background to all his thinking and constantly recurred in his thoughts and some of his later publications. Although the memex has been called the first personal workstation (*q.v.*), it is still not available in its full generality.

In terms of computing, Bush is best known for his analog devices, but he had a much more lasting impact in his work behind the scenes. He was the *eminence grise* of American science during and in the decade following World War II. In 1940 President Roosevelt appointed him to be chairman of the National Defense Research Committee, a group set up to coordinate and expand military research projects. This position led to his being named first Director of the Office of Scientific Research and Development when it was founded in 1941. In this capacity he was essentially in charge of the entire U.S. scientific research program and could command virtually unlimited budgets and work force. While not directly involved in computer developments, he started several umbrella projects in which major computational advances were to take place. In 1942 he wrote the report that resulted in the establishment of the Manhattan Project, and it was under his coordination that the development of tactical radar took place.

After the war and up until his death on 28 June 1974, he wrote of his ideas and experiences in a number of books. These were to have a profound effect on the conduct of scientific research and changed the way that basic research was done in America. One of his writings (*Science, the Endless Frontier*, July 1945, Washington, U.S. Govt. Printing Office), a report of his war-time experiences and insights into the organization of research teams, foreshadowed the 1951 establishment of the National Science Foundation. His *Modern Arms and Free Men* (1949, New York: Simon and Schuster), a discussion of how science can play a role in preserving democracy, was one of the key works that resulted in the explosive development of military research that so characterized the cold war era.

Reference

1970. Bush, V. *Pieces of the Action*. New York: William Morrow & Co.

MICHAEL R. WILLIAMS

BUSINESS DATA PROCESSING. *See* ADMINISTRATIVE APPLICATIONS; BANKING APPLICATIONS; REAL-TIME BUSINESS APPLICATIONS; and TRANSACTION PROCESSING.

C

For articles on related subjects *see* PROCEDURE-ORIENTED LANGUAGES; PROGRAMMING LANGUAGES; STRUCTURED PROGRAMMING; SYSTEMS PROGRAMMING; and UNIX OPERATING SYSTEM.

C is a general-purpose programming language featuring economy of expression, modern control flow and data structure capabilities, and a rich set of operators and data types.

C is best known as the primary language of the Unix* operating system, but is also used in several other environments. It has been used for a wide variety of programs, including the Unix operating system, the C compiler itself, and essentially all Unix applications software. In addition to systems programming, C has been used successfully for major numerical, text processing, and database programs. Although C is a high-level language, it is sufficiently expressive and efficient to have completely displaced assembly language in many environments.

C was originally designed and implemented by Dennis Ritchie in 1972–1973 for the DEC PDP-11. C has its roots in BCPL** in much the same way that, for example, Pascal springs from Algol. (C is the successor to a short-lived BCPL-like language called B that was developed at Bell Labs; thus, the very name "C" derives from BCPL.) Like BCPL, C is relatively simple, notationally compact, and makes significant use of pointer (*q.v.*) arithmetic. One major distinction between them, however, is that, while BCPL is typeless, C supports a range of data types, thus better reflecting the architecture of most current computers.

The standard reference on C is Kernighan and Ritchie (1988); more information on the philosophy of the language may be found in Ritchie *et al.* (1978).

*Unix is a Trademark of AT&T Bell Laboratories.

**BCPL ("Basic Combined Programming Language") is a systems programming language developed in 1969 by Martin Richards of Cambridge University. It has been transported to a variety of computers, and is still widely used.

Language Components

Control Flow Control flow in C is relatively conventional:

```
if (expr) stat1 else stat2
while (expr) stat
do stat while (expr)
for (exprl; expr2; expr3) stat
switch (expr) {
    case const1: stat1
    case const2: stat2
    ...
    default: stat
}
```

In each of these, *expr* is an expression, and *stat* is a statement, either simple or a group of statements enclosed in {...} (the equivalent of **begin...end**).

Within a loop, **break** causes an immediate exit and **continue** causes the next iteration to begin. There are also labels and a **goto.**

Data Types The basic data types in C are **char** (usually an eight-bit byte), **int, short**, and **long** (various sizes of integers), and **float** and **double** (floating point numbers).

In addition, there is a conceptually infinite hierarchy of derived types: If T is a type, then there are pointers to objects of type T, arrays of T's, and structures and unions (records and variant records, in Pascal terminology) that may contain T's. There are also pointers to functions, and an enumeration data type (i.e. one whose range of values is explicitly defined by the programmer).

C does not have a string data type; strings are represented as arrays of char's, usually with a null byte as terminator, and manipulated by library functions.

Pointer arithmetic is an integral part of C. If *p* is of type pointer to T, and currently points to an element of an array of T's, then *p* + 1 is a pointer to the next element of the array. That is, arithmetic operations on pointers are

151

scaled by the size of the object to which the pointer points. The programmer is (or should be) unconcerned with the actual size.

Operators and Expressions In addition to the usual +, −, etc., C has a relatively rich set of operators (except compared to APL). Two classes are worth special mention. Any binary operator such as + has a corresponding "assignment operator" (here +=) so that the statement

$$v = v + expr$$

can be more concisely written

$$v += expr$$

"+ =" is analogous to ":+ =" in Algol 68 (q.v.).

The unary operators ++ and − − increment or decrement their operand:

$$++thing$$

is the preferred way to write

$$thing = thing + 1$$

An expression may be coerced to another type by preceding the expression with a type name, as in

$$x = sqrt(\ (double)\ integer\ expression)\ ;$$

The coercion (q.v.) in this example converts the *integer expression* into double precision, the type required by the function sqrt.

Program Structure A C program is a set of declarations (q.v.) of variables and functions in one or more source files that may be compiled separately. Function declarations may not be nested; C is otherwise block structured (q.v.).

Objects—functions or external variables—at the top level are declared either global (i.e. available to all functions) or visible only within the source file where they are declared. Variables internal to a function are either automatic (i.e. they appear when the function is entered and disappear when it is exited) or static (i.e. they retain their values from one call of the function to the next). There is a **register** declaration to advise the compiler that a variable is likely to be heavily used. Normally, a compiler would attempt to store such a variable in a register for fast access, but the declaration is only a suggestion; compilers are free to ignore the advice.

All functions may be recursive. Arguments are passed by value, but passing a pointer provides call by reference when necessary. Function arguments and return values may be any basic type, pointers, structures, unions, and enumerations. Arrays are passed by passing a pointer to the first element.

A preprocessor (q.v.) provides source file inclusion, conditional compilation, and macro processing for symbolic names and short in-line functions.

Run-time Environment C does not provide input/output (I/O) statements as a formal part of the language, nor does it supply storage management or string manipulation. Similarly, even though C was originally designed for systems programming applications, it provides only single-thread control flow constructions—no multiprogramming, parallel operations, synchronization, or coroutines (q.v.). All of these higher-level facilities must be provided by separate functions; a standard I/O library provides a uniform run-time environment for most C programs.

An Example The following program computes the powers of 2 up to 2^{20}.

```
#define LIMIT 20
main( ) /* test power function */
{
  int i;
  long power( );/* power returns a long */
  for (i = 0; i < = LIMIT; ++ i)
      printf("%d %ld\n", i, power(2,i));
}
long power(x, n) /*raise x to n-th power;   n >= 0 */
    int x,n;
{
    int i;
    long p;
    p = 1;
    for (i = 1; i <= n;++ i)
        p = p*x;
    return(p);
}
```

Execution begins at *main*. The function *printf* does formatted output conversion according to the specification in its first argument. Here, %d signals an ordinary integer, and %ld a long integer; \n is a newline character.

The function *power* would normally be written more concisely by experienced C programmers as:

```
long power(x,n) /* raise x to n-th power; n >= 0 */
    int x,n;
{
    long p = 1;
    while (--n >= 0) /* decrement n before  testing */
         p* = x;
    return(p);
}
```

Portability C is not tied to any particular hardware or operating system; C compilers run on a wide variety of machines, from micros to the largest mainframes. Most of these newer compilers are based on the "portable C compiler" developed by S. C. Johnson. The language and the standard library have been kept under strict enough control that they show little variation among machines. An ANSI standard for C was defined in 1988. Accordingly, most C programs can be moved without change to any system that supports C and the run-time library. In particular, this has meant that the Unix operating system itself, which is largely written in C, can be transported to a variety of computers with relatively modest effort.

Moving the operating system overcomes the main obstacle to portability of applications programs—diversity of run-time environments on different machines.

References

1978. Ritchie, D. M., Johnson, S. C., Lesk, M. E., and Kernighan, B. W. "UNIX Time-Sharing System: The C Programming Language," *Bell Sys. Tech. J.* **57**, *6*: 1991–2019.

1978. Johnson, S. C. and Ritchie, D. M. "UNIX Time-Sharing System: Portability of C Programs and the UNIX System," *Bell Sys. Tech. J.* **57**, *6*: 2021–2048.

1988. Kernighan, B. W. and Ritchie, D. M. *The C Programming Language C* (2nd Ed.) Englewood Cliffs, NJ: Prentice-Hall.

BRIAN W. KERNIGHAN

C++. *See* OBJECT-ORIENTED PROGRAMMING.

CACHE MEMORY

For articles on related subjects *see* ASSOCIATIVE MEMORY; BUFFER; MEMORY; STORAGE HIERRARCHY; and VIRTUAL MEMORY.

A *cache memory* is an auxiliary memory that provides a buffering capability by which the relatively slow and ever-increasingly large main memory can interface to the CPU at the processor cycle time in order to optimize performance. Early computers did not have cache memories, and, in fact, the concept was not enunciated until 1965, when Maurice Wilkes (*q.v.*) attributed the idea to Gorden Scarrott. Actual cache memories were introduced in 1969 out of a necessity that could not have been foreseen in earlier times. This occurred in the following manner.

Most early computing systems consisted basically of a central processing unit (CPU), a main memory, and some sort of secondary I/O capability. In such systems, the main memory was the single most crucial and limiting element. Typically, the main memory technology was chosen first which dictated the final memory storage capacity and speed. Subsequently, the CPU was then designed to match the speed of the memory. This matching of memory cycle time to the processor cycle time is necessary for optimization of processing speed, and remains necessary even today. Historically, as technology progressed, logic circuit speeds increased, as well as the capacity requirements of main memory. However, because of the need for increasing capacity, the speed of main memory could not keep up with the ever-improving cycle time of the CPU. Thus, a gap developed between memory and processor cycle time, and this gap continued to increase with time (*see* Matick, 1977, Chapter 1, for details of this history).

Many suggestions were proposed in the late 1950s and early 1960s to bridge the degradation resulting from this gap. These suggestions consisted mainly of some form of a small "scratch pad" memory of one form or another, running at the speed of the CPU and loaded out of the main memory. However, most of these were more like an extension of the general purpose register stack so common on all computers today, rather than having the features of what are now called cache memories. The modern cache was pioneered by IBM and first introduced in 1969 in the IBM S/360 Model 85. The fundamental purpose of the cache was and still remains very simple and clear: to provide a mechanism by which the main memory can "effectively" run or appear to run at the CPU cycle time.

The Model 85 demonstrated quite conclusively the value of using a cache buffer between main memory and the CPU. Nevertheless, the organization of this first cache did not give the best possible performance. Hence, the next system to include a cache, namely the System 360/Model 195, had a modified cache organization that proved to be superior in terms of performance. This cache organization, namely a four-way set associative design discussed later, has been used for many years with few fundamental changes. Rather, only small additions have gradually been added for performance enhancement.

The fundamental principle that makes a cache effective is exactly the same principle that allows us to construct virtual memory (*q.v.*), namely "locality of reference." This is a simple principle that everyone uses quite regularly and takes for granted. This locality of reference will be illustrated below with a very easily understood example, namely that of borrowing books from a central library.

Library Example: Locality of Reference Suppose we had the task of writing an essay on the history of the American Revolution. Further, suppose we were doing this task in an office that had shelf space for a maximum of only ten books. In order to write the essay, we need some reference books, so we visit the library and take out ten books that cover various aspects of the revolution. These are placed on our shelf, which can just accomodate these ten and no more. As the work begins, we first use one book; perhaps one chapter is especially useful for the beginning. As we proceed, we may have to resort to another book for additional information and use it for some time period, then perhaps go back to the original book, and then to one or several others on the shelf. Eventually, we reach a point where the ten books do not have all the necessary information. It is necessary to visit the library once again for needed information. However, before we can borrow an additional book, one on the shelf must be removed and returned. We will naturally pick the book that has been the least recently used, since it is the one least likely to be needed in the immediate future. Thus, we replace the least needed book with one immediately needed, borrowed from the library. Once again we have all the needed information close at hand, and these books are accessed as needed. Eventually, we may have to visit the library again and replace another book, as we did previously. However, we only visit the library on rare occasions, since most of the time the information needed *is* in one of the books. The principle at work here is "locality of references." Humans organize information in a very structured manner, which is fundamental and necessary for any kind of organized thought or behavior. Imagine what it would be like to write this essay if every page of every book dealt with a totally different subject. You would have to be running to the library very often, which takes orders of magnitude longer than turning a page or accessing another book. It would become a very inefficient process.

Thus, locality of reference is a fundamental property of human behavior and is the foundation of cache (and virtual memory) design. Since the books are very close to you, they can be accessed very quickly. Also, since there are only ten, it is easy to recognize and access the next book needed. If our shelf could contain hundreds or thousands of books, both the access time and the addressing time (i.e. time to find the right one) become much longer and make the task less efficient.

A very key component in the overall task time-to-completion is the time to reload a miss. Clearly, if the time to visit the library and reload our shelf becomes very small, the number of misses is not significant in the total time to complete the task. Conversely, if the reload time is very large, then the reload time can dominate the total task time. Thus, it is desirable to minimize both the access time to books on our shelf, as well as reload time for misses. This is especially true as the actual time to process the task (i.e. do the writing) becomes smaller and smaller, which is the trend in computers (i.e. their processing speed is increasing rapidly).

A cache is analogous to the office shelf, while main memory is analogous to the library. Only a small part of the main memory library is resident in the cache office at any one time—that part containing the information needed immediately and that part most likely to be needed soon. When a time is reached for which the needed information is not in the cache, this is referred to as a cache "miss," meaning that an access to the cache does not produce the desired information. The miss ratio is defined as the percent of access misses. Thus, if 100 accesses are attempted to the cache, and 8 of them miss, requiring a reload from main memory, the miss ratio is 8 percent.

When a miss occurs, we must "cast out" one cache block, as previously, to make room for "reloading" the new one. The block picked to be cast out is that "least recently used," just as above. The old block is replaced by the new one, and the so called "replacement algorithm" is "least recently used."

The unit of data transfer and replacement, namely the books in our example, were called "blocks" in the original and early designs, but more recently are referred to as cache "lines." The size of cache blocks or lines has varied over the years and for different designs, with typical values ranging from 16 to 128 bytes. As the speed and technology of computers improves, the size of all parameters tends to increase. For example, the caches in the original Model 85 and 195 were 16K and 32K bytes with block size of 64 bytes. Both of these were very large, high-performance processors in their time. These should be compared with the Intel i860 microprocessor of 1989 vintage, which has a 4K byte instruction cache and 8K byte data cache with 32-byte blocks fabricated directly on the processor chip, the IBM RS/6000 workstation first delivered in 1990, which has a 64K byte cache with 128 byte blocks, and the largest IBM 3090 system with a 256K byte cache using 128 byte blocks.

Miss Ratios From the above discussion, it should be clear that, when a task is first started, little or none of the required information is present in the cache. Thus, the miss ratio will initially be large. However, as the desired information is reloaded, locality of reference will make the miss ratio decrease to a small value, typically a few percent. The miss ratio will vary with time in the same way and for the same reason as it did in our previous example, but after the initial startup, it will typically remain reasonably small. When the current task is completed and a new task started, we will again experience the initial startup misses.

Over a long time good cache designs typically achieve an average miss ratio of less than 10 percent, and, for many tasks, a few percent is quite common. Obviously, the more misses on average, the longer it takes to complete the task and thus the lower the overall performance of the processor. A very small task that fits into the cache will have very few misses and give the appearance of high performance. A task that is much larger than the cache will have a substantial number of misses. If the reload time has not been well designed, the performance may be very good for small problems, but very poor for large ones. Thus, in evaluating a processor with a cache, it is important to measure performance with problems at least as large as will be typically processed on the system.

Cache Organization and Addressing In order to illustrate the various possible organizations as well as the inherent problems, let us continue with our office shelf and library example, but with some small changes for expediency. Suppose our office shelf can accommodate a maximum of 26 books. We will assume for the first case that 26 books can be arranged in any order on the shelf. The title of each book is its address, or identifying tag, while the data desired is the information within the book. If we need any particular book (address) at any given moment, we will have to search through all the titles on the books to find the desired one. This is a *fully associative* mapping of book titles to physical locations on the shelf. The addressing, or accessing, of any one book requires associative compares in our brains. We compare the title of each book with the image of the desired title in our brains. Because our brains are sequential, we would do this serially, one book at a time. In the worst case, we may have to do 26 such compares, one on each book title if the desired book is the last one. In order to speed-up the search process, a computer would have 26 compare circuits in parallel, one for each title, so that all compares could be done simultaneously. It can be seen that, if the number of books on our shelf gets very large, the number of compares required increases proportionally. This can become very cumbersome, so some alternative methods for mapping and accessing the books are desirable.

We can greatly simplify the addressing by using a so-called "direct mapping." To accomplish this in our example, we divide our shelf into 26 slots and label each with one letter of the alphabet, as shown in Fig. 1. Now, any book title (address) that begins with A must be placed only in slot A, those beginning with B into slot B, etc. For simplicity, we assume all books are about the same physical size, so fitting them in the slots is not a concern. This is the equivalent of using cache blocks/lines of fixed size. If the sizes were all vastly different, an additional and even more complex problem would be encountered in trying to use all the available shelf space efficiently. All cache designs avoid this by using a fixed book (block) size.

Continuing with our example, if we now need any book title that begins with, say, R, we can find it immediately since it can only be in one location, the R slot. This makes the accessing very simple, but produces an inefficient office (cache) design for the following reasons.

Suppose we have four books that all begin with A and that are all used very frequently. Unfortunately, only one of these can be resident in our office at any one time. Under the ground rules assumed, this is the case *even* if many of the other slots are empty on the shelf. Thus, we will have to make frequent visits to the library to reload our shelf, and the effeciency of the task is greatly degraded. This is an inherent limitation of direct mapped organizations, so they are almost never used.

One simple way to improve the office cache accessing capability is to use a combination of direct and associative mapping. This can be achieved as follows, and is analogous to what was actually used for many years and is still in use. Let us combine the book slots of Fig. 1 into groups of four slots, as shown in Fig. 2. Each slot is now four times larger than previously and can hold four books, with any combination of titles and in any order, but starting only with the label above the slot. For instance, the first slot can

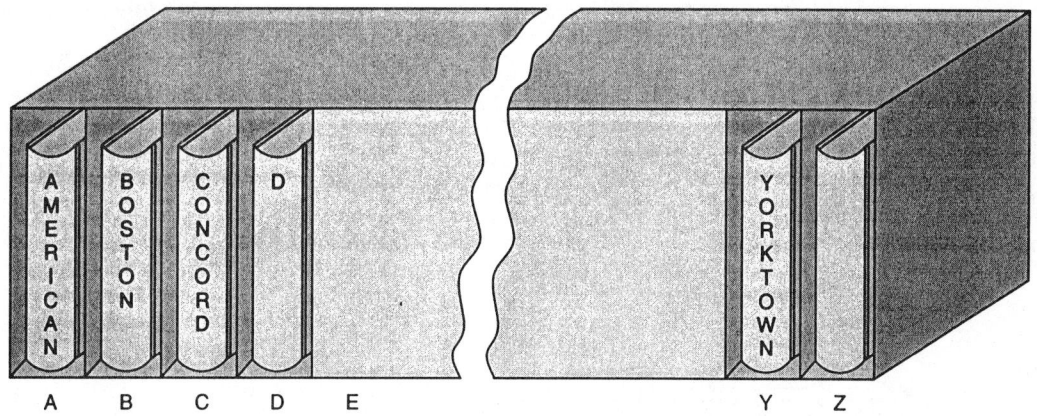

FIG. 1. Office shelf-cache, using direct mapping of one book per shelf slot.

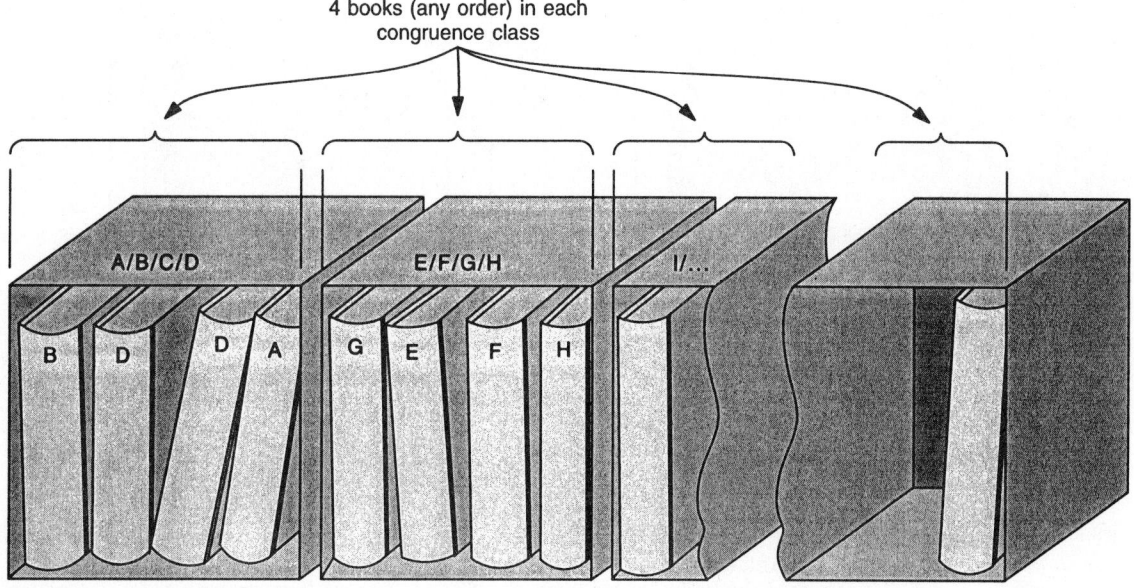

FIG. 2. Office shelf-cache using 4-way set-associative mapping.

hold any four books having titles starting with A, or B, or C, or D in any combination. Thus, at one instant, the four books could have titles starting with B, D, D, A, as shown. At some future time, after we have reloaded some new books into the first slot, the titles and their relative ordering can be different. We can have any combination of A, B, C, and D in any order. Thus, to access a book having a title starting with any of these four letters, we first do a *direct access* to the first group and then we must do four associative compares to find the desired book within the group of four. If we do not get a compare match, then a miss has occurred and a reload is necessary.

This is known as a *set associative organization* and is widely used in caches and other translation components of computers. The example above is four-way set associative because four compares must be made for each and every access. Each group of four slots is known as a *congruence class.*

Set Associative Cache Organization
Since the earliest days, caches have, with few exceptions, all been organized in a set-associative configuration. This organization is very commonly used by almost everyone at one time or another, but we are just not aware of its application elsewhere. An ordinary pop-up telephone index is a perfect analogy to a cache and thus will be used to make the concepts understandable. The phone directory we will use is the ordinary desktop type that allows us to move a pointer to some letter of the alphabet and then

push a button to access the information contained under that letter. Its use is detailed below.

Cache Example Using Set Associative Telephone Directory In our previous office example, the address of the desired information resided with the data. In a cache, the addresses are contained in a small directory, separate from the data since the latter are typically much larger. A perfect analogy can be obtained by using two ordinary, desktop telephone directories, with some minor modifications, as illustrated in Fig. 3. The addresses are contained in the Directory on the left side, while the data (phone numbers in this case) are contained in the Storage Array on the right side, as shown. There is one congruence class for each letter of the alphabet. In the Directory, each congruence class can contain four names, all beginning with the letter of the alphabet belonging to that congruence class. In a similar manner, each congruence class in the array can contain four phone numbers belonging to the addresses in the directory. There is an exact one-to-one correspondence between addresses in the Directory and data in the array.

As an example, suppose we have previously reloaded congruence class K with four names in the Directory, namely Kerr, Kagan, Knopf, and Kantor. Internal to the directory, we do not have to include the letter K with each name, since the external mechanical selector picks (translates) the letter K—the names cannot start with any other letter in this congruence class. The K congruence class in

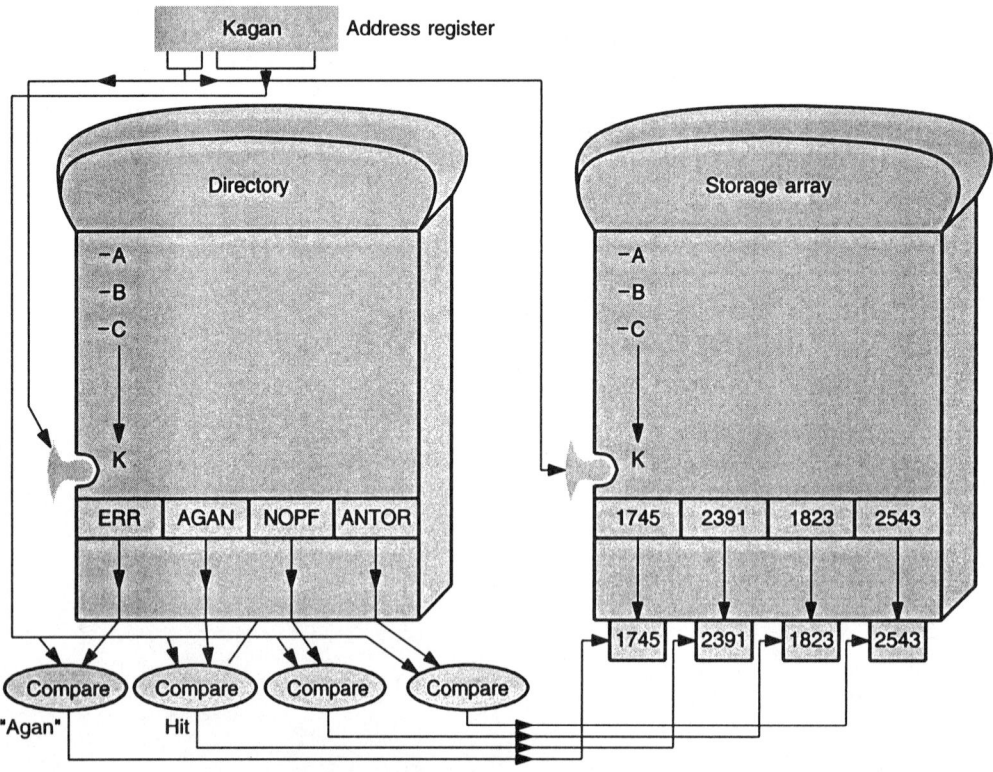

FIG. 3. 4-way set-associative, late select organization.

the array contains the numbers 1745 for Kerr, 2391 for Kagan, etc. Now suppose we wish to find the number for Kagan, which is the full address appearing in our address register at the top of Fig. 3. The first letter, K, is used to access the K congruence class in both the directory and array by moving both selectors to the letter K, as shown. We push the buttons to open both directories and retrieve four names and four numbers. The remaining portion of the starting address, namely "AGAN" (Kagan without the K), is compared simultaneously with the four names accessed. If a match occurs, the corresponding number is selected for use. In this case, a match (HIT) occurs on the second entry in the K congruence class, so the second number in the array is used. If no compare match was obtained, a MISS has obviously resulted, requiring a reload.

This example is a perfect analogy to a real cache in another very important way. Notice that in the example above, access to the array was done at the same time as access to the directory. By the time the four address compares are completed, the four possible numbers are also accessed so that it is only necessary to select one of the four using the compare signal. In an actual cache, the directory and storage array would both be arrays of static RAM devices with appropriate address decoders, sense amplifiers, etc. An address K (in binary) would be applied to both arrays, and the internal information would be latched at the edge of each array in sense amplifier/latches. The directory will have four compare circuits on the periphery of the array that will do the remaining address matching. If a match is obtained, a direct enable signal is sent to the corresponding register on the storage array and the data is gated to its destination, usually the processor.

This is called a *late-select* organization, since the data is accessed simultaneously with the addresses; if a match occurs, the late-select signal from the match only has to gate the data out of the latch on the edge of the storage array. Late-select is an extremely fast organization for accessing a cache and is used widely. If we did not use it, we might be forced to first access the directory for the match and then subsequently access the storage array for data. This serial access of first address and then data is much slower than accessing both addresses and data, and using a late-select signal.

The use of a cache to bridge the performance gap between processors and main memory has become important in the entire range of computer designs from personal computers (*q.v.*), workstations (*q.v.*), and mini and mid-range systems, up through very high performance processors. Its use in future systems will become even more important and widespread as processor speed and main memory capacity both continue to increase.

References

1977. Matick, R. E. *Computer Storage Systems and Technology.* Chapter 9, New York: John Wiley and Sons.
1991. Apiki, Steve, and Grehan, Rick. "Caching Cards Speed Data Access," *Byte,* **16**, 1 (January) 168–182.

RICHARD E. MATICK

CAD. *See* COMPUTER-AIDED DESIGN/COMPUTER-AIDED MANUFACTURING.

CAI. *See* COMPUTER-ASSISTED INSTRUCTION.

CALCULATING MACHINES

For articles on related subjects *see* BURROUGHS, WILLIAM S.; CALCULATORS, ELECTRONIC and PROGRAMMABLE; LEIBNIZ, GOTTFRIED WILHELM VON; NAPIER, JOHN; and PASCAL, BLAISE.

The art of mechanical calculation could be said to date back to whenever people first used pebbles or grains of corn to keep track of their belongings. However, the subject is usually thought of as starting when mechanical calculators were invented. A *mechanical calculator* is a device that has three properties: a mechanism that will act as a register to store a number; a mechanism to add a fixed amount to the number stored in that register; and an addition mechanism having the ability to deal automatically with any carry, from one digit to the next, that is generated during the addition process.

The first known device of this kind (Fig. 1a) was produced by the German scholar Wilhelm Schickard (1592–1635) in 1623 as a response to a request for calculating help from the astronomer Johann Kepler. Unfortunately, the machine was destroyed in a fire before Kepler ever saw it, but descriptions and drawings have been found in their correspondence that are sufficiently detailed to enable reconstructions. The upper portion of the

FIG. 1a. Schickard's calculator.

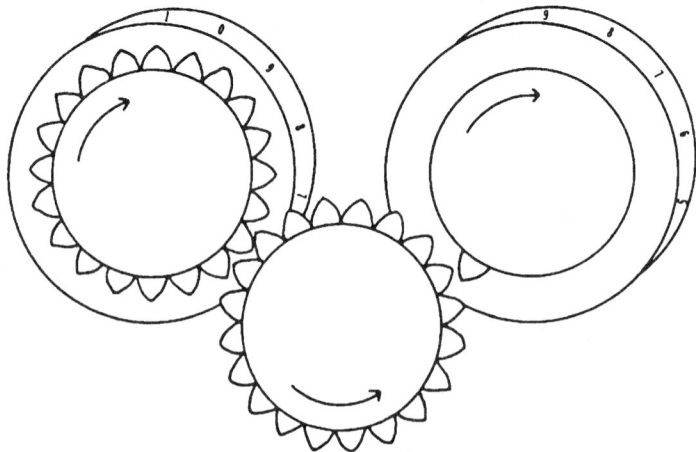

FIG. 1b. The Schickard carry mechanism.

machine contains a multiplication table in the form of cylindrical Napier's bones with slides that allow one row at a time to be seen. The lower part contains a very simple register, much like an automobile odometer, each digit of which contains a single tooth that, when it rotates from 9 to 0, will cause the next wheel on the left to rotate one digit position.

There are two major problems with this "single-tooth" carry mechanism (Fig. 1b). The first is that the addition 99,999 + 1 will result in a carry being propagated right through the register. This means that considerable force must be used in turning the units digit wheel—enough force to break gears that are not manufactured out of modern high-strength materials. The second problem is more subtle. As can be seen in the diagram, the process of carrying a one to the next digit position is done by the single-tooth gear entering the teeth of the intermediate gear, rotating it 36 degrees (1/10 of a revolution), and exiting from the intermediate gear teeth, all while rotating only 36 degrees itself. This problem led to some very interesting gear designs.

The next major advance in mechanical calculation came 19 years later when Blaise Pascal, the famous French mathematician and philosopher, invented an adding machine with a gravity-assisted carry mechanism (Fig. 2a). The two difficulties with the single-tooth carry were overcome in the Pascal machine by the simple expedient of having a weight lift up as the digits of the register rotate (Fig. 2b). When a carry was necessary, the weight would

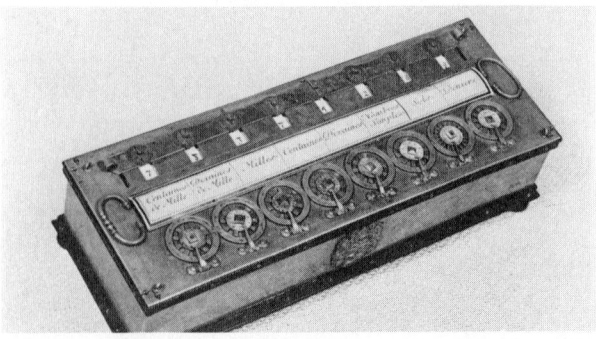

FIG. 2a. Pascal's calculating machine. (Photograph courtesy of IBM Archives.)

fall and "kick" the adjacent digit of the register over one position. By having each digit-carry mechanism driven by gravity, the problem of having to use excess force on the right-hand digit of the register to propagate a carry several digit places was eliminated. The only force needed was to turn the rightmost wheel; the carry weight would drop and that force would turn the wheel next to it, etc. Pascal was then faced with the problem of creating an "over-rotation preventer" to stop the left digit from rotating too far when a "carry-kick" was given by a digit on the right. Pascal experimented for several years with different versions of his machine, even attempting to interest people in purchasing them for help with their accounting chores. His commercial ventures were unsuccessful, but it did result in about 60 of the machines surviving to modern times.

The story now switches back to Germany and Gottfried Wilhelm von Leibniz (1646–1716). During one of his many trips to France as a diplomat, he saw a copy of the Pascal machine and became intrigued with the concept. When he attempted to add extra gearing on top in order to form a machine with which he could multiply, he discovered that the internal mechanism was not capable of simultaneous action on all digits at once. For the next 20 years he toyed with different ideas, but even after he had envisioned what is today called the *Leibniz stepped-drum principle*, he was unable to construct his machine until he encountered a French clock maker named Olivier who had the necessary skills. The Leibniz machine, which was to be the basic pattern for many mechanical calculating machines for the next 300 years, was constructed during the summer of 1674.

Leibniz's inventive genius led him to create a machine in which a number could be set up on an input mechanism and, once set, could be added to the result register by simply turing a crank. Thus, to multiply a number such as 375 by 15, it was only necessary to put 375 on the set-up mechanism and turn the crank 15 times. Leibniz saw that the more efficient way would be to have the set-up mechanism movable along the gearing that formed the result register—this allowed one to set 375 on the set-up, turn the crank five times (adding 375*5=1,875 to the result register), shift the input mechanism one place to the left (effectively making the set-up take on the value of 3750),

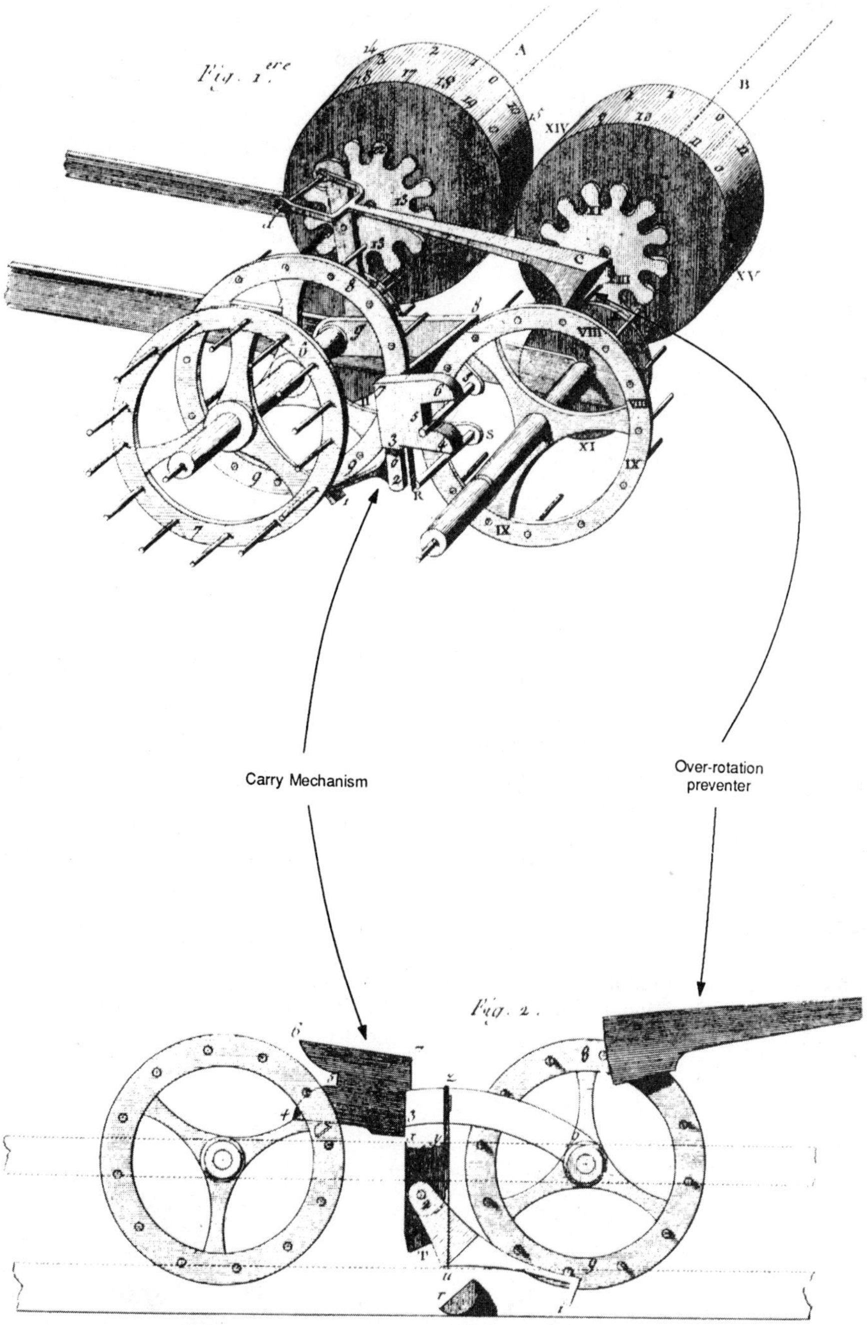

Fig. 1.ere

Carry Mechanism

Over-rotation preventer

Fig. 2.

FIG. 2b. Single-tooth carry mechanism.

and then turn the crank once (adding 3,750 to the result register). The movable set-up section is clearly visible in the picture of the Leibniz machine (Fig. 3).

The concept of how the machine functioned can be seen by noting the diagram (Fig. 4) showing a single digit of the machine (without any of the mechanical apparatus that controlled the carry operation). The result wheel, shown at the end of the square shaft, showed the current digit being stored. To add a value, say 8, to this wheel, it was necessary to rotate the square shaft 8 positions. That could be accomplished by moving the small gear up or down the square shaft until it was in such a position that, when the large drum was rotated one full revolution, 8 of its long teeth would interact with the gear on the square

shaft to move the result wheel 8 positions around. Once the mechanism had been set up to hold a number (375 being done by having the small gear on the units digit set to the 5 position, the tens gear set to the 7, and the

FIG. 3. The Leibniz calculating machine. (Photograph courtesy of IBM Archives.)

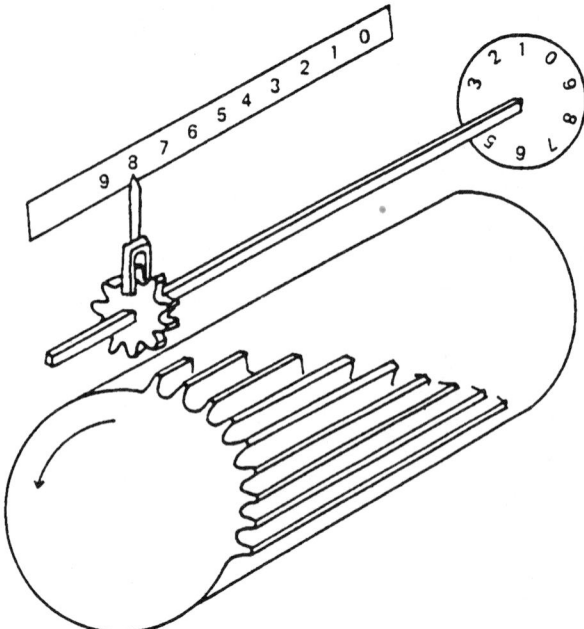

FIG. 4. A drawing of Leibniz's stepped-drum mechanism.

hundreds to the 3), a single turn of the crank would cause all the large stepped-drum gears to rotate through a full revolution and add 375 to the result wheels.

Needless to say, the entire mechanism was more complex than that shown here, the carry mechanism being the most complicated portion. Even then, it sometimes required the operator to stop and help the machine if a carry of more than two decimal places was needed. Nonetheless, this stepped-drum concept was central to most of the attempts at constructing calculating machines for the next 200 years.

Many others made calculating machines of one form or another, some fully functional, others only marginally so, but none was a commercial success. Occasional machines were actually sold by their manufacturers, but they were usually not used for anything except display purposes to show that their owners could afford the latest in scientific toys. The exception to this was the machine made by Charles Xavier Thomas, sometimes known as Thomas de Colmar, a French insurance executive. He was familiar enough with the manufacturing processes available around 1820 to design a workable mechanical calculator and create a successful business by selling them to people who actually wanted to perform computations. The Thomas Arithmometer was based on the Leibniz stepped-drum principle, but had a fully working carry mechanism. It was first demonstrated to the French Academy of Science in 1820, and several thousand were sold in Europe and occasionally elsewhere, until about 1900. This same technology was used by many other manufacturers and could be found, often in greatly modified form, in mechanical adding machines still being made in the 1970s.

The major problem with any machine based on the Leibniz stepped drum was the fact that it was both large and heavy. A machine with a many digit capacity would often require two people to move it from place to place. The Leibniz drum essentially provided a gear with a variable number (0–9) of teeth, but at the cost of size and weight. A number of attempts at producing a true variable-toothed gear that would literally change the number of teeth protruding from its surface were unsuccessful until the solution was found, essentially simultaneously, by Willigodt T. Odhner, a Swede working in Russia, and Frank S. Baldwin, an American, in about the year 1874.

As can be seen in the illustration (Fig. 5), the movement of the lever would cause the circular cam to force

FIG. 5. An illustration of the variable-toothed gear.

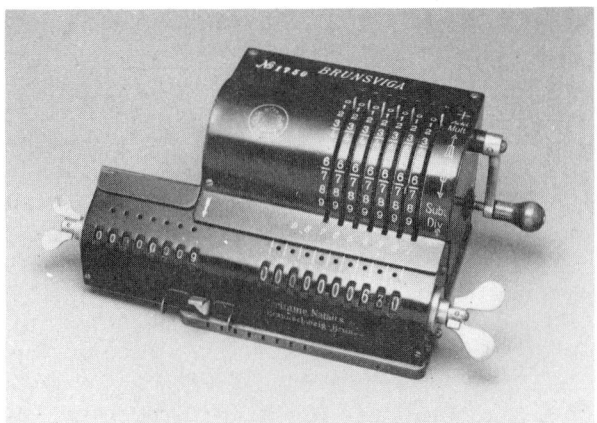

FIG. 6. A Brunsviga Calculator. (Courtesy of Smithsonian Institution.)

different numbers of pins through the edge surface of the gear, the pins acting as gear teeth when the whole mechanism was rotated about the central axis. Odhner first produced his "pin wheel" calculator in 1874 at a factory he had set up in St. Petersburg. The concept quickly spread and soon the famous Brunsviga firm was producing them in Germany, the Baldwin calculators were being made in America, and the original Odhner firm was continuing to produce them in Russia. By 1912 the Brunsviga firm alone had produced over 20,000 machines (Fig. 6) and the total worldwide production was likely many times that number.

The only significant advance on the technology of the variable-toothed gear was the key-driven adding machine. It had long been recognized that the act of moving a setting lever contained enough energy actually to perform the addition if a suitable mechanical mechanism could be invented. Dorr E. Felt, an American, produced the first workable system in 1886, which he named the Comptometer (Fig. 7). By combining the action of entering a number with the action of actually adding it to a mechanical register, the process of performing simple addition was speeded up by several orders of magnitude. This allowed the Comptometer—and similar machines

FIG. 8. The Curta. (Courtesy of Smithsonian Institution.)

made by Burroughs and others—to become practical tools for the business office.

There were, of course, many improvements to these very basic devices over the years. The addition of a printing mechanism allowed users to keep track of their computations. The replacement of human motive power by electric motors allowed both faster computation and less fatigue for the operator. The improvements in engineering technology shrunk the size and weight of the machines to the point where the Curta calculator (Fig. 8), ironically enough based on the Leibniz stepped drum, could not only be carried in pockets, but was actually used by holding it in one hand. However the speed, flexibility, and ultra–light weight of the electronic calculators began to replace the mechanical ones in the modern era. By the early 1970s, even the Curta had ceased production.

In the middle years of the twentieth century electro-mechanical desktop calculating machines manufactured by Brunsviga, Facit, Friden, Marchant and Monroe, among others, were widely used but, with the advent of the hand-held electronic calculator, they disappeared.

References

1914. Horsburgh, E. M. *Handbook of the Napier Tercentenary Celebration on Modern Instruments and Methods of Calculation.* Edinburgh: The Royal Society of Edinburgh (reprinted by M.I.T. Press and Tomash Publishers, 1982).

1921. Turck, J. V. A. *Origin of Modern Calculating Machines.* Chicago: The Western Society of Engineers.

1989. Aspray, W. (Ed.) *Computing Before Computers,* Ames, IA: The Iowa State University Press.

FIG. 7. An early Comptometer. (Courtesy of Smithsonian Institution.)

MICHAEL R. WILLIAMS

CALCULATORS, ELECTRONIC AND PROGRAMMABLE

For articles on related subjects *see* CALCULATING MACHINES; DIGITAL COMPUTERS: HISTORY: PERSONAL COMPUTERS.; and LAPTOP COMPUTERS.

It is believed that the first mechanical calculating device was the abacus. There is evidence that the abacus was invented prior to 500 B.C. Visitors to the Far East will know that the abacus is still a common form of desk calculator and is used with great dexterity and speed.

Modern calculators are descendants of a digital arithmetic machine devised by Blaise Pascal (*q.v.*) in 1642. In 1671, Gottfried Von Leibniz (*q.v.*) designed a calculating machine that could add and multiply, with multiplication being performed by repeated addition. During the late nineteenth century and early twentieth century, inventors produced calculators that were progressively smaller and less and less laborious to use.

Prior to the 1950s, desktop calculators were either key driven or used a rotating drum to enter sums punched into a keyboard. Eventually, this drum was spun by an electric motor. The invention of the transistor in 1948 and the integrated circuit in 1964 were the two events that formed the basis for the electronic calculator revolution. Minature solid-state electronics enabled calculators to progress past the basic four arithmetic functions to the point where they are capable of performing almost any function that can be expressed as a programmable sequence or a mathematical formula.

By 1974, calculators using modern electronic technology cost less than $50 and could outperform mechanical calculators that had once sold for up to $1500. Today, some handheld calculators can be purchased for less than $5; and $300 will buy an extremely sophisticated calculator.

Some electronic calculators are intended for desk use, but since 1970 numerous hand models have been available, some as small as a credit card. At the same time, solar or other long-life batteries brought about calculators that can operate for thousands of hours without energy source replacements.

Nearly all calculators have programmed microinstructions; their circuitry can do any of several different things depending on coded commands stored in the system. Some electronic calculators are programmed externally. In this case, a sequence of operations is entered into the calculator, much as occurs during the programming of a computer.

As electronic calculators, increase in capabilities, the gap closes between the capabilities of a calculator and the capabilities of an electronic computer. The programmable calculator was first introduced in 1974 by Hewlett-Packard. Today, calculators such as the Hewlett-Packard HP 48SX can translate calculus and other types of engineering problems into pictures. Punch in an equation and the calculator can draw the result, complete with annotations, on its 1-inch by 3-inch liquid-crystal display.

The HP 48SX calculator, shown in the photo in Fig. 1, includes features that make it a virtual microcomputer,

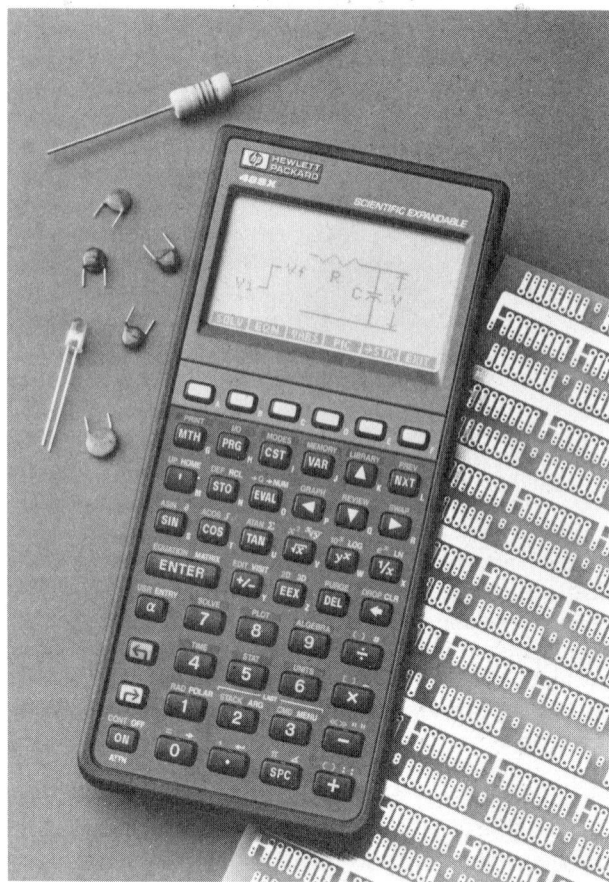

FIG. 1. The HP 48SX scientific calculator. (Courtesy of Hewlett-Packard Corpaoration.)

including 32K bytes of RAM, 256K bytes of ROM (Read-only Memory - *q.v.*), and a serial I/O interface. This calculator can be expanded up to 288K bytes and can interface with MS-DOS or Macintosh computer systems and infrared printers. One special feature of the 48SX calculator is a greatly improved 8-row by 22-column supertwist LCD display. This display provides the ability to enter equations exactly as they would be entered on paper.

Electronic calculators are designed to perform their functions using either algebraic notation or RPN, Reverse Polish Notation (*see* POLISH NOTATION). Algebraic notation permits entry of calculations as normally written (e.g. ($\boxed{2}$ + $\boxed{3}$) with the arithmetic function between the two numbers–infix notation. With RPN, the operator is placed after the two numbers, ($\boxed{2}\boxed{3}\boxed{+}$), and, therefore, the operator is input *after* both numbers have been entered (postfix notation). The former requires parenthesizing for all but the simplest calculations, whereas RPN allows any sequence of calculations to be entered without parentheses. It is unfamiliar however, and considerable learning is needed before it can be used easily. Other calculators have been programmed so that the "order of operations" rules are followed, thereby eliminating much of the need for entering parentheses. (*See* OPERATOR PRECEDENCE.)

Calculators typically compute non-zero numbers in a range from 10^{-99} to 10^{99} and print from 8 to 12 digits in the display. If the answer is larger than the display,

FIG. 2.   The TI Math Explorer calculator. (Courtesy of Texas Instruments Corporation.)

many calculators will automatically express the answer in scientific notation. A typical advanced nonprogrammable electronic caculator would normally include the following scientific functions: x^2, $\sqrt{x}$, $1/x$, y^x, x-y interchange, normal and inverse trigonometric functions, logarithms to the bases 10 and e, e^x, 10^x, $x!$, and degree to radian conversions. Statistical functions often included are summation, mean, and standard deviation. Other common calculator capabilities are the ability to store a number in memory, to add to memory, to divide into a number saved in memory, and to exchange the display with memory.

Special-purpose calculators have been designed for many professions and hobbies, including finance, statistics, business, mathematics, science, economics, accounting, real estate, sports, and time management. A relatively inexpensive calculator developed by Texas Instruments, called the Math Explorer (Fig. 2), is able to add, subtract, multiply, divide, and reduce fractions, in addition to many of the normal functions found on most calculators. Sports Page is a "pocket electronic scoreboard." Its two-line display gives the latest lineups and results of college and professional football, basketball, baseball, soccer, hockey games, and even horse racing. It gets its input from local transmitters that are fed by satellite. Sharp's DialMaster EL-6250 stores 200 names and numbers and calls one automatically when held to a touch-tone phone. It also works as a calculator and has two electronic memo pads to record appointments and make notes.

Americans have been purchasing in excess of 4 million calculators per year for nearly two decades. Texas Instruments, Casio, Sharp, Unisonic, and Novis are the leaders in total number of calculators sold each year.

JERALD L. MIKESELL

CALL.   *See* CALLING SEQUENCE; and PROCEDURE.

CALL-BY-NAME, -REFERENCE, OR -VALUE.   *See* PARAMETER PASSING.

CALLING SEQUENCE

For articles on related subjects *see* ACTIVATION RECORD, PARAMETER PASSING; and PROCEDURE.

A *calling sequence* is the precise sequence of one or more commands or statements needed to invoke a subordinate procedure. In a high-level language like Pascal, procedures are called by stating their name, followed by a parenthesized list of the actual parameters that the procedure needs to do its work. An example is

```
search(haystack,150,'needle',locations)
```

which invokes a procedure that searches an array of 150 character strings called *haystack* and places in an array called *locations* the indices (subscripts) of all *haystack* locations that contain "needle."

The single-statement calling sequence just cited is properly formed only if it contains exactly the right number of parameters expected by the called procedure, the parameters are specified in the expected order, and the data type of each parameter (integer, real, string, etc.) is what is expected.

The mechanism used for parameter passing (*q.v.*) may limit the form of the expression used to cite actual parameters. For example, if the second parameter used with procedure *search* is to be an integer passed by value, then the actual parameter used in this position could be an expression such as $n-j+2$, just as well as a particular number like 150. But if the first and last parameters are passed by reference (VAR parameters in the vocabulary of Pascal), the actual parameters used in those positions must be variable names (as they are in the example given).

The term *calling sequence* predates the use of high-level languages. In an assembly language, such as is used with the Digital Equipment Corporation VAX computer, the calling sequence for a machine-language version of *search* would be

```
PUSHAL locations   ; Push the address of
 symbol "locations"
PUSHAL item        ; Push the address of the
 1st byte of string sought
PUSHL #150         ; Push the value 150
PUSHAL haystack    ; Push the address of
                   ; symbol "haystack"
CALLS #4,search    ; Call search with 4
                   ; parameters
```

Note that, with respect to the one-statement Pascal calling sequence, parameters are pushed in right-to-left order so that the first parameter, the address of *haystack*, ends up at the top of the stack. Each push command ends with "L" because, on the VAX, both addresses and the most commonly used form of integer occupy Longwords (32 bits). The # symbol is the VAX way of specifying an immediate value. In accord with the assumptions made, only the 150 is passed by value (through use of PUSHL). The addresses of the other three parameters, not their values, are stacked through use of PUSHAL (the "A" indicating "address of") in accord with the procedure's expectation that these parameters are being passed by reference.

EDWIN D. REILLY

CAM. *See* AUTOMATION; and COMPUTER-AIDED DESIGN/ COMPUTER-AIDED MANUFACTURING.

CANADIAN INFORMATION PROCESSING SOCIETY (CIPS)

Purpose The objective of CIPS is the advancement of computer and information processing in Canada. To this end, it brings together scientists, business people, and others who make their careers in computing and information processing. The Society's activities include committees organized to pursue special interests, meetings, seminars, and conferences held at national and regional levels to exchange information, publications to disseminate information, and long-term commitments to promoting the use of computers in the best interests of society.

How Established CIPS was born in 1958 as a result of the Canadian Conference on Computing and Data Processing held in Toronto, 9–10 June 1958. The Society, established originally as the Computing and Data Processing Society of Canada, shortened its name to the Computer Society of Canada in 1965, and in 1968 its name was again amended to the present title. The current membership (1992) is over 6,700.

Presidents of the society since its inception have been:

Fred Thomas, 1958–1959
Hudson Stowe, 1959–1960
C. C. Gotlieb, 1960–1961
Otto M. Mackey, 1961–1962
J. H. Aitchison, 1962–1963
J. C. Davidson, 1963–1964
Harvey S. Gellman, 1964–1965
J. Wesley Graham, 1965–1967
Bernard Hodson, 1967–1968
B. B. Goodfellow, 1968–1969
Mers Kutt, 1969–1970
George A. Fierheller, 1970–1971
James M. Kennedy, 1971–1972
James H. Finch, 1972–1973
Grant N. Boyd, 1973–1974

Robert T. Horwood, 1974–1975
Joseph B. Reid, 1975–1976
T. Ross Jewell, 1976–1977
Glenn McInnes, 1977–1978
Wayne A. Davis, 1978–1979
Larry R. Symes, 1979–1980
Chris G. K. Bishop, 1980–1981
Alvin G. Fowler, 1981–1982
John E. Bates, 1982–1983
Bernard Hodson, 1983–1984
Gary Hadford, 1984–1985
Rod Shearing, 1985–1986
Marilyn Harris, 1986–1987
Gaylen Duncan, 1987–1988
Patricia Glenn, 1988–1989
Patricia Bewers, 1989–1990
Nelson Armstrong, 1990–1991
Normard Paradis, 1991–1992

Organizational Structure The Management of the Society is vested in the National Board of Directors consisting of six nationally elected Executive Committee members, eleven regionally elected Directors, and one elected representative from each of the Society's 17 Special Interest Groups. Members of the Executive Committee act as officers of the Society, and, together with the Regional Directors, they constitute the governing body of the Society.

The President normally holds office for one year and then remains on the Board as Past-President for an additional year. The First Vice-President automatically becomes the next president. The other three elected members of the Executive—the Second Vice-President, the Secretary, and the Treasurer—are elected as a group for a two-year period.

The various Standing Committees of the Society, which report directly to the National Board of Directors, include Publication, Constitution, Membership, Administration, Professional Standards, Government Liaison, Public Service/Public Relations, and Audit. Committee Chairs are appointed by the President and normally serve two-year terms. The Committees are guided by Terms of Reference, which have been established by the National Board of Directors.

The 17 sections of CIPS across the country continue to be the focal point of Society activities. Local executives meet on an ongoing basis to plan programs and administer section affairs. Section activities include programs of invited speakers, panels, seminars, and tours.

To foster development in specialized areas, CIPS has a number of Special Interest Groups, including the Computer Science Association, the Canadian Image Processing and Pattern Recognition Society, and the Canadian Society for the Computational Study of Intelligence.

There are six classes of membership—Active, Student, Graduated, Certified, Retired, and Honorary. Eligibility for active membership requires that the individual be engaged in the administration, practice, or teaching of computing and information processing. Student membership requires that the individual be registered full time in a recognized educational institution. Student members who graduate are called Graduated Members for two years and pay reduced fees. Certified Members are active Members who have applied for and been granted CIPS certification as an Information Systems Professional of Canada (I.S.P.). Retired Members are active members for at least 10 years who have retired from full-time employment and who pay reduced fees. Honorary membership is awarded to those who, in the opinion of the National Board, have made an outstanding contribution to computing and information processing.

The headquarters of CIPS are at 430 King Street W., Suite 205, Toronto, Ontario, M5V 1L5.

Technical Program Conferences have remained a major activity of the Society. In addition to the National Conference held each year in the early summer, CIPS also organizes one-day national seminars. Important topics, such as EDP Audit and Security and Distributed Data Processing, have been covered by these seminars. CIPS also sponsors the annual Canadian Computer Show and Conference in Toronto and the Salon de l'ordinateur in Montreal. These two events, the largest of their kind in Canada, each attract upwards of 20,000 people.

The four main publications of CIPS are:

- *CIPS Review*, a bimonthly publication which contains informative, useful, and controversial articles covering the broad spectrum of information processing. (Theme issues have included *Computers and Health, Manpower, Leasing, and Communications Policy*.)
- *The Canadian Computer Census*, the authoritative Canadian directory of computer installations in Canada, used by researchers, marketers, foreign companies, and government agencies, which has been published annually by the Society since the early 1960s.
- *The Canadian Salary Survey*, an annual publication, which is a guide to Canadian salaries at all occupational levels in the data processing industry.
- *Infor Journal*, a quarterly publication, which is the leading Canadian scientific journal in the computing field, and contains refereed technical papers. *Infor* is published jointly by CIPS and the Canadian Operational Research Society.

Additionally, the Society publishes proceedings following each conference, and from time to time publishes special material, such as *"CIPS Tips"—A Buyers Guide to Small Business Computers*.

MARION J. HART

CARD. See PUNCHED CARD; and PUNCHED CARD MACHINERY.

CASE. See COMPUTER-ASSISTED SOFTWARE ENGINNERING.

CATALOG. See DIRECTORY.

CBI. See CHARLES BABBAGE INSTITUTE.

CD-ROM

For articles on related subjects *see* MEMORY: AUXILIARY; READ-ONLY MEMORY; and VIDEODISC.

CD-ROM (*compact disc, read-only memory*) is an optical storage medium, used primarily with personal computers. CD-ROM is slow compared to electronic or magnetic storage, but the capacity is very high and the cost per bit low. The capacity of a CD-ROM disc is over 600 MB, so roughly 100 copies of this encyclopedia would fit on a single CD-ROM, exclusive of space for digitized photographs and figures.

CD-ROM storage was adapted from audio CD, developed in the mid 1970s by Sony and Philips. CD-ROM units have been available for personal computers since the mid-1980s, but sales figures were not impressive until the end of that decade. According to InfoTech, a market research firm, there were 171,000 CD-ROM drives installed, mostly on IBM PCs, and 580 CD-ROM titles in production as of 1989. The industry sales rate was $406 million per year.

CD-ROM uses the same media and disc duplication facilities as audio CDs, and the drives are modified audio drives. Information is recorded as rough pits on a polished substrate, and is read by measuring reflected laser light. CD-ROM adds error-detection information not needed with audio CDs. Information is recorded in concentric, addressable tracks, like a magnetic disk and unlike videodisc. There are two standard logical file formats for CD-ROM: ISO 9660, for MS-DOS computers, and a format compatible with the Hierarchical File System used with Apple's Macintosh computer. Since CD-ROM capacity is high, many publishers press a single version of a disc, with data recorded in both HFS and ISO 9660 formats.

CD-ROM applications were pioneered by Gary Kildall and Bill Gates. Kildall, author of CP/M, an operating system that was widely used on early personal computers, worked with Grolier to publish the Academic American Encyclopedia in 1985. Gates, founder of Microsoft, has sponsored an annual CD-ROM Conference, has spearheaded the effort leading to the ISO 9660 standard, and has published a number of CD-ROMs and books on the topic.

Being read-only, CD-ROM is a publishing medium. The first applications were the publishing of reference material and databases, many of which were on-line or in other machine-readable form. Examples are the Grolier encyclopedia mentioned, telephone directories, and financial, bibliographic, and specialized alphanumeric databases. Such applications are now common in schools, libraries, and industry.

Some organizations also use CD-ROM internally. For example, Hewlett-Packard, DEC, and Apple offer software

FIG. 1. A CD-Rom disc in front of an equivalent stack of manuals from the Hewlett-Packard 9000 Series of Computers. (Courtesy of Hewlett-Packard.)

documentation on CD-ROM as an option to printed manuals (see Fig. 1). Apple uses CD-ROM to distribute new product information, training material, software, and developer's tools and other information to field personnel and customers. Arthur Andersen auditors carry CD-ROMs with reference material, including SEC regulations, proprietary auditing procedures, and auditing software and guidelines when they go into the field.

Nearly all of the applications to date have been character-oriented; however, effort is underway to extend CD-ROM by adding sound, graphics, and motion video. CD-ROM XA (CD-ROM Extended Architecture) is a proposed extension that specifies formats for recorded sound interleaved with data. CD-ROM XA enables applications in which voice and music can play "behind" still images and data displayed on the screen.

CD-I (Compact Disc Interactive) is another CD-ROM extension. CD-I systems are not intended to be computer peripherals, but rather standalone devices interfaced to television sets. The CD-I specification includes several quality levels for sound and still pictures.

Several companies are also pursuing motion video extensions. Most prominent is Intel with their DVI (Digital Video Interactive) format. Current DVI drives and controllers compress approximately 70 minutes of full-motion video material on a CD-ROM disc. The present quality is somewhat below NTSC television, but improving rapidly. Material is compressed and recorded off-line, but played back in real time.

These and other multimedia extensions to CD-ROM open the possibility of innovative applications in education, entertainment, and merchandising (see Fig. 2, color insert page CP-2). However, the production of such material is costly and requires creativity and new skills. While multimedia applications are still in the future, character-based applications of CD-ROM are entering the mainstream.

References

1987. Brand, Stewart, *The Media Lab*. Penguin Books. This is a non-technical book of the M.I.T. Media Lab. Brand paints an

optimistic picture of the lab and the computer-entertainment-publishing industry of the future.

1989. *1990 CD-ROM Yearbook*. Compiled by Salley Oberlin and Joyce Cox. Microsoft Press. This is 640 pages of very short (1–3 pages) articles on technology, applications, the industry, and future dreams, followed by 260 pages of directory information listing vendors, CD-ROM titles, publications, conferences, and so forth.

LAURENCE PRESS

CDC. *See* CONTROL DATA CORPORATION COMPUTERS.

CELLULAR AUTOMATA

For articles on related subjects *see* AUTOMATA THEORY; and PARALLEL PROCESSING.

A *cellular automaton*, or *polyautomaton*, is a theoretical model of a parallel computer, subject to various restrictions to make formal investigation of its computing powers tractable. All versions of the model share these properties: Each is an interconnection of identical cells, where a cell is a model of a computer with finite memory—i.e. a finite-state machine. Each cell computes an output from inputs it receives from a finite set of cells forming its neighborhood, and possibly from an external source.

All cells compute one output simultaneously and each cell computes an output at each tick of a clock, i.e. after each unit time step. The output of a cell is distributed to its neighborhood and possibly to an external receiver.

A version of the cellular automaton model exists for each set of choices in the following dichotomies: an infinite or a finite number of cells; a uniform interconnection scheme (all cells have neighborhoods of the same shape, e.g. that in Fig. 1) or a non-uniform scheme (Fig. 2); deterministic or non-deterministic cells (a choice of one output value at each unit time step or one of several values chosen randomly); the absence or presence of an external input (output), and, in the case of an external input (output), the automaton is connected to all cells or to only a subset; Moore-type or Mealy-type cells (unit time steps allowed or not allowed, respectively, between inputs and the associated output); a static or dynamic interconnection scheme (neighbor-

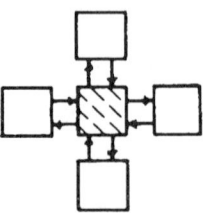

FIG. 1. A cell (hatched) and its neighborhood.

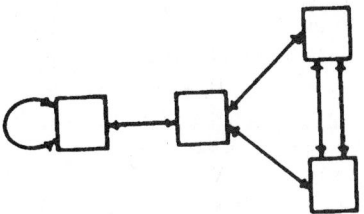

FIG. 2. A cellular automaton with non-uniform neighborhood.

hood does or does not remain fixed in time). Some of the names associated with one or more of these versions are cellular automaton, tessellation automaton, modular computer, iterative automaton, intelligent graph, Lindenmayer system, and cellular network.

The first version of the cellular automaton, historically, was the cellular space obtained by selecting the first choice in each dichotomy above, but with no external input or output. It can be visualized in two dimensions as an infinite chessboard, each square representing a cell. It has been used to prove the existence of non-trivial self-reproducing machines, is capable of computing any computable function with only three states per cell and the four nearest cells as the neighborhood (Fig. 1), and can exhibit *Garden of Eden configurations*; i.e. patterns of cell states at one time, which can never arise in a given cellular space except at time zero. If an external input is assumed distributed to each cell, then the cellular space becomes what is usually called a "tessellation" space.

The cellular automaton is obtained from the cellular space by admitting only a finite, connected set of cells on the chessboard (Fig. 3). A cell with a neighbor missing has a special boundary signal substituted instead. The cellular automaton is particularly useful as a pattern recognizer, where the pattern comprises the states of the cells at time zero, especially if non-deterministic cells are allowed. A famous problem for the (deterministic) cellular automaton, the Firing Squad problem, calls each cell a soldier with one of them as the general—i.e. all cells but one are "off" initially—and asks if all soldiers can begin firing simultaneously by going into the same state. The Firing Squad theorem, which solves this problem, guarantees an affirmative answer.

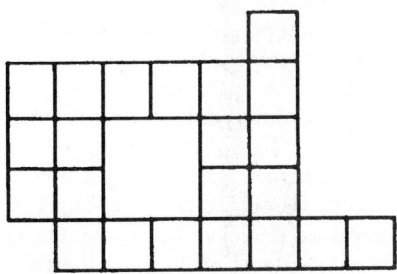

FIG. 3. A cellular automaton with uniform neighborhood of Fig. 1 assumed.

The Firing Squad theorem remains valid even when a non-uniform interconnection scheme is allowed. Thus, another version of the cellular automaton, the graphical cellular automaton (Fig. 2), requires only that the number of neighbors be fixed, not that they be in any fixed geometric relationship with a cell. They have been shown to be more powerful than the uniformly interconnected cellular automata.

The final type of cellular automaton to be mentioned, the dynamic cellular automaton, or *Lindenmayer system*, allows a cell to divide into children cells—regardless of the position of that cell in the initial array of cells—and allows the disappearance, or death, of cells. This version, with its dynamic interconnection scheme, is of interest to theoretical biologists as a model for the growth and development of living things.

The infinite chessboard cellular automaton model gained much public popularity in the 1970s as the so-called *Game of Life*. A resurgence of interest in the 1980s accompanied application of simple two-state, one-dimensional cellular automata to fractals (*q.v.*) and chaos, rich new subjects that arose during that decade.

References

1968. Codd, E. F. *Cellular Automata*, ACM Monograph Series. New York: Academic Press.
1971. Gardner, M. "On Cellular Automata, Self-Reproduction, the Garden of Eden, and the Game of Life." Mathematical Games Department, *Scientific American* 224: 112-117.
1976. Lindenmayer, A. and Rozenberg, G. (Eds.). *Automata, Languages, Development*. Amsterdam: North Holland.
1986. Wolfram, S. (Ed.). *Theory and Applications of Cellular Automata*. Singapore: World Scientific.

ALVY RAY SMITH

CENTRAL PROCESSING UNIT (CPU)

For articles on related subjects *see* ARITHMETIC-LOGIC UNIT; DIGITAL COMPUTERS; MEMORY: MAIN; and STORED PROGRAM CONCEPT.

A digital computer consists of a selection of units of various types, all interconnected and functioning harmoniously with one another under central control. Most of the units in a system are called "peripheral" devices and serve either as the means of feeding raw data or file data into the system or of receiving results or updated files from the system.

The term "peripheral" conjures up a vision in which these units surround others that serve as the focal point or center of the system (although this is rarely true physically). The name "central processor," or *central processing unit* (CPU), is used to describe elements that carry out a variety of essential data manipulations and controlling tasks at the heart of the computer.

The principal element of the CPU is the one required to carry out arithmetic and other, mainly logical, operations on data, which is usually called the *arithmetic logic unit* (ALU). It is designed to operate on a pair of numbers and carry out on them the processes of addition, subtraction, multiplication, and division. It can compare numbers and determine whether one is the greater or whether both are equal. These operations are carried out at very high speeds; even the slowest computers can do at least 100,000 such operations in a second, and the really fast "number crunchers" handle as many as 100 million.

Another important element of the CPU is the *control unit* required to supervise the functioning of the machine as a whole, calling into operation the various units as required by the program. It receives the program instructions one by one in sequence, interprets them, and sends appropriate control signals to the various units. It acts in many ways as a very sophisticated telephone switchboard operator, making interconnections between various parts of the system. When the control unit recognizes special signals (e.g. that the result of a subtraction is negative), it can depart from the strict sequence of program instructions and jump to a different part of the program that is designed to deal with those circumstances.

Both the arithmetic unit and control unit depend heavily on the third main part of the central processor, the main or central storage (or memory) unit. The arithmetic unit needs numbers on which to operate and needs to store intermediate results at some place until the end of the calculation. The control unit needs program instructions in rapid succession. Both data and instructions are held in memory. The program for a given job is read into memory from an input unit or auxiliary storage device as part of the setting-up procedure for the job. Data flows into memory from such devices as keyboards on terminals, and magnetic tape or disk units, and is manipulated while in storage to produce results that are output, for example, to a printer.

Memory is also used to store a complex of programs known as the *operating system* (*q.v.*); this system is designed to supervise the total operation of the computer in as efficient a manner as possible. These programs function in some ways analogous to "traffic controllers," as they have to monitor the flow of data around the computer, giving some streams right of way over others, opening up clearways for top priority messages, looking out for emergency signals, and generally keeping things flowing smoothly.

The central processing unit thus consists of the control unit, the arithmetic-logic unit, and the main storage. It is aptly named, since it is very much at the center of computer activity, and it completes a massive amount of processing work, both directly to produce the desired results and generally to supervise the efficient operation of the computer system as a whole. With the advent of microprocessors (*q.v.*), we now find entire CPUs contained on a single integrated circuit (*q.v.*) chip ("CPU on a chip"). These CPUs are as fast and as powerful as those that required entire cabinets of hardware only a few years ago.

GRAHAM J. MORRIS

CHANNEL

For articles on related subjects *see* BUFFER; BUS; COMMUNICATION CONTROL UNIT; DATA COMMUNICATIONS; INTERRUPT; MEMORY: AUXILIARY; MULTIPLEXING; POLLING; PORT; and SYNCHRONOUS/ASYNCHRONOUS OPERATION.

Early Design In the design of early computing systems it was usual to provide for only a minimum of input and output devices, such as paper tape or card readers and punches, and perhaps a line printer or teleprinter. All these peripherals were essentially slow. In such cases, data could be transferred to and from the peripheral, character by character, and each unit had its special input or output line. Normally, data transferred between an input/output (I/O) device and memory passed through the processor. Later it was found necessary to provide many I/O devices. With the advent of magnetic tape and disk units, which are faster devices with short crisis times (i.e. a need to be serviced very quickly if data was not to be lost), multicharacter block transfers became necessary.

In all cases, however, it was necessary to provide some indication of the status of the I/O device in use, such as "ready" or "busy." If the device called upon was busy, the program had to stop and wait for the unit to become available.

The need for block transfers and the avoidance of delays due to unsuitable peripheral conditions led to the use of *buffered* peripherals and the development of continuously operating *channels* communicating directly with memory. Additionally, the channel provides overlap of I/O processing with logical and arithmetic processing, thereby obtaining high throughput (*q.v.*) by performing different operations in parallel. The channel also provides a standard interface for a range of I/O devices that may be connected to one processor in many combinations.

Autonomous Channel Operation The eventual availability of buffered peripherals called for the fast transfer of data to and from those peripherals. If these transfers were controlled by the CPU, much time would be lost since character transfer is slow compared with other CPU operations. Methods of autonomous transfer were needed whereby a whole block of data is transferred rapidly, word by word, to and from the main store, the cycles of the storage time taken for the word transfer being "stolen" from those available to the CPU. This cycle stealing (*q.v.*) usually causes only a slight hesitation of the CPU, whose storage cycle time of 200–1,000 ns should be compared with that of a high-speed disk drive that operates at about 10 μs per byte.

To facilitate block transfers directly between the store and the peripheral units, a controller called a *data channel* was introduced. There may be more than one channel. A data channel is essentially a small, special-purpose computer. I/O operations are initiated by the processor that selects a channel and a device. The channel then accesses a unique location in main memory where the processor has stored the address of the first instruction to be issued to the channel. Usually, a list of instructions called a *channel program*, is set up in storage. Each instruction is a particular operation that the channel must execute.

The CPU sends to the channel the address of the block of consecutive storage words (or bytes) to be transferred and the number of words to be transferred. If the channel is not already busy and the channel equipment is available and ready to operate, the channel initiates the transfer.

Instructions relating to channel operations commonly consist of two or more parts. The first part will specify and initiate the action of reading or writing, will give the address to which transfer of control will be made in the case of the rejection of the operation, and will contain the address of a *control word*, the second part of the channel instruction. The control word contains the length and initial address of the block to be transferred and is that information that is actually passed to the data channel. It is also possible to allow a sequence of data blocks to be transferred by providing a chain of control words that are sent one after another to the channel.

The control word also provides a *function code* that specifies and provides for certain types of variation of the normal mode of transfer of data, such as skipping, reading, or writing zeros, or terminating data transfer before the specified number of words indicated in the control word is actually transferred. A channel unit may also receive a variety of special orders from the processor, such as channel and equipment selection and channel and equipment status inquiry.

In the case in which there is more than one channel, the channels are connected at the processor end to a scanner circuit called a *director*. The director polls the various data channels in turn, and when data is ready it is transferred, the data channel providing the address to store it in, or from which data is to be provided, and then providing or receiving the word. This scanning is done sufficiently rapidly to avoid any crisis. The director has direct access to memory and activates the input to and the output from memory. It scans the channels in a defined order of priority. One director may service as many as 16 channels.

Channel Capacity   The rate at which a channel can transmit data to or from an I/O device, or to or from main storage, is the *channel capacity*. This is usually given in bytes or kilobytes per second. The channel capacity must, of course, be great enough to service the fastest I/O device connected to it.

Computer manuals and channel specifications usually give figures for data transfer rates under the assumption of ideal conditions. Actual data transmission rates are usually lower. If the channel hardware and the CPU hardware use the same registers, the channel may have to wait on the CPU for available registers (and vice versa), thus affecting transfer rates in a manner that cannot be determined *a priori*. The maximum rates given for discrete channels will also be lowered by the operation of other channels and by relative channel priorities.

Since *multiplexer* or *selector* channels are essentially independent computers controlling I/O, they will, of course, have their transfer rates affected by the way they are programmed. If the data is entered into a contiguous area of storage, the rate of data transmission will be greater than if it is entered into a non-contiguous set of areas, where all sorts of addresses must be computed and the CPU notified as to which storage area is being affected. This use of non-contiguous memory for a data set is known as *data chaining*. Of course, data chaining creates more conflict with the CPU, slowing either data transmission or processing or both.

Channel Command   A computer program consists of a set of instructions that are decoded and executed by the CPU. Channel commands are instructions that are decoded and executed by the I/O channels. A sequence of commands constitutes a channel program. Commands are stored in the main storage just as though they were instructions. They are fetched from main storage and are common to all I/O devices, but modifier bits are used to specify device-dependent conditions. The modifier bits of the command may also be used to order the I/O device to execute certain functions that are not involved in data transfer, such as tape rewinding.

During its execution of a program the CPU will initiate I/O operations. A command will specify a channel, a device, and an operation to be performed, and perhaps a storage area to be used, and perhaps also some memory protection information about the storage area involved. All this information may appear in the command word, or the command may tell the channel in which locations in memory to seek the necessary information. Upon receipt of this information, the multiplexer channel will attempt to select the desired device by sending the device address to all I/O units (including controllers) attached to the channel. A unit that recognizes its address connects itself logically to the channel. Once the connection is made, the channel will send the executable command to the I/O device. The device will respond to the channel, indicating whether it can execute the command and make this information available to the CPU.

An I/O operation involving data transfer to or from a series of non-contiguous memory locations may involve a series of channel commands. Termination of an I/O operation involves channel-end and device-end conditions. These conditions are brought to the attention of the CPU via interrupts or programmed interrogation of the I/O device. The channel-end condition occurs when the data transmission is completed. The channel is considered busy until this condition is accepted by the CPU. The device-end signal is given when the I/O device has terminated execution of the operation. The device remains unavailable until it is cleared by the CPU.

Lockout   The memory of a computer cannot be accessed continuously, only at specific times. The time interval within which memory may be accessed by the processor or an I/O channel is known as a *memory cycle*. Most memory cycle times are measured in microseconds or nanoseconds.

The CPU is essentially involved in processing data that is in main memory, whereas channels are concerned with the flow of data between I/O devices and main memory. Main memory is a high-speed data store, whereas peripherals are comparatively low-speed data stores. The channels and the CPU are busy moving data into and out of main memory. A conflict arises if they both need access to data at the same time. Since memory behaves the same way, whether the source or destination of the data is the I/O channels or the CPU, some method is needed to resolve the conflict.

Suppose a request for memory access is initiated by a second channel while a memory cycle is being used by the first. Since all requests must eventually be granted, but some more quickly than others, a priority system must be used. It is the comparatively slow I/O devices, rather than the high-speed CPU, that must have their requests answered first. A tape speeding under the read head must give up its data before the next data passes the read head; otherwise, the data will be lost. The moving I/O devices must always have open space to accept more data and cannot be concerned with memory access problems. The CPU, on the other hand, goes from one stable state to another. Once information is in its registers, it can wait. This will slow processing, but will not lose information. Therefore, a priority lock is set whereby the CPU is locked out from access to memory at the instant that the channels want to access memory.

Selecting a Peripheral To select a particular peripheral unit, a special function code must be transferred to the channel, indicating the identity of the unit required. This is done by sending a *connect function* to the channel. Usually, a channel unit with a variety of attached equipment is connected in what a communications specialist might call *multidrop manner;* all device controllers are connected by the same communication path to the channel (see Fig. 1). Some device controllers may be connected to more than one channel, in case the channel initially selected is busy.

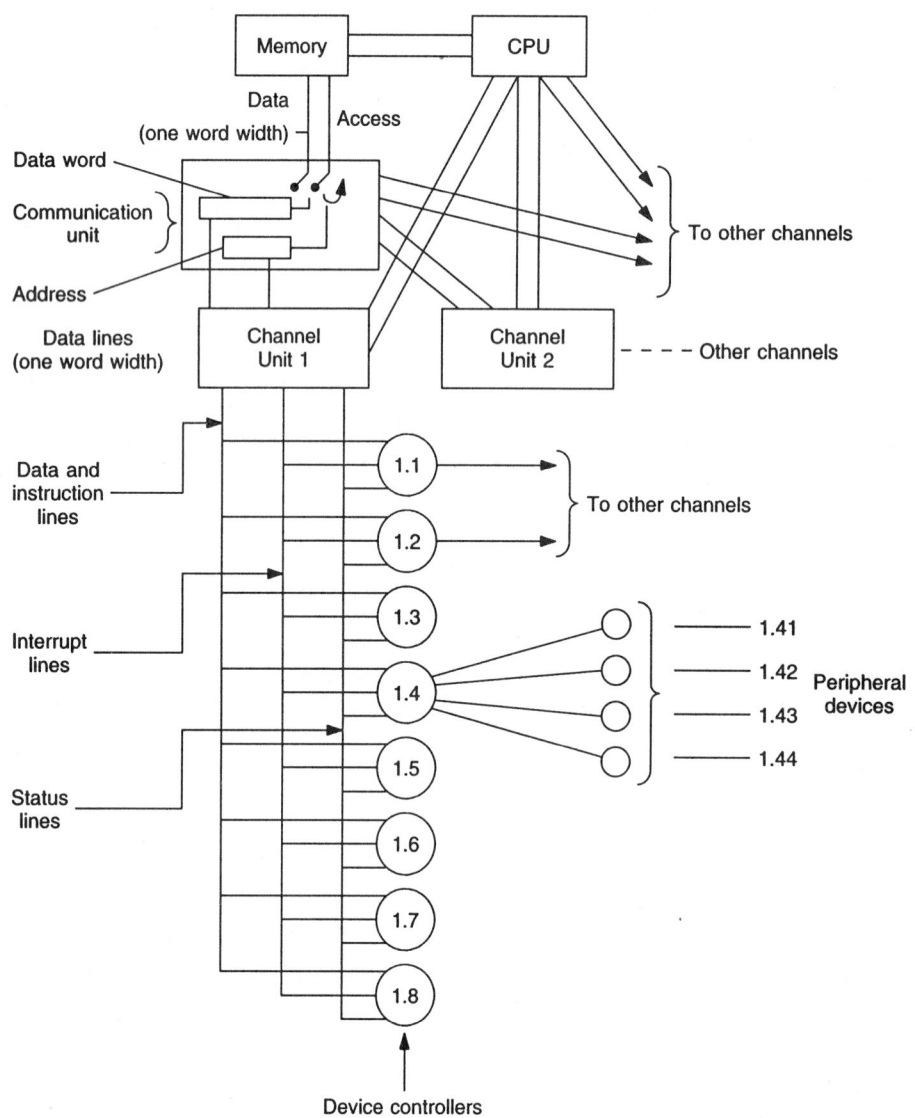

FIG. 1. Selector channel organization.

Setting a Peripheral A special function code sent to a selected peripheral by its connected channel may specify operating conditions within which the external equipment is to operate or a condition in which an interrupt may occur, such as stopping the channel activity, selecting an interrupt on detection of a parity error, or stopping the operation.

Status A channel must provide a status code to indicate its operating condition. Depending upon the kind of equipment to which the channel is connected, certain bits in the code indicate that a parity error is present, that a read or write is in progress, or that the operation is complete. Other codes in the status instruction cause the current data address and the word count to be sent to the CPU and/or the current control word address to be sent to other CPU registers.

Detection of a busy channel or equipment status may be used appropriately to transfer control to a different program until a further interrupt recalls attention to the channel and its user program.

Clear Channel When initiating a program, or starting from a dead-stop condition or a recoverable difficulty, it may be necessary (1) to clear a channel by disconnecting all equipments from the specific channel and preventing any communication until a connect instruction is provided; or (2) to disconnect all units within an equipment (e.g. magnetic tapes on a multiple tape controller) and to clear the channel control words. The *clear channel* instruction is also needed in case of difficulty with a channel operation and may be initiated by the operator.

Interrupts Selecting an interrupt condition is performed by a function instruction that can select occurrences of address and data and channel transmission parity errors. Associated with each channel, there is usually a special register in a channel unit that indicates the occurrence of one or more of these conditions. There is usually one bit in the register for each equipment condition. Additional bits are reserved for the use of the channel itself, such as an interrupt from the channel, channel data parity error, or control-word parity errors, as shown in Fig. 1.

Most systems operate in either *normal* or *privileged* mode. In the latter all interrupts are held inactive when processing an earlier interrupt. The activity state of an interrupt can be set by a special function instruction that sets interrupts active and returns the processor to the unprivileged state. The privileged status is automatically set on the detection of an interrupt when in normal state.

The structure of a channel unit is illustrated in Fig. 2. This shows the channel interrupt register, which indicates the conditions of the interrupt itself; the instruction register of the instruction which is received from the CPU; the control word, which gives the address and the number of words to be transferred; and the data word assembly registers, from which the data is to be sent from store. In addition to this, there is the status register, which is

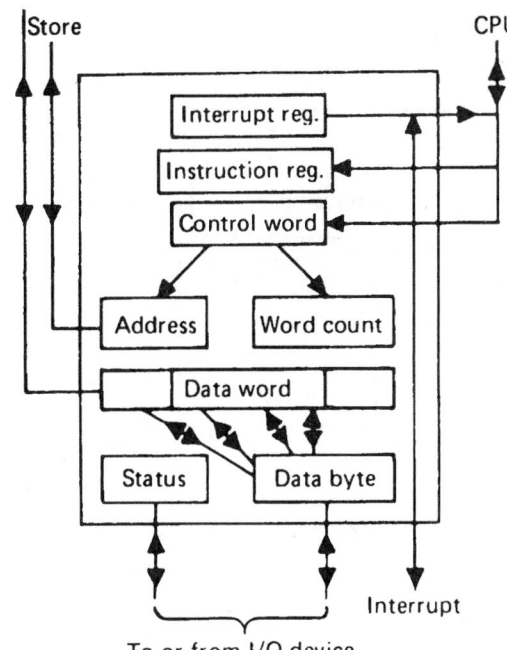

FIG. 2. Channel unit.

used to indicate the status of the connected unit of the channel.

Selector, Byte-Multiplexer, and Block-Multiplexer Channels Channels may be classified by the modes of operation they perform. The channel facilities required for an I/O operation is called a *subchannel*. The capability of a channel to perform multiplexing requires more than one subchannel.

A *selector channel* has only one subchannel and therefore forces the I/O device to transfer data in *burst mode*. The transmission of data continues uninterrupted until the whole block of data (or series of blocks of data) is transmitted. There can be only one data transfer operating at a time on a selector channel. Devices attached to the channel may be performing operations not requiring communication with the channel while data transfer is occurring in burst mode. When no data is being transferred, the selector channel monitors attached devices for status information.

The byte-multiplexer channel contains numerous subchannels and may operate in burst or in byte-interleave mode. The mode of operation is determined by the device. In burst mode, only one device on the channel may transfer data. In byte-interleave mode, more than one device may operate simultaneously, each using a separate subchannel.

The block multiplexer channel also has multiple subchannels. It forces I/O devices to transfer data in burst mode, but the burst extends over only one block of data. Multiplexing or interleaving of blocks occurs between channel commands. Multiplexing between blocks may be inhibited by appropriate channel instructions. Byte-multiplexer and block-multiplexer channels can sustain more

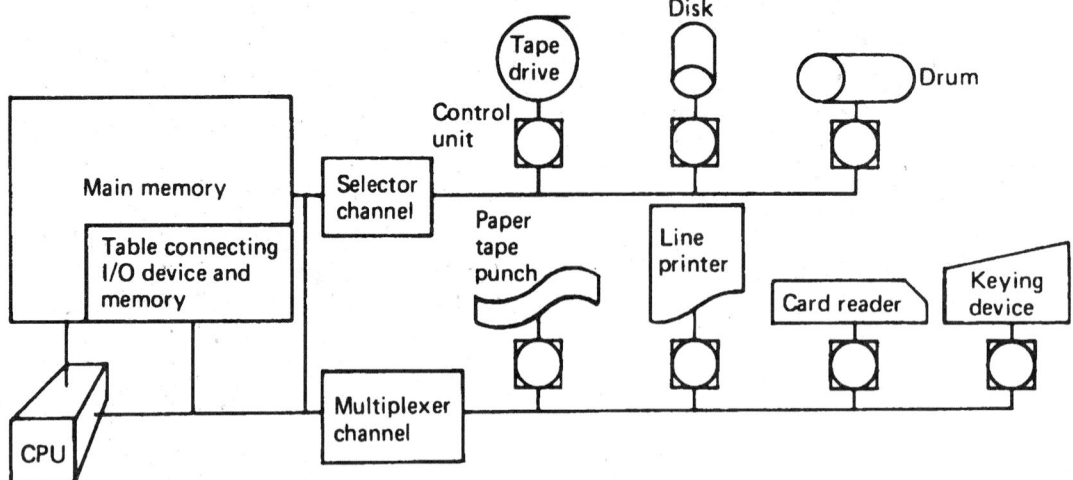

FIG. 3.   A selector and a multiplexer channel.

than one I/O operation per subchannel, provided that the total load on the channel does not exceed its capacity. Each subchannel of a multiplexer channel appears to the program as an independent selector channel. When a multiplexer channel transfers data in burst mode, the subchannel it is using controls the data-transfer facilities of the channel. Other subchannels on the multiplexer channel cannot respond to device requests until the burst is completed.

A symbolic block diagram differentiating multiplexer and selector channels is shown in Fig. 3.

Communication Channels   Some channels may be devoted to communication between memory or processor and a number of remote terminals. These terminals may either be interactive or suited only to batch processing. In either case the channel makes connection via a *multiplexer channel*, and thence (usually) via public transmission lines of specified bandwidth prescribed by the data carrier organization. The communication outlets from the multiplexer are made via *data sets*, which pass the data between the multiplexer and the transmission lines and convert signals to frequency modulation or otherwise adapt them to the communication line. Communication may be *simplex* (one direction only), *half-duplex* (transmission may take place in either direction but only one direction at a time), or *duplex* (transmission can pass in both directions at the same time).

Buffering   *Buffering* is used to gather information at a time when it is not needed so that it will be available for processing when it *is* needed. An early use of buffering was to overlap I/O and CPU operations. For example, an I/O operation is initiated to read a block of data into memory. While the channels are controlling this direct memory access (DMA) operation, the CPU continues to process unrelated information or related information read at an earlier time.

Care must be taken during programming to see that I/O is completed by the time the CPU needs the buffered information. Sometimes all I/O is directed toward a block of memory, a *buffer*, set aside just for I/O purposes by either the programmer or the supervisory program. The information is then moved to a working storage area for processing to take place; the I/O buffer is then available for more I/O.

The concept of buffering has also found a significant application in peripherals. For example, in an on-line inventory control system, a salesperson may type out a message and check it on a display device for errors and then transmit it to a computer. The message is stored in a small buffer in the remote terminal and then transmitted as a whole message to the main computer, rather than transmitting character by character as typed. In this manner the communications lines may be more efficiently used. Shrewd manipulation of buffers will greatly enhance the efficiency of its associated processing equipment by making necessary information available at precisely the appropriate moment.

Current Trends   It is apparent that the complete function required of a channel allowing for multiprogramming and time sharing far exceeds those of simply reading and writing data. It is therefore becoming more common for channel units actually to be small programmable processors or microcomputers. This facilitates extension of channel functions and provides a greater variety of conditions that can be specified by software design at a later stage of development. In this way a large CPU may be placed in charge of many small independent processors.

References

1978. Kuck, D. J. *The Structure of Computers and Communications* **1**. New York: Wiley.

TREVOR PEARCEY AND MILTON PINE

CHARACTER SET.   *See* ASCII; and EBCDIC.

CHARLES BABBAGE INSTITUTE (CBI)

For an article on a related subject *see* BABBAGE, CHARLES.

Purpose The Charles Babbage Institute for the History of Information Processing (CBI) was established in 1977 to support the study of the history of information processing and to be a clearinghouse for information about research resources related to this history, as well as a repository for archival materials. CBI conducts research on the technical and socioeconomic aspects of the history of information processing and promotes awareness of its impact on society. CBI also encourages others engaged in this and related work activities, and promotes interchange among those interested in such activities.

CBI draws together the perspectives of business administrators, scholars, technicians, computer specialists, and government officials. It is international in scope.

How Established CBI was founded in 1977 by Erwin Tomash to fill the need for an organization that would develop a broad historical view of the entire computing industry. In 1978, Paul Armer accepted the position of executive secretary. On 21 June 1979, Tomash and Albert S. Hoagland, president of the American Federation of Information Processing Societies (AFIPS) signed an agreement whereby AFIPS would become a major supporter of CBI, thus bringing the resources of both organizations to bear on the development of the history of information processing (*see also* AFIPS). Later, with an agreement between the board of CBI and the University of Minnesota to place the Charles Babbage Institute at the University, the Charles Babbage Foundation (CBF) was established. In 1987, the University assumed full responsibility for all CBI activities. The Babbage Foundation now serves in an advisory capacity to the University about CBI affairs.

Board of Trustees Members of the CBF have been vitally important to the successful launching and development of the organization. The directors and trustees groups are composed of members from academe and industry, including computer scientists, technologists, and industrial leaders, as well as historians of science. Erwin Tomash is chairman of the Charles Babbage Foundation board.

Program CBI conducts historical research of two types. General research provides background information about the history of modern computing that is useful to historians, archivists, journalists, and educators. These include, for example, survey articles on major historical topics, genealogies of computer companies, bibliographies, and review articles. Project research involves in-depth historical research on topics of current interest. Recent projects include studies of new engineering firms in the computer industry, scientific computing, and the influence of DARPA on computing.

The archives activity is divided into collection development at CBI and elsewhere, as well as archival methods

research. CBI has acquired a range of important collections which have been cataloged and are available for research. One concern of the methods research program is proper appraisal of the historic value of industry records. A major study developed a model for the industrial process in high-technology companies and the type of records produced in each aspect of the industrial process. This model will be a guide to the selection for preservation of industry records in individual cases. CBI has developed an extensive oral history program. Its oral history collection includes 200 interviews, available in tape and edited transcript form, on major business and technical decisions made by computer businesses in the 1950s and 1960s, early leading centers of computer education, computing in U.S. government organizations, and computing in major centers outside the U.S. From its beginning, CBI has offered an annual fellowship to a graduate student working in the field of the history of information processing.

CBI publishes a free newsletter and in other ways disseminates information through the data processing community. CBI's publication program also has a reprint series, now in its fourteenth volume, and occasional papers and monographs. CBI's address is University of Minnesota, 103 Walter Library, 117 Pleasant Street SE, Minneapolis, MN 55455, (612) 624-5050.

WILLIAM F. ASPRAY, JR.

CHEBYSHEV APPROXIMATION

For articles on related subjects *see* APPROXIMATION THEORY; LEAST-SQUARES APPROXIMATION; and NUMERICAL ANALYSIS.

Many computations on computers require the calculation of values of one or more functions, such as square roots, sines, cosines, logarithms, exponentials, and other elementary functions, or more complicated functions, such as Bessel functions. Since computers can only perform the operations of arithmetic, these functions cannot be evaluated directly, but must be *approximated* by some other functions that can be evaluated arithmetically. For example, a common method for computing the square root of a number A is the following application of the Newton-Raphson method:

$$x_{i+1} = \frac{1}{2}\left(x_i + \frac{A}{x_i}\right) \quad i = 0,1,2,3,\ldots \quad x_0 = A$$

It can be shown that x_i gets arbitrarily close to A as $i \to \infty$. For example, let $A = 2$. Then

$$x_0 = 2$$
$$x_1 = 1.5$$
$$x_2 = 1.41666\ldots$$
$$x_3 = 1.414215\ldots$$

whereas $\sqrt{2} = 1.414213\ldots$

The general problem we wish to consider here is: Given a function $f(x)$ and an interval $[a,b]$ on which we wish to approximate $f(x)$, find an approximation to $f(x)$ on this interval—which can be computed arithmetically—of minimum error. But what do we mean by minimum error? In many problems in mathematics this would mean minimum least squares error over the interval. But in approximating functions for computers we are more usually interested in minimizing the maximum error on the interval, for then the user of the approximation always knows that the worst possible case is as favorable as it can be. Rigorously stated, we wish to find an approximation $R(x)$, which has the property that

$$r = \max_{[a,b]} |f(x) - R(x)|$$

is smaller than for any other approximation. Such a *minimum-maximum error approximation*, or *minimax approximation*, is usually called a *Chebyshev approximation*, after the great Russian mathematician P. L. Chebyshev (1821–1894), whose name is transliterated from the Russian in a variety of other ways (e.g. Tchebycheff).

The question remains of what form $R(x)$ should have. If it is to be evaluated arithmetically, the most general function it can be is a *rational function*, i.e. the ratio of two polynomials. For example, the Chebyshev approximation to the exponential function e^x on the interval $[-1, 1]$, which is the ratio of two quadratic polynomials, is given by

$$R(x) = \frac{1.00007255 + 0.50863618x + 0.08582937x^2}{1.0 - 0.49109193x + 0.07770847x^2}$$

for which $r = 0.86899 \times \ddot{o}\ 10^{-4}$. The error, $E(x) = e^x - R(x)$, is shown in Fig. 1. It exhibits the characteristic property of Chebyshev approximations of alternating between its greatest and least values twice more than the sum of the degrees of numerator and denominator of $R(x)$ or, in the example above, $2 + 2 + 2 = 6$ times.

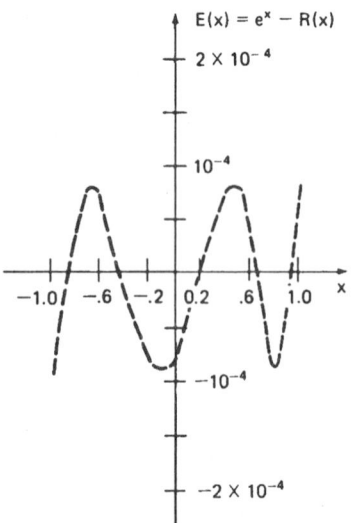

Fig. 1. Error in Chebyshev approximation to e^x on [-1,1] as a ratio of two quadratics.

Reference

1978. Ralston, A. and Rabinowitz, P. *A First Course in Numerical Analysis, 2nd ed.* New York: McGraw-Hill.
1990. Rivlin, Theodore J. *Chebyshev Polynomials: From Approximation Theory to Algebra and Number Theory.* New York: John Wiley.

ANTHONY RALSTON

CHECKPOINT AND RESTART

For articles on related subjects *see* DEBUGGING; and PROGRAMMING SUPPORT ENVIRONMENTS.

A *checkpoint* is a designated place in a program at which normal processing is interrupted specifically to preserve the status information necessary to allow resumption of processing at some arbitrary time in the future.

The primary purpose of a checkpoint is to avoid repeating the execution of a program from its beginning, should an error or malfunction occur somewhere in the middle of processing. This is especially effective in runs involving several hours of machine time. For such situations it is often appropriate to set up checkpoints at a number of strategic places in the program, either with all checkpoint information being saved, or by using a less conservative system in which the information captured at the most recent checkpoint replaces (overwrites) the previous set. Then, should difficulties arise, it is possible to take corrective action and resume processing from the last checkpoint, rather than starting over. Since the manipulations associated with checkpoint/restart procedures can consume substantial amounts of time and storage, it is possible to have situations in which it is more economical to avoid checkpoints.

A checkpoint capability is implemented by means of a procedure (often termed a *checkpoint routine*) that captures the status of the program at the particular instant when it stopped and copies it onto an auxiliary storage medium. This data includes the contents of the special registers, storage locations associated with the program, and other information relating to the status of input/output devices. Later on, another procedure (a *restart routine*) can reset the system to resume processing by reading in and restoring the checkpoint information.

In many systems the checkpoint and restart routines are prepackaged software components accessible to the high-level language programmer via ordinary CALL statements. These facilities usually include numerous options that allow the programmer to exercise some control over the type of information gathered, the form in which it is stored, and the circumstances under which the restart is to proceed.

The introduction of multiprogramming (*q.v.*) operating systems has prompted an expansion in the use of checkpoint-restart procedures beyond the context of insurance against malfunctions. Depending on the scheduling algorithm (*q.v.*) implemented in a particular system, it may occasionally be necessary to interrupt a particular run, releasing its storage for other purposes with the intent of resuming that run at some later (presumably more propitious) time. In order to handle that type of procedure without the user's involvement, the check-point/restart process must be completely automated, which, indeed, is the norm in modern operating systems.

SEYMOUR V. POLLACK

CHESS. *See* COMPUTER CHESS.

CHIEF PROGRAMMER TEAM

For articles on related subjects *see* SOFTWARE ENGINEERING; SOFTWARE MANAGEMENT; and STRUCTURED PROGRAMMING.

A *Chief Programmer Team* is a concept coupling a functionally specialized programming organization with the use of software engineering techniques, such as structured programming (*q.v.*) and top-down development, to produce effective software systems of high quality. The idea originated with Harlan D. Mills, who in 1968 was concerned about the inefficiencies apparent in large-scale software development. He believed that a structured, multi-disciplinary organization using standardized methods and tools could develop systems of higher quality and achieve improved productivity.

A team begins as a nucleus of a *chief programmer*, a *backup programmer*, and a *programming librarian*. The chief programmer is the technical manager of the organization, responsible for all aspects of the design and development of a software system. The backup programmer is the chief's alter ego, serving both as a check and balance and as an insurance policy in case of the illness or departure of the chief. The programming librarian provides clerical support for both programming and documentation activities. (In Mills's original concept, the librarian physically managed all the programming materials of the project—hence the name.) This organizational nucleus begins a project by performing systems analysis, software architecture, and top-level design work, and then develops the code needed to make the framework of the system operational. Specialists (e.g. additional programmers, testers, technical writers) are then added to complete the development, testing, and documentation of the full system. All work is viewed as the shared and public property of the team, rather than as the private property of each participant. Walkthroughs (a precursor to inspections) are performed on all elements of design, code, and documentation. The organization was consciously designed to take advantage of the methods of top-down (incremental) development and structured programming, which in 1968 were viewed as radical and untried.

The team idea was first applied on a contract that the IBM Federal Systems Division held with *The New York Times* for development of *The New York Times Information Bank*. The system was designed to be an interactive re-placement for the newspaper's internal library, both to be used by staffers and to be marketed to outside users. Use of the team organization and methodology on this contract resulted in delivery in 1971 of a system of over 83,000 source lines. The software had only 21 errors identified during five weeks of acceptance testing and only 25 errors during its first year of use, just one of which resulted in termination of operations. Productivity was 35 lines per person-day over the entire project, and 65 lines per person-day for the software development phase. Although software metrics for comparable projects were not generally available at that time, these levels of quality and productivity were viewed as significantly better than those being achieved elsewhere.

The team idea was tried on other projects, both within IBM and by outside organizations. The formal team structure, the roles of the participants, and the degree of discipline expected proved difficult for people to accept; they preferred a less formal structure. Also, while the team was well adapted to small- and medium-sized projects, it proved difficult to scale up to large ones; the chief programmer had difficulty in performing both architectural and management duties. The real value of the early experiments proved to be in demonstrating that structured programming and top-down development, which later became integral components of software engineering (*q.v.*), were in fact practical outside of the academic environment where they originated.

References

1972. Baker, F. T. "System Quality through Structured Programming," *AFIPS Proceedings of the 1972 Fall Joint Computer Conference*, Vol. 41, pp. 339–43, Montvale, NJ: AFIPS Press.

1972. Baker, F. T. "Chief Programmer Team Management of Structured Programming," *IBM Systems Journal*, 11, 1 (January), 56–73.

F. TERRY BAKER

CHIP. *See* INTEGRATED CIRCUITRY; and MICROCOMPUTER CHIP.

CHOMSKY HIERARCHY

For articles on related subjects *see* AUTOMATA THEORY; FORMAL LANGUAGES; GRAMMARS; LANGUAGE TRANSLATION; PROGRAMMING LINGUISTICS; and TURING MACHINE.

For the mathematician, an *alphabet* is a set of symbols and a language is a set, finite or infinite, of strings formed from that alphabet. A *grammar* is a finite system that characterizes a language. Customarily, grammars work by substitution (production). Take the alphabet (or, as it is usually called, the *terminal* alphabet) of the language V_T add a *nonterminal* alphabet V_N and a special symbol S that belongs to neither V_T nor V_N. A *production* or rule of substitution, R, is an ordered pair of strings, $R = T_1 \rightarrow T_2$. A grammar is a system, $G = <\ V_N,\ V_T,\ P,\ S\ >$, where P denotes the set of allowable productions. To use the grammar, start with S and find a rule (i.e. a production) $S \rightarrow T_1$ and substitute T_1 for S. Find another rule $S_1 \rightarrow T_2$, such that S_1 matches part or all of T_1, and substitute T_2 for the matched part of T_1. Continue with any member of P until the result is a string that contains only terminal symbols. This sequential process is called the *derivation* of the string, and the final string belongs to the language. The language consists of exactly the strings that can be so derived.

If, in a grammar, every rule has the form $n \rightarrow nt$ or $n \rightarrow t$, where n is a non-terminal symbol and t is a terminal symbol, the grammar is *regular* and characterizes a *regular language*.

If every rule has the form $n \rightarrow T$, where T is a string over the combined terminal and nonterminal alphabets, the grammar is *context-free* (the substitution $n \rightarrow T$ can be made wherever n occurs). A context-free grammar generates a context-free language.

If every rule has the form $S'\ n\ S'' \rightarrow S'\ T\ S''$, where S' and S'' are strings over the combined alphabet of terminal and nonterminal symbols, the grammar is *context sensitive* (the substitution $n \rightarrow T$ can be made only in the context $S'...S''$). A context-sensitive grammar characterizes a context-sensitive language.

Changing the restrictions on the forms of rules changes the power of the grammar. Without restrictions on the form of rules, a grammar can characterize any *recursively enumerable* set of strings, that is, any language that can be characterized at all (call this class of languages type 0). Not every recursively enumerable set (i.e. type 0 language) is a context-sensitive language, but every context-sensitive language is a recursively enumerable set (call the context-sensitive systems type 1). Again, the context-sensitive systems characterize all context-free languages, but the context-free systems (type 2) cannot characterize some context-sensitive languages. Finally, a regular language can be characterized by a system of any type, but regular grammars (type 3) cannot characterize all context-free languages. The hierarchy of types 0, 1, 2, and 3 is due to Noam Chomsky (1946), and is commonly called the *Chomsky hierarchy* (see Fig. 1).

Many other classes of languages have been added to the hierarchy to form a partial order. To each type of grammar corresponds a kind of machine that *produces* or *accepts* a language of the given type: Turing machines (type 0), linear-bounded automata (type 1), non-deterministic pushdown automata (type 2), and finite-state machines (type 3).

References

1946. Chomsky, Noam. "Three Models for the Description of Language." *IRE Trans. Information Theory* **IT-2**: 113-124.

1969. Salomaa, Arto. *Theory of Automata*. Oxford: Pergamon Press.

1978. Denning, Peter J., Dennis, Jack B., and Qualitz, Joseph E. *Machines, Languages, and Computation*. Englewood Cliffs, NJ: Prentice-Hall.

DAVID G. HAYS

CHURCH, ALONZO

For articles on related subjects *see* ALGORITHMS, THEORY OF; LAMBDA CALCULUS; LOGIC PROGRAMMING; and TURING, ALAN.

Alonzo Church was born in Washington, D.C., on 14 June 1903, the son of Samuel Robbins Church, Justice of the Municipal Court of the District of Columbia, and Mildred Hannah Church (née Parker). The Church family was of considerable civic and academic distinction; Church's great grandfather, also named Alonzo Church, was a professor of mathematics and later president from 1829 to 1859 of the college in Athens, Georgia, now known as the University of Georgia. Church did his undergraduate work at Princeton University, where his mathematical, logical, and foundational abilities were recognized and nurtured by Oswald Veblen, the brilliant American geometer and postulate theorist who was to become the first professor

Class of Grammar, G_i	Grammatical Characterization	Machine Characterization
Type 0	Unrestricted (or phrase structure)	Turing machine
Type 1	Context-sensitive	Linear-bounded automaton
Type 2	Context-free	Pushdown automaton
Type 3	Regular (or right linear)	Finite state machine

FIG. 1. The Chomsky Hierarchy. Each class of grammars in the hierarchy contains all lower levels. Thus $G_0 \supset G_1 \supset G_2 \supset G_3$.

FIG. 1. Alonzo Church.

of the Institute for Advanced Study at Princeton (the second was Albert Einstein). Church received an A.B. from Princeton in 1924 and was further encouraged by Veblen, then President of the American Mathematical Society, to stay on for graduate work in mathematics and logic, and in particular to study the foundational research being developed by David Hilbert and the Hilbert school. Throughout his life, Church warmly acknowledged his friendship and indebtedness to Veblen, whom he referred to as "my sponsor."

In 1927, Church received a Ph.D. for a dissertation directed by Veblen on the effects of modifying the axiom of choice in set theory. This was followed by a two-year National Research Fellowship, the first year of which was spent at Harvard working with Birkhoff and Huntington. At that time, Harvard was the institutional affiliation of such logicians as Sheffer, Lewis, and Whitehead. In the second year (1928–29), Church went to Europe. He worked at Göttingen, where he met members of the Hilbert school, including Hilbert himself and Bernays. In Amsterdam, he met Brouwer, the famous intuitionistic mathematician. On his return to the U. S. in the fall of 1929, he began teaching as an Assistant Professor of Mathematics at Princeton, a position that Veblen was instrumental in arranging. He continued teaching at Princeton as Professor of Mathematics and Philosophy, a title he received in 1961, until his "retirement" in 1967. In that year he was appointed with the same title at UCLA, where he maintained an active schedule of research, lecturing, and teaching through the spring semester of 1990, when he retired from teaching.

Church received many honors. In 1967, he was elected to the American Academy of Arts and Sciences and to the Academie Internationale de Philosophie des Sciences. In 1969, he received an honorary doctorate from Case Western Reserve University. In 1978, he was elected to the National Academy of Sciences and to the British Academy. In 1980, Princeton University awarded him an honorary doctor of science degree, and in 1990 an international symposium in his honor was held at the State University of New York at Buffalo, in conjunction with the conferral of another honorary doctorate.

Church's contributions to logic are extensive, ranging from the practical, the pedagogical, and the philosophical to the scholarly, the historical, and the mathematical. There is no area of modern logic that has not been influenced by his work. The linguistic analysis of mathematical discourse, which resulted both in his discovery of the logical form of certain propositions involving functions and in his creation of the Church Lambda Operator, which makes possible logically precise expression of such propositions, continues to exert profound influence on logic, mathematics, and computer science. He was one of the first logicians along with Hilbert, Tarski, and Gödel to grasp and exploit the syntactical, character-manipulating, and computational aspects of logic and postulate theory. He was the first person to articulate the principle, now known as Church's Thesis and widely accepted as axiomatic, that every effectively calculable number-theoretic function is recursive. This principle, which at first was highly controversial, boldly connects syntactical/computational aspects of mathematics to the abstract/numerical: while calculability has to do with string manipulation, recursiveness is abstract and numerical. Church's work on the Hilbert decision problem led to the discovery and proof of Church's Theorem—basically, that the set of formulas that do not express tautological propositions cannot be computer-generated and thus that there is no computational method for determining whether a given "conclusion" is logically implied by given "premises." Church's Theorem identifies one outer limit of what is achievable in automated theorem proving *(q.v.)* and thereby plays a role in modern computer science analogous to the role of the second law of thermodynamics in engineering. Church's lambda calculus and his formalizations of higher-order logics, including the simple theory of types, have together and separately influenced the most recent attempts by mathematically-oriented computer scientists to "computerize" mathematics.

Church was also a highly successful teacher; the list of his doctoral students is a virtual who's who of modern logic and computer science. It includes William Boone, Martin Davis, Stephen Kleene, Hartley Rogers, Barkley Rosser, Dana Scott, Raymond Smullyan, Leon Henkin, Peter Andrews, and Alan Turing *(q.v.)*.

Throughout his life, Church maintained a deep and abiding interest in the practical aspects of logic. His practical interests in logic included not only concern with applications of logic in computer science, but also concern with institutions that foster creation and dissemination of logical knowledge. He was an editor of *The Journal of Symbolic Logic* from its inception in 1936 until 1980, when he turned over the world-famous reviews section to a successor.

In the opinion of many logicians, Church's 1956 masterpiece *Introduction to Mathematical Logic* is still unsurpassed for its purpose.

References

1956. Church, Alonzo. *Introduction To Mathematical Logic.* Princeton, NJ: Princeton University Press.

1965. Davis, Martin. *The Undecidable: Basic Papers On Undecidable Propositions, Unsolvable Problems, and Computable Functions.* Hackett, NY: Raven Press.

1968. Davis, Martin. *Computability and Unsolvability.* New York: McGraw-Hill, 2nd Ed. 1982, New York: Dover.

1991. Scanlan, Michael. "Who Were the American Postulate Theorists?" *Journal of Symbolic Logic,* **56,** 981–1002.

JOHN CORCORAN AND MICHAEL SCANLAN

CIPS. *See* CANADIAN INFORMATION PROCESSING SOCIETY.

CIRCUITRY. *See* COMPUTER CIRCUITRY; and INTEGRATED CIRCUITRY.

CLASS

For articles on related subjects *see* ABSTRACT DATA TYPE; BLOCK STRUCTURE; DATA STRUCTURES; DATA TYPE; and OBJECT-ORIENTED PROGRAMMING.

The concept of *class* was introduced in the programming language Simula 67 as an extension to the block structure and procedure mechanisms of Algol 60. As a way of structuring programs, it is an alternative to the strict nesting of blocks in Algol 60.

Class Declaration   A class declaration resembles a procedure declaration in Algol 60. It was the inspiration for the *abstract data type* mechanism that is an important feature of several newer programming languages. A class may have formal parameters like a procedure. In general, a class declaration includes declarations for variables, functions, and procedures that are local to the class, followed by the body of the class, which is usually a block. An example of class declaration is given in Fig. 1. Unlike an Algol 60 procedure declaration, a class declaration does not by itself cause storage to be allocated or executable code to be compiled. A class declaration is a template that can be used to create instances of the class. In Simula 67, these class instances are called *objects*. Simula 67 allows the declaration of variables that are references to objects. The built-in operation **new** is used to create objects (class instances). For example, if Z is a variable, that is a reference to the class C declared in Fig. 1, then the statement

$$Z: = \textbf{new } C(100)$$

would create an instance of the class C. The formal parameter n of the class is used to specify the characteristics of the object created from the class (e.g. the upper bound of the array A). In Simula 67, "dot notation" is used to reference variables within objects (e.g. $Z.A$ is a reference to the array A in the object Z and $Z.A[j]$ is a reference to the j th component of A in Z).

```
class C(n);
    integer n;
    begin
        integer array A[1:n];
        integer k;
        procedure clear;
            begin
                integer i;
                for i: = 1 step 1 until n do
                    A[i]: = 0
        end;
    . . .
    comment end of declarations;
    comment execution of class object starts here;
    k := 0;
    resume;
    k := k + 1;
    . . .
    end;
```

FIG. 1.   Class declaration.

```
C class D(x);
    real x;
    begin
        real y;
        real array B[1:100];
        . . .
        comment note the use of variables from C and D;
        y:= x + A[k]
    . . .
end;
```

FIG. 2.   Subclass declaration.

Note that there may be many objects of a given class, each with its own set of variables in existence at any given time. Thus, the strict Algol 60 nesting of block invocations has been replaced by a more flexible regime.

The class concept also involves a different rule for the execution of the statements in a class. When an object is created, control is transferred to the executable statements in the body of the class. Three situations are possible: (1) Control passes through the class definition to the end of the block; the object is terminated; execution cannot reenter the object, but its local storage remains allocated. (2) A **detach** statement is executed in the body of the object; in this case, the object becomes an independently executing entity; its lifetime may exceed that of the block in which it was created, which allows objects to be used to create *processes* in a multiprocessing system; e.g. an operating system could be structured as a set of cooperating concurrently executing class objects. (3) A **resume** statement is executed in the body of the object. Execution of the body is suspended at the point of the **resume** statement until it is reactivated by a **resume** statement from outside of the object. For example, if the class C in Fig. 1 is used to create the object named Z, as shown above, then the statement

$$\textbf{resume}(Z):$$

would cause execution to continue in the body of the object Z at the statement $k := k + 1$. This allows coroutine (*q.v.*) structures to be built using objects.

Subclasses   The power and flexibility of the class concept is enhanced by the ability to declare subclasses. A subclass is formed by concatenating the formal parameters, local variables, procedures, and executable statements of an existing class with those of a class being declared. A subclass is created when the name of a class is used as a prefix to a class declaration. In the example in Fig. 2, the declaration of class D has class C as a prefix. The class D has formal parameters n and x, local variables A, k, y, and B, and a body consisting of the body of C followed by the body of D.

References

1972. Dahl, O. J. and Hoare, C. A. R. "Hierarchical Program Structures." in Dahl, O. J., Dijkstra, E. W., and Hoare, C. A. R. *Structured Programming*. London: Academic Press, 175–220.

1973. Birtwistle, G. M., Dahl, O. J., Myhrhaug, B., and Nygaard, K. *SIMULA Begin*, Philadelphia: Auerbach.

DAVID B. WORTMAN

CLIENT/SERVER ARCHITECTURE. *See* FILE SERVER.

CLONE. *See* IBM-PC and PC-COMPATIBLES.

CLOSE AND OPEN A FILE. *See* OPEN AND CLOSE A FILE.

CMI. *See* COMPUTER-MANAGED INSTRUCTION.

COBOL. *See* PROCEDURE-ORIENTED LANGUAGES.

CODASYL

For articles on related subjects *see* DATABASE MANAGEMENT SYSTEMS; PROCEDURE-ORIENTED LANGUAGES; and STANDARDS.

Codasyl (Conference on Data Systems Languages) is a volunteer organization consisting of professional computing personnel from the computing industry and from computing-systems users. It was formed in 1959 to attempt to standardize the languages used in computer programs and thus to permit such programs to be "machine independent." Initially, it was the purpose of Codasyl to choose and standardize a programming language from among the numerous common programming languages being promulgated at that time, mostly by computer hardware suppliers. A Codasyl task force, organized in 1959 to work on the technical aspects of this objective, found it impossible to achieve acceptance of any language as a standard and equally impossible to integrate features of one language with another. Therefore, in 1960, this task force published specifications for a new common language called Cobol (Common Business-Oriented Language). Initially, the only suppliers to implement Cobol were Univac and RCA. Then the U.S. Department of Defense, one of the original contributors to the standardization effort, made Cobol mandatory for all suppliers of computing hardware and software who were bidding on defense procurements. This economic pressure resulted in persuading other suppliers to implement Cobol also.

Experience gained with the initial language resulted in the publication of an improved version of Cobol in 1961. Another version, called "Cobol 61 Extended," was published in 1962, and additional features and enhancements have been added to the language almost every year since then. Cobol compilers were generally provided with all computer equipment from 1962 on. Cobol was adopted as an American standard by ANSI in 1968. An updated standard was issued in 1974 and in 1985. In 1976, a Cobol Compiler Validation System, originally developed by Grace Hopper (*q.v.*), became the standard Federal government benchmark for determining adherence of Cobol compilers to the Cobol standard.

The 1990 Codasyl organization consists of an Executive Committee and two Development Committees (1) Cobol, (2) Forms Interface Management System (FIMS).

The task of the development committees is to develop specifications for a common language in their area of assignment. These committees have common attendance and voting rules specified by the Executive Committee. The current Codasyl organization has evolved from concepts that gave recognition to the separate interests of the hardware suppliers versus the users, as well as to short-range issues versus long-range developments. As the Cobol language achieved acceptance, the disparity between the interests of the manufacturers of computers and the users of computers, which had to be recognized in the early existence of Codasyl, began to disappear, and the current organization evolved.

The development committees of Codasyl accept comments and proposals from any competent source, review these proposals, modify them, and publish the resultant actions in a *Journal of Development* (JOD) for each language in which it is currently interested. As of 1990, there are *JODs* for Cobol and for FIMS.

JODs are published at one- to two-year intervals, depending upon development activity. Only *JODs* from active development committees are maintained.

Other Codasyl publications include *An Information Algebra, Decision Tables (D-Tab), Data Base Task Group Report, A Survey of Generalized Data Base Management Systems*, and *Feature Analysis of Generalized DBM Systems, End User Function Language, Data Description Language, Operating System Control Language*, and *Fortran Data Manipulation Language*.

All Codasyl effort continues to be totally voluntary and oriented towards data processing language specifications that are common to all types of computer systems. New committees are formed when a clear need exists that is not being addressed by another organization. All resultant effort, in the form of a *JOD*, is in the public domain and offered as a candidate for standardization.

JAN PROKOP

CODE, ERROR CORRECTING. *See* ERROR-CORRECTING CODE.

CODER. *See* PROGRAMMER.

CODES

For articles on related subjects *see* ASCII; BAUDOT CODE; BINARY-CODED DECIMAL; EBCDIC; ERROR-CORRECTING CODE; and UNIVERSAL PRODUCT CODE.

The term *code* has a particular meaning in cryptography, and is also sometimes used as a synonym for *program* or part of a program. But for the purposes of this article, a code is a correspondence between a symbol of an alphabet (e.g. our alphabet of letters) and a number of digits of a number system (e.g. six bits for base 2). To be more precise, the mathematician would say that a code is a pair $(\Sigma; \Pi)$ where Σ is the symbol space and the Π are numeric combinations. Suppose that S is some symbol in the symbol space Σ and P is one of the permutations of the digits in a numeric counting system Π. We might say "S is mapped into P" or that "S is represented by P," using the symbols:

$$S \rightarrow P \quad \text{or} \quad S \equiv P. \tag{1}$$

Each P in Π is called a *combination*. Since P consists of n digits, it can be written as

$$P = P_1 P_2 P_3 \cdots P_n \tag{2}$$

where P_i is any digit of the counting system with radix r, i.e.

$$P_i = 0, 1, 2, \ldots, \text{or } r - 1. \tag{3}$$

To make this more concrete, let us examine the case where the symbol space Σ_A consists of letters of the alphabet. Let each combination P consist of two decimal digits; thus, $r = 10$ and $n = 2$. A very simple code might assign numbers consecutively to the letters so that we would have

$$A \equiv 01, B \equiv 02, C \equiv 03, \ldots, Z \equiv 26. \tag{4}$$

It is convenient here to introduce the operator v, whose action is to find the number of elements in a set. For our example,

$$v\Sigma_A = 26 \quad \text{and} \quad v\Pi = 100. \tag{5}$$

Since there are many more permutations than there are symbols in the symbol space, many permutations are unassigned. These are sometimes called *forbidden combinations*.

Need   Data is an abstraction of information in the real world. People keep this information in the form of symbols. The computer stores information in the various hardware elements that constitute it. Elements have been designed that have two or more states. An element such as the Nixie tube has ten states. But by far the most common, least expensive, and most efficient element is the *bistable device*; it has only two stable states. For the computer to represent information, it must be structured so that the devices used in the computer can accommodate it. Since there are not enough states in a single bistable device to represent each symbol as a human being uses it, the symbols are represented by a combination of these settings, i.e. by a binary code.

It might seem initially that any representation of a symbol would do. This is not so. The design of a code usually must take into account the following requirements:

1. The original order relations (i.e. A before B, $1 < 2$) that apply to the symbols within the symbol space should apply to the relation between combinations in the code.
2. Operations applied to the symbols should have analogous operations, which—when defined upon the combinations—produce a corresponding result.
3. The representation should be efficient (to minimize the number of combinations that go to waste).

Decimal Codes   A decimal code provides a representation for the decimal numbers in binary. To summarize their characteristics:

$$v\Sigma_D = 10, \quad r = 2, \quad n \geq 4. \tag{6}$$

Note that these codes use four bits or more.

There are two principal ways to associate symbols with combinations:

1. *Weighted codes* assign different weights to each bit in the combination, as discussed shortly.
2. *Transition rules* may be created to indicate how the code for the successor number is created from the code for any given number.

Four-Bit Codes

Weighted Codes   Let us label the bits of the combination that represents a decimal digit. Unlike (2), where the subscripts increase from left to right, we will now order the subscripts 1 through 4 in reverse, going from right to left. Thus, if D is a decimal digit, we have

$$D \equiv b_4 b_3 b_2 b_1. \tag{7}$$

A weighted code associates a weight W_i with each bit b_i and might be stated symbolically as

$$b_i \leftrightarrow W_i \quad i = 1 \text{ to } 4. \tag{8}$$

The requirement of the weighted code is that, when each bit is multiplied by its weight and then these are totaled, the total must be equal in value to the digit. Stated symbolically, we have

Weights / Digits	Table 1 8 4 2 1 Code	Table 2 7 4 2 1 Code	Table 3 7 4 2 –1 Code	Table 4 Excess-3 Code
0	0 0 0 0	0 0 0 0	0 0 0 0	0 0 1 1
1	0 0 0 1	0 0 0 1	0 0 1 1	0 1 0 0
2	0 0 1 0	0 0 1 0	0 0 1 0	0 1 0 1
3	0 0 1 1	0 0 1 1	0 1 0 1	0 1 1 0
4	0 1 0 0	0 1 0 0	0 1 0 0	0 1 1 1
5	0 1 0 1	0 1 0 1	0 1 1 1	1 0 0 0
6	0 1 1 0	0 1 1 0	1 0 0 1 (0 1 1 0)	1 0 0 1
7	0 1 1 1	1 0 0 0 (0 1 1 1)	1 0 0 0	1 0 1 0
8	1 0 0 0	1 0 0 1	1 0 1 1	1 0 1 1
9	1 0 0 1	1 0 1 0	1 0 1 0	1 1 0 0
*(A)	1 0 1 0	1 0 1 1	1 1 0 1	1 1 0 1
*(B)	1 0 1 1	1 1 0 0	1 1 0 0	1 1 1 0
*(C)	1 1 0 0	1 1 0 1	1 1 1 1	1 1 1 1
*(D)	1 1 0 1	1 1 1 0	—	—
*(E)	1 1 1 0	1 1 1 1	—	—
*(F)	1 1 1 1	—	—	—

*Forbidden combinations.

$$D = \sum_1^4 b_i W_i = b_4 W_4 + b_3 W_3 + b_2 W_2 + b_1 W_1. \qquad (9)$$

Some restrictions arise in setting up the weights:

1. For each digit to be encoded, there must be a combination of bits and their corresponding weights, whose total—using (9)—is equal to the value of the digit.
2. When two combinations exist that, when substituted into (9), yield the same digit, D, then another rule must be provided to decide which combination will be used.

8421 Code The weighted 8421 code is illustrated in Table 1. From left to right, weights 8, 4, 2, and 1 are assigned to the bits that make up the combination. When the bits are set to 0 or 1, the resulting number is shown in the left column of the table.

The six entries at the bottom of the table provide values 10 through 15. Of course, there are no digits to correspond to these values in the decimal system. Hence, these combinations are forbidden. If these occur, the computer should signal an error.

Note that these combinations would be legal if the base for our system were 16. Hence, we will return to this table when we discuss the hexadecimal (base 16) system.

Finally, note that the sequence of combinations for the 8421 code is the same sequence in which these binary numbers occur in the binary counting system. Hence, the appellation *binary-coded decimal*, or simply BCD for the code of Table 1.

7421 Code Table 2 presents the 7421 code. Again, there are six forbidden combinations. The bits that constitute each combination are calculated so that (9) will yield the digit value.

A problem arises for encoding the digit 7. There are two combinations, 1000 and 0111, both of which yield the value 7. An auxiliary rule is required to settle this difficulty: Use the combination with the least number of 1s in it (i.e. 1000).

742 –1 Code The code for these weights is presented in Table 3. It illustrates that one or more of the weights may be negative as long as the weights fulfill the requirement that all digit values must be created. This time we find that there are two combinations that yield the digit value 6. Since both have the same number of 1s, we choose the combination with the 1 in the least significant place.

XS 3 Code To show that not all codes require weights explicitly, we examine the XS 3 (excess-3) code presented in Table 4. The rule for generating this code requires that we use the BCD code for a digit, call it n_D, and add the binary number 0011 (i.e. 3 in decimal) to it:

$$D \equiv n_D + 0011 \qquad (10)$$

What use would there be for this code? It has two advantages:

1. No proper combination consists of all zeros; therefore, no combination will be mistaken for a null transmission or *vice versa*.
2. It is a self-complementing code.

A *self-complementing code* is very valuable because it possesses this quality: The combination for the complement of a digit is the complement of the combination for that digit. The complement of a number is needed when we do subtraction by addition and complementation. For decimal arithmetic, this requires that we subtract the value of the digit from 9. In our binary code, the complement of a combination b_D is taken with respect to the largest valued combination; for a four-bit code, this would be 1111. Then, our definition for a self-complementing code is one for which the following holds:

$$9 - D \equiv 1111 - b_D \qquad (11)$$

As an example of how XS 3 fulfills this requirement, we have

$$2 \equiv 0101, \ 9 - 2 = 7, \qquad (12)$$
$$1111 - 0101 = 1010, \ 7 \equiv 1010$$

Hexadecimal Programmers often deal with data in units of a *byte*, which consists of eight bits or two *nibbles*, each nibble consisting of four bits. If the combination for each nibble has a different symbol to represent it, then this simplifies the description. The binary values with decimal equivalents between 10 and 15 have been assigned the upper case letters A through F, as shown in Table 1 in parentheses. Thus, the programmer can describe the byte consisting of 10110101 in hexadecimal as B5.

Digits	Table 5 2-out-of-5 Code Weights 74210	Table 6 Biquinary Code 50 43210	Table 7 MBQ Code 5421	Table 8 Gray Code
0	11000	01 00001	0000	0000
1	00011	01 00010	0001	0001
2	00101	01 00100	0010	1001
3	00110	01 01000	0011	1101
4	01001	01 10000	0100	0101
5	01010	10 00001	1000	0111
6	01100	10 00010	1001	1111
7	10001	10 00100	1010	1011
8	10010	10 01000	1011	0011
9	10100	10 10000	1100	0010
10	—	—	—	1010
11	—	—	—	1110
12	—	—	—	0110
13	—	—	—	0100
14	—	—	—	1100
15	—	—	—	1000

Other Decimal Codes If we do not restrict ourselves to four-bit decimal codes, we can provide one or more of the following advantages:

1. Error detection.
2. Simplicity of combination construction.
3. Simplicity of implementation in hardware.

2-Out-of-5 Code The 2-out-of-5 code provides the first advantage and is illustrated in Table 5. Every five-bit combination that represents a digit contains exactly two 1s. Since there are ten such combinations, this works out well. To assign each combination, we establish a set of five *pseudoweights*. One of these weights, W_1, is 0, and the bit corresponding to this weight, b_1, should be set to 1 when the value of the digit being encoded corresponds to precisely one of the non-zero weights; this is true for the digits 1, 2, 4, and 7. The weights work out for all digit values except 0; this digit uses bits with weights 7 and 4, which obviously do not sum to 0; hence the term "pseudoweights."

Biquinary The biquinary code is a seven-bit code using exactly two 1s; it is illustrated in Table 6. One of the 1s is chosen from the left two bits; the other is chosen from the right five bits. The weights are used as would be expected. This code provides error detection whenever more than one 1 appears in either half of a combination, and also provides a logical progression from one combination to the next, which is useful for implementing arithmetic.

MBQ Code The modified biquinary code (MBQ) illustrated in Table 7, is derived from biquinary by replacing the first two bits by a single bit, and the last five bits (which represent 0, 1, 2, 3, or 4) by three bits, which represent them in BCD.

Gray Code The Gray code, invented and patented by F. Gray, was developed to fill a particular requirement. At one time, many devices designed to convert analog (i.e. continuous) data depended on the mechanical position of a shaft. Attached to the shaft was an encoder that produced electromechanical or optical signals corresponding to the shaft rotation. This created a transition problem. Table 1 shows that the combination for 7 is 0111 and that for 8 is 1000. As the shaft rotated, the apparatus for reading out the position could not be depended upon to change simultaneously in each bit position. Thus, totally erroneous readings occurred. If b_4 goes to 1 before the other bits change in going from 7 to 8, the output would be read as 15.

To overcome this transition difficulty, codes called *Gray codes* have been devised, whereby successive combinations change in one-bit position only, as shown in Table 8. The length in bits of each combination L is a function of the number (N) of discrete shaft positions to be encoded, as given by the formula

$$2^{L-1} < N \le 2^L = \lceil \log_2 N \rceil \tag{13}$$

Fig. 1 displays a code disk for the Gray code of Table 8, which indicates the change of one bit at a time. Whereas the transition from one code value to the next in Table 8 cannot simply be described by a rule, there are Gray codes that can be so described. For example, if B_i is the binary equivalent of the integer i, $i = 0, 1, ..., 2^n - 1$ and if B_i is the result of shifting B_i to the right one place (inserting a zero in the left), then $G_i = B_i \oplus B'_i$ where $\oplus$ represents the exclusive-OR operation, is a Gray code. A three-bit code formed this way is 000, 001, 011, 010, 110, 111, 101, 100, where, for example, 101 (which corresponds to $i = 6$) is calculated as $110 \oplus 011 = 101$.

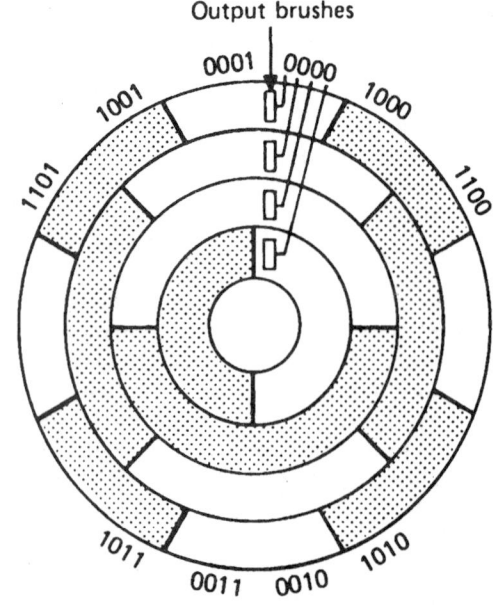

FIG. 1 The Gray code disk for Table 8. (Shading represents 1; no shading represents 0.)

Full Alphabet Thus far, we have restricted our symbol set Σ to decimal numerals. As computers went from infancy to early childhood, it was obvious they could be applied to many problems in which alphabetic output is mandatory, and where we encounter the following classes of symbols:

1. Letters: the alphabet from A to Z.
2. Numerals 0 through 9 (which we have already examined).
3. Punctuation.
4. Special symbols, such as &, @, $.

The question arose of how large or how small the symbol space should be. With six bits, we can encode 64 symbols. Why should we want more than this? The most obvious reason is to accommodate the lower case as well as upper case alphabetic characters in order to allow printed (or displayed) output to look like normal printing. Additionally, there is a need for a variety of control characters and a desire to allow for additional future requirements. Although the 128 characters allowed using seven bits seem sufficient for all needs, the convenience of using eight-bit bytes (or two four-bit combinations) has led to the development of eight-bit codes. On personal computers, for example, the additional 128 character codes made available by using eight bits instead of seven are often used to represent various graphic characters that allow interesting video display designs.

We now consider some of the main six- and eight-bit codes.

Hollerith The Hollerith card code for punched cards (which enables each column in the card to represent alphabetic, numeric, or symbolic information) is discussed in the article PUNCHED CARDS.

IBM 1401 When the second generation IBM 1401 computer was developed, it was intended to replace electronic accounting machines that rely entirely on punched cards. Therefore, as expected, the code used in the 1401 computers, as given in Table 9, corresponds closely to the Hollerith code. We note the following:

1. For digits 1 through 9, the 8421 columns are given by BCD, but 0 is represented by 1010.
2. The bits B and A represent the three zone punches 12, 11, and 0 on an IBM card as follows: $BA = 11$ for 12, $= 10$ for 11, $= 01$ for 0, and $= 00$ for no zone punch.
3. The C bit is the check bit (or *parity* bit, which is discussed in the following section, "Error Detection and Correction").

There are many other six-bit codes that are characteristic of the machine that employs them. They are generally listed in an appendix of the programmer's manual for the machine.

EBCDIC The Extended Binary Coded Decimal Interchange Code (EBCDIC) is an eight-bit code developed by IBM and is available on all IBM 360 and 370 computers. Hexadecimal may be used to convey each combination, as shown in Table 10. Thus, A is represented by $C1$, which in turn means 11000001.

ASCII The American Standard Code for Information Interchange (ASCII) is actually a seven-bit code. To make it an eight-bit code, it is often embedded into a comparable eight-bit code (ASCII-8) in which the leftmost bit is either 0 (as in Table 11) or on some computers, a parity bit. Table 11 displays the encoding of the important characters—letters and numerals.

There is no clear superiority of either EBCDIC and ASCII-8, but there are two important differences. The collating sequence for EBCDIC has the numerals follow the letters; for ASCII-8, the reverse is true. Hence, documents coded and sorted under one system would be in a different order than if they were coded and sorted by the other. Secondly, the ASCII codes for the alphabet progress consecutively by +1, whereas EBCDIC has two gaps (between

Numeric/ Alphabetic	Table 9 IBM 1401 Code							Table 10 EBCDIC in hex	Table 11 ASCII-8 in hex
	C	B	A	8	4	2	1		
A	0	1	1	0	0	0	1	C1	41
B	0	1	1	0	0	1	0	C2	42
C	1	1	1	0	0	1	1	C3	43
D	0	1	1	0	1	0	0	C4	44
E	1	1	1	0	1	0	1	C5	45
F	1	1	1	0	1	1	0	C6	46
G	0	1	1	0	1	1	1	C7	47
H	0	1	1	1	0	0	0	C8	48
I	1	1	1	1	0	0	1	C9	49
J	1	1	0	0	0	0	1	D1	4A
K	1	1	0	0	0	1	0	D2	4B
L	0	1	0	0	0	1	1	D3	4C
M	1	1	0	0	1	0	0	D4	4D
N	0	1	0	0	1	0	1	D5	4E
O	0	1	0	0	1	1	0	D6	4F
P	1	1	0	0	1	1	1	D7	50
Q	1	1	0	1	0	0	0	D8	51
R	0	1	0	1	0	0	1	D9	52
S	1	0	1	0	0	1	0	E2	53
T	0	0	1	0	0	1	1	E3	54
U	1	0	1	0	1	0	0	E4	55
V	0	0	1	0	1	0	1	E5	56
W	0	0	1	0	1	1	0	E6	57
X	1	0	1	0	1	1	1	E7	58
Y	1	0	1	1	0	0	0	E8	59
Z	0	0	1	1	0	0	1	E9	5A
0	0	1	0	0	1	0	1	0	F0	30
1	0	0	0	0	0	0	1	F1	31
2	0	0	0	0	0	1	0	F2	32
3	1	0	0	0	0	1	1	F3	33
4	0	0	0	0	1	0	0	F4	34
5	1	0	0	0	1	0	1	F5	35
6	1	0	0	0	1	1	0	F6	36
7	0	0	0	0	1	1	1	F7	37
8	0	0	0	1	0	0	0	F8	38
9	1	0	0	1	0	0	1	F9	39

I and *J* and between *R* and *S*), which prove annoying in certain programming situations.

Error Detection and Correction

In the case of biquinary, we have seen how a code can be constructed with error detection properties. This is helpful, and even necessary, in many situations, such as when:

1. Information is transmitted from one site to another along lines where noise or other signal distortion might occur.
2. The data is recorded on a medium that is not impervious to noise so that 1s may get lost and be read as 0s, or 0s may be interpreted as 1s.
3. Devices within the computer may become faulty and create or destroy information.

Parity   The simplest means for detecting errors is to attach an extra bit to each combination of the code, called a *parity* bit. This bit is set to 0 or 1, according to the scheme used: For *odd* parity, the total number of 1s, including the parity bit, must be odd, for *even* parity, the total number of 1s, including the parity bit, must be 0 or even. An example of the use of an odd parity bit (also called a "check" bit), labeled *C*, is shown in Table 9. There are two phases in the use of the parity bit: creation and checking.

In the *creation phase*, the combination is examined and a parity bit is created so that the number of 1s in the total combination is proper. Now the combination can be transmitted from one place inside or outside the computer to another place. When it arrives there, the checking action follows. Circuitry similar to that for parity creation examines the combination exclusive of the parity bit as though it were creating that parity bit. If this developed bit and the accompanying parity bit coincide, a *single* bit error could not have occurred, and the information is accepted.

Other Codes

Many different kinds of computers have been built, and there are almost as many types of codes as there are computers. Further, some peripheral devices have their own codes. Magnetic tape usually uses the same code as that employed in the computer proper, but because magnetic tape is used for transmitting at densities and speeds approaching the limit of engineering capability, these devices are prone to error. A parity bit is added for each character of information. Thus, we find seven-track and nine-track tapes used with characters represented by six-bit and eight-bit codes, respectively, with the addition of a parity bit.

Punched paper tape devices that employ five-, six-, seven-, or eight-bit codes are available. The codes are usually peculiar to these devices.

Some typewriter consoles use a printing head that looks much like a golf ball. The head can tilt and rotate to get the proper character into position to strike the paper. To tell this golf ball at what angle to tilt and what angle to rotate, a *Tilt/Rotate code* (T/R) has been developed. Characters transmitted to the type mechanism in EBCDIC must be converted to the T/R code to activate the mechanism properly. It is interesting to note that when the operator presses a key on such a typewriter, a six-bit code is produced. This is normally converted into EBCDIC for transmission to the computer; this is then translated into the T/R code to energize the print ball. The operator can verify that both translations have occurred successfully, since the key struck produces only a code character; it prints the character wanted only if the code and two translations of the code are all correct.

References

1961. Peterson, W. W. *Error Correcting Codes.* Cambridge, MA: The M.I.T. Press.
1968. Berlekamp, E. R. *Algebraic Coding Theory.* New York: McGraw-Hill.
1977. McEliece, R. J. *The Theory of Information Coding.* Reading, MA: Addison-Wesley. (Vol. 3 of the *Encyclopedia of Mathematics and Its Applications.*)
1980. Mackenzie, C. E. *Coded Character Sets: History and Development* Reading, MA: Addison Wesley. (Part of the Systems Programming Series.)

IVAN FLORES

COERCION

For articles on related subjects *see* DEFAULT CONDITION; EXPRESSION; and PROCEDURE-ORIENTED LANGUAGES: PROGRAMMING.

As a matter of convenience to the programmer, many programming languages provide a mechanism for automatically converting from one data type to another in expressions. This automatic type conversion is called *coercion.*

A familiar example of coercion occurs in arithmetic expressions containing both integer and floating point operands, as in $K + 3.5$, where K is of type integer. The integer variable K is first automatically converted to floating point, and then the addition is performed in floating point mode. If the language does not have such a coercion, the programmer must make the conversion explicit (e.g. FLOAT $(K) + 3.5$).

The kind of coercion that must be applied to an operand depends on the type of that operand, as well as on the type of operand required by the context. As an illustration, consider the expression $X + K$, where K is again of type integer. If X is also of type integer, no coercion need be performed; if X is of type floating point or complex, K must be coerced to the same type as X before the addition can be performed. Note that a language may not simultaneously provide coercions from type A to type B and also from type B to type A, since expressions of the form $A + B$ would then be ambiguous.

Coercions are not restricted to converting between integer, floating point, and complex. In Snobol4 and AWK, for example, an expression such as $K + $ '01.50' is permitted, since '01.50' may be coerced from type string to type floating point. Other common coercions are from decimal to binary (PL/I), and scalar to array (APL).

The term coercion was first used in this context Algol 68 (*q.v.*). In the revised Algol 68 report, there are six coercions—*widening* (e.g. integer to floating point), *rowing* (e.g. character to string), *deproceduring* (calling an argumentless function, e.g coercing a **proc real** to a **real**), *dereferencing* (converting a variable to its value), *uniting* (used to assign values to variables that accept several types), and *voiding* (used for discarding superfluous values).

Coercion is also used in other languages to describe the assignment of an expression of one mode to a variable of another. There is, of course, little difference between coercing as described above and then assigning or coercing *while* assigning.

ANDREW S. TANENBAUM

COGNITIVE SCIENCE

For articles on related subjects *see* ARTIFICIAL INTELLIGENCE; NEURAL NETWORKS; and PERCEPTRON.

Definition *Cognitive science* is the interdisciplinary study of cognition. Cognition includes mental states and processes such as thinking, reasoning, remembering, language understanding and generation, visual perception, learning, consciousness, emotions, etc. Some cognitive scientists limit their study to *human* cognition, though most consider cognition independently of its implementation in humans or computers. Some cognitive scientists study cognition independently of the cognitive agent's environment; others study it within the context of society or culture.

Cognitive science can also be defined as, roughly, the intersection of the disciplines of computer science [especially artificial intelligence (*q.v.*)], linguistics, philosophy, psychology, cognitive anthropology, and the cognitive neurosciences. Cognitive science contrasts with other academic disciplines, in which (usually) a common methodology is brought to bear on a multitude of problems. In cognitive science, many *different* methodologies—those of the several cognitive sciences—are brought to bear on a *common* problem: the nature of intelligent cognitive behavior.

Cognitive science's approach to the study of mind is often contrasted with that of *behaviorism*. The behaviorist approach to psychology seeks to describe and predict human behavior in terms of stimulus-response correlations, with no mention of unobservable (hence, "unscientific") mental states (including mental constructs such as symbols, ideas, or schemata) or mental processes (such as thinking, planning, etc.) that might mediate these correlations. A behaviorist who would be willing even to talk about the "mind" would view it as a "black box" that could only be understood in terms of its input-output behavior. Cognitive science seeks to understand human cognitive functions in terms of mental states and processes—i.e. in terms of the algorithms that mediate between input and output. Nonetheless, insofar as behaviorism is concerned with the "intelligent cognitive" behaviors listed above, it too is a cognitive science.

History of Cognitive Science Cognitive science can trace its origins to two major lines of investigation. (1) the development of symbolic logic at the turn of the century and McCulloch and Pitts's 1943 application of logic to the analysis of the behavior of neural networks, and (2) Turing's 1936 analysis of computation and—using the Imitation Game (now known as the Turing Test) in 1950—of whether computers could think. Cognitivism burst upon the scene in 1956. In that year, the following cognitive theories appeared: Miller's theory of human short-term memory; Chomsky's analysis of formal grammars; Bruner and colleagues' study of thinking; and Newell and Simon's Logic Theorist—the first artificial intelligence program (presented at the first artificial intelligence conference, at Dartmouth, organized by Minsky and McCarthy). This was followed a few years later in 1960 by Putnam's theory of Turing-machine (*q.v.*) functionalism as a solution to the classic philosophical problem of the relationship of mind and body. In 1979, the journal *Cognitive Science* appeared; two years later, the first annual meeting of the Cognitive Science Society was held (its proceedings are now published by Lawrence Erlbaum Associates). Other major cognitive-science journals include: *Behavioral and Brain Sciences, Cognition, Linguistics and Philosophy, Mind and Language, Minds and Machines*, and *Philosophical Psychology*; in addition, most journals in the specific cognitive-science disciplines also have articles on cognitive science. Finally, there has been a recent surge of research centers and institutes of cognitive science, as well as graduate and undergraduate degree programs, including university departments of cognitive science.

Central sources of information on cognitive science include Collins and Smith (1988), Gardner (1985), Johnson-Laird (1981), Norman (1981), Posner (1989), Pylyshyn (1985) and Stillings, et al. (1987).

Cognition and Computation The notion that mental states and processes intervene between stimuli and responses sometimes takes the form of a "computational metaphor," often used as the identifying mark of contemporary cognitive science. The mind is to the brain as software is to hardware; mental states and processes are like computer programs implemented (in the case of humans) in brain states and processes. Some cognitive scientists, however, make a stronger claim: Mental states and processes *are* expressible as algorithms: "cognition *is* a type of computation" (Pylyshyn 1985).

Thus, according to the computational view of cognitive science, (1) there are mental states and processes intervening between input stimuli and output responses, (2) these mental states and processes are algorithms (according to the strong, or literal, form)—or they are like algorithms (according to the weak, or metaphorical, form), and, hence, (3) in contrast to behaviorism, mental states and processes are capable of being investigated scientifically (even if they are not capable of being directly observed).

Insofar as the methods of investigation are taken to be computational in nature, computer science in general and artificial intelligence in particular have come to play a central role in cognitive science. It is, however, a role not without controversial philosophical implications. For if mental states and processes can be expressed as algorithms, they are capable of being implemented in non-human computers. The philosophical issue is simply this: Are computers executing such algorithms merely simulating mental states and processes, or are they actually exhibiting them? Do such computers think?

Even cognitive scientists who disagree about the weak vs. the strong computational view of the mind are usually willing to agree that computer programs force cognitive scientists "to make intuitions explicit and to translate vague terminology into concrete proposals; they provide a secure test of the consistency of a theory...; they are 'working models' whose behavior can be directly compared with human performance" (Johnson-Laird 1981: 185-186). That is, the proper methodology of cognitive science is to express one's theories about (human) cognition in a computer program (rather than, say, in English or in the languages of mathematics, logic, or statistics, as other sciences do) and then to compare the program's behavior with human cognitive behavior. Note, however, that this methodology accepts the strong form of the computational view of the mind as at least a working hypothesis. Although this methodology is consistent with the denial of the strong computational view—i.e. human cognitive behavior might be *simulable* by a computer program without itself *being* computational—such a denial is a *very* weak (if not incoherent) claim.

Varieties of Cognitive Science

Currently, there are two major paradigms of computational cognitive science. To lead up to these, several dichotomies can be made:

1. Researchers who study (human) cognitive behavior believe that either (a) there *are* mental states and processes that mediate input stimuli and output responses (this position may be called "cognitivism"), or (b) there are no such mediating states or processes (or it is unscientific to talk about any unobservable such states or processes—the position of behaviorism).

2. Cognitivists believe that either (a) all mental states and processes are computational in nature (and here there is a further dichotomy between (i) the weak and (ii) the strong computational views), or (b) at least some (and perhaps all) such processes are not computational. Position 2b is held by a number of scholars who believe that there are inherent limitations on the ability of computers to simulate or produce mental phenomena (e.g. Dreyfus 1979, Searle 1980). It is certainly a position that provides many of the most interesting and hardest challenges to the

computational cognitivists. One such challenge is the problem of the nature of consciousness. Another is the problem of subjective qualitative experiences—e.g. what kind of computational theory can account for our experience of pain or of the color green? But 2b is also a position that is often ridiculed as "mysticism" or as a contemporary version of vitalism.

3. The dichotomy between the two major paradigms is between (a) those computational cognitivists who believe that cognitive computations are "symbolic" and (b) those who believe that they are, rather, "connectionist."

Symbolic Computational Cognitive Science Symbolic computational cognitivism is often called the "Physical Symbol System Hypothesis" (PSSH) or the "Representational Theory of the Mind" (RTM). The PSSH, due to Newell and Simon, is offered as a solution to the problem of "how it is possible for mind to exist in this physical universe." Mind exists as a physically implemented "symbol system." The concept of a physical symbol system is "the most fundamental contribution...of artificial intelligence and computer science to" cognitive science (*see* Norman 1981). A *symbol system* is any effectively computable procedure—i.e. a universal machine (which, by Church's Thesis, could be a Turing machine (*q.v.*), a recursive function, a general-purpose digital computer, etc.). A *physical symbol system* is a physical implementation of such a symbol system. The PSSH states that a physical system is capable of exhibiting intelligent behavior (where intelligence is defined in terms of *human* intelligence) if and only if it is a physical symbol system. This is taken to be an empirical hypothesis, whose evidence comes from work in symbolic (i.e. non-connectionist) artificial intelligence. Newell argues that *intelligent* physical systems are physical *symbol* systems because intelligence requires *representations* of a wide variety of goals and states, and because such flexible representations require symbols. It is the first of these reasons—the requirement of representations—that is empirical; the second—that the representations must be symbolic—is challenged by connectionism. The converse claim, that physical *symbol* systems are capable of being *intelligent* physical systems, has been challenged by the non-computationalists of position 2b, above. One particularly strong form of the RTM is Fodor's "language of thought" theory (1975), which says that the mental representations are a language (sometimes called "mentalese") with a syntax (and, perhaps, a semantics). Fodor's theory of *methodological solipsism* holds that the syntax of the language of thought is all that cognitive science needs to deal with—i.e. that the input-output transducers—while important for understanding how information gets into and out of the mind—are irrelevant for understanding how the mind works.

There is, perhaps, a fourth dichotomy among the symbolic computational cognitivists, between those who are satisfied with symbolic algorithms whose input-output behavior is the same as human cognitive behavior, and those who are satisfied only with symbolic algorithms that not only are input-output equivalent to human cognitive behavior, but also are equivalent in all but the details of physical implementation (i.e. equivalent in terms of subroutines and abstract data types (*q.v.*)—a particularly strong form of this also requires the algorithms to be equivalent to human cognitive behavior at the level of space and time complexity). (Pylyshyn 1985).

According to the PSSH and the RTM, when a physical system (computer or human) executes a "cognitive" algorithm, the representations are brought to life, so to speak, and made to behave according to the rules of the symbol system; the symbol system becomes dynamic, rather than static. If cognition is representational and rule-based in this way—i.e. if cognitive behavior consists of transformations of representations according to rules—then a computer that behaves according to these rules causally applied to these representations *is* behaving cognitively and is not merely simulating cognitive behavior.

Although the PSSH and the RTM offer an answer (satisfying to most computer scientists) to Descartes's question of how mind and body can interact (namely, mind can be implemented in body), they are not without their detractors. Of particular note are the objections of Winograd (see Norman, 1981), who did pioneering work in the symbolic paradigm of artificial intelligence. Winograd cites a biologist, Maturana, who straightforwardly denies the RTM: "cognition is not based on the manipulation of mental models or representations of the world." Instead, according to Winograd and Maturana, there are cognitive phenomena that *for an observer* can be described in terms of representation, but that can also be understood as the activity of a structure-determined system with no mechanism corresponding to a representation. This view echoes the "intentional stance" theory of the philosopher Dennett (who has many more sympathies with computational cognitivism). According to Dennett, it makes sense to treat certain complex systems (e.g. chess-playing computers) as *if* they had beliefs and acted intentionally, even though there might not be anything in their structure that corresponded in any way to beliefs or intentions (Dennett, 1978).

Connectionist Computational Cognitive Science

The "connectionist" (or "neural network" (*q.v.*), or "parallel distributed processing") approach to artificial intelligence and computational cognitive science can be seen as one way for a system to (appear to) behave intelligently without being a "symbol system" and yet be computational. (For a description of connectionism, *see* NEURAL NETWORK.)

Many connectionist methods are, in fact, highly representational, but most are "distributively representational"—i.e. the kind of information that a *symbolic* artificial intelligence program would represent by using various symbolic knowledge-representation techniques is instead "represented" by the strengths and connectivity patterns of the links. Rather than having intelligence "programmed" into the system by using explicit rules and representations, intelligence is sometimes held to "emerge" from the organization of the nodes and links.

(Good surveys of connectionism are Graubard, 1988; *Cognitive Science*, Vol. 9, No. 1 (1985); and, from a critical standpoint, Pinker and Mehler 1988.

Cognitive processes that are easy to implement symbolically (e.g. problem solving, reasoning, game playing, certain aspects of linguistic competence) tend to be ones that are relatively difficult for humans or that have to be explicitly taught, while those that have proven difficult to implement symbolically (e.g. certain aspects of visual perception and learning) tend to be those that "come naturally" to humans. This paradox of (symbolic) artificial intelligence has its counterpart in the debate over connectionism. The processes that have proven difficult to implement symbolically appear to be susceptible to connectionist techniques. This complementarity may prove to be a major advance in our understanding of cognition.

Cognitive Science Research

One way of exploring the content of cognitive science is to look at research in the individual cognitive science disciplines that could just as well be considered research in cognitive science *per se*.

Artificial Intelligence

Given the computational view of cognitive science, it is arguable that all research in artificial intelligence is also research in cognitive science. Nonetheless, certain applications of artificial intelligence techniques to problems in engineering, management, etc., and, perhaps, the development of *expert systems* (*q.v.*) do not seem to fall within the scope of cognitive science. Certainly, however, those aspects of artificial intelligence research that might be considered to be "computational psychology" or "computational philosophy" are also in the domain of cognitive science. Among these are early work by Newell and Simon on problem solving (the Logic Theorist, the General Problem Solver); aspects of knowledge representation that attempt to reflect cognition; Minsky's theory of frames; Schank's theory of scripts and conceptual dependency; work on "naive" or "qualitative" physics, which attempts to develop systems that can reason about physics in ways that humans do on an everyday basis (rather than in ways that professional physicists do); machine learning; planning; reasoning; natural-language understanding and generation; and computer vision (*q.v.*). (For surveys of these and other topics, *see* Shapiro 1992.)

Linguistics

Linguistics is another discipline that is arguably wholly subsumed by cognitive science (at least, to the extent that computationalism is de-emphasized). After all, language is often held to be the "mirror of the mind"—the (physical) means for one mind to communicate its thoughts to another. But it was with the development of transformational grammar by Chomsky that cognitivism replaced behaviorism in linguistics. Subsequent work on a variety of computationally tractable "successors" to transformational grammar and work in computational and cognitive linguistics is clearly a part of cognitive science.

Philosophy Philosophers have long studied the nature of mind and language, and much recent work in the philosophy of mind, the philosophy of language, and epistemology has been informed by research in the other cognitive-science disciplines. The objections to the nature and possibility of success of artificial intelligence that have been raised by philosophers have served as research goals for artificial intelligence researchers—such criticisms must also be considered as part of cognitive science. The two major lines of criticism are those due to Dreyfus and to Searle. Dreyfus argued, on the basis of the phenomenological school of philosophy, that since computers do not have a (human) body, do not have (human) purposes or needs, and do not share the human cultural milieu, they will never be truly intelligent. Searle has argued that the Turing Test, although perhaps an indicator of the presence of intelligent *behavior*, fails as an indicator of the presence of intelligence. His "Chinese Room Argument" purports to show that a computer cannot understand natural language. Suppose that an English-speaking human who knew no Chinese was locked in a room and equipped with a program (written in English) for manipulating Chinese ideographs in such a way as to convince native Chinese speakers that they were communicating with another native speaker of Chinese. Such a person, according to Searle, would pass the Turing Test, yet (by hypothesis) would not understand Chinese.

Psychology Cognitive psychology, of course, is a central cognitive-science discipline. Among recent work by cognitive psychologists that has been influential in cognitive science are Bransford, Barclay, and Franks's (1972) findings that people actively construct mental representations of the "propositional" meaning of sentences, Rumelhart's theory of story grammars (1975), and Shepard's and Kosslyn's theories of mental imagery as a non-propositional kind of mental representation (Shepard and Judd 1976, Kosslyn 1981).

Cognitive Science Perhaps the most important research topics in cognitive science are those that are truly interdisciplinary—i.e. those in which researchers from the several cognitive sciences apply their differing methodologies to a common problem and, conversely, inform their own studies with results of investigations from the complementary disciplines. Prime examples would be research in visual perception, which has been investigated in psychology, in artificial intelligence, and in robotics (*q.v.*), not to mention in physiology and biophysics; research into mental imagery, which, in addition to the work in psychology mentioned above, has received critical philosophical attention from Pylyshyn and Dennett (*cf.* Block 1981); research on categorization, where results from psychology have largely overturned the "classical" philosophical view going back to Aristotle of there being necessary and sufficient conditions for membership in a category; and research on the logic of belief and knowledge, in which people from artificial intelligence have not only adapted, for use in artificial intelligence programs, systems of epistemic and doxastic logics developed by philosophers, but have also offered solutions to many open problems in these logics that philosophers have largely ignored.

The Future of Cognitive Science If cognitive science is to become a discipline in its own right, and not just a congeries of parts of other disciplines, perhaps its best hope lies not only in such multi-pronged attacks on common problems, as just discussed, but in single research groups whose members come from different disciplines, yet who work together on common problems of cognition. The range of disciplines and the levels of analysis are by no means settled and, indeed, are widening in scope. The two major open issues for a complete understanding of cognition are—looking inwards—how the mind is implemented and how the very fact of its implementation in particular kinds of physical or biological mechanisms influences the nature of cognition, and—looking outwards—how and to what extent the nature of cognition is shaped by the sociocultural world in which minds find themselves.

References

Items prefixed by an asterisk are central sources of information on cognitive science.

1936. Turing, Alan M. "On Computable Numbers, with an Application to the Entscheidungsproblem," *Proceedings of the London Mathematical Society*, Ser. 2, **42**, 230–265. Reprinted in M. Davis (ed.), *The Undecidable*, New York: Raven Press, 1965: 116–154.

1943. McCulloch, Warren S. and Pitts, Walter H. "A Logical Calculus of the Ideas Immanent in Nervous Activity," *Bulletin of Mathematical Biophysics* **7**:115–133; reprinted in W.S. McCulloch, *Embodiments of Mind*. Cambridge, MA: MIT Press, 1965: 19–39.

1950. Turing, Alan M. "Computing Machinery and Intelligence," *Mind* 59. Reprinted in A. R. Anderson (ed.), *Minds and Machines*, Englewood Cliffs, NJ: Prentice-Hall, 1964: 4–30.

1960. Putnam, Hilary. "Minds and Machines," in S. Hook (ed.), *Dimensions of Mind*. New York: New York University Press: 148–179; Reprinted in H. Putnam, *Mind, Language and Reality*, Cambridge, England: Cambridge University Press: 362–385.

1972. Bransford, J. D., Barclay, J. R., and Franks, J. J. "Sentence Memory: A Constructive Versus Interpretive Approach," *Cognitive Psychology* **3**: 193–209.

1975. Fodor, Jerry A. *The Language of Thought*. New York: Thomas Y. Crowell Co.

1975. Rumelhart, Donald E. "Notes on a Schema for Stories," in D. G. Bobrow and Collins, A. (eds.). *Representation and Understanding: Studies in Cognitive Science*. New York: Academic Press: 211–236.

1976. Shepard, R. N. and Judd, S. A. "Perceptual Illusion of Rotation of Three-dimensional Objects," *Science* **191**: 952–954.

1978. Dennett, Daniel C., "Intentional Systems," in D.C. Dennett, *Brainstorms*. Montgomery, VT: Bradford Books: 3–22.

1979. Dreyfus, Hubert L. *What Computers Can't Do: The Limits of Artificial Intelligence*, revised edition. New York: Harper & Row.

1980. Fodor, Jerry A. "Methodological Solipsism Considered as a Research Strategy in Cognitive Psychology," *Behavioral and Brain Sciences* **3**: 63–109.

1980. Searle, John R. "Minds, Brains, and Programs," *Behavioral and Brain Sciences* **3**:417–457.

1981. Block, Ned (ed.). *Imagery*. Cambridge, MA: MIT Press.

1981. Johnson-Laird, Philip N. "Mental Models in Cognitive Science," in D. A. Norman (ed.), *Perspectives on Cognitive Science*. Norwood, NJ: Ablex Publishing Corp: 147–191.

1981. Kosslyn, Stephen M. "The Medium and the Message in Mental Imagery: A Theory," in N. Block (ed.), *Imagery*. Cambridge, MA: MIT Press: 207–244.

1981. *Norman, Donald A. (ed.). *Perspectives on Cognitive Science*. Norwood, NJ: Ablex Publishing Corp.

1981. **Proceedings of the Annual Conference of the Cognitive Science Society*. Hillsdale, NJ: Lawrence Erlbaum Associates.

1981. Winograd, Terry. "What Does It Mean to Understand Language?", in D. A. Norman (ed.), *Perspectives on Cognitive Science*, Norwood, NJ: Ablex Publishing Corp: 231–263.

1984. *Kintsch, Walter, Miller, James R., and Polson, Peter G. (eds.). *Methods and Tactics in Cognitive Science*. Hillsdale, NJ: Lawrence Erlbaum Associates.

1985. *Gardner, Howard. *The Mind's New Science: A History of the Cognitive Revolution*. New York: Basic Books.

1985. *Pylyshyn, Zenon. *Computation and Cognition: Toward a Foundation for Cognitive Science*, 2nd edition. Cambridge, MA: MIT Press.

1987. *Stillings, Neil A., Feinstein, Mark H., Garfield, Jay L., Rissland, Edwina L., Rosenbaum, David A., Weisler, Steven E., and Baker-Ward, Lynne. *Cognitive Science: An Introduction*. Cambridge, MA: M.I.T. Press.

1988. *Collins, Allen, and Smith, Edward E. (eds.). *Readings in Cognitive Science: A Perspective from Psychology and Artificial Intelligence*. San Mateo, CA: Morgan Kaufmann Publishers.

1988. Graubard, Stephen R. (ed.). "Artificial Intelligence," special issue of *Daedalus*, **117**, No. 1 (Winter 1988); reprinted as *The Artificial Intelligence Debate: False Starts, Real Foundations*. Cambridge, MA: MIT Press.

1988. *Johnson-Laird, Philip N. *The Computer and the Mind: An Introduction to Cognitive Science*. Cambridge, MA: Harvard University Press.

1988. Pinker, Steven, and Mehler, Jacques (eds.). *Connections and Symbols*. Cambridge, MA: MIT Press.

1989. *Posner, Michael I. (ed.). *Foundations of Cognitive Science*. Cambridge, MA: MIT Press.

1992. Shapiro, Stuart C. (ed.). *Encyclopedia of Artificial Intelligence,* 2nd. Ed. New York: John Wiley & Sons.

WILLIAM J. RAPAPORT

COLLATING SEQUENCE. *See* SORTING.

COLOSSUS

For articles on related subjects *see* CRYPTOGRAPHY, COMPUTERS IN; and DIGITAL COMPUTERS; HISTORY: EARLY.

Colossus was one of the earliest programmable electronic computers. It was developed in Britain during World War II to break top-level German machine ciphers generated by the *Geheimfernschreiber*, a teletype machine manufactured by Siemens AG. The first tests with the ciphers were run successfully in December 1943. Several more Colossi were built before the end of the war. Because of engineering improvements, no two were identical. Many details about their design and performance, particularly their capacity for conditional branching, still remain secret.

As early as 1939, British cryptanalysts working at Bletchley Park, a country estate about halfway between London and Birmingham, invented an analog device to break the rotor ciphers of the German *Enigma* machine. Their success encouraged them to attack the much more difficult teletype ciphers. In 1942, when mathematics professor M. H. A. Newman arrived at Bletchley from Cambridge University, the cryptanalysts were trying to solve the *Geheimfernschreiber* ciphers with pencil and paper, using exhaustive techniques of Bayesian statistical analysis.

Newman set up a team of mathematical specialists to mechanize part of the task. Their early work led to the development of the "Heath Robinson" machines, which compared two punched paper tapes at rates of up to 2,000 characters per second. Mechanical problems with the Robinsons pushed Newman and his team toward a radical innovation. T. H. Flowers, an engineer from the Post Office Research Station at Dollis Hill, proposed to build a machine with 1,500 vacuum tubes, almost three times the number in any contemporary machine. It would execute the comparisons electronically rather than mechanically, a strategy that has guided the evolution of the computer ever since. The idea of automating the comparisons was probably influenced by Alan Turing's (*q.v.*) classic work on computability, and particularly by his notion of the Universal Turing Machine (*q.v.*). Although Turing himself worked at Bletchley Park, his exact role in the development of Colossus remains obscure.

By redesigning the tape drive and the readers used in the Robinson machines, Flowers and his colleagues at Dollis Hill greatly increased the rate at which two cipher texts could be compared. Colossus could read punched tape at 5,000 characters per second, a truly impressive speed even by postwar standards. Only one tape at a time was fed into the machine, and the results were stored in a memory consisting of gas-filled thyratron triodes. To eliminate cumulative timing errors, a clock pulse was generated by a photocell that read the sprocket holes in the tape. The necessary programming was done with plugboards. Although Flowers later noted that the prototype was probably less programmable than some contemporary IBM machines, Newman and his colleagues began to exploit the flexibility of the machine, making dynamically generated data dependent on the results of previous processing.

When installed at Bletchley, Colossus filled a large room in one of the temporary wartime huts. It operated in parallel arithmetic mode at 5,000 pulses per second and had electronic counting circuits, electronic storage resistors that were changeable by an automatically controlled sequence of operations, and typewriter output. The Mark II Colossus, completed in June 1944, had 2,400 tubes and was five times faster. The basic clock rate was the same, but five-stage shift registers increased the speed by providing access to five characters at a time. About ten of the Mark V machines were in successful operation in Bletchley Park by the end of the war in 1945.

Colossus went on-line two years before ENIAC (*q.v.*). Colossus, though built as a special-purpose logical computer, proved flexible enough to be programmed to execute a variety of tasks, though it was not quite capable of decimal multiplication. ENIAC, a much larger and faster machine, programmed with patch cords, initially was intended for solving differential equations, but was used for a variety of numerical calculations.

Although it was the ENIAC group that made the final leap toward the modern general-purpose digital computer with the design for EDVAC (*q.v.*), Colossus stands as an impressive pioneering achievement in its own right, and was a powerful stimulus to postwar computer research in Britain.

References

1974. Kahn, David. "The Ultra Secret," *New York Times Book Review*, 29 December.
1977. Randell, Brian. "Colossus: Godfather of the Computer," *New Scientist*, 10 February.
1980. Randell, Brian. "The Colossus," in *A History of Computing in the Twentieth Century*. New York: Academic Press.
1983. Hodges, Andrew, *Alan Turing: The Enigma*. New York: Simon and Schuster.

WILLIAM E. BOGGS

COMBINATORICS

For articles on related subjects *see* ALGORITHMS, ANALYSIS OF; CODES; DISCRETE MATHEMATICS; and GRAPH THEORY.

Introduction *Combinatorics* is the branch of discrete mathematics that involves the study of methods of counting how many objects there are of some type, or how many ways there are to do something. The items being counted are generally drawn from a finite system that has some structure, and the process of counting requires a detailed analysis of that structure. Such counting problems are ubiquitous in the sciences and especially in computer science; since the computer can aid in such analyses, combinatorics and computer science have developed a symbiotic relationship.

Most brain teasers, games, and puzzles are combinatorial in nature, and their solutions have often become the basis for general theories in combinatorics. Combinatorial problems have attracted the attention of serious mathematicians since ancient times. For example, magic squares (square arrays of numbers with the property that the rows, columns, and diagonals add up to the same sum) were discovered by the Chinese as early as 2200 B.C. Other similar problems resulted in important contributions by such eminent mathematicians as Blaise Pascal (*q.v.*), Pierre de Fermat, Gottfried Wilhelm von Leibniz (*q.v.*), Leonhard Euler, Arthur Cayley, and James Joseph Sylvester.

Combinatorics was once considered to embrace only disconnected ideas and tricks for solving isolated problems, most of them recreational in nature. Since the early 1960s, however, unifying principles and cross connections have helped to make combinatorics a coherent body of concepts and techniques. Widely varied applications to problems in statistics, theoretical physics, chemistry, the social sciences, communication theory, and computer science have demonstrated the generality of the techniques and have enhanced the importance of combinatorics as a branch of applied mathematics. We present as illustrations some combinatoric problems and their solutions in three areas: combinations and permutations, combinatorial designs, and asymptotics.

Most combinatoric problems can be characterized as either (1) an existence problem, in which one determines whether a problem has a solution, (2) an enumeration problem, in which one determines the number of solutions to a problem, or (3) a selection problem, in which one is to find, among all the solutions to a problem, one or more with particular properties. The selection problem is often related to efficient algorithms that produce the desired solutions.

As general references, the books by Hall (1986), Liu (1968), and Tucker (1984) are suggested.

Combinations and Permutations One of the most important areas in combinatorics is the study of the ways in which discrete objects are combined and permuted. A selection of r objects from a set of n objects is called a *combination*. An ordered selection of r objects chosen from n objects is called a *permutation*. The number of ways to select r distinct objects from n distinct objects is given by the formula $\frac{n!}{r!\,(n-r)!}$, where $i!$ denotes the product $i \cdot (i-1) \cdot (i-2) \cdots 3 \cdot 2 \cdot 1$ and is read "i factorial." The quantity $\frac{n!}{r!\,(n-r)!}$, usually written $\binom{n}{r}$, is known as a *binomial coefficient* because it is the coefficient of the term x^r in the expansion of $(1+x)^n$. The number of ordered arrangements of r distinct objects chosen from n distinct objects is $n!/(n-r)! = n \cdot (n-1) \cdot (n-2) \cdots (n-r+1)$.

There are many possible variations on permutations and combinations. For example, one might wish to select r objects from n distinct objects, allowing repeated selection of the same object. One way to solve the problem is to note that the coefficient of x^r in the expansion of $(1-x)^{-n}$ is the answer. This example illustrates *generating functions*, a technique useful in enumeration problems. The generating function of a sequence of numbers $a_0, a_1, a_2, \ldots, a_r, \ldots$ is the power series $a_0 + a_1 x + a_2 x^2 + \cdots + a_r x^r + \cdots$, where x is a formal variable (i.e. a variable without intrinsic meaning). In many enumeration problems, it is easier or more desirable to obtain the generating function of the solutions for a sequence of problems, rather than to obtain an explicit closed-form expression of the solution for a particular problem. Thus, the generating function $(1-x)^{-n}$ gives the number of ways to select, for all r, r objects from n distinct objects, allowing unlimited repetitions. For example, when $n = 3$, $(1-x)^{-3} = 1 + 3x + 6x^2 + \cdots$ and the six combinations of three objects, say a, b, and c, taken two at a time, are aa, ab, ac, bb, bc, and cc. Similarly, the number of ways to divide r distinct objects into n non-empty subsets is equal to $r!/n!$ times the coefficient of x^r in $(e^x - 1)^n$. Thus, for instance, when $n = 2$, $(e^x - 1)^2 = x^2 + x^3 + \frac{7}{12}x^4 + \cdots$ and there are

$3!/2! = 3$ ways that three objects can be divided into two non-empty sets: (a, bc), (b, ac), and (c, ab).

Generating functions are also useful in determining the number of ways to arrange n opening parentheses and n closing parentheses so that each open parenthesis is balanced by a corresponding closed parenthesis to its right. For example, $()(())$ is a well-formed arrangement, while $()((\ )$ is not. If a_n denotes the number of such arrangements, we note that $a_0 = 1$, since there is a unique empty arrangement (no parentheses) and

$$a_n = a_{n-1} + a_1 a_{n-2} + a_2 a_{n-3} + \cdots + a_{n-2} a_1 + a_{n-1},$$

since all possible arrangements on n parentheses P_n are formed without repetition by $(P_j) P_{n-j-1}$, for $j = 0, 1,..., n - 1$, with P_0 being the empty string of parentheses. This is an example of a *recurrence relation*, which, in general, is an equation relating a sequence of numbers $a_0, a_1, a_2,..., a_n,...$. Often, a recurrence relation can be solved to obtain either a closed-form expression or the generating function for a_n, so many enumeration problems can be attacked by first setting up a recurrence relation and then solving it. In this case, the generating function can be shown to be $(1 - \sqrt{1 - 4x})/2x$ and from this we can determine that $a_n = \binom{2n}{n}/(n + 1)$; these a_n are called *Catalan numbers*.

A *derangement* is a permutation of the integers $1, 2,..., n$ so that no integer i occupies the ith position. The problem of counting the number of derangements is a special case of the general problem of the permutation of objects, with restrictions on the positions each object may occupy. The number of derangements of n objects can be determined by generating functions or by a formula known as the *principle of inclusion and exclusion*, which states that for r sets $A_1, A_2,..., A_r$

$$|A_1 \cup A_2 \cup \cdots \cup A_r| = |A_1| + |A_2| + \cdots + |A_r| \\ - |A_1 \cap A_2| - |A_1 \cap A_3| - \cdots - |A_{r-1} \cap A_r| + \\ + |A_1 \cap A_2 \cap A_3| + |A_1 \cap A_2 \cap A_4| + \cdots \\ + (-1)^{r-1} |A_1 \cap A_2 \cap \cdots \cap A_r|,$$

where $|X|$ denotes the cardinality (number of members) of the set X. Thus, of the $n!$ permutations of the integers $1, 2,..., n$, let A_i denote the set of those permutations in which the integer i is the ith position. It follows that the number of derangements is equal to

$$n! - |A_1 \cup A_2 \cup \cdots \cup A_n|$$
$$= n! - \binom{n}{1}(n-1)! + \binom{n}{2}(n-2)! + \cdots + (-1)^n \binom{n}{n}$$
$$= n! \left(1 - \frac{1}{1!} + \frac{1}{2!} - \ldots + (-1)^n \frac{1}{n!}\right)$$
$$\approx n!/e,$$

where $\approx$ means "approximately equal to" and e is the base of the natural logarithms. Gian-Carlo Rota has observed that the principle of inclusion and exclusion and the well-known Möbius inversion formula of number theory are special cases of a general inversion formula for partially ordered sets. Rota's work is an excellent example of unifying results that have emerged since the 1960s.

Permutation problems also arise from the study of molecular structures. We may ask, for example, how many ways there are to place molecules at the apexes of a regular polyhedron; two placements are considered equivalent if one can be obtained from another by a rotation of the polyhedron. If there are five kinds of molecules and the regular polyhedron is a tetrahedron (a pyramid with three sides and a base), the number of placements is 75, a result that can be found using *Polya's theory of counting* (see Liu (1968)).

Graph Theory Graph theory is an area of significant importance in combinatorics, and it provides a good example of the study of the structural properties of discrete systems. Since it is discussed in a separate article, we shall not discuss it here.

Combinatorial Designs Combinatorial designs is the area of combinatorics concerned with the arrangement of discrete objects. However, unlike the enumerative problems discussed above, its main emphasis is on proof of existence and nonexistence.

Typical of such arrangements are *Latin squares*. A Latin square of order n is an arrangement of n distinct symbols in an $n \times n$ square so that each symbol appears in each row and each column exactly once. Two Latin squares are said to be *orthogonal* if, when they are superimposed, the ordered pairs of entries are all distinct. A set of Latin squares is said to be *mutually orthogonal* if every two squares in the set are orthogonal. Latin squares were first studied by Euler when he posed the so-called "36 officers problem" in which six officers of different ranks from each of six regiments are to be arranged in a 6×6 square so that no two officers of the same rank or from the same regiment will stand in the same row or the same column. This problem is equivalent to the problem of the existence of a pair of orthogonal Latin squares of order 6. It is not difficult to discover that for $n - 2$ not divisible by 4, there always exists a pair of orthogonal Latin squares of order n. For example, Fig. 1 shows a pair of orthogonal Latin squares of order 10. Euler conjectured that for $n - 2$ divisible by 4 there is no pair of orthogonal Latin squares. Indeed, there do not exist orthogonal Latin squares of order 2 or 6, but in 1960 R. C. Bose, S. S. Shrikhande, and E. T. Parker proved the falsity of Euler's conjecture by exhibiting pairs of orthogonal Latin squares for all orders $n \geq 10$, such that $n - 2$ is divisible by 4.

Of related interest is the largest number of Latin squares in a mutually orthogonal set. A mutually orthogonal set of Latin squares of order n can contain at most $n - 1$ Latin squares; furthermore, for n equal to a power of a prime, such a set exists. However, the question is still open for general n; the case $n = 10$ was settled only recently by Lam, Thiel, and Swiercz [1989]. An exhaustive computer search failed to discover a set of nine mutually orthogonal Latin squares of order 10. Various properties of Latin squares have been studied for the more restricted case in which entries in each *diagonal* or *superdiagonal*

0	4	1	7	2	9	8	3	6	5
8	1	5	2	7	3	9	4	0	6
9	8	2	6	3	7	4	5	1	0
5	9	8	3	0	4	7	6	2	1
7	6	9	8	4	1	5	0	3	2
6	7	0	9	8	5	2	1	4	3
3	0	7	1	9	8	6	2	5	4
1	2	3	4	5	6	0	7	8	9
2	3	4	5	6	0	1	8	9	7
4	5	6	0	1	2	3	9	7	8

0	7	8	6	9	3	5	4	1	2
6	1	7	8	0	9	4	5	2	3
5	0	2	7	8	1	9	6	3	4
9	6	1	3	7	8	2	0	4	5
3	9	0	2	4	7	8	1	5	6
8	4	9	1	3	5	7	2	6	0
7	8	5	9	2	4	6	3	0	1
4	5	6	0	1	2	3	7	8	9
1	2	3	4	5	6	0	9	7	8
2	3	4	5	6	0	1	8	9	7

FIG. 1. A pair of orthogonal 10×10 Latin squares.

are distinct. The superdiagonals are the diagonals formed when the square is rolled into a cylinder with the first column adjacent to the last column, and the ends of the cylinder are then joined to form a torus.

The design of statistical experiments to test the effects and interrelations of various "treatments" (medications) leads to the area of combinatorial designs known as *block designs*; most of the terminology in this area is derived from such applications. Let $T = \{1, 2, ..., v\}$ be a set of distinct objects called *treatments*, and let $B_1, B_2, ...,$ B_b be subsets of T called *blocks*. A collection of blocks is called a *design* on the treatments: a *balanced incomplete block design* is a design in which every treatment appears in exactly r blocks, every block is of size k, and every pair of treatments appears in exactly λ blocks. Since balanced incomplete block designs are characterized by the five parameters v, b, r, k, and λ, they are also referred to as (v, b, r, k, λ) designs. Most important is the question of the existence of a balanced incomplete block design for given values of v, b, r, k, and λ. This general problem is extremely difficult and has not been completely solved, although there are many results for specific sets of parameters. The special class of balanced incomplete block designs in which $v = b$ (and, consequently, $r = k$) is known as *symmetric balanced incomplete block designs*. Because of the additional constraints, more is known about such designs, although the general existence question remains a difficult one.

The construction of codes is closely related to that of block designs. Let $A = \{a_1, a_2, ...\}$ be a set of distinct symbols (letters). The set A is called the *alphabet*. A *word* is an ordered sequence of letters from the alphabet; the *length* of a word is the number of letters in it. A *code* is a collection of words (called *codewords*). If no codeword is a prefix of another codeword, the code is a *prefix code*. If all codewords are the same length, the code is a *block code*. When A is the set of elements in a finite field, a block code is said to be *linear* if it forms a vector space over the finite field $(A, +, \cdot)$. An *error* is said to occur if one of the letters in a codeword is changed into another letter. Some codes are *t-error detecting*, i.e. they can recognize when t or fewer errors occur in a codeword. A code is said to be *t-error correcting* if the original codeword can be reconstructed when t or fewer errors occur.

The three important parameters of a block code are the length of its words (short codewords yield low communication cost), the number of its codewords (a large number of codewords gives the capability of representing a large number of messages), and its error-detecting/correcting capability (detection or correction of errors means high reliability in communication). The problem of code design is to select a set of codewords so that these interdependent parameters satisfy the needs of a particular communication problem. It is also desirable that the code have efficient encoding and decoding algorithms.

Asymptotics In enumerative combinatorial problems, it is necessary to count the number of occurrences of some configuration. The derangements problem is a typical example. Frequently, the answer can be expressed by a recurrence relation, a generating function, a sum of terms, or a product of terms. In addition to an exact answer of that type, we usually would like to know an approximation in more elementary terms. *Asymptotics* is concerned with such approximations.

For example, the single most important asymptotic result of combinatorics is the answer to the question "How large is $n! = n \cdot (n - 1) \cdot (n - 2) \cdots 2 \cdot 1$?" The answer was found by James Stirling in the early eighteenth century. He showed that

$$n! \approx \sqrt{2\pi n} \left(\frac{n}{e}\right)^n.$$

Stirling's formula also gives us an approximation for the binomial coefficients since $\binom{n}{r} = \frac{n!}{r! (n-r)!}$, and for many other similar functions.

The *harmonic numbers*, $H_n = \sum_{i=1}^{n} \frac{1}{i}$, occur in many contexts in combinatorics and their approximation is also of interest:

$$H_n \approx \ln n + \gamma,$$

where $\gamma \approx 0.5772$ is known as *Euler's constant*.

Both the approximation for $n!$ and H_n are derived by

Euler's summation formula, which approximates a discrete summation, such as $\ln n! = \sum_{i=1}^{n} \ln i$ or $H_n = \sum_{i=1}^{n} \frac{1}{i}$, by the corresponding integral, $\int_{1}^{n} \ln x \, dx$ or $\int_{1}^{n} \frac{dx}{x}$. The integral is then evaluated, and the error is bounded by various analytical tecnhiques.

Connections with Computer Science The close relation between combinatorics and computer science works to the advantage of both areas. Combinatorics gains in two distinct ways. First, the computer allows large-scale testing of conjectures and generation of data that would have been impossible or infeasible only a few decades ago. Before computers, results like Appel and Haken's proof of the four-color theorem could never have been achieved. Second, the application of techniques from combinatorics to problems in computer science infuses new vigor into the study of the techniques themselves and suggests new avenues for combinatorial investigation.

Computer science gains from combinatorics the tools necessary for analyzing algorithms and data structures. The best examples are algorithms for sorting (*q.v.*) elements according to some order. The analysis of the average, best, and worst case performance of most sorting algorithms hinges critically on the structure of permutations; the classical results in this area are just what are needed to understand the relative behavior of various sorting algorithms. Similarly, results on combinations, permutations, and trees (a special type of graph) facilitate the analysis of merging algorithms and search strategies. The techniques for the solution of recurrence relations and of asymptotic analysis are used in the analysis of almost all algorithms. Without such techniques, we would never be able to answer questions about, for instance, the average number of interchanges in the bubble sort, the expected height of a search tree, or the average stack depth encountered in parsing arithmetic expressions.

Computer science also benefits from the computational problems suggested by the classical structures of combinatorics. How can we determine if a graph is planar? How do we find the shortest path between two nodes of a network? Is there an efficient way to determine whether two planar networks are isomorphic? These questions originated with combinatorics, but their algorithmic solutions came largely from computer science.

The books by Knuth (1968) and Reingold, Nievergelt, and Deo (1977) are recommended as references for the interface between combinatorics and computer science.

Concluding Remarks The topics discussed are merely representative. We have not discussed many beautiful and deep topics, such as *Ramsey theory*, which is concerned with certain generalizations of the "pigeonhole principle" (if $n + 1$ pigeons are put into n holes, then one of the holes must contain two or more pigeons), partially ordered sets (exemplified by structural results such as Sperner's Lemma and Dilworth's Theorem), the theory of matroids as generalizations of graphs, or the mathematical programming (*q.v.*) approach to optimization problems.

Combinatorial techniques will undoubtedly continue to play a crucial role in computer science. The future design of computer hardware by VLSI is but one area in which deep combinatorial problems are certain to emerge.

References

1968. Knuth, D. E. *The Art of Computer Programming Volume I.* Reading, MA: Addison-Wesley. (See also Volume II, 1969, and Volume III, 1972.)

1968. Liu, C. L. *Introduction to Combinatorial Mathematics.* New York: McGraw-Hill.

1974. Dena, J. and Keedwell, A. D. *Latin Squares and Their Applications.* London: English University Press.

1977. Reingold, E. M., Nievergelt, J. and Deo, N. *Combinatorial Algorithms: Theory and Practice.* Englewood Cliffs, NJ: Prentice-Hall.

1984. Tucker, A. *Applied Combinatorics,* 2nd edition. New York: John Wiley.

1986. Hall, M., Jr. *Combinatorial Theory,* 2nd edition. New York: John Wiley.

1988. Sedgewick, R. *Algorithms,* 2nd edition. Reading, MA: Addison-Wesley Publishing Co.

1989. Lam, C. W. H., Thiel, L. and Swierez, S. "The Non-Existence of Finite Projective Planes of Order 10," *Can. J. Math* **41:** 1117–1123.

C.L. LIU AND EDWARD M. REINGOLD

COMMAND AND JOB CONTROL LANGUAGE

For articles on related subjects *see* DIRECTORY; JOB; LANGUAGE PROCESSORS; LOGIN FILE; OPERATING SYSTEMS; SHELL; TERMINALS; TIME SHARING; UNIX OPERATING SYSTEM; and USER INTERFACE.

A *command language* (CL) or a *job control language* (JCL) is a language in which users of a computer (or data processing) system describe to that system the requirements of their *tasks* (or jobs - *q.v.*). Most computer systems operate under the control of an *operating system*. The users interact with a computer system via the command or job control language of its operating system; thus, this language is the primary interface between a computer system and its users. The term *command language* is most often used when speaking of *time-sharing* or interactive computers, while *job control language* is used primarily in relation to batch computers. Here, we will use the term *command language* to mean *both* CL and JCL.

More specifically, users of computer systems employ the command language to:

1. Identify themselves to the system for security and accounting purposes, and, in some instances, to inform the computer system about

which *directory* and data files are to be used in processing their respective tasks.

2. Inform the computer system about the particular resources required by their tasks [e.g. amount of storage needed, language translator(s) to be used, expected amount of *central processing unit* (*q.v.*) time].

3. Specify *input/output devices* required by their tasks (e.g. magnetic tapes, disks, line printer, plotter) and define the manner in which the information is or should be organized (or "formatted") on these devices.

4. Specify what action the computer system should take in exceptional cases (e.g. errors in programs, missing or incorrect input data, input-output device malfunctions).

Batch Command Languages Early batch computers had no operating systems and were capable of executing only one task at a time. As a result, users of these systems controlled the execution of their tasks themselves; while the computer was executing their tasks, such users often acted as operators of the computer and controlled the operation of the entire system.

As computers grew in complexity (and, therefore, in cost), this mode of operation became no longer economically feasible. Primitive operating systems were developed to allow the computer system to sequence automatically the tasks of the various users through the system. These early, simple batch operating systems executed one task at a time, either to completion or until some error made it impossible to continue a task (Jardine, 1975). In the latter case, the operating system would usually give the user (via a printed report) some rudimentary indication of what went wrong and would then immediately proceed to the next user's task. The user had only a very limited ability to affect the behavior of the operating system. The system simply sequenced the jobs through the computer, giving up on any task that did not behave exactly according to the user's (or, more accurately, the system's) expectations.

These systems utilized the computer more efficiently than the initial "hands-on" method, but at the price of increasing the overhead on the users' time; they also forced the users to work in a much more formal and regulated fashion, sometimes with large delays (*turnaround time - q.v.*) between the time a job was submitted by the user and the time when the user received the corresponding output.

Because of the large cost of computers, further attempts at making their use more efficient and at increasing their throughput resulted in the development of *multiprogramming* (*q.v.*) operating systems, which allow several independent tasks to use the computer simultaneously. Thus, one task might be performing calculations while a second task might be reading a magnetic tape, a third writing a disk, etc. In addition, all such concurrently executing tasks could, for instance, access the same disk (each task, of course, using only those portions of the disk that the operating system had assigned to it), or specify

that their output was to be printed on the same printer (in which case each task's output was saved by the operating system on some secondary storage device—e.g. a disk—and then printed when the printer became available). This mode of operation required the users to inform the operating system about the specific resources needed by their tasks. This evolution had several effects:

1. The computer systems became used more efficiently.

2. The users became forced to state explicitly (and a priori) the resource requirements of their tasks in a formal way through the facilities of the CL, as opposed to remembering them, writing them on pieces of paper as "instructions to the operator," or coding them directly into their programs. The users could no longer assume that each of their tasks had total control of the computer system.

3. It became possible for the users to state their requirements in a more abstract fashion. Thus, the user could say, for instance, that a task required three tape drives, but the operating systems would choose, each time that this task was executed, the actual tape drives to be used. This ability to state one's resource requirements in such an abstract fashion tends to minimize the interference between the tasks belonging to different users and allows a computer system to continue operating even when some of its resources (e.g. a tape drive) are unavailable because of failures or other reasons. In this fashion, a certain amount of independence from the actual physical configuration of the computer system is achieved.

Thus, with the passage of time, it became necessary for the users to be able to state their requirements to the operating system in a more and more rigorous and detailed fashion. Simultaneously, the complexity of users' tasks grew. Increasingly often, users want operating systems to take care of exceptional conditions (e.g. errors in input data) automatically without necessarily giving up on their tasks; to accomplish this, operating systems have to be able to make decisions based on what happens to a task while it is executing; therefore, CLs have to allow the user to state the rules and conditions for making these decisions.

As a result, the complexity of the user's interface (i.e. the CL) with the operating system has grown to accommodate these needs. As additional capabilities became needed in CLs, they were added, often in purely *ad hoc* ways, resulting in CLs that were very flexible and powerful, but also needlessly complex, difficult to learn, unnatural to use, and non-systematic (Barron and Jackson, 1972). This increase in complexity has had several results:

1. The need, in most big computing centers, for one or more (often full-time) "CL experts."

2. The development of *macroprocedure* capabilities in CLs; these facilities allow a user to invoke, in a

relatively simple fashion, a set of complex CL statements (i.e. a CL procedure) that the user, another user, or a "CL expert" has developed, debugged, and that has been previously stored in the computer system under a specific name.

3. The emergence of research aimed at developing a theory of, and designs for, more general, systematic, simpler, and easier to use CLs (Dolotta and Irvine, 1969; Gram and Hertweck, 1975; Unger in Beech, 1980).

4. The emergence of attempts at standardizing CLs. The purpose of such standardization is to make CLs less machine-dependent, just as has been done with most high-level programming languages.

Interactive Command Languages

CLs meant to be used in a time-sharing mode or used interactively on a personal computer are usually much simpler than batch CLs. There are several reasons for this:

1. Interactively, the user most often types in a *single* CL statement at a time, observes the result(s) of that statement, and then decides what to do next. Thus, the user does not have to decide and explicitly state in advance what the system is to do under *all* possible conditions; he or she can make these decisions, one at a time, while interacting with the computer system.

2. The user interacts *directly* and in real time with the computer, as opposed to having to use the computer through intermediate operators.

3. Users of a time-sharing computer are often geographically isolated from that computer (e.g. by working at home). Under such conditions, simplicity and ease of use of the CL is a very important factor (Dolotta and Irvine, 1969).

4. Because many, if not most, CL statements are typed every time they are executed, it is very important that they be simple and short.

5. The computer system can guide the user by printing prompting messages, thus making it less necessary for the user to remember all the details of the CL.

As a result, more attention has been paid to the human factors engineering of interactive CLs than to that of batch CLs. In addition, interactive CLs and computer systems have adapted the better features of batch systems. Thus, in many CLs, it is possible to construct and save cataloged command language scripts for repeated use. In interactive computers, all data files and programs are stored on-line. Editing programs allow users to create, examine, and modify on-line files of programs and data.

General Observations

Unlike programming languages, different vendors' CLs have very little in common (in fact, one often finds that the different CLs available from a *single* vendor are also incompatible); for example,

there is no compatibility between the IBM's OS/MVS and Univac's EXEC-8 CLs. In fact, even the terminology used to describe the various CL facilities is different between the two, so that, while it is relatively easy to convert a Fortran or Pascal program from one of these systems to the other, the conversion of the corresponding CL statements is difficult.

The large number of CLs in use today is, in itself, a serious problem for users of *distributed computing* (*q.v.*) facilities and of computer networks (see the paper by Hertweck in Beech, 1980, pp. 369–383). Users of such networks often have to use several CLs in a single session.

These various manifestations of the "Tower of Babel" effect provide a very strong impetus towards the development of a single, standard CL. On the other hand, because the state-of-the-art in CL design and implementation is still relatively rudimentary, it is not clear that such efforts (see the papers by Frampton *et al.*, Harris, and Newman, pp. 101–113 in Beech, 1980) are desirable at this time; quite to the contrary, it is likely that progress in CLs will be slowed significantly by such premature standardization.

A recent and very interesting trend has been toward CLs that have many, if not most, of the facilities that, until now, were available only in the traditional programming languages (see the paper by Dolotta and Mashey in Beech, 1980); such facilities, together with the ability to write and store CL procedures, allow one to perform, within a single CL procedure, tasks that previously required several separate programs to be written, compiled, debugged, etc. These new, "programmable" CLs are rapidly gaining in popularity because they make the users' work simpler and, thereby, make the users more productive.

Another very interesting recent rend affecting CLs is the extremely rapid growth of microcomputers. These computers offer limited resources relative to mainframes, while their users are often relatively unsophisticated. Therefore, it is very desirable that the CLs available on these computers be very simple (to use little of the available resources) and, at the same time, very natural and easy-to-use ("friendly"). Unfortunately, these two sets of requirements are not compatible.

We expect future CLs to be more flexible, to possess more programming power and expressiveness, to be "subsetable," and to be designed and implemented in much more systematic ways and with much better human engineering factors.

It is even conceivable that CLs, as we know them, will not survive at all. The rapidly growing alternative is use of a *graphical user interface* (GUI) as represented by the user interface (*q.v.*) of the Apple Macintosh (which is the only way to use that computer), and by such GUIs as the Microsoft Windows system for the IBM-PC and compatibles (*q.v.*). CL commands are verbal; GUI commands are pictorial. For example, to delete file STORY.TXT in the MS-DOS CL, one writes explicitly DEL STORY.TXT. On the Macintosh, the same operation is performed by using a mouse (*q.v.*) to drag the *icon* that represents the file until it is superimposed on an icon shaped like a garbage can. Then, releasing the mouse button that effectuated the dragging causes the garbage can to bulge, symbolizing completion of file disposal. A generation of users raised on arcade games may well prefer icons, though there is a remnant of older users who still enjoy using the expressiveness and precision of an English-like CL to type in the exact request desired.

References

1969. Dolotta, T. A. and Irvine, C. A. "Proposal for a Time-Sharing Command Structure," *Information Processing 68*. Amsterdam: North-Holland; 493–498.

1972. Barron, D. W. and Jackson, I. R. "The Evolution of Job Control Languages," *Software—Practice & Experience* **2**, 2: 143–164.

1975. Gram, C. and Hertweck, F. R. "Command Languages: Design Considerations and Basic Concepts," in Unger, C. (Ed.), *Command Languages*. Amsterdam: North Holland; New York: American Elsevier; 43–69.

1975. Jardine, D. A. "The Structure of Operating System Control Languages," in Unger, C. (Ed.), *Command Languages*. Amsterdam: North Holland; New York: American Elsevier, 27–42.

1978. Ritchie, D. M. and Thompson, K. "The UNIX Time-Sharing System," *The Bell System Technical Journal* **57**, 6, Part 2: 1905–1929.

1980. Beech, D. (Ed.). *Command Language Directions*. Amsterdam: North Holland.

1989. Trombetta, M. and Finkelstein, S. C. *MVS JCL and Utilities*, Reading, MA: Addison-Wesley.

TED A. DOLOTTA

COMMUNICATION CONTROL UNIT

For articles on related subjects *see* CHANNEL, DATA COMMUNICATIONS; FRONT-END PROCESSOR; GATEWAY; LOCAL AREA NETWORK; MULTIPLEXING; NETWORKS, COMPUTER; POLLING; PROTOCOL; and TELEPROCESSING.

A *communication control unit* is a unit that controls the transmission and reception of data in a computer network. It may be a complex unit, such as a front-end or network processor, or a simpler one, such as a concentrator, multiplexer, bridge, router, or terminal server. Most such units use special purpose computers or microprocessors programmed to perform the required communication functions.

Functions Performed Inside computers, workstations (*q.v.*) or other digital devices, character bits are usually transmitted in parallel, while over communication lines they tend to be transmitted serially. Communication control units that interconnect computers, workstations, terminals, and other digital devices must, therefore, perform three basic functions:

1. Convert data from parallel to serial form at the **transmitting end (serialization).**
2. Convert data from serial to parallel form at the **receiving end (deserialization).**
3. Add and/or remove control bits or characters

(packet assembly/disassembly) for data synchronization, error control, and other needed functions.

As the size and complexity of data communication networks has increased, more and more functions previously performed by mainframes are now being performed by communication control units. The advent of powerful microprocessors helped make this possible. Some of these more complex functions include:

1. Line polling.
2. Auto-baud (automatic speed) detection.
3. Automatic disconnect of inactive devices.
4. Supporting many different protocols and conversions among them.
5. Keyboard mapping and code conversion (e.g. ASCII (*q.v.*) to EBCDIC (*q.v.*) and vice versa).
6. Message buffering, storage, and forwarding.
7. Multiplexing and concentrating.
8. Transmission error detection and correction.
9. Data compression (*q.v.*).
10. Message routing and filtering.
11. Security control.
12. Collecting network traffic statistics.
13. Optimum route selection.
14. Logging transmission errors and network failures.
15. Running network diagnostics.
16. Fallback switching in case of catastrophic line or equipment failures.

Architecture Most early communication control units were hardwired, but now the vast majority are program controlled. Typically, the latter consist of a central processing unit (CPU) controlling a number of line units (LU) and some optional input/output (I/O) processors, as shown in Fig. 1.

The CPU and its memory are at the top of the hierarchy. It is programmed to perform the needed communication functions and control the overall operation of the various line units, I/O processors, and associated interfaces. In general, the CPU performs the more complex tasks, such as addressing, session establishment, error logging, and fallback switching, in case of some serious failures. It also delegates the more routine or primitive communication tasks to the other subsidiary components.

The line units handle the data transmitted or received from communication lines. They may include microprocessors programmed to perform tasks such as data serialization/deserialization, packet assembly/disassembly, synchronization, and error detection and correction under the direction of the CPU. Most units include an interface of varying sophistication that allows a human operator to monitor the performance of the communication control unit and to initiate diagnostic tests when necessary. Some communication control units include

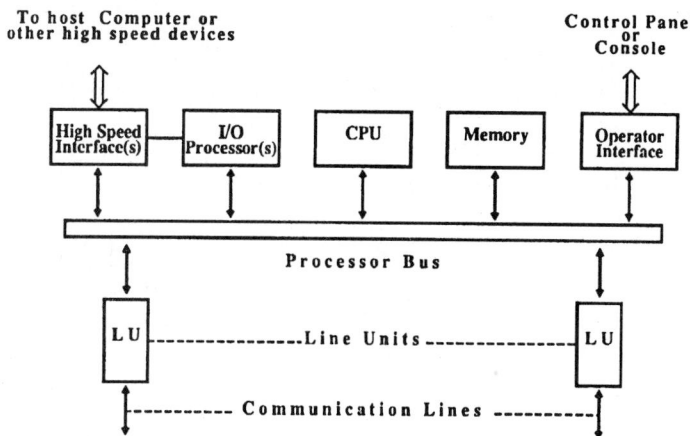

FIG. 1. Architecture of a typical communications control unit.

one or more I/O processors for high-speed data transfers between the unit and host computers or peripherals such as disks for high-capacity data storage.

Types of Communication Control Units

The advent of the microprocessor has made it possible to program controllers to perform many different communication functions concurrently, each of which was once the primary function of an individual controller. Consequently, the descriptions that follow tend to describe the major *individual* functions that such units can perform, rather than the various combinations one can encounter in practice. Their use in a typical network is illustrated in Figure 2.

Multiplexers Multiplexing permits the transmission of several low-speed data streams over a single higher-speed communication line to help reduce transmission costs. The low-speed lines are sampled, and their data are assembled and transmitted over the single higher-speed line in some deterministic fashion. They are demultiplexed into their original multiple streams at the destination. Simple multiplexers tend to be available from modem and communication system vendors, as well as from major computer system vendors.

Concentrators This term is usually reserved for a computer or microprocessor programmed to perform several communication tasks, including buffered multiplexing, as described in the previous section. Concentrators can be character-or message-oriented and can support a variety of different devices. Since, in practice, devices do not transmit or receive data at their maximum rates for sustained periods of time, the buffering capability of concentrators allow them to multiplex data more effectively than simple multiplexers with little or no buffering. The data buffers help absorb peak data loads, while sustained peak loads can be accommodated by temporarily inhibiting transmission to or from some devices. Concentrators can also be programmed to perform many other communication tasks in addition to their primary concentrating function.

Terminal Servers This is a generic term to describe devices that connect a number of terminals, workstations, or other devices with an RS-232 interface to an *ethernet* or *token ring* network. Terminal servers may support one or more protocols. An example of the latter may include support for both the TCP/IP and LAT (Local Area Transport) protocols over the same ethernet.

Front-End Communication Processors These devices provide the interface between a mainframe (or host) and its communication network. They help offload many routine and CPU-intensive tasks from the host computer by supporting a large variety of different devices and protocols and integrating many communication tasks into one unit. A distinguishing characteristic of front-end processors (q.v.) is that they have an interface to one or more host processors with the software necessary to transfer data between the host and its network.

Network Processors These devices are stand-alone units that have a large degree of autonomy in controlling a network without much direction from host computers. Their main functions are to provide a link between a large variety of local or remote user devices and the front-end or other network processors. Like front-end processors, network processors usually perform a wide variety of communication tasks, including network statistics, diagnostics, and reconfiguration, in case of serious network failures.

Message Switching Systems This term usually refers to a concentrator that stores and forwards entire messages rather than just single characters. The message can be forwarded as soon as it is assembled, or it can be stored and forwarded when requested. For this reason, such devices are sometimes called *store and forward systems*.

Repeaters *Repeaters* receive signals from one segment of a local area network (LAN), retime and amplify the signals, and forward (repeat) them to an adjacent segment of the same LAN. They are frequently used to connect two segments of an ethernet cable, to extend its length beyond the 500-meter single cable limit.

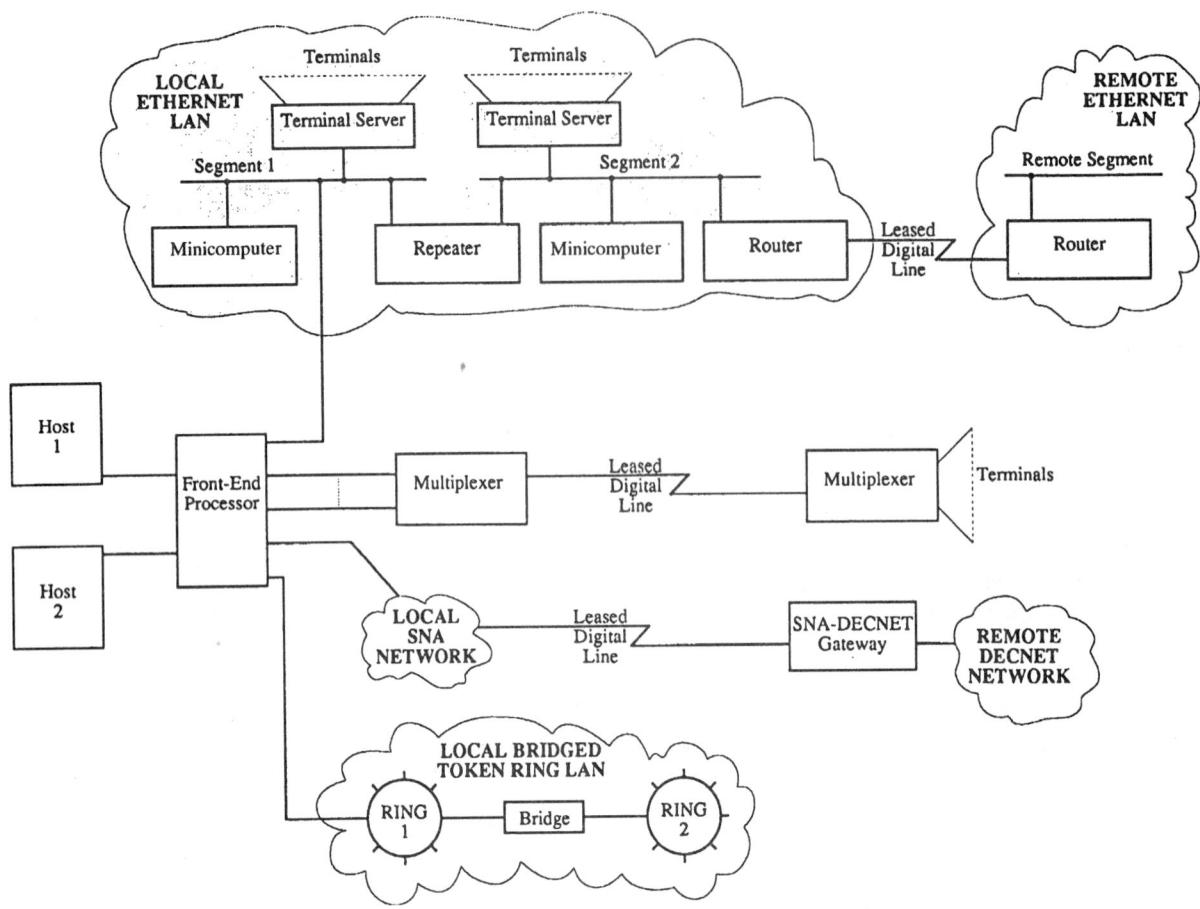

FIG. 2. Functions supported in a typical communications control unit.

Bridges *Bridges* operate at the data link layer of the Open System Interconnection (OSI - *q.v.*) model for network architecture and are used to connect two or more adjacent LANs. The interconnected LAN segments form what is called a bridged LAN. Bridges filter entire packets and pass (bridge) only those that need to cross the boundary between the LANs they connect. As such, they are often used to help reduce traffic on individual LAN segments.

Routers *Routers* work at the network layer of the OSI model. They provide translation between different network address domains and are, therefore, used to connect LANs to networks with incompatible address formats, including wide area networks. A typical application may be to connect two ethernet LANs in different cities, using the public wide area network, as shown in Fig. 2—something that a simple bridge cannot do because of the incompatibility between the 48-bit binary ethernet address and the 14-decimal digit address used on the X.25 wide area network.

Gateways The term *gateway* is used loosely to describe a variety of devices, including bridges and routers used to connect similar or dissimilar networks. When connecting networks with different architectures, gateways must per-

form message format conversion, address translation, and protocol conversion.

References

1988. Tanenbaum A. S. *Computer Networks*, 2nd Edition, Englewood Cliffs, NJ; Prentice-Hall.

JOHN S. SOBOLEWSKI

COMMUNICATIONS. *See also* DATA COMMUNICATIONS.

COMMUNICATIONS AND COMPUTERS

For articles on related subjects *see* COMMUNICATION CONTROL UNIT; DATA COMMUNICATIONS; NETWORK ARCHITECTURE; NETWORK PROTOCOLS; NETWORKS; NETWORKS, COMPUTER; and PACKET SWITCHING.

Introduction Extremely rapid technological advances in both communications and computers have created an environment that fosters increasing interaction between these two technologies, while at the same time creating entirely new legal, political, and social issues. Although the telecommunications and computer industries in the U.S. have historically been quite separate, and are prohibited by present (1991) law from merging, both groups have recognized that the common product they offer is *information handling services*. In the future, *communications, computers,* and *information* will form an inseparable trilogy.

Technology Among recent advances in the technologies of computers and communications, the most important are the increasing use of data communications as an integral part of data processing systems and the use of digital technology in communications systems, both in the digital transmission of signals and in computer-controlled communications switches.

Computers in Communication Systems Computers are used in communication systems for a number of purposes, principally for computer-controlled circuit switches and store-and-forward switches.

Computer Controlled Switches Circuit switching is used to establish a communication path between two users so that they may converse. The most common circuit switch is the telephone exchange. Fig. 1 illustrates the basic components of a circuit switch.

The line terminating equipment provides the line-oriented services, such as detecting off-hook and sending a dial tone, and receiving dialing signals. There is line-terminating equipment connected full-time (dedicated) to each line. Note that the lines are all bi-directional or *full-duplex.*

The common control equipment provides the control services that are common to all connection requests (e.g. determining if the called party is local or served by another switch or determining the connection path to be utilized). The common control equipment is shared by all lines, since it is required only during call set-up (and, possibly, breakdown).

The connecting equipment provides the physical path connecting the lines involved. This type of equipment is shared in the sense that there are usually not enough links provided to connect *all* lines *at the same time.*

Once the communication path between two lines has been established by the connecting equipment, as directed by the control equipment, the connection remains in place and there is no further requirement for control functions until a signal is received to disconnect the circuit. Digital computers are being utilized to provide the control functions required in such switches. Such switches are known as stored-program-controller switches (SPC).

Store-and-Forward Switches In a store-and-forward switching system, a dedicated path between the source and the destination of the message is not provided. A diagram of a simple store-and-forward system is shown in Fig. 2. Subscribers input their messages to the nearest node of the system, where the complete message is accepted and stored locally before further action is taken. After the complete message has been accepted by a node, the processor at that node determines to which node the message should be sent next so that it will eventually reach its destination. For example, in Fig. 2, if a subscriber of node B has a message to be delivered to a subscriber of node E, the message would first be entered into the node B processor and temporarily stored at node B. Then, depending upon the current traffic on each link, the message is routed to node C or node D for further transmission to node E. A digital computer with good communications and storage capabilities may be used as a store-and-forward switch. Store-and-forward switching systems fall into two subcategories— *message switching systems* and *packet switching (q.v.) systems*. Both forms of store-and-forward systems are used for the same general objective—to obtain better utilization of the trunks, the connections between the switches. If, in the design of the switching system, very high emphasis is placed upon minimizing the delivery delay through the systems, then the resulting system will meet the objectives of a packet-switched system. If, on the other hand, more emphasis is placed on increasing the utilization than on minimizing delivery delay, then the system will have those characteristics attributed to message switching. This difference in objectives—minimum delivery delay vs. maximizing unitization—is the key factor defining the difference between these two important classes of switching systems. For many distributed computing applications, minimum delivery delay is required, allowing the use of a packet-switched, store-and-forward system.

Communications in Computer Systems Communications have become an integral and essential part of a large number of currently installed computer systems, and the proportion of systems incorporating communications is expected to continue to increase. Communications are used to provide terminal users access to computer systems that may be remotely located, as well as to provide a means for computers to communicate with other computers for the purpose of load sharing and accessing the data and/or programs stored at a dis-

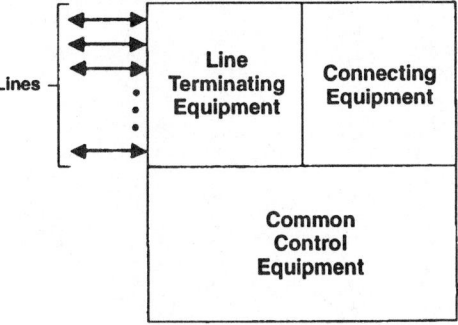

FIG. 1. Computer-controlled circuit switch.

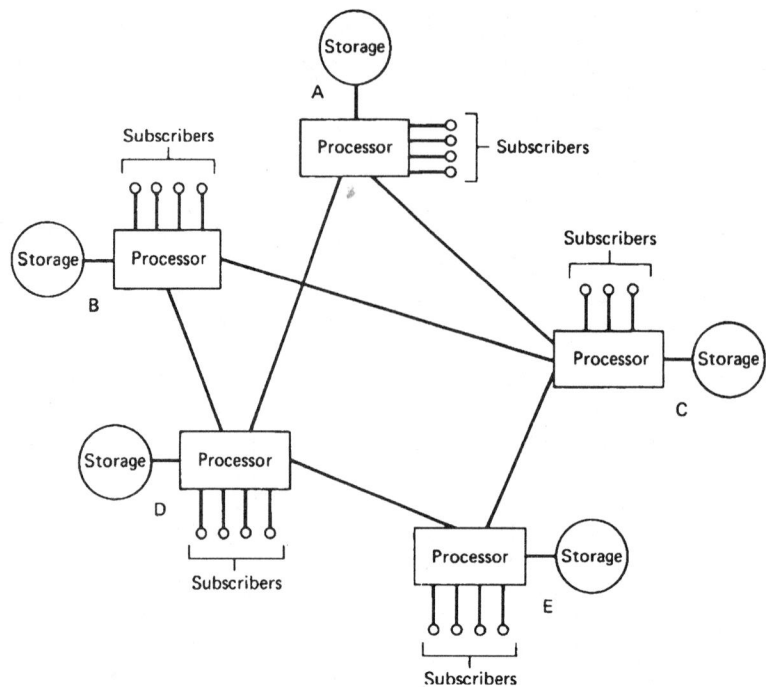

FIG. 2.   A store-and-forward switching system.

tant computer. Fig. 3 illustrates a simple computer network (*see* NETWORKS, COMPUTER).

Analog and Digital Communication   Digitally encoded signal transmission is now the standard technology for the telephone systems of the U.S. and most other countries. A completely new hierarchy of digital transmission systems has been introduced to replace those based on analog signals and frequency division multiplexing (*see* MULTIPLEXING). Analog systems require the transmission of a signal that is an *exact* replica of the waveform produced by the speaker or data device. The "standard voice channel" is 4,000 Hz, including appropriate guardbands to separate the different channels when they are each translated by an appropriate amount and "stacked" to produce the frequency division multiplexed groupings shown in Fig. 4. There are both technical and economic advantages in transmitting a digital pulse stream (i.e. the signal takes on only a small set of fixed and discrete values), rather than analog signals. Rapid progress is being made in "digitizing" the telephone transmission systems, but the frequency hierarchy of analog signals shown in Fig. 4 remains in use because of the large amount of analog equipment already installed. Fig. 4 illustrates how individual analog voice channels are combined into groups and then higher-level groupings formed to make better use of

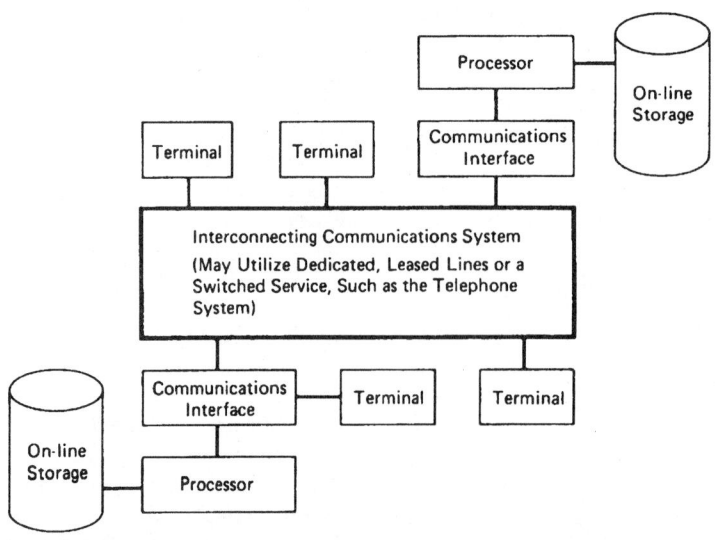

FIG. 3.   A simple computer network.

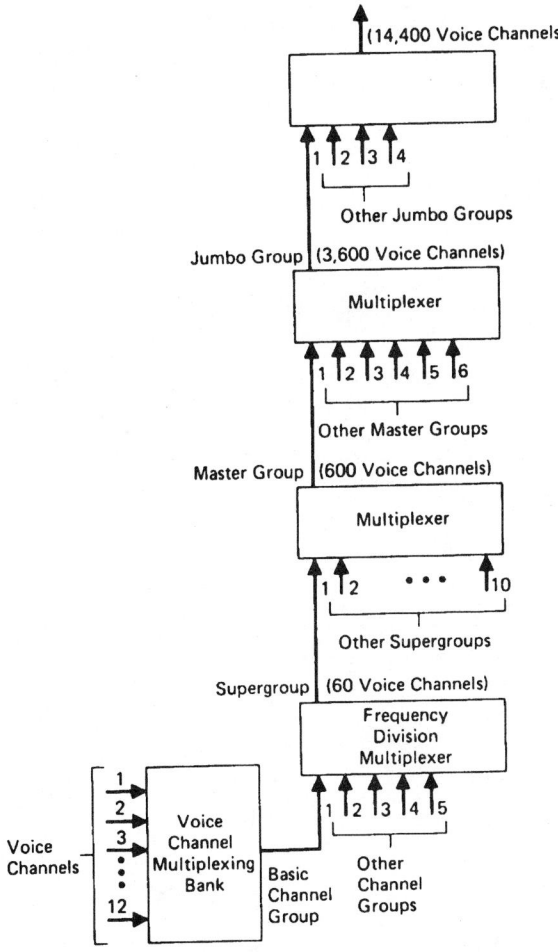

FIG. 4. The analog/frequency division transmission hierarchy.

the transmission capabilities of the intercity long-line facilities, such as microwave radio and buried coaxial cable, which provide the capability to carry extremely wide-band signals. The digital multiplexing hierarchy adopted in the United States and being implemented in Canada is shown in Fig. 5. (The numbers for the "European" digital hierarchy are 64 Kbps per channel; 30 channels form a 2.048-Mbps primary signal; 4 primaries form a 120-channel, 8.448-Mbps secondary signed; and 4 secondaries give a 480-channel, 34.368-Mpbs signal). Note that the basic message channel is now a 64,000–bit-per-second pulse stream. For normal telephone usage, the standard voice channel is converted to this digital stream through a technique known as pulse code modulation (*see* DATA COMMUNICATIONS). In pulse code modulation, the continuous (analog) waveform representing the voice signal to be transmitted is sampled 8,000 times per second, and the value of the sample is transmitted as an 8-bit binary-coded number. The transmission system required in this instance has the much simpler task of indicating only whether the signal is a "0" or a "1." The receiver detects these binary signals and reconstructs the original signal. From the point of view of computer users, the most important effect of this change in transmission is that *digital signals* may be brought directly to the user's instal-

lation. Computing devices, including both terminals and processors, communicate using binary signals, which take on only two values, "zero" or "one." In order for such equipment to use analog circuits, a device must convert the digital 0/1 signal into an analog form suitable for transmission, and a reverse conversion must take place at the other end of the circuit. The device performing this conversion is known as a *modem* (*q.v.*) and is installed as shown in Fig. 6. In the future, when the signals delivered to the customer are *digital*, modems will no longer be needed (*see* DSU/CSU).

Integrated Voice and Data   Although voice traffic and data traffic are often handled separately, as the needs for data traffic increase even further, it is almost certain that the transmission networks for voice and data will be totally integrated. Increasing demand for this will develop as businesses make better use of communications and computers to process and store all forms of data, not just numeric information. As this occurs, office communications systems handling both voice and data will need to be integrated, as shown in Fig. 7.

Legal Issues   The legal issues surrounding computers and communications fall into two general areas—regulation and privacy.

Regulation   The increasing interrelation of computers and communications has resulted in strong forces for making changes in the procedures by which the telecommunications industry is regulated.

In most countries other than the U.S., communication services are provided by a government organization that operates as a monopoly. The discussion below focuses on developments within the telecommunications industry in the U.S. Although the industry is not government owned, the legal problems it presents are not much different from those encountered in other countries in which private industry may provide remote computer services and specialized data transmission.

Separation of Computing and Communications

The first problem of the computer era that confronted communication regulators was defining the dividing line between the two technologies. Such a division is essential in order to establish which activities are subject to regulation and which are not. This question was first addressed by the Federal Communications Commission (FCC) in the late 1960s in its "Computer Inquiry I." As a result of that inquiry, the Commission defined the two end points of the spectrum— *pure* communication and *pure* data processing; however, a large area of "hybrid services" was left without further appropriate definition or distinction. A significant comment in the final decision that resulted from that inquiry was that "...Data-processing cannot survive, much less develop further, except through reliance upon and use of communication facilities and services." This observation has certainly proven to be true, as has its converse, which was not stated: Digital computing technology has also become essential to the development of

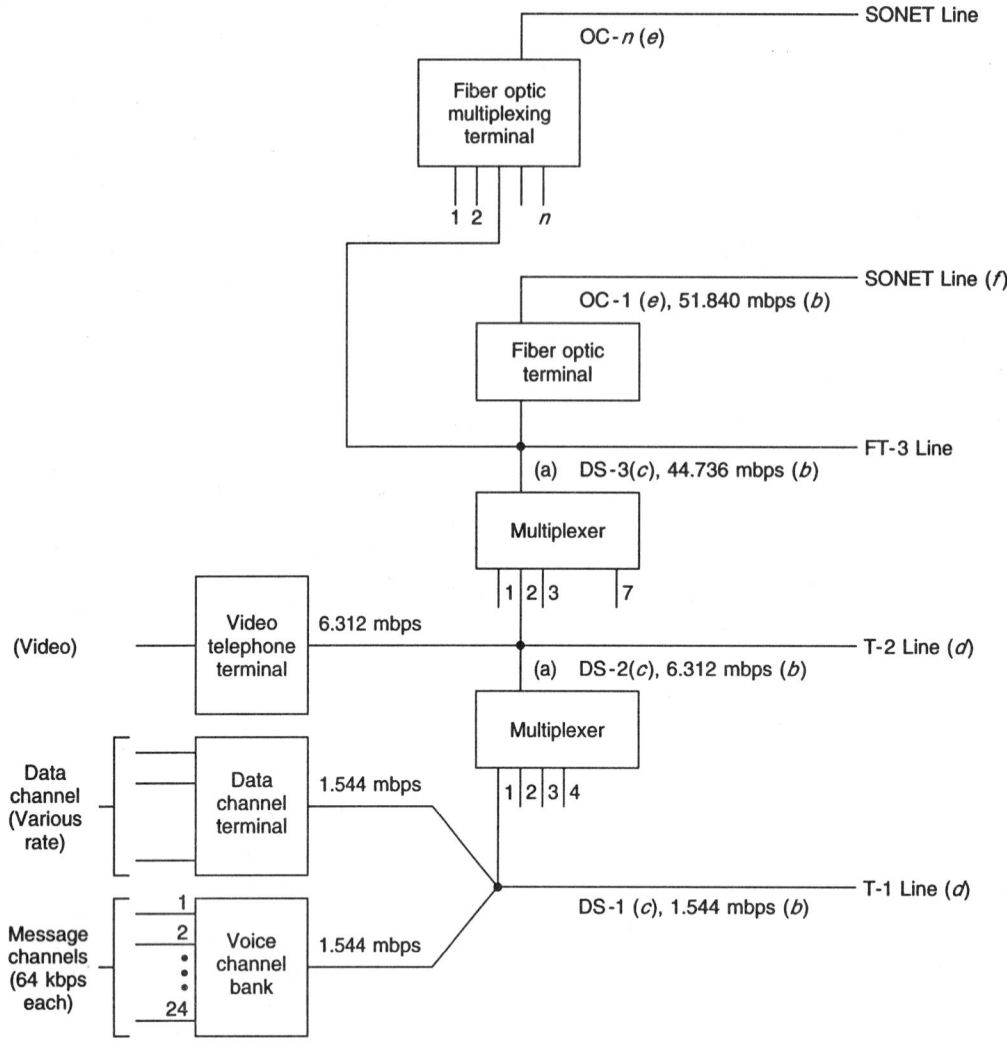

FIG. 5. The digital transmission hierarchy.

(a) These are cross-connection points or patch panels.

(b) These values are not exact multiples of the input line rates. The additional bits are required for control, timing, and speed adjustments.

(c) "DS-1" is a contraction of "digital signal number one," etc.

(d) Representative transmission media that can be utilized to carry the digital signals; T-1 and T-2 refer to standard industry transmission systems.

(e) "Oc-n" is a contraction of "optical carrier level n"; n = 1, 3, 9, 12, 18, 24, 36, 48.

(f) "SONET"— "Synchronous Optical Network."

communications. A January 1982 consent decree allowed AT&T to enter the data processing business; prior to that date, they were prohibited from doing so.

Not long after completion of the initial computer inquiry, the FCC recognized that there must be a better

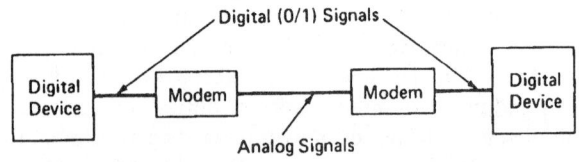

FIG. 6. Use of modems in analog transmission systems.

delineation of hybrid services. Important questions were raised as to how much data processing could be considered as "incidental" to the primary function of communications. It has long been a function of some communications systems (e.g. teletype) to store a message at a switch before forwarding it to the next switch or to the final destination. Questions are raised when the switch is used to hold the message and then deliver it at some specific time in the future, to distribute it automatically to multiple addresses, or to provide temporary storage and on-line editing capabilities for message preparation.

It was to address issues such as these that the FCC initiated "Computer Inquiry II" in 1976. In April 1980, the

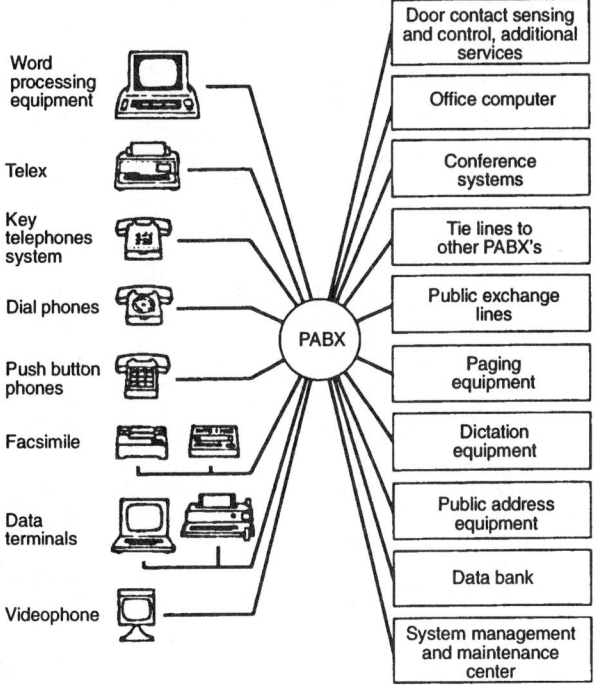

FIG 7.   The future business communication system (PABX-Private Automatic Branch Exchange). *(Courtesy Arthur D. Little.)*

FCC released its decision on this inquiry. In this ruling, the FCC reversed its earlier decision to distinguish between enhanced voice and enhanced data services. The key points in this new decision on regulation of communications and computer services are as follows:

- There are only two categories of network services— *basic* (the simple transferal of voices or data) and *enhanced* (communication services combined with data processing).
- FCC regulation will apply only to basic services. Enhanced services will be unregulated.
- Terminal equipment of all types provided by common carriers will be unregulated.

Competition

For many years, competition within the communications industry in the U.S. was almost non-existent. Rules and regulations of the FCC, as well as state and local regulatory bodies, established "regulated monopolies" within specific geographic areas. Although interconnection between the regulated common carriers was permitted, and even required to provide long-distance service, neither non-common carrier companies nor individuals were permitted to attach devices directly to the telephone system. The first change in this policy occurred in 1968 in the Carterfone Decision, in which the FCC ruled that customer-owned equipment could be connected to the telephone system as long as certain technical standards were met. Although the Carterfone case was precipitated by a desire to attach voice equipment to the telephone system, the implications for the data processing community,

with its customer-owned terminals and modems, were enormous.

The next step in introducing competition into the U.S. telecommunications industry was the establishment of specialized common carriers (SCCs) in the early 1970s. These organizations were formed in response to the anticipated demand for large increases in the volume of data traffic. The SCCs were founded on the basis that they would build and operate long-haul communications facilities (primarily microwave) between major cities and use the facilities of the local telephone company to provide the interconnection to the customer's premises. Although the SCCs were originally formed to provide only data transmission services, they later expanded their operations to include long-distance voice as well.

The 1970s also saw the introduction of *value-added carriers* as another class of supplier of communication services. As contrasted to the "common carriers," the value-added carriers do not construct transmission facilities such as microwave and coaxial cable systems. They lease transmission services from the common carriers and utilize these to implement a value-added network (VAN) in which the "added value" may be features such as switching, shared usage, error control, enhanced reliability, and transmission speed and protocol conversions. Two of the largest VANs are Telenet and Tymnet.

More recently, Congress has become directly involved in the issue of competition in the telecommunications industry. The present basis for the regulation of the communications industries is the Communications Act of 1934, which covers all forms of communications (broadcast, in addition to common-carriers). Technological advances, as well as new economic factors, have rendered the 1934 Act almost unusable, especially with regard to telecommunications. As a result, legislation has been introduced in both houses of Congress to establish a new basis for the organization and regulation of the telecommunications industry.

Privacy   Privacy has become an important public concern, both legally and socially, that encompasses individuals as well as organizations and companies. Although the interest in privacy predates the computer era, the combined effects of computer and communications are raising the topic to a high level of sensitivity.

Governments and other agencies that deal with the public, such as credit bureaus, have long maintained extensive records and files on both individuals and companies. In the past, the sheer mass of those records and the difficulty in accessing them for anything other than the purpose for which they were collected and organized have been the primary protection against unauthorized use of that material. The development of the digital computer has provided the means with which to access massive records quickly and inexpensively, extracting both specific as well as summary data. Advances in communications have allowed such information to be transferred from one record-keeping system to another so that information collected for one purpose can be used for other purposes.

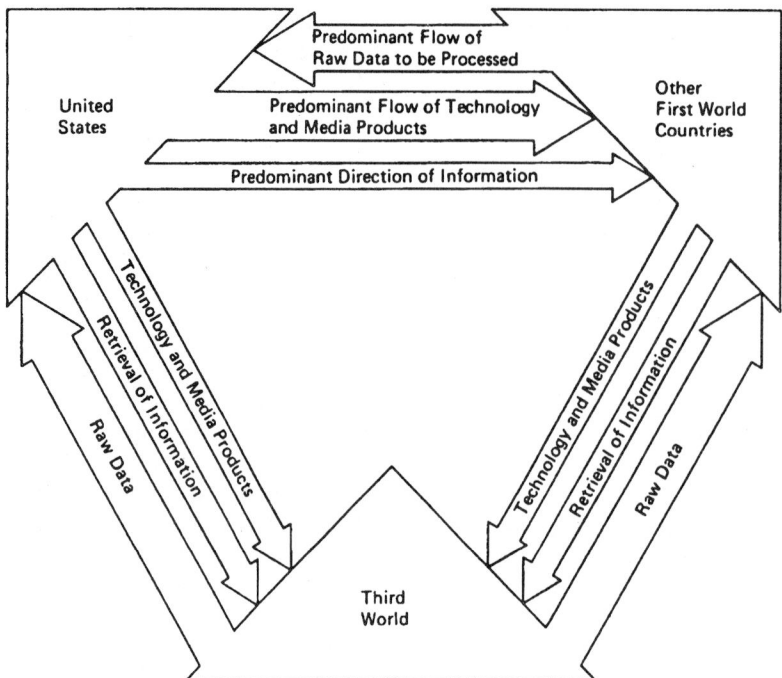

FIG. 8. The nature of transborder data flows (Turn, 1979; p. 5).

The 1970s and 1980s saw a growing awareness of the problems of privacy, and a number of privacy laws were passed at the national and state levels, as well as in foreign countries.

Political Issues The most significant political issue resulting from the wide use of computers and communications is that of *transborder data flow.* As the use of communications to transmit data to remote computer sites for processing and/or storage has become more and more prevalent, the "data exporting" countries are highly sensitized to the issues raised by data leaving their country. These concerns are threefold:

1. Concern that personal and corporate data that is exported from one country for processing on computers will not be protected by privacy laws equivalent to those in the country of origin. Similarly, there is a concern that an "illegal" database (i.e. one not permitted in the country of origin) will be assembled in another country.
2. Concern by a lesser developed country that it become "data dependent" on another country that could hold private as well as government databases "hostage" in computer systems located in the more developed country.
3. Concern that the financial motivations for the development of a local computer or data processing industry will be curtailed by having such services and products provided external to the country.

The degree of concern about each of these three aspects is related to the level of development of the country in question (see Fig. 8). Although third world countries are most worried about becoming informatics-dependent (see Fig. 9), they are not alone in their desire to insure against losing control of information vital to national sovereignty.

One result of the concerns over transborder data flow has been a number of stringent national regulations on the exportation of data. International discussions have been held primarily within the Organization for Economic Cooperation and Development (OECD), which is focusing on the protection and privacy of data crossing national borders. The Council of Europe is also very active in this area. The laws of some countries place such strong restrictions on the export of data that an international data circuit may be almost useless.

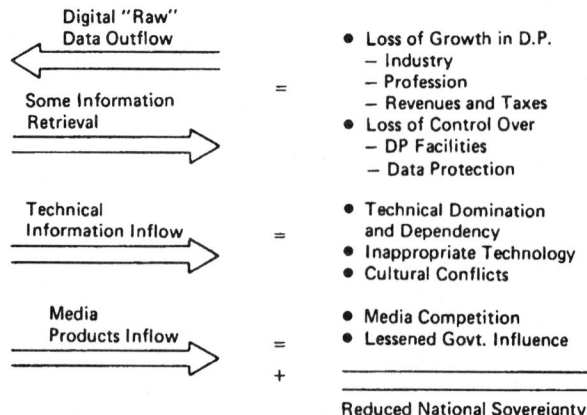

FIG. 9. The perspective of information dependent countries (Turn, 1979; p. 13).

Social Awareness As the public becomes more and more familiar with computers and their utilization and computers become even more widely available, there will certainly be changes in the means by which the general public obtains and uses information. A significant example of such a change is the action by the French telephone authorities to abolish information operators in their system. To provide the directory assistance services that are presently the responsibility of such operators, all telephone subscribers are being provided with a data terminal that will directly access the directory database and obtain the desired information. Economic studies clearly suggest that such a change would be economically justifiable.

In the U.S., the most recent computer phenomenon has been the *personal computer (q.v.)*. At first, these devices were used in a standalone mode for limited applications. However, it soon became apparent that the availability of databases that could be searched by such computers would be economically important. Such information depositories and sources as well as "personal computer networks" are beginning to appear. An isolated home computer is not going to be a very potent force, but when it is connected into a communications systems, it will undoubtedly cause fundamental changes in public information habits.

Another example of coupling between computer databases and the general public are the *videotex (q.v.)* systems, in which a portion of the television transmission time not presently required for picture transmission is used to transmit data to the home for display on the television screen. A large number of "pages" of data are available, and the local viewer can select a particular portion of the information for examination.

References

1979. Lewin, L. (Ed.). *Telecommunications: An Interdisciplinary Survey*. Norwood, MA: Artech House.

1979. Turn, Rein (Ed.). *Transborder Data Flows* **1** and **2**. Arlington, VA: AFIPS.

1979. Uhlig, R. P., Farber, D. J., and Bair, J. H. *The Office of the Future—Communication and Computers*. Amsterdam: North-Holland.

1991. Spragins, John D. *Telecommunications Protocols and Design*. Reading, MA: Addison-Wesley.

1991. Stallings, William. *Data Computer Communications* (3rd Ed.). New York: Macmillan.

PHILIP H. ENSLOW

COMPACTION. *See* DATA COMPRESSION AND COMPACTION.

COMPATIBILITY

For articles on related subjects *see* CROSS ASSEMBLERS AND COMPILERS; EMULATION; OPEN ARCHITECTURE; OPEN SYSTEMS INTERCONNECTION; PORTABILITY; SIMULATION: PRINCIPLES; SOFTWARE; and TRANSPARENCY.

Two compilers or language translators (usually on different computers) are said to be *compatible* if source programs written for a compiler on one computer will compile and execute successfully on the other. Similarly, two versions of the same compiler (on the same computer) are said to be compatible if a source program written for one version of the compiler will successfully compile and execute using the other version. If the compatibility extends in only one direction, we speak of "upward" (older to newer) or "downward" (newer to older) compatibility. Occasionally, specific programs will be said to be compatible with specific computer systems when they can be compiled or assembled and executed correctly using that computer system; but the more common use of compatibility in computing is applied to two machines, two configurations, two operating systems, or two software packages with respect to the ease with which programs or data can be converted from one to the other. The term normally applied to a program to describe the ease with which it can be converted from one system to another is *portability*.

Upward compatibility refers not only to computers with respect to the programs that run on them, but also to the data that they accept and operate on. For example, a computer software system is said to be upward compatible if identical data will produce identical results on a more recent (hence, upward) version as on an older version, even though the newer version may also accept additional forms of data. The term "identical" in this context is somewhat utopian because it almost never is realized in practice.

Manufacturers have historically extolled upward compatibility as an improvement of their small machines extended to their own larger machines, while minimizing any compatibility (especially upward) between their machines and those of their competition. However, they have been quick to point out the upward compatibility of their equipment as compared with that of the competition. In fact, computing equipment and compilers of particular manufacturers have been deliberately designed so that programs running on competitive equipment can be easily converted to run on their systems. Conversely, equipment and systems have also been designed to maximize the difficulty of converting programs so that they cannot be run on competing equipment or systems. The result has been that true compatibility is almost never achieved between equipment from different manufacturers.

Hardware component compatibility is an intensely competitive area. Since many peripheral devices are hooked to the computer by a relatively small number of cables (usually with a plug, in fact), so-called *plug-to-plug compatible* peripherals have been developed by some competitive firms. Their practice is to build one that works exactly the same (and even has identical plugs on the ends of the cables) as the original, but which can be profitably marketed at a lower price than the original. Thus, potential customers exist wherever the original equipment was installed.

In contrast to the practice of minicomputer and mainframe manufacturers who, historically, have resisted cross-vendor compatibility, the makers of personal computers (*q.v.*) and workstations (*q.v.*) often promote such compatibility through use of an *open architecture* or an *open systems interconnection* (OSI), which encourages other firms to market add-on products to their computer line.

CHESTER L. MEEK

COMPILE AND RUN TIME

For articles on related subjects *see* COMPILER CONSTRUCTION; BINDING; DIAGNOSTICS; LANGUAGE PROCESSORS; LOAD AND GO COMPILER; OBJECT PROGRAM; and SOURCE PROGRAM.

The complete process of running a program that has been written in a high-level language such as Pascal or C (*q.v.*) is accomplished in two steps:

1. Translation of the *source program* as written by the programmer into a machine executable form (a process commonly referred to as *compilation*).
2. Execution of the generated form; i.e. the *running* of the compiled or *object program*.

To distinguish between certain actions that may occur during one or another of these phases, the period of compilation is known as the *compile time* and the succeeding period as the *run time* or *execution time*. In the usual compile and execute system, these two phases are distinct and may be temporally separated. In fact, the running of a program may be accomplished many times without the need for the recompilation of the program, provided the compiled code is saved on, say, disk. In an interpretive system, however, the two phases are intertwined, since execution of each source program statement follows immediately after its "compilation" (see LANGUAGE PROCESSORS).

Typically, errors in a program are related to compile time or run time. Where the error is an error of language (i.e. incorrect syntax, such as a missing parenthesis), then the system is capable of recognizing this at compilation time; on the other hand, errors in logic or arithmetic (i.e. semantic errors) are normally discovered (if at all) at run time. Some sophisticated language processor systems allow the programmer to use certain facilities called compile-time and run-time facilities. As an example of the latter, some systems allow the programmer to specify the format of the input data and output results at run time rather than in the source program.

J. A. N. LEE

COMPILER. *See also* CROSS ASSEMBLERS AND COMPILERS.

COMPILER-COMPILER

For articles on related subject *see* COMPILER CONSTRUCTION; and LANGUAGE PROCESSORS.

A compiler is a program that, given the description of another program in a suitable language, translates it into executable form for a given computer. Similarly, a *compiler-compiler* (CC) is a program that, given the description of a compiler in a suitable notation, produces as output a compiler usable on a given target computer. Compiler-compilers can also be called *compiler-writing systems*.

A compiler is characterized by three languages: it is programmed in a writing language (WL); it translates programs written in a source language (SL) into equivalent programs written in an object language (OL). The most general CC should be able to generate the compiler (SL, WL, OL) automatically, with the only data being the descriptions of the three languages.

Parameterization of WL is too difficult, and most CCs generate compilers written in a built-in language such as Pascal, C (*q.v.*), or Ada (*q.v.*).

The compiling process is generally divided into several phases. These phases can be generated by different parts of a general CC, or by specialized generators.

Scanning is the process that understands the vocabulary of the source language. It reads the source text and combines character sequences into *tokens* (e.g. identifiers, numbers, operators, or keywords). A scanner generator accepts a description of tokens in the form of a regular grammar (or something similar), and generates a finite state automaton that represents the scanner. A good example is Lex.

Parsing is the process that understands the sentence structure of the source language. It gets token sequences from the scanner, and builds (at least implicitly) a tree structure representation of the text. A parser generator accepts a description of the source language in the form of a context-free grammar, and generates a parsing automaton. Parser generators differ by their writing language, the principles of the parsing algorithm, and the ability to handle syntax errors in source texts correctly. A well-known example is Yacc, an LALR(1) generator whose writing language is C. It has been used for generating the parser of many operational compilers running with the operating system Unix (*q.v.*). Yacc and Lex have a common interface and can be combined.

Semantic analysis is the process that checks whether syntactically correct constructs of a given program have a correct meaning, and more generally establishes this meaning. For most imperative languages, the main part of the static semantic analysis is the handling, building, and searching of a symbol table, which is a representation of the declarations (*q.v.*) of the source program. Dynamic semantic analysis deals with all aspects of program, meaning that it either depends on the target language or on the need to execute the program. It uses the information contained in the symbol table, as well as information about the target language. There are no true semantic analyzer generators, but, instead, the semantic analysis process can be described using attribute grammars (AG). Then, the relevant component of a CC can transform the given AG into a running program that gives values to all attributes. During this evaluation, all the static and dynamic semantics of the source program are computed.

Code generation uses all semantic information collected in the preceding phases, in order to translate the source program into target language. It is the part of the compiler that is the most resistant to automation, and truly general code generation generators do not presently exist. What is meant by this term, instead, is a generator for the translation between a standard intermediate language and any target language. Systems do exist that provide for the description of the target language, and that can generate the code generator from a predefined intermediate language. A system like ACK, for example, contains components for optimizing programs written in the intermediate language, as well as generators for assemblers, linkage editors, and target-oriented optimizers.

References

1988. Fischer, C. N., and LeBlanc, R. J., Jr. *Crafting a Compiler*. Menlo Park, CA: Benjamin-Cummings Publishing Co.
1990. Holub, Allen I. *Compiler Design in C*. Englewood Cliffs, NJ: Prentice-Hall.

OLIVIER LECARME

COMPILER CONSTRUCTION

For articles on related subjects *see* COMPILER-COMPILER; FORMAL LANGUAGES; GRAMMARS; LANGUAGE PROCESSORS; LINKER; and LOAD AND GO COMPILER.

Introduction   A *compiler* is a program that translates programs written in a high-level programming language into the native machine language of a digital computer. The term originated in an earlier technology, where the principal action was the combination of previously written program parts into a whole program. The collection of parts still exists in the form of a run-time library, but the modern emphasis is more on the program itself than on pre-existing parts. The language in which the program is written and the machine for which it is intended are the central points of interest. The input is called the *source program* (*q.v.*) or *source code* and the output is called the *object program* (*q.v.*) or *target code*. The definition of the translation may involve one or more intermediate encodings called *intermediate languages* (ILs).

The first step in writing a compiler is to specify the criteria upon which the compiler will be evaluated. Typical criteria relate to compilation speed (measured in statements compiled per second) and speed and memory requirements of the compiled target code. One must also obtain a definition of the source language and target machine and environment. A project plan is then written, providing staffing estimates and milestones.

The task of writing a compiler can be broken down into several simpler tasks, some of which can be done simultaneously. Documentation includes a language-user's tutorial and also a reference manual. The compiler will need a guide for users that tells how to install and run it, as well as a maintenance manual.

The principal implementation decisions for compile writers are those defining the internal data structures. The most complex of these are usually for the symbol table and the optimizer flow analysis. The compiler itself consists of several distinct parts. Some parts can be used in any compiler; other parts can be used with small changes. Each part of the compiler is specified, and interfaces are defined. Identification of reusable components is now feasible. It is not unusual for a whole new compiler to be written as a modification of an existing compiler.

All of the major parts of a compiler can be tested alone, which means they can be written and run without needing the rest of the compiler (Homer and Schooler 1989). This is convenient if more than one person is working on the compiler. Standalone test harnesses are also of great value during the maintenance stage in the life of the compiler after the original programmers are gone and new programmers must learn to change it.

Compiler construction is an engineering process. The ideal scenario presented below can usually be followed closely, but there are always departures as a consequence of complications in the programming language, the target machine, or the evaluation criteria which will be applied to the resulting compiler.

Grammatical Description   The form of a programming language is described on at least two levels: lexically and as a phrase structure. These levels correspond roughly to the structures in natural languages corresponding to, in the first case, words, punctuation, and *whitespace* (a run of one or more consecutive blank characters) and, in the second case, subjects, predicates, and sentences. Both levels of description can be expressed by grammars. The *lexical grammar* is typically simpler than the *phrase-structure grammar*. When transformations are a part of the definition of the language, the description of form may go beyond grammars. The most common transformational feature is the concept of a *macroinstruction* (*q.v.*), or *macro*.

Compiler Structure   The grammatical descriptions give rise to a *syntax analyzer,* either via an automatic constructor or hand coding. The declarative constructs of the language are analyzed to establish an association between names and attributes. The imperative constructs are analyzed to produce the executable form of the program. In most modern languages, the separation between declarative and imperative is not precise; nevertheless, the separation of concerns is valuable in understanding the functions of the compiler.

Some parts of the compiler are mostly dependent on the details of the source language; other parts are most dependent on the details of the target computer. This leads to a natural division of a compiler into a *front end* and a *back end*. Information is typically passed from front to back via an intermediate language.

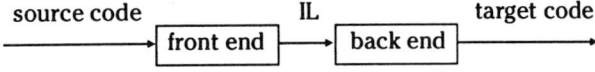

The unit of translation is generally less than a whole program. One overriding reason is that the translation of a program may consume more resources than the execution of that same program. If one had to translate it all at once, the largest translatable program might be smaller than the largest executable program. No such limitation on what the computer can accomplish is acceptable.

In any case, after all translations are complete, there is another step, called *linking*, that takes the separately prepared parts, and perhaps elements from the run-time library, and finally puts the whole together in an executable form (*see* LINKER).

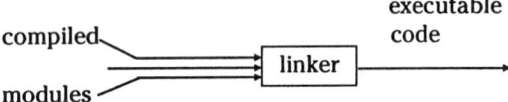

Evaluation Criteria

Evaluation Criteria The evaluation criteria for compilers have gradually changed over the last 40 years. Early compilers were experimental. The programming language evolved while the compiler was being constructed. The completed compilers were never left alone—the original authors of a compiler moved on, leaving the compiler in other hands, but these new hands fixed old errors, adding features and introducing new errors. Programming languages were what their compilers did. Compilers were desirable if they were more useable than an assembler. The evaluation of compilers was expressed as a comparison with the mythical *best hand code*. The criterion was a code quality ratio: speed of compiled code divided by speed of best hand code. A rating of 1.2 was considered excellent.

Programming Language Support

Programming Language Support The first impetus toward regularizing compiler construction came from a need to implement a wide variety of programming languages. It was felt that better languages might help high-level language programmers. The main variant was the syntax, and the main result was a rapid increase in the number of programming languages. The technical innovation was the separation of the front and back end of the compiler and the development of front-end technology. The central idea was that many front ends could be written to be used with one back end.

The lexical structure is processed by a *scanner*, which can be hand written or can be derived from a finite state model taken from the lexical grammar. The phrase structure is processed by a *parser*. As in the case of the scanner, the parser can either be written by hand (using the so-called *recursive descent* technique) or derived from a context-free grammar (variants of LR technology, where LR connotes a Left to Right scan). Front-end technology was in place by the early 1970s and has been able to handle a series of increasingly complex programming languages.

Reducing Computing Costs

Reducing Computing Costs The cost of computing provided the impetus for the second round of developments, leading to an emphasis on back-end technology. *Code optimization* is the process of taking a program that is correct and transforming it into one that is equally correct but uses computational resources such as registers (*q.v.*) and I/O devices more efficiently.

The evaluation criterion is efficiency—how fast does the compiled code run? How much memory does it use? The evaluation method, so-called *benchmarking* (*q.v.*), is a comparison between compilers over some mix of sample programs. Comparisons with hand code are only anecdotal—there is no longer any expectation that a large program can be entirely coded in assembler. Benchmarks are not particularly convincing—the results are dependent on the mix of test programs. Different application areas need different mixes, and there is a tendency to tune a compiler for the benchmark instead of for the application area.

Portability

Portability The most recent impetus toward regularizing compiler construction has come from the economic necessity to develop portable programs (*see* PORTABILITY). The essential problem is to get an application implemented on many target computers from only one development effort. One technical response has been the rise of standards activities where the definition of a programming language is a document instead of a compiler. The problem is to get many back ends for one front end.

Compiler writers must meet the standard, even when it is inconvenient or inefficient on their target machine. While, in the early days, a new feature in a programming language was seen as value added to the compiler, now a customer is more likely to consider a feature beyond the standard as a barrier to easy migration of application programs from target to target, and compiler to compiler.

Compilers have been implemented by computer manufacturers for their own products as a way of providing productivity tools for their customers. Compilers built by independent vendors, on the other hand, provide uniform implementations on many different computers. The portability evaluation criteria for a compiler are degree of conformance to the standard, often measured by a test suite, and the number of computers for which it is available.

Software Engineering

Software Engineering It is likely that integration with the software engineering (*q.v.*) process will form the next impetus in compiler construction. The size of application programs continues to grow. There are many programs approaching a million lines of source code. Often, several large programs are expected to cooperate, bringing the active code to perhaps 10 million lines. The parts of a megaprogram may be on dissimilar machines, remotely connected by a network of imperfect reliability, in places the programmer cannot go. The problems of building and testing such artifacts are formidable. It requires an engineering discipline and tools that are able to deal with both the technical definition and implementation, as well as the resource allocation and management problems that arise.

The tools of the programmer include text editors (*q.v.*), browsers, analyzers, preprocessors (*q.v.*), source code managers, builders, debuggers, test generators, and test harnesses. All of them need information that the compiler can supply. The quality of a diagnostic or the speed with which a question is answered has economic significance. The evaluation criterion is the time to make and verify a change in the source program. Integration across the toolset, and even across different programming languages—optimizing the compilers for programmer performance—conflicts with the traditional goals and structures of compilers.

The software engineer needs, in addition, tools that aid in defining, documenting, and tracking projects. Detailed history of activity within the source files, information about frequency and content of diagnostic messages issued by the compilers, and audit trails are all examples of information produced for the software engineer by integrated tools.

Front-end Technology A grammar describing the lexicon of a programming language may be 100 lines long. The scanner produces a stream of *tokens* from the source text, one for each significant lexical object, such as an identifier (*q.v.*), constant, delimiter (*q.v.*), or separator. The implementation of a scanner for the lexicon may be 1,000 lines of source code and may take a few days to implement. A scanner can also be implemented by presenting the grammar as input to a scanner generator. The output of the scanner generator is a compiler module—generally in the form of some tables and functions (*see* COMPILER-COMPILER).

The efficiency of the scanner is often critical—it is the only component that examines each source character. Generated scanners are less efficient than hand-written scanners. Thus, scanner generators are not always worth the trouble to acquire, learn, and use, and in any case the scanner is a small part of the whole problem of compiler implementation.

A grammar describing the rest of the structure of a programming language may be 300 or more lines long. While the lexical structure rarely holds surprises, the implications of a phrase structure grammar are often difficult to see. The reduction rules of the grammar are repeatedly applied to a source program, reducing it step by step until the entire program is reduced to a unique grammatical goal symbol. The part of the compiler applying the rules is called a *parser*.

The sequence of applied rules is the principal information supplied by the parser. Some abstraction of the rule sequence is presented by the front end to the back end of the compiler. The rules can be presented as a sequence of integers (the rule numbers) or as a *syntax tree*. In the former case, there must be some special mechanism to associate the contents of identifiers and constants with the rules reducing them.

There are two principal technologies for implementing parsers—*recursive descent* and an LALR(1) *parser generator* (Aho *et al.* 1986). An LALR(*k*) parser is a Look-Ahead LR grammar that may look ahead *k* characters to the right of the current character being analyzed. Looking ahead one character, hence LALR(1), is sufficient to parse the grammars of most high-level languages, without ambi-

guity. Recursive parsers are written in a systems programming language such as C (*q.v.*), with one recursive procedure for each nonterminal symbol of the phrase structure grammar. They can be tricky to get right for a complicated language. A parser generator accepts a grammar as input and generates a parser. It can be difficult to get the parser generator to accept a hand-written grammar. Once generated, the parser is guaranteed to implement the grammar.

Parser generators are particularly attractive for standard languages for which standard LALR(1) grammars are published. Recursive parsers are more attractive where the implementor needs to be flexible, since any kind of information available can be used in a handwritten parser, rather than the strictly grammatical input to the LALR(1) processors. No generator is needed for recursive descent. Some LALR(1) processors allow the user to intervene in the table generation to achieve flexibility at the cost of invalidating the guarantees.

Generated parsers have a better chance to continue parsing after a syntax error because there is an *error-repair* algorithm that is soundly based on the grammar and straightforward to implement. Both technologies are likely to continue in use. Parsers can be written so that the rest of the compiler is independent of the choice—a recursive parser can be taken out and a LALR(1) parser substituted, without making any other changes. Often, the writers of recursive parsers combine the parser and generator, which makes the later substitution of a different parser much harder.

The *generator* is a mechanism to generate an intermediate form (in an IL) of the program. The IL is designed to simplify the final steps of compilation. An IL may carry only executable information, or it may also carry declarations (*q.v.*). The generator is driven by the sequence of tokens and rules from the scanner and parser. The form of the IL is usually an *abstract syntax tree* or linear *pseudocode* with target machine addresses in symbolic form.

Back-end Technology The back end takes the information gathered during source analysis and emits the target code. The *symbol table* is a mechanism designed to collect information about the symbols in a program. The function of the symbol table is to deliver that information, properly resolved in terms of the scope rules of the language, to the code emitters. Typically, the information includes the data type of the symbol, its initialization, its machine location, and anything else of use to the rest of the compilation process. It is often convenient to record the information found in the source code as an abstract syntax tree of the corresponding declaration. The rest of the information about a symbol is derived by routines in the back end. Derived information can be tabulated by amending the tree, or alongside the tree in another data structure. A most common symbol table action is table look-up; thus symbol tables are written to make look-up fast. It is an arbitrary choice whether to generate the symbol table in the front or back end.

Emitting Target Code If a high degree of optimization is required, the IL may provide hooks for *control flow analysis*, permitting the compiler to improve the code for a statement based on knowing what statements come before and after. It also allows the compiler to locate the paths expected to be most frequently executed, enabling a choice between optimization based on which one will help most often. The output of the emitter may be assembly language, in which case an assembler (*q.v.*) will later build an *object module* acceptable to the linker, or the output may be the object module itself.

Transformations of the program for optimization may be carried out on an intermediate language form, or on the target code, or both. The transformation and analysis techniques, in order of complexity, are instruction choice, local transformations, and transformations over larger regions of the source program based on flow analysis. The most common case of a local transformation is the computation of *constant expressions* at compile time. Another local transformation eliminates repeated computations by having them done once and then providing for the result to be used more than once.

Instruction choice and local transformations can be *table driven*. The effect is to remove target machine dependency from the implemented code of the emitter, and, instead, place it in more accessible and modifiable tables external to the compiler proper. For simple target computers, the choices depend only on the costs of the individual instructions. There are more complex situations where the interactions between instructions may be the dominant effect. The most common case of interaction is the need of some one emitted instruction to wait for a result being produced by an earlier emitted instruction.

Flow Analysis The starting point for flow analysis is a branch-free segment (called a *basic block*). Basic blocks are entered at the start and exited at the end. The representation of control flow, reflecting source program structures such as loops (*q.v.*) and subroutines is a directed graph with nodes for basic blocks and transfer constructs that determine the graph branches.

Two important flow analysis regions are the bodies of loops and the bodies of procedures. Analyzing flow allows the back end to extend the kind of analysis applied to basic blocks to larger regions of code. For example, an expression that is used within a loop and does not change until the loop is exited can be computed outside the loop and, therefore, computed once instead of repeatedly.

Because the compiler is limited to compiling only part of the program at a time, the effectiveness of the optimizer is limited—flow out of the translation unit cannot be traced. The linker deals with all of the target code at once, so some optimizations, particularly interprocedural optimizations, are done on target code during linking, if at all.

Knowing how many times a loop runs on the average, as well as the frequency of each conditional branch, allows better choices to be made by the optimizer. For this, the compiler may depend on frequency profiles gathered during test executions of the program under development. This information is not perfect, but it is likely to be more accurate than a blind guess made by the optimization code. Optimizers are hand written, using tables of information about instructions, timing, and equivalences. The problem is made harder by radical changes in hardware targets. Networking, parallelism, and pipelining, for instance, introduce new problems that do not yield to the kinds of analysis developed for sequential machines.

Conclusion There are various important criteria for compiler excellence. The ideal compiler has a table-driven front end that can accept any reasonable language, a table-driven back end that can make good code for any reasonable computer, and a single universal IL to describe the interface. The engineering process to change the source or target is routine and inexpensive. The compiler is an acceptable component of software engineering environments that are designed to assist teams of programmers building complex programs.

Because these goals are to some extent in conflict, the ideal compiler does not exist, but compilers are designed to approach the ideal, perhaps giving up a little in some areas in order to attain excellence in others.

References

1976. Lewis, P. M., Rosenkrantz, D. J., and Stearns, R. E. *Compiler Design Theory*. Reading, MA: Academic Press.

1986. Aho, A., Sethi, Ravi, and Ullman, J. D. *Compiler Principles, Techniques, and Tools*. Reading, MA: Addison-Wesley.

1989. Homer, W., and Schooler, R. "Independent Testing of Compiler Phases Using a Test Case Generator," *Software—Practice and Experience*, **19**, 1, (January) 53–62.

1991. Pagan, F. G. *Partial Computation and the Construction of Language Processors*. Englewood Cliffs, NJ: Prentice-Hall.

WILLIAM M. MCKEEMAN

COMPLEMENT

For articles on related subjects *see* ARITHMETIC, COMPUTER; and NUMBERS AND NUMBER SYSTEMS.

In ordinary arithmetic, we represent negative numbers by a minus sign followed by the absolute value (i.e. magnitude) of the number (e.g. -6.42). In computers, we can represent negative numbers this way also, and sometimes this is actually done, but more often a *complement* representation is used.

To motivate the need for complements or complementers, consider the addition of two numbers expressed in sign-magnitude form. Before the operation can be carried out, the signs of the numbers must be compared. If they are the same, the two numbers can be added; if they are different, the smaller in magnitude may be subtracted from the larger and the correct sign appended to the result. As we will see, the use of complements avoids much of this complication.

Definitions There are two kinds of complements, *radix* complements and *diminished radix* complements, where *radix* refers to the base of the number system being used. Let x be a positive number in the decimal system. Then the diminished 10s complement of x, which we denote by $\bar{x}$ and which is generally called the *9s complement*, is formed by subtracting every digit of x

from 9. Thus, if $x = 426.3091$, $\bar{x} = 573.6908$. The *10s complement* $\tilde{x}$ is defined as the result of adding 1 in the least significant place of $\bar{x}$ or, equivalently, as the result of subtracting x from 10^n, where n is such that the 1 in 10^n is one place to the left of the most significant digit of x. Using the above example, $\tilde{x} = 573.6909 = 1,000.0000 - 426.3091$. Both the quantities $\bar{x}$ and $\tilde{x}$ are thus representations of the quantity $-x$.

The other complements of practical importance are those in the radix 2, or binary, system. If x is now a positive binary number, its *1s complement* $\bar{x}$ is formed by changing all 0s in x to 1s and 1s to 0s (i.e. subtracting all bits of x from 1) and the *2s complement* $\tilde{x}$ is formed by adding 1 in the least significant place of $\bar{x}$ or, equivalently, subtracting x from 2^n with n chosen as above. Thus, if $x = 10.1101$, then $\bar{x} = 01.0010$ and $\tilde{x} = 01.0011 = 100.0000 - 10.1101$.

Properties of Complements

The useful properties of complements in computers are best illustrated using the binary system. For illustrative purposes, consider a computer where the numbers on which arithmetic operations are to be performed each have eight bits, the first of which denotes the sign (0 for plus, 1 for minus) and the other seven bits are, for convenience, assumed to represent an integer. If the sign is negative, let us assume the integer is the 2s complement form. Then, to add two such numbers, we need only treat them as eight-bit positive integers (i.e. treat the sign as another bit of the number), add them, and discard any carry to the left of the eighth position (see Fig. 1). Thus, we are able to ignore both the sign and relative magnitudes of the two numbers. With negative numbers in the 1s complement form, there is the slight additional complication that carries to the left of the eighth position must be added into the first (i.e. least significant) position (see Fig. 2).

Both results given above are rather easily proved by writing complemented numbers as 2^n minus the corresponding positive number (minus 1 for 1s complements).

One interesting property of the 1s complement form is the existence, as in sign-magnitude representation, of two zeros, one with a positive sign and one with a negative sign. This follows because the 1s complement of 0000 0000 to is 1111 1111 (-0). With 2s complements, however, there is only one n-bit zero (namely, 0000 0000 for $n = 8$), since the 2s complement of 0000 0000 is 10000 0000, which has nine bits, the first of which is discarded. (Of the other 255 different 8-bit patterns, only one other is its own 2s complement: 1000 0000 $[-128]$.) In 2s complement representation, 1111 1111 is the complement of 0000 0001.

Since 1s complements are generated merely by changing 0s to 1s, and vice versa, it is very easy to build a circuit to generate the 1s complement of a number. It is somewhat more difficult, but not very hard, to build a circuit to generate 2s complements. Therefore, it is easy to perform subtraction by first complementing the minuend and then adding (see Fig. 3). This means it is not necessary to have a hardware subtracter if there is a hardware adder and a complementer.

Let $\quad x = 00001000$ (decimal 8)
$\qquad y = 00010101$ (decimal 21)
Then $\tilde{x} = 11111000$ (decimal -8)
$\qquad \tilde{y} = 11101011$ (decimal -21)

Then $x + \tilde{y} = $
$$\begin{array}{r} 00001000 \\ + 11101011 \\ \hline 11110011 \end{array}$$

which is the 2s complement of 13 in decimal (00001101 in binary); and

$$\tilde{x} + \tilde{y} = \begin{array}{r} 11111000 \\ + 11101011 \\ \hline 11100011 \end{array}$$

which is the 2s complement of 29 in decimal (00011101 in binary).

FIG. 1. Addition of numbers using 2s complements.

Let $\quad x = 00001000$
$\qquad y = 00010101$
$\qquad \bar{x} = 11110111$
$\qquad \bar{y} = 11101010$

Then $x + \bar{y} = $
$$\begin{array}{r} 00001000 \\ + 11101010 \\ \hline 11110010 \end{array}$$

which is the 1s complement of 13 in decimal (00001101 in binary); and

$$\bar{x} + \bar{y} = \begin{array}{r} 11110111 \\ + 11101010 \\ \hline 11100001 \\ \quad\longrightarrow 1 \\ \hline 11100010 \end{array}$$

which is the 1s complement of 29 in decimal (00011101 in binary).

FIG. 2. Additions of numbers using 1s complements.

Let $\quad x = 00001000$
$\qquad y = 00010101$

Then $x - y$ is found by first forming

$$\bar{y} = 11101010$$

and then adding $x + \bar{y}$, as in Fig 2, to get 11110010, which is the 1s complement of 13 in decimal.

FIG. 3. Subtraction using 1s complements.

For performing multiplication and division, there are no direct advantages to the complement form and some disadvantages. However, the adjustments to algorithms for multiplying or dividing two positive numbers to allow them to handle operands in complement form are not major. Alternatively, negative operands in multiplication or division can first be complemented and then the appropriate sign can be appended at the end.

Most modern computers store negative numbers in either 1s or 2s complement form, with the latter gradually becoming predominant, likely because of the unique 0 in 2s complement. Otherwise, which of the two forms to choose depends upon some rather subtle and by no means conclusive considerations concerning the details of computer circuitry.

ANTHONY RALSTON

COMPLEXITY. See COMPUTATIONAL COMPLEXITY; INFORMATION-BASED COMPLEXITY; and NP-COMPLETE PROBLEMS.

COMPRESSION. See DATA COMPRESSION AND COMPACTION.

COMPUTATIONAL COMPLEXITY

For articles on related subjects *see* ALGORITHMS, ANALYSIS OF; ALGORITHMS, THEORY OF; FAST FOURIER TRANSFORM; INFORMATION-BASED COMPLEXITY; MATHEMATICAL PROGRAMMING; NP-COMPLETE PROBLEMS; and TURING MACHINE.

Computational complexity is concerned with the determination of the intrinsic difficulty of mathematically posed problems that arise in many disciplines. The study of complexity has led to more efficient algorithms than those previously known or suspected. We begin by illustrating some of the important ideas of computational complexity with the example of matrix multiplication.

Computational Complexity of Matrix Multiplication
Consider the multiplication of 2×2 matrices. Let

$$A = \begin{pmatrix} a_{11} & a_{12} \\ a_{21} & a_{22} \end{pmatrix}, \ B = \begin{pmatrix} b_{11} & b_{12} \\ b_{21} & b_{22} \end{pmatrix}, \ C = \begin{pmatrix} c_{11} & c_{12} \\ c_{21} & c_{22} \end{pmatrix}.$$

Given A, B, we seek $C = AB$.

The classical algorithm computes C by

$$c_{11} = a_{11} b_{11} + a_{12} b_{21}, \quad c_{12} = a_{11} b_{12} + a_{12} b_{22},$$
$$c_{21} = a_{21} b_{11} + a_{22} b_{21}, \quad c_{22} = a_{21} b_{12} + a_{22} b_{22},$$

at a cost of eight multiplications. (The addition time is considered to be relatively trivial.)

Until the late sixties, no one seems to have asked whether two matrices could be multiplied in fewer than eight scalar multiplications. Then Strassen showed that seven scalar multiplications are sufficient by introducing the following algorithm:

$$p_1 = (a_{11} + a_{12})(b_{11} + b_{22}), \quad p_2 = (a_{21} + a_{22}) b_{11},$$
$$p_3 = a_{11}(b_{12} - b_{22}), \quad p_4 = a_{22}(-b_{11} + b_{21}),$$
$$p_5 = (a_{11} + a_{12}) b_{22}, \quad p_6 = (-a_{11} + a_{21})(b_{11} + b_{12}),$$
$$p_7 = (a_{12} - a_{22})(b_{21} + b_{22}),$$
$$c_{11} = p_1 + p_4 - p_5 + p_7, \quad c_{12} = p_3 + p_5,$$
$$c_{21} = p_2 + p_4, \quad p_{22} = p_1 + p_3 - p_2 + p_6.$$

Consider next the multiplication of $N \times N$ matrices. The classical algorithm uses N^3 arithmetic operations. (In this article, we disregard multiplicative constants in giving algorithm cost.) By repeated partitioning of $N \times N$ matrices into 2×2 submatrices, two matrices can be multiplied in $N^{\log_2 7} \sim N^{2.81}$ arithmetic operations.

After a decade, during which there was practically no progress on decreasing the number of arithmetic operations used in matrix multiplication, Schönhage and Pan [1979] showed that $N^{2.52}$ arithmetic operations are sufficient. Since then, there has been steady progress in reducing the exponent. The best result known, due to Coppersmith and Winograd [1987], is $N^{2.376}$. The exponent 2.376 is the state of our knowledge as of 1991, but researchers expect that the exponent will be further decreased.

The above results are of theoretical rather than practical value. The value of N has to be enormous before the new algorithm becomes faster than the classical one. On the other hand, there are some problems for which new algorithms have had profound influence. A good example is provided by the finite Fourier transform on N points. The Fast Fourier Transform (*q.v.*) uses only $N \log N$ arithmetic operations, compared to N^2 for the classical algorithms. Since $N \log N$ is much smaller than N^2 for even moderate values of N, and since the finite Fourier transform is often needed for a large number of points, the introduction of the Fast Fourier Transform has revolutionized computation in a number of scientific fields.

Using the matrix multiplication example, we can now introduce some basic terminology. The minimal number of arithmetic operations is called the *computational complexity* (or *problem complexity* or just *complexity*) of the matrix multiplication problem. The complexity of matrix multiplication is unknown. An *upper bound* is $N^{2.376}$. A *lower bound* is N^2. Since this lower bound is linear in the number of inputs and outputs, we say it is a *trivial* lower bound. No non-trivial lower bound is known.

Algorithm complexity is the cost of a particular algorithm. This should be contrasted but not confused with problem complexity, which is the minimal cost over *all* possible algorithms. *Fast algorithm* is a qualitative term meaning faster than a classical algorithm or faster than previously known algorithms. An *optimal algorithm* is one whose complexity equals the problem complexity.

Table 1 summarizes the present state of our knowledge concerning matrix multiplication.

TABLE 1. *Summary of Matrix Multiplication*

upper bound	$N^{2.376}$
lower boound	N^2
complexity	unknown
optimal algorithm	unknown

Computational Complexity in General

To study computational complexity requires a *model of computation* that states which "operations" or "steps" are permissible and how much they cost. Using the model, we can then ask the same questions as in the matrix multiplication example. For instance, we seek *problem complexity, upper bounds, lower bounds, fast algorithms,* and *optimal algorithms.*

Typically, an *upper bound* is the cost of the fastest known algorithm for solving the problem. A *lower bound* can be established only through a theorem that states that no algorithm exists whose cost is less than the lower bound. Not surprisingly, lower bounds are far harder to establish than upper bounds.

Numerous models of computation have been studied. In our matrix multiplication example, we counted arithmetic operations. Very significant results have been obtained for space and time complexity in a Turing Machine (*q.v.*) model. Another important model is a random access machine (RAM). The parallel random-access machine (PRAM) is used to model parallel machines. Other models are appropriate for studying asynchronous or VLSI computation.

Often, we assign a "size" N to a problem, such as, for example, the number of rows in a matrix, the number of items to be sorted, or the length of a list to be searched. If the number of operations or steps required to solve a problem is an exponential function of N, we say that the problem has *exponential time complexity.* If the problem requires a number of operations that is a polynomial function of N, we say that the problem has *polynomial time complexity.*

If a problem has exponential time complexity, we say that it is *intractable.*

Typical Applications of Computational Complexity

The complexity of numerous problems has been studied. To illustrate the variety, we exhibit ten drawn from various areas.

1. Compute the finite Fourier transform at N points.
2. Determine if an N digit integer is prime; if not, determine its factors.
3. Compute the Kendall rank correlation at N points.
4. Multiply two polynomials of degree N.
5. Prove all theorems that can be stated with at most N symbols in a certain system of axioms.
6. Solve the traveling salesman problem for N cities.
7. Solve to within ε a large sparse linear system of order N whose matrix is positive definite and has condition number bounded by M.
8. Find the closest neighbor of P points in K dimensions.
9. Compute the first N terms of the Qth composite of a power series.
10. Compute the first N digits of π (for, say, $N = 20,000,000$).

Reducibility Among Problems

There are many problems for which the best algorithm known costs exponential time. Such problems occur in operations research (*q.v.*), computer design, data manipulation, graph theory (*q.v.*), and mathematical logic. Do faster algorithms exist that solve these problems in polynomial time? We don't know. What we do know is that there is a large class of problems that are equivalent in that, if one of them can be solved in polynomial time, they all can. For technical reasons, this class of problems is said to be *NP-complete* (*q.v.*). Because no one has succeeded in devising a polynomial time algorithm for any of these problems, many researchers believe that NP-complete problems are exponentially hard. There is no proof of this, and settling this question is the most important open problem in computational complexity.

An example of an NP-complete problem is the *Traveling Salesman Problem.* Given a set of cities and the distance between them, determine the order in which the cities should be visited so that each city is visited exactly once, the tour ends in the starting city, and the distance traveled is as small as possible. The size of this problem is the number of cities. The investigation of NP-complete problems is an example of work in a very active area of research called *structural computational complexity.*

Intractable Problems

A problem is *intractable* if it has an exponential time complexity. If a problem is intractable, it can be solved for small values of the size N, but not for large values (i.e. the problem does not scale). An intractable problem cannot be solved for large values of N, no matter how much faster computer circuits become or how much parallelism is used.

All complexity results are relative to a model of computation and a setting. The setting used in the study of NP-completeness is *deterministic worst case. Deterministic* means that the algorithm does not toss coins, while *worst case* means that the answer is guaranteed for all inputs.

We cannot circumvent a negative complexity conclusion by inventing a more clever algorithm. We can change the setting, however, and see if that makes the problem tractable.

One possibility is to permit the algorithm to toss coins. Such an algorithm is said to be *randomized.* Although Monte Carlo methods (*q.v.*) have long been used for continuous problems, such as multivariate integration, it is only within the last 15 years that computer scientists have realized the power of randomized algorithms. Rabin [1976] and Solovay and Strassen [1977] showed that randomized algorithms could, at low cost, be used to determine if a very large integer is prime. However, there is a small probability that the randomized algorithm will incorrectly output that an integer input is prime. Other problems where randomized algorithms are useful include fault detection in digital circuits, routing of messages in distributed networks, interactive proofs, and coordination of processors in an asynchronous system.

Another way in which an intractable problem may be made tractable is to settle for an *average case* assurance (i.e. we consider the complexity averaged over a set of inputs). For example, Klee and Mintz showed that, in the worst case, the simplex algorithm for linear programming has exponential cost. However, Borgwardt [1982] and Smale [1982,3] showed that the average cost of the simplex algorithm is polynomial. Note that this is an algorithm cost result, rather than a problem complexity result, but it reveals the power of looking at average behavior.

Axiomatic Complexity Theory

We discuss an abstract complexity model based on two axioms. Let $T_A(x)$ denote the cost of algorithm A applied to the input of integer x. Assume that $T_A(x)$ satisfies the following two axioms:

1. $T_A(x)$ is finite if and only if algorithm A applied to input x eventually halts and gives an output. (In other words, an algorithm halts if and only if it halts after a finite number of steps.)
2. There is an algorithm that, given as inputs any integers x and y and any algorithm A, will determine whether or not $T_A(x) = y$.

These straightforward axioms are enough to imply, for example, that there are computable functions that cannot be computed rapidly by any algorithm, and that more functions can be computed if more time is allowed. They also imply a much less obvious fact, known as the "Speed-up Theorem": There is a computable function f with the property that, given any algorithm A that computes f, there is another algorithm B that computes f "much faster" than A. "Much faster" is interpreted by choosing any rapidly growing computable function such as 2^w; then, according to the speed-up theorem, there is a function f such that, if A is any algorithm for f, there is always another algorithm B for f, such that $2^{T_B(x)} \leq T_A(x)$ for all large integers x. Thus, algorithm B requires at most the logarithm of the time required by A.

Of course, since B is itself an algorithm for f, there must be another algorithm C for f that requires only the logarithm of the time for B, etc. Clearly, there is no single most efficient way to compute such an f.

Also, notice that f must be hopelessly difficult to compute even though it has faster and faster programs. Each program for f must require more than 2^x, and more than 2^{2^x}, etc, steps for all large inputs x; otherwise, the program could only be "sped up" by an exponential a fixed number of times before "hitting bottom," after which it cannot be sped up further.

These conclusions may seem to violate intuition, but they follow from the two simple axioms given above. The speed-up theorem is proved by using diagonal arguments similar to those used to establish the existence of undecidable problems.

Conclusions

Computational complexity deals with the fundamental issues of determining the intrinsic difficulty of mathematically posed problems. Through the study of complexity, it has been established that certain problems are intrinsically hard. On the other hand, for some problem areas new algorithms have been introduced that are far superior to any previously known. Problems occurring in a rich diversity of disciplines are being and will be subjected to complexity analysis.

References

1975. Borodin, A. and Munro, I. *The Computational Complexity of Algebraic and Numeric Problems*. New York: American Elsevier.
1979. Garey, M. R. and Johnson, D. S. *Computers and Intractability*. San Francisco: W. H. Freeman.
1990. Corman, T. H., Leiserson, C. E., and Rivest, R. L. *Introduction to Algorithms*. Cambridge, MA: MIT Press.

JOSEPH F. TRAUB

COMPUTATIONAL GEOMETRY

For articles on related subjects *see* ALGORITHMS, ANALYSIS OF; ALGORITHMS, DESIGN AND CLASSIFICATION OF; COMPUTER GRAPHICS; and GRAPH THEORY.

Computational geometry is the study of algorithmic problems involving geometry. Although the ruler-and-compass constructions of ancient Greek geometry were essentially algorithms for producing geometric objects, modern computational geometry began with M. I. Shamos' 1975 Ph.D. dissertation which solved several fundamental geometric problems and posed many more. Over the last ten years, computational geometry has been a very active area of algorithms research, and a recent bibliography lists over 2,000 relevant publications. The explosive growth of this field can be traced to the intuitive appeal of geometric problems and the wide range of their practical applications.

Geometric problems arise in a variety of applications, some of which would not seem to have geometric aspects. VLSI circuits are described by overlapping rectangles of different materials. To prevent wires from short circuiting, it is necessary to test designs such that no two rectangles intersect. The huge number of rectangles in a large circuit implies the need for fast intersection detection algorithms. Mobile robots must find paths to a goal through rooms full of obstacles without bumping into anything. This can be more difficult than it might appear, as anyone who tries to move a piano through a door quickly discovers. Finite element methods (*q.v.*) used to simulate the performance of physical systems such as aircraft depend upon dividing the surface of the object into triangular regions; effort spent in finding a "good" triangulation pays dividends in more efficient and accurate simulations. Database queries of the form "how many people are between 180 and 200 centimeters tall and weigh between 60 and 75 kilograms" can be thought of as asking how many plotted points lie in a given rectangle, where the *x*-axis represents the height and the y-axis the weight. Finally, the problems of eliminating hidden lines and surfaces in computer graphics is an inherently geometric problem.

Computational geometry deals with questions of how to compute various aspects of geometric structures. Many brute force algorithms for solving geometric problems can be improved by algorithmic techniques and more sophisticated data structures. To a larger extent than most traditional algorithmic problems, efficient solutions often rely on a *combinatorial* understanding of the problem—for example, knowing how many regions of a certain type can be formed by an arrangement of *n* lines.

Geometric algorithms must often cope with complications that do not occur in such related areas as graph algorithms. Even very primitive problems, such as testing whether two line segments intersect, are complicated by *degenerate* data. If two segments overlap or share an endpoint, do they intersect? The correct answer depends on the application. To avoid such problems, it is often assumed that the points representing the data are in *general position*, meaning that no three points lie on the same line.

The complexity of a geometric algorithm depends on the type and size of the geometric objects being dealt with. For example, consider determining the intersection between two polygons *A* and *B* with *n* and *m* vertices respectively. A *convex* polygon has the property that the line segment between any two points in the polygon lies completely within the polygon. The intersection between two convex polygons is itself a convex polygon (Fig. 1a).

This intersection can be computed in $O(n + m)$ time. A *star-shaped* polygon has the property that there exists a point *P* such that the line segment from *P* to any other point in the polygon lies entirely within the polygon. Fig. 1b shows that the intersection of two star-shaped polygons can produce many small polygons, in fact $O(mn)$ of them. Thus, the best algorithm to compute this intersection is doomed to being $O(mn)$ in the worst case.

Another aspect of geometric problems is *dimensionality*. Any failed artist will testify that it is easier to visualize objects in two dimensions than three. The distinction between dimensions is more substantial than just visualization, however, as objects in different dimensions have different properties. For example, polygons in two dimensions have the same number of vertices as edges, so the edges can be described by simply listing the vertices in order. In three or higher dimensions however, polyhedra have more edges than vertices, and more complicated data structures are needed to represent them.

One of the main paradigms of geometric algorithms uses a *sweep line* to process all of an object's points in a systematic way. We will illustrate such algorithms by computing the *convex hull* of a set of *n* points in two dimensions, which is the convex polygon smallest in area that contains all of the points. If we could stretch a rubber band around all the points and let go, the rubber band would "compute" the convex hull of the point set.

It is easy to see that the convex hull of any three points is the triangle they define. If we add another point to the point set, it will change the convex hull if and only if it lies outside the original hull. Any of the old hull vertices that lie within a triangle formed by two hull vertices and the new point cannot be on the hull, and must be deleted. Suppose that we sort the points in

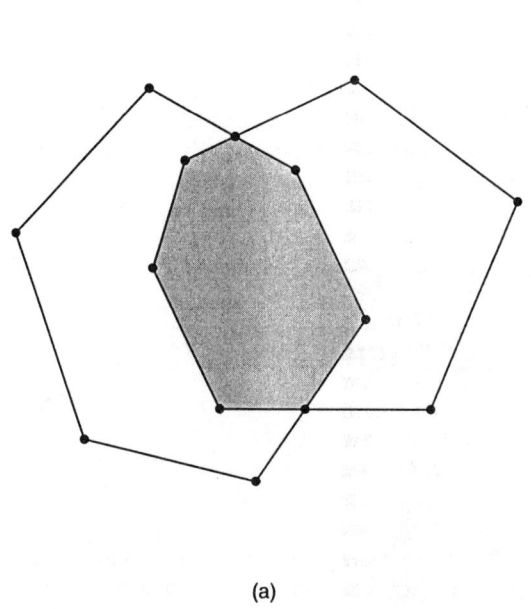

(a)

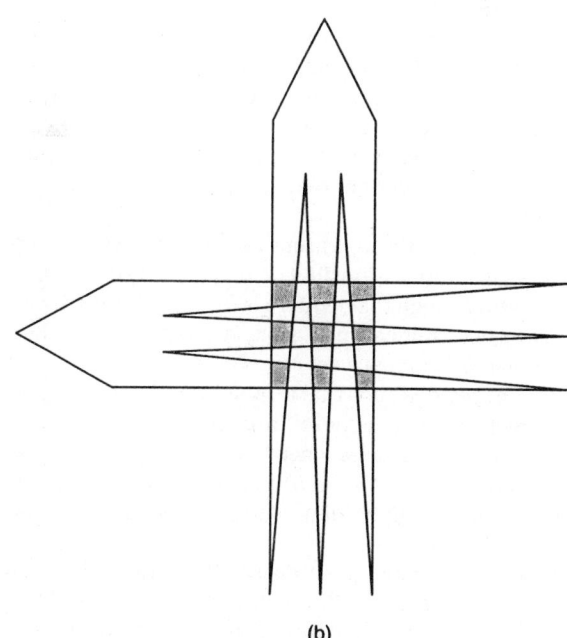

(b)

FIG. 1.   The intersection of convex and star-shaped polygons

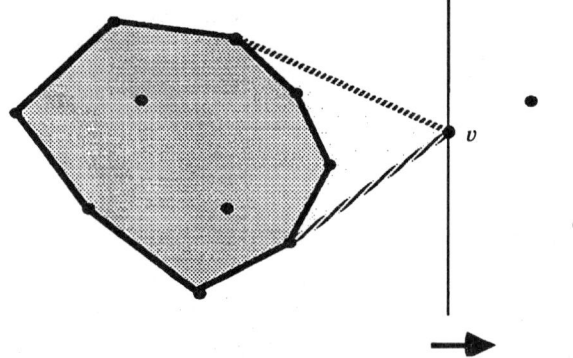

FIG. 2. Finding the convex hull

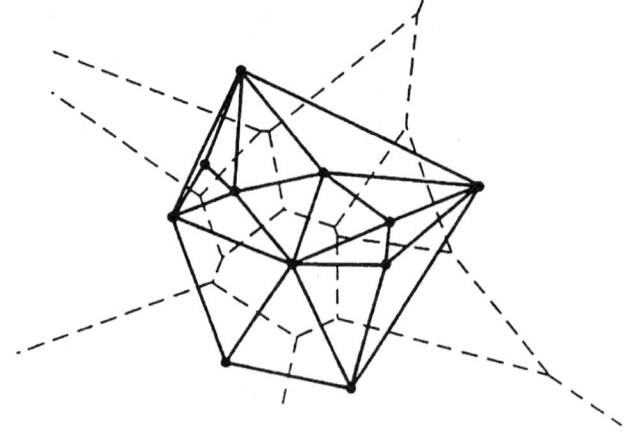

FIG. 3. A Voronoi diagram and its Delaunay triangulation. Black dots are original points. Dotted lines form Voronoi polygons and solid lines form Delaunay triangles.

increasing order by the x-coordinate (and thus process them them from left to right, as shown in Fig. 2) and store them in a doubly-linked list. When we add a new point v, we can start from the rightmost hull point and walk around the hull, deleting points from the list until the internal angle each vertex makes with v and its hull neighbor ensures convexity. Because we delete each point at most once and otherwise do a constant amount of work in each insertion, we can determine the convex hull in $O(n)$ time once we do the sorting in $O(n \log n)$ time. The sweep line permits the fast deletion by telling us where to start looking.

Another important idea in computational geometry is *duality*—that two seemingly distinct problems are really the same. For example, suppose we want to test whether any three lines in an arrangement of n lines intersect in the same point. This can easily be done using a sweep-line algorithm that moves from left to right, stopping at each point of intersection. It would appear more difficult to test whether any three of a set of n points lie on the same line, since it appears that we have to test every subset of three points. There is a simple mathematical transformation, however, that can be used to convert a point to a line and a line to a point. Thus, we can solve the three-points-on-a-line problem by transforming it to the question of three lines meeting at a point and use the sweep line algorithm to solve it. The transformation to a dual problem provides a different point of view that leads to a more efficient solution.

Other geometric algorithms involve interesting intermediate structures. Consider a dispatch system for a chain of stores such that, when a customer phones, it can quickly be determined which store is nearest to the caller. The *Voronoi diagram* of a set of n points divides the plane into convex regions such that all points in the same region are nearest to the same point from the set. (Fig. 3). Algorithms for such nearest neighbor queries build the Voronoi diagram in $O(n \log n)$ time and then do a point location query to determine which region contains the point in $O(\log n)$ time.

Voronoi diagrams have many other interesting and useful properties as well. Suppose we take a Voronoi diagram and connect all pairs of points that share an edge in the diagram. All the regions in this new construct are triangles which collectively, represent a particular way of triangulating the plane. The resulting *Delaunay* triangulation is itself useful for other geometric problems.

Computational geometry is a young field, and research is continuing. Directions of current work include more robust algorithms in the face of degeneracy, faster algorithms in higher dimensions, and algorithms that are output-sensitive (e.g. polygonal intersection problems that are faster when the intersection has only a few edges).

References

1985. Preparata, F. P., and Shamos, M. I. *Computational Geometry: An Introduction.* New York: Springer-Verlag.
1987. Edelsbrunner, H. *Algorithms in Combinatorial Geometry.* Berlin: Springer-Verlag.
1988. O'Rourke, J. "Computational Geometry," *Annual Review of Computer Science,* **3** Annual Reviews, Inc., 389–411.

STEVEN S. SKIENA

COMPUTATIONAL LINGUISTICS.
See PROGRAMMING LINGUISTICS; and SYNTAX, SEMANTICS, AND PRAGMATICS.

COMPUTER-AIDED DESIGN/COMPUTER-AIDED MANUFACTURING (CAD/CAM)

For articles on related subjects *see*; COMPUTATIONAL GEOMETRY; COMPUTER-AIDED ENGINEERING; COMPUTER ANIMATION; COMPUTER GRAPHICS; COMPUTER-INTEGRATED MANUFACTURING; FINITE ELEMENT METHOD; ROBOTICS; and WORKSTATION.

Introduction Computers have aided the closer integration of design activities with the actions required to manufacture goods, and many of the systems used to provide these aids have been called CAD/CAM systems.

Many of the functions provided by initial CAD systems were directed at the design phase (the CAD portion), with the resulting computer models used to aid manufacturing activities. As the benefits of computer aids for manufacturing (the CAM portion) were recognized, the need for tighter integration of the two functions led to CAD/CAM systems where the design result (a model of the item) can be used directly to create the manufacturing information for the item. In addition to manufacturing information, the database is often supplemented to aid in tracking inventories of materials and costs.

Design Design is primarily a creative activity in which a person takes an aesthetic or functional idea and incorporates it in some medium in a way that can be understood by someone else. The most common example is engineering design, where the ideas of the designer are put on paper as drawings that include both geometric descriptions and notes. The essence of computer-aided design (CAD) is the marriage created by applying the strengths and capabilities of computers to provide assistance for design needs.

Geometry is a vital factor in most design; description of the shape and size of an item is the essential element in most tangible representations of that item. Humans are usually able to visualize a geometric description of an item more easily than they can understand a word description of the same item, hence the old adage that a picture is worth a thousand words. Thus, a major portion of the time spent in design is often devoted to creating and modifying geometric "pictures" of the item being designed.

In most kinds of design work, a designer works with a number of previously defined elements that are selectively included in the design of the new item. For example, the designer of an electrical circuit selects circuit elements and places them into the design. Even at the level of designing the elements, geometric entities such as circles are used to "build up" the element. This selection process is well suited to computer assistance, since computers can store large numbers of elements and allow designers rapid access to them for use in design. Another characteristic of the process of design is that it is highly iterative; designers frequently make multiple changes to various elements of the design as work proceeds. This also can be conveniently assisted by computers. Further, much of design is concerned with items for which some kind of analysis must be performed after the design is proposed. The results of the analysis often lead to additional changes in the design, such as to the selection of different elements in the item being designed.

Manufacturing Manufacturing activities frequently involve the positioning of parts and subsequent operations, such as cutting, milling, drilling, forming, and finishing. In all of these operations, the geometry of the part is critical, particularly if the operations are carried out by computer-driven tools, often termed NC (for *numerically controlled*) tools. Fig. 1 shows part of a machine shop at a large aerospace company.

FIG. 1. A portion of a machine shop at a large aerospace manufacturing facility. Cables carry numerical control (NC) information from central computers to drive machine tools.

When the same basic geometry from the database is used for both design and manufacturing, parts fit together with great precision. The creation, storage, and interface of 3-D geometric data among various disciplines (e.g. engineering and manufacturing) provide communication that is helpful in both increasing the precision with which parts are made and the ease of specifying the manufacturing steps to be carried out. The same geometric model—with mathematical integrity—is accessed and used by designers, part programmers (people who describe machine tool movements to create parts), structural analysts (engineers who calculate the structural strength of parts and assemblies), tool designers, and quality assurance personnel. CAD/CAM systems allow for this data to be captured during the construction phases of design.

In addition, the manufacturing process requires lists of parts (the bill of materials, etc.) and costs for the parts and for the entire item. Most CAD/CAM systems accommodate this data as supplements to the design and manufacturing process information.

Application Areas The most obvious examples of CAD/CAM uses are connected with engineering design activities, which will be emphasized in this article. These activities include the design of structures, highways, machine parts, printed circuit boards, plants, piping, assembly lines, airplanes (see Fig. 2), and automobiles (see Fig. 3, color insert page CP-2, and Fig. 4). In addition, CAD/CAM is often thought of as including the use of computers to aid in a design and analysis process, such as structural analysis following the actual design work, although this is more properly called computer-aided engineering (CAE). Further, it is sometimes used to encompass design of computer programs themselves, patterns for clothing, architectural exterior and interior layouts, packaging containers, and management systems.

The main strengths of computers—speed, accuracy, and repeatability—are particularly well matched to these kinds of design activities. In addition, computers can store

FIG. 2. A product of the aerospace industry, designed and manufactured in large part by using CAD/CAM. Note the complicated 3-D surfaces. The high cost of parts in this kind of product, the pressure to complete the design in as little time as possible, and the need to maintain high precision in manufacturing all lead to high payoffs in using CAD/CAM.

very large amounts of information (the database) that can be retrieved rapidly and used for additional calculations or for display (including supplemental information about parts lists and costs). This database capability, by the very nature of design (geometric construction, selection, and iteration), plays an important role in CAD/CAM.

Computers—Only an Aid It is important to note, however, that computers are used only as an *aid* to design and manufacturing. The process of design involves extensive decision-making and subjective evaluation, activities that are aided greatly by using computers, but that are generally carried out by computers under human direction. The same is true of decisions about manufacturing processes.

This article will focus primarily on the area of interactive engineering design and manufacture, primarily of machine parts. Especially in this area, as part of the

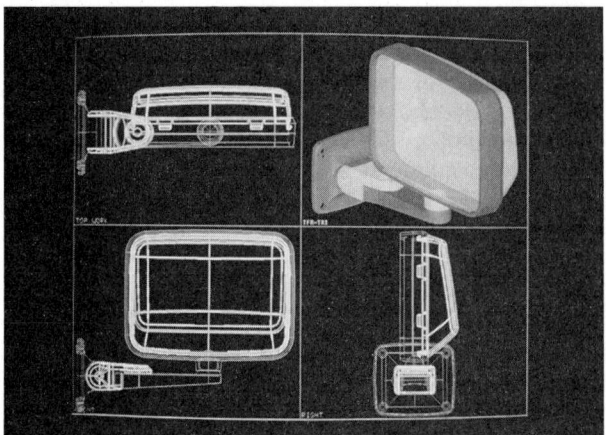

FIG. 4. An automobile mirror assembly. The screen displays three views of the part, along with a shaded model of the complete assembly.

design process, an engineer must be able to describe and communicate to others the geometric relationships of the design. The systems that assist in these needs are called interactive computer graphics systems, and they are the foundation of CAD/CAM systems. In fact, the terms are sometimes used interchangeably. However, the field of computer graphics includes many activities outside of design and manufacturing, and CAD/CAM encompasses activities outside of computer graphics.

Until about 20 to 25 years ago, almost all engineering design was done on the drafting board. Selection of elements was implemented by tracing, drawing from templates, or pasting the elements onto the drawing of the design of each element. Iteration was obtained by sequential use of pencil, eraser, pencil, eraser, etc. The only way to improve the productivity of this process was to provide better templates or paste-ons, to use less iteration, or to speed up the humans in some way. The recognition that significant gains in productivity could result from using computers to aid the process led to CAD systems.

At the same time, computers began to be used to aid in the preparation of plans for manufacturing activities, and computer controls for driving machine tools began to be used in large machine shops. These early CAD and CAM systems were very expensive and required large productivity gains to justify their cost. As prices of CAD/CAM systems have come down relative to the cost of humans doing design work, the cost benefits from productivity gains have become more significant and the variety of CAD/CAM systems has increased.

The Process As has been noted, the essence of these design functions is geometric construction. Geometric entities are typically built through repeated selection of "functions" or "tasks" to be performed from a "menu" of selection possibilities (see Fig. 3). Menus, function keyboards, data tablets, etc., are used not only for selection of *elements* for insertion and for positioning them on the design. They are also used to select tasks that permit a designer to move elements or items from location to location (translations and rotations), to create a blown-up view of a portion of the drawing (*windowing*), and to permit easy annotation or dimensioning of the drawings.

Using these and other functional capabilities, the user builds the database interactively—a database composed of both geometric and alphanumeric information. For a mechanical design, the output may take the form of a traditional drawing, showing the classical principal orthographic views (front, top, and side), with a 3-D view added. The general 3-D view (see Fig. 5) is important because it helps to avoid misinterpretation and ambiguity and thus minimizes later re-work by engineering and manufacturing personnel. Note that even though the 3-D view is quite helpful, it could have been obtained by projection from an existing 2-D database, but this would require considerably more time than would use of a 3-D system. Because this process creates lines that represent the edges of the item, these models are called *wireframe* models (*see* FINITE ELEMENT METHOD).

Construction of the design is not the only way in which data can be captured, however. An automatic laser

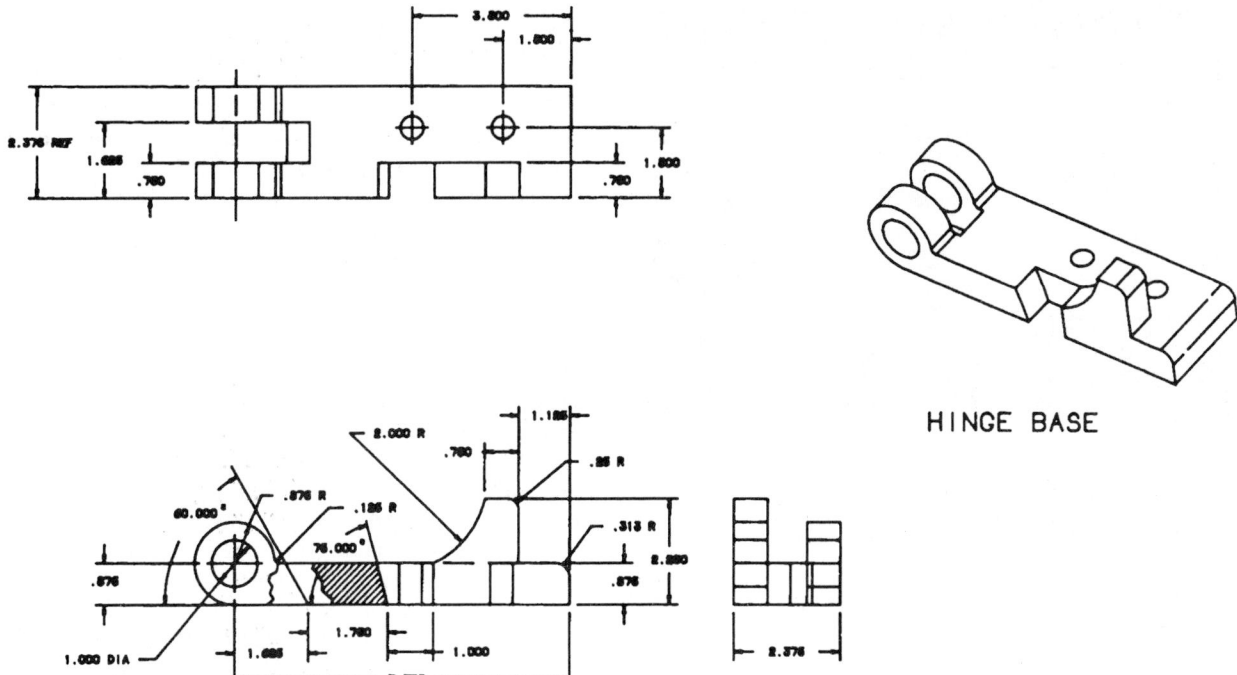

HINGE BASE

FIG. 5. A typical drawing format—three views plus a 3-D view.

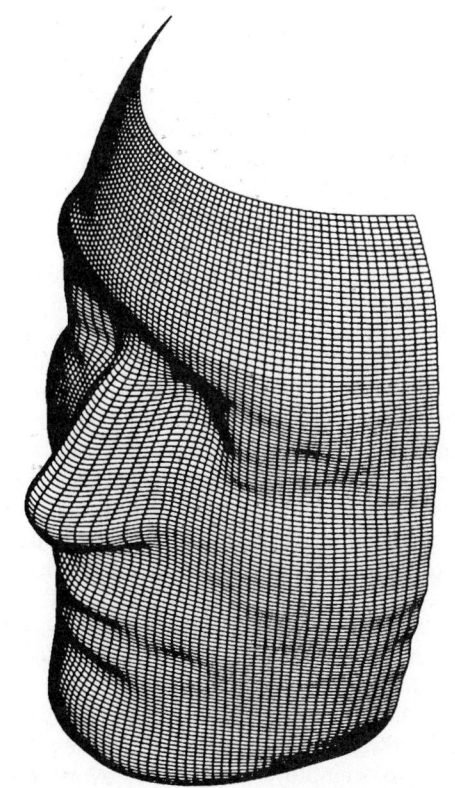

FIG. 6. A surface representation of a face, serving as the start of design of a fire protection mask. The physical sculpted model was digitized (scanned) to produce 3-D data points, which were then used to create surfaces. The display shows the computer-generated surfaces.

scanner can be used for 2-D data capture, with data automatically entered into the database. This data is then available for further modification (or editing). In addition to this type of scanner, hand-held or movable scanning (or "digitizing") devices are available. These allow the locations of points to be input. They can be moved to various points on 2-D or 3-D models. At a desired point, the user causes the device to sense the location of the point and enter it into the database. After the points are entered, CAD functions can be applied to create smooth lines, curves, or surfaces between the points. These lines, curves, or surfaces can then be used with the points for further design or for interfacing with CAM functions. Fig. 6 shows an interesting example of this technique. The key to this process is the variety of functions available to the designer to carry out actions in creating the design.

As computers and disks (used for storage of the database) have grown larger, there has been a trend to use true 3-D geometric databases and to use solid models (see Figs. 2 and 3). Manufacturing process planning must usually deal with solids and with manipulations on them, so solid models are a significant advantage in going from CAD systems to CAD/CAM systems.

The primary benefit of CAM is the use of the computer description of the part(s) to drive cutting, forming, and other operations in a manufacturing environment. Manufacturing personnel are concerned with deciding how the part will be manufactured. One of their concerns is the determination of tools, materials, and methods that will be used to cut, form, and/or finish the part. Fig. 7 shows a screen display of a tool path generation program, which aids in this process. In addition, databases for

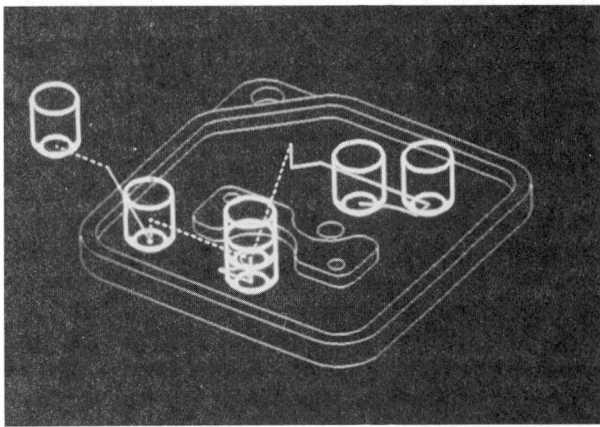

FIG. 7. A screen display of a simple tool path generation program. The position of the tool is displayed for visualization/simulation of how the part will be cut.

CAD/CAM systems need to provide information about stock to form or cut the part. Another concern is the design of fixtures to hold parts during manufacturing operations. Fig. 8 (see color insert, page CP-2) is the display of a fixture design program. Efficient utilization of material is also important. Fig. 9 shows a *nesting* program that attempts to optimize the use of sheet material.

Hardware Pioneering CAD systems were developed in the 1960s, using large mainframe computers attached to graphics terminals. These systems were primarily used in automotive and aerospace organizations, industries that required large amounts of data storage for their CAD data. The large centralized mainframe systems were the only systems that could provide this needed data storage. In addition, the large mainframes were the only source of sufficient computing power for the geometric and display calculations required. Early systems required the terminals to be located physically close to the computer in order to maintain adequate performance. As it became

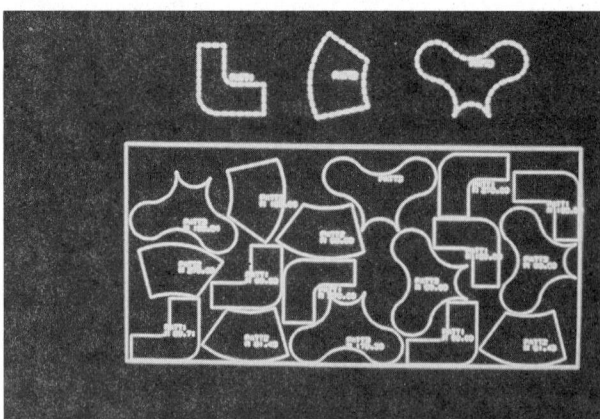

FIG. 9. The output from a program that aids in "nesting" calculations. The goal is to use as little as possible of the sheet metal material in cutting out the necessary parts.

possible to locate terminals further away, CAD and CAM capabilities became more widely used in the remote locations of large corporations.

The advent of personal computers, (*q.v.*), workstations, and supercomputers (*q.v.*) has broadened the way that CAD/CAM capabilities can be delivered. Applications are now available on every type of hardware, with the specific type of application varying depending on the computing power and sophistication of the graphics device.

The performance of personal computers has increased significantly, both in processor performance and in graphics capability; thus a generation of CAD/CAM packages have been developed for them. PC-based software provide 2-D drafting capabilities, including support of production-quality plotters. Emerging versions of PC-based software include 3-D design capabilities and manufacturing functions for generating machine tool programs. The software is available through personal computer retail outlets, making the advantages of CAD/CAM software available to a larger audience.

The technical workstation provides sufficient computing and graphics to make almost any design, manufacturing, or analysis software available on "desk-top" hardware. With the computing power available and the use of the Unix operating system (*q.v.*) on workstations, most CAD/CAM software developers have made their products available on these platforms. Hardware vendors have improved software performance through the development of graphics capabilities that increase drawing performance, the ability to display realistic shaded images with minimal impact on the compute engine in the workstation, and tools for the development of improved user interfaces. The work in realistic image "rendering" has often reduced the need for the manufacture of mockup or prototype parts, since the rendered image, with its shading, shadows, and texturing to represent different material types and surface finishes has achieved new levels of realism (*see* COMPUTER GRAPHICS). While the technical workstation became the hardware of choice for CAD/CAM systems during the late 1980s in most large industrial companies, the increasing power of personal computers in the 1990s are blurring the differences between PCs and workstations, both in raw computing power and the software that is available.

Supercomputers have emerged as tools for the analysis of complex physical systems. Uses have included the stress analysis of modern aircraft and automobiles, the analysis of internal combustion engine behavior, and the simulation of the crash-worthiness of aircraft and automobiles. This analysis is done based on the design of the parts, subassemblies, and systems described by the CAD/CAM database.

Applications need to exchange data, no matter what available hardware types are being used. Most CAD/CAM implementations employ a local area network (LAN - *q.v.*) to connect systems, allowing data sharing between personal computers, workstations, and large processors. The role of large mainframe systems continues in many implementations, largely as networked data storage and analysis nodes. These LANs are based on internationally recognized standards in order to encourage widespread data sharing and use throughout an organization. To enhance data sharing, many CAD/CAM packages allow user-written packages to access the database.

Software Common to all CAD/CAM software are the functions to store and manipulate the geometric data, or model of the part or assembly. The area of geometric modeling continues to be an area of intense development and study in an effort to define better all aspects of the object being modeled.

Initial CAD/CAM models grew from 2-D systems representing drawings to 3-D systems representing objects defined by lines, curves, circles, and points located in 3-D space. Actual surfaces on the part were defined in second generation systems in the 1970s; the surfaces allowed the design and manufacturing of more complex shapes as the CAD/CAM data was used to model smooth-flowing surfaces where accuracy was critical (see Fig. 2). The plastics-forming industry has made wide use of surfaces in the definition of aesthetically pleasing shapes and the construction of molds for their manufacture; the common desk telephone handset is a good example. See Fig. 10 (color insert page, CP-2) for another example.

Designing with solid shapes has always been attractive due to the ability of solids to define an object unambiguously and to present a complete definition of the outside surfaces used in manufacturing operations. The drawbacks of solid-based modeling systems have been the large amount of computing resources it requires and the inability to represent free-form surfaces such as those used in automotive body-panel design. With the advent of high-powered technical workstations, sufficient computing power is available, allowing solids that model systems to respond more quickly to user commands. Improvements in solids modeling techniques has allowed general surfaces to be supported, greatly increasing the types of objects that can be modeled quickly (see Figs. 3 and 4).

One advantage of a solids modeling system is the wide range of analysis programs that can be used in conjunction with the model data; common analyses include mass calculations and structural analysis. While these analyses can be done on selected models developed with surfaces, a solids model is assured to always be "well-behaved," since it is unambiguous with regard to shape and behavior. Rendering applications provided by many solids modeling systems realistically display the modeled object, with the various materials displayed with reflective parameters matching that of the metal, plastic, or surface finish used on the actual part.

Further improvements to the design process are being obtained through the use of feature-based and constraint-based modeling systems. Usually based on solids modelers, feature-based systems help in the design of standard features in parts. The nature of the features will depend on the industry of the user, but could involve standard hole sizes, specific threads on threaded parts, or standard configurations for machined pockets in an airframe structural part. By using standard features, modular manufacturing processes can be employed, improv-

ing the quality of design and the quality of the manufactured result.

There is a trend toward even tighter ties between CAD and CAM, because systems are starting to incorporate aids to enforce rules of manufacturability during the design process. These aids are inspired by artificial intelligence (q.v.) work in expert systems (q.v.). These systems ensure that manufacturing constraints are not violated, that parts can be produced by an organization with the tools it has on hand, and that classes of products can be designed once, with parameters distinguishing the individual particular members of the classes. These programs, termed constraint-based modelers, allow designs to be optimized for specific parameters. For example, a part could be designed to optimize the strength of a specific feature while minimizing part weight. Typically, the constraints are given a priority and the CAD/CAM system assists in the design of the part based on selected features required in the design.

Using CAD/CAM Data In Applications Many applications that use CAD/CAM data have introduced model-based tools in new areas of a firm. Use by people who had never before been exposed to CAD/CAM systems put special requirements on the user interface (q.v.) of the design tools. In the past, a relatively small group of designers worked with the CAD/CAM packages, and extensive training was available to help users become expert in system use. As the use of CAD/CAM systems grew, less frequent users found a need to use the systems—users who could not justify extensive training in system use. This was especially true of those systems sold through retail outlets for the personal computer market. Modern systems are increasingly easy to use, through the use of windows and pop-up menus on technical workstations and the inclusion of on-line help facilities, all in an effort to encourage additional CAD/CAM use.

The importance of CAD/CAM has increased because the use of the model data has gone beyond its original use as a record of the design. Many applications have been developed that enhance the functions that can be done by the basic system, allowing the CAD/CAM database to be used across many functional areas in the design, manufacturing, and assembly processes.

NC Applications The use of CAD data to program NC machines was one of the first manufacturing application areas. This area of activity was pioneered by the aerospace industry, using the Automatically Programmed Tool (APT) language. This is a language used to describe the operations and path of a machine tool or NC lathe in the cutting of a part from a piece of stock. Modern CAM software allows the cutter path to be programmed, using graphic aids without the use of a separate language. With increased use of surface and solid models, artificial intelligence methods are used to develop manufacturing programs with minimal user involvement. These techniques are based on the recognition of features in the object, such as drilled holes, machined pockets, and specified tolerances; the features require specific operations, which are automatically invoked.

Plastic Forming With the increased use of plastics in many products and the use of structural plastics to replace metal parts in many load-bearing structures, the design of the molds used in plastic forming has become a frequent task for CAD/CAM systems (see Fig. 10). Previously, sample molds were constructed and tested to see if the part was properly formed with a consistent thickness and structural integrity. Using applications that are a modification of structural analysis applications previously developed, many companies are able to bypass the development and testing of prototype molds. These analysis applications use the CAD/CAM data and evaluate the effectiveness of the mold in distributing the liquid plastic throughout the mold, the time required to mold a part, and the optimum temperature and cool-down period required. The advantage to the user is reduced cost by eliminating the prototype testing and redesign process.

Assemblies The initial use of CAD/CAM systems concentrated on the modeling of individual objects. In almost all cases, these individual objects are part of larger assemblies, made up of a number of objects of different materials, often from different designers and manufacturers. The assembly of a first prototype can involve time-consuming (and therefore expensive) fitting and adjustment of these individual parts so that they can become part of a more complex assembly. This problem is compounded when the assembly involves complex motions at high speeds or high stress levels, such as the paper handling mechanism in a copier or the steering and suspension of a front-wheel drive automobile. Assembly modeling lessens redesign and improves the performance of the assembly, while reducing the need for prototype test fitting. In addition, by identifying parts that make up an assembly while they are being designed, complete bill of materials processing can be performed, which later produces benefits in purchasing and scheduling. A number of companies have taken the assemblies capabilities even further, using them to simulate field service operations, thus improving the serviceability of the products.

Allied Applications Many other application areas use the computer graphics foundation of CAD/CAM systems for visualization of complex shapes and intricate designs. Examples include the analysis of the motions of robots, movement through a mechanism or building by moving the viewing point through the model, creation of animated motion sequences to illustrate maintenance or service operations, and even the creation of movie sequences for popular consumption or for training purposes. Continuing improvement in both hardware and software will make these more realistic and less expensive.

References

1988. Farin, Gerald. *Curves and Surfaces for Computer Aided Design—A Practical Guide*. New York: Academic Press.
1988. Mantyla, Martti. *Introduction to Solid Modeling*. Potomac, MD: Computer Science Press.
1989. Curry, Thomas C. "Updating Design With CAD/CAM," *Machine Design*, **61**, 10 (25 May), 218.
1989. Rogers, David F., and Adams, J. Arlan. *Mathematical Elements for Computer Graphics, 2nd Ed.* New York: McGraw-Hill.
1989. Ward, Fred. "Images for the Computer Age," *National Geographic*, **175**, 6 (June), 718.
1990. Foley, J. D., Van Dam, A., Feiner, S. K. and Hughes, J. F. *Fundamentals of Interactive Computer Graphics, 2nd Ed.* Reading, MA: Addison-Wesley.

BARRY FLACHSBART, DAVID SHUEY, AND GEORGE PETERS

COMPUTER-AIDED ENGINEERING (CAE)

For articles on related subjects *see* COMPUTER-AIDED DESIGN/COMPUTER-AIDED MANUFACTURING; COMPUTER-INTEGRATED MANUFACTURING; FINITE ELEMENT METHOD; and ROBOTICS.

Introduction The abbreviation CAE stands for *computer-aided engineering*, but common usage since the 1980s indicates that when CAE is used by itself it refers in particular to electrical and electronic engineering applications. Mechanical computer-aided engineering is frequently referred to as MCAE.

The goals of applying computer-aided engineering analysis include:

- Improved product quality.
- Improved safety.
- Reduced engineering time, achieved through fewer design iterations.
- Reduced number of prototypes, ultimately leading to the elimination of prototypes in many cases.
- Reduced product cost.

Engineering analyses can be used to evaluate and predict the behavior of new designs, as well as to evaluate the performance of existing designs. Engineers use computers for a number of tasks, including conceptual design, engineering analysis, detailed design, drafting and documentation, and manufacturing design. This article describes the application of computers to engineering analysis.

Historically, engineers analyzed designs by performing calculations by hand or with some computing aid such as a slide rule. They frequently used tabulated mathematical functions, approximation methods, and data accumulated from previous experience and physical testing to simplify their analyses. Some analyses were so time-consuming that when done at all they could only be completed for one simplified example. This frequently led to under- and overdesigned systems. In the first case, this created systems that did not work properly or failed outright. In the second case, the systems were more expensive than necessary or too heavy to meet their goals.

History The advent of analog and digital computers provided engineers with systems capable of analyzing designs much more quickly and allowed them to undertake analyses that were previously impractical to attempt. However, early computer systems were too slow and limited in capacity (memory, storage, I/O speed) to handle extremely large or complex systems. While they provided a base for new, more extensive design evaluations, many of the historical problems remained and new problems arose. These included limited access to expensive computing systems and difficulties describing the physical form of designs in a way that computers could work with them. Most early analysis programs used simplified, schematic-like descriptions of the physical system. It was impossible to describe any but the simplest systems geometry within the computing environment.

With the advent of computer-aided design and computer-aided manufacturing (CAD/CAM - *q.v.*) in the early 1970s and the rapid advancements in computer system performance from 1960 to the present, most technological barriers to CAE have fallen. An engineer can now have enough computing power on his or her desk (or next to it) to solve any but the largest of problems. For extremely complex problems, supercomputers (*q.v.*) may be employed.

Engineering *workstations* (*q.v.*) provide extensive computing power with high-resolution, high-speed graphics systems at very reasonable and continually decreasing cost (as little as $10,000 in 1991).

Three broad areas of engineering discipline are supported by CAE: mechanical, civil, and electrical. In a typical situation, an engineer will use a CAD/CAM system to develop a model of a system (be it mechanical, electrical, electromechanical, or otherwise) that is to be analyzed. Other required data, such as a finite element mesh, mechanical properties, and loading, are then developed on or linked to this geometric description of the system. The analysis software is used to analyze this combination of model and related data, with its results presented to the engineer in various forms: tabular, graphical, animation, changes to the geometric model, etc.

Mechanical Engineering Applications

Volume Properties Various volumetric properties can be computed directly for solid and surface models in most CAD/CAM systems. These properties include lengths, areas, and volumes as well as mass, centroid, first and second moments of inertia, and products of inertia. In many CAD systems the results of this analysis can be transferred directly into structural and mechanism analysis applications where they are required as data. A few systems can compute volumetric properties for components consisting of composite materials.

Finite Element Method (FEM) Finite element methods are used to perform several types of engineering analyses. These include:

- Structural analysis of a component's behavior under various kinds of applied loads and supports. Linear static, modal, dynamic, forced response,

and buckling conditions can be analyzed. Special programs also exist for analyzing beam and grid structures, such as those used in building framing, ships, bridges, and other similar systems.
- Thermal analysis of a structure's behavior when it is subjected to heating and cooling.
- Combined structural and thermal analysis.
- Plastic mold and part analysis that examines various factors having to do with mold filling and the shape of the molded part. Mold analyses include plastic flow into the mold and mold cooling. Shrinkage and warpage can be predicted for finished parts.
- Fluid mechanics analysis of the flow of fluids, such as air, water, and lubricants around the surfaces of an object. Pressure, fluid velocity, and other factors can be determined.

In the FEM, a model of a component or assembly (see Fig. 1, color insert page CP-3) is decomposed into discrete pieces called the *finite element mesh*. Loads and supporting constraints are applied at mesh locations. The finite element modeling software creates a series of simultaneous linear equations that relate each mesh element to its neighbors. Very complex problems can be analyzed by solving these simultaneous equations iteratively.

Triangular mesh elements are the easiest to create and analyze and are the most often used, but engineering workstations can process much more complex mesh types, leading to higher accuracy and, in some cases, to more easily defined models. Parts modeled as plates, surface shells, or solid models (see Fig. 2, color insert page CP-3) can be meshed with elements that include two- and three-dimensional triangular and rectangular, parabolic, tetrahedral, quadrilateral, shell, solid, and beam elements. The mesh can be created manually (usually in an interactive mode with the mesh building program) or automatically by the program with manual refinements.

Loading conditions may include point, distributed, torque, hydraulic, and others. Supports can be anchored, free, pin, hinge, slider, and most other kinds of mechanical connections (see Fig. 3, color insert page CP-3).

Several schemes are used to increase finite element analysis (FEA) accuracy and reduce computational requirements. These include *feature suppression* and *adaptive meshing*. In feature suppression, the geometry of a part model that is to be analyzed is simplified by temporarily removing features (holes, bosses, flanges, etc.) that the analyst feels are not going to have an appreciable impact on the overall validity of the FEA results. Since these types of features usually produce highly complex mesh structures that unnecessarily increase the number of simultaneous equations to be solved, their removal shortens the solution process. Adaptive FEM systems automatically refine the mesh definition in areas of detail that contribute to high stress or other qualities or coarsen the mesh in areas of less stress. These refinements provide increased accuracy and shorter processing time, respectively. This process is done as a closed-loop—analyze the object, refine the mesh, analyze, refine, etc.—until the results converge to a user-defined tolerance. A few systems offer design optimization, in which the results of the analysis are used to modify the geometric model automatically in order to match a design goal such as, for example, obtaining the lowest weight that will withstand the specified loading conditions at a particular safety factor.

Both standalone FEM/FEA systems and CAD/CAM systems support simulation and display of results. A typical display for a structural analysis might show the geometric model overlaid with stress contours, with color indicating the magnitude of the stress (see Fig. 4, color insert page CP-3). Another type of display frequently used is an animated view of the model as it deforms under cyclical loading. These types of display can be combined to produce simulations that are relatively easy for the engineer to understand, making the reading of large tables of stress values unnecessary.

Mechanism Analysis   Mechanism analysis studies the behavior of mechanical systems undergoing motion. These systems may be comprised of rigid and flexible parts and their interconnections. Typically, the geometry, mass, inertia, compliance, stiffness, and damping of the system's components as well as the forces and loads applied from outside the system must be defined. Equations of motion are developed and solved. The results of the analysis may include positions, velocities, accelerations, forces (applied, reactive, and inertial), determination of equilibrium positions, and other computed parameters. These results can be displayed as tables, charts and graphs, overlayed drawings of position vs. time, and animations (see Figs. 5 and 6, color insert page CP-3). Historically, analyzing systems of rigid bodies undergoing large-amplitude motions was impractical. Early computerized systems could handle rigid body motions involving large-amplitude rotations and translations in two dimensions. Current systems are capable of kinematic, static, and dynamic analysis of three-dimensional rigid and flexible bodies undergoing large displacements and coupled rotations and translations.

Mechanism analysis programs can accept geometric data from FEM/FEA programs, analyze the motion of a system, and return appropriate loading and force data to the FEA program for use in determining component deflections. Mechanism analysis can also be linked to control system design and analysis. The control system's responses to mechanism behavior can be programmed and fed back to control the mechanism's reaction. Control system modeling coupled with the ability of engineering workstations to compute and display real-time animation make it possible to simulate mechanisms such as robots and workcells (*see* ROBOTICS).

Human-machine interactions can be analyzed using mechanism models of the human body. The physical characteristics of the human body model can be varied according to population statistics for height, weight, age, and gender. Android models are now being used to analyze vehicles, machine tools, and other systems in which a human is an integral part of normal operation.

Rapid Prototyping   Rapid prototyping is a recently developed technology that allows a special machine tool to produce physical prototypes of very complex objects. Although several technologies are now used for this process, stereo lithography was the first and remains popular. In stereo lithography, the prototype is built up in thin layers by slicing the geometric model into cross-sections and using a computer-driven laser to harden layer upon layer of a polymer solution, each in the shape of a particular cross-section. These models are used to evaluate the appearance of the designed part and to verify its fit with other parts and its manufacturability. A few rapid prototyping systems are being evaluated as low-quantity manufacturing systems.

Civil Engineering Applications   Most of the analysis tools mentioned are also used in the field of civil engineering. However, a few special areas exist that do not have direct counterparts in mechanical engineering. These include surveying, earthworks, piping, and mapping.

In the area of piping plant design, structural engineers use systems similar to those used by mechanical engineers. In roadway design, cut-and-fill and other earth moving computations are done in combination with digital terrain mapping. Most surveying functions, such as triangulation and elevation computations, are now computerized, with data being collected in computer form in the field via electronic instruments. Map making and analysis are also largely computerized.

Electrical/Electronic Engineering Applications   Electrical and electronic engineering applications use some structural and thermal analyses, as described above; however, this discipline uses many specialized analyses for circuit design, VLSI device design, and simulation (*q.v.*). A few of the major mechanical CAD/CAM systems have some electrical CAD capabilities, but electronic CAD (E-CAD) products are the best choice for electrical/electronic analysis. Many types of electrical analog, digital, and mixed devices can be simulated. Simulations allow design engineers to test a design for a circuit board, VLSI chip, or other electrical device before it is committed to manufacturing. In some cases the computer simulation will supplant altogether the building of a prototype. Available analyses include gate level, switching, electrical level, analog-to-digital conversion, statistical (worst case), and sensitivity-based simulations. Control systems that combine electrical and mechanical or hydraulic controls can also be simulated. Other electrical analyses examine transient waveforms and signal frequency response to determine signal characteristics, such as bandwidth and rise and fall times; analyze interference between parallel traces on printed circuit boards; and determine cooling and flow requirements in forced convection systems.

E-CAD systems provide libraries of standard electrical components, including their physical characteristics as well as performance criteria and specifications. The use of these standard-parts libraries greatly simplifies the process of setting up a simulation.

Technological Trends The conceptual design loop is still not completely computerized. At this time, very few computer products are able to couple both the CAD geometric modeling and engineering analysis functions required to develop engineering concepts rapidly and easily. Detailers and draftsmen remain in the process because it is too difficult for engineers to develop sufficiently detailed models in most current CAD systems. This situation is beginning to change with the introduction of a few engineering workbench systems that are specifically tailored to create solid models easily and feed those models directly into structural and mechanisms analyses, with the results immediately available to the designer. This will allow engineers to create better developed designs without the costs incurred today.

Manufacturing engineers remain outside the early design loop. To appreciate the advantages of CAE most fully, manufacturing processes and their effects on the product (such as warpage from machining and structural integrity for clamping and handling) must be analyzed before the design reaches the detailed layout stage. As mentioned, a few systems are beginning to provide conceptual design tools coupled with sophisticated but simplified analysis tools that can be used by design engineers and manufacturing engineers, without the need for the design to be fully detailed.

Developments in parallel-processing (*q.v.*) computer architectures will bring additional power to the engineer's desktop. Many of the analysis techniques used today (most notably FEM) are good candidates for parallel processing. Faster processing will reduce the design cycle and/or allow additional design iterations, resulting in improved products.

More integration between disciplines is to be expected. In particular, several products now combine the electrical/electronic and the mechanical aspects of design and analysis.

References

1980. Timmer, H. G. and Stern, J. M. "Computation of Global Geometric Properties of Solid Objects," *Computer-Aided Design,*, **12**, *6*, 301–304.

1982. Huebner, K. H. and Thornton, E. A. *The Finite Element Method for Engineers*, 2nd Ed. New York: John Wiley.

1984. Chace, M. A. "Methods and Experience in Computer Aided Design of Large-Displacement Mechanical Systems," *Computer-Aided Analysis and Optimization of Mechanical System Dynamics*, NATO ASI Series, **F9**, Berlin: Springer-Verlag.

1984. Erdman, A. G. and Sandor, G. N. *Mechanism Design: Analysis and Synthesis*, **1**, Englewood Cliffs, NJ,: Prentice-Hall.

1988. Turner, P. R. and Bodner, M. E. "Optimization and Synthesis for Mechanism Design," Paper MS88-711, Proceedings of the Society of Manufacturing Engineers AUTOFACT 88 Conference and Exposition (October), Chicago, IL.

1989. Sapidis, N. and Perucchio, R. "Advanced Techniques for Automatic Finite Element Meshing from Solid Models," *Computer-Aided Design*, **21**, *4*, 248–253.

1991. Zeid, I. *CAD/CAM Theory and Practice*. New York: McGraw-Hill.

JOHN MACKRELL AND BERTRAM HERZOG

COMPUTER-AIDED MANUFACTURING. *See* AUTOMATION; COMPUTER-AIDED DESIGN/COMPUTER-AIDED MANUFACTURING; and COMPUTER-INTEGRATED MANUFACTURING.

COMPUTER-AIDED SOFTWARE ENGINEERING (CASE)

For articles on related subjects *see* SOFTWARE CONFIGURATION MANAGEMENT; SOFTWARE ENGINEERING, SOFTWARE FLEXIBILITY; SOFTWARE MAINTENANCE; SOFTWARE MANAGEMENT; SOFTWARE MONITOR; SOFTWARE PERSONALIZATION; SOFTWARE PROTOTYPING, SOFTWARE RELIABILITY, SOFTWARE REUSABILITY; and SOFTWARE TESTING.

CASE is an acronym for computer-aided software engineering. The purpose of CASE is to provide software engineers with tools that help them specify functional requirements and designs for software projects. The goal of CASE technology is to separate an application program's design from its coded implementation, and to automate the generation of software that is based on a design built with CASE tools (Fisher, 1988).

Structured methodologies for software engineering include, in general, structured analysis, structured design, structured programming (*q.v.*) , structured reviews, and structured testing. Together, these methods help the software engineer take a disciplined approach to building the system. At present, the main technologies associated with CASE, in particular, are structured analysis and structured design.

Structured methodologies are an attempt to replace undisciplined approaches to programming that had become entrenched in the culture. There was a time when one programmer did everything and hence tended not to document code very thoroughly. In this way, he or she created a mystique that evoked an aura of indispensability. The work tended to a low level of abstraction that made maintenance and enhancement very difficult. This was a successful approach in many ways, as much software was produced and used. However, there are many problems that managers have that are not addressed by this approach: it usually took much longer than expected to finish the project; costs ran higher than expected; it was difficult to measure project progress; and errors appeared after the software had been delivered to the customer.

CASE tools support structured methodologies and range from those that are clearly technical and logical extensions of existing compiler and support environment techniques to those that attempt to deal with many of the "softer" issues of system development, such as tracing customer requirements and design decisions. Fig. 1 shows the many levels of system development for which there now exist structured development methodologies and CASE tools.

Other tools that contribute to the CASE toolbox include general purpose tools for desktop publishing (*q.v.*),

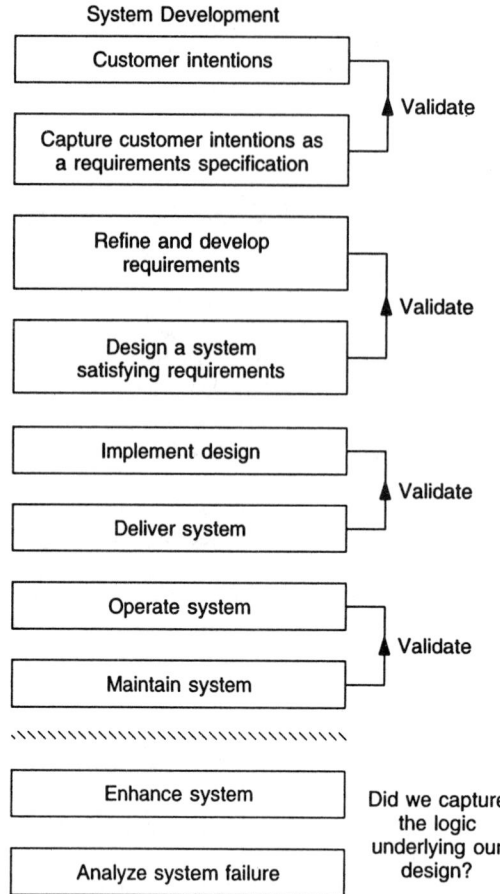

FIG. 1.   System design as supported through Computer-Aided Software Engineering (CASE).

coding and debugging, project and configuration management, prototyping and simulation, and communication and documentation.

Software quality assurance (SQA) should be applied throughout the development process. Some of the indicators of quality are correctness, reliability, testability, maintainability, portability (*q.v.*), and reuseability.

Before it is possible to implement CASE, a framework for that implementation must exist (Pressman 1988). This involves an assessment of the organizational needs and goals followed by the education of the software engineers and management. After this stage, a tool or set of tools must be selected with regard to how they will help the organization achieve its goals more easily. These must then be installed and evaluated against the requirements, and tuned or replaced as necessary. This is not a once-only process, but must be applied with feedback at each stage and reviewed and revised until it is satisfactory to all concerned.

In summary, CASE is an attempt to support modern software engineering methodologies through computer-based tools. These tools provide good person-computer interfaces to existing methodologies, such as a graphics interface for the design and keeping track of changes in the design. They may also keep track of relationships between different variables, such as data and users, and will support software design, simulation, implementation, testing, debugging, enhancement, and maintenance activities. CASE technology is an example of the evolution of problem-oriented programming languages (*q.v.*) into higher-level forms, using software to develop software that is well-organized and easy to understand and modify.

References

1979. Crosby, P. *Quality Is Free.* New York: McGraw-Hill.

1987. Pressman, R. S. *Software Engineering: A Practitioner's Approach.* New York: McGraw-Hill.

1988. Fisher, A. S. *CASE: Using Software Development Tools.* New York: John Wiley.

1988. Pressman, R. S. *Making Software Engineering Happen.* Englewood Cliffs, NJ: Prentice-Hall.

Mildred L. G. Shaw

COMPUTER ALGEBRA

PRINCIPLES

For an article on a related subject *see* SYMBOL MANIPULA-
TION.

Computer algebra is a branch of scientific computation. There are several characteristic features that distinguish computer algebra from numerical analysis (*q.v.*),
the other principal branch of scientific computation. (1)
Computer algebra involves computation in algebraic
structures, such as finitely presented groups, polynomial
rings, rational function fields, algebraic and transcendental extensions of the rational numbers, or differential and
difference fields. (2) Computer algebra manipulates formulas. Whereas in numerical computation the input and
output of algorithms are basically (integer or floating
point) numbers, the input and output of computer algebra algorithms are generally formulas. So, typically, instead of computing

$$\int_0^{1/2} \frac{x}{x^2 - 1} dx = -0.1438... ,$$

an integration algorithm in computer algebra yields

$$\int \frac{x}{x^2 - 1} dx = \frac{\ln |x^2 - 1|}{2}.$$

(3) Computations in computer algebra are carried
through exactly (i.e. no approximations are applied at any
step). So, typically, the solutions of a system of algebraic
equations such as

$$x^4 + 2x^2 y^2 + 3x y^2 + y^4 - y^3 = 0$$
$$x^2 + y^2 - 1 = 0$$

are presented as $(0,1),(\pm\sqrt{3/4}, -1/2)$, instead of
$(0,1),(\pm 0.86602\cdots, -0.5)$. Because of the exact nature of
the computations in computer algebra, decision procedures can be derived from such algorithms that decide,
for example, the solvability of systems of algebraic equations, the solvability of integration problems in a specified
class of formulas, or the validity of geometric formulas.

Applications of Computer Algebra

The Piano Movers Problem   Many problems in robotics
(*q.v.*) can be modelled by the piano movers problem:
finding a path that will take a given body B from a given
initial position to a desired final position. The additional
constraint is that along the path the body should not hit
any obstacles, such as walls or other bodies. A simple
example in the plane is shown in Fig. 1. The initial and final
positions of the body B are drawn in full, whereas a
possible intermediate position is drawn in dotted lines.
J. T. Schwartz and M. Sharir have shown how to reduce

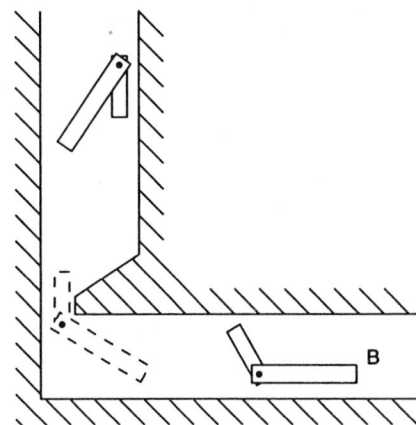

FIG. 1.

this problem to a certain problem about semialgebraic
sets that can be solved by Collins' cylindrical algebraic
decomposition (cad) method.

Semialgebraic sets are subsets of a real m-dimen-
sional space R^m that can be cut out by polynomial equations and inequalities. That is, start with simple sets of the
form

$$\{(x_1...,x_m) \mid p(x_1,...,x_m) = 0\} \text{ or } \{(x_1,...,x_m) \mid q(x_1,...,x_m) > 0\},$$

where p, q are polynomials with real coefficients, and
allow the construction of more complicated sets by
means of intersection, union, and difference. Any subset
of R^m that can be defined in this way is called a *semialgebraic set*.

Consider a two-dimensional problem, as in Fig. 1.
Starting from some fixed position of the body B (say P at
the origin, where P is the point at which the parts of B are
joined together) in R^2, obtain an arbitrary position of B by
applying a rotation T_1 to part B_2, a rotation T_2 to B, and
afterwards a translation T_3 to B (Fig. 2). Since T_1, T_2 can be
described by 2×2–matrices and T_3 by a vector of length
2, any such position of B can be specified by 10 coefficients (i.e. a point in R^{10}). Some of these possible positions are illegal, since the body B would intersect or lie
outside of the boundaries. If the legal positions $L(\subset R^{10})$
can be described by polynomial equations and inequalities then L is a semialgebraic set.

The piano movers problem is now reduced to the
question of whether two points P_1, P_2 in L can be joined by
a path in L (i.e. whether P_1 and P_2 lie in the same connected component of L). This question can be decided by
Collins' cad method, which makes heavy use of computer
algebra algorithms. In particular, the cad method uses
algorithms for greatest common divisors of polynomials,
factorization of polynomials into square-free factors, resultant computations, and isolation of real roots of polynomials.

Algorithmic Methods in Geometry   Often, a geometric
statement can be described by polynomial equations over
some ground field K, such as the real or complex numbers.
Consider, for instance, the statement *"The altitude pedal of*

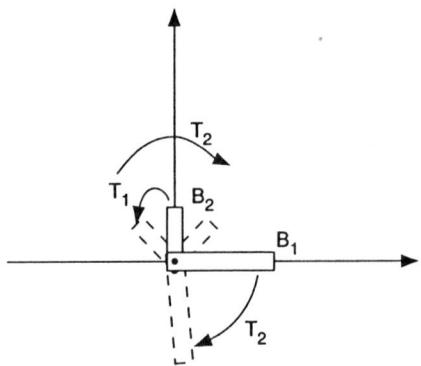

FIG. 2.

the hypotenuse of a right-angled triangle and the midpoints of the three sides of the triangle lie on a circle" (Fig. 3).

Once the geometric figure is placed into a coordinate system, it can be described by polynomial equations. For instance, the fact that E is the midpoint of the side AC is expressed by the equation $2y_3 - y_1 = 0$; the fact that the line segments EM and FM are of equal length is expressed by the equation $(y_7 - y_3)^2 + y_8^2 - (y_7 - y_4)^2 - (y_8 - y_5)^2 = 0$; and so on. In this way, the system $h_1 = \ldots = h_m = 0$ of polynomial equations in the indeterminates $y_1, \ldots, y_n$ determines the geometric figure. Call these polynomials the *hypothesis polynomials*. The equation $(y_7 - y_3)^2 + y_8^2 - (y_7 - y_9)^2 - (y_6 - y_{10})^2 = 0$ then states that the line segments HM and EM are also of equal length. Call this polynomial the *conclusion polynomial*.

The problem of proving the geometric statement is now reduced to the problem of proving that every common solution of the hypothesis polynomials (i.e. every valid geometric configuration) also solves the conclusion polynomial (i.e. the statements is valid for the configuration). Various computer algebra methods can be used for proving such geometry statements. Wu Wen-tsun has given a method using characteristic sets of polynomials; Kutzler and Stifter and Kapur have used Gröbner bases. The underlying computer algebra algorithms for these methods are mainly the solution of systems of polynomial equations, various decision algorithms in the theory of polynomial ideals, and algorithms for computing in algebraic extensions of the field of rational numbers.

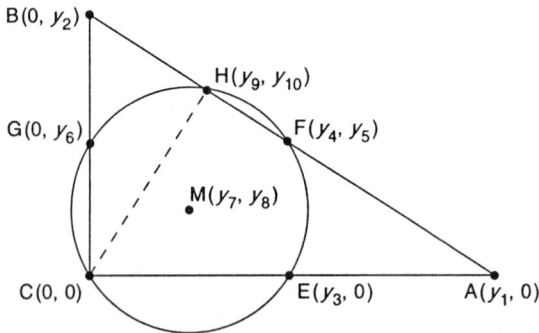

FIG. 3.

Modeling in Science and Engineering In science and engineering, it is common to express a problem in terms of integrals or differential equations with boundary conditions. Numerical integration leads to approximations of the values of the solution functions. But, as R. W. Hamming has written, "the purpose of computing is insight, not numbers." So, instead of computing tables of values, it would be much more gratifying to derive formulas for the solution functions. Computer algebra algorithms can do just that for certain classes of integration and differential equation problems.

Consider, for example, the system of differential equations

$$-6\frac{dq}{dx}(x) + \frac{d^2p}{dx^2}(x) - 6\sin(x) = 0,$$

$$6\frac{d^2q}{dx^2}(x) + a^2\frac{dp}{dx}(x) - 6\cos(x) = 0$$

subject to the boundary conditions $p(0) = 0$, $q(0) = 1$, $p'(0) = 0$, $q'(0) = 0$. Given this information as input, any of the major computer algebra systems will derive the formal solution

$$p(x) = -\frac{12\sin(ax)}{a(a^2-1)} - \frac{6\cos(ax)}{a^2} + \frac{12\sin(x)}{a^2-1} + \frac{6}{a^2},$$

$$q(x) = \frac{\sin(ax)}{a} - \frac{2\cos(ax)}{a^2-1} + \frac{(a^2+1)\cos(x)}{a^2-1}$$

for $a \notin \{-1, 0, 1\}$.

Some Algorithms in Computer Algebra Since computer algebra algorithms must yield exact results, these algorithms use integers and rational numbers as coefficients of algebraic expressions because these numbers can be represented exactly in the computer. Coefficients may also be algebraic.

Addition or subtraction of integers is quite straightforward, and these operations can be performed in time linear in the length of the numbers. The classical algorithm for multiplication of integers x and y proceeds by multiplying every digit of x by every digit of y and adding the results after appropriate shifts. This clearly takes time quadratic in the length of the inputs. A faster multiplication algorithm due to A. Karatsuba and Yu. Ofman is usually called the *Karatsuba algorithm*. The basic idea is to cut the two inputs x, y of length $\leq n$ into pieces of length $\leq n/2$ such that

$$x = a \cdot \beta^{n/2} + b, \quad y = c \cdot \beta^{n/2} + d,$$

where β is the basis of the number system. A usual divide-and-conquer approach would reduce the multiplication of two integers of length n to four multiplications of integers of length $n/2$ and some subsequent shifts and additions. The complexity of this algorithm would still be quadratic in n. However, from

$$x \cdot y = ac\beta^n + ((a + b)(c + d) - ac - bd)\beta^{n/2} + bd$$

we see that one of the four multiplications can be replaced by additions and shifts, which take only linear time. If this reduction of the problem is applied recursively, we get a multiplication algorithm with a time complexity proportional to $n^{\log_2 3}$. This is still not the best we can hope for. In fact, the fastest known algorithm is due to Schönhage and Strassen and its complexity is proportional to $n(\log n)(\log \log n)$. However, the overhead of this algorithm is enormous, and it pays off only if the numbers are incredibly large.

Polynomial arithmetic with coefficients in a field, like the rational numbers, presents no problem. These polynomials form a Euclidean domain, so we can carry out division with quotient and remainder. Often, however, we need to work with polynomials whose coefficients lie in an integral domain like the integers. Addition, subtraction, and multiplication are again obvious, but division with quotient and remainder is not possible. Fortunately, we can replace division by a similar process, called pseudo-division. If $a(x) = a_m x^m + \cdots + a_1 x + a_0$ and $b(x) = b_n x^n + \cdots + b_1 x + b_0$, with $m \geq n$, then there exists a unique pair of quotient $q(x)$ and remainder $r(x)$ such that $b_n^{m-n+1} \cdot a(x) = q(x) b(x) + r(x)$ where either r is the zero polynomial or the degree of r is less than the degree of b.

Good algorithms are needed for computing the *greatest common divisor* (gcd) of polynomials. If we are working with polynomials over a field, we can use Euclid's algorithm, which takes two polynomials $f_1(x)$, $f_2(x)$ and computes a chain of remainders $f_3(x),\dots,f_k(x), f_{k+1}(x) = 0$, such that f_i is the remainder in dividing f_{i-2} by f_{i-1}. Then $f_k(x)$ is the desired greatest common divisor. For polynomials over the integers we can replace division by pseudo-division, and the Euclidean algorithm still works. The problem, however, is that, although the inputs and the final result might be quite small, the intermediate polynomials can have huge coefficients. This problem becomes even more pronounced if we deal with multivariate polynomials. As an example, consider the computation of the greatest common divisor of two bivariate polynomials

$$f(x,y) = y^6 + xy^5 + x^3 y - xy + x^4 - x^2,$$
$$g(x,y) = xy^5 - 2y^5 + x^2 y^4 - 2xy^4 + xy^2 + xy$$

with integral coefficients. Consider y to be the main variable, so that the coefficients of powers of y are polynomials in x. Euclid's algorithm yields the polynomial remainder sequence

$r_0 = f,$

$r_1 = g,$

$r_2 = (2x - x^2)y^3 + (2x^2 - x^3)y^2 + (x^5 - 4x^4 + 3x^3 + 4x^2 - 4x)y + x^6 - 4x^5 - 3x^4 + 4x^3 - 4x^2,$

$r_3 = (-x^7 + 6x^6 - 12x^5 + 8x^4)y^2 + (-x^{13} + 12x^{12} - 58x^{11} + 136x^{10} - 121x^9 - 117x^8 + 362x^7 - 236x^6 - 104x^5 + 192x^4 - 64x^3)y - x^{14} + 12x^{13} - 58x^{12} - 136x^{11} - 121x^{10} - 116x^9 + 356x^8 - 224x^7 - 112x^6 + 192x^5 - 64x^4,$

$r_4 = (-x^{28} + 26x^{27} - 308x^{26} + 2184x^{25} - 10198x^{24} + 32188x^{23} - 65932x^{22} + 68536x^{21} + 42431x^{20} - 274533x^{19} + 411512x^{18} - 149025x^{17} - 431200x^{16} + 729296x^{15} - 337472x^{14} - 318304x^{13} + 523264x^{12} - 225280x^{11} - 78848x^{10} + 126720x^9 - 53248x^8 + 8192x^7)$
$y - x^{29} + 26x^{28} - 308x^{27} + 2184x^{26} - 10198x^{25} + 32188x^{24} - 65932x^{23} + 68536x^{22} + 42431x^{21} - 274533x^{20} + 411512x^{19} - 149025x^{18} - 431200x^{17} + 729296x^{16} - 337472x^{15} - 318304x^{14} - 523264x^{13} - 225280x^{12} - 78848x^{11} + 126720x^{10} - 53248x^9 + 8192x^8.$

The greatest common divisor of f and g is obtained by eliminating common factors $p(x)$ in r_4. The final result is $y + x$. Although the inputs and the output are small, the intermediate expressions get very big. The biggest polynomial in this computation happens to occur in the pseudo-division of r_3 by r_4. The intermediate polynomial has degree 70 in x.

This problem of coefficient growth is ubiquitous in computer algebra, and there are some general approaches for dealing with it. In the special case of polynomial gcd's, we could always make the polynomials *primitive* (i.e. eliminate common factors not depending on the main variable). This approach keeps intermediate remainders as small as possible, but at a high price: many gcd computations on the coefficients. The subresultant gcd algorithm can determine many of the common factors of the coefficients, without ever computing gcd's of coefficients. The remainders stay reasonably small during this algorithm. In fact, in our example the integer coefficients grow only to length 4.

The most efficient algorithm for computing gcd's of multivariate polynomials is the *modular algorithm*. The basic idea is to apply homomorphisms to the coefficients, compute the gcd's of the evaluated polynomials, and use the *Chinese remainder algorithm* to reconstruct the actual coefficients in the gcd. If the input polynomials are univariate, we can take homomorphisms H_p, mapping an integer a to $a \bmod p$. If the input polynomials are multivariate, we can take evaluation homomorphisms of the form $H_{x1=r1}$ for reducing the number of variables. In our example, we get

$$\gcd(H_{x=2}(f), H_{x=2}(g)) = y + 2, \quad \gcd(H_{x=3}(f), H_{x=3}(g)) = y + 3.$$

So the gcd is $y + x$. Never during this algorithm did we have to consider large coefficients.

Decomposing polynomials into irreducible factors is another crucial algorithm in computer algebra. A few decades ago, only rather inefficient techniques for polynomial factorization were available. Research in computer algebra has contributed to a deeper understanding of the problem and, as a result, has created much better algorithms. Let us first consider univariate polynomials with integer coefficients. Since the problem of coefficient growth appears again, one usually maps the polynomial

$f(x)$ to a polynomial $f_{(p)}(x)$ by applying a homomorphism H_p, p a prime. $f_{(p)}$ can now be factored by the *Berlekamp algorithm*, which involves some linear algebra and computations of gcd's. Conceivably, we could factor f modulo various primes $p_1, ..., p_k$ and try to reconstruct the factors over the integers by the Chinese remainder algorithm, as we did in the modular gcd algorithm. The problem is that we do not know which factors correspond. So instead, one uses a *p*-adic approach based on *Hensel's lemma*, which states that a factorization of f modulo a prime p can be lifted to a factorization of f modulo p^k, for any positive integer k. Since we know bounds for the size of the coefficients that can occur in the factors, we can determine a suitable k and thus construct the correct coefficients of the integral factors. There is, however, an additional twist. If $f(x)$ can be decomposed into irreducible factors $f_1(x)$, $f_2(x)$ over the integers, it could well be that, modulo p, these irreducible factors can be split even further. So after we have lifted the factorization modulo p to a factorization modulo p^k for a suitable k, we need to try combinations of factors for determining the factors over the integers. For instance, $x^4 + 1$ is a polynomial that is irreducible over the integers, but factors modulo every prime. Theoretically, this final step is the most costly one, and it makes the time complexity of the Berlekamp-Hensel algorithm exponential in the degree of the input. Nevertheless, in practice the algorithm works very well for most examples.

In 1982, Lenstra, Lenstra, and Lovász developed an algorithm for factoring univariate polynomials over the integers with a polynomial time complexity. Kaltofen extended this result to multivariate polynomials. The overhead of this algorithm, however, is extremely high.

To integrate a rational function $A(x)/B(x)$, where A, B are polynomials with integral coefficients, we could split the polynomial B into linear factors in a suitable algebraic extension field, compute a partial fraction decomposition of the integrand, and integrate all the summands in this decomposition. The summands with linear denominators lead to logarithmic parts in the integral. Computations in the splitting field of a polynomial are very expensive; if n is the degree of the polynomial, the necessary algebraic extension has degree $n!$. So the question arises as to whether it is really necessary to go to the full splitting field. For instance,

$$\int \frac{x}{x^2 - 2} dx = \int \frac{\frac{1}{2}}{x - \sqrt{2}} dx + \int \frac{\frac{1}{2}}{x + \sqrt{2}} dx =$$
$$\frac{1}{2} [\log (x - \sqrt{2}) + \log (x + \sqrt{2})] = \frac{1}{2} \log(x^2 - 2).$$

The example shows that although we had to compute in the splitting field of the denominator, the algebraic extensions actually disappear in the end. A deeper analysis of the problem reveals that, instead of factoring the denominator into linear factors, it suffices to compute a so-called *square-free factorization*—i.e. a decomposition of a polynomial f into $f = f_1 \cdot f_2^2 \cdots f_r^r$, where the factors f_i are pairwise relatively prime and have no multiple roots (square-free). The square-free factorization can be computed by successive gcd operations. Now if A and B are

relatively prime polynomials over the rational numbers, B is square-free, and the degree of A is less than the degree of B, then

$$\int \frac{A(x)}{B(x)} dx = \sum_{i=1}^{n} c_i \log v_i,$$

where the $c_1, ..., c_n$ are the distinct roots of the resultant of $A(x) - c \cdot B'(x)$ and $B(x)$ w.r.t. x, and each v_i is the gcd of $A(x) - c_i \cdot B'(x)$ and $B(x)$. In this way we get the smallest field extension necessary for expressing the integral.

The problem of integration becomes more complicated if the class of integrands is extended. A very common class is that of elementary functions. We get this class by starting with the rational functions and successively adding exponentials (exp $f(x)$), logarithms (log $f(x)$), or roots of algebraic equations, where the exponents, arguments, or coefficients are previously constructed elementary functions. Not every elementary integrand has an elementary integral (e.g. $\int e^{x^2} dx$ cannot be expressed as an elementary function). However, there is an algorithm (the *Risch algorithm*) that can decide whether a given integrand can be integrated in terms of elementary functions, and if so the Risch algorithm yields the integral. The case of algebraic functions is the most complicated part of the Risch algorithm. For a thorough introduction to the algebraic integration problem, the reader is referred to the paper by M. Bronstein in the *Journal of Symbolic Computation*, Vol. 9.

The discrete analog to the integration problem is the problem of summation in finite terms. We are given an expression for a summand a_n, and we want to compute a closed expression for the partial sums of the infinite series $\sum_{n=1}^{\infty} a_n$. That is, we want to compute a function $S(m)$, such that

$$\sum_{n=1}^{m} a_n = S(m) - S(0).$$

For instance, we want to compute

$$\sum_{n=1}^{m} n \cdot x^n = \frac{mx^{m+2} - (m+1)x^{m+1} + x}{(x-1)^2}.$$

For the case of hypergeometric functions, *Gosper's algorithm* solves this problem. There is also a theory of summation similar to the theory of integration in finite terms.

Gröbner bases are an extremely powerful method for deciding many problems in the theory of polynomial ideals. As an example, consider the system of algebraic equations

$$2x^4 + y^4 + 8x^3 - 3x^2y + 2y^3 + 12x^2 - 6xy + y^2 + 8x - 3y + 2 = 0$$
$$8x^3 + 24x^2 - 6xy + 24x - 6y + 8 = 0$$
$$4y^3 - 3x^2 - 6y^2 - 6x + 2y - 3 = 0 \qquad (1)$$

Every root of these equations is also a root of any linear combination of these equations, so in fact we are looking for zeros of the ideal generated by the left-hand sides in the ring of polynomials in x and y over Q. The left-hand sides form a specific basis of this ideal. The goal is to compute another basis for this same ideal that is better suited for solving the system. Such a basis is a Gröbner basis with respect to a lexicographic ordering of the variables. In our example, we get the following Gröbner basis, which we again write as a system of equations.

$$y^3 - y^2 = 0$$
$$yx + y = 0$$
$$3x^2 + 2y^2 + 6x - 2y + 3 = 0. \qquad (2)$$

The solutions of (1) and (2) are the same, but obviously it is much easier to investigate the solutions of (2). The system contains a polynomial depending only on y, and the zeros are $y = 0$ and $y = 1$. Substituting these values for y into the other two equations, we get the solutions $(x = -1, y = 0)$ and $(x = -1, y = 1)$ for the system of algebraic equations.

Other problems in the theory of polynomial ideals that can be solved by Gröbner bases include the ideal membership problem, the radical membership problem, the primary decomposition of an ideal, or the computation of the dimension of an ideal. Most computer algebra programs contain a Gröbner basis package.

Representation of Expressions Dynamic data structures are necessary for representing the computational objects of computer algebra in the memory of the computer. For instance, during the execution of the Euclidean algorithm, the coefficients in the polynomials expand and shrink again. Since the goal of the computation is an exact result, we cannot just truncate them to the most significant positions.

Most computer algebra programs represent objects as lists. An integer is represented as a list of digits. For more complicated objects, the choice of representation is not that clear. So, for instance, we can represent a bivariate polynomial recursively as a polynomial in a main variable with coefficients in a univariate polynomial ring, or distributively as pairs of coefficients and power products in the variables. For example:

Recursive representation:

$$p(x,y) = (3x^2 - 2x + 1)y^2 + (x^2 - 3x)y + (2x + 1)$$

Distributive representation:

$$p(x,y) = 3x^2y^2 - 2xy^2 + x^2y + y^2 - 3xy + 2x + 1$$

For both these representations, we can use a dense or a sparse list representation. In the dense representation, a polynomial is a list of coefficients, starting from some highest coefficient down to the constant coefficient. So the dense recursive representation of p is

$$((3 \ -2 \ 1) (1 \ -3 \ 0) (2 \ 1))$$

For the dense distributive representation of p, we order the power products according to their degree and lexicographically within the same degree. So p is represented as

$$\begin{pmatrix} 3 & 0 & 0 & 0 & -2 & 1 & 0 & 1 & -3 & 0 & 0 & 2 & 1 \\ x^2y^2 & x^3y & x^4 & y^3 & xy^2 & x^2y & x^3 & y^2 & xy & x^2 & y & x & 1 \end{pmatrix}.$$

If only a few power products have a coefficient different from 0, then a dense representation wastes a lot of space. In this case we really want to represent the polynomial sparsely (i.e. by pairs of coefficients and exponents). The sparse recursive representation of p is

$$((((3 \ 2) (-2 \ 1) (1 \ 0)) \ 2) (((1 \ 2) (-3 \ 1)) \ 1) (((2 \ 1) (1 \ 0)) \ 0)),$$

and the sparse distributive representation of p is

$$((3 \ (2 \ 2)) (-2 \ (1 \ 2)) (1 \ (2 \ 1)) (1 \ (\ 0 \ 2)) (-3 \ (1 \ 1)) (2 \ (1 \ 0)) (1 \ (0 \ 0))).$$

For different algorithms, different representations of the objects are useful or even necessary. The multivariate gcd algorithm works best with polynomials given in recursive representation, whereas the Gröbner basis algorithm needs the input in distributive representation. So, in general, a computer algebra program has to provide many different representations for the various algebraic objects and transformations that convert one form to another.

References

1981. Knuth, D. E. *The Art of Computer Programming, Vol. 2*, 2nd ed. Reading, MA: Addison-Wesley.

1983. Buchberger, B., Collins, G. E., and Loos, R. (eds.). *Computer Algebra— Symbolic and Algebraic Computation*, 2nd ed. Wien-New York: Springer-Verlag.

1985–present. *Journal of Symbolic Computation*. London: Academic Press.

1988. Davenport, J. H., Siret, Y., and Tournier, E. *Computer Algebra— Systems and Algorithms for Algebraic Computation*. London: Academic Press.

1989. Akritas, A. G. *Elements of Computer Algebra*. New York: John Wiley & Sons.

FRANZ WINKLER

SYSTEMS

For articles on related subjects *see* NUMERICAL ANALYSIS; and SYMBOL MANIPULATION.

What Is Computer Algebra? Computer algebra (sometimes called algebraic manipulation or symbolic computation) can be defined to be computation with variables and constants according to the rules of algebra, analysis, and other branches of mathematics, or formula manipulation involving symbols, unknowns, and formal operations, rather than the conventional computer data of numbers and character strings.

The goal of a symbolic computation language is to provide to the large and diverse community of "mathematics users" facilities for general mathematical calculations, typically including facilities such as arithmetic with exact fractions, polynomial and rational function arithmetic, factorization of integers and polynomials, exact solution of linear and polynomial systems of equations, closed forms for summations, simplification of mathematical expressions, and integration of elementary functions. Most languages also allow users to define and use facilities that supplement those primitively available.

The term symbolic computation is too vague to use in this context, since it includes other disciplines, such as text manipulation and most of artificial intelligence. We will restrict our attention to systems that perform *mathematical* manipulations over symbols and not just symbol manipulation.

Computer algebra systems can be classified as being either *general purpose* or *special purpose*. Special purpose computer algebra systems are designed to solve problems in one specific area (e.g. celestial mechanics, general relativity, group theory). As such, special purpose computer algebra systems use special notations and special data structures, and have most of their essential algorithms implemented in the kernel of the system. Such systems will normally excel in their respective areas, but would be of little use in other applications. Examples are *Cayley* for discrete algebraic and combinatorial structures, *Macaulay* for computing in algebraic geometry and commutative algebra or *Pari* intended for number-theoretic computations. We will restrict our attention to general purpose computer algebra systems. A general purpose computer algebra system is designed to cover many diverse application areas and has sufficient data structures, data types, and functions to do so.

Computation Computer algebra systems have the ability to do mathematical computations with unassigned variables. For example,

```
> t := x^2 * sin(x);
                         2
                    t := x  sin(x)
< diff(t,x);
                              2
             2 x sin(x) + x  cos(x)
```

computes the derivative of expression *t* with respect to *x*, where *x* is an unassigned variable.

Computer algebra systems have the ability to perform exact computation (e.g. arbitrary precision rational arithmetic, field extensions). For example,

$$\frac{1}{2} + \frac{1}{3} \to \frac{5}{6} \qquad \frac{1}{(\sqrt{2}+1)^3} \to 5\sqrt{2} - 7$$

(as opposed to 0.8333...and 0.07106...).

"Computation" in a computer algebra system requires a much more careful definition than in other languages. For example, compare the Pascal statement x := a/b with the Maple statement f := int(*expr*, x); Provided that $b \neq 0$, the division a/b will produce a result (a floating point number) of a predictable size and in a predictable

time. In contradistinction, the statement int(*expr*, x); may

1. Return the integral of the *expr* with respect to *x* (the size of the result is difficult to predict).
2. Return a partial answer (i.e. $f(x) + \int g(x)dx$).
3. May fail to compute because an integral does not exist (e.g. e^{x^3} does not have an integral).
4. May fail to compute because the algorithms used cannot find an integral, even though one exists.
5. May produce a symbolic result that is too long to represent even though it is computable (e.g. $\int \frac{x^{10^7} - 1}{x - 1} \, dx$).
6. May require a *very* long time to compute, making its computation not feasible for practical purposes.

The size of the result generated by the int statement is *not* predictable. This implies dynamic memory management and garbage collection (*q.v.*) for computer algebra systems. This is one of the main reasons why Lisp was used in early systems as an implementation language.

Correctness To some extent, it is surprising that there should be any incorrectness tolerated by a supposedly mathematical symbol manipulation system, and not all are convinced that this is really necessary. However, in most current symbolic computation systems, simplifications such as $\frac{(x+y)}{(x+y)} \to 1$ are performed automatically, without keeping track that *x* must not be equal to $-y$ for this to make sense. This is an example where the compromise is that the system may sometimes make a mistake in order to have efficient simplification which is almost always correct. (Notice that we are not talking about program "bugs," but rather design decisions.) Another example is the automatic simplification of $0 \times f(1000) \to 0$ before evaluation of $f(1000)$. This simplification is "obviously desirable" unless $f(1000)$ is undefined, or infinity. Performing the simplification is an efficiency that is "slightly" incorrect, while always evaluating $f(1000)$ if its value is not known beforehand is something that most users would choose to avoid. Thus, we see that many systems take the point of view that "users will tolerate some degree of deviation from rigorous correctness."

As a further example, probably more serious, of the conflict between correctness and efficiency/usability, consider the following sequence, involving a summation followed by a substitution:

```
e := sum(a[i]*x^i, i = 0..n);
subs(x=0, e);
```

If *n* is an indeterminate when this sequence is executed, the result given by several systems is 0. In contrast, if *n* has the value 5, say, then the result computed by these same systems is (correctly) $a[0]$. Mathematically, we see that the value being assigned to *e* is

```
a[0] + a[1]*x + a[2]*x^2 + ...
```

and when x is replaced by the value 0, we would expect the result to be $a[0]$ (if n is to be a nonnegative integer). However, in the case where n is an indeterminate, the system represents the call to the "sum" function as an unevaluated function and when x is replaced by the value 0, the simplifications

```
0^i -> 0
a[i]*0 -> 0
```

result in the summation

```
sum(0, i = 0..n)
```

which then simplifies to 0. It can be seen that the simplification $0^i \ -> 0$ is mathematically correct only if i is restricted to be positive, but the common practice in symbolic computation systems is to apply the rule "blindly." In exactly the same manner, it is common practice to apply the rule

```
x^0 -> 1
```

for any arbitrary expression x, but if x later takes on the value 0, for example, then this simplification may have been erroneous. The user should be aware that *all* systems will perform some simplifications which are not safe 100% of the time.

The Systems In this section, we describe some of the most important languages in more detail. We restrict our attention to either new languages or languages that are widely used. For older languages, such as Camal, Formac, or SAC-I/II, see the 2nd edition of this Encyclopedia.

All the systems that we describe are interactive general purpose computer algebra systems that provide the following three key areas:

- *Symbolic computations*—All systems support routines for expansion and factoring of polynomials, differentiation and integration (definite and indefinite), series computation, solving equations and systems of equations, and linear algebra.
- *Numeric computations*—All systems support arbitrary precision numerical computation, including computation of definite integrals, numerical solutions of equations, and evaluation of elementary and special functions.
- *Graphics*—All systems (except Reduce) allow one to plot two- and three-dimensional graphics.

Additionally, each system has a programming language that allows the user to extend the system.

For other comparisons of computer algebra systems, see Harper, Woof, and Hodgkinson (1989) and Betts (1990).

Macsyma The Macsyma project was founded by William Martin and Joel Moses of M.I.T. Macsyma was built upon a predecessor M.I.T. project, Mathlab 68, an interactive, general purpose system that was the development tool and test bed for several M.I.T. doctoral theses in algebraic manipulation and algorithms.

The Macsyma system internals were first implemented in Maclisp, a systems programming dialect of Lisp developed at M.I.T. For many years, Macsyma was available through the Arpanet on a DEC PDP-10 running the ITS system. However, in the late 1970s and early 1980s, the important features of Maclisp were recreated in Franz Lisp running in the Unix environment. Two similar versions of Macsyma (DOE Macsyma and Symbolics Macsyma) are now supported commercially on VAX Unix or VMS, Sun, PC, Symbolics 3600 systems, etc. The Macsyma kernel is over 75,000 lines of Lisp code. The executable binary file loaded at invocation time is approximately 3.6 megabytes for the Berkeley VAX/Unix version. In addition, there are user-contributed libraries that can be loaded at will. There are about 10,000 lines of Macsyma language programs in the distributed library. Macsyma is a typical algebraic manipulation language in many ways. It provides a Fortran/Algol-like notation for mathematical expressions and programming. Automatic type checking is almost non-existent.

Macsyma users can translate programs into Lisp. This allows interpretation by the Lisp interpreter (instead of the Macsyma language interpreter, which itself is coded in Lisp). The Lisp compiler can then be applied to the translation, to take the further step of compiling the program into machine code.

A user wishing to make any extensions to the functionality of the system (e.g. installing a new kind of mathematical object for which addition or multiplication must still work) must learn Lisp in order to allow its manipulation to proceed as efficiently as the rest of the built-in mathematical code. However, the language allows a large amount of extensibility without recourse to or knowledge of the Lisp internals. For example, the parser/grammar of the Macsyma language can be altered on-the-fly to include new prefix, infix, or "matchfix" operations defined by user-supplied Macsyma programs.

Another feature of Macsyma is its *assume* facility, which allows the user to define properties over the symbols. For example, one can define ASSUME(A>B) and then the system *knows* this relation between A and B. If the user then asks MAX(A,B), the answer is A.

Macsyma makes extensive use of flags for directing the computation; for example, if the flag TRIGEXPAND is set to TRUE, Macsyma will cause full expansion of sines and cosines of sums of angles and of multiple angles occurring in all expressions. There also exist non-binary flags, as for example LHOSPITALLIM, which is the maximum number of times L'Hospital's rule is used in a limit computation.

Reduce Reduce was originally written in Lisp by a team led by Anthony Hearn, to assist symbolic computation in high energy physics in the late 1960s. Its user base grew beyond the particle-physics community as its general-purpose facilities were found to be useful in many other mathematical situations. Reduce 2 was ported to several different machines and operating systems during the 1970s, making it the most widely distributed system of that time, and one of the first efforts in Lisp portability. Reduce 3, written in the dialect of Lisp called "Standard Lisp" is a further refinement and enhancement (Hearn 1983). It consists of about 4MB of Lisp code.

Reduce, like Macsyma, has a simple syntax for the basic mathematical commands (expression evaluation, differentiation, integration, etc.), and a Fortran-like programming language. Its reserved words include not only the keywords of the programming language, but also the names of the various flags that control default simplification and evaluation modes. For example, the reserved word EXP is a flag that when turned OFF, blocks the default expansion of rational function expressions.

Reduce has two programming modes—an "algebraic" mode and a "symbolic" mode. The same syntactic forms for procedure definition, assignment, and control statements are observed in both modes. In algebraic mode, data objects are manipulated through mathematical operations, such as numerical or rational function arithmetic, FACTORIZE (factor a polynomial over the integers), DF (partial differentiation), SUB (substitute an expression for a variable in another variable), or COEFF (find the coefficients of various powers of a variable in an expression). In symbolic mode, one can directly manipulate the internal representation of mathematical expressions, using Lisp-like manipulation primitives such as CAR and CDR, and routines such as LC (find the leading coefficient of a polynomial), . + (add a term to a polynomial). Most casual users of Reduce need to learn only the functionality provided by algebraic mode (programming-in-the-abstract), but since most of the basic system is coded in symbolic mode, programming in symbolic mode is sometimes necessary to augment or borrow from those basic facilities.

Numerical programs often have to be written based on a set of formulas that describe the solution of a problem in science or engineering. For that step, Reduce provides GENTRAN, an automatic code generator and translator. It constructs complete numerical programs based on sets of algorithmic specifications and symbolic expressions. Formatted Fortran, RATFOR, or C code can be generated through a series of interactive commands or under the control of a template processing routine. This package is available in Macsyma, too.

Derive Derive was developed by A. Rich and D. Stoutmeyer and is marketed by Soft Warehouse Inc. in Hawaii. It is also implemented in Lisp. Derive will run on any PC compatible (with 640K) and does not require a math coprocessor.

Derive is the successor to μMath and is menu-driven. Many commands and operations can be carried out with just two or three keystrokes.[1] In addition to μMath, it has a powerful graphics package that can plot functions in two and three dimensions. One can plot more than one function on the same graph and use multiple windows for easy comparisons. Derive supports all the basic symbolic mathematics like factorization, integration, differentiation, etc. It also understands matrices and vectors and can do basic vector calculus. Although Derive is less capable than other general purpose computer algebra systems, the extent of its power based on such minimal hardware is remarkable. Nonetheless, it lacks, for example, procedures for solving systems of nonlinear equations, computation of eigenvectors of matrices,[2] and special features such as Laplace transforms, Fourier transforms, and Bessel functions.[3]

The programming language of Derive provides only the definition of simple functions, which may be recursive. All utility files are programmed in this language.

Mathematica The development of Mathematica was started by Stephen Wolfram in 1986. The first version of the system was released by Wolfram Research, Inc. in 1988. Wolfram had previously developed the SMP computer algebra system in 1979–81, which served as a forerunner of some elements of Mathematica. Mathematica was designed to be a computer algebra system with graphics, numerical computation, and a flexible programming language.

In Mathematica, patterns are used to represent classes of expressions with a given structure. Pattern matching and transformation/rewrite rules greatly simplify the programming of mathematical functions because one need only define replacements for patterns. For example, consider the definition of the logarithm of a product or a power:

```
In[1] := log [x_ y_] := log [x] + log [y]

In[2] := log [x_^y_] := y log[x]
```

where In[k] is the kth input since the beginning of a work session. These definitions are global rules. Such a rule is applied to all expressions automatically if the left-hand side of the rule matches the expression (i.e. the heads are equal and the arguments match). This is in contrast to rewrite rules, which are applied on demand. The notation x_ denotes a pattern that matches anything and is referred to as x in the right-hand side of the rule. The structure of patterns can be very complex. For example, the pattern x:_^n_Integer?Positive matches any expression of the form a^b, where a is any expression and b is a positive integer. The exponent b is then referred to as n, and the complete object is referred to as x. Writing a definition in terms of rules for specific patterns can obviate the need for extensive checking of argument values within the body of a definition. Pattern matching is structural, not mathematical, so b^2 is not recognized as

---

[1] In the examples that follow in later sections, we denote menu options using square brackets. For example, [A]uthor means that the menu option A (Author) is chosen.

[2] Eigenvalues can be computed as roots of the determinant of A − x.I.

[3] One can define a Bessel function as an integral and calculate values, but this definition cannot be used in symbolic calculations.

the product *b b*. However, the pattern matcher recognizes that multiplication is associative:

```
In[3] := f[log [2a b^2] ]
Out[3] := f[log [2] + log [a] + 2 log [b] ]
```

Mathematica's colorful plotting features are very good. It provides two- and three-dimensional graphs, along with the flexibility to rotate and change the viewpoint easily. The plot in Fig. 1 has been generated with the command

```
Plot3D[Sin[x y], {x, 0, 3}, {y, 0, 3},
   Plot Points -> 31. Boxed -> False.
```

Mathematica's kernel consists of about 333,000 lines of C code, and there are about 56,000 lines of Mathematica code in the distributed packages. The basic functionality of Mathematica is built into the kernel or is coded in the Mathematica language in "start-up" packages. A wide variety of applications, such as statistics and Laplace transforms, are coded in Mathematica in "standard" packages that can be read in on request. On the NeXT or Macintosh computers, applications can be in the form of *notebooks*, in which one can mix text, animated graphics, and Mathematica input. This is an excellent tool for education and for the presentation of results.

Maple The Maple project was started by K. Geddes and G. Gonnet at the University of Waterloo in November 1980. It followed from the construction of an experimental system (named "wama") that proved the feasibility of writing a symbolic computation system in system implementation languages and running it in a crowded time-sharing environment.

Maple was designed and implemented to be a pleasant programming language, as well as being compact, efficient, portable, and extensible. The Maple language is reminiscent of Algol 68 (*q.v.*) without declarations, but also includes several functional programming (*q.v.*) paradigms. The internal mathematical libraries are written in the same language that users use. Maple's kernel interprets this language rather efficiently. Most higher level functions or packages, about 95% of the functionality (e.g. integration, solving equations, normalization of expressions, radical simplification, factorization) are coded in the user language. Primitive functions like arithmetic, basic simplification, polynomial division, manipulations of structures, series arithmetic, integer gcds, etc. are coded in the kernel. In principle, the user will not perceive the difference between using internal or external functions. The kernel is implemented in C and consists of 20,000 lines of code. The implementation of external functions uses about 130,000 lines of Maple code.

Maple supports a large collection of specialized data structures: integers, rationals, floating point numbers, polynomials, series, equations, sets, ranges, lists, arrays, tables, etc. All of these are objects that can be easily type-tested, assembled, or disassembled.

Major emphasis has been placed on readability, natural syntax, orthogonality, portability, compactness, and efficiency. Maple is currently being used not only for symbolic computation, but also as a tool for supporting the teaching of diverse courses (e.g., Algebra and Calculus, Numerical Analysis, Economics, Mechanical Engineering).

Maple makes extensive use of hashing tables for various purposes (*see* SEARCHING). (1) Hashing (or *signatures* of expressions) are used to keep a single occurrence of any expression or subexpression in the system; (2) Tables and arrays are implemented internally as hashing tables; (3) The "partial computation table" permits efficient (optional) remembering of function values. The motivation for remembering results lies on the observation that the same subexpression may appear repeatedly as a consequence of some computation. For example, computing the third derivative of $e^{\sin(x)}$ will compute the first derivative of $\sin(x)$ at least 5 times.

Packages in Maple are collections of functions suitable for a special area, like linalg for linear algebra or numtheory for number theory. Functions from such packages could be called with the command "*packagename[function]*". To avoid using these long names, one could set up short names for each function, so, for example, after the command with(linalg), one can use det(A) instead of linalg[det] (A). Naming conflicts are always reported to the user.

Maple V incorporates a new user interface for the X Window and Sun View Systems that includes 3-D plotting, separate help windows, allows editing of input expressions, and maintains a log of a Maple session. Figure 2 is a plot generated by the command

```
plot3d((x^2-y^2)/(x^2+y^2),
   x=-1..1,y=-1..1,labels=[x,y],axes=FRAME);
```

Axiom Axiom[4] (Davenport and Trager, 1990) is a system that was developed at IBM Thomas J. Watson Research

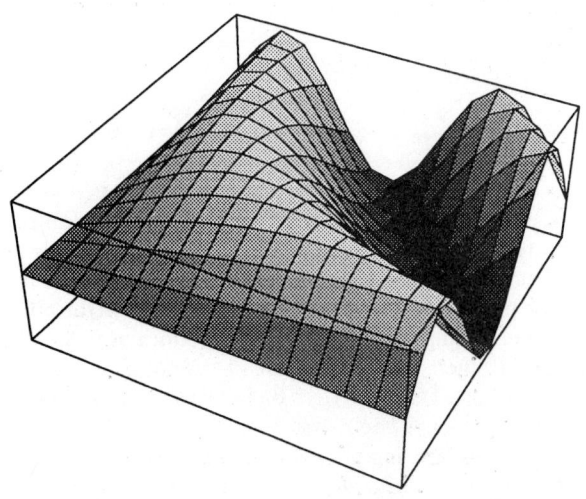

FIG. 1. Mathematica plot of the function sin(*xy*)

---

[4]Formerly called Scratchpad.

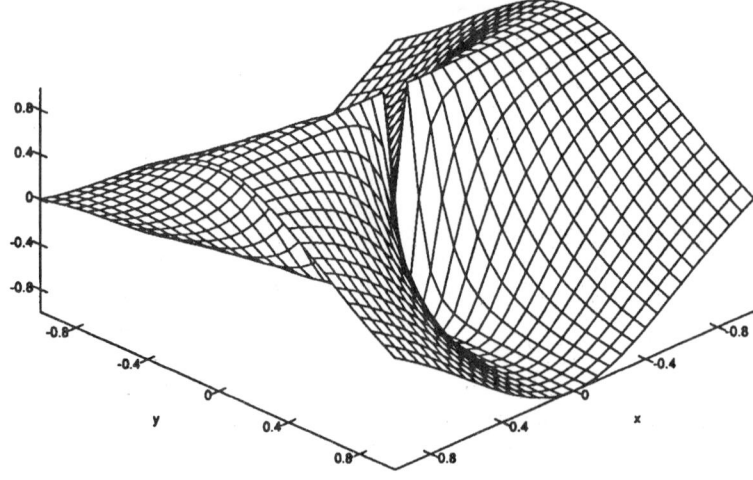

FIG. 2. Maple's surface plot of $\dfrac{x^2-y^2}{x^2+y^2}$ for $x, y \in -1..1$

Center and is presently distributed by NAG. Axiom currently runs only on the VM/CMS operating System and IBM workstations (RT/PC, RS/6000), but it has not been distributed widely outside of IBM. Axiom is implemented in Lisp.

Axiom is both a language for casual algebraic computing and a programming language complete with abstract data types and information hiding, designed to allow description and implementation of mathematical code at a high level.

Every Axiom object has an associated data type that determines the operations that are applicable to the object. Axiom has a set of 300 different data types, some of which pertain to algebraic computational objects, while others are data structures. Some are simple, like Integer $(Z)^5$, RationalNumber (Q), and Float, and some are parametrized, like Complex (C) (e.g. C Z for complex integers), UnivariatePolynomial (UP) (e.g. UP(x,Q) for univariate polynomials in x over the rational numbers), etc. However, the user may have to supply type declarations. The interpreter usually can determine a suitable type for an object, but not always. The following dialogue demonstrates this type of assignment by the interpreter. The type is always printed on a line following the object itself.

```
1/2 + 1/6 +1/12
        3
   (1)  -
        4
   Type: Fraction Integer
(5 + %i)**3
   (2) 110 + 74%i
   Type: Complex Integer
```

The portion of the Axiom language intended for programming computational procedures contains several features novel to algebraic manipulation languages, al-

though some reflect concepts developed in other languages in the past ten years—in particular, parametrized abstract data types, modules, and inheritance. The unique abstract data type design of Axiom is based on the notion of *categories*.

Categories lay out classes and hierarchies of types. Defining a category means defining its relation in the existing hierarchy, extra parameters (the category VectorField needs a parameter from the category Field to describe its scalars), operations that must be supported by its members, which are called *domains*, and properties the operations must satisfy. For example, the category OrderedSet:

```
OrderedSet(): Category == SectCategory with
  -- operations
   "<": ($,$) -> Boolean
   max: ($,$) -> $
   min: ($,$) -> $
  --   attributes
   irreflexive "<" -- not(x<x)
   transitive  "<" -- x<y and y<z => x<z
   total       "<" -- not(x<y) and not
                         (y<z) => x=y
  --   implementation
  add
   max(x,y) == (x<y => y; x)
   min(x,y) == (x<y => x; y)
```

This definition gives a category that extends (inherits) the category SetCategory by requiring three additional operations and three properties. If some operations are expressible by others, the implementation of these may also be put in the definition, like max and min in the above example. Examples of categories in Axiom are algebraic concepts, such as Group, AbelianGroup, Ring, EuclideanDomain, Field, UnivariatePolynomial-Category (R: Ring), etc.

Domains are instances of categories which means that they define an *actual* data representation and provide functions implementing the operations of a category

---

[5]The user may define abbreviations to each type in a macro file. They may then be used anywhere the full name is used.

in accordance with the stated attributes. Domains can be parametrized too; for example. `SparseUnivariate-Polynomial(R)` takes one parameter `R`, the coefficient ring, which must be of type `Ring` (a category) and the special representation used is a linked list of coefficients.

This concept also allows us to implement an algorithm only once for a given category and to use it for any values for which it makes sense. For example, the Euclidean algorithm can be used for values belonging to any domain that is a Euclidean domain (a category!). The following package takes a Euclidean domain as a type parameter and exports the operation `gcd` on that type.

```
GCDpackage(R: EuclideanDomain): with
       gcd: (R, R) -> R
  ==add
       gcd(x,y) ==
         x := unitNormal(x).canonical
         y := unitNormal(y).canonical
         while y ^= 0 repeat
           (x,y) := (y, x rem y)
           y := unitNormal(y).canonical
         x
```

This gcd operation is now polymorphic and may be used for many types (e.g. `Z`, `SUP(Q)`, `SUP(Integer Mod 11)`. It also could be put in the definition of the category `EuclideanDomain`.

Examples In this section we present some examples that define the boundaries of what computer algebra systems can and cannot do. The successful results we call "remarkable," in the sense that it is surprising that computer algebra systems can obtain them. The unsuccessful ones are likely to be beyond the frontiers of today's systems. Of course, these examples are valid now; in the future systems might evolve that will be able to solve the ones we now call "difficult/impossible."

Difficult/Impossible Problems

- For which values of n is $\int \dfrac{dx}{x^n\sqrt{1-x^3}}$ integrable in closed form?
- Let H be a Banach space...(Computer algebra systems cannot handle such abstract concepts at present.)
- Test whether the expression $\zeta(3/2)+4\pi\zeta(-1/2)$ is equal to some number or not (indeed, it is equal to 0).
- Solve the nonlinear differential equation $y''(x) + y'(x^2)/(y(x) + x) = 0$.

Remarkable Solutions

- Series expansion of
$$R(s) = \int_0^\infty \frac{\ln(1 + st)}{1 + t^2}\,dt$$

```
> series( int( ln(1+s*t)/(1+t^2), t=0..
           infinity), s=0);
```

$$(-\ln(s) = 1)\, s^2 + 1/4\, Pi\, s^4\, (1/3$$
$$\ln(s) - 1/9)\, s^3 - 1/8\, Pi\, s^3$$
$$+ (-1/5\, \ln(s) + 1/25)\, s^5 + O(s^6)$$

- We define $\{x_n\}$ to be the sequence of iterated sines, i.e. $x_{n+1} = \sin(x_n)$. What is the asymptotic expansion of x_n for $n \to \infty$?

```
> asympt(rsolve(x(n+1)=sin(x(n)),x),n);
```

$$\frac{3^{1/2}}{n^{1/2}} + \frac{\_C + 3/5\, 3^{1/2}\, \ln\!\left(\dfrac{1}{n^{1/2}}\right)}{n^{3/2}} + O\!\left(\frac{1}{n^2}\right)$$

- $\int \tan\!\left(\dfrac{\arctan(x)}{3}\right) dx$ in terms of tan's and arctan's:

$$\frac{8\, \log\!\left(3\, \tan\!\left(\dfrac{\arctan(x)}{3}\right)^2 - 1\right) - 3\, \tan\!\left(\dfrac{\arctan(x)}{3}\right)^2}{18}$$
$$+ \frac{18x\, \tan\!\left(\dfrac{\arctan(x)}{3}\right)}{18}$$

Comparative Examples In this section we present a few examples of some operations commonly done in symbolic computation. The examples are presented with all the declarations or environments settings that are necessary to perform the operations. We have used the following environments:

Maple V	Sun SPARC
Mathematica 2.0	Sun SPARC
Reduce 3.3	DECstation 3100
Macsyma 309.6	VAX 8600
Axiom	IBM RS/6000
Derive 2.01	386-based DOS system

Because of the wide variety of hardware used, timing results are not given.

1. Limit computation

The answer of $\lim_{x\to\infty} \dfrac{(e + 1)^{x^2}}{e^x}$ is obviously ∞, but L'Hospital's rule will fail to compute the limit:

Maple   `> limit ((E+1)^(x^2)/E^x, x=infinity`
Mathematica[6]   returns the limit unevaluated.

[6]If the Limit function defined in the package `Calculus/Limit`. `m` is used, then Mathematica will find the limit
```
In[1]: = << Calculus/Limit, m
In[2]: = Limit[(E+1)^(x^2)/E^x,  x,-> Infin-
          ity]
Out[2] = Infinity
```

Reduce	no evaluation of limits.
Macsyma	returns the limit unevaluated.[7]
Scratchpad	returns "failed".
Derive	[A]uthor (<ALT>−e + 1)^(x^2)/<ALT>−e^x
	[C]alculus/[L]imit <CR> inf <TAB> <space>
	[S]implify

$$\infty$$

2. Series expansion:

The series for $\tan(\sin(x))$ and $\sin(\tan(x))$ agree through several terms. Compute the series expansion of the difference up to order 13:

Maple
```
> series(sin(tan(x))-tan(sin(x)),x,14);
                 7    29   9    1913   11     95   13        14
        - 1/30 x  - --- x  - ----- x   - ---- x   + O(x  )
                    756      75600        7392
```

Mathematica
```
In[1]:= Series[Sin[Tan[x]]-Tan[Sin[x]], {x, 0, 13}]
            7        9        11        13
          -x    29 x    1913 x     95 x          14
Out[1]= --- - ----- - -------- - ------ + O[x]
         30    756      75600      7392
```

Reduce[8]
```
1: off allfac; on div;
2: taylor(sin(tan(x))-tan(sin(x)),x,13,0);

          95   13    1913   11    29   9    1   7
  - (------*X   + -------*X    +-----*X  + ----*X )
     7392         75600        756         30
```

Macsyma
```
(c1) taylor(sin(tan(x))-tan(sin(x)),x,0,13);

               7        9        11        13
             x     29 x    1913 x     95 x
   (d1)/T/   - -- - ----- - -------- - ------ + . . .
             30     756      75600      7392
```

Axiom
```
s := series(sin(tan x) - tan(sin x), x=0)

   (1)
       1   7    29   9    1913   11     95   13        14
     - -- x  - --- x  - ----- x   - ---- x   + O(x  )
       30      756      75600        7392

   Type: UnivariatePuiseuxSeries(Expression Integer,x,0)
```

Derive[9]
```
[A]uthor sin tan x - tan sin x
[C]alculus[T]aylor <CR> <CR> 13 <CR>
[S]implify
              13          11        9       7
        95 x        1913 x     29 x      x
      - ----   -   ------   -  -----  -  --
        7392        75600       756      30
```

3. Linear ODE:

Solve the second order differential equation

$$y''(x) + 2y'(x) + y(x) = \cos(x):$$

---

[7] Macsyma returns the correct result, if the input is changed to `limit(exp(x^2*log(%e11))/%e^x`.

[8] Supports no series expansion directly, but it is easy to define such a function.

[9] Using some of the IBM's special characters, Derive's output is actually prettier than this.

Maple

```
> dg1 := diff(y(x),x$2)+2*diff(y(x),x)+y(x)=cos(x);
                    /  2      \
                    |  d      |        /  d      \
         dg1 :=     |----- y(x)| + 2  |---- y(x)| + y(x) = cos(x)
                    |  2      |        \ dx      /
                    \ dx      /

> dsolve(dg1,y(x));
          y(x) = 1/2 sin(x) + _C1 exp(- x) + _C2 exp(- x) x
```

Mathematica

```
In[1]:= DSolve[y"[x] + 2 y'[x] + y[x] = Cos[x], y[x], x]

                      C[1]    x C[2]    Sin[x]
Out[1]= {{y[x] -> ---- + ------ + ------}}
                      x        x        2
                      E        E
```

Reduce   cannot solve differential equations.

Macsyma

```
(c3) deq:'diff(y,x,2)+2*'diff(y,x)+y=cos(x);

                          2
                        d y     dy
(d3)                    --- + 2 -- +y = cos(x)
                          2     dx
                        dx

(c4) ode(deq,y,x);
                        sin(x)                  - x
(d4)             y =    ------ + (%k2 x + %k1) %e
                          2
```

Axiom

```
(1) -> := operator y
   (1) y
                                             Type: BasicOperator
(2) ->deq := differentiate(y x, x, 2) +
          2 * differentiate (y x, x) + y x = cos x
        ..             '
   (2)   y  (x) + 2y (x) + y(x)= cos(x)
                            Type: Equation Expression Integer
(3) ->solve(deq, y, x)
                   sin(x)
   (3)   [particular= ------,basis = [%,   x %e   ]]
                        2
                Type: Union(Record(particular: Expression Integer,
                          basis: List Expression Integer)....)
```

Derive

```
[T]ransfer[L]oad ODE2
[A]uthor LIN2_POS(2,1,cos(x) ,x)
[S]implify
                    -x               sin x
               e  (c2 x + c1) + -----
                                    2
```

4. Symbolic integration: Integrate $(x + 1)/(x^2 + x + 1)$

Maple

```
> int((x+1)/(x^2+x+1),x];
                    2                1/2                        1/2
        1/2 ln(x  + x + 1) + 1/3 3   arctan (1/3 (2 x + 1) 3   )
```

Mathematica

```
In[1]:= Integrate[(x+1)/(x^2+x+1),x]
                    1 + 2 x
            ArcTan[-------]
                    Sqrt[3]    Log[1 + x + x ]
Out[1]= --------------- + ---------------
            Sqrt[3]             2
```

Reduce

```
1: f := int((x+1)/(x^2+x+1),x);
                    2*X + 1             2
         2*SQRT(3)*ATAN(---------) + 3*LOG(X + X + 1)
                        SQRT(3)
F := -----------------------------------------------
                            6
```

Macsyma   (c1) integrate((x+1)/(x^2+x+1), x);

$$
\text{(d1)} \qquad \frac{\log(x^2 + x + 1)}{2} + \frac{\operatorname{atan}\left(\dfrac{2x+1}{\operatorname{sqrt}(3)}\right)}{\operatorname{sqrt}(3)}
$$

Axiom[10]   integrate((x+1)/(x**2+x+1), x)

$$
\text{(1)} \qquad \frac{\operatorname{\sqrt{3}} \log(x^2 + x + 1) + 2\operatorname{atan}\left(\dfrac{2x+1}{\sqrt{3}}\right)}{2\sqrt{3}}
$$

         Type: Union(Expression Integer,List Expression Integer)

Derive   [A]uthor (x+1)/(x^2+x+1)
          [C]alculus/[I]ntegrate <CR> <CR> <CR>

$$
\frac{\operatorname{sqrt}(3) \ \mathrm{ATAN}\left(\dfrac{\operatorname{sqrt}(3)*(2x+1)}{3}\right)}{3} + \frac{\mathrm{LN}(x^2 + x + 1)}{2}
$$

5. Recurrence equations: Solve $s_n = -3s_{n-1} - 2s_{n-2}$

Maple   > rsolve(s(n) = -3*s(n-1) - 2*s(n-2), s(n));

$$
(2 \, s(0) + s(1)) \, (-1)^n + (-s(0) - s(1)) \, (-2)^n
$$

Mathematica   returns a result which is not undersandable.
Reduce   is unable to solve recurrence equations.
Macsyma   (c1) load(differ)$
               (c2) difference(s[n+2]+3*s[n+1]+2*s[n]=0, s[n]),

$$
\text{(d2)} \qquad s_n = -(-s_1 - 2 s_0)(-1)^2 - \frac{(2 s_1 + 2 s_0)(-2)^n}{2}
$$

Axiom   is unable to solve recurrence equations.
Derive[11]   [T]ransfer/[L]oad RECUREQN
               [A]uthor LIN2_CCF_POS(3,2,0,n) [S]
               [S]implify

$$
2^n C2 \cos(n\,Pi) + C1 \cos(n\,Pi)
$$
$$
+ I*(2^n C2 \sin(n\,Pi) + C1 \sin(n\,Pi))
$$

6. Programming

To illustrate the similarities and differences in the programming languages associated with the respective computer algebra systems covered, we include a procedure definition of the algorithm to compute the square free decomposition of a certain polynomial $a(x)$. This is a coding of Yun's algorithm, as presented in Knuth (1981). The algorithm involves the computation of a polynomial sequence generated from a polynomial a and its derivative with respect to x.

Maple:

```
sqrfree := proc(a, x) local d, v, w, i, t, g;
    if gcd(a, diff(a,x,), v, w) = 1 then
        RETURN(a) fi;
    t := 1;
```

[10]Axiom's output is actually prettier than this if some of IBM's special characters are used.

[11]There is no way to tell Derive that n is an integer in order to simplify the result to $C1(1-1)^n + C2(-2)^n$.

```
        d := w — diff(v,x);
        for i while d<>0 do
                g := gcd(v, d, 'v', 'w');
                d := w — diff(v,w);
                t := t * g^i
        od;
        t * v^i
end;
```

Macsyma:

```
sqrfree(a,x) : block([d,v,i,t,g],
        if (g:gcd(a, t:diff(a,x))) = 1 then
            RETURN(a),
        d : quotient(t,g) diff(quotient(a,g),x),
        t : 1,
        for i:1 while d<>0 do
        (       g : gcd(v, d),
                v : quotient(v,g),
                d : quotient(d,g) — diff(v,x),
                t : t * g^i
        ),
        t * v^i);
```

Mathematica:

```
SqrFree[a_, x_] :=
        Block[ {t,d,g,v,i},
                g=GCD[a, d=D[a,x]];
                If[g==1, Return[a] ]
                v=Cancel[a/g];
                d=Cancel[d/g]-D[v.x];
                t=1;
                For[i=1, d =!= 0, i++,
                        g=GCD[v, d];
                        v=Cancel[v/g];
                        d=Cancel[d/g]—D[v,x];
                        t=t g^i];
                t v^i
        ];
```

Reduce:

```
PROCEDURE sqrtfree (a,x);
BEGIN  SCALAR d,v,ii,tt,g;
        on exp;
        if (g := gcd(a, tt := df(a,x)) ) = 1 then
                RETURN a;
        d := tt/g df(y:=a/g, x);
        ii := 1;
        tt: = 1;
        while (d NEQ 0) do
        <<
                on exp;
                        g := gcd(v, d);
                        d := d/g — df(v:=v/g, x);
                off exp;
                tt := tt * g ** ii;
                ii := ii + 1;
        >>;
        RETURN(tt *v ** ii);
END;
```

Axiom:

```
sqrfree(p,x) ==
    g := extendedEuclidean(p,
                    differentiate(p,x))
    unit?(g.generator) => p
    t := 1
    d := g.coef2 - differentiate(g.coef1,x)
    for i in 1.. while d ^= 0 repeat
        g := extendedEuclidean(g.coef1,d)
        d := g.coef2 -differentiate(g.coef1,x)
        r := r * (g.generator) * monomial(1,x,i)
    r * g.coef2 ^ i
```

Acknowledgements We wish to acknowledge R. Corless for his assistance with Derive, K. Geddes and B. Char for the sqrfree codes, and M. Bronstein and M. Monagan for valuable discussions.

References

1981. Knuth, Donald E. *Seminumerical Algorithms, 2nd edition.* The Art of Computer Programming, vol. 2. Reading, MA: Addison-Wesley.

1981. Foderaro J. K. and Fateman, R. J. "Characterization of Vax MACSYMA." In *SYMSAC '81: Proceedings of the 1981 ACM Symposium on Symbolic and Algebraic Computation; August 5–7, 1981,* Snowbird, UT. pp. 14–19, Paul S. Wang (ed.). New York: Association for Computing Machinery.

1983. Hearn, Anthony C. *REDUCE User's Manual, Version 3.0.* Santa Monica, CA 90406: Rand Publication CP78(4/83).

1988. Wolfram, Stephen *Mathematica— A System for Doing Mathematics by Computer.* Reading, MA: Addison-Wesley Publishing Company.

1989. Harper, David, Wooff, Chris and Hodgkinson, David. "A Guide to Computer Algebra Systems." Technical report, The University of Liverpool, Brownlow Hill, P.O. Box 147, Liverpool L68 3BX.

1990 Simon, Barry "The New World of Higher Math." *PC Magazine,* **9**(10), May.

1990. Betts, Kelleyn S. "Math packages multiply." *Mechanical Engineering,* **112**(8): 32–38, August.

1990. Simon, Barry, "Four Computer Mathematical Environments." *Notices of the American Mathematical Society,* **37**(7):861–868, September.

1990. Davenport, J. H. and Trager, B. M. "Scratchpad's View of Algebra I: Basic Commutative Algebra. In *International Symposium on Design and Implementation of Symbolic Computation Systems,* volume 429 of *Lecture Notes in Computer Science,* A. Miula (ed.) 40–54, Heidelberg: Springer-Verlag.

GASTON H. GONNET AND DOMINIK W. GRUNTZ

COMPUTER ANIMATION

For articles on related subjects *see* COMPUTER-AIDED DESIGN/COMPUTER-AIDED MANUFACTURING; COMPUTER ART; COMPUTER GAMES; COMPUTER GRAPHICS; IMAGE PROCESSING; and SCIENTIFIC APPLICATIONS.

Introduction *Computer animation* refers to the use of digital computers to synthesize images that are recorded to disk, film, or videotape for later viewing. Just as in conventional animation, each frame is slightly different from its predecessor, so that playback at the proper speed gives a sense of motion.

There are two major branches of computer animation: two-dimensional and three-dimensional. In two-dimensional animation, the animator works directly with images or image portions on a screen. Images represent the final version of some particular scene, so, to obtain a different version, a new image must be constructed. If an animator decides, for example, that an arm needs to be moved just a little bit, that entire portion of the image must be redrawn. For some attributes, such as lighting, this could involve redoing the entire image.

In three-dimensional animation, the animator works with objects in a virtual space, manipulating their attributes as well as global viewing parameters. An image synthesized by incorporating all of these attributes with the geometries defining the objects is then rendered. Rather than being flat primitives, the actors actually have depth and volume. In 3-D animation, the image is comparable to a window through which one looks into a synthesized world, rather than being a primitive, as in 2-D animation.

Motion Description Points in space are defined as a vector $\mathbf{P} = (x\ y\ z)$; in its simplest form, animation becomes a matter of calculating $\mathbf{P}$ as a function of time. Technically, this is the derivative of $\mathbf{P}$ with respect to time, $\dfrac{d\mathbf{P}}{dt}$, although there are simpler methods presented below that are faster to calculate.

Hierarchical Objects A *hierarchical object* is an actor in a 3-D animation built of interrelated parts, with the relationship represented as a *tree* (*q.v.*). Transformations applied to a node are also applied to its subtree, so any particular node is subject to all of its parent's transformations in addition to its own.

Splines Given two points in space, $\mathbf{P}_0$ and $\mathbf{P}_1$, we can calculate the line between them using the linear interpolation $\mathbf{P} = \mathbf{P}_0 + \alpha(\mathbf{P}_1 - \mathbf{P}_0)$. To relate this to computer animation, we associate times t_0 and t_1 with $\mathbf{P}_0$ and $\mathbf{P}_1$, respectively, and calculate $\alpha = \dfrac{t - t_0}{t_1 - t_0}$, where t is the current time, which is usually measured by frame number in the animation.

This method can be extended to a cubic curve in space, called a *spline* (*q.v.*), be defining $P = \Psi_0 (P_0) + \Psi_1 (P_1) + \Psi_2 (P_2) + \Psi_3(P_3)$. The Ψ_i are known as *blending functions* because they yield a weighted sum of the four points used to synthesize the curve. There are many different possible combinations of weights; any particular one is known as a *basis* for the spline.

Practically, the equation is implemented as $P = (t^3\ t^2\ t\ 1)[C][G]$, where t has the same meaning as before, [C] is the conversion matrix containing the weighting coefficients for the particular basis, and [G] is the matrix of row vectors of the four points controlling the spline.

The advantage of cubic over linear splines is continuity in the first and second derivatives. A discontinuous first derivative shows up as a sudden jump in position (or in the value of whatever attribute is being animated); a discontinuous second derivative shows up as a sudden change in speed (or rate of change of the attribute).

Forward Kinematics Forward kinematics is the application of the techniques described above to calculate motion. The transformations are calculated for the root node and propagated down its subtree, and the process is applied recursively.

Inverse Kinematics In an *inverse kinematic* formulation, the positions and orientations of a hierarchical object are calculated from the bottom up (of the tree structure). Think of a human placing a hand somewhere: the position and rotation data for the forearm and upper arm and shoulder are determined by where the hand is. There are, however, an infinite number of solutions for the other parts: even though the hand is held still, the elbow can be twisted around to multiple positions. In an inverse kinematic formulation, a solution to this problem would be calculated according to some constraint, such as minimum energy expenditure, minimum angular displacement, etc.

Dynamics Formulations based on kinematic motion alone do not generally account for real life (i.e. Newtonian mechanics). This requires the inclusion of mass and acceleration to calculate motion, as expressed through the familiar relation *F=ma*. Dynamics formulations are typically expressed by systems of partial differential equations (pde's - *q.v.*) that describe accelerations and velocities in the system; these are then integrated to calculate animated motion.

The classic problem with kinematics alone is that, although it is WYSIWYG (What You See Is What You Get), it does not look real unless it is carefully designed. The classic problem with dynamics is that although it is real motion, the animator must adjust equation coefficients iteratively until the resulting motion is what is desired. Considering the turnaround time required to calculate motion using dynamics, it is not surprising that the animator might lose concentration while this is carried out.

Computer Animation System Models Computer animation systems can be categorized by the level of abstraction of motion, and by the mechanisms available to the animator for control. Zeltzer (1990, 1991) classed systems by their levels of *abstraction* and *interaction* (Fig. 1):

Abstraction refers to the level at which the animation can be described, where *machine* level would be a computer program and *task* would be a high-level description, such as "clench fist."

Interaction refers to how the animator deals with the system. *Guiding* involves showing the system how a motion is to be performed; at a basic level this is also known as *keyframe* animation and, as the level becomes more complex, *key parameter* animation. *Programming* ultimately provides the most flexibility in dealing with motion, but is also the most difficult aspect of design.

Applications

Commercial Computer Animation The predominant applications for computer animation are commercial, involving both TV advertisements and logo packages. Such productions are fairly popular, but generally use simple motion to keep design costs down.

The use of computer animation in feature films has varied over the last two decades (see Figs. 2 and 3, color insert pages CP-3, 4). In 1982 Disney Studios released *Tron*, with an unprecedented 52 minutes of computer animation from four different production facilities. Since then, feature films have used substantially less computer animation, although the imagery is of higher quality, as it was, for example, in the 1989 film, *The Abyss*.

Visualization Over the last decade, the use of computer animation to visualize scientific activity has become increasingly important. *Visualization*, including scientific visualization, can be used to make images of processes that are not normally visible, such as the temperature

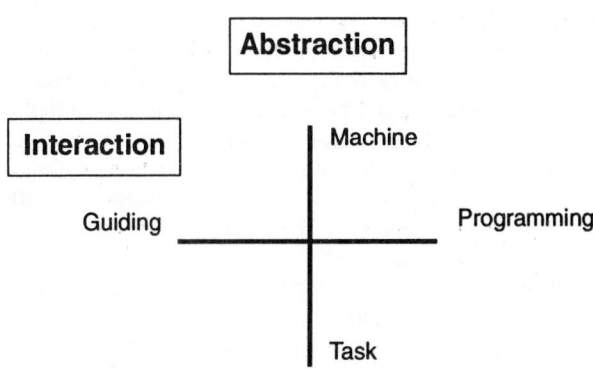

FIG. 1 Abstraction and interaction.

distribution around a reentering space vehicle, or air movement in a thunderstorm.

Because time can be treated as an informational dimension, it can be used in a variety of ways. One is to show the state of a physical system as a parameter is varied so as to provide a better understanding of how a function depends on its variables. A photographer will often *bracket* the exposure for a picture, meaning that different aperture and shutter combinations will be used, and the best one selected later. Animation provides a way to bracket experiments easily; because the system is built to vary parameters, the scientist can easily try different combinations of parameter values to see what happens to the system.

Another use of the time dimension is to show the progression of a system in a different time scale than normal, as in high speed or time lapse photography. When both of these uses are combined, the techniques help explain what is going on in a scientific experiment in a way that is difficult to do with only static images.

Visualization also plays important roles in medicine, both education and practice. Computer simulations can show in class how processes such as blood flow work. Visualization techniques are used in CAT (computer-aided tomography - *q.v.*) and MRI (magnetic resonance imaging) scans in diagnostic medicine.

Because of all these advantages, the use of visualization for education is a welcome byproduct of the emphasis on scientific visualization. In many educational circumstances, scenarios are too expensive or simply impossible to demonstrate; through visualization, they can be viewed, providing a much better understanding of the subject. Historically, the most common application has been flight simulation. There are many aerospace problem scenarios that are extremely difficult or dangerous to practice in reality; simulators provide ways to train for these without endangering anyone. The Federal Aviation Administration considers advanced simulators so realistic that airline pilots are allowed to do some of their training in them, rather than in real airplanes.

Art Computer animated short films form the majority of works in the art category. These range from homework projects to Academy Award winning animations (*Tin Toy*, 1988). Frequently, these films are rereleased in animation collections.

Other art applications include theater and dance visualization, where animation is used to give an idea of what the production will look like before it is actually staged. It is a simple matter to build an online version of a stage setting and lighting plot and animate lighting changes, although the calculation requirements for multiple light sources are usually rather drastic. There have been suggestions for systems that would read a dance notation, such as *Labanotation*, and automatically construct animations demonstrating the movements. Dance is especially difficult to animate because of the classic kinematic-dynamics tradeoff; the requirement for natural looking movement is high, indicating the use of dynamics, but animation of complex dance movements requires use of inverse kinematics.

History The first computer animations were made by Lillian Schwartz and Ken Knowlton at Bell Labs in the early and mid-1960s. The animations were two-dimensional and the motion was described by computer programs. Later in the decade, the Mathematical Applications Group, Inc. (MAGI) was formed to do contract animations using proprietary ray tracing software. Also around this time, Charles Csuri began experimenting with computer-drawn pictures as fine art at the Ohio State University.

In the 1970s, there were two important developments: hardware explicitly designed to handle 3-D graphics became a commercial product, and the University of Utah program in computer graphics developed techniques for synthesizing color images of 3-D scenes. By the end of the decade, both of these were commonplace, and the New York Institute of Technology Computer Graphics Laboratory had established a solid program for commercial applications of computer animation, as well as a research and development program.

The first half of the 1980s saw the outbreak of *character animation*, where animated actors behaved in a manner that suggested innate characters, just as in a play or a work of prose. Also, much more attention was directed to content, so animations conveyed stories as well as looking pretty. The Ohio State University, NYIT, and Pixar all were producing notable animations.

By the end of the decade, workstations (*q.v.*) had become immensely popular, so that animators would have their own station to work at instead of having to share a centrally located expensive system. Supercomputer design architectures began filtering down into the workstation design. All this was due to decreases in hardware cost, which meant that more people than ever could gain access to 3-D animation facilities that were no longer prohibitively expensive. This period also saw the emergence of other methods, such as inverse kinematics and dynamics, as well as behavioral models. Networking between computer systems became commonplace, so that animators could design an animation on their workstations, but send the heavy duty rendering calculations to larger, faster computers. Such trends are expected to continue.

References

1982. Beatty, John C. and Booth, Kellogg S. *Computer Graphics*, 2nd edition. Washington, D.C.: IEEE Computer Society Press.
1990. Foley, J., van Dam, A., Feiner, S. and Hughes, J. *Computer Graphics: Principles and Practice*, 2nd edition. Reading, MA: Addison-Wesley.
1990. Badler, Norman, Barsky, Brian, and Zeltzer, David, eds. *Making Them Move*. San Mateo, CA: Morgan-Kaufman Publishers, Inc.
1991. Gómez, Julian E. and Zeltzer, David. *Computer Animation: Principles and Practice*. San Mateo, CA: Morgan-Kaufmann.

JULIAN E. GÓMEZ

COMPUTER ARCHITECTURE

For articles on related subjects *see* ADDRESSING; ARITHMETIC-LOGIC UNIT; BASE REGISTER; BUS; CACHE MEMORY; CHANNEL; COMPUTERS, MULTIPLE ADDRESS; DIGITAL COMPUTERS: GENERAL PRINCIPLES; GENERAL REGISTER; INDEX REGISTER; INDIRECT ADDRESS; INSTRUCTION AND DATA REPRESENTATION; INSTRUCTION SET; INTERRUPT; MEMORY; MEMORY-MAPPED I/O; MICROPROGRAMMING; NETWORK ARCHITECTURE; PARALLEL PROCESSING: ARCHITECTURE; PROGRAM COUNTER; REGISTER; RISC ARCHITECTURE; VON NEUMANN MACHINE; and WORD LENGTH, VARIABLE.

Introduction *Computer architecture* is an interdisciplinary field concerned with the physical or hardware structure of computer systems, the attributes of the various parts thereof, and how these parts are interconnected. In the formative years (1940s and 1950s), the principal elements of computer architecture were numerical analysis (specifically digital arithmetic), physics (the behavior of materials), and electrical engineering (specifically the design of electronic circuits and their organization into computer systems. The 1960s saw the introduction of semiconductor devices, which greatly enhanced performance at substantially lower cost. By the late 1960s, *operating systems* (*q.v.*) and other software components were seen to play a major role in system behavior. Mainstream computer designs also began embodying software-based techniques at very fundamental levels (such as microprogramming and virtual machines). With the advent of very large scale integration (VLSI) in the early 1980s, semiconductor technology once again proved its role as a major driver of designs. The mid- to late 1980s saw the widespread introduction of *workstations* (*q.v.*) and other computer systems whose functionality is strongly influenced by human interfaces and effective use of *computer graphics* (*q.v.*). Thus, computer architecture has continued and expanded its interdisciplinary character and now contains elements of computer science, human factors (*q.v.*), numerical analysis (*q.v.*), operations research (*q.v.*), electrical and electronic engineering, and solid-state physics.

For the purposes of this article, two fundamental aspects of computer architecture will be identified:

1. *System architecture*—the functional behavior and conceptual structure of a computer system as seen by the software developer (i.e. in terms of those characteristics affecting software design and development); and
2. *Implementation architecture*—those characteristics affecting the relative cost and performance of a computer system and that are of concern to the semiconductor designer or electronic engineer, such as logic design, memory bandwidth, and device technology.

The significance of this distinction is illustrated by the Vax series of computer systems (Fig. 1). The Vax series, made by Digital Equipment Corporation (*q.v.*), is a family of computers sharing a common system architecture—that is, software written for any model in the series will operate correctly (although at varying speeds) on any other model (with certain exceptions, mostly related to operating system code). In order for this to happen, the various members of the Vax family share the same instruction set, arithmetic registers, I/O methods, memory addressing mechanisms, and such. A single document (Leonard, 1989) is sufficient to allow one to write assembly language software, compilers, loaders, and most components of an operating system for any model in the series. Software written for the original Vax systems in the late 1970s can still be run on the Vax systems of today. (In certain instances, newer members of the series have extended the architecture in an *upward compatible* way—that is, software written for the older series can run on the newer ones, but not always vice versa.)

From an implementation standpoint, the VAX series spans a variety of technologies and a processing performance range in excess of 100–1. The original vax system, the 11/780, had an effective execution speed of approximately 1 million instructions per section (1 MIP). The Vax 9000 model 440, which has four processors, is described as having a relative speed of over 100 times that of the original 11/780. Several of the Vax models are shown in the figure, along with other ways in which they differ. One of the most interesting differences is the fact that, in some

Model	VAX Station 3100	Micro VAX 3800	VAX 6000 460	VAX 9000 440
Relative Processing Performance	2.7	3.8	36	117
No. of Processors	1	1	6	4
Maximum Main Memory	32 MB	64 MB	192 MB	512 MB
Cache Size	1 KB	1 KB	2 KB/CPU	128 KB/CPU
Cache Speed	90 ns	60 ns	28 ns	16 ns
I/O Bus Capacity	1.5 MB/s	3.3 MB/s	40 MB/s	320 MB/s

FIG. 1. Various Implementations of Vax Architecture

Vax models, portions of the instruction set are implemented in software rather than hardware.

Subsystems   The three major subsystems of a computer are the storage, the processor, and the input/output and communication subsystem. We discuss each of these from both the system and implementation architecture perspectives. The classic von Neumann machine design is assumed, except where otherwise noted.

Storage   The *storage*, or *memory*, of a computer system contains both the data to be processed by the system and the instructions indicating what processing is to be performed. Three levels of storage are generally identified: registers, main memory or RAM (for random access memory), and secondary or auxiliary storage (see MEMORY). Table 1 indicates the general characteristics of each of these. Regardless of the level, the fundamental unit of digital computer storage is the *bit*, conceptually containing one of two distinct values: 0 or 1. Aggregates of bits are combined into larger units, such as *bytes* (usually 8 bits) and *words* (anywhere from 8 to 64 bits or more). As a rule, the larger its word length, the more powerful the computer. Therefore, many have tended to classify computers by their word lengths. However, there are so many ways to define word length that it should never be the sole basis for classification.

Early computer systems organized memory as follows: bits were organized into fixed-length words, where each word was referenced as a unit by a single memory address, and the individual bits of a word were transferred as a group between a computer's main memory and its registers or secondary storage. Each word would contain a single instruction or datum. The *arithmetic-logic unit* would operate on one word of data at a time.

A contemporary computer, by contrast, might address data in groups of 8 bits, transfer data to registers in groups of 16 bits, transfer data to secondary storage in groups of 64 bits, operate arithmetically on data "words" of 32 bits, have variable-length instructions ranging from 16 to 48 bits, and use a 24-bit memory address. What, then, is the computer's word length? Today's most commonly accepted system architecture definition is the length of a typical arithmetic register. This is usually equal to the number of bits operated on in parallel by the arithmetic unit, and may or may not be equal to the number of bits needed to hold a single precision integer number. The commonly accepted definition from an implementation architecture point of view is the number of bits transferred in parallel from the main memory to the processor, a quantity sometimes called the *data path*. However, if cache memories are used, this definition can be interpreted in at least two different ways. The main point is that word length can be a very misleading indicator of a computer's memory system architecture.

Registers   Registers were once the fastest and most expensive memory units in a computer. Today, due to advances in semiconductor technology, main memories and registers can be essentially equal in these characteristics, but their functions remain distinct. Registers are a computer's most frequently used memory units, playing a role in the execution of every instruction. They also tend to be few in number, both to enhance performance by keeping them physically "close" to the processing elements, and to make possible a shorter addressing scheme in the instruction format. Two fundamental categories of registers can be distinguished: registers that are directly accessible by application programs (and, therefore, are part of the system architecture), and registers that are not directly accessible from software. The former generally hold data that are actively being processed by the computer's arithmetic and logic unit(s). The latter contain information that describe the current state of the computation process, and may vary with different implementations of the same architecture family.

The minimum complement of system architecture registers is essentially one: an arithmetic register or *accumulator* which serves to hold the intermediate results of computations or other data processing activities. (Although usually part of the system architecture, accumulators may be hidden from the software in some designs such as those using a *stack* (*q.v.*) for computation). Most current computers have multiple accumulators so that several intermediate results may be maintained. Other registers usually found in contemporary computers include a *status register*, indicating the current condition of the various hardware components and computational results; and a *program counter*, indicating the location in main memory of the next instruction to be executed. In addition to these, many computers have *index registers* for counting and for "pointing" into tables; *address* or *base registers*, containing addresses of blocks of main or secondary memory; a *stack pointer*, containing the address of a special block of registers or main memory, which is treated like a pushdown stack; and various *special-purpose registers*, whose functions depend on the details of the particular computer.

Registers that are part of the implementation architecture tend to vary substantially among various designs.

TABLE 1

Type	Access Time	Capacity in Words	Use
Registers	10–50 ns	1–128	Data, status, control info, current instruction
Cache memory	10–100 ns	512–500,000	Frequently used instructions and data
Main memory	50–500 ns	16,000–1,000,000,000	Programs, data
Auxiliary memory	10–100 ms	500,000–100,000,000,000	Long-term storage

The most common among these are an *instruction register*, containing the instruction currently being executed; a *memory address register*, containing the address of the memory cell currently being read to or written from main memory; a *memory data register*, containing the data being read from or written to main memory; and similar registers pertaining to secondary memory and peripheral devices.

A major architectural issue beyond the number, accessibility, and functions of registers is that of special purpose versus *general registers*. In a special purpose design, each register has a specific, narrow function, whereas in a general purpose design, the registers may be used for a variety of purposes, as directed by the software. Real machines tend to have a mixture of both types, but none that are totally general in purpose. The flexibility of general purpose designs is attractive from a software viewpoint, but it can impose penalties in implementation efficiency because all parts of the processor require data paths to the general register set. On the other hand, a general purpose approach may be a necessity in designs where only a small number of registers can be accommodated. The structure and discipline imposed by special purpose registers may have software benefits as well, and many computer designs aimed at supporting higher-level languages tend to depend heavily on restricted use of registers. Fig. 2 illustrates the use of both general purpose and special purpose registers in the National 16032 microprocessor, which was designed to support block structured higher-level languages.

Main Memory The main memory contains programs and data that are ready for processing by the computer. It consists of a linear sequence of "words," each individually addressable and each capable of being read or written to. In some designs, different technologies will be used to implement different sections of memory. For example, a frequently used section may have higher speed memory than the others; or a section whose contents must survive power failures or should never be modified might be implemented with non-volatile *read-only memory* (ROM - *q.v.*), the contents of which cannot be altered. In recent years, the concept of different implementations for different parts of memory has been extended to include "memory" that can be addressed by the processor, but is not actually present as part of the physical main memory. We will discuss two of these concepts in the sequel: *virtual memory (q.v.)* and direct memory access (DMA) I/O.

The performance of a computer depends on the size and speed of its main memory. The total number of words in a memory is typically a configuration decision, with upper and lower limits determined by both the system and implementation architectures. The speed of memory is determined by implementation and cost factors, and is also influenced by size in the sense that very large memories must be physically more distant from the processor and therefore take longer to access. Numerous techniques have been used to increase the effective speed of a memory system. *Cacheing* and *interleaving* are probably the two most popular.

Cacheing is a technique whereby a small, high-speed memory is used to contain the most frequently used words from a larger, slower main memory. If the "hit ratio" (percent of memory references found in the small, *cache memory*) is high, the average speed of the entire memory is substantially increased.

With *interleaving (q.v.)*, two or more independent memory systems are combined in such a way that they appear as one faster memory system. In one approach, all

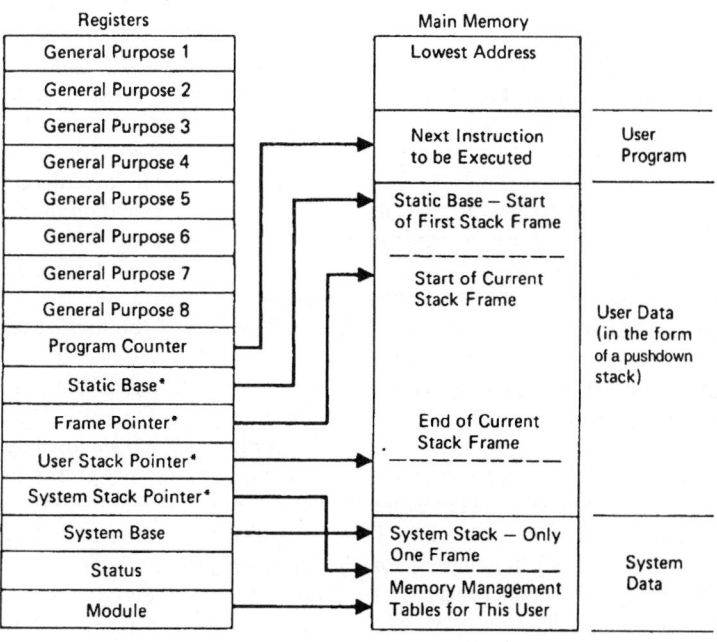

FIG. 2. Register and memory structure of National 16032 microprocessor.

words with even addresses come from one memory system, and all words with odd addresses come from another. When an even-numbered word is fetched, the next-higher odd-numbered word is fetched simultaneously from the other memory system, on the theory that it is likely to be the next word requested. If this guess is correct (as it often is), the next word's *access time (q.v.)* is essentially zero, thus nearly doubling the average memory access speed. Commercial computer systems have employed 4-way, 8-way, and even 16-way interleaving, with a variety of organization strategies. The higher degrees of interleaving are used predominantly in systems requiring access to memory by multiple, parallel processors.

The form in which memory is presented to the software by the system architecture is sometimes called the *logical address space* or the *virtual address space*. In the most straightforward designs, the logical address space is a *linear* sequence of words or bytes containing the programs being executed and the data to be acted upon. It will differ from the physical memory (implementation) mainly in size (number of words), in some cases fewer and in other cases more. Two potential drawbacks of a linear approach are that a large memory may require a large address, which costs more to implement, makes instructions bigger and generally makes processing slower (it takes n bits to address 2^n words); and that it may be awkward to partition a linear space into several parts that have different purposes.

To deal with these drawbacks, certain system architectures provide a more complex logical address space. In one design, the address space is perceived by software as a set of *pages*. Each page is a sequence of words; all pages are the same in size (usually a power of two); and each page has a distinct identification number or page number. A memory address consists of two parts: a page number and a word offset or displacement (within the page) (Fig. 3b). There may or may not be an implied spatial relationship between consecutively numbered pages.

Another approach is the *segment* design, in which there are several independently numbered blocks called segments, but with no requirement that they all be the same size. This permits each software module to be placed in whatever size segment is most suitable. Segment and page designs may be combined so that each segment contains several pages and the size of a segment is a multiple of the page size. Other concepts of logical address space have been discussed in the literature, but are only occasionally found in mainstream computers.

There are several other reasons for having a structured *virtual memory (q.v.)*, rather than one large linear sequence. From a software viewpoint, a major objective is to provide a means of organizing programs and data according to their characteristics, such as type (instructions, characters, real numbers, integers), access rules (read only, execute only, read and write), ownership (if two or more programs are simultaneously in memory), or utilization (all data used during the same phase of a process, may be grouped into one block). *Object-oriented programming (q.v.)* can be supported very effectively with a properly structured virtual memory. From a supervisory standpoint, memory structure enables efficient management of memory resources, especially among multiple tasks or multiple users (see MULTITASKING). From an implementation perspective, structured memory may allow efficiencies in memory system design, such as placement of high speed memory devices in the most frequently used segments, convenient schemes for protection against unauthorized access, or (via memory mapping) may permit a small computer to support more memory than can be conveniently addressed with one word.

Memory Mapping Memory mapping is the translation between the logical address space and the physical memory. The objectives of memory mapping are (1) to translate from logical to physical address (where these are different), (2) to aid in memory protection (q.v.), and (3) to enable better management of memory resources. Mapping is important to computer performance, both in a local sense (how long it takes to execute an instruction) and in a global sense (how long it takes to run a given set of programs). In effect, each time a program presents a logical memory address and requests that the corresponding memory word be accessed, the mapping mechanism must translate that address into an appropriate physical memory location. The simpler this translation, the lower the implementation cost and the higher the performance of the individual memory reference. However, more capable translation mechanisms permit protection of memory segments from unauthorized access and/or facilitate dynamic rearrangement of objects in physical memory. These enable efficiencies in the programming, debugging, and supervisory phases of computing, which may far outweigh the cost of slower individual instruction execution times.

Although there are many techniques of memory mapping, there are two fundamental situations to be overcome: when the logical address space is smaller than the physical address space (common on microcontrollers, microprocessors, and older mini- and mainframe computers), mapping is needed to gain access to all of physical memory; and when the logical address space is larger than the physical address space, mapping is used to assure that each logical address actually used corresponds to a physical memory cell. The latter situation is discussed below, under "Virtual Memory," although virtual memory can also be used with small logical address spaces.

The size of the logical address space is determined by the number of bits in a memory address. Typically, the size of an address is limited by the word length of the computer. On a typical computer with a 16-bit word, only 2^{16} or about 65,000 words may be addressed. Technology now permits such systems to be attached physically to many times this much memory, but there is no direct way to address it without redesigning the instruction set. Thus, the primary purpose of a memory mapping mechanism on such a system is to enable the logical address space to be assigned to a desired portion of a larger physical address space. Three such methods are illustrated in Fig. 3: relocation, paging, and segmentation.

Translation Technique

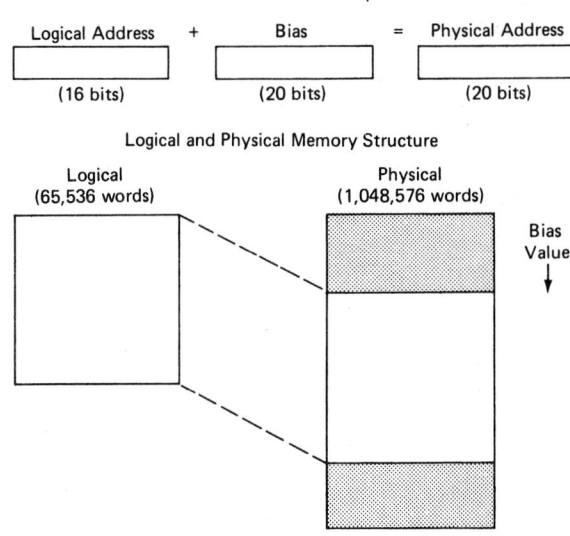

FIG. 3(a). Biased memory mapping (with sample values).

In the relocation scheme, the contents of a *bias* register are added to each logical memory address to produce a physical address. The effect is to offset the program by the biased amount in physical memory. Several different programs can coexist in the same physical memory without overlap by assigning different bias values to each of them.

In paging, the logical address space is divided into a set of equal-sized blocks called pages, and each is mapped onto a block of physical memory (called a page frame). The effect is similar to that of biasing, except that the program is broken into several separately-biased pieces (pages), and each page must begin at a page frame boundary in physical memory. The primary advantage of paging is that it allows a contiguous logical address space to be split into several noncontiguous physical frames. This makes memory management easier and also permits sharing of some of a program's pages among multiple processes without complete overlap of physical addresses. This scheme may be faster than the bias technique because it requires only a concatenation of two

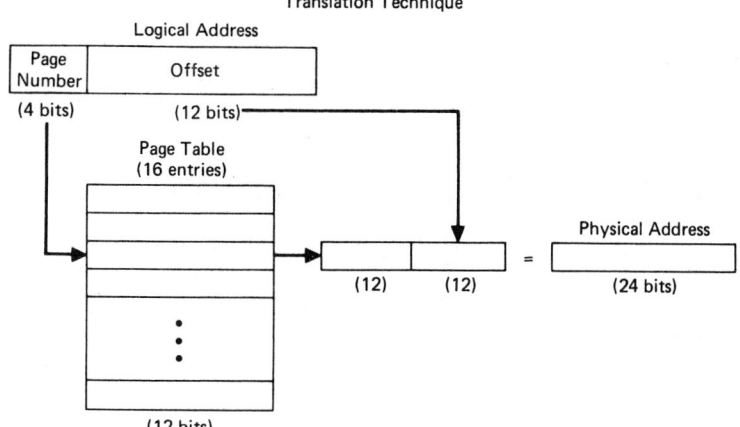

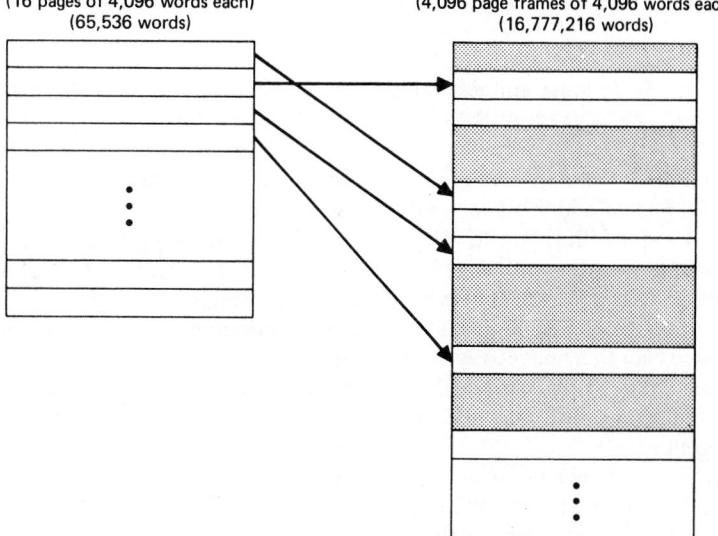

FIG. 3(b). Paged memory mapping (with sample values).

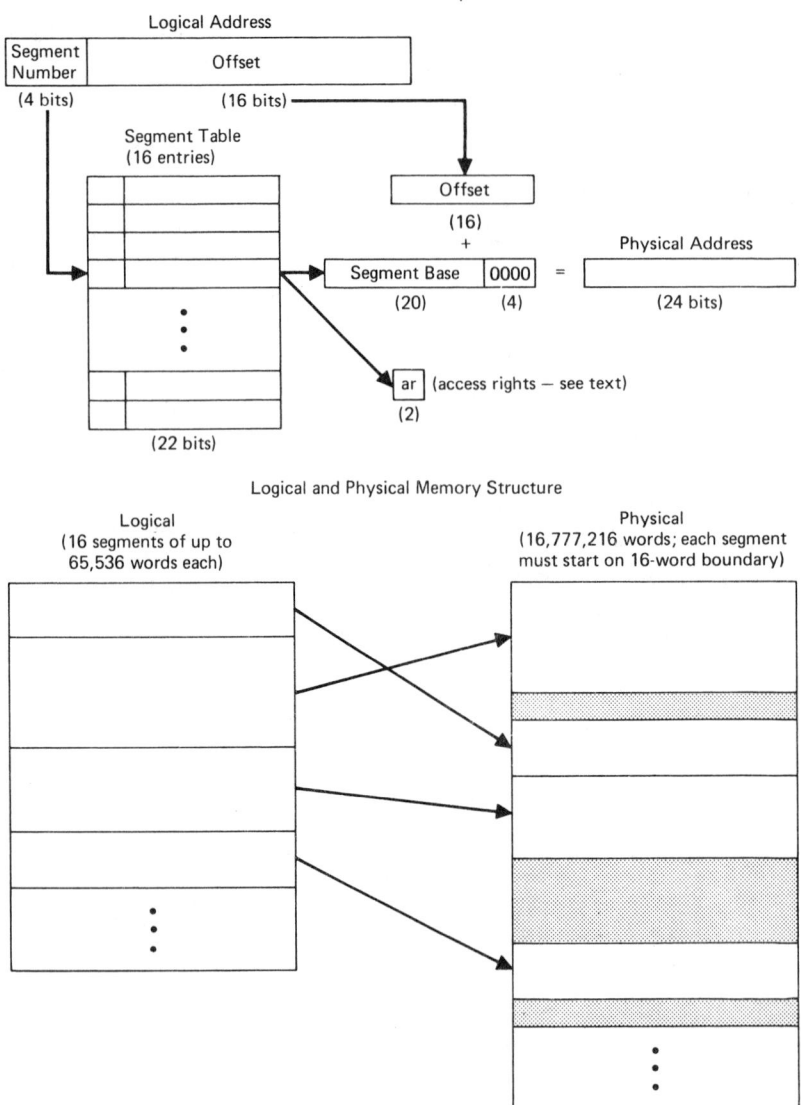

FIG. 3(c).   Segmented memory management (with sample values).

addresses instead of an addition to form the physical address. However, the page map file requires more register bits than the bias register.

Segmenting is somewhat like a combination of biasing and paging. It breaks the logical address space into several blocks, but does not require them to be of any particular size or to be mapped into any particular physical frames. Physical addresses are obtained by biasing the individual segments. As might be expected, this approach is the most flexible and also the most costly, both in hardware and performance. It requires both a file of bias values (the segment table) and an extra addition operation per memory reference.

As noted above, mapping can enable protection against unauthorized access. A typical method, illustrated in Fig. 3(c), is to incorporate a set of access rights in the segment table. The access rights indicate a mode of access that is permitted to a segment (such as "read only"

or "execute only"), and the memory mapping hardware can verify that each access to the segment fits this mode.

For more information on memory addressing and mapping, see ADDRESSING.

Auxiliary Memory (Secondary Storage).   *Auxiliary memory* is the lowest-cost, highest-capacity, and slowest-access storage area in a computer system. It is where programs and data are kept for long-term storage or when not in immediate use. Such memories tend to occur in two types—*sequential access* (data must be accessed in a linear sequence) and *direct access* (data may be accessed in any sequence). The most common sequential storage device is the magnetic tape, whereas direct access devices include rotating drums, disks, and certain low-speed semiconductor devices such as bubble memory.

Typically, a computer operates as follows. A program and its data are initially located on a secondary storage device. Program execution is achieved by copying the program and some of the data into main memory. Instructions are then executed, causing data to be copied into registers, operated on or tested, and results stored back into main memory. Occasionally, an *input* operation is generated, causing more data to be copied from secondary storage, perhaps overwriting some that were previously read. As computation proceeds, results are sent back to secondary storage via *output* operations.

Many fundamental architectural issues are related to the means by which data and programs are transferred between main and secondary storage. The basic problem is that the storage and transfer characteristics of secondary devices do not match those of main storage. Typical access times for main and secondary storage were given in Table 1; but to understand this better, we must consider the structure of a secondary storage device. Data are stored in blocks whose size is determined by the characteristics of the device (anywhere from 64 to 512 words is typical). This leads to three distinct time periods related to data access (see Table 2 for some typical values of these times for various devices):

1. *Positioning time* is the amount of time required to move the read/write mechanism to the location of a block of data. In the case of a magnetic tape, this may involve moving to the next consecutive record or spinning all the way down to the other end of the tape. On a disk, it involves moving the read/write heads to the proper track. For a drum or a "fixed head" disk, positioning time is not a factor because there is always a read/write mechanism at every track.
2. *Latency* is the amount of time for a rotational storage device to attain the correct position for data access. For magnetic tape, this is essentially null, although one generally considers the tape "start-up" time as a latency time. For disks and drums, latency varies from 0 to the time of a complete rotation, depending on the location of the data.
3. *Transfer time* is the amount of time required to transfer a block of data to or from a storage device, once the positioning and latency have been completed. For tape, disk, and drum, the transfer time is reasonably small, but it is pru-

dent to transfer an entire block at one time so as to avoid additional positioning and latency delays.

If a program is to access data sequentially, and the data are located on a secondary storage device, there is a delay for positioning and latency time, followed by a period when the data are transferred. Because the transfer rate of the secondary device is typically 5–50 times slower than that of the main storage, it is desirable to design a computer system so that the processor and main memory can carry out useful work both during the positioning and latency delays (when main storage is otherwise idle) and during the transfer period (when the main storage is only required 2–20% of the time). If a program is to access data in a non-sequential fashion, the latency and positioning delays become even more significant.

Architectural features such as interrupts and direct memory access I/O are designed to simplify the process of allowing the processor to do useful work while data are being transferred (see "Input/Output," below). Supervisory techniques such as multitasking (*q.v.*) and multiprogramming (*q.v.*) have a similar objective; thus, architectural features that support these are important to system performance.

RAM Disks Personal computer users have first-hand awareness of the speed difference between main and secondary memory. Programs on a disk generally take a while to start up (they must first be loaded into main memory) and may operate more slowly if designed to access the disk during execution. If a computer has enough main memory, it might be desirable to keep frequently used software and data in main memory for the duration of a work session. One very simple technique for this is to set aside a portion of main memory, designate it a "RAM disk," and provide software that allows one to access this portion of memory as though it were an actual disk (albeit one with zero access time, zero latency, and a very high transfer rate). This approach is very popular on personal computers and workstations. (If power is turned off between work sessions, however, information on a RAM disk is lost and will need to be reloaded.) On larger computers, a sophisticated operating system generally solves the problem in a different and more automated way that is invisible to the user.

Virtual Memory and Memory Hierarchies The idea of virtual memory is to give the programmer the illusion of a very large main memory, even though only a modest amount of main memory is actually available. This is achieved by placing the contents of the large, virtual memory on an auxiliary memory device and bringing parts of it into main memory, as required by the program, in a way that is transparent to the program. Virtual memory is prevalent on systems with large word lengths (large logical address sizes), although it is found on systems of all sizes.

Virtual memory is an excellent example of the subtle interplay between system and implementation architectures. Although the programmer with a virtual memory

TABLE 2. Data Access Comparison for Typical Devices

Storage device	Positioning Time	Latency	Transfer Time (512 bytes)
Cache memory	0	0	.01–.1 µs
Main memory	0	0	.05–.5 µs
RAM disk	0	0	.05–.5 µs
Magnetic drum or fixed head disk	0	5–50 ms	2–25 µs
Moving head disk	20–100 ms	10–50 ms	2–25 µs
Magnetic tape	0 sec–5 min	10 ms	2–25 µs

system can theoretically assume that a large amount of memory is available, seemingly minor changes in the data access pattern may have major ramifications on the amount of time required to execute programs. Thus, the programmer is driven to strive for *locality of reference*, in which consecutive references are made to objects that are physically adjacent, or nearly so; and to access multi-dimensional array data in a sequence corresponding to that used by the compiler for storing in memory. Conversely, the implementation of virtual memory calls for the architect to design hardware that "learns" (or makes good guesses at) the memory reference patterns of programs so that the data most frequently referenced will be kept in main memory. See Denning (1970) for more details.

A concept related to virtual memory is that of *hierarchical memory*. In its simplest form, this means that there is a hierarchy of memory types ranging from "large and slow" to "small and fast." The important idea, however, is to give the programmer access to only one type of logical memory (typically, "main" memory), with unseen implementation techniques making this memory appear both fast and plentiful. Caches and interleaving (see "Main Memory") are popular techniques for achieving a high apparent speed, and virtual memory techniques are used to achieve a large apparent size. In such an architecture, the registers may no longer be of concern to the programmer, who is given the view that all of main memory is fast. The real registers may be hidden from the system architecture or may be presented in the guise of designated, frequently used main memory locations for which there are special addressing modes.

In fact, as memory technology has advanced to the point where main memory is as fast as registers, actual implementation of real registers within main memory is becoming commonplace.

The ability to provide registers within main memory has additional benefits in terms of *multitasking*—a widely used method of sharing a processor among several activities. One of the most significant overhead costs of multitasking is the "context switch" time—i.e. the time required to save the contents of the registers for one task and load up new values corresponding to another task. In the past, designers have reduced this overhead by providing multiple sets of registers. But today it may be easier and cheaper to simply dispense with the distinction between registers and main memory so that no values need to be saved or loaded. Instead, the "registers" or context of a process can be assigned to a distinct block of main memory for each task. A "context switch" simply changes a "register pointer" (the only genuine register required in the system architecture). This approach has additional benefits with tightly-coupled multiprocessors, since it allows easy switching of tasks between processors (see Parallelism below).

Processing

The processing unit of a computer system consists of two parts—the control unit, which governs the operation of the system, and the arithmetic-logic unit (ALU), which carries out the computational and processing functions. In addition to the register set, key issues in processing unit architecture are the instruction set and the extent of parallelism.

Instruction Set An instruction tends to occupy one or more words of storage, and its purpose is to specify an operation to be performed by the processor. An instruction (Fig. 4) consists of an *operation code* (*op code*), which indicates the general nature of the function to be performed; possibly one or more *flags*, denoting special modes of operation; and possibly one or more *addresses*, which specify the operands or data to be operated upon. An instruction format is usually characterized by the number of such operand specifiers, and although a given processor will usually support several instruction formats, one will tend to predominate. Most common today are the "one-address" and "two-address" instruction formats.

By way of comparison, consider a typical instruction, "integer add," which requires three operands: two integer numbers to be added, and one integer result. With a three-address format, all three operands would be specified directly. With a two-address format, one of the three would be implicit—typically, a register or the top of a stack. A one-address format would have two implicit operands, and so forth.

An issue that was once a source of considerable debate among computer architects is which form of instruction has the highest "bit efficiency"—i.e. which form allows "typical" programs to be written with the fewest bits. This was deemed an important goal because smaller programs would make more efficient use of memory. As a general rule, a format calling for more addresses requires more bits per instruction, but needs fewer instructions to perform a computation and thus perhaps fewer bits for the computation. Research showed that an "optimal" instruction set would support several formats, with the most frequently used instructions being as short as possible. However, this was taken to extremes with processors that had dozens of different instruction lengths and formats. Such processors had marginally better bit efficiency, but the implementation costs and performance penalties showed the folly of focusing on a single design goal. Today, the emphasis is on achieving a balanced combination of bit efficiency, performance, and cost. In fact, some of the designs based on RISC architecture have

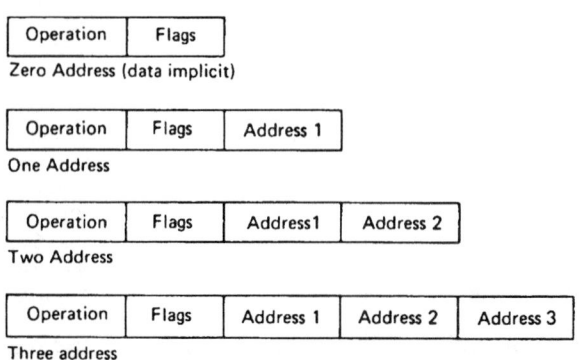

FIG. 4. Typical instruction formats.

sacrificed bit efficiency to achieve very high performance.

Operand addressing is usually more complex than is implied above. The field of an instruction that identifies an operand may contain several subfields, and may require a significant amount of computation just to determine the location of the operand. The various ways of identifying an operand are called *addressing modes*. A representative set of addressing modes is as follows.

Operand Specifier Format
(in address field of instruction)

| type | designator |

Type	Operand Class	Designator Interpretation
0	Immediate	Operand is designator itself
1	Direct	Designator is address of operand
2	Indirect	Designator is address of memory cell containing address of operand
3	Register	Designator indicates a register containing the operand

Many other operand formats have been used. The instruction set reference manual of any computer system will provide details on the specific approach used therein. (See also the articles in this encyclopedia on ADDRESSING and on specific systems such as the DEC VAX and the IBM 360/370/390 series.)

In addition to the format of a computer's instructions, the architect must consider their semantics—i.e. what functions they perform. For example, one issue is how to compare different values. In one approach, a "compare" instruction compares the values of two operands and sets a *condition code*, indicating whether the first operand is less than, equal to, or greater than the other. This code can be tested or stored for later use. An alternative approach is to simply subtract one item from the other and test the sign and value of the result. The condition code approach is more flexible, especially for comparing non-numeric quantities, but it is also more expensive to implement (*see* INSTRUCTION SET).

CISC and RISC For many years, instruction sets were designed on the basis of the register set, word length, technology characteristics, and the designer's concept of how programs would be written (generally based on assembly language programming styles). The functions performed were quite simple, such as controlling the sequence of instruction execution, shifting data, adding numbers together, and comparing values. Among the first "higher-level" features found in instruction sets were instructions to perform floating-point calculations.

In the mid-1970s, more designers began to examine what actual programs (mostly written in high-level languages) do. Initially, this work led to direct instruction set support for such "high-level" functions as procedure calling, list searching, and complex array access. As the computers of this period developed more and more complex features, they came to be known as Complex Instruction Set Computers (CISC). The trend in architectural circles was toward even more complex architectures that provide direct support for high-level languages (Myers, 1982) and sophisticated memory addressing and protection (Levy, 1984).

However, another trend was quietly developing among those trying to develop better microprocessors and microcomputers—entire processors and/or computers on a single, very-large-scale integrated circuit (VLSI) (*see* INTEGRATED CIRCUIT). The better work was done by interdisciplinary teams that combined knowledge of compilers, operating systems, the fundamental properties of VLSI, and the actual behavior of real application programs. Analysis of the frequency with which various instructions are used showed that a small number of relatively simple instructions account for most of the time spent by typical programs. Moreover, some of the more complex instructions perform functions that can be accomplished just as well, if not better, by short sequences of simpler instructions. Reduced instruction set computers (RISC), in which there are only a few carefully selected instructions, developed out of this work. Their high-performance potential made them so popular that the term RISC had become a rather abused marketing term by the late 1980s (just as the word "length" had been abused in earlier times). In the meantime, the best mainstream processors have combined the best concepts of both RISC and CISC, yielding instruction sets that are carefully chosen, based on the requirements of efficient implementation, as well as the requirements of high performance by realistic application software.

Tagged Architectures In the von Neumann type of instruction set described above, there is no distinction made in storage between instructions and data and in storage between different types of data. That is, it would be possible to perform an addition operation on a bit pattern representing an instruction and, although the results might be meaningless, the computer would not detect any problem. Such cases are the cause of numerous programming errors; thus, some computers have used *tagged architecture*, in which each memory word consists of two parts: the "data" part, which contains conventional data or instruction, and the "tag" part, which is a few extra bits that describe the data part. This enables detection of errors, and also has ramifications on instruction set design. Because the type of data is implied by the word containing the data, it is no longer necessary to have separate instructions for each data type supported by the machine. Instead of "integer add," "floating-point add," and "decimal add," a tagged architecture needs only a single "generic" instruction: "add." The tag fields indicate the specific type of addition to be performed.

Tagged architectures remain a controversial subject due to concerns about storage space efficiency, implementation cost, and the semantics of generic instructions when several different data types are used in the same instruction. They have been quite successful in symbolic processing systems, but have not made wide inroads into mainstream computer design.

Microprogamming and Writable Control Storage   One of the most popular techniques for implementation of processing units is *microprogramming*. In this technique, each instruction can be thought of as a "subroutine call" to a program written in a lower-level language, whose domain includes the data paths and registers of the processor. A major advantage of microprogramming is that hardware design errors can be corrected by simply revising the microprograms instead of changing the circuitry. This becomes a particularly important advantage in the VLSI era, where the entire processing function may be imbedded in a single silicon circuit, and where a "circuit change" is a prohibitively expensive process. Moreover, use of microprogramming allows the development of relatively complex instructions, without a substantial increase in processing unit complexity; instead, the amount of storage for microprograms is increased. While such storage is not free, it is composed of standard memory devices whose regular structure makes them relatively simple to design and build.

Normally, microprograms are stored in a "read only" memory device (ROM), both to reduce cost and to avoid loss of information during a loss of power. With *writable control store* (WCS), a part of the microcode storage is implemented with writable memory. This allows a general-purpose computer to be tailored to the requirements of a specific application by selective introduction of new instructions. The technique has achieved some use in research environments, but the complexities of software support (designing compilers that can make use of the new instructions, for example) have restricted commercial use to applications that can benefit significantly from the technique. The Burroughs B1800, for example, used writable control store to permit tailoring of the instruction set to different application areas at different times.

Parallelism   The speed with which instructions can be processed is determined by two factors: how fast the circuitry can perform a single instruction, and how many instructions can be performed in parallel. Circuit speed is largely determined by system cost, as limited by the available circuit technology, which now is limited by the fundamental laws of physics. Thus, to achieve the speed desired in high-performance systems, efforts are made to achieve high degrees of parallelism. Most of the techniques used to exploit parallelism belong to two disciplines: implementation architecture and algorithm design, although the results strongly affect system architecture (*see* PARALLEL PROCESSING: ARCHITECTURE).

Parallelism requires the use of multiple processors, and one of the first design issues is whether they should share the same main memory (tightly coupled) or have their own separate memories (loosely coupled). Either way, each processor generally has its own registers, and they generally share at least some of the secondary storage and peripherals. Which approach is better generally depends on the nature of the application.

A second issue is whether to use a small number of very powerful processors or a very large number of simple processors (massive parallelism). The latter approach generally involves tight coupling and an intricate design for the memory access mechanism. Algorithm design plays an important role in the effective use of massively parallel processors.

A third issue is whether to associate processors in a "pipeline" or "assembly line" fashion, with each stream of data passing through several processors, or whether to assign each processor to work on a separate stream of data.

Special-purpose architectures exploit parallelism in unique ways for particular applications. A case in point is *signal processing*, in which billions of operations per second may be achieved on a single microprocessor through the exploitation of specific characteristics. For example, signal processing is usually done on one bit at a time, and arithmetic overflow is generally ignored. An interesting aspect of these processors is that they deviate from conventional processors in many unexpected ways. For example, with a signal processor, it may be perfectly acceptable to ignore the higher-order digits of a multiplication, and when there is contention (*q.v.*) for memory access, the processor is given priority over peripheral devices.

Almost all issues of parallelism are strongly influenced by the nature of the problem being solved, as well as the algorithms proposed for the solution. Thus, truly general-purpose parallelism remains an elusive goal. The most dominant form of parallelism in actual commercial use is the sharing of peripherals and secondary storage through loosely coupled networks of processors (*see* NETWORK ARCHITECTURE).

Input-Output and Communication

Fundamental Issues   The remaining major architectural aspects of a computer system are related to communicating between the computer and the "outside" world. A typical computer system will be surrounded by an array of devices such as terminals, printers, and plotters, which are collectively called its *input/output (I/O)* devices. The function of such devices is to transmit data between the computer and its users, with appropriate transformations along the way. For example, a printer will transform bits and bytes into control signals for a mechanical printing mechanism; a video terminal will translate keystrokes into bytes of data, and then back into dots on a cathode ray tube.

I/O devices share certain characteristics with auxiliary storage devices; thus, both tend to be handled in similar ways architecturally. These devices have relatively low access speed and are usually capable of operating more or less independently from the processing unit. Thus, a complex, "loosely coupled" connection to the processor and main memory is required. Because of their relatively low speed, it is desirable to keep these devices in continuous operation, so that their maximum performance potential can be realized. Low speed and independent operation make it attractive to allow several devices to operate simultaneously. The fundamental issues of I/O architecture relate to the means of transferring data between these devices and main memory, and to the process of coordinating and synchronizing multiple devices, with the goal of obtaining maximum performance from each.

Communication Paths A peripheral or storage device must be connected to either the processor or main memory. A *data path* is a bundle of wires or other connecting medium that accomplishes this task. More capable data paths may involve their own special purpose processing units.

Data paths are generally grouped into three types: *simplex* paths allow data to flow in only a single direction; *half-duplex* paths allow data to flow in either direction, but only one at a time; *full-duplex* paths allow data to flow in both directions simultaneously. A simplex path might be used to connect an input-only device (e.g. a keyboard) to the computer or to connect the computer to an output-only device (e.g. a display or printer). A half-duplex path would be used to connect a device that does both input and output, but only one at a time (e.g. a tape drive). A full-duplex path is necessary when the device needs to do both input and output at the same time or requires rapid switching between input and output modes. Any of the data paths discussed below may be implemented in a simplex, half-duplex, or full-duplex manner.

A *channel* is a data path connecting a peripheral device directly to a memory system. If more than one device is required, each may be connected to a different channel, or there may be a way for several devices to share the same channel. Simple shared channels permit only one device to transmit data at a time, whereas multiplexor channels allow interleaved data transfers from several devices. *Multiplexing* (*q.v.*) can be performed by dividing the channel into several parallel sub-channels or by time multiplexing, in which units of data from different devices alternate. Two examples of time multiplexing are the byte multiplexor channel, which transmits one byte of data at a time from each device, and the block multiplexor channel, in which large blocks of data are interleaved.

The channel is a good way to achieve high performance in device-to-memory communication, but its costs can be high for resolving contention problems. Thus, it is most appropriate when all devices are similar or when there are only a few devices.

A *daisy chain* is a low cost, prioritized method of connecting several devices to the computer, but allowing only one of them to communicate. It works like certain old-fashioned decorative tree lights. The computer is connected to the first device, which, in turn, is connected to the second device, and so on. Each device has a switch that controls the link to the next device. If all switches are on, the last device in the chain can communicate with the computer. However, any device in the chain can request access to the computer by simply switching off the lower devices. The first device in the chain has top priority—it can communicate at will by simply switching off the others. The second device has next highest priority—it can communicate except when the first device has preempted it, and so on with remaining devices.

A *bus* is a data path that connects devices in parallel, more or less like a party line. Any device can use the bus, but one of the devices is designated as a master, and it controls access to the bus by issuing authorization signals. Information is transmitted across a bus in two parts: address and data. Each device is associated with a specific address or range of addresses, and when an address comes down the bus, the associated device is designated to receive or send the associated data. Buses were originally devised to allow data to flow among computer registers and between the processor and main memory. This concept was later generalized to accommodate secondary storage and peripheral devices. Today, certain forms of local area network (LAN - *q.v.*) have extended this concept to longer distances and a wider range of devices.

An advantage of the bus is simplicity in connecting things to the main memory system. Only one bus-to-memory connection need be made. All contention for memory access is resolved with the bus, rather than with the memory interface. This permits memory access to remain fast and simple, while allowing many devices to have direct access to memory. However, the interface between the device and the bus is more expensive than, for example, the daisy chain connection. Use of buses has steadily increased over the past two decades, due to advances in circuit technology that permit a bus interface to be implemented relatively inexpensively.

Control Control of input and output must accomplish initiation of the transfer, synchronization of communicating devices, and completion reporting. Three potential "players" in this process are the processor, the memory, and a peripheral or secondary storage device. The data path is the medium of communication, and it often handles much of the synchronization. Many authors have attempted to organize the various forms in which I/O control may occur, although none has been entirely satisfactory. Smotherman's taxonomy (1989) is one of the most recent, and this paper has the advantage of discussing some of its predecessors. Here we attempt to organize matters in a somewhat simpler way.

The most straightforward approach to controlling the transmission of data is *program-controlled I/O*. Under such a scheme, the processor will direct the input and output activity. In one approach, there will be an *explicit instruction* which initiates the transfer by commanding a device to accept a small amount of data (typically one word or byte) for display or storage (output) or to transmit a small unit of data to the processor (input). The instruction may wait for transmission to occur or may simply initiate the activity, with subsequent "test" instructions required to poll the device and determine when transmission is complete. Transmission usually occurs between the device and some processor register, although in some designs a main memory cell may be specified.

An alternative to use of explicit instructions is *memory-mapped I/O* (*q.v.*). This technique has the processor direct activity by writing to certain reserved cells in its logical memory space, called *control words*. Control words may actually be implemented as reserved main memory cells or may be implemented within the device itself. The act of writing into a control word causes the address of that word to be sent out across the memory bus. As previously discussed, different devices on a bus will be associated with different addresses. Thus, each device on the bus observes all addresses and intercepts those that correspond to its control words. The device reads the "data" being written to the control word and interprets it as an I/O command.

The memory-mapped approach simplifies the control interface and the instruction set. Its main drawbacks are that (1) it puts "holes" in the logical address space (i.e. sections of the address space that cannot be used as genuine memory cells), and (2) it complicates cacheing and virtual memory. Ill-conceived use of memory-mapped I/O in low cost processors has sometimes impeded the growth of their architectures into more powerful systems. However, by judicious use of memory mapping or virtual memory, the drawbacks of program-controlled I/O can be managed.

Whether through explicit instructions or memory mapping, the processor will typically initiate activity on several devices, with subsequent polling to determine when each has finished. However, in the absence of further architectural support, it is difficult (or even impossible) for the processor to be programmed in such a way that it performs useful work while the devices are busy and also responds promptly when they are finished so as to keep them in continuous operation. Since most peripheral devices are slow (by processor standards), it is desirable to reduce or eliminate the need for polling and thus free up the processor during I/O operations.

The program-controlled scheme tends to impose high overhead when the peripheral device has a relatively high data transfer rate. This is due to having the processor execute an initiation command, a repeated series of completion tests, and perhaps a transfer between register and main memory for each word or byte of data transferred. *Direct memory access (DMA)* is a technique for reducing processor involvement during the transfer of blocks of data. This technique incorporates specific concepts of both control and communication. DMA not only allows transmission directly between devices and memory, as the name implies, but, as commonly defined, it eliminates the high processor control overhead, described earlier.

With the DMA technique, the processor will initiate the transfer of a block of data, with the "completion" notification coming only when the entire block has been moved. The processor's command goes to a DMA controller—a separate, special-purpose processor—which has the independent capability to count the number of items transmitted and keep track of where they go in memory. Meanwhile, the processor can do other useful work.

Advanced DMA systems allow *chaining* of command blocks and other techniques that permit multiple blocks of data to be transmitted to different areas of main memory by a single command from the processor. Certain channels operate in essentially the same way as DMA except that DMA is generally a shared capability, whereas a channel is usually associated with a specific set of peripherals.

Interrupts and Traps   These two techniques are very similar, and some designs do not distinguish between them. Both are methods of notifying the processor of an event. A *trap* signals an abnormal event within the processor, such as an arithmetic fault, illegal instruction, or power failure. An *interrupt* notifies the processor of an external event, such as completion of an I/O operation. Traps generally force the processor to stop what it is doing and deal immediately with the event. Interrupts usually signal events that are less urgent than traps, and the processor need not always respond immediately. Recent systems have expanded the role of the interrupt to include software-detected events, such as completion of a task or emptying of a queue. While interrupts are used in many contexts, we focus here on their use in I/O applications.

An interrupt can be used by a peripheral device to notify a processor that a data transfer has been completed. This allows the processor to perform other work in the meantime, yet service the device promptly upon its completion. I/O interrupts can be used with any of the control or communication schemes described above.

Typically, the interrupt signal is generated by an I/O device that has completed its most recent request or that requires some other service. In response to the interrupt signal, a processor will usually suspend its current activity and attend to the device. In the simplest schemes, all devices share the same interrupt signal, and the processor must scan all devices to determine which has generated the interrupt. More elaborate schemes allow the processor to determine immediately which device caused the interrupt. This may be a control word that has a separate bit for each interrupting device (the processor tests to see which bit has been set) or a *vectored interrupt scheme*, in which each device causes the processor to transfer to a different address.

A typical busy processor will have many interrupting devices. In order to make order out of potential chaos, there must be a method of resolving conflicts. If two devices interrupt at the same time, which one should be serviced first? If one device is being serviced and another interrupts, should the first one be interrupted to service the second one? To deal with issues such as these, most processors support multiple levels of interrupts. In a simple scheme that suffices for most situations, a small number of levels are supported—perhaps four or eight. Each potential source of interrupts is associated with a particular level, corresponding to how quickly its requests must be responded to. Higher-level devices can interrupt lower-level ones, but not vice versa. Equal level devices cannot interrupt each other. A typical scheme might assign the highest level to events that:

- Require immediate action, such as power failures or illegal instructions;
- Could cause functional failure if not attended to promptly, such as a timing signal that must be acknowledged promptly if time is to be kept accurately;
- Could cause performance degradation, such as a disk that has rotated to a desired position and

should be accessed within a short time to avoid waiting for another rotation; or

- Have relatively minimal impact, such as notification that a task has completed and its storage is no longer needed.

More elaborate schemes assign distinct priorities to each interrupt or to small groups of similar interrupts. Vectored interrupt schemes often associate a distinct priority with each distinct interrupt address. There remains some dispute as to whether this degree of priority distinction is really necessary for most applications. Too many priority levels can lead to excessive "context switch" overhead as one device interrupts another.

Another issue stems from the fact that interrupt priorities are often built into the processor or bus hardware, with little or no flexibility. In actual applications, it might be appropriate to let priorities be controlled by the devices or by software. For example, a single device might report different kinds of events that deserve different priorities (e.g. disk has rotated to desired position, vs. disk has been turned on). Changes in system state might cause the need for software to vary priorities (normal versus emergency operation, for example). Some recent designs allow device and/or software control of interrupt priorities, but there is little agreement at this point about what type of scheme is best suited to the general case. Different programming languages call for different approaches to this problem, and, until some consensus can be reached, computer architecture will continue to be experimental in this regard.

Interrupts are a valuable architectural feature, but they tend to cause numerous problems as well. A processor may inadvertently receive an interrupt from a device that the software is not prepared to handle, or at a time when it was not expected. A faulty device may send interrupts continuously, deluging the system with interrupt response activity and blocking other devices from service. Elaborate software may be required to handle such cases correctly, and in some systems such situations may result in uncorrectable hardware or software faults ("hangups"). As a result of many years of experience with interrupts, architects have begun to refine and "civilize" the interrupt systems of computers. For example, it is now usually possible for the software to mask or block interrupts in cases where a software module requires higher priority than an external device, or where some particular device's interrupts are to be ignored. A very promising concept is to model interrupts after more general synchronization mechanisms such as messages or semaphores. This is an excellent example of how a technique developed to solve a software problem has impacted computer architecture in more fundamental ways.

Publications Certain professional publications and organizations are concerned with the advancement of computer architecture. The Association for Computing Machinery has a special interest group on computer architecture (SIGARCH) that publishes a newsletter (*Computer Architecture News* or *CAN*) several times a year. Strongly related issues are covered in *Operating Systems Review*, the newsletter of the special interest group on operating systems (SIGOPS). Another special interest group focuses on mircoprogramming (SIGMICRO). The IEEE Computer Society has several publications relating to computer architecture and design. Most important are the monthly *Computer* and *IEEE Transactions on Computers*. The IEEE and SIGARCH sponsor an annual symposium on computer architecture, usually held in the spring, the proceedings of which are available from the IEEE Publications department, and as a special issue of *Computer Architecture News*. SIGMICRO sponsors an annual microprogramming symposium in the fall, the proceedings of which are available from ACM or as a special issue of the SIGMICRO newsletter.

References

1962. Buchholz, Werner. *Planning a Computer System—Project Stretch*. New York: McGraw-Hill.

1970. Denning, Peter J. "Virtual Memory," *ACM Computing Surveys* **2**, *3*: 153–190 (September).

1973. Feustel, E. A. "On the Advantages of Tagged Architecture," *IEEE Transactions on Computers* **22** (July), 644–656.

1975. Patil, S. (Ed.). "Computer Systems Architecture," Special Issue: *ACM Computing Surveys* **7**, *4* (December).

1976. Reddi, S. S. and Feustel, E. A. "A Conceptual Framework for Computer Architecture," *ACM Computing Surveys* **8**, *2*: 277–300 (June).

1980. Baer, J-L. *Computer Systems Architecture*. Potomac, MD: Computer Science Press.

1982. Siewiorek, D. P., Bell, C. G., and Newell, A. *Computer Structures: Principles and Examples*. New York: McGraw-Hill.

1982. Myers, Glenford J. *Advances in Computer Architecture*, 2nd Ed. New York: John Wiley & Sons.

1984. Hwang, Kai, and Briggs, Faye A. *Computer Architecture and Parallel Processing*. New York: McGraw-Hill.

1984. Levy, Henry M. *Capability-Based Computer Systems*. Bedford, MA: Digital Press.

1987. Leonard, Timothy E (Ed.). *Vax Architecture Reference Manual*. Bedford MA: Digital Press.

1989. Smotherman, Mark. "A Sequencing-Based Taxonomy of I/O Systems and Review of Historical Machines," *Computer Architecture News*, **17**, 5 (September) 5–15.

1990. Hennessy, J. L., and Patterson, D. A. *Computer Architecture: A Quantitative Approach*. San Mateo, CA: Morgan-Kaufman.

DENNIS J. FRAILEY

COMPUTER ARITHMETIC. See ARITHMETIC, COMPUTER.

COMPUTER ART

For articles on related subjects *see* COMPUTER GRAPHICS; FRACTALS; HUMANITIES APPLICATIONS; and IMAGE PROCESSING.

History Efforts to create art with analog machines date back to the 1950s. However, it was not until January 1965 that the first exhibition of digital computer graphics was arranged by three mathematicians: Frieder Nake and

George Nees, both Germans, and an American, A. Michael Noll. Their goal (Franke, 1971) was to create visually pleasing images, not merely graphics representing data. This exhibition was held at the Studio Gallery of the University of Stuttgart. Several shows followed the initial one in Germany, including one in New York City at the Howard Wise Gallery. Computer art became an international movement (Reichardt, 1971) practiced in Britain, Germany, Italy, Austria, Japan, Canada, and the U.S.

Non-utilitarian use of the machine was practiced in those countries that were technologically developed. An image reminiscent of this period is a graphic by Guenther Tetz (Fig. 1) created at the University of Illinois at Chicago Circle on the PDP-11/45-Vector General Graphic System. The event that made the world really take note of computer art was "Cybernetic Serendipity" (Reichardt, 1968), an exhibition held at the Institute of Contemporary Arts in London. The catalog for the show was a special issue of *Studio International* magazine and was subsequently published as the first book of art dealing with the computer and creativity. "Cybernetic Serendipity" brought together individuals who had been working in isolation and was a source of inspiration for others to begin working in this area. Artists from France, Spain, and Holland joined in making computer-aided art. They either learned to use the computer themselves or worked with computer experts. In 1970, works created with the aid of the computer were hung alongside traditionally made artworks at the Venice Biennial. Today, computer art hangs in permanent museum collections, corporate offices, public spaces, and private homes. It is judged in competitions, along with traditional art, on its artistic merits, not on the tools that aided in its creation.

Developments in hardware have brought about changes in computer art. Towards the end of the 1960s, many artists began to use cathode ray tubes to visualize their work. This made it possible for the artist to work in a more traditional way, since artistic decisions are often made during the creation of a work. Interactive systems allow the artist to see the work immediately and to modify it. With the development of color graphics terminals, the artist could see images displayed in color. On many systems it is now possible to choose from over a quarter-million different colors. Numerical values are assigned to each color in the spectrum as well as to black and white. The consistency of the machine, moreover, makes it superior to mixing colors with the traditional artist's palette, since commercial artist's pigments sold under the same name can vary widely. Interfacing video with computer hardware has expanded the digital palette even further. Video samplings captured with the camera allow the artist to brush on a marble surface as easily as painting with color. In addition to samplings, both the video camera interface and the recently invented digital camera permit the artist to store entire pictures in memory for later use. The untitled image (see Fig. 2, color insert page CP-4) by William Tudor, artist and composer, is a good example of this technique. With higher resolution terminals and laser printers, the appearance of lines has changed as well. Today the once jagged look is gone and it is difficult to differentiate between hand-drawn and machine-drawn lines. The availability of tablets and pens to input information, accessibility to microcomputers, and the abundance of quality commercial software is making the computer in the artist's studio commonplace.

Media Conventionally, the tools of the artist define the type of work that is produced. The painter, for example, uses brushes and paint, the photographer uses a camera, and so on. The computer artist, on the other hand, finds that the machine is multifaceted. Not only is it a high-powered design tool, but its output devices make it possible for the artist to express a particular idea in various media: Drawings may be produced with a vector or raster plotter; sculptures may be milled with computer-driven milling machines; paintings may be painted with computer-driven airbrushes; video, frames of film animations, and photographs may be taken directly off the cathode ray tube; graphics are made possible by a photo transfer process of computer images; and environmental art can be created where the computer senses and accordingly activates devices in a given space.

The advantages of using the computer in each medium differ. Drawings, for example, are made both as preliminary sketches for other work and as art objects in themselves. Artists who write programs to create imagery frequently use a random number generator (Mezei, 1971). This yields two specific effects: (1) It is apt to produce variations that the artists would not ordinarily conceive of on their own, and (2) in a short amount of time, artists have a good many sketches from which they can choose to work or to use as finished pieces. The wall mural (see Fig. 3, color insert page CP-4) by Harold Cohen, a new wave British artist, is an example of producing variations by deterministic strategies. Investigating the potential of artificial intelligence (*q.v.*) and art, Cohen's program AARON simulates human freehand drawing, while providing insights into the thinking processes of creating art. Exploring questions about the perception of space, Margot Lovejoy, artist and author, outputs her drawings as slides to be used in computer-controlled projection installations (Fig. 4, color insert page CP-4), as well as prints, constructions, and artists' books.

The development of the digital camera supports the move by many photographers to experiment with imag-

FIG. 1. Untitled image by Guenther Tetz, 1979.

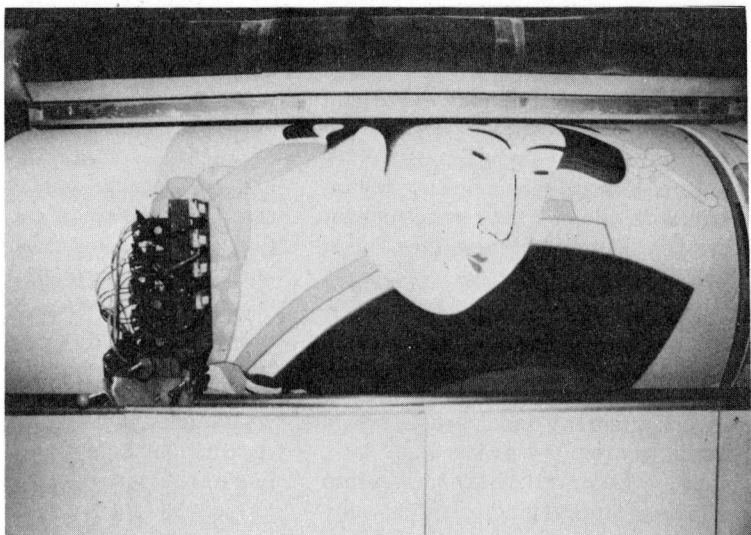

FIG. 6. Computer-controlled painting device. (Photograph courtesy of Minnesota Mining and Manufacturing Company.)

ery on the computer before entering the darkroom. Omitting the expense of chemicals and paper while increasing creative options is why photographers like Ellen Sandor are using the computer. Sandor's "Phscolograms," created with the collective group (Art)ⁿ, combines *p*hotography, *h*olography, *s*culpture, and *c*omputer graphics to create large, full-color, three-dimensional photographic images (see Fig. 5, color insert page CP-4). Intrigued by the idea of discovery through simulation, she uses the computer to aid her in creating the illusions she achieves in her work.

Paintings can be produced with computers starting from the preliminary drawings up to the final execution on canvas. The artist first utilizes the machine as a sketchpad, creating the design to be painted. This design may then, for example, be drawn by the machine onto 35 mm film by an electron beam gun through colored filters. The design on the slide is input by means of a scanning device to another computer that in turn, controls airbrushes and paint to produce the final product. Wall-sized murals are being produced by the 3M Company of St. Paul, MN with just such a machine (Fig. 6).

Sculpture can also be a fully automated process. The use of the computer in this medium is especially impressive. The machine allows the sculptor to envision a piece of work at a given location from any perspective before it is completed and installed. This permits the artist to make changes before investing time, energy, and cost of materials on a project that might not succeed. The 6-ft-high wood and plaster sculpture in Fig. 7 would not have been produced without the aid of the computer. Not only was it designed on the machine, but also a plotter produced the template for its formation. The fact that the machine mills with exact precision extends the concept of what can be created as well as what materials can be employed. Highly detailed works can now be sculptured with computer-controlled milling machines having five degrees of freedom. On these output devices, the drill bit not only moves back and forth and up and down, but is

able to make undercuts as well. The milling machine relieves artists of the physical demands of creation and allows them to concentrate on the exploration of ideas.

The evolution to a new sculptural aesthetic can be seen in the works of Stephen Pevnick, Milton Komisar, and Alan Rath. Although each artist uses different materials, all incorporate digital computers into their art. Unlike traditional sculptures, these self-contained information processing systems are capable of conveying the concept of time as a creative element, thereby providing an ever-changing perspective for the viewer. Pevnic's

FIG. 7. Untitled sculpture by Ruth Leavitt. Wood and plaster, 6' × 6', 1980, private collection.

computer-designed and -controlled fountains allow him to sculpt with falling water (see Fig. 8, color insert page CP-5). A programmable matrix of valves (each valve can generate 4,608 water droplets per second) permits the artist to translate images on the computer screen into a lyrical flow of three-dimensional objects. Milton Komisar, on the other hand, choreographs waves of light throughout structures of clear acrylic rods (see Fig. 9, color insert page CP-5). Each rod is attached to a module containing two or three tinted light bulbs and a driver translating binary code to control the current coming from a transformer. Processing up to 60 changes a second for each bulb, the artist can control such variables as time entry, duration, color, pattern, and speed, to create a myriad of sculptures from one. Whereas Alan Rath, another contemporary artist, converts video images into digital animations which he stores and displays in sculptural form (see Fig. 10. color insert page CP-5). Some of his pieces also include a digital phoneme generator that provides a synthesized spoken audio track. Previously, sculptors used the wind and simple mechanisms to exert change in their work. The ability to master the element of time was not possible. Now, as Pevnick, Rath, and Komisar demonstrate, sculptors are able to realize that vision.

The production of film animation and graphics presents difficulties that the computer alleviates. Customarily, animation is extremely expensive to create, since each frame must be drawn by hand. The artist using the computer allows the machine to draw the intermediate pictures, thus saving both time and expense. Images can be produced on color displays and filmed directly off the scope. A major problem in creating graphics is the production of color separations. In serigraphy, for example, each color must be screened separately. An inherent quality of computers that display colored images is that they automatically color-separate each picture. To display each colored design, the computer must calculate what percentage of each of three colors plus black and white is used to create the desired picture. Thus, for the animator and the graphic artist, the computer can save great amounts of time.

Interactive artists use computing equipment to invite the viewer, traditionally a passive observer, to become an active participant in creativity. Taking shape in various forms such as *environments*, *hypermedia*, *virtual reality*, and *telecommunications*, interactive art blurs the line that traditionally separates artistic expression from aesthetic experience. Myron Krueger, a pioneer of interactive art, has used computing equipment since the late 1960s to control entire rooms designed for interactivity. His environments perceive the human body in motion, analyze it, and respond in real time with visual and auditory displays. A primary computer with 2,000 storage and specialized processing chips controls 10 secondary computers that filter the main machine's input. A participant enters a room with only a computer controlled video camera and large screen. What then occurs is dependent upon the actions of the viewer. Using his own body movement, a participant is able to create a variety of pictures and sounds or simply play with the "critter" displayed with his own image on the screen (see Fig. 11, color insert page CP-5). The complexity of personally designing the hardware and software for interactive art prohibited its growth as an art discipline until the mid 1980s when Hypercard, commercial software with interactive applications, became available. Known as Hypermedia, or computer controlled multimedia, artists integrate such things as animation, still imagery, video, and audio into interactive works of art. Incorporating wearable technologies such as gloves, goggles, and suits into computer art environments can heighten a participant's experiences with realistic sensations. Moving one step closer to a totally defined interactive data space, artists can create what are termed Virtual Worlds, depicting the essence of reality in full color, three-dimensional imagery with attributes such as touch, sound, and motion. For example, a virtual reality glove can be programmed so that a viewer selects and manipulates screen objects while simultaneously feeling each one's weight and texture. Nicole Stengler, a fine artist working in collaboration with the Human Interface Technology Laboratory at the University of Washington Technology Center, has added goggles and glove to her work "Angels" to turn myth into virtual reality for museum attendees. However, telecommunication artists like Roy Ascott bypass the traditional exhibition system by using electronic space mediated by computer networks to create virtual presence environments. Collaborative art works are created interactively on electronic mail (*q.v.*) systems, offering participants from international locations (nodes) an environment that defies boundaries and alters the concept of time and space. Virtual presence will interface with virtual reality when participants have data gloves (now available by mail order) and goggles attached to their modems.

The manner in which traditional artists employ their tools creates individual styles. We often recognize artists by their styles or the styles they imitate. There is, however, no unique style that typifies works of art as "computer art" (Leavitt, 1976). The statement an artist makes in his or her work is a function of the artist and the program, not the artist and the computer. Rather than identifying a style as having originated from a particular artist, in computer-aided art we can often identify a style of work as having been created with a particular program. Commercial software paint packages exemplify this. Artwork created with commercial paint programs, although produced by different people at different locations, looks very similar because the uniqueness of the program causes it to define its own style. All computer art programs use one or more techniques, such as rotation, scaling, windowing, zooming, transformations, and picture processing, but each uses these techniques in such a way as to be stylistically identifiable. Whether the artist approaches the work in a random or deterministic manner, the program still is the overriding factor regarding style.

An artist has the option of participating in the creation of the program to be used, as well as to explore the possibilities that exist within that particular program. This allows artists to determine their own styles. A unique feature of using the computer is that the artist can create an environment that does not exist in the real world. This permits the artist to explore ideas never before thought possible. In the past, artists created work from the world around them. They translated the world in either figurative or abstract terms, but in either case, this was their sense of reality. Computer artists can create their own sense of reality, allowing them to transcend the role of the traditional artist.

References

1968. Reichardt, Jasia. *"Cybernetic Serendipity"—The Computer and the Arts*. New York: Praeger.

1971. Reichardt, Jasia. *The Computer in Art*. New York: Van Nostrand Reinhold.

1971. Mezei, Leslie. "Randomness in Computer Graphics," in Reichardt, Jasia (Ed.), *Cybernetics, Art and Ideas*. New York: New York Graphic Society.

1976. Leavitt, Ruth. *Artist and Computer*. New York: Harmony Books.

1979. Malina, Frank. *Visual Art, Mathematics, and Computers*. Selections from the journal *LEONARDO*. Elmsford, NY: Pergamon Press.

1983. Krueger, Myron W. *Artificial Reality*. Reading, MA: Addison-Wesley.

1983. Peterson, Dale. *Genesis II*. Reston, VA: Reston Publishing Company, Inc.

1984. Franke, Herbert W. *Computer Graphics, Computer Art* (2nd Ed.). New York: Phaidon.

1984. Franke, Herbert W. *Computergrafik—Galerie*. Carson, CA: DuMont.

1984. Grundmann, Heidi. *Art Telecommunication*. Vancouver: A Western Front Publication.

1984. Jankel, Annabel and Morton, Rocky. *Creative Computer Graphics*. New York: Cambridge University Press.

1986. Kerlow, Issac Victor and Rosebush, Judson. *Computer Graphics for Designers and Artists*. New York: Van Nostrand Reinhold Company Inc.

1987. Goodman, Cynthia. *Digital Visions, Computers and Art*. New York: Abrams.

1989. Lamb, D.J. "The Impact of the Computer on the Arts," *Academic Computing* (April) 22–24, 50–54.

1989. Schwartz, Lillian with Schwartz, Laurens. *The Handbook of Art, Animation and Analysis By Computer*. New York: W. W. Norton.

1989. Lovejoy, Margot. *Postmodern Currents, Art and Artists in the Age of Electronic Media*. Ann Arbor, MI: UMI Research Press.

1990. Krueger, Myron W. *Artificial Reality II*. Reading, MA: Addison-Wesley Publishing.

1990. McCorduck, Pamela. *Aaron's Code: Meta-Art, Artificial Intelligence, and the Work of Harold Cohen*. New York: W. H. Freeman.

1991. Ascott, Roy and Loeffler, Carl (Eds.). *Connectivity: Art and Interactive Telecommunications*. LEONARDO **24**, 2. New York: Pergamon Press.

1991. Brill Louis, *Virtual Reality '91 Conference*. YLEM Newsletter **11**, 11. Orinda, CA: YLEM Artists Using Science and Technology.

1991. Goodman, Danny. *Hypercard 2.0*. New York: Bantam Books.

1991. Kerlow, I.V. "Art and Design and Computer Graphics Technology," *Comm. ACM*, **34**, 7 (July) 30–39.

1991. Wilson, Stephen. *Multimedia Design with Hypercard*. Englewoods Cliffs, NJ: Prentice-Hall.

RUTH LEAVITT

COMPUTER-ASSISTED INSTRUCTION (CAI)

For articles on related subjects *see* COMPUTER-ASSISTED LEARNING AND TEACHING; COMPUTER-MANAGED INSTRUCTION; and NETWORKS FOR LEARNING.

Computer-assisted instruction (CAI) refers to the use of computers to present drills, practice exercises, and tutorial sequences to the student, and perhaps to engage the student in a dialogue about the substance of the instruction. A CAI (tutorial) dialogue is achieved between a computer program and a student when the responses derived from the program are highly responsive to the questions, answers, and directives given by the student, while at the same time the dialogue advances the goals and means established by the author of the curriculum materials.

CAI is only one part of computer assistance in the processes of learning and teaching. It has proved successful where the goals of instruction are clearly defined, achievement of those goals is highly valued by the organization providing instruction, the substance of instruction is suited to automated delivery, and the student is lacking important skills, background, or motivation for self-instruction via less expensive media. Research studies tend to show advantages for CAI in terms of shorter learning times and improved performance. Inhibitors to operational use include high costs of delivery systems and curriculum development, conflicts between individualized instruction and current educational practices, and commitment of most of the computing resources available in schools to instructional use for education about computers. An analysis of CAI effectiveness, along with other media for instruction, is given by Kulik and Bangert-Drowns (1990).

Initial Demonstration Projects A group of engineers and educators in the Computer-based Education Research Laboratory at the University of Illinois, Urbana, designed a computing system (PLATO) especially for effective and efficient teaching. It was a large system that provided instructional computing to about 1,000 simultaneous users throughout the university and also a number of other colleges and schools in Illinois. The design included notable advances in the technology for display and communications. The PLATO system has been marketed commercially by Control Data Corporation, and the curriculum materials and programming language are available for use with microcomputers.

Stanford University operated a CAI system to distribute instructional computing to a number of centers throughout the country. A large-scale service operation using long-distance telephone communications, clusters of terminals, and some standalone computer systems, the remote centers were usually associated with elementary school demonstration projects and special education institutions. The service operation was conducted in parallel with an extensive program of research and development at the Institute for Mathematical Studies in the Social Sciences, Stanford University. Curriculum materials were prepared for young children (elementary school math and reading), learners with special difficulties (for example, the deaf), and certain university courses (especially second-language learning and logic). Some of these materials have been marketed by the Computer Curriculum Corporation, along with new developments.

TICCIT (Time-shared, Interactive, Computer-Controlled Informational Television) is a name given to systems developed by the Mitre Corporation in McLean, Virginia, and since marketed by Hazeltine Corporation. The first version of an instructional system was designed especially for use in a small college. It was a medium-sized computer system with video technology to obtain low-cost operation with about 100 simultaneous users. The hardware and software design was coordinated with the development of instructional materials, carefully prepared according to rules of effective instruction by instructional design teams at Brigham Young University in Utah, to provide basic remedial instruction in mathematical and language skills at small colleges.

Areas of Application

CAI materials have been prepared for many subjects, from accounting to zoology, and from preschool through adult education. Materials can be found in selected disciplinary areas by consulting teaching publications or professional committees associated with mathematics, physics, chemistry, biology, geography, political science, history, psychology, English, business, engineering, law, and medicine, among others.

Current Status.

CAI has had many successes in military and industrial training, where the objectives are clear and a modest percentage advantage in delivery cost and trainee time adds up to considerable savings for the organization. Effective automation of training is essential in areas where new job requirements, employee turnover, and decreasing skills among those entering the workforce combine to force costs up.

Adoptions of CAI by educational institutions are not common. Even where costs of instruction via computers have been shown to be lower, institutions have difficulty shifting dollars from people to machines, adjusting schedules and rules to realize the benefits of individualized instruction, and convincing students that technology can do the job on its own. Nevertheless, some schools and colleges regularly employ CAI for second language instruction, practice of basic skills in writing, remediation in mathematics and sciences, or preparation for laboratory exercises. The early and optimistic promises for CAI have not been realized. The costs are high compared to other uses of computers in teaching and learning.

Improving technologies are increasing the capabilities of computer systems for effective delivery of instruction (seen mostly in characteristics of the display) and bringing down the price of a personal computer. Videodiscs (*q.v.*) provide a low-cost, color image storage medium under computer control, and animated graphics are practical on inexpensive color displays. Control of images and ease of access make qualitative differences in the use of computers in teaching and learning.

The locus of decisions about CAI in education has shifted from institutions to individuals. Parents are taking their children to community learning centers for automated tutoring to improve basic skills. Students and families are purchasing home computers to provide learning activities along with productivity tools and entertainment.

The installed base of personal computers now provides a market for learning materials that is large enough to justify investments by educational publishers. However, the improvements in hardware technology aren't matched by computer software and learning materials. The application of artificial intelligence techniques to tutorial CAI (e.g. for training trouble-shooting skills) holds some promise for considerable increase in flexibility and effectiveness of computer delivery with a wide range of learners. However, costs for curriculum development remain high. CAI may never get its breakthrough in software and materials development that is necessary if it is to compete with other uses of computers in learning and teaching.

References

1989. Farr, Marshall and Psotka, J. *Intelligent Instruction by Computer: Theory and Practice.* New York: Taylor and Francis.
1990. Kulik, J. A., and Bangert-Drowns, R. L. "Computer-Assisted Learning." In N. Entwistle (Ed.), *Handbook of Educational Ideas and Practices.* London: Routledge.

KARL L. ZINN

COMPUTER-ASSISTED LEARNING AND TEACHING

For articles on related subjects *see* AUTHORING LANGUAGES AND SYSTEMS; COMPUTER-ASSISTED INSTRUCTION; COMPUTER-MANAGED INSTRUCTION; LOGO; and NETWORKS FOR INSTRUCTION.

The impact of computers on *teaching and learning* activities at all levels of education is considerable, and the extent of use is increasing rapidly. Current uses in postsecondary education are quite varied. A medical student practices diagnosis and prescription on a wide variety of hypothetical patients simulated by computer programs. A senior engineering student using computer assistance solves problems in road design that ten years ago were not approached until after two years of experience on the job. A sophomore in computer science develops a program to help a professor of chemistry evaluate the effectiveness of questions on a multiple-choice quiz. A freshman in general psychology directs a computer-based information system to assemble a complete bibliography on the relation between achievement motivation and college grades, which is as current as the journals received by his or her professor. A laboratory technician tests him/herself on newly acquired skills, using a terminal on a hospital information system.

Computing is also quite visible in education outside colleges and universities. A high school science student applies wildlife management practices to a computer simulation of the American bison herds that were slaughtered in the 1800s. An English literature student programs a computer to generate poetry. A child in the fifth grade explores mathematics by writing computer programs that draw spirals or solve mazes. A second grader practices spelling or addition problems "spoken" by a computer; the computer checks the answers that the student enters on the keyboard. In some systems, the student simply speaks the answer to be "recognized" by the computer. A high school dropout improves language skills using a computer program made available on a community cable television system.

When the computer system is appropriate for educational uses and the programs are properly written, the learners should find the assistance to be responsive to their needs; patient and not punitive while they learn; accurate in assessment of answers and problem solutions; individualized in a useful way; realistic in the presentation of training or testing situations; and helpful with many information processing tasks. Teachers find computer assistance valuable for keeping accurate records, summarizing data, projecting student-learning difficulties, assembling individualized tests, and retrieving information about films or other learning resources. Authors of textbooks and other learning materials use computers to draw figures, to animate motion picture sequences, or to keep track of the introduction and frequency of occurrence of concepts throughout a text. Researchers record and analyze data, build models of student learning and performance, and administer experiments on methods of instruction. Administrators use computers for keeping records, planning, scheduling, allocating resources, and processing data.

These applications and many others are described in the references at the end of this article.

Use of the computer as a tool for problem solving in education began in graduate schools about 1955, and a few years later moved into the classroom with the initiation of curriculum development projects in engineering and science. Computer use as a teaching machine dates from 1958; early developments took place at IBM's Watson Research Center, System Development Corporation, and the University of Illinois Coordinated Science Laboratory. The topic of computers in education became popular for meetings in 1965; separate conferences were held on computers in American education, higher education, and physics teaching. In the next ten years, major conferences were organized for computers in mathematics teaching, chemistry education, computer science education, science education, undergraduate curriculum, and high school counseling.

The commercial introduction of the personal computer in 1977 reduced the cost of computers in education. Tools for desktop publishing (*q.v.*), laboratory instrumentation, music, graphic art, and manipulation of media introduced in the 1980s increased the scope and depth of applications. Instructional use of computers is a frequent topic at meetings of the contributing professions (computing, engineering, psychology, and educational research) and at meetings of teachers of most disciplines (ranging from engineering and physics to history, art, and modern languages). Various human components in effective computer use are related in Fig. 1.

Special interest groups on computers and learning have been formed by professional associations and other organizations. Newsletters, bulletins, and journals carry reports of use, development, and research.

Kind of Use Computer assistance with learning and teaching has been described by many different phrases. One could assemble an apt phrase by selecting one word or suffix from each of the following three lists:

	-aided	
	-assisted	
	-augmented	training
	-based	instruction
computer	-extended	learning
technology	-managed	teaching
media	-mediated	education
	-monitored	
	-related	
	uses in	

The most common label has been CAI: Computer-aided instruction. When "instruction" is replaced by "learning," as in CAL, the combination connotes greater emphasis on activities initiated by the learner than on the instructional materials created by a teacher-author. When "learning" is replaced by "education" to obtain CAE (or CBE, computer-based education), the implication is a greater variety of computer uses, including administrative data processing and materials production as well as student use of computers. If the role of the computer is to assist the teacher in managing instruction, for example, in retrieving and summarizing performance records and curriculum files, the label used is CMI: computer-managed instruction.

Instruction and the Learning Processth The most visible use of computers in instruction is to provide direct assistance to learners and to assist teachers, administrators, and educational technologists in helping learners. The users may work individually or in groups, using a device directly connected to a computer (on line) or using some medium later entered into a computer (off line), typing letters and numbers only (alphanumeric) or pointing and drawing diagrams for the computer (graphic), etc., through many options that vary in cost and convenience. Some typical labels within this category of use are drill, skills practice, programmed tutorial, testing and diagnosis, dialogue tutorial, simulation, gaming, information retrieval and processing, computation, problem solving, construction of procedures as models, and display of graphic constructions. A very popular use of the computer is for simulation of a decision-making situation, as in resource management, pollution control, business marketing, or medical testing. For example, college economics students study the history of a hypothetical national economy (similar to that of the U.S.), prescribe actions such as changing the prime interest rate, and observe the consequences for unemployment, inflation, and other indicators. Time is greatly compressed in the

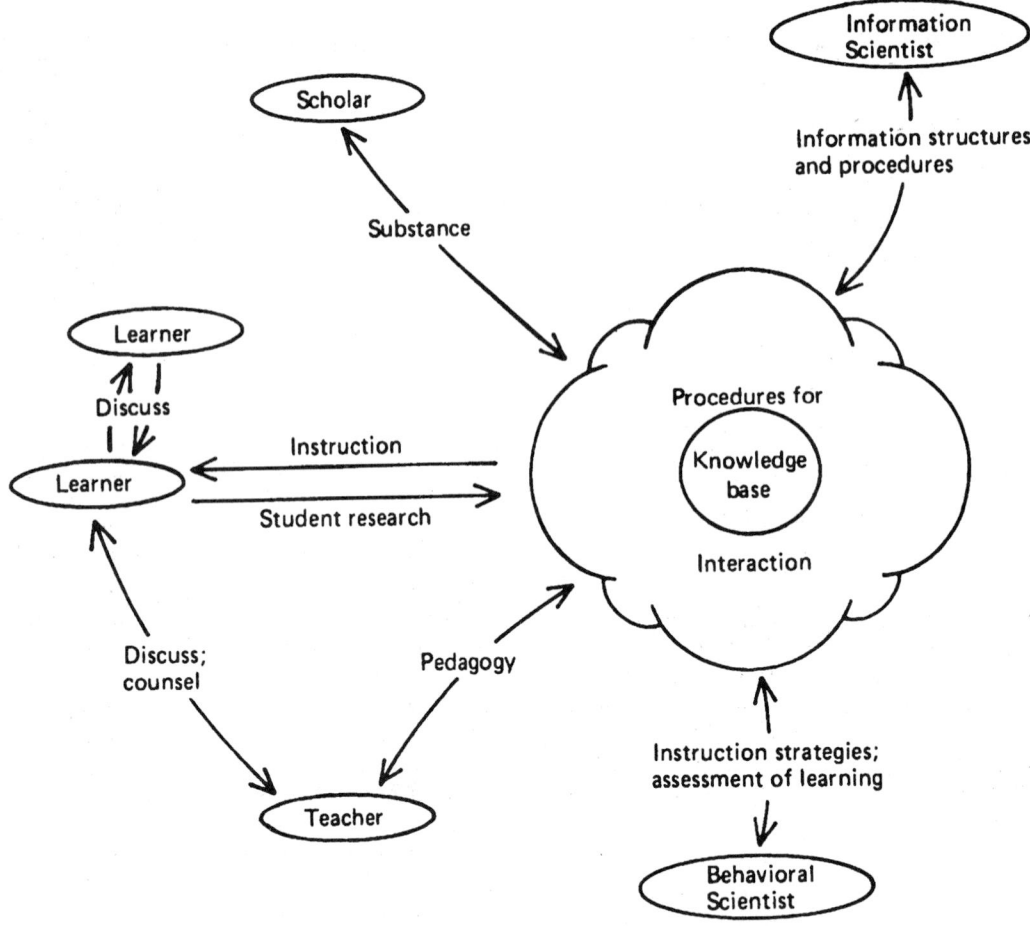

FIG. 1. Human components in effective computer use for learning and teaching.

hypothetical situation, and real-world complexities are abstracted for easier study.

Management of Instruction Resources and Process Computer aids help teachers to supervise the instructional process, and similar assistance is provided directly to students without intervention of teachers and managers. Information management services are readily extended to potential users of learning resources outside traditional educational institutions. The essential information in the various files for management of instructional resources concerns student performance, learning materials, desired outcomes, job opportunities, and student interests. For example, a student obtains information from the computer about achievement and then compares his or her own performance, interests, and goals, with averages recorded for all similar students using the information system. After interpreting the information provided, the student uses the computer further to locate and retrieve suitable learning aids from a large file keyed to goals, learning difficulties, job opportunities, and interests.

Preparation and Display of Materials Materials may be generated in "real time" (i.e. as needed by a student in a seminar or by a teacher during a lecture). Text and prob-

lems also may be assembled by computer in advance of scheduled use so that individualized material may be distributed at less expense than through on-line computing. Computers assist writers of materials in many ways—for example: procedures for generating films and graphs; on-line trial of materials under development; procedures for automatically editing and analyzing text materials for new uses, and information structures for representing new organizations of knowledge; hierarchies of instructional objectives; and libraries of learning materials. New technologies are changing the work of technicians and teachers in developing educational materials and media. Machines handle the routine tasks in drafting graphics and editing film or video.

Other Uses of Information Processing Those planning instructional uses apply computers in administration (accounting, scheduling, planning, etc.) and in research (institutional, sociological, psychological, instructional, etc.), and to the practice of various computer-related vocations in science, technology, management, banking, production, retailing, etc. The last area is especially important because of needs for preservice training. For example, most large retailing operations use computing heavily, and employees with some sensible background in computing have a better chance of coming to terms with computer assistance on the job. Indeed, a general literacy about computing and information processing is essential in the age of informatics. Educated persons should have sufficient knowledge about the practices of automated information processing to exercise on occasion effective control over the machines and data files with which they must deal.

Means and Goals

Diversity of Resources Many different kinds of computer and software systems are being used effectively. Small machines can be used by one or a few students (Fig. 2) to access stored programs (usually drills or simulations) or to write simple computer programs. Workstations offer tools for scholarly and creative work conducted by students individually and in groups. Time-sharing systems handle thousands of students accessing a variety of programs. The PLATO system at the University of Illinois was designed for up to 4,000 simultaneous users and diverse applications: self-instruction, self-testing, simulation, gaming, and problem solving. Most of the multipurpose computer systems serving general user communities at colleges and universities include instructional applications among other uses for research and administration.

Programming languages and systems (software) exhibit even more diversity than the computing equipment (hardware). More than 100 languages and dialects have been developed specifically for programming conversational instruction, although many programs have been written in general-purpose languages, such as Fortran, Pascal, C, and Basic. Different kinds of users have distinguishable requirements: students, instructors, authors, instructional researchers, administrators, and computer programmers (who work on convenience programs for any of the other users). The characteristics of different subject areas also necessitate different language features. Authoring languages and systems are described in a separate article. Appropriate design of display screens, user control, and input devices can be of great help compensating for disabilities (see Fig. 3 and COMPUTERS AND THE HANDICAPPED) and reduces the need for the user to learn computing tools and languages that are incidental to the learning and performance tasks.

Instructional materials (sometimes called *courseware*) have been written in nearly all subject areas and for many age levels. While some of the materials use the computer as an information processing device, others use it as a presentation medium in competition with less expensive modes, such as books, films, or video tapes.

Strategies of instruction associated with computer use (the name *teachware* has been proposed) have been explored. Guidelines for writing instruction-related computer programs have been derived from psychological and educational research, but most developers work from a "common sense" analysis and by trial and error. Some basis for a new science of instruction can be found in research programs at the University of Pittsburgh, Carnegie-Mellon University, Florida State University, and Brigham Young University.

Computer Contributions The value of computer assistance for self-instruction depends on many factors: organization of the subject matter, the purposes of the author or institution, convenient means for interacting with the subject, and the characteristics of the student. Self-study material in text format has been adapted for computer presentation with the following computer contributions proposed. First, the machine evaluates a response constructed by the student (the author must provide a key or standard); an automated procedure prints out discrepancies, tallies scores, and selects remedial or enrichment material. Second, the machine conceals and, to some extent, controls the teaching material so that the author can specify greater complexity in a strategy of instruction and assume more accuracy in its execution than is possible when the student is expected to find a way through the branching instructions in the pages of a large booklet (the scrambled text format for programmed instruction), perhaps starting and stopping an audio or video player as well. Third, the computer carries out operations specified by the student, who uses a simple programming language or computer-aided design system. Fourth, the author or researcher obtains detailed data on student performance (and perhaps attitude) along with a convenient summarization of student accomplishment ready for interpretation. Fifth, the author is able to modify the text on the basis of student use and prepare alternative versions with relative ease.

The prepackaged self-instruction just described can be replaced by a dynamic information system that serves as a common working ground for a scholar and a learner; they share a computer-based, primary-source "textbook," continually updated by the scholar and occasionally annotated by each student who uses it (Fig. 4). Hypertext

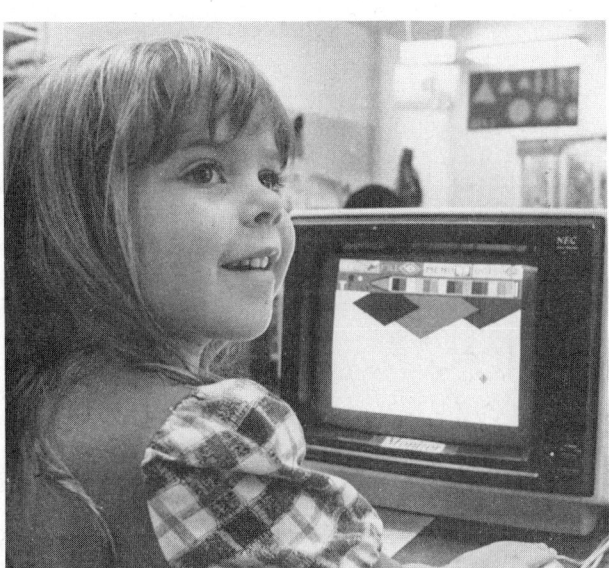

FIG. 2. This photo of a child working with a simple color paint program on an Apple IIc was provided by High/Scope Educational Research Foundation, Ypsilanti, Michigan.

FIG. 3. Adaptations to computer entry devices and displays help students participate in lab work, class discussions, and outside communications, in spite of limitations on mobility, vision, hearing, or vocalization.

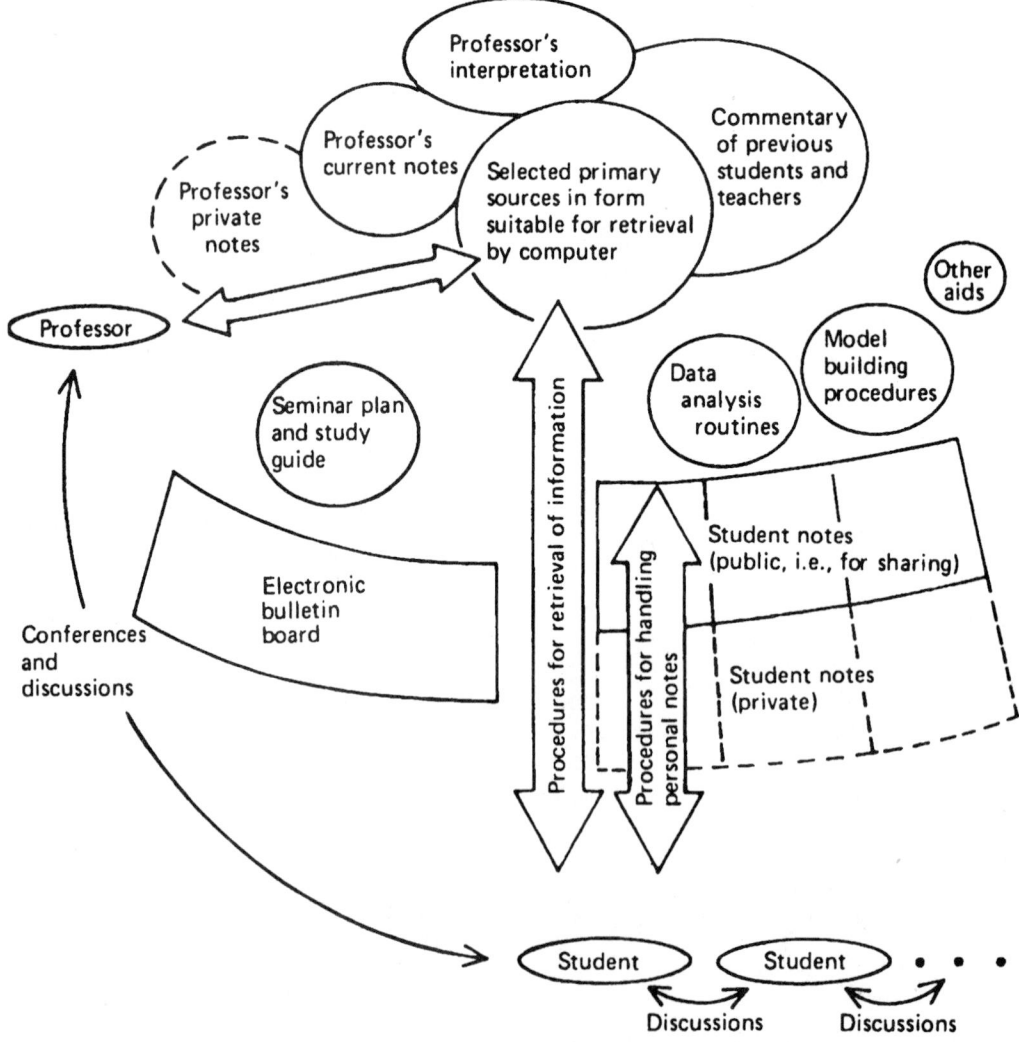

FIG. 4. A dynamic information system for scholar and learner.

was conceived by Theodor Nelson (then at Vassar College) and implemented by Andries van Dam and others at Brown University; it's most popular implementation today is through HyperCard on the MacIntosh computer. In a similar way, an automated information system helps a learner and teacher share a common working environment for hypothesis testing. The environment is sometimes artificial, as in computer simulation of physical and social processes (e.g. a model of evolution), and sometimes real in the sense of actual data from experiments (e.g. election returns or water quality measures). Increased access to information processing tools is perhaps the most important contribution of computers to instruction and learning. Many such activities, perhaps not all called computer-assisted instruction, demonstrate viable alternatives to strictly specified instructional strategies for computer use. For example, students in sociology retrieve and summarize information obtained from large-scale surveys and test hypotheses that might never have been conceived by those who executed and reported the survey. Students in physics test lens designs according to a detailed model of aberrations and corrections, perhaps finding variations on standard lens designs that better serve a particular photographic or instrumentation purpose.

Whatever the technique or philosophy of computer use, the extent of use supported by educational institutions will ultimately be determined by judgments of appropriateness by subject experts, effectiveness observed from records of student performance, and costs that must be met by administrators of schools or training programs.

Some of the limitations imposed by present computer technology involve high cost and unreliability of processing lengthy verbal constructions, and inability to interpret bodily gestures or vocal intonations. Computing costs are decreasing even while capabilities are increasing, but one of the most difficult problems remaining is lack of organization of the subject matter. Human teachers manage to be reasonably successful in spite of vague goals and material poorly organized for learning; instructional computing (and educational technology in general) seems to require specific text materials and clear guidelines (prepared by curriculum experts) for successful use.

Major Approaches

Educational Technology Educational technology and instructional psychology have been the main sources of one kind of development activity. IBM's Coursewriter programming language, one of the earliest languages for authors of computer-based lessons, characterizes this first approach to computer use. The software has built into it an implicit logic of instruction requiring the author to fit text and keywords into the following pattern: (1) the computer program presents information to the student; (2) the computer program then asks a question and waits for a response from the student; (3) the program scans a short textual response and classifies the response as right or wrong according to keywords identified within it; and (4) if the student's response matches an anticipated wrong answer, the program displays a corrective hint and, if nothing was recognized, it offers a general hint. Instances of this approach can be characterized as the computerization of programmed instruction. Careful development of a total curriculum for elementary school mathematics and reading was first carried out by teams of authors at Stanford University, directed by Patrick Suppes and Richard Atkinson.

In some curriculum development projects the content has been assembled in files separate from the logic of the computer program (the strategy of instruction). Elements of the curriculum can thereby be varied without rewriting many lines of instructions to the computer, and different strategies can be tried on the same file of learning materials. This arrangement helps the instructional psychologist give full attention to the design of effective instructional strategies and helps the subject expert avoid the distraction of programming procedures. In fact, this approach is generally pursued by a team, with each member contributing different expertise. The first such authoring teams were organized by C. Victor Bunderson at Brigham Young University to develop materials for community college courses in mathematics and English for the TICCIT system developed by Mitre Corporation.

Problems faced by the educational technology approach to computer use result from the high cost of the computer as a primary medium for exposition of learning materials, the difficulties of accurately identifying unconstrained input (text, algebraic expressions, drawings, spoken expression, etc.), and the lack of a well-developed theory of instruction.

Disciplines and Curriculum Discipline-oriented use of the computer was pursued by many institutions quite separately from the educational technology developments. Dartmouth College provides a prime instance of spreading computer uses throughout a college curriculum. The University of California at Irvine uses computing extensively in physics courses. Annual conferences were held on the topic of computers in the undergraduate curriculum from 1970 to 1978, and have since expanded to serve pre-college interests as well in the National Educational Computing Conference each year. Regional computing services, conferences, and newsletters have been established to serve the needs of colleges and schools throughout a region. In contrast to the educational technology approach, the teacher as subject expert in the discipline approach assumes the central role in determining computer use, creating materials, and persuading colleagues to use them. Computing activity is likely to include more student initiative in solving problems and more problem-orienting program packages than does expository material. Student use of simulation and modeling tools is favored; one goal is to adapt the scholar's research tools to student use.

The discipline approach to computer use has many problems; among them are sparse user documentation for instruction-related computing activities that are worthy of widespread use; lack of economic and professional incentives for the production and dissemination of programs and related materials; and difficult procedures for review and validation of programs. Educom and related groups are working to set high standards and improve incentives for quality work through an annual awards program and other activities. The purchase of hundreds of thousands of microcomputers by students and teachers as well as institutions provides a market that now has the attention of publishers and authors in addition to professional societies.

Computing and Information Sciences Some researchers suggest that major advances in instructional use of computers will occur through significant developments in artificial intelligence (*q.v.*), natural language processing (*q.v.*), speech recognition (*q.v.*), and extensible programming languages (*q.v*). Although information scientists typically are more interested in their own disciplines and related research topics than in educational techniques and practice, the tools developed may be useful to others. The results of computer science research may be an important source of suitable models for instruction strategies, information structures, and representations of knowledge. Projects giving particular attention to educational applications have adapted tools from computing and information science, and formulated new models of human learning and information processing.

Development of techniques and materials using the information science approach is very costly and time consuming; the resulting applications tend to be more expensive for students to use; skill in use of the specialized development techniques is not easily acquired by persons outside computer science. Nevertheless, the projects based in computing and information sciences continue to provide important indicators of future resources that may be essential to success of computers in education.

Computing Technology, Engineering, and "Common Sense" A fourth category includes all other approaches, particularly those characterized by the engineering of a helpful technology, perhaps involving some combination of the first three approaches. Engineers at the Computer-Based Educational Research Laboratory, University of Illinois, designed and built a computer-based education system for multiple purposes: educational technologists presenting programmed instruction, instructional psychologists conducting research on teaching and learning, professors preparing a computer presentation of a lecture or laboratory, and computer specialists building information processing aids for learning and scholarly work. Specialists in computers and education at Bolt Beranek and Newman (led by Wallace Feurzeig) and the Massachusetts Institute of Technology (Seymour Papert, the Media Lab) devised various programming languages (Logo and LogoWriter) and equipment (computer-controlled "turtle," music player, and construction kits) for computer-related learning activities.

Other groups exhibit a similar philosophy with extra attention to creative student work (e.g. the Learning Re-

search Group directed by Alan Kay and Adele Goldberg at the Palo Alto Research Center of Xerox Corporation). Children write simple programs for controlling robots, drawing and animating pictures, generating speech and music, and the like. Interest in enhancing such capabilities motivates a new approach to mathematics and heuristics in which programming languages provide a powerful conceptual framework.

Trends A major trend in the design of computer-based exercises is a shift from programmer to learner control. The designer of the exercise invests less effort in a careful diagnosis and prescription accomplished by some automated instructional strategy, and instead provides information and tools by which the student can explore the topic and assess his or her own learning.

Considerable use of graphics is typical. Pictures are an important component of the learning process, and computer-drawn pictures and animations add to the responsive uses of computing. For many topics the picture is a valuable way of representing complex relationships derived by the computer.

Computer-based education systems and designers of materials have provided an increasing variety of functions for the user. More attention is being given to interaction between student and computer program, not simply to provide a quick reply to some question, but to increase the actual responsiveness of the system to the student's needs and situation. The machine responds to the commands and questions of the student, and the exercises are designed in a way that helps the student retrieve and organize the information provided by the computer.

A very important trend concerns the role of the machine from the perspective of the individual using it. The teacher is now more likely to see computer-managed instruction as an aid to human management than as a replacement for it. Learners view the machine more as an aid to learning and performance than as a presenter and drill master. All these developments are helped along by personal ownership of computers or other personalization of use.

Naturalness of communication between learner and system is being improved day by day. Computer-based learning exercises are achieving increased relevance for the subject being studied, and the nomenclature and conventions that have to be learned in order to use the system tend to be essential to the study of the topics rather than peculiar to the requirement of the computer as a medium of presentation.

References

1985. Duncan, Karen and Harris, Diana. *Computers in Education: Proceedings of the IFIP Fourth World Conference.* Amsterdam: North-Holland.
1986. Culbertson, Jack A. and Cunningham, Luvern L. *Microcomputers and Education.* Chicago: National Society for the Study of Education.
1987. Brand, Stewart *The Media Lab: Inventing the Future at MIT.* New York: Viking.

1987. Weir, Sylvia. *Cultivating Minds: A Logo Casebook*. New York: Harper & Row.

1987. Nelson, Theodor. *Computer Lib/Dream Machines*. Redmond, WA: Tempus Books.

1987. Bork, Alfred M. *Learning with Personal Computers*. New York: Harper & Row.

1988. OTA. *Power On! New Tools for Teaching and Learning*. U.S. Congress, Office of Technology Assessment, Washington, D.C. U.S. Government Printing Office.

1990. Ambron, Sueann and Hooper, Kristina. *Learning with Interactive Multimedia: Developing and Using Multimedia Tools in Education*. Redmond, WA: Microsoft Press.

KARL L. ZINN

COMPUTER CHESS

For articles on related subjects *see* ARTIFICIAL INTELLIGENCE; and COMPUTER GAMES: TRADITIONAL.

Chess tournaments exclusively for computers have been held since 1970 (see Table 1). Until 1978, these tournaments were dominated by David Slate and Larry Atkin's program, first called Chess 3.0 and finally, after many revisions, Chess 4.9. It earned a rating of about 2050 in 1978. It was developed at Northwestern University and ran on CDC's Cyber 176 in the late 1970s. Chess 4.9 carried out a sequence of incrementally deeper exhaustive searches, examining approximately 5,000 chess positions per second. Belle, developed at Bell Laboratories by Ken Thompson and Joe Condon, ruled the world of computer chess from 1979 through 1983. It was the first program to be awarded the title of Master by the United States Chess Federation (USCF). Belle examined 150,000 chess positions/second and ran on special-purpose chess circuitry. In 1983, Cray Blitz, developed at the University of Southern Mississippi by Robert Hyatt, Albert Gower, and Harry Nelson, won the world championship while running on a 4-processor Cray XMP supercomputer. The program successfully defended its title in 1986. Hitech appeared in 1986, winning the Pennsylvania State Championship two years in a row and, while being a bit unlucky in computer tournament play, establishing new levels of performance in human play, obtaining a USCF rating in the neighborhood of 2400. Hitech, which also used special-purpose circuitry, was developed at CMU by the programming

TABLE 1. History of Major Tournaments

	ACM North American Computer Chess Championships
Year, City	Winner, Runner-up (* denotes a tie)
1970, New York	CHESS 3.0 (Slate, Atkin, Gorlen; CDC 6400) ; DALY CHESS PROGRAM (Daly, King; Varian 620/i)
1971, Chicago	CHESS 3.5 (Slate, Atkin, Gorlen; CDC 6400) ; TECH (Gillogly; PDP 10)
1972, Boston	CHESS 3.6 (Slate, Atkin, Gorlen; CDC 6400) ; OSTRICH (Arnold, Newborn; DG Supernova)
1973, Atlanta	CHESS 4.0 (Slate, Atkin, Gorlen; CDC 6400) ; TECH II (Baisley; PDP 10)
1974, San Diego	RIBBIT (Hansen, Crook, Parry; Honeywell 6050) ; CHESS 4.0 (Slate, Atkin; CDC 6400)
1975, Minneapolis	CHESS 4.4 (Slate, Atkin; CDC Cyber 175) ; TREEFROG (Hansen, Calnek, Crook; Honeywell 6080)
1976, Houston	CHESS 4.5 (Slate, Atkin; CDC Cyber 176) ; CHAOS (Swartz, Berman, Alexander, Ruben, Toikka, Winograd; Amdahl 470)
1977, Seattle	CHESS 4.6 (Slate, Atkin; CDC Cyber 176) ; DUCHESS (Truscott, Wright, Jensen; IBM 370/168)
1978, Washington	BELLE (Thompson, Condon; PDP 11/70 w/ chess hardware) ; CHESS 4.7 (Slate, Atkin; CDC Cyber 176)
1979, Detroit	CHESS 4.9 (Slate, Atkin; CDC Cyber 176) ; BELLE (Thompson, Condon; PDP 11/70 w/ chess hardware)
1980, Nashville	BELLE (Thompson, Condon; PDP 11/70 w/ chess hardware) ; CHAOS (Alexander, O'Keefe, Swartz, Berman; Amdahl 470)
1981, Los Angeles	BELLE (Thompson, Condon; PDP 11/23 w/ chess hardware) ; NUCHESS (Blanchard, Slate; CDC Cyber 176)
1982, Dallas	BELLE (Thompson, Condon; PDP 11/23 w/ chess hardware) ; CRAY BLITZ (Hyatt, Gower, Nelson; Cray 1)
1983	Not held as the ACM's NACCC that year, but as the Fourth World Championship. See below.
1984, San Francisco	CRAY BLITZ (Hyatt, Gower, Nelson; Cray XMP/4) ; *BEBE (Scherzer; Chess Engine), *FIDELITY EXPERIMENTAL (Spracklen, Spracklen; Fidelity machine)
1985, Denver	HITECH (Ebeling, Berliner, Goetsch, Paley, Campbell, Slomer; SUN w/ chess hardware) ; BEBE (Scherzer; Chess engine)
1986, Dallas	BELLE (Thompson, Condon; PDP 11/23 w/ chess hardware) ; LACHEX (Wendroff; Cray XMP)
1987, Dallas	CHIPTEST-M (Anantharaman, Hsu, Campbell; SUN 3 w/ VLSI chess hardware) ; CRAY BLITZ (Hyatt, Nelson, Gower; Cray XMP 4/8)
1988, Orlando	DEEP THOUGHT 0.02 (Hsu, Anantharaman, Browne, Campbell; SUN 3 w/ VLSI chess hardware) ; CHESS CHALLENGER EXP (Spracklen, Spracklen, Nelson; Fidelity machine with Motorola 68030 microprocessor)
1989, Reno	HITECH* (Ebeling, Berliner, Goetsch, Paley Campbell, Slomer; SUN w/ chess hardware) ; DEEP THOUGHT* (Hsu, Anantharamam, Browne, Campbell, Nowatzyk; 3 SUN 4s w/ 2 VLSI chess processors per SUN)
1990, New York	DEEP THOUGHT/88 (HSU, Anantharaman, Jensen, Campbell, Nowatzyk; SUN 4 w/ 2 VLSI chess processors) ; MEPHISTO (Lang; MEPHISTO Machine with Motorola 68030 microprocessors)
1991, Albuquerque	DEEP THOUGHT II (Hsu, Campbell; IBM RS 6000/550 w/ 24 VLSI chess processors); M CHESS (Hirsch; IBM PC w/Intel 80486 microprocessor)

TABLE 1. History of Major Tournaments (Continued)

ACM North American Computer Chess Championships	
Year, City	Winner, Runner-up (* denotes a tie)

World Computer Chess Championships	
1974, Stockholm	KAISSA (Donskoy, Arlazarov; ICL 4/70) ; CHESS 4.0 (Slate, Atkin; CDC 6600)
1977, Toronto	CHESS 4.6 (Slate, Atkin; CDC Cyber 176) ; DUCHESS (Truscott, Wright, Jensen; IBM 370/165)
1980, Linz	BELLE (Thompson, Condon; PDP 11/23 with chess circuitry) ; CHAOS (Alexander, Swartz, Berman, O'Keefe; Amdahl 470/V8)
1983, New York	CRAY BLITZ (Hyatt, Gower, Nelson; Cray XMP 48) ; BEBE (Scherzer; Chess engine)
1986, Cologne	CRAY BLITZ (Hyatt, Gower, Nelson; Cray XMP 48) ; HITECH (Berliner, *et al*; SUN workstaton w/ chess circuitry)
1989, Edmonton	DEEP THOUGHT (Hsu, Anantharaman, Browne, Campbell, Jansen, Nowatzyk; SUN w/ VLSI chess hardware) ; BEBE (Scherzer, Scherzer; Chess Engine)

World Microcomputer Chess Championships	
1980, London	CHESS CHALLENGER ; BORIS EXPERIMENTAL
1981, Travemunde	FIDELITY X ; CHESS CHAMPION MARK V
1983, Budapest	ELITE A/S ; MEPHISTO X
1984, Glasgow	Four-way tie: ELITE X, MEPHISTO S/X, PRINCESS, PSION CHESS
1985, Amsterdam	MEPHISTO AMSTERDAM I ; MEPHISTO AMSTERDAM II
1986, Dallas	MEPHISTO DALLAS 3 ; FIDELITY "2533"
1987, Rome	MEPHISTO ; CYRUS 68K
1988, Almeria	MEPHISTO ; FIDELITY
1989, Portoroz̆, Slovenia	MEPHISTO ; FIDELITY
1990, Lyon	MEPHISTO; Tie: ECHEC 1.9 and GIDEON
1991, Vancouver	Tie: MEPHISTO and GIDEON

team of Carl Ebeling, Hans Berliner, Gordon Goetsch, Murray Campbell, Andy Gruss, and Andy Paley. It searched approximately 110,000 positions per second.

By 1988, Deep Thought had established itself as the world's best program and was defeating Grandmasters in tournament competition. It won the World Computer Chess Championship in 1989. Work on Deep Thought began at Carnegie-Mellon University. Subsequently, the programming team joined IBM's T. J. Watson Research Center. The team is led by Feng-Hsiung Hsu and has included Murray Campbell, Thomas Anantharaman, Mike Browne, Andreas Nowatzyk, Joe Hoane, and Jerry Brody. The most recent version runs on an IBM RS 6500/ 550 host connected to 24 special-purpose VLSI chess processors, and searches 5,000,000 chess positions per second. Its level of play is in excess of a UCSF rating of 2600. (There are about 40 players in the world with a rating in excess of 2600. World Champion Gary Kasparov's rating has fluctuated around 2800.)

The leading microcomputer programs as of early 1992 are M CHESS, programmed by Marty Hirsch, MEPHISTO, programmed by Richard Lang, and the CHESS MACHINE, programmed by Ed Schroeder. They play at approximately a 2400 level.

In recent years, endgame databases have been created by Ken Thompson and Larry Stiller. All five-piece endgames have been solved as well as a number of six-piece endgames. The databases are built using retrograde analysis: Starting with a database of won positions and then working backwards to all other positions, each position is assigned a win, loss, or draw, and a count of the number of moves to the end of the game, or to another, simpler endgame.

In 1978, David Levy, International Master from London, won a wager of several thousand dollars by defeating Chess 4.7 in a match in Toronto. In 1968, he had wagered four computer scientists that no computer would defeat him in a match during the next 10 years. He won three games, drew one, and lost one. Following the match, *Omni Magazine* offered a prize of $5,000 to the authors of the first program to defeat Levy. The prize was won in December 1989 by Deep Thought when it won four straight games from Levy.

1989 saw the first meeting between the human world champion, Gary Kasparov, and the world computer chess champion. Kasparov defeated Deep Thought in a two-game match in New York in October 1989. A castling bug in Deep Thought surfaced during the games that, given Kasparov's strength, was a sufficient reason to cause Deep Thought to lose. The first of the two games with Kasparov is presented in Fig. 1. Several months earlier, Deep Thought split two games under tournament conditions against Grandmaster Robert Byrne, chess columnist for *The New York Times*. Its victory is presented in Fig. 2.

At the 1977 World Championship in Toronto, the International Computer Chess Association was formed to provide an international framework for activities in computer chess and to encourage advances in this field. There

Sicilian Opening

1 e2−e4 c7−c5 2 c2−c3 e7−e6 3 d2−d4 d7−d5 4 e4×d5 e6×d5 5 Ng1−f3 Bf8−d6 6
Bc1−e3 c5−c4 7 b2−b3 c4×b3 8 a2×b3 Ng8−e7 9 Nb1−a3 Nb8−c6 10 Na3−b5 Bd6−b8 11
Bf1−d3 Bc8−f5 12 c3−c4 O−O 13 Ra1−a4 Qd8−d7 14 Nb5−c3 Bb8−c7 15 Bd3×f5 Qd7×f5
16 Nf3−h4 Qf5−d7 17 O−O Ra8−d8 18 Rf1−e1 Rf8−e8 19 c4−c5 Bc7−a5 20 Qd1−d3 a7−a6
21 h2−h3 Ba5×c3 22 Qd3×c3 Ne7−f5 23 Nh4×f5 Qd7×f5 24 Ra4−a2 Re8−e6 25 Ra2−e2
Rd8−e8 26 Qc3−d2 f7−f6 27 Qd2−c3 h7−h5 28 b3−b4 Re8−e7 29 Kg1−h1 g7−g5 30 Kh1−g1
g5−g4 31 h3−h4 Re6−e4 32 Qc3−b2 Nc6−a7 33 Qb2−d2 Re4−e6 34 Qd2−c1 Na7−b5 35
Qc1−d2 Nb5−a3 36 Qd2−d1 Kg8−f7 37 Qd1−b3 Na3−c4 38 Kg1−h2 Re6−e4 39 g2−g3
Qf5−f3 40 b4−b5 a6−a5 41 c5−c6 f6−f5 42 c6×b7 Re7×b7 43 Kh2−g1 f5−f4 44 g3×f4 g4−g3
45 Qb3−d1 Rb7−e7 46 b5−b6 g3×f2+ 47 Re2×f2 Qf3×d1 48 Re1×d1 Re4×e3 49 Rf2−g2
Nc4×b6 50 Rg2−g5 a5−a4 51 Rg5×h5 a4−a3 52 Rd1−d2 Re3−e2 53 Resigns

FIG. 1.   DEEP THOUGHT (White) vs. Gary Kasparov (Black); 22 October 1989.

Sicilian Opening

1 e2−e4 c7−c5 2 c2−c3 b7−b6 3 d2−d4 Bc8−b7 4 Bf1−d3 e7−e6 5 Bc1−e3 Ng8−f6 6
Nb1−d2 Nb8−c6 7 a2−a3 d7−d6 8 Qd1−f3 g7−g6 9 Ng1−e2 Bf8−g7 10 O−O O−O 11 b2−b4
c5×d4 12 c3×d4 Qd8−d7 13 Ra1−c1 Ra8−c8 14 h2−h3 Nc6−e7 15 Be3−g5 Rc8×c1 16
Rf1×c1 Nf6−e8 17 Bd3−b5 Qd7−d8 18 Qf3−g3 h7−h6 19 Bg5−e3 d6−d5 20 f2−f3 Ne8−d6
21 Bb5−d3 b6−b5 22 Rc1−c5 a7−a6 23 Be3−f4 Nd6−c4 24 Bd3×c4 d5×c4 25 Bf4−d6
Rf8−e8 26 Rc5−c7 Bb7−a8 27 Rc7−c5 Ne7−c8 28 Bd6−e5 Bg7×e5 29 Qg3×e5 Nc8−d6 30
a3−a4 Qd8−d7 31 Qe5−f4 Kg8−g7 32 h3−h4 Ba8−c6 33 d4−d5 Bc6−a8 34 d5×e6 Re8×e6
35 a4×b5 a6×b5 36 Nd2−f1 Nd6×e4 37 f3×e4 Re6×e4 38 Qf4−f2 c4−c3 39 Ne2×c3 Re4×b4
40 Nf1−e3 Ba8−c6 41 Ne3−d5 Bc6×d5 42 Nc3×d5 Rb4−b1+ 43 Kg1−h2 Qd7−d6+ 44 g2−g3
Qd6−e5 45 Nd5−c3 Qe5−e1 46 Qf1−d4+ Kg7−g8 47 Nc3×b1 Qe1−e2+ 48 Kh2−g1 Resigns.

FIG. 2.   DEEP THOUGHT (White) vs. Robert Byrne (Black); 23 August 1989.

are currently about 500 members. It puiblishes the *ICCA Journal*, the leading publication in the field. Information on ICCA can be obtained from Professor Jonathan Schaeffer, Department of Computing Science, University of Alberta, Edmonton, Alberta, Canada T6G 2H1.

References

1950. Shannon, C. "Programming a Computer for Playing Chess," *Philosophy Magazine* **41**: 256–275.

1953. Turing, A. M. "Digital Computers Applied to Games," in Bowden, B. V. (Ed.), *Faster than Thought*. London: Pitman, 286–295.

1975. Newborn, M. *Computer Chess*. New York: Academic Press.

1977. Frey, P. (Ed.). *Chess Skill in Man and Machine*. New York: Springer-Verlag.

1979. Newborn, M. "Recent Progress in Computer Chess," *Advances in Computers* **18**: 59–117.

1980. Levy, D. N. L. and Newborn, M. *More Chess and Computers*. Potomac, MD: Computer Science Press.

1989. Newborn, M. "Computer Chess: Ten Years of Significant Progress," *Advances in Computers* **29**: 197–250.

1990. Levy, D. N. L. and Newborn, M. *How Computers Play Chess* New York: W. H. Freeman.

1991. Hsu, F-H., Avantharaman, T., and Nowatzyk, A. "A Grandmaster Chess Machine," *Scientific American*, **263**, *4* (October) 44–50.

MONROE M. NEWBORN

COMPUTER CIRCUITRY

For articles on related subjects *see* INTEGRATED CIRCUITRY: MICROCOMPUTER CHIP; MICROPROCESSERS AND MICROCOMPUTERS; SUPERCONDUCTING DEVICES; and SWITCHING THEORY.

Although the development of digital computers can be traced back to Charles Babbage, who conceived a mechanical machine with toothed wheels to perform arithmetic processes, electrical principles first found application in digital computers in the form of electromechanical relays. The most prominent examples of this type of computer are the Bell Labs relay machines (*q.v.*) and the Harvard Mark I (*q.v.*) and Mark II. Even while these machines were under construction in the early and middle 1940s, it was recognized that an *electronic* computer would offer great advantages in terms of computational speed. This pattern of improving implementation technology has continued even to the present time. In this article we will survey some of the basic concepts that are used in designing computer circuitry.

Boolean Algebra   Boolean algebra (*q.v.*) forms the theoretical cornerstone on which modern digital computers are built. Boolean algebra deals with functions and variables that take on only two values, commonly denoted by either T and F or 1 and 0. Using the axioms of boolean algebra, it can be shown that any boolean func-

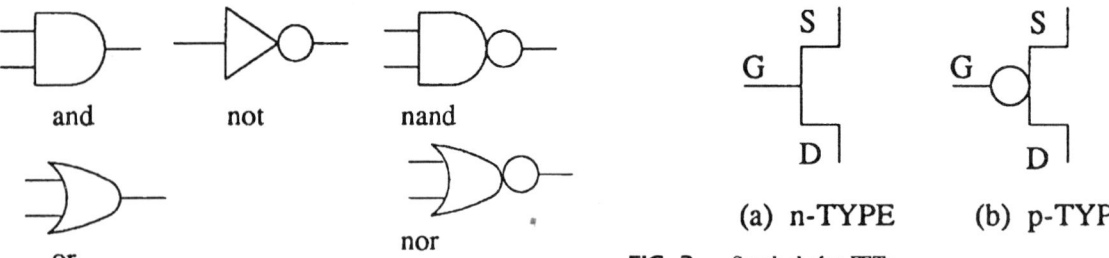

FIG. 1. Symbols for Logic Gates.

FIG. 2. Symbols for FETs.

tion (a function over boolean variables), no matter how complex, can be composed from three primitive operations: *and*, *or*, and *not*. This set of logic operations is therefore said to be *functionally complete*. In fact, there are two primitive operations, widely used in the design of computer circuitry, that are functionally complete in themselves. These are *nand* (equivalent to a *not* following an *and*) and *nor* (equivalent to a *not* following an *or*). The implication is that one only needs to design circuits for a functionally complete set of boolean operations in order to have the basic building blocks for a digital computer.

The association that is usually made between an abstract boolean operation and circuitry that implements that operation is through voltage levels. That is, digital circuitry is designed to respond to two voltage levels, designated high and low (e.g. + 5 volts and 0 volts). The conventional method uses the high voltage (or V_{dd}) to represent a 1 and the low voltage (or *Gnd* (Ground)) to represent a 0. Other associations of boolean values and circuit quantities are possible.

MOS Logic Gates

Circuits that implement the most primitive boolean functions are called *gates*. The symbols that are used to implement the commonly used gates are shown in Fig. 1. A small circle used in conjunction with any gate denotes negation of that gate's function.

Variations of *Metal-Oxide Semiconductor* (MOS) technologies are currently used to design computers. In such technologies logic gates are built using *controlled switches*. As shown in Fig. 2, such switches consist of three terminals and can be either "n-type" or "p-type." In an *n-type* switch, if *G equals 1*, terminal *S* is *connected* to terminal *D*. If *G equals 0*, then terminal *S* is *disconnected* from terminal *D*. In a *p-type switch*, if *G equals 1*, terminal *S* is *disconnected* from terminal *D*. If *G equals 0*, then terminal *S* is *connected* to terminal *D*. Physically, the "n-type" switch is an n-type field effect transistor (nFET) and the "p-type" switch is a p-type field effect transistor (pFET). For the purpose of this discussion, we will not be concerned with the physics of these devices.

As shown in Fig. 3, such switches are interconnected to form a network having two distinct terminals, *X* and *Y*. The connection pattern of Fig. 3(a) is a series connection, and the pattern of Fig. 3(b) is a parallel connection. These elementary connection patterns can be used to build larger networks, as shown in Fig. 3(c).

We say that a network *N* of switches is *activated* if and only if the two terminals *X*, *Y* of *N* are connected through a set of switches. For example, in Fig. 3(a), if *A = B = 1*, both switches are closed and *X* is connected to *Y*. Therefore, the network of Fig. 3(a) is activated by the assignment *A = B = 1*. One can verify that, if *A = B = 0*, the network of Fig. 3(c) is activated.

MOS logic gates are constructed by using networks of switches. As shown in Fig. 4, there are two distinct models of logic gates. The *type-a* gate uses two networks of switches—*pullup* and *pulldown* networks. The pullup network consists only of pFETs and the pulldown network consists only of nFETs. These gates are designed so that, for any assignment of values to the input variables, only

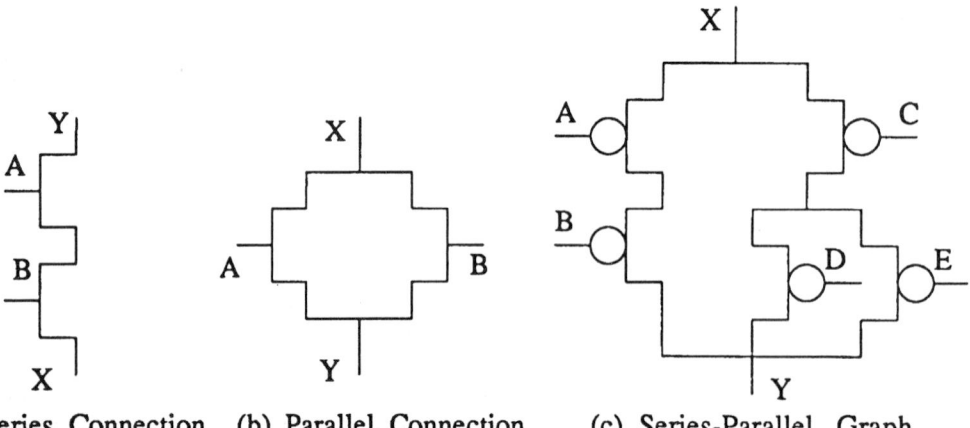

(a) Series Connection   (b) Parallel Connection   (c) Series-Parallel Graph

FIG. 3. Series-Parallel Connections.

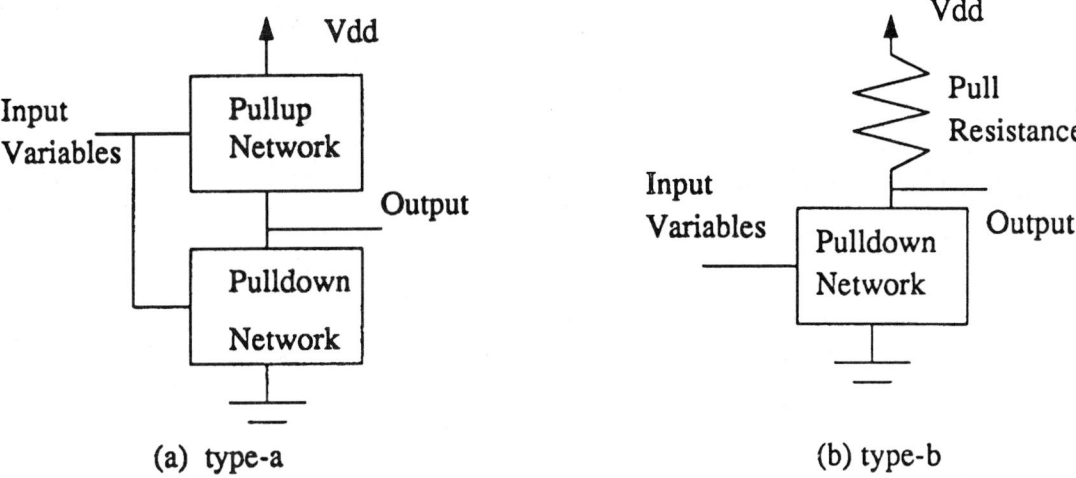

FIG. 4. Structure of MOS gates.

one of the two networks is activated. If the pullup (pulldown) network is activated, the output of the gate is set to the logic value 1 (0). Fig. 5(a) is an example of a type-a gate. If $A = B = 1$, the pulldown network is activated and the output is set to 0. If $A = B = 0$, then the pullup network is activated and the output is set to 1. One can verify that the gate of Fig. 5(a) implements the *nand* function.

For any assignment of values to the input of *type-b* gates, the output is set to 0 if and only if the assignments activate the pulldown network. One can verify that Fig. 5(b) is a type-b *nand* gate, and Fig. 5(c) is a type b *nor* gate.

Type-a gates in which the pullup network consists only of pFETs and the pulldown network consists only of nFETs are known as *CMOS (Complementary Metal-Oxide Semiconductor)* gates. Circuits consisting of CMOS gates are known as CMOS circuits. Type-b gates in which the

pulldown network consists only of nFETs are known as *nMOS* gates. Circuits consisting of nMOS gates are known as nMOS circuits.

Historically, nMOS circuits preceded CMOS circuits because nMOS circuits, unlike CMOS circuits, require only one type of switch. Therefore, it was easier to perfect the nMOS technology. However, technological innovation has made CMOS an equally feasible technology and today almost all circuits are CMOS circuits.

One of the major reasons for developing the more complicated CMOS technology can be understood by re-examining the structure of the nMOS and CMOS logic gates. Consider the *nand* gates of Fig. 5(a), (b). If $A = B = 1$, the pulldown network of Fig. 5(a) is activated. The pullup network of Fig. 5(a) is not activated. Therefore, in Fig. 5(a), there is no conducting path from V_{dd} to *Gnd*. In fact, in the gate of Fig. 5(a), there is no assignment of

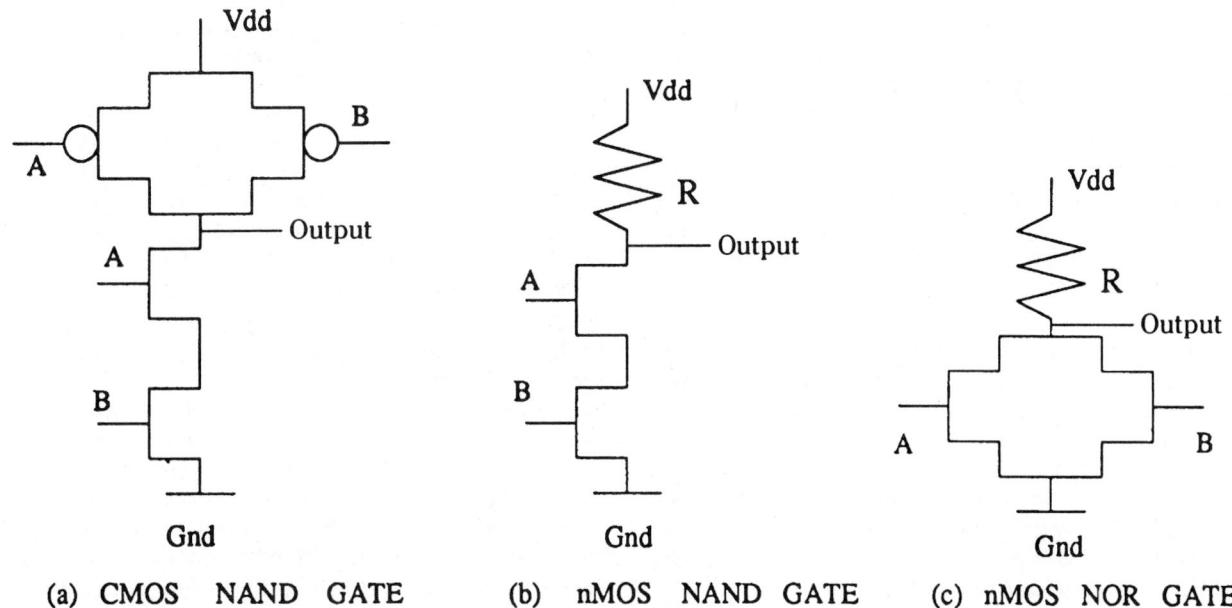

(a) CMOS NAND GATE (b) nMOS NAND GATE (c) nMOS NOR GATE

FIG. 5. Examples of MOS gates.

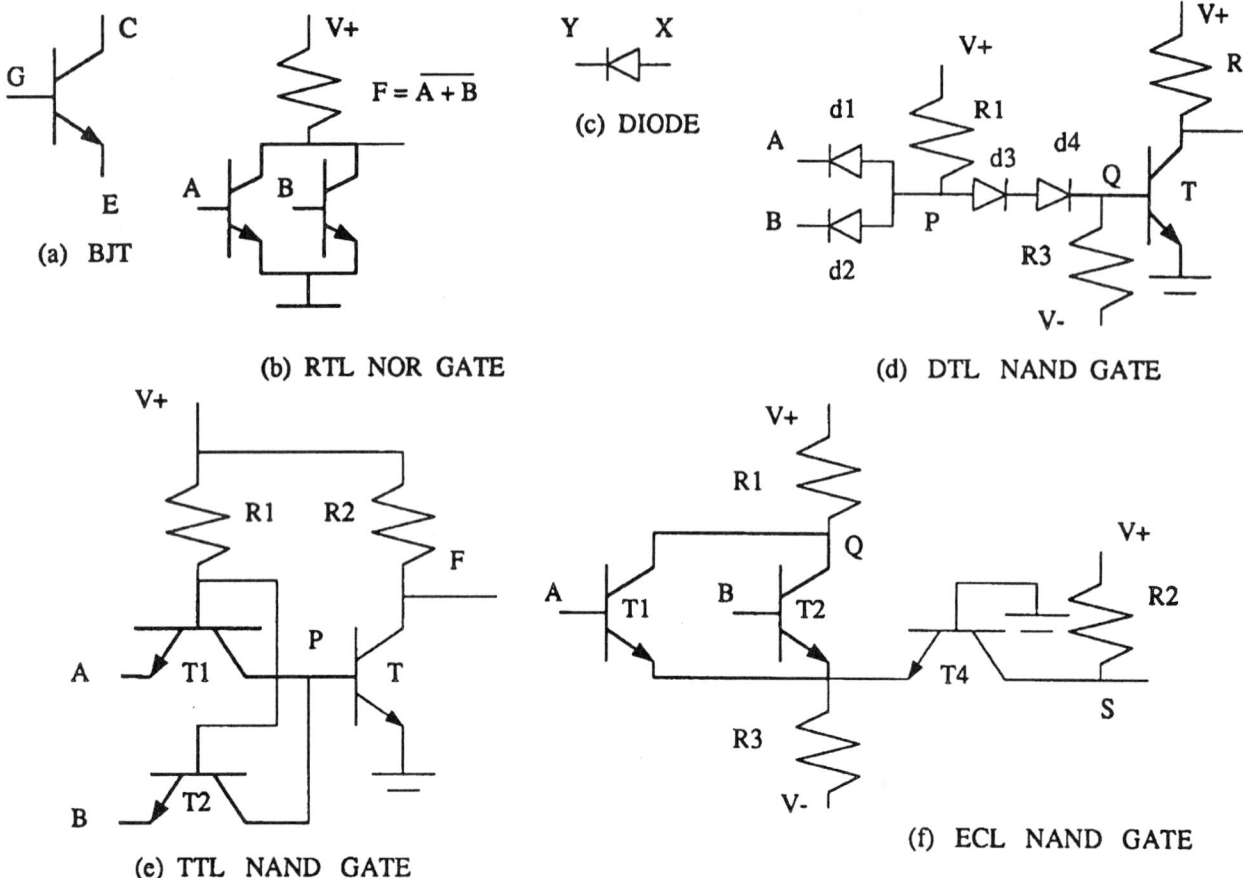

FIG. 6.   Implementation of some Universal Gates using BJT-based Logic Families.

values to the input of the gate that will result in a conducting path from V_{dd} to *Gnd*. On the other hand, in Fig. 5(b), when $A = B = 1$, there is a conducting path from V_{dd} to *Gnd*. Therefore, current flows through the pullup resistor *R*, thereby dissipating power, something that does not occur with CMOS circuits. This, in turn, hinders the integration of a large number of nMOS gates on a single chip. This is one of the many reasons for using CMOS circuits for denser chips.

Other Logic Families   Although MOS, more specifically CMOS, is now the dominant technology, a number of technologies have been used for manufacturing computers. These technologies differ in the type of switching devices used, as well as how the devices are used in the design of logic gates. The earliest computer circuits used vacuum tubes, but since they are no longer in use, we will not discuss the implementation of logic gates using vacuum tubes.

The logic families that we will discuss here use *bipolar junction transistors* (BJTs) as the switching device. Like FETs, BJTs are also three-dimensional devices. We use the symbol of Fig. 6(a) to represent a BJT where G is the *base*, E is the *emitter*, and C is the *collector*. If the voltage at C is "sufficiently higher" than the voltage at E, terminal C is electrically connected to terminal E (the switch is ON);

otherwise, terminal C is disconnected from terminal E (the switch is OFF).

Logic gates using BJTs are similar (if not identical) to type-b gates. In *register-transistor logic* (RTL), only *nor* gates are available for designing circuits. It is for this reason that RTL is said to be "nor logic." A two-input RTL *nor* gate is shown in Fig. 6(b). It is similar to the nMOS *nor* gate of Fig. 5(c).

In *diode-transistor logic* (DTL), unlike RTL, only *nand* gates are available for designing the circuits. These *nand* gates use both *diodes* and *transistors* as active devices. The symbol for a diode is shown in Fig. 6(c). A diode is a unidirectional two-terminal device. If the voltage at X is higher than the voltage at Y, terminal X is electrically connected to terminal Y; otherwise, X is disconnected from Y. A DTL *nand* gate is shown in Fig. 6(d). To understand the operation of this gate, note that if A (B) has the logic level 0 (i.e. voltage 0), diode d1 (d2) conducts. This implies that the voltage at P is 0. V- is a negative voltage. Therefore, diodes d3, d4 conduct and Q is at a negative voltage (by adjusting the resistance value R3). This cuts T, the *driver* transistor, OFF and the output F is at the logic level 1. If A = B = 1, diodes d1, d2 do not conduct. Diodes d3, d4 conduct and Q is at a positive voltage (adjusted by resistances R1, R3). The driver T is ON and the output F is pulled down to logic level 0.

In *transistor-transistor logic* (TTL), the only gates available are *nand* gates. A TTL *nand* gate is shown in Fig. 6(e). It is very similar to a DTL *nand* gate, but is faster than either RTL or DTL. If either A or B is at logic 0, there is significant base to emitter voltage difference of either T1 or T2 to turn one or both of them ON. This brings down the voltage of P to a sufficiently low value to cut T OFF. The output F is therefore at the logic level 1. When both A, B are 1, then both T1 and T2 are cut OFF and P returns to a high voltage. This turns T ON and the output F is pulled to the logic level 0.

In DTL and TTL, there is a driver BJT and circuitry is added to the base of this BJT to implement the *nand* function. In *emitter-coupled logic* (ECL), the base of the driver BJT is grounded and circuitry is added to its emitter (hence its name) to implement the *nor* function. ECL circuits are potentially faster than RTL, DTL, or TTL because, unlike those logic families, the driver BJT is never driven into saturation and can therefore switch much faster from one state to another. If either A or B in Fig. 6(f) is at a logic level 1, either T1 or T2 conducts. Therefore, there is current through R1. This brings Q to the logic level 0. The emitter of T4 is now at either 0 or a small positive voltage (depending on the values of R1 and R3) and this cuts T4 OFF. S is therefore at the logic level 1. When both A, B are 0, neither T1 *nor* T2 conducts. Q is at the logic level 1. The emitter of T4 is at a negative voltage (close to 0). T4 conducts and S is set to the logic level 0. Note that Q and S are complements.

One advantage of using logic gates implemented using BJTs is that they have faster switching speeds than gates using MOS devices. The low power dissipation of MOS gates, among other reasons, made it easier to integrate MOS devices. However, many of these logic families are still in use for special purpose circuits or where higher driving capabilities are required.

Classes of Computer Circuits

Depending on the functions they implement, computer circuits are divided into two classes: *combinational circuits* and *sequential circuits*. Combinational circuits are the simpler of the two classes and, along with other circuit elements, are used in the design of sequential circuits.

To understand the difference between combinational and sequential circuits, refer to Fig. 7(a). The time interval is divided into sub-intervals $I1, I2,...$ of equal size. The intervals are marked by a periodic logic signal known as *clock*. The *period* of clock is equal to the length of the interval. Every interval is divided into two parts. During the first part, clock is 1, and during the second part, clock is 0. We will refer to them as the *one* and *zero* periods of the interval.

Every circuit can be abstracted, as shown in Fig. 7(b). Computation proceeds as follows. During the one period, the values of the inputs change. During the zero period, the logic values at the outputs change and settle down to their steady state value. This is known as *single-phase clocking*.

Combinational circuits are circuits whose output, during any time interval, depends *only* on the values of the inputs during the current time interval and is independent of the values of the inputs during the preceding time intervals. The output of *sequential circuits*, during any time interval, on the other hand, depends on *both* the values of the inputs during the current interval, as well as the values of the inputs during the preceding time intervals. Having noted this difference, we will next look at some combinational and sequential circuits and try to understand some simple design procedures for these classes of circuits.

Combinational Circuits

Boolean functions are functions over boolean variables whose result can only be one of the two boolean values 0, 1. Combinational circuits implement boolean functions. An example of such a function is the *odd parity function* P_n of n variables. P_n equals 1 if and only if an odd number of the n input variables equal 1.

Boolean functions are defined using *truth tables*. Such a table defines the value of the function for each combination of values of the input. The truth table of the *parity function* of three variables is shown in Table 1. Circuits with multiple outputs can also be specified using truth tables.

Fig. 8 is a description of a circuit for the parity function. Such a pictorial representation is a *gate level description* of the circuit. A simple, but not necessarily efficient, way to derive a gate level description from a truth table is as follows. An input variable X_i or its complement (i.e. negation) $\overline{X}_i$ is known as an *input literal*. A conjunction of literals is known as a *term*. Corresponding to each row of a truth table, we have a term. For example, for row 1 of Table 1, we have the term $\overline{X}_1 \cdot \overline{X}_2 \cdot \overline{X}_3$ ('·' denotes the 'and' operation). The term corresponding to a row of a truth table for a boolean function f is a *one-term* for f if and only if the value of f for that input combination is 1. A *zero-term*

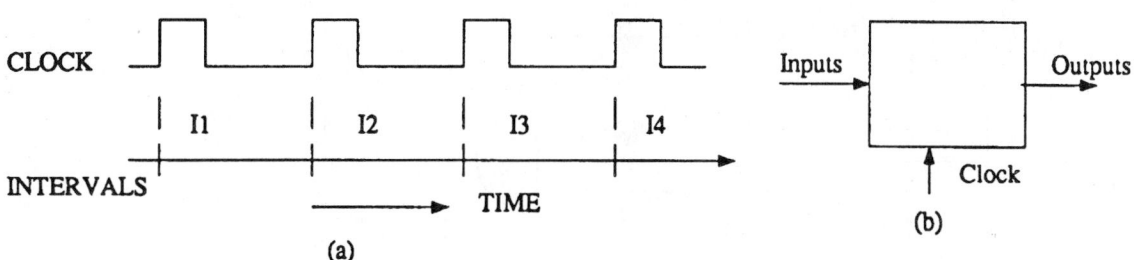

FIG. 7. Global Clock.

TABLE 1

	X_1	X_2	X_3	P_3
	0	0	0	0
	0	0	1	1
	0	1	0	1
	0	1	1	0
	1	0	0	1
	1	0	1	0
	1	1	0	0
	1	1	1	1

is similarly defined. From Table 1, $\overline{X}_1 \cdot \overline{X}_2 \cdot X_3$ is a zero-term and $\overline{X}_1 \cdot \overline{X}_2 \cdot X_3$ is a one-term for P_3.

Let $a_1,\ldots, a_t$ be the one-terms of a function f. Then, $a_1 + a_2 +\ldots+ a_t$ ('+' denotes the *or* operation) is a *sum-of-products* expression for f. From Table 1 we get the following sum of products expression P_3: $P_3 = \overline{X}_1 \cdot \overline{X}_2 \cdot X_3 + \overline{X}_1 \cdot X_2 \cdot \overline{X}_3 + X_1 \cdot \overline{X}_2 \cdot \overline{X}_3 + X_1 \cdot X_2 \cdot X_3$. From such an expression, we get the gate level description shown in Fig. 8. Note that, for each term, we have an *and* gate and there is one *or* gate that is driven by all the *and* gates.

Programmable Circuits   The gate level description is a description of the circuit that is used for fabricating the circuit. Prior to fabrication, the physical location on a silicon wafer of the devices (like FETs, resistors, etc.) has to be determined (*placement*). This is followed by determining how the devices are to be interconnected (*routing*). For circuits using a small number of devices, placement and routing can be done manually. For larger circuits, the entire process has to be automated. Many of the steps of placement and routing can be easily automated if the circuit topology is regular. Moreover, the integration process becomes simpler and more cost effective if a variety of circuits can be physically implemented

by minor variations (or *programming*) of a "master piece." These factors have led to the evolution of a number of design styles like *Programmable Logic Arrays* (PLAs), *Weinburger Arrays, Gate Matrix Arrays,* etc. Such design styles are being used extensively. To gain insight into these styles, we will have a brief look at nMOS PLAs.

Let X_1, $\overline{X}_2$, X_3 be input variables. The *nor* expression $X_1 + X_2 + X_3 (X_1 + \overline{X}_2 + X_3)$ can be logically implemented, as shown in Fig. 9(a). To implement this expression physically—if there are n input variables, we have a physical row of $2n$ nFETs. For every input variable X_i, there exists two nFETs, one driven by X_i and the other driven by $\overline{X}_i$. An example is shown in Fig. 9(b). For this row of nFETs, some of the "links" are "broken." This effectively removes some of the FETs from the circuit, resulting in the desired gate shown in Fig. 9(c). This is the basic idea used in a PLA.

A PLA is shown in Fig. 10. It consists of two parts, an AND-PLANE and an OR-PLANE. Each of these two parts are two-dimensional array of FETs. Every row of the AND-PLANE is arranged to form a potential *nor* gate. All FETs in a column of the AND-PLANE are driven by the same input literal. Every column of the OR-PLANE is arranged to form a potential *nor* gate. The inputs of the FETs in a row of the OR-PLANE are driven by the output of the same *nor* gate of the AND-PLANE. Given such an array of FETs, a set of sum of products expressions is implemented by "selectively disconnecting" some of the FETs from the circuit. For example, to implement the following boolean functions, the FETs to be disconnected are shown by 'X' in Fig. 10.

$$f_1 = X_1 X_2 + \overline{X_1 X_2}$$

$$f_2 = X_1 X_2 + \overline{X}_1 X_2$$

Sequential Circuits   We will use a simple example to illustrate how sequential circuits are designed. Consider

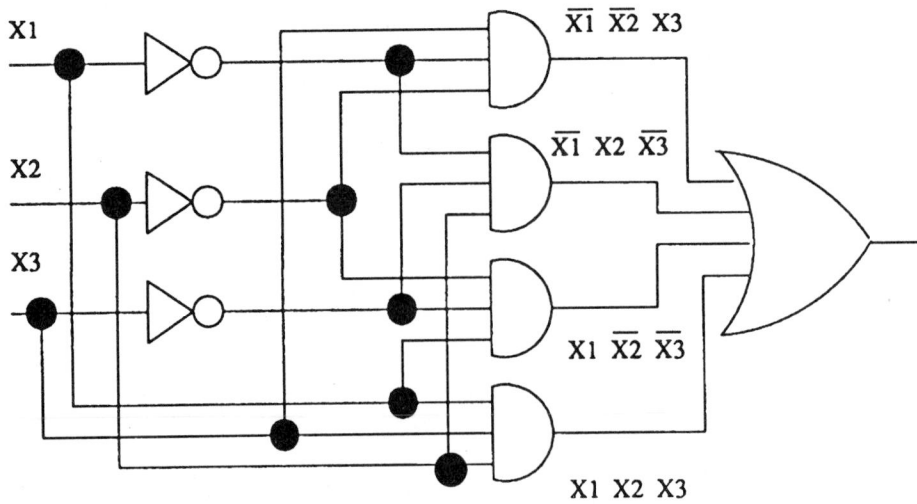

FIG. 8.   Example of Sum-Of-Product Circuits.

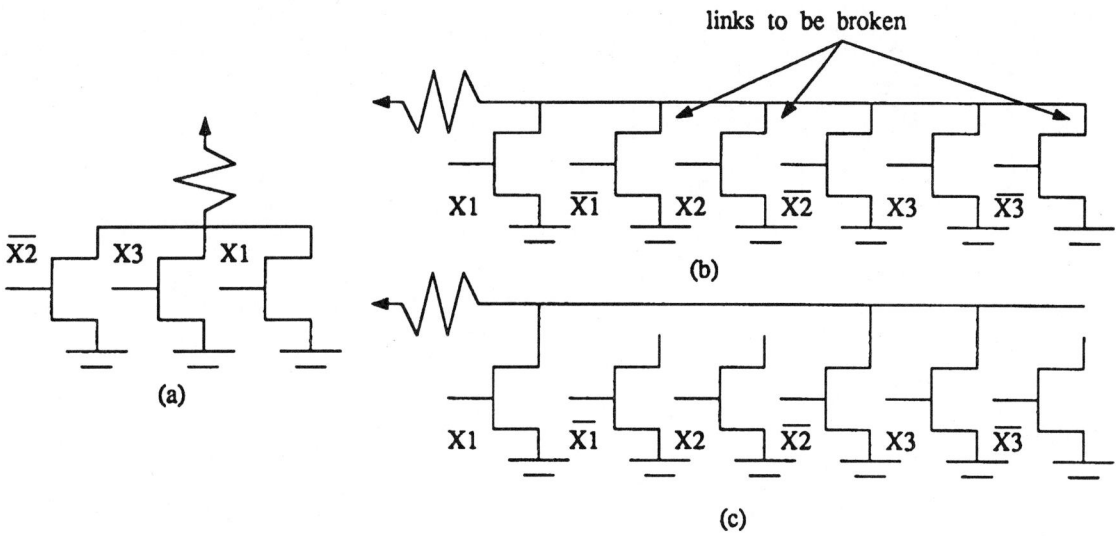

FIG. 9. Programmable NOR Gate.

a circuit with one input X and one output Y, defined as follows. Let n_j be the number of intervals, including and up to I_j, during which X had the value 1. At the end of I_j, Y is set to 1 if and only if n_j is divisible by 3. We call such a circuit *MOD-3*.

In order to compute the value of Y during the interval I_j, MOD-3 must remember some characteristics of the pattern of 0s and 1s during the intervals 1 to I_{j-1}. It is enough for the circuit to remember the value of $r_{j-1} = n_{j-1}$

mod 3, which is nothing but the remainder left after dividing n_{j-1} by 3. Also note that if X, during I_j, equals 1, then $r_j = (r_{j-1} + 1)$ mod 3; and if r_j equals 0, then Y is to be set to 1. Therefore, at the end of any interval, we need to remember if the remainder was 0, 1, or 2.

Another way to express this behavior of MOD-3 is with the help of the *state diagram* of Fig. 11(b). Since we need to know if r_j is 0, 1, or 2, we say that the circuit, at the end of I_j, is in state S0 if r_j is 0, S1 if r_j is 1, and S2 if r_j is 2.

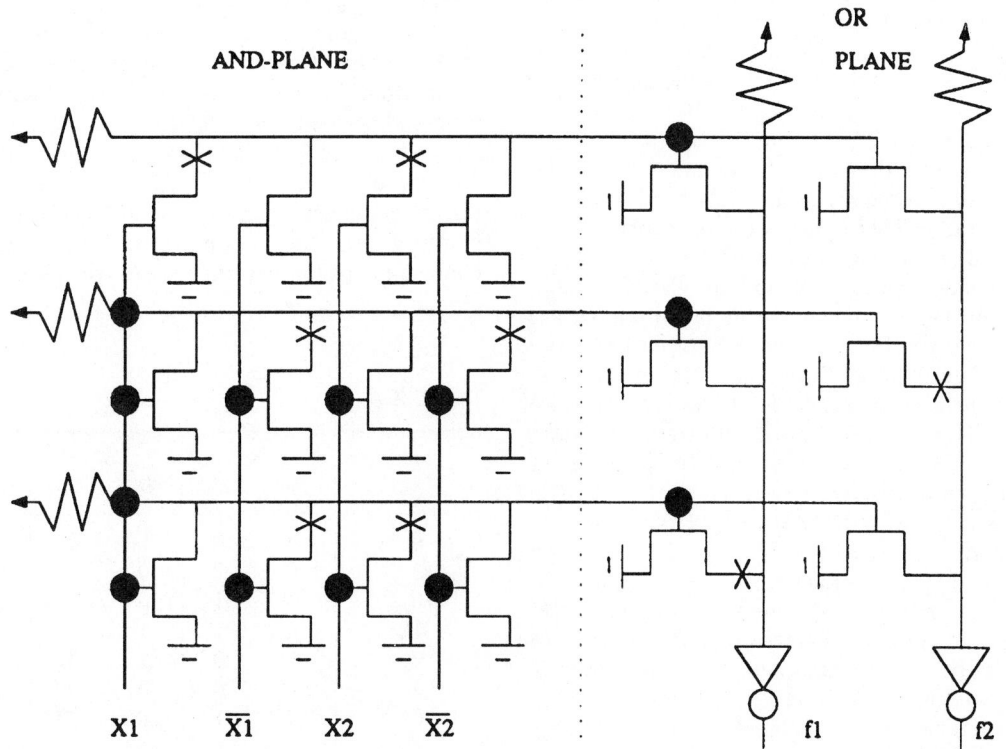

FIG. 10. Example of a programmable logic array.

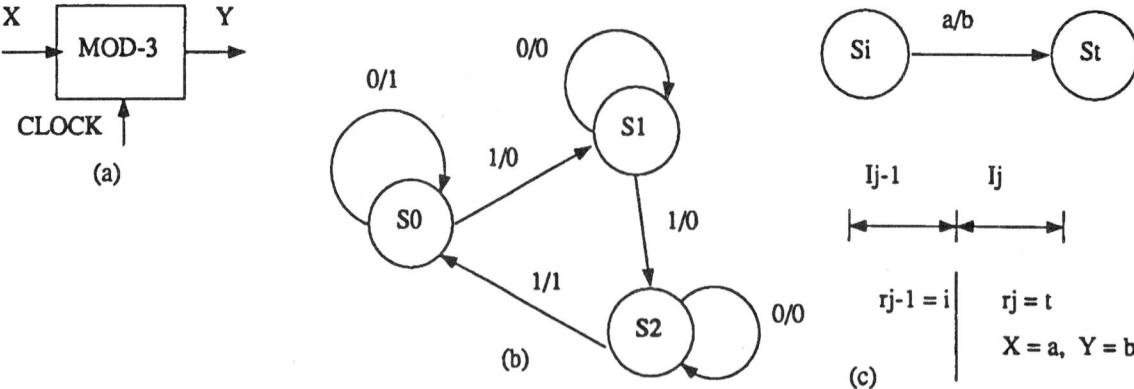

FIG. 11. Example of a state diagram.

The arrow marked a/b, which starts at Si and ends at St, is to be interpreted as follows: if, at the end of the interval I_{j-1}, r_{j-1} is i and during interval I_j the value of X is a, then, at the end of interval I_j, the value of Y should be b and r_j should be t.

While designing a circuit from a state diagram, we have to make sure that the circuit "remembers" the state of the system. In order to do that, the states are *encoded* using two *state variables* a_0, a_1 as follows: $S0 = (a0 = 0, a1 = 0)$; $S1 = (a0 = 0, a1 = 1)$; and $S2 = (a0 = 1, a1 = 0)$. The circuit now needs to remember the values of the state variables. In other words, the circuit should be capable of remembering *two bits of information*. This leads to the question: how exactly does a circuit remember two or more bits of information?

As they did for logic gates, circuit designers have devised circuit elements called *flip-flops*. A flip-flop can store (i.e. remember) 1 bit of information. The structure of a flip-flop is shown in Fig. 12(a) and we will use the symbol of Fig. 12(b) to represent such a flip-flop. Here Q is the output of the flip-flop and $\overline{Q}$ is another output, such that the value of $\overline{Q}$ is always the complement of the value of Q. D is the input to the flip-flop. When CLOCK is 1 and D is 1, Q is set to 1. When D is 0 and CLOCK is 1, then Q is set to 0. When CLOCK is 0, the value of Q or $\overline{Q}$ cannot change. What we have just described is a D *flip-flop*. There are a number of other classes of flip-flops like SR flip-flop, JK flip-flops, etc. Fig. 12(c) depicts a slight variation of a D flip-flop that uses nFETs. In this case, in order to modify the values of Q and $\overline{Q}$, both CLOCK and WR have to be 1.

To continue our discussion of the design process, we derive the *state table* from the state diagram. The state table for our example is shown in Table 2. For each edge in the state diagram, we have a row in the state table. The pair $< a_0, a_1 >$ defines the state S_i of Fig. 11(c); $< D_0, D_1 >$ defines the state S_t; X defines the value a; and Y defines the value b. Note that D_0, D_1 will become the new value of a_0, a_1 at the start of the next interval. In order for that to happen, the circuit should be of the form shown in Fig. 13(a), where C must satisfy the conditions of the state table (Table 2). The complete circuit is shown in Fig. 13(b). Note that Table 2 is like a truth table for the combinational block C of Fig. 13(a). This is a simple, but not necessarily an efficient way to implement sequential circuits.

Historical Notes We conclude the discussion with some historical notes. The earliest electronic computers were based on vacuum tubes. They are known as *first generation* computers and spanned the years 1945 to 1959. ENIAC (*q.v.*), which was built around 1945 at the University of Pennsylvania, is an example. It used about 18,000 tubes.

After the BJT was invented in 1948, it took almost 10 years for it to become a practically feasible alternative to vacuum tubes. The *second generation* of computers, which spanned the years 1959 to 1964, used BJTs. In making these computers, discrete components like BJTs, diodes, etc. were placed on a *printed circuit* wiring board and interconnected using copper wires. Since these components were much smaller than vacuum tubes and required much less power, the resulting computers were significantly smaller in size.

Unlike the clear distinction between the first and second generation of computers, there is a smaller distinction between subsequent generations. The *third generation*, exemplified by the IBM System 360, used integrated circuit technology. In integrated circuits, a number of devices like BJTs, diodes, etc. along with the interconnecting wires, are all fabricated on a single silicon wafer. These chunks of circuits were then interconnected using external wires to make the entire circuit.

TABLE 2.

Input X	S_i		S_t		Output Y
	a_0	a_1	D_0	D_1	
0	0	0	0	0	1
1	0	0	0	1	0
0	0	1	0	1	0
1	0	1	1	0	0
0	1	0	1	0	0
1	1	0	0	0	1
0	1	1	dc	dc	dc
1	1	1	dc	dc	dc

dc— don't care

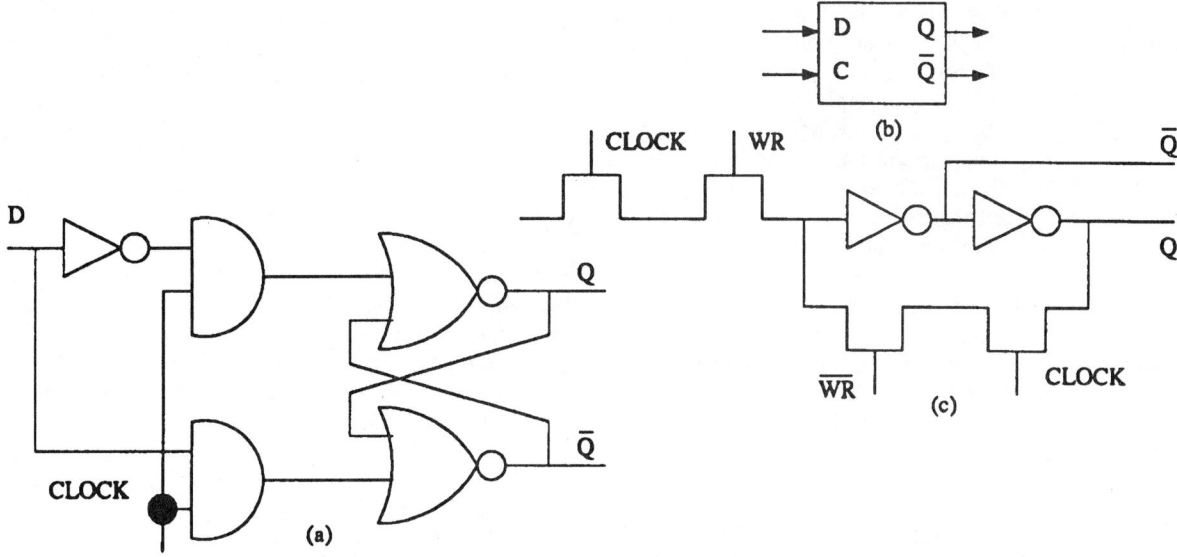

FIG. 12. Structure of a Flip/Flop.

Initially, only a few hundred devices could be integrated on a single silicon wafer. That was the era of *small scale integration* (SSI). With technological innovations, the number of devices that could be integrated on a single wafer grew. Today, a few hundred thousand devices are fabricated on a single silicon wafer. This is known as *very large scale integration* (VSLI). It is now possible to fabricate an entire processor, except for the external memory and peripheral drivers, on a single silicon wafer. These are known as *microprocessors*. Powerful computing systems that are made from these VLSI chips constitute the *fourth generation* of computers. Unlike third generation computers, these computers are almost exclusively based on MOS devices.

It would be inaccurate to leave the impression that the technological innovations in computer circuitry resulted only in smaller and more highly integrated circuits. Designers of systems to be used for special purpose ap-

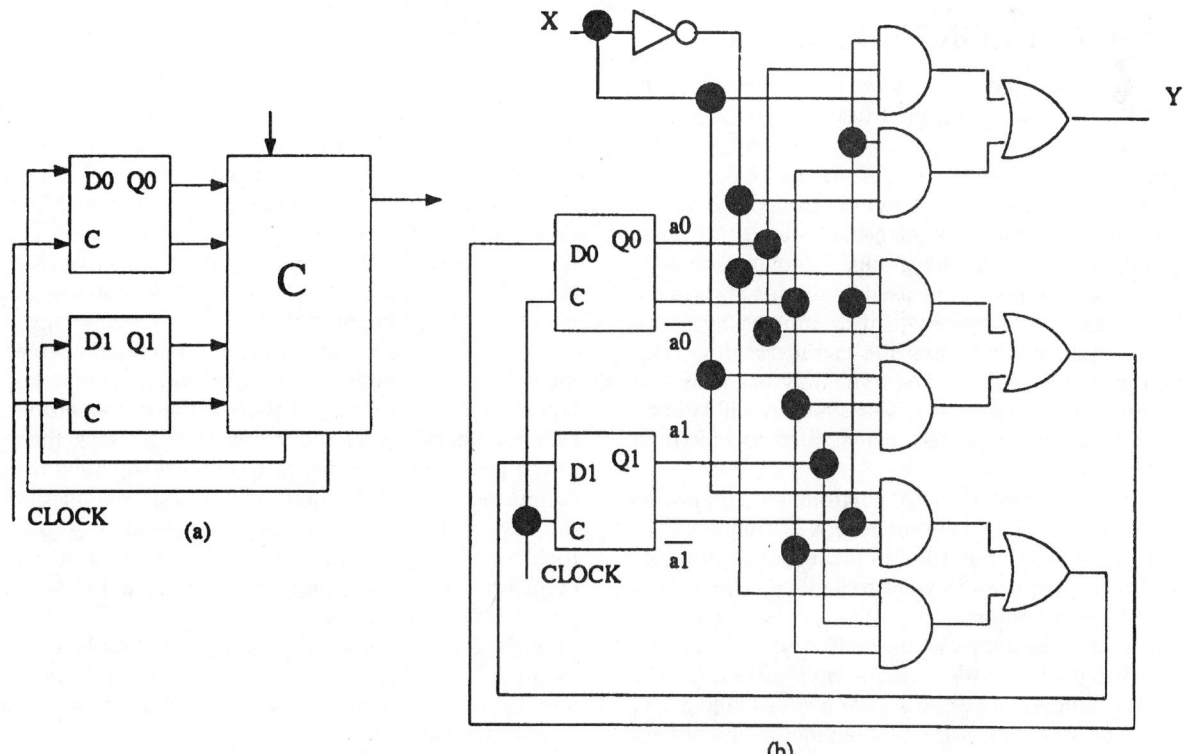

FIG. 13. Implementation of the state diagram of Figure 11.

plications like scientific applications were more interested in the speed of the circuits. So, along with increased levels of integration, faster and faster switching devices were made. The CDC 6000 was implemented using discrete components that were very fast, and yet is generally considered to be a third generation computer. Similarly, the CRAY-1, CRAY-XMP, etc., which do not use a very high level of integration but instead use very fast specialized components, are considered to belong to the fourth generation.

The classification of computing systems based on circuit technology alone has often been questioned. Of late, it is generally believed that the "nature of the computation" should be used to classify computers. Accordingly, the *fifth* and latest generation of computers consists of those that can directly execute "logic programs" (*q.v.*).

References

1977. Taub, H. and Schilling, D. *Digital Integrated Electronics*. New York: McGraw-Hill.

1978. Kohavi, Z. *Switching and Finite Automata Theory*. New York: McGraw-Hill.

1980. Mead, C. and Conway, L. *Introduction to VLSI Systems*. Reading, MA: Addison Wesley.

1985. Bartee, T. C. *Digital Computer Fundamentals*, 6th Ed. New York: McGraw-Hill.

1985. Weste, N. and Eshraghian, K. *Principles of CMOS VLSI Design*. Reading, MA: Addison-Wesley.

1989. Unger, S. H. *The Essence of Logic Circuits*. Englewood Cliffs, NJ: Prentice Hall.

SREEJIT CHAKRAVARTY

COMPUTER CONFERENCING

For articles on related subjects *see* BULLETIN BOARD; ELECTRONIC MAIL; GROUPWARE; and NETWORKS, COMPUTER.

Computer conferencing (CC) is the use of computers and computer networks to structure group communications according to the nature of the communication objectives and the nature of the group. Although computer conferencing systems can be used by groups at the same time, they are primarily designed to support asynchronous communications among the members of a group. Though most CC systems are commonly used for text-based communications, the newer systems will support graphics and other digitized media, such as electronic voice.

A given conference in a CC environment can last for years and accumulate many thousands of comments. As a result, CC systems incorporate numerous information organizing and retrieval features to facilitate the use of a dynamic "group memory."

The first CC system was the incorporation of a Policy Delphi structure into a time sharing environment in 1971. Since 1971, numerous systems have evolved, and a long list of alternative names for this technology have been introduced: groupware (*q.v.*), teamware, collaborative systems, coordination systems, electronic meeting systems, bulletin boards (*q.v.*), group decision support systems, computer supported cooperative work, etc.

Since many of these systems incorporate electronic mail (*q.v.*) subsystems, the best term that has emerged to encompass all versions of this technology is "computer-mediated communication systems" (CMCS).

Some examples of particular application structures that have undergone field trials, evaluation, and application are crisis management, project management, unpredictable information exchange, collaborative composition, group therapy, Delphi exercises, management gaming, remote education and training (e.g. virtual classroom), data validation, and general discussion.

Some features that characterize a general purpose computer conferencing system are:

- All comments in a conference (group discussion space) are signed and dated.
- Conference membership is under the control of the owner or open to the public.
- Status reports show who has read or written what.
- Availability of anonymity or pen names as alternatives to signatures.
- Keyword indexing of conference comments and use of subject headings.
- Voting and collaborative decision aids.
- Specific human roles in the group supported by the software (e.g. monitors, editors, observers, indexers).
- Specialized privileges, such as joint editing of the same entry.
- Executable programs attached to conference comments.
- Directories of members and conferences.
- Virtual addressing of all existing objects, such as comments and mail.

While computer-mediated communications allows individuals to engage in group communication processes at any time or place that is individually convenient for them, the main benefit of this technology is the possibility for these systems to provide the ability to promote "collective intelligence"—the communication objective that the result of the group process can be better than that possible by the "best" member in the group acting alone.

Individuals in a computerized conferencing environment are free to integrate their individual problem-solving abilities as an integral part of the group problems. Different members of the group may address the part of the problem about which they have the most insight or information independent of the other members. It is the objective of the structure and communication protocols provided by the computer to integrate these contributions into a group result and to aid in synchronizing the group at key points in the group process. This integration of individual and group problem-solving methods is what provides the promise of "collective intelligence" on a more consistent basis than normal face-to-face meetings.

Some of the current issues being addressed by active research in this field are:

- The trade-off between human facilitation and computer facilitation.
- Collaborative composition of Hypertext (*q.v.*).
- The impact of such parameters as the size of the group and the relationship to structure.
- Conference tailoring under control of the user or owner of a given conference.
- Decision support toolkits.
- Generalized gaming support.
- Evaluation methods for group performance.
- Appropriate models for individual and group process.
- Object-oriented systems (*q.v.*).
- Integration with other computer resources.
- Communications as an interface metaphor.
- Expert system (*q.v.*) guidance on use of available tools.

The future of this technology lies in the ability of the computer to provide structures appropriate to a given application, and in our understanding of the relationships among the structures, protocols, tools, and the individual and group problem-solving process. It is impossible to divorce the design and evolution of this technology from behavioral and social understanding. Designing human communication systems is, in effect, the designing of social systems. As a result, the technology offers the possibility of new social structures for organizations and for society.

References

1989. Turoff, Murray. "The Anatomy of a Computer Application Innovation: Computer Mediated Communications (CMC)," *Journal of Technological Forecasting and Social Change,* **36**, 107–122.
1991. Turoff, Murray. "Requirements for Group Support in Computer Mediated Communication Systems," *Journal of Organizational Computing,* **1**, 1.

MURRAY TUROFF

COMPUTER CRIME

For articles on related subjects *see* COMPUTER VIRUS; HACKER; LEGAL ASPECTS OF COMPUTING; and LEGAL PROTECTION OF SOFTWARE.

Business, economic, and white-collar crimes have changed rapidly as computers proliferate into the activities and environments in which these crimes occur. Computers have engendered a different form of crime. Computers have been involved in most types of crime, including fraud, theft, larceny, embezzlement, bribery, burglary, sabotage, espionage, conspiracy, extortion, attempted murder, manslaughter, pornography, trespassing, violation of privacy, and kidnapping.

The evolution of occupations in this field has extended the traditional categories of criminals to include computer programmers, computer operators, tape librarians, and electronic engineers who function in new environments. Although crime has traditionally occurred in ordinary human environments, some crime is now perpetrated inside personal computers in bedrooms or mainframe computers in the specialized environment of rooms with raised flooring, lowered ceilings, large gray boxes, flashing lights, moving tapes, and the hum of air-conditioning motors.

The methods of committing crime have changed. A new jargon has developed, identifying automated criminal methods such as data diddling, Trojan horses, viruses, worms, logic bombs, salami techniques, superzapping, piggybacking, scavenging, data leakage, and asynchronous attacks. The forms of many of the targets of computer crime are also different. Electronic transactions and money, as well as paper and plastic money (credit cards), represent assets subject to intentionally caused automated loss. Money in the form of electronic signals and magnetic patterns is stored and processed in computers and transmitted over telephone lines. Money is debited and credited to accounts inside computers. In fact, the computer has become an electronic vault for the business community. Many other physical assets, including inventories of products in warehouses and of materials leaving or entering factories, are represented by electronic and optical documents of records inside computer systems. Electronic data interchange (EDI), which connects trading partners for conducting contract negotiations, sales, invoicing, and collections, focuses traditional sources of business crime on computers and data communications.

The timing of some crimes is also different. Traditionally, the duration of criminal acts is measured in minutes, hours, days, weeks, months, and years. Today, some crimes are being perpetrated in less than 0.003 of a second (3 milliseconds). Thus, automated crime must be considered in terms of a computer time scale of milliseconds, microseconds, and nanoseconds because of the speed of execution of instructions in computers.

Geographic constraints do not inhibit perpetration of this crime. A telephone with an attached computer terminal in one part of the world could be used to engage in a crime in an online computer system in any other part of the world.

All these factors and more must be considered in dealing with the crime of computer abuse. Unfortunately, however, the business community, constituting all businesses, government agencies, and institutions that use computers for technical and business purposes, is neither adequately prepared to deal with nor sufficiently motivated to report this kind of crime to the authorities. Although reliable statistics are as yet unavailable to prove this, computer security studies for the business community and interviews with certified public accountants have indicated that few crimes of this type are ever reported to law enforcement agencies for prosecution.

State and federal criminal codes contain at least 50 statutes defining computer crime. Any violations of these specific statutes are computer crimes under the most strict interpretation of the term; in some contexts it is also customary to include alleged violations of these statutes as computer crimes.

Computer-related crimes—a broader category—are any violations of criminal law that involve a knowledge of computer technology for their perpetration, investigation, or prosecution. Although computer-related crimes are primarily white-collar offenses, any kind of illegal act based on an understanding of computer technology can be a computer-related crime. They could even be violent crimes that destroy computers or their contents and thereby jeopardize human lives (e.g. people who depend on the correct functioning of computers for their health or well being). The proliferation and use of personal computers make computer-related crimes potentially endemic throughout society.

Computer abuse encompasses a broad range of intentional acts that may or may not be specifically prohibited by criminal statutes. Any intentional act involving knowledge of computer use or technology is computer abuse if one or more perpetrators made or could have made gain, one or more victims suffered or could have suffered loss, or both.

The term *computer crime* has been used to refer generally to all three categories: computer crime in the strict sense, computer-related crime, and computer abuse. Where the context requires distinctions among the three categories to avoid confusion or misinterpretation, the text specifically identifies the type of crime or abuse that is intended.

Computer crime may involve computers not only actively but also passively when usable evidence of the acts resides in computer storage. The victims and potential victims of computer crime include all organizations and people who use or are affected by computer and data communication systems, including people about whom data are stored and processed in computers.

Categories All known and reported cases of computer crime involve computers in one or more of the following four roles:

- Object—Cases include destruction of computers or of data or programs contained in them or of supportive facilities and resources, such as airconditioning equipment and electrical power that allow them to function.
- Subject—A computer can be the site or environment of a crime or the source of or reason for unique forms and kinds of assets lost, such as a pirated computer program. A fraud perpetrated by changing account balances in financial data stored in a computer makes the computer the subject of a crime.
- Instrument—Some types and methods of crime are complex enough to require the use of a computer as a tool or instrument. A computer can be used actively such as in automatically scanning telephone codes to make unauthorized use of a telephone system. It could also be used passively to simulate a general ledger in the planning and control of a continuing financial embezzlement.

- Symbol—A computer can be used as a symbol for intimidation or deception. This could involve an organization falsely claiming to use nonexistent computers.

The dimensions of the definition of computer crime becomes a problem in some cases. If a computer is stolen in a simple theft where, based on all circumstances, it could have been a washing machine or milling machine and made no difference, a knowledge of computer technology is not necessary and it would not be a computer crime. However, if knowledge of computer technology is necessary to determine the value of the article taken, the nature of possible damage done in the taking, or the intended use by the thief, then the theft would be a computer crime.

The following illustrates. If an individual telephones a bank funds transfer department and fraudulently requests a transfer of $70 million to an account in a bank in Vienna, two possibilities occur. If the clerk who received the call was deceived and keyed the transfer into a computer terminal, the funds transfer would not be a computer crime. No fraudulent act was related directly to a computer, and no special knowledge of computer technology was required. However, if the clerk was in collusion with the caller, the fraudulent act would include the entry of data at the terminal and would be a computer crime. Knowledge of computer technology would be necessary to understand the terminal usage and protocol.

These examples indicate the possibilities of rational conclusions in defining computer crime. However, more practical considerations should not make such explicit and absolute decisions necessary. A classification of computer crime is based on a variety of lists and models from several sources. The classification goes beyond white-collar crimes because computers have been found to be involved in almost all types of crime. Computer crime has been categorized by types of information and information-processing loss: modification, destruction, disclosure, and use or denial of use. This classification is deceptive, however, because many other types of loss have occurred, including acts of misrepresentation, delay or prolongation of use, renaming, misappropriation, and failure to act. Therefore, a more comprehensive and usable typing is loss of integrity, confidentiality, and availability of information. These three classes define acts that are intrinsic to information (such as changing it), extrinsic to information (such as changing access to it), and external to information (by removing or copying it).

The SRI Computer Abuse Methods Model considers a classification system for computer abuses that is summarized in Fig. 1. It shows the relationships of computer crime methods. The model is more of a system of descriptors than it is a taxonomy in the usual sense, in that multiple descriptors may apply in any particular case. For visual simplicity, this model is depicted as a simple tree, although that is an oversimplification—the classes are not mutually disjoint.

The order of categorization depicted is roughly from the physical world to the hardware to the operating system (and network software) to the application code. The first abuse class includes external abuses that can take

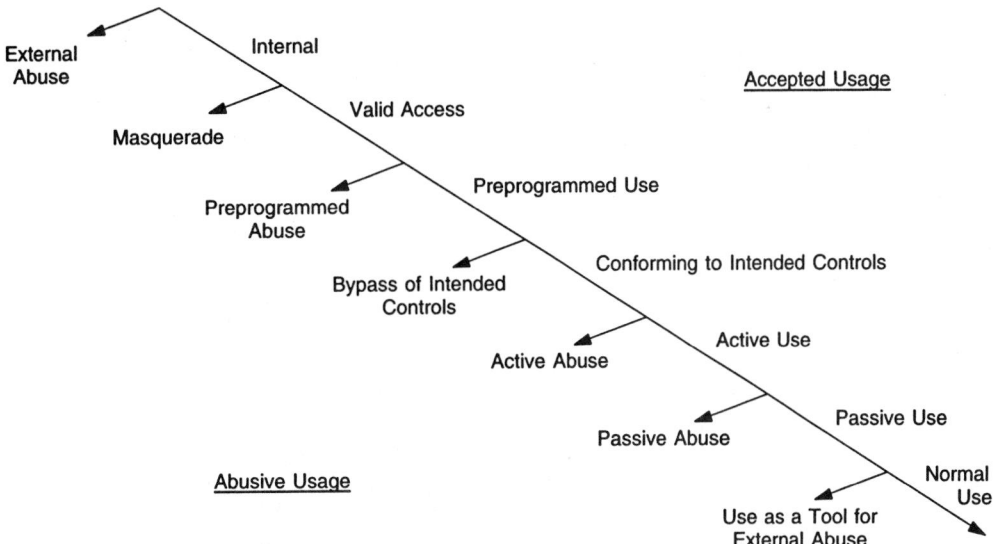

FIG 1. Computer Abuse Methods Model.

place passively without access to the computer systems. The second class includes hardware abuse, and generally requires some sort of physical access and active behavior with respect to the computer system itself. Eavesdropping and interference are examples of these two classes, respectively. The third class includes masquerading in a variety of forms. The fourth includes cases of preparation for subsequent abuses, (e.g. the planting of a Trojan horse (instructions secretly inserted into the victim's computer program)), as opposed to the abuses that result from the actual exploitation of the Trojan horse, which show up later in subsequent classes. The remaining classes involve bypass of authorization, active abuse, passive abuse, and uses that lead to subsequent abuse. The leftward branches all involve misuses, while the rightward branches represent potentially acceptable use, until a leftward branch is taken. Every leftward branch represents a class of vulnerabilties that must be defended against and detected at the earliest possible time. However, the techniques for defense and detection differ from one branch to the next.

This figure represents a classification system for types of techniques, but not a taxonomy of computer crimes. Actual violations of computer security and integrity have often involved multiple types of abuse. For example, the German Chaos Computer Club people who attacked NASA systems in 1987 utilized (at least) techniques of external abuse, masquerading, preplanned Trojan horse attacks, bypass of intended controls, and both active and passive abuses. Thus, the tree representation is merely a convenient way of summarizing the classes.

History Computer abuse started with the emergence of computer technology in the late 1940s. As the number of people in the computer field began to increase, that facet of human nature that wants to harm society for personal gain took hold; the problem of abuse became

especially acute as computer technology proliferated into sensitive areas in society, such as military systems. The abuse then spread to engineering, to science, and in parallel to business and personal applications.

The first recorded computer abuse occurred in 1958 (Parker et al. 1973). The first federally prosecuted computer crime, identified as such, was the alteration of bank records by computer in Minneapolis in 1966.

No valid, representative statistics on computer crime exist, even through several surveys have been conducted and well-known organizations and individuals have quoted various statistics. Frequency, losses per year, rate of increase or decrease, percentages of perpetrators within or outside of victimized organizations, and the number of cases discovered and prosecuted are not known. To protect themselves, victims try to deny their loss. No methods have been devised to apply uniform definitions, identify authoritative sources, or conduct surveys in any statistically valid way. The formal study of computer abuse was started in 1971. The first national conference on computer abuse and a comprehensive report were completed in 1973. Since then, many reports, papers, journal articles, and books have been published describing the research (see References).

In 1976, as a result of the increasing frequency of cases, Senator Abraham Ribicoff and his U.S. Senate Government Affairs Committee became aware of computer crime and the inadequacy of federal criminal law to deal with it. The committee produced two reports on its research (1976, 1977), and Senator Ribicoff introduced the first Federal Systems Protection Act Bill in June 1977. These legislative efforts evolved into House Bill 5616 in 1986, which resulted in the Computer Fraud and Abuse Act of 1987, established as Article 1030, Chapter 47 of Title 18 Criminal Code. On the state level, Florida, Michigan, Colorado, Rhode Island, and Arizona were the first to have computer crime laws based on the first Ribicoff bill.

Current legislation on computer crime exists in all states and several other countries.

Computer crime has been portrayed fictionally in several novels, motion pictures, and television dramas. Two comic strips, Dick Tracy and Steve Roper, have depicted fictional stories. The British Broadcasting System dramatized the computer crime aspects of a massive insurance fraud. NBC TV News and the CBS show "60 Minutes" have had special segments. The motion picture "War Games" was the first to popularize computer hacking. Several nonfiction trade books have been published, and articles have appeared in all major magazines and newspapers. Unfortunately, the public interest and sensationalism associated with computer crime, particularly the malicious hacker (*q.v.*) cases that peaked in 1982 and the 1988 computer virus cases, have made folk heroes of the perpetrators and embarrassed the victims.

References

1973. Parker, Donn B., Nycum, Susan H., and Oura, S. "Computer Abuse," SRI International, Menlo Park, California, report distributed by National Technical Information Service, U.S. Department of Commerce, Springfield, Virginia.

1975. Allen Brandt. "Embezzler's Guide to the Computer," *Harvard Business Review.* (July) 53.

1976. Parker, Donn B. *Crime by Computer.* New York: Charles Scribner's Sons.

1976. U.S. Senate Committee on Government Operations, "Problems Associated with Computer Technology in Federal Programs and Private Industry," U.S. Government Printing Office, Washington, D.C. (June).

1977. U.S. Senate Committee on Government Operations, "Staff Study of Computer Security in Federal Programs." U.S. Government Printing Office, Washington, D.C.

1983. Parker, Donn B. *Fighting Computer Crime.* New York: Charles Scribner's Sons.

1986. Sieber, Ulrich. *The International Handbook on Computer Crime.* New York: John Wiley and Sons.

1989. *Computer Crime: Criminal Justice Resource Manual.* U.S. Department of Justice Report No. NCJ118214, Washington D.C. (August).

1989. Stoll, C. *The Cuckoo's Egg.* Garden City, NY: Doubleday.

1990. BloomBecker, B., *Spectacular Computer Crimes.* Homewood, IL: Dow Jones-Irwin.

1991. Hafner, K. and Markoff, J. *Cyberpunk: Outlaws and Hackers on the Computer Frontier.* New York: Simon and Shuster.

DONN B. PARKER

COMPUTER ENGINEERING

For articles on related subjects *see* COMPUTER-AIDED ENGINEERING; and COMPUTER SCIENCE.

Computer engineering, as differentiated from *computer science,* focuses on the implementation (i.e. reduction to practice) aspects of the discipline, and the trade-offs required to produce viable systems.

Like computer science, computer engineering is also concerned with all elements of information processing systems, including the application environment (e.g. visualization of the results of a computation, artificial intelligence, computational science—harnessing the power of supercomputers, and perceptual and cognitive processes), paradigms for representing information (e.g. algorithms for numeric and non-numeric applications, symbol manipulation, and language processing), paradigms for processing information (e.g. distributed computing, software engineering, information storage and retrieval, programs for managing computing resources, programs for transforming source programs, hardware execution models, programming languages and compilers—from the standpoint that they impact an integrated hardware/software system, networks that interconnect pieces of a computer system to form one complete computer system and those that interconnect complete computer systems), and tools for designing and measuring the effectiveness of computer systems (e.g. CAD design tools and performance measurement and analysis tools).

Also like computer science, computer engineering is concerned with human/machine interfaces, vision systems, robotics, graphics, reliable computer systems, logic circuits, hardware devices and structures, and application-specific computers.

A continuing debate persists as to what is computer science and what is computer engineering and where one should draw the line between the two. It is sometimes argued that computer engineering is more concerned with hardware and computer science is more concerned with software. But that would put both hardware design and hardware models within the realm of computer engineering. Hardware design clearly belongs in computer engineering, since the element of design is central to computer engineering. Arguably, however, the development of hardware models is really computer science. Therefore, VLSI design, as a subset of hardware design, also belongs in both disciplines.

This hardware/software dichotomy also produces a problem with software engineering (*q.v.*). Certainly, formal methods (*q.v.*) for proofs of program correctness is computer science, but the practice of software engineering, getting large programs to work, falls squarely in the domain of computer engineering.

Computer engineering and computer science are not at all differentiated by whether they involve hardware or software, since each involves both. Rather, computer engineering is more concerned with the implementation of ideas, while computer science is more concerned with the formal structure of those ideas. Two examples may make the distinction clearer.

Case 1. A *compiler* is a program that transforms a source program written in a language reasonably suitable for humans into a set of directives suitable for the hardware to carry out the work specified by the source program. The taxonomy of compiler features, the functionality that each provides, and the distinction between what is doable and not doable by a compiler is more nearly computer science. The design and development of a compiler that includes performing cost/benefit trade-off analysis with respect to including or leaving out specific features vis-à-vis a specific target hardware implementation is more nearly computer engineering.

Case. 2. A *hardware execution model* is a paradigm for carrying out the directives produced by the compiler. The taxonomy of hardware execution models and their distinguishing characteristics is more nearly computer science. The design and implementation of a hardware execution model, with strong attention to the cost vs. benefits trade-offs associated with the individual features, is more nearly computer engineering.

YALE PATT

COMPUTER GAMES

For articles on related subjects *see* ARTIFICIAL INTELLIGENCE; and COMPUTER CHESS.

HISTORY

Computers weren't invented to play games. In the 1950s and 1960s, with computer time both scarce and expensive, writing games for the fun of it was actively discouraged at most computer centers.

Nevertheless, there were many other reasons than just plain fun for writing computer games. Common reasons included exploring the power of the computer, improving understanding of human thought processes, producing educational tools for managers or military officers, simulating dangerous environments, and providing the means for discovery learning.

In some sense, the association of computers and games started in 1950 when Alan Turing proposed his famous *imitation game* in the article "Computing Machinery and Intelligence," published in *Mind* magazine. Never programmed by Turing himself, a variation of Turing's game called Eliza was put in the form of a computer program 13 years later by Joseph Weizenbaum at M.I.T.

In 1952, behind a cloak of secrecy, the first military simulation games were programmed by Bob Chapman and others at Rand Air Defense Lab in Santa Monica. In the same year, a number of "formula" games (Nim, etc.) and "dictionary look-up" games (tic-tac-toe, etc.) were programmed for several early computers. Also in 1952, a computer was specially designed to play Hex, a game with no exact solution, by E.F. Moore and Claude Shannon (*q.v.*) at Bell Labs in New Jersey.

In 1953, Arthur Samuel first demonstrated his Checkers program on the newly unveiled IBM 701 computer at IBM in Poughkeepsie, NY. Later that year, the book *The Complete Strategyst* by J.D. Williams was published by RAND Corp. This was the first primer on game theory and provided the theoretical foundation for many early computer game programs.

The first computer game of blackjack was programmed in 1954 for the IBM 701 at the Atomic Energy Lab at Los Alamos, NM. Also in 1954, a crude game of pool—perhaps the first non-military game to use a video display—was programmed at the University of Michigan.

The military set the pace for simulation games for many years, and in 1955 Hutspiel, the first theater-level war game (NATO vs. USSR), was programmed at the Research Analysis Corporation in McLean, Virginia.

Although Newell, Shaw, and Simon are frequently credited with the first chess game—probably because they stayed at it for over 20 years—the first version of computer chess (*q.v.*) was actually programmed in 1956 by Kister, Stein, Ulam, Walden, and Wells on the MANIAC-I at the Los Alamos Atomic Energy Laboratory. The game was played on a simplified 6 × 6 board and examined all possible moves two levels deep at the rate of 12 moves per minute. It played similar to a human player with about 20 games experience. In contrast, Deep Thought, the 1990 computer chess champion, examined about 1.5 million moves per second and used a combination of brute force and intuitive play on a standard board. Although rated at about 2600 on the FIDE system, which places it among the top 40 human players in the world, Deep Thought was decisively defeated by Gary Kasparov in a two-game match in October 1989.

In 1958, a tennis game was designed for an analog computer at Brookhaven National Lab by Willy Higinbothan. This game, played on an oscilloscope display, was significant in that it was the first video game to permit two players actually to control the direction and motion of the object moving on the screen (the ball).

In 1959, large-scale simulation games moved into the private sector with the programming of "The Management Game" by Cohen, Cyert, Dill, and others at Carnegie Tech in Pittsburgh. This game, programmed in the language GATE on a Bendix G-15 computer, simulated competition between three companies in the detergent industry and integrated modules on marketing, production, finance, and research. Modified and updated for newer computers, but still in use at many graduate schools of business today, this game has certainly set the record for the longest life of any computer game ever written.

With the delivery in 1959 of the first Digital Equipment Corporation (DEC) PDP-1 with its 15-inch video

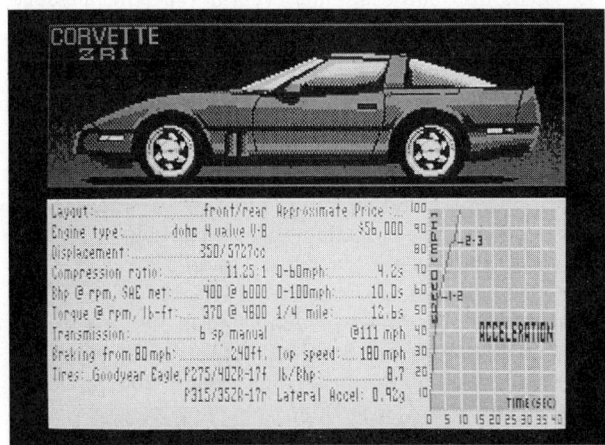

FIG. 1. In Accolade's "Test Drive" game, players can choose to drive various cars on a variety of demanding tracks and courses.

FIG. 2. In "Yeager," a typical flight simulator, players must learn to land on a carrier deck, tough even for seasoned pilots.

display, the continuing evolution from text-only games to video games was hastened. Written by Slug Russel, Shag Gratz, and Alan Kotok, the first game for the PDP-1 was "Spacewar," first demonstrated at an MIT open house in 1962.

Later in 1962, Omar K. Moore at Yale built a device called "The Talking Typewriter" for teaching reading to young children. In the device, built by Edison Electric, a computer controlled a video display, slide projector, and audio recorder. In 1964, a more general-purpose computer-assisted instruction (CAI) system using IBM hardware, including a CRT with graphics, light pen, and audio, was developed by Patrick Suppes at Stanford. Military research kept pace, and in 1964 Bunker-Ramo demonstrated a CRT display that simultaneously combined computer data with a projected background.

Artists began to realize the potential of the computer in 1964 when A. Michael Noll at Bell Labs produced the first computer art (*q.v.*) on a CRT display. Many years later, spurred by such companies as Activision, Lucasfilm Games, and Cinemaware, artists began to play a much larger role in the creation of games through computer animation (*q.v.*).

Rounding out the landmark year of 1964, the language Basic was developed by John Kemeny and Tom Kurtz on the GE 225 timesharing system at Dartmouth College. Within a few months, the first interactive educational games and simulations began to appear on the Dartmouth system.

Various types of graphics displays from many manufacturers were introduced in the mid-1960s, opening the door to new video effects. Thus, we find a video pool game developed at RCA (1967), a ball-and-paddle game by Ralph Baer at Sanders Associates (1967, later to become the Magnavox Odyssey home video game in 1972), a rocket car simulation by Judah Schwartz at MIT (1968), a graphic flight simulation by Evans and Sutherland (1969), a lunar lander game at DEC (1969), and a device to permit computer output and standard television video on the same display at Stanford (1968).

In the October 1970 issue of *Scientific American*, Martin Gardner devoted his "Mathematical Games" column to

a description of John Conway's "Game of Life." Easily programmed, it began to appear on virtually every video computer terminal in the country within weeks.

In the late 1960s, the National Science Foundation was attempting to encourage the use of computers in secondary schools to improve science education. One of the notable NSF-funded projects that produced scores of simulation games in science and social studies was the Huntington Computer Project directed by Ludwig Braun at Brooklyn Polytechnic Institute (later at SUNY, Stony Brook). In the Project's "Malaria" simulation game, for example, students must try to control an outbreak of malaria in a Central American country using a combination of various pesticides, innoculations, and treatment of the ill—all without bankrupting the country.

Also in the late 1960s, both DEC and Hewlett-Packard started major marketing efforts to sell computers to secondary and elementary schools. As a result, both companies sponsored a number of small-scale projects to write computer games and simulations in various fields, many of which were released in the early 1970s. In DEC's "King" game, for example, players decide how much land to buy, sell, and cultivate each year, how much to feed the people, etc., while dealing with problems of industrial development, pollution, and tourism.

Meanwhile, on the recreational front, in 1971, Nolan Bushnell rewrote "Spacewar" as a coin-operated arcade game called "Computer Space," which was marketed by Nutting Associates. Too complicated for the average player, only 1500 units were sold and the game was not successful. A year later, Bushnell's next project, the Pong arcade game, was considerably more successful and was the foundation of the Atari Corporation.

Also in 1972, Willy Crother and Don Woods wrote a game for the DEC PDP-10 that they simply called "Adventure." The game, the first in the interactive role-playing fantasy genre, was unbelievably addictive and players consumed vast amounts of time-shared computer time on whatever system it was loaded.

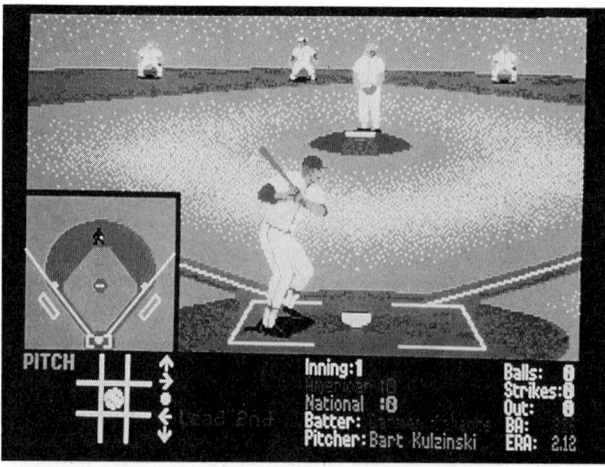

FIG. 3. "Hardball," a realistic sports simulation provides realistic player animation, instant replays, complete player and team statistics, and five field perspectives.

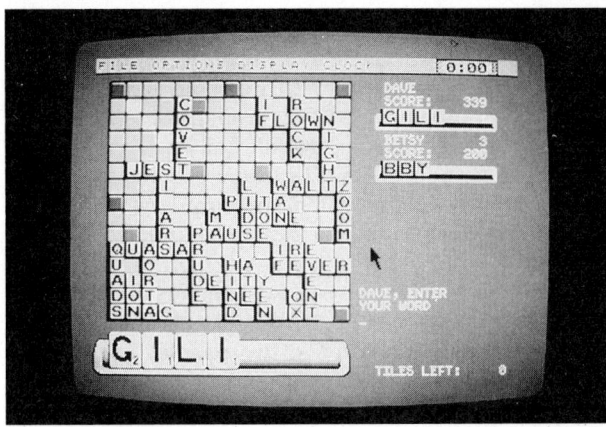

FIG. 4. Computer versions of virtually every card and board game, such as this version of Scrabble, are available for one or more players.

1972 also saw the first issue of Bob Albrecht's *People's Computer Company* newsletter, which, along with material for teachers and students, included many small Basic games in each issue. A year later, DEC published the book *101 Basic Computer Games* by David Ahl, which, in 1978, became the first computer book of any kind to sell a million copies.

Ahl left DEC in 1974 and started *Creative Computing*, the first personal computing magazine and the first magazine to publish three or four major games every issue. Also in 1974, Ted Nelson published the book *Computer Lib/Dream Machines*, while, at the MITS company in Albuquerque, NM, Ed Roberts was putting the final touches on the first mass produced personal computer kit—the Altair 8800.

With the widespread availability of affordable video game systems and personal computers, it looked as though there was no limit to the computer and video games market. Atari introduced the home version of Pong in 1975 and it was followed a year later by literally hundreds of imitators. Removable cartridge home games were first introduced by Fairchild in 1976, followed by Bally, Atari, and others a year later. By 1982, over 100 companies had entered the market with game systems or cartridges.

Also by 1982, the $6 billion in quarters put into arcade games exceeded the gross take of all professional sports combined, bouyed by such games as "Space Invaders" (1978), "Pac-Man" (1980), "Defender" (1981), and scores of other mega-hits.

The kit era of personal computers lasted only two years and by 1977 manufacturers of self-contained, assembled computers like Commodore, Apple, and Radio Shack took the market by storm. This opened the computer game floodgates as the cost of entry was so low. All one needed was a personal computer, some programming smarts, and a few hundred bucks to buy some magazine ads. In more than one case, bright teenage programmers started game companies and hired their parents as employees.

All was not well in gameland, however, and in 1983 the bubble burst. Many factors are responsible for the crash: too many me-too games, scores of companies with no management or financial expertise, jaded game players, public backlash against arcades, and just too much expansion too fast.

After a disastrous two-year downward spiral, it looked to many like computer games were in the grave. In April 1985, the Frost & Sullivan market research firm rated computer and video games as having the least potential of 24 high-technology markets. The video and home computer games market was judged to have been a passing fad, and manufacturers seeking profitable opportunities were advised to turn their attention elsewhere.

Apparently, Nintendo didn't read (or heed) the report since they chose 1985 to introduce their home game system. Also, Accolade, Electronic Arts, Strategic Simulations, and other computer game companies started to release more games in the IBM PC format, even though the PC was then considered to be primarily a "business" machine. These turned out to be wise decisions.

According to market surveys, Nintendo games were the most wanted Christmas presents three years in a row (1987–89). Two new game formats were introduced in 1990: 16-bit systems by Sega and computer/compact disc games by NEC. The home video game market—far from being a fad—was healthy and growing again.

The steep and continuing decline in the prices of PC clones put them within reach of most home users, thereby simplifying the life of game designers and manufacturers. No longer did manufacturers have to make a different game version for Apple, Atari, Commodore, and Tandy computers when a PC version would reach 90% of the users. Bouyed by a choice of new and innovative games, the market steadily rebounded from its 1985 trough.

Today, real-time flight simulation games almost exactly duplicate the situation faced by actual pilots. Tomorrow, the word "almost" will be eliminated.

New games are certain to emerge that will use the latest technology—videodiscs (*q.v.*), multi-channel sound, voice synthesis, speech recognition (*q.v.*), and much more. Where to from there is anybody's guess.

DAVID H. AHL

ARCADE GAMES

Coin-operated machines were first introduced for vending holy water in ancient Alexandria almost two thousand years ago. The origin of the coin-operated amusement industry can be traced back to an old game called Bagatelle in which marbles were propelled to the top of a sloping board. Pins in the board (from whence comes the name "pinball") deflected the marble, until it fell into one of several semicircular pockets made either of pins or strips of metal. The further the ball traveled down the board, the higher the value associated with the pocket.

Pinball as an arcade game first took advantage of electricity in about 1929, chiefly to light the game. By 1932, Harry Williams had included a "tilt" mechanism, which would cancel play if the operator applied too much force to the cabinet. The year 1932 also saw introduction of the "kickout" hole. A solenoid in the hole would cause the ball to be propelled back into play after scoring. The introduction of the flipper in 1942 added player skill to a game that formerly had been influenced only by chance once the ball was released. Pinball machines improved along with technology—printed circuits were introduced into a game called "Perky" in 1956, eliminating most of the wiring that filled the older game cabinets. Pinball machines and jukeboxes remained the basis of the coin-operated amusement business for almost 80 years, until the introduction of video games.

The first coin-operated game to be played on a monochromatic video screen was called "Computer Space." Developed in 1971, this game was a simple shoot-up in which the operator controlled the direction of a spacecraft. The object of the game was to destroy dots on the screen by firing at them. "Computer Space" was developed by Nolan Bushnell from a popular mainframe game called Spacewar. (Computer games have always fascinated programmers—there were games written for mainframes in the 1950s, even though computers of the time cost up to $1,000 per hour and supported only one program at a time.) "Computer Space" was not a commercial success, possibly because its controls were complicated. Bushnell used the small profit from the game to found Atari Corporation and, in 1972, produced a game known as "Pong." A similar game, "Paddle Ball," was produced in the same year by Williams Electronics. "Pong" was a two-player game in which a ball moved around a rectangular space. Each player rotated a knob to control a rectangular "paddle," the object being to keep the ball from moving off the player's side of the screen. Refinements to the original were made in one-man hockey and tennis simulations in which each player controlled two paddles and the ball was delivered at various speeds.

Non-electronic color was introduced to video games in 1973 when Atari introduced "Breakout," another game using a paddle in which a ball was bounced off an array of bricks, destroying those it touched. Since the bricks did not move in the original version of this game, they could be colored by attaching strips of cellophane to the screen.

In 1976, a very controversial arcade game called "Death Race" was developed by Exidy Corporation from a science-fiction story that was made into the motion picture "Death Race 2000." The story was based on a cross-country automobile race in which the participants scored bonus points for hitting pedestrians. Much of its popularity came from the controversy caused by its theme.

"Seawolf" (Bally/Midway) was introduced in 1977. The theme was submarine warfare, with the player viewing and firing torpedoes at targets through a realistic periscope.

The first game to take advantage of vector graphics was "Space Wars," introduced by Cinematronics in 1978. A more popular vector game was "Asteroids" by Atari (1979), in which the player controlled a spacecraft among a host of asteroids that were moving across the screen. The craft could turn and accelerate to escape asteroids and destroy them by shooting. Big asteroids, however, turned into many small ones when hit. "Asteroids" included good sound effects and good physics—the principle of conservation of momentum was not only evident in the performance of the spacecraft, but also in the breakup of asteroids. When an asteroid was hit, the smaller objects resulting from the impact moved faster than the original.

One of the most popular video games of its time was "Space Invaders," designed by Taito in 1978. Hordes of little aliens marched down the screen, shooting at a hapless defender who could shoot back or hide behind barricades but who always lost. The game was predictable, however, so experienced players could destroy large numbers of invaders before meeting an inevitable end.

"Atari Football" was also introduced in 1978. This two-user game was played using X's and O's to represent players, but allowed users to control one football player each by means of a trackball, an innovation in arcade games. This game was the first one to use a team sport as the basis for play. Virtually every sport has now been simulated—football, baseball, golf, soccer, track, martial arts, automobile and motorcycle racing, and even skateboarding (720 degrees, Atari, 1986), to mention a few. Sega

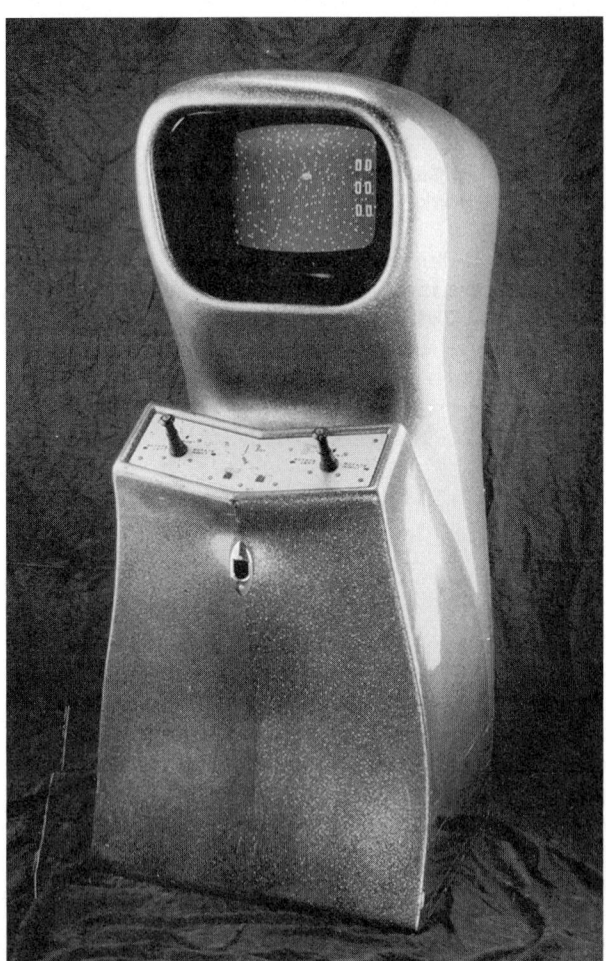

FIG. 1. "Computer Space" was the first video arcade game. (Courtesy American Museum of the Moving Image)

FIG. 2. Atari "Asteroids," which made effective use of computer graphics. (Courtesy *Play Meter* Magazine)

Enterprises, Inc., has specialized in simulations, including Hang-On (1985), in which the player sat on a motorcycle. The screen display was controlled by the operator's use of the handlebars, and the motorcycle banked appropriately from side to side. "Afterburner" (1987) added the pitch dimension to the motion of the operator's chair, and "Galaxy Force" version 2 (1988) included pitch, roll, and yaw.

"Galaxian" (Bally/Midway, 1979) was based on the same theme as "Space Invaders," but took advantage of color graphics and more versatile maneuvering by the raiders.

In 1980, the phenomenally successful "Pac-Man" was introduced. The game display represented a maze through which the player could manipulate the famous Pac-Man face by using a joystick. Pac-Man had to eat all the cookies in the maze while avoiding little ghosts that tried to trap him. This game was displayed on a color monitor. Pac-Man was partly responsible for the huge growth in video game income from 1978, when the gross first reached $1 billion, to a peak of $7 billion in 1982. By comparison, the motion picture industry estimated that its best year to date, 1989, would see a gross income of $5 billion. After 1981, income from video games declined dramatically to about $4.2 billion in 1985. There was gen-

eral recognition in the industry that it would be necessary to improve the visual quality of video games as well as their themes.

Technological improvements were part of the resurgence of arcade game popularity in the 1980s. In 1980, Atari introduced "Battle Zone," in which the operator manipulated a tank, using realistic controls. The operator's view consisted of a three-dimensional scene composed of obstacles and enemy tanks. Tanks not in the operator's field of view were indicated as dots on a round "radar screen." All enemy tanks could fire at the operator, even those outside the viewing screen. Scenes were rendered in wire-frame 3-D. Very realistic sound included varying engine noise and explosions. A modification of the game was used by the army to train tank drivers.

"Defender," introduced in 1980 by Williams, took full advantage of the current technology. The game consisted of controlling a small plane that fought various enemies. Five different controllers were used for simultaneous control of picture, sound, and player interaction, and graphics and sounds were stored in ROM. Other technical features were introduced in 1980, including good speech synthesis ("Berzerk," Stern.)

"Donkey Kong" (Nintendo, 1981) introduced improvements in automation and a game with a mission other than "senseless slaughter." A little man named Mario could be controlled by a joystick for horizontal motion and a button to cause him to jump over objects in his path. The player had to guide Mario to rescue a lady in distress from a gorilla. This explains the word "Kong" in the game's title, but there is no apparent reason for "Donkey." One theory has it that the word was meant to be "Monkey," but the game was made in Japan and the error was not detected until many units had already been sent to the U. S. In any event, this game was the beginning of a series of adventure-style games just as "Pac-Man" began a series of maze games such as "Ms. Pac-Man" (Bally/Midway, 1982) and "Dig Dug" (Atari, 1982.)

Another 1982 spinoff of "Pac-Man's" success was "Baby Pac-Man" (Bally/Midway) that was part video game and part pinball machine. When a player escaped out of an exit door in the video game, the pinball game was activated. After playing a ball, it was possible to return to the video game and continue.

Other new features were introduced in the same year. In "Robotron 2084" (Williams), two joysticks were used—one for moving and another for aiming a weapon—making it possible to fire without first facing various attacking outer space creatures. "SUBROC 3-D" (Sega) created stereoscopic 3-D effects by displaying stereo pairs of images using polarized light. Fortunately, the format of the game was a submarine fight, so the periscope viewing device could hold the necessary polarizing filters without distracting the player. "Zaxxon" (Sega/Gremlin) was the first raster image game that generated realistic 3-D effects. It was another space war simulation, but alien craft changed size as they approached or receded, and the moving spacecraft cast a shadow on the ground.

In 1983, "Star Wars" (Atari) copied the attack sequence from the motion picture of the same name in which the hero flew at high speed down a narrow corridor while under attack by laser cannons. The video game was a remarkably faithful rendition of the movie scene, requiring almost impossibly fast reflexes on the part of the player.

Another major innovation was introduced in the "Nintendo Vs" system in 1984. Two players may participate in the games ("Vs Tennis," "Vs Golf," or "Vs Baseball") while looking at separate screens not visible to the opponent.

"Karate Champ" (Data East, 1985) was the first martial arts game. In the one-player version, the machine was the opponent; however, two players could compete against each other. Arm and leg motions were controlled by the player and the motion of the game figures looked very realistic.

"Out Run" (Sega, 1986) was a high-speed automobile driving game that featured not only good graphics and sound, but also a realistic ride. The player sat in front of a steering wheel, accelerator pedal, and brake. As the wheel was turned, the "car" would react by tilting to one side. If the driver left the road, the car would move up and down as if on a rough shoulder.

"Gauntlet" (Atari, 1986) represents a departure in games that will probably be followed in the 1990s. It is a "dungeons and dragons" theme that allows up to four players to choose roles and play simultaneously. The salient feature of this game is the capability to play on after being "killed." For another quarter (of course), the player is resurrected and can continue.

The style of display used in arcade games fits naturally into coin-operated gambling games. Poker and blackjack machines, as well as the electronic equivalent of the slot machine, are supplementing the traditional "one-armed bandit" mechanical games, but have not yet replaced them.

Realism is increasing in modern games. "Narc" (Williams, 1988) was developed by using live actors and digitizing from film to produce realistic images that seem to be three-dimensional. Nintendo's "Hogan's Alley" (1988) has been used by at least one Dallas police station for target practice.

Although future arcade games will continue to use the latest technology for graphics and sound effects as well as improving the "feel" of a simulation, the games will probably continue on existing themes. Home computer and hand-held games are eroding the popularity of arcade games, while the cost of playing in an arcade is likely to increase. The game manufacturers, for instance, have lobbied Congress heavily for a popular $1 coin. (Arcade games have been played for 25 cents for years, while the cost of manufacturing games has increased, on average, 2,700%.) Nevertheless, so much creativity is poured into the development of these games that it is hard to imagine their demise. It is more likely that continuing innovation will maintain the popularity of video arcade games.

KEITH S. REID-GREEN

TRADITIONAL GAMES

When the earliest digital computers were built, scientists immediately became fascinated with the possibility of having them play such games as chess, checkers, and tic-tac-toe. Although this sort of activity proved to be a great deal of fun, the scientists were not just playing around; there are several good reasons to study game playing by computers.

The first reason relates to the popular conception of computers as "giant brains." Even the earliest digital computers could do arithmetic and make decisions at a rate thousands of times faster than humans could. Thus, it was felt that computers could be set up to perform intelligent activities, such as to translate French to English, recognize sloppy handwriting, and play chess. At the same time, it was realized that, if computers could not perform these tasks, they could not be considered intelligent by human standards. A new scientific discipline arose from these considerations and became known as *artificial intelligence. (q.v.).*

A second reason involves the understanding by humans of their own intelligence. It is conjectured that computer mechanisms for game playing will bear a resemblance to human thought processes. If this is true, game-playing computers can help us understand how human minds work.

Another reason for studying games is that they are well-defined activities. Most games use very simple equipment and have a simple set of rules that must be followed. Usually, the ultimate goal (winning) can be very simply defined. Thus, a computer can be easily programmed to follow the rules of any board or card game. This allows the computer scientist to devote more effort to the problem of getting the computer to play an intelligent game.

There is also a practical payoff from computer game-playing studies. Specific techniques developed in programming a computer to play games have been applied to other more practical problems. To cite a few, methods of searching (*q.v.*) are used to consider alternative moves in chess have been adapted to find the correct path through a switching network or the correct sequence of steps for an assembly line. Learning methods developed for a checker-playing program have been used to recognize elementary parts of spoken speech. It is felt that the mechanisms of intelligence are general purpose, and therefore the borrowing of techniques from one application to another will continue in the field of artificial intelligence.

Basic Techniques   The fundamental reason for the ability of computers to play a variety of games is that computers have the ability to represent arbitrary situations and processes through the use of symbols and logic operations. For example, one can set up a chess position inside a computer by means of an 8×8 array of integers, and tentative moves can be made by computer instructions that change the positions of the numbers in the array (Fig. 1). This capability is extremely general. That is, the symbols could represent checker pieces, or with a

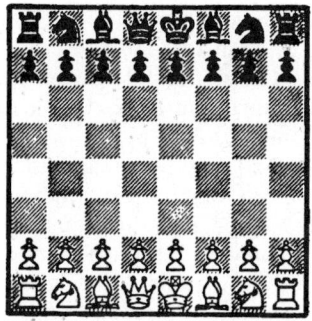 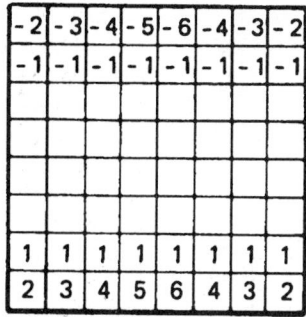 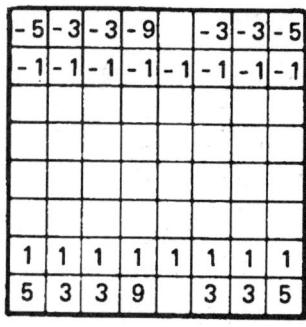

FIG. 1. Computer representation of a chess position. In the second array, numbers are used to represent the various pieces. The third array represents the values of the pieces for use by the computer in evaluating trades.

slight rearrangement, they could be playing cards for poker or bridge.

Fig. 1 also shows the representation of derived information. The values of the pieces are stored in another 8×8 array for use by the computer. In effect, they are part of the computer's "knowledge" of the values of chess pieces. (The king may be considered to have an infinitely large value.)

Since symbols can be used to represent the objects of a particular game, computer instructions can be written by a programmer to specify the procedures for playing the game according to the rules and also for playing the game according to a strategy. In order for a set of procedures to be programmable, it is usually sufficient that they be defined in enough detail so that they can be translated into a computer language. For the purposes of this exposition, several game playing algorithms will be stated using English words in place of computer language. The game of tic-tac-toe, for example, can be played perfectly by the following algorithm, in which the word "row" refers to a row, column, or diagonal.

ALGORITHM A (THE COMPUTER PLAYS X)

A1. Perform the first applicable step that follows.

A2. Search for two X's in a row. If found, then make three X's in a row.

A3. Search for two O's in a row. If found, then block them with an X.

A4. Search for two rows that intersect with an empty square, each of which contains one X and no O's. If found, then place an X on the intersection.

A5. Search for two rows that intersect at an empty square, each of which contains one O and no X's. If found, then place an X on the intersection.

A6. Search for a vacant corner square. If found, then place an X on the vacancy.

A7. Search for a vacant square. If found, then place an X on the vacancy.

The algorithm is perfect in the sense that it will find a forced win if it exists and it will never lose. This

algorithm may be called a *rejection scheme* because the first applicable step (following A1) is to be performed and all other steps are rejected (Fig. 2). A computer can be easily programmed to execute such an algorithm.

For another example, consider the following game, a special case of Nim. It is played with 13 matches; two players remove matches in turn until one player is forced to take the last match. A player may remove only one to three matches in a single turn, and the player who removes the last match is the loser. This is an algorithm for perfect play.

ALGORITHM B (THE COMPUTER PLAYS SECOND)

B1. Let n be the number of matches taken by the opponent at the last turn.

B2. Remove $(4 - n)$ matches.

B3. If the game is not over, go to Step B1.

Both tic-tac-toe and Nim are simple examples of a large number of games classed as two-person games of skill. An essential feature of these games is that both players have perfect information about the current state of the game. Chess, checkers, and GO are well-known

X	O	X
	O	2
O	1	X

FIG. 2. In the position shown here, algorithm A would choose a move at square 2 for a win rather than at square 1, to block the opponent win. This is done because step A2 precedes step A3.

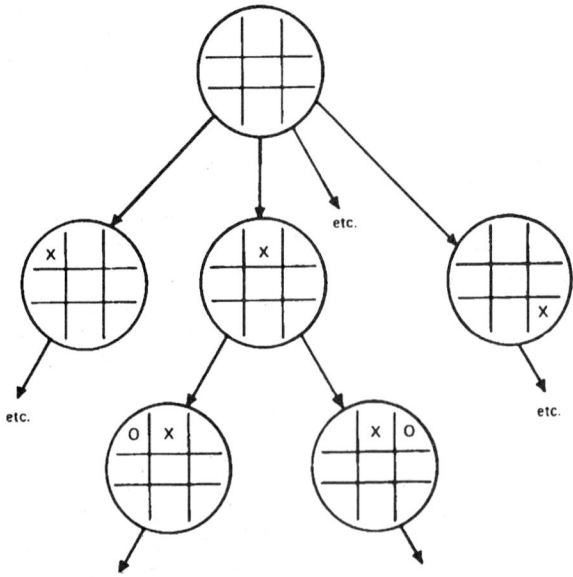

FIG. 3.   Part of the lookahead tree for tic-tac-toe. Circles represent game positions and arrows represent moves by X or O.

games of pure skill. It can be shown mathematically that there is, in principle, an optimal strategy for each player and that its application always gives the same result. In the case of tic-tac-toe, the result is a draw. In the case of the match game, the second player always wins. The possibility of playing a perfect game of chess, checkers, or GO will now be examined.

In order to show that an optimal strategy exists for two-person games of skill, the principle of *minimax* must be explained. If the state of a game is represented by a circle and the moves from that state are represented by lines (Fig. 3), then a tree (*q.v.*) can be obtained that represents the set of all possible games. The leaves of this tree (Fig. 4) can all be labeled with the terms *win, loss,* or *draw* for the first player. Now consider any node that is followed only by labeled nodes. If that node corresponds to the first player's move and it is connected to a node labeled, *win,* then it may be labeled with the term *win.* It may be labeled with a *draw,* if it is connected to a draw, otherwise, it is labeled with a *loss.* If it is the second player's move from a position, then a loss is most preferred. This procedure can be repeated to back up the values W, L, and D to the top of the lookahead tree. Optimal strategy consists of following the path taken by the letter W, L, or D, which is backed up to the top. In other words, a player makes the best move, based on the assumption that the opponent will make the best reply, and the opponent's reply assumes that the player will make the best counter-reply, etc. (The best outcome is guaranteed, of course, even if the opponent makes less than optimum moves.)

Thus, since all possible chess games can be expressed in a tree like that in Fig. 3, it is known that there is a perfect strategy for chess, that guarantees a win or a draw for one player. Of course, the strategy has never been found. It is the combinatorics of game playing that prevent the discovery of perfect strategies. In chess, when it is a player's turn to move, that player has, on the average, 30 legal moves resulting in 30 different positions. If the opponent also has 30 replies to each of those moves, then 900 positions result. This sort of calculation gives an estimate of 10^{125} as the size of the lookahead tree for chess (the number of paths from the top of the tree to the terminal positions). If a computer could examine a billion positions per second, it would still take 10^{108} years to examine the entire

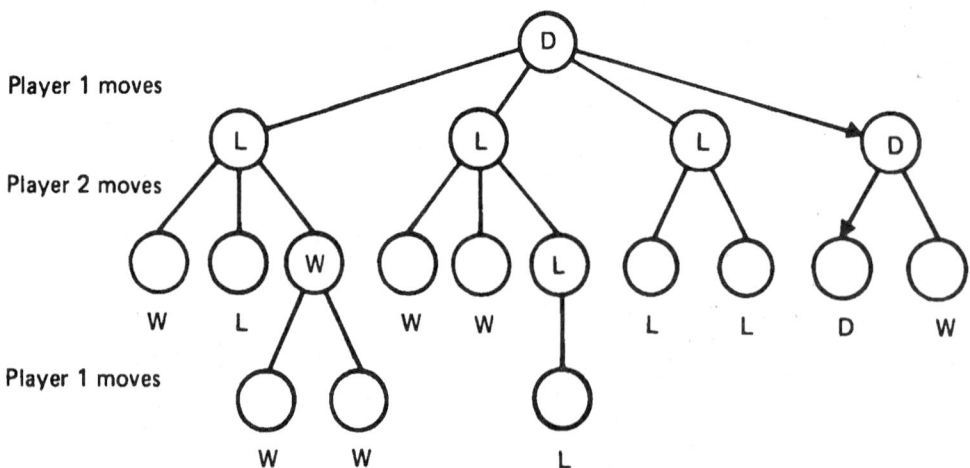

FIG. 4.   Illustration of the minimax procedure. The values at the bottom are calculated by an evaluation function. The backed-up values in circles reflect the result of optimal play. The arrows show the path of optimal play.

lookahead tree to determine the optimal strategy. It should be mentioned that the number of board positions is far smaller, approximately 10^{42}, so it is theoretically possible to store all positions together with their optimal moves in a large table. Storing one board position on an element the size of an atom would necessitate a memory of about the size of the earth. This gives a rather extreme example of the storage versus computational tradeoff that is so common to computer science.

A second class of games involves no skill at all, and a player's success depends only on chance. Examples are craps and roulette, in which the roll of dice or drop of a ball determines whether a bet is won or lost. A third and most important class of games involves a mixture of skill and chance of varying degrees. This includes games such as poker, bridge, backgammon, and Monopoly, which are affected by the distribution of cards or the roll of dice, although these randomizing features are generally overcome in the long run by the skill of a player. Computers can be set up to play these games of chance, but it is usually more difficult to represent the tree for a game when probabilistic factors are present.

Games are also categorized according to whether players have incomplete or complete knowledge of the current state. Games of pure skill, such as chess and checkers, and some games involving chance, such as backgammon and parcheesi, have no elements that are hidden from the players. But in many games, such as poker, bridge, and salvo (battleship), each player can have information that is hidden from the other players. The presence of unknown factors poses additional problems for computerization. Methods developed here may be very useful, however, since real-world problems often involve unknown and probabilistic factors.

Game-Playing Programs An early and very successful game-playing program is Arthur Samuel's (1967) checker player. Though checkers is a fairly difficult game (the game tree for checkers has an estimated 10^{40} paths), the checker program plays at a sound master level, having played a world champion to a draw. What is more amazing is that much of the program's skill is due to automatic learning procedures. In one experiment, the program was played against a copy of itself in which the copy was not allowed to "learn." As a result, the program improved itself enough to win consistently over the non-learning copy. Although the program uses a predetermined set of evaluation criteria, it learns the best means of combining these criteria to arrive at an overall evaluation of a board position. Eric Jensen and Tom Truscott of Duke University created a program that defeated the Samuel program and exhibited strong play against highly rated players.

Go-Moku has become an extremely popular subject for computerization. It is essentially a game of the tic-tac-toe type, with each player trying to achieve five in a row on a 19×19 board. Since 1975, a North American computer Go-Moku tournament has been held, and, since 1977, there has also been a European tournament.

GO, an extremely difficult game played principally in the Orient, has been the subject of an international computer tournament since 1985. The main interest here is the difficult problem of representing the derived information that humans use to play the game. GO is played by placing white and black stones on a 19×19 grid. The most important feature of play is the emergence of groups or armies of similarly colored stones. GO may well prove to be the most difficult of the pure skill games to computerize.

Bridge is an especially interesting case, since there are two distinct phases of play—bidding and trick taking. Wasserman has produced a bridge bidder that achieves an expert level of skill. An unusual feature of his program is that it knows all standard bidding conventions and therefore can be adjusted to be an ideal partner for any player. Wasserman's approach was to use a base language, Algol, to implement primitive elements of bridge bidding; for example, a routine FIVECARDMAJOR[NORTH] that returns TRUE or FALSE, depending on the north hand cards. Higher-level routines are built in layers over the primitives; for example:

IF FIVECARDMAJOR[H] AND POINTCOUNT[H]
 > 12 THEN BIDMAJOR[H]

where H is a variable that can take on the values NORTH, SOUTH, EAST, or WEST.

A research project by Findler at the State University of New York at Buffalo used poker as a model for decision-making in the real world. Instead of creating a single game-playing program, Findler created a system that allows several programs to play each other or to play against human subjects through the use of interactive graphics displays. An interesting match might pit a program that occasionally bluffs against a program that never bluffs against several human players. A large number of distinct programs have been created, some of which use learning. Each program is a specific model of human play at poker, and its success is a measure of the quality of the model.

The unusual mideastern game Kalah, played using stones and dishes, has been studied extensively. The game commences (Fig. 5) with an equal number of stones (usually three to six) in each of the side dishes (commonly six in number). The players take turns; in one turn a player takes all stones from one side dish and distributes them, one to a dish, in a counterclockwise fashion, but skipping the opponent's home dish (or Kalah). If the last stone falls in the player's home dish, then a second turn is taken. If the last stone in the first turn falls in an empty dish on the player's side, the stones in the opponent's dish on the opposite side are "captured" and placed in the player's Kalah. The game ends when all dishes on one side are empty, at which point all stones remaining on the other side are placed in that player's Kalah. A Kalah-playing program by Slagle achieved excellent results against human opponents.

Of all games programmed for computers, more time

Side dishes player A

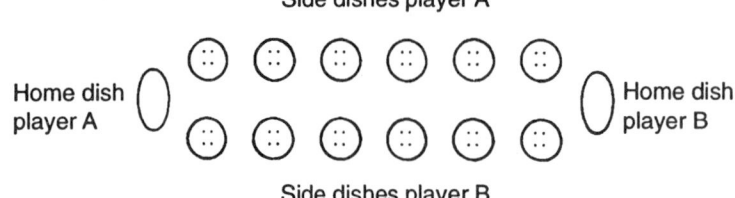

Home dish player A

Home dish player B

Side dishes player B

FIG. 5.   Start of a Kalah game with four stones in each of the side dishes.

and effort has been devoted to chess than to any other (see COMPUTER CHESS). A recent trend is the emergence of microcomputer-based games on the mass market. Quality of play varies, with backgammon, checker and chess programs playing quite well and bridge programs playing at a lower level. Rapid improvements in the quality and variety of these games may be expected.

References

1950. Shannon, C. E. "Automatic Chess Player," *Scientific American* **182**, *2*: 48-51.

1967. Epstein, R. A. *The Theory of Gambling and Statistical Logic.* New York: Academic Press, Chap. 10.

1978. Findler, N. V. "Computer Poker," *Scientific American* **239**, *1*: 144-151.

1975. Knuth, D. E., and Moore, R. W. "An Analysis of Alpha-Beta Pruning." *Artificial Intelligence* **6**: 293–326.

1987. Rivest, R. "Game Tree Searching by Min/Max Approximation," *Artificial Intelligence* **34**, *1*: 77–96.

1990. Hsu, F., Anantharanum, T., Campbell, M. and Nowatzyk, A. "A Grandmaster Chess Machine," *Scientific American* **263**, *4*: 44–50.

ALBERT L. ZOBRIST

COMPUTER GENERATIONS. *See* GENERATIONS, COMPUTER.

COMPUTER GRAPHICS

PRINCIPLES

For articles on related subjects *see* COMPUTER-AIDED DESIGN/COMPUTER-AIDED MANUFACTURING; COMPUTER ANIMATION; COMPUTER ART; COMPUTER GAMES; COMPUTER VISION; ENTERTAINMENT INDUSTRY, COMPUTERS IN THE; FRACTALS; IMAGE PROCESSING; INTERACTIVE INPUT DEVICES; MEDICAL IMAGING; PATTERN RECOGNITION; USER INTERFACE; and WORKSTATION.

Computer graphics may be defined as the input, construction, storage, retrieval, manipulation, alteration, and analysis of objects and their pictorial representation. Computer graphics in general includes both off-line input of drawings or photographs of objects via scanners, digitizers, or pattern recognition devices, and output of drawings on paper on (micro) film via plotters and film recorders. *Interactive graphics* is a term used to emphasize user-computer dialogue that takes place in real time using an online display console with interactive input devices.

The field of computer graphics (or simply "graphics") is evolving rapidly, as the speed of computers increases and the cost of the technology decreases. In the past, graphics was primarily used to convert data sets in scientific and business environments to pictures that captured detail and trends. As output devices increased in capability, graphics began to strive for realism in produced images. A current trend in graphics is the depiction of data sets that pertain to complex and chaotic natural phenomena.

The key notion of computer graphics is the process of producing pictures or images of an environment described within the computer. This environment could be based on user input or mathematical formulas. This process is the reverse of what is done in the field of *image processing*, which converts an image into a description of the elements it contains.

The balance of this article will give an overview of the major trends and issues in computer graphics. A more detailed discussion of the field can be found in graphics textbooks (e. g. Foley *et al.* (1990)), journals (*ACM Transactions on Graphics*, and *IEEE Computer Graphics & Applications*), and major conference proceedings (ACM SIGGRAPH, and Eurographics).

In discussing computer graphics, there are two different views, each with its own concerns. A graphics system user is interested in what images are produced, what they mean, and how they can be manipulated. A graphics system *programmer* is interested in how to write graphics-based applications programs for those users. The programmer can be interested in clarity of data presentation, manipulation of imagery, or realism of that imagery. Each of these requires a different programming technique, level of sophistication, and type of hardware.

Some Representative Uses of Computer Graphics

Computer graphics is used in many different areas of industry, business, government, education, entertainment, and, most recently, in the home. The list of applications is large and growing rapidly, as display devices become routinely affordable.

Visualization Computer-produced animated movies of the time-varying behavior of real or simulated objects are becoming increasingly popular. We can study mathematical models for such scientific phenomena as hydraulic flow, relativity, nuclear and chemical reactions, physiological systems and organs, and deformation of structures under load by seeing the effects of the transformations pictorially.

The increase in speed, reduction of memory cost, and improved monitor resolution have all contributed to an expansion in the application of computer graphics to scientific simulation and modeling of natural phenomena. Scientific experimentation with natural systems produces large amounts of data. Capturing this data with a computer and using visualization techniques to display it gives the scientist a better understanding of the forces at work. This can lead to a hypothesis tested by computer program, which will also produce large data sets that can be analyzed with use of visualization techniques. The goal is to use color theory and artistic principles to present animated images of multiple variable data. For example, an animated sequence of warm and cold water mixing can represent temperature by color, direction of water movement with an arrow, and water velocity by the arrow size, for various data collection locations.

Cartography Computer graphics is used for the production of highly accurate representations on paper or film of geographical and other natural phenomena. Examples include geographic maps, relief maps, exploration maps for drilling and mining, oceanographic charts, weather maps, contour maps, oil exploration maps, and population density maps.

Computer-Aided Design and Manufacturing In the design phase of computer-aided design and manufacturing (CAD/CAM), interactive graphics are used to design components and systems of mechanical, electrical, electromechanical, and electronic devices. These systems include structures such as buildings, chemical and power plants, automobile bodies, airplane and ship hulls (and their contents), optical systems, and telephone and computer networks. The emphasis is sometimes on merely producing precise drawings of components and (sub) assemblies, as in on-line drafting or architectural rendering. More frequently, however, the emphasis is on interacting with a computer-based model of the component or system being designed, in order to test, for example, its mechanical, electrical, or thermal properties. Often, the model is interpreted by a simulator that feeds back the behavior of the system to the display console operator for further interactive design and test cycles. After objects have been designed, utility programs can process the design database to make parts lists, do bill of materials processing, define numerical control tapes for cutting or drilling parts, etc.

Computer-aided manufacturing (CAM) techniques frequently make use of the database created with CAD for control of assembly line and parts fabrication machinery.

Animation The interactive production of two-and three-dimensional cartoons of very high visual quality is becoming ever more cost-effective through the use of modern computer graphics technology. Flight simulators are another sophisticated application of animation. Simulators generate views not only of the fixed world in which the vehicle is moving, but also of special effects such as clouds, fog, smog, nighttime lights, and other craft of various sizes and shapes, each on its own course.

The execution and operation of hardware or software computer systems can also be nicely simulated and displayed graphically to show how components interact and change values. Finally, arcade games and home video games simulate artificial two- or three-dimensional worlds in real time, testing hand-eye coordination and reaction time.

Process Control While a flight simulator or arcade game lets the user interact with a simulation of either a real or artificial world, many other applications enable the user to interact with some aspect of the real world itself. Status displays for refineries, power plants, and computer networks display data values from sensors attached to critical components in the system, allowing operators to respond to exceptional conditions. Flight controllers at an airport see computer-generated identification and status information along with the aircraft blips on their radar scopes and can thus control traffic more quickly and accurately than with the unannotated radar data alone. Spacecraft controllers monitor telemetry data and initiate corrective procedures as needed.

Office Automation and Electronic Publication The use of alphanumeric and graphic terminals that create and disseminate information in the office and even the home is increasing rapidly. Both traditionally printed documents (hard copy) and electronic documents (soft copy) can be produced that contain not just text but also tables, graphs, and other two-dimensional information.

Art Computer artists attempt to express artistic messages and attract the attention of the public through presentation of esthetically pleasing pictures. An artist uses a computer for tasks in the entire artistic process, from sketching or ideation, through the production of prototypes or drafts, and then the final work, which can be a traditional sculpture or painting, a computer print, or an interactive installation.

Very sophisticated mechanisms are available to the computer artist for modeling objects and for the representation of light and shadows. The range of output mechanisms available to the artist for the production of the art work allows a good deal of variation for the look of the final piece. Research into three-dimensional output will further expand the artist's options.

A Brief Historical Development of Graphics Technology Computer graphics started with graph

plotting. Crude plotting on hard-copy devices, such as teletypes and line printers, dates from the early days of computing. M.I.T.'s 1950 Whirlwind Computer (*q.v.*) had computer-driven CRT (cathode ray tube) displays for output (both for operators and for cameras to produce hard copy), while the Sage Air Defense System in the mid-1950s was the first to use "command and control" CRT display consoles in which operators identified targets by pointing at them with lightpens.

The beginnings of modern interactive graphics are found in Ivan Sutherland's "Sketchpad" drawing system. He introduced data structures for storing symbol hierarchies that are built up through replication of standard components, a technique akin to the use of plastic templates for drawing flowchart or circuit symbols. He also developed interactive techniques for using the keyboard and lightpen for making choices, pointing, and drawing, and he formulated many other fundamental ideas and techniques still in use today.

The enormous potential for partially automating drafting and other drawing-intensive activities in computer-aided design (CAD) and computer-aided manufacturing (CAM) was not lost on manufacturers in the computer, automobile, and aerospace industries, and by the mid-1960s a number of research projects and commercial products began to appear. Prominent among these were General Motors' ambitious project for multiple time-shared graphics consoles for many phases of car design, the Digigraphic design system developed by Itek for lens design (and later bought and marketed by CDC), and the IBM 2250 display system based on the General Motors prototype.

Despite this early promise, interactive graphics remained beyond the resources of all but the most technology-intensive organizations for many years. Among the reasons were:

1. The high cost of graphics hardware;
2. The significant computing resources required to support graphics applications;
3. The difficulty of writing large, interactive programs for a time-sharing environment; and
4. One-of-a-kind, nonportable software, locked into a particular manufacturer's display device.

Output Technology The display devices developed in the mid-1960s and still in use today are called *vector, stroke,* or *calligraphic* displays. They consist of a display processor, a display buffer memory, and a CRT with its associated electronics. The buffer stores the computer-produced display list or display program; this contains point and line plotting commands with coordinates as endpoint data and character plotting commands (Fig. 1). These commands are interpreted by a display processor that converts digital values to analog voltages that displace an electron beam writing on the phosphor coating of the CRT. Since the light output of the phosphor decays in hundreds of microseconds, the display processor must cycle through the list to refresh the phosphor at least 30 times per second to avoid flicker; hence

the buffer holding the display list is usually called a *refresh buffer.* Note that the jump instruction in Fig. 1 loops back to the top of the display list to provide the cyclic refresh.

Both the buffer memory required for typical line drawings (8–32 kilobytes) and a processor fast enough to refresh at 30 cycles per second were very expensive in the 1960s. Thus, Tektronix's development in the late 1960s of the direct-view storage tube (DVST), which obviated both the buffer and the refresh process, was the vital step that made interactive graphics affordable (Fig. 2). In a DVST, the image is stored (until erased) by writing it once with a relatively slow-moving electron beam on a storage mesh in which the phosphor is embedded. This small, self-sufficient terminal-sized device was ideal for an inexpensive, low-speed (300–1200 baud) telephone interface to a time-sharing system, and formed a most cost-effective alternative to the bulky, complex refresh systems attached via expensive, high-speed interfaces to input/output channels or peripheral controllers. DVSTs allowed interactive plotting for many simple applications at costs often an order of magnitude smaller than for refresh displays. Thus, they helped introduce many users and programmers not interested in complex CAD applications to interactive graphics.

The next major hardware advance was to relieve the central computer of the heavy demands of the refreshed display device by attaching it to a minicomputer. The minicomputer typically functions as a dedicated stand-alone computer for running applications programs as well as servicing the display and user interaction devices. Often, it can also run as an "intelligent satellite" to the

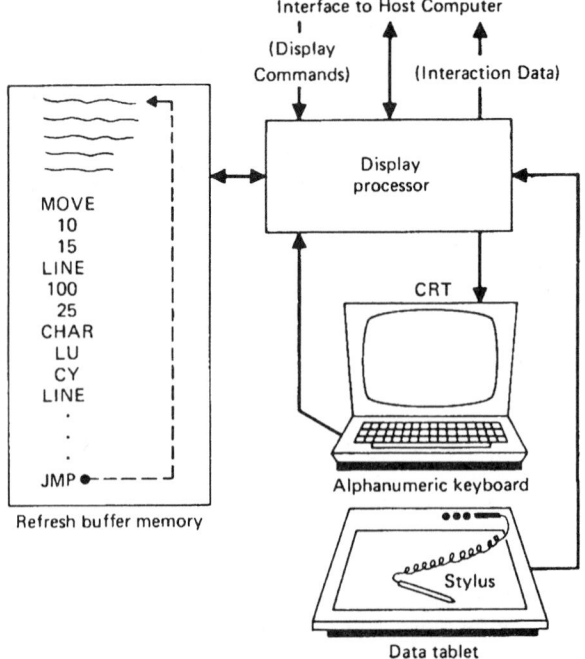

FIG. 1. Typical refresh display device.

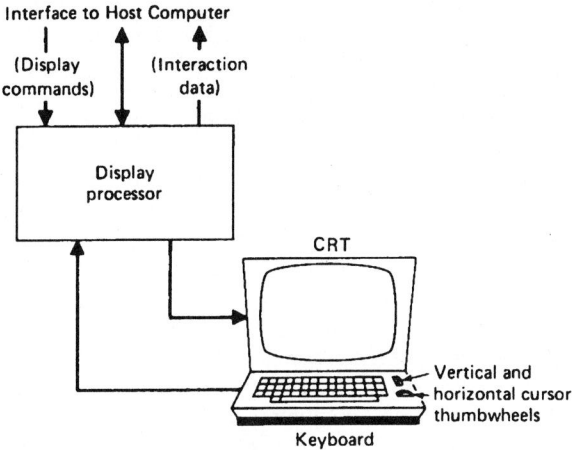

FIG. 2. Typical storage tube display.

main computer, handling user interaction but leaving large computation or large database jobs to the mainframe. At the same time, the hardware of the display processor itself was becoming more sophisticated, taking over many routine but time-consuming jobs of the graphics software.

The development of the mid-1970s which has contributed most to the development of the field is that of cheap *raster graphics*, based on television technology. In raster graphics, the display primitives, such as lines, characters, and solid areas (typically polygons), are stored in a refresh buffer in terms of their component points, called *pixels* (short for "picture elements"). The image is formed from the raster, a set of horizontal scan lines each made up of individual pixels. The raster is thus simply a matrix of pixels covering the entire screen area. 30 to 60 times per second, the entire image is scanned sequentially, one raster line at a time, top to bottom, by varying only the intensity of the electron beam for each pixel on a line (Fig. 3). The storage needed is thus greatly increased in that the entire image of, say, 512 lines of 512

pixels each, must be stored explicitly in a bit map containing only points that map one-for-one to points on the screen. On the other hand, the actual display of the simple image can then be handled by very inexpensive standard television components.

What made raster graphics possible was the development of inexpensive solid-state memory, which can provide refresh buffers considerably larger than those previously at a fraction of the price. Standard raster graphics systems are now reaching the resolution of vector systems, and will soon have hardware fast enough to provide motion dynamics for high-resolution displays. Since all pixels for the object must be transformed in the buffer, anywhere from a few hundred to more than a million pixels may have to be altered in a fraction of a second. Unlike vector graphics, raster graphics also makes possible the display of solid areas, an especially rich means for communicating information. Furthermore, the refresh process is independent of the complexity (number of lines, etc.) of the image, because each pixel in the buffer is read out on each refresh cycle, regardless of whether it represents information or background. Thus, there is no flicker. In contrast, refreshed vector displays begin to flicker when the number of primitives in the buffer grows so large that they cannot be read and processed in $\frac{1}{30}$ of a second.

Input Technology

User-Computer Interaction   When computers were slow and expensive (relative to personnel), computer interfaces were minimal. As computer costs drop and computer power and personnel costs increase, the move has been toward user interfaces that make the user's task easier to perform. Manufacturers are developing standards for their graphical user interfaces (GUI), so that all applications on their computer systems will appear and act in a uniform way.

User-computer interaction is a field of research separate from graphics in which the advantages and disad-

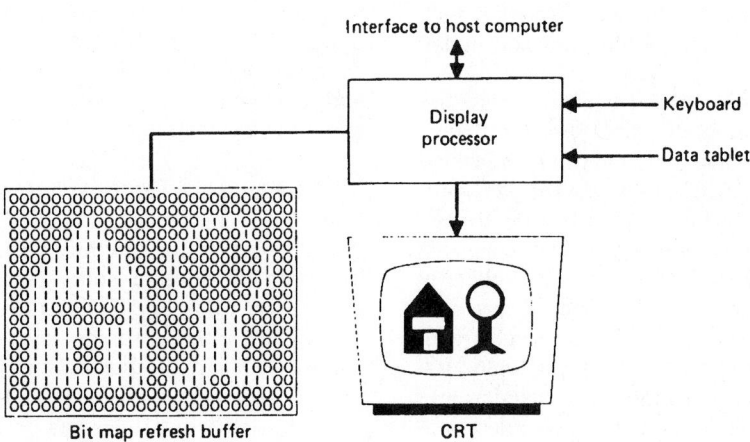

FIG. 3. Typical raster graphics display.

vantages of interaction styles for system usability, user training, and user efficiency are explored. (Brown and Cunningham, 1989)

Interactive vs. Non-interactive Graphics The choice between interactive and non-interactive computer graphics depends on the application. Interactive graphics are used for systems where the user plays a significant and active role in the system. A CAD/CAM system must be inherently interactive since the user must create the object and its components as they are viewed on the computer monitor. Visualization systems are also frequently interactive so that the user can replay animation sequences, magnify parts of the image that appear interesting (*zooming*), and alter colors used so that different phenomenon are highlighted. Applications that by their nature require frequent user input are programmed as interactive systems.

Non-interactive graphics systems are primarily those that are so computationally complex that the production of a single image takes longer than the time even the most patient user would wait. The production of realistic imagery using techniques of radiosity and ray tracing and the production of animated sequences is very time consuming. In these cases, the user will define the environment for the image (or for an animation sequence, the motions to occur) using some preprocessing system. This definition then serves as the input for the *image generator*, which can be run in batch or background mode. The resulting images are usually stored in a file, and viewed at a later time, using a device-dependent postprocessor. It is not unusual for complex animation sequences of a few minutes duration to take thousands of hours of compute time to prepare, though some simple animation sequences can be done in real time.

The Advantage of Interactive Graphics While static pictures are often an acceptable means of communicating information, dynamically varying pictures are frequently better. This is especially true when one needs to visualize time-varying phenomena, both real (e.g. shock waves caused by a sharp object penetrating a soft one) and abstract (e.g. growth trends, such as the population movement from cities to suburbs and back to the cities, as functions of time). Much of interactive graphics technology, therefore, deals with hardware and software techniques for user-controlled motion dynamics and update dynamics.

With *motion dynamics*, objects can be moved and tumbled with respect to a stationary observer. Equivalently, the objects can remain stationary and the viewer can move around them ("pan"), to select the portion in view, and "zoom" in or out for more or less detail, as if looking through the view finder of a rapidly moving camera. Flight simulators are used to train aircraft pilots by letting them maneuver their simulated craft over a computer generated three-dimensional landscape portrayed on one or more cockpit windows, which are actually large TV screens. Similarly, motion dynamics are used to let a user fly around and through buildings, molecules, two-, three-, or four- dimensional mathematical functions, or "clouds" (scatter diagrams) of data points in two- or three-dimensional space. In another form of motion dynamics, the "camera" is held fixed, but the objects in the scene are moved relative to the camera. For example, a complex mechanical linkage, such as a gear train, may be animated on the screen by rotating all the individual gears appropriately.

Update dynamics refers to the actual change of the shape, color, or other properties of the objects being viewed. For instance, one can display the deformation of a metal frame by user-applied loads, or the state changes in a block diagram of a computer in response to data and control flows. The smoother the change, the more realistic and meaningful the result. Dynamic interactive graphics offers a large number of user-controllable modes with which to encode and communicate information: the two- or three-dimensional shape of objects in a picture, their position and orientation, their gray scale (grayness value between white and black) or color, and the time variations of these properties. In the near future, digitally encoded sound will be added so that objects and feedback from the program or the operating system can be heard as well as seen.

The burgeoning fields of word processing (*q.v.*) and office automation are introducing large numbers of office workers to computer-based workstations for document preparation and electronic mail. Most of these workstations are based on high-quality display screens suitable for interactive graphics. While the emphasis until recently was on strictly alphanumeric interaction, the demand for charts and figures is sufficiently strong that systems are now expected to display them, along with surrounding high-quality text, directly on the screen as they would appear on a hard-copy output device. This "what-you-see-is-what-you-get" (WYSIWYG) design philosophy, in which the screen mirrors the printed page as much as possible, eliminates bothersome and unnatural formatting or typesetting codes whose effects are not seen until the document is printed.

Interactive computer graphics provides much better human-machine communication through use of a judicious combination of text and static and dynamic pictures than is possible with text alone. The result is a significant improvement in our ability to understand data, perceive trends, and visualize real or imaginary objects. By making communication more efficient, graphics makes possible greater productivity, higher quality and more precise results or products, and lower design and analysis costs.

Software and Portability While steady advances in hardware technology have made possible the evolution of ever better graphics display devices, one may well wonder whether software has kept pace. For example, what has happened to the early difficulties experienced with graphics systems and application software? Much of that difficulty lay in the primitive graphics software then available to application programmers. By and large, there has been a long, slow process of maturation. We have moved from low-level, device-dependent subroutine packages supplied by manufacturers for their unique display devices to higher-level, device-independent packages. These packages, typically supplied by independent developers, can drive a wide variety of display devices from plotters to high-performance vector and raster displays. The main purpose of a device-independent package used in conjunction with a high-level programming language is to induce application program (and programmer) portability. This portability (*q.v.*) is provided in much the same way that a "high-level," machine-independent language provides a large measure of portability by isolating the programmer from most machine peculiarities. The Graphical Kernel System (GKS) was accepted as a two-dimensional standard in 1985, and a three-dimensional version was standardized in 1988. PHIGS, Programmer's Hierarchical Interactive Graphics System, is an alternative to GKS that has gained in popularity recently. As technology advances and these graphics standards (*see* second part of this article) are no longer able to handle new capabilities, they will be revised or replaced.

Geometric and Windowing Transformations

Graphics becomes especially powerful through the ability to compose complicated objects from pieces suitably transformed to fit into a higher-level structure. Furthermore, these instancing transformations are mathematically identical to those used to determine which portion of an object is in view and is to be displayed on the screen.

Any object can be defined recursively in terms of its component primitives, such as points, lines, polygons, character strings, and sub-objects, each suitably sized and positioned on the coordinate system of that object. Once formulations are available that allow point transformations, a line can then be transformed simply by transforming its endpoints, and a polygon by its vertices.

Most display manufacturers supply special hardware or firmware (*q.v.*) to carry out these transformations and provide the ability to combine the basic transformations with windowing and perspective mapping. The details of two- and three-dimensional transformations can be found in most computer graphics textbooks, such as Foley *et al.* (1990).

Windowing   Since large drawings cannot fit in their entirety on small display screens, they can either be compressed to fit, thereby obscuring details and inducing clutter, or only a portion of the total drawing can be displayed. The portion of a two- or three-dimensional object to be displayed is chosen through specification of a rectangular window that limits what part of the drawing can be seen.

A two-dimensional window is usually defined by choosing a maximum and minimum value for its *x*- and *y*-coordinates, or by specifying the center of the window and giving its maximum relative height and width. Simple subtractions or comparisons suffice to determine whether or not a point is in view. For lines and polygons, a *clipping* operation is performed that discards those parts that fall outside of the window. Only those parts that remain inside the window are drawn or otherwise rendered to make them visible.

Realistic Image Generation   Assume that there is a scene consisting of several objects, each of which is defined by mathematical formulas or some other mechanism. Assume further that these objects are all visible in a certain window and that there is a light source that illuminates the scene and highlights the objects.

In most of the algorithms to be discussed, each of these objects is approximated by a set of planar pieces. The more and smaller pieces that are used, the closer the approximation will be to the actual surface, but more storage space will be required. For example, a two-dimensional equivalent would be the approximation of a circle by a series of lines. Three lines produce a triangle, four a square, and eight an octagon. Each of these is closer to a circle than the previous one.

Lighting Models   As a prelude to the discussion of shading models, it is necessary to discuss the way in which the effects of incident light can be quantified for image production. The first type of illumination to be considered is *ambient light*, I_a, present in the environment. Since ambient light has no focus or direction, this is treated as an additive factor for all objects. The second type of light is *reflected light*, which varies depending on the location of the light source, the object, and the viewer. From Lambert's cosine law of physics, we know that the intensity of the diffusely reflected light is related to the scalar (dot) product of the surface normal, N, and a unit vector pointing toward the light source, L. The last type of illumination is *specular reflection*, which causes the highlights on an object. Specular reflection (Fig. 4) depends on the angle between the reflected vector, R, and the vector pointing at the viewer's position, V. If these two correspond, the highlight is bright; the further apart they are, the dimmer the highlight.

A simplified version of the light calculation is given by the formula $I = I_a + I_s [k_d (N \cdot L) + k_s (V \cdot R)^n]$, where I_s is the intensity of the light source, k_s is a diffuse reflection coefficient, k_s is a specular reflection coefficient, and n is the specular reflection exponent (when n is 1, the highlight is broad with blurred edges,

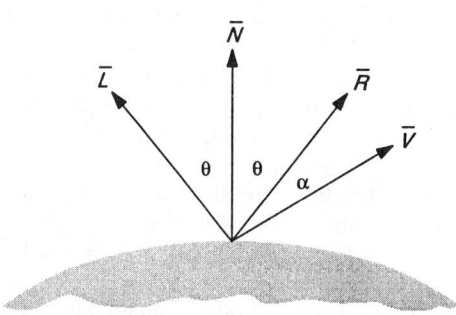

FIG. 4.   Specular reflection.

and as n gets larger, the highlight is narrowed and has sharper edges).

Painter's and Z-Buffer Algorithms   In the Painter's Algorithm, each object is broken into planar piece approximations that are, as separate units, arranged according to their distance from the viewer. The algorithm now works like a painter applying paint to a canvas—if something is blocked by an object in front, the painter just paints the foreground object over it. The piece farthest from the viewer is drawn, then the second farthest, and so on. If a piece will ultimately be visible, nothing will be drawn over it; however, if it is not entirely visible, a piece drawn later will cover all or part of it. So the picture is drawn back to front.

In the Z-Buffer Algorithm, there is a Z- or *depth-buffer* that has one value for each pixel in the frame buffer. These values represent the depth of the object of which the pixel is a part. For example, if an area of four pixels square is part of the first object, which is 4 units away from the viewer, all of the Z-buffer values for these pixels would be set to 4. As each new piece is drawn, its depth at the pixel location is compared to the Z-buffer value. If the buffer value is greater, this piece is in front and can be drawn (and the Z-buffer value is updated). If the buffer value is smaller, the old object is closer, so the current one is not drawn at that point. The benefit of the Z-buffer algorithm is that it is not necessary to sort the pieces, as the Z-buffer does that implicitly.

These two algorithms show the common space vs. time trade-off of computer science. The painter's algorithm is slower because of the sort, but it doesn't require the extremely large space of the Z-buffer.

Flat Shading   A problem with the painter's and Z-buffer algorithms is that they ignore the effects of the light source and use only the ambient light factor. Flat shading goes a bit further and includes the diffuse reflections as well. For each of the planar pieces, an intensity value is calculated based on the surface normal, the direction to the light, and the ambient light and diffuse coefficient constants. Since none of these change at any point on the piece, all of the pixels for it will have the same value. The resulting image will appear to be faceted, with ridges running along the boundaries of the pieces that comprise an object (see Fig. 5a, color insert page CP-6).

Gouraud Shading   In 1971, Henri Gouraud developed an interpolation method that removed some of the discontinuities between pieces and also produced more realistic highlighting (Fig. 5b, color insert page CP-6). The problem with the previous method is that a single normal is used for a patch that approximates a curved surface. Gouraud's method keeps a normal vector from the actual surface for each vertex of every piece. When the piece is being shaded, the intensity at each vertex is calculated, and then the system interpolates between them for the interior points of the piece. Since an edge that is shared between two pieces will have equal vertex normals, the resulting intensity values along these two coincident edges will correspond.

Phong Shading   Gouraud shading improved on the images that were produced by flat shading, but the highlighting was still off. In 1975, Bui-Tuong Phong improved on Gouraud shading by interpolating the normals across the surface, as opposed to the intensities (Fig. 5c, color insert page CP-6). This leads to finer and more precise highlights. The differences between these three shading methods can be seen in Fig. 5, color insert page CP-6.

Ray Tracing   In the methods examined so far, all objects are assumed to have a matte or dull finish. None is reflective, translucent, or transparent, because the previous methods are not able to handle these types of objects. Ray tracing takes the previous methods one step further in allowing rays of light that strike a surface to reflect and refract between all the objects in the scene (see Fig. 6, color insert page CP-6).

When the viewer location and pixel location on the screen are considered, they define a line or ray into the scene to be rendered. This ray is traced into the scene, where it can strike a matte surface object, and the pixel color is determined as in Phong shading. If the ray strikes a reflective or refractive surface, the laws of optics are used to determine the new direction of one or more rays that would result. These new rays are then traced recursively until they leave the scene or strike another surface, a computationally complex process that quickly deteriorates as the number of reflective and refractive objects increases.

Radiosity   Ray tracing improves imagery, but suffers from an inability to handle reflections between diffuse surfaces. Most people have experienced reflections between two diffuse surfaces when, in a bright room, the color of the rug makes the walls appear to be a different color or, when wearing a red shirt, one appears to be blushing.

Radiosity, developed by Michael Cohen and Don Greenberg from Cornell University, treats light as energy instead of a vector, and considers how that energy is transferred between surfaces based on their color and proximity. Radiosity is applied in three stages, and, based on what type of changes occur, only some of the stages require recalculation. If the viewing location changes, only the last rendering stage is redone. If an object in the scene is moved, all stages are recalculated. Since early stages are the most computationally complex, the less they are redone, the more time is saved. As can be seen in Fig. 7 (color insert page CP-6), radiosity produces remarkable realism.

Texture Mapping   Early computer-generated images used shaded objects that had unnaturally smooth surfaces. To produce a textured surface using the techniques discussed would require creating an excessive number of surface pieces that follow all of the complexities of the texture. An alternative to the explosion of surfaces would be to use the techniques of *texture mapping*. Texture mapping is a technique used to paint scanned images of a texture onto the object being modeled. Through an associated technique called *bump map-*

ping, the appearance of the texture can be improved still further.

Surface Painting vs. Bump Mapping

Surface painting simply adds an image to the surface of an object. If the image is itself a texture, it makes the object appear textured. This technique requires the production of a texture file containing color values that traditionally have been obtained by scanning a picture of a real object with the desired pattern.

The shading algorithm is altered to use the texture file for determining the color of points on the surface. To do this, a mapping function is produced that converts surface locations into the range of the texture. As the surface is shaded, the locations on the surface, corresponding to pixels in the image, are mapped into the texture's space, and the texture value at that point is used as the object's color. This is not normally a good solution, since specular highlights are not affected; the resulting images appear to be flat surfaces that have had pictures painted on them.

An obvious way to include specular highlighting would be to use the texture to modify the surface definition. This is complex and quickly explodes the amount of surface information that needs to be stored and accessed. The alternative is to treat the texture as a *bump map* that modifies the surface definition at a single point for only the brief instant that it is being rendered.

Where texture painting techniques alter the color of the surface based on the values in the texture, bump mapping alters the value of the surface normal at the point. When the surface normal is turned away from the light direction, this darkens the location; conversely, when it is turned toward the light, it is brightened. For example, a ridge bump map would add a highlight shaped like the ridge.

The problem with bump mapping appears with objects in profile. Since its surface is not actually changed, as an object is rotated, the highlighting of the bumps appears to be correct until the surface reaches its profile, when the bumps disappear.

Two-Dimensional vs. Three-Dimensional Textures

The foregoing discussion assumes a two-dimensional texture wrapped around a surface. This requires special conditions to be present in the map, depending on the surfaces to be textured. If cylinders are to be textured, the texture must be continuous so that, when the texture is wrapped around the cylinder, no seam appears where the ends meet. This is also required if the surface is so large that the texture needs to be repeated to cover it. The requirements for texturing a sphere are even more demanding.

One solution to this problem is use of a three-dimensional texture, as is done in the work of Peachy (1985) and Perlin (1985). Since these textures show proper changes in all directions, a surface can be textured by "placing" it into the three-dimensional texture. This is done by mapping the surface locations into the texture's three-dimen-

sional space. This eliminates the problem of texture seams, but increases the space requirements for the texture.

Static vs. Functional Maps

At this point, all discussion has assumed that the texture is static, having been scanned into a file. This places restrictions on the texture.

An alternative is a *functional texture*, i.e. the encoding of a texture in an equation-based routine. Surface indices are used as parameters for the equations. This removes the need to store the texture (a space reduction), but also reduces the speed of image production, as the function is likely to be more expensive to compute than a table look-up in an array (a time increase). This trade-off is tempered by the ability to alter system parameters dynamically, allowing the texture to evolve based on the natural demands of the image. Additionally, the texture is now potentially infinite in all directions. This eliminates scaling or cycling through a static texture that is used to cover an arbitrarily large surface.

Functional texturing has been taken to a successful extreme by Geoffrey Gardner (1985), who produces entire images based on a single formula, with parameters altered to produce mountains, clouds, and trees (see Fig. 8, color insert page CP-6).

Modeling of Natural Phenomena The main research into probabilistic models of plant growth are those of Phillipe de Reffye and his colleagues (1988), a group composed of agronomists, botanists, and computer scientists. Their model considers the growth point of a plant, as well as four possible events that can occur in one time unit. The bud can become a flower or fruit and then die; it can go into a dormant state; it can abort or die; or it can grow, producing a new branch section. All of these are controlled by predetermined probabilities that the user must specify.

The model also requires that the user provide the age of the plant and, for each branch, the rate at which the branch grows, the maximum number of buds produced by each branch, the length and diameter of the branches, and the development trend of the branch (either vertical or horizontal).

A grammar-based approach to modeling plant growth was proposed by Aristid Lindenmayer as a way to formally define the growth that was observed in filamentous organisms. These grammars (*q.v.*), now known as L-Systems, were used to define the interaction between cells in these organisms and to define branching patterns. These L-Systems are parallel string grammars that can consider any predefined context on the left and right of the symbol. Branching is incorporated by enclosing the symbols of the branch in brackets.

Pauline Hogeweg takes these L-Systems and reverses the process, using their simple parallel grammars to produce tree-like images. In her work, she generates a string from the grammar, and then renders it with simple parameters. Each symbol is represented as a vertical line, and each branch section causes a rotation of the axes.

Masaki Aono and Tosiyasu Kunii enhance these L-Systems by the addition of a geometry specified by a limited number of branching angles. This work is also interesting in that it attempts to model natural effects of sunlight and wind with "attractors" that pull the ends of the branches like magnets. Unfortunately, this technique cannot model the inhibition of growth on the shadowed side of the plant, nor can it account for environmental objects that may partially or completely block the light.

Przemyslaw Prusinkiewicz (1990) also incorporates both two- and three-dimensional interpretations by the addition of special symbols into the L-System grammars. These special symbols control a two/three-dimensional turtle that draws the plant image. In turtle geometry, a "turtle" is commanded to move in various directions, with either its pen up or down, drawing lines as it moves in the latter case. With the correct sequence of symbols, the turtle draws flowers, leaves, and entire plants.

Three-dimensional graph grammars were developed by Jeffrey J. McConnell (1989) to model growth of plants not only in an ideal environment, as most other models assume, but also in a natural environment. Because of the three-dimensional nature of the model, the positions of the branches relative to each other, the sun position, and external obstructions can be determined. Sunlight calculations can be done to find how much light falls on a particular branch, and the system can then slow the growth, if not enough light is present, or encourage growth in high light areas. The growth of a plant can also be altered by either external obstructions or other parts of the plant (internal obstructions).

Particle systems, developed by Bill Reeves, are used to model fire, explosions, and fireworks. In his research, a particle is an entity that has mass, color, velocity, direction, and duration. By combining a group of particles that start from a central point and move outward, a realistic fireworks burst can be simulated. A cylinder-shaped group rising from a plane produces a fire. Particles emanating from the top of a sinusoidal wave produce a foam-like appearance.

Physically-Based Modeling The increasing speed of computer systems allows production of high-quality computer graphics images through the use of physically-based models. Prior to the advent of reasonable computer power, animation sequences were very unrealistic, because all calculations of how objects moved had to be done with approximations to actual equations.

Images and animation sequences of cloth being draped over an object, chains dangling between two poles, and indentations of elastic objects can now be produced with amazing realism.

Computing power is available to treat cloth not as a single entity, but as a collection of constituent woven threads. Jerry Weil has developed a technique that is based on seeing the threads as lying in catenary curves (the shape of a hanging chain). To model, for example, a cloth laying over a chair, the points of the cloth that contact the chair are fixed in space. The threads between these points are then mapped into a catenary curve. Other threads intersect these catenary-shaped threads, fixing more points for these new threads. The process repeats until all of the threads have been placed. There could be thousands of threads running the length and width of even a small piece of cloth, leading to millions of intersection points on the fabric, whose locations must be determined.

Constraint-based modeling is used in computer graphics for modeling movement of the human skeleton, chains, and other physical objects. The idea is that it is difficult to specify a coordinate at which a ball would be resting on a table, but it would be simple to constrain the ball to do so and to have the computer calculate the correct location. For the human skeleton, constraints specify the connectivity of bones at joints and the directions and angles of movement. In modeling the movement of a skeleton across a terrain, the system will set bone positions to best satisfy the constraints placed on the system.

Solids Modeling In the discussion of shading methods, objects in the world were described by their outer surfaces. This is fine for applications that require only the production of images, but systems designed to manipulate or test the created objects need an alternative representation. Solids modeling treats all objects as solids, clearly identifying the inside and outside of each object, which allows tests for stress and obstruction as well as production of parts lists. This is the underlying model for CAD/CAM systems.

In solids modeling, the system has a collection of primitive objects that can be scaled, rotated, and translated. Complex objects are built by applying boolean operations to simpler objects. A washer can be created by differencing a short, narrow cylinder from a short, wide one. A door hinge pin can be created through logical union of a wide, short cylinder with a tall, narrow one.

Animation Animated cartoons were the hallmark of Walt Disney, whose studio produced a number of classic films. This work, called cel animation, first requires the production of an overall story board. From that, individual scenes are created, with the *animator* drawing only key frames, an *in-betweener* drawing the frames connecting the key frames, and an *inker* adding the proper colors. The characters are drawn on acetate sheets called cels that are laid over the background and photographed to make the animated scene. Clearly, this is a labor-intensive process.

Computers are helping to automate the animation process by taking over the in-betweening and inking processes. It is more common, however, for the computer to control the whole process (see COMPUTER ANIMATION). The animator describes the objects in the scene and how they are to move, and the computer takes over from there, moving each object to its new position before rendering the next image.

Craig Reynolds (1987) has taken this one step further. His research into flocks, herds, and schools indicated that the members follow three simple rules: 1. stay close to the center of the flock, 2. match velocity with the neighbors, and 3. avoid collisions. His system then creates a set of *actors*, each adhering to these three rules, and allows them to move based on their own limited perception of the world. The resulting animation sequences show extremely realistic flocking behavior. With systems based on independent actors, there is even less human effort. For some control over the result, it is possible to put in lead actors, whose movements are scripted, which help to direct the other independent actor motions.

Fractals Fractals are not a new area of research, but rather an old mathematical area that has received new life with the advent of computer graphics. The term *fractal* is derived from the fact that certain objects behave as if they have fractional dimensions. A line is one-dimensional, but a coast line is greater than one-dimensional and not quite two-dimensional because, at finer and finer resolutions, the coast line gets longer and longer without consuming any more outer area. As a one-dimensional line forms a tight spiral into the center of a circle, it becomes more like a plane. Mountains operate similarly between two and three dimensions, and clouds between three and four dimensions.

References

1985. Gardner, Geoffrey Y. "Visual Simulation of Clouds," proceedings of SIGGRAPH '85 (San Fransisco, CA, 22–26 July), in *Computer Graphics* **17**, *3* (July). New York: ACM SIGGRAPH.

1985. Peachy, Darwin R. "Solid Texturing of Complex Surfaces," proceedings of SIGGRAPH '85 (San Fransisco, CA, 22–26 July), in *Computer Graphics* **17**, *3* (July). New York: ACM SIGGRAPH.

1985. Perlin, Ken. "An Image Synthesizer," proceedings of SIGGRAPH '85 (San Fransisco, CA, 22–26 July), in *Computer Graphics* **17**, *3* (July 1985). New York: ACM SIGGRAPH.

1986. Weil, Jerry. "The Synthesis of Cloth Objects," proceedings of SIGGRAPH '86 (Dallas, TX, 18–22 August) in *Computer Graphics* **20**, *4* (August). New York: ACM SIGGRAPH.

1987. Reynolds, Craig. "Flocks, Herds, and Schools," proceedings of SIGGRAPH '87 (Anaheim, CA, 27–31 July) in *Computer Graphics* **21**, *4* (July). New York: ACM SIGGRAPH.

1988. Reffye (de), Philippe, et al. "Plant Models Faithful to Botanical Structure and Development," proceedings of SIGGRAPH '88 (Atlanta, GA, 1–5 August), in *Computer Graphics* **22**, *4* (August). New York: ACM SIGGRAPH.

1989. Brown, Judith R. and Cunningham, Steve. *Programming the User Interface.* New York: John Wiley & Sons.

1989. McConnell, Jeffrey J. "Botanical Models Based on Three-Dimensional Attributed Graph Grammars," proceedings of the Twentieth Annual Pittsburgh Conference (Pittsburgh, PA 4–5 May).

1989. Watt, Alan H. *Fundamentals of Three-Dimensional Computer Graphics.* Reading, MA: Addison-Wesley.

1990. Foley, James, van Dam, Andries, Feiner, Steven K., and Hughes, John F. *Computer Graphics: Principles and Practice.* Reading, MA: Addison-Wesley.

1990. Hill, Francis S. *Computer Graphics.* New York: Macmillian.

1990. Prusinkiewicz, Przemyslaw and Lindenmeyer, Aristid. *The Algorithmic Beauty of Plants.* New York: Springer-Verlag.

JEFFERY J. MCCONNELL

STANDARDS

For articles on related subjects *see* COMPUTER-AIDED DESIGN/COMPUTER-AIDED MANUFACTURING; USER INTERFACE; WINDOW ENVIRONMENTS; and WORKSTATION.

Introduction *Computer graphics standards* provide portability across computing systems and devices for interactive graphics applications. The variety of individual device characteristics that must be considered to achieve portability of graphical output are considerable (Fig. 1). Essentially, all computer graphics standards are interface definitions standardizing the protocol and information formats to the degree needed to provide portability. These interfaces may be realized as information exchanged in a communication stream between two system components or as procedural interfaces to a subroutine package. All of the computer graphics standards, with the exception of metafiles, have been primarily implemented as subroutine packages.

There are two approaches that can be followed to achieve portability. One is by defining a *virtual device* which hides individual device characteristics. Using this method, an application directs output to and manages a virtual device defined by a standard interface. Software on the device side of the interface must then interpret the information received in order to manage the output device and generate an image that is reasonably compatible with the application intent.

The second approach is that of *inquiry*. This approach allows the application to inquire about the capabilities and characteristics of the device and then manage the output to use those capabilities to meet the needs of the application. For example, the application may ask if a device supports multiple line styles or multiple line widths. Depending on the reply, the application may specify either different line styles or line widths (or use a compensating technique if neither are present) to differentiate lines that have particular application attributes.

In order to optimize the use of particular device capabilities while minimizing the overhead required to manage a large set of options, computer graphics standards combine the use of both the inquiry and virtual device approaches. But applications and computer graphics requirements vary greatly. Many applications need little more than simple line drawing capability to produce charts and graphs. Other applications require significant model synthesis—full three-dimensional (3-D) color images viewed from varying perspectives with hidden lines and surfaces removed and with light sources and surface textures realistically portrayed.

Several standards have been developed to satisfy the requirements for portability of different applications and the computer graphics capability they require. The older and more commonly used standards are best suited for display of static, two-dimensional (2-D) images and are suitable for applications having little or no user interaction. More recent standards provide support for

Output:
static vs. dynamic media,
drawing modes
    - calligraphic (line drawing) vs. raster (pixel painting),
drawing surface size,
buffering
    - frame buffers
    - display lists
resolution,
device coordinate systems,
gray scale and color capability
    - intensity control
    - gamut (number of colors possible),
available graphical primitives
    - lines, circles, fill areas, characters, etc.,
advanced graphical capability
    - hidden line removal
    - illumination and shading
    - geometric relationship modeling,
line styles
    - width
    - texture
    - joins,
text capability
    - text path
    - character orientation
    - character sets
    - fonts, styles, sizes, etc.
Input:
protocols and coding,
keyboards
    - special keys
    - modifier keys
    - function keys and buttons
    - numeric keypads
coordinates received
    - absolute vs. relative

FIG. 1. In order to achieve portability, device characteristics must either be made transparent to the application, or the particulars of the device be made available for the application to manage by means of inquiry functions.

the generation and maintenance of dynamic, geometrically-related models and their display. Standards to support windowing systems and applications designed for use in a windowed environment have been proposed, but may not be available as soon as anticipated by their proponents. The major computer graphics standards are described below.

Graphical Kernel System

Graphical Kernel System The Graphical Kernel System (GKS)[1] is the oldest of the computer graphics standards. Although the standard claims to include "all the capabilities that are essential for a broad spectrum of graphics, from simple passive output to highly interactive applications," GKS supports 2-D graphics and is best suited for display of static images and applications requiring primarily discrete input. A 3-D version of GKS has been defined as an international standard (ISO 8805).

The theoretical basis for GKS was conceived and developed well before modern windowing systems came into use, and GKS, therefore, is not directly compatible with such systems. GKS assumes that it controls the entire workstation and does not share either screen space or input devices with other applications. However, workaround modifications can be applied, allowing GKS applications to be run in a windowed environment.

Computer Graphics Metafile

Computer Graphics Metafile The Computer Graphics Metafile (CGM)[2] provides a means to store and transfer 2-D picture description information in a device- and environment-independent manner for use by graphics production systems and applications. It defines a presentation level interface and contains elements for graphical primitives and control of the appearance of the graphical primitives through the use of attributes.

CGM supports three types of encodings for picture description: character, binary, and clear text. The character encoding provides an encoding of minimum size that may be transmitted through character-oriented communications services. The binary encoding provides a representation that optimizes speed of generation and interpretation. Clear text encoding provides a representation that may be easily read and edited by humans. It is intended that CGM data will be interpreted by the application rather than by other standards, as the particular device used to render a picture may not have the exact complement of features as used for the picture description. The applications programmer, who presumably understands the class of display devices available, is then responsible for making trade-off decisions regarding the rendering of the picture.

The Computer Graphics Interface

The Computer Graphics Interface The Computer Graphics Interface (CGI)[3] is a 2-D graphics standard defining the functions for control and data exchange between device-independent (client) and device-dependent (device) parts of a graphics system. CGI is intended to provide portability at the device level

---

[1]GKS is both a U.S. national and an international standard. The American International Standards Institute (ANSI) publishes the GKS standard as ANSI X3.124-1985. The International Standards Organization (ISO) publishes it as ISO 7942.

[2]CGM is both an American standard, ANSI X3.122-1986, and an international standard, ISO 8632.

[3]CGI is an international standard, ISO 9636.

and is expected to be used by higher-level standards, such as GKS.

CGI is designed to support a wide variety of clients having very different functional scopes and quite distinct classes of devices. Although CGI is most likely to be realized as a subroutine package, a data stream encoding of CGI functionality is possible and is planned as a future standard.

The scope of CGI is quite large, and a full implementation of the standard would be overkill for most environments. In order to reduce the size of an implementation of CGI, profiles that are subsets of the CGI functions may be defined. Three standard profiles—a foundation profile, a GKS profile, and a CGM profile—are provided as part of the CGI standard.

The architecture of the CGI standard was determined well before windowing systems appeared in the marketplace, and the capability to support windows is not straightforwardly available in CGI. Unfortunately, the computer graphics systems level for which CGI was designed is the level at which most applications and other graphics standards would interact with a window system. This, along with its inherent complexity, may have already made CGI obsolete as a standard, even though it was approved only recently.

Programmer's Hierarchical Interactive Graphical System

The Programmer's Hierarchical Interactive Graphical System (PHIGS)[4] specifies a set of 2-D and 3-D functions for the definition, display, and modification of geometrically-related objects and graphical data. Whereas GKS, CGM, and CGI are oriented towards static pictures, PHIGS is designed to provide dynamic interpretation of geometrical relationships inherent in a hierarchical model. As such, PHIGS is much more suited for applications that require animated display of structured objects, particularly computer-aided design. It also is more suited to and makes better use of the advanced graphics capability of sophisticated computer graphics workstations.

PHIGS manages a central structure store in which individual structures and their geometric and hierarchical relationships to other structures may be defined and edited. A given structure may be referenced by a number of other structures. In order to display a picture, the structure is traversed from its root, and, as each structure is referenced, that structure is interpreted relative to the one referencing it. Since model transforms are attributes stored as elements in structures, they are interpreted during traversal. This allows a change in the position, orientation, or scale of a

structure to be inherited by all structures that it references.

An extension of PHIGS—PHIGS PLUS[5]—provides support for advanced computer graphics capabilities, such as light sources, shading, reflectance, and spline curves and surfaces.

Window Systems

The advent of window environments provides capabilities that are greatly desired by users of interactive graphics systems. The major utility provided by window systems is the definition of sections of a display that qualify input relative to the position of a special cursor known as the *pointer*. This capability is used to build *widgets*, interactive techniques for manipulating a display and communicating with an interaction. State-of-the-art interactive applications utilize widgets extensively, and, in order to make these applications portable, it will be necessary to define either standard widgets or interfaces to widgets.

Most windowing systems have been designed for specific workstations or personal computers. The X Window System™[6] was designed to be used with heterogeneous workstations in a network environment and is currently the base for complementary standards proposed by the Accredited Standards Committee on Computers and Information Processing, X3, and the Institute of Electrical and Electronic Engineers (IEEE).

X3[7] is currently defining the standard data stream between clients (applications including X-related support software) and the X Window System server, which is responsible for managing the workstation screen(s) and input devices. It is standardization of the data stream that enables remote applications to generate a display on a workstation and to interact with the user.

The IEEE Standards Subcommittee, P1201, has initiated an effort to define standards for interfacing to widgets and to the intrinsic software required for managing widgets. Without great care and comprehensive insight, it will be difficult, if not impossible, to develop a standard without defining carefully the appearance and behavior of the widgets themselves.

Finally, a standard is required to define interaction and communication protocols for sharing information, and between applications (and particularly with the window manager), a special application is needed that is responsible for managing the screen's display surface and for directing input to the appropriate application(s). Currently, a de facto X Window System standard—the Inter-Client Communication Conventions Manual (ICCCM)—has been defined to meet this need.

JON MEADS

---

[4]PHIGS is both an American standard, ANSI X3.144-1988, and an international standard, ISO 9592.

[5]PHIGS PLUS is Part 4 of the PHIGS international standard.
[6]The X Window System is a trademark of M.I.T.
[7]More specifically, the Technical Subcommittee on Computer Graphics, X3H3.

COMPUTER-INTEGRATED MANUFACTURING (CIM)

For articles on related subjects *see* COMPUTER-AIDED DESIGN/COMPUTER-AIDED MANUFACTURING; and ROBOTICS.

Computers in Manufacturing

Computer-integrated manufacturing (CIM) refers to the interconnection of computers to enable several organizational or functional units of a manufacturer to share computing resources and information. Using CIM, production workers responsible for building a product can electronically access product design information generated by another group, such as the engineering department. Furthermore, the initial design data may electronically drive the production equipment so that the plant floor equipment can manufacture a product automatically.

When CIM is applied most comprehensively, virtually every department in the manufacturing enterprise is interconnected via a single computer network. These departments include purchasing, logistics, maintenance, business operations, and engineering (see Fig. 1). In such a case, the overall computer system is the dominant means for communicating information and controlling the operations of the firm. The term computer-integrated enterprise (CIE) is also used to describe this intense application of information technology throughout the manufacturing enterprise. Driving the integration effort is manufacturing's need to (1) improve the quality of its products, processes, and services, (2) reduce the lead time to bring new products to markets, (3) respond faster to customer orders, and (4) reduce costs.

Information Flow in Manufacturing

Information in manufacturing is centered around two major activities: (1) creating new products, and (2) transforming customer orders and raw materials into finished, delivered products on a routine basis. The first activity encompasses not only the design of the new product, but also the design of the associated processes and equipment that enable the manufacture of that product (see Fig. 2). This can be an informationally intense undertaking. For instance, a new aircraft consists of 100,000 to 300,000 components that must be individually specified and combined into subassemblies.

Some of the software applications that help launch new products include computer-aided design (CAD), for visualizing the design of a part and specifying its geometry. Another is computer-aided engineering (CAE), for testing and simulating design ideas before building physical prototypes. Computer-aided manufacturing (CAM) defines the steps that a computer-controlled machine must follow to machine a part. Computer-aided process planning (CAPP) defines the order of operations and routings when several machine tools are required to make a single part.

The second principal activity centers on the operational aspects that begin with a customer order and culminate in the delivery of the product. Literally thousands of intermediate steps are typically required. These include acquiring raw materials, allocating equipment and personnel, operating and monitoring plant-floor equipment, and delivering the finished product.

Among the software applications employed in CIM are manufacturing resource planning (MRP) systems for production planning and control. Market forecasts drive the MRP system. Taking into account lead times and capacity constraints, the MRP system creates schedules for material procurement, sets work schedules, and determines cash-flow requirements. Communication links based on Electronic Data Interchange (EDI) alert suppliers when additional raw materials are needed. Factory management systems track work in process and gather and analyze labor and equipment utilization data. Statis-

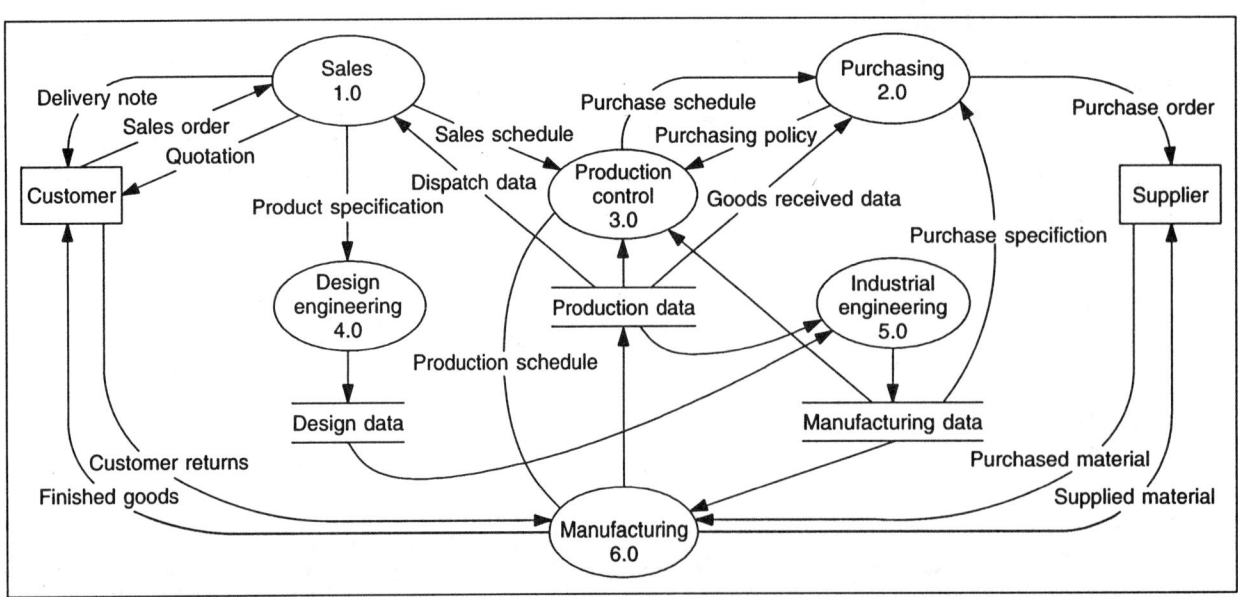

FIG. 1.

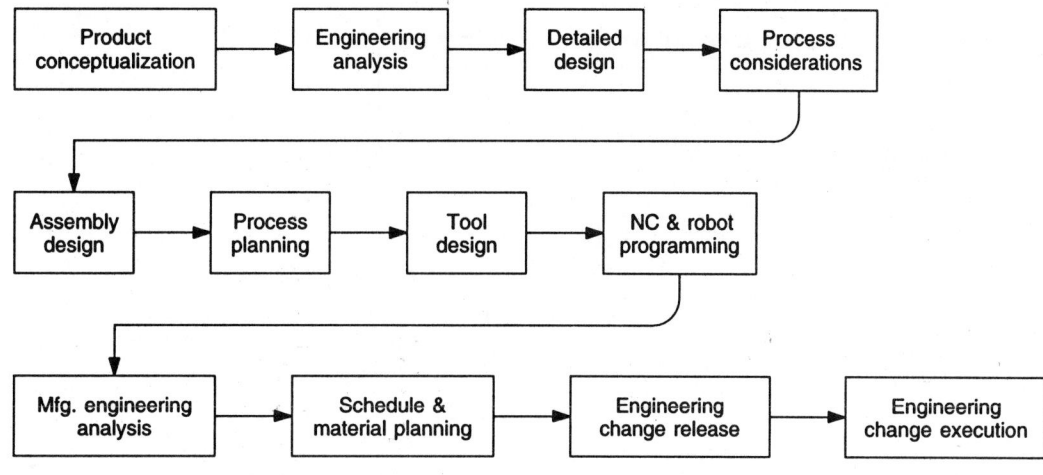

FIG. 2.

tical Process Control (SPC) and Statistical Quality Control (SQC) software detect when production equipment is beginning to drift out of specification so that closed loop control automatic corrections can be made.

History One of the earliest applications of computers in manufacturing was for industrial control. Paper mills and tobacco firms employed these precursors to digital computers as early as 1920. These process companies used hydraulically-based devices to measure temperature, pressure, and flow rates and in turn would automatically adjust processes such as closing or opening valves.

Military technology developed during World War II vastly improved industrial controls technology. New monitoring devices and electromechanical servo systems created during the war soon found their way into petroleum refineries and chemical plants. By 1950, IBM began selling small analog computers (q.v.) to the industrial world.

Among the earliest digital devices used in manufacturing were numerical control (NC) machines. John Parsons and others in the late 1940s pioneered the use of computer technology to control machine tools such as lathes. Numbers recorded on punched cards guided the movement of NC machines in cutting parts.

Between 1950 and 1980, industrial firms introduced computer technology into virtually every major manufacturing activity. General Motors applied computer-aided design techniques in 1960 to help create the tooling necessary to fabricate car body panels. Unfortunately, these industry efforts were done independently of each other, thereby creating "islands of automation." Since the various departmental computers were not interconnected, interdepartmental coordination and communication were poor. Early attempts to rectify this problem centered on creating point-to-point interfaces between pairs of computers. An example would be transforming the data directly from a CAD workstation to the software part programs that would drive an NC machine. Joseph Harrington, Jr., and others, however, recognized that the problem was far broader and that only enterprise-wide

integration would truly unify the highly fragmented computer activities in a manufacturing company. As a result, industrial firms now build massive CIM architectures and infrastructures specifically to facilitate the integration of existing technologies, as well as ease the introduction of new systems.

Communications and Data Management Communication networks and common data management systems are the core underlying technologies for integrating computer systems (see Fig. 3). Communication networks provide the physical links between computers. In addition to twisted pair and coaxial cable, the industry is moving toward fiber optics (q.v.) as the primary physical medium for data communication.

Manufacturing applications need common data in order to act cooperatively. Early integration efforts relied on the direct exchange of data between applications, but the current trend is not to use point-to-point solutions. Rather, the data that is shared across organizational boundaries is maintained and managed in independent database management systems (DBMS) (see Fig. 4).

Manufacturers rely on both disk-based relational database management systems (RDBMS) and real-time, memory-resident database management systems (RT/DBMS). In order to start and stop motors that control the actual material flow, such systems must respond in milliseconds on the plant floor. Integrating RT/DBMS-based shop-floor systems with RDBMS-based business systems is a major challenge.

Critical to data sharing and task coordination are industry-wide data and protocol standards that govern the format of shared data and the sequence of requests and responses between cooperating devices. Examples include Initial Graphical Exchange Specification (IGES), Product Data Exchange Specification (PDES), and the European Standard for the Exchange of Product Model Data (STEP). IGES, for instance, enables CAD machines to exchange part geometry information. PDES extends this sharing to include a complete product model description, including manufacturing features, tolerances, and mate-

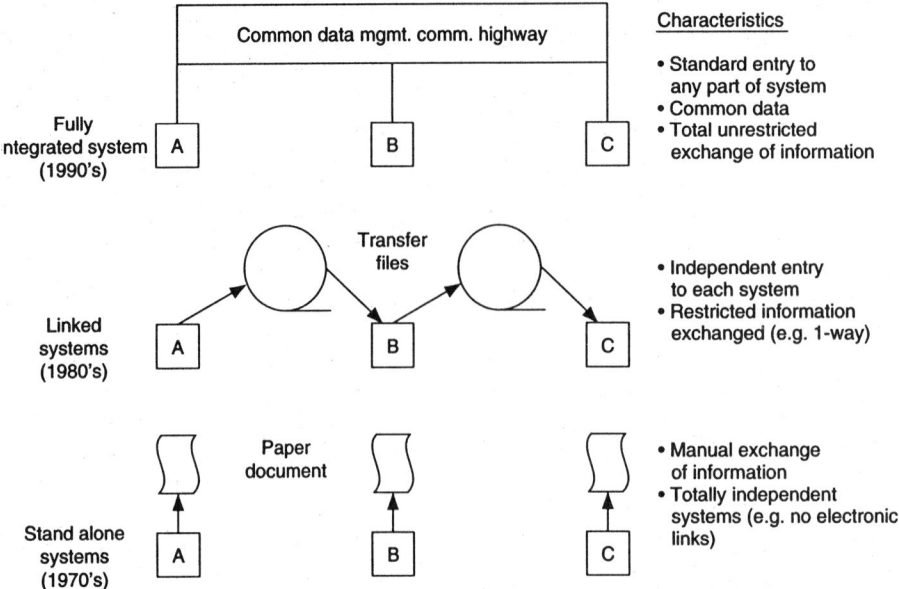

FIG. 3.

rial properties. Consistent data definitions (e.g. uniform part identification numbers) are essential to sharing data across the enterprise.

Two important communication protocols are Manufacturing Automation Protocol (MAP) and Transmission Control Protocol/Internet Protocol (TCP/IP). The manufacturing industry in general is steadily pursuing more standards in order to create a "plug and play" capability,

to diminish the need for custom integration for new systems.

The CIM Hierarchy in Plants and Mills The computational devices in a manufacturing plant are typically organized as a three-tier hierarchy. In this model, each device serves a particular level: process control, cell control, or area/plant control (see Fig. 5). The lower-level

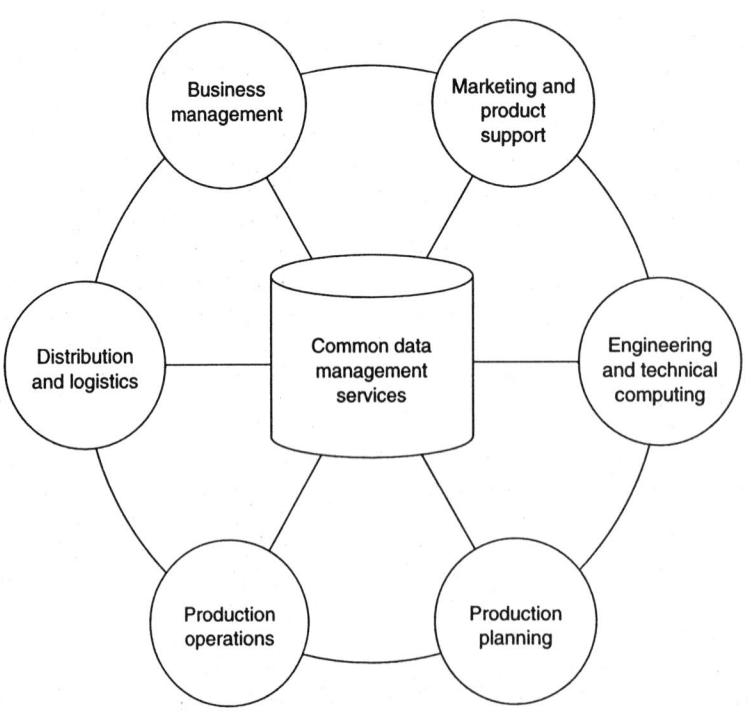

FIG. 4.

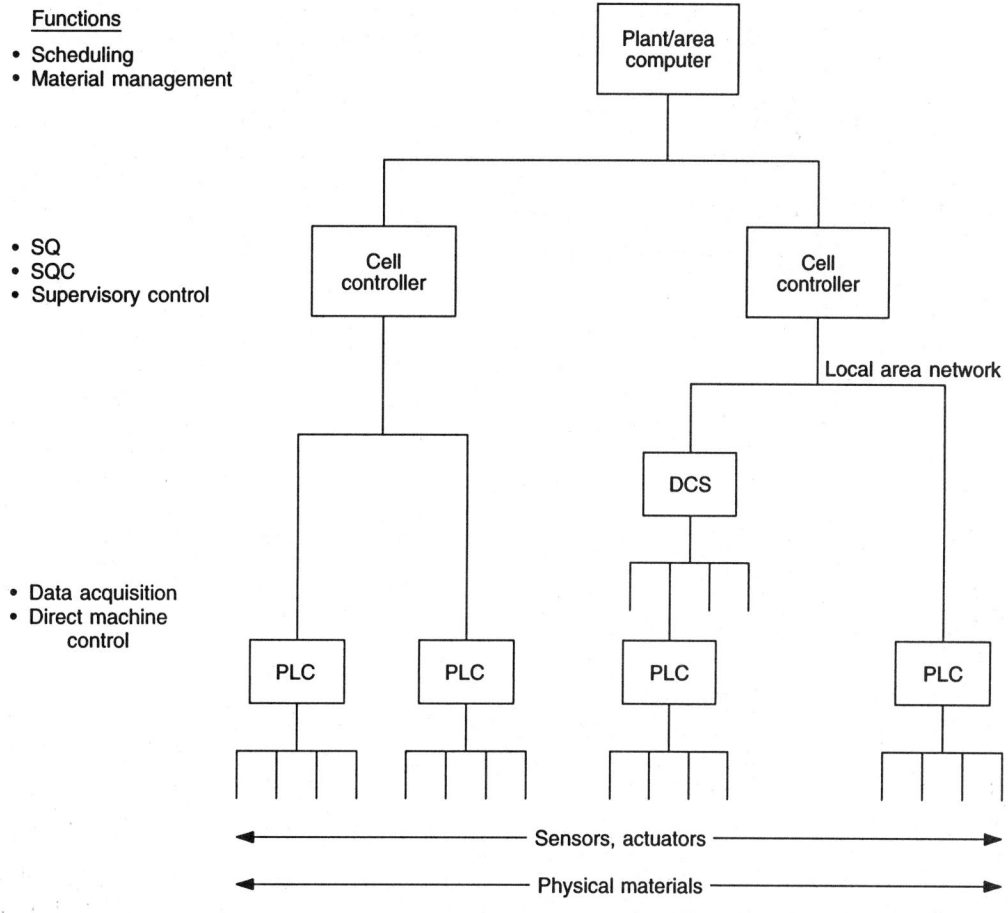

Functions
- Scheduling
- Material management

- SQ
- SQC
- Supervisory control

- Data acquisition
- Direct machine control

FIG. 5.

devices are most intimately involved with the actual handling and transformation of materials into finished goods.

At the lowest level, process-control sensors assess proximity, temperature, and other physical conditions and feed the information up the hierarchy. In a complementary but opposite direction, control information originating higher in the hierarchy determines instructions sent to actuators at the process-control level that start and stop motors, open and close valves, and control other physical actions.

The two most important types of programmable machines that gather sensory data, interpret this data, and send control signals back to actuators are programmable logic controllers (PLC) and distributed control systems (DCS). PLCs are more prevalent among discrete manufacturers such as automotive and aerospace firms. DCSs are commonplace in process and batch industries, such as petroleum refineries and food manufacturers. Both PLCs and DCSs are special-purpose, digital devices designed expressly for manufacturing environments. They are industrially hardened and optimized to handle considerable input/output traffic in a deterministic manner.

Next up the hierarchy are *cell controllers.* They coordinate the functions of multiple PLCs, DCSs, and other automated devices, such as robots, computer numeri-

cally controlled (CNC) machines, material handling systems, and machine vision systems. Cell controllers typically contain an operator interface for a worker to monitor cell activities and intervene when necessary. An example of a cell controller would be a paint cell in an automobile factory. There the cell controller would direct the paint robot, check the paint job afterwards with a machine vision system, and then signal that the cell was ready to paint another car. Cell control duties can be done on minicomputers (*q.v.*), workstations (*q.v.*), or personal computers (*q.v.*).

The highest level in the CIM plant hierarchy are the area or plant-wide computers that coordinate work among the lower-level cell controllers and serve as the interface to the external world. These area and plant-wide systems manage the overall flow of materials by assigning labor and machinery to specific production orders and by monitoring the production process. Traditionally, the larger plants have used mainframes and minicomputers as area and plant managers, but networked personal computers are beginning to serve this top level as well.

Future Trends   Higher speed networks (in excess of 100 megabytes/sec) are flattening the CIM hierarchy, and are ushering in an era of *client-server architectures* (see Fig. 6). Sensors and multi-microprocessor hardware are be-

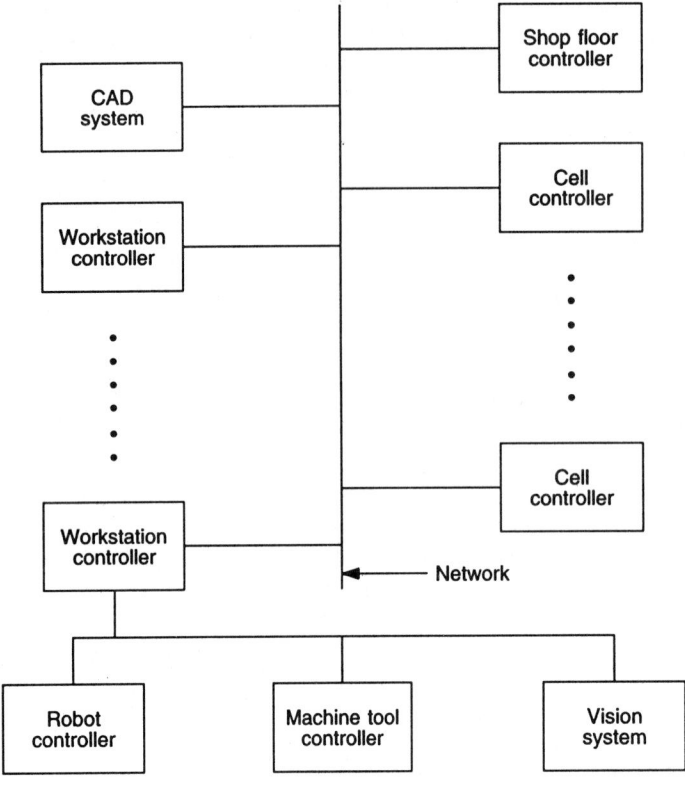

FIG. 6.

coming ubiquitous, leading to highly distributed, redundant, fault-tolerant systems (*q.v.*).

The manufacturing industry is moving toward universal access to a firm's data, regardless of the data's geographical location or the role it plays. By standardizing the definitions of data, higher-level objects, and protocols, manufacturers will be able to add new systems quickly with little customization required. For instance, a firm's engineering and manufacturing groups each have their own bill-of-materials (BOM) descriptions indicating a product's subassembly structure. Traditionally, manufacturing firms have created BOM software with little regard for sharing that data either internally or externally. In adopting industry-standard data structures for BOMs, an industrial firm could more easily move information between these two BOMs, as well as facilitate integration with other CIM subsystems.

More data sharing between customers, suppliers, and governments will lead to product model–centered databases that manage multi-company data. The U.S. Defense Department–initiated Computer-Aided Acquisition and Logistics Support (CALS) effort is promoting this capability. The intent is to manage centrally all the common data pertaining to a product over its entire life cycle—from product conception to the final termination and disposal of the product.

Greater intelligence will also be embedded in manufacturing information systems. Changes made to data in any area will automatically ripple through to other parts of the company. For instance, an engineering change to a bolt would automatically alert another engineer responsible for the engineering of the companion part, a nut; the suppliers of raw materials would be notified; product managers incorporating that bolt in their products would be alerted to the proposed change; etc. Currently, such coordination and administration is relegated to humans who move far more slowly and less accurately than a computer-driven management system.

Totally automatic "lights-out" factories are not going to predominate within this century. More probable are a growing number of "hands-off" factories that are maintained by a few highly skilled technicians. These individuals will monitor and control the plant through an intelligent, integrated computer network. Indeed, as the plant equipment becomes more integrated, the entire plant will function essentially as one large computer system, with all the manufacturing devices serving as peripherals.

References

1985. Rembold, U., Blume, C, and Dillmann, R. *Computer-Integrated Manufacturing Technology and Systems*. New York: Marcel Dekker.

1985. Savage, C. *A Program Guide for CIM Implementation*. Dearborn, MI: The Computer and Automated Systems Association of the Society of Manufacturing Engineers.

1986. Noble, D. *Forces of Production. A Social History of Industrial Automation*. New York: Oxford University Press.

1987. Jurgen, R. (ed.) *Computers and Manufacturing Productivity*.

New York: The Institute of Electrical and Electronics Engineers.

1987. Gunn, T. *Manufacturing for Competitive Advantage*. Cambridge, MA: Ballinger (Harper and Row).

1990. Piszczalski, M. *Data Management in the Manufacturing Enterprise*. Boston: The Yankee Group.

MARTIN PISZCZALSKI

COMPUTER LITERACY

For articles on related subjects *see* COMPUTING IN SOCIETY; and HUMAN FACTORS IN COMPUTING.

A *computer literate* person is one who has acquired the skills needed to use computers effectively. More important, the computer literate person is comfortable in the computer age. Technical expertise is not required. Familiarity, experience, and understanding create comfort.

Computer literacy has four characteristics:

1. The ability to use the computer as a tool for problem solving.
2. An understanding of what computers can and cannot do (the function of hardware and software).
3. Non-technical experience with computer software.
4. The ability to evaluate the societal impact of computers.

When the only effective way to use a computer was to program it yourself, programming knowledge was considered an integral part of computer literacy. With today's vast array of off-the-shelf software products, such knowledge is unnecessary. For many students, learning to program is a negative experience. They feel ill-equipped to handle this task due to a poor background in mathematics, and, as a result, they have only limited success that translates into a fear of computers.

An understanding of and experience in using readily available software is just as important as knowing how to program. The computer literate person should have experience with computer software tools for writing, communicating, and processing information. While a knowledge of programming might be useful in these endeavors, it is by no means a requirement.

Most people become computer literate through courses in schools, colleges, and community centers; however, such formal training is not required. Many individuals choose to learn on their own. They study the documentation that accompanies the machine and the software they have access to, and learn by experimentation. More and more, our youngsters amass considerable knowledge in just this way and, for all intents and purposes, are computer literate by the time they leave grammar school.

Reference

1992. Kershner, H. G. *Computer Literacy* (2nd Ed.). Lexington, MA: D. C. Heath.

HELENE G. KERSHNER

COMPUTER-MANAGED INSTRUCTION (CMI)

For articles on related subjects *see* COMPUTER-ASSISTED INSTRUCTION; COMPUTER-ASSISTED LEARNING and TEACHING; and NETWORKS FOR LEARNING.

Computer-managed instruction (CMI) refers to the use of computer assistance in testing, diagnosing, prescribing, grading, and record keeping. Some writers prefer "computer-aided management of instruction" in order to emphasize computer assistance *to* the human teacher or counselor, in contrast with management *by* the computer.

Computer assistance has been made available in many ways to those managing instruction, including aids for students managing their own instruction. The teacher of a large class finds assistance in scoring tests, keeping records, checking on which students need what kind of work, and computing grades. A manager of a self-instruction group uses the computer to obtain summary records showing where each student stands. A student or teacher may call upon the computer files and procedures to generate a test at random but according to set rules. The procedure may select from an item pool and plug in variations on standard question forms to obtain the specific test items so that they appear fresh each time. Computer-based information systems are used by students and teachers to locate instructional materials in various media according to needs, interests, and the limitations of course time and instructional budget.

Major projects using the computer for assistance in the management of instruction are based on a large amount of curricular materials, probably in modular form, and a convenient testing and record-handling system. The arguments for CMI instead of CAI include: lower cost of operation, since students spend less time at computer stations; more flexibility in learning formats, since students are referred to materials in a variety of media and learning settings apart from the computer; lower cost of development, since existing materials can be used for instruction. CMI and CAI may be used together; the management aids associated with CMI can refer the student to selected exercises that are presented by the computer (CAI) as well as to many others that do not benefit from presentation in the computer medium.

References

1985. Coburn, Peter *et al. Practical Guide to Computers in Education*. Reading, MA: Addison-Wesley.

1987. Bluhm, Harry P. *Administrative Uses of Computers in the Schools*. Englewood Cliffs, NJ: Prentice-Hall.

KARL L. ZINN

COMPUTER MUSIC

For articles on related subjects *see* COMPUTER ART; ENTERTAINMENT INDUSTRY, COMPUTERS IN THE; HUMANITIES APPLICATIONS; and SPEECH RECOGNITION AND SYNTHESIS.

Historically, the first application of computers to music resulted in compositions such as Hiller and Isaacson's famous 1957 *Illiac Suite* for string quartet. Shortly thereafter, Max Mathews and his colleagues at Bell Laboratories introduced the first programs for digital sound synthesis. Today, computers participate in all aspects of music making, including composition, live performance processing, score printing, sound production, studio editing of performance data and digitized audio signals, and sound reproduction.

Digital Sound Synthesis The foundation of computer sound synthesis is the technology of analog-to-digital (A/D) and digital-to-analog (D/A) conversion (*q.v.*). This technology transforms a continuous audio signal into a discrete sequence of *samples*. Each sample quantifies the amplitude of the signal at an instant in time. (With the recent introduction of sampling synthesizers, the word *sample* has also come to indicate a short digitized signal; e.g. of a single instrumental tone.) The number of samples per second is known as the *sampling rate*, while the number of bits accorded to one sample is the *quantization*. Both of these factors significantly affect sound quality. The frequencies represented in any digitized signal are limited to half the sampling rate **R**, since samples are required to represent both the "up" and "down" phases of an oscillation. Any attempt to digitize frequencies above this ceiling—including upper harmonics of complex timbres—leads to *foldover* (also called *aliasing*); the out-of-range frequencies are reflected back down below **R**/2. Digitized waveforms also suffer from distortions owing to imprecise quantization. Rudimentary sound synthesis, such as that used in early video games, employs 8-bit quantization at sampling rates around 10 kHz for a maximum frequency barely exceeding the highest pitch on the piano. Quality audio processing employs 16-bit quantization at 48 kHz per channel, which fully accomodates the ear's frequency limit of 20 kHz.

Early computer sound-synthesis environments, such as Max Mathews' MUSIC4 and MUSIC5 programs, implemented software simulations of devices employed in "classical" electronic music studios. Each device was simulated by a re-entrant software module, anticipating by some 20 years an important premise of object-oriented programming (*q.v.*): instantiation. In Mathews' programs and in their contemporary descendents, a control language enables the user to describe a computer music "instrument" as a coupling of signal generators (e.g. oscillators and noise generators) and signal modifiers (e.g. mixers, amplifiers, filters, and reverberators). Digital *oscillators* store a single cycle of a waveform in a digitized table; they produce different fundmental frequencies by stepping through this table at variable rates. *White noise* is simulated by generating random values for each sample; *low-pass noise* is simulated by interpolating linearly between random values chosen at a specified rate. Digital *mixers* simply add source samples together, while digital *amplifiers* multiply each source sample by a gain factor. Such a gain factor might typically be supplied by an *envelope generator*, which computes attack, decay, sustain, and release contours by interpolating between specified magnitudes over specified intervals of time. Digital *filtering* is implemented using second-order recursive difference equations (i.e. equations of the form $O[n]= aI[n]+bO[n-1]+cO[n-2]$); the very gradual roll-off resulting from these difference equations gives better simulations of formant resonances (see next paragraph) than it does of analog *band-pass* filtering. Digital *reverberation* (or *echo*, depending on the response time) is accomplished by diverting samples through a *delay line* and feeding them back into the signal. A t-second delay line is a queue of $N=t\mathbf{R}$ samples; each transit through the delay line yields one echo. Although digital reverberators were described by Schroeder in 1962, they did not begin to be incorporated into sound-synthesis packages until the mid-1970s.

Acousticians most commonly describe instrumental tone production in terms of an active *source* phase coupled to a passive *transfer* phase, and the source-transfer model provides the foundation for many sound-synthesis strategies. The source phase describes how energy is introduced into the vibrating system. Sometimes, the source is pitched, as in the glottal vibrations for the human voice or the buzzing of lips into a trumpet mouthpiece; sometimes the source is unpitched, as in the rasping of a bow against a violin string. The transfer phase accomodates the various resonances present in the system. *Harmonic* resonators, such as strings and tubes, nurture specific source overtones, thus producing clear-pitched tones. *Formant* resonators, such as the cavities of the vocal tract or the sounding body of a stringed instrument, nurture (or suppress, in *off-line* resonators, such as the nasal cavities) wider frequency bands.

The source-transfer model of tone production is sometimes known in the electronic music world as "subtractive synthesis," since the transfer phase tends to eliminate frequency components from a rich source spectrum. Early attempts to simulate natural string tones digitally coupled an oscillator, simulating the vibrating string, with several formant filters, simulating the resonances of the sounding body. In 1970, Winham and Steiglitz generated pulse waves with equal-amplitude harmonics, based upon the trigonometric identity

$$1 + 2(\cos x + \cos 2x + ... + \cos Nx) = \frac{\sin[(2N+1)(x/2)]}{\sin(x/2)}.$$

This method provided a truly neutral, foldover-proof source whose ultimate character could be shaped entirely by filtering. The feedback intrinsic to digital filtering often leads to unpredictable shifts in amplitude, especially when several narrow-bandwidth resonances are cascaded, but these amplitude shifts can be "normalized" out by dividing the signal's average power (derived by smoothing squared sample values with a low-pass filter, then calculating the square root) back into the signal. One of the more dramatic applications of the source-transfer model is the synthesis algorithm described in 1983 by Karplus and Strong; this algorithm exploits the analogy between digital delay lines and harmonic resonators such as strings and tubes.

Fourier theory suggests an alternative way of generating instrumental timbres, known among electronic musicians as *additive synthesis*. In this approach, each harmonic of a pitched tone is generated with its own independent envelope. Full-blown additive synthesis generates extremely realistic tones, but it is computationally intensive, and it provides few "handles" for timbral manipulation.

Analog-to-digital convertors provide the option of incorporating "real-world" sources into computer music compositions. The most straightforward approach—direct sampling—treats a source signal very much like a digital oscillator with an extremely long waveform. Theoretically, direct sampling has been possible from the earliest days of computer sound synthesis, but it became practical only with the introduction of large-memory computers. Source signals may be reduced and reconstituted using Fourier methods; however, most of the requirements that once led computer musicians to consider Fourier methods can now be satisfied much more efficiently by direct sampling. A more subtle way of reducing real-world sources is *linear predictive coding* (LPC), which effectively strips the pitch information from a signal, leaving only the timbre. LPC simulates the effect of a phase vocoder by using a digitized signal to "predict" a set of coefficients for an N-pole filter (an Nth-degree recursive difference equation). By analyzing segments of short duration (say 50 msec), one can extract evolving formant information from a rich source signal, such as a whispered poem. In a process sometimes referred to as *cross synthesis*, this extracted formant information may subsequently be used to make an instrumental source, such as a string orchestra "sing" the poem.

Several synthesis methods bypass psychophysical models of tone production, but nonetheless yield complex, evolving timbres. The most famous is Chowning's method of synthesis by *frequency modulation*, based on the happy coincidence that when sinusoidal carrier and modulating waves are tuned in small-integer ratios, the resulting sound will itself have a harmonic spectrum whose bandwidth varies roughly with the index of modulation. Another method, Kaegi's *vosim* system (for VOice SIMulator), exploits graphic and aural similarities between sine-squared waveforms and the waveforms generated by the human vocal tract. A third method is called *nonlinear processing* or *waveshaping*; this method extends the principle of "clipping" on an overdriven amplifier.

Since the late 1970s, mainframe programs like MUSIC4 have gradually given way to real-time digital synthesis systems. These real-time systems implement oscillators, adders, multipliers, etc., using dedicated processors or specialized digital-signal-processing (DSP) chips. All commercial synthesizers on the market today use digital technology.

The Midi Studio MIDI, or musical instrument digital interface, was established by the synthesizer industry during the mid 1980s. Initially conceived as a set of industry standards for communicating performance data between synthesizers, MIDI was quickly exploited as a means of bringing synthesizers under computer control. The key to this control has been the *MIDI sequencer*, software that enables musicians to record, play back, splice, overdub, and otherwise manipulate performance data. The MIDI sequencer does more than co-opt tasks that formerly could be undertaken using only expensive multitrack recorders. With a MIDI sequencer, one can, for example, selectively change tempo without affecting transposition and vice versa.

Among other things, MIDI established a simple but versatile encoding system for performance gestures. Central to this is the notion of the MIDI channel, the digital equivalent of a keyboard on a multi-keyboard pipe organ. Notes are initiated by *key down* commands, indicating channel, chromatic pitch, and velocity (loudness); the note sustains until the synthesizer receives a *key up* command with a matching channel and pitch. (The original MIDI specification did not concern itself with timing; however, the introduction of MIDI sequencers quickly led to supplementary negotiations among the industry so that recorded performances could be saved in a standard file format.) Also included among MIDI's repertoire of commands are the *program change*—equivalent to a stop change on an organ—a *control* command, used for sending specialized information, such as relative speaker balances, and two *continuous* commands: *pitch bend* and *channel pressure*. The latter two commands permit MIDI to transcend its keyboard origins, to some extent.

Supplementing MIDI sequencers in computer music studios are graphic score-editing programs. With today's commercial score editors, a musician can enter score data in a variety of modes, ranging from note-by-note descriptions to automatic transcription of MIDI performance data. The quality of the graphic output is competitive with scores produced by traditional engraving, with much less time investment. Additionally, the fact that all of the score data is retained in disk files means that parts can be extracted automatically and also that revisions can be easily effected. As of this writing, the only serious drawback with graphic score editors is the automated performance of score data. Score editors still do not have sufficient expertise to fill in nuances of articulation that human performers insert instinctively.

A trend that has generated much enthusiasm is the real-time processing of MIDI performance data. Performance-processing software builds upon the postwar idea of an "open score," in which details of a composition are filled in anew with each performance. In a program such as Spiegel's MUSIC MOUSE, complex passages generated by the computer are predicated entirely upon simple actions taken by a performer. Other programs, such as M and JAM FACTORY by Zicarelli, *et al*, permit the computer to undertake random choices conditioned by statistical tendencies deduced through analysis of captured MIDI sequences. (The same techniques had been used earlier in automated composing programs (see below). What is significant here is the real-time implementation.) Still other programs, such as Levitt's HOOKUP and Puckette's

PATCHER, assume no specific generative paradigm; rather, they provide repertoires of fundamental performance-processing units within an iconic programming environment (see OBJECT-ORIENTED PROGRAMMING). The environment permits users to link units together, however they see fit.

Automated Composition and Analysis

Despite a tradition of rigorous (and often explicitly mathematical) musical theory dating back to antiquity, the idea of delegating compositional decisions to a machine remains controversial, even among computer music professionals.

The first generation of composing programs, produced during the 1960s by composer/programmers such as Hiller, Tenney, and Brun in the U. S. and Barbaud, Xenakis, and Koenig in Europe, emphasized two general approaches: (1) *serialism*, in which basic motifs are subjected to a variety of systematic manipulations (e.g. inversion, retrograde, transposition, and rotation), and (2) *random selection*, including ball-and-urn–type statistical procedures and Markov-style conditional probability.

The introduction of online computer systems early in the 1970s inspired hybrid computer-synthesizer environments, such as Mathews and Moore's GROOVE, Truax's POD, and Buxton's SSSP. Such hybrid facilities greatly enhanced the rate of interaction between musicians and computers, permitting composers to evaluate a composition aurally at each stage in its genesis. Serialism and randomness were augmented by interactive score-processing and score-editing tools—the direct forerunners of today's MIDI sequencers and graphic score editors.

During the late 1970s, computer composers began looking for new ways to generate material automatically. One of the first alternatives to first-generation serialism and randomness was *top-down recursion*. Recursive concepts of musical structure had been advocated by musical theorists (e.g. Lorenz and Schenker) since the early twentieth century, and this internal tradition received added impetus from three external influences: Chomsky's formal grammars (applied to composition by Smoliar, Roads, Holtzman, Jones, and Langston), Gestalt psychology (applied by Tenney and by Ames), and fractal geometry (applied by Wuorinen, Austin, Vaggione, and Dodge) (see FRACTALS).

The ball-and-urn procedures employed by first-generation programs treated *randomness* and *distributions* as dual consequences of a single paradigm, when, in fact, statistical distributions are equally characteristic of non-random phenomena. Musically, randomness and distribution address entirely different concerns: randomness affects a listener's expectations, while distribution affects the listener's sense of compositional balance. The palette of behaviors used to "shape" musical expectations embraces not just conventional random number generation, but also Brownian, 1/f, and chaotic processes. Discrete statistical balances can now be realized deterministically, using Ames's method of *statistical feedback*. Briefly, statistical feedback maintains statistics detailing how much each available option has been used up to the present decision; the most underused options receive the greatest priorities of selection.

In the author's view, the most important innovation for composing programs during the 1980s was the adoption of AI (*see* ARTIFICIAL INTELLIGENCE) search techniques. Instances include Ebcioglu's 1980 program for species counterpoint, the programs for Ames's 1981 composition *Protocol*, Ebcioglu's 1984 chorale harmonization program (which has duplicated Bach's own harmonizations on a few occasions), Hiller and Ames's tune-writing program MIX OR MATCH (exhibited in the U.S. Pavilion at Expo '85), Thomas's 1985 VIVACE, Schwanauer's 1986 MUSE, and Ames's 1987 CYBERNETIC COMPOSER. Such programs make a significant leap by formalizing not just compositional procedures, but also the principles underlying these procedures. Such principles can be expressed either as constraints (e.g. downward resolutions of dissonances are traditionally mandatory) or heuristics (e.g. upward resolutions of traditional leading tones are not mandatory, but still desirable). Only AI composing programs are capable of prioritizing options; only AI composing programs can consider alternative solutions, should their decision making lead them into an impasse.

Much effort has also been directed toward formulating generalized utilities that facilitate implementation of automated compositional processes. Examples include Polansky, Rosenboom, and Burk's 1985 HMSL, Pope's 1986 DOUBLETALK, Desain and Honig's 1988 LOCO, Ames's 1989 COMPOSE, Camurri, Canepa, Frixione, and Zaccaria's 1990 HARP, in addition to the previously mentioned HOOKUP and PATCHER. Many of these utilities are object-oriented. In effect, they do for composition or performance what MUSIC4 and its descendents did for sound synthesis: they provide a repertory of instantiable units, each designed to perform one basic compositional task (e.g. note creation, note-parameter generation, score splicing, layering, transposition), along with standard communication protocols so that units can be freely linked into elaborate music-processing networks. Some writers cite utilities such as these as instances of musical AI, but the utilities implemented to date do not accommodate search-based strategies.

Automated musical analysis has been pursued, both as a rigorous way of verifying speculations by musical theorists and as a means of acquiring "real-world" expertise for composing programs. The most outstanding of the analysis-only programs include the harmony analysis programs of Winograd and Maxwell. Winograd's 1968 EXPLAIN parses block-chord harmonies in order to discern key schemes; Maxwell's 1988 program extends this capability to freely contrapuntal music. Both programs use searches to seek out "better" key interpretations. Efforts have also been made to parse melodic phrase structures automatically. A 1980 program by Tenney and Polansky employs a "perceptual distance metric," while Scarborough, Jones, and Miller's 1988 program applies discrete note-grouping rules. Attempts to analyze music by means of neural nets have to date yielded much less reliable conclusions than rote, rule-based, or heuristic (*q.v.*) approaches.

The five "Strophe" movements of Hiller and Baker's 1963 *Computer Cantata* were generated as Markov chains, using transition probabilities acquired through statistical analysis of a composition by Ives, and much the same approach underlies Zicarelli's 1986 JAM FACTORY. Cope's 1987 EMI scans musical input for musical patterns, which EMI compiles into an augmented transition network; the accumulated knowledge base can then be used to generate new compositions in the "same" style. Although its stylistic matches are not yet entirely convincing, EMI's sensitivity to formal structure gives Cope's synthetic examples a long-term coherence that has been entirely lacking in older Markovian approaches.

References

Journals

Computer Music Journal. Cambridge, MA: M.I.T. Press Journals. The primary source for articles on computer music.
INTERFACE: Journal of New Music Research. Lisse, The Netherlands: Swets Publishing Service. Emphasizes computer applications to composition and analysis. Articles are typically more detailed than in *CMJ.*

Books and Articles

1969. Mathews, M. V., *et al. The Technology of Computer Music.* Cambridge, MA: MIT Press. The classic book on digital sound synthesis, still valuable for its discussion of basic principles.
1983. International MIDI Association. *MIDI: Musical Instrument Digital Interface Specification 1.0.* North Hollywood, CA.
1985. Dodge, C., and Jerse, T. *Computer Music: Synthesis, Composition, and Performance.* New York: Schirmer's.
1987. Ames, C. "Automated Composition in Retrospect: 1956–1986." *LEONARDO: Journal of the International Society for Science, Technology, and the Arts* 20(2):169.
1989. Mathews, M. V., and Pierce, J. R., (ed.) *Current Directions in Computer Music Research.* Cambridge, MA: M.I.T. Press.
1991. Balaban, M., Ebcioglu, K., and Laske, O. (Ed.) *Musical Intelligence.* Palo Alto, CA: AAI Press.

CHARLES AMES

COMPUTER NETWORK. See LOCAL AREA NETWORK; METROPOLITAN AREA NETWORK; and NETWORKS, COMPUTER.

COMPUTING RESEARCH ASSOCIATION (CRA)

For articles on related subjects *see* ASSOCIATION FOR COMPUTING MACHINERY; COMPUTER SCIENCE; COMPUTER SCIENCE, ACADEMIC; EDUCATION IN COMPUTER ENGINEERING; and EDUCATION IN COMPUTER SCIENCE.

The purpose of the CRA is to represent the interests of computing research (i.e. computer science and engineering and computational science) in North America. The CRA is responsible for the annual Taulbee surveys of Ph.D.-granting computer science departments and other data collection projects studying the state of the field. It publishes *Computing Research News*, which is distributed to nearly 8,000 researchers and policy makers around the world. CRA also organizes the biannual Snowbird conference of department chairs, sponsors workshops and seminars on research priorities and trends, and maintains contact with government policy-making groups.

CRA members are academic departments and industrial laboratories that conduct research in computing-related fields. The ACM and AAAI are affiliate members. CRA is administered by a board of directors, most of whom are elected by member departments and laboratories. The ACM has two appointed members. CRA maintains a professionally staffed permanent office in Washington, D.C.

The CRA grew out of the Computer Science Board, an informal group of chairs of computer science departments that formed in 1972 and organized the first Computer Science Conference, which is now the annual national conference of the ACM.

For further information, write to the Computing Research Association, Suite 110, 1625 Massachusetts Avenue, N.W., Washington, DC 20036-2212.

FRED W. WEINGARTEN

COMPUTER SCIENCE

For articles on related subjects *see* ALGORITHMS, ANALYSIS OF; ARTIFICIAL INTELLIGENCE; AUTOMATA THEORY; COMPUTER ALGEBRA; COMPUTER ARCHITECTURE; COMPUTER ENGINEERING; COMPUTER GRAPHICS; COMPUTER SYSTEM; COMPILER CONSTRUCTION; COMPUTATIONAL COMPLEXITY; CONCURRENT PROGRAMMING; DATA STRUCTURES; DATABASE MANAGEMENT SYSTEM; EDUCATION IN COMPUTER SCIENCE; FORMAL LANGUAGES; IMAGE PROCESSING; INFORMATION PROCESSING; INFORMATION RETRIEVAL; INFORMATION SCIENCE; LIST PROCESSING; NUMERICAL ANALYSIS; OPERATING SYSTEMS; PARALLEL PROCESSING; PROGRAMMING LANGUAGES; SIMULATION; and SOFTWARE ENGINEERING.

OVERALL SCOPE

Computer science is concerned with information processes, with the information structures and procedures that enter into representation of such processes, and with their implementation in information processing systems. It is also concerned with relationships between information processes and classes of tasks that give rise to them.

The Domain of Computer Science   Even though the domain of discourse in computer science includes both human-made and natural information processes, the main effort in the discipline is now directed to *human-made* processes and to information processing systems that are designed to achieve desired goals (i.e. machines). The reason lies in the phenomenal growth of the computer field, its rapid penetration into almost all aspects of contemporary life, the resulting pressure to bring some order into what is being done in the field, and the need to educate the people behind the computing machines and to provide intellectual guidance for new developments in computer design and applications. Thus, the bulk of empirical material currently available to computer science consists of systems, processes, and operational experience that grew in the computer field during the past four decades. Clearly, the empirical corpus in the science is not stationary. It is growing with new developments in the computer field. Some of these developments are themselves stimulated by the ongoing activities in computer science.

The main objects of study in computer science are digital computers and the phenomena surrounding them. Work in the discipline is focused on the structure and operation of computer systems, on the principles that underlie their design and programming, on effective methods for their use in different classes of information processing tasks, and on theoretical characterizations of their properties and limitations. Also, a substantial effort is directed into explorations and experimentation with new computer systems and with new domains of intellectual activity where computers can be applied.

The central role of the digital computer in the discipline is due to its near universality as an information processing machine. With enough memory capacity, a digital computer provides the basis for modeling any information processing system, provided the task to be performed by the system can be specified in some rigorous manner. If its specification is possible, the task can be represented in the form of a program that can be stored in computer memory. Thus, the stored program digital computer enables us to represent conveniently and implement (run) any information process. It provides a methodologically adequate, as well as realistic, basis for the exploration and study of a great variety of concepts, schemes, and techniques of information processing.

There exist, in nature, information processes that are of great interest to computer science (e.g., perceptual and cognitive processes in humans, and cellular processes that are controlled by genetic information). An understanding of these processes is intrinsically important, and it promises to enrich the pool of basic concepts and schemes that are available to computer science. In turn, application of the current approaches and techniques of the discipline to cognitive psychology and to bioscience promises to result in important insights into natural information processes. To date, most of the work on these processes has proceeded either by modeling them on digital computers and studying these models experimentally, or by using existing theoretical models in computer science (e.g. in automata theory) for the analysis of certain properties of these processes. There is still little contribution from the study of natural information systems to the design and use of computing machines, or to the development of theoretical concepts in computer science.

Scope and Nature of Activities in Computer Science

The subject matter of computer science can be broadly divided into two parts. The first part covers information processing tasks, procedures for handling them, and a variety of related representations. The second part is mainly concerned with a variety of structures, mechanisms, and schemes for processing information. From the point of view of the practitioner in the computer field, the first part corresponds to computer applications, and the second corresponds to computer systems. There are significant connections between the two parts. Indeed, it is a major goal of computer science to elucidate the relationships between application areas and computer systems.

Computer applications can be broadly subdivided into *numerical* applications and *non-numerical* applications. Work in numerical applications is mainly oriented toward problems and procedures where numerical data are dominant, such as problems in the areas of numerical analysis, optimization, and simulation. These areas are important branches of computer science. Work in non-numerical applications is primarily concerned with processes involving non-numerical data, such as representations of problems, programs, symbolic expressions, language, relational structures, and graphic objects. Branches of computer science with major activities in non-numerical applications are artifical intelligence, information storage and retrieval, combinatorial processes, language processing, symbol manipulation, graphics, and image processing.

Computer systems can be partitioned into *software* systems and *hardware* systems. The emphasis of work in software systems is on machine-level representations of programs and associated data, on schemes for controlling program execution, and on programs for handling computer languages and for managing computer operations. Branches of computer science with major concern in software systems are programming languages and processors, operating systems and utility programs, and programming techniques. Computer architecture is concerned with software systems as well as with hardware systems. Other major branches of computer science with a main focus on hardware systems are machine organization and logical design.

Generally, applications-oriented activities in computer science are also concerned with related systems problems (e.g. with high-level languages and their computer implementation). Similarly, systems-oriented activities are also concerned with the task environments (e.g. classes of applications and modes of human-machine interaction) in which the systems operate.

We can identify two major types of activities in computer science:

1. Building conceptual frameworks for understanding the available empirical material in the discipline via an active search for unifying principles, general methods, and theories.
2. Exploring new computer systems and applications in the light of new concepts and theories.

The first type of activity is analytic in nature; the second is oriented toward syntheses, experimentation, and probing for new empirical knowledge. A continuous interaction between these activities is essential for a vigorous rate of progress in the discipline. The situation is analogous to the interaction between theoretical and experimental work in any rapidly developing natural science.

At present, the theoretical underpinnings of computer science are at an early stage of development. In some areas, theoretical work is mainly oriented toward bringing elementary order into a rapidly accumulating mass of experience via the introduction of broad conceptual frameworks and analytic methodologies. In a few areas, theoretical work is concentrating on comprehensive analysis of specific classes of phenomena for which formal models exist. Branches of computer science involved in this type of work are the theory of computation, complexity theory, analysis of algorithms, automata theory, theory of formal languages, and switching theory. In general, theoretical work in computer science has been diffused over a large number of fairly narrow phenomena. Much of this work has not yet had an appreciable impact on the complex problems of systems and applications that are encountered in the computer field. There is a growing concern, however, with the development of unifying principles and models that are appropriate for understanding and guiding the major constructive and experimental activities in the field. The work in the area of analysis of algorithms (which includes important approaches to the study of computational complexity) promises to contribute significant theoretical insights into problems that are in the mainstream of the computer field. As computer science continues to grow, theoretical work on the discipline is also likely to grow, not only in relative volume to the other activities in the discipline, but also in relevance to the significant problems in the domain of computer science.

Experimental work in computer science requires extensive use of computers, and it often stimulates new developments in computer design and utilization. Typical experimental activities may involve the development and evaluation of a new computer language or the testing of a procedure for a new class of problem. Theoretical work in the discipline relies on several branches of mathematics and logic. A typical theoretical problem may focus on the characterization of a class of computer procedures (e.g. procedures for sorting data), the analysis of their structure, and the establishment of bounds on the storage space and time that they require for execution. The objects of study in this example are computer procedures and their properties. The theoretical treatment of these objects is conducted within mathematical systems that provide the analytical framework needed to obtain desired insights and specific results. Just as mathematics is used in chemistry (say, to develop theories of certain chemical processes), mathematics and logic are used in computer science to study information processes.

Relationships Between Computer Science and Other Disciplines

The bond between computer science and mathematics is stronger than the normal bond between mathematics and the theoretical component of a science. Computer science and mathematics have a common concern with formalism, symbolic structures, and their properties. Both put emphasis on general methods and problem-solving tools that can be used in a great variety of situations. There are subjects, such as numerical analysis, that are being studied in both disciplines. These are some of the reasons why computer science is widely considered a *mathematical science*.

Computer science is also considered to be an *engineering science*. The structure of a computer system consists of physical components (the hardware) in the form of electronic or electromechanical building blocks for switching, storage, and communication of information, and programs (the software) for managing the operation of the hardware. In the logical design and the system design of a computer system, the designer is concerned with the choice of hardware and software building blocks, and with their local and global organization in the light of given operational goals for the overall system. These design activities have strong points of contact with work in electrical engineering and in the emerging field of software engineering. They are also important subjects of study in computer science.

Every transition from the specification of an information processing task to a system for implementing the task involves a design process. In many cases, these processes are highly complex, and their effectiveness is strongly dependent on the availability of appropriate methodologies and techniques that may be used to guide and support them. This is one of the reasons why computer science is concerned with methodologies of systems analysis and synthesis and with general tools for design. This concern is shared not only with engineering, but also with other decision-oriented disciplines, such as business administration and institutional planning. There is a more fundamental reason for a close coupling between computer science and a science of design. It comes from the concern of computer science with the information processes of problem solving and goal-directed decision making, which are at the core of design. Processes of this type are objects of study in artifical intelligence, a branch of computer science.

Several other disciplines are recognized as having domains of interest that overlap with computer science. One of these is library science. The problems of organizing and managing knowledge and of designing systems for its storage and retrieval (in the form of documents or facts) are shared between computer science and library science (*see* LIBRARY AUTOMATION.). The activities at the interface between these two disciplines are often identified as part of information science. The main concern of information science is with process of communication, storage, management, and utilization of information in large database systems. Thus, the domain of information science is included in the broader domain of computer science.

Another discipline whose domain of interest overlaps with computer science is linguistics, which shares with computer science a concern with language and communication. The study of linguistic processes and of related phenomena of "understanding" establishes a special bond between computer science and psychology. Psychological research in information processing models of cognition, perception, and other mental functions has a substantial overlap with work in computer science.

The study of certain theoretical questions about processes of reasoning by computer (performing deductions, forming hypotheses, using knowledge effectively in problem-solving processes) is beginning to create points of contact between certain parts of philosophy (logic, epistemology, methodology) and computer science (*see* COGNITIVE SCIENCE.).

The development of computer science has been strongly stimulated by demands for the application of computers in a wide variety of new areas. The challenges created by new computer application and the constructive attempts to meet them are important factors in the growth of computer science. The exploratory activity in the discipline, as it interacts with other disciplines in the development of computer applications, results in both a better understanding of the power and limitations of current knowledge in the computer field, and the identification of new problems of information processing that require further study. At a more practical level, the exploratory work on computer applications is contributing to the solution of significant problems in various disciplines that could not be approached without the introduction of computer methods.

There is a large *surface of contact* between computer science and the disciplines where new computer applications are being developed. Virtually all disciplines are involved in this contact. The nature of the contact is similar to the relationship between mathematics and the physical sciences; this relationship involves the representation of scientific problems in mathematical systems wherein the problems can be studied and solved. In the case of computer science, the contact involves the representation of knowledge and problems of a discipline in forms that are acceptable to computers, and the development of computer methods for the effective handling of these problems. Since computers can be made to represent and manipulate problems of enormous variety and complexity, it is likely that the extent of fruitful contact between computer science and other disciplines will be much larger than the contact between mathematics and the disciplines that use mathematics. In particular, it is likely that the role played by computer science in behavioral and social sciences, the professions, and the humanities will be similar to that played by mathematics in the growth of the physical sciences.

An important application for computers that is of special interest to computer science is in the design of more powerful, efficient, and easy-to-use computer systems. The use of computers in the study of computers and in their improvement is a powerful means for gaining the knowledge and insights that computer science seeks at the same time the field is being bootstrapped.

Computer science has two types of interface with other disciplines. The first type is characterized by a *shared concern* with subjects of study that are of intrinsic interest to computer science. Here there is an area of overlap between work in computer science and work in other disciplines. Mathematics and electrical engineering have this type of interface with computer science. To a lesser extent, such an interface exists between computer science and the decision-oriented disciplines (e.g. business administration, institutional planning), library science, linguistics, psychology, and philosophy. The second type of interface includes disciplines in which new computer applications are being explored. The main role of computer science in these activities is *to support* and enhance work in a discipline. Practically all disciplines that involve some kind of intellectual activity have this type of interface with computer science.

Major Areas of Study in Computer Science

The conception, formulation, computer implementation, analysis, and evaluation of procedures (algorithms) for a broad variety of problems constitute a major part of the activities in computer science. Closely associated with these activities are efforts to develop schemes, means, and tools for building and executing procedures, such as languages, major principles for structuring procedures, programming mechanisms, computer architectures, and design aids to facilitate these efforts.

The second part of this article concentrates on the internal structure of the discipline, and on the various types of technical activity in computer science. In what follows, we highlight a few of these internal activities that are being stimulated by challenges from other disciplines, by the recognition of special needs in the use of computing, or by the desire to understand and exploit new technological developments in the field.

Currently, there are a growing number of efforts in various specific domains of computational science and engineering (e.g. computational fluid dynamics, computational genetics, computational algebra) that are offering new challenges to computer science, and they are stimulating the development of new computational methods. Recent developments in parallel computer architectures are generating pressures for the development of computational paradigms and algorithms for handling various problem classes in parallel computing environments (*see* PARALLEL PROCESSING.).

Work in the area of software methodologies and tools deals with methods and principles for the design of programs and software systems that meet specifications, and are safe, reliable and maintainable. In recent years, this work has focused mainly on the development of programming environments and on software evaluation methods. An important goal in this area is to automate (large parts of) the program design process—from the formulation of specifications to the creation of running code. Efforts in this general area are related both to representations of computational processes in various application domains, and also to computer systems. In effect, this area constitutes a bridge between application domains—through software systems—to specific computer architectures.

Current work in the general area of computer architecture deals with such design questions as how to optimize instruction sets for various computational models and workloads. It deals with control mechanisms (and their hardware/software implementation) that allow multiple resources to be coordinated efficiently in the execution of programs. It is concerned with distributed computations and with problems of computer networking. It is also concerned with human-machine interfaces, with related problems of visualization and monitoring, and with various issues of coupling computers with other systems (e.g. robotic effectors, industrial processes). It includes research efforts towards automating the design of computers, and it is strongly related to professional activities in computer system design. Recent efforts in this area have been focusing on the exploration of very high performance computing through parallel computation. There is close coupling between work in this area and the exploration of new physical devices and microstructures (e.g. VLSI circuits) for the efficient implementation of switching, memory, and communication functions in computer systems.

Computer science is a young and rapidly expanding discipline. In a period of less than 30 years, it has succeeded in establishing its distinct identity in universities and laboratories throughout the world. One of its recognized roles is to provide the intellectual guidance needed for the understanding and development of the computer field. Another role, which is likely to grow in significance in the coming years, is to contribute to an understanding of the impact of computers on other disciplines and on society in general.

SAUL AMAREL

DISCIPLINARY STRUCTURE

The computing profession is the aggregate of people and institutions concerned with information processing. The profession contains various specialties such as computer science, computer engineering, software engineering, domain-specific applications, computer system designers, and systems architecture. These diverse specialities share a common base of knowledge, which is called the *core* of computing. The *discipline of computing* consists of the core plus the standard practices, questions, controversies, and speculations used by computing professionals in their work.

The discipline of computing is usually characterized as the systematic study of algorithmic processes that describe and transform information: their theory, analysis, design, efficiency, implementation, and application. The fundamental question underlying all of computing is, "What can be (efficiently) automated?" This discipline was born in the early 1940s with the joining together of algorithm theory, mathematical logic, and the invention of the stored-program electronic computer (*see* STORED PROGRAM CONCEPT).

This common characterization is too narrow to capture the full richness of the discipline. It does not call attention to the connections between specific elements of knowledge and the concerns of people to whom these elements contribute, notably the concerns for reliability, dependability, robustness, integrity, security, and modifiability of computer systems. It hides the social and historical context of the field, and the values of the people who practice in it.

Part one of this article examines the larger context of applications, technology, research, and society in which the discipline of computing is situated. What follows is a discussion of the major technical components of the discipline.

Paradigms Work in the discipline of computing tends to be conducted within one of three major paradigms:

1. Theory—Building conceptual frameworks and notations for understanding relationships among objects in a domain and the logical consequences of axioms and laws.
2. Experimentation—Exploring new systems and architectures and models within given application domains and in the light of new concepts and theories. (This paradigm is sometimes called *abstraction* or *modeling*.)
3. Design—Constructing computer systems that support work in given organizations or application domains.

These three paradigms come from the historical roots of the discipline of computing. Theory comes from applied mathematics; experimentation comes from the scientific method; design comes from engineering. All three are important. Continuous interaction between people in the three paradigms is important for vigorous progress in the discipline. Many controversies in the field are associated with someone in one paradigm criticizing the work of someone in another without being aware of the difference.

The theory paradigm consists of the four broad steps that should be followed in order to develop a coherent, valid theory:

- Characterize objects of study (definition).
- Hypothesize possible relationships among them (theorem).
- Determine whether the relationships are true (proof).
- Interpret results.

A mathematician expects to iterate these steps when, for example, errors or inconsistencies are discovered. In many areas of computing, theory has been used primarily to bring order into a rapid accumulation of experience, and in some it has produced new methods and models that have been used to improve practice.

The experimentation paradigm consists of four broad steps that are followed in the interpretation of a phenomenon:

- Form a hypothesis.
- Construct a model and make a prediction.
- Design an experiment and collect data.
- Analyze results.

A scientist expects to iterate these steps when, for example, a model's prediction disagrees with experimental evidence. This paradigm is most conspicuous in the interactions with other scientific disciplines (computational science), in performance evaluation of computers and networks, and in testing heuristics (*q.v.*). It nonetheless appears in all areas of computing.

The design paradigm consists of four broad steps followed in the construction of a system (or device) to solve a given problem:

- State requirements.
- State specifications.
- Design and implement the system.
- Test the system.

An engineer expects to iterate these steps when, for example, tests reveal that the latest version of the system does not satisfactorily meet the requirements. Design can be seen in all areas of computing.

The Internal Structure of Computer Science

The roots of computing extend deeply into mathematics and engineering. Mathematics imparts analysis to the field; engineering imparts design. The discipline embraces its own theory, experimental method, and engineering. This contrasts with most physical sciences, which are separate from the engineering disciplines that apply their findings as is the case, for example, in the distinctively different fields of chemistry and chemical engineering. The science and engineering of computing are inseparable because of the fundamental interplay between the scientific and engineering paradigms within the discipline.

For several thousand years, calculation has been a principal concern of mathematics. Many models of physical phenomena have been used to derive equations whose solutions yield predictions of those phenomena—for example, calculations of orbital trajectories, weather forecasts, and fluid flows (*see* SCIENTIFIC APPLICATIONS). Many general methods for solving such equations have been devised, among them, for example, algorithms for systems of linear equations, differential equations, and integrating functions. For almost the same period, calculations that aid in the design of mechanical systems have been a principal concern of engineering. Examples include algorithms for evaluating stresses in static objects, calculating momenta of moving objects, and measuring distances much larger or smaller than our immediate perception.

One product of the long interaction between engineering and mathematics has been mechanical aids for calculating. Some surveyors' and navigators' instruments date back a thousand years. Pascal and Leibniz built arithmetic calculators in the middle 1600s (*see* CALCULATING MACHINES). In the 1830s, Babbage conceived of an *analytical engine* (*q.v.*) that could mechanically and without error evaluate logarithms, trigonometric functions, and other general arithmetic functions. His machine, though never completed, served as an inspiration for later work. In the 1920s, Bush constructed a *differential analyzer*

(*q.v.*), an electronic analog computer for solving general systems of differential equations. In the same period, electromechanical calculating machines capable of addition, subtraction, multiplication, division, and square root became available. The electronic flip-flop provided a natural bridge from these machines to digital versions with no moving parts.

Logic is a branch of mathematics concerned with criteria of validity of inference and formal principles of reasoning. Since the days of Euclid, it has been a tool for rigorous mathematical and scientific argument. In the nineteenth century, there began a search for a universal system of logic that would be free of the incompletenesses observed in known deductive systems. In a complete system, it would be possible to determine mechanically whether any given statement is either true or false. In 1931, however, Kurt Gödel published his *incompleteness theorem*, showing that there is no such system. In the late 1930s, Turing explored the idea of a universal computer that could simulate any step-by-step procedure of any other computing machine (*see* TURING MACHINE). He discovered a result similar to Gödel's: some well-defined problems cannot be solved by any mechanical procedure. The importance of logic was not only its deep insight into the limits of automatic calculation, but also its insight that strings of symbols, perhaps encoded as numbers, can be interpreted both as data and as programs.

This insight is the key idea that distinguishes the stored program computer from calculating machines. The steps of the algorithm are encoded in a machine representation and stored in the memory for later decoding and execution by the processor. The machine code can be derived mechanically from a higher-level symbolic form, the programming language.

It is the explicit and intricate intertwining of the ancient threads of calculation and logical symbol manipulation, together with the modern threads of electronics and electronic representation of information, that gave birth to the discipline of computing.

Computing has grown from infancy in the 1940s to a broad discipline in the 1990s. Table 1 divides the field into nine subareas. Each of the subareas has an underlying unity of subject matter, a substantial theoretical component, significant experimental methods, and substantial design and implementation issues. Significant industries and institutions have been established in each of these areas.

TABLE 1. Nine Subareas of Computing

1 Algorithms and data structures
2 Programming languages
3 Computer architecture
4 Numerical and symbolic computation
5 Operating systems
6 Software engineering
7 Databases and information retrieval
8 Artificial intelligence and robotics
9 Human-computer communication

Theory deals with the underlying mathematical development of the subarea and includes supporting theory such as graph theory (*q.v.*), combinatorics (*q.v.*) and formal languages (*q.v.*). Experimentation deals with models of potential implementations; the models are abstractions that suppress detail, while retaining essential features, and provide means for predicting future behavior. *Design* deals with the process of specifying a problem, deriving requirements and specifications, iterating and testing prototypes, and system implementation. Design includes the experimental method, which in computing includes measurement of programs and systems, validation of hypotheses, and prototyping to extend abstractions into practice.

Although software methodology is essentially concerned with design, it contains substantial elements of theory and abstraction. For this reason, we have identified it as a subarea. On the other hand, parallel processing (*q.v.*) and distributed computing (*q.v.*) are issues that pervade all subareas and all of their components (theory, abstraction, and design); accordingly, they have been identified neither as subareas nor as subarea components.

What follows is a summary of the principal questions and concerns dealt with in each of the nine subareas.

1. **Algorithms and data structures (*q.v.*)**
   This area deals with specific classes of problems and their efficient solutions. Fundamental questions include: For given classes of problems, what are the best algorithms? How much storage and time do they require? What is the trade-off between space and time? What is the best way to access the data? What is the worst case of the best algorithms? How well do algorithms behave on average? How general are algorithms—i.e. what classes of problems can be dealt with by similar methods?

2. **Programming languages (*q.v.*)**
   This area deals with notations for virtual machines that execute algorithms, with notations for algorithms and data, and with efficient translations from high-level languages into machine codes. Fundamental questions include: What are possible organizations of the virtual machine presented by the language (data types, operations, control structures, mechanisms for introducing new types and operations)? How are these abstractions implemented on computers? What notation (syntax) can be used effectively and efficiently to specify what the computer should do?

3. **Computer architecture (*q.v.*)**
   This area deals with methods of organizing hardware (and associated software) into efficient, reliable systems. Fundamental questions include: What are good methods of implementing processors, memory, and communication in a machine?

What constitutes an efficient machine instruction set? How do we design and control large computational systems and convincingly demonstrate that they work as intended despite errors and failures? What types of architectures can efficiently incorporate many processing elements that can work concurrently on a computation? How do we measure performance?

4. **Numerical and symbolic computation** (*see* NUMERICAL ANALYSIS and COMPUTER ALGEBRA).
   This area deals with general methods for efficiently and accurately solving equations resulting from mathematical models of systems. Fundamental questions include: How can we accurately approximate continuous or infinite processes by finite discrete processes? How do we cope with the errors arising from these approximations? How rapidly can a given class of equations be solved for a given level of accuracy? How can symbolic manipulations on equations, such as integration, differentiation, and reduction to minimal terms be carried out? How can the answers to these questions be incorporated into efficient, reliable, high-quality mathematical software packages?

5. **Operating systems (*q.v.*)**
   This area deals with control mechanisms that allow multiple resources to be efficiently coordinated in the execution of programs. Fundamental questions include: At each time scale in the operation of a computer system, what are the visible objects and permissible operations on them? For each class of resource (objects visible at some level), what is a minimal set of operations that permit their effective use? How can interfaces be organized so that users deal only with abstract versions of resources and not with physical details of hardware? What are effective control strategies for job scheduling, memory management, communications, access to software resources, communication among concurrent tasks, reliability, and security? What are the principles by which systems can be extended in function by repeated application of a small number of construction rules? How should distributed computations be organized so that many autonomous machines connected by a communication network can participate in a computation, with the details of network protocols, host locations, bandwidths, and resource naming being mostly invisible?

6. **Software engineering (*q.v.*)**
   This area deals with the design of programs and large software systems that meet specifications and are safe, secure, reliable, and dependable. Fundamental questions include: What are the principles behind the development of programs

and programming systems? How does one prove that a program or system meets its specifications? How does one develop specifications that do not omit important cases and can be analyzed for safety? How do software systems evolve through different generations? How can software be designed for understandability and modifiability?

7. **Database management systems (DBMS - *q.v.*) and information retrieval (*q.v.*)**
This area deals with the organization of large sets of persistent, shared data for efficient query and update. Fundamental questions include: What modeling concepts should be used to represent data elements and their relationships? How can basic operations such as store, locate, match, and retrieve be combined into effective transactions? How can these transactions interact effectively with the user? How can high-level queries be translated into high-performance programs? What machine architectures lead to efficient retrieval and update? How can data be protected against unauthorized access, disclosure, or destruction? How can large databases be protected from inconsistencies due to simultaneous update? How can protection and performance be achieved when the data are distributed among many machines? How can text be indexed and classified for efficient retrieval?

8. **Artificial intelligence (AI - *q.v.*) and robotics (*q.v.*)**
This area deals with the modeling of animal and human (intelligent) behavior. Fundamental questions include: What are basic models of behavior and how do we build machines that simulate them? To what extent is intelligence described by rule evaluation, inference, deduction, and pattern computation? What is the ultimate performance of machines that simulate behavior by these methods? How are sensory data encoded so that similar patterns have similar codes? How are motor codes associated with sensory codes? What are architectures for learning systems, and how do those systems represent their knowledge of the world? How can computers be designed to see, hear, and speak?

9. **Human-computer communication**
This area deals with the efficient transfer of information between humans and machines via various human-like sensors and motors, and with information structures that reflect human conceptualizations. Fundamental questions include: What are efficient methods of representing objects and automatically creating pictures for viewing? What are effective methods for receiving input or presenting output? How can the risk of misperception and subsequent human error

be minimized? How can graphics and other tools be used to understand physical phenomena through information stored in data sets? (*see* COMPUTER-AIDED DESIGN/COMPUTER-AIDED MANUFACTURING; HUMAN FACTORS IN COMPUTING; and USER INTERFACE.)

Each of the nine subareas is represented by at least one and usually several major articles in this encyclopedia. The subareas also correlate to some degree with the major categories used in the classification of articles given in the front, but since taxonomy is not an exact science, correspondence is not precisely one-to-one. Nonetheless, the totality of the concerns and questions listed under the foregoing nine subareas should serve to illustrate and define the limits of what we have called the disciplinary structure of computer science.

References

1968. National Academy of Sciences. "The Mathematical Sciences: A Report," Publication 1681. Washington, DC.

1969. Hamming, R. W., "One Man's View of Computer Science," 1968 ACM Turing Lecture, *Journal of the ACM* **16**, *1* (January), 1–5.

1970. Wegner, P. "Three Computer Cultures—Computer Technology, Computer Mathematics, and Computer Science," in *Advances in Computers* **10** (W. Freiberger, Ed.). New York: Academic Press.

1971. Amarel, S. "Computer Science: A Conceptual Framework for Curriculum Planning," *Communications of the ACM* **14**, *6* (June).

1980. Arden B., (Ed.) *What can be automated?—The Computer Science and Engineering Research Study*. Cambridge, MA: The M.I.T. Press.

1989. Denning, P., Comer, D. E., Gries, D, Mulder, M. C., Tucker, A., Turner, A. J., Young, P. R., "Computing as a Discipline," *Communications of the ACM* **32**, *1* (January), 9–23.

PETER J. DENNING

COMPUTER SCIENCE EDUCATION. *See* EDUCATION IN COMPUTER SCIENCE.

COMPUTER SCIENCE, ACADEMIC

For articles on related subjects *see* COMPUTER SCIENCE; COMPUTING RESEARCH ASSOCIATION; EDUCATION IN COMPUTER ENGINEERING; EDUCATION IN COMPUTER SCIENCE; and WOMEN AND COMPUTING.

The first academic computer science departments in the U.S. were formed in the mid 1960s. Some 25 years later, in 1991, there are 137 departments of computer science that grant Ph.D.'s in North America (123 in the U. S. and 12 in Canada). In addition, 32 other departments offer a Ph.D. in computer engineering; many of these are electrical engineering departments. It is estimated that another 850 colleges and universities award undergraduate or masters degrees in computer science.

In September 1991, the Ph.D.-granting departments had 2,724 faculty members: 979 assistant professors, 774 associate professors, and 971 full professors. The greater number of assistant professors than full professors is characteristic of a young discipline. This youth has made it difficult for computer science in several ways. There is more administration for younger and less-experienced faculty members. There are relatively few people with a computer science background in policy-making positions in the state and federal governments, so the opinions of the computer scientist are not always heard. Also, as in any new field, computer science changes rapidly, making it difficult to stabilize the curriculum.

Ph.D. production in computer science grew substantially in the 1980s, with the field producing 862 in 1990–91 (see Table 1). In the past ten years, the field has produced over 4,000 Ph.D.'s, with about half of them remaining in academia.

With the current level of Ph.D. production, supply is approaching or exceeding demand, which means that new Ph.D.'s are now available in more satisfactory numbers to the smaller and newer Ph.D.-granting departments and to the non-Ph.D.-granting departments. Previously, these departments had trouble filling faculty positions and have often hired people with master's degrees or from other disciplines.

Between 10 and 14 percent of the new Ph.D.'s are women; but this percentage has been essentially constant for 10 years. The field does far worse with regard to blacks and hispanics: out of the 862 Ph.D.'s granted in 1990–91, 7 went to blacks and 19 to Hispanics. Since 1985, 40 to 45 percent of the Ph.D.'s have been awarded to foreign nationals.

At the undergraduate level, computer science saw steady growth in both service courses and majors from the early 1970s to about 1985. This growth was so strong that departments had difficulty keeping up with it. In some departments, the faculty taught two to three times as many credit hours per faculty member as in other fields. From 1985, there was a precipitous decrease in enrollments for several years. Some viewed this as a welcome technical correction that brought enrollments down to a manageable level. However, some smaller and less-well-known departments are suffering from too few students. In some places, the decrease has stopped, and enrollments are rising again.

Data in this article are taken from the Taulbee surveys of computer science, which are essentially complete surveys of the Ph.D.-granting departments. The 1990–91 Taulbee survey appeared in *Computing Research News* **4,** 1 (January 1992); the surveys also appear in Communications of the ACM each year. The surveys are performed by the Computing Research Association (CRA), which serves to represent research in computer science and engineering. Further information can be obtained by writing to the Computing Research Association, Suite 110, 1625 Massachusetts Avenue, N.W., Washington, DC 20036-2212.

DAVID GRIES AND DOROTHY MARSH

COMPUTER SECURITY. *See* COMPUTER CRIME; and DATA SECURITY.

COMPUTER SYSTEM

For articles on related subjects *see* ARITHMETIC-LOGIC UNIT; CACHE MEMORY; CENTRAL PROCESSING UNIT; CHANNEL; COMMUNICATIONS AND COMPUTERS; COMPUTING CENTER; DISTRIBUTED SYSTEMS; INFORMATION SYSTEM; INPUT/OUTPUT CONTROL SYSTEM; INTERRUPT; MEMORY; NETWORKS, COMPUTER; OPERATING SYSTEMS; PROCESSING MODES; SOFTWARE; and STORAGE HIERARCHY.

A modern computer system is one of the most wonderful and complex achievements of humankind. This is due to its incredible speed, very high reliability, and almost limitless versatility. For example, in the year 1990 a large mainframe computer could execute over 100 million instructions per second (MIPS) when processing business workloads, and certain "supercomputers" (*q.v.*) designed to handle numerically-intensive scientific and engineering work can perform close to 1,000 million arithmetic operations per second. Even small personal computers (*q.v.*) can execute millions of instructions per second.

The versatility accompanying this processing power is due to *programming*, meaning that a *single machine*, with appropriate programs (software) can do such diverse tasks as complex engineering computations pertaining to the design of high-speed aircraft, preparation of the payroll for thousands of employees, or keeping track of inventory for a whole chain of retail stores. The term "general purpose" is then a fair one to characterize the capabilities of most computers, although of course not every particular machine is actually used for such a wide variety of tasks.

Because it is most easily visualized, a description of the equipment or hardware subsystem will be discussed first, followed by the software subsystem and how it appears to users.

TABLE 1. Computer science Ph.D. production and its growth

Year	No. of Ph.D. granting depts.	No. of Ph.D's
1980–81		230
1984–85	103	326
1985–86	117	412
1986–87	123	466
1987–88	127	577
1988–89	129	625
1989–90	135	734
1990–91	137	862

FIG. 1.

The Hardware Subsystem Fig. 1 shows the exterior appearance of a typical very large system's processor complex. Fig. 2 schematically shows the major hardware components of a computer that can be classified into a number of categories:

Transducers Transducers are hardware devices that change information from one physical form to another, linking the computer with its environment. They include keyboards, video screens, printers, plotters and various interactive input devices (*q.v.*) such as the trackball and mouse (*q.v.*).

Storage Devices The same devices store two distinct types of information: 1) data, and 2) instructions (programs). The most elementary unit of stored information is the bit (a 0 or 1 value). For most purposes, a *byte*, which is a group of 8 bits representing 256 possible values, or a character of the system's character-set are treated as an elementary stored unit. Because storages can be very large, certain multiples of a byte are typically used to express storage capacities:

KB = kilobyte = 1,000 bytes (also 1,024 bytes)
MB = megabyte = 1,000,000 bytes (also 1,024 KB)

GB = gigabyte = 1,000,000,000 bytes (also 1,024 MB)
TB = terabyte = 1,000,000,000,000 bytes (also 1,024 GB)

For economical and technological reasons, storage devices come in many sizes, speeds, and costs. They range from inexpensive, low-capacity, slow devices (e.g. floppy disks - *q.v.*) to larger, more expensive, faster ones (e.g. nonremovable or hard disks (*q.v.*), and tapes), suitable for permanent storage of the information of large commercial, governmental, or educational enterprises.

From a use viewpoint, most storage, which can be hundreds of gigabytes in size, is organized into *files* (*q.v.*) that are retained in the system unless explicitly deleted or replaced. This requires nonvolatile media, such as disk or tape. "Nonvolatile" means that stored contents are retained even if electrical power is removed by shut-down or failure.

Storage with faster access (by a factor of 10,000 or more) than disk storage is physically composed of semiconductor chips and is used in the computer's *main storage* or *memory*. Although far faster than file storage, semiconductor storage is far more expensive per byte and is held to smaller capacities (megabytes). Also, semiconductor memory is *volatile*, meaning that its contents are lost when its power is removed. Although this sounds ominous, in fact it is not, since its contents are needed only during actual processing, and any information that must be retained longer is easily copied to nonvolatile file storage. Because of its speed, main storage, and a related, even faster semiconductor type, called the *cache* or *buffer*, has the special "privilege" of being directly accessible by fast central processing units (CPUs).

Central Processing Units (CPUs) The term "CPU" derives from the fact that for a long time each computer system contained only one processor, and this is the case even today for many smaller systems. The CPU is in many ways the heart of the computer system. It does its work directed by *instructions*, most of which operate on data.

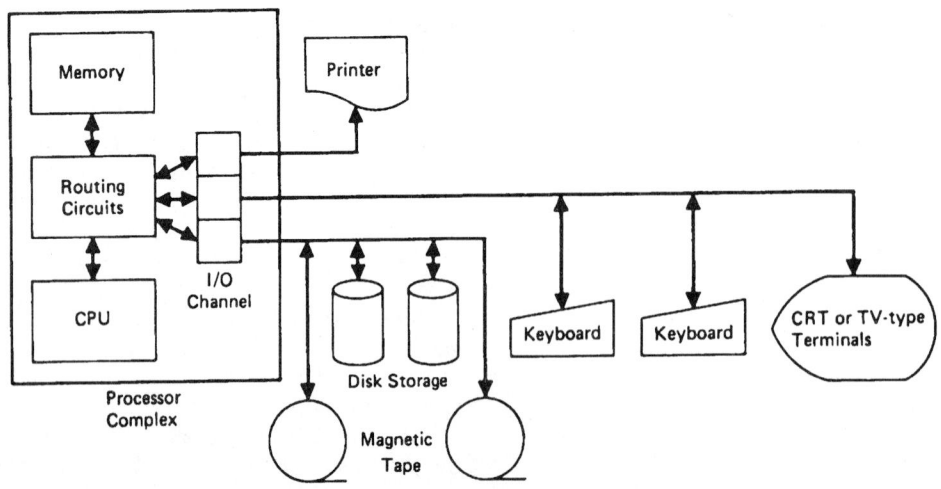

FIG. 2.

The operation performed by each instruction is usually quite primitive. The repertoire of instruction types (e.g. add, subtract, test-for-sign), is called the machine's *instruction set* (*q.v.*) or *instruction repertoire* and typically contains about 200 instructions. But some machines have as few as say 64 instructions in their set, and even this is larger than is theoretically required. The design of a machine's instruction set is an arcane subject with many speed, cost, and even esthetic factors involved (*see* REDUCED INSTRUCTION SET COMPUTER). The instruction-set and associated items constitute the native "machine language" of a computer.

Some CPU circuitry is responsible for execution of the instructions; this includes an adder, augmented by shift and control circuits that together implement the system's arithmetic and processing operations. The ability to execute all instructions, while necessary, is *not* sufficient. Also needed is a control mechanism to *sequence* from one instruction to the next in a program of instructions stored in the computer's main storage. Programs (i.e. specific instruction sequences) express the required function of the program (payroll, inventory, etc.).

Although not an exact analogy, the instruction-set is akin to a set of musical notes, as is found on a piano, and a program is like the score for a particular song. In the case of music, the human performer "reads" the next note from the score, then invokes that note from the instrument, then repeats the process for the next note, etc. In the computer case, the CPU contains *program control circuitry* that automatically reads or accesses the stored program's next instruction, and then invokes the computer's execution circuitry to execute the instruction. This cycle is then repeated automatically. During execution, many instructions call for data, which are held in the same main storage as the program. Main storage appears as a long list of memory cells, each with a unique location-number called its *address*. So main storage is addressed for instructions that in turn address it for data.

Also essential for program control are provisions for testing conditions on input or computed data and, depending on the test-outcome, *branching* or jumping in the stored program sequence from strict progression to a new program segment. Using branching, a single segment of stored program may be used repetitively thousands of times in the same program, with certain necessary program-modifiable differences in each such use.

All CPU functions use the fastest (but expensive, and hence small) kind of storage—the CPU registers—usually built from the same circuitry used for processing. The registers are a sort of scratch pad for the CPU to jot down results, especially those used frequently in local parts of the program. Some register contents are later transferred to main storage and even to file storage.

Routing and Control Circuitry Routing circuits include the networks and "buses" that direct the flow of information between various functional parts of the hardware subsystem (*see* BUS). For instance, the I/O channels control the flow of information between the transducers, peripheral storage devices, and main storage. Other routing circuits control communication between main storage and the CPU. The control circuitry generates timing signals in various arrangements that specify at what times which information is moved from place to place in the system.

Another classification scheme divides the hardware subsystem into "internal" and "external" items. The internal ones are the CPU, with its registers, instruction-execution and control units, main storage and cache storage, and I/O channels. This "internal computer," which may contain several CPUs sharing access to common main storage and sets of channels is sometimes called the "processor complex" (see Fig 1). All other hardware devices, such as transducers and file-storage disks and tapes, are referred to as the *peripheral*, or input/output, or *I/O*, subsystem.

General Hardware Organization How do the constituents of these hardware categories work together? The reader is advised to trace the following description through the paths and facilities of Fig. 2. The program (say, as a sequence of keystrokes entered by the programmer) must first be physically translated into electric-signal form, which is done by the terminal keyboard, a transducer. Once in electrical form, the typed information is stored as a file on nonvolatile disk storage for future use. Accordingly, it is moved by an I/O channel to disk storage (briefly passing through main storage in the process), where it is held until it is to be executed.

To be executed, the program must satisfy two main requirements: it must be in machine-language (object-code) form, and it must reside in main storage. As to the first, the typed form of the program (source code) must almost always be translated and then typically stored as an object-code file. Assume for the moment that this has been done, so it remains to move the object-code file from disk storage to memory via an I/O channel and routing circuits.

Once in memory, the object-code program is executable by the CPU. During execution, most storage accessing is to the memory (main store). However, the running program is capable of directing movement of data, including final results between memory and peripheral storages (disk or tape) via the I/O channels. Later, such results can be moved, again via channels to a transducer (display terminal or printer) for human inspection.

Until about 1968, most computers were *mainframes* (*q.v.*) that were expensive and required considerable floor space, electric power, and air conditioning. However, due to rapid advances in the computer technologies, especially semiconductor circuitry, by the late 1960s a genre of small-size machines termed *minicomputers* (*q.v.*) started to be produced that occupied only the space of an office desk, and were inexpensive enough to be used for the solution of a single problem, such as the control of particular industrial process as well as a variety of shared uses.

By about 1973, further rapid advances in technology led to another class of even smaller, cheaper systems based on the *microprocessor*, a complete CPU contained on a single or very few semiconductor chips. This method of manufacture eliminated most hand-wiring and separate-component manufacture of the CPU with substantial improvements, not only in cost but also reliability.

This great advance in technology was matched by corresponding advances in semiconductor memory that allowed compact, high-capacity main storage to be offered at a price hundreds of times cheaper per unit of stored information than was available only a decade earlier. By 1990, several million microprocessor-based systems, called *personal computers (PCs - q.v.)* or *workstations (q.v.)* were in common use in homes, offices, and businesses. Each supplied to an individual user computation power and main storage that had been available in shared form only from large, expensive systems a few years earlier. Furthermore, the progress in technology that has given us the microprocessor has also enhanced the cost effectiveness of the larger minicomputer and general-purpose mainframe systems.

Here, only a very brief account has been given of three main classes of computer system: mainframe, minicomputer, and microprocessor-based. These are not precise categories. Thus, many minicomputers are shared by several users and applications in the same way as are mainframe systems. Although each PC/workstation is typically used by only one person, some are being interconnected via *local area networks* (LANs - *q.v.*) that also contain *servers* that use microprocessor-based technology to permit access to large shared disk storage by the many PCs and workstations on the LAN (*see* FILE SERVER).

The Software Subsystem Unlike hardware, software (*q.v.*) is not tangible. Software, although held in a physical medium, say on a disk storage unit, is composed of programs and data arranged in logical, not physical, structures (*see* DATA STRUCTURES).

Software is usually described in two major categories, *application software* and *system software*, with subcategories:

1. Application software:
   a. Programs written by users for a particular purpose, such as payroll, inventory control, design of a product, etc.
   b. "Packaged" programs written and supplied by vendors for end-users, each for a wide but restricted range of purposes. Examples: word processors for creating text documents; spreadsheets (*q.v.*) for financial analysis work; database packages for creating, maintaining, and searching large structured data collections; statistical analysis packages, etc.
   c. Installation libraries, containing programs of types a. and b. and databases that are particular to several users at a site or an enterprise. Increasingly, a central "repository," or "data dictionary," itself an item of complex software, is used to manage access to these objects.
2. System software:
   a. Operating system.
   b. Language processors (compilers).
   c. Utilities.

The following discussion concentrates on system software, which is part of the system itself.

The *operating system* is usually the most complex software in a computer system. Two of its basic purposes are: 1) to supply common functions or "services" for use by other software, and 2) to control the orderly *sharing* of the system's hardware and software resources by several users where such sharing is done. Most of the types of system programs below are part of the operating system:

1. Device drivers (DD)—There is one per device that controls device-specific details of a video screen, a printer, a disk storage, etc. Most other software will, as needed, call on a DD when it interacts with the device. Such software sees the device as a much simpler logical unit than is seen by the DD itself, and in this way most software is shielded from onerous device-sensitive details.
2. Data management programs (DMP)—These keep track of the named storage items such as files, i.e. where each is located and the means to store and access the data efficiently. For instance, when a user's program calls for data, a DMP locates and fetches the data to the requesting program. (In so doing, the DMP may well call on the DD part of the operating system described earlier). For each file, the DMP may maintain information as to who is permitted to use the data, who is currently using it, what is being done with it, whether or not the data should be retained in the system after the job ends, etc. Some parts of DMP software are called *access methods (q.v.)*.
3. Linkers/loaders—These programs do the final preparation of object code programs prior to initiation of execution. Included may be "binding" or linking of references in one program with another using machine-language naming (addresses).
4. System control program (SCP)—This complex part of operating system software is found in *shared systems*, as is common in most mainframe and minicomputer systems, but not in many personal computers or workstations that serve single users only.
5. Language processors (translators/compilers)—Programs that are executed by the computer must be in machine-language form, which is exceedingly tedious for humans to use when creating programs. Accordingly, modern computer systems support much more convenient *higher-level languages* (HLL) for human use, along with language translators, usually compilers, to deal with them. These translate user-written programs (*source code*) from such HLL source languages as Cobol or Fortran or C (*q.v.*) into machine-language object code, the only form the machine can execute.
6. Utilities—These are programs that perform frequently required tasks, such as sorting (*q.v.*) and

merging two or more files, copying or moving files within the system, etc.

A computer system is best understood as a collection of two interrelating subsystems—hardware and software. There are, however, certain aspects that do not fall into either subsystem: an example is a microprogram, which has been termed *firmware* (*q.v.*). Microprogramming (*q.v.*), as the name implies, is a type of programming but a highly specialized one. Microprograms directly control the sequencing of the computer circuits at the detailed level of the single instruction. Organizing the control hardware in a microprogrammed structure rather than as wired circuitry has several advantages. First is economy of circuitry if the machine must have complex instructions. A second advantage is that it is possible, by microprogramming, to produce an *emulator*, a set of microprograms that makes a given machine have the same appearance to object code software as some other machine (*see* EMULATION). This permits the same machine to run programs written for either itself or the machine it is emulating at reasonable efficiency. Yet another advantage is to produce faster operations of the special functions that are microprogrammed rather than programmed in the usual manner. There are, however, some negative aspects of microprogramming, such as the highly specialized knowledge needed and the great tedium of writing microprograms. For these and other reasons, microprogramming is almost always confined to the staff of computer vendors. Also, although microprograms are faster than doing the same functions with software, they are slower than using wired control circuitry.

The User's View of a Computer System

Consider now how the system appears to a user. Suppose we are at the keyboard and screen of a small single-user system such as a personal computer (PC) or workstation. Its hardware consists of a keyboard, video screen and printer (transducers), a CPU, memory (main storage), and disk storage for files. The software subsystem consists of an operating system and application packages: a word processor, an editor, and, say, a C-language compiler. The operating system, through a set of commands that may be offered in "menu" fashion, provides the means to select from a list of particular services.

In the first and simplest case, we wish to type and edit a report. We start by issuing a command to the operating system (by typing or selecting it from a menu). In this case, the command is to start to execute the word processor program. Good software of this kind requires minimal user knowledge of the system or software, and as we use it we mainly see a collection of editing facilities that allow us to enter our document into the system by typing, then to edit (change) it, and eventually to print it. The word processor software allows the document to be stored as a named file on disk storage for later reference or further editing. We name this file "EXAMPLE.TXT".

A far more interesting case is where we wish to create and then run our own *program*. Then we typically proceed as follows:

1. Program creation—Start by creating a program, expressing it in one of the system's designated or "supported" programming languages, say C. Creating a program is a profound intellectual process, but beyond the scope of this discussion. Mechanically, at creation time, we use a pencil and paper.

2. Program entry—The next task is to enter the text of this program into the computer system. Mechanically, this is a document creation and editing process (editing is to help us correct certain errors, such as mistakes in typing), so we use software called an *editor*, which is much like a word processor. As in the case of 1. above, our C language source program is stored as a file, say "EXAMPLE.SRC", on a disk storage device.

3. Compile time—Since C is not a machine language, our C program must be translated from C into machine language by a packaged program called a C compiler. We order this done by again using the operating system command to "call" a program into execution; in this case, that program is the C *compiler*. Naturally, we must also specify the name of our source code file (EXAMPLE.SRC) as its data input. The C compiler then starts to run on the CPU, and translates each C source statement from the EXAMPLE.SRC file to machine language object code.

   As it attempts to translate, the compiler may discover syntax errors in the program due to typing errors or other reasons, and will then notify us by a message on the screen. (We can then correct the errors on the EXAMPLE.SRC file, using processes like 2. above, and then call the compiler again.)

   While translating, the compiler is "aware" not only of the machine instructions it must supply for the translation, but also of the operating system's many service programs. The compiler will, as appropriate, insert calls on such services as access methods, device drivers, etc., as needed into the object code.

   The compiler typically stores the translated program (object code) on the disk as a file named EXAMPLE.EXE for later use.

4. Load time—The next step is to prepare to run or execute the object code. The same command is used as in 3), except now we specify EXAMPLE.EXE as the program to be run rather than the compiler. To start to run this program, the operating system moves the object-code file from the disk into main storage since programs must be in main storage in order to execute. The Linker/Loader system program then does some necessary final processing of the object code, and then starts it executing.

5. Run time—As the program EXAMPLE.EXE executes, much of its action is determined by the machine instructions in its object code produced by the compiler. But recall that the compiler also

inserted calls to operating system services, say for access to data files previously stored on disk, and also to new ones to hold results for later viewing or printing or for access by other programs. Such a service call to the operating system activates a service subroutine (which may call other subroutines), which then becomes, during this time, part of the running object code.

All during the above process, the user hardly needs to be aware of the hardware subsystem, or even much of the detail of the software subsystem, such as the operating system services available to the compiler.

Shared Systems "Shared systems" refer to a mode of operation whereby several users share the CPU time, main storage space, and peripheral devices of a single system. Mainframe and minicomputers typically work as shared systems, while personal computers and workstations typically do not unless networked through use of a local area network (*q.v.*) or file server (*q.v.*).

Sharing has two motivations: 1) to provide a means of inter-user communication, and 2) to bring the processing power and storage capacity of a powerful but expensive system to many users in an economically justifiable way. Shared systems are covered in the articles DISTRIBUTED SYSTEMS; MULTITASKING; NETWORKS, COMPUTER; and TIME SHARING.

Interfaces, Architecture, and Computability

From the viewpoint of a purchaser of computers, a system appears as a coherent collection of *products*, both hardware and software. To work in a system, every product must comply with precise rules governing its intended relationships with other products, with user software, and even with user interactions. Such relationships are called *interfaces*. The totality of the interfaces of a specific product is called its *architecture*, and the totality of the architectures of a system's products plus any system-system interfaces such as *gateways* (*q.v.*) governing relationships with other systems, is the system architecture.

In many ways, interfaces and architectures are fundamentally standards, but, unlike other systems such as electric power or home entertainment, there are few universal standards in computer systems, so there are many computer architectures (*q.v.*), not just one.

One important example is the hardware-software interface specification that precisely describes all of the instructions in the CPU's repertoire. Another interface specifies the precise relationships between I/O channels and peripheral devices.

A product whose interfaces all comply with those of a given system is said to be *compatible* with that system and will work as intended in that system. Conversely, a product incompatible with a system cannot be used in that system. For example, disk storage products compatible with IBM S/370 will not work in DEC VAX systems and, conversely, even if the disk products are of comparable capacity, speed, and function.

The economic significance of compatibility (*q.v.*) is due to the dependence of the great bulk of user-developed software on the specific interfaces of a particular system architecture. Thus, the great user investment in such software and related items, such as training of staff, is preserved only if the user buys compatible products when expanding or replacing the system.

Compatibility dictates a product's external behavior but not its internal (non-interface) structure. Thus, compatible-substitutable products are not usually copies or "clones" and are typically very different in technology, circuitry, and design. They also often differ in speed, capacity, reliability, and price, and may be offered by different vendors. For example, S/370-compatible processors and disk storages are offered by IBM, Amdahl Corp., and Hitachi Data Systems, and all are of different internal designs. Customers of S/370 systems can then choose between competing products and vendors on a product basis while retaining their typically large software investments that depend on S/370 architecture.

Summary A computer system is characterized by its high speed, high reliability, and great versatility. Since its commercial beginnings in 1950, there has been remarkable improvement in the cost per unit computation and per unit storage. This is due to rapid advances in the technologies of semiconductor circuits and storage devices. The 1970s saw the maturity of mainframes and minicomputers, as well as the emergence of the personal computer and workstations based on microprocessor technology. The 1980s saw explosive growth of microprocessor-based systems with millions in use by individual workers in businesses and schools of all sizes.

Structurally, a computer system is best considered as a collection of resources of two broad classes: hardware and software. Both are served and managed by a carefully designed collection of system programs, including an operating system.

From a business perspective, a computer system is a collection of hardware and software products with precise interfaces between products and with users, especially their software. The great user investments in their self-developed software are usually dependent on compatibility with the interfaces of the specific systems for which such software was developed. In some cases, compatible products with different prices, capacities, and qualities are available from competing vendors.

References

1980. Stone, H. S. (Ed.). *Introduction To Computer Architecture (2nd Ed.)*. Chicago: Science Research Associates.
1984. Hamacher, V. C., Vranesic, Z. G., and Zaky, S. G. *Computer Organization (2nd Ed.)*. New York: McGraw-Hill.
1986. Bach, M. J. *The Design of the Unix Operating System*. Englewood Cliffs, NJ: Prentice-Hall.
1989. ___ , Intel Corp. *i486 Microprocessor*. Santa Clara, CA: Intel Corporation, 44, 92, 120.

HERBERT HELLERMAN

COMPUTER VIRUS

For articles on related subjects *see* COMPUTER CRIME; DATA SECURITY; HACKER; and LEGAL ASPECTS OF COMPUTING.

A *virus* is a piece of program code that attaches copies of itself to other programs, incorporating itself into them so that the modified programs, while still possibly performing their intended function, surreptitiously do other things. Programs so corrupted seek others to which to attach the virus, and so the "infection" spreads. Successful viruses lie low until they have thoroughly infiltrated the system, and then and only then reveal their presence by causing damage.

Viruses work by altering disk files that contain the compiled version of otherwise harmless programs. When an infected program is invoked, it seeks other programs stored in files to which it has write permission, and infects them by modifying the files to include a copy of the virus code and inserting an instruction to branch to that code at the old program's starting point. Then the virus starts up the original program so that the user is unaware of its intervention.

A virus can spread on a multi-user system with shared disk facilities, or in a personal computer environment where users download programs from bulletin boards (*q.v.*) or share floppy disks (*q.v.*) or other removable media. In the former case, file protection schemes can limit spreading the virus provided that users do not execute each other's programs. If A executes one of B's programs that is infected, A's programs risk becoming infected, since programs that A invokes normally have permission to alter its own files. Even when they never execute one another's programs, infection can spread from A to B through an intermediary. In practice, it is hard to guard against infection in an environment that encourages program sharing. In personal computer environments, viruses generally spread from one floppy disk to another by infiltrating the system disk, often a hard disk (*q.v.*).

Other Malicious Programs

The term "virus" is also a popular catch-all for other kinds of malicious software. A *logic bomb* or *time bomb* is a destructive program activated by a certain combination of circumstances, or on a certain date. A *Trojan horse* is any bug inserted into a computer program that takes advantage of the trusted status of its host by surreptitiously performing unintended functions. A *worm* is a robust distributed program that invades workstations (*q.v.*) on a network. It consists of several processes or "segments" that keep in touch through the network; when one is lost (e.g. by a workstation being rebooted), the others conspire to replace it on another processor—they search for an idle workstation, load it with copies of themselves, and start it up. Like viruses, worms spread by replication; unlike them, they run as independent processes rather than as part of a host program, and can occupy volatile memory rather than disk storage.

To escape detection, viruses normally reside in binary rather than source code and thus do not survive recompilation. Just as worms are destroyed by simultaneously rebooting all affected machines, viruses are eradicated by simultaneously recompiling all affected programs. However, under special circumstances a bug can survive recompilation even though it resides in binary rather than source code (and is thus undetectable by inspection). In a language compiler that is written in the language it compiles (a common bootstrapping practice), it is possible to implant a bug that re-inserts itself into the binary code whenever the compiler is recompiled.

History and Examples

The idea of a maliciously self-propagating computer program originated in Gerrold's 1972 novel *When Harlie Was One*, in which a computer program called telephone numbers at random until it found another computer into which it could spread. Worms were also presaged in science fiction by Brunner's 1975 novel *The Shockwave Rider*. The first actual virus program seems to have been created in 1983 as the result of a discussion in a computer security seminar and described at the AFIPS Computer Security Conference the following year. In 1984, Ken Thompson, in his Turing award (*q.v.*) lecture, showed how a self-replicating bug can infest a compiler or other language processor, as noted above.

Virus attacks were not reported until a few years thereafter, and so far have been more in the nature of electronic vandalism than serious subversion. One of the first occurred in late 1987 when, over a two-month period, a virus quietly insinuated itself into IBM-PC programs at a Jerusalem university. It was noticed because it caused programs to grow longer (due to a bug, it repeatedly reinfected files). Once discovered, it was analyzed and an antidote devised. It was designed to slow processors down on certain Fridays, and to erase all files on Friday, 13 May.

At about the same time, another PC virus invaded Lehigh University, and a much-publicized "chain letter" Christmas message spread itself by self-replication, clogging the Bitnet network. The latter was eradicated only by a massive network shutdown. Early 1988 saw a relatively harmless Macintosh virus designed to distribute a "message of peace," and a number of other viruses appeared for this and other personal computers. By that time talk about viruses had invaded the news media.

At 9 P.M. on 2 November 1988, a worm program was inserted into the Internet computer network by Cornell graduate student Robert Morris, Jr. It exploited several security flaws in SUN and VAX systems running Unix to spread itself from system to system. Although discovered within hours, it required a huge effort (estimated at 5,000 hours and $200,000) by programmers at affected sites to counteract and eliminate the worm over a period of weeks. Again, it was unmasked by a bug: under some circumstances it replicated itself so fast that it seriously slowed down the infected host. Morris was subsequently indicted on charges that exposed him to a possible sentence of five years imprisonment and a fine of up to $250,000. On 21 January 1990, Morris was convicted and in May 1990 he was sentenced to three years probation and fined $10,000. In addition, he was ordered to perform 400 hours of community service.

On 6 March 1992, the Michelangelo virus (so named because 6 March is Michelangelo's birthday), although widely heralded as a worldwide threat to computer systems, actually did little damage.

Defenses The obvious, but generally impractical, defense against viruses is never to use anyone else's software and never to connect with anyone else's computer. Another is to implement a check in the operating system that queries users whenever a program they have invoked attempts to write to disk. In practice, however, this imposes an intolerable burden because users do not generally know which files their software writes legitimately. Given a particular virus, one can write an *antibody program* that spreads itself in the same way, removing the original virus from infected programs, and ultimately removing itself too. However, this approach cannot protect against viruses in general, since it is not possible to tell whether a particular piece of code is a virus or not. *Digital signatures* have been suggested to prevent the corruption of files. Each file as it is written is sealed by appending an encrypted checksum. Also, before it is used, the checksum is decrypted and checked against the file's actual checksum. Such a scheme may engender unacceptable overhead, however, both in execution time and in the logicistics of handling encryption keys.

The only really effective defense is eternal vigilance on the part of users, and, above all, education of users to the possible consequences of their actions.

References

1989. Spafford, E. H. "The Internet Worm: Crisis and Aftermath," *American Scientist* (June).
1989. Stoll, Clifford. *The Cuckoo's Egg: Tracking a Spy Through the Maze of Computer Espionage.* New York: Doubleday.
1991. Hafner, Katie and Markoff, John. *Cyberpunk: Outlaws and Hackers on the Computer Frontier.* New York: Simon and Schuster.

IAN H. WITTEN

COMPUTER VISION

For articles on related subjects *see* IMAGE PROCESSING; NEURAL NETWORKS; MEDICAL IMAGING; PATTERN RECOGNITION; and ROBOTICS.

Computer vision is the process of using computers to extract from images useful information about the physical world, including meaningful descriptions of physical objects. For example, if an image sensor, such as a digitizing video camera, captured an image of a physical scene, and the digital image was input to a computer vision system, the desired output would be a description of the physical scene in terms that would be useful for the particular task at hand. Computer vision has many applications, including robotics, industrial automation, document processing, remote sensing, navigation, microscopy, medical imaging, and the development of visual protheses for the blind.

Terminology There are various terms used to refer to the field of computer vision: machine vision, computational vision, image understanding, robot vision, image analysis, and scene analysis. Each of these terms has a different historical perspective, and some retain a difference in emphasis. For example, the term "machine vision" is most commonly used in engineering disciplines and thus has more of an engineering and applications flavor. The term "computational vision" arose from interdisciplinary research by computer scientists, visual psychophysicists, physicists, and neuroscientists. There are two goals of computational vision: one concerns the creation of computer systems that can "see," and the other concerns understanding biological vision. The unifying principle of computational vision is the concept that it is possible to understand vision independent of whether it is implemented in computer hardware or in biological "wetware." More specifically, the goal of computational vision is to express the process of vision in terms of computations. This sense of computation is not limited to the numerical computations performed on a calculator, but includes all the more abstract computations that can be performed by an abstract algorithmic processing system.

Related Fields There are several fields to which computer vision is closely related: *image processing*, which involves image to image transformations; *computer graphics (q.v.)*, which involves description to image transformations (the inverse of computer vision's image to description transformations); and *pattern recognition*, which involves pattern to class transformations. Computer vision is a subfield of artificial intelligence (AI - *q.v.*) and the process of extracting information from images requires the same types of knowledge acquisition and cognitive reasoning as other AI subfields. However, vision requires in addition significant perceptual preprocessing of the visual input before the cognitive analysis.

Levels of Computer Vision Processing Computer vision processing is generally divided into two levels: *early vision* and *scene analysis*. Early vision, otherwise known as *low level vision*, involves the first stages of processing required for a visual task. One aspect of this first stage is *feature analysis*, whereby information about color, motion, shape, texture, stereo depth, and intensity edges are extracted. Another aspect of early vision is *image segmentation*, whereby the featural information is used to segment the image into regions that have a high probability of having arisen from a single physical cause. For example, suppose a scene consisted of a single orange resting upon an infinitely large flat white surface that is illuminated by a diffuse light source. An image of this scene could be segmented based on color information alone to form two regions—one corresponding to the orange and the the other corresponding to the flat surface.

The second level of processing, scene analysis, involves taking the featural descriptors generated by early vision and constructing higher-level descriptions of the scene. Some components of this task are *shape analysis*, *object recognition*, and *object localization*. This level is also referred to as *high level vision*, and involves more knowledge-based processing than early vision. In the example image of an orange, scene analysis would involve recognizing that the circular orange-colored region was an image of an orange. This recognition must be based on the system having knowledge about the nature of oranges, and the ability to make inferences based on the visual information.

The division between early vision and scene analysis is not firm. Many computer vision systems have partial information generated by the scene analysis processing feed back to the early vision processing to be used in refining the initial descriptions to make them more useful for the scene analysis processing. Several iterations through this feedback and feedforward process may be required to generate the final scene descriptions. Another sense in which the division is not firm is that some researchers refer to three levels of vision: low level, intermediate, and high level. Again, the exact boundaries between these three levels are not distinct.

Why Computer Vision Is Difficult
The goal of creating computer vision systems that can "see" was initially thought to be rather easy. The argument was made that computers are very powerful. For example, even though the solution of simultaneous differential equations is very difficult for humans, computers can readily solve them. So, if we take a task that is trivially easy for humans, such as vision, it should be even easier to implement it on a computer. Yet when computer scientists and engineers first attempted to give computers a visual sense, they failed completely. The problem was that there is a fallacy in the simple argument used above. While humans are conscious of most of the stages of processing involved in solving simultaneous differential equations and thus can realize the complexity involved, most of the processing involved in visual perception remains subconscious. So while the process of encountering, say, a yellow Volkswagen in the environment and using our visual sense to determine that there is a yellow Volkswagen currently present in our environment may feel like a simple process, it actually involves many interelated levels of computational processing. Uncovering just what those levels of processing are and expressing them as algorithms is one goal of computer vision.

Vision is difficult because it is an underconstrained problem. For example, an image is a two-dimensional projection of a three-dimensional scene, but there can be infinitely many three-dimensional scenes that project the same two-dimensional image. Thus, given just the single image, it is impossible to determine which of the possible scenes is depicted in the image. For example, the image in Fig. 1a appears to depict a rectangle, but the actual scene from which this image arose is seen in Fig. 1b: it consists of four thin wires that do not touch. But the image in Fig. 1a could just as well have been the projection of a scene containing a rectangle (Fig. 1c). This simple example illustrates that it is possible to have two scenes that both

Image

FIG. 1a.

project to the same image. But notice that the image in Fig. 1a does not appear to be ambiguous; we do not perceive all possible scenes. Thus, humans either use some additional high-level information about the world to interpret images unambiguously (such as knowledge about rectangles, for example), or they use some general constraints to rule out multiple interpretations. There is psychophysical evidence that humans use both strategies, but the surprising result is that the high-level knowledge appears to provide less information for disambiguating scenes than the lower-level general constraints. This can be illustrated by drawing an arbitrary squiggle and observing that it generates a single percept, even though it does not depict a familiar object. This suggests the idea that there must be some additional general constraints that humans use in perceiving images.

Determining Constraints for Vision
One of the primary tasks in computer vision is to find a set of constraints that would allow a computer to interpret images unambiguously. The constraints can be either features in the image that can be used to make inferences about the scene, or regularities of nature that can be exploited. There are four main techniques for determining such constraints: the engineering approach, the statistical approach, the biological approach, and the physical approach.

Engineering Approach to Determining Constraints
The engineering approach relies on the intuitions, introspections, and prior knowledge of the system designer as to what the important image features should be, and how such features should be interpreted. This approach was used in much of the early work in computer vision, and continues to be used in many machine vision systems. Although this approach has been successful in some applications, its lack of a theoretical basis makes it less desirable than some of the other approaches.

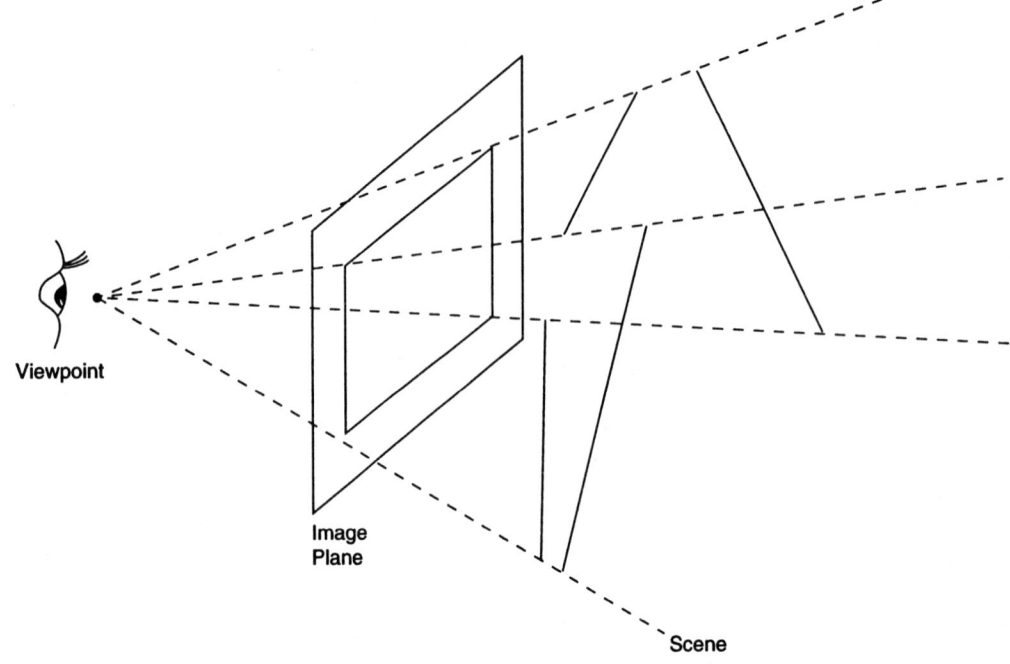

FIG. 1b.

Statistical Approach to Determining Constraints Statistical analysis provides the second approach to determining image constraints. The basic idea is that it is possible to design a system that can "learn" what the constraints are simply by observing the world through sensory input. This is the approach used in statistical pattern recognition, and more recently in artificial *neural networks*. In the statistical approach, the relevant aspects of the visual environment are sampled, and the sample statistics used to find image features that can be used to provide the necessary constraints on image interpretation. This approach can be successful when the input stimuli can be recognized from descriptions that are directly constructed from the image. However, in most vision problems, the direct descriptions are further processed into higher-level descriptions, which are then further processed into even higher-level descriptions, etc., and only after several such intervening levels of

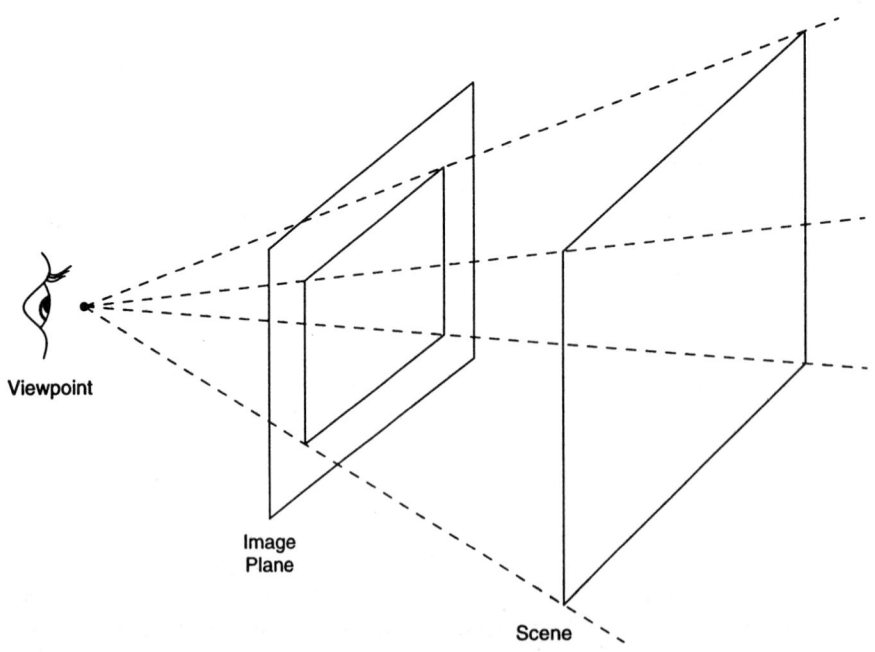

FIG. 1c.

successively more derived descriptions does recognition occur. It is not yet clear how such complex structure could emerge in an artificial system that must "learn" its structure. One solution would be to design such structure into the network, but this then begs the question of what image features are important, as at least the basic level features would have to be predetermined. So, although the statistical approaches may produce interesting results for early vision, they are not well suited for scene analysis.

Biological Approach to Determining Constraints The third approach to finding useful image constraints involves studying biological vision systems with the aim of uncovering the constraints that they use in image interpretation. In some cases, the biological solution may be constrained by the neurophysiological implementation mechanisms, and in such cases the biological approach may fail. However, in other cases the biological solution may be constrained by the general problem of vision and may provide useful insights for computer vision.

In one sense, all computer vision uses the biological approach, as vision is defined in terms of the human visual sense. But as mentioned previously, most stages of visual processing are not open to conscious introspection, so in order to use systematically the biological approach, other means of determining how the mammalian visual system functions must be used. This is possible using techniques from the disciplines of visual perception, psychophysics, neurophysiology, and neuroanatomy. Over the past ten years there has been an increasing degree of interaction between those interested in biological vision and those primarily interested in machine vision, and the contributions from each side enhance the research of the other.

Physical Approach to Determining Constraints In the physical approach, the basic idea is to determine properties of the physical world that can be used to constrain image interpretation. This has been a very successful approach and has led to many useful constraints. For example, David Marr (1982) frequently used continuity as a constraint. The continuity constraint makes use of the fact that the physical world is basically continuous; thus neighboring image points have a high probability of having arisen from the same physical entity. This constraint has been used in a simple cooperative algorithm to compute the relative depth of different image regions. Another example of a frequently used constraint is the assumption of a general viewpoint. This assumption is based on the fact that for a given scene, as the viewpoint changes slightly, there will generally be only slight changes in the projected image, and thus many properties of the projected image will remain constant over most viewpoints. So, if it is possible to determine which image properties are invariant over viewpoint, except at a limited number of viewpoints, it may be possible to make useful inferences about the scene based on these properties. For example, if several points in an image are co-linear, there is a high probability that they depict co-linear

points on a curve in three-space. This will not always be true: if an arc of a circle exists in three-space, there will be a limited number of viewpoints such that the points on the arc project onto a straight line in an image, but for the vast majority of possible viewpoints this will not be true. Vision constraints often have the property of being true only in general, yet they can be important in providing inferences useful for the correct interpretation of an image.

References

1982. Marr, D. *Vision*. San Francisco: W.H. Freeman.
1982. Ballard, Dana H., and Brown, C.P. *Computer Vision*. Englewood Cliffs, NJ: Prentice Hall, Inc.
1986. Horn, Berthold. *Robot Vision*. New York: McGraw-Hill.
1987. Fischler, Martin and Firschein, Oscar. *Readings in Computer Vision: Issues, Problems, Principles and Paradigms*. Los Altos, CA: Morgan Kaufmann.

DEBORAH WALTERS

COMPUTERS, HISTORY OF. See DIGITAL COMPUTERS: HISTORY.

COMPUTERS, MULTIPLE ADDRESS

For articles on related subjects *see* ADDRESSING; COMPUTER ARCHITECTURE; INDEX REGISTER; INDIRECT ADDRESS; INSTRUCTION SET; and MACHINE AND ASSEMBLY LANGUAGE PROGRAMMING.

In addition to an operation (command) specification and other information (e.g. indexing), a computer instruction may contain from zero to four addresses. An address usually points either to a location in the memory that stores the value of the operand or to a location involved in the control process.

Computers may be classified according to the number of addresses in most or in common (e.g. arithmetic) instructions: zero, one, two, three, and four having been used. The number of addresses depends on both the register structure and central processor organization.

Zero-Address Instructions Zero-address instructions do not require access to memory for operands. Examples include HALT and RESET OVERFLOW INDICATORS. Arithmetic zero-address instructions occur in stack-type organizations in which arithmetic expressions are conveniently evaluated by conversion to Polish form. For example, ADD would cause the two top stacked operands to be replaced by their sum, thereby shortening the stack by one item.

One-Address Instructions For many years, the high cost of hardware led to systems wherein the arithmetic operations were all associated with one particular register called an *accumulator*. Thus, the instructions to evaluate $C = A + B$ were LOAD A, ADD B, STORE C, with a natural instruction format of

```
[op code] [address]
```

where [address] points to a particular memory cell. Control instructions fitting this structure were JUMP, address; JUMP IF ACCUMULATOR POSITIVE, address; etc. In both zero-address and one-address structures, successive instructions came from sequential locations in memory as specified by a *program counter* (*q.v.*) which progressed in units of one until a jump occurred. The EDSAC (*q.v.*) was an example of a one-address computer. The IBM 700-7000 series of computers were another example.

Two-Address Instructions Early computers can be divided into two groups according to memory organization—those with random access (Williams' tube memory (*q.v.*), and somewhat later, magnetic cores) and cyclic memory (mercury delay lines, and a little later, magnetic drum memories). In mercury delay line memories (*see* ULTRASONIC MEMORY), several words (8 to 32, say) circulate in a line and are sequentially available at the output. The time from the availability of the first to the availability of the last bit of a word might be 32 microseconds, and the time to the next appearance of this word might be 300 to 1,000 microseconds. A similar relationship holds for drum memories. With this structure, faster programs could be written if each instruction had a second address specifying the location of the next instruction. This implied that instructions were no longer sequentially located but were scattered through memory so as to become available at the optimum time. This concept was used by the ACE computer at the National Physical Laboratories (England, 1946) and later in such computers as the Bendix G15 and the IBM 650. A more common use today of the two-address format, [opcode] [A] [B], has both addresses referring to memory locations for operands so that, for example, ADD [A] [B] means add the contents of A to the contents of B and place the result in B (or, occasionally, A).

Three-Address Instructions Motivated by the fact that arithmetic operations usually involve two operands and a result, a number of early computers used three addresses in arithmetic instructions. Examples include MIDAC (University of Michigan) and NORC (Naval Ordinance Research Computer). Thus, ADD [A] [B] [C] means add the contents of A to the contents of B and place the result in C.

Four-Address Instructions Some designers also specified the location of the next instruction, using three addresses for arithmetic purposes. The EDVAC, SEAC, and SWAC were examples of this structure. Thus, ADD [A] [B] [C] [D] means add the contents of A to the contents of B, place the result in C, and take the next instruction from D. Since every instruction is a potential jump, no unconditional jump instruction is needed on such computers.

In 1955, Weik reported on 65 computers giving the following distribution.

Address	Number of Systems
1	33
2	6
3	12
4	6
Combinations	8
Total	65

A similar compilation today would show a preponderance of one- and two-address systems, where often the addresses refer to *registers* rather than memory cells.

Multiple Address versus Multiple Instruction In early computers, memory was small (rarely more than 1,024 words), so addresses were ten bits or less. Ten-decimal digit precision implied word lengths of 30 to 40 bits, so the designer's problem was to fit an op code-address structure into the desired word length. Many one-address systems stored two instructions per word, whereas three- and four-address systems could efficiently have one instruction per word.

Address Modification Only one of the first computers had index registers (the B-box on the Manchester University Mark I), but designers soon realized their value. This forced designs toward one-address systems because of the word length compatibility and the pressure for simple control structures.

Since many operations in programs (particularly operations related to control) involve operations with small integers, designers sometimes provide a modifier indicating that the "address" is the actual operand (saving a memory access). Such addressing is called *immediate*. In the other direction, the address might point to a location in memory that contained a pointer (*q.v.*) to still another location, etc. (*indirect addressing*). Add to this the capability of indexing these various addresses, and we see that the address has evolved from a simple explicit integer to a potentially quite complicated function. This complexity has also been a strong force toward one-address structures. However, the utility of source-destination structures has caused continued use of two-address instructions, although, as noted above, one or both of these may refer to registers.

Short Word Length Computers. The advent of 16-bit word minicomputers in the 1960s (the earlier Whirlwind I at M.I.T. was also a 16-bit computer) and, more recently, the 8- or 16-bit microcomputer, and the decline in the cost of logic (so that multiple registers and much larger memories are prevalent) placed other pressures on designers. The PDP-11 structure represents one relatively successful approach to this problem by using one- and two-address instructions.

The PDP-11 had 8 registers (R0 to R7) with R6 being a stack pointer and R7 a program counter. Each instruction consisted of an op code (4 or 10 bits), and one or two addresses. The address consisted of a 2-bit MODE, a single bit specifying DIRECT/DEFERRED, and a 3-bit general register specification. In two-address instructions, the addresses specified source and destination.

Reference

1955. Weik, M. H. "A Survey of Domestic Electronic Digital Computing Systems." Ballistic Research Laboratories, Aberdeen Proving Ground, Report No. 971.

HARRY D. HUSKEY

COMPUTERS, PERSONAL. *See* DIGITAL COMPUTERS: HISTORY: PERSONAL COMPUTERS; and PERSONAL COMPUTING.

COMPUTERS IN SOCIETY

For articles on related subjects *see* BULLETIN BOARD; COMPUTER CRIME; COMPUTER LITERACY; COMPUTER VIRUS; DATA SECURITY; ELECTRONIC FUNDS TRANSFER SYSTEM; ELECTRONIC MAIL; ELECTRONIC OFFICE; HACKER; HANDICAPPED, COMPUTERS AND THE; HUMAN FACTORS IN COMPUTING; INFORMATION ACCESS; LEGAL ASPECTS OF COMPUTING; LEGAL PROTECTION OF SOFTWARE; PERSONAL COMPUTING; POLITICAL APPLICATIONS; PRIVACY, COMPUTERS AND; and SOCIAL SCIENCE APPLICATIONS.

Introduction Because the rapidly diminishing cost of computers over the last decade has made it increasingly cost-effective to use them in more diverse ways, computers have become ubiquitous. Computers are integral to communications, government, the military, medicine, and most everyday business. When we visit the bank, we are likely to use an automatic teller machine. If our job once required a typewriter, odds are good that we now use a word processor. When we make an airline reservation, request a telephone number from directory assistance, or even order a meal in a fast-food restaurant, a computer system is likely to be centrally involved, even if we, as consumers, are not always conscious of that fact.

As computers have become enormously useful, society has become increasingly dependent on this technology. And with increasing dependence comes increasing risks. For many years, any such risk was assumed to be insignificant in comparison to the enormous and largely self-evident promise of computing technology. However, as various incidents within the last decade have demonstrated, such risks are real, and interest in understanding them and in assessing the long-term social effect of computing technology began to grow. Many computer science programs in colleges and universities now require courses in "computers and society" or "computers and ethics," and several academic journals now explore these issues. We have also seen the creation of new organizations, such as Computer Professionals for Social Responsibility or the Association for Computing Machinery's Special Interest Group on Computers and Society (SIGCAS), dedicated to promoting the responsible use of computing technology within society.

The risks associated with computers take two principal forms. First, there is a risk of *failure*. Designing a computer-based system, particularly when it requires extensive software development, tends to be so complex that it is difficult even to understand its failures, much less to predict or prevent them. The likelihood of such failures, coupled with our growing dependence on the underlying technology, represents an important social problem. Second, there is also a risk of *success*. As computers become essential to an ever-widening range of human activity, the nature of those activities and the social relations surrounding those activities will also change.

This article looks first at the phenomenon of our growing dependence on computers and the ways in which this dependence has been shaped by technological progress. It then examines the risks of both failure and success, considering first the question of computer reliability and the social implications of computer failures and then the effects of the growing use of computers on the individual and on society as a whole.

The Growing Dependence on Computers

On a historical scale, computers are a recent technological phenomenon. Sixty years ago, no digital computer yet existed. By 1990, there were an estimated 200 million computers worldwide, and the count has been doubling every two years. Moreover, since the appearance of the first computer systems, there has been a consistent trend toward vast increases in computing power at ever decreasing cost. Robert Noyce, one of the inventors of the integrated circuit and founder of Intel Corporation, observed in *Scientific American* that, compared to the early ENIAC (*q.v.*) of 1946, the typical modern computer chip (*q.v.*) "is twenty times faster, has a larger memory, is thousands of times more reliable, consumes the power of a light bulb rather than that of a locomotive, occupies 1/30,000 the volume, and costs 1/10,000 as much."

The Personal Computer Revolution This continued improvement in price-performance ratio has had some profound effects, particularly in the last decade, most notably the development and explosive growth of the personal computer industry. The first personal computer appeared in 1975; by 1990, there were an estimated 100 million personal computers worldwide. In 1980, personal computers represented a $2 billion industry; by 1990, the total worldwide market was $45 billion. The power of the personal computer has increased as dramatically as its availability. Hardware has advanced in numerous ways: processors are faster, memory capacity has increased by several orders of magnitude, peripheral devices (including laser printers, telecommunications devices such as modems, and input devices such as the hand-held mouse) have made revolutionary progress, size has been reduced to the point that truly portable computers are commonplace (*see* LAPTOP COMPUTERS), and the price for all of these features has dropped sharply. Concurrently, software for personal computers has also been radically transformed in recent years, both in terms of the expected styles of interaction and in the way in which software is developed for popular consumption.

Based on the philosophy that computers should be sufficiently easy to understand that they can be used by nontechnical persons, the early 1980s witnessed a considerable shift in the style of computer/human interaction. Using technology pioneered at the Xerox Palo Alto Research Center in the late 1970s, Apple Computer's introduction of the Macintosh led the way to widespread acceptance of a new user-interface (*q.v.*) paradigm emphasizing extensive graphics, mouse-oriented interaction, and ease of use. As this style of interaction has been adopted by the designers of other systems (as in the Microsoft Windows product for the IBM-PC and PC-Compatibles - *q.v*), computers have become accessible to the average citizen.

Strategies for software development have also been affected by the growth of personal computing. As the product base for the dominant personal computer systems expands, there is an ever greater premium on compatibility and integration. A software application that doesn't integrate well with the existing base of tools available on a particular platform is less likely to survive in the competitive marketplace. This emphasis on integration and compatibility has led to *de facto* standardization of certain operating systems and user-interface paradigms, at the expense of others. Some industry observers have expressed the concern that this standardization threatens future innovation, but it has also certainly improved the quality and usability of the systems emerging at the top of the heap.

The widespread availability of computers to individual programmers has also led to the development of a sizable cottage industry in computer software. Private system designers have in some cases had significant success developing and marketing computer applications. The fact that such individual entrepreneurs lack access to the large-scale distribution mechanisms of large companies has led to the development of *shareware*, software distributed freely over computer networks, with users encouraged to send in voluntary contributions if they are satisfied with the products.

The Communications Explosion Another aspect of the enormous changes in computing over the last two decades, and one that has significant social impact, is the growth of communications technology in general and computer networking in particular. In 1968, Bolt Beranek and Newman Inc. of Cambridge, MA, won a contract from the Defense Advanced Research Projects Agency (then identified as ARPA, but later as DARPA) to build a network that would connect computer systems at various universities, corporate research centers, and government agencies. In late 1969, the first four nodes of this system were in operation, and by 1977 the Arpanet system had grown to include 111 host computers. In the next decade, network growth in both the public and private sector grew enormously. The Arpanet became the Internet, its structure became much more sophisticated through the creation of domains and subdomains, and by 1989 there were over 60,000 computers connected to the network.

The last decade also saw the development of several commercial networks, such as CompuServe and Prodigy, most of which offer additional services beyond standard network communications. In addition, a number of networks have also been created to further communications between individuals and groups on a non-profit basis. These include such national networks as PeaceNet or the Well (Whole Earth 'Lectronic Link). Certain cities, most notably Santa Monica, California, have made networks available to the public in order to improve communication between citizens and elected officials. As the cost of computer and network technology drops, such systems should become even more widespread.

The Integration of Computers into Other Products As microchip processors became smaller, cheaper, and more powerful, it began to make economic sense to incorporate them into a wide variety of products, from microwave ovens to automobiles, from children's toys to high-tech military weapons. The addition of computing technology to such systems means that they can perform a more sophisticated set of functions and be more flexible in their operation. It also means that the systems increase in complexity, in the sense that their detailed operation is much less transparent to their users.

Reliability and Risk Increasing reliance on sophisticated computer technology, particularly when such technology is employed in life-critical applications, carries with it the significant social risk that such technology will fail, in potentially catastrophic ways. In much of society, the idea that computers always give the correct answer is strongly embedded in the cultural mythology. Given recent advances in computer engineering, this perception is now substantially correct for the hardware itself. Machines rarely give incorrect results through any sort of physical failure, and the reliability of computing hardware has been increasing steadily. Nonetheless, hardware failures do occur, and the results can be particularly frightening. In June 1980, the failure of a multiplexer chip at NORAD led to two false nuclear alerts in four days.

Computer systems, however, are much more complex than the hardware alone. In order to perform any useful tasks, computers must be programmed; they need software to control the hardware. While engineering advances have led to dramatic improvements in hardware reliability, the problems involved in the development of reliable software have proven much more difficult to solve. Software systems are complex, and the opportunities for error are myriad. These errors may be simple oversights or typographical mistakes, or they may represent more serious failures in the conceptual design. Often, software errors are manifest only when the system encounters some unexpected or unlikely situation, or when several individually innocuous events occur in concert. In such cases, it is common for the errors to remain undetected despite years of use.

Examples of Software Failures In 1962, a single-character error in the controlling software for the Mariner 1 Venus probe sent the booster off course and forced mission controllers to destroy the launch vehicle, at a cost of $18.5 million. On 15 January 1990, the AT&T long-distance system suffered a catastrophic failure in which much of the national telephone network was out of service for nine hours. The problem was eventually traced to a problem in the routing software. In each of these instances, moreover, the error occurred in a part of the program responsible for failure recovery. These systems worked under "normal" operating conditions and had therefore passed most tests successfully. It was only when a special condition occurred, and the system needed to respond to that condition, that the software failure was triggered.

Many "computer problems" are not necessarily the fault of the computer itself. Computers are most often used as parts of larger systems that involve both people and technology. In such systems, a common source of risk is the human/computer interface. If a computer system is designed in such a way that it is difficult to use or so that people are likely to make mistakes when using it, this is in itself a risk. One instance is the failure of the first test of the accuracy of ground-based laser stations as a candidate architecture for the Strategic Defense System. An operator entered the height of the ground station in feet, but the programmer had intended that this value be entered in nautical miles. Comically, when the space shuttle received this value, it turned upside-down so that its mirror pointed out into space toward the top of a hypothetical mountain more than 10,000 miles high—well above the shuttle's orbit.

But this type of failure has had tragic consequences as well. In 1985 and 1986, several malfunctions of the Therac 25 X-ray machine left one patient dead and several others paralyzed. In later analysis, it was discovered that, although the user interface included some safety checking to avoid excessive doses, changing previously entered data in a certain way caused the program to bypass these safety checks. Poor user-interface design has also been implicated as a major contributing factor in the incorrect identification of a radar image by the *USS Vincennes*—an error that resulted in the downing of Iranian flight 655 and the death of its 290 civilian passengers.

Finally, many failures are caused by unanticipated interactions between the computer system and its environment. In 1980, a hospital patient was receiving treatment on a microwave-based arthritis therapy machine that had previously been used successfully on many patients. In this case, however, the patient died when the therapy machine inadvertently reprogrammed his pacemaker. And since 1982, there have been five crashes of the Air Force Blackhawk helicopter, resulting in 22 deaths. Each of these crashes have been traced to radio interference affecting the helicopter's computerized control system.

These examples are not isolated instances or occasional flukes. Computer systems have been implicated, for example, in the near-meltdown of the Three Mile Island nuclear power plant, in the stock market crash of October 1987, and in at least two crashes of the Airbus A320 fly-by-wire aircraft.

The Inevitability of Software Risk It is interesting to speculate as to why the discipline of software engineering (*q.v.*) has not advanced to the point at which software designers can avoid software errors and their attendant risk. For the foreseeable future, such a goal is unlikely to be reached. Most experts in software engineering believe that software errors are inevitable in any large system. When the U.S. Department of Defense convened the Eastport panel in 1985 to study the feasibility of the software required for a ballistic missile defense system, they concluded, "Simply because of its large size, the software capable of performing the battle management task for strategic defense will contain errors. All systems of useful complexity contain errors." In effect, errors are a consequence of the complexity of the problems that computers are directed to solve.

In one important respect, software engineering differs from other engineering disciplines in which technological advances and the development of appropriate standards have made it possible to eliminate the major causes of catastrophic failures. Computers are discrete systems, whereas most engineering is concerned with continuous ones. A continuous system usually degrades in a predictable and continuous way: small changes have small effects. This property is not at all true of a computational system. A single character change in a program or its data may be completely innocuous, but on the other hand, it led to the loss of the Mariner I spacecraft. Small changes can, and do, have catastrophic effects. A related problem is that most technologies permit the designer to *overengineer* a system in case of uncertainty. If a bridge designer is unsure whether a particular number of reinforcing supports will be sufficient to withstand an earthquake, it is usually reasonable, for example, to double the predicted number of supports "just for good measure." The same strategy is not available to the software designer. If that designer is unsure whether errors are lurking in a 10,000 line program, doubling the number of lines will decrease rather than increase confidence in the product. As we use computers to solve problems of increasing complexity, we need to accept a corresponding increase in risk. This observation has led some well-informed critics, including David Parnas, Charles Perrow, and Joseph Weizenbaum, to conclude that there must be limits on the level of risk that we, as a society, can accept. Moreover, limiting these risks imposes a parallel limitation on the complexity of systems that we should be willing to deploy in life-critical applications.

Software Liability That computer systems are prone to failure has not been lost on software developers. Throughout much of its history, software development has not been subjected to the same standards of strict liability as have other engineering disciplines, and software vendors have gone to considerable pains to avoid liability for products that cause damage through software error. Almost every piece of software sold includes a standard disclaimer indicating that the product is sold "as is," with no responsibility whatever accruing to the vendor should the product fail to operate as advertised. The legal status of such blanket disclaimers is open to question, and the entire issue of liability for software errors is likely to become a central legal concern in the 1990s.

The Risk of Malicious Attack The enormous proliferation of computing technology and the degree to which computers interact, either through networks or the sharing of software, has led to a new concern. The hazards described in the previous section are caused by errors, oversights, or a failure to understand the complexities of a problem. In all of these cases, the results were unintended, even if they should have been foreseen. They are not deliberate assaults.

In the last decade, however, several serious incidents have occurred in which the perpetrator was intentional, or at least reckless. Computer networks have been prime targets. In the summer of 1986, an astronomer-turned-computer-operator named Cliff Stoll discovered that someone was breaking into the computers at Lawrence Berkeley Laboratory and acquiring special privileges on that system. After more than a year of investigation, described in Stoll's book, *The Cuckoo's Egg*, the intrusion was traced through an astonishing array of networks and computers to Germany, where a group of computer "hackers" was selling U.S. military computing secrets to the Soviet KGB. In November 1988, Robert Morris, a graduate student at Cornell, unleashed a *worm* that exploited three different holes in the Unix operating system to replicate itself across the Internet computer network, eventually affecting more than 6,000 machines. The worm's author evidently did not intend his program to cause real damage, but a software error in the program caused it to replicate itself much more rapidly than intended, overwhelming many of the machines it reached.

In the personal computer world, the dominant problem has been the *computer virus*. A virus is a program that can copy itself into other programs, which then will create further copies of the virus, etc. They may or may not have malicious consequences. Viruses are usually spread from one personal computer to another when a piece of software is copied. If the source machine is infected, it is likely to infect the diskette used to make the copy, and then to go on to spread the virus to the new machine. Since the appearance in 1986 of the first virus to be transmitted outside of the laboratory (the so-called "Brain" or "Pakistani" virus), the problem quickly became increasingly severe, so that by 1990 over 100 identifiable viruses and virus variants had been detected.

The proliferation of viruses and worms, and the threat of additional attacks by computer *hackers* have led to an increase in emphasis on system security. Some response to this threat is indeed necessary, but there is also concern that defending against such attacks may adversely affect research. The existence of relatively open computer networks and the widespread availability of software have both contributed to the successes of the computer age by making it far easier than it has ever been to build upon the work of others. As these channels are restricted, some fear that the advantages of an open environment will also be lost, to the ultimate detriment of the field.

Computer Crime   While computer hackers have captured most of the headlines in recent years, most observers believe that the real threat of malicious attack lies elsewhere. The danger represented by unauthorized users is probably small in comparison to the danger posed by authorized users who exploit their authorization with criminal intent. White-collar crimes, such as embezzlement and fraud, are familiar problems in business. In the computer age, however, these age-old problems can expand in magnitude because reliance on computers creates new opportunities for economic crime.

It is very difficult to assess the actual impact of computer crime within the U.S. or world economies. Possibly out of fear that disclosure of losses might weaken the confidence of consumers or investors, few companies are willing to prosecute computer crimes, preferring instead to handle such cases internally. In any case, losses are certainly high. A 1984 report by the American Bar Association (ABA) surveyed 278 companies and public agencies, concluding that "if the annual losses attributable to computer crime sustained by the relatively small survey are, conservatively estimated, in the range of half a billion dollars, then it takes little imagination to realize the magnitude of the annual losses sustained on a nationwide basis."

A few cases of computer fraud have drawn widespread attention. In 1979, a computer consultant to the Security Pacific Bank, who had acquired in the course of his work the access codes to the electronic funds transfer (EFT) system, was able to shift more than 10 million dollars to his account in Switzerland. One of the largest computer fraud cases known is the Equity Funding scandal, uncovered in 1972. In this case, computers at Equity Funding were used to generate fraudulent insurance policies that were then resold to other insurance carriers. As a result of the scam, losses to investors and legitimate insurance companies may have been as much as 2 billion dollars. In 1987, the German Volkswagen corporation revealed that it had lost about 260 million dollars through a computer-based foreign exchange contract scheme.

Software Piracy   The examples of computer crime cited in the previous section are those in which computers are the *instruments* of crime. Computers and their software are also the *objects* of crime. Theft of computer hardware has grown in importance as the size of the computers themselves (and the concomitant difficulty of moving them) has diminished. Even so, the economic impact of hardware theft is certainly dwarfed by that of what is often referred to as *software piracy*—the act of copying proprietary software without payment of any licensing fees. Particularly after the development of the personal computer opened up the home computing market, such copying of software has become enormously widespread, to the point that software vendors estimate that two to three copies are made for every program that is sold.

Once again, the actual extent of such copying, or the attendant economic costs, are difficult to assess. Ironically, one of the best indicators of the scope of the problem is the proliferation of computer viruses (as discussed above), because such viruses are most often spread through software copying. The extent of the problem was vividly illustrated by the "Peace Virus," which was designed so that on 2 March 1988, it would display a message promoting peace. According to Richard Brandow, publisher of the Canadian *MacMag* magazine and one of the creators of the virus, the virus was transmitted to 350,000 Macintosh computers within two months.

There is considerable debate as to the ethics of such unauthorized copying. Many computer users simply do not regard such copying as theft, pointing out that classical theft denies the original owner possession of an object of value, whereas software copying does not. An organization of programmers called the League for Programming Freedom, originally formed by Richard Stallman, opposes software patents and copyrights. Critics counter that some form of protection analogous to copyright is essential in order to protect the intellectual property rights of inventors. In recent years, particularly with the introduction of lawsuits asserting protection for the "look and feel" of a particular product, this debate has quickly grown in importance so that it is now the foremost legal question facing the computing community.

The Security of Electronic Vote Tabulation While most of the concern about the threat of fraud or data tampering is focused on economic crime, there are other concerns as well. For example, computer experts have expressed increasing concern that the proliferation of electronic vote-counting systems could threaten our democratic rights. A small number of vendors supply the vast majority of voting systems for the country at every electoral level. There are many opportunities, both inside and outside those companies, to sabotage the vote tabulation software, and there are few safeguards to prohibit such tampering or even to detect it if it occurs. In most cases, election officials are not even able to review the vendor-supplied voting software, since the companies providing that software regard it as a proprietary trade secret.

Although the possibility of fraud exists, most of the known problems in electronic vote counting have to do with computer failures and undetected software errors, and not with actual fraud. In the 1985 mayoral race in Dallas, for example, there was a momentary power outage during the tabulation process. When power was restored, the candidate who had been leading up to that time quickly fell behind, which aroused enough suspicion that the problem was investigated. That investigation determined that the software supplied for the election system was incorrectly reporting vote totals for the so-called "split precincts" lying partly inside and partly outside of the city limits. Still other problems were detected during further investigation. This election fiasco, which *The New York Times* reported in five separate articles, eventually led the Texas legislature to amend the state election law and forced Dallas County to replace its entire vote-counting system.

Computers and the Changing Social Order

The preceding section focused on how computers affect society when they are either misused or fail to function as intended. This, however, is only one aspect of the social impact of computers. It is at least as interesting to consider how computers affect individuals and society when they operate entirely as advertised.

Computers and the Workplace For many people in modern society, the greatest impact of computing technology has been in the workplace. As technological innovation produces computing equipment that is faster, more powerful, and less expensive than its predecessors, there is an increasing impetus toward using computer systems in an enormously wide variety of work environments. In the office, typewriters have been almost entirely replaced by word processing systems or workstations (*q.v.*). On the shop floor, technology has led to the development of significantly more sophisticated tools, such as computer-aided design and computer-aided manufacturing systems (CAD/CAM - *q.v.*). Computers have made their mark even in the fast-food industry, with systems that allow workers to ring up orders by pushing buttons with pictures of hamburgers, french fries, and the like.

In each of these environments, the introduction of computers has profoundly transformed the nature of the work process. One of the principal effects of computerization on the labor force itself has been to increase the polarization of job categories with respect to skill levels. Some jobs require increased skill levels on the part of employees, so that they can handle the new, more sophisticated tools; office jobs that require the use of word processors are one example. Many other jobs, such as that of the fast-food clerk pushing picture buttons, require less skill as a result of computerization. Some jobs can be eliminated entirely through the introduction of computing technology, although the extent to which this has occurred has been less than either its proponents or critics predicted. Thus, while there are more jobs requiring highly skilled workers and more requiring essentially no special skills, there are fewer jobs for workers with intermediate skill levels who nonetheless seek rewarding work that validates their talent and intelligence.

It is also difficult to assess precisely the economic impact of the massive introduction of computers into the workplace. Initially, one of the goals of management was to reduce the size of the required labor force through the introduction of new technology. While employment has decreased in some job categories, it has increased in others, and the overall effect on employment is unclear. Moreover, many of the computer systems have proven to be far less effective than was originally anticipated. In some cases, the failure of computer systems to meet the needs of the work environment into which they were introduced has been traced to a failure on the part of their designers to understand the precise requirements of the job. Understanding this source of failure has led to a new philosophy of software development, *participatory design,* which encourages greater participation by employees in the design of the systems they will eventually use.

One of the work environments in which the impact of computers has been most heavily studied is the electronic office. According to a 1987 report prepared by the Office of Technology Assessment of the U.S. Congress, 20 million office workers in the U.S. use a computer as part of their job. Of these, somewhere between 4 and 6 million are evaluated on the basis of monitoring data collected by the computer system they use. This practice has raised new concerns. Electronic monitoring—the process of collecting performance statistics automatically as part of the standard operation of the computer system—is quite widespread. Although such performance statistics can be a useful tool for management in evaluating employee productivity and can help workers improve their own performance, several studies have shown that monitored workers often experience substantially increased levels of job stress. Moreover, electronic monitoring emphasizes those aspects of a job that are easily quantifiable, often at the expense of more subjective measures of the quality of job performance. Electronic monitoring has become a central question of labor policy at all levels of government, and is likely to become more important as this practice becomes more widespread.

In recent years, new concerns have been raised about possible health and safety consequences of the growing use of computers on the job. The most significant problem for the computerized workforce has been the development of an astonishing number of cases of repetitive strain injuries, a debilitating condition that usually affects the hands and wrists ("carpal tunnel syndrome"), caused by repeated keyboard motions over extended periods of time. Such conditions now account for almost half of the total occupational safety and health claims in the state of California, which led the city of San Francisco in 1990 to pass new legislation mandating special health precautions for computer workers within the city limits. In addition to these problems, workers who use computers extensively also appear to have serious problems with eyestrain, headaches, and back pain. Two studies have also found evidence linking heavy use of video display terminals (VDTs) with increased miscarriage rates. As yet, the data on these health problems remains somewhat inconclusive, but there is certainly cause for concern and need for additional study.

Privacy in the Information Age Historically, one of the principal applications for computer systems has been recordkeeping. Computers provide an ideal mechanism for storing large quantities of data in a way that makes that data easy to retrieve or to manipulate. And because it is so convenient to maintain computer databases, the amount of information stored in computers has grown enormously over the last few decades. For example, in *The Rise of the Computer State,* David Burnham reports that the U.S. maintains four billion records about its citizens in the form of IRS tax data, Social Security and Medicare records, criminal justice data, etc. Private companies also record data about individuals, most commonly in the form of credit records. Credit-reporting companies, such as TRW and Equifax, maintain records on the majority of U.S. citizens.

The existence of this vast amount of data raises important questions of privacy. Since the 1880s, the Supreme Court has recognized some constitutional protection for the right of privacy, and there is considerable concern that these rights are being eroded by the enormous growth in electronic databases. An ironic example of the danger was provided during the 1987 confirmation hearings for Supreme Court nominee Robert Bork, who disagreed with the idea of a constitutionally-based right to privacy. An enterprising reporter managed to obtain and publish the list of videotapes Bork had rented, which were maintained in the computer system of the video rental store. In response, Congress passed a Video Privacy Protection Act, but has yet to deal with many more substantial questions that arise.

The question of privacy is compounded by the fact that it is easy to use electronically stored data for purposes other than that for which it was collected. A particularly dramatic example occurred when a restaurant chain offered free ice cream cones to children on their birthdays, keeping records on those customers, presumably to ensure that only one birthday was recorded for each child per year. Allegedly, this data eventually made its way into the Selective Service system, which used the information to determine when those children had reached draft age. A more common example concerns the sale of mailing lists between companies or organizations. Ordering a magazine, for example, may result in an avalanche of unsolicited mail if that magazine sells its list of subscribers to other companies. In 1990, this problem caused a new level of concern when the Lotus Corporation announced that it would offer to sell companies a product called Household Marketplace containing information—including home addresses, buying habits, estimated income, "lifestyle" classification, and other information obtained from credit histories—on over 120 million Americans. Public pressure based on privacy concerns forced Lotus to cancel the product.

Data Accuracy Civil libertarians are not only concerned that the collection of personal data may threaten individual privacy, but also that inaccuracies or errors in the data may harm the affected person. As more and more data is collected and stored in computerized form, it has become increasingly difficult to ensure that the stored information is correct and up to date. In 1982, the Office of Technology Assessment (OTA) undertook a study of the files maintained in the National Crime Information Center (NCIC) maintained by the FBI. Of the records in the wanted person file, the OTA study found that 11.2% of the warrants were no longer valid, 6.6% were inaccurate, and 15.1% were more than 5 years old. The FBI undertook its own study in 1984, and found error rates of 6.0%. An internal review of agency operations improved the data quality somewhat, but a second study undertaken in 1988 continued to show an error rate of 3.6%. While this error rate may seem small, the impact of those errors on innocent citizens can be high. A certain Terry Dean Rogan of Michigan was arrested for crimes committed by another man using that name, and because the NCIC records indicated that the suspect was armed and dangerous, the arrest was made at gunpoint. Even after the error was discovered, it proved to be difficult to correct the erroneous entries, and Rogan was arrested four more times in the next two years.

Computers and the Security State For some critics of privacy policy, the increasing use of computing technology by law enforcement agencies raises the danger of a police state. Courts have ruled that electronic information is not subject to the same protection against wiretaps that have traditionally safeguarded telephone communication, for example. This raises fears among some people that the government may undertake extensive surveillance of electronic communication. A request submitted by Computer Professionals for Social Responsibility under the Freedom of Information Act revealed that the Secret Service has monitored electronic transmission over computer networks, and that the agency has even set up special bulletin boards that they hope will entrap hackers who openly boast of their illegal activities.

Computers and Social Power Finally, there is some concern that the proliferation of computers will affect the distribution of power in society, although opinions are divided as to whether the eventual result will be greater democratic participation or the reinforcement of existing imbalances between social classes. Those who see the computer as a democratizing force point out that personal computers have brought considerable computational power into the economic reach of common citizens. With a relatively small investment, for example, any individual or organization can use desktop publishing software to produce a high-quality newsletter or magazine. Others counter that computers are essentially a tool, and power will accrue disproportionately to those who have the economic resources to buy the biggest and best tools.

There is little quantitative data available to indicate which of these perspectives is more likely to be correct in the long run, but there are some disturbing trends. Access to computers in the educational system, out of which will certainly come the future programmers and software engineers, is clearly related to economic class. Students in private schools or those in well-funded public systems have much greater access to computers than do students in poorer districts, an imbalance of access that reinforces existing inequalities based on social class.

Conclusions Although computers still qualify as a new technology in a historical sense, they are no longer the novelty they were two decades ago. In the intervening years, computers have become integral to the functioning of society as they demonstrate their enormous promise. At the same time, we have become more aware as a culture that the use of computers, and particularly reliance on them, also involves significant risk. That risk is in part due to the fact that computer systems are susceptible to failure, usually as a result of software or design errors. Moreover, the very complexity of the tasks that these computer systems are used to solve makes it unlikely that we can eliminate such risks. But computers also have a profound, and possibly negative, effect on our lives, even when they operate as advertised.

References

1976. Weizenbaum, Joseph. *Computer Power and Human Reason: From Judgment to Calculation.* San Francisco: W. H. Freeman and Company.
1983. Burnham, David. *The Rise of the Computer State.* New York: Random House.
1983. Pool, Ithiel de Sola. *Technologies of Freedom.* London: Belknap Press.
1984. Perrow, Charles. *Normal Accidents: Living with High-Risk Technologies.* New York: Basic Books.
1985. Howard, Robert. *Brave New Workplace.* New York: Elizabeth Sifton Books/Viking Press.
1985. Johnson, Deborah. *Computer Ethics.* Englewood Cliffs, NJ: Prentice-Hall.
1987. Bellin, David and Chapman, Gary. *Computers in Battle.* New York: Harcourt Brace Jovanovich.
1987. Forester, Tom. *High-Tech Society.* Cambridge, MA: The M.I.T. Press.
1989. Stoll, Clifford. *The Cuckoo's Egg: Tracking a Spy through the Maze of Computer Espionage.* New York: Doubleday.
1990. Denning, Peter J. (Ed.). *Computers Under Attack: Intruders, Worms, Viruses.* New York: Addison-Wesley.
1990. Forester, Tom. *Computer Ethics: Cautionary Tales and Ethical Dilemmas in Computing.* Cambridge, MA: The M.I.T. Press.

Eric Roberts

COMPUTING AND THE HANDICAPPED

For an article on a related subject *see* COMPUTERS IN SOCIETY.

The legal mandate to mainstream the disabled in the public school system and efforts to increase the employability of the disabled occurred at about the same time as the development of personal computers. This serendipitous coincidence has fostered considerable effort in applying personal computers to improve the education and employability of the disabled. Widespread interest in the subject was focused at the 1980 workshop on "The Application of Personal Computing to Aid the Handicapped," held at Johns Hopkins University and cosponsored by the IEEE (Institute of Electrical and Electronic Engineers).

As initially designed, the personal computer itself presented hardware and software barriers to use by the disabled. The hardware barriers were:

- Having the keyboard attached to the processor, which precluded the optimal positioning of the keyboard to make use of the disabled person's abilities.
- The requirement to strike several keys simultaneously.
- Multiple character input due to accidental bouncing of the keys.
- Incorrect key selection due to poor motor control.

Software barriers consisted of

- Educational software with time constraints that could not be met by the disabled, or with references to life experiences not familiar to the disabled.
- Software that could not be accessed due to modifications made to the input system (keyboard), in order to eliminate input difficulties.

Solutions to the hardware problems have consisted of devices as simple as plastic keyguards that fit over the keyboard and reduce accidental key depressions and velcro strips connected in a way that allows a control key to be held down while a second key is depressed. More complex designs have involved *scanning keyboards* which use a single switch that can be controlled by any part of the body (foot, tongue, eyebrow, etc.). Another solution involves a resident program which displays the next most probable character sequence after any character is hit. The next character is then selected from a small keyboard keyed to the displayed characters. A keyboard has also been designed for those persons requiring the use of a head, mouth, or hand stick for input called the 2DOF (two degrees of freedom) keyboard. The 2DOF keyboard has key channels through which the user moves the stick to select the desired key. Two actions, *select* and *send*, are required to input a character, a process that eliminates the multiple and incorrect character input problems. In addition, up to 16 characters can be assigned to any key, and the keyboard generates audio output that speaks the character or characters selected.

Other techniques for input involve voice input, optical systems that track eye movement, light-sensitive keys selected by lightpens, and touch screens. Output capabilities include text-to-speech and braille text writers, in addition to those output devices used by the able-bodied. The most prominent user of scanning keyboard and text-to-speech devices is Dr. Stephen Hawking, the noted Cambridge physicist. Though severely disabled by Lou Gehrig's disease, Dr. Hawking communicates with students and the general public by using a PC especially adapted to his limited physical abilities. This is an excellent example of the application of using computers to allow society to benefit from contributions of the disabled.

Educational software has been written specifically for the disabled that uses their abilities and experiences for teaching purposes. Increased resolution CRTs, improved graphics capabilities, and inexpensive mass storage devices have provided new tools for preparing educational software that utilizes voice and animation in order to improve education for both the able-bodied and the disabled. An excellent resource book is available that contains listings and descriptions of both devices and software for communication control and computer access for disabled and elderly individuals (1987 reference). A resource guide for persons with mobility impairment is available from IBM (1988 reference).

Several professional organizations now have committees whose activities are directed toward the application of computing for the betterment of the disabled. Additional information on the subject may be obtained from these organizations.

IEEE Computer Society
TC on Computing and the Handicapped
1730 Massachusetts Avenue, NW
Washington, DC 20036-1903

ACM SIGCAPH
1515 Broadway
New York, NY 10036

RESNA
1101 Connecticut Avenue NW, Suite 700
Washington, DC 20036

As computers become smaller and less expensive and new disciplines such as expert systems (*q.v.*) and artificial intelligence (*q.v.*) continue to mature, new applications that will provide additional improvements to the lives, education, and employability of the disabled will surely follow.

References

1987. "Communication, Control, and Computer Access for Disabled & Elderly Persons," Resource Book 3. Boston, MA: College Hill Press.
1988. "Resource Guide for Persons With Mobility Impairments." National Support Center for Persons with Disabilities, P.O. Box 2150, Atlanta, GA 30055.

EVERETT L. JOHNSON

COMPUTING CENTER

For articles on related subjects *see* APPLICATIONS PROGRAMMING; DATA PROCESSING; DATA SECURITY; DISTRIBUTED SYSTEMS; OPERATING SYSTEMS; PROCESSING MODES; SYSTEMS PROGRAMMING; and TIME SHARING.

A *computing center* provides computing services to a variety of users through the operation of computer and auxiliary hardware, and through ancillary services provided by its staff.

Services Fundamentally, there are four services provided by a computing center: *machine operation, systems programming, application system development,* and *data control, scheduling, and quality control.*

Machine Operation The operating system and the machine operator must communicate about the running of some applications. This is accomplished via the operator's console, usually a display screen with a keyboard and a printer for hard copy. The operating system sends messages to the console indicating that operator intervention is required. For example, if the printer jams, thus inhibiting its action, it usually indicates a "turned-off" state to the operating system when a program issues a request to print. Upon noting the printer in a turned-off state (either due to a jam or other failure), the operating system would issue a message to the operator, indicating the condition. Once the problem had been cleared, the operator would key an "all clear" into the console to indicate the back-to-normal condition.

Of course, in very simple computers, the communication is much more simple-minded. The computer issues the request to print and then just waits until the information is transmitted. If the printer is jammed or turned off, everything comes to a standstill until the problem is rectified. Either way, the operator must notice that the machine is waiting for some operation, know where to look to find out what it is waiting for, and finally how to fix it. Similarly, the operator must locate and mount tapes in the correct sequence for both reading and writing, etc.

Systems Programming Systems programming deals with the writing and maintenance of programs that are part of the computer operating system. The amount of systems programming skill required in a computing center is dependent probably as much on its management philosophy as on its size. Most general-purpose computers are made available by their manufacturers, complete with *operating systems*. The earliest machines had none or only very rudimentary operating systems, whereas modern machines have very sophisticated ones. These operating systems (or just systems) are designed for use by a typical installation and provide parameters that can be varied to meet that installation's needs.

For example, one parameter in most operating systems is the number of files that will be maintained on permanent mass-storage media (e.g. rotating magnetic disks). This parameter is important because space must be allocated to catalog all the attributes of each file (such as its name and number of records it contains). Since these are permanent files, these names must be stored somewhere for ready access by the operating system. The point is that some large installations with very large numbers of files will have to allocate much space to store file-name tables, whereas a small installation will not wish to tie up a lot of valuable space for only a small file-name table.

Many such installation parameters are set to help tailor the operating system to fit a variety of needs. Often, however, the operating system, even with all of its parameters set, still falls short of the installation's needs. The usual case is that it can meet most needs, but meets some critical need only marginally or with low efficiency. For example, a computing center whose purpose is to run applications that simulate nuclear reactors will typically run a few very long jobs (on the order of hours of running time each) in a day. On the other hand, a programming school might run a very large number of very small jobs (each taking only a second or two to run). Even with a well-designed operating system, some functions are unlikely to be adequate for both installations. In such a case the installation management must decide between the costs of inadequate or inefficient operating system performance in some functional area, and the costs of systems programming talent to modify the operating system to meet its specific needs.

This decision is not nearly as simple to make as it seems on the surface. Since the computer manufacturer provides the operating system with the computer, and since such systems are made up of very sophisticated programs (even for relatively rudimentary systems), they are almost never fully debugged. Accordingly, the manufacturer provides software support (or operating system maintenance) to fix the bugs as they crop up.

Since the manufacturer has a support group of systems programmers, this group is the target of many requests for improvements and enhancements to parts of the system that perform their published tasks properly.

These requests for improvements come from the installations using the equipment and from the manufacturer's own sales organization. Regardless, if an installation does not make any changes in the operating system it receives from the manufacturer, it can expect a much more sympathetic hearing if the system supposedly fails to perform in some area. Just as in manufactured goods, the manufacturer feels much less compelled to support a device that has been "tampered" with (even by competent people) than for one that is still in its delivery state.

Principally for this reason, systems programming tends to be an all-or-nothing proposition. Either a shop has no systems programming talent or it has enough to become completely familiar with and substantially provide overall support for its operating systems.

The argument for no systems programming talent is that the costs of inefficiency or incapacity in some areas are less than the costs of learning about and maintaining an operating system. The opposite point of view is that if the operating system needs work that the manufacturer is not inclined to supply, then work on many marginal areas may as well be done too. This is usually the policy of the larger shops with specialized work loads not encountered by most users of the equipment. Systems programming, because of the relatively high level of sophistication of the programs, is usually staffed with the more experienced programmers. For this reason the systems programming function often serves as a consulting function to the applications programming staff, as well as performing the functions mentioned above. Finally, in some of the largest installations, small systems programming staffs are recruited to monitor system performance and establish parameter settings (to assure adequate response times and other performance according to policy), but without actually modifying the operating system programs themselves. These professionals also install new releases of the manufacturer's operating system.

Application System Development Applications programming is concerned with the writing and maintenance of programs that accept as input the information supplied by the users and possibly combine it with information on file to produce output for the user. In that context, applications programming is at the heart of the purpose of a computing center: making machines do what people want.

Data Control, Quality Control, and Scheduling In some cases, users will provide their own data, validate and control it themselves, schedule their use of the machine to coincide with the availability of the latest data, and check their own reports. In that case, no service of this sort needs to be offered by the computing center. In other cases, a great deal of data handling prior to the production run will often be required. Thereafter, if the reporting system is complex, or if many reports are routed to several destinations, staff must be provided by the computing center to handle all those chores.

For example, in an application where hours worked are accumulated and posted for a department each week, somebody has to verify that each person submitted a time card. All the time cards must be checked to see that employee numbers are correct, that legitimate charge numbers were used, and that the hours charged are reasonable. Some of this checking can be done using computer programs that compare those numbers to sets of numbers on file. But that does not verify that the correct numbers were used, only that legitimate numbers (i.e. numbers that are permissible to use) were used. Some parts of the checking are best done in the department. For instance, in a department with large fluctuations in personnel, somebody familiar with everyone present might most efficiently check that a time card was collected from each person.

Keeping track of what has been received and processed by the computing center can be done only by the computing center staff. This service may be divided into two categories: checking that the center processes all the data it receives and checking that it receives all the data sent by the using department. Obviously, it will do little good to check that every person in a department submits a time card if the computing center cannot determine if it got all the time cards. Accordingly, much of the checking about amounts of data is handled by both the user and the computing center. Then, before a production run is made, the user and computing center reconcile their separate control records to be sure there is agreement. Frequently, for example, in an application such as the time-card system, both the center and the user keep a written record with batch numbers, numbers of time cards, and total hours in each batch. The user counts the cards and totals the hours manually before sending the time cards to the computing center for processing. Upon receipt of the cards, the computing center converts the information into machine-readable form. Such recording equipment sometimes accumulates record counts and total hours as the data is recorded. More commonly, a special computer program is used to read each batch of time cards, count the number of entries, total the hours, and verify that legitimate numbers are used, etc. Inspection of the counts and totals verifies (or contradicts) the manual counts and totals sent by the user. Once these are reconciled, the production run can be made.

Concern that all the information received is properly processed lies exclusively with the computing center. Typically, when each batch is added to the master file, a report is generated to display the total number of entries and total number of hours (using again the preceding example) on file at the start of the run, added as a result of the run, and on file at the end of the run. In addition to file-labeling and checking by the programs, a manual record is frequently kept to show counts and totals before and after every run made to add time cards to the file. In that way, in the case of reruns, when file-label checking sometimes needs to be bypassed, files can still be checked for completeness. Curiously, one of the biggest headaches in the data control area is not in making sure that all data has been added to the file, but that it has not been added more than once. This occurs most frequently when a file is updated with bad information, requiring a rerun.

Since the references in all the programs are to the latest file when one is updated, care must be taken in the case of a rerun to update the second-from-latest file. Further care must be taken to destroy the former latest file so that it will not be confused with the one produced by the rerun. For these reasons, several generations of files are kept on hand at all times: the latest, the one before that (from which the latest was made), the one before that, and so on. Typically, four such copies are kept as backup to the latest file, but fewer are kept in applications not prone to error, and more are kept (up to six or eight) on applications subject to high error rates or many updates in a short time period. The shorter the period, the more backups are required. For example, three update runs, all in the same shift and all performed by the same operator, may be handled incorrectly. If all the backups were created using the same bad technique, the file would be in danger of being wiped out (destroyed or rendered useless for purposes of making an update run).

Notice that each time a file is brought up to date (or *updated*), an entirely new copy of the file is made, to which the new information has been added. At the end of such an update run, the old file is intact, exactly as it was prior to the run, and the new copy contains everything from the preceding file plus all the new material. On the surface, this may seem extravagant, especially when compared to manual file maintenance. Imagine the cost to copy an entire file of letters every time a new one was added to the file! But it would certainly insure that there would be adequate copies of the correspondence.

In computing, the cost of updating is nearly negligible by contrast. If the file is kept on tape, for example, a new copy can be made as each record is read, in substantially the same time as that required to simply read the file. Since there are always at least two tape drives available, the updated tape can contain a copy of the preceding generation of the file at essentially zero cost. This technique insures against operator, equipment, and program failure, since it allows for reproducibility of any update run. All that is needed to re-create any edition (or generation) of the file is the previous edition and the new material that was added. Contrast that with the case where the new edition is created by reading the old edition up to the end and then adding the new material to the end of the old file, thus making it the new one. Such a practice is not reproducible because the "end" of the old information is no longer identifiable. Accepted practice is to keep enough previous generations of files on hand so that any operator, equipment, or program error can be detected and corrected (by running the reproducible run that re-creates the faulty generation), all before either the backup or current information is discarded.

Occasionally, of course, errors are not detected in time, especially programming errors that introduce subtle errors into the files at each update. In such cases, files need to be regenerated from scratch. For this reason, current data is often stored for very long periods of times. Such a practice is called *archiving*, wherein either the cards themselves, microfilm images, or separate files on magnetic tape are stored in case it is necessary to go back to a version of the file beyond the usual backup period. To reduce the incidence of having to regenerate a file from scratch, sometimes year-end or quarter-end copies are stored separate from the usual backups. In addition, hard-copy reports are sometimes used as a starting point in the case where all file information is destroyed. At any rate, even though the data control function is supposed to keep these problems from occurring in the first place, it must be aware of how best to detect and recoup any foul-ups well before the last good copy of the file is retired.

Kinds of Computing Centers Computing centers provide service to a variety of constituents, using a variety of equipment and personnel configurations. Computing workload can be classified into two categories: batch and time sharing. Historically, the first general-purpose computers were batch machines. In that kind of computing, jobs are processed in serial fashion, one after the other. Each job had exclusive use of the computer and all its peripheral devices (card reader, printer, magnetic-tape drives, disk drives, etc.) during the time it was being executed. But the batch arrangement made very inefficient use of some resources most of the time. As faster computers evolved, ways had to be found to improve the efficiency of the computer use.

One fairly early solution was tape-oriented batch systems with two computers: The main computer and a smaller machine. All tape drives in such a system are wired to the main computer. At least one, and sometimes two, of them are also switchable to the smaller machine, to which the card reader, punch, and printer are also attached. Input jobs are loaded onto tape by the smaller machine from cards. The tape is then rewound and switched to the main computer, which is programmed to read that tape for all card input. Another tape drive is used by the main machine to write out all output destined for the printer and the card punch. After a batch of jobs has been run, that output tape is rewound and switched to the smaller machine to be read and listed and/or punched. Using this technique, processing times on the main computer are speeded up, because tape can be read faster than cards, but additional time is required to load a batch of jobs to tape. Of course, the first job cannot be started until the last job is loaded and the tape rewound and switched to the main computer.

This apparent paradox of a reduction in service (i.e. longer turnaround) with faster processing led to a search for a solution that allowed the latter without the penalty of the former. A number of schemes were developed, including the use of common disk files and two computers hooked together so that one could stoke the other's memory directly (called, variously, *direct-coupled systems* and *attached support processors*). These methods preserved the batch nature of a main machine and improved both efficiency and turnaround by providing faster transfer of information in and out of the main computer and by reducing the waiting time of information in the input and output streams. But the main computer efficiency was still low, and turnaround far from the instantaneous ideal. With a great deal of oversimplification, what was needed was a main computer that had a large enough memory to hold several jobs, and enough random access mass storage to hold files for all those jobs being processed, including one holding input and output for each job.

Some overhead in switching from job to job is required, of course, and the operating system must be much more sophisticated if it is to keep track of what portions of memory are in use and by what jobs (especially since jobs are finishing and new ones starting all the time), and what files are in use in what positions and by what jobs. This arrangement might be referred to as a sort of simultaneous batch, but it is, in fact, called *multiprogramming* (more than one program in execution at once). Although computer efficiency is greatly improved, turnaround is still far from instantaneous. Since there are only a few input and output devices on such systems, and since it is desirable to have input and output on disk or tape whenever possible (so it can be read and written faster), a job cannot be a candidate to start until all of it is on disk, nor can its output be started on the printer until all of it has been written out to the output file (called the *output queue*). If there were many I/O devices, one could be associated with each job. Then the execution of that job could be carried out piecemeal as the input was available and as any output could be printed.

As noted above, the term *multiprogramming* originated to describe the situation in which the central memory is shared by many applications at the same time, with the central processor alternating attention among them. Thus, with careful scheduling, several applications are perceived as receiving attention from the central processor simultaneously. When two or more of the applications being given simultaneous attention are in communication with (usually remote) users at simple graphical display terminals, we say that the system is providing *time sharing* (q.v.). Some early time-sharing applications followed the usual sequence previously employed in batch processing applications; namely, the reading of all the input, followed by the checking of the input, followed by the processing, and finally the preparation of reports. This sequence lent itself conveniently to the preparation of exhaustive error reports, for example, that allowed the user to correct all of the errors in the data at once. A more convenient arrangement quickly emerged, however, in which each line of input is accepted, checked for errors, and sometimes partially processed, with error messages and preliminary output reported as soon as all of the necessary components are available. Using this arrangement, the user receives error messages following the input of the line in which the error occurs. The error may be in syntax (such as a spelling error or misplaced decimal point); or it may be an error in logic (such as the use of a number that results in an attempted division by zero). The former is referred to as line-by-line syntax checking; and the latter is referred to as *partial compilation*. In either of these arrangements, the user is said to be "interacting" with the computer (i.e. the computer is examining each line of data, testing, or doing some calculations using the input, and often providing a response); hence, this arrangement is referred to as *interactive* or *conversational* or on-line computing.

In so-called computing networks, the equipment that

is located remotely from the central computer has some, perhaps quite substantial processing capability. This remote equipment is referred to as *intelligent* or *smart*; and, in some cases, the power of the remote devices rivals the power of the central or host computer. In these applications, some error checking, for example, or response to the user, can be undertaken by the processor at the remote location, and information that has been partially processed or summarized can then be transmitted to the central computer. Since there is processing capability both at the remote locations and at the central location, this arrangement is referred to as *distributed processing (q.v.)*. With the advent of moderate- and low-priced, limited-processing computers, distributed processing has become the dominant processing arrangement of the 1990s.

Kinds of Computing Center Applications

Early in the history of computing, and until about the mid-1960s, computers tended to be specialized in the kinds of applications they could handle. Some of those machines were designed and built to meet the needs of business accounting and record keeping. These applications require fast, reliable input-output devices of large capacity but with relatively small main memory and unsophisticated arithmetic capability. Records are usually processed sequentially one at a time, as when writing paychecks for one person after another. In contrast, for engineering and scientific problem solving, machines were developed with an emphasis on their arithmetic units rather than on their input-output devices. In fact, since most scientific problems used relatively small amounts of data and produced limited amounts of output—but required extensive main memory space to store both the relatively large number of programmed instructions and all the intermediate numbers in the calculation—such machines were normally equipped with the slower (and therefore less expensive) input-output devices.

Until the mid-1960s, the two kinds of machines were much more distinct than today's machines. *Scientific machines* were characterized by slow peripheral equipment, large memories, and sophisticated arithmetic instruction sets. Their arithmetic instructions often included floating-point instructions, a feature almost never required in accounting and record keeping because answers need be computed only to the nearest cent. *Business machines*, on the other hand, were characterized by relatively limited arithmetic power, character rather than word addressability and substantial I/O capability.

Accordingly, computing centers tended to be divided along the same lines. Programming and operating staff who understood the need of business users for fast reliable access to large files of information were required for the commercial or data processing centers; and technically trained programming staff who could converse with and understand the requirements of engineers and scientists were required for the scientific and university centers. In recent years, however, an increasing need by scientists and engineers for exceptional amounts of very high speed calculations has coincided with the expansion by the business users into much more sophisticated record keeping (involving a greater need for better arithmetic performance) and an increasing requirement by the engineers and scientists in their applications for large amounts of data, particularly input data. Thus, the distinction between what was known as scientific computing and business data processing has become blurred. The result is that the machines of today need many fast, reliable peripheral devices with plenty of mass storage and main computers with large memory capacity and sophisticated instruction sets.

Physical Characteristics

Depending on the amounts and kinds of services provided, a typical computing center consists of a computer room (or machine room), a data preparation/dispatching area, a file-storage area, and offices for the personnel arranged in some logical manner. The machine room is about a third of the space (with wide variations between installations), and usually has a raised (or false) floor. This floor, usually tiled with 2 by 2 ft panels, rests on 8-14 inch pedestals above the main slab. Air conditioning and heating ducts force air under these panels, and power and control cables are also housed there. The (usually) cooled air and the cables come up through holes cut in the panels, often under the equipment modules, thus allowing each module to stand free of encumbrance by cabling or ductwork. In large systems, chilled-water piping is also housed under the panels and is hooked to the equipment through similar holes in the panels.

The machine room is usually heated and cooled, using equipment that is separated from all other areas of the center. This is done primarily because of the control nightmare that is generated by heat produced by the equipment, and also as a fire safety measure. Even in moderately cold climates, more heat is produced by the equipment in a computer room than is needed to keep the room at a comfortable temperature. Humidity also must be regulated much more rigidly for reliable operation of the machine than is required for human comfort. Usually, the absolute values of temperature and humidity are not nearly as important to regulate as are their fluctuations and their differences from one side of the machine to the other. Once set in the human comfort zone, tolerances are relatively narrow, and are typically narrower for larger machines than for smaller ones. As computers are made faster and their components become smaller, the heat-dissipation problem stays about the same. The faster equipment requires narrower tolerances because of the increasing importance of timing electronic speeds in conductors at certain temperatures; the smaller components produce less heat and require shorter wires to connect them, but this does not mitigate the problem.

The data preparation/dispatching area varies from a front counter in the input-output clerk's office, in a small installation, to several rooms in a large organization for input preparation of data, file checking, and scheduling of input; and for rows, bins, and counters for dispatching output, checking updated files, and preparing the files for storage. The file-storage area is usually separated from the machine room, for security and fire protection, but is close to the equipment with which it is used (tape storage near the tape drives; disk-pack storage near disk drives, etc.).

Pricing Pricing of computing services in the early days of computing was a relatively easy task. Each job required exclusive use of the entire main processor and all peripheral equipment for a certain length of time. Virtually every job ran in exactly the same length of time if rerun with the same data. Managers simply divided total costs plus margin for a period by the number of production hours they could expect to run the machine during that period. This calculation produced a rate in dollars per hour of running time, one that appeared fair to the user because it was reproducible; running time could be controlled by varying the amount of data submitted and by specifying (or writing) programs that were more or less efficient in processing those amounts of data. Program and system development could also be fairly easily priced in dollars per person-hour for various levels of talent. Until the advent of time sharing and multiprogramming, pricing was one aspect of computing that was a fairly conventional procedure.

When time sharing and multiprogramming became available, however, the user could expect that any memory not needed by the program might reasonably be sold to another customer. The problem in multiprogramming arrangements is complicated by the fact that many measures of usage are not reproducible. For example, if a job writes a disk file, in some multiprogrammed systems the file may be written in either a large number of small blocks or a smaller number of large blocks, depending on how busy the system is (how much space is available for accumulation of large blocks, and how busy the disk storage device is). Therefore, as a result of the variability in the size of blocks that are accumulated before writing, the job can use a variable amount of computing time between writing each block. This, in turn, determines the amount of time the job spends taking up memory. The job may run in, say, 1 minute on an otherwise empty machine, and use 3 seconds of processor time during that minute (the rest being taken up by the writing out of the information on the disk file).

In a busy machine two effects are noticeable: There is less space for large blocks, so more time is spent writing a larger number of the smaller blocks; and the processor does not switch back to a particular job with any predictable regularity, since there is virtually no way to control whatever other jobs are running concurrently. The effect of both is to extend the amount of time that the job spends in main memory to perhaps 5 or 10 minutes. It still requires the same 3 seconds of processor time (because it still does exactly the steps it did before), but now they are spread over, say, 5 minutes. That is five times as long as it would take on an otherwise idle machine. In the case of pricing based on usage, this job should cost more when run on a busy machine (because it ties up memory and disk-file space longer, requires more overhead to write more blocks, and uses more overhead because it uses the processor more often, due to the reduced block

sizes). In the case of pricing based on service, this job should cost less because the turnaround time is worse.

Computing centers that are service centers (as opposed to profit centers) price their services on the basis of either service or cost. Few of the special arguments that apply to computing are not applicable to many other services within a corporate, university, or government environment. When all is said and done, the processing that can be handled most profitably by the computer is what ought to be processed. For example, if the service center that is newly installed must recover all costs from services rendered, it would have a high rate and an underutilized system. The well-heeled departments could use its services, but those not so well off (and who might be able to use the machine more profitably) could not afford the rates. The computer would be standing idle part of the time, and departments (which could use it to produce considerably more return than the incremental cost to have it running) would be doing without it. On the other hand, a computing center whose costs are fully absorbed into overhead, will be processing the unpopular chores for user departments (not necessarily the profitable ones). Since the users cannot control the costs of computing, they might as well have the computing center do whatever work the using department would like to farm out. As in any service, either pricing method has its drawbacks. The problem is further complicated by the difficulty in allocating costs in multiprogrammed and time-sharing systems. The services are a little easier to identify, but much harder to price. All things considered, computing center pricing presents about the same problem as that of any centralized service.

Chester L. Meek

CONCATENATION

Concatenation (or, sometimes, *catenation*) is an operation wherein a number of conceptually related components are linked together to form a larger, organizationally similar entity.

In the context of string processing (*q.v.*), concatenation refers specifically to the synthesis of longer character strings from shorter ones. In more recent implementations of Fortran, for example, string concatenation is indicated by a double slash (//) so that if W1 = 'CON', W2 = 'CAT', and W3 = 'ION', then W4 = W1//W2//'ENAT'//W3 is the title of this article. Turbo Pascal and Basic use plus (+) for the concatenation operator, APL uses a comma (,), and SNOBOL4 uses a blank.

Some high-level languages support string concatenation by providing a library function. For instance, in the C programming language, if S1 refers to a string variable having the value 'CAMP', then `strcat` (S1, 'SITE') produces the value 'CAMPSITE' for string S1.

Concatenation also refers to a specific technique in defining *macroinstructions* (*q.v.*), where a designated symbol may represent a character string consisting of fixed and variable segments. When such a macroinstruction is used in a program, a specified string constant is concatenated with the symbol's fixed portion during the macroexpansion process to form a complete syntactic component. (*See* MACHINE AND ASSEMBLY LANGUAGE PROGRAMMING.)

In the context of file processing, concatenation refers to the creation of a single, large (conceptual) file by linking together several smaller ones. The resulting collection can be processed as a single entity without relinquishing the identities of its components.

SEYMOUR V. POLLACK AND THEODOR D. STERLING

CONCURRENCY CONTROL

For articles on related subjects *see* CONCURRENT PROGRAMMING; DATA SECURITY; DATABASE MANAGEMENT SYSTEM; and MULTITASKING.

Whenever two or more system processes coexist, there is a potential for mutual interaction. The management of such interaction is called *concurrency control*. In database management systems (*q.v.*), the units over which such control is exercised are known as *transactions*. A transaction is a set of actions of which either all complete execution successfully or none do. For example, if money is moved from one bank account to another at a teller machine, the withdrawal from one account and the deposit in the other account are both part of one and the same transaction, guaranteeing that it is never the case that money has been withdrawn from one account but not deposited in the other. This concept of a transaction is now being adopted in other areas of computer science as well, such as in operating systems.

The standard notion used for concurrency control is *serializability*. The idea is that, even though multiple transactions could be executing concurrently, it should be possible to define a serial ordering of the transactions that would have exactly the same effect in terms of the values recorded in the database and the results produced by the transactions. For example, suppose transaction A writes a record into a buffer and transaction B reads from the buffer: irrespective of when transaction B reads, it must either find the entire record written by A (B is serialized after A), or must find none of it (B is serialized before A). It must never find part of the record.

A popular way of enforcing serializability is to use *two-phase locking*. When a transaction wishes to access a resource, it places a "lock" on it. When it is done, it releases the lock. In two-phase locking, the requirement is that each transaction obtain all the locks it needs before it releases any locks, thus having two phases to its execution: one in which it obtains locks, and another in which it releases locks. If a resource required by a transaction is locked by someone else, the transaction waits until the lock becomes available.

There are many refinements of the above scheme. For example, a transaction that is reading a data item can "share" a lock on this data item with other transactions that also wish to read the item. An "exclusive" lock is required only if a data item is to be written. Another

generalization of a lock is a *semaphore*. A semaphore, S, is a non-negative integer on which two atomic actions are defined:

[Obtain Lock] P(S): if (S = 0) then <failure>
           else S = S − 1 ;/*success*/
[Release Lock] V(S): S = S + 1;

If, to begin with, every item has an associated S = 1, then each semaphore S becomes an exclusive lock. When the item is locked, S is 0. When there is a pool of N similar resources, the entire pool is assigned a simple semaphore with, initially, S=N. Every time a resource from the pool is requested and obtained, S is decremented. Every time a resource is released back into the pool, S is incremented. Thus, S maintains a count of the number of available units of the resource in the pool.

Consider the following situation: transaction A requests resource P and obtains a lock on it, while transaction B requests resource Q and obtains a lock on it. Now transaction A requests resource Q and transaction B requests resource P. Both transactions have their requests denied on account of the other. Both transactions then wait for their respective requests to be granted. Both wait forever, a situation called *deadlock*. Sometimes it is possible to prescribe an order in which transactions request resources, making it impossible for a deadlock to occur. More commonly, deadlocks must be detected when they arise, and must be resolved by aborting one of the transactions involved. Usually, there is a choice of transactions that can be aborted to correct the deadlock. For instance, in the example above, if either transaction is aborted, the other can proceed. Which transaction to choose is a decision that depends on such factors as how time-critical the transactions are and how much work they have done until now. If transactions usually do not have to wait very long for a resource, then, rather than trying to detect deadlock, a simple "time-out" mechanism may be used. In general, however, a "wait-for" graph is constructed, with a node corresponding to each transaction and an edge from node A to node B if and only if transaction A is waiting for a resource currently locked by transaction B. A deadlock occurs whenever this "wait-for" graph develops a cycle. The deadlock is resolved by deleting a transaction that corresponds to one of the nodes in the cycle.

Thus far, we have used the term "resource" or "data item" freely, without specifying exactly what it is; indeed, exactly what it is can depend on the particular system. We could be referring to a "large" resource like an entire relation in a database or a buffer in memory, or we could be referring to a "small" resource, such as an individual word of data. The larger the granularity used, the greater the loss of concurrency due to transactions being locked out. On the other hand, the smaller the granularity, the greater the overhead (both in terms of storage and in terms of effort) to store, obtain, and release locks. An appropriate trade-off is required. Some systems permit the granularity of the lock to be adjusted dynamically, adapting to current system conditions and the access pattern of a transaction. With a view to increasing concurrency, weaker notions than serializability to ensure correctness have been proposed for concurrency control, especially in applications where transactions can be of long duration.

Reference

1987. Bernstein, P. A. Hadzilacos, V. and Goodman, N. *Concurrency Control and Recovery in Database Systems*. Reading, MA: Addison-Wesley.

H. JAGADISH

CONCURRENT PROGRAMMING

For articles on related subjects *see* ADA; CONCURRENCY CONTROL; GUARDED COMMAND; MODULA-2; MULTIPLEXING; MULTIPROCESSING; MULTITASKING; PARALLEL PROCESSING; and PETRI NET.

Introduction Concurrent programming is becoming increasingly important because multicomputer architectures, particularly networks of microprocessors, are rapidly becoming attractive alternatives to traditional maxicomputers (minicomputers and mainframes). Concurrent programming facilities allow the natural expression of concurrency, and they exploit the parallelism, if any, of the underlying computer system. Concurrent (parallel) algorithms occur in a wide variety of application domains, such as operating systems (*q.v.*), databases, simulation (*q.v.*), weather prediction, real-time system design, scientific applications (*q.v.*), artificial intelligence (*q.v.*), and robotics (*q.v.*). Specifically, concurrent programming is important for many reasons [Hoare 1978; Gehani and Roome 1989]:

- Concurrent programming facilities are notationally convenient and conceptually elegant for writing systems in which many events occur concurrently (e.g. operating systems, real-time systems, and database systems).
- Without concurrent programming facilities, programmers are forced to implement parallel systems and algorithms as sequential programs. Thus, the program does not reflect the structure of the system or algorithm implemented, and this makes the program hard to understand, analyze, and maintain.
- Efficient utilization of multiprocessor architectures requires concurrent programming.
- Concurrent programming can reduce program execution time, even on uniprocessors, by allowing input/output operations to run in parallel with computation.

The only disadvantage of concurrent programming is that it adds complexity to a programming language. For example, a concurrent programming language introduces additional syntax and semantics for defining program components that can run in parallel and for controlling how they interact. However, anyone who implements a parallel application in a sequential language must write code to simulate these concurrent facilities. The amount of work required to do this is non-trivial, and it requires knowledge of the hardware, the operating system, and the interprocessor communication facilities. Moreover, the code is likely to be difficult to port to different computer systems.

To give the flavor of a concurrent programming language, we briefly describe Concurrent C [Gehani and Roome 1989], give a summary of its facilities, and show a game-playing program written in Concurrent C.

Concurrent C Concurrent C is a superset of C (*q.v.*) that provides parallel programming facilities. It has also been integrated with C++, which extends C to provide data abstraction facilities [Stroustrup 1986; Gehani and Roome 1989]. A Concurrent C program consists of a set of components, called *processes*, that execute in parallel. Processes interact by means of *transactions*, which can be synchronous or asynchronous.(To avoid confusion with "database transactions," the term "transaction" shall mean a Concurrent C process interaction. Transactions are like remote procedure calls, with one important difference: the receiving process can schedule acceptance of the calls.) Synchronous transactions implement the extended rendezvous concept (as in Ada): two processes interact by first synchronizing, then exchanging information (bidirectional information transfer) and, finally, by continuing their individual activities. A process calling a synchronous transaction is forced to wait (unless it times out) until the called process accepts the transaction and performs the requested service. With asynchronous transactions, the caller does not wait for the called process to accept the transaction; instead, the caller continues with other activities after issuing the transaction call. Information transfer in asynchronous transactions is unidirectional: from the calling process to the called process.

Summary of Facilities Concurrent C extends C for parallel programming by providing facilities for:

- Defining processes. (A process definition consists of a process specification, i.e. a process type, and a process body.)
- Creating processes (using the `create` operator).
- Specifying the processor on which a process is to run (using the `processor` clause of the `create` operator).
- Specifying, querying, and changing process priorities (using the `priority` clause of the `create` operator and library functions).
- Synchronous transactions (for synchronous bidirectional information transfer).
- Asynchronous transactions (for asynchronous unidirectional information transfer).
- Delays and timeouts (using the `delay` statement and the `within` operator).
- Interrupt handling (using the `c_associate` func-

tion, which associates interrupts with transaction calls).

- Waiting for a set of events (using the `select` statement, which allows a process to wait for a set of events, such as the arrival of transactions and the expiration of a delay without the necessity of *polling* (q.v.).
- Accepting transactions (using the `accept` statement) in a user-specified order (with the `by` clause of the `accept` statement) and selectively (using guards of the `select` statement and the `suchthat` clause of the `accept` statement).
- Process abortion (using the `c_abort` function).
- Collective termination automatically. (When all processes in a program are waiting at a `terminate` alternative of the `select` statement, the whole program terminates automatically.)

An Example We now show a Concurrent C program that models a very simple two-person betting game [Gehani and Roome 1989]. Each person is modeled as a process of type `bettor`. The two processes take turns betting. To place a bet, one process calls the other with its bet. A player's bet is his or her opponent's last bet plus a random number between 1 and 100, provided that the total does not exceed the player's betting limit. If it does, the player gives 0 as a bet, signifying that the player has lost. One process is designated as the first bettor, and initially calls the other with a bet of 1. After this, the processes alternate between waiting for the next bet (waiting for a transaction call) and placing a bet (making a transaction call). The processes continue until one of them places a bet of 0. The first bettor prints the results.

Here is the specification of the bettor process.

```
File: bettor.h
```

```
process spec bettor(int first, int limit)
{
    trans void playwith(process bettor player);
    trans void placebet(int bet);
};
```

The `bettor` processes are created with two parameters: the first specifies whether or not the process represents the first player, and the second specifies the player's betting limit. Each `bettor` process has two synchronous transactions: `playwith` and `placebet`. The first transaction informs the `bettor` process of its opponent and the second transaction, `placebet`, is used by the opponent to place a bet:

Here is the body of the `bettor` process:

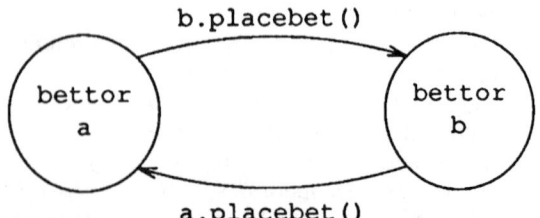

```
File: bettor.cc
```

```
#include "bettor.h"
process body bettor(first, limit)
{
    int mybet = 1, yourbet = 1;
    process bettor opponent;
    accept playwith(player)
        opponent = player;
    if (first)
        opponent.placebet(mybet);
    while (mybet > 0 && yourbet > 0) {
        accept placebet(bet)
            yourbet = bet;
        if (hisbet > 0) {
            mybet = yourbet + 1 + rand()%100;
            if (mybet > limit)
                mybet = 0;
            opponent.placebet(mybet);
        }
    }
    if (first)
        if (mybet > 0)
            printf("I won; last bet %d\n",mybet);
        else
            printf("I lost; last bet %d\n",yourbet);
}
```

Each `bettor` process first waits to get the id of its opponent `bettor` process, and then it alternates between placing a bet and accepting a bet (the first `bettor` process starts by placing a bet, while the second `bettor` process starts by accepting a bet).

Finally, here is the `main` process:

```
File: bet-main.cc
```

```
#include "bettor.h"
#define BETTING_LMT 1000
#define FIRST_PLAYER  0
main()
{
    process bettor a, b;
    srand(time(0)); /* set seed for rand() */
    a=create bettor(FIRST_PLAYER==0,BETTING
        _LMT);
    b=create bettor (FIRST_PLAYER==1,BETTING
        _LMT);
    a.playwith(b); b.playwith(a);
}
```

The `main` process creates the two `bettor` processes and records their IDs (the values returned by the `create` operator). It then calls transaction `playwith` of each `bettor` process to inform it of its opponent.

Although the program shown is quite simple, this program structure can be used for implementing more sophisticated game-playing programs.

References

1986. Stroustrup, B. *The C++ Programming Language*. Reading, MA: Addison-Wesley.

1978. Hoare, C. A. R. Communicating Sequential Processes. *CACM*, **21**, 8 (August), pp. 666–677.

1989. Gehani, N. H. and Roome, W. D. *Concurrent C*. Summit, NJ: Silicon Press.

NARAIN H. GEHANI

CONDITIONING

For an article on a related subject *see* DATA COMMUNICATIONS: PRINCIPLES.

Conditioning is the term used to describe the improvements made in the signaling characteristics of leased telephone lines over those in the normal switched telephone network. When a telephone connection is leased, certain restrictions on the frequencies that can be transmitted over the switched network because of attenuation and related problems no longer apply. Since a leased line uses the same *path* continually, special *equalizing filters* insure that its attenuation and related parameters have characteristics much closer to ideal square waves that can be guaranteed for switched connections. Standards are published of the characteristics that a telephone company guarantees for lines that have been conditioned to variously different degrees (for which there is an extra charge). In such leased lines, it is also usual to have two pairs of connections to the nearest exchange (a so-called *four-wire line*) so that the full bandwidth (*q.v.*) can be used simultaneously in the two directions. Over the interexchange links, the conversations always go on different channels, but, between the local exchange and the subscriber, the two directions of conversation share a normal switched telephone line.

Although the conditioning of a leased telephone line will considerably improve its characteristics, there will be time variations in the characteristics of the line. For this reason, the modems (*q.v.*) in high-performance data transmission systems will themselves add a further (variable) amount to equalization by use of adaptive digital filters. These currently enable switched telephone lines to be used with analog transmission at up to 9.6K bits per second (bps) and leased telephone lines at up to 19.2K bps. It is increasingly common to use digital transmission to achieve 64K bps over unconditioned telephone lines. This should be possible over most local telephone lines as part of the Integrated Services Digital Network (ISDN - *q.v.*). The use of digital filters, with the powerful arithmetic facilities of microprocessors, allows rapid compensation for differing transmission channel characteristics.

PETER T. KIRSTEIN

CONFERENCING, COMPUTER. *See* COMPUTER CONFERENCING.

CONSTANT

A *constant* is a value that remains unchanged during a computation. Various types of constants are discussed in this article—numerical, character, logical, location, and figurative (symbolic) constants. While the reference to an item of information is usually given in terms of its location or address, it is more convenient to refer to constants by their values, since these are intrinsically meaningful in an algorithm. Consequently, high-level languages allow the inclusion of actual values, specified directly in the program, rather than being read in.

The spectrum of items that may be expressed as direct literal values transcends the numbers traditionally associated with the mathematical idea of a "constant." Some of these serve as data items, while others may provide operational information for the program.

Numerical Constants Specification of numerical constants closely follows conventional forms. Thus, the constants in the familiar distance formula

$$S = v_0 t + 0.5 a t^2$$

require no special form in equivalent high-level langauge statements:

(Fortran)	S = V0*t + 0.5*a*t**2
(Pascal)	S := V0*t + 0.5*a*t*t
(C)	S = V0*t + 0.5*a*t*t;

A number of languages also recognize a form of scientific notation for numerical constants. For instance, in languages like Basic, Fortran, Pascal, and C, the constant 0.00000513 can be expressed alternatively as 5.13E-6, 0.513E-5, or even 51.3E-7.

The foregoing numerical constants (reasonably) assume an underlying base of 10. Many languages provide ways to specify other bases (2, 8, and 16) useful in computer work. For instance, the C language recognizes 0X3CF6 as the hexadecimal (base 16) integer 3CF6.

Character String Constants. Many languages recognize character string constants, distinguishing them from symbolic names through the use of special delimiters (*q.v.*). The most popular delimiter is the single quote mark ('). (The double quote mark, ", is often used as an alternative.) Thus, 'BELT' or "BELT" refers to the four characters B, E, L, and T, distinct from some item named BELT. Note that the apostrophes are not part of the string; they merely define its extent. Inclusion of an apostrophe as part of a string is handled by specifying two apostrophes. For instance, 'CAN''T' specifies the five characters C, A, N, ', T, and ' ''TIS' specifies the four characters ', T, I, S.

Logical (or Boolean) Constants Many languages offer facilities for describing and manipulating processes whose outcomes are either "true" or "false." When such support is available, the programmer can define logical (boolean) variables and use them in conjunction with appropriate operators to form logical (boolean) expressions. As part of this support, these languages recognize the two logical constants (.TRUE. and .FALSE. in Fortran, true and false in Pascal, 1 and 0 in C). Thus, for instance, the following Pascal statements

```
var
    switch : boolean;
    . . . . . . . .
    switch := true
```

declare a variable named *switch*, and assign to it a (constant) value of **true**.

Figurative (Symbolic) Constants

There are special types of constants that represent fixed values that are unlike previously discussed types in that they are not designated by their literal values. Instead, they are identified by names intended to convey the constants' meanings. Such *figurative* or *symbolic* constants may be permanent parts of a particular high-level language, or they may be defined for a specific program. Examples of the former are seen in the Cobol language, in which a value of zero has the preassigned names of ZERO, ZEROS, or ZEROES. Similarly, maxint in the Pascal language refers to the largest expressible integer value on the particular computer being used. In addition, many high-level languages support the use of programmer-defined symbolic constants. For instance, the PARAMETER statement, available in Fortran beginning with the Fortran 77 version, enables the programmer to establish a fixed association between a name and a particular data value. To illustrate, the statement

```
PARAMETER (PI = 3.14159,HANDLE ='TABMAT')
```

defines the indicated constants and thwarts any attempt (in the program) to change their associated values. The same results are achieved in Pascal via the following declaration:

```
const
    pi = 3.14159;
    handle = 'TABMAT';
```

Arbitrary Constants

While a symbolic constant's name may be arbitrary, the value associated with it must conform to one of the data types predefined for the language. However, some languages such as Pascal and Modula-2 (*q.v.*) enable the programmer to define an arbitrary data type and an associated roster of "allowable" values for it. For example, the declarations

```
type
    peach = (cling, stark, elberta, redhaven, mushchik);
var
    dessert : peach;
```

define a data type named *peach* and equip it with the five assignable values shown in the parentheses. Declaration of *dessert*, then, establishes that variable as being of the type *peach*, thereby empowering it to take on one of the five legitimate values. Accordingly, *dessert* can now receive a value via normal assignment, e.g.

```
dessert := redhaven
```

Internal representation of such arbitrary constants is a separate issue from which the programmer is insulated. As far as he or she is concerned, the *peach* data type has five values defined such that

cling < stark < elberta < redhaven < mushchik

References

1969. Sammet, J. *Programming Languages: History and Fundamentals.* Englewood Cliffs, NJ: Prentice Hall (see especially Section III.4).

1985. Jensen, K. and Wirth, N. *Pascal User Manual and Report*, Revised Edition. Berlin: Springer-Verlag.

SEYMOUR V. POLLACK

CONTENT-ADDRESSABLE MEMORY. *See* ASSOCIATIVE MEMORY.

CONTENTION

For articles on related subjects *see* COMMUNICATIONS AND COMPUTERS; CONCURRENCY CONTROL; LOCKOUT; MULTIPROCESSING; MULTIPROGRAMMING; and MULTITASKING.

Originally, the term *contention* was used to describe a communication system where the terminals, or lines, were competing for a circuit and the first one to find it free obtained it. This concept can be generalized to the case of multiple users (jobs, tasks, processes) competing for sharable resources (processors, channels, devices). For example, in a multiprogramming system, two jobs may simultaneously require the use of tape drives, thus possibly exceeding the capacity of the installation. This overflow situation would lead to contention delays, since one job would have to be put temporarily in a waiting state. Another example can be found in the case of a multiprocessing system where a process can be split into several tasks and the number of tasks ready to be processed in parallel is larger than the number of available processors.

Contention is solved by using priority schemes; the simplest one is a first-come-first-served strategy. However, all processes contending for a shared resource must be remembered so that they will, in turn, be able to use it. In addition, access to the shared resource must be synchronized. This implies the presence of queues, or buffers, with adequate synchronization mechanisms associated with each sharable resource.

JEAN-LOUP BAER

CONTROL APPLICATIONS

For articles on related subjects *see* ANALOG-TO-DIGITAL AND DIGITAL-TO-ANALOG CONVERTERS; AUTOMATION; COMPUTER-INTEGRATED MANUFACTURING; CYBERNETICS; EMBEDDED SYSTEM; ROBOTICS; and SIMULATION.

The introduction of the microcomputer chip (*q.v.*) has modified the term "control" to the extent that we need to distinguish between digital control and analog control. The inputs and outputs from a digital control system are no longer continuous with time as was the case with analog control systems. The microcomputer, and indeed any computer, must share its time domain with that of the external world to which it is interfaced. As such, input and output is sampled and/or changed in discrete time intervals. Additionally, almost-random events must be accounted for and correctly handled by the discrete nature of a digital control. Continuous, discrete, and sampled data can now be handled properly, and all are embodied in the term *automatic control*.

Control Theory *Control* refers to the function whereby the outputs of a device, a process, or a system can be maintained at a desired value by specifying only its inputs. These generally are spoken of as the input signal and the output signal. The relationship between them is defined as the *transfer function* and is represented, in its simplest form, by the block diagram in Fig. 1.

There are no guarantees that by adjusting only the input the desired output will be achieved. First, it must be determined if a static series of input settings will produce corresponding output reliably. Observations must be made to establish the relation between input and output, the *transfer function*. If these observations reveal a stable relationship, then we have succeeded in building a control system. However, in many applications both internal and external parameter variations can affect the stability of the transfer function or influence the system's output,

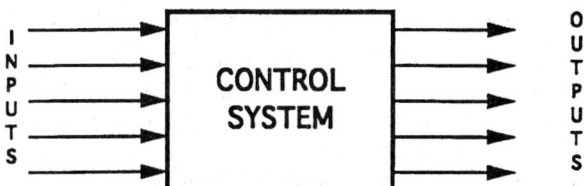

FIG. 1. Block diagram of a system.

thus requiring the modification of the transfer function. Some of these variations may be beyond the direct influence of the designer or the resulting control system.

A system such as a simple lawn sprinkler will deliver an amount of water depending upon the setting of the water faucet and the length of time the water is allowed to run. This is based on the assumption that the lawn watering process is satisfied by providing a predetermined quantity of water per unit area. Achieving this, in turn, depends upon a constant-pressure water supply. What we have just described is an *open-loop system*, (i.e. the setting of the faucet will suffice to provide the correct amount of water). If we elected to measure the amount of water descending upon a sample area of the lawn, then we could arrange for extending or reducing the duration of the sprinkling period to accommodate variations in water pressure and thus to provide the requisite amount of water.

Systems where we measure the success of reaching the target value and feed back the deviation from the target value are called *closed-loop systems*. Closed-loop systems are eminently suited for those situations where we need to overcome anticipated or random variations in the system itself or in the environment in which the system operates. The difference between the desired value and the actual value at any time is called the "error," and the objective of any closed-loop control system is to manage all the adjustable aspects of the system so as to drive the error to zero. A block diagram for a generalized closed-loop system is shown in Fig. 2.

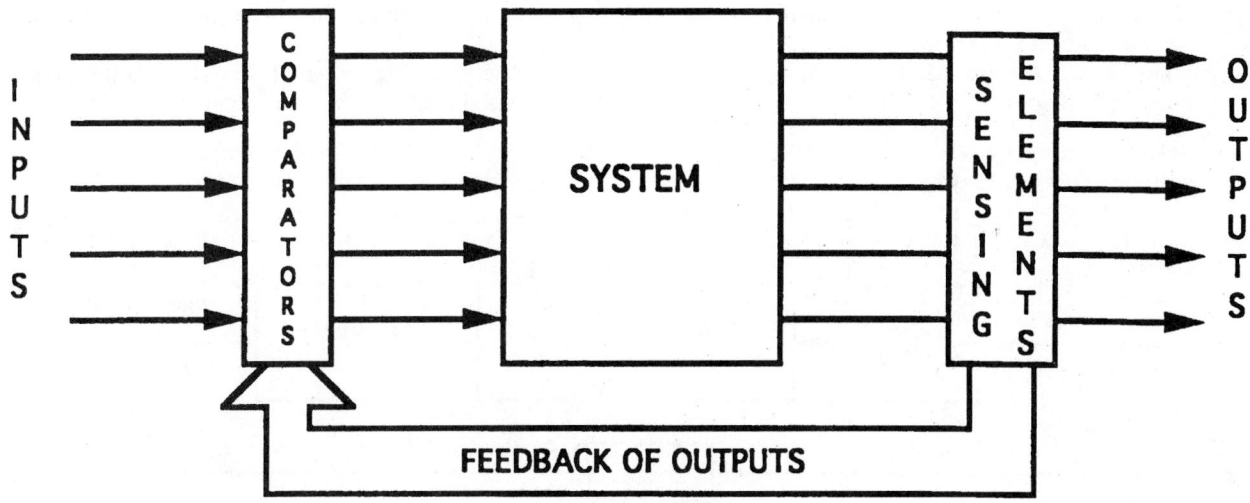

FIG. 2. Block diagram of a closed loop system.

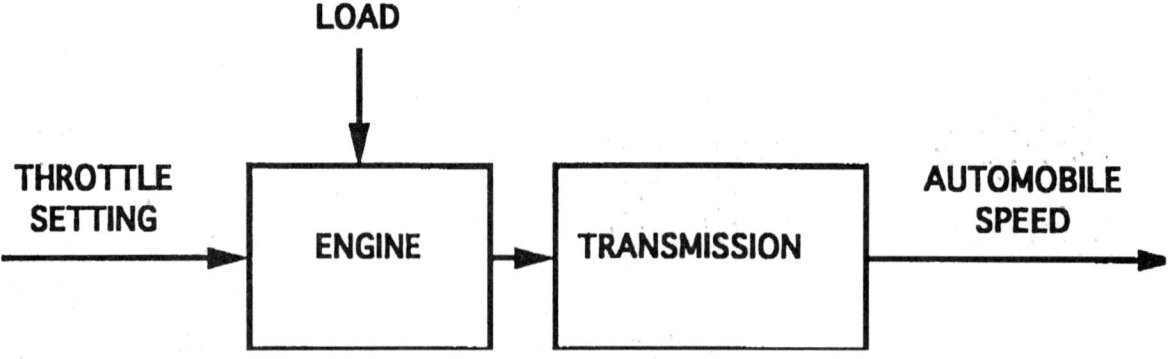

FIG. 3a. Block diagram of an open-loop automobile speed control system.

Note the important components of this system: the inputs, the outputs, the comparators that determine the error from the difference between the inputs and outputs, the output sensing elements, and the feedback loop to the comparators. This diagram shows that the controlled system may have several inputs and outputs. The task remains the same: the correct output is maintained by driving the error to zero.

Applications We encounter many open-loop systems in everyday life. As the need for improved system performance rises and the cost of microprocessors and microcomputers decrease, it is possible to take greater advantage of closed-loop control systems. In environmental and safety contexts, the impetus for improvement is driven by state and federal laws. Further, there has been a growth in the number of devices whose operational performance can be achieved only with closed-loop control systems. Current systems for the control of automotive emissions and to achieve gasoline economy are commonly seen examples.

Two different approaches to controlling the speed of an automobile serve to illustrate the distinction between open-loop and closed-loop systems. Years ago there were hand throttles on automobiles. Setting the throttle on a level highway would result in a constant speed. The automobile would be running open loop (see Fig. 3a). As one encountered a hill, the load on the engine would increase. Since the system had no capability to anticipate the extra load that the hill presented, the car would slow down.

When we introduce a human driver into the system to adjust the gas pedal, we create a closed-loop system. Here the person plays the multi-part role of output sensor (measuring the change in speed and noting the approach to a hill), the feedback loop, the comparator, and the actuator to adjust the gas pedal. The driver will note both the hill and the start of the slowing process and can depress the accelerator pedal further to maintain the desired speed.

A number of years ago the automobile industry introduced automatic constant-speed control systems ("cruise control"). These systems relieve the driver of one of these tasks: maintaining constant speed. Such a system allows the driver to bring the automobile to the desired speed, S_s, the set point, by pressing a button. The car's actual speed, S_e, is measured by a sensor. The error is the difference between the two and becomes the measure for deciding how to manipulate the accelerator pedal to maintain the desired speed. This closed-loop system is sensitive only to the actual speed of the car and is unable to anticipate a hill a mile ahead or another vehicle yards ahead. Therefore, means are provided to disengage the automatic speed control via a button or by depressing the brake pedal. On the other hand, if the driver wishes to accelerate for any reason, a temporary adjustment of the gas pedal is permitted and the control system will resume its original setting when the driver "gets out of the loop." The closed-loop version of this automobile speed control system is shown in Fig. 3b.

Early versions of automobile speed control systems were a combination of electromechanical gadgetry. The

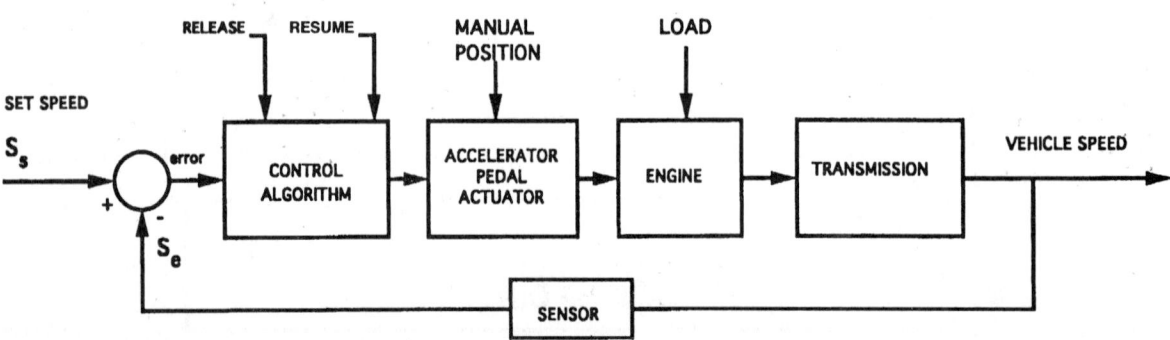

FIG. 3b. Block diagram of closed-loop automobile speed control system.

advent of inexpensive and compact microprocessors (*q.v.*) saw their introduction not only in speed controls but also in ignition and combustion systems (*see* EMBEDDED SYSTEMS). There were two advantages. First, the microprocessors played an integral role in the control system, but their function was easily simulated in larger computer systems used just for the purpose of designing and evaluating the proposed control systems. This not only reduced the amount of trial and error in the design process, but also allowed for inexpensive exploration of the performance of the intended control system and its algorithm.

The control algorithm is the plan for achieving the desired control result. It provides the schema for calculating what changes must be made in response to changing inputs and outputs. In the example just discussed, we find both continuous and discrete operations. The automatic speed controller allows: the setting of a desired speed, the set point, to be locked in; cancellation of the automatic speed control process by depressing the brake pedal; activation of the system to resume automatic operation with the original set point speed; and using the control system manually to move to a new speed and establishing that as the new set point.

The control algorithm, that is, the equations that handle the error signal, generally apply one or more of three standard control actions, although more complex forms can be defined. The net action to be taken is a combination of proportional, integral, or derivative terms, each combined with the appropriate constants (Kuo, 1991):

1. A proportional or *gain term*, with constant K_p.
2. An integral or *summation term*, with constant K_i.
3. A derivative or *difference term*, with constant K_d.

The output from the controller will be the sum of one or more of these actions. The proper values for the constants K_p, K_i, K_d are set by the control engineer to suit the particular situation.

These combined control actions are so frequently used, that the name PID (proportional, integral, derivative) is used to describe the control algorithm. This PID control action is applied in most of the control loops used in today's process control applications. Digital microprocessor versions fill catalogs (see Fig. 4). The current rapid increase in the price-performance ratio of the microcomputer, coupled with the availability of hardware interfaces to "real world" signals, has provided the control engineer with new and affordable control analysis and simulation tools to evaluate proposed solutions to control problems.

What has been described is an automobile speed control system and not an automatic automobile driving system. For example, the system does not sense that there may be a slower moving vehicle immediately in front of the automobile or even a brick wall! The system is unable to sense that the road may curve quickly to the right or left, requiring that the vehicle speed must be changed to negotiate the curve safely. To accommodate these new goals, the control system would have to be changed to allow for the additional inputs. Input signals would have to be provided about road conditions and the spacing between ve-

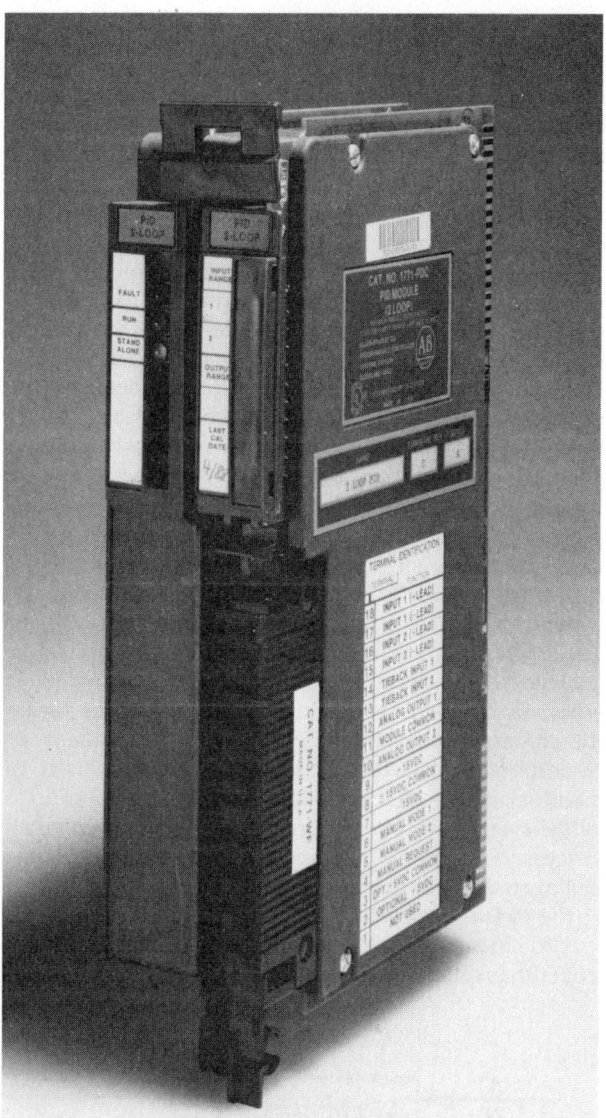

FIG. 4. The Allen-Bradley 1771-PD Microprocessor-based PID Controller. (Courtesy of Allen-Bradley)

hicles. Sensors for some of these additional inputs are available; others remain to be developed. Electronic highway or "drive-by-wire" control systems are receiving attention in many parts of the world. The complexity and cost of such systems would easily increase cost over the current speed control by an order of magnitude, but are said to provide many advantages for relieving driver fatigue and optimizing the use of the highway system. The implied complexity leads us to discuss a combination or collection of controls combined to manage a whole process.

Process control involves the automatic control of manufacturing, material handling, or treatment processes. These processes were once manually or mechanically controlled. Parameter levels were manually measured, adjustments were calculated, set points were mechanically changed, etc. As a result, a kind of "batch" process control mode prevailed.

The advent of microprocessors in the control arena allowed the digital control system to move rapidly into "process" control. The lower cost and high speed of this type of controller found an existing, responsive market. Numerous manufacturing processes were in place. In addition, many new regulations were being imposed upon industries to reduce the adverse impacts of industrial processes on the environment. At the same time, competitive pressures were forcing these same processes to reduce costs while maintaining sufficient profit margins.

The microcomputer provided a solution for these complex requirements. It was not difficult to find sufficient cost savings through a better control of the process itself to easily cost-justify the application of digital control on all or parts of the process. Thus, process control, especially in those applications involving large quantities, propelled the digital controller to its present cost-effective performance level. These applications are typically found in those industries that have developed processes to produce chemicals, steel, aluminum, plastics, food, beverages, petrochemicals, water, etc. These applications tend to be concerned with the automatic control of chemical, mechanical, and energy systems. The digital control systems are generally expected to achieve the necessary performance goals as well as adjust or compensate for inherent disturbances within the process or accommodate variations due to the input of additional material. Digital controllers are used to monitor, adjust, and hold the operational level of individual systems within the process as well as the overall process. Finally, an ever-increasing reason for using digital controllers in this application is the optimization of the overall process itself.

To illustrate these objectives, consider a digital controller that sets the position on a flow valve such that the value of a given parameter in a chemical tank is always maintained at a set point (see Fig. 5).

The particular set point may have been determined by any one of a variety of reasons (e.g. the need for a particular mixture in the tank, a level in the tank, or a chemical concentration in the tank). We are controlling an output parameter, as previously described. Again, the difference between the set point value and the sensor, called the *error signal*, is passed to the control algorithm. The microcomputer-based controller accommodates an algorithm that can either perform a calculation or a table look-up. It establishes the required signal level that must be sent to the flow valve to change the flow rate. This new flow rate adjusts the liquid level in the tank if a certain pressure head or specified level is needed, or it adds more of compound A if the mixture needs to be adjusted, or it adds more of chemical B if the concentration of that chemical needs to be adjusted, etc. At this point the set point has been reached (i.e. the process has been "controlled").

This previous description is called a "control loop." In process control applications it is not unusual to have numerous control loops operating at one time and interacting with each other. This, of course, is a dynamic interaction. It is the microcomputer based controller, with its cost advantage, that now allows the control engineer to address the dynamics of complex process control effectively.

The overall process tends to drive the system *away* from the set point, and the controller tends to drive the system *to* the set point. The rate at which this happens and the changes in the system around the set point is an important design parameter. The control engineer must

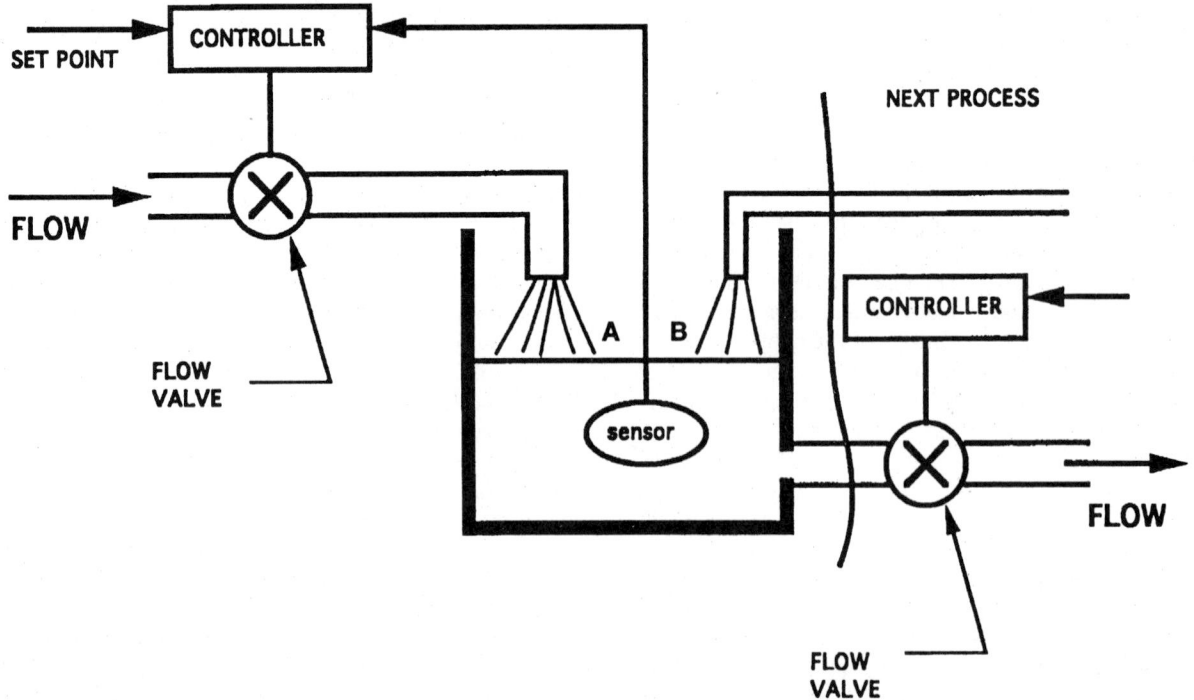

FIG. 5. Chemical tank.

design for this dynamic in the selection of the computer for the digital controller, the control methods that will be used, and the algorithms that must be written.

A block diagram of one system in an overall process can best demonstrate the interaction between the various elements in the process and the digital controller, (see Fig. 6). Note the interaction and information flowing from neighboring systems. The process shown is for a chemical tank that has two inputs and one output. The level of activity in the tank is a function of its inputs and its output. This tank is just part of the overall process. The output from the tank may be metered by another control system. The second input may also be metered by another and different control system. It is expected that the digital control system on the tank will maintain the tank contents at the proper level/state/activity/etc. The second input into the tank was chosen to illustrate an additional aspect that must be handled by a control system. This input introduces a disturbance or variance into the system. This second flow is not metered by the controller; rather, this flow may be introduced into the tank at any time. The control system, or more particularly the control loop, must be able to compensate for this almost random event. (In effect this is another reason why a control system has been placed on this tank.)

The flow valve increases or decreases the flow into the tank. This action is in the direction to reduce the error signal. Once the error signal is zero, the tank conditions have reached the set point and the flow will stop or be maintained in a steady state condition. (It is possible that the set point represent a condition of a continuous steady flow into the tank. In this case the controller is modulating the flow around this steady state flow value.)

Further, a condition of no flow may be one of several special cases in the sense that the controller receives a signal from other systems in the overall process that could represent a "starting-the-process condition," a "shutting-down-the-process condition," a "service-the-process condition," or an "emergency shutdown condition." The control algorithm senses all inputs to the controller, continuously testing this signal, and, upon sensing a change in one of the inputs, it may exit from the main control loop and go into a loop written for the above conditions. In the simplest scenario it would shut off the flow, turn on a light indicating a "standby" mode, and send a signal indicating the same to other controllers in the process.

During the normal operational mode, flow leaves the tank, which in turn forces the controller to make appropriate adjustments. A secondary but equally important activity occurs when the flow from the second input into the tank may start, stop, and/or change. As in the normal operation, the tank sensor would react to this new change in tank properties and produce an error signal. The controller would take the proper action to bring that error signal to zero, bringing the system back to the set point. Again, the process is controlled.

With the advent of the microprocessor and (hence the microcomputer), digital control systems are now the norm. If the microprocessor is powerful enough in terms of its instruction set and its execution speed, it may be able to handle numerous functions, including more than one control loop. (It is this speed that allows one to use the computer in the controller for a variety of purposes other that servicing the control loops. In the past it was this aspect that helped justify the use of digital controllers over conventional analog controllers when the latter had a cost advantage.) The computer measures input signals, computes error signals, performs computations, services the control loops, senses and services external inputs, etc. In effect, the computer's time is shared among these various functions.

The time between servicing of all these operations is referred to as the *sampling time*. Inexpensive microprocessors are leading the control engineer in the direction of being able to use a single digital computer

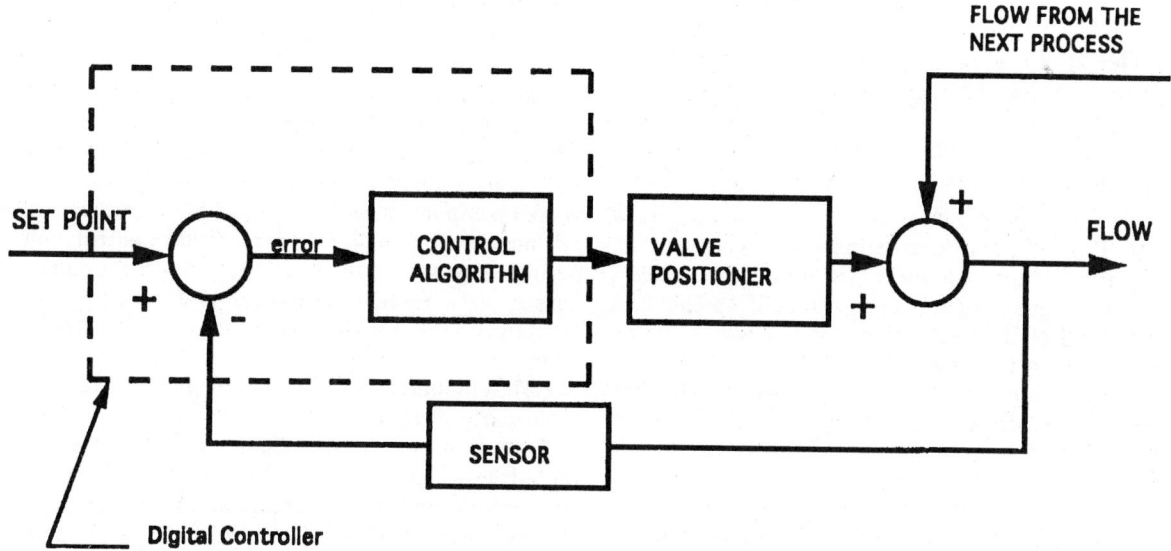

FIG. 6.   Tank control loop.

per control loop. That single digital computer will be servicing all outputs and all inputs, as well as performing any necessary computations. It still, however, is time-sharing various functions before it will again service that same function; hence, the sampling time becomes an important design consideration. The question to be asked is whether or not a given analog signal into the computer (e.g. the feedback signal from the tank sensor) will change significantly between sample periods. If we expand this description to encompass all of the components, all of the digital controllers, all of the control loops, etc., in the overall process, we will start addressing a current issue in process control applications: the need for "distributed" control (Oshman, 1991). This now includes not only the digital computers in each controlled process, but also a network tying all of these computers and control systems together, providing the basis for the beginnings of a study of process control optimization.

References

1988. Bollinger, J. G. and Duffie, N. A. *Computer Control of Machines and Processes*. Reading, MA: Addison-Wesley.

1989. Åström, K. J. and Wittenmark, B. *Adaptive Control*. Reading, MA: Addison-Wesley.

1989. Dorf, R. C. *Modern Control Systems*, 5th Ed., Reading, MA: Addison-Wesley.

1990. Franklin, G. F., Powell, J. D., and Workman, M. L. *Digital Control of Dynamic Systems*. 2nd Ed., Reading, MA: Addison-Wesley.

1990. Ogata, K. *Modern Control Engineering*. Englewood Cliffs, NJ: Prentice-Hall.

1990. Phillips, C. L. and Nagle, H. T. *Digital Control Systems Analysis and Design*. Englewood Cliffs, NJ: Prentice-Hall.

1991. Kuo, B. *Automatic Control Systems*. Englewood Cliffs, NJ: Prentice-Hall.

1991. Oshman, K. "Distributed Control," *Computer Design*, (July), 23–25.

DONALD B. GEISTER AND BERTRAM HERZOG

CONTROL DATA CORPORATION (CDC) COMPUTERS

For articles on related subjects *see* DIGITAL COMPUTERS: HISTORY; and ENTREPRENEURS.

History Control Data Corporation (CDC) opened for business in 1957 when co-founder William C. Norris and a handful of colleagues began to occupy rented warehouse space in St. Paul, Minnesota. The corporation was the first computer company to be publicly financed. Initial capitalization was accomplished through the sale of 600,000 shares of common stock priced at $1 per share.

Mr. Norris and the associates who followed him from Sperry-Rand set out to design and build the most powerful computer in the world. After the release of the 1604 computer in 1958 and the introduction of two more computers by 1960, Control Data became firmly established in scientific computing.

In 1958, the company began to grow through acquisition. It acquired Cedar Engineering, which manufactured peripheral equipment for computers. Cedar Engineering eventually grew into Imprimis Technology, Inc., the largest supplier of high-performance data storage products for the original equipment manufacturers (OEM - *q.v.*) market.

At about the time Control Data began marketing peripheral products, it also moved into data services. There were many companies with the technical sophistication to use powerful computers, but at the time, only the largest and most prosperous could afford to invest in the computers Control Data offered or to keep that equipment busy enough to make it cost-effective. In his words, Mr. Norris decided to "sell a little piece of a big computer at a time."

Control Data's involvement in computer-based services expanded in 1967 when it acquired the Arbitron Company as part of CEIR, a software company. CEIR is no longer in business, but Arbitron has been a major financial contributor to Control Data for many years.

Rapid growth began to strain Control Data's limited resources. In addition, many computer systems were leased rather than sold outright, and the debt that was incurred to finance lease buildup had an unfavorable impact on the Company's balance sheet. Control Data determined that a possible solution to both problems was the acquisition of a finance company. The Commercial Credit Company of Baltimore made overtures to which Control Data responded affirmatively, and Commercial Credit became a wholly-owned subsidiary of Control Data in 1968.

In 1968, Control Data filed an antitrust suit against IBM that was ultimately successful. As part of the settlement, Control Data acquired the Service Bureau Company from IBM. This organization was the forerunner of a number of successful Control Data businesses, the largest of which is Business Management Services, a major provider of payroll processing, tax filing, and other business administration services. The acquisition of the Service Bureau Company doubled the size of Control Data's service business, broadened its markets, and brought to the Company a first-rate management staff.

In 1967, Control Data began to found and promote businesses in which computers were used to provide education, training, and better management services to the disadvantaged. The largest of these businesses involved computer-based education, job creation, and new business incubation. By the early 1980s, Control Data was perhaps best known by many people for these small businesses, even though computers and peripheral equipment accounted for the largest share of the Company's revenues.

The computer industry underwent significant change in the early 1980s, due principally to intense competition from the Japanese and small start-up companies in the United States, as well as the advent of the microcomputer. Some of Control Data's competitors reacted to these changes more quickly than it did and, as a result, the Company's performance fell off sharply and it began to experience serious liquidity problems. It became clear that Control Data had become far too diverse and that it needed to focus much more narrowly if it was to prosper again.

Refocusing became the primary task of Robert M. Price, who succeeded Mr. Norris as chairman and chief executive officer in January 1986. When a successful public debt offering removed the most immediate pressure on the company in mid-1986, the sale of non-strategic and non-performing assets began. The Company had determined that it would concentrate on the computer business, so in late 1986 Commercial Credit was spun off as a publicly-owned company. Control Data initially retained a minority interest, but sold that to Commercial Credit a year later.

Several small businesses were sold in 1987 and 1988. In early 1989, Control Data decided to narrow its focus even further, concentrating on data services and data systems. Subsequently, Control Data has sold Imprimis (its data storage products subsidiary), closed its supercomputer operation (ETA Systems), streamlined its mainframe business, and shed its training and education businesses and several other operations.

Today, Control Data is a data solutions company. Its businesses integrate hardware and software components, to meet complex customer needs. Its Computer Products Group is the largest of Control Data's businesses.

Control Data Corporation's Computer Products Group supplies computer systems and services for engineering, scientific, and other technical markets. The group has a worldwide presence in the automotive and aerospace industries, government, and higher education. There are 1,400 customers around the world, with 1,500 mainframes and more than 2,000 workstations installed.

The group's mission is to provide high-performance computer solutions for engineers and scientists and to manage large and complex databases and distributed communications networks supported by task-specific supercomputers, super-minicomputers, and workstations.

CDC Computers

Mainframes Control Data manufactures high-performance mainframes that offer a balance of high input/output speed and capacity, very high central processor performance, real- and virtual-memory (*q.v.*) capacity, disk capacity, and transfer rates. At the high end of its line are the CYBER 2000 supermainframe and the CYBER 990 mainframe, both of which offer vector processing. In the midrange, Control Data offers the CYBER 960 series (Fig. 1) and entry-level CYBER 930 series. All four mainframe series include single- and symmetrical dual-processor models.

Departmental Computers Control Data 4000 departmental computers are built upon reduced instruction set computer (RISC) architecture (*q.v.*). They use systems software and networking components that comply with open systems standards. The four Control Data 4000 mod-

FIG. 1. Control Data CYBER 960.

els are binary-compatible and run Control Data's version of the Unix operating system (*q.v.*). The 4000 series offers single-processor performance up to 55 MIPS for technical and commercial computing. The high-end Control Data 4680 system uses the MIPS Computer Systems R6000 CPU chip tightly coupled to a floating-point unit. Multiple independent VME buses provide a cumulative 200-MB-per-second I/O bandwidth that can support hundreds of users simultaneously.

Control Data 4380, 4360, and 4340 models offer performance of 18 to 20 equivalent VAX MIPS. The 4000 series models, based on VLSI semiconductor technology, offer robust optimizing compilers, a tuned Unix port, and a wide range of third-party application software.

Workstations and Workstation Servers In high-end workstations (*q.v.*), Control Data offers a broad range of compatible workstations and powerful graphics and numeric-intensive computing capabilities.

The CYBER 910-400 series (Fig. 2) provides real-time three-dimensional graphics performance. The CYBER 910-600 and -700 series offer extremely high processing power and graphics performance for users who need exceptional computing power at the deskside. They produce computer visualizations that appear as realistic as photographs. The 700 series has a graphics architecture that unifies geometric processing with high-speed image processing (*q.v.*) in order to enhance its visualization capability.

Control Data also offers CYBER 920 systems, a series of Unix-based network servers designed to provide file servers (*q.v.*) for workstations. CYBER 920 systems function in multivendor networks, enabling users to distribute their computation workloads, consolidate file storage, and share peripheral resources. There are single- and multiprocessor models. The CYBER 920 is optimized for

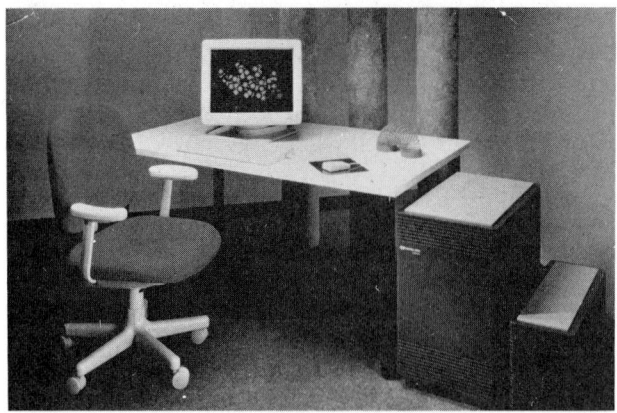

FIG. 2. Control Data CYBER 910 Workstation.

application to disciplines such as finite-element analysis (*q.v.*) and computational fluid dynamics.

CYBER 910-600/700 workstations and CYBER 920 servers may be configured with two, four, or eight 33 MHz RISC processors, providing a maximum sustained performance up to 234 MIPS and 30 double precision MFLOPS.

CYBER 910 workstations and CYBER 920 servers incorporate reduced instruction set computing (RISC) processors from MIPS Computer Systems Inc.

High-Performance Peripherals High-performance mainframe disk subsystems, including the Disk Array Subsystem, provide sustained transfer rates of up to 16.7 megabytes per second. Other CYBER peripherals include 200-inch-per-second magnetic tape subsystems, band printer technology, and optical disk subsystems. To complement information server and archiving software, CDC markets a robotic storage device called the Automated Cartridge Library, a tape storage system that offers extremely low storage costs and stores up to 19 terabytes of data.

Networking and Connectivity Control Data has adopted the International Standards Organization's Open Systems Interconnection (OSI - *q.v.*) model as its networking standard for CYBER mainframe computer systems. Control Data's intent is to move from proprietary communications protocols toward a full, native OSI network implementation in order to meet the schedules in the U.S. Government OSI Profile (GOSIP).

Specific networking and connectivity products include the following:

CDCNET—Enables customers to build local area networks by using ethernet media. In turn, customers can extend these 10-megabit-per-second local area networks (LANs - *q.v.*) into wide area networks by using appropriate CDCNET products called network device interfaces. To add multivendor connectivity, CDCNET includes such features as TCP/IP, NJE, HASP, and IBM 3270 support, as well as asynchronous terminal passthrough.

Loosely-Coupled Network (LCN)—Lets customers build a high-speed (50 megabits per second) "backbone" into their local area network for the transmission of jobs/files among connected mainframes and supercomputers. Hardware and software products support communication between CYBER mainframes, Cray Research supercomputers, Digital Equipment mainframes, and IBM mainframes, over the local backbone and at speeds up to six megabits per second between remote backbones.

NSC Product Suite—Enables customers to interconnect Control Data workstations and computer systems with computers offered by other system suppliers. Here, Control Data augments CDCNET and LCN connectivity by offering all of the local and remote networking products offered by Network Systems Corporation (NSC). Available products include HYPERchannel hardware and NETEX software.

Desktop/VE for Macintosh—Enables Macintosh users to work with NOS/VE-based CYBER mainframes and perform such functions as host-login, file manipulation, file editing, and application execution, using familiar Macintosh-like conventions such as multiple windows, pull-down menus, mouse devices, and icons (*see* APPLE COMPUTER).

CONNECT VIEW—Enables PC users to work with NOS/VE-based CYBER mainframes and perform such functions as host-login, file manipulation, file editing, and application execution, using conventions such as pull-down menus and mouse devices.

Vista Application Link—Allows users to download data from Control Data CYBER, DEC VAX/VMS, or Unix-based systems in Lotus 1-2-3, Symphony, or dBase, without rekeying any data. Micro-to-mainframe communications interfaces allow users to obtain data from PC programs without having to understand the larger system.

Complex Information Management Products

Specific information management products include:

ORACLE Relational Database Management System—Incorporates several features that promote integrated information management. For example, SQL*STAR lets users maintain an application program on one system while its related database resides on a different system. In addition, ORACLE supports the SQL standard for user/program access to databases.

IM/DM Relational Database Management System—Also supports a distributed database feature (DMNAM)that lets users maintain an application program on one system while retaining its related database on a different system.

EDL—Represents an information integrator capable of managing data generated by multiple applications programs across multivendor workstations and mainframes. End users can request data without knowing where that data resides, and they can ask for information in natural language. For example, an engineering manager can ask for "design drawings," instead of using database terminology. EDL also lets customers manage approvals, audit trails, security checks, user profiles, application processes, and network access and control.

THOMAS A. CHARLAND

CONTROL STRUCTURE

For articles on related subjects *see* COROUTINE; DATA STRUCTURES; EXCEPTION HANDLING; PROCEDURE; and STRUCTURED PROGRAMMING.

A *control structure* is a programming language construct that specifies a departure from the normal sequential execution of statements. In its broadest sense, this includes calling a procedure, resuming a coroutine, and initiating tasks, all of which involve transferring the path of execution to another program unit. (In the case of recursion, the "other" program unit is a copy of the calling program.) It also includes, in its broadest sense, the "parallel" (simultaneous) performance of two or more operations within a given program unit. In its more common usage, however, *control structure* refers to the facilities for controlling the sequence of statement execution within a given program unit, and includes special facilities for selection control, repetition control, and exception handling. The description here is limited to this more common view. Usually, such facilities are in the form of "extended" statements, involving several parts in different lines—hence, the term control *structure*.

Arbitrary Control The normal pattern of program execution is sequential control, in which statements are executed in the order they appear. If $\langle S1 \rangle$ and $\langle S2 \rangle$ are each a program statement (or self-contained sequence of statements) that performs some processing (e.g. assignment, I/O, or procedure call) then

$$...\langle S1 \rangle; \; \langle S2 \rangle \text{ or } \langle S1 \rangle$$
$$\langle S2 \rangle$$

represents the execution of $\langle S1 \rangle$, followed immediately by the execution of $\langle S2 \rangle$. A pictorial representation of sequential control is

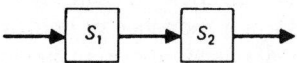

Virtually all useful programs (except those consisting only of procedure calls) involve intra-program execution path control different from sequential control, and therefore all programming languages provide facil-

ities for specifying such control. A simple and fundamental, yet powerful and "complete," set of execution control facilities consists of the ability to (1) insert a label $\langle L \rangle$ at any point in the program, for identification of that location:

$$\langle L \rangle:$$

and to (2) unconditionally or conditionally (depending upon the value of a boolean expression $[B]$) transfer execution control to such points, using **goto** (branching) statements.

$$\textbf{goto} \langle L \rangle$$
$$\textbf{if} \langle B \rangle \, \textbf{goto} \langle L \rangle$$

The conditional **goto** involves two possible paths of execution, as shown, one of which continues sequential control (if $\langle B \rangle$ is **false**) and the other ($\langle B \rangle$ **true**) transferring control to the specified label.

```
         True
  ──▶ ◇ B ────────▶ (Transfer to Specified Label)
         
         False
       ────────▶ (Continue with Next Statement)
```

With conditional and unconditional **goto** statements, arbitrary execution control may be achieved. Typically, in programming languages, labels are either numbers (e.g. in Fortran: GO TO 210) or alphanumeric identifiers (e.g. in Ada: **goto** MATCH-FOUND).

While the **goto** is, in principle, sufficient for all conceivable intra-program sequence control, in practice it is not generally the most satisfactory in a high-level language environment. Most need for execution control is limited to a few highly systematic patterns. When implemented with **gotos**, such control patterns are not especially apparent to the reader of the program, which detracts from the understanding of the program. By the same token, primary reliance on **gotos** for specifying control when writing programs tends to be error-prone. This was pointed out by Edsger Dijkstra in a now classic letter (1968). Bohm and Jacopini (1966) showed that essentially any control flow can be achieved without the **goto** by using appropriately chosen sequential, selection, and repetition control structures. Therefore, high-level general-purpose programming languages include, among their features, facilities designed expressly for optimum implementation of these and other commonly found control patterns. Software development (programming) tends to be significantly easier, and more reliable, if these control structures are used for most execution control, with **gotos** being used only in those occasional instances where the needed control has some unusual pattern.

Selection Control A very common control pattern is that of selectively executing, or not executing, a sequence of statements $\langle S \rangle$, depending upon the current value (**true** or **false**) of a boolean expression $\langle B \rangle$. The control structure for such a control pattern is as follows, with the equivalent control using **goto** shown below the pictorial representation.

if$\langle B \rangle$ **then**$\langle S \rangle$ **endif**

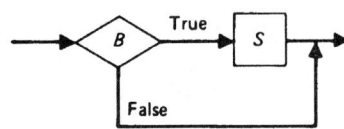

if not$\langle B \rangle$ **goto**$\langle L \rangle$; $\langle S \rangle$
$\langle L \rangle$:

Another common pattern has one group of statements, $\langle S1 \rangle$, being executed if $\langle B \rangle$ is true, and a different group, $\langle S2 \rangle$, if $\langle B \rangle$ is false.

if$\langle B \rangle$ **then**$\langle S1 \rangle$
　　　else$\langle S2 \rangle$
endif

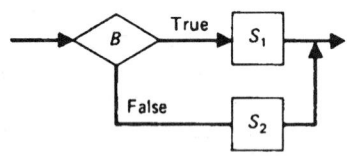

if not$\langle B \rangle$ **goto**$\langle L2 \rangle$
　　　$\langle S1 \rangle$; **goto**$\langle L1 \rangle$
$\langle L2 \rangle$: $\langle S2 \rangle$
$\langle L1 \rangle$:

This latter structure, which is simply an extension of the first one with the optional **else**$\langle S2 \rangle$ part, is known as the **if-then-else** selection control structure, and (with minor syntactic variations) is the most commonly found selection control structure in high-level languages.

Another common control pattern is that of selecting one group of statements to be executed, from among 3, 4, 5, or more different statement groups. In general, one can think of n groups of statements $(n > 0)$, $\langle S1 \rangle$, $\langle S2 \rangle$,..., $\langle Sn \rangle$, from which (at most) one group is to be selected for execution. The conditions governing the selection are formulated as a set of boolean expressions, $\langle B1 \rangle$, $\langle B2 \rangle$,..., $\langle Bn \rangle$, as may be appropriate for the needed control, so that if $\langle B1 \rangle$ is true $\langle S1 \rangle$ is selected; otherwise, if $\langle B2 \rangle$ is true $\langle S2 \rangle$ is selected and, in general, for the first $\langle Bi \rangle$ that is true, the corresponding $\langle Si \rangle$ is selected.

if$\langle B1 \rangle$ **then**$\langle S1 \rangle$
　$\langle B2 \rangle$ **then**$\langle S2 \rangle$
　　．
　　．
　　．

$\langle Bn \rangle$ **then**$\langle Sn \rangle$
　　[**else**$\langle Sn + 1 \rangle$]
endif

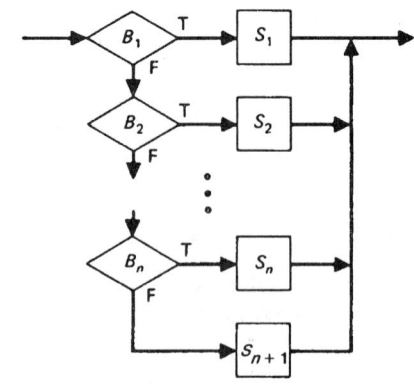

if not$\langle B1 \rangle$ **goto**$\langle L2 \rangle$
　　　$\langle S1 \rangle$; **goto**$\langle L1 \rangle$
$\langle L2 \rangle$: **if not**$\langle B2 \rangle$ **goto**$\langle L3 \rangle$
　　　　$\langle S2 \rangle$; **goto**$\langle L1 \rangle$
$\langle L3 \rangle$:
　　．
　　．
$\langle Ln \rangle$: **if not**$\langle Bn \rangle$ **goto**$\langle Ln + 1 \rangle$
　　　　$\langle Sn \rangle$ **goto**$\langle L1 \rangle$
$\langle Ln + 1 \rangle$: $\langle Sn + 1 \rangle$
$\langle L1 \rangle$:

Since there are no restrictions on the boolean expressions in this *n*-way selection control structure, more than one such expression may be true (**else** is always considered to be "true"). Still, at most one statement group is executed—that one associated with the first true boolean expression—and none may be executed (if there are no true boolean expressions and the **else** option is absent). Square brackets, as around the **else** portion of the above structure, denote optionality.

In none of the selection control structures is there any restriction on the statements that any $\langle S \rangle$ may contain. And, in particular, any $\langle S \rangle$ may contain other (nested) selection control structures. *n*-way selection control may be achieved using nested **if-then-else** structures, for example. Therefore, the above *n*-way structure provides no additional functionality over the **if-then-else**, but highly nested structures detract enough from program readability that the arbitrary *n*-way selection structure is desirable. Note that **if-then-else** is simply a special case of *n*-way selection—i.e. for $n = 1$.

The *n*-way selection structure described above is a highly sequential selection mechanism, involving an ordered evaluation of a sequence of boolean expressions. Another common selection pattern involves, conceptually, "parallel" selection of one from among several statement groups. Here, the selection conditions are disjoint relations involving constant values, so that, in principle, selection may be "immediate" and not require the evaluation of a sequence of boolean expressions. The **case** selection structure is often used to express such "parallel" selection. If $\langle X \rangle$ is an expression, and $\langle V \rangle$ is a constant value of the same data type as $\langle X \rangle$, the **case** structure has the form shown below.

```
case⟨ X ⟩
    ⟨ V1 ⟩ then⟨ S1 ⟩
    ⟨ V2 ⟩ then⟨ S2 ⟩
        .
        .
        .
    ⟨ Vn ⟩ then⟨ Sn ⟩
        [else⟨ Sn + 1 ⟩]
endcase
```

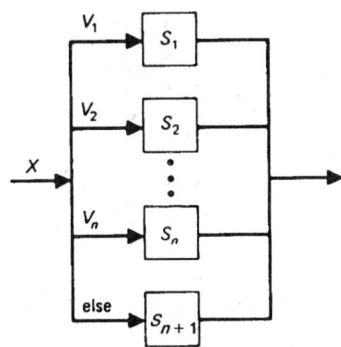

Since the $\langle V \rangle$s are disjoint, their order in the **case** structure is immaterial. Also, any $\langle V \rangle$ may consist of a set or range of values, rather than just a single value, as long as all of the $\langle V \rangle$s remain disjoint. As with the n-way **if**, there may be any number of cases in a **case** structure and the **else** part is optional. In some **case** implementations, if the value of $\langle X \rangle$ does not match any of the $\langle V \rangle$ values and the **else** part is omitted, then an error condition exists, from which recovery must be made (see exception handling below) or execution of the program is terminated.

A significant variation of the **case** structure is the replacement of the expression $\langle X \rangle$ with an arbitrary program segment $\langle S \rangle$. At various points in this program segment, the case value groups are identified for subsequent execution (e.g. with a statement such as **select** $\langle V \rangle$). Such a selection structure, generally known as a *Zahn structure*, provides for arbitrary selective execution based upon the results of an arbitrary algorithm, and has the general form given below.

```
case selection:⟨ V1 ⟩,⟨ V2 ⟩,... ,⟨ Vn ⟩
    ⟨ S ⟩
    ⟨ V1 ⟩ then⟨ S1 ⟩
    ⟨ V2 ⟩ then⟨ S2 ⟩
        .
        .
        .
    ⟨ Vn ⟩ then⟨ Sn ⟩
        [else⟨ Sn + 1 ⟩]
endcase
```

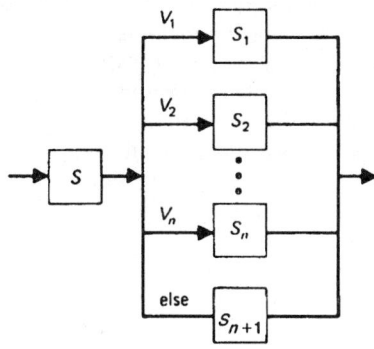

A special application of this structure is described in the next section on repetition control.

Repetition Control An extremely important aspect of programming is the specification of repetitive execution of a statement group $\langle S \rangle$. The following structure, with its **goto** equivalent on the bottom, will repeat execution of $\langle S \rangle$ indefinitely.

```
loop
⟨ S ⟩
endloop
```

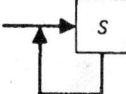

```
⟨ L1 ⟩
        ⟨ S ⟩
        goto⟨ L1 ⟩
    ⟨ L2 ⟩:
```

The above loop control results in an *infinite loop* unless execution of one of the statements in $\langle S \rangle$ causes either program termination (e.g. execution of a **stop** statement) or a branch out of the loop (e.g. **goto** $\langle L2 \rangle$). A **loop exit** statement is one whose purpose is to cause termination of loop execution, and is equivalent to **goto** $\langle L2 \rangle$. Loop exits are normally conditional, and may have a form equivalent to

if $\langle Be \rangle$ **exit**

where $\langle Be \rangle$ is the loop exit condition. A common extension of this is to allow specification of some end-of-loop processing $\langle Se \rangle$ prior to exiting the loop:

if $\langle Be \rangle$ **then** $\langle Se \rangle$ **exit**

This is useful if the loop has different end-of-loop processing requirements at different exits.

Conditional **exit** statements can provide any kind of loop control; whether or not $\langle S \rangle$ is executed again may be controlled completely by the use of **exit** statements. For often-encountered looping control patterns, however, it is convenient to be able to include, in the loop header, specification of the loop control. This usually makes writing the loop significantly easier, and makes the loop much more understandable in reading the program, both of which are highly desirable in the development and maintenance of reliable software. Therefore, loop structures often have the general form:

> **loop**$\langle C \rangle$
> $\langle S \rangle$
> **endloop**

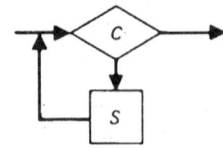

where $\langle C \rangle$ specifies the desired control of repetition. With loop control specified in this manner, the need for **exit** statements in $\langle S \rangle$ is typically much reduced (although **exit** statements may still be allowed in $\langle S \rangle$). Two of the more common types of control, $\langle C \rangle$, are:

1. Indexed: **for**$\langle I \rangle \leftarrow \langle X1 \rangle$ **to** $\langle X2 \rangle$ **[by**$\langle X3 \rangle$**]**
2. Conditional: **while**$\langle B \rangle$

where $\langle I \rangle$ is an integer variable, the $\langle X \rangle$s are integer expressions, and $\langle B \rangle$ is a boolean expression. The effect of each of these control options is as follows (Z is an "internal" integer "hidden" from the programmer).

> **loop for**$\langle I \rangle \leftarrow \langle X1 \rangle$ **to** $\langle X2 \rangle$ **by** $\langle X3 \rangle$
> $\langle S \rangle$
> **endloop**
> (if$\langle X3 \rangle$ option is omitted, + 1 is assumed)

> $Z \leftarrow \langle X3 \rangle /$**abs**$(\langle X3 \rangle)$
> $\langle I \rangle \leftarrow \langle X1 \rangle - \langle X3 \rangle$
> **loop**
> $\langle I \rangle \leftarrow \langle I \rangle + \langle X3 \rangle$
>   **if** $Z * \langle I \rangle > Z * \langle X2 \rangle$ **exit**
> $\langle S \rangle$
> **endloop**

> **loop while**$\langle B \rangle$
> $\langle S \rangle$
> **endloop**

> **loop**
>   **if not**$\langle B \rangle$ **exit**
> $\langle S \rangle$
> **endloop**

A number of variations of these loop facilities are implemented in various computer languages, and occasionally an entirely different kind of control is defined and implemented for $\langle C \rangle$. One such class of variations is

control at the bottom of the loop rather than at the top (**repeat - until**).

Loop structures may be nested, and occasionally it is necessary to exit more than one level of repetition. This may be done by using the **goto** statement, or by identifying loops with (the equivalent of) a label$\langle L \rangle$ and allowing "multi-level" **exit** statements of the form:

> **if**$\langle B \rangle$ **exit**$\langle L \rangle$

A third way to achieve multi-level exits is to "cascade" the requisite number of single-level exits. This may be done by setting a boolean "flag" and exiting one level (e.g. **if** $\langle Be \rangle$ **then** MULTILEVEL $\leftarrow$ **true; exit**), then immediately (after **endloop**) exiting again (e.g. **if** MULTILEVEL **exit**).

Another facility occasionally provided in loop structures is that of proceeding directly to the next repetition cycle of a loop:

> **if**$\langle B \rangle$ **cycle**$\langle L \rangle$

$\langle L \rangle$ refers to the desired loop identification; as with exits, the $\langle L \rangle$ may be omitted for single-level cycling. Since cycling is not needed often in practice, and may be achieved using **exit** and selection control, **cycle** is not as commonly implemented as is **exit**.

A reasonably common occurrence (some studies have indicated for about 20% of all loops) is that of multiple (more than one) single-level exits in a given loop. Normally, one can expect the post-loop processing to be somewhat different for the different exits. For example, a search loop may contain two exits, one for when the search is successful and one when it is unsuccessful. The action taken after the search is normally dependent upon whether or not the search was successful, implying different processing at each of the two exits. Selection of the proper post-loop processing routine may be achieved by flagging each exit, just prior to departure from the loop, for use in ordinary selection control following the loop. Forms of the loop control specification $\langle C \rangle$ exist that facilitate such exit flagging.

A variation of the Zahn **case** selection structure, in which the pre-selection routine is the loop, integrates a loop and its various exit-processing routines into a single control structure. The form of such a structure is:

> **loop**$\langle C \rangle$ **with exits** $(\langle E1 \rangle, \langle E2 \rangle, \ldots, \langle En \rangle)$
> $\langle S \rangle$
> **endloop**
> $\langle E1 \rangle$ **then** $\langle S1 \rangle$
> $\langle E2 \rangle$ **then** $\langle S2 \rangle$
>   .
>   .
>   .
> $\langle En \rangle$ **then** $\langle Sn \rangle$
> **endexits**

where$\langle S1 \rangle, \langle S2 \rangle, \ldots, \langle Sn \rangle$ are the different post-loop exit-processing routines corresponding to exits$\langle E1 \rangle, \langle E2 \rangle, \ldots,$

TABLE 1.

Feature	ADA	BASIC	C	COBOL	FORTRAN 90	PASCAL
1. Label example	⟨⟨LABEL⟩⟩	100	LABEL	LABEL	100	100
2. Branching	**goto** LABEL **if**⟨B⟩**then goto** LABEL **endif**	**goto** 100 **if**⟨B⟩**then** 100	**goto** LABEL **if**(⟨B⟩)**goto** LABEL	**goto** LABEL **if**⟨B⟩**goto** LABEL	**goto** 100 **if**(⟨B⟩)**goto** 100	**goto** 100 **if**⟨B⟩**then goto** 100
3. If-then-else	**if**⟨B⟩**then**⟨S₁⟩ [**else**⟨S₂⟩] **endif**	**if**⟨B⟩**then**⟨S₁⟩ [**else**⟨S₂⟩] **endif**	**if**(⟨B⟩)⟨S₁⟩ [**else**⟨S₂⟩]	**if**⟨B⟩⟨S₁⟩ [**else**⟨S₂⟩]	**if**(⟨B⟩)**then**⟨S₁⟩ [**else**⟨S₂⟩] **endif**	**if**⟨B⟩**then**⟨S₁⟩ [**else**⟨S₂⟩]
4. *n*-Way-branch	**if**⟨B₁⟩**then**⟨S₁⟩ **elsif**⟨B₂⟩**then**⟨S₂⟩ **elsif** ⋮ [**else**⟨Sₙ₊₁⟩] **endif**	**if**⟨B₁⟩**then**⟨S₁⟩ **elsif**⟨B₂⟩**then**⟨S₂⟩ **elsif** ⋮ [**else**⟨Sₙ₊₁⟩] **endif**	nested if-then-else	nested if-then-else	**if**(⟨B₁⟩)**then**⟨S₁⟩ **elseif**(⟨B₂⟩)**then**⟨S₂⟩ **elseif** ⋮ ⟨**else**⟨Sₙ₊₁⟩⟩ **endif**	nested if-then-else
5. Case	**case**⟨X⟩**of:** **when**⟨V₁⟩→⟨S₁⟩ **when**⟨V₂⟩→⟨S₂⟩ **when** ⋮ [**when others**→⟨Sₙ₊₁⟩] **endcase**	**select case**⟨X⟩ **case**⟨V₁⟩⟨S₁⟩ **case**⟨V₂⟩⟨S₂⟩ ⋮ **case else**⟨Sₙ₊₁⟩ **end select**	**switch**(⟨X⟩) {**case**⟨V₁⟩:⟨S₁⟩ **case**⟨V₂⟩:⟨S₂⟩ ⋮ **default:**⟨Sₙ₊₁⟩ }	**goto**⟨L₁⟩,⟨L₂⟩,...,⟨Lₙ⟩ **depending on**⟨I⟩	**select case**((⟨X⟩)) **case**((⟨V₁⟩))⟨S₁⟩ **case**((⟨V₂⟩))⟨S₂⟩ ⋮ [**case default**⟨Sₙ₊₁⟩] **end select**	**case**⟨X⟩**of** ⟨V₁⟩:⟨S₁⟩ ⟨V₂⟩:⟨S₂⟩ ⋮ ⟨Vₙ⟩:⟨Sₙ⟩ **end**
6. Looping	**loop** ⟨S⟩ **endloop** **while**⟨B⟩**loop** ⟨S⟩ **endloop** **for**⟨I⟩**in**⟨X₁⟩..⟨X₂⟩**loop** ⟨S⟩ **endloop**	**for**⟨I⟩→⟨X₁⟩**to** ⟨X₂⟩ [**step**⟨X₃⟩] ⟨S⟩ **next**⟨I⟩ **do** ⟨S⟩ **loop** **do while**⟨B⟩ ⟨S⟩ **loop**	**while**⟨B⟩ ⟨S⟩ **do** ⟨S⟩ **while**(⟨B⟩) **for**((⟨I⟩) = ⟨X₁⟩;⟨B⟩;⟨X₂⟩) ⟨S⟩	**perform**⟨L⟩**until**⟨B⟩ **perform**⟨L⟩**varying**⟨I⟩ **from**⟨X₁⟩**by**⟨X₂⟩ **until**⟨B⟩ ⟨L⟩:⟨S⟩	**do** ⟨S⟩ **enddo** **do**((⟨I⟩=⟨X₁⟩,⟨X₂⟩,[⟨X₃⟩]) ⟨S⟩ **enddo** **do while**((⟨B⟩) ⟨S⟩ **enddo**	**while**⟨B⟩**do**⟨S⟩ **repeat**⟨S⟩**until**⟨B⟩ **for**⟨I⟩:=⟨X₁⟩**to**⟨X₂⟩ **do**⟨S⟩

TABLE 1 (continued)

Feature	ADA	BASIC	C	COBOL	FORTRAN 90	PASCAL
7. Loop exits	**exit [when** $\langle B \rangle$**]**	*exit*	*break*	*goto* $\langle L \rangle$	*exit*	**goto** $\langle L \rangle$
8. Exception handling	**begin** $\langle S_0 \rangle$ **exception** **when** $\langle E_1 \rangle \rightarrow \langle S_1 \rangle$ **when** $\langle E_2 \rangle \rightarrow \langle S_2 \rangle$ **when** . . . [**when others** $\rightarrow \langle S_{n+1} \rangle$] **end**	*when exception in* $\langle S_1 \rangle$ *use* $\langle S_2 \rangle$ *end when* *handler* $\langle X \rangle$ $\langle S \rangle$ *end handler*	N/A	*on* $\langle E_1 \rangle \langle S_1 \rangle$. *on* $\langle E_2 \rangle \langle S_2 \rangle$. . . .	N/A	N/A

NOTES: Square brackets [] denote optional items.
The Basic above is ANSI Standard Basic.
N/A = not available in language.
$\langle B \rangle$ is a boolean (logical) expression.
$\langle S \rangle$ is a (compound) statement.
$\langle X \rangle$ is a (numeric) expression.
$\langle V \rangle$ is a variable identifier.
$\langle L \rangle$ is a label.
$\langle I \rangle$ is an integer variable identifier.
$\langle E \rangle$ is an exception condition (e.g. logical expression).

⟨ *En* ⟩, respectively. Within the loop body ⟨ *S* ⟩, a certain exit may be specified with an exit statement of the form:

if⟨ *Be* ⟩ **select exit**⟨ *Ei* ⟩.

Most programming languages do not provide a full Zahn construct as such, but rely upon the programmer to use two consecutive simpler structures, such as a simple loop structure followed by a simple case structure, with appropriate variable communication between them, to simulate the effect of a Zahn structure.

Exception Handling A number of things can happen during program execution that can prevent execution from successfully continuing. These include division by zero, subscript out of bounds, numeric overflow, **case** value missing, unavailable read-only file, wrong data type on input, insufficient storage available, and referencing an undefined value. Such exceptions, when detected, normally result in program termination without further processing unless provision is made for some other action, and possibly recovery. Such provision is called *exception handling* and, since execution control is the issue, constitutes a form of control structuring.

The structural nature of an exception handler is essentially that of a **case** selection control structure. One of a predefined set of exception values is presented to the handler, which then selects the routine that performs the action desired in the event that that particular exception occurs. If corrective action is possible, then that routine may include such action, followed by resumption of normal processing; otherwise, program execution terminates after execution of the handling routine. The form of such an exception handler is

> **exception**
>   ⟨ *E1* ⟩ **then**⟨ *S1* ⟩
>   ⟨ *E2* ⟩ **then**⟨ *S2* ⟩
>   .
>   .
>   .
>   ⟨ *En* ⟩ **then**⟨ *Sn* ⟩
> **endexception**

When an exception occurs, execution control automatically is passed to the beginning of the exception handler, along with the identification⟨ *E* ⟩ of the exception that has occurred. Selection is then made of the corresponding routine⟨ *S* ⟩ to be executed. Program execution is terminated after execution of⟨ *S* ⟩, unless⟨ *S* ⟩ specifies recovery and resumption of program execution. For example, if the last statement in⟨ *S* ⟩ is

> **recover**

then, instead of terminating, program execution would resume from the point at which the exception occurred. Presumably, the statements in ⟨ *S* ⟩ preceding **recover** would provide suitable corrective action so that resumed program execution is sensible.

In addition to the intrinsic exception cases, some implementations allow the programmer to define additional exception values, and to specify explicitly that an exception has occurred. Such programmer defined and detected exceptions may be handled in the same manner, and with the same handler control structure as intrinsic exceptions. In terms of control structure considerations, the two main differences between **case** selection and exception handling are (1) that exception handling involves some intrinsic exception values in addition to programmer-defined ones, and (2) that the location in the program of an exception handler is immaterial, with the necessary branches to and from the handler taking place automatically (whereas a **case** structure must be placed in the program at the point the selection is to be performed). Exception handlers may also be implemented as procedures.

In most instances, the logic of a problem can be expressed in a relatively straightforward manner in terms of selection and repetition control structures. Arbitrary sequencing and nesting of such structures is permitted, as is allowing any ⟨ *S* ⟩ to be empty. For example, loop bodies may contain other loops and/or any type of selection, without restriction; selection statement groups may contain additional selection structures and/or loops, without restriction. Although nesting can be carried to any level, the control logic tends to become difficult for humans to read easily after about three levels of nesting.

Control structures are major features of high-level programming languages, and a language's control structures play a major role in its effectiveness in software development. Table 1 shows the control structure features of several popular general-purpose programming languages. A concise uniform syntax is used for all constructs. Actual syntax used by particular languages will differ, but the functionality is the same.

References

1966. Bohm and Jacopini. "Flow Diagrams, Turing Machines, and Languages with Only Two Formation Rules," *Comm. ACM* **9**, *5* (May).

1968. Dijkstra, E. W. "**Goto** Statement Considered Harmful," *Comm. ACM* (March).

1974. Knuth, D. E. "Structured Programming with **goto** Statements," *Computing Surveys* (December).

1974. Kernighan, B. W. and Plauger, P. J. *The Elements of Programming Style*. New York: McGraw-Hill.

1975. Goodenough, J. B. "Exception-Handling: Issues and a Proposed Notation," *Comm. ACM* **18**, *12* (December).

JERROLD L. WAGENER

COPYRIGHTS. *See* LEGAL PROTECTION OF SOFTWARE.

COROUTINE

For articles on related subjects *see* ACTIVATION RECORD; PROCEDURE; and SUBPROGRAM.

The *coroutine* resembles the more familiar subroutine or function of most programming languages in that it encapsulates some computation and helps to break a large program into smaller parts. However, coroutines differ from subroutines in that their lifetimes are not tied to the flow of control. When a subroutine is called, a new instance of its activation record (i.e. its control information and local variables) is created. It is destroyed when control is returned to the calling program. On the other hand, when a coroutine returns control, its execution is not finished and so its activation record is preserved. Each time control reenters the coroutine, it resumes execution where it left off with its local control and data state retained.

For the simple reason that a new activation record is not created on every call, coroutines can be more efficient than subroutines. This is true, for example, in the Mesa programming language (Mitchell *et al.*, 1979). Furthermore, because coroutines can be entered directly at the appropriate point to continue some computation, their use can simplify the implementation of some algorithms. This is especially true when the processing to be done on a given call depends in a complex fashion upon previous calls. For example, a program that needs to compare the corresponding elements stored in a tree and a linear list might use a coroutine to traverse the tree. The coroutine returns the next tree element each time control is passed to it. Using a coroutine avoids the need to record in some data structure where the tree traversal should restart.

Coroutines are often used to implement logically concurrent processes (or *threads*) on a single processor. These coroutine-based threads rarely pass control to each other directly with explicit transfer operations. Instead, the transfer is normally indirect and is done as a side effect (*q.v.*) of a call on a library routine. For example, the programming language Modula-2 (*q.v.*) provides a *Processes* library module with procedures that support synchronization and mutual exclusion for coroutine-based threads (Wirth, 1985). These threads are often referred to as "coroutines" when people want to distinguish them from truly parallel threads.

Applications of coroutines include operating systems (*q.v.*), compilers, and discrete event simulation programs. For example, the language Simula 67 supports discrete event simulation with flexible coroutine mechanisms (Dahl, 1972). Coroutines are also used in text manipulation, artificial intelligence (*q.v.*), sorting (*q.v.*), and numerical analysis (*q.v.*) programs. A survey of coroutines and their uses appears in Martin (1980).

Coroutines are sometimes organized into *linear pipelines*. Linear pipelines are useful when the data transformation implemented by a program can be decomposed into several simpler transformations that are applied one after the other. The coroutines of the pipeline can be envisaged as being arranged in a line: information flows through the line in one direction, with each coroutine implementing part of the overall transformation. A coroutine obtains input items by transferring control to one neighbor (perhaps as a side effect of calling a *read* procedure), and outputs results by transferring control to the other. Each coroutine is written as if it were the main program and without concern for the implementation of the other coroutines. These linear pipelines (with buffering) appear in the Unix (*q.v.*) command language (Ritchie, 1974).

Another kind of coroutine is the *semicoroutine*. Semicoroutines have the restriction that when they are called, they must eventually return control back to the caller. Thus, semicoroutines resemble subroutines, except that their data and control state is preserved between calls. Semicoroutines are useful for the incremental generation of sequences of items, especially when each item to be returned depends in a complicated way on the items that were generated previously. Semicoroutines can be used to enumerate the items stored in data structures. As an example, a compiler might use a semicoroutine to produce, one at a time, the items recorded in a parse tree. The semicoroutine can traverse the parse tree recursively. Since it is a semicoroutine, it can directly record in its program counter where to resume the traversal each time it is reentered. The *iterators* of the programming language CLU (Liskov *et al.*, 1977) are semicoroutines that are intended to be used in conjunction with loop control structures. Iterators allow a program to process the items stored in a data object, such as a set, where details of the item generation and the data object's representation are hidden in the iterator (*see* INFORMATION HIDING.).

References

1972. Dahl, O.-J. "Hierarchical Program Structures," *Structured Programming*. New York: Academic Press, 175–220.

1974. Ritchie, D. and Thompson, K. "The UNIX Time-Sharing System," *Comm. ACM* **17**, 7: 365–375 (July).

1977. Liskov, B., Snyder, A., Atkinson, R., and Shaffert, C. "Abstraction Mechanisms in CLU," *Comm. ACM* **20**, 8: 564–576 (August).

1979. Mitchell, J. G., Maybury, W., and Sweet, R. "Mesa Language Manual," Xerox Palo Alto Research Center technical report CSL-79-3.

1980. Martin, C. "Coroutines: A Programming Methodology, a Language Design, and an Implementation," *Lecture Notes in Computer Science No. 95*. New York: Springer-Varlag.

1985. Wirth, N. *Programming in Modula-2, Third Edition*. New York: Springer-Verlag.

BRIAN T. LEWIS

CPM. *See* PERT/CPM.

CPU. *See* CENTRAL PROCESSING UNIT.

CRIME, COMPUTER. *See* COMPUTER CRIME; and COMPUTER VIRUS.

CROSS-ASSEMBLERS AND COMPILERS

For articles on related subjects *see* ASSEMBLER; COMPATIBILITY; COMPILER CONSTRUCTION; LANGUAGE PROCESSORS; and PORTABILITY.

Cross-processors, a term that includes both *cross-compilers* and *cross-assemblers*, are programs written to run on machine A (called variably the development machine, the controller, the host, or the front end), to produce programs to be run on machine B (called the target machine or the main processor). Thus, A is running a program (the cross-processor) written in a language acceptable to A. The input to this program are statements in assembly language for machine B (for a cross-assembler) or in any language for machine B for which there exists a cross-compiler.

The output of a cross-processor is machine language for machine B, which is then down-loaded from machine A to machine B. Downloading is the process by which the host computer transfers binary core images (or sometimes coded information) into the target computer so that the target computer can then proceed with program execution. The data for the program is either read directly by machine B or is part of the downloaded binary or coded image.

The two major uses of cross-processors are indicative of their versatility. Cross-processors are used for production of software for machines whose hardware is not yet available or is just being designed and evaluated. In this case, machine B may be initially a simulation rather than actual hardware, to be later replaced by actual hardware. Cross-processors are also used for production of programs for target machines whose specialized instruction set is not suitable for software production (e.g. signal processors or array processors) or whose cost may make them too expensive and thus not cost effective for compilation (e.g. vector machines, supercomputers (*q.v.*), massively parallel machines).

GIDEON FRIEDER

CRT. *See* TERMINALS.

CRYPTOGRAPHY, COMPUTERS IN

For articles on related subjects *see* COMPUTER CRIME; DATA COMMUNICATIONS; and DATA SECURITY.

Cryptography is the science of transforming messages for the purpose of making the message unintelligible to all but the intended receiver of the message. The term *data encryption* refers to the use of cryptographic methods in computer communications for the same reason, but also implies the additional goals of providing assurance to the receiver that the message is not a forgery, and/or allowing the receiver to prove to a third party that the message is not a forgery. These various aims are called, respectively, the goals of *communication security, authentication,* and *digital signatures.*

The transformation used to encipher a message typically involves both a general method, or algorithm, and a *key*. While the general method used by a pair of correspondents may be public knowledge, some or all of the key information must be kept secret. The process of transforming (enciphering) a message is to apply the enciphering algorithm to the message, where the key is used as an auxiliary input to control the enciphering. The reverse operation (deciphering) is performed similarly.

Classical encryption techniques involve such operations as substituting for each message letter a substitute letter; in this case, the key is the correspondence between message (plaintext) letters and the enciphered message (ciphertext) letters. Such *substitution ciphers* can also be based on substituting for two or more letters at a time. Another common technique is to use a transposition cipher which permutes the order of the message letters using an algorithm whose steps are determined by a *key*. Many complicated hand or mechanical ciphers have been developed in the last few centuries; see Kahn (1967) for details. These techniques are insecure in general; the breaking of the German Enigma cipher during World War II attests to the vulnerability of even complicated rotor-machine ciphers (*see* Colossus).

The *one-time pad* is a technique that provides the ultimate in security: It is provably unbreakable. To encipher a 1,000-bit message, however, requires the use of a 1,000-bit key that will not be used for any other message. Each ciphertext bit is the exclusive-or of the corresponding message and key bits. The one-time pad is used only in very important applications (like the Moscow-Washington hot-line) because of the expense in creating and distributing the large amount of key information required.

Cryptosystems, which, unlike the one-time pad, depend upon an amount of key information that is independent of message length, are breakable in theory. What makes them usable in practice is that the person trying to break the cipher (the *cryptanalyst*) must use an impractical or infeasible amount of computational resources in order to break the cipher. These ciphers are constructed so that the "work-factor" in breaking them is high enough to prevent a successful attack.

The major application of cryptography today is for data transmitted between computers in computer communication networks and for computer data encrypted for storage.

The most widely used cipher in the U.S. for the encryption of stored or transmitted computer data is undoubtedly the Data Encryption Standard (DES), which was designed at IBM and approved as a standard by the National Bureau of Standards in 1976. The DES enciphers a 64-bit message block under control of a 56-bit key to produce a 64-bit ciphertext. The enciphering operation consists of roughly 16 iterations of the following two steps.

1. Exchange the left half of the 64-bit message with the right half.
2. Replace the right half of the message with the

bit-wise exclusive-or of the right half and a 32-bit word, which is a complicated function *f* of the left half, the key, and the iteration number. The function *f* involves in part a number of substitutions of short sub-blocks using specially constructed substitution tables (*S*-boxes) and permutations of the individual bit positions. The basic DES function has been implemented by a large number of manufacturers on special-purpose LSI chips which can encipher at megabit per second rates.

Some applications (e.g. enciphering a line to a user's terminal) require that blocks shorter than 64 bits (e.g. a byte) be individually enciphered. The basic DES block can be used for this application in *cipher feedback mode:* each message byte is enciphered by an exclusive-or with the left-most byte of the result of taking the last eight ciphertext bytes and using them as input to the DES to obtain another 64-bit block of ciphertext.

Conventional cryptosystems (including DES) use the same key at both the enciphering and deciphering stations. In 1976, Diffie and Hellman proposed *public-key cryptosystems* in which the deciphering key was different from, and not computable from, the enciphering key (and vice versa). A person might create a matched pair of such keys and distribute copies of the enciphering key to friends, while keeping the deciphering key secret. The friends can send to the creator of the enciphering key enciphered mail that only the creator can read. (Even if a cryptanalyst obtains a copy of the enciphering key, it does no good.) This demonstrates the flexibility of a public-key cryptosystem for *key distribution*, an area where conventional cryptosystems are awkward because all keys must be kept secret. Public-key cryptosystems can also be used to provide *digital signatures:* A user can create a signature for a message by enciphering it with a private key. (Here the enciphering/deciphering roles of the public/private keys are reversed.) Someone else can check the validity of the signature by checking that it deciphers to the message using the signer's public key. This capability of public-key cryptosystems promises to have important applications in electronic funds transfer systems (*q.v.*).

The first proposal for a function to implement public-key cryptosystems was by Rivest, Shamir, and Adleman (1978). Their cryptosystem (the so-called *RSA cipher*) enciphers a message *M* (first coded into numeric form by, for example, setting $A = 01$, $B = 02$, etc.) using a public key (*e,n*) to obtain a ciphertext *C* as follows.

$$C = M^e (\text{mod } n).$$

That is, *C* is the remainder of M^e when divided by *n*. Here all quantities are large numbers (several hundred bits long), and *n* is the product of two very large prime numbers *p* and *q*. The security of the cipher rests mainly on the practical impossibility of factoring the number *n* into its parts *p* and *q*. The deciphering operation is similar, except that the exponent is different:

$$M = C^d (\text{mod } n).$$

As a small example of the RSA method, the word "IT" can be encrypted as follows. Using the representation $A = 01$, $B = 02,..., Z = 26$, we obtain the number 0920 for IT. Then with $n = 2773 = 47 \cdot 59$ and $e = 17$, we obtain the ciphertext:

$$C = 920^{17}(\text{modulo } 2773) = 948.$$

Using $p = 47$ and $q = 59$, a value of $d = 157$ can be derived, from which we can calculate 948^{157} (modulo 2773) $= 920$, the original message.

FIG. 1. Data encryption using the RSA method.

Since *d* depends on *p* and *q* (in a way too complicated to explain here), it is provably as hard to compute *d* from *e* and *n* as it is to factor *n*. When *n* is more than roughly 400 bits long, this becomes a prohibitively time-consuming task. Although the enciphering operation itself is quite complicated, enciphering rates of 1–10 kilobits/second are possible with a special-purpose LSI chip. An example of the RSA method is shown in Fig. 1.

The theoretical foundations of cryptography were vigorously developed during the 1980s, and the security of various encryption and signature schemes have been evaluated with respect to powerful new formal definitions of security. See Rivest (1990) for a survey of these developments.

References

1967. Kahn, D. *The Codebreakers.* New York: Macmillan.
1976. Diffie, W. and Hellman, M. "New Directions in Cryptography," *IEEE Trans. Information Theory* **IT-22**, 644–654 (November).
1977. FIPS Publication 46. *Specifications for the Data Encryption Standard.*
1978. Rivest, R., Shamir, A., and Adleman, L. "A Method for Obtaining Digital Signatures and Public-Key Cryptosystems," *Comm. ACM*, **21**, *2*, 120–126 (February).
1979. Diffie, W. and Hellman, M. "Privacy and Authentication: An Introduction to Cryptography," *Proc. IEEE* **67**, 397–427 (March).
1982. Denning, Dorothy E. *Cryptography and Data Security*, Reading, MA: Addison-Wesley.
1987. Patterson, Wayne. *Mathematical Cryptology for Computer Scientists and Mathematicians,* Totowa, NJ: Rowman and Littlefield.
1990. Rivest, R. *Cryptography* in *Handbook of Theoretical Computer Science* (J. van Leeuwen, Ed.). Amsterdam: North Holland.

RONALD L. RIVEST

CURRENT AWARENESS SYSTEM

For articles on related subjects *see* INFORMATION RETRIEVAL; LIBRARY AUTOMATION; and MEDLARS/MEDLINE.

A *current awareness system* is a system for periodically notifying users of the acquisition of selected items of information (often literature or electronic messages of various kinds) by a central file or library. Such systems are designed to respond to the problems of search selectivity and timeliness by carrying out information searches, using only small files of selected documents. Typically, user queries, or *interest profiles*, are stored on a permanent basis, to be processed periodically against small files of documents that might be newly received at a given information center. Users are notified on a weekly or monthly basis of new acquisitions that match their interest profile. Under ideal conditions, such systems for the *selective dissemination of information* (SDI) are able to retrieve information exactly tailored to meet the specific, possibly changing, needs of each user, while supplying the output directly on a periodic and dependable basis.

The rapid development of selective dissemination services is due to two main factors: First, SDI services are much less expensive to implement than on-demand searches because there is no need to include in the document collections the backlog information covering many years in the past. Second, the existence of many distributors of magnetic tape and CD-ROM databases—normally containing titles, citations, and sometimes index terms and abstracts of published articles and research—ensures the availability of the needed input data on a regular basis. Normally, the producers of the databases sell the SDI services directly on their own account, or they make the information available to third parties who, in turn, provide the dissemination service. SDI services are implemented in all areas of applied science and engineering, and in many of the natural and social sciences as well.

A flexible SDI service may be the answer to the inefficiencies now inherent in the normal publication system, in which each published item carries high publication costs and minimal readership. An improved, more economical system might then eliminate bound-volume journals entirely and restrict certain types of books to library use, while providing at the same time an efficient distribution of individual articles and citations that are tailored to specific user populations.

A flowchart outlining a typical SDI service is shown in Fig. 1. Specific SDI features are:

1. *Universal features:* User feedback; automatic or manual profile revision; option for hard copy of abstract and/or full text; and system evaluation.
2. *Optional features:* Use of free text (title or abstract) search; searching of multiple databases; incorporation of preprinted in addition to published information; incorporation of citation, author, or institution alert; and special distribution to designated recipients.

To improve services at a later time, nearly all SDI services include feedback provisions that utilize user opinions about the effectiveness of the search output. Specifically, response cards are often included with the output sent to the user population to enable the recipients to return information concerning the retrieved materials. Direct assessments of usefulness are sometimes wanted for each retrieved citation; alternatively, the return cards representing user requests for hard copies of certain retrieved documents are automatically taken by the system operators as an expression of approbation on the user's part.

In either case, the user profile statement may be updated by reinforcing or increasing the weight of profile terms that match terms included in retrieved items designated as relevant by the users. Profile terms included in documents identified as non-relevant may be similarly demoted or decreased in weight. Occasionally, the docu-

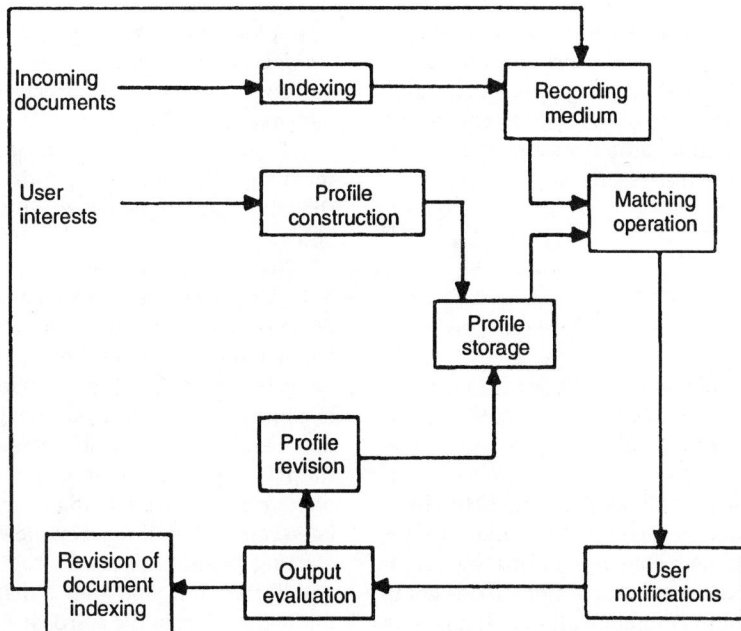

FIG. 1. Typical simplified selective dissemination service.

ment indexing may also be changed as a function of user judgment. The corresponding feedback paths are indicated in Fig. 1.

The feedback feature is particularly useful in a research environment, where user interests may change fairly rapidly. The profiles can then be adjusted little by little, as the users express satisfaction or dissatisfaction with the materials obtained from the retrieval service.

Among the useful optional SDI features is the possibility of including in the distribution service those documents in preprint form or other items that are not intended for eventual formal publication. This option provides the means for bypassing the normal publication process and for avoiding publication delays. Delays can also be avoided by having the authors of certain items provide a special distribution list of recipients to whom the corresponding documents are to be sent regardless of the profile-matching results. Finally, the participants in an SDI system can gain better service by extending their profiles to include not only subject terms, but also names of authors or of institutions whose documents they wish to receive automatically.

Another extension of optional service permits the inclusion of document citations in the user profiles so that new items citing the original profile documents will be automatically retrieved with other pertinent materials. In its simplest form, such a citation-monitoring system would alert a given participant whenever one of his or her own papers was being cited by some outside author, assuming that the users of the service include their own documents as part of their profiles. Alternatively, a citation alert system can simplify normal subject searches by eliminating the problems of vocabulary know-how and control that affect document indexing and query formulations.

An evaluation of SDI services shows that a large proportion of the materials retrieved for the user population is indeed germane to user interests. However, complaints arise because of the large volume of output continually delivered by the services. Even if the proportion of relevant items is fairly high, users receiving 30 or 40 citations every week may eventually tire of the system and revert to on-demand searches that furnish output only when specific requests for service are made.

GERARD SALTON

CYBERNETICS

For articles on related subjects *see* ANALOG COMPUTER; AUTOMATION; CONTROL APPLICATIONS; INFORMATION THEORY; SHANNON, CLAUDE; and WIENER, NORBERT.

Cybernetics is a science founded in the 1940s by a group of scientists and engineers led by Norbert Wiener and Arturo Rosenblueth, who coined the word "cybernetics" (from Greek: pilot, steersman, governor) to designate the science of "control and communication in the animal and the machine" (Wiener, 1948). This definition still expresses the substantial content of cybernetics, although there is a broad spectrum of current interpretations (Drozin *et al.*, 1973).

Cybernetic concepts cluster around three related component concepts: systems (animal or machine), communication between systems, and regulation or self-regulation of systems. Since the first two are common to nearly all fields of knowledge, it is the third component, regulation, that distinguishes the discipline. Cybernetics is the science of regulation and control—purposive regulation for adaptive system survival (Beer, 1970).

Cybernetics borrows ubiquitously from other sciences. Based on the mathematical concept, cybernetics concerns all conceivable *sets* of systems (Ashby, 1968); and from physical and psychological concepts, it "deals with all forms of behavior in so far as they are regular, or determinate, or reproducible" (Ashby, 1968, p. 1). To be of practical interest, however, cybernetic systems have two properties: (1) some aspect must provide observable data over a period of time (the *protocol*, Ashby, 1968, p. 88); (2) from the protocol it must be possible to infer some stable configuration or regularity in transformation of states. Without observable regularity in transformation, a system is said to be *unconstrained*. Without constraint, it is unpredictable; if it becomes unstable and cannot be restored to stability, it is uncontrollable. For regulation, a system must show some regularity.

Time is the principal cybernetic variable, while *variety* is the principal dependent variable. Variety is quantitatively measured by the logarithm (usually base 2) of the number of discriminations that an observer (or a sensing system) can make relative to a system (Ashby, 1968, p. 124). For example, in the phrase "take care," the variety is $\log_2 6 = 2.51$ bits if the system is the set of distinguishably different letters; $\log_2 2 = 1$ bit if the system is the set of words; and $\log_2 1 = 0$ if the system is the message considered as a unit. Because variety is based on discrimination of differences, it measures equally well all psychophysical or higher cognitive discriminations (Heilprin, 1973). For example, the variety in five psychologically discriminated shades of green is $\log_2 5 = 2.25$ bits, the same as the variety in a decision process from a choice of five abstract alternatives.

Regulation of a system has a well-defined technical meaning. What this is depends on a technical distinction, the difference between *essential* and *non-essential* variables.

To understand them, consider Fig. 1. This represents a simple physical system—a heavy solid object that looks like a triangle—resting on a horizontal table surface. The triangle may be the end of a prism or the projection of a cone. In the first position (top left), the center of mass (C) is as low as it can get relative to the table, so it will not move and is said to be in *stable equilibrium*. Now suppose the triangle is tilted, as in the next position, its bottom plane rotated through angle θ relative to the table. C has been raised, but, if the triangle is let go, it will return to its starting position. That is, the triangle is still in stable equilibrium if it will, after a displacement θ, return to its initial position. In the third case, θ is just so large that the triangle is balanced precariously in *neutral* equilibrium. Any further small displacement that increases or de-

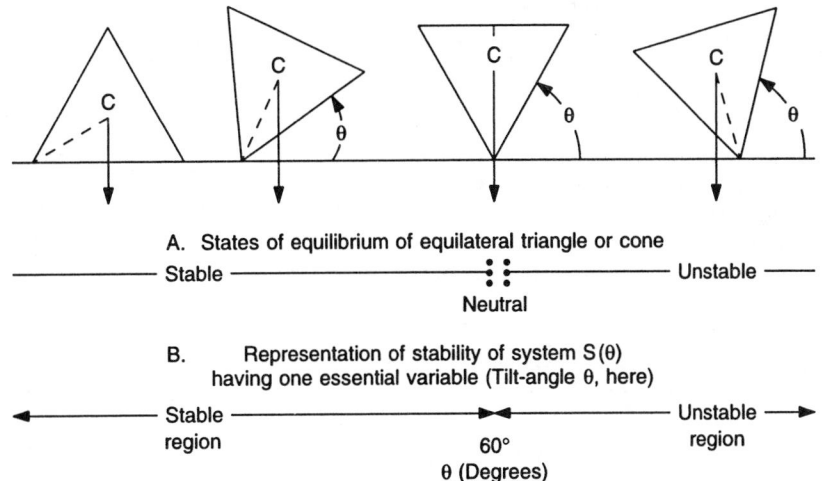

A. States of equilibrium of equilateral triangle or cone

—— Stable ———————— Neutral ———— Unstable ——

B. Representation of stability of system S(θ)
having one essential variable (Tilt-angle θ, here)

← —— Stable ———————————— Unstable —— →
region   region

60°

θ (Degrees)

FIG. 1.   A system whose stability depends on one independent variable.

creases θ will send the triangle either back to the initial position or to a new position from which it cannot return. In the last figure, the angular displacement θ is so great that, if the triangle is let go, it must fall to the new position.

Suppose we define the system "triangle in its initial position." Then this system *continues to exist* as long as, and only as long as, the variable θ (which measures the tilt) remains within the range −60° to +60°. This is shown as a region within the line at the bottom, representing values of θ.

Fig. 2 extends this idea for a system S, which depends upon two essential variables. The kidney-shaped region in the X, Y plane is the region within which the system S(X, Y) is stable. Because there are two stable ranges—one for X and one for Y—the curve or perimeter of this region is *not* the same as the more common functional curve Y = Y(X). Both X and Y are independent essential variables, and S(X, Y) depends on both. Let us suppose S is a small boat, X the wind velocity, and Y the wave height. Then the closed region in Fig. 2 could represent, in an

abstract way, all of the double displacements of wave and wind such that the boat will not capsize, but return to its initial vertical position.

If the region did not represent the region within which S will not capsize, but rather the region within which its timbers will hold so that it remains in one piece, we could say that this region represented the range of double displacements for the *existence* of the boat as a boat. If S were not an inanimate object but a living animal, we could regard the region as that within which the animal could go on living as a system—that is, could *survive*. To generalize, Fig. 2 can represent any qualitative kind of regulation, ranging from mere change (such as capsizing) to actual destruction (such as splintering and breaking up). If the system happens to be an organism, regulation can mean merely keeping it comfortable (as in maintaining its blood pressure, oxygen intake, or other variables) within certain limits. In general, organisms have many more essential variables than non-organisms, so that the "space" within which they may be represented for system survival is *n*-dimensional, where *n* is larger than that for inanimate systems.

How does one identify essential variables? Suppose that in Fig. 1 we had also been given the range of color of the triangle, or its flavor, or its temperature? It is obvious that these would not have been relevant to the question of stability under displacement. But only our own experience could tell us that. Also, we can see two things: (1) that any real system or object has an indefinitely large number of variables that can describe or identify it; and (2) that among this set of variables, only a subset is relevant to any given *goal*—in this case, regulation of the object so that it returns to equilibrium. Intuition tells us that in Fig. 1 a relevant variable is tilt angle θ. We could not regulate by using, as variables, color, temperature, size, loudness, or other variables that, for *other* kinds of displacement, might be relevant measures. To sum up: essential variables are essential, *relative to the purpose of regulation*. Since organisms have to survive in order to be said to remain in the same system, we usually think of "regulation" as keeping an organism within a region of displacements of its essen-

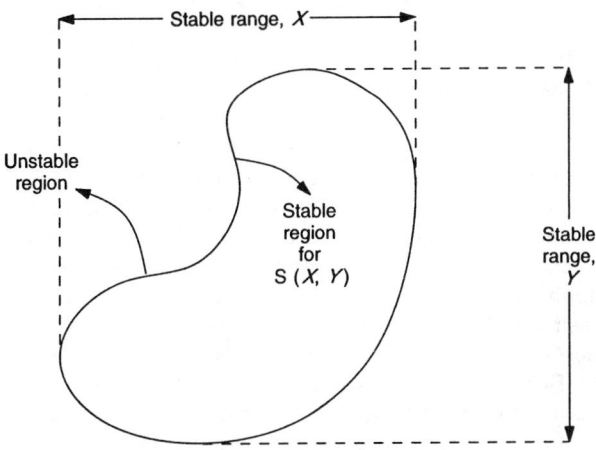

FIG. 2.   Representation of stability of a system *S*(*X, Y*) having two independent essential variables.

tial variables within which it can comfortably retain its vital functions. Therefore, in cybernetics "regulation" commonly means keeping a system not necessarily completely intact, but substantially "the same." It means keeping the system together, as a whole, and identifiable as the same system, and, if it is alive, surviving.

It is this special meaning of the word regulation that gives cybernetics its particular pattern—its paradigm. We conclude that the paradigm of cybernetics is the regulation of its essential variables for maintaining a system in states such that its identity as a system remains continuously the same, before and after displacements of the variables. Or we can say that the paradigm of cybernetics is keeping certain system variables within certain limits, such that the system survives.

The real significance of *variety* lies not in absolute amount, but in the possibility of its increase or decrease. We increase sensory variety when we gather data, decrease it when we summarize, compress, or abstract. Both processes are necessary for cognition. However, "lower" cognitive processes are associated with data gathering or increase in concrete sensory variety, whereas "higher" cognitive processes are associated with data condensation, abstraction, or decrease in concrete variety.

When the variety shown by a system under one set of conditions is less than that shown by the system under another set of conditions, the relation between the two sets of variety is a *constraint* (Ashby, 1968, p. 127). For example, suppose two couples (A and B, or four voters) can each independently vote for R or D. Then, the number of distinguishably different outcomes is $2^4 = 16$ and the variety is $\log_2 16 = 4$ bits. If, however, Mr. A always defers to Ms. A's judgment and votes the same as Ms. A, the number of different outcomes is 8, and the variety shown is $\log_2 8 = 3$ bits. If, further, Mr. and Ms. B always vote R, the variety in the outcomes is $\log_2 2 = 1$ bit. The progressive decrease in variety from 4 bits to 3 to 1 corresponds to increase in constraint on the system showing the variety. Returning to the requirement for regulation—that there must exist some constraint in order to predict the behavior of a system—it is apparent that to regulate a system is to impose a constraint on its variety.

The cybernetics of constrained and unconstrained sets was advanced by the insight of Wiener (1948), who said that "the transmission of information is impossible save as a transmission of alternatives," and by Shannon's observation that "the significant aspect is that the actual message is *selected from a set* of possible messages" (Shannon and Weaver, 1949). Thus, *regulation implies the capability to prevent occurrences of unfavorable alternatives.* Therefore, it implies *transmission* of these alternatives to the regulator, which in turn must respond with a command message directed toward preserving the stability of the regulated system.

Fig. 3 shows the basic elements of a regulatory system. The system whose essential variables (E) are to be kept within certain limits depends on communication of variety between system disturbance (D), the regulator (R), and the environment (T). The most direct regulation is DR, shown in Fig. 3(a). The signal arrives from D in time for R to act on T before T affects E. Figs. 3(c) and 3(d)

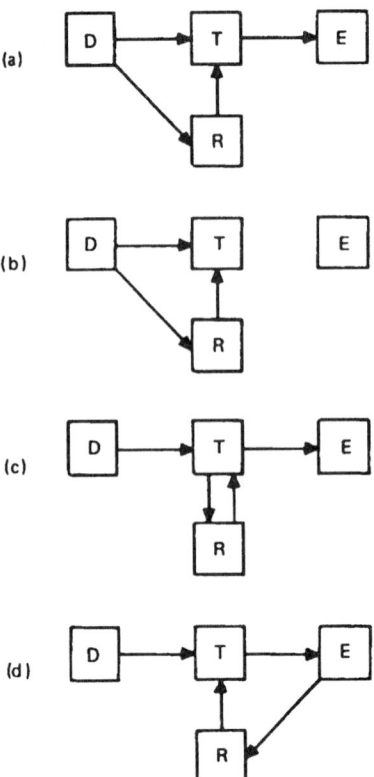

FIG. 3. Regulation of a system through Law of Requisite Variety.

show paths DTR and DTER, progressively less effective. Perfect regulation (Fig. 3(b)) would leave E isolated from external disturbance (i.e. unaware because of non-communication that a disturbance had occurred).

A system is said to be *well regulated* when, through the intervention of the regulator and the environment, a disturbance cannot permanently drive the system from a state in which it is stable (retains its structure and function—"survives"). Lack of regulation occurs when the system is transformed to a state from which it cannot return to a stable state (i.e. cannot survive).

The principal law of cybernetics (credited to Ashby, 1968, p. 206) is the *law of requisite variety*. This states that, if $\log V_d$ is the variety in the possible ways in which a disturbance D can affect a system E (to be regulated by a regulator R) and if $\log V_r$ is the variety in R's alternatives (optional ways of response to D), the variety in the possible outcomes ($\log V_o$) affecting E cannot be forced by R below the limit ($\log V_d - \log V_r$), or $\log (V_d/V_r) \geq \log V_o$.

This law applies to all forms of regulation and is independent of field of science or technology or of specific mechanism. Loosely interpreted, it means that—assuming the disturbance, environment, and the system itself are fixed and cannot be altered—the only way to increase E's probability of survival is to increase R's variety (R's versatility, or the number of different modes of response that R can make in order to protect E's stability as affected by D). However, satisfying the law by increasing V_r does not guarantee perfect regulation (i.e. perfect shielding of E). Just as the existence of constraint is necessary but not sufficient for regulation, satisfying the law of requisite variety is necessary but not sufficient for successful regulation (Heilprin, 1973, p. 24).

Space prevents discussion of many prominent cybernetic features, such as classification of cybernetic systems by intractability to control (determinate, complex, and "very large"), black-box theory, feedback and feedforward, and isomorphism and homomorphism. See the references cited and a growing list of periodicals, among which are the *Journal of Cybernetics* (American Society of Cybernetics), *Transactions on Systems, Man and Cybernetics* (IEEE), and *Soviet Cybernetic Review*.

References

1948. Wiener, N. *Cybernetics or Control and Communication in the Animal and the Machine.* Cambridge, MA: M.I.T. Press. (New York: John Wiley & Sons, 1948; 2nd ed., 1965).

1949. Shannon, C. E., and Weaver, W. *The Mathematical Theory of Communication.* Urbana, IL: University of Illinois Press, p. 3.

1968. Ashby, W. R. *An Introduction to Cybernetics.* London: Methuen (University Paperbacks, 1956, reprinted, 1968) chap. 7.

1970. Beer, S. *Decision and Control.* New York: John Wiley & Sons, chap. 15.

1973. Drozin, V. G., Fisher, R., Kopstein, F. F., Pask, G., and Toda, M. "What is Cybernetics?" *FORUM*; American Society for Cybernetics, **V**, 4 (December), 3–8.

1973. Heilprin, L. B. *Impact of the Cybernetic Law of Requisite Variety on a Theory of Information Science.* College Park, MD: University of Maryland Computer Science Center, Report No. TR-236, March, ERIC No. ED 073 777, 9–10.

1981. Conant, Roger (Ed.). *Mechanisms of Intelligence: Ross Ashby's Writings on Cybernetics.* The Systems Inquiry Series, Seaside, CA: Intersystems Publications.

LAURENCE B. HEILPRIN

CYCLE STEALING

For articles on related subjects *see* CHANNEL; and MEMORY: MAIN.

Cycle stealing is a technique for memory sharing whereby a memory may serve two autonomous masters and in effect provide service to each simultaneously. One of the masters is commonly the central processing unit (CPU - *q.v.*), and the other is usually an I/O channel or device controller. Fig. 1 illustrates two memory cycles (numbers 3 and 5) being stolen by an I/O channel (from the CPU) between two cycles of memory use by the CPU. This is possible and convenient, at least periodically, because the CPU is self-driven (except possibly between some substeps of a process it is conducting) and has no fixed time demands on memory. Furthermore, there are occasions, particularly in simpler CPU designs, where the instruction being obeyed (e.g. division) is processor-limited (i.e. uses all the processor's capabilities) and memory access is temporarily suspended.

The I/O equipment is, on the other hand, quite different. Its use of the memory, though generally less frequent than that by the CPU, is much more time-constrained. For many I/O devices, such as disks and tapes, data is produced or required at fixed intervals. The need for data transfer occurs relentlessly at fixed time intervals. In transferring data from a tape to memory, the previous byte or word must have been stored before the next arrives; otherwise, data is lost. This problem is somewhat alleviated by the use of single or multiple buffers (*q.v.*) in the device controller and/or channel, but in any case there are important recurring time demands for memory access. These can be met by the technique of cycle stealing in those CPU designs in which processor activity can be suspended for a memory cycle while a memory access is made by the I/O system.

KENNETH C. SMITH AND ADEL SEDRA

CYCLE TIME

For articles on related subjects *see* REGISTER; and SYNCHRONOUS/ASYNCHRONOUS OPERATION.

The *cycle time* of a computer is the time required to change the information in a set of registers. This is also sometimes called the *state transition time*.

The register cycle time of a processor is sometimes referred to as the *internal cycle time, clock time,* or simply *cycle time;* occasionally, confusion develops between the internal cycle time (referenced to registers) and the main memory cycle time. The memory cycle time is usually several times the internal cycle time.

The internal cycle time may not be of constant value.

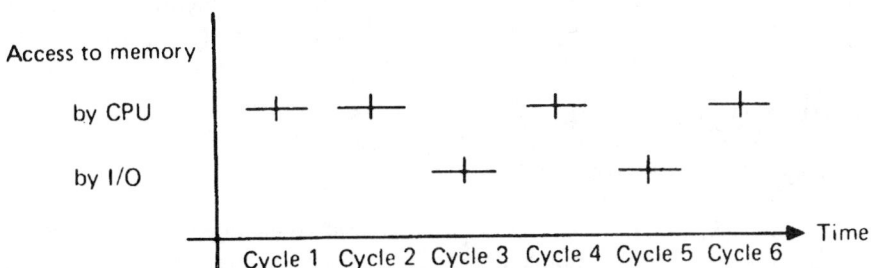

FIG. 1. Cycle stealing.

There are basically three different types of cycle-timing organizations:

1. *Synchronous (fixed):* In this scheme all operations are composed of one or more cycles, with the fundamental time quantum being fixed by the design. Such systems are also referred to as *clocked,* since usually a master oscillator (or clock) is used to distribute and define these cycles.
2. *Synchronous (variable):* This is a slight variation of the first scheme; certain long operations are allowed to take multiple cycles without causing a register state transition. In such systems there may be several different cycle lengths. For example, a register-to-register transfer of information cycle might take one cycle, while a register-to-adder and return-to-register cycle would perhaps be two or three cycles. (The fundamental difference between the fixed and variable synchronous types is that the former stores information into registers at the end of every cycle time, whereas the latter sets information into registers after a number of cycles, depending upon the type of operation being performed.)
3. *Asynchronous operation:* In a completely asynchronous machine there is no clock or external mechanism that determines a state transition. Rather, the logic of the system is arranged in stages; when the output value of one stage has been stabilized, the logic signals the input at that stage to admit new operands. (Asynchronous operation is clearly advantageous when the variation in cycle time is significant, since a synchronous scheme must always wait for the worst possible delay in the definition of the time quantum required. On the other hand, when logic delays are predictable, synchronous approaches have an advantage because several additional stages of logic are required in the asynchronous scheme to signal completion of an operation.)

In actual practice, most systems are basically synchronous (either fixed or variable), with some asynchronous operations being used for particular parts of the machine, such as handling access to main memory.

Michael J. Flynn

CYCLIC REDUNDANCY CHECK

For articles on related subjects *see* CODES; ERROR-CORRECTING CODE; and PARITY.

In modern computer systems, data is continuously transferred between the main processor and its peripherals, storage, or terminals. Errors may be introduced during the reading, writing, or actual transmission of this data. Consequently, error control has become an integral part in the design of modern computers and communication systems. The most commonly used methods for error detection involve the addition of one or more *redundancy bits* to the information-carrying bits of a character or stream of characters. These redundancy bits do not carry any information; they are merely used to determine the correctness of the bits carrying the information.

Perhaps the most commonly used method for error detection is the simple *parity check.* Parity may be even or odd, meaning that the sum of the "one" bits of any character, including the parity bit itself, will always be even or odd, depending upon which arrangement is chosen.

Fig. 1 illustrates a form of two-dimensional parity checking used on some magnetic tapes that can detect and even correct some types of errors. The six-bit characters are arranged in columns with a seventh odd parity bit, called the *vertical redundancy check* (VRC), added to make the sum of the "one" bits in each column an odd number. Similarly, an odd parity-check bit, called the *longitudinal redundancy check* (LRC), is added at the end of the block for each row of bits. As the tape is read, the VRC and LRC are regenerated and compared to the check characters read. If equal, the information is assumed correct. If not equal, the block is read again. Some types of errors, like the one shown in Fig. 1, may also be corrected by using this method.

Cyclic redundancy checking is a far more powerful error-detecting method. Here, all the characters in a message block are treated as a serial string of bits representing a binary number. This number is then divided modulo 2 by a predetermined binary number and the remainder of this division is appended to the block of characters as a cyclic redundancy check (CRC) character. The CRC is compared with the check character obtained in similar fashion at the receiving end. If they agree, the message is assumed correct. If they disagree, the receiver will demand a retransmission. This is usually called the ARQ (automatic repeat request) method of error control and is very commonly used in data communication. The CRC character is also called the *cyclic check sum,* or simply the *check sum* character. The Digital Equipment Corporation VAX computer contains, as part of its construction repertoire, a single command that computes a cyclic redundancy check character.

To show how the CRC is generated, let the message consist of k bits, $a_0 a_1 \ldots a_{k-1}$, $a_i = 0$ or 1. Then we form the $(k-1)$-degree polynomial:

$$M(x) = a_0 + a_1 x + \cdots + a_{k-1} x^{k-1} = \sum_{i=0}^{k-1} a_i x^i. \quad (1)$$

If we wish to include r CRC bits, $r < k$, $M(x)$ is multiplied by x^r (this is equivalent to shifting the message bits r places to the right). Let $G(x)$ be another polynomial—called the "generator" or "checking" polynomial—of de-

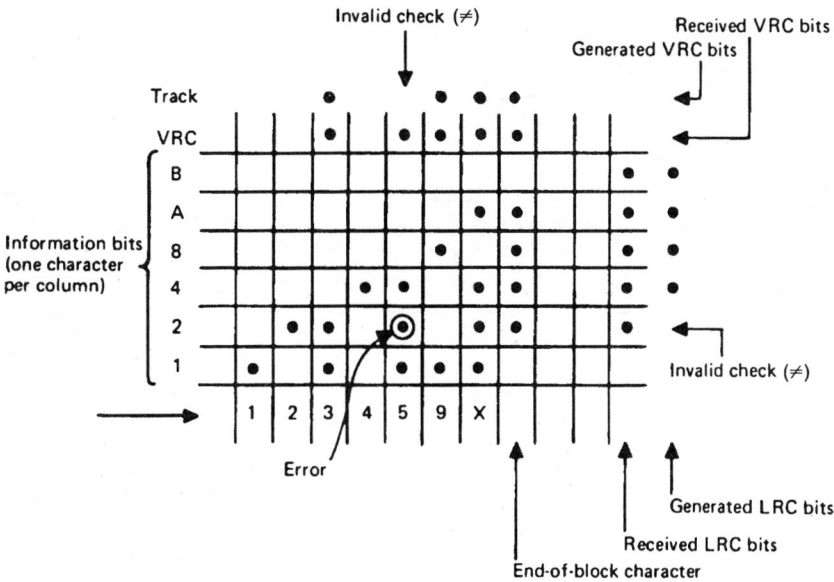

FIG. 1. Error detection using LRC and VRC bits. An extra "1" bit has been introduced in the character "5." Assuming no errors in the received check bits, the error must occur at the intersection of the invalid check column and row. The error bit must be reversed. In this case, the "1" must be changed to "0."

gree r, whose coefficients are also 0 or 1. We divide $x^r M(x)$ by $G(x)$, obtaining

$$\frac{x^r M(x)}{G(x)} = Q(x) + \frac{R(x)}{G(x)} \qquad \text{mod 2} \qquad (2)$$

where the "mod 2" indicates that all sums and differences of coefficients are taken as 0, if the result is 0 or even, and 1 if it is odd. Thus, from Eq. (2)

$$R(x) = x^r M(x) + Q(x)G(x) \qquad \text{mod 2} \qquad (3)$$

where $R(x)$ is the remainder and $Q(x)$ is the quotient. The code word $W(x)$ is

$$W(x) = Q(x)G(x) = x^r M(x) + R(x) \qquad \text{mod 2}, \qquad (4)$$

and what is transmitted are the coefficients of $W(x)$.

Note that $W(x)$, which is of degree $r + k - 1$, contains the original k message bits (the $x^r M(x)$ term) and r check bits (the $R(x)$ term). Furthermore, $W(x)$ is exactly divisible by $G(x)$. The division by $G(x)$ at the transmitting end is accomplished by an r-stage shift register with feedback paths represented by the coefficients of $G(x)$, as shown in Fig. 2. On the receiving end, $W(x)$ is also divided by $G(x)$, and the remainder in this case must be 0; otherwise, an error has occurred.

Consider the following example related to the shift register shown in Fig. 2. Let the message be 1010010001. Therefore, $M(x) = 1 + x^2 + x^5 + x^9$. With $G(x) = 1 + x^2 + x^4 + x^5$, modulo 2 division of $x^5 M(x)$ by $G(x)$ yields

$$Q(x) = 1 + x + x^2 + x^3 + x^7 + x^8 + x^9$$

and $R(x) = 1 + x$. Thus,

$$W(x) = 1 + x + x^5 + x^7 + x^{10} + x^{14},$$

and the transmitted message is

```
        |
1100    |  1010010001
CRC     |  original
bits    |  message
        |  bits
        |
```

The remainder, $R(x)$, is generated by the shift register (which is initially at 00000) as follows:

Message Bit	Shift Register Contents Stage 12345
1	10101
0	11111
0	11010
0	01101
1	00110
0	00011
0	10100
1	11111
0	11010
1	11000

The final content is $R(x)$. Each successive shift register content represents a successive stage of the division of $x^5 M(x)$, remembering that only the bits of $x^5 M(x)$, which have been already transmitted at each stage, take part in the division. When all message bits have been trans-

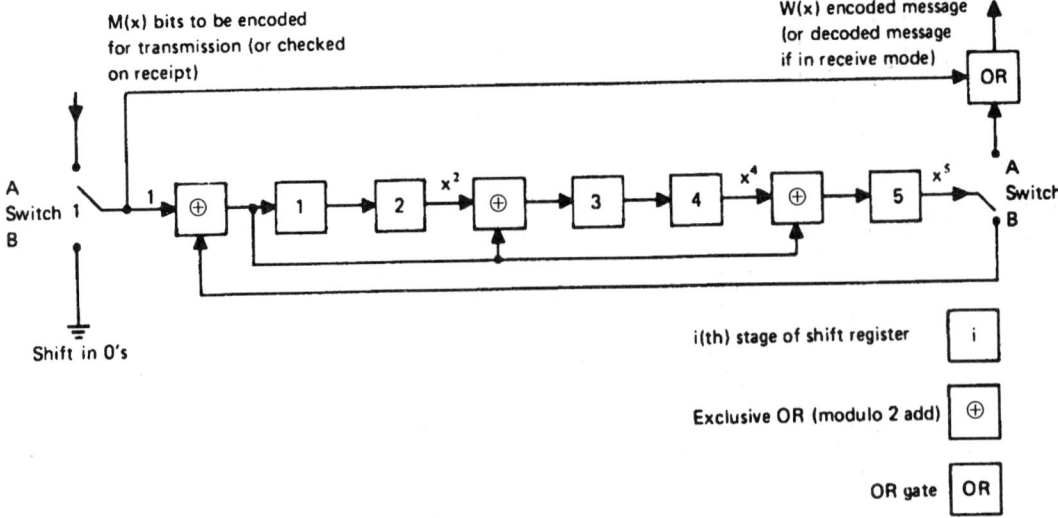

FIG. 2.   Shift register for $G(x) = 1 + x^2 + x^4 + x^5$. Initially, the register contains 00000, switch 1 is in position A, and switch 2 is in position B. When all message bits have been transmitted, the register contains $R(x)$. Switch 1 now goes to B, and switch 2 goes to A to enable $R(x)$ to be shifted out. When data is being received, the resulting $R(x)$ must be zero; otherwise, the data is in error.

mitted, the contents of the shift register are shifted out by five successive right shifts to transmit $R(x)$. Note that during this operation, the zeros are shifted into stage 1 so that after $R(x)$ is transmitted, the contents are 00000; hence, the register is automatically cleared for more transmission.

Codes developed as described above are called *cyclic codes*. Such codes are used for error detection and correction for magnetic tape, disk, and data communication. The generator polynomial $x^{16} + x^{15} + x^2 + 1$, for example, is widely used in synchronous data communication systems. It can detect all odd numbers of error bits, all possible single-error bursts not exceeding 16 bits, 99.9969% of all possible single bursts 17 bits long, and 99.9984% of all possible longer bursts. This is much better than simple parity checking, for instance, which detects only all odd numbers of error bits and no others. Note that parity checking is equivalent to having a generator polynomial $G(x) = x + 1$.

The study of cyclic codes revolves principally upon determining the code characteristics resulting from various generator polynomials. Peterson and Weldon (1972) and Tang and Chien (1969) give some applications and a thorough mathematical treatment of cyclic and other codes. A more elementary description is given by McNamara (1988).

References

1969. Tang, D. T. and Chien, R. T. "Coding for Error Control," *IBM Systems Journal* **8** *1*: 48-86.
1972. Peterson, W. W. and Weldon, E. J. *Error-Correcting Codes*, 2nd Ed. Cambridge, MA: M.I.T. Press.
1977. MacWilliams, F. and Sloane, N. J. A. *The Theory of Error-Correcting Codes*. Amsterdam: Elsevier.
1988. McNamara, J. E. *Technical Aspects of Data Communication*. Bedford, MA: Digital Press.

JOHN S. SOBOLEWSKI

CYLINDER

For articles on related subjects *see* ACCESS TIME; HARD DISK; and MEMORY: AUXILIARY.

Many rotating storage devices—drums, disks, data cells, and the like—have fewer read/write heads than recording tracks. Therefore, either the surfaces of these devices must move to position the desired information under a read/write head, or the read/write heads must move to hover above the appropriate tracks. The latter strategy is commonly used for large direct-access devices such as disks containing at least 100 million bytes.

For engineering convenience and efficient sequential processing of data, the following design has been adopted by most manufacturers of moving-head disk drives:

1. Disk surfaces are numbered from top to bottom for each horizontal position of the read/write comb.
2. During sequential writing operations, as the top track in each vertical plane becomes filled, control circuitry and system software allocate subsequent records to the beginning of the next vertical track. When this is filled, records are started on the third track, etc.

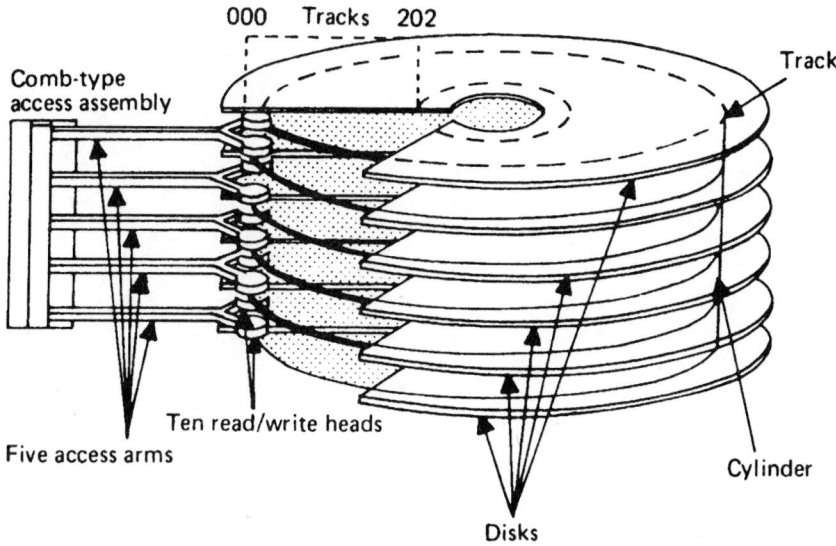

000   Tracks   202

Comb-type
access assembly

Track

Ten read/write heads

Five access arms

Cylinder

Disks

FIG. 1.

3. Therefore, during sequential reading, a maximum amount of data can be read at one time before the comb must be moved. This is considerably faster than the alternative strategy of writing all tracks concentrically on one surface before advancing to the next surface.

Each vertical set of tracks, one track per recording surface, is called a *cylinder*, after the geometrical surface outlined. There are as many cylinders per disk pack as tracks per recording surface (203 cylinders for the disk pack shown in Fig. 1.).

DAVID N. FREEMAN

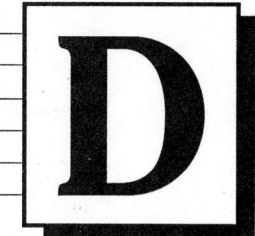

DATA ACQUISITION COMPUTER

For an article on a related subject *see* ANALOG-TO-DIGITAL AND DIGITAL-TO-ANALOG CONVERTERS.

Computers have been used for decades to acquire and analyze data generated by instruments such as voltmeters, thermocouples, and electromechanical relays in factories, refineries, missiles, or aircraft. Typical *data acquisition* (DA) *computers* have fast memory-cycle times so that bursts of signals from real-time physical processes such as video scan devices will not be lost. Although early DA computers had relatively short word lengths (16–24 bits), many now have 32-bit words and use the same architecture as general-purpose minicomputers, permitting economies of scale in manufacturing and software support. Although most DA computers lack floating-point instructions (since measured data are inherently within predefined narrow ranges), the modest incremental cost for FP hardware has encouraged its inclusion in large devices.

The main components of a data-acquisition computer are as follows:

1. Analog and digital input cables;
2. Analog to digital converter;
3. Disk or tape cassette for storage;
4. Central processor;
5. Main memory; and
6. Operator console.

For low-volume data acquisition, a floppy-disk drive may be substituted for the disk drive or tape cassette. Programs are loaded from cassettes, floppy disks, or—in some newer models—a host computer over a communications link.

Prices of data acquisition computers have decreased considerably, improving their advantage over manual methods for capturing and transcribing data in many applications. Their inherent reliability—especially the central processor, main memory, and disk/tape components—has risen to such high levels that they may operate unattended for days at a time. To raise system reliability still higher, multiple (three to five) processors are often packaged together, so that failure of one processor leaves the DA computer functionally intact (albeit slowed down)(*see* FAULT-TOLERANT COMPUTING).

Many data acquisition computers have been "ruggedized" to function in high-temperature environments, such as steel plants or high-acceleration environments such as spacecraft.

During the 1980s, powerful, low-cost, miniaturized DA computers were installed increasingly close to where the original data is generated: factory floors, cash registers, continuous-process plants, etc. They are connected by medium-speed (2,400 bits per second) telephone links to central computers which periodically poll them for data, display status reports on processing being supervised, and print hardware-reliability reports on the data acquisition computers themselves.

DAVID N. FREEMAN

DATA COMMUNICATIONS

For articles on related subjects *see* BANDWIDTH; BAUD; CHANNEL; CODES; COMMUNICATIONS AND COMPUTERS; COMMUNICATION CONTROL UNIT, CONDITIONING; CONTENTION; CYCLIC REDUNDANCY CHECK; ECHOING; ERROR-CORRECTING CODE; MODEM; MULTIPLEXING; NETWORK PROTOCOL; OPEN SYSTEMS INTERCONNECTION; PACKET SWITCHING; PARITY; PROTOCOL; SYNCHRONOUS/ASYNCHRONOUS OPERATION; TELEPROCESSING SYSTEMS; and TERMINALS.

PRINCIPLES

Introduction From the first time that data had to be passed between one register and another in a computer,

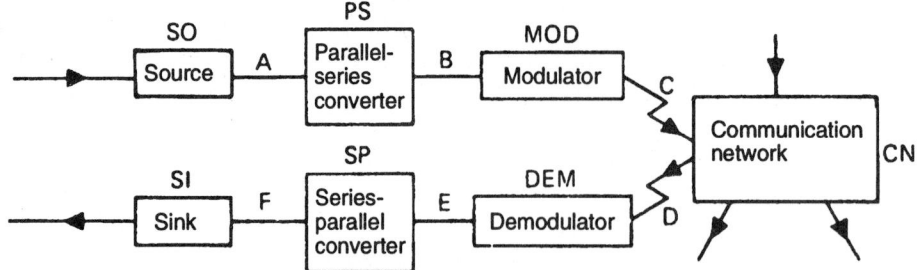

FIG. 1. Schematic of communications between source and destination.

the problem of data communications had to be addressed. This article is concerned with the transmission of data from its source to its destination, as shown in Fig. 1. Two general textbooks (Black, 1989; and Halsall, 1988) are recommended for additional reading. Other references (Tanenbaum, 1988; Proahms, 1983; and Petersen, 1972) deal with more specialized areas.

Normally (see Fig. 1), data is passed in parallel between a computer or peripheral in finite-sized chunks (e.g. 8-bit bytes) to a register, shown as SO. This data must be passed via a communications network (CN) to a sink (SI), where it is passed on in the same or different finite-sized chunks to another computer or peripheral. The communication network usually has the property that the part of it dedicated to the communication between SO and SI can carry only 1 bit at a time. Therefore, that data from the SO must be serialized in the parallel-series converter (PS) and deserialized again in the series-parallel converter (SP). The data output of PS is usually a bistable binary signal that can be interpreted as one of two states: 0 or 1. The adaption of the binary signal at B to the network at C is achieved by a *line interface unit* (LIU).

If information can flow only from SO to SI (Fig. 1), the communication is said to be *simplex*. If data can flow both from SO to SI and from SI to SO simultaneously, the communication is called *duplex*. If data transmission in these two directions does not proceed simultaneously, the communication is said to be *half-duplex*. In some cases, the communication channels themselves may be full-duplex, but either the hardware of the SO and SI or the software associated with them may restrict the communication to half-duplex.

It is usual for the communication portion of the circuit to be at least half-duplex. The communications network CN may transmit and switch either analog or digital signals. If the former, CN is a *communications system with* *analog transmission* to the end user; the line interface unit modulates or demodulates between a binary signal and an analog waveform. It is normal for the functions of the modulator and demodulator (Fig. 1) to be combined; the resulting equipment is called a *modem*, short for *modulator-demod*ulator. If CN uses *digital* transmission, the LIU is a *coder-deco*der called usually a *codec*. For local area networks (LANs - *q.v.*), the transmission is usually digital. Moreover, the LIU is usually integrated into the network interface and has the functionality of a codec.

In modern data communications equipment, the functions of the PS and the LIU are usually combined into single boards called a *communications adaptor* (CA), and most of the functionality is achieved in single VLSI chips. Often, the communications network (CN) accepts data in *blocks* or *packets*. There may then be a specific set of messages passed between the communications adaptor and the CN. This is normally called a *Network Access Protocol* (*see* NETWORK PROTOCOL and PROTOCOL). The CA carries the full communication protocol needed. Often, a character input from a terminal to a computer will be echoed back onto the terminal's printer to show it was received correctly; this mode of working is called *echoplex*. The devices SP and PS and the interfaces A and F in Fig. 1 are also often combined with additional buffers in each to permit duplex operation.

Modulation and Signalling Rates The simplest way to modulate signals is to use telegraph techniques to ensure that the channel has one of two states—with current or without current (see Halsall, 1988). An example of this form of signaling is shown in Fig. 2.

The fastest signaling rate of a communication channel is called the *baud rate*. In the system shown in Fig. 2, the baud rate is $1/t$. When only two-level signaling is used, the baud rate is also equal to the rate of information

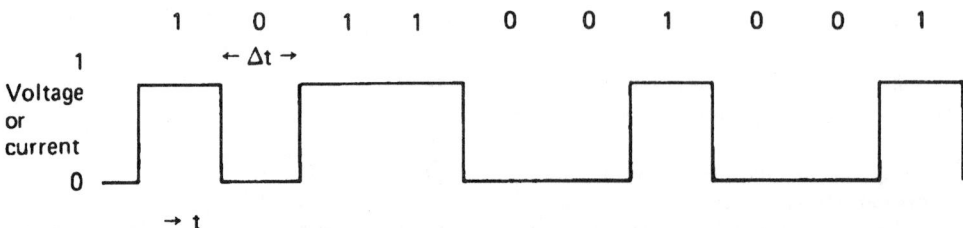

FIG. 2. Examples of telegraph modulation.

transfer in bits per second (bps). If multiple-level signalling is used, as shown in Fig. 3 for four-level coding, then the bit rate is higher than the baud rate. To obtain the signals in Fig. 3, each pair of the bits in Fig. 2 is taken together, and the four resulting combinations (00, 01, 10, 11) are each coded to one level. Clearly, this approach can be extended to *n* levels, but the circuitry required to discriminate and decode the levels becomes increasingly complex.

The form of signaling described above has problems in long-distance transmission, and it is more usual to use the pulsed signals shown in Fig. 2 or Fig. 3 to modulate the amplitude, frequency, or phase of the carrier sine wave. These forms of transmission are called *analog transmission* and are well suited for use over the conventional telephone system, which was originally designed for the transfer of analog signals. The changeover to *digital transmission* is discussed in Section 3.

When the analog facilities are used, each end-to-end channel has a certain *bandwidth* which limits the frequencies that can propagate. Typically, the signaling rate over normal telephone lines is limited by noise considerations to 2.4 Kbps. However, by the use of multilevel signaling and automatic *line conditioning*, an effective data transmission rate of 19.2 Kbps can be achieved.

The theoretical limit to the information transfer rate or channel capacity, C, has been shown by Shannon (*q.v.*) to be:

$$C = BW \log_2 (1 + S/N)$$

where *BW* is the bandwidth and *S/N* is the ratio of signal strength to noise level—*the signal to noise ratio.* If S/N is 15, this equation shows that the channel capacity is *BW* $\log_2 16 = 4 BW$, so that four-level coding (2 bits) can be used (see Fig. 3).

The mode of modulation may make it possible for the modems to generate timing pulses themselves; such a system is called *synchronous.* With these timing pulses, it is possible to synchronize the two modems and produce timing pulses in the modem, to indicate when a bit is being sent or received.

We mentioned earlier that the data format could be asynchronous with synchronous data transmission; redundant start-bits and stop-bits would be transmitted. In the same way, even an asynchronous communication system can be used to send block-orientated data by

prefacing it with an appropriate header and ending the block with appropriate end-of-block characters. A simpler modem is possible when such synchronization is not required. This will be discussed further in a later section.

Digital Transmission With the reduction in cost of digital circuitry, it is becoming more prevalent to use *pulse-code modulation* for transmission. Here, each device is given a time slot, and during this period either a pulse is put on the channel or one is not. This is a modification of the original telegraph techniques, and is the basis of the digital transmission now being deployed. This form of modulation is really two-level amplitude modulation in a synchronous system.

While the trunk portion of the telephone network in most advanced countries is largely based on digital transmission and switching, the local network is still mainly analog. With the advent of digital switching in the local network and the reduced costs of digital termination, a new generation of local digital transmission is becoming available called ISDN, the Integrated Services Digital Network (*q.v.*) (Halsall, 1988).

Asynchronous Transmission Certain human-oriented peripherals, such as keyboard terminals, need to send data only at irregular intervals. Such systems are termed *asynchronous.* In an asynchronous system, the signaling rate is predetermined, but it is necessary to indicate the start of each piece of information (usually, a byte or character) by sending a *start-bit* before and one or more *stop-bits* (of opposite polarity) after transmission of the data. Thus, a byte 145 (in octal) would be sent as shown in Fig. 4. From the arrival time of the start-bit, the bit timings of the subsequent bits can be deduced. The stop-bit is required to ensure that, for at least a one-bit time, the signal has an appropriate value by which a subsequent start-bit can be recognized.

It is even possible for the data format to be asynchronous (i.e. start- and stop-bits are included) with synchronous modems so that the transmission system itself is synchronous. Although the start-bits and stop-bits are redundant in such a system, it is often convenient to include them when the same electronics in PS and SO of Fig. 1 is to be used with different modems. As described before, an asynchronous system has a fixed-byte length, whereas a synchronous system may have a variable length (see below).

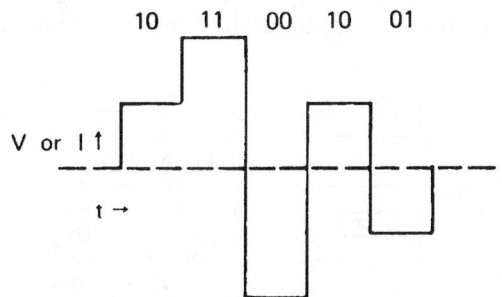

FIG. 3.   Examples of four-level coding.

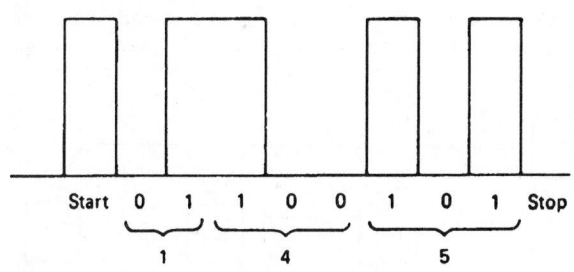

FIG. 4.   Data sent for octal 145 in an asynchronous system.

Multiplexed Communications   The communication shown in Fig. 1, in which two parties, SO and SI, are connected, is called *point-to-point*. An alternative form used in some applications is shown in Fig. 5. In the communication circuit depicted by Fig. 5, SO can send (or receive) data along the channel connecting it to SI$_1$, SI$_2$, and SI$_3$. By appropriate signaling, it is possible to ensure that the data is received at its correct destination SI1. This type of connection is called *multidrop* or *multipoint*. In some cases, it is desirable to have information received at all stations: This mode of communication is called *broadcast*.

If several devices share the same communication channel, as shown in Fig. 5, conflict for use of the channel can occur. One mode of overcoming the conflict is to allow any device to request the channel at will; its efforts to put information onto the channel will then be detected by the others, who will refrain from putting on their information until the message-sending transmitter has ceased. This mode of using a channel is called *contention*; it works well on a point-to-point basis, but reasonably complex strategies must be adopted for successful contention on multipoint channels because of the perceptible delay between information being placed on the channel and its receipt by the other parties.

Another way of resolving conflicts is particularly useful if one device, shown as SO in Fig. 5, can be used to control the others. This mode of control is called *polling* (*q.v.*); in this mode of communications, SO will ask each SI, in turn, whether it has anything to send, or will address an SI, if it wishes to send data to that device. Clearly, the polling strategy can be carried further; SO can poll one device SI$_i$, and address another one SI$_j$, to ensure that the data is sent from SI$_i$ to SI$_j$. Alternatively, it can poll to see if any device has data to send. The whole question of address control is complex and depends on the nature of the communication channel. A normal telephone channel, for example, is usually point-to-point. A satellite communication channel is fundamentally broadcast, even if it is often used in a point-to-point manner.

Just as a single byte in Fig. 4 of an asynchronous transmission system was framed by a start-bit (often a parity bit) and a stop-bit, so whole blocks are usually framed by some synchronizing bytes, a start-byte, error-detection bytes, and an end-of-block indication. This end-of-block indication always used to be a specific byte sequence or an indication at the start of the block of its length. More recently, a structure has been standardized by the International Standards Organization (ISO, 1978). Here, the normal data bits have a "0" inserted into the data stream by its transmitting communication adaptor hardware after each five consecutive "1" bits. The receiving hardware thus interprets six consecutive one-bits as signaling the end of a data block. For the case of *multiplexed*, multipoint, or polling situations, the header may also contain polling or addressing information (*see* MULTI-PLEXING). Most synchronous communication systems are synchronous at the bit level, but are asynchronous at the block level. For this reason, the header and the end-of-block bear the same relation to the block as the start-bits and stop-bits do to the single byte shown in Fig. 4. Some special synchronizing bytes are sent in the header to obtain the bit synchronization achieved by the start-bit in an asynchronous system.

Local and Long Distance Communications

To illustrate the problems of the control and synchronization required between SO and SI, we consider the interface inside a single computer system. Here, the data communication path usually has a fairly complex hardware interface with lines for passing data and control. The type of information passed is indicated in Fig. 6. This interface is for a synchronous autonomous simplex transfer, with 8-bit data lines and a parity line (PD). The AO and SO lines in Fig. 6 are to assure each device that the other is operational. The AC informs the source when new data is required, and SO then informs the acceptor when the data is ready. If an error (e.g. parity) is detected, AE informs the source, and completion of block transfer is indicated by ST.

The discussion of the interface of Fig. 6 illustrates one of the key features of data communication. In a local connection, there are a number of control lines to establish synchronization, timing, acknowledgement, error detection, end-of-transmission, etc. All such control information in the data communication system of Fig. 1 *must be carried with the data*. Moreover, in a local system, errors in transmitting data over the interface of Fig. 6 are usually rare; over long distances, noise and other phenomena will often cause bits to be lost. Since some of these bits may contain control information, care must be taken in the communication environment to ensure that the correct action will be taken in all cases on *both sides of the link*. We will discuss below how some of this control information is passed.

In the communication of Fig. 6, the data is carried across the interface in parallel; in that of Fig. 1, it must first be serialized. We discussed previously that, in some systems, the modems of Fig. 1 established synchronization with each other—the so-called synchronous systems in which the bit timings are developed in the modems. It is merely necessary to establish this synchronization at

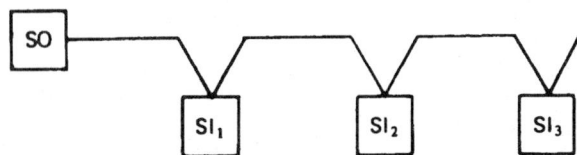

FIG. 5.   Multipoint connection between SO and SI$_1$, SI$_2$, SI$_3$.

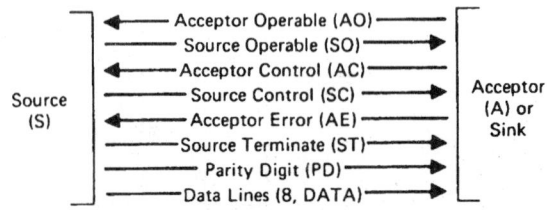

FIG. 6.   Standard peripheral interface.

the beginning of the transmission. Since this takes some time, it is usual to send data in a synchronous system in a block with some header information, followed by the data, and with some control and error detection data at the end. A synchronous system can be used only if the source SO of Fig. 5 has a buffer (*q.v.*) so that it can collect a whole block of information before transmission begins.

Error Detection And Correction

It is usual in a data communication system to send some bits additional to the actual useful data to identify the existence of, and possibly to correct, errors. The simplest error detection code is to add to each n bits of data an $(n + 1)$st bit, so chosen that the sum of the $(n + 1)$ bits is of a given parity (even or odd); such an extra bit is called a *parity* bit. In the asynchronous transmission system of Fig. 5, such a parity bit is often sent immediately before the stop-bit.

While the code is simple, it is not adequate if high information integrity is desired. Noise in transmission lines occurs fairly often; one incorrect bit in a thousand is a normal error rate on a switched line. Moreover, the nature of these errors in such that the noise that causes them often lasts more than one-bit time. For this reason, most data transmissions systems, other than those involving the simplest keyboard terminals, send their information in blocks and use more sophisticated error-detection codes that act on the whole block. One simple method considers the block as made up of n-bit bytes; it then does a parity check on the ith bits of each byte, and thus constructs the ith bit of a *block-parity check* byte. When this block-parity check is combined with a parity check on each byte, only errors that occur in rare combinations would remain undetected. A more sophisticated set of error-detection codes is based on *cyclic redundancy checks* (CRCs), which require rather more logic, but are even safer. The subject of error-detection codes is discussed fully by Petersen (1972).

Just as the interface of Fig. 6 must have an error-return line, so it is usually necessary to acknowledge the correctness of each block sent. In some cases, this acknowledgement is made before any new block can be sent. In others, a header contains a block number which is increased each time a block is sent. It is assumed that each block has been received correctly, unless a *negative acknowledgement* is sent subsequent. If that occurs, either only the faulty block or all subsequent blocks are

re-transmitted. The philosophy is particularly important when there are significant delays in the communication network (e.g. when one or more satellite hops are involved), requiring a minimum of 0.5 seconds for a round-trip signal. The standardized control procedure (HDLC) mentioned above prescribes variants at all these control functions. The control procedures for multiplexed communication over public data networks have been standardized further by the Consultative Committee on International Telephone and Telegraph (CCITT). Its procedures (X.25 to the customer, X.75 between carriers, and X.121 for international numbering) are the subject of another set of international recommendations (CCITT, 1978).

Public Data Services

It is instructive to consider what speeds and modes of data communication are offered currently by the telecommunications authorities over the telephone networks. They usually offer facilities over both switched and leased lines. In the former, it is possible to dial up any other subscriber on the switched network and to communicate with that party; in the latter, connection can be made along only one path (possibly multidrop, as in Fig. 5). On a leased line, because only one path is used, it is possible for the telecommunications authorities to *condition* the line to improve its performance; such conditioning is called *line equalization*. Alternatively, both with switched and leased lines, it is possible to arrange for the modems to adjust to line conditions; this is called *equalizing* or *balancing* the modems. On a switched line, this balancing must be done on each call.

Fig. 7 illustrates the connection between two telephones and their local exchanges. Between the exchanges (C-D in Fig. 7), there are separate channels in the two directions, ensuring duplex facilities. On a switched line, there is usually only one pair of lines, as shown in Fig. 7(a), between the telephone line and the local exchange; this is called a *two-wire circuit*. On a leased line, it is possible to order at comparatively low cost a second pair of lines to the local exchange, as illustrated in Fig. 7(b). In this case, one has a four-wire circuit, and is able to operate at maximum speed simultaneously in both directions. On a single pair, as in A-B of Fig. 7(a), it is possible to work at medium speeds in both directions simultaneously. It is also possible to work at a much higher speed in one

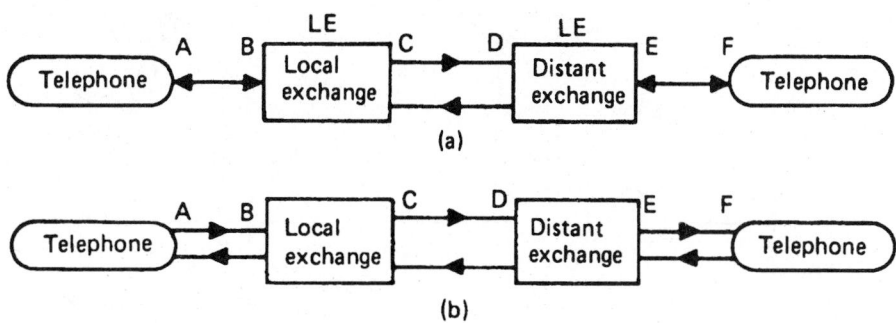

FIG. 7. Schematics of telephone networks. (a) switched telephone line (b) four-wire leased telephone line.

direction, with a lower-speed return path. Schematically, this situation is then as shown in Fig. 7(b), but only one pair of physical connections need exist between A and B or E and F. This low-speed return path is called a *supervisory return*, and varies in speed between 75 and 300 bps. It is used to turn around the line in the half-duplex situation or to signal acknowledgements or enter keyboard data in duplex. Thus, in the true four-wire case of Fig. 7(b), it is possible to have the high-speed data going simultaneously on each line, as shown in the figure, with additional reverse supervisory information. It is now customary to achieve speeds up to 2.4 Kbps duplex on Public Switched Telephone channels, and up to 19.2 Kbps in one direction (with potentially a supervisory signal in the return direction) on leased channels. For poorer quality channels, these speeds may have to be reduced. Some modems reduce their speeds automatically to adjust to the quality of the telephone channels.

The Integrated Digital Services Network, discussed above, uses the digital transmission of Section 3 to provide two information channels (at 64 Kbps each) and one signaling channel (at 16 Kbps), all running duplex over one two-wire line to the nearest switch or concentration point (see Halsall, 1989). From this point, the data is multiplexed digitally on to the standard digital data hierarchy used by the PTTs for inter-exchange transmission. The interface standards have been defined by the CCITT as the X-Series of their recommendations for ordinary data services, and the I-series for the Integrated Digital Network Services. In totally leased facilities, the transmission circuits bypass the switches on PTT premises. However, there are also switched data services. The switching can be of a *circuit-switched* type, as in the normal telephone system. Alternatively, they can be *packet-switched*. The choice of switching mode is quite separate from that of transmission mode.

Private Data Networks

Finally, a brief discussion of methods of data concentration and multiplexing is required. The situation is illustrated in Fig. 8. In Fig. 8, H represents a computer that may receive a multileaved data stream. The multileaving may be in the form of a number of streams interleaved at the transmission level by using a different frequency for each stream (*frequency division multiplexing FDM*); the bits of the different streams may be transmitted on a round robin basis by bit

or byte (*time division multiplexing TDM*); or complete blocks may be sent (packet switching). Different forms of hardware and software are needed in the switch S in each case. Terminals T supporting only one duplex data stream may also be supported in one of two ways: Either a *concentrator* C may be used (in this case, the number of terminal ports to T is greater than the number that can be supported simultaneously; statistical averaging is used to reduce the number of terminals that would be refused service to acceptable proportions), or a *multiplexer* is used, wherein each terminal can be serviced—albeit possibly at a reduced rate if all are active. The switches S in Fig. 8 will serve to demultiplex and then remultiplex the incoming streams to other switches S, concentrators C, and multiplexers M.

Note that there will usually be some limit to the number of simultaneous streams that can be handled by a switch S. If *packet switching* is used, this limit may be fixed by the header address space (e.g. defined by HDLC or X.25). If circuit switching (or even virtual call packet switching—*see* PACKET SWITCHING) is used, the limit is set by the number of simultaneous buffers for each call that can be supported. Several levels of multiplexing and concentration may be supported. This is illustrated in Fig. 9.

Moreover, the type of multiplexing between different levels may be quite different. For example, between M1 and M2, a more powerful form of multiplexing, such as packet switching, would be used.

All these techniques take advantage of one or more of the following factors:

1. Normally, not all terminals T operate simultaneously.
2. When in use, the data transmission rate between an active terminal and a network may exhibit considerable variation.
3. The cost of a long distance communication channel increases much more slowly than its data capacity.
4. The communications channels installed often have greater capacity than the average traffic.

It is often cheaper to take advantage of the *transmission savings* by incorporating more complex *switching* or *mul-*

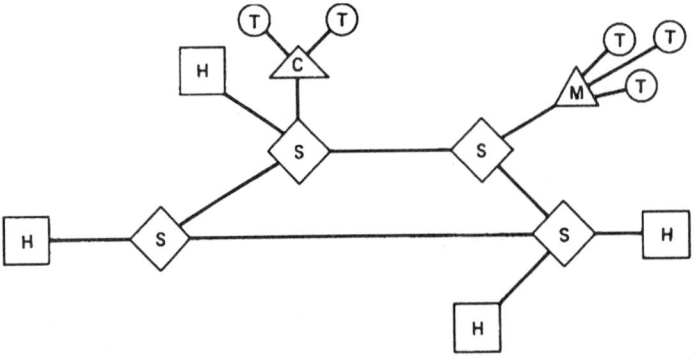

FIG. 8. Schematic of computer network.

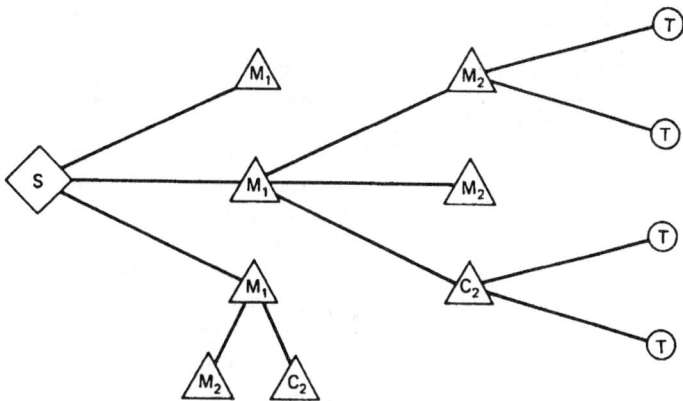

FIG. 9. Example of multilevel multiplexing.

tiplexing. In *public data networks*, the savings are partially (or entirely) enjoyed by the carriers. In *leased networks*, the customers, not the PTTs, are the main beneficiaries. Partially to ease disparities of cost and to encourage the use of public networks, some PTTs had started to raise the cost of leased circuits, charge partly by volume of traffic on the leased facilities, and restrict the switching permitted by the customer. With the advent of greater freedom of competition to the PTTs, and the difficulty of policing the nature of the traffic, some of these tactics are becoming less prevalent.

References

1972. Petersen, W. W. *Error Correcting Codes.* Cambridge, MA: The M.I.T. Press.
1978. CCITT. "Provisional Recommendations X.3, X.21, X.25, X.29, X.75, X.121." Geneva: ITU.
1978. McQuillan, J. M. *A Practical View of Computer Communications Protocols,* McQuillan, J. M. and Cerf, V. G. (Eds.) New York: IEEE EHO 137-0.
1983. Proahms, J. G. *Digital Communications.* New York: McGraw-Hill.
1988. Halsall, F. *Data Communications, Computer Networks, and OSI.* 2nd Ed. Reading, MA: Addison Wesley.
1988. Tanenbaum, A. S. *Computer Networks,* 2nd Ed. Englewood Cliffs, NJ: Prentice-Hall.
1989. Black, U. D. *Data Networks: Concepts, Theory and Practices.* Englewood Cliffs, NJ: Prentice-Hall.

PETER T. KIRSTEIN

SOFTWARE

The importance of (and the attention given to) data communications software has been increasing at a rapid pace. This growing importance is driven by an ever-increasing demand for low-cost, flexible, and powerful data communications systems.

Almost every month, a new and powerful VLSI chip is announced that performs functions that traditionally were performed by data communications software. Thus, the borderline between hardware and software is rapidly moving. Today's data communications engineer, therefore, has to be thoroughly familiar with both hardware and software problem-solving techniques.

The design of data communications software is heavily influenced by the real-time requirements associated with data communications applications. There is an endless variety in the sequence and timing in which messages and characters are to be processed. Therefore, even the most exhaustive test procedure will test only a small number of all possible interactions.

Various techniques have been developed to ensure the proper design of data communications software. The interactions between two communicating entities are normally defined by carefully specified *protocols.* The use of state-transition diagrams has proved to be a valuable tool for specifying protocols, as well as for the design of software to implement these protocols. (See as an example the state-transition diagram shown in Fig. 3.)

Another technique to deal with the complexities of data communications that has proved highly successful is the hierarchical design or layering of protocols. The advantage of the layered approach is that changes in one layer do not affect the other layers. Thus, definition, implementation, and testing of the various layers can proceed in parallel. The International Standards Organization (ISO) identified seven functional layers in the ISO reference model for an Open Systems Interconnection (OSI), as shown in Fig. 1. The first level, or physical control layer, provides the physical, functional, and mechanical characteristics of the interface. The second, or link control layer, provides for the reliable exchange of messages. In particular, it specifies the rules for overcoming transmission errors. The third level, or network control layer, provides the functions required for intra-network operation, such as addressing and routing. The fourth level, or transport end-to-end control layer, ensures the reliable transfer of data between end points across a communications network. The fifth level is concerned with the control of a session, which is the period of time during which a user is connected to a computer system. In particular, this session control layer provides for identification and authentication of the user and for control of data flow during the session. The sixth level, or presentation control layer, formats the information as required by the interacting

Level   Layer

7   Application

6   Presentation
           Control

5   Session
           Control

4   Transport
           End-to-end
           Control

3   Network
           Control

2   Link
           Control

1   Physical
           Control

FIG. 1. ISO functional layers for open systems interconnection.

entities. The applications layer, which is concerned with applications software, is beyond the scope of this article.

In the following sections, we will show which functions are typically performed by data communications software and discuss a possible software structure for implementing some of these functions.

Communication Line Characteristics

There are two main modes of transmission—synchronous and asynchronous operation. In asynchronous transmissions, the data is sent one character at a time (Fig. 2a). Each character is framed by a *start* and *stop bit*. Bits within a character occur at well-defined intervals. The number of bits per character is fixed for a given communications line. The reading of this number of fixed bits is triggered

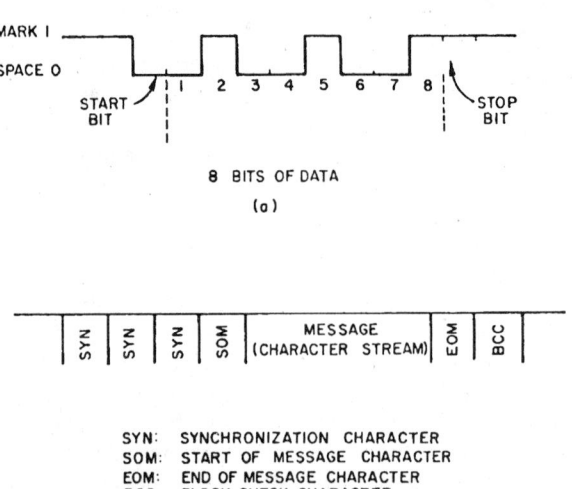

SYN: SYNCHRONIZATION CHARACTER
SOM: START OF MESSAGE CHARACTER
EOM: END OF MESSAGE CHARACTER
BCC: BLOCK CHECK CHARACTER

(b)

FIG. 2. Data transmission. a) asynchronous, b) synchronous.

by the reception of the start bit. In asynchronous transmission, characters do not recur at any predictable interval. This form of transmission is most commonly used for communication with slower-speed human-operated terminals.

In synchronous transmission, the bits of one character are followed immediately by those of the next (Fig. 2b). The stream of characters is divided into blocks. Each block is surrounded by framing characters. The reading of the sequence of characters in a block is triggered by the reception of a start-of-block framing character. Characters are received continuously until an end-of-block framing character is detected. Since there are no control bits for each character, synchronous transmissions generally result in a more efficient line utilization.

Protocol Characteristics

Since data communications software is mainly concerned with data communications protocols, it is important to understand which protocol functions are typically implemented, at least partially, in software. Therefore, the following five protocol functions will be discussed in more detail: (1) call establishment and clearing; (2) error control; (3) flow control; (4) concentration; and (5) terminal-specific procedures. This, of course, is not an exhaustive list, but it highlights some of the main issues that need to be addressed in designing data communications software.

Call Establishment and Clearing

Before any data can be exchanged over data communications facilities, there needs to be a mechanism invoked by which one end can decide whether or not the other is operating at all (i.e. able and willing to establish a connection). In other words, both parties need to agree on a procedure by which one side can indicate to the other side that it either wants to establish or break a connection. Data set signals are used to convey this information at the physical communications level. Depending on the voltage of a particular pin of the interface, each side indicates that it is either operating or not available. In case a connection is established via the public telephone network, a more complex sequence of changes in the data set signals is required. At the link level, an exchange of special initialization commands and responses is normally required before data can be transmitted. The most sophisticated call establishment and clearing procedures are used at the network control level. In this case, highly structured call request and clear request messages are sent that carry information relating to the nature of the call. In particular, the call request message may indicate who intends to pay for the call, throughput requirements, what higher level protocol is to be used, etc. The clear message may carry information about the clearing cause, duration of the call, accounting data, etc.

Fig. 3 shows a state diagram for call establishment between two stations, A and B. Normally, a station sends out a call request and waits until it receives the matching call accept message. Call collision will occur when both stations try to establish a call at the same time. Note that, in the case presented, the call request from A to B takes precedence.

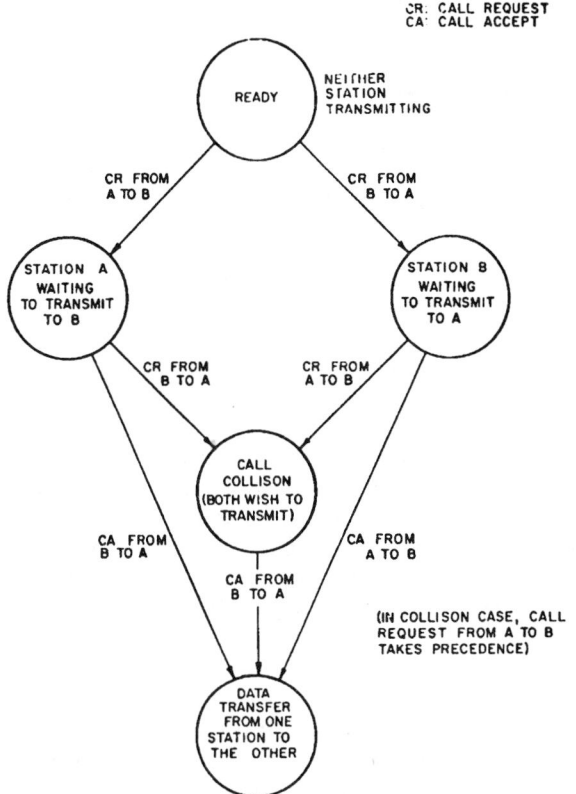

FIG. 3. State transition diagram for call establishment.

Error Control One of the most important tasks of any data communications protocol is to deal with line errors. Various error detection and correction schemes have been studied and are in use today. They range from simple even or odd parity indication per character to powerful, usually hardware-generated, checksums per transmission block. All the more advanced procedures use positive acknowledgment schemes; i.e. the sender waits for an acknowledgment from the receiver. If an acknowledgment is not received within a given time period, the block is retransmitted. Since the acknowledgment may get lost on the line due to a line error, the receiver must be able to distinguish new incoming blocks from retransmissions of previously sent blocks. This can be accomplished through the use of sequence numbers. Whenever the receiver receives two blocks with the same sequence number, it is known that the latter block is a retransmission of the first one and can be discarded as a duplicate if there was no error in the first one. The receiver will also send an acknowledgment for each duplicate to make sure that the sender eventually learns about the successful transmission.

A well-known technique for acknowledging blocks is to send back to the sender the sequence number N of the next expected block, thereby acknowledging all blocks with sequence numbers $N - 1$ or less. The range of sequence numbers is, of course, limited, since they occupy a finite space in each block. If K bits are reserved for the sequence number in the header of a block, then they are normally calculated modulo 2^K. In the simplest case, K is equal to 1; i.e. each block is labeled as block 0 or block 1. This requires only a single bit in the header for sequence control. This scheme has, however, the disadvantage that block 1 (or 0) can only be sent after block 0 (or 1) has been acknowledged. Therefore, the throughput is limited to one message per round-trip time (i.e. the time interval between sending a block and receiving its acknowledgment).

Sequence numbers are also used to detect blocks that reach the receiver out of sequence. In this case, two recovery actions are possible. The receiver discards all out-of-sequence blocks and asks the sender to retransmit all blocks from the point where the first block was missed (reject scheme). The alternative possibility is that the receiver keeps the out-of-sequence blocks and asks the sender only for the retransmission of the missed blocks (selective retransmit scheme).

Figs. 4 and 5 demonstrate the use of the reject and the selective retransmit scheme. In both cases, message 2 is assumed to get lost on the line. The reject-retransmit scheme causes messages 2, 3, and 4 to be retransmitted (Fig. 4). The selective retransmit scheme causes only message 2 to be retransmitted (Fig. 5). Messages 3 and 4 are only acknowledged after the successful retransmission of message 2.

Flow Control To avoid loss of data, the average rate at which the receiver is able to accept data must be equal to or greater than the average rate at which the sender is sending it. Alternatively, there may be a mechanism by which the receiver can let the sender know that it should

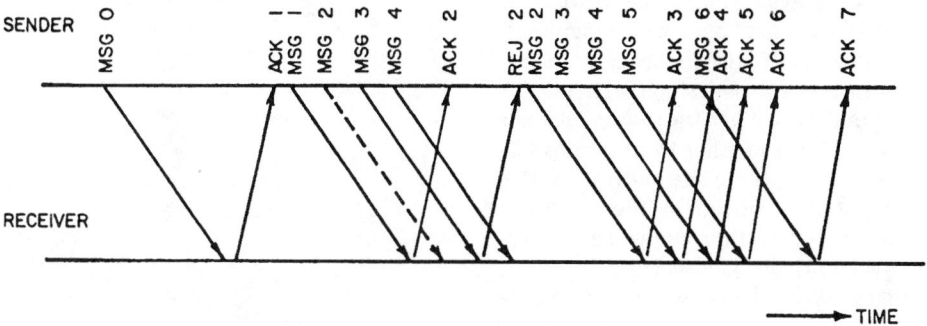

FIG. 4. Reject-retransmit scheme (each acknowledgment carries the number of the next message expected).

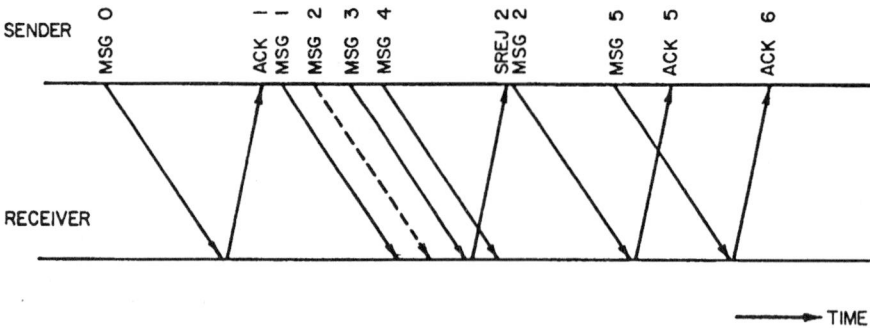

FIG. 5. Selective retransmit scheme.

stop transmitting or at least slow down. This mechanism is called *flow control.*

In simple terminal protocols, flow control is provided by means of special characters. When the receiver is not willing to accept more characters, a so-called XOFF character will be transmitted. The receipt of this character causes the sender to stop transmitting. To restart the transmission of data, the receiver sends the so-called XON character. Since the XOFF and XON characters can be garbled or even generated by line errors, this simple scheme can lead to confusion. More sophisticated protocols, therefore, use checksum-protected commands to turn off and restart the flow of data from the sender.

All acknowledgment/retransmission protocols have a built-in natural flow control mechanism. Just by not acknowledging blocks (even though they were received with a good checksum), the receiver can stop the sender. More effective, however, is an extension of the sequence number scheme to cover flow control. In this scheme, the receiver returns with the acknowledgment not only of the sequence number of the next expected block, but also of an indication as to how many more blocks the receiver is willing to accept. This indication defines to the sender a window of legal sequence numbers it can use to send data. (Therefore, this scheme is called the *window technique.*) Once all sequence numbers in this window are used up (i.e. the window is closed), the sender must stop transmitting and wait for an acknowledgment that may open up the window again.

Fig. 6 demonstrates the use of sequence numbers for flow control. The sequence number space is represented as a circle. The circle is subdivided into three sectors: (1) sequence numbers of blocks that have been transmitted but not yet acknowledged (A-B); (2) sequence numbers that are available for further transmission (B-C); and (3) illegal sequence numbers (C-A). When the sector between B and C becomes empty, the sender has to stop transmitting. Points A and C on the circle are moved by the acknowledgments; point B is moved by the transmissions. The dashed areas represent the sequence number space used up by unacknowledged messages.

One of the design goals for data communication protocols is the efficient use of the available line bandwidth; i.e. the protocol should minimize the loss of line capacity due to overhead and/or error control or flow control

restrictions. To guarantee the continuous flow of messages over a data communications link, the number of outstanding messages allowed at any time (window A-C) must be larger than the round-trip time divided by the time it takes to transmit one message. If this condition holds, the sender will never be blocked by a closed window B-C.

Concentration The flow control condition of the previous paragraph can be relaxed if the protocol supports concentration. In this case, several data streams can be sent over the same physical channel. Each block carries an identifier signifying the data stream to which it belongs. Since each data stream is driven by an independent

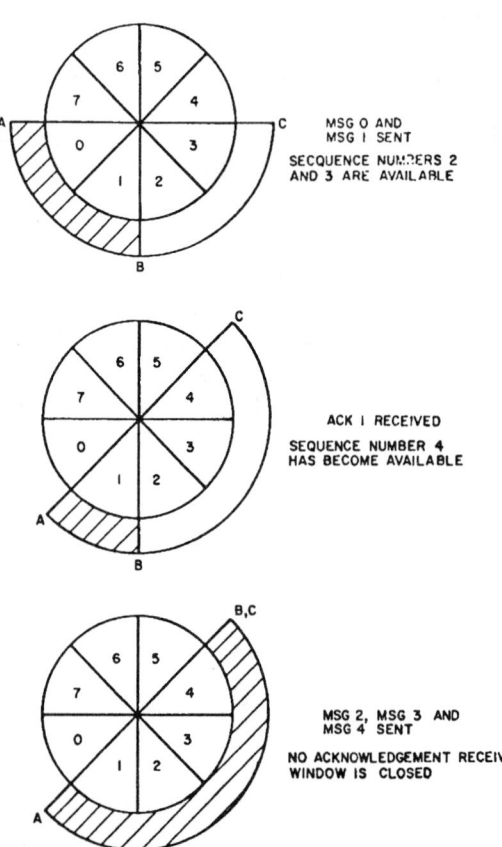

FIG. 6. Window technique.

set of sequence numbers, the sender can keep on transmitting even though some of the data streams may be blocked. The use of independent sequence numbers for each data stream is also important in order to minimize the interference between them. In particular, a protocol must ensure that one data stream being blocked does not also block the users of the other data streams.

Terminal-Specific Procedures A large variety of functions to be performed by the data communications software is common to many terminal types; others are required only for a given terminal type. Functions that are common to many asynchronous terminals are: (1) echo control; i.e. echoing of characters for full-duplex terminals and suppression of echo for half-duplex terminals; (2) padding; i.e. insertion of delay between characters to accommodate mechanical movement for characters like carriage return; (3) line folding; i.e. control of the maximum number of graphic characters that can be displayed on a single line; (4) code conversion; e.g. from EBCDIC (*q.v.*) to ASCII (*q.v.*); (5) editing; e.g. deletion of characters or lines of text; (6) keyboard control; i.e. locking and unlocking of the keyboard for certain half-duplex terminals; etc. Functions that are common to many display-type terminals are (1) cursor control (positioning of the cursor on the screen); (2) type and range checking on input data; (3) protection of read-only areas on the screen; (4) management of function keys; etc.

Network Operation Communication protocols that are used in a network environment require additional functionality. In particular, the establishment of paths through the network to any desired destination needs to be specified in detail.

Computer communication networks are either *circuit-switched* or *packet-switched*. In a circuit-switched network, the source and destination are connected by a dedicated communication path that is established at the beginning of the connection and broken at the end. This type of connection is based on the traditional telephone technology, where subscribers require continuity in voice transmission and reception.

In packet-switching (*q.v.*) networks, short messages (called packets) are handled individually by the network. Packets are stored at intermediate nodes, which switch them to the next transmission line on the path to the destination. Transmission capacity is shared among all

connections. By avoiding the transmission of long data blocks, a packet-switching system is able to ensure that short blocks of high-priority data can be rapidly transmitted through the network. In a *message switching system*, complete messages are stored at intermediate nodes, sometimes for long periods, before they are forwarded to the next node or the destination.

Software Structure In the preceding section we have shown what functions need to be performed by the data communications software. We will now turn to a discussion of software structures to implement these functions. In particular, we will present a simple communications software structure model to describe a software system for the handling of synchronous lines.

There are many ways by which data communications software can be organized. The model depicted in Fig. 7 represents a typical design that splits the entire task into functional units. Each of these functional units can be thought of as a process. The exchange of information between these processes can be done either on a shared memory basis or via a more formal message exchange procedure that is supported by the operating system.

Most of the handling of the hardware that interfaces the communications lines is normally implemented on the interrupt level to satisfy the real-time requirements of in-flow and out-flow of data. The hardware interrupts occur either on a per character or a per block basis. In the latter case, the hardware has the ability to deposit directly in memory and retrieve from memory a sequence of characters without software assistance. An interrupt is generated when this sequence has reached a predefined length or a special control character (or sequence of control characters) is encountered. Thus, if interrupts are generated only for a sequence of characters, the software is relieved of a great number of repetitive tasks. In the following discussion, we will, however, concentrate on the interrupt-per-character model, since it will allow us to describe more easily the various tasks involved in handling a communications line or terminal.

The interrupt level processes INT-IN and INT-OUT interact with the CHAR-IN and CHAR-OUT monitor level processes. The CHAR-IN process assembles characters into messages and passes the messages on to the MSG-IN process. In turn, the CHAR-OUT process receives messages from the MSG-OUT process, disassembles the mes-

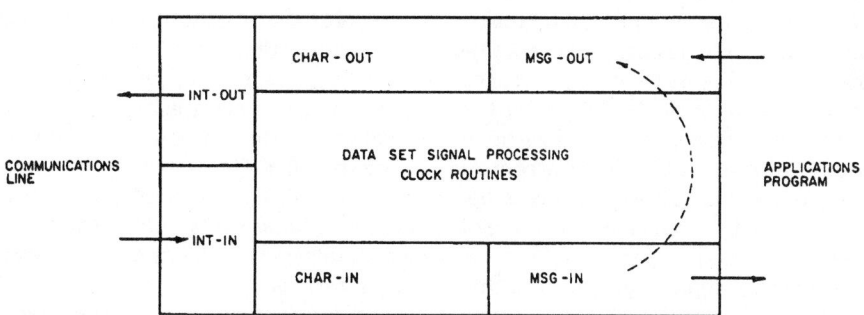

FIG. 7. Communications software structure.

sages, and passes individual characters on to the interrupt level process INT-OUT. The MSG-IN and MSG-OUT processes send messages to and receive messages from an applications program. We will now turn to a more detailed discussion of these processes for the handling of synchronous lines.

The main function of the INT-IN process is to store characters in a buffer in memory. This task involves the updating of an offset into the buffer, the detection of full buffers, and the switch-over to a new buffer. The start and end of message detection is also done by the INT-IN process. These events are either directly signaled by the hardware, or the software has to detect these conditions by searching through the stream of incoming characters for special control characters. The calculation of the checksum is almost always done by the hardware. The INT-IN process reads the result of that calculation from a control register and passes this information on to the CHAR-IN process. The INT-IN process also handles a large number of error conditions, such as underrun (i.e. a character was not received in time by the software and therefore was overwritten by the following character) and frame error (i.e. the proper message-framing characters were not detected due to line errors or transmitter errors). Whenever such an error occurs, the CHAR-IN process is informed about the condition, and all incoming characters are discarded until the start of the next message is found.

The CHAR-IN process receives from the INT-IN process buffers that contain a status indicator. Depending on this status indicator, the CHAR-IN process will build up chains of buffers if a message does not fit into a single buffer, pass these messages on to the MSG-IN process if the message was received with a correct checksum, or return the buffer to the operating system if any type of error was detected by the INT-IN process. The CHAR-IN process also has to supply the INT-IN process with buffers for the incoming messages.

The MSG-IN process ensures that messages are delivered to the applications program in correct order and without duplication. Messages that arrive out of order are either held until the missing messages are received or discarded and retransmitted later. All messages received in sequence, as well as all duplicate messages, are acknowledged. The acknowledgment information is passed on to the MSG-OUT process (dashed line in Fig. 7), which inserts it into the stream of outgoing messages. The MSG-IN process also informs the MSG-OUT process about any received acknowledgment information. This information allows the MSG-OUT process to free up buffer space that is occupied by messages that wait to be acknowledged. The main tasks of the MSG-OUT process is to accept messages from the applications program, provide them with the proper sequence number, if required, and pass them on to the CHAR-OUT process. A major part of the flow control procedure is implemented in the MSG-OUT process because it is this process that must, at any time, be aware of the ability of the receiver to receive more messages.

The CHAR-OUT process accepts messages from the MSG-OUT process. If the message is contained in a single buffer, this buffer is given to the INT-OUT process. In case the message consists of several buffers, each buffer is forwarded separately to the INT-OUT process. All buffers handed over to the interrupt level process carry a status indicator, which identifies them as either the head, middle section, or tail of a message. The INT-OUT process uses this status indicator to control proper framing of messages and the generation of the checksum. When the head of a message is received, the accumulation of the checksum is initialized. After the last buffer of the message has been emptied, the checksum is transmitted over the communications line.

Conclusion The need to access computing resources, as well as the need of these resources to communicate with one another, has become ever-more important. We are rapidly approaching the day when data terminals are as widely accessible and frequently used as telephones. In fact, single devices that can be used as a telephone, as a terminal, and as a fax machine and that, in general, can be used as a multimedia communications device are now available.

In the future, the requirements for data communications system will be coupled more closely into the overall communications requirements. Today's data communications engineer will have to be more familiar with other means of communication. Complex software systems will be required to tie the existing means of communication together into one integrated system. The data communications software will, therefore, cease to exist as a separate subject but will be folded into software systems that satisfy a far greater range of communications requirements.

References

1979. Davies, D. W., Barber, D. L. A., Price, W. L., and Solomonides, C. M. *Computer Networks and Their Protocols.* New York: John Wiley.

1979. Doll, Dixon R. *Data Communication Facilities, Networks, and Systems Design.* New York: John Wiley.

1986. Purser, Michael. *Data Communications for Programmers.* Reading, MA: Addison-Wesley.

1990. Sherman, Ken. *Data Communications: A Users's Guide*, 3rd Ed. Englewood Cliffs, NJ: Prentice-Hall.

HOLGER OPDERBECK

STANDARDS

The Need for Standards Most computer manufacturers have their own network architectures, but over recent years there has been increasing emphasis on the use of internationally agreed upon standards for communication so that systems from different suppliers can work together. The ability for machines of different types to communicate is becoming progressively more important as the focus shifts from the dedicated networks within an organization to the public networks that link separate organizations.

Networks were originally developed primarily to provide for remote access to computing facilities. For example, the airlines provided for access to seat reservation systems, and major business data processing centers, such as those operated by the banks, allowed for remote entry of data and remote printing of results. This is still an important aspect of network use and the basic principles of error-free communication have not changed. However, the major growth is now based on the exchange and sharing of information, rather than access to processing power.

Networks now support exchange of personal messages, exchange of business data, access to distributed databases, integrated manufacturing, and distributed command and control systems. They are applied in commercial activity, administration, and entertainment. Some of these new applications make additional demands on the supporting networks, but many are extensions to new fields based on existing technology. A common feature of many of these new areas of application is the sharing of information between organizations, and, in consequence, the need for communication to be effective without a single management or design authority to make it work. Data communications standards make information exchange possible in this environment.

The Organizations Involved   Two major bodies are involved in the creation of standards. These are the International Organization for Standardization (ISO), representing primarily the computer industry and its customers, and the International Consultative Committee on Telephony and Telegraphy (CCITT), representing the communication carriers via their national post and telecommunications authorities (the PTTs). Preliminary standards are also produced by the European Computer Manufacturers' Association (ECMA) and the Committee of European Posts and Telegraphs (CEPT). In the U.S., the IEEE has played a major role in drafting standards proposals, particularly in the field of local area networks (LANs - *q.v.*). Standards of general interest from ECMA and IEEE are often fed into the ISO for wider discussion and support with the option of rapid publication as an ISO standard. Many standards are now produced jointly by ISO and CCITT, with the two organizations agreeing to publish technically identical texts.

The Standardization Process   The development of a standard within the ISO involves a number of steps. The theory is as follows (see Fig. 1). Initially, a need is identified and support for a standardization project is confirmed by ballot among the national standards bodies on a new work item (NWI). A technical group then develops a working draft for the standard to the point where it is believed to be technically stable. This is approved by the controlling subcommittee and registered as a Committee Draft (CD). At this point, the national standards bodies take part in a ballot on the technical content. Each may vote "yes" without qualification, vote "yes" but give comments on possible improvements it would like to see, or vote "no" and give the reasons for its objections and an indication of what action would make the standard acceptable.

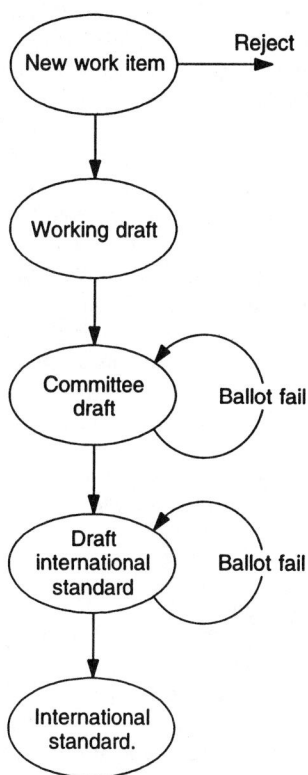

FIG. 1.   The standardization process.

If there is substantial agreement with little comment, the draft becomes a Draft International Standard (DIS). At this point it is processed editorially to conform to the ISO house style, and may need to be translated into French, although this requirement is now generally waived. A further ballot by a higher-level committee then allows it to progress to a full International Standard (IS). If any of these ballots does not show support, the document must be revised and the ballot repeated.

In favorable circumstances, the passages from CD to DIS and from DIS to IS each take about a year. Although in principle the technical content should be agreed before registration as a CD, pressure for rapid progress may result in significant instability beyond this point, making early implementation a risky business. In practice, a draft might be ready for pilot implementation by the time it reaches the DIS stage.

Major Areas of Standardization   The wide range of data communications standards is organized within the framework of the Open Systems Interconnection (OSI) Reference Model. Within the structure created by the reference model, individual service and protocol standards are defined for each of the layers except the application layer. In many layers, provision is made for choice of either a connection-oriented mode of operation, in which streams of information are sent between the communicating systems in the period during which a connection exists, and a connectionless mode of operation in which individual items of data are transmitted independently. The mode chosen depends on the application and the economics of the situation, and, in the lower layers, different families of standards have been created to meet the requirements of local and wide area networks.

The seven layers of the reference model can be considered in two groups. The three layers below the network service deal with the problems of the various network technologies, and with the use of networks in combination and the routing of information between different networks. The transport layer and the layers above it are concerned with the organization of the communication from end to end between the participating systems. Thus, the lower layers are primarily concerned with the process of data communication itself, while, the upper layers address the incompatibilities of data formats or representations (in the presentation layer) and of operating system control of communication (in the session layer) between systems.

Applications The application layer forms the top of the protocol stack, and models both the standardized applications and their users. This layer does not provide a service; all relevant aspects of the system are considered to be within it.

In consequence, the application layer has a more complex substructure than the other layers because the user activity may require a number of standard functions in combination. Separate standards cover the common functions, known as application service elements, including:

1. *Initiating and controlling the communication*—The logical linkage created when two parts of the application communicate is called an *association* and so the function is called the *association control service element.*

2. *File transfer access and management*—This one protocol can be used to access or control any passive source or sink of information, identifying the data required and organizing the data transfer.

3. *Electronic mail exchange*—(also known as interpersonal messaging)—The mail protocols support the transfer of bodies of information, possibly in a series of steps, on the basis of steering information provided by the originator, in the same way that the postal service would handle an addressed letter.

4. *Virtual terminal services*—The virtual terminal service handles problems of access and synchronization that arise when two communicating parties manipulate the same resource at the same time. It would be used, for example, to resolve conflict when a user and an application program both wish to update the terminal screen at the same time, and would ensure that their actions were interleaved in a consistent way.

5. *Transaction processing*—The transaction processing mechanisms provide a framework for applications that need to update resources in a number of different systems so that they remain consistent, ensuring, for example, that one account is debited and another credited, but that one of the actions does not take place without the other.

6. *Remote database access*—This protocol provides the means for managing database queries and responses from a remote site in a controlled and coordinated way.

7. *Job transfer and manipulation*—A job can be any free-standing task executed on a number of systems in sequence. This protocol controls the movement of jobs around a network to exploit remote resources.

8. *Directory services*—Before communication can take place, the systems involved must identify each other. The directory services provide standard location mechanisms in terms of either names or properties, just like the white and yellow page services offered in the telephone network.

9. *A wide range of network management facilities,* allowing the resources that make up the distributed system to be monitored, controlled, and accounted for. One set of mechanisms is applicable to many different classes of managed objects distributed throughout or even outside the network.

New work within ISO is currently in progress that will lead to a general standard for remote procedure call protocols.

Almost all of the application layer standards begin by defining some activity or resource that their protocol is to control. Thus, for example, the file transfer protocol begins by defining a model of file storage, and the virtual terminal protocol begins with a model of interaction and display. These models are then used when defining the service offered and the protocol that supports it in order to give meaning to the information exchanged.

Conformance The purchaser of a computer system wishes to know that the applicable standards have been implemented faithfully so that it will do the job for which it is intended. Checking that this is indeed the case is the function of *conformance testing.* Every standard that is directly implementable (and not part of a framework for other standards) contains a conformance clause that sets out exactly what behavior is required, what options exist, and what information is needed about the implementation in order to assess it.

A family of subsidiary standards has been created to define testing methodologies and then, for each of the major standards, to define a specific suite of tests that will exercise all the major features of the protocol in a systematic way. Such testing, although obviously not exhaustive, gives confidence that the standard has been correctly implemented.

TABLE 1. Representative List of ISO Data Communications Standards

ISO	CCITT	Abbreviated title
Architecture		
ISO 7498	X.200	OSI Basic Reference Model
ISO 9646	X.290	Conformance Testing Framework (5 parts)
ISO 9834		OSI Registration Procedures
ISO 10181		Security Framework
TR 10730		Tutorial on Naming and Addressing
OSI 10746	X.900 series	ODP Reference Model
Physical Layer		
—		Many connector and signalling standards
Data Link Layer		
ISO 3309, 4335,7478		High-level Data Link Control (HDLC)
ISO 7776	X.25	HDLC Procedures (X.25 compatible)
ISO 8802		Local Area Networks (7 parts)
ISO 8886	X.212	Data Link Service
Network Layer		
ISO 8348	X.213	Network Service
ISO 8208	X.25	X.25 Packet Level Protocol for DTE
ISO 8648		Internal Organization of the Network Layer
ISO 8878		Use of X.25 to Provide the Network Service
ISO 8880		Protocols to Provide the Network Service
ISO 8881		Use of X.25 in Local Area Networks
ISO 10028		Relaying Functions in an Intermediate System
ISO 9575, 9978,10030, 10589		Network Layer Routing
Transport Layer		
ISO 8072, 8073, 8602	X.214, X.224	Transport Service and Protocol
Session Layer		
ISO 8326, 8327,9548	X.215, X.225	Session Service and Protocol
Presentation Layer		
ISO 8822, 8823, 9576	X.216, X.226	Presentation Service and Protocol
ISO 8824, 8825	X.208, X.209	Abstract Syntax Notation One
Application Layer		
ISO 8649, 8650,10035	X.217, X.227	Association Control Service and Protocol
ISO 8571		File Transfer, Access, and Management
ISO 8831, 8832		Job Transfer and Manipulation
ISO 9040, 9041		Virtual Terminal Service and Protocol
ISO 9066	X.218, X.228	Reliable Transfer Service and Protocol
ISO 9072	X.219, X.229	Remote Operations Service and Protocol
ISO 9545		Application Layer Structure
ISO 9579		Remote Database Access
ISO 9594	X.500 series	The OSI Directory (9 parts)
ISO 9735		Electronic Data Interchange (EDIFACT)
ISO 9804,9805		Commitment, Concurrency, and Recovery Service and Protocol
ISO 10021	X.400 series	Message Handling and Interpersonal Messaging
ISO 10026		Transaction Processing
ISO 10166		Document Filing and Retrieval
Management		
ISO 9595, 9596	X.700 series	Common Management Information Services and Protocols
ISO 10040	X.700 series	System Management Overview
ISO 10164	X.700 series	System Management Functions (13 parts)
ISO 10165	X.700 series	Structure of Management Information

Functional Standards A system designer may be faced with a choice of options and parameters in the various general-purpose standards that make up the protocol stack to be implemented. If each designer made independent choices, it would be unlikely that an arbitrary pair of systems would communicate successfully.

To avoid this problem, a second tier of standardization has been erected, defining functional standards that give preferred values for all the choices that need to be made to support a particular user activity. These standards are produced in consultation with regional implementation groups to ensure that all requirements are taken into account.

Registration Authorities Successful communication depends on shared information. Preparing a system for connection to a network involves making a large number of choices, ranging from the names and addresses the system will be known by to the names of the types of documents it is expected to handle. This kind of information is too volatile to be the subject of standardization, but still needs to be managed and distributed.

The requirement is met by the creation of standardized procedures for the operation of registration authorities; for example, authorities exist to allocate addresses or maintain catalogs of data elements.

Some Important Standards There are now a large and growing number of data communication standards—far too many to list here in detail. Table 1 gives the ISO number (and the CCITT number where commonly referenced) and a shortened title of the major standards or groups of standards.

The Future The development of data communications standards is still going on. However, standardization of applications involves considerations outside pure communication, and aspects such as system configuration, management, and the relation of communication to other system interfaces become important. At the same time, there is growing interest in the creation of standards to support arbitrary user activity and not just selected common applications.

These considerations have led to the formulation of a new reference model within ISO, providing a framework for Open Distributed Processing (ODP), and standards resulting from it will open the way to the construction of a new generation of more flexible and powerful distributed systems.

References

1987. Knowles, T., Larmouth, J., and Knightson, K. G. *Standards for Open Systems Interconnection.* Oxford: BSP Professional Books.
1989. Tanenbaum, A. S. *Computer Networks* (2nd ed.), Englewood Cliffs, NJ: Prentice-Hall.

PETER F. LININGTON

DATA COMPRESSION AND COMPACTION

For articles on related subjects *see* CODES; CRYPTOGRAPHY, COMPUTERS IN; DATA COMMUNICATIONS; and FILE.

Many data processing applications involve storage of large volumes of alphanumeric data, such as names, addresses, inventory item descriptions, or a general ledger chart of accounts descriptions. Documents for text editors and for legal, medical, and library applications also require very high-capacity storage devices; and there is a rapid increase in the number of systems handling such material. At the same time, the proliferation of computer communication networks and teleprocessing applications involves massive transfer of data over long distance communication links.

To reduce the data storage requirements and/or the data communication costs, there is a need to reduce the redundancy in the data representation—i.e. to *compress* or *compact* the data. Data compression also reduces the load on I/O channels in a computer installation. Because of the reduced space requirements of compressed data, it may become feasible to store data at a higher, and thus faster, level of the storage hierarchy (*q.v.*).

It is also interesting to note that, since data compression techniques remove some of the redundancy in a non-compressed text, they thereby automatically contribute to data security.

Data compression can be made transparent to the user and can be implemented in either hardware, firmware, or software. The overhead involved in compression (followed later by expansion to recover the original data) is most severe in non-archival situations where the data is being actively processed rather than stored for later use.

Data compression is not without its disadvantages. Assuming compression/expansion is done in software (which is often the case), the software complexity of the system is increased. This results directly in an increase in the processing load of the system because of the additional CPU cycles needed for compression/expansion.

Another disadvantage of data compression is a decrease in portability caused by the absence of well-defined standards. Reliability is also reduced because of a decrease in redundancy that is useful for error-detection. Data compression techniques are most useful for large archival files processed by I/O-bound systems with spare CPU cycles, and for the transfer of voluminous amounts of data over long distance communication links. Data compression can achieve dramatic savings in total storage requirements, up to 80% in some cases.

Data compression techniques can be classified as being either *irreversible* or *reversible*. With an irreversible technique (usually called *data compaction*, rather than data compression, although there are no standard definitions), the size of the physical representation of data is reduced, while that subset of the information deemed "relevant information" is preserved. For example, in some data sets, "leading zeros" or "trailing blanks" may be irrelevant information that may be discarded. Data compaction techniques are, by definition, dependent on the semantics of the data.

In data compression, all information is considered relevant, and the compression is followed by an expansion that recovers the original data exactly. Reversible procedures of data compression can be divided into two groups—*semantic independent* and *semantic dependent* techniques. The semantic independent techniques can be

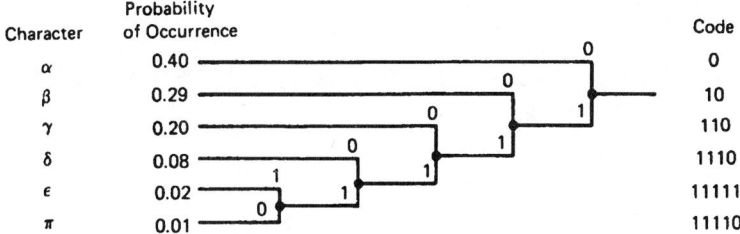

FIG. 1.   An example showing a Huffman code for the given set of characters.

used on any data with varying degrees of effectiveness. They do not use any information regarding the information content of the data. On the other hand, the semantic dependent techniques depend on (and are optimized for) the context and semantics of the data to provide for redundancy reduction.

Data compression algorithms may also be embedded in hardware. It is now possible to buy and install an electronic card into a slot in a microcomputer that intercepts data being stored to or retrieved from a hard disk (*q.v.*). Semantic independent data compression is applied to anything being stored, and corresponding expansion is applied to anything being retrieved, both without the user having to intervene in any way. The result is to allow storage of up to 80 equivalent megabytes on a nominal 40-megabyte disk.

In what follows, we briefly discuss some of the more popular techniques used for data compression and then give an example of data compaction.

Adaptive Pattern Substitution

This method does not rely on the knowledge of any existing patterns; neither does it anticipate any specific ones (i.e. it is a semantic independent technique). It scans the entire text by looking for common patterns of two or more bytes occurring frequently and substitutes an unused byte pattern for the common long one. At the same time, the substitution dictionary is updated. Note that a new substitution dictionary is created specifically for a given text. For example, the text DAABFABC can be replaced with DA*a*F*a*C where *a* stands for AB. In this case, the substitution dictionary will have only the one entry, *a* = AB.

Variable-Length Character Encoding

Character-encoding schemes in normal use have a fixed number of bits per character. Tighter packing of data can be achieved with a code that employs a variable number of bits per character. With such a code, the most commonly occurring characters would be short, and the infre-

quently occurring characters would be long. The shortest character would be only one bit.

To provide a simple illustration, suppose that it were necessary to encode only six characters: α, β, γ, δ, ε, and π. To encode these in a conventional manner would require three bits per character. Suppose the relative frequency of the characters is as shown in Fig. 1. The figure also displays a coding of these six characters, called a *Huffman code*, which minimizes the total number of bits for characters appearing with the frequency shown, under the requirement that a message with this encoding can be decoded instantaneously as the bits arrive in the data stream (i.e. there must be no ambiguity when a bit arrives as to whether or not it is the end of a character).

As an example, the data string in the top portion of Fig. 2 can be decoded immediately by reading left to right, without waiting for the end of the string, since each 0 (or the fifth 1 in a sequence of 1s) must be the end of a character. Note that it is important to start at the beginning of a data stream in order to decode it properly.

Note that the Huffman encoding scheme pays off only with a skewed character distribution. For example, if all characters in Fig. 1 were used equally often, the mean number of bits per character would be 3.33—worse than with the fixed-length character representation. For the probabilities given in Fig. 1, the average number of bits per character is 2.05.

Another example of variable-length character encoding is Morse Code, in which the most frequently occurring characters—"e" and "t"—are given one-bit codes (a dot and a dash respectively), whereas all other characters are encoded through groups of two to five dots and dashes.

Restricted Variability Codes

Because almost all computers are word-oriented rather than bit-oriented,

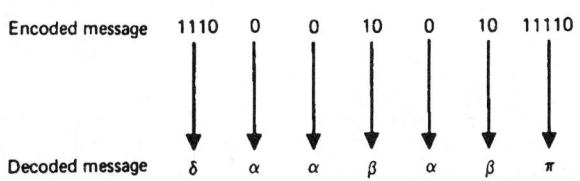

Encoded message   1110   0   0   10   0   10   11110

Decoded message δ α α β α β π

FIG. 2.   Example of decoding a data stream encoded in the Huffman code of Fig. 1.

Character	Code
α	00
β	01
γ	10
δ	1100
ε	1101
π	1110
θ	1111

FIG. 3.   The 2/4 code for encoding seven characters.

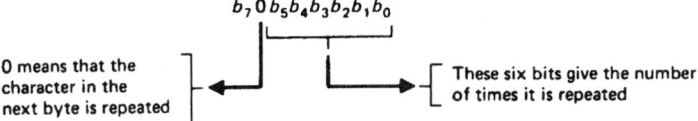

FIG. 4. Run length encoding.

the variability in length of the Huffman code for different characters is usually considered to be a drawback. This shortcoming can be avoided with the use of the restricted variability codes. It should be noted that this advantage of the restricted variability codes usually comes at the price of less efficient use of bits in representing characters.

As an example, consider the so-called 5/10 code, which can represent up to 63 characters. In this encoding scheme, the 31 most frequent characters are represented by the first 31 representations of the five-bit code. The thirty-second representation can be used as a temporary *switch* or *escape character* to indicate that the actual character is encoded in the next five bits. In other words, the thirty-second representation of the first five bits plus the second five bits provide encodings for the less frequent 32 characters. Thus, five bits are required to represent the 31 most frequent characters, while ten bits are used to denote the 32 less frequent ones. The similarity to the use of the SHIFT key on a typewriter keyboard should be noted. Clearly, for any n, there is an $n/2n$ code. As an example, Fig. 3 demonstrates an encoding of seven characters in the 2/4 code with "11" the escape character. It is assumed that a, β, and γ are more frequent than δ, ε, π, and θ.

Compact Notation   When fields are stored in the form in which humans prefer to read them, they often contain more characters than are necessary. Dates are a common example. We may write 15 DEC 1992 or, in our most compact written form, 15.12.92, and so dates are often stored as six bytes in computer files. In the machine, however, the month needs no more than four bits, the day can be encoded in five bits, and the year needs no more than seven bits if the century (e.g. 19) is taken to be fixed—a total of 16 bits, or two eight-bit bytes.

Suppression of Repeated Characters   Numeric fields in some files contain a high proportion of leading zeros; other files contain repetitive blanks or other characters. A general scheme for suppressing repeated characters is called *run-length encoding*. One such method uses the fact that, in the conventional eight-bit EBCDIC

(*q.v.*) character encoding, any character with a zero in the second position is not normally employed as a data character. Such a character is therefore employed to indicate repetition of other characters (see Fig. 4). The character in Fig. 4, therefore, indicates that the following character occurs $b_5\,b_4\,b_3\,b_2\,b_1\,b_0 + 3$ times (+3 because, if a character appears only twice, this method does not save any space).

Suppression of repeated characters is a highly desirable technique in most picture processing applications.

Avoidance of Null Fields   In some files, the fields in a record may be highly variable in length or even missing. In the latter case, *presence bits* can show which fields there are, or, if only a few fields are usually present, *tags* can be used to denote the identity of the present fields. Fig. 5 shows a record format in which the presence bits field is used to indicate whether a data item is present or not.

Dictionary Substitution   Where a quantity can have only a limited set of attribute values, there is no need to spell the item out in full; instead, a code can be used. Examples are bank account type, insurance policy type, and gender (which requires only one bit). This technique is very similar to the compact notation technique.

Exploitation of Ordered Data   By examining the relationships between successive data items, one can sometimes derive an efficient coding scheme to achieve a high level of data compression. As an example, Fig. 6 displays the first column of a list of names taken from a telephone directory. Note that, in the encoded version of the names, only the changes from the previous name in the list appear. The number in front of the trailing end of the name represents the number of characters that are the same.

Differencing   This method is similar in philosophy to the previous one and is best for files of numerical data that have small variations in magnitude between entries. As an example, rather than storing the cumulative precipitation for each day (i.e. $c_1, c_2, ..., c_{365}$), we may store the difference between entries (i.e. $c_1, c_2-c_1, ...,$

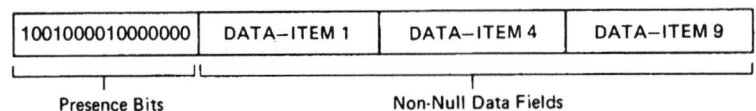

FIG. 5.   The use of the presence bits in a record that can have a maximum of 16 data items.

Name	Compressed Name
Aalbers	0 Aalbers
Aalderink	3 derink
Aamar	2 mar
Aamondt	3 ondt
Aaro	2 ro
Aarons	4 ns

FIG. 6. The exploitation of ordered data for front compression.

$c_{365}-c_{364}$). Note that c_1 is an absolute value and serves as the base. The saving in space that results is a consequence of the fact that the difference in the cumulative precipitation of two adjacent days is less than the absolute value of each of the former. In addition, we expect many of the differences to be zero. The differencing method is often highly successful in compressing digitized pictures.

Decimal to Binary Conversion Rather than storing numbers in (packed or unpacked) decimal notation (which take four and eight bits per decimal digit, respectively), binary representation can be used as a form of compact notation. As an example, numbers between 0 and 255 can be represented by using only an eight-bit byte. Decimal-to-binary conversion is a semantic dependent data compression technique.

Data Compaction As an example of data compaction, we consider a sequence of numerically ordered (i.e. sorted) keys in a directory of a file. In this example, we use *rear-compaction* to delete a rear redundant string (RRS) from a key. This string is composed of those rightmost bits of the key which are not necessary to distinguish uniquely the key from the set of all keys in the particular sequence to be rear-compacted. It can be shown that, given a set of sorted keys, to find the RRS of a key K, it is enough to look only at the previous key and the following key in the sorted sequence. Consider the following set of keys.

```
                              RRS
                            ┌────┴────┐
Key (i − 1)   1 0 1 0 1 0 1 0 1 0 1 0 1 0 1 0 1

                                      RRS
                                      ┌─┴─┐
Key i         1 0 1 0 1 0 1 1 0 1 0 1 0 1 0 1 0

                                      RRS
                                      ┌─┴─┐
Key (i + 1)   1 0 1 0 1 0 1 1 0 1 0 1 1 1 0 1 1
```

Note that key i without its RRS bits can be distinguished from both key $(i − 1)$ and key $(i + 1)$. Similarly, it is assumed that, with RRS bits deleted from the other two keys, one can still distinguish them from their adjacent keys.

In the above example, the removal of RRSs will result in compacted keys that are not of equal length. Since this is generally undesirable, the compacted keys can be forced to be of equal length by keeping a number of bits equal to the length of the longest compacted key. In the above example, this would result in:

Rear-compacted key $(i − 1)$ 1 0 1 0 1 0 1 0 1 0 1 0 1

Rear-compacted key i 1 0 1 0 1 0 1 1 0 1 0 1 0

Rear-compacted key $(i + 1)$ 1 0 1 0 1 0 1 1 0 1 0 1 1

Concluding Remarks Although the methods described have been explained separately, it may be useful to use more than one procedure for the same data set. For example, it may be beneficial to suppress the repeated characters of a text file first and then Huffman encode the resulting text.

Sometimes it is possible to reduce the need for data compression by avoiding redundant storage of information in the first place. This is one of the major objectives of database management systems. For example, one should not store a part description in both the "parts file" and the "inventory file." A somewhat related issue is that fields that are computable from others should not be stored at all. For example, store "monthly earnings" but not "tax withheld" because the tax algorithm can be used to generate the tax withheld from the monthly earnings.

This article has dealt principally with compression of data stored in databases. For information on speech and image compression, see Lynch (1985).

References

1985. Lynch, T. J. *Data Compression: Techniques and Applications.* Belmont, CA: Lifetime Learning Publications.
1987. Held, G. *Data Compression*, (2nd Ed). New York: Wiley.
1988. Storer, J. A. *Data Compression: Methods and Theory.* Rockville, MD: Computer Science Press.

H. K. REGHBATI

DATA ENCRYPTION. *See* CRYPTOGRAPHY, COMPUTERS IN.

DATA MODELS

For articles on related subjects *see* DATA TYPE; DATABASE MANAGEMENT SYSTEM; MEMORY MANAGEMENT; and RELATIONAL DATABASE.

Data models are notations for describing data. Typically, they are used to describe the structure and content of databases. As such, they have similar goals to data types that describe data within programs. At least some researchers believe that it will prove possible to use the same notations for both data types and data stored in databases.

Data Model Requirements Data models have to meet several requirements:

1. Act as a notation to be manipulated and constructed during the design of a database;
2. Provide a description that enables would-be users of the data to understand what data may be present and how to access it; and,
3. Be a major component for controlling and organizing the use of data.

Data Model Design The first two uses require notations that are *conceptual* (i.e. the level of abstraction and set of constructs matches "natural" thought processes in organizing data, such as classification). The third use requires that mechanisms, such as storage schemes, query evaluators, etc., can be implemented efficiently for large bodies of data. These implementation issues lead towards data models that pragmatically reflect memory management methods. As constructing applications from a combination of databases and programs is a serious engineering task, there is an essential requirement for precision in the description of databases, and hence in the definition of the data model. Such precision is often achieved by relating the data model to a well-defined mathematical construct. Thus, there are three forces pulling the designs of data models in different directions, as shown in Fig. 1.

Data Model Examples Actual data models are different compromises in response to these forces. A few will be illustrated. A concrete example will be used in each case, based on the task of describing the contributions to an encyclopaedia. People are *editors* or *authors*. Authors are responsible for *articles*, articles are organized within *topics*, and editors are responsible for topics.

Network Model This model was developed in the late 1960s in order to abstract various methods of organizing disk storage that were then prevalent. It therefore leans in the direction of implementation efficiency. Conceptual issues were limited to an assumption that data could be modeled in terms of *entities* and one-to-many relationships between them. These were modeled by two components—the *record type* and the *set type*. Records with a given record type all have the same format and represent similar entities. Sets were not like mathematical sets, but were ordered sequences of records *owned* by a particular record. For practical reasons, the record format was initially identical with that of Cobol, for which this model was intended as a database standard.

All data models provide a repertoire of components, out of which a specific database description, or *schema*, may be built. The two components in the network model are record types and sets (the actual model was more complex).

Data Model Diagrams Associated with most data models is a diagrammatic form, particularly beneficial to requirements 1 and 2. For the network model, these diagrams were called Bachman diagrams; boxes represent the record-types and arcs represent the sets. For the encyclopedia example, the diagram would be as in Fig. 2.

Data Description Language Also associated with a data model is a data description language that allows the full details of a schema to be expressed. For example, still using the network model:

Record Type *Article* **is**
02 *Title*: **Picture** A(40);
02 *Word Limit* : **Picture** 9(4);
...

Set *writes*; **owner** *Author*; **Member** *Article*;...

Relational Data Model This model was developed during the 1970s and is the basis of several commercial products. It is biased towards precision, as its one constructor, *a relation*, is based on the mathematical idea of a relation. This allows formal argument about and manipulation of relational data—in particular, schemata may be transformed into equivalent schemata with better prop-

**Conceptual
Naturalness**

**Implementation
Efficiency**

**Mathematical
Precision**

FIG. 1.

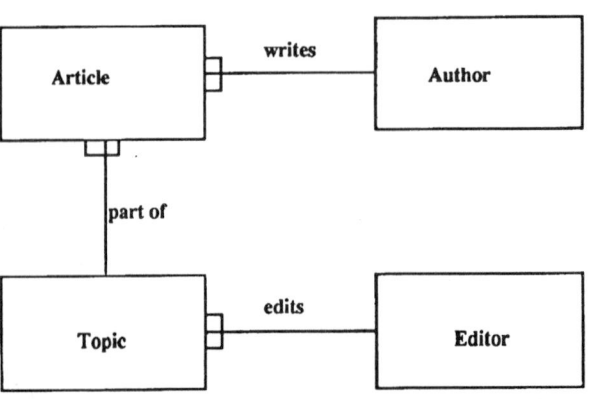

FIG. 2.

erties and queries transformed into equivalent queries that may be evaluated more quickly.

The relation is a set of *tuples* with identical format. Values in each tuple within the relation have elements taken from corresponding *domains* if they are in corresponding positions, and the positions are referred to as *attributes* and given attribute names.

Entity-Relationship Diagrams

A data model called the entity-relationship model (E-R model) has been developed with more concern for the conceptual requirement. It is used, with an associated methodology, for designing databases. For the encyclopedia example, we get the diagram in Fig. 3.

There is now a full repertoire of relationship forms, including many-to-many (the above diagram permits joint-authorship of an article) and one-to-one relationships.

Mapping E-R Diagrams to Relations

Each entity type in the E-R diagram is simply represented as a relation, with one tuple for each entity instance, and the properties of that instance represented by the attributes in that tuple. If the values of one or more of these attributes are guaranteed unique to the instance, we may call them *keys* of the relation. All four forms of relationship may then be represented by relations holding such *foreign keys*. Where the relationship is of the form one-to-many, the foreign key may be held as an extra attribute of the relation at the "many" end.

Where there is a one-to-one relationship, the relations may be merged, but at the potential cost of null values. For example, if there are special attributes for editors and only a few of the people are editors, null values would be needed for these editor's attributes.

A fragment of the relational definitions might be:

> **Relation** *Article* (*ArtNo* : *integer*,
> ! primary key underlined
> > *Title* : *char*(40);
> > *WordLimit* : integer
> > ...)
>
> **Relation** *writes* (*Author* : *PersonNo*;
> > *Article* : *ArtNo*;
> > *deadline* : *date*;
> > *delivered* : *date*;
> > *reminded* : *date*)

Commercial Relational Systems

There is a well-developed theory of relational systems, sophisticated strategies for their implementation, and query optimization techniques to achieve adequate performance. In most cases they are dependent on the formal precision with which the data model is defined. This technology, supporting a relational view of data, is available in many commercial products. A standard query language, SQL, ensures that, for straightforward use of the data, there is reasonable interchangeability between products.

Object-Oriented Data Models There are data collections that are not easily organized in a relational form (e.g. *graphs* such as arise in genealogies, *matrices* such as arise in science and engineering, and *sequences* such as the images in a video sequence). Current research and some commercial products have attempted to address these deficiencies. In object-oriented data models, two constructors are essential. The *object* is a collection of values that has identity independent of those values. So a value in one object may be the *identity* of another object. The other constructor describes an *isa* hierarchy between types of objects (classes), so that the fact that an Editor *isa* Person is modeled explicitly.

The diagram for the encyclopedia is shown in Fig. 4. and a fragment of the data language might be:

> **type** *Person* **is**
> > *name* : **string**
> > *dateOfBirth* : **date**
> > ...
> **end**
>
> **type** *Author* **is**
> > *expertIn* : **set of** *subjects*
> > *reliability* : **integer**
> **end**
> **type** *Article* **is**
> > *Title* : **string**
> > *authors* : **seq of** *Author*
> > *topic* : *Topic*
> > ...
> **end**
> ...

Some researchers have attempted to use the mathematical notion of functions as a foundation for func-

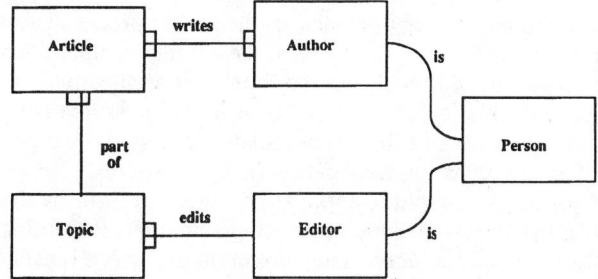

FIG. 3.

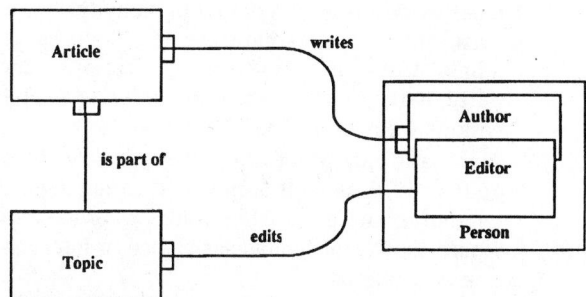

FIG. 4.

tional data models, which also provide the object-oriented features and may combine well with programs. These newer data models include several forms for bulk types (collections of instances of the same type) (e.g. *set of* and *seq of* above). They attempt to provide a wider repertoire of constructors that combine naturally. This generates new issues in formal definition and implementation. No one model yet devised is well suited to all applications.

References

1982. Tsichritzis, D. C. and Lochovsky, F. H. *Data Models*. Englewood Cliffs, NJ: Prentice-Hall.

1984. Brodie, Michael L., Mylopoulos, John and Schmidt, Joachim W. (Eds.), *On Conceptual Modelling, Perspectives from Artificial Intelligence, Databases and Programming Languages*. New York: Springer-Verlag.

1987. Hull, R. and King, R. Semantic Data Modelling: Survey, Applications and Research Issues. *ACM Computing Surveys*, **19**, 3, (September) 201–260.

MALCOLM P. ATKINSON

DATA PROCESSING

For articles on related subjects *see* ADMINISTRATIVE APPLICATIONS; INFORMATION AND DATA; and INFORMATION PROCESSING.

Data processing is a widely used term with a variety of meanings and interpretations ranging from one that makes it almost coextensive with all of computing to much narrower connotations in the general area of computer applications to business and administrative problems.

In a broad sense, data processing may be said to be what computers *do*. In this context it should be compared to *information processing*, which some prefer to data processing because "information" does not carry the connotation of "number," as "data" sometimes does. Of course, the "data" in data processing is really intended to connote any kind of information in symbolic form. Thus, information may be viewed as "knowledge," while data are the physical symbols used to represent the information.

The term "data processing" is often used with various modifiers, the most common being:

1. Electronic data processing (EDP), a term widely used to describe *all* computing activity—or, at least, the part of computing that focuses on administrative or business applications—and particularly to distinguish computerized applications from manual methods.

2. Automatic data processing (ADP), closely analogous to EDP, since it is intended to distinguish computer data processing from data processing where significant human assistance or intervention is required.

3. Business data processing (BDP) refers specifically to administrative applications (e.g. personnel, payroll, accounting) and to broader business applications (e.g. inventory control, sales forecasting).

4. Scientific data processing, which is a rather rarely used term and which is meant to imply the increasing recognition that business and scientific applications of computers have much more in common than was once realized or, indeed, than was actually the case in earlier days.

Until the 1960s it was common to divide the world of computer applications into two realms—business data processing and scientific computing—with the latter encompassing all engineering, scientific, or other technical applications of computers where the emphasis was on numerical calculations, usually extensive ones, rather than on the manipulation (sorting, organizing, etc.) of data (together with, at most, very simple arithmetic calculations), which was the province of business data processing.

Another distinct, although related contrast between the two areas was their relative dependence on the central processing unit facilities of the computer on the one hand and on the input-output facilities on the other hand. Most scientific calculations seemed to require little input data, produced relatively few numbers as results, but relied heavily on the arithmetic and logical capabilities of the CPU (*q.v.*). Indeed, computers that handled mainly large scientific calculations were, and still are, often called "number crunchers." By contrast, business data processing tasks usually involved large amounts of input data (e.g. the entire employee file of a company)—hence the name "data" processing—performed relatively few calculations, and then produced large amounts of output (e.g. all payroll checks for the company).

To a degree, this dichotomy between scientific calculations and business data processing was always misleading. If the paradigm for business data processing—much input and output, little calculation—was, in fact, a rather good generalization, the paradigm for scientific calculation was much less so. Scientific calculations involving large volumes of input data and, more commonly, large quantities of results had been common since the earliest days of computing (e.g. the production of tables of mathematical functions such as the trigonometric or Bessel functions). Still, it has only been in recent years that the dichotomy has been seen to be less and less useful for any purpose.

Increasingly, scientific calculations (e.g. meteorological and high-energy physics applications) process large amounts of input data and produce copious results. Also increasingly, although less so, business applications involve sophisticated mathematical techniques involving large amounts of calculation (e.g. various statistical and related forecasting applications). Thus, while there remain many computer applications that conform to the original business data processing/scientific computing stereotype, it is increasingly common and more reasonable to use the terms "business data processing" and "scientific data processing" to distinguish between applications areas but not between the characteristics of the applications themselves.

The past distinction between business data processing and scientific calculations was reflected in the development of computers ostensibly designed for one application area but not the other. IBM's 700 series of computers of the 1950s illustrates this point. (The 700 series comprised first-generation computers, which utilized vacuum tube technology; with the advent of transistor technology and the second generation of computers, a zero was added, and this became the 7000 series. Thus, the 7040 and 7090 were transistorized and somewhat modified versions of the 704 and 709.) There were two pairs of computers in this series, first the 701 and 702, and later the 704 and 705. (There was also a 709, more powerful but quite similar to the 704.)

Both the 701 and 704 were designed for scientific computing. Their memories were binary and word-oriented and, on the 704, floating-point arithmetic was standard. By contrast, the 702 and 705 were specifically designed for "data processing" applications, meaning business data processing. Their memories were character- and digit-oriented and only fixed-point arithmetic was possible. By the time of the advent of the IBM 360 series of computers in the mid-1960s, the previous sharp distinction between scientific computing and business data processing was becoming blurred so that the existence of separate computers for the two areas was no longer considered necessary. Nevertheless, the distinction still was considered important and, for example, one model of the 360 series, the 360/44, was specially designed for scientific computation.

In the 1970s some manufacturers still oriented their general-purpose computer line toward particular application areas, most notably Control Data, with its 6000, 7000, Cyber 70, and Cyber 170 series of computers intended mainly for scientific applications, but the trend was clearly toward computers for data processing without a distinction between scientific and business applications. In the 1980s, only supercomputers, (*q.v.*) the very largest and fastest computers, typically with only a small number of each produced, could be said to be strictly scientific computers.

The development of general-purpose high-level programming languages also parallels the history outlined in the preceding paragraph. The first such language in the mid-1950s, Fortran, was intended (and still is mainly used) for scientific calculations. Even the version used up through the 1980s, Fortran 77, lacked the significant character manipulation and good data structure facilities needed for many data processing problems. The second such language in the late 1950s, Cobol, was intended (and still is virtually always used) for business data processing problems. Its arithmetic facilities, lacking as they do a floating-point arithmetic capability, virtually preclude its use for significant numerical calculations.

The development of PL/I in the mid-1960s had, among its motivations, the desire to develop a language that could be used for both scientific and business problems because of increasing cognizance about this time of common properties in these two applications areas. PL/I's failure to achieve wide popularity cannot be ascribed to any deficiency in this viewpoint. Rather, it is due to the very large inertia among Fortran and Cobol users that prevents them from switching to a new language because of their extensive investment in programs, libraries, and expertise in the older languages.

In the future we may expect the distinctions between the scientific and business applications areas to be further blurred as the widespread use of data communications, and the increasing use of large databases further pervade all applications areas. The name "data processing," therefore, will remain an inclusive term to describe computer applications of all kinds. It will continue to be one of a few terms (information processing and symbol manipulation are others) that may reasonably be used to denote what a computer does.

Reference

1990. Senn, James A. *Information Systems in Management* (4th ed.). San Rafael, CA: Wadsworth.

ANTHONY RALSTON

DATA PROCESSING MANAGEMENT ASSOCIATION. *See* DPMA.

DATA SECURITY

For articles on related subjects *see* COMPUTER CRIME; COMPUTER VIRUS; CRYPTOGRAPHY, COMPUTERS IN; and HACKER.

Preserving the security of data (such as a payroll file or digitized graphical image) necessarily requires consideration of the security of the entire computing system—its programs, internal data, and hardware and firmware (*q.v.*) facilities. For example, it is impossible to protect just data if the programs that access and potentially modify that data have been been corrupted.

Properties of Data Security Data security is typically defined in terms of three properties:

- Confidentiality—Assurance that data, programs, and other system resources are protected against disclosure to unauthorized persons, programs, or systems.
- Integrity—Assurance that data, programs, and other system resources are protected against malicious or inadvertent modification or destruction by unauthorized persons, programs, or systems.
- Availability—Assurance that use of data, programs, and other system resources will not be denied to authorized persons, programs, or systems.

Additionally, one might also include in a definition of security the properties of authentication (the property that persons, programs, or systems are accurately identified by a computing system) and non-repudiation (the property that communications received from persons, programs, or systems can be assured to have been sent by their apparent senders).

A security flaw results from the lack, breach, or failure of confidentiality, integrity, or availability. The flaw can arise from a variety of causes, including human, mechanical, and environmental faults, as well as problems internal to the computing system. A *risk analysis* is a study to determine the susceptibility of a computing system to various kinds of security failures. Risk analysis is performed by analyzing general threats to the security of the system (such as loss of electrical power or programmer sabotage), and then determining whether the threats could affect the system in question. A threat that could affect a system adversely is called a *vulnerability*.

Computer security embraces many aspects of a computing system, including hardware design, operating systems, networks, database management systems (*q.v.*), compilers, and user applications programs and systems. Vulnerabilities of computer systems range from the possibility of a trusted employee's selling (or being forced to reveal) secrets to a competitor, disk failures that render an entire volume of data unreadable, unauthorized operating system penetration (*see* HACKER), inference of confidential data through carefully chosen queries posed to a database, loss of data because of floods or fires, acquisition of data through wiretapping or sensing the emanations of electronic equipment, or denying access to computing resources by flooding the system with other requests for service.

Protection control can be effectuated through software, hardware, physical, and procedural means, combined to provide appropriate coverage against vulnerabilities. For example, the procedural measure of creating backup copies of important data combined with the physical measure of locking the door to the computer room ensures against loss of data. Hardware features and software controls—typically portions of the operating system—combine to confine the accesses of each system user. The selection of a set of controls is based on an analysis of expected threats and available support.

Cryptography Cryptography (*q.v.*) is one important tool by which to preserve confidentiality and integrity. Confidential materials are encrypted to prevent their disclosure to unauthorized individuals (i.e. to people who do not hold the cryptographic key for the materials). Furthermore, encryption prevents unauthorized, undetected modification: someone may be able to scramble the bits of an encrypted text so that the bits decrypt to nothing meaningful, but, without breaking the encryption, no one can change a specific field of the underlying plaintext data from "1" to "2." One significant use of cryptography is to compute a *cryptographic checksum*, a function that depends upon every bit of a block of data and also upon a key used for the cryptographic function. For example, a (weak) cryptographic checksum is the parity (*q.v.*) of a string of bits; any one change to the string affects the parity. The cryptographic checksum is computed when a block of data is created and again when it is used; if the

data have been changed between origin and use, the value of the checksum at time of use will (almost certainly) not match that computed at time of origin, a signal that the data have been changed.

Cryptography is also useful in establishing reliable computer-to-computer exchanges of information. Protocols employing cryptography have been designed for such activities as voting, producing unforgeable electronic receipts for data received, providing unforgeable evidence of the authenticity of the sender of a piece of data, and storing one data item so that it can be retrieved only with the consent of several users (e.g. to make a maintenance password available only to a pair of people acting together, such as the system operator and a maintenance engineer).

Access Control Confidentiality, integrity, and availability were defined in terms of "authorized access." Two things are necessary in order to enforce "authorized" access: first, a reliable structure is needed under which authorizations to use resources are conferred (or revoked), and second, a reliable mechanism must exist to verify the authorization each time an access is attempted. Part of the authorization process is procedural, implemented outside the computing system. For example, an employee may be authorized to access certain files because of his or her job responsibilities, an individual may be authorized to access certain classified data because of having received a security clearance, a file's creator may confer access rights to a selected set of trustworthy users; or the administrator of a system may determine that data on that system may be shared with other specified systems. These permissions must be established in a reliable manner. Furthermore, the authorization data must be stored in such a way that it can be modified only by authorized administrators. These authorizations are stored in a data structure for use by the operating system or other unit that controls access. Often, the authorization data structure is encrypted, preventing it from unauthorized modification and even limiting those who can see who has been authorized access to which files.

Once the list of authorized accesses is reliably established, individuals (human users, programs, or systems acting as representatives for the individuals) will request access. All such individuals are called *subjects*; the resources, called the *objects* of a computing system, consist of files, programs, devices, and other items to which subjects' accesses are to be controlled. For each subject and each object, the system must be able to determine whether access by the subject to the object is allowable and, if so, what type of access (e.g. read, write, delete). Each requesting subject must be reliably identified by the access control system, and the requestor's identity may be verified. For example, operating systems often use passwords to ensure the authenticity of a user attempting to log in. More sophisticated authentication techniques include the use of automatic password generators, or devices that sense a physical characteristic of the user, such as a handprint or the style of a spoken phrase. Some subjects, such as certain programs or I/O devices, may be identified and authenticated by their hardware address, process identification number, or other reliable internal means. Thus, the login authorization file may be readable only by the process that performs user login.

After the computing system has verified the identity of a requesting user, it is able to implement access control decisions. The foundation of access control is the *reference monitor* concept, first documented in 1972. A reference monitor must be:

- Tamperproof, so that its functioning cannot be undermined.
- Unable to be bypassed, so that it is invoked to authorize every requested access.
- Small, so that it can be scrutinized rigorously for correctness.

One means of maintaining access authorization data is in an *access control matrix*. An access control matrix specifies, for each subject, what objects that subject can access and what kinds of access are allowed. The rows of an access control matrix represent subjects, and the columns represent objects. Each entry in the matrix indicates what types of access the subject may have, with respect to the given object. For example, subject SMITH may be allowed to read, write, and delete file A, and yet be able only to read file B. The SMITH row of the matrix would contain {read, write, delete} in the file A column and {read} in the file B column. Although an access control matrix is the most straightforward means of describing allowable accesses, in practice it is inefficient because it requires a very large amount of space. A system with 200 users, each of whom has 50 files, requires $200 \times 50 = 10{,}000$ table entries. If most users' files are private (inaccessible by other users), most cells in the access control matrix entries are empty, indicating no allowed access. An *access control list* is effectively a column of an access control matrix. For each object, there is one list that includes only those users who should be allowed to access the object and the type of access they should be allowed. For public objects, such as compilers and shared data files, a "wild card" subject can be specified; for example, the system programmer may have read and delete access, while all other users are allowed read access. Access control lists are especially effective for denoting single users who should have specific types of access to certain objects. Alternatively, a *capability list*, which corresponds to a row of the access control matrix, can be maintained to control access. The capability list indicates, for each subject, the objects that subject is allowed to access.

Other types of access control mechanisms are *capabilities*, which are, effectively, tokens or tickets that a user must possess in order to access an object, and *group authorizations*, in which subjects are allowed access to objects based on defined membership in a group, such as all employees of a single department or the collaborators on a particular project. The objects whose access is controlled in a computing system include memory, storage media, I/O devices, computing time, files, and communication paths. Although the nature of

access control to these objects is the same, access is controlled by different mechanisms. Memory can be controlled through hardware features, such as base and bounds registers or dynamic address translation (virtual memory (*q.v.*), paging, or segmentation). Access to I/O devices and computing time (i.e. to the use of the CPU) is more frequently controlled by requiring the intervention of the operating system to access the device. The operating system is assisted by the hardware, in that two or more states are present on the machine; direct access to I/O devices is permitted only from the more privileged state. Files and communications paths are typically controlled by permission to initiate access (often called "opening" the file). Such accesses are requested from the operating system.

Program Security Computers make access requests only under control of programs. Every program operates under control of or in the name of a user. Thus, the accesses of a program are presumably the result of requests from a user. However, programs are also modifiable; that is, a program is actually a series of bits in memory, and those bits can be read, written, modified, and deleted as any data can be. While a user program may be designed to read a file, the program, with minor modification to the executable code, could instead write or delete the file. Those modifications can be the result of hardware errors and failures, a flaw in the logic of the program, or a change induced by some other program in the system. Hardware errors are uncommon, and checking circuitry is built into computers to detect such errors before they affect a computation. Unintentional or malicious user errors are much more difficult to detect and prevent. Programs are stored either in files or memory (or both); thus, the first line of defense against program errors is *file and memory protection* (*q.v.*), which is designed to prevent one user from accessing files and memory assigned to another user. While these controls protect one user from another, they are less effective at protecting users from errors in their own program logic.

A second protection against program errors is careful and thorough *software engineering* (*q.v.*), including structured design, program reviews, and team programming. Such programming practices will help to protect a user from unintentional errors.

The third form of protection against program errors is *software testing* (*q.v.*). Unfortunately, testing can confirm the presence of errors, but not their absence. However, a thoroughly tested program can provide credibility to the contention that a program is error-free. Of special concern is the software that controls accesses. Presumably, the program that controls access of any subject to any object also protects itself against access by all unauthorized subjects. Nevertheless, the access control program itself represents a significant vulnerability: defeat or circumvent it, and you can obtain unhindered access to all system resources. For this reason, on more secure computing systems, the access control function is divided among several different modules: one to control access to files, one to control access to memory, etc. In this way, defeating one module does not immediately open all system resources to access.

A related question is correctness of the access control software itself, so that it will permit all and only the authorized accesses. Clearly, access control procedures are effective only if they are implemented properly. Good software engineering practices for the design and implementation of the access control software are combined with rigorous control over its modifications, once installed, to ensure the correct functioning of the access control software.

Malicious Code Computer data is vulnerable to attacks by malicious programs. Such programs range from overt attempts at accessing unauthorized data to more covert ones that attempt to subvert a benign program. While the overt, blatant attempts are typically precluded by the methods just described, the more subtle attempts may succeed.

A *Trojan horse* is a program that performs (or is made to perform) some function in addition to its expected, advertised use. For example, a program that ostensibly produces a formatted listing of stored files may actually write copies of those files on a second device to which a malicious user has access; the Trojan horse may even modify or delete the files. Or a program to produce paychecks may reduce one employee's check by an amount and add the same amount to another check. These programs represent data security flaws because they permit access to a resource by an unauthorized user. Unfortunately, the access control violation is not the Trojan horse program itself: the file listing program has legitimate access to every user's file (or, more properly, to their names—a distinction not made by most computing systems), and the paycheck program is using its legitimate access rights to query time cards and write checks, but with incorrect values. Thus, a Trojan horse is difficult to detect in operation, because it may behave ordinarily, performing only allowable accesses. The Trojan horse program may have been flawed initially, or it may have been modified during or between executions through some failure of access controls. (One serious source of Trojan horse infections is through users who fail to set access limitations to the code of their programs, so that malicious outsiders can modify otherwise innocuous and correct programs.)

A *computer virus* or *worm* is a particular type of Trojan horse that is self-replicating. In addition to performing some illicit act, the program creates a copy of itself that it can then embed in other innocent programs. Each time an infected innocent program is run, the attached virus code is activated as well; the virus can then replicate and spread itself to other previously uninfected programs.

References

1982. Denning, D. E. *Cryptography and Data Security.* Reading, MA: Addison-Wesley.
1989. Pfleeger, C. P. *Security in Computing.* Englewood Cliffs, NJ: Prentice-Hall.

CHARLES P. PFLEEGER

DATA STRUCTURES

For articles on related subjects *see* ABSTRACT DATA TYPE; FIFO-LIFO; FILE; GRAPH THEORY; LIST PROCESSING; RECORD; STACK; STRING PROCESSING; and TREE.

The term *structure* is used in many different fields to denote objects that are constructed from their components in a regular and characteristic way. Loosely, a data structure is a structure whose components are data objects. As the term is used more precisely in computer science, a *data structure* is a collection of data values, the relationships among them, and the functions or operations that can be applied to the data. If any one of these three characteristics is missing or not stated precisely, the structure being examined does not qualify as a data structure.

Example. The arithmetic expression $3 + 4 * 5$ is constructed in a systematic way from data components that are integers, such as 3, 4, and 5, and operators, such as $+$ and $*$. The structure of this expression may be thought of as either a string or a tree structure in which each operator is the root of a subtree whose descendants are operands (Fig. 1). As a string, the operations to be performed on it might include *evaluation* to obtain an arithmetic result or *concatenation* (*q.v.*) with other strings to form still longer expressions. As a *tree*, relevant operations would include insertion and deletion of objects in the tree or various kinds of tree traversal that yield either prefix, infix, or postfix equivalents of the original expression (*see* TREE).

When this data structure is stored in a computer, it must be stored so that components are readily accessible. This may be done by storing the expression $3 + 4 * 5$ as a character string A so that the ith character is retrieved by referring to the element $A[i]$ or $A(i)$, with the use of brackets or parentheses, depending upon the programming language being used. Alternatively, the string may be stored as a list structure, in which the vertex associated with $+$ has a left child 3 and a right child $*$, which in turn has left and right children 4 and 5 (Fig. 2).

Figures 1 and 2 illustrate the relation between data structures, which specify *logical* relations between data components, and *storage structures*, which specify how such relations may be realized in a digital computer. The storage structure of Fig. 2 could be represented in a digital computer by five three-component storage cells, where each cell has one component containing an operator and two components respectively containing a pointer (*q.v.*) to the left and right children. The three cells that have no successors contain special markers in their pointer fields, here indicated by the word "nil."

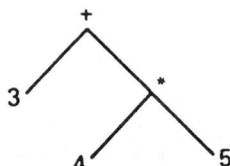

FIG. 1. A tree structure.

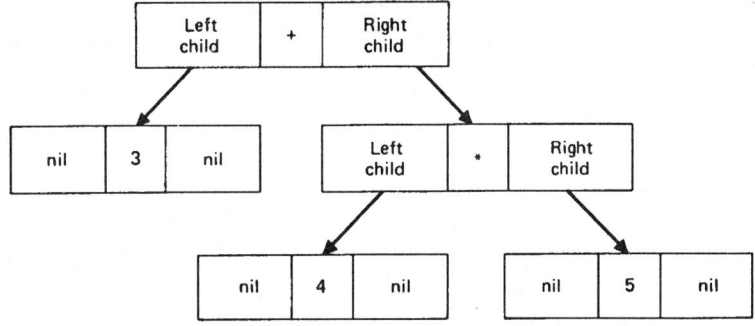

FIG. 2. Storage structure for the tree structure of Fig. 1.

In order to define a class of data objects having a common data structure, it is usual to start with a class of primitive data elements called *atoms*, or elementary objects, and to specify *construction operators* by means of which *composite objects* may be constructed from the atoms. In the preceding arithmetic-expression example, the atoms are operands (integers) and arithmetic operators. The construction operators specify how expressions are built up from operators and operands. The set of construction rules that specify how operators are built up from operands is sometimes referred to as a *grammar (q.v.)*.

In order to access and manipulate composite objects specified by a given set of atoms and construction rules, *selectors* must be defined that allow components of a data object to be accessed, and *creation* and *deletion* operators must be defined that allow components of data structures to be created and deleted. Data structures may be characterized by the nature of their accessing and their creation and deletion operators.

Some of the basic terminology relating to data structures will be mentioned by considering commonly occurring data structures, such as arrays, records, sets, lists, trees, stacks, and queues.

An *array* is a data structure whose elements may be selected by integer selectors called "indexes." If A is a one-dimensional-array data structure, then $A[3]$ (or $A(3)$ in some languages) refers to the third element of A. If B is a three-dimensional array, then $B[I, J, K]$ or $B(I, J, K)$ refers to the I, J, K element (B_{ijk}) of the array B. The set of all elements of an array are generally created and deleted at the same time by means of *declarations (q.v.)*, as illustrated by the following examples:

REAL A (1,100)	Fortran array declaration
integer array A[1:N];	Algol 60 array declaration
[1:N] **int** A;	Algol 68 array declaration
A: **array** [1..N] **of** real;	Pascal array declaration

In Fortran, the declaration "REAL A(100)" serves to reserve a block of cells for the array A at compile time. In Algol 60 or 68, declarations create an instance of the declared data structure at run time. Thus, the declaration "**integer array** $A[1:N]$" causes allocation of a block of N storage cells large enough to hold integers using the current value assigned to the variable N, and activates an accessing mechanism so that $A[i]$ will refer to the ith allocated cell.

The arrays introduced are *homogeneous* because all elements of an array have the same data type, and are *Cartesian* (rectangular) because all vectors in a given dimension have the same size. Programming languages such as Pascal, Cobol, and PL/I permit nonhomogeneous, nonrectangular arrays to be declared. The following is a PL/I declaration of a PAYROLL record with a 50-character name field, fields of the mode FIXED for the number of regular and overtime hours worked, and a field of the mode FLOAT for the rate of pay:

```
DECLARE 1 PAYROLL
          2 NAME CHARACTER(50),
          2 HOURS
            3 REGULAR FIXED,
            3 OVERTIME FIXED,
          2 RATE FLOAT;
```

If it is desired to refer to the number of overtime hours in the record PAYROLL, then this is given by PAYROLL.HOURS.OVERTIME. That is, component names rather than indexes are used to access a given element of the data structure.

Sets are a convenient form of data structure when the order of elements is irrelevant, as in (**for** x∈S **do** SUM: = SUM + x;). Sets and operations upon sets are supported in their full generality by the very high level language SETL (*q.v.*), which allows the user to make mathematical assertions using mathematical set theoretic notation. Pascal also has a data type "set" that allows us to talk about subsets and test for set membership. However, Pascal sets have an implementation-dependent maximum size, and support only operations that can be simply defined in terms of the representation of finite sets as a binary string of zeroes and ones in a computer word. The gap between abstract sets and their implementation is much greater than the corresponding gap for arrays or records. Sets are a "very high level" data structure that can be completely implemented only by "very high level languages."

List structures, just as array structures, may be characterized by their accessing creation and deletion operators. Elements of a list structure are generally accessed by "walking" along pointer chains, starting at the head of the list. In a linear list, each list element has a unique successor and the last element has an "empty" successor

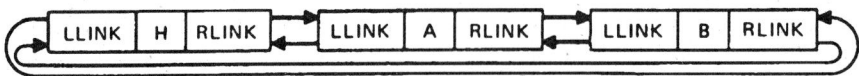

FIG. 3. Doubly linked circular list *L*.

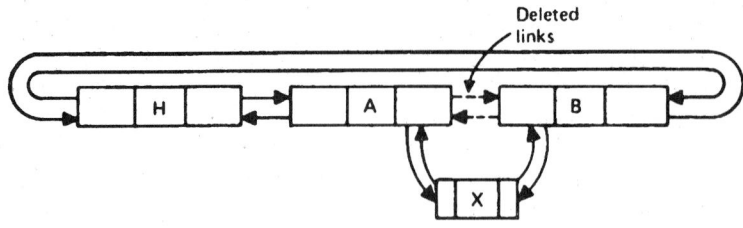

FIG. 4. Insertion of *X* into list in Fig. 3.

field, usually denoted by the symbol "nil." In general, list elements may have more than one successor, and lists may be circular in the sense that pointer chains may form cycles. Knuth (1973) introduced doubly linked lists that have forward and backward pointer chains passing through each element, and a number of other kinds of lists. Fig. 3 illustrates a doubly linked circular list named *L*, whose head element *H* is linked both to the next element *A* and to the last element *B*.

If the forward pointer is referred to by RLINK (for right link) and the backward pointer is referred to by LLINK (left link), then the second list element (labeled A) may be accessed in either of the two following ways:

```
RLINK(L)            Forward chaining
LLINK(LLINK(L))     Backward chaining
```

Insertion and deletion of elements in a list is accomplished by creation of a new list cell and by updating pointers of existing list elements and the newly created list element. Fig. 4 illustrates that the insertion of the list element *X* between the list elements *A* and *B* requires updating of the RLINK of *A*, the LLINK of *B*, and initialization of the *R* and *L* links of *X*.

The instructions to perform this insertion might be as follows (assume that *P* points to node *A*):

```
create X                    pointed at by N
RLINK(N) = RLINK(P)
LLINK(N) = LLINK(RLINK(P))
RLINK(P) = N
LLINK(RLINK(N)) = N
```

The list processing language Lisp, which was developed by John McCarthy in the late 1950s, is the most important list processing language. The list format and instruction repertoire of Lisp will be briefly illustrated. For ease of presentation, however, we will use a notation different from that actually used in Lisp.

List elements in Lisp have two components selectable by the selectors *first* and *rest*. If *L* is a list, then *first(L)* selects the first element of the list, which may be either an atom or a sublist, and *rest(L)* selects the rest of the list. The list ((*A,B*),*C*) is represented in Lisp by the list structure of Fig. 5.

For *L* = ((*A,B*), *C*), *first(L)* = (*A,B*), *rest(L)* = (*C*), *first(first(L))* = *A* and *rest(rest(L))* = *NIL*.

Lisp also has a construction operator, *cons(X;Y)*, which constructs a list *L* such that *first(L)* = *X* and *rest(L)* = (*Y*), and a predicate *atom(X)*, which is true when *X* is an atom and false otherwise. In the above example, *atom(first(L))* = *false* since *first(L)* = (*A,B*) but *atom(first(first(L)))* = *true*.

In general, any language for the manipulation of data structures has not only *selectors* for selecting components of a data structure, but also *constructors* for constructing data structures from their components and *predicates* for testing whether a given data object has certain attributes. Lisp illustrates particularly clearly the role of selectors, constructors, and predicates in a programming language.

List structures are a flexible storage structure for objects of variable sizes or tables of fixed-size objects in which insertion and deletion is frequently required. A number of special classes of list structures will now be considered in greater detail.

A *tree* is a list in which there is one element called the *root* with no predecessor and in which every other element has a unique predecessor. That is, a tree is a list that contains no circular lists, and in which no two list elements may have a common sublist as a successor. Elements of a tree that have no successor are called *leaves* of the tree. In Fig. 1, the symbol "+" is the root of the tree and the digits 3, 4, and 5 are leaves. Tree elements, just as list elements, are generally accessed by walking along a pointer chain. However, the guarantee that there are no cycles or common sublists makes it possible to define orderly procedures for insertion and deletion of subtrees.

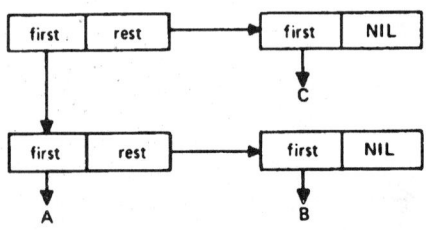

FIG. 5. Representation of a list *L*.

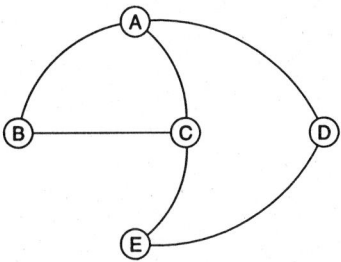

FIG. 6. A graph of five nodes and six edges.

A collection of data objects (nodes) so interconnected that their network may contain cyclic paths is called a *graph*. A typical graph is shown in Fig. 6. Such a structure is a generalization of a list structure because it can be represented by an adjacency list, a "list of lists," each of which tells which nodes are connected to the node at the head of the list (see Fig. 7). Alternatively, the same information can be represented as a generalized list (list with sublists) for processing by algorithms written in Lisp:

(A (B C D) B (A C) C (A B E) D (A E) E (C D))

For a more extensive description of graphs and operations thereon, see GRAPH THEORY.

A *stack* is a linear list in which elements are accessed, created, and deleted in a last-in-first-out (LIFO) order. In order to access an element in a stack, it is necessary to delete all more recently entered elements from the stack. Thus, only the top of the stack is immediately accessible. The two principal stack operations are *popping* and *pushing*. If S is a stack, then *pop(S,x)* causes the top element of the stack to be removed and stored at x and *push(S,x)* causes x to be placed on top of the stack.

A *queue* is a linear list in which elements are created and deleted in a first-in-first-out order. A line of people waiting to be served in a cafeteria is a queue, since the person having waited longest is always the first to be served (deleted from the queue). Similarly, employees in a large organization generally form a stack with regard to the probability that they will be fired (first-in-first-out, or FIFO). A queue in which insertions and deletions are normally made only at opposite ends, but to which an item is occasionally inserted into or removed from the interior is called a *priority queue*.

A generalization of queues and stacks in which elements may be added and deleted at both ends of a linear list is called a *deque*. A deque is said to be input-restricted

if input is possible at only one end, but deletion may occur at both ends. A deque is said to be output-restricted if output may occur at only one end, but input may occur at both ends. Fig. 8 illustrates by means of a railway-switching network the notion of a deque with input and/or output restrictions (see Knuth, 1973, p. 236). ("Deque," a shortened form of "double-ended-queue," is pronounced "deck.")

Data structures include numerical structures, such as integers that have arithmetic operations applicable to them, and nonnumerical structures, such as arrays, lists, and trees, whose primary purpose is to keep track of relations among data objects rather than to manipulate them.

Computational structures may be studied and analyzed at many different levels of abstraction. We have already remarked on the difference between logical data structures and the storage structures in terms of which they are realized. The characterization of structure by logical relations among components is clearly more abstract than the realization of the logical structure by particular configurations of cells and pointers. It is convenient to introduce an additional higher-level mathematical level of abstraction in which logical relations among components of a data structure are characterized even more abstractly by mathematical relations, and an additional lower-level "hardware" level of abstraction that specifies how storage structures are realized at the hardware level.

In programming languages, the choice of a data structure is made by selection of one of the available data types supported by the language. Usually, there are primitive data types for integers, real (floating-point) numbers, and characters; composite data types for arrays and records; and data type definition mechanisms for defining new composite types in terms of primitive constituents.

One important programming language concept is that of an *abstract data type*, which has an interface of named operators accessible to the user and which operates on a hidden internal data representation. For example, an abstract "stack" data type would provide the user with "push," "pop," and "test empty" operators, but hide from the user the stack data representation (as an array or list). The abstract data type mechanism is available in experimental languages like CLU, but is not currently available in any major production language. The language Ada (*q.v.*) has a concept called *packages* (*q.v.*) that provide collections of resources with hidden implementation to the user, but are not actually abstract data types.

Returning to the levels of abstraction listed above:

1. *Mathematical structure* is defined by specifying a set of objects and a set of operators (functions, relations) for transforming objects into other objects.
2. *Data structure* is defined by labeled, directed graphs that allow characteristic operators on data objects having the given structure to be naturally and simply defined by means of graph transformation rules. A given mathematical

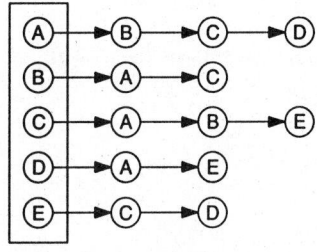

FIG. 7. An adjacency list for graph of Fig. 6.

Track closed in input-restricted deque

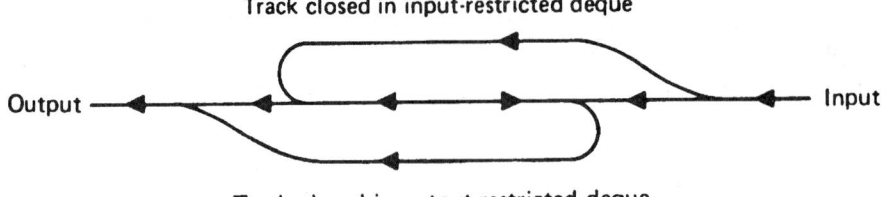

Track closed in output-restricted deque

FIG. 8.   A double-ended queue (deque).

structure may, in general, be represented in many different ways by a data structure.

3. *Storage structure* is defined by storage cells with pointers between storage cells. Storage structures, like data structures, are chosen so that operators applicable to computational objects represented by a given storage structure may be simply and efficiently defined. There are, in general, many different storage structures that realize a given data structure.

4. *Hardware structure* specifies how storage structures and transformations of storage structures may be realized at the hardware level.

Example. In modeling databases, the mathematical level of abstraction models databases as mathematical relations, the data structure level considers databases to be directed labeled graphs, the storage structure level considers how the directed graphs representing particular data configurations can be efficiently realized by storage structures, and the hardware structure level considers hardware and microprograms for realizing particular storage structures.

Although these four levels of structure specification are somewhat arbitrary, they appear to be "robust" in the sense that attempts to quantify the notion of abstraction invariably result in something similar to the above characterization. For example, in considering abstraction for program structure, we generally distinguish between mathematical structure, program structure, implementa-tion structure, and hardware realization. These distinctions are very similar to the previously discussed distinctions for the data structure case.

Classification of Data Structures   Although the range of abstract data structures is exceedingly broad, any imaginable structure can be placed into one of three categories:

1. A *static data structure* consists of a fixed number of contiguous cells arranged in a geometric pattern. That pattern usually, but not always, has a certain symmetry, such as that of a rectangular or hexagonal array.

2. An *elastic data structure* consists of a variable number of contiguous cells arranged in a geometric pattern.

3. A *dynamic data structure* consists of a dynamically changeable number of nodes, some or all of which have a stated logical connection to one another or to several others. Examples are trees and linked lists.

Static and elastic data structures are sometimes called *geometric data structures*, in contrast to dynamic ones, which are also called *topological data structures*.

Representative data structures are classified in the three categories in Table 1. In each of the three categories in Table 1, structures are arranged from simplest at the bottom to most complex at the top. This is easiest to see

TABLE 1.   Classification of representative data structures

Static Data Structures (Fixed Number of Contiguous Cells)	Elastic Data Structures (Variable Number of Contiguous Cells)	Dynamic Data Structures (Variable Number of Non-contiguous Nodes)
Non-Cartesian array	File	Graph *n*-ary tree Binary tree

Cartesian array:
    n-dimensional array
    three-dimensional array
    matrix (APL)
    two-dimensional array
    one-dimensional array
	
	n-dimensional elastic arrays (APL)
	Deque
	Queue (Simula)
	Stack (Forth)
	Variable-length string (Snobol, Icon, Turbo Pascal, APL)
		
		List with sublists (Lisp)
		simple linked lists:
		    DLCL
		    DLLL
		    SLCL
		    SLLL

Fixed-length record	Variable-length record (Cobol)	set (SETL)

DLCL –Doubly-Linked Circular List; DLLL–Doubly-Linked Linear List; SLCL–Singly-Linked Circular List; SLLL–Singly-Linked Linear List in the dynamic category. The nodes of a graph may be arbitrarily interconnected, either partially, as in Figure 6, or completely. The smallest degree of interconnection among nodes in a dynamic structure is none at all, as is exemplified by the *set*, the last entry in the dynamic category of Table 1.

Using a language such as C (*q.v.*) or Pascal, dynamic data structures have to be synthesized by using records for nodes and pointers (*q.v.*) for interconnections. Alternatively, another programming language that supports the given structure could be used. If a language does a particularly good job of supporting a certain structure, it is cited in the table. For example, Cobol might be the best choice when it is important to be able to process variable-length records. APL, noted principally for its unusual syntactic notation, is potentially valuable because it is the only language that supports elastic arrays; i.e. the dimensionality of an APL array can be changed dynamically by adding or deleting whole rows and columns, even in the interior of the original array.

Data structures capture the notion of computational structure at a level that is sufficiently abstract to emphasize logical relations among components of a data object, independently of details of implementation but at the same time sufficiently concrete to preserve some relation between a structure and its computational realization. Data structures thus represent an appropriate and practicable level of abstraction for characterizing computational structure, and it is for this reason that the study of data structures is important in computer science.

References

1973. Knuth, D. E. *The Art of Computer Programming* 1 (2nd Ed.), Reading, MA: Addison-Wesley.

1978. Gotlieb, C. C. and Gotlieb, L. R. *Data Types and Structures*. Englewood Cliffs, NJ: Prentice-Hall.

1980. Standish, T. A. *Data Structure Techniques*, Reading, MA: Addison-Wesley.

1987. Horowitz, E. and Sahni, S., *Fundamentals of Data Structures in Pascal*, 2nd Ed., Rockville, MD: Computer Science Press.

1989. Reilly, E. D. and Federighi, F. D., Pascalgorithms, Boston, MA: Houghton-Mifflin.

PETER WEGNER AND EDWIN D. REILLY

DATA TYPE

For articles on related subjects *see* ABSTRACT DATA TYPE; ARITHMETIC, COMPUTER; COERCION; DATA STRUCTURES; DECLARATION; and PROCEDURE-ORIENTED LANGUAGES.

A *data type* is an *interpretation* applied to a string of bits. Data types may be classified as structured or scalar. Scalar data types include real, integer, double precision, complex, logical ("boolean"), character, pointer, and label.

Structured data types are collections of individual data items of the same or different data types. An *array* is a data type that is a collection of data items of the same data type. *Records, structures*, or *files* are data types that are collections of data items of one or more data types.

Most programming languages provide a *declaration facility* or a standard convention to indicate the data type of the variable used. Thus, when the contents of the variable are accessed, they may be interpreted in the proper manner. This is necessary, since a string of bits may have several meanings depending on the context in which it is used.

The *real* data type is used to represent floating-point data, which contain a normalized fraction (mantissa) and an exponent (characteristic).

The *integer* (or *cardinal*) data type is used to represent whole numbers, i.e. values without fractional parts.

Double precision is a generalization of the real data type that provides greater precision and sometimes a greater range of exponents.

Complex data contain two real fields representing the real and imaginary components of a complex number $a + bi$ (where i is the square root of -1).

Logical, or *boolean*, data has only two possible values, *true* or *false*.

Character or *string*, data is the internal representation of printable characters. Some coding schemes (BCD) permit 64 characters and use six bits; others (EBCDIC and ASCII - *q.v.*) permit up to 256 characters and use 8 and 7 bits, respectively.

Label data refers to locations in the program and *pointer* data refers to locations of other pieces of data.

The commonly used operators for addition (+), subtraction (−), multiplication (*), division (/), and exponentiation (** or ↑) may be applied to real, integer, double precision, or complex data in high-level language programs, with a few restrictions. The actual operation that takes place depends on the data type of the operands. Although some language processors permit "mixed mode" expressions (i.e. expressions involving operands of differing data types), this is accomplished by converting ("coercing") the operands to a common data type before the operation is performed (*see* COERCION).

For example, to execute

$$N = (TEST + 90)/3$$

the integer value 90 is converted to a real value, 90.0, so that it may be added to the value of TEST (assumed to be real-valued). Before the resultant real value can be divided, the integer value 3 must be converted to a real value, 3.0. Finally, the real result is truncated and converted to an integer so that it may be stored in the (assumed) integer location *N*.

The logical operators *and, or, not, implies*, and *equivalence* may be applied to logical data having true or false values only. Character operations include concatenation (*q.v.*) and selection of substrings. For all data types, the assignment operator (typically, ← or :=) may be used to copy the contents of one location into another, and relational operators may be used to compare values of data items.

Certain programming languages such as Snobol, Pascal, Modula-2 (*q.v.*), and Ada (*q.v.*) are extensible in the sense that users may define new data types to suit the needs of a particular problem. Such user-defined data types are becoming increasingly popular. User programs may contain declarations of new data types, such as color, which might have a limited number of values such as *red, orange, yellow, green, blue,* and *violet.* Variable names could be declared to be of type color and could take on only the stated values. An example in Pascal would be:

type COLOR = (RED, ORANGE, YELLOW, GREEN, BLUE, VIOLET);
var CRAYON, PAINT: COLOR;

A user-defined data type might also be a subrange of a standard data type. For example, an age data type might be restricted to range from 1 to 120. An example in Pascal would be:

type AGE = 1..120;
var TREEAGE, CITIZENAGE: AGE;

The data type concept can also include sequential or random access files and complex structures such as records, arrays, or trees, that are formed from basic data types such as integers, character data, ages, or colors.

References

1976. Wirth, N. *Algorithms + Data Structures = Programs.* Englewood Cliffs, NJ: Prentice-Hall.
1978. Gotlieb, C. C. and Gotlieb, L. R. *Data Types and Data Structures.* Englewood Cliffs, NJ: Prentice-Hall.

BEN SHNEIDERMAN

DATABASE COMPUTER

For articles on related subjects *see* DATABASE MANAGEMENT SYSTEM; DEDUCTIVE DATABASE; and RELATIONAL DATABASE.

A *database computer,* a form of *backend processor,* is a highly advanced parallel processing fault-tolerant system optimized for relational database management that may be attached to one or more "host" computers, from which users can access data. A host computer may be any one of three types of computers: *mainframes (q.v.), minicomputers (q.v.)* or intelligent *workstations (q.v.)* attached to *local area networks (q.v.).* This architecture represents a major departure from conventional processing techniques because it relieves the host computer of its heavy software DBMS burden by harnessing the cost-efficient power of multiple microprocessors operating in parallel. A database computer allows concurrent access to the relational database from end-user interactive sessions, on-line transaction systems, and high-volume batch jobs, and its multiprocessor (hardware) and software provide major advances over software DBMS approaches to data management. All data is stored in relational tables and accessed via a single, high-level, nonprocedural language, SQL (Structured Query Language).

The Teradata DBC/1012 is an example of a microprocessor-based database computer that is expandable in small modules of processing and storage capacity. The minimum configuration includes a processor subsystem and a storage subsystem, providing up to 24 MIPS of processing capacity and up to 19 gigabytes of storage capacity. The system can be expanded to more than 3 BIPS and nearly 5 terabytes of data storage, all operating as a single system with a single image. The DBC/1012 is a very powerful database file server *(q.v.),* providing terabytes of data accessible from the desktop of any user. There are three types of processors that may be used with the Teradata database computer: interface processors (IFPs), access module processors (AMPs), and communications processors (COPs). A system that uses the first two of these is shown in Fig. 1. The IFP provides connection to mainframe hosts; the AMP manipulates the database, accesses disks and prepares the data results; the COP provides connection to a local area network *(q.v.),* enabling user access from minicomputers, workstations, and personal computers *(q.v.).*

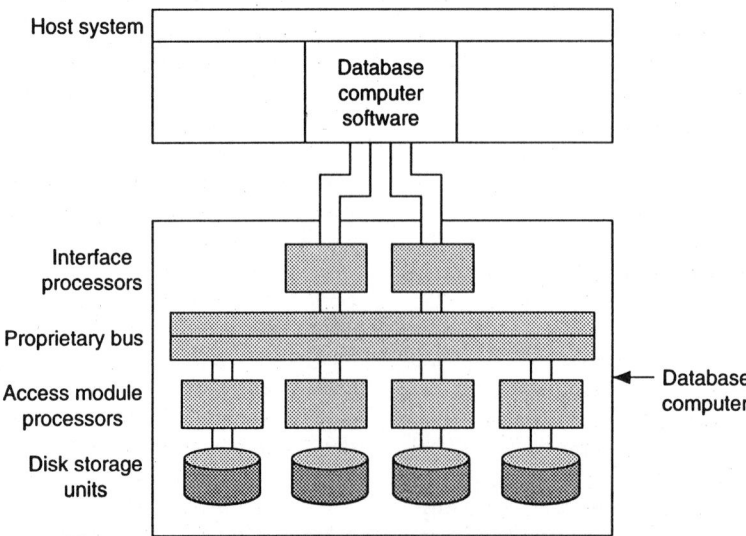

FIG. 1. Components of a database computer system used as a backend processor to a host computer.

A high-speed interconnection of processors is a very important part of the system's architecture that is designed to harness the power of 3 to 1,024 processors, while high-speed disk storage units (DSUs) can be configured to provide nearly 5,000 gigabytes of database storage.

ANSI-standard Structured Query Language (SQL) is the single, comprehensive language used for data access, definition, manipulation, and report writing on a database computer.

A database computer provides many expanded capabilities that distinguish it from a software database management system. For example:

1. The use of microprocessor technology provides cost-effective processing power that avoids costly mainframe CPU and I/O processing cycles. Parallel processing (*q.v.*) eliminates one-at-a-time bottlenecks as data is spread across a number of processors and disk storage units. The processing is performed asynchronously by multiple, independent processors. The modular design of a database computer permits growth that corresponds directly to user requirements.

2. The shared information architecture of a database computer adheres to Open Systems Interconnection (OSI - *q.v.*) standards and provides the capability to serve a heterogeneous, diverse network of mainframe computers, departmental computers, and intelligent work stations. Sharability permits all users, regardless of the application they are running, to share a common view of information, as the communication protocols and hardware platforms are transparent; a wide variety of software is fully compatible with a database computer.

3. Data protection from failure of a host computer, disk storage units, or abnormal termination of an application program is an integral part of a database computer. Fault tolerance is accomplished in hardware by providing two independent paths to the data. The duplexed access paths are always in use, assuring maximum throughput. Fallback data is stored on separate processors and separate disk storage from the primary data copy, ensuring that the data can always be accessed.

MARY O. VARGO

DATABASE MANAGEMENT SYSTEM (DBMS)

For articles on related subjects *see* DATA MODELS; DATABASE COMPUTER; DEDUCTIVE DATABASE; MANAGEMENT INFORMATION SYSTEM; and RELATIONAL DATABASE.

Database A *database* is a collection of interrelated data of different types. The term database conveys more

than the older term *file* (*q.v.*), which was carried over into data processing terminology from the pre-computer era. Unfortunately, "database" is still all too frequently used when all that is implied is a conventional file.

The difference between a database and a file, in terms used prior to the advent of data processing, is analogous to the difference between a thoroughly cross-referenced set of files in cabinets in a library or in an office and a single file in one cabinet that is not cross-referenced with any other file. The important difference between a computerized database and a thoroughly cross-referenced set of manual files is that the *database* must be stored on a direct access storage device in order for the computer's central processing unit (CPU - *q.v.*) to be able to utilize the cross references.

Along with spreadsheets (*q.v.*) and programs for word processing (*q.v.*), database programs constitute one of the three principal categories of programs in most widespread use on personal computers (*q.v.*). The leading products as of this writing are dBase IV, RBASE, FOXPRO, Q&A, and Paradox.

An important feature of a good database is that unnecessary redundancy of stored data is avoided and hence so are the consistency problems that are inevitably associated with such redundancy.

The term *cross-reference* is not normally used when talking about a database. Two terms are in common use, namely, *relationship* and *constraint*. In the last analysis, these two terms are not far apart. There are different ways of talking about databases and, consequently, different approaches and different sets of terminology. The approach that is most widely used is usually referred to as *relational*. An older but still widely practiced approach is the *network* model (*see* DATA MODELS). Relational terminology is preferred here (*see* RELATIONAL DATABASE).

Tables, Columns, and Constraints A conventional file, as definable in Cobol since the early sixties, is regarded as consisting of a collection of records of the same type or possibly of different types. In the relational approach, a file is referred to as a *table*, with several *columns* and several rows. The importance of this terminological approach is that terms are used that are easier for a person not trained in data processing to understand. For all intents and purposes, a row in a table is the same as a record in a file. A column in a table is what, in Cobol terms, would be called an item (or, more correctly, an elementary item).

Constraints The difference between the database approach and Cobol comes in the use of *constraints* in the database approach. There are different kinds of constraints in the relational approach, but it is first important to explain the role played by these constraints.

Data values that are to be stored in computerized databases (specifically in the columns of certain tables in a database) are often subjected to validation conditions. In other words, a condition may be expressed that a value has to satisfy in order to be correct at the time it is stored in the database. Such a condition is called a *constraint* in relational terms.

Uniqueness Constraints Two typical kinds of constraint can be illustrated. The simplest is that a value that is stored in a column of a table must be different from the values already stored in the same column in other rows in the same table. This is called a *uniqueness constraint*.

While it is quite common to express a uniqueness constraint on a single column in a table, it is also possible to express such constraints on any two or more columns in the same table. The term *key* (or unique key) has often been used to convey concepts very similar to that intended with "uniqueness constraint." However, the term "key" traditionally conveys the idea of some kind of mechanism being maintained and used to make it quicker to access the rows in a long table (*see* ACCESS METHODS). The term "uniqueness constraint" does not imply the provision of any kind of mechanism for this purpose. Definition of a uniqueness constraint means that a check is automatically carried out by a *database management system*, to ensure that the value being inserted in that column is not already to be found in an existing row of the same table. Examples of columns that would typically be the subject of a uniqueness constraint are employee number, social security number, supplier number, purchase order number, and pay period number.

Referential Constraints The other important kind of constraint is called a *referential constraint*. In order to illustrate this concept, consider the Tables 1 and 2.

It is important to note first that in Table 1 the column headed "Supplier No." and in Table 2 the column headed "Purchase Order No." should each be the subject of a uniqueness constraint. In fact, it is a fundamental rule in a relational database that each table should have at least one uniqueness constraint. (It is quite possible for a table to have two or more uniqueness constraints.)

The concept of a referential constraint can be illustrated using the column in the Purchase Order table that is headed "Supplier No." If expressed in narrative terms, the referential constraint would read as follows:

> The value stored in the Supplier No. column of the Purchase Order table must match a value that has already been stored in the Supplier No. column of the Supplier table.

This constraint could be expressed as a business rule, as follows:

> When the purchasing department sends a purchase order to a supplier, the supplier must already be known.

TABLE 1. Supplier Table

Supplier Number	Supplier Name	Supplier Address	Phone
43	Smith	23 South St, Walton	234567
32	Jones	12 High St, Weybridge	678912
12	Brown	17 First St, London	1234566
13	Black	23 West St, Putney	2452456

TABLE 2. Purchase Order Table

Purchase Order No.	Date	Supplier No.
74321	940406	12
74322	940406	32
74323	940408	13
74324	940408	12

Looking at Tables 1 and 2, it can be seen that supplier number 12 has been sent two purchase orders and that suppliers 13 and 32 have each been sent one purchase order. However, supplier number 43 has not been sent a purchase order. The referential constraint considered here does not require a supplier to have been sent a purchase order. It would be possible to express this condition as a separate constraint additional to the one on the Supplier No. in the Purchase Order table. The effect of expressing the constraint on the Supplier No. in the Purchase Order table is that the database management system then carries out a check each time a new row is added to the Purchase Order table. (The check on one table "refers" to another table and hence the name "referential constraint".) If the check fails, then typically the table is not updated. The tie-in between referential constraints and uniqueness constraints is that a referential constraint refers to a column in another table that is the subject of a uniqueness constraint.

Database Language SQL There is an international standard language used for defining the structure of a relational database in terms of tables, columns and various kinds of constraints. This language is called SQL, which originally meant "structured query language." In view of the fact that SQL is used for many more purposes than this, the decoded form of the acronym is to be avoided.

The latest version of the ISO SQL standard [9075: 1990] contains the definition of concrete language syntax and associated semantics that can be used for many purposes associated with database management. It provides facilities for the definition of a wide spectrum of constraints far in excess of those illustrated in this article. The importance of being able to define constraints in this way is as follows. A business rule such as the example given in this article has to be handled in a computerized system in some way or another. One alternative that has been and still is widely used is to represent the rule as a procedure using a programming language. The modern database-oriented approach is to represent the rule declaratively using a database language such as SQL. The arguments in favor of the latter approach are the following. First, it is usually quicker and hence cheaper to represent the rule declaratively and then let a database management system enforce the rule. Second, there may be several programs that update any particular table in a database. With the procedural approach, the procedure embodying the business rule has to be either repeated or possibly invoked each time. Finally, business rules change over time. It is usually easier to modify a declarative expression than to modify procedural code.

Database Management Systems

The handling of the various kinds of constraints is the capability that distinguishes a database from a file. In order to build a database, it is the normal practice to use a piece of generalized software called a *database management system* (DBMS). A DBMS that is based on the SQL database language requires the database structure to be defined in terms of tables, columns, and constraints. A typical commercial database might comprise some 50 to 100 tables, each having up to 15 columns and with one or two referential constraints on most of the tables. The resulting definition is often referred to as a *schema* or *database schema*. This database schema is referred to when defining the processes to be performed on the data. Many of the processes are fairly simple and do not need to refer to all of the tables in the database schema. It is possible in various ways to restrict the number of tables that a process is permitted to access. The statements that a DBMS uses to perform the processes on the data in the tables are called *data manipulation statements* and are typically specified as part of a database language.

Data Structure Diagrams

Diagrammatic techniques are widely used among analysts and designers to present an overall picture of the major data concepts and how they are interrelated. It is important to distinguish in this context between analysis and design. Analysis or *data analysis* is an activity carried out to discover the major data concepts in a given business area and how one or more subject experts in that business area consider these concepts to be interrelated. One of the major techniques used as a means of communication between analyst and subject expert is *data structure diagramming*. During the analysis phase, each major data concept is often referred to as an *entity type*. For example, one would refer to the entity type "supplier" and the entity type "purchase order." During the dialogue between analyst and subject area expert, it might be agreed that there is a *relationship* between these two entity types. The precise nature of the relationship could be analyzed by looking at some specific suppliers and specific purchase orders and preparing a cross reference table between the two that might appear, as shown in Table 3.

Examination of the rows in Table 3 shows that there is one cross on each row. This indicates that each purchase order is related to one supplier. No purchase order has been sent to Brown; Black has one; Smith has two; and Jones has three. Each column, however, contains zero, one, two, or three crosses, which is evidence that there may be zero, one, or more purchase orders for each supplier.

This is an example of the commonest kind of relationship that is permissible between two entity types, namely, a one-to-many relationship. The word "many" should be taken as meaning "zero, one, or more." One could represent the one-to-many relationship perceived in Table 3 using the technique shown in Figure 1. The relationship between the two entity types is not symmetric and some kind of indication is needed to depict this asymmetry.

While a rectangle is commonly used to represent an entity type, there is wide variation in practice in the number of ways used to represent a relationship between two entity types. There are, in fact, ten different kinds of relationship that can be discovered between two entity types. Several approaches to data analysis and the associated diagramming techniques also cater for relationships between entities of the same entity type and among three or more different entity types.

Data structure diagrams provide a more effective way of communicating with subject area experts and even with users than a concrete language syntax, such as that provided in SQL.

Data Analysis and Database Design

There is a close tie-in between data analysis and database design. Many experts do not choose to recognize the two as separate activities. There are some who prefer a distinctly different way of modelling data for analysis purposes from that used for design purposes. For example, some analysis techniques permit relationships among three or more entity types and this capability is not allowed in database languages such as SQL. The ISO Reference Model of Data Management [IS 10032] refers to a way of modeling data as a *data modeling facility*. It refers to a model of application data developed using a data modeling facility as an *application data model*. It has been common practice to refer to each of these with the same term, *data model*. If the data modeling facility used for analysis purposes is different from that used for design purposes, it is necessary at some point to convert the application data model of the data from the one form to the other.

TABLE 3. Cross-Reference Table Between Supplier and Purchase Order

Purchase Order	Supplier			
	Smith	Jones	Brown	Black
PO 6	X			
PO 9		X		
PO 15		X		
PO 16				X
PO 17	X			
PO 21		X		

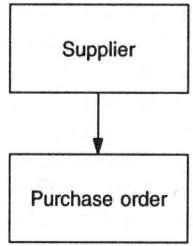

FIG. 1 Data structure diagram showing entity types and the relationship between them.

References

1988. McFadden, F. R. and Hoffer, J. A. *Database Management* (2nd Ed.). Reading, MA: Addison-Wesley.

1990. Codd E. M. *The Relational Model for Database Management: Version 2.* Reading, MA: Addison-Wesley.

1990. Date, C. J. *An Introduction to Database Systems* (5th Ed.), Vol. I. Reading, MA: Addison-Wesley.

1991. Mittra, Sitamsu. *Principles of Relational Database Systems.* Englewood Cliffs, NJ: Prentice-Hall.

1992. Date, C. J. with White, C. J. *An Introduction to Database Systems,* Vol. II. Reading, MA: Addison-Wesley.

T. WILLIAM OLLE

DATAFLOW

For articles on related subjects *see* COMPUTER ARCHITECTURE; FUNCTIONAL PROGRAMMING; GRAPH THEORY; PARALLEL PROCESSING; PETRI NET; and SUPERCOMPUTERS.

PRINCIPLES

Dataflow is a generic term that pertains to algorithms or machines whose actions are determined by the availability of the data needed for these actions. Algorithms that are expressed and executed in dataflow terms are controlled by the arrival of data at operators (called *actors*). This is to be contrasted to control flow environments where the locus of execution is based on an instruction pointer (or *program counter - q.v.*) which, identifies the operation to be performed next. Dataflow algorithms can be represented as directed graphs in which the *arcs* are data paths and the *nodes* are operations to be performed on the data tokens arriving on the incoming arcs. The graph shown in Fig. 1 is a dataflow procedure.

The names within the nodes of the graph indicate the operation to be performed. The availability of the input tokens and the ability of the output arc(s) to receive data (which will be the case when the previous output has already been used as an input to another node) are the only conditions that must be satisfied for any operation to execute. The act of performing the operation is called *firing* the node and results in the consumption of the input tokens and production of output tokens.

The node labeled "OP1" in Fig. 1 has two input arcs associated with it; nodes "OP2" and "OP4" have one input arc and node "OP3" has three input arcs. If tokens arrive on both of OP1's input arcs and its output arc is empty, then the input tokens will be consumed, the transformation OP1 will be performed on the data, and an output token will be produced. If a token had arrived on the input arc to OP2 coincidentally with the arrival of input tokens to OP1, and OP2's output arcs were empty, then both nodes OP1 and OP2 can fire simultaneously.

Node OP4 must wait only until OP2 has finished executing in order to fire, whereas node OP3 must wait for both OP1 and OP2 to complete. Thus, the synchronization of asynchronous activities is accommodated very naturally in a dataflow graph. The graph of Fig. 1 is surrounded by a dashed line (called the *procedure boundary*) and given a name, PROCA, so that it may be used in other dataflow programs. Fig. 2 shows a conventional flowchart for a sequential programming language and a corresponding dataflow program for determining the roots of a quadratic equation.

Although dataflow is a relatively new approach to computer systems organization, dataflow-related modeling techniques have been in use for quite some time. (Karp and Miller, 1969). One of the first formal methods using a dataflow-like technique is PERT/CPM (*q.v.*), developed in the 1950s for project planning and control. Another major use of a dataflow-like technique is in the simulation language GPSS V (*see* SIMULATION), developed for modeling discrete stochastic systems. The designers of logic circuits and computer hardware have used dataflow-related techniques in describing, analyzing, and testing circuits in which data items are in the form of electrical signals. Dataflow, in this context, bears a strong resemblence to Petri nets. Optimizing compilers analyze the flow of data in performing machine independent optimizations. Dataflow related techniques have also been used in microcode optimization (Lanskov *et al.*, 1980), software specification, and reliability (Fosdick and Osterweil, 1976).

There are currently several different candidate architectures proposed for executing dataflow programs. The architecture first proposed by Dennis and Misunas (1975) consists (see Fig. 3) of a collection of addressable instruction cells (IC) connected by an arbitration network to a group of operation units (transformational devices). The operation units are, in turn, connected by a distribution network back to the instruction cells. The instruction cells correspond to nodes on the graph, while operation units are merely execution units. An enabled instruction cell transmits an *instruction packet* to an operation unit via the arbitration network. The arbitration network processes instruction packets on a round robin basis. The result of a node firing is a *data packet*, which is sent to the destination instruction cells, using the distribution network. A variation of Dennis's architecture was implemented by Texas Instruments, Inc., in their Distributed Data Processor (DDP). Each operation unit in the DDP has

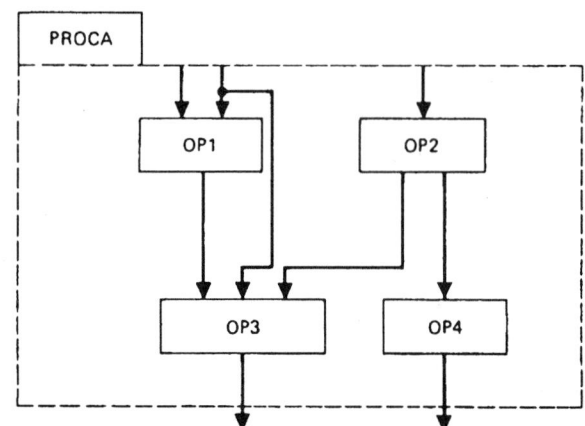

FIG. 1. Sample dataflow program and graph.

Dataflow Program

Flowchart Program

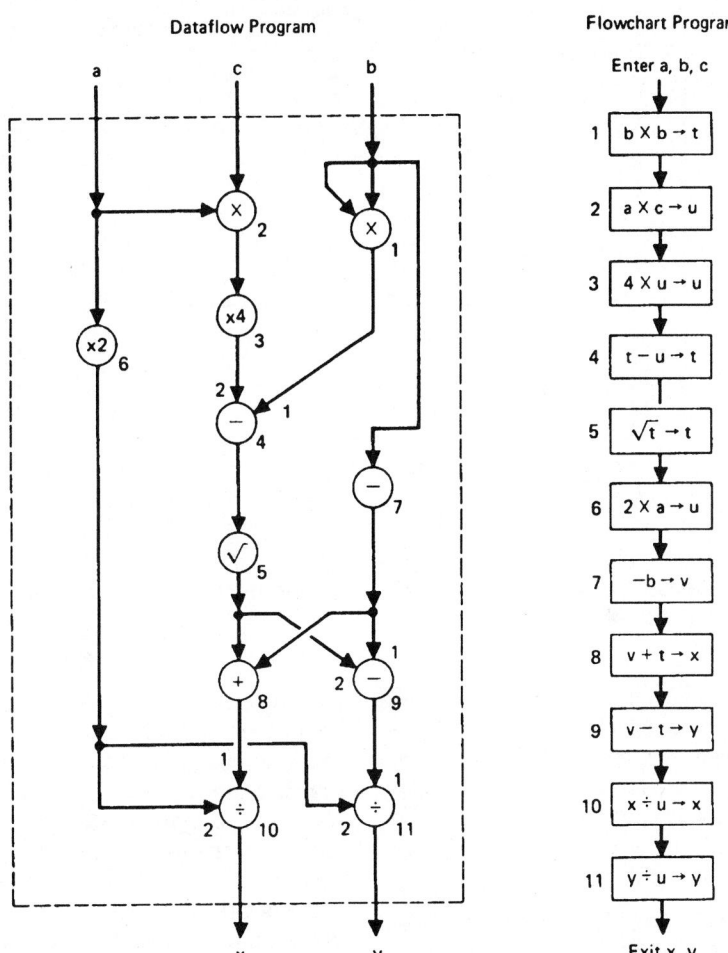

FIG. 2. Dataflow version of a sequential program to find the roots of a quadratic equation ($ax^2 + bx + c = 0$) with real roots. The labels on the lower right of the nodes of the dataflow program correspond to the labels on the boxes on the left of the flowchart. The labels 1 and 2 on the incoming arrows to the dataflow nodes indicate the order of the operands for subtraction and division.

an arithmetic/logic unit (*q.v.*) and a memory for instruction cells. The operation units are called *nodes* and are connected by a shift register interconnection network. Both the operation units and instruction cells are addressable. The primitive operations correspond to these operations used in an intermediate language for compiling Fortran to TI's ASC computer. A front-end processor (*q.v.*) accepts Fortran programs represented as dataflow graphs, identifies subgraphs having no data dependencies in the graphs, and distributes the subgraphs to various nodes of the DDP execution.

Burroughs Corporation Data Driven Machine (DDM1) executes dataflow programs using a tree structure for organizing the atomic units and a switch at each node of the tree to distribute its output. Each atomic unit consists of a processor with a number of microprogrammed functional units for manipulating data and managing storage. Like TI's DDP, this dataflow architecture also requires a front-end processor for identifying and distributing subnets in dataflow graphs.

Toulouse's LAU (for Langageá Assignation Unique) system also implements basic dataflow. The LAU system consists of a collection of processors, a central memory, and a control unit to detect all executable instructions in memory. Architectures for basic dataflow using conventional processors have also been proposed.

It is clear that dataflow languages can be used where either parallelism or communication between asynchronous processes must be accommodated. The firing semantics associated with a node and the graphical nature of dataflow enhance the overall understanding and control of these complex activities. This is to be contrasted with the traditional textual language solutions to these problems, which often increase the overall complexity of the algorithms involved. Architectures based on abstract dataflow are currently under development at various universities and industrial research laboratories. Extended abstract dataflow mechanisms that can be used in modeling and designing reconfigurable systems are being studied. Programs based on abstract dataflow are currently

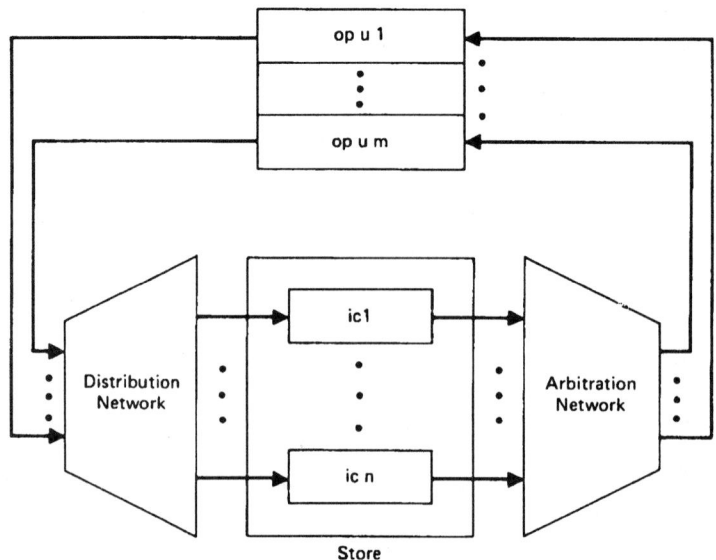

FIG. 3. Candidate dataflow architecture (ic = instruction cell; op u = operation unit).

being implemented and debugged using simulators. Several high-level textual languages for dataflow have been proposed and are in various stages of implementation. The languages are closely related to the functional (applicative) languages proposed by Backus (1978).

References

1969. Karp, R. M. and Miller, R. E. "Parallel Program Schemata," *J. Comp. Syst. Sci.* **3**, *No. 2*: 147–195 (May).

1975. Dennis, J. B. and Misunas, D. P. "A Preliminary Architecture for a Basic Dataflow Processor," *Proceedings 2nd Symposium on Computer Architecture*. New York, pp. 126–132.

1976. Fosdick, L. D. and Osterweil, L. J. "Data Flow Analysis in Software Reliability," *ACM Comp. Surveys* **8**, *No. 3*: 305–330 (September).

1978. Backus, J. "Can Programming be Liberated from the Von Neumann Style? A Functional Style and its Algebra of Programs," *CACM* **21**, *No. 8*: 613–641 (August).

1980. Lanskov, D., Davidson, S., Shriver, B., and Mallet, P. W. "Local Microcode Compaction Techniques," *Comp. Surveys* (September).

BRUCE D. SHRIVER, STEVEN P. LANDRY, AND VASON P. SRINI

LANGUAGES

A *dataflow language* is a functional programming language in which a variable may be assigned a value once and only once throughout a program. There are programming languages, such as Prolog, that also use single assignment to a variable, but are not dataflow languages. If the same variable name is used on the left side of an assignment statement in more than one place in a dataflow language program, the second and other appearances of the variable are treated as new variables. Many of the constructs found in block-structured languages, such as Pascal and C (*q.v.*), are usually supported in a dataflow language also. Data structures, such as lists, records, and arrays, are also supported along with operations on them. The single assignment rule complicates modifications to an element of a list or an array. Copying entire lists or arrays when only a single element needs to be modified is expensive. Parallel data structuring mechanisms have been devised to avoid the copying.

Since the execution of functions is free of side effects in a dataflow language, the detection of parallelism is not hard. In fact, dataflow languages and logic programming languages such as Prolog are two important classes of languages where implicit parallelism can be detected at compile time by doing a data dependency analysis and a global flow analysis.

Almost every research group that has developed a dataflow architecture has invented a dataflow language for that architecture. One of the early languages that made an impact is VAL (Ackerman, 1979). The code generated by VAL was targeted for MIT's static dataflow architectures (Dennis, 1984, Srini, 1986). One of the serious limitations of VAL was the lack of I/O and prohibition of recursive functions. Several features of VAL were used in the development of SISAL (McGraw, 1984). Compilers for SISAL have been developed for a few architectures, including the Manchester dataflow machine.

The language Id (Irvine Dataflow language), developed by Arvind and others (Arvind, 1978) to support the dynamic creation of instances of functions, is a block-structured expression–oriented dataflow language. The basic expressions are blocks, conditionals, loops, and procedure applications. An unravelling interpreter has been devised for Id that automatically unfolds loops constrained only by data dependencies. A parallel data structuring mechanism called the I-structure has been devised to avoid structure copying when elements are updated.

References

1978. Arvind, Gostelow, K. P., and Plouffe, W. *The Id Report: An Asynchronous Programming Language and Computing Machine,* TR #114, Dept. of Computer and Information Science, UC Irvine, CA 92714, September.

1979. Ackerman, W. B. and Dennis, J. B. *VAL—A Value Oriented Algorithmic Language: Preliminary Reference Manual,* TR-218, Computation Structures Group, MIT-LCS, Cambridge, MA, June.

1984. Dennis, J. B., Gao, G. R. and Todd, K. W. "Modeling the Weather with a Dataflow Supercomputer," *IEEE Transactions on Computers,* **C-33**, July, 592–603.

1984. McGraw, J., Skedzielewski, S., Allan, S., Grit, D., Oldehoft, R., Glauert, J., Hohensee, P., and Dobes, I. "SISAL Reference Manual," Technical Report, Lawrence Livermore National Laboratory, CA.

1986. Srini, V. P. "An Architectural Comparison of Dataflow Systems," *Computer,* March, 68–88.

VASON P. SRINI

DEADLOCK. *See* CONCURRENT PROGRAMMING.

DEBUGGING

For articles on related subjects *see* BUG; DIAGNOSTIC; DUMP; ERRORS; FLOWCHART; LOOP; PROCEDURE-ORIENTED LANGUAGES: PROGRAMMING; PROGRAM; PROGRAMMING SUPPORT ENVIRONMENTS; and TRACE.

In a 1966 article in *Scientific American,* the late English computer scientist, Christopher Strachey (*q.v.*), wrote:

> Although programming techniques have improved immensely since the early days, the process of finding and correcting errors in programming—known graphically if inelegantly as "debugging"—still remains a most difficult, confused and unsatisfactory operation. The chief impact of this state of affairs is psychological. Although we are happy to pay lip service to the adage that to err is human, most of us like to make a small private reservation about our own performance on special occasions when we really try. It is somewhat deflating to be shown publicly and incontrovertibly by a machine that even when we do try, we in fact make just as many mistakes as other people. If your pride cannot recover from this blow, you will never make a programmer.

Though over two decades have now elapsed since those lines were written, they still capture the essence and mystique of *debugging.*

Types of Error Mistakes (*bugs*) find their way into a computer program for many reasons, but they may generally be classified as follows:

1. An otherwise logically correct program contains one or more isolated statements or instructions that are syntactically (i.e. grammatically) incorrect in the programming language being used.
2. A potentially correct algorithm may be coded in a logically incorrect way.
3. The algorithm implemented may function correctly for some but not all data values, or, more insidiously, it may fail for just some few combinations of input values.

These three types of errors create debugging problems of increasing severity and typically require substantially different approaches to debugging.

Syntactic Errors The more flexible the syntax of a programming language, the easier it is to make syntactic errors. Thus, the simplicity and rigidity of machine language makes syntactic errors (such as illegal operation codes) relatively rare. From assembly language up through high-level language, however, it becomes increasingly easy to write a statement that is not grammatically acceptable to the language processor. Whether such statements occur because of typographical errors, imperfect understanding of language syntax, or just plain lack of concentration, such statements will prove to be only a minor annoyance, since they will produce diagnostic messages (*diagnostics*) when the errant program is assembled, compiled, or interpreted.

Language processors vary greatly in the quality of their diagnostics. For example, consider the spectrum of possible responses to the statement:

$$C = 4A$$

The message SYNTAX ERROR tells us nothing more than that the processor doesn't like it. The message ERROR 17 is annoying but at least raises the hope that if we look up ERROR 17 in some reference manual, we'll get to the root of the difficulty. Finally, the message IMPLIED MULTIPLICATION NOT ALLOWED attempts to be helpful, especially if given in conjunction with some such printout as

$$C = 4A$$
$$\wedge$$

which pinpoints the precise location of the alleged error. Note, however, that it makes the assumption that the programmer forgot to place a multiplication operator between the 4 and the *A* when, in fact, the error may have been the mistaken notion (for most computer languages) that $4A$ is a legal identifier (*q.v.*).

The type of error cited above is generally called a *fatal error* because it prevents the compiler from generating the object program needed for execution. Other situations may generate only a warning message that potentially erroneous results might be obtained; it would then be up to the programmer's judgment as to whether the offending construction really need be modified. An example is the Fortran statement

```
IF (A .EQ. 4.3567) K = K + 1,
```

which would cause many compilers to respond with:

THE TEST FOR EQUALITY BETWEEN REAL NUMBERS MAY NOT BE MEANINGFUL

(i.e. one cannot expect a computed value, A in the above, to be exactly equivalent to some other comparison value right down to the last bit of precision).

Designers of language translators intended for extensive student use try hard to make their diagnostics "friendly." However well they succeed, it is usually the case that students become unduly elated upon receipt of NO DIAGNOSTICS when, in fact, such a message is more likely to denote the real beginning of the debugging process rather than its conclusion.

Logical Errors   Logical errors are sometimes called *semantic errors* because they cause the program to have a meaning that, though syntactically valid, is other than what is needed for consistency with the algorithm being implemented. No translator will object to $C = A + B$ even if $C = A - B$ is what is needed, but such an error is virtually certain to cause incorrect results. Of course, most logical errors are more subtle. Typical errors cause programmed loops to run one time too few, one time too many, or to run indefinitely ("infinite" loops), or not at all; cause misallocation of memory relative to actual space needed; cause input data to be read with improper formats; or cause weird program behavior in any number of ways. Those errors that cause program termination with *run-time diagnostics* are easier to isolate than those that lead to infinite loops or to "normal" termination with incorrect answers. An example would be the very explicit message:

THE FOLLOWING INPUT RECORD DOES NOT CONFORM TO THE FORMAT SPECIFIED AT LINE 1023 (followed by a printout of the offending record),

but not all run-time diagnostics can be so precise.

When program execution does not lead to an easily localized error, the programmer has recourse to several debugging tools. One of the more efficient is to embed some temporary print statements at strategic places in the program flow in order to monitor the progress of intermediate results, the objective being to pinpoint the exact transition from successful progress to the point where the logic goes awry. (The information printed comprises what is sometimes called a *snapshot dump*, since, after capturing a record of conditions at a particular checkpoint, the computation continues. Of course, a prudent programmer would have had the foresight to include several such checkpoints in the program in anticipation of less than perfect initial operation, but it is almost inevitable that additional narrowing of focus will be needed. Interpretive languages can be easier vehicles for debugging in this sense, since the value of any desired variable can be solicited at the point of failure without prior inclusion of snapshot commands; this is more difficult with a compiler, since, by execution time, knowledge of the mapping between symbolic variable names and absolute memory cells has usually been lost.) At two

other extremes, the programmer may ask for extensive printout only at (normal or abnormal) program termination—a so-called *postmortem dump*—or, a last resort because of its gross inefficiency, a printout of key registers or variables after every statement (or perhaps every *n*th statement) or instruction executed; i.e. a *trace* of program flow. Narrowing the source of the error to a small section of code by one of these means or another is the necessary prelude to final identification of the error being pursued.

Algorithmic Error   When all known syntactic and semantic errors have been removed from a program, there is still a question as to whether the implemented algorithm actually solves the desired problem for all legal combinations of input values. Because so few programs are genuinely new in the sense of testing untried algorithms, this type of error is rather rare among professionals but not among students who are prone to encode, even if "correctly," some rather bizarre "algorithms." In either case, such algorithmic error can be very difficult to detect. If a program has been running satisfactorily for a sustained period, its users may place undue confidence in its output to the point where they would not detect answers that are nearly, but not quite, correct. Extensively tested programs that compute reliable results for a wide range of input values and that carefully check and reject illegal input are said to be *robust*. Programs that lack robustness are far more likely to be deficient because of logical errors (usually unchecked pathways or unverified input) rather than algorithmic error.

A program that gives correct answers for some or even many input cases may nonetheless contain huge stretches of code that have never been executed. A significant component of programming talent is the ability to devise a sufficiently comprehensive set of test cases that, at a minimum, exercise all program branches not only serially but also in such sequential combinations as to give reasonable assurance that the program will indeed be robust.

Symbolic Debuggers   Most modern assemblers and compilers are now supported by a software tool known as a *symbolic debugger*. The word "debugger," however, connotes an intelligence that does not exist. Such a debugger does not and almost certainly could not automate the debugging process. A symbolic debugger is no more than an information gatherer, one that helps the user gather evidence much more easily than having to splice gratuitous output statements into source code.

The fact that a debugger is "symbolic," however, is very valuable. When an executing program halts prematurely or emits wrong answers, it is object code that is doing so, and, at this stage, the symbolic content of the source code from which the object code was produced is not ordinarily available. What, pray tell, does it mean to find that your program has stopped at hexadecimal location 7FA3C with hexadecimal D76EA92B in general register number 7? But if, when we assemble or compile the source code we tell the language system being used that we intend to debug with a symbolic debugger, a mapping of symbols to numeric locations will be created and made available in the event that something bad happens at run time. If and when it does, we may then ask to see, for example, the current value of some variable such as *Radius* or *Volume* by those very names rather than their memory cell locations.

A second prime attribute of a symbolic debugger is that it allows us to run a program incrementally, a step at a time, rather than allowing execution to proceed as far as it can without aborting. One can take either small or large steps, whichever one chooses, by moving either from statement to statement or from one *checkpoint* to another, pausing as needed to examine key variables or machine registers.

Most debuggers support three kinds of checkpoints called, respectively, *breakpoints, tracepoints,* and *watchpoints*. The first two of these are very similar, differing only as to whether the debugger stops and awaits your further command or continues on to the next checkpoint. It will stop at a breakpoint, but merely pause (to output debug information) at a tracepoint. But a watchpoint, in some sense, is a much more clever idea. Suppose, for example, that our source program contains an identifier called *feet* whose initial value of 5,280 is not supposed to change during execution of the program. But, alas, it does. And worse, you have no idea as to what errant portion of your program is changing this value or when during execution it is being altered. What you may do is to tell the symbolic debugger that *feet* is a watchword. In essence, you are saying to it "Please keep your eye on *feet* and the instant that it changes value, stop and give me control." Simulation of such a powerful debugging technique would be very difficult without use of a commercial debugger and is one of the reasons why, to remain competitive, virtually all new language processors that run on personal computers are marketed with an associated symbolic debugger.

Correction of Errors

The correction of a serious algorithmic error might necessitate the rewriting of all or a substantial portion of a program, using essentially the same tools used to create it in the first place, but the correction of a syntactic or simple logical error is usually a trivial mechanical operation on a modern time-shared computer or even on a personal microcomputer. The principal tool is either a general text editor running under control of the computer's operating system or, in some cases, a special-purpose editor embedded in a specific language processor such as those that are typically part of Lisp and APL implementations. The programmer directs the editor to focus attention on the offending statement, which is located either by citing its line number, if known, or by asking for automatic search for the first statement that contains a particular character string, say, for example, *procedure*. After the statement that qualifies is located and displayed on the terminal by the editor, a decision is made to replace it, delete it, modify only a part of it, or add one or more new statements ahead of or after it. A still more powerful feature commonly provided is to be able to replace all occurrences of a given character string with a substitute string anywhere in the program or in specifically delineated parts of a program; e.g. changing all occurrences of INTERGER to INTEGER can get a poor speller out of a bind pretty quickly, especially if the errant word occurs 57 times.

When all corrections are made, the programmer typically asks the operating system to save the updated text segment and to retranslate this source element into a machine language object element using a particular language processor. The debugging cycle then continues iteratively until the program is deemed to be "correct." Unfortunately, saying so doesn't make it so, and the program may still need considerable exercise before it become robust in the sense discussed earlier.

Prevention of Errors

Clearly, better than finding and fixing errors would be to inhibit their introduction in the first place. In this sense, the subject of debugging is closely related to that of program design, documentation, and maintenance. Even when a program is deemed correct, it is seldom "finished"; i.e. it is almost inevitable that its sponsor will ultimately ask that it be modified. Often, the request will come well after the original programmer is still available. Experience has indicated that if certain good practices are followed during design and implementation, errors will be minimized to a degree well worth the extra original effort. Some of these are:

1. Program logic should be documented in the form of flowcharts or iteration diagrams.
2. Program variable names should be chosen mnemonically, e.g. RADIUS rather than simply R.
3. The symbolic program code should contain embedded comments that relate back to the flowchart.
4. As far as the structure of the host language permits, the principles of structured programming (*q.v.*) should be followed during program design.
5. All program input statements should be followed immediately by output statements that "echo" the input onto the output medium so that there can never be any confusion as to just which input case is being processed.
6. All output values should be carefully labeled. Two otherwise correct answers that are confused one with the other might just as well have been incorrect.

Finally, there is a growing school of adherents to a philosophy that program verification (*q.v.*) will allow programs to be "proved" correct to the point where bugs are never allowed to survive to the point where machine debugging in the sense discussed herein is needed at all. While there should be universal hope that such techniques succeed, the need for the more mundane advice cited in this article is likely to exist for some time to come.

References

1978. Van Tassel, Dennie. *Program Style, Design, Efficiency, Debugging, and Testing*. Englewood Cliffs, NJ: Prentice-Hall.
1978. Hughes, C. E., Pfleeger, C. P., and Rose, L. L. *Advanced Programming Techniques*. New York: Wiley, Chapter 1.

1988. Turbo C User's Guide Version 2.0, Scotts Valley, CA: Borland International, Chapter 4.

EDWIN D. REILLY

DEC.   *See* DIGITAL EQUIPMENT CORPORATION VAX SERIES.

DECISION TABLE

For an article on a related subject *see* CONTROL STRUCTURE.

Definition   A *decision table* is a disciplined tabular format for describing the combinations of conditions that lead to particular sequences of actions. The actions may be done by any person or any thing, such as a computer. The conditions typically take the form of data values that represent circumstances, events, policies, or characteristics. Decision tables are prepared in accord with conventions that include ways of finding errors in the resulting tables.

Fig. 1 shows an example of a decision table that describes how one organization handles the ordering of low-usage products. The stock order clerk knows that the target inventory level has been set by policy at 20 units of stock. If a particular low-usage product covered by the policy has an on-hand quantity of 18, a weekly usage of 6, and an amount already on order of 10, then the clerk is to place a regular order. This situation is shown by the third column from the right in Fig. 1. Note that only one column in the decision table exactly fits this situation, and that the matter of local vendor availability was not relevant in selecting the action in this example.

Terminology   As diagrammed in Fig. 2, decision tables have four overlapping portions (Chapin, 1967a; Pollack, 1971). The *rule counts* row (or a line) separates the upper or *condition* portion from the lower or *action* portion. On the right, the *entries* portion is arranged as a series of columns, each known as a decision rule. On the left, the *stub* portion lists briefly the identifications of the conditions and the actions.

In the condition stub quadrant, analysts may express the conditions in one of two ways. *Limited-entry* decision tables have all the conditions expressed as questions that can be answered by "yes" (Y), "no" (N), or "don't care" (-). *Extended-entry* decision tables have all the conditions expressed as questions that can be answered quantitatively or by "don't care." *Mixed-entry* decision tables, such as shown in Fig. 1, include both kinds of conditions. While analysts may list conditions in any order, decision tables are more powerful tools if analysts follow specific conventions in ordering the conditions (Hurley, 1983).

In the action stub quadrant, analysts may list actions in any order. But by convention, the "exit this table" or "return" action is always put last. In the action entry quadrant, analysts may put sequence numbers in the rules, to specify an explicit sequence of execution, as done in Fig. 1. Or analysts may indicate that the sequence of execution is immaterial by just marking the actions to be done with X, as is done in the rightmost rule in Fig. 1.

In the condition entries quadrant, analysts may list the rules in any order, but decision tables are more powerful tools if analysts follow specific conventions in ordering the rules (Hurley, 1983). If an ELSE rule is present, as it is in Fig. 1, it is a default rule and is shown always as the rightmost rule. Recognizing "don't care" situations can often result in consolidating two or more decision rules into one.

Use   In preparing decision tables, analysts must keep in mind two requirements applying to the condition entries. One is that, reading vertically within a rule, all of the conditions are logically ANDed, except for the "don't cares" (they are all ignored in the rule). The second requirement is that, reading horizontally, all of the rules are unique, mutually exclusive, and collectively exhaustive. Because of these properties, analysts can calculate a set of metrics to serve as a basis for checking decision tables for oversights, consistency, redundancy, and, to a lesser extent, accuracy (Hurley, 1983). The rule count, such as that shown in Fig. 1, is one component of the set of metrics. For each "don't care" in a limited entry rule, the rule count is 2 (i.e. the possible choices, Y or N). For each "don't care" in a mixed entry rule, the rule count is the number of possible choices (3 in row 2 in Fig. 1). The entry in each column in the rule counts row is the product of the rule counts for the "don't care"s in that column (with the ELSE entry computed differently).

As a part of systems analysis, analysts can prepare

On-hand quantity < 20	Y	Y	Y	Y	Y	Y	N	
Weekly usage amount	>15	>15	8–15	8–15	8–15	<8	-	
Local vendor available	-	-	Y	N	N	-	-	ELSE
On order quantity > 30	Y	N	N	Y	N	N	Y	
Rule counts	2	2	1	1	1	2	6	9
Place rush order		1			1			
Place regular order	1		1	1		1		
Cancel an order							1	
Exit	2	2	2	2	2	2	2	X

FIG. 1.   A decision table for low-activity stock-order procedure.

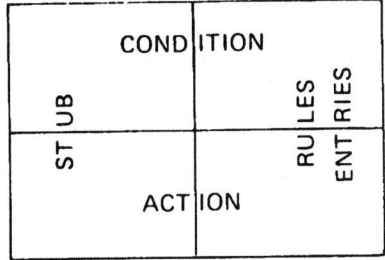

FIG. 2. Parts of a decision table.

decision tables that describe existing work practices and operations. These often reveal the presence of oversights, inconsistencies, and redundancies in the existing ways that work is done. As a part of systems design, analysts can prepare decision tables that specify the situations under which specific work is to be done by people and by computers. By using decision tables, such specifications can be made complete, self-consistent, accurate, and non-redundant.

For these reasons, analysts typically apply decision tables where the work is high in logic content—that is, the actions to be taken depend upon the complex interaction of many variables. Such situations abound in administrative and control applications of computers. Attempting to design software for such situations led in the early 1960s to the development of decision tables (Chapin, 1967a). Major users have been financial, manufacturing, and military organizations, mostly in software design, analysis, debugging and testing, programming, and documentation. Decision tables have found little use in scientific and engineering applications, when situations can be cleanly described in mathematical terms. While decision table usage declined in the 1980s, decision tables fit well with software engineering (Hurley, 1983) and offer potential in system software and expert systems (*q.v.*).

Languages Decision table languages (McDaniel, 1970) use as their input the decision table prepared during software design. Then by means of a compiler or precompiler, a computer translates the decision table into either a compilable language (such as Cobol) or, more rarely, machine language. This can directly provide the logic portion of the software, leaving the procedures for the actions to be coded by the analyst or programmer, or provided by other means. When well-checked decision tables are used as a software design tool, the use of a decision table language results in source code that is not only typically free of logic bugs, but it also can be produced very quickly.

Advantages Decision tables provide concise descriptions of logically complex situations. Decision tables can be broken or parsed into sets of smaller tables (Chapin, 1967b). Smaller tables are usually easier to prepare, since logically complex situations can become overwhelming if they have many alternatives and many variables. Also, smaller tables are easier to check.

Well-checked decision tables provide terse, accurate documentation. Such tables can also be used as input to decision table compilers or precompilers, to produce functionally correct software.

Disadvantages While decision tables have no theoretical size limit, large decision tables can become incomprehensible and difficult to modify. Fortunately, decision table size can be controlled by rule consolidation and by parsing. Also, software exists to assist in preparing, checking, and maintaining decision tables. Even so, using decision tables does not eliminate the analysis and design tasks of matching possible combinations of conditions and actions with the practices and expectations of the people who use data.

References

1967a. Chapin, Ned. "An Introduction to Decision Tables." *DPMA Quarterly*, **3**, 3: 2–23 (April).

1967b. Chapin, Ned. "Parsing of Decision Tables." *Communications of the ACM*, **10**, 8 (August).

1970. McDaniel, Herman. *Decision Table Software*. Philadelphia: Auerbach Publishers.

1971. Pollack, Solomon L., Hicks, Harry T., and Harrison, William J. *Decision Tables: Theory and Practice*. New York: John Wiley & Sons, Inc.

1983. Hurley, Richard B. *Decision Tables in Software Engineering*. New York: Van Nostrand Reinhold.

NED CHAPIN

DECLARATION

For articles on related subjects *see* EXECUTABLE STATEMENT; PROCEDURE-ORIENTED LANGUAGES; PROGRAMMING LANGUAGES; and STATEMENT.

A *declaration* (*declarative statement*) is a high-level programming language statement that provides descriptive information (contrasted with an *imperative*, or *executable*, *statement*, which specifies explicit processing operations).

Besides specifying the actual computations, decision rules, and input/output operations involved in the implementation of a particular algorithm, a high-level language program also must provide the compiler with descriptive information that allows it to perform a variety of organizational tasks directly connected with the production of an executable object program. For example, the description of a variable (its name, together with the type of data to be stored in it) enables the compiler to allocate the proper amount of storage, associate its location with the variable's name, and set up any necessary data conversion mechanisms prior to the assignment of a value to that variable. (This description also defines the set of operations that are applicable to the element.) Similarly, the definition and description of a data file makes it possible for the compiler to establish a relationship between references to that file and a particular collection of data transmitted to or from a specific input/output device.

In most languages, this type of information is supplied through a series of special statements, which often are characterized as being *non-executable* (or more properly, *declarative*). Once defined, simple variables, arrays, files, and other items can be used throughout the program simply by alluding to their properties by use of their names.

To illustrate the type of information conveyed by declarations, consider the following Pascal program, which reads a number N and uses it to compute

$$Y = \sum_{X=1}^{N} X(1 + \sqrt{X}).$$

N and Y are displayed with appropriate identification:

```
program sumup;
var I, N : integer;
    X, Y : real;
begin
    read (N);
    Y := 0.0;
    for I := 1 to N do
        begin
            X := I;
            Y := Y + X*(1.0 + sqrt(X))
        end;
    write ('N = ',N,' Y = ',Y)
end.
```

The first statement is a declaration that defines the program's name. The two statements subsumed as part of the **var** declaration direct the compiler to allocate storage for each of two integers and two real values. A subsequent reference to any of the names specified there will be automatically associated with the appropriate storage location.

SEYMOUR V. POLLACK

DEDUCTIVE DATABASE

For articles on related subjects *see* DATABASE MANAGEMENT SYSTEM; LOGIC PROGRAMMING; and RELATIONAL DATABASE.

A *deductive database* is an extended relational database that consists of a set of facts, a set of rules, and a set of integrity constraints. From the set of rules and the facts, it is possible to derive new facts not contained in the original set of facts. The integrity constraints describe the database. An example of an integrity constraint is one that specifies that all suppliers have only one store from which they sell their products. A rule might specify that, if a supplier supplies screw drivers, they must also supply screws. This rule obviates the need to list screws explicitly in the database.

A deductive database is based on logic. The set of facts is referred to as the *extensional database*, and consists of either a set of relations (or facts) whose argu-

ments are constants, or a set of positive disjuncts whose arguments are constants, or both; the set of rules are referred to as the *intensional database* and are of the form:

$$(1)\ A_1,..., A_n \leftarrow B_1,..., B_m,$$

where the A_i are atomic formulas and the B_j are literals; the integrity constraints are rules of the same kind as the intensional database. Integrity constraints are used not only to describe a database, but also to maintain the consistency of a database during updates, to permit semantic query optimization based on the meaning of the database, and to provide informative answers to a user when the integrity constraints restrict the search or provide semantic information that may explain why a query failed to find an answer. An intensional rule must have $n \geq 1$, $m \geq 0$. An *atomic formula* is a k-place predicate letter whose arguments are constants or variables. A *literal* is an atomic formula or the negation of an atomic formula. Atomic formulas evaluate to *true* or *false*.

The extensional database contains the facts or disjunctions of facts that are assumed to be *true*. An example of a disjunctive fact is: *supplier* ('abc', 'hammers') $\vee$ *supplier* ('abc', 'tomatoes'), which might mean that the abc corporation supplies *either* hammers *or* tomatoes, *or* both items. Another example of a fact in an extensional database is *supplierloc* ('abc', 'illinois'), *supplierloc* ('abc', 'virginia'). These state that the *abc* corporation is located both in Illinois *and* in Virginia. Corresponding to an atomic formula, there is a *relation* that consists of all tuples whose arguments are in an atomic formula with the same name. Thus, for the *supplierloc* predicate, there is a relation, the *SUPPLIERLOC* relation, that consists of the tuples, $< $ 'abc', 'illinois' $>,<$ 'abc', 'virginia' $>$. When the facts in the extensional database consist only of atoms, it is equivalent to a relational database.

Intensional rules are universally quantified and are an abbreviation of the formula:

$$(2)\ \forall X_1,..., X_n\ (A_1 \vee...\vee A_n \leftarrow B_1 \wedge...\wedge B_m).$$

Deductive databases restrict arguments of atomic formulas to constants and variables, whereas in first-order logic one also may have function symbols as arguments. The reason for the restriction is to assure that one has finite answers to queries. Rules are to be read either declaratively or procedurally. A declarative reading of (1) is: "A_1 or A_2 or...or A_n is *true* if B_1 and B_2 and...and B_m are all *true*." A procedural reading of (1) is "A_1 or A_2 or...or A_n are solved if B_1 *and* B_2 *and*...*and* B_m can be solved." The left-hand side of the implication, A_1 or...or A_n is referred to as the *head* of the rule, while the right-hand side, B_1 and B_2...and B_m is referred to as the *body* of the rule.

Queries to a database, $Q(X_1,..., X_r)$ are of the form $\exists X_1...\exists X_r (L_1 \wedge L_2...\wedge L_s)$ where $s \geq 0$, the L_i are literals, and the X_i, $1 \leq i \leq r$ are the variables in Q. An answer to a query has the form $< a_{11},..., a_{1r} > + < a_{21},..., a_{2r} > +...+ < a_{k1},..., a_{kr} >$ such that $Q(a_{11},..., a_{1r}) \vee Q(a_{21},..., a_{2r}) \vee...\vee Q(a_{k1},..., a_{kr})$ is provable from the database. By "provable" is meant that an inference system is used to find answers to queries.

Deductive databases are closely related to logic programs when the facts are restricted to atomic formulas and the rules have only one atom in the left-hand side of a rule. The main difference is that, in a logic program, one is searching for a *single* answer to a query, and the computation procedure is top-down, searching from the query to an answer. In the case of deductive databases, searches are bottom-up, starting from the disjunctive facts to find *all* answers to a query. A query in a logic program might ask for an item supplied by a supplier, while a query in a deductive database asks for all items supplied by a supplier. Unlike deductive databases, arguments of predicates in logic programs may contain function symbols. Deductive databases that are restricted to atoms as facts and have rules that consist of single atoms on the left-hand side of a rule and atoms on the right-hand side of a rule are referred to as *DATALOG*.

There are several different views of the relationship of an integrity constraint to the union of the database (facts and rules), and the integrity constraints. Two are noted here: *consistency* and *theoremhood*. In the consistency view, an integrity constraint must be consistent with the union of the database (facts and rules). In the theoremhood approach, an integrity constraint must be a theorem of the facts and rules—that is, it must be able to be proven from the facts and rules.

To answer queries that consist of conjunctions of positive and negated atoms requires that there be a semantics associated with negation, since one can only derive positive disjuncts from the above databases. Default rules are used to find answers to negated questions. There are several default rules used in deductive databases. Two of these rules are termed *negation as finite failure* (NFF) and the *closed world assumption* (CWA). In the NFF approach, one tries to prove the positive atom. If a proof fails in every branch of the proof search tree, one assumes the negation of the atom. In the CWA, if one fails to prove the positive atom, the negated atom may be assumed. The two approaches lead to slightly different results. They do not apply to disjunctive theories.

More expressive power may be obtained in a deductive database by allowing negated atoms on the right-hand side of a rule. The semantics associated with such databases becomes unclear in many instances. For a description of alternative semantics for deductive databases with negation in the right-hand side of rules, and a single atom on the left-hand side, see Lloyd (1987). For semantics of deductive databases when the right-hand side contains negated atoms and the left-hand side contains disjunctions, see Lobo, Minker, and Rajasekar (1990).

A historical perspective of deductive databases is given in Minker (1988). A survey of deductive databases may be found in Gallaire, Minker, and Nicolas (1984). A theoretical treatment of deductive databases and the semantics of these databases may be found in Reiter (1984). See Lloyd (1987) for alternative semantics of databases and for negation in deductive databases. Bottom-up computational methods for relational and deductive databases may be found in Ullman (1990). See Chakravarthy, Grant, and Minker (1986) for the use of integrity constraints for semantic query optimization and Gal and Minker (1990) for their use in obtaining informative answers.

References

1984. Gallaire, H., Minker, J., and Nicolas, J-M. "Logic and Databases: A Deductive Approach." *ACM Computing Surveys*, **16**(2):153–185 (June).

1984. Reiter, R. "Towards a Logical Reconstruction of Relational Database Theory." In M. L, Brodie, J. L. Mylopoulos, and J.W. Schmit, (Eds.), *On Conceptual Modelling*, 163–189. New York: Springer-Verlag.

1986. Chakravarthy, U. S., Grant, J., and Minker, J. "Foundations of Semantic Query Optimization for Deductive Databases." In J. Minker (Ed.), *Proc. Workshop on Foundations of Deductive Databases and Logic Programming*, 67–101, Washington, D.C., (August 18–22).

1987. Lloyd, J. W. *Foundations of Logic Programming*, 2nd Ed. New York: Springer-Verlag.

1988. Minker, J. "Perspectives in Deductive Databases." *Journal of Logic Programming*, 5:33–60.

1990. Ullman, J. D. *Principles of Database and Knowledge-Base Systems*. Potomac, MD: Computer Science Press.

1990. Gal, A., and Minker, J. "Producing Cooperative Answers in Deductive Databases." In P. Saint-Dizier and S. Szpakowicz, (Eds.) *Logic and Logic Grammars for Language Processing*, 223–254, New York: VCH.

1990. Lobo, J., Minker, J., and Rajasekar, A. "On General Disjunctive Logic Programs." In M. Zemankova and Z. Ras (Eds.) *Intelligent Systems: State of the Art and Future Directions*. Amsterdam: North-Holland.

JACK MINKER

DEFAULT CONDITION

For articles on related subjects *see* EXPRESSION; PROCEDURE-ORIENTED LANGUAGES; and STATEMENT.

A *default condition* or value is one set by software when a user elects not to make a choice that was available in a particular situation. Unlike its normal English usage, default carries no pejorative connotation; there is no suggestion that a person should have done something, merely that he or she *could* have. Some examples are:

1. The Fortran iteration statement DO 17 I = 1,100 behaves as if the user had written DO 17 I = 1,100, 1; i.e. The control variable I will be incremented by +1 by default, since the step size is assumed to be +1 unless otherwise specified.
2. In Basic, subscripted variable references such as LET *B* (7) = 4 may be made without dimensioning *B* explicitly, provided the maximum subscript used does not exceed 10; i.e. Basic assumes an implicit DIM *B* (10) by default unless the programmer supplies a specific alternative.
3. In APL, the origin of all arrays is 1 by default, but the programmer may overrule this by inputting)ORIGIN 0. (The only choices are 0 or 1.)
4. In Pascal, the heading **procedure** Zilch (*a,b* :

integer); begins the definition of a procedure whose arguments *a* and *b* are called-by-value by default. The programmer could have elected call-by-reference by writing **procedure** Zilch (**var** *a*, *b* : integer);. Similarly, the default parameter passage in Algol 60 is call-by-name unless call-by-value is explicitly specified.

5. The Pascal statement **while not** eof **do**—acts like **while not** eof(input) **do**—; i.e. the file whose end-of-file condition is being monitored is the "input" file by default even though another file could have been specified.

Note that, in each of these situations, the language designers chose a default condition or value that, in their opinion, would be most commonly desired. Such a practice saves the user time by making it unnecessary to state the obvious. Not all default choices are benign, however. The language PL/I employs an unusually large number of default decisions and some of these can do insidious things to an inexperienced or careless user. A notorious example is the apparently innocuous expression 4E0∗6E0, which could produce the strange result 2E1 (i.e. 4 × 6 = 20), since the default precision of the product, one significant digit, would be no more than the precision of the most precise number in the expression. Despite such occasional aberrations, the judicious use of default conditions facilitates rather than impedes programming productivity.

EDWIN D. REILLY

DELIMITER

For an article on a related subject *see* PROCEDURE-ORIENTED LANGUAGES.

A *delimiter* is an item of lexical information whose form and/or position in a source program denotes the boundary between adjacent syntactic components of that program.

As is true with natural language, the *meaning* and clarity of statements in high-level programming languages often depend on the inclusion of explicit indicators that "punctuate" the statement; such signals are termed *delimiters*. Since high-level language statements must be processed by a compiler whose analytical and interpretive facilities must function without the equivalent of human cognition, it is necessary to equip programming languages with a fairly extensive variety of such delimiters, many of them highly specific. The most common of these, naturally, is the blank space, whose function as a separator is self-explanatory. Some languages, however, like Fortran, ignore blanks; more common are languages that tolerate superfluous blanks between syntactic components. (One or more consecutive blanks constitute *whitespace*. Judicious placement of whitespace improves the esthetic appearance and readability of programs.)

Parentheses also represent a commonly used type of delimiter. One of their primary purposes in high-level

languages parallels traditional mathematical usage; i.e. to define the extent of a component in a computational expression. For example, the use of parentheses in the ordinary arithmetic expression.

$$A + B(C - 2D) \qquad (1)$$

is clearly paralleled by the equivalent in many high-level languages:

$$A + B * (C - 2*D). \qquad (2)$$

Most contemporary programming languages provide a relatively free physical format where there is no intrinsic association with a specific input medium, such as the terminal's keyboard. Consequently, in the absence of an implicit correspondence in such languages between the end of a statement and the physical boundary of the medium, it is necessary to impose explicit delimiters. The semicolon serves that purpose in the C language, and the period has a similar function in Cobol.

Another type of delimiter is used to bracket a sequence of statements when the intent is to consider that sequence as a single conceptual activity. The *compound statement* in Pascal is a case in point. For instance, the following structure

```
for i := 1 to 18 do
    begin
        read(x, y);
        sum1 := sum1 + x ;
        sum2 := sum2 + 2.7*y
    end ;
```

specifies a loop in which the sequence enclosed by the **begin…end** delimiters is to be executed during each of the 18 trips through the loop.

Pascal terminology distinguishes *separators*, such as colon (:), semicolon (;), and comma (,), which separate one language token from another, and *delimiters*, which occur in pairs in order to bracket a sequence of statements or tokens. Example Pascal delimiter pairs are ( ), [], {}, **begin…end**, **repeat…until**, and the keyword **program**, which begins a program, and the final period (.), which ends it.

SEYMOUR V. POLLACK

DESIGN, LOGIC. *See* LOGIC DESIGN.

DESK CALCULATOR. *See* CALCULATORS, ELECTRONIC AND PROGRAMMABLE.

DESKTOP PUBLISHING

For articles on related subjects *see* COMPUTER GRAPHICS; METAFONT; TEX; TEXT EDITING SYSTEMS; and WORD PROCESSING.

Desktop publishing refers to the creation and printing of high-quality documents by using a small self-contained computer system with software that allows page images to be viewed and edited on the screen before printing. This form of publishing became widespread during the late 1980s, when the three essential ingredients for a desktop publishing computer system became cheap enough to be purchased by small organizations, and the complete system became small enough to fit on a desk. The essential ingredients are:

- A small laser printer capable of printing diagrams and many different typefaces and styles.
- A computer workstation (*q.v.*) with a graphics screen and pointing device (typically a mouse - *q.v.*).
- Software with a simple interactive *user interface*, designed to support document creation and editing tasks.

Given these three ingredients, users without formal training in document design can produce complex documents quickly and without the need for outside printing or typesetting facilities. Fig. 1 shows a typical desktop publishing system.

A New Publishing Method

Desktop publishing has major advantages over traditional methods of document production and typesetting. The software is interactive and maintains a what-you-see-is-what-you-get (WYSIWYG) interface so that users see the current state of the document on the screen and manipulate it directly via the keyboard and pointing device. This allows them to experiment with the page layout and edit the content until they are satisfied with the result. They can then produce a paper copy on the laser printer.

The advantages of this interactive approach, together with the speed at which output could be produced, led to a rapid expansion in use during the 1980s. Desktop

publishing became firmly established and widely known by the acronym DTP. The term is now synonymous with the use of a particular style of interactive software package, regardless of the size of computer or output device used.

Early desktop publishing systems produced documents containing graphics as well as text in many different sizes and styles, but the quality of the printed document was poor compared to documents typeset by traditional methods. This was due partly to the relatively crude formatting methods used by the software and partly to the quality of the laser printers available at the time. Rapid advances in quality have been made as the technology has become more widespread. While it is still true that desktop publishing does not always produce the very best quality documents, the software now uses sophisticated formatting methods (better hyphenation and spacing, use of kerning, etc.), and the laser printers provide significantly better typographic quality. Where quality is particularly important, it is now common for laser printer output to be used for proofing and for typeset output produced from the computer file to be produced for the final product.

Page and Document Layout

It is convenient to classify desktop publishing software into two main types.

Page-layout packages are intended primarily for short documents that have a complex page design, such as newspapers, posters, and leaflets. These packages provide sophisticated facilities for page design and manipulation, but often have limited facilities for entering and editing text and other types of content. They typically rely on importing the document content from other software packages, such as word processors (*q.v.*), spreadsheets (*q.v.*), and drawing packages.

Document-layout packages are intended primarily for producing longer documents, such as technical manuals, journals, and books. These packages are likely to provide better built-in facilities for creating document content and for dealing with niceties, such as producing an index or table of contents. A document layout package is also effectively a word processor and a simple graphics editor.

A summary of the facilities available in typical desktop publishing software packages is given in the following sections. There is no hard-and-fast dividing line between the two types of packages, but the balance of the features varies. The page-layout packages concentrate more on flexible page design and also include provision for importing items prepared by other software, while the document-layout packages provide more built-in facilities for editing and dealing with continuous text.

The popularity of desktop publishing has produced a flood of books, especially on the more popular page-layout packages. Examples of widely used page-layout packages are Ventura Publisher (Van Engelen, 1989) and Aldus PageMaker (Matthews, 1990). Examples of document-layout packages are Interleaf Publisher and FrameMaker.

Page Design

Users typically design a page by defining rectangular areas within it to contain text or graphics. These areas are usually known as *frames*. Once users have

FIG. 1.   A typical desktop publishing system.

defined a frame, they can fill it with text or graphics, edit its contents, move it around on the page, or change its size. Different page designs can be created by placing frames corresponding to single or multiple-column text and setting aside different areas of the pages for illustrations.

In order to simplify the overall document design, a *master page* facility is usually provided. A master page contains the frames that are to appear in the same place on all pages in the document. Items like company logos, page numbers, and page headers and footers are typically dealt with in this way. Individual pages are designed by adding extra frames to the master page.

Accurate positioning of frames is essential in page design, so users are provided with simple tools to help with the positioning of frames interactively. Examples of positioning tools are:

- *Rulers*—shown across the top and down the sides of pages.
- *Grids*—shown across the whole page area.
- *Guidelines or Crosshairs*—one horizontal and one vertical line that may be positioned across the page area.

Users draw and position frames approximately by hand, and can then have them positioned and sized accurately by asking for their edges to be "snapped" to the nearest line or ruler marking. Another, less flexible method of designing pages is to use style-sheets (see *Styles* section). This method is more likely to be used by document-layout packages.

Text Handling Desktop publishing software provides all the normal hyphenation, justification, kerning, and widow and orphan control capabilities needed for text formatting. It also gives access to a wide range of character fonts and sizes and allows fine control of spacing. Several typefaces are generally available, in sizes ranging from 4-point to over 100-point at intervals of half a point or less. Users can choose any type and size and can also control the leading (spacing between lines) and tracking (spacing between words and characters) of text. Easy interactive control of these features allows users to manipulate fine details of the layout and to ensure that headlines or running text look attractive and fit comfortably into the frames provided.

Simple text editing facilities for inserting and deleting text are provided, together with some form of cut-and-paste, for moving blocks of text to different positions in the document. These may be supplemented by a variety of more complex features, like search-and-replace or a spelling checker (*q.v.*). Page-layout packages are likely to accept text prepared by a wide variety of word processors, while document-layout packages are more likely to deal with index entries, cross-references, and change-bars. Document-layout packages may also provide some help with the problems of multiple versions and multiple authors.

Styles Detailed control of the typographic and formatting requirements of text can become a tedious chore when there are so many different possibilities. To help users with this, most desktop publishing software allows *styles* or *properties* to be used. Different document constituents can be named and have particular styles attached to them. Thus, there may be different styles to cover headings, several levels of sections, and a variety of paragraph types. The styles define details of font, size, spacing, and margins, and may also include information on automatic numbering of the constituents.

To change the style of a constituent, the user calls up a style-sheet in a separate window on the screen. This shows all the options available and their current settings. These can be edited interactively, and any changes are made automatically to all occurrences of that constituent in the document. Fig. 2 shows a simple example of a style-sheet.

Styles are a great help to users in minimizing the amount of work needed and in ensuring good and consistent document layout. Libraries of standard styles are usually supplied, covering a wide variety of needs. Users without training in document design can simply select the styles they require. More experienced designers can either make minor changes to the styles in the library or create their own.

Many criticisms of documents produced by desktop publishing concern poor design and are the result of allowing users without design skills to have easy access to a wide variety of typographic facilities. The provision of styles created by experienced designers has helped to minimize this problem and also to ensure that organizations can impose their own "house-style." Problems of poor design have lead to a number of books on design for desktop publishing (Ziegfeld and Tarp, 1989; Black, 1990).

Graphics, Tables, and Equations All desktop publishing software provides simple built-in drawing facilities for lines, rectangles, and circles. Further facilities for curves, patterns, and borders may also be provided, and text may be wrapped around the graphics. In some cases, text may only wrap around graphics in a rectangular frame; in others it may be possible for text to wrap around an irregular shape within a frame. There may also be ways of "anchoring" graphics, either to a particular piece of text or to a position on a page.

Graphics and images created by other software tools can generally be imported, and facilities for scaling or cropping the graphics to fit frames are provided. A wide variety of digitized pictures called *clip-art* are sold commercially for importation into desktop publishing software. Some level of support for color is given in page-layout packages, while document-layout packages are more likely to include built-in facilities for producing tables, business graphics (bar charts, pie charts, etc.), and mathematical equations.

Printing Facilities High-quality output demands, as an absolute minimum, the availability of a laser printer operating at 300 dots-per-inch. For top quality output, a

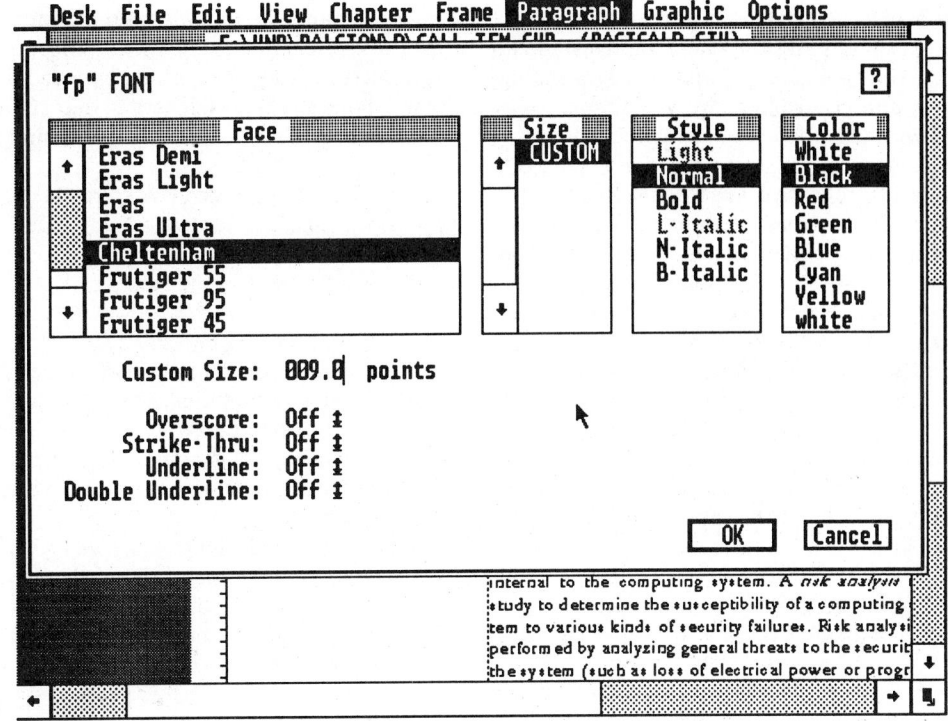

Desk File Edit View Chapter Frame **Paragraph** Graphic Options

FIG. 2.   A simple example of a style-sheet.

typesetter operating at 1000 dots-per-inch or more is required. Desktop publishing relies heavily on the use of the PostScript (q.v.) page description language (Adobe, 1985), which can be used to drive a variety of laser printers and typesetters and has all the necessary facilities needed to cope with complex text, graphics, and images. The improvement in quality of documents produced by desktop publishing packages is largely due to the dramatic improvement in digital typography (Rubinstein, 1988), which has been fueled by PostScript, the increased use of laser printers, and the popularity of desktop publishing itself.

Future Developments   Desktop publishing is now firmly established as an effective method of producing both simple and complex documents. Advances in digital typography and word processing have already found their way into desktop publishing, and advances in handling structured documents (and perhaps some elements of hypertext (q.v.) are likely to follow. One area certain to have a significant effect is the current trend towards "active documents," where document elements can have processing methods attached to them. Thus, a document element can interrogate a database and automatically include the latest version of some data, or it can send some data to another piece of software and include the processed results in the document. An active document is a means of accessing information, as well as presenting information.

References

1985. Adobe Systems Incorporated. *PostScript Language Reference Manual*. Reading, MA: Addison-Wesley.

1988. Rubinstein, R. *Digital Typography: An Introduction to Type and Composition for Computer System Design*. Reading, MA: Addison-Wesley.

1989. Van Engelen, W. *Getting Started with Xerox Ventura Publisher 2.0*. Reading, MA: Addison-Wesley.

1989. Ziegfeld R. and Tarp, J. *Desktop Publishing for the Writer: Designing, Writing, and Developing*. Los Alamitos, CA: IEEE Computer Society Press.

1990. Black, A. *Typefaces for Desktop Publishing*. London: ADT Press.

1990. Borman, J. L. *Desktop Publishing Sourcebook: Fonts and Clip-art for the IBM-PC and Compatibles*. Rocklin, CA: Prima Publishing Co.

1990. Matthews, M. S. *PageMaker 4 for the Macintosh Made Easy*. New York: Osborne/McGraw-Hill.

HEATHER BROWN

DEVICE DRIVER.   *See* DRIVER.

DIAGNOSTIC

For articles on related subjects *see* DEBUGGING; and ERRORS.

Diagnostics help determine whether there are hardware faults in a computer or errors in user programs.

Hardware diagnostics are programs designed to determine whether the components of a computer are operating properly. Circuit components are electronically exercised individually and in groups to try to induce failures. When a failure is detected, the location of the faulty element is printed and the maintenance staff can repair or replace the element. Diagnostics may test communication lines and controllers. Microcomputers may be constructed with diagnostics stored in the ROM.

Hardware diagnostic programs are run as part of a regular schedule of preventive maintenance and in the event of a failure. If a serious hardware failure has occurred, the diagnostic program may fail to operate properly, and may be useless in locating the difficulty.

Increasingly, hardware diagnostics take the form of *microdiagnostics*. A microdiagnostic program is a microprogram that tests a specific hardware component such as a bus (*q.v.*) or storage location. Microdiagnostics often provide more accurate location of a fault than hardware diagnostics written in machine language because of the addressability of individual components under microprogramming. Furthermore, these diagnostic programs are so fast that preventive maintenance testing may be interspersed transparently with other processing. Microdiagnostics, consequently, have furthered the development of self-diagnosing and self-repairing computers.

Diagnostic messages emitted by software are the error messages produced by compilers, utilities, and operating system software. These messages are designed to give programmers an indication of where their programs are at fault. Diagnostic messages at compile time may only be warnings to the programmer, or they may indicate invalid syntax, which prohibits execution. A severity level indicator is often included in the diagnostic message.

Execution-time diagnostic messages are produced by the operating system or an execution-time monitor. These messages indicate attempts to perform illegal operations, such as dividing by zero, taking the square root of a negative number, illegal operation codes, illegal address references, and so on. The diagnostic message may be followed by program termination.

Finally, application programs may produce diagnostics when erroneous data is read. The creator of the application program has complete control over these diagnostic messages and the action taken.

Diagnostic messages should avoid negative tones and be non-threatening, specific, and constructive. Instead of just pointing out what is wrong, they should also tell the user what to do to set things right.

BEN SHNEIDERMAN

DICTIONARIES, COMPUTERIZED

For articles on related subjects *see* NATURAL LANGUAGE PROCESSING; SPELLING CHECKER; and WORD PROCESSING.

A dictionary is a list of words and their corresponding definitions. Many dictionaries of natural language include additional information, such as the pronunciation, part of speech, and etymology of each word. A *computerized dictionary* is a dictionary in electronic form, suitable for searching (*q.v.*) by computer programs.

The simplest computerized dictionaries are ordered lists of correctly-spelled words. These lists are used in computerized text processing by word processors or as stand-alone spelling checkers to detect and correct spelling mistakes. Errors are caught by using simple pattern-matching algorithms.

Spelling checkers can catch mistakes only on a word-by-word basis. The sentence

"You can where a blue suit."

will pass the spelling checker's scrutiny, even though the word "where" is used in place of "wear." By adding information to the dictionaries, grammar and vocabulary mistakes can be caught as well. The grammar checker must use this information in conjunction with a word's context and sophisticated heuristics (*q.v.*) describing the rules of the language.

Computerized dictionaries can also be used as an online replacement for a printed dictionary. The human user can view words and their definitions on a screen. Given an approximate or phonetic spelling, the computer can search the dictionary for the desired word. Keywords can also be used to search for lists of synonyms, so as to form an electronic *thesaurus*, an integral part of most full-featured word processors.

Specialized dictionaries are suited to other tasks. A phonetic dictionary is used for voice synthesis, allowing the computer to read text aloud to a user. Historical dictionaries, which trace the creation and use of words, are used for language research. Encyclopedic dictionaries include sound and pictures in examples accompanying word definitions. Computerized dictionaries can also be used to derive and produce printed dictionaries, using electronic typesetting.

The most extensive dictionary computerization to date has been that of the Oxford English Dictionary (OED). The OED is widely regarded as the most comprehensive record of the English language. The first printed version was published in 12 volumes between 1884 and 1933 by the Oxford University Press (OUP). Four volumes of supplementary word definitions and changes were added between 1972 and 1986. In total, the 16 volumes contain close to 306,000 main entries. In 1984, the OUP decided to computerize the dictionary in preparation for the release of the second edition of the OED.

After the text of the original sixteen volumes was transferred into electronic form (a process that took a large group of typists and proofreaders well over a year), the OUP combined its efforts with IBM in the United Kingdom to integrate and add to the dictionary's auxiliary data. The University of Waterloo (Waterloo, Ontario, Canada) was responsible for creating the software to search the dictionary. The computerized OED was then used to prepare a new printed version, the 20-volume second edition, first released in March of 1989.

The computerized OED is a large, text-dominated database, one of a class that researchers have only recently begun to tackle. At the time of this writing, the text of the OED, together with tagging information denoting its structure, totals close to 600 megabytes in size. Indexing information to allow searches by any word or phrase requires another 300 megabytes of storage. Though the OUP plans to release the second edition on CD-ROM (*q.v.*) at some later date, currently the computerized OED is of use mostly to the OUP and university researchers.

ERIC GIGUERE

DIFFERENCE ENGINE

For articles on related subjects *see* ANALYTICAL ENGINE; BABBAGE, CHARLES; and DIGITAL COMPUTERS: HISTORY: ORIGINS.

A *difference engine* is a machine that automates the calculation of mathematical tables. Any short section of a mathematical function, such as a sine, can be approximated by a polynomial, the degree or complexity of which is determined by the accuracy required in the tables. Using the method of finite differences, the tabulation of these polynomials can be reduced to the operation of repeated addition of differences only.

The most famous attempt to mechanize this process was made by Charles Babbage in the 1820s. Frustrated by the errors made by human calculators preparing tables for him, Babbage remarked to the astronomer John Herschel, "I wish to God these calculations had been executed by steam," to which Herschel replied "It is quite possible." Inspired by this suggestion, Babbage produced a small demonstration model of a difference engine by mid-1822. Unfortunately, nothing of this model has survived, but it appears to have included six digits and to have tabulated the polynomial $x^2 + x + 41$ (whose values for integer values of x from 1 to 40 are prime numbers).

With the aid of intermittent support from the British government, Babbage then embarked on the construction of a much more extensive machine, intended to provide six orders of differences, each of 18 digits. Babbage realized that the printing of tables using movable type was as great a source of error as the calculations themselves. He therefore included in the difference engine a mechanism for automatic preparation of stereotype printing plates.

The layout of a printed page of tables is complex. Babbage made provision for the difference engine to lay out tables in either columns or rows, with spaces of variable width to guide the eye of the reader and to round off automatically all printed values. His most elaborate mechanism even allowed for the printing of only the least significant digits of each table entry—the leading digits were printed only for the first entry on each line and then only if these digits had changed from the line before.

In the design of this printing mechanism, Babbage gained valuable experience in the mechanization of complex and conditional sequences of operation. He became adept in overlapping operations in various parts of the machine, including the pipelining of the difference tabulation itself. He devised means by which the control itself did not have to transmit power to the working mechanism, but simply made connections to the main power

source. An ingenious system of "lockings" made good any lost motion or backlash in the mechanisms and ensured that the machine could not become accidently deranged and produce incorrect values. All of these ideas were essential to the subsequent rapid development of the analytical engine by Babbage in the 1830s.

The difference engine was never built. Contrary to a widely-held belief, this was not due to an inability of the mechanical technology of the day to cope with the demands of Babbage's machine. The demonstration piece, which is still in excellent working order, gives the lie to that suggestion, though the workmanship was expensive—possibly excessively so. Rather, the difficulties lay in social changes—Babbage's failure to cope with either the rapidly changing role of leading engineers or with a government that had never previously directly funded research and was itself entering an era of great social flux.

Work on Difference Engine no. 1 ceased in 1833. In 1847 Babbage produced a design for a Difference Engine no. 2, whose simpler design took advantage of ideas evolved for the analytical engine.

In the 1850s, Georg and Edvard Scheutz of Sweden built a difference engine inspired by Babbage's work, but this lacked Babbage's mechanical refinements and never worked reliably. Later nineteenth century designs by Wiberg in Sweden and Grant in the U.S.A. fared little better. In the 1930s, L. J. Comrie of the British Nautical Almanac Office adopted Burroughs and National Cash Register accounting machines for use as difference engines. These were used mainly for checking proofs of tables by applying the difference method in reverse. By then, the sub-tabulation task for which Babbage's difference engines were designed was not seen to be the major problem in the preparation of mathematical tables.

In 1991 the Science Museum in London completed the construction of a working Difference Engine No. 2 based on Babbage's drawings (Fig. 1). The machine is 10 feet long, 6 feet high, 18 inches deep and has 4,000 parts machined using modern tools but to an accuracy no greater than Babbage could have achieved.

FIG. 1.   A working difference engine.

References

1987. Bromley, A. G. "The Evolution of Babbage's Calculating Engines," *Annals of the History of Computing*, Vol. 9, pp. 113–136.

1990. Bromley, A. G. "Difference and Analytical Engines," in Aspray, W. (Ed.), *Computing Before Computers*. University of Iowa State Press.

ALLAN G. BROMLEY

DIFFERENTIAL ANALYZER

For articles on related subjects *see* ANALOG COMPUTER; BUSH, VANNEVAR; DIGITAL COMPUTERS: HISTORY: EARLY; and HARTREE, DOUGLAS.

In a paper published in the *Journal of the Franklin Institute* in 1931, Vannevar Bush described a machine (Fig. 1) that had been constructed under his direction at M.I.T. for the purpose of solving ordinary differential equations. He christened the machine a *differential analyzer*. This was what would now be called an "analog" computer, and was based on the use of mechanical integrators that could be interconnected in any desired manner. The integrator was in essence a variable-speed gear, and took the form of a rotating horizontal disk on which a small knife-edged wheel rested. The wheel was driven by friction, and the gear ratio was altered by varying the distance of the wheel from the axis of rotation of the disk. The principle is illustrated in Fig. 2.

The use of mechanical integrators for solving differential equations had been suggested by Kelvin, and various special-purpose integrating devices were constructed at various times. Bush's differential analyzer was, however, the first device of sufficiently general application to meet a genuine need, and in the period immediately before and during World War II quite a number of these devices were constructed. The one shown in Fig. 4 was installed at the Mathematical Laboratory in Cambridge, England.

In order to make a practical device, it is necessary to have some means of amplifying the small amount of torque available from the rotating wheel. Bush used a torque amplifier, working on the principle of the ship's

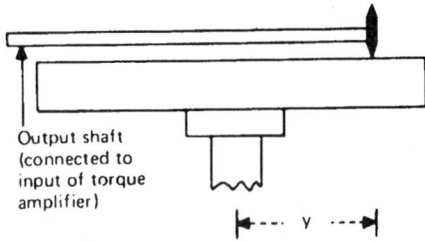

FIG. 2. Wheel and disk integrator. If the disk turns through an angle proportional to *x*, the output shaft turns through an angle proportional to $\int y\, dx$.

capstan, but adapting it for continuous rotation. Fig. 3 is taken from his report (1931) and sufficiently indicates the principle. The friction drums are rotated in opposite directions by a continuously running motor of sufficient power. When the input shaft is turned, one of the cords attached to the input arm begins to tighten on the friction drum round which it is wrapped. Which cord tightens depends on the direction of rotation of the input shaft. A very small tightening, and hence a very small tension in the end of the cord attached to the input arm, is sufficient, in view of the friction of the rotating drum, to produce a large tension in the end attached to the output arm. A small torque applied to the input shaft is thus capable of producing a much larger torque in the output shaft.

The integrators and torque amplifiers can be clearly seen in Fig. 4, together with the system of shafting used for effecting the connections. Changing the problem was a job for someone who did not mind hands covered in oil. The output table on which the results were plotted directly in graphical form can be seen in Fig. 4, which also shows a number of similar tables that were used for input, an operator being employed to turn a handle so that a cursor followed a curve. It is a comment on the primitive state of automatic control in the period in question that automatic curve-following devices were not provided until later. The accuracy attainable in a single integrator was about one part in three thousand, but of course a lower accuracy was to be expected in the solution.

FIG. 1. Vannevar Bush shown with the M.I.T. differential analyzer.

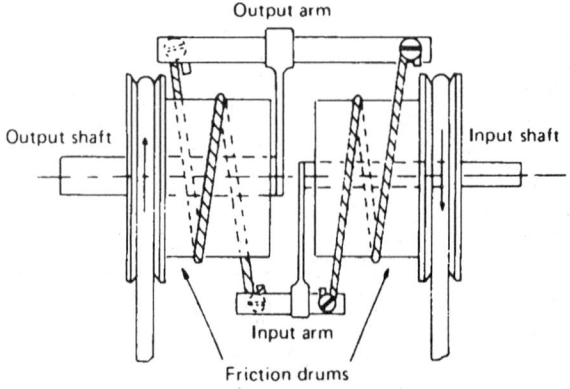

FIG. 3. Principle of torque amplifier. (*Courtesy of Journal of the Franklin Institute.*)

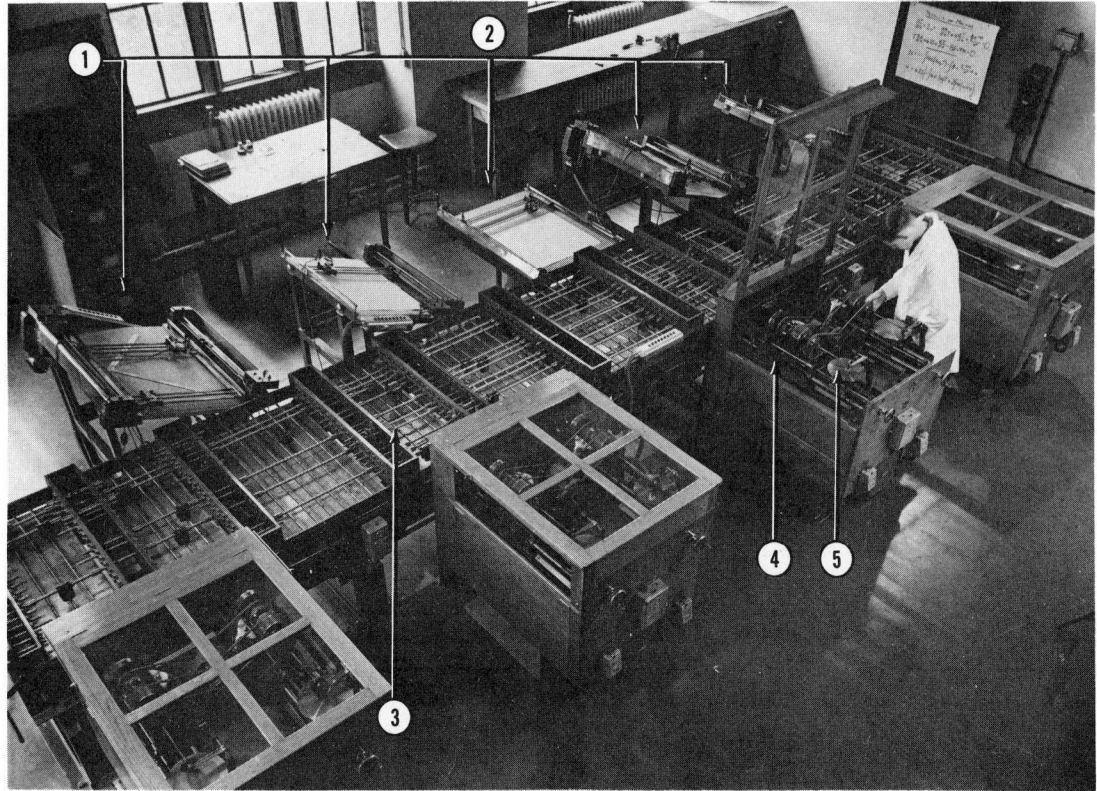

| 1 Input table | 3 Shafts and gears used | 4 Torque amplifier |
| 2 Output table | for interconnection | 5 Integrator disk |

FIG. 4.   The differential analyzer system, showing integrators, torque amplifiers, and shafting.

Fig. 5 shows the notation that was used for an integrator and Fig. 6 shows how two integrators could be interconnected to solve a simple differential equation. It was not difficult to arrive at a diagram such as Fig. 6, even for a complicated equation, but working out the gear ratios required was a distinctly tedious task calling for some experience, particularly as accuracy required that full use should be made of the available range of integrator motion.

In 1945, Bush and S. H. Caldwell described a new differential analyzer in which interconnection between the integrators was effected electrically instead of mechanically. However, during the decade that followed, competition from electronic analog computers and from digital computers began to build up, and, although the new machine ran for a number of years at M.I.T., by 1955 the mechanical differential analyzer was already obsolete.

Digital Differential Analyzer This device is based on the use of a *rate multiplier* as an integrator. In a rate multiplier, a constant quantity y is held in a register and, on the receipt of an input pulse, is added to the number standing in an accumulator. If input pulses arrive at a rate R, overflow pulses will emerge from the most significant end of the accumulator at a rate proportional to yR. If y now varies and if input pulses arrive whenever a certain other variable x increases by δx, the number of output pulses emerging is proportion to $\Sigma\, y\, \delta x$ or, approximately to $\int y\, dx$. Thus, the device serves as an integrator. Normally, δx is equal to one unit in the least significant place, and continuously updated values of the variable x can be obtained by feeding the pulses into an accumulator.

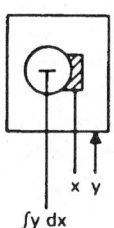

FIG. 5.   Schematic notation for an integrator.

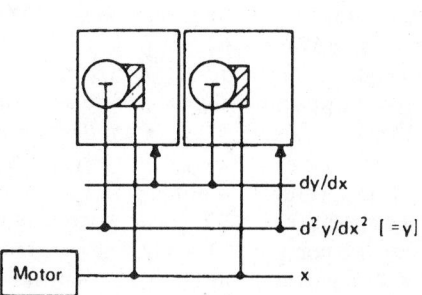

FIG. 6.   Setup for solving the equation $d^2y/dx^2 = y$.

The first digital differential analyzer was the MAD-DIDA developed in 1949 at the Northrop Aircraft Corporation. It had 44 integrators implemented using a magnetic drum for storage, the addition being done serially. There were six tracks in all on the drum, one being used for synchronizing purposes. The problem was specified by writing an appropriate pattern of bits onto one of the tracks. Compared with the digital computers then being built, the MADDIDA was on an impressively small scale. It lost some of its simplicity, however, when adequate input and output devices were added, and in the end competition from general-purpose digital computers proved too much for it. The MADDIDA and its descendants did not, therefore, have the bright future in scientific computation that was predicted for them. However, digital differential analyzers of a simple kind continue to have a place in certain control applications.

References

1931. Bush, V. *J. Frank. Inst.* **212**: 447.
1945. Bush, V. and Caldwell, S. H. *J. Frank. Inst.* **240**: 255.
1947. Crank, J. *The Differential Analyser.* London: Longmans, Green and Co.
1962. Huskey, H. D., and Korn, G. A. *Computer Handbook.* New York: McGraw-Hill.

MAURICE V. WILKES

DIGITAL COMPUTERS

GENERAL PRINCIPLES

For articles on related subjects *see* ANALOG COMPUTER; ARITHMETIC-LOGIC UNIT; CENTRAL PROCESSING UNIT; COMPUTER ARCHITECTURE; GENERATIONS, COMPUTER; HYBRID COMPUTER; MACHINE AND ASSEMBLY LANGUAGE PROGRAMMING; MEMORY; MICROPROCESSORS AND MICROCOMPUTERS; MINICOMPUTERS; PERSONAL COMPUTING; SUPERCOMPUTERS; and WORKSTATION.

A *digital computer* is a machine that will accept data and information presented to it in its required form, carry out arithmetic and logical operations on this raw material, and then supply the required results in an acceptable form. The resulting information (output) produced by these operations is entirely dependent upon the accepted information (input). Thus, correct and complete answers cannot be obtained unless correct and sufficient input data has been provided.

The sequence of the operations required to produce the desired output must be accurately determined and specified by people known as system designers (or analysts) and programmers (*q.v.*). The system designer produces a clear specification of the task to be undertaken, including elements such as clerical processing, which do not involve the computer directly. The programmer prepares the detailed set of instructions that the computer will follow automatically so as to process the work from input to output.

Computer Characteristics

The main characteristics of the computer are that it is automatic, general purpose, electronic, and digital.

Automatic   We assume that a machine is automatic if it works by itself without human intervention. But this is not the whole story. Computers are machines and have no will of their own; they cannot start themselves; they cannot go out and find their own problems and solutions. They have to be instructed. They are, however, automatic, in that once started on a job, they will carry on until it is finished, normally without human assistance.

A computer works from a program of *coded* instructions that specify exactly how a particular job is to be done. While the job is in progress, the program is *stored* in the computer, and the parts of the instructions are obeyed. As soon as one instruction is completed, the next is obeyed automatically.

By contrast, a hand-held calculator can be described as semi-automatic. The user sets up the required numbers on a keyboard and has to press a key (for example, add or multiply) to initiate each individual arithmetic operation. Today's calculators can often carry out complex arithmetic operations at the touch of a single key, but the machine is still semi-automatic.

Because a computer does not need to stop between single operations, it can take full advantage of the high-speed components that enable it to add, subtract, and perform other individual operations in millionths of a second, or even faster.

An important corollary of the automaticity of the computer is that its program has to be complete. If there is no provision for intervention by the human operator, the program must be written to provide for all possible eventualities, however rare.

General Purpose   Computers (and hand-held calculators) are *general-purpose* machines. In other words, a computer can do any job that its programmer can break down into suitable basic operations. Put a payroll program into a computer and you make it, for the time being, a special-purpose payroll machine. Replace the program by one for inverting a matrix, and you make the computer temporarily a special-purpose mathematical machine.

Electronic   The word *electronic* refers to the information processing components of the machine. It is the nature of the electronic components that make possible the very high speeds of individual operations in modern computers.

The history of electronic digital computers distinguishes a number of "generations" defined by the nature of the electronic components most prevalent in each. Thus, the first generation made extensive use of vacuum tubes, the second generation used discrete transistors, and the third used integrated circuits. There is little agreement about whether we are now on the fourth or fifth generation, or even at some midway point, as we have moved through progressively higher degrees of integration in our circuits. (*See* GENERATIONS, COMPUTER.)

Most computer users need no special knowledge of electronics, and the major practical distinctions between the generations—as far as they are concerned—are the reductions in size for a given power, the rapid increases in speed, and, above all, a substantial and continuous fall in the cost of computing.

Digital A computer may be either *digital* or *analog*. The two types do have some principles in common, but they employ different types of data representations and are, in general, suited to different kinds of work. Digital computers are so called because they work with *numbers* in the form of separate discrete digits. More precisely, they work with information that is in digital or character form, including alphabetic and other symbols as well as numbers.

In a digital machine, the data, whether numbers, letters, or other symbols, is represented in digital form. An analog computer, on the other hand, may be said to deal with a "model" of the problem, in which the variables are represented by continuous physical quantities, such as angular position and voltage. The decimal numbers 136 and 435, for instance, might be represented by 1.36 volts and 4.35 volts. Using familiar devices, we could say that a slide rule is an analog device, because numbers are represented by a linear length. The abacus, on the other hand, is a digital device, because movable counters are used for calculating.

Digital computers differ from analog computers much as counting differs in principle from measuring. Both types of machines employ electric currents, or signals, but in the analog system, a number is represented by the magnitude (e.g. voltage) of a signal, whereas, in a digital computer, it is not the magnitude of signals that is important, but rather the number of them, or their presence or absence in particular positions. Analog computers tend to be special-purpose machines designed for some specific scientific or technical application. They are frequently found useful in engineering design for such things as atomic power stations, chemical plants, and aircraft. In commercial and administrative data processing and for mathematical computation, we are concerned almost exclusively with digital computers.

Main Units Only very rarely does a computer have a unique, fixed specification. Normally, it is better described as a computer system, consisting of a selection from a wide variety of units appropriate to meet a defined need. The principal groupings of these units commonly follow the pattern shown in Fig. 1 and are defined as follows:

1. *Input units*—An input unit accepts the data, the raw material that a computer uses, communicated from outside. It is the actual means by

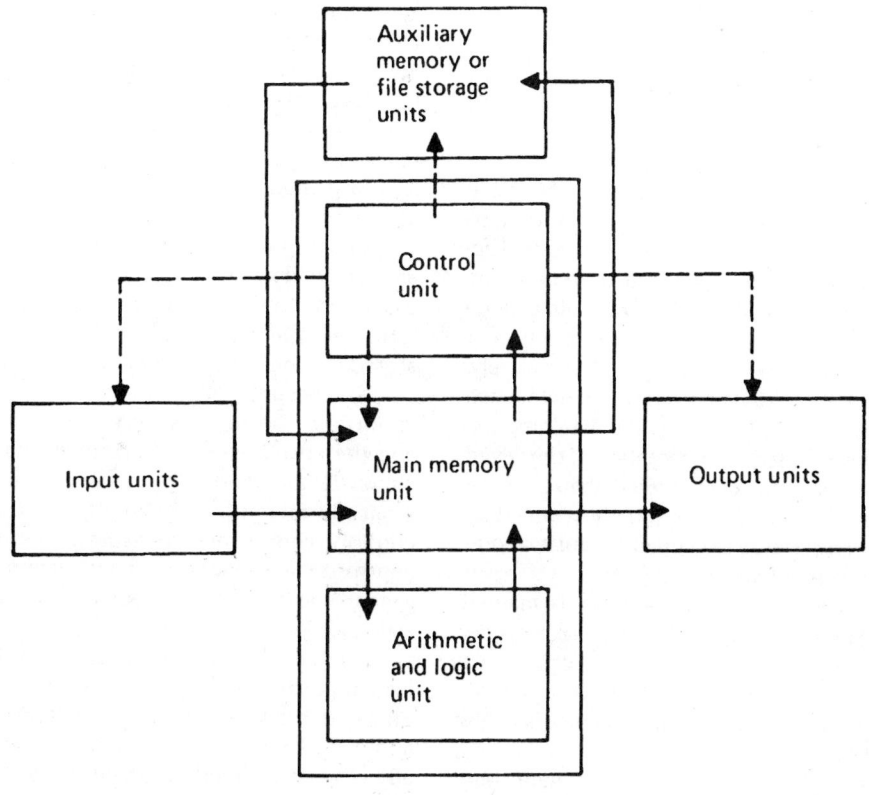

Legend:

⎯⎯→ Flow of information

- - - → Control links

FIG. 1. Central processing unit. Grouping of computer components.

which information is converted into electronic pulses, which are then fed into the machine's memory.

2. *Control unit*—The directing force of the computer, the automatic operator, is the control unit. It provides the means of communication within the machine, by moving, advancing, or transferring information. It switches and integrates the various units into a whole system.

3. *Main memory unit*—All information stored in the main memory unit is "remembered" and made available to other units as required, under the direction of the control unit.

4. *Arithmetic-logic unit*—This unit performs the four arithmetic operations of add, subtract, multiply, and divide. By determining whether one number is larger than another, whether it is zero or whether it is positive or negative, it is said to have logical abilities; i.e. it can make logical decisions. In addition, it can perform other strictly logical (Boolean) operations, such as **and** and **or**.

5. *Output units*—After information is processed, an output unit communicates it to the outside world. When needed, the results are recalled from memory under the direction of the control unit and presented by the output units in an appropriate form. A wide variety of output devices is available.

6. *File storage units*—These units store information required for reference.

We will now consider each of these main units in some detail.

Input Input devices accept data from the world outside the computer and transfer it in suitably coded form into the memory, a process frequently described as *data capture*. A very high proportion of input data is prepared by the operation of a typewriter-like keyboard. This may be linked directly to the computer either from an adjacent room or remotely over a telephone line. Alternatively, there may be some intermediate carrier of the data, such as magnetic tape or disks. In each case, the data preparation device produces a coded representation of the keyed data, which is recorded on the carrier medium in the form of magnetized blips. These are subsequently scanned by an appropriate reading device and signals transferred at high speed into the computer's memory.

A data preparation process that depends on a manual typing operation is clearly expensive and error-prone. Since most original data appears as ink on paper, devices that can read such data automatically have a great attraction and *document readers* (*scanners*) play an increasingly important part in the input process.

These readers are capable of feeding documents one by one and scanning numbers or letters printed in suitable type fonts. The first readers, developed for handling checks, read characters printed along the bottom of the check in a magnetized ink. When the characters pass the reading mechanism of the input unit, the shape of the magnetic field produced by each character is assessed by the reader and the character identified. Without such readers, the processing of today's enormous volumes of checks would be quite impracticable.

Today, there are many optical readers capable of recognizing the shape of a character from its reflected light in much the same way as humans do. They use type fonts that appear quite normal to us and, therefore, serve both the needs of people and computers. There are also readers that scan the bar codes increasingly found on packages in supermarkets and that, therefore, greatly speed up the check-out procedures (*see* UNIVERSAL PRODUCT CODE).

Some progress has also been made with voice recognition equipment that allows computers to recognize the human voice over a limited repertoire of input messages. (*See* SPEECH RECOGNITION AND SYNTHESIS.)

Central Processing Unit (CPU) The central processing unit is the focal point of the computer system. It receives data from input units and file storage units, carries out a variety of arithmetic and logical operations on this data, and transmits results to output and file units. It is traditional, and still convenient, to consider the central processor as made up of three principal parts (not necessarily easily identifiable physically): (1) the memory; (2) the arithmetic-logic unit; and (3) the control unit.

The Memory The *memory* (or *main memory*, as it is sometimes called, to distinguish it from file storage or auxiliary memory) is able to hold, for as long as desired, coded representations of numbers and letters in convenient groupings; each group is held in a uniquely addressable part of the memory, from which it can be transferred on demand. The memory may be figuratively described as a large number of pigeonholes, each identifiable by a serial number that in effect is its address.

One purpose of the memory is to hold data. Numbers and letters flow into it from input, are sent for arithmetic processing to the arithmetic unit from which the results return to the memory, and the output information is stored in it before transfer to an output unit.

The access time to data in the internal memory is important. The memory is a vital crossroad in processing, and the very high-speed arithmetic facilities of the machine demand virtually instantaneous access to data. Typically, memories can supply requested data in an incredibly short time, measured in microseconds (millionths of a second) or nanoseconds (billionths of a second); in fact, their speed is usually from 8 μs down to 200 ns or less.

The second use of the memory is to hold all the instructions of the program required to carry out a job. These instructions are normally coded in numeric form and can be read into the memory from magnetic disk or any other input medium. They remain in memory indefinitely unless they are deliberately erased.

The arithmetic-logic unit (ALU) is obviously one of the simplest parts of the machine to understand. It is that part where actual arithmetic operations are carried out. It in quite common to find a machine that can add a pair of eight-digit numbers in about one millionth of a second, and there are models that can do the job in as little as one ten-billionth of a second.

The term *logic* is used here to describe a non-arithmetic facility of the unit; e.g. an ability to differentiate between positive and negative numbers, and, as a result, to take alternative paths in the program. A simple example will illustrate its value.

In stock control, it is usual to compare a newly calculated stock balance with the preset minimum or danger level, to determine if reordering is necessary. If the "minimum" is subtracted from the "balance," then a positive (excess) result indicates that all is well; a negative result (a shortage) shows a need to reorder. In this latter case only, we can arrange for the machine to "jump to" (i.e. transfer operational control to) a part of the program that prints out reordering information on the printer for management action. If all is well, we need print nothing—one way in which the computer itself can reduce paperwork. This apparently simple facility is of fundamental significance, and a typical program of a few thousand instructions will contain many of the "test and jump to another phase of the program if negative" types of instruction.

The arithmetic and logic unit consists of one or a number of *registers* (each made up of electronic circuits), which may be termed *accumulators*. To add a number stored in address 113 of the memory to that stored in address 207, first the contents of address 113 are read into an accumulator and then the contents of address 207 are added to that accumulator. The answer is then copied to another address in memory, thereby leaving the accumulator free for the next operation.

The Control Unit This part of the central processor functions so as to cause the whole machine to operate according to the instructions in the program. Instructions are normally transferred sequentially from the memory to the control unit, where each instruction is interpreted and the appropriate circuits are activated to "execute" the instruction. This strict sequence is broken, for example, when a "test and jump" type of instruction occurs and produces an exceptional result. There is then a transfer of control to a program step in a different part of the program, from which the sequential pattern continues until again broken.

The control unit of a computer contains special circuits known as *microprograms*. One of these corresponds to each type of elementary operation (and, therefore, to each type of instruction) in the computer repertoire. It is by the inclusion of a suitable microprogram that a given operation is "built" into the computer. *(See* MICROPROGRAMMING.)

Output The output devices of the computer enable it to communicate results to the outside world. Output devices fall into two main categories:

1. Those that produce output that is readily handled and understood by human beings (printers and display units).

2. Auxiliary storage devices, which hold data intended for further processing by machine (e.g. magnetic tapes, disks, and drums).

The first group contains a number of types of devices. The most obvious of these are printers, designed to produce results in the form of printing on paper.

Most printers in current use operate on the same basic principle as the typewriter, in which a character is printed through an impact of a typeface on an inked ribbon traversing the paper. There are, however, some printers that generate and print characters electronically.

Where the volume of printing is large, it is usual to use a *line printer*, one capable of producing a whole line of print at a time (usually from 120 to 160 characters). Such printers are capable of quite high speeds, typically up to 20 or more lines per second on a continuously fed roll of stationery. It is essential, of course, to have excellent paper-handling facilities to keep pace with such speeds. Such line printers are ideal for applications requiring voluminous end-results, such as payrolls, invoices, or inventory listings, but are too often used to print more than necessary.

The output device of choice when high print quality and graphics are important is the *laser printer*. The high resolution of such printers is based on xerographic principles similar to those used with photocopy machines. A modern laser printer is shown in Fig. 2.

A related device, which is quite commonplace, is the video display unit (VDU). This has a keyboard like a typewriter, but the printing mechanism is replaced by a television-like tube on which letters or digits can be projected. Compared with the typewriter, VDUs have the advantage of displaying a large amount of information at once (often, several hundred characters), and a fresh display of additional information can be generated very rapidly. On the other hand, since they cannot produce "hard copy" (i.e. a permanent record), they are best used in circumstances where an operator needs to examine a small quantity of transient output information that does not have to be printed.

FIG. 2. The HP Laserjet III printer from Hewlett-Packard Company. (Courtesy Hewlett-Packard.)

Increasingly, *personal computers* are being used instead of VDUs. Such computers have all the capabilities of a VDU plus the added advantage of local CPU processing power, which supplements that of the *host computer* with which it communicates. A typical personal computer is shown in Fig. 3.

Video display units or personal computers can also be used to display information in graphical form or in diagrams of moderate accuracy. Associated input techniques using a lightpen (a device that effectively draws lines electronically on the face of the tube) manipulate changes or additions to drawings and diagrams. Devices such as the lightpen are increasingly being used for computer-aided design in such fields as car body or electric-circuit design.

Where a permanent record of a graph or drawing is required, or where greater accuracy is needed, a graph-plotter can be attached to the computer and can produce intricate drawings on paper.

Results from one computer operation often need to be stored temporarily and then used as an input to a subsequent process. Magnetic tape (described in detail under *Storage Media*) is frequently used for this purpose. For example, process A may produce payroll information that will subsequently be used as input to process B for a labor cost analysis. Magnetic tape may also be produced as an intermediary to carry data to other machines being operated "off-line" (i.e. not directly linked to the computer). These could include numerically controlled machine tools, printers, graph plotters, typesetting machines, etc.

File Storage (Auxiliary Memory) There are relatively few applications of computers, particularly in the field of

FIG. 3. The HP Vectra OS/20 PC from Hewlett-Packard has a 32-bit, Intel 80386 microprocessor in a desktop system. It can be configured with up to 16 Mbytes of random-access memory. It has three mass-storage shelves and seven industry-standard expansion slots. (Courtesy Hewlett-Packard.)

business data processing where the only input is fresh, raw data. For example, in inventory control, the new data consists of stock issues and receipts, but data in file storage indicates the number of items left in stock calculated at last inventory and the average value of that stock. These files also include more static information about each item, such as its name, dimensions, batch order quantity, and supplier.

Thus, the computer must also have its "filing cabinets" (albeit electronic ones) if it is to be used in business applications. It is obvious that such file storage units must act as input and output units to the computer, and as they are of special and fundamental importance in these applications, they are treated here separately.

The three most important factors relating to any filing system, whether manual or electronic, are (1) its total capacity; (2) the speed of access to required information (i.e. how long it takes to find what is needed); and (3) the cost per unit of data. The two most commonly used media for holding computer files are magnetic tapes and magnetic disks. Each system has its advantages and disadvantages, and the choice depends on the particular circumstances; many installations indeed use both.

Magnetic tape holds records in a serial fashion in a way analogous to a domestic tape recorder. Thus, if the records are in no particular sequence, the user is forced to hunt backward and forward along the tape for any desired record. Although tape moves quite quickly on a computer tape unit (up to 12 feet or so per second), a reel of tape is usually 2,400 feet long and contains many thousands of records. Thus, minutes could easily elapse between the location of succeeding required records. It is obvious, therefore, that the records in a magnetic tape file must be held in some predetermined sequence, such as employee number or customer number sequence, and that the new data being input in order to bring the file up to date (to "update" the file) must also be in the same sequence.

When used for file storage, magnetic tape units are generally operated in pairs—one carrying the brought-forward or current file, which is read by the machine; the other, a new carry-forward or updated file recorded or "written" by the machine, which, in turn, will become the brought-forward file when the job is next run. (Unaffected items on the brought-forward tape are obviously copied unchanged onto the carried-forward tape.)

Magnetic tape units (or *decks*, or *transports*, or *stations*) differ widely in performance (and price), with reading and writing speeds varying from about 10,000 characters per second through a common speed of about 60,000 characters per second to a maximum speed of over 100,000 characters per second. Obviously, a tape system offers virtually unlimited file capacity at low cost per record, but it is not an acceptable medium when immediate random access is required to every item in the file.

There are two basic forms of a mainframe *disk* unit: In one the disks are usually large (over 3 feet in diameter) and are not removable from the unit; in the other, the "removable disk," or *disk pack*, system the disks are smaller (about 20 inches in diameter) and are demountable, usually in sets of 6 to 12. This is analogous to putting six phonograph records on a player that is equipped with one pickup for each of the surfaces of the set. (Computers can "play" their disks on both sides without inverting them).

Unlike the phonograph record, which has one track spiraling from the periphery toward the center, the computer disk has a large number of concentric tracks on its surface, each capable of storing about 10,000 characters. The pick-up, or "recording head" can be moved radially across the disk surface to the desired track at very high speed. The total capacity of a set of six removable disks is usually about 60 million characters, and the recording head can move from one track to any other so quickly that direct access to any record at random can be obtained in about one-tenth of a second, or even less in some cases. For non-removable disk units, the capacity may be as large as 4 billion characters (four *gigabytes*). A typical modern hard disk system having a capacity of 767 megabytes is shown in Fig. 4.

Thus, disks offer the facility of processing data in random sequence without any undue delay in searching for a required item. However, their capacity is much more limited than magnetic tape and their cost is higher. In addition, the fact that essentially random access is possible means that, in contrast to magnetic tapes, data can be corrected or changed and the modified record can be put back on the disk in the same place that it originally occupied. One disadvantage is that the modified data could create an overflow problem, and then a way must be found to correct it.

A third type of disk is frequently used with small computers. This is the so-called *floppy disk (q.v.)*. It is somewhat like a small phonograph record, but is much thinner and very flexible. It doesn't operate to such fine tolerances as its bigger siblings and is much more robust—a floppy disk can easily be mailed in an envelope. A typical floppy disk has a storage capacity of about 1 million characters to which access can be made in about 100 milliseconds. Early floppies were 8 inches in diameter,

and then 5 1/4-inch floppies prospered for a while, but the current trend is to 3 1/2-inch diskettes stored in a solid protective case.

Personal computers also use *hard disks (q.v.)* that are similar to non-removable mainframe disks but much smaller in diameter, typically 5 1/4-inch. Capacities range from 20 MB to over 100 MB.

There are many facets to the problem of choosing between tape and disk for file storage. The simplest basis for choosing one over the other is that tape methods are in general cheaper, whereas disk systems offer greater speed and flexibility in the processing method, especially where the files must be frequently interrogated. Obviously, the choice depends on the application.

Another medium (although increasingly less important than tape or disk) used for file storage is the *magnetic drum*. Historically, it is interesting to note that, in early computers, a magnetic drum frequently provided the main memory. Its speed of access, however, was such that other processing units were frequently kept waiting for instructions and data, so it was replaced in favor by magnetic core or semiconductor stores.

However, this inherent limitation does not affect its use as a file store, now that drums of large capacity (up to 20 million characters and more) have been developed.

On a magnetic drum, the curved surface of a rapidly rotating cylinder is the recording medium. There are a large number of magnetic heads, each of which can read and write data on the drum. Each head is associated with a specific recording track that extends around the circumference of the drum. In many respects, the principles of operation and use of the magnetic drum are similar to those for the magnetic disk, but there are the following important differences.

1. Since there is usually a recording head for every track, no time is lost in the physical movement of heads to a required track.

FIG. 4. Seagate's WRENRUNNER 2-767MB, 5 1/4-inch hard disc drive; with an 11.9 msec. access time and a maximum data transfer rate of 3 megabytes per second. (Courtesy Seagate)

2. A typical drum rotates about three or four times as fast as a magnetic disk system, which means that less time is lost waiting for the required data to come around to the recording head. Since each track has its own recording head, the fast rotation means that drums have a much shorter access time than disks.

3. Drums are more expensive per record stored than are disks. Moreover, they are permanently attached and are not exchangeable.

There are a variety of other file storage devices, in addition to the more common ones discussed above (see CD-ROM). The struggle in many business applications is always to accommodate larger and larger files with an acceptable access time without paying too high a price.

Distributed Computing, Computer Networks

In the earliest days of the computer, its power was confined to the computer room. Bundles of work had to be physically brought to it and results collected. A vital step in releasing the power of the computer occurred when terminal devices, such as teletypes, were connected to the computer over telephone lines. The problems to be solved were with the physical connection of the communications equipment and the writing of very sophisticated computer programs to control and manage an ever-increasing number of terminal devices.

The development first of minicomputers and today of the microprocessor and microcomputer have made it possible to build more "intelligence" (or local computing power) into the remote terminal devices so that they have become capable of carrying out more complex operations. For example, magnetic tape, card, or document readers may be used at a distant point and results fed back for local printing (see FILE SERVER).

It is but a small step from this to the provision of computer facilities at the distant location so that many simple, routine tasks can be carried out locally and the communications facilities used either to feed results to the central installation or to make use of its greater power and wider facilities when necessary. It is then a further, relatively small step to conceive the idea of interconnecting a series of computers to form a network, passing work between themselves to be processed most economically where the most appropriate facilities are available. Again, the major obstacle was not just the physical interconnection, but also the management and control of the entire system both within the computers themselves and over the telecommunications systems. Such networks now exist on both national and international scales, frequently using satellite communication facilities, and have reached the point where a user may not know, and need not know, on which computer the work is actually being processed (see DISTRIBUTED SYSTEMS).

Microprocessors and Microcomputers

The foregoing applies in principle to all computer systems, however large or small. Under the heading *Electronic* in the section on *Computer Characteristics*, there is reference to the increasing scale of integration in computer circuits. This integration has now reached the stage where thousands of minute components and the printed wiring to interconnect them can be formed on the well-publicized "chip"—a thin slice of silicon about 0.5 cm square. The components include transistors, resistors, and capacitors, which are the raw material from which the computer's registers, arithmetic unit, control unit, and memory can be made. (*See* MICROCOMPUTER CHIP.)

The effect of achieving such a high packing density of components (or, as it is known, VLSI, very large-scale integration) is to make it possible to produce a complete processor or small memory unit on a single chip.

The implications of this are of quite fundamental importance, since, with a cost per chip ranging from tens to a few hundred dollars, it enables computing power to be built into a wide variety of devices for use in offices, factories, laboratories, and the home, and, indeed, to put a personal computer well within the range of purchase of many.

The effects of this increasing availability of cheap computing power are to cause a proliferation of more "intelligent" machines and to raise questions about the attendant social implications for both good and ill. In particular, there is great debate about the effects on employment. Word processing, (*q.v.*), for example, can greatly improve the productivity of a typist and, hence, theoretically reduce the number of available jobs. At the same time, the boring, routine aspects of many jobs, such as typing, can be eliminated and, indeed, new jobs created in the manufacture and use of new products hitherto undreamed of.

GRAHAM J. MORRIS

DIGITAL COMPUTERS: HISTORY

ORIGINS

For articles on related subjects *see* ABC COMPUTER; AIKEN, HOWARD; ANALYTICAL ENGINE; ATANASOFF, JOHN VINCENT; BABBAGE, CHARLES; BUSH, VANNEVAR; CALCULATING MACHINES; COLOSSUS; ECKERT, J. PRESPER; EDVAC; ENIAC; HOLLERITH MACHINES; HOLLERITH, HERMAN; LEIBNIZ, GOTTFRIED WILHELM VON; MARK I; MAUCHLY, JOHN W.; NAPIER, JOHN; PASCAL, BLAISE; POWERS, JAMES; STORED PROGRAM CONCEPT; TORRES Y QUEVEDO; TURING, ALAN; WIENER, NORBERT; VON NEUMANN, JOHN; ZUSE COMPUTERS; and ZUSE, KONRAD.

Mechanical aids to calculation and mechanical sequence-control devices were perhaps the earliest and most important achievements in the development of computer technology.

The first adding machines date from the early seventeenth century, the most famous of which was invented by the French scientist and philosopher Blaise Pascal, although it is now believed that his work was predated by that of William Schickard. A number of Pascal's machines, which he started to build in 1642, still exist. Even though he had intended them for practical use, their unreliability caused them to be treated mainly as objects of scientific curiosity. During the subsequent two centuries, numerous attempts to develop practical calculating machines were made by Morland, Leibniz, Mahon, Hahn, and Müller, among others. However, it was not until the mid-nineteenth century that a commercially successful machine was produced. This was the "arithmometer" of Thomas de Colmar, the first version of which was invented in 1820, and which used the stepped-wheel mechanism invented by Leibniz.

Mechanical devices for controlling the sequencing of a set of operations, such as the rotating pegged cylinders still seen in music boxes today, date back even earlier. For example, de Caus (1576–1626) used such a mechanism to control both the playing of an organ and the movements of model figures. One of the most famous designers of mechanical automata was Vaucanson. In 1736, he successfully demonstrated an automaton that simulated human lip and finger movements with sufficient accuracy to play a flute. Vaucanson was also involved in the development of what came to be known as the Jacquard loom, in which the woven pattern was specified and controlled by a sequence of perforated cards. The original idea can be traced back to Bouchon in 1725, but such automatic looms did not come into widespread use until early in the nineteenth century after the work by Jacquard.

In 1834, these two lines of development came together in the work of Charles Babbage, who had become dissatisfied with the accuracy of printed mathematical tables. Earlier, in 1822, Babbage had built a small machine, involving several linked adding mechanisms, which would automatically generate successive values of simple algebraic functions using the method of finite differences (*see* DIFFERENCE ENGINE). His attempt at making a full-scale model with a printing mechanism was abandoned in 1834, and he then started to design a more versatile machine. In the space of a few years he had developed the concept of a program-controlled, mechanical, digital computer, incorporating a complete arithmetic unit, store, punched-card input and output, and printing mechanism. The machine, which he called an analytical engine, was to have been controlled by programs represented by sets of Jacquard cards, with conditional jumps and iteration loops being provided for by devices that skipped forward or backward over the required number of cards. Internally, the machine was essentially microprogrammed by rotating pegged cylinders that controlled the sequencing of subsidiary mechanisms.

Babbage's work inspired several other people, among whom were Ludgate, who designed an analytical engine in Ireland in 1909; Torres y Quevedo, who demonstrated the feasibility of an electromechanical analytical engine by successfully producing a typewriter-controlled calculating machine in 1920; and Couffignal, who started to design a binary analytical engine in France during the 1930s. However, Babbage's pioneering efforts were apparently unknown to most of the people who worked on the various computer projects during World War II and who were unaware that the problems they were tackling had been considered and often solved by Babbage more than a hundred years earlier.

The Jacquard loom was perhaps the source of Herman Hollerith's idea of using punched cards to represent logical and numerical data. Developed for use in the 1890 U. S. National Census, his system, incorporating hand-operated tabulating machines and sorters, was highly successful and spread rapidly to several other countries. Automatic card-feed mechanisms were soon provided, and the system began to be used for business accounting applications. Following a dispute with Hollerith, the Bureau of the Census developed in time for the 1910 Census a new tabulating system involving mechanical sensing of card perforations, as opposed to Hollerith's system of electrical sensing. James Powers, the engineer in charge of this work, eventually left the Bureau to form his own company, which later became part of Remington Rand. Hollerith's company merged with two others to become the Computing-Tabulating-Recording Company, which, in 1924, changed its name to the International Business Machines Corporation.

In 1937, Howard Aiken of Harvard University approached IBM with a proposal for a large-scale calculator to be built from the mechanical and electromechanical devices that were used for punched-card machines. The resulting machine, the Automatic Sequence Controlled Calculator, or Harvard Mark I, was built at the IBM Development Laboratories at Endicott. The machine, which was completed in 1943, was a huge affair with 72 decimal accumulators, capable of multiplying two 23-digit numbers in 6 sec. It was controlled by a sequence of instructions specified by a perforated paper tape; somewhat surprisingly, in view of Aiken's knowledge of and respect for Babbage's efforts, it lacked general conditional jump facilities. After completion of the Mark I, Aiken and IBM pursued separate paths. Several more machines were designed at Harvard, the first being another tape-controlled calculator, built this time from electromagnetic relays. IBM produced various machines, including several plug-board-controlled relay calculators and the partly electronic Selective Sequence Electronic Calculator, which was very much in the tradition of the original Mark I.

Not until well after World War II was it found that in Germany there had been an operational program-controlled calculator built earlier than the Mark I, namely, Konrad Zuse's Z3 machine, which first worked in 1941. This machine, which had been preceded by two earlier but unsuccessful machines, had a mechanical store, but was otherwise built from telephone relays. It could store 64 floating-point binary numbers, and has been described as somewhat faster than the Harvard Mark I. The Z3, like several other machines built by Zuse, did not survive the war; the only one of Zuse's machines to do so was the Z4 computer, which was later used successfully for several years at the Technische Hochschule in Zurich.

Various other electromechanical machines were built during and even after World War II, including an important series of relay calculators at the Bell Telephone Laboratories. The first of these, the Complex Computer, was demonstrated in September 1940 by being operated in its New York City location from a teletypewriter installed in Hanover, New Hampshire, on the occasion of a meeting of the American Mathematical Society. The Complex Computer, or Model 1, was capable of adding, subtracting, multiplying, and dividing two complex numbers, but lacked any sequence-control facilities. Later machines in the series incorporated successively more extensive sequencing facilities, so that the Model 5 relay calculator was a truly general-purpose (tape-controlled) computer that achieved very high reliability of operation. (*See* BELL LABS RELAY COMPUTERS.)

The earliest known electronic digital calculating device was a machine for solving up to 30 simultaneous linear equations, initiated in 1938 at Iowa State College by John Atanasoff and Clifford Berry. Although the arithmetic unit had been successfully tested before the project was abandoned in 1942, the input/output mechanism was still incomplete, so the machine never saw actual use (*see* ATANASOFF-BERRY COMPUTER). Other important work on the development of electronic calculating devices was done at IBM, starting in 1942 with the building of experimental versions of various punched-card machines, including a multiplier. This machine was the origin of the electronic multipliers and calculating machines, such as the Type 604 and the Card Programmed Calculator (CPC), that IBM produced in great quantities in the years immediately following World War II and that played an important role

until stored program electronic computers became widely available.

The earliest known efforts at applying electronics to a general-purpose, program-controlled computer were those undertaken by Schreyer and Zuse in 1939, but their plans for a 1,500-valve (i.e. vacuum tube) machine were later rejected by the German government. In Britain, a series of large special-purpose electronic computers, intended for code-breaking purposes, was developed by a team at Bletchley Park, with which Alan Turing was associated. The first of these machines, which incorporated about 2,000 tubes, was operating in December 1943. It has been described as being, in a very limited fashion, a program-controlled device. Interestingly enough, several postwar British electronic computers were developed by people who had been involved with these secret machines.

However, by far the most influential line of development was that carried out at the Moore School of Electrical Engineering at the University of Pennsylvania by John Mauchly, J. Presper Eckert, and their colleagues, starting in 1943. This work, which derived at least as directly from Vannevar Bush's prewar mechanical *differential analyzer* (*q.v.*) as from any digital calculating device, first led to the development of the ENIAC, which was officially inaugurated in February 1946. This machine was intended primarily for ballistics calculations, but by the time it was completed, it was really a general-purpose device, programmed by means of pluggable interconnections. Its internal electronic memory consisted of 20 accumulators,

FIG. 1.   Family tree of computers to mid-1950s. (Courtesy of the Smithsonian Institution.)

each of 10 decimal digits, and it could perform 5,000 arithmetic operations per second—it was approximately a thousand times faster than the Harvard Mark I. The ENIAC was very much the most complex piece of electronic equipment that had ever been assembled, incorporating 19,000 tubes, and using nearly 200 KW of power. The machine was very successful, despite earlier fears regarding the reliability of electronic components.

However, even before the ENIAC was complete, the designers, who had been joined by John von Neumann, started to plan a radically different successor machine, the EDVAC. The EDVAC was a serial binary machine, far more economical on electronic tubes than ENIAC, which was a decimal machine in which each decimal digit was represented by a ring of ten flip-flops. A second major difference was that EDVAC was to have a much larger internal memory than ENIAC, based on mercury delay lines. For these reasons, the initial design of EDVAC included only one-tenth of the equipment used in ENIAC, yet provided a hundred times the internal memory capacity.

It was apparently the discussions of the various ways in which the capabilities of ENIAC might be extended, together with the knowledge of the possibility of comparatively large internal memories, that led to the realization that sequence-control information could be represented by words held in memory along with the numerical quantities entering into the computation, rather than by some external means, such as perforated tape or pluggable interconnections. Thus, EDVAC could retain the great speed of operation that had been achieved by ENIAC, but could avoid the very lengthy setup time, often on the order of a day or more, that had made it impractical to use for other than very extensive calculations. The fact that a program could read and modify portions of itself was heavily utilized, since ideas such as index registers and indirect addresses were still in the offing. Of more lasting significance was the practical and attractive proposition of using the computer to assist with the preparation of its own programs.

With EDVAC, therefore, the invention of the modern digital computer was basically complete. The plans for its design were widely published and extremely influential, so that, even though it was not the first stored-program electronic digital computer to be put into operation, it undoubtedly was the major initial inspiration that started the vast number of computer projects during the late 1940s. A family tree depicting computer development up to the mid-1950s is shown in Fig. 1.

References

1961. Morrison, P. and Morrison, E. (Eds.). *Charles Babbage and His Calculating Engines: Selected Writings by Charles Babbage and Others*. New York: Dover.

1972. Goldstine, H. H. *The Computer from Pascal to von Neumann*. Princeton: Princeton University Press.

1973. Fleck, G. (Ed.). *A Computer Perspective*. By the Office of Charles and Ray Eames, Cambridge, MA: Harvard University Press. (A profusely illustrated book, containing a vast amount of information related directly or indirectly to the history of computing.)

1982. Randell, B. (Ed.). *The Origins of Digital Computers*. (3rd Ed.). Berlin: Springer.

1983. Ceruzzi, P. E. *Reckoners: The Prehistory of the Digital Computer from Relays to the Stored Program Concept, 1935–1945*. Westport, CT: Greenwood Press.

1984. Augarten, S. *Bit by Bit: An Illustrated History of Computers*. New York: Tickner & Fields.

BRIAN RANDELL

EARLY

For articles on related subjects *see* AIKEN, HOWARD; BELL LABS RELAY COMPUTERS; ECKERT, J. PRESPER; EDSAC; EDVAC; ENIAC; MARK I; MAUCHLY, JOHN W.; STORED PROGRAM CONCEPT; TURING, ALAN; ULTRASONIC MEMORY; UNIVAC I; VON NEUMANN, JOHN; WHIRLWIND I; ZUSE, KONRAD; and ZUSE COMPUTERS.

The digital computer age began when the Automatic Sequence Controlled Calculator (Harvard Mark I) started working in August 1944. This machine was based on the mechanical technology of rotating shafts, electromagnetic clutches, and counter wheels, developed over the years for punched card tabulating machinery. It was constructed by IBM, following the ideas of Howard Aiken, whose original proposals go back at least to 1937. The shaft rotation period, and hence the time required to transfer a number or perform an addition, was 0.3 sec, while multiplication and division took 6 and 11.4 sec, respectively.

No other large machines using rotating shafts were built, but there were a number of successful magnetic relay machines. Bell Telephone Laboratories had been working in this area since 1938. Their first fully automatic computer was the one now referred to as the Bell Model V (Fig. 1), of which two examples were constructed. The first of these began to work at the end of 1946. An addition took 0.3 sec and multiplication and division took up to 1.0 and 2.2 sec, respectively. The last of the series was the Model VI, commissioned in 1949. Harvard Mark II, a relay machine designed by Aiken and following a very different design philosophy, was running in September 1948. A relay computer constructed in Sweden (BARK) was operational early in 1950. Independent work on relay computers had also been done by K. Zuse in Germany, and a Zuse Z4 was running in Zurich in 1950. Relays lend themselves to complex circuit arrangements, and all the machines just mentioned had floating-point arithmetic operations, a feature that did not appear in electronic computers until well after the period now under review here. The Bell machines had elaborate checking arrangements, including a redundant representation for stored numbers. Model VI even had a re-try feature, designed to mitigate the effect of transient relay faults.

The concept of the large-scale electronic computer is due to J. Presper Eckert and John W. Mauchly. They were already building the ENIAC when the Harvard Mark I was commissioned. The ENIAC contained nearly 19,000 vacuum tubes, more than twice as many as any later vacuum-tube computer. Because it was by far the most complex

FIG. 1.   The second Bell Model V relay calculator installed at Aberdeen Proving Ground. The first was installed at Langley Field, Virginia.

machine constructed up to that time, its construction was a great act of technological courage, both on the part of the designers and of the Office of Naval Research, which sponsored it. It was built at the Moore School of Electrical Engineering in Philadelphia. The ENIAC began to function in the summer of 1945. An addition took 200 μs and a multiplication took 2.8 ms.

The very early computers were extremely limited in the amount of internal storage that they had. Provision was usually made for tables to be held in read-only storage (banks of switches or punched paper tape) with arrangements for interpolation. It was frequently possible for the programmer to arrange that more than one arithmetic or transfer operation should take place at the same time. The ENIAC was programmed by setting up hundreds of plugs and sockets and switches, an operation that could take several hours. The other computers read their instructions from punched paper tape, endless loops being used for repeated sections of the program.

While the ENIAC was still under construction, Eckert and Mauchly began to realize that, by the application of logical principles, it would be possible to construct a machine not only much more powerful than the ENIAC but also much smaller. They were joined by John von Neumann on a part-time basis, and it was from the group

so formed that the ideas of the modern *stored-program* computer emerged. They were summarized in a document entitled "First draft of a report on the EDVAC," prepared by von Neumann and dated 30 June 1945. Because this report bore von Neumann's name only, the term *von Neumann computer* is often used as a synonym for "stored-program computer," giving the impression that the ideas were all von Neumann's own. I prefer the term *Eckert-von Neumann computer*.

Eckert and Mauchly did not stay at the Moore School to work on the EDVAC, and it was not until January 1952 that a machine bearing that name was commissioned. Instead, they founded the Eckert-Mauchly Corporation, with the object of designing and marketing the UNIVAC. This company was later absorbed into Remington Rand.

From the beginning, the UNIVAC was designed with an eye to business data processing, and the standards set for performance and reliability were very high. In March 1951, the first UNIVAC passed a rigorous acceptance test and was delivered to the U.S. Census Bureau. It was then a fully engineered machine, with magnetic tape and other peripherals required for large-scale business operations. The Eckert-Mauchly Corporation had demonstrated a smaller machine, the BINAC (Fig. 2), in August 1949, but this was not very successful and they decided to concentrate their efforts on the UNIVAC.

FIG. 2. The BINAC computer.

When the Moore School group broke up, von Neumann established a project for the construction of a computer at the Institute for Advanced Study, Princeton. Von Neumann himself, assisted by H. H. Goldstine, laid down the logical structure of this computer, and the engineering development and design was in the hands of J. H. Bigelow. It was the first parallel computer to be designed, and it introduced techniques that became commonplace, such as the register economizing device of putting the multiplier in the tail of the accumulator and shifting it out as the multiplication proceeds. Although the machine was not working until October 1952, the project had immense influence on the development of the digital computer field. The ultrasonic memory (q.v.), which had been proposed for the EDVAC, was thought to be too slow for a parallel machine, and it was planned to use instead a memory based on the Selectron proposed by J. A. Rajchman. The Selectron did not fulfill its promise, but fortunately the Williams tube memory (q.v.) came along in time to save the situation.

The experimental computers that came into action first were those that were least ambitious, both in specification and in performance. One of these was the EDSAC, a computer directly inspired by the EDVAC, designed and constructed by myself and W. Renwick in Cambridge, England. This computer did its first calculation on 6 May 1949, and was used for much early work on the development of programming techniques. Activity at Manchester University arose out of work by F. C. Williams on what became known as the Williams tube memory. In order to test this system, Williams and T. Kilburn built a small model computer with a memory of 32 words and only 5 instructions in its instruction set. The only arithmetic instruction was for subtraction. Development work continued, and by the summer of 1949 a computer with a magnetic drum as a backing memory was demonstrated. The Ferranti Mark I computer (Fig. 3), of which the first delivered model was inaugurated at Manchester University in July 1951, was based on this work.

A third center of activity in England was at the National Physical Laboratory, where the inspiration came from Alan Turing. Turing did not stay there long, leaving for Manchester University in 1948, but the Pilot ACE, which was running by December 1950, reflected very strongly his rather personal view of computer design. The Pilot ACE used an ultrasonic memory, and it was necessary for the programmer to know more of the structure of the machine and the timing of pulses within it than was required in the case of other machines.

The first of the American machines to be brought into use was the SEAC, dedicated on 20 June 1950. This was built under the direction of S. N. Alexander at the National Bureau of Standards in Washington, and the success of that group is the more remarkable, since the SEAC project started after many others. The SEAC was elegant in design and construction, and pioneered the use of small plug-in packages; each package contained a number of germanium diodes and a single vacuum tube. The SEAC used an ultrasonic memory, but a Williams tube memory was later added for evaluation purposes. Meanwhile, H. D. Huskey, who had formerly been a member of the team at the National Physical Laboratory in England and had worked on ENIAC, was completing the SWAC at the NBS Institute for Numerical Analysis at UCLA. This was a parallel machine with a Williams tube memory and was very fast by the standards of the day.

Whirlwind I was a computer with a short word length, aiming at very high speed and power, and intended ulti-

FIG. 3. The Ferranti Mark I computer at Manchester University, 1951.

mately for air traffic control and similar applications. It was designed and built under the direction of J. W. Forrester at M.I.T. and was operating in December 1950. From its specification, one would take it to be the first of the minicomputers, but in fact it occupied the largest floor area of all the early computers, including the ENIAC. The memory was of the electrostatic type, but the cathode-ray tubes were of special design and operated on a different principle from that used by Williams.

Table 1 gives brief particulars of the computers mentioned above and also of several additional ones that became operational in the same period.

TABLE 1   Characteristics of Electronic Computers as of Early 1951

Computer	Serial or Parallel	Decimal or Binary	No. of Addresses	Word length	Clock frequency KH	Memory Type	Memory No. of Words
EDVAC[b]	S	B	3 + 1[d]	44 bits	1,000	U	1,024
UNIVAC	S	D	1	12 char.	2,250	U	1,000
IAS[b]	P	B	1	40 bits	Asynch.	W	1,024
EDSAC	S	B	1	35 bits	500	U	512
Ferranti I	S	B	1	40 bits	100	W	256
Pilot ACE	S	B	—[d]	32 bits	1,000	U	360
SEAC	S	B	3	45 bits	1,000	U	512
SWAC	P	B	4	36 bits	125	W	256
Whirlwind I	P	B	1	16 bits	1,000	E	256
Harvard Mark III	S/P	D	3	16 dec.	28	D	4,000[c]
Burroughs	S	D	1 or 1 + 1[d]	9 dec.	125	D	800
ERA 1101	P	B	1 + 1[d]	24 bits	400	D	16,384

Notes: (a) U = ultrasonic delay (mercury tank); W = Williams tube; D = magnetic drum; E = electrostatic (CRT).
(b) Not commissioned until 1952.
(c) Separate 200-word memory for instructions.
(d) Provision for minimum-access coding.

References

1951. U.S. Navy, Office of Naval Research. *Digital Computer Newsletter* **1–3**.

1953. U.S. Navy, Office of Naval Research. *A Survey of Automatic Digital Computers.*

1972. Goldstine, H. H. *The Computer from Pascal to von Neumann.* Princeton: Princeton University Press.

1985. Wilkes, M. V. *Memoirs of a Computer Pioneer.* Cambridge, MA: M.I.T. Press.

MAURICE V. WILKES

CONTEMPORARY SYSTEMS

For articles on related subjects *see* APPLE COMPUTER, INC.; ATLAS; COMPUTER ARCHITECTURE; COMPUTER INDUSTRY; CONTROL DATA CORPORATION COMPUTERS; DIGITAL EQUIPMENT CORPORATION VAX SERIES; IBM 1400 SERIES; IBM 360/370/390 SERIES; IBM PC AND PC-COMPATIBLES; LIVERMORE AUTOMATIC RESEARCH COMPUTER; MINICOMPUTERS; NAVAL ORDNANCE RESEARCH CALCULATOR; NCR COMPUTERS; PERSONAL COMPUTING; STRETCH; SUPERCOMPUTERS; UNIVAC I; VON NEUMANN MACHINE; WORKSTATION.

Since 1950, computers have advanced at a pace unparalleled in the history of technology. Processing speed and memory capacity have increased, while size and cost have decreased by several orders of magnitude. The pace has not been steady on all fronts, but it has always been rapid, and it continues.

This phenomenal growth has transformed the nature of computing to the point that all but the professional historian tends to label anything that happened in computing before 1945 irrelevant "prehistory" or prologue. One can of course chronicle each dramatic advance, each "milestone" of computing that marks the passing of a certain threshold. Such listings are valuable, but do little to aid one's understanding of the subject. However, it seems impossible to make general statements about computing since 1945, as each new round of machines renders any such statement obsolete.

The notion that there were three major generations of computers, based on device technology (vacuum tubes, discrete transistors, and integrated circuits), served well to characterize machines for the beginning of this period. But even though all computers have used the integrated circuit of the "third generation" since the 1970s, advances in computing since that time have been as great as they were from 1950 to 1970. Nevertheless, the notion of generations still has explanatory power, if no longer applied to the device level. All machines, especially those tested by the rigors of the marketplace, tend to be improved or modified by their designers in incremental ways. Periodically, designers introduce more radical improvements, and when they do, it is appropriate to speak of a new generation of product. Introducing a new device technology is one of several ways this can happen; also common is a thorough redesign of the machine's architecture. Thus, the history of computing is characterized not by three or four but by many generations. Present generation cycles in the computer business can last as little as 3 or 4 years. (*See* GENERATIONS, COMPUTER.)

Given this context, the question remains: Are there general characteristics of the evolution of computing since 1950? A closer look reveals that some general trends have emerged.

The von Neumann Architecture First among these trends is the persistence of the so-called *von Neumann machine* model of computer architecture over successive waves of hardware and software advances. That model, originally conceived by J. Presper Eckert (*q.v.*), John Mauchly (*q.v.*), and John von Neumann (*q.v.*) in the mid-1940s, emerged in response to the need for a practical design for the EDVAC (*q.v.*), a machine they were proposing as a follow-on to the ENIAC (*q.v.*), then under construction. But that model's influence was to be much greater. Its persistence has come from its ability to organize and unify what otherwise would be a bewildering

Max. Memory Access Time ms	Operation Time (incl. access)			Input Output	No. of Tubes	No. of Diodes (germanium)	Aux. Memory
	Add ms	Mult. ms	Divide ms				
0.38	0.2–1.5	2.2–3.5	2.2–3.6	Paper tape	3,600	10,000	—
0.40	0.5 mean	2.15 mean	3.9 mean	Magn. tape	5,600	18,000	Magn. tape
0.025	0.062	0.44–1.0	1.1	Cards	2,300	0	—
1.1	1.5 mean	6 mean	—	Paper tape	3,800	0	—
0.64	1.2	3.36	—	Paper tape	3,800	0	Drum, 16K
1.0	—	2	—	Cards	800	—	—
0.38	1.5 max.	3.6 max.	3.6 max	Paper tape	1,300	15,800	Magn. tape
—	0.064	0.38	—	Paper tape; cards	2,300	3,000	—
0.016	0.049	0.061	0.1	Paper tape	6,800	22,000	—
4.5	5	13	100	Magn. tape	5,000	1,300	—
32	0.6–17	30–50	—	Paper tape	3,271	6,773	—
17	0.1 min.	0.35 min.	0.42 min.	Paper tape	2,200	3,000	—

range of options about computer design. It has persisted also because it could be extended and radically modified without altering its basic structure. Despite limitations, the model has served as the foundation upon which the edifice of computer science and engineering has been built, and shows signs of remaining so into the future.

Computers of the 1990s hardly resemble those sketched out by the EDVAC team in the 1940s. Yet, just as one can see in a modern automobile certain decisions made by Henry Ford seven decades ago, the ancestral lineage is there. Today it implies computers that maintain a rigid division between memory and processing units, with a single channel between the two. Instructions as well as data are stored together in the primary memory, which is configured to be large, random-access, and as fast as practical. The basic cycle of a computer is to transfer an instruction from memory to the processor, decode that instruction, and execute it with respect to data that is also retrieved from memory.

Despite all that has happened, those patterns remain. (The late Alan Perlis (q.v.) once remarked, "Sometimes I think the only universal in the computing field is the fetch-execute cycle.") From time to time, designers propose computers that radically deviate from the von Neumann model; there has been a flurry of this activity since 1985. But this architecture remains the starting point, even in the most extreme cases of massively parallel designs (some advocates of which call "non-Von machines" (see PARALLEL PROCESSING).

The ideas contained in von Neumann's 1945 report were not his alone, nor was that report the definitive statement of what has become the accepted architecture of the modern computer. A full understanding came with the cooperative effort of many persons, working on different projects, between 1945 and about 1950. The EDVAC report described a machine that economized on hardware by doing everything serially, including register addition, one bit at a time. When von Neumann moved from the EDVAC project to one at the Institute for Advanced Study at Princeton, that notion had given way to one of parallel operation on each 40-bit word. That required more hardware but simplified the design of the logical control unit and yielded faster arithmetic speeds. Transfers to and from memory, as well as processing, were done one word, not one bit, at a time. Despite this shift to a more parallel structure, memory transfer remained essentially a serial activity, since become famous as the "von Neumann bottleneck."

The notion of having the word, not the bit, as the basic unit of processing further emerged among the various one-of-a-kind computer projects in the late 1940s, as did the related notion of having a large, reliable, random access memory that could transfer a full word at a time. Most first-generation computers used serial memories, however, until reliable magnetic core memory became available in the mid-1950s.

What is most remembered about the EDVAC Report is its description of the stored program principle. That principle was much modified and extended by the time first-generation commercial computers appeared. As initially conceived, it had three features. First, storing programs in high-speed memory meant that the processor could fetch instructions at the same high speeds as data. Second, by not having a fixed barrier between data and program storage, a computer could solve a variety of problems in which the ratio of instructions to data might vary. Third, by storing instructions in the same memory unit as data, the processor could operate on and modify those instructions, especially by computing new addresses for operands required by an instruction.

By the mid-1950s it became clear that the ability to modify programs in mid-execution was the most profound innovation of all. Indeed, by allowing computers to be programmed at levels far higher than individual processor instructions, this innovation is as much responsible for the present-day "computer age" as is the invention of the integrated circuit. Although the EDVAC group hardly foresaw this, it is testimony to the originality of the team's thinking that their original concept has proved so adaptable and seminal.

Classes of Computers Computers are roughly classed, from top down, as supercomputer, mainframe, mini, workstation, and personal (or microcomputer). Other categories are developing in between these major ones, and the future may see the blurring or merging of some of the ones mentioned. These terms did not come into common use until the 1970s and (for *workstation*) the 1980s, but today they have fairly precise meanings. But a look back reveals a functional as well as price differentiation in computers almost from the beginning of commercial computing. The ENIAC, with its emphasis on numerical processing for classified military customers, was the ancestor of the supercomputer, while the UNIVAC I, optimized for business data processing, was an early mainframe. Small and relatively inexpensive computers such as the Bendix G-15, the Librascope LGP-30, and the Alwac III-E were vacuum tube machines that sold well, although their architecture was very different from that of the minicomputer of the 1960s.

Architecture is one way of assigning these classifications, but memory capacity, processing speeds, price, packaging, intended market, software, and other factors come into play as well. At any given moment, the classes are distinct and represent a descending order of computing power, but over the years each category ratchets upward. Thus, today's personal computer has the power of yesterday's mini (and the day before yesterday's mainframe), but it is still called a personal computer.

New categories, when they do arise, often bubble up from a lower level, due mainly to advances in device technology. They often begin as modest offerings designed to take advantage of a small niche poorly served by an established class, but soon grow out of that to become a full-fledged class of general-purpose computers. New classes do *not* arise from the reduction in cost and size of the machines of a higher category. For example, in 1975, Digital Equipment Corporation introduced the LSI-11, a single-board, low-cost version of its popular PDP-11 minicomputer. But the LSI-11 did not inaugurate the personal computer era. That era came instead from an upward evolution of simple 4-bit processor chips that were developed for cash resisters, adding machines, and other modest devices. As these increased in power, they took on more and more properties of general-purpose computers. In the mid 1980s, a similar phenomenon occurred as companies introduced machines ("mini-super-computers") that reached toward the performance of the supercomputer, but at far lower cost.

Upward-Compatible Families of Computers

A third pattern has emerged, and it, too, is likely to persist: the emergence of not just single products optimized for scientific, process-control, or business applications, but families of general-purpose computers that offer upward compatibility of software. This gives customers an easy path to upgrade with the same vendor as their needs increase. Offering general-purpose instead of specialized products broadens the manufacturer's customer base.

A major portion of the costs of any computing system is the software developed for it. With a family of products, a vendor can amortize these costs over a longer period of time. That in turn can justify higher initial development costs, and thus produce better software. Alternatively, it can allow a vigorous third-party software industry to flourish, especially evident with personal computers. This more than offsets the downside that one may not take advantage of new technologies in the "best" way from a hardware standpoint. Likewise, offering a family of machines based on a general-purpose architecture compensates for the fact that special-purpose architectures might work better for specific customers.

The first family of compatible processors consisted of the Philco Transac S-2000 models 210, 211, and 212, marketed over the period 1958 to 1964. Philco sold out to Ford, who subsequently left the computer business. IBM System/360, introduced in April 1964, was the first commercial system based on a family of upward compatible processors all of which were announced on the same day. Other notable families include the Univac 1100 series, the Burroughs B5000 and its successors, the CDC Cyber series, the Digital Equipment Corporation VAX series, and the Intel 8080 line of processors used in many personal computers.

The need to maintain compatibility tends to slow down the adoption of new advances in architecture or instruction set design. If improvements in device technology can be incorporated without destroying compatibility, a manufacturer will do so as soon as practical, although marketing factors come into play as well. The overall results are short, generational cycles of device technology, but less frequent cycles of changes in architecture.

Some advances in circuit technology compel modifications to a system architecture to take full advantage of it. But a good initial design can and should be robust enough to absorb advances and incorporate them while still maintaining software compatibility. The IBM System/360 used hybrid circuits, magnetic core memory, and a batch-oriented operating system. Over the years, IBM introduced integrated circuits, semiconductor memory, virtual memory (*q.v.*), time-sharing (*q.v.*), and a host of other technical innovations, all while preserving software

compatibility. The result has kept this architecture commercially competitive into the 1990s.

Whether to drop a proven architecture and adopt a new one is a decision manufacturers constantly face. Given the relentless march of device technology, a company may feel it must take that step, although it is possible to keep an obsolete design viable for a long time. When a company adopts a new architecture, its managers "bet the company" on the future design. The history of modern computing is full of examples of those who waited too long or who plunged too early into a new design. Sometimes, established firms are quickly eclipsed by other companies that make the switch effectively and at the right moment.

Following are brief descriptions of representative machines that reflect the patterns described above. Machines up to and including the IBM System/360 are classified by the traditional generations; those following it by their type: super, mainframe, mini, etc. In these descriptions the emphasis is both on the device technology as well as the overall system architecture.

The First Generation, 1950–1960

The first generation began around 1950 with the introduction of commercial computers manufactured and sold in quantity. Computers of the first generation stored their programs internally and used vacuum tubes as their switching technology, but beyond that had little else in common. Each design used a different mix of registers, addressing schemes, and instruction sets. The greatest variation was found in the devices used for memory, and this affected the logic of the processor design. Each memory technology had some sort of technical drawback, thus giving rise to a variety of machines that favored one design approach over another.

The reports describing the Institute for Advanced Study computer, written by Arthur Burks, Herman Goldstine, and John von Neumann, emphasized the advantages of a parallel memory device that could read and write a full word at a time. But the device they favored, the RCA Selectron tube, took longer than expected to appear; only the RAND Corporation's Johnniac used it. America's first commercial machine, the UNIVAC, used a mercury delay line to which words were read and written one bit at a time. The fastest machines used cathode-ray tubes (Williams tubes - *q.v.*), which were capable of parallel operation. But in practice these tubes, originally intended for other commercial applications, were notoriously unreliable. By far the most popular memory technique for first-generation machines was the rotating magnetic drum. An electromechanical device, it was slow, but its reliability and low cost made it suitable for small-scale machines like the IBM 650, Bendix G-15, Alwac III-E, and Librascope LGP-30.

By the end of this period, machines were introduced that incorporated magnetic core memory. With the advent of ferrite cores—and techniques for manufacturing and assembling them in large quantities—the memory problem endemic to the first generation was effectively solved.

nd of this period, machines were introduced that incorporated magnetic core memory. With the advent of ferrite cores—and techniques for manufacturing and assembling them in large quantities—the memory problem endemic to the first generation was effectively solved.

UNIVAC   The UNIVAC was designed by J. Presper Eckert and John Mauchly, and first delivered in 1951 (by which time their company had been acquired by Remington Rand). It was the first American computer to be serially produced and sold to commercial customers. Eventually, over 40 were built. Customers included the U.S. Census Bureau, the Lawrence Livermore Laboratory, the U.S. Army and Air Force, and the General Electric Corporation. Most customers used the UNIVAC for accounting, statistical, and other applications that would later fall under the term *data processing* (q.v.).

The computer used serial, binary-coded-decimal arithmetic performed in four general-purpose accumulators. Word length was 45 bits; each word could represent 11 binary-coded-decimal (BCD) digits plus a sign, or 6 alphabetic characters (6 bits per character plus 1 parity bit). Basic clock speed was 2.25 Mhz, and the multiplication time was about 2 msec. Mercury delay-lines stored 1,000 words in high-speed memory, while magnetic tape units stored up to 1 million characters on reels of ½-inch wide metal tape.

The UNIVAC was ruggedly designed and built. Its central processor contained over 5,000 tubes, installed in cabinets that were arranged in a 10-foot × 14-foot rectangle. Inside this rectangle were placed the mercury delay-line tanks. Many design features that later became commonplace first appeared with the UNIVAC: alphanumeric as well as numeric processing, extra bits for error checking, magnetic tapes for bulk memory, and buffers that allowed high-speed data transfer between internal and external memories without CPU intervention.

IBM 701, 650   At the time of the UNIVAC's announcement, IBM was not committed to electronic computation and was vigorously marketing its line of punched card calculators and tabulators. But, responding to the competitive threat, IBM introduced two machines, one on a par with the UNIVAC, the other more modest.

In 1952, IBM announced the 701 computer, originally called the Defense Calculator after its perceived market. True to that perception, of the 19 models installed, most went to U.S. Defense Department or aerospace customers. Initial rental fees were $15,000 a month; IBM did not sell the machines outright. For primary memory, the machine used IBM-designed Williams tubes that could store up to 4,096 36-bit words. Magnetic oxide-coated plastic tape was used for back-up memory, and a magnetic drum for intermediate storage. It could perform about 2,000 multiplications/second, but unlike the UNIVAC, the 701's central processor handled control of the slow input/output facilities directly. At about the same time, IBM also developed a character-oriented machine, the 702, for business customers. These machines began IBM's transition to a company that designed and built large-scale electronic digital computers.

Also, at about the same time, IBM developed a smaller machine that had its origins in proposals for extensions of punched card equipment. In the course of its development, its nature shifted to that of a general-purpose, stored program computer, using a magnetic drum for primary memory. IBM's acquisition of drum memory technology from Engineering Research Associates in 1949 was a key element in this shift. The machine, now called the IBM 650, was delivered in 1954, rather late relative to objectives. But it proved to be very successful; eventually, there were over a thousand 650 installations at a rental of about $3,500 per month.

By the time of its announcement, the 650 had to compete with a number of other inexpensive, drum-memory machines. But it outsold them all, partly because of IBM's reputation and existing customer base of punched card users, and partly because the 650 was perceived to be easier to program and more reliable than its competitors. The 650's drum had a faster access time (2.4 msec.) than other drum machines. But that was still slow, a limitation that precluded the use of drum-based machines for many important applications. Ironically, the 650 had less impact among the business customers for

FIG. 1.   UNIVAC 1. (Photo: Lawrence Livermore Laboratories.)

whom it was intended than it had at universities, who were able to acquire the computer at a deep discount. There it frequently became the first machine available to the nascent "computing centers" that were just getting underway in the late 1950s.

ERA 1103   Another important first-generation computer was the ERA 1103, developed by Engineering Research Associates, the St. Paul, Minnesota firm that Remington-Rand bought in 1952. This machine was geared toward scientific and engineering customers, and thus represented a different design philosophy from Remington-Rand's other large machine, the UNIVAC.

The machine used binary arithmetic, a 36-bit word length, and parallel arithmetic operation. Internal memory (1K words) was supplied by Williams tubes, with an ERA-designed drum for backup. It employed a two-address instruction scheme, with the first six bits of a word used to encode a repertoire of 45 instructions. Arithmetic was performed in an internal 72-bit accumulator.

In late 1954, the company delivered to the National Security Agency and to the National Advisory Committee for Aeronautics an 1103 that employed magnetic core in place of the Williams Tube memory—perhaps the first use of core in a commercial machine. (Core had by that time already been installed in the Whirlwind (*q.v.*) at M.I.T. and in a few other experimental computers.) Following customer advice, ERA modified the machine's instruction set to include an interrupt facility for its I/O, another first in computer design. Interrupts and core memory were later marketed as standard features of the 1103-A model.

IBM 704, 709   In late 1955, IBM began deliveries of the 36-bit 704, its successor to the scientifically-oriented 701. It was the most successful of the large first-generation computers. The 704's most notable features were core memory (initially 4K words, up to 32K by 1957)

and a rich instruction repertoire. In addition, the 704 CPU used hardware floating-point arithmetic and three addressable index registers. Both were major advances over the 701. To facilitate the use of floating point, an IBM team led by John Backus developed Fortran. Backus has said that he had not envisioned Fortran's use much beyond the 704, but of course it became and has remained, with Cobol, one of the two most successful programming languages of all time. IBM produced 123 704s between 1955 and 1960.

In January 1957, IBM announced the 709 as a compatible upgrade to the 704, but it did not enjoy the same success. Shortly after it was introduced, it became clear that after a ten-year development phase transistors were finally becoming a practical replacement for vacuum tubes. Indeed, the transistorized Philco Transac S-2000 and Control Data 1604 had already beaten IBM to the punch. IBM quickly withdrew the 709 from the market and replaced it with the transistorized 7090. The new machine was architecturally identical to the 709, so IBM engineers used a 709 to write software for the as-yet-unbuilt 7090. The first delivery of the 7090 in late 1959 marked the beginning of IBM's entry into the solid-state era.

The first-generation computers established a beachhead among commercial customers, but even considering the success of the IBM 650, they did little more than that. Punched card accounting equipment still did most of the work for businesses, while engineering and scientific calculating was done with slide rules, desk calculators, or analog computers. Machines like the ERA 1103 were too big, too expensive, and required too much maintenance to be found anywhere but at the largest aerospace firms or government research laboratories. Many still spoke of the total world market for large computers as being limited to very small numbers, much as one might speak of the demand for particle accelerators or wind tunnels. As reliable magnetic core and transistor technology developed, that perception would change.

FIG. 2.   IBM 704. (Photo: IBM.)

The Second Generation, 1960–1965

The second generation of computing lasted from about 1960 to 1965, and was characterized by the use of discrete transistors for switching elements and coincident-current ferrite core planes for internal memory. In software, this era saw the acceptance of high-level programming languages like Fortran and Cobol, although assembly language programming remained common.

From the perspective of the 1990s, the second generation appears to have been more of a transitional period than a major era in computing. The term "revolution," as applied to the invention of the integrated circuit, obscures the fact that the IC's inventors saw their work as an evolutionary outgrowth of their work in materials, circuits, and packaging pioneered in the discrete transistor era. This evolutionary approach hastened the acceptance of the otherwise exotic technology among computer designers. It was during the transistor era when some of the toughest challenges were faced, especially regarding the serial production of reliable transistors with consistent performance. It took from 1949 to 1959 to bring transistors from the laboratory to commercial production and use in computers. But the basic knowledge gained during that period hastened the advent of the IC, which went from invention to commercial use in half that time.

Transistors, replacing vacuum tubes on a one-to-one basis, solved the problems of a tube's unreliability, heat, and power consumption. As they solved those problems, they exposed another, which proved to be more fundamental: the complexity of interconnecting many thousands of simple circuits to obtain a system that had reasonable computing power. This tyranny of numbers—brought to the fore by transistorized computers—would eventually be solved by the integrated circuit.

IBM 1401

The most successful transistorized computer was the IBM 1401, introduced in 1960. Based on an initial concept developed at IBM's laboratory in France, the machine employed a character-oriented, variable-length data field, with one bit of each character code reserved to delimit the end of a field. As with the 650, the 1401's design evolved from a plug-wired, punched card calculator to a stored-program, general-purpose computer that utilized magnetic media (tape) as well as punched cards for its I/O. Ferrite cores provided a central memory of from 1,400 to 4,000 characters, while transistorized circuits supported a multiplication speed of about 500 numbers/sec.

IBM engineers took pains to make the machine easy to program, especially by those who were comfortable with punched card tabulators, but who knew nothing of stored program computers. A simple language called "Report Program Generator" (RPG) facilitated processing and printing of tabular data much as punched card equipment was formerly used to perform those tasks. With the 1401, IBM also introduced the Type 1403 printer, a rugged and fast printer that carried type on a moving chain. The system's relatively small size meant that a customer could install it in the same room that was already used for punched card accounting equipment. This combination of features, renting at $2,500 a month for a base system, made the 1401 attractive to many small- and medium-sized businesses.

Eventually, over 10,000 1401s were installed—ten times as many as the 650. Its success marked the ascendancy of IBM over Univac as the dominant computer supplier. Not only did the 1401 broaden the base of potential customers, it finally dispelled lingering doubts over whether the world could absorb more than a small number of electronic computers. Together with the 650, the 1401 made a forceful argument for general-purpose, stored program machines over special-purpose designs. Concurrently with the 1401, IBM also offered the 1620, a like-sized machine intended for scientific applications. Meanwhile, in 1962 the company introduced the 7094, an upgrade to the 7090. It, too, sold well and became the standard large-scale scientific computer of the time.

By the mid-1960s, the IBM Corporation had seized and was vigorously defending a dominant share of the U. S. computer market. Univac, Burroughs, NCR, RCA, Control Data, Philco/Ford, General Electric, and Honeywell were its chief competitors. Each produced machines that were comparable in price and functionality to the IBM machines, although they had different architectures. By 1970, GE, Ford, and RCA had left the computer business, their places taken by new companies offering computers of a different nature than the classic mainframes of this era.

LARC, Stretch, Atlas, B5000

The second generation was a time when a number of architectural innovations first appeared, but were premature. That is, the features saw only limited use until the next generation, when they became commonplace.

In 1955, Remington Rand Univac contracted with the Lawrence Livermore Laboratory to produce a high-performance computer for weapons design. Design and development of the LARC (Livermore Automatic Research Computer) were beset with problems, but in 1960 the first

FIG. 3. IBM 7094. (Photo: IBM.)

model was completed and accepted by Livermore, with a second model delivered to the Navy's David Taylor Model Basin soon thereafter. The LARC achieved high processing speeds by having a separate processor whose only job was to handle I/O. Logic circuits used Surface Barrier Transistors, developed by Philco in 1955, but already obsolete by 1960. A great deal of effort was spent on packaging the circuits. Getting the backplane wired proved to be a major challenge, ultimately solved by developing special tools that resembled those used by surgeons. The LARC was an impressive performer, but after delivering the two models for a total price of $6 million, Univac stopped production and absorbed a $20 million loss.

At about the same time IBM undertook a similar project called "Stretch," implying that it would dramatically extend the state of the art. Work began in 1956, with the first delivery (to Los Alamos Laboratory) in 1961. Like the LARC, the Stretch introduced a number of innovations in both architecture and device technology. Among the former was its use of a pipelined processor; among the latter was its use of very fast transistors and Emitter-Coupled Logic (ECL). A total of seven other machines, by now called the IBM 7030, were delivered, before the company withdrew the product line. As with Univac's experience with the LARC, IBM absorbed a huge financial loss on the project.

The Atlas computer, introduced in 1962 by the British firm Ferranti, Ltd., employed virtual memory (*q.v.*) with paging, and provision for multiprogramming (*q.v.*). Whereas most first- and second-generation computers had at best only a rudimentary job control facility, Ferranti provided the Atlas with a "Supervisor" program that foreshadowed the operating systems (*q.v.*) common after 1965.

In 1962, Burroughs introduced the 5000 series of computers that incorporated innovations similar to the Atlas. This series was further designed for optimal execution of programs written in a high-level language (Algol). The design of its processor was also novel in its use of a stack-oriented addressing scheme rather than the accumulator-oriented architectures of the first generation. Neither of these two features would prevail in the marketplace, but two others—multiprogramming and virtual memory—would become common a generation later.

The Third Generation, 1965–1970   The IBM System/360, announced on 7 April 1964, inaugurated the third generation of computers. This series of machines did not use integrated circuits, but rather small modules consisting of discrete devices laid onto a ceramic substrate. IBM had considered using the newly invented IC for the 360, but went instead with what they called Solid Logic Technology, in part because they had a better grasp of its manufacture in large quantities than they had with ICs.

The initial announcement was for a series of six machines, offering upward compatibility over a range of 25:1 in performance. The 360 machines were intended to be applicable to the full circle of applications (hence the name), rather than having a separate character-oriented line of products for business and a word-oriented line for scientific use. Eventually, over ten models were offered, plus additional models announced but not delivered or else withdrawn soon after initial delivery. The series even-

FIG. 4.   IBM System/360 Model 44. (Photo: IBM.)

tually offered a several hundred-fold range in computing power.

The 360's designers achieved compatibility over that range by adopting several design innovations. The first was the use of base-register addressing, whereby an instruction referred to a short address (*see* BASE REGISTER). This address was added to a base address (stored in a register) to yield the actual location in core of the desired data. This kept the cost of address-decoding circuits low for the low-end models.

A second innovation was the use of microprogramming (*q.v.*) to achieve compatibility. Except for the Model 75, initially at the top of the line, each model of the 360 obtained its instruction set from a read-only memory (ROM - *q.v.*) containing a microprogram. That allowed designers for each model to aim for optimum cost/performance without being unduly constrained by the specifics of the 360 instruction set. The concept of microprogramming was first suggested by Maurice Wilkes in 1951, and had been implemented in the design of the Ferranti Atlas. Another British computer, the KDF-9, used microprogramming; 360 engineers later acknowledged that this machine inspired their decision to adopt it. The 360 established microprogramming firmly in the mainstream of computing, and led the way for its use in the minicomputer and microcomputer classes that followed.

A third innovation was the use of input-output *channels* (*q.v.*)—small, independent processors—that handled the transfer of data between primary memory and peripheral devices. This allowed IBM to market a common set of I/O equipment to all customers, regardless of model. (The proliferation of incompatible peripherals for previous lines of products was one of the main forces behind the decision to develop the 360.)

By all accounts the 360 series was very successful. IBM sales personnel recorded over a thousand orders for systems within a month of the April 1964 announcement, and by 1970 there were over 18,000 installations worldwide. The architecture did, however, have serious shortcomings that were later corrected to varying degrees. Chief among them was its lack of dynamic address translation, which, among other things, made it difficult to use the machine in a time-shared environment. When IBM upgraded the 360 series to the System/370 in 1970, its architecture was extended to provide this feature and virtual memory as well. A further extension of the 360 architecture was made in 1981, when the number of addressing bits was increased from 24 to 31. The basic architecture, much extended, is still being used in the 1990s in two lines of IBM products, the 43xx series and the 30xx series which together have evolved into the System/390 series.

The success of the 360 spawned competitors. In 1965, RCA began deliveries of a series of four machines, the Spectra Series, that were software compatible to the equivalent 360 models. These had the distinction of being built with true integrated circuits instead of the 360's Solid Logic Technology. But RCA was unable to sustain the line and sold its computer business to Univac in 1971. By that time other companies were offering computers built with integrated circuits and semiconductor memory

instead of magnetic core. Shortly after the 370's announcement, IBM offered models with these as well.

Because semiconductor memory, unlike core, loses its information when power is switched off, the 370 needed a way to store its microprogrammed instructions in a non-volatile fashion. IBM engineers invented the *floppy disk* (*q.v.*) for this purpose. The floppy became the pivotal technology for establishing the personal computer class later that decade.

The notion of a compatible family of machines was not the only 360 innovation that later became widely copied. The 360 adopted the 8-bit byte as the standard for representing characters, and multiple-spindle disk systems with removable disk packs. Microprogramming soon became the most common way to implement architectures. From the marketing of the system came the acceptance of many terms now used in computing: "byte," "architecture," and "generation," among others.

Minicomputers   The term "minicomputer" was coined in the mid-1960s by a Digital Equipment Corporation salesman to describe the PDP-8. The term really has two meanings, one informal and the other specific. Informally, a minicomputer is low in cost, small in size, and intended for use by a single individual, small department, or for a dedicated application. That concept was expressed as early as 1952, when several companies introduced computers aimed at such a market.

But producing such a machine with adequate performance was another matter. First-generation computers like the Bendix G-15, Alwac III-E, or Librascope LGP-30 achieved low cost by using a drum memory, which is incapable of high-speed random access to data. The resulting low-processing speeds meant that these computers were ill-suited for process control, laboratory instrumentation, or other similar applications where minicomputers first found wide use.

A more specific definition recognizes the technical constraints that have to be overcome for a compact and inexpensive computer to be useful. By this definition, a mini is a compact, solid-state computer, with random-access electronic memory, whose internal structure is characterized by a short word length and a variety of memory addressing modes.

This definition also requires that a minicomputer be small and rugged enough to fit in a standard equipment rack and thus serve as an embedded controller for other systems. It was substantially smaller and more rugged than what many people previously thought practical; its realization had to await advances in integrated circuit technology as well as circuit board fabrication, power supply design, and packaging techniques.

This definition makes sense only in the context of the era in which the machines appear. Minicomputers, with microcomputers following close behind, have evolved to mainframe-class word lengths of 32 bits and they now come in all sizes, including some that require a full-sized computer room. But the category has persisted. (32-bit minicomputers are now called "superminis," but the differences are not yet so great as to constitute a separate class.)

The M.I.T. Whirlwind (*q.v.*), completed in the early 1950s, used a 16-bit word length, and was envisioned for real-time simulation and control applications. It was housed in several rooms of a building on the M.I.T. campus, and in its initial configuration used fragile and sensitive electrostatic tubes for memory. As such, it was hardly a minicomputer, although it was used like one. Many of the M.I.T. students and faculty who worked on it would later become founders of the minicomputer industry located around the Boston suburbs.

In 1960, Control Data Corporation introduced a transistorized, 12-bit machine called the CDC 160. The 160 was intended primarily as an input/output controller for its larger, 48-bit model 1604. But the 160 could be used as a computer on its own, and as such, was one of the first machines to fit the definition of a mini. Unlike Whirlwind, it was very compact—in fact, it was built into an ordinary office desk. Both the 160 and the 1604 sold well and helped establish CDC as a major computer manufacturer. The company continued building small machines, but concentrated more on very fast, long-word computers— later called supercomputers—for which the 160 was designed as an I/O channel. Thus it failed to establish a minicomputer niche.

The Digital Equipment Corporation PDP-8, a 12-bit computer announced in 1965, made the breakthrough. Up to that time, DEC had produced and sold a variety of machines with varying word lengths, including the 36-bit PDP-6 (later PDP-10), a full-size mainframe widely used in a time-sharing environment. But the success of the PDP-8 established the minicomputer as defined above, with DEC as the leading supplier. The success of the PDP-8 spawned a number of competitors: Varian, Hewlett-Packard, Computer Automation, and other companies. Data General, formed by ex-DEC employees, brought out the 16-bit Nova

in early 1969, and it quickly became DEC's main competitor. The Nova had a simple but powerful instruction set and was the first to use medium-scale-integrated (MSI) circuits. It led the trend toward minis having word lengths that were multiples of the 8-bit byte. DEC countered with their 16-bit PDP-11 in 1970.

The mini's low cost, ruggedness, and compact packaging made it attractive for so-called "original equipment manufacturers" (OEMs - *q.v.*), who purchased minis and embedded them into specialized systems for typesetting, process control, and a host of other applications. Having others develop the specialized software and interfaces was well-suited to small, entrepreneurial minicomputer firms who did not have the resources to develop such specialized applications in-house. Several of the mainframe companies, including IBM, introduced minicomputers at this time, but the smaller firms propelled the industry.

A typical mini was microprogrammed and transferred data internally over a high-speed channel called a *bus* (*q.v.*). To gain access to more memory than could be directly addressed by a short word, their central processors contained sets of registers for base-offset, indirect, indexed, and other types of addressing. These designs made optimum use of the medium-scale integrated memory and logic circuits then becoming available.

The machines offered considerable processing power for the money, and it was not long before customers began using them for general-purpose computation. As they did, the need for more address bits soon became pressing, in spite of the innovative addressing techniques the machines employed. Interdata, Systems Engineering Laboratories, and Prime all introduced machines with a 32-bit word length in the mid-1970s. These machines quickly became popular with NASA and other aerospace

FIG. 5.   CDC 160-A. (Photo: Control Data Corporation.)

customers, who needed that power for computer-aided design and manufacture (CAD/CAM - *q.v.*) and real-time data reduction. DEC responded to this trend in 1978 with its VAX-11, a 32-bit "Virtual Address Extension" to the PDP-11. Data General announced its 32-bit Eclipse MV/8000 in 1980.

These minicomputers thus had the same word length, 32 bits, as the mainframes of the IBM 360 class. At first the 32-bit machines were called "superminis," but as 12- and 16-bit minicomputers became scarce, this distinction became unnecessary. There were still differences, however, in the minicomputer's instruction set and use of buses instead of the mainframe's I/O channels.

The VAX soon began outselling the other 32-bit minis and went on to become one of the most successful computers of all time. Part of the reason was DEC's existing market position, but success was also due to the software compatibility the VAX had with the large installed base of PDP-11s. Internally, the VAX was a different machine, but it contained within it an emulation mode, accessed by setting a bit, that executed PDP-11 programs (eventually this feature was dropped). Also crucial to success was the VAX's ability to be networked through Ethernet, the Xerox-developed networking system that DEC chose in 1980. The VAX was further blessed with having available not one but two good operating systems: Digital's own VMS (Virtual Memory System) and Unix (*q.v.*), developed by AT&T and originally offered on a PDP-11. The combination of inherently good design, an adequate supply of semiconductor memory chips, networking, and software support enabled the VAX to compete with all but the largest mainframe computers, whose designs were beginning to look dated by 1980.

The VAX's success thus followed that of the IBM 360, in which a microprogrammed architecture allowed a wide range of models all running the same software. DEC has continued supporting the system by offering a range of VAX machines that merge into the mainframe at the high end and the micro at the low end. The machine continues to be popular into the 1990s, although its dominance is being threatened by the 32-bit microprocessor-based systems to be described later.

Supercomputers On several occasions throughout the history of digital computing, there has been a desire to push the state of the art to obtain the highest performance possible. Indeed, one sees this force driving Charles Babbage, who in 1834 abandoned work on his promising difference engine (*q.v.*) to attempt a far more powerful analytical engine (*q.v.*), which he never was able to complete. The various "Giant Brains" of the late 1940s and early 1950s reflect this desire as well.

In 1954, IBM built a fast computer called the Naval Ordnance Research Calculator (NORC - *q.v.*) for the Naval Proving Ground in Dahlgren, Virginia. At its dedication, John von Neumann spoke of the tremendous advances in computer speeds, ending his talk with the hope that computer companies would continue from time to time "...to write specifications simply calling for the most advanced machine which is possible in the present state of the art."

IBM's Stretch (1961) and Univac's LARC (1960) both fit this category. And in the late 1960s, Burroughs built the ILLIAC-IV, a parallel-processing machine based on a design by Daniel Slotnik of the University of Illinois. The computers that resulted were often well regarded by the customers who bought them, but they usually incurred huge financial losses for the companies that manufactured them, even with the government subsidies each of these machines enjoyed.

It remained for Control Data Corporation to find a way, not only to make reliable and practical supercomputers, but to sell them profitably as well. The machine that brought the term "supercomputer" into common use was their 6600, designed by Seymour Cray and delivered in 1964.

The CDC's architecture employed a 60-bit word central processor, around which were arranged ten logical 12-bit word peripheral processors each having a memory of 4K words. (Physically, there was only one such processor, but it was ingeniously time-shared to provide users the illusion of ten independent logical processors.) Within the central processor were ten "functional units," which contained specialized circuitry that performed the operations of fixed- or floating-point arithmetic and logic. Logic circuits, taking advantage of the high-speed silicon

FIG. 6. CDC 6600. (Photo: Control Data Corporation.)

transistors just then becoming available, were densely packed into modules called "cordwood" from the way they looked.

The functional units permitted a measure of parallel processing, since each unit could be doing a different specialized operation at the same time. Added parallelism was provided through "lookahead," a process (pioneered on the Stretch) by which the CPU examined the instruction stream and determined to what extent operations could be fetched in advance of the time the functional units needed them. (Interestingly, this made a branch instruction that actually branched the most time-consuming operation on the machine.) Likewise, the peripheral processors could each be busy handling I/O, while the central processor was executing program steps that did not require connection with the outside world.

The 6600 went against the trend of using microcode to build up an instruction repertoire. Curiously, it resembled the approach taken by the first digital computers, including the electromechanical Harvard Mark I (1944) and the ENIAC (1946). In the Mark I, for example, there was no operation to "multiply." Instead, lines of paper tape were punched to route numbers to a multiplying unit. While doing the multiplication, the Mark I could be coded to do something else as long as it did not need that product (or the multiplying unit). The 6600 had two floating multiply units, each of which could perform a multiplication in 1 microsecond, but no integer multiply command. Seymour Cray believed in a very sparse instruction repertoire, and his ideas presaged in many ways the current trend toward reduced instruction set computers (RISCs - *q.v.*).

Cray-1 Control Data upgraded the CDC 6600 with the 7600 in 1969 and produced an incompatible supercomputer called the STAR in 1972. The latter machine was capable of parallel operations on vector data—a feature also used in the design of the Texas Instruments Advanced Scientific Computer (1972). Around that time, Seymour Cray left CDC and formed Cray Research, whose goal was to produce an even faster machine.

In 1976, Cray Research announced the Cray-1, with the first delivery in March to the Los Alamos National Laboratory. Preliminary benchmarks showed it to be ten times faster than the 6600. Like that machine, the Cray-1 had 12 functional units and extensive buffering between the instruction stream and the central processor. Memory options ranged from 250K words to 1 million 64-bit words. The chief difference between the 6600 and the Cray was the latter's ability to process vector as well as scalar data.

The Cray-1 also achieved high speeds through innovative packaging. The computer used only four types of chips, each containing only a few circuits that used emitter-coupled logic (ECL). The circuits were densely packed and arranged in a three-quarter circle to reduce interconnection lengths. Circuit modules were interconnected by wires, laboriously soldered by hand. The modules were cooled by liquid Freon, which circulated through aluminum channels that held the circuit cards. Large power supplies located at the base of each column supplied power. These design decisions resulted not only in a fast

FIG. 7.   CRAY-1. (Photo: Cray Research, Inc.)

machine, but also one that had a distinctive and deceptively small size and shape.

Prices for a Cray-1 were on the order of $5 million and up. The Cray-1 sold well and the company prospered. Control Data continued offering supercomputers for some time, but eventually withdrew from the business. IBM had countered the announcement of the 6600 with its own 360 Model 91 (1967), which, however, was a commercial failure. However, other machines based on the 360/370 architecture in the late 1980s established IBM as a competitor in the class. Cray research announced the X-MP, a multiple processor version of the Cray-1, in 1982, the Cray-2 in 1985, and the Y-MP in 1988. Several Japanese firms, including NEC and Fujitsu, entered the arena with machines in the supercomputer class in the mid-1980s. In the U. S., several start-up companies entered the field in the late 1980s with machines with performance approaching the Crays, but selling at lower cost.

Beginning in the mid-1960s, the supercomputer was established as a viable class of machines, rather than as specialized, one-of-a-kind experimental machines. The persistence and ingenuity of one man, Seymour Cray, had a lot to do with that. Although the class is well established, the design of these machines tends to be idiosyncratic, with the personal preferences of individual designers playing a much larger role than it does in other classes. Each designer seeks the fastest device technology and pays close attention to packaging, but various architectural philosophies are followed. In contrast to Cray's approach, for example, Thinking Machines, Inc. of Cambridge, Massachusetts introduced a computer in the mid-1980s called the Connection Machine, which is characterized by a massively parallel architecture. All agree that a degree of vector processing and other parallelism is necessary, but just how much—therefore, how far to stray from the classic von Neumann concept—is far from settled.

Personal Computers Many persons in the computer business saw the trend of lower prices and smaller packaging occurring through the 1960s. They also recognized that lowering a computer's price and making it smaller opened up the market to new customers who would never have been considered to be reasonable prospects during an earlier generation.

Seen in this light, and with the hindsight of a decade of furious growth of the industry, it seems inevitable that a computer company would introduce the personal computer. The truth is more complex: The personal computer's invention was the result of a conscious effort by individuals whose vision of the industry was quite different from that of the established companies.

An understanding of the invention and subsequent growth of the personal computer must begin with an understanding of the technical and social components of a true "personal" computer. Some of the first electronic computers of the late 1940s were operated as personal computers in the sense that all control and operation of a machine was turned over to one user at a time. Prospective users had to take their place in line with others waiting to use the machine, but there were no supervisory personnel or computer operators between them and the machine. This mode of operation and very low cost are the defining characteristics of what constitutes a personal computer.

As the industry matured into the third generation, a style of access arose that became known as a "computer utility": computing power made accessible to individuals through remote terminals accessing a centralized, timeshared mainframe. Control over the physical location and supervision of the mainframe was left to computer specialists and technicians. The user had the impression that the full resources of the mainframe were available to him or her, with few of the administrative headaches. This approach had many advantages, but its very appeal and its analogy to an electric power utility created for some companies a mental block that prevented them from marketing a personal computer.

Throughout the late 1960s, the semiconductor manufacturers were continuing to place even more circuits on single chips of silicon. Around 1970, these developments led to the first consumer products: digital watches, games, and calculators. Four-function pocket calculators, priced near $100, appeared around 1971, and the following year Hewlett-Packard introduced the HP-35, which offered floating-point arithmetic and a full range of scientific functions. The HP-35 sold for $395 and was an immediate success for Hewlett-Packard, a company that had not been part of the consumer electronics business.

Some individuals within DEC, Xerox, HP, and IBM proposed to build and market an inexpensive, general-purpose personal computer around this time, but their proposals were either turned down or only weakly supported. At the same time, radio and electronics hobbyist magazines were publishing articles on how to build sophisticated digital devices using the TTL chips then becoming available at low prices. By 1973, the space that the personal computer would eventually fill was being nibbled at from above, by cheaper and cheaper minicomputers, and from below, by pocket programmable calculators and hobbyist's kits.

In January 1975, *Popular Electronics* published a cover story on a computer kit that sold for less that $400. The machine, called the Altair, was designed for the magazine by MITS, a company consisting of about ten employees located in Albuquerque, New Mexico. The Altair filled the space perfectly. It was inexpensive, less than an HP-35. It was designed around the Intel 8080 microprocessor, a chip that offered a rich instruction set, flexible addressing, and a 64 Kbyte addressing space. Also, Ed Roberts, the head of MITS, had designed the Altair along the lines of the best minicomputers, with a bus architecture and plenty of slots for expansion.

There were many things the Altair lacked, however, including decent mass storage and I/O. As delivered, it represented the minimum configuration of circuits that one could legitimately call a "computer." But hobbyists were tolerant. In fact, these hobbyists were the key to the launching of the personal computer, and the reason why the PDP-8 and the other machines proposed or offered by the established companies did not inaugurate this class of machines.

Those who bought the Altair did so not because they had a specific computing job to do, but rather because they understood the potential of owning a general-purpose, stored program computer. They understood, as the mini and mainframe makers did not, the social implications of the word "personal." As such they were in the tradition of Alan Turing (*q.v.*), who asked whether a computer could think at a time when few could run more than an hour without failing, or John Mauchly (*q.v.*), who set out to create a commercial computer industry at a time when nearly everyone else believed that the total world market for them would be on the order of ten. The

FIG. 8. Altair 8800. (Photo: Smithsonian Institution.)

personal computer's social appeal was that its owner could do as he or she wished with it; it became an extension of the owner's mind and hands, a tool like a pocket knife. Further details on the history of the personal computer are given in the next part of this History article.

Personal Workstations Beginning in the late 1980s, a number of companies introduced personal workstations, whose architecture reversed the trend set by the 360, VAX, and 8080-series. Instead of using a complex, microcoded instruction set, these workstations are *Reduced Instruction Set Computers* (RISC - *q.v.*), which use a small instruction set applied to many fast registers. These computers are intended for use by a single individual, and provide high-resolution graphics, fast numerical processing, and networking capability. As such they combine the attributes of the personal computer with those of the higher classes. Their performance reaches into the low end of the supercomputer range, but their prices, currently ranging from $100,000 down to $10,000, touch the high end of the personal computer class.

Future Trends The future may see the industry stabilize around networks of these workstations (*see* FILE SERVER). Should this happen, all other classes of machine will be subordinate to this one. On the networks connected to these workstations, other types of computers will continue to exist and evolve: mainframes to provide mass storage or database management, minis for network or process control, and supercomputers for intensive numeric processing. These computers may incorporate

FIG. 9.   IRIS Personal Workstation. (Photo: Silicon Graphics.)

new architectures that radically deviate from the classic von Neumann model. But both their architecture and even their existence will be transparent to the user. The situation is similar to the way someone using the telephone neither sees nor is aware of the specialized switching, billing, and signal-processing equipment connected to the modest telephone on one's desk (unless one of the computers malfunctions).

In the above scenario, the generational and class distinctions that characterized the history of computing since 1950 would come to an end. But in computing, any attempt to predict the future is bound to fail. The rapid pace of innovation is likely to continue, with the future bringing surprises that no one can predict. A simple extrapolation of existing trends points to an even smaller class of computers, and indeed such may have already appeared in the form of "laptop" (*q.v.*), notebook, or even palm-sized computers. But this time smaller size alone will not produce a qualitatively new class. If another class of machines should appear, it is likely to be as novel and unexpected as were the mini- and personal computer in their day. Looking at what seems to be missing from present computers, two needs stand out: ease of use and communications. Current products meet neither very well.

Despite the penetration of personal computing into the workplace, many areas of work have yet to benefit from their introduction. Computers remain difficult to use, frustrating, and overly complex in the way they present software to their owners. Manufacturers are already devoting large resources to developing graphical user interfaces (GUIs), best exemplified by the Apple MacIntosh, introduced in 1984. But, even with this computer, many of the frustrations of casual computer users remain.

There is little doubt that there is a need for systems that better integrate communications and general-purpose computing—witness the explosive growth of cellular telephones, pocket pagers, and facsimile (fax) machines beginning in the mid-1980s. It is illustrative of the need and of the problem to note that the comparatively simple fax technology, which sends an image of a page over ordinary telephone lines, has rapidly eclipsed the packet-switched networks such as Internet for general use, mainly due to the former's ease of use.

In the early 1980s, many believed that the marriage of computing and communications was imminent. The breakup of the AT&T monopoly in 1984 was seen as the pivotal event that would hasten this event. AT&T lost no time in marketing a line of computers, while IBM acquired communications technology. But to their mutual frustration, the marriage did not happen. The fundamental reasons why it should happen are still valid. There have been successes in establishing large digital networks under private control, such as the SABRE system for airline reservations or automatic teller machines for personal banking. But the vast majority of computers in use today are unable to communicate with one another. Depending on the products to be marketed, the surprising joint venture of IBM and Apple Computer called Taligent announced in 1991 may address this need.

Progress depends partly on technology, but also in

establishing communications standards, uniform government regulations, "open systems" of architecture, and protocols. The universal acceptance of networked personal workstations, as compelling as it may seem, will not happen without such standards taking hold. Also, people have to feel as comfortable using these networks as they do with the telephone system.

Conclusion The word "revolution" is overused, but by the metric of computing speeds, price, size, and power consumption, there has indeed been a revolution in computing technology since 1950. But that is not the only way to measure what has been happening, nor does it give one a reliable guide to future trends. The persistence of certain patterns of development, based on architectural features, has given some structure to these events. Future development may depend on that as well as other factors.

References

1982. Siewiorek, Daniel P., Bell, C. Gordon, and Newell, Allen. *Computer Structures: Principles and Examples.* New York: McGraw-Hill.

1986. Bashe, Charles J., Johnson, Lyle R., Palmer, John H., and Pugh, Emerson W., *IBM's Early Computers.* Cambridge, MA: The M.I.T. Press.

1989. Smith, Richard E. A historical overview of computer architecture. *Annals of the History of Computing,* **10**, 277–303.

PAUL E. CERUZZI

PERSONAL COMPUTERS

The Beginnings By 1970, a few computer visionaries saw that the new IC technologies not only solved the tyranny of numbers, but might even make it possible for small, relatively inexpensive computers to find their way into the individual home or office. The way was paved by electronic enthusiasts and hobbyists. It was not an unreasonable hope, because the increasingly small minicomputers of the 1960s, such as the later PDP-8 versions, were in fact no larger than many of the microcomputers of the mid-1970s or the later IBM PC (*q.v.*). Increasingly powerful yet ever shrinking integrated circuits and the invention of electronic calculators in the early 1970s moved the dreams along. There was scattered talk in one or two large companies about building small computers for individuals using the new chip technology. However, the first to realize the fantasy of owning their very own computer were a handful of electronics enthusiasts.

A few computer kits based on the new integrated circuit chip technology were available in the early 1970s. They appeared as kits or in electronics magazines as construction projects for electronics professionals or advanced hobbyists. These early kits created interest and awareness of the possibilities of owning one's own computer which was important to the personal computer movement.

The first known example was the "Kenbeck" which was advertised and sold in *Scientific American* around 1973. Like several such early machines, it was limited to

showing the principles of computing, but it was a working machine.

An example of a more usable machine is the "Mark-8," first advertised in the July 1974 Issue of *Radio-Electronics*. The electronics magazines usually made arrangements with electronics suppliers and manufacturers so that at least the key parts needed for the construction project could be purchased through the mail. The parts kits could include anything, but usually contained the circuit board and those parts that were not easy to get in a TV or electronics hobby shop. The prototype of the Mark-8 was designed and built by Jonathan Titus, then with the chemistry department of Virginia Polytechnic Institute in Blacksburg, Virginia. The "brain" of this and several other such machines was the Intel 8008, the next commercial version of the original microprocessor developed for calculators, the 4004. Several hundred of the machines were built by enthusiasts, and a club or "users' group" with its own newsletter was formed for mutual help and support.

From these machines and later ones produced by the new microcomputer entrepreneurs, the legend arose that the microcomputer was exclusively a grassroots movement created by individuals or small groups working in garages or recycled sandwich shops. The claim was that large companies couldn't really innovate. But there are two dramatic examples that contradict this romantic and comfortable mythology.

Xerox Alto Xerox Corporation had established its Palo Alto Research Center, more famous as "Xerox PARC," in the 1960s. Here, several research groups were given considerable freedom and funds to create high-technology machinery in various areas. One result was the "Alto," a personal computer in every sense of the word, which became operational in 1973. It was well ahead of any of the machines then available from kits. It featured high-resolution graphics on a full-page screen, a mouse (*q.v.*), high-capacity (for the time) 8-inch drives, and some excellent software. Though widely used within the Xerox Parc facilities, there was confusion and controversy about marketing the machine and it appeared publicly only as the elegant and expensive Xerox 850 dedicated word processor. The Alto caught the attention of many people, including Steve Jobs, who hired Larry Tessler and others from Xerox to work on projects for Apple Computer (*q.v.*), which included the unsuccessful Lisa machine and its popular and influential successor, the MacIntosh.

IBM SCAMP The sleek and attractive portable prototype machine called SCAMP was designed and built in the last few months of 1973 by a project team headed by Paul Friedl of the IBM Palo Alto Science Center. It was originally conceived by IBM as a vehicle to spread the use of its APL language by engineers. Heavier and slightly larger than the later "luggables" of the early 1980s, it was a personal computer in every respect, including a handle and even software that functioned as a spreadsheet (*q.v.*). Although this prototype also preceded anything offered by the small entrepreneurs, the production model (the IBM model 5100) did not reach the market until late 1975 and then as a rather expensive machine for engineering use. The Scamp and the Alto demonstrate that large companies *can* innovate; what they seldom do is commit large resources before they see a market. Despite many claims after the fact, few, if any, realized that America had a remarkable number of people who wanted *their own computer.*

The "Altair Age"   Although few, if any, predicted it, the market was ready for a complete computer kit by early 1975 and it came in the form of the now famous Altair. The Altair was produced by a small entrepreneurial company in Albuquerque, New Mexico called Micro Instrumentation and Telemetry Systems (MITS), which had been formed to make electronic instruments for model rockets. Like the Mark-8, the Altair came to many people's attention as the subject of an article in an electronics magazine, *Popular Electronics* (January 1975), where it was shown on the cover. No one predicted the great response to the Altair kit; it was hoped that perhaps 200 (a projected break-even point) would be sold, but thousands of orders poured in during the first year.

Though potentially a genuine computer and a real bargain at $397, the Altair required a great deal of work in assembly and trouble-shooting just to get it up and running. Though it was marketed as a complete kit, it was not a project for the faint of heart, much less the technical novice. Yet many novices did attempt to build the machine and many succeeded.

When built, the Altair did nothing more than produce patterns of lights on its front panel in response to a "program" that the owner put into the machine with the switches on the front panel. Serious applications required many additional and expensive additions, both inside and outside the machine, such as a keyboard and television screen. A key technical feature of the Altair was its provision of *slots* on the main circuit board in the bottom of the machine. These allowed additional electronic circuit boards to be plugged into the Altair that could be manufactured by companies other then MITS. Most early microcomputer companies got their start by making new or improved Altair circuits boards; the *open architecture* (*q.v.*) spawned an industry.

The Homebrew Club   The early computer kits like the Mark-8 and the Altair were very difficult to build, maintain, and operate. Because of this, owners of these early machines soon began to band together into clubs or "users' groups." Although the groups were truly amateur, the core of most of them consisted of people who worked in one phase or another of the established computer industry. These people wanted their own computer because they were dissatisfied with the limitations placed on them by those who managed large systems and wanted more direct access to computing power. The first users' group, the Homebrew Club, was located in the Santa Clara Valley south of San Francisco (now better known as "Silicon Valley"). Founded in March 1975, it was a cradle for early entrepreneurial efforts to build microcomputers or their components.

The Processor Technology Sol   A good example of an early entrepreneurial machine is the Sol. This machine was designed by Homebrew member Lee Felsenstein in 1976 for a new company called Processor Technology which had just been started by two other members of the Homebrew Club, Bob Marsh and Bob Curry. The Sol was designed with its keyboard and electronics in a single unit. A later example of this style was the Apple II, which used the same type of plug-in electronic circuit boards as the Altair. Many other companies adopted the Altair plug-in approach, called the "S-100" bus system because there were 100 connectors in each slot and on every board that plugged into the slot.

Apple I   The Apple I was designed and manufactured in 1976 by two other members of the Homebrew Club, Steve Jobs and Steve Wozniak. The Apple I was actually only an electronic circuit board. The case and other parts had to be bought or made by the owner. Relatively few Apple I boards were made and sold, but they gave the company its start (*see* APPLE COMPUTER).

The Hidden Enterprise: Computer Publications   As suggested by the racks of magazines, books, and software in stores that supported personal computers, publications about the microcomputer were a business arguably as large as the microcomputer industry itself. Before the great shakeout of 1983–85, there were well over one hundred periodicals (magazines, newsletters) devoted to the subject. Books on microcomputers and related subjects grew into the largest single nonfiction area in publishing.

Godbout Compupro   Machines that used the Altair's original S-100 bus circuit board system continued to be built well into the 1980s and many survive today. The well-constructed machines designed by Bill Godbout were widely admired and were among the first to be used in heavy-duty industrial and professional commercial tasks. For example, a Compupro system did all of the large-screen graphics for the movie "War Games."

Word processing (*q.v.*) was one of the earliest and most important uses of the microcomputer. For example, science fiction writer and microcomputer columnist Jerry Pournelle used a Godbout whimsically named "Zeke II" for several novels and many columns in *BYTE* magazine.

The Osborne   Conceived by computer commentator Adam Osborne and designed by Lee Felsenstein, the 1981 Osborne was the first personal computer that was truly portable and that came "bundled" with a large set of application programs, such as word processing, spreadsheets, databases, etc. Although the programs that came with the machine varied over the lifetime of the company, all of them were close to the best then available in terms of power and usefulness.

Like the Godbout and most other personal computers of the S-100 (Altair) type, the Osborne's programs all worked exclusively with a supportive software system called CP/M written by Gary Kildall in the early 1970s.

Though written originally for the use of computer programmers, CP/M was just easy enough to learn and use that it became the standard for this generation of machines. We have mentioned only a few of the many CP/M machines made from 1976 to the early 1980s when they were displaced by the IBM PC and competitive compatible machines.

The Computer as Appliance

The Tandy TRS-80 Model 1 Along with the Apple II and the Commodore Pet, the TRS-80 (Fig. 1) was introduced in 1977 as an "appliance" computer. That is, unlike the machines of the kit era of the previous few years, it was built and tested and ready to be turned on. It came with a built-in computer programming language, Basic, stored in ROM (*q.v.*), and an excellent instruction manual for that language written by David Lein. The TRS-80 had no arcane flashing lights to be interpreted; it came with a screen and a keyboard and used ordinary letters and words to communicate with the user.

The Apple II The Apple II, which was announced in the Spring 1977, was still available in several forms in the late 1980s, making it the longest lived design in the history of microcomputing. In many ways, the Apple was a model for successful microcomputers. It had open architecture (like the Altair), flexible pricing practices (book prices were fairly high, but dealers could discount within reason), encouragement of third-party software, an add-on card system (like the Altair), and a strong relationship with its users. In addition, Apple offered color and relatively high resolution graphics which made for marvelous sales demonstrations.

The Commodore 64 The Commodore 64, introduced in the spring of 1982, became the most popular home computer in history. It achieved its popularity partly because of its technical merits and partly because it was aggressively marketed in a wide variety of outlets, including toy stores. The Commodore 64 was inexpensive and had very good color graphics which allowed it to act as a game machine.

Like the CP/M machines described earlier, there were many small start-up companies that produced appliance computers. Many had their own operating systems and thus their software could not be used on other brands of computers. The situation reminded many observers of the biblical Tower of Babel. What was needed for the software industry was to have no more than a few dominant operating systems.

Social Computing Though no longer marketed in a kit form that appealed only to the electronics hobbyist, the next generation of personal computers were still relatively expensive and forbidding machines that were usually poorly explained in the documentation supplied. The standard joke in the early days of microcomputing was that the machines were not delivered, they were abandoned on your doorstep. Because of this, owners of these early machines soon banded together into clubs or users' groups, similar in form to the earlier more technical groups such as Homebrew. The largest computer group in the world and one of the oldest, the Boston Computer Society, was started by Jonathan Rotenberg when he was only 13. The BCS has been dispensing help and information to its members since 1977. Other major social institutions included conferences and computer shows where vendors demonstrated their hardware and software and sometimes sold them at discounts.

FIG. 1. A Tandy TRS-80 microcomputer system.

The Field Matures

The IBM PC The IBM Personal Computer was announced in the late summer of 1981. The announcement was particularly significant because the entry of IBM into this market signaled to the larger corporations that microcomputers were a legitimate part of the commercial computer landscape (*see* IBM PC and PC-COMPATIBLES; Fig. 2 is a picture of a compatible made by Compaq.) Unexpectedly, IBM produced a machine that used mostly standard parts and had many of the open architecture features of the Altair and the Apple. IBM allowed and even encouraged hardware and software by non-IBM firms. This openness, along with IBM's strong reputation for quality and service, quickly brought acceptance from both business people and the existing microcomputer culture. Soon the IBM-PC was the largest-selling personal computer on the market.

The Apple MacIntosh The Apple MacIntosh (*see* Fig. 3) project directed by Steve Jobs was completed during a period when Apple's fortunes were uneven. The special project team worked more than four years to produce the "Mac." As originally delivered, the new machine had very limited memory and was slow in operation. But it had a brilliant *user interface* (*q.v.*) that, along with Apple's general aura and the machine's quaint appearance, made it a favorite among college students. In any case, sales of the Apple II were strong enough to support the MacIntosh until it was improved. The most important factor in the Mac's survival was Apple's adaptation and development of *desktop publishing* (*q.v.*). This application gave the Mac credibility in the corporate marketplace and greatly increased sales (*see* APPLE COMPUTER).

The Sun-1 From the beginning, engineering applications pushed the new computer technology to its limits. Engineers' first needs were for calculating power and

FIG. 2.   COMPAQ Deskpro 486/33L (courtesy of COMPAQ).

FIG. 3.   Apple MacIntosh Plus (courtesy of Apple Computer).

then, later, for computationally intensive graphics for design and manufacture. As microprocessors grew more powerful, it appeared that engineers could have their own personal *workstations* (*q.v.*) that were especially built for technological work. Using special, fast processors, large memories, and fast, high-resolution graphics on large screens, engineers have established new and much higher standards for the young technology. The first company to make this dream into a commercial reality was Sun Microsystems, which produced the Sun 100 in 1984. Since then, other manufacturers have joined the market and personal computers have begun to offer many of the features of the workstation for general use.

For coverage of the current generation of personal computers, see PERSONAL COMPUTING.

JON EKLUND

DIGITAL EQUIPMENT CORPORATION VAX™ SERIES

For articles on related subjects *see* DIGITAL COMPUTERS: HISTORY; MINICOMPUTER; and VIRTUAL MEMORY.

Digital's VAX systems comprise a broad family of compatible computers. The first VAX system, the VAX-11/780; was introduced in 1977 at an entry price of about $200,000. Since then, the product family has been extended with models offering either higher performance or lower cost, spanning the range from small desktop systems to large mainframes. The VAX-11/780, a very successful "super" minicomputer, is still used as a norm for performance ratings. The term VAX Unit of Performance (VUP) is often used to rate other systems relative to the VAX-11/780 computer.

VAX Architecture The VAX architecture defines the common attributes of the VAX family, such as the instruction set, data types, memory management, interrupt handling, exception handling, and other programmer-visible behavior. Standardizing the architecture allows all hardware implementations to be compatible so that the same software runs on all models.

The VAX series embodies a 32-bit architecture with 32-bit virtual addresses and 32-bit general registers. There are 16 general purpose registers, including the program counter, stack pointer, frame pointer, and argument pointer. The VAX architecture features variable-length instructions, from 1 byte to over 50 bytes. Opcodes can be 1 or 2 bytes long. The number of operands varies from 0 to 6. Each operand is specified using a general operand specifier that allows 1 of 13 addressing modes, including true post-indexing. Several data types are supported, including 8-, 16-, and 32-bit integers; single, double, and quadruple precision floating-point numbers; and decimal string, numeric string, character string, 0- to 32-bit fields, and queues.

Its architecture makes the VAX a classic *complex instruction set computer* (CISC). Special instructions are provided for procedure call and return, saving and restoring process context, array index computation, polynomial evaluation, character string manipulation, transformation of packed decimal strings to character strings, etc. It also includes a PDP-11 compatibility mode for emulation of PDP-11 user code.

VAX virtual memory management uses 512-byte pages for address mapping and protection. Four modes (kernel, executive, supervisor, and user) are supported. Each mode has its own stack pointer.

The original VAX architecture included 244 instructions when it was announced in 1977. Four queue instructions for manipulating queues in a multiprocessor system were added in 1978 and retrofitted to all VAX-11/780s in the field. In 1980, 56 new instructions were added to support a new extended range double precision data type (G_floating) and a quadruple precision data type (H_floating). These new instructions were implemented as microcode options on the VAX-11/780 and VAX-11/750. Software emulation was provided to achieve compatibility of systems that did not include the microcode option.

The next major change to the VAX architecture occurred in 1984, with the definition of the MicroVAX subset, which was intended to allow single-chip VLSI microprocessor implementations. Decimal string instructions, certain character string instructions, and PDP-11 compatibility mode were excluded from the MicroVAX and relegated to software emulation. In 1988, a small number of additional instructions were removed from the required subset and replaced with software emulation.

In 1989, 63 new instructions were added to the VAX architecture to support vector register-based integrated vector processing. The vector architecture specifies 16 vector registers, each with 64 elements that are 64 bits wide. The vector instruction set supports integer and floating point arithmetic, logical operations, and stride-based load/stores, as well as scatter/gather. Operations under the control of a mask register allow selected elements of a vector register to be modified.

Operating Systems DEC supports three operating environments for VAX systems: VAX/VMS™, VAX/Ultrix™, and VAXELN™.

The VAX/VMS operating system is Digital's principal operating system. It provides multi-user time-sharing, batch, real-time, and transaction processing capabilities. It supports symmetric multiprocessing, loosely coupled VAXcluster systems, and wide area multivendor networking. It supports all major programming languages, computer-aided software engineering tools (CASE - *q.v.*), information management tools, networking, and security controls.

The Ultrix operating system is based on Unix™ Berkeley Software Distribution 4.2 with 4.3 extensions and AT&T's System V.2 enhancements. It complies with industry standards such as POSIX and X/OPEN.

The VAXELN Real-time Software Tool kit supports dedicated real-time applications, such as process control, simulation, or high-speed data acquisition.

Processors Though the VAX began as a minicomputer, the VAX series now includes a wide range of architecturally compatible processors whose performance spans a range from that typical of workstations through minis to mainframes. A summary of the mini and mainframe VAX products marketed as of 1990 is given in Table 1. A VAX Unit of Performance, one VUP, is approximately 0.5 MIPS. For multi-processor models, the performance cited is that attainable from the maximum processor configuration.

VAX Workstations

VAXstation I With the introduction of the MicroVAX I in 1984, it became technically feasible to enhance the VAX product line with a single-user, graphics-based workstation known as the VAXstation I. The VAXstation I takes the existing MicroVAX I packaging and adds to it a 1-bit frame buffer attached to a 1024 × 864 monochrome monitor. Input/output is accomplished through both a keyboard and a mouse (*q.v.*). The frame buffer remaps a portion of VAX physical memory to the frame buffer, and software routines manipulate this memory to create a basic *window environment* (*q.v.*).

VAXstation II and VAXstation II/GPX The MicroVAX II, like version I, contains graphics capabilities. The same

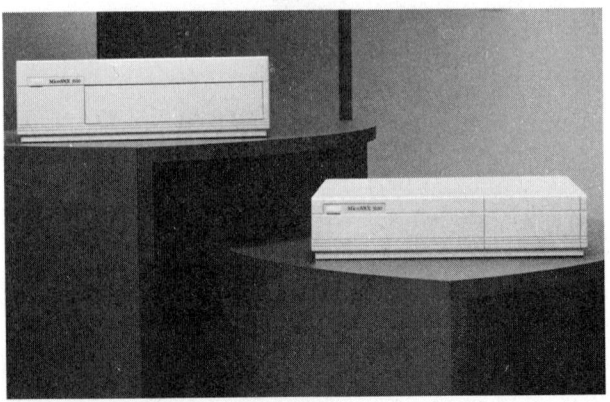

FIG. 1. The MicroVAX 3100 Models 10e and 20e.

TABLE 1.   The DEC VAX Series of Digital Computers

Model	Date	Comments	Circuitry	Bus	Cycle Time	Cache	Performance
VAX-11/780	1978		Schottky TTL	Unibus/ Massbus	200 ns	8 KB	1.0 VUP
VAX-11/750	1980		TTL gate array	Unibus/ Massbus	320 ns	4 KB	0.6 VUP
VAX-11/730	1982		TTL bit-sliced	Unibus/ Massbus	290 ns	none	0.25 VUP
VAX-11/782	1982	Dual-processor 780					2.0 VUP
VAX-11/725	1984	Repackaged 730					0.25 VUP
VAX-11/785	1984	Field updgraded 780	TTL	Unibus/ Massbus	133 ns	8 KB	1.5 VUP
VAX 8600	1984	First pipelined VAX	ECL gate-array		80 ns	16 KB	4.0 VUP
MicroVAX-I	1984	First subset VAX	TTL	Qbus	250 ns	none	0.2 VUP
MicroVAX-II	1985		Single chip	Qbus	200 ns	none	0.9 VUP
VAX 8650	1985	Field updgraded 8600	ECL gate-array		55 ms	16 KB	6.0 VUP
VAX 8200	1986		VLSI NMOS chip	VAXBI	200 ns	8 KB	1.0 VUP
VAX 8300	1986	Dual-processor 8200					2.0 VUP
VAX 8800	1986	Dual-processor 8600	ECL gate-array	VAXBI	45 ns	64 KB	12.0 VUP
VAX 8700	1986	Uniprocessor 8800					6.0 VUP
VAX 8500	1986	Slower 8700					3.0 VUP
VAX 8550	1986	Faster 8500					6.0 VUP
VAX 8250	1987	Faster 8200			160 ns		1.2 VUP
VAX 8350	1987	Dual-processor 8250					2.4 VUP
VAX 8530	1987	Faster 8500					4.0 VUP
MicroVAX 2000	1987	Repackaged uVAX II		SCSI			0.9 VUP
VAX 88x0	1987	1-4 processor 8700					24.0 VUP
MicroVAX 3600	1987		CMOS chip	Qbus	90 ns	64 KB	2.7 VUP
MicroVAX 3400	1988		CMOS chip	Qbus	90 ns	1 KB	2.5 VUP
VAX 6200	1988	1-4 processors	CVAX chip	VAXBI	80 ns	256 KB	11.2 VUP
MicroVAX 3800	1988		CVAX chip	Qbus	60 ns		4.0 VUP
VAX 6300	1988	1-6 processor 6200	CVAX chip	VAXBI	60 ns		24.0 VUP
MicroVAX 3100	1989		CVAX chip	Qbus	90 ns		2.5 VUP
VAX 6000-400	1989	1-6 vector CPUs	CMOS chip	VAXBI	28 ns	128 KB	42.0 VUP
VAX 9000	1989	1-4 pipelined CPUs	ECL gate-array	XMI	16 ns	128 KB	500 Mflops
VAX 4000-300	1990		CMOS chip	Qbus	28 ns	128 KB	8.0 VUP

monochrome frame buffer found on the VAXstation I is used on the MicroVAX II platform, forming the basis for the VAXstation II. In January 1986, Digital introduced its first graphics processor-based subsystem, the GPX. The VAXstation II/GPX is a 1024 × 864 8-bit color or gray scale graphics subsystem using a graphics processor developed by Digital.

VAXstation 2000 In February 1987, Digital introduced its first desktop workstation, the VAXstation 2000, based on the same processor found in the MicroVAX II. This was the first VAX-based system designed from the outset as a workstation. The VAXstation 2000 supported a mono-

chrome frame buffer and a 4-bit (later, 8-bit) color or gray scale graphics subsystem.

VAXstation 3200/3500 Introduced in July 1987, the VAXstation 3200/3500 uses the same CPU as the MicroVAX 3500/3600. The VAXstation 3200 was packaged in a small deskside pedestal, while the VAXstation 3500 used the same deskside enclosure as the MicroVAX 3500. The VAXstation 3200/3500 uses the same graphics options found on the VAXstation II and VAXstation II/GPX.

VAXstation 8000 The VAXstation 8000, introduced in February 1988, was Digital's first true three-dimensional workstation. Based on the VAX 8200 CPU packaged in a deskside enclosure, the VAXstation 8000 used a sophisticated 3-D graphics subsystem designed with Evans and Sutherland. This graphics subsystem consisted of the complete 3-D graphics pipeline and additional hardware support for such features as hardware anti-aliasing of vectors and depth queuing.

VAXstation 3100 In January 1989, Digital introduced the successor to the VAXstation 2000, the VAXstation 3100. The VAXstation 3100 supports both a monochrome frame buffer and an 8-bit Dragon graphics subsystem. The VAXstation 3100 came in two variants. The Model 30 is a small desktop enclosure that supports two internal SCSI-based mass storage devices. The Model 40 supports five internal SCSI-based devices. The Models 38 and 48 represented new CPU/FPU combination and enclosures. In January 1990, Digital further enhanced the VAXstation 3100 family with the introduction of the SPX graphics option. This graphics option supported the X-windows system and offered up to 10 times the performance of GPX graphics.

VAXstation 3520/3540 This is a multiprocessor VAXstation introduced in January 1989. The VAXstation 3520 offered two CPUs, while the 3540 offered four. In addition to supporting multiprocessing, the VAXstation 3520/3540 also offered follow-on 3-D graphics capability to the VAXstation 8000 and the first 1280 × 1024 monitor.

RISC Workstation and System Family

In January 1989, Digital announced its first RISC workstation based on a microprocessor designed by MIPS Computer Systems, Inc. These new systems run the Ultrix operating system and mark Digital's entry into the open systems market (*see* OSI).

DECstation 3100 This workstation, announced in January 1989, features a 64 KB instruction cache and a 64 KB data cache. The system is configurable up to 24 MB of parity memory. It can be configured with monochrome or eight color planes of 1024 × 864 frame-buffer graphics. It has a SPECmark performance rating of 11.3. (*See* BENCH-MARKS.)

DECstation 2100 Announced in July 1989, this workstation is the same as the DECstation 3100 except that it has a lower SPECmark performance rating of 8.3.

DECsystem 3100 This was DEC's first RISC-based multiuser/server system. The DECsystem 3100 was introduced in March 1989. This system allowed terminal users or networked-based server computing for a very attractive entry-level price. This system is based on the DECstation 3100 and offers all of the same features except that it does not support graphics.

DECsystem 5400 Announced in July 1989, this system uses a 64 KB instruction cache and 64 KB data cache. It has a SPECmark performance rating of 11.8.

DECsystem 5800 This multiprocessor system was also announced in July 1989. It can be configured with up to four processors. It uses the memory, I/O, and packaging of the VAX 6000 family. The uniprocessor version is rated at 11.3 SPECmarks. The fully-configured quad processor system achieves a SPEC throughput rating of 39.

DECstation 5000 Model 200 This workstation, announced in April 1990, uses a 64 KB instruction cache and 64 KB data cache. The desktop system is expandable on the desktop to 120 MB of ECC memory and up to 21 GB of disk I/O. It is offered in several different configurations, ranging from simple frame buffer graphics to hardware accelerated high-performance animation quality 3-D graphics. The DECstation 5000 is also available in a multiuser/network server configuration as the DECsystem 5400. It has a performance rating of 18.5 SPECmarks.

References

1983. Bell, C. G. and Bell, J. R., *Digital Equipment Corporation PDP Series, Encyclopedia of Computer Science and Engineering, 2nd Ed.*, Ralston, A. and Reilly, E. D., Ed. New York: Van Nostrand Reinhold. pp. 554–561.

1989. Levy, H. M. and Eckhouse, R. H. Jr. *Computer Programming and Architecture: The VAX, 2nd Ed.* Englewood Cliffs, NJ: Prentice Hall/Digital Press.

1991. Brunner, R. A. *VAX Architecture Reference Manual 2nd Ed.* Englewood Cliffs, NJ: Prentice Hall/Digital Press.

1991. Federighi, F. D. and Reilly, E. D. *VAX Assembly Language.* New York: Macmillan.

FIG. 2. The VAXstation Model 76 workstation.

DILEEP P. BHANDARKAR

DIRECT ACCESS

For articles on related subjects *see* ACCESS TIME; FILE; and MEMORY: AUXILIARY.

Early hardware, developed for the storage of large files in a data processing system, depended on two media—punched cards (in the very early days) and magnetic tapes on the early computers. Although widely different in physical characteristics, they had something in common—they forced the user to store file records in some predetermined sequence and to process them in that same order.

Punched-card users had had no option but to accept the limitations of their equipment, but there seemed to be something quite out of balance between the short time a computer took to update a file record and all the sorting, collating, etc., necessary to find the record in the first place. Worse, although users often could learn to live with these limitations, there were certain types of commercial and industrial operations where they were quite unacceptable. In processing banking transactions, for example, it is often very desirable to be able to update each record as and when each transaction is made. In any system that calls for the interrogation of a file, such as airline seat reservations, it is obviously imperative to be able to handle each separate transaction as and when it occurs in a random sequence.

Records in magnetic tape files are stored in the sequence of some key identifier, and access to them is therefore "serial", i.e. item by item in that sequence. The terms *sequential access* and *serial access* are therefore used. What is required is a system for access directly to any desired record; the term usually given to this is *direct access* or *random access*.

Not until the late 1950s was suitable hardware developed to permit files to be stored in such a way that access to any desired record could be obtained in the same time as to any other, and in an acceptably short time. The machine that first accomplished this was the IBM 305 RAMAC (Random Access Method for Accounting and Control), and the storage device was the magnetic disk file.

The magnetic tape unit is in many ways like the domestic tape recorder, where we often have to run through many feet of tape to find the recording we want. The magnetic disk file is in many ways like the phonograph, where the recording head can be moved very quickly (given a steady hand) to any desired position on the surface of the disk to select the desired piece of recording. In practice, the computer disk file is usually equipped with a number of disks, with a separate recording head for each disk surface. In this way, the selection of a desired record at random can usually be made in a fraction of a second, and the computer system can therefore respond in an acceptable time scale to the input item, usually in about one-third of a second.

Where higher speeds are required (measured, say, in hundredths of a second), magnetic drums (Fig. 1) are used. These are fast, rotating cylinders with file information stored on tracks along the surface and with a recording head for every track. There is no need, therefore, to move the heads (as with disk files), and the time for access to required information depends only on the speed of rotation of the drum.

The need for speed in accessing file records is clear. What is even more obvious is the requirement for ultrarapid access to program instructions and data held in the computer's main memory. These are required with an access time measured in millionths of a second or less so that the speed of the arithmetic unit is not wasted.

It is an interesting paradox that one of the fastest devices currently used for random access to files, the magnetic drum, was used in some of the earliest computers for the main memory and was rejected because it was too slow for random access to instructions and data!

It was replaced by magnetic core and then semiconductor memory units, which form the majority of main memories in today's computers. These are capable of providing required data or instructions in times ranging from a few microseconds (millionths of a second) down to a few nanoseconds (billionths of a second), speeds compatible with those of arithmetic and control units. Main memory is therefore also classifiable as direct access memory or, as more commonly called, *random access memory* (RAM).

GRAHAM J. MORRIS

DIRECTORY

For articles on related subjects *see* FILE; LOGIN FILE; and USER INTERFACE.

A *directory* (or *catalog*) is a file of file names. More specifically, a directory contains the names of all files that reside on a particular *volume* (*q.v.*). A volume, in turn, is a unit of mass storage, such as the diskette in a particular floppy disk (*q.v.*) drive or a portion (called a *partition*) of a hard disk (*q.v.*) drive.

The directory itself—a file of stored information—is to be distinguished from that portion of the directory selected for display. In the MS-DOS operating system used on the IBM-PC and PC-compatibles (*q.v.*), for example, the command

dir B:

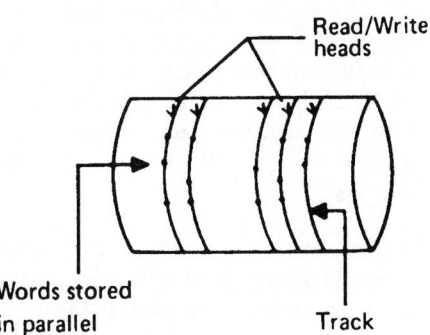

Read/Write heads

Words stored in parallel

Track

FIG. 1. Magnetic drum.

is a request to display all files of volume B (most probably, all files on the diskette currently in drive B). Typically, drives labeled A and B are floppy disk drives, and the letters C and above refer to partitions of a hard disk. On PCs that boot and reboot (*q.v.*) from hard disk partition C, C is the *default drive* whose directory is displayed if no argument is supplied to the command "dir." But, since the hard drive is likely to contain many more file names than fit on a screen, the more usual directory request is qualified so as to elicit a manageable response. For example, the request

    dir de*.*

asks for display of just those file names whose primary name starts with "de," regardless of the secondary name (file extension) that follows the period. (The "*" is a "wild card" character that matches any actual character string of any length, including the null string.) The displayed response might be that shown in Fig. 1. Note that there are three files whose primary name is DECPOS, but, as is shown in column two, they have the distinctively different full names—DECPOS.PAS, DECPOS.MAR, and DECPOS.COM. Column three shows the size of each file in bytes, and columns four and five show the date and time that the file in question was created or last revised.

Continuing to refer to Fig. 1, we see that two of the files have an "extension" of <DIR>. This notation indicates that files DERIVE and DELTA are themselves directories, or more properly, subdirectories of root directory C. To display the files on subdirectory DELTA, the proper command is

    dir \DELTA (or dir \delta since case is
              irrelevant)

and if DELTA, in turn, has a subdirectory called TOWNS, the command to display all files in the sub-subdirectory that have extension "txt" would be

    dir \delta\towns*.txt.

(The notation in the Unix operating system (*q.v.*) is similar, except that the solidus (/) is used instead of the backslash (\).) This ability to form subdirectories to subdirectories to any (reasonable) depth implies that MS-DOS and Unix directories are *hierarchical* (i.e. they have

the data structure of a tree - *q.v.*). More particularly, the tree is a dynamic *n*-ary tree (where *n* is the current maximum number of subdirectories that currently report to the root or any other subdirectory). The tree is dynamic because subdirectories may be added or deleted from the master directory (possibly changing the value of *n*, but that is of no concern to the user).

MS-DOS provides several tools that facilitate navigation through a directory tree. In order to avoid continual specification of a long chain of prefixes, the user may name any subdirectory as the *default directory*, no matter how deeply nested. For example, the "change directory" (CD) command

    CD \alpha\beta\gamma

will thereafter allow use of such commands as

    TYPE roster.txt

instead of

    TYPE \alpha\beta\gamma\roster.txt

But then file turbo.com in, say, subdirectory delta can no longer be executed by typing just turbo (because prefix \alpha\beta\gamma\ would inevitably be applied), unless the user has previously given a clue that the file is not in the default directory. The command to do this is

    PATH \delta

which may very well be part of the login file (*q.v.*) AUTOEXEC.BAT. (The PATH command is usable only to reach *executable* files in other subdirectories; i.e. files with an extension of .COM, .EXE, or .BAT. Data files in other subdirectories can be accessed only through specification of their full path in each DOS command issued.)

Keeping track of the current structure of a complex hierarchical directory can be sufficiently daunting that a sharper tool is needed than any provided by MS-DOS itself. The commercial product XTREE, for example, displays the directory tree explicitly (see Fig. 2.). Arrow keys on the keyboard (or a mouse - *q.v.*) can be used to navigate through the tree, with initially unseen parts of the tree displacing other branches as needed. The figure shows that the user has highlighted subdirectory SNOBOL, whose first 12 files are shown in the box at the lower left. But one can also see that subdirectory C (not to be confused with drive C, which is always followed by a colon) contains more deeply nested subdirectories, INCLUDE and LIB, the first of which contains a still more deeply nested subdirectory called SYS.

As hard disks increase in capacity—up to 800 megabytes on a PC is now possible—the task of finding a particular file on a full disk becomes taxonomically formidable. This concern was anticipated in a work of fiction over 30 years ago:

> The Rx (abstract records) in the new storage systems could be scanned only...by means of a code number arranged as an index to the Rx. Clearly the index itself had to be kept representational and macroscopic else a code number would become

```
Volume in drive C has no label
 Directory of C:
DEBUG    COM  15786   4-01-86    9:10a
DETECT   COM  17522  12-10-86   10:37a
DEBUGGER TXT   3258   5-24-87   11:56p
DECPOS   PAS    490  11-01-91    9:08p
DECPOS   MAR   1053  11-01-91    9:28p
DERIVE   <DIR>        6-23-91   11:29p
DELTA    <DIR>        8-31-89    7:31p
DECPOS   COM  11705   2-12-92    3:53p
        8 Files(s)  702464  bytes free
```

FIG. 1. Response to the request dir de*.*.

Path: \SNOBOL

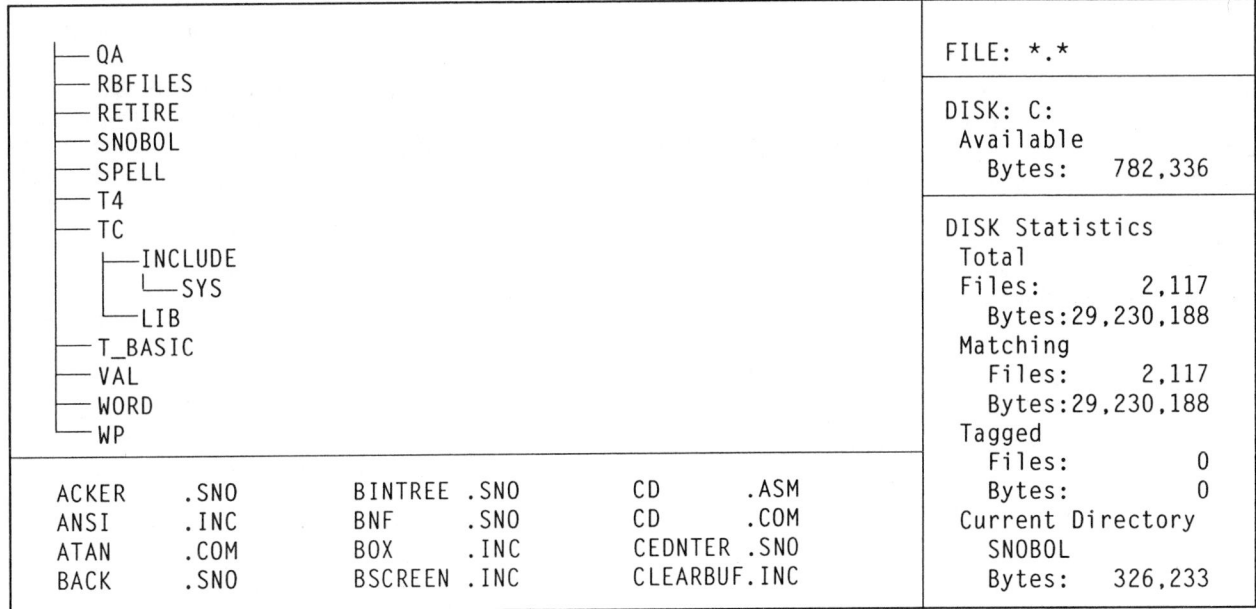

FIG. 2. An XTREE screen showing hierarchical directory structure.

necessary to activate *it*. By the time of the super-micros there were several Indexes to Indexes to Indexes (I^3), and work had already started on an I^4.

These were the innocent days before the problem became acute. Later, Index runs were collected in Files, and Files in Catalogs—so that, for example, $C^3F^5I^4$ meant that you wanted an Index to Indexes to Indexes to Indexes, which was to be found in a certain File of Files of Files of Files of Files, which in turn was contained in a Catalog of Catalogs of Catalogs. Of course actual superscripts were much greater; the structure grew exponentially. The process of education consisted solely in learning how to tap the Rx for knowledge when needed [so that] although hardly anybody knew anything any longer, everybody knew how to find out everything.

Hal Draper, "Ms Fnd in a Lbry," 1961 (long before micros, much less supermicros)

EDWIN D. REILLY

DISASSEMBLER

For related articles *see* ASSEMBLERS; MACHINE AND ASSEMBLY LANGUAGE PROGRAMMING; and SOFTWARE MAINTENANCE.

A *disassembler* is a language processor that accepts machine language object code as input and produces assembly language source code as output. Suppose that

a valuable object file exists whose corresponding source file has been lost or accidentally destroyed. The object code can be executed indefinitely, but the time will inevitably come when modifications are called for. There are ways to "patch" the object code to add new or modified code, but doing so is very tedious and error prone. What else might be done?

Most real-world processes are inherently irreversible, but a few are not. With the right scanning equipment, printed text can be read and converted back to a text file virtually identical to the one from which it was printed. Might something similar be done with orphaned object code? The answer is yes, but certain concessions must be made. If the original (but lost) source code contained the instruction ADD ACE,KING, which an assembler turned into the hexadecimal sequence A7 3B80 DFF7, then a disassembler that encounters this sequence might output something like ADD P04,S12. The "ADD" can be reconstructed, but the disassembler, having no way of knowing what symbols the original programmer used as operands, must synthesize alternative symbols. In this example, the disassembler being used invents symbols in the order A00, A01, A02, etc., up through Z99, and has reached (at least) S12.

The disassembler must be consistent, of course. If hexadecimal address 3B80 is assigned symbol P04 the first time it is encountered, then it must be replaced with the same symbol every later time it is encountered. Moreover, the disassembler must allocate a particular piece of memory of appropriate size to correspond to symbol P04, a size that is determined from knowledge that the computer's ADD command must be applied to operands of a certain type (such as integers or real numbers).

None of the comments that were embedded in the original source code can be reconstructed, and the synthesized source code will usually be far less readable than the original. What we hope to obtain through disassembly, however, is a new source file that is *logically* equivalent to the original, one that, when assembled and executed, will produce the same answers as the original. When the new source code does assemble cleanly and function as stated, it then provides a platform for modification and maintenance. The process is shown in Fig. 1.

Reference

1991. Federighi, F. D., and Reilly, E. D. *VAX Assembly Language Programming*. New York: Macmillan Publishing Company.

EDWIN D. REILLY

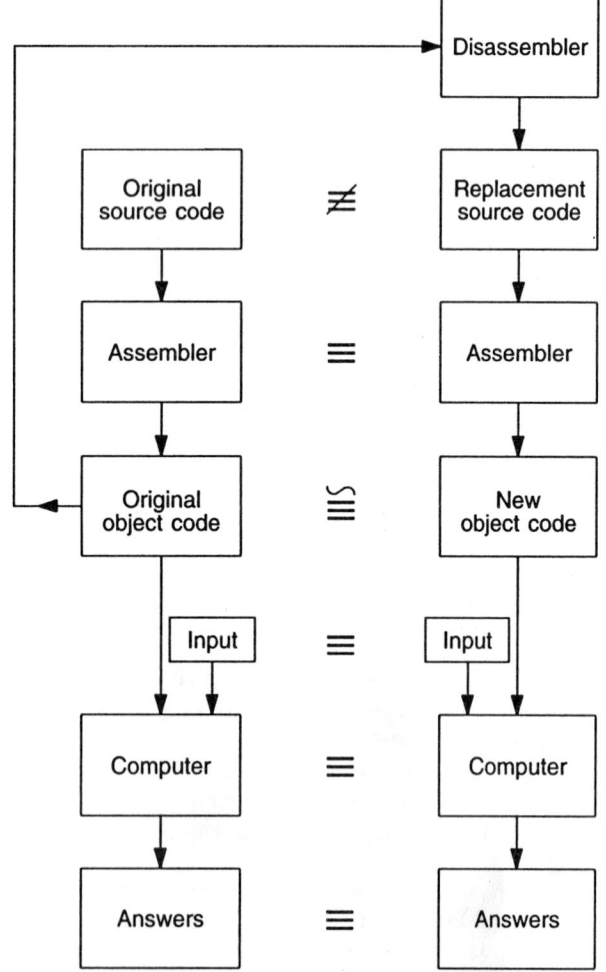

FIG. 1.   The interrelation of assembly and disassembly. The symbols ≡, ≢, and ≅ are to be read "is identical to", "is not identical to," and "is close to identical to," respectively.

DISCRETE MATHEMATICS

For articles on related subjects *see* ALGORITHMS, ANALYSIS OF; ALGORITHMICS; AUTOMATA THEORY; BOOLEAN ALGEBRA; CODES; COMBINATORICS; COMPUTATIONAL COMPLEXITY; COMPUTER ALGEBRA; ERROR ANALYSIS; FORMAL LANGUAGES; GRAPH THEORY; LOGIC DESIGN; LOOP INVARIANT; MATHEMATICAL PROGRAMMING; MATRIX COMPUTATIONS; NUMBER THEORETIC CALCULATIONS; NUMERICAL ANALYSIS; PROGRAM SPECIFICATION; PROGRAM VERIFICATION; QUEUEING THEORY; SEARCHING; and SORTING.

Discrete mathematics encompasses those branches of mathematics that deal with discrete objects, in contrast to other branches, such as calculus and analysis, whose main concern is with continuous functions. Some branches of mathematics, such as numerical analysis and linear algebra, have both continuous and discrete components. Another but somewhat simplistic perspective on the contrast between discrete and continuous mathematics is that the underlying number system in continuous mathematics is usually the real numbers, while for discrete mathematics it is the integers. Because problems in discrete mathematics often involve the integers, which form an infinite set, discrete mathematics is not necessarily *finite* mathematics.

The importance of discrete mathematics has increased rapidly over the past two decades. The reason for this is simply that digital computers are discrete engines, since all calculations done on them are effectively based on the integers. Even floating-point numbers form a discrete system because the floating-point numbers representable in any computer are a *discrete* set of points on the real line.

Discrete Mathematics and Algorithms   Although algorithms play an important role in continuous as well as discrete mathematics, they are much more a part of the warp and woof of discrete mathematics, mainly because algorithms are so closely related to computer programs. Moreover, *algorithmics*, the systematic study of algorithms, which is concerned with the development, analysis, and verification of algorithms, is a much more important subject in discrete mathematics than in continuous mathematics. This is true also because of the close relationship of algorithmics to the solution of problems on computers. Algorithms are a crucial component of most of the examples later in this article.

Proof in Discrete Mathematics   Proof is just as important in discrete mathematics as in any other branch of mathematics. But a striking feature about discrete mathematics in contrast to continuous mathematics is that, while many different methods of proof are applicable in discrete mathematics, one method of proof—mathematical induction—is quintessentially the most important. In its most basic form, mathematical induction proves the truth of a proposition $P(n)$, which depends on some integer parameter n, for all $n \geq n_0$ by first proving the *basis case* $P(n_0)$ by any available proof method. Then, assuming the truth of $P(n)$ for any unspecified value of n

and again using any available method, $P(n+1)$ is proven to be true. These two things together suffice to prove the truth of $P(n)$ for all $n \geq n_0$ (*see also* under "Mathematical Logic," below).

The above form of mathematical induction is often called *weak* induction. Mathematical induction also comes in several other flavors—*strong* induction, which is a generalization of weak induction, and induction on more than one integer parameter, among others. Together, the variants of mathematical induction suffice to prove many results and theorems in discrete mathematics, particularly those involving the analysis and verification of algorithms.

The Content of Discrete Mathematics As judged by the syllabuses of courses on discrete mathematics for college freshmen and sophomores and by the more than 40 textbooks published since 1985 for such courses, there is no universally agreed upon set of topics included under the discrete mathematics rubric, and certainly no agreement similar to that on courses in calculus. However, there is general agreement that various branches of mathematics are clearly part of discrete mathematics. Most of the remainder of this article is devoted to brief descriptions of these branches. The reader should also refer to the list of articles under Discrete Mathematics in the Classification of Articles on p. xxi for a further perspective.

Graph Theory The "graph" in graph theory is not the familiar graph of high school mathematics, which is a "picture" of a continuous function, but rather a collection of *vertices* (or nodes) and *edges* (or branches) joining pairs of vertices. Since graph theory is the subject of a separate article in this Encyclopedia, we content ourselves here with one example of its application.

Fig. 1 displays a *weighted digraph*, weighted because of the weights associated with each edge and a digraph because each edge has a *di*rection. The problem is to find the path (i.e. sequence of edges) from v_0 to v_7 that is shortest (i.e. for which the sum of the edge weights is smallest). There are many practical applications of this situation where the number of vertices is in the hundreds or more.

Fig. 2 displays a sketch of *Dijkstra's algorithm* for the solution of this problem for a graph of $n+1$ vertices, where we want the shortest path from v_0 to v_n. The distance function $d(v)$ is the length of the shortest path from v_0 to vertex v of the graph that passes through only vertices in the set U. Thus, initially, all distances are ∞ except for $d(v_0)$, which is 0. Fig. 3 shows how the computation proceeds for the graph of Fig. 1, with the first row giving the initial values and each subsequent row giving the results after the kth passage through the loop of Fig. 2. The shortest path is $(v_0, v_1, v_3, v_5, v_6, v_7)$, whose length is 11.

Graph theory is one of the most important branches of discrete mathematics and the source of many algorithms of practical importance. In particular, we note the importance of *trees* (*q.v.*), which are special cases of graphs.

Combinatorics Combinatorics is about counting the number of objects of some type or about how many ways there are to do something. It, too, is the subject of a separate article in this Encyclopedia, so again we just present a single example.

A *permutation* $P(n, r)$ is an ordered arrangement of n objects taken r at a time. It is sometimes necessary to generate permutations in lexical order so that if the objects are $1, 2,..., n$, each permutation represents the next number larger than its predecessor). Fig. 4 displays an algorithm to accomplish this when $r = n$ for the objects 1, 2,..., n. It is based on the idea that, given a permutation, the next larger one can be found by beginning at the right and going left, as long as the digits are increasing. When the first digit is reached that is less than its neighbor to the right, exchange it with the smallest digit to its right greater than it and then reverse the order of the previously increasing digits. Thus, starting with 4257631, we identify 5 as the first decreasing digit from the right, exchange it with 6, and reverse 7531 to obtain 4261357.

Applications of combinatorics play a major role in the analysis of algorithms. For example, it is often necessary in such analyses to count the average number of times that a particular portion of an algorithm is executed over all possible input data sets.

Difference Equations Another name sometimes used for this subject is *recurrence relations*. Two main sources

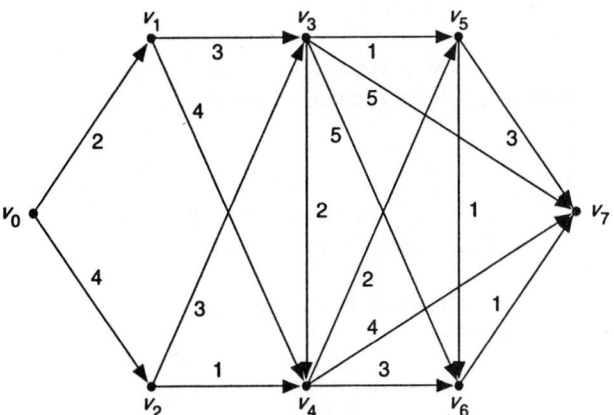

FIG. 1. The Shortest Path Problem. Object: Find the shortest path from v_0 to v_7.

Initialize $d(v_0)$ to 0 and $d(v_i)$ to ∞, i = 1,..., n
$U \leftarrow \{v_0\}$
repeat
    Update the current distance function.
    Find the vertex u not in U for which $d(u)$ is a minimum;
        if there is a tie choose u arbitrarily.
      $U \leftarrow U \cup \{u\}$
endrepeat when $u = v_n$

FIG. 2. A sketch of Dijkstra's Algorithm.

k	$d(v_1)$	$d(v_2)$	$d(v_3)$	$d(v_4)$	$d(v_5)$	$d(v_6)$	$d(v_7)$	Vertex Added to U
0	∞	∞	∞	∞	∞	∞	∞	v_0
1	2	4	∞	∞	∞	∞	∞	v_1
2	2	4	5	6	∞	∞	∞	v_2
3	2	4	5	5	∞	∞	∞	v_3
4	2	4	5	5	6	10	10	v_4
5	2	4	5	5	6	8	9	v_5
6	2	4	5	5	6	7	8	v_6
7	2	4	5	5	6	7	8	v_7

FIG. 3. Applications of Dijkstra's Algorithm to the graph of Fig. 1. k represents the count of the passages through the loop with $k = 0$ the initial state.

of these equations are the *discretization* of differential equations for solution on a computer and the analysis of algorithms (*see* ALGORITHMS, ANALYSIS OF). We shall focus on the latter here. (For the former, *see* both the NUMERICAL ANALYSIS and PARTIAL DIFFERENTIAL EQUATIONS articles.) In general, a difference equation of *order k* has the form

$$y_n = f(y_{n-1}, y_{n-2}, \dots, y_{n-k}) \tag{1}$$

$$y_i = b_i, \quad i = 1, \dots, k,$$

where (1) is the difference equation itself and below it are the *initial conditions*. By far, the most important difference equations are *linear*:

$$y_n + a_1(n)y_{n-1} + a_2(n)y_{n-2} + \dots + a_k(n)y_{n-k} = g(n),$$

where each $a_i(n)$ can be any function of n. When $g(n) = 0$, we call the equation *homogeneous*, otherwise, it is *nonhomogeneous*. When each $a_i(n)$ is a constant a_i, we speak of *linear, constant coefficient difference equations*, which are the easiest to solve.

The solution of a homogeneous, linear, constant coefficient difference equation of order k has the form

$$y_n = \sum_{i=1}^{k} c_i r_i^n \tag{2}$$

where the r_i's in (2) are the roots of the polynomial equation

```
Input n
Algorithm ALLPERM
        for i = 1 to n                                      [Generate first permutation]
            Perm(i) ← i
        endfor
        repeat                                              [Main permutation loop]
            print Perm
            b ← n − 1                      [b will be position of leftmost digit to be changed]
            repeat until b = 0 or Perm(b) < Perm(b+1)
                b ← b − 1
            endrepeat
            if b = 0 then stop                              [All permutations found]
            c ← n              [c will be position of leftmost digit to be exchanged with b]
            repeat until Perm(c) > Perm(b)
                c ← c − 1
            endrepeat
            Perm(b) ↔ Perm(c)                               [Exchange digits]
            d ← b + 1 ; f ← n                               [Initialize for reversal]
            repeat until d ≥ f
                Perm(d) ↔ Perm(f)                           [Reverse by exchanging]
                d ← d + 1; f ← f − 1
            endrepeat
        endrepeat
Output All n! permutations of 1,2,...,n
```

FIG. 4. Algorithm to generate all the permutations of 1, 2,..., n.

$$r^k - \sum_{i=1}^{k} a_i r^{k-1} = 0$$

and the c_i's are found using the initial conditions. The reader familiar with homogeneous, linear, constant coefficient differential equations will see a close analogy between the solution of those equations and the solution of similar difference equations.

Other classes of difference equations, such as first-order linear equations without constant coefficients and some nonhomogeneous equations, can also be solved in closed form but, as with differential equations, most difference equations cannot be solved in closed form. However, when a difference equation cannot be solved in closed form, we can always just compute as many values of the solution of (1) as we wish by brute force. That is, with $n = k + 1$, we can just plug the initial conditions into (1) and compute y_{k+1}, with $n = k + 2$ we can compute y_{k+2}, etc.

As an example of the use of difference equations in analyzing algorithms, consider the algorithm for binary search in the article SEARCHING. If we count the worst case of the number of comparisons c_m of the search item with items on a list of length 2^m (where we choose a power of 2 as the list length to keep things simple), we obtain the difference equation

$$c_m - c_{m-1} = 1, \quad c_o = 1$$

whose solution is $c_m = m + 1$. This is just the solution given in the article on SEARCHING, if you set the list length $n = 2^m$.

Mathematical Logic   Mathematical logic (hereafter just *logic*) has become an accepted part of discrete mathematics. One reason for this is that all efforts at the verification of algorithms inevitably involve the notation and methods of logic. The other is that mathematical logic has always played an important role in the design of computers and is playing an increasingly important role in various branches of computer science, particularly artificial intelligence (*q.v.*). One component of logic that is always part of discrete mathematics courses is the *propositional calculus*, which is concerned with the analysis of propositions that can be stated in English (e.g. traditional syllogisms), as well as those that arise in the verification of algorithms (e.g. the assertion of a *loop invariant* in an algorithm).

As an example of the latter, Fig. 5 displays an algorithm to multiply two integers by repeated addition together with the *assertions* to be used in the proof of the algorithm. Focusing on the one labeled *loop invariant*, we note that the proposition *prod* = *uy* can be proved to be true when the loop is first entered and at each subsequent entry into the loop. The proof is essentially by mathematical induction (actually a *finite* induction, which is very common in proofs of algorithm correctness). Since $u = x$ when the loop is finally exited, the final value of *prod* is xy as desired.

Propositional logic is used in the design of computers in its form as Boolean algebra (*q.v.*), wherein it is used to design logical circuits that realize particular Boolean functions (*see* LOGIC DESIGN). Such logical circuits can then be fabricated on chips.

In more sophisticated attempts at the verification of algorithms than that shown in Fig. 5 and in most applications of logic elsewhere in computer science, it is not the propositional calculus but its more sophisticated cousin, the *predicate calculus*, that must be used. The predicate calculus deals with *predicates*, which are propositions containing variables so that whether a predicate is true or false depends upon the values of its variables. Thus, "x is a feminist" is a predicate that would be true if x is Gloria Steinem and false if x is Phyllis Schafly. The crucial concept in the predicate calculus is that of a *quantifier*. The *universal quantifier* is written $\forall$ and read "for all" so that

$$(\forall n)\, P(n)$$

is true if $P(n)$ is true for all values of n and false otherwise. (Except when the domain of n is given—see the examples below—the domain is normally the positive integers or the nonnegative integers.) Using the universal quantifier, we may express formally the idea of proof by (weak) mathematical induction. That is, to prove

$$(\forall n: n \geq n_0)\, P(n),$$

```
Input x                                    [Integer ≥ 0]
      y                                     [Integer]
Algorithm MULT
    {x≥0}                                   [Input specification]
    prod ← 0; u ← 0
    {prod = uy}                             [Loop invariant]
    repeat until u = x
        prod ← prod + y
        u ← u + 1
    endrepeat
    {prod = uy ∧ u = x}                     [Loop termination condition]
    {prod = xy}                             [Output specification]
Output prod                                     [=xy]
```

FIG. 5.   A multiplication algorithm with assertions.

it suffices to prove

$$P(n_0) \wedge (\forall n: n \geq n_0 \, [P(n) \Rightarrow P(n + 1)]).$$

The other significant quantifier is the *existential quantifier*, which is written $\exists$ and read "there exists" so that

$$(\exists n) \, P(n)$$

is true if $P(n)$ is true for *any* n and false otherwise.

Here is an example of the use of quantifiers in an algorithm verification context. Suppose you wish to write the output specification for an algorithm (or program) whose purpose is to sort in ascending order m numbers, $a_1, a_2, \ldots, a_m$. You could write something like

$$a_1 \leq a_2 \wedge a_2 \leq a_3 \wedge \ldots \wedge a_{m-1} \leq a_m,$$

or perhaps

$$a_1 \leq a_2 \leq \ldots \leq a_m,$$

but it is much prettier to write

$$(\, \forall i{:}1 \leq i \leq m)(\, \forall j{:} \, 1 \leq j \leq m \, [i < j \Rightarrow a_i \leq a_j],$$

where the finite domain of each quantifier is indicated explicitly.

Other Branches of Discrete Mathematics Here are brief descriptions of areas of discrete mathematics that are sometimes but not always found in discrete mathematics courses.

Discrete Probability

This deals with the familiar notions of probability where the *sample space* (i.e. the space of possible *events*) is finite or countably infinite. The probability distributions of discrete probability include the familiar binomial and Poisson distributions. The former may, for example, be used to solve the following problem.

Consider a multiple choice exam with five possible choices on each question (such as the SATs), where you score 1 point for each correct answer and lose 1/4 for each incorrect answer. What is the probability of improving your score if you make pure guesses on 5 questions? What is the *expected* change in your score if you make pure guesses on 5 questions?

For the first question, we need to compute

$$1 - [\text{the probability of getting 0 or 1 answers correct}]$$

since you improve your score only if you get 2 or more of the 5 correct. (When you get one answer correct, your score is unchanged.) Since the probability of a pure guess being correct is 1/5, using the binomial distribution, the answer is

$$1 - (4/5)^5 - 5(4/5)^4 \, (1/5) = .263$$

where the second term on the left is the probability of 5 bad guesses and the third is the probability of 4 bad guesses and 1 good one. Despite the fact that the probability of improving your score is only just greater than 1/4, the answer to the question about expected change of score is 0 because, although the probability of losing points (which happens when all 5 guesses are wrong, which occurs with probability .328) is greater than that of gaining them, when you win, you win relatively big (e.g. 5 more points when all 5 guesses are correct), but when you lose, you don't lose so much (only 1 1/4 points when all 5 guesses are wrong). Thus, whether or not you should make pure guesses on a test like the SATs is more a psychological matter than a mathematical one. If you can rule out one of the choices so that the probability of guessing correctly is now 1/4, the probability that you improve your score is .367, the probability of a worse score is .237, and the expected gain is now .312. So, mathematically, you should guess if you can eliminate one answer, but there are still psychological considerations that might make you decide not to guess.

Discrete probability is an important tool in the analysis of algorithms because generally average case analyses require that you consider all possible input data and the *probability* that each occurs.

Sequences and Series

Although a standard part of freshman and sophomore calculus courses, sequences in their entirety and series, except for power series, are bona fide discrete mathematics. Some aspects of sequences and series are particularly pertinent to computers and computer science. For example, whereas mathematicians are usually most interested in convergent sequences, computer scientists are more interested in divergent sequences, in particular those that represent the *execution sequences* of algorithms and programs. For example, the sequence $\{n^2/4\}$ is the average case execution sequence of insertion sort (*see* SORTING), which means that, on the average, $n^2/4$ comparisons of elements on a list of length n will be needed, in order to sort it into lexical order. Thus, we say that insertion sort is an $0(n^2)$ (read "order n^2") algorithm. By determining the execution sequences of various algorithms for the same task, you can judge when one algorithm is to be preferred over another. Sometimes through analysis it is possible to determine the best possible algorithm for a task (*see* COMPUTATIONAL COMPLEXITY) by determining the slowest possible divergent execution sequence. In the case of sorting by comparisons, this sequence is known to be $\{cn \log n\}$, where c is a constant.

A powerful idea in discrete mathematics (and in continuous mathematics, as well) that arises from the study of series is that of *generating functions*. If $\{a_k\}$ is a sequence, its generating function $G(s)$ is defined to be

$$G(s) = \sum_{k=0}^{\infty} a_k \, s^k \, .$$

Using this *formal power series*, many problems in discrete mathematics, including many kinds of difference equations, can be solved. So can a variety of combinatorial problems. For example, the number of combinations a_{nmk} of n distinct objects, k at a time with up to m repetitions of each object can be found by determining that the generating function of the sequence $\{a_{nmk}\}$ is

$$(1 + s + s^2 + \ldots + s^m)^n$$

with a_{nmk} the coefficient of s^k. For example, with $n = 3$, $m = 2$, $k = 3$, a_{323} is given by the coefficient of s^3 in $(1 + s + s^2)^3$, which is easily determined to be 7. If we denote the three objects by a, b, and c, the seven combinations are

aab, aac, abb, abc, acc, bbc, bcc.

Abstract and Linear Algebra Algebras generally deal with discrete objects and are, therefore, a natural part of discrete mathematics. Abstract algebra has many applications in computer science. For example, semigroups have application to formal languages and automata theory, and groups have important applications in coding theory. A particularly important application is the use of finite state machines in compiler construction (*q.v.*) for the *recognition* of syntactically correct language structures (*see* AUTOMATA THEORY). Topics in abstract algebra are now found less frequently in freshman or sophomore discrete mathematics courses than heretofore, in part because they require a considerable amount of mathematical sophistication and in part because abstract algebra is a natural subject of more advanced mathematics courses and its applications are naturally discussed in advanced computer science courses.

Linear algebra (and linear programming) are uncommon topics in discrete mathematics, but are also quite natural, since, although the variables in linear algebra are normally real variables, the structures (e.g. matrices) and manipulations are generally discrete. Moreover, linear algebra is a highly algorithmic subject and is perhaps more effectively taught initially from this perspective than from an abstract vector space perspective. For example, the basic theorems on the solution of systems of linear equations are simply and elegantly derived from a consideration of Gaussian elimination (*see* ERROR ANALYSIS and MATRIX COMPUTATIONS). Fig. 6 displays an algorithm for the solution of $n \times n$ linear systems by Gaussian elimination, which assumes that diagonal elements never become 0. This algorithm can be used as the starting point for the design of a general algorithm for $m \times n$ linear systems, which takes into account all possible difficult and degenerate cases. The algorithm in Fig. 6 may also be used to analyze Gaussian elimination, as shown in Fig. 7.

Conclusion This has been quite a brief survey of discrete mathematics. We have not even touched upon

```
Input Â                       [n ×(n+1) augmented matrix [A|b], with entries aij]
Algorithm GAUSS-SQUARE                              [Works if no 0 pivots]
    procedure DOWNSWEEP(i)      [Subtract multiples of row i from lower rows]
        for k = i+1 to n                          [k varies over rows below i]
            m_k ← a_ki /a_ii
            a_ki ← 0                      [Assigning saves a step over computing]
            for l = i+1 to n+1                      [l varies over entries in row k]
                a_kl ← a_kl − m_k a_il
            endfor
        endfor
    endpro
    procedure Scale (i)
        a_{i,n+} ← a_{i,n+1}/a_ii
        a_ii ← 1
    endpro
    procedure Upsweep(i)        [Subtract multiples of row i from higher rows]
        for k = i–1 downto 1
            a_{k,n+1} ← a_{k,n+1} − a_ki a_{i,n+1}
            a_ki ← 0
        endfor
    endpro
    for i = 1 to n                                          [Main algorithm]
        Downsweep(i)
    endfor
    for i = n downto 1
        Scale(i)
        Upsweep(i)
    endfor
Output Â                                          [Last column is solution]
```

FIG. 6. Algorithm to find the solution of $A\mathbf{x} = \mathbf{b}$ when A is an $n \times n$ matrix, by Gaussian elimination.

	Coefficient Matrix A	Constant Column $\mathbf{b}$
Scale(i)	0	1
All Scaling	0	n
Usweep(i)	0	$i - 1$
All Upsweeping	0	$\dfrac{n^2 - n}{2}$
Downsweep(i)	$(n - i)^2 + (n - i)$	$n - i$
All Downsweeping	$\dfrac{n^3 - n}{3}$	$\dfrac{n^2 - n}{2}$
Total	$\dfrac{n^3 - n}{3}$	n^2
Combined Total	$\dfrac{n^3 + 3n^2 - n}{3}$	

FIG. 7.   Analysis of Algorithm Gauss-Square. Each entry represents the count of multiplications and divisions in the indicated portion of the algorithm.

the basic topics of sets, relations, and functions that underlie all discrete mathematics. Also, we have not mentioned such an important branch of discrete mathematics as number theory, which has recently seen important applications to coding (*see* NUMBER THEORETIC CALCULATIONS). For more information on these areas, the reader is referred to the references. One thing that can be said with certainty about discrete mathematics is that the importance of its various branches will continue to grow as the applications of computers permeate more and more aspects of science, technology, and everyday life.

References

1976. Roberts, F. R. *Discrete Mathematical Models.* Englewood Cliffs, NJ: Prentice-Hall. (Contains many applications of discrete mathematics to the social and biological sciences.)
1985. Doerr, A., and Levasseur, K. *Applied Discrete Structures for Computer Science.* Chicago: Science Research Associates. (Written specifically for computer scientists, with more on logic and automata theory than most discrete mathematics books.)
1988. Bogart, K. P. *Discrete Mathematics.* Lexington, MA: D.C. Heath. (A modern approach with plenty about algorithms.)
1989. Graham, R. L., Knuth, D. E., and Patashnik, O. *Concrete Mathematics.* Reading, MA: Addison-Wesley. (A relatively advanced book, mainly on discrete mathematics, but with a spirited discussion of areas where a combination of the CONtinuous and disCRETE is just what you need.)
1990. Epp, Susanna S. *Discrete Mathematics with Applications.* Belmont, CA: Wadsworth. (Well written and with good coverage of classical discrete mathematics topics.)
1990. Skiena, S. *Implementing Discrete Mathematics—Combinatrics and Graph Theory with Mathematica.* Reading, MA: Addison-Wesley. (How discrete mathematics capabilities can be added on to a well-known computer algebra system.)
1991. Maurer, S. B., and Ralston, A. *Discrete Algorithmic Mathematics.* Reading, MA: Addison-Wesley. (A book that emphasizes the algorithmic approach to discrete mathematics.)

ANTHONY RALSTON

DISK.

DISK.   *See* FLOPPY DISK; HARD DISK; AND MEMORY: AUXILIARY.

DISKETTE.

DISKETTE.   *See* FLOPPY DISK.

DISTRIBUTED SYSTEMS

For articles on related subjects *see* COMMUNICATIONS AND COMPUTERS; DATA COMMUNICATIONS; and NETWORKS, COMPUTER.

Distributed systems are a natural outgrowth of the development of computer networks (*see* NETWORKS, COMPUTERS). Computer networking focused on having a number of processors communicate with one another, as well as on the utilization of such systems by remote users, whether the "user" was a terminal or another computer. With distributed data processing systems, we apply the results of the work in networking to the design of applications systems. A distributed data processing system is characterized by having both the processor and storage facilities physically dispersed and interconnected by data communications facilities, as shown in Fig. 1. Distributed processing systems have been proposed as a means to provide a large number of highly desirable user and operational benefits. Some of these benefits are listed in Table 1.

What is Distributed   There are three activities of a data processing system that may be distributed: (1) processing functions; (2) storage of the database(s); and (3) system control. In order to achieve an appreciable portion of the benefits of distributed systems listed in Table 1, it is essential that the system exhibit a high degree of distribution for all three of these activities.

Distributed and Decentralized Systems   Although the term *centralized* has a very clear meaning

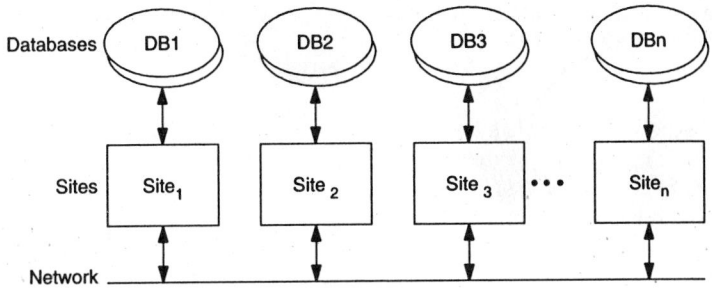

Databases   DB1   DB2   DB3   DBn

Sites   Site₁   Site₂   Site₃ • • • Siteₙ

Network

FIG. 1.   A typical distributed computing system.

almost irrespective of the context in which it is used, the terms *distributed* and *decentralized* have acquired quite different meanings when used in discussing distributed systems. *Distributed* means the *physical distribution* of a component (or components) of the system, such as the operating system code or the database. *Decentralized*, on the other hand, describes an activity in which decisions are made at different physical locations in the system.

Distributed System Requirements

A typical distributed computing system would have a structure such as that shown in Fig. 1. The network is likely to be a wide area network (WAN) having some complex topology that provides moderately reliable inter-site message delivery services with moderate bandwidth and low signaling rate. There may be a significant delay between sending a message and receiving a reply even when no processing is required to generate the reply. Occasionally, the message service is provided through a *local area network* (LAN - *q.v.*).

The sites constitute one or more computers to be treated as one component from the point of view of the system. Usually, each site is connected internally by a local area network if it involves several computers, but it may itself be a distributed system. The wide area network is used to transfer data, coordinate tasks, and share load.

TABLE 1.   Benefits of Distributed Systems

High system performance—fast response
High throughput
High system reliability/high system availability
Graceful degradation (fail-soft capability)
Reduced network transmission costs
Ease of modular and incremental growth
Configuration flexibility
Automatic resource sharing
Automatic load distribution
High adaptability to changes in workload
Incremental replacement and/or upgrading of components
  (hardware and software)
Easy expansion in both capacity and function
Easy adaptation to new functions
Good response to temporary overloads

The traffic on this network will need to be organized via protocols (*q.v.*) associated with network requirements, and higher-level protocols for distributed system requirements. A good example of a higher-level protocol is a mechanism to provide *distributed commit*. In database terminology, a commit is an arrangement to record changes to the database atomically so that either all related changes are recorded or none are. In a distributed system, a distributed commit ensures that all changes at all sites that have cooperated in a task are performed or that none are recorded. For example, in an electronic funds transfer (*q.v.*), it ensures that either both the debit of one account and the credit of the other are recorded or that neither of them is.

A distributed system requires mechanisms for distributed management. Examples are: to find out how the load is distributed across the system; to allow local changes to be made without requiring all sites to stop or coordinate change; to find services; or to choose between alternative equivalent services. A particular problem is to propagate change, such as installing a new version of commonly used software and protocols.

In distributed systems, security has to be provided via protection and authentication mechanisms. For example, data encryption should be used to prevent eavesdropping on network traffic (*see* CRYPTOGRAPHY, COMPUTERS IN). Authentication prevents a site from masquerading as a legitimate or different site, and other controls prevent sites from using resources qualitatively or quantitatively different from those to which they are entitled.

The high-level protocols must support the data exchange, coordination, security, and management of the total distributed system. This requires agreements between participants that may depend partly on data communications standards (*q.v.*). Additional protocol agreements concern the representation of application-specific information (e.g. diagnosis and treatment in a health care management system). Such protocols are difficult to develop; invariably, achieving agreement requires most participants to commit resources to revising or extending their local system. A managerial limit to the scale of distributed systems occurs when this difficulty impedes the evolution of the function and business of the organization that the distributed system was intended to support.

Capabilities of Distributed Systems   A good distributed system should provide at least the following capabilities:

- The user should view the system in the same manner as a centralized or uniprocessor system.
- The selection of the specific resources to be utilized in servicing a user's request should be transparent to the users (i.e. occur without his or her knowledge), unless a specific designation of the resources to be used is desired.
- The distributed operating system should automatically distribute and balance the load over the resources available.
- The distributed database manager should control concurrent access to data files by different processors and should ensure that the contents of redundant copies of the database are at all times consistent.
- The system should be able to continue in operation despite the failure of individual components.

Example Applications   Applications of distributed computing are common in commerce, financial institutions, industry, government, the health care field, and the military. A situation in which a distributed system might be especially appropriate is in a company with dispersed operations, such as a national warehouse system or branch sales offices. The important characteristic is that there be a combination of storage and data processing that can be performed locally while generating only a relatively small amount of external activity that must be sent to other locations for further processing. It should be noted, however, that decisions on the distribution of both processing and data are more often than not based on management or organizational factors rather than on the technical characteristics of the operation. Fig. 2 illustrates a simple example of what might be a portion of a complete distributed system. Branch office computers handle all local activities, while the headquarters' system processes aggregated data at the corporate level.

Another example would be a national chain of supermarkets in which local inventory and point-of-sale accounting may be supported at each market by a single computer system. These can be interconnected to allow common financial management, and they can be connected to warehousing and the transport fleet to organize restocking. They may also be connected to computers at their suppliers to organize reordering, billing, and dispatch. While a consistent regime may operate in all markets, it is unlikely that all of their suppliers will run similar systems; hence, inhomogeneity is inevitable.

When many companies cooperate on a manufacturing task—aircraft production for example—they will share design data, test cases, and test results among their computers. Later, they will manage scheduling, inventory, and marketing via their shared distributed computing system.

Airline reservation systems are only one aspect of an airline management system that may form a worldwide

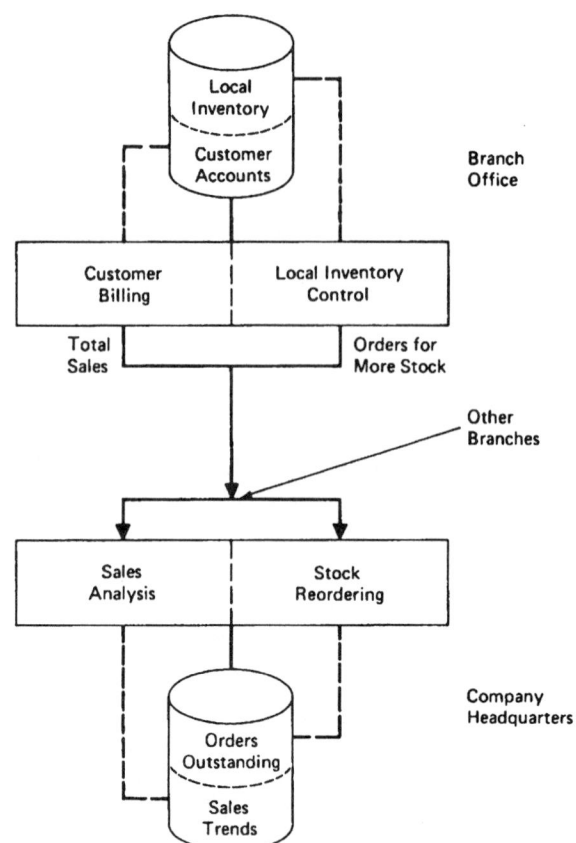

FIG. 2.   An example of a distributed application.

distributed system. These airline systems need to work together to organize passenger transfers, crew management, recovery from aircraft failure, etc.

A system currently being built will be used to collect data from meters and other instrumentation and convey it to utility companies. Individual meters will transmit readings and receive control signals, using low power radio. The data will be relayed by message concentrating computers, each serving an area about 100 meters in radius, passing messages on, by radio, until they reach the computers holding company databases, or sending disconnect and reconnect messages. In a limited application operating within the United Kingdom alone, it is anticipated that 4 million computers will be involved in the distributed system. Similarly, the system supporting brokers and stock exchanges and other financial institutions also forms a worldwide distributed computing system.

Depending on the application, we may find either a uniform, tightly-coordinated system with very specific goals, such as a bank and its state- or country-wide branches, or else a system with considerable variation of goals and interests at each site and that functions in only a partial, loosely coordinated, collaborative way, such as the international collection of stock exchanges and dealers. A system with such partial collaboration is called a *federated* system. Since a company may participate in several distributed systems using the same computers and exchanging data between them (e.g. a power utility that collects meter readings via one system and directly debits accounts by another), it is difficult to give these systems precise boundaries.

References

1984. Ceri, S. and Pelagatti, G. *Distributed Databases: Principles and Systems.* New York: McGraw-Hill.

1988. Coulouris, G. F. and Dollimore, J. B. *Distributed Systems: Concepts and Design*, Reading, MA: Addison-Wesley.

1989. Mullender, S. (Ed.). *Distributed Systems.* Reading, MA: Addison-Wesley.

MALCOLM P. ATKINSON and PHILIP H. ENSLOW

DIVIDE AND CONQUER. *See* ALGORITHMS, DESIGN AND CLASSIFICATION OF.

DOCUMENTATION

For articles on related subjects *see* ADMINISTRATIVE APPLICATIONS; DECISION TABLE; FLOWCHART; PROGRAM SPECIFICATION; SOFTWARE ENGINEERING; STANDARDS; and STRUCTURED PROGRAMMING.

Documentation is a vital part of developing and using a computer-based system and an integral part of what is now called *software engineering.* In some commercial organizations, 20% or even more of the total development effort goes into the documentation of the new system, recording how it is to work and how it was developed. Documentation of a computer project falls into two broad categories—development documentation and control documentation. Development documentation records how a computer-based system is structured and what it is supposed to do and gives the background information upon which the design is founded. Control documentation, on the other hand, serves an administrative function: It records the resources used in developing and implementing the system, and includes such documents as project plans, schedules, resource allocation details, and progress reports.

Functions of Documentation Documentation serves four main functions:

1. Intertask/interphase communication.
2. Historical reference for modification and correction.
3. Quality and quantity control.
4. Instructional reference.

The relative importance of each of these depends on many factors. For example, one of the most important is the scope and type of the project; it may be a large-scale commercial system, or a scientific problem-solving program used by one or two technicians on a limited amount of data. Within each category, there are variations in project size, problem complexity, organization of staff, and the time scale for development and use. Each function of documentation is described below.

Intertask/Interphase Communication This operation records what has been done at each stage of the project so that instructions can be issued for the next phase of work, or so that all people involved in the project can agree what has been done before work proceeds to the next step. The amount of time and effort that must be devoted to documentation for this reason is a function of the scope of the system and the number of people involved.

In the development of a major commercial system, which requires procedures such as invoicing, inventory control, payroll, or production control, many people will be involved. In a production control system, for example, the business functions involved could include, among others:

1. Sales forecasting (linking with sales accounts).
2. Parts explosion and production batching/netting (linked with engineering design).
3. Plant resource allocation and scheduling.
4. Materials ordering/tooling and allocation.
5. Monitoring job progress.
6. Scrap and bonus reporting (linking with payroll).
7. Job costing (linking all systems).

Most of these functions are closely interrelated. Some 20 or 30 separate job functions or organizational units may be involved with the development, implementation, and running of the computer system. In addition to job functions such as those described, different levels of user staff will involve senior or executive management, line management, and supervisors and operators. Similarly, a number of job functions will be performed by personnel in the data processing or management services department; for example:

1. Business analysts, internal business consultants who advise management on business methods and who identify areas for improvement.
2. Systems analysts (*q.v.*), who investigate, analyze, and specify a new system.
3. Systems designers, who design the new system (computer and manual procedures) in detail.
4. Programmers, who design, code, and test the computer programs for the system.
5. Operators, who are responsible for the day-to-day running of the system.

There may also be general support or service staff within data processing, such as maintenance programmers, software support people, forward planners, and standards analysts. In a small installation, many of the job functions listed above may be performed by one person or a small group; in a large installation, each job function may be performed by a specialist group. Keeping people informed, passing on information and ideas for approval, and giving instructions involves a complex communications network in which formal documentation plays a vital role.

A failure of communication through poor documentation (or a lack of it) can prove very expensive indeed. The documentation will also help to insure project continuity should staff changes occur.

The use of documentation for intertask/interphase communication is equally important in large technical or scientific projects. Where the development of a program or group of programs can be done by only a limited number of technicians who are quite often both problem proponents and solution programmers, the importance of documentation during the project diminishes. However, the documentation of what has been done and how the programs work will be important for historical or instructional reference, as described below.

Historical Reference   The reference function is relevant to both commercial and scientific work. It is the documentation of how the system works that makes it easily changed after it is implemented. All systems are subject to change. Maintenance of business systems and programs will be required because the nature of a business and its methods change, or because the organization is restructured, new types of products are developed, management reporting requirements change, etc.

In scientific work, programs may have to be altered because the nature of the problem to be solved changes, possibly as a result of further research. A system may have to be changed because of new software or hardware. It may be desirable to change the processing methods because new techniques become available. The reason for the change may lie outside the organization altogether, as is the case with legal requirements and statutory changes.

A system can be maintained efficiently only if the existing operation of all procedures and programs is clearly known and understood. The documentation of the system provides this knowledge. For example, a program written a year ago is to be changed today; the program consists of 2,000 instructions, with many branches and nested loops. The programmer who originally wrote it is no longer available. The modifications require that logic of the program be understood; the new programmer must ensure that errors are not introduced by overlooking the impact of some of the changes.

The documentation of a system may also be reviewed for performance purposes. Many installations develop performance standards based on records of time and resources budgeted and used in developing a system, as compared with system type, scope, and complexity. The control documentation is used for details of resources, and the development documentation for a description of the system. By formally capturing details of all projects, estimates of resources for future projects can be improved.

Quality/Quantity Control   As a system develops, various elements of documentation are completed as each step is finished. Management can use this documentation to evaluate project progress and individual performance.

Instructional Reference   The development documentation can be reviewed during and after development for many general purposes. For example, documentation will enable trainees to study a system developed by experienced technicians. This is particularly important for instructional reference to generalized systems or general-purpose software. Another benefit of documentation is that an outside party can evaluate the system and its method of operation to determine if the package is suitable for use in another environment. In this case, sufficient information must be given to enable the user to apply the software to other problems and requirements.

Instructional reference thus includes all literature provided by a software supplier, such as the reference manuals for all languages, utilities, operating systems, subroutines, and application packages. it also includes the documentation and library facilities in a large organization that produces its own software.

Types of Documentation   In the development of a system, whether it is a large-scale commercial system or a group of scientific programs for analyzing data, certain categories of documentation must be considered. These are:

1. Analytical documentation.
2. Systems documentation.
3. Program documentation.
4. Operations documentation.
5. User/management aids.

Each of these categories is described below, along with the major factors that influence the form of the documentation in any particular organization.

Analytical documentation   consists of all the records and reports produced when a project is initiated. For all projects except those that require a single, one-time, problem-solving program, some form of initial briefing is required. In most organizations, the technicians who design, program, and test a system are grouped into a computing or data processing department, and the users who commission work from the data processing department must define the nature and objectives of the project. In some technical or scientific environments, the user is capable of specifying in very exact terms what is required in the way of processing and outputs. Generally, for any type of project, the initial briefing should consist of a *user request,* stating the problem (i.e. what the user needs to achieve); a *feasibility study* that evaluates possible solutions (in outline); and a *project plan* that estimates the time and resources required to develop and implement the system. Failure to produce and agree upon these three statements in the briefing will result in much wasted effort later in the project. They are vital whenever a user commissions work from computer technicians, and must be provided before money is actually committed to the more time-consuming tasks of system design and programming.

Systems documentation encompasses all information needed to define the proposed computer-based system to a level where it can be programmed, tested, and implemented. The major document is some form of *system specification*, which acts as a permanent record of the structure, its functions and work flow, and the controls on the system. It is the basic means of communication between the systems design, programming, and user functions. In a major project, the system specification comprises a number of documents. A sample outline of specification documentation for a major project is shown in Fig. 1. If the project will result in the development of only one or two programs for restricted use, then only the *program (processing) specification* would be produced.

Program documentation comprises the records of the detailed logic and coding of the constituent programs of a system. These records, prepared by the programmer, aid program development and acceptance, troubleshooting, general maintenance, machine/software conversion at a later date, and programmer changeover.

Program documentation covers both specific applications programs and general-purpose or in-house developed software. In addition to documenting *how* a program works, instructions for *using* the program must be written for packaged software.

Operations documentation specifies those procedures required for running the system by operations personnel. It gives the general sequence of events for performing the job and defines precise procedures for data control and security, data preparation, program running, output dispersal, and ancillary operations.

User/management aids consist of all the descriptive and instructive material necessary for the user to participate in the running of the operational system, including notes on the interpretation of the output results. Where a software package is produced, this category includes all material necessary to evaluate the programs and all instructions for its use.

Every installation should establish documentation standards (i.e. rules for the completion of certain documents at certain times) that define the content, format, and distribution of the documents. Many factors influence what documents are to be produced, how, when, and by whom. For example, the extent of *management commitment* is indicated by how much the management of the installation is prepared to allocate time and resources, not only for developing a system, but also for its documentation. Another controlling factor may be *project characteristics,* which consist of the number of projects and their scope, complexity, and duration. Crucial to any set of standards is *the organization structure* of both the institution as a whole, and the development and operations departments in particular. This, in turn, is affected by *the technical environment:* the hardware/software techniques used, such as the level of programming language, the quality of documentation produced by the software, and the use of special-purpose documentation programs (flowcharters, etc.).

From this broad picture of the total documentation of a project, we select one type to review in detail: program documentation. We focus on this because the limits of the tasks of programming can be clearly defined, and because this function in programming is similar in many organizations.

Program Documentation Fig. 2 shows the flow of documentation in designing, coding, and testing a program, respectively. The starting point is a program specification. Typically, this is a statement of *what* the program must do; the programmer's task is to determine *how* the program will do it. How much the data formats are predefined and how much is left to the discretion of the programmer depends on installation policy and the project. Other inputs to the programming phase include literature—which describes the software available for the project (either from outside suppliers or from an internal library)—and the programming standards, which give the rules and techniques for programming in that installation.

The outputs include a program manual which describes the programs in detail (construction, coding, and testing), instructions for use (for a generalized program), and computer operating instructions for day-to-day running. In many cases the task of documenting a program is one of adding to the initial program specification in order to build up the program manual. The various elements of program documentation are discussed below.

Program Specification This is a statement of the data available for processing, the required outputs, and the details of the necessary processing. The specification can be prepared by the problem proponent, a specialist systems analyst/designer, or the programmer. It must be complete, accurate, and unambiguous; changes to the specification after programming begins can be very expensive. The specification usually contains the following information:

1. Input.
2. Output.
3. Major functions performed.
4. The means of communication between this program and previous and following programs.
5. Logical rules and decisions to be followed, including statements of how the input is to be examined, altered, and used.
6. Validation and edit criteria.
7. Actions to be taken on error or exception conditions.
8. Special tables, formulas, and algorithms.

The description of the processing rules (item 5 in the list), can be given in narrative, flowchart, or decision-table form.

SYSTEMS SPECIFICATION

Title and Administrative Material

1.0 Systems Summary
   1.1 User Summary
      1. Purpose and Function
      2. Files Maintained and Affected
      3. Input and Input Sources
      4. Output and Output Uses
   1.2 System Flowchart
      1. Flowchart
      2. Reference Lists
   1.3 Narrative Description
      1. Definitions
      2. System Flow
      3. General Timing and Size Estimates

2.0 File Specifications
   2.1 File Identification and Characteristics
      1. General Description
      2. File Abstract
   2.2 Record Format
   2.3 Data Element Descriptions
   2.4 Appendices
      1. Layouts
      2. Edit Lists
      3. Cross-Reference Lists
              cont./

3.0 Input Specifications
   3.1 Identification and Purpose
   3.2 Transaction Listing (media purpose, programs affected, frequency, volume and source)
   3.3 Input Layouts and Samples

4.0 Output Specifications
   4.1 Identification and Purpose
   4.2 Output Listing (program no., media, frequency, volume, no. of copies, and destination)
   4.3 Output Description
   4.4 Output Formats

5.0 Program (Processing) Specifications
   5.1 Program Specification 1
   5.2 Program Specification 2
          .
          .
   5.n Program Specification n

6.0 Systems Test Plan
   6.1 Identification
   6.2 Test Organization
   6.3 Validity Criteria (control, processing, and output)
   6.4 Test Schedule
   6.5 Test Cases

7.0 Implementation Plan (timing, resources, responsibilities, and method)

FIG. 1. Sample outline of specification documentation. Note that items 2.0, 3.0, and 4.0 are repeated for each file. Data common to a number of programs may be defined in a Data Specification section (not shown). An added section might include a final cost-benefit analysis.

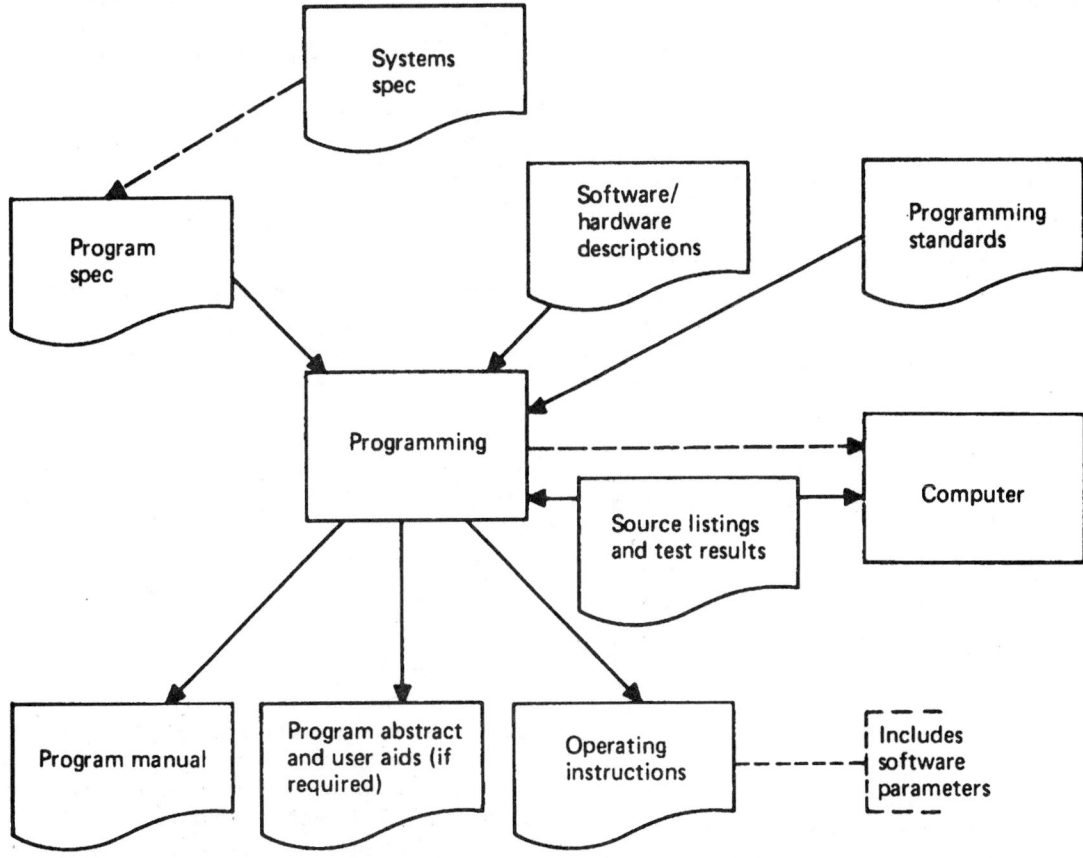

FIG. 2. Documentation flow.

Program Manual From the program specification, the programmer designs, codes, and tests the program. The output of this exercise is the program manual. The form of the logic design and the source program listing will depend on the type of application and the software used. For example, if a high-level decision-table *preprocessor* (*q.v.*) is used, the tabular program together with the data descriptions and final source listing will be complete enough without the preparation of a flowchart. Similarly, some installations use software for the final documentation; e.g. flowcharters that produce detailed flowcharts, statement by statement from the source program.

One of the advantages of high-level languages such as Cobol is that the source listing itself forms the major part of the final documentation. The programmer must insure that the source program not only is logically correct and follows the rules of the language, but also that the program coding is neat and easy to understand. By using meaningful data names and comments embedded in the program, it is possible to make a source program almost self-explanatory. In this case, a flowchart can be used as a general "route map" to the detailed coding in the source listing. When altering an operational program, many programmers refer directly to the source listing and then to the flowchart only if the required change is not immediately obvious from the listing.

Flowcharts and cross-reference lists (produced by the compiler or other software) can be used to check that an alteration has not erroneously disturbed other coding. The advantage of using comments in the source listing is that it minimizes references to other documents. The comments are not compiled as part of the program, but merely appear on the source listing. Source program comments should be kept brief while at the same time being descriptive and meaningful.

Note that the final documentation will show not only how the program works, but also how it was tested (for quality control and later retested after changes were made), operating instructions for running it, and any special parameters that are to be given to the operating system.

Although the program manual is the major output of the program specification, the programmer will use (and can produce) other types of documentation. If the program(s) being developed are for general use, either within or outside the organization, then additional user instructions will be needed. They should enable the prospective user to answer the following questions:

1. What does it do?
2. Do we want to use it?
3. Can we use it?

4. How do we use it?
5. What do we do if it changes?
6. What are its basic limitations?

For internally produced software, one approach is to produce a program abstract that can be held in a central documentation library. If, on first inspection, the user feels that it fulfills the needs, the detailed documentation can then be consulted. The form of this detailed documentation depends on the scope and complexity of the software. For example, a user's guide may be produced to give a general description of the program(s), the facilities available, the hardware environment required, and example uses of the software. The user's guide may contain instructions for using the software, or a programmer's reference manual may be supplied, giving detailed information. Most software is constructed so that the user programmer supplies parameters for a particular job. The parameters may be as simple as specifying an address of data to be processed or as comprehensive as a complete list of processing requirements. The programmer's reference manual will describe the construction of the program(s), together with all parameters required (their format, interdependence, and usage), operating instructions, and error conditions and diagnostics.

Programs ready for operational use and that are to be run repeatedly are assigned to the automated program library, usually stored on magnetic disk. The documentation for these programs is usually held in some form of central records library, together with the master reference copies of all software descriptions.

Documentation Maintenance and Control

Once a program has been implemented, the documentation must be retained for subsequent reference. When the system is changed, the documentation will be consulted and altered accordingly. It is vital to revise the documentation so that it completely and accurately reflects the operation of the system at all times. If the documentation is not so revised, then further maintenance will be very difficult. After any major amendment, all affected programs will have to be retested to prove that the changes have been made correctly and that they do not disrupt or invalidate other processing.

It is necessary, therefore, to insure that the appropriate control procedures are used. All changes should be properly recorded and all copies of the documentation updated. There is a strong case here for restricting the number of copies of the documentation to reduce the time spent in revising records and to minimize the risk of out-of-date copies being used by mistake. All copies should show current parameter requirements for the operating system, language rules, limitations and parameters for utility programs, and operating error messages produced by all software programs. A large installation will not only create a central records library, but also appoint a full-time librarian to cope with amendment distribution control. This is sometimes handled by a "software support" department, which will insure that both programming and operations departments are informed of changes in software availability and operation, such as the introduction of a new release of the operating system.

Though some form of documentation practice has been necessary since the advent of programming, there is a recent trend toward a more disciplined methodology, whereby system and program documentation is produced as an integral by-product of system and program design activities. Typical of such methods is the HIPO system (Hierarchy plus Input-Process-Output).

The thrust of this new philosophy is that structured design and implementation methodologies such as HIPO will produce nearly all of the desired analytical, systems, and program documentation in a form far superior to other, less integrated forms of documentation. In 1976, Informatics Inc. used the HIPO methodology for the analysis, system design, and program design for its ShopFloorControl/80 product. At the end of the implementation, it was concluded that only operations and user manuals need be produced. The HIPO documentation developed continues to serve its intended purpose, even though HIPO (and other similar structured) documentation is, unfortunately, no easier to maintain than the more traditional forms. But it is not any more *difficult* to maintain either, and it retains its usability longer and more reliably than many other forms of documentation. This is true because the methodology tends to enforce a functionally structural similarity between the design documentation and the programs themselves. If you understand what the system does, it is easier to find the function and its implementation.

Summary Documentation is a vital element in developing and running any computer project, whether in a government, business, academic, or military installation. It must not be handled in a haphazard fashion; formal documentation standards must be laid down and enforced. These standards must cover all areas—users, systems, and programming and operations. In a modern computer installation, the flow of documentation can be complex, encompassing in-house systems and programs as well as externally produced software.

References

1963. Brandon, D. *Management Standards for Data Processing.* New York: Van Nostrand Reinhold.
1972. Van Duyan, J. *Documentation Manual.* Philadelphia: Auerbach.
1973. London, K. *Documentation Standards* (Rev. Ed.). Philadelphia: Auerbach.
1980. *Basic Concepts of HIPO Programming.* Delpan, NJ: DATAPRO.
1990. Roetzheim, W. H. *Structured Design Using HIPO-II.* Englewood Cliffs, NJ: Prentice-Hall.

KEITH R. LONDON

DPMA (DATA PROCESSING MANAGEMENT ASSOCIATION)

For articles on related subjects *see* AMERICAN FEDERATION OF INFORMATION PROCESSING SOCIETIES; and INSTITUTE FOR CERTIFICATION OF COMPUTER PROFESSIONALS.

Purpose   The Data Processing Management Association is one of the largest worldwide organizations serving the information processing and computer management community. It comprises all levels of management personnel and, through its educational and publication activities, seeks to encourage high standards of performance in the field of data processing and to promote a professional attitude among its members. Its specific purposes, as stated in its association bylaws, are as follows:

- To foster, promote, and develop education and scientific inquiry in the field of data processing and data processing management.
- To inculcate among its members a better understanding of the nature and functions of data processing, and to engage in education and research in the technical methods pertaining thereto with a view to their improvement.
- To collect through research and to disseminate generally, by all appropriate means, all fundamentally sound data processing principles and methods.
- To study and develop improvements in equipment related to data processing.
- To supply to its members current information in the field of data processing management, and to cooperate with them and with educational institutions in the advancement of the science of data processing.
- To encourage and promote a professional attitude among its members in their approach to an understanding and application of the principles underlying the science of data processing and in their relations to others similarly engaged.
- To foster among executives, the public generally, and the members of the Association a better understanding of the vital business role of data processing, and the proper relationship of data processing to management.

How Established   Founded in Chicago as the National Machine Accountants Association, DPMA was chartered in Illinois on 26 December 1951. At this time the first electronic digital computer had yet to come into commercial use, and the name "machine accountant" was chosen to identify those associated with the operation and supervision of punched card accounting machines. Twenty-seven chapters were organized during the Association's first year. By 1955, the organization had taken on an international character with the admission of Montreal as the first Canadian chapter.

With the rapid advances in information processing techniques brought about by the introduction of comput-ers, the nature of the Association further changed as membership swelled from the ranks of computer management. In step with this trend, the Association assumed its present name in 1962. The roster of past presidents includes the following:

Robert L. Jenal, 1952	James Sutton, 1973
Gordon C. Couch, 1953	Edward J. Palmer, 1974
Richard L. Irwin, 1954	J. Ralph Leatherman,
Robert O. Cross, 1955	1975–1976
Donald L. Gerighty, 1956	Robert J. Marrigan, 1977
Willis L. Daniel, 1957	Delbert W. Atwood, 1978
Lester E. Hill, 1958	George R. Eggert, 1979
D. B. Paquin, 1959	Robert A. Finke, 1980
L. W. Montgomery, 1960	P. Roger Fenwick, 1981
Alfonso G. Pia, 1961	Donald E. Price, 1982
Elmer F. Judge, 1962	J. Crawford Turner Jr., 1983
Robert S. Gilmore, 1963	Carroll L. Lewis, 1984
John K. Swearingen, 1964	Eddie M. Ashmore, 1985
Daniel A. Will, 1965	David R. Smith, 1986
Billy R. Field, 1966	Robert A. Hoadley, 1987
Theodore Rich, 1967	Christian G. Meyer, 1988
Charles L. Davis, 1968	Georgia B. Miller, 1989
D. H. Warnke, 1969	Terence Felker, 1990
James D. Parker, Jr., 1970	Louis J. Berzai, 1991
Edward O. Lineback, 1971	Ralph E. Jones, 1992
Herbert B. Safford, 1972	

Organizational Structure   Individual chapters are organized geographically into 13 regions, each of which holds business meetings, conducts regional conferences and educational seminars, and carries on various types of interchapter educational activities. Governing authority is vested in the Association's Board of Directors, which consists of one representative from each chapter. An annual meeting of the Board is held in conjunction with the Association's Data Processing Conference & Business Exposition. Association directors, appointed by chapters, also represent their chapters at regional meetings.

Implementation of policy established by the Board is carried out by an Executive Council consisting of 21 members: President, Executive Vice-President, Secretary-Treasurer, Immediate Past President, 4 Association Vice-Presidents with various areas of responsibility, and 3 regional Presidents. The Corporate Operations Committee manages administrative matters.

The local chapter is the heart of the Association. Every member must belong to a chapter, except for those applying for an individual international membership, which is granted to qualified individuals living outside North America upon approval by the Executive Vice-President. Extensive educational programs are carried on by the local chapters through regular monthly meetings, seminars, and other activities.

Regular membership is granted by the individual chapter Board of Directors to persons engaged as (1) managerial or supervisory personnel in EDP installations; (2) systems and methods analysts, research specialists, and computer programmers employed in executive, administrative, or consulting capacities; (3) staff, managers, educators, and executive personnel with a direct interest in data processing; and (4) holders of the Certificate in Data Processing (CDP).

A computer-equipped association headquarters with modern facilities, located in Park Ridge, Illinois, serves as the administrative nucleus of the Association. It provides a wide range of programs and services to local chapters and contributes to regional educational programs. Major departments are Membership Programs and Services, Publications, Education, Public Affairs, and Financial and Administrative Services.

Programs and Services DPMA members attend meetings, seminars, and conferences at the local chapter, and at regional and international levels. A major educational event is the Annual DPMA Data Processing Conference & Business Exposition, attended by members and nonmembers from all parts of the U.S., Canada, and other countries.

The Association was the first to introduce (in 1962) a certification program for computer management personnel. The Certificate in Data Processing (CDP) examination program is dedicated to the advancement of data processing and information management and to this end has established high standards based on a broad educational framework and practical knowledge. In 1970, DPMA also introduced the Registered Business Programmer examination, which seeks to identify those reaching the level of senior business programmers. Both examinations were developed by the DPMA Certification Council and are given annually in test centers at colleges and universities in the U.S. and in Canada. In 1974, DPMA transferred ownership of these examinations to the Institute for Certification of Computer Professionals (ICCP). Other programs offered to the membership include the Business and Management Principles one-day seminar, the videotape Management Development seminar, and Educator's Night for improving communications with the education community. DPMA encourages and provides assistance to student organizations interested in data processing in colleges and universities. It also offers the Future Data Processors Program for high school students, and provides counseling aid for Boy Scouts seeking the computer merit badge.

Other programs are being constantly developed to keep the membership abreast of changing developments in effective EDP management techniques and in technological advances.

Among DPMA publications are the quarterly *Information Executive* magazine and the monthly *Inside DPMA* (included in membership dues).

The audiovisual program includes films and slide presentations ranging from technical to general management subjects. In 1969, DPMA originated the Computer-Science-Man-of-the-Year Citation (called, since 1980, the Distinguished Information Sciences Award), which in that year was presented to Commander Grace Murray Hopper, USNR. Subsequent recipients have been

Frederick Phillips Brooks, Jr. 1970
Robert C. Cheek, 1972
Carl Hammer, 1973

Prof. Edward L. Glaser, 1974
Willis H. Ware and Donald L. Bitzer
  (co-recipients), 1975
Gene M. Amdahl, 1976
J. Daniel Couger, 1977
Irwin J. Sitkin, 1978
Ruth M. Davis, 1979
John Diebold, 1980
David Packard, 1981
Jerome W. Geckle, 1982
Paul M. Pair, 1983
H. Ross Perot, 1984
Harlan D. Mills, 1985
Joseph T. Brophy, 1986
John T. (Jay) Westermeier, Jr., 1987
Emmett Paige, Jr., 1988
No award presented in 1989
Mitchell Kapor, 1990
Robert Campbell, 1991

ISAAC L. AUERBACH

DRIVER

A *driver* is a program or subprogram that is written to control either a particular hardware device or another software routine. The term originates from the concept of harness race drivers or automobile drivers putting their steeds or cars through their paces to see what they can do. The most common examples of drivers that control hardware are those that pertain to particular brands and models of printers attached to personal computers. One speaks of having or needing, for example, a printer driver that allows a word processor to communicate with a particular model dot matrix printer or laser printer.

In another context, we may have written a procedure that is to play an important role in conjunction with some large main program that is not written yet. To test the procedure while we wait, we might write a simple main program that calls the procedure with sufficiently realistic parameters to test it. The temporary main program whose only role is to provide a test bed for the new procedure may also be called a driver.

EDWIN D. REILLY

DSU/CSU

For articles on related subjects *see* CHANNEL; MODEM; and NETWORKS, COMPUTER.

A *Data Service Unit/Channel Service Unit* (DSU/CSU) serves the same function for digital data service communication (DDS) lines as a modem does for conventional analog communication lines. As shown in Fig. 1, it provides the interface between computing equipment conforming to the CCITT V.35 standard and four-wire leased

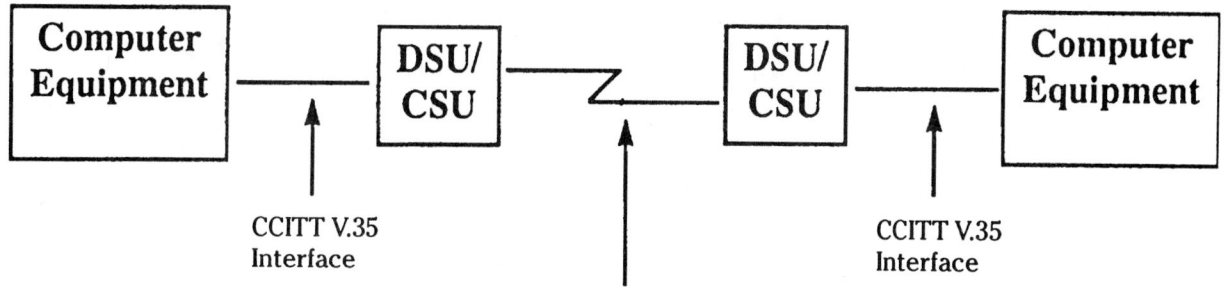

FIG. 1. Typical application of a DSU/CSU.

lines provided by an all-digital transmission facility conforming to AT&T Publication 62310. The DSU converts the digital data stream from the computer equipment into a format suitable for transmission over the digital communication line. The CSU terminates the digital line and performs line conditioning functions, ensures network compliance to FCC rules and responds to remote commands for control and loop back testing.

JOHN S. SOBOLEWSKI

DUMP

For articles on related subjects *see* BUG; DEBUGGING; MACHINE AND ASSEMBLY LANGUAGE PROGRAMMING; and TRACE.

A *dump* is a printed representation of the raw content of a computer storage device, usually main memory, at a specified instant. "Raw" means that little or no interpretation is performed on the content; it is taken simply as a number of bit strings and presented to the reader as such.

A few refinements are found in even the simplest dumps that keep them from being mere one-to-one bit maps: The representation is usually in octal or hexadecimal, reducing the dump's bulk by a factor of 3 or 4. The segmentation of memory into words or bytes is reflected in the print format; the address of the leftmost word or byte on each printed line is given; and long stretches of identically filled memory segments (typically, zero-filled) are not printed verbatim, but replaced with a message such as LOCATIONS 4000–4177 ALL ZERO. Simple dumps often offer the further amenities of permitting bounds to be set on the area of storage to be printed, and of automatically including the contents of the principal registers in the CPU.

Dumps may generally be classified as *post-mortem dumps* or *snapshot dumps*. The post-mortem dump, which occurs only when a program terminates (usually abnormally or prematurely), is the most primitive of debugging devices. It corresponds in vintage and sophistication to machine-language programming, and hence its use in debugging high-level language programs is virtually nil.

While it is far more commonly employed in debugging assembly-language programs than those written in high-level languages, it is still the last resort for programs of all descriptions, including those in high-level languages.

On-line debugging sessions do not involve extensive dumps, nor are the snapshot dumps that are involved so bit-oriented, but the representations of memory contents that are produced share the dump's essential characteristic of being instantaneous descriptions of a moving object, and of requiring the programmer to shift into another language, almost into another discipline, when debugging.

The crudeness of debugging with the sole aid of dumps, program listings, and mother wit is due not merely to the dump's being a record of a single instant only, but to its being, usually, a record of the *wrong* instant. By the time an observer, human or programmed, has detected something wrong with a running program and ordered a dump taken, it is probable that some or all of the evidence that would enable the programmer to find the underlying bug has been erased or changed.

The total replacement of the dump—or, what is equivalent, the realization of "source-language debugging"—has proved to be more difficult to achieve than had initially been expected. It may require the abandonment of the notion of "debugging"—i.e. curative, after-the-fact treatment of faulty programs—in favor of preventive or prophylactic approaches, such as those suggested in the references.

References

1965. Halpern, M. I. "Computer Programming: The Debugging Epoch Opens," *Computers and Automation* (November).
1971. Worley, W. S. "Toward Automatic Debugging of Low Level Code," IBM Technical Report TR 00.2211.

MARK HALPERN

DYNAMIC PROGRAMMIMG. *See* ALGORITHMS, DESIGN AND CLASSIFICATION OF.

E-MAIL. *See* ELECTRONIC MAIL.

EBCDIC

For articles on related subjects *see* ASCII; BINARY-CODED DECIMAL; CODES; and PUNCHED CARDS.

The Extended Binary Coded Decimal Interchange Code (EBCDIC) was developed by IBM for use on the IBM 360-370-390 (*q.v.*). In order to remain compatible with IBM mainframes, certain other computers also use EBCDIC, but the IBM-PC and most new computers now use ASCII).

Fig. 1 shows the 256 ($= 2^8$) combinations for EBCDIC, many of which are unassigned. The leftmost four bits (or first hexadecimal digit) of the eight-bit code are shown across the two rows at the top of Fig. 1 and the rightmost four bits (or second hexadecimal digit) in the first column on the side. Table 1 gives an example.

Also shown in Fig. 1 are the punches on an IBM card corresponding to each of the characters of the code. Zone punches (12, 11, 0, and occasionally 9) for characters above (below) the heavy black lines are shown at the top (bottom). Digit punches (1 to 9) for characters to the left (right) of the heavy black line are shown on the left (right). Table 2 gives an example.

TABLE 1.

Symbol	Code	
	Binary	Hexadecimal
4	11110100	F4
Y	11101000	E8
c	10000011	83
=	01111110	7E

TABLE 2.

Character	Card Punches
4	4
Y	0-8
c	12-0-3
=	8-6
IL	11-9-7

The meanings of the control characters and special graphics, as well as the card-punch patterns of characters that do not conform to the rules above, are shown in Fig. 1.

IVAN FLORES

ECHOING

For articles on related subjects *see* DATA COMMUNICATIONS; and MODEM.

In computing, an *echo* is a character or message retransmitted by the recipient fast enough to give assurance to the sender that it was received correctly. When communicating over phone lines to a distant computer using a video display terminal (VDT) or a personal computer, echoing relates to whether the characters that appear on the screen as you type are merely those that correspond to the keys struck or whether they correspond to a round trip that the characters make: keyboard over the phone to the distant computer that sends them back over the transmission line to the screen. The truly echoed character gives assurance of accurate receipt; the character that appears because of a local path from keyboard to screen does not. When using a simplex (one-way) line such as might be attached to a teletype, echoing is not an issue. When using a half-duplex line (two-way transmission, but only one way at a time), true echoing

489

Top header (column groupings):

Bit Positions 0,1															
00	00	00	00	01	01	01	01	10	10	10	10	11	11	11	11

Bit Positions 2,3															
00	01	10	11	00	01	10	11	00	01	10	11	00	01	10	11

First Hexadecimal Digit → columns 0 1 2 3 4 5 6 7 8 9 A B C D E F

Zone / Digit Punches (top):

	0	1	2	3	4	5	6	7	8	9	A	B	C	D	E	F
12	12				12	12		12	12	12		12	12			
11		11				11	11	11		11	11	11		11		
0			0		0		0	0	0		0	0		0		
9	9	9	9	9	9	9	9	9								

Main code table:

Bit Positions 4,5,6,7	2nd Hex	Digit Punches	0	1	2	3	4	5	6	7	8	9	A	B	C	D	E	F	Digit Punches
0000	0	8-1	NUL (1)	DLE (2)	DS (3)	(4)	SP (5)	& (6)	– (7)	(8)					(9)	(10)	(11)	0 (12)	8-1
0001	1	1	SOH	DC1	SOS				/ (13)		a	j			A	J	(14)	1	1
0010	2	2	STX	DC2	FS	SYN					b	k	s		B	K	S	2	2
0011	3	3	ETX	TM							c	l	t		C	L	T	3	3
0100	4	4	PF	RES	BYP	PN					d	m	u		D	M	U	4	4
0101	5	5	HT	NL	LF	RS					e	n	v		E	N	V	5	5
0110	6	6	LC	BS	ETB	UC					f	o	w		F	O	W	6	6
0111	7	7	DEL	IL	ESC	EOT					g	p	x		G	P	X	7	7
1000	8	8		CAN							h	q	y		H	Q	Y	8	8
1001	9	8-1		EM							i	r	z		I	R	Z	9	9
1010	A	8-2	SMM	CC	SM		¢	!	(15)	:									8-2
1011	B	8-3	VT	CU1	CU2	CU3	.	$	,	#									8-3
1100	C	8-4	FF	IFS		DC4	<	*	%	@									8-4
1101	D	8-5	CR	IGS	ENQ	NAK	(	)	_	'									8-5
1110	E	8-6	SO	IRS	ACK		+	;	>	=									8-6
1111	F	8-7	SI	IUS	BEL	SUB	|	¬	?	"									8-7

Zone Punches (bottom):

	0	1	2	3	4	5	6	7	8	9	A	B	C	D	E	F
12	12				12				12	12		12	12	12		12
11		11				11				11	11	11		11	11	11
0			0				0		0		0	0	0		0	0
9	9	9	9	9									9	9	9	9

Card Hole Patterns

(1)	12-0-9-8-1	(5)	No Punches	(9)	12-0	(13)	0-1
(2)	12-11-9-8-1	(6)	12	(10)	11-0	(14)	11-0-9-1
(3)	11-0-9-8-1	(7)	11	(11)	0-8-2	(15)	12-11
(4)	12-11-0-9-8-1	(8)	12-11-0	(12)	0		

Control Character Representations

ACK	Acknowledge	EOT	End of Transmission	PF	Punch Off	
BEL	Bell	ESC	Escape	PN	Punch On	
BS	Backspace	ETB	End of Transmission Block	RES	Restore	
BYP	Bypass	ETX	End of Text	RS	Reader Stop	
CAN	Cancel	FF	Form Feed	SI	Shift In	
CC	Cursor Control	FS	Field Separator	SM	Set Mode	
CR	Carriage Return	HT	Horizontal Tab	SMM	Start of Manual Message	
CU1	Customer Use 1	IFS	Interchange File Separator	SO	Shift Out	
CU2	Customer Use 2	IGS	Interchange Group Separator	SOH	Start of Heading	
CU3	Customer Use 3	IL	Idle	SOS	Start of Significance	
DC1	Device Control 1	IRS	Interchange Record Separator	SP	Space	
DC2	Device Control 2	IUS	Interchange Unit Separator	STX	Start of Text	
DC4	Device Control 4	LC	Lower Case	SUB	Substitute	
DEL	Delete	LF	Line Feed	SYN	Synchronous Idle	
DLE	Data Link Escape	NAK	Negative Acknowledge	TM	Tape Mark	
DS	Digit Select	NL	New Line	UC	Upper Case	
EM	End of Medium	NUL	Null	VT	Vertical Tab	
ENQ	Enquiry					

Special Graphic Characters

¢	Cent Sign	–	Minus Sign, Hyphen
.	Period, Decimal Point	/	Slash
<	Less-than Sign	,	Comma
(	Left Parenthesis	%	Percent
+	Plus Sign	_	Underscore
|	Logical OR	>	Greater-than Sign
&	Ampersand	?	Question Mark
!	Exclamation Point	:	Colon
$	Dollar Sign	#	Number Sign
*	Asterisk	@	At Sign
)	Right Parenthesis	'	Prime, Apostrophe
;	Semicolon	=	Equal Sign
¬	Logical NOT	"	Quotation Mark

FIG. 1. EBCDIC code combinations.

can be done only at great loss of speed. With a full-duplex line (simultaneous transmission in both directions), echoing can be done very efficiently because the echo of one character can cross the transmission of the next without inhibiting the fundamental data transmission rate of the communications channel (*q.v.*) being used.

There is also a software meaning of echo. When input is supplied to a running program by typing it at an interactive terminal, it will show on the screen, but not on whatever printed output results from the computation being done. To be sure that printed output represents the answers to the correct problem, programmers may include in their programs explicit write statements that "echo" input to the output file as soon as it is received. The echo may be a literal image of the incoming data, or it may be presented more usefully in labeled form. A fragment of Pascal code that illustrates the latter usage might be:

```
write('Enter value of radius: ');
                        {Ask for input}
readln(radius);         {Read input value}
writeln('radius = ',
            radius)     {Echo the input}
```

EDWIN D. REILLY

ECKERT, J. PRESPER

For articles on related subjects *see* DIGITAL COMPUTERS: HISTORY: EARLY; ENIAC; MAUCHLY, JOHN W.; and UNIVAC I.

J. Presper Eckert, co-inventor of ENIAC, was born in 1919 in Philadelphia. He received a Bachelor of Science degree in electrical engineering from the University of Pennsylvania's Moore School of Electrical Engineering in 1941, and his Master's degree under a graduate fellowship from the Moore School in 1943.

Dr. Eckert collaborated with Dr. John W. Mauchly, of the Moore School's staff, on developing ENIAC (Electrical Numerical Integrator and Computer) for Army Ordnance between 1943 and 1946. This was the world's first all-electronic general-purpose digital computer, and could perform 5,000 additions or subtractions per second. Its development launched the computer industry as we know it today.

In 1947, Dr. Eckert and Dr. Mauchly incorporated their venture as the Eckert-Mauchly Computer Corporation. They developed BINAC, the first electronic and fully self-checking computer, in 1949. Their next project, UNIVAC (Universal Automatic Computer), was well under way when Remington Rand acquired the Eckert-Mauchly firm in 1950.

Dr. Eckert became director of engineering for Remington Rand's Eckert-Mauchly Division, which completed UNIVAC I. He became vice-president and director of research in 1955, vice-president and director of commercial engineering in 1957, vice-president and executive assistant to the general manager in 1959, and vice-president and technical advisor to the president of Sperry-Rand, Univac division, in 1963.

FIG. 1.   J. Presper Eckert.

Dr. Eckert received an honorary degree of Doctor of Science in Engineering from the University of Pennsylvania in 1964. In 1969, he was awarded the National Medal of Science, the nation's highest award for distinguished achievement in science, mathematics, and engineering.

A Fellow of the Institute of Electrical and Electronics Engineers and a member of the National Academy of Engineering, Dr. Eckert is listed as the inventor or co-inventor on 87 patents.

MICHAEL M. MAYNARD

ECKERT, WALLACE J.

For an article on a related subject *see* DIGITAL COMPUTERS: HISTORY: EARLY.

Wallace John Eckert was born in Pittsburgh, PA, 19 June 1902 (d. Englewood, N.J., 24 Aug. 1971). Much of the credit for the introduction of machine computation into astronomy belongs to him. The significance of the computer impact on astronomy is comparable to that of the introduction and use of the telescope and photography.

Eckert was raised on a farm in Albion, PA, the second of four boys born to John and Anna (Heil) Eckert. He received his A.B. degree from Oberlin College in 1925 and his M.A. from Amherst in 1926. In 1931, he was awarded his Ph.D. in astronomy by Yale University. He joined the Columbia University Department of Astronomy as an assistant instructor in 1926.

In 1928, Professor Ben Wood formed the Columbia University Statistical Bureau using punched-card equipment donated by Thomas Watson, Sr., of IBM. It was here that Eckert was first exposed to the possibility of using machines to facilitate computation. From 1929 to 1933, he used the machines in Prof. Wood's laboratory for the interpolation of astronomical data, the reduction of ob-

FIG. 1. Wallace J. Eckert (photo courtesy of International Business Machines Corporation).

servational data, and the numerical solution of planetary equations. In 1933, with the encouragement of Ben Wood, he convinced Watson to install punched-card equipment and a control unit for astronomical calculations. This led to the formation of the T. J. Watson Astronomical Computing Bureau, jointly operated by Columbia, IBM, and the American Astronomical Society (1937–1945). During this period he published his landmark work (1940), "Punched Card Methods in Scientific Computation."

He was director of the U.S. Nautical Almanac Office in Washington, D.C., from 1940 to 1945. He introduced machine methods to data handling in the Naval Observatory as well as the Almanac Office. During the war he designed the "American Air Almanac," a great navigational influence that is still in use with only minor modifications.

In 1945 he was appointed head of IBM's Pure Science Department and became director of the Watson Scientific Computing Laboratory. The Laboratory not only performed needed computations, but also provided a training ground in machine computation for more than a thousand scientists in crystallography, geology, chemistry, statistics, optics, and solid-state physics, as well as astronomy.

Eckert was instrumental in the construction of IBM's Selective Sequence Electronic Calculator (SSEC, 1949) and the Naval Ordnance Research Calculator [NORC, 1954 (*q.v.*)]. Using the SSEC, Eckert, Dirk Brouwer of Yale, and G. M. Clemence (1951) of the U.S. Naval Observatory computed the precise positions of Jupiter, Saturn, Uranus, Neptune, and Pluto for the period 1653–

2060. This work still serves as the Ephemeris predictions for these planets.

Eckert's most important purely astronomical contributions were in relation to the moon's orbital motion. This and later work in the area of lunar coordinates and orbital parameters (1966) provided the operational basis for NASA's Surveyor, Lunar Orbiter, and Apollo projects.

He retired from IBM in 1967 and as Professor of Celestial Mechanics at Columbia in 1970.

References

Anon. "Dr. Wallace J. Eckert" (publications by W. J. Eckert, 38 items), and "Outstanding Contribution Award Report" (n.d.), IBM Archives.

1940. Eckert W. J. *Punched-Card Methods in Scientific Computation.* New York: Columbia University Press.

1951. Eckert, W. J., Brouwer, D., and Clemence, G. M. "Coordinates of the Five Outer Planets, 1653-2060," *Astronomical Papers*, NORC *12*. Washington, D.C.: U.S. Government Printing Office.

1966. Eckert, W. J. "Transformations of the Lunar Coordinates and Orbital Parameters," *Astronomical Journal* (June).

1971. J. A. "A Great American Astronomer," *Sky and Telescope* (October).

1984. Eckert W. J. *Punched-Card Methods in Scientific Computation.* New York: Columbia University Press. CBI Reprint Series #5. Introduction by John McPherson. Cambridge, MA: The M.I.T. Press.

HENRY S. TROPP

EDITOR. *See* TEXT EDITING SYSTEMS; and WORD PROCESSING.

EDUCATION IN COMPUTER ENGINEERING

For articles on related subjects *see* COMPUTER ENGINEERING; COMPUTER SCIENCE, ACADEMIC; and EDUCATION IN COMPUTER SCIENCE.

A computer engineering education is the academic preparation provided to students to prepare them with a broad and well-integrated background in the concepts and methodologies that are needed for the analysis, design, and utilization of information processing systems in a world of rapidly changing technology. Such education differs from a computer science education (when it is important to make the distinction between the two) in the sense that science is different from engineering, and relevant education should reflect the preparation required to prepare the student for work in the corresponding discipline. Nominally, science is more concerned with understanding underlying principles, and engineering is more concerned with the cost-effective harnessing of those principles. As such, a computer engineering education has a much stronger emphasis on the basic mathematical sciences and insistence on training and experience in design.

Like all engineering disciplines, an education in computer engineering requires the following three critical ingredients:

1. A foundation in engineering analysis that enables the graduate to analyze trade-offs and make design choices.
2. A foundation in mathematics and the basic quantitative sciences so that this analysis and the design choices that follow are based on rigorous understanding of fundamentals.
3. Experience in design so that students can practice their craft and develop the experiences associated with good engineering practice.

The three elements of an engineering education identified all contribute to the preparation of a computer engineer. For the computer engineer, the foundation in engineering analysis includes engineering science courses across the breadth of computer science and engineering. This breadth in engineering and in computer engineering should include engineering science courses outside of computer science and engineering. It also should include a balanced view of hardware, software, and application trade-offs, and the basic modeling courses used to represent the computing process. In addition to breadth, a computer engineering education should include the in-depth study of at least one major area of computer engineering.

The computer engineering student should be prepared in both hardware and software. Laboratory experiences dealing with each should involve problem solving, design, implementation, and documentation. The student should acquire substantive experience with the advanced features of at least one major operating system (*q.v.*). The fact that computer engineers are being prepared for a profession where the base technologies are expected to change dramatically during their professional careers dictates that a computer engineering education should focus on basic engineering sciences.

The second element of a computer engineering education is a foundation in mathematics and the basic sciences. Mathematics preparation should include the calculus through ordinary differential equations, discrete mathematics (*q.v.*), probability and statistics, and linear algebra and matrices or numerical methods. Basic science courses should include both physics and chemistry.

The third and final element of a computer engineering education is design experience. Because the practice of computer engineering involves examining issues, evaluating alternatives, and making tradeoffs, a critical component of a computer engineering education is experience in design. Preparation for doing design must be nurtured throughout a student's education. For example, a student should learn the tools of design early in the curriculum; open-ended problems should be presented throughout the program, increasing in complexity as the student matures; and documentation standards should be emphasized throughout the course of study. Finally, a comprehensive design experience should come sufficiently late in the student's program

of studies that the student has acquired the tools to understand the underlying issues and rigorously evaluate the alternatives. The design problem should not have a pre-formulated answer, nor is the answer usually precise. The experience must provide the opportunity for the student to do individual work and have that work carefully evaluated.

The Accreditation Board for Engineering and Technology (ABET), a federation of 26 engineering societies, is responsible for the accreditation of engineering programs in the U.S. Many of the specific educational guidelines identified in this article are taken from ABET guidelines for accreditation.

YALE PATT

EDUCATION IN COMPUTER SCIENCE

For articles on related subjects *see* COMPUTER LITERACY; COMPUTER SCIENCE; COMPUTER SCIENCE, ACADEMIC; and EDUCATION IN COMPUTER ENGINEERING.

UNITED STATES

The forerunners of the modern electronic computer were first developed at U.S. universities in the 1940s, mainly in response to military needs during World War II. However, a lengthy gap then ensued between the conception of computers at universities and their attendant application to the host of educational, research, and administrative processes at these universities. The beginnings of the university computing center date only to the mid-1950s; in fact, it was only during the period from 1960 to 1965 that the "computer revolution" really took hold at U. S. institutions of higher education. In some cases, the computing center began as a separate organization, but more generally it evolved from a computer facility initially installed in a department of mathematics or school of engineering to support the research projects of the departmental faculty.

Higher Education Programs: History The academic programs in computing at institutions of higher education began in the mid-1950s under pressure from early users of computing equipment, or from the computing center staff deluged with questions about the use of these new devices. Initially, the "educational program" might have consisted only of a short, non-credit course given by the computing center staff. Such a course mainly emphasized hardware characteristics, binary arithmetic, and how to program a problem for computer solution (usually in machine or assembly language). At times, some of the instructional material was absorbed into an existing course in mathematics or engineering, generally in three or four lectures. However, with the rapid growth of broadly-based university computing installations during the 1960–1965 period, and with the growth of an organized body of knowledge, it became necessary to establish more formal educational programs in computing.

One of the most influential early efforts took place at the University of Michigan, and subsequently at the University of Houston, during the period 1959–1962. These efforts, conducted jointly by the Computing Center and the College of Engineering, were aimed less at establishing computer science as a distinct academic discipline than at the "Use of Computers in Engineering Education" (University of Michigan Study, 1960 and 1961, and University of Houston Study, 1962). At approximately the same time, Stanford University, through the joint efforts of its computing center and department of mathematics, was establishing the discipline of computer science as an optional field of study in the department of mathematics.

These early efforts were capped by the creation of separate departments of computer science. In 1962, Stanford University established a Department of Computer Science in the School of Humanities and Sciences; in the same year, Purdue University created a Department of Computer Science in the Division of Mathematical Sciences. In each case, the bond between the service and academic functions of computing was made evident by the fact that one person was both director of the computing center and chairman of the department; this pattern was followed subsequently by other universities. Another pattern established by Stanford and Purdue was that of initially offering only graduate programs in computer science at the master's and doctorate levels. The thinking at the time was that there could be no well-defined undergraduate program in computer science, and that specialization in computing should start only at the graduate level. (It also reflected the fact that there were few professors qualified to teach computing at the time.)

By the mid-1960s, events in computer science education were proceeding at a dynamic pace. Governmental and quasi-governmental reports made recommendations that spurred the growth of computer science academic programs. Two were of particular importance. The National Academy of Sciences report on "Digital Computer Needs in Universities and Colleges" (Rosser et al., 1966) recommended, among other things, that campuses should "increase as rapidly as possible the number of specialists trained annually as computer specialists and the support of pioneering research into computer systems, computer languages, and specialized equipment." The President's Science Advisory Committee report on "Computers in Higher Education" (Pierce et al., 1967) recommended that "the Federal Government expand its support of both research and education in computer sciences." These reports helped obtain government and university support for the new discipline.

During the same period, university-sponsored conferences produced reports and books, such as "University Education in Computing Science" (Finerman, 1968), indicating that computer science was truly an emerging academic discipline and not a short-lived curiosity. Indeed, the "intellectual respectability" of computer science was a controversial issue in the 1960s. Many educators argued that the computer was just a tool, and that a body of study based upon a tool was not a proper academic discipline;

others took the position that computer science was not a coherent discipline but rather a collection of bits and pieces from other disciplines; still others felt that computers were not that important and were not proper objects of academic interest. By and large, however, this skepticism was short-lived.

At the same time, computing, mathematics, and engineering professional societies sponsored studies of the curricular effects of the new discipline. Reports of the Mathematical Association of America (Committee on the Undergraduate Program in Mathematics) and the Commission on Engineering Education (Cosine Committee) recommended changes in existing academic programs to assure that students in mathematics and engineering received adequate preparation in computing. This preparation was necessitated by the fact that a growing number of mathematics and engineering majors found themselves working in the computing field soon after graduation. The studies of the Association for Computing Machinery (ACM - q.v.) had the most widespread effect. ACM chartered a Curriculum Committee on Computer Science to recommend necessary academic programs. The subsequent report of the Committee, "Curriculum 68" (Atchison et al., 1968), defined for the first time the scope and content of a recommended undergraduate program in computer science. Subsequently, the Committee considerably revised and updated the recommended undergraduate program in its report, "Curriculum 78" (Austing et al., 1979). ACM also chartered a Curriculum Committee on Computer Education for Management. This Committee issued two principal reports on undergraduate and on graduate programs in information systems.

Separately, the Computer Society of the Institute of Electrical and Electronic Engineering (IEEE - see IEEE-CS) chartered a Model Curricula Subcommittee of the Education Committee, which published guidelines and curricula for programs of computer science and engineering in 1979 and 1983 (IEEE Computer Society Reports, 1979, 1983). The ACM and IEEE also cooperated in a joint curricula task force that presented its first report in 1989 (Denning et al., 1989) and will publish its final curricula recommendations in 1991. The two societies joined to publish accreditation guidelines in 1983 (Mulder et al., 1984) and to form a Computer Science Accreditation Commission (CSAC) of the Computing Sciences Accreditation Board (CSAB) in 1984. As of 1990, 80 programs in computer science had been accredited; for more information, contact the Computing Sciences Accreditation Board, Inc., 345 E. 47th St., New York, NY 10017.

ACM also chartered Curricula Committees for masters level programs in computer science (Magel et al., 1981), undergraduate and graduate degree programs in information systems (Nunamaker et al., 1983), and related computer science programs in vocational-technical schools, community and junior colleges, and health computing (ACM, 1983). ACM has also published curricula recommendations for secondary school programs in computer science and for teacher certification (ACM, 1985).

The effect of all these studies, conferences, and reports was a proliferating and seemingly endless number of academic programs in computer science and engineering. From the early graduate programs have come myriad graduate and undergraduate programs that abound at two-year colleges (associate's degree), four-year colleges (bachelor's), five-year colleges (bachelor's and master's), and universities (bachelor's, master's, and doctorate); these programs are in addition to the numerous computing service courses available to students majoring in other disciplines. Furthermore, there are a multitude of vocational courses given by technical schools. More recently, computing courses have been introduced into the educational programs of many secondary schools.

University Educational Programs

Higher education programs in computing go by different names, such as computer science, computer engineering, computer science and engineering, information science, data processing, and information systems. Each name also has come to denote a particular emphasis and origin. For example, *computer science* usually indicates a mathematical and scientific emphasis generally found at universities; *information systems* usually indicates computing applied to organizational systems generally related to the business administration programs at universities; and *data processing* usually indicates computing applied to administrative and commercial applications generally taught at two-year colleges. The programs may be housed in a department of computer science, computer engineering, computer and information science, or data processing, or given as an option in mathematics, engineering, or business administration.

Higher education programs in computing go by different names. A recent paper (Hamblen, 1989) lists the 1984–1985 output by degree for ten different programs. However, the majority of degree programs fall into two categories: computer science/computer and information science (C&IS) and business data processing. Generally, programs in the first category (C&IS) lead to an associate degree or higher, while programs in the second category often lead to a certificate or to an associate degree. Table 1 shows the number of certificate and associate degrees awarded from 1982–1989 in each category.

There was an explosive growth in computer science and related degree programs from 1970 to 1985. As shown in Table 1, the number of certificates and associate degrees started to decline around 1985.

Table 2 shows the number of higher-level degrees (bachelor's and beyond) awarded in C&IS during 1970–1989. Although the number of master's and doctor's degrees has continually increased during this period, the number of bachelor's degrees peaked in 1985–86 and has declined by approximately 27% since then.

The Taulbee Survey reports on the production of graduate degrees in the U.S. and Canada that grant Ph.D. degrees in computer science or computer engineering from 1970–1985. The most recent (1989-1990) report (Gries, 1992) provides figures from 167 of 170 Ph.D.-granting institutions. It gives the number of master's degrees awarded in 1989–1990 as 4,239 for computer science and 949 for computer engineering. These figures are lower than those shown in Table 2 because they survey a narrower population. The 1989–1990 Taulbee report gives the number of Ph.D. degrees awarded in 1989–1990 as 734 for computer science and 173 for computer engineering. (The as yet unpublished figures for 1990–91 are 862 Ph.D.s in computer science and 211 in computer engineering.)

The growth at institutions of higher education generally parallels corresponding growth in demand in industry. Until recently, students graduating with a bachelor's, master's, or Ph.D. degree in computer science or a related field have had little difficulty in finding employment. At the current time, supply and demand have approached equilibrium and some new graduates are experiencing difficulty in finding their first jobs in industry. However, the demand is still strong for experienced computer scientists.

There is a more limited demand for graduates of a two-year college and even less demand for vocational school and high school graduates to fill professional positions, although many technician positions are available, especially for graduates with associate's degrees. The bachelor's (and, increasingly, the master's) degree has rapidly become the entry-level degree for suitable professional positions in industry. In recent years, new Ph.D. graduates been actively recruited by universities, research organizations, and manufacturers of computing equipment.

Non-University Educational Programs

Computer science educational programs originated at universities and spread downward, from graduate to undergraduate to two-year colleges and then to high

TABLE 1. Certificate and Associate Degrees: 1982–1989

Year	C&IS		Business data processing	
	Certificate	Associate	Certificate	Associate
1982–83	1,960	10,065	4,005	16,307
1983–84	2,327	12,824	4,768	18,709
1984–85	2,453	12,677	4,363	18,835
1985–86	1,889	10,704	4,179	15,926
1986–87	1,977	9,098	3,213	13,294
1987–88	1,800	8,628	3,135	10,255
1988–89	1,534	7,914	2,711	9,673

Source: U.S. Department of Education, National Center for Educational Statistics

TABLE 2.   Earned Degrees in Computer and Information Sciences[1] Conferred by Institutions of Higher Education, By Level of Degree and Sex of Student: 1970–71 to 1988–89

Year	Bachelor's degrees			Master's degrees			Doctor's degrees		
	Total	Men	Women	Total	Men	Women	Total	Men	Women
1970–71	2,388	2,064	324	1,588	1,424	164	128	125	3
1971–72	3,402	2,941	461	1,977	1,752	225	167	155	12
1972–73	4,304	3,664	640	2,113	1,888	225	196	181	15
1973–74	4,756	3,976	780	2,276	1,983	293	198	189	9
1974–75	5,033	4,080	953	2,299	1,961	338	213	199	14
1975–76	5,652	4,534	1,118	2,603	2,226	377	244	221	23
1976–77	6,407	4,876	1,531	2,798	2,332	466	216	197	19
1977–78	7,201	5,349	1,852	3,038	2,471	567	196	181	15
1978–79	8,719	6,272	2,447	3,055	2,480	575	236	206	30
1979–80	11,154	7,782	3,372	3,647	2,883	764	240	213	27
1980–81	15,121	10,202	4,919	4,218	3,247	971	252	227	25
1981–82	20,267	13,218	7,049	4,935	3,625	1,310	251	230	21
1982–83	24,510	15,606	8,904	5,321	3,813	1,508	262	228	34
1983–84	32,172	20,246	11,926	6,190	4,379	1,811	251	225	26
1984–85	38,878	24,579	14,299	7,101	5,064	2,037	248	223	25
1985–86	41,889	26,923	14,966	8,070	5,658	2,412	344	299	45
1986–87	39,664	25,929	13,735	8,491	5,995	2,496	374	322	52
1987–88	34,548	23,347	11,201	9,166	6,702	2,464	428	380	48
1988–89[2]	30,637	21,221	9,416	9,392	6,769	2,623	538	457	81

[1]Includes degrees in computer and information sciences, general; information sciences and systems; data processing; computer programming; systems analysis; and other information sciences.
[2]Preliminary data.
SOURCE: U.S. Department of Education, National Center for Educational Statistics.

schools. Although subsequent sections of this article deal almost exclusively with university and college programs (undergraduate and graduate), in this section, we discuss briefly other educational programs in computing, specifically those offered by private technical schools or institutes and by two-year colleges. The latter are in some ways similar to those at technical schools and in other ways different, offering a preparation for four-year undergraduate work.

Technical School Programs   Private schools for training technicians have been operating for years. In many fields, they serve a worthwhile function by preparing people for jobs as secretaries, dental technicians, TV repairers, and the like. When the computing industry started expanding rapidly, a large number of private schools began offering educational programs in computing. There are many jobs in industry for which training as a technician is worthwhile, and the technical school graduate should be qualified to assume such jobs.

Unfortunately, some computing institutes intimate that their training will prepare students for well-paying professional jobs in the computing industry, but their graduates often discover too late that most such positions are filled by college graduates. The professional career path in computing, as in most other fields, requires a college education.

Community College Programs   Two-year community (or junior) colleges have grown phenomenally in recent years, both in quantity and in scope of offerings. Thirty

years ago, the community college was rather rare, usually specializing in such areas as agriculture, forestry, and mining. Today, the community college has become as broadly based and diversified as its university cousin.

The community college serves a twofold purpose. One is to train the student for a position as a technician. For these graduates, the two-year associate's degree is proof of better standards than those usually maintained by the technical school; the degree is also proof of a more well-rounded education. The second purpose of the community college is to serve as a bridge between the high school and the four-year college or university, especially for those students uncertain of their desire or ability to continue with higher education. For these students, the associate's degree may be an intermediate step on the way towards a bachelor's degree.

Students terminating after two years and entering industry often suffer the same identity problem as do the technical school graduates. Indeed, they are more than technicians, but not the same as college graduates. More often than not, the career paths open to them are technician-oriented. On the other hand, graduates wishing to continue toward a bachelor's degree sometimes find the transition quite difficult. Community college standards are not always the same as university standards; community college courses are not always identical or even similar to corresponding courses at the university.

Some of these difficulties are being addressed; for example, community colleges and universities have been cooperating in facilitating the transfer process by making courses more compatible. Transfer still remains a problem, however, as does the technician versus professional issue. Increasingly, as the "computer profession" evolves and becomes better defined, the broader educational scope of a bachelor's degree becomes a prerequisite for a professional career.

We will not separately detail the usual curricula at two-year colleges. In some cases, these are similar to freshman and sophomore level computing courses at universities. In other cases, the differences are more visible. By and large, university programs are more theoretically oriented, emphasizing both the theoretical underpinnings of computing and the scientific or engineering applications. Two-year college programs tend to emphasize the practical aspects and the business applications of computing. The four-year university program allows more time to take courses unrelated to computing, mathematics, and associated technical disciplines. Because of their shorter time span, community college programs, are more intensely oriented to courses in computing, business mathematics, accounting, and other technical areas. Accordingly, graduates of community colleges do not possess the broader educational background of graduates of four-year programs.

The Undergraduate Curriculum The undergraduate program varies from university to university, depending upon such factors as the resources available, the amount of specialization deemed useful, and the interests of the faculty. Even the content of specific courses is, in some cases, quite variable. As noted earlier, the most comprehensive attempts made to date in defining the scope and content of an undergraduate program in computer science have been the works of the ACM Curriculum Committee, "Curriculum 68" and "Curriculum 78." In particular, the 1968 report had a profound effect on shaping the direction of computer education in the then still emerging discipline.

The program prescribed in Curriculum 68 reflects the viewpoint of those advocating a strong specialization in computing at the undergraduate level; as such, it follows the traditional pattern of most scientific and engineering undergraduate programs. The large component of computer and mathematics courses recommended (between one-half and two-thirds of the total undergraduate course load) plus technical electives in computer-related disciplines, leaves little room for non-technical subjects in the humanities and the social sciences within the normal four-year program.

As noted earlier, "Curriculum 78," revised the recommendations for the undergraduate program. The revision reflects the significant developments that occurred within computer science education during the intervening decade. Curriculum 78 provides somewhat greater flexibility than Curriculum 68 in the content of courses, emphasizing the objectives of such a program and the subject matter to be covered. Aside from the proposed curriculum, the report discusses such topics as service courses, continuing education, computing facilities, and staff.

Curriculum 78 proposed the following requirements for computer science majors:

- acore of eight computer courses which would be taken by all majors
- four elective courses chosen from a group of ten advanced courses described in the report
- five mathematics course (calculus, mathematical analysis 1 and 2, linear algebra, discrete structures, probability and statistics)

Curriculum 78 has been criticized because of its reduced number of mathematics courses and the fact that those mathematics courses required are not prerequisite to the computer courses—and therefore are not as integral a part of the prerequisite structure as in Curriculum 68 (see, for example, Ralston and Shaw, 1980).

In 1984, an ACM Task Force revised the first two courses in the curriculum, CS1 and CS2, providing an increased emphasis on problem solving, structured design, and software engineering (Koffman *et al.* 1984 and 1985). Subsequently, a model curriculum for a liberal arts bachelor's degree in computer science was published (Gibbs *et al.*, 1986) that consists of three introductory courses (CS1, CS2, and discrete mathematics) followed by four core courses in computer science:

CO1: Principles of Computer Organization
CO2: Algorithms
CO3: Theory of Computation
CO4: Principles of Programming Languages

The program requires a second course in mathematics selected from discrete mathematics II, calculus, and linear algebra, and three remaining computer science electives. A strong laboratory component is considered essential for CS1, CS2, and CO1, and is desirable for CO4 and many of the electives.

Computer Science and Engineering (IEEE) The Educational Activities Board of the IEEE developed two model curricula for accreditable programs in computer science and engineering in schools of engineering (Cain, 1977 and 1983, IEEE Computer Society). The 1983 report updates the original curriculum and expands it to cover all resources needed to define a high-caliber undergraduate program in computing, including guidelines for the development of faculty, adminstration, and material.

The general requirements for an accreditable curriculum are:

- One-half year of mathematics beyond trigonometry.
- One-half year of basic sciences.
- One year of engineering sciences.
- One-half year of engineering design.
- One-half year of humanities and social sciences.

For the requirements in computer science and engineering, the report lists a core of 13 subject areas that map into 33 semester hours (11 3-credit courses). In addition, a course in discrete mathematics (*q.v.*) is a prerequisite or corequisite for all subject areas in the core except for SA1. Three additional professional electives in computer science are required. The 13 subject areas in the core are:

SA1 Fundamentals of Computing
SA2 Data Structures
SA3 System Software and Software Engineering
SA4 Computing Languages
SA5 Operating Systems
SA6 Logic Design
SA7 Digital Systems Design
SA8 Computer Architecture
SA9 Interfacing and Communications
SA10 Introduction to Computing Laboratory
SA11 Software Laboratory
SA12 Digital Systems Design Laboratory
SA13 Project Laboratory

The 13 subject areas can be mapped into courses in a variety of ways, and some subject areas may be covered in more than one course. The criteria for selecting the subject areas included in the core was that they comprise fundamental concepts that span the field. A curriculum based on them would give the student a broad engineering background as well as an in-depth knowledge of the hardware, software, and application trade-offs, and the basic modeling techniques used to represent the computing process. In all the subject areas, there is a strong emphasis on problem solving and the use of analytical, heuristic, and experimental techniques as an integral part of problem-solving.

Joint Curriculum Task Force (ACM and IEEE) In the spring of 1988, the ACM and IEEE Computer Society formed a joint curriculum task force whose charter was to present recommendations for the design and implementation of undergraduate curricula in the discipline of computing. A motivation for this effort was the recognition that, despite strong and fundamental differences among institutions that house the departments offering undergraduate programs, these departments share a substantially large curriculum in common. Any curriculum recommendations that attempt to speak for the entire discipline must not only identify the shared subject matter, but also suggest ways in which it can serve as the basis for building undergraduate programs in different kinds of institutions.

The task force proceeded in two stages. The first stage report (Denning et al., 1989) focused on: defining the field of computer science, proposing a teaching paradigm for computer science that conforms to traditional scientific standards, and giving an example of a three-semester introductory course sequence based on this model and the definition of the field. The report outlines nine fundamental areas of computer science and the three basic processes (*see also* COMPUTER SCIENCE: DISCIPLINARY STRUCTURE). The nine areas are:

Algorithms and Data Structures
Architecture
Artificial Intelligence and Robotics
Database and Information Retrieval

Human-Computer Communication
Numerical and Symbolic Computation
Operating Systems
Programming Languages
Software Methodology and Engineering

The three basic processes and their elements (in parentheses) are:

- theory (definitions and axioms, theorems, proofs, interpretation of results),
- abstraction (data collection and hypothesis formation, modeling and prediction, design of an experiment, analysis of results),
- design (requirements, specification, design and implementation, testing and analysis)

The second stage report (Tucker et al., 1991) discusses how to develop a curriculum based on the model of computer science developed in the first stage. It contains the following parts:

- A collection of fifty-five subject matter modules called knowledge units that comprise the common requirements for all undergraduate programs in the field of computing ensuring breadth of study. Each knowledge unit contains a list of lecture topics, relations to other knowledge units, recommended hours of coverage, and suggested laboratories.
- A collection of advanced and supplementary curriculum material that provides depth of study in several of the subjects.
- A list of twelve recurring concepts that occur throughout the discipline.

Besides the computing requirements, the report discusses requirements in science (one-half year including a year-long course in a laboratory science) and mathematics. The mathematics requirements are a minimum of the equivalent of one-half academic year of mathematics courses including discrete mathematics, calculus, and at least one of the following subjects: probability, linear algebra, advanced discrete mathematics, mathematical logic.

Rather than provide a single, definitive curriculum for all programs in computing, the report discusses how to develop curricula which incorporate all the components above and how to map the knowledge units into courses. It also describes the role of laboratories in the curriculum. The appendix to the report describes eight sample curricula which differ in their emphasis and assumed institutional constraints.

Information Systems Curricula The ACM also chartered a curriculum committee on computer education for management that has developed curricula for undergraduate and graduate programs in information systems. Students of these programs learn how to apply computer technology to meet the information needs of an organization. The first graduate report was published in 1972 (Ashenhurst, 1972), and the first undergraduate report was published in 1973 (Couger, 1973).

This committee was superseded by a curriculum committee on information systems that published their recommendations in the report "Information Systems Curriculum Recommendations for the 80s: Undergraduate and Graduate Programs" (Nunamaker *et al.* 1983). The committee updated the curricula and its requirements, stressing the inclusion of the American Assembly of Collegiate Schools of Business common body of knowledge as a major component of the program and introducing an MIS policy course as a capstone to the program. There are eight required information systems courses for the undergraduate student, and ten for the graduate student. The ten courses for the program are listed below; most of the graduate courses contain a difference in emphasis, depth, and content.

Information Systems Technology
IS1 Computer Concepts and Software Systems
IS2 Program, Data, and File Structures
IS4 Database Management Systems
IS6 Data Communication Systems and Networks
IS7 Modeling and Decision Systems (graduate program only)
Information Systems Concepts in Organizations
IS3 Information Systems in Organizations
IS5 Information Analysis
IS8 Systems Design Processes
IS9 Information Systems Policy (graduate program only)
IS10 Information Systems Projects

Courses for Non-Majors Many undergraduate courses in computer science attract not only the major in computer science (or information systems) but also students majoring in other disciplines who complete a minor in computer science. For those who do less, the introductory course in programming is still a popular option, especially for students majoring in mathematics, science, or engineering, but the liberal arts or business student will often instead take a course in computer literacy, computers and society (*q.v.*), or management information systems (*q.v.*) that emphasizes the development of computer literacy through the use of microcomputer packages rather than through actual computer programming.

Graduate Curricula in Computer Science

Graduate programs in computer science preceded the introduction of undergraduate programs, the earliest programs appearing in the early 1960s. Although concentrating on undergraduate computer science, Curriculum '68 also provided recommendations for master's programs.

In 1981, the ACM Curriculum Committee on Computer Science published recommendations for master's programs (Magel *et al.*, 1981). This report recognizes the emergence of two kinds of programs with different goals: academic programs designed to prepare students for Ph.D. study, and professional programs designed to prepare students for business and industry. However, the committee rejected the idea of a purely terminal program and believes that all programs should prepare students for study beyond the master's level.

Although early master's programs in computer science did not require a bachelor's degree in computer science or even substantial prior study in the field, students entering a master's program should now have a B.S. in computer science or at least the equivalent of the material included in CS1 through CS8 of Curriculum '78, and mathematics through calculus, linear algebra, discrete structures, and one course in probability and statistics. Maturity in both abstract reasoning and the use of models, as well as one or more years of practical experience in computer science, are desirable.

According to this report, the master's program should provide both breadth in several areas and depth in a few. In addition, it should allow a degree of flexibility to address individual needs. The typical program will consist of 30 to 36 semester hours in courses from the following subject areas:

1. Programming languages
2. Operating systems and computer architecture
3. Theoretical computer science
4. Data and file structures
5. Other topics

The report lists 30 courses in these five areas with brief descriptions.

The program should include at least two courses from A, two courses from B, and one course from each of C, D, and E. Each student's program should contain at least four computer science courses that are for graduate students only. Beyond coursework, each student should be required to participate in some summary activity, such as a thesis, project, internship, seminar, or comprehensive examination.

Doctoral programs in computer science are intended for students with theoretical or research interests, and most such programs reflect the research interests of the faculty members. In general, courses are similar to those in the master's degree programs. Of course, the doctoral thesis lies at the heart of the doctoral program. It is the means by which the student demonstrates the capability for original contribution to knowledge. This demonstrated capability is the fundamental requirement for the doctorate.

Summary Formal education in computer science and technology is quite new, dating back only to the early to mid-1960s. Educational programs originated at universities, resulting from the increasing use of computers by students, faculty, and administrators. Today, most colleges and universities offer academic programs in computing, either as a separate discipline or as an option in a related discipline. As can be expected in such a new field, the educational program still has fuzzy edges; at times, it overlaps applied mathematics, electrical engineering, business administration, and other disciplines. Yet, in just a few short years, it has become a visible and influential area of study. Computer science undergraduate programs also provide a service function by offering courses to the student majoring in other disciplines. Usually, these students require some computer courses so that they can better apply computing methods to their fields. Often, however, these students become computing practitioners after graduation.

In earlier days, entry into the computer field was always through some other discipline; there simply were no academic programs in computing. People learned by doing—by using computers, by programming, and by absorbing knowledge in this more informal manner. Today, many enter with a degree in computer science, information systems, or related programs. Furthermore, in earlier days, a university or college degree was not required for many professional positions in the computing organization (especially administrative data processing). Increasingly, prospective employers today require at least a bachelor's degree (in computing or some other field with concentration in computing) to qualify for the professional position. In many cases, a master's degree in computing is preferable. The graduate with a doctorate in computer science was, until very recently, in short supply, both at universities and at industrial research organizations; this shortage, however, ended in 1991-92 and considerable numbers of doctoral degree holders in computer science now experience difficulty in finding positions.

Although the discussions in this article apply primarily to computing education in the U. S. and Canada, experiences in other countries are quite similar. The major difference is that computer science educational programs in other countries were introduced later than those in North America. For example, with some exceptions, universities in Western Europe and Israel initiated such programs around the late 1960s, in South America around the early 1970s, and in Southeast Asia around the mid-1970s. In Europe, especially, the title of the academic program usually is a variation of the term *informatics*, derived from the French "informatique." (*See* the two following parts of this article.)

There is now an increasing awareness that the use of the computer stimulates and modifies intellectual processes, and as a result makes it possible for people to expand their intellectual capabilities. This added dimension—the extension of human intellect—must be part of any program in computer science or information systems.

References

Early efforts to bring computing methods into engineering education are described in three related volumes:

1960. University of Michigan Study. "Electronic Computers in Engineering Education." Ann Arbor: University of Michigan.

1961. University of Michigan Study. "Use of Computers in Engineering Education, Second Annual Report." Ann Arbor: University of Michigan.

1962. University of Houston Study. "Use of Computers in Engineering Education—A Report of the Advanced Science Seminar." Houston: University of Houston.

There were two principal government-sponsored studies on computing in universities during the mid-1960s. Both gave background information on the use of computers in universities and recommended government financial support for computer education:

1966. Rosser, J. B. *et al.* "Digital Computer Needs in Universities and Colleges." Washington, DC: National Academy of Sciences/National Research Council.

1967. Pierce, J. *et al.* "Computers in Higher Education," The President's Science Advisory Committee, The White House. Washington, DC: U.S. Government Printing Office.

Undergraduate and graduate programs

1968, Finerman, A (Ed.). "University Education in Computing Science," ACM Monograph. New York: Academic Press.

1968. Atchison, W. *et al.* "Curriculum '68," *CACM* **11**: 151–197(March).

1972. Ashenhurst, R. (Ed.). "Curriculum Recommendations for Graduate Professional Programs in Information Systems," *CACM* **15**: 363–398 (May).

1973. Couger, J.D. (Ed.). "Curriculum Recommendations for Undergraduate Programs in Information Systems," *CACM* **16**: 727–749 (December).

1977. Cain, J. T. (Ed.). "A Curriculum in Computer Science and Engineering," IEEE Publication EHO 119-8 (January).

1979. Austing, R. *et al.* "Curriculum '78," *CACM* **22**: 147–165 (March).

1981. Magel, K. *et al.* "Recommendations for Master's Level Programs in Computer Science," *CACM* **24**: 115–123 (March).

1981. Nunamaker, J. F. (Ed.). "Educational Programs in Information Systems," *CACM* **24**: 124–133 (March).

1982. Nunamaker, J. F. *et al.* "Information Systems Curriculum Recommendations for the 80s: Undergraduate and Graduate Programs," *CACM* **25**: 781–806 (November).

1983. IEEE Computer Society. "The 1983 Model Program in Computer Science and Engineering," IEEE Publication EHO 212-1 (December).

1984. Mulder, M. and Dalphin, J. "Computer Science Program Requirements and Accreditation—Interim Report of the ACM/IEEE Joint Task Force," *CACM* **27**: 330–335 (April).

1984. Koffman, E. *et al.* "Recommended Curriculum for CS1: 1984," *CACM* **27**: 998–1001 (October).

1985. Koffman, E. *et al.* "Recommended Curriculum for CS2: 1984," *CACM* **28**: 815–818 (August).

1989. Denning, P. *et al.* "Computing as a Discipline," *CACM* **32**: 9–23 (January).

1991. Tucker, A. *et al. Computing Curricula 1991—Report of the Joint (ACM/JEEE) Curriculum Task Force.* New York: ACM Press, Los Alamitos, CA: IEEE Computer Society Press.

For a bibliography on the subject, see "A Survey of the Literature in Computer Science Education since Curriculum '68" by Austing, Barnes, and Engel, *CACM* **20**: 13–21 (January 1977). In addition, the quarterly SIGCSE Bulletin of the ACM Special Interest Group on Computer Science Education contains articles of interest on a continuing basis.

The case for less specialized undergraduate programs in computer science is presented in:

1970. Finerman, A. and Ralston, A. "Undergraduate Programs in Computing Science in the Tradition of Liberal Education," IFIP World Conference on Computer Education 2: 195–199.

1986. Gibbs, N. and Tucker, A. "A Model Curriculum for a Liberal Arts Degree in Computer Science," *CACM* **29**: 202–210 (March).

The mathematical background of the undergraduate student in computer science is examined in:

1980. Ralston, A. and Shaw, M. "Curriculum '78—Is Computer Science Really that Unmathematical?" *CACM* **23**: 67–70 (February).

1981. Ralston, A. "Computer Science, Mathematics, and the Undergraduate Curricula in Both," *Am. Math. Monthly* **88**: 472–485 (Aug.–Sept.).

1984. Ralston, A. "The First Course in Computer Science Needs a Mathematical Corequisite," *CACM* **27**: 1002–1005 (October).

The ACM has compiled curricula recommendations for a variety of educational programs in computer science. The first item below is a paper. The remaining items are booklets that may be ordered from the ACM Order Department, P.O. Box 64145, Baltimore, MD 21264.

1981. ACM. "Recommendations and Guidelines for an Associate Level Degree Program in Computer Programming," J. C. Little, Editor, ACM Order #201812.

1983. ACM. "ACM Curricula Recommendations for Computer Science, Volume I," ACM Order #201831.

1983. ACM. "ACM Curricula Recommendations for Information Systems, Volume II," ACM Order # 201832.

1983. ACM. "ACM Curricula Recommendations for Related Computer Science Programs in Vocational-Technical Schools, Community and Junior Colleges, and Health Computing, Volume III," ACM Order # 201833.

1985. ACM. "Curricula Recommendations for Secondary Schools and Teacher Certification," ACM Order #201850.

There have been several national surveys on computers in higher education and computer manpower conducted by Hamblen. These report on computing facilities and related expenditures, and computer science and related degree programs. Two of these (which reference earlier publications) are listed below:

1979. Hamblen, J. and Baird, T. "Fourth Inventory of Computers in Higher Education 1976–1977," New Jersey: Educom.

1989. Hamblen, J. "Computer Manpower: Through 1984–1985," Computer Science Education **1**, 93–98.

From 1970–1984, Orrin E. Taulbee prepared annual reports giving data on Ph.D. academic programs. Since 1984, David Gries has written these reports, the latest of which appeared in the CACM in 1992.

1992. Gries, D. and Marsh, D. "The 1989–90 Taulbee Survey Report," *CACM* **35**: 133–143 (January).

AARON FINERMAN AND ELLIOT B. KOFFMAN

EUROPE

The teaching of computer science and technology has developed in Europe along more or less the same lines as in the U. S. and for the same reasons.

Some of the first computers in Europe were installed or built in universities: Cambridge and Manchester in the U. K.; Göttingen, Munich, and Darmstadt in Germany; and Paris, Grenoble, and Toulouse in France. They were used mainly for research purposes in departments of applied mathematics and sometimes in electrical engineering, but these research projects led to the development of academic programs.

By the mid-1950s, optional courses had started at the universities that had their own computers or could afford to rent a computer mainly for students in mathematics or physics. At that time, a curriculum in computer science was usually divided into three parts—numerical analysis, hardware, and programming.

In England, in 1965, there was only one university offering a B.Sc. degree in computer science, but there were no degrees in computer science in Germany before 1970, despite a rather extensive teaching program at a number of Hochschulen (schools of engineering). In France, degrees in computer science were given by the Institut de Programmation starting in 1964, although the teaching of computer science started much earlier at the University of Grenoble (1956), Toulouse (1957), and Paris (1957). It was also in France that computer science and technology was very early given the status of an autonomous scientific discipline because of the definition of the word "informatique" by the Académie Française in 1966. Except in English-speaking countries where computer science is still the normal designation, *informatique* or its variants in other languages is the standard name for the discipline.

In the late 1950s, there was the European Computer Manufacturer Association (ECMA), which played a role in the definition of the language Algol 60, but its action was restricted to defining technical standards and it has played no role in education. There has been no European group (up to 1990) that has tried to define a "European curriculum" and in each country the national "Computer Science Society" set up a specialized group to discuss the curriculum problem. In all countries, the discussions were based on what was known in that time about what was going on in U. S. universities, and therefore the ACM "Curriculum 68" had a tremendous influence on European curricula, as did subsequent ACM curricula.

In 1990 the teaching of informatics in Europe is not very different from what it is in the U. S. The curricula are more or less the same, and the differences come mainly from the differences in the administrative organization of education in each country. In the U. K., a number of universities offer traditional degrees in computer science (undergraduate, masters, and Ph.D.). Degrees in computer science are also offered at the colleges of technology and at the polytechnics.

In Germany, education is under the responsibility of the different "Länder" (i.e. states), but, in January 1976, a law was passed under which the federal government has been able to unify education at the university level. All post-secondary institutions are now called "Hochschulen." The scientific Hochschulen are the former universities and the "technische Hochschulen" are schools of engineering with the "Fach Hochschulen" being for vocational education. There are 19 scientific and technical Hochschulen delivering degrees in computer science, but in most Hochschulen there are optional credits in informatics for degrees in electrical engineering, law, economics, medicine, etc.

In the schools of engineering which, in France, are completely separate from universities, optional credits in informatics started in the early 1960s and are today the rule in every school of engineering. In 1969, the first department of informatics was created at the Instituts Universitaires de Technologie with a degree for analysts and programmers at the vocational level. Today there are 19 of these departments, with an output of about 2,000 per year. In 1972, an M.Sc. in applications of data processing to management was created; this degree is now offered at 10 universities and the M.Sc. in informatics is offered at 20 universities. About 10 universities award Ph.D. degrees, which require three to four years after the M.Sc. degree.

There are, of course, also computer science programs in the other countries of Western Europe, but they are all, with some local variations, strongly inspired by the various ACM curricula.

JACQUES HEBENSTREIT

JAPAN

The teaching of computer science and engineering has developed in Japan along lines similar to the U.S., though with a time lag. This article describes the education in information science and engineering in universities, high schools, the industrial world, and technical schools. Also it describes the examination for information processing engineers.

The contents and objective of education have changed with the times. In the latter half of the 1950s, several universities and research institutes developed their own computers, and researchers and graduate students did research in computer hardware and its programming. They organized short courses that emphasized hardware characteristics, binary arithmetic, and programming in machine or assembly language (*q.v.*). In the 1960s, computers were commercialized and were installed in many national universities for research purposes. They were used mainly for research, but more formal educational courses in computing were established in various departments of science and engineering of many universities. Courses for Fortran programming started in those days, and various educational courses for users were offered by computer makers, technical schools, and public educational organizations. At the end of the 1960s, the Minister of Education organized the Council on Information Processing Education. At the beginning of the 1970s, in response to the growth in computing in industry, the council recommended the establishment of both professional education in information science and engineering and the expansion of education in computer literacy (*q.v.*) for all students in universities and vocational high schools. .

University Programs   No degrees in computer science and engineering were granted before 1970. After 1970, many departments of information science or engineering were established in accord with the council recommendation. At present, more than 80, 50, and 30 universities offer undergraduate, masters, and doctoral degrees in computer science or engineering, respectively. The curricula of many of these computing departments are strongly influenced by ACM Curriculum '78 or the Model Program of Computer Science and Engineering of the IEEE. However, each department establishes its own curriculum independently; there is no standard. Also, according to whether the origin of a department is in mathematics, electrical (electronic) engineering, or management science, it has a tendency to place emphasis on theoretical foundations and software, hardware, or application to organizational systems related to business administration, respectively. Recently, several Japanese departments developed curricula that place emphasis on knowledge engineering. In 1989, the Minister of Education and the Information Processing Society of Japan organized a committee to investigate educational programs for information processing in universities. And now a core curriculum for a department of information science is under consideration and will be published before long.

Some universities have large computing centers for education. Education in computer literacy is prevalent for students of science and engineering, but not for others because of the lack of curricula, teachers, and methods of teaching. Also, the contents of programming courses did not advance after the 1960s; most centered on Fortran programming. However, the shortage of computers has been mitigated because cheap microcomputers of high quality are now used very widely.

High School Programs   After 1970, on the council's recommendation, courses for information technology and information processing were established in many technical and commercial high schools, respectively. At present, many vocational high schools have computers, and computing is one of the key subjects. But so far, most teachers in middle schools and liberal arts high schools have been indifferent to both the computer itself and to using computers in education. However, some changes are beginning to take place. During the latter half of the 1980s, various educational councils were organized to revise primary and secondary education, and it was planned to introduce education for computer literacy into them. Recently, microcomputers have been installed in many of those schools, and they are beginning to be tentatively used in various subjects.

Education in the Industrial World   The shortage of software engineers has been pointed out for more than 20 years. The shortage of senior engineers is especially serious. In 1986, the Minister of International Trade and Industry set up a committee to study how to cope with the situation. To develop a proposal from the committee, several subcommittees and working groups were organized. According to their job descriptions, engineers were divided into four kinds: an *application engineer*, to construct an information processing system for a business section, a *technical engineer*, to play the role of a bridge between users and makers and construct an optimal system for users, a *development engineer*, to construct basic software, and a *production engineer,* to design a program and manage a project of developing programs. They also established the concept of senior engineer and guidelines for fostering development of such engineers. The list that follows gives the knowledge or techniques that these senior engineers must have in common:

Computer architecture
Communication networks
Software engineering
Analysis and design of information processing systems
Information systems and the human factor
Project management
Database management
Operation of information processing systems
Communication techniques
Related knowledge, such as fundamental theory, pattern matching, and applications of artificial intelligence

Technical School Programs   There are many private schools for training information processing technicians. Most of them are post-secondary two-year schools that give no degree for graduation. These schools have increased rapidly in the last ten years. In 1980, there were about 40 such schools and nearly 10,000 students, but in 1990 there were about 300 schools and 70,000 students. Curricula are diversified, but most of them emphasize computer programming. The schools supply a large number of technicians to the software industry. But the industrial world expects them to supply engineers, rather than technicians. In order to answer the expectation, a public educational organization has retrained their teachers under the support of the government.

Examination for Information Processing Engineers

In 1969, the Minister of International Trade and Industry established an examination for an information processing engineer in order to encourage software engineers to improve their skills. At first, these were only for junior and senior programmers, but now there are examinations for system engineers, engineers of on-line data processing, and engineers of system auditing besides the above two. In 1990, there were 544,250 applicants, and the cumulative number of successful candidates was 323,057 (245,378 junior programmers, 61,596 senior programmers, 12,025 system engineers, 2,166 engineers of on-line data processing, and 1,892 engineers of system auditing).

TOSHIO NISIMURA

EDSAC

For articles on related subjects *see* DIGITAL COMPUTERS: HISTORY: EARLY, and ORIGINS; EDVAC; ENIAC; ULTRASONIC MEMORY; and WILKES, MAURICE V.

The EDSAC (Electronic Delay Storage Automatic Calculator) was built in England during the late 1940s at the Mathematical Laboratory of the University of Cambridge. It was designed according to the principles expounded by J. Presper Eckert, John W. Mauchly, and others at the summer school held in 1946 at the Moore School of Electrical Engineering in Philadelphia, and which the author of this article was privileged to attend. The objectives from the beginning were (1) to show that a binary stored-program computer could be constructed and operated; (2) to develop programming techniques, even then seen to be a subject of more than trivial content; and (3) to apply the techniques developed in a variety of application fields.

In order to accelerate the attainment of the first objective, it was decided to ease the circuit design problems by choosing a conservative pulse repetition frequency (500 KHz compared with 1 MHz used in most contemporaneous projects) and to bias the logical design in the direction of simplicity rather than speed. This policy was successful, and by May 1949 the project had reached the stage at which the development of programming techniques and the running of practical programs could begin.

The EDSAC (Fig. 1) was a serial binary computer with an ultrasonic memory (*q.v.*). The mercury tanks used for the main memory were about 1 ½ meters long and were built in batteries of 16 tanks. Two batteries were provided. A battery, with the associated circuits, could store 256 numbers of 35 binary digits each, one being a sign digit. An instruction occupied a half-word of 17 bits, and it was also possible to use half-words for short numbers. Numbering of the storage locations was in terms of half-words, not full words. The instruction set was of the

FIG. 1 The EDSAC.

single-address variety, and there were 17 instructions. Multiplication was included, but not division. Input and output were by means of five-channel punched-paper tape. The input and output orders provided for the transfer of five binary digits from the tape to the memory, and vice versa.

Operation of the machine could not start until a short standard sequence of orders, known as the *initial orders*, had been transferred into the ultrasonic memory from a mechanical read-only memory formed from a set of rotary telephone switches. The space that the initial orders occupied in the memory could be re-used when they were no longer required for reading the input tape. The initial orders determined the way in which the instructions were punched on the paper tape, and this was quite an advancement for the period.

One row of holes, interpreted as a letter, indicated the function; this was followed by the address in decimal form, with leading zeros omitted and terminated by a code letter. In the first set of initial orders to be used, this code letter merely determined whether the address referred to a short or a long location; before the end of 1950, however, these initial orders had been replaced by a more elaborate set in which the terminating characters were used to provide relocation facilities for blocks of instructions or data punched on the tape.

The EDSAC did its first calculation on 6 May 1949, and ran until 1958, when it was finally switched off.

References

1950. Wilkes, M. V. "The EDSAC (Electronic Delay Storage Automatic Calculator)," *MTAC* 4: 61.

1956.—. *Automatic Digital Computers*. London: Methuen; New York: Wiley.

MAURICE V. WILKES

EDVAC

For articles on related subjects, *see* DIGITAL COMPUTERS: HISTORY; ECKERT, J. PRESPER; ENIAC; MAUCHLY, JOHN W.; STORED-PROGRAM CONCEPT; ULTRASONIC MEMORY; VON NEUMANN, JOHN; and VON NEUMANN MACHINE.

The EDVAC (Electronic Discrete Variable Automatic Computer), the first stored program computer, was a direct outgrowth of work on the ENIAC. During the design and construction of the ENIAC in 1944 and 1945, the need for more storage than its 20 10-decimal digit numbers was realized. The experience with acoustic delay lines for radar range measurement led to the concept of recirculating storage of digital information. The group at the Moore School of Electrical Engineering at the University of Pennsylvania started development work on mercury delay lines for such storage, and initiated the design of the EDVAC.

As the first stored program computer, EDVAC instructions that controlled the computational process were stored in the same way that its data was stored. The basic logical ideas are described by von Neumann (1945), and

computers based on such designs have come to be known as *von Neumann machines*, even though most historians question whether von Neumann deserves such exclusive credit for the stored program concept. In the spring of 1945, J. Presper Eckert described the mercury delay line (ULTRASONIC MEMORY - *q.v.*) to the author. In answer to the question of how to control the operations, he replied that the instructions would be stored in the delay lines just like numbers. Once he said it, the solution was obvious. There is no doubt that Eckert deserves credit for the delay line memory, and though there is no proof that he first thought of putting instructions in the delay lines, it seems probable that he and/or John Mauchly thought of it before von Neumann came on the scene. What von Neumann should get credit for, of course, is that his interest in and support of computer activity significantly increased government and academic support. Therefore, following a suggestion of Maurice Wilkes, it is proposed that stored program computers following the EDVAC design be called *Eckert-von Neumann computers*.

The principles involved in the EDVAC design exerted a strong influence on the computers that followed it. The EDVAC had about 4,000 tubes and 10,000 crystal diodes. It used a 1,024-word recirculating mercury delay-line memory, consisting of 23 lines, each 384 microseconds long. The words were 44 bits long. Instructions were of the four-address type (4-bit operation code and four 10-bit addresses). The arithmetic unit did both fixed and floating-point operations. Input and output were via punched paper tape and IBM cards. Information was all handled as serial pulse trains and the clock frequency was 1 MHz.

Although the conceptual design of the EDVAC was complete in 1946 and was delivered to the Ballistic Research Laboratories at Aberdeen, Maryland, by 1950 the entire computer had not yet worked as a unit and was still undergoing extensive tests (Stifler, 1950, pp. 200–201). The delay in completing the EDVAC was primarily due to the efflux of computer people from the Moore School in 1946. Eckert and Mauchly resigned and launched a commercial venture (UNIVAC). Herman Goldstine and Arthur Burks went to Princeton to work with von Neumann, and the author left to work with Turing in England. T. K. Sharpless was put in charge, but he, too, left later to go into business for himself.

The EDVAC finally became operational as a unit in 1951. An Aberdeen Proving Ground report states that during 1952 the EDVAC "began to operate on a production basis." For nine months of 1952, the average available time per week was 47.4 hours (23.3 for code checking and 24.1 for production), and the average "engineering" time was 104.8 hours. Approximately 70.4 hours of this was unscheduled maintenance; 10,000 defective tubes (over twice the complement) and about 3,000 (of 10,000) germanium diodes were replaced. In a later Aberdeen report, Weik notes that during 1956 the average error-free running period was approximately 8 hours, and that out of a run time of 8,728 hours, 6,752 were good (78%). This gave approximately 130 hours of "good time" per week. The EDVAC was used until December 1962 (Knuth, 1970, p. 259).

References

1945. von Neumann, John. "First Draft of a Report on the EDVAC," Contract No. W-670-ORD-4926, U. S. Army Ordnance Department, Philadelphia: University of Pennsylvania, Moore School of Electrical Engineering (June 30).

1946. Chu, C., Davis, J., Huskey, H., Lukoff, H., Merwin, R., Sharpless, T., Shaw, R., and Sheppard, C. *Progress Report on the EDVAC, vol. II.* University of Pennsylvania, Philadelphia (June 30).

1950. Stifler, W. W., Jr. (Ed.). *High Speed Computing Devices.* New York: McGraw-Hill.

1970. Knuth, Donald E. "Von Neumann's First Computer Program," *Computing Surveys* **2**, 4: 247–260 (December).

HARRY D. HUSKEY

EFT. *See* ELECTRONIC FUNDS TRANSFER SYSTEMS.

ELECTRONIC CALCULATOR. *See* CALCULATORS, ELECTRONIC AND PROGRAMMABLE.

ELECTRONIC FUNDS TRANSFER (EFT) SYSTEMS

For articles on related subjects *see* BANKING APPLICATIONS; COMMUNICATIONS AND COMPUTERS; COMPUTING AND SOCIETY; DATA SECURITY; DISTRIBUTED SYSTEMS; ELECTRONIC MAIL; NETWORKS, COMPUTER; and PRIAVCY, COMPUTERS AND.

An *Electronic Funds Transfer (EFT) System* is a system that involves the electronic movement of funds and fund information between financial institutions. The transfer is coupled with minimal amounts of data to facilitate that transfer. There are two major worldwide EFT networks: the Clearinghouse Interbank Payments System (CHIPS) and FedWire (the oldest EFT system in the U.S.). In 1991, these networks moved an estimated $1.29 billion each banking day. A third major network, the Society for Worldwide Interbank Financial Telecommunications (SWIFT), is capable of handling nearly 1 million messages per day.

The Evolving Forms and Extensions of EFT

The original expansion of EFT was stimulated by the standardization of magnetic ink character recognition (MICR) technology in the mid-1950s. EFT systems were anticipated to be a lower-cost alternative to paper transactions. EFT has progressed through four various forms: automated teller machines (ATMs), automated clearing houses (ACH), electronic funds transfer point of sale systems (EFTPOS) and debit cards, and electronic funds transfer electronic data interchange systems (EFT-EDI).

Automated Teller Machines (ATMs) provide the basis for the most familiar EFT system in current use. These target the consumer market. ATMs are installed by financial institutions to provide unattended, on-line computerized banking "teller" services. ATMs are user-activated through a magnetic strip on a plastic card. ATMs read account information, verify a valid user by the customer's entering of a personal identification number (PIN), and then allow cash withdrawals, deposits, transfer of funds between accounts, and balance inquiry. More extensive services are offered by some ATM-based systems.

In 1990, it was estimated that, for some users, EFT saved more than $1 per transaction. Generally, however, the anticipated impact in lowering overall volume of paper transactions due to these systems has not occurred. Further, the number of ATM manufacturers has gone from eight to six within the last two years, suggesting that the domestic market may have peaked and the industry may be consolidating.

The *automated clearing house* (ACH) network is a nationwide system that processes pre-authorized electronic payments on behalf of depository financial institutions. ACH networks resulted from a joint effort by the Federal Reserve System and the banking industry in the mid-1960s.

The National Automated Clearing House Association (NACHA) is a trade association representing 42 regional ACH associations whose members comprise over 15,500 depository financial institutions. Expanding direct deposits of payroll and similar services should increase the volume of transactions substantially in the 1990s.

Electronic funds transfer at point of sale (EFTPOS) is the blending of electronic point of sale technology with EFT, usually accomplished with a "debit" card that is similar to those used for ATMs. Electronic point-of-sale advantages such as better pricing and inventory planning and control are thus enhanced by the characteristics of EFT such as convenience of cash and the security of a credit card.

EFTPOS systems involve a network of retail-based terminals linked on-line to a financial institution's computer. Payments rendered at retail operations can then be debited from a customer's account and credited to the retailer's automatically. Information about the transaction may also be entered into the retailer's information system and used for inventory management purposes.

In 1989, a one-year pilot program, EftPos UK, was begun in the United Kingdom to determine the viability of EFTPOS systems on a large scale. Though this program was terminated in April 1990 after only six months of operation, EFTPOS systems are still forecast to have potential on a less ambitious scale. The lukewarm reception to EftPos UK by fewer than the desired level of subscribers appeared to be due to uncertainty about who would pay the relatively high costs of installation of the service.

Electronic funds transfer and electronic data interchange (EFT-EDI) is the direct, rapid, computer-to-computer transmission and translation of business information (e.g. invoices, purchase orders, claims forms) in a standard format. No human intervention is necessary in order to link the transmission to other parts of a company's information system. For example, EDI-transmitted invoices can update inventory orders and generate exception reports for backorders.

EDI messages are non-proprietary and non-copyrightable, while those from EFT systems have substantially more security requirements. Combining EFT and EDI technologies offers substantial synergistic benefits, such as lower personnel costs, greater accuracy, and reduced lead time. While the cost savings with EFT are estimated to be $1 per transaction, some combined EFT-EDI systems yield savings in the range of $5 to $25 per transaction.

Architectural Requirements EFT suggests several hardware and software requirements to preserve system integrity and security in expanding regional, national, and international networks. Fault-tolerant computing (*q.v.*) systems for reliability need to be used which, if hardware-based, preserve the integrity of the network better than older, independent computer systems that were merely patched together. Authentication requirements for messages (for both PC and mainframe users) entails a watchword generator and controller, a security card, and a mainframe peripheral security module. The U.S. Data Encryption Standard (DES) has traditionally been the encryption algorithm used to secure EFTPOS systems (*see* CRYPTOGRAPHY, COMPUTERS IN). As transaction volumes increase, however, the algorithm's effectiveness tends to decrease.

While there is still not complete agreement on a standard application program interface (API), there is movement towards resolution of the issue. The X.400 Gateway API and X.400 Application API were created in 1989 by the Application Program Interface Association (APIA). APIA is a consortium of 24 vendors in the electronic mail and messaging industry. The APIs will spur the development of X.400 technology to link wide and local area networks (LANs - *q.v*). X.400 (which is a store-and-forward messaging architecture) has been recommended by the International Standards Organization (ISO).

Switching networks (such as France's X.25 packet-switching network) with add-on applications packages to handle EFT execution orders, language translations, and currency conversions are needed to handle the growing number of international message formats used by EFT systems.

EFT Trends and Issues The recent changes in EFT hardware and software technology have a number of implications for the future and growth of the methodology. Electronic benefits transfer (EBT) is the government's use of EFTS technology to automate programs such as Social Security, child support, Medicaid, and food stamp distribution. The use of EFT tax payment programs are just starting to expand. Forecasts are that, in 1992, 39 states will have such systems. The Internal Revenue Service is seeking to use EFT-EDI for refunds. Off-site mainframe computers can now deliver EFT advances automatically through facsimile transmission (fax).

Security and interface/interconnection issues are becoming more important as the industry matures. Currently, cryptographic protocols are used for security at the applications level. *Smart cards* (invented in 1974 by Roland Moreno) are beginning to be used to identify users. Smart cards have embedded integrated chips with 8K, 16K, or 32K of indelible memory. A microcom-

puter on the chip executes unalterable programs, thus making such cards more secure than the plastic, magnetic-striped cards currently in use. Different technologies will still need to be used to address compatibility problems.

A particularly troublesome issue facing EFT technology centers around legal questions. Banks and other financial institutions face legal risks that are partially protected if the EFT system used is part of CHIPS or the FedWire system (since these are underwritten by the Federal Reserve System). However, liability issues are still somewhat unsettled, with many different acts and regulations coming into play.

The Federal Reserve Board has changed Regulation CC (which implements the Expedited Funds Availability Act) to regulate time periods by which banks must make check-deposited funds available to customers. Efforts continue to revise Article 4A of the Uniform Commercial Code to address commercial EFT and integrate it with both Regulation CC and the Electronic Funds Transfer Act of 1979, which governs most consumer transactions.

As of 1990, there was no precedent for EFT-EDI documents in law except for those laws applicable to paper documents. Legal documents in the area generally require paper forms and proofs of signature in order to be binding, which tends to lessen the attractiveness of the technology to an organization considering an investment in EFT-EDI. Business documents in EFT-EDI are processed in electronic and heavily coded formats, making audit trails difficult.

Changes of terms and error resolutions associated with credit or debit card disputes are regulated by the Federal Reserve Board's Regulations Z and E, respectively. Efforts continue to reconcile the impact of those regulations on EFT.

The most current concern is the Treasury Department's effort to reformulate portions of the Bank Secrecy Act to address issues raised by EFT operations. Government has an understandable desire to trace and intercept illicitly derived monies. To provide the information necessary, the federal government is floating proposals that would impose detailed record keeping requirements directly related to EFT operations, possibly impeding progress or, at least, ease of use.

References

1987. Kirkman, Patrick. *Electronic Funds Transfer Systems, The Revolution in Cashless Banking and Payment Methods.* Oxford: Basil Blackwell, Ltd.

1989. Fuentebella, Cielo. "NACHA Pitches ACH Minus and Mystique and Mystery," *Bank Systems and Equipment,* **26**, 4 (April), 16.

1989. Organisation for Economic Co-Operation and Development. *Electronic Funds Transfer, Plastic Cards and the Consumer.* Paris: OCED.

1991. Ahwesh, Philip C. "Who Pays for Risk in Worldwide EFT Networks?" *Information Strategy: The Executive's Journal,* **7**, 3, (Spring) 21–26.

1991. Anonymous. "Smart Cards: When the Price is Right," *Banking World,* **9**, 6 (June) 36.

1991. Barr, Robert E. "Are EDI and EFT in Your Tax Filing Future?" *Journal of Systems Management,* **42**, 4 (April) 32–34.

1991. Bove, Richard X. "Bank Technology Reshapes Industry," *Bankers Magazine*, **174**, *3* (May/June), 17–20.

1991. Intriago, Charles A. "Bankers Challenge Proposed Wire Transfer Rules," *Bankers Magazine*, **174**, *4*, (July/August), 55–59.

JANICE F. CERVENY

ELECTRONIC MAIL (E-MAIL)

For articles on related subjects *see* BULLETIN BOARD; COMPUTER CONFERENCING; GATEWAY; and LOCAL AREA NETWORK.

Electronic mail (E-mail) is the electronic transmission of messages, letters, or documents. E-mail may be transmitted by means of point-to-point systems or computer-based message systems. Point-to-point systems link two specific terminals for the duration of the message. Point-to-point E-mail includes telegrams and mailgrams, Telex and TWX, and facsimile systems (fax).

Fax, which sends copies of written, printed, and graphic information over ordinary phone lines, has seen an enormous growth in popularity as the price of fax machines has decreased. Fax boards inserted into expansion slots and used with laser printers and scanners have become a popular personal computer accessory. The chief disadvantages of facsimile are the requirement to establish a point-to-point connection between the machines and, for computer-generated text, the fact that the information is converted into and received as an image rather than text suitable for a word processor. But for maps and other pictorial information, fax is exactly what is needed.

Computer-based message systems, also known as *store-and-forward* or *mailbox* systems, store messages in a computer database for later retrieval. Computer-based messaging may take place on a single computer, a network of computers, or across different computer networks linked by *gateways*. Unlike users of point-to-point systems, computer-based message system users are not location bound. Users may send and receive messages at any hour of the day and from any location that offers access to the message system, even something as simple as a phone that allows dialing in with a portable terminal. Computer-based message system users can broadcast to many users, read and discard messages, file and retrieve messages, and move messages to and from the messaging system.

Most multiuser computer systems and local area networks (*q.v.*) support some kind of computer-based messaging utility. Another alternative is to use a microcomputer based *bulletin board*. Bulletin boards are popular in both hobbyist and business settings as they represent the least expensive way to implement computer-based messaging.

Computer-based messaging is also available over wide area networks (WANs). The prototype for these is the ARPANet, established by the Department of Defense in the 1970s to link major computer research sites. Computer-based messaging quickly became ARPANet's major application. Other wide area networks include USENET, linking Unix-based systems; Internet and Bitnet which serve academic, industrial and governmental institutions, FIDONET, which links hobbyist bulletin boards; and commercial information services such as MCI, CompuServe, Prodigy, BIX and GENIE. Many software companies have found it useful to maintain mailboxes on such systems to aid communication with their user bases.

Attainment of successful electronic mail usage presents a classic "chicken and egg" problem. To be successful, a critical mass of users is required, but individuals are not motivated to use the system until that critical mass of other users exists; users quickly lose motivation to log in if there are no messages for them. Computer-based messaging is most easily established among user groups who are already using the system for other purposes. Other problems with electronic mail include determining the electronic addresses of other users and problems of etiquette with regard to using the new medium. *Electronic junk mail* consisting of unsolicited advertisements has been a particular problem with fax where the receiver has to pay the cost of paper. *Flaming*, intemperate responses to others messages, has been a problem with computer-based messaging and conferencing systems. Sending a computer-based message does not require the time for reflection that sending a conventional letter does and computer-messaging lacks the interpersonal feedback found in conversation.

References

1982. Kerr, Elaine B., and Hiltz, Starr R. *Computer-Mediated Communication Systems: Status and Evaluation* (P. R. Monge, Ed.). Human Communication Research Series. New York: Academic Press.

1985. Vervest, Peter. *Electronic Mail and Message Handling*. Westport, CT.: Quorum Books.

1990. Quarterman, John S. *The Matrix: Computer Networks and Conferencing Systems Worldwide*. Bedford, MA: Digital Press.

ROBERT G. RITTENHOUSE

ELECTRONIC OFFICE

For articles on related subjects *see* ADMINISTRATIVE APPLICATIONS; COMPUTER CONFERENCING; DATA PROCESSING; DESKTOP PUBLISHING; ELECTRONIC MAIL; TEXT EDITING SYSTEMS; and WORD PROCESSING.

The concept of the electronic office (*office automation*) encompasses the application of computer and communications technology to improve the productivity of all types of office workers, including clerical, administrative, professional, and executive. In the mid-1950s, office automation was used as a synonym for *data processing* (*q.v.*) and referred to the ways in which bookkeeping tasks were automated. After some years of disuse, the term was revived in the mid-1970s to describe the interactive use of word and text processing systems, which would later be combined with powerful computer tools leading to a so-called "office of the future" that, inevitably, would be an *electronic office*.

In its first iteration in the early and mid-1980s, this integrated electronic office employed a mainframe or minicomputer (or some part of its processing power) plus video display terminals, keyboards for input, and formed-character or high resolution dot matrix printers for "letter quality" printing. The software functionality of these early office automation systems was based on electronic mail as a kind of "glue," underlying all of the other components and permitting information to be passed from application to application and from user to user. Other major functions included word processing, information retrieval (*q.v.*), various personal assistance functions such as a personal calendar and a group meeting scheduler, and the ability to manage tasks.

Early systems offered by major manufacturers, such as IBM, Sperry Univac, and Burroughs (later merged into Unisys), Digital Equipment Corporation, and Xerox, offered little more than word processing and simple records processing (the management of small sequential files, such as names and addresses, that can be sorted and merged into letters). They were aimed at clerical and secretarial workers and offered little opportunity for substantial customer savings, since the underlying salaries of the workers employed in such jobs was relatively low.

By the mid-1980s, attention was focused on systems that directly supported professional workers and managers by emphasizing the managerial communications function. As personal computers became ubiquitous and local area networks (LANs - *q.v.*) became the accepted methodology for joining personal computer workstations to form workgroups, this more flexible and modular hardware replaced the minicomputer as the preferred office automation platform. When the PC at the desktop became known as the "client" and the shared system unit, with its storage and software, became known as the "server," client/server computing was born (*see* FILE SERVER). Host-based office automation had been used by only a small percentage of all office workers; it was too difficult to cost justify. But with millions of personal computers already in place, the client/server model permitted the implementation of office automation by the simple technique of attaching existing desktop personal computers to local area networks and servers. For a small incremental cost, significant value could be added to the workgroup. The vast majority of electronic office users in the future will use a client/server environment.

Functionality

The functionality of office automation, in the meantime, has been shifting. Electronic mail is the backbone function for all office automation systems, regardless of their underlying hardware architecture. But electronic mail based on terminals and hosts tied into networks (which was once the *only* choice) has subtly changed. The overall concept is very close: Messages can be sent to people in the same organization or to those in other companies or countries, making use of compatible networks, institutional (*de jure*) and marketplace (*de facto*) standards, and electronic mail gateway (*q.v.*) software, which provides translation services between unlike networks. But some of the processing now occurs on the PC desktop and some on a local server. Address lists and software for connection to remote systems may be stored locally, or local servers may address a central hub for such information.

Users may select mail services with substantial sophistication: Delivery may occur immediately, or it may be delayed to take advantage of multi-message bundles or lower rates at off-peak hours; mail may be marked for personal receipt only or delegation might be permitted; password protection and even full message encryption may be available.

A special and rapidly growing form of electronic mail is computer conferencing. In this format, a group of users with access to a particular electronic mail system and a common interest take turns writing, reading, and (if permitted) editing a commonly owned file. Special software facilitates viewing the file in different ways: by subtopics, by author, by date, and so forth. In a computer conference, verbal skills and speed do not count; intelligence and writing skills become more important. Such groups are often *ad hoc* in nature and disband when their task is completed or their interest wanes. The completed file could become archival material, a book on the topic, or simply be discarded.

As of 1991 there were more than 6,000,000 electronic mail users and the number is growing rapidly. About half are on host-based systems and about half on LAN-based systems. Much of the future growth is expected to be LAN-related.

Automating filing is more difficult. The filing of one's own electronically created documents can be readily automated, but much mail, especially external mail, is still received on paper. Some of that paper can be integrated into the electronic filing system by optically scanning it. One can then save it as an image file, identifying it by an index or by indexable keywords. Because image files require large amounts of storage, users may choose to limit their use of these files, except on a temporary basis, or they may choose to use optical disk hardware, for its high-capacity storage capability. Alternatively, Optical Character Recognition (OCR) software algorithms can be applied that transform images of text characters into digital codes, as if the paper document were keyboarded into the electronic system. It can then be indexed and managed just like any other electronic file using a variety of indexing and search techniques.

Recently, new search techniques have been developed that permit much more sophisticated retrieval; this insures the return of a smaller number of more precisely matched answers. Also, *search engines* are available that look for either *changes* in state or for certain events to occur, and which then notify the appropriate system user. A user might, for example, want to be notified as soon as a certain number exceeds $10,000.

Personal computers provide a variety of personal calendar schemes to record and display individual calendars and to produce reminder or "To Do" lists. Workgroup systems offer group calendars, which may be simply systems to display multiple individual calendars, or more complex software can merge calendars in order to schedule meetings for members of a group. Some software can now schedule meetings across multiple systems or local area networks. Software called *groupware* (*q.v.*) can coordinate workgroup tasks as well as meetings.

Sometimes, the term *paperless office* has been used to describe a goal of office automation, but that goal is elusive. A computer screen is not yet a suitable substitute for all the different kinds of information one might simultaneously be using in a work environment (since it is neither big enough, nor of high enough resolution). This is so partly because the screen handles only electronic information and not paper, and partly because it is on the desk. Whenever the worker leaves the office, the computer workstation is left behind. Now, however, portable personal computers are becoming small and inexpensive. By 1993, we expect that one-half of the new personal computers purchased will be portables (*see* LAPTOP COMPUTER). In combination with new pen interfaces, which permit the user to "write" on the screen of the computer rather than use a keyboard, mouse, or other pointing device, such computers can be used anywhere. Then, with an ability to send and receive information (probably via cellular telephone) to and from the office base, the paperless office will be closer to reality. Voice input is now possible for some applications, but continuous speech voice input with full natural language processing (*q.v.*) that allows users to talk and the computer to understand and act is still some way off.

While some impact printing remains in the office, almost all electronic offices now make use of high-quality laser printing at resolutions of 300 dpi (dots per inch) or higher. Color printing also makes extensive use of ink jet and a melted color wax technology. In all cases, the output may include type of any size or style, with an appearance near, if not at, (depending on resolution) a typeset page. Pages may also include forms, tables, graphics, and reproductions of half-tone photographs, although with some lessening of quality.

Future Trends Each of the elements discussed is an example of a tool designed to take an individual human task and make it more efficient. But office automation has a more important goal, namely, to look beyond mere tasks to process and to automate the processes applied to them. This *process automation* is referred to early in the history of office automation in Zisman's (1978) description of using Petri nets (*q.v.*) to describe production systems for office work. Examples are reviewing a technical paper submitted to a journal, applying for a home mortgage, and a budget approval cycle. This work has since been furthered by work at Xerox PARC and by the work of Tom Malone at M.I.T. The new groupware products, which attempt to facilitate cooperation, coordination, and negotiation in groups, are examples of this kind of process automation, as are some of the new procedural processing products being used in conjunction with image processing hardware and software to manage large document processing applications not unlike those imagined by Zisman.

With the advent of very inexpensive personal computers and cheap memory, it is now clear that the device on the desktop (or in the briefcase) will be a fully capable personal computer rather than a semi-intelligent terminal that requires attachment to another computer for any useful processing to occur. Workers are now in the process of moving from character-based, single window personal computers, to graphical user interface, multi-window, multitasking (*q.v.*) personal computers. These new devices will support more complexity and support it with less skill and training. It will change the nature of how people work in offices, what a workgroup looks like, and where, in fact, work is performed.

References

1978. Zisman, M. *The SCOOP Office Reminder System*, Working papers of the Wharton School of Business, University of Pennsylvania.

1987. Crowston, K. and Malone, T. *Information Technology and Work Organization* Cambridge, MA: M.I.T. Sloan School of Management, Center for Information Systems Research, Working Paper No. 165 (December).

1988. Malone, T., *What Is Coordination Theory?* Cambridge, MA: M.I.T. Sloan School of Management, Center for Coordination Science, Working Paper No. 2051–88 (February).

AMY D. WOHL

EMBEDDED SYSTEM

For articles on related subjects *see* ADA; MICROCOMPUTER CHIP; and MICROPROCESSORS AND MICROCOMPUTERS.

In some sense, every computer system is *embedded* within some larger system, such as a business. But the term in computer science and engineering has come to denote a computer that is physically embedded within a larger system and whose primary purpose is to maintain some property or relationship between the other components of the system in order to achieve the overall system objective. Embedded computers are now used in a wide variety of systems, such as aircraft, automobiles, appliances, weapons, and medical devices.

As opposed to computer applications that primarily provide information or computation facilities to the user or those that provide transaction processing (e.g. an airline reservation system or automated teller), the embedded computer reads data from sensors and provides commands to actuators in order to ensure that the goals of the overall system are achieved. It accomplishes this by maintaining some property or relationship between the components of the larger system at some specified value over time or by effecting some sequence of state changes over time. The required relationship between state variables for which the computer is responsible will involve fundamental chemical, thermal, mechanical, aerodynamic, or other laws, as embodied within the nature and construction of the larger system.

Embedded systems usually have certain characteristics that greatly complicate the process of constructing software:

Real-time—The correctness of the outputs is dependent not only on their value, but also on their timing. Outputs that are too early or too late may be incorrect even though they may have the desired computed value. In real-time systems, the required timing behavior of the software is dictated by external events, rather than by internal processing speed.

Reactive—The embedded computer interacts and responds to its environment during execution. Execution is in response to external events or at fixed time frequencies and is often continuous and cyclic (rather than executing once and ending).

Process-control—The computer is responsible for monitoring and partially or completely controlling mechanical devices and physical processes. Control variables in the process are measured to provide input and feedback to the computer, which uses this information to effect changes in the process through outputs to actuators that manipulate the physical properties of the process.

Critical—Often, there is a high cost associated with errors and failures of the computer. In safety-critical embedded systems, a run-time error or failure can result in death, injury, loss of property, or environmental harm.

Embedded software presents unique problems and requires a different type of development strategy than other types of software, such as data processing or transaction systems where the computer is at the center of the application. In the computer-centralized system, peripheral equipment with which the computer interacts, such as input, storage, and output devices, is there to serve the needs of the computer and not vice versa. In this type of system, the behavior of the other components of the system are usually known and often designed or chosen with the needs of the computer as the guiding feature. In the embedded system, the computer is used to service the needs of the other components; thus, its behavior and design is usually severely constrained by the external process being controlled. Furthermore, the knowledge about the behavior of the physical processes may only be partially known and is often continuous and stochastic and therefore difficult to incorporate into the usually discrete and deterministic computer software models. Instead of having the freedom to select external devices that satisfy the requirements of the computer, the other system components usually dictate the requirements for the embedded computer. Furthermore, the order, timing, and required handling of input events by the computer is completely controlled by the other system components, rather than by the software designer. Events that occur in large numbers in a short time or simultaneously must be handled by the computer software in ways that will satisfy the needs and requirements of the larger system. Software requirements for embedded systems are allocated during the system engineering process. The language Ada was designed to be particularly effective for development of embedded system software.

Errors must be handled differently in embedded systems. In most other computer systems, providing information that an error has occurred and discontinuing the processing of the erroneous transaction is satisfactory and perhaps even desirable. A human can then intervene to analyze the error and determine the appropriate recovery procedure. Although the computer system needs to provide correction procedures (e.g. for erroneous entries in an electronic database), the decision to make the correction can be handled externally and often off-line. In embedded systems, errors and failures must be dealt with immediately, and often the detection and recovery from errors must be automated. The computer must be *robust* (must continue to operate in a specified manner), even though other components of the system may fail. Also, the other components must be made robust in the face of computer errors and failures. Finally, embedded computer software must provide facilities to detect and recover from its own errors or, at the very least, to fail gracefully in a way that minimizes damage to the overall system.

References

1986. Elbert, T. F. *Embedded Programming in Ada*. New York: Van Nostrand Reinhold

1991. Leveson, Nancy G. "Software Safety in Embedded Computer Systems," *Comm. ACM*, **34**, 2 (February) 34–46.

1991. Cook, R. "Embedded Systems in Control," *Byte*, **16**, 6 (June) 153–160.

NANCY G. LEVESON

EMULATION

For articles on related subjects *see* FIRMWARE; HOST SYSTEM; MICROPROGRAMMING; READ-ONLY MEMORY; and SIMULATION.

The most common meaning of *emulation* is the ability of one digital computer to interpret and execute the instruction set of another computer. To see how this can be done, it is necessary first to note that the control unit of a computer contains the necessary information for the sequence of operations (*microoperations*) that are to be performed when a particular operation code (op-code) is to be executed. The op-codes may be referred to as *macroinstructions* (not to be confused with the more common usage of macroinstruction - q.v.).

The control unit can consist of either *hard-wired logic* (that is, special-purpose digital logic circuitry for each op-code) or *microprogrammed* control. With microprogrammed control, the control unit contains a sequence of instructions (*microinstructions*) that, when decoded, control the gate operations in the central processing unit (*q.v.*) that will cause the op-code to be executed. This *microprogram* is stored in read-only memory (ROM - *q.v.*).

The microprogram in the control unit may simply be the sequence of microinstructions that will instruct the CPU to perform operations according to an instruction set that a computer designer wishes. For instance, if a computer designer desires an ADD Register-to-Register macroinstruction, the microinstruction sequence will consist of gating operations that gate each of the registers to the arithmetic-logic unit (ALU - *q.v.*) (and then the output of the ALU back to the appropriate register). Another possibility, however—and this is the essence of emulation—is to place a set of macroinstructions of another computer into the hardware of the given computer. That is, one encodes the macroinstruction set of the first computer by microprogramming those instructions on the hardware of the second computer. What we have then is an implementation of the macroinstruction set of one computer on hardware that differs from the originally intended hardware.

Another use of the term emulation concerns the possibility that one may wish to allow the replacement of one circuit board in the control unit by another in order to change the macroinstruction set. In fact, such approaches have been used to design, say, a Cobol machine or a Fortran machine. This is done because certain macroinstructions are more useful in some languages than in others.

Lately there has been a great deal of interest in moving certain portions of software systems into the microprogrammed control portion of the machine to effect increased speed. This has created the opportunity to experiment on trade-offs between software and hardware and between software and microcode. Such implementation of software in hardware is called *firmware* and is still another type of emulation.

References

1988. Habib, S. (Ed.). *Microprogramming and Firmware Engineering*. New York: Van Nostrand Reinhold.
1989. Milutinovic, V. (Ed.). *Introduction to Microprogramming*. Englewood Cliffs, NJ: Prentice-Hall.

STANLEY HABIB

ENCAPSULATION

For articles on related subjects *see* ABSTRACT DATA TYPE; CONCURRENT PROGRAMMING; INFORMATION HIDING; MODULA-2; OBJECT-ORIENTED PROGRAMMING; and SOFTWARE REUSABILITY.

Encapsulation is a technique used to isolate some of the decisions made in writing a program. To encapsulate decisions, a program is organized into an interface, such as a set of procedures, and an internal part. All access to the program's services are available only through the interface. As a result, programs that use those services cannot reference variables internal to the program or arbitrarily transfer control to its internal part.

Decisions that are typically encapsulated are the representation of data, the way that hardware facilities are accessed, and the way in which algorithms are implemented. A typical entity suitable for encapsulation is an abstract data type, such as a stack (*q.v.*). The program that manages physical changes to the stack provides the interface to it. Programs that merely use the stack (through execution of the familiar push-and-pop operations) cannot access the mechanisms and data structures used within the encapsulated stack manager and need have no knowledge of those data structures and their associated algorithms.

One reason for encapsulation is to provide a mechanism for information hiding. If, for example, the storage structure used to implement the abstract concept of a stack is changed to provide greater efficiency, the programs that use the stack have no need to know that the hidden structure was changed. The programs would, presumably, run more efficiently without their creators having to change a single line of source code.

Another reason to encapsulate is to enforce a particular access discipline—e.g. using monitors to enforce access to critical sections of a program so that only one user program can gain access to such a section at the same time (*see* CONCURRENT PROGRAMMING).

A third reason to encapsulate is to provide compatibility among programs that were not written with the intent that they be used together. Such compatibility is sometimes achieved by an interface that translates control and data into a form that can be used by the encapsulated program. The encapsulated program can then be reused without change. This approach is often favored when there is a considerable investment in a large, complex program that is poorly documented or not designed well for change. For example, suppose that some authority decrees that the message format of a message processing program be changed in a way that was not anticipated. An encapsulated interface that transforms the messages from the new format to the old might be written as an alternative to rewriting the message processor itself to recognize the new format.

A fourth reason to encapsulate is to provide an abstraction for a resource that is particularly difficult to use. For example, many of the features of the control structure of a computer are provided to programmers through an operating system interface that makes those features both safer and easier to use. The interrupt handling code for the computer is an example. Programmers can write programs that perform input/output without having to write the interrupt code. Such code is usually carefully encapsulated (note that it is an example where there is no procedural interface). It is invoked only by the occurrence of interrupts in the computer's circuitry. In essence, the interrupt handler is a section of code that is executable for anyone, but readable and writable only by authorized persons. Encapsulation of the interrupt code prevents inexperienced or malicious programmers from corrupting it and allows often-used code to be developed once by those with the experience and knowledge to do it.

DAVID WEISS

ENIAC

For articles on related subjects *see* DIGITAL COMPUTERS: HISTORY: ORIGINS, and EARLY; ECKERT, J. PRESPER; and MAUCHLY, JOHN W.

The ENIAC (Electronic Numerical Integrator and Computer) was developed at the Moore School of the University of Pennsylvania in Philadelphia between 1943 and 1946. It was the first electronic general-purpose automatic computer, and it was certainly a landmark leading to the

FIG. 1.   ENIAC. (Courtesy of Smithsonian Institution.)

development of many automatic computer designs. The logical design of the system was based on the ideas of John Mauchly, and credit for the engineering goes to J. Presper Eckert, Jr. Eckert and Mauchly were granted a patent on the ENIAC in 1964. After a lengthy trial (Honeywell vs. Sperry Rand), this patent was declared invalid on the grounds of public use and publication more than one year prior to the application date. (The ENIAC was demonstrated to the public in February 1946 and the patent application was filed in June 1947.) The court further ruled that Eckert and Mauchly did not themselves invent the automatic electronic computer, but instead derived that subject matter from John V. Atanasoff (q.v.). Whatever the provenance of ideas between Mauchly and Atanasoff, it seems clear that Babbage (q.v.) invented the programmed mechanical general-purpose computer, that Atanasoff invented the automatic electronic computer (though his work was little known and made no contribution to the mainstream of computer development), and that the ENIAC was the first programmed general-purpose electronic computer.

The ENIAC was literally a giant. It contained more than 18,000 vacuum tubes, weighed 30 tons, and occupied a room 30 by 50 ft. The computer consisted of 20 electronic accumulators, multiplier control, divider and square root control, input, output, two function tables, and a master program control. Each accumulator could store, add, and subtract 10-decimal digit numbers. Two accumulators could be interconnected to perform 20-digit operations. Addition and subtraction took 200 μs. Multiplication involved six accumulators and took 2,600 μs.

Decimal digits were stored in ten-stage ring counters, and signed decimal numbers were transmitted in parallel over 11 lines. Each digit was represented during transmission by a train of 0–9 pulses. Clock rates were 100 KHz and pulse widths about 2 μs. All logic was accomplished with direct-coupled vacuum tube circuitry.

As initially designed, programming was by patch panel interconnection, with a wire being required for each event at each unit. Data paths were programmable, using 11 wire cables. The data paths were like a party-line telephone—many units could listen, but only one could transmit. Various units could operate in parallel, being initiated from the same program signal and perhaps using distinct data paths. Interlocks were provided so that independent actions of indeterminate length (e.g. card reading) could complete before follow-on actions were initiated. Signs of results could change the flow of control.

The ENIAC was converted later to a card-programmed computer. In this scheme, certain standard operations were set up in the patch-panel wiring, and sequences of these macro operations were initiated from the card reader.

The ENIAC was designed to integrate ballistic equations, and a significant accomplishment at its dedication in February 1946 was the computation of the trajectory of a 16-in. naval shell in less than real time. ENIAC was formally accepted a few months after its dedication by the U. S. Army Ordnance Corps, but was still operated at the Moore School until late 1946, when it was dismantled and shipped to Aberdeen Proving Ground in Maryland. It became operational again in 1947, and was operated until 2 Oct 1955 (Weik, 1961, p. 575).

The first significant computation on the ENIAC involved atomic energy. Since World War II had ended, there was no longer urgent need for the firing tables that had motivated its design and the support of the Army Ordnance Corps. Among the problems first computed on it, in addition to those involving atomic energy, were random number studies, roundoff error analysis, cosmic ray studies, thermal ignition, wind tunnel design, and weather prediction. It was the major instrument for the computation of all ballistic tables for the U. S. Army and Air Force (Weik, 1961).

Aberdeen Proving Ground reported that during 1952 the "total machine time" for the ENIAC was 7,247 hr, divided as follows: production, 3,491 hr; problem setup and code-checking, 1,061 hr; idle, 195.3 hr; scheduled engineering, 651 hr; and unscheduled "engineering," 1,847.8 hr. The major portion of the scheduled engineering was preventive servicing, the remainder being for improvements and additions; 90% of the unscheduled engineering was devoted to locating and replacing defective tubes. During 1952, approximately 19,000 tubes were replaced (more than 100% of the tube complement).

The ENIAC proved that, with careful engineering, it was possible to build extremely complex logical devices that would perform at electronic speed, without error, for significant periods of time. This was the landmark leading to the development of many automatic computer designs, and paving the way for the "computer revolution." As modestly noted by the Ordnance Corps in *Army Ordnance* (1946), the ENIAC "established the fact that the basic principles of electronic engineering are sound." It was indeed "inevitable that future computing machines of this type would be improved through the knowledge and experience gained on this first one."

Portions of the ENIAC are now in the Smithsonian Institution in Washington, DC. Other ENIAC materials are in the custody of the Historical Services Division of the Department of the Army in Washington.

References

1946. U. S. Army Ordnance Corps. "Mathematics by Robot," *Army Ordnance* **XXX**, 156: 329–331 (May–June).

1950. Stifler, W. W., Jr. (Ed.). *High Speed Computing Devices*. New York: McGraw-Hill.

1961. Weik, Martin H. "The ENIAC Story," *Army Ordnance* **XLV**, 244: 571–575 (January–February).

1974. Larson, Earl. "Findings of Fact, Conclusions of Law and Order for Judgement, *U. S. Patent Quarterly 180* (March 25), 673–773.

1981. Burks, Arthur W. and Alice R. "The ENIAC: First General-Purpose Electronic Computer," *Annals of the History of Computing*, **3**, 4, 310–399 (October).

HARRY D. HUSKEY

ENTERTAINMENT INDUSTRY, COMPUTERS IN THE

For articles on related subjects *see* COMPUTER ANIMATION; COMPUTER ART; COMPUTER GAMES; COMPUTER GRAPHICS; and IMAGE PROCESSING.

Introduction Computer technology has revolutionized what is known as entertainment. In the home, video cassette recorders and televisions grow more powerful due to computer assistance, providing multiple windows, programmed recording, and digitally enhanced images. Computer technology has also introduced digital audio and video technologies that provide higher quality recordings. The new technology allows one to record desired material, to view it when desired, and to see it on sets of very high quality. If that isn't enough, there are now any number of home video games, also computer-controlled. Computer-controlled video games are also popular in arcades and public entertainment centers (*see* COMPUTER GAMES). Theme parks and other entertainment centers are using computer control in *simulator rides*, and other forms of public entertainment and education, such as multimedia presentations, multi-projector slide presentations, and multi-tube video displays, are also computer controlled.

For all the impressive advances in viewing and home entertainment due to computer technologies, the most impressive advances may be found in the material we see on the screen in the form of film and television programming. Computer control of traditional processes found in film and television production, as well as the development of new techniques such as computer graphics has revolutionized this imagery. The impact of these technologies may be seen daily in the world of video and television, and truly amazing images are shown in feature films.

Computers in Feature Films Many applications of computer technology in the film industry are similar to those employed in any other business: word processing (*q.v.*), budgeting, and scheduling. One especially interesting application of computer technology, however, is in the creation of imagery. In 1968, Stanley Kubrick's *2001: A Space Odyssey* helped reintroduce the world of special visual effects to the motion picture industry, and in 1977, George Lucas's *Star Wars* made such special effects a box office hit. This increased emphasis on visual effects spawned a new generation of effects techniques based on the application of computer technology.

Design of visual effects begins with the *storyboard*, created from descriptions in the shooting script and conversations with the film's producer or director. The storyboard is a visual reference of a proposed shot for all members of the filmmaking team (see Fig. 1). The storyboard is traditionally hand drawn by an artist and includes background and effects elements. Storyboards often use background and foreground elements that are scanned into a computer and combined digitally. This composite image may then be further manipulated or drawn on by the storyboard artist to complete the boards. As technology and software develop, producing the storyboard on computers will become a more complete process, enabling the storyboard artist to produce precise renditions of shots, thus further helping the director to visualize a scene.

Production of visual effects has centered around a few core techniques. They include *motion control, animation, model building, creatures,* and *optical compositing*. Of these techniques, motion control, animation, creatures, and optical effects have advanced rapidly since the introduction of computer technology.

Motion control enables the filmmaker to move the

FIG. 1. A *storyboard* and *element list* from *Return of the Jedi*. Copyright © 1983 Lucasfilm Ltd. All rights reserved. Courtesy Industrial Light & Magic.

camera in a precise and repeatable manner. Camera controls are connected to stepper motors or potentiometers which allow a computer to record and/or play back camera motions, freeing the filmmaker to design motion that would otherwise be impossible to use in effects shots (see Fig. 2). Motion control allows an actor to be filmed multiple times in different locations using the same camera move, to create the illusion of self-interaction. This technique is also used to record and control camera movement when filming both scale models and live action sets. The filmmaker can create multiple pieces of film from different scale originals and combine them seamlessly. Most motion control systems allow the camera shutter to remain open during movement of the camera and subject, thus recording movement as a blurred image. Motion blur is natural in other cinematography, but was almost impossible to achieve in effects work prior to the introduction of computer technology.

Creature creation, the building and animation of synthetic characters, has also benefitted from the introduction of computer technology. One of the great advancements in creature work was the development of *go-motion* photography by Industrial Light and Magic (see Fig. 3). This was a refinement of stop-motion photography, the process by which a model, puppet, or any object is filmed one frame at a time and moved slightly between frames by an animator. Go-motion differs from stop-motion in that puppets are moved by rods and cables controlled by computer-directed motors. This technique permits the puppets to move while the camera shutter is open, creating the natural blurring of moving parts, and avoids the jerky and stroboscopic movement often associated with stop-motion animation. While go-motion allows the animator to produce work of higher technical quality, it is still the artistic skills of the animator that create the illusion of life.

Computer technology is used in a number of aspects of traditional and effects animation. Traditional animation, as exemplified by the work of the Walt Disney studio, and effects animation (see Fig. 4, color insert page CP-6), such as the creation of lightning bolts, is usually drawn on paper or animation *cels* and filmed on an *animation stand* (see Fig. 5, color insert page CP-6). Computer control of the animation stand provides the same advantages, repeatability and refinement of moves, as does motion control of stage cameras. Older techniques such as pans, tilts, zooms, spins, fade-ins, fade-outs, cross-dissolves, and wipes are all made much easier with the use of computer technology. In addition, computer-assisted techniques such as slit-scan and pin-blocked animation have been made practical and integrated into the field of effects animation.

Optical composites are the heart of visual effects. An optical composite is a shot composed of two or more images that have been combined on an optical printer to create the illusion of a single image (see Fig. 6, color insert page CP-7). Optical composites may be as simple as placing a single element into a scene or as complex as placing a hundred individual elements into a scene.

FIG. 2. The *Vista-Glide* motion control camera system. The camera is located on a motorized dolly system and its motion is recorded on the computers located in the background. Copyright © 1990 LucasArts Entertainment. All rights reserved. Courtesy Industrial Light & Magic.

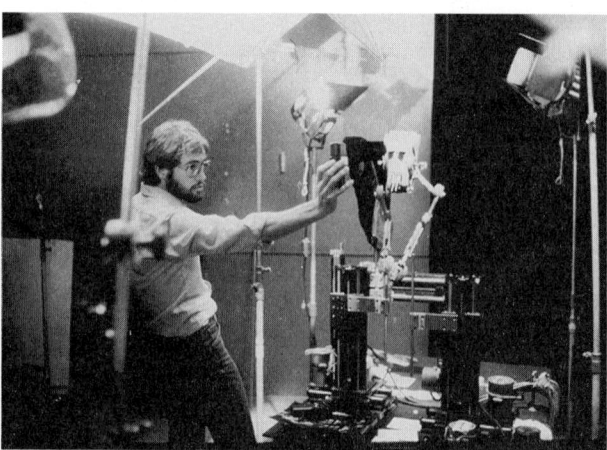

FIG. 3. An animator working with a *go-motion* set up. This is one of the Imperial Walkers from *Return of the Jedi*. Copyright © 1983 Lucasfilm Ltd. All rights reserved. Courtesy Industrial Light & Magic.

The most common application is the placing of actors, photographed on a stage, into an imaginary environment that is impractical, impossible, or too dangerous to actually film.

Optical printers are cameras that rephotograph and combine separate images onto a single piece of film. Basic optical printers consist of at least one projector and a camera facing it with lenses that focus the projector images on the film of the camera. Typical optical printers move the camera only a few thousandths of an inch; this allows for the changing of focus and slight adjustments in the position of an image, but not for creating movement or changing the size of elements.

Modern optical printers are controlled by computer and allow for movement of both the camera and the projectors (see Fig. 7). Simple optical printers use a computer with the power of a pocket calculator. This computer can run *loops* (repeat the playing or filming of a section of film), typically looping two projectors and one camera. Multiple *passes* are achieved by rewinding the film completely and restarting the camera, thus exposing multiple *elements* onto the film. The camera operator adjusts the controls, resets any filters, or inserts new film into the projector and runs the next pass.

A motion control printer offers more advanced computer-controlled features. Individual projectors are able to translate and rotate during a pass, providing actions more complex and extreme than those allowed in a simple printer. The computer also controls the position of the camera and the lens. Compensation curves programmed into the computer can adjust for irregularities in the mechanics. One use of a compensation curve provides automatic focus adjustments as the camera moves in and out. Shutter timing may also be programmed to adjust the exposure during the move. Computer control enables the camera to return reliably to positions and settings within several hundred thousandths of an inch, allowing for intricate combinations of elements and many passes. These printers have many functions similar to those of animation stands.

FIG. 7. An optical printer. Note the control panel in the operator's hands and computers located below the printer itself. Copyright © 1990 LucasArts Entertainment. All rights reserved. Courtesy Industrial Light & Magic.

Computers in Television and Video All of the techniques described in film production may be applied to television production as well; the major difference is that television production is often recorded on videotape. Computer technology was essential in the development of a number of real-time video production tools, including Quantel's Paintbox and Harry. Devices such as these have practically eliminated the use of film opticals in the area of video production. In addition, the introduction of digital video formats have eliminated the problem of generation loss (the degradation of an image due to layering or copying), allowing previously impossible effects.

Other uses of computer technology in television include weather presentation, digitally assisted slow motion, interactive chalkboards, and news graphics. Most of these technologies are now sufficiently inexpensive to allow their use by even the smallest of television stations.

Computer Graphics Computer graphics, a newcomer to the world of entertainment, is revolutionizing the industry. Examples of this work range from the first video games (such as Pong) to Academy Award–winning animation (such as *Tin Toy* - see Fig. 8, color insert page CP-7) and Academy Award–winning visual effects (as in *The Abyss*).

Video game graphics have increased in image complexity and animation quality since their introduction. The quality of these graphics is defined by the limited capability of the computer chip and display technologies to handle the real-time interaction required. They are traditionally two-dimensional and based on the ability of the system to draw small prestored images on the screen. As the technology has developed, modern computer games have become interactive stories, allowing the player to see, hear, and interact with a synthetic world (see Fig. 9, color insert page CP-7). As technologies develop further, we should expect to see three-dimensional images in video games and more sophisticated interactions with this synthetic world.

Traditional film animation has also been aided by computer graphics. The drawing, inbetweening, inking, and opaquing of two-dimensional drawings, traditionally done entirely by hand, is usually very expensive due to the large number of people required by the process. Most successful applications of computer graphics in this area have been in assisting the inking, opaquing, and compositing of drawings, as well as the generation of special animation effects.

Fully computer-generated animation is often used by the film and television industries. This work is usually categorized as either two-dimensional or three-dimensional animation. Two-dimensional computer animation is essentially identical to traditional cell animation in that key-frame drawings are made, in-betweens are generated, and the resulting images are colored. The range of computer involvement in each of these steps is great and very dependent on the cost of the system used. Some systems are simple, image-based systems that allow the animator to create, ink, store, and retrieve images. They offer the animator an easier method of refining each drawing, but

FIG. 10. A computer graphics animator examining a facial model from *The Abyss*. Copyright © 1990 LucasArts Entertainment. All rights reserved. Courtesy Industrial Light & Magic.

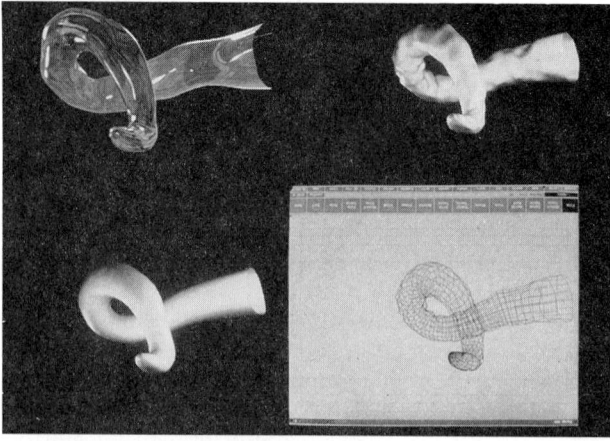

FIG. 12A. Stages in the development of a computer graphics element for the film *The Abyss*. The final element, the *pseudopod*, was either digitally or optically composited into the final scene. Copyright © 1990 LucasArts Entertainment. All rights reserved. Courtesy Industrial Light & Magic.

no other shortcuts. Other systems attempt to save the animator time by computing in-betweens and controlled movement of elements, the camera, or effects such as fades and dissolves.

Three-dimensional computer animation is different in that computer *models* (numerical descriptions) are built and animated, and a *synthetic camera* (also a numerical description) generates the resultant images (see Fig. 10). The computer models used range from very simple spheres and corporate logos to very complex models of working machinery. Animation also ranges from simple object and camera moves to simulation of natural phenomena and highly artistic character animations (see Fig. 11). These animations may be used as a method of previewing a scene, as an animated storyboard, as a guide for traditional animators, to show perspective and guide motion, or as the final imagery itself.

Computer graphics in television runs the gamut from high-end effects and commercials through national logos and station identifications to low-end "visuals." As in the

video game industry, developing technology is continually revolutionizing the look of what we see. The development of workstations (*q.v.*) and more powerful personal computers (*q.v.*) has assisted the development of more realistic imagery.

Current uses of computer graphics in film range from the generation of creatures and synthetic environments to invisible uses such as digital compositing (see Fig. 12), reduction of film grain, and the removal of unwanted objects from a scene (see Fig. 13, color insert page CP-7). No feature length film to date has been made solely with computer graphics, but many short subjects have been created in this way.

References

1969. Miller, Arthur, ASC, and Strenge, Walter, ASC. *American Cinematographers Manual*. Hollywood, CA: The ASC Press.
1983. Fielding, R. *A Technological History of Motion Pictures*. Berkeley, CA: University of California Press.

FIG. 11. A holographic shark prepares to attack Michael J. Fox in *Back to the Future, Part 2*. Copyright © 1989 Universal City Studios, Inc. All rights reserved. Courtesy Industrial Light & Magic.

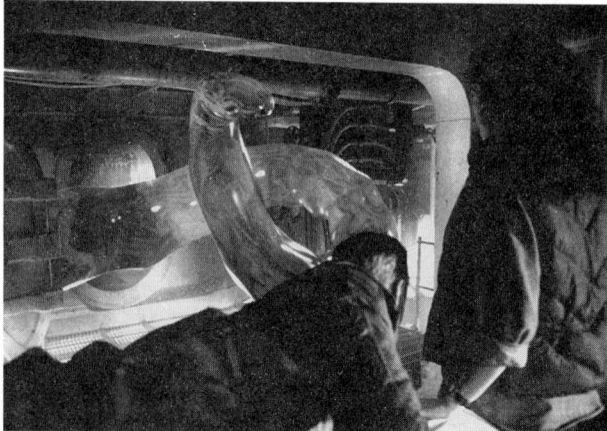

FIG. 12B. The pseudopod as seen in *The Abyss*, winner of the 1990 Academy Award for Best Visual Effects. Copyright © 1989 Twentieth Century Fox Film Corporation. All rights reserved. Courtesy Industrial Light & Magic.

1985. Magneat-Thalmann, N. and Thalmann, D. *Computer Animation*. New York: Springer-Verlag.

1986. Smith, Thomas G. *Industrial Light & Magic: The Art of Special Effects*. New York: Ballantine Books.

1989. Bernard, W. MBKS, *The Technique of Special Effects in Television.*, 2nd Ed. New York: Focal Press/Hastings House.

1990. Foley, J., van Dam, A., Feiner, S., and Hughes, J. *Computer Graphics: Principles and Practice*. Reading, MA: Addison-Wesley.

SCOTT E. ANDERSON

ENTREPRENEURS

For articles on related subjects *see* BURROUGHS, WILLIAM S.; ECKART, J. PRESPER; HOLLERITH, HERMAN; MAUCHLY, JOHN WILLIAM; WATSON, THOMAS J. SR.; and ZUSE, KONRAD.

With the exception of the early pioneers cited above (who have been accorded separate biographies), computer entrepreneurs have flourished only in the last half of the twentieth century. These individuals captured the imagination and admiration of a whole generation. Their vision and daring spawned one of the most sweeping technological revolutions humankind has seen. They gave birth to new technologies, new industries, and new ways of life.

No other field of endeavor has experienced as rapid a growth as computer technology. New products and concepts have been introduced at a dizzying pace. Computer *entrepreneurs* are dedicated and intelligent risk takers willing to create new markets rather than exploit existing ones. In many instances they nurtured ideas that others had rejected. Most became very wealthy, very fast. Short biographies of 19 computer entrepreneurs of particularly significant accomplishment appear alphabetically in the paragraphs that follow.

Gene Myron Amdahl
Best known as the man who designed the IBM Series 360 (*q.v.*) mainframe computer, arguably the most successful business machine of all time, Gene Amdahl built the Amdahl Corporation into a company that, during its peak in 1978, grossed more than 320 million dollars.

Amdahl was born in Flandreau, South Dakota, in 1922. He completed his B.S. in electrical engineering at South Dakota State in 1948 and his Ph.D. at the University of Wisconsin in 1952.

Amdahl began working at IBM in 1952. He had already developed a powerful computer, WISC (Wisconsin Integrally Synchronized Computer), to perform the extensive calculations related to the theoretical physics problems needed to complete his Ph.D. at the University of Wisconsin. At IBM he worked on the IBM 704, the first widely used computer to use indexing, floating-point arithmetic, and a high-level programming language (Fortran). He also worked on the 709/7090 series, but was denied an opportunity to work on the new and powerful IBM 7030 (Stretch - *q.v.*).

He left IBM having developed a taste for new ventures. Returning to IBM in 1960, he developed the 360 series mainframe computer. His most bitter disagreement with IBM was economic, not electronic. IBM had always priced its large systems based on their computational power rather than on their actual production cost. Amdahl, who disagreed with this marketing strategy, left IBM in 1970. At that time he was an IBM fellow working at the IBM Advanced Computing Systems Laboratory in Menlo Park, California, which he founded and directed.

In October 1970, Amdahl started his own company and gave it his name. He set out to build mainframes that were plug-to-plug compatible with IBM's popular machines. This meant that a customer could slide an Amdahl machine right next to selected IBM cabinets and use the same software and peripherals. It was a bold and risky concept that many feel only Gene Amdahl could have pulled off. His 470/V6 computer was compatible with IBM's 370/165. It used large-scale integration for processing, which was unheard of at the time. Only memory devices had been so tightly integrated in the early 1970s. The 470/V6 was one-fourth the size and four times as powerful as the corresponding IBM machine, yet it was priced at the same 3.5 million dollars. It was a major engineering and personal triumph. Orders poured in and, temporarily at least, IBM sales dropped noticeably.

Soon, however, rumors of IBM advances in power and changing trends in computer leasing dried up cash flow. This, coupled with a diminishing financial interest in the company he founded, led Amdahl to move on and pursue other dreams of powerful architectures through Trilogy and Elxsi, two companies involved in making high-performance VAX clones.

Gene Amdahl was the first to show the computer world that money could be made by cloning IBM products. This lesson would not be lost on later entrepreneurs.

Dan Bricklin
The classic entrepreneurial success story involves development of a product that was feasible long before the date of its actual invention. A case of necessity giving birth to invention, Dan Bricklin developed VisiCalc, the first spreadsheet (*q.v.*) program.

Born in Philadelphia in 1951, Bricklin earned a BS from M.I.T. in electrical engineering and computer science, but it was his graduate work at the Harvard Business School that inspired him to see the need for a "word processor for numbers." A chance encounter with schoolmate Dan Fylstra led to the loan of an Apple II computer. Using the model of the journal ledger sheets widely used by accountants, he divided the computer screen into labeled cells and allowed numbers, labels, and formulas to be assigned to those cells. Drawing on his own experience and the advice of professors and fellow students, he worked with another programmer, Bob Frankston, to develop a simple user interface (*q.v.*) written in machine language so that user feedback would be immediate. The success of VisiCalc led to the sale of more Apple II computers by far than any other software product was ever able to do for a competitive computer.

Developers scurried to develop competing products, and hardware manufacturers learned that $100 software could sell hardware worth 30 times that much. Dan Bricklin formed Software Arts in January 1979. At its peak the company was worth more than $50 million. A lawsuit between Fylstra's distribution company, VisiCorp, and Bricklin's Software Arts delayed the sale of the company and ultimately kept Bricklin from realizing his fortune.

The spreadsheet has changed the way that business does business. But something in the entrepreneurial mind does not harken well to authority. Despite attractive offers to work for others, Dan Bricklin struck out on his own again. His new company, Dan Bricklin's Software Garden, markets a program for on-screen demonstration and training of software products developed by others. It is a small operation run out of his home.

Nolan Bushnell

Nolan Bushnell was born in Clearfield, Utah in 1943 and grew up a tinkerer and a lover of all things electrical. His mother would not enter his bedroom for fear of being electrocuted. Bushnell is the father of the arcade computer game (q.v.). He took the simplest graphic concept, two bars and a dot, added the most rudimentary sound effects and a scoreboard and let people play table tennis on a TV. Bushnell showed how painlessly America could be separated from its loose change.

In 1972, Bushnell parlayed $500 into the Atari Corporation, a computer and video game giant that he would ultimately sell for $28 million dollars. Using his newfound fortune, he developed a chain of pizza parlors where people would while away the time usually spent waiting for food by pouring quarters into computer video games. Bushnell showed that game software could sell hardware to mainstream customers far better than any salesperson. He eventually tired of the fast-food business, but not before pocketing an additional $50 million. His idea for a simple and inexpensive computer game that could be played in bars as well as at home had to wait for the development of the microcomputer chip (q.v.). His dream would not prove economically feasible until large-scale integration made the component count very small and the price tag reasonable.

Bushnell provided one of the gateways for the entry of personal computing into the home of the average person. Games became an excuse to compute. He is still in the business of packaging computers and fun. Robots, talking stuffed animals, better TV resolution, and even computer maps for electronic navigation in automobiles are some of his current projects.

Seymour Cray

Because he designed so many of them, Seymour Cray is considered the father of the supercomputer (q.v.). Able to perform billions of floating-point operations per second ("gigaflops"), these "dumb things," as Cray calls them, are essential for the complex computing needs of modern society. Government, military, and educational research institutions rely heavily on the massive computing power these machines provide.

Born in Chippewa Falls, Wisconsin in 1925, Cray was educated as an electrical engineer and did advanced graduate work in applied mathematics. He worked for Engineering Research Associates (ERA) and set to work building the first scientific computer worthy of the name,

the ERA 1101. Cray had unusual aptitude in circuit analysis, logic, and software design. He was noted for the foresight, knowledge, and confidence to work alone.

ERA eventually became Sperry-Rand, for whom Cray worked on the Univac 1103. But, since he perceived that Sperry was more interested in computer sales than computer power, he left Sperry in 1957 to join his friend William Norris who had founded Control Data Corporation (CDC - q.v.). Though vacuum tubes were then still in vogue, the first CDC product, the CDC 1604, was one of the first transistorized computers. Soon, Cray was given free reign to design supercomputers, which was all he ever really liked to do. Largely on the strength of his designs, CDC showed a profit after only two years in business. Cray would eventually tire of administrative duties and retire to the solitude of a specially built laboratory on family land in his home town of Chippewa Falls. Proud of having banished telephones from his laboratory, he designed the CDC 6600, the most powerful computer of its time. A typical CDC 6600 sold for $7.5 million. He went on to design the CDC 7600 and 8600, but the latter was never built, as CDC began to emphasize commercial rather than scientific computer sales.

In 1972, Cray struck off on his own and founded Cray Research. Dedicated entirely to supercomputers, Cray Research raised needed capital solely on the reputation of its founder. With not a single product in inventory, no sales, and no earnings, Cray was able to sell 600,000 shares of stock and realize 10 million dollars to capitalize his new enterprise. He shipped the Cray-1 to Los Alamos National Laboratory in 1976. The first practical vector processing supercomputer, the Cray-1 epitomized Cray's emphasis on design and layout to achieve performance. The computer's cylindrical design allowed short wiring paths and a clock speed of 12.5 nanoseconds.

With the Cray-2 that followed, Cray Research became comfortably profitable. Tiring once again of administrative work, Cray turned over the administration to others and became the sole head of research and development for his company, the role he loves best.

Marylène Delbourg-Delphis

Marylène Delbourg-Delphis, born in France, is president and CEO of ACIUS, Inc., the largest independently owned software company in the U.S. An ex-journalist, she has written for such French publications as *Vogue* and *Le Monde*, once taught philosophy, and has written several books on nineteenth century social history.

Delbourg-Delphis's interest in computing stems from a 1983 assignment that called for the writing of a history of the French perfume industry. Needing to analyze data on over 6,000 perfumes, she sought the help of a Paris service bureau where she met programmer Laurent Ribardiére. The bureau folded, and since she felt that no existing database product could serve her needs, she proposed to Ribardiére that if he would write a suitable program to her specifications she would see that it was marketed properly. After naming their fledgling company ACI—letters having no admitted meaning—they sold 300,000 copies of their first Macintosh product, an advanced relational database called 4th Dimension (4D). At the opposite end of the scale, their entry-level database FileForce was also highly successful.

In 1987, Delbourg-Delphis and Ribardiére established ACIUS (ACI-US) in Cupertino, California, one of the few French-owned computer firms in Silicon Valley. ACI (and ACIUS) specializes in developing multi-lingual documentation for its products, with Delbourg-Delphis herself meticulously supervising preparation of documentation customized to each of the many countries in which ACI does business. To supervise her growing company, whose 1990 sales exceeded $13 million, Delbourg-Delphis now spend 60% of her time in the United States and 40% in France. At the time of this writing (1992), she had no plans to take her company public and hence has not yet realized a windfall comparable to most of the other computer entrepreneurs. But she is still young.

Michael Dell   Michael Dell, the youngest of the 19 entrepreneurs profiled in this article, was born in Houston, Texas, in 1966. He is founder, chairman of the board, and CEO of Dell Computer Corporation of Austin, Texas. He started his company in 1984, capitalizing it with $1,000 of personal savings, by building and selling computers out of his University of Texas dormitory room.

Dell's premise was that high-quality IBM-PC compatible computers could be sold exclusively through mail order, eliminating the overhead necessarily incurred by computer stores. By undercutting the prices of rivals such as IBM itself and Compaq, he managed to earn a modest but profitable share of the PC marketplace. By 1987, three years after its founding, Dell Computer's sales were $69.5 million. In 1990, annual sales reached $546 million, making the company one of the ten largest producers of PCs in the United States. The company's product line is being diversified to include notebook and desktop computers, workstations (q.v.), and network file servers (q.v.).

Dell's interest in computing began with exposure to programming in junior high school in Houston. After acquiring an Apple II of his own, he became fascinated by its communications capabilities and developed and operated his own bulletin board (q.v.) system. To this day he enjoys browsing and contributing to such commercial systems as CompuServe, which he monitors in order to sample the degree of customer satisfaction with Dell products. Those who note that his biographical sketch is somewhat shorter than those of the other 18 entrepreneurs profiled should realize that (as of 1992) he is only 26.

William Gates   As president and CEO of Microsoft, the powerful and influential microcomputer software firm, Bill Gates is the computer industry's youngest billionaire. Born in 1955 in Seattle, Gates was a most precocious teenager. Mischievous and a devoted hacker (q.v.), he knew how to make computers work and make money at it as early as age 15. A system he designed for traffic control earned $20,000 for his fledgling company, Traf-O-Data. He dropped out of high school for a year to make $30,000 working for TRW and bought a speedboat with the money.

In 1975, while a freshman at Harvard, he was struck by the cover article in *Popular Electronics* about the MITS Altair home computer (*see* DIGITAL COMPUTERS: HISTORY: PERSONAL COMPUTERS and PERSONAL COMPUTING). He recognized immediately that these computers would need software and that much money could be made writing it. Along with his friend Paul Allen, he developed a full-featured Basic language interpreter that required only 4K of memory. Basic made the Altair an instant hit, and in 1977 Allen and Gates formed the Microsoft Corporation.

Apple, Commodore, and Radio Shack all introduced computers with Microsoft software. Gates's big break came when IBM decided to enter the personal computer business. IBM's initially secret personal computer effort was called Project Chess. Sworn to secrecy that other firms had rejected, he convinced IBM that his small company could write an operating system from scratch that would take advantage of the disk drives and other peripherals that IBM had planned. Gates also convinced IBM to make the machine specifications public as part of an open architecture (q.v.). This single decision may have been responsible more than any other for the phenomenal success of the IBM-PC and PC-compatibles (q.v.). Microsoft's operating system, MS-DOS, and its applications software are at the heart of almost all of the hundreds of compatible designs that have emerged since the introduction of the original PC.

Much to the chagrin of his parents, Gates dropped out of Harvard to pursue his software development dreams. Unlike several of the other entrepreneurial stories, there has as yet been no downside for Microsoft. Gates holds Microsoft shares worth over a billion dollars. When he took Microsoft public in 1986, he was only 31.

Steven Jobs   Orphaned shortly after birth somewhere in California in 1955, Steve Jobs was adopted and raised in Los Altos. His interest in electronics started in high school. He begged for parts for his projects, even going so far as to ask William Hewlett, president of Hewlett-Packard, for those he needed to build a frequency counter. His boldness earned him a summer job at H-P. Jobs and his friend Steve Wozniak, an electronic wizard who worked for H-P, built a single board computer from inexpensive and readily available parts in Jobs's garage.

Up until that time, only computer kits were available and hence only electronics hobbyists had computers. But Jobs supplied fully assembled computers to the *Homebrew Computer Club*. Using money from the sale of his Volkswagen and Wozniak's programmable calculator, they built 50 computers in 29 days and sold these "Apple I"s, as they called them, to the *BYTE Shop* in Mountain View, California. During the early 1970s, Jobs worked for Nolan Bushnell at Atari designing video games. By 1976 he had talked Wozniak into leaving H-P and forming Apple Computer (q.v.). From the day it opened for business in 1977, Apple prospered and quickly grew into a multi-million dollar company. At one point, Jobs's stock was estimated to be worth $400 million.

Jobs had discovered that a computer in every home was not such a crazy idea. More than 2 million Apple II computers were sold. The introduction of VisiCalc whetted the appetite of the business world for these little machines.

But IBM proved a more formidable opponent than Jobs had envisioned. When sales of Apple computers dropped off after the introduction of the IBM-PC, Jobs turned his attention to a new and innovative technology that ultimately resulted in the introduction of the Macintosh.

Soon after Jobs hired John Sculley from Pepsi-Cola to manage Apple, the two had a falling out. Brash, abrasive, stubborn, hardworking, and intelligent were words variously used by Sculley loyalists to describe the young entrepreneur. Jobs left Apple under less than desirable circumstances in September 1985. He sold all but one share of his Apple stock, realizing a profit of hundreds of millions of dollars. He used part of the proceeds to fund a new company, NeXT, Inc., and part to purchase Pixar, Lucasfilm's computer graphics division. He is now building workstations (*q.v.*) for university and business environments, where a premium is placed on ease of use and high-quality graphics.

There can be no doubt that the Apple I spawned the home computer revolution and gave vision to a host of entrepreneurs. It was Jobs, however, who got there first. The world will never be the same because of the chances he took and the ideas he unleashed.

Phillipe Kahn

Phillipe Kahn, founder, president, and CEO of Borland, Inc., was born in France in 1952. Although little has been published regarding his education and early years, he was sufficiently credentialled to have been teaching math at the University of Grenoble in 1981. He and some friends who liked to write software for the Apple II had developed a very fast Pascal compiler that Kahn decided to market. Noticing that most successful U.S. computer firms had addresses in Silicon Valley, Kahn moved to Scotts Valley, California, in 1982. He made a concerted effort to shed his French accent by listening to talk radio and trying to talk Texan.

The venture capitalists whom Kahn approached shunned him, possibly because his management team included a former manager of a Japanese restaurant, a salesman for Campbell Soup in Mexico, and a cocktail waitress. So, with little or no capital, he rented a two-room $600/month office over a Jaguar garage, took orders by day, and shipped by night. Until that time, the most popular version of Pascal was UCSD Pascal. That product was noted for portability, but not for speed; compilation produced an intermediate "p-code" language that was then interpreted. Kahn's compiler, now rewritten for IBM-PC compatibles, compiled directly to machine language and was startlingly fast with regard to both compilation and execution of generated code. Most orders for this "Turbo Pascal" came from an ad in *Byte* magazine, whose salesman, spellbound by Kahn rhetoric, agreed to run the ad on credit. His ad was bound to catch the reader's eye, since it promised (and he delivered) a breakthrough product at the then unheard of price of $49.95, one-sixth of the going rate for a good language compiler.

Initially, Kahn's company was called MIT: Market In Time. "I noticed," he said, "that if I had the MIT initials in my letterhead, people would return my calls." But when the real MIT threatened to sue, Kahn changed the name to Borland. Sometimes he says that the name is meaningless; other times he says that it is a play on the name of former astronaut Frank Borman, or that it is Celtic for "deep forest."

When Kahn overstayed his initial visa and thus became an illegal alien, someone reported this to the *Wall Street Journal*, who did a feature story on his dereliction—just as he received the green card from U.S. Immigration that granted him resident alien status.

By 1988, Borland had 350 employees and its stock was being traded publicly on a London exchange. By 1990, its sales had reached $226 million and Kahn was being paid $1.6 million per year exclusive of stock options. In 1991, through a swap of stock valued at $440 million, Borland acquired rival Ashton-Tate and its large base of customers for its dBase products. That product line plus Borland's own database product, Paradox, now give Borland three-fourths of the microcomputer database market. Other popular Borland products include Sidekick, a pop-up calendar and calculator, the Quattro-Pro spreadsheet and compilers for Basic, Prolog, C (*q.v.*), and C++ .

Kahn runs Borland much by remote control from his 40-acre estate in the mountains overlooking Scotts Valley. He plays the saxophone at company toga parties, but is also proficient in flute, guitar, piano, and drums. Since he frequently loses his driving license because of too many speeding tickets, he spends much time racing sailboats and still holds a share of the record for the fastest time from San Francisco to Hawaii. And no one is likely to break his record of going from math teacher in France to head of one of the four largest U.S. software firms in nine years.

Mitchell D. Kapor

Born in Brooklyn in 1950, Mitch Kapor is a former Yale University student of linguistics who along with Jonathan Sachs brought the most successful software product of all time to the microcomputer world—the Lotus 1-2-3 spreadsheet program. Kapor started as a child of the 1960s, lover of the Beatles, and protester of the Vietnam War. In the 1970s, he worked as a disk jockey, taught transcendental meditation, and earned a master's degree in psychology.

The success of the earlier VisiCalc led to a growth industry in marketing the product. In the early 1980s, Kapor was selling the related products VisiPlot and VisiTrend under a royalty arrangement. It was clear to Kapor that as spreadsheets, word processors, and other applications software were gaining in popularity, users wanted to take the output from one program and pass it on to another. The original idea behind 1-2-3 was to integrate the operation of a spreadsheet, a graphics program, and a word processor. Sachs suggested that a database management program (DBMS - *q.v.*) would be easier to write than a word processor and would be more useful. The product, starting as *Tiny Troll* but renamed 1-2-3 at Kapor's suggestion, was originally supposed to be a programming language with a spreadsheet capability. Kapor realized the marketing problems that this would pose, so the programming language was disguised as a macro capability in order to emphasize the spreadsheet. Sachs did the programming and Kapor the marketing, and together they founded the Lotus Corporation, the most successful single-product company in the microcomputer universe.

Kapor had seen the needs of the business community and met them head on. His $495 Lotus 1-2-3 product sold almost half a million copies in a few short months. While Lotus has diversified, it is still primarily dependent on the income from 1-2-3. Kapor had made promises to investors about the software with great confidence, and his instinct turned out to be correct. Users wanted an easy way to produce documents with pictures without learning two pieces of software.

Like many gifted entrepreneurs, it is the founding of the enterprise and not its daily management that keeps the adrenaline flowing. Kapor tired of Lotus by the summer of 1986 and moved on to establish ON Technology of Cambridge, Massachusetts, which aims to build computers that are closer to being intelligent assistants than they are to being merely powerful calculators. He left Lotus a multi-million dollar international enterprise and a major force in the microcomputer marketplace.

Gary A. Kildall

Gary Kildall founded Digital Research and was the developer of CP/M, the world's first disk operating system for home computers. He was born in 1942 in Seattle, the son of a merchant marine barge captain, and began tinkering with automobiles and electronic devices while still in high school. He began working at the family-operated Kildall Nautical School, established in 1927. While teaching there, he used early microcomputer devices to develop ways to compute navigational triangle solutions. Later, he earned degrees in mathematics and computer science, finishing his Ph.D. in computer science at the University of Washington in 1972.

The first rudimentary computer kits were only a year or two away from hitting the hobbyist market. Kildall began programming navigational applications on the Intel 4004 chip and exchanged the programs he developed for a prototype personal computer called the Sim-04. He was one of the first persons to own a microcomputer. One of the first programs he developed was PL/M, a Programming Language for Microcomputers that would allow him to do the kinds of tasks that an operating system is expected to perform. PL/M was used to create CP/M (Control Program for Microcomputers), which had as its principal feature the ability to write and read information to and from a disk drive. CP/M was the first practical operating system for personal computers. Kildall began selling the program by mail for $75 through ads in *Dr. Dobb's Journal*.

In 1976, Kildall established Intergalactic Digital Research, a name that he soon shortened to Digital Research, Inc. CP/M quickly became the most popular operating system and dominated the market through the 1970s. Hundreds of different machines ran CP/M. Each had to use a modified form of the operating system that took advantage of the non-standard way in which peripherals and their bus (*q.v.*) were addressed. Kildall conceived of the idea of separating CP/M into two components: one would contain that portion of the operating system that was the same from machine to machine,

and the other would be coded into a read-only memory (ROM - *q.v.*) chip and contain vendor-specific code. In effect, Gary Kildall was the inventor of the BIOS (*q.v.*) concept.

By 1981 sales reached $5.3 million and later peaked to almost $45 million. Kildall was doing well, but events in 1981 conspired against him. IBM was looking for the rights to CP/M for its new and secret PC. They approached William Gates, founder of Microsoft, in the mistaken belief that he owned the rights to CP/M. Gates sent them off to see Kildall, who happened to be out of the office on the fateful day. In his stead, another corporate officer balked at the terms of a proposed IBM non-disclosure agreement that essentially would have allowed IBM to use whatever they learned from the experience, but permitted Digital Research to disclose nothing. IBM went back to Gates who said he could develop something and would be happy to sign the non-disclosure agreement. Digital Research had missed a billion dollar opportunity, and MS-DOS became the primary personal computer operating system of the 1980s. Because of its similarity to CP/M, Kildall believes to this day that there is a great deal of CP/M in MS-DOS.

Kildall currently works on projects involving optical disk publishing for his new company, the KnowledgeSet Corporation. He can also be seen as a regular on the PBS series *The Computer Chronicles*.

William H. Millard

William Millard developed and marketed the IMSAI 8080 home computer and established the first chain of retail computer stores, eventually to be known as Computerland. Millard was born in Denver in 1932 and moved with his parents to the West Coast four years later. He worked at a wide variety of jobs as a youth, many involving door-to-door sales. He started but did not finish college. He was a driven, hardworking man who soon became interested in mainframe computers. While working for Pacific Finance he worked on only the 26th UNIVAC mainframe ever built and took an instant liking to the machine. In 1961, he became the first chief of data processing for Alameda County, California. He was instrumental in the development of terminal-based information systems for municipalities. After repeating his success in developing Management Information Systems (MIS - *q.v.*) for the City of San Francisco, Millard set out to do business on his own. In 1969, he and his wife Pat formed Systems Dynamics and began marketing telecommunications software. By May 1972, the firm was bankrupt. By 1975, he was broke.

Just at the time the home computer was emerging, Millard formed Information Management Sciences and began marketing the IMSAI 8080 computer in kit form. From just one ad in an electronics magazine, he sold almost 3,500 kits at prices between $400 and $500. Millard decided to offer the machines in assembled form in 1976. He opened a computer store in Hayward, California and called it Computer Shack. After complaints from lawyers at Radio Shack, he changed the name of his store to Computerland and began selling franchises, allowing individuals to own their own stores.

Millard soon decided that, contrary to the practice at

competitive stores, he would sell other computers in addition to his own, a fateful decision. In 1977, he began selling the Apple II. In 1981, when IBM introduced its PC, Computerland had exclusive resale rights for six months. Growth was phenomenal. Business doubled each year, and by 1983 Computerland was doing $983 million in sales, with each outlet averaging $2 million. Millard still owned 96% of the stock and had no intention of taking the company public. Bad experiences with previous enterprises had convinced him to retain control. However, it was one of his previous entanglements that would ultimately prove his undoing. IMS had taken out a five-year loan for $250,000 in 1976 from Mariner Company, owned by the family of Phillip Reed III. The loan contained an obscure clause allowing Reed Mariner to convert the note into 20% of the stock in any enterprise that Bill Millard might start. Millard was offered the opportunity to buy back the note for $300,000. In characteristic fashion, he stubbornly refused. This would ultimately cost him in excess of $140 million and his stake in Computerland.

By July 1986, Millard had left the U.S. to live on the Pacific island of Saipan in the Marianas with his family. He is not retired, but is investigating markets around the Pacific Rim. Millard created the concept of marketing computers directly to business and consumers and more than any other individual was responsible for putting the new technology within the practical grasp of the consumer.

William Norris Iconoclastic and unconventional, William Norris was the founder of Control Data Corporation (q.v.), makers of some of the most powerful mainframe and supercomputers of its era.

William Norris was born in 1911 in Red Cloud, Nebraska. Like many of the early computer pioneers, he had an interest in electronics and amateur radio. He was granted a degree in electrical engineering from the University of Nebraska soon after the death of his father in 1932. After working the family farm for a few years, he went to work for Westinghouse selling X-ray equipment. After Pearl Harbor was attacked, he joined the Navy and worked with mathematicians, physicists, and engineers from the scientific and academic community to apply recent electronic advances to the breaking of Japanese codes. He rose to the rank of Commander.

At the end of the war, with the Navy reluctant to disband its code breaking group, Norris suggested forming a company to continue the work. Despite the secret nature of the work, he rounded up a number of investors and formed Engineering Research Associates in 1946. With himself as vice-president and John E. Parker as president, ERA concentrated on making high-speed digital electronic equipment and had revenues of $1.5 million the first year. ERA quickly earned a reputation for building reliable equipment and delivering it on time. But then president Parker decided to sell ERA to James Rand, head of Remington-Rand, for $1 million, 85 times its original worth. ERA was rich in talent and by 1952 had built over 80% of all American-built electronic computers.

Norris continued to work for Remington-Rand, but felt troubled by the lack of support. Named vice-president

of the St. Paul division after the merger in 1955 with Sperry, he headed the Univac division of Sperry-Rand. IBM had still not made a major commitment to building computers, and Norris felt Sperry-Rand should. He tried to push in that direction, but to no avail. Highly frustrated, he left in 1957 with eight colleagues to pursue the opportunity to make big machines. He formed Control Data Corporation, using $75,000 of his own money and $615,000 raised from a large group of friends. He would publicly finance his new company from day one. None of the 300 stockholders had controlling interest, not even Norris. He yearned to take on IBM. His shrewdest move was to hire Seymour Cray from Univac and give him the creative freedom and solitude he required. Cray's creative mind produced some of the most powerful machines ever developed. CDC quickly became the industry leader in powerful machines for scientific, military, and engineering work. By 1959 CDC had sales of $4.5 million, and a year later sales would exceed $28 million. Success was based primarily on the CDC 1604 mainframe and, later, its successor, the CDC 3600. In the mid-1960s, the CDC 6600 supercomputer was recognized as the computer marvel of the age. CDC followed with the 7600 and then the Cyber series. One triumph followed another. By 1965, only two computer companies were operating in the black—CDC and IBM. In 1968, when IBM announced its intent to add an allegedly powerful model 360/80 to its 360 series line, sales of the 6600 dropped precipitously. Norris accused IBM of unfair business practices for announcing computer models far in advance of their realization. Norris saw these as tactics designed to hurt sales of his machines. He took IBM to court and won. He realized more than $100 million dollars in the suit and became a hero to all of IBM's competitors.

Norris used the proceeds of his successful suit to expand the former IBM Service Bureau, ceded to CDC in the settlement. The Bureau allowed people who couldn't afford a whole machine to buy slices of time as needed. CDC ran one of the first time-sharing services and became the world leader in peripheral manufacturing through the 1970s. Ironically, most such devices were plug-to-plug compatible peripherals used with IBM mainframes.

The 1980s saw the departure of Seymour Cray and the emergence of the personal computer, a market in which CDC completely missed out. During 1985 alone, CDC lost $567 million. Criticism focused on Norris and his expensive Plato educational project. Norris stepped down in January 1986.

Norris played a critical role in the development of high-speed powerful machines at a time when the industry might have concentrated on making merely profitable machines. Were it not for CDC, America's preeminence in the computer field might not have come to pass and IBM might have come closer to building a true monopoly.

Robert Noyce Robert Noyce was a co-inventor of the integrated circuit and founder of the Fairchild Semiconductor and Intel Corporations. The integrated circuit has been the basic building block of all computing devices since the early 1960s. This was the most important development in technology during the twentieth century.

Noyce was born in Burlington, Iowa, in 1927. Fond of tinkering at an early age, he studied physics at Grinnel College. After graduating in 1949, he went on to a Ph.D. in physics from M.I.T. in 1953. He then joined the Philco Corporation, but soon became frustrated with their seeming lack of interest in the transistor. He joined Nobel Laureate and inventor of the transistor, William Shockley, in 1956 and moved to what would become known as Silicon Valley. Shockley's management style and his concentration on diodes to the exclusion of transistors led Noyce to leave Shockley's employ. Along with a group of other former Shockley scientists and with funding from Fairchild Camera and Instrument, he formed Fairchild Semiconductor in 1957. Fairchild Camera provided funding with an option to buy the new venture for $3 million at any time during the next eight years.

It was while at Fairchild that Noyce developed the process of making multiple transistors along with wiring and other components on a single layer of silicon. The planar process, which he developed, made it possible to make components small, light, fast, inexpensive, and in fewer steps. The Russians had just launched Sputnik, and the Kennedy administration was eager to boost America's prestige in science. The government became Fairchild's best customer. Since Fairchild components were at the heart of all Apollo spacecraft and Minuteman II missiles, Noyce had created a whole new industry.

By 1968 Noyce was a millionaire, but just barely. Defections from Fairchild to other Silicon Valley startups were cutting into Fairchild's business. Noyce left in June 1968 to begin a new venture over which he could have more control.

Although Jack Kilby is also credited with being a co-inventor of the integrated circuit because of independent work done at Texas Instruments, Noyce had some 12 integrated circuit patents to his credit when he formed Intel in 1968. Along with Gordon Moore and Andrew Grove, who followed him from Fairchild, he set out to make memory chips. Core memory manufacturing disappeared virtually overnight. Intel's first chip was the 1103 RAM chip. Sales reached $23.4 million by 1972. After Intel's Ted Hoff developed the microprocessor, Intel's stock tripled in value in two years. Sales reached $66 million by 1978 as microprocessor and memory chip orders poured in. By 1982 Intel could claim 16 of the 22 major breakthroughs in microelectronics technology. Even today, almost every personal computer contains chips made or inspired by Intel. By the tenth anniversary of its founding, Intel sales had reached $300 million.

As Intel entered the 1980s, Noyce became known as the "Mayor of Silicon Valley." As the founder and the spirit of Intel, the flagship company of the valley, he was the region's elder statesman and eloquent spokesman. In 1980, he was awarded the National Medal of Science and three years later was inducted into the National Inventor's Hall of Fame.

Intel sales reached $1.3 billion by 1985. Though no one dared estimate the size of Noyce's fortune, the size of his contribution to the computer industry cannot be overestimated. In 1988, he played a prominent role in the formation of the Sematech Corporation, a unique attempt to foster cooperation among semiconductor companies and the U.S. government, in order to increase competitiveness in manufacturing. When a search committee that he chaired failed to identify a suitable candidate for CEO, he agreed to accept that position himself.

Noyce loved scuba diving, hang gliding, and piloting his own airplane. On the afternoon of 3 June 1990, he was scheduled to pick up a new jet capable of flying nonstop from his home in Austin, Texas to either Washington, D.C. or Silicon Valley. But he died that morning.

Kenneth Olsen   Kenneth H. Olsen is the founder of Digital Equipment Corporation (DEC - *q.v.*), the second leading manufacturer of computer equipment in the world. He broke the mainframe's dominance of the market during the 1960s when he introduced a line of powerful minicomputers (*q.v.*) which were much less expensive than mainframes.

Olsen was born in 1926 in Bridgeport, Connecticut. He served in the Naval Reserve during World War II, completing bachelor's and master's degrees in electrical engineering at M.I.T. after the war. During the early 1950s, he worked at the M.I.T. Lincoln Laboratory. He was involved in the development of the Whirlwind (*q.v.*) computer, one of the first to abandon vacuum tube storage in favor of magnetic ferrite cores. He also worked on the SAGE military project.

When Olsen left M.I.T. in 1957 to form DEC, he had a great deal of computer experience and he knew what engineers and scientists wanted from a computer company. He set out to build small, powerful, and relatively inexpensive minicomputers and sell them in the scientific and engineering market. His sales force, who were not paid commissions, was made up of engineers who would sell face to face to other scientists. It was a controversial concept, but remarkably successful. His first computer sold for $20,000 in 1960, a full $900,000 less than a comparable mainframe. His PDP-series machines would also allow direct access by terminal or teletype, signaling the beginning of the end for punched cards. He plowed large sums of money into research and development, which led to DEC having one of the widest variety of products of any company in the industry. Its products were well built, well supported, current, practical, and well received. He took a decentralized approach to management and allowed his designers to work on all phases of computer development and to participate actively in product development decisions.

The PDP series of computers paved the way for smaller machines and legitimized the minicomputer business. By 1985, DEC sales reached $6.7 billion. DEC phased out the era of huge, intimidating machines stored in glass-enclosed, air conditioned boxes communicating only through skilled attendants. The minicomputer was the next necessary step toward the evolution of computing for the masses.

Unlike many entrepreneurs, Olsen stayed with the company he started for more than 33 years but he announced his retirement as chairman in 1992. Though an engineer at heart, he was a creative and effective manager—a rare quality for the engineer/entrepreneur. His egalitarian style of management was popular with his staff and made DEC one of the most productive and stable forces in the marketplace.

Adam Osborne   Adam Osborne is the founder of Osborne Computer Company, the manufacturers of the world's first portable computer (*see* LAPTOP COMPUTER). The Osborne I was also the first computer to be sold with several software packages bundled into one price.

Osborne was born in 1939 in Thailand to British parents and spent some of his childhood in India. He moved to Great Britain at age 11 and graduated from Birmingham University in 1961 with a bachelor's degree in chemical engineering. By this time he had developed an interest in writing. He moved to the United States and worked while completing his Ph.D. in chemical engineering at the University of Delaware. He used a computer to shorten the time needed for research on his Ph.D. He worked for Shell Oil after completing his doctorate and moved to California.

Osborne found the corporate world unsuitable and confining. He began to do freelance technical writing and in 1972 formed Osborne and Associates to write simple, easy-to-read manuals for a minicomputer firm called General Automation. It was during this time that he wrote *The Value of Power*, which he would later title *An Introduction to Microcomputers*. Since it was rejected by an established publisher, Osborne decided to publish it himself. The world was hungry for information about the new personal computers and very few books were available. He sold 300,000 copies. He began to write in earnest, and his little publishing house put out over 40 books on computers during the next five years, 12 of them written by himself. In 1979, he sold the business to McGraw-Hill and although the price was never made public, estimates are that he realized in excess of $5 million.

Osborne's writing skills and reputation as a computer guru (*q.v.*) earned him a chance to write a column in several influential periodicals, including *Infoworld*. He was critical and opinionated, but often accurate in his portrayal of the needs and wants of the consumer. He had always argued that computers, to be truly useful, should be able to go where the people are. In 1979, he set out to design and market a computer that was portable, rugged, easy to use, affordable, and that would include some of the software that users would normally buy elsewhere. The Osborne I sold for $1,795 and came with software valued at over $2,000 at retail. When Osborne introduced the machine at the West Coast Computer Faire in San Francisco in Spring 1981, it was the smash hit of the show. It weighed only 24 pounds, had a built-in monitor and disk drives, and an affordable price. The first machines were shipped that summer. By September, Osborne was enjoying his first million-dollar month, and between August and December his company had achieved $6 million in sales. Second year sales were $70 million.

Soon thereafter, however, sales of the Osborne I dropped. IBM had announced its new PC, Osborne I's were experiencing a 15% failure rate, and the announcement of the new Osborne *Executive* machine was premature. Sales of the Osborne I dropped precipitously and the $10-million-a-month business, now in the hands of professional management, was in trouble. With more than $45 million in debts, the Osborne Computer Company declared bankruptcy in September 1983. Ever the author, Osborne wrote about the experience in the book *Hypergrowth*, which he co-authored with fellow guru John Dvorak.

By Spring 1984, Osborne was back in the publishing business. With $150,000 of his own money and sales of six million shares on the penny stock market, Osborne raised more than a half million dollars, largely on his reputation and the slightness of the risk. He formed his *Paperback Software* and is dedicated to publishing inexpensive software packages in the hopes that many copies of low-priced software will realize larger gains than small quantities of high-priced software. It is also his intention to bring software prices into line with the cost of a good book.

Osborne is still running *Paperback Software* and still fighting industry forces. His *VP Planner* software, which emulates *Lotus 1-2-3* and is priced under $100, has run afoul of Lotus lawyers and he is being sued once more. Never far from controversy, this one-time *enfant terrible* is still fond of the limelight.

David Packard   David Packard is one of the founders of Hewlett-Packard Corporation, one of the most prosperous, innovative, and respected companies in the computer industry. Born in Pueblo, Colorado, in 1912, Packard, like many engineers of his day, became interested in ham radio and all things electronic at an early age. He graduated from Stanford University in 1934 and began work as an electrical engineer in the vacuum tube engineering department of General Electric in Schenectady, NY. In 1938, along with his long-time friend William Hewlett, he founded the Hewlett-Packard Company in Palo Alto, California, in an area that would later become the principal home of America's computer industry. Its founding date of 1938 makes H-P one of the oldest computer firms.

Hewlett-Packard's roots actually go back to 1931 when, as a sophomore at Stanford, Packard met Hewlett. They played football together and shared an apartment as well as an interest in ham radios and other gadgets. Both studied engineering and talked often about starting a company together upon graduation. While Packard was at GE, Hewlett was finishing up at M.I.T. They then did graduate work together at Stanford, building electronic devices in their spare time. With a loan of $538 from a Stanford professor, they built and marketed a commercial version of a variable frequency oscillator. Their base of operation was a Palo Alto garage. After many small projects they began doing work for the defense department and in the 1950s branched out into the civilian electronics field. During the 1970s, H-P moved from instruments to small computers and calculators. The H-P 3000 minicomputer was their best-known product. By the mid-1980s, sales had reached $4.4 billion and H-P had 68,000 employees. By then, Packard's share of the company—he had 18.5% of the stock—was valued at $2.1 billion.

Today, H-P is active in the personal computer field and makes a very popular and reliable line of laser printers. Because of their high quality and performance, their personal computers carry an above-average price. This has made them less than competitive in the CPU market, but they are a major force in the peripheral arena with printers and plotters.

Packard was H-P president from 1939–1946, chairman of the board from 1947–1964, and CEO from 1964–1968 and beyond. Between 1969 and 1971, he was Deputy Secretary of the United States Department of Defense. He is still extremely active in public affairs. He has served on numerous presidential commissions, the U.S.-U.S.S.R. Trade and Economic Council, and the boards of directors of many universities and public organizations.

H-P is known for its quality products and its great respect for its employees. There is a democracy of ideas that transcends rank. Work hours are flexible, dress casual, and benefits generous. Many Silicon Valley companies who have successfully implemented this model point to H-P as the standard. These notions can be credited to David Packard, one of those rare entrepreneurs with an engineering degree who knew how to manage and treat people with respect and dignity.

H. Ross Perot In 1962, H. Ross Perot founded Electronic Data Systems, the world's largest and most influential computer service bureau, with $1,000 he borrowed from his wife, who was then a teacher. He virtually created the market for servicing the computer needs of corporate America. His service bureau provided computer processing power for the many industrial, governmental, and business enterprises that chose not to establish an in-house computing center.

Perot was born in Texarkana, Texas in 1930 and grew up during the Depression. He and his family struggled to make ends meet. He sold seeds, Christmas cards, and newspapers door-to-door. He was so talented a salesman that he was able to sell newspapers to largely illiterate cotton pickers, who earned only $9 a week, by convincing them that they could use the newspapers as cheap insulation for their homes. When the director of circulation thought he was making too much money, his commission was lowered. Perot went directly to C.E. Palmer, the publisher, to complain. Palmer immediately had the original arrangement restored.

Perot claimed to be acquiring a business education in the marketplace that was more valuable than one gained at Harvard. After graduating from Texarkana High School and then Texarkana Junior College, he received an appointment to the U.S. Naval Academy, where he distinguished himself as a student and a leader. He was twice elected president of his class and named battalion commander. He graduated from the Academy in 1954 and commissioned an ensign. He served aboard both destroyers and aircraft carriers.

While a navigation officer on the aircraft carrier *Leyte*, he met an IBM executive who was so impressed with his style and demeanor that he offered Perot an interview. After four years in the navy, he was hired by IBM as a $500-a-month computer salesman in the Dallas region. Ross finished first in his sales training course and usually made his monthly quota before the 19th of the month. In fact, he was making more money than most of his bosses, and his success was a bit of an embarrassment to them. He made so much that it was difficult to

promote him. His IBM manager would refuse to give him assignments for months at a time. It was during a six-month hiatus in 1962 that he formulated the idea for EDS. He tried to interest IBM in selling time on its 7070 series of computers, but IBM feared it would cut into equipment sales and rejected the idea.

Although it is not clear why his success with IBM did not provide sufficient capital, he borrowed money from his wife and set off on his own in August 1962. He purchased time for $70 an hour on computers he did not own and resold it at a profit. After landing his first service contract from Collins Radio, he began hiring specialists to program and provide support for various businesses. EDS pioneered the idea of facilities management, a concept whereby EDS would become the data processing department for insurance firms, banks, government agencies, and manufacturers. The rise of EDS was rapid during the 1960s. Insurance and medical claims processing provided heavy income. By 1969, Perot's stock was worth more than a billion dollars.

There was a downturn in 1973 when Perot tried to computerize the Wall Street brokerage community, but EDS recovered during the 1980s with lucrative federal contracts, some worth more than a half billion dollars. EDS brought the military's computer systems into the twentieth century. By 1984, total corporate revenue was more than $800 million and income in excess of $70 million. EDS was spread across all 50 states and nine countries. It was the largest computer service firm in the world.

In 1984, Perot sold EDS to General Motors for more than $2.5 billion. While GM helped triple EDS business, Perot, as a member of the GM board, was to prove a most unacceptable thorn in GM's side. He was constantly critical of GM management and GM policy. In the fall of 1986, GM was so upset with his criticism that they paid more than $700 million for Perot's EDS shares—more than twice their market value.

More than an entrepreneur, Perot is also a superpatriot and a philanthropist. In 1985, he purchased one of the four original copies of the Magna Carta and donated it to the National Archives. He worked tirelessly on behalf of prisoners of war in Vietnam. He even financed a successful rescue mission to Iran when two of his employees were taken hostage while trying to assist Iran with computerization.

A man of sweeping vision and grand ideas, Perot has realized his dream of providing the corporate world with the tools and services it needed during the fast moving times of the late twentieth century. His latest venture has been an investment in the NeXT, Inc. enterprise started by Steven Jobs. He maintains a simple life, is close to his family, and is immensely proud of the role he played in the development of an industry. After appearing poised in the spring of 1992 to announce his independent candidacy for the presidency of the United States, he withdrew in July.

An Wang An Wang was the founder of Wang Laboratories, once the world's leading makers of free-standing word processing equipment. He is also credited with inventing magnetic core memory for early digital computers.

Wang was born in 1920 in Shanghai, China, the oldest of five children. His father was an English teacher. He lived in China until after World War II. He received his bachelor's degree in electrical engineering and communications from Chiao Tung University in Shanghai. During the war he worked for the Chinese government designing radio transmitters and receivers. He was sent to the United States after the war as part of the reconstruction effort. He enrolled at Harvard and completed both his master's and Ph.D. degrees in applied physics by 1948.

As a research fellow at the Harvard Computation Laboratory from 1948 through 1951, Wang worked under Howard Aiken (q.v.). Aiken challenged him with a most difficult problem. The design of Aiken's binary digital relay computer, the Mark I (q.v.), needed a non-mechanical memory storage system. Wang's design stored information with magnetic flux changes in tiny magnetic metal doughnuts or cores. Wang conceived the notion of reading information, which he knew would destroy it, and then re-writing the same information into the compromised location. As digital computers became popular, his invention was to prove viable for the next 20 years.

After finishing work on the Mark IV computer, Wang decided to leave Harvard Labs as it phased out basic research. Recognized for his expertise in digital electronics, he decided to manufacture and sell memory cores. With $600 in savings, he rented office space in Boston and, as sole proprietor, opened Wang Laboratories in June 1951. On that day he had no contracts, no orders, no office furniture, and a staff of one. He concentrated on small-scale applications involving counting, sorting, storing, and displaying data. As business increased he moved to Cambridge, Massachusetts, and in 1955 Wang Labs became a corporation. He sold his memory core patent to IBM for $400,000 and suddenly had the capital he needed to expand.

Wang Labs began to manufacture electronic counters, machine tool controls, telecoders, and typesetting equipment. In 1962, Wang introduced the first electronic scientific desk calculator. As slide rules became obsolete, sales reached $6.9 million by the end of the 1966 fiscal year. In 1967, Wang Labs went public. Its stock, easily the hottest offering of the year, raised an incredible $79 million.

In 1968, Wang branched out from calculators to computers. Ironically, Wang was one of the first to abandon magnetic core storage in favor of smaller, faster, and less complex semiconductor devices. As the 1970s arrived, Wang was determined to merge the dual office needs of word processing (q.v.) and data processing. He went head-to-head in the smart typewriter market with IBM. His WCS series was priced below IBM and had more options.

In 1975, he took back control of his company by a stock transfer to Class B Common. The following year he launched the WPS system, which was based on the cathode ray tube, a revolutionary development. This word processing system vaulted his company onto the Fortune 1000 list. From that moment, Wang became known as "The Word Processing Company."

By 1986, revenues of $2.6 billion produced earnings of $50.9 million. Wang's personal fortune was estimated at $1.6 billion. It had been estimated that Wang Labs would be a $5 billion company during the 1990s, but after turning company control over to his son in the late 1980s, Wang had to watch sadly as the fortunes of his former company turned sour. One contributing factor was that the ease of converting a personal computer into a word processor through software made free-standing, single-purpose word processing equipment obsolete.

An Wang, dapper, bright-eyed, soft-spoken, yet steel-willed, managed to combine an uncanny ability to anticipate market changes with a flair for innovation. His determination to return to the world more than he had taken made him a noted philanthropist. On 3 July 1986 at the relighting of the Statue of Liberty, he was awarded the Medal of Liberty as one of twelve outstanding naturalized citizens.

An Wang died at his home in Boston on 24 March 1990. In his lifetime, he had been awarded 40 patents and 23 honorary degrees. At the time of his death, *Forbes* magazine estimated that he was the fifth richest man in the U.S. Since the fortune of H. Ross Perot is likely to be slightly more, and the fortune of Bill Gates only slightly less but growing, at least three of the five largest personal fortunes accumulated in the U.S. have been earned by computer entrepreneurs.

References

1984. Levering, Robert, Katz, Michael, and Moskowitz, Milton. *The Computer Entrepreneurs: Who's Making it Big and How in America's Upstart Industry.* New York: New American Library.

1986. Lammers, Susan. *Programmers at Work.* Redmond, WA: Microsoft Press.

1986. Cortada, James. *Historical Dictionary of Data Processing Biographies.* Westport, CT: Greenwood Press.

1987. Littman, Jonathan. *Once Upon a Time in Computerland: Bill Millard's Computerland Empire.* Los Angeles: Price Stern Sloan, Inc.

1987. Slater, Robert. *Portraits in Silicon.* Cambridge, MA: The M.I.T. Press.

1988. Rifkin, Glenn and Harrar, George. *The Ultimate Entrepreneur: The Story of Ken Olsen and Digital Equipment Corporation.* Chicago: Contemporary Books.

1990. Mason, Todd. *Perot: An Unauthorized Biography.* Homewood, IL: Richard D. Irwin.

1992. Wallace, J. and Erickson, J. *Hard Drive: Bill Gates and the Making of the Microsoft Empire.* New York: John Wiley.

STEPHEN J. ROGOWSKI and EDWIN D. REILLY

ERGONOMICS. See HUMAN FACTORS IN COMPUTING.

ERROR ANALYSIS

For articles on related subjects *see* ARITHMETIC, COMPUTER; ERRORS; INTERVAL ARITHMETIC; MATRIX COMPUTATIONS; NUMERICAL ANALYSIS; ROUNDOFF ERROR; and SIGNIFICANCE ARITHMETIC.

In general, the basic arithmetic operations on digital computers are not exact but are subject to rounding or truncation errors. This article is concerned with the cumulative effect of these errors. It will be assumed that the reader has read the article on MATRIX COMPUTATIONS, since the results will be illustrated by examples from that area.

Definitions

There are two main methods of error analysis, known as *forward analysis* and *backward analysis*, respectively. They may be illustrated by considering the solution of an $n \times n$ system of linear equations by Gaussian elimination. In this algorithm, the original system is reduced successively to equivalent systems $A^{(r)}\mathbf{x} = \mathbf{b}^{(r)}$, $r = 1, 2,\ldots, n - 1$. In the final system the matrix of coefficients, $A^{(n-1)}$, is upper-triangular, and the solution is found by back substitution.

In a forward analysis, one adopts the following strategy: Because of rounding errors, the computed derived system $\overline{A}^{(r)}\mathbf{x} = \overline{\mathbf{b}}^{(r)}$ differs from that which would be obtained by exact arithmetic. It seems reasonable to assume that, if the algorithm is stable, $\overline{A}^{(r)} - A^{(r)}$ and $\overline{\mathbf{b}}^{(r)} - \mathbf{b}^{(r)}$ will be small, and, with sufficient ingenuity, bounds would be found for these "errors." This is perhaps the most natural approach.

Alternatively, one could adopt the following strategy: If the algorithm is stable, presumably the computed solution $\overline{\mathbf{x}}$ is the *exact* solution of some system $(A + E)\overline{\mathbf{x}} = \mathbf{b} + \mathbf{e}$, where E and $\mathbf{e}$ are relatively small. Of course, there will be an infinite number of sets of which $\overline{\mathbf{x}}$ is the exact solution. A successful error analysis will obtain satisfactory bounds for the elements of E and $\mathbf{e}$. Such an approach is known as *backward* error analysis, since it seeks to replace all errors made in the course of the solution by an *equivalent* perturbation of the original problem. It has one immediate advantage. It puts the errors made during the computation on the same footing as those arising from the data. Hence, when the initial data is itself inexact, no additional problem is posed.

Early Error Analysis of Elimination Processes

In the 1940s, the imminent arrival of electronic computers stimulated an interest in error analysis, and one of the first algorithms to be studied was Gaussian elimination. Early analyses were all of the forward type, and typical of the results obtained was that of Hotelling, who showed that errors in solving an $n \times n$ system might build up by a factor 4^{n-1}. The relevance of this result was widely accepted at the time. Writing in 1946, Bargmann, Montgomery, and von Neumann said of Gaussian elimination: "An error at any stage affects all succeeding results and may become greatly magnified; this explains why instability should be expected." The mood of pessimism was very infectious, and the tendency to become enmeshed in the formal complexity of the algebra of the analysis seems to have precluded a sound assessment of the nature of the problem. Before giving any error analyses, we discuss fundamental limitations on the attainable accuracy.

Norms and Floating-Point Arithmetic

We will need some way of assessing the "size" of a vector or a matrix. Such a measure is provided by vector and matrix *norms*. A norm of a vector $\mathbf{x}$, denoted by $\| \mathbf{x} \|$, is a non-negative quantity satisfying the relations

$$\| \mathbf{x} \| \geq 0 \quad \text{and} \quad \| \mathbf{x} \| = 0 \quad \text{iff } \mathbf{x} = \mathbf{0},$$
$$\| \alpha \mathbf{x} \| = | \alpha | \, \| \mathbf{x} \|,$$
$$\| \mathbf{x} + \mathbf{y} \| \leq \| \mathbf{x} \| + \| \mathbf{y} \|.$$

We will use only two norms, denoted by $\| \mathbf{x} \|_2$ and $\| \mathbf{x} \|_\infty$ and defined by

$$\| \mathbf{x} \|_2 = (\Sigma | x_i |^2)^{1/2}, \qquad \| \mathbf{x} \|_\infty = \max | x_i |.$$

Similarly, a norm of a matrix A, denoted by $\| A \|$, is a non-negative quantity satisfying the relations

$$\| A \| \geq 0 \quad \text{and} \quad \| A \| = 0 \quad \text{if } A = 0,$$
$$\| \alpha A \| = | \alpha | \, \| A \|,$$
$$\| A + B \| \leq \| A \| + \| B \|,$$
$$\| AB \| \leq \| A \| \, \| B \|.$$

We will use only two norms, denoted by $\| A \|_2$ and $\| A \|_\infty$ and defined by

$$\| A \|_2 = (\text{max eigenvalue of } AA^H)^{1/2}, \text{ where } A^H \text{ represents the conjugate transpose of } A$$
$$\| A \|_\infty = \max_i (\Sigma_j | a_{ij} |).$$

It may be verified that

$$\| A\mathbf{x} \|_2 \leq \| A \|_2 \, \| \mathbf{x} \|_2$$
$$\| A\mathbf{x} \|_\infty \leq \| A \|_\infty \, \| \mathbf{x} \|_\infty \simeq$$

Most of the early error analyses were for fixed-point computation, but, since virtually all scientific computation is now done in floating point, we restrict discussion to this case. We use the notation $\text{fl}(x \times y)$ to denote the product of two standard floating-point (fl) numbers as given by the computer under examination, with an analogous notation for the other arithmetic operations. We have the following results for each of the basic operations, using a mantissa of t digits in the base β:

$$\text{fl}(x \times y) = xy(1 + \varepsilon), | \varepsilon | \leq m\beta^{-t},$$
$$\text{fl}(x \div y) = (x/y)(1 + \varepsilon), | \varepsilon | \leq d\beta^{-t},$$
$$\text{fl}(x \pm y) = x(1 + \varepsilon_1) \pm y(1 + \varepsilon_2),$$
$$| \varepsilon_1 |, | \varepsilon_2 |, \leq s\beta^{-t}$$

where m, d, and s are constants on the order of unity, depending on the details of the rounding or chopping procedure. Described in the language of backward error analysis, we might say, for example, that the *computed* sum of two numbers x and y is the *exact* sum of two numbers $x(1 + \varepsilon_1)$ and $y(1 + \varepsilon_2)$, each having a low relative error. On well-designed computers,

$$\text{fl}(x \pm y) = (x \pm y)(1 + \varepsilon), \quad | \varepsilon | \leq s\beta^{-t}.$$

For convenience, from now on we assume that all ε in the above satisfy the bound $| \varepsilon | \leq k \cdot \beta^{-t}$, where k is of the order of unity.

By repeated application we have, with an obvious notation,

$$\text{fl}(a_1 + a_2 + \cdots + a_n)$$

$$= a_1(1 + E_1) + a_2(1 + E_2) \cdots + a_n(1 + E_n),$$
$$(1 - k\beta^{-t})^{\,n-1} \le 1 + E_1 \le (1 + k\beta^{-t})^{\,n-1}$$
$$(1 - k\beta^{-t})^{\,n+1-r} \le 1 + E_r \le (1 + k\beta^{-t})^{\,n+1-r}$$
$$r = 2, 3, \ldots, n.$$

The bounds on the errors are reasonably realistic, and examples can be constructed in which they are almost attained. Naturally, when n is large, the statistical distribution can be expected, in general, to result in some cancellation of errors and, thus, in actual errors substantially less than the bounds.

One of the most important elements in elimination methods is the computation of expressions of the form

$$p = \text{fl}(a - x_1 \times y_1 - \cdots - x_n \times y_n).$$

The computed p and the error bounds are dependent on the order in which operations are performed. If the operations are performed in the order written above, we obtain

$$p = a(1 + E) - x_1 y_1 (1 + F_1) - \cdots - x_n y_n (1 + F_n),$$

where

$$(1 - k\beta^{-t})^n \le 1 + E \le (1 + k\beta^{-t})^n,$$
$$(1 - k\beta^{-t})^{\,n+2-i} \le 1 + F_i \le (1 + k\beta^{-t})^{\,n+2-i}.$$

If one computes

$$p = \text{fl}(- x_1 \times y_1 - x_2 \times y_2 - \cdots - x_n \times y_n + a),$$

then

$$p = - x_1 y_1 (1 + E_1) - \cdots - x_n y_n (1 + E_n) + a(1 + F),$$
$$(1 - k\beta^{-t})^{\,n+3-i}(1 + E_i) \le (1 + k\beta^{-t})^{\,n+3-i},$$
$$|F| \le k\beta^{-t}$$

In describing the last result in terms of backward error analysis, we might say, for example, that it is exact for data $x_i(1 + E_i)$, y_i and $a(1 + F)$, putting all the perturbations in the x_i and a. Alternatively, we could say it is exact for data, x_i, $y_i(1 + E_i)$, and $a(1 + F)$.

Note that although the errors made can be equated with the effect of small relative pertubations in the data, the relative error in the computed p may be arbitrarily high, depending on the degree of cancellation that takes place. Indeed, if the true p is zero, one may have an infinite relative error. One would not think of attributing this to some malignant instability in this simple arithmetic process; it is the natural loss to be expected.

Inherent Sensitivity of the Solution of a Linear System

For any computational problem, the inherent sensitivity of the solution to changes in the data is of fundamental importance; yet oddly enough the early analyses of Gaussian elimination paid little attention to it. We consider in a very elementary way the effect of perturbations δA in the matrix A. We have

$$\bar{\mathbf{x}} = (A + \delta A)^{-1}\mathbf{b} = (A^{-1} - A^{-1}\delta A A^{-1} + \cdots)\mathbf{b}$$

$$= \mathbf{x} - A^{-1}\delta A\mathbf{x} + (A^{-1}\delta A)^2\mathbf{x} - \cdots,$$

giving

$$\|\bar{\mathbf{x}} - \mathbf{x}\|/\|\mathbf{x}\| \le \|A^{-1}\delta A\|/(1 - \|A^{-1}\delta A\|),$$

provided $\|A^{-1}\delta A\| < 1$. The relative error in $\bar{\mathbf{x}}$ will not be low unless $\|A^{-1}\delta A\|$ is small. Writing,

$$\|\delta A\| = \eta \|A\|,$$

we see that

$$\|\bar{\mathbf{x}} - \mathbf{x}\|/\|\mathbf{x}\|$$
$$\le \eta \|A\|\|A^{-1}\|/(1 - \eta \|A\|\|A^{-1}\|).$$

The inherent sensitivity is therefore dependent on $\|A\|$ $\|A^{-1}\|$, and this is usually known as the *condition number* of A (for the given norm), with respect to inversion or to the solution of linear systems.

We might now ask ourselves what sort of limitation we should expect on the accuracy of Gaussian elimination even if it had no menacing instability. The solution of $Ax = b$ requires $n^3/3$ multiplications and additions, an average of $\frac{1}{3} n$ per element. From the elementary discussion given so far, we might risk the following prophecy: Even if Gaussian elimination is a stable process, then we can scarcely expect to obtain a bound for the resulting error, which is less than that resulting from a perturbation δA in A satisfying, say,

$$\|\delta A\| \le \tfrac{1}{3} kn\beta^{-t} \|A\|.$$

In fact, this bound for the effect is usually reasonably realistic, provided that pivoting is used. Indeed, the advantages conferred by the statistical distribution of rounding errors is such that the error is usually less than the maximum error that could be caused by such a perturbation.

Backward Error Analysis of Gaussian Elimination

Gaussian elimination provides a very good illustration of the power and simplicity of backward error analysis. The elimination process may be described as the production of a unit lower triangular matrix L and an upper triangular matrix U such that $LU = A$. The solution of the system $Ax = b$ is then carried out in the two steps:

$$L\mathbf{y} = \mathbf{b}, \qquad U\mathbf{x} = \mathbf{y}$$

In the backward error analysis, one shows that the computed L and U satisfy the relation $LU = A + E$ and obtains bounds for the elements of E. One then shows that the computed solution $\mathbf{y}$ and $\mathbf{x}$ of the triangular systems satisfies the equations.

$$(L + \delta L)\mathbf{y} = \mathbf{b}, \qquad (U + \delta U)\mathbf{x} = \mathbf{y}$$

and obtains bounds for the elements of δL and δU. The computed $\mathbf{x}$ therefore solves *exactly* the system

$$(L + \delta L)(U + \delta U)\mathbf{x} = \mathbf{b}$$

or

$$(A + E + \delta L\, U + L\delta U + \delta L\delta U)\mathbf{x} = \mathbf{b}$$

Hence, it is the exact solution of $(A + F)\mathbf{x} = \mathbf{b}$, where

$$\begin{aligned}\| F \| &= \| E + \delta L\, U + L\, \delta U + \delta L\, \delta U \| \\ &\le \| E \| + \| L \| \| \delta U \| \\ &\quad + \| U \| \| \delta L \| + \| \delta L \| \| \delta U \|,\end{aligned}$$

and from the bounds for E, δL, and δU, one obtains a bound for F.

The simplicity of the technique may be illustrated by presenting the analysis of the solution of the system $Ly = \mathbf{b}$. We first make the following observations:

1. The relevant system to be analyzed is that with the computed matrix L, not the L that would have resulted from exact computation.
2. Since during the course of the analysis we do not attempt a direct comparison between computed and exact values, there is no need to denote computed quantities by bars. It is to be understood that all symbols refer to computed quantities.
3. It is only at the final stage when we have expressed the computed solution as the exact solution of $(A + F)\mathbf{x} = \mathbf{b}$ and have obtained a bound for $\| F \|$ that we attempt to compare the computed $\mathbf{x}$ with the true $\mathbf{x}$, and at this stage we can use the result of the previous section.

At a typical stage in the triangular solution, $y_1, y_2 \ldots, y_{r-1}$ have been computed and y_r is determined from the relation

$$y_r = \mathrm{fl}(- l_{r1} y_1 - l_{r2} y_2 - \cdots - l_{r,r-1} y_{r-1} + b_r),$$

using, of course, the computed values of the y_i. Hence,

$$\begin{aligned}y_r = &- l_{r1} y_1 (1 + E_{r1}) - l_{r2} y_2 (1 + E_{r2}) \\ &- \cdots - l_{r,r-1} y_{r-1}(1 + E_{r,r-1}) + b_r(1 + F_r),\end{aligned}$$

where the factors $1 + E_{ri}$ and $1 + F_r$ are of the type discussed in connection with the computation of p above. Hence, the computed y_i satisfy exactly the relation

$$\begin{aligned}l_{r1}(1 + G_{r1}) &+ l_{r2} y_2(1 + G_{r2}) \\ &+ \cdots + l_{r,r-1} y_{r-1}(1 + G_{r,r-1}) \\ &+ y_r(1 + G_{rr}) = b_r,\end{aligned}$$

where

$$(1 + G_{ri}) = (1 + E_{ri})/(1 + F_r),$$
$$i = 1, \cdots, r - 1,$$
$$1 + G_{rr} = 1/(1 + F_r).$$

Notice that by dividing through by $1 + F_r$, we are able to restrict ourselves to pertubations in L. The computed $\mathbf{y}$ therefore satisfies exactly the relation $(L + \delta L)\mathbf{y} = \mathbf{b}$, where $\delta L_{ij} = L_{ij}\, G_{ij}$.

We certainly have

$$(1 - k\beta^{-t})^n \le (1 + G_{ij}) \le (1 + k\beta^{-t})^n$$

most of the factors, of course, satisfying much better bounds. Bounds of the above type are cumbersome to use, and we observe that, if $kn\beta^{-1} < 0.1$, as will usually be the case, then, using the binomial theorem,

$$(1 + k\beta^{-t})^n \le 1 + (1.06)\, kn\beta^{-t},$$
$$(1 - k\beta^{-t})^n \ge 1 - (1.06)\, kn\beta^{-t}.$$

Hence, we have

$$| \delta L_{ij} | \le (1.06)\, kn\beta^{-t} | L_{ij} |,$$

giving, for example,

$$\| \delta L \|_\infty \le (1.06)\, kn\beta^{-t} \| L \|_\infty.$$

The analysis is almost trivial, though earlier error analyses of the solution of triangular systems were extremely complicated.

If the computation of y_r had been expressed in the form

$$y_r = \mathrm{fl}(b_r - l_{r1} y_1 - \cdots - l_{r,r-1} y_{r-1}),$$

then we could still obtain a relation of the form $(L + \delta L)\mathbf{y} = \mathbf{b}$, but in this case the bounds on the elements of δL would be appreciably larger.

On many computers it is possible to accumulate either of the expressions for y_r in double precision, rounding to single precision only on completion. If this is done, then we again obtain a relation of the form

$$\begin{aligned}l_{r1} y_1 (1 + G_{r1}) &+ l_{r2} y_2 (1 + G_{r2}) \\ &+ \cdots + l_{r,r-1} y_{r-1}(1 + G_{r,r-1}) \\ &+ y_r(1 + G_{rr}) = b_r,\end{aligned}$$

but now the quantities $| G_{ri} | (i < r)$ have bounds of order β^{-2t} and can therefore virtually be neglected, while $| G_{rr} |$ has the bound $k\beta^{-t}$. We therefore have a result that might well be described as best possible, having regard to the precision of computation. Indeed, the residual vector $\mathbf{b} - L\mathbf{y}$ corresponding to the computed $\mathbf{y}$ will almost certainly be smaller than that corresponding to the correctly rounded solution!

The analysis of the solution of $U\mathbf{x} = \mathbf{y}$ is almost identical to that of $L\mathbf{y} = \mathbf{b}$, while the analysis of the factorization process is only marginally more complicated. If the L and U are produced as in classical Gaussian elimination, then one can show that $LU = A + E$, where, denoting the maximum modulus of any element arising during the decomposition by g, we certainly have

$$\begin{aligned}| e_{ij} | &\le (3.02)\, igk\beta^{-t} \quad (i \le j), \\ | e_{ij} | &\le (3.02)\, jgk\beta^{-t} \quad (i > j).\end{aligned}$$

If the factors L and U are determined directly, using the relations

$$l_{ij} u_{jj} = a_{ij} - l_{i1} u_{1j} - \cdots - l_{i,j-1} u_{j-1,j} \qquad j = 1, \ldots, i-1$$

and

$$u_{ij} = a_{ij} - l_{i1} u_{1j} - \cdots - l_{i,i-1} u_{i-1,j} \qquad j = i, \ldots, n,$$

and the expressions on the right are accumulated in double precision, an even more satisfactory bound may be determined for E. Indeed, ignoring quantities of the order of magnitude of β^{-2t}, we certainly have $|e_{ij}| \le gk\beta^{-t}$, where g is now the element of maximum modulus in the computed U. Again, we have what may be regarded as a "best possible" result.

The reader may be surprised that no reference has been made to pivoting or to the size of the l_{pq}. The importance of pivoting is concealed. If any of the multipliers is large, g will usually be much larger than $\max |a_{ij}|$. When pivoting is used $|l_{pq}| \le 1$, and there will not *usually* be much growth in the size of the elements of the reduced matrices or of U relative to the initial set of a_{ij}. When A is positive definite or diagonally dominant, *no* growth can take place, and we have a guaranteed a priori bound for $\|E\|$ in terms of A.

In 1947, von Neumann and Goldstine considered the special case of the inversion of a positive definite matrix with pivoting, and obtained a result for fixed-point computation that is only marginally weaker than can be obtained by arguments of the above type, though the analysis was far more complicated. Their analysis is often described as a forward error analysis, but it is in fact of the backward type, although at no stage are results expressed in a form such as to emphasize this. The final result of an analysis of the above type for the solution of a positive definite system is to guarantee that it is the exact solution of $(A + E)\mathbf{x} = \mathbf{b}$ and to give a bound for E of the type

$$\|E\| \le f(n)k\beta^{-t}\|A\|,$$

where $f(n)$ is a modest function of n, depending a little on the details of the arithmetic. When backward error analysis is applied to matrix inversion, one cannot show that X is the exact solution of $(A + E)X = I$, with a similar bound for E, because it is not true. However, the rth column, x_r of X is the exact solution of some $(A + E_r)\mathbf{x}_r = \mathbf{e}_r$, where $\mathbf{e}_r$ is the r th column of I; the E_r are all different, but have the same satisfactory uniform bound. This result is implicit in that of von Neumann and Goldstine, but it is well concealed!

Orthogonal Transformations

Experience with error analyses of matrix processes gradually exposed the fact that control of *growth* in derived matrices is the key to stability. If orthogonal transformations Q are used, then, since $\|QA\|_2 = \|AQ\|_2 = \|A\|$, no general growth *can* take place. Although the algebra is a little complicated, a fairly general analysis can be given of whole classes of algorithms based on orthogonal transformations, both for the solution of equations and the eigenvalue problem. One can show, for example, that for a sequence of r orthogonal similarity transformations, the final computed transform $A^{(r)}$ satisfies *exactly* a relation of the form

$$A^{(r)} = Q^T(A + E)\,Q,$$

where Q is *exactly* orthogonal and

$$\|E\| \le rf(n)\|A\|k\beta^{-t},$$

where $f(n)$ is some quite innocuous function of n. Hence, the eigenvalues of $A^{(r)}$ are exactly those of $A + E$, and we are back with perturbation theory.

A Posteriori Error Bounds

The bounds discussed so far are of the a priori type. The main function of such an analysis is to show whether or not an algorithm is stable and, if not, to pinpoint the reasons for its instability.

When a solution has been determined, one can usually obtain much sharper backward error bounds. For example, from a computed eigenvalue λ *and an eigenvector* $\mathbf{u}$, such that $\|\mathbf{u}\|_2 = 1$, one can compute the residual defined by $\mathbf{r} = A\mathbf{u} - \lambda\mathbf{u}$. This may be written in the form $(A - \mathbf{ru}^H)\mathbf{u} = \lambda\mathbf{u}$, showing that λ *and* $\mathbf{u}$ are exact for the matrix $A - \mathbf{ru}^H$. When A is Hermitian, this implies that A has an eigenvalue in the interval $\lambda - \|\mathbf{r}\|_2, \lambda + \|\mathbf{r}\|_2$. Similarly, when solving linear equations, one can compute $\mathbf{r} = \mathbf{b} - A\mathbf{x}$. If $\mathbf{r}$ is computed accurately, it can then be used to obtain an improved solution by solving $A\delta = \mathbf{r}$. This process is called *iterative refinement*.

Iterative Methods

It was at one time thought that iterative methods for solving linear equations or the eigenvalue problem would give far greater accuracy than direct methods, since one works with the initial A throughout. In fact, this advantage is largely illusory. In Jacobi's method for linear equations, one derives an improved $x_i^{(r+1)}$ from the relation

$$a_{ii} x_i^{(r+1)} = b_i - \sum_{j \ne i} a_{ij} x_i^{(r)},$$

but the right-hand side cannot be computed exactly. From the above analysis it is clear that one is really working with a matrix with elements $a_{ij}(1 + e_{ij})$, where the e_{ij} are different in each iteration. When iterative methods are used in practice, iteration is usually terminated before attaining the accuracy given immediately by a direct method, *even without iterative refinement*. Since, as we mentioned earlier, the results obtained with good direct methods are almost "best possible," this is to be expected.

Interval Arithmetic and Significant Digit Arithmetic

Attempts have been made to obtain error bounds for computed quantities on the computer itself. In *interval* arithmetic, an ordered pair $[a_l, a_u]$ of floating-point numbers is stored at each stage in the computation, and it is guaranteed that the true number a lies in the interval $a_l \le a \le a_u$. Used in a direct manner, the results achieved are very pessimistic; in fact, the computer merely performs numerically the analog of what was done algebraically in the early forward error analysis of the Hotelling type. The intervals become very large. The apparently reasonable assumption that in stable algorithms the computed quantities will be close to those arising in exact computation is frequently quite false. This is particularly true of algorithms for the eigenvalue problem.

In *significant digit* arithmetic, one does not work with normalized floating-point numbers, on the grounds that when cancellation takes place, the zeros introduced are non-significant. The possibilities of significant digit arithmetic have been well exploited by Metropolis and Ashenhurst.

The realization that neither interval arithmetic nor significant digit arithmetic provides an automatic answer to error analysis led to an overreaction against them. The provision of the relevant hardware facilities should make them economic, and when combined with a more general appreciation of theoretical error analysis, they have an important role to play.

References

1963. Wilkinson, J. H. *Rounding Errors in Algebraic Processes.* London: Her Majesty's Stationery Office and Englewood Cliffs, NJ: Prentice-Hall.

1965. Wilkinson, J. H. *The Algebraic Eigenvalue Problem.* Oxford: Clarendon Press.

1967. Forsythe, G. E. and Moler, C. B. *Computer Solution of Linear Algebraic Systems.* Englewood Cliffs, NJ: Prentice-Hall.

1971. Wilkinson, J. H. "Modern Error Analysis," *SIAM Review* 13: 548–68.

1979. Moore, R. E. *Methods and Applications of Interval Analysis,* Philadelphia: SIAM Publications.

1989. Kahaner, D., Moler, C., and Nash, S. *Numerical Methods and Software.* Englewood Cliffs, NJ: Prentice-Hall.

JAMES H. WILKINSON

ERROR-CORRECTING CODE

For articles on related subjects *see* CODES; ERRORS; and PARITY.

Error-detecting and error-correcting codes arose from the well-known phenomenon that if anything can go wrong, it will. Rather than try to do everything perfectly the first time, error-detecting and error-correcting methods use some form of redundancy to handle the inevitable errors. Feedback is one way of correcting errors; error correcting codes use *feedforward* so that the receiving end has the necessary information to make the corrections.

Error detection has a long history. For example, suppose we have a block of n binary digits and add an $(n + 1)$st digit, chosen so that the whole message has an even (or odd) number of 1s in it. This is called an even (odd) *parity check*. At the receiving end, the complete block is checked. If there are not the proper number of 1s in the message, then there must be an odd number of errors in the message. Suppose that p is the probability that an isolated bit is in error. If the block is chosen to be sufficiently short, then np is small, and if we assume that errors are independent, then, approximately, there is a probability $(n + 1)p$ of a single error, and a probability $[n(n + 1)/2] p^2$ of two errors.

Upon the detection of an error, the receiver can request that the message be retransmitted, and generally this will produce an error-free message. In some circumstances, especially where it is suspected that the source is slightly defective (say, a magnetic recording), several retrials may be used before giving up. The retrial system is not entirely satisfactory because it takes extra time when errors occur and also requires two-way signaling to call for message repetition. However, if the error is in the original recorded form of the message before encoding, nothing can be done about the error.

To overcome these difficulties, including delays, error-correcting codes are often used. They are based on the use of a higher level of redundancy (i.e. several parity checks).

There are various ways of explaining how an error-correcting code works. In the algebraic approach, a parity check is assigned to those positions in the code that have a 1 in the rightmost position of their binary representation, a second parity check for those positions that have a 1 in their second to right position, etc. Thus, when a single error does occur, exactly those parity checks will fail for which the binary expansion of the position of the error has 1s. Thus, the pattern of the parity-check failures points directly to the position of the error; in a binary system of signaling, it is easy to change that bit to its opposite value and thus correct the error, with 000 meaning "no error."

As an example, consider the binary encoding of the decimal digits into an error-correcting code. In Table 1, positions 1, 2, and 4 are used for the check positions, leaving positions 3, 5, 6, and 7 for the message (where we find the binary coding of the corresponding decimal digit).

The check positions are calculated by even parity checks as follows.

Parity check column 1
Columns 1, 3, 5, 7 (columns with a 1 in the rightmost position of their binary representation).
Parity check column 2
Columns 2, 3, 6, 7 (1 in second rightmost position).
Parity check column 4
Columns 4, 5, 6, 7 (1 in leftmost position).

TABLE 1

Decimal	Position						
	1	2	3	4	5	6	7
0	0	0	0	0	0	0	0
1	1	1	0	1	0	0	1
2	0	1	0	1	0	1	0
3	1	0	0	0	0	1	1
4	1	0	0	1	1	0	0
5	0	1	0	0	1	0	1
6	1	1	0	0	1	1	0
7	0	0	0	1	1	1	1
8	1	1	1	0	0	0	0
9	0	0	1	1	0	0	1

Let any line be copied and a single error inserted as a simulation of an error in message transmission. When the three parity checks are applied, we will find that if we write a 0 for successful parity check and a 1 for a failure (writing from right to left), the three digits we get will be *exactly* the position of the inserted error. Thus, for example, if 1110110 is received instead of 1100110(= 6), the 4, 2, 1 parity checks are 011 (= 3) which identifies the third column as the one in error.

A second way of looking at the codes is a geometric approach. If an error is to be detected, the distance between two messages (which we define to be the number of positions for which they differ) must be at least two for every pair of messages. Otherwise, there would be a message that a single error would carry over into another acceptable message, and that error could not be detected. For error correction, the minimum distance must be at least three (as in Table 1); for double error detection, the minimum distance must be at least four; etc.

The encoding process can thus be extended further in protecting against errors. As an example of double-error detection, consider the code in Table 1 with an additional bit added to each message, so chosen that the entire message will have an even number of 1s. If there were a *single* error, the original set of checks would indicate the position, but the last check would fail. If there were a *pair* of errors, the last check would not fail, but some of the original checks would, indicating a double error. The minimum-distance argument can be applied to show that the additional check made each minimal distance one greater, namely, now four.

The preceding examples are the simplest cases. The theory has been highly developed and now makes use of much of abstract algebra, including Galois theory.

References

1968. Berlekamp, E., Jr. *Algebraic Coding Theory*. New York: McGraw-Hill.

1977. MacWilliams, F. and Sloane, N. J. A. *The Theory of Error Correcting Codes*. Amsterdam: Elsevier.

1977. McEliece, R. J. *The Theory of Information and Coding*. Reading, MA: Addison-Wesley.

1986. Hill, R. *A First Course in Coding Theory*. Oxford: Clarendon Press.

RICHARD W. HAMMING

ERRORS

For articles on related subjects *see* BUG; DEBUGGING; DIAGNOSTIC; ERROR ANALYSIS; ROUNDOFF ERROR; STRUCTURED PROGRAMMING; and SYNTAX, SEMANTICS, AND PRAGMATICS.

The indignant customer who receives an incorrect bill from a department store probably does not care what the source of the error was or even that, almost certainly, the fault was not the computer's but rather that of its data entry personnel or programmers. Neither is the astronaut who is descending toward the surface of the moon very concerned about the precise source of the error that caused the on-board computer to fail. But an understanding of the sources of errors in computers is important to anyone who wishes to use or comprehend digital computers.

Taxonomy of Computer Errors When a computer produces an incorrect result, the error may come from one or more of a number of sources. These sources can be fairly readily grouped under five headings:

1. *Hardware errors*, which result from a malfunction of some physical component of the computer.
2. *Software errors*, which result from a coding error in *some* program, but not necessarily in the program that seemed to produce the wrong results (see below).
3. *Algorithm errors*, which result when the algorithm or method used to solve a problem does not produce correct results, perhaps only under certain conditions and/or for certain input data.
4. *Data entry errors*, probably the most common of all, which occur when the operator of a data entry terminal makes an error, usually by pressing the wrong key.
5. *User errors* occur whenever a user invokes an undesired action, such as entering a command whose syntax or semantics is unacceptable, entering a value out of range, or making the wrong menu selection.

Data entry errors can be reduced by using good equipment, by careful training of personnel, and by verification techniques, such as repetition of the data entry by another operator and then a comparison between the two. Because the other four types of errors are more subtle and, therefore, more difficult to recognize and/or correct, we shall focus on them in this article. However, before proceeding to discuss these types of errors in some detail, we should stress that, whereas in the early days of computing it was usually rather easy to determine which of the categories above was the source of an error, it is sometimes very difficult indeed to do this today. To give one example, the increasing use of microprogramming in contemporary computer systems makes it possible for hardware errors to manifest themselves in ways that look like software errors, and vice versa. The difficulty of determining the source of a computer error has heightened the need for good diagnostic techniques, a subject we consider in the last section of this article.

Hardware Errors Considering the staggering complexity of modern computer systems, it is amazing that they work at all. The fact that they are designed to, and often do, operate for hundreds or thousands of hours without failure is even more startling. Modern computers contain literally millions of circuit elements, the failure of any one of which might cause failure of the entire system. This high level of reliability is a tribute to the careful work of circuit designers and the meticulous attention to detail and to testing on the part of the manufacturers. Still, computers are not perfect and the hardware occasionally does fail. The source of a failure may be difficult to determine, since the number of possible faulty components is so large.

A frequent source of errors is in the electromechanical peripheral devices that provide input or output for the central processing unit. The mechanical components of these peripheral devices are likely to wear out as a result of the stresses of frequent use. For example, the staccato motion of movable disk arms or the rapid rotation of disk packs are possible sources of failures.

The recording medium associated with various devices is fragile and consequently a potential source of errors. The delicate magnetic coating of magnetic tapes, disks, or drums can be easily scratched, rendering the information incorrect or inaccessible. A speck of dust or dirt can mar these coatings easily, or tension can stretch a piece of magnetic tape. The failure of these media may not be fatal to the entire computer, but individual peripheral units may be disabled or data items may be entered incorrectly or lost. Telecommunication devices attached to a computer may also be faulty. Since the quality of the voice-grade telephone lines often used for communication with computers is low, special leased lines are sometimes used to reduce the frequency of errors.

The central processing unit (*q.v.*), arithmetic and logical unit (*q.v.*), and the high-speed memory are built entirely from electronic components, thereby reducing the chance of failure inherent in mechanical devices. The technology for creating the circuit elements involved in these components is extremely complex. Early computers used vacuum tubes (first generation) as the primary circuit element. These large devices were relatively slow, generated a large amount of heat, required a large amount of power, and wore out easily. The invention of the transistor (second generation) in 1948 made it possible to construct smaller, faster, and much more reliable computers. Combining many transistors and other electronic elements into a single component, called an *integrated circuit* (third generation), enabled designers to create still faster and more reliable computers.

At present, computers are built from a smaller number of very large-scale integrated circuits (VLSI). These highly reliable circuits contain thousands of discrete circuit elements built into a single replaceable component. These devices are carefully tested during the many stages of a sophisticated fabrication process. Still, they may fail as a result of temperature changes, humidity, shock, or electrical surges. When failure occurs, the faulty circuit component must be located and replaced. This sounds simple enough, but the problem may be hard to locate, since the failure may be intermittent, occurring only when a complex combination of conditions exists. To minimize the deterioration of circuit elements, computer rooms are air conditioned to keep the temperature and humidity within acceptable ranges. The failure of the air conditioning would lead to overheating of circuit elements and to an increased chance of failure.

Modern computers are designed to monitor their own performance and constantly test themselves to assure that each operation has been performed properly.

When a fault occurs, a machine interrupt is issued, and the hardware and software attempt to identify and locate the error. Depending on the severity of the error, the control programs may shut down the entire machine, avoid use of the faulty component, or simply record the fact that an error has occurred.

Software Errors Anyone who has written a computer program knows that debugging can be difficult and tedious. Professionals writing even short programs (say, fewer than 100 lines of code) expect some difficulties and accept the fact that long programs, requiring many person-years of effort, may never be completely debugged. When writing programs in a high-level language, which requires the services of a compiler, utility programs, and an operating system, the number of software modules that come into play is large. Great effort is applied to debug the system software, but it is not currently possible to insure the correctness of such sophisticated programs. If an application program does not operate correctly, the most likely source of the error is in the application program itself. Only after a thorough and careful analysis of the situation can we begin to consider the possibility that the compiler, system utilities, or operating system are at fault. Locating the bug in the system software requires a deep understanding of the code and the expertise of a systems programmer. (*See* SYSTEMS PROGRAMMING.)

Application program errors fall into two basic categories: syntactic and semantic. The syntactic errors include typographic errors, incorrectly spelled keywords and variable names, incorrect punctuation, and improper statement formation, all of which result from violations of the programming language syntax. These errors are normally recognized by the language processor, and diagnostic messages are printed to assist the programmer in making corrections. Although some processors will attempt to fix improper syntax, programs with syntactic errors will generally not be permitted to execute.

Assuming all the syntactic errors have been fixed, the program will execute, but there is no guarantee that it will perform as the programmer intended. Semantic errors are a result of an improper understanding of the function of certain operators or mistakes in coding of an algorithm. Typical programming mistakes include exceeding the bounds of an array; failure to initialize variables; overflow or underflow; failure to account for special cases; attempted division by zero; illegal mixing of data types; and incorrect transfers of control. Isolating and locating the error can be a long, tedious process and is a skill learned mainly through much experience.

Current research is being directed at reducing the possibility of semantic errors. Improved programming language design and sophisticated compilers are one possible answer. Educating programmers to proper program design techniques such as modularity, structured programming, and object-oriented programming (*q.v.*) does, indeed, simplify the debugging process. Finally, attempts are being made to prove the correctness of programs through the use of formal mathematical techniques (*see* PROGRAM VERIFICATION).

Algorithm Errors Computer programs can be viewed as models or representations of real-world situations. Unfortunately, not all aspects of the real-world situation can be represented accurately inside a computer. Decimal quantities such as 1.2 or 6783846.678492104 may have to be approximated when stored in the memory of a binary computer. Since the initial representation is not precise, subsequent operations performed on these values may produce invalid results. The difficulty in locating such faults is that the error will manifest itself only for some sets of data. Thus, the program will produce reasonable results in most cases, but may produce erroneous results erratically.

The heart of this problem is the machine representation of values. While a 60-bit word length may provide a more accurate representation than a 36-bit word or a 32-bit word, a longer word length is not a guarantee of correctness. Since we are limited to the finite length of a computer word, the representation must be rounded off to the closest approximation possible. With each addition or multiplication, the result must also be rounded off to fit the representation scheme; hence the name *roundoff error*.

Another flaw in the representation of the real world occurs when an infinite process must be approximated by a finite series of steps. In summing an infinite series, repeating an iterative process (e.g. the Newton-Raphson method), or approximating derivatives by differences, the result may become increasingly exact, but is never precisely correct. Since in all these cases an infinite process is cut short and represented by a finite process, this error is called *truncation* or *discretization error*.

One of the central concerns of numerical analysis (*q.v.*) is to estimate the roundoff and truncation errors for various algorithms. This analysis can then be used to select and design the optimum strategy for a given problem. A major goal of numerical analysis is to avoid *unstable* algorithms that operate erratically and to identify *ill-conditioned* data sets that are difficult to deal with. The use of double or multiple precision representations and operations may reduce the error, but not eliminate it.

Another type of algorithm failure is the attempted use of an algorithm to solve a problem other than that for which it is intended. An example of this would be the use of an algorithm designed for the solution of a system of linear simultaneous equations with a symmetric coefficient matrix to solve a system with a non-symmetric coefficient matrix, resulting in an inevitably wrong result.

All too common is the development and use of an algorithm that just will not solve the problem at hand for any set of data, due to a design error, for example, or a failure to understand the underlying mathematics. A vital aspect of the avoidance of such errors is the careful debugging of all newly developed programs using data sets for which the results are known.

User Errors Computer users may make a large variety of errors, examples of which are mentioned earlier in this article. Two further examples are inadvertently opening, moving, resizing, or closing a window or making unin-

tended movements in a painting program. (*See* WINDOW ENVIRONMENTS.) Such user errors may be classified as physical motion mistakes, syntactic errors, logical errors, or just failures due to a lack of knowledge of the functioning of the computer. A key goal of the designer of a user interface (*q.v.*) is to reduce the possibility of some of these errors and to provide appropriate error messages that facilitate error recovery.

Errors can generally be reduced by permitting menu selection in place of data entry and by constraining illegal actions, just as automobile transmissions prevent engagement of reverse gears while the car is moving forward. When errors do occur, the messages should be specific, constructive, positive in tone, user-centered (avoiding technical terminology), comprehensible, and brief.

When major user actions would be irreversible (e.g. deletion of data or control of physical processes), the user should be required to confirm the action before it actually takes place.

Coping with Errors Since errors are a fact of life in computing, much has been done to assist programmers in locating errors. Syntactic errors are dealt with by the compiler and are not the source of serious difficulty. Although work remains to be done in the area of improving compile-time diagnostics, most compilers provide a reasonably lucid explanation of what has gone wrong. The programmer must then fix the mistake.

Execution-time errors that result from semantic errors are more difficult to deal with. If the program runs to completion, but does not produce the output that is expected, the programmer must carefully examine the output and attempt to locate the fault. The input data should be checked for validity, and then a careful step-by-step analysis of the program must be performed. If the output does not contain sufficient information to determine what the program was doing, an additional run with detailed printouts must be made. Special *trace* (*q.v.*) packages that print out the execution of the program on an instruction-by-instruction basis can be used. Alternatively, only the transfers of control or subprogram references can be printed. If desired, a particular location can be monitored to indicate when the value was set or referenced. Since the amount of output may be voluminous, the programmer must carefully select which features to use. Armed with this material and a thorough understanding of the program, the programmer must perform a careful analysis to locate the flaw.

If the program does not run to completion, but is interrupted as a result of an attempt to perform an illegal instruction, the operating system will (or, at least, should) print a meaningful message. However, since the operating system has no knowledge of what the application program was attempting to do, these messages can be difficult to interpret. Some programming language systems contain an execution-time monitor to produce more meaningful diagnostic messages when an abnormal termination occurs.

If a program successfully executes for a given set of data, there is no guarantee that the program will always perform properly. To verify the correctness of a program, multiple sets of test data should be constructed to exercise the program as much as possible. (*See* SOFTWARE TESTING.) As many as possible of the reasonable sets of input data should be run to validate the program. Unfortunately, there are many well-documented cases of programs that have run correctly for many years until a particular set of input data was run and resulted in failure. There is no way to guarantee the correctness of large programs, and programmers must accept the possibility of *bugs* in their programs. Large programs such as operating systems are continuously being modified as faults are located. Perfection in programming is illusory.

The diagnosis of hardware errors has become more complex with the advent of sophisticated hardware architecture constructs, such as virtual memory and microprogramming. When it is suggested that a particular error may be a result of malfunctioning hardware, a set of hardware diagnostic programs may be run to assist the maintenance engineer in locating the fault. These programs exercise each of the circuit components and print out the location of the faulty element. This technique is not always successful, since the diagnostic program may not run properly because of the fault. Individual components may have to be removed and tested electrically, or components may be replaced until the machine operates properly.

References

1963. Wilkinson, J. H. *Rounding Errors in Algebraic Processes.* Englewood Cliffs, NJ.: Prentice-Hall.
1977. Gilb, Tom and Weinberg, Gerald M. *Humanizing Input.* Cambridge, MA: Winthrop.
1978. Van Tassel, Dennie. *Program Style, Design, Efficiency, Debugging and Testing* (2nd Ed.). Englewood Cliffs, NJ: Prentice-Hall.
1988. Norman, Don. *The Psychology of Everyday Things.* New York: Basic Books.

ANTHONY RALSTON AND BEN SHNEIDERMAN

EXCEPTION HANDLING

For articles on related subjects *see* INTERRUPT; SOFTWARE ENGINEERING; and TRAP.

Exception handling deals with mechanisms and techniques for avoiding, recovering from, and documenting errors that arise during program execution. Exception handling mechanisms are features of programming languages that permit error recovery from exceptional or anomalous situations. Exception handling techniques are used by programmers to make programs *robust* and *user friendly.* Exceptions arise when illegal operations are requested or the operands of an operation are inappropriate. For example, dividing by zero will cause an error in some systems. Robust programs deal gracefully with exceptions, whereas fragile programs stop or produce erroneous results when exceptions are encountered.

In a batch program, exception handling techniques include checking the validity of data, skipping anomalous data, resetting control parameters, undoing prior opera-

tions, and reporting exceptions to exception report files. In an interactive program, exception handling techniques include checking that users are asking for legal operations before performing them, providing users with an *undo* command that cancels the result of the last operation, allowing users to save their work and restore any previously saved state, alerting users to exceptions when they occur, and allowing users to continue from exceptions without losing much work.

It is often impractical to check all the conditions that must hold in order to guarantee that an operation will be successful. To handle cases in which exceptions cannot be avoided, some programming languages provide limited backtracking, undo, or unwind protection mechanisms. Instead of backtracking, more often exceptions are reported to an exception file to be analyzed later. The exceptions are analyzed and code is added to the program so that in the future the exception can be avoided, recovered from, or documented in more detail.

JAMES C. SPOHRER

EXECUTABLE STATEMENT

For articles on related subjects *see* DECLARATION; and PROCEDURE-ORIENTED LANGUAGES: PROGRAMMING.

An *executable statement* is a procedural step in a high-level programming language that calls for processing action by the computer, such as performing arithmetic, reading data from an external medium, making a decision, etc. In describing the structure and features of high-level languages, it is convenient to distinguish between executable statements and nonexecutable *declarations* that provide information about the nature of the data or about the way the processing is to be done without themselves causing any processing action.

Executable statements are sometimes called *imperative* statements because their form often closely resembles that of an imperative sentence in a natural language. For example, the formula

$$Y = a + bx + cx^2$$

follows an imperative form that persists in corresponding structures in programming statements:

[Pascal] $y := a + b * + c * x * x;$

[Fortran] $Y = A + B * X + C * X ** 2$

[PL/I] $Y = A + B * X + C * X ** 2;$

This correspondence is emphasized more explicitly in some languages, namely,

[Basic]   LET $Y = A + B * X + C * X \uparrow 2$

[Cobol]   COMPUTE $Y = A + B * X + C * X ** 2.$

Specifications for data transmission between internal storage and an external medium are constructed along similar lines:

[Fortran]   READ (5,12) HERE
            WRITE (6,21) HERE

[Cobol]   READ INFILE INTO HERE.
            WRITE OUTFILE FROM HERE.

[PL/I]   READ FILE (INFILE) INTO (HERE);
            WRITE FILE (OUTFILE) FROM (HERE);

The numerical specifications in the Fortran example are coded references to additional information about the source (for input), destination (for output), and format of the data to be transmitted.

Sometimes, executable statements are subdivided into imperative and conditional statements because the latter, such as the IF statement in Fortran, specify alternative imperative actions linked through a decision mechanism.

A language implementation may have rules about the relative placement of executable and nonexecutable statements. Usually, it is required that all declarations appear before the first executable statement of a program; in other cases it is required only that declarations appear before any information in them is required by an executable statement. One of the distinguishing features of Cobol is its total separation of executable statements (in the *Procedure* division) from nonexecutable statements (in the *Environment* and *Data* divisions).

DANIEL D. MCCRACKEN AND SEYMOUR V. POLLACK

EXECUTION TIME.   *See* COMPILE AND RUN TIME.

EXECUTIVE.   *See* OPERATING SYSTEM.

EXPANSION SLOT.   *See* MOTHERBOARD.

EXPERT SYSTEMS

For articles on related subjects *see* ARTIFICIAL INTELLIGENCE; and KNOWLEDGE REPRESENTATION.

Most applications of artificial intelligence (AI) science and technology are of a type called *expert systems*. An expert system (ES) is a computer program that *reasons*, using *knowledge*, to solve *complex problems*. This overly brief caricature will be expanded upon below, but it serves to indicate an alignment of ES with AI's long-term goals. Traditionally, computers solve complex problems by arithmetic calculation (not logical reasoning), and the *knowledge* needed to solve the problem is known only by the human programmer and is used to cast the solution method in terms of algebraic formulas.

The Emergence of the Principles and the Technology
One way to approach an understanding of the principles of expert systems is to trace the history of the emergence of ES within AI. Perhaps AI's most widely shared early goal had been the construction of extremely intelligent computers. That is, in addition to other goals (such as learning and language understanding), most researchers shared a goal to produce programs that performed at or beyond human levels of competence. For example, an early (late 1950s) program took the N.Y. State Regents Examination in plane geometry to validate its human-level abilities in this domain. Also, a famous prediction was made regarding the year in which an AI program would be chess champion of the world. A scientific viewpoint about knowledge representation, *declarativism*, was formulated by McCarthy during this period, and proved to be robust and important. Declarativism insists that a program's knowledge about objects and relations be encoded explicitly so that other programs can access and reason with that knowledge.

In the early 1960s, the focus of AI shifted from performance to generality—how one problem-solving mechanism can solve a wide variety of problems. The most well-known AI efforts of the time were the general problem solvers, both heuristic programs and theorem provers. While these programs exhibited considerable generality, the actual problems these were able to solve were very simple, essentially toy, problems: i.e. the programs had high generality but low power.

In 1965, Feigenbaum, Lederberg, and Buchanan at Stanford University initiated a project in modeling scientific reasoning, for which the goal of high performance was once again given prominence. The task of this program, called DENDRAL, was to interpret the mass spectrum of organic molecules in terms of a hypothesis of the structure of the organic molecule that was present in the instrument (Lindsay *et al.* 1980).

The intent of DENDRAL's designers was that the program was to perform the difficult mass spectral analysis task at the level of competence of specialists in that area. As it turned out, AI's problem-solving methods (primarily search-based methods) were useful, but not sufficient. Most important in achieving the goal of expert-level competence was knowledge of chemistry and mass spectroscopy. The key empirical result of DENDRAL experiments became known as the *knowledge-is-power hypothesis* (later called the *knowledge principle*), stating that *knowledge of the specific task domain in which the program is to do its problem solving was more important as a source of power for competent problem solving than the reasoning method employed* (Feigenbaum, 1977).

The knowledge that DENDRAL needed was provided by scientists of the Stanford Mass Spectrometry Laboratory, in an intense collaboration with the AI scientists. Such efforts at codifying the knowledge of specialists for use in expert systems later came to be called *knowledge engineering*. The first use of the term "expert" in connection with such programs was made in an article analyzing the generality vs. power issue in the light of the results of DENDRAL computational experiments (Feigenbaum *et al.*, 1971).

In short, the DENDRAL program was the progenitor of the class of programs subsequently called expert systems, and the development of DENDRAL illustrated the major principles, issues, and limitations of expert systems that will be discussed later. A case has been made that an M.I.T. project of the same era, Macsyma, that built a program to assist people in doing complex symbolic mathematics, shared with DENDRAL the same underlying view of the primacy of domain-specific knowledge and the same motivation to achieve high levels of competence in performance (McCorduck, 1979). However, the Macsyma papers and extended work were focused on the domain of symbolic mathematics, whereas the DENDRAL papers and extended work actually provided the foundation for most of the subsequent ES technology.

Extensions of DENDRAL, done in the 1970s, were of two types. First, many pioneering expert systems were built by AI researchers to explore and extend the new technology and, by the sheer weight of accumulating evidence of capability, to lend credibility to the ES technology and to knowledge engineering. The earliest and most famous of these was the MYCIN system, which showed the first integrated architecture for interactive consultation between an expert user and an ES, including explanation of the line of reasoning and was the first of a fruitful line of applications of ES to medical diagnosis (Buchanan and Shortliffe, 1984). Second, the underlying programming systems and languages of these ESs, that embodied the reasoning procedures and the framework for representing knowledge, were generalized so that they were no longer domain-specific and therefore could be used as programming systems and languages for the construction of new, albeit similar, ESs. Such software came to be known as ES "development environments" or "ES tools" or "ES shells." The pioneering tool/shell, derived from MYCIN, was EMYCIN, the prototype for literally dozens of commercially available ES shells (Van Melle *et al.*, 1984).

Transfer of ES Technology into Practice

As the 1970s came to a close, so did the decade of laboratory exploration of the first-generation ES ideas and techniques. A period of transfer of the technology to industrial use began and is still underway (1991). The two best-known early industrial applications were XCON from Digital Equipment Corporation and the Dipmeter Adviser from Schlumberger Ltd.

XCON's task was the configuration under constraints of a DEC minicomputer from a large number of component subassemblies. The configuration task was done so fast and so accurately by XCON that DEC saved tens of millions of dollars per year in manufacturing and sales operations. XCON configures minicomputers about 300 times faster than human engineers and does it virtually error-free. XCON has been extended to many different families of DEC computers and other equipment, and was generalized into an ES called XSEL to assist DEC salespeople to correctly configure and price equipment sales at the time of customer contact. XCON had an immediate effect outside of DEC: most other computer manufacturers copied the idea for their own operations. More important, the success of XCON opened the way to a broader generalization: most devices that are engineered and manufactured are built out of component subassemblies; hence, the XCON idea could be used to realize a new generation of CAD, or "intelligent CAD," as it is called.

Schlumberger's Dipmeter Adviser (DA) is typical of programs that analyze streams of data (with or without real time considerations) and propose hypotheses to account for and explain the data. DA interprets the data taken from instruments lowered into bore holes during the search for oil and gas. It offers hypotheses about the tilt, or so-called "dip," of the rock layers far beneath the earth's surface. Knowing the dip of each of the hundreds of rock layers in a bore hole is valuable in oil exploration.

Another example of a program that interprets signal data to produce hypotheses is the Charley program of General Motors, for analyzing vibrations of machinery as a means of troubleshooting mechanical equipment, particularly automotive and manufacturing equipment (Bajpai and Marczewski, 1989). This ES is a model of the expertise of a senior GM specialist in vibrational analysis whose retirement was imminent, and is an instance of a very important class of ESs that are done to capture and preserve rare corporate expertise.

With similar motive, an ES was built by DEC for Lend Lease, the largest construction firm in Australia, for the task of estimating the time to completion of high-rise buildings with an accuracy of ±10 percent from just the first few hours of preliminary discussions with the customer. Similarly, also, NKK Steel Co. in Japan modeled the expertise of one of their senior specialists in blast furnace operations (he is called at NKK "the furnace god") in an ES that predicts in near–real time the probability of two different types of catastrophic failures of blast furnace operations. This ES was built with the intention of selling it to buyers of NKK blast furnaces. (NKK makes equipment as well as steel.)

The use of an ES to improve the quality of human decisions was the motive behind the well-known Authorizers' Assistant (AA) of American Express. To assist a human authorizer with the decision to allow or disallow a customer charge, AA analyzes a large amount of customer data from the database files that AmEx keeps on the customer; then AA issues a recommended decision, offers the explanation or rationale for its recommendation, and gives the human authorizer a screenful of the data that supports its recommendation. The payoff in terms of avoiding bad debt and fraud amounts to millions of dollars per year.

ESs have been built to assist people with the accurate and timely processing of "cases" in the context of very complex systems of bureaucratic laws, rules, and regulations. A system done for the British Social Security Administration assists clerks in answering the written queries of citizens concerning their pensions. The Taxpayers' Assistant Expert System of the U.S. Internal Revenue Service helps IRS personnel to give accurate tax information in response to telephoned queries from taxpayers (usually in the few months before tax returns are due). And in both Fresno and Tulare Counties of California, ESs assist social welfare case workers with the decision about whether a person applying for welfare qualifies under the complex rules.

There are major applications of ES across the complete spectrum of human professional and semi-professional work: in medicine, law, manufacturing, sales, maintenance, engineering, architectural design, finance, insurance, and so on. Presently (1991), there are tens of thousands of operational ESs, in the U.S., Japan, and Europe primarily, though increasing numbers are seen in Australia, Singapore, and India (which has a National Center for Expert Systems in Hyderabad).

Expert System Technology The word "expert" in expert system refers to the intention of the ES designer to have the system achieve a level of competence of problem solving in some domain of work that rivals the performance of human specialists (experts) in that domain. To accomplish this, the ES must be given the knowledge that such human experts have that distinguishes experts from novices and enables experts to perform well. To acquire and represent that knowledge is the job of the knowledge engineer. Increasingly, with the advance of ES development tools, experts are able to be their own knowledge engineers. ESs are almost always used as *interactive intellectual aids* for human decision makers and almost never as autonomous unsupervised agents.

Every expert system consists of two principal parts: the *knowledge base* and the *reasoning* or *inference engine* (see Fig. 1). The knowledge base contains both factual and heuristic knowledge. The factual knowledge is that knowledge widely shared in the domain and commonly agreed upon by experts. The heuristic knowledge is the non-rigorous, experiential knowledge, the rules-of-thumb, the knowledge of good judgment. Heuristics (*q.v.*) constitutes the "art of good guessing" in the domain.

Knowledge representation formalizes and organizes the knowledge for use by the inference engine. One widely used representational form is the *production rule*, or simply the *rule*. A rule consists of an IF part and a THEN part (also called a *condition* and an *action*). The IF part lists a set of conditions in some logical combination. The piece of knowledge represented by the rule is relevant to the line of reasoning being developed if the IF part of the rule is satisfied; consequently, the THEN part can be concluded, or its action taken. Expert systems whose knowledge is represented in rule form are called *rule-based systems*. This kind of representation is *action-oriented*.

Another widely used representational form, called the *unit* (or *frame*, or *schema*) is based upon a more passive *object-oriented* view of knowledge. Systems of units (sometimes called *frame-based systems*) are siblings of the object-oriented systems common in computer science. Typically, a unit consists of a symbolic name, a list

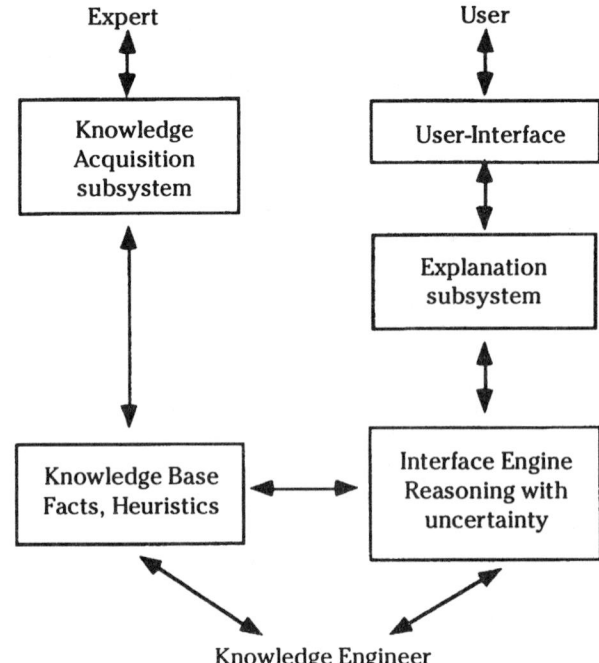

FIG. 1. Basic structure of an expert system.

of attributes of some entity, and the values associated with the attributes. That is, the unit is a complex symbolic description of an entity that the ES needs to know about. There is a *knowledge base management system*, akin to a database management system, associated with the units. One of its important functions is to handle automatically some routine inference functions for knowledge updating and knowledge propagation. The automatic handling is called *inheritance*.

Another general and powerful formalism for representing knowledge is the "standard" mathematical way, given by the symbols and formulas of *mathematical logic*, particularly first order predicate logic and some higher-order logics (Genesereth and Nilsson, 1987).

In addition to naturalness and expressiveness of the representational form, a representation needs to be very modular and flexible. The process of building a knowledge base is an iterative one that has been called "an incremental approach to competence." The knowledge is teased out of the expert and the problem domain little by little on each iteration. The "module size" needs to match these little pieces, and the knowledge "modules" need to be easily integrated into the existing, growing knowledge base, with virtually no incremental reprogramming of the knowledge base.

In every expert system, the inference engine (embodying the problem-solving method or procedure) uses the knowledge in the knowledge base to construct the line of reasoning leading to the solution of the problem. The most common method (the method of choice in rule-based systems) involves chaining of IF-THEN rules. If the chaining starts from a set of conditions and moves toward some (possibly remote) conclusion, the method is called *forward chaining*. If the conclusion is known (e.g. it is a goal to be achieved) but the path to that conclusion is not known, then *backward chaining* with rules is employed, seeking conditions under which a particular line of reasoning will be true.

Sometimes, an inflexible commitment to either forward or backward chaining is not optimal, especially if new data is arriving needing interpretation, and if a changing situation demands that goals change. In these cases, an opportunistic strategy that allows the flexible mixing of some forward chaining with some backward chaining is used. Opportunistic problem solving strategies are the hallmark of *blackboard systems* (Nii, 1989).

Other procedures commonly found in expert systems are procedures for *reasoning with uncertain information*, as well as knowledge and procedures for *explaining* the line of reasoning to the user.

Knowledge of a domain and of a particular problem is almost always incomplete and uncertain. To deal with uncertainty, a rule may have associated with it a *confidence factor (CF)*, or weight. A standard calculus for using CFs to construct and evaluate lines of reasoning is available. In an alternative method, called *fuzzy logic*, uncertainty is represented by a distribution of values, and another standard calculus is available for handling these distributions. Finally, where sufficient statistical data is available, Bayes' Theorem and its associated calculations have been used (Buchanan and Smith, 1989).

Since ESs explicitly build lines of reasoning, there is little difficulty in responding to users' questions about the line of reasoning: how and why did it take the form that it has? Typical questions that can be answered by the explanation procedure are: "Why are you asking me that (particular) question?," or "How did you conclude (something)?" Also, "Show me your line of reasoning (main conclusions, intermediate and final)." The explanation procedure answers these questions by looking back at what rules were examined, which were selected and why, and what conclusions were drawn.

From the applications viewpoint, the AI science offers only a small number of practical techniques for representing knowledge, for making inferences (certain and uncertain) and for generating explanations. Commercial software systems are offered that carefully integrate various selections from this small menu to assist knowledge engineers who do not want to program the techniques themselves to build their expert systems. These are the hybrid commercial tools or shells of the ES software industry, with representative names like KEE (Knowledge Engineering Environment) and ART (Advanced Reasoning Tool). The use of these tools/shells is very widespread—indeed, the method of choice in building expert systems. Powerful tools/shells are available on all platforms from PCs to mainframes.

Note, however, that although tools/shells simplify programming ESs, they do not usually help with the crucial bottleneck problem of *knowledge acquisition*. As the Knowledge Principle informs us, the choice of reasoning method is important, but not nearly as important for the ES's ultimate performance as the accumulation of high-quality knowledge. It might be asked why automatic methods of extracting knowledge from experts, from textbooks, and from real world data have not

destroyed this bottleneck. Stating the question in another way, where do we stand with *machine learning for ES applications*? Although the field of machine learning research is quite vigorous and exciting, virtually no techniques have emerged to help with ES knowledge acquisition (with the exception of a few simple inductive algorithms that allow the inductive formation of some kinds of rules from data sets (Finebaugh, 1988)). In the early 1990s, the size of a typical ES was 10^2–10^3 rules and/or objects. Some ESs were of order 10^4. Only a few (perhaps even just one or two) were of order 10^5.

Research Aimed at Removing Limitations

The techniques that made first generation ESs work at all were also responsible for the key limitations of the technology. These are *narrowness* (or *overspecialization*) and its sibling, *brittleness*. The Knowledge Principle tells us that an ES has little competence outside of the domain of specialization for which its knowledge base has been carefully and systematically built. Since the ES knows only **that**, and has no ability to generalize, analogize, or in any other way extend knowledge, it can only solve problems of **that** kind—thereby exhibiting narrowness. If a problem posed by a user is simply beyond the boundary of what the ES knows about, the ES's performance degrades ungracefully (with brittleness), falling from expert levels of competence to complete incompetence. The boundaries of an ES's knowledge, hence the margins of its competence, are almost never represented explicitly so that this knowledge can inform the user and also be available to the reasoning process.

First generation ESs usually represent associational or phenomenological knowledge (i.e. knowledge near the surface of events), not the knowledge of what is deep below the surface, causing the events. Such deeper knowledge is called "*first principles*" knowledge or *model-based knowledge*. Methods for representing such knowledge and procedures for the inference engines of model-based reasoners are important topics being vigorously researched by the AI community. It is readily seen that this kind of knowledge helps to remove the limitations of narrowness and brittleness, since the use of principles and models generalizes much more readily than does the phenomenological description of events (e.g. on the IF side of a rule).

The breadth of an ES's competence can also be extended with cases (i.e. "worked examples") that have been experienced in the past. Human experts know a great many particulars not necessarily in the rule form but in the case form. A major branch of second-generation ES research is concerned with the representation of case libraries and methods for reasoning from cases that are fundamentally different from the earlier methods based on logical chaining, fuzzy logic, or Bayes' Theorem.

Finally, there is the engineering economics of ES construction. Each ES is built from scratch. In first generation ESs, there is almost no reuse of knowledge and there is no systematic way in which a community of knowledge engineers cooperate to allow their ESs to share knowledge. The conceptual infrastructure of *knowledge sharing* and reuse is presently a major topic of research, and will be heard from during the 1990s under such names as knowledge interchange formats (KIF), ontolingua, shared ontologies, national engineering knowledge bases, and national "common sense" knowledge bases.

References

1971. Feigenbaum, E. A., Buchanan, B. G., and Lederberg, J. "On Generality and Problem Solving: A Case Study Using the DENDRAL Program," in *Machine Intelligence 6*, B. Meltzer and D. Michie (Eds.) Edinburgh: Edinburgh University Press.

1977. Feigenbaum, E. A. "The Art of Artificial Intelligence: Themes and Case Studies of Knowledge Engineering," *Proceedings of the International Joint Conference on Artificial Intelligence.* Cambridge, MA: The M.I.T. Press.

1979. McCorduck, P. *Machines Who Think*, San Francisco: Freeman.

1980. Lindsay, R. K., Buchanan, B. G., Feigenbaum, E. A., and Lederberg, J. *Applications of Artificial Intelligence for Organic Chemistry: The DENDRAL Project*, New York: McGraw-Hill.

1984. Buchanan, B. G. and Shortliffe, E. H. *Rule-Based Expert Systems: The MYCIN Experiments of the Stanford Heuristic Programming Project.* Reading, MA: Addison-Wesley.

1984. van Melle, W., Shortliffe, E. H., and Buchanan, B. G. "EMYCIN: A Knowledge Engineer's Tool for Constructing Rule-Based Expert Systems," in *Rule-Based Expert Systems: The MYCIN Experiments of the Stanford Heuristic Programming Project*," B. G. Buchanan and E. H. Shortliffe (Eds.) Reading, MA: Addison-Wesley.

1987. Genesereth, M. and Nilsson, N. *Logical Foundations of Artificial Intelligence.* San Mateo, CA: Morgan Kaufmann.

1988. Feigenbaum, E., McCorduck, P., and Nii, H. P. *The Rise of the Expert Company.* New York: Times Books.

1988. Firebaugh, M. W. *Artificial Intelligence: A Knowledge-Based Approach.* Boston, MA: Boyd and Fraser.

1989. Bajpai, A. and Marczewski, R. "Charley: An Expert System for Diagnostics of Manufacturing Equipment," in *Innovative Applications of Artificial Intelligence*, H. Schorr and A. Rappaport (Eds.) Cambridge, MA: AAAI Press/The M.I.T. Press.

1989. Buchanan, B.G. and Smith, R.G. "Fundamentals of Expert Systems," in *The Handbook of Artificial Intelligence, Vol. IV*, A. Barr, P.R. Cohen, and E.A. Feigenbaum (Eds.). Reading, MA: Addison-Wesley.

1989. Nii, H. Penny. "Blackboard Systems," in *The Handbook of Artificial Intelligence, Vol. IV*, A. Barr, P. R. Cohen, and E. A. Feigenbaum (Eds.). Reading, MA: Addison-Wesley.

EDWARD A. FEIGENBAUM

EXPRESSION

For articles on related subjects *see* COERCION; CONSTANT; OPERATOR PRECEDENCE; PARSING; PROCEDURE-ORIENTED LANGUAGES, PROGRAMMING IN; and STATEMENT.

An *expression*, one of the fundamental constituents of high-level language syntax, is a character sequence that specifies a rule for calculating a value. That value may be either numeric, as in the Pascal expression $a + 6$, or alphanumeric, as in the Basic expression LEFT$(A\$, 5) (whose value is the leftmost 5 characters of string A\$). An expression may appear to the right of the replacement symbol (usually = or := or ←) in statement-oriented languages such as Pascal or Fortran, or

may stand alone and be evaluated immediately to yield a particular value in expression-oriented languages such as Lisp or APL.

A *statement-oriented language* is one in which sentence-like statements calculate and save intermediate values but (except for specific I/O statements) do not print them. In Pascal, for example, the statement $p := a * b + c$ is composed of an *identifier* (variable name) p, a *replacement symbol*, :=, and the *expression* $a * b + c$. Such an expression makes sense to the Pascal compiler if all of its identifiers have been previously declared as to type (real, integer, etc.) and if it is *well formed* according to the grammatical rules of the language. The expression will make sense at execution time if, by the time it is reached during program flow, all of its identifiers have been assigned specific values that enable evaluation of the expression and storage of the result at the identifier specified to the left of the replacement symbol.

An *expression-oriented language* is one in which expressions may stand alone such that, when encountered during program flow, their value is calculated and printed immediately. Thus, if the expression $3 + 4$ is presented to APL at an interactive terminal session, APL will respond immediately by outputting 7.

An expression that is valid in one high-level language might be invalid in another or, even if valid, produce a different result. Thus, $a**b$ is a valid Fortran expression, but is not valid in Pascal, which does not have an exponentiation operator. The upper-case equivalent of the expression used earlier, $A*B+C$, would be acceptable to APL, but would have an entirely different meaning because of different interpretations of the $*$ operator (multiplication in Pascal, exponentiation in APL) and different operator precedence. To obtain the same meaning, the APL programmer would write $(A \times B)+C$ or $C+A \times B$ and the Lisp programmer would write (PLUS (TIMES A B) C) because that language uses a fully-parenthesized notation in which operators precede their operands (prefix form).

Most high-level languages allow use of expressions in contexts other than replacement statements. A typical use is for subscript selection. For example, the Pascal statement

$$k := 3 * a + b[round(j + sqrt (x))]$$

will calculate and use the integer closest to the value of the expression $j + sqrt(x)$ to select a particular member of the one-dimensional array b. The sum of the selected value and the value of $3 * a$ is then assigned to k. In Algol and Pascal, a subscript may be any valid expression; other languages are more restrictive.

Expressions may also be classified as being either *homogeneous* (all constituents of the same type) or *mixed-mode*. An example of the latter is $A + J * Z$ where, perhaps, A has been declared as being real (floating-point), J as being integer, and Z as being complex. What should be done? Early dialects of Fortran declared such expressions syntactically illegal and refused to process them. Almost all current languages accept mixed-mode expressions whenever reasonable type conversions can be inferred (e.g. automatic conversion of A and J to complex prior to evaluation of the cited expression), which allow calculation to proceed. (*See* COERCION.)

An expression may be very simple as well as complicated. In most languages, the single digit 7 or the single-letter variable Q are valid expressions. Thus, the Pascal statement cited earlier, $k := 3 * a + b[round(j + sqrt(x))]$, contains ten recognizable expressions:

1-4. 3, a, j, and x are expressions.
5. $3 * a$ is an expression.
6. The function $sqrt(x)$ is an expression.
7. $j + sqrt(x)$ is an expression.
8. The subscript $round(j + sqrt(x))$ is an expression.
9. The subscripted variable $b[round(j + sqrt(x))]$ is an expression.
10. The entire right-hand side is an expression.

The rules for recognizing a well-formed (syntactically valid) expression in any given language may be stated quite rigorously in a notation such as Backus-Naur Form (BNF - *q.v.*) or perhaps in the increasingly popular equivalent *syntax diagram* form commonly used to define Pascal. Consider the following example of the use of such diagrams (Fig. 1) to define first <operator> and then <expression> in a very simple hypothetical language (where we assume that the intuitive concepts of <variable> and <number> were defined earlier).

Using such diagrams, one can readily ascertain that such character sequences as

$$(a + b) * (c - d)$$
$$(5 * 9/(h + 7)) \quad \text{and}$$
$$r * s - t/u$$

are valid expressions, but that others, such as $a*(b$ and $* a + b$ are not well formed.

References

1975. Pratt, T. W. *Programming Languages: Design and Implementation.* Englewood Cliffs, NJ: Prentice-Hall, 123–136.
1973. Wirth, N. *Systematic Programming: An Introduction.* Englewood Cliffs, NJ: Prentice-Hall.

EDWIN D. REILLY

EXTENDED BINARY CODED DECIMAL INTERCHANGE CODE. *See* EBCDIC.

EXTENSIBLE LANGUAGE

For articles on related subjects *see* ADA; ALGOL 68; MODULA-2; PROCEDURE-ORIENTED LANGUAGES; and PROGRAMMING LANGUAGES.

The concept of an *extensible language* was evolved to permit the user to modify a programming language by adding new features to it or by modifying existing ones. One of the goals was to let the user mold the language to the requirements of the particular area of application and thus improve the efficiency of the programmer and the clarity of the product.

Extensible languages consist of two basic components:

1. A *base language*, which provides a complete but minimal set of primitive facilities, such as elementary data types and simple operations and control constructs.
2. *Extension mechanisms*, which allow the definition of new language features in terms of the base language primitives.

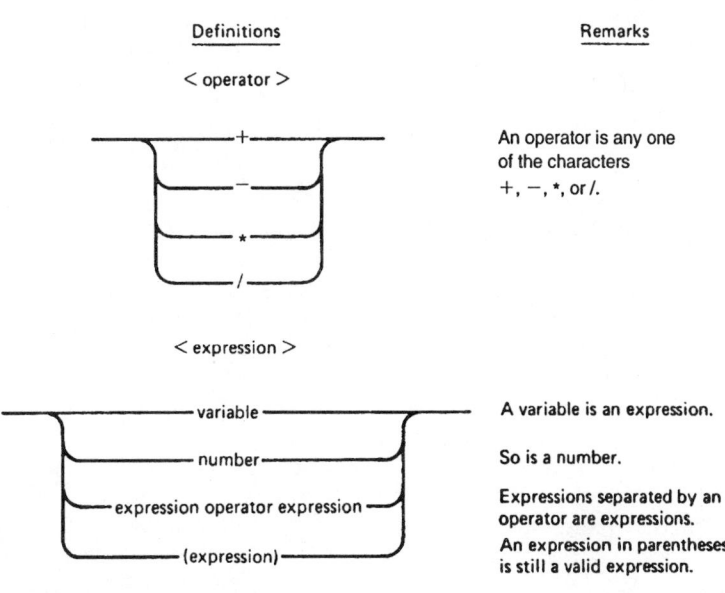

FIG. 1.

The extension mechanisms can be further subdivided into *semantic extension* facilities and *syntactic extension* facilities.

Semantic extensions introduce new kinds of objects to the languages such as additional data types or operations, whereas syntactic extensions create new notations for existing or user-defined mechanisms.

Among others, Ada, Algol 68, Basel, EL1 (Extensible Language 1), GPL (General Purpose Language), PPL (Polymorphic Programming Language), Proteus, and Snobol4 are languages that are extensible to a higher or lower degree.

Languages such as Fortran and Cobol are not extensible in the technical sense, although they have been enhanced over the years by the addition of new features. However, these enhancements are, in fact, modifications of the language definitions and not extensions accomplished by an extension mechanism that is part of the language and, thus, accessible to the user.

As an example of semantic extensibility, consider the mode (i.e. type) and operator definition facilities provided by Algol 68 as demonstrated by the following program segment:

mode point = **struct** (**real** x, y);

Comment: A new object of the mode **point** is being defined as a structure of two real components. The components are accessed by the selectors x and y.¢

priority – – = 6;

Comment: The symbol – – is declared to be an infix operator symbol of priority level 6, i.e. the level of addition.¢

op – – = (**point** p1, p2) **real:**
sqrt ((x **of** p1 – x **of** p2) ↑ 2 + (y **of** p1 – y **of** p2) ↑2);

Comment: The symbol – –, if applied to operands of the mode *point*, is defined to denote the Euclidean distance between the two points p1 and p2.

The following segment demonstrates how the newly defined objects may be used.¢

begin real a, **point** u, v;
u:= (.0,.0), v:= (3.0,4.0); a:= u – – v **end**

Comment: a is set to 5.0.¢

It should be noted that all operators so defined are generic, i.e. the same operator symbol may be defined for and used with different operand modes, evoking different computations. This is accomplished by checking and matching modes during the compilation.

The above example gives a glimpse of the power of the concept. In a similar fashion, these facilities could be used to define polynomials or logical formulas as objects for programs that manipulate formulas, with operations that, for example, add, multiply, intersect, or unite these objects in a formal rather than a numeric way. In computer graphics applications, pictures could be defined as new objects with operators that overlay, scale, or rotate them, etc.

Both mechanisms demonstrated use only notational patterns that are part of the language Algol 68, namely, the mode declaration and the infix operator notation. Algol 68 does not allow the user to redefine the *syntactic form* of a statement; thus, it does not provide syntactic extensions.

Where syntactic extension mechanisms are available, they usually have the general form

phrase α means β

Here, α is a new syntactic pattern defined to invoke the program segment β. For more detail, see Schuman and Jorrand (1970) and *SIGPLAN Notices* (1971).

Extensible languages are mainly of historical importance. Together with the work in structured programming in the late 1960s and early 1970s, they furthered efforts to reexamine and generalize programming language primitives that have led to the more recent research in the area of abstraction mechanisms. As one result, for example, the importance of devices for the specification of what are now called abstract data types (*q.v.*) has been widely recognized. These devices, pioneered by Simula 67 (1967) with its *class* (*q.v.*) concept, have hence become central features of such later languages as CLU, Alphard, Euclid, Modula, and Ada.

References

1970. Schuman, S. A. and Jorrand, P. "Definition Mechanisms in Extensible Programming Languages," *AFIPS Conference Proceedings* **37**. AFIPS Press, 9–20.

1971. "Proceedings of the International Symposium on Extensible Languages" (September 1971, Grenoble, France), *SIGPLAN Notices* **6**, *12* (December).

1976. Melkanoff, M. A. "Extensible Languages," in *Formal Languages and Programming*, R. Aguilar (Ed.). Amsterdam: North-Holland.

JOHANNES J. MARTIN

FACTORING INTEGERS

For articles on related subjects *see* CRYPTOGRAPHY, COMPUTERS IN; and NUMBER THEORETIC CALCULATIONS.

The theory of numbers is primarily concerned with the properties of the *natural numbers* 1, 2, 3,....The fundamental theorem of arithmetic states that each natural number greater than 1 can be expressed uniquely as a product of *prime numbers*. A prime number is a natural number greater than 1 having no divisor other than 1 and itself. A natural number that is not prime is called *composite*. Proofs of the fundamental theorem provide no efficient method for obtaining the unique prime factorization of a natural number. The discovery of such methods is an important and difficult problem in number theory. This article will describe some of the best algorithms known for factoring integers.

Trial Division   If the number to be factored has only a few decimal digits, we can factor it by trying to divide it by 2, 3, 5, 7,...(the first few prime numbers). Every composite number must have a prime factor less than its square root. When a factor is discovered by this method, divide it out and continue recursively while trying to factor the remaining cofactor, but starting with the most recently used trial divisor. When the trial division reaches the square root of the cofactor, we are done because the cofactor must be prime. The prime factors are discovered in increasing order of size.

The algorithm will remain correct if the sequence of trial divisors is replaced by any superset of the set of the first few primes. For example, one may use 2 and all the odd numbers after 2 as the trial divisors with only a moderate loss of efficiency.

Although trial division will succeed in factoring only small numbers, it is a good first step for trying to factor an unknown number of any size. This is so because a large random integer is likely to have one or more small prime factors.

The Pollard Methods   In the 1970s, Pollard invented two factoring algorithms that can find small factors of large numbers and that are more powerful than trial division. His Rho or Monte Carlo method (*q.v.*) finds a prime factor p of n in roughly $\sqrt{p}$ steps. Let $f(x)$ be a quadratic polynomial with integer coefficients. Choose a random integer x_0 and define the sequence of iterates of f as $x_i = f(x_{i-1})$ for $i \geq 1$. The sequence $x_i \bmod p$ is periodic with period $\leq p$. If $f(x)$ is neither x^2 nor $x^2 - 2$, then the period is usually near $\sqrt{p}$ for most values of x_0.

To factor a number n, compute $g_i = \mathrm{GCD}(x_{2i} - x_i, n)$ for $i = 1, 2,....$When i reaches the period, p will divide g_i and, probably, g_i will equal p and n will be factored. The number of steps needed to find p is roughly $\sqrt{p}$ steps.

Pollard's $p - 1$ factoring algorithm finds a prime factor p of a larger number n quickly when all prime factors of $p - 1$ are small. The number of steps it takes to find p usually is proportional to the largest prime factor of $p - 1$. Here is one simple (but slightly slower) version of the algorithm. Choose a random starting value y_1. For $i > 1$, define $y_i = (y_{i-1})^i \bmod n$ and $g_i = \mathrm{GCD}(y_i - 1, n)$. Then p will appear as a factor of g_i as soon as $p - 1$ divides $i\,!$. One can raise y_{i-1} to the i power (mod n) in roughly $\log_2 i$ steps by a doubling and squaring procedure (see Lehmer, 1969, p. 126).

There is also a $p + 1$ algorithm that finds a prime factor p of a larger number n quickly when all prime factors of $p + 1$ are small. See Guy (1976) for examples of factoring with these and similar methods.

The Elliptic Curve Method   This factoring algorithm was announced by H. W. Lenstra, Jr. in 1985. It is the first to use twentieth-century mathematics. It is similar to Pollard's $p - 1$ algorithm discussed above. The multiplicative group of $GF(p)$ in that algorithm is replaced by the group of a random elliptic curve modulo p. A random point P on the elliptic curve is added to itself repeatedly to form $(i\,!)\,P$ for $i = 1, 2,....$During these additions, whose arithmetic is performed modulo n, one must invert a certain number modulo n. With a little luck, this number will have a factor p in common with n. When this happens, the inversion modulo n will fail and n will be factored.

When a number of random elliptic curves are tried, this algorithm will discover a factor p of n in about $\exp(\sqrt{2}\log p\,\log\log p)$ operators. It has been used with great success to find prime factors in the 10- to 30-digit range, with a few larger successes.

Quadratic Residue Methods The methods described so far usually discover small prime factors of n before large ones, and their running times increase with the size of the factor found. In contrast, the methods described below have running times that increase with the size of n and are independent of the size of the factor discovered. They are most effective for factoring numbers without small factors. They are used when the earlier methods fail.

In the quadratic residue methods, many quadratic residues modulo n are generated. These are solutions to the congruence $A^2 = Q \pmod{n}$. The prime factors of the Q's are matched up (by Gaussian elimination over GF(2)) to form squares. Then subsets of the congruences are multiplied to produce several congruences of the form $X^2 \equiv Y^2 \pmod{n}$. Each congruence like this gives a chance to factor n, as $\mathrm{GCD}(X - Y, n)$ may be a proper factor of n. The methods differ in the way the factored quadratic residues Q are produced.

The Continued Fraction Algorithm of Morrison and Brillhart derives the congruences $A^2 \equiv Q \pmod{n}$ from the simple continued fraction expansion of $\sqrt{n}$. The Q's are factored by trial division by a fixed set of small primes called the *factor base*. The Q's are more likely than random quadratic residues to have only small prime factors because they are smaller than $2\sqrt{n}$. This method has been used to factor numbers as large as 62 digits.

The Quadratic Sieve Algorithm of Pomerance generates the Q's as part of the range of a quadratic polynomial. The regularity of their rule of formation allows them to be factored by a sieve rather than by trial division, which is slow. This method has been used to factor numbers as large as 111 digits.

A related algorithm, the Number Field Sieve, was developed in 1990. It works best on numbers of the form $b^n \pm c$, where b and c are small positive integers. This method has been used to factor numbers as large as 148 digits, but only ones of the special form.

References

1969. Lehmer, D. H. "Computer Technology Applied to the Theory of Numbers," *Studies in Number Theory*, MAA Studies in Mathematics, Vol. 6, Englewood Cliffs, NJ: Prentice-Hall.

1976. Guy, R. K. "How to Factor a Number," *Congressus Numerantium XVI, Proceedings of the Fifth Conference on Numerical Mathematics*, Winnipeg, 49–89.

1981. Knuth, D. E. *The Art of Computer Programming*, **2**, *Seminumerical Algorithms*, 2nd Ed. Reading, MA: Addison-Wesley.

1985. Riesel, H. *Prime Numbers and Computer Methods for Factorization*. Progress in Mathematics, **57**, Boston, MA: Birkhauser.

SAMUEL S. WAGSTAFF, JR.

FAST FOURIER TRANSFORM

For Articles on related subjects *see* ALGORITHMS, ANALYSIS OF; DISCRETE MATHEMATICS; and NUMERICAL ANALYSIS.

The Discrete Fourier Transform The *Fast Fourier Transform* (FFT) refers to a family of numerical algorithms for computing the Discrete Fourier Transform (DFT). In complex notation, the DFT is defined by

$$a(n) = \sum_{j=0}^{N-1} x(j) W_N^{nj} \qquad (1)$$

where $x(j)$, $j = 0,1,2,\ldots, N-1$ is a given sequence of complex numbers and

$$W_N = \exp(-2\pi i /N) \qquad (2)$$

This can be written as a series of sines and cosines by making the substitution

$$W_N^{nj} = \cos(2\pi nj/N) - i\sin(2\pi nj/N) \qquad (3)$$

Most of the important applications of the FFT involve the inversion theorem and the convolution theorem. The inversion formula is

$$x(j) = N^{-1} \sum_{n=0}^{N-1} a(n) W_N^{-nj} \qquad (4)$$

and can be computed by the same algorithm that computes Eq. (1). A direct calculation according to the defining formula (1) would require N^2 complex multiplications and $N \times (N-1)$ complex additions. If $N = N_1 N_2 \ldots N_m$, an FFT algorithm can compute the same DFT in $N(N_1 + N_2 + \ldots + N_m)$ complex multiplications and $N(N_1 + N_2 + \ldots + N_m) - m)$ complex additions. For simplicity, approximate expressions will be used, and this will be referred to as

$$N(N_1 + N_2 + \ldots + N_m) \qquad (5)$$

multiply-adds or just "operations." For $N > 4$, this is much smaller than N^2 operations required by direct calculation of the sums in (1). For N equal to a power of 2, very simple efficient programs can compute the DFT in $N\log_2 N$ operations, yielding a speed-up factor of $N/\log_2 N$. Other choices of N with small factors lead to simple programs with comparable efficiency and a broad selection of possible N-values.

The *convolution theorem* permits one to use the FFT to compute convolution and covariance functions. The theorem states that given two periodic sequences $x(j)$ and $y(j)$ with period N, the DFT of the cyclic convolution

$$z(j) = \sum_{n=0}^{N-1} x(k) y(j-k) \qquad j = 0, 1, \ldots, N-1 \qquad (6)$$

is the product sequence

$$c(n) = a(n)b(n), \quad n = 0,1,...,N-1 \qquad (7)$$

where $b(n)$ is the DFT of $y(j)$. Thus, the DFT method can compute the convolution in a number of operations proportional to $N \log N$ instead of N^2.

The DFT is used extensively in digital signal processing, statistical analysis, and in the solution of differential and difference equations.

The General Arbitrary Factor Algorithm

Although the basic idea in the FFT algorithm had been used earlier (Cooley *et al.*, 1967, and Heideman *et al.* 1984), it was not generally known and used until the mid-1960s (Cooley and Tukey, 1965, and Cooley *et al.*, 1969). It may be described as follows: Consider N with two factors, $N = N_1 N_2$ and the mapping from one-dimensional to two-dimensional indices:

$$x(j) = x(j_2, j_1), \quad j = j_2 + j_1 N_2 \qquad (8)$$

$$a(n) = a(n_1, n_2), \quad n = n_1 + n_2 N_1 \qquad (9)$$

This maps $x(j)$ into an $N_2 \times N_1$ array and $a(n)$ into an $N_1 \times N_2$ array as follows: The one-dimensional DFT is expressed as a two-dimensional DFT:

$$a(n_1, n_2) = \sum_{j_2=0}^{N_2-1} \sum_{j_1=0}^{N_1-1} x(j_2, j_1) W_N^{jk} \qquad (10)$$

where

$$W_N^{jk} = W_N^{(j_2 + j_1 N_2)(n_1 + n_2 N_1)} = W_N^{j_1 n_1 N_2} W_N^{j_2 n_1} W_N^{j_2 n_2 N_1} W_N^{j_1 n_2 N} \quad (11)$$

Since $W_N^N = 1$ and $W_N^{N_2} = W_{N_1}$, substitution in Eq. (10) gives

$$a(n_1, n_2) = \sum_{j_2=0}^{N_2-1} \left\{ \sum_{j_1=0}^{N_1-1} x(j_2, j_1) W_N^{j_1 n_1} \right\} W_{N_2}^{j_2 n_2} \qquad (12)$$

The inner sum, in braces, may be computed first:

$$a_1(j_2, n_1) = \sum_{j_1=0}^{N_1-1} x(j_2, j_1) W_{N_1}^{j_1 n_1} \qquad (13)$$

It is multiplied by the "twiddle factor," $W_N^{j_1 n_1}$ and a second set of Fourier transforms is computed:

$$a_2(n_2, n_1) = \sum_{j_2=0}^{N_2-1} \left\{ a_1(j_2, n_1) W_N^{j_2 n_1} \right\} W_{N_2}^{j_2 n_2} \qquad (14)$$

This is a 2-dimensional DFT with a twiddle factor multiplication applied to the intermediate array $a_1(j_2, n_1)$. Finally, it is noted that the resulting array $a_2(n_2, n_1)$ has the required values of the result, $a(n_1, n_2)$, but they are in a transposed array, or in "digit-reversed" order, as it is

called. It is often advantageous to transpose all arrays to obtain an algorithm that starts with data in permuted order and gives results in correct order.

If N has more than two factors, one may iterate with the above algorithm and obtain an algorithm requiring the number of operations in (5).

The Radix 2 FFT

When $N_1 = N_2 = ... = N_m = 2$, the mapping to m dimensions expresses each data element in terms of the bit representation of its index. The transpose mentioned above is a bit-reversal permutation defined by

$$a_0(j_0, j_1,..., j_{m-1}, j_m) = x_0(j_m, j_{m-1},..., j_1, j_0) \qquad (15)$$

The radix 2 algorithm assumes the form of a series of two-point DFTs:

$$a_1(0, j_2, j_3,..., j_m) = a_0(0, j_2, j_3,..., j_m) + a_0(1, j_2, j_3,..., j_m)$$

$$a_1(1, j_2, j_3,..., j_m) = a_0(0, j_2, j_3,..., j_m) - a_0(1, j_2, j_3,..., j_m)$$

$$a_2(n_1, 0, j_3,..., j_m) = a_1(n_1, 0, j_3,..., j_m) + a_1(n_1, 1, j_3,..., j_m) W_4^{n_1}$$

$$a_2(n_1, 1, j_3,..., j_m) = a_1(n_1, 0, j_3,..., j_m) - a_1(n_1, 1, j_3,..., j_m) W_4^{n_1}$$

$$a_3(n_1, n_2, 0,..., j_m) = a_2(n_1, n_2, 0,..., j_m) + a_2(n_1, n_2, 1,..., j_m) W_8^{n_1 + 2n_2}$$

$$a_3(n_1, n_2, 1,..., j_m) = a_2(n_1, n_2, 0,..., j_m) - a_2(n_1, n_2, 1,..., j_m) W_8^{n_1 + 2n_2}$$

$$\cdots \cdots \qquad (16)$$

$$a_m(n_1, n_2, n_3,..., 0) = a_{m-1}(n_1, n_2, n_3,..., 0) + a_{m-1}(n_1, n_2, n_3,..., 1) \times W_{2^m}^{n_1 + 2n_2 + ... + 2^{m-1} n_{m-1}}$$

$$a_m(n_1, n_2, n_3,..., 1) = a_{m-1}(n_1, n_2, n_3,..., 0) - a_{m-1}(n_1, n_2, n_3,..., 1) \times W_{2^m}^{n_1 + 2n_2 + ... + 2^{m-1} n_{m-1}}$$

The Fortran program listing in Fig. 1 for the radix 2 algorithm demonstrates the use of the above algorithm. Written to explain the algorithm rather than to achieve efficiency, it is referred to as the "decimation in time algorithm." A slight change in the factoring of W^{jn} leads to the form referred to as the "Sande Tukey" or "decimation in frequency" form of the algorithm. A radix 4 algorithm saves one out of four complex multiplications and has an advantage on RISC architecture (*q.v.*) machines, where more calculations can be done in registers without intermediate store load operations.

The Mutually Prime Factor Algorithm

If N_1 and N_2 are mutually prime factors of N, one can use a different mapping from one-to-two dimensional indices:

$$j = j_1 N_2 + j_2 N_1 \mod N \qquad (17)$$

```
    DO 20 L = 1, M
        LE = 2**L
        LE1 = LE/2
        U = (1.,0.)
        ANG = 3.14159265358979/LE1
        W = CMPLX (COS(ANG),SIN(ANG))
        DO 20 J = 1, LE1
            DO 10 I = J,N,LE
            IP = I 1 LE1
            T = A(IP)*U
            A(IP) = A(I) - T
10          A(I) = A(I)+ T
20  U = U*W
```

FIG. 1. Fortran subroutine for FFT with $N = 2^m$, starting with bit-reversed data.

$$n_1 = n \bmod N_1 \quad n_2 = n \bmod N_2 \quad (18)$$

The solution of these two congruences is given by the *Chinese Remainder Theorem* (CRT):

$$n = n_1 Q_1 + n_2 Q_2 \bmod N \quad (19)$$

where Q_1 and Q_2 are idempotents under multiplication mod N, i.e.

$$Q_1 = 1 \bmod N_1, \quad Q_2 = 0 \bmod N_1 \quad (20)$$

$$Q_1 = 0 \bmod N_2, \quad Q_2 = 1 \bmod N_2 \quad (21)$$

Then

$$W_N^{jn} = W_N^{j_1 N_2 n} W_N^{j_2 N_1 n} = W_{N_1}^{j_1 n_1} W_{N_2}^{j_2 n_2} \quad (22)$$

where n may be replaced in the exponents of W_{N_1} and W_{N_2}, respectively, by n_1 and n_2. The DFT can then be written:

$$a(n_1, n_2) = \sum_{j_2=0}^{N_2-1} \left[\sum_{j_1=0}^{N_1-1} x(j_1, j_2) W_N^{j_1 n_1} \right] W_{N_2}^{j_2 n_2} \quad (23)$$

In iterated form, this is written

$$a_1(n_1, j_2) = \sum_{j_1=0}^{N_1-1} x(j_1, j_2) W_N^{j_1 n_1} \quad (24)$$

$$a(n_1, n_2) = \sum_{j_2=0}^{N_2-1} a_1(n_1, j_2) W_{N_2}^{j_2 n_2} \quad (25)$$

The advantage of the mutually prime factor algorithms is that there is no twiddle factor between iterations. The disadvantage is in the increased complexity of the addressing of the data. C. S. Burrus has published a series of papers on the index mappings and has produced programs written in a neat modular fashion with separate and independent routines for each of the possible factors of N (Burrus, 1977, Burrus and Johnson, 1984).

Rader's DFT Algorithm The FFT algorithm requires an N that is factorable. Rader (1968) addressed the challenge of being able to use the FFT algorithm for N equal to a prime number. For example, consider $N = 7$. The DFT may be expressed

$$\begin{bmatrix} a_0 \\ a_1 \\ a_2 \\ a_3 \\ a_4 \\ a_5 \\ a_6 \end{bmatrix} = W_7 ** \begin{bmatrix} 0000000 \\ 0123456 \\ 0246135 \\ 0362514 \\ 0415263 \\ 0531642 \\ 0654321 \end{bmatrix} \begin{bmatrix} x_0 \\ x_1 \\ x_2 \\ x_3 \\ x_4 \\ x_5 \\ x_6 \end{bmatrix} \quad (26)$$

where the matrix contains the exponents of W_7.

The integers under multiplication mod 7 form a group with the generators of the whole group. This permits the use of an index permutation defined by

$$j = 3^{j'} \bmod 7 = 1, 3, 2, 6, 4, 5, \quad j' = 0, 1, 2, \ldots, 5 \quad (27)$$

$$n = 3^{n'} \bmod 7 = 1, 3, 2, 6, 4, 5, \quad n' = 0, 1, 2, \ldots, 5 \quad (28)$$

which puts the DFT matrix in the form

$$W_7^{jn} = W_7^{3^{j'+n'}} \quad (29)$$

Therefore, the 6 by 6 block of the DFT matrix of non-zero exponents becomes a cyclic skew-symmetric matrix:

$$\begin{bmatrix} a_0 \\ a_1 \\ a_3 \\ a_2 \\ a_6 \\ a_4 \\ a_5 \end{bmatrix} = W_7 ** \begin{bmatrix} 0000000 \\ 0132645 \\ 0326451 \\ 0264513 \\ 0645132 \\ 0451326 \\ 0513264 \end{bmatrix} \begin{bmatrix} x_0 \\ x_1 \\ x_3 \\ x_2 \\ x_6 \\ x_4 \\ x_5 \end{bmatrix} \quad (30)$$

The block of W's with non-zero exponents is a 6-point cyclic convolution, or "correlation" to be precise, which can be computed by the Fourier transform method described above in $O(N \log N)$ operations, where $O(f(N))$ denotes a quantity proportional to $f(N)$ for large N. Thus, the DFT for a prime number can be computed in $O(N \log N)$ operations. However, the crossover point in the number of operations (i.e. the point where the DFT beats brute force) for the two methods is high, at around $N = 100$.

The Winograd Fourier Transform Algorithm
Shmuel Winograd has developed a theory of computational complexity, which he has applied to the calculation of convolutions and DFT's (Winograd, 1974; and Silverman, 1977). To apply this to the calculation of the DFT, he uses mutually prime factors of N to reduce the DFT to a set of small DFTs that can be expressed as convolutions. He also schedules the calculation so that all sinusoidal factors are combined into one set of factors, further reducing computation. Others have found it efficient to take

more multiplications and schedule the calculations as was done above for the prime factor algorithm and use Winograd's efficient small DFT algorithms for each of the factors (Kolba and Parks, 1977).

Very efficient general-purpose FFT subroutines combine all of the above algorithms and permit the efficient calculation of the DFT for a wide selection of N values. When the data is real, or real and symmetric (cosine transform) or real and anti-symmetric (sine-transform), special efficient algorithms can be used to avoid redundant calculations.

References

1965. Cooley, J. W. and Tukey, J. W. "An Algorithm for the Machine Calculation of Complex Fourier Series," *Mathematics of Computation*, **19** (April) 297.

1967. Cooley, J. W., Lewis, P. A. W., and Welch, P. D. "Historical Notes on the Fast Fourier Transform," *IEEE Trans. Audio Electroacoustics*, **AU-15** (June), 76–79.

1968. Rader, C. M. "Discrete Fourier Transforms When the Number of Data Samples is Prime," *Proc. IEEE (Letters)*, **56** (June) 1107–1108.

1969. Cooley, J. W., Lewis, P. A. W. and Welch, P. D. "The Fast Fourier Transform Algorithm and its Applications," *IEEE Trans. on Education*, **E-12**, (March) 27–34.

1974. Winograd, S. "Arithmetic Complexity of Computations," CBMS-NSF Regional Conference Series in Applied Mathematics, Philadelphia: SIAM.

1977. Burrus, C. S. "Index Mappings for Multidimensional Formulation of the DFT and Convolution," *IEEE Trans. Acoust. Speech and Signal Processing*, **ASSP-25**, *3* (June), 239–242.

1977. Silverman, H. F. "An Introduction to Programming the Winograd Fourier Transform Algorithm (WFTA)," *IEEE Trans. Acoust. Speech, Signal Processing*, **ASSP-25**, *2* (April), 152–164.

1977. Kolba, D. P. and Parks, T. W. "A Prime Factor FFT Algorithm Using High-Speed Convolution," *IEEE Trans. Acoust. Speech, Signal Processing*, **ASSP-25**, *4* (August) 281–294.

1984. Heideman, M. T., Johnson, D. H. and Burrus, C. S. "Gauss and the History of the Fast Fourier Transform," *The ASSP MAgazine*, **1**, *4*, (October).

1984. Burrus C. S. and Johnson, H. W. "An In-Order In-Place Radix-2 FFT," *Proceedings of the International Conference on Acoustics Speech and Signal Processing*, p. 28A.2.1.

JAMES W. COOLEY

FAULT-TOLERANT COMPUTING

For articles on related subjects *see* ERROR-CORRECTING CODE; and ERRORS.

Fault-tolerant computing is the art of building computing systems that continue to operate satisfactorily in the presence of faults (i.e. hardware or software failures). An extensive methodology has been developed in this field over the past two decades. Several fault-tolerant machines have been developed, and a large amount of supporting research has been reported.

The majority of fault-tolerant designs have been directed toward building computers that automatically recover from faults occurring in internal hardware components. The techniques employed to do this generally involve partitioning a computing system into modules. Each module is backed up with protective redundancy so that, if the module fails, others can assume its function. Special mechanisms are added to detect errors and implement recovery. Recent research has centered on making software more dependable.

Two general approaches to hardware fault recovery have been used: 1) fault masking, and 2) dynamic recovery. Fault masking is a structural redundancy technique that completely masks faults within a set of redundant modules. A number of identical modules execute the same functions and their outputs are voted to remove errors created by a faulty module. Triple modular redundancy (TMR) is a commonly used form of fault masking in which the circuitry is triplicated and voted. The voting circuitry is also triplicated so that individual voter failures can also be corrected by the voting process. A TMR system fails whenever two modules in a redundant triplet create errors so that the vote is no longer valid. Hybrid redundancy is an extension of TMR in which triplicated modules are backed up with additional spare modules, which are used to replace faulty modules. When a module disagrees within a triplet, the two remaining good machines command its replacement with a spare. A triplet, backed up with N spares, can tolerate $N + 1$ module failures. Voted systems require greater than three times as much hardware as non-redundant systems due to replication of modules and the further addition of voter circuits, which is the price of automatic fault recovery.

Dynamic recovery involves automated self-repair. As in fault masking, the computing system is partitioned into modules backed up by spares as protective redundancy. In the case of dynamic recovery, a special mechanism detects faults in the modules, switches out a faulty module, switches in a spare, and instigates those software actions (rollback, initialization, retry, restart) necessary to continue the ongoing computation. The few existing uniprocessors of this type depend upon special hardware to carry out this function of automated recovery. This special hardware is made as simple as possible and is protected by TMR or hybrid redundancy. In multiprocessors and distributed computing systems (*q.v.*), the special recovery function is usually implemented by one of the other non-faulty machines in the system.

Recent efforts to attain fault-tolerance in software have used static and dynamic redundancy approaches similar to those used for hardware faults. One such approach, *N*-version programming, uses static redundancy in the form of independently written programs (versions) that perform identical functions and are executed concurrently. The goal is to vote out any error in one of the versions. They are voted at special checkpoints to remove errors from a faulty version, and the faulty version is resynchronized with the others. An alternative dynamic approach is based on the concept of recovery blocks. Programs are partitioned into blocks and acceptance tests are executed after each block. If an acceptance test fails, a redundant code block is executed.

An approach called *design diversity* combines hardware and software fault-tolerance by implementing a fault-tolerant computer system using different hardware *and* software in each of several different channels. Each channel is designed to provide the same function, and a method is provided to identify if one channel deviates unacceptably from the others. The goal is to tolerate both hardware and software design faults by using a redundant channel if one should fail. This is a very expensive technique, but it is useful in very critical applications.

History The SAPO computer built in Prague, Czechoslovakia was probably the first fault-tolerant computer. It was built in 1950–1954 under the supervision of A. Svoboda, using relays and a magnetic drum memory. The processor used triplication and voting (TMR), and the memory implemented error detection with automatic retries when an error was detected. A second machine developed by the same group (EPOS) also contained comprehensive fault-tolerance features. The fault-tolerant features of these machines were motivated by the local unavailability of reliable components and a high probability of reprisals by the ruling authorities should the machine fail.

Over the past 25 years, a number of fault-tolerant computers have been developed that fall into three general types: 1) long-life, unmaintainable computers, 2) ultradependable, real-time computers, and 3) high-availability computers.

Long-Life, Unmaintained Computers Applications such as spacecraft require computers to operate for long periods of time without external repair. Typical requirements are a probability of 95% that the computer will operate correctly for 5–10 years. Machines of this type must use hardware in a very efficient fashion, and they are typically constrained to low power, weight, and volume. Therefore, it is not surprising that NASA was an early sponsor of fault-tolerant computing. In the 1960s, the first fault-tolerant machine to be developed and flown was the on-board computer for the Orbiting Astronomical Observatory (OAO), which used fault masking at the component (transistor) level.

The JPL Self-Testing-and-Repairing (STAR) computer was the next fault-tolerant computer, developed by NASA in the late 1960s for a 10-year mission to the outer planets. The STAR computer, designed under the leadership of A. Avizienis was the first computer to employ dynamic recovery throughout its design. Various modules of the computer were instrumented to detect internal faults and signal fault conditions to a special test and repair processor that effected reconfiguration and recovery. An experimental version of the STAR was implemented in the laboratory and its fault-tolerance properties were verified by experimental testing. Following the STAR, the Raytheon Corporation developed a similar but higher performance machine for the United States Air Force, designated the Fault-Tolerant Spaceborne Computer (FTSC). During the 1970s, it was implemented and tested in the laboratory, but the program was halted due to the unavailability of specialized components.

Ultradependable Real-Time Computers These are computers for which an error or delay can prove to be catastrophic. They are designed for applications such as control of aircraft, mass transportation systems, and nuclear power plants. The applications justify massive investments in redundant hardware, software, and testing.

The first operational machine of this type was the Saturn V guidance computer, developed in the 1960s. It contained a TMR processor and duplicated memories (each using internal error detection). Processor errors were masked by voting, and a memory error was circumvented by reading from the other memory. The next machine of this type was the space shuttle computer. It was a rather ad-hoc design that used four computers that executed the same programs and were voted. A fifth, non-redundant computer was included with different programs in case a software error was encountered.

During the 1970s, two influential fault-tolerant machines were developed by NASA for fuel-efficient aircraft that require continuous computer control in flight. Since these machines were intended for life-critical applications, they were designed to meet the most stringent reliability requirements of any computer to that time. Both machines employed hybrid redundancy. The first, designated Software Implemented Fault Tolerance (SIFT), was developed by SRI International. It used off-the-shelf computers and achieved voting and reconfiguration through software. The second machine, the Fault-Tolerant Multiprocessor (FTMP) developed by the C. S. Draper Laboratory, used specialized hardware to effect error and fault recovery. A commercial company, August Systems, was a spinoff from the SIFT program. It has developed a Can't Fail 300 system intended for process control applications. The FTMP has evolved into the Fault-Tolerant Processor (FTP), used by Draper in several applications.

The new generation of fly-by-wire aircraft are using fault-tolerant computers of this type for flight control. The Boeing 757 and 767 airliners use a triplicated Flight Control Computer and a duplex Flight Management Computer. The Boeing 737-300 and Airbus Airliners use redundant diverse channels in their flight control architectures.

The Advanced Automation System, the largest fault-tolerant computing project to date, has recently been initiated. It is being designed to replace the entire aircraft control system throughout the U.S.

High-Availability Computers Many applications require very high availability but can tolerate an occasional error or very short delays (on the order of a few seconds), while error recovery is taking place. Hardware designs for these systems are often considerably less expensive than those used for ultradependable real-time computers. Computers of this type often use duplex designs. Example applications are telephone switching and transaction processing.

The most widely used fault-tolerant computer systems developed during the 1960s were in electronic switching systems (ESS), which are used in telephone switching offices throughout the country. The first of these AT&T machines, No. 1 ESS, had a goal of no more than two hours downtime in 40 years. The computers are duplicated, to detect errors, with some dedicated hardware and extensive software used to identify faults for manual replacement. These machines have since evolved over several generations to No. 5 ESS (which uses a distributed system controlled by the 3B20D fault tolerant computer) and are possibly the most widely used fault-tolerant machines in the world.

The largest commercial success in fault-tolerant computing has been in the area of transaction processing (*q.v.*) for banks, airline reservations, etc. Tandem Computers, Inc. was the first major producer and is the current leader in this market. The design approach is a distributed system using a sophisticated form of duplication. For each running process, there is a duplicated backup process running on a different computer. The primary process is responsible for checkpointing its state to duplex disks. If it should fail, the backup process can restart from the last checkpoint. Recently, Stratus Computer has become a major producer of fault-tolerant machines for high-availability applications. Their approach uses duplex self-checking computers with error detection provided by internal duplication of processors and memories. A pair of self-checking computers are run synchronously so that if one fails, the other can continue the computations without delay.

Validation of Fault-Tolerance One of the most difficult tasks in the design of a fault-tolerant machine is to verify that it will meet its reliability requirements. This requires creating a number of models. The first model is of the error/fault environment that is expected. Other models specify the structure and behavior of the design. It is then necessary to determine how well the fault-tolerance mechanisms work by analytic studies and fault simulations. The results, in the form of error rates, fault-rates, latencies, and coverages, are used in reliability prediction models.

A number of probabilistic models have been developed using Markov and semi-Markov processes to predict the reliability of fault-tolerant machines as a function of time. These models have been implemented in several computer-aided design tools. Some of the more recent tools are:

ARIES—Automated Reliability Interactive Estimation System (UCLA)
CARE III—Computer-Aided Reliability Estimator (NASA)
HARP—Hybrid Automated Reliability Predictor (Duke)
SAVE—System Availability Estimator (IBM)
SHARPE—Symbolic Hierarchical Automated Reliability and Performance Evaluator (Duke)

Future Development Through the use of VLSI technology, the cost of hardware is decreasing dramatically compared to the costs of software, operation, and maintenance of computing systems. Thus, the cost of protective redundancy for fault-tolerance is also a rapidly decreasing fraction of system costs. At the same time, the degree of dependence of people upon computing systems is increasing. These trends are leading to an increased use of fault-tolerant machines. Fault-tolerant computers have already become common in telephone systems as well as banking and transaction applications. They are used for airplanes and mass transit control, and they are now appearing in automobiles. A large future market has been predicted, and a number of major computer makers are announcing plans for fault-tolerant products.

Two of the most important areas of future research are 1) dependable software, and 2) high-performance parallel systems. As systems become more complex, software errors dominate the causes of failure. This has become the most serious and difficult problem in current fault-tolerant designs. A relatively new area of research is fault-tolerance in large, high-speed multicomputers and multiprocessors. These evolving architectures are aimed at ultra–high performance using state-of-the-art VLSI design techniques. These designs are expected to require extremely dense packaging, making manual repair difficult. The high complexity of the design together with the high-density of the chips is also expected to increase the frequency of computing errors. New fault-tolerance techniques are required that can provide error and fault recovery in a hardware-efficient fashion, and that do not significantly degrade performance.

References

1978. *Proceedings of the IEEE* (Special Issue on Fault-Tolerant Computing) **66**, *10* (October).

1980. *Computer* (Special Issue on Fault-Tolerant Computing) **13**, *3* (March).

1980. Ng, Y.-W. and Avizienis, A. "A Unified Reliability Model for Fault-Tolerant Computers, " *IEEE Trans. Computers* **C-29**, *11*: 1002–1011 (November).

1982. Siewiorek, D., and Swarz, R. *The Theory and Practice of Reliable System Design.* Bedford, MA: Digital Press.

1985. Anderson, T. (Ed.). *Resilient Computing Systems Vol. 1*, New York: John Wiley and Sons.

1987. Avizienis, A., *et al.*, (Ed.). *Dependable Computing and Fault-Tolerant Systems Vol. 1: The Evolution of Fault-Tolerant Computing*, Vienna: Springer-Verlag.

1987. Nelson, V. P. and Carroll, B. D. (Eds.), *Tutorial: Fault-Tolerant Computing*, Washington, DC: IEEE Computer Society Press.

1990. *Computer* (Special Issue on Fault-Tolerant Computing) **23**, *7* (July).

DAVID A. RENNELS

FFT. *See* FAST FOURIER TRANSFORM.

FIBER OPTICS

For articles on related subjects *see* DATA COMMUNICATIONS; MULTIPLEXING; and NETWORKS, COMPUTERS.

Optical fibers are thin, flexible strands of clear glass or plastic that can serve as a transmission medium capable of carrying up to several gigabits of information per second over short or long distances. They perform the same basic functions as copper wires or coaxial cables in carrying voice, data, or video information, but they transmit light instead of electrical signals. An optical fiber transmission system, shown in Fig. 1, is similar to a con-

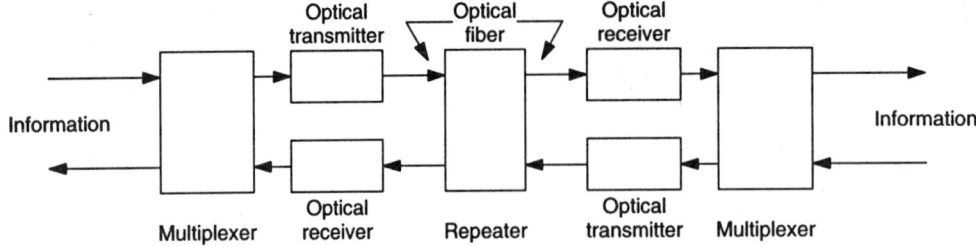

FIG. 1.   Typical optical fiber communication system.

ventional transmission system, except that the transmitter uses a light-emitting or a laser diode to convert electrical information signals to light signals while the receiver uses a photodiode to convert the light back into electrical signals.

Optical fibers offer so many distinct advantages that they are rapidly replacing older transmission media in applications ranging from telephony to computers and automated factories. These advantages include:

1. *Large bandwidth*—Modem optical fibers can have bandwidths 10 to 100 times greater than the best coaxial cables. With currently available technology, a 10-fiber cable can accommodate 241,920 voice channels, and this will increase as technology improves.

2. *Low loss*—The attenuation or loss of an optical fiber is essentially independent of the transmission rate, whereas other media exhibit increasing attenuation with increasing transmission rates. The implication is that signal repeaters need not be placed so close together, which reduces the cost of fiber optics systems.

3. *Electromagnetic immunity*—Because they are made of insulators, optical fibers are not affected by ordinary stray electromagnetic fields. Consequently, fiber optics systems have the potential for reducing costs associated with complex error checking and correction mechanisms that must be used with media subject to electromagnetic interference.

4. *Small size and light weight*—A fiber with a 0.125 mm diameter and 3.5 mm protective jacket has the same information carrying capacity as 900 twisted copper wire pairs with an 8 cm outer diameter and weighing 100 times as much. Size and weight are important factors when considering overcrowded conduits running under city streets.

5. *Security*—Unlike electrical conductors, optical fibers do not radiate energy; eavesdropping techniques that can be used on the former are useless with fibers. Tapping a fiber is very difficult, since this usually affects its light transmission capability enough to be detected.

6. *Safety and electrical insulation*—Because optical fibers are insulators, they provide electrical isolation between the source and the destination. Therefore, optical fibers present no electrical spark hazards and can be used where electrical

codes and common sense prohibit the use of electrical conductors.

Types of Fibers   Optical fibers are made of plastic, glass, or silica. Plastic fibers are the least efficient, but tend to be cheaper and more rugged. Glass or silica fibers are much smaller, and their lower attenuation makes them more suited for very high capacity channels.

The basic optical fiber consists of two concentric layers—the inner core and the outer cladding, which has a refractive index smaller than that of the core. The characteristics of light propagation depend primarily on the fiber size, its construction, the refractive index profile, and the nature of the light source.

The two main types of refractive index profiles are *step* and *graded*. In a step index fiber, the core has a uniform refractive index n_1 with a distinct change to a lower index, n_2, for the cladding. Multimode step index fibers usually have a core diameter from 0.05 to 1.0 mm. With a light source such that the light injected always strikes the core to cladding interface at an angle greater than the critical angle, the light is reflected back into the core. Since the angles of incidence and reflection are equal, the light continues to propagate down the core of the fiber in a zig-zag fashion by total internal reflection, as shown in Fig. 2a. In effect, the light is trapped in the core and the cladding not only provides protection to the core, but may be thought of as the "insulation" that prevents the light from escaping. Since some rays follow longer paths than others, their original relationship is not preserved. The result is that a narrow pulse of light has a tendency to spread as it travels down the fiber. Such spreading is known as *modal dispersion*; fibers with high modal dispersions tend to be used over short to medium distances.

When the core diameter is made small enough (between 0.002 and 0.01 mm), the fiber propagates light efficiently only at the lowest order mode along its axis, as shown in Fig. 2b. Since the zig-zag pattern associated with multimode step index fibers is eliminated, modal dispersion is very low and such fibers are, therefore, very efficient for high-speed, long distance transmission. Their small size, however, makes them relatively difficult to work with.

Modal dispersion can also be reduced by using graded index fibers, as shown in Fig. 2c. The core in such fibers consists of a series of concentric rings, each with a lower refractive index as we move from the core to the cladding boundary. Since light travels faster in a medium of lower refractive index, light further from the fiber axis

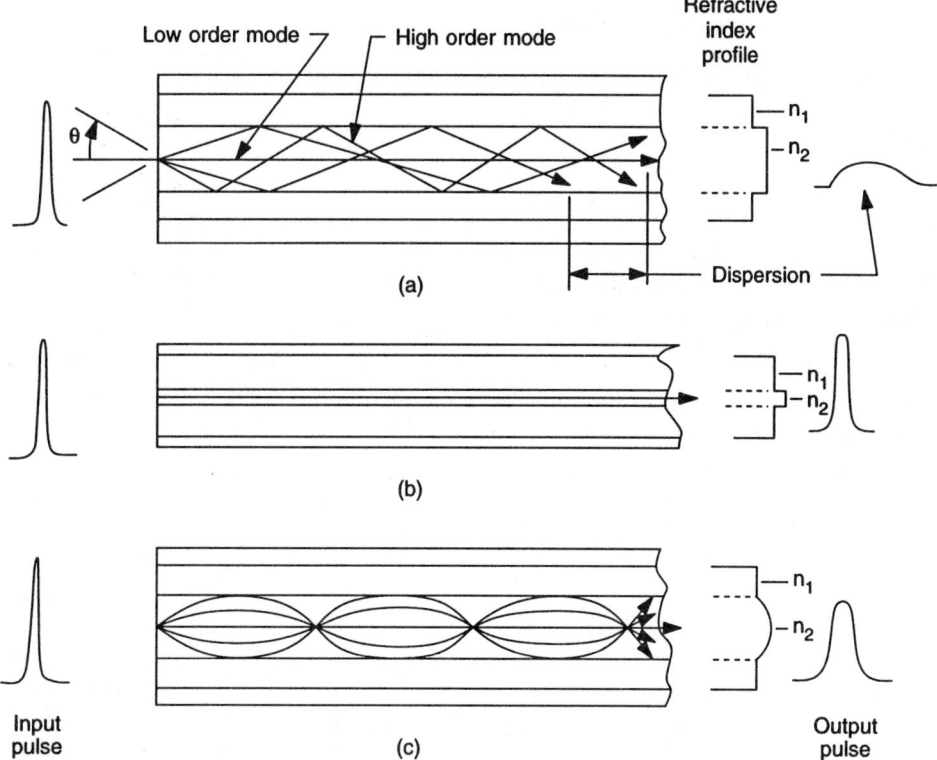

FIG. 2. Characteristics of common optical fibers—(a) multimode step index; (b) single-mode step index; (c) multimode graded index.

travels faster. The result is that light is refracted successively by the different layers of the core and appears to follow a nearly sinusoidal path with all modes arriving at any point at nearly the same time. Such fibers have a modal dispersion that lies between multimode and single-mode step index fibers.

As in the case of electrical conductors, optical fibers are usually cabled by enclosing many fibers in a protective sheath made of some material, such as polyvinyl chloride or polyurethane. The cable is strengthened by adding steel wire or Kevlar aramid yarn to give the cable assembly greater tensile strength. Cables are also available containing both optical fibers and electrical conductors, with the latter used to provide power for remote equipment.

Signal Degradation in Fibers Signal degradation in optical fiber systems is caused by one or more of the following:

1. *Attenuation* or *transmission loss* (dimming of light intensity), which is caused by absorption and scattering. Absorption is the equivalent to electrical resistance and is usually caused by fiber impurities that absorb light energy. Scattering usually results from imperfections in fibers.
2. *Dispersion*, which is a measure of the widening of light pulses as they travel along the fiber and is usually expressed in nanoseconds per kilometer. Dispersion limits the information carrying capacity of fibers, since input pulses must be sepa-

rated enough in time that dispersion does not cause adjacent pulses to overlap at the destination to ensure that the receiver can distinguish them. Modal dispersion arises from the different lengths of paths traveled by the different modes. Material dispersion is due to different velocities of different wavelengths of the light source.
3. *Other causes*—Fibers must be connected or spliced to provide a low-loss coupling through the junction. Precise alignment results in low loss, but the small size of fiber cores, together with dimensional variations in core diameter and alignment, make this a difficult task.

Light Sources and Detectors In fiber optics communication systems, the light source must efficiently convert electrical energy (current and voltage) into optical energy in the form of light. A good source must be:

1. Small and bright to permit the maximum transfer of light into the core of the fiber.
2. Fast to respond to rapidly changing signals encountered in high-bandwidth systems.
3. Monochromatic (i.e. produce light within a narrow band of wavelengths) to limit dispersion.
4. Reliable with a lifetime in the hundreds of thousands of hours of operation.

The most commonly used light sources are gallium arsenide light emitting diodes (LEDs) and injection laser diodes (ILDs). Both devices come in sizes compatible with the cores of fibers and emit light wavelengths in the range of 800–900 nm, where fibers have relatively low loss and dispersion. LEDs are not monochromatic, which limits their upper bit-rate capacity to about 200 Mbits/sec. ILDs produce light that is almost monochromatic and can transfer almost 100 times more light energy into the core than the LEDs, allowing fibers to be driven at Gbit/sec rates.

Optical detectors convert optical energy into electrical energy. Devices most commonly used for this purpose include silicon photodiodes because of their sensitivity to light in the 750–950 nm wavelength region.

Applications of Optical Fibers As the world moves towards an *integrated services digital network* (ISDN - *q.v.*) in which voice, video, and data can be seamlessly transmitted over public and private networks, the need for more and higher bandwidth communication channels will continue to grow. Optical fibers offer capacities well beyond those of copper cables or microwave radio at lower cost and will play a major role in the implementation of the new "information highways" that will continue to affect us all.

Fibers are already widely used to carry voice and television signals across the country and continents and connect computers and workstations in local area networks, and are replacing cables to interconnect computers and their peripherals. Their advantages and the fact that they represent a relatively new technology with much potential for improvement will make them the transmission medium of choice for many applications in the future.

References

1987. Sterling, D. J. *Technician's Guide to Fiber Optics*. Albany, N.Y.: Delmar Publishers Inc.

1987. Sobolewski, J. S. "Data Transmission Media," *Encyclopedia of Physical Science and Technology*, **4**, 136–164. San Diego: Academic Press.

JOHN S. SOBOLEWSKI

FIFO-LIFO

For articles on related subjects *see* DATA STRUCTURES; LIST PROCESSING; and STACK.

The terms FIFO and LIFO refer to two techniques for dealing with collections of items to which additions and deletions are to be made. The acronyms FIFO and LIFO stand for *first-in-first-out* and *last-in-first-out*, respectively. Derived from business accounting and inventory management notions, these techniques have found widespread application in computer science.

The FIFO concept is based on the simple idea of people waiting in line to be serviced at a bank teller's window, a supermarket checkout counter, or a bus stop. The first person to arrive is serviced and, if there is a line of customers, the order of entry to the rear of the line is the order of

FIG. 1   FIFO queue; additions at back; deletions at front.

service given at the front of the line. The same concept can be applied to ships waiting to unload at a dock, to jobs waiting to be run in a computer system, or to airplanes waiting to be serviced by a repair shop. The line of people or items waiting to be serviced is called the *queue* (Fig. 1).

There are a number of variations to the basic theme of FIFO arrangement. *Multiple-server queues* have a single queue but several facilities that provide service. Many banks and airline ticket counters have adopted this technique by having a single line that feeds to a group of teller windows. *Priority queueing* permits persons with high priority to move up to the front of the queue. Bounded-length queueing puts an upper limit to the number of persons in the queue.

The LIFO concept is based on the notion that the most recently arrived item is dispatched first. Thus, the freshest vegetables in the grocery are sold first and the inventory items most recently put on the shelf are the first to be sold. This idea is familiar to card players in some games (gin rummy, for example), who may take a card from the top of the pile or place another card face up on the pile. The stack of plates on the spring-loaded dispenser found in cafeterias is another common example of the LIFO principle. The usual definition of this principle includes the specification that only the top element of the collection may be removed and that new items may be placed only on the top of the collection. A collection that has these rules for addition and deletion is called a *stack* (*q.v.*) or a *pushdown list* (Fig. 2). Automata theorists distinguish between these two terms: In a stack, the interior items may be examined; in a pushdown list, they may not be.

The LIFO technique has widespread application in computer science, particularly in the parsing techniques employed by compilers and in the searching of data structures.

BEN SHNEIDERMAN

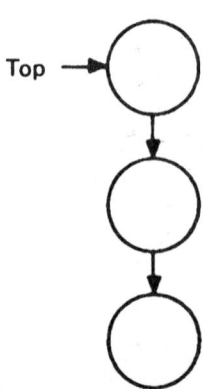

FIG. 2   LIFO stack; additions and deletions at top.

FILE

For articles on related subjects *see* ACCESS METHODS; BLOCK and BLOCKING FACTOR; DATABASE MANAGEMENT SYSTEM; DIRECT ACCESS; DIRECTORY; FILE SERVER; OPEN AND CLOSE A FILE; RECORD; and SCRATCH FILE.

The term *file* was used even before the advent of computers and was one of the first to be incorporated into data processing terminology. There are various definitions of the term in use; those given below are typical. In general, a *file* is a collection of data representing a set of entities with certain aspects in common and that are organized for some specific purpose. An *entity* is any data object, such as *employee* or *part*, and is represented in a file by a record occurrence. A punched card deck containing information on automobile parts and a cabinet drawer filled with manila folders containing data sheets on employees are examples of (non-computer) files.

Definitions In computing, the word *file* can be defined in various ways and the definition depends on the level at which the file is being viewed. From an abstract viewpoint, a file can be considered to be a data object having certain attributes and a set of operations for creating and manipulating it. A file has also been defined as a data structure stored in external memory. Perhaps the most common definition of file is that a file is an organized collection of data records, possibly of different types, stored on some external storage device, such as magnetic tape, disk, drum, charge-coupled device, magnetic bubble memory, etc.

Storage Devices The variety of external storage devices on which files can be stored has been increasing in recent years. New storage technologies, such as charge-coupled devices and magnetic bubble memories, are being used to replace the magnetic disk in certain situations. These new memory technologies have begun to fill the so-called "access time gap" that existed for several years between fixed head disk and drum devices and core memory. While these new memories are appealing because of their relatively low access time, the cost per bit is still considerably above that of disk and drum. For this reason, magnetic disk remains the most popular device for storing large files on line. Magnetic tape, because of its high access time, its portability and compactness characteristics, and its relatively low cost, has been relegated in many computer installations to serving as a storage medium for archival files and for backup copies of files.

File Structure A file has structure that determines how the records in the file are organized. Structure can be subdivided into logical structure and physical structure. The *logical structure* of a file is essentially the application program's (i.e. the user's) view of the file (see Fig. 1). A file declaration that appears in a high-level language such as Cobol or Pascal is basically a logical structure specification and usually involves defining the attribute(s) of the record type(s) and possibly specifying a relationship (e.g. an ordering relationship) on the record occurrences. *Physical structure* is associated with how a file is actually organized on the storage medium on which it resides. This normally involves pointers (*q.v.*), indexes, etc., and how the records are "laid out" on the external storage device (see Fig. 1). The application program should have to be aware of only the logical structure of the file, whereas the access methods must know about the physical structure. *Access methods* are embodied in programs that satisfy user requests against a file; they provide the interface between a user program and a file.

Files can be structured and accessed in various ways. The earliest and most common type of file organization was sequential because computer files were first stored on inherently sequential storage media such as magnetic tape. To access a record in a sequential file, the preceding records must be passed over. The appearance of random access storage devices such as magnetic disk and drum

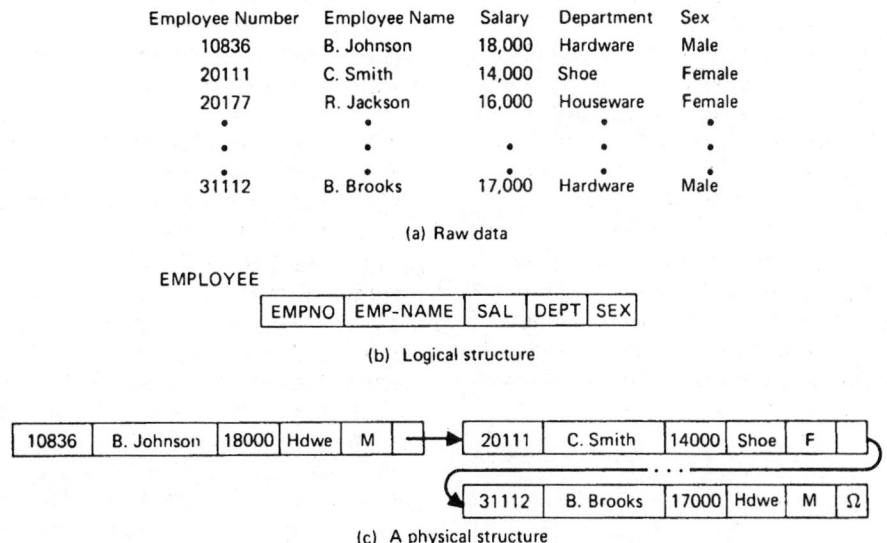

Employee Number	Employee Name	Salary	Department	Sex
10836	B. Johnson	18,000	Hardware	Male
20111	C. Smith	14,000	Shoe	Female
20177	R. Jackson	16,000	Houseware	Female
•	•	•	•	•
•	•	•	•	•
31112	B. Brooks	17,000	Hardware	Male

(a) Raw data

EMPLOYEE

| EMPNO | EMP-NAME | SAL | DEPT | SEX |

(b) Logical structure

(c) A physical structure

FIG. 1. Raw data to logical file structure to physical file structure.

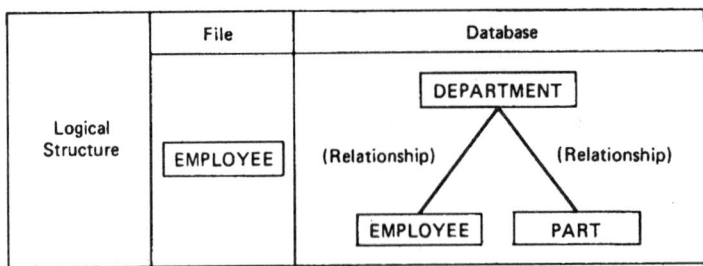

	File	Database		
Logical Structure	EMPLOYEE	(Relationship)	DEPARTMENT	(Relationship)
		EMPLOYEE		PART

FIG. 2.   Logical structure.

provided the capability not only for sequential accessing but also for random (or direct) accessing of records. With *direct access (q.v.)*, any record in a file can be retrieved without looking first at the records preceding it. Techniques for implementing direct access usually involve some method for translating a *key* (or a composite of several keys) that identify the record sought into the address (absolute or relative) of the corresponding record on the device on which it is stored. This translation is normally done via an index (or indexes) or a key-to-address transformation function (sometimes called a *hashing* function) that computes the address of the record from the key (or keys) (*see* SEARCHING). Among the various access methods that have been developed are the sequential, indexed sequential, and direct access methods.

Files and Databases   The popularity of database management systems and the rather loose use of the term *database* has led to some confusion between a file and a database. One basic difference is their usage pattern. The use of a file is usually limited to one user or a few users, and there is only one logical view of the file, which is shared by the (usually small number of) application programs that access the file. On the other hand, a database brings together a variety of data and integrates it in such a way that it is available for a variety of users, with each user possibly having a different logical view of the database. In trying to make a clear distinction between a file and a database, some define a file as a collection of occurrences of records of one type and a database as a collection of occurrences of records of several types with specific relationships among the record types. Fig. 2 illustrates this distinction.

Kinds of Files   The word *file* is used in many ways in data processing. Examples are input file, output file, master file, scratch file (*q.v.*), temporary file, card file, job file, and program file. Although the unmodified use of the term *file* usually means a data file holding data on "real-world" entities, some files are specifically called *program files*, since they contain programs stored in source or object form.

BILLY G. CLAYBROOK

FILE COMPRESSION.   *See* DATA COMPRESSION AND COMPACTION.

FILE SERVER

For articles on related subjects *see* CACHE MEMORY; DISTRIBUTED SYSTEMS; LOCAL AREA NETWORK; and WORKSTATION.

The increasing power of low-cost computers has brought about a revolution in computing. The traditional computing center of the 1970s, characterized by a small number of centralized mainframe computers shared by all users in an organization, has been supplanted by workstations (*q.v.*) and personal computers located in departmental user rooms and private offices. With the increased number of machines came the need to move data and files from one machine to another. One approach to solving the file transfer problem is to connect the machines to a network and provide primitives that allow users to copy files from one machine to another. This approach works best when the number of files that need to be exchanged is small. A second approach is to place shared data on a *file server* and have individual machines access data files located on the remote file server rather than on a local disk.

The file server approach is an example of *client-server* interaction. Clients executing on the local machine forward all file requests (e.g. open, close, read, write, and seek) to the remote file server. The server accepts a client's request, performs its associated operation, and returns a response to the client. Indeed, if client software is structured *transparently*, the client need not even be aware that files being accessed physically reside on machines located elsewhere on the network (*see* TRANSPARENCY).

The file server approach has several benefits. First, multiple machines can access shared files concurrently. Files are no longer stored on individual machines; they are stored on the file server where they can be accessed by all client machines. Thus, a user can run the same programs on the same data files regardless of which client machine is being used. This has the advantage that users can use any of a set of machines, rather than just the machine on which their files reside. Second, the cost of supporting and maintaining one large file server is less than the corresponding cost of maintaining separate file systems on each machine. Indeed, client machines need not even have disk drives. Larger disk drives have a lower cost per megabyte than smaller drives, and it is easier to perform such maintenance functions as file backups on one machine than on many.

The use of file servers on a network raises many design issues. A server can either be a *disk server* or a *file server*. A disk server presents a raw disk interface through which client machines read and write disk sectors. Disk servers are primarily useful as a backing store for swapping (*q.v.*) or paging. In contrast, a file server provides access to files. Clients open files, read and write file contents, etc. All details about how the file system is represented on the physical device is hidden within the server. When a client opens a file, the client's operating system forwards the open request across the network to the file server and waits for the server's response.

Because files are accessed across a network, the performance of remote operations is generally lower than when accessing a local disk. To improve performance, network file systems use *cacheing* techniques (*see* CACHE MEMORY). The client, server, or both maintain a cache of recently used file pages. Before the client forwards a request to the remote server, it checks to see if the request can be satisfied using information in the local cache. If the information resides in the cache, the file pages are retrieved directly from the cache, and the request need not be sent to the server at all, reducing latencies (access times - *q.v.*). Likewise, the server consults its local cache before issuing input-output commands to the disk device. Because file reference strings display similar locality to page reference strings in virtual memory systems (*q.v.*), caches can improve average access times by an order of magnitude or more.

Although cacheing improves access time performance, it also raises *cache coherency* issues. For example, suppose that two machines have been accessing a file at the same time, and the contents of the file resides in both client caches. If a user on one machine deletes the file, a user on the other machine may find that the file still exists because the client finds it in its local cache. To keep caches consistent, changing or deleting a file on one machine must update the caches on all other machines in the distributed network. Special protocols are used to solve such problems. For example, a server may specify that a file can be cached by only one client at a time, or disable caching completely for those files that are being shared.

File servers must also address the problem of *authentication*. That is, if a client requests file pages, how can the server be sure that the client is really who he or she claims to be? In a networked environment, an unauthorized client may masquerade as another in an attempt to access sensitive data stored on the file sever. Authentication is handled by using cryptographic techniques (*see* CRYPTOGRAPHY, COMPUTERS IN). Before authorizing access, the file server forwards the request to an *authentication server*. The messages exchanged by the file and authentication servers are encrypted using keys that only the two servers share, insuring that the authentication server can be trusted. The authentication server verifies access rights of the client (perhaps by exchanging messages directly with the client, using another set of private keys), and then returns its response to the file server.

Another aspect of file server design is whether the server should be *stateful* or *stateless*. Upon machine reboots, a stateless server retains no knowledge about the files client machines are using. When a client makes a request, each request contains complete information needed to service it. For example, when reading a file sequentially, each request contains the starting and ending byte offsets of the desired information rather than requesting "the next 1,024 bytes." In contrast, stateful servers keep track of which clients are using files and in what ways. Such information is important for maintaining cache consistency and for providing such services as exclusive file locks. The main drawback of stateful servers is that rebooting the server interrupts all client applications that were accessing files at the time the server went down. The server must reject all requests related to file accesses initiated before the server rebooted.

Refererences

1988. Tanenbaum, Andrew. *Computer Networks*, 2nd Ed. Englewood Cliffs, NJ: Prentice-Hall.

1990. Comer, Douglas E. *Internetworking with TCP/IP: Principles, Protocols, and Architecture*, 2nd Ed. Englewood Cliffs, NJ: Prentice-Hall.

THOMAS NARTEN

FINITE ELEMENT METHOD

For articles on related subjects *see* COMPUTER-AIDED ENGINEERING; NUMERICAL ANALYSIS; PARTIAL DIFFERENTIAL EQUATIONS; SCIENTIFIC APPLICATIONS; and SPLINE.

The *finite element method* applies to a broad range of engineering problems and attracts theoreticians and practitioners from many disciplines. It provides the formalism for reducing the continuum to a finite-dimensional space for numerical resolution of complicated field problems with digital computers. The space of interest is partitioned into a finite number of nonoverlapping elements (Fig. 1). A basis is defined within each element, and the field within the element is determined from a stationarity condition with the basis-function combining-coefficients as free parameters. The element parameters are constrained to yield appropriate interelement continuity consistent with the underlying stationarity principle. Engineering problems are thus reduced to systems of

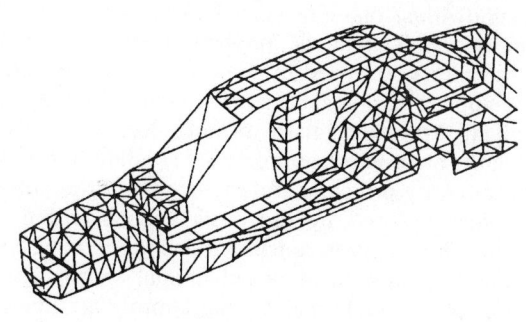

FIG. 1   Idealization of a car body using finite elements.

algebraic equations that are solved by a variety of methods.

The finite element method encompasses representation of the physical situation by some differential, integral, or integro-differential equation, partitioning of the space of interest into elements, developing a stationarity principle and an associated approximation space in terms of element basis functions, generating a system of algebraic equations satisfied by the basis function expansion coefficients, solving these equations, and displaying the phases of the computation for evaluation.

The finite element method is an outgrowth of analysis and computation in the 1940s. Some early finite difference formulations based on integration over elements are equivalent to finite element methods. The term "finite element" and modern development was introduced in the field of structural mechanics. Two- and three-dimensional structural problems were solved with a finite element formalism based on a variational principle relating to energy minimization over a continuous approximation space. The remarkable success of this formalism together with the explosion in computer capabilities led to rapid expansion of the method to include more general principles with relaxed continuity constraints. The method was applied to virtually all scientific investigation involving field functions. Analysis was generalized from linear statics to nonlinear and time-dependent problems and to interaction of different fields.

Hundreds of millions of dollars are spent worldwide each year on finite element analysis. There has been an exponential growth of publications on finite element topics. Hundreds of user-oriented program packages are available. An outstanding reference work is the *Finite Element Handbook*, edited by H. Kardestuncer, which describes the roles of various scientific disciplines in finite element analysis and implementation. The ubiquity of finite elements in scientific research is evidenced by the broad spectrum of scientists contributing to its development and application.

Mathematicians concerned with formulation and error estimation apply techniques of functional analysis, classical approximation theory, and the theory of partial differential equations. This may either guide practitioners in use of existing techniques or suggest new procedures. The functional analysis draws heavily on theory related to Sobolev Spaces. A priori error estimates guide selection of approximation spaces and stationarity principles. A posteriori estimates facilitate adaptive refinement by either subdividing or increasing the degrees of freedom within identified elements. Mapping theorems and algebraic geometry are used in analyzing the relationships among approximation spaces and element geometry. An underlying theme in mainstream finite element analysis is relating the error in the approximate solution to the chosen stationarity principle and the degree of the polynomial space spanned by the basis vectors within the elements. Thus, a prime consideration in generating basis functions is achievement of polynomial approximation within elements while maintaining appropriate interelement continuity. The "isoparametric" element (introduced by engineers and subsequently analyzed by

mathematicians) is the most prevalent device for accomplishing this with elements other than the simple triangles, rectangles, tetrahedra, and rectangular bricks shown in Fig. 2.

Engineers examine element geometry and appropriate stationarity principles for specific application and often introduce new formalisms that are then analyzed with greater rigor by mathematicians. Among the areas investigated with finite elements are: solid mechanics, fluid mechanics, biomechanics, heat transfer, geomechanics, aeromechanics, coupled systems (fluid-structure-thermal interaction), chemical reactions, neutron flux, plasmas, acoustics, materials processes, and electric and magnetic fields. The early finite element development was used almost exclusively by engineers in analysis of structures. As the applications have expanded, the engineers responsible for simulation of physical phenomena have developed and analyzed new methods and have guided much of the growth in technology. As techniques have matured, the role of theoreticians has become more pronounced. This interplay of theoretical and practical development has enhanced adoption of finite elements in almost every area of scientific computation.

Computer scientists and numerical analysts address data structuring, automatic mesh generation (see Fig. 3), and efficient software generation as a function of hardware and interactive computer graphics (*q.v.*). All have addressed methodology for efficient numerical solution of the finite element equations that are characteristically large banded systems. Although the earlier finite element

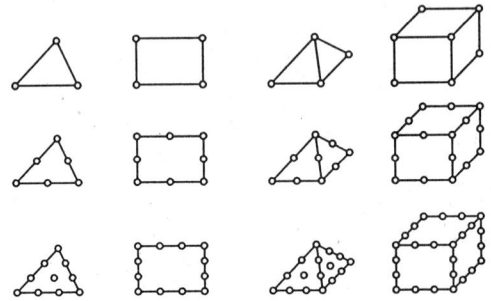

FIG. 2   Some common two-dimensional and three-dimensional finite elements.

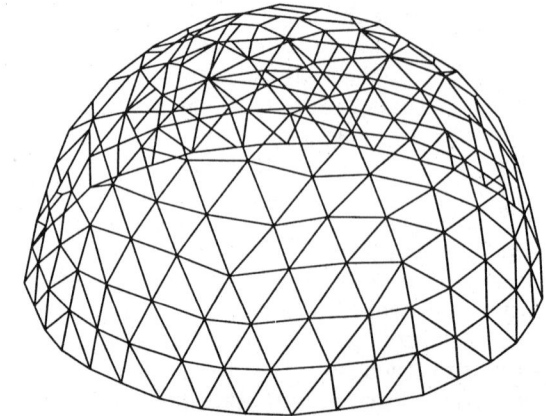

FIG. 3   Computer-generated mesh pattern.

programs and many of the existing software packages use direct solution techniques, increased size of problems solved has led to more extensive application of iterative methods. A popular family of solution techniques entails iteration on the difference between an approximate sparse factorization and the actual sparse system. This balances direct and iterative techniques as a function of complexity and computer characteristics. The current area of greatest concern is parallel computation on emerging architectures.

References

Handbooks

1983. Noor, A. K., and Pilkey, W. D. *State-of-the-Art Surveys on Finite Element Technology*, ASME (with a list of textbooks and monographs on finite element technology).

1987. Kardestuncer, H. and Norrie, D. H. *Finite Element Handbook*. New York: McGraw-Hill.

Bibliographies

1975. Whiteman, J. R. *A Bibliography for Finite Elements*. New York: Academic Press.

1976. Norrie, D. and deVries, G. *Finite Element Bibliography*. New York: Plenum Press.

1985. Noor, A. K. "Books on Finite Element Technology," *J. Finite Elements Anal. Design* **1** (1).

Selected Texts on Fundamentals and Foundations

1972. Aziz, A. K. and Babuska, I. *The Mathematical Foundations of the Finite Element Method with Applications to Partial Differential Equations*. New York: Academic Press.

1973. Fix, G. J. and Strang, G. *An Analysis of the Finite Element Method*. Englewood Cliffs, NJ: Prentice-Hall.

1974. deBoor, C. *Mathematical Aspects of Finite Elements in Partial Differential Equations*. New York: Academic Press.

1978. Ciarlet, P. G. *The Finite Element Method for Elliptic Problems*. Amsterdam: North Holland.

1978. Norrie, D. H. and deVries, G. *An Introduction to Finite Element Analysis*. New York: Academic Press.

1979. Desai, C. S. *Elementary Finite Element Method*. Englewood Cliffs, NJ: Prentice-Hall.

1981. Becker, E. B., Carey, G. F., and Oden, J. T. *Finite Elements: An Introduction*. Englewood Cliffs, NJ: Prentice-Hall.

1981. Cook, R. D. *Concepts and Applications of Finite Element Analysis*. 2nd ed. New York: John Wiley.

1982. Bathe, K. J. *Finite Element Procedure in Engineering Analysis*. Englewood Cliffs, NJ: Prentice-Hall.

1982. Huebner, K. H. and Thornton, E. A. *The Finite Element Method for Engineers*, 2nd ed., New York: Wiley Interscience.

1983. Carey, G. F. and Oden J. T. *Finite Elements: A Second Course*. Englewood Cliffs, NJ: Prentice-Hall.

1983. Irons, B. and Shrive, N. *Finite Element Primer*. New York: John Wiley.

1989. Zienkiewicz, O. C. *The Finite Element Method: Basic Concepts and Linear Applications*, 4th ed. New York: McGraw-Hill.

EUGENE L. WACHSPRESS

FINITE-STATE MACHINE. *See* SEQUENTIAL MACHINE.

FIRMWARE

For articles on related subjects *see* EMULATION; MICROPROGRAMMING; READ-ONLY MEMORY; and SOFTWARE.

Early in the history of digital computation, the useful distinction was made between *hardware*, the tangible componentry of a computing system, and *software*, the collection of instructions that directed what was to be computed. While it was true that software had to be recorded on some tangible medium, such as punched cards or paper or magnetic tape (early), or, later, hard or floppy disks (*q.v.*), the software itself was considered to be pure information and hence intangible. Supporting the "softness" of this interpretation was the fact that, when recorded on a magnetic medium, software could be modified with ease.

The question soon arose as to what to call programs recorded indelibly on a medium such as read-only memory (ROM) or embodied in hard-wired computer circuitry. The result was no longer "soft" enough to be modified, but, since it was so intimately bonded to hardware, the term coined was *firmware*.

Early personal computers (*q.v.*), such as the Apple and the Radio Shack TRS-80 maintained firmware copies of an interpreter for the language Basic in ROM so that the language was on tap immediately upon booting (*see* BOOT and REBOOT), but the term firmware originated as far back as the mid-1960s. In order to help the large base of IBM 1400 series (*q.v.*) users convert to the new but incompatible IBM 360 series (*q.v.*) with minimum disruption, IBM provided optional firmware that could be added to the 360 that allowed it to execute 1400 series programs through *emulation*, hardware-assisted simulation. Given adequate memory, any general purpose digital computer can execute programs written for any other through use of a *simulator*, a program that interprets each target machine instruction and executes whatever sequence of host machine instructions is needed to do the same thing, bit for bit. Interpretation is naturally slow, but implementation of key parts of the simulator as firmware provides a significant increase in speed of execution.

EDWIN D. REILLY

FLOATING-POINT ARITHMETIC. *See* ARITHETIC, COMPUTER.

FLOPPY DISK

For articles on related subjects *see* HARD DISK; LATENCY; and MEMORY: AUXILIARY.

The *floppy disk*, once called a minidisk, is the primary medium for getting voluminous information into and out of a microcomputer system. Such a disk is called a *floppy disk* in distinction to a *hard disk* (*q.v.*) because the earliest floppy disks, themselves flexible, were encased in a square cardboard envelope that preserved the flexibility of the ensemble.

The floppy disk subsystem consists of a controller card that is inserted into a *slot* connected to the expansion bus, a disk drive to read and write the disk itself, and a cable that connects the card to the disk drive and is used to pass data and control signals between the two.

Floppy disks are used to load programs into a computer, to exchange data between computers that use a compatible format, and to back up information stored on hard disks and other high-capacity storage devices. On systems with no hard disk, the floppy disk contains the operating system, which boots the computer as well as application programs and associated data.

Floppy disks are made by depositing a metallic oxide material on a mylar substrate. The oxide coating is ferromagnetic and responds to the magnetic fields generated by the heads in the disk drive. For this reason, care must be taken when handling floppy disks in the presence of strong magnetic fields.

The disks come in a variety of sizes. The 8-inch disks used with early 8-bit CP/M personal computers are now obsolete. Currently, the most popular sizes are 5.25-inch and 3.5-inch. Depending on their formatting and on the drive they are used on, 5.25-inch disks have capacities of either 360 kilobytes or 1.2 megabytes, while 3.5-inch disks are available in 720KB and 1.44MB capacities. Unlike 5.25-inch disks, the 3.5-inch disk is encased in hard plastic and accessed inside the disk drive through a movable metallic slide. Since, externally at least, such disks are no longer flexible, the name *diskette* has now become more common than floppy disk.

On a 5.25-inch diskette, a square notch is covered with an adhesive tab to prevent accidental erasure of information. A sliding plastic tab covers a square hole to make a 3.5-inch disk read-only.

Each of these formats uses both sides of the disk and are hence known as double-sided formats. Each disk drive must therefore have two read/write heads. Information is layed down in concentric *tracks* that are magnetically etched by a formatting program that comes with the operating system. Typically, each track is subdivided into *sectors* and each sector into bytes. On the IBM-PC and PC-compatibles (*q.v.*), the double-sided double density (DSDD) 5.25-inch floppy has 40 tracks of nine sectors each, on both sides of the diskette. Each sector holds 512 bytes of information. The smaller 3.5-inch diskettes typically squeeze 80 tracks onto a disk and also double the number of sectors per track to 18 and retain the 512 bytes per sector count. This means that the highest density 3.5-inch diskettes can hold 1.44 million characters (1.44 Mb).

The disk drive consists essentially of two motors and some controlling circuitry. One motor drives a spindle that spins the disk usually at about 300 RPM. Control circuitry, either optical or electronic, precisely regulates this speed. A second precision *stepping motor* incrementally moves the heads from track to track to read and write information. It actually counts the number of tracks as it moves. It is slower than the *voice coil actuator*, which flies right to the proper track, but drives built with the latter technology, while faster, require more complicated electronics and are thus more expensive and prone to problems.

It was in the 1960s that floppy disks first appeared. IBM used them in its System 30 series minicomputers. These 8-inch floppies could hold almost a million bytes and made the computers easy to use and enormously flexible.

The physical size of the disk drive soon became a consideration as computers got smaller. Even 3.5-inch drives are too big, heavy, and power hungry to satisfy the manufacturers of portable laptop computers (*q.v.*). A 2-inch diskette was introduced in the late 1980s, but it is not yet clear that this standard will catch on.

The floppy disk has made it very easy to share information and programs. The process of making copies is quick and inexpensive. Diskettes are easy to mail and carry; the 3.5-inch floppy even fits in a shirt pocket. Software piracy and the spread of computer viruses (*q.v.*) are a direct consequence of the ease of copying. Even the greenest user can learn to make copies without the assistance and scrutiny of others.

It isn't likely that diskettes will get much smaller, but the computer industry is experimenting with storage techniques that do not involve moving parts. The motors, coils, spinning hubs, and flying heads are the first parts to fail or go out of alignment. They are the primary source of disk drive problems. Semiconductor devices must be made reliable, inexpensive, and interchangeable before they replace the floppy disk, but potential replacements hold the prospect of higher-capacity "diskettes," or whatever replaceable units of storage will be called, whose contents can be accessed without rotational delay (latency - *q.v.*).

STEPHEN J. ROGOWSKI

FLOWCHART

For articles on related subjects *see* DATAFLOW; and DOCUMENTATION.

Definition   A *flowchart* is a graphic means of documenting a sequence of operations. Flowcharts serve as a pictorial means of communicating from one person to another the time-ordering of events or actions. As a pictorial format, flowcharts have been the subject of both an International and an American National Standard (ANSI, 1970, and Chapin, 1979). Flowcharts go by many other names, including block diagram, flow diagram, system chart, run diagram, process chart, and logic chart.

Format   The two main varieties of flowchart are the *flow diagram* and the *system chart*. A flow diagram gives a detailed view of what is shown as a single process in a system chart. Flow diagrams and system charts use different pictorial conventions, but also share certain conventions. The basic outlines shown in Fig. 1 are common to both. Also common is the reading convention—top to bottom, left to right—and the practice of labeling the

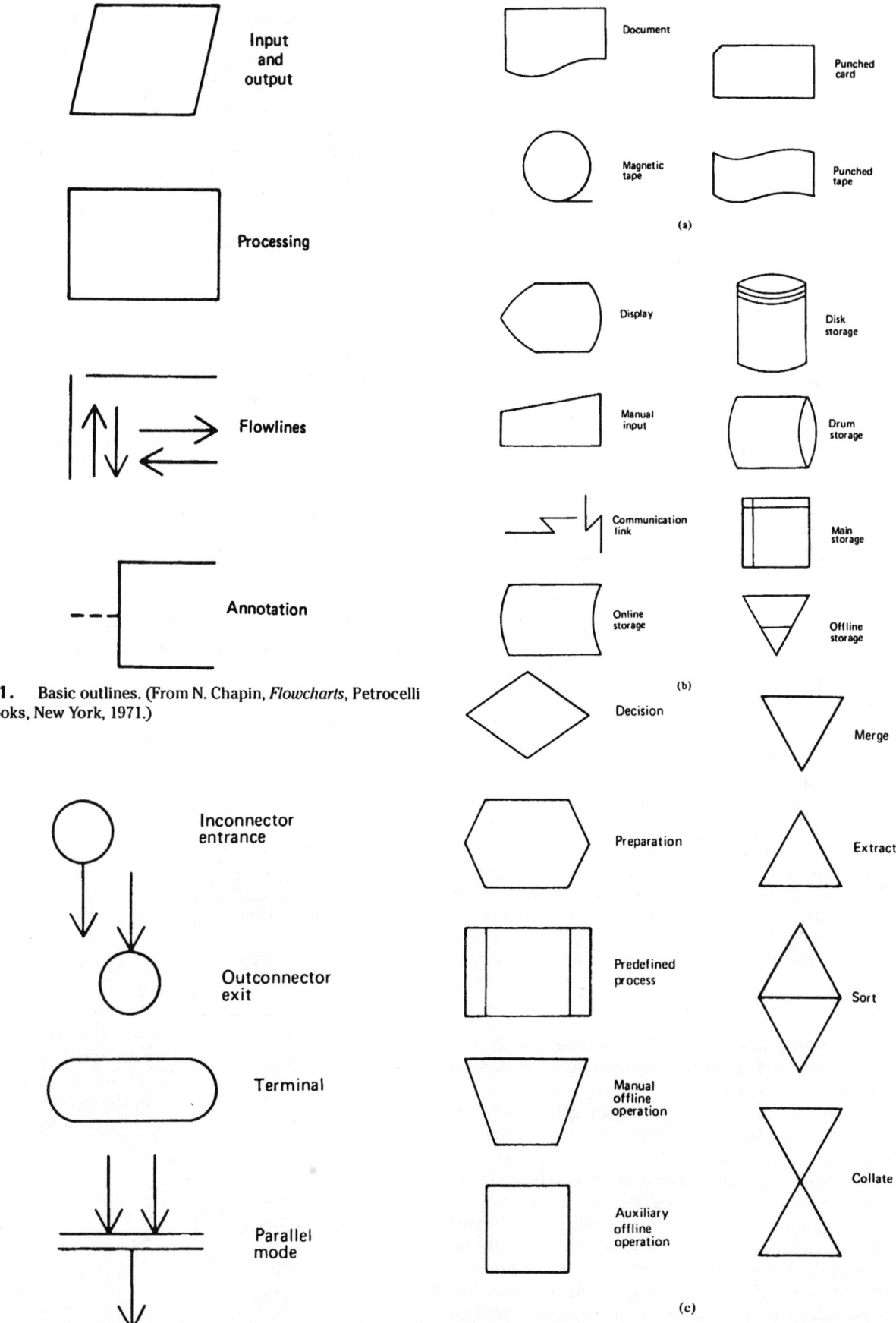

FIG. 1. Basic outlines. (From N. Chapin, *Flowcharts*, Petrocelli Books, New York, 1971.)

FIG. 2. Additional outlines. (From N. Chapin, *Flowcharts*, Petrocelli Books, New York, 1971.)

FIG. 3. Specialized outlines. (a) Media. (b) Equipment. (c) Processes. (From N. Chapin *Flowcharts*, Petrocelli Books, New York, 1971.)

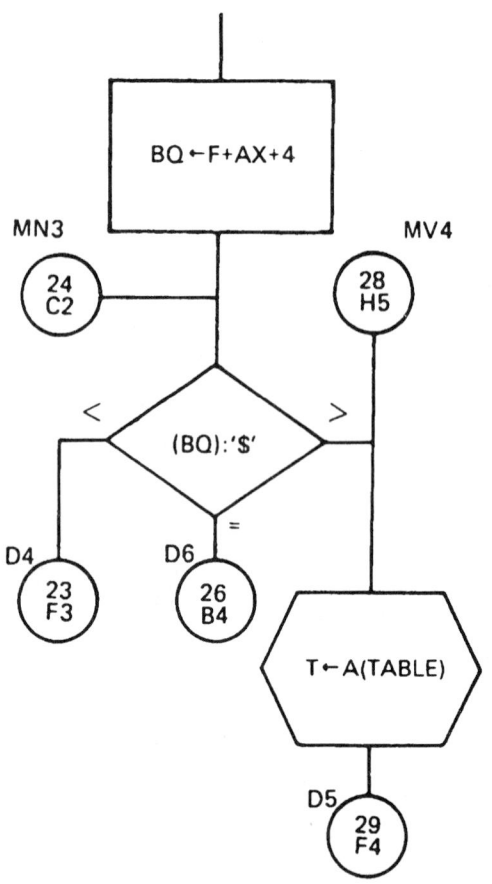

FIG. 4. Entry and exit flowlines in a flow diagram. (From N. Chapin, *Flowcharts*, Petrocelli Books, New York, 1971.)

outlines internally to identify data and processes (Chapin, 1971). The additional outlines shown in Fig. 2 are all used in flow diagrams. The parallel mode outline also finds some use in system charts.

System charts are pictorially richer. While analysts can prepare system charts using only the basic outlines of Fig. 1, analysts often selectively substitute some of the specialized outlines for media, equipment, and processes, as shown in Fig. 3. Except for the decision and predefined processes, the specialized outlines are not used in flow diagrams.

Use: System Chart Analysts most commonly prepare system charts to show graphically the interactions in execution among the programs of a system. The inputs and outputs of each program are shown, either in a generalized form using the basic outlines, or in a particularized form using the specialized outlines. Analysts may prepare system charts at a logical level (using the basic outlines) or at a physical level (using the specialized outlines).

In preparing a system chart, analysts usually regard each program's execution as a single process with the respective inputs above and connected to the process, and with the respective outputs below and connected to the process. This gives a sandwich-like arrangement to the outlines in a system chart: a layer of input data (bread), followed by a process (the filling), followed by a

layer of output data (bread). Often, the output data of one process becomes the input data for a subsequent process, giving a multi-layer sandwich effect (a compound system chart). A simple system chart shows only a single process, which could be for any level of software from system to subroutine.

Analysts also may prepare system charts for other situations that are characterized by an alternation of data and action. Some general examples are the situations where a dataflow diagram could be used, or where an integrated data engineering facility diagram (IDEF) could be used, or where a state transition diagram could be used.

Use: Program Flowchart Analysts most commonly prepare program flowcharts or flow diagrams to describe in step-by-step detail the time-sequence of functions, actions, or events. Such sequences usually comprise a process that takes in input data and produces output data. A flow diagram (not to be confused with a dataflow diagram) begins and ends with a labeled terminal outline (Fig. 2) to mark each entrance and exit. Then successive outlines connected by flow arrows depict the ac-

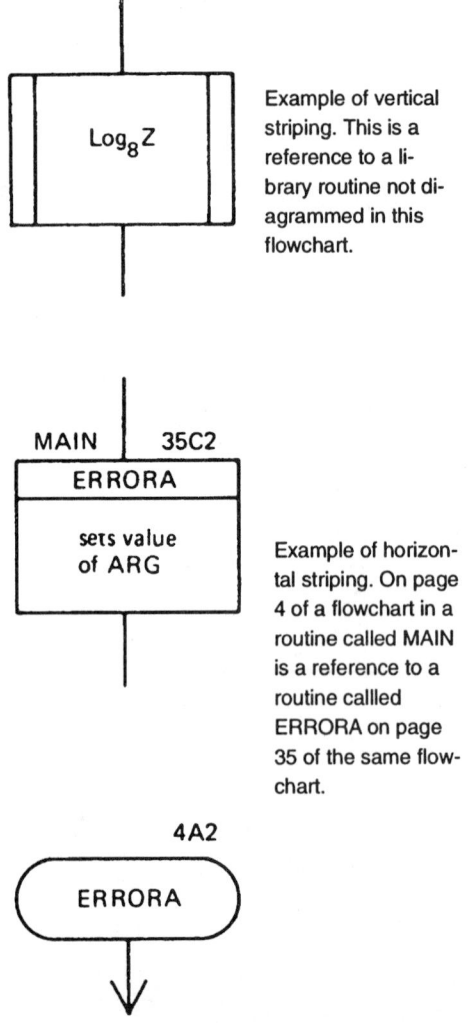

FIG. 5. Conventions for striping and references. (From N. Chapin, *Flowcharts*, Petrocelli Books New York, 1971.)

ceptance of data as input, the processing steps taken, and the disposition of data as output. No sandwich convention applies, and decisions are shown explicitly, as illustrated in Fig. 4. Also as shown there, analysts often use connectors to reduce clutter (since flow diagrams often get large) and to provide cross-referencing and location annotation. Thus, in Fig. 4, the inconnector marked 28H5 refers to the outconnector H5 on page 28, and the H5 itself refers to a grid pattern on the page. Analysts often show software component or entry names, such as the MV4 or D6 in Fig. 4. Two forms of reference to more detail are also provided by striping conventions, as shown in Fig. 5.

Alternatives Historically, analysts drew flowcharts by hand. Currently, some popular CASE (*q.v.*) software tools facilitate drawing and revising flowcharts. Flowcharts have been declining in favor as alternatives have appeared, such as the dataflow diagram and IDEF noted earlier. The term *structured flowchart* usually refers to either Chapin charts (Chapin, 1974) or to Nassi-Shneiderman diagrams (Nassi, 1973) (*see* STRUCTURED PROGRAMMING). Warnier-Orr diagrams provide a way of depicting both data and software structures hierarchically (Warnier, 1974), as do *tree charts* (*see* TREE).

References

1970. Chapin, Ned. *et al.* "Full report of the Flowchart Committee on ANSI Standard X3.5–1970," *SIGPLAN Notices,* **14**, 3:16–27 (March).

1971. Chapin, Ned. *Flowcharts.* New York: Petrocelli Books.

1973. Nassi, Isaac, and Shneiderman, Ben. "Flowchart techniques for structured programming," *SIGPLAN Notices,* **8**, 8:12–26 (August).

1974. Chapin, Ned. "New format for flowcharts," *Software Practice and Experience,* **4**, 4: 341–357 (October–December).

1974. Warnier, Jean Dominique. *Logical Construction of Programs.* New York: Van Nostrand Reinhold.

1979. ANSI. *American National Standard Flowchart Symbols and Their Usage in Information Processing, X3.5–1970.* New York: American National Standards Institute.

NED CHAPIN

FONT. *See* DESKTOP PUBLISHING; METAFONT; and TEXT EDITING SYSTEMS.

FORMAL LANGUAGES

For articles on related subjects *see* AUTOMATA THEORY; BACKUS-NAUR FORM; CHOMSKY HIERARCHY; GRAMMARS; LANGUAGE PROCESSORS; LANGUAGE TRANSLATION; METALANGUAGE; REGULAR EXPRESSION; TURING MACHINE; and WELL-FORMED FORMULA.

Languages and Grammars Formal languages are abstract mathematical objects used to model the syntax of programming languages or (less successfully) of natural languages such as English. For example, consider a simple English sentence, such as

THE MAN ATE THE APPLE.

Let us assume that individual English words are indecomposable objects. Then the study of English syntax attempts to answer the question: When is a string of words a grammatically correct English sentence? And when it is a sentence, how can it be parsed into its grammatical components?

To model this situation, we let V be a finite set of symbols, called a *vocabulary.* In the previous example, V contains the four indecomposable words (in this context, called *symbols* or *letters*): APPLE, ATE, MAN, THE. More generally, V might contain all English words and punctuation marks. Let V^* denote all finite-length strings of symbols from V. (It is mathematically convenient to include in V^* the *empty string* of length zero.) Then a *formal language* L is simply a set of strings from V^*. For example, if V^* is the set of all finite sequences of English words, then L could be the subset of V^* consisting of all grammatically correct sentences. Although V is always finite, in most cases of interest L will be infinite, and we will wish to have a finitely specified way of generating, or recognizing, or *parsing* the strings in L.

The sample sentence given earlier can be parsed by the treelike diagram in Fig. 1, where $\langle S \rangle, \langle NP \rangle, \langle VP \rangle, \langle A \rangle, \langle N \rangle,$ and $\langle V \rangle$ are six variables ranging over all *sentences, noun phrases, verb phrases, articles, nouns,* and *verbs,* respectively. Using the *rewriting* rules in Fig. 2, it is possible to generate our sample sentence from the variable $\langle S \rangle$. The generation proceeds as follows:

$$\begin{aligned}
\langle S \rangle &\Rightarrow \langle NP \rangle \langle VP \rangle \Rightarrow \langle A \rangle \langle N \rangle \langle VP \rangle \\
&\Rightarrow \langle A \rangle \langle N \rangle \langle V \rangle \langle NP \rangle \Rightarrow \langle A \rangle \langle N \rangle \langle V \rangle \langle A \rangle \langle N \rangle \\
&\Rightarrow \text{THE} \langle N \rangle \langle V \rangle \langle A \rangle \langle N \rangle \\
&\Rightarrow \text{THE MAN} \langle V \rangle \langle A \rangle \langle N \rangle \\
&\Rightarrow \text{THE MAN ATE} \langle A \rangle \langle N \rangle \\
&\Rightarrow \text{THE MAN ATE THE} \langle N \rangle \\
&\Rightarrow \text{THE MAN ATE THE APPLE}
\end{aligned}$$

With these rules, we can also generate various improbable but grammatically correct sentences such as THE APPLE ATE THE MAN, and with more rules we could generate more sentences. Rewriting schemes of this sort were introduced by the linguist Noam Chomsky, who called

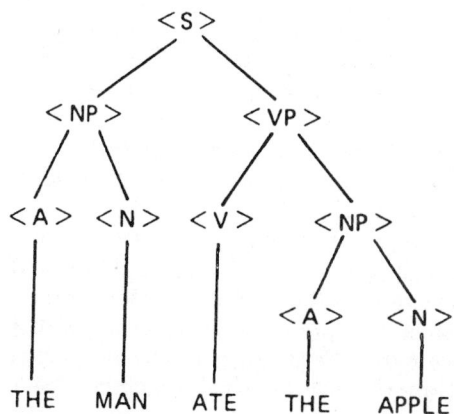

FIG. 1. Tree for parsing sentence.

$$
\begin{array}{rcl}
<S> & \rightarrow & <NP><VP> \\
<NP> & \rightarrow & <A><N> \\
<VP> & \rightarrow & <V><NP> \\
<A> & \rightarrow & \text{THE} \\
<V> & \rightarrow & \text{ATE} \\
<N> & \rightarrow & \text{MAN} \\
<N> & \rightarrow & \text{APPLE}
\end{array}
$$

FIG. 2.   Rewriting rules.

them *context-free grammars*. Chomsky observed that these grammars are not good models for the syntax of natural languages, but it was soon discovered that they do closely model the syntax of programming languages, and for this reason they have been studied in great detail.

To see a simple example of context-free rewriting rules that give rise to an infinite language, suppose that the vocabulary consists of two abstract symbols a and b, and let S be a variable. Then, using the rules $S \rightarrow aSb$ and $S \rightarrow ab$, we can generate the infinite language

$$
L = \{a^n b^n \mid n \geq= 1\} = \{ab, aabb, aaabbb, \ldots\} .
$$

Rewriting rules of this type are called "context free" because they permit any occurrence of a variable within a string to be rewritten without regard to the context in which that variable occurs. By contrast, a rewriting rule like $aXab \rightarrow aYZcab$ is not context-free. It is called *context sensitive*, since it allows X to be rewritten as YZc only when X occurs in the context $s_1 a\_abs_2$, where s_1 and s_2 are arbitrary strings.

To describe different kinds of grammars more precisely, let us define a *phrase-structure* grammar to be a quadruple $G = (V_N, V_T, P, S)$, where

1. V_N is a finite vocabulary of non-terminal symbols or variables.
2. V_T is a finite vocabulary of terminal symbols.
3. P is a finite set of rewriting rules (also called *productions*) of the form $a \rightarrow \beta$, where a is a nonempty string of variables and β is an arbitrary string of variables and terminal symbols.
4. S is a particular variable called the *start* variable.

For all strings s_1 and s_2 we may write $s_1 a s_2 \Rightarrow s_1 \beta s_2$ if $a \rightarrow \beta$ is a production of the grammar G. Then the language generated by G is the set of all strings t of *terminal symbols* such that

$$
S \Rightarrow s_1 \Rightarrow s_2 \Rightarrow \ldots \Rightarrow s_n \Rightarrow t
$$

for some choice of intermediate strings $s_1, s_2, \ldots s_n$. The intermediate strings may consist of both variables and terminal symbols.

Let a, a_1, and a_2 denote arbitrary strings of variables and terminal symbols, and let A and B denote variables. If the productions in G have the specialized form $a_1 A a_2 \rightarrow a_1 \beta a_2$, where β represents any non-empty string, then G is a *context-sensitive* grammar. (Frequently, a grammar is called context sensitive if the productions merely have the form $a \rightarrow \beta$, with β at least as long as a. These two definitions are in fact equivalent in the sense that the

same collection of languages is generated.) If the productions in the grammar G have the form $A \rightarrow a$, then G is context free. If the productions have the form $A \rightarrow w_1 B$ or $A \rightarrow w_2$, where w_1 and w_2 are strings of terminal symbols, then G is right-linear. A language is called a "phrase-structure" language, or a "context-sensitive," "context-free," or "right-linear" language, if it can be generated by a phrase-structure grammar, or a context-sensitive, context-free, or right-linear grammar, respectively.

The four types of grammars (phrase-structure, context-sensitive, context-free, and right-linear) are also known as type 0, type 1, type 2, and type 3 grammars, respectively. They form a grammatical hierarchy, called the *Chomsky hierarchy*. Among the four corresponding families of languages, the smallest family, the right-linear languages, is important because it turns out to consist precisely of those languages that can be recognized by finite-state automata. These languages arise in many different contexts, and they have the advantage of being very easy to parse.

The next family in the hierarchy, the family of context-free languages, is important because context-free languages are good approximations to the syntax of programming languages, even though this syntax is usually a little too complicated to be completely captured by context-free grammars. Context-sensitive languages are powerful enough to encompass any complications in syntax that may have been missed by the context-free model, but they are so general that they are difficult to work with. As a result, they have been studied less than the other models, and various attempts have been made to add to the power of context-free grammars without resorting to the full strength of context-sensitive productions. These efforts have produced various kinds of grammars that are more powerful than context-free grammars, although they are unfortunately more complicated as well: programmed grammars, macro grammars, indexed grammars, and others.

The largest family of languages in the Chomsky hierarchy, the family of phrase-structure languages, is an important family because it represents the largest class with which one is likely to be concerned when modeling natural or artificial languages. This is so because the family of phrase-structure languages is in fact the same as the family of all recursively enumerable languages—i.e. of all languages L such that membership of a string w in L can be verified by some algorithm (or, more precisely, by some Turing machine).

Languages and Equations   We have noted that context-free languages are good approximations to the syntax of many programming languages. Consider the following very simple example of syntax specifications in *Backus-Naur form*, or *BNF*:

⟨*digit*⟩ : : = 0 | 1 | 2 | 3 | 4 | 5 | 6 | 7 | 8 | 9
⟨*unsigned integer*⟩ : : = ⟨*digit*⟩ | ⟨*unsigned integer*⟩⟨*digit*⟩

This means that ⟨digit⟩ and ⟨unsigned integer⟩ are the smallest sets of strings satisfying the following conditions: 0, 1,..., 9 are digits (i.e. they are in the set ⟨digit⟩);

any digit is an unsigned integer; and any unsigned integer followed by a digit is an unsigned integer. Rewriting these equations in a more algebraic form, we obtain:

$$D = \text{"0"} + \text{"1"} + \cdots + \text{"9"}$$
$$U = D + U \cdot D$$

Consider these as abstract equations. What is their meaning? The unknowns U and D are variables whose values are languages; $X + Y$ denotes the union of the languages X and Y; $X \cdot Y$ denotes the product of the languages X and Y, obtained by concatenating the strings in X with those in Y : $X \cdot Y = \{xy \mid x \, \varepsilon \, X, y \, \varepsilon \, Y\}$; and "0," "1," etc., are constants denoting the languages consisting of just the single symbol 0, 1, etc. In general, the equations corresponding to BNF syntax descriptions can be more complicated than in our example. A typical equation might have the form

$$A = abBAAaAb + BaC + ba.$$

(The letters a and b are terminal symbols; A, B, and C are variables; and we have omitted the dot in products.) The operations $+$ and $\cdot$ are roughly analogous to addition and multiplication of numbers; only $\cdot$ is not commutative. (If X and Y are languages, $Y \cdot X$ is not generally the same as $Y \cdot X$.) If the product of languages were commutative, we could write the term $abBAAaAb$ as $aabbA^3B$. This would be similar to a fourth-degree term in a polynomial expression, except that the variables range over languages rather than numbers and the coefficient $aabb$ is a string of symbols instead of a number. Since the product of languages is not commutative, we cannot rearrange terms in this way, but we can still regard these equations as polynomial equations in non-commuting variables. In general, the right-hand side of each equation will be a finite sum of terms, and each term will be a string of variables and terminal symbols. A set of such equations always has a unique smallest solution, so it always makes sense to speak of the "smallest sets of strings" U and D satisfying equations like those in our original example. The languages definable in this way by polynomial equations turn out to be precisely the context-free languages.

As a simple example, the language $\{a^n b^n \mid n \geq 1\}$ can be specified either as the language generated by the context-free productions $S \rightarrow aSb$ and $S \rightarrow ab$ or as the smallest solution of the equation $S = aSb + ab$. Incidentally, note that this equation is a first-degree or "linear" equation, since each summand contains at most one occurrence of a variable. Languages defined by such equations are called "linear" context-free languages. They can also be characterized as the languages generated by linear context-free grammars; i.e. by context-free grammars having productions of the form $A \rightarrow a$, where the string a contains at most one occurrence of a variable. It should now be clear why right-linear grammars are so named.

In view of the preceding discussion, any programming language whose syntax can be specified in BNF is context-free. Generally, most but not all of the syntax of a programming language can be specified in BNF. So languages such as Pascal and Fortran are not quite context-free, but they are close to being so, and context-free languages are useful approximations to their syntax.

Languages and Automata The four families of languages in the Chomsky hierarchy can be obtained from automata as well as from grammars (*see* AUTOMATA THEORY). The phrase-structure languages are the languages accepted by Turing machines; the context-sensitive languages are the languages accepted by linear-bounded automata or *lba's*; the context-free languages are the languages accepted by pushdown automata; and the right-linear languages are the languages accepted by finite-state automata. For this reason, right-linear languages are sometimes called *finite-state* languages. Usually, however, right-linear languages are known as regular languages or regular sets. This terminology comes from Kleene's theorem, which states that a language is a finite-state language if and only if it can be represented by a *regular* expression. A regular expression is an expression that can be built up from individual strings by using the three operations $+$, $\cdot$, and $*$. The operations $+$ and $\cdot$ are the operations of union and product introduced earlier. (The symbol U is sometimes used instead of $+$, and the $\cdot$ may be omitted.) The operation $*$ is called the *Kleene closure* operation. If L is any set of strings, then L^* is defined to be the set of all strings that can be formed by concatenating sequences of strings from L: $L^* = \{s_1 s_2 \ldots s_n \mid n \geq 0, \text{ each } s_i \varepsilon L\}$. (By convention, the empty string is always in L^*.) For example, $(a + b)^* \cdot aaa \cdot (a + b)^*$ is a regular expression representing the set of all strings of a's and b's containing at least three consecutive a's.

Let us consider the relation between context-free languages and pushdown automata a little more closely. A pushdown automaton is a non-deterministic device having a memory consisting of a finite-state control and a pushdown stack. It receives its input one symbol at a time on request. Every context-free language L is the set of input strings accepted by some pushdown automaton P. In fact, we can always find a pushdown automaton P for L that operates in real time; i.e. one that uses up one input letter on every move. This means that P recognizes strings in L very quickly—in fact, in an amount of time proportional to the length of the input string. The catch is that P is a non-deterministic device. It is credited with accepting an input string w if there is *any* sequence of choices of moves (i.e. any sequence of "guesses") it can make while processing w that will lead it to an accepting mode, even though there may be other choices that do not lead to an accepting mode. But if we want to simulate P in the real world, we would systematically have to test every sequence of choices that P could make.

Since P might have several choices available to it on each move, this simulation could take exponentially more time than P does. This might suggest that the task of parsing a context-free language can be prohibitively time consuming, but in fact it is not. General-purpose, context-free parsing algorithms can be designed to require only time n^3, where n is the length of the input by using *dynamic programming* (*see* ALGORITHMS, CLASSIFICATION OF). One of the most popular such algorithms is *Earley's algorithm*. It takes time n^3 in the worst case, but for many context-free grammars it takes only a linear amount of time. The n^3 bound for an all-purpose, context-free parser can be improved slightly, but it is not yet known how much improvement is possible.

A non-deterministic pushdown automaton is a theoretical construct that is time consuming to simulate in the real world. So, in searching for classes of context-free languages that are easy to parse, it is reasonable to consider *deterministic* context-free languages—those languages that can be recognized by a deterministic pushdown automaton. As one might expect, all deterministic context-free languages can be parsed rapidly, in fact, in a linear amount of time. But not all context-free languages are deterministic. For example, the set of all binary strings (strings of 0s and 1s) that are palindromes is context-free but not deterministic because a pushdown automaton for this language must of necessity operate something like this: Store the first half of the input string on the stack, *guess* when half the input has been read, and use the stack to verify that the second half of the input agrees symbol by symbol, in reverse order, with the first half.

So, non-deterministic pushdown acceptors are more powerful than deterministic ones. Are the corresponding statements true for the other kinds of automata used to characterize the families of languages in the Chomsky hierarchy? For finite-state automata and for Turing machines, the answer is no. It is easy to show that the non-deterministic versions of these devices are no more powerful than the deterministic versions. In other words, the ability to make guesses may enable these devices to do their jobs more quickly, but it will not let them do anything that they could not have done without guessing. But for linear-bounded automata, it is still not known whether the non-deterministic version (which corresponds to the context-sensitive languages) is more powerful than the deterministic version.

This question, called the *lba* problem, can be recast in the following form: Can a Turing machine that performs a computation with the aid of guessing (i.e. of non-determinism), using just a linear amount of storage space, always be simulated by a comparably efficient Turing machine that does not need to guess? The analogous question for Turing machines that use a polynomially-bounded amount of computation time rather than a linear amount of storage space is the very important P = NP problem (*see* COMPUTATIONAL COMPLEXITY; NP-COMPLETE PROBLEMS). In both cases, the answer is thought to be no, but such questions are notoriously difficult and have so far resisted all efforts at solution.

References

1972. Aho, A. V. and Ullman, J. D. *The Theory of Parsing, Translation and Compiling.* Englewood Cliffs, NJ: Prentice-Hall.

1973. Salomaa, A. *Formal Languages.* New York: Academic Press.

1978. Harrison, M. A. *Introduction to Formal Language Theory.* Reading, MA: Addison-Wesley.

1979. Hopcroft, J. E. and Ullman, J. D. *Introduction to Automata Theory, Languages, and Computation.* Reading, MA: Addison-Wesley.

1988. Moll, R. N., Arbib, M. A. and Kfoury, A. J. *An Introduction to Formal Language Theory.* New York: Springer-Verlag.

JONATHAN GOLDSTINE

FORMAL METHODS FOR COMPUTER SYSTEMS

For articles on related subjects see HARDWARE VERIFICATION; PROGRAM SPECIFICATION; and PROGRAM VERIFICATION.

Formal methods used in developing and verifying software and hardware systems are mathematically-based techniques for describing and reasoning about system properties. Such formal methods provide frameworks within which people specify, develop, and verify systems in a systematic, rather than ad hoc, manner. Formal methods include the more specific activities of program specification, program verification, and hardware verification.

A method is formal if it has a sound mathematical basis, typically given by a formal specification language. This basis provides the means of precisely defining notions like consistency and completeness and, more relevantly, specification, implementation, and correctness. It provides the means of proving that a specification is realizable, proving that a system has been implemented correctly and proving properties of a system without necessarily running it to determine its behavior.

A formal method also addresses a number of pragmatic considerations: who uses it, what it is used for, when it is used, and how it is used. Most commonly, system designers use formal methods to specify and/or verify a system's desired behavioral and structural properties. However, anyone involved in any stage of system development can make use of formal methods. They can be used in the initial statement of a customer's requirements, through system design, implementation, software testing (*q.v.*), debugging (*q.v.*), software maintenance (*q.v.*), program verification, and evaluation.

Formal methods are used to reveal ambiguity, incompleteness, and inconsistency in a system. When used early in the system development process, they can reveal design flaws that otherwise might be discovered only during costly testing and debugging phases. When used later (e.g. in verification), they can help determine the correctness of a system implementation and the equivalence of different implementations.

For a method to be formal, it must have a well-defined mathematical basis. It need not address any pragmatic considerations, but a lack of such considerations would render it useless. Hence, a formal method should possess a set of guidelines or a "style sheet" that tells the user the circumstances under which the method can and should be applied, as well as how it can be applied most effectively.

One tangible product of applying a formal method is a formal specification. A specification serves as a contract, a valuable piece of documentation, and a means of communication between a client, a specifier, and an implementer. Because of their mathematical basis, formal specifications are more precise and usually more concise than informal ones.

Since a formal method is a method and not just a computer program or language, it may or may not have software tools to support it. If the syntax of a formal method's specification language is made explicit, providing standard syntax analysis tools for formal specifications would be appropriate. If the language's semantics are sufficiently restricted, varying degrees of semantic analysis can be performed with machine aids as well. For example, under certain circumstances in hardware verification, the process of proving the correctness of an implementation against a specification can be completely automated. Thus, formal specifications have the additional advantage over informal ones of being amenable to machine anaylsis and manipulation.

For more on the benefits of formal specification, see Meyer (1985). For more on the distinction between a method and a language, as well as what specifying a computer system means, see Lamport (1989).

References

1985. Meyer, B. "On Formalism in Specification," *IEEE Software*: **2**: 6–26 (Jan.).
1989. Lamport, L. "A Simple Approach to Specifying Concurrent Systems," *Communications of the ACM*, **32**: 32–45.

JEANNETTE M. WING

FORTH

For articles on related subjects *see* POLISH NOTATION; POST-SCRIPT; PROGRAMMING LANGUAGES; and REAL-TIME BUSINESS APPLICATIONS.

History   *Forth* is an interpretive programming language and environment invented in 1970 by Charles H. Moore, who founded the first Forth vendor, Forth, Inc. Forth was designed to be both the development and run-time environment for real-time applications such as controlling radio telescopes. Today, most of its commercial use continues to be in the fields of real-time business (*q.v.*), scientific, and hardware control applications.

Forth's early acceptance was due to its small size, interactive access to all of its components, and the ease with which a single user could understand the entire system and leverage it into a succinct application-oriented environment. Early implementations packaged the interpreter, the compiler, a disk operating system, a multitasking (*q.v.*) executive, an editor, and an assembler into resident memory of less than 16K bytes.

In 1978, the Forth Interest Group (FIG) was formed. Its members developed a model implementation of the language and, for a few dollars, distributed source code for the microprocessors that were common at the time. The FIG model demonstrated the accessibility of Forth by showing how it could be ported to new platforms with very little effort. The FIG model was widely embraced by hobbyists.

One consequence of this ease in implementing the language was an early and rapid proliferation of dialects. Subsequent standardization efforts culminated in differing standards established by equally influential users in 1979 and again in 1983. These standards were increasingly ignored, both because they were silent on important issues (e.g. vocabulary structure and search order) and too restrictive for emerging technologies.

In recent years, Forth has been shedding some of its handicaps. The proportion of non-commercial users and advocates has diminished, and there have been some notable commercial successes: a hand-held package tracker used by Federal Express, the VP Planner spreadsheet (*q.v.*), and Sun Microsystem's Open Boot PROM firmware (*q.v.*), delivered in all its SPARCstations. A far more serious standardization effort began, and a draft ANSI Standard was released for public review in October 1991.

The Language   As a language, Forth is both interpreted and compiled, is extensible, and uses postfix syntax and implicit parameter passing through a data stack (*q.v.*). A Forth development environment typically includes a large and varied set of pre-defined "words." Any word may be executed from the keyboard or combined with others in the definition of a new word. This means that Forth has no syntactic model and no grammar. The underlying Forth model is semantic. Each word has an action, and the meaning of a sequence of words is the sequence of actions implied by the ordering of the words.

Programming   Programming in Forth consists of simply adding new words that are defined in terms of previously defined words. Most implementations provide an assembler "vocabulary" (a list of words) so that new primitives may be added. At the other end of the scale, there are words that allow the creation of "defining" words. These are words that, when executed, define other words. New defining words and new primitives can be defined as easily as any other kind of word. Applications written in Forth tend to be factored into much smaller pieces than in other languages. The definition of a Forth word is typically just a few lines long.

The Interpreter   The Forth interpreter identifies a *token* as any sequence of printable characters delimited by spaces or the end of a line. The interpreter simply gets the next token from the input stream, looks in its vocabularies for one whose name matches the token, executes the word if a match is found, attempts to interpret it as a numeric constant if a match is not found, and, failing both of these, complains. This process is repeated until the input stream is exhausted.

For example, one may enter

```
1 3 + .
```

and press the return key. When the interpreter sees "1" it pushes the integer value 1 to the stack and takes a similar action when it sees "3." When it sees " + " it executes the Forth word named " + " which is defined as a command to remove the top two values from the stack, add them, and push the result to the stack. When it sees "." the interpreter executes the Forth word named ".", which removes the top integer from the stack and prints it out. Thus, like the language PostScript (*q.v.*), Forth expressions are written in postfix form in which operands precede the operator (*see* POLISH NOTATION).

The Compiler Strictly speaking, there is no such thing as *the* Forth compiler. Compiling actions are performed by many Forth words, and new compiling words are commonly defined either in terms of existing ones or, rarely, as new primitives. Compiling actions are invoked by "defining words."

New words are most commonly defined with a "colon definition," such as

    : Bump 3 + . ;

which defines a new word named "bump." All the interpreter does, however, is fetch the word named ":" from the input and execute it. This word's action is to create a new word with the name that follows the ":" (one of Forth's prefix anomalies) and then compile all of the following words as part of the new word's definition up to the first semicolon.

Bump can be used immediately by entering

    17 bump

and pressing the return key which results in "20" being printed.

Defining Words An integer variable (e.g. TEMP) is defined in Forth with

    VARIABLE TEMP

which leads to VARIABLE being referred to as a defining word. VARIABLE causes TEMP to be added to the list of available words and sets TEMP's action to be the standard action of a variable, which is to push the address of its "data field" to the stack. The data field is that portion of memory that holds the current value of the variable.

A value is stored into the data field of a variable with

    20 TEMP !

which sets the value of TEMP to 20. The value in a variable's data field is fetched to the stack with

    TEMP ©

and once the value is on the stack it can be printed or used as a parameter by any other word.

The defining word VARIABLE could be defined this way:

    : VARIABLE CREATE 0 , DOES> ;

and when this line is interpreted, the colon is executed, which defines VARIABLE as a new word. When VARIABLE is subsequently executed, the word CREATE is executed, which fetches the next name in the input stream and creates a new word with that name. Then zero is pushed to the stack. The comma removes the value on the top of the stack and compiles it into the data field of the word being created. The comma's action allocates memory for the variable and initializes it at the same time.

When DOES> executes, it terminates the definition of the new word (TEMP, in our example) and specifies that the words that follow it, up to the semicolon, are executed whenever TEMP (or any other word defined by VARIABLE) is executed. In this case there are no words between DOES> and the semicolon, so all that happens when TEMP is executed is the default behavior of pushing the address of TEMP's data field to the stack.

Forth has been mastered when one not only understands the difference between (1) what happens when the definition of VARIABLE is compiled, (2) what happens when VARIABLE is executed, and (3) what happens when a word defined with VARIABLE is executed, but sees the power in being able to stipulate and exercise all three of these actions interactively.

Forth Literature The *Journal of Forth Applications and Research* is a refereed journal published by the Institute for Applied Forth Research, Inc. *FORTH Dimensions* is published six times a year by the Forth Interest Group. The ACM has a Forth special interest group, SIGForth, which publishes a quarterly newsletter.

Availability Commercially supported Forth implementations are available from many vendors for most common hardware platforms. There are also numerous public domain versions of varying quality and complexity. For more information, contact the Forth Interest Group, Box 1105, San Carlos, CA 94070.

References

1984. Brodie, Leo. *Thinking Forth*. Englewood Cliffs, NJ: Prentice-Hall. A sophisticated exploration of Forth and ways to use it effectively.

1987. Brodie, Leo. *Starting Forth* (2nd Ed.). Englewood Cliffs, NJ: Prentice-Hall. The most accessible introduction to Forth.

1987. Pountain, Dick. *Object-Oriented Forth*. San Diego, CA: Academic Press. A readable discussion of one way to add object-oriented constructs to Forth.

CHARLES EAKER

FORTRAN. *See* PROCEDURE-ORIENTED LANGUAGES.

FRACTALS

For articles on related subjects *see* COMPUTER ART; COMPUTER GRAPHICS; IMAGE PROCESSING; PATTERN RECOGNITION; and SCIENTIFIC APPLICATIONS.

Introduction The greater part of the applied scientific research of the past consisted of the analysis of human-made machines and the physical laws that govern their operation. The success of science relies on the predictability of the underlying experiments. Euclidean geometry—based on lines, circles, etc.—is the tool to describe spatial relations, where differential equations are essential in the study of motion and growth. However, natural shapes such as mountains, clouds, or trees do not fit well into this framework. The understanding of these phenomena underwent a fundamental change in the last two decades. *Fractal geometry*, as conceived by Mandelbrot, provides a mathematical model for many of the seemingly complex forms found in nature. One of Mandelbrot's key observations was that these forms possess a remarkable statistical invariance under magnification. This may be quantified by a *fractal dimension*, a number that agrees with our intuitive understanding of dimension but need not be an integer. These ideas may also be applied to time-variant processes. Another important discovery has been that even in very simple nonlinear dynamical systems, such as the double pendulum, long-term predictions are not possible despite exact knowledge of the underlying governing equations. Such systems exhibit behavioral patterns that we can conceive only as erratic or chaotic, despite their very simple and deterministic generating mechanisms. Arbitrarily small perturbations of solutions are blown up by such systems until the perturbed solutions have lost all correlation with the original solution. This phenomenon has been termed *sensitive dependence on initial conditions* and is the trademark of what became known as *chaos theory*. There is a strong connection between chaos and fractal geometry, namely that, as one follows the evolution of the states of a chaotic nonlinear system, it typically leaves a trace in its embedding space that has a very complex geometric structure: This trace is a fractal.

Fractals are of particular interest to computer scientists because of their use in computer graphics to depict landscape and vegetation in a very natural way. This and other scientific applications are discussed in the last section of this article.

Random Fractals Fractal geometric structures exhibit a self-similarity when the distance at which they are viewed is changed. This self-similarity may be either exact or statistical. An exact self-similar fractal is the snowflake curve devised by the Swedish mathematician Helge von Koch in 1904 (see the construction in Fig. 1). The curve is self-similar: Magnifying one quarter of the snowflake curve by a factor of 3 produces another complete snowflake curve.

When a self-similar object is given as N copies of itself, each one scaled down by a factor of r, the *self-similarity dimension* of the object is defined as

$$D = \frac{\log N}{\log 1/r}.$$

This definition assigns a dimension 1 to straight lines and 2 to squares, as expected. Fractals typically have a non-integer dimension. The snowflake curve has a dimension $D = \log 4/\log 3 \approx 1.262$.

The notion of self-similarity dimension is extended to sets that do not have *exact* self-similarity. Let A be a set in n-dimensional Euclidean space R^n, and define $N(r)$ as the minimal number of n-dimensional cubes necessary to cover the set A. Then the (box-counting) *fractal dimension* is

$$D_f(A) = \lim_{r \to 0} \frac{\log N(r)}{\log 1/r}$$

This quantity can be estimated from a given data set by drawing a graph of the function $N(r)$ on doubly logarithmic paper. The negative slope of the resulting line fit is an estimate for D_f. There are other definitions of dimension (e.g. the Hausdorff-Besicovitch dimension, the mass dimension, and the correlation dimension).

The mathematical model for a statistically self-similar object is given by *fractional Brownian motion* (fBm). In one dimension, fBm is a random process $X(t)$ with Gaussian increments $X(t_2) - X(t_1)$. The variance of these increments is proportional to $|t_2 - t_1|^{2H}$ where $0 < H < 1$. The increments of X are *statistically self-similar with parameter H*. This means that, after setting $t_0 = 0$ and $X(t_0) = 0$, the two random functions $X(t)$ and $r^{-H}X(rt)$ are statistically indistinguishable. For a given number X_0, we have that the points t that satisfy $X(t) = X_0$ will constitute a fractal point set, which is statistically self-similar. Its dimension is $D_f = 1 - H$. The graph of $X(t)$ is not self-similar, since we must scale in the t- and X-direction by *different* factors r and $1/r^H$ to obtain statistically equivalent graphs. This form of similarity has been termed *self-affinity* (properties are invariant under affine transformations). The graph of $X(t)$ has a fractal dimension of $2 - H$. Spectral analysis of fBm yields the spectral density $S(f)$ of the process $X(t)$. The density $S(f)$ is proportional to $1/f^\beta$, where the *spectral exponent β* equals $2H + 1$. Thus, β is in the range from 1 to 3.

The generalization of fractional Brownian motion to higher dimensions is a multidimensional process (a *random field*) X and $(t_1, t_2,..., t_n)$, with the properties analogous to the above. The random field X has *stationary increments* and is *isotropic* (i.e., all points $(t_1, t_2,..., t_n)$ and all directions are statistically equivalent). The random fields can also be characterized by their spectral density function or, equivalently, by their autocorrelation function.

Let us consider the case $n = 2$, where $X(t_1, t_2)$ may be plotted as height over the point (t_1, t_2) in the plane. The result is a fractal surface, the graph of X. It is a self-affine fractal whose dimension is $D_f = 3 - H$. The sets of points $\{(t_1, t_2)$ satisfying $X(t_1, t_2) = X_0\}$ are collections of curves interpreted as coastlines, assuming a water level X_0. These curves are statistically self-similar with dimension $2 - H$.

The above models describe *uniform fractals* (i.e. fractal properties are essentially global properties). In non-uniform fractals, the dimension may require different values. These *multifractals* have received wide attention in the study of aggregation problems.

Another topic of interest here is the *lacunarity* of a fractal. It is a property independent of the fractal dimension, but has an effect on the texture or appearance of the fractal and thus is a useful additional parameter for algorithms for the simulation of natural shapes (see below).

Algorithms for Random Fractals There have been many algorithms developed that generate finite approximations of random fractals. Initially, methods have been judged primarily with respect to the quality of the approximation and raw compute speed, two conflicting goals. More recently, with the advent of increased availability of workstation (*q.v.*) computing power as well as very good built-in graphics capabilities, research emphasis is more on flexibility and control of the fractals. For example, local control of the fractal dimension is desir-

FIG. 1. Construction of the von Koch snowflake curve. The interval [0,1] is given initially (not shown here). In each stage (going from bottom to top), line segments are replaced by the generator curve, which consist of four lines as shown in the bottom curve (stage 1). As stages are added, the total length of the curve tends to infinity, although the curve is confined to a finite region.

able to model "smooth" valleys surrounded by rough mountains in a landscape scene.

In this section we present a few selected algorithms, first for the one-dimensional case and then for two or more dimensions. One of the first and most widely known methods is the *midpoint displacement method*. Assume that values $X(0) = 0$ and $X(1)$ are given. $X(1)$ may be obtained as a sample of a Gaussian random variable of variance σ^2. The interval [0, 1] is partitioned into two subintervals [0, ½], [½, 1], and $X(½)$ is defined as the average of $X(0)$ and $X(1)$ plus a displacement D_1—i.e.

$$X(½) = ½[X(0) + X(1)] + D_1.$$

The displacement D_1 is computed as a sample of a Gaussian random variable with variance Δ_1^2 proportional to $\sigma^2/2^{2H}$. The process is repeated with the two intervals—i.e. more precisely, we set in this second stage

$$X(¼) = ½(X(0) + X(½)) + D_2,$$
$$X(¾) = ½(X(½) + X(1)) + D_2,$$

where D_2 is Gaussian with variance Δ_2^2 proportional to $\sigma^2/(2^2)^{2H}$. Note that the two samples of D_2 in the above formulas may be different. The process is continued with displacements D_n having variances Δ_n^2 proportional to $\sigma^2/(2^n)^{2H}$ in the n-th stage. This method is fast, but lacks mathematical purity, since the process X does not have stationary increments for $H \neq ½$.

One method that improves on the stationarity of the increments of X is called *successive random additions*. Assume that $X(t)$ is already approximated on an interval at equidistant points with grid size Δt, and let $r > 1$ be a fixed number denoting a reduction factor. In the next step, the grid size is reduced to $\Delta t/r$ and values at the new equidistant points are defined by an interpolation procedure (e.g. linear interpolation). Additionally, all values are offset by a sample of a Gaussian random variable with a proper choice of variance. This procedure is repeated until the desired resolution is achieved (e.g. if we start out with just two values of X as in the midpoint displacement algorithm, then in order to obtain an appropriate random fractal with N points, we must exercise n stages of the successive random additions method, where $n \geq \log N / \log r$). The variance Δ_n^2 of the displacement in the n-th such stage of the algorithm must be proportional to $1/r^{2nH}$. The parameter $r > 1$ controls the lacunarity of the fractal. With a large value of r, only a very few stages are necessary and the lacunarity is especially drastic.

An alternative method is to sum

$$X(t) = \sum_{k=k_0}^{k_1} \frac{S(r^k t)}{r^{kH}},$$

where $r > 1$, $0 < H < 1$ and S is an auxiliary function similar to the sine and cosine functions (e.g. S may be defined as a smooth interpolant of random data at integer points $t = 0, \pm 1, \pm 2, \ldots$ For $k_0 = -\infty$, $k_1 = \infty$, we obtain a random fractal whose graph has a fractal dimension $2 - H$ and $r > 1$ determines lacunarity. In practice, the numbers k_0, k_1 are chosen to reflect the upper and lower *crossover scales* of the fractal (i.e. basically $r^{-k_0 H}$ and $r^{-k_1 H}$ will define the largest and the smallest structures seen in $X(t)$. This method is a summation of band limited functions and is also called the "rescale-and-add-method", and in this one-dimensional formulation is almost the same as the Mandelbrot-Weierstrass function.) The parameters r and H determine lacunarity and fractal dimension ($D = 2 - H$) of the graph of $X(t)$. They need not be fixed globally, but may change depending, for example, on t or even $X(t)$.

The generalization of the methods to random fields $X(t_1, t_2)$ is as follows: In the midpoint displacement method we start out with an equilateral triangle and random values of $X(t_1, t_2)$ at the three vertices. Each side is subdivided into two halves and the displacements are done on each side just as in the one-dimensional case. This yields four smaller equilateral triangles with sides half as long. This procedure is iterated until the desired resolution is achieved. It can be modified to operate on squares in place of triangles.

The method of successive random additions is also very easy to implement in the two-dimensional case. One works with grids where the grid sizes are given by $1/r^n$ and multilinear interpolation may be applied.

In the rescale-and-add-method we set

$$X(t_1, t_2) = \sum_{k=k_0}^{k_1} \frac{S(r^k t_1, r^k t_2)}{r^{kH}}.$$

Nothing is changed except that the auxiliary function now has two arguments and must be modified accordingly.

Comparing the above methods, we deduce that the midpoint displacement method and its variants are the fastest. However, increments are not stationary and, in consequence, one obtains the so-called *creasing effect*, which disturbs the natural look of the fractal. For a small extra expense, the method of successive random additions offers improved results. The rescale-and-add-method is relatively slow in one dimension, but it is superior in three dimensions, in which case the other methods suffer from storage problems and time complexity. Moreover, dimension and lacunarity may be changed not only globally, but also locally.

The output of the methods discussed is a two-dimensional array of heights. There are several computer graphics methods available for a rendering. Squares or triangles may be shown as shaded polygons with z-buffer or scanline techniques. When many data are given, a floating horizon method can be applied. For most realistic images, ray tracing techniques are suitable. Generally, it is the case that the rendering of fractal surfaces takes more compute time than the generation process for the fractal itself.

Deterministic Fractals Random fractals involve an element of chance. In contrast, deterministic fractals are given by means of exact formulas. In this section we consider those deterministic fractals that arise from *discrete dynamical systems* (i.e. the iteration of mappings). These may be derived, for example, from *population dynamics* in biology and yield maps that describe growth of population from one generation to the next. Iteration of the maps simulates the dynamics over longer time periods. Other mappings are motivated by time-variant processes described by differential equations and associated *Poincaré sections*.

The first system of differential equations discovered for which a fractal structure is central consists of the Lorenz equations (1963):

$$\dot{x} = \sigma(y - x),$$
$$\dot{y} = Rx - y - xz,$$
$$\dot{z} = xy - bz.$$

These equations, named after the meteorologist E. Lorenz, were motivated by the problem of weather forecasting and represent a much simplified model of Rayleigh-Bénard convection in fluids. As solutions are followed, they tend to a set in 3-space with a complicated fractal structure, a *strange attractor* (see Fig. 2).

One way to study the dynamics given by a system of three differential equations, such as the Lorenz equations, consists of reducing the description to a two-dimensional map called the Poincaré section. A model for the Lorenz system has been suggested by Hénon and Pomeau in 1976

$$x_{k+1} = 1 + y_k - ax_k^2, \quad a = 1.4,$$
$$y_{k+1} = bx_k, \quad b = 0.3.$$

Given an initial point (x_0, y_0), the formula defines a successor point (x_1, y_1) and all following points iteratively. Again, there is a strange attractor with self-similar fractal structure (see Fig. 3). It is remarkable that important

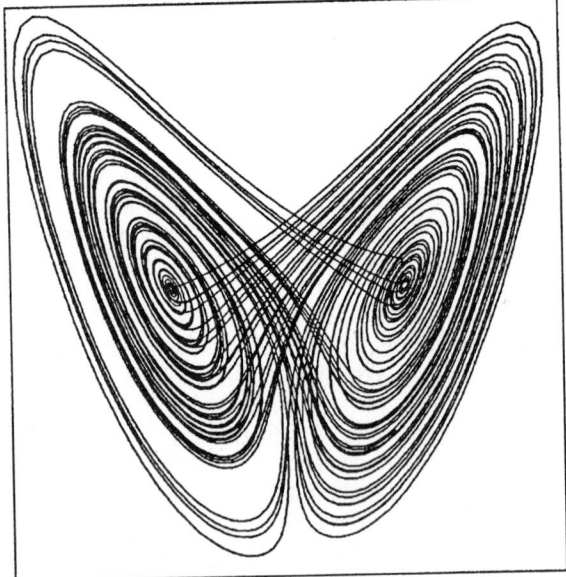

FIG. 2. The Lorenz attractor for parameters $R = 28$, $\sigma = 10$, $b = 8/3$.

aspects of complex dynamical behavior found in nature can be captured in such simple discrete maps.

A related discrete model is the quadratic mapping

$$z_{k+1} = R_c(z_k) = z_k^2 + c,$$

where z_k, $k = 0, 1, 2,...$ are complex numbers, and c is a complex parameter. This iteration has found widespread interest, not only in the scientific community, but also among amateur scientists, due to its computer graphical potential. It is the iteration procedure that yields the Mandelbrot set

$$M = \{\, c \in C \mid \lim_{k \to \infty} z_k \neq \infty \text{ with } z_0 = c \,\}$$

and the Julia set J_c that is the minimal completely invariant closed subset of C (i.e. we have that $z \in J_c$ if and only if $z^2 + c \in J_c$ except in the special case $c = 0$ where the Julia set is the unit circle).

The self-similarity of the Julia set is as follows. As in the case of exact self-similar fractals, any small neighborhood of a point in the Julia set can be mapped onto the complete Julia set. However, the necessary similarity mapping is not affine, but *nonlinear*. The fractal dimension of J typically is a non-integer value between 0 and 2. The theory of Julia sets has been carried out not only for the quadratic map, but also for polynomials and rational maps (e.g. Julia sets naturally arise when a complex polynomial equation $p(z) = 0$ is solved numerically by Newton's method). This amounts to the iteration of $N(z) = z - p(z)/p'(z)$. The roots of the equation $p(z) = 0$ are attractors for the rational map $N(z)$, and the Julia set is the boundary that separates the corresponding basins of attraction (see Fig. 4). It is the locus of instability: In any arbitrarily small neighborhood of a point in J, one finds points that converge to different roots of $p(z)$.

Most phenomena that occur in context with rational maps already appear in the quadratic map $R(z) = z^2 + c$. The Mandelbrot set reflects qualitative aspects for all parameters c of this map, namely it collects all parameters c whose Julia set J_c is a connected set. Outside of the Mandelbrot set, corresponding Julia sets are not connected; they are just clouds of points. The Mandelbrot set (see Fig. 5) itself is also a fractal with a certain self-similarity: Any small neighborhood of a boundary point of M contains a complete copy of M. The conjecture that the

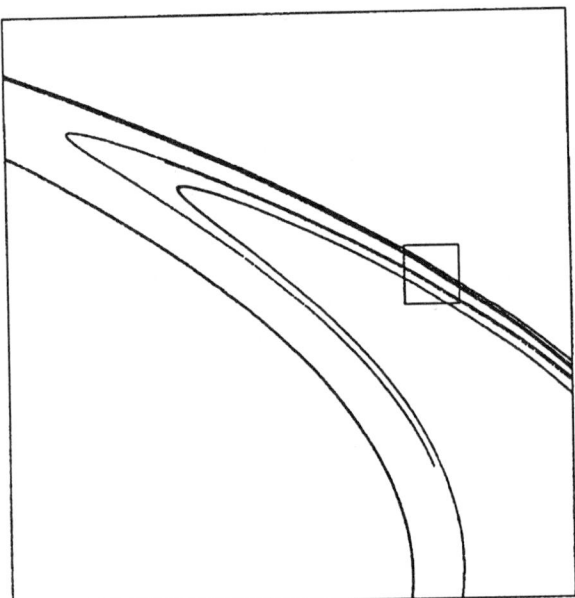 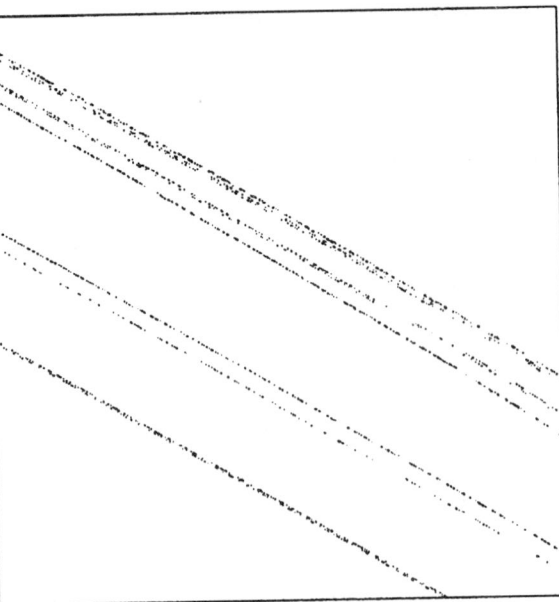

FIG. 3. The Hénon chaotic attractor in two enlargements, computed from a run of 100,000 points. The regions shown are $[0,1] \times [0,0.3]$ (left) and $[0.7,0.8] \times [0.15,0.18]$ (right). The small square in the left figure corresponds to the enlargement on the right. The self-similar structures are clearly visible.

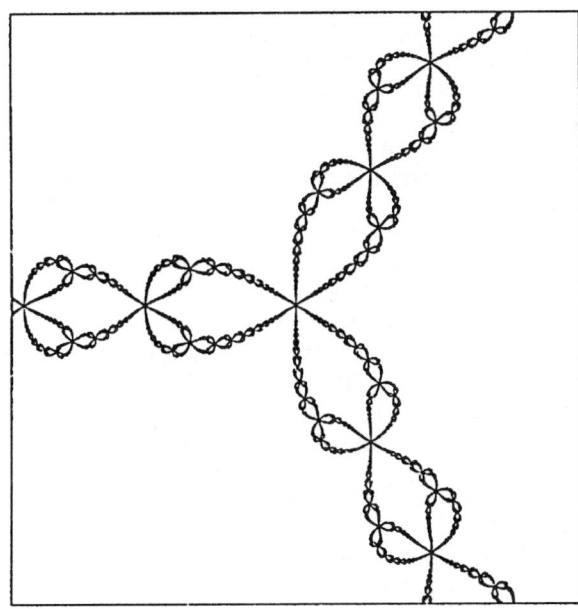

FIG. 4. The Julia set corresponding to Newton's method for the solution of $z^3 - 1 = 0$. The thick points indicate the three roots of the equation.

boundary of M has a dimension equal to 2 has recently been proved.

The computer code to generate the data for an image of the Mandelbrot set is very short, it implements the integer-valued function

$$L(c) = \begin{cases} \ell = \min\{k: |R_c^k(c)| > R_{max}\} & \text{if } \ell \le L_{max} \\ \infty & \text{otherwise} \end{cases}$$

Here $R_c^k(c)$ denotes z_k, the k-th iterate of $z \to z^2 + c$, starting at $z_0 = c$; L_{max} is the maximal number of allowed iterations per point; and R_{max} is a large number (≥ 2). Thus, $L(c)$ is the number of iterations necessary to detect that the critical value c of R_c escapes to ∞. The computation of $L(c)$ is carried out once per pixel of the image, each

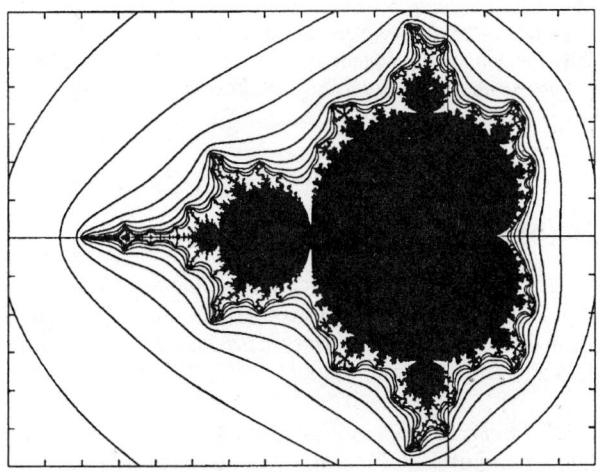

FIG. 5. The Mandelbrot set with some equipotential lines.

pixel representing a small region in complex parameter space. Colors are assigned using a color look-up table.

$L(c)$ is an integer-valued function. It is possible to define a smooth version by means of the potential function of the Mandelbrot set. For points $c \notin M$, the *potential* is given by

$$G(c) = \lim_{k \to \infty} \frac{\log |R_c^k(c)|}{2^k}.$$

The expression in the limit converges rapidly once $|R_c^k(c)|$ is large.

The values of $G(c)$ can be used in an image again in connection with a color look-up table, or they are interpreted as a third spatial coordinate (i.e. height, see Figs. 6–11, color insert pages CP-8, 9).

An alternative measurement for points $c \notin M$ is the distance $d(c, M)$ of c to M, which can be estimated according to

$$\frac{\sinh G(c)}{2\, e^{G(c)} |G'(c)|} < d(c, M) < \frac{2 \sinh G(c)}{|G'(c)|}$$

This estimate gives rise to different pictures (see Fig. 12, color insert page CP-9) and also to a new, fast algorithm to compute the Mandelbrot set: Once the lower estimate on the left side has been computed for a point $c \notin M$, a disk with that radius can be eliminated from further computation, since it is guaranteed that this disk does not intersect M. A speed-up factor of 10 or higher may result, depending on the region of the image and the resolution.

The algorithms for the computation of color images of Julia sets are very similar to the above. For details, see the literature.

Applications Fractal phenomena are found almost everywhere in nature, from the very large scales of clusters of galaxies down to the microcosmos of molecular particles. Although the mere description of these shapes and forms in terms of fractals does not explain anything, it is clear that the fractal "dialect" is the appropriate language and, thus, will likely evolve to become a lasting element of science.

Obviously, wherever nature is to be *simulated*, fractals are of value. Because of the difficulty of depicting them realistically, landscapes and clouds were two of the first natural phenomena discussed in the computer graphics community. Research is now incorporating effects such as erosion of a fractal landscape, allowing rivers and river networks to be included in the long list of simulated phenomena.

Fractal geometry applied to spatial relationships provides one way to achieve visual complexity. Another method used in computer graphics is called *solid texturing*, which is usually given as a functional model (e.g. in Fig. 8, which shows a fractal planet, the geometry is very simple and not fractal: it is merely a sphere). But the texturing function, which determines the coloring, is constructed using the laws of random fractals. As demonstrated, there is a balance between geometry and texture.

No visual complexity is lost if one of the two is relaxed while the other one is enhanced.

One of the most important aspects of fractals is that their visual complexity is very high in contrast to their intrinsic complexity, as measured in terms of the length of the shortest computer program that can generate them. Typically, such programs are quite short. This is called *database amplification* and is important where large, detailed databases are too big or too costly to be used (e.g. in flight or driving simulators, or in telecommunication).

A systematic analysis of images using self-similarity by means of affine maps has been carved out by Barnsley and his coworkers in an approach called *iterated function systems*. One grayscale or color image (e.g. a rasterized photograph or a transmitted satellite image) may be encoded as an object that is invariant under a collection of affine maps. These affine maps may be stored in much less memory than the original image. Compression ratios of 10,000 to 1 are reported. In turn, these affine maps may again be used to reconstruct the image, or at least a close approximation of it. There is promising evidence that sophisticated implementation of a further development of the method will allow real-time transmission of video quality images over low-speed channels such as phone lines.

There are numerous other applications of fractal geometry in image processing and pattern recognition. Two of them are:

1. Automatic segmentation of images based on fractal dimension, lacunarity, etc., which is useful in differentiating objects in an image such as man-made structures, forest, and sky.
2. Optimization of camouflage methods based on fractal analysis of the surroundings.

A method to generate fractal shapes that grow in space is based on *Lindenmayer systems*. Objects are represented as strings of symbols that are generated from an *axiom* (initial short string) and a set of *production rules* that are applied recursively to the symbols of the axiom and the resulting strings. The geometric representation of these strings is obtained through *turtle graphics*. Classic fractal curves, such as the snowflake curve, Hilbert's space filling curve, the Sierpinski gasket, etc., are easily and compactly formulated as L-systems. The main application is the modeling of growth and form of trees, bushes, and plants. These results stem from an interdisciplinary effort in computer science and biology.

These aforementioned applications are relevant to computer science and engineering. Perhaps the most important uses are in the physical sciences. One area of application is given by *percolation processes* describing a fluid spreading randomly through a medium that supplies a network of narrow pores and channels for the fluid flow. This includes seepage of (possibly contaminated) water through the cracks and fractures of rock formation.

Another application is diffusion-limited aggregation in which "sticky" particles move about randomly and eventually attach to a cluster of particles. In this process, the cluster grows into a fractal characterized by its fractal dimension. There is a strong coincidence with forms generated by viscous fingering in porous media, which is an important issue for oil recovery.

It is no surprise that molecular surfaces are fractal; thus, fractal geometry will prove useful in chemical engineering (catalysis) and other areas where surface/volume relations are crucial (e.g. wetting and powder technology).

Deterministic fractals typically arise from dynamical systems that are motivated by numerous models for natural phenomena (e.g. the production of red blood cells in the bone marrow may be modelled using a delay differential equation, which exhibits chaotic attractors, which in turn may be interpreted as serious irregularity in the red blood cell concentration in patients with leukemia).

The Mandelbrot set plays a central role as a *paradigm* for the transition from order to chaos in such models. As the parameter c is decreased along the real axis, the system $z \to z^2 + c$ undergoes a series of *period doubling bifurcations*, a phenomenon that has also been discovered in several physical laboratory experiments. Moreover, it has been revealed that the Mandelbrot set is in some sense a *universal object*. It appears also in the study of rational and so-called polynomial-like maps.

As a side effect due to their beauty, Julia sets and the Mandelbrot set have provided inspiration for computer art and serve as a pleasing demonstration object on computer trade shows. Another unforeseen but possibly relevant side effect of the colorful Mandelbrot set images is that they convey a hint at the beauty that lies within mathematics. Thus, they supply motivation to support the assertion that mathematics is a worthwhile and, in fact, important part of human culture.

References

1982. Mandelbrot, B. B. *The Fractal Geometry of Nature*. New York: W. H. Freeman and Co.,

1986. Peitgen, H. O. and Richter, P. H. *The Beauty of Fractals*, Heidelberg: Springer-Verlag.

1987. Gleick, J. *Chaos—Making a New Science*. New York: Viking.

1988. Barnsley, M. F. *Fractals Everywhere*. New York: Academic Press.

1988. Peitgen, H. O. and Saupe, D. (Eds). *The Science of Fractal Images*. New York: Springer-Verlag.

1990. Hao B. L. *Chaos II*. Singapore: World Scientific.

1990. Prusinkiewicz, P. and Lindenmayer, A. *The Algorithmic Beauty of Plants*. New York: Springer-Verlag.

1991. Peitgen, H. O., Jügens, H, and Saupe, D. *Fractals for the Classroom, Part One and Part Two*. New York: Springer-Verlag.

DIETMAR SAUPE

FRONT-END PROCESSOR

For articles on related subjects *see* CHANNEL; COMMUNICATION CONTROL UNIT; COMMUNICATIONS AND COMPUTERS; DATABASE COMPUTER; HOST SYSTEM; INTERRUPT; MODEM; MULTIPLEXING; and PROCESSING MODES.

A *front-end processor* is a small, limited capability, digital computer that is programmed to replace the hardwired input and output functions of a central computing system (e.g. for the control of remote terminals in a time-sharing system). The front-end processor thereby permits the host computer to perform its primary functions with little regard for the slower input/output activities associated with large-scale multiprogrammed or time-shared computing systems.

In addition to receiving and transmitting all data passing through a computing system, front-end processors may also support a wide variety of functions, such as:

1. *Data and/or format conversion*—the conversion of one or more incoming data codes and formats to that of the host system.
2. *Polling (q.v.)*—the determination by a front-end processor of a terminal's readiness to send or receive data.
3. *Assembly of characters and messages*—the assembly and disassembly of all data, which may be input at varying line speeds and in synchronous or asynchronous formats, to insure that the host system receives only complete messages.
4. *Error control and editing*—the detection and possible correction of transmission errors, as well as corrections initiated at the terminals prior to reception by the host system.
5. *Fail-soft functions*—the ability of the front-end processor to keep parts of the system operating (such as terminals) when a major element of the host system has failed.
6. *Queueing*—placing incoming messages in transmission order for processing by the host system, or in some cases queueing messages on auxiliary storage devices (*spooling*).
7. *Message switching*—a function of front-end processors that service more than one central processing unit.
8. *Direct response*—the front-end processor may have the ability to respond to simple inquiries directly without contact with the host system.

The basic components of a typical front-end processor system are:

1. *Processor*—a stored program digital computer that has main memory that may vary in size from several hundred words to many thousands of words depending on the complexities of the specific application. Two important qualities required of a front-end processor are good facilities for bit manipulation and handling interrupts (*q.v.*). The processor may or may not have its own on-line peripheral devices, depending on the particular application.
2. *Central processor interface*—the hardware interface that allows the front-end processor to connect directly to an input/output channel of the host system. The host system is then able to communicate with the front-end processor as if it were a standard peripheral device controller.

3. *Communication multiplexer*—a device with programmable or hard-wired logic that produces logically independent data channels into the front-end processor's main memory from each transmission line serviced. The coordination of the data flow between the multiplexer and processor is handled by the front-end processor's interrupt system.
4. *Line interface units*—the hardware devices that link the communication multiplexer with the modems that terminate each of the communication lines.
5. *Software*—the programs that integrate the functions of the various hardware components of the front-end processor. Included in the software package are such functions as terminal, line and message control, system interface procedures, and whatever other functions are required by a particular installation.

The front-end processor can be a powerful and economical means of relieving a central processor of its time-consuming overhead activities by placing these activities under the control of an independent and parallel processing unit, but the need for front-end processors has been declining as mainframe I/O units have become more powerful.

ARTHUR I. KARSHMER

FUNCTION. *See* PROCEDURE; and SUBPROGRAM.

FUNCTIONAL PROGRAMMING

For articles on related subjects *see* LAMBDA CALCULUS; LIST PROCESSING: LANGUAGES; PROCEDURE-ORIENTED LANGUAGES; and RECURSION.

Functional programming, sometimes also called *applicative programming*, is a style that uses function application as the only control structure (*q.v.*). Rather than conditional statements, one uses conditional expressions to yield alternative results; rather than an assignment statement, one uses binding of parameter to argument to place a name on a value; rather than explicit sequencing or looping of control flow, one uses patterns of nested invocations to direct the generation of an result. Of immediate importance for general problem-solving is that, just as a function may take several arguments, a result can have several components.

There are various approaches to a pure applicative style. Some are restricted to functions that can only receive and return elementary data objects, respectively, as arguments and as results. Examples of this class include primitive recursion, pure expressions in Iverson's APL (its infamous one-liners) and Backus's FP. APL is rich in primitive operators and naming conventions, which Bird has refined into a powerful calculus of programs (Turner, 1990); FP is quite spartan in both respects (Hudak, 1989).

More contemporary examples allow functions themselves to be data objects and to be passed throughout the system. Examples include very pure versions of John McCarthy's Lisp (Henderson, 1980) and Backus's Formal Functional Programming (FFP), Miranda, ML, and Haskell (Hudak, 1989). These are closer to the theoretical foundations of functional programming because the domain of data objects includes everything computable, including the very function that a user requires; it is only necessary that it be identified.

Church's *Lambda Calculus* is one such foundation language; it is commonly used to relate many topics from logic and computer science. It forms the foundation for pure Lisp, for much work in theorem proving (including program correctness), and for the work in denotational semantics by Scott and Strachey. Under their approach, a program must be expressible as a function, since the only way that any looping program has meaning is through the mathematical concept of the *fixed point* of a functional interpretation of its definition (Stoy, 1977). For this reason, Lisp is chosen as the medium for a first example. The description of Lisp and the example in the article LIST PROCESSING: LANGUAGES (*q.v.*) are useful starting points for understanding this code, especially car and cdr. Consider a program that reads a list of triples and returns a list of pairs; a triple contains the coefficients of a quadratic equation, and the pair is its computed roots.

Using the language Scheme, which uses a Lisp notation akin to Lambda calculus, we might write the definition:

```
(define solveQuads (lambda (listOf3s) (cond
((null? listOf3s) () )
(else    (cons (  quad (car listOf3s))
        (solveQuads (cdr listOf3s)) )) ))))
```

If the list of triples is empty, so is the answer. Otherwise, build up a new list whose first element is the root of the first triple and whose remainder solves the remaining triples.

```
(define quad (lambda (triple)
            (roots (a triple) (b triple)
                    (c triple)) ));
```

Thus quad applies roots to the three elements of a triple:

```
a = (lambda (x) (car           x))   ;
b = (lambda (x) (car      (cdr x)))  ;
c = (lambda (x) (car(cdr (cdr x))))) ;
```

that is, a, b, and c are functions that return, respectively, the first, the second, and the third elements of a list.

```
(define roots (lambda (a b c)
        (twoRts (neg b)
                (sqrt (- (* b b) (* 4 a c)))
                (+ a a))))
```

Here, a, b, and c are local parameters. From them, three terms are assembled and passed to twoRts, which computes the pair of roots.

```
twoRts = (lambda (term1 term2 denominator)
        (cons (/ (+ term1 term2) denominator)
        (cons (/ (- term1 term2) denominator)
        () )) )
```

which forms a list of the two roots.

The arithmetic functions +, −, *, /, neg, and sqrt are primitive and have their obvious meaning. While a necessary example of elementary primitives and style, this code is unwieldy; it would have been better rendered in Scheme as

```
(define solveQuads (lambda (listOf3s)
                        (letrec
    ((quad (lambda (listOf3s) (apply
                    roots listOf3s)))
    (roots (lambda (a b c) (let
    ((term1 (neg b))
    (term2 (sqrt (- (* b b) (* 4 a c))))
    (denominator (+ a a)) )
    `(  ,(/ (+ term1 term2) denominator)
        ,(/ (- term1 term2)
                denominator)) ))) )
    (mapcar quad listOf3s) )))
```

A similar solution, an APL expression, is more concise, but uses the far richer primitives of that language.

$$\nabla\ Q \leftarrow SOLVEQUADS\ M$$
$$Q \leftarrow 1\ 2\ 1\ 1\ \phi\ ((-M[;2]) \circ . + 1\ -1 \circ . \times$$
$$((M[;2] * 2) - 4 \times M[;1] \times M[;3]) * .5)$$
$$\circ . \div 2 \times M[;1]$$
$$\nabla$$

This declares SOLVEQUADS as a function of one argument on an $n \times 3$ array. $M[;i]$ extracts the ith column of M as a vector—either all values of a, of b, or of c. The operator $\circ.\otimes$ is an outer product in which $\otimes$ is applied pairwise to all components of each operand for any dyadic operator $\otimes$; in this example, $\circ.+$, $\circ.\times$, and $\circ.\div$ are used, each operating on a vector and an array of dimension d, yielding an array of dimension $d+1$. One may identify the outer products on the vectors composed of all values, respectively, of $-b$, of $(b^2 - 4\ ac)^{0.5}$, and of $2a$. The two-element vector $\langle +1\ -1 \rangle$ is used with an outer product to effect the alternative sum or difference of twoRts, above. The apparent, intermediate result is a four-dimensional $n \times 2 \times n \times n$ matrix, of which only one diagonal plane, that with equal first, third, and fourth indices, selected by the prefixed 1 2 1 1, is the desired answer.

In Haskell, the same same algorithm would be rendered as follows:

```
solveQuads = map (quad where
    quad(a,b,c)= ((-b+term2)/denominator,
                    (-b-term2)/denominator)
            where term2 = sqrt(b*b - 4*a*c)
    denominator = a+a
```

Although both Lisp and Scheme are untyped languages that require full run-time type checking, Haskell is strongly typed. The type information is implicit in the primitives or literals, like (+) and tt sqrt. In fact, Haskell will determine that the type of solveQuads is

```
solveQuads :: (Floating a) => [(a,a,a)]->
                [(a,a)]
```

That is, it maps a list of floating-point triples into a list of floating pairs. A slight modification reveals another difference from Lisp.

```
solveQuads = map (quad where
    quad(a,b,c) = ((-b+term2)/denominator,
                    (-b-term2)/denominator)
        where denominator = a+a
              term2 = case b*b - 4*a*c of
                      discriminant
| discriminant<0.0  -> error "No quad soln"
| otherwise-> sqrt discriminant
)
```

The test, illustrating patterns with guards, generates a post-mortem error message when there is no real solution. (However, Haskell also has provision for complex numbers.)

With or without this test, both Haskell and Lisp will crash when sqrt is applied to a negative radicand, but the manner in which they crash is far different. Lisp and Scheme use *applicative order* to evaluate expressions; i.e. all arguments are fully, strictly evaluated as a function is invoked. Thus, if any of the triples yields a negative radicand, then the entire program crashes; no pairs at all are returned.

However, Haskell uses *lazy evaluation*, semantically the same as *normal order* evaluation. Arguments are necessarily evaluated when and *if* they are *necessary* to the output of the system. Therefore, a negative radicand would never be evaluated where the "printer" does not depend on that answer; even when the list of pairs itself is being printed, its prefix up to that error will be computed before the error "occurs."

The previous paragraph stumbles on the issue of time—i.e. exactly when does an error actually occur? Since the semantics of many functional languages, like Haskell, require no unnecessary sequentiality (because of lazy evaluation), it become difficult to describe their run-time behavior in terms of event ordering. While at first confusing to the sequential programmer, this property is highly desirable for parallel processing. Such temporal under-specification there allows the system to implement a program using far more latitude to isolate and to schedule mutually independent processes. Indeed, on a multiprocessor, that negative radicand can cause an error on one processor even while the printer-process continues to completion on another, as described next.

Lazy evaluation provides another insight to reconcile the equivalence between these solutions and iterative Fortran code. It is possible to represent a data structure—in this case the list of pairs, or matrix of results—without it being represented all at once in the computer's memory. Landin (Henderson, 1980) specified a *stream* to be a (perhaps infinite) list, of which only the first element need be explicit. The rest of the list becomes explicit only as it is accessed. Each result of solveQuads above may be perceived as a stream that becomes explicit only while it is traversed. A typical use of such a stream is to print it, and the preorder traversal during printing forces more pairs to be generated. Moreover, since an already-printed pair is immediately abandoned by such a traversal, its explicit representation can be erased as it is printed. Under that operational philosophy, only one pair at a time is generated, made explicit, printed, and abandoned. Since solveQuads is "tail recursive," the traversal can be done without using a recursion stack. In APL, the large intermediate result is not necessarily generated—only the diagonal plane, a pair at a time.

The analogs of input values to a program are files passed as multiple arguments to a function; the analog of output is the (multiple) result returned from such an application. Just as each output file is implemented as a stream, so also may the input files be streams (here, a stream of triples) so that only a finite prefix of unbounded input is ever represented within the computer. Thus, the code above can run using constant space and time proportional to the length of the input file—just as Fortran code would.

The quadratic example was selected for comparison with a procedure-oriented language. It is a poor example for applicative programming because the code generates a very simple stream of involved, but algebraically trivial, results. A problem that better exhibits the facility of functional programming and its use of recursion is testing the equality of two arbitrarily complex structures. Within the constraints of the data domain of each language, the solutions follow.

The Lisp function equal for lists, although primitive in Scheme, might be defined as

```
(define equal? (lambda (x y) (cond
              ((not (pair? x)) (eq? x y))
              ((pair? y) (and(equal?
                     (car x) (car y))
                            (equal?
                     (cdr x) (cdr y)) ))
          (else       false)  )))
```

If the first argument is atomic, check if it equals the second in a primitive sense. Otherwise, if the second argument is also a list, then equality distributes to equality of both their prefixes and suffixes, using the equal? predicate recursively. Otherwise, equality fails.

In APL (where X and Y are formal parameters), the solution is:

$$\nabla\, E \leftarrow X\,EQUAL\,Y\,M$$
$$E \leftarrow ((,X)\wedge.=(\rho,X)\uparrow,Y)\wedge$$
$$((\rho X)\wedge.=(\rho\rho X)\uparrow\rho Y)\wedge((\rho\rho X)=\rho\rho y)$$
$$\nabla$$

APL has only homogeneous arrays as data types. Thus, equality exists if the content of the two arrays is equal, and if their shapes are the same, and if they have the same dimension. Because APL is strict, it evaluates all conjuncts and because operands *must* be conformable, the "simpler" expression

$$E \leftarrow ((, X) =, Y) \wedge ((\rho X) = \rho Y) \wedge ((\rho X) = \rho \rho Y)$$

cannot be used. Parsing of the more complicated expression requires knowledge of APL's convention on binary operators, all of which have uniform precedence and associate to the right.

Haskell's prelude derives built-in list equality:

```
instance (Eq a) => Eq [a] where
    [] == []               = True
    (x:xs) == (y:ys)       = (x==y) && (xs==ys)
    _ == _                 = False
```

This code follows the logic of the Scheme code, above. Of particular note is the pattern matching, displacing the explicit conditionals, and the use of the wildcard pattern, underscore. The code for equality is bound to the infix operator (==) and integrates homogeneous lists into Haskell's typing system via instance.

Functional programming offers much expressiveness for machine architectures beyond that used by conventional procedure-oriented languages. Since results are defined without sequential imperatives, much of a functional program can be adapted to use available parallelism (e.g.

multiple or pipelined processors) without tailoring it to a particular machine. Moreover, much of the notation for *program verification (q.v.)* has a functional foundation, and so functional programs usually can be read as their own proofs. Finally, the natural modularity of function definitions provides for facile, piecewise testing and maintenance of large programs.

References

1977. Stoy, J. E. *Denotational Semantics.* Cambridge, MA: The M.I.T. Press.

1980. Henderson, P. *Functional Programming, Application and Implementation.* Englewood Cliffs, NJ: Prentice-Hall.

1987. Peyton Jones, S. L. *The Implementation of Functional Programming Languages.* New York: Prentice-Hall.

1988. Bird, R. and Wadler, P. *Introduction to Functional Programming.* New York: Prentice-Hall.

1989. Hudak, P. "The conception, evolution, and application of functional programming languages." *ACM Computing Surveys* **21**, 359–411.

1990. Turner, D. A. *Research Topics in Functional Programming.* Reading, MA: Addison-Wesley.

1991. Szymanski, B. K. (Ed.) *Parallel Functional Languages and Compilers.* New York: ACM Press.

1988. Bird, R. and Wadler, P. *Introduction to Functional Programming.* New York: Prentice-Hall.

1991. Szymanski, B. K. (Ed.) *Parallel Functional Languages and Compilers.* New York: ACM Press.

1992. Hudak, P., Peyton Jones, S, and Wadler, P. (Eds.). "Report on the Programming Language Haskell." SIGPLAN *Notices* **27**, 3.

DAVID S. WISE

GAMES. *See* COMPUTER GAMES.

GARBAGE COLLECTION

For articles on related subjects *see* LIST PROCESSING; STRING PROCESSING; and VIRTUAL MEMORY.

Many programming languages and systems provide for dynamic as well as static allocation of memory storage to abstract data objects. The performance of these systems relies on their ability to reclaim and re-use storage for dynamically allocated objects after they are no longer needed by the executing program.

Some language systems (Pascal, for example) require programmers to return unneeded objects (*garbage*) to the memory system explicitly. Although this permits precise and efficient recycling of storage when done carefully, the extra conceptual burden it places on the programmer often results in objects being recycled prematurely or being forgotten and thus lost to the system. Other systems reclaim abandoned objects automatically through a process called *garbage collection*. Reclaiming storage automatically in this way is both a convenience to the programmer and a means of ensuring that every object's storage is recycled correctly.

Garbage collection was first developed for list processing languages like Lisp, then adapted to Smalltalk and other high-level integrated language systems. More recently, it has started to appear in implementations of more traditional languages that support dynamically allocated data, including Modula-3, C++, and Ada.

Garbage collection occurs in two phases: identifying unneeded objects, and then making their storage available for reallocation. We say that an object in a program is needed, or *live*, at a given time if the program might access that object in the future; otherwise, it is *dead*. In practice, garbage collectors consider an object to be dead only if the program has abandoned all pointers to it,

making future access impossible. The two principal approaches to garbage collection differ primarily in the way they detect abandoned objects: *Reference counting collectors* maintain a count for each object of the number of pointers to it; an object is known to be dead when its count falls to zero. *Tracing collectors* identify as live those objects that are accessible either directly or indirectly from a set of root cells (essentially, the registers and named variables of the program). Objects that are not encountered during the trace are dead.

Tracing collectors are further distinguished by whether they copy or merely mark objects found to be live. *Copying collectors* relocate live objects into a new memory area as they are encountered during the trace. They then scan the objects in the new area, replacing the pointers to old objects with their new values. Finally, they reclaim the entire area from which the objects were copied. *Marking collectors*, on the other hand, simply flag live objects during the trace, then scan the memory area afterwards to find and reclaim unmarked objects.

Since garbage increases rapidly with memory size, large memory systems pose two critical problems. Long pauses for garbage collection are intolerable for interactive and real-time applications and may well dominate the execution time of large programs. Second, tracing garbage collectors access all of a program's live objects within a very short period of time. This severely violates the presumption of locality of reference that underlies virtual memory systems, so it usually results in excessive page thrashing (*q.v.*).

These problems have prompted the development of area-based *compacting collectors*. These copying collectors arrange for related live objects to be clustered into relatively small areas of memory that may be processed separately. If there are few instances of references between objects in different areas and if each area is small enough to fit within the working set (*q.v.*) of the program, then the garbage collection process itself is well-behaved with respect to the virtual memory and each pause is relatively short. It is important to note, however, that clustering also improves the locality of reference for the application program as well. Indeed, this property has become the prime motivation for incorporating compacting garbage collectors into many large-memory systems.

The performance of an area-based collector depends most critically on the principles by which it clusters objects into particular areas. The most successful techniques rely on two empirical observations concerning the lifetimes of objects: (1) newly created (young) objects tend to die quickly, while old ones are likely to continue living; and (2) objects seldom reference objects that are younger than themselves. *Generational scavenging* clusters objects into areas called *generations*, according to their ages. In this method, a scavenger process collects the younger (typically smaller) generations frequently. When an object has survived several collections in one generation, the scavenger relocates it to the next older generation, which it scavenges much less frequently.

Lifetime-based collectors are well-suited to interactive and soft real-time applications because they may be configured so that the pause to collect the youngest generation is well below one second. Garbage collection with hard real-time constraints is much harder to accomplish, however, and is the focus of ongoing research.

Garbage collection for languages that lack run-time typing of data objects is hampered by the difficulty of distinguishing pointers from the other possible contents of variables and data objects. Collectors for these languages usually rely on conservative variants of marking algorithms. During the tracing phase, they assume that if a cell contains the same bit value as a pointer to an object, then that object is live. This works well for systems with large, sparsely occupied address spaces and when pointer values are distinct from most small integers and floating point values.

References

1981. Cohen, J. "Garbage Collection of Linked Data Structures," *ACM Computing Surveys* **13**,3: 341–367.

1983. Lieberman, H. and Hewitt, C. "A Real-Time Garbage Collector Based on the Lifetimes of Objects," *Communications of the ACM* **26**,6 (June): 419–429.

1973. Knuth, D. E. *The Art of Computer Programming, vol. 1: Fundamental Algorithms*. Reading, MA: Addison-Wesley.

1980. Standish, T. A. *Data Structure Techniques*. Reading, MA: Addison-Wesley.

DAVID H. BARTLEY

GATEWAY

For articles on related subjects *see*: DATA COMMUNICATIONS; LOCAL AREA NETWORKS; METROPOLITAN AREA NETWORK; NETWORK PROTOCOLS; NETWORKS, COMPUTER; OPEN SYSTEMS INTERCONNECTION; and PACKET SWITCHING.

A *gateway* is a communications device that interconnects networks. There are two common ways in which networks can be interconnected, and the term gateway is used to describe both.

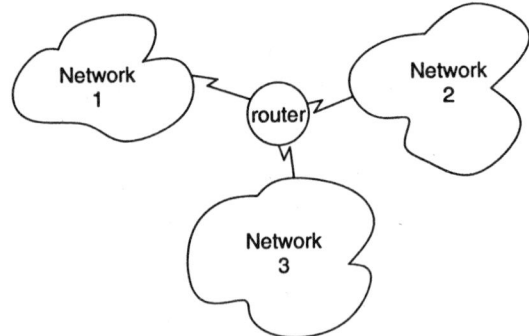

FIG. 1. Gateway: internetwork router.

1. A gateway can interconnect two or more network services. Fig. 1 shows a simple device that takes packets from one network and forwards them on another. The underlying technology and formats of packets may be different. The essential service/protocol are the same. Alternative terms for this device are *router, switch,* and network or internetwork level relay.

2. A gateway can convert between two different ways of providing a particular communications application. (See Fig. 2). Alternative terms for such a gateway are application level relay, application protocol convertor, and application protocol translator. An example of this is a device that takes electronic mail from one system and converts and forwards it to another.

Both of these devices are distinct from *repeaters* and *bridges*. In the OSI model of service layering, a gateway operates either in layer 3 or layer 7. A repeater operates at layer 1, physically interconnecting similar or identical transmission media, while a bridge operates at level 2, forwarding identical frame formats, but potentially over very different media with possibly different access protocols.

A gateway that interconnects networks at the packet forwarding level can operate in two different ways de-

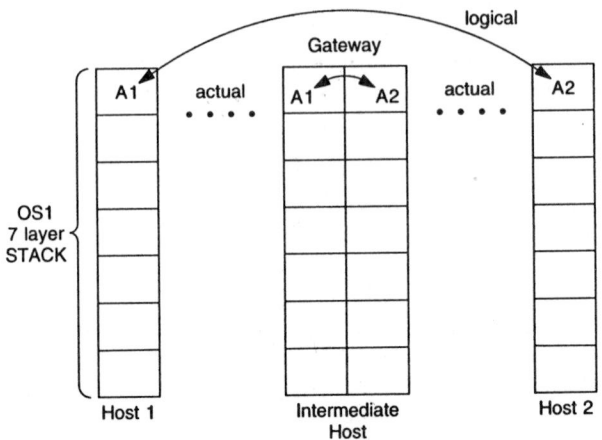

FIG. 2. Application level gateway.

pending on the underlying network services it is interconnecting:

 a. *Datagram router*
 This functions by receiving connectionless mode network protocol data units (*datagrams,*) and forwarding them on the basis of some routing table. Many such devices employ distributed algorithms to provide. "Dynamic Routing," whereby each datagram is routed independently. When there are failures of networks, links, or routers, new routes are calculated.
 b. *Virtual circuit switch*
 The networks interconnected by such a device provide a connection-oriented network service, often by using a protocol such as X.25. A gateway interconnecting two different X.25 networks does so on a "per connection" basis. This means that each end system establishes a path across a number of networks and gateways, and this is used for the duration of the communication. Routing is usually calculated no more frequently than for each path establishment.

Networks that employ different network services cannot be connected using network level relay type gateways. Instead, they must employ application level gateways, or else use some ad hoc means such as a Transport Service Bridge (Rose, 1990).

References

1990. Rose, M. T. *The Open Book*. Englewood Cliffs, NJ: Prentice-Hall.
1990. Stevens, W. Richard. *Unix Network Programming*. Englewood Cliffs, NJ: Prentice-Hall.

JON CROWCROFT

GENERAL REGISTER

For articles on related subjects *see* ARITHMETIC-LOGIC UNIT; BASE REGISTER; INDEX REGISTER; and REGISTER.

A *general register* is a storage device that holds the input (operands) and the output (results) of the various functional units of a computing system. It is also used for temporary storage of intermediate results. The functional units referred to in the definition usually include the arithmetic/logic unit (ALU), memory (*q.v.*), the control unit, and various I/O processors.

The width of the register in bits is directly related to the precision of a binary integer as it appears to the programmer, and does not necessarily reflect the width (data path) of the main-memory addressable unit. Thus, in the IBM/370 and its successors, for example, the general registers are 32 bits wide, although the memory is addressed in 8-bit bytes and accessed in 16-, 32-, or 64-bit units, depending on the model.

The registers operate at a speed that is directly matched to the speed of the units they serve. Their speed must be such that they do not slow down the functional units connected to them. In this sense they are the highest-speed storage in the storage hierarchy (*q.v.*) present in a computer.

Among the reasons for the presence of general registers, one should note their role in reducing the average number of bits needed to specify operands in a computer program. For example, one of 16 general registers can be addressed with four bits, whereas a main memory address for a memory of 1 million locations requires a 20-bit address.

General registers may serve as arithmetic or logical registers, in which case they function as dedicated parts of the arithmetic/logic unit. If we denote registers by R, then a typical arithmetic or logical instruction will be $R_i \leftarrow R_j \circ R_k$, where o stands for any arithmetic or logical operation, and i, j, k may be either distinct or equal (e.g. $R_2 \leftarrow R_2 + R_3$). In some machines, the specification of a register as part of an instruction can automatically increment or decrement its value by an amount that may vary by the operand type. Thus, for a byte, the change may be 1; for a 32-bit operand, the change may be 4. This attribute is particularly useful if the register is used as an *index register*.

The general registers may also serve as shift registers; index registers, in which case they serve as input to the memory unit; input/output registers, in which case they hold parameters that specify channels (*q.v.*), or channel command registers, etc.

The number of general registers varies widely between 0 to 256 (as of 1990). The numbers represent current architecture and hardware trade-offs, and are not to be taken as magic numbers. There are also computers that possess more than one set of general-purpose registers, computers that possess no general registers at all, and computers that possess specialized registers (such as vector registers, segment registers, address registers, etc.)

GIDEON FRIEDER

GENERATIONS, COMPUTER

For articles on related subjects *see* DIGITAL COMPUTERS; and GROSCH'S LAW.

In discussions of the history of electronic computers, it is convenient to refer to at least three computer generations.

The first generation is characterized by the use of vacuum tubes as active elements. This generation started with one-of-a-kind computers in university and government research laboratories. Mercury-delay lines and electrostatic storage tubes were the typical memory devices in the early systems.

The development of a reliable magnetic core memory was a major turning point in the first generation. The IBM 704 is an impressive example of the advanced hardware and software technology of that period. The latter part of the first generation also saw the introduction of many computers that used magnetic drums as their main storage.

The second generation is characterized by the use of transistors as active elements. The first important transistorized computers were delivered in 1959, and vacuum tubes rapidly disappeared from computer systems. The second generation was characterized by some powerful computers: Larc (*q.v.*), Stretch (*q.v.*), IBM 7090, Philco 2000, CDC 3600, etc. and many small systems such as the IBM 1401, RCA 301, and CDC 160A.

The distinction between the second and third generation is not nearly as clear-cut as that between the first and second. Computers that use integrated circuit technology are by definition, third-generation computers, but some of the most powerful computers of the third generation use discrete component technology. It is capability and performance rather than circuitry that makes a large computer a member of the third generation. They are characterized by their ability to support multiprogramming (*q.v.*) and multiprocessors with a rather elaborate disk-based operating system. A typical third-generation operating system on a large computer handles multiple local and remote job streams and can support a variety of remote on-line terminals.

The third computer generation is generally considered to have started in 1964. Third-generation systems introduced by the largest computer manufacturers around that time and in the 10 years or so thereafter include the IBM 360 and 370 series, the Univac 1108 and 1110, the Honeywell 6000 series, the Control Data 6000, 7000, Cyber 70, and Cyber 170 series, the Burroughs B5700 and B6700, the Digital Equipment Corporation PDP-10 and PDP-20, and many others.

Some of the smaller computer manufacturers have claimed that one or another of their computers represents a fourth generation, but as of 1992 there is still no generally accepted definition of a fourth generation of computers. Most authorities consider the computers introduced since 1969 to be "late third generation" computers. They look for a more significant breakthrough, such as an electronic peripheral storage system to replace disk storage, to characterize a fourth generation. Since the introduction of their third-generation systems, most computer manufacturers, especially the large ones, have been very reluctant to make any major changes in the logical organization of their computer systems. They feel that it is necessary to protect the enormous investment in systems and applications software by manufacturers and by users. Thus, it can be argued that we are still in the third computer generation and will probably remain there for a long time to come.

Even though logical organization has changed very slowly since the mid-1960s, circuit technology has continued to advance at a very rapid rate. From the point of view of circuit technology, vacuum tubes and germanium diodes characterize a first generation, discrete transistors a second, simple integrated circuits a third, medium scale integration a fourth, and large scale integration a fifth generation.

Some authorities suggest that microprocessors, which represent the most impressive achievement of large-scale integration technology, also represent a fourth or perhaps even a fifth computer generation. If the concept of computer generation is tied directly to advances in technology, we are faced with an anomalous situation in which the most powerful supercomputers would have to be assigned to the third generation, while the most trivial of hobbyist computers would be a fourth- or fifth-generation system, a clearly untenable system of nomenclature.

With two exceptions, there is no longer much attention accorded the concept of a computer "generation." One is in the area of software, where the highly structured Pascal-like languages such as Clipper that are typically supplied with microcomputer database packages are called "fourth generation languages" (4GLs). Another is a massive effort backed by the government of Japan that aspires to the development of a "fifth generation" computer whose supporting software makes extensive use of the concepts of Artificial Intelligence (*AI* - *q.v.*).

SAUL ROSEN

GEOMETRY, COMPUTATIONAL. *See* COMPUTATIONAL GEOMETRY.

GLOBAL AND LOCAL VARIABLES

For articles on related subjects *see* BLOCK STRUCTURE; PROCEDURE-ORIENTED LANGUAGES; and SIDE EFFECT.

The quantity (or quantities) referred to by a given variable name in a computer program can generally be accessed (i.e. used or changed) only in certain parts of the program. The domain of the program during which a variable name can be accessed is called the *scope* of the variable.

In a *block-structured* language, the scope of a variable is the block in which it is declared, but excludes any subblocks that are internal to the defining block *and* in which the same variable name is declared. This is illustrated in Fig. 1, which shows the schematic of an Algol program with an outer block L1 and an inner subblock L2, which in turn contains two further subblocks L3 and L4. Also shown in Fig. 1 is the scope of each variable. Note in particular that a variable like C, defined in the outer block, has a scope L1 but without L4 because C is declared again in L4.

A variable in a block in which it is defined, like G in block L4 in the example, is said to be *local* to that block, and is therefore a local variable. Correspondingly, variable A is *global* to block L4, since it is defined outside this block, although it may be referred to in the block. The variable C defined in the outer block is also global to block L4, but it cannot be referred to in L4 because of the declaration of C in block L4, the latter (but different) C being local to L4.

Experience suggests that global variables should be used sparingly, if at all, because of the risk of unfavorable *side effects*.

```
L1:  begin
       real A, C, D; real array B[1:10];
         L2:  begin
                real D, E; real array F[-4:-6,1:12];
                  L3:  begin
                         real F, G;
                              .
                              .
                              .
                         end L3;
                  L4:  begin
                         real B, C, G;
                              .
                              .
                              .
                         end L4
                end L2;
       end L1
```

Variable Name	Label of Defining Block	Scope of Name
A	L1	L1
B	L1	L1,~L4
C	L1	L1,~L4
D	L1	L1,~L2
D	L2	L2
E	L2	L2
F	L2	L2,~L3
F	L3	L3
G	L3	L3
B	L4	L4
C	L4	L4
G	L4	L4

Note: L1,~L4 means for example, that the variable's scope holds throughout block L1 except for block L4.

FIG. 1.   Scope of variable names.

Reference

1978. Peterson, J. L. *Computer Organization and Assembly Language Programming.* New York: Academic Press.

J.A.N. LEE AND ANTHONY RALSTON

GRAMMARS

For articles on related subjects *see* BACKUS-NAUR FORM; CHOMSKY HIERARCHY; COMPILER CONSTRUCTION; FORMAL LANGUAGES; LANGUAGE PROCESSORS; METALANGUAGE; PRODUCTION; PROGRAMMING LINGUISTICS; and SYNTAX, SEMANTICS, AND PRAGMATICS.

A *grammar* is an algebraic system describing the processes by which instances of a language can be constructed. A grammar consists of four elements—a set of *metavariables* or *nonterminal* symbols V_T (usually called *parts of speech* when dealing with natural languages); an alphabet V_T (or character set), often called the *terminal symbols*; a set of rules or *productions P*, which describe how a sequence of substitutions can be made for each metavariable; and a special metavariable *S* called the *starting* or *root* symbol, which is the starting point for the substitution process to be described below. These four elements are often represented by the quadruple $\{V_N, V_T, P, S\}$.

Grammars are most commonly classified into two groups—*context-sensitive* and *context-free*. In the case of context-sensitive grammars, the rules are applicable only when a metavariable occurs in a specified context—for example, the modification of verbs to their plural form in the context of plurality in the rest of the sentence in natural languages. By contrast, in a context-free grammar, any occurrence of a metavariable may be replaced by one of its alternatives, irrespective of the other elements in the language. Most programming languages appear at first glance to be describable by context-free grammars until consideration is given to the effect of declarations, such as the dimensions of an array or the specification of a procedure to support a procedure reference. In the discussion that follows, we will restrict ourselves to context-free grammars.

Grammars for high-level programming languages are called *generative* because, given a starting metavariable such as *sentence*, they specify a sequence of replacements or substitutions that can be applied to that name to form an instance (in this case, a sentence) in the language. For example, consider the following small grammar:

> *sentence* : : = *noun–phrase verb–phrase*
> *noun–phrase* : : = *article noun*
> *verb–phrase* : : = *verb noun–phrase*

and

> *article* : : = the, a
> *noun* : : = cat, milk
> *verb* : : = drank

where the italicized elements are metavariables and the non-italicized elements are from the alphabet of the language. Using these rules, the sentence

> The cat drank the milk.

can be generated by the following sequence:

> *sentence* → *noun-phrase verb-phrase.*
> → *article noun verb-phrase.*
> → the *noun verb-phrase.*
> → the cat *verb-phrase.*
> → the cat *verb noun-phrase.*
> → the cat drank *noun-phrase.*
> → the cat drank *article noun.*
> → the cat drank the *noun.*
> → the cat drank the milk.

Equally, the sentences "the milk drank the cat" and "the cat drank the cat" can be generated, since they have the required underlying syntactic (grammatical) structure.

Similarly, consider the following grammar for simple forms of arithmetic expressions in high-level languages (where the vertical bar is to be read "or"):

add-op : : = + | −
mult-op : : = * | /
exp-op : : = **
primary : : = *constant* | *variable*
factor : : = *primary* | *primary exp-op primary*
term : : = *factor* | *factor mult-op factor*
arithmetic-expression : : = *term add-op term*

and where constants and variables then have usual definitions in computer languages. Then the expression

A + B*C**D

could be generated as follows:

arithmetic-expression
$\rightarrow$ *term add-op term*
$\rightarrow$ *factor add-op term*
$\rightarrow$ *primary add-op term*
$\rightarrow$ *variable add-op term*
$\rightarrow$ A *add-op term*
$\rightarrow$ A + *term*
$\rightarrow$ A + *factor mult-op factor*
$\rightarrow$ A + *primary mult-op factor*
$\rightarrow$ A + *variable mult-op factor*
$\rightarrow$ A + B* *factor*
$\rightarrow$ A + B* *primary exp-op primary*
$\rightarrow$ A + B* *variable exp-op primary*
$\rightarrow$ A + B*C *exp-op primary*
$\rightarrow$ A + B*C** *primary*
$\rightarrow$ A + B*C** *variable*
$\rightarrow$ A + B*C**D

During the compilation process for high-level programming languages, we are interested not in generating the allowable strings in a language, but rather in syntactically analyzing or *parsing* the strings presented to the compiler. The function that performs this analysis is naturally called a *syntactic analyzer*. Grammars for high-level programming languages are commonly classified according to the types of syntactic analyzers used to parse them.

Syntactic analyzers can broadly be classified into two types: (1) the predictive types, which, starting from the root symbol, attempt to predict the means by which the string was generated; and (2) the reductive types, which attempt to reduce the string to the root symbol. These methods are loosely termed the *top-down* and *bottom-up* methods, respectively. The direction implied by these terms is related to the *syntactic trees* that may be generated by the analysis wherein the root symbol is at the top of the page and the string at the bottom. It may then be seen that a predictive (top-down) method starts at the top of the (yet unconstructed) tree and builds down toward the string, whereas the bottom-up (reductive) method starts at the string and attempts to develop a tree that converges onto the root symbol.

For example, consider the grammar with

$$V_N = \{A, B, C, X\}$$
$$V_T = \{a, b, c, d, x, y\}$$

and the production rules

$$S : : = AX$$
$$A : : = aB$$
$$B : : = b$$
$$X : : = xC$$
$$X : : = yC$$
$$C : : = cd$$

which generates the language L with two strings {*abxcd*, *abycd*}. Note that, when a particular metavariable, such as *X* in this example, has more than one possible substitution for it, the productions are sometimes written

$$X : : = xC | yC$$

with the vertical bar being read as "or." When *X* is to be substituted for in a string, the syntactic analyzer must then choose one of the possible substitutions and, if this does not leads to a successful parse, try another. Typically, the possibilities are tried in left-to-right order when the production is written using the vertical bar.

The above grammar can be analyzed in either a top-down or bottom-up manner. For the string *abxcd*, we have

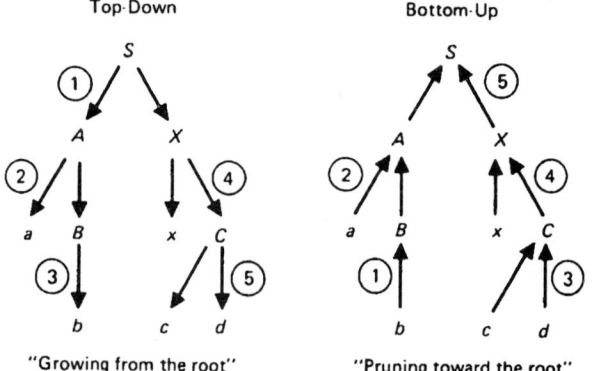

"Growing from the root"   "Pruning toward the root"

The top-down tree corresponds to the derivation

$$S \rightarrow AX \rightarrow aBX \rightarrow abX \rightarrow abxC \rightarrow abxcd$$

so that the numbers in the tree correspond to the steps in the derivation. Similarly, in the bottom-up case, the reduction shown in the tree corresponds to

$$abxcd \rightarrow aBxcd \rightarrow Axcd \rightarrow AxC \rightarrow AX \rightarrow S.$$

Since each metavariable appears on the left side of some production, in the top-down approach any metavariable in the string can always be replaced by the corresponding right side of a production. When going bottom-up, however, metavariables in the string may not correspond to right sides of productions (e.g. *A* in *Axcd* above). The bottom-up procedure is conveniently visualized by imagining a left-to-right scan across the string with successive characters put on a *stack* (q.v.) until a production can be applied. For the example above, this is illustrated as follows, where the symbol ∇ signifies the bottom of the stack.

Symbol Scanned	Stack	Comments
a	$\nabla\, a$	
b	$\nabla\, aB$	Using $B \rightarrow b$
	$\nabla\, A$	Using $A \rightarrow aB$
x	$\nabla\, Ax$	
c	$\nabla\, Axc$	
d	$\nabla\, Axcd$	
	$\nabla\, AxC$	Using $C \rightarrow cd$
	$\nabla\, AX$	Using $X \rightarrow xC$
	$\nabla\, S$	Using $S \rightarrow AX$

Notice, in particular, the ability to search down from the top of the stack (or, if you will, "remember" the previous contents of the stack) in order to determine if the top elements of the stack contain the right side of some production.

In the top-down derivation for the example above, whenever the derived string contained more than one metavariable, the leftmost one was used to generate the next string, thus leading to a *leftmost derivation*. Similarly, in the bottom-up derivation, the rightmost nonterminal was always replaced (indeed, in this example, there was no choice), thus leading to a *rightmost derivation*.

Studies of the development of parsers for programming languages have led to the definition of specialized grammars that are parsable by certain classes of analyzers. These can be divided into two classes that correspond directly to top-down (*predictive*) and bottom-up (*reductive*) analyzers and are known as either LL or LR grammars, respectively. LL grammars are defined by a parser which scans the input string from left-to-right (the first L in the name) and produces a parsing that corresponds to a leftmost (the second L) generation of the string. Where such a grammar (and corresponding parser) can accomplish the analysis with the examination of a single symbol in the string at each stage of the predictive process, then this is known as an LL(1) grammar; where up to k symbols may be required, it is called an LL(k) grammar. There exist languages that are LL(0); i.e. the predictor does not have to look at the string at all

except to confirm conformance with the prediction in order to analyze the string. Obviously, a degenerate LL(0) grammar is one containing only a single production rule; other simple LL(0) grammars can be constructed, such as

$$A :: = aBe$$
$$B :: = bC$$
$$C :: = c.$$

LR grammars are reductive in processing style and are much more reliable in their analysis of complex languages once the generated parser tables have been optimized. As with LL, the LR system scans the string from left to right, but, because of the use of reductive analysis, the derived syntactic structure is equivalent to the rightmost generation (the R in the name LR). As with LL grammars, an LR(k) grammar must examine up to k symbols in the analysis. Whereas the amount of processing to analyze a language by means of an LL(k) system increases rapidly as the number of symbols (k) to be examined at each stage increases, to the point where it is very uncommon to consider symbol groupings of more than one character at a time (i.e. LL(1) systems), the increase in complexity for increasing symbol groupings in LR systems is much smaller. Thus, it is more common to use LR(k) systems where k is greater than 1 to improve the efficiency of analysis and to minimize the changes that have to be made to a context-free grammar in order to convert it to an acceptable LR(k) grammar.

Simply because a grammar is context-free, there is no guarantee that it can be converted into either an LL(k) or an LR(k) type grammar by simple transformations. At each stage of either an LL or LR analysis, there must exist a unique relationship between the next k symbols in the string and a specific production in the grammar. If this

TABLE 1. Grammars and Languages of Various Types

LR, left-parsable, not LL	$S :: = A \mid B$ $A :: = aaA \mid aa$ $B :: = aaB \mid a$
LR, not left-parsable	$S :: = Ab \mid Ac$ $A :: = AB \mid a$ $B :: = a$
Left- and right-parsable, not LR	$S :: = Ab \mid Bc$ $A :: = Aa \mid a$ $B :: = Ba \mid a$
Right-parsable only	$S :: = Ab \mid Bc$ $A :: = AC \mid a$ $B :: = BC \mid a$ $C :: = a$
Left-parsable only	$S :: = BAb \mid CAc$ $A :: = BA \mid a$ $B :: = a$ $C :: = a$

TABLE 2. Attributes of LL and LR Grammars

Attribute	LL	LR
Grammars	Can be hard to construct; rather awkward/ unnatural. Class of LL grammars is small.	Rather straightforward. Can express virtually all programming constructs naturally.
Languages	Like the grammars, class is small but is adequate for the normal syntactic features of programming languages.	Can find an LR(1) grammar for *every* deterministic context-free language.
		Some examples of LR but not LL languages: $\{a^n b^n \mid n \geq 1\}$ $\cup \{a^n c^n \mid n \geq 1\}$ $\{a^n b^m \mid 1 \leq m \leq n\}$ $\{a^n O b^n \mid n \geq 0\}$ $\cup \{a^n O b^{2n} \mid n \geq 0\}$

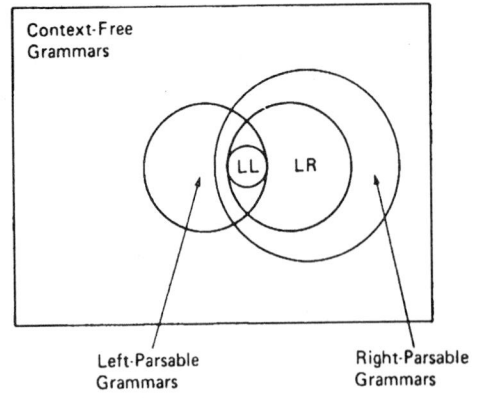 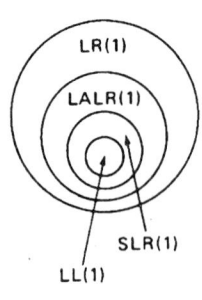

FIG. 1. Relationships between grammars.

relationship cannot be determined, then the grammar cannot be converted into one of the desired forms. Thus, there are grammars that are LL and not LR and others that, though parsable to either a left or right derivative form by the addition of further information about the string, are not LL or LR, respectively. The set of grammars in Table 1 are examples of each of these cases.

Although LR parsing techniques have been known since 1965, the parsers produced were far too large to be practical. However, optimizing techniques were discovered by DeRemer in 1969, resulting in modified grammars known as SLR (Simple LR) and LALR (Look-Ahead LR) parsers. Each of these is defined in terms of the optimization techniques that are used and are virtually impossible to construct by hand except in trivial cases. Basically, given an LR(1) system, the optimization process develops an LALR parser, while an LR(0) grammar can be converted into an SLR system. However, this process is not guaranteed for all LR grammars and, thus, the set of languages that can be optimized in this way is much smaller than that which may be represented by the LR system of grammars.

Table 2 lists some of the characteristics of LL and LR grammars and provides a comparison of the qualities of each grammar system. Fig. 1 illustrates some relationships of the grammars discussed in this article. Both the table and figure are due to N. Tindall.

References

1978. Lewis, P. M. 2d, Rosenkrantz, D. J., and Stearns, R. E. *Compiler Design Theory*. Reading, MA: Addison-Wesley.
1979. Aho, A. V. and Ullman, J. D. *Principles of Compiler Design*. Reading, MA: Addison-Wesley.

J. A. N. LEE

GRAPH THEORY

For articles on related subjects *see* ALGORITHMS, ANALYSIS OF; COMPUTATIONAL COMPLEXITY; DATA STRUCTURES; DISCRETE MATHEMATICS; NP-COMPLETE PROBLEMS; and TREE.

A *graph* is a set of points (commonly called *vertices* or *nodes*) in space that are interconnected by a set of lines (called *edges*). For a graph G, the edge set is denoted by E and the vertex set by V, so that $G=(V,E)$. Common nomenclature denotes the number of Vertices $|V|$ by n and the number of edges $|E|$ by m. Fig. 1 shows a graph G with $V=\{v_1, v_2, v_3, v_4, v_5\}$, $E=\{e_1, e_2, e_3, e_4, e_5, e_6, e_7\}$, $n=5$, and $m=7$. If, within E, each edge is specified by its pair of endpoints (e.g. for the example of Fig. 1, e_1 is replaced by (v_1, v_2) etc), the figure can be dispensed with.

If, as in most applications, the values of both n and m are finite, G is said to be a *finite* graph. The *degree* of a vertex v (denoted by $d(v)$) is the number of edges that have v as an endpoint. An elementary theorem (with an easy inductive proof) is that within a finite graph there are always an even number of vertices with odd degree. For example, in the graph of Fig. 1 there are two vertices (v_1 and v_2) of odd degree (both have degree 3). A *self-loop* is an edge (v_i, v_j) where $v_i=v_j$. Two edges (v_i, v_j) and (v_r, v_s) are *parallel edges* if $v_i=v_r$ and $v_j=v_s$. A *simple graph* is a graph without self-loops and without parallel edges. A *multigraph* contains parallel edges but no self-loops. A *path* between vertices v_1 and v_s is a sequence of vertices $(v_1, v_2, v_3..., v_s)$ such that $(v_i, v_{i+1}) \in E$ for $1 \le i \le s-1$. If $v_i = v_s$, the path is a *circuit* (or cycle). If no vertex appears more than once on a path, then the path is a *simple path* (similarly, a *simple circuit* passes through any vertex at most once). A *component* of a graph is defined by stating that a path exists between any pair of vertices if and only if the two vertices belong to the same component of the graph. A graph consisting of a single component is said to be a *connected graph*. A *tree* is a connected graph containing no circuits. For any tree T with n vertices and m edges, $m=n-1$ and there exists precisely one path between any pair of vertices of T.

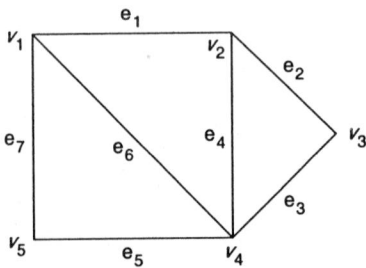

FIG. 1.

In many applications it is natural to associate a direction with each edge of the graph. The graph is then said to be a *directed graph* or *digraph*. In specifying any edge of a digraph by its end-points, then (by convention) the edge is understood to be directed from the first vertex towards the second. The *indegree*, $d^-(v)$, of any vertex v is the number of edges directed towards v. Similarly, the *outdegree*, $d^+(v)$, of v is the number of edges directed from v. A digraph G is *strongly connected* if, for any pair of vertices u and v of G, there exists a path from u to v and a path from v to u.

Any *subgraph* of a graph G can be obtained by removing vertices and edges from G. It is understood that the removal of an edge leaves its endpoints in place, whereas the removal of a vertex necessitates the removal of any edges with that vertex as an endpoint. An *articulation point* of a connected graph is any vertex whose removal produces a subgraph with two or more components. Any graph with no articulation point is said to be *2-connected*. In a 2-connected graph there are at least two vertex-disjoint paths between any pair of vertices. Two paths are *vertex disjoint* if (apart from the ends of the path) they do not share a vertex. A 2-connected component (sometimes called a *block*) of a graph G is a maximal subgraph G' of G (maximal in the sense that no additional edges or vertices of G can be added to G') such that there are at least two vertex-disjoint paths between every pair of vertices of G'.

Many applications require a number to be associated with each edge of a graph. Such a graph with associated *edge weights* is said to be a *weighted graph*. For any edge (u,v), $w(u,v)$ denotes the edge weight, which is also sometimes called the *length* of (u,v).

In a *complete graph*, there is an edge between every pair of vertices. The complete graph with n vertices is denoted by K_n. Fig. 2 shows K_3 and K_4. In a *regular* undirected graph, every vertex has the same degree; if this is k, the graph is *k-regular*. Note that K_n is $(n-1)$-regular.

If, for a graph G, it is possible to partition the vertex set v into two disjoint subsets, V_1 and V_2 $(V_1 \cup V_2 = V)$, such that every edge of G connects a vertex in V_1 to a vertex in V_2, then G is a *bipartite graph*. If there is an edge between every vertex of V_1 and every edge of V_2, then G is said to be a *complete bipartite graph*, which is denoted by $K_{i,j}$ where $|V_1|=i$ and $|V_2|=j$. Fig. 3 shows two representations of $K_{3,3}$. In this figure, dots distinguish vertices from edge crossings. The graphs of this figure are said to be *isomorphic*. Two graphs are isomorphic if there is a one-to-one correspondence between the vertices of one and

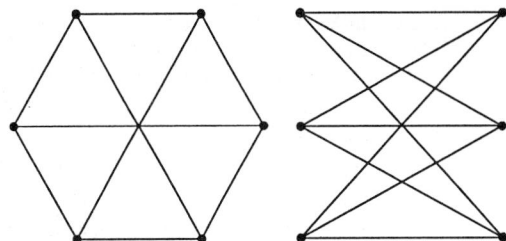

FIG. 3.

the vertices of the other such that the number of edges between any two vertices of one is equal to the number of edges between the corresponding vertices in the other.

Computations involving graphs require that the graph be represented somehow within computer storage. The choice of data structure may have important implications for the complexity of the algorithm. A natural form of representation is provided by a so-called *adjacency matrix*. An adjacency matrix A is an $n \times n$ matrix where $A(i,j)=1$ if $(v_i,v_j) \in E$ and is 0 otherwise. Such a representation requires $O(n^2)$ storage space and consequently requires $O(n^2)$ time to initialize. Adjacency matrices are very useful for algorithmic questions concerning paths in graphs. For example, it is not difficult to show that there is a path of length r (i.e. having r edges) from v_s to v_t if and only if $A^r(s,t)=1$, where A^r is the r-th matrix product. Another common data structure for graphs is the so-called *adjacency list* representation. In this representation, for every $v \in V$, $L(v)$ is a pointer to a list of vertices adjacent to v. Fig. 4 shows the adjacency list representation of the graph of Fig. 1. The adjacency list representation of a graph requires $O(n+m)$ space and thus $O(n+m)$ time to initialize. From the point of view of complexity considerations, this is usually an improvement compared with adjacency matrices.

Graph Algorithms Many graph algorithms are structured by systematically searching (or *traversing*) the graph subjected to the algorithm. Consider the following technique for traversing a (connected) graph. Initially mark all vertices as being "unvisited." Now start the search at some arbitrarily chosen vertex and, when visiting any vertex v, proceed as follows. If v has not been previously visited, mark v as "visited." Next, visit an "unvisited" vertex in the adjacency list for v. If no such vertex exists, return to the vertex visited just before v was visited for the first time. The visit terminates when all vertices adjacent to the initial vertex have been visited and the search has returned to the initial vertex.

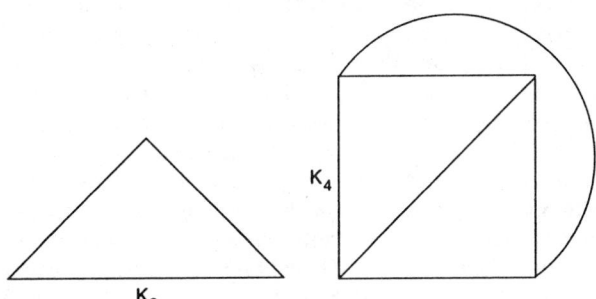

FIG. 2.

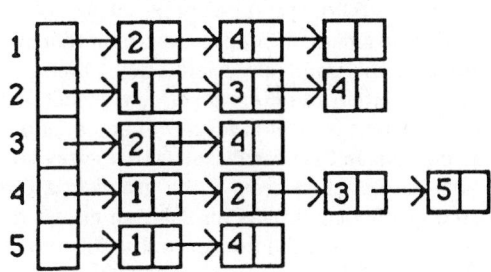

FIG. 4.

Such a search is called a *depth first search* (DFS). A DFS of a graph G has certain useful properties: (a) the set of edges by which vertices are visited for the first time form a tree (called the DFS tree and rooted at the initially visited vertex), (b) edges of G not belonging to the DFS tree connect two nodes, one of which is a decendent of the other in the DFS tree, (c) DFS can be achieved in $O(n + m)$ time. Another frequently employed traversal method is *breadth first search* (BFS). In a BFS, some arbitrary vertex is visited first, and this vertex is placed on an initially empty queue (first-in, first-out data structure), Q. At any point in the traversal, visit next some vertex v' that is "unvisited" and is in the adjacency list of the vertex v at the head of the queue (if v has not been visited before, add v to the queue). If no such vertex as v' exists, remove v from the queue and repeat the process. The traversal stops when the queue becomes empty. A BFS of G has the following properties: (a) the edges by which vertices are first visited form a BFS tree rooted at the initially visited vertex, (b) those edges of G not in the BFS tree connect vertices, neither of which is an ancestor of the other in the BFS tree, (c) BFS can be achieved in $O(n + m)$ time.

Particular types of traversals of a graph such as those just described have individual properties that make them appropriate for particular algorithmic application. For example, the properties of DFS leads to a classic $O(n + m)$ algorithm to find the blocks of a graph. Similarly, application of DFS to digraphs provides an $O(n + m)$ algorithm to find the strongly connected components of a digraph. In a BFS of an undirected graph, the depth of a vertex v in the BFS tree rooted at v' is precisely the shortest distance from v to v' in the original graph. This leads to an $O(n + m)$ algorithm for finding distances between a single vertex and all the other vertices in a graph (which is the so-called *single source shortest paths problem*). Such a search, however, is not useful when shortest paths in weighted graphs are required. In such graphs, distances are measured as the sum of the edge weights (rather than in numbers of edges) on a path, and there are several classic algorithms for the single source shortest paths problem (such as *Dijkstra's algorithm*, which operates in $O(n^2)$ time with simple data structures that can be improved to $O(m+n\log n)$, using sophisticated structures). There now follows a catalog of commonly occuring graph problems with some indication of their algorithmic complexities. Algorithms for these problems can be found in the references or in the primary sources cited therein. Many problems concerning graphs are intractable, being NP-complete (*q.v.*). (Garey and Johnson, 1979).

An *Eulerian circuit* of a graph is a circuit that contains every edge of the graph precisely once. Of course, not every graph contains an Eulerian circuit. In fact, a necessary and sufficient condition for a connected, undirected graph to contain an Eulerian circuit is that every vertex of the graph is of even degree. If the graph is a directed connected graph, it contains an Eulerian circuit (such a circuit traces each edge in the sense that it is directed) if and only if for each vertex v, $d^+(v)= d^-(v)$. Eulerian circuits can be found in $O(m)$ time. Eulerian circuits, for the

special class of graphs that contain them, are solutions of the *Chinese Postman problem*. Given a weighted graph or digraph, the Chinese Postman problem is to find a (not necessarily simple) circuit of shortest length (the length is given by $\Sigma_{\text{all edges } e}\, w(e)r(e)$, where $w(e)$ is the weight of e and $r(e)$ is the number of occurrences of e in the circuit) that traverses each edge of the graph at least once. Every connected undirected graph contains a solution to the Chinese Postman problem, whereas a connected digraph has a solution if and only if the digraph is strongly connected. There are low-order polynomial-time algorithms for the Chinese Postman problem for both undirected and directed connected graphs.

A *Hamiltonian circuit* of a connected graph is a circuit that passes through each vertex precisely once. Such a circuit can be defined for both directed and undirected graphs (of course, in the case of digraphs, edges are traversed in the same sense as they are directed). Not every graph contains a Hamiltonian circuit and (unlike the case for Eulerian circuits) there seems to be no polynomial time test for whether such a circuit exists for a given graph. In fact, the problem of determining whether a graph contains a Hamiltonian circuit is a classic NP-complete problem. If the graph is weighted, the problem of finding a shortest Hamiltonian circuit is one variation of the well-known *Traveling Salesman* problem. Another variant is to find the shortest circuit that passes through each vertex *at least* once. In this second form, a solution to the problem always exists, whereas for the former specification the graph of course has to contain a Hamiltonian circuit. In both these forms, the Traveling Salesman problem is NP-complete.

A *(transport) network* is a connected digraph in which one vertex x (called the *source*) has $d^+(x)>0$ and one vertex y (the *sink*) has $d^-(y)>0$. A flow of the network associates a weight $f(e)$ with each edge e such that, for all vertices v other than x or y, $\Sigma_{(u,v)\in E}f(u,v)=\Sigma_{(v,u)\in E}f(v,u)$. Clearly, a network is a model for the flow of material leaving a single departure point (the source) and arriving at a single point (the sink). The equation ensures a conservation of flow at all other vertices. It is usual to associate (apart from $f(e)$) another parameter (called the *capacity* of e and denoted by $c(e)$) with each edge, which is the maximum value that $f(e)$ can attain. Thus, $0 \le f(e) \le c(e)$ for all e. For a network N, $F(N)$ denotes the value of the flow that is defined to be the net flow leaving the source: $F(N) = \Sigma_{(x,v)\in E}f(x,v) - S_{(v,x)\in E}f(v,x)$. A standard problem in network theory is to find a set of $f(e)$ such that $F(N)$ is a maximum. This is called the *maximum flow problem*. The problem of finding a maximum flow has a low-order, polynomial-time solution. The value of such a flow is given by the classic theorem of Ford and Fulkerson (called the *max-flow, min-cut theorem*), which states that $F(N)$ has a maximum value equal to the minimum capacity of all cuts of the network. A *cut* of the network is a minimal set of edges whose removal from the network separates the network into two components, one containing x and the other containing y. The capacity of the cut is the sum of the capacities of those edges in the cut that are directed from the component containing x and directed towards the component containing y. Many other problems can be posed for networks. For example, if yet another parameter (called the cost of e and denoted by $a(e)$) is associated with each edge, the *minimum cost flow problem* is to find (for a given value $F(N)$) a set of $f(e)$ such that the sum $\Sigma_{(u,v)\in E} f(u,v)a(u,v)$ is minimized. Again, there are low-order, polynomial-time algorithms to solve this problem.

Planar graphs are an important subclass of graphs. A graph is planar if it can be arranged on a planar surface (the arrangement is called an *embedding*) so that, at most, one vertex occupies or, at most, one edge passes through any point of the plane. There exists algorithms that can test whether a graph is planar (such algorithms normally generate an embedding) in $O(n)$ time.

Scheduling and time-tabling problems, among others, generate problems equivalent to coloring graphs. A *vertex coloring* of a graph is the assignment of a color to each vertex of the graph in such a way that no two adjacent vertices have the same color (vertices are adjacent if there is an edge connecting them). Normally, the interest is to find a vertex coloring that employs a minimum number of colors, this number is called the *vertex-chromatic index*. Similarly, an *edge coloring* is an assignment of colors to the edges in such a way that no two edges sharing an endpoint have the same color. The minimum number of colors required to do this is the *edge-chromatic index*. Problems involving the coloring of graphs are notoriously intractable. For example, the problems of determining whether the vertex- or the edge-chromatic index are less than some fixed constant are both NP-complete.

A *matching* of a graph is a subset of its edges such that no two elements of the subset have a common endpoint. The question of determining matchings arises in many guises. Common problems concern finding *maximum cardinality matchings* (such a matching has a maximum number of elements) and *maximum weight matchings* (which occur for weighted graphs; the sum of the edge weights of such a matching is maximized). Efficient (polynomial-time) algorithms are known for both of these problems.

A *spanning tree* of a connected graph G is a connected circuitless subgraph of G that contains every vertex of G. The *connector problem*, a classic problem of graph theory, is to find a spanning tree of a weighted connected graph such that the sum of the edge weights of the tree is a minimum. Such a solution is also called a *minimum weight spanning tree*. Spanning trees can be found in $O(m+n)$ time (e.g. a depth-first-search tree). Prim's or Kruskal's algorithms provide classic solutions to the connector problem at low-order polynomial-time cost.

The *vertex-connectivity* $K_v(G)$ of a connected graph G is the minimum number of vertices that have to be removed from G in order to produce a subgraph of two or more components. If a graph has $K_v(G)=k$, there are k vertex disjoint paths between every pair of vertices. The *edge-connectivity* $K_e(G)$ is similarly defined. Also, if

$K_e(G)=k$, there are k edge disjoint paths between every pair of vertices. There exists polynomial-time solutions to the problems of finding $K_v(G)$ and $K_e(G)$ for an arbitrary graph G.

Given two graphs G_1 and G_2, many applications of graphs require one of the following two problems to be solved. (a) Is G_1 isomorphic to G_2? (This is called the *graph isomorphism problem*.) (b) Is G_1 isomorphic to a subgraph of G_2? (This is the *subgraph isomorphism problem*.) Both of these problems are notoriously costly to solve, and no polynimial-time solution is known for either if G_1 and G_2 are arbitrary graphs.

Given the intractability of many problems in graph theory, it is natural that this area has given rise to the development of many approximation algorithms. An *approximation algorithm* is an algorithm that runs in polynomial-time but that provides an approximation (within known bounds) to the problem in hand. A classic example is provided by *Christofides' algorithm*, which finds a solution to the Traveling Salesman problem that guarantees that the solution found is no more than a factor of 3/2 longer than an optimum solution. While this approximation may not seem to be very tight, no approximation algorithm is presently known that provides a better guarantee. Another example provides an approximation for the edge-chromatic index of a graph and is the polynomial-time algorithm implicit in the proof of *Vizing's theorem*. This algorithm gives an edge-coloring, using no more than one more color than is necessary, a very good approximation. Unless there are polynomial-time solutions for the NP-complete problems (an unlikely possibility), it has been proved that there can be no polynomial-time solution that gives a vertex coloring of an arbitrary graph that guarantees to use less than twice the minimum number of colors required.

References

1979. Even, S. *Graph Algorithms*. Potomac, MD: Computer Science Press.

1979. Garey, M. R., and Johnson, D. S. *Computers and Intractability: A Guide to the Theory of NP-Completeness*. San Francisco: Freeman.

1985. Berge G. *Graphs*. Amsterdam: North-Holland, (2nd Rev. Ed.).

1985. Gibbons, A. M. *Algorithmic Graph Theory*. Cambridge: Cambridge University Press.

1990. van Leeuwen, J. *Graph Algorithms*. Chapter 10 of the *Handbook of Theoretical Computer Science*, Volume A (Algorithms and Complexity), J. van Leeuwen(Ed.), New York: Elsevier.

ALAN M. GIBBONS

GRAPHICAL USER INTERFACE (GUI). *See* USER INTERFACE.

GRAPHICS. *See* COMPUTER GRAPHICS.

GROSCH'S LAW

For articles on related subjects *see* BENCHMARKS; PERFORMANCE MEASUREMENT AND EVALUATION; and PERFORMANCE OF COMPUTERS.

In the late 1940s, Herbert R. J. Grosch formulated *Grosch's law* concerning economies of scale in computers; namely, that computing power increases as the square of the cost, or

$$p = kc^2$$

where p = computing power, k = a constant, and c = system cost (either lease price or purchase price) so that, for example, for twice the money one obtains four times the computing power.

Grosch developed the "law" by hand on semi-log paper two or three years before the delivery of mass-produced machines. The data points he used "...were hand calculations, log tables, desk calculators, punched card machines (IBM 601, 602A, 604), relay calculators, ENIAC, the SSEC, NORC, the Harvard Mark I and Mark II and rumors of the SEAC. Speeds were not known yet for the Eckert-Mauchy machine (later UNIVAC I) or for the Defense Calculator and Tape Processing Machine (later IBM 701 and 702), let alone prices, and costs of one-off machinery were the wildest kind of guesswork." (Grosch, 1975, p. 9). This was a rather casual beginning for a "law" that has given rise to a great deal of research and speculation.

While Grosch did not originally publish his law, it became part of the oral tradition of the computer industry. It was quoted both seriously and humorously, and eventually gained respectability through numerous journal citations. The earliest presentation by Grosch himself was in the *Journal of the Optical Society of America* in 1953 (Grosch, 1953).

The pricing implications inherent in Grosch's law led to serious attempts to ascertain its validity. While several earlier studies lent empirical validity to its assumptions, it is not clear whether this reflected a true value in relation to users' costs or if computer manufacturers used its widespread acceptance in pricing (Bertean, 1975). Most studies performed since the late 1970s question whether it still holds.

Regardless of whether Grosch's law still holds, there are limits to the extent that economies of scale can be realized and there is some point—the state of the art—beyond which computing power can only be increased at great cost. Also, the calculations of Grosch's law reflect a given instant in that they are concerned with new computers only. The existence of a used computer market, short- and long-term leases, third-party leases, and the emergence of the personal computer all limit applicability of the law.

Grosch felt that, if the considerations include "total cost"—CPU, memory, peripheral devices, software, and operations, then "...my old law still gives useful guidance." (Grosch, 1975) However, Grosch and other authors would agree that, regardless of the truth in the law, "...real computing power comes from the smarter use of computers...," not from raw power alone (Jones, 1985).

References

1953. Grosch, H. R. J. "High Speed Arithmetic: The Digital Computer as a Research Tool," *Journal of the Optical Society of America*, **43**, *4* (April) 306–310.

1975. Bertean, D. "Letter," *Computerworld*, **8**, *12* (16 March) 13.

1975. Grosch, Herb. "Grosch's Law Revisited," *Computerworld*, **8**, *16* (16 April) 9.

1985. Jones, Jeremy. "On Grosch's Law Revisited," in "Letters, ACM Forum," Robert L. Ashenhurst, editor, *Communications of the ACM*, **28**, 5 (May) 453.

ROBERT P. CERVENY AND KENNETH E. KNIGHT

GROUPWARE

For articles on related subjects see BULLETIN BOARD; COMPUTER CONFERENCING; and ELECTRONIC MAIL.

Groupware is the software written to support a class of applications arising from the integration of computation and communication. Groupware must be able to support two or more users engaged in a common task and provide the users with an interface to a shared environment (Ellis, 1989). Thus, groupware is an area of organizational computing, the field of study and practice concerned with discovering and developing useful fits between computing possibilities and organizational (in contrast to individual) needs (Applegate, 1991). In practice, groupware denotes human-machine systems that support multi-agent communication, cooperation, collaboration, and coordination in the course of organizational activity.

Groupware has become important because in the setting of diverse, interdependent, and competing organizational forms, improvement of organizational effectiveness is a paramount concern. This requires more than improving intrinsic individual productivities. It entails the creation, use, and maintenance of both structural and dynamic configurations of interaction such that the organizations' productivity is maximized or improved on a continuing basis. Groupware is concerned with the ways in which computing technologies can facilitate such efforts.

Groupware is a multi-disciplinary research area that draws on theories from distributed computing (*q.v.*), parallel processing (*q.v.*), cognitive engineering of interactive software, model management, social psychology, sociology, organizational design, and economics. Thus, groupware is the next step in the progression from electronic data processing to decision support systems by way of management information systems (*q.v.*).

There is a fundamental difference between groupware and other systems that support multi-user activity, such as database management systems (*q.v.*). The aim of the database approach to information locking is to create the impression that users are working on a single, isolated task. The underlying design philosophy is that each user should work independently of others and remain unaware of their actions. In groupware systems, the fundamental design philosophy is that group processes must be actively supported and that users must be made aware of the context in which their tasks are being executed. Hence, weak locking mechanisms like *telepointers* (cursors that appear on more than one display and that can be moved by different users) are used.

An early advance in groupware systems was the development of meeting room technology and group decision support systems (GDSS). These efforts concentrated on augmenting the efficiency of meetings and small group discussions, with an emphasis on single-party, co-located, same time interaction. Since then, groupware has made enormous strides. Systems have been designed and built to support business case discussions (CATT), collaboratory work (COLAB), real time structured discussion (rIBIS), group editors (GROVE), group writing tools (QUILT), and organizational coordination (Coordinator).

Groupware is still very much in Kuhn's pre-paradigm stage. The grand challenge facing groupware researchers and developers is to create theories that bind research streams from multiple disciplines. At the theoretical end, there is the need for the identification and/or creation of mathematical frameworks and models of group, team, and organizational roles, tasks, and procedures. From a systems development perspective, the key research issues include the development of multiuser, multi-media interfaces, distributed concurrent architectures for shared objects, and a variety of flexible interaction locking mechanisms.

References

1989. Ellis, C. A., Gibbs, S. J., and Rein G. L. "Groupware: The Research and Development Issues," *MCC Technical Report STP-414-88*, 3 March.

1991. Applegate, L. M., Ellis, C. A., Holsapple, C. W., Radermacher, F. J., and Whinston, A. B. "Organizational Computing: Definitions and Issues," *Journal of Organizational Computing*, *1*, *1*, 1–10.

Clyde W. Holsapple, Sukumar Rathnam, and Andrew B. Whinston

GUARDED COMMAND

For articles on related subjects *see* CONTROL STRUCTURES; PROGRAMMING LANGUAGE SEMANTICS; and PROGRAM VERIFICATION.

The term *guarded command*, as defined by Dijkstra (1975), is synonymous with a conditionally executed statement. More precisely, a guarded command is the combination of a condition (boolean expression) B and the (possibly compound) statement S whose execution is controlled by B. In a sense, B "guards" the execution of S. In Dijkstra's notation, a guarded command is represented as

$$B \rightarrow S.$$

In more common notation, the meaning of a guarded command is very much like that of the simple selection structure (**if** statement):

$$\textbf{if } B \textbf{ then } S.$$

Unlike the **if** statement, however, a guarded command, by itself, is not a complete statement in a programming language. Rather, it is one component of a more extensive control structure containing one or more guarded commands. The most interesting applications of guarded commands are those involving a set of n of them, for $n > 1$.

$$
\begin{aligned}
B_1 &\rightarrow S_1 \\
B_2 &\rightarrow S_2 \\
&\;\;\vdots \\
B_n &\rightarrow S_n
\end{aligned}
$$

Here there are n boolean expressions, each guarding a different statement. When a structure containing a set of guarded commands is executed, the guards are evaluated; the fashion in which they are evaluated is completely immaterial. Upon evaluation, a subset (which may be empty) of the guards will have the value **true**. Of this subset, one is chosen *at random*; it is the corresponding S that is selected for execution.

If all of the guards in a given guarded command set are disjoint—that is, if no more than one guard is **true** at any given time—then the selection of S is well-defined despite the unspecified and random nature of guard evaluation and selection. If, however, the guards are not disjoint, with the possibility that more than one may be true simultaneously, then selection of S is not well defined (and indeed may be different from one execution of the program to the next). For this reason, guarded command sets are fundamentally nondeterministic. The nondeterminism places increased emphasis on abstract specification of the desired computation, with corresponding de-emphasis of algorithm implementation details. This encourages more systematic, and hence reliable, program development.

Guarded command sets may be incorporated into control structures in a number of ways. The two following examples, together with simple illustrative applications, have been described by Dijkstra. In each case, the control structure syntax is the guarded command set, as formulated above, enclosed in a pair of key words.

A *selection* control structure has the syntax

$$
\begin{aligned}
&\textbf{if} \\
&\quad B_1 \rightarrow S_1 \\
&\quad B_2 \rightarrow S_2 \\
&\quad\;\; \vdots \\
&\quad B_n \rightarrow S_n \\
&\textbf{fi}
\end{aligned}
$$

The semantics of this structure are that after execution of an S, execution of the **if-fi** terminates. Only one execution of an S is performed, the selection of which is as described above. If no B is true in an execution of an **if-fi** structure, then execution of the **if-fi** does not terminate, causing the program to abort. In a multitasking (*q.v.*) environment, an alternative might be to wait for a guard to become true.

This **if-fi** structure is very much like the classical **case** control structure (*see* CONTROL STRUCTURE), in that only one statement group is executed and the order of the statement groups is immaterial. Unlike the usual **case** structure, however, the guards in the **if-fi** structure may be non-disjoint arbitrary conditions. In the **case** structure, the "guards" are disjoint sets of constants. Thus, the **case** structure is completely deterministic, whereas the **if-fi** is in general non-deterministic.

The following program is a simple application of the **if-fi** structure.

$$[\text{determine } max\ (P,Q)]$$

if
$$P \geq Q \rightarrow \text{MAX} \leftarrow P$$
$$Q \geq P \rightarrow \text{MAX} \leftarrow Q$$
fi
$$[\text{MAX} = max(P,Q)]$$

Note in this example that one of the two guards must be true, so that execution of this **if-fi** is guaranteed to terminate. Note also that both guards may be true (when $P = Q$), and that in this case execution of either statement gives the same result. Thus, at termination of execution of the **if-fi**, MAX $= max(\text{P,Q})$.

A *repetition* control structure involving guarded commands has the form

do
$$B_1 \rightarrow S_1$$
$$B_2 \rightarrow S_2$$
$$.$$
$$.$$
$$.$$
$$B_n \rightarrow S_n$$
od

The semantics are that a statement S is selected in the manner described above, and, after execution of S, this entire process is repeated. Execution of the **do-od** structure terminates only when all guards evaluate to **false**. By constructing the appropriate guards, any desired repetitive control can be achieved.

The following program for calculating the greatest common divisor of two positive integers illustrates the use of **do-od** for specifying repetition control.

$$[\text{determine } gcd(P,Q)]$$

$$X \leftarrow P, Y \leftarrow Q$$
do
$$X > Y \rightarrow X \leftarrow X - Y$$
$$Y > X \rightarrow Y \leftarrow Y - X$$
od
$$[X = Y = gcd(P,Q)]$$

Note that the two guards in this program for *gcd* are disjoint, so that this example is completely deterministic. In principle, the guards for a given control pattern can always be devised so that no two are true simultaneously, although this restriction often (unnecessarily) complicates guard construction and evaluation.

It is well known that **if-then-else** selection control and **do while** repetition control are sufficient to construct any conceivable execution control in a program. Special cases of **if-fi** and **do-od** are identical to **if-then-else** and **do while**, as shown in the following constructs.

if B **then** S_1	**if**
else S_2	$B \rightarrow S_1$
endif	$\neg B \rightarrow S_2$
	fi
do while B	**do**
S	$B \rightarrow S$
endloop	**od**

These particular forms of **if-fi** and **do-od** are completely deterministic, and the **if-fi** is guaranteed to terminate.

Therefore, **if-fi** and **do-od**, as defined here in general, are quite versatile control structures. The inefficiencies of guard evaluation, however, currently discourage their use as practical control structures in programming languages. This could change with the advent of highly parallel architectures and corresponding language support—**if-fi** and **do-od** are inherently "parallel," and concurrent guard evaluation would resolve the efficiency issue. Because **if-fi** and **do-od** are simple and systematic and therefore relatively amenable to formal description and analysis, guarded commands could increase in practical importance in situations requiring more formal analysis, such as highly parallel algorithm development.

References

1975. Dijkstra, E. J. "Guarded Commands, Nondeterminancy and Formal Derivations of Programs," *Communications ACM*, **18** (August).
1976. Dijkstra, E. J. *A Discipline of Programming*. Englewood Cliffs, NJ: Prentice-Hall.

JERROLD L. WAGENER

GURU

For articles on related subjects *see* POWER USER; and WIZARD.

The term *guru* is used more frequently in computing than in most other phases of human activity, but with its conventional meaning: a wise person—a teacher, perhaps—who knows or claims to know a great deal about a particular subject and who is readily available and anxious to share his or her knowledge with others. Some early computer gurus were Jackson Granholm, who held forth in *Datamation* and who coined the term "kludge" (*q.v.*), and H. R. J. Grosch, who promulgated, among other precepts, Grosch's Law (*q.v.*). The era of the personal computer has spawned more gurus than mainframe computers ever did, current exemplars being John Dvorak and Jim Seymour of *PC Magazine*, Esther Dyson of EDventure Holdings, Stewart Alsop of *InfoWorld*, and Jerry Pournelle of *Byte* magazine.

Gurus, who *know* much, are not necessarily programmers and hence not usually *wizards*, who can *do* much, though they may very well be *power users* of particular operating systems, user interfaces (*q.v.*), or applications software.

EDWIN D. REILLY

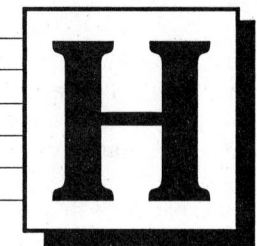

HACKER

For articles on related subjects *see* BULLETIN BOARD; COMPUTER CRIME; COMPUTER SECURITY; COMPUTER VIRUS; PROGRAMMER; and WIZARD.

A *hacker* is a person obsessed with computers. At the heart of the obsession is a drive to master the computer. The classic hacker was simply a compulsive programmer. It is only recently that the term hacker has become associated with computerized vandalism. The best known description of hackers comes from Weizenbaum (1976):

> bright young men of disheveled appearance, often with sunken glowing eyes, can be seen sitting at computer consoles, their arms tensed and waiting to fire their fingers, already poised to strike, at the buttons and keys on which their attention seems to be as riveted as a gambler's on the rolling dice....They work until they nearly drop, twenty, thirty hours at a time....If possible they sleep on cots near the computer. But only for a few hours—then back to the console or the printouts. Their crumpled clothes, their unwashed and unshaven faces, and their uncombed hair all testify that they are oblivious to their bodies and to the world in which they move. They exist, at least when so engaged, only through and for the computers.

The majority of hackers are young men, often teenagers, who have found within the computer a world that they can mold to their desires, a world far less threatening and more rewarding to them than the world of conventional social relations. Many of them are social misfits—shy, inarticulate young men with few fulfilling personal relationships. Turkle (1984) describes hackers as "trapped" in a quest for control and mastery with the computer as their medium.

Early hacker communities developed around accessible interactive computer systems at places such as M.I.T. Today, hacker communities are often linked through bulletin board and message systems, and their members may never have met or even know each others' real names, only their aliases.

A hacker gains status by demonstrating his or her mastery of the system. This may be done by writing clever programs (hacks), "cracking" a system by penetrating its security, crashing a system, or accessing supposedly secure information. The highest accolade for a hacker is to be termed a *wizard* by other hackers.

The Hacker Ethic The hacker's obsession with computing leads to impatience and intolerance with anything that stands in the way. Levy (1984) codifies the resulting *hacker ethic*:

> Access to computers—and anything which might teach you something about the way the world works—should be unlimited and total. Always yield to the Hands-On Imperative!
> All information should be free.
> Mistrust Authority—Promote Decentralization.
> Hackers should be judged by their hacking, not bogus criteria such as degrees, age, race, or position.
> You can create art and beauty on a computer.
> Computers can change your life for the better.

Noticeably missing from this ethic is respect for personal property, security, and privacy. While they may be scrupulously honest and law abiding in other aspects, hackers let no one and nothing come between them and their pursuit of computing. This leads to conflict between those who follow the hacker ethic and the larger community of users.

Types of Hackers Most early hackers were programmers. Hacking, as a programming style, is distinguished by its lack of apparent method. Hackers are impatient with structured design, systematic development, and documentation. Instead, the hacker spends long hours at the terminal developing programs and debugging them interactively. Hackers believe that programs should be built "straight from your mind" (Turkle, 1984). They prize concise, efficient, elegant, and even tricky code. Although this programming style is frowned upon by more conventional programmers, many hacker-developed projects, such as the text editor EMACS and the Incompatible Timesharing System (ITS) (both developed at M.I.T.), are prime examples of the programming craft.

Traditionally, hackers have been a valuable resource to computing centers. Their knowledge of the machine and their programming skills are prized. Typically, hackers work only on programs that interest them; are reluctant to take on assigned projects, particularly if they offer no opportunity to demonstrate mastery of the computer; are reluctant to document their work; and are endlessly tinkering and adding "features," which may result in products that are never finished or unstable.

Some hackers demonstrate their proficiency in socially unacceptable ways. *Crackers* penetrate computer systems. They see computer system security as a challenge and a puzzle to solve. Cracking is almost as old as hacking itself. Hackers are commonly intolerant of anything that limits their access to information. They are driven by curiosity and see a lock, whether physical or part of a computer system, as a challenge to be met. Thus, many M.I.T. hackers were skilled lock pickers and were more than willing to apply their skills wherever there was a locked door (Levy, 1984; Turkle, 1984). Fortunately, most hackers are not malicious. Many of the computer break-ins that have caused such concern were motivated by curiosity on the part of the cracker. While the original intent was not malicious, many crackers cannot resist leaving some mark of their presence, and many trade methods of access to systems among themselves (Landreth, 1989). The original trespass by a curious cracker may be followed by serious damage by other, more malicious, hackers.

Phone phreaks are hackers who are fascinated with the telephone system. The primary motivation for the phone phreak is not the free phone call, but the opportunity to master a complex system. For example, the legendary phone phreak Cap'n Crunch, John Draper, once routed a phone call around the world and back to himself (Turkle, 1984). Draper's early phone phreaking activities were carried out with the aid of a promotional whistle from a box of Cap'n Crunch cereal that he used to generate control tones for the phone systems switching computers. Later phone phreaks used electronic "blue boxes" for similar activities. Today's phone phreaks rely upon stolen long distance access codes.

The hackers that have caused the greatest concern are the *computer vandals*. Computer vandals turn their skills toward damaging computer systems. *Crashers* demonstrate their mastery of computer systems by causing them to *crash*—i.e. to behave so erratically that they are incapable of continuing to provide service. Being able to shut down a supposedly crashproof system is a challenge many hackers cannot resist.

Other hackers create programs that interfere with system operations or destroy data. They may modify programs to create *trojan horses* that masquerade as useful software but actually destroy or corrupt data, create *virus* programs that "infect" or hide in other programs and awaken at unpredictable times to damage the system, and devise *worms* that transport themselves between computers in a network. Since trojan horses and virus programs inhibit the spread of public domain software and shareware, the hackers who create such programs are clearly working against the hacker ethic.

Worms have disrupted both the IBM internal computer network and the Internet (a group of connected computer networks, including ARPANET, BITNET, and CSNET) that links thousands of research and educational computing centers (see CACM (1989) for a detailed discussion). Fortunately, neither of these worms appear to have been particularly malicious. The IBM worm was apparently an attempt to spread Christmas cheer that succeeded beyond its creator's expectations, and the sole purpose of the Internet virus seems to have been to spread itself. Despite this, both caused major disruptions in the affected networks.

Hackers in Perspective

The public has become fascinated by hackers. Depictions in books such as Brunner's *The Shockwave Rider*, movies such as *War Games*, and television series such as *Whiz Kids* show the hacker in a sympathetic light. The hacker is usually portrayed as a boy genius. System break-ins by crackers, the activities of crashers, and even such disruptive activities as the IBM and Internet Worms have been excused as harmless pranks or even praised as valuable lessons in the need for system security. This tolerance is fading rapidly, however, and the perpetrators of both have been identified and punished.

There is some truth to this depiction. Many hackers are brilliant. Many are not malicious, merely curious or showing off. Many of the founding fathers of modern computing are former hackers: Bill Gates of Microsoft and Steve Jobs and Steve Wozniak of Apple Computer fame are prime examples.

Some authors have expressed concern about the mental well-being of hackers. Certainly, computers can be addictive (see Turkle (1984) and Weizenbaum (1976)), and such addictions can lead to problems in susceptible individuals. Most hackers do eventually outgrow their addiction, just as many have outgrown similar addictions to video games and "Dungeons and Dragons."

Unfortunately, hacking appears to have taken a damaging turn over the last several years. While the original hackers were certainly fond of pranks and had little respect for system security, they were primarily interested in developing elegant and powerful programs. Many of today's hackers seem more interested in gaining a name for themselves by damaging and disrupting systems than in developing new and useful software. In response to this new breed of hackers, there has been an increased call for the teaching of computer ethics and the redirecting of such activities into less harmful pursuits.

References

1976. Weizenbaum, Joseph. *Computer Power and Human Reason.* San Francisco: W. H. Freeman.

1984. Turkle, Sherry. *The Second Self: Computers and the Human Spirit.* New York: Simon and Schuster.

1984. Levy, Steven. *Hackers: Heroes of the Computer Revolution.* New York: Anchor Press/Doubleday.

1989. Landreth, Bill. *Out of the Inner Circle.* Redmond, Washington: Tempus Books of Microsoft Press.

1989. CACM Special Section on the Internet Worm. *Communications of the ACM,* **32**, 6 (June) 677–710.

1989. Stoll, Clifford. *The Cuckoo's Egg: Tracking a Spy Through the Maze of Computer Espionage.* New York: Doubleday.

ROBERT G. RITTENHOUSE

HANDICAPPED. *See* COMPUTING AND THE HANDICAPPED.

HANDSHAKING

For articles on related subjects *see* BUS; COMMUNICATIONS AND COMPUTERS; DATA COMMUNICATIONS; PROTOCOL; and TELEPROCESSING SYSTEMS.

The exchange of predetermined sequences of control signals or control characters between two devices or systems to establish a connection, to break a connection, or to exchange data and status information, is commonly referred to as *handshaking*. This is best illustrated by means of examples.

Consider first Fig. 1, which shows the sequence of signals on the input-output bus of a small computer when writing a character to a device connected to the bus. The computer first places the device address on the DATA OUT lines and raises the ADDRESS control line to tell the device that the data on the DATA OUT lines is an address. The device recognizes its address and raises the control line OK, informing the computer that the device is aware that it has been selected. This causes the computer to drop ADDRESS and DATA OUT. The device responds by dropping OK, upon which the computer places the character on the DATA OUT lines and raises the control line WRITE to tell the selected device that the character is on the bus. The device then accepts the character and raises OK, signifying that it has accepted it. The computer then drops DATA OUT and WRITE, which causes OK to go down. This completes the handshaking sequence for transferring a character from the computer to the device.

Fig. 2 (on the next page) shows an example of handshaking between a computer and a remote batch terminal using synchronous communication. Here the connection is established by a special sequence of control characters (SYN, SOH, STX, etc.). Such handshaking between remote terminals and a computer is often called a *communication protocol*, or simply a *protocol*.

JOHN S. SOBOLEWSKI

HARD DISK

For articles on related subjects *see* CYLINDER; FLOPPY DISK; LATENCY; and MEMORY: AUXILIARY.

A *hard disk* is a high-capacity, high-speed rotational storage device. Hard disks are sometimes called *fixed disks* because they usually cannot be removed from the computer. Hard disk drives are also called *Winchester drives*, a name derived from an IBM model 3030 drive that stored 30 megabytes of information on each side of a single platter. The model number 3030 was reminiscent of the famed Winchester 3030 rifle.

A hard disk consists of a rigid aluminum alloy disk that is coated with a magnetic oxide material, much like a floppy disk. Because the disks are rigid, they can be spun much faster than a floppy—up to 3,600 RPM. The drive itself may contain a number of platters mounted on a rotating spindle (see Fig. 6 of MEMORY: AUXILIARY). Each platter surface has its own read/write head. The head actually floats above the surface of the disk on a cushion of air. The heads on hard disks are designed like small airfoils so that they can be efficiently lifted and landed. The heads float very close to the disk surface. The gap is about 1/100,000 of an inch. The disk case is assembled in a controlled and ultra-clean environment because con-

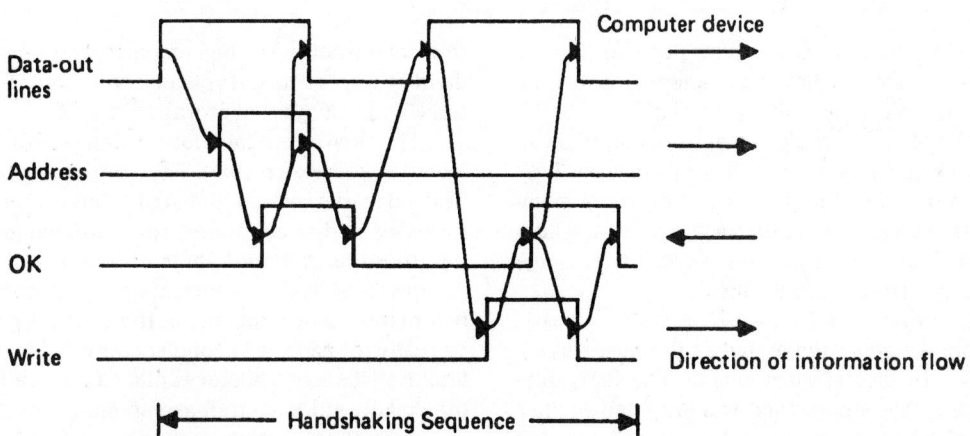

FIG. 1. Example of handshaking sequence. The arrows are used to indicate which control signal causes which response during sequence.

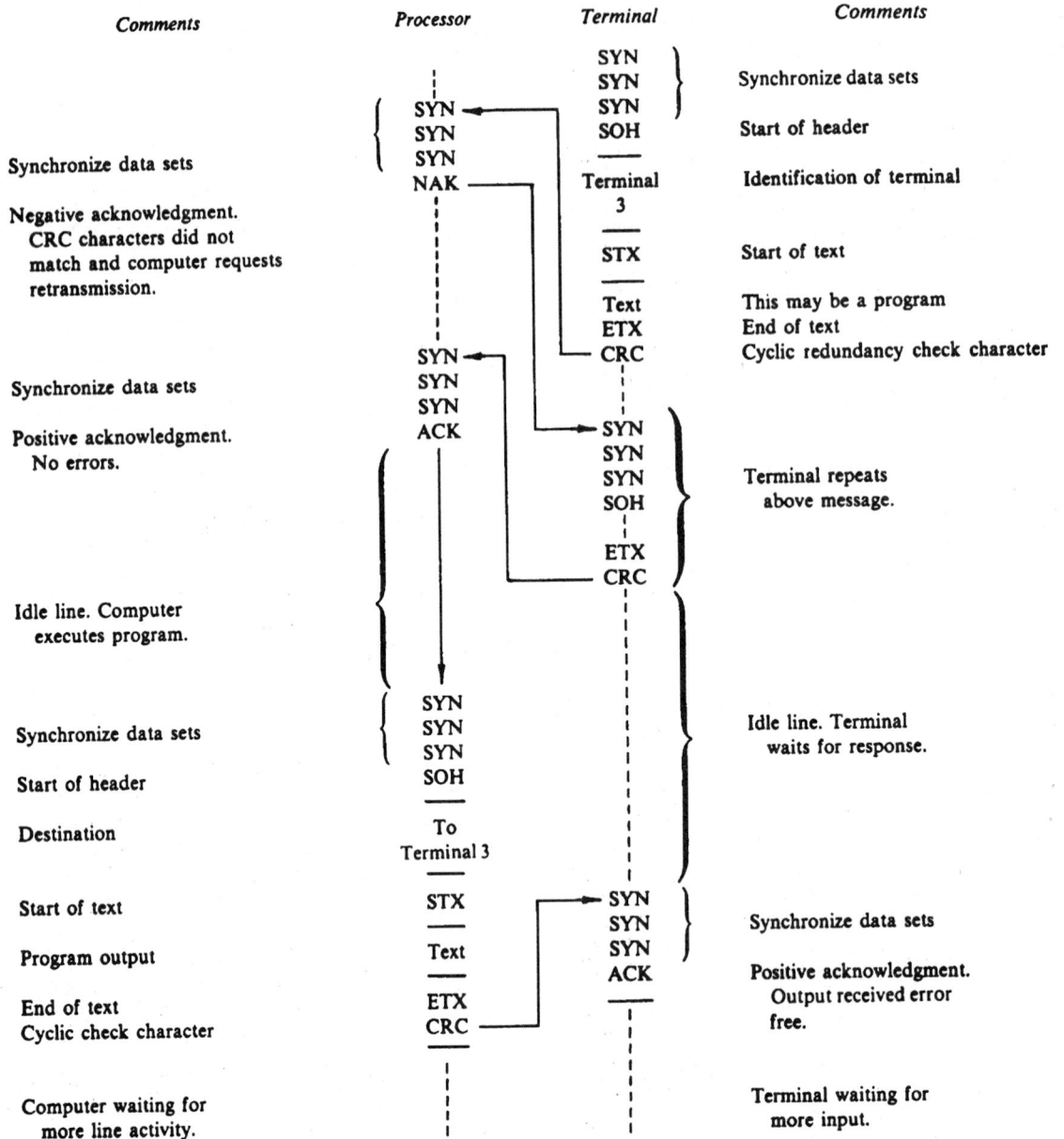

Comments	*Processor*	*Terminal*	*Comments*
		SYN	
		SYN	
	SYN	SYN	Synchronize data sets
	SYN	SOH	Start of header
Synchronize data sets	SYN		
	NAK	Terminal 3	Identification of terminal
Negative acknowledgment. CRC characters did not match and computer requests retransmission.		STX	Start of text
		Text	This may be a program
		ETX	End of text
	SYN	CRC	Cyclic redundancy check character
Synchronize data sets	SYN		
	SYN	SYN	
Positive acknowledgment. No errors.	ACK	SYN	
		SYN	
		SOH	Terminal repeats above message.
		ETX	
		CRC	
Idle line. Computer executes program.			
	SYN		
Synchronize data sets	SYN		Idle line. Terminal waits for response.
	SYN		
Start of header	SOH		
Destination	To Terminal 3		
Start of text	STX	SYN	
		SYN	Synchronize data sets
Program output	Text	SYN	
		ACK	Positive acknowledgment. Output received error free.
End of text	ETX		
Cyclic check character	CRC		
Computer waiting for more line activity.			Terminal waiting for more input.

FIG. 2. Handshaking between a computer and a remote batch terminal. The arrows indicate the sequence of line activities.

taminants in the form of airborne particles can be very destructive. The inside of a disk drive cannot be a vacuum because the heads need air to lift off and land.

Because the platters are rigid, magnetic material can be densely packed so that hard disks have very high capacities. With a large number of platters, some mainframe hard disks can hold more than a gigabyte—a billion characters. Hard disks used with microcomputers range in storage capacity from 20Mb to 200Mb.

Each disk surface has its own head and all heads move in unison. A *stepper motor* moves the heads along the disk surface in discrete increments. The individual stopping points for the stepper motor represent a circular path that the disk traces out under the head. The trail of magnetically oriented particles or domains that is left behind is called a *track*. There may be as many as a

thousand tracks on a high-capacity hard disk. Tracks are divided into *sectors*. Typically, there are 17 sectors per track and 512 bytes of storage per sector.

The sectors are laid down when the disk undergoes a low-level software format. The formatting program identifies and marks sectors that are bad and lays out the sector locations and stores them. The low-level format also establishes the *interleave factor* for the disk. Because a disk is capable of feeding information to an operating system before it is ready to accept it, the controller card may not be ready to read the second sector of a file right after the first. If that second sector is placed right next to the first, the disk would have to make an entire revolution before the second sector came around again (*see* LATENCY). Since files sometimes consist of hundreds of sectors, a tremendous amount of time can be wasted. If consecutively numbered sectors are interleaved according to the average time it takes to read data, the disk can operate more efficiently.

On hard disks used with the IBM-PC and compatibles (*q.v.*), track zero is dedicated to system files. A high-level format is performed by DOS, using the FORMAT command. This copies some code into the boot sector and starts to expand the File Allocation Table (FAT). The FORMAT command also writes the special command file and two hidden system files that DOS needs to operate. The *boot sector* is a special area used by the computer to start the process of booting the computer (*see* BOOT AND REBOOT). The file allocation tables are the most important files on a hard disk. The FAT contains information about which sectors are assigned to which files. When a file is written to a hard disk, it is not written in consecutive sectors. Sectors are scattered all over the disk, organized as a linked list. The disk *directory* (*q.v.*) knows how big a file is and when it was created. It also stores the location of the first sector for a given filename. After that, only the FAT knows where the others sectors are. Destroy the FAT and the hard disk is useless.

The collection of tracks with the same number arranged vertically on all platters is called a *cylinder*. Since the heads are connected to only one actuator arm, all heads move in unison. For example, when the head is over, say, track 15 on the top platter, it is over track 15 on all platters. For that reason, DOS, through programmed directions to the hard disk controller, tries to store all sectors belonging to the same file on the same cylinder to minimize head movement. There are also two track numbers that serve a special purpose. The *landing track* is a track where data is never written. This is where the heads go to land when the system is powered down or the heads are "parked" by a utility program prior to shipment of the disk drive. Some disks have self-parking heads while others require user intervention through software.

As tracks get closer to the center of the disk, their circumference necessarily gets smaller. But since the number of sectors stays the same and so does the number of bytes per sector (for most drives), the data is therefore more densely packed. The controller must therefore compensate for this increase in magnetic intensity when it is a certain number of tracks from the center of the disk. This *precompensation factor* is usually stored as a track number at which to begin sensing the increased magnetic density.

Hard disks are now moving away from the magnetic and towards optical mechanisms. Hard disks are likely to get much faster and to be able to store a *terabyte*—a trillion characters—by the year 2000.

STEPHEN J. ROGOWSKI

HARDWARE. *See* COMPUTER CIRCUITRY; COMPUTER SYSTEMS; HARDWARE RELIABILITY; and entries under MEMORY and STORAGE.

HARDWARE DESCRIPTION LANGUAGES

For articles on related subjects *see* COMPUTER SYSTEMS; INSTRUCTION SET; LOGIC DESIGN; NONPROCEDURAL LANGUAGES; and PROCEDURE-ORIENTED LANGUAGES.

Hardware description languages (HDL) are notations and languages that facilitate the documentation, design, simulation, and manufacturing of digital computer systems. A digital system can be described at many different levels of detail in order to depict structural or behavioral aspects. Thus, a system can be described at the gate level as a network of logic gates and flip-flops whose behavior is specified by timing diagrams, boolean equations, or truth tables. Typical gate level information is shown in Fig. 1. While a complete digital computer can be described at this level, the amount of information to be conveyed can be too extensive for a human designer to comprehend, and higher-level notations are often used to abstract or hide details.

Above the gate level, standard or predefined networks of gates and flip-flops are often used as building blocks at the register transfer level. Typical components are registers, multiplexers, and arithmetic-logic units (ALUs - *q.v.*). Systems may be decomposed into a data part and a control part, operating in discrete steps, and some of the lower-level details, such as gate interconnection, placement, individual gate delays, etc., are suppressed.

While structure is normally depicted by block diagrams, a wide variety of conventions exist for describing the behavior of the system. Thus, in addition to truth fables and boolean equations (used mostly for combinational networks), timing and state diagrams are also used. Special-purpose programming languages (called register transfer languages) permit the use of digital computers as design aids, and a number of such RT-languages have been proposed (Barbacci, 1975).

The existence of digital components capable of interpreting instructions stored in memory (i.e. instruction set processors) motivates the existence of the programming level of description. At the programming level, the basic components are the interpretation cycle, the machine instructions, and operations (all of which are defined as register transfer level operations). The programming level arises from the need to describe the behavior rather

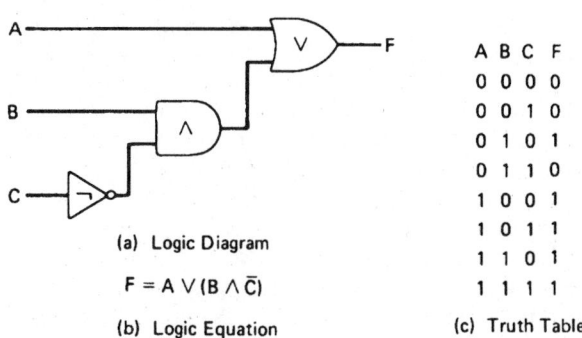

	A	B	C	F
	0	0	0	0
	0	0	1	0
	0	1	0	1
	0	1	1	0
	1	0	0	1
	1	0	1	1
	1	1	0	1
	1	1	1	1

(a) Logic Diagram

$$F = A \vee (B \wedge \bar{C})$$

(b) Logic Equation

(c) Truth Table

FIG. 1.   Gate level descriptions.

```
**Memory.State**
M\Memory [0:4095]<0:11>,
        P.0\Page.Zero [0:127]<0:11>              := M[0:127]<0:11>,
        A.I\Auto.Index[0:7]<0:11>                := P.0[8:15]<0:11>,


**Processor.State**
L\Link<>,
AC\Accumulator<0:11>,
PC\Program.Counter<0:11>,

**Instruction.Format**
i\instruction<0:11>,
        op\operation.code<0.2>    := i<0:2>,
        ib\indirect.bit<>         := i<3>,
        pb\page.0.bit<>           := i<4>,
        pa\page.address<0:6>      := i<5:11>,

**Effective.Address**
last.pc<0:11>,
eadd\effective.address<0:11> :=
        Begin
        Decode pb  =>
                Begin
                0 := eadd = '00000 @ pa,        ! Page Zero
                1 := eadd = last.pc<0:4> @ pa   ! Current Page
                End Next
        If Not ib => Leave eadd Next
        If eadd<0:8> Eqv #001 =>
                M[eadd] = M{eadd] + 1 Next      ! Auto Index
        eadd = M[eadd]
        End

**Instruction.Interpretation**
interpret :=
        Begin
        Repeat  Begin
                i = M[PC]; last.pc = PC Next
                PC = PC + 1 Next
                execute() Next
                End
        End,


execute :=
        Begin
        Decode op =>
                Begin
                #0\and :=        AC = AC And M[eadd()],
                #1\tad :=        L@AC = L@AC + M[eadd()],
                #2\isz :=        Begin
                                 M[eadd] = M[eadd()] + 1 Next
                                 If M[eadd] Eql 0 => PC = PC + 1
                                 End,
                . . . . . . . .
                End
        End,
```

FIG. 2.   ISP level description.

than the structure of processors—in particular, the behavior as seen by the programmers of the machine.

In the Instruction Set Processor (ISP) notation (Bell, 1971) and its successor, ISPS (Barbacci, 1981), a processor is described by declarations of carriers and procedures specifying the behavior of the system:

1. *Information carriers*—registers and memories used to store programs, data, and other state information.
2. *Instruction set*—procedures describing the behavior of the processor instructions.
3. *Addressing modes*—procedures describing the operand and instruction fetch and store operations.
4. *Interpretaton cycle*—typically, the main procedure of an ISP description. It defines the fetch, decode, and execute sequence of a digital processor.

Fig. 2 shows an abridged description of the Digital Equipment Corporation PDP-8 processor. Declarations are grouped into sections as an organizational device; thus, **Memory.state**, **Processor.state**, **Instruction.Format**, etc., are suggestive of the role of the declarations in the overall description of the machine. For instance, the main memory of PDP-8 is described in the Memory.state section and consists of 4,096 12-bit words. The Processor.state section describes those registers used to preserve the status of the processor between instructions. It includes the program counter (*q.v.*), an accumulator, and a "link" (arithmetic carry) register. The

instruction format section describes the different fields of an instruction (e.g. operation code, address, and indirect bit, etc.). The behavior of the PDP-8 is specified via three procedures, specifying the instruction interpretation cycle, the effective address computation algorithm, and the instruction set proper (the execute algorithm).

Beyond the programming level, other notations are used to provide concise descriptions of the physical structure of a digital system. The Processor Memory Switch (PMS) notation (Bell, 1971) is a graphical notation, and makes use of only a few primitive components:

M—A *memory* holds or stores information over time.
L—A *link* transfers information from one place to another in a system between fixed ports of other components.
K—A *control* evokes operations of other components in a system.
S—A *switch* enables links between other components.
T—A *transducer* is used to interface a system with the external world.
D—A *data operation* produces or alters information according to algorithms describing logical and arithmetic operations.
P—A *processor* interprets programs in order to execute a sequence of operations.

Components of these types can be connected to make computers and other digital systems, as shown in Fig. 3. Components are classified as belonging to one of several categories (processors, memories, switches, links, etc.) characterizing their generic function (e.g. stor-

C := M[primary; 32K words; 16 bits/word; core] —— P[central] —— T[console]—— X

$$C := Mp^1 — K — T \mid Ms^2 — X$$
$$\qquad\qquad\quad\mid$$
$$\qquad\qquad D^3$$

1 Mp[256K bytes; access-time 256 nanoseconds]
2 Ms[magnetic tape; 9 tracks]
3 D[arithmetic-logic-unit; floating point]

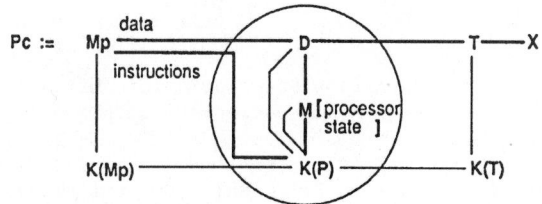

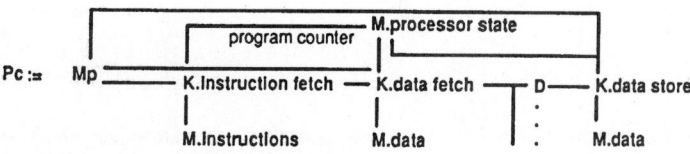

FIG. 3. PMS level descriptions.

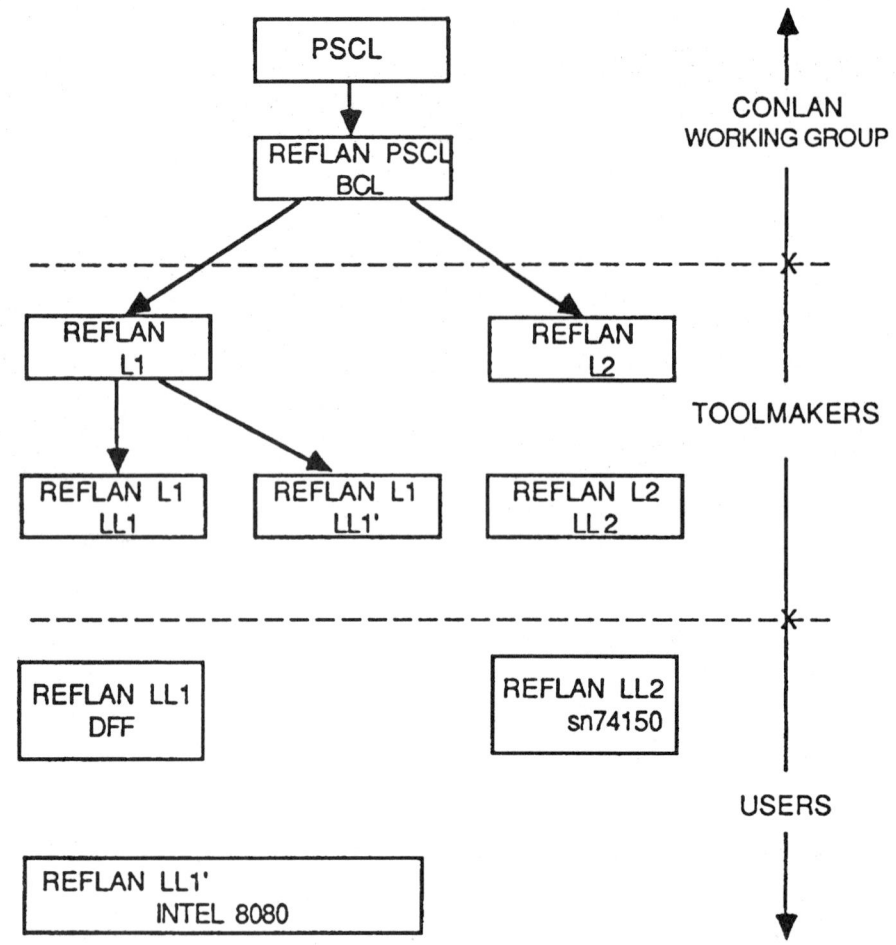

FIG. 4. CONLAN text structure. This example is taken from Piloty et al (1983).

```
entity FULL_ADDER is
  port (X, Y, CIN: in BIT; SUM, COUT: out Bit):
  CIN : in BIT : = '0';
end FULL_ADDER;
                                Interface of the Full_Adder


architecture DATA_FLOW of FUll_ADDER is
  signal C : BIT;
begin
  SUM  <= X xor Y xor CIN after 5 NS;
  C    <= (Y and CIN) or (X and CIN) or (X and Y);
  COUT <= C after 6 NS;
end DATA_FLOW
                        Data-flow Description of FULL_ADDER
                            (a representative BODY)


architecture Structure_View of Full_Adder is
 Component Half_Adder port (I1, I2: in BIT;CARRY, SUM: out BIT);
 Component Or_Gate     port (I1, I2: in BIT;0: out BIT);
begin
 C1: Half_Adder port map (X,Y,a,b);
 C2: Half_Adder port map (b,CIN,c,SUM);
 C3: Or_Gate    port map (a,c,COUT);
end Structure_View;
                        Structural Description of FULL_ADDER
                            (a representative BODY)
```

FIG. 5. VHDL description of a full-adder. This example is taken from "An Interface Between VHDL and EDIF," Proceedings of the 24th Design Automation Conference, 28 July–1 August 1987, Miami Beach, Florida, by Moe Shadad.

```
(edif edifname
   (edifVersion 2 0 0)
   (edifLevel 0)
   (keywordMap (keywordLevel 0)
   (status (written (timestamp 1988 12 15 16 53 42)
       (author "Mentor Grpahics Corporation")
       (program "EDIFNET V6.0_1.13 Wednesday, July 29, 1987 9:26:17 am(PDT)")))

(library libraryname (edifLevel 0)
   (technology (numberDefinition (scal 1 (e 1 -9) unit time)))

(cell (rename buf "/user/gen_lib/$buf")
   (CellType generic)
   (view v (viewType netlist)
   (interface
       (port (rename OUT "OUT") (direction output))
       (port (rename IO "IO")   (direction input)))))

(cell (rename inv "/user/gen_lib/$inv")
   (cellType generic)
   (view v (viewType netlist)
   (interface
       (port (rename OUT "OUT") (direction output))
       (port (rename IN "IN")   (direction input)))))
        . . . . . . .

(cell (rename ja374 "ja374")
   (cellType generic)
   (view v (viewType netlist)
   (interface
       (port (rename OEN "OEN") (direction input))
       (port (rename O "O")   (direction output))
       (port (rename D "D")   (direction input))
       (port (rename CP "CP")   (direction input)))
   (contents
       (instance (rename I44 "/I$44") (viewRef v (cellRef buf)))
       (instance (rename I121 "I$121") (viewRef v (cellRef inv)))
       (instance (rename I23I84 "/I$23/I$84") (viewRef v (cellRef buf)))
            . . . . . . . .
       (net (rename CP "CP")
           (joined (portRef CP)   (portRef IO (instanceRef I44))))
       (net (rename N103 "N$103")
           (joined (portRef CLK (instanceRef I289)) (portRef CLK ...))
            . . . . . . . . .
       ))))))
```

FIG. 6.   EDIF netlist example. This example is taken from "EDIF, The Electronics Design Interchange Format—An Introduction," Proceedings of ELECTRO 89, 11–13 April 1989, New York City, New York, by John Andrews.

age). In addition, each component specifies its specific function (e.g. primary memory, abbreviated Mp), its technology (e.g. core), its speed, capacity, cost, size, etc. The notation allows for the specification of a limitless amount of information characterizing or describing a component.

PMS components are hierarchical in nature, and can be decomposed and described by simpler PMS diagrams. For instance, processors typically consist of networks of components of the other types, as shown in the figure. Computers consists of processors, memories, and other PMS components. Computer networks consist of computers and transmission links, etc.

The proliferation of HDLs in the 1960s and 1970s led to the definition of CONLAN. CONLAN (CONsensus LANguage) was more an attempt to design a language con-

struction mechanism rather than a specific hardware description language. Thus, the effort centered around the definition of a primitive notation and a powerful extension mechanism. The intention was to build hierarchies of languages with the same underlying semantic model (Fig. 4). Two types of users were envisioned. *Toolmakers* design languages, taking as a base of reference an already existing language. The extension mechanisms in CONLAN are used by the toolmaker to extend the syntax of the base language and to remove constructs that are not allowed to the final users (these extension mechanisms are not allowed in a user description). The second class of users are hardware designers who write descriptions using the syntax of a language provided by a tool maker. CONLAN provides mechanisms to specify the behavior and structure of a digital system. An interpreter is responsible for the correct sequencing of the operations. Toolmakers have facilities to extend the interpreter by specifying functions and procedures to be invoked by the interpreter.

The languages mentioned so far have been used mostly in research and academic environments, as input notations for experimental simulation, analysis, or synthesis tools. In the industrial world, however, there are many additional requirements to consider in the definition of a design.

Creating, modifying, supporting, and managing complex electronic systems are dependent upon the ability to communicate the design details from one design discipline to another and to integrate the various types of data representing the many facets of the product description. The reliability of complex electronic systems is equally dependent on the ability to communicate the necessary data, throughout a product's life-cycle, among those who design and maintain the product. To address these requirements, several industry-supported efforts have sought to establish means to represent product data in a standard format that will be useful to product designers, maintainers, and managers (Waxman, 1989). Two of these efforts are the Very High Speed Integrated Circuits Hardware Description Language (VHDL) and the Electronic Design Interchange Format (EDIF). VHDL and EDIF became standards in 1987.

In VHDL, the hardware entities are modeled as abstractions of the real hardware, called *design entities*. As in real hardware, each design entity has an *interface* and a body or *architecture*. The interface description allows one to describe input and output ports and various attributes associated with the interface, such as pin names, timing constraints, etc. The body description allows one to describe the function or the structure of the design. The body may be written as an abstract algorithm or as a less abstract architectural description made up of algorithms and real hardware representations (e.g. gates, arithmetic-logic units) or made up totally as a structure of real hardware representations. Alternative approaches (i.e. alternative bodies) to the functional representation of a particular design entity may be associated with a given interface, just as in real hardware where equivalent components may be interchanged as long as the interfaces are identical functionally and structurally (Fig. 5).

EDIF provides a hierarchical syntax for data necessary for chip and printed circuit board fabrication. Note that EDIF is a *format*, not a *language*. EDIF's primary application is as a means of transferring design data from the design environment to the fabrication environment. The format provides for libraries, cells, views, interfaces, and information on the content within each cell. Test data, mask layout data, physical layout data, connectivity data, and simulation data can be represented in EDIF.

In EDIF there are ten "view types": The *behavior* view (compiled simulation model); the *document* view (supports text documentation); the *graphic* view (supports portions of artwork repeatedly used); the *logic model* view (definition of primitive simulation logic models); the *mask layout* view (artwork and fabrication data); the *net-list* view (netlist data); the *PCB layout* view (similar to the mask layout view, but for printed circuit boards); the *schematic* view (netlist plus graphics providing a graphic schematic); the *stranger* view (an escape hatch for two party special agreements); and the *symbolic* view (a virtual grid somewhere between a schematic and a mask layout). Fig. 6 illustrates the *netlist* view in EDIF.

These industry standards attempt to answer the needs of the various product life-cycle activities. However, the development of these standards have not been coordinated, and users still need a thorough understanding of the objectives and uses of each standard. The technology of HDLs has not matured to the point that one standard language or format can satisfy the wide diversity of product description requirements, at least for the foreseeable future.

References

1971. Bell, C. G. and Newell, A. *Computer Structures: Readings and Examples.* New York: McGraw-Hill Book Company.
1975. Barbacci, M. R. "A Comparison of Register Transfer Languages for Describing Digital Systems," *IEEE Transactions on Computers*, C-24, 2 (February).
1981. Barbacci, M. R. "Instruction Set Processor Specifications (ISPS): The Notation and Its Applications." *IEEE Transactions on Computers*, C-30, 1 (January).
1983. Piloty, R., Barbacci, M. R., Borrione, D., Dietmeyer, D., Hill, F., Skelly, P. *CONLAN Report.* Lecture Notes in Computer Science, 151. Berlin: Springer-Verlag.
1987. EIA/EDIF/IS-44 Specification, Electronic Design Interchange Format, Version 2.0.0, May.
1987. IEEE, VHDL Language Reference Manual, Standard 1076-1987, December.
1989. Waxman, R., and Saunders, L. "The Evolution of VHDL." Proceedings of the IFIP Congress (August). San Francisco, California.

MARIO R. BARBACCI AND RONALD WAXMAN

HARDWARE MONITOR

For articles on related subjects *see* PERFORMANCE MEASUREMENT AND EVALUATION; and SOFTWARE MONITOR.

A *hardware monitor* is a device for measuring electrical events (e.g. pulses, voltage levels) in a digital computer. It is useful for gathering data for measurement and evaluation of computer systems, particularly when used in conjunction with software monitoring, a technique using programmed steps that lead a computer to examine its own internal operation. Most hardware monitors are external general-purpose devices, but in principle they could be—and now often are—built into a computer if economically justifiable.

Fig. 1 illustrates the elements of a hardware monitor. The various components are discussed below.

General probes—Probes consist of a set of signal sensors designed for minimum interference with the host machine and able to drive relatively long cables so that signals can be picked up from various

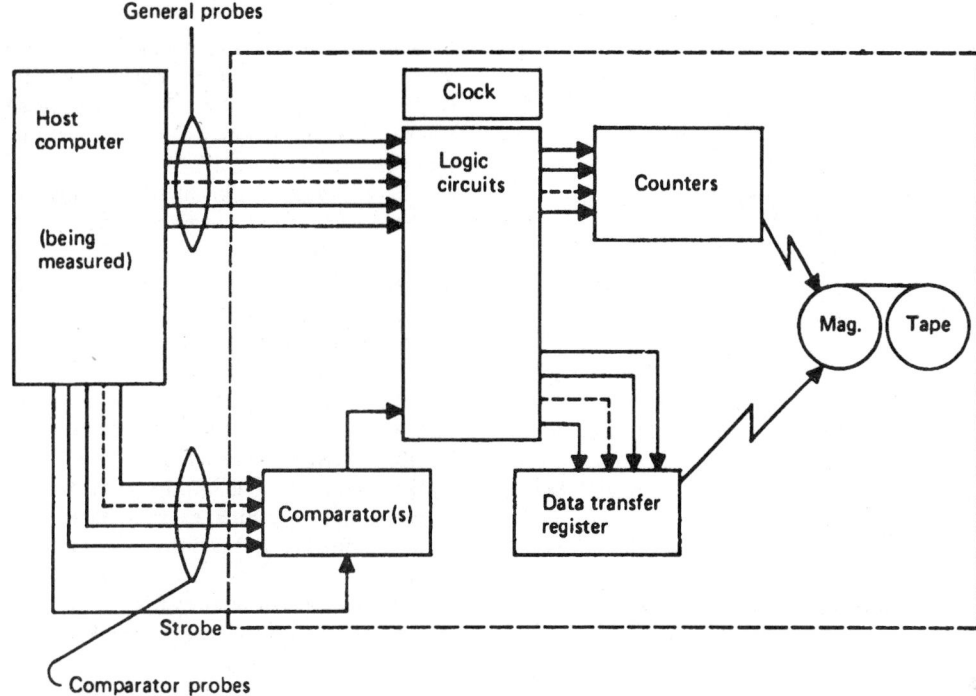

FIG. 1. Elements of a hardware monitor.

points physically distant from each other and from the central monitor console.

Logic circuits—The logic circuits accept signals from the general probes and allow logical combinations of the signals (AND, NOR, INVERT, etc.) so that events of interest can be defined.

Counters—Counters are used to count·the occurrence of various events or to measure the time between events by counting the number of intervening clock pulses.

Comparator probes—The comparator probes are similar to the general probes. They are used to sense a number of bits that appear in parallel (e.g. as in an address register).

Comparator—This component provides means for comparing the parallel bits with some preset value at an instant defined by a signal on the strobe line.

Data transfer register—The transfer register provides means for passing data directly from the host computer to a recording device. This register could be combined with the counter functions or with the comparator functions.

As an example of use, a hardware monitor might be connected to measure the busy time for a CPU and an I/O channel controller and their overlap, or the time they are simultaneously busy. Too little overlap might alert one to examine the operating system (*q.v.*) to see if opportunities for overlap are being lost, causing a decrease in efficiency of the system. As another example, a hardware monitor might count the number of accesses to several disks to see if, over a period of time, there is reasonable balance in demand for the various disks. However, a much better diagnosis of the system might result from also knowing what kinds of calls to disk were being made—e.g.

calls to load parts of the operating system, calls for user files, or calls caused by page faults in a paging system. Since hardware monitors usually cannot detect the difference between these types of calls, one could usefully combine a software monitor to identify the types of events and a hardware monitor to observe their frequency and duration.

In addition to refining the basic functions of gathering data, current development in hardware monitors shows a trend toward using microprocessors for processing data during collection and for allowing the host computer and the monitor to alter each other's measurement functions during operation. From the user's viewpoint, the principal differences between hardware and software monitors are:

1. Software monitors can provide more information on cause and effect by relating measured data to the program steps being executed; however, care must be. exercised to avoid disruption of time relationships caused by the addition of the measurement programs.
2. Hardware monitors measure only electrical events at predetermined physical points; hence, it is more difficult to relate measurements to program activity. However, with reasonable care, data may be gathered without interfering with the system being measured.

References

1978. Ferrari, D. *Computer Systems Performance Evaluation.* Englewood Cliffs, NJ: Prentice-Hall, 32–40.

1979. Borovits, I. and Neumann, S. *Computer Systems Performance Evaluation.* Lexington, MA: Lexington Books, D. C. Heath and Co., 39–56.

1981. Plattner, B. and Nievergelt, J. "Monitoring Program Execution: A Survey," *IEEE Computer* **14**, *11* (November).

JERRE D. NOE

HARDWARE RELIABILITY

For articles on related subjects *see* DATA SECURITY; FAULT-TOLERANT COMPUTING; MAINTENANCE OF COMPUTERS; REDUNDANCY; and SOFTWARE RELIABILITY.

Reliability engineering involves all aspects of design, development, and fabrication that minimize the chance of equipment breakdown. Neglect of reliability considerations can prove to be very costly, from the loss of consumer acceptance of the product to the possibility of endangering human life. The success of complex missions such as space probes depends heavily on reliability engineering, since failure of a single component, such as an O-ring, can and has resulted in total loss of the system.

Reliability in a qualitative sense can mean a host of different things relating to the confidence in the quality of the equipment, and is closely connected but often confused with the concepts of maintainability, availability, safety, and even security of the system. Quantitatively, reliability can be formulated mathematically as the probability that the system will perform its intended function over the stated duration of time in its specified environment.

As equipment becomes more complex, the chance of system unreliability becomes greater, since the reliability of any equipment depends on the reliability of its components. The relationship between parts reliability and the system reliability can be formulated mathematically to varying degrees of precision, depending on the scale of the modeling effort. The mathematics of reliability is based on parts failure-rate statistics and probability theoretic relationships. The mathematical theory of reliability is used to model, simulate, and predict proneness of the equipment to failure under expected operating conditions.

There have been two distinct and viable approaches taken to enhance system reliability. One is based on component technology; i.e. manufacturing capability of producing the component with the highest possible reliability, followed by parts screening, quality control, pretesting to remove early failures (infant mortality effects), etc. The second approach is based on the organization of the system itself (e.g. fault-tolerant architectures that make use of protective redundancy to mask or remove the effects of failure, and thereby provide greater overall system reliability than would be possible by the use of the same components in a simplex or nonredundant configuration).

Fault tolerance is the capability of the system to perform its functions in accordance with design specifications, even in the presence of hardware failures. If, in the event of faults, the system functions can be performed, but do not meet the design specifications with respect to the time required to complete the job or the storage capacity required for the job, then the system is said to be *partially* or *quasi fault-tolerant*. Since the number of possible hardware failures can be very large, in practice it is necessary to restrict fault tolerance to prespecified classes of faults from which the system is designed to recover.

Faults may be classified as *transient* or *permanent, deterministic* or *indeterminate, local* or *catastrophic*. The first category refers to the duration of the fault, the second to its effect on the values of the system design parameters, and the third to the propagation of the fault to its neighboring elements.

Fault tolerance is provided by the application of protective redundancy, or the use of more resources so as to upgrade system reliability. These resources may consist of more hardware, software, or time, or a combination of all three. Extra time is required to retransmit messages or to reexecute programs; extra software is required to perform diagnosis on the hardware; and extra hardware is required to provide replication of units.

Hardware redundancy may be of the *fault-masking* or *self-repair* types, or a hybrid of these two. In fault masking, redundancy is of a static nature; faults are masked instantly and the operations of fault detection, location, and correction are indistinguishable. In self-repair, redundancy is used dynamically; faults are selectively masked and are detected, located, and subsequently corrected by replacing the failed unit with an unfailed replica. Examples of the former are triple modular redundancy (TMR) and quadding (see below), and (of the latter) standby-replacement (SR) systems and reconfigurable systems. Schemes using a combination of these two basic approaches are called *hybrid* or *adaptive* redundancy.

Some Fundamental Principles A fundamental principle of reliability is that it must be not only inherent, but also a function of how the component is used. Another important principle is that, to achieve reliability by means of protective redundancy, the redundancy must be applied to the lowest level of component complexity in the system in order to maximize gain in reliability. This is the idealized state; in practice, trade-offs due to overhead are required in using redundancy techniques (e.g. providing *voters* in TMR systems and detection-switching requirements in standby systems). The application of the mathematical theory of reliability in modeling such systems provides quantitative design guidelines that make such trade-offs and optimizations possible and practicable.

In addition to the foregoing first and second principles of fault tolerance, a third principle is that a system may be made arbitrarily reliable provided the degree of redundancy is made high enough (i.e. a sufficiently large number of replicas are provided). Again, this principle holds only in an idealized situation; in practice, since the probability of detecting a failure and correctly switching over to a spare is less than unity, this parameter, called *coverage*, limits the advantages postulated by the third principle.

A fourth principle concerns the problem of requiring the checking elements (those elements that are used for

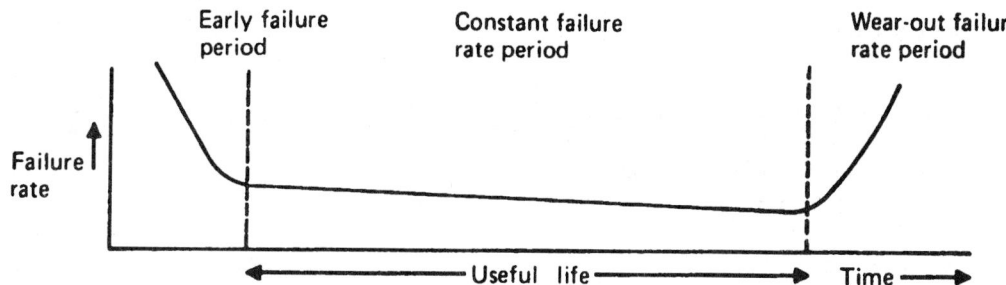

FIG. 1. Bathtub curve of failure rate.

the diagnosis of the rest of the system and the subsequent reconfiguration of the system units) also to be checkable. This is the problem of "checking the checker." Thus, the fourth principle states that any system using protective redundancy will have major and minor "hard cores" (i.e. unprotected system elements), and that these cannot be totally eliminated from the system design. They may be made arbitrarily small, however, by judicious use of a mixture of different, protective redundance techniques.

Mathematical Theory of Reliability Certain relationships exist among reliability parameters and their underlying probability theoretic relationships. If a fixed large number N_o of identical items are being tested, of which N_s is the number of items surviving after time t and N_f is the number of items that failed during time t, then $N_o = N_s + N_f$ for all t. Now, for a sufficiently large N_o, the reliability $R(t)$ of an item is N_s/N_o. The failure rate $\lambda(t)$, which is defined to be the rate at which the population changes at time t, can be shown to be given by

$$\lambda(t) = -\frac{1}{R(t)}\frac{dR(t)}{dt}, \tag{1}$$

so that

$$R(t) = \exp\left(-\int_0^t \lambda(t)\, d\tau\right) \tag{2}$$

The reliability function $R(t)$ is often called the *survival probability function*, since it measures the probability that failure of an item does not occur during the time interval $[0,t]$.

Failure Rate Statistical data on equipment failure yield a characteristic "bathtub" curve, as shown in Fig. 1. When the equipment is first put into service, inherently weak components fail early. Subsequently, the failure rate stabilizes quickly to a relatively constant value; this period is called the "useful life period." After much usage,

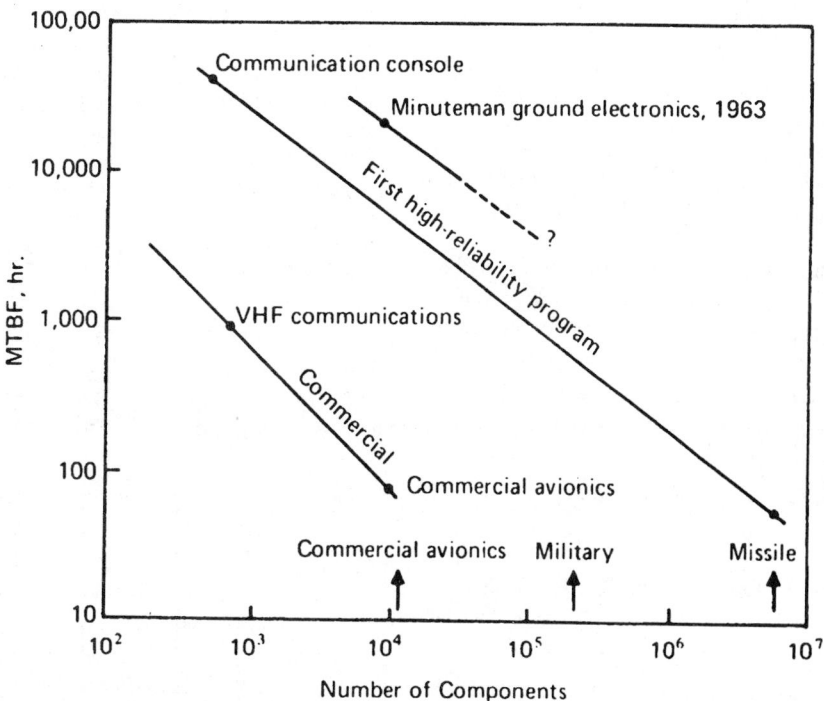

FIG. 2. Comparison of mean time between failures for commercial equipment and high-reliability military equipment. (From E. J. Nalos and R. B. Schultz, "Reliability and Cost of Avionics," *IEEE Trans. Reliability*, October 1965. By permission.)

failure rate begins to increase rapidly as a result of deterioration and wear.

Exponential Failure Law   In general, the failure law of a component is the probability distribution effective from the moment at which a component enters service up to the moment of its failure. In practice the most commonly used failure law is the exponential law, which applies when a component is subject only to failures that occur at random intervals and the average number of failures is the same for equal time periods. These constraints are valid for a component that is no longer subject to early mortality failure and whose failure rate is a constant within the "useful life" span. Thus, for operating periods within the useful life, the component reliability over a period of time t can be expressed as $R(t) = e^{\lambda t}$, where λ (usually expressed in failures per hour or per million hours) is the constant failure rate of the device. A characteristic of the exponential failure law is that the reliability of the device within the useful life period is the same for operating times of equal duration.

From the definition of $R(t)$ it follows that the mean time between failures (MTBF) or the mean time to first failure (MTTF), usually expressed in hours (Fig. 2), are given by $\int_0^\infty R(t)\,dt$; i.e. it is the area underneath the reliability curve $R(t)$ plotted versus t. This is true for any failure distribution. For the specific case of the exponential failure law, the MTBF, m, is equal to $1/\lambda$. Further, when the product λt is small, the equation for $R(t)$ may be approximated by $R(t) \approx 1 - \lambda t$. Thus, if $\lambda t = 0.01$, $R(t) = e^{-0.01} = 0.99$., or 99.0%. The product λt is often referred to as the "normalized" time, since $\lambda t = t/m$; i.e. the mission time t is normalized with respect to the MTBF.

Series Reliability   If a system is composed of elements in such a way that the failure of any one element causes a failure of the system, then these elements are considered to be functionally in series. For the system to survive, each element must survive. The probability of survival for the system cannot be better than the element with the lowest probability of survival; i.e. a chain is no stronger than its weakest link. When these series elements are independent of each other, then, by the probability multiplication law, the system survival probability is the product of the individual survival probabilities of the elements. This is known as the product rule:

$$R_{\text{system}} = \prod_{i=1}^{n} R_i,$$

where R_i is the reliability of the ith element of an n-element system (Fig. 3).

Parallel Reliability   Parallel reliability is an illustration of protective redundancy. The system is composed of functionally parallel elements in such a way that if one of

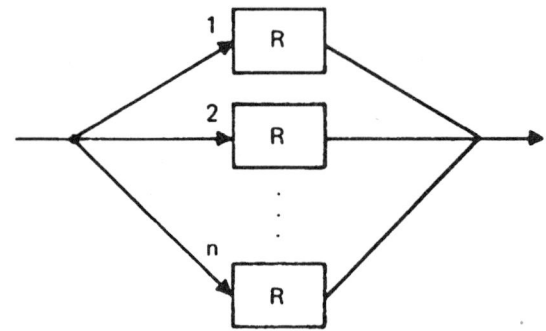

FIG. 4.   System composed of elements in parallel.

the elements fails the parallel unit will continue to do the system function. See Fig. 4. The system reliability, under the assumption of independence of failure of the elements, is expressed by

$$R_{\text{system}} = 1 - (1 - R)^n,$$

which is the probability that not all n elements have failed. The term $(1 - R)$, known as the unreliability of a unit, is the probability that a unit will fail. The term $(1 - R)^n$ by the product rule is the probability that all n units will fail and one minus that is the probability that not all units will have failed. An example of parallel reliability is given by electronic diodes in parallel; if one diode open-circuits, the other will still provide the function.

Triple Modular Redundancy (TMR)   TMR is also known as the *multiple-line voting* system. One of the earliest and most influential schemes was developed by John von Neumann (*q.v.*). The simplex unit is triplicated and each of the three independent units feeds into a majority voter, which outputs the majority signal (*see* Fig. 5). The system fails if more than one unit fails, in which case the failed units outvote the good one. This scheme is generalized to N-modular redundancy (NMR), where N is any odd number of units. Various schemes of protecting the voter are available, and also various other variants of the basic TMR strategy have been developed. The TMR system reliability is expressed as

$$R_{\text{system}} = [R^3 + 3R^2(1 - R)]\,R_v,$$

which is the product of the reliability R_v (the voter reliability) and the reliability of the idealized TMR system. The

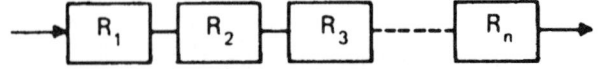

FIG. 3.   System composed of a series of elements.

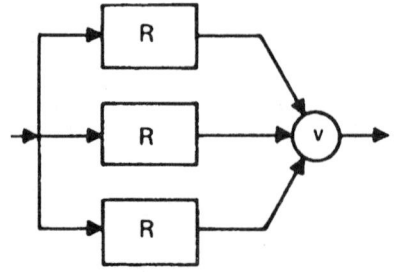

FIG. 5.   Triple modular redundancy.

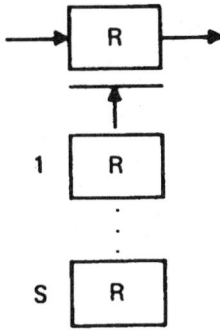

FIG. 6.   Standby replacement redundancy.

idealized TMR system reliability is the sum of the probabilities of two events: (1) that all three units survive, R^3; and (2) that any two units survive so that only one unit fails, $3R^2 (1 - R)$.

Quadded Redundancy   Quadding is a method of component redundancy applicable to circuits with alternating AND and OR gates. It is similar in concept to TMR, with the major difference being that the voting or restoration of fault-masking functions are distributed into the network and are not separable, as in TMR. In general, the quadding procedure requires that each logic gate be quadruplicated and that each of the gates in a quad stage will have twice as many inputs as the nonredundant gate replaced. The outputs of a stage are interconnected to the inputs of the succeeding stage by a connection pattern in such a way that the effects of errors in earlier stages get subsequently "restored" in the latter stages; i.e. the originally intended "good" signal is restored.

Standby Replacement Redundancy   In standby replacement redundancy (Fig. 6), only one unit is operational at a time, unlike TMR. When the active unit fails, this event is detected by additional circuitry, and a spare unit from a reserve of spares is switched in as a replacement of the failed unit, thereby restoring the system to its operational state. The reliability of this system is expressed as

$$R_{\text{system}} = 1 - (1 - R)^{S + 1},$$

which is the probability that not all S units have failed.

Hybrid Redundancy   Hybrid redundancy is a synthesis of TMR and standby replacement redundancy (see Fig. 7). It consists of a TMR system (or, in general, an NMR —for N-Modular Redundancy—system), with a bank of spares so that when one of the TMR units fails, it is replaced by a spare unit. Failure detection is achieved by means of disagreement detectors which compare the individual outputs of each of the triple modular redundancy units with the system output. If there is a difference, the disagreement detector signals the switching network to replace the failed unit by a spare unit. When all spares are utilized, the hybrid redundancy system reduces to a TMR system. Variations of hybrid or adaptive redundancy schemes are possible. The system reliability in its simplest terms may be expressed as

$$R_{\text{system}} = 1 - [(1 - R^{S + 3} + R (S + 3) (1 - R)^{S + 2}],$$

which is the probability that not all $S + 3$ units fail and that not any $S + 2$ units fail with one not failing.

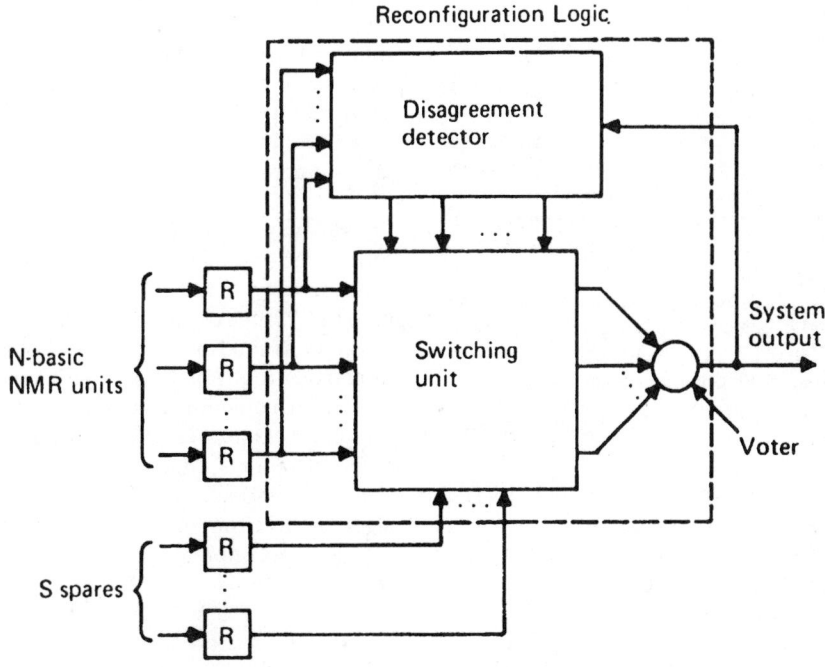

FIG. 7.   Hybrid redundancy.

Summary Redundancy as a procedure for designing more reliable systems than allowed by the intrinsic reliability of the constituent components is as old as the discipline of engineering itself. In fact, even the evolutionary processes of life use it (e.g. in the human body there are two kidneys, two lungs, etc.).

Examples of the use of redundancy in ancient times are provided in the construction of temples and bridges, where more than the absolutely required number of pillars is provided to support structure; thus, should one pillar sustain damage, the remaining pillars would still be able to share the load successfully.

In the computer age, all the basic techniques described have been applied, with varying degrees of sophistication, to the design of ultrareliable computing systems. TMR has been successfully applied in designing the guidance and control computer of the Saturn V launch vehicle. Quadding is used to a great extent in the design of the spacecraft computer of the Orbiting Astronomical Observatory (OAO). Standby replacement redundancy was extensively used in the Raytheon RAY-DAC computer and in the Jet Propulsion Laboratory's self-test and repair (STAR) computer. The latter also used hybrid redundancy to protect the monitor sub-system of the self-repairing computer.

In addition, these techniques are also finding application in protecting the automated computerized controls of modern high-speed transit systems and in other applications where the cost of using redundancy is justifiable because it minimizes danger to human life, or increases the continuous availability of services that, if interrupted by failure and subsequent repair, would cause severe consumer dissatisfaction. An example of the latter is the present-day automated telephone switching system. In an expanding society where products become more sophisticated and projects proliferate, the scope of reliability engineering, protective redundancy, and fault-tolerant computing will continue to grow.

References

1956. von Neumann, J. "Probabilistic Logics and the Synthesis of Reliable Organisms from Unreliable Components," in *Automata Studies*. Princeton, NJ: Princeton University, 43–98.

1971. IEEE. *Transactions on Computers: Special Issue on Fault-Tolerant Computing* **C-20,** *11* (November). *Digest of the IEEE Annual Symposium on Fault Tolerance.*

1986. Pradhan, D. K. (Ed.). *Fault-Tolerant Computing: Theory and Techniques*, Vols. I and II. Englewood Cliffs, NJ: Prentice-Hall.

1987. Nelson, V. P. and Carroll, B. D. *Tutorial: Fault-Tolerant Computing*, Los Alamitos, CA: IEEE Computer Society Press.

FRANCIS P. MATHUR

HARDWARE VERIFICATION

For articles on related subjects *see* HARDWARE DESCRIPTION LANGUAGES; and PROGRAM VERIFICATION.

What Is Hardware Verification? *Hardware verification* typically involves demonstrating that an *implementation* of a system is "consistent" with respect to its *specification*, where these descriptions tend to be at different levels of abstraction. Somewhat more generally, hardware verification involves comparing two descriptions of a (hardware) design for "consistency." This requires (1) the two descriptions; (2) formal models for each (since these may or may not be the same); (3) a formal notion of the "consistency" relation between them; (4) some way of checking or proving the consistency relation. We note that such a proof need not necessarily directly resemble a "traditional" logic proof (e.g. it may simply be a mechanical enumeration of all possibilities). It should, however, be something that could always be translated into a logical proof. Thus, for instance, simulation cannot be used for formal verification unless it is feasible to simulate exhaustively all the possibilities of interest.

Techniques Used In Hardware Verification

Specification and Formal Models A system description may be given in a "hardware description language" (HDL), such as VHDL (IEEE 1987) or a "broad-spectrum" system description language (encompassing both hardware and software subsystems). Alternatively, it may be expressed directly in the syntax of the underlying formal model.

The formal models that underlie system descriptions typically use some form of algebra or logic. Common examples of useful models include boolean or propositional logic (for combinational circuits), finite state machines (for sequential circuits), and state graphs. Other examples of formal models include various flavors of temporal logic (e.g. Computational Tree Logic (Burch *et al.* 1990) used for stating properties of finite state systems); logics that incorporate the notion of dense real-time intervals, enabling properties of timed systems to be expressed; various flavors of "process algebras" that are used to provide semantics for ensembles of processes (e.g. CCS (Milner, 1980); infinitary languages (and automata that accept them); and Petri Nets - *q.v.*).

Consistency The notion of consistency depends on the properties of the system that are deemed relevant; while this normally includes "observable" functional behavior, other attributes of interest include timing characteristics, power consumption, and testability. Even when restricted to considering "functional" behavior, there are considerable (and sometimes subtle) variations in the precise notion of "consistency" that is used in the context of different models, and sometimes even within the same "family" of models (e.g. within models based on process algebras or within models based on temporal logic).

Some examples of the consistency relation between two descriptions S and I include:

- Equality: $S = I.$
- Equivalence: $S \Leftrightarrow I.$
- Logical implication: $I \Rightarrow S.$

- Conditional logical implication: $C(input) \Rightarrow (I \Rightarrow S)$; where the predicate $C(input)$ is designed to ensure that the system's environment behaves properly.
- Homomorphism: This may loosely be expressed as $R(\varphi(I), S)$, where a homomorphic function φ is used to represent (or relate) different levels of abstraction, and the relation R embodies an appropriate notion of consistency between $\varphi(I)$ and S. Examples of useful abstractions include structural abstraction (enabling the "hiding" of internal signals or wires), temporal abstraction (enabling different granularities of timing); data abstraction (consisting of relating "abstract" objects to more concrete "representation" objects); and event abstraction (the abstraction of events that are not relevant to the specific task in hand).

Further differences result from viewing concurrent computations as having a tree-like (branching) structure, in contrast to being linearized in some fashion. The former view is reflected in branching time temporal logics and process algebras like CCS. The latter view is reflected in linear time temporal logics, trace theory and systems that model communicating sequential processes (e.g. CSP (Hoare, 1985)).

Checking for Consistency The techniques used for checking equivalence are closely related to the formal models used. There is a wide spectrum of logics and related systems that perform manipulations relevant to the logics. In general, the simpler logics (e.g. boolean logic) are typically less expressive and more tractable, while the richer logics (e.g. formulations of higher-order logic that permit variables to range over functions and predicates, and quantification over such variables) are more expressive and less tractable. Various flavors of temporal logics and enhancements of first-order logic fall between these extremes.

It is often possible to exploit the special properties and idiosyncrasies of certain logics to develop specialized data structures and algorithms to support the manipulations required by the logic. A good example of this is a graph-based canonical representation of boolean expressions, called Typed Ordered Binary Decision Diagrams and abbreviated BDDs (Bryant, 1986). BDDs enable very efficient implementations of boolean operations, such as conjunction, disjunction, and negation of expressions, as well as checks for satisfiability of a formula and the equivalence of two boolean formulas (and therefore two combinational logic networks). BDD-based systems have also been used to show equivalence between deterministic Moore machines by performing a *symbolic* exploration of the state space determined by the product of the two machines. Other methods use BDDs in "symbolic" simulation, and also combine graph-based and theorem-proving/assertion-based proof techniques.

Temporal logics enable reasoning about the order of events in time without introducing time explicitly. Although a number of different temporal logics have been studied, most have an operator like $G(f)$ that is true in the present if f is always true in the future (i.e. if f is **G**lobally true). To assert that two events e_1 and e_2 never occur at the same time, one would write $G(\neg\,e_1 \wedge \neg\,e_2)$. The meaning of a temporal logic formula is usually determined with respect to a labelled state transition graph (sometimes called a *Kripke structure* for historical reasons). To check if a system described by a state graph satisfies a certain property (the "specification") expressed by a temporal logic formula, the state space denoted by the state graph has to be explored; this can be done in time linear in the size of the state graph and the temporal logic formula being checked.

A logic called the μ-calculus can be used as a general framework for describing a variety of verification methodologies. A *model checking* algorithm for the μ-calculus can be used to decide, among other things, the validity of branching-time and linear-time temporal logic formulas with respect to a finite model, strong and weak observational equivalence of finite transition systems, and language containment of finite ω-automata.

Graph-based verification methods include temporal logic model checking, formal language containment, trace theory, and the calculus of communicating systems (CCS). While these have different computational models and differ in their notions of verification, they generally involve decision algorithms that explicitly represent some relational quantity over the domain of the model. By using a binary encoding of the domain of the model and efficient representations of the relational quantities using BDDs, the complexity of the decision algorithms can be greatly reduced *in practice*. Some empirical results show that the method can be applied in practice to verify models with in excess of 10^{120} states.

Another approach involves checking *inclusion* between two automata on infinite tapes. The first machine represents the system that is being verified; the second represents its specification. Automata on infinite tapes are used in order to handle fairness.

A desired goal (or "theorem") is obtained ("proved") in a logic by the application of an appropriate sequence of inference rules of the logic. A mechanization of a logic provides support for mechanical application of the inference rules of a logic. In interactive proof-based systems, such as the HOL system supporting Higher Order Logic (Gordon, 1988), additional support is typically provided for concisely encoding strategies and high-level tactics that drive the lower-level mechanical inferences needed to carry out large and complex proofs. Further, several forms of "bookkeeping" support are also provided by such systems to facilitate the development, browsing, and subsequent modification of proofs and proof strategies.

The Boyer-Moore theorem prover is based on the Boyer-Moore logic (Boyer and Moore, 1988), which augments first-order predicate calculus with a semi-automated induction scheme and axioms for data types, such as natural numbers, strings, and lists.

As and when the representations and algorithms for relevant classes of logical manipulations evolve and mature, mechanized systems based on such logics will naturally evolve along with them. Recently, there has been dramatic progress in the complexity of systems that can be addressed by special-purpose logics and automata. General-purpose proof and theorem prover technology has also evolved considerably over the last 20 years, although the relative progress here has been slower, since it is comparatively difficult to discover "universally applicable" tricks.

Current Status—What Can We Expect from Formal Verification?

There are some areas where verification is useful even today, (e.g. the verification of the function of "medium size" combinational circuits (100K transistors) and the function of small(er) control circuits (possessing on the order of 2^{20} states); further, the sophistication of these techniques has been rapidly improving of late. Other, more powerful (but less automatic) techniques and tools are being explored that address much broader classes of circuits. For example, interactive techniques based on theorem provers have been used to verify certain aspects of the functional behavior of simple microprocessors. Similar techniques are being used to verify "vertically integrated systems" (e.g. operating systems running on robust hardware) as well as compilers and application programs based on these. It should be noted that totally automated verification for arbitrary circuits is (theoretically) impossible in general.

Often, even *attempting* formal verification of hardware designs—by striving to provide formal specifications of the desired system attributes such as behavior and performance—can be quite beneficial; a high proportion of ambiguities and inconsistencies tend to be exposed during such an exercise. While verification can improve the quality and cost-effectiveness of many designs, it is certainly not a panacea. Verification involves two or more models, where the models typically bear an uncheckable (and possibly imperfect) relationship, both to devices and the designer's intentions. It is important to distinguish the limitations and capabilities of the model from those of the tools and techniques.

Hardware verification should be deemed useful if it reduces the cost and time of developing a new product and/or improves the reliability or the degree of confidence in a product sufficient to justify any increased costs. Sometimes, verification is not needed because other strategies are sufficient. At other times, it may be needed but not practical, in that the techniques available may be too expensive to be cost-effective for a given application. Nevertheless, such advanced techniques can be justified in the context of designing life-critical applications (e.g. systems used in medicine for life-support, civil avionics, and nuclear reactors), as well as systems where replacement is either very expensive (e.g. oil pipelines and some embedded applications), or impossible (e.g. space probes).

References

1980. Milner. R. *A Calculus of Communicating Systems*. New York: Springer-Verlag, LNCS 92.

1985. Hoare, C. A. R., *Communicating Sequential Processes*. Engle-wood Cliffs, NJ: Prentice-Hall International Series in Computer Science.

1986. Bryant, R. E. "Graph Based Algorithms for Boolean Function Manipulation," *IEEE Transactions on Computers*, C-35(8): 677–691.

1987. IEEE *IEEE Standard VHDL Language Reference Manual*. New York: IEEE Press.

1988. Boyer, R. S., and Moore, J. S. *A Computational Logic Handbook*. In Perspectives in Computing, **23**, New York: Academic Press.

1988. Gordon, M. "HOL: A Proof Generating System for Higher Order Logic," in *VLSI Specification, Synthesis and Verification*, G. Birtwistle and P. A. Subrahmanyam (Ed.) C. M. Kluwer Academic Publishers.

1990. Burch, J. R., Clarke, E. M., Dill, D. L., McMillan, K. L., and Hwang, L. J., "Symbolic Model Checking: 10^{20} States and Beyond," in Proc. of the IEEE Conference on *Logic in Computer Science*.

EDMUND M. CLARKE, JR. AND P. A. SUBRAHMANYAM

HARTREE, DOUGLAS R.

For articles on related subjects *see* DIFFERENTIAL ANALYZER; and MANCHESTER UNIVERSITY COMPUTING.

Douglas Rayner Hartree was born on 27 March 1897. During the First World War, he did scientific work in anti-aircraft gunnery and afterwards began research in wave mechanics, then a new subject. He pioneered a method of computing molecular wave functions by what he called the method of the self-consistent field. This was long before the days of digital computers and Hartree used a desk calculator for the heavy numerical calculations that were involved. He became attracted by the potential of numerical computation in scientific research, and it was as a specialist in that field that he became known rather than as a physicist.

In 1931, Vannevar Bush (*q.v.*) published his description of the differential analyzer. Hartree was impressed by the possibilities of this machine and in the summer of 1934 spent a month studying it at M.I.T. On his return, he set about raising funds for the installation of a similar machine at Manchester University, where he was Professor of Applied Mathematics. The machine was duly installed and during the Second World War constituted a valuable computing resource. Under Hartree's direction, it was used for a number of wartime problems, relating notably to the radar magnetron and to anomalous propagation of radio waves in the troposphere.

At the time, there were only a handful of people in the world who could be described as specialists in numerical computation. This put Hartree in a strong position to advise when the early digital computers became available. In May or June 1945, he paid an official visit on behalf of the British government to the United States, where he saw the Automatic Sequence Controlled Calculator at Harvard and the ENIAC (*q.v.*), then still incomplete, at the University of Pennsylvania. Through the interest of Colonel Paul Gillon, he paid another visit in 1946 to advise on non-military uses to which the ENIAC might be put. He was able to get personal expe-

FIG. 1.

rience of the use of the machine by running on it a problem in compressible fluid flow. In 1948, Hartree again visited the U.S. and spent three months as acting chief of the newly founded Institute for Numerical Analysis of the National Bureau of Standards on the UCLA campus. On his way back to the East Coast, he delivered a series of lectures at the University of Illinois. These were published under the title "Calculating Instruments and Machines." At the time, a number of the new stored-program computers were under construction, but none was actually operating. The lectures give a most interesting picture of the world of scientific computation on the very eve of the computer revolution.

In October 1946, Hartree had moved from Manchester to the Cavendish Laboratory in Cambridge. The Mathematical Laboratory (later called the Computer Laboratory) was then beginning to get into its postwar stride. From the beginning, Hartree gave it his whole-hearted support. He volunteered to give a course of lectures in numerical analysis, which he later published as a book. When the EDSAC (*q.v.*) began to be used on scientific problems, his experience with numerical computation was of the greatest value. He became a key member of the committee that interviewed applicants who wished to use the machine and, if their projects were approved, gave them advice on how to proceed.

By 1958 the credibility of digital computers had been established and the foundations of the computer field as we now know it were being established. Hartree was making many contributions and it was a serious loss to the field when, on 12 February 1958, he collapsed in the street from heart failure and died almost immediately.

References

1950. Hartree, D. R. *Calculating Instruments and Machines*. Illinois University Press; Charles Babbage reprint series 6. Tomash-M.I.T. Press (1984).
1958. Darwin, C. G. "D. R. Hartree," *Biographical Memoirs of the Royal Society* 4: 103.

MAURICE V. WILKES

HASHING. *See* SEARCHING.

HEURISTIC

For articles on related subjects *see* ALGORITHM; ARTIFICIAL INTELLIGENCE; EXPERT SYSTEM; and KNOWLEDGE REPRESENTATION.

The ancient Greek word *heuriskein* means "to find out, to discover." The English adjective "heuristic" and the more recently coined noun came into being via the Latin adjective *heuristicus*. According to the *Random House Dictionary:*

> *heuristic* adj. *1.* serving to indicate or point out, stimulating interest as a means of furthering investigation. *2.* (of a teaching method) encouraging the student to discover for himself.—n. *3.* a heuristic method or argument.

In the general sense, we talk of the "heuristic power" of a technique, the "heuristics in somebody's reasoning," and so on. Pólya (1954) has written several entertaining books that show how to approach problems in mathematics and geometry via heuristic ideas. Also, Hadamard's essay (*The Psychology of Invention in the Mathematical Field*, Dover, 1974) on discovery in mathematics yields an interesting insight—a much too rare phenomenon—into how one of the great mathematicians tackles problems.

How does all this concern us in computing? The reason is simple, but its application leads to an area that is completely open-ended. Let us consider, for example, a standard task in programming. We wish to find the roots of a higher-order algebraic equation. There are several methods of approximation that yield the solution with estimatable error bounds. We have the formulas to follow, step by step, and eventually we obtain the results. This is the *algorithmic approach*.

Let us now consider a so-called ill-defined problem, and we have many of them in everyday life. For example, say we want to balance our household budget by following a program. Although our basic needs are reasonably well known (food, shelter, clothing, medical items, transportation, entertainment, etc.), neither the relative weight of the components nor their unit prices are determinable completely. Also, our needs, desires, and tastes change continually. Our interaction with the environment represents a significant modifying factor. Because this problem is terribly ill-defined, no mathematical technique by itself has a chance to solve it. The computerization of the solution requires all those vague, hard-to-quantify ideas that humans in fact make use of in doing this problem. ("Either I go on vacation or buy that new car....Let's see, how much longer can I drive my old bomb?") The collection of these rules of thumb, sometimes referred to as insight, intuition, or experience with a particular task, represents what computer scientists call "heuristics" (plural noun). Any one such rule is thus a *heuristic* (singular noun).

We resort to *heuristic programming* whenever an algorithmic solution is prohibitively expensive or impossible to follow, or is unavailable. The role of heuristics is to cut down the time and memory requirements of search. On the average, it should result in appreciable savings when programming our budget to satisfy our basic needs. Heuristic methods are not foolproof; they can fail a certain proportion of the time. (Algorithms are not supposed to fail....However, the fact that a technique is not foolproof does not render it heuristic.)

The larger the range in which a heuristic can be applied, the more powerful it is considered to be. Also, its level of performance should be at least comparable to that of an exhaustive strategy (an algorithm, in fact) or of a random search for a solution.

The following example, originally reported by Simon, should shed some light on the concept under discussion. Nontrivial games cannot be played by humans *or* by machines algorithmically (because there does not exist an algorithm) or exhaustively (because the memory and time requirements far exceed any available ones). The classical example of an intellectual game, chess, has been programmed by several groups of researchers. (*see* COMPUTER CHESS). In all these, heuristic ideas occupy a central role in move selection and position evaluation. In fact, de Groot and other psychologists have shown that the basic difference between excellent and merely good players is not in their memory capacity or even in their data processing ability *in abstracto*. All players analyze practically the same number of board positions, but not always the same ones. Excellent chess players have developed very powerful heuristics for the *selection* of game continuations to be considered. They may go down to a depth of, say, 20 half-moves along one path and disregard others below a depth of 2 or 3, for reasons of their own.

One often used heuristic in chess is to leave as little freedom of move selection for the opponent as possible. If all other techniques of comparison assign an equal score to two moves considered, a chess expert usually selects the one that restricts the opponent's mobility to a larger degree. This technique, being a heuristic, works most of the time. There was a famous game, however, between two international masters in which the winner used this heuristic to *his disadvantage*. It has been shown by game analysts that in a particular position, the optimum move (overlooked for the reasons discussed) could have led to an earlier victory. A supplement to this story is that the MATER program by Baylor and Simon (1966), which incorporates the heuristic of fewest-replies, was presented the same particular near-end position and duplicated the mistake made by the international master.

Outlook   Except for some introductory efforts (Waterman, 1970; Findler *et al.*, 1971), present heuristics are all preprogrammed in artificial intelligence projects. In other words, it is not the machine that discovers, selects, and optimizes the rules that play an increasingly important role in many problem-solving programs. Therefore, the performance level of these programs is determined by the researcher's experience, insight, and perhaps even luck.

A much more desirable situation would be the one in which heuristic processes are automated. Learning programs, initially inefficient and possibly even random in their actions, would gradually formulate more and more heuristics on the basis of experience. These heuristics would assume a flexible, or parametric, format so that subsequent optimization processes could raise the overall level of performance.

References

1954. Pólya G. *Mathematics and Plausible Reasoning:* **I.** *Induction and Analogy in Mathematics,* **II.** *Patterns of Plausible Inference.* Princeton, NJ: Princeton University Press.
1966. Baylor, G. W. and Simon, H. A. "A Chess Mating Combinations Program," *Proc. SJCC* **28**: 431–447.
1970. Waterman, D. A. "Generalization Learning Techniques for Automating the Learning of Heuristics," *Artificial Intelligence* **1**: 121–170.
1971. Findler, N. V., Klein, H., Gould, W., Kowal, A., and Menig, J. "Studies on Decision Making Using the Game of Poker," *Proc. IFIP Congress, Book TA-7:* 50–61. Ljubljana, Yugoslavia.
1978. Waterman, D. A. and Hayes-Roth, F. (Eds.). *Pattern-Directed Inference Systems.* New York: Academic Press.

NICHOLAS V. FINDLER

HIERARCHY OF OPERATORS.   See OPERATOR PRECEDENCE.

HIGH-LEVEL LANGUAGE.   See PROBLEM-ORIENTED LANGUAGES; and PROCEDURE-ORIENTED LANGUAGES.

HISTORY.   See DIGITAL COMPUTERS: HISTORY; and SOFTWARE HISTORY.

HOLLERITH, HERMAN

For articles on related subjects *see* DIGITAL COMPUTERS: HISTORY; PUNCHED CARDS; and WATSON, THOMAS, SR.

Herman Hollerith (b. Buffalo, NY, 1860; d. Washington, DC, 1929) was the inventor of punched-card data processing and founder of a firm that evolved to become IBM.

For the quarter-century from 1890 to World War I, he had a virtual monopoly on punched-card data processing. He held the foundation patents on the field (U. S. Patents

395 781-395 783) and nearly 50 other U. S. and foreign patents on basic techniques and equipment. He developed applications of punched-card data processing to many fields of endeavor, including the U.S. Census, medical and public health statistics, railroad and public utility accounting, stock and inventory control, and factory cost accounting.

Many basic decisions he made at, or before, the turn of the twentieth century persist today. Punched cards today are the size of dollar bills of that era because Hollerith found it economical to buy cabinets and drawers subdivided in that size. The positional coding used on punched cards (Hollerith code) has evolved directly from decisions he made about card design when designing the first column-by-column keypunch for the 1901 Census of Agriculture. Even the practice of IBM and other firms of leasing and maintaining their own data processing equipment originated in Hollerith's decisions made prior to 1900.

Upon graduation from Columbia University in 1879, Hollerith took a job with the Census, where he became the protégé of Colonel John Shaw Billings, an Army surgeon who was also serving as director of the division of vital statistics for the Census. Billings suggested to Hollerith that a good machine to do the purely mechanical work of tabulating population and similar statistics was badly needed and that a technique of using cards with the description of each individual punched into them was a good approach to the problem. Intrigued by this suggestion, Hollerith made a study of the problem and determined to his own satisfaction that it was feasible.

In 1882, Hollerith followed General Francis Walker from the Census to M.I.T., where he became an instructor in mechanical engineering. While there he worked hard on his "Census machine" invention, concentrating initially upon a variant of an earlier machine developed by Colonel Charles W. Seaton, chief clerk for the 1870 Census. This prototype had used a player-piano roll type of feed mechanism rather than individual cards.

By the end of his first year at M.I.T., Hollerith decided that his true vocation was invention. He returned to Washington and secured a position with the Patent Office to learn the arts of invention and patent protection. After a year, he left the Patent Office and set up shop as a "Solicitor and Expert on Patents" to earn his living while he gave his primary attention to invention. Soon he applied for several patents; included among them was the first application for the foundation patents on punched-card data processing.

Considering this to be the most promising of his inventions, he concentrated upon it and developed the experimental test systems used for vital statistics tabulations in Baltimore, New Jersey, and New York City. During this period, his system evolved from a simple machine with cards punched by a conductor's ticket punch to a complete system. This system included a pantograph-like punch, a tabulating machine with a large number of clocklike counters (each capable of counting up to 10,000 occurrences), and a simple, electrically actuated sorting box for classifying and grouping cards in accordance with the categories punched into them.

In 1889, his system was installed in the Army Surgeon General's office to handle Army medical statistics. A description of this system and his plans for the Census was accepted by Columbia as a doctoral dissertation, and he was awarded a Ph.D. "for achievement" in 1890. Also in 1889, a comparative test made of the Hollerith and two competitive systems caused the Hollerith system to be chosen for use in the 1890 Census. Austria, Canada, Italy, Norway, and Russia were soon investigating and adopting Hollerith equipment for their population censuses. These early systems could tally totals one at a time but could not add or accumulate.

Shortly after 1900, Hollerith began developing a second generation of his equipment. A new type of card design arranged numeric information in columns and permitted development of a simple, new kind of keypunch, an automatic-feed card sorter, and an automatic-feed tabulator of vastly improved performance. These new systems could accumulate numbers of any size, and thus were obviously applicable to many situations other than census and similar statistical work. Hollerith soon spread their use to an amazing variety of industries. They even went overseas with the American Expeditionary Forces in World War I.

About 1905, the management in the Census Bureau began to object to Hollerith's profits and sponsored alternative developments designed to break his monopoly. These competitive systems were widely adopted, once Hollerith's fundamental patents expired, and often led the data processing industry into new developments. Because this competition resulted in a need for increased capitalization, Hollerith sold his patent and proprietary rights to a holding company in 1912. This relieved him of day-by-day management chores and he became a highly paid consultant. Before long, Thomas J. Watson, Sr., was brought in to head Hollerith's old company, but Watson's commercialism and Hollerith's devotion to purely inventive objectives caused dissension. Watson's interests prevailed, and Hollerith's contributions and achievements were soon absorbed into the greater representative image of IBM.

Reference

1971. Hollerith, Virginia. "Biographical Sketch of Herman Hollerith," *ISIS* **62**, *210*: 69–78.

WILLIAM F. LUEBBERT

HOLLERITH'S MACHINE

For articles on related subjects *see* HOLLERITH, HERMAN; PUNCHED CARDS; and PUNCHED CARD MACHINERY.

The first practical electric tabulating system, developed and patented by Herman Hollerith in the late 1880s, received its widest initial use, encouragement, and greatest impetus from the 1890 census of the United States. On short notice, he produced 50 tabulating machines and related equipment that were used to tally the population and dwelling counts and later to tabulate and cross-tabu-

FIG. 1.

late the characteristics for nearly 63 million persons. The Census Bureau employed later versions of this system for the next 60 years, or until electronic tabulation appeared in the form of UNIVAC I (*q.v.*).

Hollerith's system was based on a card-punching device that a clerk, reading a census return, used to record up to 17 different characteristics for one person by choosing among 240 possible punching positions and punching holes in a 6 5/8-inch × 3 1/4-inch card. (Certain standard codes, such as for a particular enumeration district, could be set on another punch and transferred to stacks of cards.) The completed cards then were fed, one at a time, into a "circuit-closing press" on the tabulating machine. This press was equipped with rows of spring-loaded pins in the top jaw and tiny matching pots of mercury in the bottom jaw. The pins were wired for an electric current; the mercury pots were connected to 40 counter dials. When a clerk inserted the punched card in the press and closed the jaws, the pins finding holes were able to descend into their mercury pots. The current passed through these pins and pots to their related electromagnetic counter dials on the machine, advancing the unit hand on each dial one place. (When the unit hand made a complete revolution on the dial, it activated a hundreds pointer one place.) The clerk then released the jaws, removed the card and dropped it into an open pocket on a sorting box connected to the machine, and repeated the entire operation with the next card. At the end of the run, the dials were read and reset for the next run and the sorting box was emptied. The dials could also be con-

nected through relays, to deal with combinations of characteristics such as "foreign-born white males."

Since clerks in the 1890 census were now able to punch an average of 700 cards each in an 8-hour day and a tabulating-machine operator could handle 7,000 cards in the same period, the Hollerith system represented a considerable advance in speed over the past. One machine now could process 250 items (characteristics) per minute once the cards had been punched. A clerk in the 1880 census (when there were just 50 million people in the United States), with the help of a fairly crude mechanical device, could tally (but not cross-tabulate) 20 characteristics per minute, but even that was about four times faster than was possible with the big census schedules and tally sheets used in earlier years. Even so, census data processing was labor intensive and time consuming—so much so that, allowing for budget constraints, some tabulations could not be published until 1889—a year before the next census began.

For vital statistics agencies, insurance companies, railroads, and other organizations—but especially the Census Bureau—that needed to process quantities of data and produce timely results, the Hollerith machine and the punched cards it required broke most of the nineteenth century labor and time barriers they faced. In computer history, the Hollerith system was the technological advance that for 60 years bridged the gap between marks on paper and the electronic age.

Reference

1965. Truesdell, L. E. *The Development of Punch Card Tabulation in the Bureau of the Census, 1890–1940.* Washington, DC: Govt. Print. Off.

FREDERICK G. BOHME

HOPPER, GRACE MURRAY

For articles on related subjects *see* AIKEN, HOWARD; DIGITAL COMPUTERS: HISTORY: EARLY; and MARK I.

Grace Brewster Murray Hopper was born in New York City on 9 December 1906. She received her B.A. in Mathematics and Physics from Vassar College in 1928, where she was elected to Phi Beta Kappa. She continued her graduate studies in mathematics at Yale University, where she was awarded her M.A. (1930) and Ph.D. (1934). From 1931 to 1943, she was a member of the mathematics faculty at Vassar College. In December 1943, she joined the United States Naval Reserve and attended Midshipman's School at Northampton, Massachusetts.

She graduated in 1944 with a commission in the U.S. Navy (Lt. J.G.) and was assigned to the Bureau of Ordnance's Computation Project under the direction of Howard Aiken at Harvard University. It was at Harvard that Dr. Hopper was first exposed to the world of automatic digital processing. There she joined Robert Campbell and Richard Bloch as a "coder." In her words: "I became the third programmer on the world's first large-scale digital computer, Mark I." At the end of World War II, Dr. Hopper

FIG. 1.   Grace Murray Hopper.

resigned from Vassar and was appointed to the Harvard faculty as a Research Fellow in the newly founded Computation Laboratory.

In 1949, she joined, as senior mathematician, the fledgling Eckert-Mauchly Corporation, where BINAC and UNIVAC were under construction. She remained with the organization after its acquisition by Remington Rand, through the merger with Sperry Rand, and until her retirement from the Univac division in 1971. Throughout this period, she maintained her activity in the U.S. Naval Reserve and was promoted successively through the ranks until her retirement as a Commander in 1966. In 1967, she was recalled to active duty and, in 1973, promoted to the rank of Captain. In 1985, she was advanced in rank to Commodore. The title of that grade was changed to Rear Admiral in 1985. She continued on active duty until her forced retirement in 1987.

For more than three decades, Captain Hopper was an innovator and major contributor to the development of programming languages. Inspired by John Mauchly's "Short Order Code" (BINAC, 1949) and Betty Holberton's first Sort-Merge Generator (UNIVAC I, 1951), she developed the first compiler, A-0 (1952), and the first compiler to handle mathematical computations, A-2 (1953). This work, coupled with her view of what the world of programming languages ought to be like, led her to the development of the first English language data processing compiler, B-0 (Flow-Matic), which was in use as early as 1957. In April 1959, Dr. Hopper and five others (I.E. Block, B. Cheydleur, S. Gorn, R. Rossheim, and A. E. Smith) met to plan a formal meeting whose object would be " to develop the specifications for a common business language for...automatic digital computers" (Sammet, 1981, p. 200).

This meeting triggered a sequence of events that resulted in "Initial Specifications for a Common Business Language" (DoD, April 1960). Flow-Matic, along with AIMACO and Commercial Translator, provided the main inputs in influencing the early development of Cobol (Sammet, 1981, p. 217).

Dr. Hopper's awards, honors, and professional publications are much too numerous to detail here. Most notably, she received honorary degrees from the Newark College of Engineering (D. Engr., 1972); C. W. Post College, L.I.U. (D. Sci., 1973); The University of Pennsylvania (LL.D., 1974); and the Pratt Institute (D. Sci., 1976). She has also received almost every major award in her profession. These include DPMA's "Man-of-the-Year" (1969); AFIPS' Harry Goode Memorial Award (1970); and Yale University's Wilbur Lucius Cross Medal (1972). In 1971, the Univac Division of Sperry Rand Corporation created the Grace Murray Hopper Award, which is awarded annually by ACM to a distinguished young computer professional. In 1991 she was awarded the National Medal of Technology.

Clearly, Grace Hopper belongs to that select group of computer professionals whose talent, vision, dedication, and constant persistence has laid the foundation for the continuing information processing explosion. Throughout her career, she saw herself as a teacher and as one who always battled entrenched attitudes of those she referred to as the "establishment." The phrase "but it's never been done that way" was anathema to her. As a visual reminder of her personal creed, she kept a ship's clock in her office. It appeared to be a typical ship's clock until you looked carefully: It ran backward.

Grace Hopper died on 1 January 1992.

References

1971. "Grace Murray Hopper," *ACM '71: A Quarter Century View*, pp. iii–iv.
1981. Wexelblat, Richard (Ed.). *Proceedings, History of Programming Languages Conference*. New York: Academic Press. (See Sammet, J. "Introduction of Captain Grace Murray Hopper," 5–7; Hopper, G. "Keynote Address," 7-24; and Sammet, J. "COBOL," 199–278.)
1984. Tropp, H. "Grace Hopper: The Youthful Teacher of us All." *Abacus* **2**, 6–18.
1988. Hopper, Grace Murray. "The Education of a Computer," *Annals of the History of Computing* **9** (3/4), 271–281. Reprint of a 1952 ACM Publication. Introduction by David Gries.

HENRY S. TROPP

HOSPITAL INFORMATION SYSTEM (HIS)

For articles on related subjects *see* BIOCOMPUTING; COMPUTERIZED TOMOGRAPHY; INFORMATION SYSTEMS; INTENSIVE CARE, COMPUTERS IN; MANAGEMENT INFORMATION SYSTEMS; MEDICAL APPLICATIONS; MEDICAL IMAGING; and MEDLARS/MEDLINE.

Computers in hospitals perform a wide range of activities, such as processing and storing the data necessary to support daily operations, facilitating clinical and financial decision making, and satisfying internal and external documentation requirements. These computer systems are variously referred to as hospital, health, and medical information systems. The term *hospital information system* (HIS) encompasses both patient care and patient management systems, which support health care delivery, and financial and resource management systems, which support the business and strategic operations of a hospital. In countries that have hospital-based health care systems, the term HIS can imply information systems with broader functions, including applications that support ambulatory (outpatient) care.

Hospital staff spend as much as 20 to 30 percent of their time collecting, analyzing, disseminating, and otherwise handling information. Most hospitals use some form of computer system to assist in these activities. The core HIS applications perform basic hospital functions, including patient registration and admission, discharge, and transfer (ADT). These fundamental systems maintain the inpatient census, as well as store patient identification information and critical demographic data that are acquired during the registration process. In addition, the patient registry functions as a reference base for HIS components, such as the medical records and patient billing systems. When an HIS is extended to the pharmacy, laboratory, and other ancillary departments, the core systems serve as a repository for shared data, thus minimizing the need for redundant data entry.

The department-specific components of an HIS perform a variety of clinical and operational tasks:

- Pharmacy systems typically prepare work lists for drug preparation and distribution, generate prescription labels, and monitor drug inventories. They may also keep an on-line record of patients' medication orders and perform drug interaction checking.
- Laboratory systems create specimen collection schedules, store results generated by automated instruments or via manual testing procedures, and print patient-specific laboratory reports, with flags to indicate abnormal results. In addition, they often provide tools to measure the productivity of laboratory personnel and may promote quality control by monitoring the accuracy of the instruments used.
- Radiology information systems facilitate examination scheduling, film library management, and transcription of examination interpretations. Many of the newest imaging techniques, such as computerized tomography (CT) and magnetic resonance imaging (MRI), are inherently digital; thus, the radiology department has become a growing area for computer-based medical applications. Although currently too costly for widespread use, sophisticated picture archiving and communication systems (PACS) have been developed to store, communicate, and display digitized medical images.
- A variety of additional systems are available to support other departments in the hospital. Typical

applications include inventory tracking and supplies purchasing, operating room management, staff scheduling, nursing care plan development, diet planning, quality assurance, professional credentialing, and risk management.

Among the most common HIS applications are traditional financial functions such as payroll administration, patient billing, and accounts receivable management. To cope with increasing competition and complex reimbursement mechanisms, a growing number of hospitals are acquiring cost accounting systems and financial decision support tools designed to help administrators make investment decisions, manage costs, set charges, and respond to bids from third-party payers.

Communications and networking systems allow the integration of the various HIS components. Communication of physicians' orders is critical because most hospital activities, including drug distribution, test performance, and charge capture for patient billing, are initi-

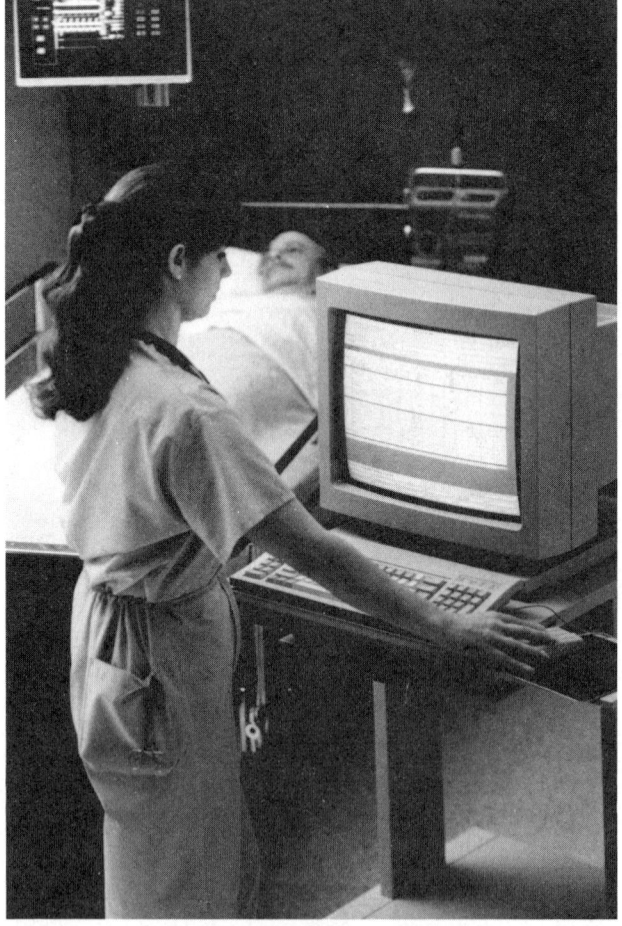

FIG. 1. A bedside data management system. Using such a system, physicians and nurses in an intensive care unit can enter physicians' orders and clinical observations, and gain assistance in developing care plans, progress notes, and nursing assessments. Interfaces to patient monitoring instruments and laboratory information systems eliminate much of the need for redundant data entry. (Courtesy of EMTEK Health Care Systems, Tempe, AZ.)

ated by these orders. In non-automated hospitals, orders are conveyed by using slips of paper. Automated order entry and results reporting capabilities allow communication with ancillary areas electronically, thus eliminating the easily misplaced paper slips and minimizing delays in communication. As an additional advantage, the information is then available on line, where it can be accessed by health professionals who wish to review a patient's drug profile or previous laboratory test results.

The medical record is the key to coordinating the various health professionals who participate in providing patient care. It integrates diverse patient information, provides a mechanism for communication, and serves as a legal document of a patient's experiences during hospitalization. Current hospital information systems, however, typically store only limited clinical information and provide little support for true patient care—a paper medical chart continues to serve as the primary repository for clinical data. Although the more sophisticated systems can assist nurses in creating care plans and charting patient progress notes, in the vast majority of hospitals, ward clerks and nurses enter only the information necessary for performance of operational tasks and record keeping.

To affect patient care to a greater extent, an HIS must store a more complete on-line medical record. The advantages of an electronic medical record include rapid access to pertinent information, simultaneous access by multiple users, improved legibility, and, when the data are stored in a structured manner, assistance in searching for pertinent information. Furthermore, when the clinical components of an HIS are well developed, clinical assistance is possible. Systems that use the stored information can be developed to monitor patients and issue alerts, make diagnostic

suggestions, recommend patient-specific drug dosing regimens, and provide limited therapy advice.

Steady decreases in the costs of on-line storage and computer processing power have removed major barriers to the feasibility of an electronic medical record. Entry of information into the computer remains an enormous bottleneck, however. For ease of data entry, most HI systems have minimal keystroke or menu-driven interfaces, and many support touchscreen, lightpen, or barcode data entry devices. Timely and accurate data capture is also facilitated by direct interfaces with patient monitors and other medical instruments. Recently, there has been growing interest in the implementation of point-of-care systems. Using bedside terminals or handheld devices, care providers are able to enter and review patient information, such as vital signs, clinical observations, and medication administration data at the time care is delivered (see Fig. 1).

A related area of exploration is the development of workstations (*q.v.*) that facilitate clinical decision making by physicians. A simple function of such a workstation is the graphical or tabular display of trends in laboratory test values. More sophisticated clinical decision aids are possible when physicians' observations and other detailed patient data are stored on line. These data, when combined with formal categorizations, such as problem statements and diagnoses, will allow automated summarization of a patient's history and clinical progress and provide support for therapy planning and medical diagnosis. Although decision aids for physicians have been pursued by researchers since the 1960s, commercial HIS developers have only recently begun to develop true clinical applications.

Hospitals may choose from a host of alternatives

VENDOR NAME/SYSTEM DESCRIPTION	BELL ATLANTIC HEALTHCARE SYSTEMS	GERBER ALLEY	SHARED MEDICAL SYSTEMS	TDS HEALTHCARE SYSTEMS
Headquarters Location	Greenbrae, CA	Norcross, GA	Malvern, PA	Atlanta, GA
System Name	StatLAN	The Precision Alternative	Invision	TDS 7000 Series
System Type	Applications Integration and Networking	Integrated HIS	Integrated HIS	Integrated HIS
Hardware Platform	SUN Microcomputers and Local Area Network	DEC, HP Minicomputer	IBM Mainframe (In-house or Remote)	IBM Mainframe (In-house or Remote)
Bedsize of Target Hospital	300+ Beds	150-500 Beds	250+ Beds	250+ Beds
Number of Sites	~10	~65	120	125
Major Applications	Network Gateway; Order/Results Communication; Clinician Workstation	General Accounting; Patient Accounting; ADT; Registration; Medical Records; Order/Results Communication; Nursing Notes; Laboratory; Pharmacy; Radiology	General Accounting; Patient Accounting; ADT; Registration; Scheduling; Medical Records; Order/Results Communication; Nursing Notes; Laboratory; Pharmacy; Radiology	Patient Accounting; ADT; Registration; Scheduling; Medical Records; Order/Results Communication; Treatment Notes; Nursing Care Plans; Pharmacy; Radiology; Point of Care Terminals

FIG. 2.   Examples of available HIS. A large number of systems have been developed to support the information processing needs of hospitals, including these products, which exemplify alternative systems delivery modes.

when acquiring an HIS (see Fig. 2). Available modes for HIS delivery range from shared processing services to custom-developed in-house systems and to networked configurations of specialized systems. The most common HIS model combines a central mainframe- or minicomputer-based system that supports institutional applications (ADT, medical records index, order entry, results reporting, general accounting, patient billing, etc.) with minicomputer- or microcomputer-based systems for ancillary management and other specialized functions. Mainframe HI systems, which are designed to support larger and more complex institutions, typically provide richer functions than do minicomputer-based systems. Due to the difficulties of developing an HIS from scratch and the need for institutional control over information processing, most new and replacement HI systems are "turnkey" (ready to install) systems that have been tailored to accommodate the specific needs of the institution.

Data integration is critical to avoiding redundant data entry and storage, and thus to promoting data consistency among independent systems. Traditionally, information exchange has been accomplished through magnetic tape or on-line interfaces. With the emergence of network communications technology, it became possible to exchange data electronically, avoiding the need to develop and maintain cumbersome direct system interfaces. Because of their ability to distribute processing to local users and to provide common access to shared resources

such as databases, computer programs, and printers, the local area network (LAN - *q.v.*) has rapidly gained prominence in hospitals during the late 1980s (see Fig. 3).

The development of industrywide standard network protocols (*q.v.*) has eased the technical problems of electronic communication. Still, many obstacles to system integration remain, such as an agreement on standard coding schemes and formats for medical data and definition of minimum data sets to collect. The development of data standards is currently an active area of endeavor. Examples are the American Society of Testing Materials (ASTM) standard for representing, storing, and transmitting laboratory information; the American College of Radiology and the National Electronic Manufacturers' Association (ACR-NEMA) standard for transmission of digital radiologic imaging data; the Medical Information Bus (MIB) standard for interconnecting patient monitors and other bedside devices; and the Health Level Seven (HL-7) and Medical Data Interchange (MEDIX) standards for transmitting billing data, updating the census, and communicating orders and results within hospital networks.

In the coming years, the integration of myriad diverse computer systems will remain a challenge for health care institutions and information systems vendors alike. Increasing pressure to provide high-quality health care at the lowest possible cost has fueled hospital needs to relate costs to patient outcomes and to identify the most cost-effective means of providing care. From a hospital management perspective, the ability of an HIS to analyze internal financial and clinical data, as well as comparative information from external databases, may provide the edge necessary for long-term survival. From a patient care perspective, linkage of information systems in hospitals, physicians offices, outpatient facilities, and other affiliated institutions will enhance continuity and consistency of care across providers. Furthermore, an integrated on-line medical record will support development of guidelines for appropriate care, quality assurance activities, cost management, clinical research, and technology assessment.

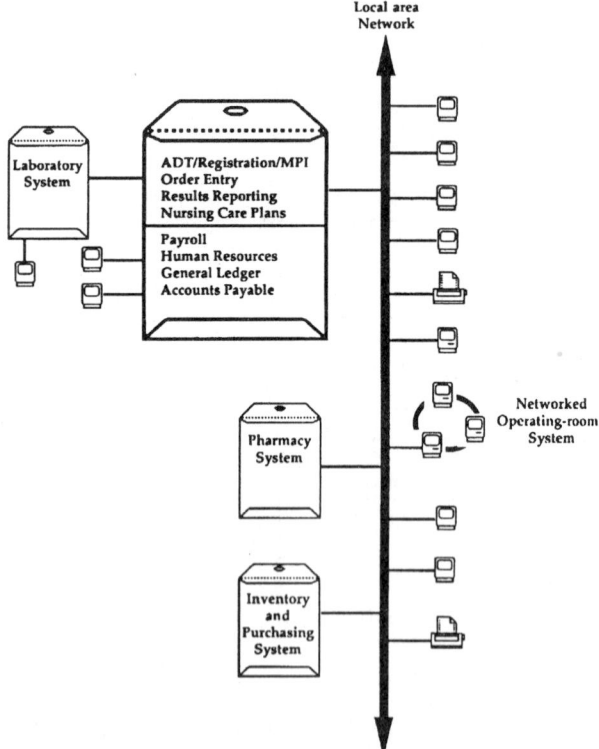

Local area Network

Laboratory System

ADT/Registration/MPI
Order Entry
Results Reporting
Nursing Care Plans

Payroll
Human Resources
General Ledger
Accounts Payable

Networked Operating-room System

Pharmacy System

Inventory and Purchasing System

FIG. 3. Components of a LAN-based HIS. The most common HIS model combines a mainframe- or minicomputer-based system running central institutional applications with stand-alone systems for ancillary management and other specialty applications. Information exchange among independent systems may be accomplished via network connections or direct interfaces.

References

1986. Blum, B. I. *Clinical Information Systems*. New York: Springer-Verlag.

1987. Anderson, J. G. and Jay, S. J. (Eds.). *Use and Impact of Computers in Clinical Medicine*. New York: Springer-Verlag.

1988. McDonald, C. J. (Ed.). "Computer-stored medical record systems." *M.D. Computing*, **5**(5): 1–62.

1989. Orthner, H. F. and Blum, B. I. (Eds.). *Implementing Health Care Information Systems*. New York: Springer-Verlag.

1990. Bakker, A. R. "An integrated hospital information system in the Netherlands." *M.D. Computing*, **7**(2): 91–7.

1990. Miller, R. A. (Ed.). *Proceedings of the Fourteenth Annual Symposium on Computer Applications in Medical Care*. Los Alamitos, CA: IEEE Computer Society Press.

1990. Scherrer, J., *et al.* "An integrated hospital information system in Geneva." *M.D. Computing*, **7**(2): 81–9.

1990. Shortliffe, E. H., Perreault, L. E., Wiederhold, G., and Fagan, L. M. (Eds.). *Medical Informatics: Computer Applications in Health Care*. Reading, MA: Addison-Wesley.

LESLIE E. PERREAULT

HOST SYSTEM

For articles on related subjects *see* DISTRIBUTED SYSTEMS; FILE SERVER; FRONT-END PROCESSOR; MICROPROGRAMMING; MULTIPROGRAMMING; and MULTITASKING.

A *host system* or a *host computer* is the physical system that interprets a program. The program is written on a *logical machine*, which is usually not the same as the physical machine (host system). These differences arise because the physical system either does not possess or does not allocate all features or resources directly requested by the logical machine (program). The distinction between host system and logical system is especially notable in two areas: multiprogramming systems and microprogrammed (emulated) systems.

In multiprogramming systems, the host system is responsible for allocating storage and I/O resources to each of the logical machines (i.e. in effect, active programs), which are usually called *virtual* machines, as they are required. This allows a number of virtual machines to share the physical resources without logical conflict (i.e. without any programmer intervention in the source programs) and at the same time more effectively use the resources of the physical host system.

In microprogrammed systems, the notion of host system applies to the physical machine that interprets (*emulates*) the programs written in other machine languages. The machine being emulated by the host machine is said to be the *image* machine (sometimes the term "virtual" is also used to describe this situation).

Another use of the term *host system* is in time sharing or remote computing, where the *host* is the central computer providing service to terminals or satellite computers.

MICHAEL J. FLYNN

HUMAN FACTORS IN COMPUTING

For articles on related subjects *see* INTERACTIVE INPUT DEVICES; INTERACTIVE SYSTEM; USER INTERFACE; and WINDOW ENVIRONMENTS.

Introduction   Satisfied users of interactive computer systems often experience a sense of competence, clarity, and even power as they do their work. For many other users, however, frustration and anxiety are a part of daily life. They struggle to learn complex command languages or confusing menu selection systems that are supposed to help them do their jobs. Some users develop such serious cases of computer shock, terminal terror, or network neurosis that they go to great lengths to avoid computers. With the proliferation of personal computers, these electronic age maladies are growing more common, but help is on the way.

Proper design of the human-computer interface can make a substantial difference in training time, performance speed, error rates, user satisfaction, and the human retention of operations over time. The poor designs of the past are giving way to elegant systems. Descriptive taxonomies of users and tasks, predictive models of performance, and explanatory theories are being developed to guide designers and evaluators. Haphazard and intuitive development strategies with argumentation about "user friendliness" is yielding to a more scientific approach. Measurement of learning time, performance, errors, and subjective satisfaction is now a natural part of the design process.

Interaction Styles   The central concern of designers is the interaction style of a system. Each style has its merits for particular user communities or sets of tasks. Choosing a style or a combination of styles is a key step, but within each there are numerous minute decisions that determine the efficacy of the resulting system. The primary styles currently being applied are menu selection, form fill-in, command language, and direct manipulation. We will examine each in turn.

Menu Selection   Users read a list of items, select the one most appropriate to their task, type or point to indicate their selection, verify that the selection is correct, initiate the action, and observe the effect. If the terminology and meaning of the items are understandable and distinct, the users can accomplish their tasks with little learning or memorization and few keystrokes. The greatest benefit may be that there is a clear structure to decision making, since only a few choices are presented at a time. This interaction style is appropriate for novice and intermittent users. It can also be appealing to frequent users if the display and selection mechanisms are very rapid.

For designers, menu selection systems require careful task analysis to ensure that all functions are supported conveniently and that terminology is chosen carefully and used consistently. Dialogue management software tools to support menu selection are an enormous benefit in ensuring consistent screen design, validating completeness, and supporting maintenance.

Form Fill-in   When data entry is required, menu selection usually becomes cumbersome, and form fill-in (also called fill-in-the-blanks) is appropriate. Users see a display of related fields, move a cursor among the fields, and enter data where desired, much as they would with a paper form for an invoice, personnel data sheet, or order form. Seeing the full set of related fields on the screen at one time in a familiar format is often very helpful.

Form fill-in interaction does require that users understand the field labels, know the permissible values, are familiar with typing and editing fields, and are capable of responding to error messages. These demands imply that users must have some training or experience.

Command Language   For frequent users, command languages provide a strong feeling that they are in charge and that they are taking the initiative rather than responding to the computer. Command language users must learn the syntax, but they can often express complex possibilities rapidly, without having to read distracting prompts. However, error rates are typically high, training is necessary, and retention may be poor. Error messages and on-line assistance are hard to provide because of the diversity of possibilities and the complexity of relating tasks to computer concepts and syntax. Command languages and lengthier query or programming languages are the domain of the expert frequent users ("power users" - *q.v.*) who often derive great satisfaction from mastering a complex set of concepts and syntax.

Direct Manipulation   When a clever designer can create a visual representation of the world of action, the users' tasks can often be greatly simplified by allowing direct manipulation of the objects of interest. Examples include painting programs such as MacPaint or PC Paintbrush, electronic spreadsheets (*q.v.*), manufacturing or process control systems that show a schematic diagram of the plant, air traffic control systems, some educational and flight simulations, and video games.

In the PacMan video game, the joystick is used to move the PacMan icon through a maze to consume power dots, avoid ghosts, and eat fruits. Another playful example is the Music Construction Set, which enables the user to pick up notes, drag them onto a staff, and then play the music. Several chemistry simulations allow the user to assemble laboratory equipment and run experiments just by touching the beakers, burners, and thermometers. A popular application of direct manipulation is in display editors that have the WYSIWYG property (what-you-see-is-what-you-get).

By pointing at objects and actions, users can rapidly carry out tasks, immediately observe the results, and, if necessary, reverse the action. Keyboard entry of commands or menu choices is replaced by cursor motion devices, such as a lightpen, joystick, touchscreen, trackball, or mouse (*q.v.*), to select from a visible set of objects and actions. Direct manipulation is appealing to novices, is easy to remember for intermittent users, encourages exploration, and with careful design can be rapid for power users.

Fig. 1 offers a comparison of these four interaction styles. Blending several styles may be appropriate when the required tasks and users are diverse. Commands may lead the user to a form fill-in where data entry is required or *pop-up* (or *pull-down*) *menus* may be used to control a direct manipulation environment when a suitable visualization of operations cannot be found.

The hope that computers will respond properly to arbitrary natural language sentences or phrases has engaged many researchers and system developers, but with limited success thus far. Natural language interaction usually provides little context for issuing the next command, frequently requires "clarification dialog," and may be slower and more cumbersome than the alternatives. Still, where users are knowledgeable about a task domain whose scope is limited and where intermittent use inhib-

INTERACTION STYLE	ADVANTAGES	DISADVANTAGES
Menu selection	shortens learning reduces keystrokes structures decision-making permits use of dialogue management tools easy to support error handling	danger of many menus may slow frequent users consumes screen space requires rapid display rate
Form fill-in	simplifies data entry requires modest training assistance is convenient shows context for activity permits use of form management software tools	consumes screen space
Command language	flexibility appeals to "power" users supports user initiative potentially rapid for complex tasks	poor error handling requires substantial training difficult to retain
Direct manipulation	visually presents task concepts easy to learn easy to retain errors can be avoided encourages exploration	may be hard to program may require graphics display

FIG. 1.   Advantages and disadvantages of interaction styles.

its command language training, natural language interfaces have their place (though form fill-in or direct manipulation may be more attractive).

Within each of the interaction styles, there are hundreds of design decisions that critically affect the user's success. For menus and form fill-in, each screen title should guide the user, items should be familiar, distinctive, and arranged in a logical order, instructions should be comprehensible, error correction should be easy, return to previous menus or screens should be rapid, and some mechanism should exist to enable frequent users to speed traversal.

For command languages, each command name should be distinctive and meaningful. A regular and logical pattern of formation aids learning and retention. Symmetric pairs of instructions such as BACKWARD/FORWARD or OPEN/CLOSE, instead of UP/NEXT or OPEN/RESTORE, are also helpful. When a keyboard is used to enter commands, a simple strategy of abbreviation (such as truncation to the shortest unambiguous character string) speeds the work of frequent users.

With direct manipulation systems, the visual presentation should be comprehensible to users familiar with the task. Actions should be rapid, incremental, and reversible. Visual feedback after each action assures users that they are making progress towards completing their task.

Response Time

Critical to every interactive system is the time it takes to complete a task. User expectations are rising, and excessive delays are perceived as an annoying impediment. While novices may appreciate a slower speed, the desire for rapid response grows as experience increases. Many researchers have demonstrated a strong correlation between the computer's response time and the user's thinking time. With long response times, users reflect carefully about each action, in part because they wish to reduce errors and the number of interactions. With short response times, the pattern of work changes and users will issue many brief commands. In short, users respond to the pace of the system.

When the task is cognitively challenging, error rates may increase with shorter response times. This is acceptable in many tasks, because errors are apparent and correction is simple. However, with life-critical or irreversible operations, there may be an advantage in encouraging more careful consideration of the user's actions by slowing the pace. Too rapid a pace may increase stress. Since long response times can also increase frustration, empirical tests are necessary to determine a reasonable pace. Users should be informed of progress during long response times. An open problem is to predict performance and error rates as a function of user experience, task, and response time.

Error Messages

With many contemporary menu selection and command languages, errors are common, even for frequent users. Harsh messages such as FATAL ERROR - RUN ABORTED, vague comments such as SYNTAX ERROR or ILLEGAL DATA, or cryptic responses such as IEH219H TRANS CTL ERROR are disruptive and annoying. In five experimental studies, merely altering diagnostic messages led to measurable improvement in performance and subjective satisfaction. Moreover, with specific, constructive, and positive messages such as MONTHS RANGE FROM 1 TO 12 or PERMISSIBLE COMMANDS ARE SAVE OR LOAD, users began to make fewer errors, since they were learning about the system in a relaxed supportive environment.

Writing effective error messages is a reasonable goal, but a more appealing strategy is to prevent users from making errors. This seems natural in direct manipulation systems where the syntax is eliminated and the visual feedback guides the user. For example, when the PacMan is against the right wall and the user moves the joystick to the right, error messages are unnecessary. The user quickly recognizes the situation and soon chooses a different direction. In menu selection, simple typographic errors can be avoided if instead of typing a number or letter, the users simply point at items using their finger, a mouse, or other pointing device. Similarly, selecting a command or file name from a list eliminates typing errors.

Input Devices

Input tasks range from open-ended word processing or painting programs to simple repeated ENTER key presses for page turning in an electronic document. While keyboards have been the standard computer input device, there are increasingly attractive alternatives for many tasks. The mouse has gained prominence in many environments because of the convenience in pointing, even though additional desk space is required. High-precision touchscreens have made this durable device more attractive for public access, home control, process control, and other applications. Joysticks, trackballs, and data tablets with styluses with numerous variations all have their devotees.

Human interface evaluations have demonstrated the advantages of each device for certain tasks and have led to refinements to reduce pointing time and increase accuracy. Speech input for voice mail and speech recognition for commands are effective, especially over the telephone and for the handicapped. Novel approaches using foot pointing devices, data gloves, eye tracking, and whole body motion are being explored in many laboratories.

Output

The output mechanisms must be successful in conveying to the user what the current state is and what actions are currently available. The CRT display has become the standard approach, but flat panel (LED, LCD, plasma, electroluminescent, etc.) and hardcopy devices are alternatives. In recent years, the pressure has been strong for larger and higher resolution devices (at least $1,024 \times 1,024$ pixels) that accommodate graphics and color. Higher-resolution displays can improve the readability of textual displays so that performance can match that of typewritten documents.

Within the display, there has been substantial research on methods for organizing text, numerical data, choosing fonts, color, polarity (black on white vs. white on black), spacing, capitalization, scrolling vs. paging, and cursor movement. Multiple window displays have become common, and their benefits for complex tasks requiring multiple sources of information have been studied. There are many strategies for dealing with multiple windows, and this is a topic of active research and experimentation.

Synthesized or digitized voice output is effective and economical, especially in telephone applications and for the handicapped. Voice mail systems that store and forward digitized voice messages continue to grow in popularity.

The Syntactic/Semantic Model Cognitive theories and models of human behavior are being adapted to accommodate the complexities of human-computer interaction. Most models present a multi-leveled view starting from high-level tasks or intentions and going down to low-level details of which keystrokes or pointing actions the user must perform.

The syntactic/semantic model separates task and computer concepts (semantics) from the syntax for carrying out the task. For example, the task of writing a scientific journal article can be decomposed into the subtasks for writing the title page, the body, and the references. Similarly, the title page might be decomposed into a unique title, one or more authors, an abstract, and several keywords. To write a scientific article, the user must understand these task semantics. Then, to use a word processor, the user must learn about computer semantics, such as directories, filenames, files, and the structure of a file. Finally, the user must learn the syntax of the commands for opening a file, inserting text, editing, and saving or printing the file.

Novices often struggle to learn how to carry out their tasks on the computer and to remember the syntactic details. Once learned, the task and computer semantics are relatively stable in human memory, but the syntactic details must be frequently rehearsed. A knowledgeable user of one word processor who wishes to learn a second one only needs to learn the new syntactic details.

The syntactic/semantic model is descriptive and is helpful in design as well as training. It needs refinement to make it predictive. The goal would be to allow designers to predict learning times, performance rates, error rates, subjective satisfaction, and human retention over time.

An Emerging Science and Technology Human engineering, which once was seen as the paint put on at the end of a project, is now more often becoming the steel frame on which the structure is built. Academic and industrial researchers are rediscovering the power of the traditional scientific method. They make sure that they:

- Begin with a lucid and testable hypothesis.
- Explicitly state the independent variables that are altered.
- Carefully choose the dependent variables to be measured.

- Judiciously select and randomly assign subjects to groups.
- Control for biasing factors.
- Apply statistical methods to data analysis.

The classic experimental methods of psychology are being applied to deal with the complex cognitive tasks of human performance with information and computer systems. The transformation from Aristotelian introspection to Galilean experimentation that took two millenia in physics is being accomplished in two decades in the study of human-computer interaction.

A reductionist approach required for controlled experimentation yields small but reliable results. Through multiple replications with similar tasks, subjects, and experimental conditions, generality and validity can be enhanced. Each small experimental result becomes a tile in the mosaic of human performance with computerized information systems.

At the same time, holistic approaches of participant observation, also known as *usability* or *action studies*, are contributing insights that can be immediately applied to designs and hypotheses that lead to controlled experiments. The simple notion of asking users to "think aloud" as they use a computer system yields great benefits. Videotapes of users struggling with a system make a strong impact on designers and identify at least some of the flaws in a design.

Such research in industrial and academic centers leads to practical guidelines for future developers. Empirical techniques are also beneficially applied for informal evaluations of early prototypes and rigorous acceptance tests before delivery. User Interface Management Systems are emerging as powerful tools that not only reduce development effort, but also encourage exploratory prototyping.

Conclusion One vision of successful design is that computer-related idiosyncrasies vanish and users are free to concentrate on their task. Designers are seeking to reduce the burden of complex syntax and awkward computer concepts, but much work remains. Empirical studies produce many important small results, provide the basis for refining the emerging theories, and contribute to practical guidelines. Commercial system designers apply the guidelines and their intuition to create elegant systems, but must thoroughly test their designs with real users.

References

1987. Shneiderman, Ben. *Designing the User Interface: Strategies for Effective Human-Computer Interaction.* Reading, MA: Addison-Wesley Publishing Co.

1988. Brown, C. Marlin. *Human-Computer Interface Design Guidelines.* Norwood, NJ: Ablex Publishing Co.

1988. Hartson, H. Rex and Hix, Deborah, (Eds.). Advances in *Human-Computer Interaction: Volume 2.* Norwood, NJ: Ablex Publishing Co.

BEN SHNEIDERMAN

HUMANITIES APPLICATIONS

For articles on related subjects *see* Computer Animation; Computer Art; Computer Music; Computerized Dictionaries; Desktop Publishing; Hypertext; Language Translation; Natural Language Processing; and Text Editing Systems.

Historical Overview The rapid changes in the use of computers in humanities research and instruction in recent years parallel the evolution of computing itself. While the computing humanist was still a rarity as late as 1980, within a decade a sizable number of academic humanists were using computers for writing, research, instruction, publication, communications, and project simulation.

At the lowest levels, computers became nearly universally employed to compile bibliographies and to replace typewriters as a basic writing tool. Word processing (*q.v.*) became widely used in student writing courses, and drill-and-practice programs became common in foreign language instruction. Computer-aided projects abounded in humanities research and professional activity in many unpredicted ways.

In the 1970s, word processing meant a dedicated or proprietary computer with built-in software and printer to imitate an electric typewriter. In the 1980s, however, word processing came to mean a software module usable on a general-purpose computer connected to a laser printer whose output is of book or studio quality. Moreover, many highly advanced features, some of them once belonging to the provinces of artificial intelligence (*q.v.*), natural language processing, and typographic design, were widely integrated and taken for granted in the leading word processing packages: spelling checker (*q.v.*), thesaurus, grammar checking, arithmetic, laser fonts, page layout, graphical review, textbase, foreign language character support for both Roman and non-Roman alphabets, internal macros and programming, outlining and numbering, text format conversion, and support for academic apparatus, including footnotes, table of contents, and indexing.

If the 1970s was an era of mainframe computing and the 1980s an era of desktop computing, the 1990s promised to reintroduce connectivity in the form of local area networks (LANs - *q.v.*), wide area networks (WANs), and whole-site computer integration. A new class of workgroup and network-capable software appeared that acknowledged the teamwork behind many humanistic enterprises (*see* Groupware). New connectivity features began to erase the difference between the mainframe terminal and the microcomputer as stations to be used in global remote access to such resources as library catalogs, periodical databases, dictionaries, thesauri, and other reference works, often without cost to the user. Many humanists enjoyed the increasing integration of several information services, including computing centers, libraries, and special research projects that shared the common goal of information literacy. Although long available as e-mail (electronic mail - *q.v.*) electronic connectivity took on added life in the rise of dozens of specialist *listservs* (list servers) and newsgroups in the humanities, the growth of text projects with remote access features, and the wider sharing of electronic information. Some journals and newsletters began to appear in electronic form; editors of the all-electronic journals accomplished the processes of peer review, editing, and distribution in months instead of years. Some electronic journals were never printed on paper; one scholar even issued regular lists (distributed electronically of course) of the current "e-journals."

Large Databases for Humanities Research As computer capacity and speed rapidly increased and as computer size and prices rapidly decreased, replaceable hard disks (*q.v.*) and optical storage media began to mean limitless capacity for humanists working with very large texts. The character-based monochrome monitor was replaced by graphical color monitors of high resolution, and for those who required them, advanced monitors were available that could display an entire page of text or perhaps even two or more pages at one time. The graphical user interface (GUI), a luxury for some computing humanists, came to be regarded as a necessity by others. For those engaged in time-consuming processes, such as downloading texts, multitasking (*q.v.*) made it possible to conduct foreground and background operations simultaneously. The humanist could purchase a desktop computer at moderate cost that was more powerful than the minicomputers (*q.v.*) of a generation before. And the more venturesome humanists could take notes while doing research on site and write while traveling thanks to portable, laptop (*q.v.*), and notebook computers and a new class of pocket and miniature note jotters.

The economics of academic publishing were transformed by two new computer-assisted forms. Since many humanists wrote using word processing software and had access to laser printing services, smaller humanities presses could request camera-ready copy from authors, thereby reducing their editorial and typesetting costs for smaller scholarly editions. Meanwhile, the very high capacity, wide availability, microcomputer connectability, and relatively low mastering cost of the compact disk made it a natural candidate for high-volume electronic text publishing. Single CD-ROM (*q.v.*) disks were used to reissue entire encyclopedias, bookshelves of classics, massive bibliographies, major reference works, multiple volume dictionaries, and sweeping collections of literary and historical texts.

But the printed texts that the humanist requires in the fields of literature, history, language, and philosophy are not hospitable to computer use until certain necessary steps are taken. A generation ago this required laborious re-keying and verifying, sometimes on machines that lacked lower case characters. Today there are expanding machine-readable libraries embracing many of the hundreds of texts that constitute the working materials of humanistic study and teaching. These computer-readable texts, also called "electronic texts," are gradually becoming more readily available, more convenient to use, and less expensive. Although scanning hardware and software were showing considerable improvement in handling standard or contemporary book and office fonts, the new technology did not always serve the scholar interested in historical editions.

Natural language research in the humanities has encouraged efforts at automated language translation and at machine-assisted instruction. Although complete reliance on machine translation is still a vision for the future, partial processing by computer greatly speeds up the work of organizations with enormous translation output, such as the United Nations, where professional speakers already use a vocabulary and syntax in their utterances that is designed to resist the vagaries of the translation process.

The use of graphical databases has real promise for art history, where it is now possible to integrate slides and lecture notes in customized multimedia presentations. Applied art, of course, follows the widespread introduction of graphical computers for design, layout, and typography. In the field of musicology, it is possible to use the computer as copyist, performer, and editor—not to mention its functions in the analysis and synthesis of sound wave forms. But humanities computing has often excelled more in recent years in practical work than in theoretical breakthroughs. Although the statistical methods of the social sciences may have lured some pioneering scholars into humanistic computing, fairly few reports have offered convincing statistical evidence for reattributing disputed authorship or redating a writer's work.

Applications of Networking, Holography, and Multimedia

As computers become more accepted as commonplace tools for academic research, three technological advances—networking, holography, and multimedia—provided special impetus to the nonverbal disciplines. For art historians, a major problem has been simply comparing large agglomerations of objects. With paintings, sculpture, and all the other subjects of their study scattered around the world in a multitude of public and private collections, these scholars must rely on published reproductions representing only a limited selection of an artist's work or of a genre. The growth of communications like the Museum Computer Network has overcome the inadequate budgets of art and science museums to create a scholarly link among all the extant collections in the world. A second technology, holography, may in the future allow any museum to possess satisfactory simulacra of the art objects its visitors wish to view. In theory, any museum could be a museum of all the world's art, not just the flower of industrial nations but also creativity from non-industrial parts of the world.

The Canadian Heritage Information Network, a consortium of 11 museums and research centers, suggests some of what such a network could provide globally. Its listing of about 12 million objects is accessible to over 400 museums and similar institutions in 22 countries and, of course, to all parts of Canada. In addition to its databases, the network provides collections management, electronic mail, specialized training, and advice on information standards and new technology. With the participation of specialists in the arts as well as the sciences, a constantly revised data dictionary defines data fields and supports sharing of information in standardized documents. Perhaps it will begin to distribute CD-ROMs of museum holdings (think of the treasures from the Northwest Indians), and thereby illustrate the immense benefits from linking all institutions that share a common goal.

The third technology of promise for humanists, after networking and holography, is multimedia—the interactive integration of text, images, and sound. A new generation of computer-controlled CD-ROMs permit the viewer both to hear the music and to interrogate the system about aspects of it, such as the libretto of an opera (with English translation, if necessary), the life of the composer, the structure of the music, other works by the same composer, or similar works by other composers.

Although literary scholars are becoming more aware through explorations of multimedia that documents are physical artifacts (a consideration of prime importance with poets like Blake, who created unified works incorporating both illustrations and poetry), the area in which success has been most visible is one that dates back to the late Middle Ages, and has merely been upgraded technologically. An amazing number of concordances have been published in the last 25 years, using at first the output from the primitive line printers of the 1960s and now capitalizing on the advantages of desktop publishing (*q.v.*). As soon as it became known that computers could sort verbal data, hundreds of these alphabetized keys to literature were published, most of them as books, some as microfiche. Unlike the hand-compiled concordances of previous centuries, machine-generated ones could include every word of the base text and supply all the lines in which they appeared.

Textual Analysis and Concordances

The traditional limits of this heretofore laborious industry could be expanded in several imaginative ways: concordances were compiled for categories of literature, such as the Elizabethan sonnets, or for prose works previously considered too long, such as *Moby Dick*, which has been honored with no less than three of these reference works. Complexities were introduced like indicating for *Paradise Lost* the speaker and location for each concorded word. Unique among these efforts is the monumental work of Father Roberto Busa and his Jesuit associates, who have produced, in many volumes, a multidimensional concordance to the works of St. Thomas Aquinas and to all the authors who are cited in his writing.

Textual indexes and concordances are no longer exotic things. Preparing a word count, long a standard exercise of beginners who study a programming language, is now also possible with software packages that require no knowledge of programming. These packages can generate not only a count of each word but also an index giving the location and even a concordance that displays the surrounding text. They can also be used to inquire into the frequency with which a word is distributed in the several parts of a text, the collocations of a given word and other words of interest, and other patterns of clustering or density. These functions, which once required mainframe programming, can now be done on a desktop computer by someone with comparatively little computer experience.

Text retrieval using an index or concordance program can be either a simple matter of qualitative readings of the text (e.g. an author's use of color words and the objects connected with them) or a highly complex matter of quantitative analysis (e.g. statistical patterns of marked parts of speech). Apart from stylistics, the retrieval of indexed texts makes it possible to do content analyses of how authors treat political, social, religious, and philosophical ideas. In the humanities, of course, vocabularies of a given subject are rarely standardized, so the researcher in concepts must learn to use word groups (e.g. not just "liberty," but also "freedom" and "independence" and perhaps even "license" and "autonomy").

Around the world, major initiatives have been undertaken to employ the computer to compile various national dictionaries. Sometimes functioning as a governmental effort to enhance the stature of specific languages (and perhaps indirectly the economic competitiveness of its speakers), many of these dictionaries have appeared in both conventional print and machine-readable formats. So neatly do the data-handling and photocomposition capabilities of computers mesh with the needs of lexicographers that no dictionary today is produced by any other means. Abbreviated dictionaries, spelling lists, and traveller's translation aids are casually bundled into handheld devices that are almost as cheap as pocket calculators. The availability of the historic *Oxford English Dictionary* on CD-ROM, providing access to the history of English with examples, obviously holds great potential for literary and linguistic scholarship.

The creation of textual databases for research, originally a byproduct of concordance projects, has begun to develop as an independent operation. At first, efforts were made (as at the Oxford Text Archive of Oxford University) to create a scholarly collection of computer-readable texts that had been produced for other purposes. Researchers at Rutgers and Georgetown Universities assembled bibliographic information regarding computer-readable texts and text projects. An initiative at Rutgers and Princeton led to the formation of the Center for Electronic Texts in the Humanities, to provide leadership and information on the collection and dissemination of texts. The huge verbal database—1,600 volumes spanning a century and a half—created to support the French national dictionary, the *Tresor de la langue français*, has been converted into a library available in Nancy and Chicago.

Since almost all the computer-encoded material up until now has been intended for another purpose—namely, the production of a printed work according to the proprietary style rules of its publisher—little care was taken to follow any standard encoding. To remedy this defect in future projects, the Text Encoding Initiative (TEI) is developing and promulgating a uniform method of presenting and marking the contents of text materials. If this coding is universally adopted, the interchange of texts among many professional users will be greatly facilitated. At the same time, the needs of the undergraduate student and general reader are being addressed by initiatives such as the Gutenberg Project, designed to make public domain texts available electronically for the mere cost of duplication.

Specialized Databases *Text corpora* are databases designed specifically for linguistic research. Generally modeling themselves after the one constructed for edited American English by W. Francis Nelson and Henry Kucera of Brown University, a goodly number of these represent various categories of writing (sports writing, technical writing, poetry, mystery novels, etc.) in samples proportionate to their quantity as published. Some of these corpora are now being manually tagged with their parts of speech, to provide a more definitive baseline for measuring other samples. One unusual computer database of 20 million English words from different regions, nationalities, and media, is the *Cobuild Dictionary*, jointly produced by the University of Birmingham and Collins, the first dictionary based on an actual field study of English phrases and idioms.

The *Thesaurus Linguae Graecae* (TLG), also designed from the outset as a database for computer investigation, is a vast undertaking directed by Theodore Brunner at the University of California, Irvine. Encompassing the entire body of Greek writing from the earliest days to about A.D. 600, when the dominance of this language in the Mediterranean Basin began to wane, this project provides access to not only a major literary resource but to the means of studying the economic, social, and cultural history of the civilized world at that time. Requiring much larger funding and management than are customary for humanities projects, the TLG has become a model for a parallel initiative in Latin undertaken by the Packard Humanities Foundation in Los Altos, California.

Another humanistic application, emerging more recently as the computer has been recognized as an on-line storage device, has been the compilation of critical databases. Among literary efforts, the Dante Project, distinguished by having been conceived from the beginning as an on-line resource, has updated a classic scholarly tool, the variorum edition, in which all significant commentary on a single work (in this case the *Divine Comedy*) is appended to the individual passages it pertains to. The desirability of developing such a tool in an interactive mode presages a number of similar efforts for other literary monuments.

Textual collation, once limited to the optical and mechanical comparisons of the Hinman Collating Machine for comparing the quartos and folios of Shakespeare, is now commonly done by computer. Once reference marks are set for lines or verse, the variant editions (even multiple variants) of a text are compared to a base version, the "copy text." The editor uses the computer to compare the versions, line by line, make a selection, comment when necessary, and then output everything (final text, variants and annotative apparatus) to a laser printer or typesetting device.

At present, several projects under development at major universities are capitalizing on the potential to incorporate not only words but pictures and sound into databases that might reveal aspects of the humanities that even the developers were not themselves aware of.

At Brown University, for example, English literature is being presented to students in a hypertext environment that encourages exploring the lives of poets and writers, their social milieu, their literary affiliations, and similar intersecting lines of inquiry. In hypermedia mode, the boundaries between scholarship and instruction begin to erode. The Perseus Project at Harvard is creating a similar database for Classical Greek culture.

Communication Among Humanists A growing link among computer-using humanists, even more important as newly accessible colleagues in Eastern Europe gain capacity for Internet communication, is the growing variety of listservs and newsgroups. The largest of these in the field, a conference on Bitnet called HUMANIST, originally established at the University of Toronto, now operates from Brown University. Although some of its conversation deals with computer applications, this conference accepts exchanges on almost any humanistic topic. Many others are much more constricted in their range, concentrating, for example, on the problems of computational linguistics or those involved in dealing with text in a single language.

For more traditional communication, computer-using humanists rely on several conventional media. They can utilize several print journals, like *Computers and the Humanities* and *Literary and Linguistic Computing*. Various newsletters emanate from such sources as the Association for Computers and the Humanities (ACH) and several centers for computer-aided humanistic research. Biennial meetings of the ACH alternate with those of the Association for Literary and Linguistic Computing (ALLC). Associations in classical and modern languages allocate time on their programs for special interest groups in this area. The Modern Language Association (MLA) supports computing by endorsing and distributing software, providing space in its newsletter, publishing books on humanities computing applications and computers in composition, and supporting programs on current computer use at its annual conferences.

In Europe, many countries have established national centers to develop new applications, to study the national culture, and to train students and faculty in the new technology. In France, Norway, Belgium, Italy, Germany, and elsewhere, full-time staff are compiling national dictionaries, concording the works of major writers, analyzing texts, tagging lexical corpora, and holding conferences (both national and international) to learn what is happening elsewhere and to publicize their own progress.

Progress in theoretical areas such as artificial intelligence (*q.v.*), natural language processing, text scanning, machine translation, the paperless office, the electronic classroom, videotex (*q.v.*), the computer-human interface, voice-operated computers, and universal access to information seems to more gradual, more local, and more personal than was expected in the sweeping projections and predictions of the 1960s and 1970s. Some of this change is mirrored in the image of the computer in fiction, which has gone from HAL in Arthur C. Clarke's *2001: A Space Odyssey* (1968) to the cyberpunk biotechnology of William Gibson's *Neuromancer* (1984).

References

1980. Hockey, Susan. *A Guide to Computer Applications in the Humanities*. Baltimore: Johns Hopkins University Press.

1982. Campbell, Jeremy. *Grammatical Man: Information, Entropy, Language, and Life*. New York: Simon & Schuster.

1984. Bolter, J. David. *Turing's Man*. Raleigh, NC: University of North Carolina Press.

1984. Oakman, Robert. *Computer Methods for Literary Research*. Athens, GA: University of Georgia Press.

1985. Olsen, Solveig (Ed.). *Computer-Aided Instruction in the Humanities*, MLA.

1985. Hockey, Susan. *Snobol Programming for the Humanities*. Oxford: Oxford University Press.

1985. Porush, David. *The Soft Machine: Cybernetic Fiction*. New York: Methuen.

1987. Feldman, Paula R. and Buford, Norman. *The Wordworthy Computer: Classroom and Research Applications in Language and Literature*. New York: Random House.

1987. Heim, Michael. *Electric Language: A Philosophical Study of Word Processing*. New Haven, CT: Yale University Press.

1987. Ide, Nancy. *Pascal for the Humanities*. Philadelphia: University of Pennsylvania Press.

1987. Rahtz, Sebastian (Ed.). *Information Technology in the Humanities*. New York: Halstead (John Wiley).

1987. Rudall, B. H. and Corns, T. N. *Computers and Literature: A Practical Guide*. Kent: Tunbridge Wells, and Boston: Abacus.

1990. —, "Computer Applications in the Humanities: A Reading List," *Canadian Humanites Computing Quarterly* (May).

JOSEPH RABEN AND HEYWARD EHRLICH

HYBRID COMPUTERS

For articles on related subjects *see* ANALOG COMPUTER; ANALOG-TO-DIGITAL AND DIGITAL-TO-ANALOG CONVERTERS; and SIMULATION.

Overview *Hybrid computers*, incorporating at least one stored-program digital processor linked with a multiplicity of analog computing units, have been successfully used since the late 1950s for the solution of a wide range of engineering simulation studies. In addition, the continuous parallel computing capability of analog devices in combination with the sampling and storage facilities of the digital computer has proven to be very efficient for complex signal processing. Many large industrial and government organizations with major research and development programs have at least one active hybrid computing center. In some fields, such as guided missiles and space vehicles where real-time, high fidelity simulation is essential, hybrid computers have been necessary for successful system development.

The relative usefulness of continuous analog simulation versus numerical digital techniques has been subject to continuous review over the last 30 years. The proponents of analog techniques have often been successful in demonstrating the desirability of these methods. The main rationale is that digital computers capable of real-time engineering simulation of very complex systems cost many millions of dollars and cannot be realistically dedicated in real time. In most applications, a hybrid computer capable of real-time solution has been much less expensive than an equivalent digital computer. In certain real-time applications demanding unusually high frequency performance, no single digital computer is capable of the task. Also, standard multiprocessor systems supported by appropriate software for real-time simultaneous computation are still not available. Multiple CPU systems beyond the complexity of two or three processors require a level of overhead for synchronization that obviates the speed advantage.

A new generation of automatic hybrid computing multiprocessor systems called SIMSTAR was introduced in 1983 by Electronic Associates, Inc. of West Long Branch, New Jersey. Over 40 of these multiprocessors are presently in use throughout the world. Of course, during the same time period, there has been an explosion of high-speed, low-cost digital processors that have encroached upon the previous hybrid computer application areas. However, there are still a variety of high-frequency, real-time applications that can be handled only by hybrid methods.

Hybrid computing methodology spans a continuum ranging from all-digital numerical analysis to all-analog continuous electrical solution. Since all-digital and all-analog solution methodologies are covered in other articles, we will discuss only the techniques and the systems that have been developed to exploit the combined computation schemes.

Architecture The modern hybrid computer is a digitally-based system in which the users interact primarily with the digital computer through alphanumeric and graphic terminals. All programs and data for the complete hybrid programs are maintained as mass memory files to provide automatic program set-up and operation. The analog computer(s) serve as high-speed parallel computing devices under direct control of the master digital program. This is in contrast to earlier hybrid laboratories, where the digital computer was often used only as an adjunct to the analog computers to perform special computations.

As shown in Fig. 1., the hybrid simulation laboratory is usually composed of a master stored program digital computer to which a variety of local and/or remote terminals are interfaced. The digital computer may include a multiplicity of secondary digital processors, such as minicomputers (*q.v.*) or array processors to handle specific tasks. A data and control interface is required for communication between the digital computer and one or more analog processors. This includes a multiplexed analog-to-digital converter (ADC) and a set of digital-to-analog converters (DAC). In many systems, the DACs are actually digital-to-analog multiplying (DAM) devices that obtain the analog product of an analog signal and a rapidly updated digital coefficient.

The control interface provides both communication of logical data and facilities for real-time synchronization of the digital subsystems and the analog processors. In some more sophisticated systems, logical control signals from the analog processors can control the sequencing of data transfer through the interface directly to/from the main memory, as well as independent control of specialized digital processors such as those used for function generation.

Analog processors, as used in SIMSTAR hybrid systems, are automatically loaded from the digital computer. Older analog computers required manual preparation of a *patchpanel*, which was then inserted into the machine. All control and monitoring functions available to the analog computer user are now digitally controlled through a terminal in the SIMSTAR system.

Finally, as shown in Fig. 1, this complex of processors can be connected in real time to various test facilities and analog graphic devices through a trunking system. The trunking system, in its simplest form, may be a set of cables, while in multi-purpose laboratories, it is a programmable interconnection system. Graphic devices include CRTs, strip-chart recorders, and analog plotters. Test facilities often require both parallel analog/logic signals and digital bus signals. Using the latest multiprogrammed operating systems, it is feasible to provide non-

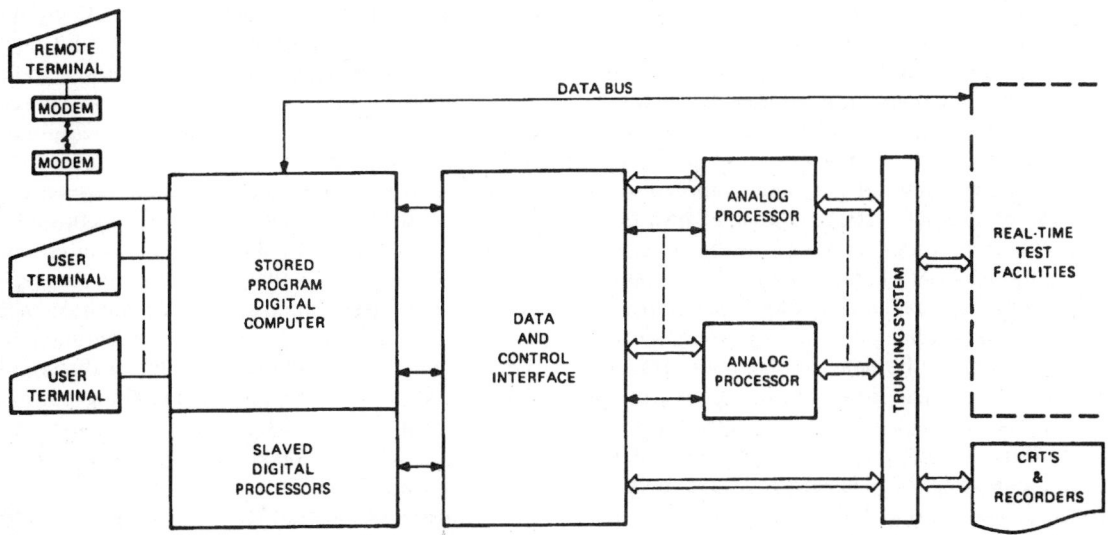

FIG. 1. Hybrid simulation laboratory structure.

FIG. 2.   Grumman Aerospace Corporation of Bethpage, NY EAI HYSHARE 2000 computer for dynamic systems simulation.

real-time user operation on terminals, while real-time simulation studies are running on the test facilities.

Fig. 2 shows a typical manual patch hybrid computer of the 1970s, an EAI Hyshare 2000 installed at Grumman Aerospace. This system was used for many studies, including the design of the X-29 Forward Swept-Wing fighter.

Electronic Associates, Inc., (EAI) of West Long Branch, N.J. is the last manufacturer of general-purpose hybrid computing systems as exemplified by the SIMSTAR installations. In the past, other manufacturers were Applied Dynamics International (ADI) and Dornier in Germany. In addition, a number of small educational analog computers are built by small companies like Comdyna, Inc., but these are seldom used in hybrid configurations.

The SIMSTAR Multiprocessor Since the early 1960s, there have been studies and proposals to replace the manual patchpanel of analog computers with switching matrices. However, the many thousands of switching contacts needed, coupled with the lack of an appropriate switching element, had made the implementation of such a computer rather impractical except for small prototype systems. A high-level compiler has always been considered an essential element of such an automatic system, but this did not become available until the late 1970s.

Development of solid-state, high-accuracy analog switching elements in the late 1970s made the implementation of a matrix for analog processors an economic and technical reality. These switching elements, using Complementary Metal Oxide Semiconductor (CMOS) technology, have been developed both as multiplexers for analog-to-digital converters and as matrix elements for solid-state PBX systems. Combined in a three-stage matrix architecture with voltage following

differential output amplifiers, a practical large-scale matrix switch was constructed by EAI for the SIMSTAR system.

A second dimension to the implementation of the SIMSTAR automatic analog processor was to replace the patched logic and switching components of the earlier analog/hybrid computer capability. Programmable logic arrays (PLAs) and logic signal matrix capability in the form of high-speed memory elements were combined with logic storage elements (flip-flops and registers) in the SIMSTAR hybrid system to meet this requirement. This approach, set up from a digital computer, provides speeds comparable to wired components in earlier analog computers.

The architecture of the SIMSTAR processor is shown in Fig. 3. The high-speed microprocessor controller acts as a format converter between CPU floating-point data in memory and the multiplicity of fixed-point devices in the various processing units. This interface translation also includes automatic optimization for the setup of each analog computing element to insure maximum accuracy. The 16-bit control bus (*q.v.*) allows the microprocessor to set up a block transfer between the main memory and the various storage elements of the analog/logic processor. The 30-bit counters/interval timers have a built-in clock and buffer register so that a multiplicity of precisely timed sequences can be established. Communication from the analog computing blocks to the logic subsystem is through a set of threshold comparators, while logic to analog switching control goes directly from the outputs of the PLAs to the electronic switches and mode control gating of the analog computing blocks.

A portion of the SIMSTAR Hybrid System installed at Martin Marietta Aerospace in Orlando, Florida is shown in Fig. 4. This facility, which has six SIMSTAR PSP's, is capa-

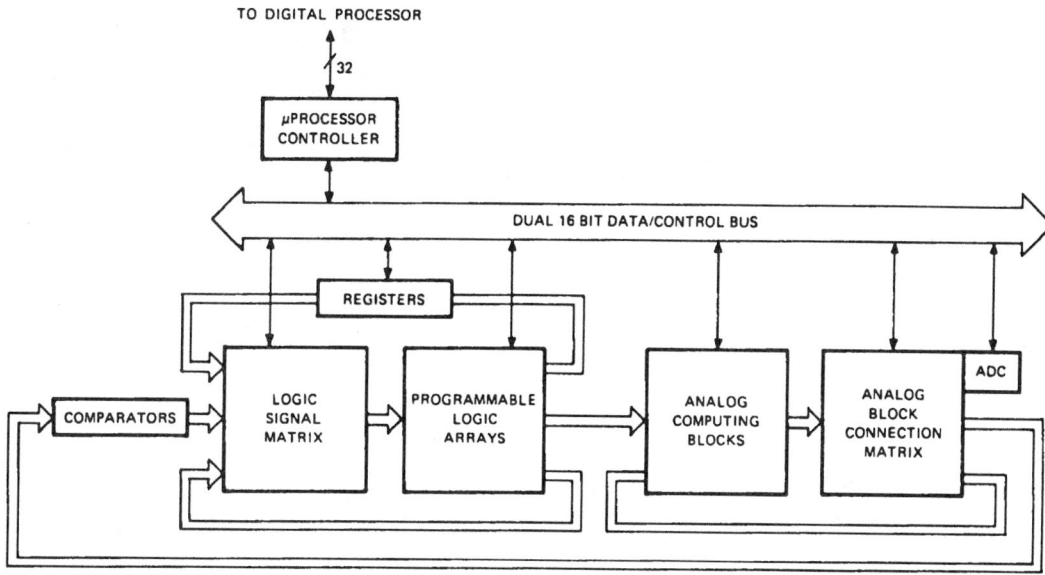

FIG. 3.   Architecture of SIMSTAR parallel analog/logic processor.

ble of simultaneously performing three real-time, hardware-in-the-loop engineering simulations.

Operating Systems Hybrid computation places unique demands upon the digital computer operating system for both communication and sequence control. A variety of tasks must be handled with different timing priorities:

1. Time-critical CPU operation for hybrid closed-loop operation.
2. Real-time data storage/retrieval for graphic display, forcing functions, iterative computation, curve fitting, etc.
3. Non-real-time analog processor automatic iterative control.
4. Hybrid system interactive operation.

FIG. 4.   SIMSTAR facility at Martin Marietta Aerospace. (Courtesy of Martin Marietta).

5. Loading and calibration of the analog processor.
6. Diagnostic testing of the analog processor.

Of all these tasks, only the first demands true real-time operation of the central processing/arithmetic units. Time-critical operation, which means that the CPU must perform a specified task within a given frame time, can be defined on the basis of a repetitive frame time or a random event basis. For dedicated single-task operation, the repetitive frame time operation and appropriate multiframe sequencing can be programmed by polling a real-time control signal. Interrupts (*q.v.*) could also be used, but this is wasteful simply for synchronizing to real time.

Most real-time data communication tasks, such as data storage/retrieval, can be preprogrammed for direct memory transfer during the analog processor run.

For random events, as typified by exception conditions such as overflow or block transfer termination, interrupt-oriented operation is most efficient. In some cases, these interrupts do not need to be handled on a time-critical basis, and the usual task activation procedure will suffice. In other situations, there is a maximum interrupt response time requirement, and "directly connected" vectored interrupts are required. In this case, the only operating system overhead permitted is for saving and restoring of register stacks.

The most demanding requirement is for time-critical processing in a multiprogramming (*q.v.*) environment. However, this type of operation provides for the most efficient system utilization and user access/convenience. Both repetitive frame time and random solution events demand directly connected interrupts. One of the complications for the time-critical processing of directly connected interrupts is the relative priority of I/O interrupts, which usually have higher priority in operating systems than the user interrupt levels. For buffered I/O devices operating on a record basis, CPU processing is needed only between records and is not a time-critical function. Therefore, the directly connected hybrid interrupts are given a higher priority than I/O interrupts.

There are two basic methods for implementing analog/digital interprocessor communication. In a single-user hybrid environment, the complete set of I/O instructions for the analog processor can be executed directly in the user's program since there are no questions about user program integrity. The problem with most digital processors and operating systems is that, in this mode of communication, the operating system must allow the user to execute the entire set of I/O instructions. This can destroy other users' programs if not the operating system itself.

Implementation of hybrid computation in a multiprogramming environment requires that the basic hybrid communication be performed by resident routines as a part of the operating system. Users can then request allocation of resources and the operating system can maintain integrity. A large portion of the analog processor set-up and control functions are not time-critical—the extra time required to perform these functions through the operating system is not significant. For time-critical

functions, however, special handling of the operating system traps is required. When the communication sequence can be preprogrammed prior to real-time operation, time-critical operating system response is often not needed.

In the SIMSTAR system, specialized processors (e.g. function generators) and the SIMSTATION run-time display also operate on a shared memory basis to avoid operating system overhead. Of course, the hybrid operating system must support the setup of these devices while run-time operation is performed directly by the user program. The operating system is used to process any failures. The remaining tasks require the operating system to provide rather sophisticated data/logical communication with the analog processor, but there are no special priority processing demands. For iterative control of the analog processor, the digital computer need only read the value of an objective function at the end of a run, charge appropriate parameters on the analog console, and initiate another run. This type of operation is often nested in a real-time simulation to represent constrained motion or boundary conditions.

Finally, the digital processor must have full access to all control and monitoring features of the parallel processor for user interactive operation, program loading, calibration, and automatic diagnostics. This is most critical for the SIMSTAR stored program hybrid computer since the previous parallel access of the patchpanel is not available.

Programming Languages Hybrid computers have always been recognized as the fastest computation tool for solution of sets of differential equations. Prior to SIMSTAR, the manual programming procedures were much more difficult and specialized than corresponding procedures for digital computer programming. Using the STARTRAN programming environment with SIMSTAR, the tasks of preparation and operation are very comparable to the use of real-time simulation languages on a digital system.

Through the 1970s and early 1980s, Electronic Associates adapted the earlier APSE (Automatic Programming and Scaling of Equations) compiler for analog computers to develop the present Parallel Translator (PTRAN). This work, which was started in England at the British Aircraft Company, was partially funded by the U. S. government. The source language is based upon ACSL (Advanced Continuous Simulation Language), developed by Mitchell and Gauthier Associates.

Programming the Digital Arithmetic Processor in SIMSTAR is also done in the ACSL language, using a modified version of the ACSL compiler that supports real-time, interrupt-driven operation. With appropriate targeting statements and extended mathematical and logic operators, complete flexibility for a non-homogeneous multiprocessor solution is provided

All of these program elements are brought together under a sophisticated interactive executive called SIMRUN, which has access to the complete SIMSTAR system. Working with the generated programs, SIMRUN can provide a flexible graphic display of solution results.

Computing Methodology Most studies to which hybrid computers are applied include two fundamental elements: first, a mathematical model or analysis requirement and, second, an experimental procedure. For relatively simple problems, this leads to a natural problem split where the analog processor handles the mathematical analysis and the stored program digital processor implements the experiment. The programming, setup, and check-out of the analog processor are also performed by the digital computer.

As seen from the digital computer, the analog processor is a very high speed processor to handle those parts of a task that would consume an inordinate amount of CPU processing. But, as seen from the analog real-time program, the digital processor looks like a set of real-time functions that are not available on the analog processor or for which there are insufficient analog components. Another way of using the hybrid scheme is to split the problem so that the lowest frequency (longest time constant) components of a model are solved digitally while the highest frequency (stiff equations) are solved using continuous parallel analog methods.

Applications Hybrid computers are used by an engineer for the analysis of dynamic systems, much as an oscilloscope or spectrum analyzer and a breadboard circuit implementation may be used. For system design and evaluation, an engineer needs to express the mathematical laws governing the system operation, test a set of design parameters and logical sequences, and observe the results. This kind of symbiotic relationship between the creative mind of the engineer and the realization of a physical system as embodied in the computer model is very different from the structured business information processing or statistical analysis functions of a typical data processing system.

A major class of application for hybrid computers has been and continues to be the design of controllable liquid-fueled rocket engines for space vehicles, such as the space shuttle and heavy launch vehicles. Faithful models of the engine dynamics in real time requires equivalent computing speeds that exceed 300 MIPS. This is due to the flow equations, which have time constants as low as 200 microseconds.

Hybrid computers were also used extensively for the development of the space shuttle subsystems such as hydraulics and flight control. Future development of the aerospace plane will also use hybrid simulation methods.

As shown in Fig. 5, hybrid computation has been used in nearly all fields of engineering design and evaluation. There are hundreds of older active hybrid computing laboratories throughout the world. SIMSTAR is presently in use in over 25 installations in many different fields, ranging from space vehicles and heavy machinery to education. The powerful digital processors in many of these installations permit simulation of much more complex, high-performance systems than possible with earlier hybrid computers.

Conclusions Combined digital and analog computing methods have proven to be very effective for a range of engineering studies over the last 30 years. The newest automatic hybrid multiprocessing systems have proven to follow the tradition of being the fastest available tool for real-time simulation of complex systems.

As more powerful and economical digital processors become available, the hybrid computer will continue toward more digital computation and smaller analog processors will be needed. If new methods are developed for employing multiple digital processors for these applications, it is likely that analog processors will no longer be needed by the year 2000. Of course, if the application requirements continue to be more demanding and if new, faster, and more accurate analog ICs are developed, we may see a whole new hybrid product developed over the next 10 years.

Aerospace
Real-time missile system design/evaluation
Space vehicle stabilization
Space vehicle human factors analysis
Helicopter dynamics
Shuttle hydraulics system design
Shuttle mission evaluation
High-performance fighter aircraft human factors

Rotating Machinery
Turbine engine control
Centrifugal compressor dynamics/control
Synchronous motor control

Chemical
Distillation column controller design
Tubular reactor control/optimization
Heat exchange analysis/control

Electrical/Nuclear
Nuclear power plant
Three-phase inverters/rectifiers
Electric car power conversion/storage
Transmission line overvoltage transients
Communications system design

Automotive
Directional control/stability
Ride quality analysis
Microprocessor engine control
Real-time off-highway vehicle simulator
Crash data signal processing
Military tank human factor studies

Biomedical
Biomechanical studies for prosthetic design
Cardiovascular system simulation
Pulmonary system modeling

FIG. 5. Classes of hybrid computer applications.

References

1974. Bennett, A. W. *Introduction to Computer Simulation.* New York: West Publishing Co.

1977. Landauer, J. P. "Stored Program Hybrid Processing System," *Simulation* **77**, 127–191.

1980. Holmes, W. M. and Hall, K. L. "MICOM's Advanced Simulation Center and Digital Computer Boundness," *Symposium on Very High-Speed Computing Technology* (September), I.3–I.18.

1988. Landauer, J. P. "Real-Time Simulation of the Space Shuttle Main Engine on the SIMSTAR Multiprocessor." Long Branch, NJ: Electronic Associates.

1989. *SIMSTAR User Guide & Programming Manual*, Long Branch, NJ: Electronic Associates Publ. # 827.0123-1, March.

J. PAUL LANDAUER

HYPERTEXT

For articles on related subjects *see* CD-ROM; DATABASE MANAGEMENT SYSTEM; INFORMATION RETRIEVAL; KNOWLEDGE REPRESENTATION; and VIDEODISC.

Introduction Just as books have a linear logical structure (sequential chapters or alphabetically sequenced articles as in this encyclopedia) represented in a physical structure (font size, margins, pages, binding, etc.), hypertexts have network structures. There may be a logical structure of interrelated ideas (as in this encyclopedia), high-level notions plus low-level details, concepts with examples, expansions of knowledge frameworks, tree-like procedures, and even sequentially related components. The physical structures of hypertext include nodes containing text, graphics, or videodisc images, and links to connect the nodes. Other physical hypertext attributes include screen formats (margins, spacing, justification, fonts, etc.) and link markers with the accompanying mechanism for following them (the look and feel of using the hypertext).

Hypertext is a new way of writing and reading that simultaneously offers opportunities and dangers. By replacing the largely linear format of printed materials with a computer-supported branching format, hypertext enables authors to structure information in novel ways. Effectively designed hypertexts can help readers rapidly locate specific facts, encourage felicitous browsing, read at multiple levels of detail, follow diagnostic, office, or cooking procedures, explore travel destinations, and pursue multiple policy scenarios. However, the same branching format can lead to disorientation, lack of closure, unpredictable behavior, and additional perceptual/cognitive/motor loads for the reader. The designers of hypertext software and the authors of hypertext databases are developing appropriate strategies for creating new works or converting existing ones to fit the hypertext medium.

Hypertext nodes can contain a single word or name, a paragraph, an article with graphics, a videodisc image or segment, or a full book. The granularity of nodes varies depending on the system. Sometimes, nodes are used to match physical structures, such as single screens or 3 × 5 cards and sometimes larger logical nodes are used that match concepts (e.g. an article in this encyclopedia might be a single node or possibly several related nodes). Other variations across systems deal with whether links should have multiple types (indicating physical destinations, such as a graphic or videodisc image, or logical destinations, such as a map, biography, or book reference) and how they should be shown on the screen (strategies include a standard link marker, such as a box, highlighted text, or author-defined graphic symbols).

As the field matures, researchers are more accurately recognizing which features support fact finding versus browsing in differing genres of writing. Hypertext is proving to be most effective when there is a large body of information organized into numerous fragments, the fragments relate to each other, and the user needs only a small fraction of the information at any time.

Potential applications include:

- Product catalogs and advertisements.
- Organizational charts and policy manuals.
- Annual reports and orientation guides.
- Resumés and biographies.
- Contracts and wills.
- Newsletters and news magazines.

TABLE 1. Implementations

Commercial systems on personal computers:

- Hypercard
- Hyperties
- Guide

Commercial systems on larger computers:

- Knowledge Management System (KMS)
- NoteCards
- Augment

Research systems:

- XANADU
- Intermedia
- Neptune
- Writing Environment (WE)

Special purpose applications:

- Navitext
- Superbook
- NLM medical project

Personal information managers:

- SearchExpress
- askSam
- IZE
- Lotus Agenda

- Software documentation and code.
- Encyclopedias, glossaries, and dictionaries.
- Medical and legal reference books.
- Religious and literary annotations.
- College catalogs and departmental guides.
- Travel and restaurant guides.
- Scientific journals, abstracts, and indexes.
- Instruction and exploration.
- Repair and maintenance manuals.
- Time-lines and geographical maps.
- On-line help and technical documentation.
- Cookbooks and home repair manuals.
- Mysteries, fantasies, and jokebooks.

There are a multiplicity of commercial hypertext systems on personal computers, mainframes, and networks of distributed systems, a profusion of research systems, and a still wider set of variant forms of hypertext features that have been added to word processors or desktop publishing systems, database management or information retrieval systems, expert system shells, computer-based training tools, or on-line assistance facilities (Conklin, 1987; Shneiderman and Kearsley, 1989). A list of implementations known to this author as of 1991 is given in Table 1. Hyperties (Fig. 1) on the IBM PC and compatible computers and HyperCard (Fig. 2) on the Apple Macintosh offer interesting contrasts in commercial hypertext systems. Hyperties was developed for museum viewers and encyclopedia construction, thereby leading to a strong separation in the author and browser components, powerful article management features for authors, ease of use for the browser, and a stronger dependence on text. Nodes are called *articles* (containing text, color graphics, or videodisc segments), and links are shown by highlighted phrases embedded in the text. Alphabetical lists of article titles, tables of contents, path histories showing article titles, and lists of article titles generated by string searches complement the link following strategy.

In HyperCard, nodes are called *cards* and links are shown by a variety of graphical buttons that can be

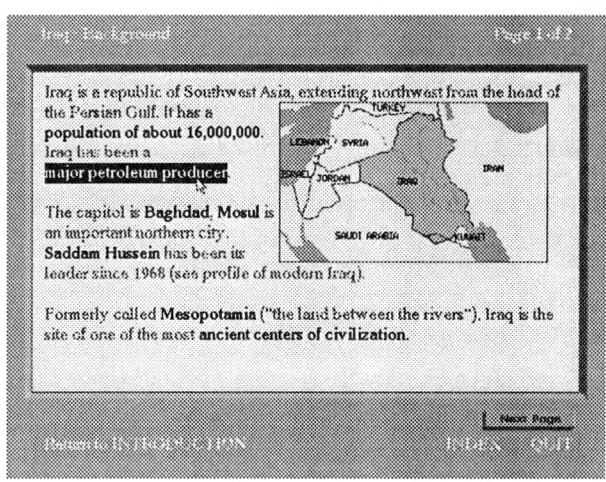

FIG. 2. Customizable "buttons" provide automatic return-path navigation ("Return to INTRODUCTION") and special functions ("INDEX" "QUIT").

rectangular boxes, standard icons, or user-defined shapes. Selecting a button by a mouse click can produce another card with text and graphics or a videodisc segment. The programming language HyperTalk enables construction of a wide variety of facilities limited only by the programmer's imagination. HyperCard collects cards into *stacks* and provides a HomeCard, which acts as a table of contents for the stacks. Path history is shown through miniaturized versions of the most recent 42 cards. A limited string search facility enables users to move to the next card containing a specified string of text.

Other important systems include NoteCards (Fig. 3), KMS, Intermedia, Guide, and Document Examiner/Concordia. New systems and hypertext additions to other packages appear regularly. In assessing these different systems we consider three domains: user interface (*q.v.*)

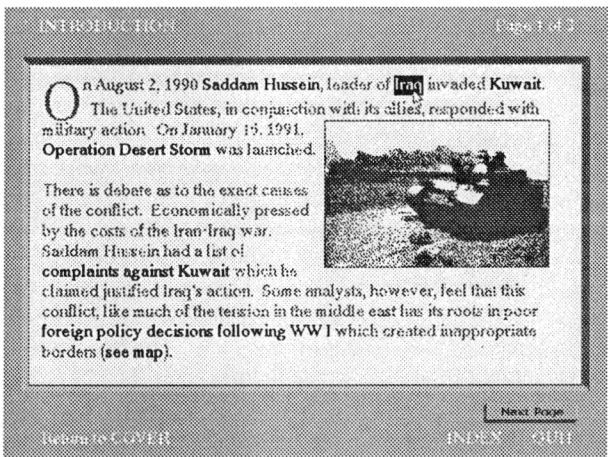

FIG. 1. A typical Hyperties application. Text flows around imbedded graphics in multipage documents called "articles." Links are indicated by a specified highlight color.

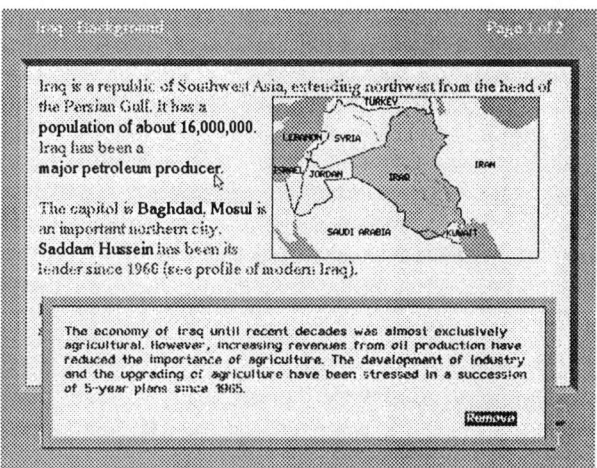

FIG. 3. Links in Hyperties can reveal summary information or definitions, without leaving the current document. This brief description can also serve as an introduction to in-depth information available through a "SEE MORE" link on the pop-up.

for browsing, support for authoring, and system design aspects.

User Interface for Browsing

The key determinants of success of a hypertext system and database are the user interface design and the browsing facility. Browsing issues include:

Node contents (e.g. text, graphics, video)—Hypermedia designers often pursue the most advanced media, such as video images, graphic animation, high fidelity stereo, or even environmental experiences, but many important projects can be accomplished with simple monochrome textual displays.

Formatting capabilities—Flexibility in formatting can contribute to more appealing and effective hypertext projects. Control over fonts, font sizes, boldface, underscore, italic, inverse, blinking, and color is useful. Margin settings, justification, indentation, centering, and screen layout are also important influences. Increasingly, hypertext designers recognize the need to deal with full-screen layouts, just as book or magazine designers consider the physical limits of their media. Dynamic attributes such as scrolling, text replacement, popover windows, outlining strategies, and user controls (page turning or scroll bars) are very closely studied.

Screen resolution, size, and color—The physical display devices are getting greater attention because designers are aware of the potential for substantial improvement over current devices. Higher resolution displays or high-quality fonts can improve readability, reduce eyestrain, and lessen fatigue. Larger displays (more pixels) can reduce the need for distracting scrolling, page turning, and window manipulation. (*See* WINDOW ENVIRONMENTS.)

Window size and management—Since hypertext systems are predicated on traversal of multiple nodes, it is natural that multiple window design issues are frequently considered. Single window strategies are appreciated for their simplicity, but with larger displays the allure of multiple window strategies is great. While overlapped windows are visually attractive, it may turn out that tiled strategies with system-or user-controlled replacement are more effective.

Response time and display rate—One of the pleasures of hypertext is the ability to explore and return rapidly to previous nodes. Therefore, rapid response times (a few seconds for most nodes) and high display rates (9,600 baud or higher) that fill a screen in less than a second are especially appreciated.

Annotation and exportation—Many hypertext users are eager to record their reactions to retrieved information or to export that information for printing or use in other electronic environments. Sharing annotations among multiple users and exportation of portions of the database are useful features.

Links (typed vs. single type)—The essence of hypertext is the link to jump to a new node. Some systems pursue simplicity and have only one type of link, while others emphasize the flexibility of having multiple link types to jump to a variety of logical or physical destinations. Links may be represented by a standard icon, by highlighting text or graphic regions, or by user-defined buttons.

Selection mechanism (e.g. touch, mouse, keys)—While touchscreens are the most rapid pointing device, the mouse (*q.v.*) is more widely available. Still more widely available are arrow keys, which can be quite rapid if the cursor can be made to jump among the links. Trackballs, tablets, and an on-screen stylus are also applicable.

Structure of graph—Some hypertext systems limit information structures to trees, while others encourage largely linear patterns with some links, but most hypertext systems allow arbitrary linking. While unlimited freedom is appreciated by users, there can be a great benefit in restrictions that enhance modularity.

Multiple tables of contents—An *overview* is often very helpful in conveying the structure and scope of the contents of a hypertext. Alphabetic lists, high-level overviews, conceptual indices, and detailed indices are available in many systems.

Graphic vs. tabular overviews—Node-link diagrams can be used as a graphic overview but the appeal of this approach fades as the size grows, since it is difficult to deal with a large diagram. Tabular textual overviews in the form of tables of contents are an effective alternative in many situations.

Indexing vs. keyword search—Instead of an author-constructed table of contents, some systems provide a lengthy, automatically generated index of terms (except for common words that are filtered out). Other systems enable users to type keywords and receive a list of nodes containing those keywords.

Path history and bookmarks—To help keep track of where the user has been, some systems provide a history of the nodes visited or enable the user to mark nodes so that they can be relocated easily.

Support for Authoring

Authoring tools can speed development and improve quality. Authors should be able to import, edit, export, and print either a single article, a subset of articles, or the entire database. Authoring processes should be rapid, reliable, flexible, extendible, and secure. Maintenance of multiple versions is a benefit, as is implementation in a multiple-user, distributed network environment that supports collaboration.

System Design Aspects

Although the browser and author facilities are primary in the mind of most people who consider hypertext, the underlying system structure must be effective. The data management system must support very large information spaces with rapid data transfer to enable use of color graphics, animation, and video images. At the same time, data compression (*q.v.*) is necessary if distribution on portable media (floppy disks, compact disks, etc.) is anticipated. Security control and encryption are sometimes additional requirements.

Other system design concerns include integration with other software/hardware systems, distribution licenses for the browsing software, standard data interchange formats, and portability (*q.v.*).

References

1987. Conklin, Jeff. "Hypertext: A survey and introduction", *IEEE Computer* **20**, 9, (September), 465–472.

1989. Shneiderman, Ben. "Reflections on authoring, editing, and managing hypertext," in Barrett, Edward, *The Society of Text*. Cambridge, MA: M.I.T. Press, 115–131.

1989. Shneiderman, Ben and Kearsley, Greg. *Hypertext Hands-On!* Reading, MA: Addison-Wesley.

1992. Landow, G. P. *Hypertext*. Baltimore, MD: Johns Hopkins Press.

BEN SHNEIDERMAN

I/O BUS. *See* Bus.

I/O CHANNEL. *See* Channel.

IBM 1400 SERIES

For articles on related subjects *see* Digital Computers: History; and Generations, Computer.

The IBM 1400 series data processing systems, introduced in 1959, had a dramatic impact on the business world. The first of the 1400 series machines, the 1401, rapidly made the older vacuum tube and electromechanical *unit record* systems obsolete. The 1400 system enjoyed widespread use in data processing applications from 1959 until "third-generation" equipment became available in the mid-1960s.

The 1400 line consisted of five basic computers: 1401, 1440, 1460, 1410, and 7010. The basic mainframe, the 1401, was a second-generation, fully-transistorized machine with a magnetic core memory having original capacity options of 1.4K, 2K, 4K, 8K, 12K, and 16K characters. Internally, data was represented in six-bit BCD (*q.v.*) code, with additional parity check and *word mark* bits. The memory cycle was 11.5 μs per character access.

Instruction formats were variable from one to eight characters, and data fields and records could be variable length within the constraints of peripheral device characteristics and memory size. Instruction and data fields were defined by the presence of a word-mark bit set beneath the leftmost character of the instruction or data field.

The instruction format consisted of a single character op-code, two optional three-character addresses, and an optional single character "d-modifier." The instruction set provided for internal data transfer, input/output con-trol, add-to-storage decimal arithmetic, condition testing, and branching operations. Indirect addressing (*q.v.*) could be accomplished using any of three standard index registers (*q.v.*).

The 1401 (Fig. 1) had an I/O interface that permitted only one I/O operation at a time, regardless of the number of devices on-line. I/O operations interlocked the central processor, although some overlap of processing and I/O operation could be gained by the addition of special features.

Although a wide variety of peripheral devices was available for the 1400 series, including MICR and optical character readers, paper-tape readers, remote transmission devices, etc., the principal devices in use were:

1402 Card Reader/Punch—This unit was capable of reading 800 cards per minute (cpm) and punching 250 cpm.

1403 Chain Printer—This device had a maximum rated speed of 1100 alphanumeric lines per minute (lpm), was reliable and comparatively quiet, and had excellent print quality.

729 Magnetic Tape Units—Seven-track units with speeds ranging from 15,000 to 62,000 characters per second (cps), depending upon the model and the recording density, which could be 200, 556, or 800 characters per inch (cpi).

7330 Magnetic Tape Units—These were relatively slow and inexpensive units (7,200 cps at 200 cpi density).

1405 Disk Storage Units—These were fixed-disk units with 50,000 or 100,000 directly addressable 200-character records. Average access time was 600 ms.

1311 Disk Storage Units—These replaced the 1405-type units with modular disk-pack storage. Each pack stored 2 million characters in the form of 20,000 100-character records. Average access time was 250 ms per record.

Several languages were available for the 1401. A basic assembly language, SPS (Symbolic Programming System),

FIG. 1. The IBM 1401 System.

permitted the use of mnemonic operation codes, symbolic addresses, and indirect addressing. A significantly enhanced version of SPS, called "Autocoder"—analogous to basic assembly language for third-generation computers—became the predominantly used language. Autocoder used SPS constructs and employed macroinstructions for initiating I/O operations. Fortran and Cobol compilers existed, but were not widely used because of either excessive compilation time or limited memory. Various Report Program Generator (RPG) packages were available, as was a complete set of basic utility packages. Operating systems were not used with the 1401, 1440, or 1460, but many users developed monitors to permit a rudimentary form of job control.

The 1440 system was initially a disk-oriented 1401 with slower peripherals and lower cost. Internally, the 1440 was, for all practical purposes, identical to the 1401 except that the memory cycle was 11.1 μs as compared to 11.5 for the 1401, and the printer and reader-punch buffers were relocatable in memory. The 1460 was also basically a 1401 except that it had a 6 μs memory expandable to a 32K capacity.

The 1410 systems, while having the same basic architecture as the 1401, were significantly more powerful. Memory sizes were 10K, 20K, 40K, 60K, or 80K characters. The memory cycle was 4.5 μs per character. The instruction set was similar to the 1401, but included a table-lookup instruction and 64 different data-move instructions. Fifteen index registers were available. The basic system had a single I/O channel, but a second could be installed. Like the 1401, the processor was interlocked during any I/O operation, though special features were available to provide limited overlap. Autocoder was the predominantly used language, although Cobol and Fortran were widely used. All peripheral equipment was the same as that used in other 1400 series systems except for 1301 and 1302 disk files, which were large fixed-disk units similar to the 350 units that had been used with the IBM 305 RAMAC, an (incompatible) predecessor to the 1400 series. The 1410 could be operated in emulated 1401 mode, which provided almost total compatibility with 1401 programs.

The 7010 system was functionally, although not architecturally, an advanced 1410. It used the 1410 instruction set and, like the 1410, had a 1401 compatibility feature. The 7010 accessed two characters in parallel on each 2.4 μs cycle. Four I/O channels could be installed. Memory protection, an interval timer, and a program-level interrupt feature were available. All 1400 compatible I/O devices could be used on the 7010. Comparatively few of these systems were installed, as the system was introduced shortly before the System 360 was announced.

There were approximately 14,000 of the 1401 systems and over 1,000 of the 1410 systems installed. A typical 1401 system rented for $8,000 per month and the range was from $4,000 to $12,000 per month. A typical 1410 system rented for $11,000 per month and the range was from $8,000 to $18,000 per month.

The high-speed card reading and tape and printing ability of the 1401 systems ideally suited them for use as peripheral I/O systems to IBM 7000 series computers.

G. DAVID BAER

IBM SYSTEM 360/370/390

For articles on related subjects *see* DIGITAL COMPUTERS: HISTORY; IBM 1400 SERIES; and IBM PC and PC-COMPATIBLES.

The IBM System/360 and System/370 comprise an architecture that has been the basis for all intermediate and large mainframe processors produced by IBM since 1964. This architecture has also become the basis for machines produced by other manufacturers. Currently, the IBM System/390 architecture is the upward compatible successor to IBM's System/360 and System/370 systems. These systems have been so widely used and so many of the features have been so widely imitated that it is important to describe the essential aspects of their architecture and their hardware and software systems.

During the past quarter century, IBM has introduced the System/360 (S/360) architecture, System/370 (S/370) architecture, System/370 Extended Architecture (370-XA), Vector Extensions to S/370 and 370-XA architectures, Enterprise System Architecture/370 (ESA/370), and, most recently, the Enterprise Systems Architecture/390 (ESA/390), also known as System/390 (S/390) architecture.

The *architecture* of a system defines its attributes as seen by the programmer, i.e. the conceptual structure and functional behavior of the machine, as distinct from the organization of the data flow, the logical design, the physical design, and the performance of any particular implementation (*see* COMPUTER ARCHITECTURE). Several dissimilar machine implementations may conform to a single architecture. The current IBM implementation of the S/390 architecture is the Enterprise System/9000 (ES/9000) series of processors.

Logically, a system consists of main storage, one or more central processors (CPUs - *q.v.*) operator facilities, a channel subsystem, and I/O devices. I/O devices are attached to the channel subsystem through control units. The communication between the channel subsystem and a control unit is called a *channel path*. A channel path employs either a parallel-transmission protocol or a serial-transmission protocol and, accordingly, is called a parallel or serial channel path. Expanded storage may also be available in a system, and vector or cryptographic units or both may be included in a CPU.

The physical identity of the above functions may vary among implementations, called "models." Specific processors may differ in their internal characteristics, the installed facilities, the number of subchannels, channel paths, and control units that can be attached to the channel subsystem, the size of main and expanded storage, and the operator facilities.

The basic unit of information in these systems is the 8-bit byte. Four bytes comprise a word. Some instructions operate on bytes, and others operate on half-words (2 bytes), words, double words (8 bytes), and on strings of bytes. An instruction or operand address is always a byte address, the leftmost or most significant byte when a group consisting of more than 1 byte is being addressed. In the early S/360 and S/370 systems, a 24-bit address field in index registers permitted the direct addressing of 2^{24} or 16,777,216 bytes. In 1981, IBM announced a significant architecture change to System/370: the System/370 Extended Architecture (370-XA). This provided 31-bit addressability which extends the real and virtual address space from the 16M bytes addressable with 24-bit addresses to 2 gigabytes (2^{31} or 2,147,483,648 bytes). Bimodal operation (S/370 or 370-XA mode) permits concurrent execution of programs using either 24-bit or 31-bit addresses.

Memory The magnetic core memories of the early S/360s were severely limited in size, from a 64K-byte maximum (K = 1024) on the Model 30 to a maximum of IM bytes (M = 1,048,576) on the top-of-the-line Model 75. The larger S/360 models could use auxiliary (though slower) large-core memory of up to 8M bytes. Maximum memory was gradually increased into the millions of bytes on even the small S/370 models, and up to the 24-bit addressing limit of 16M bytes on the larger ones. These large memories became economical and practical with the use of MOS large-scale integration memory technology on models of the S/370 introduced after 1972. Today's S/390 processors employ an advanced three-level storage hierarchy comprised of a high-speed (cache) buffer, cen-

tral storage, and expanded storage. Central storage capacity in an ES/9000 multiprocessing complex can be up to 1 billion bytes (1 gigabyte) and expanded storage can be up to 8 gigabytes.

Main storage, which is directly addressable, provides for high-speed processing of data by the CPUs and the channel subsystem. Main storage may include a faster-access buffer storage, sometimes called a *cache* (*q.v.*), and each CPU may have an associated cache that is used to improve performance. Expanded storage may be available on some models. It can be accessed by all CPUs in the configuration by means of instructions that transfer 4K-byte blocks of data from expanded storage to main storage or from main storage to expanded storage. Each 4K-byte block in expanded storage is addressed by a 31-bit block number.

Certain models of the ES/9000 employ a two-level high-speed (cache) buffer design. Each processor in a multiprocessor configuration contains a 256 KByte first-level high-speed buffer (HSB) divided into two independent HSBs of 128 KBytes each. One holds instructions, the other data. This design permits both instructions and data fetching to take place in the same machine cycle. A second-level HSB contains 4,096 KBytes of data and is used to match the speed of the processor, including the first-level HSB, with the speed of the processor storage hierarchy to achieve better system-level performance.

Expanded storage is a logically separate storage under control of the operating system, providing performance up to 28 times faster than physical I/O to cached direct access storage devices and up to 200 times faster than physical I/O to non-cached direct access storage devices. It is designed for electronic block transfers of 4-KByte pages directly to and from central storage.

System/390 is designed to be used with a control program or interrupt-driven operating system that coordinates the use of system resources and executes all I/O instructions, handles exceptional conditions, and supervises scheduling and execution of multiple programs. This was also the case for systems based on the earlier architectures. The system provides for automatic storage in main memory and for automatic loading from a different area of main memory of the contents of essential control registers in response to an interrupt. The contents of these control registers may be considered to form a control word, which is referred to as the *program status word*. The program status word contains the address of the next instruction to permit resumption of a program after an interrupt. It also contains interrupt masks, the storage protection key, and a number of special control fields and control bits. One of these control bits distinguishes between system (or supervisor) state and problem state.

Instruction Set The S/390 series has a large and varied instruction set made up of 229 instructions. Instructions fall into five classes: general, decimal, floating-point, control, and I/O instructions. Instructions may be one, two or three half-words long. There are three types of arithmetic: fixed point, floating point, and a special decimal arithmetic that uses strings of four-bit binary-coded decimal digits as operands. There is a set of *privileged instructions* (*q.v.*) that can be executed only in supervisor state.

A S/390 series computer has general-purpose registers that serve as base registers (*q.v.*) and index registers (*q.v.*), and that also serve as fixed-point accumulators and as temporary storage registers. The general registers are 32 bits long, and the most significant 8 bits are ignored in physical address calculations when 24-bit addressing is used. For 31-bit addressing, only the most significant bit is ignored. The use of the general registers as base and index registers permits the direct addressing of 16,777,216 bytes or 2,147,483,648 bytes, depending on whether 24-bit or 31-bit addressing is being used, without requiring that each instruction contain a 24-bit or 31-bit address field. This is illustrated by the RX (register-and-indexed-storage) instruction format, one of several instruction formats used in the S/390. The RX format uses two half-words as follows:

```
OP–code    R1   X2   B2   D2
--------   ---- ---- ---- ------------
```

The 8-bit op-code specifies the instruction. There are two operands. The first is in the general register, specified by the 4-bit field R1. The second is in memory, at a location determined by adding the 12-bit displacement D2 to the contents of the two general registers specified by B2 and X2.

In addition to the general-purpose registers, the S/360, S/370, and S/390 have four 64-bit floating-point registers that can be coupled for expanded (128-bit) precision in floating-point operations. ESA/370 and ESA/390 provided 16 access registers for fast access to hundreds of different operand address spaces and allows programs and data to reside in different address spaces.

ES/9000 systems include multiple instruction execution units supporting arithmetic and logical operations, I/O activity, systems management functions, and other tasks. The central processor has only very rudimentary I/O instructions to start and stop I/O, and to determine the status of an I/O operation that has been started or stopped. Input and output can proceed simultaneously with computing under control of channels that can directly access main memory and which can execute *channel programs*. Block multiplexer channels control devices, such as tapes and disks for fast, high-volume data transfers. Byte multiplexer channels can control large numbers of lower-speed devices.

ES/9000 systems include a channel I/O processor, an independent instruction processing unit developed to offload I/O handling from central processing elements by communicating directly with I/O devices. The channels, using Reduced Instruction Set Computer (RISC) microprocessors, offload I/O instruction processing to the channel subsystems for improved system throughput. Standard high-speed (4.5 MBytes/second) parallel channels provide high bandwidth channel attachment capabilities and complete compatibility with standard System/370 control units for workstations, disks, tapes, and communications. Serial channels using fiber optic (*q.v.*) links can deliver the highest bandwidth (10 MBytes/second) channel capacity,

for longer distance (up to 9 km) data transmissions between systems or to I/O devices. The largest water-cooled systems can transfer data at 17 MBytes/second over even greater distances using channels with fiber optic media.

IBM's original lines of computers, the S/360 and S/370 models, were introduced in 1964 and 1970, respectively. During the late 1970s and 1980s, IBM announced an increasingly powerful series of processors: the 303Xs; the intermediate-sized, air-cooled 43XXs; and the large-scale water-cooled 308Xs and 3090s. The 43XX series included both uniprocessors and dyadic processors, while the 308X and 3090 series included uniprocessors, dyadic and triadic processors, and N-way multiprocessors.

A Vector Facility was announced as an optional feature of the 3090 series, which included Vector Extensions to the S/370 and 370-XA architectures. The Vector Facility is an extension of the central processor's instruction and execution elements that allows the central processor to execute vector arithmetic and logical operations on up to 128 sets of operands with a single instruction. The Vector Facility, used for scientific and engineering applications such as structural analysis and computational fluid dynamics, adds 191 new instructions and 16 vector registers, each containing 128 elements. The Vector Facility extends the power of the ES/9000 processors allowing high-performance processing of multiple pairs of operands (arrays of data). It operates as a compatible extension of the S/370, 370-XA, ESA/370, and S/390 architectures. Two IBM 3090 Model 600S processors with 12 CPUs and 12 Vector Facilities are the base for Cornell University's National Supercomputer Facility. Cornell's National Supercomputer Facility is one of six supercomputing centers (*q.v.*) established by the National Science Foundation's Office of Advanced Scientific Computing in 1986 to provide supercomputer access to researchers.

IBM's current processors conforming to the System/390 architecture are the Enterprise System/9000 (ES/9000) family of processors (see Fig. 1). This family ranges from small systems for departmental computing to very large systems used for commercial applications, such as airlines reservations systems and engineering/scientific applications requiring supercomputer power. The

FIG. 1.

entire family of processors from the smallest to the largest employ the same architecture, use the same operating systems, and are completely upward compatible. The ES/9000 family includes three series: the small, air-cooled rack-mounted 9221 series; the intermediate, air-cooled frame 9121 series; and the large, water-cooled frame 9021 series. Each series has a number of models with varying levels of performance. The largest ES/9000 Model 900 system is a 6-way multiprocessor with six central processors and up to six optional Vector Facilities, which can be physically partitioned into two 3-way systems.

A list of the current S/390 models and an estimate of their relative performance is presented in Table 1, with the performance of the S/370 Model 158-3 taken as equal to 1.0. The central processor speed of the Model 158-3 is roughly estimated to be 1 million instructions per second (1 MIPS).

Operating Systems

The original S/360 concept assumed that only one major operating system would be required, which was given the name OS/360 (Operating System/360). It became apparent that many small- and intermediate-sized S/360 systems needed a reasonably sophisticated operating system, but could not afford the high memory space and processor overhead of OS/360. This led to the early development of DOS (Disk Operating System), which was very widely used. IBM also provided an alternative system, CP-67, which ran on the S/360 Model 67. At that time, the Model 67 was unique in that it provided dynamic address translation hardware and was a virtual memory system (*see* VIRTUAL MEMORY). In 1972, virtual storage became a standard feature of all S/370 and future IBM systems. Another alternative was MTS (Michigan Terminal System), developed by the University of Michigan.

With the announcement of dynamic address translation and virtual storage as standard for the S/370 line, IBM introduced its VS (Virtual Storage) operating systems. These include VSE (Virtual Storage Extended), a replacement for DOS, VS1 (Virtual Storage 1), in which users shared a 16-megabyte address space, and MVS (Multiple Virtual Storages), a more sophisticated system in which each user had a 16-megabyte address space. Today, MVS, IBM's largest and most functional operating system, provides each user with a 2-gigabyte address space. The VM (Virtual Machine) system, a successor to the earlier CP-67 system, provides the Conversational Monitor System (CMS), a widely used time-sharing system. The VM system also provides a virtual machine capability that permits users on the same hardware system to use different operating systems concurrently, including, for example, an older and newer MVS system. This great flexibility is achieved at some cost in system overhead. Today's systems offer a broad range of partitioning options, including physical and logical partitioning in addition to VM's software partitioning.

Physical partitioning enables a multiprocessor to be divided and operated as two logically independent complexes. The resulting images can be asymmetric, with each image controlling a different set of resources: processors, channels, central and expanded storage, and vector facilities. For logical partitioning, the Processor Resource/Systems Manager (PR/SM) feature provides hardware support for partitioning of a uniprocessor or multiprocessor into multiple logical partitions or systems images. These logical partitions, designed as independent systems images, can be defined with processor resources allocated as required according to workload requirements. Each of the partitions can run the same or dissimilar operating systems.

IBM's current operating systems include MVS, VM, VSE, and AIX. AIX, the Advanced Interactive Executive, is IBM's implementation of Unix. Each of these operating systems has gone through an evolution in the form of various versions over the past 25 years to support the evolution in architectures.

NORMAN LAYER

TABLE 1. Relative Throughput* of IBM System/390 Series Computers Manufactured in 1990–1991

ES/9000-9021 Water-Cooled Frame			ES/9000-9121 Air-Cooled Frame			ES/9000-9221 Air-Cooled Rack-Mounted		
Model No.	No. CPUs	Relative Performance	Model No.	No. CPUs	Relative Performance	Model No.	No. CPUs	Relative Performance
330	1	20	190	1	8	120	1	2.0
340	1	23	210	1	12	130	1	3.5
500	2	45	260	1	16	150	1	5.0
520	1	45	320	1	21	170	1	6.5
580	3	66	440	2	31			
620	4	85	480	2	40			
640	2	85	490	2	39			
660	2	86	570	3	60			
720	6	124	610	4	78			
740	3	121						
820	4	160						
860	5	194						
900	6	225						

*Relative performance is taken from tables published by Computer Price Watch, October 1991.

IBM CARD. *See* PUNCHED CARD.

IBM PC AND PC-COMPATIBLES

For articles on related subjects *see* APPLE COMPUTER; DIGITAL COMPUTERS: HISTORY: PERSONAL COMPUTERS; and PERSONAL COMPUTING.

The conceptual and practical foundation for the personal computer was developed at M.I.T., the Stanford Research Institute, and the Xerox Palo Alto Research Center, beginning in the 1940s; however, the personal computer industry did not begin until 8-bit microprocessors that had the ability to address at least 32K bytes of memory became available. In 1975, the Intel 8080, MOS Technology 6502, and Motorola 6800 microprocessors were incorporated into dozens of commercial personal computers beginning with the Altair from Micro Instrumentation and Telemetry Systems (MITS).

The first of these 8-bit machines were targeted at the hobby market and were generally sold in kit form. Soon, companies such as Processor Technology, Compal, Commodore, Radio Shack, and Apple recognized the demand for pre-assembled computers. These systems broadened the market from electronic hobbyists to some schools, homes, and small businesses.

In 1977, Digital Microsystems introduced a computer designed for the business and professional market. It was pre-assembled with an Intel 8080 CPU, 64K memory, two floppy disk drives (most early systems used paper or audio cassette tape for storage), and built-in I/O ports. Most important, it used a disk operating system called CP/M (control program for microprocessors), which had been developed by Gary Kildall, a consultant to Intel. While Digital Microsystems did not survive, CP/M and Kildall's company, Digital Research, did.

The CP/M operating system and the bus structure of the MITS Altair, later called the S-100 Bus, became de facto standards for high-end business and professional personal computers during the late 1970s. The CP/M platform encouraged application software developers, and thousands of programs, including Microsoft's language processors, dBase, and WordStar, were developed. While some major manufacturers (e.g. Xerox, Wang, and DEC) entered the CP/M market, IBM did not.

The PC-1   IBM waited for the next generation machine, made possible by 16-bit microprocessors. In order to move quickly, they formed an "intrapreneurial" special business unit called the Entry Systems Division (ESD) to design the PC. A group of about a dozen people, headed by Phillip "Don" Estridge, was chartered to develop a personal computer and bring it to market within a year. The short time limit meant that the PC would be IBM's first product built from off-the-shelf components and third-party software.

Nearly all of the hardware—the disk drives, monitors, memory, CPU, printer, etc.—were purchased from outside vendors. Adopting the standard ASCII code for representing alphanumeric data was a first for IBM because they had used EBCDIC (*q.v.*) on their mainframes for years. System software also came from outside. IBM turned to Microsoft for consultation on the system architecture and a Basic interpreter, as well as to three vendors for operating systems.

IBM chose an Intel CPU because its architecture was close to that of the Intel 8080 used in CP/M-based machines, making it easy to upgrade application software. (IBM later bought a share of Intel.) Intel had two CPUs, the 8086 and 8088. They were software compatible and had 16-bit registers and instructions; however, the 8088 was somewhat slower because of its multiplexed 8-bit data path. To lower system cost, the 8088 was used.

The minimum configuration had only 16K memory. Memory could be expanded to 64K by plugging 16K-bit memory chips into sockets on the system board. Further expansion entailed plugging add-in boards into the five bus expansion slots on the system board. This PC bus soon became the industry standard.

Disk drives were optional on the first PCs, which came standard with an audio cassette interface. The original floppy disk drives used only one side of 5 1/4–inch media and had a capacity of 160K. IBM did not offer a hard disk at first.

There were two display adapters, the monochrome display adapter, (MDA) and a color graphics adapter (CGA). The MDA was a character display with a monochrome monitor. Resolution and character quality were excellent by the standards of the time, and the MDA was targeted to character-oriented applications like word processing (*q.v.*), spreadsheets (*q.v.*), and software development. The CGA delivered color and graphics on a more expensive RGB monitor. Character resolution was significantly lower than with the MDA, so it was targeted at applications like education, games, and business graphics.

The operating system was more problematic than the hardware. CP/M could not be used directly because the 8088 architecture was not identical to that of the 8080. Furthermore, the 8088 could address 1MB of memory, as opposed to the 64K limit of the 8080, and IBM chose to allow up to 640K of contiguous memory for programs. (The rest of the address space was reserved for I/O adapters, ROM, and future use.)

Digital Research was working on an operating system for the new Intel CPUs (CP/M-86), but so were other companies. One was Softech Microsystems, which had acquired the P-System, an operating system and software development environment developed by Ken Bowles at the University of California at San Diego. Another was Seattle Computer Products, headed by Tim Patterson, who wrote DOS, a CP/M-like operating system, for use on their early 8086-based system. Microsoft acquired the rights to market and further develop Patterson's DOS, although there was later litigation over the transaction. IBM eventually decided to offer three operating systems: DOS, CP/M-86, and the P-System. However, DOS was priced much lower than the others, and eventually became the standard.

The IBM-PC was announced in April 1981, with forecast sales of 250,000 units over five years. By the end of 1983, the IBM-PC had become a de facto standard and had an installed base of a million machines. IBM eventually recognized the strategic importance of personal workstations (q.v.), integrated the ESD into the marketing mainstream of the corporation, and defined a System Application Architecture (SAA) to integrate distributed computing (q.v.) and workstations.

Evolution Since its introduction, the PC has undergone three major upgrades (see Table 1). The first was the PC-XT. The XT was a response to the needs of business and professional customers, who had clearly emerged as the major market. With the XT, IBM added a hard disk and expanded the amount of memory on the system board. Even before the introduction of the XT, they had upgraded the floppy disk drives to 360K by using both sides of the media and writing in a higher density (9-sector) format.

The next major upgrade was the PC-AT. The AT used Intel's 80286 CPU, as had Tandy in marketing the excellent but short-lived Tandy 2000. The 80286 was faster than the 8088, and had a 16-bit data bus; therefore, the PC bus was extended by adding additional data lines. The AT bus was upward compatible with the PC bus, so PC and XT add-in cards worked in the AT. The AT bus is also known as the ISA (industry standard architecture) bus.

The 80286 is capable of addressing 16MB of memory; however, to retain compatibility with commercially available software, it is almost always run in its limited "real"

mode, in which it acts as a fast 8086. The AT came with more memory on the system board, and today nearly all PCs are sold with at least 640K. The AT also introduced a high density 5 1/4–inch disk drive with 1.2 MB capacity, and hard disk sizes continued to grow. With the AT, IBM also introduced the EGA (extended graphics adapter) video controller. EGA, a color controller that exceeded CGA in resolution and color palette, became widely used and copied. EGA controllers are compatible with MDA and CGA software. (Tragically, Don Estridge was killed in a plane crash in 1985 just shortly after introduction of the AT.)

The AT was followed by the PS/2 line in 1987. The original line consisted of six models, using the 8086, 80286, and 80386 CPUs. Models using the 80386 SX and the 80486 CPU have been announced subsequently. The 80386 is upward compatible with the earlier CPUs, has 32-bit registers and instructions, and can address 4.3GB of memory. The 80386 SX is software-compatible with the 80386, but uses a multiplexed 16-bit data path. The 80386 SX is to the 80386 as the 8088 was to the 8086. Intel predicts that the 80386 SX will eventually make the 80286 obsolete. The 80486 is compatible with the 80386, but it is faster due to a design that integrates previously off-chip functions and enhances internal caching and parallelism (see CACHE MEMORY).

The low-end (8086-based) PS/2 used the AT bus, but the others used the new microchannel architecture (MCA) bus. The 80386-SX- and 80286-based PS/2s used a

TABLE 1. *Major Steps in the Evolution of the IBM-PC Family*

		PC	PC-XT	PC-AT	PS/2
Year introduced		1981	1982	1984	1987
CPU chip[1]		8088	8088	80286	80386 80386-SX 80486
Bus[2]		PC	PC	AT	MCA
Bus data bits		8	8	16	16 32
Memory on system board[3]		64KB	256KB	512KB	1–2MB
Typical memory		320KB	512KB	640KB	2–8MB
Floppy disk	5 1/4": 3 1/2":	160KB —	360KB —	1.2MB —	1.44MB 760KB
Typical hard disk		n/a	10MB	20MB	40MB
Display adapter		MDA CGA	MDA CGA	EGA	MCGA VGA 8514

[1]The 8086 and 80286 CPU chips were used in some PS/2 models.
[2]Some PS/2 models used the AT bus.
[3]Depends upon model.

16-bit version of the MCA bus, and the 80386- and 80486-based PS/2s used a 32-bit version. The MCA bus was incompatible with the AT bus, but offered advantages, including greater speed and the ability to add cards without having to set switches.

The PS/2s introduced 3 1/2–inch floppy disk drives with 1.44MB capacity on all but the low-end model, which used 760KB drives. The minimum hard disk for the PS/2 was 20MB.

Three new display controllers were also announced for the PS/2 line. The MCGA (multicolor graphics array), an enhanced version of the CGA adapter, was available on the low-end model. Other models came with the VGA (video graphics array)—a color graphic controller exceeding EGA resolution and color palette. VGA controllers use analog monitors and have displaced EGA as a standard. They are compatible with EGA software. The 8514 is a higher resolution controller, but it has not enjoyed the success and emulation of VGA.

IBM and Microsoft also announced OS/2, a new operating system, with the PS/2. OS/2 is not compatible with DOS, but adds features including multitasking, multiple threads, a graphical user interface, and extended file and communication management. OS/2 is designed for machines with at least 2MB of memory, and IBM and Microsoft are committed to supporting both it and DOS for the foreseeable future. Microsoft also markets Windows, a DOS extension that adds a graphical user interface (GUI) and limited multitasking. The product was only moderately successful until the windows 3.0 and 3.1 versions suddenly became very popular in the early 1990s.

The machines described above were IBM's main line, designed primarily for business and professional work. There were also several less successful machines along the way. These included the PCjr (which was targeted to the school and home market), a transportable PC, and a PC with add-in boards to emulate the IBM 370 mainframe instruction set. These have all been withdrawn from the market.

The Competition   IBM was able to bring the PC to market quickly because they used commercially available components, rather than building their own. This also opened the way for competition.

FIG. 1.

A number of companies marketed 8086-based computers before IBM. These included small firms like Seattle Computer Products and Godbout and large ones like Victor Business Machines; however, the market did not take off until IBM entered and established a standard.

There were several gaps in the original PC offering, so IBM's entry was followed almost immediately by a wave of add-in board makers. IBM used 16K-bit memory chips at first, allowing companies using 64K-bit chips to compete effectively in memory upgrades. The value of competitive memory cards was often augmented by including additional I/O ports and calendar chips, making them far superior to IBM memory. The limitations of the CGA and MDA display controllers created a niche filled by a higher-resolution, monochrome, graphic controller from Hercules Graphics. The Hercules controller has become a widely emulated standard. Several companies also developed hard disk subsystems for the PC before IBM did.

By 1982, several companies were marketing PC-compatible computers. One of these, Compaq, combined PC-compatibility with transportability (along the lines of the Osborne CP/M-based computers), a high resolution display, and quality workmanship. Compaq, Zenith, and Tandy have since emerged as major challengers to IBM in the personal computer market. Early PC-compatibles like the Compaq were soon joined by very low cost systems made possible by off-shore design and manufacturing. The August 1991 issue of *PC Magazine* either discussed or carried advertisements for no fewer than 50 different manufacturers of PC-compatible computers. Clearly, they cannot all survive, but the small companies receiving the most attention include Advanced Logic Research, CompuAdd, Dell, Leading Edge, Northgate, Swan, TriStar, and Zeos. More established companies still competing for a share of the PC-compatible market include AT&T, Epson, Hewlett-Packard, Hyundai, NEC, NCR, Packard-Bell, Panasonic, and Texas Instruments. It would appear that one of the reasons IBM abandoned the PC and AT buses in favor of the incompatible MCA bus was to avoid competition with low-overhead producers of commodity computers. IBM protected MCA with many patents, and charges royalties for its use.

In response, leading competitors, headed by Compaq and Hewlett-Packard, banded together to define the EISA (extended industry standard architecture) bus. EISA is a 32-bit bus that is compatible with the AT and not controlled by IBM. The IBM PC set de facto standards that enabled the personal computer market place to grow as it has. In doing so, they attracted many competitors and their market share has declined; however, they remain the largest manufacturer of personal computers.

References

1990. Bradley, D. J. "The Creation of the IBM-PC," *Byte*, **15**, *9* (September) 414–420.

1991. Sheldon, K. M. "You've Come a Long Way, PC: the 10th Anniversary of the IBM-PC," *Byte*, **16**, *8* (August) 336.

ICCP. *See* INSTITUTE FOR CERTIFICATION OF COMPUTER PROFESSIONALS.

ICON. *See* STRING PROCESSING: LANGUAGES; and USER INTERFACE.

IDENTIFIER

For articles on related subjects *see* CONSTANT; EXPRESSION; PROCEDURE-ORIENTED LANGUAGES; PROGRAMMING LANGUAGES; and STATEMENT.

In a programming language, an *identifier* is a string of characters used as a name for some element of the program. This element may be a statement label, a procedure or function, a data element (such as a scalar variable or an array), or the program itself.

Most commonly, the word *identifier* is used almost synonymously with *variable name*. In a system where the location of a program's data remains fixed throughout program execution, the identifier associated with a scalar variable is related to a memory address, which in turn references a physical location within the memory of the machine, which in turn contains a value representation. The intermediate relationships between the identifier and a value are usually transparent to a programmer, and thus some confusion arises in practice between the *name* of a variable (i.e. its identifier) and its *value*, which is the current contents of the memory location assigned to that identifier.

In the majority of programming languages, identifiers may be formed from any alphanumeric string, often of some restricted length, provided the leftmost character is alphabetic. Some languages also permit the use of special characters, the dollar sign ($) and underscore (_) being typical. In Pascal, letter-case does not matter, so TAXRATE, taxrate, and TaxRate are all the same identifier, but in certain other languages such as Modula-2 (*q.v.*) these identifiers would be distinct.

J. A. N. LEE

IEEE—CS. *See* INSTITUTE OF ELECTRICAL AND ELECTRONIC ENGINEERS—COMPUTER SOCIETY.

IFAC. *See* INTERNATIONAL FEDERATION OF AUTOMATIC CONTROL.

IFIP. *See* INTERNATIONAL FEDERATION FOR INFORMATION PROCESSING.

IMAGE PROCESSING

For articles on related subjects *see* COMPUTER GRAPHICS; COMPUTER VISION; MEDICAL IMAGING; PATTERN RECOGNITION; and TOMOGRAPHY, COMPUTERIZED.

Introduction   Digital *image processing* deals with the systematic manipulation of an input image to produce an output image that is better suited for viewing or subsequent analysis. The processed images are either examined by a human observer, such as a radiologist viewing an X-ray, or they form inputs to an automatic machine vision system. The machine vision system then analyzes the image to derive an interpretation of the scene. A digital image is represented as a discrete two-dimensional array of numbers. Each element in the array is known as a *pixel* (for picture element). These pixels are assigned values that correspond to the relative brightness of the tiny portions of the image that they depict. These values are known as *gray levels*. Digital image processing deals with the systematic manipulation of the pixel gray levels and their distribution.

Digital processing of images requires three basic capabilities. First is the ability to form digital images, second is the ability to store and manipulate these images, and third is the ability to display such images. Digital image processing technology traces its origin to the technologies associated with the above three capabilities. Electronics and optics technologies provided the ability for image acquisition; digital computers and associated technologies provided the abilities to store and manipulate these images; and television and communication technologies effected the display and storage abilities.

Growth and Applications of the Technology   It was only about three decades ago that serious research in digital image processing could begin. During this relatively short span, digital image processing technology has proved its importance and utility over a broad spectrum of applications. For example, modern medicine, weather forecasting, manufacturing, surveillance, and video entertainment have all greatly benefitted from image processing technology.

Digital image processing has experienced a steady and sustained growth ever since its inception in the early 1960s. By its very nature, the field is application-oriented. The main objective is to develop tools and techniques for analyzing pictorial data generated in a diverse range of application domains. Initial research and development revolved around the image processing needs of the space program. In the late 1960s and the early 1970s, image processing was introduced to medical imaging. In the early development stages, the hardware environment required for performing image processing was quite expensive and specialized. With the introduction of high-quality imaging cameras and computing workstations at relatively low costs, image processing applications are sprouting in a variety of domains, such as electronics fabrication and testing, document processing and analysis, automotive and aerospace engineering, food processing, and pharmaceutical manufacturing. With the availability of good, affordable cameras and image processing hardware boards, a personal computer can be converted into a complete image processing workstation at a very affordable cost. These developments make it reasonable to expect further rapid growth of the image processing field.

In the early phases of its development, digital image processing was used primarily for image enhancement, restoration, and compression tasks. This period saw the development of some interesting and useful mathematical approaches for solving these problems. More recently, image processing is increasingly viewed as the front-end processing module of a complete machine vision system.

Image Processing Approaches

Image processing methods can be classified in two groups: *spatial domain approaches* and *transform (or frequency) domain approaches*. The spatial domain techniques work directly on the two-dimensional digital images, whereas the transform domain techniques require an image to be transformed into another domain. Characteristics of these transformed images are analyzed to accomplish a specific image processing task. Linear systems theory had allowed treatment of one-dimensional signals in both time and frequency domains. This experience played a major role in developing theories and techniques for processing two-dimensional signals (i.e. images). For several important image processing functions, one can find an appropriate technique from either the spatial domain or the frequency domain. Typically, results of the spatial domain analysis are easier to interpret than those of the frequency domain. Some of the more commonly used transforms for image processing include Fourier, cosine, Hadamard, Harr, and Walsh transforms. Approaches based upon the Hough transform for detection of specific types of structural details like lines, circles, or curves are also finding increasing utility.

Image Quantization and Sampling

Quantization and sampling deal with the issues underlying the formation of a digital image that can be processed by a computer. Digital images are two-dimensional discrete representations. This digitization of the signals is performed to allow subsequent processing of these signals by a digital computer. Conversion of the continuous analog signals into their digital form involves two considerations. First is the digitization of the amplitude of the signals, a process referred to as *quantization*. The second is *sampling*, the formation of the two-dimensional spatial grid associated with an image. Typically, a uniform quantization scheme and a rectangular (or square) sampling grid are used.

Image Registration

One of the important requirements in many image processing and analysis tasks is to extract information from multiple image copies of the same scene. These copies could be acquired in different wavelengths or at different times or from a slightly different perspective or resolution. In order to perform a systematic analysis of such a data set, one requires an ability to match these copies accurately to a standardized grid so that the images are in perfect spatial registration. This involves corrections for rotational, translational, and scale differences present in the images, a process called *image registration*. Development of registration techniques was mainly due to the satellite and aerial image processing studies.

Image Compression

Transmission and storage of digital images poses challenging problems due to the vast amounts of data involved. *Image compression* deals with efficient encoding and decoding of digital images for either transmission or storage (*see* DATA COMPRESSION AND COMPACTION). The initial thrust for image compression studies came from the imaging requirements of the space program in the early 1960s. Recently, after a low level of relevant research activity, there has been renewed interest in this topic. There is a definite cost associated with the storage, processing, and transmission of the data. Images typically contain a significantly large amount of redundant information. In many applications, such redundant information can be eliminated without adversely affecting the original objective of an image processing task. Image compression methods allow reduction of image storage, processing, and transmission requirements without sacrificing the image quality.

Compression techniques are divided into two categories: (1) *reversible (or lossless) techniques*, and (2) *irreversible (or lossy) techniques*. One can achieve a much larger compression ratio by using lossy methods as compared to the lossless methods. Two important types of compression, *predictive* and *transform coding*, use the high correlation between the gray levels associated with neighboring pixels to achieve compression. Typically, predictive coding schemes are relatively simpler to implement but are not robust (i.e. they suffer from high sensitivity to various statistical parameters). Transform coding schemes achieve higher compression ratios as compared to the predictive approaches, but are more complex to implement. Hybrid coding schemes combine the best features of the predictive and transform coding approaches. In the case of the compression of multiple frames of images (such as those involved in television transmission), one can use the high correlation between the successive frames to achieve compression.

Image Enhancement

The goal of *image enhancement*, one of the most widely used image processing functions, is to highlight or enhance a particular type of image feature. Suppression of image detail that is not of interest for a particular task is also a part of the image enhancement process. These techniques are used in the following types of problems:

1. Object/background contrast stretching.
2. Modification of the dynamic range of an image.
3. Removal of false contours introduced through inadequate quantization levels.
4. Reduction of additive, multiplicative, or "salt-and-pepper" noise.
5. Enhancement of edge features ("edge sharpening").

6. Image smoothing ("image blurring").
7. Display of image detail by pseudo-color (or "false color") enhancement.

In Figs. 1 and 2, two examples of image enhancement are presented. In Fig. 1, the objective is to reduce the additive and multiplicative noise in an image. A nonlinear neighborhood operator has been iteratively applied to reduce the high contrast noise. This spatial domain enhancement operation can be viewed as a low-pass adaptive filtering operation. The example in Fig. 2 deals with the enhancement of a neutron radiographic image of a nuclear fuel rod. The original image is corrupted by a nonuniform intensity pattern imposed by the nonuniform flux of neutrons from the cylindrical fuel rod. This nonuniformity is independent of the vertical position, so that a simple column-by-column gray-level averaging operation allows us to isolate the intensity pattern, which is then subtracted from the original image. As the second step in enhancement, a nonlinear spatial domain filter for contrast stretching is applied to highlight the pellet interfaces and the casing structure.

Image Restoration

The objective of image restoration is to undo the effects of any degradation that might have affected an image. In a sense, image restoration can be considered a special kind of image enhancement. In image restoration, it is assumed that the mathematical model of the degradation process is available or can be accurately derived by examining the input images. Image restoration offers many problems that can be examined in a nice mathematical framework. However, applying these techniques to solve real-world problems is difficult. In order to derive useful results in practical situations, one must consider approaches where the assumed mathematical models are satisfied. Image restoration techniques use an image formation model. In most cases, one assumes that the image formation is a spatially invariant and linear process. With these assumptions, it is possible to describe image formation by an integral equation in-

FIG. 2. Enhancement of a neutron radiograph of a nuclear fuel rod. A two-step enhancement procedure was used to eliminate the nonuniform illumination variations and to enhance the contrast highlighting fuel pellets and casing. (Courtesy of Dr. G. Mastin, Sandia National Laboratory.)

volving the original ("ideal") image convolved with the point spread function (PSF) of the imaging system, a model for the electro-optical sensor, and a random noise term. The most straightforward image restoration method is known as the "inverse filter" approach. It involves use of the noise model and the knowledge of the PSF to estimate the original image from the recorded image. For many practical problems, the PSF may not be known. In such cases, it may be possible to analyze the power spectrum of the recorded image to deduce the parameters of the PSF. This can be explained with the help of the examples shown in Fig. 3. Parts (a) and (b) of this figure show recorded images that are corrupted by defocus and uniform motion blur, respectively. Part (c) shows the Fourier domain signature of the image of Fig. 3(a). The diameter of the visible ring is equal to the circular aperture PSF used to describe the lens defocus. Similarly, part

FIG. 1. Reduction of additive and multiplicative noise by applying a nonlinear neighborhood operator in the spatial domain. (Courtesy of Dr. G. Mastin, Sandia National Laboratory.)

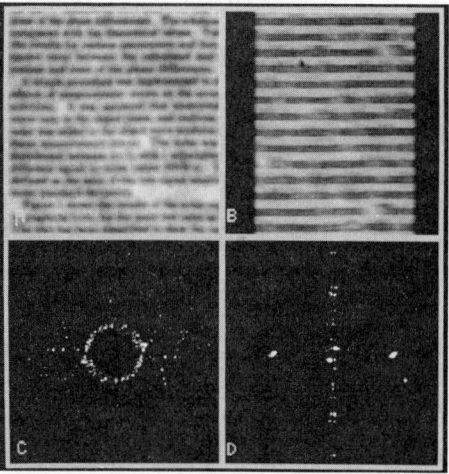

FIG. 3. Part (a) shows an image blurred due to defocus. Part (b) shows an image with uniform motion blur. Parts (c) and (d) show their respective Fourier domain blur signatures. (Courtesy of Dr. G. Mastin, Sandia National Laboratory.)

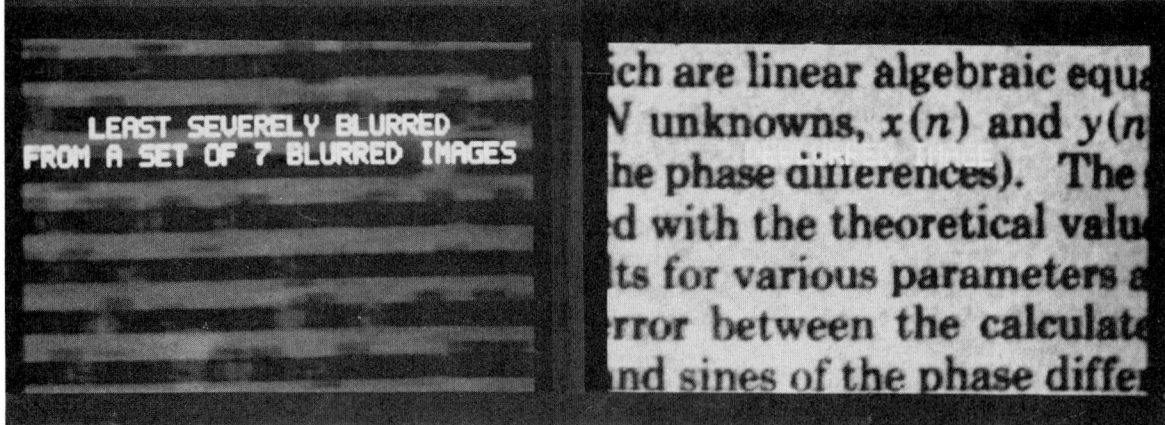

FIG. 4. Example of restoration of a motion blurred image. Part (a) shows one of the seven images affected by motion blur. Part (b) shows the restored image. (Courtesy of Drs. D. Ghiglia and G. Mastin, Sandia National Laboratory.)

(d) shows the uniform motion blur signature. The strong intensity spikes located in a horizontal plane indicate the blur direction. The spacing of these components is equal to twice the blur width and can be used to create a transfer function describing horizontal motion.

Examples of image restoration of two images affected by motion blur are presented in Figs. 4 and 5. Fig. 4(a) shows one of the seven images recorded with motion blur. Fig. 4(b) shows the restored image. Details of the restoration technique are described by Ghiglia (1984). Fig. 5(a) shows an image blurred by an object moving in a perspective plane. Fig. 5(b) presents the results of a linear Weiner restoration technique by first invoking a geometric transformation to remove the perspective (Ghiglia and Jakowatz, 1985).

Image Reconstruction This topic deals with the problem of reconstructing a digital image given a set of image projections. There are several important applica-tion areas where the only practical way to acquire two-dimensional or three-dimensional images of an object is by utilizing a set of image projections. For example, image reconstruction is an important requirement in medical imaging, geophysical exploration, underwater exploration, and radio astronomy.

Image Segmentation Segmentation deals with the partitioning of an image into parts for further processing. There are basically two types of approaches to accomplish image segmentation: edge-based and region-based. The edge-based segmentation approach utilizes properties of dissimilarity between adjacent pixels to identify all edge pixels in an image. Various operators can be developed to detect such discontinuities in the properties of the pixels. While developing such operators, issues such as accuracy in detection and localization are considered. For each edge pixel, the *strength* of the edge (magnitude of the discontinuity value) and the *direction* of the edge

FIG. 5. Image with severe blurring from a van moving in a perspective plane (left). Image after applying Weiner restoration to the perspective corrected image (right). Note that the stationary objects in the scene, such as trees and grass, are now blurred, while the van is deblurred. (Courtesy of Drs. D. Ghiglia and G. Mastin, Sandia National Laboratory.)

are evaluated. Once edge pixels in an image are identified, the task is to form boundaries that segment the image into distinct regions. This task can be quite difficult for most real-world images. Basically, it requires tracing of the global object contours based upon very localized information that is highly susceptible to error and inaccuracy. Such a boundary formation task can also involve complex computations. In situations where the boundaries are linear or of a specified parametric form, techniques such as Hough transforms have proved to be quite useful.

The region-based approach to segmentation utilizes properties of similarity among image pixels. There are three different implementations of the basic region-based approach. The first is called *segmentation by region merg-*

ing, where a region is merged with its neighboring region if they share some uniformity or homogeneity property. This can be considered a bottom-up approach, where one begins with individual pixels to form homogeneous regions. The second approach is known as *segmentation by region splitting.* One starts with a large region which is then split into homogeneous subregions using a uniformity or homogeneity test. This can be considered a top-down approach, where one begins with a large region and keeps splitting it into smaller homogeneous regions. Finally, one can also develop a *split-and-merge* technique for segmentation, where one can use either a merge or split decision at a given level to segment an image efficiently. Region-based approaches have proved to be more effective in practical situations than edge-based approaches,

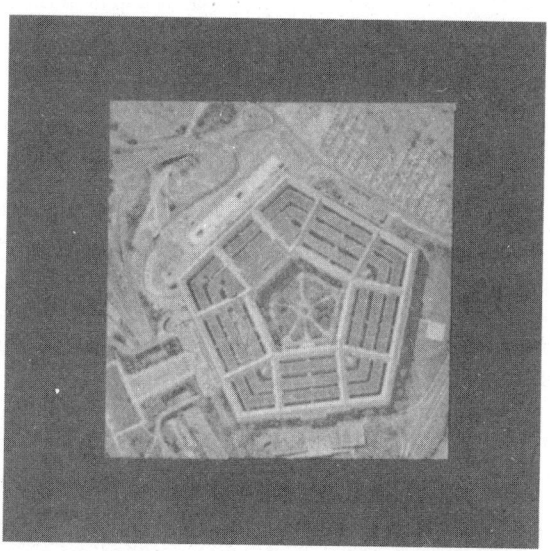

(a)

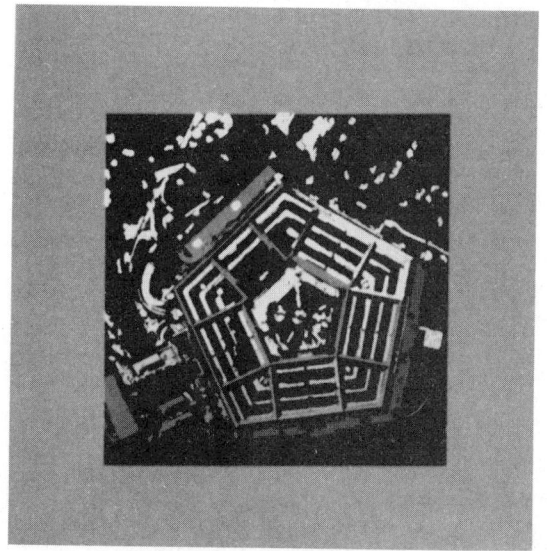

(b)

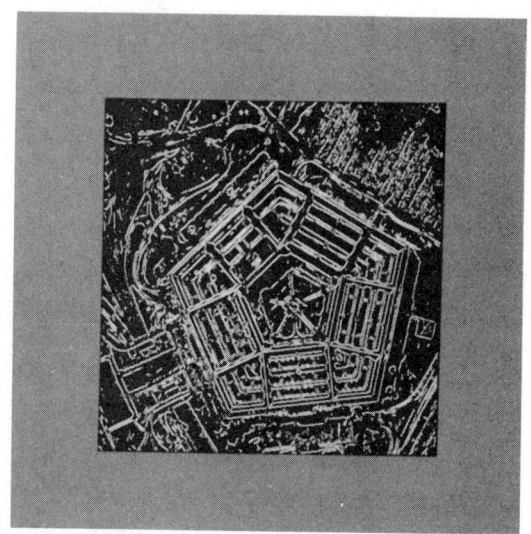

(c)

FIG. 6. Image segmentation: Part (a) shows a high-resolution aerial image of the Pentagon. Part (b) shows the results of applying a region-growing algorithm to identify homogeneous regions. Part (c) shows the results of applying an edge operator to identify the intensity discontinuities.

as they exhibit better noise immunity, and are more efficient. There are also a number of studies where both the edge and region-based techniques are used in a complementary fashion.

Examples of image segmentation are presented in Fig. 6. Fig. 6a shows a high resolution aerial image of the Pentagon. Fig. 6b shows the results of applying a region-growing segmentation algorithm (Levine, 1985). The basic premise is to merge pixels belonging to the same statistical distribution in a region. From a perceptual psychology viewpoint, region-growing is based upon two important criteria of perceptual grouping. The criterion of *proximity* is observed by evaluating each pixel with pixels in its neighborhood, and the *similarity* criterion is observed due to the fact that the above evaluation requires comparison of a specified pixel property with that of its neighbors. If the pixels are judged to be similar, they are merged; otherwise they are assigned to different regions. In Fig. 6c, results of applying an edge operator are shown. A 5 × 5 kernel was used in the edge operator, and a threshold was used to reject weak edges.

Image Processing Hardware Efficient processing of images requires specialized hardware for image acquisition, storage, manipulation, and display. Advances in image processing hardware are derived directly from dramatic advances made in fields such as electro-optics, electronics, VLSI, and computers. There are several ways in which an image can be digitized. A scanning microdensitometer or a flying spot scanner can be used to digitize a photograph or a transparency. Devices using semiconductor technology represent the most popular image acquisition mechanism. They use charge-coupled devices mounted in a rectangular array to sense a full image field.

Digital outputs generated by these devices are linearly proportional to the intensity of the light falling on the sensors. The image processing workstation utilizes a high-speed memory storage board ("frame grabber") to acquire a full image frame for processing. Typically, the size of these frames is 512 × 512 or 1,024 × 1,024, with a 64, 128, or 256 gray-level dynamic range. The frame grabber acquires these frames at video rates (1/30 of a second per frame). The workstations also provide specialized functions for performing common image processing operations. In addition, algorithms can be programmed for the general-purpose computer that forms part of each workstation. For display, a high-resolution color graphics monitor is used. Typically, these monitors can handle 1,000 × 1,000 color images and provide graphics overlay capabilities. Most image processing development is accomplished in an interactive computing environment.

References

1984. Ghiglia, D. C. "Space-Invariant Deblurring Given N Independent Blurred Images of a Common Object," *Journal of Optical Society of America*, **1**, April, 398–402.
1985. Ghiglia, D. C., and Jakowatz, C. V. "Some Practical Aspects of Moving Object Deblurring in a Perspective Plane," *Applied Optics*, **24**, *22*, 15 November, 3830–3837.
1985. Levine, M. D., *Vision in Man and Machine*. New York: McGraw-Hill.
1989. Jain, A. K. *Fundamentals of Digital Image Processing*. Englewood Cliffs, NJ: Prentice-Hall.
1990. Trivedi, M. M. (Ed.). *Selected Reprints on Digital Image Processing*, Milestone Series, **17**, Bellingham, WA: Optical Engineering Press.
1990. Kasturi, R. and Trivedi, M. M. (Ed.) *Image Analysis Applications*. New York: Marcel Dekker.

Mohan M. Trivedi

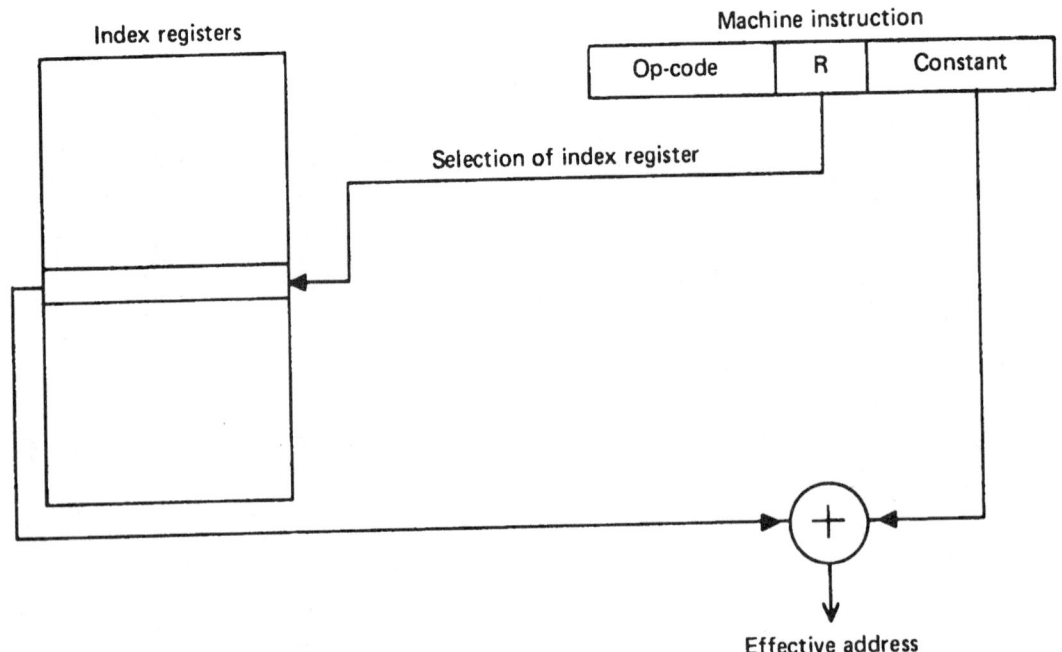

FIG. 1.   Example of the formation of an effective address.

INDEX REGISTER

For articles on related subjects *see* ADDRESSING; BASE REGISTER; GENERAL REGISTER; INDIRECT ADDRESS; INSTRUCTION SET; and REGISTER.

An *index register* is a storage device most often used in the determination of an operand address, but that may be used for other purposes, mainly as a counter.

In the process of the formation of the address of an operand, one can distinguish three basic parts. Consider, for example, the ADD instruction in a program loop computing the sum of the elements of a vector. The operand address of the ADD instruction is formed from:

1. The address of the base of the vector (its first element) relative to the beginning of the program module. This address is known when the program is being written.
2. The memory address into which the program module is loaded. This address is known at load time.
3. The offset from the base of the vector, which depends on the element that is currently being added and which is known only at execution time.

Index registers are normally involved with the last of the three parts of the address.

The address computed with an index register is referred to as the *effective address*. The index register accomplishes its role of forming the effective address in one of two ways: Either the address is formed from a constant in the address field of an instruction plus a changing offset in the index register, or the address as a whole is contained in the index register. In the former case, shown in Fig. 1, the index register is used as a counter.

The number of index registers in a machine and the number of index registers used in the formation of the effective address and other attributes of the index registers are highly dependent on the particular architecture. Thus, one finds machines with a single index register, one index register and one dedicated base register, multiple index registers and/or base registers, and machines in which the general registers may be utilized for indexing and base addressing.

Index registers are also used as counters. In this role, they are typically used as loop-control instructions that increment/decrement their values and test against a constant (typically zero) to cause a conditional branch. Some computers also possess the capability to increment or decrement registers as a side effect of data access using that register. In that case, the value by which the register is incremented or decremented usually depends on the byte-size of the operands being processed—1 for 8-bit bytes (that typically hold characters), 2 for 16-bit integers, 4 for 32-bit integers, etc. (*see* GENERAL REGISTER).

Special care must be exercised in the use of index registers when the computer possesses an indirect addressing mode. In this case, the index register can be used either to compute the location of the indirect address (*pre-indexing*) or as an offset to the indirect address itself (*post-indexing*). When more than one index register is involved in the formation of the effective address, both pre- and post-indexing may be present. Again, the availability of either of the modes varies widely among different machines.

GIDEON FRIEDER

INDIRECT ADDRESS

For articles on related subjects *see* ADDRESSING; INSTRUCTION SET; and MACHINE AND ASSEMBLY LANGUAGE PROGRAMMING.

A simple one-address computer instruction contains an operation code (op code) and an address that points to a location in memory. The contents of that location may be the data required by the operation, or may be an address that points to another location in memory. In this latter case, the address in the instruction itself is called an *indirect address* (or *deferred address*), since it references data indirectly by pointing to the address of the data rather than to the data itself.

In some computers, the instruction itself contains a control field (one bit per address is enough) that specifies that the corresponding address is an indirect address. In other computers, tag bits are associated with data words, and these tag bits determine whether the word is to be treated as data or is to be used as an address that points to data.

Many systems support multilevel indirect addressing (see Fig. 1). The address retrieved in the memory word may itself be an indirect address that points to another memory location, which in turn may be an indirect ad-

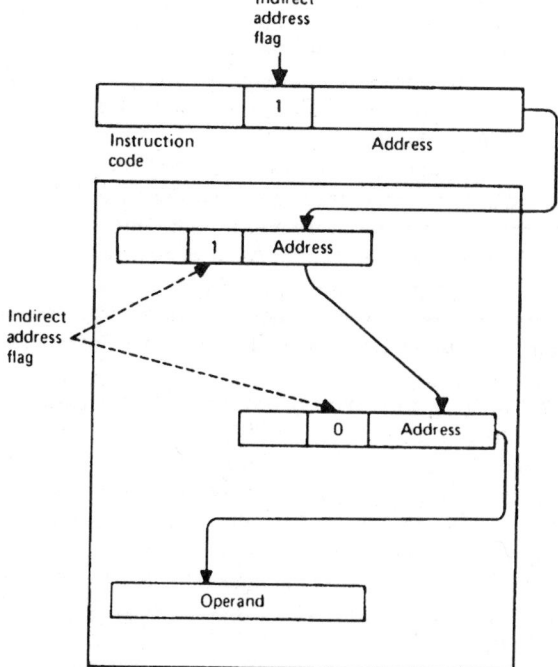

FIG. 1. Two-level indirect addressing.

dress, etc. Computers that allow multilevel indirect addressing usually have a time-out interrupt facility that causes an interrupt to occur in the case of a non-terminating indirect addressing loop.

There are many uses for indirect addressing. It has been used most effectively in those systems that require a longer address field than can be conveniently or reasonably provided in each instruction. Many small computers use indirect addressing in this way, but it is also used on many larger ones. Thus, the *descriptors* on large Burroughs systems were indirect addresses in which the address word contains the origin and size of an array that is addressed to permit an automatic check for out-of-bounds addressing. The Multics system used two-word indirect addresses to permit the addressing of its very large virtual memory.

SAUL ROSEN

INFORMATICS. *See* COMPUTER SCIENCE; EDUCATION IN COMPUTER SCIENCE; and INFORMATION SCIENCE.

INFORMATION ACCESS

For articles on related subjects *see* COMPUTERS IN SOCIETY; LEGAL ASPECTS OF COMPUTING; NETWORKS, COMPUTER; and SOCIAL SCIENCE APPLICATIONS.

During the 1970s and 1980s, government agencies across the U.S. computerized information systems. At the same time, public and academic libraries developed computer networks to promote public access to information, and a new industry for electronic information services emerged. This rapid transformation of the nation's information resources has raised new public policy questions about the dissemination of "electronic" information, the future role of libraries, and the application of information laws, such as the Freedom of Information Act, to computerized information.

The impact of computer technology on government record systems is far-reaching. According to a 1987 Office of Technology Assessment report, computer technology is eliminating the distinctions between government reports, publications, databases, and records. Computer technology has also made possible the rapid dissemination of government information, in some instances at substantial cost savings.

This transformation of government information systems creates new questions about the appropriate roles for the public and private sectors. Traditionally, the U.S. government encouraged the distribution of government publications at little or no cost to the general public through the Government Printing Office and the Depository Library Program. At the same time, there is an opportunity for private sector firms to develop information products.

The Depository Library Program is administered by the Government Printing Office. The DLP was established by the Depository Library Act of 1895 for the purpose of providing free public access to government information. The DLP provides access to federal agency publications through approximately 1,400 libraries across the U.S. The libraries, in turn, maintain the documents and provide public access free of charge. Public libraries and library associations, such as the American Library Association and the Association of Research Libraries, work closely with the GPO and the DLP to promote public access to information.

Many private firms also promote public access to government information, though on a cost basis. The Information Industry Association was established in 1968 to "promote the development of private enterprise in the field of information and...gain recognition for information as a commercial product." Its membership includes large information companies, such as Dow Jones, McGraw-Hill, and Dun & Bradstreet, as well as smaller, newly formed information companies and services. The information industry is one of the fastest growing industries in the U.S. A 1986 Department of Commerce report estimated annual income for the 900 firms at about 2 billion dollars.

The competing interests of the public information providers and the private sector came to a head in 1985. In that year, the Office of Management and Budget issued Circular A-130, "Management of Federal Information Resources," which recommended that federal agencies place "maximum feasible reliance" on the private sector in the dissemination of government information in electronic formats. This policy was opposed by many library organizations. They believed that the policy would diminish public access to government information and result in a gap between information haves and have-nots. As the U.S. enters the 1990s, the appropriate roles of the public and private sectors is still hotly debated.

Another consequence of computerized record systems is the applicability of information laws, such as the Freedom of Information Act. This law requires that federal agencies provide public information upon request and is designed to promote public access to the records of government. The FOIA is often credited with uncovering government waste and mismanagement, public health hazards, and business fraud. The law was passed in 1966 and strengthened significantly in 1974.

Some federal agencies contend that the Freedom of Information Act does not require agencies to disclose information in electronic formats, since the law was enacted before the development of current record-keeping systems. Others say that the purpose of the law, to provide public access to the records of government activity, does not change because the technology changes. This debate may be resolved in either the courts or the Congress. The courts may be asked to decide how to apply current laws to new technologies. The Congress may be asked to develop new laws specifically for new technologies. Both efforts are currently underway.

At present, there are great opportunities to promote public access to information through the development of computer systems and networks. Whether these opportunities are realized will depend largely on the ability of the various policy stakeholders to put aside short-term concerns for institutional security and profitability and consider the long-term opportunities that computer networks provide.

MARC ROTENBERG

INFORMATION AND DATA

For articles on related subjects *see* DATA MODELS; DATA STRUCTURES; DATA TYPE; INFORMATION RETRIEVAL; INFORMATION THEORY; KNOWLEDGE REPRESENTATION; SYMBOL MANIPULATION; and SYNTAX, SEMANTICS, AND PRAGMATICS.

Although the layperson typically uses the terms *information* and *data* interchangeably, to the information scientist or the information systems designer, the distinction between them is important. Among the several existing points of view about this distinction, this article presents one with considerable current and, more important, increasing support.

The term *information* has a number of different meanings and is used in a number of different contexts. It is one of the more overused words in our language, a word considered to be synonymous with knowledge or intelligence. Computer and information scientists and systems designers are broadly concerned with this meaning of the term. The same meaning is also implied when a layperson says, "May I have some information, please?" However, in a scientific and engineering sense, it is desirable to establish a somewhat more formal, useful, and precise definition.

The word *information* is also frequently used rather narrowly, specifically in the sense that Shannon (*q.v.*) and Weaver (1949) have established in their treatment of *information theory*. In this sense, the context of the message is of no significance; instead, the theory is concerned with the probability of the receipt of any particular message from among many for various conditions of the transmission system. While this interpretation may indeed be of interest in designing information systems, it is certainly not the major, nor even *a* major, concern. Such a treatment does not consider the really important areas of interest, almost all of which involve the context, meaning, and effectiveness of the message.

Shannon and Weaver identify three levels of information problems:

1. The technical problem. (How accurately can the symbols of communication be transmitted?)
2. The semantic problem. (How precisely do the transmitted symbols convey the desired *meaning*?)
3. The effectiveness (or behavioral) problem. (How effectively does the received meaning *affect conduct* in the desired way?)

These three levels of communication research are perhaps most clearly and most simply described by these questions: (1) What is the message? (2) What does the message mean? (3) What are the effects of the message on the recipient?

Problems at the first level are essentially attacked by the use of Shannon's information theory, which is concerned primarily with the *communication* problem.

The semantic problem has been of interest for some time. Early productive ideas were suggested by Carnap and Bar-Hillel in 1952. Since then, many others have studied this problem. More recently, for example, Winograd (1972) and Woods (1978) and others have attacked the problem of the meaning of transmitted symbols.

And yet, ultimately, it is the level 3 consideration, namely how the message *affects* the *behavior* of the recipient with which information scientists and systems designers are primarily concerned. That is, what is the effectiveness of the information? This is a much more difficult problem than the other two. It has been approached by MacKay (1969), Marschak (1964), and Yovits and colleagues (1969, 1981), as well as a number of others. This third level may be said to deal with *pragmatic information*, or just *pragmatics*.

Information and Data   Even among professionals engaged in the design and use of computerized information systems, there is a difference of opinion as to how to define and categorize information and data, all generally within the framework of equating information essentially with knowledge or intelligence of some type. See, for example, Langefors (1972). There are those who suggest that information is somehow connected with the way in which data is displayed. It is suggested that the information is a function of the ease with which the data can be comprehended by the user.

Then there are those who suggest that information is "smoothed" as opposed to "raw" data. This smoothing permits a user to make decisions more easily than might be possible from the unsmoothed data. The suggestion has been made that information consists of appropriate aggregation of data; or perhaps information can be defined as the appropriate interconnection between various pieces of data, thus making it possible to use the data readily.

Several common characteristics run through most of these definitions. First, information is a *subset* of *data* or perhaps inferred from data. It is also generally either explicitly stated or at least implied that the ultimate concern is that somehow the information must eventually be *used*. Thus, a user is involved. Generally, the concern is with the *effectiveness* with which the information is used. In other words, the general interest is with the problems of level 3—the pragmatics of the message. The *value* of the information in a message is the important criterion.

Information: A Definition   Many information scientists accept the standard definition: *Information is data which is used in decision-making* (Yovits and Ernst, 1969; McDonough and Garrett, 1965). This definition has a number of significant derived implications. One is that information is a *relative* quantity—relative to the situation, to the time at which a decision is made, and to the decision maker and the decision maker's background and history.

What is of considerable importance in one situation is very possibly totally useless in another. What may be of considerable value to one decision maker at a particular time may likely be useless to another decision maker or even to the same decision maker at a different time or in a different situation. This differs from the physical world, where the quantities involved are generally absolute; i.e. one second is (almost) always one second.

A second implication is that information and decision making are closely intertwined. Information is used *only* for decision making, and decision makers have *only* the resource of information available to them. Consequently, to understand these properties of information in this context, the process of decision making must also be studied.

The objective of information system design then becomes principally the design of a system that makes available the information needed for making a variety of decisions obtained from among all the data the system has stored. Such a system must capture and store as much as possible of the information that may be needed, and *only* this information. An information system should make available most readily the most valuable data. The *value* of information in some sense is a major criterion.

Data: A Definition We have defined information in terms of data. It is, accordingly, desirable to define data in somewhat more fundamental terms. We first quote from Webster's Unabridged Dictionary, which offers the following partial definition for *datum*.

> Something that is given either from being experimentally encountered or from being admitted or assumed for specific purposes; a fact or principle granted or presented...

In other words: *Data are facts or are believed to be or are said to be facts that result from the observation of physical phenomena.*

The Generalized Information System Model
Yovits and Ernst (1969) have proposed a generalized model or a *generalized information system* (G.I.S.) that explicitly indicates the interrelationship between data, information, decision making, and other important quantities. This is shown in Fig. 1.

This model can be used to describe and understand any information-dependent activity of the level 3 type—that is, information involved in the decision-making process. Information is presented to the decision maker (DM) by the information acquisition and dissemination (IAD) module. Information enters the IAD module either as external or feedback (internal) data. Feedback provides information to the decision maker about prior decisions. It is the mechanism available to the DM by which the DM's assessment of the decision-making situation can be updated. Repetitive or similar types of decisions enable the DM to benefit from prior decisions by updating and modifying the DM's current personal model of the situation.

The DM makes a decision (selects a course of action) that the *execution* module carries out. The decision making will generally have uncertainty with regard to the execution function (*executional uncertainty*) and with re-

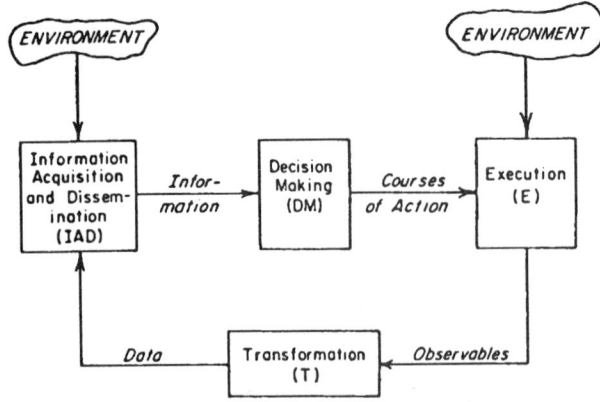

FIG. 1. The generalized information system model.

gard to the specific environmental conditions prevailing (*state of nature uncertainty*). The *transformation* module converts or transforms the results of the decisions that are physical and observable into feedback *data* for the IAD. Note that the decision maker has *transduced* information into observable quantities. The observables are in turn transformed into data.

The model makes explicit not only the relationship between information and decision making but also the relationship between data and observable physical quantities as well as the sometimes overlooked but necessary feedback property found in useful information/decision-making systems.

Although it is beyond the scope of this article, it is possible using the framework established by the G.I.S. to establish precise and quantitative definitions of *quantity of information* in terms of *binary choice units* (which is a deterministic choice from a pair of alternatives); *decision-maker effectiveness* in terms of expected values and probabilities of choice; *value or effectiveness of information* in terms of the change which will result in decision-maker effectiveness; as well as other important quantities. (*see* Yovits, *et al.* 1981).

More recently, a conceptual framework has been established to determine the value of the information contained in a message or document used in a particular situation (*see* Yovits, *et al.* 1987).

References

1949. Shannon, C. E. and Weaver, W. *The Mathematical Theory of Communication.* Urbana, IL: University of Illinois Press.

1952. Carnap, R. and Bar-Hillel, Y. *An Outline of a Theory of Semantic Information,* Technical Report No. 247. Cambridge, MA: Research Laboratory of Electronics, M.I.T.

1964. Marschak, J. "Problems in Information Economics," in Bonini, C. P., Jaedicke, R. K., and Wagner, H. M. *Management Controls.* New York: McGraw-Hill, 38–74.

1965. McDonough, A. M. and Garrett, L. J. *Management Systems, Working Concepts and Practices.* Homewood, IL: Richard D. Irwin.

1969. MacKay, D. M. *Information, Mechanism, and Meaning.* Cambridge, MA: The M.I.T. Press.

1969. Yovits, M. C. and Ernst, R. L. "Generalized Information Systems: Consequences for Information Transfer," in Pepinsky, H. P. (Ed.). *People and Information.* New York: Pergamon Press.

1972. Langefors, B. *Theoretical Analysis of Information Systems.* Philadelphia, PA: Auerbach (also Lund, Sweden: Studentlitteratur).

1972. Winograd, T. "Understanding Natural Language," *Cognitive Psychology* **3.**

1978. Woods, W. A. "Semantics and Quantification in Natural Language Question Answering," in Yovits, M. C. (Ed.). *Advances in Computers.* **17.** New York: Academic Press.

1981. Yovits, M. C., Foulk, C. R., and Rose, L. L. "Information Flow and Analysis: Theory, Simulation, and Experiments," *Journal of the American Society for Information Science,* **32,** 3, May, 187–202.

1987. Yovits, M. C., de Korvin, A., Kleyle, R., and Mascarenhas, M. "External Documentation and Its Quantitative Relationship to the Internal Information State of a Decision Maker: The Information Profile," *Journal of the American Society for Information Science,* **38,** 6, November, 405–419.

Marshall C. Yovits

INFORMATION-BASED COMPLEXITY

For articles on related subjects *see* Computational Complexity; and NP-Complete Problems.

A very simplified view of an important scientific paradigm is as follows. A mathematical formulation of a natural phenomenon is created. Computations stemming from the mathematical formulations lead to understanding and predictions. The relation between a real world phenomenon, a mathematical formulation, and the computation are schematized in Fig. 1.

Mathematical formulations of scientific problems are often infinite-dimensional and continuous. They are expressed, for example, as systems of ordinary or partial differential equations (*q.v.*), integral equations, or optimization problems.

Information-based complexity (IBC) studies the computational complexity of infinite-dimensional continuous problems. These are problems where either the input or

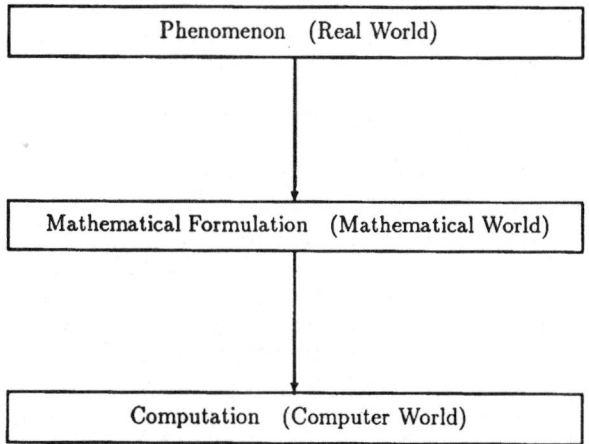

FIG. 1. Three worlds.

the output are elements of infinite-dimensional spaces. It is a branch of *computational complexity* that studies the minimal computer resources (typically, time or space) needed to solve a mathematically posed problem.

Computational Complexity of Integration

We illustrate some of the important ideas of information-based complexity with the example of integration. Consider the computation of $\int_0^1 f(x)\,dx$. For "most" integrands, this integral cannot be computed symbolically. Therefore, we must integrate numerically. The input to the integration problem is the function $f(x)$. All we can enter into the computer are some numbers that represent $f(x)$. Often, the available information is the values of f at a number of points. This information is *partial* because there are many integrands that are indistinguishable using this information. If the information has errors (due, for example, to roundoff errors), it is *contaminated.* It is clear that partial or contaminated information causes *uncertainty,* say ε, in the integral. This uncertainty is intrinsic and caused by the limited information. Furthermore, we assume that the information is priced.

To introduce computational complexity, we first define the *model of computation.* The model of computation states which operations are permitted and how much they cost. The model of computation is based on two assumptions:

1. We can perform arithmetic operations and comparisons on real numbers at unit cost.
2. We can evaluate a function f at any point x at cost c, where c is independent of f and x.

We comment on these assumptions. The *real number model* (Assumption 1) is used as an abstraction of the floating-point model typically used in scientific computation. Except for the possible effect of roundoff errors and numerical stability, complexity results will be the same in these two models.

The real number model should be contrasted with the *Turing Machine* (*q.v.*) *model,* typically used for discrete problems. The cost of an operation in a Turing Machine model depends on the size of the operands. But the cost of a floating-point operation is independent of the size of the operands, which is why we use the real number model. Whether a real number or Turing Machine model is used can make an enormous difference. For example, Kachian showed that linear programming is polynomial in the Turing Machine model. In 1981, Traub and Wozniakowski showed that Kachian's algorithm is not polynomial in the real number model and conjectured that linear programming is not polynomial in this model. This conjecture is still open.

It would be more realistic to replace Assumption 2 by the assumption that the cost of a function evaluation depends on f or x or both, but this would complicate the theory.

A *quadrature algorithm* is any procedure for approximating the integral using the available information. Any such algorithm must have error at least as large as the intrinsic uncertainty. The *computational complexity* of the integration problem is the minimal cost of computing the integral to within error ε.

The concept of computational complexity permits us to introduce the fundamental concepts of optimal information and optimal algorithm. Information and an algorithm that uses the information are called *optimal information* and an *optimal algorithm* if the error of the approximation is at most the intrinsic uncertainty and the cost of computing the approximation equals the computational complexity.

General Formulation

We have used the integration example to introduce basic concepts of IBC. Generally, IBC is characterized by three assumptions, namely that information is *partial*, *contaminated*, and *priced*. A general formulation and extensive bibliography may be found in Traub, Wasilkowski, and Wozniakowski (1988).

IBC has been used for numerous applications, including partial differential equations, ordinary differential equations, integral equations, approximation, nonlinear optimization, control theory, computer vision (*q.v.*), and edge detection.

Although the focus has been on infinite-dimensional problems, there has been some work on finite-dimensional problems. Examples are large linear systems and eigenvalue problems, as well as the discrete problem of synchronizing clocks in a distributed system (*q.v.*).

Intractable Problems

In applications, the inputs are often multivariate functions. For example, we might want to integrate a function of d variables. Let the smoothness of the class of inputs be r. Then to guarantee an error of at most ε,

$$\text{comp}^{\text{wor-det}}(\varepsilon) = \Theta((1/\varepsilon)^{d/r}).$$

The symbol on the left-hand side indicates this is the complexity in the worst case deterministic setting. Worst case means that we guarantee an error of at most ε for every input in a class of inputs. Deterministic means that we do not toss coins. The capital theta notation means that the upper and lower bounds on the computational complexity differ by at most a constant.

We comment on this result:

1. It holds for many problems, including integration, approximation, nonlinear optimization, systems of nonlinear equations, linear elliptic differential equations, and Fredholm integral equations of the second kind.
2. For ε and r fixed, the complexity is exponential in d.
3. Hence, any problem with this complexity is *intractable*. We can regard the dimension as the *size* of the input. (The number of variables and dimension are used interchangeably.) This may be contrasted with discrete problems, where the size of the input is typically the number of objects.

4. The worst case deterministic setting is the same as the one used in the theory of *NP-complete problems*.
5. Since we have an exponential lower bound, these problems are provably intractable. This may be contrasted with the theory of NP-complete problems, whose intractability is conjectured.
6. Because the information is partial, we are able to obtain lower bounds on a problem's computational complexity, using adversary arguments at the information level. That is why this branch of computational complexity is called *information-based complexity*.
7. Even for rather small values of d, the problem may be very hard. For example, let $\varepsilon = 10^{-8}$ (single-precision), $r = 1, d = 3$. Then the complexity is proportional to 10^{24}. Take the units to be function evaluations. No digital computer now or in the future can perform 10^{24} function evaluations in a reasonable amount of time.

Very high dimensional problems occur in supercomputing and in the foundations of physics. For example, computational chemistry, computational design of pharmaceuticals, and computational metallurgy involve computation with huge numbers of particles. Since the specification of each particle in classical physics requires six dimensions and in quantum physics requires three more dimensions, this leads to very high dimensional problems. Economic modeling can involve a large number of variables. Path integrals, which are of great importance in physics, are infinite-dimensional, and therefore invite high-dimensional approximations.

This motivates our interest in breaking the exponential dependence of complexity on dimension. Since this is a complexity result, we cannot get around it by a clever algorithm; we must change the setting. We might break intractability by permitting randomization or by settling for an average case assurance. We consider these in turn.

Randomization

The first significant use of randomization was the Monte Carlo method (*q.v.*), introduced in the 1940s. As indicated above, multivariate integration is exponential in dimension if coin tossing is not permitted, even if the integrand is evaluated at optimal points. However, if the integrand is sampled at random points,

$$\text{comp}^{\text{wor-ran}} = \Theta(1/\varepsilon^2).$$

Hence, the symbol on the left-hand side indicates this is the complexity in the worst case randomized setting.

This is a truly remarkable result. If one evaluates at random rather than at optimal deterministic points, the complexity is independent of the number of variables d! Furthermore, this holds even if the class of integrands consists of functions that are only continuous (i.e. $r = 0$). For this class, $\text{comp}^{\text{wor-det}}(\varepsilon) = \infty$.

Thus, randomization can be very powerful for continuous problems, just as for discrete problems (*see* COMPUTATIONAL COMPLEXITY). Not all intractable problems can be

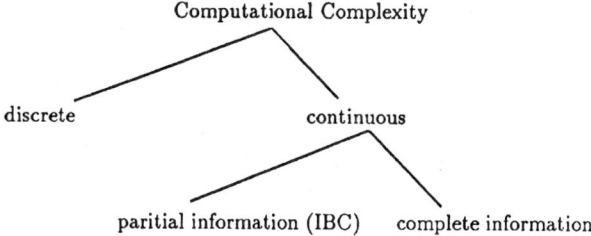

FIG. 2. Structure of computational complexity.

broken by using randomization. It is an open question to characterize the class of problems for which intractability is broken by randomization.

Average Case Another way we can try to break intractability is to settle for an average case assurance. That is, we consider error and cost averaged over a set of inputs.

Recall that for multivariate integration

$$\text{comp}^{\text{wor--det}}(\varepsilon) = \Theta((1/\varepsilon)^{d/r}).$$

A question that has been open for 20 years until settled by Wozniakowski in 1991 is the complexity of integration in the average case deterministic setting. Let the class of inputs be continuous functions with a Wiener measure. (A Wiener measure is a Gaussian measure, which is a generalization of a Gaussian distribution.) Let the domain of integration be the unit cube in d dimensions. Wozniakowski showed that

$$\text{comp}^{\text{avg--det}}(\varepsilon) = \Theta((1/\varepsilon) \ [\log (1/\varepsilon)^{\frac{d-1}{2}}])$$

Thus, the complexity depends only very weakly on dimension.

It is an open question to characterize the class of problems for which intractability is broken by the average case setting.

Computational Complexity for Continuous Problems with Complete Information We briefly discuss the complexity theory introduced by Blum, Shub, and Smale (1989). They also consider continuous problems, but those whose inputs are characterized by a finite number of parameters. Thus, they can assume that information is complete and exact. They adopt the real number model. One of their results is that the problem of determining whether a system of n real number polynomials of degree at most four has a real zero is NP-complete.

Fig. 2 schematizes the relation between IBC and other branches of computational complexity.

References

1988. Traub, J. F., Wasilkowski, G. W., and Wozniakowski, H. *Information Based-Complexity*. New York: Academic Press.
1989. Blum, L., Shub, M., and Smale, S. "On a Theory of Computation and Complexity Over the Real Numbers: NP-Completeness, Recursive Functions and Universal Machines." *Bulletin AMS* **21**, 1–46.
1991. Traub, J. F. and Wozniakowski, H. *Theory and Applications of Information-Based Complexity*. Lectures in Complex Systems, Santa Fe Institute Studies in the Sciences of Complexity, Lect. Vol. III (L. Nadel and D. Stern, Eds.). Reading, MA: Addison-Wesley.
1991. Werschulz, A. G. *The Computational Complexity of Differential and Integral Equations*. Oxford: Oxford University Press.
1991. Wozniakowski, H. "Average Case Complexity of Multivariate Integration." *Bulletin AMS* **24**, 185–194.

JOSEPH F. TRAUB

INFORMATION HIDING

For articles on related subjects *see* ABSTRACT DATA TYPE; ENCAPSULATION; MODULAR PROGRAMMING; OBJECT-ORIENTED PROGRAMMING; and TRANSPARENCY.

Three major problems in developing complex software systems are:

- Decomposing the task of writing software into work assignments for programmers.
- Preparing for and accommodating change.
- Managing complexity.

Collections of programs whose implementations are work assignments for individual programmers or teams of programmers are often called *modules. Information hiding* is a principle used to divide software into such modules. The objectives are to produce software that accommodates change and to help manage complexity during both development and maintenance. To achieve these objectives, software designed using information hiding is structured into modules that are intended to be independently changeable and understandable.

The information-hiding principle states that information that is likely to change should be hidden (or encapsulated) in a single module (*see* ENCAPSULATION). The information to be hidden includes decisions such as data structures (*q.v.*), hardware characteristics, and behavioral requirements. Since modules are work assignments, a decision has been hidden successfully if it can be revised without requiring a change to other work assignments. Such a module is known as an information hiding module; the hidden information is often known as the *secret* of the module.

An example often used to illustrate the principle is a *stack* (*q.v.*). When designed as an information-hiding module, the stack's secret is the data structure used to represent its state. Two possibilities are (1) as an array and (2) as a linked list. If properly designed, the module that implements the stack conceals the decision, and changing the implementation from array to linked list should require no changes in any of the programs that use the stack.

A primary goal of the designer of an information hiding module is to provide services to the module's users without revealing the module's secret. Accordingly, the module provides an interface to the external environment, analogous to a black box that has a set of switches that the user may operate and a set of dials that the user may observe. The device can be used without knowing how its internals operate. Much as the owner of a wristwatch need not know how the watch's mechanism operates to read or set it, the user of the services of an information-hiding module need not know how those services are programmed to use them. In the stack example, the stack module need only provide to its users an interface that allows them to push items onto the stack, pop items from the stack, read the top item on the stack, and determine how many items are on the stack.

Because information-hiding modules have independently changeable implementations, their internal structures are independently understandable and verifiable. The internal structure of a module can be understood and verified without considering the implementation details of other modules. Limiting the information required to understand the implementation simplifies program verification (*q.v.*) and makes the software easier to understand and change. For the stack, the verifier must show that the implementation obeys the specification for the stack—e.g. that it obeys the characteristic behavior of a stack (i.e. that a push followed by a pop does not change the state of the stack).

Because modules are work assignments, the assumptions that the programmer of one module may make about another module form the interface between the two. Those assumptions may be embodied in a variety of mechanisms, such as procedures that a user may call, signals that the module may send, or macros that users may include in their own programs. Guidelines for designing such interfaces, and example specifications may be found in Britton *et al.*, 1981. For the stack, the module may offer to its users procedures or macros called PUSH, POP, TOP, and DEPTH.

The specification of a module's interface must include the complete set of assumptions that the module's users need to make about it. Such assumptions include both the syntax used to invoke the module's services and the semantics of those services. The semantics includes the externally visible effects on the module of invoking its services (including undesired events that may result), and specifications for the types of input and output data supplied to and by the module.

Although the use of information hiding may be seen in the design of many software systems since the advent of electronic digital computers, the earliest description of the principle was given in Parnas (1972). A more detailed explanation of its systematic use in the design of complex systems may be found in Clements *et al.* (1984).

Much of the current activity in developing software design methods relies on the use of the information-hiding principle. It is the basis for object-oriented programming design methods, wherein software is organized into *objects* that perform services for each other without being dependent on each other's implementations. Each object may be considered an implementation of an information-hiding module; many objects of the same type may be implementations of the same module. The principle is also the basis for organizing the data used by a program into abstract data types. The secret of the abstract data type is the representation of the data and the way that operations on the data are implemented. The stack may be considered to be an abstract data type whose representation is hidden and whose operations are PUSH, POP, TOP, and DEPTH.

A number of programming languages provide support for creating and using information-hiding modules and their interfaces. Prominent examples include *packages* in Ada (*q.v.*), *modules* in Modula-2 (*q.v.*), and *objects* in Smalltalk. In each case, the language separates the specification of the syntax of invocation of a module's operations from the specification of their implementation. Unfortunately, few languages provide any support for specifying the semantics of the module's services in other than comment form. The difficult task of creating those specifications and checking them for consistency and completeness is left to the developers and users of the software. No special language is needed to apply information hiding; early examples were done in Fortran.

Although organizing software using information hiding has the benefits of encouraging the developer to design software that is changeable and understandable one part at a time, there are also potential drawbacks to its use. Preserving the secret of a module requires that its services be available only through its interface. Progress through a computation may require the use of the services of many different modules. When procedures or subroutines are used as the only interface mechanism, considerable overhead may be incurred in switching among different modules. The solution generally suggested to this problem is to use inline procedures or macros rather than closed subroutines as the interface mechanism.

Where the number of modules in a system is large, it pays to introduce a hierarchical structure—for organizing them (Clements *et al.*, 1984). The relation defining the hierarchy is "part of"—i.e. lower-level modules are part of higher level modules, or, equivalently, higher-level modules are the union of their submodules (Parnas, 1984). The "part of" relation defines a design decomposition. Put another way, the information hidden by a higher-level module is distributed among lower-level modules. For example, a module whose secret is the representation of data structures could be decomposed into submodules, one of which has as its secret the representation of stacks. The hierarchy provides a roadmap that guides developers and maintainers when they make changes to the software.

Although an information-hiding decomposition makes clear what decisions are easy to change, it should not be considered a complete design description. Concerns such as the run-time operation of a system, the organization of a system into subsets, or the flow of data through a system are better addressed by examining other design structures.

Information hiding is another view of two other software design principles. It is one way to separate concerns, so that developers and maintainers may concentrate on one concern at a time, and it is a means for achieving abstraction, since an information-hiding module provides its users with an abstraction of the decision that it hides.

References

1972. Parnas, D. L. "On the Criteria To Be Used in Decomposing a System Into Modules," *Communications ACM*, **15**, *12* (December), 1053–1058.

1974. Parnas, D. L. "On A 'Buzzword': Hierarchical Structure," Proc. IFIPS Congress.

1981. Britton, K. H., Parker, R. A., and Parnas, D.L. "A Procedure for Designing Abstract Interfaces for Device Interface Modules," Proc. of 5th International Conference on Software Engineering, 195–204.

1984. Clements, P. C., Parnas, D. L., and Weiss, D. M. "The Modular Structure of Complex Systems," Proc. of 7th International Conference on Software Engineering, March, 408–417.

DAVID M. WEISS

INFORMATION PROCESSING

For articles on related subjects *see* ACCESS METHODS; ARTIFICIAL INTELLIGENCE; COGNITIVE SCIENCE; DATABASE MANAGEMENT SYSTEM; INFORMATION AND DATA; INFORMATION THEORY; INFORMATION RETRIEVAL; INFORMATION SYSTEMS; MANAGEMENT INFORMATION SYSTEMS; and SYMBOL MANIPULATION.

Information processing might, not inaccurately, be defined as "what computers do." In fact, the broadest professional organization concerned with computer science is named the International Federation for Information Processing (*q.v.*).

For information to be processed by a computer or by any other information processing system, it must somehow be represented or symbolized. Hence, information processing is essentially synonymous with symbol manipulation, but we will approach the topic in a somewhat more philosophical, less technical, vein than in the article SYMBOL MANIPULATION.

The phrase *information processing* is often used in preference to *computation* or *data processing*, to emphasize the generality of computers—the fact that they are in no way limited to manipulating just symbols that designate numbers, but can operate in any domain, numerical or non-numerical, where information is represented in symbolic form. The term *information*, in turn, carries allusions to Shannon-Wiener *information theory*, which emphasizes the role of symbol structures as designating one particular state of affairs out of some larger set of possible states. Thus, if we are dealing with the class of flowers, the symbol "rose" conveys the information that we are concerned with a particular subclass of that class.

Information has other aspects besides the selective aspect emphasized in the Shannon-Wiener theory. However, this selective aspect is closely connected with the way in which information is used by information processing systems such as computers. Information processing systems are capable of executing a *conditional branch* or transfer operation. The conditional branch operation detects which of several different states of affairs prevails (e.g. which of several symbol structures is stored in the working memory of the computer), and sends the subsequent computation along different paths, depending on which state is detected. Thus, on the basis of the selective information available to it, the information processing system behaves in a selective, or informed, fashion.

The use of selective information by conditional branch processes lies at the root of everything complex or clever that a computer can do. In the simplest case, the conditional branch detects when an iteration is done (e.g. when the adding of a column of figures has been completed), and transfers control to the next process. (It was with this use in mind that Babbage first invented the conditional branch.) In more complex situations, conditional branching processes enable information processing systems to engage in all kinds of intelligent problem-solving behaviors (whether the intelligence be artificial or natural).

Effective information processing often depends crucially on substituting a high degree of selectivity (i.e. a high degree of dependence on selective information) for a large amount of brute-force search through immense spaces of possible alternatives. Popular accounts of the computer often emphasize the impressive speed of its basic arithmetic processes and the vast number of computations it can perform in a short time. In actual fact, apart from the *number crunching* that is typical of scientific and engineering applications, the arithmetic speed of the computer is far less important than its capability for selectivity, using information interpreted by the conditional branch processes.

Empirical research on human chess-playing skill, for example, shows that masters do not explore more alternatives than ordinary players—and probably do not even usually look more moves ahead. Instead, their superior performance almost certainly rests on looking at the *right* things—i.e. using information effectively to explore selectively. Similarly, artificial intelligence applications of the computer, whether for chess playing or in other tasks, always require the use of information to behave selectively, rather than relying primarily on the speed of the machine to carry out extensive searches.

We can illustrate this trade-off between selectivity and speed in information processing by two examples: programs for retrieving information from large stores, and programs for solving problems.

Information Retrieval Whenever we have a large store of data—say, a set of customer records—it becomes expensive to search the entire store sequentially to find a particular piece of data. We would like, instead, to be able to go directly to the point where the relevant data is to be found and to extract it without a lengthy search. A memory that allows us to do this is often called *random access*. A better description for it is *addressable, direct access*, for there is nothing random about the way in which we approach it. The store is to be *addressable* so that each record in it can be designated, or pointed to, by a symbolized address (name). It is to have *direct access* so that the information processor can be switched to read the desired record directly, once its name is known, without requiring a search.

Now it is well known that to select a particular item from a set of n ordered items requires approximately $\log_2 n$

binary switching operations (*see* SEARCHING). Suppose we have a store of 64 records. Since $64 = 2^6$, we can use strings of 6 binary digits each (e.g. 100110) to provide distinct addresses for the 64 records. An appropriate switching device would have to perform six switching operations—one for each digit—to select a desired record. With such a system, the number of switching operations required to select a record increases only with the logarithm of the number of records—6 binary operations, as we have seen, for 64 records; 10 operations for 1,024 records; and 20 operations for more than a million records.

An unindexed book (or a non-alphabetized encyclopedia) frustrates human information processors because it provides no means to find a desired item of information without linear search. Thick books are proportionately more frustrating in this respect than thin books. A good index converts the book into an addressable, direct access store. The cost of retrieving an item can now be expected to increase only with the logarithm of the size of the book.

Problem Solving

To illustrate how information permits selectivity in solving problems, we will examine a trivially simple example.

How do we use an information processor to solve the algebraic equation

$$5X + 3 = 2X + 7$$

for X.

If we depended only on the processor's speed, we might try a simple *generate-and-test* method: Generate various values of X and substitute them in the equation; then test whether the two sides are equal. The futility of this approach is evident as soon as we ask, "Over what class of values shall we generate—integers, rational numbers, real numbers—and in what order?" Of course, a very fast computer might solve such problems in a reasonable time, if only problems involving small numbers were presented and possible solutions involving fractions with small numerators and denominators were generated first.

A second approach might be to write the equation as

$$5X + 3 - 2X - 7 = 0.$$

Then we could generate a possible solution and test to find if it gave a positive or negative value to the left side. If the values were positive, this information, communicated to the generator, could cause it to next generate a smaller possible solution or, if the values were negative, a larger solution. In this way, the feedback of information could guide the generator to the correct solution by a process of successive approximations. Computational algorithms that employ successive approximations use information in this general way to reduce the amount of search.

Of course, a far more effective way to solve the original equation is to observe that the solution is an expression of the form $X = K$, with no constant on the left side, no term in X on the right side, and X having unity as its coefficient. By subtracting 3 from both sides of the origi-

nal equation, then subtracting $2X$ from both sides, and then dividing the resulting equation through by 3, we obtain the final result, $X = 4/3$, without any search whatsoever. This was accomplished by comparing the given equation with the form of the desired solution, and taking specific actions to bring it into the desired form based on the specific differences noted. Thus, when the constant 3 is found on the left side, where no constant is wanted, it is removed by subtracting 3 from both sides.

At each step, specific information extracted from the problem expression is used to choose a specific action that will alter the expression in the desired way. Since all the required selectivity is provided by the information embedded in the given symbolic expression, no search is required to find the answer. The safe can be opened, so to speak, by reading off the correct combination, rather than by spinning the dials to try different settings. Simple as it is, this example is a prototype for the most sophisticated artificial intelligence systems, and contains in rudimentary form the information processes needed for carrying out *means-ends analysis*. (Means-ends analysis involves deleting one or more differences between an actual and a desired situation and then applying operators to reduce one or more of the remaining differences as described in the algebra example above.)

A basic reason, then, why we refer to computers as information processors is that they have not only to provide us with information—by performing a numerical computation, retrieving data from a store, or in some other way—but also to respond to new information, enabling them to substitute a high degree of selectivity for brute force search speed as a means of solving problems.

References

1972. Newell, Allen and Simon, Herbert A. *Human Problem Solving.* Englewood Cliffs, NJ: Prentice-Hall, Chap. 4. (This work discusses selective search, and describes a number of general search methods, including means-ends analysis and their properties.)

1972. Simon, Herbert A. and Siklóssy, Laurent (Eds.). *Representation and Meaning.* Englewood Cliffs, NJ: Prentice-Hall. (Further examples of sophisticated search in information processing systems that use information to guide search in sophisticated ways.)

1989. Posner, Michael I. (Ed.). *Foundations of Cognitive Science.* Cambridge, MA: The M.I.T. Press.

HERBERT A. SIMON

INFORMATION RETRIEVAL

For articles on related subjects *see* CD-ROM; CURRENT AWARENESS SYSTEM; DATABASE MANAGEMENT SYSTEM; DATA SECURITY; DATA STRUCTURES; INFORMATION AND DATA; INFORMATION SCIENCE; INFORMATION SYSTEMS; LIBRARY AUTOMATION; MANAGEMENT INFORMATION SYSTEM; MEDLARS / MEDLINE; NATURAL LANGUAGE PROCESSING; and SEARCHING.

Information retrieval (IR) is concerned with the structure, analysis, organization, storage, searching, and dissemination of information. An IR system is designed to make available a given stored collection of information items to a user population desiring to obtain access. The stored information is normally assumed to consist of bibliographic items such as the books in a library or documents of many kinds; by extension, an IR system may also be used to access collections of drawings, films, museum artifacts, patents, and so on. In each case, the IR system is designed to extract from the files those items that most nearly correspond to existing user needs as reflected in requests submitted by the user population.

IR has become increasingly important in recent years because of the large amount of information that is potentially available for access—the production of printed materials, for example, is thought to increase yearly at a rate of about 10%; because of the difficulties of assembling large stores of bibliographic records in easily accessible forms and locations; and because of the increasing technical problems that arise in the selective distribution of large volumes of materials to heterogeneous user populations.

Most operational retrieval services are implemented on-line using console terminal devices to introduce search queries and to obtain retrieval output. In that case, the information searches may take place *interactively* in such a way that information supplied by the users during the search operation is used to obtain improved search output. Furthermore, networks of information centers may be created by supplying suitable connections between individual centers, thereby affording the user population a chance to access the resources of the whole network.

The establishment of information nets raises complicated legal and social problems, connected in part with the propriety of unlimited duplication and transmission of information that may be subject to legal restrictions (as is the case for patented and copyrighted information), and in part with the preservation of information privacy, where this may be warranted.

Retrieval operations and techniques used in conjunction with library or text processing systems are also of interest in a variety of different information processing systems, including database management systems, selective information dissemination systems, and fact retrieval or question-answering systems.

Indexing and Content Analysis

In most operational retrieval situations, information analysis is carried out manually by using subject experts or trained indexers to assign content identifiers to information items and search requests. Such information identifiers are known variously as *keywords*, *index terms*, *subject indicators*, or *concepts*, and the search operation often consists in matching sets of keywords assigned to stored information items with keywords representing the search requests. The matching is followed by the retrieval of those items whose content indicators exhibit a sufficiently high degree of similarity to the query indicators.

A typical set of words, or word portions, indicative of the notion of "toxicity" is contained in Fig. 1. Such terms

toxic ... , poison ... , lethal dose, LD, side effect, drug allerg ... , drug reaction, drug sensiti ... , intoxicat ... , venom ... , side action, side reaction, adverse effect, adverse reaction, ill effect, idiosyncra ... , overdos ... , overtreat ... , intoleran ... , contraindicat ... , salicylism, goitrogen ... , nephrotoxic ... , neurotoxic ... , hypervitaminosis, untoward, undesirable, deleterious, irritat ... , irritan ... , harm ... , risk ... , danger ... , hazard ... .

FIG. 1. Terms denoting notion of toxicity that may be assigned during document and query analysis.

might then be assigned for purposes of content identification to documents and queries in the area of toxicity.

In "full-text" retrieval systems, the assignment of keywords and content identifiers is completely avoided by assuming that the words that occur in the document texts can serve adequately for content representation. In these cases, a given item is retrieved if its text contains a given combination of words suggested in the information request.

While the indexing practice is still largely manual, automatic indexing methods are becoming increasingly popular. The following types of operations are often used.

1. Expressions are chosen from document or query texts, consisting variously of words, word stems, noun phrases, prepositional phrases, or other content units, which exhibit certain specified properties.
2. Weights may be assigned to each expression on the basis of the frequency of occurrence of the given expression, or the position of the expression in the document, or the type of entity.
3. The expressions originally assigned may be replaced by new ones, or new "associated" expressions may be added to those originally available, based on information contained in stored dictionaries, or on statistical co-occurrence characteristics among the terms in a document collection, or on syntactical relations among words.
4. Additional relational indicators between terms may be supplied to express syntactical, or functional, or logical relationships among the entities available for content identification.

Such an automatic indexing process then produces for each stored item a set of *terms* representing information content. In operational systems, the automatic indexing practice is still largely restricted to the analysis of document *titles* only—the resulting search products being called "permuted" title indexes or "keyword in context" (KWIC) indexes. However, as larger text portions are made available in machine-readable form, content analysis will extend to abstracts, summaries, or full texts, with results equivalent to, or exceeding in effectiveness, those now obtainable in manual systems.

Instead of using ordinary index terms for the representation of document content, it is also possible to describe bibliographic items by using lists of bibliographic citations related to the particular item to be described. The citations may consist of the reference lists that normally appear at the end of a given technical article or book. Alternatively, the citations may comprise outside documents that themselves cite the particular item under consideration. A *citation index* can be used to identify the lists of outside documents that all refer to a given document. An example is shown in Fig. 2. The representation of document content through the use of citations is indirect: A document dealing with toxicity is described by citing other toxicity-related documents from the literature.

File Organization and Search Strategies

Several classes of file organizations are commonly used, the simplest of which is the *serial file*. Here, no subsets of the file are defined, no directories are provided affording access to any subsections of the file, and no particular file order is specified. A search is then performed by a sequential comparison of the query with the identifiers of all stored items. Such a serial file organization is most economical in storage space, since no overhead is incurred for the storage of directories or links between items. Furthermore, access is equally convenient with respect to all keyword classes such as document authors, dates of publication, or content indicators. Unfortunately, a sequential search operation is time consuming and is thus unusable if search output is expected rapidly.

An equally small storage overhead may be incurred in the *computed-access* or *scatter storage* files, where the stored information is grouped into sets of items mathematically related in some way. In this case, a computation is performed on the set of terms used for accessing, and the *hashed* result of the computation is transformed into one or more storage addresses corresponding to the locations where the requested information may be stored. The search time is very small for computed access files, and no directories may be needed in addition to the main file. However, it is difficult in practice to construct good hashing functions that produce few collisions between distinct items mapping into the same storage address (*see* SEARCHING).

Chained files are characterized by the fact that all items exhibiting a given common identifier are "chained" together by appropriate links, or pointers; a directory normally provides access to the first item in each chain, and the file is searched by following the pointers within the individual chains. Chained files provide faster access than do serial files, but considerable storage overhead may be incurred to store pointers and directories, and a problem arises when the chain lengths become excessive for certain terms.

The best known and most universally used file organization in information retrieval is the so-called *inverted file*, where a large inverted directory is used to store for each applicable keyword or content identifier the corresponding set of document or item identifications and locations. The file is thus partitioned into sets of items with common keywords, and a search in the document file is replaced by the directory search. To identify the documents indexed by term *A* as well as term *B*, it is sufficient

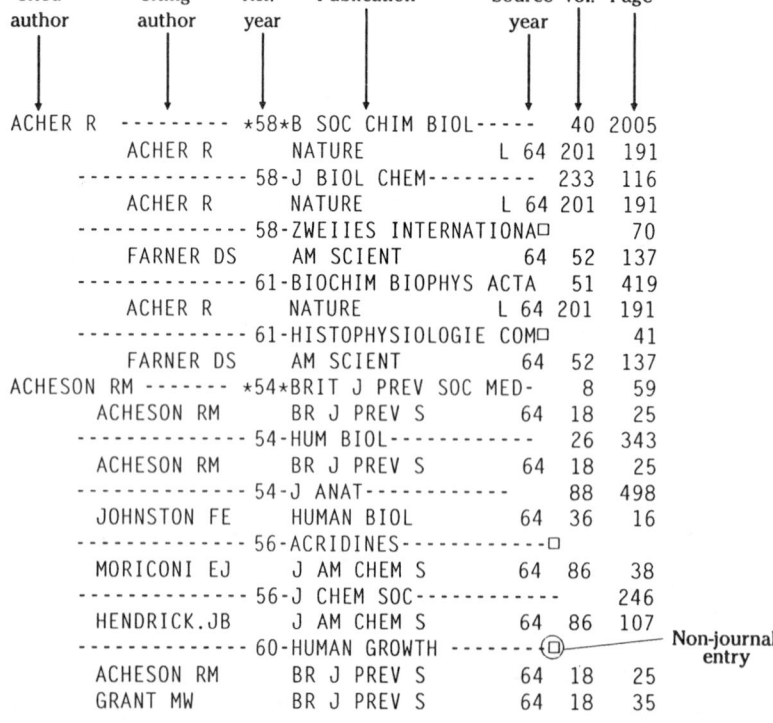

FIG. 2. Typical excerpt of science citation index.

to retrieve from the inverted directory the list of document identifications appearing under term *A* as well as term *B*. References contained on both lists represent the answers to the query. Since only small portions of the directory need to be accessed for any given query, acceptable search times are generally obtainable. For this reason, inverted files are currently used with almost all operational on-line retrieval systems.

Inverted file organizations are advantageous in a static environment where the set of terms usable for content identification is not subject to many changes, and where access to the complete term set pertaining to a given stored item is not normally required. In a dynamic situation where changes are made to the content indicators attached to queries and documents, a *clustered file* organization may be preferable. In a clustered file, items that exhibit similar sets of content identifiers are automatically grouped into common classes, or clusters, and a search is performed by looking only at those clusters that exhibit close similarity with the corresponding query identifiers. A clustered file produces fast search output, and the file-updating operations are relatively easy to implement.

Retrieval Operations In many conventional retrieval situations, a search request is constructed by choosing appropriate keywords and content terms and appropriately interconnecting them by boolean connections (*and, or, not*) to express the intent of the requestor. For example, a request covering "tissue culture studies of human breast cancer" may then be transformed into the statement shown in Fig. 3.

Searches may be conducted *off line*, in which case a sequential file search may be used to obtain responses within several days, or weeks, from the time of query submission; alternatively, an *on-line* search can be carried out directly from a terminal device using an inverted file organization. If an *on-line* console search is used, various optional displays may be available to help the user in obtaining acceptable search output. Thus, tutorial sequences may be included to inform the operator about the features of the system; displays of the available term vocabulary may be used during the generation of the query statement; finally, displays of previously retrieved information—i.e. titles or abstracts of items retrieved earlier—may help the user in constructing improved

query formulations. Such *feedback operations* are particularly helpful in obtaining more effective retrieval output. A typical on-line search protocol is given in Fig. 4.

Retrieval failures may be due to the analysis and indexing policy—i.e. the assignment of too many, or too few, or of a number of incorrect content indicators—or to the indexing language itself (i.e. to the type of vocabulary available for assignment to queries and stored information items); or to the search strategy used; or, finally, to problems arising during user-system interaction. The use of natural language indexing systems may ease some of the restrictions inherent in a controlled indexing language in that it creates many diverse avenues for obtaining access to the stored information. On the other hand, new problems may be introduced by ambiguous or nonstandard uses of the vocabulary. Many of the retrieval problems arising in standard systems from the lack of appropriate user-system interaction are eliminated in modern real-time search systems.

In addition, *networks of information systems* which are starting to be created may relieve the inadequacy of local data banks, provide access to a greater variety of services, and furnish economy and improved use of technical competence.

The question of *information privacy*, involving the right of individuals to obtain access to a given piece of information under specified conditions, is most complex, and no solution acceptable to all user classes is likely to emerge soon. On the other hand, it is relatively easy, at least conceptually, to provide *file security* by implementing any given set of privacy decisions. Elaborate systems of user authentication by means of special passwords and of monitoring devices designed to detect unauthorized access are now in use in most installations.

Retrieval Applications The most common type of retrieval situation is exemplified by a *reference retrieval* system performing "on demand" searches submitted by a given user population. Normally, only the bibliographic information is stored for each item, including authors' names, titles, journals or places of publication, dates, and applicable keywords and content identifiers. Often, only the keywords are usable for search purposes. Sometimes, the words of the document titles can also be searched. Less commonly, more extended text portions such as abstracts, summaries, or even full texts may be stored, in which case a text search (as opposed to a simple keyword search) becomes possible.

In any case, the responses provided by the system consist of references to the bibliographic items that match the user queries. In most conventional situations, the retrieved information is submitted to the users in no particular order of importance. An ordering in decreasing query-document similarity can, however, be obtained in the more advanced systems, which can then be used advantageously for search negotiation and feedback purposes. A sample search output in decreasing query-document similarity order is shown in Fig. 5.

In a standard reference retrieval system, a search is conducted only when a user actually submits a search request. However, systems also exist which permanently

$$\left\{ \begin{array}{c} \text{Breast neoplasm} \\ or \\ \text{Carcinoma, ductal} \end{array} \right\} \quad and \quad \left\{ \begin{array}{c} \text{Human} \\ or\ not \\ \text{(any term} \\ \text{indicating} \\ \text{animal or} \\ \text{disease)} \end{array} \right\}$$

$$and \quad \left\{ \begin{array}{c} \text{Tissue culture} \\ or \\ \text{Culture media} \\ or \\ \text{Chick embryo} \end{array} \right\} \quad and \quad \text{English}$$

FIG. 3. Typical boolean query formulation.

```
•••••USER::
FIND INFORMATION RETRIEVAL

++++CONIT:
YOUR SEARCH HAS BEEN NAMED S1 WHICH CONIT WILL GET BY DOING: COMBINE S1A AND S1B WHERE
      S1A = FIND INFORM:
      S1B = FIND RETRIEV:
RESPONSE NOT YET RECEIVED FROM RETRIEVAL SYSTEM.
SHOULD CONIT WAIT FOR A RESPONSE ANY LONGER? (ANSWER YES OR NO)
•••••USER::
YES
SEARCH S1A (FIND INFORM:) FOUND 15867 DOCUMENTS.
      NOTE THAT CONIT ORDINARILY SEARCHES EACH WORD IN YOUR SEARCH
SEPARATELY AS INDICATED BY THE COMBINE COMMAND FOR THE SEPARATE
SUB-SEARCHES.
      NOTE ALSO THAT CONIT ORDINARILY SEARCHES FOR ALL TERMS BEGINNING
WITH YOUR SEARCH WORDS AS INDICATED BY THE TRUNCATION SYMBOL (:).
USUALLY, THIS KIND OF SEARCHING GIVES THE BEST RESULTS.
FOR INFORMATION ON OTHER TYPES OF MORE EXACT SEARCHING, TYPE:
      E EXACT
RESPONSE NOT YET RECEIVED FROM RETRIEVAL SYSTEM.
SHOULD CONIT WAIT FOR A RESPONSE ANY LONGER? (ANSWER YES OR NO)
•••••USER::
YES
SEARCH S1B (FIND RETRIEV:) FOUND 1464 DOCUMENTS.
SEARCH S1 (COMBINE 1A AND 1B) FOUND 1093 DOCUMENTS.
TO SEE REFERENCES TO THE FIRST 5 DOCUMENTS TYPE:
      SHOW
•••••USER::
SHOW
-1-
ACCESSION NUMBER        A79036851
TITLE                   STATISTICAL FEATURES OF PHASE SCREENS FROM SCATTERING
                        DATA
AUTHORS                 ZARDECKI, A.; BALTES, H.P., ED.
ORGANIZATIONAL SOURCE   DEPT. DE PHYS., UNIV. LAVAL, QUEBEC, CANADA
SOURCE                  INVERSE SOURCE PROBLEMS IN OPTICS, ISBN
                        3-540-09021-5, SPRINGER-VERLAG, BERLIN, GERMANY,
                        PP.155-89, 1978, 240 REF.
TO SEE THE SAME INFORMATION ON THE NEXT 5 DOCUMENTS, TYPE:
      SHOW MORE (ABBREVIATED: SM)
TO SEE HOW TO GET OTHER INFORMATION ON YOUR SEARCH RESULTS, TYPE:
      E SHOW
```

FIG. 4.   On-line search protocol.

store (and update) user "interest profiles" (i.e. dummy queries that express the principal areas of interest for a given user population). Any new information items coming into the system are then periodically matched against the stored interest profiles, and the relevant output is supplied directly to each individual on a dependable, continuous schedule.

Some of the operational systems for such a *selective dissemination of information* (SDI) use responses submitted by the user population following receipt of a retrieved document to update automatically the stored user profiles. Thus, as users become more or less interested in some areas, the positive or negative responses of the recipients are used to add or upgrade (or, correspond-

ingly, to delete or downgrade) the respective terms from the profiles.

The rapid development of SDI systems is due in large part to the production and availability of a variety of databases containing titles, references, and sometimes index terms of the published information in various fields.

Data management, or *management information systems* normally provide general file processing capabilities together with user interface methods to simplify the manipulation and analysis of the stored data. In general, such systems include simple record-keeping provisions, together with exception reporting, and output-generating capabilities based on the use of statistical packages and plotting facilities.

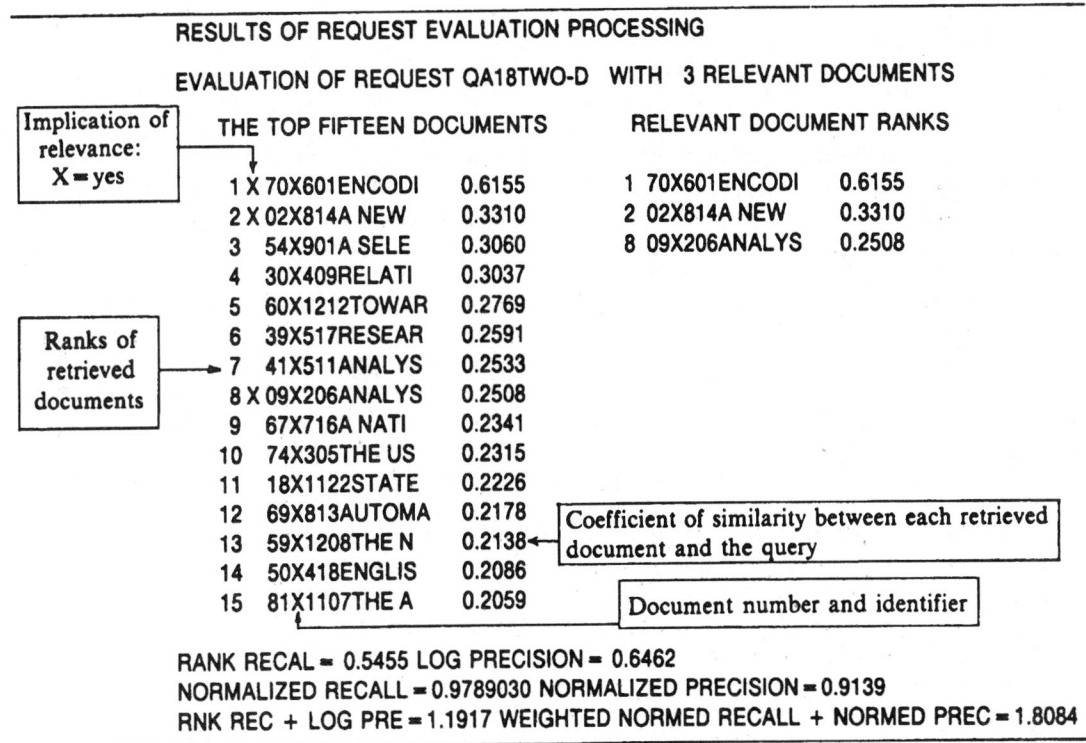

FIG. 5. Search output in query-document similarity order.

Some management information systems also include query capabilities, permitting the user to obtain answers to certain types of submitted queries. In that case, a search-and-retrieval component of the type previously described must be included.

A final class of language processing applications of interest in retrieval are the language-understanding, or *question-answering*, systems, wherein a direct answer is expected in response to a submitted query (instead of only a set of references that may in turn contain the answers). The depth and complexity of the document-and-query analysis must be much greater in question-answering than in standard reference retrieval, since a precise and detailed understanding of the queries is needed before the answers can be supplied.

Normally, question-answering systems include syntactic components based on a stored grammar and dictionary; a semantic interpreter that transforms the syntactically analyzed input into a formal query statement acceptable to the program; and, finally, a deductive component that can generate responses by comparing the formalized query statement with information included in the database.

Several experimental text-based question-answering systems have been designed, but for the moment their coverage is limited to a small discourse area and a restricted subset of the natural language. Until more is known about language understanding and semantics, the question-answering application is likely to remain a laboratory pursuit rather than a practical possibility.

References

1979. Lancaster, F. W. *Information Retrieval Systems—Characteristics, Testing and Evaluation* (2nd Ed.). New York: Wiley.
1979. Van Rijsbergen, C. J., *Information Retrieval* (2nd Ed.). London: Butterworths.
1983. Salton, G. and McGill, M. J. *Introduction to Modern Information Retrieval.* New York: McGraw-Hill.
1989. Salton, G. *Automatic Text Processing—The Transformation, Analysis, and Retrieval of Information by Computer.* Reading, MA: Addison-Wesley.

GERARD SALTON

INFORMATION SCIENCE

For articles on related subjects *see* COMPUTER SCIENCE; INFORMATION AND DATA; INFORMATION PROCESSING; and INFORMATION RETRIEVAL.

The term *information science* was coined to designate an interdisciplinary field initially concerned with the exponential growth of recorded scientific information. In 1950, the 81st U. S. Congress authorized the National Science Foundation to "foster an interchange of scientific information among scientists in the United States and foreign countries." Applied information science received a major impetus with the enactment of the National Defense Education Act of 1958, by the 89th Congress, which directed the National Science Foundation to establish a

Science Information Service through which the Foundation "shall (1) provide, or arrange for the provision of, indexing, abstracting, translating, and other services leading to a more effective dissemination of scientific information, and (2) undertake programs to develop new or improved methods, including mechanized systems, for making scientific information available."

In the 1960s, the thrust of information science was applied rather than theoretical, focusing primarily on the handling of bibliographic records and textual information. Two major foci of effort received considerable attention: the study of communication processes in the communities of science and industry; and the development of computer-aided techniques and systems for more efficient organization, storage, and dissemination of recorded scientific information. France coined for these two areas of activity the term *informatique*, popularized after its adoption by the Soviet bloc. (Since then, *informatics* has come to designate, in Western and Eastern Europe as well as in the Orient, the broadest domain of intellectual activity that the U.S. increasingly refers to as *computer science - q.v.*)

Subsequently, the preoccupation of applied information science with the control of recorded information and communication in the scientific sector has been broadened to encompass concern with information handling in other professions as well: management, education, medicine and health care, government, law, the military, and others. The initial premise of applied information science—that the cost effectiveness of scientific and engineering work can be raised by improving the communication among its practitioners—has been formulated into a broader assumption that the cost-effectiveness of the human information processes that characterize these professions (e.g. problem solving, decision making, learning) can be significantly improved through their formalization and gradual delegation to symbol processing machines.

From this assumption, present-day information science and its professions derive their current social mission and long-term objective: the design of information processing systems that augment the human mind and purposeful activities. The significance of the social mission of information science lies in its extending the historic human concern with the efficiency and effectiveness of physical processes into the domain of the symbolic processes of the human mind. So formulated and interpreted, information science subsumes or provides linkages among directions and aspects of other disciplines and professions, including those of applied computer science. Indeed, to the extent that both computer science and information science share these logical aspects of an engineering discipline (an interest in the design and use of information processing engines and systems), they are considered by many to be synonymous.

As reflected in its principal review publication (*Annual Review of Information Science and Technology*) and the programs of its professional societies (in the U.S., the American Society for Information Science), the dominant character of recent information science has been that of a social science and/or an engineering science (technol-

ogy). Some, however, have realized early that significant progress in the social mission of information science may depend on its ability to develop a natural science branch of the discipline to be devoted to basic research on the nature and properties of "information" as a fundamental phenomenon, and on primitive information processes. Such a realization motivated the establishment of academic departments of information science in colleges of science and engineering (in contrast to librarianship-affiliated departments in colleges of arts and humanities), the first of which opened in 1963 at the Georgia Institute of Technology, under sponsorship of the National Science Foundation. Exemplary of the perceived need for a theory of the field was the 1979 research agenda of the NSF Division of Information Science and Technology (later amalgamated into the Directorate of Information and Computer Sciences).

As a basic science, information science has only begun its search for content and structure. One early direction of this incipient effort in the U.S., the (former) USSR, and western Europe is that of *empirical semiotics*, the study of sign phenomena. (Signs are entities that signify some other thing, called the "object" of the sign, and can be interpreted by a sign interpreter.) This direction includes investigations of the static structure of signs—as represented by fields such as semantics, information theory, and complexity theory—and the study of dynamic sign processes (semiosis) that transfer or transport sign phenomena. In this setting, information science is of metadisciplinary import, due to the semiotic nature of the non-physical sciences (linguistics, psychology, sociology, history, and others) in which the essential phenomena studied are sign phenomena.

Another direction of current research in basic information science attempts to explicate the nature of information through *empirical* studies of various information-based phenomena and processes. This effort has already led to formulations of various laws, theories, and hypotheses. Nevertheless, there is agreement that as yet a scientific basis for a general science of information remains wanting.

References

1980. Slamecka, V. and Borko, H. (Eds.). *Planning and Organization of National Research Programs in Information Science.* New York: Pergamon Press.

1983. Machlup, F. and Mansfield, U. (Eds.). *The Study of Information: Interdisciplinary Messages.* New York: John Wiley & Sons.

1989. Heilprin, L. B. and Williams, M. E. "Foundations of Information Science Reexamined," in Williams, M. E. (Ed.). *Annual Review of Information Science and Technology,* 343–372. Amsterdam: Elsevier Science Publishers.

VLADIMIR SLAMECKA AND CHARLS PEARSON

INFORMATION SYSTEM

For articles on related subjects *see* ADMINISTRATIVE APPLICATIONS; BULLETIN BOARD; COMPUTER INTEGRATED MANUFACTURING; DATABASE MANAGEMENT SYSTEM; DATA PROCESSING;

DISTRIBUTED SYSTEMS; DISTRIBUTED SYSTEMS; ELECTRONIC MAIL; KNOWLEDGE REPRESENTATION; MANAGEMENT INFORMATION SYSTEM; MEDLARS/MEDLINE; and SYSTEMS ANALYST.

An *information system* is a collection of people, procedures, and equipment designed, built, operated, and maintained to collect, record, process, store, retrieve, and display information.

In practice, the term *information system* is used in a very general sense, both in technical literature and in general publications. For example, in *Computing Reviews*, information systems is a major category that has subcategories: models and principles, database management, information storage and retrieval, and information systems applications. *Computerworld* (1990) contains a list of the most effective users of information systems. Sometimes the term *information processing system* is used when the focus is on the "processing" of information rather than on its use. The term *data processing system* is frequently used synonymously with *information processing system*. A difference arises when an attempt is made to distinguish between data and information. One journal concentrating on the latter is *Information Systems*.

An information system may utilize various technologies; Sage (1968) describes the historical development of information systems in organizations from Babylonian times. Systems that contain digital computers as integral parts are sometimes called computer-based information systems (CBIS) to distinguish them from earlier (i.e. manual) systems.

Structure An information system itself may be viewed as shown in Fig. 1. Information systems accept (as input), store (in files or a database), and display (as output) strings of symbols that are grouped in various ways (digits, alphabetical characters, special symbols). Users of the information systems attribute some value or meaning to the string of symbols. In this article, the emphasis is on the characteristics of systems rather than on the meaning attached to the output.

One component is machines, or hardware, of which the most important is the CPU (central processing unit) and various input and output devices, such as terminals, personal computers, workstations, readers, printers, etc. In distributed systems, the hardware also includes communication equipment. Next is a set of system software (hard software), including operating systems, utility programs, database management systems, etc. The hardware

and software constitute the computer system or *computer platform*. In addition, there are programs specially prepared for the particular system, frequently known as *application software*, which are prepared in some high-level programming language or acquired from other sources. The data stored in and maintained by the system is called the *database* and is stored on auxiliary memory devices such as disks and tapes. In some systems, a distinction is made between data, applications software, and knowledge. In these systems, there may be a *knowledge base* separate from the "facts" database and a software package known as the *inference engine*. Even in a computer-based information system, the processing is usually supplemented by manual (non-computerized) procedures. Interaction between the system and its users is provided through an *organizational interface*.

Classification of Information Systems Information systems may be classified in different ways for different purposes. One method of classification is by the application area, such as manufacturing, payroll, voter registration, accounting, and airline reservation. There is no standard, generally accepted taxonomy for this type of classification. Another classification is by type of service rendered, where the following categories are typical:

1. *Computing service* systems that provide a general computing service to a number of users. Common examples are university computing centers, computing centers in research institutions, and commercial time-sharing services.

2. *Information storage and retrieval* systems designed to store data (or documents) and retrieve it in response to queries. Examples are the medical information retrieval system MEDLARS (*q.v.*), various services providing financial data, and services providing bulletin boards (*q.v.*).

3. *Command and control* systems built to monitor some given situation and provide a signal when predefined conditions occur. Examples are various military systems, systems built by NASA for space programs, and the Federal Aviation Administration system for air traffic control.

4. *Transaction processing* (*q.v.*) systems designed to process predefined transactions and produce predefined outputs, as well as maintain the necessary database. Examples are order-entry billing systems and airline reservation systems.

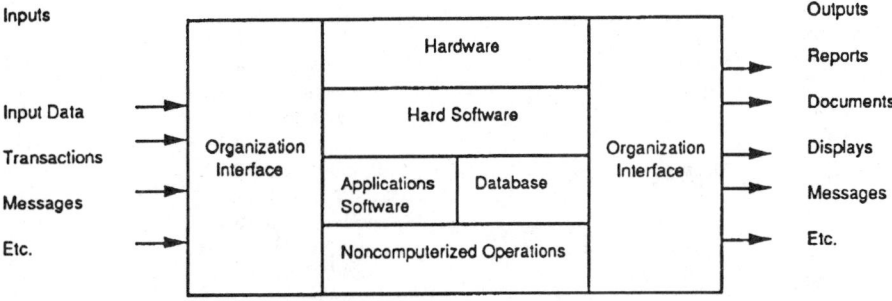

FIG. 1. Structure of an information system.

5. *Message switching* systems such as electronic mail (*q.v.*).
6. *Process control* systems designed to control physical processes by monitoring the conditions and signaling appropriate action to the machines. Common examples are systems to control chemical processes and oil refineries.

A summary of the inputs, database contents, and outputs for these six types of systems is given in Table 1.

Information systems may also be classified by the type and degree of interaction with the user and/or the environment in which the system is embedded.

Batch or sequential processing—Requests are grouped into batches on the basis of common processing requirements, and each batch is processed as a unit, often at a predetermined time. The individual user therefore gets results at the conclusion of all operations on the batch in which the request is included.

Store and forward—Each resource in the system has a queue, consisting of the jobs that require that resource. When a job is finished at that resource, it is sent to the queue at the next resource needed, and the next job in the queue is processed. The user gets results when all the operations on a job have been performed.

In-line or random processing—Jobs are selected for processing according to some priority scheme; once a job has been started, it is processed completely through to the final result. All the necessary files in the database are updated.

Interactive—The user communicates with the computing facility via terminals or personal computers, and requests are processed as they arrive. The user gets quick responses, which may be used to prepare the next input. In order to accomplish this, it is usually necessary to provide some method of time sharing (*q.v.*) unless the system is dedicated to a single user.

Real time, or on-line—When a request is received, it is acted on as soon as possible, so as to provide a response within a given time period.

Each of the types of systems has certain characteristics that affect its structure, the measures of performance that are appropriate, and the process of designing, building, and operating the system. Many systems are mixtures of the basic types; some examples are:

Business data processing systems—These are basically transaction processing systems, but usually are designed to serve users distributed over a geographical area; hence, they include communication and message-switching capabilities.

Management information systems (MIS)—These are a combination of information storage and retrieval systems and command and control systems. They usually draw a substantial part of

TABLE 1. Typical Inputs, Database Contents, and Outputs by Type of System

Type	Input	Database	Outputs
Computing service	Both programs and data supplied by users.	Created by individual users for their own purposes. System maintains minimal database for control and allocating charges.	Specified by users for their own purposes.
Information storage and retrieval	Determined by system designers on basis of what is relevant to inquiries to be answered.	Contains all input received.	Produced in answer to user inquiries.
Command and control	Obtained from sensors and monitors.	Built up from data received by inputs; contains system state.	Warning and action notices obtained by periodic processing of inputs and system state.
Transaction processing	Predefined transactions.	Contains all data necessary to process transactions and produce outputs.	Specified by system designer to accomplish system objectives.
Message switching	Messages.	Minimal. Contains data on status of nodes in network.	Messages sent to specified location.
Process control	Obtained from sensors and monitors.	Status of all processes under control of system.	Signals to control operator of physical devices.

their data from business data processing systems. These systems may include subsystems that are termed decision support systems (DSS) or executive information systems (EIS).

Computer-integrated manufacturing systems (CIMs)— These systems integrate business data processing, manufacturing control, and factory floor control systems.

Computer networks (q.v.) and distributed systems— These provide computing service and message switching over a geographical area. They may also provide transaction processing capability. The users of systems may be geographically distant from the physical hardware. Users initiate different types of requests or jobs to be processed. The system has a number of different types of resources, and may have more than one of each type. Any given request or job may need more than one type of resource, possibly given in some order. There are different ways of organizing the resources to accomplish the requests, and systems may therefore be classified by the type of system organization.

Common Features of Information Systems

The various classifications described above are useful in identifying common features of systems that may appear in more than one type. All information systems have certain characteristics in common:

1. Information systems are human-made; i.e. they have to be designed, constructed, operated, and maintained. This is a nontrivial task and has led to the need for methods of system development, operation, and maintenance often called system development methodologies. An introduction to the topic is given by Benjamin (1971); an evaluation of a number of methodologies is given by Blank and Krijger (1982). The process of system development is being formalized through the discipline of software engineering (*q.v.*). Information systems to support software engineering have been given the acronym CASE (computer-aided software engineering - *q.v.*).

2. In the development and operation of information systems, both the software and the database are important.

3. Because of the large cost involved in developing information systems, there is an economic need for systems to share hardware, files, and software.

4. The systems tend to be large and costly to develop, operate, and maintain. This arises because of economies of scale involved in larger hardware and in economies of scale involved in operation and maintenance of systems.

5. The systems involve human-machine communication at various levels, and problems of design and operation include both problems of communication among individuals, of communica-

tions with the machine, and of the communication among the various units of the machine. Therefore, documentation is an important aspect.

6. The uses of the systems and the technology on which the systems are developed are continuously changing, as are the organizations using them; consequently, the systems themselves are seldom if ever static.

Information systems are expensive to develop and operate; consequently, analyses to determine whether they are serving the desired needs of users, as well as the measurement of their performance, continue to receive considerable attention. Performance evaluation must be considered at a number of levels. At the top level, the value of the output of the system to the organization that supports it must be determined. Once these specific outputs have been justified, the performance of the physical system in achieving these outputs must be measured. This performance is a combination of the performance of programs, software, and the hardware equipment itself. The process of developing user requirements and designing systems to achieve them effectively is known as *systems analysis and design*.

References

1968. Sage, S. M. "Information Systems: A Brief Look into History," *Datamation*, 63–69 (November).

1971. Benjamin, R. I. *Control of the Information System Development Cycle.* New York: John Wiley & Sons.

1982. Blank, J. and Krijger, M. (Eds.). "Evaluation of Methods and Techniques for the Analysis, Design and Implementation of Information Systems," Dutch Computer Society (NGI), Academic Service.

1990. *Computerworld.* "The Premier 100 Most Effective Uses of Information Systems," 8 October, Section 2.

DANIEL TEICHROEW

INFORMATION SYSTEMS METHODOLOGY

For articles on related subjects *see* DATABASE MANAGEMENT SYSTEM; INFORMATION SYSTEM; MANAGEMENT INFORMATION SYSTEM; and SOFTWARE ENGINEERING.

Information System   The term *information system* is used in many branches of computer science, with significantly different meanings. In the world of commercial data processing, an information system is a system, typically but not necessarily computerized, that provides information to persons working in an enterprise. Such persons may be managers on various levels whose information needs are varied and unpredefinable in specific terms. At the other end of the spectrum, a user of an information system may require the same kind of information with intense regularity several times per minute. An example of such a user is an information operator in a telephone company.

An information system may be wholly computerized such that it performs a set of predefined operations on a regular basis. Examples of such information systems include a payroll system and an invoicing system. Alternatively, an information system may be assisting users by keeping track of a large mass of data and presenting it in different forms at different times on request. Examples of such systems are those for seat reservations at theaters and on airlines.

Information Systems and Software Software is a necessary part of any computerized information system. However, many argue about the significance of its role. The view that designing computer programs is the major task in information systems design is slowly losing acceptance. On the other hand, for many people, the term "software" and the term "system" are treated as essentially synonymous.

In this article, a broader view of the concept of information system is adopted. An information system comprises the hardware, communications networks, systems software, applications software, and human procedures required to provide the information necessary to support the business activities in a given business area.

Information Systems Life Cycle In common with other complex artifacts, an information system goes through a life cycle. While the life cycle view is widely accepted, there are varying opinions about the breakdown of this life cycle into stages (or phases).

One example of an information system life cycle breakdown has been given by an international task group of IFIP Working Group 8.1 (Design and Evaluation of Information Systems). Their life cycle has the following 12 stages.

1. Strategic study.
2. Information systems planning.
3. Business analysis.
4. System design.
5. Construction design.
6. Construction and workbench test.
7. Installation.
8. Test of installed system.
9. Operation.
10. Evolution.
11. Phase out.
12. Post mortem.

It should be noted that terms such as "development" and "implementation" are not used in this breakdown. Development covers roughly the stages from 3 to 6. Implementation covers either the stages 5 and 6 or else 7 and 8, depending on the use of the term.

A *strategic study* is the preliminary stage in which it is determined whether new information systems are needed at this time and, if so, how to proceed. *Information systems planning* is a stage that covers a large business area (possibly the whole enterprise) and includes a broad analysis of information requirements. On the basis of this stage, it is possible to subdivide the business area for more detailed analysis.

The *business analysis* stage is the one in which the business is analyzed in detail to determine which business activities are performed and the detailed information requirements of each. Business analysis is more concerned with the business than with considerations of computer hardware and software.

The differences separating *system design* and *construction design* are as follows. System design covers the specification of the external features of the system (the users' view). It is independent of any considerations attributable to the construction tools (DBMS, dictionary system, programming language) that are to be used to build the system. In some situations, construction tools may not be selected until the system design is completed. Construction design, on the other hand, is concerned with the system internals (which the users do not see). Furthermore, construction design depends heavily on the construction tools to be used.

The term *construction* is used in preference to programming because, with recent advances in technology, programming is only one of a number of alternative ways of constructing the computerized part of an information system. It is already commercially viable for a system to be constructed automatically from the system design specifications.

The *evolution* stage is being recognized as of increasing importance, and various distinct approaches exist for changing a system after it has been in the operational stage for some time. Typical distinct approaches are referred to as restructuring, re-engineering, and reverse engineering.

Information Systems Methodology Just as there are many different views of the *information systems life cycle*, there are also many different views on how one should progress through the life cycle towards an operational information system. Many approaches have been the subject of considerable formalization (usually not in the mathematical sense). The term *methodology* is used to refer to such an approach. It is noted that this term is etymologically incorrect, since "methodology," strictly speaking, means "a study of methods." For this reason, some approaches carry the name "method," but the majority prefer "methodology."

Most methodologies cover only a few stages in the information systems life cycle. The stages in the above information systems life cycle that have received the most attention from methodology designers are the following:

1. Business analysis.
2. System design.
3. Construction design.

However, the information systems planning stage and the evolution stage are also supported in some methodologies.

Each information system methodology uses a number of what are here called techniques. Examples of techniques are data flow diagramming and data structure diagramming. It should be noted that the term "methodology" is occasionally applied to a single technique.

Many methodologies are referred to as *system development methodologies*. This usually indicates that the methodology covers the construction design stage and an activity preceding that which is often labelled "requirements definition." This view of the life cycle either combines or fails to differentiate between the business analysis stage and the system design stage.

Information systems methodologies have their origins is different aspects of data processing technology. Some methodologies spring from a programming language background and emphasize the processing that needs to do be carried out by the computerized information system. Others have evolved from the use and misuse of database management systems and focus more heavily on the data used in the business area and on a database that is central to the design of the system. More recently, there have been claims that the events that can happen in the business area and the events that happen in the computerized system are critical to a successful methodology.

These various views are now converging and it is increasingly recognized that a good methodology should be able to support the three perspectives of data, process, and event.

Reference

1991. Olle, T. W., Hagelstein, J., Macdonald, I. G., Rolland, C., Sol, H. G., van Assche F. J. M., Verrijin-Stuart, A. A., *Information Systems Methodologies: A Framework for Understanding* (2nd ed.) Reading, MA: Addison-Wesley.

T. WILLIAM OLLE

INFORMATION THEORY

For article on related subjects *see* BANDWIDTH; ERROR-CORRECTING CODE; and SHANNON, CLAUDE E.

Information theory entered the world of engineering, science, and mathematics through the paper, *A Mathematical Theory of Communication*, published by Claude Elwood Shannon in the Bell System Technical Journal in 1948, and, together with material by Warren Weaver, republished in a book of the same name by the University of Illinois Press in 1949. The book is still in print and gives an excellent presentation of Shannon's revolutionary ideas.

According to Shannon, communication resolves uncertainty. If we toss an honest coin, communicating the outcome takes one bit (binary digit) of information: a *heads* or *tails*, a *yes* or *no*, a *1* or a *0*. But with a biased coin for which *heads* comes up more often than tails, the sequence of *heads* and *tails* is *redundant* and can be encoded in less than one bit per toss.

A message source may produce text, speech, or other messages. Shannon models a message source as *stochas-

tic* or *probabilistic* in nature. He defines a quantity called *entropy*, which is a measure of the unpredictability of messages from the source. Entropy can be expressed in terms of bits per symbol, bits per message, or bits per second. He gives formulas for entropy in terms of joint probabilities.

Shannon deals with continuous signals through use of the *sampling theorem*. A signal of bandwidth B can be *exactly* and *recoverably* represented by $2B$ numbers per second, each giving an instantaneous amplitude of the signal. To avoid an infinite entropy for completely undistorted continuous signals (audio waveforms or TV signals, for example), Shannon uses a *fidelity criterion*.

Information from a *message source* is transmitted over a *communication channel*. For actual channels, there is always some noise or uncertainty, some random difference between what goes into and what comes out of the channel. Despite errors or noisiness in transmission, communication channels have a *channel capacity* measured in bits per character or bits per second. Shannon gives formulas for the capacities of various channels in terms of either probabilities of errors in transmitting characters, or in terms of signal power, noise, and bandwidth. The historic Shannon formula for the channel capacity C of a channel of bandwidth B with a signal power P and added gaussian noise power N is

$$C = B \, \log_2 (1 + P/N) \text{ bits per second}$$

Shannon's crucial theorem is that if the entropy of a message source is less than the channel capacity of a noisy channel, messages from the source can be transmitted over the channel with less than any assignable error rate through the use of *error correcting codes*.

The equation for channel capacity can be used to find the absolute minimum power needed to send one bit of information. The noise power N is considered to be the unavoidable thermal noise power kTB associated with a source of temperature T degrees Kelvin (degrees above absolute zero); k is Boltzmann's constant; and the bandwidth B is made very large. Then the minimum energy needed for transmission is $kT/\ln2 = .95 \times 10^{-23} T$ joules per bit. The superbly engineered microwave links from spacecraft such as Voyager and Galileo come very close to this.

References

1949. Shannon, C. and Weaver, W. *A Mathematical Theory of Communication*. Urbana, Illinois: U. of Illinois Press.

1977. McEliece, R. J. *The Theory of Information and Coding*. Reading , MA: Addison-Wesley.

JOHN R. PIERCE

INHERITANCE. *See* OBJECT-ORIENTED PROGRAMMING.

INPUT-OUTPUT CONTROL SYSTEM (IOCS)

For articles on related subjects *see* ACCESS METHODS; BIOS; CACHE MEMORY; CHANNEL; FILE; LOGICAL AND PHYSICAL UNITS; MEMORY: AUXILIARY; MULTIPROGRAMMING; and OPERATING SYSTEMS.

One of the earliest and most fundamental reasons for the initial development and subsequent growth of operating systems concerns the handling of input/output (I/O) operations. The transfer of responsibility for I/O operations from the programmer to the operating system was undertaken for several reasons. First, the construction of code for handling I/O is one of the more difficult aspects of programming a computer. By not requiring a programmer to know primitive I/O details, computing services have become accessible to a greater number of casual programmers. Second, as assemblers, compilers, sort packages, and other utilities became available, it was necessary that each of these utilities be provided with I/O services, and that user programs be prevented from overwriting areas where these utilities or their work spaces are stored.

A common set of I/O routines that is used by all system facilities and user programs, saves duplicated effort. Moreover, a simple, carefully debugged set of routines provides some measure of protection against destruction of important files. The problem of accidental destruction of stored data was further compounded in operating systems that permitted users to construct and maintain private files of programs and/or data. In such systems, the denial of direct I/O capabilities to the user became even more important.

A common set of I/O routines also facilitates interleaved execution of unrelated programs. When a program issues a request for I/O, the appropriate I/O routine is called. If the I/O operation cannot be completed immediately, further execution of this program can be suspended and control given instead to some other program that is ready to execute. This interleaved or multiprogrammed execution of programs makes more efficient use of the central processor without necessitating detailed planning of overlapped I/O operations by individual programmers.

For all of these reasons, the handling of I/O operations has become almost exclusively the province of the operating system, more specifically, the province of its *I/O control system* (IOCS).

Programmer Communication with the IOCS

Typically, a programmer will communicate with the IOCS by calling various modules as subroutines. The assembly language programmer will generally have available a number of predefined macros, which will be expanded into subroutine calls to IOCS modules, using predefined calling sequences. Similarly, I/O commands in high-level languages will generally be compiled into subroutine calls to appropriate IOCS modules. In more recent systems, these requests for I/O service take the form of *supervisor calls* (*q.v.*).

The Function of the IOCS   The global function of an IOCS is to perform I/O operations upon request of programmers. This function may be refined to include the following tasks:

1. Interpretation of I/O requests.
2. Execution of I/O requests, once interpreted.
3. Location of the data to be transferred and where it is to be transferred to.
4. Initialization of transfer parameters.

These four topics will be discussed in subsequent sections.

Interpretation of I/O Requests   Each of the various I/O requests that a user may make (e.g. READ, WRITE, INSERT, DELETE, REPLACE, REWIND, OPEN, CLOSE) must be decoded and the parameters checked. This process is accomplished by an I/O request interpreter. The interpreter will check such things as (1) the name of the operation, (2) the name of the logical unit involved, and (3) the parameters specified for the operation. Once checked, the interpreter will enter the parameters into the appropriate table and initiate execution of the I/O request.

The I/O request interpreter can initiate a variety of actions, depending on the particular I/O request. For ex-

TABLE 1.   Division of Logical and Physical IOCS Requests

Request	Logical IOCS	Physical IOCS
Get the next record.	Deblock the next record. If buffer empty, get next buffer. If no more buffers and file not ended, get the next series of file blocks.	Deliver next block from device.
Find a record in a randomly accessed file.	Request index tracks. Search index to find block of record. Request block of record. Find record and deliver to calling program.	Deliver index tracks. Deliver requested track.
Store a new record in a randomly accessed indexed file.	Add new record to proper block if there is space. Otherwise, write new record in a separate area. Update the index to reflect the new data values.	Write updated block. Write a new record. Fetch index blocks and write index blocks.

ample, a request to read a file that has not yet been opened might cause an error condition or simply cause the open request to be generated by the interpreter. Similarly, requests to write on a read-only device such as an optical disk can be trapped at this level.

Execution of I/O Requests Execution of I/O requests involves various tasks:

1. Maintenance of correspondences between logical and physical devices.
2. Generation of physical I/O commands based on requests.
3. Coordination of peripheral activities and maintenance of status information.

Following the usual distinction between logical and physical units, it is convenient to divide the portion of the IOCS that is directly concerned with I/O transfers into two parts—logical IOCS and physical IOCS. Logical IOCS will contain routines for managing data on logical units, while physical IOCS will perform analogous functions with respect to physical units. Thus, physical IOCS will contain routines for every physical I/O device attached to the computing system (actually, these routines may be shared among devices that are all of the same type, such as all disk drives). These routines will handle interrupts from the device and control the execution of I/O transfers without regard for the logical content, format, or organization of the data being transferred. Physical IOCS will also contain routines for handling errors and exceptional conditions received from the device. Extensive re-try schemes are often included to mask failures from higher levels of the system.

The logical IOCS contains routines that perform functions associated with the logical unit, as declared by the programmer (or as predefined by the system). Thus, the logical IOCS will contain routines to handle space allocation and freeing, blocking and deblocking, index mainte-

nance, control error handling and recovery, sense end-of-file and other exceptional conditions, etc., depending on the characteristics associated with a given logical unit. Clearly, logical IOCS will communicate with physical IOCS when transfer of data is necessary. Table 1 illustrates the division between logical and physical IOCS for several I/O requests.

Tables for Logical IOCS and Physical IOCS The information that is particular to a given I/O unit is usually organized into a table. The table (or more precisely, a pointer to it) is then passed to the particular IOCS routine as a parameter. Two types of tables may be distinguished: logical device tables and physical device tables.

Physical Device Tables

Each physical I/O unit (device) will have an associated table containing information such as the following:

1. The device type and an indication of the data paths that may be used to transfer data to or from the device.
2. Status information concerning whether the device is busy, which data path is being used if the device is indeed busy, and whether the device is reserved though perhaps not busy.
3. The I/O operation currently pending on this device.
4. If the device contains storage that can be allocated and freed (e.g. the device is a disk), an indication of which areas are available.
5. The address of the routine that can construct commands for initiation of I/O transfers for this device.
6. The address of the routine that handles interrupts from the device.
7. The address of the routine that processes errors from the device.
8. Pointers to logical device tables associated with

Device Status Table (DST) Entry

Unused	Driver name	Inst.	Entry count	Alternate channel	Primary channel
Head 1 position	Head 2 position	Exit count	Inst.	Device busy/ not busy

Explanation:
Driver name: Name of subroutine that issues physical I/O commands.
Inst: Current physical I/O instruction being executed by the driver.
Entry count: Counts the number of requests on this device.
Primary-Alternate channels: Naming of channels that can be used in conjunction with this device.
Head 1-2 positions: Status information on read/write head positioning.

FIG. 1. A portion of a physical device table. (Adapted from *SCOPE 3.1 Manual,* Control Data Corp.)

this physical device, with an indication of the currently active logical device.

9. Pointers to other physical device tables that share a data path with this physical device.

Fig. 1 gives an annotated version of a portion of a physical device table.

Logical Device Tables

The logical device table is used to keep track of information pertaining to an I/O operation on a logical device. Since several logical devices may share a single physical device (e.g. a disk), there may be several I/O operations outstanding on a given physical device. The current operation on the physical device is, of course, contained in the physical device table (see Fig. 1). The information concerning the various logical device I/O operations will reside in the logical device table. A logical device table will contain information as follows:

1. The symbolic name of the logical unit.
2. The logical device type and name of the file currently attached to this logical device.
3. The logical I/O request currently pending on this logical device.
4. A pointer to the buffer(s) associated with the logical device, with indications of each buffer's status.
5. The address of the routine used for transferring data to and from buffers.
6. The address of the routine that can process interrupts, errors, and exceptional conditions for this logical device.
7. An indication of which data areas on a shared device belong to this logical device (if appropriate).
8. A pointer to the physical device table for this logical device.

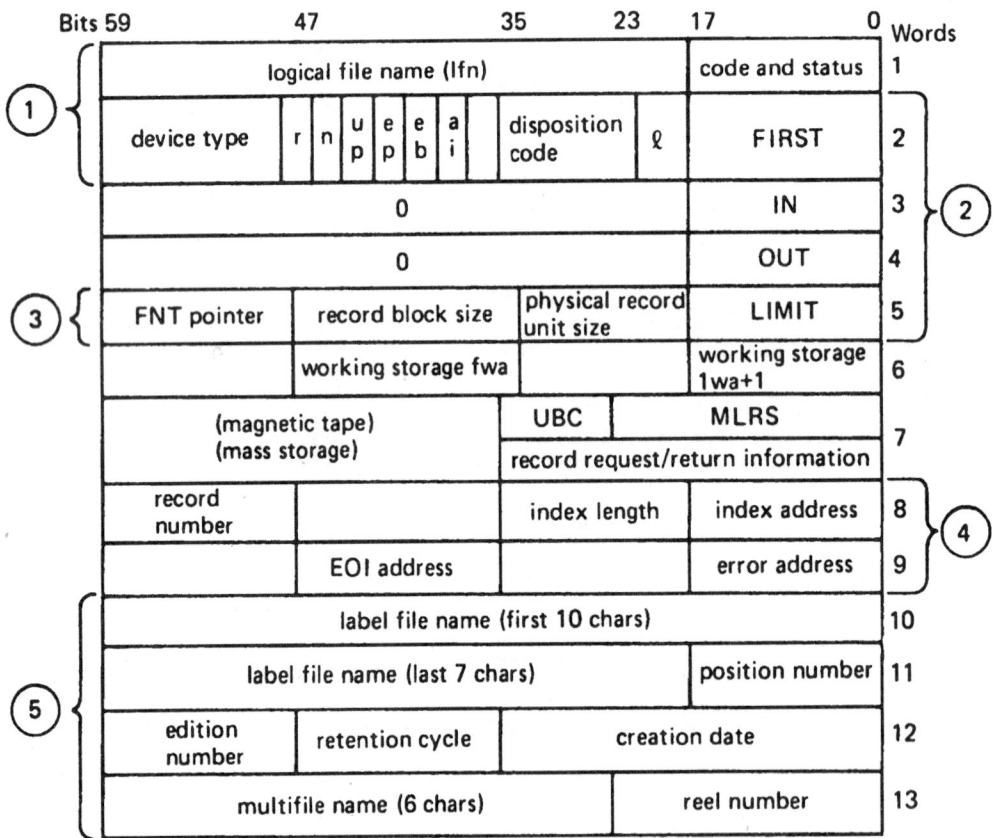

Explanation:
1. Name of the file and information concerning its corresponding physical device.
2. Buffer pointers for circular buffering.
3. Information concerning blocking factors for blocking/deblocking operations.
4. Indications of index locations for indexed sequential file organization.
5. Label information for verification and future mount requests.

FIG. 2. Annotated logical device table. (Adapted from *SCOPE 3.0 Manual 60189400*, Rev. I, Control Data Corp.)

9. Status information concerning the "current" address or position of the logical device, the "current" record number processed, the number of records in a buffer, etc.

Fig. 2 shows an annotated logical device table.

Both the logical device tables and the physical device tables contain pointers to routines that perform various functions. Typically, a programmer is not allowed to provide routines to replace those in the physical IOCS. To do so would impinge on the integrity of data stored on the physical device. It is common, however, to allow programmers to supply their own routines to perform:

1. Blocking, deblocking, and buffer management.
2. Processing of exceptional conditions such as *end-of-file* or other error conditions on the logical device.
3. Label verification of non-standard file labels (see below).

In either case, it is clear that substitution of different processing routines in place of the standard ones is simply a matter of changing pointers in the tables (and having the routines available). A programmer effects these changes by declaring that a substitution will be made and by supplying the routine. The IOCS then replaces the pointers in the logical IOCS table with pointers to these user-supplied routines.

As shown in Fig. 3, pointers are also used to maintain the correspondences between logical and physical devices. By using the pointers from logical to physical units, it is possible to discover the physical device associated with a given logical device. Moreover, a change in logical/physical device correspondence is easily accomplished by changing a pointer in the logical device table.

Coordination of Peripheral Activities and Maintenance of Positioning Information   The scheduling and coordination of peripheral activities is an especially important IOCS function. In a large computer system, there will often exist a variety of data paths from the central processors through the data channels to particular devices. Fig. 4 illustrates a typical situation.

Notice in Fig. 4 that a given device may be "attached" to more than one control unit and/or channel in order to form a path that can deliver data to or take data from main storage. This does not imply that data flows to or from the device over two paths simultaneously; only one path to or from a device is used at a given time. The multiple paths exist in order that devices may be kept busy as long as there exists at least one unused path to the device. The multiple paths also allow for continued operation should certain units in a data path break down temporarily. However, the IOCS must keep track of what data paths are currently in use and prevent new requests from using these paths. When a unit signals that a certain component of a path is no longer needed, the IOCS will search the pending requests to see if one can be initiated over the freed path.

In deciding on the next request to be serviced, it is convenient for physical IOCS to have information concerning the current position of read/write heads relative to the position of the data. This is particularly true with

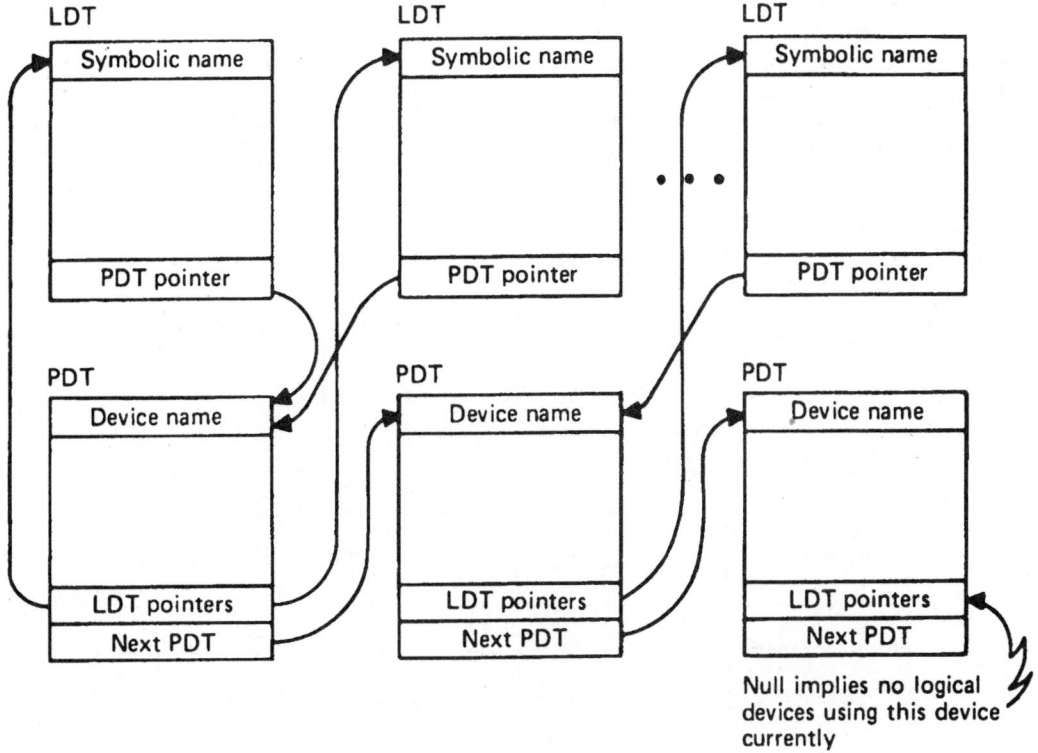

FIG. 3.   IOCS table links.

disks, which involve movable read/write heads. Requests for data near the current head position can be serviced more quickly than requests that require considerable head movement. Thus, in the scheduling of I/O operations, it is not unusual for physical IOCS to have as part of its status information an indication of current read/write head position. Using this information, it can attempt to optimize requests serviced per unit time (or some similar measure) by scheduling I/O operations based on "nearness" of data to the heads. Note also that the chain of physical device tables in Fig. 3 defines an ordering of physical devices that can be used for deciding which of a number of devices will be started first when more than one device could be started.

Location of the Data and Initialization of Transfer Parameters Before I/O requests can be interpreted and executed, the storage area that contains or will contain the data must be located and made accessible to the IOCS. Moreover, various parameters in the logical and physical device tables must be specified. The location and initialization functions are responsible for these tasks.

The location function involves routines for finding the physical devices on which the storage area to be processed resides. This storage area may or may not be directly accessible, depending on the particular computer system involved. If, for example, the programmer has attached a logical device to a tape drive on which a specified tape is to be mounted, then the IOCS must make sure that the tape is indeed mounted. This will typically involve a request to the computer system operator to mount the specified tape. It also usually involves a *label verification* routine. In order to check that the operator has indeed mounted the correct tape, a tape label in a prespecified format will usually exist on the first record of the tape. The label will contain information that identifies the tape, and the label verification routine will match the identification on the tape with the identification information given on the request for tape mount. Lack of a match

indicates an error, and an appropriate message will be issued.

If the storage area resides on a disk or other sharable device, a somewhat different kind of location function usually takes place. There will generally exist a directory (*q.v.*) or catalog of all files that have been created in the system, and a request to attach a logical device to one of these files will trigger a search of this catalog. The catalog will indicate on which disk pack(s) the storage area has been allocated. Each disk pack will typically have a table of contents, which is essentially a collection of file labels for files on this pack. By searching this table of contents, the file is located.

Initialization Once the data have been located, the initialization function can be executed. In order for I/O requests to be executed, various entries in the logical and physical device tables must be filled in. These parameters may be specified on a system control card or by the programmer during execution, but in certain cases they may reside with the data itself, usually as part of the file label. Thus, if it is appropriate, the initialization routines will move a copy of these parameters to the appropriate table entries.

When the file is no longer needed, a final set of IOCS routines will restore the file to a state in which it can be used at a later time. This will involve such things as marking the end of a tape, rewinding it, and informing the operator that it may be dismounted, or updating the table of contents for a file on a disk.

Recent Trends In recent years, the trend has been for I/O control systems to become even more sophisticated. This is necessary primarily because the rate at which central processing units can process data is increasing, while the rate at which I/O devices can access and transfer data (while also increasing) is not keeping pace. This implies that more sophisticated buffering strategies will have to be incorporated into the IOCS in order

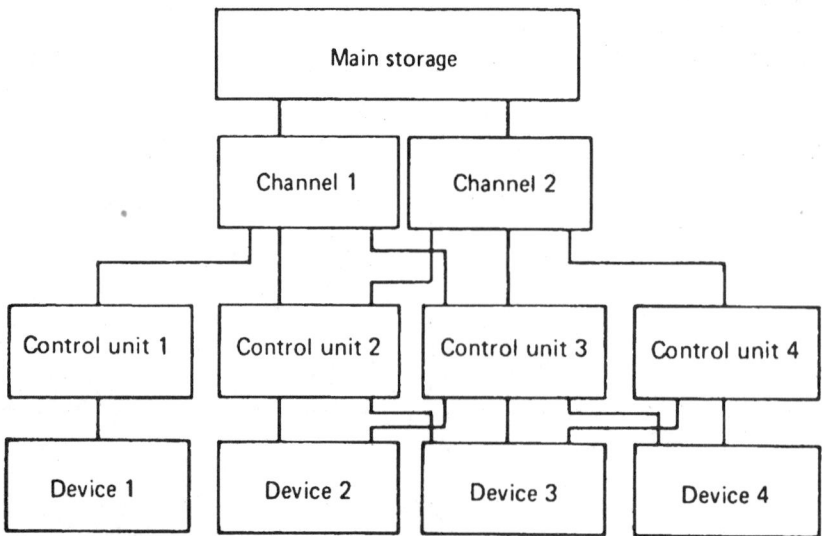

FIG. 4. Data paths to I/O devices.

that the data be ready when needed by the processor. One approach is to have the IOCS anticipate what data a program will need (based on an analysis of reference patterns) and transfer this data to a higher-speed storage device in order to reduce access time when the data is actually referenced. The extra processing power to do this reference analysis is often placed in an enhanced channel. The program within the enhanced channel can be regarded as a portion of the IOCS that has been moved to a special IOCS processor. The effect is to improve performance with minimal impact on the rest of the operating system and allow other functions such as reorganization of the data for increased efficiency to be performed, with the main processor not becoming involved.

Another recent trend is to duplicate data to enhance reliability. This technique, called *mirroring* or *shadowing*, allows systems to continue operation in spite of media, controller, or channel failure. Sophisticated systems also take advantage of the extra I/O path to enhance throughput. On-line reconstruction ("re-mirroring") of a new second copy when one of the original two is lost is also common.

References

1974. Madnick, S. E. and Donovan, J. J. *Operating Systems.* New York: McGraw-Hill, 337–373.
1974. Tsichritzis, D. C. and Bernstein, P. A. *Operating Systems.* New York: Academic Press, 123–145.

ROBERT W. TAYLOR

INPUT-OUTPUT INSTRUCTIONS

For articles on related subjects *see* CENTRAL PROCESSING UNIT; CHANNEL; DIRECT ACCESS; INPUT-OUTPUT CONTROL SYSTEM; INSTRUCTION SET; and MEMORY-MAPPED I/O.

Input-output (I/O) *instructions* cause transfer of data between peripheral devices and main memory, and enable the central processing unit (CPU) to control the peripheral devices connected to it.

In order to discuss such instructions, two rudimentary models of the logical structure of an I/O setup are presented. The models used here are purely logical; i.e. in any actual computer organization, some of the units to be mentioned may be physically non-existent, with their function being integrated into the other existing units. This will not change the description of the I/O procedures and operations that will be presented in this article.

In Fig. 1, we present the first of the two models, the channel model. The central processor and its memory are connected to *channels*. The number of possible channels is variable. Each has an identifying name (i.e. number). Each channel can accommodate a number of peripheral device controllers. Each controller will control one or more identical, or very similar, devices such as line printers of different speeds, disks, and drums.

In the area of I/O processing, the distinction between hardware and software is extremely vague. In certain cases, vendors of computing equipment include in their hardware manuals a description of I/O instructions, which in reality are parameters to subroutines that incorporate the actual hardware I/O instructions. The questions of the physical existence of channels and controllers must be kept in mind when trying to apply the following discussion to an actual computer.

Nomenclature The sequence of I/O operations needed to perform an actual data transfer will be called an *I/O procedure*. In an I/O procedure, all devices present in the I/O setup (i.e. the central processor, the channels, and the controllers) take part. They operate as independent processors, each performing its own type of operation. We distinguish between I/O *instructions* performed by central processing units, I/O *commands* performed by the channel, and I/O *orders* performed by the controllers. The degree of independency and concurrency of these operations will be dealt with later.

I/O Operations I/O operations are of two classes: control operations and data transfer operations. Control operations perform the following tasks:

1. Establish the *data path* between the main memory and the peripheral device.

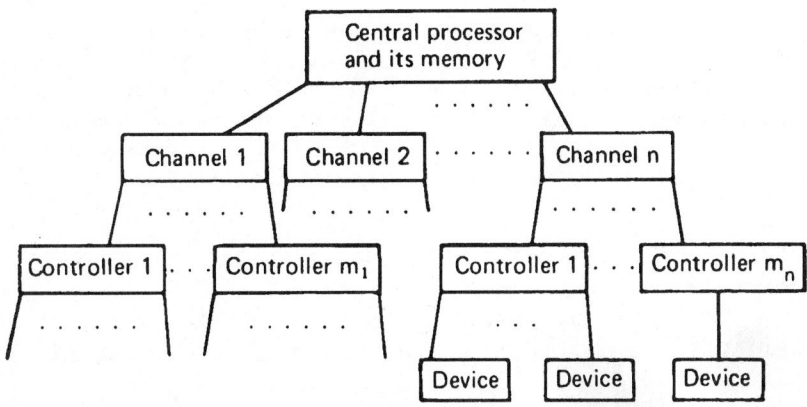

FIG. 1. The channel model.

2. Check to verify that the path is legally established and that all devices in the path are operational.

3. Diagnose the success or failure of all data transfer and control operations.

Data transfer operations initiate and terminate the actual data transfer through the preestablished path.

I/O Instructions These are regular machine instructions in one of the formats acceptable to the computer. They are decoded and performed by the central processor in the same manner as any other instruction, such as an arithmetic instruction. Examples of such instructions are: START I/O (e.g. on the IBM/3000 series), which initiates a channel operation; TEST I/O, which returns status information about the conditions on an I/O path; HALT I/O, etc. The number of basic I/O instructions is usually low, but there are many variants, which may have different meanings for different devices. These variants are usually defined by the address fields of the instruction or deferred to the channel command (see below).

While performing these instructions, the whole central processor is tied up, in the same way that any other type of instruction ties up the CPU.

Channel Commands Channel commands, sometimes referred to as *channel control words*, or *I/O descriptors*, are bit strings that contain control information for the channel. They are interpreted by the channel, which can therefore be viewed as an independent processor whose instructions are the channel commands, and which is operating in parallel to the central processor. From such a description of the channel, it is clear why the role of the channel can, in certain configurations, be performed by the central processing unit.

The channel commands can be contained either in arbitrary or fixed memory locations (as in most large-and medium-scale computers), or in special registers (as in most minicomputers and microcomputers). In each case, the channel operation is initiated by a central processor instruction that passes the location of the channel commands to the channel, or that notifies the channel to start under the assumption that the channel commands are already resident in a predefined, fixed memory location or in predefined registers.

The structure of channel commands is very similar to the structure of regular machine instructions. Fig. 2 contains a particular example of channel commands, taken from IBM. The meaning of the various fields is almost self-explanatory. The code (or "opcode") is the actual operation to be performed by the channel: READ, WRITE,

READ BACKWARD (in the case of magnetic tape), MOVE (the recording) HEADS (in the case of disks), etc.

The flags and options are usually short fields, sometimes as short as one bit, indicating specific demands and conditions. These may include indications of the course of action to be taken on normal or abnormal completion of the channel command, additional information needed to support some opcodes, enabling or disabling options like command and data chaining (see below), modes of automatic character conversion (if applicable), etc.

The starting address and count serve to identify the data on which the operation is to be performed. In certain cases, where the amount of information is limited by the nature of the device (i.e. the length of the line on a line printer), it is enough to indicate the beginning of the information.

Once the channel is started, it processes its own commands which cause the transfer of data to and from the peripheral device controllers. This data, in turn, can be interpreted by the controller, either as an actual data item or as an order to the peripheral device controller. The distinction between data and order can be done in different ways. The transferred item may have identifying information associated with it, or the sequence of arrival of the items will define them to be either orders or actual data.

I/O Orders Orders to controllers may be: START, STOP, TRANSFER status information, GET a data item, MOVE HEADS, REWIND, etc. The orders obviously must reflect the nature of the controlled device.

Each step in the sequence instruction-command-order causes, in addition to its normal operation, the creation and storage of status information. This information is usually of two types. One is the setting of the condition codes or status bits of the central processor itself, as expected after each CPU instruction. The other is the creation of a *channel status word*, sometimes also referred to as a *result descriptor*. Whereas the condition codes describe the state of the CPU, the channel status words describe the control information that is presented to the channel by the controller (together with data specifying the device itself), and the status of the channel itself.

The structure of the result descriptors varies widely among manufacturers. The reader is advised to consult the manual of any particular computer of interest.

The various status information items are used to determine the success, or failure, of the I/O process. In the case of failure, the program that initiated that I/O operation can take either corrective or merely diagnostic steps.

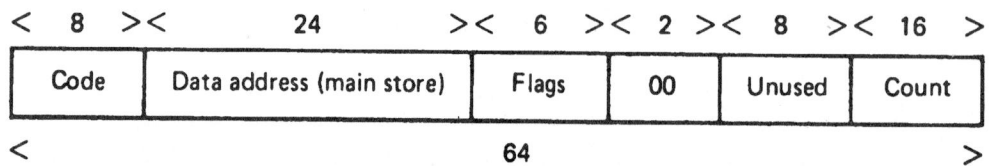

FIG. 2.   Channel commands for an IBM/3000 series computer. Field lengths are given in bits.

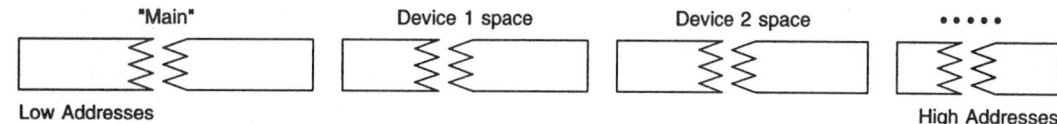

FIG. 3.   One-level memory-device data mapping.

A complete I/O procedure will therefore consist of the following steps.

1. Prepare a set of channel commands that will cause the proper set of orders for the device to be activated.
2. Issue instructions that will activate the channel. In this sequence of instructions, one should first check to see if the channel is available, i.e. not busy with previous operations or physically disabled.
3. After completion of the I/O operation, check for success and take necessary steps in case of failure.

Procedures of this type are sometimes called *I/O drivers*.

In an actual I/O process, it may be desirable to perform a whole program built from channel commands. The sequencing through the program can be driven by the end of each command, or by the exhaustion of the data to be transferred, without the command being actually finished. These two methods of sequencing channel commands are called *command chaining* and *data chaining*, respectively. Not all computers possess this capability. When present, this option is controlled by the flag and option fields of the channel command.

In actual computer systems, the channels are sometimes physically integrated into the CPU. It also happens more and more frequently that the controllers are integrated into the devices themselves. This by no means changes the description of the I/O procedures. The channel commands merely turn into computer instructions. The actual transfer of data, made by the channel, will be done by the central processor hardware. Whether this process will or will not tie up the computer is dependent on the sophistication of the hardware.

There exist computer configurations in which not only are the channels not integrated into the CPU, but (as in the CDC Cyber 170 series) are turned into full-fledged computers. In this case, one needs a whole layer of software in these computers to interpret the I/O request posted by the central processor. In other solutions to the question of channels the vendors supply factory microprogrammable channels which, on one hand, have the advantage of programmable computers, but on the other hand do not burden the user with software maintenance.

Memory-Mapped I/O   The second I/O model that we shall present is called *memory-mapped I/O (q.v.)*. We shall describe two variants and compare it to the channel model, limiting the comparison to the question of I/O instructions and I/O procedures.

In the purest form (Fig. 3), memory-mapped I/O maps all data that is present in the peripheral devices to a single memory space, a *one-level memory*. This is usually done dynamically, only for those items in peripheral memory that are of interest at the moment. Note that one can map also some "write only" devices as printers and plotters. Although it is not necessarily visible on the user level, such methodology is used, for example, in the IBM AS/400 machines. I/O procedures and instructions are therefore not visible at the user level, as they are subsumed below the level of the operating system (*q.v.*). Some types of peripheral memory (cached disks) have a memory interface built into them, and are therefore easy candidates for incorporation into single-memory systems.

In the more widely used memory-mapped I/O—implemented, for example, in the Motorola 68000 series or in the Digital VAX system—all the control part of the devices, such as control, command, and status registers are mapped onto memory locations (Fig. 4). Therefore, there are no I/O instructions per se—their function is performed by a combination of regular instructions such as moves and tests (*see* INSTRUCTION SET) and the values that are set into the dedicated memory locations for each device.

The memory locations for each device can be loosely divided into four categories: command, control, status, and data.

The command and control locations parallel the operation of the channel command. They provide the function to be performed and the variants of each function. As opposed to channel commands, there are no predefined

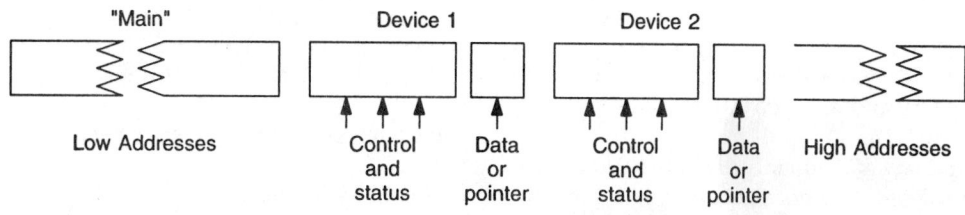

FIG. 4.   Memory mapped I/O device control, status and data pointer map.

sequences of command/control—these have to be issued one at a time in a sequence that is defined by the I/O driver, which is now composed entirely of central processor instructions.

The status locations are identical in function to the previously discussed channel status. The data locations are of two types—either the actual data or a pointer to data. This model of I/O relies on an underlying hardware support, commonly known as direct memory access (DMA - *q.v.*) controllers. These devices absorb the data transfer functions that are performed by the channel.

Note that these I/O models are not the only ones. For example, the Data General MV series possesses a number of dedicated I/O registers that serve a function similar to the dedicated memory locations (with the noted difference that they are not dedicated to a single device).

Finally, it is necessary to indicate that, no matter which of the former hardware alternatives and I/O models are present, the I/O process is basically an asynchronous one in which the channels or their variants are operating in parallel with the CPU. Thus, one needs a synchronization procedure by which the CPU and I/O operations are coordinated. This procedure involves either *interrupts* (*q.v.*) or *polling* (*q.v.*).

GIDEON FRIEDER

INSTITUTE FOR CERTIFICATION OF COMPUTER PROFESSIONALS (ICCP)

For articles on related subjects *see* ASSOCIATION FOR COMPUTING MACHINERY; DATA PROCESSING MANAGEMENT ASSOCIATION; and PERSONNEL IN THE COMPUTER FIELD.

The Institute for Certification of Computer Professionals (ICCP) is an organization of computing societies, established in 1973, for the purpose of sponsoring activity in the areas of testing and certification of knowledge and competence of computing personnel. It is intended to pool the resources and interests of individual societies so that ultimately the full attention of the industry may be focused on the vital tasks of developing and recognizing qualified personnel.

The purposes of the Institute are:

1. To foster, promote, develop, and conduct scientific inquiry and research into any of the several activities related to the development and recognition of knowledge and competence among personnel in the computer and information systems industry.
2. To foster, promote, develop, and conduct scientific inquiry and research into standards of good practice.
3. To formulate and administer testing and evaluation programs designed to determine the aptitude, level of knowledge, and competence of individuals engaging in or desiring to engage in

disciplines directly related to applied computer and information science.
4. To foster, promote, and develop internationally the purposes of the corporation, including, without limitation, (a) the establishment of reciprocal standards with, and reciprocal membership for and cooperation with, organizations having similar aims and purposes; (b) the establishment of international standards of good practice in the worldwide computer and information systems industry; and (c) the formulation and administration of reciprocal testing and evaluation programs.

How Established The ICCP was incorporated as a not-for-profit corporation in the State of Delaware on 13 August 1973. Its establishment was the outgrowth of several years of study by committees of the Data Processing Management Association (DPMA) and the Association for Computing Machinery (ACM) during which the concept of a "computer foundation" to foster testing and certification programs was formulated. An open invitation was extended to other societies to support an organizational period. The organizations that served on the Computer Foundation Organizing Committee and then became members of the Institute were:

Association for Computing Machinery
Association of Computer Programmers and Analysts
Association for Educational Data Systems (now International Society for Technology in Education)
Automation 1 Association (now the Association for Information Management)
Canadian Information Processing Society
Data Processing Management Association
IEEE Computer Society
Society of Certified Data Processors (now the Association of the Institute for Certification of Computer Professionals)
Society of Professional Data Processors

Subsequently, the Association of Computer Programmers and Analysts and the Society of Professional Data Processors disbanded, and the following organizations have become members:

Association for Systems Management
Association for Women in Computing
COMMON (a user's group for IBM computers)
Hong Kong Computer Society
Independent Computer Consultants Association
The Microcomputer Industry Association
Data Administrators Management Association
Independent Systems Consultants Association
Federation of NCR User Groups

Presidents of ICCP to date have been:

John K. Swearingen, CDP	1973–1975
Fred H. Harris	1976
G. Gary Casper, CDP, CSP	1977–1978

Merton R. Walker, CDP	1979–1980
Roland D. Spaniol, CDP, CSP	1981–1982
Robert P. Campbell, CDP	1983–1984
Thomas W. Briggs II, CCP, CDP, CSP	1985–1986
James R. Shackleford III, CCP, CDP, CSP	1987
Mike Maier, CDP, CSP	1988–1989
Anderson H. Vaughan, CDP, CSP	1990–1991
Michael R. Fitzpatrick, CDP	1992–

Organizational Structure The Institute is governed by a Board of Directors to which each member society designates two directors. Officers of the Institute are elected from the Board at its annual meeting and include a president, vice-president, secretary, and treasurer. The officers constitute an Executive Committee, which may act for the Board between its regularly scheduled meetings. Standing committees advise the Board and assist in the management of the Institute, while ad hoc committees are established from time to time to investigate, evaluate, and recommend action on potential programs.

As programs are authorized by the Institute, councils with appropriate technical and professional expertise are established to oversee them and to provide the competence necessary to ensure high standards. Councils have policy-making powers as well as responsibility for quality control, within the domain of their programs. Presently, there are four certification councils: General Certification, Information Systems Test Management, Technical Specialties Test Management, and Languages Test Management, which have jurisdiction over the testing and certification programs described in the next section.

Programs of the Institute The Institute's highest priority is the improvement of existing certification programs and the establishment of new examinations for various specialties. In 1974, the Institute acquired the testing and certification programs of the DPMA, including the Certificate in Data Processing (CDP) examination, which the DPMA began in 1962. Additional programs have subsequently been established to meet professional and industry needs.

The Institute has recently modified and updated its examinations to reflect more accurately the changing nature of the computer profession. The new examination structure for experienced professionals consists of three parts:

1. A mandatory core examination that tests general knowledge and expertise. Question topics range from management science and systems concepts to data architecture and statistics.
2. The choice of one of three specialty examinations that best reflects career expertise, and that determines the professional designation: Certified Computer Programmer (CCP), Certified Data Processor (CDP), or Certified Systems Professional (CSP).
3. A choice of one of eight additional specialty examinations (including those of the three specialty examinations of CCP, CDP, or CSP not chosen as the certification designation) that further tests specialized skills gained in the computer industry.

For example, to obtain designation as a Certified Data Processor, one would need to take the core examination, plus the specialty examination required for CDP, plus one additional specialty examination. All three examinations must be completed within 24 months or four testing sessions, whichever comes first, from initial test date.

The ICCP certification programs are directed to senior level personnel in the information processing industry. Any person may take any examination. However, they will not receive a certificate and be entitled to the use of the corresponding designation until the following experience requirement is met.

Experience A candidate must have at least 60 months of full-time (or part-time equivalent) direct experience in computer-based information systems. The 60 months need not be consecutive or in a single position. Acceptable forms of experience include that in data processing systems, programming, management, and teaching computer-based information systems. Systems and programming experience gained while employed by computer equipment manufacturers, service centers, management consulting firms, or educational institutions may be applied toward this requirement. Clerical, data entry, or experience gained in connection with formal classwork will not be considered acceptable.

Academic and Other Certification Alternatives Candidates having less than 60 months work experience may substitute post-secondary academic work for up to 24 months of experience on the following basis, provided official transcripts of academic work are submitted to ICCP:

- 24 months—Bachelor's degree or graduate degree in information systems or computer science.
- 24 months—Any candidate who holds the Certified Computer Programmer (CCP) certificate or passes the Associate Computer Professional (ACP) Examination.
- 18 months—Bachelor's or graduate degree in related area, including accounting, business, engineering, mathematics, sciences, or statistics.
- 12 months—Bachelor's or graduate degree in non-related areas.
- 12 months—Associate degree or diploma (2-year program) in information systems or computer science.

The maximum credit for academic alternatives toward the experience requirement shall not exceed 24 months.

Professional Qualifications Each candidate is required to obtain the signature of a responsible person who can verify both the candidate's work experience and professional qualifications through personal knowledge or access to the necessary information. An ICCP certificate holder is to make this verification whenever possible. The candidate's immediate supervisor may be accepted as an alternative when an ICCP certificate holder is not in a position to provide the required verification.

ICCP also provides the Associate Computer Professional (ACP) Examination, an examination program that measures qualifications of entry-level personnel. The ACP program is designed for students or recent graduates of computer programs within one-, two- and four-year colleges; graduates of technical computer institutions; and individuals who have been working in the computer field only a short period of time.

The American Council on Education (ACE) has evaluated and approved the awarding of college credit for successful candidates who pass ICCP examinations with a minimum 68% passing score. Successful candidates may earn up to 24 credit hours. Through 1991, the ICCP has certified 45,000 persons.

The ICCP historically tests on the second Saturday of May and the second Saturday of November. For further information contact ICCP Headquarters, 2200 E. Devon Ave., Suite 268, Des Plaines, IL 60018, call 708-299-4227, or fax 708-299-4280.

FRED H. HARRIS

INSTITUTE OF ELECTRICAL AND ELECTRONIC ENGINEERS—COMPUTER SOCIETY (IEEE-CS)

For an article on a related subject *see* AMERICAN FEDERATION OF INFORMATION PROCESSING SOCIETIES.

Purpose The IEEE Computer Society was formed to advance the theory and practice of computer and information processing technology. Its objectives are to promote cooperation and exchange of technical information among its members. To achieve this, the Society holds meetings for the presentation and discussion of technical papers, publishes technical journals, and through its chapters and technical committees studies and provides for the professional needs of its members. The scope of the Society encompasses all aspects of design, theory, and practice relating to digital and analog devices, computation, and information processing.

How Established The IEEE Computer Society was so-named in 1972, having originated in October 1951 as The Computer Group of IRE (Institute of Radio Engineers), which, on 1 January 1963, merged with the American Institute of Electrical Engineers and became the Institute of Electrical and Electronics Engineers (IEEE). The IEEE represents over 300,000 electrical and electronics engineers throughout the world.

With so many special interests among its members, it was natural for members who wished to concentrate in one area of electronics, or who wanted to exchange knowledge with those of similar interest, to create special interest groups. The Computer Society, with over 100,000 members, is one of these special interest groups. The IEEE-CS headquarters address is 1730 Massachusetts Ave. NW, Washington, DC 20036-1903.

Organizational Structure The IEEE Computer Society has a Governing Board consisting of a maximum of 24 voting members, including the President, two Vice-Presidents, the Junior Past-President, and 20 elected members of the Board. The Society membership annually elects the President and two Vice-Presidents. The President-elect appoints three additional Vice-Presidents, a Secretary, and a Treasurer for a one-year term coextensive with his or her term. The President, under direction of the Board, has general supervision of the affairs of the Society.

Technical Program Members of the IEEE Computer Society receive *Computer* magazine, "the voice of the computer systems design profession," which contains tutorial and survey articles, practical applications ideas for the computer professional, and various other pertinent departments. In addition, they have the choice of receiving the *Transactions on Computers,* which contains papers of archival quality on the theory, design, and practices related to digital and analog computation and information processing; the *Transactions on Software Engineering,* which contains archival research papers on all aspects of the specification, development, management, test, maintenance, and documentation of computer software; the *Transactions on Pattern Analysis and Machine Intelligence,* which contains archival materials on all aspects of pattern analysis and manipulation; or the *Journal of Solid State Circuits,* which covers devices and systems affecting circuit design.

The IEEE Computer Society sponsors three annual Computer Society Conferences and numerous specialized conferences.

The IEEE Computer Society's technical committees include Computer Architecture, Computer Communications, Computer Elements, Data Acquisition and Control, Design Automation, Data Base Engineering, Distributed Processing, Fault-Tolerant Computing, Oceanic Engineering and Technology, Machine Intelligence and Pattern Analysis, Mass Storage Systems, Math Foundations, Microprogramming, Mini/Micro Computers, Operating Systems, Optical Processing, Packaging, Security and Privacy, Simulation, Software Engineering, and Test Technology. Their aim is to promote technical excellence in specific areas by sponsoring seminars, symposia, and sessions at professional conferences.

Other activities of the IEEE Computer Society include Standards, and Education and Professional Development, which are concerned with curriculum and continuing education, and the Distinguished Visitors and Tutorial Programs, which arrange for leading computer professionals to speak to local chapters of the Society.

Chief officers of the IEEE-CS since its inception (9 October 1951) include the following persons.

Chairmen:
Morton M. Astrahan, 1951–1952

Jean H. Felker, 1953–1954
H. T. Larson, 1954–1955
Jerre D. Noe, 1955–1957
Werner Buchholz, 1957–1958
Willis H. Ware, 1958–1959
R. O. Endres, 1959–1960
A. A. Cohen, 1960–1962
W. L. Anderson, 1962–1964
K. W. Uncapher, 1964–1965
R. I. Tanaka, 1965–1966
Samuel Levine, 1966–1967
L. C. Hobbs, 1968–1970
E. J. McCluskey, 1970–1971

The Society's name changed to the IEEE Computer Society on 1 January 1971.

Presidents:
E. J. McCluskey, 1971
A. S. Hoagland, 1972–1973
S. S. Yau, 1974–1975
D. B. Simmons, 1976
M. G. Smith, 1977–1978
Tse-yun Feng, 1979–1980
Richard E. Merwin, 1981
Oscar N. Garcia, 1982–83
Martha Sloan, 1984–1985
Roy L. Russo, 1986–1987
Edward A. Parrish, Jr., 1988
Kenneth R. Anderson, 1989
Helen M. Wood, 1990
Duncan H. Lawrie, 1991
Bruce D. Shriver, 1992

ISAAC L. AUERBACH

INSTRUCTION.   See INPUT-OUTPUT INSTRUCTIONS; INSTRUCTION SET; and PRIVILEGED INSTRUCTION.

INSTRUCTION AND DATA REPRESENTATION

For articles on related subjects *see* ADDRESSING; COMPUTERS, MULTIPLE ADDRESS; INPUT-OUTPUT INSTRUCTIONS; INSTRUCTION SET; and MACHINE AND ASSEMBLY LANGUAGE PROGRAMMING.

If information is to be stored in a computer system, a representation must be chosen to be used internally. The internal representation of the information as stored in main memory (*q.v.*) may be chosen to be quite different from its external form, as long as there are unique transformations from one to the other. In fact, this freedom to use various internal forms has created problems in situations where information generated on one computer system must be processed on another system.

Assuming a two-state representation, one can treat a collection of such states (or *bit string*) as a unit as well. From the early interpretation of such bit strings as representing numbers with two states in each digit position (i.e. 0 or 1), these digits have become known as binary digits, or *bits*. This interpretation regards a string of zeroes and ones as an integer expressed in *base* 2 form. The term "bits" has now been generalized to include zeroes and ones found in strings that are not interpreted as binary integers.

Information other than binary integers must also be represented in storage. In some computer systems (in particular, those involved with monetary computations), there is a perceived need for representing decimal digits per se and for doing decimal arithmetic on these digits. (This need arises from the different roundoff effects generated in binary and decimal arithmetic.) In other situations, it is necessary to represent alphabetic characters and punctuation symbols so as to process ordinary text, names, etc. In such cases, each alphabetic, numeric, or punctuation character is assigned a particular string of bits as its representation. Part of one such assignment, which uses seven-bit strings and has received wide support, is called the American Standard Code for Information Interchange (ASCII - *q.v.*). Earlier computers tended

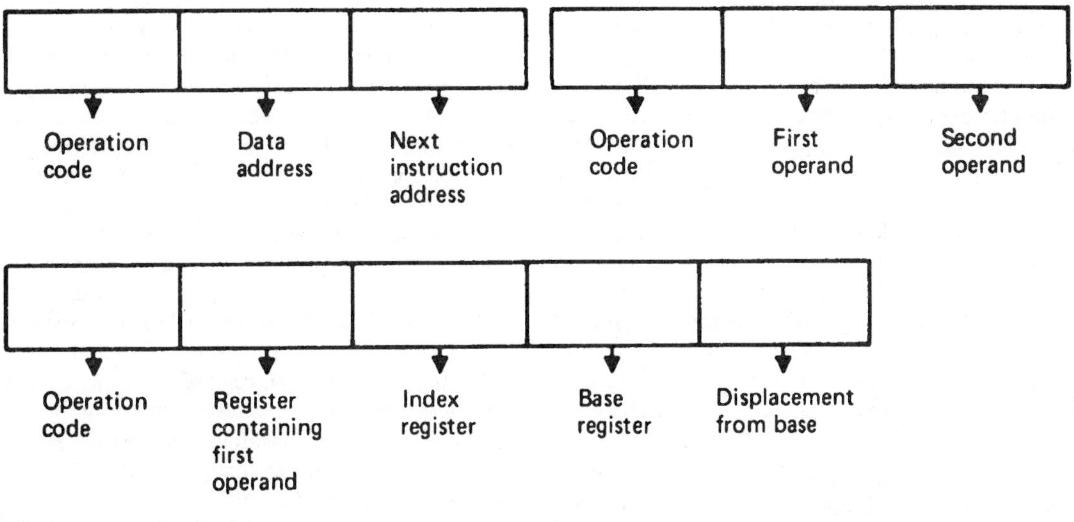

Operation code | Data address | Next instruction address

Operation code | First operand | Second operand

Operation code | Register containing first operand | Index register | Base register | Displacement from base

FIG. 1.   Typical instruction formats.

to use six-bit strings to represent symbols, but it became clear that this was too restrictive, and in recent years eight-bit strings have become standard. The 7-bit ASCII characters are usually embedded in 8-bit fields in contemporary computers, so that the 128-character ASCII code can be expanded to a 256-character set in the future. The alternative EBCDIC (*q.v.*) character set already uses 8-bit strings. The term *byte* is used in referring to a bit string that is of the size corresponding to the symbol representation in a particular system. Thus, there are older computers with six-bit "bytes," but eight-bit bytes are now the norm.

We have seen that a string of bits can have more than one interpretation, so that 01000001 might represent the letter A or the binary form of the decimal integer 65. Yet another interpretation of a string of bits may be as a computer instruction. In this case, some of the bits in the string are interpreted in the control unit of the system as a code for the operation to be performed. The remaining bits might be used to indicate registers (either special registers or storage locations), whose contents are to be used as input to the operation, or that are to receive the results of the operation as new contents. Several formats of instructions from typical computers are shown in Fig. 1.

Some early computers had separate storage for instructions and for data, but this did not last long because it proved costly to provide separate arithmetic processors for two kinds of storage, especially when many operations involved with modifying instructions were so similar to ordinary arithmetic operations. However, the development of microprogramming (*q.v.*) and *read-only* memory (ROM - *q.v.*) has somewhat restored separation of instructions and data.

Once separate storage for instructions and data was abandoned, it became necessary to find ways to store and access any kind of information from any part of storage. Very often, storage was divided into fixed-length strings called *words*, usually from 32 to 64 bits long.* Each word would contain one or more instructions or numbers in fixed- or floating-point form such that the word length was always a multiple of the byte length of the instruction(s) or number(s) packed into the word. Addresses in such computers usually specified individual words, and one could access separate bytes only by shifting (*q.v.*) or masking operations (*q.v.*).

Computers intended for commercial applications, on the other hand, were typically designed to facilitate operations on variable-length strings of characters, since so much of their data exhibited this variability. Thus, one found computers in which both instructions and data were of variable length, with an address specifying the beginning of a string of characters, and a special *word mark* symbol signaling the end of a string.

Recently, computers have been designed to try to reflect both kinds of needs: fixed-length words to represent numbers, and variable-length strings of characters. In these cases, addresses usually specify a particular byte

(occasionally even a particular bit) in storage, and a word is treated explicitly as a multiple of the byte length. Instructions may vary in length also, depending on the number of addresses they need to reference. This is to be contrasted with the fixed-word-length machine, where all addresses typically had to fit into the word, but where many bits were wasted if fewer addresses were needed in particular instructions.

Reference

1969. Rosen, S. "Electronic Computers: A Historical Survey," *Computing Reviews* **1**, *1*: 7–36 (March).

BERNARD A. GALLER

INSTRUCTION COUNTER. *See* PROGRAM COUNTER.

INSTRUCTION SET

For articles on related subjects *see* ADDRESSING; BOOLEAN ALGEBRA; COMPUTERS, MULTIPLE ADDRESS; GENERAL REGISTER; INPUT-OUTPUT INSTRUCTIONS; INTERRUPT; MACHINE AND ASSEMBLY LANGUAGE PROGRAMMING; MASKING; MICROPROGRAMMING; OPERAND; PRIVILEGED INSTRUCTION; RISC ARCHITECTURE; and SHIFTING.

A machine *instruction* is a string of digits in the base in which the machine operates which, when interpreted by the hardware, causes a unique and well-defined change in the state of the computer.

Most computers are based on the binary system. For most cases, therefore, the "string of digits" will be a string of bits, each having the value 0 or 1. In what follows, we will refer only to bit-oriented instructions, although we will express those bits using hexadecimal notation.

In the definition given, the words "interpreted by the hardware" really mean "used by the hardware." The change in state of the machine is, in fact, a change in the contents of various registers or memory locations. The changed registers may be those explicitly or implicitly referred to by the instruction, or they may be some internal registers not directly known to the user. For example: The 16-bit string 1010000100100001 (hexadecimal A121), when interpreted by the hardware of one of the IBM ES/3000 computers, causes the contents of general register 1 to be added to general register 2, the result replacing the previous contents of register 1. In this case, the change of state is apparent to the user of the machine. On the other hand, on the same machine, the bit string 0000011111110001 (hexadecimal 07F1) causes an inaccessible internal register, the *program counter* (*q.v.*), to set its value to that of general register 1, thus causing the next instruction that has to be interpreted by the hardware to be taken from the location whose address is the contents of register 1. Thus, a bit string such as 07F1 acts as a *jump* or *branch instruction*.

Each computer model possesses its own unique in-

---

*Smaller computers, particularly minicomputers and microcomputers often intended for applications in which long numbers are not needed, usually have from 8–32 bits in a word.

struction set. The same bit string may mean completely different things on two different computers, even if the number of bits needed for expressing an instruction is the same on the two machines. For example, the bit string A121 (hexadecimal), which we used as an example on the IBM ES/3000, caused addition of the contents of two registers. But when interpreted by a Data General Corporation MV computer, the same bit string will decrement by one the contents of the memory location whose address is in location 18 and skip the next instruction if the result is zero. This different interpretation for the same bit string makes it clear that bit strings are not a good basis for classification of machine instructions. We will therefore introduce categories based on other criteria in order to be able to find some patterns in the multitude of instructions available on various computers.

Classification of Machine Instructions

There is usually a simple relation between the length of the computer word or addressable unit and the instruction length. Thus, we find up to four instructions per word in the B5500 and CDC Cyber series, but one instruction per word in most minicomputers and microcomputers.

The length of the instruction need not be fixed. For example, in the IBM ES/3000 we find instructions whose length is 16, 32, or 48 bits. In most minicomputers we have single-length (i.e. one word) instructions and double-length instructions.

The bit string representing a machine instruction is generally divided into two major fields: the operation (or "op-code") field and the operand(s) field, usually referred to as the address field(s). Note that this is completely analogous to the way a mathematician denotes a function; i.e. $g(x, y, z)$ means the function (operation) g on the variables (operands) x, y, z. The number of operands available in each instruction is generally different, not only between different machines but also in the same machine between different operation types. However, neither the question of the number of operands nor the question of the way they are addressed will be discussed here. The interested reader is referred to the articles ADDRESSING; and COMPUTERS, MULTIPLE ADDRESS. This article concentrates on the operation field only.

The types of operations available on contemporary machines are roughly divided into arithmetic, logical, data move, and control operations.

Arithmetic Operations Arithmetic operations are usually confined to the four basic ones (plus, minus, multiply, and divide) and to the "compare" operation, which serves to record status information about the relative magnitude of operands compared. These arithmetic operations may operate on different types of operands, such as integers and floating-point numbers with different precision (half-, single-, or double-word length numbers). The operands may assume various bases. Binary is usual, but decimal is also common. In specialized machines, one may find arithmetic operations of a more sophisticated nature, such as exponentiation or square root, but this is rare.

An example of an arithmetic operation is the IBM ES/3000 instruction A121 (hexadecimal) used at the be-

ginning of this article. Fig. 1 gives the structure of most ES/3000 instructions, and from it we can gain some preliminary insight into the actual structure of a machine instruction. Thus, in our example, the first eight bits (i.e. hexadecimal A1) are the actual operation code and the last eight bits (i.e. hexadecimal 21) are the address field. In this particular instruction, the address field specifies register 2 with the first four bits and register 1 in the last four bits. On a Data General Corporation MV computer, the instruction for the same task has the hexadecimal code CE10. Not only is the code different, but the breakdown of the instruction into fields is also completely different.

Logical Operations The logical operations usually involve boolean operations on the bit values of the operands. Although there are 16 possible boolean operations between two operands, usually only a subset of these (typically AND, OR, and NOT) is available. This subset is sufficient to reproduce all other boolean operations.

Boolean operations are used for the manipulation of parts of words, for decision processes, and for nonnumerical processing. As an example, consider the following problem: Given a data item in a register, isolate the last six bits of it. By inspecting the AND operation truth table, one finds that the result of an AND with 0 is always zero, whereas the result of an AND with 1 reproduces the operand. Thus, an AND operation between the given data item and an operand that has 0 in all places except in the last six bits (all of which are one) will isolate the last six bits of the given data item. Thus:

Given data item:	Arbitrary bit string
Second operand:	0...0111111
Result of AND:	0...0 6 last bits of given data item.

Operations like this are called *masking* operations. Note that the bit string representing the instruction is completely independent of the actual data. On an IBM ES/3000, assuming that the first operand is in register 3 and the second in register 4, the instruction will be hexadecimal 1434.

In the logical operations, one also usually includes the various possible shift instructions, although, in some classifications, these form a category of their own. Shifting operations, as their names implies, shift the bits in a word to the left or right. The differences between types of shifts affects what happens to the bits being shifted out

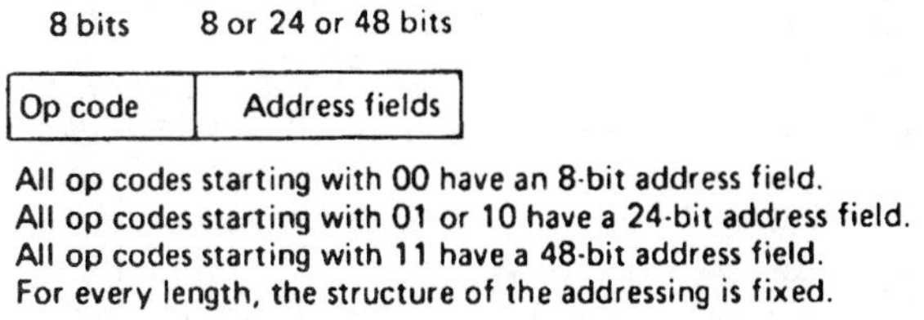

8 bits	8 or 24 or 48 bits
Op code	Address fields

All op codes starting with 00 have an 8-bit address field.
All op codes starting with 01 or 10 have a 24-bit address field.
All op codes starting with 11 have a 48-bit address field.
For every length, the structure of the addressing is fixed.

FIG. 1. Typical structure of a vertical instruction set (IBM ES/3000).

of a word and what bits are shifted in. For example, in logical shifts, the bits shifted out are lost and the bits shifted in are zeros. In an instruction that will shift two places to the left logically, the leftmost two bits of a data item are lost, and the last vacated two positions are filled with zeros (*see* SHIFTING).

Data Move Operations   The data move instructions include moves (copying) of data between memory locations and registers, and the input/output instructions necessary for communication between the central processor and peripheral devices. Examples of the former operations are instructions to load and store a register and to move data from one location in memory to another. The input/output operations are of such a complexity that no useful example can be given without an extensive explanation; *see* INPUT-OUTPUT INSTRUCTIONS. Some data move operations may be quite complex, in particular those that were designed to support graphics operations.

Control Operations   The control instructions include those operations that are necessary for the proper sequencing of the instructions so that the programmed task can be performed correctly. These include conditional and unconditional branches, test instructions, and status-changing instructions.

As an example of this category of instructions, there may be instructions like BRANCH (or JUMP) to a given address (to begin a new sequence of instructions) when the result of the last operation is negative, or if there was an arithmetic overflow. There are also instructions that swap the contents of the user accessible registers with internal registers, thus causing a change in the state of the computer; in particular, this may cause execution of a completely different sequence of instructions. Note also that program flow can be affected not only by explicit control instructions issued by the programmer, but also by special conditions known as *interrupts* (*q.v.*).

This rough division of instructions into types is not necessarily mutually exclusive. Referring to an earlier example, the MV bit string hexadecimal A121 will perform both an arithmetic operation (decrement; i.e. subtract 1) *and* a control operation (skip the next instruction if the result is zero).

Different instruction types usually possess different numbers of operands. Whereas arithmetic operations usually refer to three operands (two for the data locations and one for the result location), either explicitly or implicitly, certain control instructions may have one or no operands at all. For example, an unconditional BRANCH has one operand, but a HALT instruction has none. In addition to the operands involved in the instruction execution, there are also *condition codes* involved. Generally speaking, condition codes are indicators, usually one-bit long, which describe the properties of the results and the validity of the operation performed.

Examples of condition codes are explicit indications of (1) the sign of the result, (2) whether or not an overflow has occurred, (3) what the relative magnitudes of the operands are, (4) whether there is a parity error in read-ing or writing to memory. Similar to the instruction repertoire, the variety of condition codes differs among computers. There is also a difference in the way that condition codes are used. In some computers they are incorporated directly in the instructions, especially conditional branches (like BRANCH ON OVERFLOW), and in others they can be transferred into registers and then manipulated as data.

Machine Language and Instruction Formats

The *instruction repertoire* or *command set* of a computer is defined to be the set of all possible operations that the computer can perform. In a computer of the type discussed previously, the instruction repertoire boils down to the set of all possible operation codes (op codes). There are, however, other types of computers such as *tagged architecture* machines in which the operation code *does not* fully describe the operation to be done. In such a computer, part of the operation performed is defined by the type of the operand. For example, there is only *one* ADD operation, and this is done in floating-point or integer mode depending on the type of the operand. The instruction repertoire of such a computer is still the set of all possible operations. However, it is now defined not just by the set of all op codes, but by both op codes and operand tags. A coherent program consisting of a sequence of such operations is said to be written in *machine language*.

We now go further into the question of the format of the instruction, but again without treating addressing in any detail. A machine instruction can be written, using mathematical notation, as $g(x_1, x_2, ..., x_n) \equiv g(x)$, where g is the operation performed on the n operands:

$$x_1, ..., x_n \equiv x.$$

The natural question to ask is: Can we have multiple operation instructions in the form

$$g_1(x_1)\, g_2(x_2)\, g_3(x_3)...g_n(x_n) \tag{1}$$

where the operations g_i are performed on the operands x_i and the operand sets are either identical, partially overlapping, or distinct from each other? The answer is that machines with such instruction sets do, in fact, exist. Roughly speaking, we can divide instruction sets into *vertical* and *horizontal*. Vertical instructions are those of the type $g(x)$, where a single operation (or a time-ordered series of a *fixed* number and *type* of operations) is performed on a single set of operands. Vertical instructions are usually highly coded (see below).

Horizontal instructions are those of the form (1). Here the functions g_i are *independent* and are performed on the respective operands in parallel or in a well-defined time sequence.

The instruction set of an IBM ES/3000 computer is an example of a vertical instruction set (see Fig. 1). Vertical instructions are found in most machines today. Horizontal instructions are mainly found in microprogrammed machines and are rare outside them.

The structure of the operation code itself (i.e. the

structure of the contents of the operation field) is also of interest. In principle, if one wants a certain number of instructions, it seems sufficient to associate a function with each number expressible in the operation field. The operation then is determined by *all* the digits (in the binary case, the bits) in the field. By inspecting a part of that field, we generally have no meaningful information about the operation. We call such an arrangement a *highly coded* one. In the highly coded arrangement, the number of possible instructions is equal to the total information contents of the field. In a field of n bits, this means a total of 2^n possible instructions.

On the other hand, one can envision a completely different situation in which each part of the instruction code conveys some information about the type of the operation. For instance, the first bit in the field may determine if the instruction is arithmetical or non-arithmetical. The second bit may determine the length of the operands; the third, the arithmetic mode (real or integer); etc. In this case we speak about a *low level of coding*. The number of instructions expressible in this case is smaller than the total information content of the op code field, since some of the combinations may be unused. For example, if the instruction is logical, the arithmetic mode may be irrelevant. The low decoding level needed for this type of instruction and the strict interpretation of the various bits enable a high degree of parallelism in the decision process that the hardware has to go through in order to decide which instruction has to be performed.

Up to this point we have assumed that the operation field is of fixed length and, in the case of a low decoding level, the bits have fixed meaning. Neither of these assumptions is necessary.

Coding theory teaches that it may be advisable to have codes of different lengths, utilizing short ones for the more frequently used combinations and long ones for the least used. Indeed, one can design a "tree-structured" instruction code—i.e. the operation field is divided into parts and each part is interpreted in sequence, with the meaning attached to it dependent on the results of interpretation of the preceding parts. This not only solves the problem of meaningless bit settings that we encountered in the low decoding level combinations, but it also enables us to terminate the op code interpretation at a different point for different instructions.

With the advent of very large memories, the attractiveness of this coding scheme, which conserves memory but is more time consuming, has diminished. It is currently used mainly as a mechanism for extending an instruction set. Instructions sets can be expanded, enhanced, and augmented by different methods. One of those is the addition of an augmenting prefix. For example, in the Intel 80*x*86 instruction set, one finds a repeat prefix, which causes the next instruction to be iterated several times.

The other most prevalent method for instruction set extension is the addition of co-processors which have instructions not present in the original set. These may be single chip (in the case of floating-point operations in single-chip processors) or can be quite complex, as in the case of addition of vector instructions to large-scale machines.

General Remarks   This article has described single machine instructions according to their length, operation type, the degree of parallelism in the specification of the operation, the number of operations specified, and, finally, the degree of coding. We conclude with some general remarks on the capabilities of machine instruction sets. The emergence of single-chip processors, with both their promise and limitations, the shift to high-level languages, which distanced the programmer from the details of the instruction sets, and, finally, the change in the speed ratios of processor and memory cycles, caused the price/performance/utility consideration of various instruction sets to shift from their established 1960s and 1970s values. In general, this shift was toward simpler instruction sets (*see* REDUCED INSTRUCTION SET COMPUTER (RISC)). At the same time, success of machines like the IBM AS/400 and the need for vector machines emphasized the utility of large, complex structures; these opposing trends are too intricate to cover here.

GIDEON FRIEDER

INTEGRATED CIRCUITRY

For articles on related subjects *see* COMPUTER CIRCUITRY; LOGIC DESIGN; MICROCOMPUTER CHIP; MICROPROCESSORS AND MICROCOMPUTERS; and SUPERCONDUCTING DEVICES.

Introduction   On 29 December 1939, William Shockley wrote in his notebook, "It has today occurred to me that an amplifier using semiconductors rather than vacuum is in principle possible." It has been a long and exciting journey since the time that this statement was written, a time that has witnessed an unprecedented number of applications of the transistor and the integrated circuit (IC) chip. In the opinion of the present authors, two technological events will go down in the history of the twentieth century as the most profound and far reaching, having revolutionized the way of life on this planet: mass production of the automobile, and the design and manufacturing of the integrated chip. The latter is truly the catalyst that led from the birth of the information processing industry to become the driving force which fueled its growth and evolution. The genesis of the IC is described herein, along with its evolutionary progress, technological aspects, and processing details.

IC history began with John Bardeen, Walter Brittain, and William Shockley of AT&T Bell Laboratories, who did the pioneering work that led to the invention of the point-contact transistor, the basic building block of the IC, in 1947. In recognition of their invention, the team was awarded the Nobel Prize in Physics in 1956. What made the first transistor possible was a semiconductor material, the element germanium. Unlike metals, which conduct electricity with relative ease, and insulators, which almost always block any motion of electrons (the universal carriers of electricity), *semiconductors* can conduct *or* insulate, and there are a variety of ways these conductive properties can be controlled and exploited. At first, the introduction of the transistor elicited very little excitement outside the electronics industry. Throughout the 1950s, transistors were refined and simply used as replacement devices for vacuum tubes in everything from hearing aids to radar systems. But in 1958 and 1959 came the developments that truly launched the IC age. Within a few months of each other, Jack Kilby of Texas Instruments and Robert Noyce of Fairchild invented different versions of the IC. Both inventors filed for patents in 1959, and Texas Instruments and Fairchild were each offering ICs commercially by 1961.

As Kilby tells it, he sought to make resistors, capacitors, and diodes—all elements of electronic circuits—out of the same material as transistors, namely germanium. At that time, germanium was easier to work with than silicon, the semiconductor material that is presently the material of choice for ICs. He placed the components on a single holder, called a *substrate*, to make the device that is generally credited as being the first IC. The trouble with Kilby's invention was that it was cumbersome and costly to produce in large quantities. Workers had to solder the circuits by hand with tiny gold wires, used for electrical connections. Four months after Kilby built his germanium IC, Noyce found a way to join the circuits by printing the circuit board using lithography. He used a silicon substrate. The commercial devices that followed showed the advantages of silicon over germanium in the integration of multiple components in a single chip. The ease with which conductivity was controlled in different components and the concomitant ease with which interconnections were traced between components in a silicon chip resulted in the final triumph of silicon over germanium. The fabrication techniques developed by Noyce are the forerunner of current IC fabrication technologies.

Primitive as they were, those initial chips truly launched a revolution. Over the last three decades, ICs have pervaded almost all aspects of our daily lives, from television sets and wristwatches to rockets and the ubiquitous computer in various flavors. "Very few things have changed the world as dramatically as the IC," said Robert N. White, President of the Academy of Engineering, when he announced in 1990 that Kilby and Noyce would receive the academy's top prize in recognition of their accomplishments.

Integrated Circuits: Basic Principles An *integrated circuit* is a functioning assembly of various elements or "devices"—transistors, resistors, capacitors, diodes, etc.—all electrically connected and packaged to form a completely functioning circuit with a specific function. ICs fall into two major categories: hybrid circuits and monolithic circuits.

In a hybrid circuit, all the IC elements are wired together on a ceramic substrate, somewhat similar to a printed circuit board (PCB), and are packaged and sold as a single functioning unit with input/output (I/O) leads. In essence, a hybrid circuit is a miniaturized version of the PCB. However, the elements used in PCB assemblies are pre-encapsulated for protection from moisture and im-

purities in the atmosphere. For example, an individual transistor used on a PCB board actually consists of a protective capsule containing the transistor proper, with its leads connected to the external leads on the capsule. Hybrid ICs, on the other hand, use bare elements wherein the whole package is assembled first and then the entire unit is encapsulated in a protective polymer material. Due to longer wiring distances between circuit elements, the realized signal transmission speeds in hybrid ICs are low, although higher than those achieved in PCBs. Consequently, hybrid circuits have limited applications in digital electronics, and their use is mostly limited to analog circuitry.

In a monolithic circuit, which is the major IC in a modern computer, the circuit elements are formed on a silicon monolith using advanced materials and sophisticated fabrication and lithography equipment and techniques. In this case, the silicon substrate serves not only as a support for the circuit elements, but also as one of the materials that forms the components of the circuit. The nature of processing allows the arranging of circuit elements in close proximity, thereby reducing the wiring lengths by orders of magnitude as compared to a hybrid IC. As a result, monolithic ICs offer higher signal speeds than hybrid or PCB assemblies. The remainder of this article will focus on the basics, design, and fabrication of monolithic ICs.

Monolithic ICs are thus silicon-based, and the key to IC formation is the proper treatment of silicon in such a way as to form the desired circuit components. The basic notion is that selected impurities, when introduced into a pure polycrystalline silicon matrix in a precisely controlled manner using a process called *doping*, can appreciably alter its electrical properties in a pre-designed way. These impurities actually settle in the silicon matrix and lead, in the case of elements such as arsenic or phosphorus, to an excess of electrons within the matrix, thus yielding what is known as *n-type* silicon. The introduction of elements such as boron, on the other hand, causes a deficit of electrons, thus producing *p-type* silicon. Consequently, although pure silicon is a semiconductor, the conductivity of n- and p-type silicons can be made to vary over a wide range of conductivities, with the latter being an increasing function of impurity concentration (known as the doping level). The physics of current motion and the nature of the charge carriers is different for the two types of silicon. In the case of n-type silicon, electrons (which possess negative charge) are considered as the main contributors to the motion of flowing charge. Alternatively, because of the deficit of electrons in p-type silicon, *holes* (which are positively charged and are caused by the absence of electrons) are considered as the major charge carriers.

The presence of the two types of charge carriers is fundamental to the design and function of ICs because important physical phenomena occur when n- and p-type semiconductors are placed in contact with each other to form a p-n junction, the simplest semiconductor structure. In this case, the completed junction is formed of three distinct semiconductor regions, as shown in Fig. 1(a): a p-type region, a depletion region, and an n-type

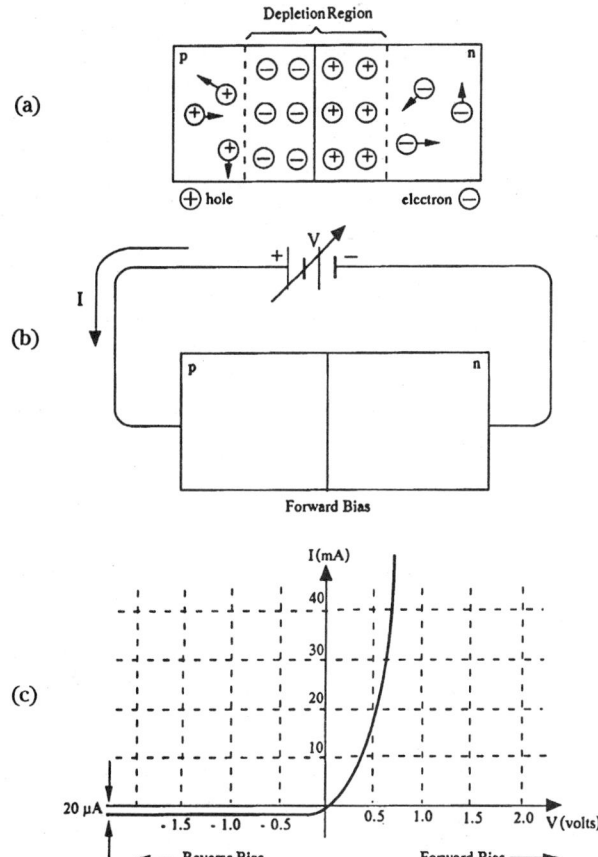

FIG. 1. (a) Physical arrangement of a p-n junction. (b) A diode (p-n junction) under forward bias. (c) The characteristic current curve for a real diode.

region. The depletion region may be visualized as arising when the two regions are placed in contact and holes diffuse to the n-side of the junction while electrons diffuse to the p-side of the junction. (Serway *et al.*, 1989). The region extending a few microns from the junction is called the *depletion region* because it is depleted of mobile charge carriers, namely, electrons and holes. It forms a potential barrier that prevents the further diffusion of holes and electrons across the junction and ensures zero electrical current when no external voltage is applied.

The most notable feature of this p-n junction is its ability to pass current in only one direction. Such diode action is due to the fact that when a positive external voltage from a battery is applied to the p-side of the junction, as shown in Fig. 1(b), the overall barrier is reduced, resulting in a current that increases rapidly with increasing forward voltage or bias, as displayed in Fig. 1(c). For reverse bias (a positive external voltage from a battery is applied to the n-side of the junction), the potential barrier is increased, resulting in a very small reverse current that quickly reaches a saturation value.

Transistors are based on similar, although more complex, n- and p-type semiconductors. ICs presently use two important device (transistor) technologies: the Bipolar Transistor, whose function is based on phenomena at the p-n junctions, and the Field Effect Transistor (FET), particularly the Metal Oxide Semiconductor FET (MOSFET),

which depends on the physical phenomena occurring close to the surfaces. The bipolar transistor is basically an n-p-n (or p-n-p) junction as shown in Figure 2. Its operation is based on exploiting the voltage of the base (the p-type region) to control the flow of current between the collector and the emitter (the two n-type regions). For instance, if the collector is made more positive than the emitter, no current will flow because of the diode effect between the base and the collector unless the base is also made more positive than the emitter, in which case current will flow from the base to the emitter and, subsequently, from the collector to the base. The device is called *bipolar* because both electrons and holes, and consequently two polarities (positive and negative), are involved in the flow of current.

The operation of the FET transistor, shown in Fig. 3, is also based on exploiting the voltage of the gate with respect to the source. For instance, if the drain is made more positive than the source, no current will flow because of the diode effect between the drain and the source, due to the existence of the p-type region, unless a positive voltage is applied to the gate. In this case, the insulator region blocks the flow of current and forms a capacitor that has its negative charge, or electrons, in the p-type region just below the insulator, and its positive charge, or holes, on the gate. At sufficiently high gate voltages, the electrons in the p-type region form a thin n-type channel beneath the insulator, which connects with the n-type regions of the source and drain, thus allowing current to flow easily through this channel. The FET is also known as a unipolar transistor, because only one type of charge, namely electrons, is involved in the flow of current. Since the gate is normally fabricated of metal and the insulator out of silicon dioxide, the FET is also commonly referred to as a metal-oxide-semiconductor (MOS) transistor. Also, a prefix is frequently employed to indicate the type of charge carrier in the FET. For example, the device shown in Fig. 3 is referred to as an NMOS transistor, while a p-n-p–based FET would be

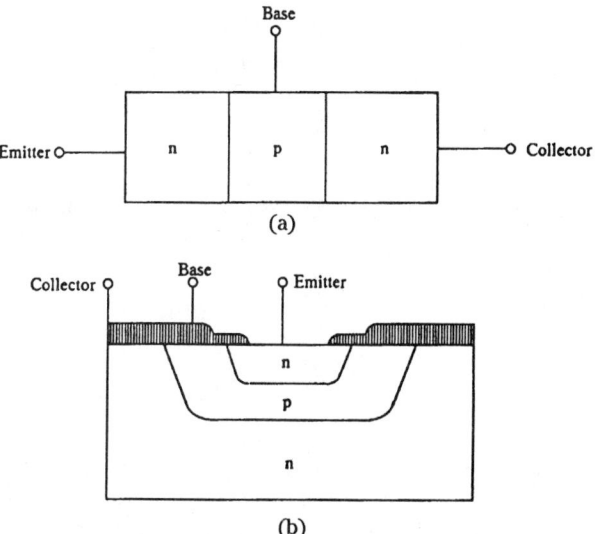

FIG. 2. (a) A bipolar transistor. (b) Cross-section of a bipolar transistor.

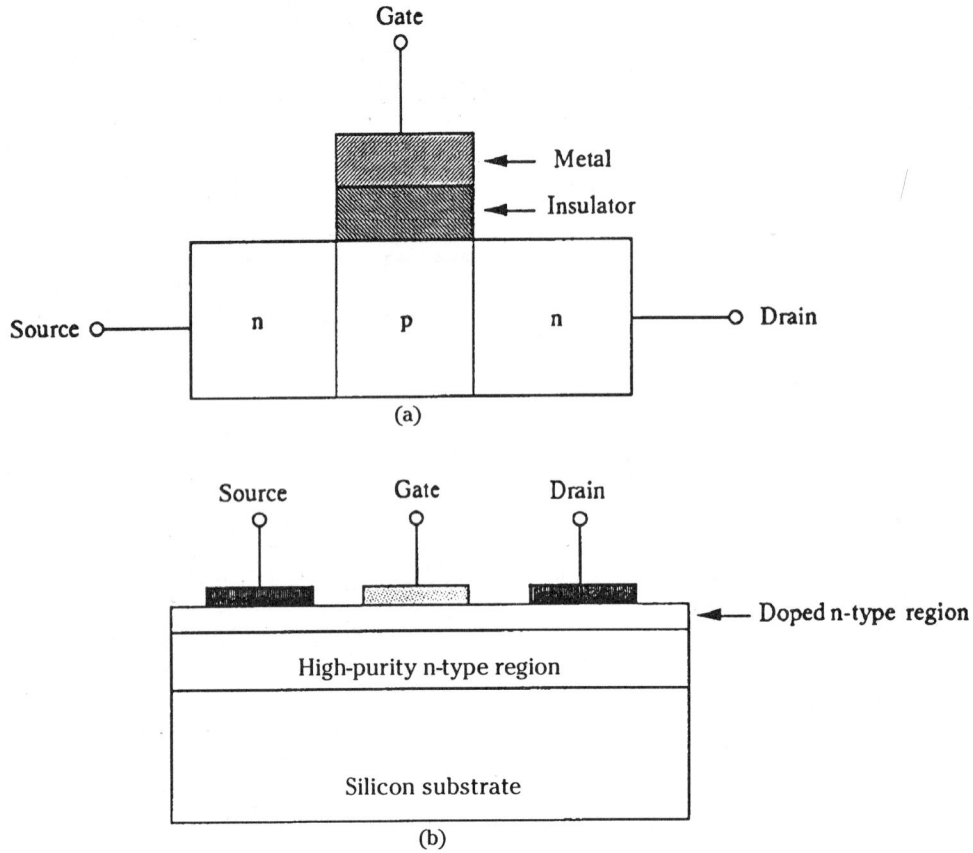

FIG. 3.   (a) A field-effect transistor (FET). (b) Cross-section of a field-effect transistor.

known as a PMOS transistor. Historically, PMOS transistors were used initially because of ease in manufacturing and impurity control. However, present technology employs NMOS transistors because of their inherently higher speed than PMOS devices.

At present, bipolar devices are the mainstay of the high-speed computer logic circuits, while FET-based transistors are used largely in memory components. Due to the high density requirements of memory circuits, innovations in FET devices have traditionally led many technological breakthroughs. Although the bipolar ICs, not as densely wired, have inherently higher speeds than MOSFETs, it is projected that some of the advanced CMOS (complementary MOS) devices will begin to encroach significantly upon the bipolar territories by the year 2000. For example, in 1986, the ratio of bipolar to MOSFET ICs

TABLE 1.   **Prevalent Device and Circuit Technologies**

Bipolar Devices	FET Devices	Bipolar Logic Circuits	FET Memory Circuits
NPN	NMOS	ECL—Emitter coupled logic	RAM—Random access memory
PNP	PMOS	TTL—Transistor-transistor logic	ROM—Read-only memory
BiCMOS	CMOS	IIL—Integrated injection logic	SRAM—Static RAM
	BiCMOS	STL—Schottky transistor logic	DRAM—Dynamic RAM
			EEPROM—Electrically erasable programmable ROM

BiCMOS: Bipolar CMOS

sold was 45% to 55%. This ratio is expected to be 32% to 68% by the mid-1990s.

IC Devices and Families. Evolution of IC Integration

The prevalent device and circuit technologies used in ICs at present are summarized in Table 1. MOSFET devices, as pointed out earlier, are the pacesetter and barometer for technological innovations and development. The number of circuit elements that can be integrated on a chip and the minimum lithographically definable dimensions are often employed as an indicator of progress in technological evolution. This measure is used for two reasons: (1) higher circuit densities per chip lead to smaller wiring lengths between elements and, subsequently, faster signal propagation (faster devices), and (2) improved resolution capabilities of patterning technologies allow denser circuit elements per chip.

Fig. 4 displays the evolution of memory circuits, the MOSFET/DRAM, since the time of the invention of the MOS transistor in 1960. The various generations of circuits shown in the figure are classified according to the degree of integration, or number of bits (there are traditionally 10 bits per basic functional unit), and are summarized in Tables 2 and 3 in terms of, respectively, bit size and physical dimensions per basic functional unit (Rymaszewski, 1989; Schumay, 1989, Larrabee and Chatterjee, 1991). The key ingredient and leverage in semiconductor technology is that each generation of smaller scale devices defines the materials and processes required and, subsequently, drives the research and development efforts to provide the fabrication, lithography, and other manufacturing techniques needed.

IC Fabrication Processes

Present integrated circuit fabrication involves a large array of advanced materials, complex processes, and sophisticated equipment.

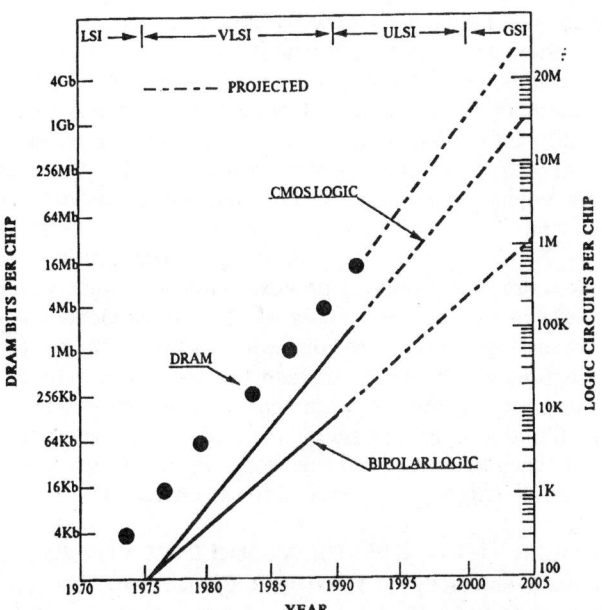

FIG. 4. Dynamic random access memory (DRAM) bits per chip and logic circuits per chip as a function of years.

TABLE 2. Generations of IC Families

IC Generation	Size, Bits
SSI—Small-scale integration	1–10^2
MSI—Medium-scale integration	10^2–10^3
LSI—Large-scale integration	10^3–10^5
VLSI—Very large scale integration	10^5–10^6
ULSI—Ultra-large scale integration	10^6–10^9
GSI—Giga-scale integration	$> 10^9$

TABLE 3. Emerging Microelectronic Technologies

Technology (μm)	0.6	0.4	0.3	0.2	0.15
Expected Development	1991	1994	1997	2001	2005
DRAM (size, bits)	16M	64M	256M	1024M	4096M

Due to the high complexity and level of integration of these circuits, quality control on incoming materials, process control, and equipment cleanliness are critical if acceptable levels of product yield are to be realized. Some of the major steps used in the present IC fabrication process are discussed briefly in what follows. However, the requirements for emerging submicron technologies in the 1990s and early 2000s are dramatically redefining the materials and reshaping the processes that constitute the building blocks of electronic devices and are thus expected to lead to radically different R&D and manufacturing strategies and approaches from those described herein.

A flowchart of a process used in the fabrication of the NMOS/FET transistor, a key constituent of RAM and ROM circuits and its derivatives, is shown in Fig. 5. The processing principles also apply to other fabrication technologies. Fabrication begins with two components: A pure silicon wafer and a set of photolithographic patterns known as *masks*. The silicon wafer is a thin, about 0.5-1 mm thick, disc of a single crystal of silicon that is doped (with boron in the example given herein). Wafers expanded from 25–50 mm in diameter in the early days of IC manufacturing, to 150–200 mm at present, a size that could reach 300 mm in the next few years. The masks define the areas within the wafer that need to be treated (e.g. etched or implanted) and are employed to define circuit configuration and device topology. The minimum definable mask dimensions have witnessed a continuous size decrease in order to keep up with circuit dimensions. Present mask features are in the submicron range.

As can be seen in Fig. 5, device manufacturing is achieved in a series of processing steps. The key process technologies that have made high levels of integration and density possible are indicated in the flow chart: lithography (*), ion implantation (**), and reactive ion etching (+). These technologies are important because they are employed repeatedly in a device fabrication line and are briefly described in what follows.

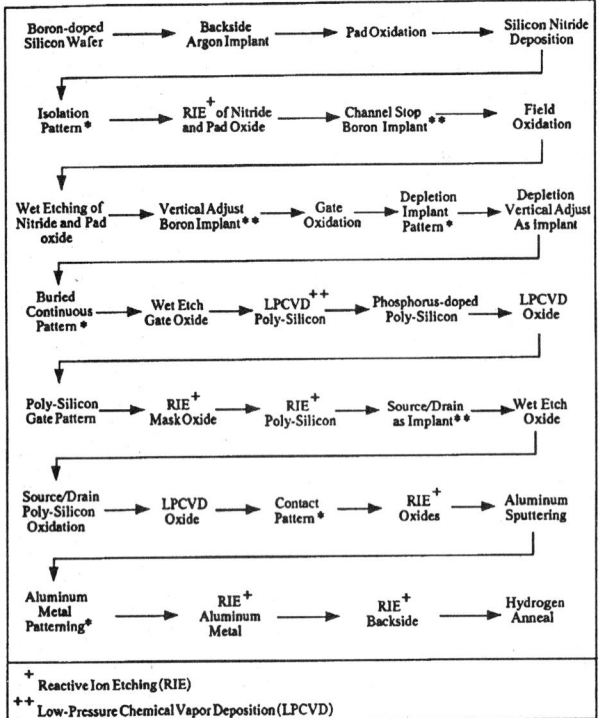

FIG. 5. NMOS process description.

Lithography *Lithography* is the process of imaging and image development of a circuit pattern onto a radiation-sensitive polymer (mask). Successful lithography requires an optimal performance of several elements simultaneously: resist materials (which resist etching), exposure tools, and lithographic processes. The net outcome of the lithographic process is to transfer a desirable device pattern from the mask to the silicon wafer, a process known as *patterning*. Most presently used patterning techniques employ optical techniques for pattern generation in combination with conventional optical printing methods to produce the desired circuit. These techniques might be limited to large feature sizes (> 1 mm) and could be replaced over the next 10 to 15 years, with new techniques for submicron (less than 0.5 mm) and nanometer (less than 0.15 mm) lithography. Some of these new techniques are: phase shift optical techniques that would extend current optical lithographic capabilities, electron beam lithography (currently electron beams are used mostly to produce high-resolution optical masks), ion beam lithography, and X-ray beam lithography.

Ion Implantation *Ion implantation* is the process by which energetic impurities can be introduced in a controlled manner into the silicon material in order to alter its electronic properties. Implantation is ordinarily performed with voltages in the range of 50,000–500,000 volts (ion energies in the 50,000–500,000 electron-volts range). Basic requirements for implantation systems are ion sources and processes to generate, accelerate, and purify them. Impurity introduction is achieved through a bombardment process that inserts ions of the desirable elements into the silicon matrix. This leads, in the case of

elements such as arsenic or phosphorus, to the formation of n-type silicon, while implantation with boron ions, on the other hand, produces p-type silicon.

Reactive Ion Etching *Reactive ion etching* is a transfer process in which a lithographically developed circuit pattern in resist is transferred onto an underlying film by the removal of undesirable sections from the film through the use of low-temperature, weakly ionized gaseous processes. The undesirable material is removed from the unmasked areas of the film by conversion to a volatile gaseous state through chemical reactions with one or more reactive ionic and neutral energetic species that are produced in the gaseous plasma.

These plasma processes have become a key for manufacturing high-density ICs due to their ability for high-fidelity transfer of submicron and nanometer scale mask images. Because of the need for low-pressure, low-energy, high-density plasmas for etching high-resolution images, today's plasma reactor technology has become highly sophisticated. It features quite exotic techniques of plasma generation like magnetic field enhancement, electron-cyclotron-resonance-induced plasmas, and radio-frequency (RF) and helicon sources.

Low-Pressure Chemical Vapor Deposition Deposited metal and dielectric thin films are widely used in the fabrication of ICs. These films provide conducting paths, like a wire, electrical insulators between electrically active areas of the device, like a dielectric, and protection from the ambient, like a passivation layer which prevents corro sion. Among the numerous techniques used for thin film deposition, low-pressure chemical vapor deposition (LPCVD) has been pivotal in the production of VLSI and ULSI circuits. As compared to the earlier atmospheric-pressure CVD (APCVD), LPCVD offers cleaner films with low pin holes and reduced defects, smoother films, improved conformality in gap filling, and superior deposition uniformity. Low pressure also reduces the deposition temperature, a desirable feature in IC fabrication. Currently, LPCVD systems come in many flavors, which includes batch and single wafer systems and hot and cold wall reactors. Many advances have been achieved in recent years to improve film uniformity over 200 mm wafers, reduce particulates, and efficiently deliver the gaseous reactants to the reaction zone.

Fig. 6 displays examples of typical end products of the wafer manufacturing process, namely 127 mm wafers made of two different types of VLSI chips. Once wafer processing is complete, the wafer is tested for proper functioning. The lines between the various circuits are then marked and the wafer cut along these lines. The resulting IC chips are then packaged (i.e. mounted on a chip carrier, attached to the proper leads, encapsulated, and tested again) and shipped to the customer.

Circuit Yields, Reliability, and Cost The ICs that have been discussed so far have to meet two important requirements: (1) the circuits must function properly throughout their intended life, and (2) they should be produced in quantities that are competitive with alterna-

FIG. 6. 127 mm wafers made of two different types of VLSI chips.

tive methods of production. The first requirement is related to circuit reliability and the second to yield and cost. The optimum size of an IC, as related to the number of circuit functions, is a compromise between many competing factors: architecture and partitioning of the overall IC, expected yield of good circuits, packaging cost, and the overall reliability of the complete assembled system.

In an ideally produced wafer, 100% of the circuits will be functioning. In reality, however, the number of good circuits (the *yield*) depends upon the process maturity, circuit design, and random defects in the circuit. Achieving high-process yields requires robust processes (a wide process window) and tolls (e.g. high uptime, stability, on-line diagnostics). Many innovative designs have been implemented to achieve these goals like computer control of process parameters, vacuum processing, vacuum load locks, and in-line diagnostic measurements. Proper design of circuits requires recognizing the tool/process capabilities and assessing circuit sensitivities to specific process parameters to assure high yields.

In spite of proper design of circuits and robust processes, the yields will be less than 100% due to random point defects (areas of the wafer that are small compared

to chip size) generated by imperfect processing, particles, stacking faults, mask defects, etc., the negative effect of these defects on yield increases as the minimum dimensions in the circuit continue to shrink. Whereas an IC with a 1mm minimum dimension can tolerate a particle 0.1 mm in size, a submicron device with 0.25 mm feature size can tolerate only a 0.025 mm particle. This implies that materials, process gases and chemicals, and tools and facilities must be controlled to contain fewer and smaller particles.

Since the ULSI technology requires finer dimensions, larger chip area, complex processes and tools, and new material systems, the problems of achieving and maintaining high yields and reliability are undoubtedly exacerbated. Factory management to achieve these high levels of performance will mean high cost of fabricating advanced ICs. At present, the fabrication facilities for the production of ULSI circuits (e.g. 64M DRAM) are estimated to cost upwards of $1 billion U.S. In spite of such high capital investments, the ever expanding applications and the demand for faster and more cost-effective computers are sure to keep the factories of advanced ICs humming for a long time to come.

References

1989. Rymaszewski, E. J. "Dense, Denser, Densest," *J. Electronic Matter*, **18**, 217–220.
1989. Serway, R. A., Moses, C. J., and Moyer, C. A. *Modern Physics*. Philadelphia: Saunders.
1989. Schumay, W. C. Jr. "Materials for High Density Interconnects", *Advanced Materials and Processes*, **135**, 43–47.
1991. Larrabee, G. and Chatterjee, P. "DRAM Manufacturing in the 90's—Part I: The History Lesson," *Semiconductor International* **14**, 84–92.

ALAIN E. KALOYEROS AND G. SWAMI MATHAD

INTEGRATED SERVICES DIGITAL NETWORK (ISDN)

For articles on related subjects *see* COMMUNICATIONS AND COMPUTERS; DATA COMMUNICATIONS, MULTIPLEXING; NETWORK PROTOCOLS; NETWORKS, COMPUTER; and OPEN SYSTEMS INTERCONNECTION.

History The *Integrated Services Digital Network* (ISDN) is a telephonic system that can support a variety of digital services (including digitized voice) through a limited set of standard interfaces. A very complete description can be found in Griffiths (1990); a brief description follows.

The principle factor that led to the development of the ISDN was the adoption of digital transmission by many public telephone systems. This was due both to the ease with which digital signals could be regenerated without deterioration and the availability of VSLI-based technologies for the processing of digital streams. Voice traffic in such networks is encoded using pulse-code modulation at 64 Kbps. Naturally, these networks could also carry data, resulting in integrated digital networks (IDN).

Although an IDN integrates many different kinds of traffic internally, the services it supports are accessed through unrelated interfaces. For example, data services might be accessed via the X.25 interface, while telephony is accessed via normal analog lines ("local loops") between the customer's premises and the telephone exchange. In order to produce an ISDN, a unified interface to the IDN is required. Since this interface will itself be digital, a key requirement is the digitization of the local loops.

Local loops are mainly copper and of variable quality, some having been in the ground for many years. However, they represent a huge investment that could not lightly be discarded. One requirement of the narrow-band ISDN has always been that it should operate over the existing local loops. Digitization of these at reasonable bit rates and at reasonable cost has only recently become feasible.

Standardization The standardization of the ISDN has been carried out by the CCITT (Comité Consultatif Internationale Télégraphique et Téléphonique) and is specified in a series of recommendations, the most important of which are the "I-Series," which specify the interface to users (CCITT - 1988). Firm recommendations exist for the narrow-band ISDN, which operates over the existing infrastructure. Recommendations are now being developed for broad-band ISDN, which will operate mainly over optical fibers.

Signaling IDNs use "common channel signaling" (CCS). This means that the messages that pass between exchanges (to control the setting up of calls for example) are carried in dedicated signaling channels. This contrasts with earlier analog systems, in which signaling was carried along with the speech channel to which it related. The principle advantage of CCS is a great reduction in the number of signaling terminations at an exchange. Naturally, digital signaling is used.

ISDN also employs CCS at the user-network interface. A very much wider range of signaling messages is available than was possible with the old analog systems. This enables a much greater range of services to be offered.

Narrow-Band ISDN The ISDNs currently available are based on the transmission and switching capabilities of the existing IDN. This is based on 64 Kbps bit-streams that are combined into higher-capacity "trunks" using Time Division Multiplexing. In Europe, the first multiplex combines 32 64-Kbps channels into one 2-Mbps channel, while in the U.S. 23 64-Kbps channels form one 1.544-Mbps channel.

User Interfaces The user interfaces reflect the 64 Kbps and 2 Mbps infrastructure, and CCS.

The basic rate interface (BRI) offers two 64-Kbps "B-Channels" for data or voice and one 16-Kbps "D-Channel" for signaling. In principle, this is available to all subscribers through the existing local loops. The presence of two B-Channels means that it is possible to offer subscribers two telephone connections where previously they had only one. Up to eight pieces of equipment may be attached to a basic rate ISDN interface in a bus configuration, though only two may be used at once.

The primary rate interface (PRI) offers 30 (23 in the U.S.) 64-Kbps B-channels and one 64-Kbps D-Channel. Data channels at higher rates (H-channels) are also defined. This interface is intended for the connection of PABXs and large computer installations. Various services may be offered over the B-channels, the simplest being an unstructured 64 Kbps bit-stream (a physical layer service in OSI terms). Packet services as well as "telematic" services such as facsimile (FAX) will also be offered. Packet services include an X.25-based service and "Frame Relay," which is a Datalink Layer service. The signaling protocols used on the D-channels resemble those specified for the X.25 interface.

There are always two stacks of protocols to consider for the ISDN. The signaling protocols (in the so-called "control-plane") are always structured as three layers, and the data protocols (in the so-called "user-plane") may be one, two, or three layers, depending on the service selected. Higher-layer protocols may operate end-to-end in the user plane, but these are transparent to the ISDN itself.

Broad-Band ISDN The narrow-band ISDN cannot support the requirements of the newest types of service. For example, the bandwidth required for full-definition digital video is in the 100 megabit per second range. To handle this sort of traffic, as well as bursts of traffic from computers, a completely new infrastructure will be needed. This will be based on optical fibers and asynchronous time-division multiplexing (ATM). In ATM, all data is divided into a series of fixed-length frames of approximately 32 bytes. Each frame carries a destination address and is switched as a separate entity. The advantage over conventional TDM is that it allows the total bandwidth available to be divided between contending activities in a much more flexible way.

References

1988. CCITT *Integrated Services Digital Network: Overall aspects and functions*, ISDN User-Network Interfaces. Melbourne, Australia. Blue-book Vol. III, Fascicle III.8. November.
1990. Griffiths, J. M. (Ed). *ISDN explained*. New York: John Wiley.

GRAHAM KNIGHT

INTENSIVE CARE, COMPUTERS IN

For articles on related subjects *see* BIOCOMPUTING; EMBEDDED SYSTEM; MEDICAL IMAGING; MUMPS and TOMOGRAPHY, COMPUTERIZED.

Digital computers have proven themselves to be able assistants to the medical staff in a hospital's intensive care unit (ICU). The principal reason for the initial introduction of computers into the ICU was to improve patient care through the automated management of patient data on a long-term basis. Such a computer system can vary in size, configuration, cost, complexity, and function, depending on the degree of sophistication of the monitoring and analysis required, and the number of patients to be monitored in a particular ICU. A pioneering computerized

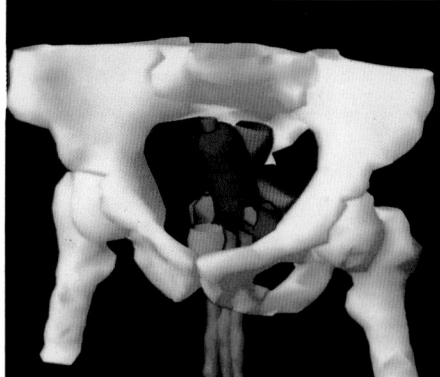

FIG. 1. Interactive surface-based rendering on Pixel-Plane 4 of female pelvis with vaginal inserts for radiation sources. The long bulbous object surrounding the tip of the three vertical shafts is a polygonally defined radiation isodose surface (CT data courtesy of North Carolina Memorial Hospital. Image courtesy of Henry Fuchs and Stephen M. Pizer, University of North Carolina).

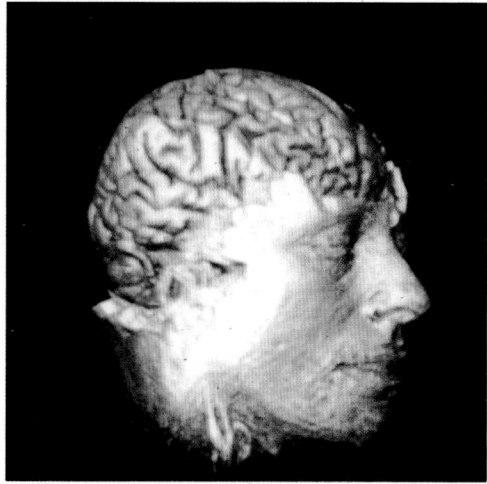

FIG. 2. Volume rendering of edited magnetic resonance data set. The apparent mottling of the facial surface in the volume rendering is due to noise in the acquired data. Note that the user was not called upon to define surface geometry, but merely to isolate a region of interest (MR data courtesy of Siemens AG, edited by Juiqi Tang. Image courtesy of Mark Levoy, University of North Carolina).

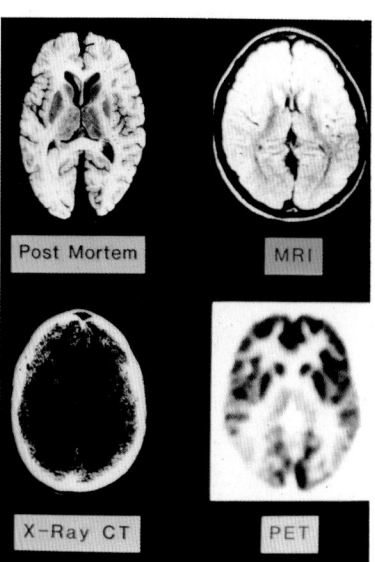

FIG. 3. An illustration of four mechanisms for viewing biological tissue. Upper left is an anatomical cross-section of the brain. Upper right is a magnetic resonance image of the same cross-section. Lower left is an X-ray CAT scan. Lower right is a positron emission tomography scan (PET scan) (Image courtesy of John C. Mazziotta, UCLA School of Medicine).

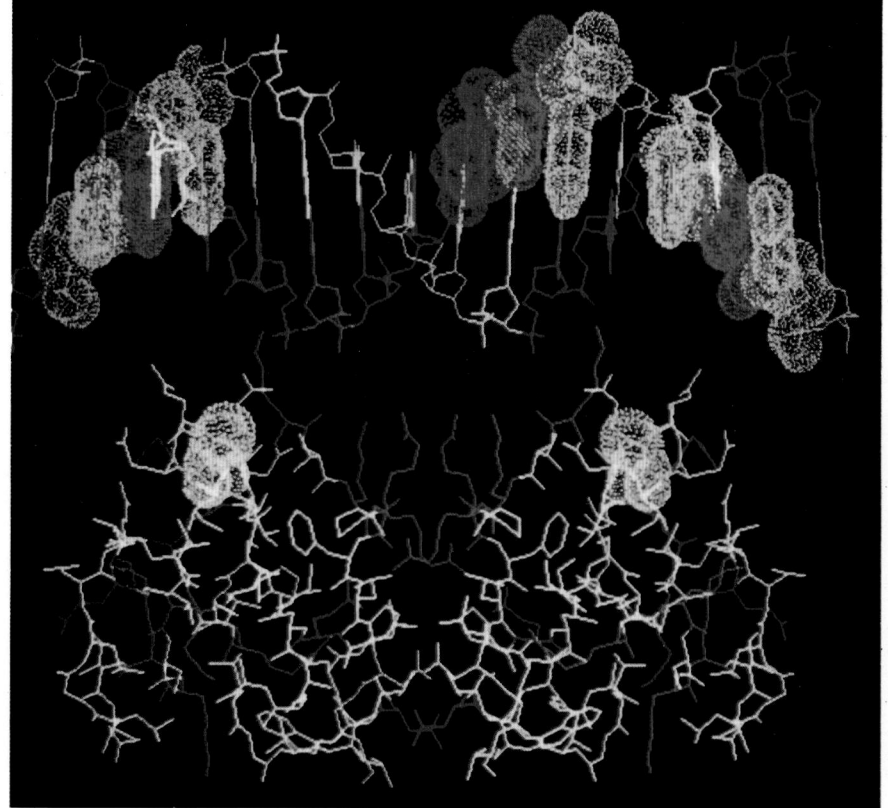

FIG. 4. Molecular modeling image of a DNA molecule docking with a protein. The DNA helix can be seen in the upper portion of the figure (Image courtesy of Lester Harris, Abbott-Northwestern Hospital).

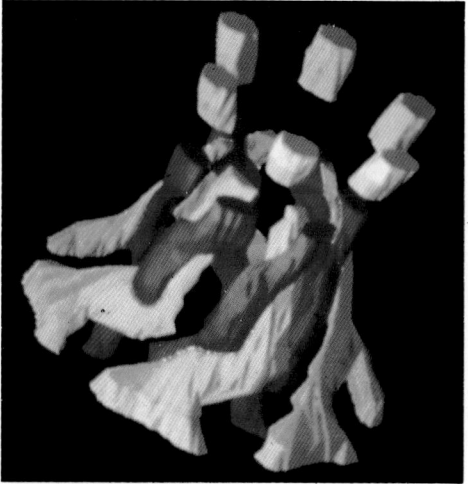

FIG. 5. Computer-aided design reconstruction of the head and neck element of the bacteriophage φ 27 (Image courtesy of D. Carrascosa).

FIG. 2. A view from "Palenque," Bank Street College's education disc on the Mayan ruin, Palenque. (Courtesy of Intel.)

COMPUTER-AIDED DESIGN AND MANUFACTURING

FIG. 3. A typical CAD/CAM workstation (A UNIGRAPHICS system from McDonnell Douglas). A function keyboard is shown on the left, with the CRT displaying an assembly model of an automobile dashboard, along with menus for the designer. Dials to move, rotate, and scale the display are on the right, as is a mouse, used for pointing to the display feature or menu item desired.

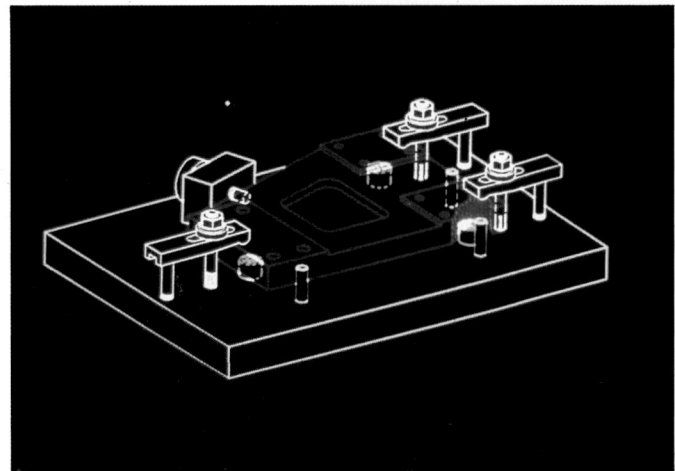

FIG. 8. A screen display of a fixture design program. The illustration provides visualization of the positions of the fixtures to hold the part while it is being manufactured.

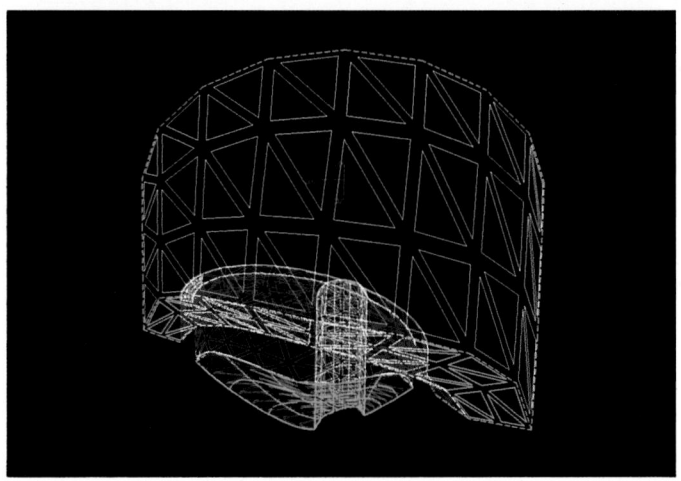

FIG. 10. A plastic cap, modeled for a molding flow analysis. The mesh represents elements used in the analysis.

COMPUTER-AIDED ENGINEERING

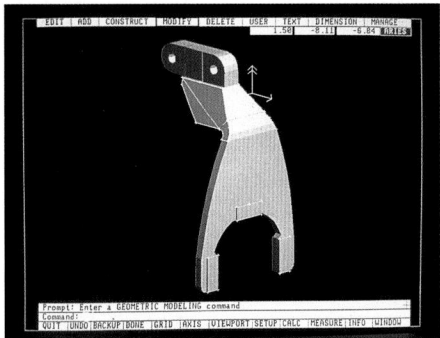

FIG. 1. A shaded image of a geometric model of a bracket. (Courtesy of Aries Technology Corporation)

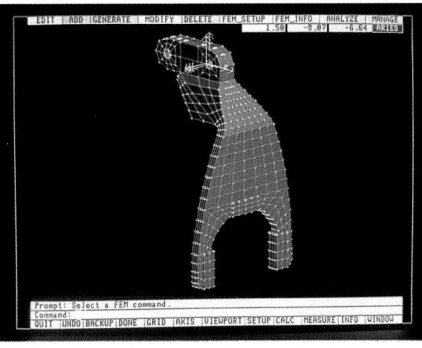

FIG. 2. The bracket shown in Figure 1 with the Finite Element Mesh applied. (Courtesy of Aries Technology Corporation)

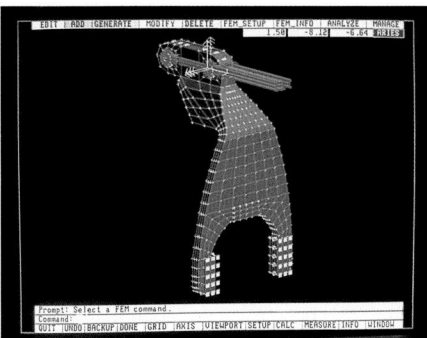

FIG. 3. The meshed bracket from Figure 2 with loads and constraints. (Courtesy of Aries Technology Corporation)

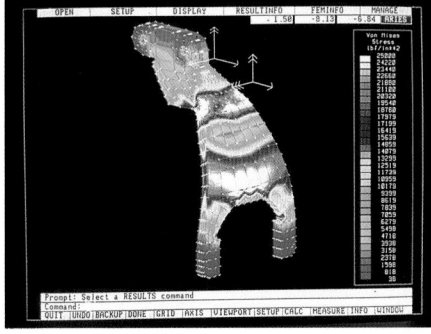

FIG. 4. The results of Finite Element Analysis displayed as stress contours for the bracket shown in Figures 1 through 3. The bar down the right-hand side of the display is a key relating color to level of stress. (Courtesy of Aries Technology Corporation)

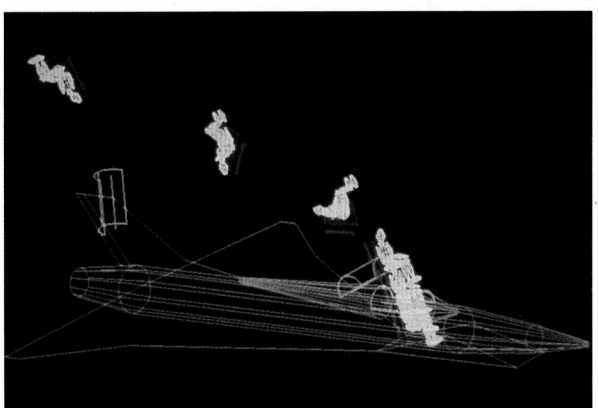

FIG. 5. This overlay drawing shows the positions of the pilot, seat, canopy, and aircraft during an ejection sequence. (Courtesy of Mechanical Dynamics, Inc.)

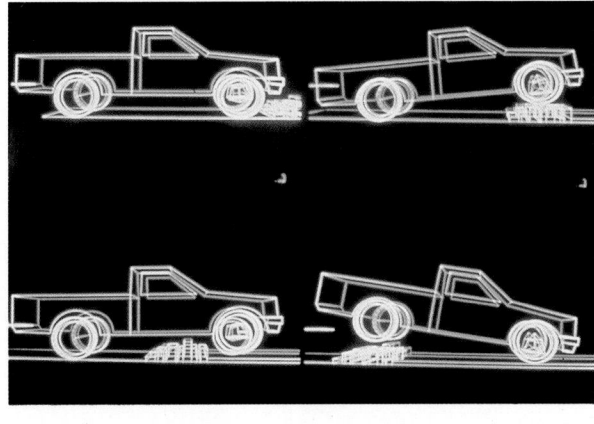

FIG. 6. A time series of the positions of a truck, its suspension, and wheels, as it passes over a bump. (Courtesy of Mechanical Dynamics, Inc.)

COMPUTER ANIMATION

FIG. 1. A wireframe image from a computer animation and its corresponding rendered image. From Panspermia. (Copyright © 1990 Karl Sims, Thinking Machines Corp., Cambridge, MA.)

COMPUTER ANIMATION (CONT.)

FIG. 2. Rendered images from the computer animation **Tuber's Two Step.** (Copyright © 1985 Chris Wedge, Ohio State University. Computer Graphics Research Group.)

COMPUTER ART

FIG. 2. Untitled Image by William Tudor, 1989.

FIG. 3. Untitled wall mural by Harold Cohen, 1984.

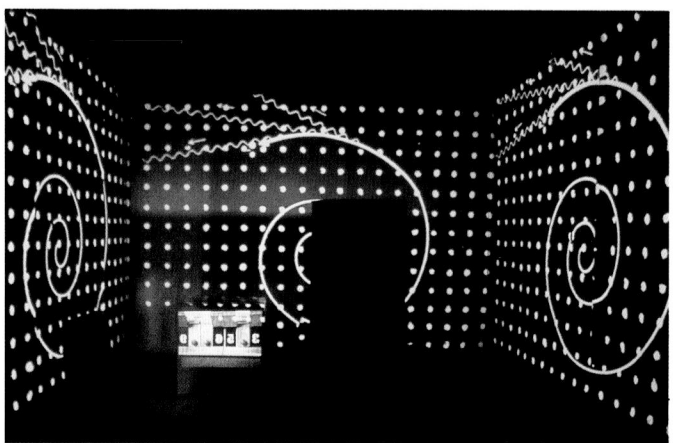

FIG. 4. "Azimuth XX" by Margot Lovejoy, a projection installation, 12′ × 12′ × 12′, 1986.

FIG. 5. "Battle To The Death" by Ellen Sandor (ART)^n, 3-D transparency mounted on a light box, 32″ × 48″, 1983.

FIG. 8. "Rainfall" by Stephen Pevnick, Fountain Project, 18' × 18' × 26', 1984.

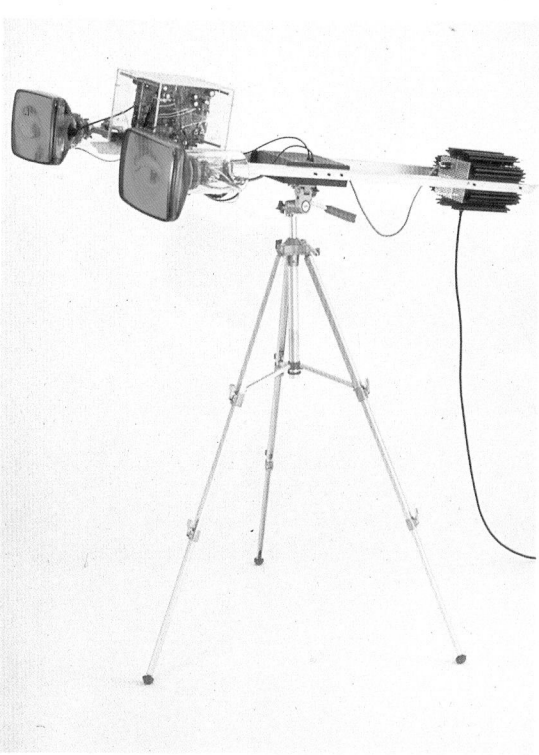

FIG. 9. "Swirling Helix" by Milton Komisar, plexiglas, polystyrene, and Apple computer, 25' high, 1982.

FIG. 10. "Voyeur" by Alan Rath, 12 × 29 × 59" plus tripod, 1986.

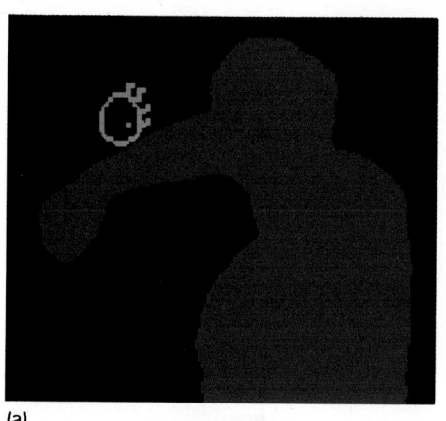

(a)

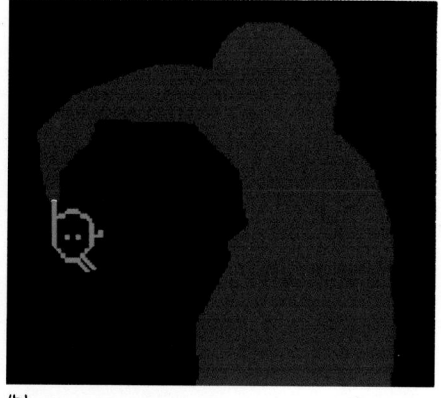

(b)

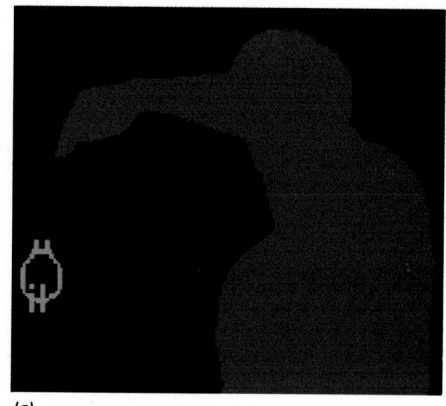

(c)

FIG. 11. ""Critter Interaction in Videoplace" by Myron Krueger, 1983.

COMPUTER GRAPHICS

(a)   (b)   (c)

FIG. 5. (a) Flat shading, (b) Gouraud shading, (c) Phong shading. (Courtesy of David Weimer and Gary Bishop, AT&T Bell Laboratories.)

FIG. 6. A ray-traced image using the Hall Illumination model. Notice the inclusion of refraction in the glass ball (front right) and reflection in the metallic sphere (left). (Courtesy of R. Hall, Program in Computer Graphics, Cornell University.)

FIG. 7. Simulated steel mill.

FIG. 8. Forest fire simulation. This realistic visualization of a forest fire is modeled with textured quadric surfaces.

ENTERTAINMENT INDUSTRY, COMPUTERS IN THE

FIG. 5. A computerized animation stand. Note the specialized controller in the animator's hand and the motors mounted on the camera itself. (Copyright © 1990 LucasArts Entertainment. All rights reserved. Courtesy Industrial Light & Magic.)

FIG. 4. An example of effects animation. The **time-slice effect**, from **Back to the Future, Part 3**, was animated by hand and then optically composited over the car. Copyright © 1990 Universal City Studios, Inc. All rights reserved. Courtesy Industrial Light & Magic.

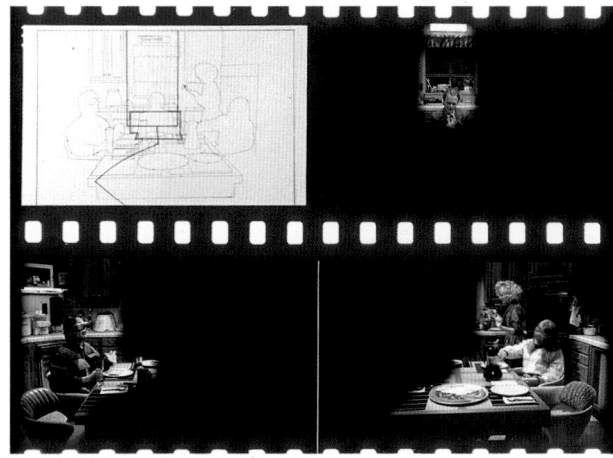

FIG. 6a. Storyboard and three elements of a *split shot*. Use of motion control allows the director to move the camera, adding interest and believability to the shot. (Copyright © 1990 LucasArts Entertainment. All rights reserved. Courtesy Industrial Light & Magic.)

FIG. 6b. The completed split shot as it appeared in **Back to the Future, Part 2**. Michael J. Fox plays all three characters at the dinner table. (Copyright © 1989 Universal City Studios, Inc. All rights reserved. Courtesy Industrial Light & Magic.)

FIG. 8. Tinny, the wind-up toy, from *Tin Toy*, winner of the 1989 Academy Award for Best Short Animated Film. (Copyright © 1988 PIXAR.)

FIG. 9. An image from the computer-based video game, **The Secret of Monkey Island**. Controls located below the image direct the lead character through an imaginary world. (Copyright © 1990 LucasArts Entertainment. All rights reserved. Courtesy Lucasfilm Games.)

FIG. 13a. A shot from **Back to the Future, Part 3** showing a wire-rig supporting the pink hoverboard. (Copyright © 1990 Universal City Studios, Inc. All rights reserved. Courtesy Industrial Light & Magic.)

FIG. 13b. The shot as it appeared in the film, the wire-rig has been removed using computer graphics software, creating the illusion of a working hoverboard. (Copyright © 1990 Universal City Studios, Inc. All rights reserved. Courtesy Industrial Light & Magic.)

FIG. 6. Electrostatic potential around a small satellite Mandelbrot set. The Julia set that belongs to the parameter c from the center of this Mandelbrot set is pictured on the (Riemann) sphere in the background. Cover picture of **The Beauty of Fractals**. (© 1986 H. Jürgens, H.-O. Peitgen, D. Saupe.)

FIG. 7. The potential function near the Mandelbrot set. The rendering of the sky is by means of random fractals (method of successive random additions). Cover picture of **The Science of Fractal Images** (© 1988 H. Jürgens, H.-O. Peitgen, D. Saupe.)

FIG. 8. Fractal planet generated with the rescale-and-add method. The fractal dimension depends on the latitude: Near the equator, the dimension of the coast lines is close to 1.0, whereas near the poles it is close to 2.0. The planet is rendered as a perfect sphere. However, the texturing function is based on the random fractal (pseudo) height and, for the polar caps, also depends on latitude. (© 1988 H. Jügens, H.-O. Peitgen, D. Saupe.)

FIG. 9. Random fractal in three variables rendered as a cloud with a fractal moon generated via the random cuts method and a background motivated by the filigrees of the Mandelbrot set. (from **The Science of Fractal Images**, © 1988 R. Voss.)

FIG. 10. Random fractal landscape with haze. (© 1989 F. K. Musgrave, B. Mandelbrot.)

FIG. 11. Fractal mountain scene with tree grown by L-systems. (© 1989 F. K. Musgrave, C. Kolb, B. Mandelbrot, P. Prusinkiewicz.'

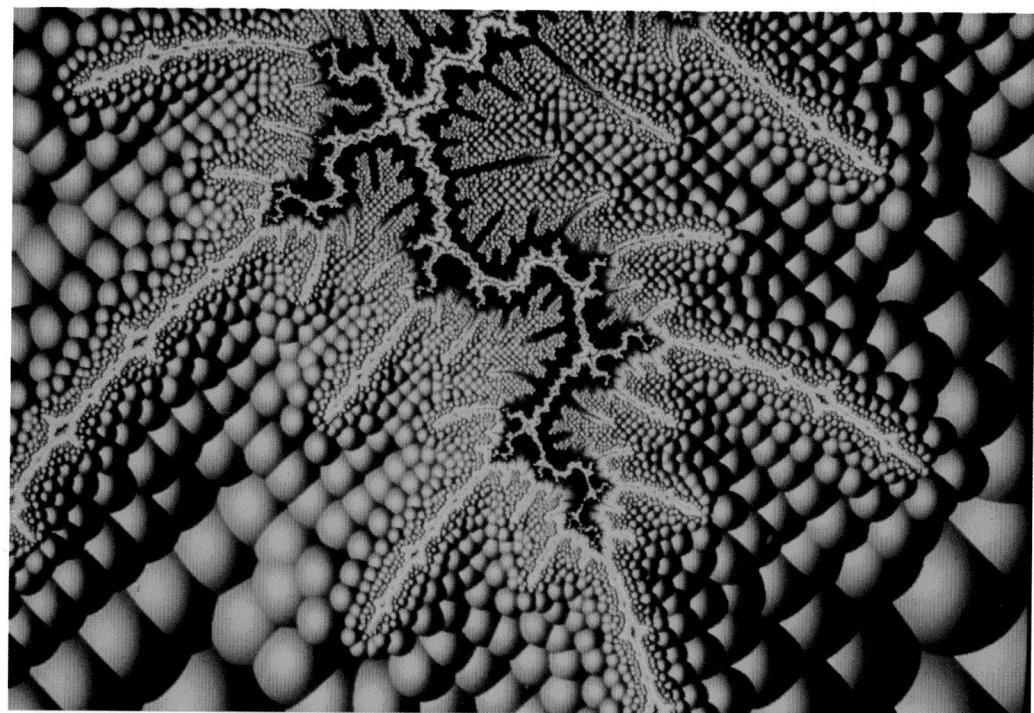

FIG. 12. Spheres filling the exterior of the Mandelbrot set. They are computed using the distance estimate formula. (© 1988 H. Jürgens, H.-O. Peitgen, D. Saupe.)

MEDICAL IMAGING

FIG. 3 h, i, j. (h) Mapping of the brain function to anatomy. The gray level image is from the MR; the color is from the PET of the same patient. Red color shows high metabolic rates. Registration of these two images required sophisticated mathematics and computer programming. (Courtesy of D. Valentino). (i) A longitudinal section Doppler ultrasound image of the abodomen. Red color shows the blood flow; arrow indicates that flow in the portal vein is hepatopetal. (Courtesy of E. Grant). (j) 3-D reconstruction of the lumber spine from sectional CT images.

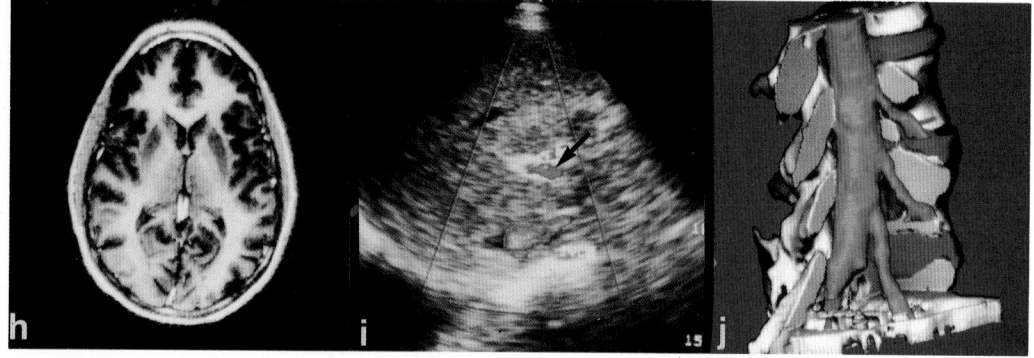

FIG. 1. Artist's view of QCD simulation on a lattice used to approximate field interactions between colored quarks that build up a hadron. (From K.M. Bitar and W. M. Heller, Florida State University in Computers in Physics, **6**, 1, Jan/Feb 1992, p. 34, permission of AIP.)

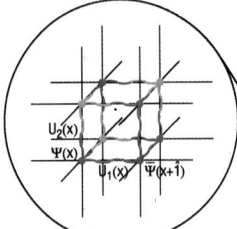

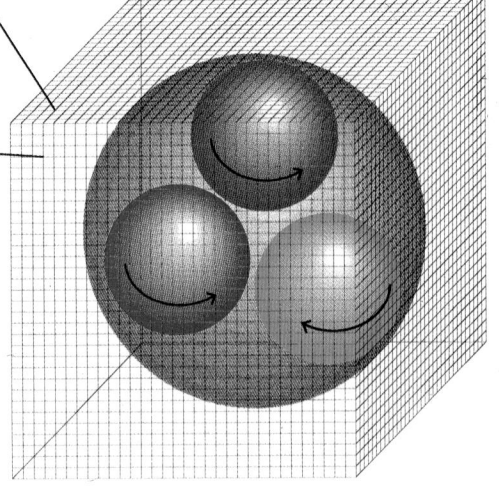

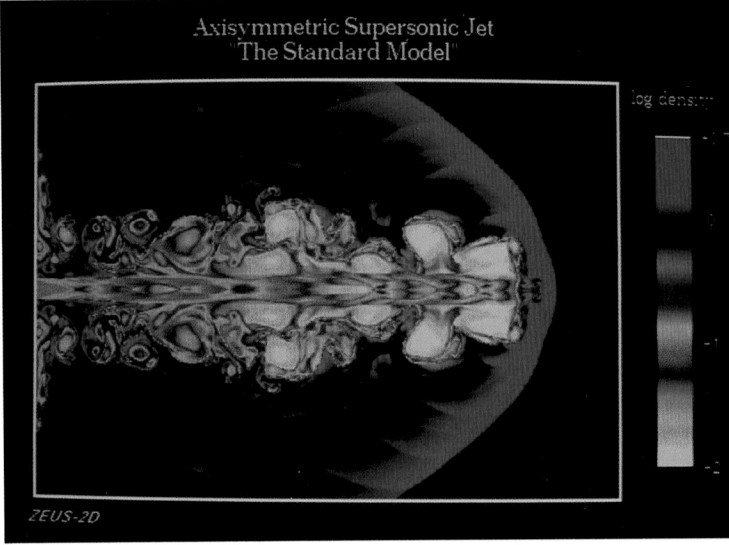

FIG. 8. Computer-generated astrophysical jet. (From Science **253**, 5019 2 Aug 1991 (cover), © 1991 AAAS, reprinted by permission of AAAS and Dr. Jack O. Burns, New Mexico State University.)

FIG. 9. Fermi surface of $YBa_2Cu_3O_7$. (From W. E. Pickett and R. E. Cohen, Naval Research Laboratory.)

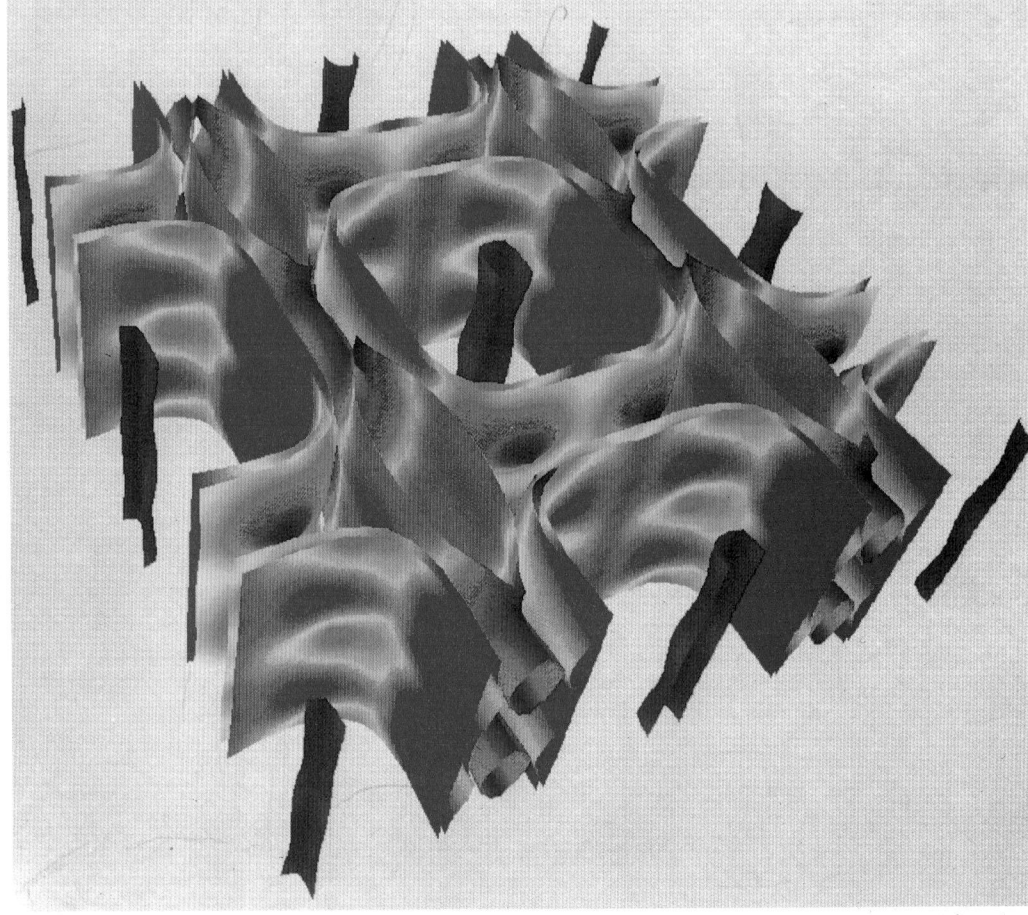

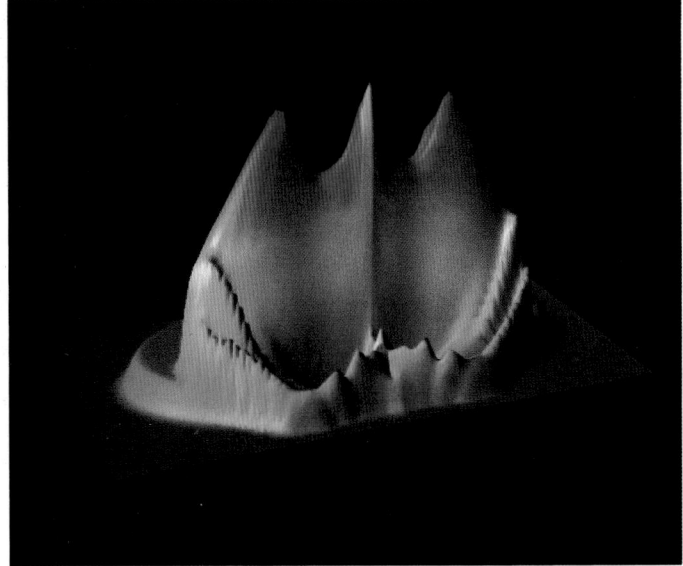

FIG. 10. Mass density and energy density rendered on the same frame using the apE2.0 program Terrain to render the mass density as the height and the energy density mapped onto the density surface as colors. Blue corresponds to cooler and red to hotter gas elements. (From G. C. Duncan, Bowling Green State University.)

FIG. 11. Magnetic strange attractors. (From Jennifer Johnson, Autodisk Inc.)

FIG. 12. Convergence patterns of Newton-Raphson iteration of $Z^4 - 1 = 0$ (page 114f of Gleick's Chaos, 1987).

STAMPS, COMPUTING ON

Colombia

West Germany

Great Britain

Norway

Switzerland

Poland

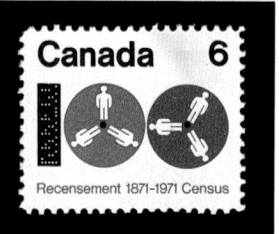
Canada

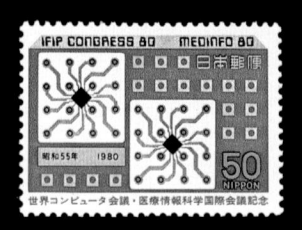
Japan

Great Britain

Ivory Coast

East Germany

TOMOGRAPHY, COMPUTERIZED

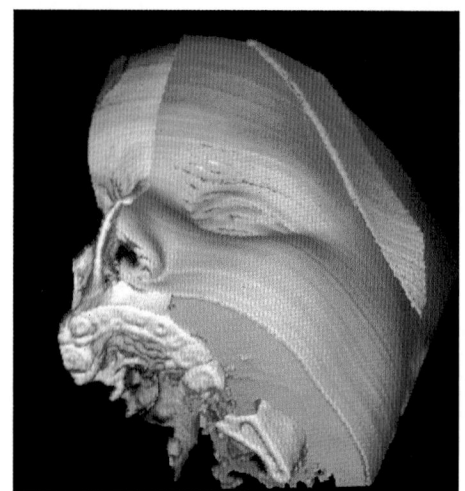

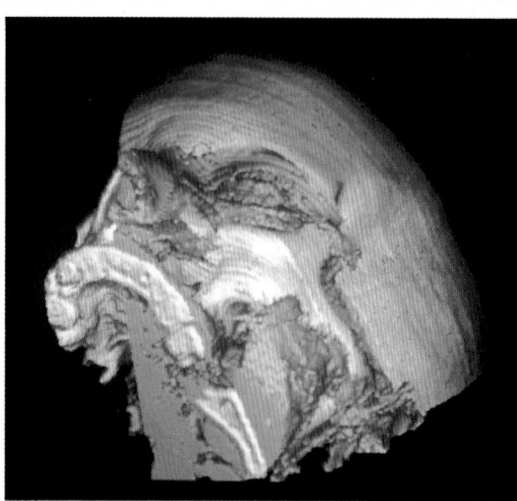

FIG. 4. Three-dimensional computer graphic display of a patient's head obtained from a series of two-dimensional CT scans. On the left we see the skin and a constraining strap as well as part of the skull, while on the right we see some of the muscles and the skull. (Illustration provided by Dr. J. K. Udupa, University of Pennsylvania).

surgical ICU is shown in Fig. 1. This system remains today as a benchmark upon which advanced therapeutic techniques have been developed.

Computers are currently distributed through many components within an intensive care unit, in addition to their use for patient data management. During the 1980s, virtually all bedside physiologic monitoring devices were converted from analog or hybrid designs to total digital systems with embedded microprocessors. *Local area networks* (*q.v.*) are typically used to connect bedside monitoring devices to each other, to the central nurses' station display systems, and to the patient data management system. The central patient data management software may reside on a powerful minicomputer (*q.v.*) or an advanced scientific workstation (*q.v.*), or may be distributed between many dedicated bed-specific workstations. Limited data management capability is also contained within some bedside physiologic monitoring devices.

Physiologic signal analysis begins within the many parameter-specific plug-in modules that customize the microprocessor-based bedside physiologic monitors. Containing microprocessors themselves, these plug-in modules provide analog-to-digital conversion (*q.v.*) of monitored waveforms, as well as initial signal processing and feature extraction. The digitization process is of critical concern because physiologic data is usually developed at the patient/transducer interface as an analog signal (i.e. a voltage that varies as a function of time) and inaccuracies at the digitization stage will corrupt the data for all subsequent analyses.

Improved patient care can be achieved through computerization for several reasons. First, nurses are able to concentrate on direct patient care when computers take over the repetitive and time-consuming measurement and record-keeping functions. The least sophisticated patient-monitoring systems should fulfill this role by logging the measurements provided by the multitude of commercially available bedside physiologic monitoring devices. These instruments typically provide average values of such parameters as heart rate, blood pressure, respiration rate, and body temperature on front panel digital displays for visual inspection by the medical staff.

Second, uniformity and reproducibility in data collection from shift-to-shift and day-to-day improve the reliability and completeness of the medical record. The more sophisticated systems maintain a database on each patient which is reviewable upon request in tabular or graphical formats.

Third, a continuous vigil is maintained for measured parameters that are out-of-tolerance. In advanced systems, trend analyses and multiparameter diagnostic algorithms contribute to a further increase in system capability by providing the physician with an immediate indication of many undesirable and correctable events, such as the presence of abnormal heart rhythms.

Finally, continuous computer adjustment of therapeutic interventions is possible and can provide a level of control unattainable by the periodic human supervision of these interventions. For example, the use of sophisticated computer hardware has been shown to allow the implementation of automated infusion of blood or drugs, under closed-loop control, in response to needs signaled by changes in monitored parameters.

The method by which patient monitoring is physically implemented depends upon the situation in question. In many research environments, or when certain cardiovascular or respiratory monitoring functions are to be performed, it is sometimes advantageous to analyze physiologic variables on a "heartbeat-by-heartbeat" or "breath-by-breath" basis. The data management computer must, in these situations, process the basic time-varying physiologic waveform. The necessary computer programs are generally written by personnel with medical backgrounds or under medical staff supervision. These *pattern recognition* (*q.v.*) programs represent a more complex level of programming than that usually required in other than the beat-to-beat situation.

The software used in intensive care monitoring systems can vary as widely as the system hardware. At one end of the spectrum, all monitoring and analysis tasks are performed by a relatively simple program that sequentially analyzes each of the signals being monitored on a particular patient, permanently records its findings, and then cyclically switches to the next patient before the program repeats its analysis.

At the other end of the software spectrum are re-entrant monitoring and analysis programs that exist in a *multiprogramming* (*q.v.*) environment. These programs use a hardware, priority interrupt system to respond dynamically to the needs of many simultaneously monitored patients. In such a computer installation, data retrieval can be carried out interactively from many independent terminals, using sophisticated data analysis and graphics software. In addition, low-priority background processing of non-real-time tasks is possible to a limited extent.

An open-ended area in the development of patient monitoring systems is that of diagnostic and statistical analysis programming. The ultimate extent to which computers will contribute to patient care depends upon the growth of techniques used in the analysis and extrapolation of all available data. The application of cluster analysis, correlation techniques, nonlinear transformations, artificial intelligence (*q.v.*), and expert systems (*q.v.*) offer the potential to improve the accuracy of diagnostic and trend detection functions. The continuing development of diagnostic methods will provide the new criteria to be implemented on ICU computer systems in the future.

A hospital can currently obtain physiologic monitoring devices, nurses' station displays and patient data management systems from many commercial vendors. These systems can be tailored to the hospital's requirements and will provide a majority of the capabilities discussed, except for research-oriented features such as automated infusion therapy, without the need for an in-house software development effort. Computerized bedside monitoring and nurses' station components are used in virtually all hospitals today. However, the current high cost and recent commercial availability of most patient data management systems tend to limit their widespread use.

References

1986. Gardner, Reed M. "Computerized Management of Intensive Care Patients," *M.D. Computing*, **3**, *1*: 36–51.

1988. Leyerle, Beverly J., LoBue, Mark, and Shabot, M. Michael. "The PDMS as A Focal Point for Distributed Patient Data," *International Journal of Clinical Monitoring and Computing*, **5**: 155–161.

KENNETH M. KEMPNER

INTERACTIVE INPUT DEVICES

For articles on related subjects *see* COMPUTER GRAPHICS; HUMAN FACTORS IN COMPUTING; MOUSE; USER INTERFACE; and WORKSTATION.

Input devices connected to a computer system allow the user to enter data or interact with running programs, and are used for activities ranging from editing computer programs to playing video games. Input devices can be separated into five classes: *keyboards, locators, picks, valuators,* and *buttons*. The classification is determined by the distinct functions performed. In many cases, these divisions are blurred because a device of one class can simulate the functions of another. This simulation allows a workstation to have full functionality without having to use a large number of different input devices.

Keyboards   A *keyboard*, the most common input device, is used for entering textual data into a computer file under control of an editor or word processor (see Fig. 1).

Keyboard keys are usually arranged similar to those of a standard typewriter, the so-called QWERTY keyboard (named for the sequence of keys in the top row). This is an historical artifact, since early typewriter keys had to be arranged to allow typists to work quickly without the keys jamming. To do this, frequently used keys were placed far apart, slowing down the typist. Because of the speed and electronic nature of the computer, other keyboard designs have been explored that group frequently used keys together. An example of this is the Dvorak keyboard (see Fig. 2).

When data is being entered at a keyboard, the user's CRT (cathode ray tube) screen provides visual feedback indicating where new data will be placed with respect to characters already typed. This is done with a *cursor*, which is usually an underscore, a reverse video character, or a bright or blinking square. The type of cursor is dependent on the application package being used.

Locating Devices   *Locators* are used for indicating a position for placing objects on the screen or quickly moving the cursor in a text editor. Visual feedback of the current position is provided with an arrow or a crosshair displayed on the screen. A digitizing tablet, mouse, trackball, and joystick are examples of location devices.

The *digitizing tablet* is a flat surface, sometimes illuminated, that has a fine grid of horizontal and vertical wires embedded into it (see Fig. 3). There is an attached stylus or *puck* that produces a magnetic field and is centered at the location to which it points. The magnetic field will induce a current on the wires of the tablet. By sensing

FIG. 1.   A computer keyboard, with attached function keys. The function keys to the left and right have specific functions. The function keys labeled F1 through F12 are programmable, and their function will vary with the application. (Photograph courtesy of Sun Microsystems, Inc.)

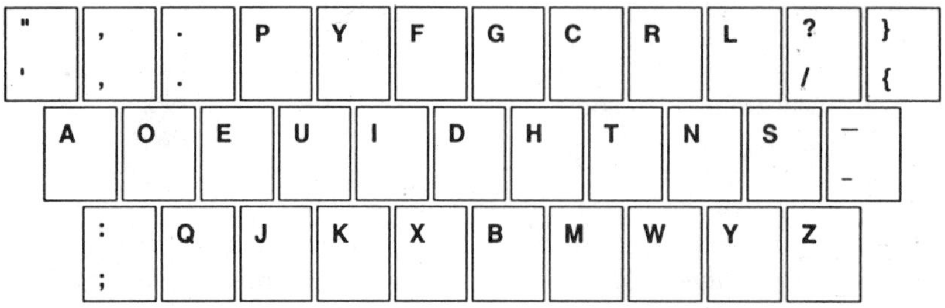

FIG. 2.   Dvorak keyboard.

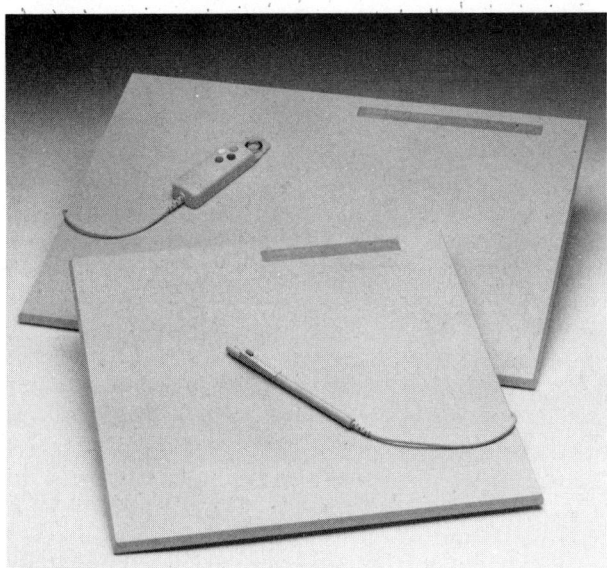

FIG. 3. Two digitizing or graphics tablets. The foreground shows a stylus, and the background shows a puck. (Photograph courtesy of Summagraphics Corporation.)

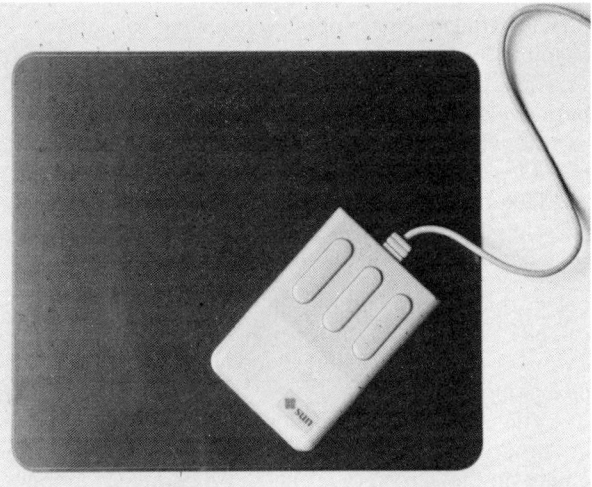

FIG. 4. An optical mouse. The grid of lines can be faintly seen on the left side of the mouse pad. (Photograph courtesy of Sun Microsystems, Inc.)

the strength of the current on a set of neighboring wires, the tablet can determine where the stylus or puck is and whether it is touching the tablet or being held above it.

Digitizing tablets are very precise and can be used to enter line drawings—maps, for example—into the computer through the input of key points in the drawing. Since the same signal is produced each time the stylus is placed in a particular position (e.g. the center of the tablet), the digitizing tablet is considered an *absolute locator*.

A *mouse* is a small hand-held device that is used to indicate a position or movement. Typical uses for a mouse include quickly repositioning the cursor in a word processor, and moving an object by "dragging" it to a new location. A mouse will also include one to three buttons on its top that can be "clicked" to start or stop an operation, or indicate a chosen position.

A mouse can be either a physical or an optical mouse. A *physical mouse* has a ball that protrudes from its bottom. When the mouse is moved, friction will cause the ball to move at a rate proportional to the movement of the mouse. Inside the mouse, there is a set of potentiometers that sense the direction and rate of movement of the ball. These are then converted into electrical signals that are interpreted by the computer as signifying that the mouse is in motion.

An *optical mouse* (see Fig. 4) uses a light emitting diode (LED), a light sensor, and a special mouse pad instead of the ball and potentiometers. The mouse pad is key to the operation of the mouse. It has a reflective surface and a set of light and dark horizontal and vertical lines. As the mouse is moved, light from the LED is reflected off the mouse pad to the sensor. When a vertical line is crossed, the reflected light is slightly darkened, and when a horizontal line is crossed, it is significantly darkened. By sensing these pulses of light, the direction and rate of movement can be determined.

A mouse is good for gross movement, but is not very useful for operations that require high precision. Also,

since a mouse can be lifted off its surface or mouse pad and be moved without disturbing the current location, the mouse is considered a *relative locator*. A related device is the trackball, which is nothing more than a mouse turned upside down so that the ball can be directly manipulated by the palm of the hand rather than rolling it over a flat surface.

A *joystick* (see Fig. 5), popular among those who play video games, is also used to indicate position. The joystick has a rod that protrudes from a base. Inside the base are a set of potentiometers that can sense when the rod is deflected from a vertical position. In spring-loaded joysticks, the rod will always return to center when released. These joysticks indicate a change of position by the direction of the push, and a change of speed by the amount of deflection. When in the center position, no change takes place. These are, therefore, relative loca-

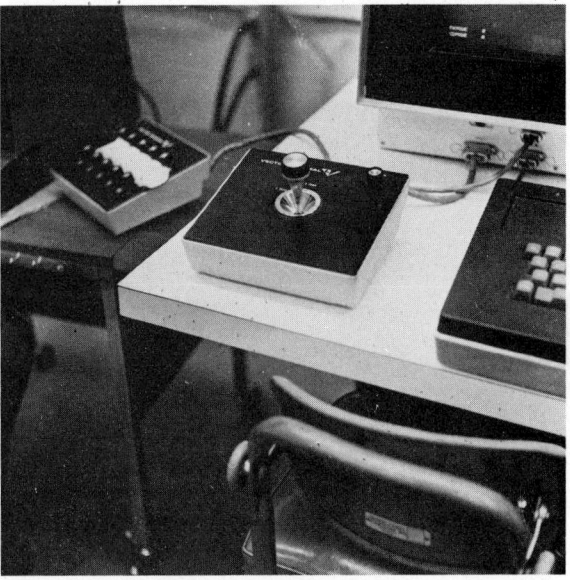

FIG. 5. A joystick on table below screen.

tors. Joysticks that are not spring-loaded will indicate an absolute location based on where the rod is positioned. Joysticks usually indicate only two-dimensional positions by moving the rod laterally, but there are also three-dimensional joysticks in which the third dimension is indicated by rotation of the rod. Like a mouse, a joystick is good for gross movement, but not precision work.

Picking Devices A *pick device* is used to choose an object that appears on the screen, whether it be graphical, like a line in an architectural drawing, or textual, like a word or sentence. *Lightpens* and *touch screens* are examples of pick devices.

The name *lightpen* is a misnomer, since the pen does not produce light, but rather senses light produced by an object on the screen (see Fig. 6). All computer monitors use phosphor to display their image. The phosphor is excited by an electron beam and, as it decays to its normal state, it produces the light that creates the image. Since the decay process also causes the light produced to dim, an image on the screen is constantly being redrawn (about 30 to 60 times a second). Each part of the image on the screen is, therefore, constantly getting darker until it flashes bright when refreshed, but this happens so frequently that the human eye cannot sense this change.

When an object or part of an object is refreshed, it becomes brighter, and it is this brightening that triggers the lightpen. When this flash of light is sensed by the lightpen, it sends a signal to the computer. The computer can then determine which object was picked by determining which was being refreshed when the flash occurred.

The basic idea of a *touch screen* is that the user need only point at an object on the screen with a finger to choose it; there is no special device that the user must hold (see Fig. 7). The sensing mechanism of a touch screen is either built into the monitor or placed over the monitor screen. Touch screens are based on either beams of light or electrical currents. In the first case, a series of LEDs are placed

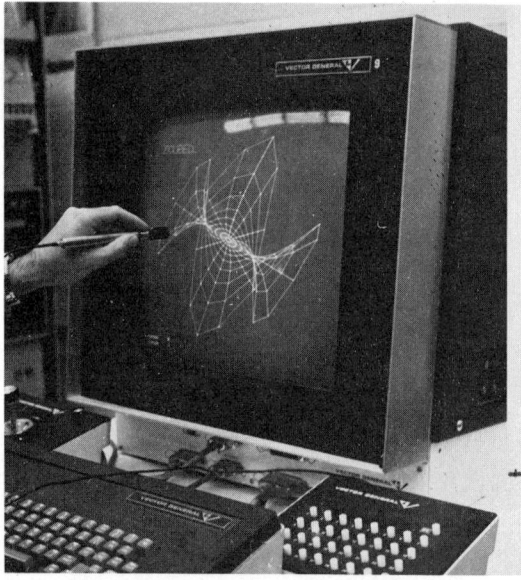

FIG. 6. A lightpen pointing to a picture on a display screen.

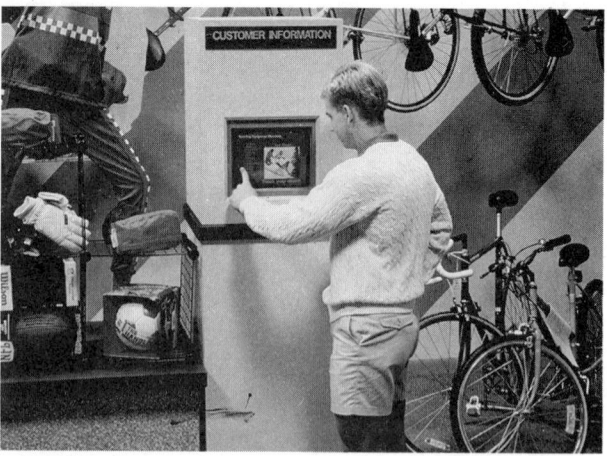

FIG. 7. A user at a touch screen. (Photograph courtesy of IBM, Inc.)

along a vertical and horizontal edge of the screen and a series of light sensors are lined up on the two opposite edges. When the user touches the screen, one or more lights are blocked in the vertical and horizontal directions. By checking which lights have been blocked, the computer can determine an approximate position. In the second case, when the user makes contact with the screen, two films placed over the screen are pushed together. The first has a conductive surface and the second has a resistive surface, and when they make contact, there is a change in voltage that determines where the touch was made. Touch screens appear to be very similar to locating devices. They are, however, of even lower resolution than the worst locating device, and this restricts them to picking functions. Their use is popular in public settings, such as libraries, where, over the course of time, users do much less damage by merely touching the surface of a CRT screen than they would by pounding on the keys of a keyboard.

Valuator Devices *Valuators* are used to indicate a real (non-integral) numeric value over a specific range. These are implemented as slide and dial potentiometers that work in the same way as a rheostatic light dimmer. When the valuator is all the way to the left, it produces high resistance, when it's all the way to the right, it produces low resistance. The resistance is then converted to a real value over some specified range. For example, the lowest resistance could represent a value of 5.0 and the highest a value of 10.0. A resistance value halfway between these two would then represent a value of 7.5.

Button Devices *Buttons* are special-purpose function keys that are frequently attached to a keyboard. For use with word processors, some of these are marked with arrows (arrow keys) and are used to move the cursor. Others can be used to delete or insert a character, word, sentence, or paragraph. Because the design of computer keyboards typically includes arrow keys and a set of function keys, users usually consider them to be an integral part of the keyboard device, but there is a conceptual difference. Whereas the conventional keys of the keyboard produce one ASCII character each time they are pressed, function keys produce a group of two or three character codes per stroke. This allows the computer to differentiate them from keyboard keys.

Function buttons are used to choose options with one key stroke and will perform a function that is specific to the application program that is running. For this reason, they are also referred to as *programmable function keys*.

Other Devices Input devices and user interaction are active topics of research. Work is being done to recognize voice data entry and handwritten data entry and will undoubtedly lead to new devices and device classes.

Simulation of Logical Functions If a workstation were to be designed such that all classes of input devices had to be included, the user's desktop could become quite cluttered with a keyboard, mouse, lightpen, button pad, and valuator dials. To reduce the number of devices without reducing the functionality of the workstation, computer systems will often simulate a device from one class with a device from another. While it is possible to simulate a device from any of the classes with one from another, some of these simulations are quite logical, but others are quite nonsensical. Some examples of device class simulation follow.

A keyboard is the most versatile input device, since it may easily simulate devices from other classes. A locator or valuator function can be simulated by the user typing in an (x,y) coordinate location or a real value. Objects can be numbered or named, and the user can pick an object by typing that object's name. Instead of function buttons, the user can type the function name on the keyboard, as is done with most operating systems.

Locating devices can perform a pick function by indicating a location on the object to be picked. A lightpen (pick) can simulate a locator by having the user drag a crosshair on the screen to the correct position. Displaying a menu of commands on the screen allows the user to use a keyboard as a simulated button with which a particular menu item can be selected.

In an extreme example, a pick device can be used to simulate a keyboard by displaying a picture of a keyboard on the screen as a series of objects. A lightpen would then be used to "hunt and peck" at the keyboard on the screen, picking the keys to be typed. Other simulations are possible and allow workstations to provide a wide range of functions without the clutter of multiple input devices.

References

1989. Brown, Judith and Cunningham, Steve. *Programming the User Interface*. New York, NY: John Wiley & Sons.

1990. Foley, James D., Van Dam, Andries, Feiner, Steven K., and Hughes, John F. *Computer Graphics: Principles and Practice*. Reading, MA: Addison-Wesley.

JEFFREY J. MCCONNELL

INTERACTIVE SYSTEM

For an article on a related subject *see* TIME SHARING.

An *interactive system* is a computing system that allows the user to interact with a running program by giving it data or control directions through a video display terminal (VDT) or personal computer. This mode of operation is in contrast to a *batch processing* system, which requires that all input be placed in a file that is readied for reading before beginning execution of the program that will process it. The obvious advantage of interactive use is that the user can choose input and control directions based on partial results received from an early phase of program execution, whereas batch processing requires that data be prepared with all eventualities in mind. The difference is most acute when debugging a new program.

A stand-alone personal computer is naturally interactive because its only user sits right at its keyboard and screen as computation proceeds. A terminal or personal computer becomes interactive with respect to a remote *host computer* (q.v.) only if it is "hard wired" to the host or is equipped with a modem (q.v.) that allows calling the host over telephone lines.

EDWIN D. REILLY

INTERLEAVING

For articles on related subjects *see* ACCESS TIME; and MEMORY: MAIN.

In systems with more than one autonomous memory module, considerable advantage in system speed may be acquired by arranging that sequential memory addresses occur in different modules. By this means the total time taken to access a sequence of memory locations can be much reduced, since several memory accesses may be overlapped by a high-speed CPU. Two-way and four-way *interleaving* are commonly encountered.

Assume, for example, a memory with 0.6 μs access time (i.e. the time to get a word from memory to the processor) and a 1.2 μs cycle (i.e. the time after the initiation of an access before the memory can be accessed again), and a processor requiring 0.2 μs to prepare a memory request and a further 0.2 μs to handle the result. Also assume processor and memory overlap.

Under these conditions, as illustrated in Fig. 1, a sequence of four memory accesses would take 4.6 μs with no interleaving, 2.4 μs with two-way interleaving, and 1.6 μs with four-way interleaving. Notice in this example that four-way interleaving provides a smaller incremental advantage than does the two-way. This is a result of the particular choice made of CPU and memory timing, which happens to be fairly well suited for two-way interleaving. Notice further that four-way interleaving leaves the CPU fully occupied (at least as far as the example goes). The result is that more than four-way interleaving in this example will provide no increase in speed. The system speed for four-way (or more) interleaving has become CPU-limited rather than memory-limited, as is the case shown in Fig. 1(a).

For very high speed CPUs (particularly those involv-

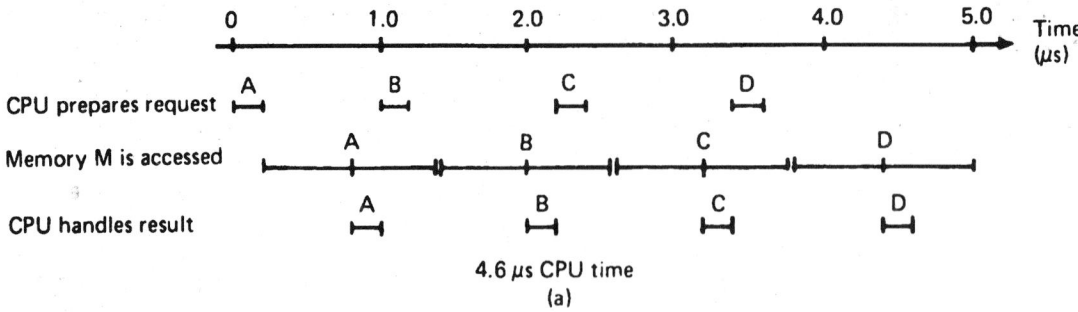

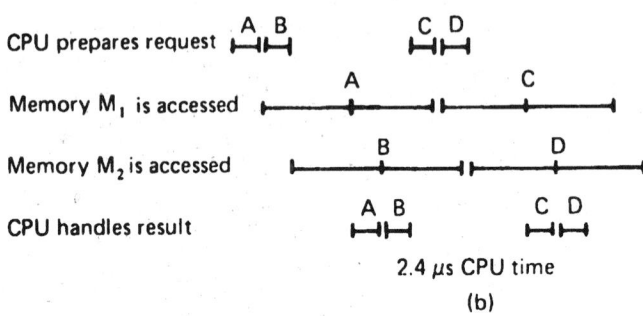

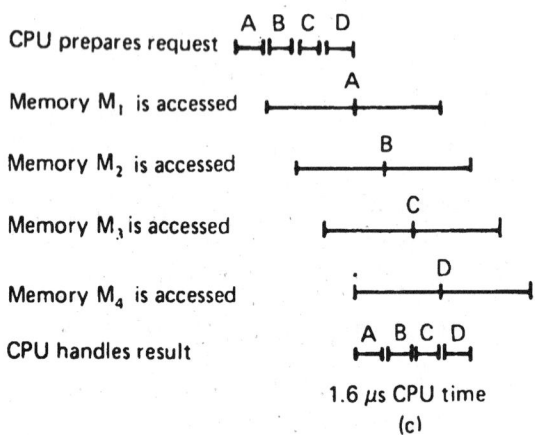

FIG. 1.   Timing diagram, showing a sequence of four memory accesses (A,B,C,D) in a speed-limited memory system with (a) no interleaving, (b) two-way interleaving, and (c) four-way interleaving. (Time scale is 0.2 μs per division.)

ing *instruction lookahead*), for multiple CPUs, and for block transfers to cache memory (*q.v.*), it is possible to keep many modules busy simultaneously. Up to 32 interleaved modules have been reported.

KENNETH C. SMITH AND ADEL S. SEDRA

Reference

1978. Hamacher, V. C., Vranesic, Z. G., and Zaky, S. G., *Computer Organization.* New York: McGraw-Hill, 243–245.

INTERLOCK

For articles on related subjects *see* CONCURRENT PROGRAMMING; CONTENTION; MEMORY: MAIN; and PETRI NET.

Interlock is a mechanism implemented in hardware or software that is intended to coordinate activity of two or more processes within a computing system. This mechanism generally insures that one process has reached a suitable state such that the other may proceed. In the event that two processes use a common resource (memory, for instance), interlock will guarantee that only one

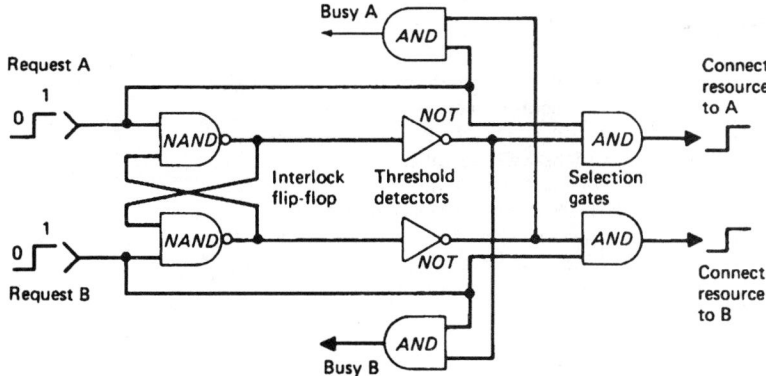

FIG. 1. A high-speed interlock mechanism for arbitrating between two asynchronous requests for a single resource.

request is honored at a time, and perhaps that some discipline, such as first-come-first-served, is observed.

In many cases, the mechanism communicates with each process using *flags*, which are memory elements set and read either through software or hardware. A common problem concerns the relative timing of setting and interrogating the flags, and of the start of subsequent action. The problem is further complicated by the fact that asynchronous (time-uncoordinated) processes may be observing each other and must decide on a future course of action based on a snapshot observation. Often, the interlock mechanism is an important part of the timing of each process; hence, it should be very fast.

One solution to interlock incorporates a polling (*q.v.*) mechanism where the appropriate conditions of each process are interrogated in turn and decisions are reached in a corresponding fixed order or priority. This scheme, though easily implemented either in hardware or software, requires a separate polling device or program and is wasteful of time, particularly when conflict is unlikely.

A hardware approach to arbitrating between requests from two processes (e.g. CPUs) for a shared resource (e.g. memory) is shown in Fig. 1. Normally, both inputs (request A and request B) are zero, setting the interlock flip-flop into the (1,1) output state and inhibiting both selection gates via the inverting threshold elements. When either request A or B is raised *separately*, the flip-flop establishes the corresponding (0,1) state, selecting the corresponding selection gate and generating a signal connecting the resource to the requester. If, for example, request B is raised while A is up, the connection to A is unaffected, and a suitable busy signal is returned to process B.

If both A and B requests occur *simultaneously*, the effect is to change both outputs of the interlock flip-flop from one to zero at once. By virtue of the feedback, shown in Fig. 1, an oscillation will be produced in which the outputs of the interlock flip-flop change in phase at a very high frequency. The amplitude of the oscillation is so small that the threshold of the detectors following can be set to ignore it.

Eventually, due to minute timing differences in the inputs, random electrical noise, circuit asymmetry, etc., the circuit will establish a stable state in which one and only one of the requests is honored. In practice, this oscillatory decision process occurs very rarely. In one study conducted using 10 ns logic, oscillation of any significance was observed only when input signals were within 100 ps of simultaneity. For signals within 10 ps of simultaneity, oscillation was maintained for about 1 μs before a decisions was reached.

ADEL S. SEDRA AND KENNETH C. SMITH

INTERPRETER. *See* LANGUAGE PROCESSORS.

INTERNATIONAL FEDERATION OF AUTOMATIC CONTROL (IFAC)

For article on related subject *see* INTERNATIONAL FEDERATION FOR INFORMATION PROCESSING.

The International Federation of Automatic Control (IFAC) is a multinational federation of national member organizations, each one of which represents the engineering and scientific societies that are concerned with automatic control in their respective countries. At present, 44 countries (see Table 1) have formed appropriate national member organizations and joined IFAC.

IFAC is concerned with advancing the science and technology of control—which in the broad sense includes engineering, physical, biological, social, and economic systems—and in promoting the dissemination of information about such systems throughout the world. The primary means for accomplishing these aims are:

1. International congresses, held every three years.
2. Between congresses, symposia covering particular aspects of control systems, with topics rang-

TABLE 1. IFAC National Member Organizations

Argentina	Asociación Argentina de Control Automático (AADECA)
Australia	The Institution of Engineers Australia
Austria	Arbeitgemeinschaft für Automatisierung
Belgium	Federation IBRA/BIRA
Brazil	Sociedade Brasileira de Automatica (SBA)
Bulgaria	The National Council of Automation
Canada	Canadian National Committee for IFAC, National Research Council
Chile	Asociation Chilena de Control Automatico (ACCA)
People's Rep. of China	Chinese Association of Automation
Commonwealth of Independent States (formerly USSR)	National Committee on Automation Control
Cuba	Centro de Automatización Industrial
Czechoslovakia	Czechoslovak National Committee for IFAC
Denmark	Danish Automation Society
Egypt	Egyptian High Commission of Automatic Control
Finland	The Finnish Society of Automatic Control
France	Association Française pour la Cybernétique Economique et Technique (AFCET)
Germany	Gesellschaft Mess- und Automatisierungstechnik
Greece	Technical Chamber of Greece
Hungary	Computer and Automation Institute, Hungarian Academy of Sciences
India	The Institution of Engineers (India)
Israel	Israel Association of Automatic Control
Italy	GNASII-CNR
Japan	National Committee of Automatic Control
Dem. People's Rep. of (North) Korea	The Korean General Federation for Science and Technology
Rep. of (South) Korea	Korean Association of Automatic Control
Kuwait	Kuwait Society of Engineers
Mexico	Mexican Association for Automatic Control (Asociación Mexicana de Control Automatico-AMCA)
Morocco	Association Marocaine pour le Développement de l'Automatique (A.MA.D.E.I.A.)
Netherlands	Koninklijk Instituut van Ingenieurs
Nigeria	IEEE Nigeria
Norway	Norsk Forening for Automatisering.
Pakistan	The Institution of Engineers
Poland	Polski Komitet Pomiarow i Automatyki, Naczelna Organizacja Techniczna w Polsce
Portugal	APDIO
Romania	Comisia de Automatizare
Singapore	Instrumentation and Control Society
South Africa	South African Council for Automation and Computation
Spain	Comité Español de la IFAC
Sweden	Svenska Kommitten för IFAC
Switzerland	Schweizerische Gesellschaft für Automatik
Turkey	Türk Otomatik Kontrol Kurumu
United Kingdom	United Kingdom Automation Control Council
U.S.A.	American Automatic Control Council
Yugoslavia	Yugoslav Committee for Electronics and Automation

ing from "Automatic Control in Space," to "Systems Approaches to Developing Countries."

3. The IFAC Journal *Automatica,* which publishes both selected papers from symposia in expanded form, and original material of particular interest.

IFAC is also concerned with the impact of this advancing technology on society. The technical committee on the Social Effects of Automation acts as the focal point for the collection and dissemination of information in this field.

IFAC takes an active role in public affairs, making its broad technical expertise available to the United Nations and other international and regional organizations.

How Established IFAC came into existence because scientists and engineers working in the field of automatic control realized their need to become more closely associated to exchange information regarding their activities. In 1956, at an International Symposium on Automatic Control at Heidelberg, V. Broida (France), O. Grebe (FGR), A. M. Letov (USSR), P. J. Nowacki (Poland), R. Oldenburger (U.S.), and J. Welbourn (U.K.) formed the Organizing Committee of IFAC, with Dr. Broida as president and Dr. G. Ruppel as secretary. A general assembly was convened in Paris, France, and on 12 September 1957, IFAC became a reality with 19 member organizations. The constitution and bylaws were adopted in London on 21 June 1966.

The presidents of IFAC have been:

Dr. Harold Chestnut (U.S.), 1957–1959
Prof. Dr. A. M. Letov (USSR), 1959–1961
Prof. E. Gerecke (Switzerland), 1961–1963
Prof. J. F. Coales (U.K.), 1963–1966
Dr. P. J. Nowacki (Poland), 1966–1969
Dr. V. Broida (France), 1969–1972
Mr. J. C. Lozier (U.S.), 1972–1975
Mr. U. A. Luoto (Finland), 1975–1978
Prof. Y. Sawaragi (Japan), 1978–1981
Prof. T. Vamos (Hungary), 1981–1984
Prof. M. Thoma (FRG), 1984–1987
Acad. B. Tamm (SU), 1987–1990
Prof. B. D. O. Anderson (Australia), 1990–

Organizational Structure   IFAC is governed by a general assembly, consisting of delegates from each national member organization, which meets during the triennial congresses. Between congresses, the federation is run by a Council, headed by the president, and elected for three years. The day-to-day work of IFAC is administered by the secretariat, whose address is IFAC, Schlossplatz 12, A-2361 Laxenburg, Austria. The legal seat of IFAC is in Zurich, Switzerland.

Technical Program   The technical activities of IFAC are carried on primarily by technical committees which play a major role in the generation of the technical program for the triennial congresses. The initiative for generating symposia on appropriate topics in their respective fields also lies with the technical committees. The list of technical committees is as follows:

1. Applications
2. Biomedical Engineering
3. Components and Instruments
4. Computers
5. Developing Countries
6. Economic and Management Systems
7. Education
8. Manufacturing Technology
9. Mathematics of Control
10. Social Effects of Automation
11. Space
12. Systems Engineering
13. Terminology and Standards
14. Theory.

Conferences and Symposia   IFAC has had 11 congresses: in Moscow, 1960; Basel, 1963; London, 1966; Warsaw, 1969; Paris, 1972; Cambridge, MA, 1975; Helsinki, Finland, 1978; Kyoto, Japan, 1981; Budapest, 1989; Munich, 1987; and Tallinn, Estonia, 1990. Full proceedings of the congresses and most of the symposium papers have been published.

ISAAC L. AUERBACH

INTERNATIONAL FEDERATION FOR INFORMATION PROCESSING (IFIP)

For articles on related subjects *see* AMERICAN FEDERATION OF INFORMATION PROCESSING SOCIETIES; and INTERNATIONAL FEDERATION OF AUTOMATIC CONTROL.

The International Federation for Information Processing (IFIP) is a multinational federation of professional-technical societies (or groups of such societies) concerned with information processing. In any country, only one such society or group—which must be representative of the national activities in the information processing field—can be admitted as a full member. As of 1 January 1992, 42 national societies were members of the federation, as shown in Table 1.

The aims of IFIP are:

1. To promote information science and technology.
2. To advance international cooperation in the field of information processing.
3. To stimulate research, development, and application of information processing in science and in human activity.
4. To further the dissemination and exchange of information on information processing.
5. To encourage education in information processing.

IFIP is both a catalyst and a focal point for conceptual and technological developments that advance the state of the information processing art, thereby accelerating technical and scientific progress. It also performs a vital function in working toward the maximum dissemination of significant information about the digital computer and its applications.

How Established   The genesis of IFIP took place in June 1959 at the UNESCO-sponsored First International Conference on Information Processing in Paris. As conference chairman, Professor Howard H. Aiken (*q.v.*) stated at the conference in his closing speech, "The suggestion to hold this meeting was originated by Mr. Isaac L. Auerbach on behalf of the (U.S.) Joint Computer Committee in the form of a letter to Professor Pierre Auger, UNESCO. The importance of the subject and of the proposal made was such that UNESCO acted immediately and this conference was called."

Even before the success of this conference was confirmed, it was apparent in the planning sessions that future international meetings and other activities were essential to the worldwide development of information sciences. A committee was organized under the leadership of Isaac L. Auerbach (U.S.), to draft appropriate statutes and lay the foundation for future activities. The members of this committee were: J. Carteron, France; S. Comet, Sweden; A. Panov, USSR; J. G. Santesmases, Spain; A. Walther, West Germany; A. van Wijngaarden, Netherlands; M. V. Wilkes, U.K.; and H. Yamashita, Japan.

TABLE 1.

Country	Society
Andorra	Centre Nacional d'Informatico d'Andorra (CNIA)
Argentina	Sociedad Argentina de Informática
Australia	Australian Computer Society
Austria	Austrian Computer Society
Belgium	FAIB-FBVI
Brazil	Sociedade dos Usuários de Computadores e Equipamentos Subsidiários (SUCESU)
Bulgaria	Bulgarian Academy of Sciences
Canada	Canadian Information Processing Society (CIPS)
China, Peoples Rep. of	Chinese Institute of Electronics
Commonwealth of Independent States (formerly USSR)	The Computing Centre of the Academy of Sciences
Cuba	Academia de Ciencias de Cuba
Czechoslovakia	Czechoslovak Committee for IFIP
Denmark	Danish Federation for Information Processing (DANFIP)
Egypt	Egyptian Computer Society
Finland	Finnish Information Processing Association
France	Association Française pour la Cybernétique Economique et Technique (AFCET)
Germany	Gesellschaft fur Informatik (GI)
Greece	Greek Computer Society
Hungary	John von Neumann Society
India	Computer Society of India
Iraq	Planning Board/National Computer Centre
Ireland	Irish Computer Society
Israel	Information Processing Association of Israel (IPA)
Italy	Associazione Italiana per il Calcolo Automatico (AICA)
Japan	Information Processing Society of Japan
Korea, Rep. of	Korea Information Science Society (KISS)
Malaysia	Malaysian National Computer Confederation
Netherlands	Nederlands Genootschap voor Informatica
Nigeria	Computer Association of Nigeria (CAN)
Norway	Norwegian Computer Society
Poland	Polish Academy of Sciences
Portugal	Associacão Portuguesa de Informática (API)
Singapore	Singapore Computer Society
South Africa	The Computer Society of South Africa
Spain	Federacion Espanola de Sociedades de Informatica (FESI)
Sweden	Swedish International Federation for Information Processing (SIFIP)
Switzerland	Swiss Federation of Information Processing Societies
Syria	Syrian Scientific Studies and Research Centre
Tunisia	Centre National de l'Informatique
United Kingdom	The British Computer Society
U.S.A.	Focus on Computing in the United States (FOCUS)
Zimbabwe	Computer Society of Zimbabwe

During the First International Conference on Information Processing, Paris, in June 1958, representatives of 18 national computer societies met to formulate the preliminary structure of IFIP. Statutes for the federation were reviewed and, in the months that followed, were ratified by 13 national societies—6 more than the minimum required. IFIP came into official existence on 1 January 1960.

The Presidents of IFIP have been the following:

Isaac L. Auerbach (U.S.) 1960–1965
Ambros P. Speiser (Switzerland) 1965–1968
A. A. Dorodnicyn (USSR) 1968–1971
Heinz Zemanek (Austria) 1971–1974
Richard I. Tanaka (U.S.) 1974–1977
Pierre A. Bobillier (Switzerland) 1977–1980
K. Ando (Japan) 1983–1986
A. W. Goldsworthy (Australia) 1986–1989
Bl. Sendov (Bulgaria) 1989–1992
A. Rolstadås (Netherlands) 1992–

Organizational Structure The supreme authority of IFIP is the General Assembly, which meets annually. It is made up of one representative from each of the member societies; the presidents of two Associate Members, IAG (IFIP Applied Information Processing Group) and IMIA (International Medical Informatics Association); the presidents of two Affiliate Members, IAPR (International Association for Pattern Recognition) and IASC (International Association for Statistical Computing); and three Honorary Life Members, Isaac L. Auerbach, Heinz Zemanek, and Richard I. Tanaka.

The executive body of IFIP is composed of the officers: The president, three vice-presidents, the secretary, and the treasurer. These officers are elected by the General Assembly. The day-to-day work of IFIP is administered by a Secretariat, whose address is 3 rue du Marche, 1204 Geneva, Switzerland.

The Council, consisting of the officers and up to eight elected trustees, meets twice a year and makes decisions that become necessary between General Assembly meetings.

Technical Committees   In a continuing program devoted to a common basis for the worldwide development of the information sciences, IFIP has established a number of Technical Committees (TC) and Working Groups (WG), the influence of which are strongly felt at international as well as national levels.

Each Technical Committee is composed of representatives of the IFIP Member Societies (one per society), whereas Working Groups, under the supervision of a Technical Committee, consist of specialists in the field who are appointed as individuals independent of nationality.

The following Technical Committees and Working Groups are currently (1991) in operation:

TC 2 SOFTWARE: THEORY AND PRACTICE
- WG 2.1 Algorithmic Languages and Calculi
- WG 2.2 Formal Description of Programming Concepts
- WG 2.3 Programming Methodology
- WG 2.4 System Implementation Languages
- WG 2.5 Numerical Software
- WG 2.6 Database
- WG 2.7 User Interface Engineering
- WG 2.8 Functional Programming

TC 3 EDUCATION
- WG 3.1 Informatics Education at the Secondary Education Level
- WG 3.2 Informatics Education at the University Level
- WG 3.3 Research on Educational Applications of Information Technologies
- WG 3.4 Vocational Education and Training
- WG 3.5 Informatics in Elementary Education
- WG 3.6 Distance Learning

TC 5   COMPUTER APPLICATIONS IN TECHNOLOGY
- WG 5.2 Computer-Aided Design
- WG 5.3 Computer-Aided Manufacturing
- WG 5.4 Computerized Process Control
- WG 5.6 Maritime Industries
- WG 5.7 Computer-Aided Production Management
- WG 5.8 Product Specification and Product Documentation
- WG 5.9 Computers in Food Production and Agriculture
- WG 5.10 Computer Graphics
- WG 5.11 Technology for the Environment

TC 6   COMMUNICATION SYSTEMS
- WG 6.1 Architecture and Protocols for Computer Networks
- WG 6.4 Local and Metropolitan Computer Networks
- WG 6.5 Application Layer Communication Services
- WG 6.6 Network Management for Communication Networks

TC 7   SYSTEM MODELLING AND OPTIMIZATION
- WG 7.1 Modelling and Simulation
- WG 7.2 Computational Techniques in Distributed Systems
- WG 7.3 Computer System Modelling
- WG 7.4 Discrete Optimization
- WG 7.5 Reliability and Optimization of Structural Systems
- WG 7.6 Optimization-Based Computer-Aided Modelling and Design
- WG 7.7 Stochastic Optimization

TC 8   INFORMATION SYSTEMS
- WG 8.1 Design and Evaluation of Information Systems
- WG 8.2 The Interaction of Information Systems and the Organization
- WG 8.3 Decision Support Systems
- WG 8.4 Office Systems
- WG 8.5 Information Systems in Public Administration

TC 9   RELATIONSHIP BETWEEN COMPUTERS AND SOCIETY
- WG 9.1 Computers and Work
- WG 9.2 Social Accountability
- WG 9.3 Home-Oriented Informatics and Telematics (HOIT)
- WG 9.4 Social Implications of Computers in Developing Countries
- WG 9.5 Social Implications of Artificial Intelligence Systems
- WG 9.6 Computer Security Law

TC 10   COMPUTER SYSTEMS TECHNOLOGY
- WG 10.2 System Description and Design Tools
- WG 10.3 Concurrent Systems
- WG 10.4 Dependable Computing and Fault-Tolerance
- WG 10.5 Very Large Scale Integration "VLSI" Systems

TC 11   SECURITY AND PROTECTION IN INFORMATION PROCESSING SYSTEMS
- WG 11.1 Information Security Management
- WG 11.2 Office Automation
- WG 11.3 Database Security
- WG 11.4 Crypto Management
- WG 11.5 Systems Integrity and Control
- WG 11.7 Legislation
- WG 11.8 Information Security Education

Affiliations of IFIP   IFIP was founded under the auspices of UNESCO and has had official relationships with UNESCO since its inception. IFIP has the status of category B ("able to advise in a particular field"). IFIP was admitted into official relations with the World Health Organization in February 1972 and maintains informal relationships with most other members of the UN family, including the UN in New York.

IFIP has the status of a Scientific Affiliate of the International Council of Scientific Unions (ICSU). ICSU on its behalf maintains relations with UNESCO in category A ("proven competence in an important field of UNESCO's work").

In 1970, IFIP together with four related federations, IMACS, IFAC, IFORS, and IMEKO, established the "Five International Associations Coordinating Committee" (FIACC), which is the basis for cordial and successful coordination of activities and a yearly opportunity for the exchange of thoughts and experiences.

IFIP also participates in an advisory capacity in the work of CCITT, the Comité Consultatif International Télégraphique and Téléphonique.

IFIP Congresses   A major event in the IFIP program of activities is the Congress, held every three years. An IFIP Congress is an international occasion that attracts information scientists, managers, and administrators from all over the world to listen, to learn, and to exchange ideas with their colleagues from other countries.

The first Congress was held in Paris, and subsequent events have been in Munich, New York, Edinburgh, Ljubljana, Stockholm, Toronto, Tokyo, Melbourne, Paris, Dublin, and San Francisco. The 1992 Congress will be held in Madrid.

IFIP Congresses have attracted up to 5,000 participants from as many as 55 countries and have a good reputation both for scientific excellence and for relevance to the day-to-day application of computers. Every Congress includes a major exhibition of computer systems and services.

IFIP also organizes a triennial series of World Congresses on medical informatics called MEDINFO. The last such event was held in Beijing from 16-20 October 1989.

In addition to these major Congresses, IFIP's Technical Committees organize many international conferences on their specialized subjects, ranging in size from small working conferences to major international events. An example of the latter is a series of World Conferences on Computers in Education. The most recent was held in Sydney, Australia, in August 1990.

ISAAC L. AUERBACH

INTERNATIONAL SOCIETY FOR TECHNOLOGY IN EDUCATION (ISTE)

The *International Society for Technology in Education* (ISTE) is a non-profit professional organization for educators who use computers. ISTE is the merged society of the International Council for Computers in Education and the International Association for Computing in Education. This merger took place in June 1989.

ISTE is dedicated to the improvement of education through the use and integration of technology. The goals of ISTE include:

- Providing a prominent information center and source of leadership to communicate and collaborate with educational professionals, policy makers, and other organizations worldwide.
- Maintaining a strong geographical/regional affiliate membership to support and be responsive to grassroots efforts to improve the educational use of technology.
- Fostering an active partnership between businesses and educators involved in the field of computer-based technology in education.

In support of educators who use computers, ISTE publishes *The Computing Teacher* journal, *Update* newsletter, the *Journal of Research on Computing in Education*, the journals and newsletters of several *Special Interest Groups*, and ISTE books and courseware.

The following have served as presidents of ISTE: Dennis Bybee and Paul Resta (jointly), 1989–1990; Gary Bitter, 1990–1991; Bonnie Marks, 1991–1992. David Moursund is the chief executive officer and editor-in-chief of *The Computing Teacher* journal. Dianne Martin is the associate executive officer and heads the Washington DC office. ISTE's international headquarters are located at the University of Oregon, 1787 Agate Street, Eugene, OR 97403-9905; phone 503-346-4414. ISTE's national office is located at School of Engineering & Applied Science/Tompkins Hall, The George Washington University, Washington, DC 20052; phone 202-994-8238.

ISAAC L. AUERBACH

INTERRUPT

For articles on related subjects *see* CHANNEL; INTERVAL TIMER; OPERATING SYSTEMS; PRIVILEGED INSTRUCTION; SUPERVISOR CALL; TIME SHARING; and TIME SLICE.

The capability to *interrupt* a program, an important feature of most modern computer systems, permits them to respond quickly to exceptional events that can occur at unpredictable times. Some events of this type are signals generated by instruments or sensors monitoring some industrial or laboratory process, or a user at a teletype or video terminal signaling the end of a typed message that requires computer analysis and response. The response to an interrupt is the invocation of a responding program and, in this respect, an interrupt resembles other means of changing the flow of program control, such as a linkage to a subroutine. The essential difference in the case of interrupt is the great diversity of interrupt events and their unpredictability.

An interrupt facility is very common in most operating systems and real-time applications. It not only enables a computer to communicate with a rich variety of external devices, but is also helpful to the system in managing its own device and program resources. Although basically implemented by hardware, the logical power of interrupts is also provided in a convenient form to users of some modern programming languages, as by the ON statement in PL/I.

Each event that can cause an interrupt generates an "interrupt request" that can be visualized as a 1 or 0 signal on a physical line indicating whether the request is active or not. To respond to an interrupt request, the current CPU (central processing unit) program must be stopped gracefully (i.e. *interrupted*) and the CPU then switched to a program designed to service the interrupt request. Interrupts are thus a mechanism that enables several logically unrelated programs to time-share a single CPU and, thereby, other computer resources.

General Functional Features There are many computer architectures, each with its own interrupt scheme. Despite this great diversity in detail and also in terminology, there are certain commonalities:

1. Storage of interrupt requests.
2. Program-controlled enabling and masking.
3. Saving the program state.
4. Forced branch to a new program.
5. Cause identification.
6. State restoration.

Item 1 refers to the need to store requests until serviced, since the CPU can respond to only one request at a time. Item 2's purpose is to provide a means for the program to "paralyze" the interrupt-response mechanism at certain awkward times, such as when a previously recognized interrupt is already being serviced. Item 3 refers to the graceful suspension of the current program, "graceful" meaning that the program is stopped in such a way that it can be easily resumed later. This involves storing certain CPU registers that must be used by every program, including the one performing the interrupt response. The program address register (PA) is the most vital such register, since it holds the address of the next instruction to be executed. Item 4 is the essence of an interrupt—the forced branch to the new responding program. Item 5 refers to the need to be able to identify the cause of the interrupt. Item 6 is required for eventual resumption of the interrupted program.

Microprocessor Example A *microprocessor* is a CPU whose circuitry is wholly contained on a single semiconductor chip. Our specific example is the Intel i486, a powerful 32-bit microprocessor chip that can handle up to 256 causes-of-interrupt. The i486 (or 80486) is the latest in a line of Intel Corporation's microprocessors dating back several years (8088, 8086, 80386, etc.), and its architecture, including the popular "vectored" interrupt scheme is an extension of the earlier models. The fact that the architecture is extended means that software written for previous models will still run on the 80486.

The interrupt-related items are:

Lines into the i486 chip:
INTR—One interrupt request line (Pin A16) that can be enabled/disabled (see EFLAGS (9) below).
NMI—One interrupt request line (Pin B15) that cannot be disabled (used for severe events like power failures).
DATA—Data bus lines into the microprocessor.

Registers/items internal to the i486 CPU chip:
IF—Bit 9 of the CPU's EFLAGS register enables/disables INTR-signaled interrupts.
PA—Program address register (address of next instruction).
IDTR—Interrupt descriptor table register (memory address of first item in an interrupt descriptor table (IDT)).
IDT—Interrupt descriptor table containing up to 256 entries, each 64 bits, that includes the memory address of an interrupt service routine.

Assume that an interrupt request, as an appropriately timed signal on the INTR line, is sent to the i486 CPU by an external device (or chip) such as an I/O channel or interval timer. Then, at the end of the current instruction, if its IF bits specifies "enabled," the i486 CPU starts the interrupt response by saving the CPU's current basic state information for later restoration, by storing (pushing) the PA and EFLAGS register into the stack (an area of memory). In the process, further interrupts are disabled by automatic setting of the IF flag to "disabled." The interrupt service routine is then selected using 8 bits called an "interrupt vector" supplied by the requesting device on the DATA lines. This 8-bit item in effect identifies the cause of interrupt, since it is used to select its service routine. The i486 does this by using the 8 bits as an address increment to IDTR, thus addressing one item in the IDT table. Part of that IDT table entry then replaces the PA, thus becoming the starting address of the interrupt service program selected by the vector.

During an interrupt-service program, the program may reset the IF flag to "enable" permitting interrupts (nested interrupts are then possible). At the end of the service program, the old program state is usually restored by the program executing the i486 instruction "IRET" (interrupt return). This "pops" the stack into the PA and EFLAGS registers, thus restoring them to the pre-interrupt state.

Apart from external interrupts, the i486 handles certain classes of internally caused events by much the same scheme, only now the 8-bit vector is supplied on-chip rather than externally on the DATA lines. One class of this type are unusual conditions encountered as a part of instruction processing ("exceptions" like illegal operation codes or addressing mishaps). Another class is the "software interrupt" that can be initiated by programs executing the CPU instruction "INT n". In this latter case the parameter "n" is used as the interrupt vector.

A Large Machine Example A large computer tends to have a more elaborate interrupt scheme than, say, a microprocessor, in keeping with the greater number, variety, and complexity of its peripheral (I/O) devices and its need for high speed.

Fig. 1 shows a highly simplified version of the scheme used in the IBM 360/370/390 (*q.v.*) systems. The large number of interrupt request lines are subdivided into several mask-groups, the members of each group sharing one mask bit. A mask bit controls whether the request will be permitted to cause an interrupt or not. The mask bits are intended to give the program control over which requests can be allowed to cause an interrupt at any given time. A special case occurs when all mask bits are 0, which inhibits all interrupts. This might be done by the operating system during certain interrupt response activities.

The interrupt mask bits, the PA (called the instruction address), and several other items relating to program sequencing and interrupt are "packaged" into a single 64-bit quantity called the PSW (program status word) that can be stored and reset in one operation (as will be seen shortly).

The circled numbers in Fig. 1 indicate relative time of events in the interrupt process. The request lines are combined with their mask bits at time 1. If any unmasked pending requests are found, this generates a master interrupt request. Also, the priority logic acts during this interval to select the highest priority request, which is then identified by the encoder logic, and this identity is then stored in the PSW at time 3. The CPU will respond to the master request at the end of the current instruction (but, in System 370, interrupts are permitted before the end of

certain long-duration instructions). The interrupt itself consists of storing the PSW into a fixed area of memory called the "Old-PSW" (at memory location 1 in this example). Then the PSW is reset from the "New-PSW" (at memory location 0). Since the New-PSW respecifies the mask bits as well as the instruction address PA, any mask can be set by prestoring its bits into location 0. The cause of interrupt is available to the response program in the Old-PSW at location 1.

Interrupt Request Classes Interrupt requests may usually be categorized as follows:

1. Processor operations
2. Privileged operations
3. Software-call instruction
4. Machine malfunction
5. Input/output
6. Timer
7. External device

Class 1 includes register overflows, divide-checks, illegal operation codes, and address-out-of-bounds. Class 2 refers to those conditions that may arise because many computers reserve certain instructions for a privileged mode of the machine, so that key resource-scheduling and storage-protection instructions can only be executed

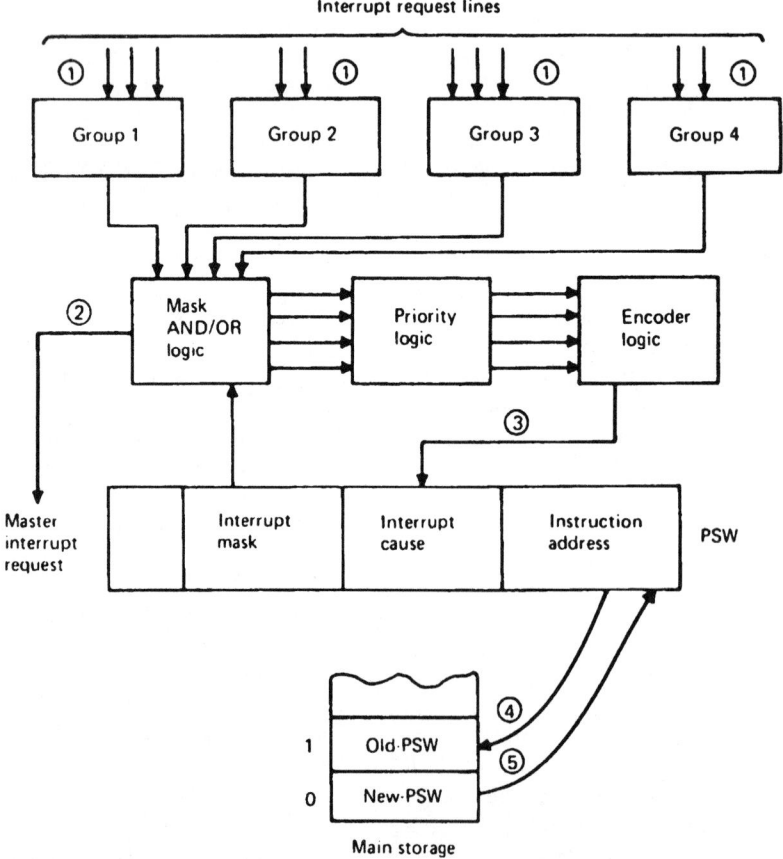

FIG. 1.   A simple interrupt system. The circled numbers indicate relative event times.

by the operating system. A class 2 interrupt occurs if execution of any of these privileged instructions is attempted while the machine is not in the privileged mode. Class 3 refers to the ability to initiate an interrupt explicitly by software executing a special instruction designed to call directly operating system routines. Classes 4 and 5 are rather obvious in principle and will not be discussed further. Class 6 refers to an interval timer that can be set to any reasonable positive value by a machine instruction. Circuitry is provided to decrement this value automatically at regular time intervals and generate an interrupt request when the value reaches zero. Class 7 refers to interrupt requests that may be typically generated by sensor devices, instruments, or relay closures.

The term *synchronous interrupt* is sometimes used for one whose cause is associated with the currently executing instruction, while other interrupts are called *asynchronous*. Thus, classes 1, 2, and 3 are synchronous and the remaining ones asynchronous. (See SYNCHRONOUS/ASYNCHRONOUS OPERATION.)

The complete problem of interrupt-handling is always solved by a combination of hardware and software. In general, the more done in hardware, the greater can be the speed of response, but the higher the cost and the less the flexibility to accommodate changes in interrupt logic. Because of these economy-speed relationships, systems differ greatly in the choice of which interrupt functions to implement in hardware.

One theme in many computer systems is that interrupts and subroutine linking have much in common, since in both cases one program or subprogram is "put to sleep" while another is "awakened" and provision must be made to return to the first program later. This idea, especially evident in microprocessors and other recent computers, leads to both mechanisms sharing common hardware and software logic. Unique aspects of interrupts, due to their time-unpredictability, necessitate hardware support for request-handling (masking, priority, cause identification).

Much of the complexity of interrupt-handling is in the software servicing the interrupt. The software is usually a part of the operating system program that manages the assignment of all hardware/software resources to workload demands. In fact, most operating systems are *interrupt-driven* i.e. the interrupt system is the mechanism for reporting all changes in resource states; and such changes are the events that induce new assignments. Incidentally, this fact makes interrupt handling an excellent place for monitoring resource-use for performance analysis and billing. Many performance monitors called *tracers* do their jobs by intercepting each interrupt and recording the cause and time of occurrence as a trace record. A stream of such records is a comprehensive log of system activity.

Because of the very close relationship between interrupts and the operating system that handles them, and the very great diversity in operating system logic, it is difficult to discuss the software aspects of interrupt implementation in any generality. For this reason, most of the following discussion is confined to options that appear in hardware implementations in some systems.

The number of request lines is clearly a logic-design decision. Some systems offer a small number as standard; the customer may add more at a modest cost.

The grouping structure is subject to hardware/software/speed trade-offs. We will call each source of New-PSW an interrupt level. Thus, for example, the case of Fig. 1 represents a one-level system. Since each level, which points to the start of an interrupt service program, constitutes a partial decoding of the interrupt cause, fast response requires a large number of levels. On the other hand, as long as the cause is recorded, only one level is logically essential, since the interrupt-handling program can use the cause-field of the Old-PSW to determine the response routine.

Another implementation issue is the amount of information to be stored automatically (by hardware) at each interrupt. The result of an interrupt is the initiation of a new program that will require the same kind of CPU facilities as the interrupted program. The PSW represents the near-minimum of such facilities; a scheme that stores only the PSW automatically will have to store other components of the state of the CPU by program instructions during the interrupt response. This has two deleterious effects on response time. First is the actual time to store the registers and to reload them for the new program. Second is the fact that during this time the system cannot be interrupted, and it is therefore possible that later interrupts might be lost. Maximum speed is attainable by supplying multiple sets of important CPU registers, and this is done in some systems. Sometimes the sets are made available in increments at incremental costs. The optimum number of register sets will, of course, depend on the interrupt speed specifications.

Finally, we should mention a hardware/software feature that is most desirable but is often lacking in an interrupt system. This is the ability to set any interrupt request line by a program instruction, although, of course, normally many such requests are generated by natural events. Such program control over requests is a desirable feature for system testing and debugging.

References

1983. IBM Corp. *IBM System/370 Extended Architecture Principles of Operation* SA22-7085. Chapter 6 "Interruption."
1984. Hamacher, V. C., Vranesic, Z. G., and Zaky, S. G. *Computer Organization (2nd Ed.)*: New York: McGraw-Hill.
1989. Intel Corp. *i486 Microprocessor*. Santa Clara, CA.: Intel Corporation, pp. 44, 92, 120.

HERBERT HELLERMAN

INTERVAL ARITHMETIC

For articles on related subjects *see* COMPUTER ARITHMETIC; ERROR ANALYSIS; NUMERICAL ANALYSIS; and SIGNIFICANCE ARITHMETIC.

The essence of *interval arithmetic* is that:

1. Closed, real intervals are substituted for computational data in which there is uncertainty.

2. Each such interval is represented by a pair of floating-point numbers that are known to be lower and upper bounds for the "true" (unknown) value of its corresponding datum.

3. In place of each arithmetic operation in a numerical algorithm, a corresponding interval arithmetic operation computes the interval containing all possible results of performing the original operation on any values taken from the interval operands.

Numerical computations have little value absent some assessment of accuracy. Computational errors can arise from any or all of: (1) measurement error in the input data, (2) propagation of rounding errors in floating-point arithmetic operations, and (3) approximation of an infinite computational sequence by a finite one. For many common numerical procedures, *a priori* error analysis can be employed either to bound the error in the computed results (forward analysis) or to show that the computed results are the exact solution for a bounded perturbation of the input data (backward analysis). In other cases, *a posteriori* computations can estimate the accuracy of a previously computed approximate solution. Each such error analysis is customized for a particular numerical algorithm. In computations for which analyses do not exist or in which the resulting error bounds are not acceptably small, other techniques must be used to estimate accuracy. Interval arithmetic is one such technique, a type of forward error analysis carried along with the computation.

Suppose, given variables x and y, we wish to compute $z = x + y$. If exact values of x and y are not available, but we know instead that $a \leq x \leq b$ and $c \leq y \leq d$, then the rules of arithmetic inequalities tell us that $a + c \leq x + y \leq b + d$. If we now designate by X, Y, and Z the intervals in which x, y, and z are known to be contained, we could write $X = [a, b]$, $Y = [c, d]$, and $Z = X + Y = [a + c, b + d]$. This definition of interval addition is consistent with the computational goal previously stated and provides the narrowest possible interval that can guarantee *rigorous* upper and lower bounds for the computed result.

Error may be introduced into the endpoint computations of $a + c$ and $b + d$, since these will not necessarily be representable floating-point values, even if a, b, c, and d are. To insure that error bounds remain valid at each computational step, it is necessary to modify the rounding rules when computing interval endpoints so that the computed value of $a + c$ will be rounded to a numerically lower value (towards minus infinity) and the computed value of $b + d$ will be rounded to a numerically higher value (towards plus infinity), *but only when they must be rounded at all*. These "directed rounding" floating-point operations have not been widely available until recently.

Interval analysis, the generalization of interval arithmetic, is concerned with problems of the following type: If bounds on the input data are known, how can we compute results in which rigorous bounds are of realistic width? This question is easily answered in the case of the elementary arithmetic operations. The rules of interval arithmetic are:

$$[a, b] + [c, d] = [a + c, b + d];$$
$$[a, b] - [c, d] = [a - d, b - c];$$
$$[a, b] \cdot [c, d] = [\min (ac, ad, bc, bd),$$
$$\max (ac, ad, bc, bd)];$$
$$[a, b] \div [c, d] = [\min (a/c, a/d, b/c, b/d),$$
$$\max (a/c, a/d, b/c, b/d)],$$
$$(\text{provided } 0 \notin [c, d]).$$

For example, we have the following correspondences:

$-1 \leq x \leq 2$	$X = [-1, 2],$
$1 \leq y \leq 3$	$Y = [1, 3],$
$0 \leq (x + y) \leq 5$	$X + Y = [0, 5],$
$-4 \leq (x - y) \leq 1$	$X - Y = [-4, 1],$
$-3 \leq (x \cdot y) \leq 6$	$X \cdot Y = [-3, 6],$
$-1 \leq (x \div y) \leq 2$	$X \div Y = [-1, 2].$

Each inequality is sharp, so each corresponding interval endpoint can be attained, provided that x and y are independent. If they are not, the inequalities will certainly still be valid, but may not be sharp. If for example,

$$-1 \leq x \leq 2 \quad \text{and} \quad y = 1 + |x|,$$

then while $1 \leq y \leq 3$ as above, in place of the previous correspondences, we have instead:

$1 \leq (x + y) \leq 5$	$[1, 5] \subset [0, 5],$
$-3 \leq (x - y) \leq -1$	$[-3, -1] \subset [-4, 1],$
$-2 \leq (x \cdot y) \leq 6$	$[-2, 6] \subset [-3, 6],$
$-1/2 \leq (x \div y) \leq 2/3$	$[-1/2, 2/3] \subset [-1, 2].$

Since the outcome of each interval arithmetic operation as defined above does not depend on past or future computational context, mathematical relationships that hold for exact operands (intervals of zero width) are not necessarily honored by interval arithmetic. For example, the evaluation of the expressions $X \cdot (Y + Z)$ and $(X \cdot Y) + (X \cdot Z)$ in interval arithmetic will not always produce the same result, since the equivalence of the two occurrences of X is not taken into account. In practice, interval analysis is concerned with finding computational sequences that minimize the excess interval width that this phenomenon induces.

Interval arithmetic is directly applicable in cases in which an *a priori* forward error analysis gives realistic bounds. However, it is not a panacea for rounding error problems, because of spurious widths introduced by neglecting mathematical dependencies such as exemplified above. Problems that are inherently sensitive to small variations in initial data will likewise invariably lead to wide interval results. In the case of problems of mathematical origin, an algorithmic restructuring can sometimes provide acceptable results. In cases that model chaotic behavior of physical systems, there are often relationships among the results that significantly constrain the nature of the solution. In these cases, interval analysis is of little help; at best, it can find bounds on each component, but even then only in conjunction with a careful algorithmic formulation.

Any computation that is inherently ill-conditioned

in floating-point arithmetic or any algorithm that induces instability will behave similarly in interval arithmetic. In these cases, the computed interval results will be so wide as to contain only the negative information that something is wrong someplace. Because this often happens when interval arithmetic is applied naively, it has long been supposed that it is hopeless to do nontrivial calculations in intervals. Nevertheless, good interval methods have been found for the evaluation of rational functions, roots of polynomials, solutions of linear and non-linear algebraic equations, the algebraic eigenvalue problem, and the solution of ordinary differential equations. Professor U. Kulisch and his colleagues at Karlsruhe University have systematized much of this work by extending the fundamental interval arithmetic operations to include an inner product ($\Sigma_i\, x_i\, y_i$) without intermediate roundings and by using a series of algorithms based on contraction mappings. Many of these interval applications are based on algorithms related to *a posteriori* error analyses, in which the initial approximation is computed using a conventional algorithm and interval methods subsequently ensure that the computed error bounds are themselves not misleadingly optimistic.

Three significant barriers to the use of interval arithmetic have been: (1) the difficulty of obtaining directed roundings for interval endpoint computations, (2) the increased overhead in both computation and storage that interval arithmetic implies, and (3) the lack of high-level language support for interval data types. The first of these has disappeared with the widespread introduction of implementations of the IEEE/ANSI binary floating-point standard (*see* COMPUTER ARITHMETIC), which requires provision of directed rounding modes in addition to the "round-to-nearest" default mode. Problems of computational and storage drag are becoming significantly less severe with the advent of very high performance scientific workstations (*q.v.*). The high-level language problem remains, but user-extensible, object-oriented languages (*q.v.*) such as C++ may in time provide solutions to overcome this remaining barrier.

As a diagnostic tool, interval arithmetic can save much human effort that might otherwise be spent doing (or accepting the consequences of not doing) error analysis. It is also useful in laboratory and engineering environments in which physical measurements subject to error are used to compute other quantities. If variation of the output as a function of the input is critical, interval arithmetic is a natural tool.

Sensitivity of results to input variation can also be estimated by the use of various forms of significance arithmetic, including unnormalized floating-point arithmetic or by repeated computations with perturbed data. While such methods may offer some confidence, none offers complete reliability, and so results obtained from these styles of computing range from difficult to impossible to interpret. By contrast, interval results are very easily understood. When a computation produces narrow intervals, the drudgery of an error analysis is not required to know with certainty what accuracy has been obtained.

References

1951. Dwyer, P. A. *Linear Computations.* New York: John Wiley & Sons. (The idea of carrying error bounds along with the underlying computation predates floating-point hardware. In Chapter 2 of this book, Dwyer explains the motivations for the use of interval arithmetic and provides a good introduction to the issues raised in approximate computation. Primarily of historical interest.)
1966. Moore, R. E. *Interval Analysis.* Englewood Cliffs, N.J.: Prentice-Hall. (This is the standard reference by the individual who has been most closely associated with the field for more than 25 years.)
1988. Moore, R. E. (Ed.). *Reliability in Computing: The Role of Interval Methods in Scientific Computing.* (Volume 19 in the series *Perspectives in Computing.*) Boston: Academic Press. (A collection of topical papers by many of the key contributors to the field.)

FREDERIC N. RIS

INTERVAL TIMER

For articles on related subjects *see* ACCOUNTING SYSTEM, COMPUTER; INTERRUPT; MULTIPROGRAMMING; and OPERATING SYSTEMS.

An *interval timer* (sometimes called a *real-time clock*) is a mechanism whereby elapsed time can be monitored by a computer system. In most systems, a word in memory is set aside to be used as the interval timer. This word, usually at the low end of memory, cannot be used for anything else, since the computer is wired to increment it automatically by one interval every millisecond (or other fixed period).

For timing purposes it is useful to have a timer capable of monitoring the execution of a few thousands, or tens of thousands, of instructions. Hence, in a computer with some instructions requiring only 1 μs, a millisecond timer will be incremented once for every thousand of those instructions, which is about as low a rate as can be tolerated. If the system stores the time of day (say, at start-up time) in another word, then any program needing to report the current time of day need only read the start time and add to it the number of milliseconds in the timer to obtain the current time of day.

The timer is useful for reporting the date and time of execution of various parts of a job or for checking the timing for segments of a routine. In multiprogrammed systems, care must be taken to maintain interval timings with each job. The time of day will be global to all jobs, of course, but for timing purposes, the interest is usually in time elapsed only while the CPU is assigned to a particular job (as opposed to running other jobs or performing input/output operations for the job in question or other jobs). An interval timer is essential for timing components of multiprogrammed systems, since time may be allocated to jobs in increments of only a few hundreds (or even tens) of milliseconds.

CHESTER L. MEEK

IOCS. See INPUT-OUTPUT CONTROL SYSTEM.

ITERATION

For articles on related subjects *see* CONTROL STRUCTURES; NUMERICAL ANALYSIS; PROCEDURE-ORIENTED LANGUAGES; RECURSION; and STRUCTURED PROGRAMMING.

To *iterate* means to do repeatedly. In computer programming, *iteration* is the repeated execution of lines of code or statements until some condition is satisfied. For example, ten numbers A(1), A(2), A(3), ..., A(10) can be summed using the following Basic program:

```
10 L = 10
20 I = 1
30 S = 0
40 S = S + A(I)
50 I = I + 1
60 IF I <= L THEN 40                    (1)
```

The statements 40 – 60 are executed repeatedly until I becomes 11.

In contrast, the sum could be computed by

$$S = A(1) + A(2) + A(3) + A(4) + A(5) + \\ A(6) + A(7) + A(8) + (9) + A(10) \qquad (2)$$

which does not involve iteration. This last statement is more efficient in the example given, since the sum is obtained with fewer program steps. However, if more elements are to be summed, then statement (2) must be changed by adding more terms. In the first program, however, to sum more elements, only the value of L (which could be an input quantity) need be changed. Therefore, when the number of elements to be summed increases, a point is eventually reached where the effort to write the program in form (2) becomes greater than for form (1). This illustrates the use of iteration to reduce the effort of the programmer at the price of using more computer time. At some point, of course, (2) will require more time to compile than (1).

All worthwhile computer programs are iterative in some way. For example, in the time that one can write program (2) above, one could perform the actual summations by hand. Thus, solving a problem by computer is worthwhile only if: (1) the programming effort is small compared with the amount of computing (which means that some of the program is executed repetitively), or (2) the program is applied to a succession of input data values. Although this last process is less often called "iteration," the program is repeatedly executed.

Another advantage of the iterative approach is the greater ease of generalization. For example, the first program could be part of a subroutine, and the control of the iterations could be done by means of a parameter. The following example uses Fortran:

```
    SUBROUTINE ABC(L)
    ...
    I = 1
```

```
    SUM = 0
15  SUM = SUM + A(I)
    I = I + 1
    IF (I.LE.L) GO TO 15
    ...
```

Calling the subroutine with

```
CALL ABC(10)
```

would compute the sum of ten elements.

Control of Iteration DO, FOR, and WHILE statements may be used to control an iteration. For example, the Basic program

```
10 S = 0
20 FOR I = 1 TO 10
30 S = S + A(I)
40 NEXT I                              (3)
```

accomplishes the same effect as program (1).

In PL/I, the program can be written as

```
SUM = 0
DO I = 1 TO 10;
  SUM = SUM + A(I);
END;                                   (4)
```

In Pascal, this same program would be

```
SUM := 0;
for I := 1 to 10 do
    SUM := SUM + A[I];                 (5)
```

In the language APL, the same summation can be written as just

```
+/A                                    (6)
```

Here, at the source language level, no iteration appears to be involved. However, at the level of the interpretive program that evaluates the APL statement, iteration will occur.

The iteration may be repeated a number of times, depending upon the values involved. For example, a summation may be terminated as soon as a zero data value is encountered, as is done in this Fortran program:

```
    SUM = 0.
    DO 5 I = 1, 10
      IF (A(I) .EQ. 0.) GO TO 6
      SUM = SUM + A(I)
5   CONTINUE
6   ...                                (7)
```

Another example is illustrated by a Newton-Raphson square root function written in Pascal:

```
function SQROOT (X: REAL): REAL;
    const
        EPSILON = ... ;
    var
        ROOT: REAL;
    begin {SQROOT}
        if X = 0.0 then
            SQROOT := 0.0
                else
            begin
                ROOT := X;
                while ABS(ROOT*ROOT – X) >=
                            EPSILON do
                    ROOT := (X/ROOT + ROOT)*0.5;
                SQROOT := ROOT
            end
    end {SQROOT};                                    (8)
```

The heart of the **while** statement computes an improved approximation to the square root. If X = 1.0, no iterations occur (assuming epsilon is of appropriate size relative to the arithmetic precision of the system). Otherwise, the number of iterations depends both on the value of X and on the value of epsilon.

Iteration in Numerical Methods

Many numerical problems can be solved by iterative techniques. Here, a succession of values for one or more variables are computed. It is hoped that the successive values approach the true values. The iterative process is terminated when some error criterion is satisfied. The square root program (9) above is an example of an iterative numerical procedure. Although the successive partial sums of the first example (1) do approach the final sum, this procedure is not usually called an iterative numerical procedure. Thus, numerical iteration is usually characterized by the use of successive approximations and termination depending upon error bounds.

Hardware Iteration

The distinction between hardware and software activity is less and less clear as more complex processors are designed. This is particularly true in using microprogramming techniques and read-only memories.

In a simple example, a number in a register (Register 2 of Fig. 1) may need to be shifted a number of binary positions determined by a number stored in a second register (Register 1). The shift circuits of Register 2 are repeatedly pulsed until the contents of Register 1 are counted down to zero. Although the activity of the shift circuits are iterative in character, very few logical designers would use the term.

In more complex processors, the term may be more appropriate. For example, the summation of the elements of a vector (as discussed above) may be done entirely by hardware. This involves a complex sequence of events including: incrementing an address register to access successive components; performing a floating-point addition, which itself involves comparing exponents; shifting mantissas; and perhaps normalizing results. Thus, the

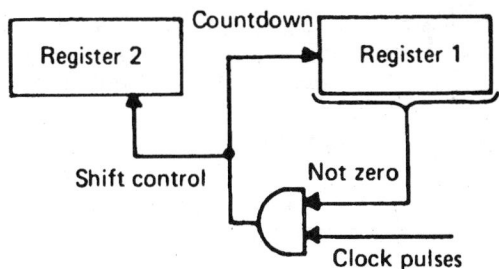

FIG. 1.   Simple example of hardware iteration.

same pattern of activities is performed iteratively until all components of the vector are accounted for.

Iteration versus Recursion

A program is *recursive* if at least one of its executable statements refers to the program itself. For example, in Pascal one may write

```
function ABC(X:integer):integer;
    . . .
    . . .
    . . .
    Z : = ABC(Y);
    . . .
    . . .
    . . .
end;
```

That is, the function calls itself. This requires a so-called STACK mechanism to keep track of parameters, and RETURN locations for each level of call. Needless to say, other statements in the program must in some way limit the levels of calling. A frequently used example is the factorial (Wirth, 1976, p. 129):

```
function FACTORIAL (X:integer):integer;
    if X < 2 then FACTORIAL := 1
        else FACTORIAL := X*FACTORIAL(X – 1)
end;                                            (10)
```

Although portions of the code (10) are executed repetitively, the control is by reference to the named procedure. Therefore, this example is said to be recursive, and not iterative.

The factorial of N can be computed iteratively:

```
function FACTORIAL (N:integer):integer;
var I, T:integer;
begin
    T := 1;
    for I := N downto 2 do
        T := T*I;
    FACTORIAL := T
end;                                            (11)
```

In the iterative example, the function does not call itself and, therefore, does not have to save the parameter X each time it is called, as the recursive function must do.

In general, when a straightforward iterative algorithm is available, it is both faster and uses less memory than a corresponding recursive algorithm. But when recursion is more natural than iteration (*see*, for example, Quicksort in the article STRUCTURED PROGRAMMING), it is often preferable to use it.

References

1970. Acton, F. S. *Numerical Methods That Work*. New York: Harper & Row.
1976. Wirth, N. *Algorithms + Data Structures = Programs*. Englewood Cliffs, NJ: Prentice-Hall.

HARRY D. HUSKEY

JCL. *See* COMMAND AND JOB CONTROL LANGUAGE.

JOB

For articles on related subjects *see* ACCOUNTING SYSTEM, COMPUTER; MULTIPROGRAMMING; OPERATING SYSTEM; PROCESSING MODES; and TASK.

A *job* is a task or group of tasks to be performed by a computer. The number of tasks (or steps) per job is usually a preference of the programmer, but is also subject to the conventions of the operating system. For example, many empty temporary files supplied by the operating system are automatically closed and released at the end of a job. If a programmer wishes to use one of these temporary files to store some intermediate information between two steps, then the two steps must be contained within the same job. On the other hand, if the programmer uses a permanent file, then there may be a step that creates the file in one job and a step that reads it in another job. In a batch-processing environment, where jobs are run one at a time, the programmer needs only to insure that the job that reads the file is *submitted* to be run after the job that creates it. But in a multiprogrammed environment, where several jobs are run concurrently, there is need to insure that the jobs are *executed* in sequence. To accomplish this automatically, many multiprogramming operating systems allow job sequencing, which allows the programmer to specify that a job cannot be selected for execution until its predecessor has been completed.

A job is also the smallest accounting unit on most machines. That is, computer resources are normally charged against one account number per job.

CHESTER L. MEEK

JOB CONTROL LANGUAGE. *See* COMMAND AND JOB CONTROL LANGUAGE.

JOSEPHSON JUNCTION. *See* SUPERCONDUCTING DEVICES.

JOURNALS, COMPUTING. *See* LITERATURE OF COMPUTING.

JOYSTICK. *See* INTERACTIVE INPUT DEVICES.

JUMP. *See* MACHINE AND ASSEMBLY LANGUAGE PROGRAMMING.

JUSTIFICATION

For articles on related subjects *see* DESKTOP PUBLISHING; TEXT EDITING SYSTEMS; and WORD PROCESSING.

In the context of programming, *justification* refers to the left or right alignment of a piece of data, typically a bit or character string, in a field that is assumed to be larger (i.e. greater in length) than the data. Thus, *right justifying* a bit string of length 2 in an 8-bit byte means that the rightmost of the two data bits is placed in the rightmost position of the byte. Remaining positions in the field are usually occupied by as many copies as needed of a specified or assumed *fill character*. These non-data characters or bits *pad* the data on the left if the data is right-justified, or on the right if the data is left-justified.

In the context of text processing, justification pertains to left- and/or right-margin alignment. Conventionally, typeset text such as that found in books and magazines appears with straight (justified) left and right margins. By contrast, typewritten letters usually have a left-justified ("flush left") margin but a "ragged right" margin. On some output devices such as computer line printers, where each character in the print line has a uniform size (monospace), computer-based typesetting algorithms can force alignment by inserting additional blanks between words or after punctuation. Typesetting for proportionally spaced devices involves inserting variable width spaces between words; with such devices, each character has its characteristic width as a function of font, size, etc.

ANDRIES VAN DAM

KERNEL

For articles on related subjects *see* INPUT-OUTPUT CONTROL SYSTEM; MEMORY MANAGEMENT; OPERATING SYSTEMS: PRINCIPLES; SCHEDULING ALGORITHM; SWAPPING; TASK; and VIRTUAL MEMORY.

The term *kernel* (and sometimes *nucleus*) is applied to the set of programs in an operating system that implement the most primitive of that system's functions. The precise interpretation of kernel programs depends on the system. Typical kernels contain programs for four types of functions:

1. *Process management*—Routines for switching processors among processes; for scheduling; for sending messages or timing signals among processes; and for creating and removing processes.
2. *Memory management*—Routines for placing, fetching, and removing pages or segments in, or from, main memory.
3. *Basic I/O control*—Routines for allocating and releasing buffers; for starting I/O requests on particular channels or devices; and for checking the integrity of individual data transmissions.
4. *Security*—Routines for enforcing the access and information-flow control policies of the system; for changing protection domains; and for encapsulating programs.

In some systems, the kernel is larger and provides for more than these classes of functions; in others, it is smaller. Each of the classes of kernel programs contains routines for handling interrupts pertaining to its class. For example, clock interrupts are handled in class 1, page faults in class 2, channel completion interrupts in class 3, and protection violations in class 4. Some systems order the classes hierarchically (e.g. in order: 1, 2, 3, 4) so that programs in the given class can invoke services of programs of lower classes. For example, memory manage-

ment (class 2) can be implemented by a collection of processes, the coordination of which is managed by process management routines (class 1).

The system kernel should not be confused with the portion of the operating system that is continuously *resident* in main memory. Two criteria determine whether a particular system module (either routine or table) should be resident—its frequency of use, and whether the system can operate at all without it. For example, file directories can be maintained in address spaces so that they can be swapped out of main memory when not in use. Status information for inactive processes can similarly be swapped out. The resident part of an operating system is a subset of its kernel.

PETER J. DENNING AND DOROTHY E. DENNING

KEY. *See* CRYPTOGRAPHY, COMPUTERS IN; and SORTING.

KEYBOARD STANDARDS

For articles on related subjects *see* ASCII; EBCDIC; INTERACTIVE INPUT DEVICES; and STANDARDS.

The most important reasons for specifying *keyboard standards* are to save manufacturing costs by standardizing both the keyboards and the interfaces with other equipment, to save operator training costs and achieve higher operator efficiency in keying, to minimize input errors into data processing systems by operators, and to make it possible to use several national alphabets in the same information system as the use of international computer networks grows.

Despite the problem posed by the large investment in current keyboard equipment, progress toward keyboard standardization is steadily being made. Two international bodies are involved: The International Standards

Organization (ISO), and the European Computer Manufacturers Association (ECMA). ISO standards are binding on all countries that have voted for their introduction, and to a degree also for those that have not; ECMA standards are, however, recommendations only.

Based upon the standard ECMA-23, the ISO issued the IS 2530 standard, "Keyboards for international information processing interchange using the ISO 7-bit coded character set—Alphanumeric area." This international standard defines layouts for the alphanumeric area of a keyboard implementing the 95 graphics positions of the ISO 7-bit coded character set, complying with ISO 646, "7-bit coded character set for information processing interchange," comprising 128 characters, of which 95 are graphics, leaving the remaining 33 for control purposes. These layouts conform to ISO/R 2126, "Basic arrangements for the alphanumeric section of keyboards operated with both hands."

The ISO 2530 standard specifies the pairing of the characters (upper and lower case) and their allocation to the keys. Out of the 95 graphics positions, one is reserved for spacing, with a special key assigned to it; the remaining 94 graphic positions are handled one of two ways: either paired to give upper and lower case positions of a 47-key layout; or, only 92 are paired on 46 keys with the remaining two—the UNDERLINE and the ZERO—assigned to two different keys for more convenience to the operator (see Fig. 1), thus giving a 48-key layout.

In addition to the basic alphabetic graphics layout, the keyboard shown in Fig. 1 has an area reserved for shift-free keys that generate the code combinations and associated characters. Rules and recommendations are given in IS 2530 on the most suitable way of contracting the standard 47-key graphic area in cases where not all of the 95 graphic characters are required.

The advent of the personal computer era has introduced a healthy ferment into the realm of keyboard standards. For some years now, vendors have been experimenting with variants of the keyboard layout shown in Fig. 1. The basic QWERTY layout tends to be retained, but specialized keys are sometimes inserted near the shift keys, and special "function keys" are often placed along either row F or column 99 or both. Such keys are very useful to the creators of software such as word processors and spreadsheets; the keys are used to provide such aids as one-stroke requests for help or for invoking special functions, such as calling up a sub-menu or exiting the system. Vendors are also prone to experiment with the ergonomic aspects of keyboards, such as the distance between keys, the sculpting of the key caps, and the "touch" of the keys. Standardization efforts are likely to continue, but perhaps only after a breathing spell that brings some degree of stabilization to the rate at which new personal computers and workstations (*q.v.*) are being introduced.

JIRI NECAS AND EDWIN D. REILLY

KILBURN, THOMAS

For articles on related subjects *see* ATLAS; MANCHESTER UNIVERSITY COMPUTERS; WILKES, MAURICE; WILLIAMS, SIR FREDERICK C.; and WILLIAMS TUBE MEMORY.

Tom Kilburn was born on 11 August 1921 in Dewsbury, Yorkshire, England. Along with F. C. Williams and M.V. Wilkes, Kilburn dominated the field of British computer engineering in its formative years. He was educated

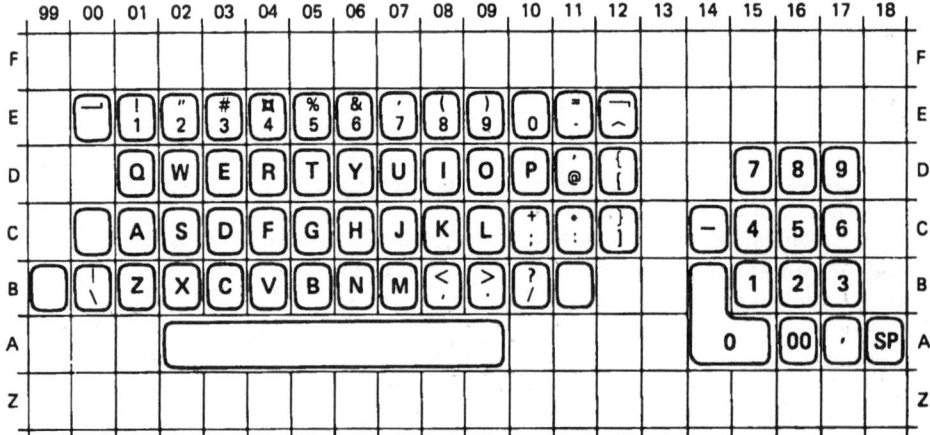

FIG. 1. The keyboard layout depicted is the ECMA-23 Standard (2nd Ed.) for predominantly numeric data. It comprises an alphanumeric area and, in addition, a numeric area consisting of shift-free keys. Only the alphanumeric area 48-key layout corresponds with the IS 2530 standard; the numeric area layout is discussed solely in the ECMA-23 standard. In both standards, the 47-key layout of the alphanumeric keyboard is derived by transmitting the UNDERLINE character from the shifted position of key E00 to the shifted position of key E10. Several allowable modifications to these layouts are discussed in detail in both standards. (The three blank single keys—B99, C00, and B11—do not count; the blank keybar is assigned to the SPACE character, which is regarded as a non-printing graphic.)

at Cambridge University, where he graduated in 1942 with a BA degree in mathematics. During the war in 1942–1945, he joined the Telecommunications Research Establishment (TRE) at Great Malvern, where he was engaged in radar work. In 1946, he was seconded from the TRE to the Electrical Engineering Department at the University of Manchester to work under F. C. Williams on research into cathode ray tube (i.e. electrostatic) storage. The result of their work was the Williams tube—the first random access digital storage device—which formed the basis for the Manchester Mark I computer. A prototype of this machine ran the world's first stored program on 21 June 1948. Collaboration with Ferranti Ltd. followed both for the Mark I and other machines such as the Mercury and Atlas computers, with Kilburn assuming direction of the projects after about 1952. Although Kilburn was involved with other important Manchester University computers such as the MU5, the Atlas project, begun in 1956, perhaps represented his finest achievement. Atlas pioneered many modern concepts, such as paging, virtual memory, and multiprogramming, and on its official inauguration in 1962 was considered to be the most powerful computer in the world.

Tom Kilburn was Professor of Computer Science at Manchester University from 1964–81 and is now Emeritus Professor. A member of numerous government committees and technical societies, he was elected Fellow of the Royal Society in 1975. Some of his other honors include CBE (1973), Computer Pioneer Award (1982), and the Eckert-Mauchly Award (1983).

References

1947. Papers of Manchester University Department of Computer Science, National Archive for the History of Computing, Manchester University.
1975. Simon H. Lavington. *A History of Manchester Computers.* Manchester: National Computer Centre.

GEOFFREY TWEEDALE

KLUDGE

The word "kludge" as used in computing was coined by Jackson Granholm in an article "How to Design a Kludge," in *Datamation* (February 1962). The definition is given as "an ill-sorted collection of poorly matching parts, forming a distressing whole." The design of every computer contains some anomalies that prove to be annoying to the users and that the designer wishes had been done differently. If there are enough of these, the machine is called a *kludge*.

By extension, the term has now come to be applied to programs, documentation, and even computing centers, so that the definition is now "an ill-conceived and hence unreliable system that has accumulated through patchwork, expediency, and poor planning."

The first kludge article triggered five others ("How to Maintain a Kludge," etc.) in subsequent issues of *Datamation*. Four of the articles may be found in the book, *Faith,*

Hope and Parity, edited by Jack Moshman, Washington: Thompson Book Company, 1966.

FRED GRUENBERGER

KNOWLEDGE REPRESENTATION

For articles on related subjects *see* ARTIFICIAL INTELLIGENCE; COMPUTER VISION; DEDUCTIVE DATABASE; EXPERT SYSTEMS; HEURISTIC; LOGIC PROGRAMMING; NATURAL LANGUAGE PROCESSING; NEURAL NETWORKS; ROBOTICS; and THEOREM PROVING.

Artificial Intelligence (AI) programs often need to use information about the domain in which they are supposed to exhibit intelligence. For example, a program that plans methods of distributing fresh bread will need access to information about the distances between the bakery and the stores, the likely times of travel, etc. The more general-purpose the program, the wider the scope of the knowledge that it might need to consult, so that, for example, a natural language comprehension system might need to use a variety of spatial, temporal, social, and physical concepts in order to help it understand the variously different meanings of "up" in the phrases "up the hill," "shut up," "catch up," and "tighten up." *Knowledge representation* is concerned with what information is needed and methods of expressing it.

The idea of using represented knowledge is controversial. Many *connectionists* and some philosophical critics of AI believe that knowledge should emerge from the dynamics of a neural network rather than being represented explicitly. Others emphasize how complex behaviors of insect-like creatures might arise from interactions of a state-free machine with a complex environment, avoiding internal representations altogether. It is widely thought, however, that cognitive abilities require access to represented information. In particular, "common sense," (i.e. the general ability to act successfully in the everyday world) seems to require a wide range of knowledge[1] at varying levels of generality, including knowledge about the physical world, about actions and their effects, and about other agent's beliefs. All of these still present problems for research.

Planning work in AI has grown out of this area and has inherited many of the problems of reasoning about actions and their effects on complex domains. Natural language work also faces a very general-purpose knowledge representation problem, since the meaning of many words involves a large variety of intuitive concepts that have not yet been formalized adequately. While robotics and computer vision seem less concerned with knowledge representation, it can be argued that the techniques used by some vision programs to arrive at descriptively adequate accounts of the scenes they examine amount

---

[1]From a strict philosophical perspective, the word "knowledge" is used illegitimately in the AI literature, since much common sense "knowledge" is, of course, false.

to the use of knowledge, some of it "compiled" for reasons of efficiency. Since there is no sharp distinction between the representation of knowledge and the general use of data structures (*q.v.*) throughout computer science to encode information, the boundaries of this area are not well-defined.

Knowledge Representation Formalisms

Most knowledge representation formalisms describe their worlds by asserting that certain *relations* hold between *individuals*, (e.g. *Loves(Harry, Sally)* or *HasMeeting(Joe, DepartmentOf(Mathematics), ThreePM(May 14))*. A knowledge representation formalism must also have some way of expressing general facts, such as that gods are immortal or that spherical objects placed on a sloping surface roll downwards.

Three common ways to organize knowledge are as collections of assertions or concepts or as a network. The first considers the knowledge representation language as being a logic, usually first-order predicate calculus (FOPC or 1PC or FOL). This formalism was developed by philosophers at the turn of the century, and its properties are very well understood. The basic unit of FOPC is an atomic assertion like those in the previous paragraph. These can be combined by connectives such as *and, or, not*, and *implies*, and general facts can be expressed by replacing some names by variables bound by the quantifiers *ForAll* and *Exists*. This recursive syntax can produce complex expressions, such as:

(Forall x)(IsBabyOf(x, me) implies

  (Forall y) (Loves(y,x) and

   (Forall z)(not(Equal(z,me))implies notLoves(x,z))))

Many equivalences hold between FOPC expressions, allowing the use of certain standard forms of which the most common is a conjunction of *clauses* i.e. implications of the form *(atom and atom and..) implies (atom or atom or...)*) where all the variables are assumed to be universally quantified. Inference then proceeds by forming links between clauses by *matching* or *unifying* atoms. The above expression becomes two clauses:

IsBabyOf(x,me) implies Loves(y,x)
(IsBabyOf(x,me) and Loves(x,z)) implies Equal(z,me)

where the two *Loves* atoms can be unified. The space of inferences generated by quite simple clauses can grow very rapidly, and the resulting general search problem is very difficult.

These are both examples of *Horn clauses* in which the disjunctive consequent has at most one element. Not all assertions can be expressed as Horn clauses, but they produce search spaces that can be searched straightforwardly. Their computational properties are so advantageous that the slight restriction on expressive power is often accepted.

There is a basic tension that runs throughout knowledge representation: There is a trade-off between the expressive power of a formalism—what it can say about

the world—and the computational difficulty of searching through the space of inferences it supports. Quite small changes to the design of a language can have very dramatic effects on where it sits on this expressiveness/tractability curve, the so-called "computational cliff" (Levesque, 1985).[2] Most knowledge representation systems have tried to find a workable compromise between the very intractable nature of FOPC and the impoverished expressive power of many ad-hoc schemes. In order to overcome this, many have suggested that part of the knowledge should be in some way about the process of reasoning itself, expressed perhaps in a *metalanguage* (*q.v.*), or merely by providing several versions of each connective, each associated with a different search strategy in the inference space. The resulting languages are often thought of as programming languages, so that the task of representing knowledge is identified with that of organizing and controlling the inference process. Indeed, Horn clauses can themselves be thought of as a style of programming language called *logic programming* (*q.v.*). This, however, produces new tensions (e.g. between different accounts of what the formalisms mean). Should the composer of representations be concerned with what they say about some external world or their effect on the state of the inference process? This *procedural-assertional debate* has been an ongoing controversy in AI and is still not resolved. More recent approaches seem to move away from either strong position, regarding knowledge representation as essentially assertional, while using many procedural devices.

The second approach organizes the knowledge base around individuals rather than propositions. The resulting structures, called *frames* or *units*, represent either an individual or a certain type of individual (e.g. *Chris* or *Human*). Each unit has associated with it a number of *slots* that encode all its relationships to other individuals. The slots may consist of simply a name of a relationship and a list of units to which this individual bears the relation, or it may be associated with a more elaborate piece of code. Units form a hierachy of individuals and types, so that we might have *Chris* being an instance of *Man*, which is itself a subtype of *Human*, of *Mammal*, and also of *Agent*, etc., forming a directed acyclic graph. Each unit is understood to inherit the slot values of units above it, so that the fact that all mammals have warm blood can be expressed by attaching the relevant information about warmbloodedness to the unit *Mammal*.

This unit-based style of representation, due originally to Minsky (1975), has been very influential and is the basis of several commercial *expert system (q.v.) shell* languages.

---

[2]The crucial issue seems to be whether the language allows expressions of incomplete knowledge, typically expressed by a disjunction. If it is known that *A* or *B* holds, but not which, the search process must somehow keep track of both possibilities. When each might involve different instantiations of variables, there is no compact way of encoding this choice as an expression in the language itself, so the search process has to keep track of them explicitly. Through recursion, this branching can result in an explosively difficult search problem. Forcing the representation to be clear sometimes improves this dramatically.

One of the first, KRL, (Bobrow and Winograd, 1977), was also one of the more complex. In KRL an individual can have several associated units representing different *views* of it, and slots contain complex expressions defining mappings between them, such as the following definition of the *admission* slot of a *CinemaTicketHolder* unit, where *PersonThisOne* refers to the *Person* view of the unit itself:

<admission ((XOR Junior Senior General)
      (using (the age from Person ThisOne) selectFrom
         (which isLessThan 13) ~ Junior
         (which isGreaterThan 65) ~ Senior
         otherwise General))>

KRL was consciously designed to be like a programming language[3], but other unit-based languages such as CYCL (Lenat and Guha, 1990), use logic as the slot language.

The third main idea in representational formalisms is a *semantic network*.

The edges of a directed graph represent two-place relations holding between individuals labeling the nodes. Semantic networks usually come with a particular set of conventions on how certain kinds of nodes or arcs are to be used, amounting to a syntax for a network language. A common device is the use of *is-a* arcs to express general statements of a type hierarchy of the kind described above, which was first developed in network languages (see Fig. 1). Any link attached to a type represents something true of all instances of that type, and can be inherited back along an *is-a* link. These instantiation links can form hierarchies of more and more general types, allowing a limited form of universal quantification.

Both units and networks can express only one- and two-argument predicates naturally, but more complex assertions can be encoded with some ingenuity. For example, the use of a three-place predicate, such as *Meeting (Bill, Harry, 5pm)*, can be replaced by a unit or node representing the event itself with slots or binary links to the arguments (see Fig. 2). The use of *case markers* in natural language parsing is a similar device.

While networks and frame systems are intuitively appealing, the basic assertions they make can usually be translated fairly directly into subsets of FOPC[4] so they can be regarded as attempts to locate a reasonable compromise between expressiveness and efficiency. However, most frame and network systems provide other mechanisms (Findler, 1979), and languages as complex as KRL or the more sophisticated network languages can encode all of FOPC (e.g. by encoding expressions as terms or by extending the graphical notation by allowing a subgraph to be treated like a single node so

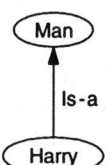

FIG. 1.

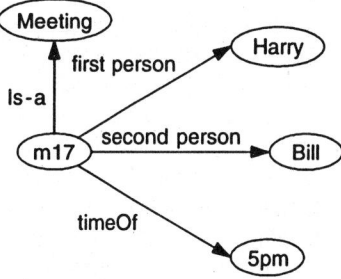

FIG. 2.

that it can represent the scope of a quantifier). Moreover, these ways of organizing the information suggest alternative strategies (e.g. analogical reasoning by partial matching of units, or the use of graph-search algorithms to seek connections between different topics in a semantic network).[5]

In addition, some common inferences fall outside the scope of FOPC, notably the use of the *is-a* hierarchy to express *defaults*. The usual convention is that a link to a lower node in the hierarchy blocks the inheritance of properties from above, so that the inheritance is only "by default." Thus, we might attach a network meaning " has legs" to the *Mammal*-type node, allowing *Whale is-a Mammal* while also consistently asserting that the whale is legless. This kind of *nonmonotonic inference* is not consistent in FOPC, although logics have been extended to allow this and other more complex nonmonotonic inferences (Schank and Reiger, 1974). Inheritance hierarchies can become intricate if, for example, exceptions to exceptions are allowed, and it is not always clear what the "correct" result should be. Since *is-a* hierarchies are often thought of as defining the meanings of the terms in the language, this issue has received a lot of attention.

Semantics and Meaning   One must be careful in interpreting formal expressions. For example, the two Horn clauses shown earlier have the rather surprising consequence

IsBabyOf(x,me) implies Equal(x,me)

---

[3]Object-oriented programming (*q.v.*) languages are based on this idea of hierarchies of units with named slots, which are thought of now as senders and recipients of messages corresponding to the values bound to variables during a matching process.

[4]Simple networks, for example, can be defined as a restriction on logical syntax to the use of only binary or unary predicates and clauses of the forms: *A(a), B(a,b), A(x) implies B(x)* and *A(x) implies R(x,y)*.

[5]In fact, these graphical representations have their historical roots in simpler graphs where adjacency modeled word association.

which follows from our asserting that *everybody* loves my baby: in particular, therefore, she loves herself; but since she doesn't love anybody but me, she must be me. Clearly, the universal quantifier made a stronger statement than intended. Such phenomena are quite common, and writing realistically complex knowledge bases requires developing a sensitivity to them. It is important to avoid the *gensym*[6] *fallacy* of assuming that symbols in a knowledge base must have a meaning that is somehow inherited from their English meaning.

What do the various formalisms mean? Most attempts at an exact answer to this question are based on *model theory* for FOPC, which defines the structure of a possible world and the conditions under which an expression would be true in it, and takes the meaning of a logical expression to be the constraint on this structure imposed by insisting on its truth. Similar accounts can be given for unit and network languages, and model theory is widely used as a tool in the analysis of more complex phenomena. For example, much nonmonotonic reasoning can be explained as the selection of the minimal model in some ordering, so that some relation of *abnormality* is asserted to be "as false as possible."

However, this entire approach to giving formal meaning is controversial. Proceduralists often argue that *any* such precise theory is an inappropriate restriction on the experimental freedom that is required at this stage in the development of AI. Others argue that the strict true/false dichotomy that classical model theory imposes is not suitable for much knowledge representation, and should be replaced by some more quantitative account of truth. Examples of this include *fuzzy logic* and *probabilistic reasoning* of various kinds. This has become a very active area, and much work has been done on the use of Bayesian reasoning to put together pieces of evidence from a wide range of sources (e.g. in attempting to diagnose faults in machinery). Probabilistic representations typically have similar syntax to assertional ones, but the sentences have associated numerical values. The probability of a sentence often depends on a larger set of assumptions than the truth of a logical consequence, so that probabilistic representations sometimes capture context dependence in a more satisfactory way, although with an increased computational cost.

Several have suggested that large parts of "ordinary" knowledge might be reducible to some small number of *primitive* relations or concepts. Probably the most influential such idea was *conceptual dependency* (Schank and Reiger, 1974), which formed complex network fragments from a vocabulary of only about 25 primitive relations. For example, "Harry wants a book" is rendered as the network shown in Fig. 3, which can be roughly transliterated as "*Harry's long-term memory contains the idea that if someone were to transfer ownership of a book to Harry, that would increase Harry's happiness.*" Simple inferences can be achieved by a process of network matching.

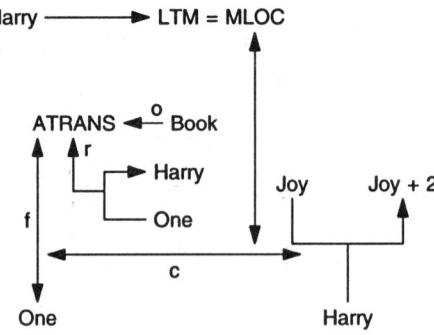

FIG. 3.

While schemes such as this have proved inadequate to handle large parts of ordinary knowledge, the idea of restricting the representational vocabulary to simplify the inference process is still appealing. However, model theory suggests that the meanings of the symbols used in a knowledge base are more tightly defined as its size increases, so that a very large, organized collection of concepts can support more plausible consequences. There is an important research issue here concerning the extent to which a knowledge base can or should be organized in a modular way, and how the boundaries between modules can be determined. While several AI projects, notably CYC (Lenat and Guha, 1990), have been inspired by this idea of size, it is notable that many of the most successful practical applications of AI have been in expert systems, where, almost by definition, the range of the concepts used in the system is limited to a fairly small set, perhaps a few hundred at the most. This suggests that perhaps large knowledge bases can be thought of as consisting of clusters of relatively tightly coupled concepts with somewhat looser connections between the clusters. This whole subject of large-scale structure of large knowledge bases is still unexplored.

Ontology and Vocabulary   All the knowledge representation formalisms distinguish between individuals and relations between them, but they do not specify which individuals and relations are to be used to represent some piece of knowledge. This is a huge topic, in many ways a central one throughout AI, and we have space only to point at some of the issues that have arisen.

Time and Change   One basic idea is the use of states to encode change. To describe a dynamic world, the representation adds a state parameter to each relation that is liable to change, so that in a logical system we might write *IsWearing(Susan,PinkDress3,ThursdayEvening)*. The results of events or actions can be described by a function from these things and states to new states:

IsDressing(x,s) implies IsWearing(x,y,result(x,putOn(y),s))

where the term *result(x,putOn(y),s)* describes the state after *x* performs the action *putOn(y)* in state *s*. This style of writing axioms is called the *situation calculus*, and supports a form of planning by inference, since proving that

---

[6]Named after a Lisp function that generates meaningless names.

a state with some desired properties exists automatically generates a term whose structure of nested *result* terms encodes a way to achieve it. There are many problems, the most difficult being the *frame problem*—how to state neatly that all the many things that do *not* change as a result of performing an action are still true in the new state.

Similar tricks can be used in other notations, of course, but since the addition of state parameters would make a binary relation have more than two arguments, network and frame-based representations often use units or nodes that represent the fact that a certain relation holds during a state, so that *IsWearing(John,pants,result(John,putOn(pants),s))* might become the network fragment shown in Fig. 4, where ACTION23 stands for the *result* term and WEARING45 for the atom. The task of designing inheritance hierarchies to handle structures like this can become very complex and subtle.

States are typically thought of as essentially static, but other approaches to describing change focus instead on time intervals during which some process is happening. This has been used especially in an approach to *qualitative physics*, which models intuitive physical reasoning by classifying processes in terms of the signs of the temporal derivatives of the positions of the objects they contain (Bobrow, 1985).

Beliefs   Another common idea is that of using the representational framework itself to describe the content of *agents beliefs*, so that the fact that Joan believes that all of Harry's friends are fools might be expressed in a logical framework by writing

Believes(Joan, (Forall x)(Friend(x,Harry)
implies Fool(x)))

where one argument of the *believes* relation is a whole logical assertion. A similar technique can be used in network and unit-based formalisms. Such expressions go beyond FOPC and have been studied in depth in philosophical logic.

There are problems in properly interpreting expressions of the form

(Forall x)(Believes(a,....x....)).

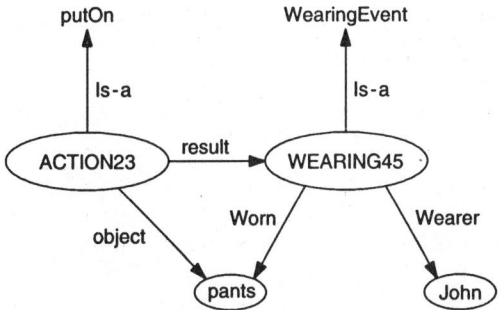

FIG. 4.

These are sometimes made illegal, but they seem to be the only natural way of expressing the idea of believing something *about* an object.

Space and Shape   Natural language uses spatial imagery extensively. Attempts to understand systematically, for example, the structure of spatial prepositions in European languages have led to complex systems of geometric concepts and relationships between them. It is not easy to formalize these in consistent ways, and some have argued that these systems are essentially metaphorical, so that some kind of best-fit structural matching is the most appropriate way to use this kind of information.

We can typically see shapes that are very hard to describe, and much of AI has been concerned with what information is needed to support such spatial intuition and how it can be represented. The problem is to find a representation in which an object has the same shape no matter what its orientation or position, or even perhaps size. Two basic ideas include the use of approximations in terms of simpler shapes with simple geometry (e.g. the human body as a series of linked cylinders), and the use of very general parameterized shapes such as "generalized cylinders," which can be "fitted" to a wide variety of shapes, the parameter settings then regarded as being the representation. Other ideas include describing shapes in terms of the relative positions of their extrema, or describing the shapes of ordinary objects as a small collection of typical views. This whole area merges into those of machine perception, computer graphics, and robotics, and has a much more mathematical flavor than the rest of knowledge representation (Koenderick, 1990).

Open Problems and Research Issues   While some topics, such as the semantics of nonmonotonic logic, are now quite well understood, many classical problems are still not fully solved—e.g. the frame problem was first noted in 1963, but is still the subject of active research (Hayes and Ford, 1992).

Probably the most important new issue is that of *scale*. Much of the earlier work in knowledge representation was motivated by very simple examples and domains, such as the "blocks world," and even commercial applications were of limited size. But more recently the accelerated progress in computing power and especially memory size and communication bandwidth (*q.v.*) have made it possible to plan very large knowledge bases containing tens or even hundreds of thousands of facts.

There are usually many ways in which some facts or processes can be represented in a formalism, and while the resulting decisions are often somewhat arbitrary, they have important consequences. One response to this is to rejoice in the freedom it gives. But if one is striving for generality, this freedom can be embarrassing. Those who attempt to make large-scale knowledge bases often find it hard to maintain a consistent framework, especially when many people contribute to the knowledge base.

Similarly, those who attempt to merge or interconnect different knowledge bases often find incompatibilities between the ways they represent some basic ideas. The problem of *standardization*, or interconnection between knowledge bases, is currently a topic of very active research, two common themes being the idea of a standardized *knowledge interchange formalism*, and the attempt to compose "standard" sets of concepts for expressing knowledge of various industrial and engineering areas. Of course, whether standardization is the right approach is itself controversial.

References

1974. Schank, R. and Reiger, C. J. "Inference and the Computer Understanding of Natural Language," *Artificial Intelligence* **5**, *4*.

1975. Minsky, M. "A Framework for Representing Knowledge," *Memo 36*, M. I. T. Artificial Intelligence Laboratory. Reprinted in Brachman and Levesque, 1985.

1977. Bobrow, D. G., and Winograd, T. "An Overview of KRL, a Knowledge Representation Language," *Cognitive Science* **1**, *1*.

1979. Findler, N. V. (Ed.). *Associative Networks: Representation and Use of Knowledge*, New York: Academic Press.

1984. Levesque, Hector J. "A Fundamental Tradeoff in Knowledge Representation and Reasoning," *Proc. CSCSI-84*, London, Ontario. Reprinted in Brachman and Levesque, 1985.

1985. Brachman, R. and Levesque, H. J. (Eds.). *Readings in Knowledge Representation*. San Mateo, CA: Morgan Kaufman.

1985. Bobrow, D. G. (Ed.). *Qualitative Reasoning about Physical Systems*. Cambridge, MA: The M.I.T. Press.

1990. Lenat, D. B. and Guha, R. V. *Building Large Knowledge-Based Systems*. Reading, MA: Addison-Wesley.

1990. Koenderick, J. J. *Solid Shape*. Cambridge, MA: The M.I.T. Press.

1992. Hayes, P. J. and Ford, K. (Eds.). *Reasoning Agents in a Dynamic World: The Frame Problem*. Boston: JAI Press.

PATRICK J. HAYES

LABEL. *See* MACHINE AND ASSEMBLY LANGUAGE PROGRAMMING; and PROCEDURE-ORIENTED LANGUAGES.

LAMBDA CALCULUS

For articles on related subjects *see* BINDING; FUNCTIONAL PROGRAMMING; GRAMMARS; LIST PROCESSING: LANGUAGES; PRODUCTION; PROGRAMMING LINGUISTICS; PROGRAM VERIFICATION; and SYNTAX, SEMANTICS AND PRAGMATICS.

The *lambda calculus* (or λ-calculus) is a mathematical formalism developed by the logician Alonzo Church (*q.v.*) in the 1930s to model the mathematical notion of substitution of values for bound variables. Consider the definition $f(x) = x + 1$, which defines f to be the successor function. The variable x in this definition is a *bound variable* in the sense that replacement of all instances of x by some other variable (say, y) yields a definition $f(y) = y + 1$, which is semantically equivalent. In the λ-calculus, the successor function f may be defined by the λ-expression $\lambda x\,(x + 1)$. The subexpression $(x + 1)$ is referred to as the *body* of the λ-expression. The subexpression λx is referred to as the *bound variable part* and specifies that x is to be regarded as a bound variable in the body with which λx is associated.

The application of $\lambda x\,(x + 1)$ to the integer argument 3 may be specified by the λ-expression $f(3) = \lambda x\,(x + 1)\,(3)$. The subexpression $\lambda x\,(x + 1)$ is referred to as the "operator part" of this lambda expression; the subexpression 3 is referred to as the "operand part" of this lambda expression. The substitution rules (reduction rules) of the lambda calculus specify that the operator part $\lambda x\,(x + 1)$ may be applied to the operand part 3 to yield the value $(3 + 1) = 4$.

Consider next the lambda expression $\lambda h\,(h(3) + h(4))\,(\lambda x\,(x + 1))$. The substitution rules of the λ-calculus specify that $\lambda x\,(x + 1)$, which is the operand part of this expression, is to be substituted for all instances of h in the

body of the operator part, yielding the λ-expression $(\lambda x\,(x + 1)(3) + \lambda x\,(x + 1)(4))$, which on further substitution yields $((3 + 1) + (4 + 1)) = 9$.

The binding of h to $\lambda x\,(x + 1)$ in $h(3) + h(4)$ may be expressed in one of the following ways.

1. Let $h = \lambda x\,(x + 1)$ in $h(3) + h(4)$.
2. $h(3) + h(4)$ where $h = \lambda x\,(x + 1)$.

The notations (1) and (2) are said to be syntactically "sugared" versions of the original λ-expression in the sense that they are semantically equivalent to the original λ-expression but are easier to read. The above syntactically sugared specifications illustrate that certain notational conventions of real programming languages may very easily be converted into semantically equivalent lambda notations.

The following example illustrates even more clearly that the bound variable h of the λ-expression given above represents a procedure that is initialized to the successor function $\lambda x\,(x + 1)$ at the time of binding, and is then called with the arguments 3 and 4:

> procedure $h(x)$; result$\leftarrow x + 1$;
> value$\leftarrow h(3) + h(4)$;

This example also illustrates that, in order to realize the functions determined by lambda expressions in a conventional programming language, it is necessary to introduce the assignment operator and to realize binding and substitution in terms of assignment.

In the preceding examples, λ-expressions were allowed to contain extraneous symbols, such as $+$, which allow arithmetic operations to be embedded in the substitutive mechanism of the λ-calculus. The pure λ-calculus does not contain such extraneous operators, and requires all transformations to be substitutions of values for bound variables. In the remainder of this article we will be concerned with the pure λ-calculus.

The pure λ-calculus may be thought of as a programming language with a very simple syntax and semantics. The syntax of λ-expressions may be defined by a BNF grammar whose terminal symbols are λ, (,), and a class V of variable names, and whose productions are $E \rightarrow V|$ $\lambda VE|(EE)$, where E denotes the class of λ-expressions. An expression of the form λVE (say, λxM) denotes a one-parameter function and has a bound variable part λx and a body part M. An expression of the form (EE) [say, $(M_1 M_2)$] is referred to as an operator-operand combination, and has an operator part M_1 and an operand part M_2. An occurrence of a variable x in a λ-expression M is said to be bound in M if it occurs within a subexpression of the form λxM_1 within M, and is said to be free otherwise.

Note: The above syntactic definition requires application of an operator f to an operand x to be specified as (fx) rather than as $f(x)$.

The "computational semantics" of the λ-calculus may be defined by transformation rules that specify how λ-expressions may be converted into "semantically equivalent" λ-expressions. The principal computation rule is the *reduction rule* (sometimes called the "β-rule").

Reduction Rule

An operator-operand combination of the form (λxMA) may be transformed into the expression $S_A^x M$, obtained by substituting the λ-expression A for all instances of x in M, provided there are no conflicts of variable names. The condition that there be no conflicts of variable names may be explicitly specified as follows:

1. M contains no bound occurrences of x.
2. M contains no bound variables that occur free in A.

A second transformation rule called the "renaming rule" (α rule) allows conflicts of variables to be eliminated.

Renaming Rule

A bound variable x in a λ-expression M may be uniformly replaced by some other bound variable y, provided y does not occur in M.

Any λ-expression of the form (λxMA) may be converted into a λ-expression of the form $(\lambda xM'A)$ satisfying conditions (1) and (2) above by renaming of the bound variables of M, using the renaming rule, and may then be reduced to $S_A^x M'$ using the reduction rule.

Example

$$(\lambda x\,(x\lambda xx)(pq)) \xrightarrow{a} (\lambda x(x\lambda tt)(pq)) \xrightarrow{\beta} ((pq)\lambda tt).$$

A λ-expression P that has no subexpressions of the form (λxMA) is said to be in *reduced form*. A λ-expression that cannot be converted to a reduced form by a sequence of renaming and reduction rules is said to be *irreducible*.

Example. $P = (\lambda x(xx)\lambda x(xx)$ is irreducible, since it is of the form (λxMA) with $M = (xx)$ and $A = \lambda x(xx)$, and application of the reduction rule produces $(\lambda x(xx)\lambda x(xx))$.

The question of whether an arbitrary λ-expression P has a reduced form is *undecidable*; i.e. there is no algorithm that, given an arbitrary λ-expression E, can always determine in a finite number of steps whether or not E has a reduced form.

The notion of a reduced form corresponds to the intuitive notion of a value in arithmetic computation. For example, the arithmetic computation $(3 + (4 * 5)) \rightarrow (3 + 20) \rightarrow 23$ is accomplished by two applications of operators to their operands, corresponding to reductions in the λ-calculus. The result, 23, corresponds to a reduced expression because it contains no more instances of operators that can be applied to their operands.

If a λ-expression contains more than one sub-expression of the form (λxMA), then there is more than one "next step" in the computation, and the evaluation process becomes non-deterministic. The following important theorem states that, for any λ-expression, all sequences of computation that yield a value will yield the same value.

Church-Rosser Theorem

If a given λ-expression is reduced by two different reduction sequences, and if both reduction sequences yield a reduced form, then the reduced forms are equivalent up to renaming of bound variables.

However, there are λ-expressions that give rise to both terminating and non-terminating sequences.

Example. The λ-expression

$$(\lambda x\lambda yy(\lambda x(xx)\lambda x(xx)))$$

has the form (λxMA), where $M = \lambda yy$ and $A = (\lambda x(xx)\lambda x(xx))$. If A is substituted for occurrences of x in M before A is evaluated, then the value of λyy is obtained, while if an attempt is made to evaluate A before substituting it in M, then an infinite reduction sequence is obtained.

The choice among different orders of evaluation in the λ-calculus has its counterpart in function evaluation for real programming languages. For example, in evaluating $f(g(x))$, we can choose to evaluate $g(x)$ and use the resulting value in the evaluation of f, or we can pass the unevaluated function $g(x)$ to f and evaluate $g(x)$ whenever it is needed in f. The first alternative is referred to as "inside-out" evaluation and corresponds to *call-by-value* in Algol 60 (Naur *et al.*, 1963), while the second alternative is referred to as "outside-in" evaluation and corresponds to *call-by-name* in Algol 60. Call-by-value is more efficient than call-by-name when the value of $g(x)$ is used more than once during the evaluation of f, but it is less efficient if $g(x)$ is never used during the evaluation of f. In particular, if $g(x)$ results in an infinite computation sequence but is never used in f, then the call-by-value strategy results in disaster, whereas the call-by-name strategy is always adequate.

The λ-expression

$$(\lambda xMA) = (\lambda x\lambda yy(\lambda x(xx)\lambda x(xx)))$$

is of the form $f(g(x))$, where $f = \lambda x\lambda yy$ has a function body with no occurrences of the parameter x, and $g(x) = (\lambda x(xx)\lambda x(xx))$ results in an infinite computation. The call-by-name evaluation strategy for λ-expressions corresponds to always reducing the instance of (λxMA) whose component λx occurs farthest to the left. This strategy is called the "leftmost" evaluation strategy. The universal adequacy of the call-by-name strategy is captured by the following theorem.

THEOREM. If for a lambda expression E there is a terminating reduction sequence yielding a reduced form E, then the leftmost reduction sequence will yield a reduced form that is equivalent to E up to renaming.

The λ-calculus is equivalent in computational power to the class of Turing machines (*q.v.*) in the sense that any computable function may be represented as a λ-expression. However, the notation and computation mechanism of the λ-calculus is closer to that of programming languages than in the case of Turing machines. This has led to attempts to model programming languages such as Algol 60 in terms of the λ-calculus (Landin, 1965). Such models capture certain concepts, such as nested block structure, binding of variables, and the order of evaluation, but have difficulty in capturing other concepts, such as assignment, sharing of values by references, side effects, and unconditional branching. Thus, although the λ-calculus is useful for gaining insights into certain computational mechanisms arising in real programming languages, it appears to be unnatural as a framework for modeling complete programming languages. In order to model complete programming languages in a natural way, it is appropriate to introduce (as a primitive notion) cells whose values may be updated and that may be referred to by references.

The λ-calculus is of computational interest because it allows us to factor out certain aspects of computational structure and study these features independently of the complexity of real programming languages. It is of mathematical interest because it provides a framework for characterizing the substitution of values for bound variables and for studying the notion of function application. The λ-calculus thus provides a bridge between mathematics and the theory of computation. However, since the λ-calculus is a natural model for only a very restricted class of computational mechanisms, it is likely to remain of limited value as a tool in the analysis of computing systems. Nevertheless, it should be noted that the programming language Lisp is closely modeled on the λ-calculus (*see* LIST PROCESSING: LANGUAGES).

References

1951. Church, A. "The Calculi of Lambda Conversion," *Ann. Math. Studies, No. 6.* Princeton, NJ: Princeton University Press.
1963. Naur, P. *et al.* "Revised Report on the Algorithmic Language ALGOL 60," *Comm. ACM* (January).
1965. Landin, P. J. "A Correspondence Between Algol 60 and Church's Lambda Notation," *Comm. ACM* (February and March).

PETER WEGNER

LANGUAGE PROCESSORS

For articles on related subjects *see* ASSEMBLER; BINDING; COMPILE AND RUN TIME; COMPILER-COMPILER; COMPILER CONSTRUCTION; DEFAULT CONDITION; DELIMITER; DISASSEMBLER; EXPRESSION; GLOBAL AND LOCAL VARIABLES; GRAMMARS; MACHINE AND ASSEMBLY LANGUAGE PROGRAMMING; OBJECT PROGRAM; PREPROCESSOR; PROGRAMMING LANGUAGES; PROGRAMMING LINGUISTICS; REENTRANT PROGRAM; SOURCE PROGRAM; and SUBPROGRAM.

Overview There exists a formidable barrier between the average person who desires to solve some problem using the computer and the description of the solution in terms of *machine language* (*see* MACHINE AND ASSEMBLY LANGUAGE PROGRAMMING). Although the ability of some programmers to communicate in terms of machine language is exceptional, the minute attention to detail required to develop a program is beyond the scope of most computer users. Thus, early in the history of computer development, there was a drive to moderate this communications gap. The initial trend was toward providing codes that would reference specialized routines that were to be drawn from a library of such routines. Only later, when these codes took on the character of alphabetic phrases, did they become known as *languages* (Hopper, 1981).

The primary efforts toward simplification led to a symbolic form of machine language in which code sequences were represented by mnemonic character sequences (such as ADD for the operation of addition, or JMP for the instruction to break normal sequential processing and "jump" to some other designated instruction), and where references to data elements were in terms of symbolic names instead of through the memory address of the data element. This language development led to the requirement for a processor (program) that would convert programs represented by a symbolic code into their equivalent machine language representation. This process is known as *assembly*, and the processor known as an *assembler*.

Such assemblers perform no task other than the generation of an equivalent machine language program based on a symbolic language program and, in particular, take no part in the actual execution of the generated program.

The development of symbolic language and assemblers was followed closely by the development of *autocoders*, in which the programmer's language was more closely related to mathematical notation than to the machine operations. Most of the first autocoders were primitive by current standards, permitting only simple one-operator expressions and restricted naming of data elements. However, the autocoder required the development of more sophisticated conversion processors, thus leading to a study of the general translatory process. An interesting comparison and effective history of the development of autocoders and other primitive languages may be found in Knuth and Pardo, 1980.

The methods of program conversion and subsequent execution of a user's program can be classified into two basic techniques: 1) compilation and execution, or 2) interpretation. Both systems use a translatory system in which the original program (the *source program*) is converted into some other language (*target language*). In the case of the compilation process (performed by a *compiler*), the target language is either machine language or its corresponding symbolic language. In the latter case, the compiler must be supplemented by an assembler in order to complete the conversion process. Once the compiler has generated the equivalent program in machine language, the resulting *object program* may then be executed independently. In the case of interpretation (performed by an *interpreter*), the two steps of conversion and execution are continuously interleaved so that the generated code corresponding to a portion of the source program is executed as it is produced. In this manner the interpreter maintains control over both conversion and execution.

In the preceding exposition, the term "conversion" has been used in place of the term "translation," since we wish to reserve the latter for a very specific purpose (*see also* LANGUAGE TRANSLATION). The American National Standard Vocabulary for Information Processing (ANSI, 1970) provides a strict definition of this term:

> **Translate**—To *transform statements* from one *language* to another without significantly changing the meaning.

In this sense, a programmer must insist that a compiler or the conversion process within an interpreter be a translator, since the meaning associated with a source program must be carried over to the target language program. The ANSI Vocabulary also provides definitions associated with the process of compilation and interpretation:

> **Compile**—To prepare a *machine language* program from a *computer program* written in another *programming language* by making use of the overall logic structure of the program, or generating more than one *machine (language) instruction* for each symbolic *statement*, or both, as well as performing the function of an *assembler*.
>
> **Interpreter**—A *computer program* that *translates* and executes each *source language* statement before translating and executing the next one.

In practice, there rarely exists a compiler or an interpreter that adheres precisely to these definitions; most languages possess certain features that cannot be compiled, and most interpreters initially preprocess the source program into some intermediate form and operate upon that code rather than the original program (*see* PREPROCESSOR). The three possibilities are shown in Fig. 1.

Part (a) of Fig. 1 illustrates pure compilation in which the source program is compiled into machine language for machine *M*. The circuits of *M* that execute the machine language instructions, known as *M*'s *hardware interpreter*, then execute the compiled code. Pure compilation is often used for languages such as Pascal, C, and Fortran. Its major advantage is fast execution.

Part (b) of Fig. 1 illustrates a combination of compilation and interpretation in which the source program is translated into an intermediate language that is interpre-

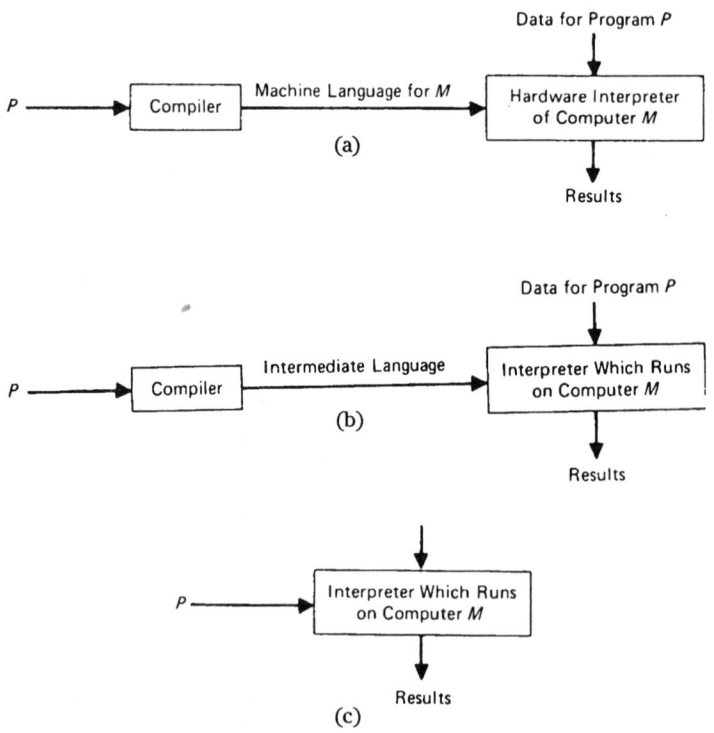

FIG. 1.   Three possibilities in compilation and interpretation. (a) Pure compilation (hardware interpreter) (b) Mixed compilation and interpretation (interpretation of intermediate language) (c) Pure interpretation (interpretation of source language)

ted by a *software interpreter*, which runs on computer *M*. Often, the intermediate language is the machine language of a hypothetical "ideal" computer that is simulated on a real machine. An example of a programming system based on this method is the UCSD Pascal system (Bowles, 1978). Because the semiconductor industry is evolving new equipment very fast, it is becoming a practical necessity to have (nearly) machine-independent software. The UCSD Pascal system is built on a small hypothetical machine known as the P-machine, which was originally developed at ETH Zurich. Therefore, to transfer the system to a new computer essentially involves only writing the P-machine interpreter in the machine language of the new computer.

Part (c) of Fig. 1 illustrates pure interpretation, in which the source program is interpreted directly by a software interpreter that runs on computer M. This method is often used for languages such as APL, Snobol, Forth (*q.v.*), Lisp, and Prolog, although optional compilation or mixed compilation and interpretation is becoming more common for these languages. Pure interpretation is also used for languages such as command and job control languages (*q.v.*). The major advantages are memory economy (no machine or intermediate code has to be stored) and the relative simplicity of programming, but the execution is slow (Calingaert, 1979).

The Translatory Process The steps that comprise the process of translation of the statements of a high-level programming language into machine language are shown in Fig. 2. The processor portions of the translation system are shown in rectangular blocks and the data groups upon which they operate and develop are in ovals. This diagram is extremely formalized, the individual processors not being readily recognizable in most translatory systems. Nor is it necessary, as may be inferred from this diagram, that each phase of translation be completed before the next is entered.

The lexical analyzer used in the lexical scan performs the task of preparing the source text (the user's program in machine-readable form) for the syntactic analyzer phase. At the same time, it attempts to condense the text so as to improve the efficiency of later examinations of the text. For example, in Fortran 77, the inclusion of blanks in statements is tolerated by the language so as to provide a more readable text for the programmer. In fact, except within literal strings, blanks may be inserted randomly.

Such niceties, however, can considerably slow the statement scanning routines that must examine each and every character of the statement. Hence, one of the assigned tasks of a Fortran lexical scan will be to eliminate nonsignificant blanks and condense the statements to their "raw" symbolic content. Further, to save later work for the syntactic analyzer, the delineation of the statements into words or phrases can often be accomplished during the lexical scan.

Once having recognized a symbol or a phrase, the lexical analyzer may then replace that item in the source text by a *token* that is more easily identifiable by the syntactic analyzer. At the same time, the lexical analyzer places the recognized element into the symbol table for later reference. For example, in Basic, the design of the language (to ease implementation) is such that the first three characters following the line number are a unique characterization of the type of statement that follows. Thus, if the lexical analyzer separates these characters into, say, one word, the recognition of the type of statement by the syntactic analyzer can be facilitated.

Further, considering Basic as a simple language for compilation, it is possible to recognize variables and language constants by simple lexical rules (as opposed to syntactic rules). Any string that starts with (has as the leftmost character) an alphabetic character is a candidate for recognition as a variable. The right delimiter of such a string is any non-alphanumeric character, except in the case of FOR statements, where special character sequences (TO and STEP) are of importance. However, it is possible in a lexical scan to recognize about 90% of all instances of variables and constants and to collect the characters that comprise those language elements into words or other well-defined units. By this means, for example, punctuation in Basic READ and PRINT statements can be eliminated, the language elements now being delineated by logical boundaries in the representation of the text. The process of lexical analysis is accomplished by the use of algorithms for finite state machines (*see* AUTOMATA THEORY).

The syntactic analyzer of a translatory process completes the task of analyzing the input text by converting the text into a completely specified (*parsed*) text in which the grammatical components of the language are appropriately connected with the elements of the text. Syntactic analyzers may appear in one of two possible forms: a generalized analyzer, which uses a set of syntactic specifications to direct the analysis of a text; or a specialized analyzer, specifically designed for the analysis of text related to one specific language. Even though the lexical analyzer has "worked over" the text on the basis of readily recognizable characters such as punctuation, the syntactic analyzer must still determine the structure of the text based on the grammar (syntax) of the language.

Lexical and syntactic analysis can be distinguished by the spatial relationships that exist between the elements over which they can operate. While it is true that in the Chomsky hierarchy (*q.v.*) of grammars (and hence of representable languages), lexical properties are a subset of syntactic properties, a useful distinction is that lexical relationships exist only between juxtaposed symbols, whereas the scope of a syntactic analyzer permits relationships between more distant symbols.

"Pure" syntactic analysis of a text develops only a parsed version of the text, but the syntactic analyzer in a translatory process (as we will consider it here) also acts as a "collection agency" by adding to the symbol table of recognized elements (such as variables and constants) the attributes assigned (or implied) to those elements by the language.

The form in which a syntactic analyzer provides the parsed text to the next process is by no means fixed. It is necessary that the output from this analyzer be in the form of a structure that conveys the nested nature of the

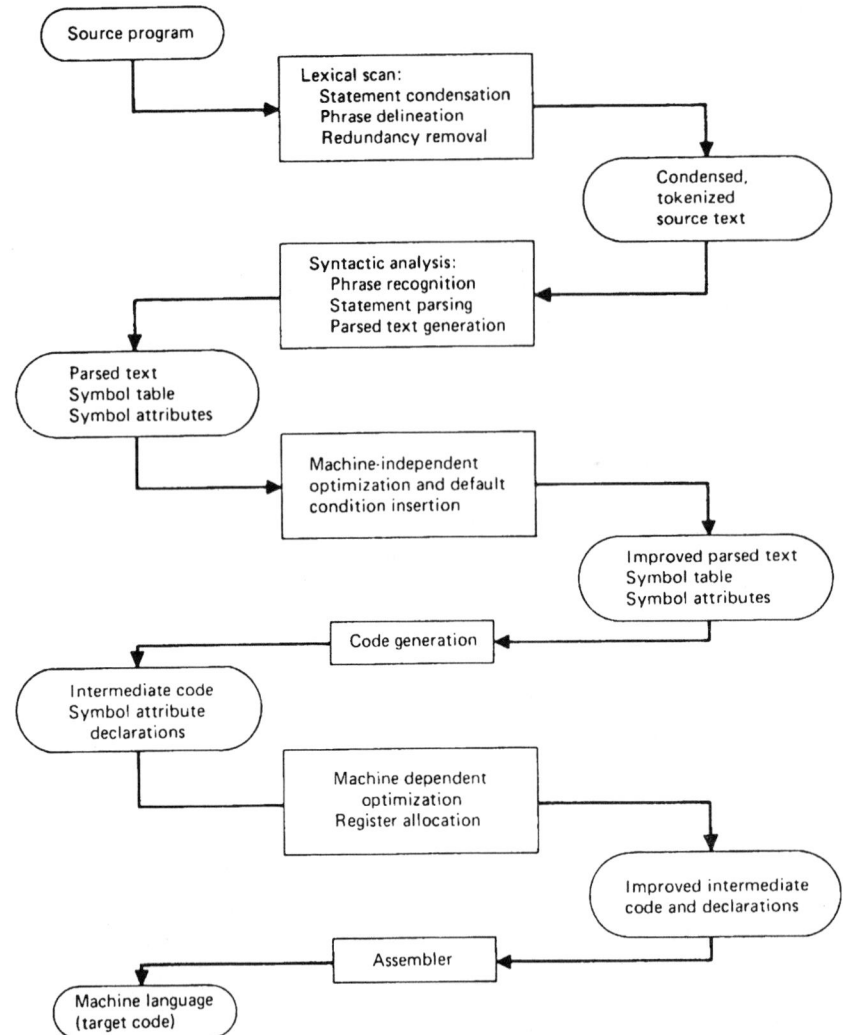

FIG. 2. The detailed process of language translation more closely related to the problem (a high-level programming language) than to a machine language.

language to the succeeding processes. Syntactically parsed texts are typically displayed as *trees* (*q.v.*), though a linked list or linear form may be more appropriate for machine representation.

Once the text has been scanned by the syntactic analyzer and the parsed test is developed, a machine-independent optimization process may be used over the text to improve the anticipated code to be generated in a later phase. Machine-independent optimization can be distinguished from the later stage of machine-dependent optimization not only by the fact that the domains of the two optimization processes are different but also by mechanisms of optimization. In the case of machine-dependent optimization, it is the general intent to eliminate instructions that are redundant (i.e. instructions that would have no effect on computed results).

If this latter type of optimization were to be applied to self-modifying code, it would not always be possible to reorganize instruction sequences and be assured that the optimizing changes do not affect the result. On the other hand, at the level of a language such as Fortran, no state-ment is subject to modification. Thus, any change made within a single Fortran statement does not affect any other statement. For example, the recognition of common subexpressions, which has been the subject of several papers in the literature, is a process that provides optimization at the machine-independent level. For example, the Fortran statement

```
X = A*B + 5/(A*B)
```

may be reduced to the sequential statements

```
Z = A*B
X = Z + 5/Z
```

which will develop the desired value of X.

On a larger scale, machine-independent optimization of statements that occur in loops can have a significant effect on the resulting execution time of the generated program. An analysis of the changes in the values of variables within loops can reveal that certain operations are repeated on each pass through the loop, and hence can be moved out of the loop to some initialization phase.

Knuth (1971) has reported that, in one typical analyzed program, almost 18% of the execution time was due to the repeated conversion of a constant from integer to real mode. In this particular program, the constant was contained in an assignment statement in which the variable on the left-hand side was invariant during the repeated execution of the loop. Thus, the movement of this statement outside the loop gave a total execution time improvement of approximately 30%. Machine-independent optimization is, however, generally language-dependent, since, although the techniques of optimization may be common across languages, the ability to apply these techniques may be different for each language.

On the other hand, optimization of the type where one specified operation is replaced by another known to be faster on a particular machine is necessarily machine-dependent. For example, on a certain machine it was found that the subroutine to perform the operation A**I (A^I) took longer than successive multiplication when the exponent I was an integer less than 15. Thus, a compiler written for that machine took this knowledge into account and transformed the Fortran phrase A**I into the optimally minimum number of multiplications needed in those circumstances. On the other hand, optimization of an expression to eliminate sign reversals, and thus minimize the number of operators in the expression, is not machine-dependent. This later process of replacing operators by simpler operators is known as *strength reduction*.

After initial code generation, the developed code is subjected to a machine-dependent optimization process that is independent of the original source language. Here, the optimization process is highly dependent on the characteristics of the target processor. An example of a highly machine-dependent optimization would be the assignment of index registers to code that had been developed on the basis of a supposed infinite availability of registers.

Definitions of the techniques of compiler code generation optimization are included in Allen and Cocke (1972), and include:

> Procedure integration (making procedures into in-line code).
> Loop transformation.
> Common subexpression elimination.
> Code motion (moving code to a location where it is less frequently used).
> Constant folding (computing constant expressions at compile time).
> Dead code elimination.
> Strength reduction.
> Instruction scheduling (especially in multiprocessor environments).
> Register allocation.
> Storage mapping (reuse of storage).
> Special case code optimization.
> Peephole (or limited domain) optimization.

Binding Time   Given a program in (almost) any language and the derivation therefrom of the set of identifiers, constants, references, and other language elements, there must occur at some time a mapping from this user's set of elements onto the available storage of the computer that is to execute or that is executing the generated program. Most high-level languages do not allow the programmer to describe explicitly the organization of memory at object time (except in the case of Fortran COMMON), and rarely (with the exception of Fortran EQUIVALENCE) do they allow the user to specify relationships between identifiers and other language elements. Thus, the implementer is free to devise some mapping algorithm between the language elements and their assigned storage locations (at object time), provided a certain criterion is met. This criterion is that the values assigned to some identifier (variable, array element, statement identifier, etc.) should be retrievable at some later (possibly restricted) time.

The instant at which all the information is available that is necessary to permit the allocation of object time storage to some language element is one of the bounds on the *binding time* of that element (*see* BINDING). That is, there must exist two bounds (which in certain instances may be identical) on the time during which storage may be assigned to a language element. The latest time (bound) available to assign a storage location to a language element is obviously the instant prior to its first usage in the program.

Conversely, if all the attributes of a language element are not only known but are also known to be fixed (i.e. static) at the instant that the element is first encountered in the translatory process, then it is possible to assign (allocate) storage at this earliest time. This period may be further subdivided by considering the type of memory referencing to be performed. For instance, if the earliest binding time is taken as that instant when an absolute address can be assigned to a language element, then actual binding might be defined as load time (i.e. the time at which the program is loaded into storage).

Binding time may be a language feature or it may be implementation-defined. For example, in APL, the left-arrow (assignment operator ←) operation has the effect of assigning the attributes of the expression to its right to the variable on its left. Thus, the instant at which all the information is available to enable the assignment of storage to the variable on the left is the instant of executing the assignment operation. Hence, APL has dynamic attribute specifications, and binding time (earliest and latest) is execution time. Lacking explicit (and static) declarations of attributes, the APL interpreter itself determines attributes at execution time. Conversely, Basic, in the case of missing (omitted) array-size declarations, inserts default attributes so as to permit compile-time binding of variables.

In choosing a binding time, the implementer is free to choose any particular instant *within the bounds allowed by the grammar of the language at hand*. However, the later that binding takes place, the greater the difficulty in generating effective code and the more time it will take to both store and retrieve the values of language elements. For instance, if an absolute address had been assigned to a variable, then all references to that variable in the generated code may be made directly. However, if the binding time is delayed until (say) the last moment, then each reference to that variable will require the system to look up the assigned location. Thus, the work of the symbol table is delayed until execution time and may be performed repeatedly rather than just once, as would be the case for compile time binding of variables. In any case, it should be a general principle that when speed of object code execution is most important, the earliest possible binding times should be used, and when flexibility of programming logic is more important, the latest possible binding times should be used. In the development of the language Ada (*q.v.*), it was established as a language design principle that the attributes of each language element should be determinable (bound) at compile time, thus making storage assignment effectively a static activity.

Compilation vs. Interpretation Many factors must be considered by a language implementer before decisions are made to compile or interpret, to optimize code, to develop a load-and-go compiler (*q.v.*), or to separate completely the translation and execution phases. The environment within which the system is to operate may help to determine the type of system to be developed. For example, if it is expected that the system will be used primarily for education, then an interpretive system may be advantageous, provided error reports are directly related to source code. Or, in a mixed education and research environment where many programs will run but few will ever become production programs and be run repeatedly, a load-and-go system may suit the needs best. That is, the code developed by a compiler is stored directly in the memory of the computer instead of being output on some intermediate storage system and control is transferred to the first executable statement in the compiled program after compilation is complete; developed code is not saved for subsequent executions. But when the number of compiles is high, an extremely efficient (or fast) compiler is necessary, and thus the optimization phases may be omitted on the basis that the overall cost of compilation does not justify the cost of execution. Conversely, in an environment where compiled programs are to be developed into production systems and one compile may result in many thousands of runs, then a methodical compiler that develops highly optimized machine code is of great importance.

Whether to compile or to interpret may depend on factors that are less easy to express in quantitative terms. With regard to storage, the amount required by a compiler is not substantially different from that required to perform the same tasks within the interpreter; in fact, the interpreter will contain additional features to perform the execution phase of the problem solution. On the other hand, while it is obvious that there need be no significant differences between user data storage requirements in an interpretive system as compared to a compiler system, nor differences between the storage requirements for the symbol tables of the two systems, a judicious design of the interpretive symbol table can substantially reduce the combined storage requirements of the symbol table and the user data storage.

Conversely, the interpreter must be self-sufficient

and, except in comparatively large computer systems with fast access ancillary storage facilities, the interpreter should also have, readily available in memory, all anticipated library routines. On the other hand, the compiler can take advantage of the hiatus between compilation and execution to load into memory only those that are needed by this particular program. It has been shown empirically that the amount of storage required by the compiled code of a source text is not substantially different (but usually less) than that needed for the source text itself.

The question of whether a program written in a certain language can be compiled or can be interpreted is not directly related to the question of whether to interpret or to compile, except as related to available storage. Obviously, if the average-size program (determined by some undefined means) cannot be interpreted because of a lack of available storage, there is a possibility that it may be compiled, and thus the question of whether to compile or to interpret is answered. However, it may be that some languages are not susceptible to compilation and must, therefore, be interpreted; conversely, it would seem that any language that can be compiled can also be interpreted (storage requirements aside). There are some languages that contain elements that cannot be compiled but that must be interpreted, thus raising the possibility of "hybrid" translator systems. In this context, it is necessary to define *interpretive code* as code that is parametrized to the extent that differing attributes of the operands can be inserted (accessed) at run time, and are not statically specified during the compilation phase. Typically, references to dynamically defined data elements take the form of calls upon generalized routines that can respond to the differing data organizations.

The Symbol Table In the organization of any translatory system in which several subprocesses of translation take place (such as lexical analysis, syntactic analysis, and code generation), the vehicle for the transference of extracted or deduced information regarding the text is the *symbol table*. The symbol table provides a base for the coalescence of data relating to the various elements of the source text and provides a possibility for describing certain relationships between the text and the target machine, such as the assigned (possibly relative) addresses of variables. In a static environment, the symbol table will serve the purpose of providing, for example, assigned addresses to the compiler's code generator for substitution into instruction masks, while the symbol table in a dynamic environment may exist also at run time to provide a key to currently allocated memory space. Between the time of ending compilation and beginning the execution of the generated program (assuming that the generated code is not resident), the symbol table will provide necessary data to the loader for the acquisition of library-provided subprograms and will in turn, during run time, act as a transfer vector for the linkage of the generated code and those subprograms.

The compile-time symbol table of an algebraic language processor will contain entries pertinent to the various data elements that may occur within the source text. In general, these may include variables (both simple and n-dimensional), statement identifiers, subprogram (or block) names, and constants. Among this data will appear not only the deduced (or defined) attributes of the language element, but also data pertinent to the compilation of the statements in which they either appeared or are expected to appear.

In some language systems, the symbol table may play an extremely important part of the run-time characteristics of the system. For example, in any system that includes the ability to allocate and free storage, or in a system that is implemented so that storage is dynamically controlled, the symbol table is the key between the executable code and the data set. During the various phases of compilation or interpretation, in any procedural or block-structured (q.v.) language, there may exist several differing symbol tables, each relating to a particular block or procedure.

The purpose of a symbol table is to provide a common data source to the various components of a translatory system relating to the elements of the source text and, in particular, to provide a source of data pertinent to the specified or deduced attributes of those elements. The symbol table is thus being accessed by many routines during the process of translation and therefore must be amenable to rapid access and data retrieval. The routine that organizes the symbol table directs a number of tasks, among them the following:

1. Post an item and its associated data.
2. Retrieve the data associated with any item.
3. Delete an item and its associated data.

All these activities involve the searching of the table to locate the item or to recognize the absence of that item, and hence the efficiency of this search affects the efficiency of the whole compiler (*see* SEARCHING).

References

1966. Ingerman, P. Z. *A Syntax Oriented Translator*. New York: Academic Press.

1967. Lee, J. A. N. *The Anatomy of a Compiler*. New York: Van Nostrand Reinhold.

1969. Hopgood, F. R. A. *Compiling Techniques*. New York: American Elsevier.

1970. American National Standards Institute. *Vocabulary for Information Processing*, Doc. No. X3.12-1970. New York: ANSI.

1970. Association for Computing Machinery. "Proceedings of a Symposium on Compiler Optimization," *SIGPLAN Notices* 5, 7, July.

1971. Knuth, D. E. "An Empirical Study of FORTRAN Programs," *Software—Practice and Experience* 1: 105–133.

1972. Gries, D. *Compiler Construction for Digital Computers*. New York: John Wiley.

1972. Allen, F. E. and Cocke, J. "A Catalog of Optimizing Transformations," Courant Computer Science Symposium. Englewood Cliffs, NJ: Prentice-Hall, 1–30.

1976. Lewis, P. M., Rosenkrantz, D. J., and Stearns, R. E. *Compiler Design Theory*. Reading, MA: Addison-Wesley.

1978. Bowles, Kenneth L. "UCSD Pascal," *Byte*, 46 (May).

1979. Calingaert, Peter. *Assemblers, Compilers, and Program Translation*. Potomac, MD: Computer Science Press.

1980. Knuth, D. E. and Pardo, L. T. "The Early Development of Programming Languages," in Metropolis, N. *et al.* (Eds.), *The History of Computing in the Twentieth Century*. New York: Academic Press.

1981. Hopper, G. M. "Early Days," Keynote Presentation, *Proc. History of Programming Languages Conference*. New York: Academic Press.

1986. Aho, A. V., Sethi, R., and Ullman, J. D. *Compilers: Principles, Techniques, and Tools*. Reading, MA: Addison-Wesley.

ADRIENNE G. BLOSS AND J. A. N. LEE

LANGUAGE TRANSLATION

For articles on related subjects *see* ARTIFICIAL INTELLIGENCE; and NATURAL LANGUAGE PROCESSING.

History of Machine Translation (MT) Within a few years of the first appearance of "electronic calculators," research had begun on using computers as aids for translating natural languages. The major stimulus was a memorandum of July 1949 by Warren Weaver who, after mentioning tentative efforts in Great Britain (by Booth and Richens) and in the U. S. (by Huskey and others), put forward possible lines of research. His optimism stemmed from war-time success in code breaking, from developments by Shannon in information theory (q.v.), and from speculations about universal principles underlying natural languages, "the common base of human communication." Within a few years research had begun at many U. S. universities, and in 1954 the first public demonstration of the feasibility of machine translation (MT) was given, a collaboration of IBM and Georgetown University. Although the demonstration used a very restricted vocabulary and grammar, it was sufficiently impressive to stimulate massive funding of MT in the U. S. and to inspire the establishment of MT projects throughout the world.

The earliest MT systems consisted primarily of large bilingual dictionaries where entries for words of the source language (SL) gave one or more equivalents in the target language (TL) and some rules for producing the correct word order in the output. It was soon recognized that specific dictionary-driven rules for syntactic ordering were too complex and increasingly ad hoc; more systematic methods of syntactic analysis were needed. A number of projects were inspired by contemporary developments in linguistics, particularly Zellig Harris's and Noam Chomsky's ideas on syntactic transformations. Other models, such as dependency grammar and stratificational grammar, also seemed to offer the prospect of greatly improved translation.

Optimism remained at a high level for the first decade of MT research, with many predictions of imminent breakthroughs, but disillusion grew as researchers encountered "semantic barriers" for which they saw no straightforward solutions. There were some operational systems—the Mark II system (developed by IBM and Washington University) installed at the USAF Foreign Technology Division, and the Georgetown University system at the U. S. Atomic Energy Authority and at Euratom in

Italy, but the quality of output was disappointing (even though it satisfied many recipients' needs for information). By 1964, the U.S. government sponsors, becoming increasingly concerned at the lack of progress, set up the Automatic Language Processing Advisory Committee (ALPAC). In its famous 1966 report, the committee concluded that MT was slower, less accurate, and twice as expensive as human translation and that "there is no immediate or predictable prospect of useful machine translation." Seeing no need in the U.S. for further investment in MT research, it recommended instead the development of machine aids for translators, such as automatic dictionaries, and continued support in basic research in computational linguistics.

The ALPAC report was widely condemned as narrow, biased, and shortsighted, but the damage had been done. It brought a virtual end to MT research in the U.S. for over a decade, and it had great impact elsewhere, particularly in the Soviet Union and in Europe. MT research did continue, however, in Canada, France, and Germany. Within a few years, Peter Toma, one of the members of the Georgetown University project, had developed Systran for operational use by the USAF (1970) and by NASA (in 1974/5), and shortly afterwards Systran was installed by the Commission of the European Communities for translating English into French (1976) and later between other Community languages. At the same time, another successful operational system appeared in Canada—the METEO system for translating weather reports, which was developed at Montreal University.

In the 1960s in the U.S. and the Soviet Union MT activity had concentrated on Russian-English and English-Russian translation of scientific and technical documents for a relatively small number of potential users, most of whom were prepared to overlook mistakes of terminology, grammar, and style in order to be able to read something that they would otherwise not have known about.

Since the mid-1970s, the demand for MT has come from quite different sources with different needs and different languages. The administrative and commercial demands of multilingual communities and multinational trade have stimulated the demand for translation in Europe, Canada, and Japan beyond the capacity of the traditional translation services. The demand is now for cost-effective machine-aided translation systems that can deal with commercial and technical documentation in the principal languages of international commerce.

The 1980s has witnessed the emergence of a variety of system types from a widening number of countries. There are a number of mainframe systems. Best known is Systran, now installed worldwide and operating with many pairs of languages. Others are: Logos for German-English translation and for English-French in Canada; the internally developed systems for Spanish-English and English-Spanish translation at the Pan American Health Organization; the systems developed by the Smart Corporation for many large organizations in North America; and the recently marketed METAL system from Siemens for German-English translation. Major systems for English-Japanese and Japanese-English translation have come from the Japanese computer companies Fujitsu,

Hitachi, and Toshiba. The wide availability of microcomputers and of text processing software has led to a commercial market for cheaper MT systems, exploited in North America and Europe by companies such as ALPS, Weidner, Linguistic Products, Tovna, and Globalink, and by many Japanese companies, e.g. Sharp, NEC, Oki, Mitsubishi, and Sanyo. Other microcomputer-based systems have appeared from China, Taiwan, Korea, Bolivia, Eastern Europe, and the Soviet Union.

Throughout the 1980s research on more advanced methods and techniques has continued. The dominant strategy is now that of "indirect" translation via intermediary representations, sometimes interlingual in nature, involving semantic as well as morphological and syntactic analysis and sometimes non-linguistic "knowledge bases." There is increasing emphasis on devising systems for particular subject areas and particular specific purposes, for monolingual users as well as bilingual users (translators), and for interactive operation rather than batch processing. The most notable projects have been the GETA-Ariane system at Grenoble, SUSY and ASCOF at Saarbrücken, Mu at Kyoto, DLT at Utrecht, Rosetta at Eindhoven, the knowledge-based MT project at Carnegie-Mellon University (Pittsburgh), and two ambitious international multilingual projects: Eurotra, supported by the European Communities, involving teams in each member country; and the Japanese CICC project with participants in China, Indonesia, and Thailand.

Linguistic Problems of MT   The basic processes of translation are the analysis of the source language (SL) text, the conversion (transfer) of the meaning of the text into another language, and the generation (synthesis) of the target language (TL) text. There are basically three overall strategies. In the *direct translation* approach, adopted by most of the early MT projects, systems are specifically designed for one particular pair of languages. Vocabulary and syntax are not analyzed any more than strictly necessary for the resolution of ambiguities. TL equivalents are output in correct word order; hence, the processes of analysis and synthesis are combined in single programs, that often have monolithic intractability (e.g. the Georgetown system).

The second strategy is the *interlingua* approach, which assumes the possibility of converting SL texts into (semantic) representations common to a number of languages, from which texts can be generated in one or more TLs. In interlingua systems, SL analysis and TL synthesis are monolingual processes independent of any other languages, and the interlingua is designed to be language-independent or "universal." (A current example is the DLT system based on modified Esperanto.)

The third strategy is the *transfer* approach, which operates in three stages: from the SL text into an abstract *intermediary* representation, which is not language-independent but oriented to the characteristics of the SL (analysis); from such an SL-oriented representation to an equivalent TL-oriented representation (transfer); and from the latter to the final TL text (synthesis). (Major examples of the transfer approach are the GETA, SUSY, Mu, and Eurotra systems.)

The principal linguistic problems encountered in MT systems may be treated under four main headings: lexical, structural, contextual, and pragmatic (situational). In each case, the problems are primarily caused by the inherent ambiguities of natural languages and by the lack of direct equivalences of vocabulary and structure between one language and another. Some English examples are:

Lexical: Homonyms (*tear* as "cry" or "rip", *bank* as "edge of river" or "financial institution") require different translations (*crier: dechirer; rive: banque*).

Structural: Nouns can function as verbs (*control, plant, face*) and hence are ambiguous, since the TL may well have different forms (*contröle: diriger, plante: planter, face: affronter*).

Contextual: Other languages make distinctions that are absent in English. *River* can be French *rivière* or *fleuve*, German *Fluss* or *Strom; blue* can be Russian *sinii* or *goluboi*.

Often, all linguistic ambiguities combine. The word *light* can be a noun meaning "luminescence," an adjective meaning "not dark," another adjective meaning "not heavy," or a verb meaning "to start burning." In French, the meanings are conveyed by four different words, *lumière, léger, clair, allumer*. An analysis of English must therefore distinguish the four possibilities by (1) recognizing the grammatical categories of words in sentences (nouns, verbs, adjectives, adverbs, prepositions, conjunctions, etc.) and the structures in which they take part, and (2) by recognizing the lexical and semantic contexts in which the words occur. At the transfer stage, this information must be used to convert the identified meaning into those lexical units and structures with equivalent meanings in the target language.

In many cases, differences between the vocabulary of the source and target languages are also accompanied by structural differences. A familiar example involves the translation of the English verb *know* into French or German, where there are two verbs that express "knowledge of a fact" (*connaître* and *kennen*) and "knowledge of how to do something" (*savoir* and *wissen*):

1. I know the man—Je connais l'homme; Ich kenne den Mann.
2. I know what he is called—Je sais ce qu'il s'appelle; Ich weiss wie er heisst.

The choice of TL form involves a restructuring with effects on the translation of other lexical items (*what* as *ce que* and *wie*). A more radical, but no less common, instance of restructuring may be illustrated by the German sentence:

3. Das Mädchen spielt gern Tennis, translated as:
4. The girl likes to play tennis.

The German adverb *gern* corresponds to an English finite verb *like*, and this choice entails the shifting of the finite verb *spielt* to a subordinate infinitive (*to play*).

The resolution of many linguistic problems transcends sentence boundaries. A common and persistently difficult one involves the use of pronouns. Following 3, this might occur:

5. Es geht jede Woche zum Club, for which the English should be:
6. She goes to the club every week.

However, *es* is normally translated as *it*. To ensure the correct selection of *she*, the preceding noun referent of the pronoun must be identified and the different practices for pronominalization must be taken into account (in German according to the "grammatical" gender of the preceding noun, and in English according to the "natural" sex of the object referred to). However, the identification of the noun referred to can often be more complex than this example. Frequently, it depends on (non-linguistic) knowledge of events or situations:

7. The soldiers killed the women. They were buried next day.

We know that the pronoun *they* does not refer to *soldiers* and must refer to *women* because we know that "killing" implies "death" and that "death" is followed (normally) by "burial." This identification is crucial when translating into French where the pronoun must be *elles* and not *ils*. Grammatical and linguistic information is insufficient in such cases.

Various aspects of syntactic relations can be analyzed. There is the need (1) to identify valid sequences of grammatical categories, (2) to identify functional relations—subjects and objects of verbs, dependencies of adjectives on "head" nouns, etc. and (3) to identify the constituents of sentences—noun phrases, verb groups, prepositional phrases, subordinate clauses, etc. Each aspect has given rise to different types of parsers. The *predictive syntactic analyzer* of the 1960s concentrated on sequences of categories (it was developed subsequently by Wood (1970) as the Augmented Transition Network parser). The *dependency grammar* (of Tesnière, Hays, etc.) concentrated on functional relationships, and the *phrase structure grammars* have been the models for parsers of constituency structure. Each have their strengths and weaknesses, and modern MT systems often adopt an eclectic mixture of parsing techniques, now often within the framework of a *unification grammar* formalism (Kay, 1984).

The most serious weakness of all syntactic parsers is precisely their limitation to structural features. An English prepositional phrase can in theory modify any preceding noun in the sentence as well as a preceding verb:

8a. The camera was purchased by the man with dark glasses.
8b. The camera was purchased by the man with a tripod.
8c. The camera was purchased by the man with a cheque.

A syntactic analysis can go no further than offer each possibility; later, semantic or pragmatic analysis (e.g. involving lexical and situational context) has the task of specifying the intended relationship.

Many parsers now include the identification of case relations, e.g. the fact that in

9. The house was built by a doctor for his son during the war.

the agent of the action ("building") is *a doctor*, the object of the action is *the house*, the recipient (or beneficiary) is *his son* and the time of the action is *during the war*. Many languages express these relations explicitly, such as, for example, through use of suffixes to Latin, German, Russian nouns (*-ibus, -en, -ami*), prepositions in English and French (*to, à*), and particles (short words or endings) of Japanese (*ga, wa*), but they are often implicit (as in English direct objects). There are rarely any direct correspondences between languages and most markers of cases are multiply ambiguous in all languages. Compare, for example, the three uses of *with* expressing *attribute* (8a.), *concomitant* (8b.), and *instrument* (8c.), respectively, in the sequence of sentences cited earlier. Nevertheless, there is a sufficient regularity and universality in such "case relations" to have encouraged their widespread adoption in many MT systems.

There is also some agreement about the use of "semantic features,"—i.e. the attachment of such categories as "human," "animate," and "liquid" to lexical items and their application in the resolution of ambiguities. For example, in:

10. He was beaten with a club.

the "social" sense of *club* found in 6. above is excluded by the verb-type that requires an "inanimate" instrument. In:

11. The sailor went on board.
12. The sailor was examined by the board.

the "physical" sense of *board* in 11 is confirmed by the verb-type (motion) and the preposition of location, and the "social" sense in 12 is confirmed by the verb *examine*, which requires an "animate" agent.

Few operational MT systems involve deeper levels of semantic or pragmatic analysis. Nevertheless, as examples 7 and 8 demonstrated, disambiguation and correct selection of TL equivalents would seem to be impossible without reference to knowledge of the features and properties of the objects and events described. This was used by Yehoshua Bar-Hillel (1960) in arguing that fully automatic translation of high quality is impossible. His famous demonstration involved the sentence *The box was in the pen*. We know that *pen* can refer here only to a "container for animals or children" and not to a "writing implement," from our knowledge of relative sizes of (writing) pens and boxes. For Bar-Hillel, the incorporation of encyclopedic knowledge and the associated inference mechanisms was "utterly chimerical." However, subsequent advances in artificial intelligence have encouraged later MT researchers to investigate the possibility of knowledge-based systems (e.g. at Carnegie-Mellon University), at least for systems restricted to specific domains. The general feasibility of AI approaches has yet to be tested on large-scale systems, however, and most MT researchers prefer to develop "linguistics-based" systems capable of incorporating AI methods as adjuncts to more traditional techniques of syntactic and semantic analysis, transfer, and generation.

MT in Practice The complexities and difficulties of linguistic analysis and the problems of incorporating appropriate semantic and extra-linguistic knowledge have persuaded many researchers that, for the foreseeable future, it is unrealistic to attempt to build fully automatic systems capable of the translation quality achieved by human translators. The growing demands for translations must be met by MT systems that involve the active assistance and expertise of natural language speakers.

The most obvious course, which has been adopted since the first MT systems, is to employ human translators to revise and improve the crude and inaccurate texts produced by MT systems. Initially, "post-editing" was undertaken manually; later systems incorporate on-line revision and in some cases special facilities for dealing with the most common types of error (e.g. transposition of words, insertion of articles). Revision for MT differs from the revision of traditionally produced translations. Unlike the human translator, the computer program is regular and consistent with terminology, but typically it contains grammatical and stylistic errors that no human translator would commit.

The development of powerful microcomputer text editing facilities has led to the introduction of interactive MT systems. During the translation process, a human operator (normally a translator) may be asked to help the computer resolve ambiguities of vocabulary or structure, e.g. whether the *club* in (13) is a "society" or not, and what relationship is expressed by *with* in 11a., 11b., and 11c. Many Japanese systems demand considerable assistance from operators, particularly with the "pre-editing" of Japanese scripts (identifying word and phrase boundaries, punctuation, etc.)

A third possibility is to constrain the variety of language in the input texts. There are two approaches: either the system is designed to deal with one particular subject matter, or the input texts are written in a vocabulary and style known to be comprehensible to a particular MT system. The former approach is illustrated by the METEO system, introduced in 1976, which translates weather forecasts from English into French for public broadcasts in Canada. The latter approach has been taken by the Xerox Corporation in its use of the Systran system. Manuals are written in a controlled English using unambiguous vocabulary and restricted syntactic patterns that can be translated with minimal revision into five other languages. Other examples are the Smart systems installed at a number of large U. S. and Canadian institutions that combine on-line editing to ensure clear documentation in

English and "restricted language" MT to produce translations for subsequent editing.

MT systems are now being used in the production of a wide range of translations of different quality and status. The raw output of both mainframe systems (Systran, Logos, Fujitsu) and microcomputer systems (Weidner, NEC) may be used as (1) a draft version for full revision to the level of human-quality products (e.g. for later publication), (2) a first draft for subsequent wholly human translation, (3) a version offered completely unedited to those who are prepared to tolerate the grammatical and stylistic errors for the sake of cheap access to information, or (4) a version for light editing for similar information purposes. It may be noted, however, that few unedited microcomputer-based translations are adequate, even for purely informational purposes.

The development of computer-based aids for translators have had a significant impact on the translation profession. These aids, which may justly be regarded as commercial by-products of MT research, include facilities for multilingual word processing, for creating in-house glossaries and termbanks, for receiving and sending texts over telecommunication networks, for accessing remote sources of information, for publishing quality documents, and for using interactive or batch MT systems when appropriate. Systems that integrate various facilities of this nature are being developed as translators' workstations.

The languages of the earlier systems were mainly Russian and English, reflecting the political situation of the time. In the 1970s, the main impetus was for systems to deal with the administrative needs of countries such as Canada and the European Communities, hence systems for English, French, German, and other Community languages. During the 1980s, the main focus has been the languages of international trade and communications (English, Japanese, French, German, Spanish, and, to a lesser extent, Chinese and Italian). On the other hand, the needs of Third World countries for scientific and technical textbooks in their own languages are still not being fully met, although a start has been made by some individual projects (notably GETA) and by the Japanese multinational project.

The Future of MT

In the immediate future, there will clearly be continued expansion and improvement of systems for the business and administrative communities. As at present, the MT market will include both microcomputer and mainframe systems. The cheaper microcomputer systems will produce relatively poor output needing substantial revision, but that can nonetheless be applied cost-effectively in commercial services. More expensive mainframe (or minicomputer) systems will be developed using transfer and interlingua approaches with some use of AI techniques. These will produce higher-quality output that, although still requiring revision for publication, will satisfy basic informational needs.

Nearly all current systems require users to know both source and target languages, generally to the level expected of regular translators. There is clearly a need for systems that can be used by those ignorant of the source language in order to obtain translations giving at least the gist of document contents. At a further stage, these systems should be integrated with other documentation systems (information retrieval, abstracting, paraphrasing, etc.). There is an equally clear need for systems for those ignorant of the target language, e.g. business persons (and others) wanting to convey simple messages to make travel arrangements, to book hotel accommodations, to arrange meetings, etc.

There has been recent research on systems that use *interactive analysis*. The computer would seek to obtain from the author of a text information that would resolve ambiguities and thus enable the generation of appropriate translated text. The interaction would be conducted in the user's own language.

The most obvious area of future development will be speech translation. Research is already in progress in Japan and elsewhere on systems for international telephone communication. Such systems, initially restricted to standard business messages, will combine voice interpretation and voice production with machine translation. Given the problems of speech recognition in addition to the peculiarities of conversational language, operational prototypes are regarded very much as long-term objectives.

Nearly all developments depend on improvements in the automation of the basic translation processes. The ultimate ideal of fully automatic high-quality translation may remain, but seems increasingly unrealistic. MT suffers still from what appear to be low-level problems: incorrect uses of pronouns, prepositions, and verb tenses, and erroneous translations of common vocabulary. Progress is slow, but developments in artificial intelligence, in linguistic theory, in computational linguistics, and in computer technology promise future improvements in general quality.

At a more basic level, much progress depends on the continued efforts to standardize terminology, both within and across languages, which is of benefit to translators and technical writers generally. More specifically, the wasteful duplication involved in the creation of large MT dictionaries calls for inter-project cooperation, a process that has already started in Japan with the Electronic Dictionary Research project.

MT is already seen not as a threatening replacement of translators but as an aid to multilingual communication. The future development of MT rests on fruitful interaction between the researchers of experimental systems investigating new methods and theories, the developers of commercial systems exploiting well-tested methods in cost-effective practical systems, and the perception of the real needs of translators and other potential users of translation systems.

Further Reading

For a general introduction to MT, see Lehrberger and Bourbeau (1988); for the general history of MT, see Hutchins (1986); and for descriptions of current systems and developments, see Hutchins (1988), Slocum (1988), and Vasconcellos (1988).

References

1960. Bar-Hillel, Y. "The Present Status of Automatic Translation of Languages," *Advances in Computers* **1**: 91–163.

1966. ALPAC. *Language and Machines: Computers in Translation and Linguistics*. A report by the Automatic Language Processing Advisory Committee. Washington, D.C.: National Academy of Sciences.

1970. Wood, W. "Transition Network Grammars for Natural Language Analysis," *Communication of the ACM* **13**: 591-606.

1984. Kay, M. "Functional Unification Grammar: A Formalism for Machine Translation" in *Coling 84*, Stanford, CA: Stanford University, 75-78.

1986. Hutchins, W. J. *Machine Translation: Past, Present, Future.* Chichester: Ellis Horwood, New York: Halsted Press.

1988. Hutchins, W. J. "Recent Developments in Machine Translation: A Review of the Last Five Years. In *New Directions in Machine Translation*, D. Maxwell *et al.* (Ed.) (Dordrecht: Foris), 7–62.

1988. Lehrberger, J. and Bourbeau, L. *Machine Translation: Linguistic Characteristics of MT Systems and General Methodology of Evaluation.* Amsterdam: Benjamins.

1988. Slocum, J. (Ed.) *Machine Translation Systems.* Cambridge: Cambridge University Press.

1988. Vasconcellos, M. (Ed.) *Technology as Translation Strategy.* Binghamton, NY: State University of New York.

1992. Hutchins, W. J. and Somers, H. L. *An Introduction to MachineTranslation.* London: Academic Press.

W. JOHN HUTCHINS

LANGUAGES, NATURAL.   *See* NATURAL LANGUAGE PROCESSING.

LANGUAGES, PROGRAMMING.   *See* PROCEDURE-ORIENTED LANGUAGES; and PROGRAMMING LANGUAGES.

LAPTOP COMPUTER

For an article on a related subject *see* PERSONAL COMPUTING.

Laptop computers comprise one subset of the genre of personal computers known as "portable computers." A portable computer is small in size, light enough to be carried from place to place with relative ease, and usually can be operated by an internal battery. Although many portables do not need a separate source of electrical power, they can use one when available. Running a portable on AC power can recharge the battery as well as power the computer.

Portable computers can be classified as being either hand-held, or *palmtop*, computers, laptop, or *notebook*, computers, or luggable computers. Hand-held computers resemble pocket calculators, but possess some of the functionality of a computer (i.e. the ability to run programs). Laptop (notebook) computers offer complete personal computer functionality in a size convenient for holding on a person's lap. Luggable computers furnish fully functional machines in a small-suitcase-sized package.

The enabling technologies for the laptop computer, the most prevalent type of portable computer, include flat-panel displays, electronic and mechanical components that use very little power, and long-life, rechargeable batteries. Compact, sometimes detachable keyboards are a frequent addition to this list of essential components.

Evolution of Portable Computers   The first portable computers weighed 28–33 pounds and were packaged in a ruggedized case very similar to the housings used for their desktop counterparts. This modified case provided a handle for carrying the machine, and frequently used a detachable keyboard that doubled as a cover for the display and front panel area. The Osborne 1 Portable, the first portable computer, was introduced in 1981. It used a standard cathode ray tube (CRT) screen that measured a scant 5 diagonal inches—a screen very similar to that of an oscilloscope. This small screen, which displayed only 40 characters by 15 lines, was difficult to read. The machine came with dual built-in floppy disk drives and a detachable keyboard. It required AC power, and used CP/M, the standard operating system of the day.

That same year, Epson America introduced the first laptop computer. The HX-20 used a 20-character by 4-line liquid crystal matrix flat-panel display (LCD). The com-

FIG. 1.   ZEOS International's Notebook 286. It weighs less than 7 pounds and has 1 megabyte of memory, a 20-megabyte hard disk drive, and a 1.44-megabyte floppy disk drive.

puter ran on standard lead/acid batteries. It even sported a built-in printer very similar to a cash register tape printer. The built-in software and small display made the machine only marginally useful.

In 1983, Radio Shack proved the usefulness of the laptop computer concept with the introduction of the TRS-80 Model 100. This 4-pound, battery-operated computer used a 40-character by 6-line LCD screen and provided useful built-in text editing and communications software. The machine soon became a favorite of newspaper and magazine journalists who found that its small size and easy-to-use text creation and transmission software made the computer an ideal writing tool to take on the road. A later version, the Model 200, provided a built-in disk drive, a larger screen, and a "clamshell" design (adopted by most subsequent laptops), in which the screen folded onto the keyboard when the computer was not in use.

The evolution of the laptop computer accelerated in response to the success of the Model 100. The IBM-PC and its MS-DOS operating system rapidly became the standard for business personal computing after 1982, and laptops touting IBM PC-compatibility sprang up from many sources. Through this period, portable computers, such as the Compaq portable (introduced in 1982), acquired 9-inch CRT screens while dropping in weight to the 17–22–pound range. Portable computers started providing hard disk capacity in 1985, and laptops later added first floppy disk and then hard disk storage. In 1988, the NEC UltraLite machine heralded the arrival of the "notebook" computer, a laptop the size of a notebook that weighed under 5 pounds, and provided all the functionality of an IBM-PC AT-class computer.

In 1991, the state-of-the-art in notebook computers provides a fast Intel microprocessor, hard disk storage, a high-resolution, flat-panel monochrome or color screen, built-in telecommunications capability, and the ability to run almost all MS-DOS desktop computer applications. Battery powered, these machines can run for 3–7 hours between battery charges. This functionality comes packaged in a notebook-sized machine that weighs from 4 to 6 pounds. The prices of the machines range between $2,000 and $5,000.

Enabling Technologies One of the most important of the enabling technologies for laptop computers resulted from improvements in semiconductor fabrication. A fabrication technique called complementary metal-oxide semiconductor (CMOS) allowed the building of integrated circuit (IC) components that required very small amounts of electrical power and produced negligible amounts of heat. CMOS-based microprocessors, memory chips, and other circuits along with design innovations like surface mounting of ICs let laptop manufacturers pack more computing power into a smaller space. Furthermore, CMOS components drew small enough quantities of electricity that they could be powered by a battery for extended periods of time.

Another key component of laptop computers—the flat-panel display—evolved rapidly in the 1980s due to heavy research and development by the Japanese. LCD technology evolved from low-contrast, narrow viewing angle twisted-nematic LCDs in 1984, through supertwist LCDs in the late 1980s, to the dual supertwist displays that have become standard on the high-end laptops of the early 1990s. Each of these technologies increased the resolution and the readability of the machine's screens, but also increased their cost and decreased the between-charge life of the computer's battery.

Battery technology improved to keep pace with the increased power demands of higher-resolution displays and the addition of floppy and hard disk drives. Some early laptops used flashlight batteries, but the later, more sophisticated machines use rechargeable lead/acid or nickel cadmium batteries. The nickel cadmium battery has become the standard in the 1990s because of its good weight-to-power ratio and its nearly constant power output voltage, regardless of charge.

Tomorrow's Laptops Improved display and battery technologies are on the horizon for notebook computers. Display improvements include film double-twist and active-matrix displays, both of which use significantly less power than current technologies. Battery innovations include nickel hydride, which produces more than twice the energy of its nickel cadmium cousin, and polymer substrates impregnated with solid chemical components that will be extremely light, possibly as small as one-fifth the size of current batteries while producing the same power.

These improved technologies and a further reduction in IC chip counts will allow manufacturers to produce future laptop computers that will be thinner and lighter than current machines. Display and keyboard sizes will prevent the machines from getting much smaller except in height. The 1-inch thick notebook machine should be the standard by 1994.

By the end of this decade, more innovative technologies, such as stylus and pen-based input devices coupled with character-recognition software in a palm-sized package, may create a whole new generation of machines that truly mimic a notebook.

G. MICHAEL VOSE

LATENCY

For articles on related subject *see* ACCESS TIME; CYLINDER; DIRECT ACCESS; FLOPPY DISK; HARD DISK; and MEMORY: AUXILIARY.

Latency is the rotational delay in reading or writing a record to a direct-access auxiliary memory device such as disk or drum (see Fig. 1). *Maximum* latency is the time for an entire revolution of the recording surface. A program suffers maximum latency—generally undesirable from an efficiency standpoint—if it requests a record whose starting point has just passed under the read/write heads. *Minimum* latency is zero delay, by definition. *Average* latency is half the maximum.

Newer direct-access devices often have a *rotational*

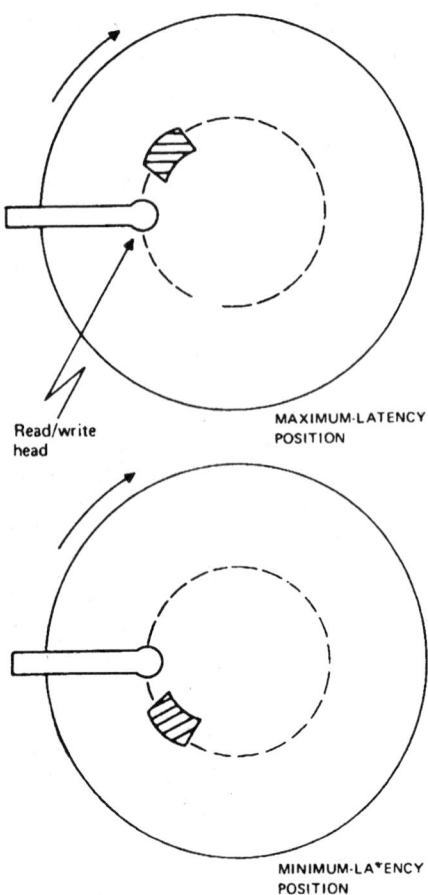

FIG. 1. Maximum and minimum latencies for various head-record orientations. Time: just after channel commences search for record indicated by cross-hatching.

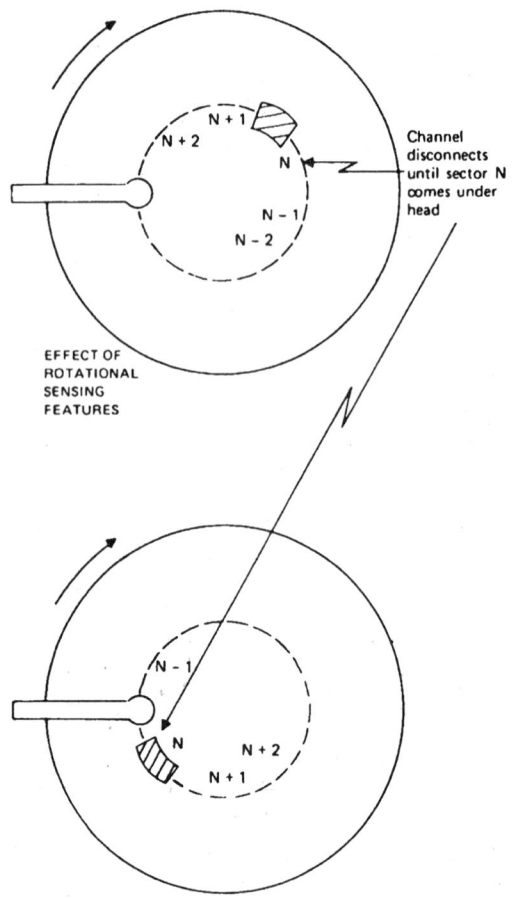

FIG. 2. Latency for direct-access devices having rotational position sensing feature.

position sensing (RPS) feature; they do not attempt to access a record until it is almost under their heads, as shown in Fig. 2. By dividing each track into N equal-sized *sectors* (N typically is 128), disk drives having the RPS feature reduce *channel latency*, but not *drive latency*. Channel latency blocks activity on all drives attached to the channel; while the channel awaits correct positioning of the record on one drive, no other drives can be active. The RPS feature permits a channel to service other drives while the requested sector is rotating toward the read/write head, as shown in Fig. 2.

DAVID N. FREEMAN

LEAST-SQUARES APPROXIMATION

For articles on related subjects *see* APPROXIMATION THEORY; CHEBYSHEV APPROXIMATION; and NUMERICAL ANALYSIS.

Least-squares approximation refers to a wide variety of mathematical optimization problems in which the objective is to make a residual vector small in the sense of minimizing the sum of squares of its elements or to make a residual function small in the sense of minimizing the integral of the squared residual function.

For definiteness, and because of its frequent occurrence as a real-life computational problem, we will describe the real discrete linear least-squares problem and its analysis and solution. In this problem, one has real numbers a_{ij}, $i = 1,\dots, m$, $j = 1,\dots, n$ ($m > n$) and b_i, $i = 1,\dots, m$. One has some reason to believe that the b_i are approximately representable as linear combinations of the a_{ij} (i.e. that there exist numbers $\bar{c}_j$, $j = 1,\dots, n$, such that $\sum_{j=1}^{n} \bar{c}_j a_{ij}$ is approximately equal to b_i for $i = 1,\dots, m$). In matrix-vector notation, this may be stated as the assumption that there is an n-vector $\bar{c}$ such that $A\bar{c}$ is approximately equal to $\mathbf{b}$.

Mathematical Theory The purely mathematical, real, discrete, linear, least-squares approximation problem, which we will refer to as problem LS, is to find an n-vector $\tilde{c}$ such that $\|\mathbf{b} - A\tilde{c}\| = \min \|\mathbf{b} - A\mathbf{c}\|$, where the *norm* of a vector $\mathbf{v}$, $\|\mathbf{v}\|$, is defined as the square root of the sum of the squares of the components of $\mathbf{v}$. A solution for this problem always exists. It is unique if and only if the rank of A is n.

A vector $\tilde{c}$ is a solution vector for problem LS if and only if the associated residual vector, $\tilde{\mathbf{r}} = \mathbf{b} - A\tilde{c}$, is orthogonal to all column vectors of A. This orthogonality condition may be written as $A^T(\mathbf{b} - A\tilde{\mathbf{c}}) = A^T\mathbf{b} - A^T A\tilde{\mathbf{c}} = 0$. From this latter expression, one obtains the system of equations, $A^T A\mathbf{c} = A^T\mathbf{b}$, called the *normal equations* for problem LS. Forming the normal equations and solving them by the Cholesky algorithm is a common method of computing a solution for problem LS.

Other solution methods providing superior numerical reliability at a cost of about twice as many arithmetic operations are based on the *QR decomposition* of A. Thus, A can be written as

$$A = Q^T \begin{bmatrix} R \\ 0 \end{bmatrix} = [Q_1^T : Q_2^T] \begin{bmatrix} R \\ 0 \end{bmatrix} = Q_1^T R$$

where Q is an $m \times m$ orthogonal matrix and R is an $n \times n$ upper triangular matrix. The orthogonality of Q assures that

$$\begin{aligned} \|\mathbf{b} - A\mathbf{c}\|^2 &= \|Q(\mathbf{b} - A\mathbf{c})\|^2 \\ &= \left\| \begin{bmatrix} Q_1 \\ Q_2 \end{bmatrix} \mathbf{b} - \begin{bmatrix} R \\ 0 \end{bmatrix} \mathbf{c} \right\|^2 \\ &= \|Q_1\mathbf{b} - R\mathbf{c}\|^2 + \|Q_2\mathbf{b}\|^2 \end{aligned}$$

for all n-vectors $\mathbf{c}$. Thus, a vector $\tilde{\mathbf{c}}$ is a solution of problem LS if and only if $R\tilde{\mathbf{c}} = Q_1\mathbf{b}$. The matrix R and the vector $Q_1\mathbf{b}$ needed here can be computed in a numerically stable manner by Householder transformations, Givens plane transformations, or modified Gram-Schmidt orthogonalization.

Practical Considerations

In practice, the given data, particularly the components of the vector $\mathbf{b}$, generally arise from observations or measurements and are therefore known only to some limited precision. One generally knows a priori the approximate size of the uncertainty in the vector $\mathbf{b}$. In addition, one often has some a priori notion about reasonable values for components of the solution vector.

We will say that problem LS is *ill-conditioned with respect to data uncertainty* if changes in the data matrix $[A:\mathbf{b}]$ of the order of magnitude of the uncertainty in this data can cause changes in the solution vector that are regarded as significant by the problem originator. In such a case, even though the rank of A may be n, there will commonly be a set of significantly different n-vectors that are almost as good as the unique best-solution vector if "goodness" is measured only by the criterion of reducing the residual norm.

In practice, it is desirable to have a systematic way of recognizing the occurrence of an ill-conditioned problem, of identifying the data dependencies that cause the ill-conditioning, of quantitatively characterizing a set of candidate solutions, and of selecting from the candidate solutions one that is suitable for the application at hand. Singular-value analysis and Levenberg-Marquardt analysis (also known as *ridge regression*) provide practical means for obtaining this information.

Singular-value analysis makes use of a matrix decomposition of the form $A = USV^T$, where U and V are orthogonal matrices and S is a diagonal matrix. The Levenberg-Marquardt analysis studies solutions of the augmented least-squares problem

$$\begin{bmatrix} A \\ \lambda I \end{bmatrix} \mathbf{c} \cong \begin{bmatrix} \mathbf{b} \\ 0 \end{bmatrix}$$

as a function of the parameter λ.

As an example of an ill-conditioned least-squares problem, consider the problem $A\mathbf{c} \cong \mathbf{b}$ with

$$A = \begin{bmatrix} 0.780 & 0.563 \\ 0.913 & 0.659 \\ 0.133 & 0.096 \end{bmatrix}, \quad \mathbf{b} = \begin{bmatrix} 0.481 \\ 0.560 \\ 0.082 \end{bmatrix}$$

The exact mathematical solution for this problem is

$$\tilde{\mathbf{c}} = [477, -660]^T$$

with a residual vector $\tilde{\mathbf{r}} = \mathbf{b} - A\tilde{\mathbf{c}} = [0.0010, --0.0010, 0.0010]^T$ and residual norm $\|\mathbf{r}\| = 0.0017$.

By either singular-value analysis or Levenberg-Marquardt analysis, one can find that there are other candidate solution vectors that are much smaller in norm than $\tilde{\mathbf{c}}$ and that have residual norms only slightly greater than the minimal norm $\|\tilde{\mathbf{r}}\|$. For instance, the vector $\hat{\mathbf{c}} = [0.404, 0.292]^T$ gives a residual vector

$$\hat{\mathbf{r}} \doteq [0.0015, -0.0013, 0.0002]^T$$

whose norm is $\|\hat{\mathbf{r}}\| \doteq 0.0020$.

In most practical situations, particularly where there is uncertainty in some of the data defining A and $\mathbf{b}$, the vector $\hat{\mathbf{c}}$ would be preferred in place of the vector $\tilde{\mathbf{c}}$, whose components are larger by three orders of magnitude. The reason for preferring smaller solution vector components will be different in different contexts, but often this is related to the preference for a simpler, more economical explanation of the real-world phenomenon being modeled.

References

1973. Stewart, G. W. *Introduction to Matrix Computations*. New York: Academic Press.
1974. Lawson, C. L., and R. J. Hanson. *Solving Least Squares Problems*. Englewood Cliffs, NJ: Prentice-Hall.
1989. Golub, G. H., and Van Loan, C. F. *Matrix Computations* (2nd Ed.). Baltimore: Johns Hopkins Press.

CHARLES L. LAWSON

LEGAL APPLICATIONS OF COMPUTERS

For articles on related subjects *see* LEGAL ASPECTS OF COMPUTING; LEGAL PROTECTION OF SOFTWARE; and PRIVACY, COMPUTERS AND.

Although many law firms and courts still make minimal use of computers, computers have had a significant impact on the practice of law. According to American Bar Association estimates in 1989, private firms spend an average of $4,400 per attorney for new technology, yet many small firms and perhaps the majority of courts are not using computers, or using them only for basic clerical work such as word processing (q.v.).

Lawyers generate large quantities of documents both apart from and in connection with litigation. Even relatively simple litigation can involve hundreds of exhibits, pleadings, briefs, and thousands of pages of transcripts and other written materials, not counting photographs, tape and video recordings, and the like. Optical scanning devices can be used to enter typed or printed documents directly into mass storage. Computers aid in assembling these documents, as well as being a mechanism for storing them and indexing them so that key passages can be located quickly whenever needed. Computers can also assist attorneys in constructing contracts, wills and other estate planning materials, tax returns, demand letters, and a host of other legal documents.

Document creation goes well beyond basic word processing. For example, appellate briefs that once had to be sent to a printer to be typeset can be produced in-house using appropriate software and laser printers.

Computers have also facilitated billing for legal services. Lawyers generally bill for their services by the hour, and different attorneys in the same firm often bill at different rates. Moreover, clients will also be billed for out-of-pocket expenses such as filing costs, long distance phone tolls, and the reporter's charges for providing a transcription of a deposition. Computers are also used to help attorneys keep track of the fees to be charged their various clients and to keep the records so that clients can be provided regular, itemized bills.

Commercial software packages are available for law office accounting, scheduling, checking for conflict of interests within a firm, litigation support, and a host of other practice-related functions. The American Bar Association has a program that permits developers of software intended for the legal market to apply for a "Statement of Approval" from the ABA's Legal Technology Advisory Council (LTAC). Such certification means that the software meets the guidelines set by the LTAC.

A 1988 survey by Price Waterhouse indicated the following percentages of law firms using various software applications: expert systems (q.v.), 4%; stock/dividend recordkeeping, 21%; stockholder mailings, 24%; litigation support, 33%; document assembly, 42%; document indexing and retrieval, 50%; electronic mail (q.v.), 50%; outside counsel fees, 56%; automated legal research, 71%; and word processing, 99%.

Although more than 97% of the nation's largest law firms were using computers in 1986, according to a survey conducted by the IIT Chicago-Kent College of Law, a 1985 survey conducted by the *ABA Journal* revealed that only 56.4% of small firms with a median of four lawyers had computers. Moreover, most courts had not computerized their calendars and document-generation systems as of the time this article was written.

Those larger law firms that use computers, according to the survey, use them for timekeeping (85%), accounting (80.5%), and personnel functions (56%). Almost 75% of the responding firms indicated that lawyers themselves used computers for word processing, legal research, and telecommunications.

Access to judicial opinions, federal and state statutes and regulations, and a host of other reference materials is essential to the successful practice of law and to legal research. Computers have facilitated access to such materials through on-line and CD-ROM (q.v.) services. The availability of reference materials on CD-ROM can save a firm or law school large amounts of space because each and every month scores if not hundreds of volumes of new materials are generated. The most popular on-line services are Lexis, Nexis, Westlaw, and Dialog. The principal means of querying such services' extensive databases is by keyword and by keyword in context (KWIC). Expert systems that can perform more intelligent functions, such as suggesting cases that support the point of view the legal research wishes to defend or that propose strategies to minimize estate taxes while conforming to the testamentary wishes of the testator, are under development. To date, however, these have had limited success even in areas of the law such as taxation where there are relatively precise rules to guide practitioners.

Computers are finding increasing use as instruments for effecting legal transactions such as transferring ownership of property. Computers are also used to store data that has legal ramifications, such as records of ownership of stock and negotiable instruments. To date, paper documents have been required in many areas of legal practice (e.g. to record deeds to real property, to serve as wills, and as pleadings in litigation). Many title insurance companies keep their own records of real estate transactions so that they do not have to depend on the official system which is difficult to use and sometimes unreliable. Computers are also used to transfer large sums of money via telecommunications links. The law concerning liability in case someone is injured economically because a transaction fails or an important record is lost because of a computer malfunction is unsettled, as is the acceptability of electronic records and signatures in lieu of the paper records and physical signatures the records represent.

Software exists that enables laypersons to create legal documents such as wills or simple contracts. Even laypersons can act as their own attorneys, but there remains the question of whether the dissemination of such tools itself constitutes the unauthorized practice of law. To date, the matter has not been addressed by the courts. Also unsettled is the liability of the vendor or author of an expert system sold to attorneys to assist them in their practices that, through a defect in the program or the database, causes an attorney to make a mistake that injures a client.

Computer applications in the practice of law are certain to increase in number and sophistication in the future. Already, some courts are experimenting with computerized trial transcripts that allow attorneys instant access to prior testimony. More and more legal documents will exist solely or primarily as electronic records. But the transition to the electronic law office or courtroom is far from complete, and there are many questions that will have to be answered as the transition proceeds. At some point, an attorney may find that a disappointed client will have a prima facie case for malpractice because the attorney did not use an on-line service to research the case, or did not use document retrieval software to find a key point in a deposition. Attorneys may well communicate with one another and with the courts via wide area networks, filing papers electronically. The computer may well become as indispensable an instrument for the practice of law as the scalpel is for the surgeon or the hammer for the carpenter, but that time is still years in the future.

References

1980. Arentowitz, F. Jr., and Bower, W. *Law Office Automation and Technology*. New York: Matthew Bender. (with annual updates)

1988. Perritt, H. Jr. *How To Practice Law with Computers*. New York: Practicing Law Institute.

MICHAEL GEMIGNANI

LEGAL ASPECTS OF COMPUTING

For articles on related subjects *see* COMPUTER CRIME; ELECTRONIC FUNDS TRANSFER SYSTEMS; LEGAL APPLICATIONS OF COMPUTERS; LEGAL PROTECTION OF SOFTWARE; and PRIVACY, COMPUTERS AND.

Introduction   Given the youth of the computer industry, much of its legal landscape is still shrouded in uncertainty despite the heavy volume of computer-related cases now reaching the courts. The law concerning areas covered in this article is changing rapidly even as this article is being written.

Contracts   A *contract* is a promise or agreement that the courts are willing to enforce. Several kinds of contracts are commonly employed in the computer industry: purchase agreements, licenses, software development contracts, maintenance agreements, to mention but a few. A contract requires an offer, an acceptance, and consideration. *Consideration* is some form of duty or obligation that a party voluntarily assumes.

If a contract involves A's transfer of ownership of item T to B in return for payment, there has been a sale. If item T is tangible (i.e. if T is "goods"), then the transaction is covered by Article 2 of the Uniform Commercial Code (UCC). The UCC has been adopted in every state except Louisiana.

The UCC, however, may not apply to many computer-related contracts because such contracts do not involve either a sale or goods, or either. Licenses and leases confer limited rights defined by the contract, rather than conveying full ownership rights; hence, they are not contracts for sale. A software development contract is a contract for services, even though the end product belongs to the buyer. Some courts have applied UCC principles by analogy to leases and licenses, but other courts

have reverted to classical contract law to decide contract disputes that do not clearly fall under the UCC.

Although a contract may not involve a sale, we will still designate the party who acquires goods, services, or rights as the "buyer," and the party who receives payment as the "seller." Preliminary to executing a contract, the buyer may issue a Request for Proposal (RFP) that describes his or her needs. Potential sellers will then respond to the RFP with proposals that state what they are willing to furnish and under what terms. The buyer must insure that the terms wanted are included in the actual contract itself; for example, the RFP can be included in the agreement by reference. Most contracts have "merger" or "integration" clauses that state that all of the terms of the contract are contained in the written agreement itself. If the merger clause is effective, the buyer may find that the RFP, promises of salespersons, and even written promises that precede the actual execution of the contract are null and void.

If what the buyer receives does not conform to the terms of the contract, or if the seller provides nothing at all, the contract has been breached. If what the seller delivers fails to perform as warranted, then there is a breach of warranty.

If there is breach of contract, a court may award various kinds of damages; the most important damages are actual and consequential. Actual damages are those losses that can be calculated precisely and that are directly caused by the defendant's wrongful action. Consequential damages are losses that are less directly caused by the wrongful action.

Suppliers of software and hardware have provided few guarantees for their products; for many years, they would not even warrant that software would do anything at all, or that hardware would do more than pass the vendor's own self-defined tests. Some limited warranties are provided now by most sellers. Sellers and licensors of computer-related products still usually include disclaimer of warranty and limitation of remedy clauses in their contracts, including provisions to limit the amount of actual damages that an aggrieved buyer can recover. Almost all computer-related contracts still disclaim any liability for consequential damages because of the open-ended nature of such damages and the large economic losses that can stem from a major computer failure. Such disclaimers and limitations are usually upheld by the courts, who assume that the parties to a contract understood and bargained for the provisions. Many contracts also provide that a dispute stemming from the contract be brought to an arbitrator rather than to a court of law.

Torts   A *tort* is an act, other than a breach of contract, by which one party injures another and because of which the injured party can seek a personal remedy in a court of law. A crime is an act forbidden by statute and for the commission of which the state may punish the actor. An act can, but need not, be both a tort and a crime. Computer crimes are discussed later in this article.

One of the most common grounds for litigation in tort is negligence. Negligence involves a breach of a duty of care to someone that causes injury to that person.

Whether a duty of care has been breached depends on the standard of care to which the actor must be held. The law will generally ask what a reasonable, prudent person would have done under the circumstances. If P has represented possession of special expertise, P will be held to the standard of care of someone who has that level of expertise.

However, there are as yet few standards in the computer industry to guide courts concerning what to expect from a reasonable, prudent programmer. Computer professionals are not required to be licensed, and there are no minimum educational qualifications to set oneself up as a programmer, systems analyst, or database manager. Given the uncertainties inherent in large-scale hardware or software design, not to mention the complex interaction between the hardware and software components of a computer system, proving that a hardware or software developer did not exercise an appropriate degree of care, or even showing that the developer made an error and that it was that error that led to the alleged injury is a formidable task.

Acting on the basis of erroneous information and even mindless action on the basis of accurate information can lead to liability in negligence and on other grounds, such as failure to accord a party due process. In several cases, credit companies have been held liable for wrongful repossession based on a computer-generated report that the debtor was delinquent, even though all payments were in order. In another case, a utility company was held liable for shutting off heat in an unsold new home in the middle of winter because its computer sent delinquency notices to the empty house when the company should have known that the notices should have been sent to the builder.

The damage that can stem from malfunction of a mainframe or a network is so great that the law will have to find a method to allocate the risk at least for catastrophic failures. One such mechanism, not as yet applied by courts to situations involving purely economic losses, is strict liability in tort. In an action in negligence, the plaintiff must prove that the defendant failed to exercise reasonable care. In an action in strict liability in tort, all the plaintiff need show is that the defendant is a manufacturer or supplier of a product that had a defect that made it unreasonably dangerous, that the defect caused the plaintiff's injuries, that the defendant is engaged in the business of selling such products, and that the product is expected to and did reach the consumer without substantial change in the condition in which it was sold. If these facts are established, the defendant firm is liable even if it used all possible care in the design and manufacture of the product. Although losses from computer failures are almost exclusively economic, the policies that led courts to adopt strict liability as a theory for recovery are generally applicable to computer systems as well; therefore, this is an area to watch in computer law.

Defamation is a wrongful injury to a person's reputation. To maintain an action in defamation, a plaintiff must prove that the defendant published a defamatory communication of fact concerning the plaintiff, and that the person to whom the communication was addressed understood that it was defamatory and concerned the plaintiff. The plaintiff is often also required to prove that the communication was false, that the defendant was negligent or guilty of fault, and that the defamatory statement actually harmed the plaintiff. The "publication" necessary for defamation is communication to a third party; a defamatory statement made only to the person defamed is not actionable at law. To protect the press, the courts have placed additional burdens on plaintiffs who are public figures or where the defamation concerns a matter of public concern.

Computers raise questions with regard to defamation that are still unanswered. Examples of such questions include: Do on-line database services or electronic bulletin boards (q.v.) have the status of the "press" in terms of what a plaintiff must prove to show defamation? Does publication occur, and, if so, who should be held liable if defamatory information is placed in mass storage and is accessed by a third party, even without authorization?

Given the enormous amount of data that computer systems can store for indefinite lengths of time, there is an increasing chance that stale or incorrect information can be disseminated more widely and for longer periods of time than if the same information had merely been published in a newspaper. Moreover, the computer system's owner may be found to be at fault for failing to update files, failing to check data entered for accuracy and completeness, or having security so inadequate that it allowed unauthorized persons to access supposedly confidential and privileged information.

Somewhat related to defamation are the group torts classified broadly as invasion of privacy: physical intrusion upon a person's seclusion; appropriation of a person's name or likeness; unreasonable publication of information concerning a person's private life; and publication of true information that portrays a person in a false light. Only the latter two are ever likely to come up in a computer context. Stale or incomplete data, even though true, for example, may convey an inaccurate impression about a person or may be highly personal in nature.

The torts of fraud or negligent misrepresentation could arise through reliance on inaccurate data files or programs that produce incorrect or misleading estimates of a customer's needs or of product performance. Buyers sometimes allege fraud and negligence as part of a breach of contract action in order to try to avoid the seller-protective restrictions in the contract, but courts are often unwilling to see a contract action transformed into an action in tort.

Protection of Intellectual Property Although legal protection of intellectual property is an important area of computer-related law, it is covered elsewhere, so we touch on it only briefly here (see LEGAL PROTECTION OF SOFTWARE). The law, both state and federal, provides mechanisms to protect intellectual property by, in effect, giving the originator of the property a monopoly on rights to that property, subject to limitations that vary according to the type of property protected and the type of protection selected.

The four principle means for protecting intellectual

property are copyrights, patents, licenses, and trade secrets. Other mechanisms for protection are found in the law of trademarks, unfair competition, and various aspects of antitrust law. Copyrights and patents are creatures of federal law alone, while trade secrecy is entirely a matter of state law.

According to Section 102(a) of the Copyright Act, the subject matter of copyright is "original works of authorship fixed in any tangible medium of expression, now known or later developed, from which they can be perceived, reproduced or otherwise communicated, either directly or with the aid of a machine or device." The Copyright Act makes it clear that computer programs are copyrightable.

However, the Act also makes clear that "[i]n no case does copyright protection...extend to any idea, procedure, process, system, method of operation, concept, principle, or discovery, regardless of the form in which it is described, explained, illustrated, or embodied in such work." Thus, the mathematical algorithms and general ideas that underlie a program are not copyrightable. Ideas are not copyrightable; only the expression of an idea is copyrightable.

A human author must make some original contribution to gain a copyright in a work. Copyright protection covers the original contribution of the author. Copyright protection accrues automatically to the author once the original work is created, even if the work is not registered with the Copyright Office and, with recent changes in the law, even if no notice of copyright is affixed to the work.

A copyright confers certain rights on the author, among them the right to make copies of and prepare derivative works from the copyrighted work, as well as to distribute copies of the copyrighted work to the public. Congress has stipulated that persons who own a legitimate copy of software can make at least one backup copy as well as modify the software, so long as the modification is an "essential step" in using that software. The rights granted by law to owners of copies of software may conflict with the rights granted to a licensee of software, because a licensee does not necessarily own a copy of the software. A licensee gains only such rights in the software as the license confers, and the copyright owner may claim retention of ownership of all copies of the software. Licenses can also require the licensee to preserve the confidentiality of any source code provided under the license, forbid the licensee from disassembling machine code (*see* DISASSEMBLER), and prescribe penalties if the licensee breaches these conditions.

Courts are now considering the scope of protection conferred by a copyright. Some courts have found that the "structure, sequence, and organization" is protected. Other courts have been willing to protect a program's "look and feel."

Copyrights are easy to obtain and protect only the original contribution of an author. If a work is written independently of another work, there is no infringement even if the works are nearly identical. There is also reason to believe that one can legitimately "reverse engineer" another program to determine the underlying unprotectible ideas and algorithms embodied in that program and then use those ideas and algorithms in building a competing program.

Patents represent a much stronger form of legal protection; they grant the patent holder a legal monopoly on the patented invention. Patents, however, are much more time-consuming and expensive to obtain than copyrights.

Computer-related inventions are usually patented, either as machines or processes. Ideas, scientific principles and laws of nature, mathematical formulas, and mental processes are not patentable. To be patentable, an invention must be useful, novel, and unobvious. To be novel, the invention must not be found in the prior art existing at the time it was invented. To be unobvious, the invention must not have been obvious to someone skilled in the prior art at the time of the invention, even if the invention itself had not actually been created yet. Infringement will be found if someone else creates an equivalent invention, even if done independently and with no knowledge of the patented invention.

To obtain a patent, the inventor must fully disclose the invention by filing a description of the invention so complete that someone knowledgeable in the art would be able to build one and would understand how it works.

Trade secrecy has up to now been the primary mechanism for the protection of intellectual property. Trade secrecy can be used to protect essentially anything that can be kept secret.

A trade secret is information of almost any kind that is used by a particular business and that provides it an opportunity to obtain an advantage over competitors who do not have the information. No precise definition of a trade secret is possible, and even the law of trade secrecy varies from one state to another. In determining whether certain information is a trade secret of the party that has it, a court will consider various factors—e.g. the extent of the measures taken by the owner of the information to keep it secret and limit the scope of those who know it, and the secret's commercial value to the owner.

Trade secrets can be legally obtained—e.g. through careless disclosure by the owner, and by reverse engineering, including disassembling machine language code, although the latter method may be forbidden by copyright law or the terms of a license. A competitor, however, cannot hire away employees who have been entrusted with the trade secret in order to learn it because employees who gain trade secrets in the course of their employment have a duty in law to keep such secrets confidential even when they go to work for another employer, at least so long as the information remains a trade secret.

Evidence   Because computer-generated and stored information may be required in litigation, operators of computer systems must be sensitive to the rules of evidence, lest they find that the credibility of their information can be successfully attacked by an adverse party, or that it may not be admissible on their own behalf.

In order to introduce computer-generated data into evidence, a party generally must first show that the data is what is claims to be (e.g. records showing sales in September), and that there is sufficient reason to believe that the data is sufficiently reliable to warrant its consideration by the court. An expert might testify to the reliability of the equipment used and the adequacy of the data processing procedures. If the equipment consistently failed, or the procedures often failed or yielded inaccurate results, the opposing party will be able to attack the credibility of the data even if the court chooses to admit it.

Because they are inherently suspect as being self-serving, reports generated by a party specifically in anticipation of litigation are inadmissible, although the data on which they are based may be admissible. Computer-generated data is almost always hearsay. Hearsay is defined as "a statement, other than the one made by the declarant while testifying at the trial or hearing, offered in evidence to prove the truth of the matter asserted." Because computer-stored data is almost always a statement of someone other than the one testifying at trial, it is hearsay if the data is produced at trial to assert the truth of the data itself.

The general rule is that hearsay is not admissible. However, there are many exceptions to this rule, the business records exception being the most widely used for computer-generated data. To be admissible under the business records exception, the data must have been kept in the course of a regularly conducted business activity and entered at, or near, the time of the events that gave rise to it, from information transmitted by a person with knowledge, and it was the regular practice of the business to compile such data, all shown by the testimony of the custodian of the data or other knowledgeable and reliable witness. Computer-generated data is also subject to the Best Evidence Rule, but a computer printout of stored data is held to be an "original" for purposes of the rule, so there is usually no problem concerning admissibility on this score.

Computer-stored data is also generally subject to disclosure on the request of a party opponent, even if no hard copies are made. Data must be provided in a form that is comprehensible and usable, and not, for example, in a format that makes the data essentially inaccessible. The party seeking the data may be asked to pay for the costs of collecting it, or converting it to the format desired, if this represents an undue burden.

Computer Crime and Security
There are disagreements as to what forms of activity qualify as computer crime, and estimates of the extent of computer crime vary widely from about $40 million to $2 billion a year. A number of computer abuses are punishable as traditional crimes; for example, if a programmer instructs a bank's computer to transfer money to which he or she is not entitled into a personal account, that programmer has still committed theft, even though a computer was the instrument of the crime. There have been some instances of computer abuse that were not covered by any criminal statute, but, now that the federal government and every state have computer crime statutes of one sort or another, such instances are likely to be extraordinarily rare.

A more significant issue has been the unwillingness of prosecutors and the courts to treat computer crime seriously. Even convictions often brought nominal punishments, and several convictions were overturned on appeal seemingly because the appellate court did not consider the computer-related activity to be serious enough to warrant punishment. According to an American Bar Association poll, even computer professionals do not consider computer crime to be much more of a threat than shoplifting. The special expertise and the additional preparation time that computer-related prosecutions require, coupled with the relatively light sentences that even those convicted are likely to receive, it is no wonder that computer crimes are not high on most district attorneys' lists of priorities. Nevertheless, with the increasing visibility of computer abuse (e.g. the Internet virus of 1989 that brought down a large, sophisticated network - *see* COMPUTER VIRUS), one may expect both more legislation and greater enforcement of existing criminal laws aimed at preventing computer crime.

Miscellaneous Issues There are numerous important issues and concepts that cannot be covered in a brief article. The interested reader is advised to consult one of the references listed in the bibliography. Someone having a specific legal problem should seek assistance of qualified counsel. We conclude by touching on several other issues that are currently in a state of flux.

Taxation Annual changes in federal tax law and the continuing stream of rulings of the Internal Revenue Service make this an unstable area of law. In addition, how states tax software and hardware varies according to the state and the nature of what is being taxed. Computer equipment has even been taxed as real estate. Whether software is subject to sales tax depends in many states on the degree to which it is customized or developed expressly for the customer. When the investment tax credit was repealed, many thought that this would bring a major restructuring and scaling back of the computer leasing market, but, to date, this has not occurred.

Privacy and First Amendment Rights According to a slightly modified definition due to Meredith Mendes of Harvard University, privacy is a condition in which individuals, groups, or institutions can determine for themselves when, how, and to what extent information about them is communicated to others. Computers have been used to "match" files of one government agency against files in another agency in order to catch "welfare cheats" and other persons suspected of criminal activities, although some commentators believe such activity is illegal. The National Crime Information Center (NCIC) receives data from 60,000 law enforcement agencies, but this data contains many errors. In 1985, the FBI admitted that at least 12,000 invalid or inaccurate reports on suspects wanted for arrest were being transmitted among the 400,000 daily responses to queries to the NCIC by federal, state, and local law enforcement agencies. The harm that these inaccurate reports may cause innocent parties must be balanced against the increased probability the NCIC provides of apprehending real criminals, but Congress and the courts have not yet arrived at a consensus concerning what an appropriate balance might be.

There are, however, various federal and state laws aimed at safeguarding the accuracy and confidentiality of databases that contain personal information or that open up certain government files to public scrutiny. Among the federal laws are the Right to Privacy Act of 1974, the Freedom of Information Act, the Fair Credit Reporting Act, the Bank Secrecy Act, the Trade Secrets Act, the Equal Credit Opportunity Act of 1976, the Right to Financial Privacy Act of 1978, and the Privacy Protection Act of 1980.

Electronic Funds Transfer   Transfers of substantial assets via computers gives rise to questions of who is liable if the transfer is improperly made (e.g. if the transfer is not completed in a timely fashion, or not completed at all). Although most of the issues concerning computer-to-computer electronic funds transfer are covered by the Uniform Commercial Code, some are not. For example, checks require a signature to be honored, but there is no agreement as yet concerning how this requirement is met with many wire transfers. Computerized transfers of assets will be an important area for the development of new law.

Electronic Records and Legal Requirements   The law has traditionally required the existence of and often a formal recording of paper documents of various sorts to testify to the authenticity of certain transactions—e.g. deeds in connection with the transfer of rights in real property, and security agreements with respect to certain kinds of liens. Generally, such documents must be signed by the party making the transfer or the person liable for a debt. More and more transactions are now recorded in computer memory, and the trend may be toward electronic record keeping and away from paper. The law must either adapt to the new technology, or else make it clear that paper is here to stay. The transient nature of even long-term mass storage may also threaten the reliability of records of transactions over a long period of time.

Future Issues   Some of the other issues that will have to be decided in the future include liability for catastrophic computer-related disasters, ownership of intellectual property created primarily or exclusively by a computer, and liability for mistakes of expert systems (q.v.).

References

General

1978. Bender, D. *Computer Law*. New York: Matthew Bender. (Originally published as *Computer Law: Evidence and Procedure*; annually updated; now two volumes covering most aspects of computer law.)

1985. Nimmer, R. *The Law of Computer Technology*. New York: Warren, Gorham & Lamont.

1985. Gemignani, M. C. *Computer Law*. Rochester: Lawyers Cooperative Publishing Co.—Bancroft-Whitney. (With annual supplements.)

1989. Gemignani, M. C. *A Legal Guide To EDP Management*. Westport, CT: Quorum.

Specific Areas

1987. Kutten, L. J. *Computer Software: Protection/Liability/Law/Forms*. New York: Clark Boardman. (With annual supplements.)

1987. Bigelow, R. *Computer Contracts: Negotiating and Drafting Guide*. New York: Matthew Bender.

1988. Arkin, S. *et al. Prevention and Prosecution of Computer and High Technology Crime*. New York: Matthew Bender.

Periodicals

Computer Industry Litigation Reporter. Andrews Publications, P. O. Box 208, Edgemont, PA 19028.

Computer Law Monitor. Research Publications, 92 Fairway Dr., P. O. Box 9267, Asheville, NC 22815.

Computer Law Reporter. 1519 Connecticut Ave., NW, Washington, DC 20036.

Software Law Reporter. 175 Strafford Ave., #1, Wayne, PA 19087.

MICHAEL GEMIGNANI

LEGAL PROTECTION OF SOFTWARE

For articles on related subjects *see* LEGAL APPLICATIONS; and LEGAL ASPECTS OF COMPUTING.

Computer software is expensive to develop and maintain. It has high monetary value to its owners, both because it can give them a competitive advantage when used internally to do tasks more cheaply or quickly and because it can be licensed for use by others. Software, however, is very easy to copy at a trivial cost and is, therefore, very susceptible to pirating. Because of its value and its vulnerability to misappropriation, ownership interests in software must be protected.

For the purpose of legal protection, software is categorized as *intellectual property*. Intellectual property is a form of intangible personal property comprised of ideas, processes, information, or symbols. Intangible personal property contrasts with tangible personal property, such as hardware or supplies, and real property, such as office buildings and other structures affixed to the land. Intellectual property is protected in one of five principal ways: by patent, copyright, trade secret, trademark, or contract.

Patent   In the U.S., patent protection is a federal statutory right that gives an inventor or his or her assignee exclusive rights to make, use, or sell products or processes within the scope of the patent for 17 years from the issuance of the patent.

To be patentable, inventions must meet several tests. They must be of statutory subject matter—physical methods, apparatus, compositions of matter, devices and improvements—but not mere ideas. Further, they must be new, useful, and not obvious. They must be described in a properly filed and prosecuted patent application.

The two statutory subject matter categories that are generally applied to patent claims involving programs are *process* (or method) and *machine* (or apparatus). In an appropriate case, a program-related invention might be claimed as an article of manufacture.

The courts have held that a mathematical algorithm is like a law of nature (which is not patentable subject matter) and has evolved a two-step process for determining whether a computer program is patentable subject matter. First, does the claim recite such an algorithm, and, if so, does it in its entirety wholly preempt that algorithm? Claims that do both of the above are deemed to be unpatentable subject matter. A negative response to either test permits the claim to be evaluated on the basis of the other tests of patentability.

Copyright Copyright protection is governed by federal law. Copyright is one of the powers granted to Congress under the U.S. Constitution. Under the Copyright Act of 1976, as amended, the protection extends to original works of authorship. These include, for example, literary works (including computer programs), musical works, dramatic works, pantomime and choreographic works, pictorial, graphic and sculptural works, motion pictures and other audio-visual works, and sound recordings. Exclusive rights are granted to the owner of the copyright to reproduce the copyrighted work; prepare derivative works based on the work; distribute copies of the work by sale, rental, lease, or lending; perform the work publicly if it is literary, musical, dramatic or choreographic, pantomime, or a motion picture and other audio-visual works; and display each of those works and pictorial, graphic, or sculptural works publicly.

To be eligible for copyright protection, a work must be original and must be fixed in a tangible means of expression, such as a book, tape, disk, or phonograph record. Protection arises automatically for protected works upon fixation and covers the expression in the work (but not the underlying ideas). Protection lasts for the life of the author plus 50 years and, in the case of works made for hire, for 75 years from first publication or 100 years from creation.

Until 1 March 1989, notice was required on all copies of published works, and registration was required for all works prior to commencement of an infringement action.

On 1 March 1989, the U.S. became a member of the Berne Convention. Under the Berne Implementation Act, which also became effective 1 March 1989, for works first publicly distributed after that date, a copyright notice is no longer required on all publicly distributed copies of a work as a condition of protection. Recordation with the Copyright Office is no longer required prior to commencing litigation for infringement if the country of origin of work is a foreign nation adhering to the Berne Convention or if the work is first published simultaneously in a Berne country and a nation not adhering to Berne. Works publicly distributed prior to 1 March 1989, must still comply with the notice and recordation requirements. Works of U.S. origin must still be registered prior to commencement of an infringement action. Works of U.S. origin include works (1) first published in the U.S. or simultaneously in another Berne member country granting equal or greater years of protection than the U.S.; (2) simultaneously in the U.S. and a non-Berne member country; or (3) in a non-Berne member country, providing that all authors of the work are "nationals, domiciliaries or habitual residents of the U.S."

There are certain advantages for those copyright owners who do comply with the formalities of placing a copyright notice on a work and registering the work with the U.S. Copyright Office. Notice, which consists of placing the legend: "© [author's name] [date of first publication of the work]" serves to defeat claims that an infringement was innocent. Registration provides eligibility for statutory damages without the need to show actual damages, in the amount of $500 ($200 to innocent wrongdoers) to $20,000, with a possible award of up to $100,000 against willful infringers. Those who register their works before the infringement takes place are also eligible to obtain their attorneys' fees in the case.

Registration of a work is accomplished by execution of the appropriate application form, which varies depending on the type of work to be registered (e.g. form TX for computer software programs), payment of a minimal fee (currently $20), and deposit of two copies of the work with the U.S. Copyright Office. For computer programs, one deposit is required and, for large programs, it can be less than all of the program, preferably the first and last 25 pages of source code.

Copyright protection can be used with other forms of protection, such as trade secret protection and trademark to retain or enhance the value of intellectual property rights.

Trade Secret A trade secret is a right that is protected state by state rather than by a federal law and is defined in the Uniform Trade Secrets Act, adopted in many states, as information, including a formula, pattern, compilation, program, device, method, technique, or process that:

1. Derives independent economic value, actual or potential, from not being generally known to the public or to other persons who can obtain economic value from its disclosure or use; and
2. Is the subject of efforts that are reasonable under the circumstances to maintain its secrecy.

In a number of court cases, computer programs have qualified as trade secrets; e.g. *University Computing Corporation* v. *Lykes-Youngstown Corporation*, 504 F.2d 518 (5th Cir. 1974), *MSA* v. *Cyborg Systems, Inc.* 6 CLSR 921 (N.D. Ill. 1978), and *Com-Share, Inc.* v. *Computer Complex, Inc.*, 338 F. Supp. 1229 (E.D. Mich. 1971). The absolute requirement for trade secret status is that the item be kept secret from all except those bound to keep it confidential by virtue of their relationship or by contract. If the secret becomes known to others, the protection vanishes. If it remains secret, the protection can last forever. Confidential relationships include employees and agents in a fiduciary or trust relationship and thieves, who are held to be in a constructive trust relationship so that they cannot use their ill-gotten knowledge. Contract is used to bind licensees and joint venture partners or investors. (In some states, these people are bound even without an express contract.) However, once the secret is disclosed without a requirement of confidentiality or is disclosed to one who did not know of its secret character, the trade secret status is lost forever. Places where trade secrets are often disclosed carelessly are user group meetings and technical meetings.

Employees may need to learn the secret in the course of their employment. These people are bound not to misappropriate the trade secret by virtue of their position of trust with respect to the secret. Many employees do not realize the parameters of that trust and should consult their lawyers before using software developed for an employer for their own purposes. Trade secrets can also be lost through "reverse engineering" (i.e. through the legitimate process of buying a product and "taking it apart" to learn how it works); this encourages many software owners to encrypt their code. Trade secret protection has been held by the U. S. Supreme Court to be compatible with patent protection, *Kewanee Oil Co. v. Bicron Corp.*, 416 U.S. 470 (1974). Many vendors of software choose between the copyright and trade secret methods of protection; yet many others have both a copyright notice on their software and also treat it and license it as a trade secret. Cases have held that, so long as the rights claimed are not identical to copyright protection, those rights are not preempted by the federal copyright law.

Many software owners place a label on their software stating: "This software is proprietary to (name of Company)." That notice serves as a no trespassing sign to observers and a reminder to users who have acquired the software under an agreement to keep the software confidential.

Trademark Trademark embodies the exclusive use of a symbol to identify goods and services. As distinguished from a patent, which does not exist until issued by the Patent Office, or a copyright, which exists as soon as the work is fixed in a tangible form, a trademark arises upon use, or, if one has a bona fide intent to use the mark, one may acquire rights by filing a federal application to register the mark. Trademark protection exists at both the federal and state levels. The symbol protected can be both a name and a logo, such as *17 Mile Drive*. However, one cannot trademark an entire program, only its identifying symbol(s).

Contract Because copies of software are ordinarily transferred to others in the course of business and sometimes transferred in source form, disclosure of the software is frequently made under an agreement to keep the secret confidential. Patented and copyrighted software can be transferred via contracts that may have more restrictive provisions than the law requires simply by the status accorded by the patent or copyright. One may, for example, contract with another not to disclose a copyrighted piece of software. One may also agree to remedies for disclosure or unauthorized copy, set up complex formulas for royalty payment for legitimate use, and agree to the ownership of enhancements and changes to the software.

Reference

1982. Nycum, S. H. *Protection of Proprietary Interests in Software.* Reston, VA: Reston Publishing Company.

SUSAN S. NYCUM

LEIBNIZ, GOTTFRIED WILHELM VON

For articles on related subjects *see* CALCULATING MACHINES; DIGITAL COMPUTERS: HISTORY: ORIGINS; and PASCAL, BLAISE.

Gottfried von Leibniz (b. Leipzig, 1646; d. Hanover, 1716) had obtained an excellent education in his father's library before entering the University of Leipzig at fifteen years of age and receiving a bachelor's degree at seventeen. At twenty he received a doctorate in jurisprudence from Altdorf, and for six years thereafter pursued a career of law and diplomacy, working to create an effective defense for the German states against Louis XIV. These diplomatic intrigues took him to Paris (1672), where he spent the four most fecund years of his mathematical career. Under the tutelage of Huygens, Leibniz systematically studied mathematics, especially the work of Descartes and Pascal (*q.v.*).

Pascal's calculating machine stimulated Leibniz's interest. By adding a movable carriage operating on wheels utilizing an active-and-inactive pin principle and a delayed carry mechanism, Leibniz modified Pascal's machine so that it would multiply and divide directly (i.e. without the operator having to use an algorithm). However, in the only extant Leibniz machine (Hanover Museum), a later model, Pascal's ratchet-carry mechanism is replaced by a primitive Geneva gear system that accomplishes the discontinuous carry of digits by a series of five-point star gears. Eliminating the ratchet mech-

FIG. 1.   Gottfried Wilhelm von Leibniz, from a painting by A. Scheits. (Photograph by courtesy of the Herzog Anton Ulrich-Museum.)

anisms made subtraction and division possible by simply reversing the rotation of the addition and multiplication mechanisms.

In 1673, Leibniz made discoveries in differential calculus and observed (in 1675) that the summation process of integration was equivalent to reversing the operation of differentiation, the fundamental theorem of calculus. Newton had also made this observation in the 1660s, but Leibniz was apparently unaware of it.

In 1676 Leibniz left Paris for Hanover, where for the next 40 years he was a historian and librarian actively pursuing philosophy, theology, diplomatic missions, and scientific correspondences, and intermittently working on his calculating machines. In 1700, he organized the Berlin Academy of Science (an idea he first articulated in 1668) and at his death was carrying on the now-famous correspondence with Clarke about the theological implications of Newton's *Principia* and *Opticks*.

CHARLES V. JONES

LIBRARY AUTOMATION

For articles on related subjects *see* HUMANITIES APPLICATIONS; HYPERTEXT; and INFORMATION RETRIEVAL.

Library automation had its genesis in the 1950s and has been rapidly evolving since that time. Once seen in fiction as a fantastic scenario, libraries now routinely provide computerized access to their collections and the information contained within them. Library automation has evolved to encompass all phases of library operations: collection development and acquisitions (determining which materials to add to a collection and the process of obtaining them); cataloging and classification (the description and subject analysis of materials so that they may be retrieved); retrieval (identifying a particular item or set of materials in response to a query); circulation (loaning of requested materials to individuals or organizations); and reference (provision of information contained within the material itself).

Early on, libraries established mechanization committees to study the application of automated techniques to the problems of information storage, retrieval, and dissemination. Early implementations focused on information retrieval. The goal was to enhance access to a library's holdings, not only to books and journals, but also to other materials, such as maps, sound recordings, and microforms. Printed keyword-in-context (KWIC) and keyword-out-of-context (KWOC) indexes and lists of journal holdings were typical early applications, but there was no standardization among processes or data formats to enable libraries to share machine-readable data.

A problem encountered in handling all types of library records is that the data (e.g. names of authors, titles of works, or listings of content) varies in length. Any truncation of this data to a fixed length makes it difficult to identify an item uniquely. Libraries must continue to maintain older materials as well as add new materials, so that the number of machine-readable records representing items in the collection is constantly growing and is available for retrieval at all times. Records for older material may be requested as frequently as records for newly acquired material. A large storage capacity must be available both for storing and maintaining the data. The records are also dynamic and subject to frequent update. Therefore, there is a significant requirement in library systems to enable long records containing variable-length data to be updated and maintained in an on-line transaction environment.

The MARC (MAchine-Readable-Cataloging) format was developed to facilitate the exchange of bibliographic data among libraries in a standardized record format. Since many of the functions of libraries are dependent upon the data describing an item in terms of its bibliographic and physical attributes and its subject matter (which together make up the cataloging records), the Council on Library Resources (CLR) supported a study of methods for converting this data to machine-readable form. This study led to a project at the Library of Congress (LC) funded by CLR that became known as the MARC Pilot Project (see Fig. 1 and Avram, 1968). Upon the successful completion of the pilot project in 1969, LC began the MARC Distribution Service, which is still in existence (Avram, 1988).

The MARC project was a fundamental building block leading to future development of the automation of many library functions, since 1) it provided the vehicle for the establishment, adoption, and increased usage of standards so that libraries could exchange and share machine-readable bibliographic data; 2) the adoption of standards provided the environment for the building of information systems to manipulate data based on the standards; 3) the MARC format documentation resulted in savings by organizations all over the world in implementing library automation projects; and 4) the machine-readable records from LC provided a database upon which to build shared cataloging and other library automation projects so that each individual organization did not have to assume the costs associated with cataloging all of its materials and/or the retrospective conversion of all of its cataloging data.

Libraries were quick to adopt the MARC format as the standard for encoding cataloging data in bibliographic records. They were eager to share bibliographic data with the goal that a bibliographic record describing a particular item need only be created once and then shared among networks and individual systems to describe like items held by other organizations. The ability to exchange information about resources is a goal fundamental to library systems development. Standardization of the bibliographic record gave rise to the ability to create shared bibliographic records that were then used as the basis for library systems and the development of library networks that began to occur in the 1970s. On-line networked systems were developed in which the database was both built and used by multiple organizations.

The earliest and still the most advanced network was OCLC (formerly the Ohio College Library Center). Nearly 12,000 OCLC member libraries, using some 10,000

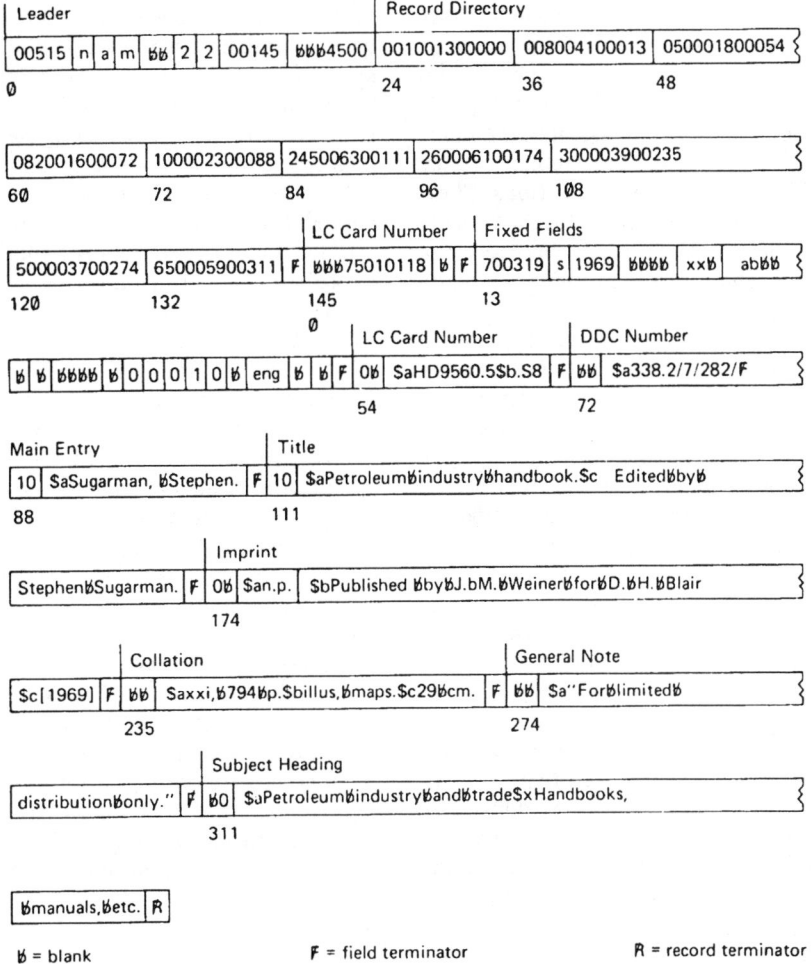

FIG. 1. Sample record in the MARC format.

terminals or workstations extending over almost all of the 50 states and into Canada and 38 other countries, receive a variety of products and services from a resource database that includes data contributed by the participating members and the MARC data distributed by LC. Several similar systems also developed, among them the Research Libraries Information Network (RLIN) and the Western Library Network (WLN) in the U. S., the University of Toronto Library Automation System (UTLAS) in Canada, and the British Library Systems (BLAISE) in the UK.

This networking activity for library technical services (principally cataloging) activities evolved into the concept of the "bibliographic utility," enabling hundreds of libraries to have access to shared cataloging, and promoted shared access to and interlibrary loan of dispersed library resources. To enhance the effectiveness of the bibliographic utilities, large-scale retrospective conversion of card catalog data to MARC format was undertaken by libraries as members of networks and by network and commercial ventures on behalf of libraries. Databases of millions of records denoting millions of points of access to research material were established by the library networks.

These large systems have remained disparate, how-ever. They developed independently and, although they were based around the common MARC record standard, contained incompatible approaches to retrieval and input. A Network Advisory Committee was formed by LC and issued a planning paper (1977) that included a recommendation for assigning a high priority to the linking of various library systems in the U.S. The Linked Systems Project (LSP) developed as an effort to link LC and the bibliographic utilities in order to avoid duplication of records among them and to enable LC records to be distributed on-line. LSP uses Standard Network Interconnection (SNI) based upon the Open Systems Interconnection (OSI - *q.v.*) seven-layer protocol. An application layer for information retrieval was developed to support the retrieval and exchange of bibliographic records. The initial LSP implementation was bibliographic authority record interchange—i.e. the exchange of information concerning the standardization of the access points used to retrieve bibliographic records. The LSP effort continues to evolve with the objective of exchanging bibliographic record information among the networks and LC.

To complement the national networks, a number of commercial vendors began to offer systems to the majority of libraries that did not possess the resources to undertake their own local systems development. At first, these systems were based around a single function (e.g. circulation control) with truncated records that could not be interchanged. As vendor systems became more sophisticated, they expanded to encompass multiple functions, integrating acquisitions, on-line public access catalog (OPAC), and circulation control functions. They also standardized around the full MARC format record. With such systems, libraries began to incorporate records from the bibliographic utilities in order to create databases tailored to their own needs.

At the same time that the large networks developed, commercial information providers began to furnish published information (e.g. journal indexes and abstracting services) in machine-readable form on value-added networks. On-line database searching increasingly began to be used to provide library reference service and quickly gained acceptance as an important tool for providing timely access to the journal literature. Customized bibliographies could now be assembled from a wide variety of sources to meet the needs of individual users.

During the 1980s, microcomputer workstations evolved. With the ability of a workstation (*q.v.*) to download bibliographic records from bibliographic utilities or remote on-line library catalogs and to manipulate the records locally, libraries could retrieve information to upload into local systems or databases, create local catalogs, and produce bibliographies and other products. Developments in CD-ROM (*q.v.*) technology have provided stand-alone databases for information to be used in cataloging activities, OPACs, journal indexes, and reference materials. Libraries are working on networking CD-ROMs in order to provide an array of information to library users from a single workstation.

Library collections represent items written in many languages, using a variety of alphabets and scripts. Therefore, the capability must exist to input, manipulate, and output multiple character sets (to include, for example, Cyrillic, Greek, Hebrew, Arabic, and Chinese in addition to expanded Roman). The original MARC development included an extended ASCII (*q.v.*) character set to accommodate diacritics and special characters for languages written in the Roman alphabet. The ability to work with non-Roman character sets was pioneered by the Research Libraries Group (RLG). Terminals with the ability to input Chinese, Japanese, and Korean (CJK) scripts were made available, and later, as workstations predominated, software to accommodate Hebrew and Arabic characters was developed. OCLC also developed its own system for CJK scripts. However, not every system can accommodate or display these vernacular character sets. Development work continues in this area. Expanded public display of vernacular character sets stored in local databases will enable researchers to conduct searches directly in the vernacular scripts of interest.

Local and national databases created to provide access to bibliographic data about items, indexes to the journal literature, holding locations for interlibrary loan, and text storage are now being tied together for the individual user through networks such as the Internet. Remote access by a library user to a wide variety of library systems/databases from a personal workstation can now be accomplished. Many local OPACs are available on the Internet for public searching. Libraries have welcomed the National Research and Education Network (NREN) initiative and are considering the implications: that of greatly facilitated sharing of databases and access to collections. Network access to full text has taken on new importance as the electronic publishing industry develops and as more professional and scholarly journals are published in electronic form.

Libraries and their networks are researching enhanced front-end system interfaces. Public front-ends to OPACs eliminate the need to learn the query syntax of a particular system and provide a view of the bibliographic data in a form readily intelligible to the library user. Front ends oriented toward the librarian eliminate the need to learn the individual command language and file structure of each local or remote system.

The focus of library automation remains the bibliographic record. Current research focuses on enhancing the basic bibliographic record to deliver more information, ranging from a summary of contents to full text information. Hypertext systems, providing traditional bibliographic data as well as related textual, visual, and aural information in a unified package, promise enhanced access to shared information resources.

The history of library automation is a rich one, and rapid advances in technology have opened a wide array of possibilities for librarians and end users alike. Further advances are expected, offering new opportunities and challenges.

References

1963–. *Proceedings of the Clinic on Library Applications of Data Processing.* Urbana-Champaign, IL: University of Illinois at Urbana-Champaign, Graduate School of Library Science.

1968. Avram, Henriette D. *The MARC Pilot Project: Final Report on a Project Sponsored by the Council on Library Resources, Inc.*, Washington, DC: Library of Congress. (For sale by the Superintendent of Documents, U. S. Government Printing Office, Washington, DC 20402.)

1969. *Library Automation; A State of the Art Review.* Salmon, Steven R. (Ed.). Chicago: American Library Association.

1975. Avram, Henriette D. *MARC, Its History and Implications.* Washington, DC: Library of Congress. (Based on an article entitled "Machine-Readable Cataloging (MARC) Program," which appeared in the *Encyclopedia of Library and Information Science* **16**.)

1975. *Library Automation; The State of the Art II.* Martin, Susan K. and Butler, Brett, (Ed.), with a bibliography compiled by West, Martha W. Chicago: American Library Association.

1978. Buckland, Lawrence F. *The Role of the Library of Congress in the Evolving National Network.* (A study commissioned by the Library of Congress Network Development Office and funded by the National Commission on Libraries and Information Science.) Washington, DC: Library of Congress.

1978. "LITA Library Automation: State of the Art III, Held in Chicago on June 22–23." *Journal of Library Automation*, **11**, 4:285–337.

1983–. *Library Hi Tech.* Ann Arbor, MI: Pierian Press.

1988. Avram, Henriette D. "Machine-Readable Cataloging (MARC): 1986." *Encyclopedia of Library and Information Science* **43**, Suppl. 8. New York: Marcel Dekker.

1988. *The Linked System Project: A Networking Tool for Libraries.* Fenley, Judith G. and Wiggins, Beacher (Eds.). Dublin, OH: OCLC Online Computer Library Center.

1989. Crawford, Walt. *MARC for Library Use; Understanding Integrated USMARC*, 2nd Ed. Boston: G. K. Hall.

JOHN GRAVES, ANDREW LISOWSKI AND JENNIFER MARILL

LIBRARY, PROGRAM. *See* MATHEMATICAL SOFTWARE; and SOFTWARE LIBRARIES.

LIFO. *See* FIFO-LIFO.

LIGHTPEN. *See* INTERACTIVE INPUT DEVICES.

LINE EDITOR. *See* TEXT EDITING SYSTEMS.

LINEAR PROGRAMMING. *See* MATHEMATICAL PROGRAMMING; and SIMPLEX METHOD.

LINGUISTICS. *See* PROGRAMMING LINGUISTICS.

LINKED LIST. *See* LIST PROCESSING.

LINKER

For articles on related subjects *see* ASSEMBLER; LOADER; and OBJECT CODE.

The function of the *linker* (sometimes called the *consolidator* or *composer* or *collector*) is to combine into a single module a number of program segments that have been independently compiled or assembled. Some of the segments may be held in a library (on disk or tape), and the linkage editor will normally provide facilities for the automatic incorporation of any library segments that have been referenced. The output of the linker is usually a relocatable binary program suitable for loading by a relocating loader.

If a section of program has been independently compiled, there will be three kinds of items in the compiler output:

1. Constants (absolute items whose value does not depend on the ultimate position of the segment in memory).
2. Items (usually addresses or address constants) whose value is known relative to the value of a specified location counter at the start of the segment.
3. External references, whose value cannot be determined until all segments are present.

The complete output of the compiler will therefore typically consist of:

1. A "code" block consisting of binary words tagged to show their absolute, relative, or external character, and, in the case of relative items, the appropriate location counter.
2. A table of external references, containing for each reference the (relative) address in the code section at which it occurs and its symbolic form.
3. A table of external (global) symbol definitions, containing the name and (relative) value of each symbol globally defined in the segment.

The linker operates in a number of passes. The first pass determines which segments are missing, by comparing the external reference tables with the global definition tables. If there are "missing" segments, the directories of specified library files are scanned. If the relevant names are found, the corresponding segments are added to the program. Pass 2 scans the segment headers and computes the sizes of the blocks corresponding to the various location counters. This information is placed in a header block for the use of the loader. Pass 3 performs relocation of all subsequent segments relative to the first segment so as to produce a relocatable program based on a single set of origins.

The process is simple: The location counters are all set to zero at the start of the first segment. Their values at the start of segment *n*, together with the information in that segment's header block, determine their values at the start of segment *n* + 1. During this pass, the entries in the global symbol definition tables and in the external reference tables are relocated relative to the origin of the first segment, and the entries from the tables associated with each segment are merged to give a single global symbol table and a single table of external references. Finally, these two tables are used to fill in all the unresolved external references, and the end result is a single module of relocatable binary.

The operation of linking is commonly done as a disk-to-disk operation, using temporary work files as necessary. It is evident that it is a trivial extra complication to perform the final relocation at the same time, thus producing an executable binary module. Such a system is called a *linking loader*.

References

1972. Barron, D. W. *Assemblers and Loaders*, 2nd Ed. New York: American Elsevier.

1972. Presser I., and White, J. R. "Linkers and Loaders," *Computing Surveys* 4: 149–168.

DAVID W. BARRON

LISP. *See* LIST PROCESSING: LANGUAGES.

LIST PROCESSING

For articles on related subjects *see* ABSTRACT DATA TYPE; ARTIFICIAL INTELLIGENCE; COMPUTER ALGEBRA; DATA STRUCTURES; DATA TYPE; FUNCTIONAL PROGRAMMING; GARBAGE COLLECTION; GRAPH THEORY; LAMBDA CALCULUS; POINTER; STORAGE ALLOCATION; STRING PROCESSING; SYMBOL MANIPULATION; and TREE.

PRINCIPLES

The two elements of a computer program are the computations (the actions we want done) and the data (the things we want the actions done upon). The computations are defined using expressions in a computer language, combined to form procedures, which are in turn combined to form compound procedures and eventually programs. The ability to combine simple expressions into procedures is the key to using computer programs to model processes in the real world. Data are defined in a similar way: compound data objects are built from simple parts, like numbers, and combined to represent real-world objects that have complex properties. Compound procedures and compound data are used for the same purposes: to improve the modularity of the program and to raise the conceptual level of its design. One of the simplest and most widespread form of compound data is the *linked list*.

Any data object that contains other objects is a compound data object. On one end of the spectrum is the *homogeneous array*, a collection of objects, all of the same type, with an implicit relationship defined by the indices of the elements of the array. Further along the spectrum in complexity is the *structure*, a collection of data objects, not necessarily all of the same type, into a single unit whose representation is hidden. (A Pascal *record* is such a structure.) Typically, one can access the elements of a structure by name, but has no idea how those elements are stored. At the extreme end of the spectrum is the sort of object implied by the phrase *object-oriented programming* (*q.v.*), an object also called an *abstract data type* (*q.v.*). These objects are also collections of data objects whose representation is hidden, but they go farther in that all access to the elements of an object is through operations defined by the program. In all these compound objects, except arrays, the relationship between the elements is explicit. The linked list occupies a point in this spectrum somewhere between the array and the structure: it is the simplest compound data object that has an explicit relationship among its elements. Hereinafter, by *list* we shall mean *linked list*.

List Basics The basic element of any list is the *node*. In its commonest form (also called a *pair*), a node has two fields. Each field can contain another data object: a number, a symbol, or even another node. (Since arbitrary data may not fit in a field, the field will actually contain a *pointer* to the object instead of the object itself.) A program can manipulate the node as a single object, and it can extract the contents of either field. Arbitrarily complex structures can be built from these simple building blocks.

A list is a simple sequence of nodes, with a list element in the first field of each node (variously called the *head*, *first*, *car*, etc.) and a pointer to the next node in the second field (*next*, *rest*, *cdr*, *link*, etc.). For example, the list of three numbers, 5, 8, 9, could be represented by three nodes. The first node has a pointer to a 5 in its head and a link to the second; the second has a pointer to an 8 and a link to the third; the third has a pointer to a 9 and its next field is empty.

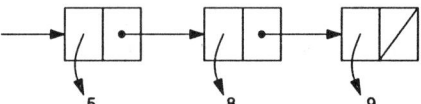

Two issues arise in this kind of list manipulation. First, while insertion and deletion are easier for a list than for an array, there's a catch: the pointer to the list points only to the first element, and all the intermediate links must be followed to reach a particular element. So the trade-off is that access is slower. Sometimes that doesn't matter—rarely does one need to access the middle elements of a stack or queue implemented as a list—but sometimes it does, and the choice of structure must depend on the application.

Second, what happens to those nodes that are deleted, and where do new nodes come from? These questions are related, in that new nodes are taken from *free storage*, (also called the *heap*, or the *list of available space*) and deleted nodes must be returned to free storage or it will run out. The process of making new nodes is part of *storage allocation*, and the process of reclaiming unused nodes is called *garbage collection*.

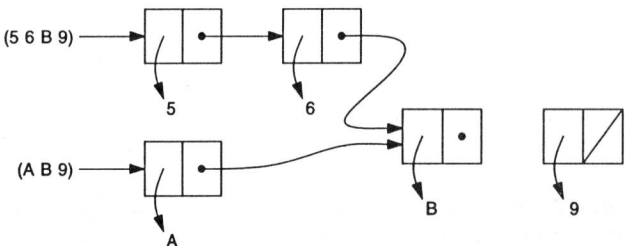

FIG. 1. Sharing parts of a list.

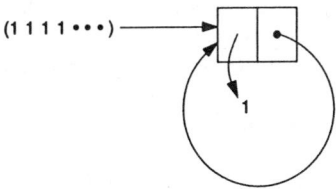

FIG. 2.   A circular list of 1s.

Since list nodes contain pointers that can point to any data object, the possibility exists that more than one node might point to the same object. When this happens, multiple lists can share parts of themselves, with the obvious consequences: identical data is not duplicated, and if part of the shared data is changed as part of operating on one list, all the sharing lists see the changes (see Fig. 1). Whether these are advantages or disadvantages depends on the application: some programs might use the common data to communicate between parts of the program, while others might have problems with data mysteriously changing for no apparent reason.

Similarly, a list may be *circular*, sharing structure with itself: a node somewhere in the list may contain a pointer to a node elsewhere in the list. The single node containing a 1 and a pointer to itself (Fig. 2) is such a list, and in some contexts behaves like an infinite list of 1's—the first element is a 1, and so is the "second" (found by following the link), the "third," etc.

Data Abstraction with Lists   This kind of power makes lists ideal for implementing all sorts of data structures. One simple structure is the *property list*, so called because it associates keys, called *properties*, with values. A property list is simply a list of alternating properties and values. Order is not important: to look up the value for a given property, one looks at the first, third, fifth, etc., element of the list, and when a match is found, the very next list element is the value. New associations are formed by attaching the new key and value to the front of the list.

The simplicity of lists gives them their power and flexibility. Complicated nested objects can be built, and these can be manipulated as a single, compound object. While some languages provide lists as a basic data structure, and are therefore called *list-processing languages*, any language that provides pointers and simple structures can be used to build lists. For example, the operations *cons* (to build a node—short for construct), *car* (to examine a node's head—the name is historical), and *cdr* (to examine its link) are basic to Lisp, because of its origin as a list-processing language. However, any language in which one can build a node, access its fields, and link nodes with pointers can be used for list processing. Examples are Pascal, C (*q.v.*), Ada (*q.v.*), Modula-2 (*q.v.*), and Snobol-4. Languages that contain list processing operations as primitive (integral) parts of the language are covered under "LANGUAGES," the second part of this article.

Since the relationship between elements of a list, represented by separate nodes, is explicit, it is very easy to insert and delete elements (see Fig. 3). Given the list of 5, 8, 9, from above, it is simple to insert the number 6 in order: make a node containing 6 as its head with its link pointing to the node containing 8, and then change the first node's link to point to the new node. The corresponding insertion for a one-dimensional array would require moving the 8 and 9 up one element and writing the 6 in the emptied location. Similarly, deleting an element from a list simply involves changing a link to one node to point to the next node, and splicing out the deleted node. The corresponding array deletion again requires copying. This principle can be extended to more than one connected node; thus, entire lists may be spliced in and out and combined.

Note that the key-value association of a property list lies in its use, not in a particular arrangement of nodes and pointers. A property list is simply a list whose elements are interpreted in a particular way, and whose purpose is to serve as a table pairing keys and values. A different kind of list, the *association list*, can perform the same function with a different structure. An association list is a list of pairs; each pair contains a key and its associated value (remember that a node field, even the usual link field, can contain any data object). To look up the value for a given key, one looks at each pair in the list, comparing the pair's key with the desired key. When a match is found, the value is the other field of the pair.

Both property lists and association lists can be used as tables, and there is no real advantage in choosing one over the other. The important idea is that they can be used to implement the "table" concept, and if the lookup procedures are written well, programs that use them will not need to know what kind of structure lies beneath the table. Indeed, some versions of "table" may change internal representation from lists to trees to hash tables as the table grows.

The explicit sequencing of lists can be used to implement sparse arrays, arrays in which the majority of the elements are zero. If the array is large, substantial space can be saved if the zeroes can be omitted. Using lists,

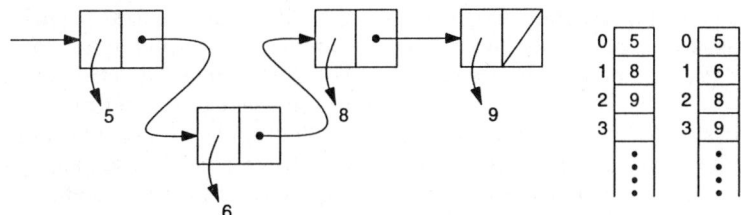

FIG. 3.   Insertion in a list and a one-dimensional array.

either as a table or in some more specialized structure, with one node per nonzero element, the array can be built in such a way that it appears as if all elements are present, but that occupies much less storage. It is also flexible: as elements become nonzero, new nodes are added, and as elements become zero, nodes are removed. There will be a cost in access time, but for some problems that cost will be outweighed by the ability to fit the problem into the computer at all.

Lists can also be used to implement trees and other graph structures (*see* GRAPH THEORY). Pair nodes can be linked into simple binary trees, and larger nodes into trees of greater degree or with data at the nodes of the tree. Larger nodes can even be simulated by lists built from pair nodes. Since list nodes can contain pointers to arbitrary data objects—even other nodes in the same list—graph structures of all complexities can be built by connecting nodes together.

Two other structures easily built with lists are the *stack* (*q.v.*) and the *queue*. A stack is just a list of elements (sometimes called a pushdown list); again its utility comes from its interpretation, not its particular structure. To push an object onto the stack, make a new node containing the object, link it to the stack, and then use that new node as the new head of stack. To pop an object off, change the stack pointer to point to the next element and discard the old head. Since, by the definition of "stack," only the first element of a stack may be accessed, only the internal sequencing of the list nodes is needed.

Similarly, queues can be built as lists of elements, with insertion defined as attaching a new node to the end of the list and deletion the same as a stack's. To attach new nodes to the end of the list, it is often most efficient to keep a pointer to the last node as well as the pointer to the first node; in fact, one might keep both pointers in another node, thereby combining all the parts into one compound data object.

Extensions of the List Concept

Note that insertion and deletion require a handle on the two nodes on either side of the insertion or deletion point. This requirement is a consequence of the single pointer between nodes—the sequencing information contained therein is in one direction only. *Doubly-linked lists*, in which each node contains three fields, a datum, and two pointers, do not have this requirement. Each node in a doubly-linked list has a pointer to both its successor and its predecessor, so an insertion or deletion requires only the knowledge of one node. This idea can be generalized into lists whose nodes have any number of pointers to nodes considered neighbors for one reason or another, and at least one list-processing language had this feature. In general, though, singly-linked lists are sufficient for most purposes, with doubly-linked lists common in some applications.

For some problems, simple lists are not enough. Sometimes one wants to represent truly infinite lists, such as a list of all the prime numbers. This kind of infinite structure can be built with an extension to the list concept, *lazy evaluation*. The idea of lazy evaluation is to create only those elements that are actually accessed. If a program looks at the first 10 primes, or the first 20, only that many will be created, but the list appears to contain them all. The key is to put a procedure in the last node of the list that will calculate the next element when it is accessed. Each time a program looks at the next element, the procedure will calculate it, attach it to the list, and attach itself to the end. If no one accesses beyond a certain point, those elements are not calculated; all elements up to that point are calculated once and left in the list. As far as the program using it is concerned, the list is indeed infinite.

References

1976. Horowitz, E. and Sahni, S. *Fundamentals of Data Structures*. Potomac, MD: Computer Science Press.
1985. Abelson, H. and Sussman, G. *Structure and Interpretation of Computer Programs*. Cambridge, MA: The M.I.T. Press.

PAUL FUQUA

LANGUAGES

A list processing language is a computer language that facilitates the processing of data organized in the form of lists. Lisp, Comit, Sail, and Pop-2 are typical list processing languages.

External List Representation   We begin with some simple examples to show what kinds of problems are solved by list processing and also how the lists look as they are used for input and output.

Traditional Notation	List Notation
French to English translation:	
Où est le Métro?	(OU EST LE METRO?)
Symbolic integration:	
$\int xe^{x^2}\,dx$	(INT X * (E ** (X ** 2)))
Logic:	
$(\supset x)(Q(x)\vee \sim P(x))$	(ALL X (QX) OR (NOT(PX)))
Automatic question answering:	
Who is on first?	(WHO IS ON FIRST?)

The list is a convenient way of representing nonnumerical data, such as English sentences, mathematical formulas, a position in a game, logic theorems, or computer programs. The structure of a list is a natural way to represent the structure of data for the computer. By nesting sublists, sub-sublists, etc. one can create list structures of arbitrary complexity. List processing techniques are especially useful for data that has variable structure, such as languages.

Some of the terms used in connection with list processing are used in slightly different ways by different writers. Some rough definitions are as follows.

An *atom* is the basic list element. It is not a list. An atom corresponds to a word in English. In the examples above, EST, INT, **, X and WHO are some of the atoms.

An *element* is one item on a list. It may be an atom or another list. Synonyms sometimes used for element are *node, item, record, entity,* and *bead.*

A *list structure* is a list whose elements may be atoms or lists or list structures.

A list is represented externally to the computer in terms of characters, and internally in terms of memory cells. The external representation (shown in the tabulated examples above) is designed for the convenience of the user and is used by the computer for input and output operations. The exact rules for writing a list vary from one language to another. In the preceding examples we have used the notation of Lisp. Parentheses indicate the beginning and end of a list, and blanks separate atoms.

Internal List Representation

The internal representation of a list is the way in which the computer stores the list in its memory cells. This varies from one language to another.

An important part of list processing concerns the way that lists are stored in memory. To clarify this point, a comparison will be made between the way lists might be stored in a conventional language such as Fortran and the way lists are usually stored in a list-processing language such as Lisp.

Fig. 1 is a simple list—(SEE (THE BIG) DOG)—as it might be stored in a Fortran array and also as it might be stored in the memory of a Lisp system. Each rectangle represents one memory cell or word. In the Fortran array, the list is stored in the conventional form of coded characters, one atom to a memory word. We assume here that the words are filled with blanks and are right-justified. Parentheses indicate the beginning and end of sublists.

The same list is represented in a Lisp system in the form of *pointers.* A pointer is the address of a memory word. Other terms sometimes used for pointer are *link*

and *reference.* In this example, each memory word is divided into a front half and a rear half. Each half contains the address of another memory word. Each such address is represented in the diagram as an arrow pointing to the word to which it refers. The characters of the atoms are located in a special part of the memory reserved for characters. The arrow pointing to SEE represents the address of a special memory word that represents the atom SEE. The other arrows pointing to atoms have similar meanings. The special atom NIL is used to mark the end of a list.

This type of memory organization has several advantages:

1. When adding or deleting items in the Fortran array representation, it is necessary to move down or move up all elements below the point at which the addition or deletion is made, whereas in the pointer type of organization, one can add or delete an element by changing only two pointers. If a list is large, this is an important saving of time.

2. If a single sublist appears in many main lists, it can be represented by one pointer in each main list, instead of repeating the entire sublist many times. This can save considerable memory space.

3. In Lisp, a sublist of any size can be added to or deleted from a main list by changing just two pointers. Thus, the processing of large sublists is more efficient.

4. In the Fortran array, adjacent elements of the list are physically adjacent in memory. In Lisp, adjacent elements are linked by pointers, so the memory cells need not be adjacent. This means that any available memory word can be used in any list. This allows more efficient use of memory space.

5. The Fortran programmer must estimate the maximum size of each list and then reserve that number of words for each array. In Lisp, the computer decides where to store lists while the problem is being run. This is called *dynamic storage allocation* and saves programmer effort.

6. Another advantage of Lisp representation is that, when searching a main list, one can easily skip over the sublists if this is desirable, but in the Fortran representation, one must search through each sublist in detail.

The Lisp Language

Data   The best way to gain a good understanding of list processing is to describe a typical list processing language in considerable detail. Lisp (short for LISt Processing) is the most popular of such languages. Lisp was developed by John McCarthy and his associates at M.I.T. during the late 1950s and early 1960s. Many details will be omitted.

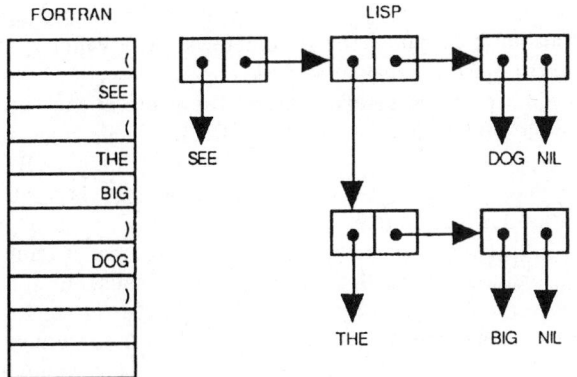

FIG. 1.   A simple list in Fortran and Lisp.

First we will define the data language that is used in Lisp. An "S-expression" (short for symbolic expression) is the general name for legal input data in Lisp. An S-expression is either an *atom* or a *list structure*. An atom is a string (sequence) of characters other than blanks or parentheses. The start and finish of each atom is indicated by parentheses or blanks. Numbers are atoms. A list structure consists of a left parenthesis followed by any number of atoms or list structures, followed by a right parenthesis. For example, each of the items below is an S-expression.

```
DOG
1984
(WHERE IS TURING NOW)
((MCCARTHY) IS MASTER OF (THE DARK TOWER))
(LIST STRUCTURE ((((CAN))) BE (((VERY)))
    ((((((DEEP)))))))
```

Let us consider how data is represented internally in the computer memory. The memory is divided into two parts: free storage and full-word space. The free storage contains the list structure in pointer form, as described earlier. The full-word space contains the characters in atoms.

An atom is represented internally as a special list in free storage space. The second half of the first word of an atom is a pointer to the *property list* of the atom. This property list contains information about that particular atom. Some typical properties are *print name* (a pointer to the characters of the atom name in full-word space), *value* (if the atom is a variable), and *function definition* (if the atom is a function name). Also, the programmer can add properties to any atom at will. For example, an atom that is an English word might be given ADJECTIVE or NOUN as a property. The Lisp reading routine checks each newly read atom against a list of all atoms known to the system. If the atom is already known, a pointer to the existing atom is used. Otherwise, a new atom is created.

Numbers may also be used in Lisp. They may be integers, fixed-point, or floating-point numbers. All Lisp functions that operate on numbers automatically test the number type and perform needed conversions. The word NIL is a special atom in Lisp and is used to mark the end of a list. By itself, NIL just means the "empty list" ( ).

Programs The language for writing programs in Lisp is actually a subset of the data language. Therefore, it is easy to write Lisp programs that operate on other Lisp programs (e.g. compilers, optimizers, interpreters).

Lisp has a reputation among programmers as being a difficult language to use. This is an illusion caused by the unconventional syntactic style of Lisp. Actually, by any measure of complexity, Lisp would have to be judged one of the simplest computer languages extant. The basic unit of a program in Lisp is the *form*. A form is usually a function with its arguments. Almost all Lisp forms follow the basic format: (function arg$_1$ arg$_2$...arg$_n$). Other kinds of forms are variables and constants, which are just atoms. The only other kind of form is the conditional expression, which has the format: (COND (arg$_1$ arg$_2$) (arg$_3$ arg$_4$)...). Since one form can be the argument for another, large programs can be built by nesting.

Lisp has few special rules and exceptions. It was designed by mathematicians and therefore has the virtues of mathematical elegance and simplicity. The semantics of Lisp are also straightforward. The Lisp system contains a program called the *interpreter*. The interpreter reads a Lisp form and then prints the value of that form. To understand a Lisp program (a form), one must know what value the interpreter will produce when evaluating that form.

The simplest form is a *variable*. A variable is any atom to which a value has been assigned. The value is a pointer to some S-expression. For example, a variable X may have as value a list of three elements (A B C). The other atomic Lisp form is the *constant*. A constant is simply a variable that has been assigned itself as a value. Typical constants are numbers, T, and NIL. The constant T means "true," and NIL means "false" and also "end of list." The QUOTE form is written (QUOTE a), where "a" can be any S-expression. The value of (QUOTE a) is "a." The argument is not evaluated. This is how data is put into a program.

The next kind of Lisp form is the SUBR form (short for subroutine). CAR is a SUBR function that returns the first element of a list. If X has the value (A B C), then (CAR X) has the value A. A companion to CAR is CDR, which returns the rest of the list. The value of (CDR X) is (B C). One can use nested CARs and CDRs to isolate any fragment of an S-expression. The names CAR and CDR are historical fossils. They relate to assembly language on the IBM 704 computer, the first machine on which Lisp was implemented. The term CAR is short for "Contents of the Address part of Register," and CDR is short for "Contents of the Decrement part of Register."

The SUBR function CONS (short for construct) is used to build S-expressions. CONS takes two arguments. The second is an existing list, and the first is a new element for that list. If Y has the value A, then (CONS Y X), with X as above, has the value (A A B C). Lisp also contains predicates: ATOM is a predicate of one argument. A predicate is either true or false: (ATOM X) has the value T for truth if X is an atom; otherwise, NIL for false.

Predicates are particularly useful in conditional forms, the Lisp equivalent of a branch instruction. The following is a typical conditional form:

```
(COND ((ATOM X) X) (T (CAR X)))
```

The arguments of a conditional form come in pairs. In each pair, the first is the predicate part and the second is the value part. The interpreter evaluates conditional pairs from left to right. If the predicate has the value T, the interpreter then evaluates the second portion of the conditional pair and returns this as the value of the entire conditional form. If (the value of) the predicate is NIL, the interpreter starts to work on the next pair. If X is (A B C), the value of the sample conditional form above is A, since (ATOM X) is NIL and (CAR X) is A.

The LAMBDA form is a way of assigning local or temporary values to variables. (The name is reminiscent of the *lambda calculus*, on which Lisp is based.) The LAMBDA form consists of a LAMBDA function followed by some arguments. A LAMBDA function is a list of three elements, for example,

```
(LAMBDA (X Y) (CONS Y X))
```

The second element is a list of LAMBDA variables, the third is a form that uses those variables. Arguments may be added to a LAMBDA function to make a complete form according to the usual syntactic rule: (function arg$_1$ arg$_2$...arg$_n$).

The results look more complex than other forms, since the LAMBDA function is a list of three elements, instead of just one atom like the other functions. An example of a complete LAMBDA form is:

```
((LAMBDA (X Y) (CONS Y X)) (QUOTE
   (A B C)) (QUOTE A))
```

The interpreter first evaluates the arguments. These values are then assigned to the corresponding variables on the LAMBDA variables list. The form in which the LAMBDA variables appear (the internal form) is then evaluated, and this value is then the value of the entire LAMBDA form. In the preceding example, X will have the value (A B C) and Y will have the value A. Thus, the internal form, (CONS Y X), will have the value (A A B C), and this will be the value of the entire LAMBDA form.

An EXPR function is a function written by the Lisp programmer. The programmer can make any atom into a function by assigning to that atom a suitable Lisp expression. Below is an example of a simple EXPR function being defined and then used. In this example, TIMES means multiply and DEF means DEFINE.

```
(DEF SQUARE (X) (TIMES X X))
(SQUARE 9)
```

The DEF form in the preceding example will assign, to the atom SQUARE, an EXPR property with the value (LAMBDA (X) (TIMES X X)). When evaluating (SQUARE 9), the Lisp interpreter will first look up the definition of the EXPR function, as given on the property list of the atom, and then evaluate the LAMBDA form. Thus, the value of (SQUARE 9) is 81.

Recursive Functions. A useful property of Lisp is the ability to evaluate a recursively defined function, i.e. a function that uses its own name as part of its definition. For example,

```
(DEF LAST(X) (COND
   ((ATOM (CDR X)) (CAR X))
   (T (LAST (CDR X)))))
```

where LAST searches a list of one or more elements and returns the last element of that list. (ATOM (CDR X)) is true only if X is a list of just one element. If X is a list of two or more elements, LAST calls itself and shortens the list by removing the first element. Eventually, the list is shortened to just one element. Then (CAR X) is returned, which is the last element of a one-element list.

How can a recursively defined function be evaluated? When the Lisp interpreter is evaluating an EXPR function and it encounters another call of the same function, it simply obtains a pointer to the definition from the property list of the atom. The interpreter saves its place in the old definition by putting a pointer on an internal structure known as the *pushdown stack*. The evaluation procedure is exactly the same, whether the function happens to be the same as the one being evaluated or a different one. In the preceding example of the function LAST, the recursion depth will be equal to the number of elements in the list being searched.

A Lisp function may also call itself at several different places in its definition (possibly with different arguments). A Lisp function may also call itself implicitly. For example, function FNA may call FNB, which then calls FNA again. One must take care that a recursive function is not given a circular definition.

The Reclaimer The *reclaimer*, or *garbage collector*, aids the dynamic storage allocation in Lisp. It periodically searches memory to locate list structures that are no longer needed. The memory cells in this *garbage* are then added to the *list of available space* (free storage) to be used in making new list structures. Reclaimers are also used in most other list processing languages.

A Practical Lisp Program As a practical example to illustrate the use of Lisp, we will now write a program to differentiate algebraic expressions. Polish prefix notation is used for the algebraic expressions. Variables may be indicated by letters of the alphabet, such as X, Y, and Z. Constants may be indicated by other letters or by numbers. These may be added or multiplied by the special symbols PLUS and TIMES, as used in polish prefix notation:

(PLUS X A) means $X + A$
(TIMES 3 X) means $3X$

Larger expressions may be built up by nesting:

(PLUS 3 (TIMES X X)) means $3 + X^2$

The program will carry out four mathematical rules of differentiation:

1. $dX/dX = 1$.
2. $dc/dX = 0$.
3. $d(\text{PLUS Y Z})/dX = (\text{PLUS } (dY/dX) (dZ/dX))$.
4. $d(\text{TIMES Y Z})/dX = (\text{PLUS } (\text{TIMES } dY/dX \ Z)$ $(\text{TIMES } dZ/dX \ Y))$.

The program to carry out these rules is straightforward. The top-level function, call DIF, takes two variables—E, the expression to be differentiated, and X, the variable of differentiation. Also, DIF uses a conditional form to decide which of the four rules should be applied. The fifth alternative is an error message, in case none of the four rules applies.

The subfunction DIF1 applies rule three above. DIF2 applies rule four. DIF1 and DIF2 each take three arguments—E2, E3, and X. E2 and E3 are the second and third elements of the expression E, which was given to DIF. The form (CAR (CDR E)), which occurs in DIF, obtains the second element of E. The form (CAR (CDR (CDR E))) obtains the third element of E. The last subfunction, DIF3 is called by DIF2 to handle the innermost part of the TIMES differentiation rule.

Note that DIF1 and DIF3 call DIF, the top-level function. Thus, DIF is a recursive function. This recursive design allows DIF to differentiate expressions that are nested to any depth. Thus, this simple program can handle algebraic expressions of arbitrary complexity. Here is the program listing.

```
(DEF DIF (E X) (COND
  ((EQ E X) 1)
  ((ATOM E) 0)
  ((EQ (CAR E) (QUOTE PLUS))
    (DIF1 (CAR (CDR E)) (CAR (CDR (CDR E))) X))
  ((EQ (CAR E) (QUOTE TIMES))
    (DIF2 (CAR (CDR E)) (CAR (CDR (CDR E))) X))
  (T (CONS (QUOTE ERROR) E))))
(DEF DIF1 (E2 E3 X) (CONS (QUOTE PLUS)
  (CONS (DIF E2 X)
  (CONS (DIF E3 X) NIL))))
(DEF DIF2 (E2 E3 X) (CONS (QUOTE PLUS)
  (CONS (DIF3 E2 E3 X)
  (CONS (DIF3 E3 E2 X) NIL))))
(DEF DIF3 (E2 E3 X) (CONS (QUOTE TIMES)
  (CONS E2
  (CONS (DIF E3 X) NIL))))
```

Below is a use of the DIF and the value that is returned by the computer. The problem is to differentiate $3X^2$:

```
(DIF (QUOTE (TIMES 3 (TIMES X X))) (QUOTE X))
```

to get the result $6X (= 3(X + X) + X^2 \cdot 0)$

```
(PLUS (TIMES 3 (PLUS (TIMES X 1) (TIMES X
 1))) (TIMES (TIMES X X) 0))
```

It is obvious that this program could use a subroutine to simplify the answers.

Other List Processing Languages

IPL-V is the grandparent of all list processing languages. It was developed by Allen Newell and his associates at the RAND Corporation and later at Carnegie-Mellon University. IPL is an acronym for Information Processing Language, a choice that reflects the lack of competition when the name was selected. IPL-V is the fifth member of the IPL family. IPL-V was the first language to use lists made of memory cells linked with pointers, but garbage collection was the programmer's responsibility.

The programming language Comit (*see* STRING PROCESSING) was originally designed for research on the mechanical translation of Russian into English. It was based on the notations used by some linguists working on this problem. Comit was generalized into a general-purpose language sufficiently powerful to perform any data processing task. In addition to the usual list processing advantages of automatic storage allocation and efficient manipulation of strings, Comit has pattern-matching capability.

The language Slip differs from other list processing languages in two main ways: It is embedded in Fortran and uses symmetric lists. Embedding in Fortran means that, except for a small number of assembly language subprograms, all Slip primitive functions are written in the form of Fortran subprograms. Slip programs are written as a series of Fortran subroutine calls. This makes it easy to use standard Fortran subroutines with a Slip program.

Data is represented in memory by Slip cells. A Slip cell is two or three memory words (depending on the implementation) that are physically adjacent. The cell represents one element of a list. It contains a pointer to the next cell on the list, a pointer to the preceding cell on the list, and some alphanumeric data. The data may be an atom or the name of another list.

Since Slip cells contain pointers in both directions, it is as easy to search a Slip list backward as it is to search it forward. This is why Slip lists are called *symmetric*. Many Slip functions come in pairs—one forward and one backward. In most other list processing languages, the programmer must save a pointer to the start of a list and start from there if any backtracking is necessary.

The language Pop-2 is a descendant of Lisp and Algol. It was developed by R. J. Popplestone in the Department of Machine Intelligence and Perception at the University of Edinburgh. Programs written in Pop-2 look very much like Algol. Pop-2 is a very general language with many ingenious features. It might be described as a combination of Algol and Lisp. The pushdown stack is accessible to the programmer. The compiler is a subroutine that can be called by a program. An automatic reclaimer is available. Pop-2 is also extensible with little difficulty in terms of data structures and the programs to handle them.

Extensions and Applications

1. *Data types*. The programmer is allowed to define new data types in a convenient way. Examples are *n*-tuples, unordered sets, etc.

2. *Control structures*. Multiarchies are now replacing hierarchies. In a hierarchy, the program control structure is like that of a tree. Multiarchies allow greater freedom. In some languages, any subroutine may call any other. Two subroutines may be executed simultaneously (simulated). Conditional interrupts, known as *demons*, are sometimes used.

3. *Deduction*. Built-in deductive mechanisms allow the programmer to specify what result is desired without telling the computer exactly how to do it. Planner, Conniver, MicroPlanner, and Popler are four languages with powerful deductive capabilities.

4. *Pattern matching*. The style of matching found in Comit has been extended in other languages, such as Snobol-4 and Icon (*see* STRING PROCESSING). Patterns for matching are known as "skeletons," or "templates."

5. *Knowledge representation* (*q.v.*). Special features make it easy to put domain-specific knowledge into the computer. One example is KRL (Knowledge Representation Language), developed by Bobrow and Winograd.

6. *Symbolic mathematics*. For example, the programs Macsyma, Mathematica, Reduce, Derive, and Maple are used by researchers all over the

world to perform symbolic mathematical operations, such as integration, differentiation, expansion, simplification, and solving differential equations (*see* COMPUTER ALGEBRA).

7. *Hardware execution.* Computers have been built for the direct hardware execution of Lisp programs. Such computers are known as Lisp machines.

8. *Automatic programming.* Research continues on automatic program synthesis from axiomatic specifications, from information specifications, or from examples. Automatic documentation and proving programs to be correct are other active research areas.

9. *Common Lisp.* Common Lisp (Winston and Horn, 1989; Koschmann, 1990; Steele, 1990) combines the best features of previous dialects of Lisp. It is the commercial standard and is supported by many computer manufacturers.

References

1961. Newell, A. (Ed.). *Information Processing Language-V Manual.* Englewood Cliffs, NJ: Prentice-Hall.

1971. Burstall, R. M., Collins, J. S., and Popplestone, R. J. *Programming in POP-2.* Edinburgh: Edinburgh University Press.

1971. Findler, N. V., Pfaltz, J. L., and Bernstein, H. J. *Four High Level Extensions of Fortran IV: SLIP, AMPPL-II, TREETRAN and SYMBOLANG.* New York: Spartan Books.

1989. Winston, P. H. and Horn, B. *LISP, 3rd Edition.* Reading, MA: Addison-Wesley.

1990. Koschmann, T. *The Common LISP Companion.* New York: John Wiley and Sons.

1990. Steele, G. L. *Common LISP, 2nd Edition.* Bedford, MA: Digital Equipment Corporation.

JAMES R. SLAGLE

LITERACY, COMPUTER. *See* COMPUTER LITERACY.

LITERATE PROGRAMMING

For articles on related subjects *see* DOCUMENTATION; MACROINSTRUCTION; METAFONT; STRUCTURED PROGRAMMING; and TEX

Literate programming is a system of combining program and internal documentation so that they may be co-developed with ease. A literate programming system provides automatic aids to readability such as substantial cross-referencing, indexing, and pretty-printing. Special macro processing allows the program to be written in any order to improve and simplify the exposition. Macros are numbered automatically so that their usage is easily cross-referenced.

A literate programming system converts documentation and code into beautifully typeset material with no additional effort by the programmer. All features combine to simplify and encourage the documentation process and to keep it in very close correspondence with the

actual program. Efficient means are provided to extract the program code from the literate program so that it may be compiled or processed in the usual way. Consider the following extract from the source of a literate program that illustrates interleaving of code, documentation, and macros. The @ signs are a system convention for introducing various literate programming features.

```
.
.
.
@*Insertion sort
This is the standard insertion sort
    algorithm.
Assumes a sentinel at $a[0]$.
@p
for i := 2 to N do
begin v := a[i]; j := i;
@⟨Insert...@⟩
end
@
@⟨Insert $v$ in the array@⟩=
while a[j-1] > v do
begin a[j] := a[j-1]; j := j-1 end;
a[j] := v
.
.
.
```

The example shows the use and definition of a macro called <Insert v in the array>. Note also that macro names may be abbreviated (e.g. <Insert...>), which encourages programmers to use mnemonic names. The $ symbols tell the literate programming system to typeset and cross-reference certain text as code rather than as commentary. The result of processing the example fragment is shown in Fig. 1.

Literate programming need not be confined to programming languages and conventional documentation of programs written in those languages. The idea of combining different types of text to make them easier to maintain together is quite general. Kurokawa [1985] exhibits a runnable Pascal program documented in Japanese, and another obvious application is the combination of formal specification with conventional program. The symbolic mathematics system *Mathematica* uses a form of literate programming in its "notebooks" (see Wolfram, 1988). *Mathematica* allows mathematical articles to be written, mixing text with mathematical formulas that can be evaluated. No cross-referencing is provided, but, as with literate programming, the very close proximity of "documentation" and "code" helps ensure their mutual correspondence. Other possibilities and advantages are suggested in Thimbleby (1986).

Literate programming was developed by D. E. Knuth in the late 1970s and has been used most successfully in the implementation and documentation of his large typesetting system, TEX. The clarity resulting from the technique has been instrumental in the range of its successful implementations. Knuth's programs are unique in being published in their entirety as readable books (*see* Knuth 1986). Other programs have also been published, of

```
for i:=2 to N do
begin v:=a[i];j:=i;
while a[j−1]>v do
begin a[j]:=a[j−1];j:=j−1 end;
a[j]:=v
```

Generated code.

31. Insertion sort. This is the standard insertion sort algorithm. Assumes a sentinel at $a[0]$.

for $i := 2$ **to** N **do**
begin
  $v := a[i]$; $j := i$;
  ⟨Insert v in the array. 32⟩
end
32. ⟨Insert v in the array. 32⟩≡
  while $a[j - 1] > v$ **do**
  begin $a[j] := a[j - 1]$; $j := j - 1$ **end**;
  $a[j] := v$;
Used in section 31.

Typeset program.
Excluding automatically generated table of contents, index etc.

FIG. 1.

course, but they are not as readable, nor are they in *exactly* the form in which they may be compiled and run.

References

1984. Knuth, D.E. Literate Programming, " *Computer Journal*, **27**, *2*, 97–111.

1985. Kurokawa, T. "Literate Programming," *BIT* **17**, 4, 426–450. (pub. Kyoritsu Shuppan). Japanese translation of Knuth (1984).

1986. Knuth, D. E. "Computers and Typesetting Series," TₑX: *The Program*, Vol. **B**; *METAFONT: The Program*, Vol. **D**. Reading, MA: Addison-Wesley.

1986. Thimbleby, H. W. "Experiences of 'Literate Programming' Using cweb (A Variant of Knuth's WEB)," *Computer Journal*, **29**, *3*, 201–211.

1988. Wolfram, S. *Mathematica*. Reading, MA: Addison-Wesley.

1989. Knuth, D. E., Larrabee, T., and Roberts, P. M. "Mathematical Writing," *MAA Notes*, 14. Washington, DC: Mathematical Association of America.

1991. Cordes, David and Brown, Marcus. "The Literate-Programming Paradigm," *Computer* (IEEE), **24**, *6* (June) 52–61.

HAROLD THIMBLEBY

LITERATURE OF COMPUTING

Before 1947, the only computing literature concerned analog computers (then called "analyzers"), punched card machines, and calculations made with pencil and paper or desk calculators. No periodicals were devoted to the subject. The literature was sparse, entirely technical, and was scattered through the publications of mathematics, statistics, physics, electrical engineering, and other sciences, especially astronomy. At that time a few books (for instance, Whittaker and Robinson's *Calculus of Observations*, Scarborough's *Numerical Mathematical Analysis*, and Eckert's *Punch Card Methods in Scientific Computation*) could, in retrospect, be said to have dealt exclusively with computing, although their subject matter was then considered to be part of applied mathematics. Contrary to legend, science fiction literature did not foreshadow the stored program digital computer, and except for the machine for writing books discovered by Captain Lemuel Gulliver on the flying island of Laputa (as reported in 1726 by Jonathan Swift), did not mention computers at all.

Since then, the situation has changed completely. We encounter computers and their literature everywhere and every day. Chain bookstores have several shelves exclusively devoted to computer books and special magazine racks displaying current issues of the most popular computer periodicals. More than 500 magazines and newspapers are published worldwide, covering everything from Artificial Intelligence (*q.v.*) to Unix (*q.v.*). Only doctors have more professional periodicals. Computer books in print exceed 5,000. In addition, there is a wide variety of constantly replenished other literature such as research reports, trade publications, theses, patents, proceedings of conferences, abstracts and indexes, dictionaries, encyclopedias, data compilations, and product catalogs. Each year, many thousand technical and popular articles about computing are published. The computer is a common part of the background of all current writing, reporting, fiction, non-fiction, stage and TV drama, and movies.

The literature of computing, especially original technical publication, is almost entirely in English. In the past half-century, the few commercial efforts to provide English translations of Russian and Japanese computing literature have failed for lack of source material as well as customers.

Bibliographic and Basic Literature

Guides and Lists There are no overall summaries or lists of all computer literature, other than the usual library references such as *Books in Print*, which contains several dozen categories relative to computing and programming.

Since 1960, the Association for Computing Machinery (ACM) has published annual indexes to the technical literature, *ACM Guide to Computing Literature*. The *Guides* include references to everything reviewed in the monthly *Computing Reviews* plus 15,000 to 20,000 additional citations from all major publishers in the computing field, including scholarly journals and trade magazines. They provide the most comprehensive coverage of the technical literature for the year. The *Guides'* emphasis on the technical and neglect of the popular, including personal computing, reflects the orientation of the ACM. The *Guide* is available in printed form, as a CD-ROM product, as well as on-line on *Dialog* through the *Math/Sci* file and on the *CompuScience* file of STN.

Lists of several hundred technical periodicals giving addresses are printed annually in *Computing Reviews* and quarterly in *Computer Literature Index*. These lists are added to but seldom thinned out and consequently include too many titles of the deceased.

The abstract journals listed below publish bibliographies on specific subjects at irregular intervals. The articles in *Computing Surveys* will often include reference lists that amount to comprehensive subject bibliographies. The ACM Special Interest Group newsletters will sometimes publish bibliographies. Now and then, some intrepid librarian will attempt to publish a list for a narrow fashionable specialty (e.g. Expert Systems (*q.v.*) or Networks (*q.v.*)), but the flood of material soon overwhelms and outdates all efforts.

There is no comprehensive listing of miscellaneous literature. Publication catalogs of the principal computer societies list their available conference and symposia proceedings and reports of their technical and special-interest divisions.

Abstracts Although most of the significant original technical material on computing appears in a relatively small number of core journals, there is some relevant material in the journals of other disciplines. Computing is now recognized as a science and a technical art in its own right, but it is also an important service discipline, and thus much computer literature is interdisciplinary. Current abstracting services ameliorate this problem of volume and scatter of computer literature to some extent. The principal abstract services listed below overlap in their coverage of periodicals, conference proceedings, research reports, patents, books, movies, and academic theses. No one service attempts to cover everything. All but one are issued monthly, have indexes, and regularly publish cumulative indexes.

> *Computer Abstracts*—U.K. and international orientation. Strong in applications.
> *Computer and Control Abstracts*—U.S. and U.K. orientation. Strong in computer hardware, control technology, and subjects related to electrical engineering.
> *Computer Literature Index*—A quarterly devoted to U.S. trade publications, general business and management periodicals, and the less esoteric and academic publications of the professional societies. Most entries include a one-sentence abstract.
> *Computing Reviews*—U.S. orientation. Strong in programming, software, and theory. Unique in that reviews are critical and signed. Occasionally compares several books in a single review.

Glossaries, Dictionaries, and Encyclopedias The glossary that should be on the shelves of all serious computer users is *A Glossary of Computing Terms: An Introduction*, edited by the British Computer Society and published by Cambridge University Press, 1989. Its 92 pages are beautifully produced and illustrated and its definitions are concise and accurate. *The Computer Glossary* by Alan Freedman, AMACOM, 1989, is a longer alternative that is more directed toward personal computing.

The best current dictionary is *Que's Computer User's Dictionary* by Bryan Pfaffenberger, published by Que Corporation, 1990. It is written to be read with informative as well as advisory entries. The book you are reading was the only one or two-volume encyclopedia until 1992 when *Encyclopedia of Computers*, edited by Gary G. Bitter, was published by Macmillan. It contains about 210 articles in 1,000 pages in two volumes. The only possible alternative to these is a badly outdated 12-volume giant, the *Encyclopedia of Computer Science and Technology*, edited by Jack Belzer *et al.* (Dekker, 1975–1979).

Annual Reviews The publication of annual review volumes, popular when computers were new, has apparently proven unprofitable, the only survivor being *Advances in Computers* (Academic Press), which started in 1960.

Introductory Books Out of the hundreds of introductions to computers for laypeople, the best combination of easy reading, accuracy, and attractive illustrations is the first volume of the Time-Life series, *Understanding Computers*. The later volumes are less satisfactory.

Texts and Professional Books

Introductory Texts Any of the following four books will give a good, well balanced introduction to academic computer science. They all use Pascal. Detailed critiques appear in *Computing Reviews* for June 1990:

> *Introduction to Computer Science: A Structured Problem Solving Approach*, by Ali Behforooz and Onkar Sharma (Prentice-Hall).
> *Principles of Computer Science: Concepts, Algorithms, Data Structures, and Applications* by M. S. Carberry, A. T. Cohen, and Hatem M. Kahalil (Computer Science Press).
> *Introduction to Computer Science (3rd Ed.)* by Neill Graham (West Publishing Co.).
> *Computer Science 2: Principles of Software Engineering, Data Types, and Algorithms*, by Henry M. Walker (Scott Foresman).

Classic Texts Several hundred publishers produce college textbooks on computing, at least half amounting to instructional manuals on programming, with Fortran, Cobol, Basic, Pascal, and C being the most popular languages. Since 1980, publishers have given up publishing general computing books and have focused narrowly on machines, systems, particular software packages, and languages, but some of the older texts are classics that have stood the test of time and are still fully accepted and often referenced. They are:

> *The Art of Computer Programming,* by Donald E. Knuth (Addison-Wesley, 1968–1973), is a three-volume omnibus survey of computer science written with style and wit. It has been recognized for two decades as the definitive statement of the fundamentals of computer science.
>
> *The Psychology of Computer Programming,* by Gerald Weinberg (Van Nostrand Reinhold, 1971), was the first to suggest that programmers are people, that they have egos, and that people and their behavior are as important to a project as technical issues.
>
> *Software Engineering Economics,* by Barry Boehm (Prentice-Hall, 1981), is crammed with 767 pages of encyclopedic information on measuring, modeling, and estimating almost every aspect of systems development.
>
> *The Mythical Man-Month,* by Fred Brooks (Addison-Wesley, 1975), is the classic identification of the root-problems of software project management, problems that are so fundamental that every new manager must discover them anew, in spite of Brooks.

Professional Books The great book editor, the late Karl Karlstrom, once pointed out that the average programmer must own less than one computer book, since the total number of serious professional books sold was less than the number of serious programmers. Knuth or one of the following programming classics should be that single volume:

> *Programming Languages: History and Fundamentals,* by Jean E. Sammet (Prentice-Hall, 1969), is complete and accurate in its history and surprisingly still definitive and reliable in spite of its age. Its author promises a revision.
>
> *Structured Programming,* by O.-J. Dahl, Edsger Dijkstra, and C. A. R. Hoare (Prentice-Hall, 1972).
>
> *The Elements of Programming Style,* by Brian Kernighan and P. J. Plauger (McGraw-Hill, 1974).
>
> *Algorithms + Data Structures = Programs,* by Niklaus Wirth (Prentice-Hall, 1976).
>
> *A Discipline of Programming,* by Edsger Dijkstra (Prentice-Hall, 1976).

Periodicals

Three types of periodicals may be distinguished according to their character, objectives, and intended beneficiaries. Academic periodicals report original results, are refereed, and are published for the benefit of the authors and their peers. Commercial periodicals interpret original results for practitioners, report and evaluate new products and practices, are professionally edited for clarity and interest, and are published to sell the products of their advertisers. News publications are a form of commercial publication in which content currency is the most significant criterion.

Academic Periodicals The best are those of the principal societies. None have circulations of more than 100,000, the size of the two major societies, and most have less than 10,000. They are: *The Journal, Communications,* and *Transactions* (on *Mathematical Software, Database Systems, Programming Languages and Systems, Information Systems, Computer Systems, Graphics, Software Engineering and Methodology,* and *Modeling and Computer Simulation*) of the ACM; *Transactions* (on *Computers, Software Engineering, Knowledge and Data Engineering, Parallel and Distributed Systems,* and *Pattern Analysis and Machine Intelligence*) of the IEEE Computer Society, as well as the magazines *Computer, IEEE Computer Graphics and Applications, IEEE Micro, IEEE Software, IEEE Expert,* and *IEEE Design and Test; The Computer Journal* of the BCS; *Mathematics of Computation* of the AMS; and the *SIAM Journals* on *Computing, Applied Mathematics,* and *Numerical Analysis.* In addition, the many subgroups of the societies publish unrefereed newsletters of variable quality.

Some academic periodicals are published commercially; for example, *Journal of Computer and System Science* and *Journal of Algorithms* (Academic Press), *Information Science, Artificial Intelligence,* and *Theoretical Computer Science* (Elsevier), *Acta Informatica* (Springer-Verlag), *Information Processing and Management* (Pergamon), and *BIT* (Data A/S, Copenhagen). The best of the academic periodicals published by industrial organizations, because of rigid reviewing, outstanding editing, and intracorporate rewards to authors, are the *IBM Journal of Research and Development,* and the *IBM Systems Journal,* which are equal in content quality to the best of the society journals.

Appendix III lists over 50 research journals and their publishers.

Commercial Periodicals The split between dispersed personal computers and centralized mainframes is reflected in commercial periodicals for which readers pay more than $100 million a year and advertisers pay almost $700 million. The PC end-user publications, many of which started as hobbyist journals, are consumer publications with large circulations and low buying power per subscriber. *PC Magazine,* with a circulation of 700,000, is the biggest, followed by *BYTE, PC World, Personal Computing,* and *PC Computing,* each with close to half a million subscribers. They focus chiefly on the description and analysis of PC-ware, both hard and soft. By fielding two magazines, *PC Magazine* and *PC Week,* Ziff Communications manages to hold almost half of the U.S. market. The principal magazines devoted to the Apple Macintosh family are MacWorld and MacUser.

A major contributor to the worldwide proliferation of computer magazines is International Data Group, which has some 150 titles in 49 different countries, including a dozen in Russia and Eastern Europe, each slightly different from the other.

The commercial periodicals directed at mainframes (*q.v*) are specialized business publications with lower circulation numbers, sent free to qualified subscribers who are selected for their control of major purchases, but referred to by the publishers as "computer professionals." The oldest, *DATAMATION*, another part of the Ziff empire, leads with a circulation of almost 200,000, followed by *Information Week, MIS Week, Computerworld*, and a string of more narrowly specialized magazines and newspapers whose numbers and page counts rise and fall with the advertising budgets of the vendors of the computing world. Bi-weekly *DATAMATION*, like its monthly competitors, looks like a magazine and mixes simplified technical articles with market surveys, news, and comment. The weeklies look like newspapers and mix news with interminable crusading and repetitive didactic articles.

On the basis that the technical content is not limited to original results, *The Computer Bulletin* of the BCS, *Data Management* of DPMA, *The Journal of Systems Management* of the ASM, *Computer* of the IEEE Computer Society, and *Communications* and *Computing Surveys* of the ACM might be categorized with commercial periodicals. In each case, refereeing procedures are applied to the technical content, resulting in dramatically superior contents. Furthermore, in contrast to commercial publications, the number of pages of text far exceeds those of advertisements.

Conference Proceedings Publication of papers in proceedings of professional computing conferences often takes the place of publication in academic periodicals. Although conference refereeing is seldom as strict as that of the leading academic journals, the published material is sometimes significant. The important regular technical conferences are those of the principal computer societies and their subgroups (i.e. the ACM), largely concerned with programming and the mathematics of computing, and the IEEE Computer Society, slightly more concerned with hardware than with software. Their conference publications, several hundred a year, are listed in *Communications of the ACM* and *Computer*.

Collections of Computer Data

Hardware and Software Information Services Auerbach Publishers, Faulkner Technical Reports, Information Age Publishing, and several others publish reports on hardware and software, giving specifications, prices, characteristics, comparisons, and advice. Some of the periodicals mentioned above do the same thing, at lower cost to the reader, for the more varied personal computing facilities.

Each software vendor publishes its own product list. Lists of free software or software for sale are out of date, incomplete, or limited to a narrow specialty and valid only for a brief moment. Periodical advertisements are a more up-to-date guide. Programs themselves on floppy discs are available from some personal computer periodicals. Since 1960, the ACM has offered the quarterly *CALGO*, (*Collected Algorithms from ACM*), which gives code listings of some of the shorter algorithms from ACM journals.

Directories The field is so large that there is no complete directory of all U.S. computer installations, or of vendors of computers and computer services, or of people in the entire computer field. Available directories are limited in their coverage to niches, like Artificial Intelligence or Local Area Networks (*q.v.*).

History and Biographies

The history of computing is already being written. Some pioneers have recorded their memoirs; for example, *The Computer from Pascal to von Neumann*, by Goldstine (Princeton University Press, 1972), *Memoirs of a Computer Pioneer*, by Maurice Wilkes (M.I.T. Press, 1985), *A Few Good Men from Univac*, by David E. Lundstrom (M.I.T. Press, 1987), *From Bits to Dits*, by Herman Lukoff (Robotics Press, 1979), and *Models of My Life*, by Herbert Simon (Basic Books, 1991). Three excellent early collections of papers and conference proceedings are *The Origins of Digital Computers: Selected Papers*, B. Randell, ed. (Springer-Verlag, 1973), *A History of Computing in the Twentieth Century*, N. Metropolis *et al.*, eds. (Academic Press), and *A History of Programming Languages*, R. L. Wexelblat, ed. (Academic Press, 1981). Since 1979, the scholarly quarterly, the *Annals of the History of Computing*, now under the aegis of the IEEE Computer Society, has encouraged the study and documentation of the history of computing by providing a refereed publication outlet for those who will write on the subject.

The best of the shorter biographical accounts are published in *Annals*. There are several book-length biographies of Charles Babbage (*q.v.*), Babbage's own *Passages from the Life of a Philosopher*, the Morrison's *Charles Babbage and His Calculating Engines*, Mabeth Moseley's *Charles Babbage, Irascible Genius*, and Anthony Hyman's *Charles Babbage, Pioneer of the Computer*. Dorothy Stein has written a life of Augusta Ada Byron, later Countess of Lovelace (*q.v.*) and Babbage's interpreter, in *Ada, A Life and a Legacy* (M.I.T. Press, 1985), chiefly to tell how badly women were treated. *John von Neumann and Norbert Wiener: from Mathematics to the Technologies of Life and Death*, by Steven J. Heims, is a double biography plus an account of science in their days. Alan M. Turing (*q.v.*) was first memorialized by his mother, Sara, in *Alan M. Turing*, and more recently popularized by Andrew Hodges in *Alan Turing, the Enigma*. The early biographies of Thomas J. Watson, Sr., (*q.v.*) the authorized version, *The Lengthening Shadow*, by the Beldens, and the unauthorized version, *THINK*, by William Rodgers, have now been corrected and expanded by his son, Thomas J. Watson Jr., in his own autobiography, *Father, Son, and Co.*

The histories of a few firms and their machines have been written, most notably in the M.I.T. Press Series in the History of Computing: *Memories that Shaped an Industry*, by Emerson W. Pugh, 1984; *IBM's Early Computers*, by Bashe, Johnson, Palmer, and Pugh, 1986; and *IBM's 360 and Early 370 Systems*, by Pugh, Johnson, and Palmer, 1991. An Wang tells his story in *Lessons* (Addison-Wesley, 1988), and James C. Worthy tells about ERA in *William Norris, Portrait of a Maverick* (Ballinger, 1987). The Apple story so far is available in several versions, chiefly John Sculley's *Odyssey* (Harper and Row, 1987) and Frank Rose's *West of Eden* (Viking, 1989). Tracy Kidder in *The Soul of a New Machine* (Little, Brown, 1981) intended to tell the history of one machine, but may have told the history of Data General. *Project Whirlwind* (Digital Press, 1980), by Redmond and Smith is a somewhat uncritical account of this breakthrough machine. Beyond these there is little corporate history worthy of note. (*See also* ENTREPRENEURS.)

The fight over who was the first true inventor of the electronic digital computer was stimulated by Nancy Stern's *From ENIAC to UNIVAC* (Digital Press, 1981), and has since produced one polemic biography, *Atanasoff, Forgotten Father of the Computer*, by Clark R. Mollenhoff (Iowa State University Press, 1988), an excellent account of the ENIAC in *The First Electronic Computer, The Atanasoff Story*, by Alice R. Burks and Arthur W. Burks (University of Michigan Press, 1988), and a continued flurry of dispute in *Annals* and elsewhere.

In 1988, ACM Press launched a History Series with Adele Goldberg's *A History of Personal Workstations*.

The Charles Babbage Institute (*q.v.*) is performing a remarkable service for historians by reprinting the key literature of early computing, including long out-of-print textbooks, reports, collections of papers, and conference proceedings. To date, they have published almost two dozen volumes.

Miscellaneous Literature

Standards The significant computing standards are produced by the American National Standards Institute (ANSI) and the National Bureau of Standards (*Federal Information Processing Standards*) in the U.S. and the British Standards Institution and the National Computing Centre in the U.K. International standards, usually derivative from those of the U.S. and the U.K., are published by the International Standards Organization (ISO).

The National Bureau of Standards annually publishes a *Federal Information Processing Standards Index*, which summarizes standard publications at all levels—federal, national, and international. (*See* STANDARDS.)

Trade Literature Vast quantities of free descriptive and promotional material are distributed by vendors. The purely factual, descriptive, and instructional manuals are valuable and important. The remaining trade literature is a form of commercial advertising and is usually worth what the vendor charges for it. There is no general listing or abstracting of such literature, each vendor maintaining its own listing, often in an uncoordinated fashion. IBM is the exception. It has a comprehensive but overwhelming list of its own literature.

Patents Although, in principle, patents (available by mail for $1.50 each from the U.S. Patent Office) should provide complete and comprehensive descriptions of the devices, methods, processes, or programs patented, their titles are deliberately vague and uninformative, and the disclosures themselves are written in an arcane, wordy, and laborious jargon that makes them generally useless as informative literature.

Fiction, Drama, Movies, and TV The computer figures naturally and importantly in technology-oriented literature and drama. Occasionally, a computer takes a major role, as with HAL in *2001, A Space Odyssey*, but literary works dealing with computers are chiefly limited to a lot of average quality science fiction. Computer people are stereotypical nerds or hackers (*q.v.*) as in John Updike's *Roger's Version* and the movie *Wargames*. Clifford Stoll playing himself in the made-for-TV-movie of his own book, *The Cuckoo's Egg*, appears to be a caricature of a computer-besotted hacker, but probably conveys true picture.

The only Broadway play about a computing person was *Breaking the Code*, by Hugh Whitemore about Turing's tragedy, in which the title referred both to the Enigma machine and homosexuality.

Philosophy Essayists and social science writers are attempting to grapple with the philosophical and humanistic implications of computers and computing. Early anthologies by Taviss (*The Computer Impact*—Prentice-Hall, 1970) and Pylyshyn (*Perspectives on the Computer Revolution*—Prentice-Hall, 1972) have been succeeded by more recent works by authors who attempt to deal with the question, "Can computers think?" while knowing little or nothing about either subject. There are some exceptions. A few well-conceived and thought-provoking books of this genre amount to works of scientific criticism addressed to computing. Worth mentioning are *What Computers Can't Do*, by Hubert L. Dreyfus (Harper & Row, 1972), *Computer Power and Human Reason*, by Joseph Weizenbaum (W. H. Freeman, 1976), and most recently *The Emperor's New Mind*, by Roger Penrose (Oxford University Press, 1989).

Donn B. Parker has published three volumes on computer crime (*q.v.*): *Crime by Computer* (Scribner, 1979), *Ethical Conflicts in Computer Science and Technology* (AFIPS, 1980), and *Ethical Conflicts in Information and Computer Science, Technology, and Business* (QED, 1990). Douglas R. Hofstadter's effort to rectify the average person's ignorance of Gödel's Theorm, *Gödel, Escher, Bach, an Eternal Golden Braid* (Basic Books, 1979), won a Pulitzer Prize and must be classified as being related to the philosophy of computing.

Critical Literature *Computing Reviews* provides the only regular critique of the current literature, although other computer publications publish a few critical book reviews in each issue. Computer books are sometimes reviewed as trade books by the usual book reviewing mechanisms.

Humor Computer humor is generally represented by cartoons in the technical and popular press. Some of this material has been collected in the now out-of-print *Faith, Hope, and Parity*, Jack Moshman, ed. (Thompson Book Company, 1966).

Computing literature has contributed new words to the language. Some of those new words now accepted into the Oxford English Dictionary are *personal computer, backslash, boot, CD-ROM, clone, hacker, transportable, user,* and *WYSIWYG,* (although the first usage of "What You See Is What You Get" was most likely on the TV show, "Saturday Night Live," perhaps not watched in Oxford).

Is Software Literature? Computer programs are legally accepted as "writings" subject to the copyright law. Other than that, their status as literature is similar to that of pre–World War I movies; not yet culturally accepted, but maybe next year.

If the criterion for acceptance is quality of performance, the widely used PC operating system MS-DOS and PC application packages like WordPerfect and Lotus 1-2-3 are candidates. If quality of expression is the criterion, there are, as yet, no candidates.

ERIC A. WEISS

LIVERMORE AUTOMATIC RESEARCH COMPUTER (LARC)

For an article on a related subject *see* STRETCH.

The *LARC* (Livermore Automatic Research Computer) was one of the first of the high-performance giant computers. It was developed at the Sperry Univac engineering facilities in Philadelphia during the 1959–1960 period. LARC represented a manyfold increase in speed over any existing computer of that period.

Two LARC computers were manufactured. One was supplied to the Lawrence Radiation Laboratory in Livermore, California; the other was delivered to the former David Taylor Model Basin (now the Naval Ships Research and Development Center) located near Washington, DC. Both computers were phased out of service in the period 1968–1969. The consensus was that LARC was a technical success, but the high costs of manufacture did not justify further sales effort.

The basic LARC system was composed of two units. One was an input/output processor designed primarily to provide flexible, parallel, and coordinated control of the input/output equipment. The second was a computing unit designed to perform the arithmetic functions of the system. If increased computing capacity was required, the basic system could be expanded to include an additional computing unit. The computing unit was a parallel computer capable of both fixed and floating-point arithmetic operation. The number system was binary-coded decimal. Except for certain intercommunication facilities, the computing units and the input/output processor operated independently. Additions were performed in 4 μs, multiplications in 8 μs.

LARC had a high-speed magnetic core memory shared by the I/O processor and computing units. The memory was divided into units, each of which was capable of storing 2,500 computer words of 11 decimal digits plus a sign digit. Each unit of the memory contained all the necessary switches, read-write regenerate circuits, and intermediate storage to operate independently and in parallel with other units. The high-speed memory could be expanded to a maximum of 39 units, equivalent to 97,500 words. Eight units were used in the basic system

FIG. 1.   The LARC computer.

on a high-speed bus to provide an effective rate of one word every 1/2 μs.

The high-speed memory was backed up by a magnetic drum-file memory. Up to 24 magnetic drums could be included in the system. Each drum was capable of storing 250,000 computer words of 11 decimal digits. The magnetic drums featured an air-floated read/write head assembly, which achieved high reliability with high pulse densities because of the absence of mechanical contact between the head and the drum surface. A continuous data-transfer rate of 2,500 words every 83 ms was achieved between the drums and the computing unit by interlacing the sequential operation of the two drums.

LARC was the largest *decimal* computer ever built and is likely to retain that distinction forever.

MICHAEL M. MAYNARD

LOAD-AND-GO COMPILER

For articles on related subjects *see* COMPILER CONSTRUCTION; LANGUAGE PROCESSORS; LINKER; LOADER; and OBJECT PROGRAM.

The process of running a computer program is generally a two-step sequence: the process of translating the program (compilation) from its human-like source language into executable machine code, and then execution of that code. Where the program is expected to be used many times without modification, such as in an accounting or payroll situation, the cost of repeated compilation can be avoided by separating the two processing steps: 1) a single compilation stage (which provides an *object program* that is stored on some auxiliary storage medium such as disk), and 2) (at later times) the repeated execution of the resultant code. In this situation, the compiler should be as efficient as possible in generating the minimal code for the program. Therefore, additional computer time is justified at the compilation stage in order to save considerably more time during the succeeding execution runs.

In a debugging (*q.v.*) or educational environment, on the other hand, where the expectation of repeated runs of the same compiled program is minimal, the cost of highly efficient compilation and its consequent time consumption must be weighed against the time used in executing the generated code. In general, in this type of environment, the time used in generating efficient code far outweighs the time saved by that code, and thus a fast compilation is more desirable than a quick execution.

Further, since the compilation is expected to be followed immediately by the execution of the generated code, the two phases can be permanently linked together. Where possible, the generated code is retained in the working memory (as contrasted with the process of generating an intermediate output onto a scratch tape or disk area and then requiring the reentry of the code prior to the execution phase) so that, as soon as the compilation is complete, control can be transferred to the generated code without delay. This process is known as *load* and *go*

and was the basis for many university systems, such as WATFOR (University of Waterloo Fortran) and its successor, WATFIV, and PUFFT (Purdue University Fast Fortran Translator). The most widely used commercial load-and-go compilers are those for the languages Pascal and C (*q.v.*) marketed by the Borland and Microsoft corporations for use in IBM PC and PC-Compatible computers (*q.v.*).

References

1965. Rosen, S. *et al.* "PUFFT—The Purdue University Fast Fortran Translator," *Comm. of the ACM* **8**, 11: 661–666 (November). (Also contained in Rosen, S. (Ed.), *Programming Systems and Languages*. New York: McGraw-Hill, 1967).

1967. Shantz, P. W. *et al.* "WATFOR—The University of Waterloo Fortran IV Compiler," *Comm. of the ACM* **10**, 1: 41–4 (January).

1980. Wilder, W. L. Comparing Load and Go and Link/Load Compiler Organizations," *AFIPS Conference Proceedings* **49**: 823–826.

J. A. N. LEE

LOADER

For articles on related subjects *see* ASSEMBLER; BOOT AND REBOOT; LINKER; and OBJECT CODE.

The function of a *loader* is to transfer a program held on some external storage medium such as magnetic disk into the main memory of the machine in a form suitable for execution. There are three main types of loaders: *binary, relocating*, and *linking*. An important variant of the binary loader is the *bootstrap loader*, which is used for the initial loading of a program into an empty machine (*see* BOOT AND REBOOT).

Binary Loaders For a *binary loader*, the external form of the program to be loaded is an exact image of the binary pattern to be established in main memory. Thus, the loading process consists of one or more read transfers, and such complication as there is resides mainly in the checksums or longitudinal parity checks used to verify correctness of the transfers.

There must be room in memory for both the loader and the program being loaded. The loader may be kept in a reserved area, or it may be placed in a position where it is known that no program will be loaded. A more sophisticated solution is to include in a header block not only the address at which loading is to commence, but also the size of the program to be loaded. The loader, which is itself written in relocatable form, reads these items and then copies itself into a place in memory outside the area to be loaded.

Relocating Loaders A relocating loader differs from a binary loader in that some of the addresses in the program to be loaded are expressed relative to the start of the program rather than in absolute form. These addresses have to be adjusted by the loader by adding a suitable constant to put the program into an executable form. This type of source material, commonly called

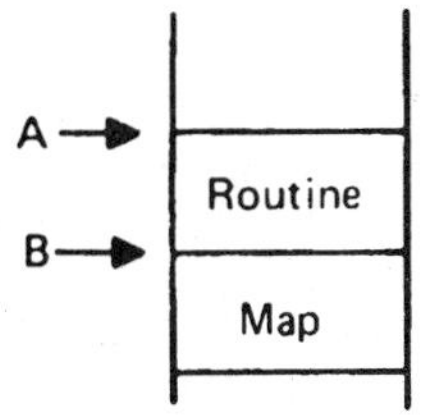

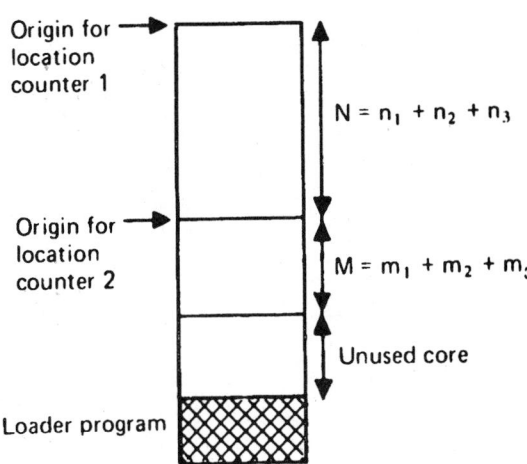

FIG. 1. Initial action of loader.

relocatable binary, is typically produced as output by a linker.

If the machine in question uses a base-and-displacement addressing system (as, for example, the IBM System/370), only address constants will need relocating. If the architecture is such that instructions include absolute addresses (strictly speaking, absolute in the virtual address space), then all memory reference instructions will require relocation. The relocation information may be concentrated in one place in a *relocation map* that contains in coded form the positions of all the addresses requiring relocation, or each individual word may be tagged to show whether or not it is to be relocated.

In the first case, the loader first reads the routine and its map into storage, as shown in Fig. 1. (The routine is preceded by a header block giving its length, thus allowing address B to be computed.) The map is then scanned and the specified words in the routine are relocated by having the address A added to them. If individual words are tagged, the loader examines the flag associated with each incoming word to decide whether or not to add the relocation constant (i.e. the address of the start of the routine). When the routine is completed, the relocation constant is updated (i.e. set to B) and the process continued by reading the next routine and its map into core, starting at B.

A more elaborate form of relocating the loader will deal with multiple location counters. [For example, an assembler output (Fig. 2) may contain code and literal constants: At run time, the literal constants for the entire program must be in a contiguous block, so they are conveniently described as being relative to a different *location counter* (Fig. 3). Similarly COMMON areas in Fortran can be dealt with conveniently using additional location counters.]

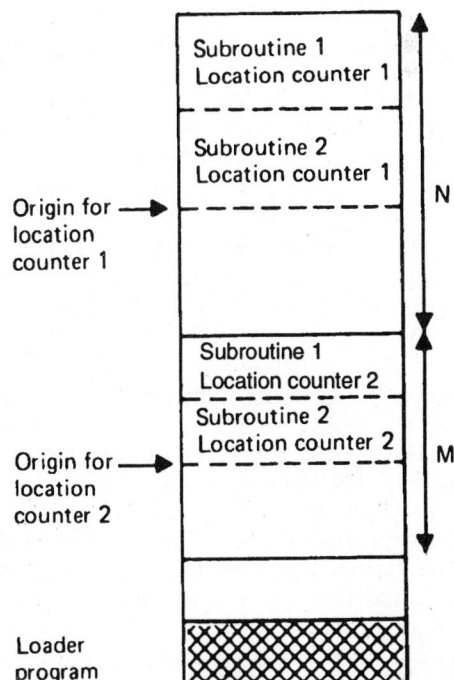

FIG. 3. Output of the assembler. Storage allocation after first pass.

In this case, each instruction is tagged to show to which location counter (if any) the address in that item is relative. The loader now becomes a two-pass process: The first pass computes the sizes of the blocks for each location counter and determines the displacement of their origins, and hence the appropriate relocation constants. The second pass loads and relocates, using the origins determined in the first pass. This process is illustrated in Figs. 2, 3, and 4. Observe in Fig. 4 that the loader is now performing a storage-allocation function.

Linking Loaders A *linking loader* combines the functions of a relocating loader and a linker. It combines into an executable program a number of program segments

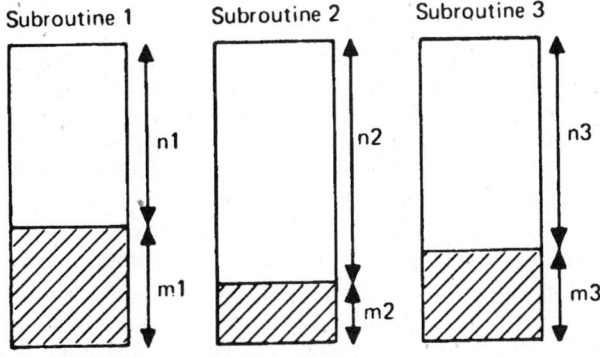

FIG. 2. Output of the assembler. White areas denote code and shaded areas denote literal constants to be stored relative to a second location counter, as in Fig. 3.

FIG. 4. Output of the assembler. Storage map after first two subroutines have been loaded.

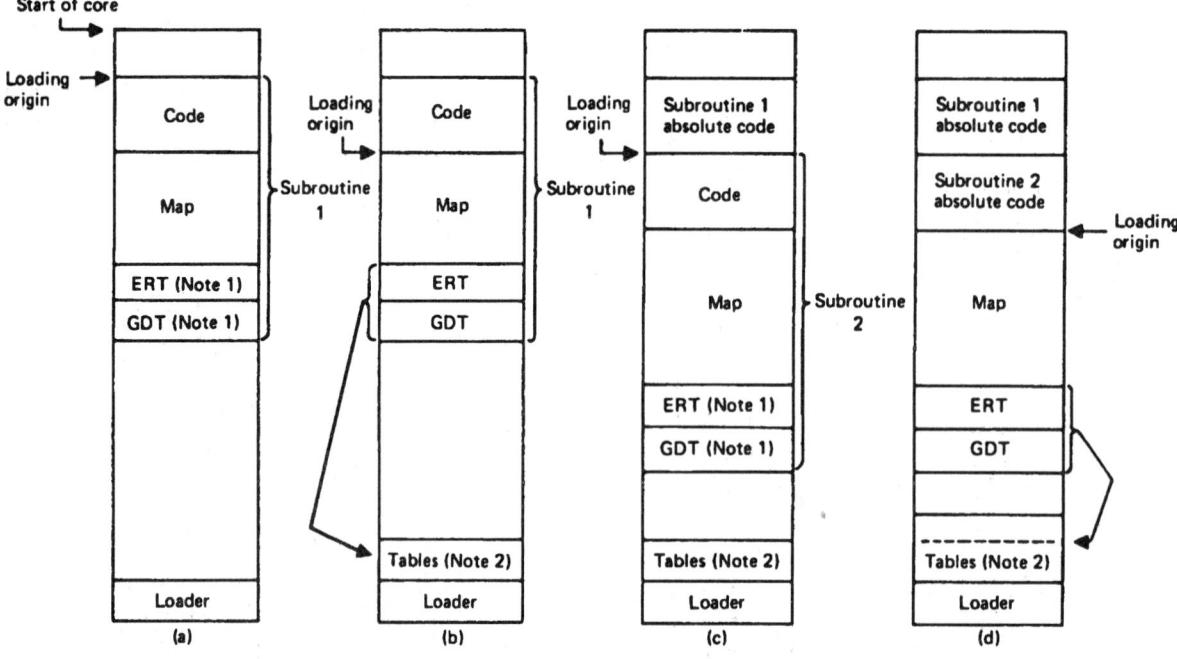

Notes:

(1) External reference table (ERT) and global definition table (GDT) entires have values relative to start of subroutine.

(2) Table entries now have values relative to start of core.

FIG. 5.   Stages in link loading: (a) after first subroutine read-in, (b) immediately prior to reading of second subroutine, (c) immediately after reading second subroutine, (d) immediately prior to reading third subroutine.

that have been independently compiled or assembled; thus, in addition to relocation, it must resolve the cross-references between the segments.

An independently compiled segment contains three kinds of information: *absolute information*, which is independent of the final position in memory (e.g. operation codes); *relative addresses*, which are expressed as displacements from the start of the segment; and *external references*. The output of the compiler will typically consist of a number of binary words, a relocation map as before, a table of external references, and a table of global symbol definitions. The external reference table contains the (relative) address of each external reference together with the symbolic form of the reference, and the table of global definitions contains the symbolic form and value (as a relative address) of each defined symbol.

The linking loader reads the first segment and its tables, noting the origin of the segment. This origin is used to adjust all relative addresses in the segment (via the relocation map), and in the external reference and definition tables. The entries from these two tables are copied to form the start of consolidated external reference and definition tables in some safe place (e.g. the top of the memory). The relocation origin is then reset to the end of the segment, and the next segment is read in, overwriting the tables of the preceding segment. The process of relocation is repeated and the external reference and definition tables are merged into the consolidated tables. (In order to conserve space in the consolidated tables, external references to symbols that are already defined can be filled in immediately.) The

process is repeated for all subsequent segments: After the last segment, all outstanding external references are filled in from the consolidated global definition table. Any unresolved references may be treated as errors or may be used to trigger the automatic scanning of a library of precompiled segments. The process is illustrated in Fig. 5.

Bootstrap Loaders   It is apparent that, to get a program into memory, we require a loader. But the loader is itself a program: How is it loaded? This is the function of the *bootstrap loader*, which is a very simple, small loader. Originally it had to be small enough to make it feasible to enter it into memory via the hand switches on the console. Today it has to be small enough to fit into a small read-only memory (ROM). The term "bootstrap" is appropriate because this loader is used to load a more elaborate loader (which may in turn load an even more elaborate loader...).

A typical system might consist of an eight-word program held in a read-only memory that is capable of reading 64 words of absolute binary from an unalterable peripheral device into a fixed place in memory (e.g. words 0 to 63). This is used to load a 64-word program that is capable of reading the first track (say, 256 words) on the first surface of the first disk found to be on line. This, in turn, can be a program that conducts a dialogue with the operator concerning available options, and then loads the "real" loader, which in turn loads the application program.

The most common use of a bootstrap loader on a large machine is for the initial loading of the operating system, but on a microcomputer the bootstrap loader is used to load most items of software.

References

1972. Barron, D. W. *Assemblers and Loaders*, 2nd Ed. New York: American Elsevier.
1980. MacEwen, G. H. *Introduction to Computer Systems Using the PDP-11 and Pascal* (Chapter 9: Linking, Loading and Interpretation.), New York: McGraw-Hill.

DAVID A. BARRON

LOCAL AREA NETWORK (LAN)

For articles on related subjects *see* BANDWIDTH; CONTENTION; CYCLIC REDUNDANCY CHECK; DATA COMMUNICATIONS; FIBER OPTICS; FILE SERVER; NETWORK ARCHITECTURE; NETWORK PROTOCOLS; NETWORKS, COMPUTER; PACKET SWITCHING; and WORKSTATION.

Origins and Taxonomy Early computer networks were developed during the late 1960s and the beginning of the following decade, a well-known example being the ARPAnet in the U.S. These networks were based on packet-switching principles, used telephone lines for the transmission media, and interconnected computers on a national and international scale. Typical line speeds ranged from 1,200-bit/s to 9.6 kbit/s, with some use of 50 kbit/s lines; the bit-error rate on such lines (which used analog transmission techniques) was of the order of 10^{-5}. As an example, on such networks it would take from one to ten hours to transfer the encoded text of Jane Austen's novel *Emma* from one computer to another.

During the early 1970s, a new kind of computer network was developed, the *local area network*, which restricts interconnection distances to a few kilometers and uses comparatively good cable to achieve transmission rates 10 to 1,000 times faster, with bit-error rates typically a million times better. More generally, a *local area network*, or *LAN*, is characterized by a number of attributes in which it differs from other networks. Of prime importance among these attributes is that all devices are directly connected to the cable or other transmission medium used by the LAN. Each packet transmitted by any station is seen by all the others, each of which examines the destination address field of the packet to determine whether it should receive it. As a consequence, the LAN does not have to perform any routing. Moreover, LANs are intrinsically capable of supporting broadcast communication by any station to all others (though this mode may not necessarily be offered by a particular product). Since there are no switching elements or buffers in the network, the only network resource for which stations have to contend is the transmission medium itself. A station also has to contend for the attention of the other station with which it wishes to communicate. All such contention and associated buffering takes place in the stations, not the network.

Size and Use The smallest LAN might typically be used in a classroom or small laboratory to allow a number of personal computers to share peripherals such as disks and printers. The length of cable in such an arrangement may be no more than 50 m. For larger installations, such as an office block, a LAN can be used to support a range of professional scientific, engineering, and administrative workstations requiring communal access to shared information storage and processing, and interchange of documents. LANs also have application in the manufacturing industry for controlling and co-ordinating individual processes in a production line. In such examples, several kilometers of cable might be needed. The largest practical LAN installations cover a whole site or campus, having, for example, a diameter of some 5 km and requiring 10 or 20 km of cable. In this case, the LAN is often used to interconnect a set of building or departmental LANs; as such, it is sometimes referred to as a *spine* or *backbone*.

Cost A variety of factors contribute to the cost of a LAN, the most obvious being the cost of cabling and the unit cost of connecting a device. The latter may range from little more than, say, a chip cost of $10, to a node cost in excess of $1,000. While the complexity of a LAN is largely contained in the circuitry of its node and the driving software in the host, the cost of a large installation can easily be dominated simply by the cost of installing the cables.

Speed Current data transmission rates for LANs range through three orders of magnitude from 100 kbit/s to 100 Mbit/s. An important property of a LAN is the low delay experienced by data traversing the network, a consequence not only of its limited range and high transmission rate, but also of the absence of any form of buffering in the network. Typical delays are in the range 10 to 100 μs. A design choice made in each type of LAN is the means by which the total transmission capacity of the LAN is apportioned among all active stations. This is intimately connected with the mechanism by which a station gains access to the transmission medium and has a direct bearing on the point-to-point data transmission rate achievable between any pair of stations.

Error Rate The most common forms of cable used for LANs are twisted pairs, coaxial cable, and optical fiber. As the price continues to drop, the last of these is becoming increasingly popular because of its good immunity to electromagnetic interference and its high bandwidth. Since in all cases the cable is both short and of good quality, it is comparatively easy to achieve high signal-to-noise ratios on the transmission medium and this leads directly to the low bit-error rates (BER) associated with LANs: 10^{-9} is considered acceptable, though 10^{-11} (or better) is more typical. Such rates are some 10^4 to 10^6 times better than those commonly obtainable using analog telephone lines and have a profound influence on the choices to be made about error recovery mechanisms used in LAN protocols.

Principles of Operation The two most common topologies that form the basis of LAN designs are the *bus* and the *ring*, shown in Fig. 1. The *star* topology, which connects a number of stations by bilateral links to some sort of

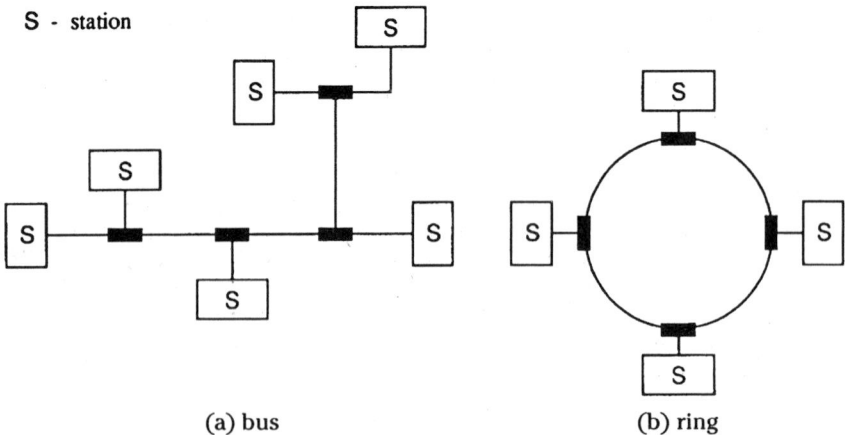

FIG. 1. LAN topologies.

central node, though discussed, is not in general use for LANs. A great variety of wiring topologies exist as derivatives of the basic bus and ring, engendered by requirements for practical and flexible cabling arrangements and for increased reliability, ease of operation, and expansibility. Considerable debate has occurred on the merits or otherwise of the fundamental topologies upon which LANs depend for their operation. The issues are blurred by the fact that practical forms of LAN can have wiring arrangements that effectively transform the topology. The classic example of this is the use of *wiring centers* in a ring (Fig. 2), which effectively transforms the installed cabling topology from a ring (Fig. 1(b)) to a bus (Fig. 1(a)). The variety of LAN designs is much too great to cover here. Instead, the basic principles of three designs, *ethernet, token ring,* and *empty-slot ring,* are described, which illustrate many of the features of current LAN technology. A more extensive treatment is to be found in Hopper *et al.* (1986).

Ethernet   This type of LAN was originally designed at the Xerox Palo Alto Research Center (Metcalfe and Boggs, 1976). In its simplest form, it uses a single length of coaxial

cable, terminated at the ends to prevent signal reflections, to which stations are attached by passive taps. A station wishing to transmit a packet first senses the transmission medium to see if another station is transmitting; if not, it begins its own transmission. There is a delay while the beginning of the packet propagates along the cable before all the other stations become aware that a transmission is in progress. During this *acquisition time,* another station may begin to transmit, resulting in a *collision.* The originating station listens to its own transmission and if a collision is detected, it aborts transmission of the packet and transmits a *jamming signal* to reinforce collision detection at other transmitters. For this scheme to work, packets must be long enough, at the transmission speed in use, that a station cannot finish transmitting before a collision has been detected. The length of this minimum-size packet is determined by the round-trip delay of the network, which increases with the size of the LAN. For the ethernet standard specified by DEC, Intel, and Xerox (known as the DIX ethernet), the worst-case configuration has a round-trip delay of 45 μs, or 450 bits at the specified 10 Mbit/s data transmission rate. When a collision occurs, the transmit-

Local Area Networks

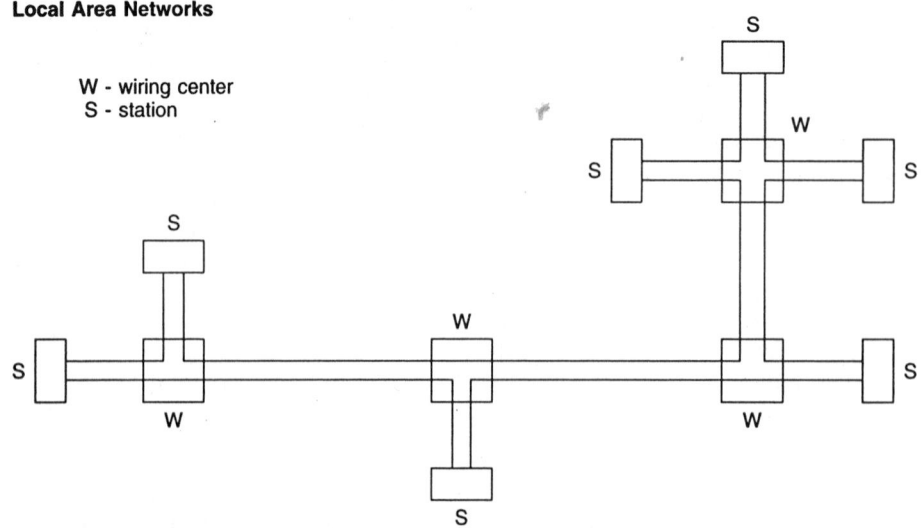

FIG. 2.   Use of wiring centers for ring.

ters involved wait for random lengths of time before retrying the transmission, in order to reduce the probability of further collisions. Nevertheless, under heavy traffic loading, the average time to transmit a packet can be long, and the worst-case time is unbounded.

Token Ring An alternative scheme for allocating access to the transmission medium is based on the use of a *token*. A station can transmit only when it holds the token. When it finishes transmitting, it passes the token on to the next station according to some appropriate algorithm. The usual arrangement for determining which is the next station is to define a cyclic ordering of the stations that are currently active. By restricting the maximum size of a packet that can be transmitted before the token must be relinquished, it is possible to specify the maximum time that a station may have to wait before being able to transmit. This single fact constitutes the main advantage that token-passing schemes have over the ethernet. Such advantage, however, is gained at the cost of a considerable increase in the complexity of the node circuitry, much of it associated with ensuring that the token is not lost, duplicated, or corrupted.

In the token ring, adopted by IBM, stations are arranged in a physical ring (Fig. 1(b)) and stations pass the token to the next active station in the ring. An alternative form of a token-passing scheme is implemented in the token bus by ordering stations that are active according to their node addresses. Each station passes the token to the station with the next higher address; the station with the highest address passes the token to the station with the lowest address. The token bus is favored for use in automated manufacturing; however, the station access circuitry is complex, dealing not only with token management but also the addition and deletion of nodes in the logical ring as they are switched on and off (a more complicated operation than the ring framing operation necessary for all physical rings). The access time associated with the token bus is generally longer than for the token ring because there is no relation between the address of a station and its situation on the bus, leading to a longer delay in passing the token.

Empty-Slot Rings Another way in which access to the transmission medium may be organized on a ring is by arranging to have a few continuously circulating small frames or *slots*, a few tens or hundreds of bits long. Each slot is marked full or empty. Any station at which an empty slot arrives may fill it with data, set the source and destination addresses, and mark it full. Variations are possible in the schemes for emptying the slot. One possibility is for the receiver to empty the slot, as is done in the Orwell ring developed by British Telecom (Adams and Falconer, 1984). Another variation, adopted in the designs developed at the University of Cambridge (Hopper *et al.*, 1986), is to allow the receiver to mark the slot and for the transmitter to note this response and empty the slot. The design trade-off is between superior data rate (Orwell) and providing information to the sender about the fate of a packet (Cambridge). An important property of empty-slot rings, not shared by the ethernet or token-passing

designs, is the potential for frequent, rapid, and regular access with small variation (jitter) in these parameters. Though currently not widely deployed, LANs with these properties may receive significantly more attention if LANs evolve as a segment of multi-service network provision. In this context, the ability to carry time-critical traffic will be of increasing importance.

Packet Format The general format of the packet or *frame* used for LANs is shown in Fig. 3. The first item is a *preamble*, which indicates the start of the frame; it may also be used to enable the receiver to synchronize. The preamble varies from as little as 2 bits for empty-slot rings, to 64 bits for 10 Mbit/s ethernets. The preamble is followed by destination and source addresses. These may be as short as 8 bits, but are more typically 48 bits. The data carried by the frame may be of fixed length, as for empty-slot rings, or of variable length. In the latter case, the length of the data can be indicated by terminating the frame with a delimiter (token bus and ring), by including a length field, or by detecting the end of a frame by the absence of signal (the ethernet, in effect, uses a combination of the last two). For the ethernet, padding is added at the end of the data field, if necessary, to ensure that the frame size (excluding the preamble) is never less than 512 bits. The frames for all types of LAN include some form of check to protect the integrity of the address and data fields. The check may be as little as a parity bit, but is more commonly a 32-bit checksum, typically a cyclic redundancy checksum (CRC). Any response bits follow the checksum and precede any frame-end delimiter.

Protocols and Standards

LAN standardization has been pursued primarily under the auspices of the IEEE 802 committees and has resulted in a series of standards covering ethernet, token ring, and token bus LANs. Owing to the fundamentally different ways in which LANs operate at the link and physical levels of the seven-layer reference model for open systems interconnection (OSI - *q.v.*), promulgated by ISO, an additional sublayer was introduced, known as the media access control (MAC) layer, which forms the lower of two sublayers in the OSI data link layer. It essentially encapsulates the principles of operation for the various forms of LAN described above. The upper sublayer is called the logical link control (LLC) layer. It provides essentially two modes of service: connectionless and connection-oriented. The former just caters for stations to exchange single packets, with as much indication about the success or otherwise of the operation as the MAC layer may provide. In connection-oriented mode, its purpose is to set up, maintain, and close down an orderly, flow-controlled, error-free logical link between two stations on a LAN. The mechanism and structure employed for this is similar to HDLC operating directly on a physical link. The mechanisms of the physical layer for LANs are quite diverse. The ethernet uses baseband signaling with

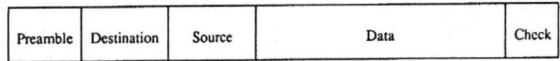

FIG. 3.   General format of LAN frame.

Manchester encoding and the main complication is in the detection of collisions. Rings have the property that they are constructed from unidirectional, point-to-point links and can easily use a variety of media, the commonest being twisted pairs and optical fibers. Signaling is usually baseband and commonly uses differential Manchester encoding. Frame synchronization typically relies upon phase-locked loop techniques and requires careful design to achieve stability. The token bus uses coaxial cable and is based on single- or dual-cable broadband cable TV technology; a number of different modulation and encoding schemes are used. In common with the token ring, ways of encoding symbols other than binary data are present and are used to encode network management and control signals. Further details of these topics may be found in Tanenbaum (1988) and Stallings (1987).

LAN Interconnection   LAN interconnection can take place at a number of levels of the ISO OSI model. Physical layer interconnections are peculiar to each type of LAN and do not exist in every case. Interconnection at layer three and above is the same as for other networks. At level two, the introduction of the MAC layer has given rise to a new technology and range of products known as MAC-layer bridges, an additional topic of standardization by IEEE 802. The possibility of such bridges arises from the intrinsic broadcast properties of LANs, as a consequence of which a node may operate in a *promiscuous* reception mode whereby it receives all packets on a LAN. A bridge is formed by a station having promiscuous connections to two (or more) LANs. By observing the source addresses of all packets on each LAN, the bridge develops tables of addresses located on each of its sides. In operation, if a packet is received on one side, destined for an address known from the tables to be on the same side, no action is taken; all other packets are forwarded to the other side and transmitted on the other LAN. This mechanism requires all LAN addresses to be distinct and of similar format, a possibility for IEEE-standard LANs. The effect of such bridging, which can include remote links between bridge halves, is to connect LANs so as to give the appearance of a single, large LAN. This is achieved without flooding the constituent LANs with every packet from each LAN. However, adjustments are needed in implementations of higher-level protocols to take account of end-to-end delays that are larger than normal. Considerable care is also required in the management of routing tables associated with higher layers.

Status   LANs conforming to the IEEE 802 (and corresponding ISO) standards are now in volume production and widely dispersed throughout the world. There are also a large number of proprietary LANs available. Currently, there is considerable activity concentrated around developing the technology and standards for LANs having data rates in the range 100 to 1,000 Mbit/s, an early example of which is the fiber distributed data interface (FDDI) defined by ANSI for a 100 Mbit/s token ring. Applications of such LANs are anticipated to include increasing use to communicate images, requiring increased capacity, and the provision of multi-service networking, requiring low delay and jitter characteristics for time-critical communication such as speech. A related application is in the interconnection of LANs by means of a spine or backbone LAN. Developments in this area include extending the range of the LAN to urban scales, a concept entitled the metropolitan area network (MAN - *q.v.*), which is being pursued for standardization purposes within IEEE 802.

References

1976. Metcalfe, R. M. and Boggs, D. R. "Ethernet: Distributed Packet-Switching for Local Computer Networks." *Comm. Assoc. Computing Machinery*, **19**, 7, 395–403.

1984. Adams, J. L. and Falconer, R. M. " 'Orwell': A Protocol for Carrying Integrated Services on a Digital Communications Ring." *Electronics Letters*, **20**, 23, 970–971.

1986. Hopper, A., Temple, S., and Williamson, R. C. *Local Area Network Design*. Reading, MA: Addison-Wesley.

1987. Stallings, W. "Local Network Standards." *Handbook of Computer-Communications Standards, Volume 2*. Indianapolis, IN: Howard W. Sams/Macmillan.

1988. Tanenbaum, A. S. *Computer Networks (2nd Ed.)*. Englewood Cliffs, NJ: Prentice-Hall.

CHRISTOPHER COOPER

LOCAL STORE

For articles on related subjects *see* GENERAL REGISTER; INDEX REGISTER; MEMORY: MAIN; and REGISTER.

The term *local store* (or *local registers*) is used to describe a relatively small number (usually less than 32) of high-speed storage elements that may be directly referred to by the instructions. In some systems these registers, because of their general-purpose usage, are called *general registers*. The contents of a cell in a local register is presumed to be readily available to the execution resources (the adder, etc.). By use of local registers, the main memory access time required for operand fetch can be reduced, thus minimizing the instruction execution time and improving the performance of the system. In addition, the size of the instruction can be reduced since fewer bits are required to identify one of the local registers than to identify a word in main storage.

Of course, not all operand references can be conveniently arranged in a single local store. Machines that use the local register concept may operate with a variety of instruction formats. This is illustrated by the System/370 RR and RX instructions, as shown in Fig. 1. In the RR instruction, the contents of register 1 (R_1) operate on register 2 (R_2), with the result replacing the contents of register 2. In the RX instruction, the contents of register 1 operate on an operand located in main memory, with the result replacing the contents of register 1. The RR instruction requires only 16 bits of storage, whereas the RX instruction requires 32 bits. In addition, the RX instruction requires the additional fetch of an operand from memory, which the RR instruction does not.

Similarly, machines that use RISC architecture (*q.v.*) may use a format to load or store a register value from or

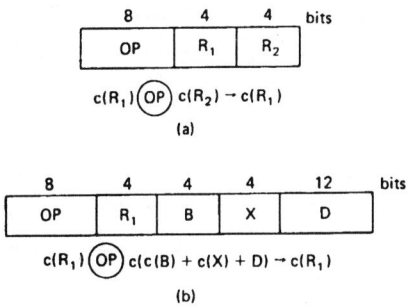

$$c(R_1)\ \boxed{OP}\ c(R_2) \rightarrow c(R_1)$$
(a)

$$c(R_1)\ \boxed{OP}\ c(c(B) + c(X) + D) \rightarrow c(R_1)$$
(b)

FIG. 1. System/370 instructions. (a) RR, register to register. (b) RX, register to memory; B, base register; X, index register; D, displacement.

to memory and a separate register-to-register format for all ALU-based operations.

Usually, local registers are implemented so that several may be accessed simultaneously. This allows two operands to be gated simultaneously into separate inputs of an adder. In most implementations, access to a local register is directly controlled by the instruction decoder through a simple gating scheme which requires only two logic delay units to retrieve the information from the register.

MICHAEL A. FLYNN

LOCAL VARIABLE. *See* GLOBAL AND LOCAL VARIABLES.

LOCKOUT

For articles on related subjects *see* CONCURRENCY CONTROL; CONCURRENT PROGRAMMING; CONTENTION; MULTIPROCESSING; MULTIPROGRAMMING; and MULTITASKING.

When several processes are executing simultaneously, it may happen that two (or more) of these processes want to access the same data. For example, in a system with multiple CPUs, two processors can be idle and request a new task at the same time. If no precaution is taken, both will access the table where the list of waiting tasks is stored, and both may initiate the same task. In a multiprogramming system a READ process and a WRITE process might share the same buffer area, so that the writer has to be protected from having its data garbled by the reader before the output is completed. To circumvent this problem, means must be provided to protect the shared data from unorderly changes. Such means are usually called *lockout*, or *mutual exclusion*. The portion of code in a process that accesses a shared area is called a *critical section* of that process.

At the hardware level, one can use instructions such as TEST AND SET and RESET, or the equivalent pair, LOCK/UNLOCK. Similar schemes have been proposed for high-level languages. In order to allow programs to be more independent, Dijkstra (1968) has defined a new type of variable, called a *semaphore*, which can take only non-negative integer values. Dijkstra's elegant solution is based on two primitive and indivisible operations on semaphores, namely:

$V(S)$ defined as: $S \leftarrow S + 1$.
$P(S)$ defined as: **if** $S = 0$ **then** block process
                         else $S \leftarrow S - 1$.

Basically, the philosophy behind the use of semaphores is as follows: For purposes of clarity we restrict the semaphore S protecting a shared database to take only the values 0 and 1. Initially, the semaphore is set to 1. Before entering a critical section, the process performs a P operation. If S is 1, the process decrements S and enters its critical section. Since S is now 0, no other process may enter its critical section. If S were 0, the process would be blocked and would remain so as long as another process was executing in a critical section. When a process terminates its critical section, it performs a V operation, setting S to 1 and thus allowing another process to enter its critical section.

The semaphore concept is now widely recognized as an efficient means of protection between cooperating processes and has been implemented in various forms in most operating systems.

Reference

1968. Dijkstra, E. W. "Cooperating Sequential Processes," in Genuys, F. (Ed.), *Programming Languages*. New York: Academic Press.

JEAN-LOUP BAER

LOGIC DESIGN

For articles on related subjects *see* ARITHMETIC-LOGIC UNIT; BOOLEAN ALGEBRA; CODES; COMPUTER ARCHITECTURE; COMPUTER CIRCUITRY; INTEGRATED CIRCUITRY; SEQUENTIAL MACHINES; and SWITCHING THEORY.

The term *logic design* refers to the process of specifying an interconnection of logic elements in digital computer hardware so that a desired function is performed. Examples of this process might be the design of a circuit that would accept data representing numbers in a gray code and convert this data into a binary-coded decimal representation, or the specification of the gates and interconnections required to implement the arithmetic unit of a computer. Both formal and ad hoc techniques are used to achieve the desired design.

All digital logic networks in current use operate on signals that are restricted to two possible values only, and are thus called *binary* values. While it is theoretically possible to design logic networks in which a larger number of discrete values are allowed for the signals (so-called multiple-valued logic networks), the discussion here will be restricted to binary logic networks, since these are the only type of networks in current use. For some binary networks, it is possible to specify the desired performance by means of a *table of combinations* (also called a *truth table*), as shown in Table 1, which lists each possible combination of binary signals on the inputs to the network and the corresponding combination of desired output signals.

In Table 1, (a) shows the table of combinations for a network having one input and one output. The output of this network will have a signal representing the zero value on it whenever the input signal represents a 1, and will have an output signal representing a 1 value whenever the input signal has a zero. Such a network is called an *inverter*, and the symbol used to represent it is shown in Fig. 1(a).

Actually, a network having such a simple performance as that of an inverter is usually realized as a single logic element and is not constructed out of more elementary subnetworks. An inverter is thus one of the basic building blocks from which more complex logic networks are constructed. Other basic building blocks, or *elementary gates*, are shown in Table 1 as (b), (c), (d), (e), and (f), with the corresponding logic symbols shown in Figs. 1(b), 1(c), 1(d), 1(e), and 1(f).

The table of combinations for a more complex logic network is shown in Table 2. This network has four input signals and four output signals. If the four input signals appearing on the network inputs represent one decimal digit encoded in the 8-4-2-1 code (i.e. binary-coded decimal (*q.v.*), or BCD), the four output signals will represent the encoding of the 9s complement of the input digit. Notice that in addition to having entries of 1 or 0, there are

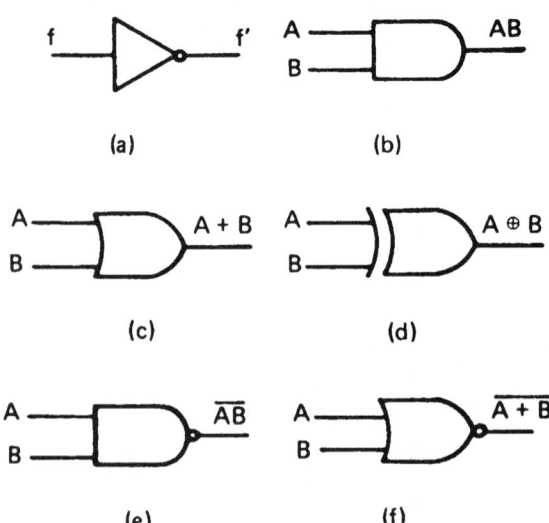

FIG. 1. Elementary gate symbols: (a) inverter; (b) AND gate; (c) OR gate; (d) XOR gate; (e) NAND gate; (f) NOR gate.

also entries in this table that are represented by a "d." This notation is used to indicate the fact that certain input combinations would not be expected to appear at the input of the network. Such entries are called "don't cares." A table of combinations that contains "don't care" entries is an *incompletely specified table of combinations*.

An incompletely specified table of combinations is actually a representation for a whole family of completely specified tables of combinations that would satisfy the given design requirements. Techniques exist that effectively choose a completely specified table of combinations that leads to the most efficient network design. An efficient network to realize the specifications of Table 2 is shown in Fig. 2. Using Table 2, the reader may verify that the equations given in Fig. 2 are correct.

The types of networks described thus far all have the

TABLE 1. Tables of Combinations for Elementary Gates

(a) Inverter		(b) AND gate		
Input f	Output f	Inputs A	B	Output f
0	1	0	0	0
1	0	0	1	0
		1	0	0
		1	1	1

(c) OR gate			(d) XOR (exclusive OR) gate		
Inputs A	B	Output f	Inputs A	B	Output f
0	0	0	0	0	0
0	1	1	0	1	1
1	0	1	1	0	1
1	1	1	1	1	0

(e) NAND (not AND) gate			(f) NOR (not OR) gate		
Inputs A	B	Output f	Inputs A	B	Output f
0	0	1	0	0	1
0	1	1	0	1	0
1	0	1	1	0	0
1	1	0	1	1	0

Note: See Fig. 1.

TABLE 2. Table of Combinations for Generating the 9s Complement of a BCD (8421) Digit.

	Inputs				Outputs			
	b_8	b_4	b_2	b_1	c_8	c_4	c_2	c_1
(0)	0	0	0	0	1	0	0	1
(1)	0	0	0	1	1	0	0	0
(2)	0	0	1	0	0	1	1	1
(3)	0	0	1	1	0	1	1	0
(4)	0	1	0	0	0	1	0	1
(5)	0	1	0	1	0	1	0	0
(6)	0	1	1	0	0	0	1	1
(7)	0	1	1	1	0	0	1	0
(8)	1	0	0	0	0	0	0	1
(9)	1	0	0	1	0	0	0	0
	1	0	1	0	d	d	d	d
	1	0	1	1	d	d	d	d
	1	1	0	0	d	d	d	d
	1	1	0	1	d	d	d	d
	1	1	1	0	d	d	d	d
	1	1	1	1	d	d	d	d

Note: See Fig. 2.

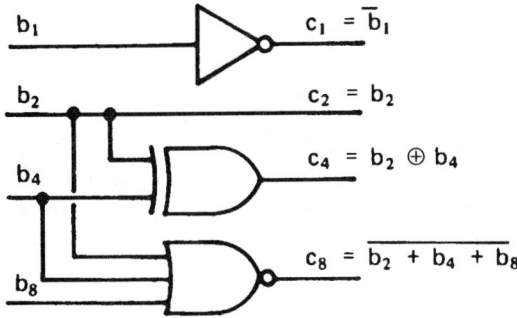

FIG. 2. Network for Table 2.

property that the output values at any given instant are dependent solely upon the input values present at the same time. Such networks are called *combinational logic networks*. The other type of logic network is called a *sequential logic network* or a *sequential circuit*. These networks have the property that their outputs are dependent not only on their present inputs, but also on the inputs that may have been present previously.

An example of a sequential circuit is a network whose input is a series of pulses on a single lead and whose outputs display the count modulo n of the number of input pulses. Such a circuit is called a *counter* (McCluskey 1986). Since the output of a sequential circuit at any particular time may depend on previous inputs, there must be contained in the circuit some mechanism for recording some information about these previous inputs. This function is achieved by providing feedback loops in the circuit that are capable of storing information in them. The most commonly used type of feedback loop consists of two gate elements interconnected, as shown in Fig. 3.

This type of circuit is called a *set-reset (S-R) latch* and operates as follows. The input combination $S = R = 1$ is not permitted. When input $S = 1$ and input $R = 0$, it follows from Table 1(f) that $Q' = 0$ and, therefore, $Q = 1$. Conversely, when $S = 0$ and $R = 1$, $Q = 0$ and $Q' = 1$. When the input that was 1 is changed to 0 so that both inputs are zero, the output remains equal to the value it had for the last non-zero input. Thus, when the inputs are both zero, the circuit "remembers" the last non-zero input. The circuit can thus be used to "store" information.

Fig. 3 is an example of a whole class of memory elements in which information is stored in interconnected gates. Such elements are known as *latches* or *flipflops*. Just

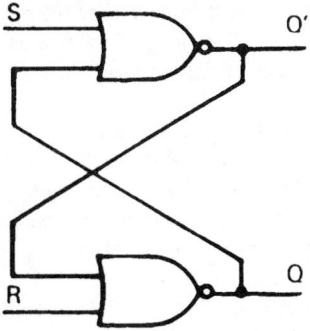

FIG. 3. Interconnected NOR gates forming an SR latch.

as a table of combinations is a formal representation for the performance of a combinational circuit, *flow tables* or *state diagrams* or *regular expressions (q.v.)* are used as formal specifications for the action of a sequential circuit (see McCluskey, 1986).

Formal techniques exist for determining logic networks that correspond to specifications given in the form of a table of combinations or a flow table. These formal techniques are the subject of the discipline known as *switching theory* (Kohavi, 1970). Classical switching theory is concerned mainly with the problem of designing optimum networks that correspond to given formal specifications. Algorithms have been developed for designing networks that contain a minimum number of gates under certain constraints; e.g. the condition that there be no more than two gates connected in series between any input and any output. While a great deal of attention has been devoted to the *minimization problem*—that of obtaining minimum element networks—this problem has been solved only for networks having very specific constraints, such as those mentioned above. General design algorithms with flexible constraints have proved to be very difficult to discover.

Formal techniques for the design of logic networks have an inherent limitation in that the size of the table of combinations, or flow table, tends to be proportional to 2^n, where n is the number of network inputs. A logic network with ten inputs is not a particularly large one, but a formal specification for such a network would require over 1,000 entries. The approach taken to overcome this difficulty is to partition logic networks into subnetworks of a convenient size. The overall network is then structured by interconnections of the subnetworks, the interconnections being determined by ad hoc rather than formal techniques.

Other motivations besides design convenience also lead to the use of building blocks more complex than elementary gates. With present-day integrated circuit technology used to realize the logic elements, much of the cost of an element is in its packaging and interconnections, and thus it pays to minimize the number of such packages and external connections. The way in which this can be done is by incorporating in an individual package a circuit more complex than an elementary gate. Two general approaches have been taken to determine the nature of the complex building blocks to be used. One approach is to attempt to identify the more common types of subnetworks that occur, and to manufacture individual integrated circuit packages incorporating the functions performed by these subnetworks. This approach is commonly called "medium-scale integration" (MSI). Some typical MSI elements are:

1. Full adder
2. Arithmetic-logic unit
3. Parallel binary multiplier
4. Magnitude comparator
5. Odd/even parity generator
6. Shift register
7. Register file (8 words of 2 bits, 4 words of 4 bits)

8. Data selector/multiplexer
9. Decoder/demultiplexer
10. Counter
11. Priority encoder

Each of the major manufacturers of integrated-circuit logic elements publishes its own manual on techniques for interconnecting the MSI elements, perhaps making use of some elementary gates (called "SSI," small scale integration), in connection with the MSI elements.

The integrated circuit industry now has the ability to manufacture chips containing hundreds of gates (LSI, large scale integration) or even a million transistors (VLSI, very large scale integration). Some modifications in logic design techniques are required to handle such complex chips. One technique used is to store a table of combinations like those in Tables 1 and 2 or a flow table in a read-only memory (ROM - *q.v.*). A particular combination of values of the input variables is used as an address for the ROM and the contents read out of the addressed memory location are the corresponding values of the output variables. A disadvantage of this technique is that the size of the ROM is doubled for each additional input variable. This problem can be avoided by using a PLA (Programmed Logic Array). A PLA is physically similar to a ROM, but logically is like a two-stage network in which the inputs are connected to AND gates, which are connected to OR gates whose outputs form the circuit outputs. Classical techniques of two-stage circuit minimization can be applied to the problem of designing efficient PLAs.

Efficient gate network design requires the ability to handle much more complex structures than two-stage designs. Until recently, the computational complexity of this problem prohibited the use of automatic synthesis techniques, and gate networks were designed using ad hoc methods. With the increased power of modern design workstations and improved heuristic design procedures, it is now possible to use switching theory synthesis techniques to carry out a major portion of the design of new computer systems. The current trend is to specify a system design using a high-level hardware description language (*q.v.*) such as VHDL to confirm the correctness of the design by simulation and then to use synthesis programs to derive the gate or transistor level implementations. Hierarchical design has now become practical.

References

1970. Kohavi, S. *Switching and Finite Automata Theory.* New York: McGraw-Hill.
1986. McCluskey, E. J. *Logic Design Principles.* Englewood Cliffs, NJ: Prentice-Hall.

EDWARD J. MCCLUSKEY

LOGIC PROGRAMMING

For articles on related subjects *see* DATAFLOW; DEDUCTIVE DATABASE; FUNCTIONAL PROGRAMMING; KNOWLEDGE REPRESENTATION; PROGRAM VERIFICATION; and THEOREM PROVING.

PRINCIPLES

Origins   Logic programming emerged in the early 1970s from a convergence of work in the fields of automated theorem-proving, artificial intelligence (*q.v.*), and formal languages (*q.v.*). In the field of automated theorem proving, for example, it was noted that the behavior of the SL-resolution theorem-prover developed in Edinburgh by Kowalski and Kuehner in 1971 resembled the execution of procedural programming languages. SL-resolution, in turn, was based upon Robinson's resolution principle and Loveland's model elimination proof procedure.

In the field of artificial intelligence, in 1969 Hewitt at M.I.T. developed the programming language PLANNER, based on logic, but emphasizing the procedural rather than the declarative representation of knowledge. At about the same time, both Green at Stanford and Elcock and Foster at Aberdeen showed how programs could be expressed declaratively in first-order logic. Elcock and Foster devised a purely declarative language, ABSYS, based on the equality relation and the logical connectives "and" and "or." Hayes in Edinburgh argued that controlled deduction in a declarative language like ABSYS could be viewed as a form of computation.

In the field of formal languages, in 1971 Colmerauer in Marseilles investigated with Kowalski how formal grammars could be represented in logic and how parsing could be performed by theorem-proving. In 1972, Colmerauer and Rousell incorporated these ideas into the first Prolog implementation based on SL-resolution. Warren in Edinburgh subsequently showed that Prolog could be implemented with an efficiency similar to that of Lisp, and implemented a compiler for Prolog in Prolog.

Many of these related ideas can be summarized by the characterization of logic programming as the *procedural interpretation* of Horn clauses (Kowalski, 1974): A sentence of the form

$$A \text{ if } B_1 \text{ and } B_2 \dots \text{ and } B_n, \, n \geq 0$$

can be interpreted as the procedure

to solve A, solve B_1 and solve $B_2 \dots$ and solve B_n.

The theorem proving method that treats such sentences as procedures is called SLD (SL-resolution for definite clauses, i.e. Horn clauses with exactly one conclusion, "A"). Clark (1978) extended the procedural interpretation to allow negative conditions. The resulting theorem-proving method is called SLDNF (SLD with negation by failure). SLDNF is the basis for most work in logic programming today.

SLDNF is the foundation, not only for Prolog, but for the closely related field of deductive databases, for the concurrent logic programming languages (Parlog, concurrent Prolog, and GHC), and to a lesser extent for the constraint logic programming languages (Prolog 2 and 3, CLP, and Chip).

In the remainder of this article, we shall consider in greater detail the relationship between the declarative and procedural styles of logic programming. We shall also discuss the contribution of logic programming to program specification and deductive databases.

Declarative Versus Procedural Knowledge Representation

Arguments over the relative merits of declarative versus procedural knowledge representation were a major theme in artificial intelligence in the 1970s. The outcome of those arguments has been a general view that both kinds of knowledge representation are desirable. The most popular way of combining them has been to include them in hybrid knowledge representation systems.

In contrast to hybrid systems, logic programming combines declarative and procedural knowledge in the same representation. For example, logic programming automatically converts the declarative statement

> X is a potential customer for product Y
>   if   Y is useful for activity of type Z
>   and   X has work of type Z

into both the procedure

to   find a potential customer X for a given product Y, find a type of activity Z for which Y is useful, and find an X which has work of type Z

and the procedure

to   find a product Y for a given potential customer X, find the type of work Z which X has, and find a Y which is useful for activity of type Z.

In this example, the declarative statement is more abstract and corresponds to several distinct procedures. Indeed, several other procedures are also possible, depending on which of X and Y are given, and which of X and Y are to be found.

Although the syntax of logic programs is biased towards their declarative reading, for many applications it is more natural to think procedurally first. Thus, for example, a salesperson might find it easier to articulate a procedure for finding customers for his or her products than to express a more abstract, declarative statement of that knowledge.

Later, we will consider alternative formulations of the sorting (*q.v.*) problem. One formulation, based on a specification of the problem, is most naturally understood declaratively. The other, a formulation of quicksort, is most naturally understood procedurally. Both can be formulated as logic programs and therefore both can be understood declaratively as well as procedurally.

The Syntax and Declarative Interpretation of Logic Problems

A *Horn clause logic program* is a collection of statements

$$A \text{ if } B_1 \text{ and...and } B_n, \quad n \geq 0$$

Each such statement is also called a *definite clause*. In the case where $n = 0$, the statement is usually written as a *fact*:

$$A$$

without the implication sign "if".

The *conclusion*, A, and the *conditions*, B_i, are *atomic formulas*—i.e. expressions that are usually written in the form

$$p(t_1,...,t_m), \qquad m \geq 0$$

where p is a *predicate symbol* and the t_i are *terms*, consisting of *variables, constants,* or *function symbols* applied to other terms. Variables, e.g.

$$X, Y, \text{Fred}$$

are distinguished from constants by their initial upper case letter. Where appropriate, atomic formulas may also be written informally, as in the examples of the previous section.

This syntax reflects the *declarative interpretation*. A definite clause is understood as a universal statement;

> for all X_1 and...and X_k
> A if B_1 and...and B_n

where $X_1,..., X_k$ is a list of all the variables occurring in the statement. Predicate symbols are understood as names of relations, and variable-free terms are understood as names of individuals.

Problems to be solved or queries to be answered can be posed in the form of a conjunction of conditions

$$B_1 \text{ and...and } B_n? \quad n \geq 1$$

In the declarative interpretation, such a problem or query is understood as an existential statement

> there exist X_1 and...and X_k such that
> B_1 and...and B_n

which is a candidate theorem to be proved from the collection of statements constituting the program. $X_1,..., X_k$ is a list of all the variables occurring in the problem. A proof of the theorem constructs a substitution

$$X_1 = t_1, \ldots , X_k = t_k$$

of terms for variables. The substitution constitutes a solution to the problem or an answer to the query.

Later, we shall consider the case where conditions B_i in program statements and in problems or queries can be negations of atomic formulas.

The Sorting Problem

The sorting problem illustrates some of the subtleties of the relationship between declarative and procedural knowledge representation in logic programming. At the topmost level, the statement

> sort(X,Y) if permutation(X,Y)
>   and ordered(Y)

can be used as the definition of the sorting predicate. The syntax of the statement favors a declarative reading:

for all X and Y,
Y is the result of sorting X
    if Y is a permutation of X
    and Y is ordered.

As a simple case, the variables X and Y can range over all terms that can be constructed from a constant symbol "nil" as the name of the empty list and a two-place function symbol "cons." As in Lisp, the term cons(s, t) names a list

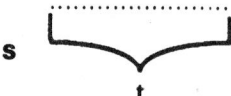

whose first element is s followed by the list t. Thus, for example, the term cons(2, cons(1, nil)) names the list of numbers, 2,1.

Given appropriate definitions of the lower-level predicates, "permutation," "ordered," and $\leq$, the definition of sort can be used to solve such problems as

sort(cons(2, cons(1, nil)), Y)?
sort(X, cons(1, cons(2, nil)))?
sort(X, Y)?

The first problem merely asks that the list supplied as first argument be sorted, so that it has the unique answer

Y = cons(1, cons(2, nil))

The second problem has a variable as first argument, so it is asking what values of X (lists) would, when sorted, produce the list cited as a second argument. The two answers are

X = cons(1, cons(2, nil))
X = cons(2, cons(1, nil)).

The third problem, since both arguments are variables, has infinitely many solutions. Queries of the third kind, where all terms are variables, are especially useful for validating logic programs because they generate all instances of the defined relations.

The Procedural Interpretation The SLD theorem-proving method treats definite clauses of the form

A if B_1 and...and B_n

as procedures

to solve A, solve B_1 and...and solve B_n.

Facts, of the form A, are treated as procedures that solve problems of the form A without introducing further subproblems.

Conditions B_i, whether in queries or in definite clauses, are treated as procedure calls. Procedure calls

can be executed in any order and even in parallel. Prolog executes procedure calls in the order in which they are written. The concurrent logic programming languages can execute procedure calls in parallel (if the underlying machine is capable of such parallelism).

Given an initial problem to be solved, the SLD theorem prover searches a tree of possible derivations (or computations) having that problem as root. At every node in the tree, each of which has the form

B_1 and...and B_n? $\quad n \geq 1$

one of the conditions is selected. Without loss of generality, by reordering conditions if necessary, we may assume that the selected condition is the first condition B_1. The condition is executed by unifying it with the conclusion of some procedure

B if C_1 and...and C_m

in the program. A successor node is created having the form

$(C_1$ and...and C_m and B_2 and...$B_n)$ θ

where θ is the unifying substitution that makes B_1 and B identical. We shall discuss unification in greater detail later.

If $m = n = 0$, then the branch from the root to the node successfully terminates, solving the problem at the root. If no conclusion unifies with the selected condition, then there are no successor nodes, and the branch to the node with no successors is said to *terminate in failure*. If more than one conclusion unifies with the selected condition, then there are successor nodes for each such conclusion.

In the latter case, the selected condition (or procedure call) is said to be nondeterministic. The different procedures whose conclusions unify with the procedure call can be executed in any order and even in parallel. Prolog executes different procedures in the order in which they are written.

Applied to the top-most level of the statement of the sorting problem, SLD converts the statement into a procedure:

to   sort X with result Y,
       find a permutation Y of X, and
       show that Y is ordered

where procedure calls are executed in the order in which they are written. The first procedure call is nondeterministic. Given a list X of length n, it will eventually generate $n!$ permutations Y of X. Thus, the sorting procedure has complexity of the order $n!$ compared with $n \cdot \log n$ for many sorting algorithms, such as quicksort.

If the two procedure calls were executed in the opposite order, the procedure would be still more inefficient, first generating ordered lists Y and then testing whether they are permutations of X.

The inefficiency that arises from executing the specification of the sorting problem shows how ambitious, and possibly impossible, is the hope that purely declarative representation of knowledge might be adequate for knowledge representation and problem solving.

In response to these problems of efficiency, some researchers have advocated the development of improved theorem-proving techniques and of parallelism in particular. Others have proposed the use of program transformation and derivation techniques to derive efficient programs from clear but inefficient specifications. Still others have suggested that logic programming be restricted to the execution and therefore to the testing of program specifications. Although all of these proposals have great merit, most practicing logic programmers solve the problems of efficiency differently, namely, by programming in a procedural way.

The Procedural Style of Logic Programming

Although the specification of the sorting problem as the problem of finding an ordered permutation is not an efficient program, the following representation of quicksort is:

    quick(nil, nil)
    quick(cons(X, Y), Z) if   partition (X, Y, Y_1, Y_2)
                             and quick(Y_1, Z_1)
                             and quick(Y_2, Z_2)
                             and append (Z_1,cons(X, Z_2), Z).

Arguably the most natural way to understand the second statement is to interpret it as a procedure:

to quicksort a non-empty list cons(X, Y) obtaining result Z,
   partition the tail of the list Y
   into the list Y_1 of all elements $< X$
   and the list Y_2 of all elements $\geq X$,
   quicksort Y_1 obtaining result Z_1,
   quicksort Y_2 obtaining result Z_2,
   append Z_1 followed by cons(X, Z_2) to obtain Z.

This example shows that, although the declarative syntax of logic programs encourages their declarative reading, the programmer might prefer to think procedurally first. This giving temporal precedence to the procedural representation of knowledge contradicts the view that logic programming is, or ought to be, nonprocedural.

The importance of procedural knowledge representation and its compatibility with logic programming could be given greater emphasis by employing a procedural syntax. Thus, logic programmers might be allowed to write procedures in the form:

to solve A, solve B_1 and...and solve B_n

where the A and B_i are suitably constrained so that the declarative interpretation

A if B_1 and...and B_n

makes logical sense. We could then think of logic programming as a way of giving a declarative interpretation to procedural statements.

Even when logic programming is used for procedural knowledge representation, the declarative interpretation is invaluable for program verification (q.v.). The declarative reading can give an informal check on the correct-

ness of the procedure. Moreover, given a specification, it can also facilitate a more rigorous proof of program correctness. The correctness of quicksort, for example, can easily and naturally be demonstrated in this way.

Unification and the Logical Variable   Viewed procedurally, nondeterminism, unification, and the logical variable are possibly the most characteristic features of logic programming.

Given a problem of the form

B_1 and...and B_n?

with selected procedural call B_1 and a procedure of the form

B if C_1 and...and C_m,

unification generates a most general substitution θ of terms for variables, such that

$B_1 \theta = B \theta$.

SLD generates the new problem

$(C_1$ and...and C_m and B_2 and...and $B_n)$ θ.

The unifying substitution θ passes input from the procedure call B_1 to the new procedure calls $C_1,..., C_m$. It simultaneously passes output from the conclusion B to the old procedure calls B_2 and...and B_n. The output may also contain (logical) variables.

Consider, for example, the recursive program

member (X, cons(X Y))
member (X, cons(X Y)) if member (X, Y)

which defines the membership relation between elements and lists.

Given the procedure call

member (2, cons(1, cons(2, nil)))?

SLD uses the second procedure to replace the call by the new call

member (2, cons (2, nil))?

and uses the first procedure to solve the new call without introducing further subproblems. All unifying substitutions in this example pass input from procedure calls to procedures.

Given, on the other hand, the procedure call

member (X, cons(1, cons (2, nil)))?

the first procedure solves the call with output

$X = 1$

and the second procedure, followed by the first, solves the call with output

$X = 2$

In this example, the unifying substitutions pass both input and output.

An outstanding characteristic of unification is that output can contain *logical variables*. For example, the call

member (2, X)?

has infinitely many outputs:

$$X = \text{cons}(2, Y)$$
$$X = \text{cons}(Z1, \text{cons}(2, Y))$$
$$X = \text{cons}(Z1, \text{cons}(Z2, \text{cons}(2, Y)))$$
etc.

each of which contains variables. The occurrence of variables in output is a powerful programming feature which corresponds in many respects to programming with higher-order functions in functional programming languages. The output

$$X = \text{cons}(2, Y),$$

for example, behaves like a function, which, given a list Y as input, returns the list $\text{cons}(2, Y)$ as output.

Negation by Failure

An important example of procedural knowledge representation in logic programming is the interpretation of negative, variable-free conditions, not A, (in program statements or queries) as holding when the attempt to show the corresponding positive condition, A, finitely fails. In general, a problem A *finitely fails* if (and only if) every branch of an SLDNF search tree having A as its root terminates in failure. Otherwise, not A finitely fails if A succeeds. Much research in logic programming has been devoted to finding an appropriate, declarative meaning for such *negation by failure*. The earliest and simplest of these, due to Clark, is to interpret each program statement as expressing one clause of the if-half of an implicit if-and-only-if definition of the predicate symbol of the conclusion of the statement.

Thus, for example, the two clauses

parent(X, Y) if father(X,Y)
parent(X, Y) if mother(X,Y)

together represent the if-half of the definition

parent(X, Y) if and only if [father (X,Y) or mother(X,Y)].

Negation by failure can be justified as reasoning implicitly with the only-if half of the definition.

Negation by failure works *incorrectly* if the negative condition contains variables at the time of execution. Given, for example, the definition of "parent" above and the additional statements

father(john, fred)
mother(mary, fred)

negation by failure correctly solves the problems

| not parent(fred, fred)? | yes |
| not parent (john, fred)? | no |

However, it incorrectly solves the problem of finding an X such that

not parent (john, X)?,   no.

A correct solution would generate the solutions

$$X = \text{john},$$
$$X = \text{mary}.$$

Failure by programmers to ensure that any variables occurring in a negative condition are completely instan-

tiated before execution of the condition is a common source of error in logic programming. The extension of negation by failure to allow execution of negative conditions containing variables is a current topic of research.

Another common error is to use negation by failure when the program contains an incomplete definition of a predicate. Negation by failure works correctly only when all clauses in the if-half of a definition have been given.

Despite these dangers, negation by failure is an extremely powerful knowledge representation and problem-solving feature. With its help, it is possible, in particular, to obtain the expressive power of allowing any formula of first-order logic as a condition of any program statement or query. For example, the statement

subset (X, Y) if for all Z [member (Z, Y) if member (Z, X)]

can be re-expressed in logic programming form by introducing an auxiliary predicate symbol:

subset (X, Y) if not nosub(X, Y)
nosub(X, Y) if member (Z, X) and not member (Z, Y).

Deductive Databases

Having emphasized that there are many applications for which procedural knowledge representation is most appropriate, it is important to note that, for certain applications (e.g. within the class of deductive databases) a purely declarative representation can be both natural and efficient. Relational databases are a special case.

A *relational* database (*q.v.*) can be regarded as the special case of a logic program where all statements have the form of conclusions without any conditions, variables, or function symbols. For example:

father(john, fred)
mother(mary, fred).

A *deductive database* can be regarded as a logic program that does not contain function symbols. The general rules

parent(X, Y)	if father(X, Y)
parent(X, Y)	if mother(X, Y)
ancestor(X, Y)	if parent(X, Y)
ancestor(X, Y)	if parent(X, Y)
	and ancestor(Z, Y)

are typical of a deductive database.

Because deductive databases contain no function symbols, their domain of discourse is finite. As a consequence, the problem of determining whether or not a query has an answer is *decidable*. The backward reasoning mode of inference associated with SLDNF, augmented with loop-checking strategies, is a decision procedure. Efficient query evaluation methods can also be based upon forward reasoning.

Rules and Regulations

Statutes can often be represented in deductive database form. The following rules are typical of those that might be used to represent part of a simplified citizenship law:

citizen(X, usa) if   born(X, usa)
citizen(X, usa) if   not born(X, usa)
                        and parent(Y, X)
                        and citizen(Y, usa).

Not only is the declarative reading of such rules the programmer's most important concern, but the procedural interpretation of the rules is often efficient enough for an implementation.

Incremental Program Development

Because individual statements of a logic program can be understood independently of one another, logic programming encourages incremental program development. Programs can be developed incrementally in both the vertical and horizontal dimensions.

Vertical development can be top-down, with high-level predicates defined before lower-level ones, as in structured programming (*q.v.*). It can also be bottom-up, middle-out, or mixed.

Horizontal development means that different clauses defining different cases of a predicate can be developed at different times. This facilitates implementing expert systems(*q.v.*), where additional heuristics for solving additional cases of a problem can be accumulated incrementally.

Other Developments in Logic Programming

Some of the more important issues not dealt with in this article are:

Parallelism—As noted earlier, logic programming offers many opportunities for parallelism. Several concurrent logic programming languages and parallel implementations of logic programming have been developed.

Constraints—It is possible to improve efficiency significantly by manipulating certain conditions as constraints. Several logic programming languages incorporating constraints have been developed.

Objects—An important area of research has been the development of systems that combine logic programming and object-oriented programming (*q.v.*) or object-oriented knowledge representation. One such approach is based upon an interpretation of objects as processes in concurrent logic programming languages.

Metaprogramming—This is a common and powerful logic programming technique for implementing more powerful theorem-provers (sometimes called "inference engines").

Types, functions, metalogic, higher-order logic, non-classical logic, integrity checking and abduction—Many proposals have been made to extend or modify logic programming by incorporating these features.

Conclusion

We have emphasized the relationship between declarative and procedural knowledge representation in logic programming. We have done so, because misunderstanding about the nature of this relationship can cause great difficulties for theoreticians and programmers alike.

References

1974. Kowalski, R. "Predicate Logic as Programming Language," in *Proceedings IFIP Congress.* Stockholm: North Holland Publishing Co., 569–574.
1978. Clark, K. L. "Negation as failure," *Logic and Data Bases*, H. Gallaire and J. Minker (Eds.). New York: Plenum Press, 293–322.
1984. Hogger, C. J. *Introduction to Logic Programming.* New York: Academic Press.
1987. Lloyd, J. W. *Foundations of Logic Programming.* (2nd Ed.). New York: Springer Verlag.

ROBERT KOWALSKI

LANGUAGES

This article is divided into two sections. The overview section is a general discussion of the range of current logic programming languages, describing their key features and differences. It contains no example programs. The second section describes five LP languages, with example programs. There is a fairly detailed description of Prolog, because it is the most widely used LP language, with many commercial implementations. This is followed by briefer descriptions of Nu-Prolog, Prolog II, Prolog III, and Parlog.

Overview   The SLD and SLDNF schemes described in the companion article (LOGIC PROGRAMMING: PRINCIPLES) are abstract evaluators for Horn clause logic programs. Logic programming languages, such as Prolog, are restricted implementations of such evaluators, augmented with a wide range of primitive predicates. The changes made in moving from the abstract SLD evaluator to Prolog are analogous to those made in moving from the lambda calculus (*q.v.*) to Lisp. The primitives invoke routines written in machine code or C (*q.v.*). Some of them are just efficient implementations of relations that could be defined using Horn clauses—e.g. a relation to evaluate arithmetic expressions or one to sort lists. Others, such as those to read and write terms, or to manipulate graphical images, have side effects that cannot be defined in logic.

Restrictions of Prolog   Prolog has:

1. Strict left-to-right evaluation of calls in queries and the bodies of clauses.
2. Backtracking depth first search of the tree (*q.v.*) of alternative evaluation paths for a query. The clauses for each call are tried in the order in which they are given in the program.

These restrictions allow for the fast evaluation of queries on conventional computers. Prolog's primitives for arithmetic, terminal I/O, file handling, etc., allow the implementation of significant applications with user interaction. But the restrictions and primitives incur a penalty. Because of the fixed left-to-right order of evaluation of calls in clauses, and restrictions on the modes of use of the primitives, Prolog programs can rarely be used in all the different generate and test modes that the SLD evaluator allows. For example, the Prolog < primitive for comparing numeric values will generate an error if the call $X<9$ is selected for evaluation with X unbound; it will not generate candidate values for X. So, if < is used in a clause, this usually restricts its modes of use.

Delaying Calls and Coroutining More modes of use of the Horn clauses of a logic program are retained if the query evaluator can delay the evaluation of some call if certain arguments are unbound. One use of this is dynamic reordering of the calls of clauses. It also allows dataflow (*q.v.*) coroutining, where the transfers between calls is triggered by the binding of shared variables. Some successors of Prolog (e.g. Nu-Prolog and Prolog II) allow such delaying of calls.

Constraint Logic Programming Languages Even more generality of use is retained by having primitives that automatically delay and are capable of being called and solved for more than one mode of use. An example is a primitive to solve simple equations such as $X = Y + 4$, which delays if X and Y were both unbound, but which will solve the equation as soon as either becomes bound. The constraint logic programming languages such as Prolog III, Chip, and CLP(R) do this. At some implementation cost, they actually do much more. If $X + Y = 12$ is delayed, and then later $X + 2Y = 17$ is delayed, the two will be combined to give $X = 7$, $Y = 5$. This involves having linear equation solving algorithms embedded in the implementation. Checking delayed sets of equations for solvability and partially solving them where possible is a costly operation, so constraint logic programming languages are much slower in execution than Prolog. But for certain applications, such as search problems that involve finding solutions of equations, they compensate by generating a much smaller search tree of alternative evaluation paths that need to be explored.

Or-Parallel Evaluation An obvious way to parallelize Prolog is to allow for parallel search of the tree of alternative evaluation paths. This is called *or-parallelism*. Or-parallel versions of Prolog have been implemented on multiprocessor machines. One such language, Aurora Prolog, has the useful feature that it will run existing Prolog applications, often with considerable speed-up.

Independent And-parallelism In some or-parallel implementations, independent calls are also evaluated in parallel. These are adjacent calls, the first of which is just about to be evaluated, that share no unbound variable.

Communicating And-parallelism Allowing the parallel evaluation of calls that share variables is a much more radical step. If this is coupled with delaying of calls when certain variables are unbound, it allows concurrent dataflow programming, the parallelization of dataflow coroutining. Concurrent Prolog, GHC, Parlog, and Strand are concurrent dataflow LP languages. To retain efficient implementation, the concurrently evaluating calls are allowed to generate only a single binding for each shared variable. They do this by incorporating the control concept of committed choice, as with Dijkstra's *guarded commands* (*q.v.*) and Hoare's CSP. That is, each call must commit to the use of just one clause before any bindings for its variables are generated. This means that the concurrent LP languages have no built-in search capability. But a parallel search can be programmed, using the and-parallelism of the languages.

Some Logic Programming Languages

Prolog The backtracking search and strict left-to-right evaluation of calls of Prolog derive from its first implementation as an interpreter by Colmerauer's research group in the University of Aix-Marseille in 1972. The syntax and most of the standard set of primitives of current commercial Prologs derive from the 1977 Edinburgh University compiler implementation by Warren and colleagues. Clocksin and Mellish (1981) was the first of many textbooks on Prolog.

Syntax

Everything in Prolog is a term. A *term* is a number, an atom, a variable, or a compound term of the form $f(t1,..,tn)$, $n > 0$, where f is an atom and $t1,..,tn$ are terms. The f is the *functor* of the term. *Atoms* are alphanumeric, symbolic, or quoted. Alphanumeric atoms begin with a *lowercase letter*.

apple tom bill_gates	are alphanumeric atoms,
+ * ^^ ++ :− !	are symbolic atoms,
'X' 'Tom' 'hello there'	are quoted atoms.

Variable names are alphanumeric character sequences beginning with an *uppercase letter* or with _ (underscore).

Tom _2 Man_in_Charge are variable names.

Operators

Prolog has an operator precedence (*q.v.*) syntax. Atoms can be declared as associative or non-associative, prefix, postfix, or infix operators. Atoms such as $> < * + : −$, are predefined infix operators. With operators, compound terms such as $>(X, Y)$ can be written as $X > Y$, and normal arithmetic expressions such as $2*X + 6$ can be used instead of $+ (*(2, X),6)$.

Clauses

In Prolog a *clause* is an atom or a compound term. (When written in a program, it must be followed by a full stop immediately followed by a whitespace character—space, tab, or newline). If the compound term has :− as outermost functor, it is a clause with preconditions. The :− is read as "if"; commas separating the preconditions are read as "and."

Example Program 1

```
parent_of(mary,fred).
parent_of(john,fred).
is_male(john).
```

```
father_of(F,C) :- parent_of(F,C),is_male(F).
grand_parent_of(Gp,Gc) :- parent_of(Gp,P),
    parent_of(P,Gc).
sibling_of(C1,C2) :- parent_of(P,C1),
    parent_of(P,C2),C1≠C2.
```

The first three clauses are *facts*. The last three are *rules* defining the father_of, grand_parent_of, and sibling_of relations. The facts about father_of and is_male can be viewed as the tuples of a relational database (*q.v.*). Usually, we would have many more such facts in the program, and more rules for relations such as mother_of, ancestor_of, grand_father_of, etc.

Because :- and the comma (,) are predefined infix operators, the rule for father_of is the compound term :- (father_of(F,C),','(parent_of(F,C),is_male(F)). (Comma needs to be quoted when not used as an operator or separator.) The fact that clauses are just terms of a certain form is important for meta-level programming. Prolog shares with Lisp the ability to treat programs and fragments of programs as data that can be manipulated and then executed. In this, as in its imperative primitives, Prolog goes beyond the pure concept of logic programming.

By optionally declaring is_male as a non associative postfix operator and parent_of, and father_of as non associative infix operators, the father_of rule can be written:

```
F father_of C :- F parent_of C,F is_male.
```

User-declared operators can be used to good effect to allow program rules to be written in a form suited to the application.

Lists

There is a special syntax for list terms. Lists are compound terms built from the empty list written [ ] using ".". The period is a predefined right associative infix operator. Thus

```
2.3.4.[] which is 2.(3.(4.[ ])) and
X.[]
```

are lists and

```
H.T
```

is a list pattern in which H is the head and T is the tail. But lists and list patterns can also be written in a more conventional notation. The above can be written

```
[2,3,4]
[X]
[H|T]
```

where the | is read as "followed by."

Programs 2 and 3 are full Prolog versions of the sort programs discussed in the LOGIC PROGRAMMING: PRINCIPLES article.

Program 2

```
sort(L,SortL) :-
 permutation(L,SortL),ordered(Sort,L).

permutation([],[]).
permutation([H|T],[V|PermL]):- delete
    V,[H|T],L), permutation(L,PermL).

delete(H,[H|T],T).
delete(V,[H|T],[H|DelT]):- delete(V,T,DelT).

ordered([ ]).
ordered([X]).
ordered([X,Y|T]):- X=<Y,ordered([Y|T]).
```

Program 3

```
quick([],[]).
quick([H|T],Sort):-
     partition(H,T,LessH,NotLessH),
     quick(LessH,SortLessH),
     quick(NotLessH,SortNotLessH),
     append(SortLessH,[H|SortNotLessH],Sort).

partition(P,[],[],[]).
partition(P,[H|T],[H|Less],NotLess) :-
    H<P,partition(P,T,Less,NotLess).
partition(P,[H|T],Less,[H|NotLess]):-
    P= <H,partition(P,T,Less,NotLess).

append([],L,L).
append([H|T],L,[H|T_L]):- append(T,L,T_L).
```

Prolog Query Evaluation

Prolog's backtracking search and left-to-right evaluation of calls means that the query

```
father_of(X,fred)
```

to Program 1 will be evaluated as follows. First, it will be reduced using the only clause for father_of to the conjunction

```
parent_of(X,fred),is_male(X)
```

The first call will now be selected and the clauses for parent_of will be unified with the call in turn, in the order in which they are written in the program.

The call will unify with the first clause, making X = mary. As the clause has no preconditions, this solves the call. Prolog now tries to solve

```
is_male(mary)
```

which fails to unify with the single is_male clause. This causes Prolog to backtrack to try the next clause for father_of in order to find an alternative solution for father_of(X,fred). This gives the binding X = john.

The second call is now `is_male(john)`, which does unify with its clause, so `X = john` is the solution to the query.

Consider now the definition for `grand_parent_of` in Program 1. Given a much larger database of `parent_of` facts, Prolog will handle queries `grand_parent_of(Gp,Gc)` in which Gp is given much more efficiently than those in which only Gc is given. In the latter case, it will still try to solve the first call, `parent_of(Gp,P)`, of the `grand_parent_of` rule with both arguments unbound variables. Prolog will unify this, in turn, with each `parent_of` fact, and for each solution test if it has found a parent of the given Gc by checking `parent_of(P,Gc)`. It would be much more efficient in this case to solve the calls in reverse order. To take the given Gc, find a parent P, and then find a parent of P.

This is an example of the usefulness of dynamic reordering of calls depending on the mode of use. Using meta-level primitives, var, and !, the solution can be programmed in Prolog, but with a loss of logical purity. We need two rules:

```
grand_parent_of(Gp,Gc) :- var(Gc,!,
    parent_of(Gp,P),parent_of(P,Gc).
grand_parent_of(Gp,Gc) :- parent_of(P,Gc),
    parent_of(Gp,P).
```

The first rule will be used only for calls in which Gc is a variable because of the `var(Gc)` test. The second will be used for all other calls. The ! following the `var(Gc)` test is Prolog's backtracking control primitive. Once evaluated in a clause, it stops Prolog from backtracking to use as yet untried clauses for the call.

In Programs 2 and 3, only the definitions for *append* and *delete* are truly flexible programs; *append* can be queried with such diverse queries as:

```
append ([1,2,3],[4,5],X)
                answer   X = [1,2,3,4,5]
append(X,Y,[1,2])
                answers  X = [],Y = [1,2],
                         X = [1],Y = [2],
                         X = [1,2],Y = []
append(X,[Z],[1,2,3])
                answer   X = [1,2],Z = 3
```

and many more. Because of this versatility, we can use *append* to define many other relations on lists, as in Program 4.

Program 4

```
on(X,L) :- append(F,[X|B],L).
                %X an element on list L
adjacent_on(X,Y,L) :- append(F,[X,Y|B],L).
                %X,Y are adjacent on L
sublist_of(S,L) :- S = [X|T],
                %S is a non-empty
            append(BeforeS,S,FrontL),
                % sublist of L.
            append(FrontL,BackL,L).
```

In contrast, the ordered definition of Program 2 can be used only for testing. This is because =< is a primitive, which, in Prolog, requires both arguments to be bound by the time it is evaluated. Therefore, the potential use of the sort definition mentioned in the PRINCIPLES portion to generate instances of the relation, is not possible using Prolog. We can use the sort and quick programs only for calls in which the list to sort is completely given. The second argument—the sorted list—can be given, be partially given, or be an unbound variable. That is, we can have calls such as sort([2,3,1,],[1,2,3,]), sort([2,3,1], [H|T]), sort([2,3,1],S), but not sort([X,Y,Z],[X1,Y1,Z1]).

Other Logical Features of Prolog   In addition to negation of calls, implemented as *negation as failure* (see PRINCIPLES), Prolog has *disjunction*, a *forall* construct, and primitives for wrapping all solutions to a query into a list.

Program 5

```
person(P) :- male(P);female(P).
            %;is the disjunction operator
ordered(L):- forall(adjacent_on(X,Y,L), X =<Y)
            % alternative defn of ordered
children_of(P,L) :- setof(C,parent_of(P,C),L)
            %L is a list of all children of P
```

The `children_of` definition of Program 5 is very powerful, for it can be used even if P is not given. A query `children_of(P,L)` will find each parent in the database and, for each, bind L to a lexically ordered list of names of their recorded children.

More Meta-level Features   Prolog has primitives for retrieving, adding, and deleting individual clauses of a relation definition. A call in a clause can also be a variable—the so-called meta-call. The variable must be bound to a call term before the left-to-right evaluation reaches the meta-call. Program 6, using the clause retrieval primitive and the meta-call, is the Prolog query evaluator defined as an interpreter in Prolog.

Program 6

```
eval(Call) :- primitive(Call),Call.
            % Call is call to a primitive
eval((Call,MoreCalls)) :- eval(Call),
    eval(MoreCall).
            % eval a conjunction
eval(Call) :- clause(Call,Body),
            % find unifying clause and
                eval (Body).
            % eval its body
eval(true).
            % an empty body is returned
                as true by the clause
                primitive
```

More elaborate interpreters have been used for building expert systems (*q.v.*) that use Prolog's clauses to represent rules and its unification for pattern matching, but that have more sophisticated evaluation strategies.

Primitives Standard Prolog has over 50 primitives. Some implementations of Prolog, (e.g. MacProlog) have over 500. These augment the standard primitives with facilities for creating menus, dialogues, window environments (*q.v.*), formatted I/O, and graphics.

Nu-Prolog Nu-Prolog (Thom and Zobel 1986), from Melbourne University, has the same syntax and standard set of primitives as Prolog. It also has backtracking search. The major difference is that it allows the delaying of calls until certain conditions on their arguments are satisfied, and many of the primitives automatically delay rather than raise an error if their arguments are underspecified. So Nu-Prolog does not have strict left-to-right evaluation of calls. Program 7 is a Nu-Prolog coroutining version of Program 2.

Program 7

```
:- ordered(L) when L.
sort(L,SortedL) :- ordered(SortedL),
    permutation(L,SortedL).
ordered([X,Y|L]):- X=<Y,ordered(L).
ordered([X]).
ordered([]).
```

The permutation program is as in Program 2. The declaration `ordered(L) when L` delays all calls to `ordered`, in all programs, until its argument is a non-variable. The `=<` primitive of Nu-Prolog automatically delays until both its arguments are variable-free terms. Given a call, `sort([2,1,3,0,8],SortedL)`, the `ordered(SortedL)` call will delay because `SortedL` is unbound. Then, when permutation binds `SortedL` to `[X|S']` using its second clause, the ordered call will resume using its first clause. This will bind `S'` to `[Y|S"]`. However, both calls `X=<Y` and `ordered (S")` of the clause body will delay allowing the `permutation` call to resume. `X=<Y` will be resumed, and fail, when `permutation`, after two recursive calls, binds `X` to 2 and `Y` to 1. In the Prolog Program 3, which does not coroutine between the two calls of the sort program, this failure is detected only when the permutation call has generated a complete first permutation. The early detection of lack of order by the Nu-Prolog program means that the backtracking search will find the ordered permutation much more quickly.

In Nu-Prolog, one can also delay calls of a specified form (i.e. with arguments that match certain patterns), and until variables have bindings that are variable-free terms, not just any term.

Prolog II Colmerauer's team modified their original Marseille Prolog into an implementation of a variant language, Prolog II. There are minor syntactic differences between it and standard Prolog. The user cannot declare operators, → is used instead of :-, clauses are terminated with ; rather than full stop, and the variable/non-variable convention is reversed. However, the major differences are in the operational and logical semantics. Giannesini *et al.* (1986) is the standard reference for Prolog II.

Delaying Calls As with Nu-Prolog, a significant feature of Prolog II is the ability to delay the evaluation of a call until one or more argument variables of the call are bound. This is not done by a declaration, which delays all calls that match the declaration. In Prolog II, each individual call that should be delayed must be designated as a delayable call. To delay a call C until some variable X is bound (to any non-variable term), the call is written `freeze(X,C)`. The following is a Prolog II definition of `grand_parent_of`, which will delay the `parent_of(P,Gc)` call if Gc is unbound. To avoid confusion, we have used Prolog syntax.

```
grand_parent_of(Gp,Gc) :-
freeze(Gc,parent_of(P,Gc)),parent_of(Gp,P);
```

It has the same effect as the two clause Prolog definition given above. Program 8 is the Prolog II equivalent of Nu-Prolog's Program 7.

Program 8

```
sort(L,SortedL) :- freeze(SortedL,ordered
    (SortedL)),permutation(L,SortedL).
ordered([X,Y|L]) :-freeze(X,freeze(Y,X=<Y)),
    freeze(ordered(L)).
ordered([X]).
ordered ([]).
```

Unification for Infinite Terms The unit of computation of the SLD evaluator is the unification of call and clause head, where the unification is that of resolution inference. Prolog uses an unsound relaxation of this unification, which significantly speeds up this crucial operation. Prolog will incorrectly allow a binding X = f(a,X) in which variable X appears in its binding term. For the most part, this presents no problem, for Prolog evaluations rarely generate such bindings. If one *is* generated, however, the binding cannot be displayed, and it may cause a subsequent unification to loop. Prolog II uses a similar relaxed unification, but one that handles such bindings correctly. The abstract model for Prolog II is really a variant of SLD in which the unification of resolution inference is replaced by "unification" for infinite but finitely representable terms (i.e. cyclic term structures). Giannesini *et al.* (1986) contains elegant examples of the use of such cyclic structures.

Inequality Constraints All uses of the inequality primitive $t_1 \neq t_2$ automatically delay if its two arguments are unifiable by a Prolog II unification that *generates bindings for variables*. (It succeeds if they are not unifiable, and fails if they are syntactically identical.) In Prolog II, we could define `sibling_of` using

```
sibling_of(C1,C2) :- C1 ≠ C2,
    parent_of(P,C1),parent_of(P,C2).
```

Given a call, `sibling_of(peter,C2)`, the `peter ≠ C2` call will immediately delay, because `peter` and `C2` are unifiable with `C2 = peter`. It will be resumed after the execution of the two `parent_of` calls, when `C2` will be bound.

Inequality ($\neq$) conditions can also be returned in answers. Given a query `absent_from(X,[E1,E2,E3])` to Program 9, Prolog II will return the answer, $X \neq E1$, $X \neq E2$, $X \neq E3$. The automatic delaying of calls to and its appearance in answers makes $\neq$ a constraint primitive.

Program 9

```
absent_from(X,[]).
absent_from(X,[Y|L]):- X≠Y,absent_from (X,L).
```

Prolog III Prolog III (Colmerauer, 1990) extends PRO-LOG II in that it has a far richer set of constraint primitives. In addition to $\neq$, inequalities ($<$, $>$, $\geq$, $\leq$) boolean equations, and linear arithmetic equations such as $2X + 5Y = 45$ are handled as constraint conditions. When selected by left-to-right evaluation, they will be solved or will fail if their variables are sufficiently instantiated. If arguments are not sufficiently instantiated, they will be delayed. Where possible, delayed constraint calls will be combined to give bindings for their common variables, or to fail. For example, if $X < 0$ is delayed, and later $X > 2$ is delayed, that branch of the evaluation will immediately fail. The overview section has an example of equation combining to generate bindings.

As a Prolog III program, the sort definition of Program 2 can be queried with `sort([X,Y,Z],[Z,X,Y])`. It will return as an answer-the-constraint conjunction $Z = <X, X = <Y$.

Parlog The Parlog version of Program 3 is given in Program 10. Parlog actually uses $<-$ instead of :–, but we have retained the latter for uniformity.

Program 10

```
mode quick(?,^).
{same clauses for quick as in Program 3}
mode partition(?,?,^,^).
partition(P,[],[],[]).
partition(P,[H|T],[H|Less],NotLess) :-
   H<P: partition(P,T,Less,NotLess).
partition (P,[H|T],Less[H|NotLess]):-
   P = <H: partition(P,T,Less,NotLess).

mode append(?,?,^).
{same clauses for append}
```

The only difference from the Prolog program is the mode declarations and the : in the two recursive partition clauses. The behavior, however, is very different. The mode declarations are similar to the *when* declarations of Nu-Prolog. They specify a delay for a call that does not satisfy certain conditions on its arguments. The difference is that they specify delays in an and-parallel evaluation.

Given a query `quick([2,3,1,8, 2 4…],S)`, Parlog will reduce this to the *parallel* conjunction

```
partition(2,[3,1,..],LessH,NotLessH),
quick(LessH,SortLessH),
```

```
quick(NotLessH,SortNotLessH),
append(SortLessH,[2|SortNotLessH],S)
```

Parlog will immediately begin to evaluate these four calls. However, the data flow specified by the mode declarations will cause the two `quick` calls and the `append` call to suspend. The `quick(?,^)` mode means that no `quick` call can proceed if it has an unbound variable as its first argument. More precisely, the ? in the first argument position says that before a clause R for `quick` can be used to evaluate a call C, the first argument of C must be a substitution instance of the term in the first argument position of the head of R. So the call `quick(LessH, SortLessH)` will suspend until either `LessH` is bound to [ ] (the first argument of the first clause), or until it is bound to a term that is an instance of the pattern [H|T] (the first argument of the second clause). A binding for `LessH` will be generated by the partition call, for `LessH` appears in an output argument position, designated ^ of the partition (?,?,^,^) mode declaration.

The `partition (2,[3,1,..], LessH,Not LessH)` call is the only one that satisfies the input argument constraints of its mode declaration, for [3,1,..] is a substitution instance of [H|T]. In parallel, an attempt is made to unify each clause head with the call, *on its input argument positions only*, which are the first two arguments. No attempt is made at this stage to unify the third and fourth arguments. The first clause fails to unify, but the other two do unify, giving H=3 and P=2 in each clause. Parlog still has to determine which clause to use, by evaluating the calls H<P and P=<H. This is because they are separated from the other call in the body by a ":", which makes them *guard calls*. Guard calls must be evaluated before Parlog commits to using any clause and before any output argument unifications. Parlog will try each test, in parallel, but only the 2=<3 test will succeed. In this case, there is only one clause that Parlog can use; it commits to the use of the third clause, reducing the partition call to `partition(2,[1,..],LessH,Not Less)`. At the same time, it unifies the output arguments of the call. This unification generates the bindings `Less = LessH` and `NotLessH = [3|NotLess]`.

Now, both the recursive partition call and the second quick call can be reduced in parallel. The call `quick(Notless,SortNotLess)` now has `NotLess = [3|Notless]`, which satisfies the input mode constraints of the second clause. It is reduced to the parallel conjunction

```
partition(3,NotLess,LessH1,NotLessH1),
quick(LessH1,SortLessH1),
quick(NotLessH1,SortNotLessH1),
append(SortLessH1,[3|SortNotLessH1],
   SortNotLess)
```

all the calls of which will initially suspend, waiting for bindings from other calls. The top level quick (LessH, SortLessH) call will be reduced as soon as the parti tion(2,[1,..],LessH,NotLess) call commits to the use of its second clause binding `LessH` to [1|Less1]. The evaluation continues in this way, with calls evaluating in parallel where possible, and with the quick calls forking into new parallel conjunctions. Bindings are always communicated from `partition` calls to `quick` calls, and from these to `append` calls. Calls will suspend, if necessary, waiting for bindings to be communicated. This is the data flow specified by the mode declarations.

Committed Choice In this program, there is always only one clause that can be used to reduce each call. That is, there is only one clause that successfully matches the input arguments of the call and has a successful guard call, where there are such calls. (Only the partition program has guard calls.) Such a clause is called a *candidate clause* for the call. More generally, there may be several candidate clauses for a call. Parlog will nonetheless commit to using just one of these candidate clauses. There will be no back-tracking on the choice, and no attempt to pursue the use of each candidate call in parallel. There is no or-parallelism beyond the or-parallel attempt to find a candidate clause. Unification on the output argument positions is always delayed until this commitment to use some candidate clause. Since there is communication only on commitment, there is never any need to rescind a communicated binding of a shared variable. This property allows for efficient implementation on multiprocessor machines.

Clark (1990) further illustrates the use of Parlog, comparing it with the other main concurrent dataflow languages. It also describes recently proposed LP languages that have communicating and-parallelism without committed choice. Another new development is concurrent constraint LP languages.

References

1981. Clocksin, W. F. and Mellish, C. S. *Programming in Prolog*. New York: Springer-Verlag.

1986. Giannesini, F., Kanoui, H., Pasero, P., and van Canegham, M. *Prolog*. Reading, MA: Addison-Wesley.

1986. Thom, J. A. and Zobel, J. *Nu-Prolog Reference Manual*. Technical Report 86/10, Dept. of Computer Science, University of Melbourne.

1990. Clark, K. L. "Parallel Logic Programming," *Computer Journal* **33**, 6.

1990. Colmerauer, A. "An Introdution to Prolog III," *CACM*, **33**, 7.

KEITH L. CLARK

LOGIC, COMPUTATIONAL. *See* LOGICS OF PROGRAMS.

LOGICAL AND PHYSICAL UNITS

For articles on related subjects *see* INPUT-OUTPUT CONTROL SYSTEM; MEMORY: AUXILIARY; and OPERATING SYSTEMS: GENERAL PRINCIPLES.

A *physical* (input/output) *unit* is an input/output device and its associated recording medium. Thus, tape units, disks, drums, keyboards, and printers are all examples of physical units. A *logical unit* is a convenient abstraction of a physical unit, an extra level of naming of input/output devices that gives both the programmer and the system added operational flexibility.

The usage of a two-level naming scheme may be compared to the use of call numbers in a library card catalog. The call number of a book is sufficient to identify the book, but it bears no permanent relationship to the location of the book on the shelves. Rather, to locate a book physically, knowing only its call number, it is necessary to consult a directory that tells (for example) on which floor a particular collection of call numbers is located. The library staff is then free to change the physical location of the books, provided the directory is updated accordingly.

A similar two-level naming scheme is used for input/output operations on a computer. Each physical input/output unit has associated with it a physical unit name (number) in order that communication with the central processor can be established. When data is being transferred, these physical unit names are ultimately used. However, a programmer frequently finds it convenient to use logical unit names in place of these physical unit names, and to provide a correspondence (i.e. directory) between logical and physical units. Thus, for example, in the Fortran statement

```
READ (5,100) X,Y,Z
```

the number 5 is a logical unit name that indicates where the data (X, Y, and Z in the format given in the statement numbered 100) is to be found. Elsewhere, the programmer (or the operating system, by default) will provide the correspondence that logical unit 5 is currently associated with physical unit 007, which might be a file residing on disk, for example. Data will then be transferred from that file.

This two-level naming provides a number of advantages, both to the programmer and to the operating system. First, it is possible to reassign the physical unit associated with a given logical unit without recompilation of the program, since the program is written in terms of logical units only, and the correspondence is made during program execution by looking in the directory (*q.v.*). This process is called *I/O redirection*, and a program that is written to capitalize on the technique is said to be *device independent*.

Similarly, a programmer processing various files using the same program can accomplish this without recompilation by changing the correspondence between logical device and file name. The correspondence between logical and physical units is very often declared in job control statements or an operating system shell language prior to program execution.

ROBERT W. TAYLOR

LOGICS OF PROGRAMS

For articles on related subjects *see* FORMAL LANGUAGES; FUNCTIONAL PROGRAMMING; GRAMMARS; LAMBDA CALCULUS; LOOP INVARIANT; PROGRAM VERIFICATION; and SYNTAX, SEMANTICS, AND PRAGMATICS.

A program logic is a *language* in which properties of programs can be expressed unambiguously, a *semantics* that specifies the meaning of the expressions of the language, and *rules* for manipulating those expressions in a meaning-respecting way in order either to calculate or demonstrate the truth of assertions in the language. The study of logics of programs is of value in understanding how both people and computers may reason about software, either autonomously or in cooperation with each other. Applications include *program verification*, automatic programming, and program analysis for optimization and auditing purposes.

In some logics, the semantics will be omitted and assumed to be either understood intuitively or implied by the rules; alternatively, only the semantics may be given and the choice of appropriate rules left open. Sometimes, the rules will be non-deterministic and intended as criteria to be met by formal proofs in the tradition of mathematical proof systems; sometimes, they will be deterministic and intended for use in an algorithm in the tradition of logical decision methods.

A number of logics of programs have been proposed, each of them owing some debt to the subject of mathematical logic, with most of them making additional program-specific contributions of their own. The subject started with the seminal papers of McCarthy (1963), Floyd (1967), and Hoare (1969).

McCarthy's approach modeled programs as recursive functions. An example is supplied by the recursively defined list processing function $x @ y$, which denotes the list that is the "append" $[x_1 x_2...x_m y_1 y_2...y_n]$ of the two lists $x = [x_1 x_2...x_m]$ and $y = [y_1 y_2...y_n]$. We write $[\,]$ for the empty list and $a.x$ for the list $[a \, x_1 x_2...x_m]$ in the following recursive definition:

$$@1: \quad [\,] @ y \quad = y$$
$$@2: \quad (a.x) @ y = a.(x @ y)$$

Append is associative; i.e. $x@(y @ z) = (x @ y)@ z$. We may prove this formally by induction on the length of x, assuming that every list x is either $[\,]$ or of the form $a.u$, where u is a shorter list than x. For the basis case, $x = [\,]$, we have

$$\begin{aligned}[\,] @(y@z) &= y@z \quad &(by \, @1) \\ &= ([\,] @ y)@ z \quad &(by \, @1).\end{aligned}$$

For the inductive case, $x = a.u$, we take as our induction hypothesis that $u@(y@ z) = (u@ y)@ z$ and argue thus:

$$\begin{aligned}(a.u)@ (y@z) &= a.(u@(y@z)) \text{ (by @2)} \\ &= a.((u@y)@ z) \text{ (by the induction} \\ &\qquad\qquad\qquad\text{hypothesis)} \\ &= (a.(u@y))@ z \text{ (by @2)} \\ &= ((a.u)@y)@ z \text{ (by @2)}.\end{aligned}$$

This completes the proof that the operator @ is associative.

It is possible to construct large systems of software entirely from recursively defined functions, and to establish many of the key properties of those systems by inductive proofs of this form on a correspondingly much larger scale. However, though some programmers find it a pleasure to program in this style, the bulk of the software that is produced in practice is written in an imperative style, involving assignments, begin-end-bracketed sequences of statements, conditional statements, and while-loops. To prove such programs correct, it would be most inconvenient to have to translate them into recursively defined functions.

To meet the needs of imperative programming more directly, Floyd developed a logic of flowcharts. The main feature of this method was the use of the *tag*, a logical assertion placed on an arc of the flowchart and guaranteed to hold whenever control passed along that arc. Floyd's principal contributions were to work out the details of a formal system based on these tags, to address aspects of the proof-theoretic completeness of his systems, and to consider the problem of proving termination of programs. He also introduced the concept of the verification condition, consisting of a component of a flowchart and tags at its entrances and exits. To prove a tagged flowchart correct, it sufficed to prove, for each component of the flowchart, the verification condition consisting of that component and its associated tags. From the correctness of the verification conditions, a local property, the rule is that one may infer the correctness of the flowchart, a global property. This inference rule could well be called *Floyd's induction rule*. The logic was intended by Floyd both for calculation and semantics; in fact, the title of his paper, "Assigning Meanings to Programs," implied that the latter was the primary application.

Shortly thereafter, Hoare developed a logic similar to Floyd's, but for "algebraic" programs rather than flowcharts, in which flow of control is represented not with a graph of assignments and decisions but with the constructs **begin** $a_1; a_2;...; a_n$ **end** (we will omit the **begin** and **end** below), **if** p **then** a_1 **else** a_2, and **while** p **do** a. Assignments are as in Floyd's system. Hoare introduced the notation $p\{a\}q$ corresponding to Floyd's verification conditions and expressing "if p (the *precondition*) holds before executing a, then q (the *postcondition*) holds when and if a terminates."

Hoare gave a set of proof rules closer in form than Floyd's to traditional logical systems, though in content similar to Floyd's rules inasmuch as every Hoare proof of an algebraic program could be readily translated to a Floyd proof of the corresponding flowchart program. The reverse translation is also possible, though complicated by the difficulty of translating flowcharts to algebraic programs. Unlike Floyd, Hoare did not address the question of completeness of any aspect of his system. Like Floyd, Hoare regarded his proof rules as being for both proofs and semantics.

Hoare's proof system for assignments, begin-end, conditional statements, and while loops amounted to the following rules (to within irrelevant details) together with whatever rules are appropriate for proving ordinary (non-Hoare) assertions of the form $p \rightarrow q$. The rules take the form of zero or more premises written over a conclusion.

1. $$\frac{p' \to p \quad p\{a\}q \quad q \to q'}{p'\{a\}q'}$$ [If $p\{a\}q$ and also $p' \to p$ and $q \to q'$, then also $p'\{a\}q'$]

2. $$\frac{}{p(e)\{x:=e\}p(x)}$$ [If p holds of e ($p(e)$ is true) before assignment of e to x, p holds of x afterwards]

3. $$\frac{p\{a\}q \quad q\{b\}r}{p\{a;b\}r}$$ [The transitive rule for sequential constructs]

4. $$\frac{p \wedge r\{a\}q \quad p \wedge \sim r\{b\}q}{p\{\textbf{if } r \textbf{ then } a \textbf{ else } b\}q}$$ [The if–then–else rule where the value of r in the precondition determines which construct is executed]

5. $$\frac{p \wedge q\{a\}p}{p\{\textbf{while } q \textbf{ do } a\}p \wedge \sim q}$$ [In a while–loop, p is the loop invariant and q the condition that becomes false]

The second rule, for assignment, is really an axiom, since it has no premises. It says that if p holds of e, then, after executing $x := e$, p holds of x. With these rules, we may prove that the following program computes $n!$, the factorial of the initial value of n of y, provided n is nonnegative.

$$A: x := 1; B$$
$$B: \textbf{while } y > 0 \textbf{ do } C$$
$$C: x := y \times x; y := y - 1$$

The following Hoare assertions about this program may all be seen to be true; moreover, they are all provable in Hoare's system. The last asserts the property we want. Together, these assertions form a correctness proof of the program, in the sense that they show that the program computes the factorial of the initial value of y.

i. $y > 0 \wedge x \times y! = n!\{x := y \times x\} y > 0 \wedge x \times (y-1)! = n!$
   [First $y > 0 \wedge x \times y! = n! \to y > 0 \wedge (y \times x) \times (y - 1)! = n!$; then apply (2), substituting x for $y \times x$]

ii. $y > 0 \wedge x \times (y-1)! = n!\{y := y-1\} y \geq 0 \wedge x \times y! = n!$
   [Similarly using (2)]

iii. $y > 0 \wedge x \times y! = n!\{C\} y \leq 0 \wedge x \times y! = n!$
   [Applying (3) to (i) and (ii)]

iv. $y \geq 0 \wedge y = n \wedge x = 1\{B\} x = n!$
   [Since $y = n \wedge x = 1 \to x \times y! = n!$ and since $y \geq 0 \wedge x \times y! = n! \wedge y \leq 0 \to y = 0 \wedge x = n! \to x \times y! = n!$ (since $0! = 1$), (5) with (iii) gives (iv) with $q = y > 0$ and $p = y \leq 0 \wedge x \times y! = n!$]

v. $y \geq 0 \wedge y = n\{x := 1\} y \geq 0 \wedge y! = n \wedge x = 1$
   [Since $p\{x := 1\} p \wedge x = 1$]

vi. $y \geq 0 \wedge y = n\{A\} x = n!$
   [Applying (3) to (v) and (iv)]

Since the precondition in (vi) is just the initial condition on n and the postcondition gives the desired result, the program A is thus proved to compute $n!$

To discover this proof, one might start with the last line and work backwards. Discovering line (iii) is the one truly creative step here. The formula $y \geq 0 \wedge x \times y! = n!$

is the *loop invariant* (*q.v.*) or the *induction hypothesis,* and plays an analogous role to the more readily discovered induction hypothesis encountered above in connection with the associativity of append.

In more recent years, there has arisen an interest in decision methods for logics of programs as an alternative to proof systems for reasoning about programs. In general, even the simple logics considered above are undecidable (*see* UNDECIDABLE PROBLEMS); their theory (set of valid formulas) is not only not recursive but not even recursively enumerable. However, there exist various fragments of program logic that are decidable, just as propositional logic is a decidable fragment of the predicate calculus. The fragment of program logic analogous to propositional logic is the system of propositional dynamic logic developed by Fischer and Ladner (1979), which they have shown to be decidable. From this, it is possible to deduce that program logic without binding (everything but assignments, quantifiers, and procedure definitions) is also decidable, and that the inclusion of any one of these binding mechanisms makes it undecidable. For reasoning about parallel programs, there is A. Pneuli's temporal fragment of logics of programs, which is also decidable (see Gabbay *et al.* 1980).

Current research into logics of programs addresses a variety of questions. What are appropriate semantics, proof rules, and decision methods for other programming language constructs, including recursion, parameter passing, manipulation of complex data structures, parallelism, non-determinism, and probabilistic programs? What is the computational complexity of the decidable fragments of program logic? What alternative forms may the semantics and rules take? What are the obstacles to applying program logics to enhancing software reliability via program verification? The reader interested in recent developments in this area should consult Harel (1984) and Kozen and Tiuryn (1989). Much of the most recent work may be found in the theoretical computer science journals and annual conferences, in particular the Symposia on Logic in Computer Science, the ACM Symposia on Theory of Computation, the ACM Symposia on Principles of Programming Languages, the IEEE Symposia on Foundations of Computer Science, the European Association for Theoretical Computer Science International Congress on Automata, Languages and Programming, and the Czech-Polish Symposium on Mathematical Foundations of Computer Science.

References

1963. McCarthy, J. "A Basis for a Mathematical Theory of Computation," in Braffort, P. and Hirschberg, D., *Computer Programming and Formal Systems*. Amsterdam: North Holland, 33–70.

1967. Floyd, R. W. "Assigning Meanings to Programs," in Schwartz, J. T. (Ed.), *Mathematical Aspects of Computer Science (Proceedings of a Symposium in Applied Mathematics)* 19. Providence, RI: American Mathematical Society, 19–32.

1969. Hoare, C. A. R. "An Axiomatic Basis for Computer Programming," *Comm. ACM* 12: 576–580.

1979. Fischer, M. J. and Ladner, R. E. "Propositional Dynamic Logic of Regular Programs," *JCSS* 18, 2: 194–211 (April).

1980. Gabbay, D., Pnueli, A., Shelah, S., and Stavi, J. "The Temporal

Analysis of Fairness," *7th ACM Symp. on Principles of Programming Languages,* Las Vegas (January).

1984. Harel, D. "Dynamic Logic," in *Handbook of Philosophical Logic. II: Extensions of Classical Logic,* 497–604. Boston: D. Reidel.

1989. Kozen, D. and Tiuryn, J. "Logics of Programs," in J. van Leeuwen (Ed.), *Handbook of Theoretical Computer Science.* Amsterdam: North Holland.

VAUGHN R. PRATT

LOGIN FILE

For an article on a related subject *see* BOOT AND REBOOT.

A *login file* is a stored file of operating system commands and definitions that are obeyed automatically upon start-up of a personal computer or workstation or upon logging on to a multiprogrammed mainframe or minicomputer. In the latter environment, login files are unique to each user, although the files of most users will contain many common elements. To enable such customization, the login file is kept in the mass storage space allocated to the particular user and, since it has the same format as any other text file, may be edited as often as desired.

With the DEC VMS operating system, the login file must be named *login.com.* A typical login file might look like Fig. 1.

The leading $ symbols are operating system prompt characters that must be a physical part of the login file. Ordinarily, the commands placed in a newly edited login file will not be obeyed until the user logs off and then logs on again, but they can be executed by typing @*login* at any system prompt.

On personal computers that use the MS-DOS operating system, users must separate system definitions from system commands through use of two login files that work in tandem. Definitions are placed in *config.sys* and commands in *autoexec.bat* (where the file extension *.bat* signifies a BATch file). An example of a typical *config.sys* file is shown in Fig. 2. A typical *autoexec.bat* file is shown in Fig. 3.

When booted (*see* BOOT AND REBOOT), the computer will first establish the definitions in *config.sys* and then obey the operating system commands in *autoexec.bat.*

EDWIN D. REILLY

LOGO

For articles on related subjects *see* COMPUTER-ASSISTED INSTRUCTION; COMPUTER-ASSISTED LEARNING AND TEACHING; COMPUTER-MANAGED INSTRUCTION; FUNCTIONAL PROGRAMMING; and LIST PROCESSING.

Logo is a dialect of Lisp designed for educational use. Like other dialects of Lisp, Logo is a general-purpose programming language with special emphasis on symbolic computing and on functional programming. Three things give Logo its special educational focus: a simplified syntax, detailed attention to the programmer's metaphors for computational processes in the naming of primitive procedures and the wording of error messages, and a collection of application areas (of which the most famous is *turtle graphics*) that combine inherent interest with open-ended intellectual content.

The first version of Logo was developed in 1967 at Bolt, Beranek, and Newman, Inc., by Wallace Feurzeig, Seymour Papert, and others. The project grew out of their experience teaching junior high school students with a more conventional algebraic programming language; many students were uninspired by the numeric emphasis, and so a language was designed with tools to manipulate English words and sentences. (The name "Logo" is derived from the Greek word λογος, meaning "word.") Papert

```
$ set terminal/device = vt100       ; Specify kind of terminal being used
$ prepare emacs                     ; Enable use of the EMACS screen editor
$ home :== set default sys$login    ; Create a synonym for the word "home"
$ set directory/version_limit = 2 [csi.reilly]; Keep only two versions of
$                                   ; each file in directory
```

FIG. 1.

```
FILES = 20          ; Allow a maximum of 20 simultaneous open files
BUFFERS = 10        ; Allocate 10 disk buffers upon start-up
DEVICE = ANSI.SYS   ; Install a particular device driver
```

FIG. 2.

```
path rbfiles ; Set a directory path to subdirectory rbfiles
cd dbfiles   ; Change active directory to dbfiles
rbase        ; Execute the rbase program
```

FIG. 3.

later established a Logo research group at the Massachusetts Institute of Technology, where the language was redesigned and the robot turtle was introduced.

Educational Goals Logo's developers were not interested primarily in the training of professional computer programmers. Instead, the goal was to provide an environment for mathematical thinking in the context of concrete projects. Developmental psychologist Jean Piaget argued that people learn mainly by *construction*—fitting new ideas with already-understood ideas. Much of traditional school mathematics is abstract and disconnected from a child's ordinary experience, so this incremental learning process is difficult. Writing a computer program gives the learner practice in formal, mathematical reasoning, but each Logo application area is connected with things children do outside the context of computers or mathematics.

For example, consider the difference between Logo's turtle graphics and the Cartesian graphics traditionally used in other languages. In the latter, a fixed pair of coordinate axes is associated with the display screen; a line segment is drawn by specifying the coordinates of its endpoints. In Logo, the metaphor is that segments are drawn by a pen controlled by a robot turtle. At any moment this turtle is in some position and facing in some direction; a segment is drawn by moving or turning relative to this position and heading. Since absolute coordinates are not used, a single procedure can draw a given shape anywhere and in any orientation. But the real reason for turtle graphics is not its technical convenience. Turtle graphics is considered easier to assimilate than conventional graphics because it is *body-syntonic*. The way the turtle moves in drawing some shape is the same way that a person would move in walking over that shape on the floor. As an analogy, consider that street directions are generally given in the form "go straight three blocks, then turn left" and not "go to latitude 46 degrees, longitude 62 degrees, then go to latitude 47 degrees, longitude 59 degrees."

The ability to draw a picture at any position and heading is particularly convenient for the exploration of fractals (*q.v.*), in which an overall picture is made by including several smaller versions of the same picture (see Fig. 1.).

Logo Syntax Lisp, Logo's parent language, was designed in part to facilitate formal reasoning about computer programs. For this reason, syntactic uniformity was valued above ease of use. Each Lisp expression represents the application of a procedure to arguments; the notation is a list in parentheses, in which the first element is the procedure and the other elements are the arguments, which are themselves Lisp expressions in the same form:

```
(DEFINE FACTORIAL
    (LAMBDA (N)
        (IF (= N 0)
            1
            (* N (FACTORIAL (- N 1)))))))
```

```
TO TREE :SIZE :LEVEL
IF :LEVEL = 0 [STOP]
FORWARD :SIZE/3
LEFT 20
TREE 2*:SIZE/3 :LEVEL-1
RIGHT 20
FORWARD :SIZE/6
RIGHT 15
TREE :SIZE/2 :LEVEL-1
LEFT 15
FORWARD :SIZE/4
LEFT 15
TREE 2*:SIZE/3 :LEVEL-1
RIGHT 15
FORWARD :SIZE/8
RIGHT 10
TREE :SIZE/3 :LEVEL-1
LEFT 10
FORWARD :SIZE/8
BACK :SIZE
END
```

FIG. 1. An example of a fractal-tree.

A Logo version has the same logical structure, but the notation is more relaxed. Parentheses are not required for every procedure call, and conventional infix notation is allowed for arithmetic operators:

```
TO FACTORIAL :N
IF :N = 0 [OUTPUT 1]
OUTPUT :N * FACTORIAL (:N - 1)
END
```

Despite the difference in notation, Logo maintains the Lisp idea that everything is done by procedure calls. For example, the word IF in the procedure above is not a special syntactic keyword as it would be in most languages. It is an invocation of the IF procedure with two arguments. The first argument (in this example, computed by an invocation of the = procedure) must be the word TRUE or the word FALSE. The second argument is a list (indicated by the square brackets) containing instructions that will be carried out if the first argument is TRUE.

The use of Lisp as a vehicle for formal reasoning about programs led to one other characteristic that is compromised in Logo: the emphasis on functional programming style. In Lisp, every procedure is a function that returns a value. The use of procedures that make permanent changes in the environment (such as assigning a value to a variable) is possible but discouraged. Logo does support this functional programming style (the FACTORIAL procedure above is an example), but in Logo a distinction is made between *operations* (procedures that return a value) and *commands* (procedures called for effect), like the distinction between functions and procedures in Pascal. The use of commands in Logo allows the more traditional sequential style for applications in which that style is more natural, such as this conversational program:

```
TO GREET
PRINT [WHAT'S YOUR NAME?]
MAKE :RESPONSE READLIST
PRINT SENTENCE [PLEASED TO MEET YOU,]
    :RESPONSE
END
```

In most other respects, Logo follows traditional Lisp ideas. There are no type declarations; data types are associated with values rather than with the variables to which those values may be assigned. The main data aggregation mechanism is the variable-length, heterogeneous list rather than the more conventional fixed-length, homogeneous array. Variables obey dynamic scoping rules; procedure definitions are never lexically within other procedures. In each case the design decision is made to promote flexibility, ease of programming and debugging, and simple computational metaphors. By contrast, each of these design decisions is reversed in many other languages to reflect conventional machine architectures that value program execution speed above ease of use.

Attention to Computational Metaphors Logo teachers use the metaphor of "teaching the computer" to describe procedure definition. The keyword that announces a definition is TO, rather than Lisp's DEFINE, to suggest the sentence "I'm going to teach you how TO GREET" (in the example above). Also, following English syntax, the keyword TO suggests that the procedure name is a verb, as befits an action we are teaching the computer. The same metaphor is supported by the error message for invoking an undefined procedure:

```
I DON'T KNOW HOW  TO GARPLY
```

The extra space in the message reminds the user how to correct the problem, without destroying the meaning of the message as an English sentence.

Some versions of Logo provide two different commands to assign a value to a variable:

```
MAKE name value
NAME value name
```

These two versions have exactly the same effect; they differ only in the order of the arguments. The older MAKE supports the traditional metaphor of a variable as a box that can contain different values at different times. However, Logo's support of functional programming style minimizes the need for such reassignment. Instead, a common use of assignment is to provide names for global constants. For example, many computers use small integers to represent the colors they can display on the screen. An assignment like

```
NAME 3 "BLUE
```

is best understood not as putting the value 3 into a box, but rather as attaching a nametag to 3. "Whenever I say BLUE, I mean 3."

The attention to metaphor extends beyond the choice of names. One application of Logo is in natural language processing; an English sentence is represented as a list of words. As in Lisp, the underlying selection operations that can be applied to a list are to select the first element of a list or all but the first element. (Lisp calls these CAR and CDR; Logo calls them FIRST and BUTFIRST.) In Logo, however, the same operations can also be used to extract the first letter, or all but the first letter, of a word. It is natural to use the same tools to manipulate words and sentences, even though the representations inside the computer are different. By similar reasoning, Logo provides symmetrical LAST and BUTLAST operations even though the underlying representation of lists is asymmetrical and these latter operations are slower than FIRST and BUTFIRST. The rules for forming the plural of an English word depend on its last letter or letters; here is a partial implementation:

```
TO PLURAL :WORD
IF MEMBERP LAST :WORD [O S X] [OUTPUT WORD
  :WORD "ES]
IF EQUALP LAST :WORD "Y
  [IF NOT MEMBERP LAST :WORD [A E I O U]
      [OUTPUT WORD BUTLAST :WORD "IES]]
OUTPUT WORD :WORD "S
END
```

This says that a word ending in O, S or X forms its plural by adding ES; a word ending in Y forms its plural by changing the Y to IES unless the letter before the Y is a vowel; otherwise, the plural is formed by adding S.

Continuing Research and Development Much of the development effort in the Logo community goes into inventing new application areas, with a new set of primitive procedures and often new peripheral hardware, rather than into the core control structures of the language. Examples from the 1970s were music synthesis and special animated graphics hardware. (The latter allowed multiple turtles, with state information, including shape and velocity as well as the traditional position and heading.) A current example uses computer-readable sensors, such as photocells and pressure switches, mounted on Lego™ blocks so that Logo programs using these sensors can control motors in robots and similar Lego machines.

Several recent versions of Logo have included more or less elaborate forms of object-oriented programming (q.v.), usually with a message-passing syntax something like

```
ASK :TURTLE3 [FORWARD 40]
```

in which the first argument to ASK is an object and the second is an instruction to be carried out by that object. Other projects have developed new languages, inspired by Logo but substantially different. One impetus for such development is the desire to take advantage of high-resolution graphics capability to express program control structure, as in Boxer (M.I.T. and Berkeley) and Function Machines (BBN).

References

On Logo's educational significance:
1980. Papert, Seymour. *Mindstorms: Computers, Children, and Powerful Ideas.* New York: Basic Books.
On technical details:
1985. Harvey, Brian. *Computer Science Logo Style, Volume 1: Intermediate Programming.* Cambridge, MA: The M.I.T. Press.

BRIAN HARVEY

LOOP

For articles on related subjects *see* CONTROL STRUCTURES; INDEX REGISTER; ITERATION; LOOP INVARIANT; and STRUCTURED PROGRAMMING.

A *loop* is a program fragment designed to be executed repeatedly during a single execution of the containing program. This ability to re-use the same instructions, normally with fresh operands at each iteration, is the great advantage offered by the stored-program computer (*q.v.*) and is what makes possible virtually all programs of practical value.

The creation of a loop, whether accomplished explicitly by an assembly-language programmer or implicitly by a programmer using a higher-level language, involves three steps beyond those required by non-iterative or straight-line programming: *initialization* (putting appropriate registers and memory locations in the proper state for starting the execution of the loop), *address modification* (to select fresh operands for each iteration of the loop), and *index modification and testing* (to record the number of times the loop has been traversed since its most recent initialization, and to exit from it when this variable reaches the user-specified value).

The assembly-language programmer has to write code to accomplish each of these tasks, usually using registers provided for the purpose that have just the decrementation and testing properties needed for loop control—for example, the CX register in the 80xxx microprocessors, or the index registers in the old IBM 704/7094

machines. Loop initialization requires loading such a register—we will use the term "index register," or IR, for convenience—with a value that is equal to, or a simple function of, the number of desired iterations. In the general case, it is necessary also to initialize another IR with the quantity by which data addresses are to be modified at each iteration. Address modification is accomplished by including a reference to the appropriate IR in each instruction in the loop whose apparent address is to be modified to select a new datum at each iteration. Index modification and testing, finally, are accomplished by instructions that test the loop-controlling IR to see if it has reached its terminal value, and cause either an exit from the loop, or another iteration of it with a decremented IR value, depending on whether or not that terminal value has been reached.

The higher-level language programmer is relieved of much of this detail, since an HLL almost always offers at least one statement type that, given the necessary parameters—the range of statements forming the loop, and the name, initial value, terminal value, and step size of the index or *control variable*—will generate all the necessary code. To illustrate, Fig. 1 shows a Fortran loop whose function is to find the largest number in an array $A(1)...A(n)$ of n numbers. In Fig. 2, the same loop is specified in C (*q.v.*).

The C version is typical of current languages, whose loop-creation statements typically begin with FOR, WHILE, UNTIL, and other such words that tell the compiler how and when to test the index variable, sparing the programmer the working out of that logic.

Loops can be nested—i.e. contain other loops—to a depth usually limited only by storage capacity, with the number of times an inner loop is iterated being the product of its own iteration count and those of all the loops it nests within. This gives code within a deeply nested loop great leverage in determining the performance of the program as a whole; 90% of a program's execution time may be consumed in iterating some deeply nested loop, and if any code within that loop is redundant, the consequent waste of time is proportionately greater.

The requirement, economic or psychological, of

Fortran statement	Comment
BIG = A(1)	BIG will hold the answer; equate it initially to the value of the first number in the array.
DO 4 I = 2,N	Set up loop: its body is all statements from the DO to the one labelled "4" (label is arbitrary); the index (control variable) is I; the value of I ranges from 2, by steps of 1 (by default; if it were other than 1, it would be given as the last parameter) to N (whose value will have been assigned elsewhere).
IF (A(I) .GT. BIG) BIG = A(I)	Compare next number in array to present value of BIG; if bigger than BIG, it becomes new BIG.
4 CONTINUE	Label "4" identifies the statement ending the loop; effect is to (a) test whether I has reached its terminal value of N (in which case, all numbers in the array have been tested, and the biggest is in BIG, so the loop is done, and control drops through to the next instruction), or it has not yet reached N (in which case it is modified by the specified or default step size, and control passes to the first instruction of the loop again to test another array element against BIG).

FIG. 1. Fortran loop to find largest of an array of numbers.

```
for (big = a[1], i=2; i<=n; i++
    if (a[i] > big) big = a[i];
```

FIG. 2. C loop to find largest of an array of numbers.

avoiding such extreme penalties for small coding lapses is the motivation for the inclusion of optimization phases in compilers, whose most fruitful efforts are those devoted to moving instructions out of inner loops and into the less frequently executed loops in which they are nested. The techniques for performing optimization have been the subject of much study, and form a significant discipline within computer science (*see* COMPILER CONSTRUCTION).

MARK HALPERN

LOOP INVARIANT

For articles on related subjects *see* CONTROL STRUCTURE; LOOP; PROGRAM VERIFICATION; and STRUCTURED PROGRAMMING.

Consider a loop **while** B **do** S, where B is a boolean expression and S a statement. This form of loop appears in most modern high-level languages. Let P be some true-false statement about the variables of the program in which the loop appears. P is a *loop invariant* if execution of the loop body S begun in any state in which P and B are true terminates with P true. For example, consider the loop

while $i \neq 10$ **do begin** $i := i + 1$; $x := x + i$ **end**

and the following assertions about the loop variables:

$P0$: $1 \leq i \leq 10$ **and** $x = 1 + 2 + ... + i$,
$P1$: $1 \leq i \leq 10$ **and** $x = 1 + 2 + ... + i$ **and** $x \leq 10$,
$P2$: $i = i$.

$P0$ is a loop invariant, since execution of $i := i + 1$; $x := x + i$ beginning with $i \neq 10$ and $P0$ true terminates with $P0$ true. $P1$ is not a loop invariant, since execution of the body of the loop with $i = 4$ and $P1$ true (so that $x = 10$) sets x to 15, thus falsifying the third conjunct of $P1$. $P2$ is a loop invariant since it is always true.

Using an Invariant to Prove Partial Correctness of a Loop

Suppose P is an invariant of a loop. Suppose further that P is true when execution of the loop begins. Since each iteration of the loop is guaranteed to keep it true, and since we assume that evaluation of an expression changes no variable, we conclude that P is still true when execution of the loop terminates. Further, B is false when the loop terminates. This gives a basis for proving a loop correct.

To prove that postcondition R is true when a loop **while** B **do** S terminates, find an assertion P that satisfies the following:

(0) P is true when execution of the loop begins,
(1) P is a loop invariant,
(2) (P **and not** B) => R.

For example, to prove that the program segment

$i := 1$; $x := 1$; **while** $i \neq 10$ **do**
  begin $i := i + 1$; $x := x + i$ **end**

terminates with R: $x = 1 + 2 + ... + 10$, we use the invariant

P: $1 \leq i \leq 10$ **and** $x = 1 + 2 + ... + i$

and note that (0) P is true just before the loop, with $x = i = 1$, (1) P is a loop invariant, and (2) (P **and** $i = 10$) => R.

Proving Total Correctness of a Loop

We have just shown the *partial* correctness of the loop: if and when it terminates, R is true. Proving *total* correctness means also showing that the loop terminates. This we do by exhibiting a *bound function* t, which is an upper bound on the number of iterations still to be performed. In this case, the bound function t: $10 - i$ gives the exact number of iterations, while the bound function $20 - i$ provides a grosser upper bound. An integer function of the variables of the program is a bound function of the loop if

(0) Each iteration of the loop decreases t, and
(1) If another iteration is to be performed, $t > 0$; i.e. (P **and** B) => $t > 0$.

If in part (1) the expression $t > 0$ is replaced by $t > c$ for some constant c, then t is called a *variant* function. For example, $-i$ is a variant function, since $-i > -11$ always holds and $-i$ is reduced by each iteration. Termination can be shown using a variant function, but in general a bound function provides more information about the execution time of the loop. One can also prove termination using more general well-founded sets.

Developing Loops Using Invariants

Some computer scientists have the opinion that it is a programmer's duty to provide documentation for a program that serves as an outline of its proof of correctness, and this means providing a suitable invariant and bound function for each loop. However, it is far too difficult to find the invariant after the fact. Rather, it is felt that the loop invariant and loop should be developed hand-in-hand, with the invariant—or an approximation to it—leading the way. A number of heuristics for the development of the loop invariant based on the shape of the pre- and postconditions have been developed, and there is much evidence that the heuristics (*q.v.*) are indeed practical. In the hands of an experienced person, they can lead to simple and efficient programs. Those most familiar with the method believe that it is superior to the more conventional, ad hoc approach to programming—that its use provides for more effective presentations of programs, and that it offers significant insight to the teacher of programming.

We illustrate this method of programming using a trivial example. We desire a program segment that stores the sum of the first ten positive integers in variable x, i.e.

a segment with precondition *true* and postcondition *R*: *x* = 1 + 2 + ... + 10. Having decided that a loop is to be written, invariant *P* is found by generalizing the postcondition, by replacing the constant 10 by a fresh variable *i* and placing suitable bounds on it:

$$P : 1 \leq i \leq 10 \text{ and } x = 1 + 2 + ... + i.$$

(The technique of replacing an expression of the postcondition by a fresh variable is one of the more effective methods of finding an invariant.) The goal of the generalization is to have an invariant that is easily established, and in this case the initialization *x,i* := 1,1 does nicely. Next, the loop condition *B* is found by solving the formula (*P* **and not** *B*) => *R* for *B*, giving *i* ≠ 10. The loop body has yet to be developed. It must decrease the bound function and maintain the invariant. A glance at the initialization, invariant, and loop condition leads to the bound function 10 − *i*, and from this we decide that *i* := *i* + 1 should appear in the body of the loop. Thus far, the body of the loop can be written as

$$\{P \text{ and } i \neq 10\} \ S; \ i := i + 1 \ \{P\}$$

where statement *S* is to be determined. Now, *P* is true after execution of the assignment to *i* exactly when *P*, with all occurrences of *i* replaced by *i* + 1, is true before, so we are left with finding a statement *S* that satisfies

$$\{P \text{ and } i \neq 10\} \ S$$
$$\{1 \leq i + 1 \leq 10 \text{ and } x = 1 + 2 + ... + (i + 1)\}.$$

The statement *S*: *x* := *x* + (*i* + 1) will do, so the loop body is *x* := *x* + (*i* + 1); *i* := *i* + 1, which can be simplified to *i* := *i* + 1; *x* := *x* + *i*. Thus, we end up with the segment

$$i := 1; x := 1; \textbf{while } i \neq 10 \textbf{ do}$$
$$\textbf{begin } i := i + 1; x := x + i \textbf{ end}$$

In this example, a trivial problem has been used so that difficulties with the problem would not overwhelm understanding of the developmental strategies. Far more complicated problems have been tackled with the method, with sometimes surprising results. Here is an example of an algorithm that is very difficult to understand without the loop invariant. The algorithm stores a^b in integer variable *z*, where *a* and *b* are integers. The loop invariant is $P : 0 \leq y$ and $z * x^y = a^b$ and a bound function is *t* : *y*.

$$\{0 \leq b\}$$
$$z := 1; x := a; y := b;$$
$$\textbf{while } y \neq 0 \textbf{ do if } even(y)$$
$$\quad \textbf{then begin } x := x * x; y := y \textbf{ div } 2 \textbf{ end}$$
$$\quad \textbf{else begin } z := z * x; y := y - 1 \textbf{ end}$$

Since, in the worst cases, *y* counts down to zero one unit at a time, there are never more than *y* more iterations to do, so that *t* : *y* is a safe bound function. Also, when the loop terminates with *y* = 0, $z * x^y = a^b$ reduces to $z * x^0 = a^b$ and hence $z = a^b$, which is what we wanted.

History   The basic ideas of proving a program (actually, a flowchart) correct, including total correctness, was given by Floyd (1967). Floyd says that the ideas were not original, but were based on ideas of Perlis and Gorn. The formulation of partial correctness in terms of a loop invariant, as described above, as well as the first definition of a language fragment in terms of correctness-proof rules, was given by Hoare (1969). The term *invariant* was not used in this paper, but it became popular soon after. The basic methods for developing proof and program hand-in-hand, with the former leading the way, were given in the monograph *A Discipline of Programming* (E.W. Dijkstra, 1976). A text on the topic is Gries (1981). Dijkstra is responsible for the term *variant function* and Gries for *bound function*. Methods of proving correctness using invariants have also been developed for the conventional **for** and **repeat** loops (*see* STRUCTURED PROGRAMMING).

References

1967. Floyd, R. W. "Assigning Meaning to Programs," *Proceedings of the American Mathematical Society Symposium on Applied Mathematics* **19**, 19–31.

1969. Hoare, C. A. R. "An Axiomatic Basis for Computer Programming," *Comm. ACM* **12**, October, 576–583.

1976. Dijkstra, E. W. *A Discipline of Programming*. Englewood Cliffs, NJ: Prentice-Hall.

1981. Gries, D. *The Science of Programming*. New York: Springer-Verlag.

DAVID GRIES

LOVELACE, COUNTESS OF

For articles on related subjects *see* ANALYTICAL ENGINE; BABBAGE, CHARLES; DIFFERENCE ENGINE; and DIGITAL COMPUTERS: HISTORY: ORIGINS.

Augusta Ada Byron was born in London on 10 December 1815. She was the daughter of Lord Byron and Annabella Milbanke Byron, whose separation a little over a month after her birth was followed by Lord Byron's leaving England, never to return. She married William, eighth Lord King, in 1835, and three years later, on his elevation to an Earldom, became known as the Countess of Lovelace, and hence Lady Lovelace.

Ada, as she was known in the family circle, was educated by governesses and tutors, and later by much self-study. Dr. Augustus De Morgan, professor at the University of London, helped her in her advanced studies, and formed a very high opinion of her abilities: "The tract about Babbage's machine is a pretty thing enough, but I could I think produce a series of extracts, out of Lady Lovelace's first queries upon new subjects, which would make a mathematician see that it was no criterion of what might be expected from her." (*Lovelace-Byron Papers.*) Her correspondence with contemporary scientists, such as Michael Faraday, Mary Somerville, and Sir John Herschel, reveals her deep interest in varied scientific topics. She was also an accomplished musician, particularly on the harp.

ADA, COUNTESS of LOVELACE

FIG. 1.   By courtesy of the Rt. Hon. Earl of Lytton, OBE.

Lady Lovelace, fascinated by Babbage's machines after first viewing his difference engine in 1833, translated L. F. Menabrea's paper on Babbage's analytical engine from French into English. Babbage suggested that she add some notes to the translation, which she did with such enthusiasm that they extended Menabrea's paper to about three times its original length. Of particular interest is her description in these notes of the repeated use of a set of cards with a purpose similar to that of subroutines in today's computer programs. With the help of Babbage, she worked out a nearly complete program to compute Bernoulli numbers, as complete as was consistent with

the state of the design of the engine at that time. Because of this, she has been called the first female computer programmer and, in 1979, a new language was named Ada (*q.v.*) in her honor. Recent books have both disparaged and praised Ada's place in computer history, depending in part on what standards they apply.

Babbage's high regard for Lady Lovelace's notes is expressed in his autobiography: "Their author has entered fully into almost all the very difficult and abstract questions connected with the subject." Also, in a letter to her son, Viscount Ockham, in 1857, Babbage wrote, "In the memoir of Mr. Menabrea and still more in the excellent Notes appended by your mother you will find the only comprehensive view of the powers of the Anal. Eng. which the mathematicians of the world have yet expressed." (*Babbage Correspondence.*)

All of her life, Lady Lovelace was plagued by ill health. She died on 27 November 1852, less than a fortnight before her 37th birthday.

References

Lovelace-Byron Papers. Bodleian Library, Oxford (Courtesy of Earl of Lytton and Viscount Knebworth).

Babbage Correspondence. Additional Ms., British Library, London.

1843. Lovelace, Ada Countess of. "Sketch of the Analytical Engine Invented by Charles Babbage, Esq. by L. F. Menabrea, of Turin, Officer of the Military Engineers: With Copious Notes by the Translator," *Scientific Memoirs* III: 666–731. Taylor, R. (Ed.). London: R. & J. E. Taylor. (Reprinted in 1953. Bowden, B. V. *Faster Than Thought.* London: Sir Isaac Pitman & Sons.)

1864. Babbage, C. *Passages from the Life of a Philosopher.* London: Longmans, Green, & Co.

1977. Moore, Doris Langley. *Ada, Countess of Lovelace.* London: Harper & Row.

1980. Huskey, V. and Huskey, H. "Lady Lovelace and Charles Babbage," *Annals of the History of Computing* 2, 4, 299–329 (October).

1986. Stein, D. *Ada, A Life and a Legacy.* Cambridge, MA: M.I.T. Press.

1986. Baum, J. *The Calculating Passion of Ada Byron.* Hamden, CT: Shoe String Press.

VELMA R. HUSKEY

MACHINE AND ASSEMBLY LANGUAGE PROGRAMMING

For articles on related subjects *see* ADDRESSING; ASSEMBLER; BINDING; COMPUTERS, MULTIPLE ADDRESS; DEBUGGING; DISASSEMBLER; DUMP; GENERAL REGISTER; INDEX REGISTER; INDIRECT ADDRESS; INSTRUCTION SET; LINKER; LOADER; MACROINSTRUCTION; MICROPROGRAMMING; NO-OP; PROGRAM COUNTER; REGISTER; RISC ARCHITECTURE; and STORED PROGRAM CONCEPT.

Notation and Conventions   Throughout this article, ML stands for machine language, and AL for (symbolic) assembly language. For the sake of clarity, the coding examples offered throughout are for a now obsolete machine family (the IBM 704-709-7090-7094 series), which lends itself to piecemeal elementary presentation better than its successors. This can be done without loss of generality because today's machines, though faster, bigger, and far more complex, embody no essentially new principles.

Definition of ML   Machine language has traditionally meant that particular representation of instructions and data directly interpretable by the central processing unit (*q.v.*) of the machine in question. It was a *low-level language*—indeed, the lowest possible—meaning that it was far more reflective of the machine's internal structure than of the purposes to which most users would want to put the computer. It was also *hard-wired*, meaning that it was the hardware's native language of discourse and hence needed no software translator.

But as the variety of implemented machines grows, it becomes increasingly difficult to give a simple and precise definition of ML. It no longer suffices to call it the language of the hardware now that microprogramming (*q.v.*) and other forms of multi-level processing have become common. It will suffice for our purposes to say that ML is that programming language that is executable, without prior software translation, by the CPU of some speci-fied machine, and whose typical statement consists of a single operator and its operands.

The operand part of such a statement or instruction is typically an *address*, i.e. a binary integer designating one of the storage segments called either *words* or *bytes*. (*Byte* is the usual term for a segment designed to hold one 8-bit alphanumeric character; *word* is usually reserved for the addressable segments of machines specialized for numerical computation, and hence anywhere from 8 to 64 bits long, with 32 being perhaps both mean and mode.) For convenience, we will use the term "word" hereafter when referring to an addressable memory segment.

The operator part of an ML statement will typically call for one of the following:

- An arithmetic or logical operation upon the contents of the addressed word or upon the addressed word and any of the CPU registers in which these operations can be carried out.
- The movement (copying) of data between one of these registers and a word.
- The movement of data from or to one of the machine's input/output devices.
- Transfer of control (branching), either conditionally or unconditionally, to the address cited in the operand field.

The bit pattern in an addressed word will, if the operator is an ordinary arithmetic one, be treated as the representation of a scalar quantity in base 2 (or an integral power of 2, such as hexadecimal).

The foregoing describes a typical one-address ML instruction. Some computers use *multiple-address* instructions that include the addresses of two or more operands, such as the augend and addend of an addition operation. Many machines offer some instructions whose operand parts are *immediate*, i.e. they are themselves the data to be operated on, not the addresses of that data. Other instructions interpret their address field as an *indirect address* that takes the value in that field not as the address of the data, but as the address of the address of the data. Many instructions can be *indexed*, i.e. they contain a field that can be used to designate some register whose contents are to modify the present contents of the address field (the *apparent address*) to form the *effective address* that will actually be used to access the operand.

All machines include instructions, variously called *jumps*, *transfers*, or *branches*, whose purpose is to change the standard sequential order in which the instructions in a program are executed. Some jumps are absolute (unconditional): when executed, they always force program execution to continue at the programmer-specified point in the program, rather than at the normal point which would be the next instruction following the jump itself. Other types of jumps are conditional: they call for the execution of some test and change the order of instruction execution only if the test result satisfies some specified condition. Unconditional jumps and conditional jumps whose test is met effectuate a change in flow of control by resetting the machine's program counter (*q.v.*) to the address specified in the operand field of the jump instruction.

Regretably, ML is sometimes used loosely as a synonym for "assembly language." In this article, the terms *machine language* and *assembly language* will be kept quite distinct, with ML standing solely for that language (characterized above) which requires no software to translate it and makes no concession whatever to human readability or convenience.

Example of ML

In the IBM 704 architecture, the register in which addition and subtraction are done is called the *accumulator*. The instruction that causes the quantity in a specific word—the word whose address is decimal 100, say—to be brought to the accumulator is in binary

$$000101000000000000000000001100100 \qquad (1)$$

The leftmost 12 bits of this instruction contain the *operation code* (op-code), which in this case specifies that a quantity in memory is to be brought to the accumulator. The rightmost 15 (the *address field*) specify that the word whose contents are to be fetched is that at address 100 (binary 1100100 is decimal 100). The other bits in this instruction type are not used in the present example.

The instruction that adds the quantity in word 101 to the quantity in the accumulator is

$$000100000000000000000000001100101 \qquad (2)$$

and the instruction that stores the quantity in the accumulator into word 102 is

$$000110000001000000000000001100110 \qquad (3)$$

These three instructions constitute a tiny program. If they were loaded into the computer at locations n, $n+1$, and $n+2$, and the computer were directed to execute the program starting at location n, then the sum of the quantities that were the contents of words 100 and 101 would be formed in the accumulator and stored in word 102.

Uses of ML

Many programmers have to be able to recognize and interpret ML when they see it in memory dumps and assembly listings, but very few have occasion to use it as source language, since assembly language is so much easier to use. The occasions that still arise for its use are virtually limited to the patching of a program that is available only in ML, or to the implementation of the first assembler for a new machine. In the latter case, the usual approach is to write the assembler in its own language, as if it already existed, and then assemble it by hand.

Often, it will be sufficient to hand assemble only a certain essential core of the new assembler, after which the rest of it can be written in the now-implemented subset of the new assembler language, and assembled by the part already running. A curious result of this technique is that the first ML version of a new assembler, the largely handwritten one, usually has its own assembly language image for its first source program and is usually discarded after assembling that one source program, since the version that it has just assembled is both richer in facilities and freer from bugs than it is itself (*see* BOOT and REBOOT).

A third role for ML—one that may be disappearing with the increasing rationalization of computer design and the coming of RISC architecture—lies in the discovery and exploitation of the undocumented instructions that enterprising programmers used to delight in finding among a new machine's capabilities, although not advertised or even perhaps known to its designers or the authors of its assembler. (The modern equivalent of finding undocumented operation codes is finding undocumented DOS Function Calls; see Schulman, 1990, Angermeyer, 1989, pp. 741–8; and Hogan, 1988, pages 142–3.)

For programmers of the IBM-PC and compatibles (*q.v.*), ML is by no means a dead language. Many PC effects are best achieved (or achievable only) by using ML, made available through its DEBUG facility. DEBUG, a part of the PC's suite of system software originally intended for the purpose indicated by its name, is no longer much used for debugging—far better tools are now available for that—but has become instead a general ML-level tool for investigating and modifying all PC software, from DOS itself to utilities and applications. See Somerson (1988).

Features of AL

ML is not a convenient language for human use. During the 1950s, some early programmers whose names are mostly lost in the mist of computing prehistory started developing more congenial notations as well as programs for translating them into ML. In doing so, they created not only AL and the assembler (*q.v.*), but founded that large branch of computer science and software development that is devoted to improving the operating systems (*q.v.*) or user interface (*q.v.*).

The earliest assemblers were little more than routines for translating some more convenient representation of ML instructions into ML proper, with none of the additional features now expected in AL as a matter of course. The primitive assembler offered the programmer at most a symbolic representation of operators (e.g.

"ADD" instead of 000101000000), with decimal or octal representation of operand addresses.

AL now, however, is a fully symbolic language, one in which all operators and virtually all operands are normally represented by names chosen for their explanatory and mnemonic power. Some of these names, particularly those for the operators, will have been chosen by the AL designers (although many modern assemblers allow users to rename operators); operands are left for the user to name.

Example of AL The three instructions given in ML form earlier (Examples 1, 2, and 3) would appear in AL as

```
CLA 100
ADD 101          (4)
STO 102
```

or, if the programmer cared to assign names (by means defined later) to the words containing the operands, they could be

```
CLA AUGEND
ADD ADDEND       (5)
STO SUM
```

This more convenient form for writing instructions is, however, only one part, and perhaps the less important part, of the advantage offered by AL. In introducing a software intermediary—the assembler—between the programmer and the computer, AL provided a vehicle in which all kinds of new conveniences and features could be offered.

Among those substantive new features are those that allow data to be introduced in octal, decimal, hexadecimal, character string, and other "natural" forms; those that reserve execution-time storage space; and those that produce a printed, cross-indexed listing of the program, with programmer-written comments and assembler-generated warnings of known or suspected errors.

The way in which operand names such as those used in example (5) would be defined is through the use of one or another of the new assembler features. These features are usually called either *assembler directives* or *pseudo-operations,* since they look, in their AL representation, like the AL representation of actual operation codes (or instructions), but are really artifacts introduced by the assembler. They do not represent instructions to be translated into ML as part of the program, but rather directives to the assembler as to how it is to do its job. The distinction between pseudo-ops and real instructions is analogous to that between an author's marginal notes to a typist (such as "double space the next paragraph") and the manuscript to be typed. The *symbolic addresses* AUGEND, ADDEND, and SUM, for example, would have been assigned their respective values by means of pseudo-ops like these:

```
AUGEND PZE 0
ADDEND PZE 0     (6)
SUM    PZE
```

or

```
AUGEN  DZE 0
ADDEND DEC 1     (7)
SUM    PZE 0
```

where "PZE" is a pseudo-op standing for "Plus ZEro," meaning that the word in question is to contain the machine's representation of plus zero, which is 36 binary zeros, and that any symbol to its left is to be recorded as the symbolic name of that word. "DEC" is for "DECimal," meaning that the number to its right is to be interpreted as decimal (rather than binary or octal, the other two possibilities in the machine we are dealing with) and that any symbol to its left is to be similarly recorded as the word's name.

Example (6), then, reserves the next three available words in memory (the next available word being that whose address is greater by one than that last used, unless the programmer directs otherwise), assigns them the names given in their left-hand column, and sets their contents to zero. (Non-zero values will presumably be stored in at least one of AUGEND and ADDEND by some earlier part of the program before they are added together.) Example (7) does the same thing (6) does, but adds one more feature: it assigns ADDEND the initial value of 1. The pseudo-op "DEC" directs the assembler to interpret the number that follows it as a decimal number and to put the binary representation of that number in the word being reserved.

As assembly proceeds, it will often be the case that a symbolic operand is encountered that has not yet been defined. To deal with this, the assembler can adopt either of two strategies: (1) it can make two complete "passes" over the program text, collecting all definitions in the first pass, and using them in the second; or (2) it can adopt a more complex but time-saving technique, in which it makes only one pass, but notes while making it all locations at which undefined symbols are used, and goes back to replace them as soon as their definitions are found.

Each of the names assigned to a word or memory location is entered into a *symbol table* or *dictionary* created by the assembler during its first pass, along with the numerical address of the location to which it has been assigned. Then, whenever the assembler encounters a symbolic address in the program during its second pass, it substitutes the numerical equivalent of that symbol. By doing so, it frees the programmer to use a symbol ("AUGEND," for example) that is meaningful, and leaves it to the assembler to see that "AUGEND" is replaced by its binary equivalent throughout the ML program that the assembler will produce. (It should be noted that a programmer-chosen mnemonic name for a value is, to the assembler, simply an arbitrary string of characters, and it is up to the programmer to see to it that the value in a word actually mirrors its name. There is nothing, for example, to prevent the programmer from calling a location "ONE," and storing a value of two or two thousand in it.)

Probably the most important of the unexpected advantages of programming in symbols rather than bit patterns is the control it gives the programmer over *binding* (*q.v.*): the act of reducing a variable or expression in the program to a specific, fixed value. Symbolic programming allows the programmer to defer such binding and leave appropriate parts of a program on a generalized, somewhat abstract level until it is convenient to make it perfectly concrete and specific. Since the computer cannot execute a program until all of its symbols are bound, a narrow concept of efficiency would dictate that it be reduced to ML form as quickly as possible, but the forced deferral of ML form that is entailed by the use of AL turns out to carry advantages more important even than those originally sought for AL.

Programming in a symbolic language both enables the programmer to see the potential generality of a program and encourages and facilitates the realization of this generality. If the program computes a payroll, for example, the fact that AL will encourage the programmer to represent a tax rate as "TAXRATE" rather than as 17.25% and will allow it to be numerically defined just once by use of a "DEC" pseudo-op allows it to survive a change in the tax rate at no greater cost than a reassembly with a new definition of "TAXRATE."

Furthermore, by forcing the programmer's mind to the slightly elevated abstraction of the symbolic level, AL tends to suggest treating as variables other quantities that almost certainly would have been treated as constants in ML: the total number of paycheck deductions to be allowed for, the number of jurisdictions for which tax was to be withheld, etc. If the possibility of change has occurred to the programmer while writing the program, it can be provided for in any of several ways:

1. Assign a new value to a symbolic variable by substituting a new definition of it in the source program and reassemble.

2. Design the program to accept a possibly new value for the variable from data given at execution time.

3. If the program is being run interactively, prompt the user to enter such a new value or let the user take the initiative by interrupting the running of the program to introduce a new value.

The degree of control offered by a modern multi-pass assembler working in conjunction with a linking loader and an indulgent operating system is very substantial. Symbols can be defined in terms not only of final numerical values, but of elaborate expressions containing other symbols that may themselves be as yet undefined, to form an indefinitely deep regression, with the resolution of the most primitive layer of symbols deferred until the end of the source program or even, in the limit, until load or execution time.

A loader prepared to handle so-called object programs (q.v.) in which so much binding remains to be done is misnamed, in fact, since its loading function is by this point incidental. It is actually the last (and sometimes the longest) pass of the assembler it works with, and its use amounts to a return to the "load-and-go" concept in which final assembly is followed immediately by loading and execution, rather than simply the production of an object program that is to be executed later. The object program produced by the assembler part of such an assembler-loader partnership is not in ML, but in some nameless intermediate language dictated by the needs of the loader.

Through the use of *external symbols* resolved by the linker (q.v.), variables in one program can be bound to values assigned in another. This makes it possible for a number of independently written and separately assembled programs to become in effect one large program, and in doing so to greatly extend the usefulness of the constituent programs.

Important as it is, binding-time control is only one aspect of a broader and more fundamental principle that was introduced into programming along with AL: *decoupling*. This is the technological equivalent of the military principle "divide and conquer." As applied to programming, it means the isolation of potential problems so that they can be separately dealt with and so that errors cannot propagate from one module to another. Binding-time control permits decoupling the writing of an expression (q.v.) that may relate many variables in elaborate ways from the task of giving those variables specific numeric or other computable values.

AL programming permits and promotes many forms of decoupling. The symbols used in an AL program for things other than instruction locations, for example, will probably be defined by the programmer in a group, at the end of the source program; if there are many of them, they will probably be divided further into subgroups of constants, storage reservations, error messages, etc, creating something very like Cobol's Data Division. In doing this, the AL programmer is led naturally into applying decoupling, not merely on the level of the individual expression and its component variables, but also on that of the entire program algorithm and the data it operates on. The strikingly superior manageability of programs so organized—their greater intelligibility to those who have to study and maintain them, their amenability to revision, their resistence to obsolescence as circumstances and specifications change—collectively amount to an enormous advantage over ML programming, one probably far more important than the convenience that AL offers in simply getting a program running. Such modularization, pioneered in AL, is now also commonplace in high-level language programming.

Subroutines and Macroinstructions Decoupling can be seen again in the practice of subroutinizing, in which routines that have been written once are preserved so that they need not be written again: the decoupling is between work done and work yet to do. The occasion for creating a subroutine arises when a programmer notices that essentially the same routine (for example, one that converts external-representation numerals to internal, computable form) has been written over and over, possibly with minor variations. Creating a subroutine for the function in question will obviate the need ever to do it again, and this promise gives its author incentive to invest great care in generalizing it, debugging it, optimizing its performance, documenting it, and otherwise perfecting it (*see* SUBPROGRAM).

Subroutinizing is not the same thing as modularizing, with which it is often confused. Both subroutines and macros (macroinstructions - q.v.) are chunks of code that have been deliberately isolated and packaged, but for quite different, even opposed, reasons. The ignorance of context that is a corollary of this packaging is, for the subroutine, its major liability; in the module, this trait is the very reason for its existence. The success of a subroutine is often dependent on the degree to which it can overcome its isolation and be made sensitive to its context each time it is used; it needs to approximate the efficiency of the tailor-made code it has replaced.

A module, on the other hand, like a member of a cloistered religious order, is supposed to remain ignorant of the world it lives in for the sake of higher things. The module is intended to limit the area of concern of any one programming-team member, and—most important—to minimize the impact on the program of later changes to its environment or specifications. It does this by isolating and formalizing the channels of communication, or *interfaces*, between itself and other program components (*see* ENCAPSULATION). A typical application: a module through which all of a program's input/output requests are funnelled, and that alone makes direct requests on the operating system or hardware. If the I/O facilities of the system later change in ways that affect a program that has been so modularized, only its I/O module need be revised, rather than an indefinite number of I/O operations that would have been scattered throughout the program in unrecorded places, with varying assumptions about their contexts silently built into them. Modularization, then, like the water-tight compartmentalization of a ship, is a damage-limiting and responsibility-limiting device; restricting intercourse between a part of a program and its environment (code or hardware) is its purpose in life. A subroutine, on the other hand, will often succeed to the extent that it can adapt to the state of the calling program at each call; it should be as worldly as the module should be sequestered.

Once created, a subroutine need only be assembled along with a calling AL program (or loaded with its object program) to be available as often as needed throughout that program. At whatever points in the program the function performed by the subroutine is required, a *calling sequence* (q.v.) to the subroutine is inserted by the programmer, and a transfer to it will be made when that point is reached in program execution. After the subroutine has been executed, a return jump from it is made to a point some fixed number of words from the most recent call, and the calling program continues. The subroutine itself need never be written again, nor need it appear more than once in a program, no matter how often its services may be required.

Subroutinizing is useful even when practiced by a solitary programmer within one program; its advantages grow enormously if subroutines can be freely traded within the community of programmers working with one type of computer or operating system. The possibility of doing so depends on the observance of a number of conventions for creating and using subroutines that are usually set forth in the AL manual of each computer. These conventions, while necessary for the exchangeability of subroutines within the community of users, are responsible also for many of the unsatisfactory features of subroutines, and account at least in part for the rise of an alternative form of software packaging, the *macroinstruction*.

Like the subroutine, the macro (short for macroinstruction) is a way of packaging common routines for later use, but the conventions governing both its creation and its use differ greatly from those of the subroutine. The root of the difference is that the macro facility is made possible by a special processor that is either embedded within an assembler (yielding a macroassembler) or provided as a separate piece of software (a macroprocessor). If separate, it will be given as input a source program consisting of a mixture of macros and AL statements, transform the macros into AL, and pass the resulting program to a simple assembler. The consequent differences between programming with macros and with subroutines may be summarized under four heads: locus of creation, calling format, trapping ability, and code-generation efficiency.

Locus of Creation   A new macro can be created or defined at any point in any program that will be processed by a macroassembler or macroprocessor. Since the macroprocessor, whether embedded in an assembler or not, is put into a special macro-defining mode when it encounters a macro definition, the creation of a macro generates no instructions in the program; only an explicit call on the macro (an *invocation* of the macro) does that.

Until called, the instructions constituting a macro definition are stored in an area under the control of the macroprocessor, and do not appear in the object program being generated. In contrast, the defining of a subroutine, since it is indistinguishable from ordinary programming as far as the assembler is concerned, causes the insertion of its constituent instructions into the host program at the point of definition. If the programmer wants the subroutine to be stored at the end of the object program when it is loaded, as is usual, the definition itself must appear at the end of the source program.

A subroutinized version of the miniature program given in example (5), for example, would take a form like this:

```
TRISUM   CLA*   1,4
         ADD*   2,4                    (8)
         STO*   3,4
         TRA    4,4
```

In this (trivial) subroutine, which we have given the name TRISUM, some new programming features are used.

The addresses of the four instructions refer respectively to the first, second, third, and fourth words following the instruction that has just called TRISUM. The "4" following the comma in each of these instructions is the designation of an *index register*—a specialized register, one of whose principal uses is to record the location of an instruction calling on a subroutine. Its action is such that an address within the subroutine of the form "$n,4$" will refer to the nth location following that calling instruction.

Another item of notation new to this example is the "*" following each of the first three instructions, denoting *indirect* use of the address that follows in each case. This means that the assembler is being directed to interpret the address (first modified if necessary by any index register used) not as the location of the data, but as the location of the address of the data. Accordingly, the interpretation of "CLA* 1,4" is "Bring to the accumulator the quantity whose address is one word below that in which the instruction calling on this subroutine is located." Using the calling sequence in (10) below as an example, the quantity specified would be that in LOCA.

An equivalent macro would take the form:

```
TRISUM  MACRO  A,B,C
        CLA    A
        ADD    B              (9)
        STO    C
        END
```

The first line of this macro definition declares that TRISUM is its name and that this name, when used to call the macro, will be accompanied by three values (*parameters*) that are to replace A, B, and C (the *dummy parameters*, or just *dummies*), respectively, wherever those dummies occur in the definition. The precise way in which the TRISUM subroutine and the TRISUM macro are called is explained in the next section.

Form of Call The subroutine is traditionally called by a stereotyped series of AL instructions (see (10) below) known as a *calling sequence*. This consists of (1) an instruction that jumps to the subroutine while recording its own location (in index register 4, in our example machine) so that the subroutine will know how to reach back for parameters, and where to return to the calling program when it is done; (2) a number of words reserved for the parameters that are to be passed to the subroutine with each call; and (3) one or more locations for the subroutine to transfer back to when it has completed execution, depending on the number of exit conditions that its author has decided to distinguish and handle separately. This is the general form; each subroutine will have its own specific calling sequence requirements, and it is the responsibility of the subroutine user to construct a correct calling sequence when he or she wishes to call upon a subroutine. An example of a simple calling sequence is

```
TSX   TRISUM,4
PZE   LOCA
PZE   LOCB              (10)
PZE   LOCC
<return location>
```

The first of these instructions, TSX (Transfer and Set indeX), is the special transfer instruction referred to earlier that transfers control to TRISUM while marking its own location in an index register (4, in this case). The three PZE pseudo-ops that follow are simply place holders whose function is to hold in their address fields the addresses at which parameters A, B, and C can be found by the subroutine. Each call upon the subroutine, then, would cost the execution time of the TSX and the return

transfer at the end of the subroutine, plus the storage space for these two instructions and the three PZEs.

To call the functionally equivalent TRISUM macroinstruction, the programmer simply uses its name as if it were a simple AL operation code. The parameters to replace the dummies will usually follow the macro name, starting in the same field where an ordinary AL op code's address would be given, and in the same order as that of the dummies they are to replace. In more advanced macroprocessors, the difference in notational friendliness may be greater yet; at least one would permit the user to give the parameters accompanying a call on a macro as part of a readable English language statement, and in an order that need not mirror that in which the dummies were given when the macro was defined (see Halpern, 1990, chapter 3). A simple, conventional call on TRISUM would take the form:

```
TRISUM ALPHA, BETA, GAMMA          (11)
```

where ALPHA, BETA, and GAMMA are the values the user wants inserted in the code wherever A, B, and C appeared in the macro's definition. The macroprocessor would make these substitutions, and generate into the program, at the point where the user called the macro, the wanted instructions:

```
CLA   ALPHA
ADD   BETA              (12)
STO   GAMMA
```

The superiority of the macro over the subroutine in this example is due to our use of an unrealistically brief piece of code as the core of each. In particular, the example is unfair to the subroutine in making it so trivial that it is actually shorter than the calling sequence that connects it to the main program. A more realistic evaluation would result if we stipulated that TRISUM were a routine of 50 to 100 instructions. On the other hand, the macro, too, can do better than this example would suggest; see the section below on "Code-Generating Economy."

Trapping Ability A property of the macroinstruction that has no counterpart in the subroutine is that of trapping and reinterpreting AL operation codes. Since the macroprocessor that makes possible the use of macros looks for macros before it looks for and handles simple AL input, the user can define what would ordinarily be an AL op code (e.g. "CLA" or "STO") as a macro and thereby transform it into something else before the assembler proper sees it, or can act upon it in any way desired by the user, without letting the assembler see it at all. (Such a name remains known to the assembler as that of one of its op codes, but the fact that the macroprocessor gets first crack at it makes it effectively a macro only.)

This feature makes possible some useful tricks. For example, it enables the user to (1) trap every transfer (branch) instruction in a program, or some specified portion of it, and generate instead (or in addition) instructions that compute at execution time the actual addresses to which control is being ordered transferred; (2) compare those addresses with limits set by the user; and (3) allow the transfer to be executed only if its actual target is within those limits. Depending on how strict these limits are, this prevents the execution of most or all "wild" transfers—those whose actual addresses, because of a bug somewhere in the program, are effectively random numbers. This constraint on the behavior of the executing program greatly eases debugging, whose difficulties are compounded many times over if a wild transfer has been allowed to execute, with the usual consequences: the destruction of the evidence that a bug hunter would need to find the original error.

For example, a macro that would trap and test the effective address of an ordinary unconditional transfer instruction (TRA) is shown below. .

```
.TRA OPSYN  TRA         Clone TRA instruction as
                        '.TRA'
TRA  MACRO  X,Y         Name macro 'TRA', dummy
                        parameters X & Y
     LOCAL  A,B         Demand new labels at each
                        call on TRA
A    NOP    Y,X         Acquire TRA's address and
                        tag fields
     SXA    B,4         Save C(IR4) in address of B
     SDC    *+2,X       Store —C(X) in decrement of
                        TXI below
     LXA    A,4         Apparent address of TRA to
                        IR4
     TXI    *+1,4,**    subtract C(IR4) to get
                        effective address
     TXL    *+2,4,LOWLIM-1 if address too
                        low, skip one instr.
     TXL    B,4,HILIM   not too high, skip one
                        instruction
     TSX    AERROR,4    too hi/low; mark place,
                        go to error routine
B    AXT    **,4        Restore value of IR4 as
                        at time of call
     .TRA*  A           Execute the calling TRA
                        instruction
     END                Terminate macro
                        definition            (13)
```

The macro as presented omits some housekeeping instructions and makes a few simplifying assumptions, for the sake of clarity and brevity; none of these simplifications affects the generality of the concept. The new instructions introduced in this example are not explained in full, like those in earlier examples, but their effects in this context are described in the comments given alongside each of them. Also, the notation C(n) means "contents of n"; e.g. C(IR4) means "contents of index register 4." Recall too that "apparent address" means the value of the expression in the address-field of an instruction, before account is taken of any indirect addressing or index register modification called for in other fields.

First, this macro defines a new mnemonic for the TRA instruction (.TRA) so that the instruction can still be used within the macro itself without recursively calling on the macro again. Then it defines the AL operation code "TRA"

to be the name of a macroinstruction. This causes every occurence of the "TRA" mnemonic in the program that follows to be caught by the macroprocessor and replaced by the instructions in the macro, rather than simply to be passed unchanged to the assembler and there translated to its ML equivalent. When the macro is invoked by the appearance of a TRA, the body of the macro computes the effective address of that instruction—i.e. it computes the value of the instruction's address-field expression, modified by the contents of any index register specified in the "tag" field of the instruction (we ignore, for simplicity, the further possibility of indirect addressing). It then compares the resulting effective address with the limits of a permissible range of transfer addresses supplied elsewhere by the user when the variables LOWLIM and HILIM were defined.

If the address lies outside that range, the original TRA instruction is not executed; instead, control is passed to an error routine, where it is reported and handled by whatever means the programmer has directed there. If the address falls within the permissible range, the TRA instruction is executed as originally given and the program proceeds.

Code-Generating Economy The macroinstruction and the subroutine differ most obviously in that each use of a macro causes a fresh copy of its defining instructions to be inserted into the text of the program being generated, while a subroutine appears in the program using it just once, no matter how often called. This distinction should not, however, be taken to mean, as it frequently is, that macro usage entails a wasteful repetitive generation of code that could be avoided by the use of subroutines instead.

The economics of programming is such that the advantage sometimes lies with generating the substantive code as many times as it is to be executed, sometimes with generating only multiple calling sequences to a single copy of that code. The decision will hinge on such considerations as the length of the calling sequence versus that of the routine to be executed, and the relative importance of memory and time during execution. While a decision to save time clearly points to the macro as the instrument of choice, a space-saving strategy does not point to the subroutine; it merely suggests that the macros to be employed should generate not the entire routine, but only a calling sequence to a subroutinized version of it.

In short, if both macros and subroutines are available to do a job, there is no hard choice to be made: a macro facility incorporates the ability to use subroutines as well, and also to call them by means of macros, with the superior writeability and readability of that feature. In at least one macroinstruction processor based on assembly language (see Halpern, 1990, chapter 3), the user is enabled to include within a macro definition both a subroutine and its calling sequence. At the first use of the macro, the processor copies both the calling sequence and the subroutine into the object program—the former at the point where the macro is invoked and the latter at the end of the program (or wherever the user chooses). Subsequent uses of the macro cause only the calling sequence to be copied, the processor recalling that is has already incorporated the subroutine into the program. Graphically:

Macro definition:

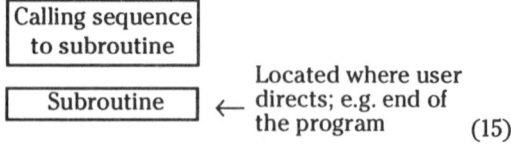

$$(14)$$

Result of first call:

| Calling sequence to subroutine |
| Subroutine | ← Located where user directs; e.g. end of the program

$$(15)$$

Result of second and each subsequent call:

| Calling sequence to subroutine |

$$(16)$$

Roles and Applications of AL　It has long been expected that compiled high-level languages and other forms of communication between human and machine would completely supplant AL, but this replacement has not occurred. Not only AL, but even ML, to a more limited extent, survive and flourish. This should no longer surprise us.

The fundamental reasons for AL's indispensability are clear: it is a completely general programming language, standing to the various compiler languages as English stands to the jargons of the various trades and professions. AL allows the programmer to do with the computer anything it can do at all, while high-level languages trade this universality of application for superior applicability to a limited range of problems.

During the years between the second and third editions of this *Encyclopedia*, the microprocessor burst from the laboratory into our kitchen appliances, our children's toys, and our wristwatches—its use in personal computers, ubiquitous though they are, is almost incidental. This explosion of small processors has brought back the circumstances that had, decades before, made every programmer an AL programmer: small memories, limited addressability, much slower (if any) secondary storage. (A recent development that has encouraged AL programming is the emergence of good debuggers; the last time AL was in common use, debugging aids consisted of octal memory dumps and black coffee.)

The result has been a near-recapitulation on the PC of the history of software development on the mainframe. It has not been due, this second time around, to doubts about the merits of high-level languages on the part of entrenched skeptics; the major high-level languages are available and widely used on processors that can be carried in an attache case (*see* LAPTOP COMPUTERS). Nevertheless, the microprocessor has caused an outburst of AL and ML activity and will probably continue to provide an op-

portunity for programming in those languages for many who would otherwise never have had that experience.

Beyond these general grounds for the survival and flourishing of AL/ML lie several specific roles for which it seems uniquely well suited—ecological niches into which it fits so well as to insure its survival against any competitor now visible. Among these are at least five that are worthy of being noted and named: fine tuning, early responsiveness, machine exploitation, pioneering, and craftsmanship.

Fine Tuning　Because only AL/ML programmers directly and consciously determine the machine-language instructions that are to be executed and the bit-by-bit internal representation of the data upon which they are to operate, they alone can guarantee that a program will fit within a given chunk of memory or will execute within a given period of time. They, too, are the only programmers who can plausibly claim that a program has been so written as to occupy the least possible space or to execute as fast as possible.

Programs may be arbitrarily restricted as to the time in which they are to execute because they are real-time applications (i.e. processes directly linked to other processes that are executing fast enough so that even a computer is pressed to keep up with their demands). An example of such demanding processes is the evaluation of radar returns to produce target-tracking displays and antenna-steering commands. Like all such processes, it involves computer linkage to equipment that, based on the same technology that supports the computer itself, demands inputs and generates outputs at rates comparable to the computer's. With only a slight stretching of terminology, it may be said that in such applications the computer is pushed to its limits because it is trying to satisfy another computer.

Programs may be arbitrarily restricted as to the memory space available to them because they are to be executed under control of a multiprogramming (*q.v.*) system in which each process is allocated a partition of memory within which it must run; this is becoming an increasingly common strategy of computer resource allocation, as attempts are made to keep all components of a computing system productively busy by having them deal concurrently with several distinct programs. In PCs, the space constraints are likely to be due to the absolute size of the machine. Especially where a microprocessor is embedded within a missile or similarly weight- and space-limited environment, its storage size may be such as to make a program hard to fit in, even though the processor may be dedicated to that one task.

Whatever the cause and the circumstances, a requirement that a program be executable within tight time or space constraints generally implies that it, or at least critical parts of it, should be written in AL. (It is possible to write such a program in a compiler language, if one is available, and then, if the object program exceeds the limits, to rewrite parts of it in AL so as to make it fit. This approach requires, if the hand-written code being introduced is to work smoothly with its host, a very detailed knowledge of the way in which the compiler generates its object code. The difficulty of integrating the hand-written code into the compiler-generated code, and the uncongeniality to programmers of having to revise others' code rather than write their own, make this a seldom-chosen alternative.)

An example of AL fine-tuning that is brief enough to include here is offered by an episode that occurred in the development of the original Fortran compiler for the IBM 704. It was discovered at a late stage in the development of that compiler that a quantity had been stored in the wrong index register, and if the error were to be rectified without extensive re-coding, it would have to be done under drastic constraints. These constraints dictated that space for only two additional instructions was available to load the proper index register with the quantity and that this two-instruction sequence had to be absolutely autonomous. It could not affect any memory or register contents, nor could it make any assumptions about the state of the machine other than that the value that should have been in index register 2 (say) was presently in index register 1. The following two instructions accomplished this seemingly impossible task:

$$
\begin{array}{ll}
\text{LXD} & *+1,2 \\
\text{TXI} & *+1,3,0
\end{array}
\tag{17}
$$

The first of these instructions (Load indeX from Decrement) loads the target index register, IR2, with the quantity, 0, in the so-called decrement field of the following instruction ("*+1" means "this location plus one"). This needs to be done because the contents of the target index register is unknown, and the logic of this patch requires that it be zero. The precise function of the second instruction (Transfer with indeX Incremented) is unimportant—any of several others would do as well. Its only functions here are (1) to contain a value of 0 in its decrement field so that the preceding LXD knows where to find one (recall that this patch cannot take for granted the contents of any location outside itself), and (2) to address index register 3—an index register whose usefulness lies in the fact that it does not exist.

The 704 had but three index registers (1, 2, and 4); if the numbers 3, 5, 6, or 7 were used where an index register designation was expected, the index registers affected would be those whose numerical designations summed to form the number given. The effect on the actual index registers so designated was to OR their contents and store the logical sum thus formed into each of them. It should be apparent how the storing of a zero into the target index register (IR2), followed by the execution of an instruction that referred to a mythical IR3, can achieve the desired movement of the value in IR1 into IR2. A compiler language (such as Fortran itself, the beneficiary of this *coup*) would not have permitted the programmer to specify the index register into which a quantity was to be loaded, let alone specify a non-existent register. Solving this problem was made possible only by a combination of intimate knowledge of the machine and the availability of AL to exploit that knowledge.

Another common fine-tuning application of AL is the writing of segments of code that are to be executed so often as to make their time- or space-optimization economically worthwhile, if not strictly necessary. These include practically every routine that has been turned into a subroutine, practically all systems software, and the critical parts of big, long-lived, compiler-language application programs. This last category is worth some examination because its hazards are seldom appreciated until they produce a serious problem.

The compiler-language application programs that are candidates for this treatment are those whose execution consumes a substantial part of the total computing resources at their installations, and hence offer real payoffs for any improvement in execution time. In such circumstances, a clever programmer who is familiar with the code the compiler has turned out, and also with the purpose of the program in hand, is very likely to be able to improve it significantly by rewriting in AL some small but critical section of it. It would not be very unusual for that programmer to be able to improve the program's performance by an order of magnitude by rewriting a few dozen, or a few hundred, instructions. This can often be accomplished, in fact, by essentially negative actions involving no significant new code at all: just the re-ordering of some file searches to reflect the programmer's knowledge of the probable contents of those files, or the removal from an inner loop of some calculations not needed in the present application, may be enough to produce dramatic improvements in execution time.

With such potential rewards, an installation manager may be strongly tempted to relax the edict that only Fortran (or Cobol, or whatever) is to be used, and allow at least a few programmers to fine-tune the most time-consuming programs. If the manager succumbs to this temptation, however, those big programs will tend to become hand-written AL programs that use a thin shell of compiler-generated code just to interface with the operating system. The danger of this practice is sometimes unrecognized until the installation that has permitted it decides to replace its computers with some newer, incompatible model.

Early Responsiveness To ensure that their development will be carried on in a thoughtful and orderly way, and in a way that will not jeopardize their machine independence, the specifications of the standard compiler languages have been entrusted to various national and international standards organizations (in the United States, chiefly to the American National Standards Institute—ANSI). These organizations, which attempt to include or at least consult all concerned parties, issue formal specifications of the languages entrusted to their care and invite and evaluate proposals for their revision. Part of the price that must be paid for this elaborate and necessarily slow-moving apparatus of consultation and deliberation is that additions to the compiler languages, even if approved at every stage of review, are a very long time in coming. Usually, years pass between the first proposal that a new feature be incorporated and the actual appearance of that feature in manufacturer-supplied software. This gap between programmer requirements and vendors' response leaves another opening for AL, which, under the sole control of the manufacturer of the machine concerned, can be used to meet the need quickly.

Machine Exploitation   As early responsiveness reflects AL's ability to yield an immediate answer to requirements generated by application programmers, so machine exploitation refers to its unique ability to permit full access to all features built into a machine, whether ever available through a compiler language or not. Providing such access may be virtually impossible for compiler languages, which—again, because of their need to remain machine-independent—cannot refer to any machine facility not common to all on which they are to run. If some, but not all, of the machines on which a compiler is to run include, say, a program-testable clock, the compiler language cannot offer statements that let users refer to that clock, without either restricting the transferability of programs that do so or forcing the compiler to generate coding that simulates such clocks on those machines not having it in their hardware.

Since neither of these penalties is acceptable (the second is not always physically possible), the outcome is that such non-universal features are often simply ignored in the standard compiler languages. For most purposes, this partial disabling of the machine is tolerable; for a few, and most particularly for systems programming (*q.v.*), it is not. Whatever distinctive features a machine offers must be usable by its fundamental software, or they may as well not exist. System software itself is a major consumer of machine time, and time spent on its execution is felt to be non-productive overhead, so it is especially important that that layer of software be as fast as possible. This requirement means that systems software has to be written in a language that permits access to all machine features, and thus often rules out standard compiler languages other than, perhaps, C (*q.v.*). For the foreseeable future, AL remains an indispensible part of the building of systems software.

Pioneering   AL is almost always involved when a wholly new computer application is being pioneered, even though it may later turn out not to be needed. When it is uncertain what the demands of a new species of program are going to be, the safest course is to use the language that imposes no constraints. After a number of AL programs have been written for the new application, it may turn out that one of the existing compiler languages (often, with some modification) is adequate for the task (e.g. generating programs for parallel computers), or it may be found that the new application is sufficiently different, and economically important, to warrant the development of a language tailored to its needs (e.g. page layout programs such as PostScript (*q.v.*) for desktop publishing (*q.v.*)). AL programming experience forms, among other things, a breeding ground for specialized language development.

Craftsmanship   Another reason for the continued use of AL is that AL programming is widely felt to be the most professional and demanding kind, and many career programmers will seek to use it even when none of the reasons discussed above apply. To a considerable extent, the programmer's wish to use AL can coincide with the best interests of the installation. No matter how adamant management may be about running a pure Ada or Pascal shop, there must always be a few programmers behind the scenes who can read dumps, help the application programmers with special debugging problems, understand the operating system, and deal as equals with the computer manufacturer's systems engineers.

Furthermore, a knowledge of AL often helps the programmer to use compiler languages more efficiently, clarifying the relationship between source code and what the compiler has generated, and warning about the hidden points in compiler-language usage where the price of execution may suddenly rise tenfold because the code compiled has exceeded some buffer size or other critical system constraint. And if AL specialists in what is nominally a pure compiler-language shop are to keep their skills sharp, they must be allowed to practice them. This instinct to practice one's craft at the highest possible level is a perennial one that will, independent of economic considerations, continue to turn many programmers toward AL.

Acknowledgements   I am indebted to Richard Goodell of Tandem Computers, Inc. for a code inspection that greatly improved the sample macro offered in the "Trapping Ability" section.

ML programming seems to have generated no literature, and AL has had little of consequence written about it. On most topics the reader may want to pursue further, the relevant articles in this encyclopedia will probably be the best recourse. On the loading of programs that have been assembled into ML, as well as the linking together of separately assembled programs when they refer symbolically to each other, see Presser and White (1972). For the internal workings of assemblers, see Barron's lucid explanation. There are countless books explaining AL programming for the Intel and Motorola chips that power most PCs; that by Crayne and Girard starts from scratch and is clearly written.

References

1972. Barron, D. W. *Assemblers and Loaders*, 2nd Ed.. New York: American Elsevier.

1972. Presser, L. and White, J. "Linkers and Loaders," *Computing Surveys* **4**, 3 (September), 149–167.

1985. Crayne, Charles and Girard, Dian. *The Serious Assembler*. Baen Publishing Enterprises.

1988. Hogan, Thom. *The Programmer's PC Sourcebook*. Redmond, WA: Microsoft Press.

1988. Somerson, Paul. *DOS Power Tools: Techniques, Tricks and Utilities*. New York: Bantam Books.

1989. Angermeyer, John, *et al. The Waite Group's MS-DOS Developer's Guide* (2nd Ed.). Howard W. Sams & Co.

1990. Halpern, Mark. *Binding Time*. Norwood, NJ: Ablex Publishing Co.

1990. Schulman, Andrew. *Undocumented DOS: A Programmer's Guide to Reserved MS-DOS Functions and Data Structures*. Reading, MA: Addison-Wesley.

1991. Federighi, F. D. and Reilly, E. D. *VAX Assembly Language*. New York: Macmillan.

MARK HALPERN

MACHINE LANGUAGE. *See* INSTRUCTION AND DATA REPRESENTATION; INSTRUCTION SET; and MACHINE AND ASSEMBLY LANGUAGE PROGRAMMING.

MACHINE-READABLE FORM

For articles on related subjects *see* MEMORY: AUXILIARY; OPTICAL CHARACTER READERS; OPTICAL MARK READERS; PAPER TAPE; PUNCHED CARDS; and UNIVERSAL PRODUCT CODE.

Machine-readable form refers to the form in which information is encoded for direct, automatic input into a computer. Keyboard input is machine-readable, for example, because the machine senses which keys are depressed in which order. Information handwritten in script is typically not machine-readable because devices are not yet generally available that can handle the wide variations in style. One exception to this is carefully handprinted characters on certain forms (e.g. social security numbers on driver's license renewals), which are read directly by optical scanning devices.

In general, keyboard inputs, bar codes, punched cards, magnetic tape, disks, drums, etc., carry information in machine-readable form for the express purpose of being read exclusively by computers. Some printer and typewriter fonts can be machine-read by optical scanners, and are also directly readable by humans, unlike the magnetic coding on tape or disk. Magnetic-ink characters, used principally for coding bank-accounting information on checks, are readable by humans (optically) and by machines (magnetically). Such magnetic-ink character recognition is often referred to by its abbreviation, MICR.

CHESTER L. MEEK

MACHINE TRANSLATION. *See* LANGUAGE TRANSLATION.

MACROINSTRUCTION

For articles on related subjects *see* ARGUMENT; ASSEMBLER; MACHINE AND ASSEMBLY LANGUAGE PROGRAMMING; MACRO LANGUAGES; PROGRAMMING LANGUAGES; and SUBPROGRAM.

In its simplest form, a *macroinstruction* (which is usually called, simply, a *macro*) is a single computer instruction that stands for a given sequence of instructions. This can be illustrated by taking an analogy from the English language. Originally, people working with computers spoke of a "binary digit," but since this is a frequently used term, people got tired of saying it and coined the more concise word "bit" to use instead. The word "bit" is therefore a macro that stands for "binary digit."

To implement macros, it is necessary to have a piece of software called a *macro processor*, which is often itself part of an assembly language software system. Macro processors are available on almost all computers, but there has been no standardization in their design. The job of a macro processor is simple. The programmer supplies some macro definitions, which define the macros and what is to replace them, and the macro processor then replaces any occurrence of the macro accordingly.

This is best illustrated by an example which will be taken from the assembly language of a hypothetical computer. Assume, for instance, that at several points in a program a programmer needs to increase a variable, whose name is COUNT by 1. Assume further that this takes three assembly-language instructions:

```
LOAD    COUNT
ADD     ONE
STORE   COUNT
```

It would be wasteful of a programmer's time to keep writing out these three instructions in full. It would be much better to choose a single name (BUMPCOUNT, say) to stand for these instructions, and then to write the name each time it was necessary to specify the three instructions. The source program would then be processed according to Fig. 1.

The macro definitions define BUMPCOUNT and the instructions that are to replace it. In practice, there would probably be several other macro definitions as well. The macro processor then scans the program, replacing each occurrence of BUMPCOUNT by its expanded form. It would similarly process any other macros that had been defined. As a result of this, the program is then in pure assembly language and can be passed on to the assembler, which processes it in the normal way.

The reader may wonder why the assembler itself cannot be adapted to deal with BUMPCOUNT, thus obviating the need for the two-part process illustrated above. The answer is that assembly languages, like almost all other computer languages, are inflexible, and the ordinary programmer is not allowed to change them. To return to the earlier analogy, the assembler is akin to a person who has been taught about "binary digits," and is not going to understand anyone who calls them "bits." Hence, if anyone does speak of bits, an interpreter—the analogy of the

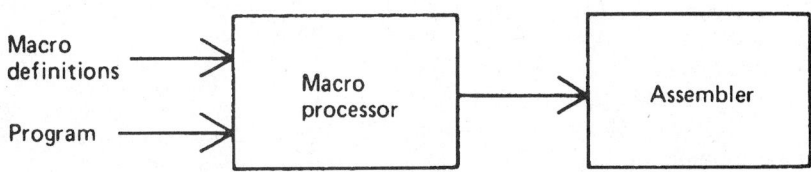

FIG. 1.

macro processor—is needed to convert to the assembler's style of language. In summary, therefore, computer languages are intrinsically inflexible, but with a macro processor to act as interpreter, this need not inconvenience the programmer.

Thus far our picture of macros has been an oversimplified one in that the most important and powerful aspect has not been mentioned. This concerns macros with variable elements.

To return to the example of the BUMPCOUNT macro, the defect of this macro as it stands is that it works only for one variable, COUNT. In practice, it would be much more useful to have a general macro (called, say, BUMP) that could be used to increment *any* variable by 1. This can, in fact, be done. The name of the variable to be incremented is written immediately after BUMP, and is called the *argument* of the macro. The macro processor can be told to insert the argument at various points in the replacement of the macro. Thus,

```
BUMP (name)
```

would be replaced by

```
LOAD  (name)
ADD   ONE
STORE (name)
```

where any name of a variable could occur as *name*.

It is possible to have more than one argument to a macro. For example, it would be possible to specify a macro of the form

```
PRODUCT X, Y, Z
```

which for any *X*, *Y*, and *Z* would compute *Z* to be the product of *X* and *Y*.

Beginners at programming often find it hard to distinguish between the concept of a macro and that of a subroutine. The difference is, in fact, clear-cut. A macro is actually replaced by its expanded form. Hence, if a program contains *n* occurrences of a macro, then *n* copies of the instructions it stands for are inserted into the program. (Note, however, that, if the macro possesses arguments, the instructions need not be identical in all the cases.) A subroutine, on the other hand, involves a break in the flow of a program. If a sequence of instructions occurs frequently in a program, then these can be written as a subroutine, and each occurrence in the program is replaced by an instruction to jump to this subroutine, execute it, and then return. There is then only one copy of the sequence of instructions. (Viewed at a more fundamental level, a subroutine is a run-time replacement and a macro a replacement at the time of translation.)

Macros are most often used to represent relatively short sequences of instructions or sequences that involve a relatively large number of insertions of arguments. But sometimes macros are quite long sequences of instructions, in which case the macroprocessor will normally generate a calling sequence to a subroutinized version of the macro. Often, a set of macros is combined into a library; a very common example of this is a library of macros to aid communication with an operating system.

Looked at from another viewpoint, a macro is a way of extending a language. Thus, once the BUMP macro has been defined, a programmer can treat BUMP as an extra assembly language instruction. It is common practice to build an extensive group of macros, and it often happens that a program is built entirely of macros and devoid of true assembly-language instructions. In this case, the macros can be thought of as forming a new language in their own right. Macros are therefore a useful tool for constructing programming languages, though they are not normally powerful enough to build up from assembly languages to such high-level languages as Pascal.

Needless to say, such relatively sophisticated uses of macros require more facilities than have been described here. In particular, it is necessary for macro processors to contain a decision-making facility so that the instructions to replace the macro can depend on the form of a macro argument and the context in which it occurs.

The examples considered so far have shown macros for assembly language, as this is the most popular use of macros. Indeed, a macro processor is often combined with an assembler to make it appear to the programmer as if the two are a single unit called a *macro assembler*. However, macros can be used with any programming language and, perhaps most interestingly of all, as an end in themselves.

As an example of the latter, assume that a computer is being used to print invitations. Each invitation is identical except for the name of the person to be invited. One way to do this would be to define a macro called, say, INVITE, that generates the invitation, inserting the argument at the necessary places. This macro could then be used by writing

```
INVITE STAN JONES
INVITE MONICA SMITH
...etc.
```

In more general applications, macros can be used to provide a replacement facility in any written text. At the simplest level, macros may be used to replace one word by another throughout a document, and can therefore be used to correct systematic errors or make systematic changes. To deal with applications such as this, there exist so-called *general-purpose* macro processors.

References

1960. McIlroy, M. D. "Macro Instruction Extensions of Compiler Languages," *Comm. ACM* **3**, 4: 214–220 (April). (This is a classic early paper on macros and gives a good insight into their potential power.)

1969. Kent, W. "Assembler Language Macroprogramming," *Computing Surveys* **1**, 4: 183–196 (December). (A tutorial paper on macro assemblers, particularly the macro assembler for IBM System/360.)

1971. Macleod, J. A. "MP/I—A FORTRAN Macroprocessor," *Computer Journal* **14**, 3: 229–231 (August). (One example of a macro facility designed for a high-level language.)

1974. Brown, P. J. *Macro Processors and Techniques for Portable Software.* New York: Wiley.

PETER J. BROWN

MAGNETIC DISK. *See* Floppy disk; Hard disk; and Memory: Auxiliary.

MAGNETIC DRUM. *See* Memory: Auxiliary.

MAGNETIC TAPE. *See* Memory: Auxiliary.

MAIN MEMORY. *See* Memory: Main.

MAINFRAME

For articles on related subjects *see* Central Processing Unit; and Memory: Main.

The *mainframe* of a computer system is the cabinet that houses the central processor and main memory. It is, therefore, separate from the peripheral devices (disks, printers, tape drives, etc.) and device controllers. Typically, it is the largest component in size and cost, but modern electronics have allowed great reductions in both in recent years. The mainframe usually has many indicator lights (sometimes as part of the operator's console) to show fault conditions, memory contents, etc. The central processor and main memory are housed together as an aid in increasing processing speeds (cable lengths will be short) and improving reliability (e.g. both will be at similar temperatures and humidities). The term *mainframe* comes from the use of "frame" as a device to hold electronics (rack is also frequently used), and the frame holding the electronics that do the computing might reasonably be the main frame.

In modern systems with very large main memory, some memory modules are housed in cabinets separate from the mainframe. Frequently, they are attached and thus become part of the mainframe cabinet. Multiprocessor systems with more than one central processor (CPU) are referred to as two- or three-mainframe systems, in which case the mainframe refers only to the CPU and not to the main memory.

The term *mainframe* as a single word has come to be used as a designation of medium- and large-scale computers that contain a "main frame" as defined in this article; thus, we speak of a *mainframe* computer in contrast to a *microcomputer, minicomputer* (*q.v.*), *personal computer* (*q.v.*), or *workstation* (*q.v.*).

Chester L. Meek

MAINTENANCE OF COMPUTERS

For articles on related subjects *see* Computing Center; Fault Tolerant Computing; Hardware Monitor; Performance of Computers; Redundancy; and Reliability, Hardware.

This article focuses on the *maintenance* of minicomputers and larger systems. By their nature, microprocessors (*q.v.*) require specialized, automatic testing techniques.

Like all sophisticated equipment, computers undergo the cycle of repair, check-out, operational readiness, failure, and back to repair. When the cost of a machine's not being in service is high, methods must be applied to reduce these out-of-service, or *downtime,* periods. The cost of downtime is not simply the lost revenue when the computer is not used, but also the cost of having to rerun programs that were interrupted by the ailing system, perhaps loss of real-time data, loss of control of external processes, opportunity costs, and costs related to user inconvenience, dissatisfaction, and reduced confidence in the system. Other costs are related directly to the diagnosis and corrective repair actions, and associated logistics and bookkeeping.

Due to the complexity of the equipment, as well as managerial judgment, many users, even some sophisticated computer-knowledgeable users, often decide not to maintain the system (processors, memory, system software, peripherals) themselves, but rather to have a maintenance contract with the system manufacturer. The cost of a maintenance contract over the useful life of the equipment in relation to its capital cost is quite high. It is also a good indicator of the expected unreliability. High costs due to unreliability and maintenance needs are a strong argument for designing dependability, maintainability, and serviceability into the equipment.

Decisions such as whether to have one's own maintenance personnel, what spare parts to stock and in what quantities, what test instruments are required, etc., have to be faced. Mathematical tools offered by operations research, such as dynamic programming and others, are often used to model the system in an attempt to arrive at optimal solutions to this complex problem.

Preventive Maintenance One means of reducing the direct cost associated with an unexpected system failure is to provide scheduled downtimes for the purpose of preventive maintenance. Obviously, a deliberate scheduled shutdown is less disruptive than that due to an unexpected system failure. During the downtime the general idea is to tune up the system so that things that are in marginal working condition will be identified and remedied. Diagnosis should be made by exercising all aspects of the system to catch latent failures and those that may have already occurred but have been lying undetected. Failed portions of the system are likely to be undetected if they have never been called into service, and therefore their operational readiness would not have been verified.

Typically, most computing centers use a few hours every week, (say, Saturday mornings) for scheduled preventive maintenance. Especially prepared diagnostic programs may be run to exercise the hardware, benchmark (*q.v.*) programs may be run to verify timing and accuracy considerations, and peripherals may be serviced by oiling, removing dust, replacing ribbons, etc. The typical cyclical behavior of a maintained system is shown in Fig. 1.

Maintainability For the purposes of better understanding and for controlling maintenance requirements, we will attempt to quantify the foregoing considerations by defining the applicable terms, such as *maintainability* and *availability,* as well as other related terms. A qualitative definition of maintainability *M* is given by Goldman and Slattery (1967) as

> ...the characteristics (both qualitative and quantitative) of material design and installation which make it possible to meet operational objectives with a minimum expenditure of maintenance effort (manpower, personnel skill, test equipment, technical data, and maintenance support facilities) under operational environmental conditions in which scheduled and unscheduled maintenances will be performed.

The preceding qualification, like the qualitative definition of reliability, can also be expressed quantitatively by means of probability theory. Thus, quantitatively, according to Goldman and Slattery.

> ...maintainability is a characteristic of design and installation which is expressed as the *probability* that an item will be restored to specified conditions within a given *period of time* when main-

tenance action is performed in accordance with prescribed procedures and resources.

Mathematically, this can be expressed as

$$M = 1 - e^{-t/\text{MTTR}}$$

where *t* is the specified time to repair, and MTTR is the mean time to repair.

Availability Availability refers to the probability that a system will be operative (up), and is expressed as

$$A = \frac{\text{up time}}{\text{downtime} + \text{up time}}$$

or equivalently as

$$A = \frac{\text{MTBF}}{\text{MTTR} + \text{MTBF}}$$

where MTBF = mean time between failures
       MTTR = mean time to repair

The quantitative definition of availability assumes a system model where all faults are immediately detected at the time of their occurrence, and fault location and repair action are initiated immediately. More complex availability models have also been developed that do not make these simplifying assumptions.

Methods for Predicting Maintainability The military handbook *Maintainability Prediction Techniques* describes a "check-list" method of predicting maintainability. Three check lists are used: the first for physical design factors, the second for personnel factors, and the third for support factors. The physical design factors

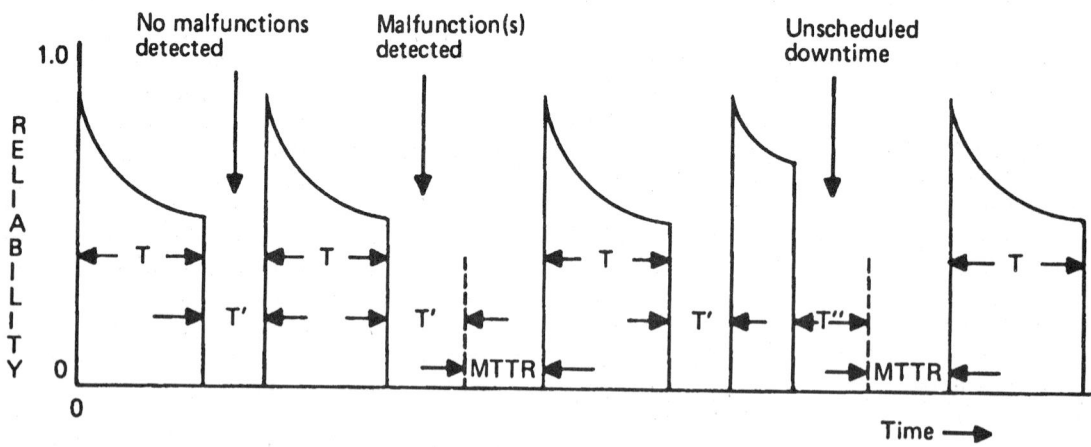

T = maximum allowed "up" time
T' = downtime due to preventive maintenance
T'' = unscheduled diagnosis
MTTR = mean time to repair

FIG. 1. Cyclical behavior of a maintained system.

encompass such equipment features as physical aspects and tool requirements, and its check list has items such as accessibility, packaging, test-points, internal latches, and built-in test equipment. The personnel factors include skill level, attitudes, and experience of the system operators. The support factors cover logistics and maintenance organization.

These check lists are used to evaluate each step essential to maintenance. A series of questions are raised: e.g. "Is external access adequate for visual inspection and manipulative action?" The answer is given a score of between 4 and 0, inclusive, where a "4" represents an unqualified yes, and a zero an unqualified no, with intermediate values to represent intermediate situations. The scores in the three check lists are then totaled to give a score for check list A, check list B, and check list C. Having obtained the scores for A, B, and C, the necessary predicted maintenance time (M) is then given by the following empirical formula:

$$M = \exp(3.54651 - 0.02512A - 0.03055B - 0.01093C).$$

The preceding description is a very brief summary of the MIL-HDBK-472 check list method.

Other institutions and companies have also developed their own check lists, scoring criteria, and empirical formulas appropriate to their equipment. In the absence of check lists specifically tailored to one's own equipment, experience has shown that the procedures and equations given in MIL-HDBK-472 serve as a good approximation.

References

1969. Blanchard, B. S., Jr. and Lovery, E. E. *Maintainability Principles and Practices.* New York: McGraw-Hill.

1972. Cunningham, C. E. and W. Cox. *Applied Maintainability Engineering.* New York: Wiley-Interscience.

1988. Morris, S. F. *et al.* "RADC Reliability Engineer's Toolkit: An Application Oriented Guide for the Practicing Reliability Engineer." Rome Air Development Center Air Force Systems Command, Griffis Air Force Base, NY 13441-5700, (July).

IEEE *Proceedings of the Annual Reliability and Maintainability Symposium.*

FRANCIS P. MATHUR

MANAGEMENT INFORMATION SYSTEMS

For articles on related subjects *see* ADMINISTRATIVE APPLICATIONS, COMPUTER SYSTEMS; DATABASE MANAGEMENT SYSTEM; DISTRIBUTED SYSTEMS; INFORMATION SYSTEMS; and SIMULATION: PRINCIPLES.

A *management information system* (MIS) is a system for providing information and information processing to support organizational activities, competitive strategy, and management functions. The system utilizes information technology; manual procedures; models for analysis, planning, control, and decision making; and databases. The portfolio of MIS applications covers a wide variety of organizational needs, including applications that indirectly support management activities and applications that directly serve management users. Since management applications frequently need data that is best provided by a database, databases and database management software are generally part of an MIS.

Evolution of the MIS Concept The term *management information system*, or MIS, is the most widely used title for a management-oriented information system. However, many organizations refer to their computer-based information system as just a data processing system or information system. The organizational function responsible for management of information systems is termed the MIS, information systems, or information management function.

The use of the term MIS to describe a computer-based information system having applications in support of management activities began in the mid-1960s. Another term, *decision support systems* (DSS), is sometimes used to describe those MIS applications that directly support specific decision making. An executive support system (ESS) is a specialized system in an MIS.

The names of academic programs in organizational information systems reflect business practice. There are a number of different names in use, but central tendencies can be observed. Masters degree programs (usually in business) with emphasis or concentration in organizational information systems most frequently are termed MIS programs; undergraduate programs are more likely to be called *information systems* or *data processing.*

The evolution of the use of computers in organizations may be traced as a function of type of applications (see Nolan 1979). In the first stage, applications are mainly transaction processing (*q.v.*) of such fundamental transactions as sales orders, billing and receipts, payables, and inventory accounting. These applications are at a clerical level—displacing clerical personnel and supporting basic operations in accounting, marketing, manufacturing, etc. The transaction processing applications generally include simple operations summaries. The next stage of information system development is the preparation of management control reports summarizing and analyzing the transaction data for management control purposes. The third stage is the data resource stage, in which stored data is made readily available to analysts and decision makers through organizational databases and database management software. The fourth stage is the use of retrieval software, analytical software, planning models, and decision models to obtain, analyze, and manipulate data for support of analysis, planning, and decision making.

The four stages of evolution have emphasized support for organizational activities and management functions. A major development in information systems has been the use of information systems to support organizational strategies, including those for competitive advantage. These systems include inter-organizational

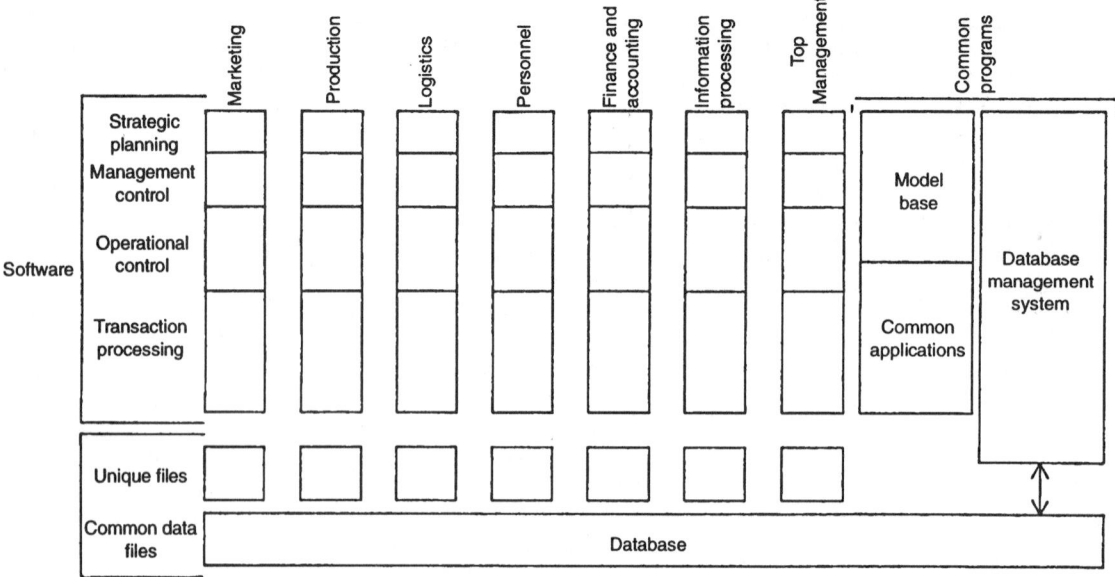

FIG. 1. The organizational MIS. (Reprinted by permission from Gordon B. Davis and Margrethe H. Olson, *Management Information Systems: Conceptual Foundations, Structure, and Development,* 2nd Ed. New York: McGraw-Hill, p. 46 (1985).

applications that automate interactions between the organization and its suppliers and customers.

The Structure of an MIS

An information system consists of a number of elements—hardware, system software, application software, databases, procedures, and personnel. Data communication (*q.v.*) facilities are also included in most systems of more than modest complexity. For the purpose of defining the structure of an MIS, the basic components are the application systems, each consisting of a set of application programs, plus related procedures for data entry, system operation, and information distribution. Applications may incorporate expert system (*q.v.*) modules and knowledge bases. The set of existing application systems (the *application portfolio*) defines the current capabilities of an information system.

The structure of an MIS is based on the structure and activities of the organization. Organizations are divided into functional areas (such as marketing, manufacturing, accounting, and finance). Within each function, management activities can be classified into three levels: operational control, management control, and strategic planning (see Anthony, 1965). There are sets of applications that apply to each specific functional area. For example, a group of applications process the finance transactions and provide reports and analyses to support finance management. These applications form the finance information system, which is a subsystem of the organization's MIS. The MIS for an organization, therefore, can be described as a federation of functional-area subsystems, each of which is divided into four major sections: transaction processing, operational control, management control, and strategic planning. This structure is illustrated in Fig. 1.

Each of the functional subsystems of the MIS has unique data files that are used only by that subsystem (Fig. 1). There are also files that need to be available for general retrieval. These are organized into a general database under the control of a database management system. There may be common applications used by more than one subsystem; there are also decision models and analytical software that can be termed the *model base.*

The applications in the cells of Fig. 1 differ in several respects. The transaction processing applications support lower-level management and clerical personnel. Any decisions included in transaction processing computer programs are programmed decisions that can be described by straightforward algorithms. Applications supporting higher-level activities are less structured, and decisions incorporated in the applications tend to be less programmable and require human/machine interaction to arrive at a result. There are considerably more feasible applications in support of transaction processing and operations than there are in support of strategic planning. Therefore, the structure of an MIS is sometimes described visually as a pyramid (Fig. 2).

MIS Applications to Support Management Activities

The classification of management activities into operational control, management control, and strategic planning is based on the commonly used classification by Anthony (1965). The applications associated with each of the levels of management activity have different characteristics.

Operational Control Operational control is the process of ensuring that operational activities are carried out effectively and efficiently. Operational control makes use

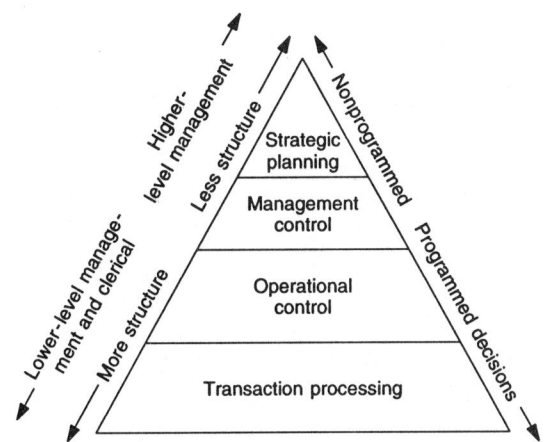

FIG. 2. The management information system as a pyramid. (Reprinted by permission from Gordon B. Davis and Margrethe H. Olson, *Management Information Systems: Conceptual Foundations, Structure, and Development,* 2nd Ed. New York: McGraw-Hill, p. 48 (1985).

of fairly stable pre-established procedures and decision rules. The decisions and actions cover short time periods. The information system support for operational control consists of transaction processing, operational report processing, and inquiry processing. Some examples of information processing in support of operational decision making are the following:

- When an inventory withdrawal is made the system not only records the transaction and produces a transaction document but also, using pre-established algorithms, examines the balance on hand to see if a replenishment order should be placed. If so, order quantity is calculated. An action order document is produced for review by an analyst before the order is placed.
- An analysis of orders still outstanding after 30 days is produced periodically for manual follow-up.

Management Control Management control information is needed by managers of departments, profit centers,

etc., to measure performance, to decide on control actions, to formulate new decision rules, and to allocate resources. Management control reporting generally requires some standard of performance in order to calculate variances from standard and to analyze the causes of the variances. MIS applications include planning models to assist in preparing plans and budgets, variance analysis programs, problem analysis modules, and inquiry capabilities. An example of management control information is a performance report with planned and actual performance, plus an analysis of reasons for variances. Fig. 3 illustrates a management control report for a sales manager.

Strategic Planning Strategic planning develops the strategy with which an organization will attempt to achieve its objectives. Data requirements are generally for summary data rather than for detailed transaction data. The data needs include both external and internal data and projections of future demand. An example is a report describing past demand and past market share, plus a forecast of future demand (Fig. 4).

MIS Support for Decision Making and Planning

The MIS support for decision making in an organization can be described in terms of Simon's (1977) three phases of the decision-making process: intelligence, decision design, and choice. The intelligence phase is for discovering problems and opportunities. The MIS support for this phase requires a database plus methods for search and discovery. Structured search may use predefined search algorithms; unstructured search requires flexible access to the database. The decision design phase is for the generation of alternatives. This involves inventing, developing, and analyzing possible courses of action. The MIS support for decision design consists of statistical and analytical software and model-building software. The final step in the decision-making process is choice. The MIS support for the choice phase consists of various decision models, sensitivity analysis, and choice procedures. Expert systems can support all phases of decision making. Fig. 5 gives examples of MIS support for the three phases of decision making.

Demo Company
Report of Sales and Gross Profit on Sales
Month Ended 31 March 1991

	Sales Dollars (000) Actual/		Gross Profit (000) Actual/		Analysis of Gross Profit Variance (000)		
	Planned	Variance	Planned	Variance	Volume	Price	Mix
Jan	3,791	19*	1398	122*	61*	12*	49*
Feb	3,142	42	1290	50	21	5*	34
Mar	3,761	239*	1173	210*	159*	38*	13*
Apr	4,050		1620				
May	4,100		1640				

*Unfavorable variance.

FIG. 3. Management control report for sales manager using variance analysis.

Demo Company
Market Share Analysis
for Past Five Years and
Five-Year Demand Forecast
for Squidgits

		Total Units (000)	Estimated Market Share [Units (000) and Percent]			
			Demo Co.	Svarto, Inc.	Vito Co.	Andra
Past	1986	12,500	1,900 (15.2)	3,137 (25.1)	6,313 (50.5)	1,150 (9.2)
	1987	13,300	2,168 (16.3)	3,724 (28.0)	6,198 (46.6)	1,210 (9.1)
	1988	12,000	2,100 (17.5)	3,384 (28.2)	5,376 (44.8)	1,083 (9.5)
	1989	15,600	2,652 (17.0)	4,555 (29.2)	6,864 (44.0)	1,529 (9.8)
	1990	14,900	2,742 (18.4)	4,232 (28.4)	1,586 (44.2)	1,340 (9.0)
Forecast	1991	16,200				
	1992	16,900				
	1993	17,500				
	1994	17,500				
	1995	17,000				

FIG. 4. Strategic planning report showing past and projected demand and past market shares.

The planning process requires future expectations to be quantified and classified. A planning model is prepared as a method of structuring, manipulating, and communicating expectations and plans. Computational support for the planning process consists of historical data analysis techniques, planning data generation techniques, and financial planning computations. The preparation and testing of organizational plans can be aided by planning software.

Issues in the Design and Implementation of MIS Some MIS applications have been implemented with great success; others have been failures. The failures, which are often instructive, have usually been due to one of the following factors:

- Failure to identify correctly or completely user requirements. (Systems were designed to meet re-
quirements that turned out to be incorrect or incomplete when the systems were implemented.)
- Rigidity in the application development life cycle. (MIS applications often need an iterative or experimental development life cycle because many of the requirements emerge during development. Use of a rigid, linear cycle that ensures complete specification of requirements in the first stage has resulted in systems that have not been accepted.)
- Making systems too complex. (The designs typically attempted to integrate processes too tightly to use a computer-based system.)
- Lack of attention to human and social factors in the design of the system. (Technical factors have often dominated during design, and the systems as designed have met resistance from the organization.)
- Lack of attention to implementation processes. (Management information systems cause changes

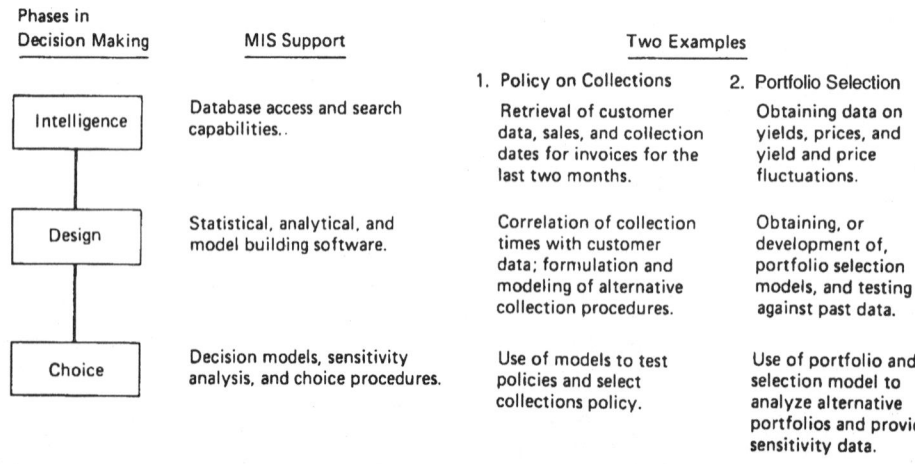

FIG. 5. MIS support for phases in decision making with examples from finance subsystem.

in organizational structure, power relationships, etc. Where the procedures for change have been inadequate to obtain organizational willingness to change, the systems have not received adequate support to succeed.)

The above causes of failure suggest some of the issues in MIS design and implementation. Other MIS design issues are listed below:

- How can cost-effective information systems be designed to support relatively unstructured management activities such as strategic planning?
- How can applications be designed so as to achieve desired organizational behavior? (The issue arises from experience that indicates that information systems applications have substantial impact on organizational behavior.)
- How much control should be given to users, and how should this control be achieved? (Technology changes and user awareness of the power of information technology have made many users demand greater control over their information resources.) This issue includes how to incorporate microcomputers and end user computing into the MIS.
- How should the functions between computer and user be allocated and what should be the characteristics of the user interface? (The design of user interfaces in applications and the allocation of functions between the computer and the user affect both the user performance and the user willingness to accept the application).
- How should expert systems be assimilated into application design?

Note that the MIS design and implementation issues are usually not technical; rather, they relate to cost and effectiveness and to the impact of design and implementation on human and organizational behavior.

Sources of Information on MIS
The Society for Information Management (SIM) is a professional society for MIS whose members are mainly MIS executives and MIS planners. Formerly known as the Society for Management Information Systems (SMIS), it holds an annual convention and publishes a quarterly bulletin plus the *MIS Quarterly* (jointly with the Management Information Systems Research Center at the University of Minnesota). The Data Processing Management Association (DPMA) is a broad-based organization oriented to information processing in organizations.

The major conference for information systems researchers and academics is the annual International Conference on Information Systems (ICIS). Its proceedings are distributed through the Association for Computing Machinery. The most important international scholarly body is Technical Committee 8 (Information Systems) of the International Federation for Information Processing (IFIP).

The general computing literature contains articles on MIS. Important sources are the *MIS Quarterly*, *Information Systems Research*, *Data Base* (published by the Special Interest Group for Business Data Processing of ACM), *Datamation*, and *Journal of Management Information Systems*. A European journal in English is *Information and Management*. Articles on MIS appear with reasonable frequency in *Management Sciences*, *Communications of the ACM*, *Decision Sciences*, and the *Harvard Business Review*. *Computing Reviews* of ACM reviews some MIS articles under the section titled, "Information Systems Applications."

The Future of MIS
The implementation of systems embodying MIS concepts dominates the design or redesign of almost all organizational information systems. Technology improvements in hardware and software make many MIS applications both feasible and cost-effective. For example, improved terminals at lower cost make terminal-based management applications more cost-effective, and improved database management systems make it feasible to implement applications involving management inquiry and retrieval from databases.

References

1965. Anthony, Robert N. *Planning and Control Systems: A Framework for Analysis*. Cambridge, MA: Harvard University Press.

1971. Gorry, G. A. and Scott Morton, M. S. "A Framework for Management Information Systems," *Sloan Management Review*, Fall 1971. One of the most significant framework articles.

1977. Simon, Herbert A. *The New Science of Management Decision* (Rev. Ed.). Englewood Cliffs, NJ: Prentice-Hall.

1985. Davis, Gordon B. and Olson, Margrethe H. *Management Information Systems: Conceptual Foundations, Structure, and Development*, 2nd Ed. New York: McGraw-Hill. (The most widely cited conceptual text on MIS and noted as a classic in the field.)

1987. Emery, James C. *Management Information Systems: The Critical Strategic Resource*. New York: Oxford University Press, 1987. A good managerial-level, non-technical book.

1988. Loehlein, Patricia. *Management Information Systems: An Information Sourcebook*. Phoenix, AZ: Oryx Press. A comprehensive annotated list of important literature in the field.

1989. Boyer, Glen L. and Carlson, Gary. "Characteristics of Periodical Literature for the Potential Reader or Author in Information Management," *MIS Quarterly*, **13**:2 (June) 221–229. A summary of key characteristics of 110 periodicals that publish information systems articles.

GORDON B. DAVIS

MANCHESTER UNIVERSITY COMPUTERS

For articles on related subjects *see* ATLAS; BUSH, VANNEVAR; HARTREE, DOUGLAS R.; KILBURN, THOMAS; WILKES, MAURICE; and WILLIAMS, SIR FREDERICK C.

Manchester University has played an important role in the development of computer science. As early as the 1930s, Douglas R. Hartree (1897–1958) had constructed a differential analyzer (*q.v.*), a mechanical calculating machine based upon the theoretical ideas of Lord Kelvin and the designs of the American engineer, Vannevar Bush. This was an analog device. After the Second World War, these machines were overtaken by electronic stored-program digital computers.

In 1946, Professor (Sir) F. C. Williams (1911–1977) and Professor Tom Kilburn began work at Manchester University with the intention of developing a novel form of computer storage using cathode ray tubes. The system, which involved the use of the "Williams tube" (*q.v.*) to store binary digits of information, was perfected during 1947. Kilburn reported the results, together with the outline design for a hypothetical computer in December of that year. The team was also joined by G. C. Toothill, who, like Williams and Kilburn, had previously worked at the Telecommunications Research Establishment at Malvern. A prototype—the "baby machine," the forerunner of the Manchester Mark I—was built, and on 21 June 1948 became the world's first operational stored-program digital computer. The successful running of its first program, recorded Williams, "was the breakthrough and sparks flew in all directions."

The Manchester group doubled its size in 1948 by taking on two research students, D. B. G. Edwards and G. E. Thomas. Besides Williams and Kilburn, who provided the electrical engineering skills, Professor M. H. A. (Max) Newman (1897–1984) and Alan Turing (*q.v.*), who joined the mathematics department in 1948, gave theoretical support. Turing, for example, with Edwards and Thomas, designed a paper tape input/output system and also wrote a programming manual.

In 1948, the attention of Sir Ben Lockspeiser, the then Government Chief Scientist, was drawn to the Mark I. The result was a government contract with Ferranti Ltd. to make a production version of the machine "to Professor Williams' specification." The first Ferranti Mark I was installed at Manchester University in February 1951, thereby becoming the world's first commercially available computer to be delivered. A subsequent version was named the Mark I Star. The government's involvement with Manchester University proved worthwhile: Royalties from Williams's patents (the first of which had been filed on 11 December 1946 by the Ministry of Supply) gave an important boost to the National Research Development Corporation (NRDC), a government body set up to advise on and support developments in British industry.

Initially, hardware design tended to dominate the development of Manchester University computers. However, software development for the Mark I gained considerable momentum after the appointment of R. A. Brooker in 1951. His high-level programming language, the Mark I Autocode System, was available by 1954, pre-dating Fortran by two years.

Besides building the world's first stored-program computer, as well as the world's first commercially available computer, Kilburn and his group can be credited with building the first proper transistorized computer in 1953. The Metropolitan Vickers Company later built a commercial version of the design, the MV950, which was completed in 1956.

The University's involvement with Ferranti continued into the 1950s when the design team (increasingly headed

FIG. 1.

by Kilburn as Williams' interest turned to other engineering matters) was working on a Mark II computer nicknamed MEG (megacycle engine). The production version of MEG was known as the Ferranti Mercury, and the first machine was delivered in August 1957. Collaboration in these years eventually resulted in the Atlas computer, an ambitious project that pioneered many concepts in storage and addressing that are in common use today. On its official inauguration on 7 December 1962, it was considered to be the most powerful computer in the world.

By the end of the 1960s, developments elsewhere, particularly in the United States, had eroded Manchester University's lead. Nevertheless, innovation continued into the 1960s and beyond, when, with the help of the Science Research Council and the British computer firm, ICL, the MU5 was built between 1969 and 1974. The MU5 heavily influenced the architecture of the ICL 2900 series computers. During the 1980s, the University has been active in dataflow computing (*q.v.*) and in parallel declarative architecture.

Both in commercial and technical terms, the legacy of these vintage years of computing was immense (42 computer patents emanated from Manchester University during 1948–50). Through development of their computers, Manchester University pioneered the teaching of the wholly new subject of computing within the British university system. Finally, all these developments established an important link between the University and the computer industry that has lasted through various projects to the present day.

References

—. Papers of Manchester University Department of Computer Science, National Archive for the History of Computing, Manchester University.

1975. Lavington, Simon H. *A History of Manchester Computers*. Manchester: National Computer Centre.

1980. Lavington, Simon H. *Early British Computers* Manchester: Manchester University Press.

GEOFFREY TWEEDALE

MARK I

For articles on related subjects *see* AIKEN, HOWARD; DIGITAL COMPUTERS: HISTORY: EARLY; and HOPPER, GRACE MURRAY.

The Harvard *Mark I*, also called the IBM Automatic Sequence Controlled Calculator, was the first large-scale, automatic, digital computer produced in the U.S. The gift of the International Business Machines Corporation to Harvard University in August 1944, Mark I marked the beginning of the era of the modern computer.

The Mark I was the brainchild of Howard Hathaway Aiken, who conceived the idea for a general-purpose computing machine for scientific calculations while working on his Ph.D. at Harvard. In 1937 he approached IBM with this idea. Thomas J. Watson, Sr. (*q.v.*) supported the plan to adapt the components and techniques of IBM statistical machines to an automatic scientific calculator.

The machine was designed in collaboration with IBM engineers Claire D. Lake, Francis E. Hamilton, and Benjamin M. Durfee (U.S. Patent 2,616,626) at the IBM Research Laboratory at Endicott, New York. Final construction of the machine was delayed by U.S. entrance into World War II. When placed in operation at Harvard in 1944, the Mark I was operated round-the-clock for the Navy's Bureau of Ships, under the supervision of Professor Aiken, then Commander, USNR.

The Mark I was a parallel, synchronous calculator with a word length of 23 decimal digits, plus the algebraic sign. It was 51 ft long (see Fig. 1), stood 8 ft high, and weighed approximately 5 tons. It used many standard components from IBM equipment, including relays, counters, cam contacts, typewriters, card feeds, and punches. The sequence mechanism, the primary innovation of the Mark I, governed the automatic operation of the machine from instructions encoded on punched paper tape. By much the same method, Babbage envisioned the control of his Analytical Engine (*q.v.*) by Jacquard cards. The fundamental time cycle of the Mark I was 300 ms, the time necessary to advance the sequence tape. One cycle was sufficient for addition; multiplication, division, and functional computations required from 10 to 200 cycles.

FIG. 1. The Mark I, or Automatic Sequence Controlled Calculator.

The machine consisted of 60 constant registers set by dial switches, 72 storage counters used for arithmetic operations and temporary storage, a multiplying/dividing unit, functional counters for computing logarithmic and trigonometric functions, three interpolators capable of interpolation from tables of previously computed values punched on paper tape, and the sequence mechanism. Input was by interpolator tape, punched cards, and constant registers; output, by punched cards or IBM Electromatic typewriters. A 4 hp, 25 Kw motor provided the mechanical drive for the counters and functional units through electromagnetic clutches controlled by relays.

The principal task of the Mark I for many years was the computation of Bessel functions. Later electronic machines out-rivaled the Mark I in speed, but its suitability for the computation of tables insured its continued operation until 1959. After more than 15 years of service in the Harvard Computation Laboratory, the Mark I was retired and dismantled. Pieces of the machine may still be seen at Harvard, IBM headquarters in New York, and the Smithsonian.

References

1946. Computation Laboratory, Harvard University. "Manual of Operation for the Automatic Sequence Controlled Calculator," *Annals of the Computation Laboratory* **1**, Cambridge, MA: Harvard University Press.

ELIZABETH L. STOLL

MASKING

For articles on related subjects *see* INSTRUCTION SET; INTERRUPT; MACHINE AND ASSEMBLY LANGUAGE PROGRAMMING; and SHIFTING.

The items of information required by a computer program may be of lengths that are not matched to the usually fixed length of the storage unit (cell) in the computer memory. Therefore, either an item may require several storage units or several items may be packed into one unit. In the latter case, a mechanism is necessary in order to retrieve the item needed without interference from other items that are stored in the same memory unit. *Masking* is the procedure that enables one to do so by accessing the desired information while suppressing or "masking out" the undesired information.

The basis of the masking operation is the boolean operation AND, which, for two variables D and M, is defined as follows.

D	M	D AND M
0	0	0
0	1	0
1	0	0
1	1	1

From the truth table, we see that

when $M = 1$, D AND $M = D$
when $M = 0$, D AND $M = 0$.

The variable M, therefore, functions as a *mask*. Whenever its value is 1, the result of the AND operation is to duplicate the value of D, whereas if $M = 0$, the value of D is masked out.

As an example, let us assume that in an eight-bit byte we would like to gain access to the middle four bits. The necessary mask is 00111100. The AND operation of this mask with the data byte produces a result in which the first two and last two bits are masked out. This result can then be aligned to the byte boundary (or any other boundary) with the aid of shift operations.

There are other masking operations concerned with control information. Various control items can be grouped; those that are required can then be chosen by masking all non-required items with a zero mask. For example, a user of an IBM ES/3000 may choose one of four possible condition codes by structuring a mask of four bits, with values of one and zero corresponding to the selection or masking of the appropriate condition. The same type of masking is used in order to mask out undesired interrupt conditions, control bits, etc. In these cases, one cannot use shift operations as an alternative to masking because the information to be masked is not data in the usual sense, that is it does not lie in a register whose contents can be shifted.

GIDEON FRIEDER

MASS STORAGE. *See* MEMORY: AUXILIARY.

MATHEMATICAL PROGRAMMING

For articles on related subjects *see* DISCRETE MATHEMATICS; NUMERICAL ANALYSIS; OPERATIONS RESEARCH; OPTIMIZATION METHODS; and SIMPLEX METHOD.

This article provides an overview of *mathematical programming*—its scope, its methods, and the associated computer feasibility and efficacy of the methods. Mathematical programming as discussed here has nothing inherently to do with computer programming. Although mathematical programming is usually done by computer, this term refers to mathematical *optimization*, with or without constraints. A mathematical programming problem can be written without loss of generality as

Maximize: $c(x_1, \ldots, x_n)$,
Subject to: $a_i(x_1, \ldots, x_n) \le 0$ $(i = 1, \ldots, m)$ (1)

In the formulation (1), $x_1, \ldots, x_n$ are real decision variables for which values are desired that will maximize the objective function $c(x_1, \ldots, x_n)$, subject to the m constraints $a_i(x_1, \ldots, x_n) \le 0$. There may be further restrictions requir-

ing that the values of x_j $(j = 1, \ldots, n)$ are a proper subset of those values that satisfy the constraints. For example, all or some of the variables may be required to be integers.

With some imagination, one can see that almost any well-defined deterministic optimization problem (a problem in which all numbers in the functions of expression (1) are known constants) can be formulated as a mathematical programming problem. Many non-deterministic problems (those in which some numbers in the functions of expression (1) are probabilistic, i.e. are random) can be formulated in this manner as well. Solving mathematical programming problems in general is quite another matter. Although certain classes of problems are relatively inexpensive to solve computationally, others are very expensive.

Methods of mathematical programming may be divided into three groups: linear programming, integer linear programming, and nonlinear programming. Linear programming methods solve the problem for which the functions $c(x_1, \ldots, x_n)$ and $a_i(x_1, \ldots, x_n)$ are linear and the x_j may take on any values that satisfy the constraints. Linear programming problems are relatively easy to solve, and computers have great capability for solving such problems. Integer linear programming problems are those in which some or all variables must be integers. Nonlinear programming is literally everything else in mathematical programming. As might be expected, because of the availability of computer programs to solve large linear programming problems efficiently, there has been a great incentive to find nonlinear programming problems that are in some manner similar or reducible to linear programming problems so that linear programming methods can be used to solve (or approximately solve) them. In addition, special methods have been developed to solve certain nonlinear programming problems that have special features.

This article discusses linear and nonlinear programming problems and methods for their solution. Also discussed are some useful necessary conditions for an optimal solution to a nonlinear programming problem that are also sufficient under restrictive circumstances. Finally, integer programming problems and methods are discussed, and some comments on computational feasibility are presented.

Linear Programming Problems Linear programming is used to solve problems of resource allocation in which the employment of a resource in different activities has proportionately constant returns. This means that, for example, if four units of a resource can be employed to produce one unit of a product, then eight units of the resource can be used to produce two units of the product. Similarly, each unit of a product produced contributes the same amount to cover profits and overhead.

The general linear programming problem may be written as follows (minimization problems may be solved by maximizing the negative of the objective function, and variables unrestricted in sign may also be handled):

Maximize $\quad c_1 x_1 + \ldots + c_n x_n$

subject to: $a_{i1} x_1 + \ldots + a_{in} x_n \leq b_i, \quad i = 1, \ldots, m$

$$x_1, \ldots, x_n \geq 0 \qquad (2)$$

The a_{ij}, c_j, and b_i are constants. The above problem is solved by first converting the inequalities into equalities as follows: $a_{i1} x_1 + \ldots + a_{in} x_n + x_{n+1} = b_i, x_{n+1} \geq 0$, $i = 1, \ldots, m$. The variables x_{n+1} are called *slack variables* ($\geq$ type constraints are converted to equalities by subtracting nonnegative variables, and these are called *surplus variables*. Equality constraints are also permitted.) Adding slack variables to equation (2) yields an underdefined system of m equations in $(n + m)$ variables. A *basic solution* to this system is obtained by setting n variables to zero, and solving the set of m equations for the remaining m variables. The variables set to zero are called *non-basic* and the remaining variables are called *basic*. If a basic solution is feasible to the problem, it is called a *basic feasible solution*. If the problem has an optimal solution, then it can be shown that there is at least one basic feasible solution that is optimal. A naive way to solve linear programming problems would be to enumerate all basic solutions and choose one that is optimal.

A practical way to solve linear programming problems is to begin with a basic feasible solution and then find a sequence of basic feasible solutions such that the objective function monotonically increases in the sequence and terminates at an optimal solution. Each solution in this sequence is obtained from its predecessor solution by increasing the value of one non-basic variable until a basic variable becomes zero. The non-basic variable whose value is increased now becomes basic, and the basic variable that drops to zero becomes non-basic in the new solution. In this procedure, a non-basic variable is chosen if an increase in its value would lead to an increase in the problem's objective function value. This is the essence of the simplex method that has been widely used to solve linear programming problems.

Applications Linear programming has been used for a number of years by business, government, and industry to solve certain resource allocation problems. Some examples of applications include the following:

1. *Blending problems* in which a lowest-cost blend is desired to satisfy certain requirements subject to material availability, etc. The blending of animal feeds, peanut butter, gasoline, and specification of foods in hospital diets are examples of blending problems that have been solved using linear programming.
2. *Product-mix problems* in which the maximal-profit mix of products is desired consistent with facility and material limitations, sales commitments to customers, and sales potential of products. Product-mix problems in the aluminum, manufacturing, oil, and steel industries (among others) have been solved by linear programming.

3. *Distribution problems* in which least-cost procedures are desired for distributing products from plants or warehouses to customers.
4. *Dynamic production planning* over a time projection.

Example of a Linear Programming Problem We will now develop an example of a linear programming problem that will also illustrate related concepts.

A small shop has two machines used to make two products. Both machines are each operated 12 hours each day. Product 1 requires 2 hours on machine A and 1 hour on machine B, and produces a net profit (above the costs of materials) of \$15. Product 2 requires 0.25 hour on machine A and 0.5 hour on machine B, and produces a profit of \$10. The proprietor of the shop wants to maximize total profits. Assume that raw materials are abundantly available, and that all production will be saleable. To formulate the problem, let x_1 and x_2 be the number of units of product 1 and product 2 produced on a given day, respectively.

We formulate the problem as a linear program as follows.

Maximize $\quad 15 x_1 + 10 \quad x_2 \qquad (3)$

subject to: $\quad 2 x_1 + 0.25 \ x_2 \leq 12 \qquad (4)$

$\qquad\qquad\quad x_1 + 0.5 \ x_2 \leq 12 \qquad (5)$

$\qquad\qquad\qquad\quad x_1, \ x_2 \leq 0 \qquad (6)$

The objective function gives the total profit from producing x_1 units of product 1 and x_2 units of product 2. Constraint (4) stipulates that the total amount of machine A time required for this production should not exceed 12 hours, and constraint (5) stipulates a similar restriction with regard to machine B. Constraint (6) stipulates that the number of units of a product to be produced must not be negative.

The problem may be solved graphically by plotting x_1 and x_2 as coordinates and graphing the constraints. A graph for the example is given in Fig. 1, in which the shaded area represents the set of feasible solutions to the problem. The feasible region is bounded by line segments (see Fig. 1), and the points at which these segments intersect are called *corner points* (or basic feasible solutions). The corner points of the feasible set are indicated as A, B, C, and D in Fig. 1. The dashed lines of the form $15x_1 + 10x_2 = K$ are lines of constant profit K. These lines are called *isoprofit lines*. We desire the line having the greatest value of K that intersects the shaded area. As can be seen, $K = 240$ is the maximum value of profits for which the associated isoprofit line intersects the solution set. This line intersects the shaded area at point D, and isoprofit lines having $K > 240$ do not intersect the feasible region. Accordingly, point D ($x_1 = 0$, $x_2 = 24$) is the optimal solution. If we wish to maximize $x_1 + 0.5x_2$ in the above example, the isoprofit lines would be parallel to the constraint $x_1 + 0.5x_2 \leq 12$. The isoprofit lines $x_1 + 0.5x_2 = 12$ coincides with this constraint, and every point along the line segment between points C and D would be optimal. This analysis shows that the optimal solution to a linear programming problem always occurs on the boundary of the feasible region. The optimal solution is either a unique

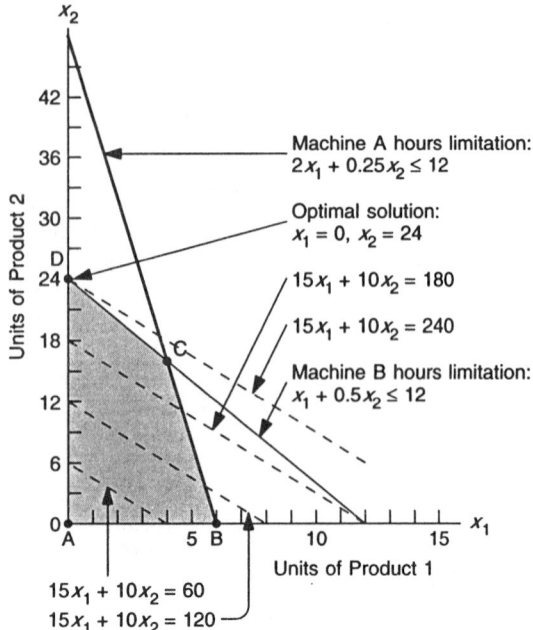

FIG. 1.   Graphical representation of example.

corner point, or there may be multiple optimal solutions along the boundary.

Problems having more than two variables cannot be solved graphically. Such problems are solved algebraically using the simplex method, which was outlined earlier. For more information on the simplex method and its variants, see Bazaraa *et al.* (1989). The simplex method is efficient, and computer programs capable of solving problems with a very large number of variables and constraints are available.

Duality   Closely associated with the preceding problem is another linear programming problem called the *dual* problem. This is a pricing problem, as opposed to a resource allocation problem, and has both practical and theoretical importance.

Example of a Dual Problem   Suppose the owner of the machine shop has been approached by an individual who would like to rent the facilities of the shop for one day. The assets of the shop consist of hours on machine A and hours on machine B. Designating the rental rate for each kind of hour as y_A and y_B, respectively, the owner will receive a daily rental of $12\,y_A + 12\,y_B$. However, if the *owner* were to use the shop to produce one unit each of products 1 and 2, a profit of 15 and 10, respectively, would be made. Hence, whatever rental price is decided on, the owner would not be willing to rent the machines unless

$$2y_A + y_B \geq 15 \tag{7}$$

$$0.25y_A + 0.5y_B \geq 10 \tag{8}$$

$$y_A, y_B \geq 0.$$

That is, the value that we place on the resources going into a unit of product must be as least as large as the profit that could be generated by making the product. For (7), recall that product 1 requires 2 hours on machine A and 1 hour on machine B; for (8), apply a similar argument for product 2. The *owner* wants to know the minimum rent he or she should accept, consistent with the alternatives of production. Thus, we want to solve the following linear programming problem.

$$\text{Minimize:} \quad 12y_A + 12y_B$$
$$\text{Subject to:} \quad 2y_A + y_B \geq 15$$
$$0.25y_A + 0.5y_B \geq 10$$
$$y_A, y_B \geq 0. \tag{9}$$

The solution to (9) that may be found graphically is $y_A = 0$, $y_B = 20$, with a total rental of \$240. It should not be surprising that the minimum acceptable rental is the same as the maximum level of profits that can be achieved. The owner should accept any offer of more than \$240 rental per day, reject any offer of less than \$240 per day and be indifferent to an offer of \$240. (The reader may wonder why someone would be willing to pay a rental of more than \$240 per day. Such a person might have other options that the owner does not have available.)

Individual rental rates are of interest, too. Those rates (sometimes called *shadow prices* or *dual variables*) are the values of a unit of each resource. Recall that in the optimal solution to the owner's problem, only 6 machine A hours were used $(2(0) + 0.25(24) = 6)$ and all 12 machine B hours were used $(1(0) + 0.5(24) = 12)$. The dual variables, $y_A = 0$, $y_B = 20$ reflect the fact that the owner's profit will decrease by \$20 if 1 hour of machine B time is lost. Similarly, the owner's profit may increase as the amount of available resources increases. The dual variables will vary in general as a function of the number of units of resource lost or added. Dual variables give valuable measures by which to gauge the cost of resources. Fortunately, the solution of the dual problem is obtained as a by-product of solving the resource allocation problem.

The dual theorem of linear programming sums up the relationship between the two problems in a formal manner.

The Dual Theorem of Linear Programming   Given two linear programming problems:

$$\text{Maximize:} \quad c_1x_1 + \ldots + c_nx_n$$
$$\text{Subject to:} \quad a_{11}x_1 + \ldots + a_{1n}x_n \leq b_i$$
$$\vdots \qquad \vdots \qquad \vdots$$
$$a_{m1}x_1 + \ldots + a_{mn}x_n \leq b_m$$
$$x_1, \ldots, x_n \geq 0$$

and

Minimize: $b_1 y_1 + \ldots b_m y_m$

Subject to: $a_{11} y_1 + \ldots + a_{m1} y_m \geq c_1$

$$
\begin{array}{ccccc}
\cdot & \cdot & \cdot & \cdot & \cdot \\
\cdot & \cdot & \cdot & \cdot & \cdot \\
\cdot & \cdot & \cdot & \cdot & \cdot
\end{array}
$$

$a_{1n} y_1 + \ldots + a_{mn} y_m \geq c_n$

$y_1, \ldots, y_m < 0.$

1. If one problem has an optimal solution, so does the other, and the objective function values of the solutions to the two problems are identical.
2. If one problem has an infinite optimal solution (i.e. the constraint set is not bounded and the optimal solution is infinite), then the other problem does not have any feasible solutions.

As a corollary to the dual theorem, there are the complementary slackness conditions, which we now state informally and give examples of from our problem. (The word "resource" is used in a general sense; every constraint is assumed to limit a resource. Similarly, the word "product" is used in a general sense; every variable is assumed to be a product.)

1. If the value of a resource (as measured by its dual variable) is positive, it should all be used ($y_B = 20$ implies that machine B has no idle hours: $x_1 + 0.5 x_2 = 12$).
2. If a resource is not all used, its value is zero. (That machine A is not fully utilized or that $2x_1 + 0.25 x_2 < 12$ in the optimal solution implies that $y_A = 0$.)
3. If the value of resources required to produce a unit of product exceeds the profit of producing that product, the product will not be produced. (For product 1, $2y_A + y_B > 15$ implies that $x_1 = 0$.)
4. If a product is produced, the value of the resources used to produce the product exactly equals the profit associated with producing the product. (That product 2 is produced, or $x_2 > 0$, implies that $0.25 y_A + 0.5 y_B = 10$.)

Karmarkar's Method Karmarkar (1984) developed a unique new approach for solving linear programming problems. The simplex method finds an optimal solution by examining a sequence of corner points (which are points on the boundary of the feasible region). In contrast, Karmarkar's method finds the optimal solution by examining the interior of the feasible region. In this method, an artificial variable is added to the problem and the problem is rescaled. The artificial variable is used to ensure that the point (say P_0) having all the decision variables $(x_1, \ldots, x_n)$ equal to 1 is feasible. By construction, such a point lies in the interior of the feasible region. Then, Karmarkar's method obtains a new point P_1 by moving from P_0 in a direction for which the objective function improves. The point P_1 is obtained using a linear transformation of the problem. Point P_1 therefore has the same properties as point P_0. This procedure is repeated from P_1 in an iterative manner until an optimal solution is found.

Karmarkar's method has been shown to be a "polynomial time" algorithm (*see* NP-CCOMPLETE PROBLEMS). If a linear programming problem of size n is solved by this method, then the order of computation required is an^b, where a and b are positive numbers. In contrast, the simplex method is an "exponential time" algorithm, whose order of computation is $c2^n$ where c is a positive number. Given a, b, and c, for sufficiently large n, $c2^n > an^b$. Therefore, a polynomial time algorithm is superior to an exponential time algorithm for sufficiently large n. Although actual empirical evidence is still inconclusive, preliminary testing indicates that Karmarkar's method can be as much as 50 times faster than the simplex method in solving large linear programming problems.

Nonlinear Programming Problems A mathematical programming problem of the form

Maximize: $c(x_1, x_2, \ldots, x_n)$

Subject to: $X \equiv (x_1, x_2, \ldots, x_n)$ in S, (10)

which is not a linear or integer programming problem, is classified as a nonlinear programming (NLP) problem.

If the function, c, in (10) is concave and the set S is closed, bounded, and convex, then an optimal solution occurs either at the global maximum of c or a boundary point of S. A function, c, is concave if for all $X \equiv (x_1, x_2, \ldots, x_n)$ and $Y \equiv (y_1, y_2, \ldots, y_n)$ and $0 < \lambda < 1$,

$$
\begin{aligned}
c(\lambda(x, x_2, \ldots, x_n) &+ (1 - \lambda)(y_1, y_2, \ldots, y_n)) \\
&\geq \lambda c(x_1, x_2, \ldots, x_n) \\
&+ (1 - \lambda) c(y_1, y_2, \ldots, y_n).
\end{aligned}
$$

Intuitively, if the function is concave, then if a line is "stretched" between any two points on the function's surface, that line will be at or below the surface.

A set, S, is called convex if for any X and Y in S, the point $\lambda(x_1, x_2, \ldots, x_n) + (1 - \lambda)(y_1, y_2, \ldots, y_n)$ is also in S. If either c is not concave or S is not convex (or both), then an optimal solution could occur anywhere within S.

Methods for solving NLP problems exist, but many methods apply only to certain subsets of problems because they assume certain conditions about c or S (e.g. concavity or convexity). The problem of solving a general NLP problem can be compared to the problem faced by a person trying to walk to the highest point in the State of New York on a foggy day. From any point, the person can only see a short distance in any direction and hence never knows for sure if the "hill" on which he or she is standing is the highest hill.

Most algorithms used for solving general NLP problems involve some sort of neighborhood search method analogous to the method of the hiker in New York. There are four problems that such a method must overcome:

1. How can a local optimum be identified?
2. Which direction from a given point leads to an improvement in the function value?
3. If several directions improve the function, which is the "best" direction?
4. How far can the searcher move in the improving direction and still remain within S?

In the case of an NLP problem of form (1) in which the functions c, a_1, a_2,..., a_m are differentiable, an important theoretical result known as the Karush-Kuhn-Tucker conditions provides necessary conditions for a point to be a local optimum (see Bazaraa and Shetty, 1979). The Karush-Kuhn-Tucker conditions characterize local optimality by use of the gradient vectors of c and a_i. The gradient vector, c, is the vector of partial derivatives of c, $\nabla c = (\partial c/\partial x_1, \partial c/\partial x_2,...,\partial c/\partial x_n)$. This vector also provides an analytic tool for determining which way is "up." If a point X is a local optimum, then it must satisfy the following *Karush-Kuhn-Tucker conditions*.

1. X must be in S.
2. There exist $y_1 \geq 0$ such that

$$\partial c/\partial x_j = \sum_{i=1}^{m} y_i (\partial a_j /\partial x_j) \qquad j, = 1,2,...,n.$$

3. $y_i\, a_i(X) = 0$.
4. The Karush-Kuhn-Tucker constraint qualification holds at X.

Condition 4, whose precise statement is beyond our scope here, is a condition that ensures that the feasible region is "well behaved" at the point. The Karush-Kuhn-Tucker conditions are the basis for determining local optimality in NLP algorithms.

Intuitively, what the first three conditions state is the following: If we construct the normal vectors to the binding constraints at the optimal solution "pointing out" of the feasible region, we can define the cone determined by the vectors. For the point to be optimal, the objective function vector at that point must lie in the cone. The fourth condition states that the surface at that point must not have any peculiar cusps.

The gradient, ∇c, indicates the direction of increase of c. The method of "steepest ascent (descent)" is an algorithm that begins at a point X_0 in S, and moves through S in "small" steps by computing

$$X_i = X_{i-1} + a\nabla c(X_{i-1})$$

where $a > 0$ is a (usually small) real constant that determines the size of the movement. Under certain conditions, this procedure converges to a local optimum and the rate of convergence can be computed. The problem with this approach is that the sequence of points generated by such a method may lead to points not in S. Two methods, known as penalty and barrier methods, attempt to overcome this problem.

A penalty function, $P(X)$, has the property,

$P(X) < 0$ if X is not in S
$P(X) = 0$ if X is in S.

Thus, the constrained optimization problem (10) can be converted to the unconstrained optimization problem,

$$\text{Maximize: } c(X) + \theta\, P(X). \qquad (11)$$

If θ is very large, then the maximum must occur at a point X for which $P(X) = 0$. Therefore, by solving (11) for successively larger values of θ, a solution to (10) can sometimes be obtained.

A barrier function, $B(X)$, has the property,

$B(X) \geq 0$ for all X
$B(X) \to \infty$ as X approaches the boundary of S from a feasible point

For example, if S is defined by the m constraints,

$$g_i(X) \geq 0 \qquad i = 1,2,...,m.$$

Then,

$$B(X) = \sum_{i=1}^{m} [g_i(X)]^{-1}$$

is a barrier function, since it becomes infinite as the boundary $g_i(X) = 0$ is approached.

A constrained optimization problem can be converted to the unconstrained problem,

$$\text{Maximize: } c(X) - \theta B(X),$$

if a barrier function can be found.

Integer Linear Programming   Solving linear programming problems with the stipulation that some or all variables be integer-valued might seem to be a rather useless activity, particularly if we are concerned with determining the optimal number of four-door sedans General Motors should produce next year. It would appear that rounding a solution value such as 102,376.35 to a nearby integer value would make a neglible difference in the objective function value. On the other hand, if a variable represented the number of new bridges to be built across the Niagara River between the U. S. and Canada, and the optimal linear program solution value were 0.53, rounding to 0 or 1 would indeed make a great deal of difference in the objective function value.

We may infer from the above that, generally, large integer variables may be rounded arbitrarily, whereas small integer variables may not; this seems most reasonable. In addition, the use of integer variables may be made to assure that certain logical conditions are fulfilled [e.g. of two alternatives (x_1 and x_2), exactly one must be selected: $x_1 + x_2 = 1$, where $x_1, x_2 \geq 0$ and integer], or that certain peculiar nonlinear functions are involved that do not correspond to maximizing a concave function over a convex set.

Thus, there are many applications for integer variables in addition to the obvious one that the number of units to be produced is to be integer. Integer programming methods have been successfully utilized to solve problems of airline-crew scheduling, capital budgeting, and bank-check clearing for large companies, as well as other problems.

In general, integer programming problems are difficult to solve, and no polynomial time algorithm exists for solving them. Usually, moderate-sized problems are solved to optimality using exponential time search procedures, and large problems are solved using heuristics (*q.v.*). Heuristics are used to obtain "good" and not necessarily optimal solutions. The performance of a heuristic is assessed using theoretical worst-case analyses and empirical investigations (see Parker and Rardin, 1988). We briefly describe the optimal integer programming methods in terms of four categories, as follows:

1. Cut methods.
2. Group theoretic methods.
3. Branch-and-bound methods.
4. Implicit enumeration methods.

Further, we will refer to the problem as an all-integer problem if all variables are required to be integer valued, and as mixed integer if only some of the variables are required to be integer valued.

Cut Methods Cut methods, which were among the first methods developed, employ cut constraints derived from the original problem. Cut constraints have the desirable property that they exclude or cut off parts of the feasible solution space without cutting off any integer solution points. Some cut methods first require the solution of the linear programming problem before cut constraints are added; others do not. If the linear programming optimal solution should happen to have the required variables integer, it is optimal. Otherwise, a cut constraint is added and a new optimal solution to the augmented problem is found. The procedure is continued until an integer solution is obtained. Other cut methods do not first solve the linear programming problem; instead they generate and utilize a cut constraint at every step of the solution process. There are cut methods for both all-integer and mixed-integer problems.

In recent years, an approach to the efficient solution of certain integer programming problems using cuts derived from polyhedral geometry has been developed. Cut constraints derived from polyhedral considerations are known as "valid inequalities" (see Parker and Rardin, 1988). Several specially structured large problems have been successfully solved to optimality by this approach.

Group Theoretic Methods Group theoretic methods can be used only for problems in which all variables are required to be integers. The method begins by solving the linear programming problem. Assuming that the solution is not integer, the method then systematically constructs an integer solution to the problem by increasing to positive integer values certain variables that were set equal to zero in the optimal linear programming solution. Quite often, the constructed solution will be the optimal solution to the integer programming problem; where it is not, additional construction is required to generate the integer optimum. The method is based on mathematical group theory and works reasonably well on some problems. Although there is little available data on the efficiency of the methods, commercial computer codes using the technique are in use.

Branch-and-Bound Methods Branch-and-bound methods are generally the most successful for solving integer programming problems—both for all integer and mixed integer. We outline one of a number of variations of the branch-and-bound procedure.

First solve the linear programming problem. If the solution does not satisfy the integer requirements, choose a variable in the solution that should be integer but is not. Supposing that the variable chosen has a solution value of 3.4, two new linear programs are solved, one stating that the variable must not exceed 3, and the other stating that the variable must be at least 4. Then the two problems and their solutions are stored in a list. The following procedure is then used.

Pick the best solution from the list; if it is integer, it is optimal. Otherwise, as above, choose a variable in that solution that is not integer but should be, and solve two linear programming problems, storing the resulting solutions in the list. Then the best solution on the list is chosen, a variable is branched upon, etc. The method is particularly successful because feasible integer solutions are usually found early in the solution process. Once such a solution has been found, the solution can be terminated at any time, as is often done in practice. A bound on how far the solution can be from optimal is known; it is the difference between the objective function value of the best-known integer solution and the objective function value of the best non-integer solution on the list. In addition, the cost of altering and resolving the problem is usually quite low.

Implicit Enumeration Methods Implicit enumeration methods are methods for solving all-integer problems. Most of the successfully implemented variations also require that all integer variables be zero or one, but more general methods have been developed. The idea of the method is straightforward: if there are n variables, there are 2^n possible solutions to enumerate; explicit enumeration would require explicit consideration of each of them. By using tests that follow conceptually from using implied upper and lower bounds on variables, generally only a tiny fraction of all possibilities need to be considered with the implicit treatment of all possibilities. Some auxiliary techniques used to accelerate implicit enumeration have been derived from linear programming.

Putting the Computational Considerations into Perspective We conclude this article with a few comments about the current state of computational efficiency in mathematical programming. Very large linear programming problems (having thousands of constraints) may be solved and have been solved, inexpensively, although it is certainly possible to dream up problems that are too large for solution. Fairly large non-linear programming problems (including quadratic programming and separable programming) that employ methods based on linear programming methods may be solved at reasonable cost. Beyond that, linear constraints are much easier to handle than nonlinear constraints, and the size capabilities of the remaining methods are somewhat smaller. In integer programming, although some fairly large problems have been and are being solved on a routine basis, there are still many relatively small problems that are computationally difficult to solve.

In perspective, mathematical programming gives a potentially very powerful means for formulating and solving optimization problems. Numerous methods have been developed and implemented in many computer systems, and are becoming a viable means of solving all kinds of optimization problems.

References

1979. Bazaraa, M. S. and Shetty, C. M. *Nonlinear Programming—Theory and Algorithms*. New York: John Wiley.

1984. Karmarkar, N. "A New Polynomial Time Algorithm for Linear Programming," *Combinatorica*, 4, 373–395.

1988. Nemhauser, G. L. and Wolsey, L. A. *Integer and Combinatorial Optimization*. New York: John Wiley.

1988. Parker, R. G. and Rardin, R. L. *Discrete Optimization*. New York: Academic Press.

1989. Bazaraa, M. S., Jarvis, J. J., and Sherali, H. D. *Linear Programming and Network Flows*. New York: John Wiley.

STANLEY ZIONTS AND RAMASWAMY RAMESH

MATHEMATICAL SOFTWARE

For articles on related subjects *see* ALGORITHM; APPROXIMATION THEORY; COMPUTER ALGEBRA; INFORMATION-BASED COMPLEXITY; MATHEMATICAL PROGRAMMING; MATRIX COMPUTATIONS; NUMERICAL ANALYSIS; and SYMBOL MANIPULATION.

Mathematical software is software that implements algorithms that have a basis in mathematics. The scope of the term is generally accepted to include algorithms whose primary interest or motivation is mathematical and not merely the application of mathematics. Thus, a computer program to solve a system of first-order differential equations is considered to be mathematical software. A program to solve a chemical reaction problem is not mathematical software, even though the essence of the program might be an algorithm for solving differential equations. The scope of the term is much broader than a pure mathematician's view of mathematics; it includes some aspects of programming languages and computer systems. The scope is also much broader than traditional *numerical analysis*, for it includes such areas as statistics, symbolic mathematical analysis, and linear programming, which are clearly mathematical in nature.

The origins of mathematical software came with the advent of modern computers. A Mark I routine for $\sin(x)$ was published in 1944, and the first operational electronic computer (EDSAC) had a well thought out subroutine library in 1950. Activity and interest in the area grew steadily, and by 1970 mathematical software began to be recognized as a separate subdiscipline of the mathematics–computer science area.

Classification Mathematical software can be classified from several points of view, and one of the most natural is according to complexity or mathematical level. At the bottom are algorithms for arithmetic; i.e. addition, subtraction, multiplication, and division. In many instances, these algorithms are more appropriately called *mathematical hardware*, since they are carried out by the hardware of central processing units. The wide variety of algorithms here stems from the different representations and types of numbers used. Not only are there different radices (base 2, 10, and 16 are common), but there are also different lengths (6 to 15 equivalent decimal digits are common), plus multiple-precision, fixed- and floating-point (or integers and reals), and complex numbers. More specialized arithmetics include interval arithmetic (*q.v.*) and significance arithmetic (*q.v.*). Each combination of these representations and types requires algorithms for the basic arithmetic operations.

The next higher mathematical level includes the evaluation of the functions of algebra, trigonometry, and analysis (e.g. roots and powers, sines and cosines, exponentials, logarithms, and a selection of "higher" functions). These are the *elementary functions* that are commonly included as the built-in mathematical routines of higher-level languages such as C, Ada, Algol, Fortran, Pascal, and PL/I. These built-in routines allow one to write statements such as the following:

```
X   = SIN(3.2) + ALOG(4.7)/5.1 (Fortran)
X  := sin(3.2) + ln(4.7)/5.1    (Algol or
                                 Pascal)
X   = SIN(3.2) + LOG(4.7)/5.1   (PL/I)
```

The following algorithm illustrates how an efficient evaluation is made for the sine function $\sin(x)$.

Set $Y = X \bmod (2\pi)$
If $Y > \pi$ **then set** $Y = Y - \pi$, SIGN $= -1$
      else set SIGN $= 1$

If $Y > \dfrac{\pi}{2}$ **then set** $Y = \pi - Y$

Set $Z = Y/3$
Compute SIN(Z) using a cubic polynomial accurate to 10 decimal places
Set $\text{SIN}(X) = \text{SIGN} * \text{SIN}(Z) * (3\text{-}4\,\text{SIN}^2(Z))$

One may obtain 20-decimal-digit accuracy by replacing the cubic polynomial by an appropriate sixth-degree polynomial. The state-of-the-art for this software is such that high-quality programs are tailored to exploit the specific characteristics of each computer's arithmetic logic unit, (ALU - *q.v.*).

The next level of mathematical software includes the algorithms of linear algebra (e.g. solving linear systems of equations) and the operations of calculus and advanced calculus (e.g. integration, differentiation, and solving nonlinear equations). These mathematical problems are of an order of magnitude more difficult than those discussed above. This software is distinguished from the previous level by two other characteristics. First, it is well known that it is impossible to solve most of the underlying mathematical problems in complete generality. Thus, given any algorithm for integrating functions, one can construct a function for which the algorithm fails. This is true whether the integration algorithm is symbolic or numerical or a combination. Second, one should expect to discover new algorithms that are much superior to currently known ones.

The highest level of mathematical software is an integrated system for a particular branch of mathematics or all of mathematics up to a particular level. Several experimental systems of this type, such as *Mathematica*, are described in the article COMPUTER ALGEBRA. Mathematica attempts to provide numerical, graphic, and symbolic capability up through calculus. When it matures, one can expect it to allow one to do mathematics at this level in ordinary mathematics terms, not using lower level, specialized algorithmic languages like Fortran, Pascal, Ada, or C. There are two primary goals of these mathematical systems. The first is to use standard mathematical notation; the system is to communicate with users in their own terms. Such systems allow statements like

$$A = \int_{0}^{1.8} \cos{(x^2 + 1)}\sqrt{x + 2}\,dx$$

$$\text{SOLVE } Bx^2 - 3.1\,e^{-x} = \text{HBAR}$$

$$F(T) = A'(T) + \int_{0}^{T+1} \sin(x)/(A(x) + 1)\,dx$$

The second goal is to incorporate high-quality, robust algorithms and software to carry out the mathematical procedures allowed in the language. These algorithms are integrated with one another and the overall system so that the results of one are automatically compatible with the others. The development of mathematical systems involves a broad range of mathematics and computer science. The computing areas involved most directly are symbolic manipulation, numerical methods, computational geometry, and expert systems (*q.v.*), all supported by programming languages, operating systems, graphics, and powerful computers. These systems are examples of *problem-solving environments.*

Mathematical algorithms can also be divided into two classes, according to whether the algorithm is "static" or "deterministic," or whether it is "dynamic" or "heuristic." This division is not precise, but it serves a useful intuitive purpose. An algorithm is said to be *static* if its operation is known fully in advance. Examples of static algorithms are those of arithmetic, symbolic differentiation, Simpson's rule for quadrature, and the evaluation of sin(*x*). The ambiguity of this classification arises from the word "known," and the division depends upon how much one knows. An algorithm is *dynamic* or heuristic or *adaptive* if its operation is somewhat unpredictable in advance.

Unpredictability normally comes from logical decisions that are made on the basis of quantities computed during the operation of the algorithm. An example of such software is a *polyalgorithm*, which is set of static algorithms plus a strategy for choosing and switching among them. Polyalgorithms were first introduced in the late 1960s with attempts to automate numerical analysis. Only a small portion of current mathematical software is dynamic, but this is an area with great potential significance and growth. As computing power increases and as knowledge about problem solving increases, these methods will gradually blur the distinction between algorithmic problem solving (where the programmer is certain about all aspects of the method) and artificial intelligence (where the system itself has helped perfect aspects of the method).

Another common division of mathematical software is between *symbolic, numerical,* and *geometric* algorithms. This division is easily seen in simple cases. Integer addition and symbolic differentiation of polynomials are symbolic; the exact results are obtained after a finite number of symbolic operations. Newton's method for polynomial zeros and Simpson's rule for integration are numerical. Approximate results are obtained, but they can be made as accurate as one pleases with sufficient effort and precision in the arithmetic. The constructions of Euclidean geometry are graphical. Perhaps one could call them symbolic, but they are symbols very different from algebra. Geometric mathematical software is still in its infancy compared to symbolic and numerical software. The algorithms of arithmetic are symbolic, but—unfortunately and unavoidably—they are incorrect due to the fixed precision of arithmetic. The algorithms of geometry are implemented using arithmetic, so they too are incorrect beyond a certain level of precision. This incorrectness introduces ambiguity in the distinction between symbolic, numerical, and geometric algorithms. For example, many of the algorithms of linear algebra are symbolic (e.g. Gaussian elimination for solving linear equations), but are considered to be part of numerical analysis. This is perhaps because one of the most important questions is the effect that incorrect arithmetic has upon these algorithms. On the other hand, polynomial manipulation is considered to be symbolic, and yet some programs for this take $(2X + 3) + (1/2) * (3X - 4)$ to be $3.5X + 1$, and thus are also subject to incorrectness due to the arithmetic. The depth and difficulty of understanding this distinction is much greater than one might conjecture. For example, there is a well-known formula to express the roots X_0 and X_1 of $ax^2 + bx + c = 0$ in terms of a, b, and c. However, given that a, b, c, X_0 and X_1 are representable in a particular computer, as yet there is no known program to produce X_0 and X_1 from a, b, and c, which will always be correct (for this computer).

General Problems Mathematical software contains three general problems and areas of great importance. One of these is the *dissemination of software*, and while it may be a somewhat mundane problem, it is also a very difficult one. The objective is simple: Make the best and most effective software available to *everyone* in a natural, efficient, and automatic manner. Materials that fall into this area include *subroutine libraries, textbooks, published algorithms*, and *reference manuals*. All these materials are prone to weaknesses in documentation, effectiveness, efficiency, ease-of-use, and ease-of-access. The best solution to the dissemination problem is the creation of problem-solving environments for mathematics where the problem-solving knowhow and abilities are incorporated by the builders of the system.

A second problem area of great theoretical and practical interest is the *evaluation of algorithms*. The problems here range from the foundations of mathematics to experimental investigations. Symbolic algorithms have been studied from the point of view of pure mathematics, and a variety of proof techniques of a very rigorous nature have been used. Complex and/or numerical algorithms are much less tractable for rigorous and mathematical proofs, and new techniques (both mathematical and experimental) are needed.

Finally, we come to the *resource allocation* aspect of mathematical software. A simple example of this is the trade-off between computation time and memory used. There are frequent instances in which significantly faster execution results by using significantly larger amounts of memory. The advent of sophisticated multiprogramming systems and parallel computers with hierarchies of memories has introduced another dimension to the creation and evaluation of mathematical software.

Libraries High-quality collections, libraries, and packages of mathematical software first appeared in the 1970s. These include two commercial libraries of algorithms and several systematized collections—the BLAS (Basic Linear Algebra Subroutines), EISPACK (56 routines for matrix eigensystems), FUNPACK (covers a number of the more difficult, higher transcendental functions), and LINPACK (linear systems of equations). All these collections are available for a modest handling fee. The Association for Computing Machinery *Transactions on Mathematical Software* and a few other journals regularly publish mathematical software; over 600 ACM algorithms have appeared, and those published since 1975 are available in machine-readable form from the ACM Algorithms Distribution Service at 1515 Broadway, New York, NY 10036. Other packages appeared in the 1980s, covering a dozen or so subareas of mathematics (e.g. ordinary differential equations, partial differential equations, numerical quadrature, homotopy maps). Initial problem-solving environ-

ments have appeared for calculus-level mathematics and for statistics.

References

1980. Rice, J. *et al.* "Numerical Computation," Chapter 3 in Arden, B.(Ed.), *What can be Automated?* Cambridge, MA: The M.I.T. Press, 51–136.
1984. Cowell, W. R. *Sources and Development of Mathematical Software*. Englewood Cliffs, NJ: Prentice-Hall.
1987. Ford, B. and Chatelin, F. *Problem Solving Environments for Scientific Computing*. Amsterdam: North-Holland.
1991. Houstis, E., Rice, J., and Vichnevetsky, R. *Intelligent Scientific Software Systems*. Amsterdam: North-Holland.

JOHN R. RICE

MATRIX COMPUTATIONS

For articles on related subjects *see* ERROR ANALYSIS; LEAST-SQUARES APPROXIMATION; MATHEMATICAL SOFTWARE; NUMERICAL ANALYSIS; and SCIENTIFIC APPLICATIONS.

A large proportion of the scientific calculations performed on computers involves *matrices*. Partly, this is because of the ubiquity of matrices in the mathematics of scientific problems, but it is also partly due to the fact that the use of matrices is ideally suited to the iterative type of calculation in which computers realize their full power.

Notation and Definitions From the point of view of this article, a *matrix* is defined to be a rectangular array of elements, each of which will generally be a real or complex number. An $m \times n$ matrix will be denoted by a capital Roman letter, and the elements of such a matrix A will be denoted by a_{ij}, $i = 1,..., m$, $j = 1,..., n$. If $n = 1$, the matrix is called a *column vector* and a lower case Roman letter will be used. The elements of a vector x of order m are denoted by x_i ($i = 1,..., m$). The *transpose B* of an $m \times n$ matrix A is an $n \times m$ matrix defined by $b_{ij} = a_{ji}$. It is commonly denoted by A^T or A'. Similarly, the $1 \times m$ transpose of a column vector is denoted by x^T, and is called a *row vector*. The *Hermitian transpose B* of an $m \times n$ matrix A is defined by $b_{ij} = \bar{a}_{ji}$, where the bar over $\bar{a}$ denotes the complex conjugate, and is commonly denoted by A^H or $A^\star$; x^H is defined similarly.

If A and B are of the same dimension, their sum C is defined by $c_{ij} = a_{ij} + b_{ij}$. The product C of an $m \times k$ matrix A and a $k \times n$ matrix B is defined by

$$c_{ij} = \sum_{s=1}^{k} a_{is} b_{sj}.$$

The definition applies immediately to the product y of an $m \times n$ matrix A and an $n \times 1$ column vector x; we have

$$y_i = \sum_{s=1}^{n} a_{is} x_s.$$

Finally, the product C of a matrix A by a scalar a is defined by

$$c_{ij} = aa_{ij}.$$

A matrix or vector is said to be *null* if all its components are zero. Either "null" or "zero" will be denoted by the same symbol used for the zero scalar, the context providing adequate identification.

The classes of square matrices defined below are of special interest in matrix computations.

Symmetric: $A = A^T$ (i.e. $a_{ij} = a_{ji}$).

Positive definite: A real, symmetric and $x^T A x > 0$ for all real $x \neq 0$.

Hermitian: $A = A^H$ (i.e. $a_{ij} = \bar{a}_{ji}$).

Orthogonal: A real and $AA^I = A^T A = I$.

Upper (lower) triangular: $a_{ij} = 0$, $i > j$ ($i < j$).

Tridiagonal: $a_{ij} = 0$, $|i - j| > 1$.

Upper-Hessenberg: $a_{ij} = 0$, $i > j + 1$.

The *identity matrix* of order n is denoted by I_n, or by I if the order is obvious, and is defined by

$$i_{kk} = 1, \quad i_{kl} = 0 \quad (k \neq l).$$

The elements are usually denoted by δ_{kl} rather than by i_{kl}. From the definitions, $IA = A = AI$ whenever the dimensions are such that these exist.

It will be assumed that the reader is familiar with the concept of the scalar function of a square matrix A, known as its *determinant* and denoted by $\det(A)$. A square matrix A is said to be *singular* if $\det(A) = 0$; otherwise, it is *nonsingular*. The matrix formed by the elements at the intersection of any collection of rows and columns is called a *submatrix*. The determinant of a square submatrix is called a *minor*; if the submatrix is formed from the intersection of the first r rows and columns, its determinant is called a *leading principal minor*. The *cofactor* A_{ij} of the element a_{ij} of an $n \times n$ square matrix A is defined by

$$A_{ij} = (-1)^{i+j} \det(\text{matrix formed by omitting} \\ \text{row } i \text{ and column } j).$$

The $n \times n$ matrix X with $x_{ij} = A_{ji}$ is called the *adjoint* of A, and it follows from the elementary properties of determinants that

$$AX = \det(A) I = XA.$$

Hence, if A is non-singular, the matrix Y defined by $Y = X/\det(A)$ satisfies the relation $AY = YA = I$; Y is called the *inverse* of A and is denoted by A^{-1}.

The *rank* r of an $m \times n$ matrix A is defined to be the highest order of nonzero minor. Clearly, $r \leq m, n$.

A set of matrices $A^{(1)}, \ldots, A^{(k)}$ is said to be *linearly dependent* if there exists a set of scalars a_i, not all zero, such that

$$\sum_{i=1}^{k} a_i A^{(i)} = 0;$$

otherwise, they are said to be *linearly independent*. The concept is of particular interest when the $A^{(i)}$ are row or column vectors. If A is of rank r, then it has r independent rows and r independent columns; any k rows (or columns) with $k > r$ are linearly dependent.

The Solution of Simultaneous Linear Algebraic Equations

Perhaps the most fundamental of all computations is the solution of a system of m simultaneous linear equations in n unknowns:

$$\sum_{j=1}^{n} a_{ij} x_j = b_i \quad (i = 1, \ldots, m) \text{ or } Ax = \mathbf{b},$$

where A is the $m \times n$ matrix (a_{ij}), and $\mathbf{x}$ and $\mathbf{b}$ are column vectors of order n and m, respectively. The mathematical theory is well known, the following being a brief summary.

Solutions exist if and only if rank $(A, \mathbf{b}) = $ rank (A). The general solution is based on the ability to solve any $r \times r$ system $Cy = \mathbf{d}$, where C is nonsingular. Such a system has the unique solution

$$\mathbf{y} = C^{-1} \mathbf{d},$$

the inverse C^{-1} existing since C is assumed to be nonsingular.

If rank$(A, \mathbf{b}) > $ rank(A), then there is no solution. If rank$(A, \mathbf{b}) = $ rank$(A) = r$ (say), then the solutions are determined as follows: Since A is of rank r, there is a nonsingular $r \times r$ submatrix of A; arrange the order of the equations and the order of the variables so that the leading principal $r \times r$ matrix is nonsingular. Then any solution of the first r equations is automatically a solution of the remainder. The first r equations may be written in the form

$$a_{i1} x_1 + \ldots + a_{ir} x_r \\ = b_i - a_{i,r+1} x_{r+1} - \cdots - a_{in} x_n \\ = d_i \text{ (say)} \quad (i = 1, \ldots, r),$$

or

$$C\mathbf{x}^{(r)} = \mathbf{d}^{(r)},$$

where C is a nonsingular $r \times r$ matrix and $x^{(r)} = (x_1, \ldots, x_r)^T$. Hence, $x_{r+1}, \ldots, x_n$ may be chosen arbitrarily, and for each such choice $x_1, \ldots, x_r$ are given uniquely as the solution of $C\mathbf{x}^{(r)} = \mathbf{d}^{(r)}$. If $r < n$, there is an $(n - r)$-fold infinity of solutions. If $r = n$, the solution is unique.

Of particular importance is the case $\mathbf{b} = \mathbf{0}$; the system is then called *homogeneous*. For such systems, rank $(A, \mathbf{b})$ certainly equals rank(A), and hence they are necessarily compatible, but if $r = n$, the only solution is $\mathbf{x} = \mathbf{0}$, the *null* solution. If $r < n$, there is an $(n - r)$ fold infinity of non-null solutions.

The Practical Solution of a Nonsingular n × n System

The difficulties involved in solving a system of equations are almost entirely of a practical nature. It is essential that a method should be stable with respect to rounding errors and be as economical as possible. Since the fundamental problem is the solution of a system with a square nonsingular matrix of coefficients, we now concentrate on this case. There are two main classes of methods. In *direct* methods the solution is obtained in a finite number of operations; without the intervention of rounding errors, it would be exact. In *iterative* methods a sequence $\mathbf{x}^{(k)}$ of solutions is obtained such that $\mathbf{x}^{(k)} \to \mathbf{x}$ the true solution, as $k \to \infty$. In practice, iteration is terminated after a finite number of steps.

Direct Methods The best-known direct method is *Gaussian elimination*, which is merely a systematic version of the high-school method of successive elimination of variables. We denote the original set of equations by

$$a_{i1} x_1 + a_{i2} x_2 + \cdots + a_{in} x_n = b_i \qquad (i = 1,\dots,n).$$

The variable x_1 is eliminated in each of equations $i = 2,\dots, n$ by subtracting a multiple $m_{i1} = a_{i1}/a_{11}$ of the first equation from it. This gives the first derived set:

$$a_{11} x_1 + a_{12} x_2 + \cdots + a_{1n} x_n = b_1$$
$$a_{22}^{(1)} x_2 + \cdots + a_{2n}^{(1)} x_n = b_2^{(1)}$$
$$\cdots \qquad \cdots \quad \cdots \qquad \cdots$$
$$a_{n2}^{(1)} x_2 + \cdots + a_{nn}^{(1)} x_n = b_n^{(1)}$$

The variable x_2 is now eliminated from each of equations $i = 3,\dots, n$ by subtracting a multiple $m_{i2} = a_{i2}^{(1)}/a_{22}^{(1)}$ of the second row from it. After $n - 1$ such steps, we obtain an *equivalent* derived system of the following form:

$$a_{11} x_1 + a_{12} x_2 + a_{13} x_3 + \cdots + a_{1n} x_n = b_1$$
$$a_{22}^{(1)} x_2 + a_{23}^{(1)} x_3 + \cdots + a_{2n}^{(1)} x_n = b_2^{(1)}$$
$$a_{33}^{(2)} x_3 + \cdots + a_{3n}^{(2)} x_n = b_3^{(2)}$$
$$\cdots \qquad \cdots \cdots \cdots \qquad \cdots$$
$$a_{nn}^{(n-1)} x_n = b_n^{(1)}$$

or, in matrix form, $U\mathbf{x} = \mathbf{b}^{(n-1)}$, where U is *upper triangular*. This triangular set may now be solved by *back substitution*, computing x_n from the nth equation, x_{n-1} from the $(n - 1)$st equation,..., x_1 from the first.

The process breaks down if at any stage $a_{r+1,r+1}^{(r)} = 0$. This may be avoided by a simple modification. In the rth derived system, the last $n - r$ equations involve only the last $n - r$ variables. Any of these equations may be used to eliminate x_{r+1} from the remaining $n - r - 1$. We may choose that equation that has the largest coefficient of x_{r+1}. It is convenient to think of terms of interchanging this equation with equation $r + 1$. This modified process is known as Gaussian elimination with *partial pivoting*. Breakdown cannot now occur unless A is singular. (More accurately,

unless A, modified by the rounding errors, is singular.) With this modification $|m_{ij}| \le 1$. A more sophisticated form of pivoting is sometimes used. In the rth reduced set, the largest element $|a_{ij}^{(r)}|$ $(i,j \ge r + 1)$ is determined. If this is $a_{st}^{(r)}$, then equation s is used to eliminate x_t from the remaining $n - r - 1$ equations. This is best thought of in terms of interchanging the appropriate rows and columns. This process is *complete pivoting*. In general, Gaussian elimination with pivoting is remarkably stable with respect to rounding errors, but without pivoting it may be arbitrarily unstable.

If a matrix L is constructed from the multipliers m_{ij} by taking $l_{ij} = m_{ij}$ $(i > j), l_{ii} = 1, l_{ij} = 0$ $(j > i)$, then the resulting unit lower triangular matrix (i.e. lower triangular with diagonal 1s) is such that $LU = A$. (In the case where partial pivoting has been used, the relation is $LU = \tilde{A}$, where $\tilde{A}$ is A with its rows suitably permuted; with complete pivoting, $LU = \tilde{A}$ where $\tilde{A}$ is A with both rows and columns suitably permuted.) The factorization $A = LU$ may be derived directly without producing the intermediate matrices $A^{(k)}$, and it is not difficult to combine this direct factorization with the equivalent of partial pivoting. The solution of $A\mathbf{x} = \mathbf{b}$ is then achieved by solving $L\mathbf{y} = \mathbf{b}$, $U\mathbf{x} = \mathbf{y}$. There is an analogous factorization in which U is unit upper triangular.

An important class of direct methods is based on the factorization of A into the product of an orthogonal matrix Q and an upper triangular matrix R. (The notation R is used rather than U, for historical reasons.) If $A = QR$, then $Q^T A = R$, where Q^T is of course also orthogonal, and the factorization is commonly achieved in this way. Q^T is not derived directly, but as the product of a number of simple orthogonal matrices. Such factorizations are associated with the names of Givens and Householder. The QR factorizations have slightly more reliable numerical stability than the LU factorization with pivoting, but since they involve more work, the LU factorization is more commonly used for solving linear equations. However, the QR factorizations are of fundamental importance in connection with the eigenvalue problem and the least squares problem.

Iterative Methods Basically, the simplest iterative methods for solving linear systems are those of Jacobi and Gauss-Seidel. The relations are most simply expressed if we write $A \equiv D - E - F$, where D is the set of diagonal elements, $-E$ is the set of subdiagonal elements, and $-F$ the set of superdiagonal elements. Jacobi's method may then be expressed in the form

$$D\mathbf{x}^{(k+1)} = b + E\mathbf{x}^{(k)} + F\mathbf{x}^{(k)}.$$

Clearly, the method can be applied only if the diagonal elements are non-zero. Writing $D^{-1}E = L$, $D^{-1}F = U$, this becomes

$$\mathbf{x}^{(k+1)} = D^{-1}\mathbf{b} + (L + U)\mathbf{x}^{(k)}.$$

If $\mathbf{x}$ is the true solution, then

$$\mathbf{x} = D^{-1}\mathbf{b} + (L + U)\,\mathbf{x}.$$

and writing $\mathbf{e}^{(k)} = \mathbf{x} - \mathbf{x}^{(k)}$, we have

$$\mathbf{e}^{(k+1)} = (L + U)\mathbf{e}^{(k)} = P\mathbf{e}^{(k)},$$

giving $\mathbf{e}^{(k+1)} = P^k \mathbf{e}^{(1)}$.

The process is therefore convergent if $P_k \to 0$ as $k \to \infty$ which is true if all the eigenvalues of P are less than unity in modulus (see later sections of this article). In the Gauss-Seidel method, the most up-to-date value of each component is used at each stage, the relevant relations being

$$D\mathbf{x}^{(k+1)} = \mathbf{b} + E\mathbf{x}^{(k+1)} + F\mathbf{x}^{(k)},$$

giving

$$(I - L)\,\mathbf{x}^{(k+1)} = D^{-1}\,\boldsymbol{b} + U\boldsymbol{x}^{(k)}.$$

The error matrix now satisfies the relations

$$(I - L)\,\mathbf{e}^{(k+1)} = U\mathbf{e}^{(k)}$$

or

$$\mathbf{e}^{(k+1)} = (I - L)^{-1}\,U\mathbf{e}^{(k)} = Q\mathbf{x}^{(k)},$$

and the process is convergent if $Q^k \to 0$. When both methods are convergent, one might expect the Gauss-Seidel to converge faster, since it always uses the most recent information; this is true generally, but not always.

Research on iterative methods has mainly been concerned with *sufficient* conditions for convergence and methods for *accelerating* the rate of convergence. If A is real and symmetric with a positive diagonal, then a *necessary* and *sufficient* condition for Gauss-Seidel to converge is that it be positive definite. If L and U are non-negative, then Gauss-Seidel and Jacobi are either both convergent or both divergent. In the former case, Gauss-Seidel converges the more rapidly.

A class of matrices that arises frequently in the study of partial differential equations (*q.v.*) is that for which the equations and variables can be reordered so that $L + U$ is of the form

$$\begin{bmatrix} 0 & P \\ Q & 0 \end{bmatrix}$$

where the null submatrices are square. These are said to have *Young's property A*. For matrices of this kind, when Gauss-Seidel converges, it does so twice as fast as Jacobi.

Acceleration of convergence of Gauss-Seidel can be achieved by making a change in each component that is ω times as great as that determined by Gauss-Seidel itself. The relevant relation is therefore

$$\mathbf{x}^{(k+1)} - \mathbf{x}^{(k)} = \omega\,[\,D^{-1}\,\mathbf{b} + L\mathbf{x}^{(k+1)} + U\mathbf{x}^{(k)} - \mathbf{x}^{(k)}],$$
$$(I - \omega L)\,\mathbf{x}^{(k+1)} = \mathbf{x}^{(k)} + \omega\,[\,D^{-1}\,\mathbf{b} - (I - U)\,\mathbf{x}^{(k)}],$$

giving

$$\mathbf{e}^{(k+1)} = (I - \omega L)^{-1}\,[(1 - \omega)\,I + \omega U]\,\mathbf{e}^{(k)}.$$

If $\omega > 1$ (<1), the method is known as *successive over-relaxation* (*under-relaxation*). The effectiveness of the method depends on a judicious choice of ω. Young has

investigated fully the case when A has property A, and has shown that the optimum choice of ω is $2/(1 + (1 - \theta^2)^{1/2})$, where θ is the largest eigenvalue of $L + U$.

In iterative methods, one works throughout with the original matrix A, and for this reason it was at one time thought that such methods would be much more stable with respect to rounding errors than would direct methods. This advantage has proved to be less important than was thought. Much more important is the fact that if A has a high percentage of zero elements, then it is easy to take advantage of this and thereby reduce the storage requirements and the number of arithmetic operations. In direct methods, such as Gaussian elimination, the zero elements in the original matrix do not persist in the successive derived matrices.

The Algebraic Eigenvalue Problem

The practical importance of the algebraic eigenvalue problem springs mainly from its relation to the problem of solving a system of n simultaneous linear differential equations of first order with constant coefficients. In standard form such a system may be written as

$$\frac{d\mathbf{x}}{dt} = A\mathbf{x},$$

where A is an $n \times n$ matrix and $\mathbf{x}$ a vector. By substitution, $\mathbf{x} = \mathbf{u}^{\lambda t}$ is a solution if $\lambda\mathbf{u} = A\mathbf{u}$. Conversely, if λ and $\mathbf{u} \neq \mathbf{0}$ satisfy $\lambda\mathbf{u} = A\mathbf{u}$, then $\mathbf{x} = \mathbf{u}^{\lambda t}$ is a solution. The *algebraic eigenvalue problem* is the determination of such λ and $\mathbf{u}$. From the theory of linear algebraic equations, nonnull solutions exist if and only if $\det(\lambda I - A) = 0$. This is a polynomial equation of degree n, the coefficient of λ^n being unity. It is known as the *characteristic equation* of A. The roots of this equation are called the *eigenvalues, latent roots,* or *characteristic values* of A. Taking into account multiplicities, there are always precisely n eigenvalues. Corresponding to each eigenvalue there is at least one non-null solution $\mathbf{u}$, and this is known as a corresponding *eigenvector*. The number of independent eigenvectors corresponding to a given eigenvalue λ may be less than its multiplicity; it is equal to $n - k$, where k is the rank of $A - \lambda I$.

Since the calculation of the eigenvalues is equivalent to finding the roots of the characteristic equation (an *apparently* simpler problem), early methods were based on the explicit determination of this equation. All such methods are inherently unstable, since very small errors in the coefficients of the equation may correspond to large changes in its roots even when the eigenvalues are not unduly sensitive to changes in the elements of A.

If the transformation $\mathbf{x} = P\mathbf{y}$ is made in the system of differential equations, it becomes $d\mathbf{y}/dt = (P^{-1}AP)\,\mathbf{y}$, assuming that P is nonsingular. The matrix $P^{-1}AP$ is said to be *similar* to A. Since $\det(P^{-1}AP - \lambda I) = \det(A - \lambda I)$, the eigenvalues of A are the same as those of any similar matrix. This is intuitively obvious from consideration of the differential equations. Many of the most effective methods for finding eigenvalues are based on determining a similarity transformation such that eigenvalues of $P^{-1}AP$ are readily available. The eigenvalues of a triangular matrix are its diagonal elements, hence, reduction to this form gives the eigenvalues immediately.

The theory of similarity transformations shows that, for any A, there exists a nonsingular P such that $P^{-1}AP$ is upper-triangular. In fact, such a transformation is always possible, even if P is restricted to the class of *unitary* matrices, i.e. matrices such that $PP^H = P^HP = I$. A real unitary matrix satisfies $PP^T = P^TP = I$ and is therefore orthogonal. Unitary similarity transformations are numerically very stable, and several of the best algorithms are based on their use. For such matrices, $P^{-1}AP = P^HAP$.

When A has distinct eigenvalues, there is always a P such that $P^{-1}AP = \text{diag}(\lambda_i)$, the diagonal matrix with λ_i on the diagonal. If A has any multiple eigenvalues, reduction to diagonal form is not generally possible, hence, *general* algorithms are not usually based on such a reduction.

Real Symmetric Matrices When A is symmetric, there is an advantage in taking P to be orthogonal, since P^TAP is still symmetric. It is known that a real symmetric matrix is always reducible to diagonal form via an orthogonal P; Jacobi's method, one of the most effective algorithms, is based on such a reduction. P is not determined directly, but as a product of a sequence of elementary orthogonal matrices of the form R_{pq}, where

$$r_{pp} = r_{qq} = \cos\theta$$
$$r_{pq} = -r_{qp} = \sin\theta;$$
$$r_{ij} = \delta_{ij} \quad \text{(otherwise)}$$

This is known as a rotation in the p,q plane. Denoting the successive derived matrices by $A^{(k)}$, if $a^{(k)}_{p_k,q_k}$ is the off-diagonal element of largest modulus, then the next transformation is given by

$$A^{(k+1)} = R^T_{p_k,q_k} A^{(k)} R_{p_k,q_k}$$

with the angle θ being chosen so that

$$a^{(k+1)}_{p_k,q_k} = 0.$$

In general, an infinite number of transformations are needed to give the diagonal form, and iteration is terminated when the off-diagonal elements are all negligible. To reach this point, approximately $1 - n^3$ multiplications and additions are required.

A real symmetric matrix can be reduced to symmetric tridiagonal form by $(1/2)\,n(n-1)$ elementary orthogonal similarities of the above type, involving less than 10% of the computation in Jacobi's method. This algorithm is due to Givens; an alternative reduction involving orthogonal similarities and requiring half as much work is due to Householder.

The calculation of the eigenvalues of a symmetric tridiagonal matrix is a very economical process. Two

methods are widely used. The first is due to Givens and is based on the fact that if T is tridiagonal, the leading principal minors p_r $(r = 0,...,n)$ of $(T - \lambda I)$ can be computed from the relations

$$p_0(\lambda) = 1,$$
$$p_1(\lambda) = t_{11} - \lambda,$$
$$p_r(\lambda) = (t_{rr} - \lambda)p_{r-1}(\lambda) - (t_{r,r-1})^2 p_{r-2}(\lambda).$$

For any given value of λ, the number of agreements in sign between consecutive members of the sequence $p_0, p_1,..., p_n$ equals the number of eigenvalues greater than λ. Any individual eigenvalue may be found by repeated bisection using this property, given only an initial upper and lower bound. The second method is described in the next section.

Eigenvalues of General Matrices The most efficient method for general matrices is based on the unitary similarity reduction to upper-triangular form. For real matrices, an analogous *real* reduction may be achieved, using only orthogonal similarities to give a triangular matrix apart from 2×2 diagonal blocks corresponding to complex conjugate pairs of eigenvalues. This reduction is much more economical if the original matrix is first reduced to upper-Hessenberg form, which can be done by $(1/2)\,n(n-1)$ elementary orthogonal similarities, as in Givens' reduction of a symmetric matrix to tridiagonal form. Again, Householder has given an alternative requiring only half as much computation.

The Hessenberg matrix is then reduced to the quasi-triangular form by the Francis QR algorithm. In the basic QR algorithm, a sequence of similar matrices A, is produced via the relations

$$A_s - k_s I = Q_s R_s, \qquad R_s Q_s + k_s I = A_{s+1},$$

where Q_s is orthogonal, R_s is upper-triangular, and the k_s are chosen so as to accelerate convergence. The matrix A_s tends to the quasi-triangular form, the speed of convergence being extraordinarily satisfactory. Upper-Hessenberg form is preserved by this algorithm, which greatly reduces the volume of computation.

The QR method is also extremely effective for finding the eigenvalues of a real symmetric tridiagonal matrix. The symmetric tridiagonal form is preserved, giving great economy in the volume of work. For finding all the eigenvalues, it is the most efficient of known methods.

Software The most successful algorithms for computation with dense, stored matrices have been implemented in efficient, portable, standard Fortran software. LINPACK has subroutines for computing factorizations and solving simultaneous linear systems involving square general matrices, symmetric matrices, positive definite matrices, band matrices, and triangular matrices, as well as subroutines for computing orthogonal factorizations and solving least-squares problems for rectangular matrices. EISPACK has subroutines for solving various forms of the algebraic eigenvalues problem for several different types of matrices.

Software for iterative methods on large, sparse matrices, particularly those arising in finite difference and finite element methods for partial differential equations, is usually closely coupled to particular applications and so is not organized in general-purpose packages.

The Main Areas of Research   In the solution of linear systems, the main areas of research are devoted to the economical solution, by both direct and iterative methods, of large, sparse systems. The work on direct methods concentrates on the development of efficient data structures for representing and manipulating sparse matrices, and on the development of pivoting strategies that reduce the number of new non-zero matrix elements created during factorization.

Much of the research work on iterative methods for linear systems is focused on refinements of the conjugate gradient method, particularly in connection with pre-conditioners that significantly accelerate the convergence.

In the eigenvalue field, there is active research on special matrix problems that occur in system theory, control theory, and signal processing. The singular value decomposition is a particularly effective tool in dealing with least squares data fitting problems and principal component analysis in the presence of noise and near-linear dependence.

References

1965. Wilkinson, J. H. *The Algebraic Eigenvalue Problem.* Oxford: Clarendon Press.

1971. Wilkinson, J. H. and Reinsch, C. *Handbook for Automatic Computation, Volume II: Linear Algebra.* Berlin: Springer-Verlag.

1971. Young, D. M. *Iterative Solution of Large Linear Systems.* New York: Academic Press.

1973. Stewart, G. W. *Introduction to Matrix Computations.* New York: Academic Press.

1974. Smith, B. T., Boyle, J. M., Dongarra, J. J., Garbow, B. S., Ikebe, Y., Klema, V. C., and Moler, C. B. *Matrix Eigensystem Routines—EISPACK User's Guide* (2nd Ed.). Berlin: Springer-Verlag.

1977. Garbow, B. S., Boyle, J. M., Dongarra, J. J., and Moler, C. B. *Matrix Eigensystem Routines—EISPACK Guide Extension.* Berlin: Springer-Verlag.

1979. Dongarra, J. J., Bunch, J. R., Moler, C. B., and Stewart, G. W. *LINPACK Users' Guide.* Philadelphia: SIAM Publications.

1980. Parlett, B. N. *The Symmetric Eigenvalue Problem.* Englewood Cliffs, NJ: Prentice-Hall.

1981. Hageman, L. A. and Young, D. M. *Applied Iterative Methods.* New York: Academic Press.

1986. Duff, I. S., Erisman, A. M. and Reid, J. K. *Direct Methods for Sparse Matrices.* Oxford: Clarendon Press.

1989. Kahaner, D., Moler, C., and Nash, S. *Numerical Methods and Software.* Englewood Cliffs, NJ: Prentice-Hall.

1989. Golub, G. H. and Van Loan, C. F. *Matrix Computations,* (2nd. Ed.). Baltimore: The Johns Hopkins University Press.

J. H. WILKINSON AND CLEVE B. MOLER

MAUCHLY, JOHN WILLIAM

For articles on related subjects *see* DIGITAL COMPUTERS: EARLY; ECKERT, J. PRESPER; ENIAC; and UNIVAC I.

John Mauchly (b. Cincinnati, OH, 30 August 1907, d. Philadelphia, PA, 8 January 1980) was one of the major visionaries and pioneers of our current electronic digital computer era. The dedication of his brainchild, ENIAC, in 1946 totally changed the scientific and commercial information processing environment.

In 1925, Mauchly received a scholarship to attend the engineering school of The Johns Hopkins University. After two years, however, he decided that he didn't care for engineering and switched to physics. His Ph.D. was awarded in 1932 with a thesis on an analysis of the carbon monoxide molecule. He remained at Johns Hopkins the following year as a research assistant to Professor Joseph Eachus, where his work included calculating the energy levels of the formaldehyde spectrum. This research project, as well as his thesis work, involved a great deal of calculation, and Mauchly began to be interested in devising special techniques to cut down on the work involved.

He taught physics at Ursinus College from 1933 to 1941. During this period he developed an interest in the problem of weather prediction, and built an analog computer to do harmonic analysis of weather data. This work led to a paper (1940) on the quasi-periodicity of precipitation. He spent the summer of 1940 with H. Helm Clayton, who was interested in long-range weather forecasting, and he also presented a paper during this period to the

FIG. 1.   John William Mauchly

Geophysical Union, using a statistical approach to the causes of sunspots.

In the summer of 1941, with war impending, he attended a defense training course in electronics at the Moore School of Electrical Engineering (University of Pennsylvania). He was subsequently invited to join the faculty of the Moore School as an instructor. The Moore School had long had a contract with Army Ordnance to calculate ballistics tables, and Mauchly was assigned this work in addition to his regular teaching duties. All of his work of the past decade seemed to come together in these ballistics calculations, and in 1942 he wrote a memorandum proposing that an electronic calculator be constructed to perform these vital computations. This original proposal was rejected, but it was revived a year later by Herman Goldstine, who had been assigned to Aberdeen Proving Ground to expedite the production of the firing data. Thirty months later, ENIAC, conceived by Mauchly and engineered by J. Presper Eckert, was publicly demonstrated (February 1946).

ENIAC, now retired to the Smithsonian Institution, operated successfully at Aberdeen Proving Ground for ten years. It well deserves its description as the first truly electronic, general-purpose computer and the precursor of all that was to come.

Mauchly and Eckert left the Moore School in 1946 to found the Electronic Control Co., which became the Eckert-Mauchly Corporation in 1947. The company's first contract was to design a small binary computer for the Northrop Aircraft Corporation (BINAC, 1949). UNIVAC I followed, and the Bureau of the Census received the first completed model in 1951. In that same year, the Eckert-Mauchly Corporation became a division of the Remington-Rand Corporation, and Mauchly remained with it in various capacities until 1959, when he formed Mauchly Associates.

Mauchly was a founder of both ACM and SIAM. He served ACM as its first Vice-President and second President. He was a member of many other learned societies, including the American Physical Society, the Franklin Institute, and the National Academy of Engineering. He has received numerous awards, including the Howard Potts Medal of the Franklin Institute (1949), the John Scott Award (1961), and (jointly with J. P. Eckert) the Philadelphia Man of the Year Award (1973). ACM's Eckert-Mauchly award is partially named in his honor. His scientific papers are housed in the Van Pelt Library of the University of Pennsylvania.

References

1946. Kennedy, T. R., Jr. "Electronic Computer Flashes Answers, May Speed Engineering," *New York Times* (February 15), 1,16.

1969. Rosen, Saul. "Electronic Computers: A Historical Survey," *Computing Surveys*, **1**, *1* (March). Reprinted in "A Quarter Century View," *ACM*, 7–36.

1980. Stern, Nancy. "John William Mauchly: 1907–1980." *Annals of the History of Computing* **2**, *2*, 100–103.

1982. Mauchly, John "Unpublished Remarks" *Annals of the History of Computing* **4**, *3*, 245–256.

HENRY S. TROPP

MCDOWELL AWARD WINNERS

For an article on a related subject *see* TURING AWARD WINNERS.

The W. Wallace McDowell Award is made annually by the IEEE Computer Society for outstanding professional work in the computer field. The award, which currently includes a prize of $2,000, honors a former IBM vice-president. As might be expected for an electrical engineering society, the award is most often given for hardware and management achievements, but there is some intersection with the set of Turing award winners. The award is named in honor of William Wallace McDowell (1906–1985), who, in his 38-year IBM career, went from a designer in 1931 to Director of Engineering in 1950 and retired as a vice-president. His major computing contribution was to direct IBM's transition from electro-mechanical techniques to electronics and finally to solid state devices. Awards made since inception in 1966 have been:

1966
Fernando J. Corbató (1926–), for his leadership in time sharing (*q.v.*).

1967
John W. Backus (1924–), for Fortran.

1968
Seymour R. Cray (1925–), for his series of supercomputers (*q.v.*).

1969
Herman Lukoff (1923–1979), for his contributions to early computers.

1970
Frederic P. Brooks, Jr. (1931–), for his contributions to computer architecture, programming, and education and for skewering the myth of the man-month.

1971
Thomas Kilburn (1921–) (*q.v.*), for his work on early powerful computers.

1972
Jean A. Hoerni (1925–), for inventing the planar process of semiconductor fabrication.

1973
David A. Huffman (1925–), for his solution of sequential circuit problems and coding theory and for his teaching.

1974

Shmuel Winograd (1936–), for pioneering in computational complexity and the efficiency of algorithms.

1975

C. Gordon Bell (1934–), for his work in technical design, education, and publication.

1976

Gene M. Amdahl (1922–), for his contributions to computer architecture and design and his business enterprise.

1977

Robert S. Barton (1925–), for stack processing, data stored with self-describing tags, and the direct execution of higher-level languages, as in the B-5000 computer and its successors.

1978

Gordon E. Moore (1929–), for his development of semiconductor components and the microprocessor.

1979

Grace Murray Hopper (1906–1992) (*q.v.*), for her single-minded drive for the acceptance of high-level programming languages.

1980

Donald E. Knuth (1938–), for his contributions to software engineering and education and for the scholarship and creativity of his classical texts that have made the essentials of computer science accessible to all.

1981

Maurice V. Wilkes (1913–) (*q.v.*), for his innovative contributions to software engineering (*q.v.*), structured programming (*q.v.*), distributed computing (*q.v.*), database structures, time sharing (*q.v.*), storage hierarchies, paging, and microprogramming (*q.v.*).

1982

Rex Rice (1918–), for the invention of the dual-in-line semiconductor component package and LSI semiconductor memories.

1983

Daniel L. Slotnik (1931–1985), for the centrally controlled parallel computer, ILLIAC IV.

1984

Thomas M. McWilliams (1952–) and Lawrence Curtis Widdoes, Jr. (1952–), for Structured Computer-Aided Logic (SCALD).

1985

William D. Strecker (1944–), for VAX architecture and contributions to local area networks (*q.v.*), high-performance interconnects, cache memory (*q.v.*), and memory hierarchies.

1986

No award was made because no nomination was considered worthy.

1987

Sidney Fernbach (1917–1991), for pushing for U.S. supercomputers.

1988

John W. Poduska, Sr. (1937–), for hardware and software developments and management expertise.

1989

Edward B. Eichelberger (1934–) and Thomas W. Williams (1943–), for the level-sensitive scan technique of testing logic circuits.

1990

Lawrence G. Roberts (1937–), for packet switching (*q.v.*) technology brought into practical use through the ARPA network.

ERIC A. WEISS

MEDICAL APPLICATIONS

For articles on related subjects *see* BIOCOMPUTING; COMPUTERIZED TOMOGRAPHY; HOSPITAL INFORMATION SYSTEMS; INTENSIVE CARE, COMPUTERS IN; MEDICAL IMAGING; MEDLARS/MEDLINE; and MUMPS.

Computers have made significant inroads in the health care industry, and computing systems are now commonplace in many medical settings. Products are available for individual physicians, as well as for hospitals, and applications can be found throughout clinical practice, medical research, and medical education. The applications themselves are varied, spanning sophisticated instrumentation used for patient monitoring, hospital information systems that coordinate communication and support clinical and financial management functions, analytical tools used by clinical researchers, specialized programs designed to assist physicians in clinical decision making, and instructional programs to augment provider and patient education.

Clinical Uses Because of their superior accuracy, memory, and processing capacity, computers have replaced manual methods for performing many repetitious and time-consuming clinical tasks. In addition, continuing increases in the speed and power of computers and corresponding reductions in the costs of processing power and storage have promoted the development of new applications that were not practical without computers. In particular, the availability of powerful, inexpensive, and easy-to-use microcomputers has made computer technology accessible to individual health practitioners and spurred the development of diverse medical applications.

Patient Monitoring Patient monitoring is a prime medical computing application. Computer-based patient monitors are commonly used to collect and display physiological parameters such as heart rate, respiratory rate, blood pressure, and blood-oxygen content, and to sound alarms when intervention is required. Analysis of electrocardiograms (ECGs) to detect arrhythmias is one of the most sophisticated and difficult bedside monitoring tasks. Because this task is also among the most tedious and is unreliably performed by humans, computer-based arrhythmia analysis has gained widespread acceptance. Patient-monitoring devices are useful particularly in settings where frequent assessment of patient status is essential to effective therapy. Thus, patient monitors are standard equipment in intensive care units, operating rooms, and trauma centers.

Although the earliest patient monitoring systems, developed during the late 1960s and early 1970s, relied on expensive mainframes or minicomputers to analyze the physiological measurements acquired from sensors, modern monitoring devices are based on microprocessor technology, in which the computer is an integral component of the instrumentation (*see* EMBEDDED SYSTEMS and MICROCOMPUTER CHIP). State-of-the-art monitoring devices not only sample and convert biological signals to digital data, but also store the results, calculate derived variables that cannot be measured directly, format and print reports, flag abnormal values, and provide interpretations of data (Fig. 1).

Automated monitoring allows nearly continuous assessment of physiological parameters. The large amount of data collected, however, threatens to overload providers' capacity for interpretation. For this reason, some commercial vendors have designed data management systems that integrate, organize, and display data collected from multiple devices, as well as medication-administration records and patient observations. To facilitate integration, researchers are working to define standards for a medical information bus (MIB) that would allow the interconnection of multiple bedside devices (Fig. 2). Prototype versions of the developing MIB specify requirements for physical connections, data communication protocols, medical terminology, and data formats.

Closed-loop drug delivery systems are another application of computers in patient care. Functioning much like the thermostat of a heater, closed-loop control devices use a computer to sense and control a physiological variable by altering therapy directly. Commercial systems currently are available for controlling the infusion of oxytocin during labor, and of insulin and dextrose to regulate blood-glucose level. The effectiveness of closed-loop technology in regulating blood pressure has also been

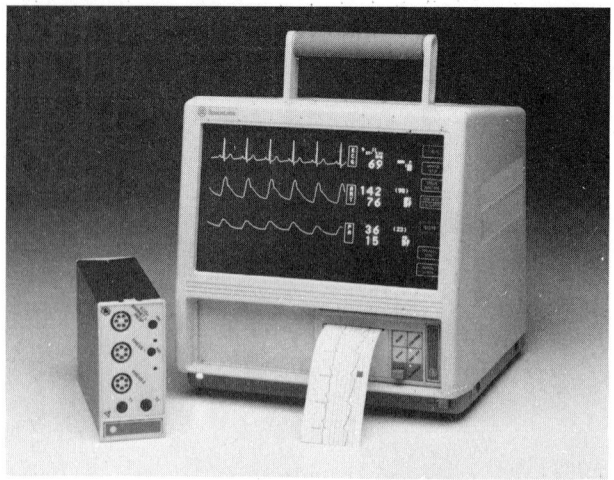

FIG. 1. A computer-based patient monitor. These are common features of intensive care units and other critical care settings. Commercially available monitors collect, store, and evaluate physiological data, thus freeing nurses to perform other patient care functions. (Courtesy of SpaceLabs, Inc.)

demonstrated, and similar systems may become available to control the administration of anesthesia and to manage patients on ventilator therapy.

Pharmacy Computers are used in pharmacies to maintain accessible, legible, and up-to-date medication records, playing an important role in providing safe and effective drug therapy. Contemporary pharmacy systems also assist physicians and pharmacists more directly by screening patients' computer-stored medication profiles, to identify drug allergies, potential drug interactions, and prior adverse reactions. With the development of integrated clinical databases, more sophisticated support is possible. The HELP system developed at LDS Hospital in Salt Lake City, for example, identifies abnormal chemistry levels, concurrent diseases, and other patient conditions that should be considered when particular drugs are prescribed. HELP also has been used to monitor the use of prophylactic antibiotics, to evaluate surgical-scheduling records, and to identify patients who could benefit from preventive drug therapy as well as patients who are receiving antibiotics unnecessarily.

A number of computer programs have been developed to assist physicians in dosing and timing drug administration. Most drugs may be safely prescribed in accordance with dosing guidelines developed for broad classes of patients. The effects of some drugs, however, are extremely sensitive to variability among patients, and dosing regimens must be individually tailored. These programs use mathematical models that relate measured drug concentration levels in the blood over time to drug-specific parameters (e.g. rate of drug elimination from the body) and patient-specific parameters (e.g. age, gender, ideal body weight, and concurrent disease factors). Physicians use these programs to forecast future drug levels and to choose the amount and timing of drug doses that will achieve target levels.

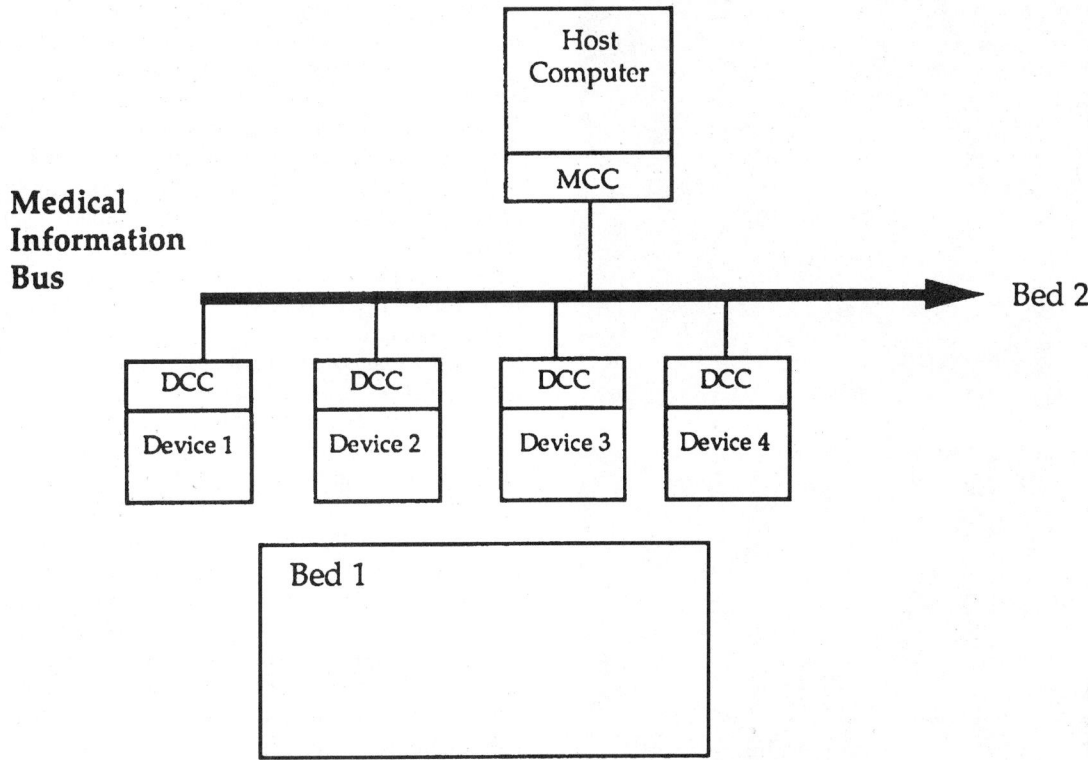

FIG. 2. The developing medical information bus (MIB) standard will facilitate the interconnection of multiple bedside devices by defining the hardware connections, data communications protocols, and data formats necessary for integration. Communication controllers connected to individual devices convert MIB instructions into device-specific instructions and translate instrument outputs into the MIB protocol.

Radiology Medical imaging is an active area for medical computing research. Many of the newest imaging modalities, such as computerized tomography (CT) and magnetic resonance imaging (MRI) are inherently digital. Rather than depicting a directly measurable parameter (such as the attenuation of an X-ray beam as it travels through body tissues), the computer creates a "functional image" by performing complex calculations on measured data. Because of the enormous number of calculations to be performed, these modalities are only practical with powerful computers that perform computation rapidly. Conventional X-ray images also can be captured directly or scanned and stored in digital memory, rather than on film.

Images stored in digital format provide an opportunity for improved viewing and interpretation. For example, a variety of image enhancement techniques can be applied to enhance edges, to sharpen blurry images, and to otherwise improve the quality of images for human visualization. Digital images also are accessible for computer-assisted quantification of measurable parameters, such as the volume of a heart or the diameter of a fetus's head. Collection and storage of multiple, closely stacked image slices supports additional capabilities, such as displaying image slices on planes other than those originally collected, and displaying three-dimensional (3-D) images. Three-dimensional imaging is particularly valuable for

localization of lesions for radiation therapy, interventional radiological procedures, and surgery (Fig. 3). Reconstructions from 3-D images have also been used to design and guide the creation of joint prostheses.

The development of powerful and relatively inexpensive computers capable of performing computation-intensive data transformations in real time, high-resolution graphics monitors, and high-density storage media such as videodiscs (*q.v.*) enables ongoing research in the creation of picture archiving and communications systems (PACS) for image management and analysis. Specialized workstations (*q.v.*) are now available to replace the traditional lightboxes used for viewing radiology films. With these workstations, radiologists can view multiple images for comparison, zoom in to examine subregions at greater magnification, alter image contrast, rotate images to alternative perspectives, and annotate images on screen. Other current programs support transcription of radiologists' interpretive results, providing modifiable templates for common findings and selectable text strings for assembly of textual reports. Because of its fairly circumscribed vocabulary, radiology has also served as an initial domain for voice-recognition systems designed to capture physicians' dictated notes.

Laboratories One of the earliest areas of clinical application, clinical laboratories first used computers in the

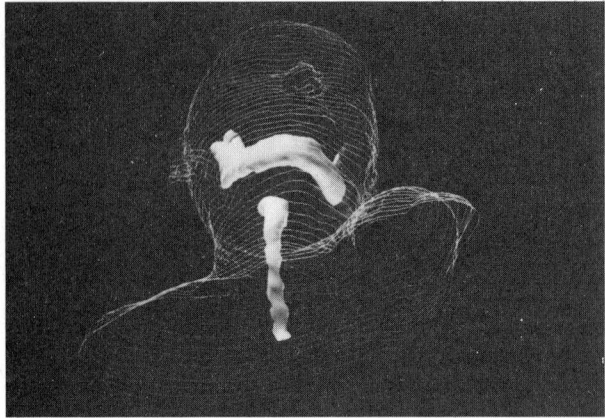

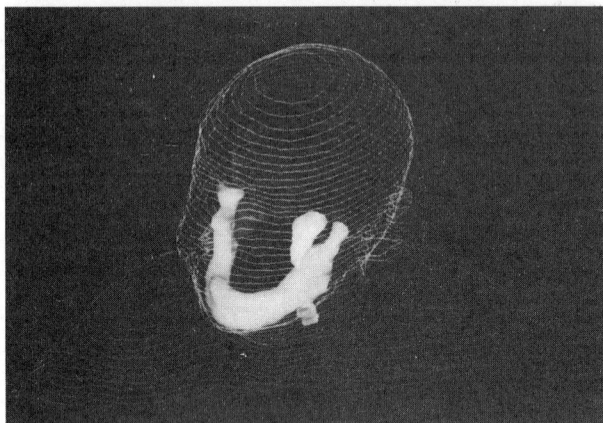

FIG. 3.   The FOCUS Treatment Planning System assists radiation oncologists in planning radiation therapy by evaluating competing plans to optimize parameters such as beam angle and radiation dose. Three-dimensional MRI and CT data can be displayed and rotated through different viewing planes, thus enhancing the radiation oncologist's ability to visualize the treatment beam in relation to the lesion and surrounding healthy tissues. (a) and (b) show two views of the same imaging data. (Courtesy of Computerized Medical Systems, Inc. and Hewlett Packard Corporation.)

late 1950s to meet the growing demand for laboratory testing. Manual procedures were adequate when test volumes were low, but automated instruments became necessary to perform high volumes of repetitious tasks quickly and accurately, and the laboratory information system (LIS) was developed to manage the large amount of data generated. Most modern laboratory instruments can perform panels of tests on a single specimen. These instruments contain preprocessors (*q.v.*) that convert raw data to digital format and transmit numerical results to the LIS for storage and report generation. Many instruments contain dedicated microprocessors that facilitate all phases of the testing process, including instrument calibration, association of results with individual specimens, and reporting of results. LISs commonly perform a number of administrative and managerial functions, including specimen tracking, productivity analysis, and quality control. Many have optional subsystems to meet the unique needs of the microbiology and anatomical

pathology divisions and to satisfy the stricter information management and reporting requirements of blood banks.

Computer-based tools have also been developed to support the professional functions of laboratory personnel. For example, programs are available to facilitate chromosome analysis and interpretation of some specialized laboratory tests, such as certain immunoassay tests. The Intellipath system, developed at Stanford University School of Medicine and the University of Southern California School of Medicine, integrates an expert system (*q.v.*) for pathology diagnosis with a videodisc library of cell slides. Intellipath uses encoded probabilities to form a differential diagnosis of plausible diseases based on the histological features that have been entered into the system. Pathologists can recall images from the slide library to view cases that illustrate particular diseases and histological features (Fig. 4).

Physician Tools   The past decade has seen a proliferation of microcomputer-based programs that support physicians in various aspects of medical practice. Examples of the many applications available include programs to assist in management of hypertension and diabetes patients, interpretation of diagnostic exercise test results in coronary heart disease patients, health risk appraisal and evaluation of cardiac risk factors, interpretation of laboratory tests such as blood gases and blood counts, neurological assessment, and evaluation of physical impairment. A number of medical records systems allow physicians to record patient histories, maintain problem lists, and track diagnoses, procedures, and prescriptions.

The development of computer-based tools to support clinical decision making has been an area of research since the 1960s. Multiple approaches have been pursued, including the application of simple algorithmic logic, symbolic processing techniques, and numerical approaches based on comparative analysis and probability theory.

Researchers have demonstrated a number of systems that assist physicians with clinical tasks such as diagnosis and therapy planning. For example, computer-based consultations regarding acid-base and electrolyte disorders are routinely available at Beth Israel Hospital in Boston, using an acid-base advisor developed by Bleich, which is one of the best known examples of an algorithmic approach. During the early 1970s, Shortliffe at Stanford University developed the MYCIN system, one of the first rule-based expert systems. MYCIN was designed to assist physicians in selecting appropriate antibiotic therapy for patients with meningitis and bacterial infections of the blood. One of the first systems founded on the use of Bayesian probability theory, a program for diagnosis of abdominal pain, was developed by de Dombal at the University of Leeds. The system used sensitivity, specificity, and disease-prevalence data for various signs, symptoms, and test results, to calculate the probabilities of seven possible explanations for acute abdominal pain.

Clinical decision-support systems have been slow to achieve acceptance because of the complexity of medical domains, the potentially dire consequences of providing incorrect information, and resistance by the medical community. Decision-support tools are beginning to be

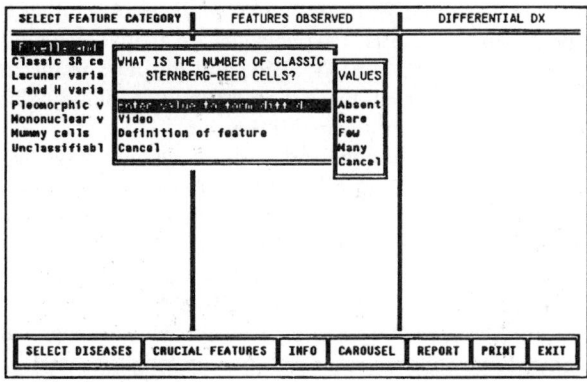

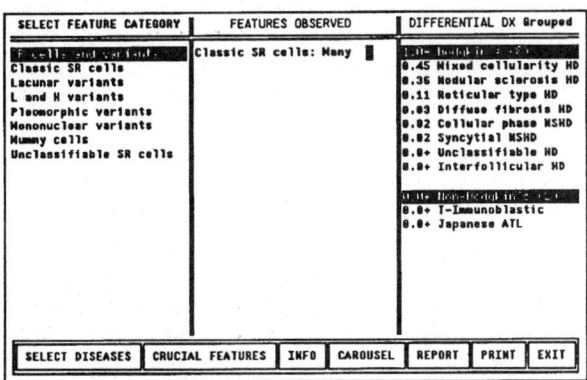

FIG. 4. Pathologists using the Intellipath educational system can explore the relationships between diseases and their histological features. (a) The user enters one or more findings into the system (in this case, the number of classic Sternberg-Reed cells). (b) The system then uses encoded probabilities to determine the most plausible diseases that account for the findings (the differential diagnosis). The pathologist can use other system functions to identify crucial features that will distinguish among diagnoses and to recall images from a videodisc library of slides to view cases that illustrate diseases and histological features. (Courtesy of Intellipath.)

used clinically, however, and a number of diagnostic support systems are commercially available. For example, the DXplain system, developed by Barnett and colleagues at Massachusetts General Hospital, is available nationally on the American Medical Association's network, AMA/NET. DXplain evaluates patients' signs, symptoms, and test results, to suggest differential diagnoses and to indicate additional information that would help to narrow the diagnostic possibilities.

QMR, one of several microcomputer-based diagnostic systems, was developed by Miller and colleagues at the University of Pittsburgh School of Medicine. Building on research that began in the early 1970s, QMR's large internal medicine knowledge base contains information on approximately 600 diseases, including measures of the strength of the relationship between each disease and related findings and manifestations. QMR can be used in consultation mode to determine the best diagnosis to account for the symptoms and findings that are entered, as an electronic textbook that relates patient characteristics to diseases, or as a medical spreadsheet (*q.v.*) that

suggests potential causes for multiple symptoms or diseases (Fig. 5). The current knowledge base reflects the encoded knowledge and experience of the physicians and students who worked on the Internist-1/QMR project for nearly two decades.

More widespread than diagnostic aids are computer-based tools that assist health professionals with patient management by providing access to the biomedical literature and to detailed information in particular domains. Drug information bases are widely used, allowing physicians to retrieve comprehensive information on drug effects, interactions, contraindications, and dosing guidelines. Online bibliographic indexes are replacing conventional manual indexes, because complex online searches, infeasible when using printed indexes, can be performed rapidly and comprehensively. MEDLINE, the National Library of Medicine's major bibliographic database, contains roughly one million references to the recent biomedical literature and additional backfiles to 1966. In addition, a variety of bibliographic databases is available for specific topic areas, such as psychology, toxicology, health planning, cancer research, and AIDS. Traditionally, these databases were accessed by specially trained librarians or search intermediaries. End-user searching has rapidly gained popularity, however, and many commercial products can assist users in formulating appropriate queries. A growing number of publishers and database distributors market biomedical information in CD-ROM (*q.v.*) format, with selected abstracts, complete journal articles, and entire books becoming available on optical disc.

Relationships
  Contains 16 Hypotheses arranged by relative score (1-100)
  Urination Frequency and Polydipsia Hx

98 Analgesic Nephropathy
98 Diabetes Insipidus
98 Diabetes Insipidus Nephrogenic
98 Diabetes Mellitus
98 Diabetes Ketoacidosis
98 Glomerulonephritis Advanced Chronic
98 Hyperparathyroidism Primary
98 Hypokalemic Nephropathy
98 Polycystic Renal Disease
98 Pyelonephritis Chronic
98 Renal Tubular Acidosis Distal
98 Tubular Necrosis Acute
92 Diabetic Nephropathy
92 Renal Tubular Acidosis Proximal (Fanconi Syndrome)
56 Medullary Cystic Kidney
56 Sarcoidosis Chronic Systemic

FIG. 5. A physician using Quick Medical Reference (QMR) can enter one or more key findings to view a differential diagnosis of diseases that can account for those findings. QMR provides a variety of tools for exploring a diagnosis, including the ability to view a disease profile, to list simple and expensive tests that will help to rule out or rule in a disease, and to identify diseases with similar presentations. (Courtesy Camdat Corporation.) (QMR ® Knowledge Base, Copyright © 1988, 1990 Univ. of Pittsburgh 7-12-91.)

Hospital Management Computers perform an array of activities in hospitals, processing and storing data to support patient management and patient care, as well as daily business operations and longer term strategic planning (*see* HOSPITAL INFORMATION SYSTEMS). The most common applications of a hospital information system (HIS) are traditional financial functions such as payroll, billing, and accounts receivable management. Complementing the financial components of an HIS are modules designed to support health care delivery, including patient registration, order entry, results reporting, and management of ancillary areas such as the clinical laboratory, pharmacy, and radiology departments. In addition, specialty systems are available to support other hospital departments, assisting in inventory tracking and supplies purchasing, operating room management, staff scheduling, and diet planning. A large number of commercial vendors market complete HISs or stand-alone specialty systems on hardware platforms, ranging from mainframes to networked microcomputers. Similar systems are also available to manage information in nonhospital settings, including outpatient clinics, nursing homes, physicians' group practices, and individual physicians' offices.

Until recently, HISs performed mainly administrative and financially-oriented functions. Currently, however, there is growing emphasis on enhancing clinical functions. The most sophisticated HISs provide integrated interfaces for ordering medications, procedures, and tests, performing contraindication checking, displaying on-line patient preparation instructions, and performing multilevel verification of orders. Nursing care modules assist in initial and ongoing patient assessment, development of nursing care plans based on patient problems, documentation of medication administration, and charting of nursing progress notes. Many health professionals believe that clinical systems can yield improvements in both the quality of patient care and the productivity of care providers and that significant benefits can be gained through the use of point-of-care systems such as bedside terminals. Although cost justification studies have been generally inconclusive to date, bedside terminal technology has gained the interest of the hospital industry. As of yet, the immaturity of the technology and the high cost per bed have discouraged widespread adoption. The development of an integrated clinical database in HISs represents one step toward the long-term goal of achieving a fully on-line medical record. In the meantime, some hospitals are experimenting with imaging technologies that would allow them to scan and digitally store copies of paper medical records.

Biomedical Research A fundamental task of clinical research is the analysis of patient data that has been collected either retrospectively from medical records or prospectively during clinical trials. Computer-based clinical research systems provide investigators with tools for acquiring, maintaining, and analyzing such data sets to attain a better understanding of diseases and disease manifestations and of the relationships between medical interventions and clinical outcomes. Since the late 1950s, researchers have used the computer's superior computational power to perform statistical analyses. A number of general purpose statistical packages are available, including SAS, MEDLOG, SYSTAT, SPSS, and BMDP. The microcomputer-based systems generally include high-quality graphical presentation capabilities.

Specialized database and analysis systems have also been developed to support clinical research. For example, ARAMIS, a nationwide database system developed by researchers at the Stanford University Medical Center, includes not only clinical data, but also an evolving set of programs to manipulate this data. Developed in the belief that solutions to the problems of chronic diseases will require large collections of high-quality longitudinal data, ARAMIS databases contain information about the long-term clinical courses of patients who have arthritis and rheumatic disease. Similarly, researchers at Duke University Medical Center have developed a clinical research database for patients with documented or suspected ischemic heart disease. The stored records can be used to explore general research questions, as well as to improve the care of individual patients by identifying the expected outcomes for alternative interventions based on the recorded experience of similar patients.

The highest quality clinical databases typically are those collected during prospective clinical trials. The increasing complexity of experimental protocols in such trials, however, has produced a need for computer systems to support direct management of experiments. Current research systems for clinical studies include features such as audit trails, patient tracking and scheduling to minimize attrition, and automated randomization and treatment assignment tools.

The construction of computer-based simulation models provides an alternative method for studying disease processes. Models can be developed that represent various disease states and the risk factors that influence transitions among states. Disease development is then modeled as a series of state changes over time. Such compartmental modeling techniques have been used to study infectious disease and coronary heart disease in patient populations. By manipulating the parameters of computer-based simulation models, researchers are able to study interactions among variables and the effects of interventions on health outcomes, thus reducing the need for expensive and time-consuming real-world experiments. Simulations are useful for planning full-scale clinical trials and for focusing on the most promising programs when planning health services.

A current area of biomedical research is the ongoing Human Genome Project sponsored by the National Institutes of Health. The primary goal of the project is to map the structure and function of human DNA. Computers are used to analyze the inheritance patterns of extended families in genetic linkage analyses that are designed to determine the chromosome locations of genes for inherited traits. Computers also support physical mapping experiments by executing algorithms used for genetic sequence comparison and for identifying possible overlaps in DNA fragments. In addition, database management systems (*q.v.*) will play a key administrative role in managing the operation of clone libraries, maintaining databases of information on clones and known DNA segments, and integrating data contributed from the multiple sites pursuing genetics research agendas.

Medical Education Physicians can perform a large number of diagnostic procedures and choose from a wide array of alternative drugs. Many of these diagnostic and therapeutic choices have implications not only for patients' physical outcomes, but also for health care costs. To practice medicine effectively, physicians must have a firm foundation of knowledge and experience and continue to build and refine this base as medical science advances.

The use of computers in medical education offers one means for avoiding the shortcomings of traditional teaching methods. Advantages of computer-aided instruction (CAI - *q.v.*) include the abilities to provide a medium for interactive learning, to offer immediate, student-specific feedback, to support individually tailored instruction, and to form a basis for objective testing. Computer-based simulations, in particular, provide a forum for learning to manage both typical and unusual cases, and for experimentation without danger or inconvenience to real patients.

During the past decade, CAI programs have proliferated. Virtually all medical schools and many nursing schools use computers to facilitate education. A number of publishing firms and specialty software companies are distributing educational programs on floppy disks (*q.v.*). Programs are currently available to teach clinical skills such as neurological assessment and interpretation of laboratory-test results and ECGs, and to address case management problems, such as the treatment of trauma and shock victims, advanced cardiac life support, and management of patients with diabetes (Fig. 6). CAI programs have also been developed to educate patients regarding their diseases and treatments. Examples of current CAI programs include the TIME project of the Lister Hill National Center for Biomedical Communications, which combines interactive videodisc and speech recognition technologies to create realistic simulations, and HeartLab, developed by researchers at the Harvard Medical School, which teaches students to interpret the results of auscultation of the heart through a combination of computer-generated heart sounds and graphical depictions.

Organizational Support The federal government has played a key role in funding medical computing research in the U.S., mainly through the National Library of Medicine, the National Institutes of Health, and the National Center for Health Services Research (now subsumed by the Agency for Health Research and Policy). These agencies have promoted more general applications of computer technology in medicine, complementing the specific mission-oriented grants of organizations such as the National Cancer Institute. In Europe, much activity has been sponsored through national health maintenance organizations. Hospital computer systems have had specific governmental encouragement in Scandinavia, France, and Germany. As initial research approaches have proven feasible, commercial developers have moved to

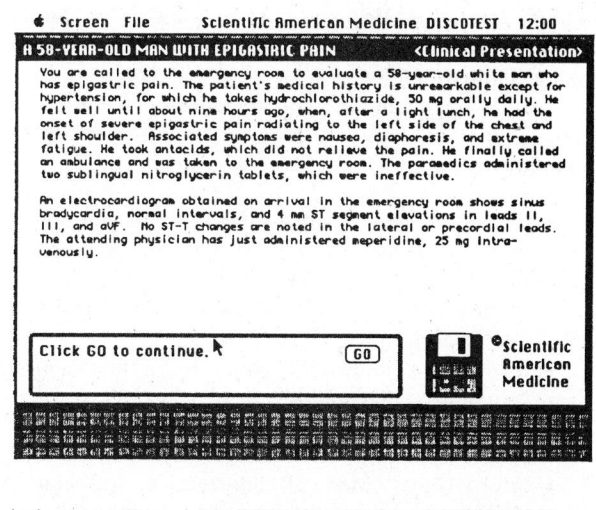

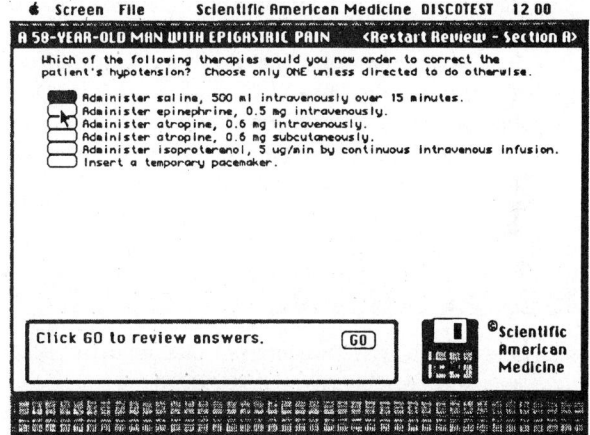

FIG. 6. DISCOTEST interactive programs present physician users with specific case management problems in internal medicine. (a) Initial screens summarize the patient's history of present illness and physical examination. (b) In subsequent screens, the user can interview the patient, order diagnostic tests, prescribe therapies, and assess the patient's progress. Each case can be run once for Continuing Medical Education credit and rerun for practice and review. (Courtesy of Scientific American Medicine.)

refine and market similar systems. In some areas, such as medical imaging, hardware manufacturers have played an important role in technology development.

Sources For current information on specific applications, the journals *M.D. Computing* and *Computers in Healthcare* publish annual surveys of commercially available medical computing systems and current vendors.

Journals devoted to medical informatics (the study of biomedical information and the applications of computers in medicine) include *Computers and Biomedical Research, Methods of Information in Medicine, Computer Methods and Programs in Biomedicine, M.D. Computing, Computers in Healthcare, Artificial Intelligence in Medicine,* and the *Journal of Medical Systems.* Selected articles are also published in medical journals, such as *JAMA* (the *Journal of the American Medical Association*), the *New*

England Journal of Medicine, and the *Annals of Internal Medicine*, as well as the literatures of specific medical subspecialties.

In addition, a number of organizations provide a focal point for medical and health care computing, including the following:

- American Medical Informatics Association (AMIA), which sponsors the annual Symposium on Computer Applications in Medical Care (SCAMC).
- Artificial Intelligence in Medicine (AIM), American Association for Artificial Intelligence.
- Engineering in Medicine and Biology Society, Institute of Electrical and Electronics Engineers.
- Healthcare Information and Management Systems Society (HIMSS), American Hospital Association.
- International Medical Informatics Association (IMIA), which sponsors the triennial international MEDINFO conference jointly with a special interest group of the International Federation for Information Processing (IFIP).
- Special Interest Group on Biomedical Computing (SIGBIO), Association for Computing Machinery.

LESLIE PERREAULT

MEDICAL IMAGING

For articles on related subjects *see* BIOCOMPUTING; IMAGE PROCESSING; and TOMOGRAPHY, COMPUTERIZED.

History and Background   *Medical imaging* is the study of human functions and anatomy through pictorial information. In order to generate this pictorial information, multidisciplinary knowledge, including anatomy, physiology, chemistry, computer science, optical science, radiological science, electrical engineering, mathematics, and physics are required. Generally speaking, medical imaging studies methods and procedures of:

1. Converting a medical image, or synthesizing some anatomical or physiological information, to a digital image.
2. Analyzing the digital image according to clinical need.
3. Extracting key results and casting them into a format suitable for presentation, archiving, and decision making.

Some successful medical imaging applications in the early 1970s were the blood cell analyzer and the gamma camera in nuclear medicine. The development of the computed tomography (CT) scanner resulted in the award of the Nobel Prize in Medicine to Allan M. Cormack and Godfrey N. Hounsfield in 1979. Major medical imaging developments in the 1980s were electron microscopy (EM) and laser microscopy (LM), digital subtraction angiography (DSA), magnetic resonance imaging (MRI), positron emission tomography (PET), computed radiography (CR), doppler ultrasound, and picture archiving and communi-

cation systems (PACS). EM can reveal minute details in biological infrastructures as small as a few angstroms in size. LM yields thin serial images providing three-dimensional morphology of living cells. DSA allows real-time subtraction to enhance the vascularities in angiograms. Without the use of ionizing radiation, MRI reveals high-contrast images of anatomical structures in any plane of the body. MRI is the method of choice for neuroradiological, vascular, and musculoskeletal diagnosis.

PET provides chemical and physiological images of the human body that complement anatomical images obtained using MRI and CT. The registration of MRI or CT with PET head images provides an insight into the specific function of various parts of the brain. CR allows an X-ray image to be recorded directly as a digital image, opening new avenues for using digital image processing as an aid in medical diagnosis.

PACS is a novel concept for medical image management and communication. When fully implemented, the system will revolutionize the practice of radiology. PACS storage technology includes parallel transfer disks and optical disk libraries. In the former, a conventional X-ray image of 6 megabytes can be stored or retrieved from the parallel transfer disks within one second. In the latter, an optical disk library that occupies a footprint of no more than 3×6 ft. allows the storage of one terabyte of information, equivalent to about two years worth of all MR and CT examinations conducted in a large teaching hospital.

In communication components, fiber optics systems with specially designed fiber optic transmitters and receivers can transmit images at a rate up to 1 gigabit per second. A conventional 6-megabyte X-ray can be transmitted between two points in about one second. For display, 2000×2000 pixel monitors are readily available that display a conventional X-ray without loss of diagnostic quality. Three-dimensional display stations are used in various clinical applications.

Medical Image Detectors and Recorders
Medical image detection and recording methods can be categorized as being either photochemical or photoelectronic. An example of a photochemical method is the phosphorous screen and silver halide film combination system used for X-ray detection. The television camera and display monitor used in fluorography is a photoelectronic technique. The photochemical method is a direct process; it has the advantage of combining image detection and image recording in a single step. The screen/film system simultaneously detects and records the attenuated X-rays. A photoelectronic system, on the other hand, usually involves a two-step process; the image is detected first and then recorded in a subsequent step.

In the case of DSA, an image intensifier tube (II) is used as the X-ray detector instead of a screen/film combination. The detected X-rays are converted first into light photons and then into electronic signals that are recorded by a video camera. The images from the video camera can be displayed on a TV monitor, and the video signal can be digitized to form a digital image. The photoelectronic system, while clearly more complicated, has one important advantage: the output information can be easily converted to digital format for image processing.

Fig. 1 shows an example of medical image detectors and recorders. In this case, an image of blood cells from a blood sample on a glass slide is to be recorded. The glass slide is first placed under the microscope. If a 35mm camera is attached to the microscope, an image of the blood cells can be recorded on film. On the other hand, if a television camera is attached to the microscope, then the blood cells are seen as an electronic image on a TV monitor. In either case, the recorded image is in analog form. For a digital computer to process these images, they must first be converted to digital form, a step called analog to digital conversion (*q.v.*).

Digital Images   A digital image $P(x,y)$ is defined as an integer function of two variables x,y such that

$$0 \leq P(x,y) \leq N \text{ where } 1 \leq x \leq m, 1 \leq y \leq n$$

and x, y, m, n, and N are positive integers. For simplicity, we let $m = n$ (i.e. $P(x,y)$ is a square image). Given (x,y), $P(x,y)$ is called a picture element, or *pixel*. The computer memory requirement for storing the image $P(x,y)$ is $n \times n \times k$ bits where $k = \log_2 (N + 1)$. Thus, $n \times n \times k$ means that the image has n lines, each line has n pixels, and each pixel can have a discrete gray-level value that ranges from 0 to $2^k - 1$.

Spatial and Density Resolution   Once an object of interest has been digitally recorded, we would like to know its image quality. Image quality is characterized by three parameters: spatial resolution, density resolution, and signal-to-noise ratio. Spatial resolution is a measure of the number of pixels used to represent the object, and density resolution is the total number of discrete gray level values in the digital image. It is apparent that n and N are proportional to spatial resolution and density resolution, respectively. A high signal-to-noise ratio means that the image is very pleasing to the eye and hence is a better-quality image. Fig. 2 demonstrates the concept of spatial and density resolution of a digital image of a lymphocyte. The left-hand column in Fig. 2 shows digitized images of the lymphocyte with a fixed spatial resolution (21×15) and variable density resolutions (from top to bottom: 16, 4, and 2 gray levels). The right-hand column depicts the digital representation of the same analog image with a fixed density resolution (16) and variable spatial resolutions (from top to bottom: high, medium, low). It is clear from this example that the upper right corner digital image has the best quality (highest spatial and density resolutions), whereas the lower left corner image has the lowest spatial and density resolutions. Depending on the diagnostic requirement, the spatial resolution, density resolution, and signal-to-noise ratio of the image should be adjusted properly during image acquisition. A high-resolution image requires a larger memory capacity for storage and a correspondingly longer time for image processing than a lower-resolution image.

Sources of Medical Images   By far, the richest source of medical images is radiology. In radiology, about 75% of the examinations, including those that involve skull, chest, abdomen, and bone, produce images that are acquired and stored on X-ray film. These images have a spatial resolution of about 5 lp/mm. Line pair per millimeter "(lp/mm)" is a measure of spatial resolution; one line pair represents two pixels. These films can be converted to digital format using a film digitizer. Among various types of digitizers, the laser scanning digitizer is consid-

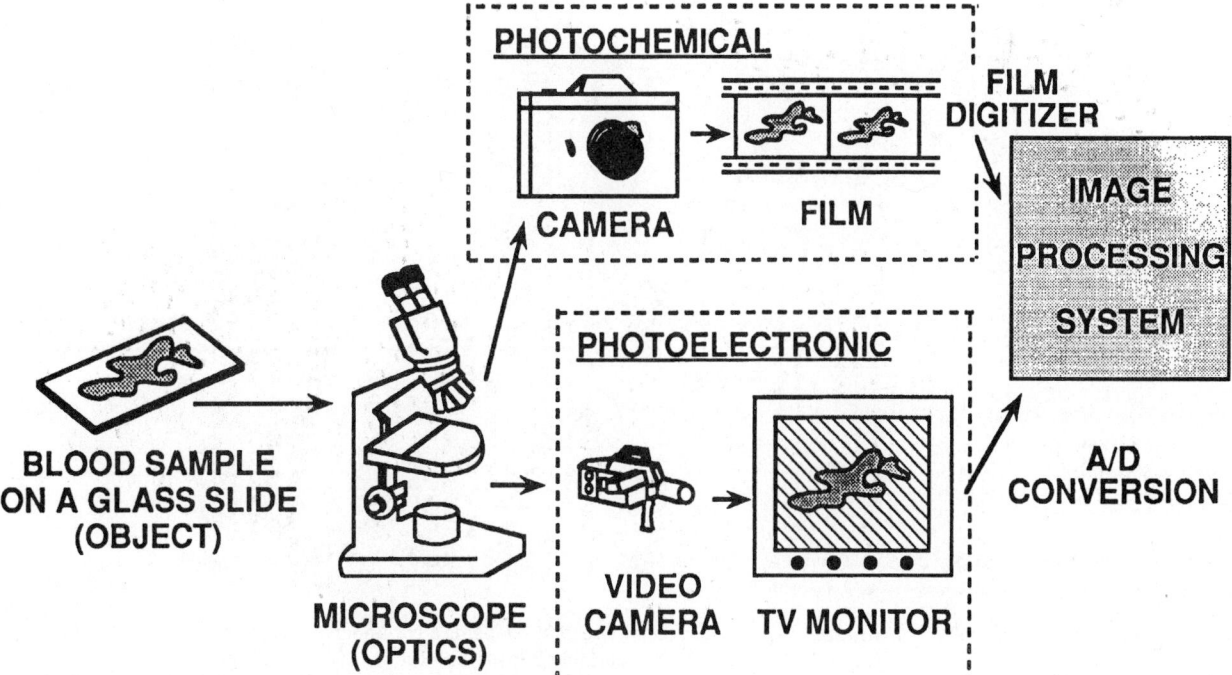

FIG. 1.   An example of biomedical image detectors and recorders.

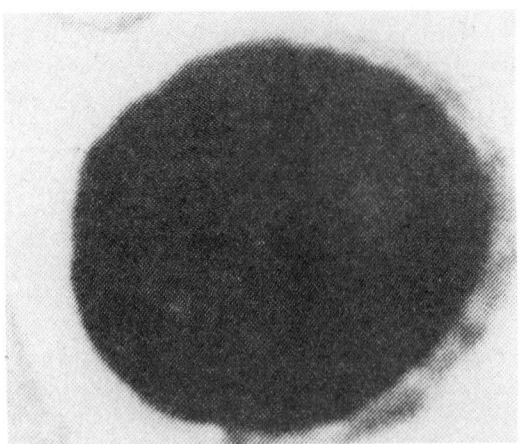

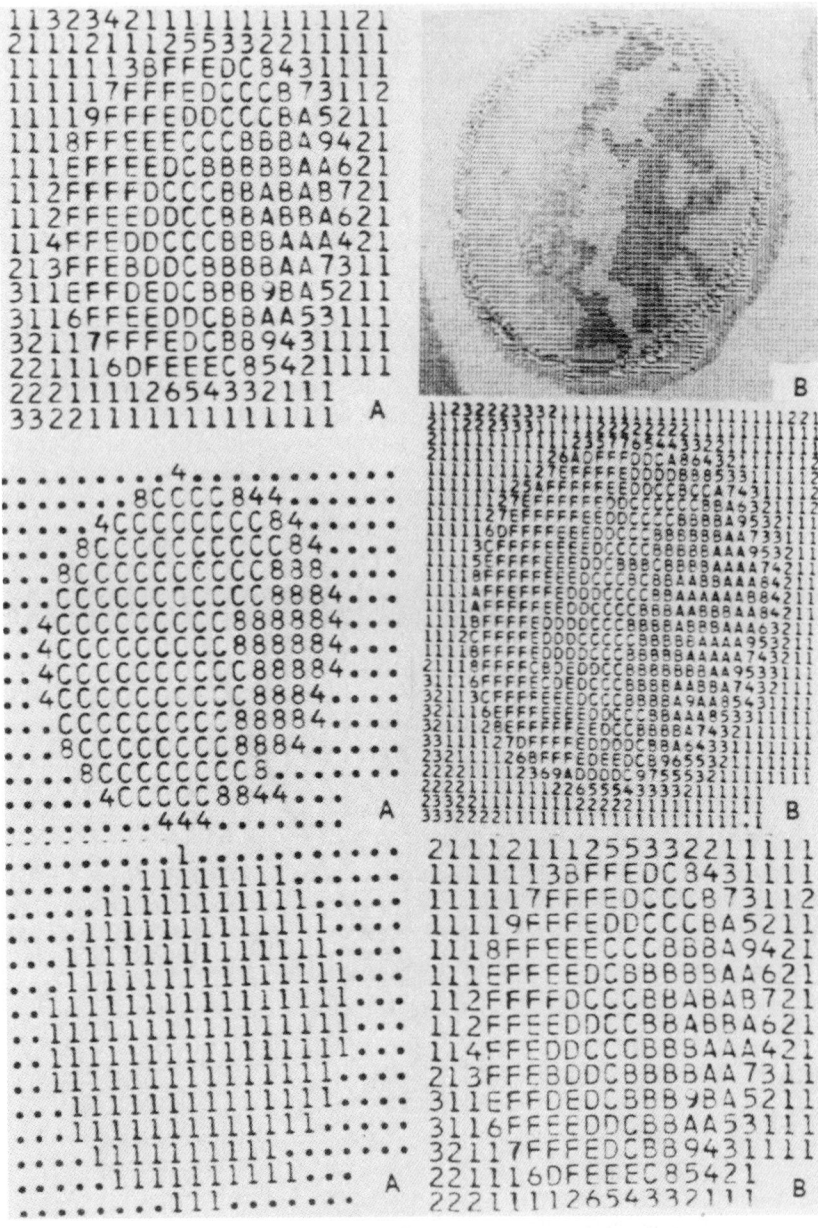

FIG. 2.   Illustration of spatial and density resolution, using a lymphocyte image as an example. (a) Fixed spatial resolution, variable density resolution: 16, 4, and 2 gray levels. (b) Fixed density resolution (16 levels), variable spatial resolutions. The 16 levels are represented by: 0, 1, 2, 3, 4, 5, 6, 7, 8, 9, A, B, C, D, E, and F.

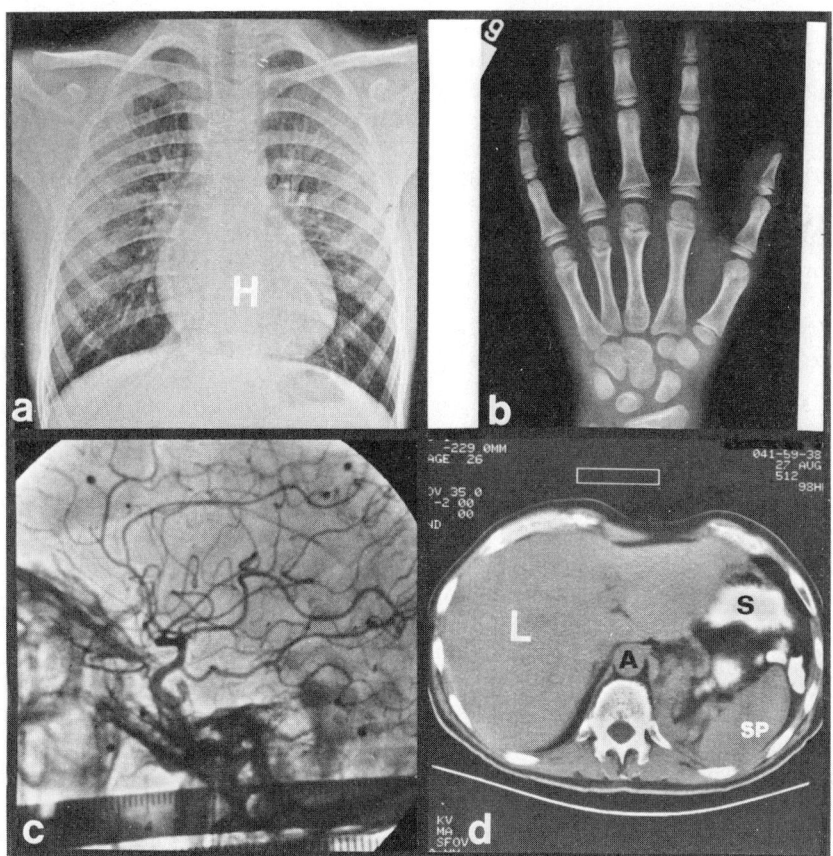

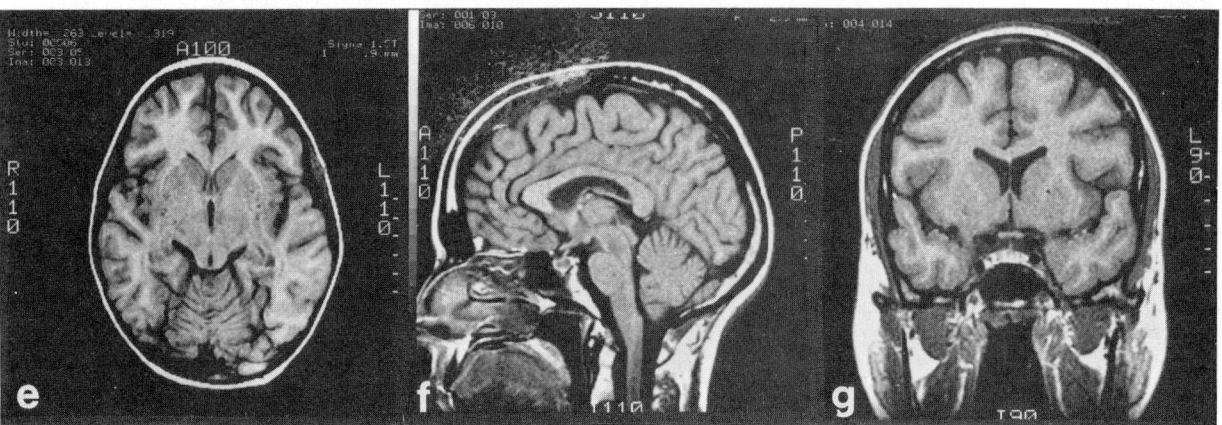

FIG. 3. Examples of medical images obtained from various sources. (a) CR image of the chest; the image is 2000 × 2500 pixels and 10 bits/pixel. Excellent delineation of the blood vessels behind the heart (h). (b) CR image of the hand. Both soft tissues and the detail of the bones are seen very clearly. (c) DSA of the brain showing contrast enhanced blood vessels. (Courtesy of E. Pietka.) (d) CT image of the upper abdomen. Contrast media is shown in the S: stomach, L: liver, SP: spleen, A: descending aorta. (e, f, g) MR images of the head from the same patient in the transverse, sagittal, and coronal plane. Images show fine structures of the brain. (Courtesy of S. Sinha.)

ered superior because it can best preserve the resolution of the original analog image. A laser film scanner can digitize a 14″ × 17″ X-ray film to 4000 × 5000 pixels (about 5 lp/mm), using 12 bits per pixel. At this density, the quality of the original analog image and the digitized image is essentially equivalent. In practice, however, we digitize an X-ray film to just 2,000 × 2,500 pixels. Computed radiography (CR), which uses a laser stimulable luminescence phosphor imaging plate as a detector, is gradually replacing the screen/film combination as the image detector. In this case, a laser beam is used to scan the imaging plate that contains the latent X-ray image. The latent image is excited and emits photons that are detected and converted to digitized electronic signals that form a digital X-ray image.

The other 25% of radiological examinations—those that involve computed tomography (CT), ultrasonography (US), magnetic resonance imaging (MRI), and digital subtraction angiography (DSA)—produce images that are already in digital format. A CT, US, MRI, PET, DSA image has sizes of 512 × 512 × 12, 512 × 512 × 8, 256 × 256 × 8, 128 × 128 × 12, and 512 × 512 × 8, respectively. These techniques use different energy sources and detectors to generate images and are complementary to each other with regard to clinical requirements. CT uses X-rays as an energy source and gas or scintillating crystals as detectors. US uses an ultrasonic transducer both as the energy source and detector. MR uses two energy sources, magnetic fields and radio-frequency electromagnetic waves, and a radio-frequency receiver as the detector. DSA uses X-rays as an energy source and an image intensifier tube as the detector. Conventional X-ray examinations and DSA produce a projectional image, whereas CT, US, PET, and MRI give sectional images. All radiologic images are monochromatic.

Other medical image sources used in anatomy and pathology are light and electron microscopes. Images from these sources are collected with a video camera and then digitized to a 512 × 512 × 8 image. Light microscopy produces true color images, using red, green, and blue filters for color separation. Thus, a color image after digitization yields three digital images, the combination of which produces a true-color digital image encoded at 24 bits/pixel. Fig. 3a–g shows some examples of medical images (for Figs. 3h–3j, see color insert page CP-9).

Image Processing Systems   After a medical image is formed, it is analyzed by an image processing system. The architecture of an image processing system (IP) consists of three major components: image processor(s), image memories, and video processor(s). They are connected by internal buses to form an integrated system. Fig. 4 shows the general block diagram of an integrated image processing system. For this particular system, only the system controller is connected to the host bus. The image processor is a high-speed array processor. It is

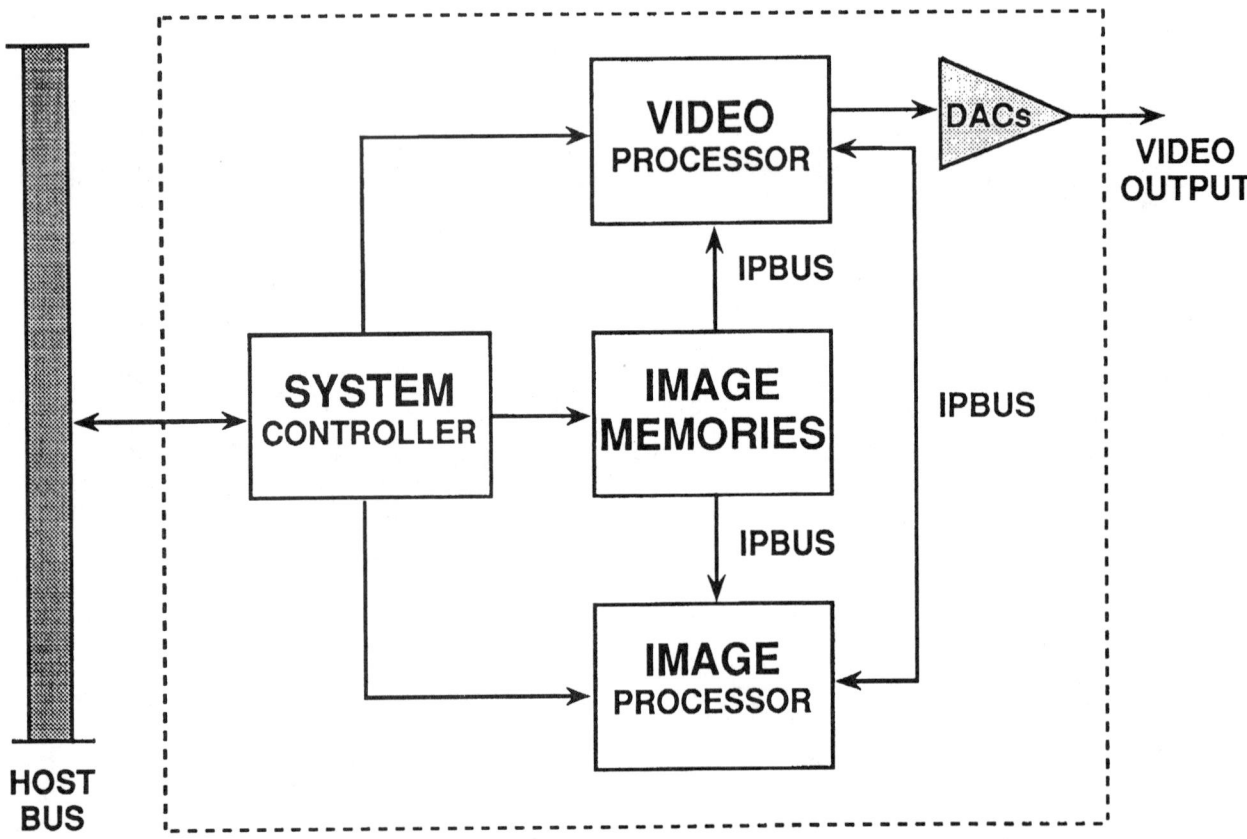

FIG. 4.   A general architecture of an integrated image processing system. Only the system controller is connected to the host bus.

composed of arithmetic-logic units, multipliers and shifters, comparators, and look-up tables. The image memories can be partitioned into various sizes for efficient storage of image data. The video processor takes the images from the image memories and selectively displays them on video monitors.

An IP system requires extensive software support. The trend in IP software development is towards portability. Fig. 5 shows the general organization of IP software. Portability is preferred in the three higher levels of software so that they can be used in future hardware architecture. The two lower levels are machine dependent and have to be rewritten for every new hardware architecture. IP functions include pixel, local, global, and statistical operations. IP functions also consist of image database manipulation and image display. In the past, Fortran was used in most IP software development, but C (*q.v.*) running under Unix is now standard.

In medical imaging applications, contour extraction of an object of interest is important because it leads to quantitative measurements. Despite many years of research and development, resolution of soft-tissue segmentation in radiologic images is still a very difficult task. Advances in medical image processing remain largely in the domain of quantization. Fig. 6 shows the levels of sophistication in medical image processing.

Future Trends The use of medical imaging in the radiological sciences is expected to increase about 40% in the next 5 years. The method for producing medical images will not change drastically, but image quality will continue to improve. Traditionally, medical imaging is used only for diagnostic purpose, but ultimately it will expand to cover therapeutic applications as well, especially in interventional radiology. PACS will be established as a vital image database management system. This will lead to the development of an image knowledge database that will require new kinds of IP hardware and software. The leading candidate in hardware design for medical image processing will be a modified parallel processing architecture that will shorten the time required for interprocessor communication. Mathematical advances may provide a new approach for image segmentation. Fractal

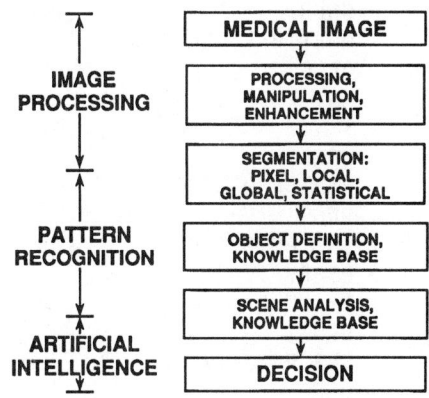

FIG. 6. Levels of sophistication in medical image processing. Pattern recognition and artificial intelligence will be two major research topics in the 1990s.

(*q.v.*) analysis shows promise for image feature extraction and object definition. Neutral networks (*q.v.*) may prove useful for medical pattern recognition, and other artificial intelligence techniques may bring medical imaging to the threshold of a mature science.

References

1981. Huang, H. K. "Medical Image Processing," *CRC Critical Reviews in Bioengineering*, 5, 3, 185-271.

1987. Huang, H. K. *Elements of Digital Radiology*. Englewood Cliffs, NJ: Prentice-Hall.

1988. Huang, H. K., Mankovich, N. J., Taira, R. K., Cho, P. S., Stewart, B. K., Ho, B. K. T., Chan, K. K., and Ishimitsa, Y. "Picture Archiving and Communication Systems for Radiological Images: State-of-the-Art," *CRC Critical Reviews in Diagnostic Imaging*, 28, 4, 383-427.

1990. Huang, H. K., Aberle, D. R., Lufkin, R., Grant, E. G., Hanafee, W. N., and Kangarloo, H. "Advances in Medical Imaging," *Annals of Internal Medicine*, 112, 3: 203-220.

H. K. HUANG

MEDLARS/MEDLINE

For articles on related subjects *see* BIOCOMPUTING; CURRENT AWARENESS SYSTEMS; INFORMATION RETRIEVAL; MEDICAL APPLICATIONS; and MEDICAL IMAGING.

The National Library of Medicine initiated a program for access to the biomedical literature over 100 years ago under the guidance of Dr. John Shaw Billings. *Index Medicus*, a guide to the medical literature, was first published in 1879. In 1962, the library began to develop a computerized system for the production of *Index Medicus*; the system went into operation in January 1964. This computer system, called MEDLARS (Medical Literature Analysis and Retrieval System), incorporated the first operational photocomposition system. As a by-product, the system could provide partially individualized bibliographies ("demand searches") for a requesting health professional. The demand for such services grew with time and with the size

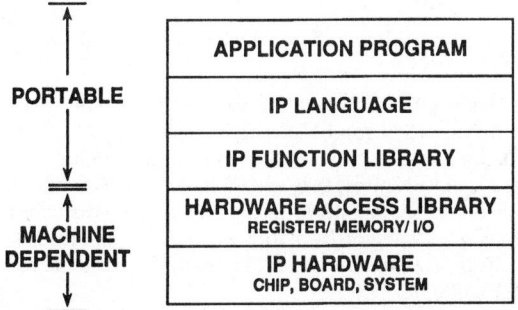

FIG. 5. Organization of image processing software. The three higher levels should be portable so that they can be used for any future hardware architecture.

```
USER:                    [User is to type command]
MULTIPLE SCLEROSIS       [Command to search for this term]
PROG:
SS1 PSTG (1183)          [Number of articles (postings) of this
                         term in the current MEDLINE file]
USER:
VISION DISORDERS         [Command to search for this term]
PROG:
SS2 PSTG (592)           [Number of articles found]
USER:
1 AND 2                  [Command to find articles with both]
PROG:
SS3 PSTG (7)             [Number of articles found]
USER:
PRINT                    [Command to print one citation]
PROG:
AU - Regan D
TI - To what extent can visual deficits caused by multiple sclerosis
be understood in terms of parallel processing?
SO - Res Publ Assoc Res Nerv Ment Dis 1990;67:317-29
```

FIG. 1. Excerpt from a search of the MEDLINE file (last 2–3 years). AU=Author; TI=Title; SO=Source. The entire record has many more printable fields. It is possible to search MEDLINE for references back to 1966.

of the computer file, reaching a peak in 1970 with a total of 24,000 searches in the U.S. and participating foreign centers. The search service was provided, at times, from 10 computers in the U.S. and 11 computers in foreign countries.

On 29 October 1971, NLM initiated a nationwide, on-line, bibliographic retrieval system as a general service for the biomedical community. This service, called MED-LINE, now allows almost instantaneous, interactive searching of over 600,000 citations from the world's biomedical serial literature. This service has superseded the MEDLARS-batch demand search service. The service now supports a maximum of 250 simultaneous users, 24 hours/day, 7 days/week. In 1990, about 4.5 million on-line searches were processed.

Access to the MEDLARS/MEDLINE network is by telephone communications networks. The central computers (IBM 3084-Q) are located at the National Library of Medicine in Bethesda, MD. There are over 40,000 institutions and individuals in the U.S. with MEDLINE access, located at medical schools, hospitals, research institutions, government agencies, commercial organizations, and private practices. In addition, MEDLINE is available in Australia, Canada, China, Colombia, Egypt, France, Germany, Great Britain, Italy, Japan, Kuwait, Mexico, South Africa, Sweden, Switzerland, and Taiwan and at the Pan American Health Organization Regional Medical Library in Sao Paulo, Brazil.

MEDLINE is the largest and most important of the Library's on-line databases, containing recent references (most with abstracts) to journal articles published in over 3,000 biomedical serials. There are a number of other important on-line databases, however, available over the network: CATLINE (books catalogued at NLM), AVLINE (audiovisuals), CANCERLIT (cancer literature), and SER-LINE (serial records), to name just several. A separate MEDLARS on-line network, TOXNET, permits searching of several specialized data banks containing factual information about environmental pollution, toxic spills, and hazardous substances. Altogether, the MEDLARS databases contain some 13 million records. Fig. 1 is an excerpt from a MEDLINE search.

In 1986, the Library introduced "Grateful Med." This is a user-friendly mode of access to NLM's major databases for users of personal computers (IBM or Macintosh) equipped with a modem. The user is not required to know the formal search language of the NLM system; Grateful Med also handles all telecommunications procedures and search commands. References and abstracts identified during the search are automatically downloaded to the user's PC and may be reviewed and printed at leisure. The increasing use of Grateful Med by health professionals and students is changing the composition of the MEDLARS on-line network from overwhelmingly institutional to one in which about half the searching is by individual users.

References

1973. McCarn, Davis B. and Leiter, Joseph. "On-line Services in Medicine and Beyond," *Science,* **181** (27 July): 318–324.

1977. Leiter, Joseph. "On-Line Systems of the National Library of Medicine," in Shires, D. F. and Wolf, H.: *MEDINFO 77: Proceedings of the Second World Conference on Medical Informatics. Toronto, 8-12 August.* New York: North-Holland, 349–353.

1978. *Medical Informatics* **3**, *3* (September). (Issue devoted to MEDLARS/MEDLINE.)

1987. Haynes, Brian R. and McKibbon, Ann K. "Grateful Med," *M.D. Computing,* **4**, Sept/Oct: 47–57.

ROBERT MEHNERT

MEMORY

For articles on related subjects *see* ASSOCIATIVE MEMORY; CACHE MEMORY; CD-ROM; FLOPPY DISK; HARD DISK; READ-ONLY MEMORY; REGISTER; STORAGE HIERARCHY; ULTRASONIC MEMORY; and VIDEODISC.

MAIN

Different levels of storage (or memory) are usually employed in a computer system. At one extreme are very fast and relatively small storage units used as fast access registers by the central processing unit (CPU - *q.v.*). At the other extreme are relatively slow, large capacity units of *auxiliary storage*. The auxiliary storage devices are typically tape and/or disk drives. The characteristics of *main memory* lie between these two extremes. In general, the main memory will contain instructions and data that are accessed by a program while it is executing.

In this article the key terms related to main memory are described and illustrated. The logical components, organizations, and techniques of main memory are described. Finally, the technologies employed in main memory systems are described.

Memory performance and cost have evolved rapidly since the 1970s. These advances have come about primarily through miniaturization brought on by improvements in the integrated microelectronic technologies used to fabricate the storage devices. The availability of fast, inexpensive memory has had enormous impact on computer technology.

Definitions and Terminology Digital computers store data as a representation of binary digits. Each digit is called a *bit*, the minimum storage element. A bit may assume the value "1" or "0," nothing else. Data may be both read from and written to any location in main memory. This type of memory is known as random access read/write memory, or RAM. To access the data in main memory, some element of the computer system must first provide the memory system with an *address* (*q.v.*) which describes the location of the data in memory. The address may come from the CPU, from a cache memory, or from a memory mapped I/O (*q.v.*) device. This address is a binary representation placed on the *address bus* of the memory system (*see* BUS). After an *access time* (*q.v.*), the memory system will return the selected data on its *data bus* where it can be captured by the computer system. Alternatively, the computer system can write data into the memory by signaling a write operation to the memory system and placing data on the data bus and addresses on the address bus. The data bus is called *bi-directional*, as it can serve to write data to and read data from the memory system. New data can be read or written from the memory system every *cycle time* (*q.v.*). The access and cycle times are a function of both the technology and organization of the memory system.

Typically, each memory address refers to more than one bit of data in the memory system. The minimum uniquely addressable unit of data in main memory is typically eight bits, or a *byte*. However, the size of this addressable quantum, often called a *word*, depends upon the computer system, the memory unit, and the access mode. The choice of a *data path*, the number of bits simultaneously transferred per memory access, is governed by the trade-off between performance and cost. A wider data path will allow a greater rate of transfer of data in and out of the memory, but is accompanied by additional expense, power consumption, and system complexity.

An alternative technique for increasing the memory system data rate is the use of *interleaving* (*q.v.*). An interleaved memory system is physically implemented using a number (M) of independent memory subsystems of similar size and performance. Adjacent memory addresses are assigned to different physical subsystems. Hence, if the processor accesses sequential memory locations, each memory subsystem can be activated concurrently. The peak memory system cycle time can be reduced by a factor M from the memory subsystem cycle time, using this technique. Implementation of an interleaved memory system requires the use of a memory control function, which analyzes the memory access address stream and determines the availability of the various memory subsystems to adjust the memory system timing. In the case of a nonsequential address access, the memory system cycle time must be lengthened. A portion of the memory address will be used to select the individual memory subsystem to read or write from.

Even small computer systems have relatively large main memories. Since the memory addressed is represented by a binary word, the memory size is typically related to a power of two and described in units of kilobytes (KB), megabytes (MB), or gigabytes (GB). A kilobyte is 2^{10} or 1,024 bytes. A megabyte is 2^{20} or 1,048,576 bytes. A gigabyte is 2^{30} or 1.074×10^9 bytes. Computer main memory sizes range from a few KBs to several GBs. To translate the binary address provided by a computer system on the memory bus, the memory system makes use of *decoders,* which accept as input a binary address and, as output, activate one signal line chosen by the address. For example, a 6-bit address decoder would have 6 input bits and 2^6 or 64 output signals. One of these 64 would be activated in response to each unique input address. Information inside the memory system is stored in *memory cells.* An individual memory cell can be uniquely selected by a signal from the decoder. However, in this simple realization, a moderately sized memory would require an unrealistically large decoder circuit and associated signal wiring. To solve this problem, main memory addressing typically uses a hierarchical scheme. This is most easily understood in the case of a three-level hierarchy by visualizing the memory space as a three-dimensional cube with numbered lines containing integers starting with 0 on each axis of the cube. Separate memory cells are logically located at each cartesian coordinate within the cube thus forming a three-dimensional matrix of memory cells. The "address" of any cell is given by its cartesian triplet (i.e. its "*x, y, z*" ordered triplet). The length of each axis is selected to be a power of two. In this way the entire address space may be represented by assigning specific bits from the address data word to a separate decoder for each axis that effectively chooses a specific position along that axis. In this three-level example, one portion of the address bits will choose a "plane" of cells, another portion of the address chooses a "row" of cells in the plane, and the final portion of the address bits choose a column within the row. Use of an hierarchical address decoding scheme reduces the required number of decoded signals into the memory array. For example, a 1MB memory system requires 20 bits to address. A one-level decoder would require 1,048,576 output signals. A two-level addressing scheme can be partitioned in a number of ways. A "square" representation would assign 10 address bits to one axis and the other 10 address bits to the other. This scheme would require two decoders, each with 1,024 output signals. A significant reduction in the number of decoded signal lines can result from this hierarchical addressing scheme. The choice of the number of levels in the addressing hierarchy and the number of unique addresses in each level depends on the desired cost, performance, power, and size of the memory system. The details of these trade-offs also depend upon the technology with which the memory cell and the decoders are realized. In a typical memory system using semiconductor memory, decoder cost and its associated signal wiring is much reduced when it can be integrated into the integrated circuit chip itself rather than being used to choose between chips or boards.

Memory Technologies

Memory cells for main memory may be realized by a number of technologies and designs that are distinguished by their unique characteristics of density, performance (access and cycle time), power dissipation, and volatility. Density is important to the system through its impact on cost, size, and performance. A significant part of the delay in modern, high-speed computers comes from the delay along signal lines. Smaller, denser components allow use of shorter signal lines and therefore improve performance. In integrated semiconductor technologies, the cost of the memory is strongly influenced by the density of the storage element. The smaller the memory cell, the cheaper the integrated memory chip and the cheaper the memory system. Power becomes a concern as it affects the overall system density, or portability of the technology. Due to the large number of storage elements in a main memory system, if significant power is used by each individual memory cell, special cooling structures will be required to remove the heat from the system. This increases the cost and reduces the density of the overall system.

Memory volatility refers to the ability (or lack thereof) of the memory to retain its data after the power is removed from the system. Most main memories are volatile, (i.e. information is lost when power is removed). However, in some applications that require rapid restart after power failure or maintenance of data for intervals of power-off, specialty nonvolatile memories are available. In general, nonvolatile magnetic medium auxiliary storage devices are used to hold programs and data in the absence of system power. Table 1 describes the relative characteristics of popular main memory technologies.

Semiconductor Technologies

Main memory systems are most often realized using semiconductor technologies. To achieve high density and low cost, semiconductor memories use very large scale integration (VLSI) to integrate many memory cells as well as decoder and detector circuits on the same semiconductor chips. Typically, each memory chip receives an address as input and outputs 1 to 8 bits corresponding to this address. Several memory chips will be activated at the same time to access an entire byte or memory word.

MOSFET Dynamic RAM

Metal Oxide Semiconductor Field Effect Transistor Dynamic Random Access Memory (*MOSFET DRAM*) is the dominant main memory technology. MOSFET DRAMs are chosen primarily for their characteristics of low cost, low power, and moderate performance, that make them an ideal choice for large main memories. DRAMs achieve their low cost through use of a relatively simple semiconductor technology (CMOS) and a small memory cell consisting of a single transistor and a single capacitor. The CMOS technology provides both n-channel and p-channel field effect transistors. The equivalent circuit of a DRAM memory cell, called the one device cell, is shown in Fig. 1. This one-device memory cell was invented by Dennard in 1967. The value of the memory bit is represented by voltage stored on the cell's capacitor. This voltage is written into the storage capacitor by asserting the *word line* such that the transistor is turned "on." The desired data state is then imposed on the *bit line*. Typically, this will be either 5V to represent a "1" or 0V to represent a "0." Since the transistor is on, this voltage will be transferred onto the capacitor. Next, the word line voltage is returned to a low voltage, which turns the transistor off, isolating the charge on the capacitor. To read

TABLE 1. Relative Characteristics of Technologies Used in Main Memories

Technology	Density	Performance	Power	Volatile
Semiconductor MOSFET dynamic RAM	4	3	2	yes
Semiconductor MOSFET static RAM	3	2	3	yes
Semiconductor bipolar static RAM	2	1	4	yes
Magnetic core	1	4	1	no

1 (high) → 4 (low)

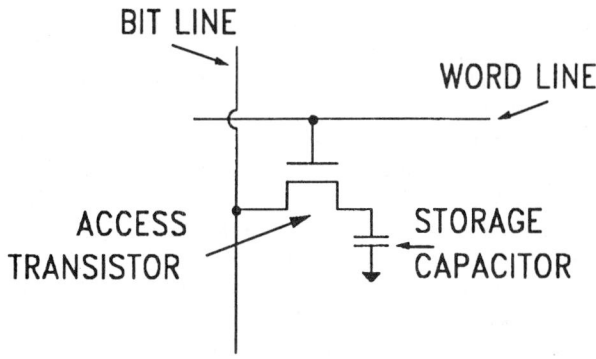

FIG. 1.   Equivalent circuit of a one-device DRAM memory cell.

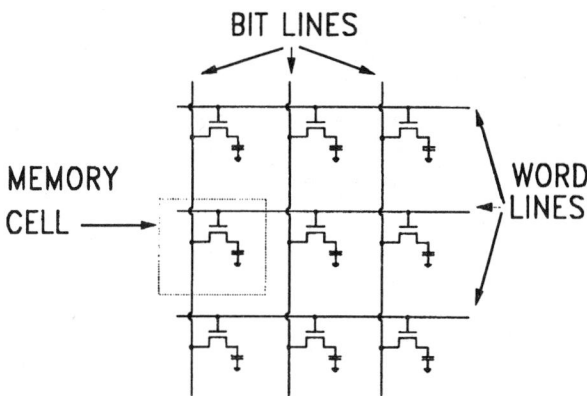

FIG. 2.   Schematic of a DRAM memory array.

the information from the cell, the word line is again asserted after the bit line has been connected to the input of a sense amplifier circuit. The charge from the capacitor is then transferred to the amplifier, where it can be detected as a "1" or a "0." This readout procedure is destructive, since it disturbs the information in the storage capacitor. Hence, the read operation must be followed by a subsequent write operation. Charge stored on the memory cell's capacitor does not remain on the capacitor indefinitely. Due to a variety of leakage paths, the charge can eventually leak off the capacitor, causing the memory cell to loose its information. To alleviate this problem, each memory cell in the memory must be periodically read, sensed, and re-written to a full level. This *refresh* requirement distinguishes the "dynamic" RAM from a "static" RAM. The implication of the refresh requirements on the operation of the memory system are described below.

Using modern integrated circuit technologies, a large number of one-device memory cells can be fabricated on a single integrated circuit chip (*see* INTEGRATED CIRCUITRY). By 1991, chips containing 4M bits were commonly available in large quantities. Chips containing 64M bits have been demonstrated in the laboratory. To provide high packing density of the cells and to allow hierarchical addressing, the memory cells are physically configured in a square or rectangular array on the integrated circuit chip. A single bit line is shared by many memory cells. Also, a single word line is shared by many cells. By running the word and bit lines in orthogonal directions, only one memory cell shares the combination of a given word and bit line, as shown in Fig 2. This orthogonal configuration of control lines allows a two-level hierarchical addressing scheme. One level selects a single word line (often called a row). The second addressing level selects a single bit line (often called a column). Theoretically, a 4M DRAM array could be constructed of 2K word lines and 2K bit lines. However, to improve array performance and signal margins, the 4Mb chip will typically be segmented into a number of sub-arrays, with each sub-array having fewer word and bit lines.

The important elements of a DRAM sub-array are shown in Fig. 3. The *row decoder* accepts as input a portion of the data address presented to the chip. From

this address, the row decoder activates one of the word lines. When this word line is activated, all of the memory cells located on this line are selected and the charge from their capacitors will be placed on the bit lines. Since this is a destructive read out, each bit line must be equipped with *sensing write-back* circuitry. Once the signal on each of the bit lines is sensed and amplified, the *column decoder* uses as input a separate portion of the data address to select which sense amplifier output to connect to the *data bus*. Finally, if the array is segmented into a number of sub-arrays, the remainder of the address will be used to determine which segment data bus(es) to select as output from the chip. A single chip may output one or several bits. Typically, several memory chips will be activated at the same time to access an entire byte or memory word.

The sense amplifier and write-back circuitry are typically merged into one cross-coupled sense amplifier circuit, as shown in Fig. 4. Successful operation of this circuit requires the use of a *reference cell*, which is often implemented as an extra row of cells that store a voltage between a "1" and a "0." Whenever a memory cell is

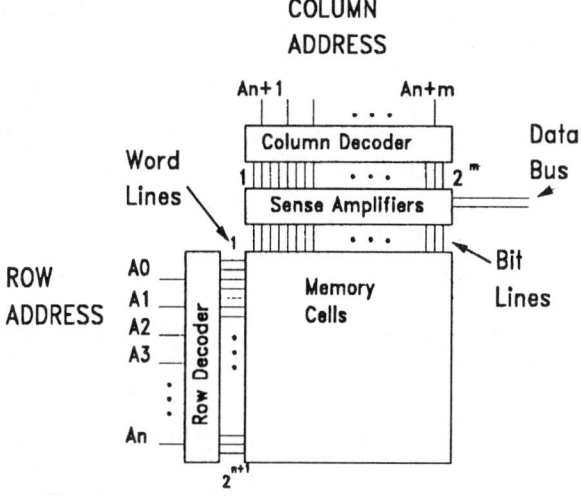

FIG. 3.   Important elements of a DRAM sub-array.

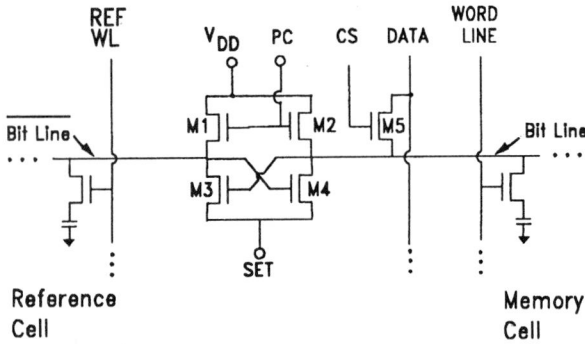

FIG. 4.   Cross-coupled sense amplifier circuit.

accessed, a reference cell on a separate bit line is also selected. The sense amplifier compares the voltage on the reference bit line to the voltage on the memory cell bit line in order to determine the logical state of the memory cell. The detailed operation of the sense amplifier circuit is described in Fig. 5. Initially, the bit lines are precharged to a high level by transistors M1–M2 during time period t1. Next, the word line selected by the row decoder circuit is activated at time t2. At the same time, the reference word line is activated. The signal stored on the memory cell capacitor will be partially transferred to the bit lines during time period t3. Since the bit line capacitance is large compared to the memory cell capacitance, only a fraction of the memory cell voltage is transferred. During time period t4 the cross-coupled sense amplifier made up of transistors M3–M4 is activated by lowering the voltage on node NSET. This action will amplify the voltage difference present on the bit lines. This amplified level can now be transferred to the data bus during time period t5 through transistor M5, which is selected by the column decoder circuitry. If it is desired to change the state of the cell, a voltage can be impressed on the data bus during time period t6. This voltage is transferred to the selected bit lines through FET M5 and to the selected memory cell capacitor through the access transistor. Finally, during time period t7 the word line is returned to ground and the signal is stored in the cell. In the case of unselected bit lines, the transistor M5 remains off and the information read from the cell is simply amplified and rewritten into

the cell. This is the refresh operation. Hence, to refresh the array, one simply selects a word line, activates the sense amplifiers, and deselects the word lines. This must be repeated for all word lines in the chip at least once every refresh cycle. A typical refresh cycle time is 16 ms. The chip refresh operation occupies only a small fraction of this 16ms cycle.

The sequencing of the operations described above is controlled by circuitry on the DRAM chip. The typical signal sequences required to operate the 4Mb DRAM chip are shown in Fig. 6. The address pins are multiplexed to serve as both the row and column addresses. When the $\overline{RAS}$ (row address strobe) signal falls, the chip accepts the signals present on the address lines as the row address. Next, when the $\overline{CAS}$ (column address strobe) signal falls, the chip accepts the signals present on the address lines as the column address. The $\overline{WE}$ (read/write enable) pin signals to the chip that the present operation is a read or a write. Data is transferred in and out of the chip via the data pin.

Several additional modes are typically implemented on the DRAM. For example, memory chips often contain a refresh address register. When the $\overline{CAS}$ signal falls before the $\overline{RAS}$ signal, the chip increments the refresh address counter and then automatically refreshes the cells on the wordline indicated by this register. This features simplifies the supporting functions that the memory system must supply. A second feature called *fast page mode* allows reduced cycle time for data bits present in the same row. In this mode, a single row address is latched in by a

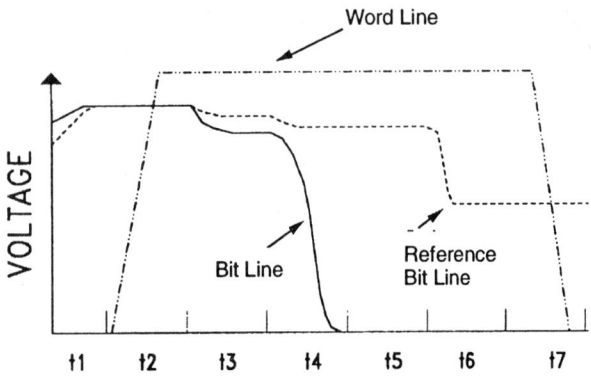

FIG. 5.   Operation of the cross-coupled sense amplifier.

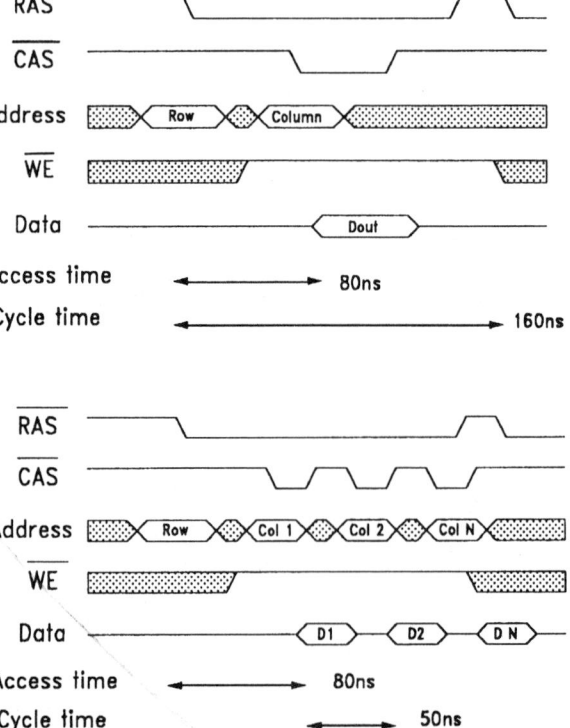

FIG. 6.   Typical signal sequence for a 4Mb DRAM chip. (a) Normal mode (b) fast PAGE mode.

falling $\overline{RAS}$ signal, and then different column addresses can be presented accompanied by a falling $\overline{CAS}$ signal. Column addresses can be changed rapidly with new data resulting from each cycle. A third mode is called the static column mode. In this mode, a single row is addressed, and any column on that row can then be accessed by merely changing the signals on the address pins. This is also a fast cycle mode of operation.

The technology employed in the fabrication of silicon MOSFET dynamic RAMs has progressed at a rapid pace throughout the 1970s and 1980s. In 1991, 4Mb DRAMs are commonly available from a number of manufacturers worldwide. The number of bits per DRAM chip have quadrupled every generation, with a new generation of DRAMs becoming available approximately every 3 years. This density increase has been brought about through steady advances in three major elements: (1) manufacturing quality has improved, allowing fabrication of larger chips each generation; (2) fabrication tools have improved, allowing the individual elements of the DRAM cell to be smaller each generation; and (3) invention of new memory cell structures each generation has allowed the elements of a DRAM cell to be placed closer to each other, allowing higher packing density. Each of these three elements contributes approximately an equal share to the increase in the number of bits per DRAM chip.

The first dynamic RAMs made use of a planar storage capacitor. Here the memory cell capacitor is formed between the semiconductor substrate and an electrode called the plate. To assure reliable operation of the memory cell, the capacitance of the memory cell's storage capacitor must be maintained above a minimum value of approximately 40fF. In order to make the memory cell smaller while maintaining a large storage capacitor, modern dynamic RAM cells employ three-dimensional storage capacitor structures in the form of either a *stacked* or *trench* capacitor. In a stacked capacitor cell, the memory capacitor is stacked above the access transistor of the cell, thus allowing sufficient area for the memory capacitor. In the trench capacitor DRAM cell, the storage capacitor is placed inside a trench that is etched into the silicon substrate. Use of a deep trench allows a large storage capacitor area. Fig. 7 shows the cross-section of a 4Mb trench DRAM cell manufactured by IBM.

MOSFET Static RAM To reduce the cycle time of the main memory, some computer designs choose to use static memory technologies. These circuits have the characteristics of not requiring refresh operation and can be read out non-destructively. Since the memory cell need not be rewritten after every read, the memory cycle time can be reduced. The static RAM cell consists of cross-coupled inverter circuits (also known as flip-flops), as shown in Fig. 8, as well as two access transistors. The cross-coupled inverters possess two stable states. In one state, the right transistor (M2) is on and the left transistor (M1) is off. The second stable state has M1 on and M2 off. Each stable state represents a binary value. The memory cell's state is probed by raising the word line, turning on the access transistors. This transfers the state of the cross-coupled inverters onto the bit lines. The bit lines selected

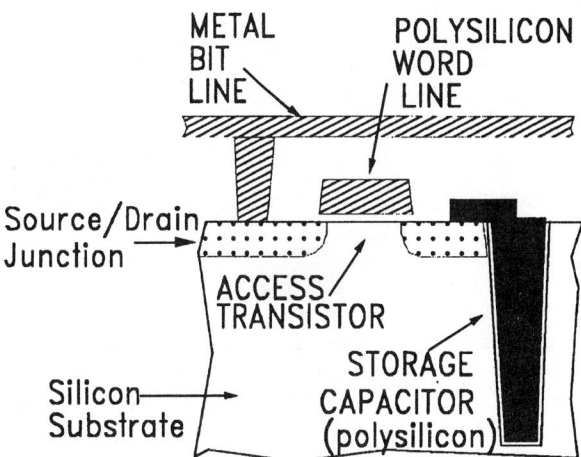

FIG. 7.   Cross-section of a typical trench capacitor DRAM cell.

by the column decoders can then be sensed and the data transferred onto the data bus and eventually off chip. Data is written into the cell by simply forcing a voltage onto the bit lines and turning on the access transistors. The memory cell's transistor characteristics are chosen such that the state of the bit lines can overcome the data state stored in the cross-coupled inverters to change the state of the cell.

Since each static memory cell requires either 4 FETs and 2 resistors or 6 FETs, the size of a static RAM cell is large compared to a dynamic RAM cell. For comparable technologies, SRAM chip densities tend to be approximately a factor of 4 less than that of DRAMs. This density is traded off for the improved performance of static RAMs.

Recently the performance of static RAMs has been enhanced by using a hybrid technology base called BiCMOS that integrates bipolar devices and CMOS devices on the same chip. BiCMOS static RAM chips use the CMOS technology to implement the memory cells. This is chosen as it results in a small memory cell with minimal power dissipation while the cell is storing its state. The

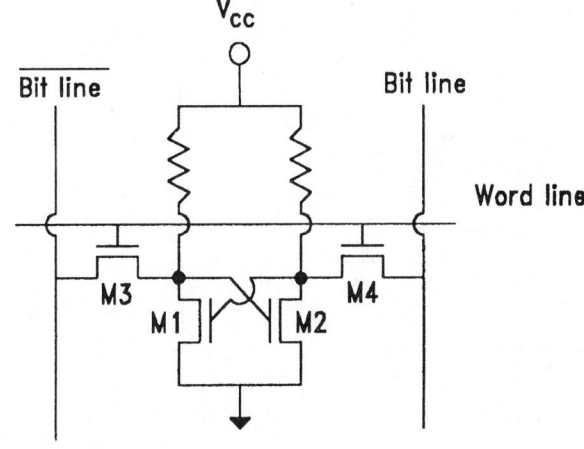

FIG. 8.   CMOS Static RAM cell.

TABLE 2. *Sampling of Static RAM Integrated Circuits Available in 1991*

Vendor	Part No.	Organization	Access Time (ns)	Technology	Power (mW)
Micon Tech.	MT5C1008	128K × 8	25	CMOS	350
Hitachi	HM6787	64K × 1	15	BiCMOS	300
Fujitsu	MBM10C514	256K × 4	15	BiCMOS	990
Fujitsu	MBM10474	1K × 4	3	Bipolar	1700

bipolar devices are used to enhance the speed of the decoders, line drivers, and amplifiers on the chip. Table 2 lists the characteristics of several static RAM chips available in 1991.

Bipolar Static RAM   The first integrated semiconductor memory to be used in computer systems was the bipolar static RAM. Early IBM system 360 computers employed 64-bit bipolar static RAM chips. While this cell affords the fastest speed when compared to the previously discussed technologies, its high power dissipation makes it unusable for large main memory systems. The bipolar static ram cell, shown in Fig. 9, is configured as cross-coupled inverter circuits. The load devices for the inverters include a resister as well as a diode to improve speed. The cell access to the bit lines is provided through one of the emitters of a split emitter transistor. In store mode, the voltage on the word line is low, and the current through the cross-coupled inverter flows through the emitter of the transistor into the word line. To access a cell, the word line voltage is raised above the bit line voltage of the selected cell. In this case, the cross-coupled inverter current flows onto one of the bit lines or the other, depending on the state of the cross-coupled inverter. This current flow in the bit lines is detected to read the status of the cell.

Ferrite-Core Memory   Ferrite-core memory was the first widely used technology for computer main memory.

The idea of using magnetic loop toroids was first discussed by Jay Forrester in 1950. His concept of using Permalloy tape-wound cores was quickly extended to the use of mass-produced ferrite material. Fig. 10 shows a schematic representation of a single ferrite-core memory cell. The ferrite core has the characteristic of hysteresis in its *remanence* shown in Fig 10, which is used to represent the digital state of the cell. The remanence of the cell can be changed by passing a current through wires passing through the center of the toroid. The toroid's remanence exhibits a threshold behavior whereby if a current less than a critical value is passed through the toroid and

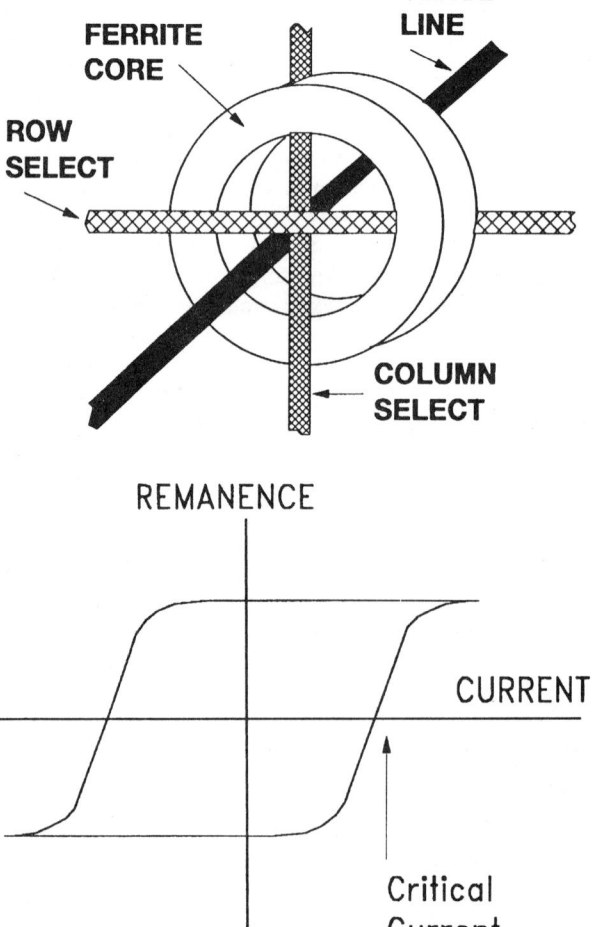

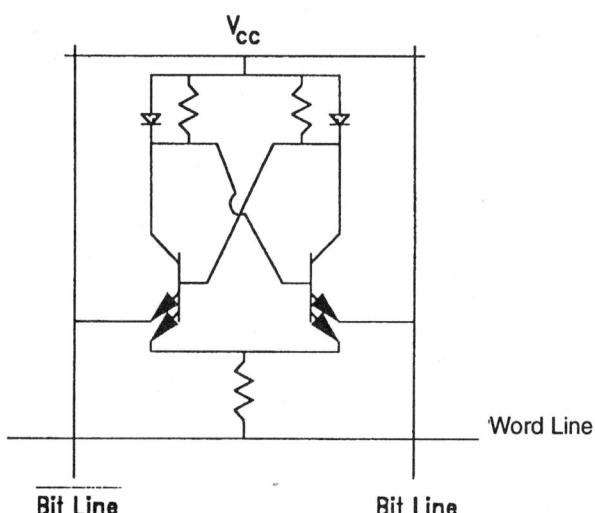

FIG. 9.   Bipolar SRAM cell.

FIG. 10.   Ferrite core memory. (a) schematic of a single memory cell (b) remanence curve of a single ferrite core.

then removed, no change in remanence results. If the current exceeds the threshold value, the remanence can be switched. Remanence can be returned to the original state by passing a current greater than the threshold value in the opposite direction. This threshold behavior can be used to provide a *cross-point* addressing scheme in a core memory. In this case an array of ferrite cores is constructed. Each row of cores has a common wire passing through the cores. This wire is selected by the row decoder. When selected, a current greater than one-half the critical current but less than the critical current flows through the wire. Also, each column of cores has a common wire selected by the column decoder. One column wire will carry a current similar to the selected row wire. Only one core that has both the selected row and column wires passing through it will have a total current passing through the toroid greater than the critical value. Hence, this selected cell is the only one that can switch remanence. The data state of this cell is detected by examining the current flow through the sense line. If the remanence of the core is switched by the select currents, a characteristic signal will be induced on the sense line. Since this read-out is destructive, the memory cell must be rewritten after sensing.

References

1964. Renwick, W. *Digital Storage Systems*. London: SPON.

1986. Chuang, K. et al. "A 1.0ns 5-kbit ECL RAM," *IEEE Journal of Solid-State Circuits* **SC-21** (October), 670–675.

1990. Itoh, Kiyoo, "Trends in Megabit DRAM Circuit Design," *IEEE Journal of Solid-State Circuits* **SC-25**, 778–789.

1991. Yoshinori, O. *et al.* "7ns 4Mb BiCMOS SRAM with Parallel Testing Circuit," *1991 International Solid-State Circuits Conference Digest*, 54.

MATTHEW R. WORDEMAN

AUXILIARY

Auxiliary memory (AM) is distinguished from main memory (MM) by the fact that only from the latter are instructions taken for execution. In most computers, the arithmetic logic unit (ALU - *q.v.*) and MM comprise a carefully designed pair of machine components, matched for speed and data path width. AM comprises all other memories, whose contents (instructions and data) must be fetched into the MM before processing by the ALU.

Most AM is rewritable, i.e. it can be written, read, rewritten; etc. many times without deterioration. Certain types of optical AM is read-only. AM generally uses electromagnetic or optical digital technology for storing data.

There are some nine different types of AMs in use and their variety and number continue to grow:

Magnetic tapes
Cassette tapes
Drums
Floppy disks
Fixed-head hard disks
Moving-head hard disks
Video-recorded cartridges
Large solid-state memories
Optical and laser disks (*see* CD-ROM; and VIDEODISK).

Magnetic Tapes Magnetic tapes are long narrow ribbons (typically 2,400 feet long and 0.5 inch wide) of plastic film coated with iron oxide and wound on hard plastic reels approximately 1 foot in diameter. Information is stored transversely on tape, usually 7 or 9 bits per *frame* (character or byte of data recorded on tape; see Fig. 1). Several frames are consecutively recorded as a *block* of data; blocks are separated by *inter-record gaps* (IRGs), and files of such blocks by inter-file gaps usually called *tape marks*. Newer high-density tapes are recorded in 18-bit frames on chromium-dioxide-coated substrates.

Longitudinally, data is typically stored at one of the following densities: 800, 1,600, or 6,250 bits per inch. Thus, a fully written reel of tape, recorded at 1,600 frames per inch (or, on each track, "bits per inch," normally abbreviated to bpi), contains over 40 million bytes: 2,400 feet by 12 inches/foot by 1,600 bytes/inch = 46,080,000 bytes, although normally inter-record gaps would reduce this by about 1/3. Some newer tapes are recorded at 38,000 bpi.

Data is read from a magnetic tape AM into MM via a *tape drive* depicted in the photo in Fig. 2 and the schematic in Fig. 3. Referring to Fig. 3, the tape is pulled from the supply reel to the take up reel by motors driving the two hubs. These motors operate independently, so that the length of tape between the two reels varies from instant to instant. This permits the takeup reel to accelerate quickly at the start of each read/write (R/W) operation without requiring synchronized acceleration of the supply reel. The interhub strand of tape droops into two vacuum columns in most tape drives, where it is held lightly taut by air-pressure differences. As the loop drops below a vacuum-sensing hold in the takeup column, an electric signal engages the takeup motor with the corresponding reel. The motor disengages as soon as the loop is pulled above a second vacuum-sensing hold. Analogous controls keep a varying-length loop suspended in the supply column.

The foregoing describes *forward* R/W operations; *backward* R/W operations are commonly available on tape drives manufactured since the early 1960s. Supply and takeup reels reverse roles; the two motors are capable of driving the reels in either direction.

Reading and writing are performed by a pair of *heads* (seven to nine transformers) aligned transverse to tape motion. During reading operations, the *write head* is inactive; the *read head* senses the flux produced by electromagnetic spots on the tape as it moves past the transformers. During writing operations, the write head furnishes strong electromagnetic signals at precisely timed instants. Whether the prior content of each frame is logical 0, 1, or "no value" (i.e. blank tape), the write signal creates a new frame of 0s and 1s (predetermined voltage levels). The read head checks newly written data a split second later by reading back the pattern of bits and comparing it to the pattern originally transmitted to the write head. These patterns should be identical; if not, a "write error" signal is sent by the tape drive to the com-

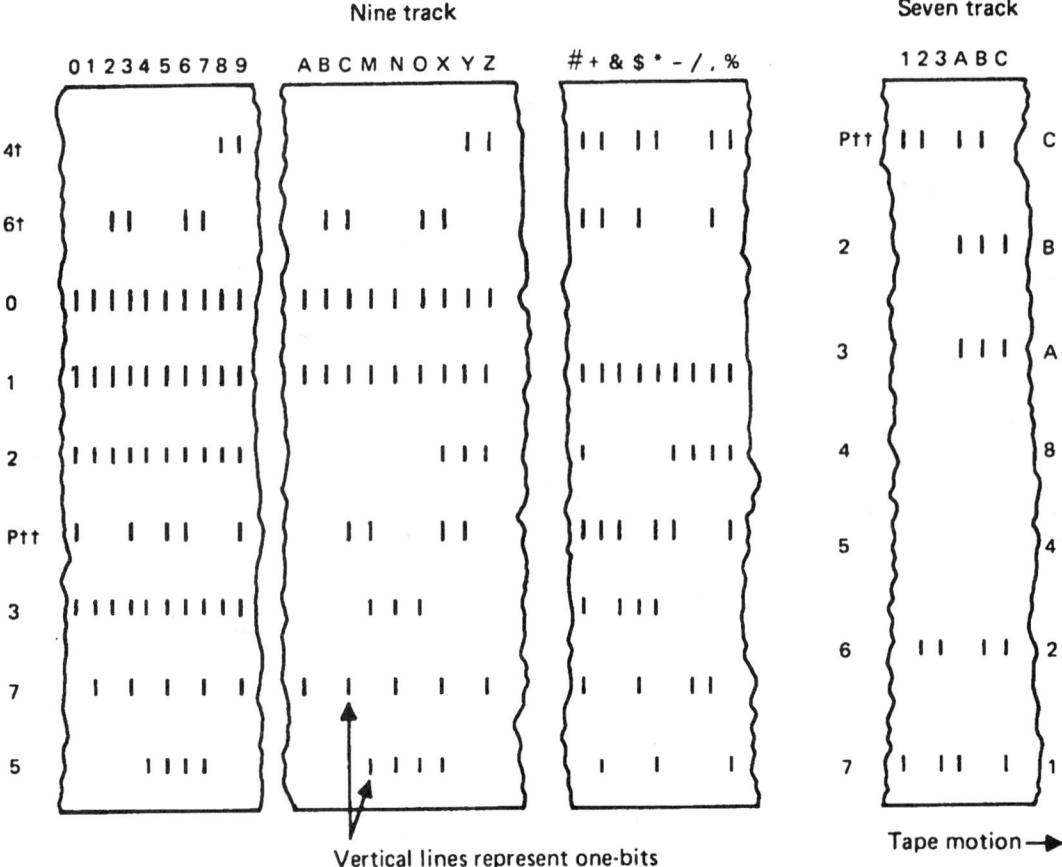

FIG. 1. Nine- and seven-track tape data format. Notes. †Track numbering shows order in which bits are accumulated into bytes (characters); bit 0 is leftmost character and bit 1 is next, etc. Therefore, the character 0 has the bit representation 11110000 on a nine-track tape. ††The parity bit.

puter. Error-retry operations follow, as described in the following paragraphs.

To detect (and, in some advanced tape drives, to permit logical correction of) recording errors, two sets of check bits are written—*parity bits* and *longitudinal check bits* (Fig. 4). One or two parity bits are furnished per frame on almost all tape drives, permitting detection of all *single-bit* errors (substitution of 0 for 1, or *vice versa*). At the end of each block of data, several frames of check bits are written, typically two (with their own parity bits, of course). The *tape subsystem* (one or more drives plus control unit) contains sophisticated checking logic that determines during each R/W operation if all frames have been correctly transmitted to/from the tape. If a parity error is sensed during reading of one or more frames, the subsystem sets an internal latch; when the end of this block is reached, the subsystem sends status bits to the ALU (via an I/O channel) so that rereading may be attempted.

Two different approaches to formatting and using magnetic tape data are prevalent, exemplified by tape drives furnished by IBM and DEC. IBM-compatible drives create variable-length blocks and cannot be updated/overwritten in place; DECTAPE drives create fixed-length blocks that can be updated/overwritten with new infor-

mation. To update a tape file using an IBM-compatible system, the old master file must be completely copied onto a new master file, with transaction data merged in as appropriate. With DECTAPE drives, the master file need only be spaced forward to blocks requiring updating. In this respect, DECTAPE drives can be used like direct-access devices (see next section). However, it is often desirable in commercial data processing (and certain scientific applications) to continually create backup copies of tape master files. In such environments, recopying required by IBM-compatible drives is consistent with local data security practices. The old master file is called the "parent," the new master file the "child"; when the next updating is performed, a new generation of this file is created; the "parent" file becomes the "grandparent," the "child" becomes the "parent," etc. Often, 30 or more generations are kept for vital corporate master files; e.g. daily updatings for a month.

Typical Usage Until the early 1960s, magnetic tape was the prevalent AM for scientific and commercial data processing; direct-access devices were used only for executable programs and data (e.g. drums on the IBM 650 and Burroughs 205 computers), or for on-line real-time applications, such as inventory control and satellite monitor-

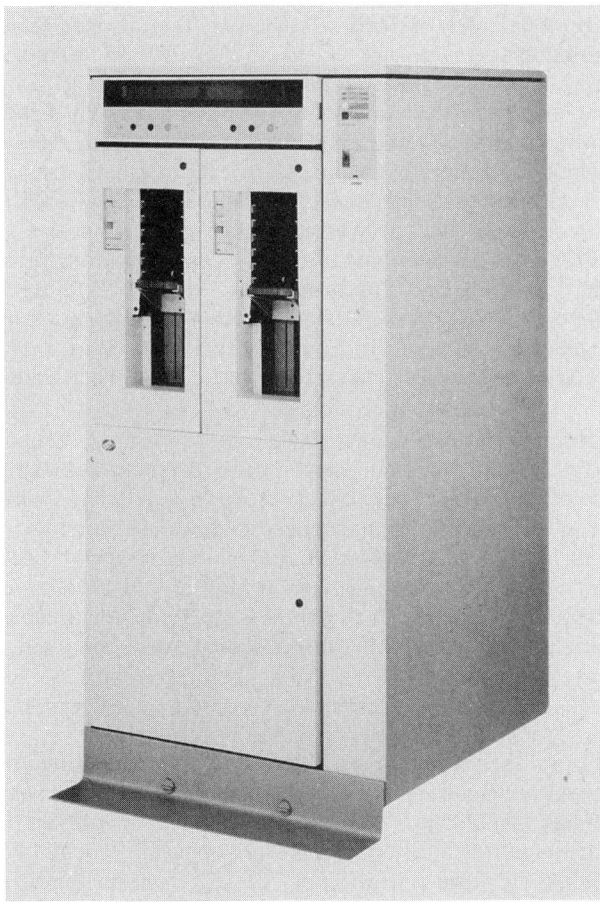

FIG. 2. An IBM 3490 magnetic tape unit.

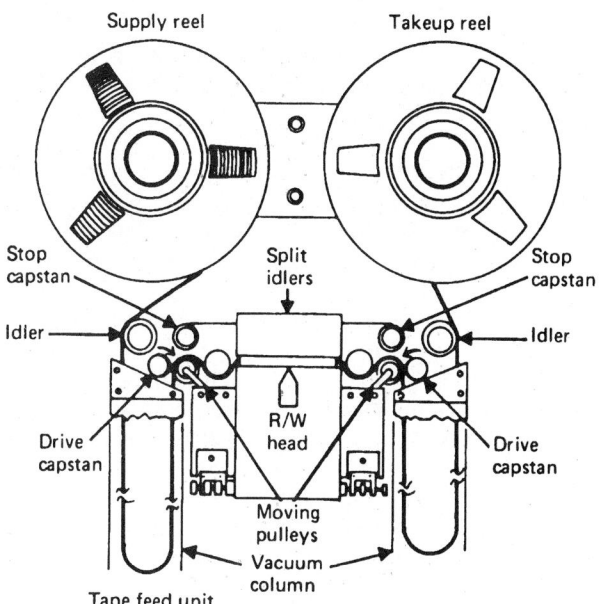

FIG. 3. Tape-drive schematic.

ing. From 1963 to 1968, many sequentially stored files were transferred from magnetic tape to direct-access devices. Allocated to tape drives on second-generation computers, *scratch files* (*q.v.*) (intermediate storage required by compilers, sort and utility programs, and application programs) were typically allocated to disk and drum devices on third-generation computers.

Nonetheless, magnetic tape drives are found on most third-generation systems (and their successors), where they fulfill the following roles:

1. Retention of low- and medium-activity master files. Common practice is that "high activity" files are accessed over 300 times annually, "medium activity" files at least 50 times, "low activity" files less than 50.
2. Backup of direct-access device contents (1–3 reels are required to back up each disk pack containing 20–100 million bytes).
3. Initial capture of key-entered data and its subsequent presentation for computer processing. Floppy disks are replacing magnetic tapes and cassette tapes for most data-capture functions nowadays.
4. Interchange of data among computer installations by courier or mail service.

Magnetic tape is one of the cheapest ways to store machine-readable information indefinitely, and it is far more compact than punched cards or paper records, tradition-

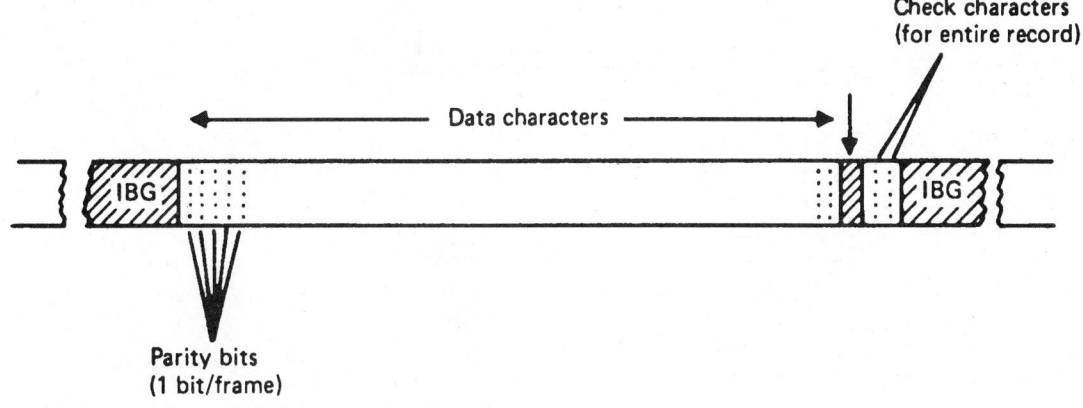

FIG. 4. Data and checking bits for typical magnetic tapes.

ally used for data archives. Many medium-sized businesses have vaults containing a thousand or more tape reels; a large insurance company may store over 50,000 reels.

Cassette Tapes The preceding section described magnetic tapes created and used primarily *within* computing centers. Cassette tapes are increasingly used for data originating *outside* computing centers, as follows:

1. *Acquisition of data from laboratory instruments*— Analog voltages are digitized and written onto a cassette. Paper tape punches have performed data acquisition for decades; cassette and floppy disk devices have generally displaced paper tape for these functions.
2. *Cash register, gasoline, credit card, and other retailing applications.*—Some cassette-oriented devices are small and light enough to be hand-held.

Typically, cassette tapes are 1/4-inch wide and store 10^5 characters, in contrast to full-sized tapes, which are 1/2-inch wide and store $10^6 - 10^9$ characters. Many minicomputers and some full-sized third-generation computers use cassette drives as supplemental I/O devices. For many minicomputers used in data acquisition environments, cassette tapes are often the principal AM, used both to load programs into MM and to capture data. On other computers, cassette readers serve primarily for original entry of data. Cassette drives are often installed on terminals, serving as a local data-capture AM. After all data are on the cassette, the user dials up a computer and transmits cassette contents through the terminal-computer link.

Cassette reels should not be confused with short-length reels of conventional computer tape; some of the latter are only 5 inches in diameter and wind 50–200 feet of 1/2-inch tape.

Direct-Access Devices Drums, hard disks, floppy disks, video-recorded cartridges, and optical/laser disks

are collectively termed *direct-access* (DA) devices (also sometimes *random-access devices*), for their ability to access blocks of data at random without sequentially passing over a major portion of their contents. Thus, DA devices can be contrasted with magnetic tape drives, which are generally cost-ineffective for random retrieval of data (but see the preceding discussion of DECTAPE). DA devices cannot access individual words as fast as MM devices, the former having access times in the range 5×10^{-3} seconds and the latter in the range 10^{-8} to 10^{-6} seconds. Most DA devices are suitable for software storage; video-recorded storages, however, have undesirably long random-access characteristics for system software.

Drums The earliest DA devices were magnetic drums (Fig. 5), built since the early 1950s by a number of major manufacturers. A cobalt-nickel substrate is coated with iron oxide, which is magnetized and sensed much as in magnetic-tape operations. Drums are typically 8–20 inches in diameter, 2–4 feet in length, and revolve at 1,500–4,000 rpm. Each character is stored on one or more tracks circumferentially, blocks of characters being separated by inter-record gaps of several thousandths of an inch. Densities of 4,000 bpi are commonplace, yielding R/W rates of 1–3 million characters per second.

As with magnetic tape, two types of formatting are possible: *fixed-length blocks* (often called *sectors*) and *variable-length blocks*. With either format—and in contrast to conventional magnetic tape—it is possible to update blocks in place (i.e. without copying their contents to another part of the device). This facility is vital to the updating activities commonly performed during random retrievals from master files. In fact, all AMs except certain magnetic tapes and the photocopy/laser-holography devices permit updating in place.

Drums hold considerably less data than do disks, magnetic tapes, etc. However, they can access blocks of data at random more quickly than other DA devices, 5–8 ms on the average. Since a drum is a narrow cylinder, its typical rotational speed of 3,600 rpm is considerably higher than that of disk drives, typically 2,400 rpm. A

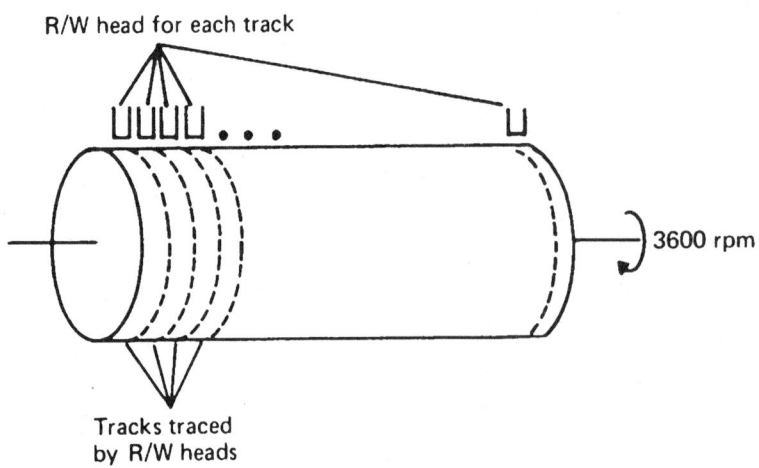

FIG. 5. Magnetic drum.

speed of 3,600 rpm means an average rotational time of 16.7 ms. This compares to 12–80 ms for disk drives. Therefore, drums have typically been used for the following functions:

1. Prior to the development of magnetic-core memories in the mid-1950s, drums were used as MMs (e.g. on the IBM 650 and Burroughs 205 computers).
2. Thereafter, frequently needed software (interjob monitors, portions of the I/O-error and program error supervisors, compilers and sort programs, etc.) has been stored permanently on drums. Since drum storage is *nonvolatile*—electric power can be turned off and on without disturbing its contents—it is well suited for permanent storage of continually used software.
3. High-activity scratch files for the operating system, compilers, and other software are often allocated to drums.
4. Backing storage for virtual-memory (VM) machines has been a major role for drums since the Ferranti Atlas systems of the late 1950s. Thousand-word blocks of MM contents are shuttled to/from drums by the VM control program.
5. In many airborne computers (and similar high-stress environments), drums are used for MMs, or AMs because of their high reliability, insensitivity to sudden force changes, and relatively light weight and small bulk.

Disks Two major varieties of disk drives are widely used:

Fixed-head, multiple-platter (Fig. 6)

Although their geometry is considerably different from that of drums, fixed-head (FH) disks (Fig. 6) have comparable access times and transfer rates and greater storage capacity—up to a gigabyte.

Each FH drive contains several steel platters coated with iron oxide aligned vertically on a common spindle. R/W heads extend between the platters, facing up and down from the *comb* suspending the heads and containing signal cables. Since there is a head for each track, the only delay in accessing a data block is due to *rotational latency* (0–15 ms required for the block to revolve beneath the corresponding R/W head). Although track *lengths* vary linearly with distance from the spindle, R/W heads are calibrated in such a way that track capacities are all identical. Therefore, there is a universal transfer rate for data, whether read from inner or outer tracks. The average delay for reading a random block is half the maximum rotational latency, although recent hardware/software developments in *rotational position sensing* (RPS) considerably reduce inefficiencies caused by I/O, as follows.

The I/O supervisor keeps the queue of disk requests (i.e. R/W operations pending for one or more programs) ordered by angular displacement from an *index point,* a universal logical origin for the tracks. Index points for all platters are vertically aligned (Fig. 7). As each R/W operation terminates, the I/O supervisor searches its queue for the nearest request in terms of angular position. This request may reference any track in the FH file, not necessarily that from which the preceding block was read. If N requests are enqueued with uniformly distributed angular displacements—a reasonable assumption for most

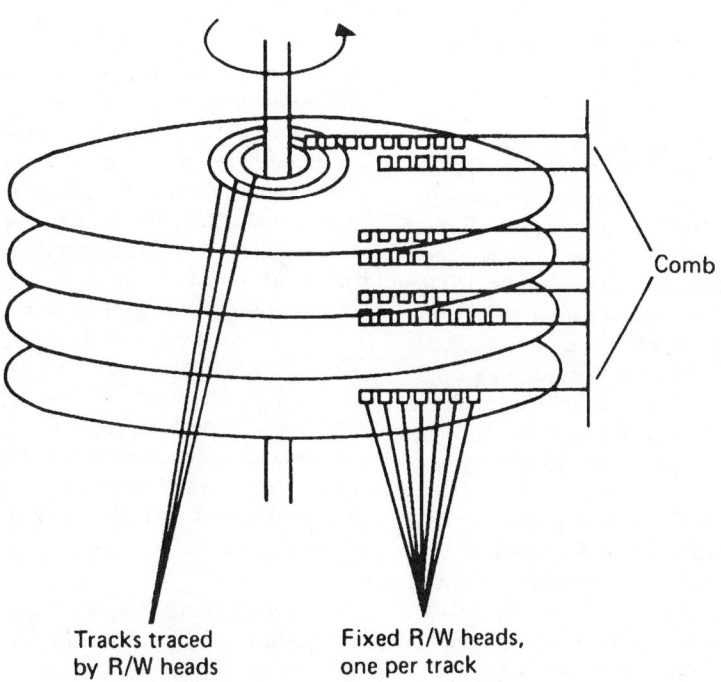

Tracks traced by R/W heads   Fixed R/W heads, one per track

FIG. 6. Fixed-head disk drive.

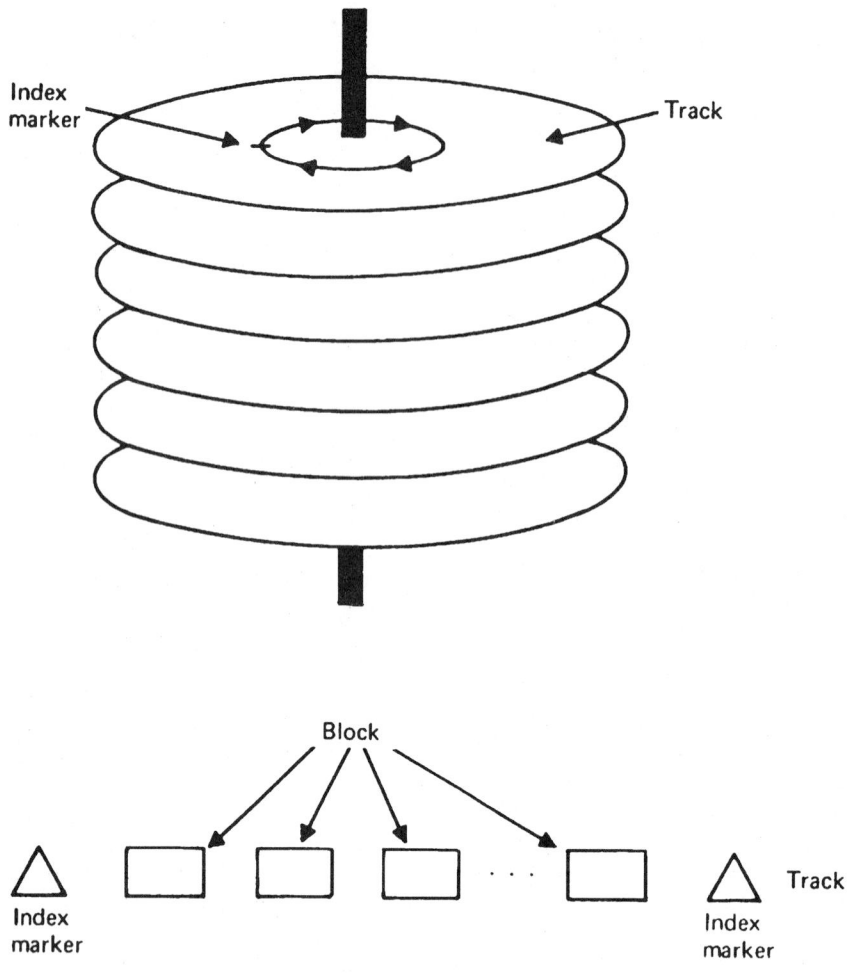

FIG. 7. Track format for disk storage.

computer environments—the average *interoperation latency* is only $(1/(N + 1)) \times$ (max. latency).

Moving head

Since only two heads and associated electronics are required per platter, moving-head (MH) drives are considerably cheaper to build than FH drives, although the former require sophisticated servomechanisms to move their read/write heads over the platters. Per-character cost for MH storage is typically 10–15% of the cost for FH storage. Some MH drives permit removal of their disk-and-spindle socket assemblies: *a disk cartridge* in the case of a single platter, a *disk pack* in the case of multiple platters. An installation can store an indefinite number of cartridges/packs off line to be mounted as required by various applications programs.

The *Winchester architecture* for disk packs has now superseded most conventional disk-and-spindle socket assemblies (*see* HARD DISK). Winchester drives (derived from IBM's pre- announcement product name) do not themselves contain R/W heads, the latter being manufactured together with the platters they access: *Winchester modules.* Winchester drives with the highest storage capacities (3×10^8 to 12×10^8 bytes) do not have removable

modules; small Winchester drives permit shelf storage and mounting of the modules, although the latter are considerably more expensive than conventional disk packs.

Most batch-processing installations with MH drives designate one subset as *resident* (also called *permanently mounted*, although this is a logical designation rather than a physical attribute), containing the operating system, scratch storage, and frequently referenced data files. Another subset of drives is designated *mountable*, where cartridges/packs are set up as required.

Most on-line installations (i.e. devoted to real-time and telecommunications applications) keep cartridges/packs resident, since data requests originate unpredictably and generally require responses within a few seconds (or milliseconds), too short for a computer operator to retrieve and mount an off-line cartridge/pack. Moving-head drives may be either single platter or multiple platter.

Moving Head Single Platter (MHSP) This type is shown in Fig. 8. Typically, the *fork* (two-tined comb) contains two R/W heads; it is inserted/withdrawn radially according to the track address furnished with each I/O request.

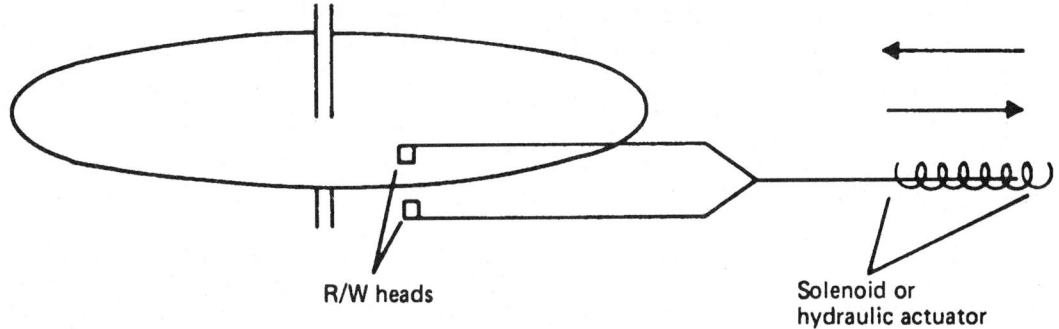

FIG. 8.   Moving-head single-platter drive.

Moving Head Multiple Platter (MHMP) The MHMP (Fig. 9) drives generalize the MHSP type, with combs containing *2P-2* heads, *P* being the number of platters. (The top surface of the top platter and bottom surface of the bottom platter are not used on MHMP packs, since they are much more exposed to scratches and dust contamination than are interior surfaces.) Widely used drives have $P = 6$ or 11, corresponding to pack capacities of approximately 50×10^6 and $100 - 1,200 \times 10^6$ characters. (The wide range of the latter figure is due to recent doublings of both radial and circumferential bit densities.)

After optical/laser disks, MHMP drives have the largest capacity of all hard-surface DA devices. Floppy disks, tapes, and video-recorded cartridges have flexible substrates and hence an inherently higher error rate—both *hard errors* (unrecoverable errors), where a small recording area becomes permanently defective, and *soft errors,* where rereading or rewriting successfully brushes off (or avoids) small oxide flecks. Hard-surface devices may operate for weeks or months without experiencing hard or soft errors—especially FH and Winchester drives, which

have an air-sealed environment, in contrast to non-Winchester MH drives, in which cartridges/packs are exposed to dust during handling and off-line storage.

From 4–100 MHMP drives are installed in most third-generation installations performing scientific and business data processing. Large installations oriented to on-line operations, such as air traffic control and real-time inventory, often have over one hundred drives. Growth in their usage was rapid between second-generation (1962) and third-generation (1968) computers. As operating systems evolved toward more comprehensive control of programs and data during this period, they made increasing use of program and data *libraries,* accessed through catalogs, directories, and indices. For most third-generation systems, catalogs and directories were stored exclusively on DA devices, generally disks and drums. Increasingly, libraries themselves are being stored on disk drives, to take advantage of their superior transfer rates, random access, and reliability versus soft-surface AMs.

Soft-Surface DA Devices   Floppy disks (also called *diskettes*), video-recorded cartridges, and similar devices

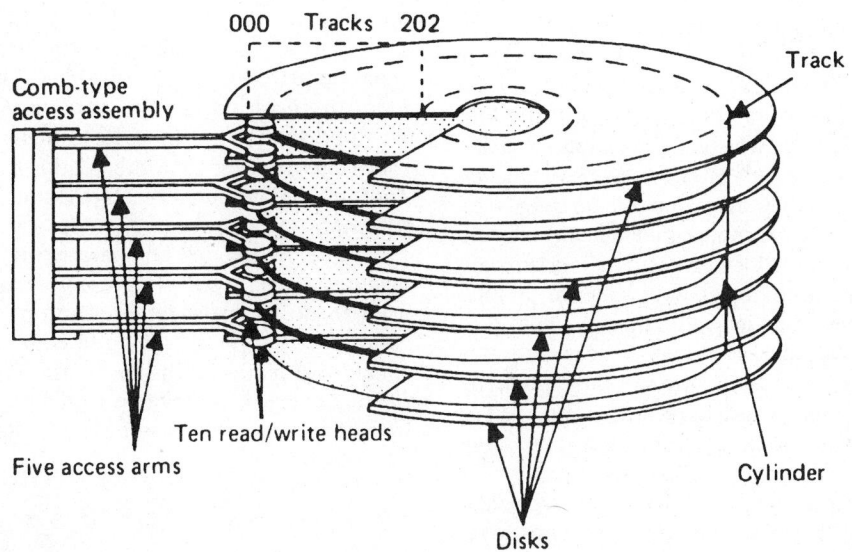

FIG. 9.   Moving-head multiple-platter drive.

TABLE 1. Typical Capacity, Speed, and Cost of Memory Devices

Memory	Device Cost ($ per Megabyte)	Capacity (Megabytes)	Random Access Time (Milliseconds)	Transfer Rate (Megabytes/sec)
Main (mainframe)	2,000	20	.0001	100
Main (micro)	200	8	.0004	25
Drum	10,000	4	5	2
FH disk drive	2,000	10	10	2
MHSP (mainframe)	200	100	100	.10
MHMP (mainframe)	40	400	10	1
Hard disk (micro)	5	100	100	.25
Floppy disk (micro)	200	1	200	.05
High-density floppy	50	20	100	.50
MSS	4	100,000	8,000	.80
Videodisc*	1.5	1,000	1,000	.20
CD-ROM*	1	650	500	.15
EO (erasable optical)	8	600	500	.20
WORM drive	6	800	500	.20
Magnetic tape drive	10	1000	—	1
Cassette tape drive	50	1	—	.001

*Read-only

compete against MH disk drives for selected application areas. *Floppy disks* are structurally similar to MHSP hard-surface disk drives, except that their recording medium is a flexible plastic substrate—3 1/2, 5 1/4 or 8 inches in diameter—coated with iron oxide. Information is recorded and read back just as for an MHSP hard-surface drive. Unlike the latter, a floppy disk can be easily handled (within its protective cardboard jacket) and even sent through the mails without extraordinary protective wrapping. Floppy disks are inexpensive, less than a dollar per mid-size diskette (5 1/4-inch diameter), each of which can hold approximately one million characters. Smaller diskettes (3 1/2 inches in diameter) which store either 700 kilobytes or 1.44 megabytes have become the *de facto* standard but they are not "floppies," externally at least, since their recording surface is enclosed in hard plastic.

During the 1970s, several manufactures developed *mass storage systems:* Trillion-bit (terabit) storage devices based on reels, cartridges, or cassettes of videotape or wide magnetic tape. In late 1974, marketing of these MSS devices to commercial users commenced with the IBM 3850 Mass Storage System, whose on-line capacity is 50–500 billion bytes $(0.4–4 \times 10^{12}$ bits). A mass storage system typically has a large magazine of cartridges or cassettes from which a transport mechanism extracts requested units. Each cartridge or cassette contains approximately 50 million bytes, comparable to a fully packed reel of conventional magnetic tape. A full MSS of this type contains 500–5,000 cartridges or cassettes, together with transports and read/write stations. Often, the transports and R/W stations are duplexed or triplexed to assure continuity of operation should one of these complex electromechanical devices malfunction.

The dominant trend in MSS design is toward *virtual direct access storage* whereby data are automatically retrieved at the start of a batch job and transcribed onto a conventional MH disk drive. The MSS performs this transcription (*staging*) asynchronously with respect to other computing on the host computer. It utilizes neither the main memory nor CPU power of the host, since the MSS controller contains one or more minicomputers and its own memory. The principal interface of the MSS to the host computer is through disk storage controllers. Via the latter, the host computer and the MSS alternatively read and write to the same disk drives. This provides to the host computer an on-line database whose unit storage cost is comparable to conventional magnetic tape, but whose accessibility—after transcription to disk—is approximately the same as for a 100-megabyte disk drive (8.4 milliseconds average sequential access time, transfer rate exceeding 800KB).

Average random access time to MSS units is 10–20 seconds. However, this delay is essentially invisible to the host computer, since MSS devices are not generally used for servicing on-line transactions submitted to the host.

CD-ROM and Videodisc memories are discussed in separate articles with those titles. These are read-only AMs, prerecorded by the vendor. A variant called a WORM drive (Write Once, Read Many times) allows the user (once) rather than the vendor to do the recording. Another variant, an Erasable Optical (EO) drive, is a true AM.

Table 1 provides comparative data for the various memory types, also giving cost/benefit comparisons of using these memories for large and small computer applications. Costs per megabyte in column two include reasonable estimates for the cost of the supporting drive. For AM that comes in removable segments, the cost per megabyte of a segment itself would be far less.

DAVID N. FREEMAN

MEMORY ADDRESSING. *See* ADDRESSING.

MEMORY ALLOCATION. *See* STORAGE ALLOCATION.

MEMORY MANAGEMENT

For articles on related subjects *see* CACHE MEMORY; DATA TYPE; DATABASE MANAGEMENT SYSTEM; GARBAGE COLLECTION; LIST PROCESSING; OPERATING SYSTEMS; POINTER; STACK; STORAGE HIERARCHY; STORAGE ORGANIZATION; VIRTUAL MEMORY; and WORKING SET.

Memory management is concerned with the organization of the storage in which data is placed in a computer and with the identification and enforcement of the rules for interpreting and assigning meaning to the bits in the storage. Thus, it is closely related to database management. While there is no agreed division, the principle differences are that database management is concerned with data of longer persistence (that is, the data exists for more than the execution time of one program), shared data, and data design in the context of planning large-scale systems, whereas memory management is primarily concerned with data used within a program for periods up to the duration of the program's execution. Since some of this data may have been obtained from sources outside the program, or may be left in a database, the two regimes interact closely, and the distinction may be unhelpful, though it is often enforced in current implementation environments.

Since data is not of use unless it can be manipulated, memory management interacts strongly with programming languages. Most languages provide some space allocation to hold the values of variables, as well as the values that are *dereferenced*, which are held in an area, called a *heap*, with a particular data management regime. Programming languages have also developed the notion of *type* to identify the interpretation of the data bits, and of *strong typing* to ensure that operations on the data are consistent with its type declaration. Further development of this aspect of data management has occurred in providing facilities to define types, leading to comprehensive definition facilities, such as Simula classes (*q.v.*) and abstract data types.

Languages with modern type systems: Quest, Modula-3, Napier-88, and Oberon, for example, require very sophisticated implicit data management. Particular problems are the representation of multiple inheritance structures and other values of polymorphic type. Languages with higher order functions: Lisp, Miranda, Quest, Napier-88, etc., require complex memory management to represent environments.

Requirements for Storage Regimes

A Discipline of Interpretation If one is working in a language that does not provide or enforce data types, then it is necessary for the programmer to adopt some such discipline. But whether the discipline is adopted or enforced, it remains necessary for the programmer to manage the provision of storage space (i.e. to adopt a *storage regime*).

Programming languages have supported the provision of storage space by using one of two policies. *Static allocation* is a policy in which the provision of space is determined at compilation time. Fortran is a language adopting this policy. If the programmer requires space to be allocated in ways that change as the computation progresses, then routines must be written that administer a policy within one of the statically allocated spaces. *Dynamic allocation* is a policy in which the provision of space is linked to the progress of a computation. The language Algol 68 (*q.v.*) and its derivations adopt this strategy. For example, they use a stack allocation scheme (see below) to provide local variables.

Dynamic storage regimes may be categorized by the demands made upon them both by the objects stored and by the sequences of operations by which space is claimed and freed. The space required by an object to be stored is called a *cell*. A cell is, therefore, a contiguous sequence of words or bytes in the computer memory. The cells may be of only one size, of a variety of sizes, or of varying size (i.e. an object once stored may change its size). The interaction of claims on and return of space gives rise to the following patterns of demand.

1. The space may be claimed by successive demands and then all relinquished.
2. The space may be claimed by successive demands and be explicitly returned in reverse order, or in blocks that are subsequences of the original claims in reverse order.
3. The space may be claimed by a sequence of demands and returned in random order.
4. The space may be claimed in sequence, and no space is explicitly returned, but the storage management algorithm is expected to discover (from time to time) which space is now unreachable and retrieve that space for reuse.

A Stack Regime for Space Allocation With a constant size or a variety of sizes, and with demand patterns (1) and (2) above, a space allocation strategy is straightforward. The total area of space available for allocation is viewed as a sequence of cells. A pointer records a position in this space indicating the start of the *next* place to allocate—the free cell. On making an allocation, the value of the pointer is returned as the address of the new cell, and the pointer is moved on, by the length of the space allocated, to the remaining cells. Such a scheme is shown in Fig. 1.

Such a regime is simple to implement and reasonably fast to operate. It is the basic strategy normally provided in Pascal, for example. If space is relinquished in the reverse order from which it is claimed, noting the return of space is achieved merely by subtracting from *next* the size of the space returned. For safe operation, the correct size of the returned space must be available.

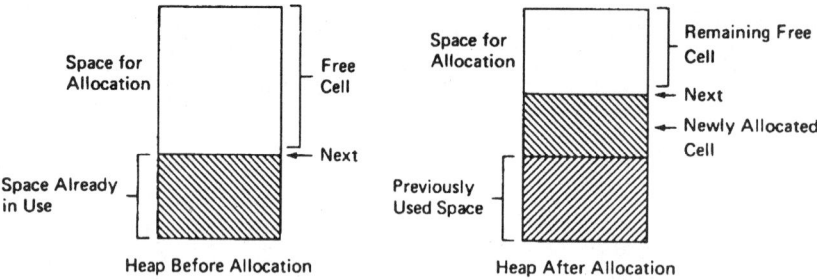

FIG. 1. The operation of a stack regime.

Blocked Return of Space Where the space is provided in blocks to be returned in the reverse order, the value of *next* may be recorded with the block. When the block is returned, *next* is reset to that recorded value. Such a strategy is used in many Pascal implementations, and is the normal way of allocating space for local variables in block-structured languages not supporting higher order functions.

Regimes for Handling Random Return of Space When demand is interspersed with return in some random sequence—case (3) above—then different strategies are appropriate, depending on whether or not all the cells are of the same size. In either case, a list (or some more complex structure that is faster to search) is kept of all the cells available for issue. When a cell is returned, it is added to the list. This list is called the *free list* or, sometimes, the *list of available space*. If all cells are the same size, when a cell is requested, the first one on the list is allocated.

In Pascal and other languages that support pointer-based objects, data memory is divided dynamically into three regions. Local variables are allocated on a stack that grows (and recedes) from one end of memory, and data *nodes* that comprise linked structures are allocated from the other. The collection of allocated nodes is called the *heap*; thus, available space at any given time is just the region that lies between the stack and the heap.

Strategies for Choosing the Best Cell to Allocate When the cells vary in size, it is likely that the first cell in the list will not be large enough, or will not be the optimum one to allocate. Thus problem arises both in compiler construction (*q.v.*), where the cells are interrelated nodes of pointer-based data structures, and in operating systems (*q.v.*), where the "cells" are the respective blocks of unrelated processes (programs) being managed by the system. Many algorithms are known for performing cell allocation. In choosing one, it is necessary to choose a suitable compromise between the computational cost of finding the cell and the optimality of the cell found. The optimality depends on the rate of *fragmentation*; that is, on the proportion of small cells generated that are not contiguous and therefore cannot be amalgamated and that are too small to be useful. Three examples of this compromise are presented.

The Best Fit Strategy The best fit algorithm requires a search of all cells available for allocation until one is found that is the correct size or is the smallest that is sufficiently large. When a cell is returned, it is placed at the start of the free list. These operations are shown in Fig. 2. It is possible to introduce more complex structures to hold the free list, such as a tree, a sorted list, or many lists corresponding to defined ranges of cell size. Such structures accelerate the search for the optimum cell, but increase the cost of returning a cell. In the example cells of Fig. 2(a), *B*, *A*, *C*, and *D* form the free list. If a cell of size 3 were requested, cell *D* would be allocated after a search of the entire free list.

Suppose that a cell is now returned consisting of the four words between *C* and *B*. Then the system could coalesce *B*, *E*, and *C*, as shown in Fig. 2(b), into a single cell. However, since the algorithm to coalesce cells is usually expensive to run, some systems do not implement it.

The First Fit Strategy The first fit algorithm scans the list and allocates the first cell that is large enough, retaining the fragment left over. This takes minimal computation, but may promote fragmentation (though the fragments produced may be large enough to be useful). Return of cells is similar to best fit. The operations involved in allocating a cell are shown in Fig. 3.

The Buddy System Strategy The buddy system is based on the hypothesis that the sizes of cells requested are not random, but that, if a cell is requested, it is likely that other cells of that size will also be requested. It also takes advantage of the binary form of addresses to reduce the cost of coalescing returned cells with their neighbors. Separate lists are maintained for cells of each size that is a power of two; i.e. 1, 2, 4, 8, etc. When a request is made, the next larger power of two is the size of the space actually allocated. This results in some internal waste. If the list of cells of this size is empty, a cell from a list of double that size is split, and so on. Minimal searching is needed to allocate space. This allocation process is illustrated in Fig. 4.

On return of a cell, it may be coalesced with its neighbor, if that is also free, using an efficient algorithm. Only cells of the same size need be considered. It is possible to compute the address of the neighboring cell of the same size without a search, since the addresses of

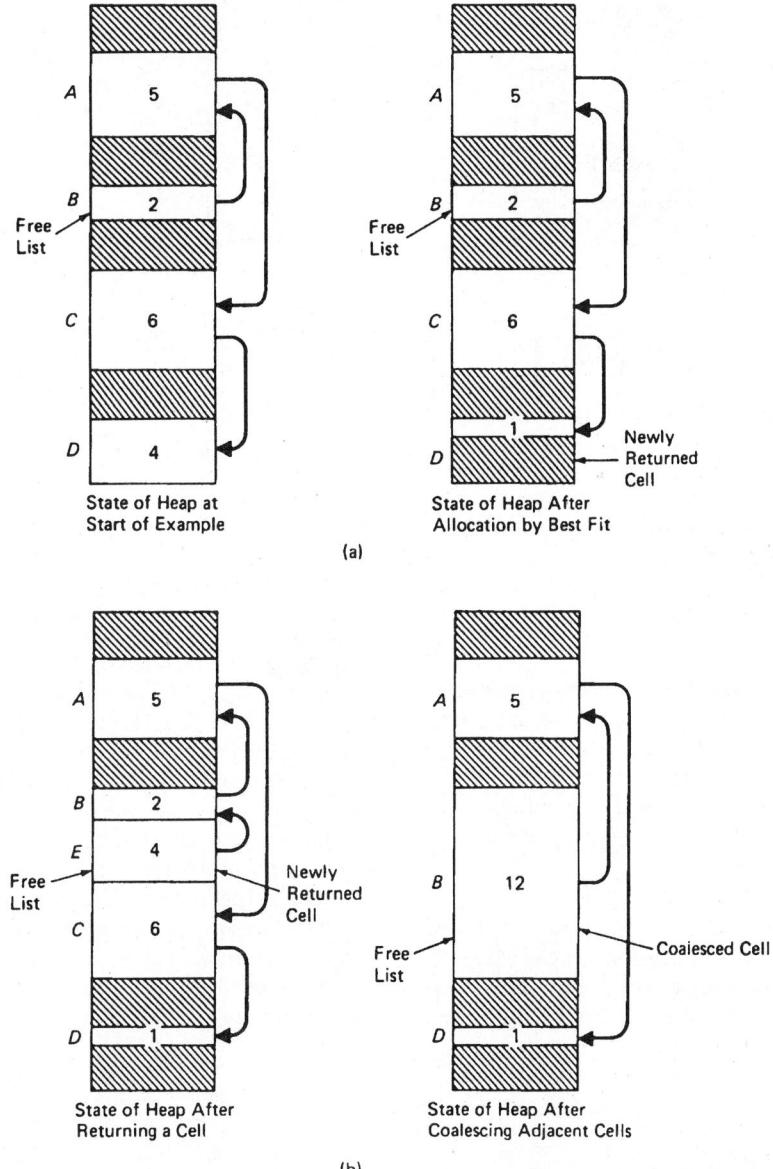

State of Heap at
Start of Example

State of Heap After
Allocation by Best Fit

(a)

State of Heap After
Returning a Cell

State of Heap After
Coalescing Adjacent Cells

(b)

FIG. 2. The operation of a best fit strategy.

the two cells will differ by only one bit. If that cell is marked free, the list pointers in the cell can then be used to remove the cell and join it to the returned cell. (Using a doubly-linked list for the free list makes this removal easier.) If a pair of cells is coalesced, the new cell formed is then considered for coalescing with the cells of its own size, and so on. Fig. 5 shows the return of a cell that causes buddy cells to coalesce twice.

Garbage Collection to Form the Free List

When storage space is not explicitly returned, then, if the free list becomes empty (or does not contain a cell large enough to meet the current request), it is necessary to gather up the space that is no longer accessible to the program. To do this, all the accessible space is found and marked. The unmarked space can then be assembled into a new free list. This process is called *garbage collection*. It

is necessary to know all the places in the program that may refer to data, and to follow those references to mark the accessible data. If the data itself may contain further references to other data, a scanning and searching algorithm is required. Such a search is only possible if there is a reliable type discipline so that the location of all references is known. Note that the criteria for invoking garbage collection may be different in a virtual memory system.

Compaction When the new list has been formed, it may be used for allocation as before. However, it is possible that the space collected is large enough to satisfy a request, but not contiguous. It is then necessary to shuffle the data in use to make contiguous space. This process is known as *compaction*, and may be computationally ex-

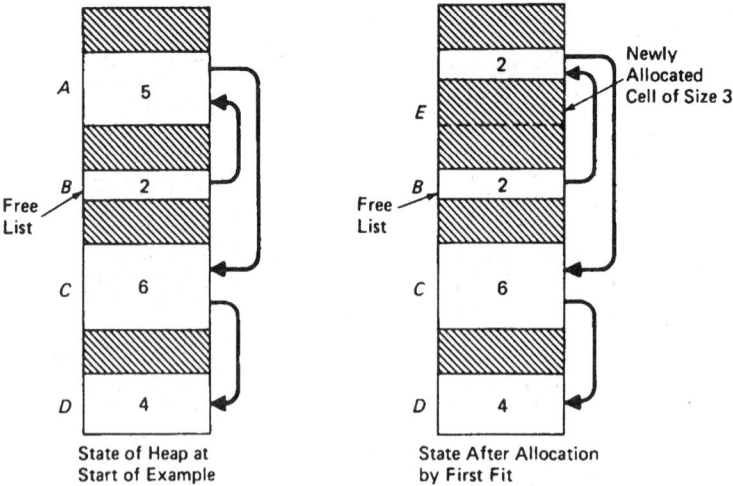

FIG. 3. The operation of a first fit strategy.

pensive, as it is necessary to adjust all the references to refer to the new locations.

Some systems reclaim space, performing garbage collection and compaction by copying to a new space. These are called *semi-space* algorithms. A refinement of these are the *generation-based* algorithms. Recently, incremental and concurrent data management algorithms have been developed to avoid processing pauses using large stores.

Storage for Varying Size Objects The problem of providing for data cells that vary in size during use is more complex. One approach is to divide them into a linked list of fixed size fragments, since to allow them to change size

in situ is expensive, as it involves similar reference adjustment costs to compaction. An alternative is to arrange that all references to cells be indirect; for example, by a page and line number. The allocatable space is then divided into pages. At the beginning of each page is a set of "line pointers" which refer to the start of the data object corresponding to that line. As objects grow or shrink, the line parameters are adjusted accordingly. Thus, compaction within a page involves adjusting only the affected line pointers on that page and hence is of reasonable cost. The overheads are the space taken by line pointers, the cost of following them, and some extra fragmentation (the wastage left unused on each page). This technique, shown in Fig. 6, is used in many database systems.

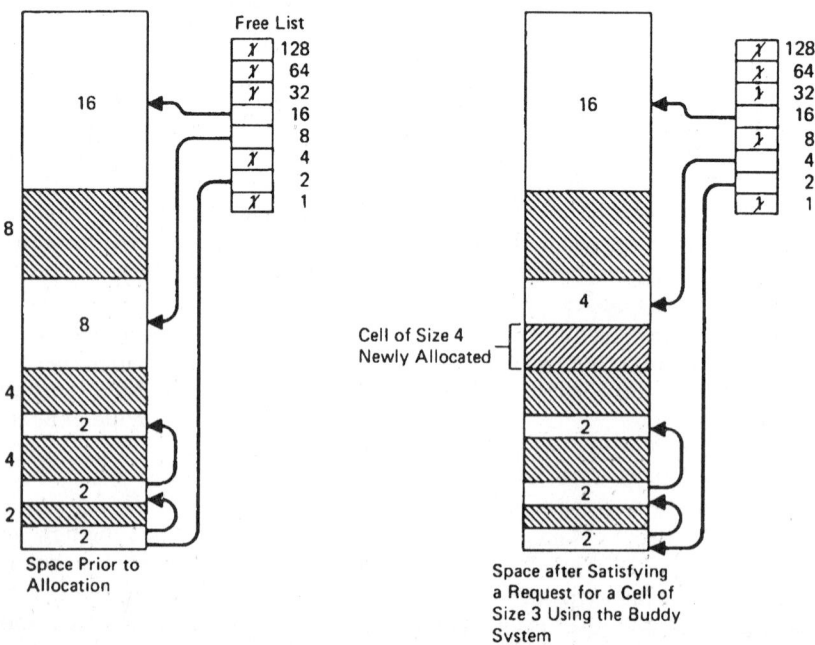

FIG. 4. Space allocation using the buddy system.

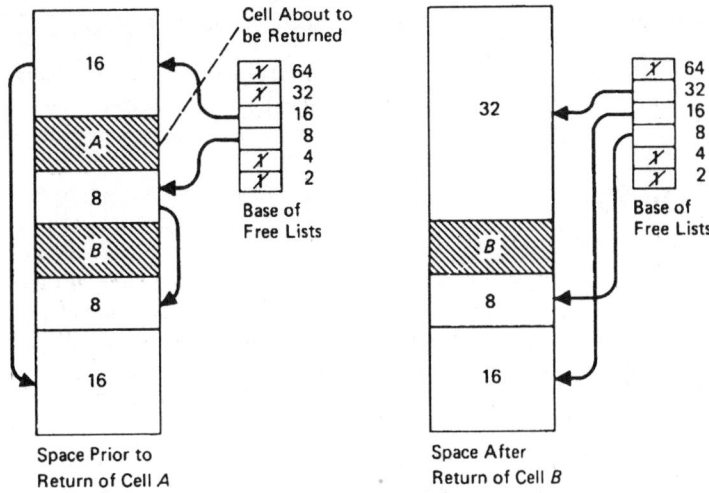

FIG. 5. Return of a cell in the buddy system.

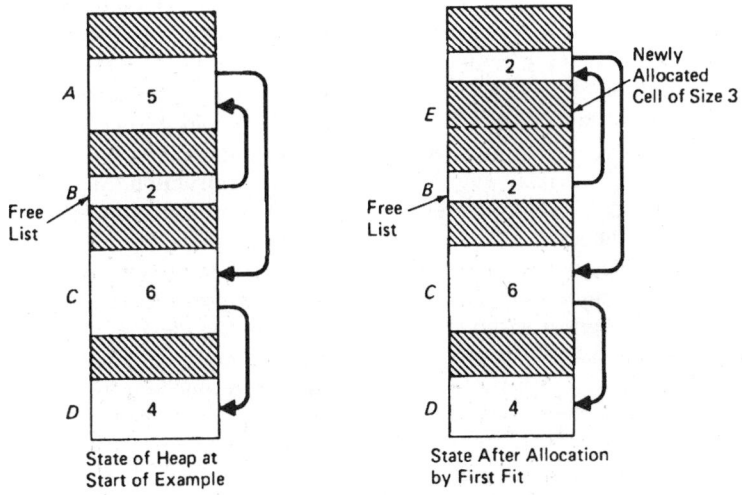

FIG. 6. Organization of a page to allow varying sized objects.

Trends in Data Management As the cost of memory is decreasing and the power of processors is increasing, the volume of data to be managed is increasing substantially, but the compromises which have to be made using the available algorithms remain fundamentally the same. With the increasing predominance of interactive computing, the unpredictable delays of garbage collection become less acceptable. This has led to experiments in concurrent garbage collection, and to an increased use of the page-based structures which permit incremental space management. Some language machines have been built which perform all the operations of space management using hardware.

With respect to the IBM-PC and PC compatibles (*q.v.*), *memory management* has come to be associated with software that helps the operating system and applications programs cope with three different classes of main memory, that lying in the address space below 640K, that

lying between 640K and 1MB (*expanded memory*) and that lying above 1MB (*extended memory*).

References

1972. Knuth, D. E. *The Art of Computer Programming* **1**: *Fundamental Algorithms*. Reading, MA: Addison-Wesley, Section 2.5.

1977. Wiederhold, G. *Database Design*. New York: McGraw-Hill.

1978. Gotlieb, C. C. and Gotlieb, L. R. *Data Types and Structures*. Englewood Cliffs, N. J.: Prentice-Hall.

1978. Coleman, D. *A Structured Programming Approach to Data*. New York: MacMillan.

1983. Henry Lieberman and Carl Hewitt. "A Real-time Garbage Collector Based on the Lifetimes of Objects." *Communications of the ACM*, **26**, 6: 419–429; (June).

1984. David Ungar. "Generation Scavenging: A Non-disruptive High Performance Storage Reclamation Algorithm." *ACM SIGPLAN Notices*, **19**, 5 (May).

1988. Hyde, Randall L. "Overview of Memory Management," *Byte* **13**, 4 (April) 219–225.

1988. Anderson, Alan. "Macintosh Memory Management," Byte **13**, *4* (April) 249–254.

MALCOLM P. ATKINSON

MEMORY-MAPPED I/O

For articles on related subjects *see* MEMORY: MAIN; MICROPROCESSORS AND MICROCOMPUTERS; and PERSONAL COMPUTING.

In a conventional computer equipped with a graphic display device, a programmer must direct characters to such a display in much the same way as output is directed to a tape or disk or other on-line I/O device; i.e. the program must execute an I/O statement that (typically) names the channel to which the display device is attached, the number of characters to be transmitted, the screen location where they are to be displayed, and the starting address in memory where the data to be transmitted may be found. Most popular microcomputers, however, are now using a much simpler and more flexible system known as *memory-mapped I/O*, whereby individual character positions on the screen are mapped one-to-one to bytes in the computer's main memory. For example, suppose that a certain (hypothetical) 32×128 character display screen is mapped onto the 4,096-byte memory segment starting at hexadecimal address A000. This has a twofold advantage. First, to display, say, HELLO in the middle of the screen, one would merely store the five-byte ASCII (*q.v.*) equivalent of HELLO at hexadecimal memory locations A83E to A842 which correspond to the desired portion of the screen. Instantaneously and automatically, the desired message will appear without need for any further instructions. Second, unlike the programmer of a conventional system whose programs cannot detect what is currently on the screen, the programmer of a memory-mapped system need only check the current contents of the memory map area to ascertain what is being displayed. If a user at the console changes it through keyboard action, the storage map will change to conform.

Not only the display device but also the keyboard is memory mapped in some of the newer microcomputers. This allows the software to use simple memory accesses to be able to sense at any given time which keys (or combination of keys) are being depressed and to take appropriate action. Such mapping systems are so obviously flexible and useful that the concept is likely to endure and be applied to additional I/O interface situations.

EDWIN D. REILLY

MEMORY ORGANIZATION. *See* STORAGE ORGANIZATION.

MEMORY PORT. *See* PORT, MEMORY.

MEMORY PROTECTION

For articles on related subjects *see* ADDRESSING; BASE REGISTER; MULTIPROGRAMMING; OPERATING SYSTEMS; READ-ONLY MEMORY; STORAGE ALLOCATION; and VIRTUAL MEMORY.

Memory protection, as used in this article, is a hardware mechanism that limits or prevents access to specified areas in the central or main memory of a computer.

Memory protection first became important when systems became capable of permitting or requiring more than one program to be resident in memory at the same time. The possibility then existed that, while one of the programs was running, it might inadvertently (e.g. because of a bug) write in the area occupied by the other program and thus invalidate that program.

In *uniprogramming* operating systems (i.e. most first-generation systems), there were typically two programs resident in memory—an executive program and a user program. The earliest memory protection mechanism provided a switch register that could be set to a memory address that marked the upper limit of a protected area. The lower limit was zero. No program running outside the protected area could write into any location inside the protected area. The executive routine, presumably debugged, would reside *in* the protected area. The user program would run on the outside, and if it did anything improper, it could hurt only itself. The execution of a user program instruction that would result in a write into the protected area would abort the user program, and then, either automatically or through operator intervention, control would be returned to the executive, which could proceed to the next user program.

With the development of *multiprogramming* (*q.v.*) systems, more elaborate memory protection mechanisms were needed. In such systems, supervisory programs and a number of user programs may reside in memory simultaneously. While a user program is running, it is important to be able to designate the areas that belong to that program and to limit its access to other areas. The supervisory programs must be able to designate and change the areas under protection, and the user programs must be denied this capability. Although some systems limited themselves to *write protection* (i.e. a program could *read* from any area in memory, but could not *write* outside its own area), it was recognized quite early that a more general access protection was desirable.

The first effective memory protection mechanism for a multiprogramming system used a *base register* (*q.v.*), also called a *relocation register*, and a *limit register*. A program must reside in a contiguous area of memory; when that program is to run, the executive places the program's origin (i.e. its lowest address) in the base register and its length in the limit register. Any attempt by a program to access a memory location outside its own area causes control to go to the executive routine.

It is, however, often desirable for a program and its associated data to reside in disjoint areas of memory. In such cases, it is nevertheless necessary to protect the program and data as a unit. In the IBM 360/370/390 series (*q.v.*), for example, each block of 2,048 consecutive bytes has an associated protection code register that holds a four-bit *protection key* set by an executive routine operating in *supervisor* state. A running program runs under its protection key, and an interrupt results from any attempt to access a block whose protection key is different from that of the running program. Protection code 0000 is reserved for executive routines and has special significance in that a program with protection code 0000 has access to all memory.

Memory protection is an important feature of multiprogramming systems, but it does create problems in systems in which routines and data are to be shared among programs simultaneously present in memory. *Virtual memory* (*q.v.*) systems have been designed to permit and encourage such sharing.

Memory protection can be important within a single program. One of the most usual of program bugs occurs when a program calculates a subscript that causes a value to be stored outside the array that is being referenced. Automatic checking of array boundaries can be an extremely useful memory protection feature. This type of checking is often done in software. The run-time systems provided by many compilers provide a routine check for references outside of the bounds that have been declared for arrays.

SAUL ROSEN

MEMORY, CACHE. *See* CACHE MEMORY.

MENU. *See* USER INTERFACE.

MERGING. *See* SORTING.

METAFONT

For articles on related subjects *see* DESKTOP PUBLISHING; and TEX.

METAFONT is a computer-controlled system for specifying the shapes of letters and other symbols. It was designed by Donald E. Knuth at the same time as TEX, a computer-controlled typesetting system, and it shares the same goals of quality and portability. Like TEX, METAFONT was written in the WEB language and has been placed in the public domain.

Traditionally, a type designer has worked out the shape of each character by making many large-scale drawings. Then the scale is reduced to the desired size, and the type designer can see how the letters work together as blocks of text. Needless to say, it takes years of tedious work to develop a single new typeface with this method.

METAFONT allows the type designer to make changes in the shapes of letters almost instantly, and to see the letters in various sizes and combinations at will. The user can ask METAFONT to draw strokes with a specific kind of pen point—sharp, broad, round, rectangular, slanted. The pen point can be instructed to make an image either by following the center of a curve or by filling between the edges of a region that has been outlined. There are also erasers, which act like pens except that they remove parts of strokes.

METAFONT doesn't have any built-in information about the shapes of letters; it is just a robot draftsman, able to follow instructions about how to move pens and erasers. It is also a programming language; the user writes a program for every letter, stating how that letter should be drawn.

Most statements in the METAFONT language are equations that express the designer's intentions about key parts of a shape to be drawn. For example, the designer may want one point to be one-third of the way between two other points. If the designer specifies a sequence of points, METAFONT will draw a smooth curve through them.

The design can be stated in terms of absolute physical dimensions, or it can be stated in terms of variable quantities or parameters that can be changed to produce a series of related fonts. For example, some parameters of a design could be the thickness of stem strokes and hairlines, the x-height of lowercase letters and the heights of ascenders and descenders; the length of serifs, the width of an "em," the amount of oblique slant, etc. If a designer has written a METAFONT program in terms of such parameters, rather than in terms of absolute dimensions, other users can quickly and easily use the resulting

```
z1=(15u,16u); 1/2[z1,z2]=1/2[z3,z5]+(0,10u);
z3=(0,5u); z4=1/3[z3,z5]-(0,10u); z5=(50u,10u);
pickup pencircle xscaled 10u yscaled 3u rotated 30;
drawdot z1; drawdot z2;
draw z3..z4..z5;
```

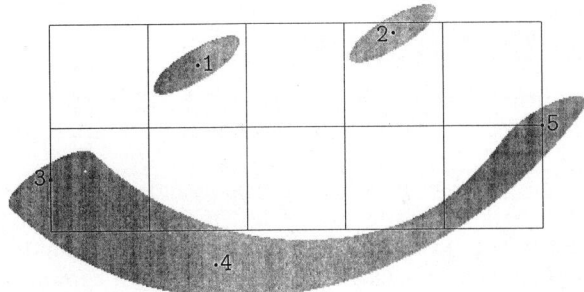

FIG. 1. This METAFONT program defines five points $z_1,...,z_5$, by specifying algebraic relations that they must satisfy. (The notation "$1/2[z_1, z_2]$" used in the second equation stands for the point halfway between z_1 and z_2.) Then the computer is told to pick up a pen whose tip has an oval shape, holding it at an angle of 30° from the horizontal. The machine draws dots of this oval shape at points z_1 and z_2; then it uses the pen to draw a curved line from z_3 to z_4 to z_5.

design to generate a large family of fonts, simply by specifying different sets of numerical values for the parameters. Knuth has constructed an example of such a "meta-design," called the Computer Modern family of typefaces. Computer Modern fonts are based on traditional styles of type that had been used in his series of books, *The Art of Computer Programming*.

With an almost infinite set of possibilities, type designers must use their esthetic sense and professional experience to choose shapes that are beautiful and robust under a variety of parameter settings. Thus, the design of a complete typeface family is still a major undertaking, even though the amount of non-creative labor has been reduced.

Many uses of METAFONT are much simpler. Individual special characters and a wide variety of geometric symbols and decorations can be created quickly and used immediately within typeset documents.

The METAFONT language is of interest to designers of programming languages because it is a declarative language that combines a macro capability with structured types, much as SIMULA 67 combines procedures with structured types.

Information about METAFONT is regularly published in *TUGboat*, the journal of the TEX Users Group.

References

1982. Knuth, Donald E. "The Concept of a Meta-font," *Visible Language* **16**, 3–27.

1985. Knuth, Donald E. "Lessons Learned from METAFONT," *Visible Language* **19**, 35–53.

1986. Knuth, Donald E. *The METAFONT book*, Volume C of *Computers & Typesetting*. Reading, MA: Addison-Wesley.

1986. Knuth, Donald E. *METAFONT: The Program*, Volume D of *Computers & Typesetting*, Reading, MA: Addison-Wesley.

1986. Knuth, Donald E. *Computer Modern Typefaces*, Volume E of *Computers & Typesetting*, Reading, MA: Addison-Wesley.

1989. Billawala, Neenie. *Metamarks: Preliminary Studies for a Pandora's Box of Shapes*. Stanford University Computer Science Report STAN-CS-89-1256, May.

DONALD E. AND JILL C. KNUTH

METALANGUAGE

For articles on related subjects *see* BACKUS-NAUR FORM; GRAMMARS; and PROGRAMMING LINGUISTICS.

A *metalanguage* is a set of symbols and words used to describe another language in which these symbols do not appear. The most common application is in the definition of programming languages. The first and best known example was the definition of Algol 60, and a small section of this follows as an example.

The metalanguage used in this case, Backus-Naur Form, consists of the symbols ⟨ , ⟩, |, :: =, together with a number of metalinguistic variables that are used to define the elements of Algol. The brackets ⟨ ⟩ are used as delimiters for the metalinguistic variables, the vertical stroke | has the meaning "or," and the symbol :: = means "is defined as." The following extract from the report on Algol

60 gives the definition of an integer and illustrates the use of the symbols:

```
⟨digit⟩ ::= 0|1|2|3|4|5|6|7|8|9
⟨unsigned integer⟩ ::= ⟨digit⟩
          |⟨unsigned integer⟩⟨digit⟩
⟨integer⟩ ::= ⟨unsigned integer⟩
          | + ⟨unsigned integer⟩
          | − ⟨unsigned integer⟩
```

The complete definition of Algol 60 in this form, together with some semantic interpretation, takes about 26 pages.

Note that in order to define the symbols of the metalanguage, we had to make use of another language, namely, English. This causes no confusion in the present case, but might do so if we were to try to define English itself by a metalanguage.

In the example above we made use of three metalinguistic variables: digit, unsigned integer, and integer. In defining the complete language, there will normally be one metalinguistic variable that is never used in the definition of any other variable; this is known as the *starting type*. In programming languages, this would normally be ⟨program⟩, and in natural languages it might be ⟨sentence⟩.

The digits 0, 1...9 and the signs + and − are *terminal symbols* of the language; i.e. they will appear in statements written in the language. For this reason they are often printed in heavy type to distinguish them from the *nonterminal symbols* (digit, integer etc.), sometimes called *defined types* or *metavariables*.

References

1969. Sammet, J. E. *Programming Languages*. Englewood Cliffs, NJ: Prentice-Hall.

1980. Hill, I. D. and Meek, B. L., New York: (Eds.) *Programming Language Standardisation*. New York: John Wiley (Ellis Horwood).

KATHLEEN H. V. BOOTH

METROPOLITAN AREA NETWORK (MAN)

For articles on related subjects *see* DATA COMMUNICATIONS; GATEWAY; INTEGRATED SERVICES DIGITAL NETWORK; LOCAL AREA NETWORK; NETWORK PROTOCOLS; and NETWORKS, COMPUTER.

Data communications networks have traditionally been divided into local area networks and wide area networks. This division actually represents two ends of a range of a number of parameters for a network:

1. Geographical (local = up to several buildings, wide = up to worldwide).
2. Organizational (the larger, the more organizations involved).
3. Technological (the larger, the older).
4. Topological (redundancy of routes).
5. Performance (throughput, delay, errors).

A *metropolitan area network* (MAN) can be placed at the midpoint of each of these ranges:

1. 1–100 km in diameter.
2. Building-wide to city-wide.
3. Fiber optic cable plant, electronic switching.
4. At least dual route—some redundancy.
5. 100 Mbps throughput, delay in the milliseconds, one bit in ten billion in error.

The motivation for the development of a clear standard way of implementing MANs came from the confluence of new ideas from digital telecommunications and telephony, with old ideas from data communications. Digitized speech (and video) are best carried over a network in fixed-size packets called *cells*. These are small (53 bytes, made from 5 bytes of control information and 48 bytes payload/user data). The 5 bytes also contain the source and destination addresses of the cell. The fixed size means that the network can offer a predictable service time, which is vital so as not to confuse the end human user. These ideas are embodied in the Broadband ISDN Asynchronous Transfer Mode service (ATM). Such networks are also designed to carry data.

Local area networks use variable sized-packets ranging from 50 to 4,000 bytes. Wide area networks have offered recovery from outages and efficient use of the network bandwidth by using statistical multiplexing of variable-sized packets from many end users.

The main algorithms used with a MAN are:

1. The Distributed Queue, Dual Bus (DQDB) architecture (defined by the IEEE 802.6 Committee), also known as Queued Packet Switched eXchange, used at 150Mbps.
2. Fiber Distributed Data Interface (FDDI) I & II.

With method 1 (see Fig. 1), physical recovery from loss of a cable can be effected by bypassing it until it is repaired. The physical length of the bus is constrained so that cells are not delayed more than 1.5 msecs. The head nodes generate empty cells and transmit them down each bus.

DQDB offers three types of service to the user:

1. Connection-oriented service—This is designed to carry compressed video service, with buffering to match the synchronous video stream to ATM cells.
2. Connectionless data service (like the LLC service of a LAN)—Here, just as on ethernet or Token Ring, large packets are carried from one station to another on a best effort basis. The large packets are built out of a collection of cells (see Fig. 2).
3. Isochronous, equal time segments, fixed bandwidth service. Digitized video or voice are often sampled in the way that fits this service. Once an isochronous channel is established, the end system nodes know which cells map into it from the cells time slot position.

Types 1 and 2 are arbitrated by a distributed queue algorithm. Type 3 is non-arbitrated and is allocated on a fixed basis by a "head-end" specially designated station.

Operation of the Distributed Queue Algorithm Access to each bus is requested by sending out requests on the other bus, which transmits in the reverse direction. Each node keeps a counter of requests seen for each bus. Whenever empty packets are seen (neither requests nor those that contain data), the counter is

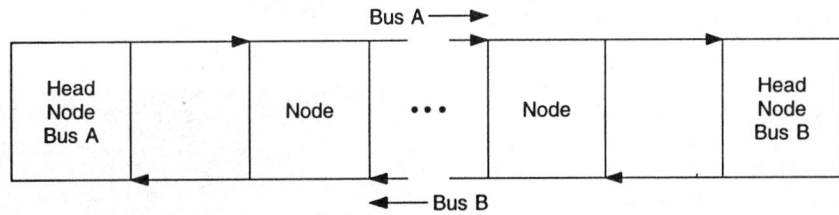

FIG. 1. Distributed Queue Dual Bus (DQDB) architecture.

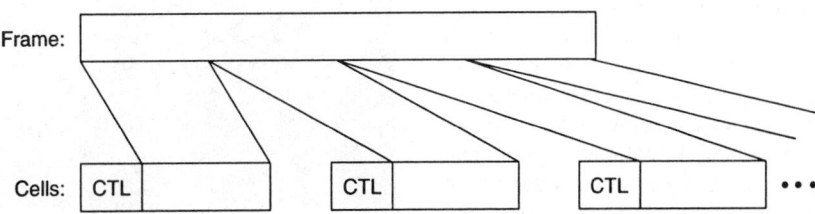

FIG. 2. Mapping a large frame into cells by segmentation.

decremented. Empty cells must be for a "downstream" node, so they will have resulted from earlier requests. When a node has data ready to send and its counter is zero, it simply copies the data into the next empty slot that passes.

This algorithm ensures fairness of access to the MAN since, at worst, every other node has sent out a request just before a given one. Thus, the given node will have access after all the others have had just one access. For an N node DQDB, it has to wait $N-1$ cell service times.

FDDI—100 Mbps, Dual Fiber Optic Ring
FDDI is a token ring standard for MANs similar to the LAN 802.5 standard. It has been proposed to extend the services available to include connection-oriented services to carry compressed video, voice, and other services. This is a far less popular option than DQDB. FDDI runs over either a single fiber optic ring or a dual ring system.

References

1989. IEEE 802.6, Draft Standard for Metropolitan Networks.
1989. *Data Communications Magazine*, Special Issue, December.

JON CROWCROFT

MICROCOMPUTER CHIP

For articles on related subjects *see* INTEGRATED CIRCUITRY; MICROPROCESSORS AND MICROCOMPUTERS; MINICOMPUTERS; and PERSONAL COMPUTING.

A *microcomputer chip* is an integrated circuit component that is the building block of a computer system. A microcomputer chip is often simply referred to as a *microchip*, or just *chip*. Typically, microcomputer chips are very large scale integrated circuit components (VLSI) containing tens of thousands of transistors. The largest such components contain over a million transistors. A computer will typically contain a large number and variety of such components or chips. A typical personal computer will contain about 200 microcomputer chips of about 50 different varieties. The best known example of a microcomputer chip is the microprocessor, but "microcomputer chip" is a very broad term that refers to thousands of different kinds of such components. Furthermore, the boundaries and distinctions between the particular forms is constantly changing.

Physical Description Silicon wafers are typically 6 inches in diameter and thinner than cardboard. During semiconductor manufacturing, a single such wafer contains tens and possibly hundreds of individual microcomputer chips. The wafers are cut or diced into individual chips that are the size of a little fingernail. The surface of each chip is covered with transistors that are etched into the surface of the silicon through a complex sequence of superimposed, photographically developed layers. The photographic layers provide a stencil for sequences of carefully controlled chemical procedures. The chemical procedures create metal lines for signal flow, transistors,

and the interconnections between various metal lines and transistors. The chips themselves are then typically placed into a package. The package provides a mechanically sound structure to keep the chip from being cracked. In addition, the package has pins that allow it to be connected to a circuit board that subsequently allows interconnection to other components. The individual signals of the chip are connected to the package with gold wires that are finer than hair. Packages contain 50 to 300 pins (see Fig. 1). For a considerably more detailed analysis of integrated circuits and their fabrication process, see INTEGRATED CIRCUITRY. Over three decades, the number of transistors that can be fabricated as a single integrated circuit has more than doubled every 2 years. The largest microprocessor of 1990 had over 1 million transistors. Chips containing 50 to 100 million transistors are expected to exist by the year 2000.

History The precursor to the first microcomputer chip was the integrated circuit invented simultaneously by Jack Kilby of Texas Instruments and Robert Noyce, then of Fairchild Semiconductor, in 1959. The microcomputer chip traces its origin to the microprocessor invented in the early 1970s (*see* MICROPROCESSORS AND MICROCOMPUTERS). Prior to the microprocessor, integrated circuits were rather simplistic, performing a single function on an individual chip. The breakthrough of the microprocessor was the combination of several different computing elements or functional units of a computer into a single integrated circuit. The first such microprocessor was the 4004 invented by Marcian (Ted) Hoff of Intel Corporation in 1972. In the case of the microprocessor, the functions combined onto a single chip were those that constitute most of a central processing unit (*q.v.*), the heart of a computer. These functions include items such as the arithmetic unit for addition and subtraction, register file, and memory address generation. The first significant variation following the microprocessor was the *microcontroller* developed in the mid-1970s. The microcontroller combined memory with the

FIG. 1. Packaged microcomputer chip.

microprocessor. The memory typically contains the program or sequence of instructions the microprocessor is to execute. In this way, the microcontroller can be embedded into a host system and perform a function repetitively, as needed, for extended periods of time. A trivial example might be a traffic light controller whose memory is loaded with a program indicating what sequence of lights should be used for each conceivable configuration (*see* EMBEDDED SYSTEMS).

Integrating functions into a single chip has three significant advantages. First, the size of a system diminishes as functions are integrated. Thus, systems built with microcomputer chips can provide much greater functionality in a smaller size. Second, signals travel smaller distances when combined into a single chip, so that the functions implemented on the chip operate at a higher speed. Finally and most important, new techniques are possible when functions are integrated that are not possible when implemented discretely. For instance, when several functions are implemented as individual components, a designer is constrained to implementations that require a much smaller number of pins then would be the case with a single chip.

The move from the microprocessor to a microcontroller is demonstrative of the evolution of the microcomputer chip. Due to the increasing transistor budget provided by integrated circuit technology, designers have been choosing different functions or inventing new functions to integrate into a single chip ever since.

Types of Microchips

Microprocessors Microprocessors combine all the capabilities of a central processing unit onto a single chip and perform tens of millions of instructions per second. The chip acts as the orchestra leader of the computer. Microprocessors have typically integrated new functions as required to remove bottlenecks that inhibit the performance of a microcomputer system. This is seen by examples such as the integration of memory management, cache memory (*q.v.*), and floating-point operations that have occurred in the two most significant microprocessor families, the Intel 80x86 and Motorola 68000 microprocessor families. Currently, however, dramatic steps are being taken in the integration of many microcomputer chips onto the microprocessor itself to reduce system size. The Intel 80386SL microprocessor allows an entire personal computer to be built in 10 square inches (see Fig. 2). A highly integrated microcomputer chip such as the 386SL is particularly targeted to portable laptop computers (*q.v.*), where physical size is at a premium. It is projected that by the mid-1990s an entire personal computer will be built as a single microcomputer chip.

Microcontrollers A single modern car may have as many as 25 microcontrollers that perform tasks ranging from ignition control to suspension balancing. As microcontrollers have become very powerful (tens of millions of instructions per second) at very low costs (about $20), they have begun to replace many special-pur-

FIG. 2. Die photo of Intel 386SL Microprocessor.

pose microcomputer chips. For example, a powerful microcontroller may perform a computer's disk control function. In addition to simply coordinating the disk accesses requested by the microprocessor, it also performs numerous other tasks, such as searching for disk errors and correcting them, caching frequently used information, and compressing and encoding information stored on the disk to increase security and the amount of information that can be stored on the disk (*see* DATA COMPRESSION and COMPACTION). Another example of a microcontroller is the network controller that can interpret higher-level communication protocols, perform network monitoring, and transfer information without any intervention from the microprocessor.

In many ways it appears that the microprocessor and microcontroller are on a collision course. Should computational power be increasingly placed in the various microcontroller-based subsystems of the computer system or in the microprocessor-based central processing unit? The outcome of this debate is unlikely to be unclear for several years.

Graphics Another microcomputer chip of interest is the *graphics controller*, whose function is to display information upon the screen. The gradual transition from monochrome to higher-resolution color displays has been a direct result of the increasing capabilities allowed by the larger transistor budget of integrated circuits. As the graphics chip combines more functions and runs faster, it is able to update more pixels, draw lines more quickly, or display more information. Over the next decade, it is expected that displays will move upward in resolution to the point of photographic realism—resolution that exceeds what the human eye can detect—and that such displays will allow photographs and motion video to be played in real time. Three-dimensional displays will be more prevalent. All of these capabilities will require substantial increases in function of the graphics chip.

Future As the number of transistors that can be integrated onto a single piece of silicon grows, potentially reaching 100 million by the year 2000, the pervasiveness of microcomputer chips is certain to increase. Amazing levels of computation will be found in very small packages. A credit card size personal phone book that recognizes your spoken requests for addresses and names is just one possibility. Currently, the list of different types of microcomputer chips is long and growing. It seems likely, however, that the number of transistors available will begin to surpass the number of different functions that need to be performed in a computer system. Then, the number of variations of microcomputer chip will begin to diminish as a single chip combines a substantially growing variety of functions.

References

1987. Crawford, J. and Gelsinger, P. *Programming the 80386*. Alameda, CA: Sybex.

1990. Hennessey, J. and Patterson, D. *Computer Architecture—A Quantitative Approach*. San Mateo, CA: Morgan Kaufmann.

1991. Bell, T. "Incredible Shrinking Computers," *IEEE Spectrum*, May 1991, 37–41.

PATRICK P. GELSINGER

MICROPROCESSORS AND MICROCOMPUTERS

For articles on related subjects *see* COMPUTER CIRCUITRY; EMBEDDED SYSTEM; INTEGRATED CIRCUITRY; and MICROCOMPUTER CHIP.

A *microprocessor* is a single-chip integrated circuit (IC) implementation of a general-purpose central processing unit (CPU - *q.v.*). It contains a controller to direct the execution of program instructions, registers to store control and data values temporarily, and an arithmetic logic unit (ALU - *q.v.*) to calculate results. A microprocessor chip is a (very) large-scale integrated (LSI or VLSI) circuit fabricated on a sliver of silicon less than 5 mm (1/5 in.) square and 0.5 mm (1/50 in.) thick, about the size of a baby's fingernail.

There are many different kinds of microprocessors, designed for many different applications. In 1990, there were about 50 different microprocessor families, including 995 varieties of CPU chips, each containing the equivalent of between 4,000 and 2,000,000 transistors. A transistor-equivalent is able to make one simple logic decision or to store one binary digit (0 or 1). A popular CPU categorization is based on the width in bits of its internal datapath, commonly 8-bit, 16-bit, or 32-bit. The circuit densities, in transistors per chip, of commercially available CPUs have been increasing by a factor of 10 every 4 to 6 years.

A *coprocessor* is an optional function unit on a separate chip that can execute certain complex instructions

rapidly. The most common coprocessors implement floating-point arithmetic (*see* COMPUTER ARITHMETIC).

Processor architecture, such as the Sun SPARC family, is sometimes distinguished from a particular implementation. Architectures specify programmer-visible functions. Microprocessors realize these specifications economically. A flexible architecture takes advantage of technological progress that allows ever faster, more highly integrated microprocessors.

A *bit-sliced microprocessor* is an older design in which fast functional blocks of a CPU have been packaged individually. By selecting, combining, and programming the components, it is possible to create many different processors. The term *bit-slicing* (*q.v.*) describes the blocks for handling data within the CPU; they are 1 to 32 bits wide, but can be connected in parallel to form processors with any desired word width.

A *microcomputer* is a more complete system than a microprocessor, containing not only the CPU logic, but also memory for storing programs and data plus input/output (I/O) interfaces for exchanging data with peripheral devices (see Fig. 1). In 1990, most microcomputers combined a CPU chip with 1 to 200 other support chips on a single circuit board no larger than a double book page. Most extra chips contained from 262,144 (2^{18}) to 4,194,304 (2^{22}) bits of memory. A 100-chip microcomputer most likely controlled a workstation (*q.v.*), with I/O interfaces for a graphics display, mouse (*q.v.*), input keyboard, disk store, loudspeaker, and network communications; it executed from 64 to 300 different operations at rates between 500,000 and 80,000,000 operations per second and contained 9 to 36 million bytes of memory, including the display image. A memory byte consists of eight bits and can store one alphabetic character, two decimal digits, eight display dots, one color value, or part of a large binary number.

The term "microcomputer" is somewhat misleading, since it has a connotation of low performance left from the early days of microprocessors. Now, microcomputers range in processing speeds from slow, tiny appliance controllers to near-supercomputers (*q.v.*). Many expensive, performance-driven minicomputers use microprocessor CPUs.

The ever-increasing number of transistors that a single integrated circuit can hold makes possible *single-chip microcomputers* (see Fig. 2), smaller and faster systems with new application areas and larger markets. A *digital signal processor (DSP)* is a microcomputer specially designed for high-throughput (*q.v.*) numerical processing ("number crunching"). DSP chips are very useful for speech analysis and synthesis (*q.v.*) to produce computerized speech. Their fast operations on arrays of numbers will find many other scientific applications.

A *microcontroller* is a single-chip microcomputer targeted for embedded system control applications. A microcontroller typically has on-chip permanent program memory, a small amount of data memory for temporary values, and an assorted selection of interfaces and peripheral units such as serial and parallel ports, timers, and analog-to-digital converters (*q.v.*). Embedded applications usually do not require high performance, but need

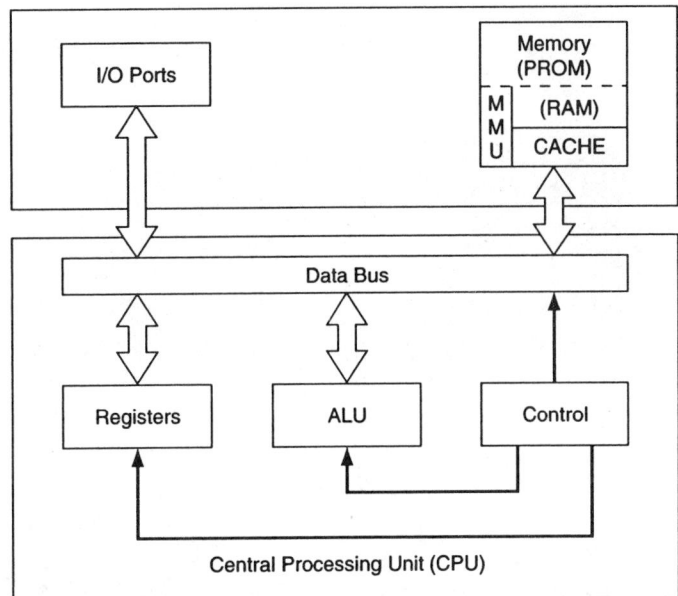

FIG. 1. Basic components of computer system compressed onto a single microcomputer chip, as in the Intel 8748. In this block diagram, "control" includes control logic for decoding and executing the program stored in "memory" (PROM or RAM). "Registers" provide temporary storage for data. Random-access memory (RAM) provides longer term primary storage for data. The "ALU" (arithmetic logic unit) carries out arithmetic and logic operations at times specified by the control circuitry. "I/O ports" provide access to peripheral devices, such as a keyboard, a graphics display unit, and a disk storage device.

identical chips in huge quantities at very cheap prices. Over 99% of all microprocessors and microcomputers sold in 1990 were 4-bit and 8-bit chips intended for dedicated control.

Organization A (micro) computer is organized into the three major subsystems inherited from the von Neumann stored-program design: processor, memory, and input-output. This model has stood the test of time surprisingly well, kept alive by improving implementation technology, even though it has an inherent speed limitation in exchanging data between the CPU and memory. Newer experimental architectures, such as massively parallel machines that intersperse CPUs and input-output devices among memory modules, have the potential for much greater performance, but have yet to achieve standardization and widespread use.

The *central processing unit (CPU)* contains the control units, execution units, and data registers that perform the instructions in a computer program. It can fetch instructions and data from the memory system, can store results back into memory, and can exchange output with the input-output subsystem.

The *control unit* is in charge of decoding instructions and sequencing the actions of the different functional units. It resolves conflicts between on-chip resources, and responds to internal and external interrupts. Control units are simple state machines, implemented by fixed logic circuitry (hard-wired) or by state table lookup

(microprogrammed). Microprogrammed control is more flexible, but is slower than hard-wired control. Processors with many complex instructions and a complex state table are microprogrammed; processors with simple internal architectures are controllable by relatively simple circuits needing less IC space.

A *bus interface unit* controls instruction and data transfers to and from the CPU. (*See* Bus). Architectures that have separate instruction and data busses need two bus interface units—one for instruction fetch and one for data read and write. Sophisticated interfaces improve performance by prefetching instructions, buffering memory writes, and predicting instruction branches.

There can be many *execution units*, commonly including an *arithmetic logic unit (ALU), floating-point unit (FPU)*, and special-purpose units to execute graphics or vector instructions. The ALU executes most instructions on integer data types, such as add, subtract, shift, rotate, and bitwise logical operations. If present, the FPU has specialized hardware to speed the execution of instructions for complicated floating-point arithmetic. FPUs often include distinct addition, multiplication, and division units, and have a separate register set for operands and results. A few CPUs have a graphics function unit to execute special graphics primitives.

A *register (q.v.)* is a storage location within an execution unit capable of holding one number. It is often part of a register file—a small on-chip data array that is explicitly or implicitly addressable by program in-

FIG. 2.   Photomicrograph of an Intel 8748 single-chip 8-bit microcomputer first marketed in 1977. It is a large-scale integrated circuit containing approximately 20,000 transistors. The major subunits of the 8748 are roughly in the same positions as Fig. 1 and include two I/O ports, 1,024 bytes of EPROM, 64 bytes of RAM, two sets of 8-bit registers, and a stack for subroutine returns. The 8748 can execute about 400,000 instructions per second. By 1990, very-large-scale integrated (VLSI) circuits allowed 1,200,000 transistors in the Motorola 68040 microprocessor, which executes about 20 million instructions per second. (Courtesy Intel Corporation.)

structions. Registers provide storage with the fastest possible access time, and are included in all major microprocessors. They enable high performance even when processing rates exceed slow off-chip memory access times.

Registers are classified by function. *General-purpose registers* hold data values temporarily during computations. Instructions access these locations directly as operand sources or result destinations. A homogeneous register set is a collection of general-purpose registers with no predefined functions; all can be used equivalently by programs.

Because reading a value from a register is much faster than reading from a memory location, keeping needed values in registers can greatly improve execution speed. Recent high-performance architectures all have dozens or hundreds of general-purpose registers. Opti-

mizing compilers must carefully allocate registers to values for fast execution.

Dedicated registers play specific roles during the execution of some instructions. For instance, the stack pointer in the Motorola 68000 is one of the general-purpose registers, but is implicitly modified by instructions that access the stack. Many architectures place the program counter and condition codes in dedicated registers. Some older architectures use a single *accumulator*, a register that provides one operand for each operation and receives all results.

Floating-point registers are general-purpose registers accessible by only floating-point and data transfer instructions. They provide additional storage space for lengthy floating-point numbers, freeing the integer registers. Having them as separate registers simplifies control of instruction pipelines. When the FPU is implemented as a coprocessor, putting the floating-point registers on the coprocessor greatly speeds FP execution by not requiring slow off-chip data transfers.

To the CPU, the *memory* subsystem appears to be a large array of locations that can hold data values or program instructions. *Random access memory (RAM)* has become synonymous with "computer main memory." "Random access" means that any location can be referenced in the same time and manner. RAM can be dynamic (DRAM) or static (SRAM). DRAM is denser and needs much less power; SRAM is significantly faster, but more costly. The densities achieved by DRAMs have made multi-megabyte primary memories affordable.

Read-only memory (ROM) is a simple type of memory with contents that cannot be changed, even by loss of electrical power. The contents are programmed during manufacture and are inalterable afterwards. ROMs are used for very high volume control applications where simplicity and low per-unit cost, gained from mass producing the program within the memory chip, are critical.

Other common non-volatile memories are PROMs, EPROMs, and EEPROMs. A *programmable read-only memory (PROM)* can be programmed by the user through an irreversible process; once written, a PROM cannot be changed. An *erasable PROM (EPROM)* allows the programming to be reversed by exposure to intense ultraviolet light. An *electrically erasable PROM (EEPROM)* is alterable by using a large current to reset the internal memory cells. EPROMs and EEPROMs are very useful because they can survive power losses; however, they can be reprogrammed (written) only very slowly and for a limited number of times. Ongoing research is exploring technologies for *non-volatile random access memory (NVRAM)* that solve these two writing problems and offer comparable speeds and densities to DRAMS.

High-performance microprocessors need fast memory subsystems, which do not cost much more than simple DRAM arrays. The most important methods to improve price-performance are *cache memory (q.v.)* and paged *virtual memory (q.v.)*. Caches greatly lower the average access time of system memory; virtual memory increases capacity. Both are part of a general memory storage hierarchy *(q.v.)* that encompasses all storage, from registers to magnetic tape.

Memory hierarchies rely on the temporal and spatial locality of code and data references in running programs: after a new memory location is accessed, it and nearby locations usually will be needed many times. A large, cheap, slow memory can be combined with a small, expensive, fast memory to get both low cost and fast access. Currently needed regions are copied into the faster memory and unneeded locations are moved back to the slower one.

Cache memories are very fast SRAMs accessed directly by the processor and filled with copies of data from slower but cheaper DRAMs. Mappings between official DRAM addresses and actual SRAM locations are maintained by a cache controller. Average access times for memory with caching are less than half those for DRAMs alone. Paged *virtual memory* is a similar selective copying scheme that makes a slow disk appear to be a very large capacity RAM. Multitasking systems also use virtual memory to give each process its own separate memory, apparently starting at location zero. The virtual memory mappings of RAM to disk locations are maintained by the *memory management unit (MMU)*.

The *input-output (I/O)* subsystem includes all interfaces that connect the CPU to external peripherals, usually via controllers that translate general commands from the CPU into specific details. A CPU may exchange I/O commands and data via direct I/O by using special I/O instructions, memory-mapped I/O *(q.v.)* by accessing controller registers as if they were memory locations, or direct memory access (DMA) by using an interface sophisticated enough to control the memory bus and transfers of large blocks of data without CPU help. There are many types of I/O controllers, reflecting the many application areas for microprocessors. Most controllers themselves contain an inexpensive microprocessor.

The most common input-output units are serial and parallel interfaces or *ports (q.v.)*. *Serial interfaces* accept parallel data, such as 8-bit bytes, convert them into one-bit-at-a-time serial form, and send them over an optical fiber or a wire pair. The I/O interfaces must generate light or voltage signals corresponding to the data bits. *Parallel interfaces* are similar, but send or receive 8 or more bits of data simultaneously on multistranded wire cables.

Network interfaces, such as those for Ethernet and token ring, allow computers to exchange data over communication networks. They convert data to and from the special formats used in the network. All network devices have addresses. Propagation delays are longer than within a single computer system (*see* DATA COMMUNICATIONS).

Programmable *timers* interrupt the processor after a delay specified as a number of fundamental microcomputer clock cycles. They are very useful in real-time systems for providing a constant time delay between actions. *Analog to digital (A/D)* and *digital to analog (D/A)* converters *(q.v.)* are often provided on single-chip microcomputers, to transform analog input signals into digital form for processing, or vice versa.

Direct memory access (DMA) controllers can autonomously and rapidly transfer large blocks of data. They free the CPU to execute other tasks; they run transparently, without interfering with the CPU, by using the memory bus only when not needed by the CPU, in a process called cycle-stealing *(q.v.)*. Fast disk controllers provide DMA block transfers.

Disk controllers are common peripheral interface units, one of the earliest kinds of unit to be produced in single-chip form. They convert I/O read and write requests into the right sequence of seeks, delays, and data transfer operations. Some disk interfaces—those following the small computer system interface (SCSI) standard, for example—assume an intelligent controller in the disk drive that accepts high-level commands to access stored data.

Video controllers pack the electronics for a video display into one chip. Typically, they repeatedly read image data from memory, convert the data to pixels and colors, and send it to the screen. They calculate data addresses, look up colors, position pixels, and generate timing signals for the monitor. Some video controllers are general-purpose programmable microcomputers that also perform a number of different drawing primitives. Other specialized controllers for speech synthesis, speech recognition, and three-dimensional imaging are topics of current research.

History Microprocessors and microcomputers are products of a microelectronic revolution characterized by ever-shrinking costs and sizes for information processing devices. The history of microprocessors is tightly interwoven with the histories of integrated circuits and the semiconductor industry.

Microelectronics began with the development of the transistor in 1948 at Bell Laboratories. This tiny amplifier was formed on the surface of a semiconductor material, such as pure germanium or silicon (sand and glass are mainly silicon dioxide). It was hundreds of times smaller than the vacuum tube, which it replaced for building computers by the late 1950s. After learning how to use photographic masks to control diffusion of critical trace impurities into tiny regions of silicon, by the mid-1950s engineers could produce batches of hundreds of individual transistors from a single, thin wafer of silicon.

In 1959, Fairchild marketed a planar transistor, the first device using integrated circuit (IC) technology. In 1960, TI produced a special military IC. In 1961, Fairchild marketed the first commercially available IC, a flip-flop with four transistors and two resistors. Transistor, resistor, and capacitor circuit elements in an IC are insulated by layers of silicon dioxide and connected by thin films of evaporated metal. After hundreds of ICs have been photographically reproduced upon a wafer, they are tested to eliminate defective copies, cut into individual circuits about 5 mm (1/5 in.) square, and mounted in standard plastic or ceramic packages. The first ICs were single-logic gates or single flip-flop (1-bit) memory circuits. The maximum number of elements per silicon circuit has roughly doubled every year since 1959. As of 1990, gallium arsenide (GaAs) is starting to supplant silicon to create very fast ICs.

In 1967, ex-Fairchild executives formed Intel. In 1969, engineers at Intel began developing a general-purpose chip set for inexpensive hand-held calculators. They abstracted the control mechanism into a programmable unit—the 4004 chip. The idea of a controller on a chip was borrowed from Gilbert Hyatt, a California entrepreneur. Hyatt had the first microprocessor prototype running in 1968, but told his investors too much. After they attempted a takeover in 1971, his business failed.

The Intel 8080 Family The microcomputer revolution started in 1971 when Intel marketed its 4004 controller, the first microprocessor chip sold. The 4004 contained 2,100 transistors, addressed 256 8-bit instructions, and operated on 4-bit data, each enough for a decimal digit (0..9).

The direct descendants of the 4004 are used today by millions of people all over the world. The 4004 was followed soon by the 4040 and several processors for 8-bit data: 8008, 8080, and 8080A. The 8008 (1972) was designed to control video display terminals and keyboards. The 8080 and faster 8080A (1974) provided more registers, a stack for calling subroutines, and rudimentary 16-bit arithmetic. They executed 8-bit instructions, operated on 8-bit data with provisions for 16-bit values, and had eight limited-use registers: a stack pointer (SP), three pairs of 8-bit registers (B, C, D, E, H, L), and an arithmetic accumulator (A). A register pair formed a primitive index register addressing 2^{16} (65,536) bytes of memory. The 8080 and 8080A became the first widely used microprocessors. They were popular in embedded control applications and in the hobbyist systems that preceded personal computers.

Improvements continued in 1978 with the 8086 and 8088, internally identical chips for 16-bit operations. The 8088 retained a narrow 8-bit external data bus for circuit compatibility. The 8086 used segmentation to extend the memory address range to 1 megabyte (2^{20} bytes). The 80186 (1981) was an 8086 with on-chip peripheral circuits for embedded controller applications. Subsequent improvements to 8086 performance were made through the 80286 (1982), 80386 (1985), and the 80486 (1989) chips.

Starting with the 80386, the architecture was radically upgraded to form a 32-bit microprocessor, supporting a non-segmented 4-gigabyte (2^{32} bytes) address space, virtual memory, and many new instructions. Compatibility with previous versions was provided by retaining the same register structure and supporting a virtual 8086 mode. Although having few registers hurts its performance, Intel has committed to developing this architecture for the foreseeable future. The 80486 (i486) is essentially identical to the 80386, but with greatly improved performance.

By the end of the 1990s (see Fig. 3), future chips in the Intel 4004 family may include multiple CPUs with large caches, multimedia interfaces, and floating-point, graphics, and vector function units, all on a one 1-inch square (625 mm^2) chip containing over 50 million transistors and operating at over 250 million clock cycles per second (250 MHz).

Other Early Microprocessor Families Eight-bit microprocessors were important because they were the first to address enough memory and to be powerful enough for general-purpose computing. Seeing the 8080 gaining acceptance, other electronics companies introduced 8-bit and 16-bit microprocessors.

Zilog was founded by designers of the Intel 8080A. The Z80 (1976) was upwardly compatible with the 8080A, but faster. It had more instructions, more addressing modes, and an alternate register set for fast interrupt responses. Its support chips were less expensive. It was used for most personal computers before the IBM PC adopted the 8088. The Z80 moved to embedded applications, where it was again successful. Although Z80 descendants (Z8, Z180, Z280 controllers; 16-bit Z8000(1979); 32-bit Z80000) are not so famous as the 8080 family, they are well respected for their technical merits.

The 6800 from Motorola (1974) was very different from the 8080. It had two accumulators, a stack pointer, and an index register (*q.v.*), but no data registers; it relied on powerful addressing modes to process data efficiently in main memory. Programs for the 6800 were more com-

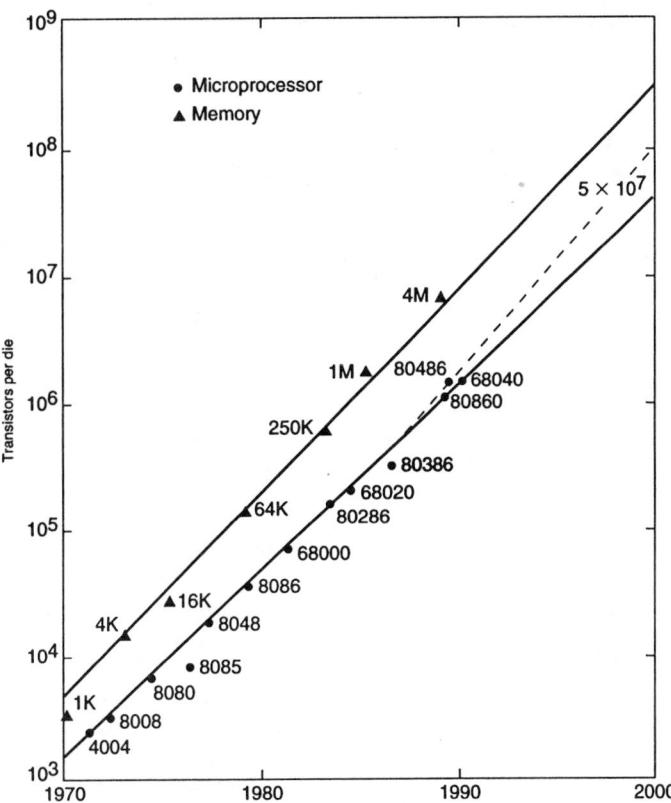

FIG. 3.   Annual doubling of transistors per chip for microprocessors and memories. The graph shows the densest memory chips and microprocessors from Intel (4004, 80xx, 80xxx) and Motorola (680xx). As microprocessors are built with more on-chip memory for fast access, the two lines will merge, as indicated by the dashed line. (Source: Intel Corp.)

pact than for the 8080, saving expensive memory and execution time. The 6802 added a small, fast on-chip RAM. The MOS Technology 6502, created by ex-Motorola engineers, was inexpensive and popular for home computers. The 6809 was the last 8-bit architecture from Motorola. It added two registers for base-page relative addressing, but sacrificed binary compatibility so that the developers could introduce a very sophisticated instruction set to improve code density and execution speed. The 6809 is a good example of instruction set design based on measured instruction usage patterns.

The Motorola MC68000 (1980) was significantly different. It used a 16-bit data bus to access 32-bit values and had eight data registers, eight index registers, two security levels, an orthogonal instruction set (one in which operand addressing modes may be chosen independently of the instruction in which the operands appear), and a non-segmented 16-megabyte address space. Although it was designed only about one year after the 8086, it was much more elegant and powerful. It was adopted for many personal computers, and is still widely used in embedded applications. The 68010 (1982) supported virtual memory by allowing instructions to be restarted after receiving page fault interrupts. The 68020 (1984) was a full 32-bit architecture with a 4-gigabyte address range, an on-chip

memory cache, and many powerful new instructions and addressing modes. It quickly became the standard CPU for high-performance Unix workstations. The 68030 (1989) added an on-chip MMU for mapping virtual addresses. The 68040 (1990) has large on-chip caches, integrated floating-point, and very aggressive pipelining; it runs four times faster than the 68030, an admirable achievement. Motorola has also introduced a RISC architecture (*q.v.*), the 88000 (1989), and pledged full commitment to it, but its future is unclear.

Microcontroller Families   For microprocessors, the 1980s were a time of remarkable architectural innovation and performance advances, but also a time of market consolidation. By 1980, hundreds of types of microprocessor chips had flooded the market. Eight-bit microprocessors dominated, but some 16-bit minicomputer architectures had been put onto chips used to build single-board microcomputers. In 1973, National Semiconductor sold the IMP-16C, the first *single-board* 16-bit microcontroller; it had a CPU, 256 bytes of RAM, 512 bytes of ROM, and I/O drivers. In 1975, Digital Equipment (DEC) introduced the LSI-11, a single-board version of its popular PDP-11 minicomputer; it was soon followed by the TM990 card from Texas Instruments (TI) and the

MicroNova board from Data General. In the late 1980s, single-board microcomputers became inexpensive workstation cards.

Single-chip microcomputers include, on the chip, all CPU, memory, and I/O subsystems, permitting very small, flexible, and inexpensive control circuits for consumer products. Many controller varieties have been developed, targeting many different functionality/performance/price points. In 1974, TI introduced the first single-chip 4-bit microcomputer, the TMS1000, which at $2 was by far the most widely sold microprocessor in the world by 1980. In 1977, Intel introduced its first microcomputer family—the 8-bit 8048 with factory-masked ROM and 8748 with EPROM—followed soon by the 8051. By 1980, microcontroller cards had been supplanted by single-chip microcomputers. Intel targeted the 16-bit 8096 and 32-bit 80960 microprocessors for fast embedded control. The 80960 is an example of Intel's future controller architecture, intended for very high performance applications. Its architecture provides for optional function units, floating-point, pipelining, superscalar execution, message passing, context switching, and multiprocessing.

Microcontrollers using existing microprocessor designs have good software tools available. Examples based on the 68000 family include the 68070 and 93C110 from Philips, plus the 68200 and 68300 from Motorola. Other designs focus on performance. The Harris RTX is a very fast, very small 4000-gate hardware implementation of Forth (*q.v.*), a popular language for real-time control. The choices of on-chip support circuits and memory varieties decide suitability for many applications; for this reason, very many different microcontrollers can coexist. There were 424 varieties of single-chip microcontrollers for sale in the United States in 1990.

Although the 68000 and 8086 prospered, most other families of general-purpose high-performance microprocessors disappeared from new system designs during the 1980s. Some found niches in the low-cost microcontroller market, which is large in volume, low in profile, and tolerant of diversity.

Fast Reduced Instruction Set Computer Chips   The UC Berkeley "Reduced Instruction Set Computer" (RISC) project, started in 1980, popularized simplification of architectures as it explored overlapping register windows and instructions for fast Smalltalk and Lisp programs. The 1981 Stanford "Microprocessor without Interlocked Pipe Stages" (MIPS) project developed compiler methods to improve instruction pipeline performance. Both the RISC and MIPS efforts recognized that simplifying instruction decoding allows fast, compact hardwired control, which frees valuable chip area and allows fast processors to be built as single IC chips.

Early RISC chips had small, regular, hard-wired instruction sets that differentiated them from complex instruction set computers (CISCs) with large microcoded instruction sets. RISC is becoming less a set of architectural features and more a design philosophy that seeks elegant, simple solutions with provable benefits. By the late 1980s, RISC architectures had produced several very fast commercial microprocessors.

The term RISC is recent, but the principle is older. The Control Data CDC 6600 of 1964 had simplified instructions that could be executed in efficient pipelines. To solve scientific problems as fast as possible, the 6600 had a load-store architecture, simple instructions in a uniform three-address format, pipelined instruction execution, multiple function units, and a scoreboard to execute instructions out of order to avoid data conflicts.

The IBM 801 project, started in 1974, used simplification to design a low-cost, extremely fast computer. It pioneered many design decisions that characterize RISC systems today: 32 general-purpose registers, 32-bit three-address instructions, pipelined single-cycle instructions, a delay slot to execute one instruction during each jump, and compiler reordering of instructions to improve performance. It also used sophisticated simulations to evaluate instruction set alternatives. The first prototype was built in 1980, but was not revealed until 1982.

The Berkeley RISC project commanded attention in 1980 with the claim that higher performance could be achieved with lower cost, less complexity, and quicker design times. The Berkeley RISC-II chip was designed by students in a few months, yet outperformed commercial microprocessors and minicomputers.

The key to high performance is efficient instruction pipelines that are made possible by a simple architecture. The second most important factor for fast processors is fitting the entire CPU on a single chip, since communication between chips is significantly slower than high-speed data exchanges within a chip.

Seeing the success of the RISC-II project, Hewlett-Packard started working on its high-performance precision architecture (HPPA) in 1983. In 1984, engineers trained at Stanford founded Mips Computer Systems to develop a commercial chip—the MIPS R2000—released in 1986. In 1985, Sun Microsystems started to design its own SPARC processor family based on the RISC-II, and widely licensed the technology for chips delivered in 1987. Many commercial RISC processors followed: Advanced Micro Devices (AMD) 29000 in 1986, Motorola 88000 in 1988, Intel's 80960 controller in 1988, MIPS R3000 in 1988, Intel's 80860 graphics accelerator in 1989, and the IBM RS/6000 with a powerful "post-RISC" superscalar architecture in 1989.

The foreseeable future for microprocessors is driven by increasing levels of integration and the rational use of RISC design methods to select on-chip features. For high-performance designs, greater circuit density allows on-chip parallelism and fast special-purpose circuits; for microcontrollers, it permits more interfaces and input-output units; for computers, it allows placing more of the entire system onto a single chip. By 1995, high-performance chips will have many millions of transistors operating at hundreds of megahertz, with aggregate computing power of 100 to 400 million instructions per second, a hundred times faster than at the start of the commercial RISC revolution in 1985.

Applications   Microprocessors are most visible as the central processors of general-purpose computing systems. The vast majority of computers use commercial microprocessor CPUs because of their low cost and increasingly unmatchable performance.

Microprocessors offer greatly reduced size, power, and cooling requirements, compared to processors implemented from discrete components. Only the very highest performance computers have architectures too complex or use implementation technologies too sparse to fit the CPU on one chip. In 1990, supercomputers resorted to fast but sparse emitter-coupled logic (ECL) and gallium arsenide (GaAs) circuits to maintain their performance lead.

In addition, microcomputers play supporting roles within more complex computers, as smart controllers for peripherals: displaying graphics, controlling disks, and monitoring keyboards. However, the great majority of microcomputers are dedicated to controlling everything from consumer appliances to cars to missiles to space probes. In embedded applications, the microprocessor in effect serves as a cheap replacement for an otherwise very complicated control circuitry and often offers functionality not feasible with alternative methods. Only in the late 1980s did annual shipments of 8-bit microprocessors pass the volume of 4-bit chips. In 1988, 99% of all microprocessors shipped were 4- and 8-bit chips intended for embedded control applications.

One of the earliest application areas for many new technologies is the defense industry, since it is less constrained by development costs when new methods make previously infeasible tasks possible. Modern defense systems are unimaginable without microprocessors. They operate automatic tracking and targeting systems in planes, guns, missiles, and smart bombs; in fighter jets, they run the displays, navigation, weapons, radar, and controls; they identify the sound signatures of enemy ships for smart mines; they guide ground-hugging missiles with the aid of stored maps; they control radar arrays that track and identify aircraft, and they aim antiaircraft guns and missiles.

Microprocessors are playing an increasingly important role in the transportation industry, from automobiles to airplanes to traffic regulation. The automotive industry has found a number of uses for microprocessors: controlling fuel and air delivery to the engine for optimal performance, fuel efficiency, and exhaust emissions; monitoring brakes to prevent skidding; controlling shock absorbers to give more comfort under varying road conditions and better handling by leaning into turns; tracking road surface markings to warn when a car strays from its lane; and processing traffic information to recommend shortcuts that avoid traffic jams. Microprocessors also regulate traffic by counting local vehicles and adjusting signal light timings accordingly. In aircraft, there is an even greater reliance on light-weight microprocessors. They monitor and operate many flight systems, like inertial navigation, and report status to flight computers that display summaries on video screens. Newer "fly-by-wire" planes are increasingly controlled by computer.

Personal electronics is a ready match for microprocessors. Many household electric appliances now have computerized controls, replacing mechanical ones with fewer choices. Digital keypads on microwave ovens allow programmed cooking sequences; an unattended video cassette recorder (VCR) can tape several programs at different times on different channels; a digital chess game can itself provide challenging moves; digital wristwatches can calculate and play music; and telephones can store frequently dialed numbers. There are exercise stations that report calorie losses and monitor heartbeat to help maintain optimal exercise rates. Appliances such as washers and dryers have benefited from the replacement of complex electromechanical systems with simpler and more reliable electronic ones. Devices such as compact disc players and cellular phones, autofocus cameras, hand-held calculators, television game machines, and personal computers have been made possible by inexpensive microprocessors.

Industry has embraced microprocessor technology. On the factory floor, microcomputers store shapes to guide automated manufacturing machinery, control component placement, guide robot arms that insert components, and keep track of parts inventory. In buildings, microprocessors control air conditioners, turn off lights in empty rooms, and maintain security by logging all door openings and limiting access.

In offices, they handle small business accounting and inventory, generate payrolls, and run word processors. In home offices, they control personal computers, facsimile (fax) machines, and modems that increasingly let people work in pleasant locations instead of commuting to centralized offices. On the salesroom floor, microprocessors process product bar codes, update inventory databases from point-of-sale terminals, and enable just-in-time inventory methods to keep overheads low. In the field, microprocessors control instruments and log data to be downloaded to larger computers. In medicine, microprocessor-controlled scanners generate three-dimensional images of the body. In outer space, microcomputers control satellites, spacecraft, and interplanetary probes.

Future applications are even more wide ranging. The most interesting and revolutionary are the ones related to information management and sharing among the population. Microcomputers can distribute information, make large central databases easily accessible, and allow for a wide exchange of ideas. Notebook-sized, radio-linked microcomputer displays may supersede printed media and allow users to select items of interest from electronically distributed news updates. Pocket-sized portable cellular telephones are becoming common. High-definition television and its three-dimensional "virtual reality" extensions will be heavily dependent on fast microprocessors for local reconstruction on compactly encoded complex images.

Microcomputers and microprocessors are leading a true revolution in manufacturing, communications, information management, and personal services. They will profoundly affect society.

References

1977. Toong, H. M. D. "Microprocessors," *Scientific American* (Special Issue on Microelectronics) **237**, **3**: 146–161 (September).

1980. Patterson, D. A., and Sequin, C. H. "Design Considerations for Single-Chip Computers of the Future," *IEEE Transactions on Computers* (Special Issue on Microprocessors and Microcomputers) **C-29, 2:** 108–116 (February).

1989. Almasi, George S., and Gottlieb, Allan. *Highly Parallel Computing.* Redwood City, CA: Benjamin-Cummings.

1989. Gelsinger, Patrick P., et al. "Microprocessors circa 2000," IEEE Spectrum, **26,** 10: 43–47 (October).

1989. Slater, Michael. *Microprocessor-Based Design: A Comprehensive Guide to Effective Hardware Design.* Englewood Cliffs, NJ: Prentice-Hall.

1990. Dewar, Robert. *Microprocessors: A Programmer's Guide.* New York: McGraw-Hill.

1990. Hennessy, John L., and Patterson, David A. *Computer Architecture: A Quantitative Approach.* San Mateo, CA: Morgan Kaufmann.

LARRY D. WITTIE AND ANDRAS RADICS

MICROPROGRAMMING

For articles on related subjects *see* COMPUTER ARCHITECTURE; CYCLE TIME; DIGITAL COMPUTERS; EMULATION; FIRMWARE; HOST SYSTEM; INSTRUCTION SET; LOGIC DESIGN; READ-ONLY MEMORY; and WILKES, MAURICE V.

Microprogramming is a technique used by designers to implement the control functions of a computer. The collection of control microprograms is sometimes called the *firmware* of the computer. As with the case of a number of other terms relating to computer systems, microprogramming has gradually evolved and broadened its meaning—as, in fact, the understanding of the term "control" has also broadened. Microprogramming, as originally conceived by M. V. Wilkes in 1951, was a specific technique "to provide a systematic approach and an orderly approach to designing the control section of any computing system." In Wilkes' context, the term "control" is taken to mean the interpretation and execution of a machine instruction. The timing for this is shown in Fig. 1.

The interpretation and execution of the instruction involves four phases:

1. Fetching the instruction into the instruction register (IR).
2. Decoding the instruction and generation of the data address.
3. Fetching the data.
4. Final execution of the instruction.

Each of these phases is broken into a number of steps. The steps are defined by the notion of a *cycle*: One cycle is the smallest time quantum in the control process. Generally, it is the time required to reconfigure (i.e. change the contents of) the data registers of the system. Thus, the notion of step or cycle is roughly equivalent to the notion of a register-state transition. Several cycles are required to execute one machine instruction; usually between 2 and 5 cycles are required per phase or between 6 and 20 cycles per instruction execution for even a simple instruction.

The machine, exclusive of control, consists of register and combinatorial execution resources (adders, shifters, etc). Each register in the system can be directed to one of a number of other registers during one cycle. The registers, interconnections, and resources are referred to as the *data paths*. The output of each register drives a series of AND gates, which are directed to each of the destinations that may be reached from the source register in one cycle. See Fig. 2.

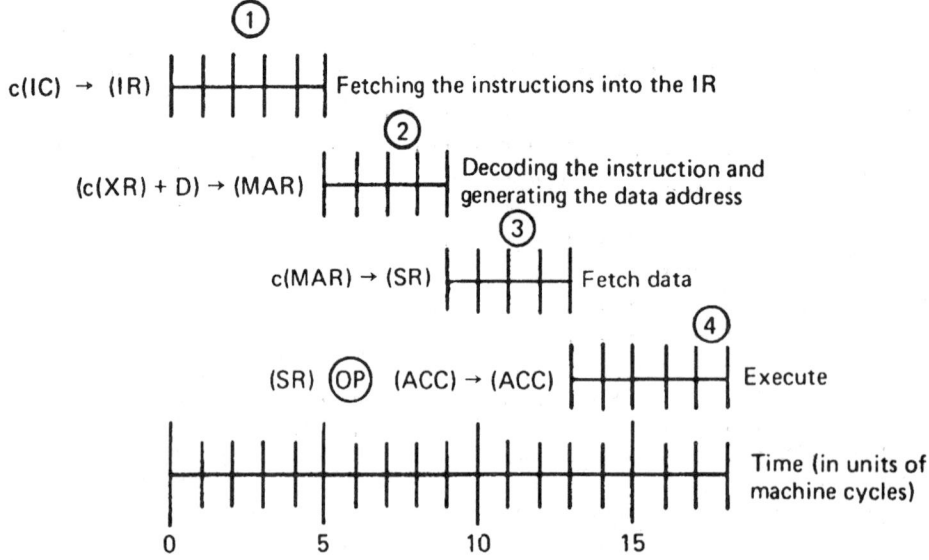

FIG. 1. Sequencing through a simple instruction. Instruction in the form c(c(XR) + D) OP (ACC)→(ACC), where c() = contents of; SR = storage register; MAR = memory address register; IR = instruction register; XR = index register; OP = operation specified by the instruction; D = address displacement; ACC = accumulator; IC = instruction (program) counter.

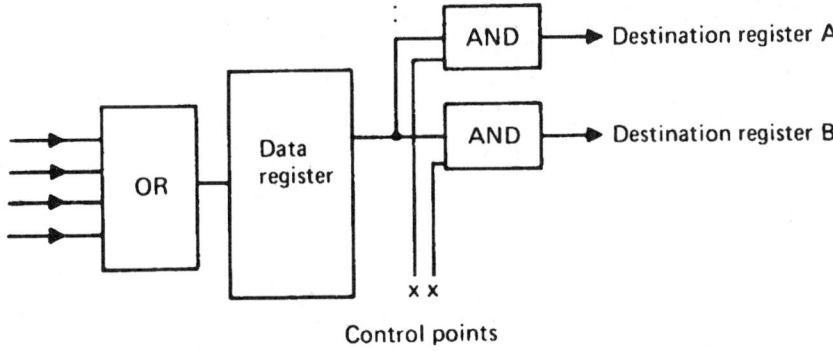

FIG. 2. Gating logic.

The gates on the output of the registers, which direct the flow of information along the data paths, are called the *control points* of the system. Every bit of every register will have at least one control point. More commonly, however, there will be between five and ten control points per register bit, each corresponding to a possible destination point. However, control points are not handled independently; i.e. the control unit that is responsible for specifying data movement does not signal each point independently, but rather many (e.g. the control points associated with different bits of the same register) are ganged together and treated as one point by the control unit. This defines an *independent control point*, or ICP (Fig. 3). Each of the ICPs must be specified as an output from the control unit. The sum value of all ICPs determines the complete control state of the system—i.e. which data register is connected to which and through what resource. Thus, the set of all ICPs represents the output of the control unit. Primary input to the control unit is the *op-code* (operation code) of the instruction.

The op-code specifies the operation to be performed; by itself, it is insufficient to specify multiple ICP steps for the execution of an instruction. Some additional counting mechanism is also required. If the control implementation is to be done with *hardwire* implementation using a combinational network (Fig. 4), then the counting mechanism will be a sequence counter. This counter identifies the particular step of the instruction that is executed at any moment. The combination of the sequence count and the operation is the input to the network, which then describes the exact state of each ICP on each cycle of every instruction.

The microprogramming technique to implement the control function substitutes storage for the boolean combinational network and sequence counter. This serves as both a sequence and a combinational translator. The op code specifies the first microinstruction. The next microinstruction in the sequence, which interprets the instruction, may lie "in line" (i.e. following the address of the first microinstruction) or, alternately, the successor microinstruction may have its address contained in one of the fields of the first microinstruction.

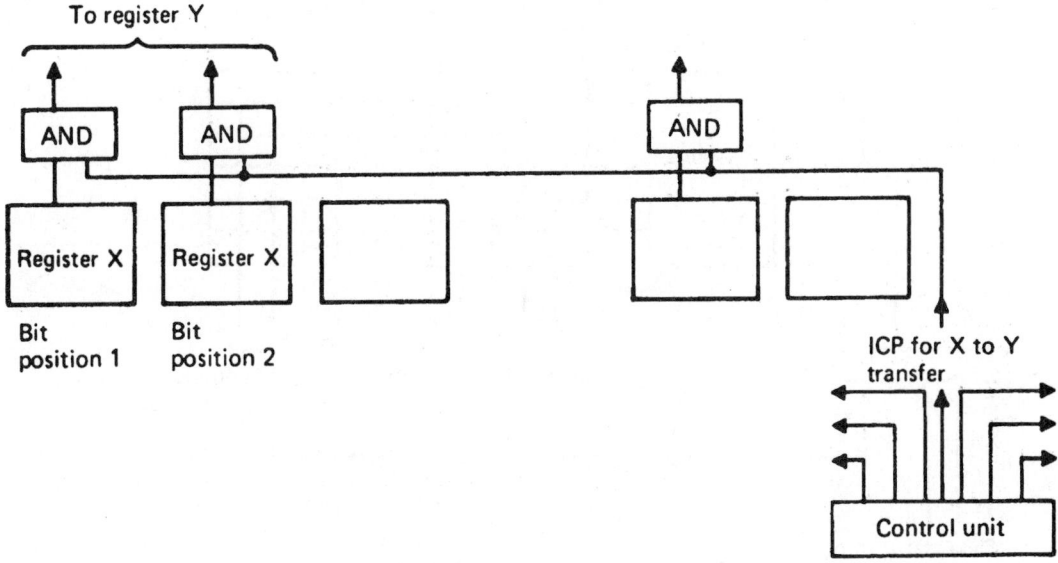

FIG. 3. Independent control points (ICPs).

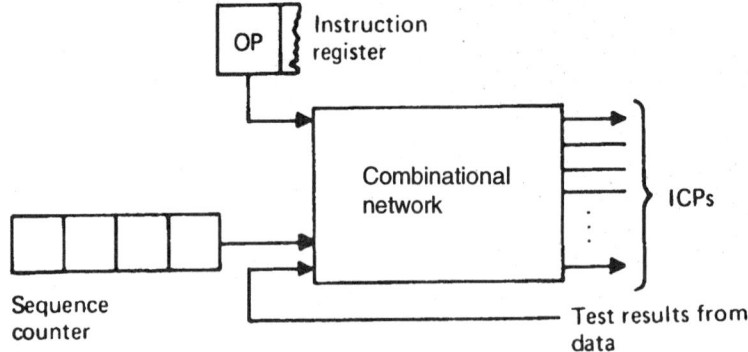

FIG. 4. Hardwire control.

The Evolution of Microprogramming

Initially, microprogramming was used for engineering convenience. The storage contained the ICPs for each cycle. Ease of engineering change and design were important considerations. For these early microprogram implementations, diode matrix technology was well suited. Microprogrammed implementations of control during this era are best illustrated perhaps by Wilkes' ideas (Fig. 5). Wilkes viewed the microprogrammed control store as consisting of two diode matrices. The first matrix would determine the control information for the data paths, while the second matrix would determine, at least in part, the next microinstruction selected to continue the interpretation of the given instruction. The next microinstruction could be influenced by some selected datum (e.g. the sign bit of an accumulator). If the sign were negative, one microinstruction would be called; if the sign bit were positive, another might be invoked. This was required so that proper complementation rules could be used for addition and subtraction.

A decoding tree has the function of transforming a pattern of n bits into a unique selection of 1 out of 2^n possible outputs. Thus, for example, a four-bit binary input into a decoder tree would have four input variables. These would define 16 possible configurations, from 0000 to 1111. The output of the tree would be 16 lines or possible events. Each output line would correspond to one and only one of the input configurations. When an output line is activated, it would also activate all lines out of the matrix that are connected to it (via diodes). The diode action essentially allows current to pass from the drive or input line into the output line. Of course, if no diode connects an input line to an output line, no current will be transmitted, and that line will remain in a "down state." These diode arrays give a simple and regular implementation to the control function. However, speed could be a problem.

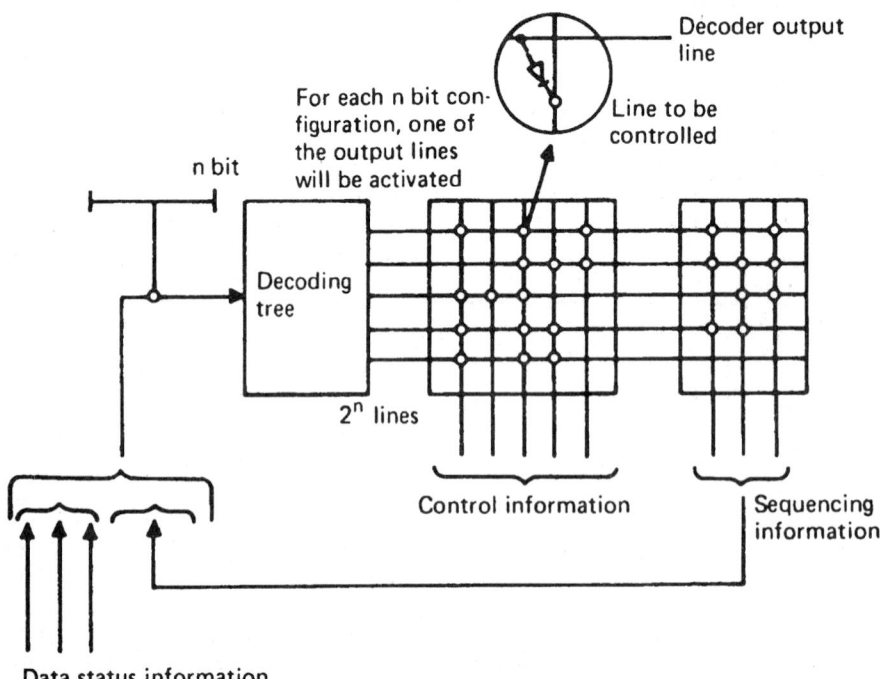

FIG. 5. Wilkes's microprogrammed control storage.

In early implementations, no speed problems developed because main memory was quite slow, on the order of 10 µs cycle time, and the diode matrix had an access time of under 1/2 µs. The ratio of control access time to the main memory access time was an important one; namely, as long as there was a large number of internal cycles in each memory cycle, the microprogramming task was relatively simple and straightforward. One register-to-register transformation was performed per internal cycle, and performance was essentially limited by the main memory cycle. As the main memory access time decreased, however, microprogramming techniques became correspondingly more sophisticated. If only one or two internal machine cycles are available for each main memory cycle, it is necessary to have multiple data transfers in each machine cycle. That is, the microinstruction has to control simultaneously a number of resources internal to the system. This gave rise to a type of internal parallelism within the processor.

The second generation of microprogrammed systems was distinguished by its small number of internal machine cycles per main memory cycle. By the early 1960s, main memory speed had dropped below 1 µs, yet the technology for control store had not noticeably improved, and the best access for read-only store varied between 200 and 400 ns. In addition, the read-only storage technologies tended to be exotic. The technology was not common with any other part of the machine and not always reliable. However, by this time the arguments for using microprogramming went well beyond the reasons cited by Wilkes. In the beginning of 1964, with the announcement of the IBM System 360, an important application for microprogramming was added—*emulation* of multiple machines on a single host system. This was intended to make the customer's transition from an old to a new system much more palatable, in that the customer could, with one system, support old software as well as develop new applications with new programming languages and facilities (Husson, 1970).

The third generation of microprogramming dates from about 1970, with the advent of fast read-write control store. The development of bipolar monolithic technology created a storage medium with the same access time as combinational decisions, since essentially they are made out of the same material. The writable capability of control store represents an important transition, since now the control store becomes a true member of the memory hierarchy. It is unnecessary for control store to contain dynamically all interpretations for each and every instruction for each and every machine that must be emulated. Rather, emulated routines may be overlaid, as required, into a common microstorage. Similarly, the same storage may be used to hold parameters and buffer data values. Where the flexibility of high-performance operation over a variety of machine languages is not required, the data buffering function can be split off into a separate memory, again with the same technology. Here, references to main memory are anticipated by transferring blocks of data into the buffer, giving rise to cache memory (*q.v.*) systems.

Microinstructions The *microinstruction* is the control mechanism that causes a single data-register state transition; i.e. it actuates an internal cycle. One can view this as the action of two separate machines: (1) a control machine whose output activates the data, and (2) an operational machine. The flexibility of these activations gives rise to a variety of possible microinstructions; terms such as horizontal, vertical, nanoinstruction, and packed or unpacked microinstructions have been used to describe the diversity of activations. These terms arise, sometimes ambiguously, to describe certain differences (Fig. 6):

1. If the microinstruction contains a separate description of each independent control point in the resource (i.e. the true description of the control gating), that activation is said to be an *unpacked* or *exploded form* of the microinstruction. This form is most expensive in terms of space, but it provides the ultimate flexibility in that any combination of ICP values may be specified at any time in the future. As an alternate to this unpacked form, a specific number of combinations of ICPs may be chosen. These combinations are coded into a smaller number of control points, and through the use of a decoder can be regenerated when the microinstruction is executed. Thus, only the packed form of the microinstruction is stored, in effect saving space at the expense of flexibility. Occasionally, the distinction between packed and unpacked forms of microinstructions are referred to as *vertical* and *horizontal* microinstructions, respectively.

2. If the resources of the system are partitioned into a number of independent units that can be simultaneously activated, then the microinstruction that activates each of these resources simultaneously contains separate control information. Thus, in Fig. 6(c), a resource might be an adder, a shifter, or a unit for loading and/or storing information into a register or a test and branch unit. Notice that each of these could be operated at the same time, as long as they did not make conflicting use of a data operand.

The distinction between the control of the single resource through the use of ICPs [whether packed or unpacked—Figs. 6(a), (b)] and the multiple resource control situation [Fig. 6(c)] should be noted. Of course, the control for an adder still requires a set of ICPs, whether or not a microinstruction is specifying only the adder action or multiple units. This simultaneous use of resources gives rise to a type of internal parallelism that is explicit (visible to the microprogrammer) within the single instruction stream. This is unlike the type of internal parallelism of certain highly overlapped machines, such as the IBM S/390, whose parallelism is transparent to the programmer. In any event, this use of the microinstruction for identification of pos-

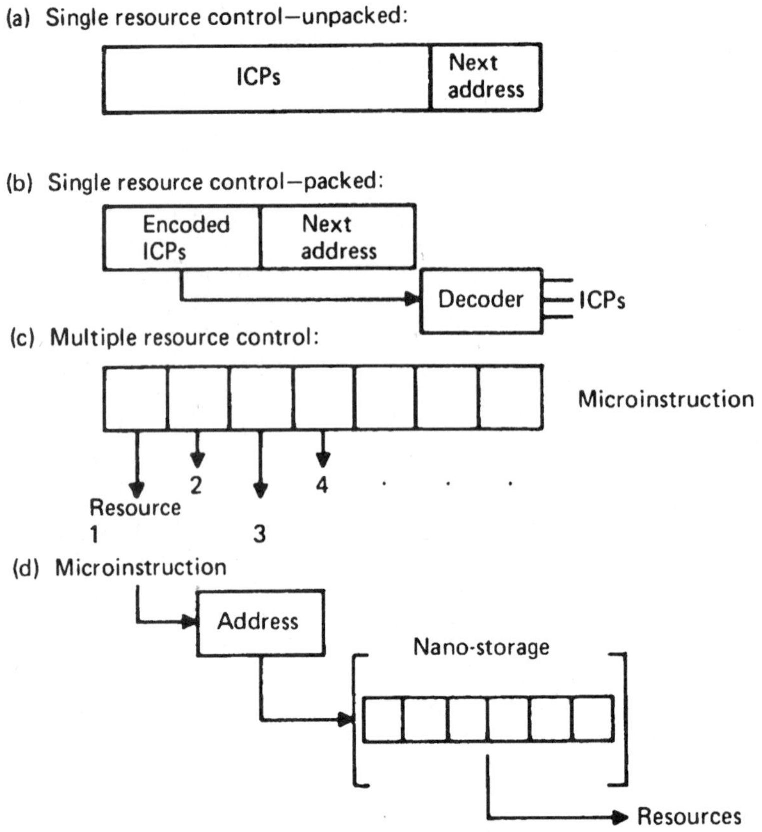

(a) Single resource control—unpacked:

ICPs	Next address

(b) Single resource control—packed:

Encoded ICPs	Next address

Decoder —— ICPs

(c) Multiple resource control:

Microinstruction

Resource 1   2   3   4   .   .   .

(d) Microinstruction

Address

Nano-storage

Resources

FIG. 6.   Some concepts used in microinstruction formats.

sible simultaneous use of resources in conjunction with a partitioned set of resources has also been referred to as a "horizontal" microinstruction. The alternative is to use a universal single resource (unpartitioned); its corresponding control mechanism is sometimes referred to as a "vertical" microinstruction.

These two notions are independent; i.e. one can have an unpacked single resource microinstruction or a packed parallel-control-type microinstruction. In any event, a "vertical" microinstruction is a short form of a microinstruction, usually using a coded (packed) specification of an operation and also usually referring to only one type of operation. The "horizontal" microinstruction usually has either an unpacked specification or an operation and/or specification of multiple simultaneous operations.

3. There is an allied notion relating to the structure of a microinstruction called a *nanoinstruction*. In this mode, a packed instruction (the microinstruction), with usually only one or two fields, is used as the basic control mechanism. However, instead of driving the resources directly, it indirectly refers to the resources through another storage level, the nanoinstruction. The nanoinstruction is the "horizontal" instruction that contains the exploded form of the control description.

Fig. 6(d) illustrates this concept in which the microinstructions are a sequence of addresses in which each address points to a nanoinstruction. A microinstruction may be horizontal and may have multiple resource specifications. The purpose of this technique is to reduce the size of the storage needed to represent the program. Use of a two-level control strategy requires both *microprogramming* and *nanoprogramming* to complete the interpretation.

Emulation   An *emulator* (Rosin, 1969; Husson, 1970, Habib, 1988) is the collection of routines and programs that interprets a language. Languages that are efficiently interpreted are said to have the directly executable language property. "Efficiency" in this sense is a relative measure, and includes factors such as the amount of storage required to represent a statement in a language, as well as the amount of time required to interpret that statement (Fig. 7).

In the past, emulation has mainly involved the interpretation of machine language with the use of microprogramming techniques for instruction interpretation. It is relatively easy for a single physical system to interpret more than one machine language. The physical machine, as defined by its microinstructions and their actions, is called a *host machine*. Machine languages that are emulated by sets of microprogrammed routines are called *image machines*. It is, of course, possible to write an

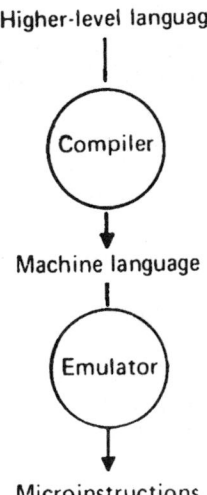

FIG. 7. Emulation.

TABLE 1. Emulation of 7090 Instructions

7090 Instruction	360 Emulation Routine	
AXT address to index true	EAXT DIL	Microroutine that does AXT Microroutine that does fetch and interpretation of next instruction
AXC address to index complemented	LCR	360 instruction that complements the address
	EAXT	Microroutine (see above)
	DIL	Microroutine (see above)
TMI transfer if minus	ESTO	Microroutine that puts the value into a work area of the 360 (the simulated accumulator)
	TM	360 instruction, test under mask (to get the sign bit)
	EBC	Microroutine that does a 7090 branch if the test is satisfied

emulator for one image machine in terms of another image machine language; thus, one can conceive of layers of emulators. However, more common usage of the term *emulator* implies that the interpretive set of programs is written in the microlanguage of the host processor.

Probably the most widely known use of emulation is that of IBM System/360. Most of the models of System/360 and System/370 are microprogrammed. Each model of the System/360 and System/370 is quite a distinct machine, with widely differing performance characteristics, data path size, etc. However, each has the common machine language of System/360. In all the microprogrammed models of the System/360, the interpretation of the machine language is done by an emulator that resides in microstorage. This emulator consists of a series of routines; each routine represents a particular System/360 instruction.

The emulation of a non-360 machine on a 360 machine is not so straightforward. Consider a Model 65 that emulates a 7090 (Table 1—see Tucker, 1967). The "emulation" of a 7090 on a Model 65 is more accurately described as a simulation of the 7090 using a combination of techniques, which includes 360 instructions, special instructions, and 7090 type instructions. The hybrid approach to emulation reduces the size of microstorage needed to provide emulation for both the 360 and the 7090. In the Model 65, each 7090 instruction is interpreted by an emulation subroutine that is contained in main memory (Fig. 8). This subroutine uses special instructions as well as conventional System/360 instructions. One of the most notable of the special instructions is the DIL (Do Interpretive Loop), which is a microprogrammed routine that does a fetch and interpretation of the next 7090 instruction. In addition to the DIL routine, a number of other subroutines are added to the microstorage to assist in emulating specific 7090 instructions. The configuration of main storage and microstorage during emulation is shown in Fig. 8.

Microprogramming and Computer Architecture
The development of large, high-speed read-write storage technology is now widely recognized for its at-

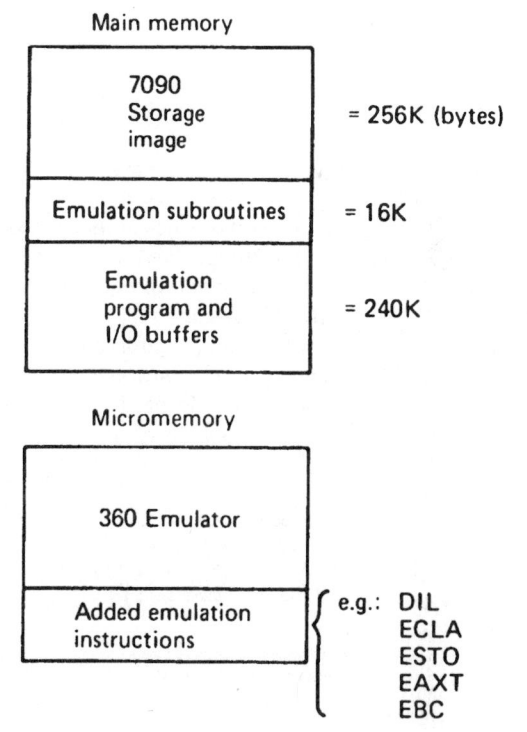

FIG. 8. Configuration of main memory and micromemory in a 360 Model 65 that is emulating a 7090 (Tucker, 1967).

tractiveness in microprogram storage implementations. Presently, there are two important trends in computer architecture arising from this use of microprogram storage: (1) enriching the capability of traditional machine

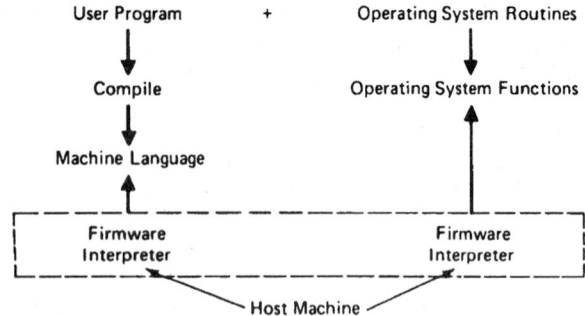

FIG. 9. Expanding operating system function and efficiency through emulation using firmware interpreters.

implementations (Fig. 9) and special language machines (Fig. 10).

An important trend in recent implementations of general-purpose computers is the use of large microprogram storage to support additional functionality in the instruction set. The large microprogram storage actually represents an extension mechanism that allows portions of the operating system and the diagnostic support system to be implemented efficiently in microprogramming. The user's investment in traditional program representations prohibits extensive changes to the user's instruction set and thus only small extensions are made at this level. However, instructions executed in the supervisory state, entered by calls to the operating system, such as special memory management functions, can be microcoded and emulated to improve the overall performance of a virtual storage system as well as improve file handling capabilities.

Microcoding parts of the operating system are especially interesting in the area of security detection, since usually the microprogram storage lies outside the addressable memory space of the problem state program. This prevents accidental contamination of the operating system by a problem state program.

Machine diagnostics for fault location are already a widely accepted use of microprogram storage. With a conventional instruction, the diagnostic program must pro-

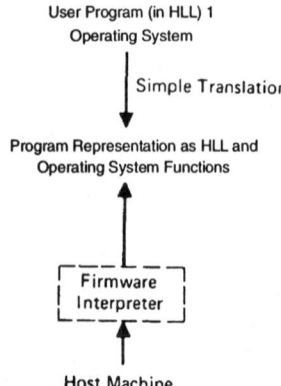

FIG. 10. High-level language (HLL) machine emulation.

ceed through a large number of state transitions before a result can be evaluated and a determination made as to whether or not a fault has been encountered. The microinstruction, on the other hand, by its nature, executes in exactly one state transition. Therefore, the diagnostic resolution through the use of microinstructions is much finer than by the use of traditional machine instructions. Thus, higher resolution and more efficient diagnostic routines can be implemented by the use of microprogram storage.

High-Level Language Machines By redefining the instruction set to make it cater to particular high-level language environments, one may realize an additional degree of representation efficiency (see Fig. 10). Of course, the resulting architecture is necessarily more limited in its flexibility. It is efficient only for one particular high-level language. However, in those cases where the emulators can be easily changed, so too can the interpreter for a particular high-level language.

In the high-level language machine, the instruction set is designed around the actions in the high-level language itself. A translation process still exists, but it is now a simple one- or two-pass process to bind the variable values to names before program interpretation is done. Of course, more efficient coding of all objects used in the program may be accomplished during the same translation. In a well-designed, directly executable language form (which has been called a DEL), the instructions to be interpreted lie in one-to-one correspondence with the actions called for in the high-level language program. Further, no new names or objects are introduced into the representation; thus, unique names in the high-level language are preserved uniquely in the DEL form. Coding of objects in the intermediate form can be done much more concisely than in a traditional image program, since the translator will know the number of objects used by the program or used within the scope of a subroutine and may use field sizes to represent these objects that are appropriate to the number of unique objects used (of the order of the logarithm to the base 2 of the number of objects in the scope of definition).

In a typical object code produced by standard compilers for familiar high-level language programs, there is an expansion factor of between 3 and 10 to 1 in the number of instructions in the object form when compared to the number of actions in the high-level language source form. But by the creation of efficient DEL representations, one can effectively reduce the number of instructions to be interpreted by exactly this factor and obtain a further program representation reduction by efficient coding of object names.

The result of all the above is very concise program representations that have been created with a minimum compilation time. Since the number of objects to be interpreted has been reduced by a substantial factor, so too is the interpretation time provided that an efficient host implementation for the emulator is available.

An opposite approach used by RISC (*q.v.*) microprocessors is to rely heavily on compilers to map applications onto very simple high-speed processors. It is structurally similar to compiling applications into microinstructions, bypassing the intermediate instruction level. This has been successful for microprocessors, as it optimizes the use of silicon area for processor implementations. This approach comes at the expense of memory bandwidth. As microprocessors increase in speed, it is expected that the bandwidth problem will be addressed by more complex memory hierarchies and/or increased attention to instruction encoding.

References

1967. Tucker, S. G. "Microprogram Control for System 360," *IBM Sys. J.* **6**: 222–241.
1969. Rosin, R. F. "Contemporary Concepts in Microprogramming and Emulation," *Computing Surveys* **1**: 197–212 (December).
1970. Husson, S. S. *Microprogramming: Principles and Practices.* Englewood Cliffs, NJ: Prentice-Hall.
1988. Habib, S. *Microprogramming and Firmware Engineering Methods.* New York: Van Nostrand Reinhold.

MICHAEL J. FLYNN

MINICOMPUTER

For articles on related subjects *see* ADDRESSING; COMPUTER SYSTEMS; DIGITAL COMPUTERS: CONTEMPORARY SYSTEMS; INSTRUCTION SET; MICROPROCESSORS AND MICROCOMPUTERS; and MICROPROGRAMMING.

A *minicomputer* is a digital computer whose price and capability lies above that of a personal computer or workstation (*q.v.*) and below that of a mainframe (*q.v.*). What distinguishes a workstation from a minicomputer is not its processing engine (although typically it is a microprocessor) but rather its graphics orientation and dependence on a network that supplies missing resources, such as disks and printers. While a minicomputer system can include both graphics devices and network connections, it more often is relegated to the task of either providing time-sharing services to a large class of users, or it is used as a standalone real-time processor.

Minicomputers can be broadly classified as having 12-, 16-, 18-, 24-, or 32-bit word lengths with memory sizes of 256K–128M bytes provided in modules of 256K or 1MB. Nearly all minicomputers employ a parallel internal processor structure with a high-speed bus and a clock rate of 4–40 MHz. The basic configuration ranges in price from $4,000–$500,000, with the cost of peripheral devices usually far outstripping the cost of the machine. The use of low-cost LSI and VLSI logic has removed many of the initial design constraints, such as:

1. Limited addressing capability.
2. Lack of general-purpose registers and accumulators.
3. Elementary I/O processing and devices.
4. Limited interrupt schemes.

Although it is becoming increasingly difficult to distinguish differences in the range of applications of minicomputers and larger-scale (mainframe) computers, there are some differences in usage which are worth mentioning.

1. For minicomputers with word lengths shorter than 32 bits, precision is limited without use of multiple-precision software.
2. Although high-level languages are available, the use of assembly language for writing user application-specific programs is more common than on mainframes.
3. Although some minis are run in a closed-shop, production environment, many are still run in an open-shop environment, with the user acting as operator, programmer, and application analyst. A typical installation is shown in Fig.1.
4. A substantial number of minis operate in a dedicated environment for which the system has been specifically configured.
5. For other than standard applications, the mini user must, in general, be more sophisticated and ingenious, since minicomputer operating systems do not necessarily provide the kind of environment (e.g. real-time) that a mini is often used for.

The trend of the minicomputer market has shifted from an OEM (*q.v.*) to an end-user market, and, as a result, more sophisticated software (requiring additional hardware) is being developed. This allows the user to buy a turnkey minicomputer system that has a complete operating system capable of supporting one or many users simultaneously. Indeed, the new breed of 32-bit machines look increasingly like their mainframe counterparts.

The languages available on these machines usually include Fortran, Basic, APL, Cobol, PL/I, C, and Pascal, besides other proprietary dialects of these standards. As we go through new generations of minicomputer systems, the mini and large computer are beginning to appear as one, at least from the point of view of the applications programmer.

Differences Among Minicomputers Despite basic similarity of appearance, not all minicomputers

FIG. 1. An HP 3000 minicomputer system (Courtesy of Hewlett-Packard).

are alike. Thus, although two manufacturers may provide similar capabilities on their 16- or 32-bit minis, the machines may differ in such minor things as use of octal or hexadecimal notation and a number of accumulators/index registers to other considerations, such as addressing techniques, I/O methods, interrupt structures, and instruction code assignments.

With so many types of minicomputers being produced by different manufacturers, the amount of variation seems unlimited. The same manufacturer will have different "families," whose commonality is achieved by machines that have a given word length and an essentially similar instruction set. Because of the similarities and differences, the user must choose a mini both on its external characteristics (software and support) and on its internal characteristics (word length, I/O structure, etc.) in light of the intended primary focus—namely, the tasks to be performed.

Internal Characteristics   As with most larger computers, the basic instruction in any minicomputer may be divided into three fields—the operation to be performed, the address mode to be used, and the address field (see Fig. 2). Often, the last two fields are repeated if more than single operand instructions are allowed. The size of each field is very important in that it determines much of the internal machine characteristics (e.g. how many registers, how much memory may be referenced directly, how many distinct op codes will exist).

Operation Codes   Since the size of the op code field of an instruction is often limited by the short word length of older minis, the number of distinct op codes is increased by a simple trick. Instructions that do not reference memory do not have address fields. Instead, these instructions are lumped together under one basic op code, and the address field is used as an extension of the basic op code so as to specify a particular operation within the group.

On some machines, the extension field is likened to horizontal microprogramming, where the individual bits can be used independently to perform such functions as clearing the accumulator, skipping if a register is zero (or positive or negative), and shifting the contents of a specified register/accumulator. As a result of these instruction extenders, most minicomputers have large instruction sets when all the various legal combinations are considered, though RISC (*q.v.*) machines are beginning to appear.

New machines, with their longer word lengths, allocate 1 byte for the instruction codes. This simplifies instruction decoding and allows for a large combination of op codes. If 1 byte isn't enough, one op code can be reserved to indicate a second instruction code byte.

Addressing Characteristics   Part of the basic instruction word is the *address mode field*. Possible addressing options include absolute/relative addressing, direct/indirect addressing, and indexed/no-indexed addressing. These different modes allow the programmer to expand the range of possible addresses that programs can generate. Since the number of bits available for specifying the address is small in 12- or 16-bit minis, it is absolutely essential that various addressing options be part of the addressing structure.

Although newer minis may address all of memory directly and absolutely, such is not the normal case in older machines. Instead, it was more common to be able to address only 256 (8 bits) or 4,096 (12 bits) memory locations. As a result, the address field of the instruction is used relatively to address small portions of memory by combining its value with the current program counter value, resulting in a floating page of fixed-size, or with a page-register value, such as the high-order bits of the program-counter value, resulting in a fixed page of a fixed size.

Fig. 3 depicts both the floating and fixed page addressing schemes. In Fig. 3(a), the program-generated address X is added algebraically to the program-counter value, generating the effective memory address. In Fig. 3(b), only the page bits of the program counter are used with X to generate the effective address. In this second case, the value of X is always assumed to be positive, so that the page is fixed in both size and position.

One advantage of relative addressing is the position independence of the generated code. Since only the relative distance between instructions and data are preserved as part of the instruction word, the word can be easily moved around in memory without requiring the services of a relocatable assembler and loader.

When indirect addressing is used, the entire word pointed to as the address field can be utilized, thus expanding significantly the addressing space of the instruction. The level of indirectness may be single or multilevel, of course, depending on whether the indirect bit is associated with the instruction or the address field.

Current technology has produced minicomputers with truly general-purpose registers that may be used as index registers, accumulators, program counters, and stack registers. When used as index registers (and when implemented in active logic rather than as special-purpose memory locations), general-purpose registers allow large blocks of memory to be referenced without requiring additional instruction execution time. Additionally,

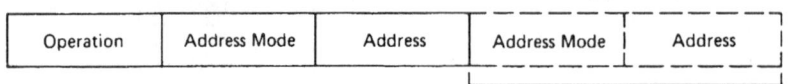

Operation	Address Mode	Address	Address Mode	Address

Repeated for Multi-Address Instructions

FIG. 2.   Instruction format.

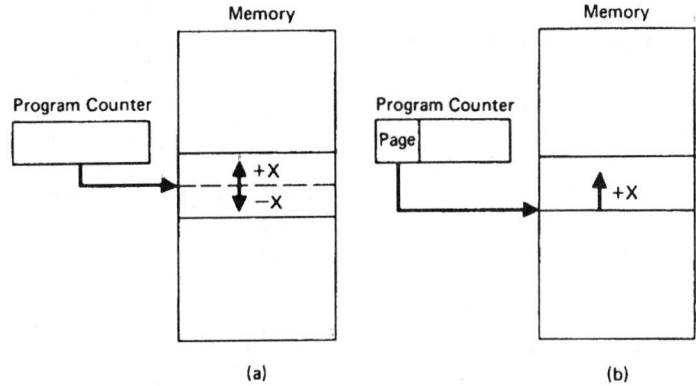

FIG. 3.   Fixed and floating pages. (a) Floating page: effective address = PC $\pm$ X. (b) Fixed page: effective address = Page + X.

these registers (whether part of memory or separate hardware locations) may be used in an auto-indexing fashion such that, when utilized indirectly, their contents are automatically incremented (or decremented). Auto-indexing is useful for loops that step through arrays.

When it is possible to use all the addressing modes described, the order of execution for calculating the effective address becomes quite important. Depending on the size of the address field, post- or pre-indexing is performed after "derelativizing" the address field. For small address field machines, post-indexing is preferred, since the indirect address field can address a larger portion of memory, which is then indexed. On the other hand, for a large address field where more of memory can be addressed, it is particularly convenient to perform indexing before indirect addressing for such things as subroutine parameter passing, where the parameters may be addresses that have to be indirectly referenced.

There is another type of addressing scheme, which is associated with the variable-length instruction minicomputer. These machines use an extra memory word for the address field (when necessary) and specify that the instruction is more than one word long by setting the appropriate bits in the address-mode field. These machines require extra memory cycles for fetching the extra words, but clearly the time is no more than the time required to perform indirect addressing.

Finally, the larger minicomputers use 24- and 32-bit addressing, thus allowing for the direct specification of enormous amounts of memory (up to 4 gigabytes). These minis don't actually contain that much real memory, but use a virtual memory (*q.v.*) addressing technique to collapse or map the virtual memory address into its physical memory location. Since not all of virtual memory can be resident in physical memory, a large portion of it must reside on secondary storage. When needed, this copy of what would have been in physical memory is swapped with what currently resides there.

Input/Output   The range of peripheral devices that may be connected to a minicomputer is quite large and includes graphic displays, line/page printers, disks, cassette tapes, magnetic tapes, plotters, and telecommunica-

tion equipment. Because of the sophistication of the minicomputer I/O bus, a large number of peripheral devices may be attached.

Data and control information is transferred to the I/O device either through the mini's accumulator or through special device registers. Once initiated (by making a request to the device controller), the I/O device is capable of operating concurrently with the CPU. Indeed, it is often possible to have several devices running simultaneously with the CPU, stealing memory cycles as needed.

Many minicomputers include a direct memory access (DMA) feature as part of the computer's structure. A DMA port allows an I/O device to communicate directly with memory without tying up the I/O bus or the CPU. Typical devices for which a DMA port would be useful are high-speed mass-storage devices and special-purpose interfaces to time-critical processes, such as color graphic displays.

One of the key features of a minicomputer is its interrupt structure. Depending on the application, the sophistication of the interrupt system may be more important than machine speed or instruction repertoire. The interrupt structures commonly found on minis range from single-level without priority to multi-level with priority.

A direct consequence of the multilevel interrupt structure is the automatic stacking of the processor state words. By means of a stack register, any level of interrupt nesting is possible. In addition, by using the stack register for the automatic stacking of state words during subroutine activation, recursive programming and co-routine (*q.v.*) structures are more easily facilitated. Further, by introducing trap instructions into the instruction set, it is possible to link independently written software routines and/or emulate/simulate hardware features (e.g. multiply/divide, floating point) not part of the basic instruction set.

Software   The range of software packages available for most minicomputers is quite large. At the very minimal level, all systems include an assembler, a loader, and editor, an I/O programming system, a debugging tool, and a mathematical utilities package. Each of these programs can be executed on the basic or minimal hardware configuration.

As the size of memory is increased, more sophisticated software becomes available to the user. This software includes high-level and special-purpose languages, as well as database software and networking.

By adding a mass-storage device, such as a disk, to the minicomputer system, the minicomputer user gains the flexibility of a single-user disk operating system, or a batch operating system. In addition, by adding memory hardware for protection and relocation, background/foreground programming becomes possible, or even time-sharing systems capable of supporting up to 256 simultaneous users.

As a result of the recent trend to provide more sophisticated software, it is becoming more common to find minicomputers serving as general-purpose computing machines. On the other hand, the number of potential applications is almost limitless, and minicomputers can be found in a wide range of environments.

Applications The greatest use of minicomputers has been in areas other than general-purpose computing. These areas include:

1. Industrial applications, such as control of power generation, petrochemical systems, data acquisition, and testing of equipment and devices.
2. Biomedical control for experiment monitoring.
3. In larger computer systems for communication and peripheral control, such as data concentrators, satellite peripherals, and intelligent terminals.
4. Intelligent graphic terminals and interactive graphic systems that may be part of general-purpose, graphic-oriented computing.
5. Microprogrammable minicomputer systems that are capable of being tailored to specific applications and/or environments.

It is important to distinguish between microprogrammable computers and the simple operation-code extension mentioned earlier. The value of the microprogrammable machine can be found in its compatibility with other different machines by emulation of the same instruction set, in its ability to allow the user to tailor a machine at the most primitive level to accommodate particular requirements, or in its ability to allow the user the flexibility of experimenting with new ideas and designs.

Another distinction occurs between microprogrammable minis and minis with read-only memories (ROM - q.v.). Although ROMs are often used to hold microprograms, they may also be used to store programs for minicomputer applications that do not change and where the instructions may be locked into memory, providing decreased memory cycle time and greater integrity against accidental destruction.

Future Developments As the cost of the hardware goes down with new technological advances, the cost/performance ratio of minicomputer hardware will continue to improve more dramatically than for large computer systems, where cost has remained fairly constant and performance has changed only slightly. As a result, there will be an increasing use of minicomputers in new applications areas (e.g. hospital record keeping, retail inventory management, and specialized commercial applications areas). Indeed, as the sophistication of the software improves, it will become increasingly difficult to distinguish minicomputers from larger ones.

References

1979. Eckhouse, Richard and Morris, Robert. *Minicomputer Systems: Organization, Programming and Applications (PDP-11).* Englewood Cliffs, NJ: Prentice-Hall.
1984. Tanenbaum, Andrew, "Structured Computer Organization" 2nd Ed. Englewood Cliffs, NJ: Prentice-Hall.
1989. Levy, Henry and Eckhouse, Richard. *Computer Programming and Architecture: the VAX*, 2nd Ed. Bedford MA: Digital Press.

RICHARD H. ECKHOUSE, JR.

MODEM

For articles on related subjects *see* BANDWIDTH; BAUD; CYCLIC REDUNDANCY CHECK; DSU/CSU; and NETWORKS, COMPUTER.

A *modem* is a device used to transmit data between computers, workstations, and other peripheral devices interconnected by means of conventional communication lines supporting analog transmission. Modems transform (modulate) data from a digital device to analog form suitable for transmission over such lines. Since, in general, data flows in both directions, modems are also able to receive an analog signal from some remote device and restore (demodulate) it back to its original digital form, as shown in Fig. 1. The word modem stems from the *modu*lation-*dem*odulation process performed. In addition to performing the basic transformation between digital and analog signals, modems also can perform a variety of control functions that coordinate data flow over the analog communication link. Terms usually used synonymously for modems include *data set* or *data phone*. A DSU/CSU (data service unit/channel service unit) performs the same function as a modem, but is used on communication lines supporting digital transmission conforming to ATT publication 62310.

Modem Types Many different types of modems are available, depending on their transmission speed, whether they are installed internally or connected externally to the computer with which they are used, and their mode of use:

- Serial or parallel transmission;
- Synchronous or asynchronous transmission;
- Simplex, duplex, or full duplex operation;

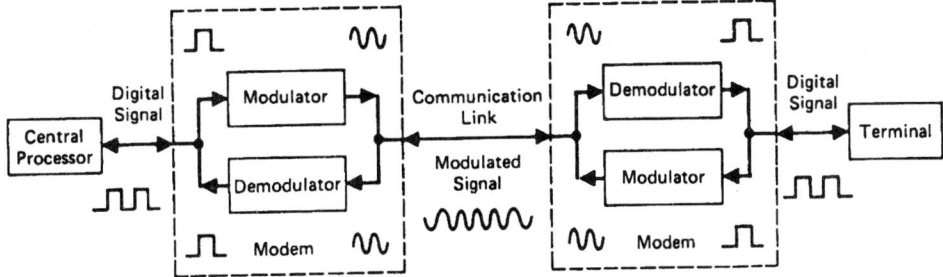

FIG. 1.

- Long distance (long-haul) or limited distance (short-haul) operation; and
- Operation over dedicated or dial-up lines.

Most modems transmit characters serially, bit by bit, but others are designed to transmit a character in one-bit time by receiving or transmitting its bits in parallel over several lines in order to increase the effective transmission rate. Some modems, called *acoustic couplers*, can be acoustically coupled to the telephone handset. Since parallel modems are not very common and since use of acoustic couplers is now rare, further comments will be confined to serial modems that do not use acoustic coupling.

Internal modems are built into computing equipment such as personal computers. External modems have their own separate case with independent power supply and are connected to the computer by cable.

In synchronous transmission, the characters are transmitted at a fixed rate, usually at or in excess of 2,400 bits per second (bps). This mode of transmission is used primarily for high-speed communication between buffered systems. Synchronization between receiver and transmitter is achieved by using special SYNCH characters at the beginning of each block or message. In asynchronous transmission, the characters are sent one at a time and the interval between them can vary arbitrarily. Synchronization is accomplished by adding *start* and *stop* bits to each character to allow delineation of adjacent characters. This mode is used primarily for transmission between unbuffered devices. Synchronous transmission is more difficult to implement but is more efficient, since no start and stop bits are needed. Software for simultaneous support of many asynchronous devices, however, is generally much easier to implement than for a similar number of synchronous devices.

Most modern modems can operate in simplex, half duplex, and full duplex modes. *Simplex* refers to one-way transmission only and hence is rarely used. *Full duplex* refers to simultaneous transmission in both directions, while in *half duplex* systems the data may flow in both directions but not at the same time.

Initially, most modems were long-haul; i.e. they would function satisfactorily for unlimited distances over the public telephone network. Today, one may obtain limited-distance, or short-haul, modems. These are specifically designed to work on short (usually 50 miles or less) point-to-point dedicated lines and, in general, offer higher transmission speeds than their similarly priced long-haul counterparts.

Modems that must operate over the public switched (telephone) network must have a dialing unit or auxiliary set to allow dialing from the originating device to establish a connection with the destination. The dialing unit may be manual, automatic (controlled by the computing device), or both. A conventional telephone suitably connected to a modem can perform this function.

Modulation Techniques Conventional telephone lines have a bandwidth of about 3,000 hertz (cycles per second). Data transmission over such lines is limited to 2,400 baud or state changes per second. To modulate a digital signal over such a communication channel, a modem may use amplitude modulation (AM), frequency modulation (FM), or phase modulation (PM), as shown in Fig 2. The type of modulation used depends upon the transmission speed. FM, in the form of *frequency-shift keying* (FSK), is used almost exclusively for asynchronous communication up to 1,800 bits/second. A form of PM is used for synchronous communication at 2,000 to 2,400 bits/second. A combination of AM and PM, called *Quadrature Amplitude Modulation* (QAM), is used for speeds between 2,400 and 9,600 bits/second. At 9,600 bits/second, for example, 4 bits are encoded as one of 16 possible combinations of phase and amplitude, and 2,400 of these combinations are sent each second to achieve the desired 9,600 bits/second. Another sophisticated technique is *Trellis Code Modulation* (TCM) in which several data bits and one or two redundancy bits are encoded as one of 64 or 128 phase and amplitude combinations to achieve transmission rates of up to 14,400 bits/second over conventional telephone lines.

Modem Design Modems are continuously becoming smaller, cheaper, faster, and smarter. Relatively inexpensive programmable modems operate at up to 2,400 bits/second and include features such as auto-dial, automatic speed detection of the modem being called, and automatic switching to that speed. More expensive, higher-speed modems may include additional features such as improved diagnostics, multiple modulation techniques (e.g. FSK at 300 and 1,200 bits/second, QAM at 2,400, 4,800, and 9,600 bits/second), error detection and correction, data compression, fall back to a lower speed to reduce the number of retransmission errors, automatic

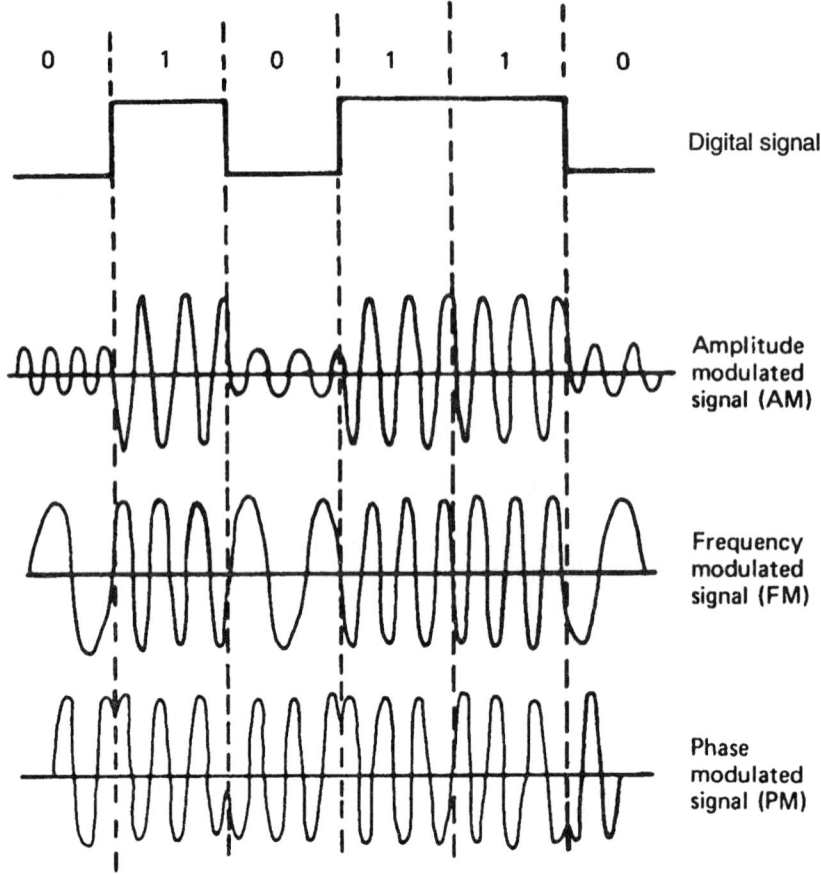

FIG. 2.

equalization to allow for the wide variation encountered on telephone lines, call back security, fax reception and remote configuration.

Many of the more sophisticated modems use the Microcom Networking Protocol ™ (MNP) to achieve the highest rate of error-free transmission for interactive and file transfer applications. The modem buffers the data and automatically appends a cyclic redundancy check to transmitted blocks for error detection and correction through retransmission. Data compression hardware in the modem can provide an effective transfer rate up to 300% greater than conventional modems of the same speed. When the rate of retransmissions due to detected line errors exceeds a certain threshold, both the transmitting and receiving modems may automatically reduce the transmission speed to minimize the effect of adverse line conditions.

Call back security provides a mechanism of protecting networks from unauthorized access. The modem can include a list of valid phone number–password combinations with routines for automatic password check and call back. Host sites can use this feature to call back remote sites immediately after being called by them. In addition to security, this feature can also redistribute and possibly reduce phone line costs through host site call origination.

Remote configuration and diagnostic capabilities provide network management features that allow a cen-

tral site to configure modems at remote sites and to run a variety of line and modem diagnostics.

Most modems in the United States use the EIA (Electronic Industries Association) Standard RS-232 specifications to define the interface between the modem and computing device. The international version of this interface is CCITT (Comite Consultatif Internationale de Telegraphie et Telephonie) recommendation V.24. Other standards define frequency assignments for compatibility among modems and specifications for error control as well as data compression and decompression.

The newest modems use microprocessor technology, which allows them to provide some of the features discussed above at relatively low cost. All indications are that the number and sophistications of these features will continue to increase in the future. The goals are to simplify network management, improve its security and reliability, and maximize the effective (error-free) data transmission rate.

References

1972. Davey, J. R. "Modems," *Proc. IEEE* **60**, *11*: 1284–1292 (November).

1988. McNamana, J. E. *Technical Aspects of Data Communication*, 3rd Ed. Bedford, MA: Digital Press.

JOHN S. SOBOLEWSKI

MODULA-2

For articles on related subjects *see* ABSTRACT DATA TYPE; ENCAPSULATION; INFORMATION HIDING; PROCEDURE-ORIENTED LANGUAGES; and SOFTWARE REUSABILITY.

Modula-2 is one of the programming languages designed by the Turing Award (*q.v.*) scientist Niklaus Wirth. The name was derived from the term "module," which was used to describe the three forms of Modula-2 compilation units—the *program module*, the *definition module*, and the *implementation module*.

Wirth defined Modula-2 based on his earlier design experiences with Pascal and Modula ("Modula-1"), as well as with the Alto computer. In 1976–77, Professor Wirth took a sabbatical leave at the Xerox Palo Alto Research Center to work with the Alto computer design team. The next year, Wirth started the Lilith personal computer project at the Institut fur Informatik of the Swiss Federal Institute of Technology (ETH). The guiding principle in the project was that Modula-2 would be the systems programming language for the Lilith and the Lilith would be the architecture for Modula-2. Since there would be no assembler, the language had to be suitable not only for high-level, application programming but also for low-level, machine-dependent coding, such as device handling and storage allocation.

Both the language and the Lilith architecture embody design principles that stress elegance and simplicity. During the lifetime (1978–88) of the Lilith project, operating systems, graphics packages, database systems, network protocol suites, file servers, and innumerable other system and application modules were all developed in Modula-2. Within a few years of its introduction on the Lilith, Modula-2 was in use worldwide.

Pascal was designed so that its users could code and exchange programs. Modula-2 was designed so that program components (modules) could be reused. The changes to Pascal involved a simplified syntax, a reduction in features, and a new emphasis on interface design. Modula-2 avoids language complexity by providing libraries of mechanisms for standard programming abstractions, such as exception handling, string processing, I/O, and concurrent programming (*q.v.*). Standardization is achieved by selecting a single interface and the implementation semantics for every abstraction. For example, text I/O procedures are defined in the "InOut" module. There is also a standard module called "SYSTEM" for machine dependencies that support low-level programming. The SYSTEM module defines a WORD type that can be used to store any other type that occupies one machine word. It also provides the ADDRESS type that is compatible with any pointer type.

A Modula-2 DEFINITION module defines the interface specification for a data abstraction. A DEFINITION module is compiled separately from its corresponding IMPLEMENTATION module and, once compiled, it need never change. A DEFINITION module may contain only declarations of constants, types, variables, and procedure headings. Only those procedure headings intended for use by other programmers are listed in the DEFINITION module.

The corresponding IMPLEMENTATION module contains local constant, type, and variable declarations as well as the procedure definitions both for the external (DEFINITION) procedures and for those used internally in the implementation. Programs can be developed in a top-down fashion by first creating several DEFINITION modules and then elaborating the implementation parts as needed. Every IMPLEMENTATION module can contain statements that initialize its local data structures before the module is invoked elsewhere in a program. In addition to this consistency feature, Modula-2 semantics require the detection of IMPLEMENTATION modules that are out-of-date with respect to their DEFINITION modules.

Fig. 1 lists a subset of the DEFINITION and IMPLEMENTATION parts for a string-handling module. The text between the "(*" and the "*)" is treated as a comment. The type specification, "ARRAY OF", is a feature of Modula-2. The omission of the array bounds causes the formal parameter type to match any shape array that has a matching component type ("CHAR" in the Fig. 1). The lower bound of the resulting parameter is zero, and the upper bound can be accessed with "HIGH(i)". This flexible array notation makes it easy to define generic interfaces that would be impossible to specify in Pascal.

There is nothing in the interface that binds the user to a particular implementation of the "String" abstract data type. The binding can be accomplished by substituting one implementation module for another. This can be contrasted with the approach of other languages in which the implementation binding occurs when a program is compiled.

Fig. 2 illustrates the use of another Modula-2 innovation, the *opaque type*, to define a communication channel abstraction. An opaque type is not bound to a data structure until the corresponding IMPLEMENTATION module is defined. This provides perfect *information hiding* (*q.v.*). As a result, the implementation can be changed arbitrarily and recompiled without inducing recompilations in any dependent modules. For example, the sample implementation uses an end-of-string sentinel. An alternative would be to keep the length in the zeroth array position, which could improve the efficiency of a number of the string operators. Either alternative could be substituted without recompiling dependent modules.

The channel abstraction is similar to that provided by the Occam programming language. Channels implement interprocess communication via synchronous message passing. The use of the "ARRAY OF WORD" type for the "message" parameter causes it to be type compatible with any argument type. As a result, processes can send messages composed from scalar types, records, or arrays. The example illustrates the ease with which different models of computation, such as a concurrent programming model in this case, can be made available to the application programmer. This can be contrasted with the approach of other languages in which the user is restricted to a single model of computation.

Modula-2 deserves a place in the history of computer science for three reasons. First, the integrated design of a computer architecture, language, and operating environ-

```
DEFINITION MODULE String;
  (*  A string is a vector of characters, typically 8 bits.
      A string is indexed from left to right, [0..HIGH(s)].
  *)
  CONST FIRST = 0;                    (* denotes the beginning of a string *)
        LAST  = MAX(CARDINAL);  (* denotes the end of a string *)

  PROCEDURE Insert (VAR s : ARRAY OF CHAR; what : ARRAY OF CHAR; at : CARDINAL);
  (* Inserts "what" before position "at" in "s", shifting "s" to the right as necessary.
     The result when characters are shifted off the right end of "s" is implementation
     dependent. FIRST or LAST can be used for "at" to effect concatenation on the left or
     right, respectively.
  *)
  PROCEDURE Length (VAR s : ARRAY OF CHAR):CARDINAL;
  (* Returns the length in characters of string "s" *)
END String.

IMPLEMENTATION MODULE String;
  (* The implementation assumes that strings shorter than their storage area are
     terminated by a marker character, usually OC. Result strings longer than their
     storage area generate an error.
  *)
  IMPORT Character;
  FROM Errors IMPORT SoftwareError;

  PROCEDURE Length(VAR s : ARRAY OF CHAR):CARDINAL;
  BEGIN (* implementation not shown *)
  END Length;

PROCEDURE Insert(VAR s : ARRAY OF CHAR; what : ARRAY OF CHAR; at : CARDINAL);
    VAR lengths, lengthw, i, j : CARDINAL;
  BEGIN
    lengths := Length(s);                        (* range is [0..HIGH(s) + 1] *)
    lengthw := Length(what);
    IF at > lengths THEN at := lengths; END;  (* concatenate on the right *)
    IF lengths + lengthw > HIGH(s) + 1 THEN
      SoftwareError ("String.Insert:inserted string doesn't fit");
    ELSIF lengths + lengthw # HIGH(s) + 1 THEN
      s[lengths + lengthw] := Character.EOS;   (* update end-of-string marker *)
    END;
    IF lengths > 0 THEN
      j := lengths + lengthw - 1;
      FOR i := lengths-1 TO at BY - 1 DO     (* shift target to the right *)
        s[j] := s[i];    DEC(j);
      END;
    END;
    j := 0;
    FOR i := at TO at + lengthw-1 DO          (* copy the inserted string *)
      s[i] := what[j];   INC(j);
    END;
  END Insert;

END String.
```

FIG. 1.

ment is a revolutionary ideal that is seldom attempted in practice. Second, Modula-2 challenges the programmer to put as much effort into interface design as is invested in implementation. A good interface specification can last forever; implementations change as new technology is introduced or when application requirements are modified. Finally, Modula-2 encourages elegant and simple designs for data abstractions.

```
DEFINITION MODULE (*Occam*) Channels;
  FROM SYSTEM IMPORT WORD;              (* ARRAY OF WORD matches any type *)

  TYPE Channel;                                (* opaque type; declaration is hidden
                                                  in the implementation module *)
  PROCEDURE Parallel (p, q : PROC);
  (* Transforms procedures p and q into processes and runs them in parallel
     The caller is delayed until both p and q terminate
  *)
  PROCEDURE Open(VAR c : Channel);
  (* Initializes a message-passing channel for use by processes *)
  PROCEDURE Close(VAR c : Channel);
  (* Terminates an idle channel so that it cannot be used *)
  PROCEDURE Send(c : Channel; message : ARRAY OF WORD);
  (* Sending process is delayed until the receiver picks up the message *)
  PROCEDURE Receive(c : Channel; VAR message : ARRAY OF WORD);
  (* Receiving process is delayed until a message arrives *)
  PROCEDURE Status(c : Channel; VAR blockedSenders, blockedReceivers :
   CARDINAL);
    (* Count the number of blocked processes *)
END Channels.


MODULE TimingTest;
(* Send 30,000 messages between two processes to compute the average time necessary to
   send a simple message.
*)
FROM Channels IMPORT Channel, Parallel, Open, Send, Receive;
FROM InOut IMPORT Read, Write;

VAR n : CARDINAL;                       (* repeat count to collect
                                           performance statistics *)

    ch: CHAR;
    c : Channel;

  PROCEDURE P;                          (* started as a process *)



    VAR k : CARDINAL;                   (* runs in parallel with Q *)
  BEGIN
    REPEAT Receive(c, k) UNTIL k = 0;   (* loop until last message *)
  END P;                                (* procedure exit kills the process *)

  PROCEDURE Q;                           (* runs in parallel with P *)
  BEGIN
    REPEAT n := n − 1; Send(c, n); UNTIL n = 0;    (* send n messages and exit *)
  END Q;

BEGIN
  n := 30000;                    (* runs in 5.5 seconds on a Lilith *)
  Open(c);                       (* initialize the message channel *)
  Write("["); Read(ch);          (* let user start timing *)
  Parallel(P, Q);                (* creates processes; waits for completion *)
  Write("]");                    (* stop timing; difference/30000 is the average *)
END TimingTest.
```

FIG. 2.

References

1984. Wirth, N. "Schemes for Multiprogramming and Their Implementation in Modula-2," Technical Report #59, Institut fur Informatik, ETH.
1985. Wirth, N. *Programming in Modula-2*, 3rd Ed. Berlin: Springer-Verlag.
1987. Stubbs, D. F. and Webre, N. W. *Data Structures with Abstract Data Types and Modula-2*. Monterey, CA: Brooks/Cole.

ROBERT COOK

MODULAR PROGRAMMING

For articles on related subjects *see* ENCAPSULATION; INFORMATION HIDING; OBJECT-ORIENTED PROGRAMMING; PROGRAM VERIFICATION; SOFTWARE ENGINEERING; and STRUCTURED PROGRAMMING.

A program or system *module* can be defined as a logically self-contained and discrete part of a larger program. A complete program can thus be considered to be a collection of modules. A properly constructed module accepts input that is well defined as to content and structure, carries out a well-defined set of processing actions, and produces output that is well defined as to content and structure. A properly constructed module, as the term is normally used, has only one entry point and only one exit point. If it is a subroutine, it always returns only to the statement following the one that called it into play.

In many languages, a subroutine is functionally equivalent to a module, although most languages permit violations of the guidelines just stated, such as allowing multiple entry and exit points.

The purpose of *modular programming* is to break a complex task into smaller and simpler subtasks which, among other things, facilitates writing correct programs. A program consisting of modules of properly designed scope (typically a page or two of coding at most) is much simpler to design, write, and test than is the same program when it is not so modularized. Further, the interactions between parts of a program or system can be rigidly restricted to the interactions between modules, which greatly simplifies the understanding of how a program works. In the rapidly developing methodology of *object-oriented programming*, the concept of a module has been perfected to encompass modern ideas of *data encapsulation* and *information hiding*.

In the development of large software systems by teams of programmers, good modularization is essential if the portions written by different programmers are to mesh effectively in a reasonable period of time. Finally, since all programs and systems that are used over a period of time have to be maintained and modified, good modularization also aids in doing these chores more quickly and accurately.

Good program design starts with the most general definition of the function of the program, and proceeds through a sequence of increasingly detailed specifications. This technique, called *top-down design*, is an aspect of structured programming and is greatly enhanced by modular programming.

DANIEL D. MCCRACKEN

MONITOR. *See also* HARDWARE MONITOR; and SOFTWARE MONITOR.

MONITOR

For articles on related subjects *see* ABSTRACT DATA TYPE; CLASS; CONCURRENT PROGRAMMING; and OPERATING SYSTEMS.

The term *monitor* denotes a control program that oversees the allocation of resources among a set of user programs. It was, along with *supervisor* and *executive,* an early synonym for *operating system*. An old example is the Fortran Monitor System (FMS), which appeared on the IBM 709 series beginning in the late 1950s to provide run-time support for Fortran programs. A more modern example is the Conversational Monitor System (CMS) for the IBM VM/370; CMS is a single-user interactive system that runs on a virtual machine (VM) implemented by the control program (CP) of the VM/370 operating system.

In the early 1970s, the term *monitor* was applied to a formal program construct used to simplify operating systems by providing a separate scheduler for each class of resources. This kind of monitor has a syntactic form that generalizes the idea of an abstract data type; it defines a set of procedures for manipulating a set of objects concurrently. As with abstract data types, the monitor's procedures enable the caller to perform high-level operations on the monitor's resources; the details of resource status and structure are hidden inside the monitor. Unlike abstract data types, monitors have internal locks that permit only one process to execute monitor instructions at a time. Other processes must wait in a queue to enter the monitor. If a process in the monitor stops to wait for a resource to become available, the monitor must be unlocked so that another process (e.g. one that will release the desired resource) can gain access.

The following example of a resource manager is adapted from Hoare's 1974 paper on monitors. Monitor RM handles the allocation of a set of resources whose indices $1, \ldots, N$ are initially in the set UNITS.

```
type RM = monitor:

    var nonbusy: condition;
    type unitnumber = 1..N;
    type UNITS = set of unitnumber;

    function entry acquire: unitnumber;
    var i: unitnumber;
    begin
        if UNITS = [ ] then nonbusy.wait;
                                  ([ ] denotes empty set)
```

```
    i: = "any member of UNITS";
    UNITS := UNITS – i;
                            (Deletes i from UNITS)
        return i;
    end acquire;


    procedure entry release (i: unitnumber);
    begin
        UNITS := UNITS + i;
                            (Inserts i in UNITS)
        nonbusy. signal;
    end release;

begin
    UNITS := [1..N];
end RM;
```

The condition "nonbusy" can be regarded as an (initially empty) queue of processes each awaiting a unit of resource. To acquire a unit of resource, a process executes the call:

$$i: = RM. \ acquire;$$

As soon as this procedure returns, the caller has control over the ith unit of resource and the monitor is unlocked. If other processes come while there are no available units of resource, they will be enqueued when they perform the operation "nonbusy.wait." To release unit i, the holder executes the call

$$RM. \ release(i);$$

The operation "nonbusy.signal" during this call permits one of the queued processes to proceed from its stopping point (at the statement "nonbusy.wait"). The monitor lock is held as long as any process is executing in the monitor; it is released either when a process exits from the monitor or gets queued for a condition.

Monitors in their modern context are increasingly used as tools for structuring operating systems.

References

1974. Hoare, C. A. R. "Monitors: An Operating System Structuring Concept," *Comm. ACM* **17**, *10*: 549–557 (October).

1977. Brinch Hansen, P. *The Architecture of Concurrent Programs.* Englewood Cliffs, NJ: Prentice-Hall.

PETER J. DENNING AND WALTER F. TICHY

MONTE CARLO METHOD

For articles on related subjects *see* RANDOM NUMBER GENERATION; SCIENTIFIC APPLICATIONS; and SIMULATION.

In applied mathematics, the name *Monte Carlo* is given to the method of solving problems by means of experiments with random numbers. This name (after the casino at Monaco) was first applied around 1944 to the method of solving deterministic problems by reformulat-ing them in terms of a problem with random elements, which could then be solved by large-scale sampling. But, by extension, the term has come to mean any simulation that uses random numbers.

A classical example of what we would now call the Monte Carlo method is that of Buffon, who in 1733 pointed out that π could be determined experimentally by repeatedly throwing a needle onto a ruled surface and counting the number of times the needle crossed a line (see Fig. 1). The idea is more remarkable for its sophistication in geometric probability than for its practicality—a more accurate evaluation of π could be done with a piece of string, a ruler, and the plates and saucers in your kitchen. But the idea of Monte Carlo had been conceived, although the difficulty of using physical devices for sampling and the lack of suitable statistical theory made it little more than a curiosity until the advent of large-scale computers.

The development and proliferation of computers has led to widespread use of Monte Carlo methods in virtually all branches of science, ranging from nuclear physics (where computer-aided Monte Carlo was first applied) to astrophysics, biology, engineering, medicine, operations research, and the social sciences.

The Monte Carlo Method of solving problems by using random numbers in a computer—either by direct simulation of physical or statistical problems or by reformulating deterministic problems in terms of ones incorporating randomness—has become one of the most important tools of applied mathematics. A significant proportion of articles in technical journals in such fields as physics, chemistry, and statistics contain articles reporting results of Monte Carlo simulations or suggestions on how they might be applied. Some journals are devoted almost entirely to Monte Carlo problems in their fields. Studies in the formation of the universe or of stars and their planetary systems use Monte Carlo techniques. Studies in genetics, the biochemistry of DNA, and the random configuration and knotting of biological molecules are studied by Monte Carlo methods. In number theory, Monte Carlo methods play an important role in determining primality or factoring of very large integers far beyond the range of deterministic methods. Several important new statistical techniques such as

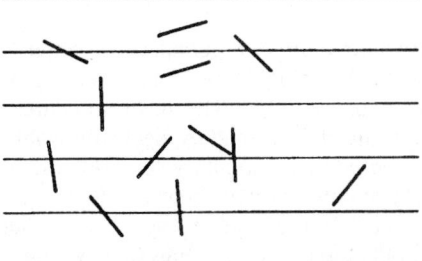

FIG. 1. Buffon's needle problem. If a needle of length L (≤ 1) is dropped on a ruled surface of parallel lines spaced one unit apart, the probability that the needle will cross a line is $2L/\pi$. If the needle is dropped N times, the number of line crossings (say, X) should be about $2NL/\pi$, and hence, $2NL/X$ us a Monte Carlo estimate of π.

"bootstrapping" and "jackknifing" are based on Monte Carlo methods.

The use of Monte Carlo methods is so widespread that literature on it tends to be focused on particular fields. Interested readers will find Monte Carlo references spread throughout most technical journals. Calls such as "subject = monte carlo" or equivalent to the databases of most libraries will show numerous entries relating to such applications as artificial intelligence, creep life prediction, hurricane wind speeds, polymer science, three-dimensional flow, microstructural lattices, statistical physics, economics, neutron transport, integrated circuits, and prediction of stock returns. Also listed will be a wide variety of proceedings of various conferences on Monte Carlo methods in special fields.

The references below list a few of the many books on Monte Carlo methods. Knuth's book describes and gives references for Monte Carlo methods for factoring and determining primality. It and those of DeVroye and Ripley give excellent discussions of methods for producing the random variables used in Monte Carlo simulations. The text of Hammersly and Handscomb was one of the first on Monte Carlo methods, and is still one of the best. Even by 1964, it listed several hundred references to Monte Carlo applications; by now a full list of references would number in the tens of thousands.

References

1964. Hammersley, J. M. and Handscomb, DC. *Monte Carlo Methods*. London: Methuen & Co.

1981. Knuth, Donald J. *The Art of Computer Programming: Volume 2/Seminumerical Algorithms*, 2nd Ed. Reading, MA: Addison-Wesley.

1986. DeVroye, Luc. *Non-uniform Random Variate Generation*. New York: Springer-Verlag.

1986. Kalos, Malvin H. and Whitlock, Paula A. *Monte Carlo Methods*. New York: John Wiley.

1987. Ripley, Brian D. *Stochastic Simulation*. New York: John Wiley.

GEORGE MARSAGLIA

MOTHERBOARD

For articles on related subjects *see* BUS; and OPEN ARCHITECTURE.

The *motherboard* of a personal computer is its main logic board containing its central processing unit (CPU - *q.v.*) and memory chips. The term antedates personal computing since it was used by electronic hobbyists who often connected small ancillary "breadboard" circuits to a larger, principal circuit board, which was dubbed "motherboard" to the smaller ones. On computers such as the IBM-PC and PC-compatibles (*q.v.*) which employ an *open architecture*, the motherboard has attached *slots* into which specialized supplemental logic cards can be inserted to augment the primitive functions supported by the minimum configuration of the computer system.

EDWIN D. REILLY

MOUSE

For an article on a related subject *see* INTERACTIVE INPUT DEVICES.

In computing, a *mouse* is a small hand-held interactive input device that, when rolled over a flat surface, controls placement of the cursor on a computer's terminal display screen. The palm-sized device has roughly an oval shape (or at least rounded corners) and is connected to the computer by a wire that is suggestive of a tail, hence the semi-affectionate name "mouse." (What to call two or more of them, however, is still evolving: "mice" or "mouses" ?) A typical mouse is shown in Fig. 1, and a newer one that deliberately exploits comparison to a live mouse is shown in Fig. 2.

The earliest mouse has been credited to Douglas Englebart and his colleagues at the Stanford Research Institute in 1965, but mouse technology has changed considerably since then. The Englebart mouse used a wooden housing with wheels placed at right angles to track cursor movement. The modern mouse uses either tiny wheels, mechanical rollers placed at right angles, optical signals requiring a reflective-grid *mouse pad,* or optomechanical methods that Logitech, the leading mouse manufacturer, considers optimal.

The mouse used with the Apple Macintosh is a one-button device. After positioning the cursor by moving the mouse, single or multiple clicks of its only button select a course of action from a menu or, in word processing, affect whether a word is to be highlighted for additional processing. Items such as screen *icons* (little pictures that stand for program applications) can be "dragged" across

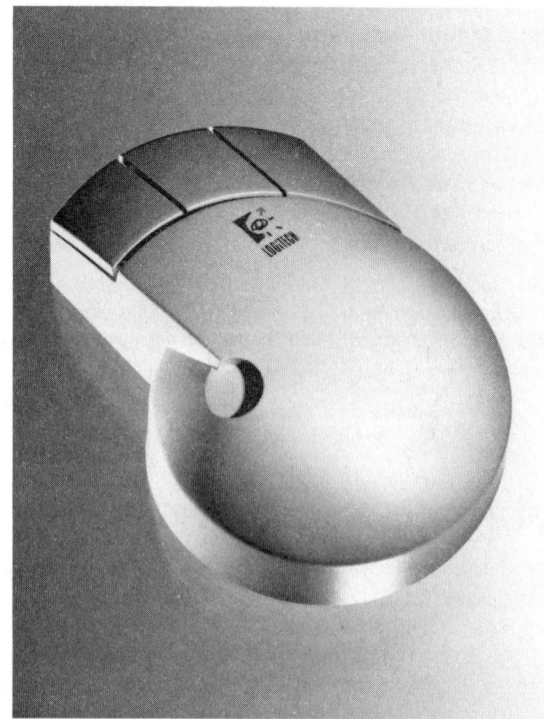

FIG. 1. The Logitech Cordless MouseMan (courtesy Logitech).

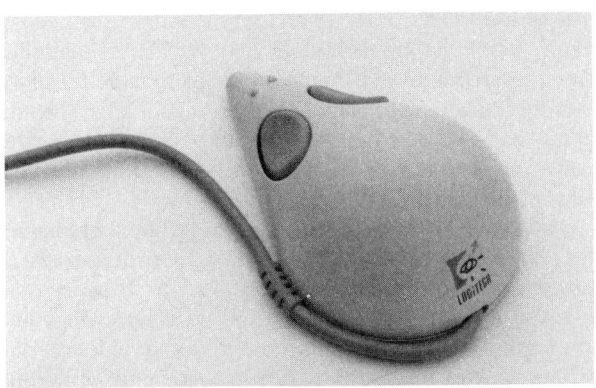

FIG. 2. The Logitech Kidz Mouse (courtesy Logitech).

the screen by moving the cursor over them, holding the mouse button down, and moving the icon to a new position by moving the mouse and then releasing the button. The mouse used with the IBM-PC and PC-compatibles (*q.v.*) (and with workstations - *q.v.*) is usually a two- or three-button device, but few applications use more than one (see Miller 1992).

References

1992. Miller, M. J. "The Riddle of the Right Mouse Button," *PC Magazine*, **11,** *1* (14 January), 81–82.
1992. Soberanis, Pat. "Of Mice and Trends," *CompuServe Magazine*, **11,** *2* (February), 29–30.

EDWIN D. REILLY

MULTIMEDIA. *See* COMPUTER ANIMATION; and PERSONAL COMPUTING.

MULTIPLEXING

For articles on related subjects *see* BANDWIDTH; CHANNEL; COMMUNICATION CONTROL UNIT; CONTENTION; MODEM; NETWORKS, COMPUTER; PACKET SWITCHING; POLLING; and TIME SHARING.

Multiplexing is a technique that allows a number of lower bandwidth communication channels to be combined and transmitted over a higher bandwidth channel.

At the receiving end, *demultiplexing* recovers the original lower bandwidth channels. The main reason for multiplexing is to make efficient use of the full bandwidth of the communication channel and to achieve a lower transmission cost.

The three basic multiplexing methods in use are *space division multiplexing* (SDM), *frequency division multiplexing* (FDM), and *time division multiplexing* (TDM). The words *multiplexing* and *concentration* are sometimes used synonymously. Concentration, however, is a TDM technique in which statistics, buffering, and querying play an important role. It usually involves a *concentrator*, a small computer programmed to perform the function of a time division multiplexer.

Space Division Multiplexing Space division multiplexing refers to the physical grouping of many individual channels or transmission patterns to form a channel with a high aggregate bandwidth. Hundreds of twisted wire pairs, coaxial cables, and/or optical fibers can be grouped to form a larger diameter cable. Each wire pair, coaxial cable, or fiber in the main cable is an individual communication channel capable of being frequency- or time-division multiplexed. Such cables have enough total bandwidth to carry tens of thousands of two-way voice channels of 4,000 Hz each in a cable diameter of under 3 inches.

Frequency Division Multiplexing As shown in Fig. 1, frequency division multiplexing (FDM) divides a higher bandwidth channel into many individual smaller bandwidth channels. Signals (data, voice, or video) on these channels are transmitted at the same time but at different carrier frequencies. *Guard bands* are needed between the channels to help reduce interchannel interference.

A familiar example of FDM is television broadcasting. Stations broadcast programs continuously, each at a different frequency, the atmosphere being the transmission medium. The tuning circuits in the television tuner select and separate one channel from the others.

Time Division Multiplexing In time division multiplexing, the entire bandwidth of the channel is dedicated to one low-speed channel for a short period of time, and then to the other low-speed channels in round-robin fashion or some other predetermined sequence (see Fig. 1). In effect, the low bandwidth channels

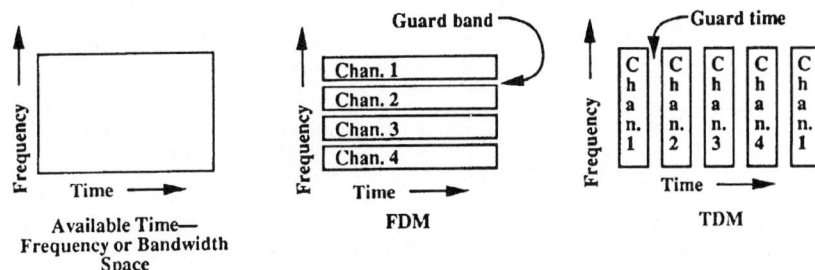

FIG. 1. Relationship between frequency or bandwidth and time in FDM and TDM.

are accommodated on the high bandwidth channel by interleaving the former in the time domain. Guard times are used to separate time slices, and the transmitting and receiving ends must be synchronized. A familiar example of TDM is the input-output bus (*q.v.*) of a computer servicing many peripherals, one at a time for short periods of time.

The time slots may be allocated on a fixed, predetermined (*a priori*) basis or on a demand basis. TDM is, therefore, usually subdivided into the following categories:

1. Synchronous time division multiplexing (STDM).
2. Asynchronous time division multiplexing (ASTDM).
3. Message switching multiplexing (MSM):
    a. Polling type; and
    b. Contention type.

The time slots in STDM are allocated on a fixed basis, usually in a round-robin fashion, as shown in Fig. 2. The data stream may be bit or character interleaved, depending on whether each time slot within the frame is devoted to a bit or a character, respectively. Each channel is sampled one by one for 1 bit or character time, and the samples are assembled into a serial stream. At the receiving end, the stream is disassembled and the original streams are reconstructed.

A time slot in STDM is allocated for a channel even in the absence of data on that channel. ATDM (sometimes also called *statistical multiplexing*) overcomes this inefficiency by allocating time slots only for active channels. This requires a special control header in each frame to identify the active channels. Despite this header, the efficiency and effective throughput can be improved significantly, since much of the time some channels are idle. This is illustrated in Fig. 3.

STDM and ATDM may be interleaved by bit or character. The interleaving may also be on an entire message, in which case it is sometimes called *message switching multiplexing* (MSM). Fig. 4 shows one communication line connecting a computer or master station to remote terminals or slave stations. Each slave is assigned a unique address and the master performs the multiplexing function by *polling* or *contention*. In a polled environment, each slave is addressed in turn to determine whether it has data to send or needs access to the master. If it does, the master authorizes the access for a finite period, and only one slave is permitted to receive or transmit data over the communication line at any one time. In a contention system, any slave device needing to communicate waits until there is no traffic on the line and then seizes the line to transmit its message. The line is then released to give another slave device the opportunity to seize the line. In such a system, the transmitted messages must be short to avoid unduly long wait times by the other devices on the line.

Computer-based communication controllers are used extensively to multiplex or concentrate many lower-speed devices onto a higher-speed line, since they can be

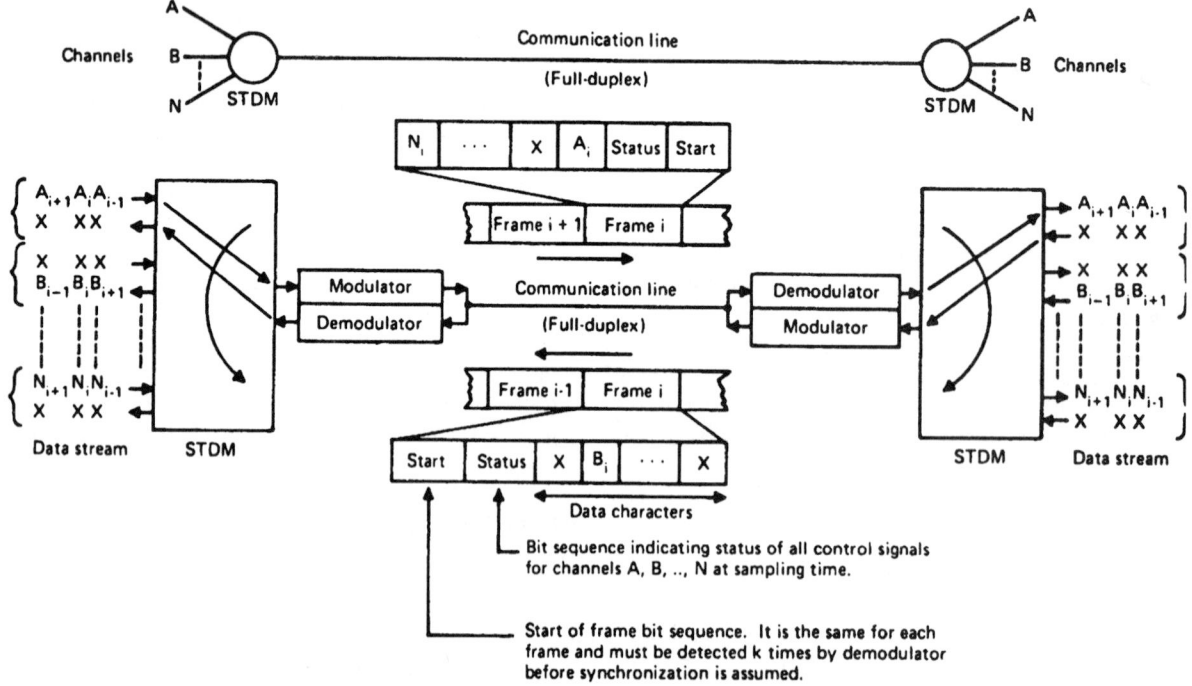

FIG. 2. Typical character-interleaved STDM and associated frame format. After sending the start and status bit sequences, the STDM in effect connects in turn each channel to the line for a very short time, forming the stream of data characters for each frame. A full-duplex line is shown to enable simultaneous data transfer in both directions. The X's represent an idle-line condition.

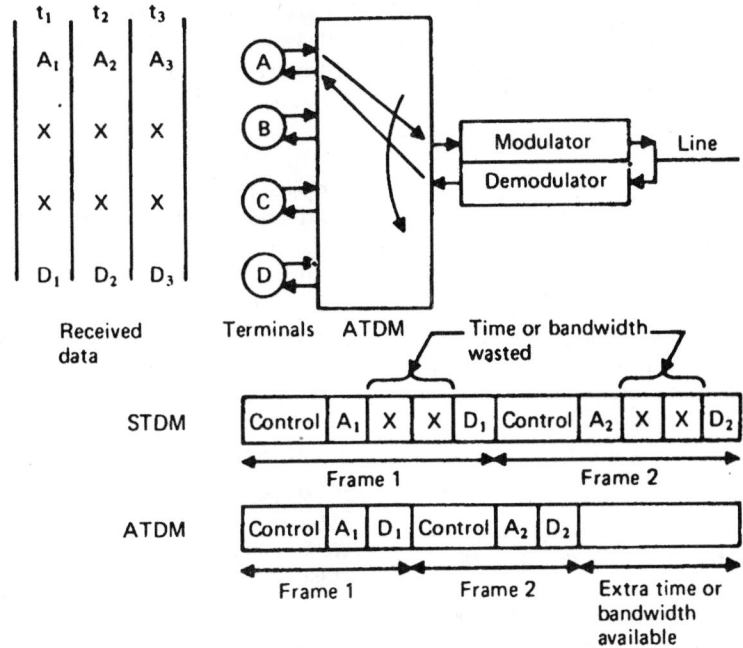

FIG. 3.   Comparison of STDM and ATDM. The example shows reception of data on channels A and D, with B and C being idle, as indicated by the X's. By assigning time slots only to the active terminals, ATDM results in less wasted bandwidth. The control signals in ATDM contain the addresses of the active terminals and the order in which they are sent.

programmed to perform the ATDM or MSM function. They may also perform many additional tasks such as code conversion, error detection and correction, line polling, and other control functions at little additional cost. Computers programmed to perform the function of a multiplexer are sometimes called programmable multiplexers or concentrators if they use buffering and querying for the ATDM or statistical multiplexing functions.

Circuit and Packet Switching   A circuit switch refers to equipment that can convert any one of m input lines to any one of n output lines or trunks ($m > n$), as

shown in Fig. 5. Once established, the connection is typically held for the duration of the entire transmission of data or voice call in the case of the telephone network. At the end of the transmission, the trunk is freed and is available for assignment to the next input line needing a trunk connection. An input can be connected to a trunk if at least one trunk is not being used. This technique is mainly used in telephone networks to establish an end-to-end circuit for the entire duration of a call and, although it has sometimes been called space division multiplexing, it is more appropriate to call it circuit or line switching. This should be contrasted with packet switching, in

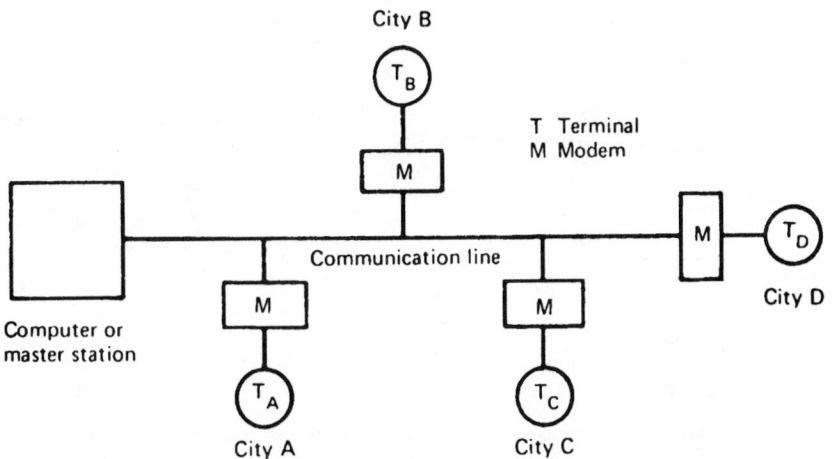

FIG. 4.   Multiplexing by polling or by contention.

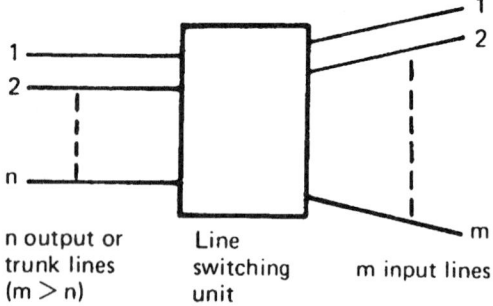

FIG. 5.   Line or circuit-switching unit connects any one of *m* input lines to any one of *n* trunk lines. This is widely used where the probability of all input lines being used at a given time is small, resulting in more efficient usage of the trunk lines.

which the trunk is used only for the duration of the transmission of a packet rather than the entire duration of the call or transmission. By limiting the length of packets, wait times for other users are limited. Packet switching is, therefore, very effective for transmitting data for interactive computing over a wide area network. Packet switching is a form of MSM and, therefore, TDM.

Multiplexer Hierarchies   As networks grow and get more complex, hierarchies of multiplexing are required in which low bandwidth channels are multiplexed onto higher bandwidth channels, which in turn are multiplexed on even higher bandwidth channels, etc. In the FDM hierarchy, multiplex levels correspond to increasingly higher frequency bands. In the TDM hierarchy, they correspond to increasingly higher pulse rates. For example, 24 voice channels can be time division multiplexed on a T1 carrier operating at 1.54 Mbps (millions of bits per second), 4 T1

carriers can be multiplexed onto a T2 carrier operating at 6.312 Mbps, while 42 T2 carriers can be multiplexed onto a T4 carrier operating at 274.176 Mbps (*see* COMMUNICATIONS AND COMPUTERS).

Economics of Multiplexing   The basic reason for multiplexing is that the cost to transmit a fixed amount of data decreases as the total capacity of the communication channel increases, provided that the amount of traffic justifies the higher capacity. Multiplexing is especially advantageous when there is a need for many connections between two points or when multiple data paths parallel each other for long distances. The economics are illustrated in Fig. 6.

References

1985. Meadow C. T. and Tedesco A. S. *Telecommunications for Management.* New York: McGraw-Hill Book Co.
1988. Tanenbaum, A. S. *Computer Networks*, 2nd Ed. Englewood Cliffs, NJ: Prentice-Hall.

JOHN S. SOBOLEWSKI

MULTIPROCESSING

For articles on related subjects *see* CONCURRENCY CONTROL; CONCURRENT PROGRAMMING; CONTENTION; LOCKOUT; MULTIPLEXING; MULTIPROGRAMMING; MULTITASKING; PARALLEL PROCESSING; and PETRI NET.

Multiprocessing is the simultaneous processing of two or more portions of the same program by two or more processing units. Among the latter, the I/O processors are normally excluded, since the asynchronous operation of a CPU and I/O processors is called *buffering* and the par-

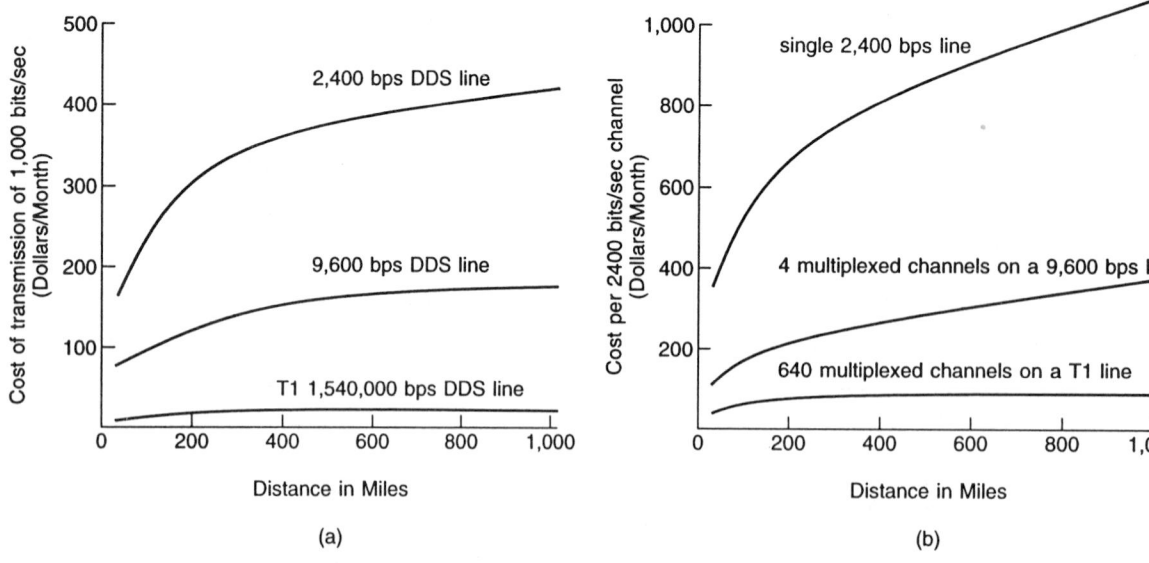

(a)   (b)

FIG. 6.   Comparative cost showing economics of multiplexing. (a) Cost of transmitting 1,000 bits/sec using low-, medium-, and high-speed interstate channels. Note how costs decrease on higher-speed channels. (b) Reduction in costs for a 2,400 bps channels using multiplexing.

allel operation of two or more I/O processors is called *multiplexing*. Similarly, the simultaneous processing of different programs on a system with several CPUs (one program/CPU) sharing a common memory is considered here as an extension of multiprogramming rather than true multiprocessing.

With this definition, multiprocessing involves a departure from the classical von Neumann machine (*q.v.*) organization in which there is a single instruction stream (single program counter) and a single data stream (unique communication channel between CPU and memory). From an architectural viewpoint, extensions to this Single Instruction Single Data (SISD) organization will yield Single Instruction Multiple Data (SIMD) architectures and Multiple Instruction Multiple Data (MIMD) architectures.

In SIMD architectures, exemplified by the ILLIAC IV and more recently by the Connection Machine, a single control unit, or host computer, fetches and decodes instructions. Then the instruction is either executed in the control unit itself (e.g. a Jump instruction) or is broadcast to multiple parallel processing elements that perform the same operation on different sets of data. Pipeline or vector computers, such as the CRAY machines and CDC Cyber 205, can also be considered of the SIMD type since a single instruction allows the simultaneous processing of aggregates (vectors) of data.

MIMD architectures are differentiated according to whether they are shared-memory machines (tightly coupled) or operate according to a message-passing paradigm (loosely coupled). In the former case, further differentiation arises when one considers the switching structure between processors and memory modules. Typical switching structures are a common single shared bus, a multistage interconnection network, and a cross-bar.

In the shared-bus architecture (often called a *multi*; see Fig. 1), processors have access to a common *bus* (*q.v.*). Global memory, common to all processors, is also attached to the bus. Since the single bus is a major source of contention for access to memory, each processor will need its own private cache memory (*q.v.*). This gives rise to the *cache coherence problem*, which is solved by having each cache controller "snoop" the bus on every cache transaction. Commercial multis (Sequent Symmetry, Encore Multimax) are limited to 30 processors.

Larger multiprocessors (e.g. on the order of several hundred processing elements) require another switching structure. Multistage ($O(\log n)$ stages for n processor and memory modules) interconnection networks have been used to connect processors (and/or memory modules) to other processors. Examples of such systems are the NYU Ultra computer and its successor, IBM RP3 (using an Omega network, cf. Fig. 2) and the BBN Butterfly (using a butterfly network). Memory latency and network traffic need to be minimized. This requires either the presence of private caches (but without a snoopy mechanism, since there is no single shared bus any more) or of local memory managed by software. Another possibility is to use a combining network where accesses to common

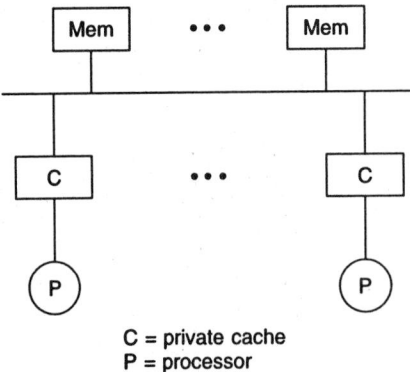

C = private cache
P = processor

FIG. 1. Multi: multiprocessor with a shared bus.

memory locations are combined in the switches of the interconnection network.

Cross-bars allow maximum concurrency for interconnecting processors and memory modules. However, since the number of switches grows as n^2, their cost becomes rapidly prohibitive. A typical system is limited to 16 or, at most, 32 processors.

In contrast with shared-memory architectures, where all processes share a global address space and a common memory, processing elements of a message-passing architecture consist of a processor, local memory, and communication links. All communication and synchronization among processes is via messages that must be explicitly sent—and received—by the communicating processes. Message-passing architectures can have various topologies, the most familiar being based on a *hypercube*, where each processor can communicate with its neighbor in each dimension of the cube. Six- or seven-dimension cubes are available commercially (e.g. Intel iSPC, Ncube).

In multiprocessing systems, the increase in performance resides mainly in path parallelism (i.e. the concurrent execution of two different parts, or of the same part with different data, of the program). Explicit indication of

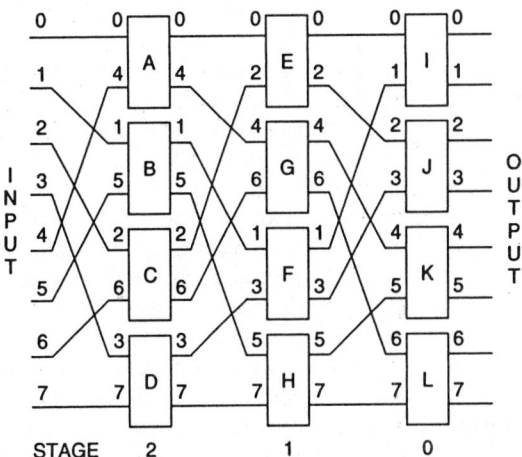

FIG. 2. Example of a multistage interconnection network: the Omega network.

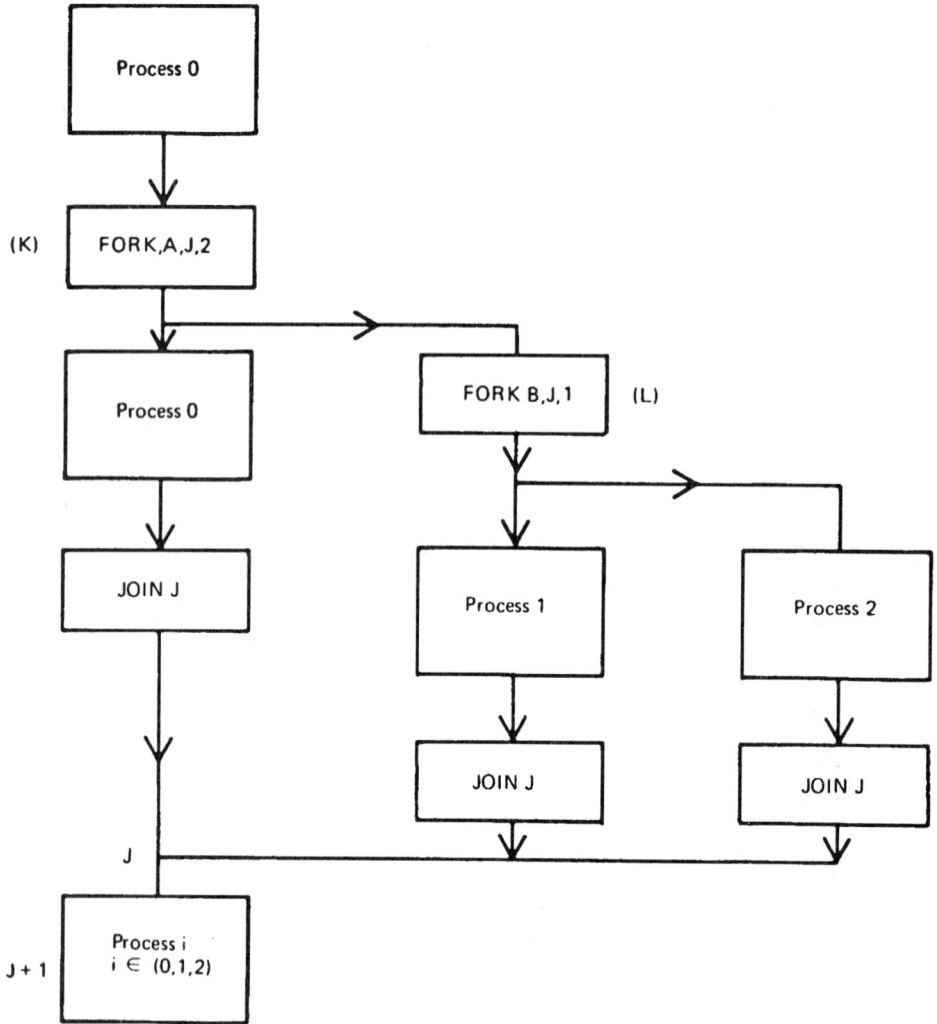

FIG. 3. FORK-JOIN concept. FORK *A,J,N*: (1) Initiate process at address *A*; (2) continue current process at next instruction; (3) increment counter at address *J* by *N*. JOIN *J*: (1) Decrement counter at address *J*; if zero, initiate processing at address *J* + 1, else (2) release the processor executing

this parallelism is done by FORK and JOIN or equivalent constructs for distinct paths, and by DO ALL statements for replication of loops. In Fig. 3, we show how one process is FORKed (or multitasked) into three concurrent paths (at points *K* and *L*) and how these latter three JOIN at point *J*. Instructions starting at point (*J* + 1) cannot begin execution prior to the termination of the three processes. This is also called *barrier* synchronization.

In MIMD architectures, control, synchronization, and scheduling of the processors are sensitive areas. Two types of control can be implemented: a fixed mode, whereby one or more processors are dedicated to execute the operating system; and a floating, or decentralized, mode, where each processor can have access to the operating system and schedule itself. In this latter, more common case, and more generally when a task is split into concurrent paths, it will happen that two concurrent processes will wish to access the same data. Hence, there must be some means of preventing disorderly changes in the shared database. This has been referred to as the

lockout or *mutual exclusion* problem. The portion of code—in a path—that accesses the shared data is called the *critical section* of that path.

One way to provide the necessary protection is by having instructions of the form TEST AND SET/RESET or the equivalent pair LOCK/UNLOCK. A possible realization is to associate a one-bit lock indicator *w* with each shared data object. The effect of the LOCK instruction is shown in Fig. 4(a). The lock bit is set to 1 by the current process when the data object has not been locked by any other process. The effect of the UNLOCK instruction is to reset the bit indicator to 0 [Fig. 4(b)]. The synchronization of concurrent processes cycling through their critical sections can be done through software, with integer and boolean variables. By using a new type of variable called a *semaphore*, elegant and efficient solutions can be obtained.

The presence of several CPUs adds a new dimension to the scheduling problem. In almost all cases, optimal schedules cannot be attained even with an *a priori* knowledge of the exact time requirements of each task. Models

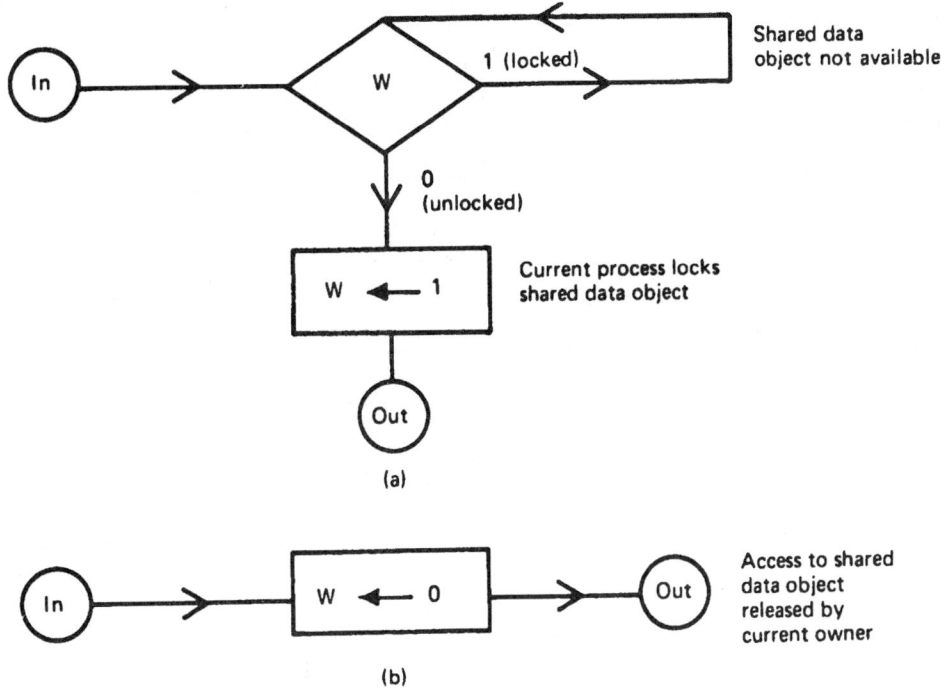

FIG. 4. LOCK/UNLOCK concept. (a) LOCK instruction; (b) UNLOCK instruction.

have been devised, analytical solutions have been investigated, and a number of heuristic methods have been proposed to assess the performance of multiprocessing systems. This performance can be improved not only by an explicit expression of parallelism, but also by compiler-detected parallelism (loop replication principally for SIMD machines) and by designing new algorithms for parallel environments.

References

1980. Baer, J. L. *Computer Systems Architecture.* Potomac, MD: Computer Science Press.

1987. Stone, H. *High-Performance Computer Architecture.* Reading, MA: Addison-Wesley.

JEAN-LOUP BAER

MULTIPROGRAMMING

For articles on related subjects *see* CONCURRENCY CONTROL; CONCURRENT PROGRAMMING; DATA SECURITY; INPUT/OUTPUT CONTROL SYSTEM; MULTITASKING; OPERATING SYSTEMS; OVERHEAD; PARALLEL PROCESSING; PRIVILEGED INSTRUCTION; PROCESSING MODES; SCHEDULING ALGORITHM; SWAPPING; TASK; TIME SHARING; and VIRTUAL MEMORY.

Most modern computer systems can provide more resources than one typical program requires. By *multiprogramming*—i.e. overlapping and interleaving the executions of more than one program—an attempt is made to keep all the resources of a modern computer system working as much as possible.

Early computer systems executed only one program (or *job*) at a time. It was quickly observed that certain jobs were *input/output* (I/O) *bound*; i.e. their rate of progress was limited by the speed of input/output units, such as tape drives or card readers. Other jobs rarely used these I/O devices after they began calculating; these *central processing unit* (CPU) *bound* jobs performed mostly numerical calculations, with little input/output. Neither of these types of jobs fully utilized the power of the computer system. But it was found that if we can multiprogram, and thereby concurrently execute more than one job, better utilization of the available equipment could be realized.

In modern computing systems, many resources can be active simultaneously. For example, once a computer has begun to read data from a disk, the processor can execute instructions while data is being transferred into an area of memory that is being used as a *buffer*. If we have a single CPU, then it can perform work for many different jobs by switching from one to another while being devoted at any one moment to a particular *task*. Each program requires memory space to hold the data and instructions to be executed, and this memory cannot be simultaneously occupied by two different jobs. If sufficient memory and other resources exist and can be allocated to many programs in a manner such that each makes effective progress, then we can consider using a multiprogrammed computer system.

Fig. 1 is an example of how two programs can be interleaved and overlapped by multiprogramming. The first program (shown in Fig. 1(a)) is heavily input/output-bound, and uses the CPU only 10% of the time. The second program, shown in Fig. 1(c), has the opposite nature, and

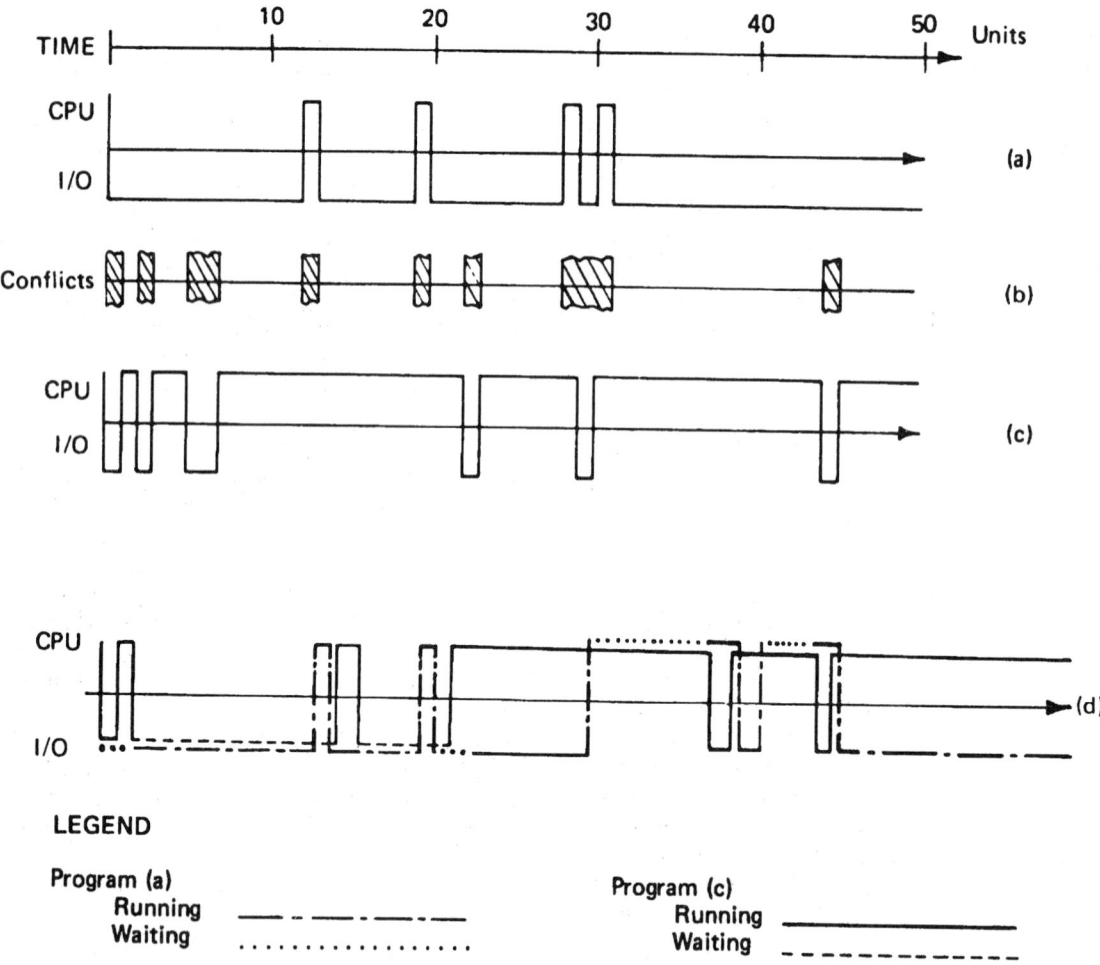

FIG. 1. An example of the advantages of multiprogramming. The area of overlap between the I/O-bound program (a) and CPU-bound program (c) is shown in (b). In (d), one way of multiprogramming these two programs is shown.

would like to use the CPU 90% of the time. If these programs were executing alone, each would behave as shown in Figs. 1(a) and 1(c), respectively, but Fig. 1(b) shows how often the demands of the first program and those of the second conflict because each wants to use the same resource. Notice that this happens about 20% of the time. We could have calculated this number by realizing that the program in Fig. 1(a) would like to use the CPU 10% of the time, but that the program in Fig. 1(c) probably wants to do the same. Conversely, the program in Fig. 1(c) wants to do some input/output about 10% of the time, when it is very likely that the program in Fig. 1(a) does also. Thus, we estimate that for 20% of the time there is a conflict for resources, while for 80% of the time the programs might be able to overlap by using different resources [Fig. 1(d)].

Fig. 1(d) shows one way in which we can multiprogram these two programs. The following rules are used to determine which program will be active and which resource it can use: Whenever both programs request the use of the same resource, the CPU-bound program is allowed to proceed, and the I/O-bound program must wait, subject to the restriction that once an input/output operation is begun, it cannot be stopped and must be finished. (These decision rules are shown only as an ex-

ample and are not necessarily the "best" rules to use for the types of jobs shown.) We see that, in the 50 units of time displayed, either the CPU or an I/O device is in use for 71 units. Since together we have resources for 100 units of work (50 from the CPU and 50 of I/O), we are achieving 71% *utilization* of the system. Separately, the program in Fig. 1(a) or Fig. 1(c) would use only 50% of the available resources, so we have improved utilization of the system by about 40%. We could not expect utilization to go much beyond 90% (excepting some unusually favorable circumstances), since we calculated that for 80% of the time both resources could be in use, and that for 20% of the time only one resource is busy while one program waits for the other.

Multiprogramming does not require a large operating system in order to coordinate the demands of each program. On a small computer, such as is used for process control, it is common to provide a *background/foreground* system that permits two programs to execute. The foreground, or real-time, program may consist of a job to monitor periodically a number of instruments and perform some corrective adjustment. In between each measurement, the system may have sufficient resources to permit a background program to execute, doing compilations or calculations. These two programs might cooperate by mutual understanding; i.e. the programmers could insure that each would not interfere with the use of the system by the other.

While in very simple situations it may be feasible to multiprogram cooperatively, often we must be sure that, if one program somehow violates the rules of the system, it does not corrupt the whole environment. Thus, most multiprogramming systems require a *monitor* (also called an *executive* or *supervisor*).

It is the responsibility of the monitor to maintain the integrity of the system. In the case of the background/foreground system used as an example, we would like the monitor to guarantee that the foreground real-time program will be able to take its measurements, even if the background program goes into a loop and never voluntarily relinquishes control. Thus, our computer system must have the capability to preempt a resource (such as the CPU) from a program and to insure that the foreground program or the monitor gains control. The monitor must be *protected* from accidental or malicious destruction by a program (which we refer to as a *user* program, in contrast to the supervisor itself); and user programs must be protected one from the other by intercepting, usually through hardware features, attempts to change or access memory that is "out of bounds" to a particular program.

In order to control resources effectively such as space for data or file storage, modern systems centralize all input/output operations in an *input/output control system* that performs services on behalf of the user programs. In this manner the users of the multiprogrammed system cannot corrupt each other's data or invade the privacy of secure information. The multiprogrammed operating system may provide accounting information for the management of the computer system, and this information should not be destroyed by a user program.

To permit the construction of a monitor with these capabilities, computer systems generally possess *privileged instructions* that user programs cannot execute. For example, all input/output instructions, or those instructions associated with the protection of one area of memory from a program executing in a different area, are reserved for the monitor. When the computer is executing in monitor (or *master*) mode, these functions are permitted. The monitor has the responsibility of insuring that when control is given to a user program, the system is switched to user (or *slave*) mode. In slave mode, any attempt to execute privileged instructions will give control back to the monitor without permitting any violations of resource control.

In addition to the monitoring function, the executive of a multiprogrammed operating system must implement a *scheduling algorithm*. If too many jobs are begun, they can interfere with each other and waste resources. In fact, it is even possible to cause a *deadlock* to occur when a number of programs have begun but cannot continue until additional resources are available, and yet those resources are tied up by other jobs. The algorithm used for scheduling must have enough information to avoid such situations, or should possess the means to "untan-

gle" them if they occur; otherwise, system performance degrades as it enters a very active but non-productive state called *thrashing* (*q.v.*).

Scheduling in a multiprogrammed environment is often complex. The concept of multiprogramming entails the *global* optimization of the resources of the entire system. However, users are generally concerned with their own tasks, and attempt to optimize *locally*; i.e. they try to make their programs perform better or faster, without regard to the total environment.

Consequently, it is common to find the ultimate scheduling performed external to the system itself, either by administrative decisions concerning the categories (or *classes*) of jobs that are permitted at certain times of day, or by the operator of the system. The operator may be able to start or suspend programs from an operator's console based on the performance of the system. Meanwhile, the scheduler program of the multiprogrammed operating system performs the microscopic decisions such as initiating input/output operations or deciding which program is to be given the resources of the central processor.

One common form of scheduling is provided by a *priority* assigned to each job or task within the system. The actual value of the priority may be based on external factors, such as the fact that the results are needed quickly (or the converse), or it may be based on the overall resource requirements of the job when submitted to the computer system. This priority may change dynamically as the program evolves, or it may increase as time progresses if the job is not making effective progress. It may also be changed by an operator from a console. The detailed nature of scheduling depends heavily on the nature of the service the system is expected to provide.

Multiprogramming of modern computer systems can be done in a variety of fashions. Some systems, such as the IBM 370/390 Operating System Multiprogramming a Fixed number of Tasks (OS/MFT), allocate certain resources in a static fashion. Memory is divided into *partitions* of fixed size, and each job submitted to the system must specify which partition is to be used. Other systems, such as OS/MVT (the IBM System/370 Operating System with a Variable number of Tasks), distribute the memory space according to the request of the user. This additional flexibility requires extra complexity and possibly extra *overhead*, but may be critical in the effective use of a system where many users submit programs of widely differing sizes.

Multiprogramming may also take place within a single job. For example, the system may be able to overlap the computational needs of a single program with its input/output needs. In IBM's OS/MVT or Unix (*q.v.*), a program may spawn (or create) additional tasks (user processes) that are to be multiprogrammed as if they were jobs, but that possess a filial relationship to the parent task. Each of these tasks may have differing requirements for resources, and may cause concurrent utilization of system facilities.

Multiprogramming is accepted as the standard means of using all but the smallest of today's computer systems. A computer utility that provides service to many users who may be sitting at remote consoles, communicating with an executing program in an interactive fashion, can serve many individuals while others are thinking or responding. Such a *time-sharing* system attempts to provide rapid response to the interactive requests of users at consoles; a *multiprogrammed* system may be required in order to provide time-sharing facilities, but multiprogramming connotes, in itself, a concern with resource utilization and not with rapid response time. The advantages offered by multiprogramming are now filtering down to even very small systems, and may be found on a large number of computers that until recently were used in a dedicated, one-user environment.

References

1972. Lorin, H. *Parallelism in Hardware and Software: Real and Apparent Concurrency.* Englewood Cliffs, NJ: Prentice-Hall.

1976. McKeag, R. M. and Wilson, R. *Studies in Operating Systems.* New York: Academic Press.

1978. Kuck, D. J. *The Structure of Computers and Computations.* 1: 521–535. New York: Wiley.

1991. Miller, D. D. *Operating Systems Concepts: A Practical Approach Using VAX/VMS.* Englewood Cliffs, NJ: Prentice-Hall/Digital Press.

HARRY J. SAAL

MULTITASKING

For articles on related subjects *see* CONCURRENCY CONTROL; CONCURRENT PROGRAMMMING; MULTIPLEXING; MULTIPROCESSING; MULTIPROGRAMMING; OPERATING SYSTEMS; PARALLEL PROCESSING; TIME SHARING; and TIME SLICE.

Multitasking refers to an operating system's ability to support multiple processes simultaneously. A *process* is a program in execution. Support for multiple processes is necessary in applications where several computations must proceed in parallel. In time-sharing systems, multiple users share a single computer system and all processes created by them should, at least in principle, execute simultaneously. Real-time systems that control multiple devices also need to support multiple processes. For instance, an avionics computer on board an airplane runs processes for monitoring the engines, updating the flight instruments, processing radar signals, and keeping the airplane on course. Batch operating systems depend on multitasking for overlapping computation with I/O operations: When a process performs I/O, the operating system runs another process to avoid idling the central processor for long periods of time.

Modern operating systems distinguish between two types of processes. *Primitive processes* or *threads* are described by their stateword or statevector (i.e. the contents of the processor registers, such as program counter, stack pointer, general-purpose registers, condition codes, etc.). A *user process*, also called a *task*, is a significant extension. It includes at least one primitive process, a virtual memory (*q.v.*) containing a program (instructions and data), and context information such as descriptors for open files and communication channels (Accetta *et al.*, 1986; and Tanenbaum, 1987). Multitasking must be supported on both the thread and task levels.

Thread-level Support for Multitasking The simplest way to execute multiple threads simultaneously is to assign each thread to its own processor in a multiprocessor system. If the number of threads exceeds the number of processors, then processors must be multiplexed among threads. Processor multiplexing implements quasi-parallelism: By switching a processor rapidly from one thread to the next, it appears to the observer as if all threads are making progress, even though the processor can execute only one instruction at a time.

Processor multiplexing works as follows. Time is divided into disjoint intervals called *time slices*, and the processor is assigned to at most one thread during each interval. At the end of a time slice, the operating system performs a *context switch*: It switches the running thread off its processor by first saving the processor registers into memory, and then loads the stateword of the next thread into the processor registers.

There are two major techniques for determining the end of a time slice. In simple batch operating systems, a time slice ends when the thread must wait for an event, such as the completion of an I/O operation or a signal from another thread. Whilst this approach assures high processor utilization, it allows a thread performing little or no I/O to monopolize the processor. In order to give all threads a fair share, most operating systems additionally implement a limit on the maximum period during which a thread may run continuously. When a thread begins its time slice, a timer in the processor is set to a standard value and decremented during every instruction cycle. When it reaches zero, the timer generates an *interrupt* (*q.v.*). The interrupt handler then performs a context switch.

The choice of thread to be loaded onto the processor by a context switch is determined by a scheduling policy. Most scheduling policies simply select the thread with the highest priority. To ensure adequate response time in time-sharing systems, interactive threads are usually given higher priority than compute-intensive threads. This setting works well, since interactive threads spend most of their time waiting for input and do not need much compute time, but can regain the processor quickly when needed. In real-time systems where threads must meet specified deadlines, priorities are not sufficient. Instead, a schedule for the entire set of available threads must be computed. (Xu and Parnas, 1990).

While processor multiplexing implements only quasi-parallelism, peripheral devices can provide true parallelism even if the computer system contains only a single, central processor. Peripheral devices can be regarded as specialized processors that operate concurrently with the central processor. A device runs a single process specialized, for example, for printing a line or writing a disk block. The device receives commands from a device driver process that itself runs on the central processor. After a device driver has issued a command to a device, the driver waits for a completion signal (implemented by the interrupt system). During this wait, the main processor switches its attention from the device driver to other threads. With multiple processors (devices and CPUs), the potential for true parallel processing is increased.

Task-level Support for Multitasking At the task level, memory management (*q.v.*) is an important issue. A simple approach is swapping (*q.v.*): The operating system keeps only a single task's program in main memory at a time; the programs of other tasks are stored on secondary storage (usually disk). As part of a context switch, the operating system must first unload its memory to disk and then reload it with the program of the next task. In order to reduce I/O traffic, a multiprogrammed operating system keeps programs or program segments of several tasks in main memory simultaneously. Multiprogramming reduces the number of reads and writes to secondary storage, provided main memory is large enough to hold the working sets (*q.v.*) of several tasks. Multiprogramming is facilitated by virtual memory (*q.v.*), a mechanism that simulates an address space much larger than the physical memory available to each task; it is discussed in detail elsewhere in this encyclopedia.

If tasks contain several threads, then thread management becomes an issue as well. The threads of a task form a team and share memory and context information. To ensure rapid progress of tasks, the operating system must perform co-scheduling (i.e. schedule the threads of a task together). A task may also create and manage sub-tasks containing independent teams of threads and virtual memories.

For specifications of the operating system functions provided at the thread and task levels, see OPERATING SYSTEMS.

References

1986. Accetta, M. *et al.* "Mach: A New Kernel Foundation for Unix Development," Proceedings of USENIX 1986 Summer Conference (Summer) 93–112.
1987. Tanenbaum, Andrew S. *Operating Systems—Design and Implementation.* Englewood Cliffs, NJ: Prentice-Hall.
1990. Xu, Jia and Parnas, David L. "Scheduling Processes with Release Times, Deadlines, Precedence, and Exclusion Relations." IEEE Transactions on Software Engineering, **16**(3) (March) 360–369.

WALTER F. TICHY

MUMPS

For articles on related subject *see* HOSPITAL INFORMATION SYSTEMS; MEDICAL APPLICATIONS; and STRING PROCESSING.

The *MUMPS* programming language, alternatively named M in 1990, was developed in the 1960s at the Massachusetts General Hospital for handling multiuser access to medical database systems. MUMPS is an acronym for Massachusetts General Hospital Utility MultiProgramming System. Originally designed to run on small

minicomputers, MUMPS, now runs on IBM mainframes, the DEC VAX, and most personal computers and workstations. Applications in standard MUMPS are portable without modifications. The current language standard is ANSI standard X11.1-1990.

MUMPS is a general-purpose high-level language that is suitable for most information management needs. It has a very simple and highly regular syntax and uses only one data type, the character string. This makes MUMPS easy to learn and maintain. An extensive array of string manipulation functions makes MUMPS highly suited to text processing.

The following characteristics distinguish MUMPS from other high-level languages:

- Equivalence of data and program code.
- Run-time binding of symbols and values.
- Data persistence after programs terminate.
- Arrays with string subscripts and sparse storage.

These features make MUMPS a powerful language, particularly in the problem domain of database management systems.

Equivalence Of Data and Code As in Lisp and machine language, MUMPS makes no distinction between data and program code; data can be executed as a program. The command used to do this is spelled XECUTE and pronounced *execute*:

```
XECUTE "READ X SET Y = X*4/1.2"
```

The literal string within quotes will be executed as MUMPS code. The XECUTE command can be abbreviated as "X" and the operand can be a symbol:

```
X CODE
```

This MUMPS phrase will interpret the value of CODE as MUMPS code. The XECUTE command allows MUMPS to be used to write programs that are very general. Such utilities can be *table driven* by data that is in permanent storage.

Run-Time Binding When the argument of the XECUTE command is a symbol, the value is not assigned until run time. Thus, components of the program logic are added when it is executed. The program takes the value from data in permanent storage, and the XECUTE command exploits the binding of symbols to values at run-time.

Indirection A MUMPS program may be designed to let another program assign a string to CODE. When this is done, the host program must not execute the value of CODE itself. Instead, the program will use the value of CODE as a *reference* to data that should be executed, an *indirect* reference. To make an indirect reference, CODE is introduced by the "@" (at-sign) character, as follows:

```
XECUTE @CODE
```

Now, the value of CODE is used as a storage reference. The value found at the location referred to by the value of CODE is executed. Execution of strings and the deferred binding of symbols until run time are critical requirements for writing general-purpose utilities. These properties of the MUMPS language support writing resuable programs that can function in many different contexts.

Data Persistence

Symbolic references and data manipulated by a MUMPS program can persist after the program terminates. Thus, the MUMPS language includes a standard way of controlling *named system storage* in the system that does not rely on any other external data management facilities. To assign the value "BAPTIST" to the symbol RELIGION, and force the assignment to persist after the program terminates, we write:

```
SET ^RELIGION = "BAPTIST"
```

Prefixing the "^" (up-arrow) character to RELIGION causes the MUMPS system to place the symbol and its value into permanent storage. When some other program executes the following phrase:

```
WRITE RELIGION
```

the string "BAPTIST" will be sent to the current output device.

Permanent storage may contain the following references and values:

```
^PERSON("John", "RELIGION") = "BAPTIST"
^PERSON("Mary", "RELIGION") = "CATHOLIC"
^PERSON("Joe", "RELIGION") = "JEWISH"
```

These assignments use symbols that can be referred to as *named vectors*. These named vectors specify logical locations in permanent storage. Each vector is named PERSON and has two values that define fixed associations between persons and the string "RELIGION", and such vectors have assigned values that are literal strings.

Array References

These symbolic references have the form A(S1,S2), which is called an *array,* with the name A and with dimensions S1 and S2. In this sense, MUMPS data references are arrays. However, the similarity to conventional arrays in other programming languages ends there.

A dimension statement to declare the array PERSON is never needed in MUMPS, nor is subscript size ever declared. The number of subscripts is not logically limited, either. The PERSON array can be referenced with added dimensions,

```
SET ^PERSON("Joe", "HOBBY", 3) = "Chess"
```

An existing value stored at the "Joe", "HOBBY", 3 location in the PERSON array is replaced by the value "Chess". Otherwise, a new symbolic location is created, and the value is stored.

Sparse Arrays

Arrays in MUMPS are sparse storage structures. As array references are assigned values, only the amount of storage needed is allocated. A logically unlimited storage space in MUMPS uses only the amount of space that has actually been assigned values.

Arrays Are Public

The MUMPS array in permanent storage is public. Any MUMPS process can refer to the symbol ^PERSON("Joe", "HOBBY", 3). Therefore, array values are *globally* available. The permanent storage in MUMPS is referred to as *GLOBAL* storage, and the array ^PERSON is called a *global*. Globals can be manipulated simultaneously by many processes. To prevent illogical operations, the LOCK command is used to gain access to a global location. When another MUMPS process attempts to LOCK that location, it will pause until the first process releases the LOCK.

Subscripts

The individual elements of the global reference are called *subscripts*. Most languages restrict subscripts to numeric integers; globals can have *string* subscripts. Meaningful literal values and actual data values may be used in the subscripts. For example, the global reference

```
^PERSON("Roosevelt, Franklin Delano")
```

can be used to designate storage for all of the information about this person.

Collation of Subscripts

New references are inserted into existing globals in a predictable manner. References are placed into the position determined by the ASCII collating sequence of the subscript values. When the new reference ^PERSON("Jill", "BIRTHDAY") is added to the following PERSON global:

```
^PERSON("Jack", "BIRTHDAY")
^PERSON("Joe", "BIRTHDAY")
```

it is logically inserted between the "Jack" and "Joe" references. Thus, sorting of data in MUMPS is not necessary.

References

1969. Greenes, R. A., Pappalardo, A. N., Marble, C. W., Barnett, G. O. "Design and Implementation of a Clinical Data Management System." *Computers in Biomedical Research* **2**. 469–485.

1977. Munnecke, T., Walters, R. F., Bowie, J., Lazarus, C. B., and Bridger, D. A. "MUMPS: Characteristics and Comparisons with other Programming Systems." *Medical Informatics* **2**, 173–196.

1989. Lewkowicz, John. *The Complete MUMPS.* Englewood Cliffs, NJ: Prentice-Hall.

1989. Walters, Richard F. *The ABC's of MUMPS: An Introduction for Novice and Intermediate Programmers.* Englewoood Cliffs, NJ/Bedford, MA: Prentice-Hall/Digital Press.

RICHARD G. DAVIS

MUSIC.   *See* COMPUTER MUSIC.

NAPIER, JOHN

For an article on a related subject *see* CALCULATING MACHINES.

John Napier, the eighth Laird of Merchiston, was born in Merchiston, Scotland in 1550. He is best known for his invention of logarithms, but he also took an active part in the development of other forms of computational methods and instruments, was very active in the religious controversies arising out of the Scottish reformation, and invented a great many devices for agricultural and military use.

Logarithms are, undoubtedly, his most famous invention simply because they were the fundamental basis for all serious computation from the early 1600s until the invention of the electronic computer. Napier's original 1614 publication, *Mirifici Logarithmorum Canonis Descriptio*, contained 90 pages of logarithm tables and an introduction describing how they were to be used. The tables were not the common base 10 logarithms that are used today, but were actually logarithms of sines, whose base was a fractional quantity (different from what are known today as 'Napierian logarithms') that arose naturally by reason of the method by which they were computed. Henry Briggs, a professor at Gresham College in London, suggested to Napier that the tables be changed to the common base 10 logarithms. Although Napier agreed to the change, his advanced years and ill health prevented his taking part in the production of the new tables. Henry Briggs published the first book of modern base 10 logarithms in 1624.

In 1617, three years after the publication of his first book on logarithms, Napier published a small volume entitled *Rabdologia*, which contained a description of three other devices that could be used to aid the process of multiplication and division. These were specifically designed for people who preferred to work with the natural numbers, rather than the logarithms of numbers.

The first and most famous of these devices is the one that Napier called rabdologia, but almost everyone else called *Napier's bones*. They obtained this nickname because the better quality sets were made from bone or ivory. In essence, they were simply vertical strips cut from a 10 by 10 multiplication table which could then be rearranged into the order required to produce a single-digit multiplication table for a multidigit number.

The other two devices never gained any popularity, primarily because they were either too difficult to manufacture or involved concepts that were unintelligible to most. His second device, the *multiplicationis promptuarium*, was a more complex version of the bones. It consisted of two sets of strips, to be stacked on top of and at right angles to one another, to create a multiplication table for any two multidigit numbers. The third was a form of a table abacus that was set out on a chessboard, the rows and columns of which represented places within the binary number system.

Napier died in 1617 in Merchiston, the same town in which he was born 67 years earlier.

References

1914. Horsburgh, E. M. *Handbook of the Napier Tercentenary Celebration or Modern Instruments and Methods of Calculation.* Edinburgh: The Royal Society of Edinburgh (reprinted by The M.I.T. Press and Tomash Publishers, 1982).

1983. Williams, M. R. "From Napier to Lucas, the use of Napier's Bones in Calculating Machinery 1617–1900," *The Annals of the History of Computing,* **5**, *3*, 279–296.

1988. Hawkins, William F., Tomash, E., and Williams, M. R. "The Promptuary Papers," *Annals of the History of Computing,* **10**, *1*, 35–67.

MICHAEL R. WILLIAMS

NATURAL LANGUAGE PROCESSING

For articles on related subjects *see* GRAMMARS; HUMANITIES APPLICATIONS; KNOWLEDGE REPRESENATION; LANGUAGE TRANSLATION; LOGIC PROGRAMMING; and RELATIONAL DATABASE.

Natural language processing (NLP) refers to computer systems that analyze, attempt to understand, or produce one or more human languages, such as English, Japanese, Italian, or Russian. The input might be text, spoken language, or keyboard input. The task might be to translate to another language, to comprehend and represent the content of text, to build a database or generate summaries, or to maintain a dialogue with a user as part of an interface for database/information retrieval. This article addresses issues in natural language comprehension and generation from text or keyboard input. Similar techniques can be used for spoken language by adding a system for speech recognition (*q.v.*).

It is extremely difficult to define how we would ever know that a system actually "understands" language. All we can actually test is whether a system appears to understand language by successfully performing its task. The Turing test, proposed by Turing (1950) [reprinted in *Computers and Thought* (1963)], has been the classical model. In this test, the system must be indistinguishable from a human when both answer arbitrary interrogation by a human over a terminal. This test has the unfortunate property that, while it sets the ultimate goal, it provides for no intermediate evaluation of work along the way. A growing concern in NLP is with developing more sensitive models of evaluation that can measure progress, given current performance levels. The usual approach is to develop evaluation tests within limited domains to test specific capabilities. For example, in the area of natural language interfaces for database query, statistical performance measures can be determined based on test sets of human-generated questions collected in protocols that use another human to simulate the system. It remains an area of active concern, however, as to how more complex systems that can handle extended dialogue can be evaluated.

The principal difficulty in processing natural language is the pervasive ambiguity found at all levels of the problem. For example, all natural languages involve:

- Simple lexical ambiguity (e.g. "duck" can be a noun (the animal) or a verb (to avoid something thrown).
- Structural or syntactic ambiguity (e.g. in "I saw the man with a telescope," the telescope might be used for the viewing or might be held by the man being observed).
- Semantic ambiguity (e.g. "go" as a verb has well over ten distinct meanings in any dictionary).
- Pragmatic ambiguity (e.g. "Can you lift that rock?" may be a yes/no question or a request to lift the rock).
- Referential ambiguity (e.g. in "Jack met Sam at the station. He was feeling ill...," it is not clear who is ill, although the remainder of the sentence might suggest a preferred interpretation).

Of course, all these forms of ambiguity may interact, producing an extremely complex interpretation process. It is the prevalence of ambiguity that distinguishes natural languages from precisely defined artificial languages, such as logic and programming languages. It also makes most of the techniques developed in programming language grammars, parsing, and semantics ineffective unless significantly modified.

Natural Language Database Query Systems: Syntax and Semantics

The most successful NLP systems to date have been front ends to databases. These systems can understand isolated questions dealing with the content of the database; several systems that do so are commercially available. While they have not been precisely evaluated, these systems provide a wide coverage of English questions, including quite complex quantified database queries. The LUNAR system was the first system to develop this technology and serves as the prototype for many current-day commercial systems. The core of the LUNAR system was a syntactic grammar in a formalism called an Augmented Transition Network (ATN) Grammar (see Woods, 1970). An ATN is a graphical notation that can be shown to be equivalent to context free grammars. The exception is the augmentation: each arc in the grammar may have a procedurally defined augmentation that can enforce non-context-free restrictions that provide a representation of the sentence convenient for semantic interpretation. The principle contribution of the LUNAR system was to demonstrate that such augmented systems could retain the efficiency of pure context-free parsing algorithms, yet handle the context-sensitive aspects found in natural language. The architecture of a typical NLP database query system is shown in Fig. 1. Examples of state-of-the-art natural language interfaces are TEAM (Grosz et al., 1987) and IRUS (Bates et al., 1986). An example of a natural language query to TEAM is *Which employees earn more than their manager's salary?*, which, after syntactic and semantic processing would result in a query, such as the following, to a relational database:

```
(IN $E EMPLOYEE) (IN $D DEPT) (EQ ($E
DEPT) ($D NAME)) (IN $M EMPLOYEE) (EQ ($M
NAME) ($D MANAGER)) (GT ($E SALARY) ($M SAL-
ARY)) (? ($E NAME)).
```

The other major development in the area of grammars and parsing for natural language was the development of definite clause grammars (DCGs) based on Prolog. Prolog offers an efficient mechanism for parsing

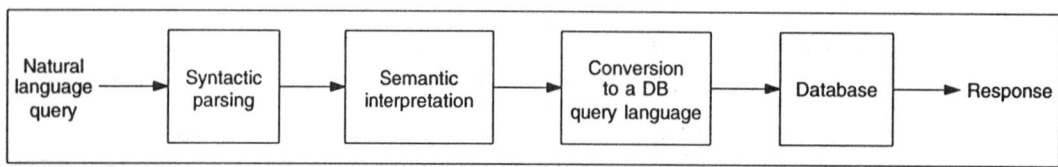

FIG. 1. The architecture of an NL database query system.

context-free grammars simply by writing each context-free rule as a Prolog clause. The additional power required to handle natural language is obtained by using variable bindings and unification to add additional restrictions and to build a convenient representation of the sentence for semantic interpretations. Prolog-based systems have the additional advantage that the semantic processing and the database itself, for that matter, can be represented within the same notation. Pereira and Warren (1980) describe this approach in some detail.

New grammatical formalisms that slightly extend context-free grammars are an active area of research in both computational and theoretical linguistics. These theories require finer distinctions than found in the traditional Chomsky Hierarchy (*q.v.*) to characterize their generative power. A good survey of such formalisms has been given by Perrault (1984).

As for semantic processing, the technology is at a considerably less developed stage, and most work is still being done within research prototypes of limited scope; there are very few commercial applications. Within limited-scope domains, such as database query applications, the semantic component is not much more than a translation program from the output of the parser into a database query language. In the more general research systems, the semantic interpretation phase produces a mapping from the parser output to a knowledge representation that supports inference and the later stages of pragmatic interpretation.

Semantic interpreters can be placed into two major classes: the *compositional* and the *non-compositional*. The non-compositional allows arbitrary transformations from the parser output to the final form. The compositional requires that interpretation rules are applied in accordance with the structure of the parser output. In its strongest form, compositional semantics requires a single semantic interpretation rule for each syntactic rule, and can support simultaneous syntactic and semantic processing while parsing. While non-compositional schemes were common in early systems because of their greater power and flexibility, the compositional approaches are now more frequently used because they are significantly more modular and extendable. However, by working within the stricter constraints that a compositional approach imposes, difficult problems arise that require solutions when the syntactic structure of the sentence differs significantly from the structure of the final meaning representation. For example, consider the form of quantification in language versus quantification in a logic in Fig. 2. The structure of the English sentence *Every boy loves a girl* is quite different from the structure of the logic formula $\forall b \, \exists \, g \, Loves(b,g)$. English puts the quantifiers within the noun phrases, whereas in logic all the quantifiers are outside the scope of the proposition representing the sentence. In addition, there is no natural subpart of the logical formula that corresponds to the interpretation of the noun phrase *a girl*. Rather, the interpretation is spread between the quantifier outside the scope of the predicate and the variable within the scope of the predicate. Proposals for handling this problem within the compositional framework involve introducing an intermediate form of representation that can be built compositionally from the syntactic structure. This representation is then used as input for a second interpretation phase called *quantifier and operator scope determination* that produces the final meaning representation. This identifies yet another source of ambiguity in language: the scope of quantifiers and sentential operators.

Most current NLP systems use a knowledge representation (*q.v.*) expressively equivalent or weaker than the first order predicate calculus (FOPC). But significant aspects of language appear to remain outside the range of first order logic, and considerable basic research into more expressive formalisms is required before systems will be able to represent the meaning of a significant subset of natural language.

Text Understanding: Pragmatics and World Knowledge Understanding extended text, such as newspaper articles, paper abstracts, or books, requires significant additions to the capabilities required for question-answering systems discussed above. In particular, there is a strong pragmatic component as well—namely, the use of common everyday knowledge about the world

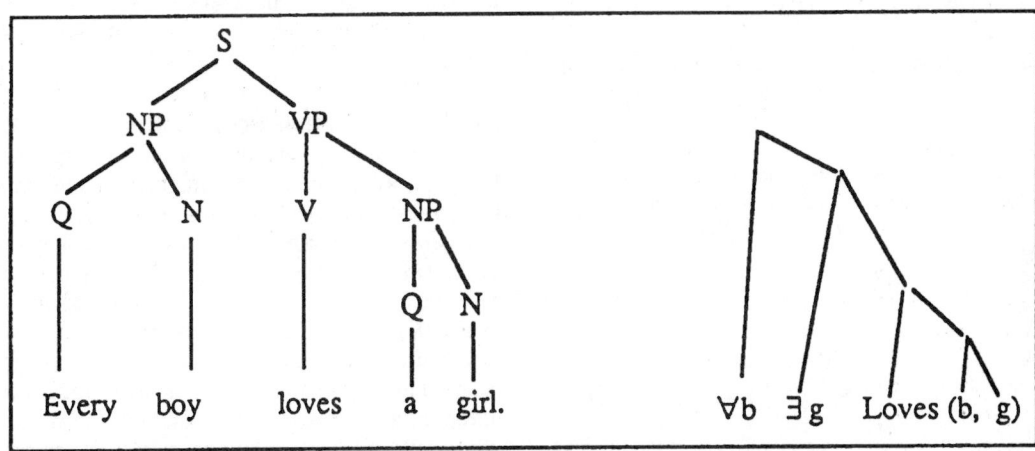

FIG. 2. The Structure of natural language compared with FOPC quantification.

in order to determine the relationships between the sentences in the text. There is a need for significant world knowledge even within single sentences. For example, the sentence *Jack couldn't drive to work because he lost his keys* requires knowledge about cars and keys (e.g. you need a key to start a car, driving to work requires starting the car, etc.). Without this basic knowledge, a system will not be able to determine why Jack couldn't drive to work. The need for using large amounts of common knowledge for natural language understanding was a major focus of the work by Roger Schank and his students. This work focused primarily on representing general knowledge about everyday actions and using this knowledge in interpreting language. These systems could understand simple stories about everyday activities, such as eating in a restaurant or taking public transit. To demonstrate this, they answered questions that required information necessary to understand the story, but not explicitly given in the story. A good description of the techniques is Schank and Reisbeck (1981).

The same motivations were used in the development of the GUS system (Bobrow et al., 1977), which used a representation based on encapsulated knowledge about a specific task called Frames (*see* Knowledge Representation) to capture knowledge about planning airplane trips. Using the predefined knowledge that captured the structure of the information involved in planning trips, the system "understood" requests in this domain by instantiating the general knowledge to the specific knowledge described in the sentences. Such frame-based approaches still play an important role in current text-understanding systems. Typical application areas for current research systems include understanding messages regarding equipment failures, and extracting the key facts (i.e. those for which slots are defined in the frame) from newspaper articles about takeover attempts in the financial market. The following is an example of the analysis of an article by the SCISOR system, developed by GE Labs (Jacobs and Rao, 1990):

PILLSBURY SURGED 3 3-4 TO 62 IN BIG BOARD COMPOSITE TRADING OF 3.1 MILLION SHARES AFTER BRITAIN'S GRAND METROPOLITAN RAISED ITS HOSTILE TENDER OFFER BY $3 A SHARE TO $63. THE COMPANY PROMPTLY REJECTED THE SWEETENED BID, WHICH CAME AFTER THE TWO SIDES COULDN'T AGREE TO A HIGHER OFFER ON FRIENDLY TERMS OVER THE WEEKEND[1]

The system extracts the following information from the story:

Corporate-takeover-event:
Target:	Name:	Pillsbury-Corporation
Suitor:	Name:	Grand-Metropolitan
	Country:	United Kingdom
Type:	Hostile	
State:	Rejected-offer	
Price:	$63/share	
Stock-exchange:	NYSE	
Volume:	3.1 million	
Subevent:	Increased-offer:	

	Effect-on-stock:	
	Increment:	3 3-4
	Direction:	Up
	Type:	Surge
	Final-Value:	$62/share
Previous-state:	Negotiated-offer:	
	Type:	Friendly

It is realistic to expect 90% (combined recall and precision) accuracy for certain useful, carefully constructed tasks, but unrealistic to expect much higher. Many difficulties in reading texts appear when trying to achieve better results, but the most common limitation seems to be the degree of real inference required for understanding. In spite of its fairly sophisticated methods for combining linguistic and world knowledge, SCISOR has very little of the latter.

Dialogue Systems: Discourse and Communication

Systems that can engage in extended natural dialogue present particular challenges in addition to the issues described above. In order to account for dialogue phenomena, a model of conversational interaction needs to be developed. In addition, significant reasoning is required, both to recognize the other speaker's intentions and to produce reasonable responses. The most promising model so far has been based on the notion of speech acts—actions that are performed by speaking, such as requesting, informing, warning, etc. Computational speech act models have been developed by using models of actions and planning developed in work in knowledge representation (Cohen and Perrault, 1979). Plan recognition becomes an important technique for understanding the underlying motivations behind questions. These models can be used to generalize question-answering systems so that the answers generated are more useful and appropriate. These models, however, are not yet capable of explaining dialogues longer than a few sentences. In addition, structural models of discourse are being developed (see Grosz and Sidner, 1986) that appear promising. There are currently no systems that come close to having human dialogue capabilities, which involves considerable clarification and correction subdialogues, topic change, and other complexities. It is reasonable to expect that prototype systems will be developed in the next few years that can handle dialogues within limited-topic application domains.

Machine Translation

Machine translation (language translation) was one of the first applications that led to AI work on natural language processing. Machine translation is a very active area of research, especially in Europe and Japan, and is now undergoing a resurgence in the United States. There are two primary approaches. The first is based on defining corresponding lexical, syntactic, and semantic correspondences between a pair of languages, and defining a transducer based on these rules. The second is based on a notion of a language independent representation or *interlingua*. To translate, one would parse one language into the interlingua and then from that generate text in the second language.

---

[1]From the Dow Jones News Service, 12 December 1988.

While the second is the more general approach, the most successful systems to date are based on the former techniques. It seems commonly accepted that, except in limited technical domains, high-quality machine translation of general text is either impossible or a very long way off in the future. What is feasible currently, however, is the development of machine translation tools to aid human translators, and the development of translation systems that then require post-editing by a human. While this might seem a failure, using such techniques can in practice significantly increase the productivity of each human translator. There are commercial systems available that offer these abilities, and we can expect considerable growth in the use and development of machine-translation "workstations" in the next decade.

Generation An issue that arises in dialogue systems, in text summarization applications, and in many machine translation systems is natural language generation (i.e. the production of sentences to describe a given body of knowledge). There are two primary problems in generation: deciding what content needs to be communicated and then deciding how to realize that content in language. The former problem is related to the reasoning abilities of the system, say those required for participating in a dialogue, whereas the latter is related to inverting the parsing and semantic interpretation processes. Typically, generation systems have been developed independently of the understanding component because each component faces a different set of issues. Present-day generation systems can generate paragraph-length text to describe a prespecified body of information in some knowledge representation. The issue of intelligently choosing what knowledge needs to be realized is just beginning to be addressed.

Speech Another active area of research is aimed at developing natural language systems that use spoken, rather than written, language (*see* SPEECH RECOGNITION AND SYNTHESIS). But there is more to building a spoken language system than combining a speech recognizer with a natural language system. In particular, new uncertainty and ambiguity is introduced, since the parser does not know precisely what the input words are. On the other hand, other sources of information, such as intonation and prosody, are available to aid the interpretation. It is believed that such information will greatly aid discourse processing, as there appear to be strong intonational clues to discourse structure and communicative intent. To solve these problems and to take advantage of the additional information found in spoken language, new methods of integrating speech recognition and natural language systems must be developed.

Prospects Natural language processing should make considerable strides in the 1990s. Large-scale grammars of natural languages are being written, and there is considerable effort in building large English lexicons using automatic techniques. We can expect to see the emergence of quite sophisticated question-answering systems if there is sufficient economic demand for such technology. In the area of text skimming and summarizing, substantial progress should be made in identifying and capturing a specific set of predetermined topics (e.g. a brief summary of the major financial transactions described in the *Wall Street Journal*). Such a system could automatically read the newspaper and build a database of the transactions described, which could then be searched and used to generate short paragraph summaries of the information extracted. We can also expect considerable progress in the area of dialogue systems, although such systems in realistic-sized domains will remain as research prototypes. Highly constrained dialogue systems, using speech input, will probably be feasible by the end of the decade.

References

1963. Feigenbaum, E. A. and Feldman, J. (Eds.) *Computers and Thought*. New York: McGraw-Hill.

1970. Woods, W. A. "Transition Network Grammars for Natural Language Analysis," *Comm. ACM* **13**, *10*: 591–606.

1977. Bobrow, D., Kaplan, R., Kay, M., Norman, D., Thompson, H., and Winograd, T. "GUS: A Frame Driven Dialog System," *Artificial Intelligence* **8**, 155–173.

1979. Cohen, P and Perrault, C. R. "Elements of a plan-based model of speech acts", *Cognitive Science, 3, 3,* 177–212.

1980. Pereira, F. C. N. and Warren, D. H. D. "Definite Clause Grammars for Language Analysis—A Survey of the Formalism and a Comparison with Augmented Transition Network Grammars," *Artificial Intelligence, 13, 3,* 231–278.

1981. Schank, R. C. and Reisbeck, C. K. *Inside Computer Understanding*. Hillsdale, NJ: Lawrence Erlbaum.

1984. Perrault, C. R. "On the Mathematical Properties of Linguistic Theories," *Computational Linguistics* **10**, 165–176.

1986. Bates, M., Moser, M. G., and Stallard, D. "The IRUS Transportable Natural Language Database Interface," in Kershberg, L. (Ed.) *Expert Database Systems*, Menlo Park, CA: Benjamin/Cummings Pub. Co.

1986. Grosz, B. and Sidner, C. "Attention, Intentions, and the Structure of Discourse," *Computational Linguistics, 12, 3,* 175–204.

1986. Grosz, B., Sparck-Jones, K., and Webber, B. *Readings in Natural Language Processing*. Los Altos, CA: Morgan Kaufmann Publishers, Inc.

1987. Allen, J. *Natural Language Understanding*. Menlo Park, CA: Benjamin/Cummings Pub Co.

1987. Grosz, B. J., Appelt, D., Martin, P., and Pereira, F. "TEAM: An Experiment in the Design of Transportable Natural-Language Interfaces," *Artificial Intelligence* **32**, *2*, 173–244.

1990. Jacobs, P. S. and Rau, L. F. "SCISOR: A System for Extracting Information from On-line News." Comm. of the ACM **33**, *11*, 88–97.

JAMES F. ALLEN

NAVAL ORDNANCE RESEARCH CALCULATOR (NORC)

For articles on related subjects *see* DIGITAL COMPUTERS: HISTORY: EARLY; and ECKERT, WALLACE J.

The *NORC* was built by IBM for the U.S. Navy Bureau of Ordnance under a non-profit research and develop-

FIG. 1. The NORC computer.

ment contract to build the most powerful and effective calculator that the state of the art would permit (as of 1951). It was designed for the rapid and convenient solution of the very largest computational problems of science, including partial differential equations in three space dimensions and time. It was the outgrowth of a research project under Byron L. Havens at IBM's Watson Scientific Computing Laboratory at Columbia University, where Dr. Wallace J. Eckert had assembled a group of electronic specialists in 1946 to further the development of electronic computers. Early in the project, Havens developed a fundamental circuit, the microsecond delay unit, which operated reliably at 1,000,000 steps a second. The NORC was designed and built at the Laboratory. Assembly started in late 1953 and it was demonstrated and turned over to the Navy on 2 December 1954, at which time it calculated pi to over 3,000 places. It was installed at the Naval Proving Grounds, Dahlgren, VA in the summer of 1955 and remained in highly productive use until replaced by an IBM Stretch computer in 1968.

NORC was based on the use of the Havens microsecond delay unit, diode switching, a 3,600-word cathode ray tube storage unit with 8-microsecond access, and high-speed 4-channel magnetic tape units (which transferred 71,340 decimal digits per second). The calculator operated on decimal numbers of 13 digits precision and a range of 10^{-30} to 10^{30}.

Computing speed was 15,000 three-address instructions per second. Each instruction provided for modifying each address by any of three modifiers, fetching two operands from electronic storage, carrying out a floating point, specified point, or fixed decimal point (i.e. integer) arithmetic operation, checking the result with an independent modulo-9 arithmetic unit, and storing the result. The arithmetic unit featured fast multiplication using serial digit-by-digit addition and serial generation of the nine multiples of the multiplicand. A pipeline of 12 decimal adders, each of which introduced a microsecond of delay while adding, combined a digit from each one-digit product and output, one digit of the result every microsecond. The product of two 13-digit numbers required 31 microseconds.

Checking of the operation of the calculator was continuous. In addition to the mod-9 arithmetic check, a check digit accompanied each word of instruction or data. This check digit was calculated when the data was read from punched cards, and verified each time it was read from tape or in storage or refreshed in storage and after printing by echo pulses generated during printing. The cathode ray tube storage was further checked by an independent check on each bit column of storage. These two orthogonal checks pinpointed for correction any single bit in storage that was in error.

The instruction set took advantage of the three-address format to perform arithmetic (including multiple precision numbers), modification of the address modifiers, machine and operator interrupts, and three-way transfer of control with a single instruction wherever possible. Reading tape forward or backward or writing tape with a variable length block of words was done with a single instruction.

The microsecond delay unit that was used throughout the calculator for the registers, arithmetic units, and logical control functions acted as a storage unit with an output that regenerated a full pulse the microsecond following the receipt of an input pulse. It was highly reliable and facilitated maintenance off-line of the pluggable units of which the machine was composed. 50% of the total circuitry employed only six types of units, and 80% employed only 18 types.

The peripheral equipment for the NORC was built by the IBM Poughkeepsie and Endicott laboratories. It included eight tape units operating at 70,000 characters per second reading or writing, two 150 line-per-minute printers with buffered input permitting calculation to proceed during printing, and a card-to-tape-to-card machine for card input and output.

One of the early uses of the NORC was computing the exact positions of the moon, earth, and other planets in space at all times to the year 2000 for Project Vanguard. This was done by Dr. Paul Herget, Director of the Cincinnati Observatory in a 10-hour run on the NORC. Another was a simulation of neutron motion in a nuclear reactor. Mathematical models of various aspects of the earth satellite programs, evaluation of various guided missile designs, and study of the re-entry of satellites into the earth's atmosphere were other early uses of the NORC. One of its last jobs was a tremendous astronomical calculation for which the answers could be rigorously checked. The NORC run lasted 65 hours, performing over 75 billion operations without error.

References

1954. Anon. *IBM Business Machines* **37**, *26*: 1, 4–11 (23 December).
1955. Eckert, W. J. and Jones, R. *Faster, Faster.* New York: McGraw-Hill.
1963. von Neumann, J., *Collected Works* **5**: 238–247 [Taub, A. H. (Ed.)]. New York: Oxford University Press.
1971. Brennan, J. F. *The IBM Watson Laboratory at Columbia University: A History.* Armonk, NY: IBM, 18, 26–29.

JOHN C. MCPHERSON

NCR COMPUTERS

For an article on a related subject *see* DIGITAL COMPUTERS: HISTORY.

Introduction   NCR Corporation was founded as the National Cash Register Company by John H. Patterson in 1884 in Dayton, Ohio. Patterson built the company around the mechanical cash register, developed by James Ritty. In 1926, NCR became publicly owned and was incorporated in Maryland. Today, the company is known as NCR Corporation and specializes in business information systems development, production, sales, and service. NCR products range from point-of-sale systems to automated-teller machines, supermicrocomputers, personal computers, and networking and microelectronic products.

Computing and NCR   NCR began its experimentation with and exploration of electronics in the company's electrical department in 1938. By 1942, a team of researchers had produced a counting device that used vacuum tubes. Late in the decade, NCR engineers created magnetic memory drums attached to accounting machines, various electronic digital displays and indicators, and signature-verification systems that used video signals.

In 1952, NCR acquired Computer Research Corporation (CRC) of Hawthorne, California. The firm had been innovative in its use of diodes, which significantly reduced the number of vacuum tubes required for computing, cutting costs and power needs for the new technology. CRC became the NCR Electronics Division in 1953.

NCR entered the business-information-systems market in 1957 with the announcement of the NCR 304, the industry's first solid-state business computer. Manufactured by General Electric Corporation and developed and marketed by NCR, the 304 consisted of a central processor, magnetic tape memory units, media converters, and high-speed input and output equipment. The first NCR 304 was installed at Camp Pendleton, California, in 1959, for use by the U.S. Marine Corps.

Following the NCR 304, the company developed computers for small and midsize businesses and the financial services industry, and committed extensive resources to research in microelectronics. In 1960, NCR introduced the NCR 390, the first low-cost, mass-marketed computer, which used punched-tape recorders for original data entry. In 1967, NCR introduced the Century Series of computers, targeted at financial institutions. Other significant products followed, among them the NCR 280 retail terminal and the NCR 270 financial terminal. These products incorporated MOS-LSI (Metal Oxide Silicon-Large Scale Integration) circuitry, developed through NCR's research in microelectronics, and were announced in 1969.

In 1970, NCR established the NCR Microelectronics Division (now known as the NCR Microelectronic Products Division). By the mid-1970s, NCR had discontinued its electromechanical products and had become a computer vendor. To strengthen its position in the computer industry in the late 1970s and early 1980s, NCR made several acquisitions: Data Pathing, Inc. in 1976, giving NCR a position in factory data entry and processing systems; Quantor Corporation in 1978, giving NCR computer output microfiche capabilities; Comten, Inc. (renamed NCR Comten, Inc. and now known as the NCR Network Products Division) in 1979, a leading force in data communications technology; and Applied Digital Data Systems, Inc. (ADDS) in 1980, a supplier of high-quality video display computer terminals.

The introduction of the Criterion Series 8550 and 8570 met the needs of medium- and large-scale users beginning in 1976. In 1981, NCR entered the word processing market with the WorkSaver product line. In 1982, NCR introduced the first member of its TOWER supermicrocomputer line, based on AT&T's Unix operating system. In 1983, the company delivered the industry's first externally programmable, 32-bit very-large-scale integration (VLSI) mainframe computer, the NCR 9300.

By the mid-1980s, NCR had centered its marketing on three open systems product lines: the NCR 9800 series, the NCR TOWER family, and a series of IBM-compatible workstations. The NCR 9800, a microprocessor-based system that supports the SQL relational database query language, replaced the company's 8000 mainframe series in 1986. While the 9800 runs VRX/E (NCR's proprietary operating system), it can attach to standard peripheral interfaces and provides interfaces to OSI (*q.v.*) and SNA communications protocols. The 9800 is a collection of microprocessors operating in tandem, delivering more computing power per dollar than a single large computer. Microprocessors can be added in "slices" to meet the computing needs of users who need enhanced capacity.

The NCR TOWER family is a series of open, Unix-based microcomputers. The NCR TOWERs, which range in power from a 16-bit machine accommodating up to eight users to the TOWER 32/800 line configured for more than 120 users, are able to run software written for machines made by other vendors and can tie personal computers into a mainframe.

The NCR Personal Computer Division (now known as the NCR Workstation Products Division) was formed in 1985. The division launched a series of IBM-compatible personal computers. NCR was the first company to introduce a machine based on Intel's 486 chip. The NCR System 10000, a family of computers that use NCR's 32-bit processor technology and ITX operating system, was introduced in 1989, and in 1990 NCR introduced the NCR System 3000, a seven-tiered family of computers having laptop to mainframe power, cooperation software, and open network environment products.

In 1991 NCR merged with AT&T and combined its operations with the AT&T Computer Systems Group although the NCR name will be retained.

ALAN J. BUDDENDECK

NETWORK ARCHITECTURE

For articles on related topics *see* LOCAL AREA NETWORK; NETWORKS, COMPUTER; NETWORK PROTOCOLS; and OPEN SYSTEMS INTERCONNECTION.

Modern computer networks may consist of thousands of computing devices of various kinds, often made by different vendors and interconnected by many types of transmission media, including standard telephone lines, satellites, digital microwave radio, optical fibers, or digital data lines. They may include local or wide area configurations. For such a group of heterogeneous devices to be linked, either the hardware and software need to be compatible or else complex interfaces need to be built to allow meaningful communication to take place. *Network architecture* helps achieve this compatibility.

Objectives A network architecture defines the message and data formats as well as the protocols and other standards to which hardware and software must conform to meet desired network objectives. Most network architectures are designed to achieve the following objectives:

1. *Connectivity* to permit diverse hardware and software built in conformance with the architecture to intercommunicate with each other over the network.
2. *Flexibility* to permit easy modification as user needs change or available technologies improve. These modifications should be possible without

the need for costly new interfaces or program modifications.
3. *Modularity* to permit mass production of hardware and software modules (building blocks) that can be used in a wide variety of devices.
4. *Reliability* to permit error-free communication by providing appropriate error detection and correction capabilities.
5. *Simplicity* to permit easy implementation, installation, and reconfiguration of the network and its services.
6. *Diversity* of network services that can be easily used and yet isolate users from the details of network structure or implementation.

Implementation Although the above objectives may seem straightforward, designing a network architecture to achieve them is a difficult task given the many trade-offs that are possible. Furthermore, a modern network architecture must support a wide variety of functions. Consequently, the common set of rules for generating and interpreting messages sent and received by the communicating devices to implement these functions can be large and complex. For this reason, the entire set of rules is often partitioned into groups or layers of manageable size, with each layer containing only those rules needed to perform some specific set of functions. By making the functions in each layer independent of those in other layers, new functions or enhancement of existing functions can be implemented with little or no disruptions to other layers. This layered approach, therefore, helps reduce design complexity and offers the advantages of ease of modification and flexibility.

The Reference Model for Open Systems Interconnection (often referred to as the OSI model) is shown in Fig. 1 and is an example of a model for a layered network architecture. It has been widely adopted and its primary purpose is to provide the basis for coordinating standards for interconnection of systems using data communication facilities. The term "open" denotes the ability to transfer information between any two systems that conform to the model and its associated standards. The actual transfer of data occurs through the physical medium (telephone line, coaxial cable, or some other transmission medium) located just below layer 1 of the model. The seven layers collectively provide all the functions necessary for communication between two systems, with each layer providing a service to the layer above and enhancing the service provided by the layer below. With this approach, a process initiated at the highest layer has the full set of services at its disposal. For a more extensive discussion, *see* OPEN SYSTEMS INTERCONNECTION.

Virtual and Physical Data Transmission in the OSI Model For two machines to communicate, the same set of layered functions must exist on each machine. Each layer, *n*, on one machine can be thought of as communicating with the corresponding layer on the other machine as a peer process using the appropriate layer *n* protocol. This is illustrated by the dotted horizontal lines

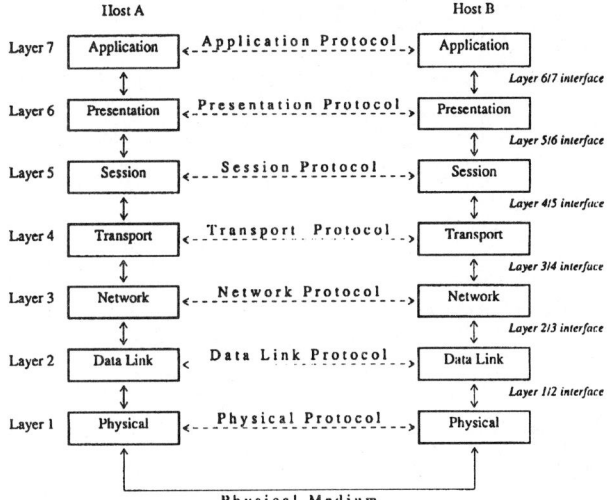

FIG. 1. Information exchange between two systems in the seven layer OSI model showing the peer-to-peer protocols and interfaces between the layers.

in Fig. 1. An application on machine A requiring a file transfer from machine B, for example, will invoke a file transfer process on machine A that will communicate with its peer process on machine B, using a file transfer protocol (part of the application layer suite of protocols) designed to communicate the name of the file and other needed details of the request. If compression/decompression is used for data transmission, the application layer on machine B will pass the file to its presentation layer (via the level 6/7 interface) to perform the data compression, while the peer process on machine A will perform the corresponding decompression and pass the decompressed data through its application layer to the application that made the original request. Again, the compression/decompression can be thought of as being performed by communication between peer processes, using the appropriate presentation layer protocols.

The above example helps illustrate the relation between virtual and actual data transmission within the model. While the peer processes in layer n think of their communication as being horizontal using the layer n protocol, no data are directly transferred from layer n of one machine to layer n of another machine. Instead, during transmission each layer passes data and control information to the layer below until the lowest (physical) layer is reached. Below this layer is the physical medium through which the actual transmission occurs. Conversely, on the receiving end, each layer passes data and control information to the layers immediately above. In Fig. 1, the virtual communication between peer processes is shown by the horizontal dotted lines, while the actual or physical communication is shown by the solid vertical lines between layers and the solid horizontal line denoting the physical medium.

With this model, the set of functional layers and corresponding protocols defines the network architecture. Their specifications must contain enough information to allow design and implementation of the necessary hardware and software to ensure that each layer obeys the

appropriate protocols. Neither the specification of the interfaces between the layers nor the implementation details are part of the architecture, to ensure the designer has full implementation flexibility. All that is needed is to ensure that all machines can correctly use all the protocols.

References

1988. Tanenbaum, A. S. *Computer Networks*, 2nd Ed. Englewood Cliffs, NJ: Prentice-Hall.
1989. Keiser, G. E. *Local Area Networks*, New York; McGraw-Hill Book Co.

JOHN S. SOBOLEWSKI

NETWORK PROTOCOLS

For articles on related subjects, *see* HANDSHAKING; NETWORK ARCHITECTURE; NETWORKS, COMPUTER; and OPEN SYSTEMS INTERCONNECTION.

A *protocol* is the set of formal operating rules, procedures, or conventions that govern a given process. A *communication* or *network protocol*, therefore, describes the rules that govern the transmission of data over communication networks. These rules are designed to help provide needed network services or to solve operating problems, including:

1. Formatting, or *framing*, which defines which group of bits or characters within a frame or a packet constitutes data, control, addressing, or other information.
2. *Error control*, which refers to the acceptance of correct messages, the detection of errors (usually by means of cyclic redundancy checks - *q.v.*), and the retransmission of messages in which errors were detected.
3. *Sequence control*, which defines the method of numbering (or sequencing) messages to detect loss or duplication of messages, and to identify correctly messages that are retransmitted by the error control mechanism.
4. *Flow control*, which defines the mechanisms used to ensure effective utilization of network resources without causing traffic congestion.
5. *Initiation and termination control*, which define how connections are established, maintained, and terminated across the network.
6. *Recovery control*, which defines mechanisms used for graceful recovery in case of abnormal conditions, such as loss of a message or an inquiry or cessation of information flow that may be caused by line, equipment, or software failures.

Types of Protocols Protocols may be divided into three general categories, depending upon the technique used for message framing. These are illustrated in Fig. 1 and include:

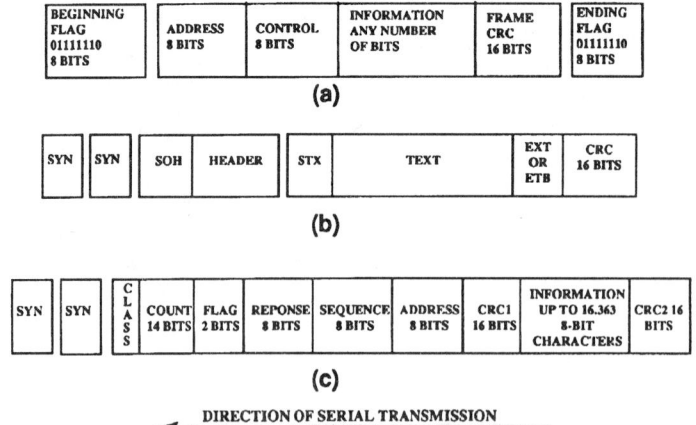

FIG. 1. Frame formats for (a) SDLC, (b) BISYNC, and (c) DDCMP protocols.

1. *Bit-oriented protocols*, in which a unique flag character, such as 01111110, delineates individual frames. An example is IBM's Synchronous Data Link Control (SDLC) protocol, illustrated in Fig. 1a, in which a frame consists of the 01111110 beginning flag, followed by an 8-bit address, an 8-bit control field, information bits, a 16-bit cyclic redundancy check, and an ending flag. The address bits identify the secondary station to which the information is being sent, while the control field defines whether the information field consists of data or commands and the type of commands. It should be noted that this protocol specifies that there shall never be six consecutive 1 bits except for the transmission of the flag character. This requires insertion of a binary 0 by the transmitter after any five consecutive 1s. The receiver, in turn, removes every 0 that follows reception of five consecutive 1s. (Such 0s do not contribute to the calculation of the cyclic redundancy check.)

2. *Character-oriented protocols*, which use special characters to delineate the various fields of a message and to provide needed control functions. An important example is IBM's Binary Synchronous Communications (BISYNC) protocol, whose message format is shown in Fig. 1b. It consists of two or more SYN characters (to synchronize the receiver and transmitter), followed by an SOH (start of header) to delineate the optional header, an STX (start of text) to delineate text, and an ETB or ETX character to delineate the end of a block of data or end of text (no more text coming) and inform the receiver that the subsequent two characters are the cyclic redundancy check characters for error control. BISYNC uses a rigorous set of rules for establishing, maintaining, and terminating transmission, including shorter formats for control that begin with two or more SYN characters followed by special control characters, such as positive or negative acknowledgements, inquiry, wait, or

end transmission (*see* HANDSHAKING for a typical exchange between a computer and a remote device on a private line using this protocol).

3. *Byte count-oriented protocols*, which keep track of the number of bytes transmitted. Digital Equipment Corporation's DDCMP protocol is an example, and its message format is shown in Fig. 1c. As with BISYNC, two or more SYN characters are used for synchronization, followed by:
   a. A class character to denote whether this is a control, data, or maintenance message.
   b. A 14-bit count field, indicating the number of characters that follow the header in a data message or the command for a command message.
   c. A 2-bit flag field, used for additional control and synchronization.
   d. A response field to indicate the number of the last message correctly received.
   e. A sequence field for added control messages and the message sequence number for data messages.
   f. An address field.
   g. A 16-bit cyclic redundancy check for the header.
   h. The number of data characters, specified by a 14-bit count field, and the data itself.
   i. A 16-bit cyclic redundancy check field for the data characters.

Byte count protocols have been implemented to help overcome problems encountered with the other two types of protocols in transmitting transparent data where special precautions must be taken when the data fields contain special characters, such as 01111110, SOH, STX, ETX, and others used to delineate and format messages.

TCP/IP TCP/IP (Transmission Control Protocol/Internet Protocol) is a widely used set of byte count-oriented routing protocols that evolved from the implementation of the ARPA network, an early packet switching network. The Internet Protocol (IP) allows data packets to be sent and received across networks, while the Transmission Control Protocol (TCP) provides flow control and reliable transmission using cyclic redundancy checking. TCP/IP is supported by the Unix operating system (*q.v.*) and, therefore, is one of the more popular communication protocols in use today, especially for scientific and engineering applications.

Protocol Implementation Besides specifying the frame and message formats, network protocols specify the type of control messages needed for establishing and terminating connections, transmitting data, and recovering from various error conditions, as well as their sequence and allowable responses. This kind of "handshaking" between the transmitting and receiving stations over the network can be quite complex and is outside the scope of this article. To help reduce this complexity, a 7-layer model for network architecture has been developed and a variety of protocols have been implemented to define and provide the services at each layer of the model (*see* OSI).

References

1988. McNamara, J. E. *Technical Aspects of Data Communication.* Maynard, MA: Digital Press.
1989. Keiser, G. E. *Local Area Networks.* New York: McGraw-Hill.

JOHN S. SOBOLEWSKI

NETWORK, LOCAL AREA. *See* LOCAL AREA NETWORK.

NETWORK, METROPOLITAN AREA. *See* METROPOLITAN AREA NETWORK.

NETWORK, WIDE AREA. *See* NETWORKS, COMPUTER.

NETWORKS FOR LEARNING

For articles on related subjects *see* COMPUTER-ASSISTED INSTRUCTION; COMPUTER-ASSISTED LEARNING AND TEACHING; COMPUTER CONFERENCING; and COMPUTER-MANAGED INSTRUCTION.

Networks that extended student access to computing played a major role in the development of instructional uses from the middle 1960s through the 1970s. Authors of instructional software found a larger audience for their programs and related materials, and obtained more feedback from users, since the applications were used on a network. Users benefited from access to the most current version of a program at the originating site or a central library. Increasing capability and decreasing cost of personal computers during the 1980s replaced networks as a source of programs for instruction. CONDUIT, which began as a consortium of regional computing services, and EDUCOM, the Inter-university Communications Council, continue to distribute software and provide service on computers in education. The National Science Foundation sponsored NSFNET which, although primarily for researchers, provides service for teachers and students as well. The National Research and Education Network will provide high-speed, fiber optic communications to link researchers to supercomputing centers (*q.v.*), and link educators to one another more efficiently.

Research and development projects in the 1970s (e.g. those at New Jersey Institute of Technology, University of Illinois, and University of Michigan) established computer-based conferencing and other electronic aids to educational communications as a major justification of

remote access to computers as information systems for teaching and learning. Access to databases and other information services, along with communications among groups of learners, is now common at all levels of education.

Local area networks (LANs - *q.v.*) provide for group work within a school building or on a college campus. Collaborative writing and group research projects are common applications. Students find others with whom to discuss their schoolwork as well as to organize special school projects and extracurricular activities. Databases related to local organizations and projects may be available to students, and members of the community may be be encouraged to dial in to the local network to participate in discussions.

National and international data networks link students from schools throughout the world. Kids Network was established by Technology Education Research Center (TERC) and National Geographic in 1985, to explore science projects such as might be accomplished with data on acid rain from throughout the world. The Star Schools network set up by TERC is used to exchange data and ideas about math, weather, alternative energy, and environmental concerns. The Interactive Communications Simulations project at the University of Michigan provides a variety of activities for students at schools throughout the world. After much success with role-playing (e.g. as a basis for study of international conflicts) and electronic publication (as in poetry stimulated and collected through international links among students), two of the staff members set off on an odyssey across Europe and North Africa, with students at participating schools posing questions for and collecting information from the two travelers (see Fig. 1).

Some commercial networks offer special rates to schools for use at off-hours, usually providing special services and orientation packages as well. Some networks promote sales of their services to families to help children in school through on-line encyclopedias.

The costs of network communications require some subsidy to be affordable by schools. Sometimes, assistance comes from the government in the form of a contract with the organization providing the service. Some commercial organizations (e.g. AT&T and Apple Computer) have subsidized network projects by making their own services available directly to schools to support communications among students in different parts of the world.

Uses of networks for learning are emerging as a major part of computers in education, providing students with electronic mail (*q.v.*), bulletin boards (*q.v.*), computer-based conferences, access to databases, on-line tutoring, discussions with experts, and other resources that extend learning opportunities.

References

1989. ISTE. *Proceedings of the International Symposium on Telecommunications in Education: Learners and the Global Village.* Eugene, OR: International Society for Technology in Education.

1990. Harasim, Linda M. *Online Education: Perspectives on a New Environment.* New York: Praeger.

KARL L. ZINN

NETWORKS, COMPUTER

For articles on related topics *see* COMMUNICATION CONTROL UNIT; LOCAL AREA NETWORK; METROPOLITAN AREA NETWORK; NETWORK ARCHITECTURE; NETWORK PROTOCOL; and OPEN SYSTEMS INTERCONNECTION; and TELEPROCESSING SYSTEM.

A *computer network* consists of a set of communication channels interconnecting a set of computing devices or nodes that can communicate with each other. The nodes may be computers, terminals, workstations (*q.v.*), or communication units of various kinds distributed over different locations. They communicate over communication channels that can be leased from common carriers (e.g. telephone companies) or are provided by the owners of the network. These channels may use a variety of transmission media, including optical fibers, coaxial cable, twisted copper pairs, satellite links, or digital microwave radio. The nodes may be distributed over a wide area (distances of hundreds or thousands of miles) or over a local area (distances of a hundred feet to several miles), in which case the networks are called wide area (WAN) or local area (LAN) networks, respectively. Combinations of LANs and WANs are also possible in the case of widely separated LANs in branch offices connected via a WAN to the LAN in corporate headquarters.

Over the past decade, modern computer networks have greatly increased in number and geographical area, in the number and variety of devices interconnected, and in the scope of applications supported. A modern network may consist of thousands of computing devices made by various manufacturers connected by a variety of transmission media spanning international and intercontinental boundaries. Design, operation, and management of such complex systems is a challenge. The sections that follow briefly describe network applications, design objectives, types of transmission media used, commonly used topologies, and standards, as well as some well-known networks that have been implemented.

Network Applications The basic reasons for the explosive growth in computer networks include:

- *Resource sharing*—Networks can provide users with convenient access to special computing resources, regardless of the physical location of the resources and the users. These resources may include specialized computers, software, or other devices that are expensive or unique and must be shared. An example is access to a corporate supercomputer (*q.v.*) from workstations at remote research laboratories.
- *Data sharing*—Networks can provide local and remote users with access to unique databases. Ex-

amples include remote access to stock exchange data or hotel and airline reservation systems.

- *Communication and data exchange*—Networks allow users to exchange data, graphs, or documents and to communicate with each other using electronic mail (*q.v.*) or bulletin boards (*q.v.*), irrespective of their location.

In effect, networks can be considered as the information roads and highways over which data is transported to support the above applications.

Network Objectives
The various types of networks that have evolved share a common set of objectives. They include:

- *Connectivity* to permit various hardware and software products to be connected and communicate with each other in a seamless way.
- *Simplicity* to permit easy installation and operation of all network components.
- *Modularity* to enable building of a wide variety of network devices from a relatively small set of mass-produced building blocks.
- *Reliability* to permit error-free transmission by providing appropriate error detection and correction capabilities.
- *Flexibility* to permit the network to evolve as new needs arise or new technologies become available.
- *Diversity* of network services that can be easily used yet isolate users from the technical details of network structure and implementation.

Network Architecture
While the above objectives may appear to be simple, their implementation is very complex since many trade-offs are involved. Moreover, linking a wide variety of computing devices made by different vendors requires hardware and software compatibility for seamless communication. A number of network architectures have evolved to help ensure this compatibility.

A network architecture defines the protocols, message formats, and other standards to which communication hardware and software must conform to achieve the network objectives. Computing devices complying with a given network architecture can intercommunicate. Communication between devices that conform to different network architectures is possible only through complex gateways (*q.v.*) designed to translate the protocols between them.

Some popular implementations of network architectures include the Xerox Network Systems (XNS) architecture, IBM's System Network Architecture (SNA), DEC's Digital Network Architecture (DNA), and the Department of Defense suite of protocols (notably TCP/IP). In 1978, the International Standards Organization (ISO) recognized the importance for a standard for the exchange of information within and between networks and issued a recommendation for a standard network architecture. This recommendation is now becoming widely accepted and is in the form of a seven-layer model known as the

Open Systems Interconnection (OSI) Reference Model. The term "open" denotes the ability to transfer information between any two systems that conform to the reference model and its standards.

Network Topology
Two important network parameters are its topology and the transmission media used. The topology refers to the geometrical arrangement and connection of network nodes. The basic topologies are illustrated in Fig. 1 and include the:

- *Point-to-point connection*. It has the advantage of simplifying routing decisions among nodes, but the reliability of the network depends on the reliability of the weakest links.
- *Linear bus* (*q.v.*), in which all network nodes have unique addresses and are connected to a common transmission medium. When a device transmits data onto the bus, it is received by all devices and is ignored, except by the one that is addressed. Local area networks based on the *ethernet* use this topology.
- *Ring connection*, in which consecutive nodes are connected by point-to-point links arranged to form a closed path (ring). Information is passed from node to node around the ring until it arrives at the node that is addressed.
- *Star connection*, in which all nodes are connected to a node called the central node or hub. The central node can be active or passive. If it is active, it is usually used to control the entire network and performs all the routing. This topology is used in applications where a central computer communicates with remote terminals or workstations.
- *Multiconnected networks*, in which nodes are connected by point-to-point links in an arbitrary fashion, with each node connected to at least two others. This improves reliability and reduces the likelihood of congestion, but makes routing much more complex since many paths are possible between any two nodes.

Large and complex networks may use various combinations of these basic topologies.

Transmission Media
Data transmission media provide the physical communication channel to interconnect nodes in a network. Commonly used media for computer networks include:

- *Twisted wire pairs*, usually made of insulated copper wire, which are commonly used for connections within buildings and between nodes separated by 10 miles or less. This medium is commonly used because it is relatively inexpensive and easy to install. Although it can support transmission rates of up to 10 Mbits/sec over distances of 100 feet or less, its main disadvantage is that the effective transmission rate decreases very rapidly with distance.
- *Shielded twisted pairs*. These have similar proper-

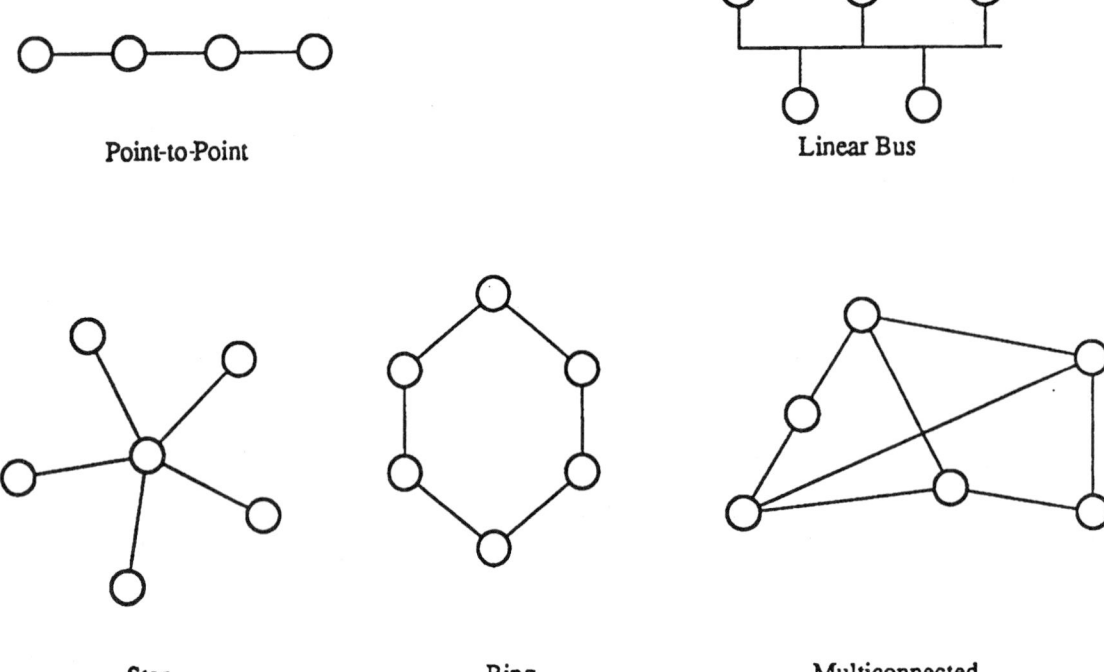

FIG. 1.   Basic methods of interconnecting nodes in a network. The circles represent computing devices or network nodes.

ties as simple twisted pairs, but include a metallic shield around both conductors to enhance reliability by reducing susceptibility to electromagnetic noise.

- *Coaxial cables,* which can be used over short (tens of feet) or long (hundreds of miles, with appropriate repeaters to help amplify the signal) distances, with bandwidths of up to 500 MHz. They are easy to install and are very popular, especially for local area networks. Such cables consist of an inner conductor completely surrounded by an outer conductor, with a layer of insulation in between.

- *Optical fibers,* which are thin, flexible glass or plastic fibers through which light is transmitted (*see* FIBER OPTICS). Although they are more difficult to work with than twisted pairs or coaxial cables, their use is increasing very rapidly, since they can support transmission rates of up to 16 gigabits/sec over short or long distances using currently available technologies.

- *Microwave radio,* which uses highly directional antennas for line-of-sight transmission between repeater stations. These spacings may vary from several hundred feet (e.g. from building to building) to 20 to 30 miles, depending upon the geographical terrain and the transmitter power permitted by regulatory agencies. Microwave radio links can support very high transmission rates and compete with coaxial cables as a transmission medium. They are particularly effective in

rough terrain or cities where laying coaxial cable can be very costly.

- *Satellite links,* which consist of line-of-sight propagation paths from a ground station to a communication satellite (up link) and back to a ground station (down link) that is the destination. The satellite is usually placed in a geosynchronous orbit about 22,300 miles above the earth so that it appears stationary at any point from which it is visible. In effect, the satellite acts like a repeater in the sky. This medium is usually used for very high transmission rates over long distances, and its use for transmission of voice, data, and video signals is increasing very rapidly.

Networks usually use a combination of the above media. A corporate network, for example, may use twisted pairs within buildings, optical fibers between local buildings, microwave radio to access buildings within 20 miles, and satellites to access branches distributed across the nation. Special hardware interfaces are required to interconnect the different media. In general, the wiring within buildings and between buildings on a corporate campus is owned by the corporation, while the links to distant branches are leased from common carriers, such as telephone companies.

Communication Control Units   The nodes connected by the network include a variety of communication control units that serve as the interfaces between the computing devices and the physical transmission medium over which data are actually transmitted. These control units vary in function and complexity, from a simple ethernet card that connects a personal computer and a local ethernet to a large front-end processor that performs a variety of complex network functions in front of a mainframe computer. Such control units include devices such as bridges, to interconnect local area networks and routers, or gateways, to interconnect different network architectures using different protocols. An example of the latter includes the use of routers to interconnect two widely separated local area networks using lines leased from the telephone company.

Types of Networks   Networks can be characterized as local area networks (LANs), metropolitan area networks (MANs - *q.v.*), or wide area networks (WANs). As their names imply, the former are usually limited to a geographical area that extends no more than a few miles between the extremities. Because of the smaller distances involved, LANs usually operate at relatively high speeds of between 100 kilobits/sec to 100 Mbits/sec. The ethernet, the token ring, and FDDI (fiber distributed data interface) are examples of commonly used LANs operating at speeds up to 10, 16, and 100 Mbits/sec, respectively. WANs can cover distances of hundreds or thousands of miles and, in general, use a variety of transmission media leased from common carriers. Sometimes, networks are also characterized as:

- *Private*. Such networks are usually owned by some corporation or other entity that confines access and use of network services to its staff.
- *Public*. This usually refers to entities that offer networking or network services to any organization or individual that wishes to subscribe. The telephone system is an example of a public network. Besides providing basic telephone services, telephone companies also sell or lease a variety of local and wide area communication services to their customers.
- *Cooperative*. This refers to networks that are supported and managed by their users. BITNET is an example of a cooperative network.

Internets   Despite the growing acceptance of the OSI reference model for network architectures, the current abundance of incompatible network types will not go away very soon. The need arises, therefore, to interconnect two or more compatible or incompatible networks to form an *internet* (network of networks). This is usually done by using communication control units called *routers* or *gateways* whose complexity depends mostly on the similarity of the networks connected in terms of frames, messages, and protocols.

Network Planning and Design   Planning, implementing, and operating a computer network can be a very complex task because of the number of often conflicting requirements that need to be satisfied and the variety of potential solutions that must be considered.

The objective is to satisfy all, or at least most, of the requirements at the lowest total cost. Factors to consider in planning include the:

- Type of applications for which the network will be used.
- Number and geographical distribution of the nodes.
- Amount and distribution of data to be transmitted.
- Access and response times required.
- Type of equipment that needs to be connected.
- Expected reliability and availability of network services.
- Need for future expansion.
- Needed compatibility with existing hardware and software.
- Simplicity in terms of ease of use.
- Security and management needs.

The design process includes the choice of the appropriate architectures, topologies, transmission media, communication control units, and software so that all devices can intercommunicate seamlessly and transparently.

Examples of Networks   Tens of thousands of networks of various kinds are currently operating around the world. They differ in the services provided, the users they serve, the technologies used, and their administration. The sections that follow describe some well-known and large networks that have played an important role in modern networking.

The ARPANET   In the late 1960s, the Advanced Research Projects Agency of the U. S. Department of Defense (DoD) began funding research in computer networks. This research led to an experimental four-node network in late 1969, which expanded to include almost 1,000 computers by the mid 1980s. Although the ARPANET, as it was called, spanned half the globe from Hawaii to Sweden, most of these systems were located at U. S. universities and research laboratories that had DoD research contracts.

When the ARPANET technology had proven itself by years of reliable operation, MILNET (Military Network) was implemented, using the same technology, and extended to Europe. It was connected to ARPANET, but the traffic between the two was tightly controlled to ensure MILNET security. Since many user organizations connected their own local area networks to ARPANET and MILNET, the resulting ARPA internet included thousands of interconnected computing devices and a total of about 100,000 users by 1985. After 1985, ARPA continued to support MILNET, but began phasing out support of the ARPANET.

Much of our present knowledge about computer networking is a direct result of the ARPANET project. The major nodes or local area networks were interfaced to the network through communication processors known as IMPs (interface message processors) and TIPs (terminal interface processors), connected mostly with 56 Kbps leased lines, with some operating at rates as high as 230.4

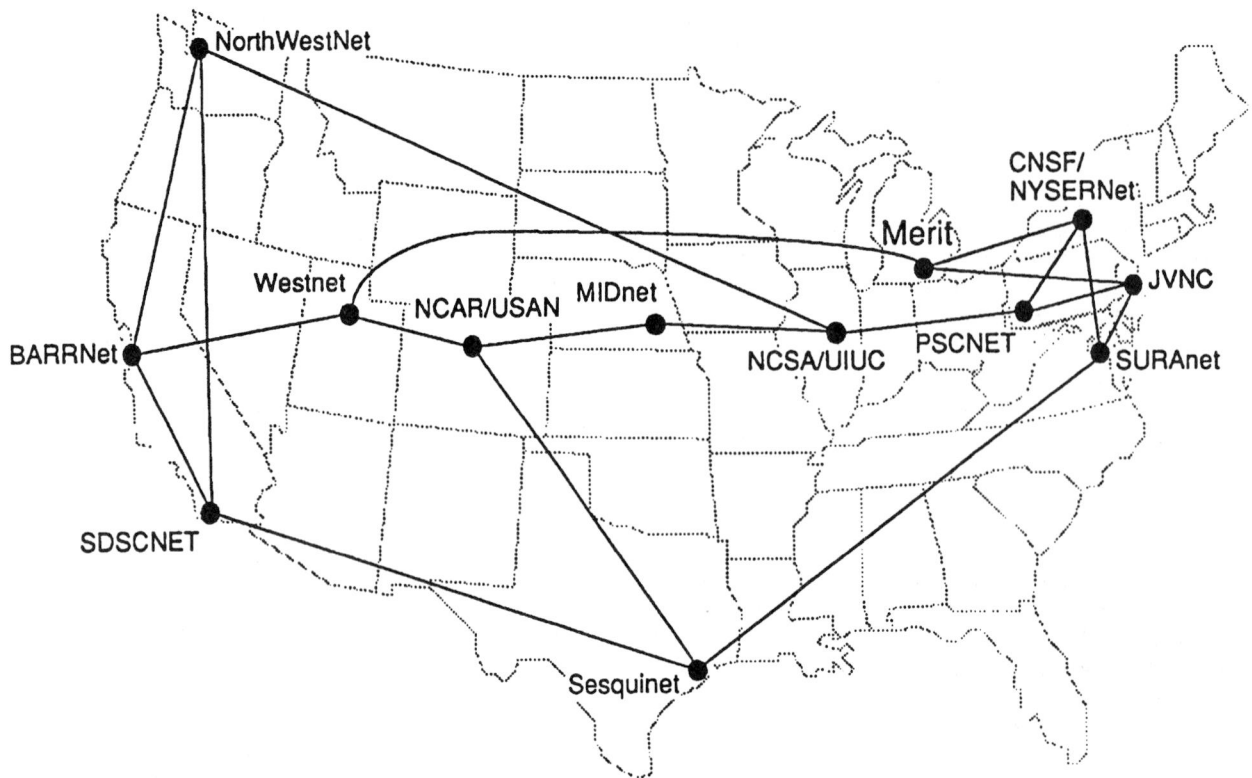

FIG. 2. NSFNET backbone topology. Besides routing, the nodes shown connect regional or mid-level networks (not shown) to the backbone. In March of 1992. NSFNET interconnected 4,071 local area networks at universities and research laboratories.

Kbps. The project led to the development of the TCP/IP (Transmission Control Protocol/Internet Protocol) family of protocols now used so widely to interconnect nodes using the Unix operating system (*q.v.*). The IP protocol was designed to handle the interconnection of the vast number of LANs comprising the ARPA internet. Other important ARPANET protocols include the File Transfer (FTP) and Simple Mail Transfer (SMTP) protocols, as well as TELNET, which supports login to a remote computer.

NSFNET In the early 1980s, the importance of the ARPANET for sharing resources and information among academic researchers had become obvious. Unfortunately, ARPANET was funded by the Department of Defense, and its use was therefore restricted to academic departments with DoD research contracts. As the DoD began phasing out its support for ARPANET after 1985, the National Science Foundation (NSF) began funding a number of network initiatives to ensure that university researchers could continue to communicate with each other and have convenient access to the national supercomputer centers established to help support NSF funded research.

The network that emerged from these initiatives in the late 1980s is known as NSFNET. It is based on the TCP/IP suite of protocols and consists of a high-speed multiconnected backbone network (see Fig. 2) designed to handle expected traffic patterns and provide reliability through redundant paths. Initially, this backbone con-

sisted of 56 Kbps leased lines, but these were upgraded to 1.54 Mbps (T1 lines) by 1990 because of the exponential growth in data traffic. Current plans are to expand the backbone to 45 Mbps and eventually to gigabit per second speeds by the late 1990s.

The NSFNET backbone nodes, shown in Fig. 2, serve two main purposes. They help route backbone traffic towards the appropriate destination and also provide the interface between the backbone and regional or mid-level networks. These regional networks (not shown in Fig. 2) connect universities and research laboratories in the states they serve. Westnet, for example, serves institutions in the states of Arizona, Colorado, Southern Idaho, New Mexico, and Wyoming. In this respect, NSFNET is an internet connecting local area networks at universities and research laboratories to form regional networks, which in turn are interconnected via the backbone using appropriate routers. Gateways are used to connect NSFNET to other national and international networks.

By March 1992, 4,071 local area networks at universities and research laboratories in each of the 50 states were interconnected by the NSFNET backbone and its regional networks. That month the backbone carried a data traffic of 8.4 billion packets or 1,533 billion bytes, with the data traffic growing at a rate of about 100% per year.

BITNET BITNET (Because It's Time NETwork) was started in 1981 by City University of New York and Yale University. The goal was to create an inexpensive mechanism for university departments to communicate with their peers at other institutions through electronic mail and file transfer.

The network uses an old IBM protocol designed to transmit 80-column punched card images. Besides IBM mainframes, this protocol has been ported to run on mainframes of other vendors. When electronic mail or a file is transmitted, it contains the address of its final destination and is stored and forwarded from system to system across the network until the destination is reached. Consequently, it is suited for file transfer, but not for interaction with a remote computer. This is in contrast with NSFNET, which supports both file transfer and interactive remote login quite effectively.

In November 1990, BITNET connected about 3,000 nodes at universities located in the U. S., Europe, Central and South America, Canada, the Middle East, Japan, and Southeast Asia. Some gateways were available to connect with Australia and other networks, including NSFNET. The popularity of BITNET stems largely from the unusual financing mechanism used. To join, a university must pay for the cost of a leased line to some other BITNET node (usually a nearest neighbor) and also permit some other university to connect to it, should that be needed in the future. It must also agree to allow BITNET traffic to pass (i.e. to be stored and forwarded) through its node at no cost to others. The net result is that for the cost of a leased line to its nearest neighbor and some loss of computing power for processing other traffic, university users can communicate with their peers at 3,000 other institutions worldwide. Furthermore, this cost is constant and independent of the volume of traffic sent. The latter is limited primarily by the transmission line speed. This is usually 9,600 bps, which is adequate for the store and forward applications for which the network is used. Although there is a central board to set BITNET policies, the network is effectively managed and financed by its users and is an example of a worldwide cooperative network.

References

1985. Meadow, C. and Tedesco, A. *Telecommunication for Management*, New York: McGraw-Hill.
1988. Tanenbaum, A. S. *Computer Networks*, 2nd Ed. Englewood Cliffs, NJ: Prentice-Hall.
1989. Martin, J. *Local Area Networks*, Englewood Cliffs, NJ: Prentice-Hall.
1990. Robertazzi, T. G. *Computer Networks and Systems*. New York: Springer-Verlag.

JOHN S. SOBOLEWSKI

NEURAL NETWORKS

For articles on related subjects *see* ARTIFICIAL INTELLIGENCE; COMPUTER VISION; EXPERT SYSTEMS; PATTERN RECOGNITION; PERCEPTRON; ROBOTICS; and SPEECH RECOGNITION AND SYNTHESIS.

Introduction The human brain performs perceptual tasks such as visual pattern recognition and speech understanding remarkably well. Historically, such cognitive tasks have been very difficult for digital computers to accomplish. The promise of neural computing relies on the rapid solution of such problems through massive parallelism, where information is not transferred between computing units, but is encoded through patterns of interconnectivity in a distributed fashion. The study of *neural networks* includes the notions of *connectionism, parallel distributed processing, self-adaptive systems,* and *self-organizing systems.*

Neural network processing has been inspired by the biological knowledge of the brain. Neural systems have been investigated by creating simplified theories and modeling those theories by simulation on conventional computers and VLSI implementation. By studying neural models, researchers hope to gain the insight needed to build machines with perceptual and cognitive capabilities that can understand what we say, read what we write, and recognize what we see. Such capabilities could complement existing computing systems and allow us to use machines more naturally, making them more effective in handling real-world tasks.

In general, neural net or parallel distributed processing (PDP) models are specified by network topology, node characteristics, and training or learning rules. Networks are comprised of a large number of simple processing units, each interacting with others via excitatory and inhibitory connections. Distributed representation over a massive number of units, together with local interconnectedness among processing units, provides for fault-tolerance. Learning is achieved through a rule that adapts connection weights in response to input patterns. Alterations in the degree of interconnectedness (i.e. the weight associated with a connection) permits adaptability to new situations. Recent developments in net topologies and learning algorithms have led to a resurgence in the field of neural computing and has inspired new applications for neural networks.

Historically, the study of artificial neural systems has been interdisciplinary, exciting the interest of scientists from the fields of neurobiology, psychology, computer science, and physics. The development of mathematical models for neural computing began more than 40 years ago with the work of McCulloch and Pitts (1943), Hebb (1949), Rosenblatt (1959), Widrow (1959) and others. While some researchers have closely adhered to known biological mechanisms, others have evolved new computational paradigms using simpler models. Such models have been successful in solving difficult optimization problems (Foo and Szu, 1989; Kirkpatrick, 1983) and in implementing associative memories (1984). Researchers have also combined conventional symbolic and heuristic approaches of artificial intelligence (AI) with new parallel distributed approaches. Unlike traditional expert systems, where knowledge is made explicit in the form of rules, neural networks generate their own "rules" by learning encounters. Established techniques may be used in conjunction with neural networks. For example, in the recognition of characters, one might use a Fast Fourier Transform (FFT - *q.v.*) to reduce a large input representation to a smaller set of vectors from which a neural net may be trained.

Current estimates place the number of neurons in the human brain at 100 billion (10^{11}). In contrast to the accuracy and high speed of modern-day digital computers, the brain is relatively slow and imprecise. But even with electronic circuit switching times a million times faster than neurons, artificial neural models face severe size constraints. Conventional chips typically have an average fan-out of five, while single cortical neurons can have from 1,000 to 100,000 synapses (connections) on their dendrites and can make from 1,000 to 100,000 synapses on the dendrites of other neurons. Thus, while biologically motivated massive parallel solutions may offer important insights, their practical implementations may require reformulation to make them realizable with respect to existing technology.

The remaining sections of this article provide an overview of a framework for neural computing and describe a neural network capable of arbitrary mapping.

Framework for Neural Computing
Rumelhart and McClelland (1986) identify eight major aspects of a parallel distributed model:

1. A set of processing units.
2. A state of activation.
3. An output function for each unit.
4. A pattern of connectivity among units.
5. A propagation rule for propagating patterns of activities through the network.
6. An activation rule for combining the inputs on a unit with its current state to produce a new level of activation.
7. A learning rule whereby patterns of connectivity are modified by experience.
8. An environment within which the system must operate.

A set of N processing *units* may represent distinct objects, such as features, letters, and concepts (*local representation*), or abstract elements over which meaningful patterns can be defined (*distributed representations*). In the latter case, each entity is represented by a pattern of activity distributed over many units, and each unit may be involved in representing several entities. As shown in Fig. 1, the architecture of neural networks distinguishes between three types of units: *input, output,* and *hidden.* Input units receive information from the outside world, such as sensory, or from other parts of the system in which the model is embedded. Output units transmit information out of the system, either directly affecting motor control or driving other systems. Hidden units are those contained within the input and output layers and are not "seen" outside the system.

The state of the system at time t may be defined by a vector of N real numbers representing the pattern of activation over a set of processing units, $\mathbf{a}(t)$. The activation of unit u_i at time t is $a_i(t)$ (see Fig. 2). It is the pattern of activation over the set of units that identifies what the system represents at time t. Activation values may be continuous or discrete, bounded or unbounded. Assump-

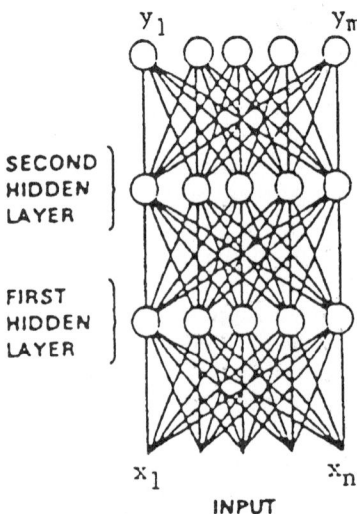

OUTPUT

FIG. 1. A three-layered network.

tions concerning the domain and range of activation values account for most differences among neural models.

Each unit communicates with its neighbors via the strength of its output signals. For each unit u_i, output $o_i(t) = f_i(a_i(t))$. Output functions f may simply be an identity function, $f(x) = x$ (linear), a threshold function (nonlinear) or a stochastic function in which its output depends in a probabilistic fashion upon its activation values.

The pattern of connectivity among units specifies *what* the system represents and *how* it responds to arbitrary input. In a simple model, signals coming into a unit are multiplied by weights and summed to produce an output signal. Typically, positive weights represent excitatory types of input and negative weights represent inhibitory types of input. For weight matrix W, each entry w_{ij} represents the connection strength (magnitude) and type (sign) from unit i to unit j.

A propagation rule sends patterns of activities throughout a network. Signals may flow unidirectionally or may feed back to other units within a network. In a *feed-forward* model, activations are computed in sequence starting with the input layer and propagated towards the output layer. The structure of communication links is reflected by the connectivity matrix of each layer. In general, a propagation rule combines an output vector $\mathbf{o}(t)$ with its associated connectivity weight matrix to produce a resultant input to the next layer. Let net_j be the resultant input connections to unit j. Typically, the propagation rule is simply the weighted sum of the input (i.e. $\mathbf{net}(t) = \mathbf{Wo}(t)$).

An activation rule $\mathbf{F}$ combines all net inputs of a unit with its current activation value to produce a new level of activation. The activation is formulated by the expression $a_i(t + 1) = \mathbf{F}(net_i(t)) = \mathbf{F}(\Sigma_j w_{ij} o_j)$ (see Fig. 2). For most neural models, each unit sums its weighted input and passes the result through a nonlinearity. Activation rules may be characterized by an internal threshold parameter and by the kind of nonlinearity. Fig. 3 shows three representative nonlinear activation functions: hard limiters,

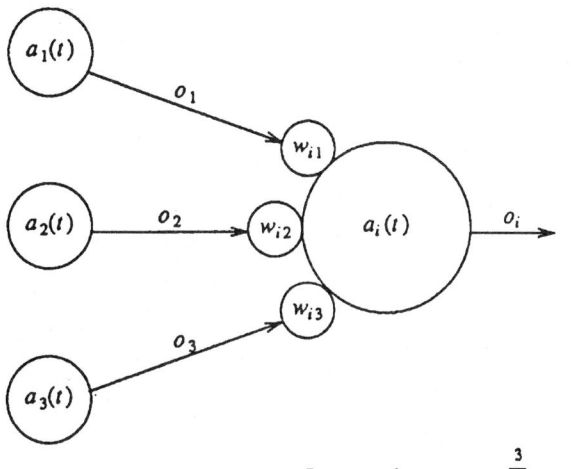

Propagation: $\text{net}_i = \sum_{j=1}^{3} w_{ij} o_j$

Activation: $a_i(t) = F_i(a_i, \text{net}_i)$

Output: $o_i(t) = f_i(a_i)$

FIG. 2. The basic components of a neural computing system.

threshold logic, and sigmoidal functions. In the case of the hard limiter (Fig. 3 (a)), if the weighted sum of inputs is greater than or less than zero, the input pattern will be mapped onto the values +1 or −1, respectively. The earliest neurons (McCulloch-Pitt neurons) were such binary threshold devices. Timing of the activation rule may be driven synchronously or asynchronously. In models where updates are asynchronous and random, the network is more likely to avoid oscillations (Hopfield and Tank, 1986).

Learning strategies are the focus of much research in the field. In the next section, we describe two paradigms by which networks may be trained: *supervised* and *unsupervised* learning.

Learning Paradigms Changing the processing and/or knowledge stored in a network may involve three kinds of modifications to the pattern of interconnectivity: developing new connections, losing existing connections, and modifying the strengths of existing connections. The modification of interconnections is accomplished by adjusting the weights between connections whenever the neural net learns something in response to new inputs (experience or changes in the environment). In general, most learning rules increase or decrease synaptic weights in proportion to a reinforcement signal.

Networks may be trained with or without supervision. In *unsupervised learning*, no information concerning correct class is provided to reinforce training patterns. The

earliest example of unsupervised learning is the Hebbian learning rule: if cell A persistently participates in firing cell B, then A's efficiency in firing B is increased (Hebb 1949). This rule may be approximated by $w_{ij}(t+1) = w_{ij}(t) + \eta\, a_i(t)\, o_j(t)$, where η is a gain parameter for the rate of learning. However, using this simple rule, networks can learn only orthogonal input patterns. A more sophisticated form of unsupervised learning is a variant of Hebb's rule called *competitive learning* $\Delta w_{ij} = (a_j(t) - w_{ij}(t))\, a_i(t)$, where changes are balanced against previously established clusters. Kohonen's feature-map-forming sets (1984) and Grossberg's ART (Adaptive Resonance Theory, 1986) have evolved from competitive learning models.

Supervised learning requires a teacher, reinforcing correct associations between inputs and outputs by providing the correct or desired output during training periods. For example, consider the *Widrow-Hoff* rule, $\Delta w_{ij} = \eta\, (u_i(t) - a_i(t))\, o_j(t)$. In this rule, the reinforcement signal is proportional to the difference between the desired activation provided by a "teacher" u_i and the current activation signal a_i. Using this error correcting rule (or *delta rule*), it is possible to train a network to recognize patterns that are linearly independent rather than strictly orthogonal. Models using methods of supervised learning, such as Hopfield's (1986), perceptrons, and Boltzman's Machine, may be described as associative memories or classifiers (see Fig. 4).

Network models may be classified based on their learning paradigms and goals. The goal of *pattern associators* is to map one set onto another. *Auto associators* can be used to recover a pattern from a degraded version. *Regularity detectors* discover useful features of an input population. *Reinforcement learning* provides feedback on input stimuli. Hebb's ideas remains a common thread in these paradigms. In the next sections, we describe how these goals may be achieved in the context of linear and nonlinear models.

Linear Models In linear models, activation values are unbounded real numbers and consist of two sets of units—input and output. There is no need for hidden

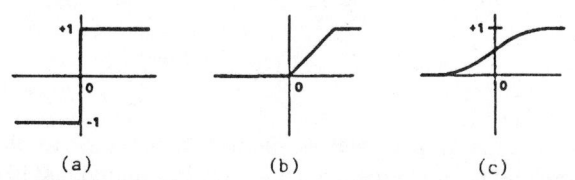

FIG. 3. Three nonlinear activation functions: (a) hard limiter, (b) threshold logic, and (c) sigmoidal.

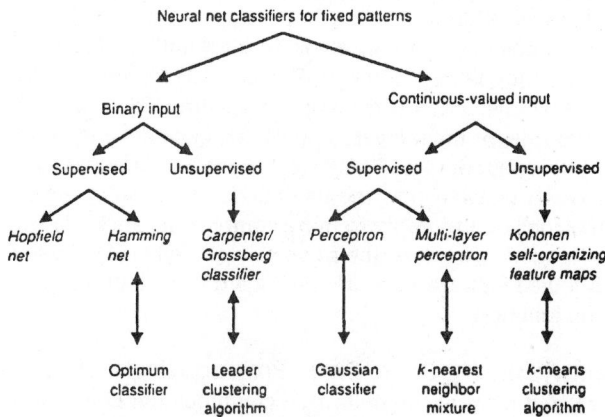

FIG. 4. Neural net classifiers for fixed patterns. (From R. Lippman, "An Introduction to Computing with Neural Nets," *IEEE ASSP Magazine*, April 1987. © 1987 IEEE.)

units in linear systems because all multiple step computations may be accomplished in a single step. Units may be fully connected, and all connections are of the same type. A linear model with a simple Hebbian rule is called a *linear associator*. As a pattern associator, the presentation of one pattern makes the network produce a previously learned pattern associated with the input. The new pattern may be associated with itself (auto-association). In this case, when presented with a portion of the input, a trained network generates a completed version of that pattern. Thus, in terms of function, these networks can accomplish *mapping* and *pattern completion*.

The orthogonal constraint of linear systems may be overcome by using nonlinear units within multi-layer systems. In the next section, we describe a nonlinear model, the perceptron, and discuss its significance with respect to the evolution of a learning rule for multi-layered networks called the *generalized delta rule*.

Nonlinear Models The simplest nonlinear system consists of linear threshold units. As shown in Fig. 3(b), if the weighted sum of inputs is greater than some threshold, the activation value is 1, otherwise, it is 0. A *perceptron* is a single-layer network of linear threshold units without feedback. Rosenblatt (1959) studied perceptrons, using a learning rule similar to the delta rule described earlier. The Perceptron convergence theorem claims that such a system is guaranteed to find a set of weights that correctly classifies a set of input vectors *if such a set of weights exists*. Unfortunately, as Minsky and Papert pointed out in their 1969 book, *Perceptrons*, such a set of weights does not always exist. Perceptrons can solve only the class of functions that are *linearly separable*. (If the input patterns are not linearly independent, they cannot be discriminated by a simple linear network.) The simplest example of a function that cannot be computed by a single-layered perceptron is exclusive-or (XOR), shown in Fig. 5(a). A multi-layered perceptron capable of computing the XOR function is shown in Figure 5(b).

The perceptron (nonlinear) and delta-rule (linear) provided a simple guaranteed learning rule for all problems solvable without hidden units. Unfortunately, no such learning rule existed for networks with hidden units. A revitalization in neural computing was sparked by the development of learning algorithms for multi-layered networks. Rumelhart (1986), Werbos (1984), and Parker (1985) independently developed a generalized form of the delta rule for multi-layered networks, capable of learning arbitrary mappings. Their work remains significant because it showed that the limitations of single-layer perceptrons do not apply to more complex networks. In the next section we describe a generalized delta rule applied to a feed-forward network having a differentiable activation function.

Learning by Back Error Propagation The generalized form of the delta rule combines the benefits of nonlinear perceptron-like classification capability with a method of minimizing an error measure for learning called *gradient descent*. Widrow and Hoff (1960) first used gradient descent for learning in linear systems by the least-

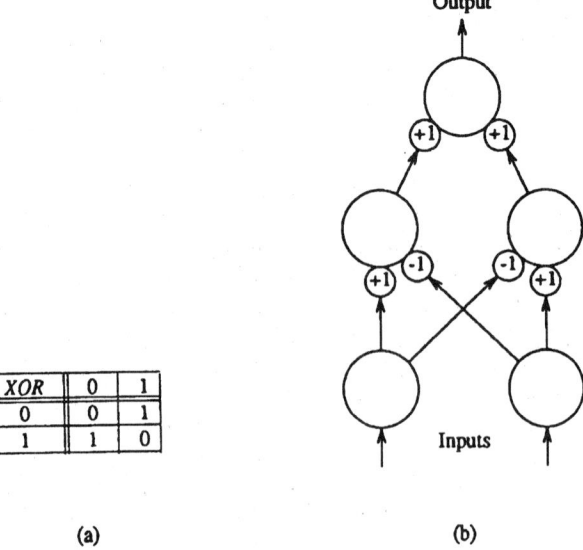

XOR	0	1
0	0	1
1	1	0

(a)   (b)

FIG. 5. A multi-layered network of linear threshold units configured to compute the XOR function. Each unit has zero threshold, and responds only if the input is greater than zero.

mean-square (LMS) method. The LMS procedure finds a set of connection weights that minimize the mean-squared-error between desired output and actual output over a set of input patterns, using gradient descent.

Similarly, learning by back error propagation exploits the method of gradient descent: Changes in weights are made in proportion to the negative of the derivative of an error term, as measured on a current pattern with respect to existing weights. For example, given pattern *p*, the learning rule becomes

$$\Delta w_{ij} = -k \frac{\partial E_p}{\partial w_{ij}}, \tag{1}$$

where k is a proportionality constant. Computing the derivative of Eq. (1) shows that the generalized rule takes the same form as the original delta rule, $\Delta w_{ij} = \eta \delta_{pi} o_{pj}$. Thus, the delta rule implements gradient descent in E (see Fig. 6). Each connection weight is changed by an amount proportional to the product of an error term called δ times the output signal of the unit sending activation along each connection.

The generalized delta rule requires *semi-linear* activations. A semi-linear activation function is a non-decreasing differentiable function of net output, such as the sigmoid logistic function shown in Fig. 3(c).

$$o_{pj} = \frac{1}{1 - e^{-net_{pj}}},$$
where $net_{pj} = \sum_i w_{ji} o_{pi} + bias_j.$

The parameter *bias* is similar in function to the threshold of the perceptron and may be treated just like any other weight. The linear threshold function (Fig. 3(b)) on which the perceptron is based is discontinuous, and

$$F : R^n \rightarrow I^m$$
$$\text{where} \quad R = (-\infty, \infty) \quad I = (0,1)$$

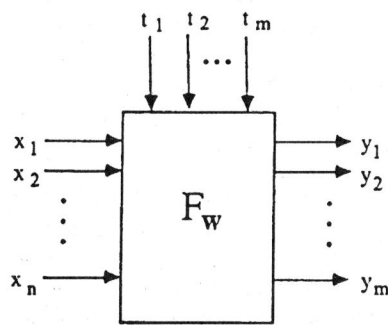

$$F_W : R^n \rightarrow I^m$$

$x \in R^n$: input signal $y \in I^m$: output signal

$t \in I^m$: teaching signal $w \in R^p$: connection weight

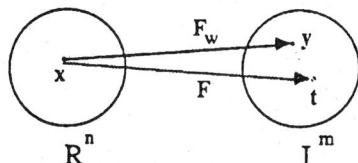

FIG. 6. A backpropagation net as a mapping device. Learning rule: Search for w such that $F = F_W$ by (1) Select training set $T \subseteq R^n$. (2) Minimize error function $E = \dfrac{1}{|T|} \sum\limits_{x \in T} \| F(x) - F_W(x) \|$ with $\Delta w = -\eta \dfrac{\partial E}{\partial w}$ by method of gradient descent. (From T. Kimura, Department of Computer Science, Washington University, St. Louis, MO. © 1989 Class notes. Reprinted with permission.)

cannot be used since the new learning rule requires that the derivative of the activation function $f_i'(net_i)$ exist.

For purposes of back-propagation, the error signal δ is computed in two distinct ways. The error signal for output units is similar the the standard delta rule and is computed by

$$\delta_{pi} = (t_{pi} - o_{pj}) \, f_i'(net_{pj}), \qquad (2)$$

where f_i' is the derivative of the activation function. The error signal for hidden units for which there is no specific target is computed recursively in terms of the δ values of units to which it directly connects and the weights of those connections. That is,

$$\delta_{pi} = f_i'(net_{pj}) \, \Sigma_k \delta_{pk} \, w_{kj}. \qquad (3)$$

Thus, learning by back-propagation requires that the generalized rule be applied in two phases. In the first phase, an input is presented and propagated forward through the network to compute an output value o_{pj} for each unit. Output unit values are then compared with the target

pattern associated with the input, and a δ term is computed for each output unit using Eq. (2). In the second phase, a backward pass through the network allows the recursive computation of δ as shown in Eq. (3).

The network is trained by initially selecting small random weights and internal thresholds and presenting training input patterns repeatedly. Weights are adjusted after each pattern set until the weights converge and the cost function (E) is reduced to an acceptable value. Finding the global minimum is not guaranteed (Hinton et al. 1984). Convergence is sometimes faster and escape from local minima is possible if a momentum term is added, smoothing the weight changes.

Concluding Remarks The potential of artificial neural computing has yet to be reached. The back-propagation network described above is an example of a functional component that may be part of more complex systems in the future. Current research is focused on analyzing learning and self-organizing algorithms used in multi-layered networks, on building complete systems for image understanding and speech recognition, and in exploring different VLSI implementation strategies (Mead, 1986; Graf et al. 1986). Research in achieving high-speed processing through massively parallel VLSI implementations holds the promise of success and could lead to practical real-time neural net systems.

References

1943. McCulloch, W. S. and Pitts, W. "A Logical Calculus of the Ideas Immanent in Nervous Activity," *Bulletin of Mathematical Biophysics*, **5**, 115–133.

1949. Hebb, D. O. *The Organization of Behavior*, New York: John Wiley & Sons.

1959. Rosenblatt, R. *Principles of Neurodynamics*, New York: Spartan Books.

1960. Widrow, B., and Hoff, M. E. "Adaptive Switching Circuits," *1960 IRE WESCON Conv. Record, Part 4*, 96–104, August.

1969. Minsky, M., and Papert, S. *Perceptrons: An Introduction to Computational Geometry*, Cambridge, MA: M.I.T. Press.

1982. Hopfield, J. J., "Neural Networks and Physical Systems with Emergent Collective Computational Abilities," *Proc. Natl. Acad. Sci.* USA, **79** (April) 2554–2558.

1982. Feldman, J. A., and Ballard, D. H., "Connectionist Models and Their Properties," *Cognitive Science*, **6**, 205–254.

1983. Anderson, J. A., "Cognitive and Psychological Computation with Neural Models," *IEEE Trans. Sys. Man, Cyb.*, **SCM-13**, 799–815.

1983. Kirkpatrick, S., Gellatt, C. D., Jr., and Vecchi, M. P., "Optimization by Simulated Annealing," *Science*, **220**, 671–680.

1984. Hinton, G. E., Sejnowski, T. J., and Ackley, D. H., "Boltzman Machines: Constrained Satisfaction Networks that Learn," CMU-CS-84-119, Carnegie Mellon University (May).

1984. Kohonen, T. *Self-Organization and Associative Memory*. Berlin: Springer-Verlag.

1984. Werbos, P. *Beyond regression: new tools for prediction and analysis in behavioral sciences*. Ph.D. Dissertation, Harvard University.

1985. Parker, D. B. *Learning-logic*, (TR-47), Center for Computational Research in Economics and Management Science, Cambridge, MA: The M.I.T. Press.

1986. Rumelhart, D. E. and McClelland, J. L. *Parallel Distributed*

Processing: Explorations in the Microstructure of Cognition, Cambridge, MA: The M.I.T. Press.

1986. S. Grossberg, *The Adaptive Brain I: Cognition, Learning, Reinforcement, and Rhythm*, and *The Adaptive Brain II: Vision, Speech, Language, and Motor Control*, Amsterdam: Elsevier/North-Holland.

1986. Hopfield, J. J., and Tank, D. W. "Computing with Neural Circuits: A Model," *Science*, **233** (August), 625–633.

1986. Mead, C. A. *Analog VLSI and Neural Systems*, Course Notes, Computer Science Dept., California Institute of Technology.

1986. Graf, H. P., Jackel, L. D., Howard, R. E., Straughn, B., Denker, J. S., Hubbard, W., Tennant, D. M., and Schwartz, D. "VLSI Implementation of a Neural Network Memory With Several Hundreds of Neurons," in Denker, J. S. (Ed.) *AIP Conference Proceedings* **151**, *Neural Networks for Computing, Snowbird Utah*, AIP.

1988. *Science*, **242**, Special Issue: Frontiers in Neuroscience," 633–828 (November).

1989. Foo, Y. P. S., and Szu, H. "Solving Large-Scale Optimization Problems By Divide-and-Conquer Neural Networks," *International Joint Conference on Neural Networks*, Washington D.C., 18–22 June.

1989. Szu, H. "Reconfigurable Neural Nets by Energy Convergence Learning Principle Based on Extended McCulloch-Pitts Neurons and Synapses," *International Joint Conference of Neural Networks*, Washington D.C., 18–22 June.

1990. Diederick, J., Morgan, N., and Vemuri, V., (Ed.) *Artificial Neural Networks* (3 volumes), Los Alamitos, CA: IEEE Society Press.

ANDREW LAINE

NO-OP

For articles on related subjects *see* ASSEMBLER; INSTRUCTION SET; and MACHINE AND ASSEMBLY LANGUAGE PROGRAMMING.

A *no-op* ("no operation") is a machine language instruction that can safely be placed in the flow of control of a program but that does nothing to advance the computation in progress. A true no-op does not change the status of any bit or register in the computer other than the program counter (*q.v.*), which, when control reaches the no-op, advances to the next meaningful instruction (or another no-op). The usual reasons for embedding a sequence of one or more no-ops in the flow of control are that the programmer wants to introduce a deliberate delay in processing for the sake of either time or address synchronization (to reach an even-numbered address, perhaps), or that space must be reserved in the object code that will be overwritten with a meaningful instruction at some point during execution of the program. (The latter practice is now discouraged because the resulting code would not constitute a reentrant program (*q.v.*).)

The instruction sets (*q.v.*) of a CISC (complex instruction set computer) often include one op code (operation code) that is itself a no-op, but newer computers built in accord with the reduced instruction set (RISC-*q.v.*) philosophy cannot usually afford to devote one of its precious few op codes to such a (non-) function. But a no-op can be synthesized on virtually any computer by writing such instructions as adding zero to a register, shifting a register zero places left, or branching to the next instruction.

EDWIN D. REILLY

NONPROCEDURAL LANGUAGES

For articles on related subjects *see* DATAFLOW; FUNCTIONAL PROGRAMMING; LOGIC PROGRAMMING; PROBLEM-ORIENTED LANGUAGES; PROCEDURE-ORIENTED LANGUAGES; and PROGRAMMING LANGUAGES.

Basic Concepts

Nomenclature This article describes some of the basic characteristics of the class of programming languages commonly referred to as *nonprocedural* or *very high level* (see Leavenworth and Sammet, 1974). Some of the descriptive terms that have often been applied to the word "language" to convey essentially the same concept are the following:

Nonprocedural
Very high level
Less procedural
Goal-oriented
Problem-oriented
Pattern-directed
Declarative
Functional
Relational
Problem statement
Problem definition
Problem description
Specification
Result specification
Task description

The most common term used has been *nonprocedural*, which is employed by a user to indicate the goals to be achieved (i.e. *what*), rather than the specific methods used to achieve them (i.e. *how*).

Properties of Programs It is not possible to state that a given programming language is nonprocedural in any absolute sense because it is a relative term that changes as the state of the art changes. We can, however, say that a language possesses certain nonprocedural features. In order to see why this is so, we review briefly some fundamental properties of programs and programming languages.

In general, a *program* is a prescription for solving a particular problem. A *procedure* (*q.v.*) is a series of steps followed in a regular, orderly, definite way. Procedural programming is based to a great extent on the necessity to conform to the inherent sequential organization of the conventional digital computer. Therefore, a possible definition of a nonprocedural program is that it is a prescription for solving a problem without regard to any arbitrary sequencing requirements. More generally, we will say that a nonprocedural program is a prescription for solving a problem without regard to details of *how* it is solved. That is, the solution should be specified in terms of structures or abstractions that are relevant to the problem rather than those operations, data, and control structures that are based on some particular machine organization.

Relative Nature of the Term "Nonprocedural" In many ways, the term *less procedural* is better than nonprocedural because it makes clear the relative nature of the concept. An examination of Fig. 1 should make this clearer. A comparison of Figs. 1(a) and (a*) shows the difference between assembly language and Fortran-like languages. Prior to the existence of Fortran, the expression A = (B + C) * D + E * F could have been considered nonprocedural because it could not be directly translated by any language processor. Similarly, Figs. 1(b) and (b*) indicate another level of relativity, since the Fortran program to do matrix multiplication can be handled by one statement in APL. The use of a subroutine in Fortran would not give additional nonprocedurality, since the procedurality is based on the language primitives. Finally, the illustration of Fig. 1(c*), which is a program to CALCULATE THE SQUARE ROOT OF THE PRIME NUMBERS FROM 3 TO 95 AND PRINT IN TWO

COLUMNS, cannot be handled by any translating system known today, but, if it could be, the language would be considered nonprocedural by the standards of 1992. [It is essential to realize that the two forms shown in Fig. 1(c*) are logically equivalent, and the desirability of one form over the other (i.e. formal notation versus English) is a matter of personal preference.] The ability of a system to "understand" English is not at issue here; phrases that look like English may really depend on specific programming techniques (e.g. pattern matching and macro expansion), rather than English grammar. It is entirely possible to design a formal language for doing mathematical problems in which the statement CALCULATE THE SQUARE ROOT OF THE PRIME NUMBERS FROM 3 TO 95 AND PRINT IN TWO COLUMNS is acceptable. At the other extreme, a natural and elegant looking phrase such as FIND X SUCH THAT X**2 = 5 is really equivalent to invoking a square root routine. Thus, nonprocedurality and English notation are completely independent issues.

We actually have two types of relativity: One involves the problem or application area as described above and one involves the actual hardware. In the case of the hardware, we can only use as the base from which to measure some particular hardware or class of machines. As the machine changes, so does the relativity. The reason that one must consider the hardware is that certain features or facilities that might be available on one machine are not on another. Thus, prior to the availability of floating-point instructions in essentially all hardware, the capability to perform floating-point arithmetic had to be included explicitly in the programming language, and thus would be considered higher level with respect to the machine. Once floating-point became virtually universal on computers, it was removed from serious language consideration.

Sequencing There is a difference between sequencing across statements and sequencing within one statement. The former requirement tends to be obvious in a problem. However, sequencing within a single statement may or may not be explicit, and this affects the nonprocedurality of the statement. Moreover, it is not always obvious from looking at a statement whether sequencing information is embedded in it. For example, sequencing is inherent in any mathematical expression that has precedence among its operators. Any data dependencies that are inherent in the problem statement may also affect the sequencing by requiring the data to be obtained in the correct order. A trivial illustration of this is obvious by merely noting that one cannot produce outputs until after one has performed calculations on the inputs.

As another illustration of the significance and relevance of sequencing, consider the problem statement shown in Fig. 1(c*). This calculation could actually be performed in several ways. One way is to follow each number through the three "computations"; i.e. test for primality, and if the number is prime, then compute its square root and print it. However, depending on the particular hardware and software, it might be more efficient first to determine all the primes, then to calculate all the square roots of the identified primes, and then to do all

```
       (a)                        (a*)
(Assembly Language)            (Fortran)

CLA B                     A = (B + C) * D + E * F
ADD C
MPY D
STO T
CLA E
MPY F
ADD T
STO A


       (b)                        (b*)
    (Fortran)                    (APL)

  DO 7 I = 1,M               A ← B +.× C
    DO 8 J = 1,N
      C(I,J) = 0
      DO 9 K = 1,L
        C(I,J) + A(I,K) * B(K,J)
9       CONTINUE
8     CONTINUE
7   CONTINUE


       (c)                        (c*)
    (PL/I)

DO 1 = 3 TO 95 BY 2;        PRINT 2, SQR (PRIME (3,95))
  IF PRIME (I)
    THEN PUT SKIP LIST
      (I, SQRT (I));               or
    ELSE RETURN;
END;                       CALCULATE THE SQUARE
                           ROOT OF THE PRIME
                           NUMBERS FROM 3 TO
                           95 AND PRINT IN 2
                           COLUMNS
```

FIG. 1.

the printing. This is a prototype of a calculation involving a sequence of tasks, each of which supplies data to the next, but where each input datum is independent of the others. The program given in Fig. 1(c) chooses only one of the alternatives; no discretion is left to the translator, whereas the statement in Fig. 1(c*) could—as indicated above—be translated in several significantly different ways that could have a major impact on efficiency. The explicit sequencing used in the program of Fig. 1(c) is not required for solution of the problem. One way of characterizing nonprocedurality is to say that the specification of sequencing of any information by the programmer (except that which is inherent to the logic of the problem) is irrelevant.

History

In the very early stages of programming (i.e. in the first half of the 1950s), the phrase *automatic programming* was used to mean the process of writing a program in some high-level language. In that context, "high-level" was by comparison with machine code. As time went on, it became clear that the coding was only a portion of the entire problem-solving task, and therefore the phrase *automatic coding* came into use as meaning the use of a language such as Fortran. Thus, even in the very early days, the proper distinction was made between coding (which is one aspect of the entire programming task) and the larger activity of specification and design. One of the first significant accomplishments was the work of the Codasyl Language Structure Group (1962) in the development of the Information Algebra. This was essentially a mathematically-oriented way of describing a data processing application in terms of the input/output relationships; these were actually defined by means of transformations on sets of entities called *areas* (analogous to files). As another example, we note that a string and pattern directed language such as Snobol or Icon are much less procedural for those features than a language such as Fortran or Cobol.

Features of Nonprocedural Languages

We discuss three features that are considered of major importance for inclusion in a programming language that claims to be nonprocedural. Some examples of languages possessing some of these features are included.

Associative Referencing We will use the term *associative referencing* to refer to the accessing of data based on some intrinsic property of the data. Associative referencing is usually provided in those languages that contain sets as a data structure. The operation of selecting elements from previously defined sets, and of defining new sets from old based on some property of the members, is sometimes called the *set former* (see, for example, SETL – *q.v.*). An example of the power of SETL can be seen by the following expression, which specifies the prime numbers between 2 and 100.

```
{P,2 <= P <= 100↑
          (∀2 <= N < P ↑ (P//N)NE. 0)}
```

This can be read as "the set of P's between 2 and 100 such that for every N greater than or equal to 2 and less than P,

the remainder of P/N is not equal to zero." (This specification is obviously not an efficient one; a practical algorithm would at the very least consider the odd numbers from 3 to 100.)

The importance of associative referencing in nonprocedural languages is that the programmer does not have to specify access paths explicitly or program an algorithm to conduct a search for a specific data structure. Associative referencing is also used in database management languages.

Codd (1972) defines algebraic operations on *relations* that give a measure of the relative power of a language with respect to this type of data structure. In addition to the traditional set operations of Cartesian product, union, intersection, etc. he defines the relational operations of projection, join, division, and restriction. These operators (see *Aggregate Operators*, below) effectively provide various types of associative referencing. (*See* RELATIONAL DATABASE.)

Aggregate Operators It is possible to avoid writing loops in some programming languages that provide aggregate operators. The + operator in APL is the simplest example of an operator that applies equally to scalars and aggregates. For example, the addition of two vectors x, y is obtained merely by writing x + y, whereas, in most programming languages, the elements of the result vector would have to be obtained one at a time under the control of a loop. Another example of an aggregate operator in APL is the use of the reduction operator to sum the elements of a vector x, as shown in the following expression: +/x.

There seems in general to be a close relationship between associative referencing and the aggregate operators we are discussing. It is certainly clear that the algebraic operators defined by Codd (1972) on relations are aggregate operators. Certainly, the elimination of explicit sequencing by this means is a nonprocedural feature.

Elimination of Arbitrary Sequencing We will define *arbitrary sequencing* as any sequencing that is not dictated by the data dependencies of the application.

A pure functional programming language is one that does not contain either assignment or goto statements. As such, "functional" appears to be a synonym for "nonprocedural," since it is more involved with specifying the outcome desired as a function of the inputs, rather than indicating a step-by-step sequence of program steps. A program in a functional language such as pure Lisp avoids side effects (*q.v.*), which are a concomitant of procedural programming. A side effect may be caused in procedural languages during expression evaluation by the modification of memory by an assignment statement (e.g. during evaluation of a function in the expression). Pure functional languages produce no side effects, since they have no assignment operation and cannot modify memory during expression evaluation.

One example of functional programming would be APL "one-liners" (without assignments, or without function calls with side effects). The following APL one-line function will delete leading elements from a vector X where Q represents a quoted character string or a numeric vector that contains examples to be deleted.

$$\nabla R \leftarrow Q \text{ DELETE } X$$
$$[1] \quad R \leftarrow (\sim \wedge \backslash X \in Q)/X$$
$$\nabla$$

The Prolog language (Clocksin and Mellish, 1986) is another example of a language that possesses some of the attributes we have been describing (*see* LOGIC PROGRAMMING: LANGUAGES). Prolog allows one to describe known facts and relationships about a problem, rather than prescribing a sequence of steps. Prolog uses pattern matching and "backtracking" to infer new facts from given facts. It therefore satisfies the associative referencing and lack of arbitrary sequencing criteria for nonprocedurality. For example, if the following relationship (rule) is declared:

X is mortal if X is human.

and the following simple fact is also declared:

Socrates is human.

then Prolog can "infer" that Socrates is mortal, even though this fact is not declared explicitly. Moreover, Prolog may be used to model a relational database from which retrievals may be made by pattern matching. For example, if the following facts are asserted:

s(s1,smith,20,london),
s(s2,jones,10,paris),
s(s3,blake,30,paris),

then the query to find s# and status for suppliers in Paris (*see* "Database Languages" below) could be written

?-s(S#,_,Status,paris),

where lowercase names denote constants, uppercase names denote variables, and "_" represents a "don't care" value. The result of this query would be:

S# = s2
Status = 10;

S# = s3
Status = 30;

no (meaning no further solutions).

The ultimate expression of lack of arbitrary sequencing is a pure *dataflow* programming language. In this formalism, an application is decomposed into a set of modules such that one module can only consume (i.e. get as its input data) a particular value after it has been produced by another module, and conversely. The sequencing is governed strictly by data dependencies [see, for example, Fig. 1(c*)]. An example of a well-known dataflow programming language is GPSS (General-Purpose Systems Simulator), in which sequencing of a simu-

lation program is controlled by transactions (data) moving through the model.

Database Languages Database languages have many of the characteristics we have been discussing. We will give one example from relational algebra (Date, 1986), which may be considered to be representative of a class of languages rather than a specific implementation. The special issue of *ACM Computing Surveys* (1976) gives examples of the different database approaches and data management languages. The relational algebra, which was developed originally by Codd (1972), consists of the operators SELECT, PROJECT, and JOIN, among others. Each operation of the relational algebra takes either one or two relations as its operand(s) and produces a new relation as a result. A relation has a precise mathematical definition, but can be considered to be a *table* for our purpose. An example of a relation (table) called S is shown below:

S

S#	SNAME	STATUS	CITY
S1	Smith	20	London
S2	Jones	10	Paris
S3	Blake	30	Paris

The heading SNAME stands for supplier name, and the first row can be interpreted as the supplier Smith who has supplier number (S#) S1, has status 20, and is in London. The SELECT operator constructs a new relation by taking a horizontal subset of the argument table (i.e. all rows that satisfy some condition) and the PROJECT operator constructs a new relation by taking a vertical subset of the argument table. As an example, consider the query to find S# and STATUS for suppliers in Paris. This can be determined in two stages:

TEMP ← SELECT S WHERE CITY = 'PARIS'

This returns the table:

TEMP

S#	SNAME	STATUS	CITY
S2	Jones	10	Paris
S3	Blake	30	Paris

We then do a projection:

RESULT ← PROJECT TEMP OVER S#, STATUS

The result is the relation:

RESULT

S#	STATUS
S2	10
S3	30

Note that the SELECT operator uses associative referencing and is an aggregate operator. PROJECT is an aggregate operator, too.

It is not necessary to break up the retrievals into two distinct steps as indicated above. We could combine the query into one operation using the following syntax.

```
SELECT S#, STATUS
FROM S
WHERE CITY = 'PARIS'
```

Many of the newer database languages, such as SQL (Date, 1986), have extensive data manipulation capabilities in addition to their retrieval function.

Relation of Other Systems to Nonprocedural Language

RPGs (report program generators) are often mentioned when discussing nonprocedural languages. It is certainly true that the output format of an RPG is specified by stating what is wanted rather than how it should be produced. It should be noted, however, that the Calculation section of an RPG program is decidedly low-level. This confirms our statement that no language is nonprocedural in any absolute sense. A particular language may possess a certain feature in one area and lack other features in that area or it may possess a certain feature in one area and lack the same feature in another area.

Spreadsheets are related to nonprocedural languages in the following sense. A spreadsheet (*q.v.*) is a two-dimensional grid of cells, where a cell may contain a datum (number or string) or a formula for computing a number based on values computed in other cells. There is no notion of sequencing other than dependencies that are implicit in the cell formulas. Spreadsheets therefore are nonprocedural using the criteria already established.

Fourth-generation languages (4GLs) are rather poorly named and not clearly defined; most tend to have both procedural and nonprocedural components. It is only the latter that are of concern here. The major nonprocedural elements of a fourth-generation language are generally similar to database languages and report writers, and thus do *not* represent a new nonprocedural concept. Some of the fourth-generation language systems actually generate code for procedural languages such as Cobol, and/or link to them.

Summary

It is not possible to state that a given programming language is nonprocedural in any absolute sense because it is a relative term that changes as the state of the art changes. However, it can be said that a language possesses certain nonprocedural features relative to a specific time. The best examples of languages in 1992 that possess the "most" nonprocedural features are probably Prolog, Miranda (Turner, 1986), and many of the database query languages. APL has high-level operators, but does not have the concept of associative referencing as a primitive notion. However, the elimination of arbitrary sequencing can be achieved in APL programs by exploiting the power of the aggregate operators.

References

1962. Codasyl Language Structure Group. "An Information Algebra Phase I Report," *Comm. ACM* **5**, *4 (April).*

1972. Codd, E. F. "Relational Completeness of Data Base Sublanguages," in Rustin, R. (Ed.), *Data Base Systems.* Courant Computer Science Symposia Series, Vol. 6. Englewood Cliffs, NJ: Prentice-Hall.

1974. Leavenworth, Burt M. and Sammet, Jean E. "An Overview of Nonprocedural Languages," *Proc. ACM SIGPLAN Symposium on Very High Level Languages, ACM SIGPLAN Notices* **9**, *4* (April).

1976. Special Issue on Data Base Management Systems. *ACM Computing Surveys* **8**, *1* (March).

1986. Clocksin, W. F. and Mellish, C. S. *Programming in Prolog* (2nd Ed.). New York: Springer-Verlag.

1986. Date, C. J. *An Introduction to Database Systems*, Volumes 1 and 2. Reading, MA: Addison-Wesley.

1986. Turner, D. A. "An Overview of Miranda," *ACM SIGPLAN Notices* **21**, *12* (December).

BURTON M. LEAVENWORTH AND JEAN E. SAMMET

NP-COMPLETE PROBLEMS

For articles on related subjects *see* ALGORITHMS, ANALYSIS OF; ALGORITHMS, THEORY OF; COMBINATORICS; COMPUTATIONAL COMPLEXITY; DISCRETE MATHEMATICS; GRAPH THEORY; and MATHEMATICAL PROGRAMMING.

There are many practical computational problems for which no effective computer algorithms have been devised. Many of these seemingly intractable problems belong to a class of problems known as the *NP-complete problems*. NP stands for *non-deterministic polynomial*, a concept discussed below. The only known algorithms for these problems require an amount of time that is an exponential function of the problem size (measured by some parameter, n, on which the problem depends). Such algorithms are called *exponential time algorithms*. Technically, problem size is measured by the number of bits in the problem description, but often the running time of an algorithm is more conveniently expressed in terms of some other (roughly equivalent) measure of the amount of input data. For problems of size n, exponential time algorithms may take time $2^n, 2^{n^{1/2}}, 3^{n^2}$, etc. In contrast, many problems can be solved by algorithms that require an amount of time that is a polynomial function of the problem size. These algorithms are called *polynomial time algorithms*. For problems of size n, they may take time n, $n \log n, n^2, n^3$, etc. Because polynomials grow more slowly than exponentials, polynomial time algorithms (even with a large exponent) are efficient in comparison with exponential time algorithms. As a first cut at categorizing algorithm complexity, polynomial time algorithms are regarded as "efficient," and exponential time algorithms as "inefficient."

Computer scientists have proved that if one efficient (i.e. polynomial time) algorithm can be found for *any* of the NP-complete problems, then efficient algorithms can be devised for *all* of these problems. Conversely, if any of these problems requires exponential time, they all do. Most computer scientists are pessimistic about the possibility that non-exponential algorithms for these problems will ever be found, and so proving a problem to be NP-complete is now regarded as strong evidence that the problem is intrinsically intractable. If, however, an efficient algorithm can be found for any one (and hence all) NP-complete problems, it would be a major intellectual breakthrough with immense practical implications.

We illustrate these concepts with three NP-complete problems—one from graph theory, one involving summing numbers, and one involving sets.

Clique Problem

A *graph* is a set of nodes with edges connecting certain pairs of nodes (such as the graph in Fig. 1). A *clique* is a set of nodes from a graph where every pair of nodes in the set is connected by an edge. In the figure, {1, 3, 7} is a clique set. Set {2, 4, 5, 6} is not because nodes 5 and 6 in this set are not connected by an edge.

Problem. Given a graph and a "clique size" k, decide if the graph has a clique of size k. For the problem given in Fig. 1 and $k = 4$, the answer is "YES" because {1, 2, 4, 5} is a clique of size 4. If, instead, the clique size in the problem were 5, the answer would be "NO."

Knapsack Problem

Given a list of numbers and a "knapsack size," determine if some subset of the listed numbers adds up to the knapsack size. For the problem given in Fig. 2, the answer is "YES" because

$$4 + 18 + 25 + 42 = 89.$$

If, instead, the knapsack size were 90, the answer would be "NO."

Set Covering Problem

For a given set, a collection of subsets is said to *cover* the given set if each member of the given set belongs to at least one set in the collection.

Problem. Given a set to be covered, a list of available subsets, and a "cover size" k, determine if k of the available subsets can be chosen so that the collection of chosen subsets covers the given set. For the problem given in Fig. 3, the answer is "YES" because the three subsets S_3, S_6, and S_7 can be chosen. If, instead, the cover size were 2, the answer would be "NO."

The three problems illustrated have the common property that, if the answer is "YES," there is a short, easily verified demonstration of this fact. For the clique problem, the demonstration is a list of nodes, equal in number to the clique size, that form a clique. For the

List of Numbers: 4 7 13 18 25 32 42 49
Knapsack Size: 89

FIG. 2. Example of a knapsack problem.

knapsack problem, the demonstration is a subset of the listed numbers whose sum equals the knapsack size. For the set covering problem, the demonstration is a collection of the available subsets that contain every element of the set to be covered. This common property suggests a common approach to solving these problems; namely, enumerate the potential demonstrations and check each potential demonstration to see if it is an actual demonstration. For the knapsack problem, this means enumerating the subsets of the given numbers and adding the numbers in each subset to see if their sum is the knapsack value. Unfortunately, these enumerate-and-check algorithms require exponential time due to the number of things to be enumerated. In the knapsack case, with n numbers, there are 2^n subsets to be checked.

The preceding problems are called *recognition problems* because the answer for a given problem example is "YES" or "NO." A recognition problem is called *non-deterministic polynomial* (or *NP*) if, whenever the answer is "YES," there is a "polynomial" demonstration of this fact. A problem is considered to have polynomial demonstrations if there are constants c and k such that a problem example of size n with answer "YES" has a potential demonstration that can be verified correct in cn^k steps. Thus, if the answer is "YES," a lucky person might guess a correct demonstration and verify his or her guess, all in polynomial time. However, the word *non-deterministic* is not meant to imply randomness or any use of probability. *Non-deterministic* signifies only that no rule is given for determining what the guess should be.

The key concept in relating problems to each other is *polynomial-time reducibility*. Problem A is said to be *reducible* to problem B if problem A can be solved using as a subroutine an algorithm that solves problem B. In particular, problem A is *polynomial-time reducible* to problem B if there is a polynomial bound on the number of steps taken by a main program to solve problem A, where the main program can call a subroutine for problem B. Note that the number of steps taken by the subroutine is not counted. If there is an efficient (i.e. polynomial-time) algorithm for solving problem B, then using that algorithm as the subroutine produces an efficient algorithm for problem A. Conversely, if problem A is intrinsically hard (i.e. cannot be solved in polynomial time), then no efficient subroutine for B can exist, and so problem B is also intrinsically hard.

To illustrate a polynomial-time reduction, Fig. 4 outlines a main program for reducing the clique problem to

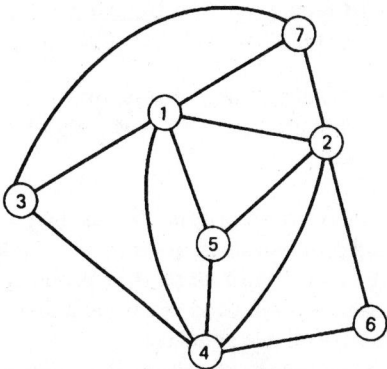

FIG. 1. Example of a clique problem. Is there a clique of size 4?

Set to be Covered: {a, b, c, d, e, f, g, h}
Available Subsets: $S_1 = \{d\}$, $S_2 = \{a\}$, $S_3 = \{a, b, c\}$
$S_4 = \{f\}$, $S_5 = \{b, e, g\}$, $S_6 = \{c, d, e, h\}$, $S_7 = \{f, g, h\}$

Cover Size: 3

FIG. 3. Example of a set covering problem.

Main Program for Clique Problem
Step 1
Input graph G and clique size k
Step 2
Construct new graph $\overline{G}$ with:
    (a) The same nodes as G
    (b) An edge between two nodes if an only if there is no edge between these two nodes in G.
    (c) A unique name for each edge in $\overline{G}$
Step 3
Let S = set of edges in graph $\overline{G}$
(S is set to be covered)
Step 4
For each node x in graph $\overline{G}$, let S_x = members of S with endpoint x (each S_x is an available subset)
Step 5
Let cover size = number of nodes − clique size
Step 6
Call subroutine for set covering problem, passing it the problem example constructed in steps 3, 4, and 5
Step 7
If subroutine answers "YES," then output "YES"
If subroutine answers "NO," then output "NO"

FIG. 4. Reduction of clique problem to set covering problem.

the set covering problem. If step 1 of the main program is given the clique problem example of Fig. 1 as input, the graph $\overline{G}$ constructed in step 2 is the graph of Fig. 5. For instance, the edge named b appears in $\overline{G}$ because G does not contain an edge between nodes 3 and 5, and $\overline{G}$ has no edge between 1 and 3 because G does have an edge between 1 and 3. Steps 3, 4, and 5 construct the set covering example of Fig. 3. Notice that set S_3 has members a, b, and c because a, b, and c are the edges of $\overline{G}$ having node 3 as an endpoint. The subroutine returns with answer "YES" (because of cover S_3, S_6, and S_7), and the main program outputs "YES."

The reason the program works is that for a graph with n nodes, there is a direct relationship between the nodes that form the clique of size k and the $n\text{-}k$ covering subsets that solve the constructed set covering problem. Specifically, the clique consists of the nodes corresponding to the available subsets that are not part of the cover. In the example, it is the available subsets S_1, S_2, S_4, and S_5 that

are not in the cover { S_3, S_6, S_7}, and it is nodes {1, 2, 4, 5} that form the clique.

A problem is said to be *NP-complete* if it is an NP-problem and every NP-problem is polynomial-time reducible to it. Thus, an algorithm for an NP-complete problem is universal in that it can be used as a subroutine for any NP-problem.

To show that a new problem is NP-complete, it suffices to show that it is an NP-problem, and that any one problem already known to be NP-complete is polynomial-time reducible to it.

As the number of problems already known to be NP-complete increases, there are more problems available for showing other problems NP-complete, and so the task of proving NP-completeness becomes easier and easier. In 1971, Cook formulated the concept of NP-completeness and showed that the problem of testing a logical formula for satisfiability is NP-complete. Shortly thereafter, Karp (1972) extended the set of known NP-problems to include about 20 other problems of practical interest. This gave momentum to the search for NP-complete problems and now thousands are known (see, for example, Garey and Johnson, 1979). It is now routine for a computer scientist confronting an apparently hard problem to investigate whether the problem is NP-complete.

The concept of NP-completeness is relevant not only to recognition (i.e. YES-NO) problems, but also to optimization problems. This is because optimization problems have closely related recognition problems. The clique problem above is the recognition problem closely related to the optimization problem of finding the largest size clique in a graph. The knapsack problem above is the problem closely related to the optimization problem of finding a subset of listed numbers that has the largest sum not exceeding the knapsack size. The set covering problem above is the problem closely related to the optimization problem of finding the smallest collection of available subsets that cover a given set. In each case, the answer to the optimization problem also provides an answer to the recognition problem. For example, if the answer to the clique optimization problem is a clique of size n, the clique recognition problem has answer "YES" if $k \leq n$ and "NO" if $k > n$. Thus, optimization must be at least as hard as recognition. Some well-known optimization problems with closely related NP-complete recognition problems are the traveling salesman problem, integer programming, job-shop scheduling, and graph coloring.

What does a computer scientist do when confronted with an NP-complete problem? A variety of approaches have been taken.

1. Develop an algorithm that is fast enough for small problem sizes, but that would take too long if presented with larger size problems. This approach is often used when the anticipated problems are all of a small size.
2. Develop a fast algorithm that solves a special case of the problem, but does not solve the gen-

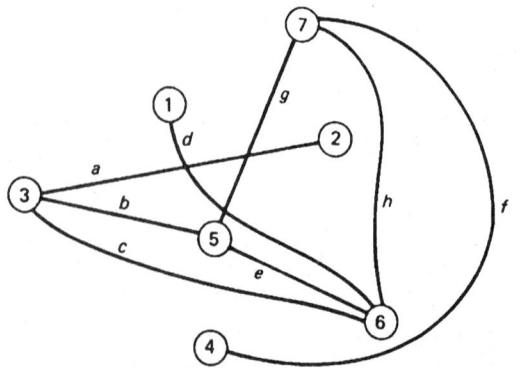

FIG. 5. The graph $\overline{G}$ related to the graph G of Fig. 1.

eral problem. This approach is often used when the special case is of practical importance.

3. Develop an algorithm that quickly solves a large proportion of the cases that come up in practice, but in the worst case may run for a long time. This approach is often used when the problems occurring in practice tend to have special features that can be exploited to speed up the computation.

4. For an optimization problem, develop an algorithm that always runs quickly, but produces an answer that is not necessarily optimal. Sometimes, a worst case bound can be obtained on how much the answer produced may differ from the optimum, so that a reasonably close answer is assured. This is an area of active research, with sub-optimal algorithms for a variety of important problems being developed and analyzed.

5. Work on some other problem. This is often done when there are no users who really care about the problem.

In general, NP-completeness effectively eliminates the possibility of developing a completely satisfactory algorithm. Once a problem is seen to be NP-complete, it is appropriate to direct development efforts towards a more achievable goal.

References

1971. Cook, S. A. "The Complexity of Theorem-Proving Procedures," *Proc. Third ACM Symposium on Theory of Computing*, 151–158.

1972. Karp, R. M. "Reducibility Among Combinatorial Problems," in Miller, R. E. and Thatcher, J. W. (Eds.), *Complexity of Computer Computations*. New York: Plenum Press, 85–104.

1979. Garey, M. R. and Johnson, D. S. *Computers and Intractability: A Guide to the Theory of NP-Completeness*. San Francisco: W. H. Freeman and Co.

1989. Dewdney, A. K. *The Turing Omnibus*. Rockville, MD: Computer Science Press (Chapters 31, 38, 50).

DANIEL J. ROSENKRANTZ AND RICHARD E. STEARNS

NUMBER THEORETIC CALCULATIONS

For articles on related subjects *see* CRYPTOGRAPHY, COMPUTERS IN; and FACTORING INTEGERS.

The theory of numbers is primarily concerned with the properties of the *natural numbers* 1, 2, 3,.... The fundamental theorem of arithmetic states that each natural number can be expressed uniquely as a product of *prime numbers*. A prime number is a natural number greater than 1 having no divisor other than 1 and itself. A natural number that is not prime is called *composite*. Much of the research in number theory, both theoretical and computational, has dealt with properties of the primes. This article will report some major advances in computational number theory made during the past 10 years.

Prime Testing This is the problem of deciding whether a number n is prime or composite (*see* FACTORING INTEGERS). If n has only a few decimal digits, we can show that it is prime by trial division up to its square root. If n is composite, then it must have a prime divisor $\leq \sqrt{n}$.

A better procedure is needed for larger numbers. A simple test is based on Fermat's little theorem, which states that if n is prime and n does not divide a, then

$$a^{n-1} \equiv 1 \pmod{n}, \qquad (1)$$

(i.e. n divides evenly into the difference $a^{n-1} - 1$). Although the converse of this theorem is false, very few composite numbers satisfy (1). Odd numbers n that satisfy (1) for several randomly chosen values of a are called *industrial grade primes*. One can raise a to the $n-1$ power (mod n) in roughly $\log_2 n$ steps by a doubling and squaring procedure (see Lehmer, 1969, p. 126).

More computation than (1) is needed to obtain a rigorous proof that n is prime, but (1) often is used to decide whether to attempt a rigorous prime proof or to try to factor n. If (1) holds and if one can factor either $n-1$ or $n+1$ completely, then there is a quick method for proving that n is prime via more calculations like that in (1). This method works well for large numbers n for which either $n-1$ or $n+1$ has only small prime factors. The largest known primes (see below) all have this special form. For general n, the method becomes impractical at about 50 digits because some numbers of that size take a while to factor.

In 1983, Adleman, Pomerance, and Rumely published an algorithm that uses algebraic number theory to decide whether n is prime in about $n^{\log \log \log n}$ steps. A practical version of it can test a 100-digit number for primality in a few seconds.

In the past few years, Goldwasser, Kilian, and Atkin have invented powerful prime tests that use elliptic curves. They work well for most primes, but may fail to work or be very slow for certain primes. Morain has used these methods to find primes without special form having more than 1,000 digits.

Recently, Adleman and Huang have invented a polynomial time prime test that uses *abelian varieties*, but this test has not been programmed yet.

Largest Known Primes There is an especially simple prime test for *Mersenne numbers*, numbers of the form $2^p - 1$, where p is prime. For most of the past 400 years, the largest known primes have had this special form. There are 32 known Mersenne primes. The largest one is $2^{756,839} - 1$, which has 227,832 digits. It was discovered in 1992 by Slowinski and Gage. *See* Ribenboim (1988, 1991) for more on this subject.

At this writing (1992), the largest known non-Mersenne prime is $391,581 \times 2^{216,193} - 1$. It has 65,087 digits and was discovered in 1989 by John Brown, Landon Curt Noll, Bodo K. Parady, Gene Ward Smith, Joel F. Smith, and Sergio Zarantonello.

Fermat's Last Theorem This conjecture asserts that if $n > 2$, then the equation

$$x^n + y^n = z^n$$

has no solution in positive integers. This conjecture has resisted proof for three centuries, since Fermat noted it in the margin of his copy of a book of Diophantus. Although Fermat claimed he proved it, apparently he did not. Computers may be used to check the conjecture for particular n. In 1987, Tanner and Wagstaff verified the conjecture for all n up to 150,000. See Ribenboim (1977) for a very readable exposition on the subject.

Waring's Problem Waring conjectured that for every integer $k > 1$ there is an integer r so that every natural number can be expressed as the sum of r exact kth powers. For example, every positive integer is the sum of four squares, nine cubes, etc. Hilbert proved this conjecture in 1909. Let $g(k)$ denote the smallest such r, so that $g(2) = 4, g(3) = 9$, etc. It has been proved that for $k \geq 6$ we have $g(k) = 2^k + q - 2$ provided $r + q \leq 2^k$, where q and r are the quotient and remainder when 3^k is divided by 2^k. (There is a different formula for $g(k)$ when this condition fails.) In 1989, Wunderlich and Kubina used a Cray-2 to verify the condition for all $k < 470,000,000$.

The Riemann Zeta Function Our final topic concerns the function

$$\zeta(s) = \sum_{k=1}^{\infty} \frac{1}{k^s}$$

of the complex variable $s = \sigma + it$. The formula

$$\zeta(s) = \prod_{p} \left(1 - \frac{1}{p^s}\right)^{-1},$$

where the product is taken over all prime numbers, shows the connection between $\zeta(s)$ and prime number theory. From this relationship and the fact that $\zeta(1 + it)$ is never zero, one can prove the *prime number theorem*, which says that the number of primes $\leq x$ is asymptotic to $x/\log x$. The celebrated Riemann Hypothesis conjectures that all zeros of $\zeta(s)$ with $\sigma > 0$ satisfy $\sigma = 1/2$. Many important results in number theory would follow if this conjecture were proved. In 1986, van de Lune, te Riele, and Winter verified that the first 1,500,000,001 zeros of $\zeta(s)$ have real part 1/2. See Ribenboim (1988, 1991) for more on this subject.

References

1969. Lehmer, D. H. "Computer Technology Applied to the Theory of Numbers." *Studies in Number Theory*, MAA Studies in Mathematics, **6**, Englewood Cliffs, NJ: Prentice-Hall

1977. Ribenboim, P. *13 Lectures on Fermat's Last Theorem*. Berlin: Springer-Verlag.

1985. Riesel, H. *Prime Numbers and Computer Methods for Factorization*. Progress in Mathematics, **57**. Boston, MA: Birkhauser.

1988. Ribenboim, P. *The Book of Prime Number Records*. Berlin: Springer-Verlag.

1991. Ribenboim, P. *The Little Book of Big Primes*. New York: Springer-Verlag.

SAMUEL S. WAGSTAFF, JR.

NUMBERS AND NUMBER SYSTEMS

For articles on related subjects *see* ARITHMETIC, COMPUTER; COMPLEMENT; INTERVAL ARITHMETIC; NUMERICAL ANALYSIS; PRECISION; and SIGNIFICANCE ARITHMETIC.

The representation in which we normally write decimal numbers, for example

$$276.1069 \tag{1}$$

is nothing more than shorthand symbolic representation for the precise mathematical equivalent

$$2 \times 100 + 7 \times 10 + 6 \times 1 + 1 \times 0.1$$
$$+ 0 \times 0.01 + 6 \times 0.001 + 9 \times 0.0001 \tag{2}$$

or

$$2 \times 10^2 + 7 \times 10^1 + 6 \times 10^0 + 1 \times 10^{-1}$$
$$+ 0 \times 10^{-2} + 6 \times 10^{-3} + 9 \times 10^{-4} \tag{3}$$

Equations (2) and (3) express clearly that the decimal system we use has a *base*, or *radix*, 10. By analogy, therefore, the *binary*, or *base 2*, system so commonly used with computers can become immediately understandable, as presented below. The notation (1)—often called *positional notation* because the position of a digit specifies the power of 10 in (3), which is associated with it—effectively hides the real mathematical content of a number.

Radix Representation The notation in (2) or (3) above is called the *radix representation* of a number. The general form of any decimal number may be written

$$\sum_{i=-m}^{n} d_i \cdot 10^i \qquad 0 \leq d_1 \leq 9 \ (d_1 \text{ an integer}),$$

which in the case of (3) specializes to

$$
\begin{aligned}
m &= 4, & n &= 2 \\
d_{-4} &= 9, & d_{-3} &= 6 \\
d_{-2} &= 0, & d_{-1} &= 1 \\
d_0 &= 6, & d_1 &= 7, & d_2 &= 2
\end{aligned}
$$

The three other number systems most important in computers are *binary*, *octal*, and *hexadecimal*.

1. In binary, numbers are represented by

$$\sum_{i=-m}^{n} b_i \cdot 2^i \qquad b_i = 0 \text{ or } 1. \tag{4}$$

2. In the octal, or base 8, representation, we have

$$\sum_{i=-m}^{n} o_i \cdot 8^i \qquad 0 \leq o_1 \leq 7 \ (o_1 \text{ an integer}).$$

3. In the hexadecimal, or base 16, system, numbers are represented by

TABLE 1. Binary Addition and Multiplication Tables

+	0	1		×	0	1
0	0	1		0	0	0
1	0	10		1	0	1

$$\sum_{i=-m}^{n} h_i \cdot 16^i \qquad 0 \le h_i \le 15 \qquad (h_i \text{ an integer}).$$

We will now consider the characteristics of each of these systems briefly.

Binary The rule for generating successive numbers in a number system of radix R, whose digits range from 0 to $R - 1$, is as follows:

1. When the rightmost digit of the number whose successor is desired is less than $R - 1$, increase that digit to its successor digit.
2. When the rightmost digit of the number whose successor is desired is equal to $R - 1$, replace $R - 1$ by 0, "carry" a 1 to the second radix position from the right, and repeat this two-step process until carries no longer need be propagated to the left.

If $R = 10$, this algorithm will generate successfully the familiar sequence of decimal numbers. But, if $R = 2$, we get the sequence of binary numbers, the first few of which are

0	1	10	11	100	101
110	111	1000	1001	1010	1011
1100	1101	1110	1111	1000	10001

The addition and multiplication tables for binary numbers are particularly simple (Table 1) and, once learned, so is binary arithmetic using these tables. Fig. 1 gives examples of all four arithmetic operations in binary, with the corresponding decimal arithmetic also given. Finding the decimal integer equivalent to a given binary integer is very simple using equation (4). Thus, for example,

$$\begin{aligned}
1011010 &= 1 \times 2^6 + 0 \times 2^5 + 1 \times 2^4 + 1 \times 2^3 \\
&\quad + 0 \times 2^2 + 1 \times 2^1 + 0 \times 2^0 \\
&= 64 + 16 + 8 + 2 \\
&= 90
\end{aligned}$$

Later on in this article, we will consider the general problem of conversion from a number in one system to another.

Octal The octal system was once used widely in computing (but is rather seldom used now) only because of its simple relation to binary. To convert a binary number to octal, it is only necessary (since $8 = 2^3$) to group the binary digits in sets of three and convert each set to its binary equivalent. (Note that three binary digits—hereafter we will use the common contraction *bits* for binary digits—can represent the digits from 0 to 7 or one octal digit.) Thus, the binary equivalent of one million in decimal is

Addition

```
Carries    10011

           11001     25
         +10011     +19
          ------    ----
          101100     44
```

Subtraction

```
Borrowing       10    1    1
           0     0    10   10   10
           1     1    0    0    0    24
          -0     1    1    0    1   -13
          --------------------------  ----
                 1    0    1    1    11
```

Multiplication

```
      1101        13
    ×1110       × 14
    ------       ----
    11010         52
   1101           13
  1101            ----
  1101            182
 --------
 10110110
```

Division

```
           11               3 1/9
     1001| 11100          9| 28
        1001
        ----
        1010
        1001
        ----
           1
```

FIG. 1. Binary arithmetic.

11 | 110 | 100 | 001 | 001 | 000 | 000
$\downarrow$ $\quad\downarrow$ $\quad\downarrow$ $\quad\downarrow$ $\quad\downarrow$ $\quad\downarrow$ $\quad\downarrow$
3 $\quad$ 6 $\quad$ 4 $\quad$ 1 $\quad$ 1 $\quad$ 0 $\quad$ 0

and the octal equivalent is 3641100. Correspondingly, to go from octal to binary, each octal digit is converted into its binary equivalent. Thus,

$$647.0534$$
$$\downarrow$$
$$110100111.000101011100$$

The advantage of octal over binary is shown clearly by the preceding two examples. For all large numbers or numbers with a significant number of binary places, the octal representation is much more compact, and therefore is easier to write and manipulate than its binary equivalent. Table 2 gives the octal addition and multiplication tables.

Hexadecimal This system became important with the advent of the IBM 360/370/390 systems, (*q.v.*), which, while binary internally, from the user's point of view, use hexadecimal floating-point arithmetic. Because hexadecimal requires 16 distinct characters, 6 characters in addi-

TABLE 2 Octal Addition and Multiplication Tables

+	0	1	2	3	4	5	6	7	×	0	1	2	3	4	5	6	7
0	0	1	2	3	4	5	6	7	0	0	0	0	0	0	0	0	0
1	1	2	3	4	5	6	7	10	1	0	1	2	3	4	5	6	7
2	2	3	4	5	6	7	10	11	2	0	2	4	6	10	12	14	16
3	3	4	5	6	7	10	11	12	3	0	3	6	11	14	17	22	25
4	4	5	6	7	10	11	12	13	4	0	4	10	14	20	24	30	34
5	5	6	7	10	11	12	13	14	5	0	5	12	17	24	31	36	43
6	6	7	10	11	12	13	14	15	6	0	6	14	22	30	36	44	52
7	7	10	11	12	13	14	15	16	7	0	7	16	25	34	43	52	61

tion to 0, 1,..., 9 are needed to represent "10", "11",..., "15". These are usually taken to be *A, B, C, D, E, F*.

Just as octal is related to binary using three-bit groups, hexadecimal is related to binary using four-bit groups. Thus,

$$111 \mid 1010 \mid 0001 \mid 0010 \mid 0001$$

becomes

$$7 A 1 2 1$$

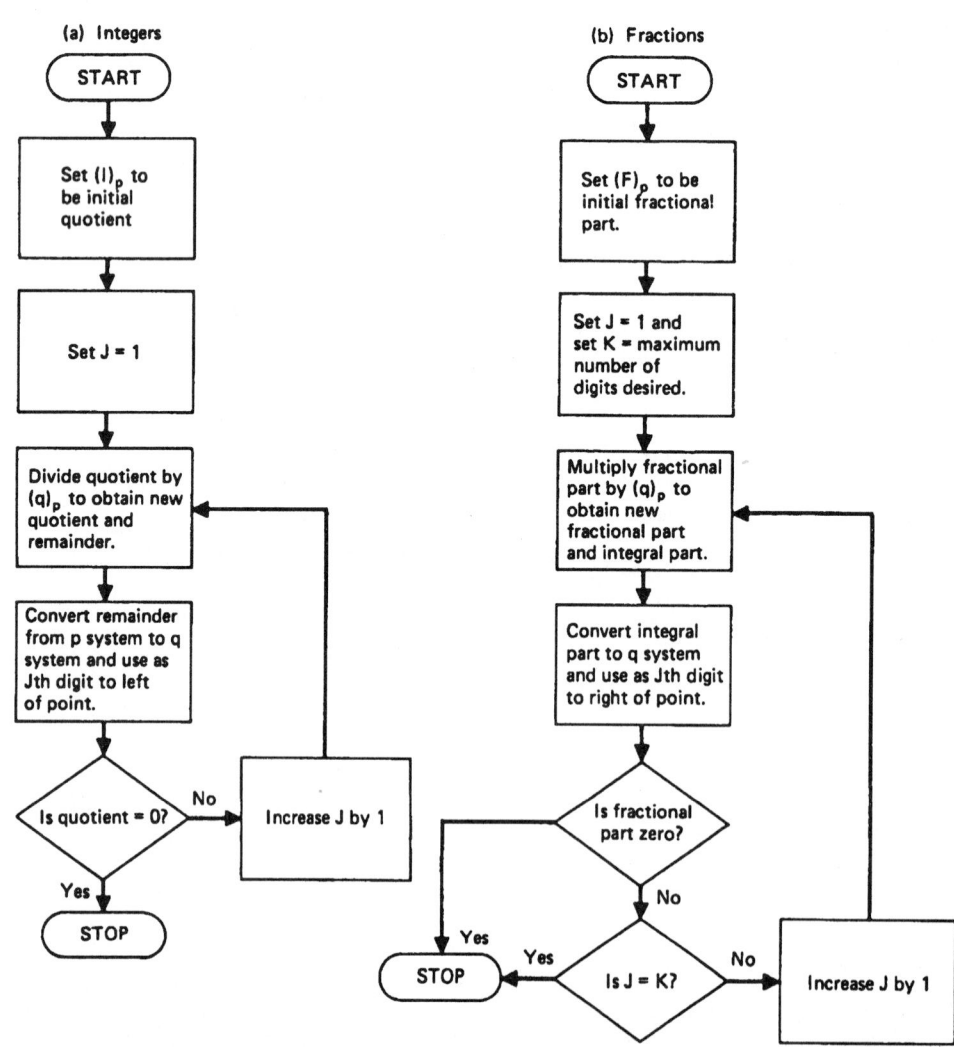

FIG. 2. Radix conversion.

in hexadecimal. Since the preponderance of computers in current use—IBM mainframes, the DEC VAX series (*q.v.*), and all popular personal computers (*q.v.*)—have word lengths that are divisible by four but not three (16 or 32 bits), use of hexadecimal notation for binary numbers has become much more common than use of octal.

OTHER NUMBER SYSTEMS

Balanced Digit Systems In a balanced digit system the allowable digits in each position range in value from $-s$ to $+s$, with negative numbers usually denoted by an overbar. Thus, a balanced binary system might have digits $-1, 0, 1$ with -1 written as $\bar{1}$. In this system,

$$10\overline{11} = 2^3 - 2^1 - 2^0 = 5$$

and

$$\bar{1}101 = -2^3 + 2^2 + 2^0 = -3.$$

One property of such a system, sometimes useful in the design of arithmetic units in computers, is the *redundancy* that occurs when a number has more than one possible representation. For example, in the system described above, 5 may, as in the usual binary system, also be represented by

$$101$$

In any balanced digit system where s is less than the base, the leftmost digit gives the sign of the number so that no explicit sign is needed. In addition, given any number A, its negative may be found by changing all digits to their negatives (i.e. removing all overbars and inserting overbars where there were none). Thus, for example,

$$10\bar{1}10 = 2^4 - 2^2 + 2^1 = +14$$

and

$$\overline{10}1\overline{10} = -2^4 + 2^2 - 2^1 = -14.$$

A particularly interesting balanced digit system which does not yet appear to have been applied in computers, is *balanced ternary* (Knuth, 1969), which has radix 3 and where, as above, the digits, called *trits*, are 1, 0, and $\bar{1}$. This system is nonredundant and, in addition to the properties mentioned above, has the additional useful property that a number may be rounded to the nearest integer merely by deleting its fractional part. Thus,

$$10\overline{1.11} = 3^2 - 3^0 - 3^{-1} - 3^{-2} = 7\tfrac{5}{9}$$

and

$$10\bar{1} = 8.$$

Residue Systems A residue system is one in which (1) each digit position corresponds to a different radix; (2) all pairs of radices are relatively prime; i.e. the only common

divisor of any two radices is 1; (3) the value of the digit d_i for integer A in position i corresponding to radix r_i is given by $d_i = A$ modulo r_i, i.e. the remainder when A is divided by r_i.

For example, if $r_2 = 5$, $r_1 = 3$, $r_0 = 2$, then 13 is represented by

$$311$$

and 29 is represented by

$$421.$$

Because of property (2), the range of values that can be expressed is from 0 to 1 less than the product of the radices used.

Radix Conversion We now consider how to take a number in a system with base p and convert it to a number in base q. To do this, we consider the integer and fractional parts of the number separately. Let $(I)_p$ and $(F)_p$, respectively, be the integer and fractional parts of the number in base p, which we wish to convert to base q; let $(q)_p$ be the expression of q in the p system (e.g. to convert from binary to decimal $(q)_p = (10)_2 = 1010$). Figures 2(a) and 2(b) are flowcharts to perform the conversions of the integer and fractional parts, respectively. We illustrate these algorithms with two examples.

Example 1. Convert 6753.31 in decimal to binary. Here $p = 10$, $q = 2$, $(I)_p = 6753$, $(F)_p = 0.31$, and $(q)_p = 2$. From Fig. 2(a) we calculate the integral part and find it to be 1101001100001.

	Quotient	Remainder
6753/2	3376	1
3376/2	1688	0
1688/2	844	0
844/2	422	0
422/2	211	0
211/2	105	1
105/2	52	1
52/2	26	0
26/2	13	0
13/2	6	1
6/2	3	0
3/2	1	1
1/2	0	1

From Fig. 2(b), with $K = 6$, we calculate the fractional part, and find it to be 010011.

	Fractional Part	Integral Part
0.31×2	0.62	0
0.62×2	0.24	1
0.24×2	0.48	0
0.48×2	0.96	0
0.96×2	0.92	1
0.92×2	0.84	1

Thus, 6753.31 in decimal is equivalent to

$$1101001100001.010011\cdots$$

in binary.

Note that the binary fraction is nonterminating (i.e. not expressible in a finite number of bits), even though the decimal fraction is finite.

Example 2. Convert 1001100.011 in binary to decimal. Here, $p = 2$, $q = 10$, $(I)_p = 1001100$, $(F)_p = 0.011$, and $(q)_p = 1010$, which is the binary representation of 10 in decimal. From Fig. 2(a),

	Quotient	Remainder
1001100/1010	111	110 → 6 in decimal
111/1010	0	111 → 7 in decimal

Thus, the integral part of the decimal number is 76. From Fig. 3(b),

	Fractional Part	Integral Part
0.011 × 1010	0.110	11 → 3 in decimal
0.110 × 1010	0.100	111 → 7 in decimal
0.100 × 1010	0.000	101 → 5 in decimal

Thus, the decimal equivalent of 1001100.011 is 76.375. In this instance a finite binary fraction became a finite decimal fraction. This is always the case because all the negative powers of 2 have finite fractional expansions in the decimal system.

Because of our natural facility with decimal arithmetic, an easier way to do Example 2 is to apply expression (4) directly:

$$\begin{aligned} 1001100.011 &= 1 \times 2^6 + 1 \times 2^3 + 1 \times 2^2 \\ &\quad + 1 \times 2^{-2} + 1 \times 2^{-3} \\ &= 64 + 8 + 4 + 0.25 + 0.125 \\ &= 76.375 \end{aligned}$$

The conversions illustrated in Examples 1 and 2 are indeed precisely those performed when

1. A program written in a high-level language in decimal notation is compiled into the machine language of a binary computer.
2. The results computed in that binary computer are printed out as decimal numbers.

References

1969. Knuth, D. E. *The Art of Computer Programming* **2**. Reading, MA: Addison-Wesley.
1969. Menninger, K. *Number Words and Number Symbols.* Cambridge, MA: (This book, subtitled "A Cultural History of Numbers," is a fascinating account of the history and uses of numbers in many natural languages.)

ANTHONY RALSTON

NUMERICAL ANALYSIS

For articles on related subjects *see* ALGORITHM; APPROXIMATION THEORY; DISCRETE MATHEMATICS; ERROR ANALYSIS; FAST FOURIER TRANSFORM; FINITE ELEMENT METHOD; INTERVAL ARITHMETIC; MATHEMATICAL PROGRAMMING; MATHEMATICAL SOFTWARE; MATRIX COMPUTATIONS; PARTIAL DIFFERENTIAL EQUATIONS; ROUNDOFF ERROR; SCIENTIFIC APPLICATIONS; and SPLINE.

Numerical analysis is concerned with the development, analysis, and use of algorithms that simulate physical and social processes. It is a practical science, involving as it does the production of numbers that approximate the solution of mathematical models of physical and social systems. It is a very old science. Many famous mathematicians from the eighteenth and nineteenth centuries—including Gauss, Newton, and Fourier, to mention a few—developed numerical algorithms that are still widely used. The advent of computers provided a tremendous impetus to the study and development of numerical analysis, and indeed led to so many new advances that it is now common to refer to the period from 1950 to the present as the era of "modern numerical analysis." High-speed computers have made it possible for us to solve ever more complex problems and, as a result, to gain much better insight into complex processes. Modern technological achievements in such areas as space and atomic energy would have been impossible without high-speed computers and advances in numerical analysis.

Computers have affected the direction of numerical analysis in several important ways. They have forced numerical analysts to search for algorithms that are computationally fast and efficient, and to search for a better understanding of error analysis. Algorithms that produce speed-up factors on the order of 100 or more have been discovered in such areas as harmonic analysis, the solution of large linear systems by iterative methods, and matrix eigenvalue problems, to mention a few. Computers have also generated new problems for numerical analysts. For example, because computers work with finite word lengths and because of the inexactness of conversion from one number base to another, roundoff errors are inevitably introduced. These errors in turn propagate in very complicated ways. Numerical analysts are concerned about the effect of the totality of such errors on the accuracy of the results. Statistical methods of error analysis held some promise in this area, but the most effective approach to date is that of backward error analysis, due to Wilkinson (1960).

In backward error analysis, one shows that the *computed* results are the exact solutions of a perturbed problem and that the bounds for the perturbations can be obtained numerically. By comparing the perturbed problem and the given problem, one can then decide on how much confidence one can place in the computed results.

Another problem introduced by computers is that of numerical instability. Errors introduced into a computation, from whatever source, propagate in different ways. In some algorithmic processes, these errors tend to grow exponentially, with disastrous computational results. An algorithm that exhibits such exponential error growth is said to be numerically unstable. Numerical analysts therefore seek algorithms that are not only fast and efficient, but also stable.

The complexity of error analysis has also led to the development of automatic error analysis procedures. In such automatic error procedures, an attempt is made to have the computer monitor the error at each stage of the computation and to adjust parameters automatically so as to reduce the error in subsequent computations. The adaptive integration schemes for quadrature, which will be described in a later section, provide one example of such automatic error-monitoring algorithms.

In recent years aspects of the implementation of algorithms have become of increasing importance. Teams of specialists have produced computer programs that implement the best available algorithms for important standard problems, such as the solution of linear equations, integration of differential equations, and evaluation of important functions of physics and chemistry. These programs, usually written in Fortran, have gone a long way toward making high-quality standardized algorithms readily available. The most famous example is the LINPACK project, a collection of programs for matrix computation developed at the Argonne National Laboratory. See Dongarra *et al.* (1979).

An important new trend in numerical analysis is the construction of algorithms to take advantage of specialized computer hardware. Some new computers can perform simultaneous calculations, such as multiply and add. On several multiprocessing and parallel processing (*q.v.*) computers, it is possible to divide a computation into pieces, each of which will be done on a separate computing "node" with an overseer program synchronizing and combining the results. As computer networks improve, it will also be possible for the nodes to be widely separated. Developing efficient algorithms becomes much more difficult in these cases and is an active topic of current research.

In the early days of computers, the graphical representation of data was secondary to the calculation, which was thought of as the major task. Today this view has largely been replaced by the realization that the representation of results is often as important as what is calculated. By examining pictures, plots, and animated sequences, scientists can often analyze the output of computer runs much more effectively than by reading tables. However, displaying graphical data presents its own demands on computer resources. The graphical output device must be able to translate commands and numbers into pictures. In addition, the numerical description of a picture often requires that a large amount of data be generated and moved rapidly from the computer to the graphics device, implying the need for "high bandwidth" communication paths. Nevertheless, a recent trend in numerical analysis is the use of sophisticated interactive graphics, in which the scientist views partial solutions to the posed problem and then advises the computer, graphically, on how to proceed. A related development has been the increasing use of "user friendly" programs that assist scientists who have little or no programming knowledge.

Traditional numerical analysis usually deals with some aspects of the following topics:

1. Root-finding methods for a single equation or for systems of equations.
2. Interpolation.
3. Approximation.
4. Least squares calculations.
5. Numerical differentiation.
6. Numerical integration.
7. Solution of linear equations.
8. Matrix eigenvalue problems.
9. Solution of ordinary differential equations.
10. Boundary value problems.
11. Solution of partial differential equations.
12. Generation of pseudo-random numbers.
13. Fourier analysis and the Fast Fourier Transform.

In an article of this length, one cannot provide more than a brief glimpse into some of these areas. In what follows are elementary discussions of root finding, interpolation, numerical differentiation, quadrature, and ordinary differential equations. More detailed treatments are given in Ortega and Rheinboldt (1970), Golub and Van Loan (1983), Kahaner, Moler, and Nash (1989), and Shampine and Gordon (1975). Topics 4, 7, 8, 11, 12, and 13 above are discussed in separate articles in this encyclopedia.

Roots of Equations We consider first the problem of finding the roots of equations of one variable. Some examples of equations that arise in physics and engineering are:

1. $x^3 - x - 1 = 0$.
2. $e^x - \cos x = 0$.
3. $2x - \tan x = 0$.

It is only rarely possible to find roots of such equations explicitly, and we must therefore rely on numerical methods that produce approximate solutions.

The simplest of all methods for finding a simple real zero of a continuous function $f(x)$ is the *bisection method*. The process begins by finding an interval (a_0, b_0) which contains the desired zero α. If the zero is simple, then $f(a_0)$ and $f(b_0)$ must be opposite in sign, the usual test for this being based on the inequality

$$f(a_0)\, f(b_0) < 0 .$$

The next step is to bisect the interval (a_0, b_0); i.e. compute $m = 1/2\,(a_0 + b_0)$. We then evaluate $f(m)$ and form the product $f(a_0)f(m)$. If this product is negative, then we know that the zero lies in the interval (a_0, m); otherwise, it must be in the interval (m, b_0). Of course, if $f(a_0)\, f(m) = 0$, then m is the desired zero. We now bisect the smaller interval, which is known to contain the zero α, and the entire process is repeated until the zero is obtained to the accuracy desired. The procedure is summarized in algorithmic form below.

The Bisection Algorithm   Given a function $f(x)$ continuous on the interval (a_0, b_0) and such that $f(a_0)\,f(b_0) \le 0$.

> For $n = 0, 1, 2, \ldots$, until satisfied, do:
> Set $m = (a_n + b_n)/2$.
> If $f(a_n)\,f(m) \le 0$, set $a_{n+1} = a_n$, $b_{n+1} = m$;
>   otherwise, set $a_{n+1} = m$, $b_{n+1} = b_n$.
> Then $f(x)$ has a root in the interval (a_{n+1}, b_{n+1}).

The phrase "until satisfied" used in this algorithm must be made precise in a program and is usually based on one of the following criteria.

1. $|f(m)| < \epsilon$;
2. $|b_{n+1} - a_{n+1}| < \delta$

where ϵ, δ are selected to achieve the desired accuracy.

As a simple example, consider the function $f(x) = x^3 - x - 1$. It is easy to verify that

$$f(1) = -1 < 0 < 5 = f(2).$$

Hence, there must be at least one zero of $f(x)$ on the interval $(1,2)$. In fact, there is exactly one zero on $(1,2)$. We call this zero α. The midpoint of the interval $(1,2)$ is 1.5, and we know that $\alpha \approx 1.5$ with an absolute error of at most 0.5. Now $f(1.5) = 0.875$ and $f(1)\,f(1.5) < 0$; hence, the zero lies in the interval $(1, 1.5)$. Therefore, $\alpha \approx 1.25$, with absolute error less than 0.25. After 20 steps of this algorithm we find that

$$1.3247175 = a_{20} \le a \le b_{20} = 1.3247184,$$
$$f(a_{20}) = (-1.857 \cdots)\,10^{-6},$$
$$f(b_{20}) = (2.209 \cdots)\,10^{-6}.$$

At this point we have six significant digits of accuracy. As this example shows, the bisection method always brackets the zero and provides an automatic bound on the approximation. Its simplicity makes it ideal for computer solution. On the other hand, it usually converges very slowly. If the function is complicated, this method is not very efficient and we are led to a search for methods that converge faster.

One such method is due to Newton. The algorithm for Newton's method is also quite simple.

Newton's Algorithm   Given $f(x)$ continuously differentiable and a starting approximation x_0. For $n = 0, 1, 2, \ldots$, until satisfied, do:
> Calculate

$$x_{n+1} = x_n - \frac{f(x_n)}{f'(x_n)}. \tag{1}$$

Geometrically, Newton's method takes as a next approximation the intersection of the tangent to the curve $f(x)$ at the point x_n with the x-axis (see Fig. 1). We note that

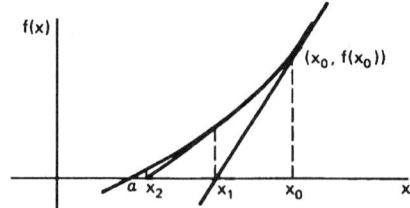

FIG. 1.   Newton's method.

Newton's algorithm requires that the derivative $f'(x)$ be available.

For the example used above, $f(x) = x^3 - x - 1$, we have $f'(x) = 3x^2 - 1$, and Newton's algorithm leads to the iteration

$$x_{n+1} = x_n - \frac{x_n^3 - x_n - 1}{3x_n^2 - 1}$$

Starting with $x_0 = 1$, we obtain the values in Table 1. Since the iterates x_4, x_5 agree to seven significant digits, we take x_5 as an approximation to α, which is correct to at least that many digits.

The rapidity of convergence in this problem, even considering the fact that we do more work per step, shows that Newton's method is much more efficient than the bisection method. The tabular results also illustrate another important feature of this method. The number of correct digits, those underlined in Table 1, appears to double with each iteration. This observation is made more precise by the following theorem.

Theorem: Newton's Method. Let $f(x)$, $f'(x)$, $f''(x)$ be continuous and bounded on an interval containing the zero α. If x_0 is picked sufficiently close to α, then the iteration of Eq. (1) converges; moreover, for n large enough,

$$(x_n + 1 - a) \approx K(x_n - a)^2, \tag{2}$$

where K is a constant that depends on the derivatives of $f(x)$ at the point α.

The last inequality shows that the error of the $(n + 1)$st iterate is proportional to the square of the error at the nth iterate, and demonstrates the eventual quadratic convergence of Newton's method. For this reason it is a very popular method. The most important disadvantage of Newton's method is that it will sometimes diverge or that it will converge to some zero other than the one

TABLE 1   Newton's Method Applied to $f(x) = x^3 - x - 1$

n	x_n
0	1.0
1	1.5
2	1.3478261
3	1.3252004
4	1.3247182
5	1.3247180

desired. While the theorem guarantees convergence if x_0 is sufficiently close to α, it is difficult in practice to know what "sufficiently close" implies. A second disadvantage of Newton's method is that it requires that $f'(x)$ be computable. In many cases we may know $f(x)$ but not $f'(x)$.

A method that retains most of the advantages of Newton's method, but that does not require knowledge of $f'(x)$, is the secant method. It can be derived directly from Eq. (1) by replacing $f'(x_n)$ by a difference quotient:

$$f'(x_n) \approx \frac{f(x_n) - f(x_{n-1})}{x_n - x_{n-1}} \tag{3}$$

We know from calculus that this difference quotient is a reasonable approximation to $f'(x_n)$, provided x_{n-1} is sufficiently close to x_n. Substituting expression (3) into Eq. (1), we obtain the secant iteration:

$$x_{n+1} = x_n - f(x_n) \frac{x_n - x_{n-1}}{f(x_n) - f(x_{n-1})} .$$

Here is the statement of the secant method in algorithmic form.

The Secant Algorithm Given a function $f(x)$ and two points x_{-1}, x_0. For $n = 0, 1, 2, \ldots$ until satisfied do: Calculate

$$x_{n+1} = x_n - f(x_n) \frac{x_n - x_{n-1}}{f(x_n) - f(x_{n-1})}. \tag{4}$$

Geometrically, as shown in Fig. 2, the secant method takes x_{n+1} as the intersection with the x-axis of the secant passing through the points (x_n, f_n) and (x_{n-1}, f_{n-1}).

This method converges much more rapidly than the bisection method, but less rapidly than Newton's method. Its primary advantage is that it requires no knowledge of $f'(x)$.

There are many other methods that could be considered, including fixed-point iteration, the modified regula falsi, Steffensen iteration, etc. Those mentioned above are, however, used most commonly in practice. Moreover, each of these methods can be generalized to apply to systems of nonlinear equations. As applied to systems, however, these methods frequently fail to converge, and in fact a great deal of research remains to be done to produce an effective computational method for finding zeros of nonlinear systems.

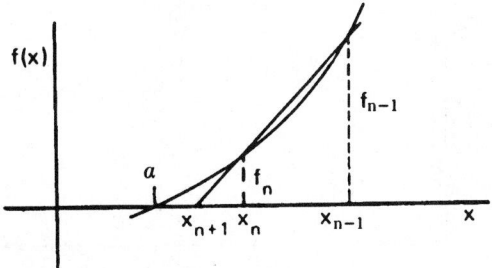

FIG. 2. Secant method.

Interpolation We now describe briefly the process of interpolation. In its simplest form, we are given the values of a function $f(x)$ at a selected set of points $\{x_i\}$ ($i = 0, 1, \ldots, n$). The function $f(x)$ is usually not known explicitly, but its values at the selected points can be obtained either from a table of values or experimentally. The problem is to estimate the value of $f(x)$ at some non-tabular point $\bar{x}$. In Table 2, for example, we are given the values of an unspecified function $f(x)$ at the indicated points. We may now be required to estimate the value of $f(x)$ at, say, $\bar{x} = 2.1$, or at any nontabular point. To do so, it is customary to select a simple class of functions, most commonly polynomials, that agree with the function $f(x)$ at the tabular points. We can then evaluate this polynomial at the point $x = \bar{x}$ to obtain the desired estimate. The simplest case is that of linear interpolation. Here we are given two points $\{x_0, x_1\}$ and the corresponding values $\{f(x_0), f(x_1)\}$. The equation of the linear polynomial (a straight line) that passes through the points $(x_0, f(x_0))$ and $(x_1, f(x_1))$ may be written in the following equivalent forms:

$$y = f_0 + \frac{f_1 - f_0}{x_1 - x_0}(x - x_0), \tag{5a}$$

$$y = f_0 \frac{x - x_1}{x_0 - x_1} + f_1 \frac{x - x_0}{x_1 - x_0}, \tag{5b}$$

where we have used the notation $f_0 = f(x_0), f_1 = f(x_1)$. From either form it is easily verified that when $x = x_0, y = f_0$; and when $x = x_1, y = f_1$. Hence, the line passes through the two tabular points (x_0, f_0) and (x_1, f_1). Linear interpolation is pictured geometrically in Fig. 3.

To estimate $f(2.1)$ for the data in Table 2, using linear interpolation, substitute $x = 2.1$ into Eq. (5a) to obtain

$$y = 0.30103 + \frac{0.34242 - 0.30103}{2.2 - 2.0}(2.1 - 2.0)$$

$$= 0.30103 + 0.020695 = 0.321725.$$

This result "appears" to be reasonable, but we cannot say much about its accuracy. If the function varies greatly over the interval $[x_0, x_1]$, linear interpolation will generally give poor accuracy. It is reasonable to expect that, if the actual function $f(x)$ is smooth, interpolation based on a higher degree polynomial will give better results than that based on lower-degree polynomials.

If we are given $n + 1$ values of x and $f(x)$, say $\{x_i, f_i\}$ ($i = 0, 1, \ldots, n$), then we can pass a polynomial of degree n through these points. It can be proved that if the points x_i are distinct, the interpolating polynomial of degree less than or equal to n is unique. However, it can be expressed in many different forms. One such form is the Lagrangian form defined by

TABLE 2.

x	2.0	2.2	2.4	2.6
$f(x)$	0.30103	0.34242	0.38021	0.41497

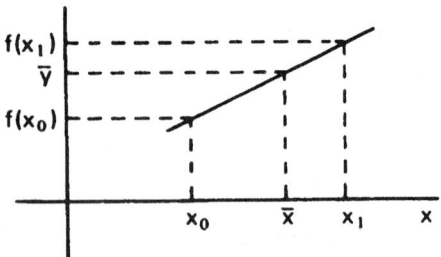

FIG. 3.   Linear interpolation.

$$P_n(x) = \sum_{k=0}^{n} f(x_k) l_k(x), \qquad (6a)$$

where the $l_k(x)$, $k = 0, 1, \ldots, n$ are defined by

$$l_k(x) = \prod_{\substack{i=0, \\ i \neq k}}^{n} \frac{(x - x_i)}{(x_k - x_i)}.$$

Since each $l_k(x)$ is a polynomial of degree n, it is obvious that $p_n(x)$ is a polynomial of degree *at most* n and, furthermore, it is evident by direct substitution that $p_n(x_j) = f(x_j)$ ($j = 0.1, \ldots, n$). Another form of the interpolating polynomial that is more convenient than the Lagrangian form is the "Newton Divided Difference Polynomial." It is defined by

$$p_n(x) = a_0 + a_1(x - x_0) + a_2(x - x_0)(x - x_1)$$
$$+ \cdots + a_n(x - x_0) \cdots (x - x_{n-1}). \qquad (6b)$$

In order for this polynomial to interpolate properly at the $n + 1$ distinct points $[x_k, f(x_k)]$, the coefficients a_k, $k = 0, 1, \ldots$ must be chosen properly. This can be done conveniently by use of a *divided difference table*; see for example Conte (1972). For the data of Table 2 the interpolating polynomial (Eq. 6b) now becomes

$$p_3(x) = 0.30103 + 0.20695(x - 2)$$
$$- 0.04500(x - 2)(x - 2.2) \qquad (7)$$
$$+ 0.011875(x - 2)(x - 2.2)(x - 2.4).$$

To find an estimate for $f(2.1)$, we set $x = 2.1$ in (7) to obtain

$$f(2.1) \approx p_3(2.1) = 0.30103 + 0.020695$$
$$+ 0.00045 + 0.000035625 = 0.3222106. \qquad (8)$$

This example illustrates two important features of Newton polynomial interpolation. First, we can increase the degree of the interpolating polynomial by simply adding on additional terms. No recalculation of coefficients once obtained is necessary. Second, the error of the interpolating polynomial of a given degree can be estimated by examining the next term. Thus, in Eq. (8) the error in linear interpolation is approximately 0.00045, while the error in second-degree interpolation is 0.000035625. No-

tice that each term decreases in magnitude. A thorough study of the error in the interpolating polynomial is beyond the scope of this article.

Although an interpolating polynomial is guaranteed to reproduce its input data, (e.g. the points in Table 2), what happens for other values of x is much more diffiucult to predict. It is known that polynomial interpolants often "wiggle" or oscillate between the data points, and this is rarely desirable. One approach that often works better is to use a "piecewise" polynomial as an interpolating function. The idea is that in practice, it is usually better to use a low-degree polynomial over a smaller range of the points than to use a high-degree polynomial over a larger range. For example, if successive data points in Table 2 were connected by a straight line, the result would be a piecewise linear interpolant. Between each pair of points the interpolant is linear. This is simple, but the interpolant has "corners" (*see* Fig. 4). To make the interpolant smoother, one can use higher-degree polynomial "pieces." It is common to allow the interpolant to be a different cubic between each pair of points, and to force them to join together smoothly. If, at each joint the cubics on the right and left side have the same first derivative, the interpolant is called an Hermite cubic. If they have the same first and second derivatives at these points (continuous curvature), the interpolant is called a *cubic spline* (*see* SPLINE). Piecewise polynomials can be very successful in representing physical data and have become an indispensable part of most programs for computer-aided design (*q.v.*).

Numerical Differentiation   We turn next to a consideration of numerical differentiation. In the calculus differentiation is a well-defined process if the function to be differentiated is given explicitly. Thus, if $f(x) = \sin x$, $f'(x) = \cos x$ and if $f(x) = x \sin x$, then $f'(x) = \sin x + x \cos x$. Often, however, the function is not known explicitly. $f(x)$ may, for example, only be known at a set of tabular points. How do we then obtain an estimate of the derivative at a point? One answer is to rely on finite difference approximations to the derivative. The simplest of these

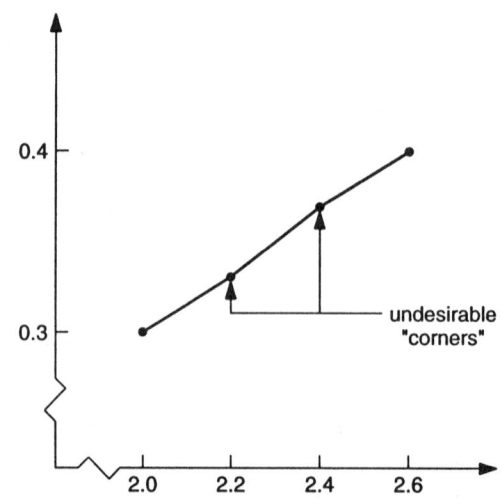

FIG. 4.   Precewise linear interpolation.

approximations is the "forward difference formula," given by

$$f'(x0) \approx \frac{f(x_0 + h) - f(x_0)}{h} = \frac{\Delta f_o}{h}. \qquad (9)$$

where the forward difference operator Δf_0 is defined by (9) as $f(x_0 + h) - f(x_0)$.

Since the limit on the right as $h \to 0$ is the definition of $f'(x_0)$, if it exists, then we can expect that for h small enough, the difference quotient will be close to $f'(x_0)$. Geometrically, as shown in Fig. 5, the difference quotient is the slope of the chord joining the points $(x_0, f(x_0))$ and $(x_0 + h, f(x_0 + h))$.

It can be shown that the error in the forward difference formula is proportional to h. Hence, the approximation (9) is generally quite poor unless h is very small. If, however, h is taken very small, then there is a possibility of serious loss of accuracy due to the fact that we will be subtracting two quantities, $f(x_0 + h)$ and $f(x_0)$, which are nearly equal in magnitude. This type of error arises because computers have fixed word lengths. It is usually referred to as a "loss of significant digits due to subtraction." For example, if $f(x_0) = 0.76482122$ and $f(x_0 + h) = 0.76482333$, then $f(x_0 + h) - f(x_0) = 0.00000211$, which in floating-point arithmetic will be written as $0.211 \cdot 10^{-5}$. Even if $f(x_0)$ and $f(x_0 + h)$ were correct to eight significant digits, the difference will be correct to only three significant digits. How, then, do we avoid this loss of significance? One way is to use a formula that has a smaller error term and hence will not require so small a value of h for a desired accuracy. One such formula is the "central difference formula":

$$D(f,h) = \frac{f(x_0 + h) - f(x_0 - h)}{2h} \qquad (10)$$

The error term for this formula is of the order h^2 ($0(h^2)$); i.e.

$$f'(x_0) - D(f,h) = ch^2 \qquad (11)$$

for some constant c, while the error for the forward difference formula is only $0(h)$. An even more accurate formula is

$$D^2(f,h) = -\frac{1}{12h} \{f(x_0 + 2h) - 8f(x_0 + h) \\ + 8f(x_0 - h) - f(x_0 - 2h)\} \qquad (12)$$

The error of this formula is given by
$$f'(x_0) - D^2(f,h) = 0(h^4). \qquad (13)$$

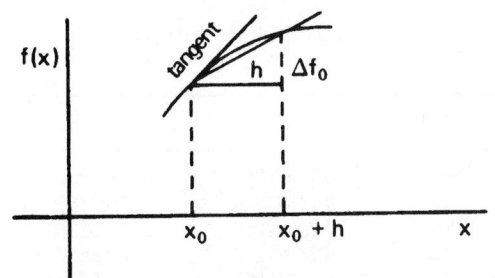

FIG. 5. Numerical approximation to $f'(x_0)$.

Of course, Eq. (13) requires more information about the function. Nevertheless, there is much less danger of loss of significance from subtraction, since we can use a considerably larger value of h.

To illustrate these formulas, consider the data in Table 3. Suppose that we wish to find an estimate of $f'(1)$, using this data. The function tabulated in Table 3 is $f(x) = e^x$, and since $f'(x) = e^x$, $f'(1) = e \approx 2.7183$. Using the forward difference formula (9) with $h = 0.1$, we get

$$f'(1) < \frac{f(1.1) - f(1.0)}{0.1} = \frac{3.0042 - 2.7183}{0.1} = 2.8590,$$

while for $h = 0.01$, we get

$$f'(1) \approx \frac{f(1.01) - f(1.0)}{0.01} = \frac{2.7456 - 2.7183}{0.01} = 2.7300.$$

Neither result here is very good.

If we now use the central difference formula (10) with $h = 0.1$, we obtain

$$f'(x_0) < \frac{f(1.1) - f(0.9)}{0.2} = \frac{3.0042 - 2.4596}{0.2} = 2.7230,$$

while for $h = 0.04$ we obtain

$$f'(x_0) < \frac{f(1.04) - f(0.96)}{0.08} = 2.7188.$$

Finally, for $h = 0.01$ we find that

$$f'(x_0) < \frac{f(1.01) - f(0.99)}{0.02} = 2.7200.$$

These results are clearly better than those for the forward difference formula, but notice that the results for $h = 0.01$ are worse than those for $h = 0.04$. This is again due to loss of significance. If we now use formula (12) with $h = 0.1$, we obtain

$$f'(x_0) < \frac{-1}{.12} \{f(1.2) - 8f(1.1) + 8f(0.9) - f(0.8)\}$$

$$= 2.7185,$$

TABLE 3

x	$f(x)$
0.80	2.2255
0.90	2.4596
0.96	2.6117
0.98	2.6645
0.99	2.6912
1.00	2.7183
1.01	2.7456
1.02	2.7732
1.04	2.8292
1.10	3.0042
1.20	3.3201

a greatly improved result even with a rather coarse step h.

As this example shows, numerical differentiation is an unstable process. Even under the best of circumstances, it is often difficult to obtain good accuracy. A technique that sometimes works is to compute a spline interpolant through the data and then differentiate the spline analytically. If the data are equally spaced, it is also possible to use Fourier techniques to compute a smoothed derivative. For a discussion of these methods, see Atkinson (1989) or Weaver (1983).

Numerical Integration

We turn now to a consideration of numerical integration. In contrast to numerical differentiation, integration is usually a very stable process. The problem here in its simplest form is to compute an approximation to the definite integral

$$I = \int_a^b f(x)\, dx. \qquad (14)$$

Geometrically, we can interpret this problem as that of finding the area between the curve for $f(x)$ and the x-axis on the interval (a,b) (see Fig. 6).

The simplest usable formula based on equally spaced points for this purpose is the *trapezoidal rule*. This rule in its composite form consists of subdividing the interval (a,b) into N equal parts, each of length h, so that $Nh = b - a$. Also let $x_0 = a$, $x_1 = a + h, \dots, x_N = b$, and $f(x_0) = f_0$, $f(x_1) = f_1$, etc. The area of a trapezoid over one panel (say, the first) is

$$T = \frac{h}{2}(f_0 + f_1).$$

Adding the areas over each panel leads to the composite trapezoidal formula

$$T_N = \frac{h}{2}(f_0 + 2f_1 + 2f_2 + \dots + 2f_{N-1} + f_N).$$

How good is T_N as an approximation to the integral I? It is impossible to answer this question for all integrable functions $f(x)$. Sometimes the results are remarkably accurate, in some cases even exact. If we assume that the class of functions we are considering is sufficiently smooth, then we might try to answer the question by examining the error in the approximation T_N. It can be shown that the error is given by

$$E = I - T_N = \frac{h^2(b - a)}{12} f''(\eta), \quad a < \eta < b$$

The error here is called the *discretization error*. In general, we will not know $f''(\eta)$, but we see that the error in T_N is proportional to h^2, where $h = (b - a)/N$. We can achieve any desired accuracy, at least mathematically, by taking h sufficiently small. As we decrease h, however, the required number of function evaluations will increase and the danger of roundoff error accumulation will also increase.

We have thus encountered a situation that arises frequently in numerical computations. The total error comes from two sources: a discretization error caused by using an approximate expression for the true mathematical operator, and a roundoff error. To achieve good accuracy in the mathematical sense (i.e. to reduce the discretization error), we need to take smaller divisions of h. Roundoff error, however, is inversely proportional to h. Hence, decreasing h increases roundoff error. The numerical analyst must therefore seek algorithms that in some sense minimize the totality of errors, those due to the sum of the absolute values of the discretization and roundoff errors.

Table 4 presents the results of applying the trapezoidal rule for various values of N to the integral

$$I = \int_0^1 e^{-x^2}\, dx$$

calculated using both single precision (SP) and double precision (DP) arithmetic.

The correct value of I to eight significant figures is 0.74682413. As N increases from 50 to 400, $T_N(\text{SP})$ approaches the correct result. However, for $N = 800$, the results are worse. The difference between the single precision result and the double precision result shows that the poorer results are due entirely to roundoff error. Thus, for this example, the optimum single precision result would be obtained for a value of N considerably less than $N = 800$. Even $N = 400$ requires considerable computational effort. This effort can be reduced by using a formula with a smaller discretization error.

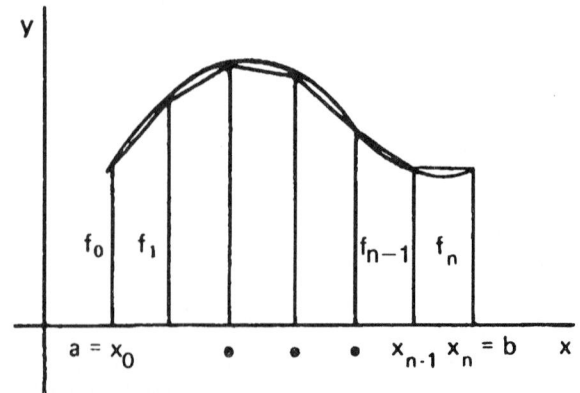

FIG. 6.   The trapezoidal rule.

TABLE 4   Trapezoidal Rule Results for $I = \int_0^1 e^{-x^2}\, dx$

N	$T_N(\text{SP})$	$T_N(\text{DP})$
50	0.74679947	0.74679961
100	0.74681776	0.74681800
200	0.74682212	0.74682260
400	0.74682275	0.74682375
800	0.74682207	0.74682404

One such formula is known as *Simpson's rule*. It begins by subdividing the interval (a,b) into $2N$ equally spaced panels, each of length h. Hence, $2Nh = b - a$. Again the subdivision points are labeled x_i $(i = 0,1,..., 2N)$ and the functional values $f(x_i) = f_i$ $(i = 0,1,..., 2N)$. Over each panel of width $2h$, one now assumes that the function $f(x)$ can be approximated by a polynomial of degree 2 passing through the points (x_{2j}, f_{2j}), (x_{2j+1}, f_{2j+1}), (x_{2j+2}, f_{2j+2}), $(j = 0,1..., N - 1)$. Integrating the polynomial over this panel then yields an approximation to the integral of $f(x)$ over this panel. Adding these approximations over all subpanels of width $2h$ leads to Simpson's quadrature formula S_{2N}.

$$S_{2N} = \frac{h}{3}(f_0 + 4f_1 + 2f_2 + 4f_3 + \ldots + 4f_{2N-1} + f_{2N}). \quad (15)$$

The error of this formula is given by

$$I - S_{2N} = \frac{-h^4(b-a)}{180} f^{\text{iv}}(\xi), \quad a < \xi < b.$$

Again, we do not in general know $f^{\text{iv}}(\xi)$, but the error is proportional to h^4. Thus, for functions that are sufficiently smooth, Simpson's formula should require fewer subdivisions, at least theoretically, to obtain a required accuracy compared with the trapezoidal rule. In fact, for the example considered above, Simpson's rule with $N = 50$ yields the result 0.74682400 in single precision and the result 0.74682413 (which is correct to eight significant figures) in double precision. Obviously, Simpson's rule is computationally much more efficient than the trapezoidal rule in this case, and this remains true in general for most functions $f(x)$.

Having selected a method and a step h in either Simpson's formula or the trapezoidal rule, we are faced with the question: "How good are the results produced?" The error term normally provides little help, since we usually cannot evaluate the derivatives involved. One way to build some confidence in the results is to solve the same problem several times with different values of h and then compare the results. Thus, if one uses Simpson's rule with a step h and then with a step $h/2$, one will have two approximations to the integral. If these two approximations agree to s significant figures, the assumption is then made that the results are correct to s significant figures. This method, while not conclusive mathematically, does provide some basis for confidence in the results. Each halving of the step size doubles the

amount of work, however, and if the function $f(x)$ is not "smooth," the halving process may have to be repeated many times. We will not precisely define "smoothness" of a function here. However, a function that wiggles a great deal on part of an interval will be harder to integrate than one that does not, and some functions may even have singularities within the interval. In Fig. 7 we exhibit a function of this type.

A finer subdivision will be required over the interval (a,c) than over the interval (c,b). At the point c there is a discontinuity in the function. If this is known to the user, then it is reasonable to write

$$\int_a^b f(x)\,dx = \int_a^c f(x)\,dx + \int_c^b f(x)\,dx.$$

The user, however, may not know that c is a point of discontinuity. An automatic approach, which has been used to handle such a situation in an efficient manner, is known as *adaptive integration*. It can be based on any basic integration formula, but we choose Simpson's rule for illustrative purposes. We are given an interval (a,b), the function $f(x)$, and an error ϵ, and a starting step size h.

The procedure for adaptive integration is as follows:

Denote by $S(I)$ the result of applying Simpson's rule to the integrand on an interval I, and by ϵ the user-requested accuracy, such as 10^{-4}. Denote by $E(I)$ the magnitude of the difference between $S(I)$ and $S(I_1) + S(I_2)$, where I_1 and I_2 are the left and right halves of I.

The procedure for adaptive integration is as follows:

1. Initialize Q to $S([a,b])$ and E to $E([a,b])$.
2. If $E < \epsilon$ stop. Report Q as the best estimate of the integral, and report E as the best estimate of the error in Q.
3. Otherwise, select the subinterval I with largest $E(I)$. (At the first step, there is only one interval $([a,b])$. Bisect I into I_1, I_2 and compute $S(I_i)$, $E(I_i)$, $i = 1,2$.
4. Update, $E = E - E(I) + E(I_1) + E(I_2)$, $Q = Q - S(I) + S(I_1) + S(I_2)$.
5. Delete interval I and add I_1, I_2 to the collection of intervals.
6. Go to 2.

The advantage of adaptive schemes is that they do only as much work as necessary on each subinterval. Even discontinuities can be handled reasonably well by this approach.

Among other formulas based on equally spaced points, one should mention the *Newton-Cotes formulas* and *Romberg integration*. These quadrature formulas are capable of producing higher order error terms and thus hold the promise of further reduction in computational error.

Somewhat different in nature are integration formulas of the Gaussian type. All the formulas considered above are based on equally spaced points. In Gaussian formulas, one attempts to select the integration points as well as the weights so as to produce a "best" integration formula. Such formulas have the form

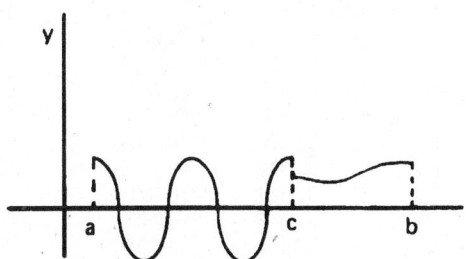

FIG. 7. A discontinuous function.

$$I = \int_a^b f(x)\, dx \approx \sum_{i=0}^{n} w_i f(x_i),$$

where the points x_i as well as the weights w_i are to be determined. Such formulas, for a given number n of points, are capable of much higher accuracy. Gaussian methods can also be used to treat integrals with singularities.

The points x_i and weights w_i of most Gaussian formulas are irrational numbers that can only be obtained after substantial calculation; programs incorporating these formulas use embedded tables. Also, until recently, there was no practical way to estimate the error in Gaussian integration rules, a disadvantage if the program is to be automatic. In 1968, the Russian computer scientist Kronrod developed a technique that pairs a Gaussian rule with a new rule utilizing all the Gaussian points as well as others. For example, a common pair is the 7-point Gaussian rule, G_7, and the 15-point "Kronrod" rule, K_{15}. The difference between these is a good estimate of the error in G_7. Pairs such as these are at the heart of many automatic integration programs such as Quadpack. See Piessens *et al.* (1983).

A more complete discussion of integration formulas can be found in Davis and Rabinowitz (1984).

Differential Equations Now we consider methods for solving ordinary differential equations. In this section, we restrict ourselves to a first-order initial value problem; i.e. we are given an equation involving a function $y(x)$ and its derivative

$$y' = f(x,y) \tag{16a}$$

and an initial value such as

$$y'(x_0) = y_0. \tag{16b}$$

We seek a continuous function $y(x)$ that satisfies Eq. (16a) subject to the initial value (16b). The theory of differential equations tells us that Eqs. (16a) and (16b) have a unique solution provided certain conditions on $f(x,y)$ are satisfied. Closed-form solutions are sometimes, but not very often, possible. For example, the differential system

$$y' = y, \quad y(x_0) = y_0$$

has the solution $y(x) = y_0(\exp(x - x_0))$. More often we must rely on numerical methods to obtain an approximation to the solution over a given interval.

Let a solution be required over an interval (x_0, b). We first subdivide the interval (x_0, b) into N equal parts of length h so that $Nh = b - x_0$, and we label the subdivision points $x_n = x_0 + nh$ $(n = 0,1..., N)$ with $x_N = b$. We will consider several methods that yield approximations y_n to the true solution $y(x_n)$ at the subdivision points. The simplest of all methods is that of Euler, depicted in Fig. 8.

Geometrically, we find an approximate value of y at x_1 by extending the tangent to $y(x)$ at x_0 to the line $x = x_1$ and

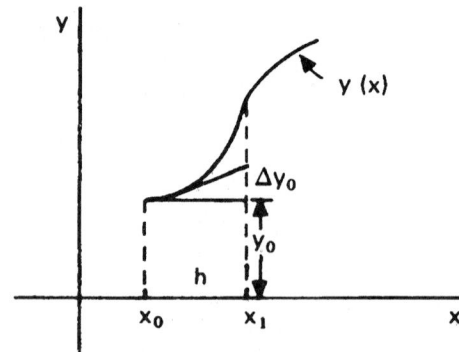

FIG. 8. Euler's method.

then adding to y_0 the increment $\Delta y_0 = hf(x_0, y_0)$. We thus obtain

$$y(x_1) \approx y_1 = y_0 + hf(x_0, y_0).$$

Note in Fig. 8 that the slope to the curve $y(x)$ is available immediately from the given equation $y' = f(x,y)$. Now that we have an estimate y_1 at $x = x_1$, we can calculate $y' = f(x_1, y_1)$, and thus we can step ahead to obtain

$$y(x_2) \approx y_2 = y_1 + hf(x_1, y_1).$$

The general formula, which yields y_{n+1} when we know x_n and y_n, is

$$y_{n+1} = y_n + hf(x_n, y_n), \quad n = 0,1,...,N-1. \tag{17}$$

As an example, consider the equation

$$y' = -y^2 \quad y(1) = 1 \tag{18}$$

We choose $h = 0.1$ and apply formula (17) over the interval $(1,2)$. The results are given in Table 5. The exact solution of Eq. (18) is $y = 1/x$. The results of Euler's method with a step $h = 0.1$ produces about one-digit accuracy.

An estimate of the error in Euler's method can be obtained by expanding $y(x_n + h)$ about x_n. Thus, application of Taylor's theorem with remainder yields

TABLE 5

n	x_n	y_n	$y(x_n) = 1/x_n$	$f(x_n, y_n) = -y_n^2$
0	1.	1.	1.	-1.
1	1.1	0.0	0.9090	-0.81
2	1.2	0.819	0.8333	-0.6708
3	1.3	0.7519	0.7692	-0.5654
4	1.4	0.6954	0.7143	-0.4836
5	1.5	0.6470	0.6667	-0.4186
6	1.6	0.6051	0.6250	-0.3661
7	1.7	0.5685	0.5882	-0.3232
8	1.8	0.5362	0.5555	-0.2875
9	1.9	0.5074	0.5263	-0.2575
10	2.0	0.4817	0.5000	-0.2320

$$y(x_n + h) = y(x_n) + hy'(x_n) + \frac{h^2}{2} y''(\xi), \qquad x_n < \xi < x_n + h.$$

Hence, the error in one step of Euler's method is

$$y(x_n + h) - \{y(x_n) + hf(x_n, y_n)\} = \frac{h^2}{2} y''(\xi_n).$$

This is called the *local error*, since it is based on the assumption that x_n and $y(x_n)$ are known exactly. Errors committed at each step will themselves propagate, and the global or total error at the end of N steps will be considerably larger. In fact, the global error of Euler's method can be shown to be of order h instead of h^2. To achieve any kind of accuracy for the problem presented above will clearly require a much smaller value of h. As we decrease h, however, the amount of work increases because we must evaluate $f(x,y)$ once for each step and, in addition, our roundoff error problems will increase. In practice, therefore, it is advisable to use formulas that are of higher order; i.e. we seek formulas for which the error is $0(h^p)$ with p greater than 1.

A direct use of Taylor's theorem carried to more terms would yield a formula of the form

$$y(x_n + h) = y(x_n) + hy'(x_n) + \frac{h^2}{2} y''(x_n)$$
$$+ \ldots + \frac{h^k}{k!} y^{(k)}(x_n) + \frac{h^{k+1}}{(k+1)!} y^{(k+1)}(\xi_n) \qquad (19)$$

If we use the first $k + 1$ terms of this formula to predict $y(x_{n+1})$, then the error would be of order h^{k+1}. Taylor's theorem in this form is difficult to use because the higher derivatives of $y(x)$ are generally not easily computable. Runge first discovered formulas that achieve agreement with the Taylor expansion for different values of k, but that depend only upon the evaluation of $f(x,y)$. One such formula is

$$y_{n+1} = y_n + \frac{h}{6}(k_1 + 2k_2 + 2k_3 + k_4), \qquad (20)$$

where:

$$k_1 = hf(x_n, y_n),$$
$$k_2 = hf\left(x_n + \frac{h}{2}, y_n + \frac{k_1}{2}\right)$$
$$k_3 = hf\left(x_n + \frac{h}{2}, y_n + \frac{k_2}{2}\right)$$
$$k_4 = hf(x_n + h, y_n + k_3).$$

The local error of this method is $0(h^5)$ and the global error is $0(h^4)$. It is called a *Runge-Kutta fourth-order method*; no derivatives of y other than $y' = f(x,y)$ are required. We note, however, that we must evaluate $f(x,y)$ at four different points for each step of the integration. By comparison with Euler's method, this Runge-Kutta method is far more efficient and, in addition, roundoff error is considerably less for the same accuracy. For the example presented in

Eq. (18), again using $h = 0.1$, at $x = 1.1$ we obtain $y_1 = 0.090909$, which agrees with the exact result 1/1.1 to all digits shown, indeed a remarkable improvement over the Euler result. The Runge-Kutta method and variations of it are very popular. It provides good accuracy, it is simple to program, it requires minimum storage, and it is stable. Its principal disadvantage, compared to methods based on finite differences, is that it requires four function evaluations per integration step.

Next we discuss the so-called multistep methods, which make it possible to achieve comparable accuracy with about half the amount of work. Runge-Kutta methods are called "one-step" methods because they use information at a single point to estimate y at the next point. Let us suppose that we have already estimated $y(x)$ at several successive subdivision points. For definiteness, assume that we know

$$(x_n, y_n, f_n), \quad (x_{n-1}, y_{n-1}, f_{n-1}),$$
$$(x_{n-2}, y_{n-2}, f_{n-2}), \quad (x_{n-3}, y_{n-3}, f_{n-3}),$$

where f_n represents $f(x_n, y_n)$, etc. How can this information be used to extrapolate a value for y at x_{n+1}? The theory of interpolation suggests one possible approach. If we integrate the equation $y' = f(x,y)$ from x_n to x_{n+1}, we obtain

$$y(x_{n+1}) - y(x_n) = \int_{x_n}^{x_{n+1}} f(x, y(x)) \, dx.$$

Since we know the value of f at the four successive points $x_n, x_{n-1}, x_{n-2}, x_{n-3}$, we can pass a polynomial of degree 3 through these points. Integrating the resulting polynomial and evaluating it between the limits x_n to x_{n+1} will then yield an approximate formula for $y(x_{n+1})$. One such formula is that of Adams, which after simplification, takes the form

$$y_{n+1} = y_n + \frac{h}{24}(55f_n - 59f_{n-1} + 37f_{n-2} - 9f_{n-3}). \qquad (21)$$

The local error of this formula is $0(h^5)$ and the global error $0(h^4)$, just as for the Runge-Kutta method of order 4, discussed earlier. Notice that only one new function evaluation is required to compute y_{n+1}. It would thus appear that a formula of this type should be computationally more efficient than the Runge-Kutta method. It turns out that the accuracy of Adams' formula (21) is not quite so good as that of the Runge-Kutta method, even though both are of the same order, because the coefficient in the error term is somewhat larger. It is customary to consider the result of applying Eq. (21) as a predicted value and to correct it by using the formula

$$y_{n+1}^c = y_n + \frac{h}{24}\{9f(x_{n+1}, y_{n+1}^p)$$
$$+ 19f_n - 5f_{n-1} + f_{n-2}\}, \qquad (22)$$

where y_{n+1}^p is the value obtained from Eq. (21). The global error of Eq. (22) is also $0(h^4)$. The pair of formulas (21) and

(22) is called a *predictor-corrector* pair. It yields results comparable in accuracy to the Runge-Kutta method with about half as much work. Multistep formulas such as (21) and (22) have the disadvantage of requiring special techniques for starting, since initially we have information at one point only. Some multistep methods also suffer from numerical instability, a phenomenon that can lead to disastrous results, and hence they should not be used indiscriminately.

Two important issues have propelled recent research in ordinary differential equations. The first is the need to develop reliable programs that can be used by non-specialists. The second is the need to solve "stiff" problems.

Programs for solving differential equations usually accept as input an error request ϵ and deliver a solution to the appropriate accuracy, much as for numerical integration. This implies the need to assess the accuracy of each integration step. If the estimated error is too large, the step is not accepted and a smaller one is tried instead. If the estimated error is sufficiently small, the step is accepted and an estimate is made to see if a larger step could be used from this point forward. A great deal of work has been done recently on estimating errors and developing variable step and variable order algorithms that are reliable and efficient. Nevertheless, the best programs, such as LSODE by Hindmarsh (1980) or DEABM by Shampine and Gordon (1975), still blend theory and experience. The reader is referred to Gear (1971), Shampine and Gordon (1975), or Shampine, Watts, and Davenport (1975) for a discussion of these methods.

When a differential equation is modeling two interrelated phenomena, with one changing rapidly and one changing slowly, difficulties can arise. An example might be a model of a drum beat where there are rapid vibrations corresponding to the tone of the drum, along with a slow decay in the volume of the sound. Many small integration steps would have to be used to model the rapid vibrations, leading to a great many calculations. However, a short time after the drum is struck, these rapid vibrations will be less important than the general decay, which can be approximated well by using only a few steps. Such a problem is called "stiff." The traditional numerical methods described in the early portion of this section have difficulty with stiff problems, since they slavishly follow the rapid motions even when they are less important than the general trend in the solution. Special algorithms have been devised for solving stiff problems. See Aiken (1985).

Boundary Value Problems   Differential equations of order higher than one are classified either as *initial value problems* or as *boundary value problems*. In general, a differential equation of order n that can be expressed in the form

$$y^{(N)}(x) = f(x, y(x), y'(x), ..., y^{(N-1)}(x))$$

requires N conditions if it is to yield a unique solution. If these N conditions are all specified at one point, say $x = x_0$, then we have an *initial value problem*. If these conditions are specified at more than one point, then we have

a *boundary value problem*. The methods previously considered for a single differential equation can be directly adapted to apply to initial value problems of any order. Boundary value problems are more complicated and require a different approach. Among the methods most commonly used for such problems are *finite difference methods*, the *finite element method, shooting methods,* and *collocation methods*. We shall restrict our discussion to a consideration of the finite difference method as applied to a second order equation. We assume a second order equation in the form

$$y''(x) + f(x)y'(x) + g(x)y(x) = q(x) \qquad (23)$$

subject to the boundary conditions

$$y(a) = \alpha, \quad y(b) = \beta, \qquad (24)$$

where $f(x)$, $g(x)$, and $q(x)$ are given coefficient functions with sufficient continuity requirements. The problem is to find an approximate solution of Eq. 23 over an interval (a,b) that satisfies the boundary conditions (Eq. 24) at $x = a$ and $x = b$.

We first divide the interval (a,b) into N equal parts of width h so that $Nh = b - a$. We set $x_0 = a$, $x_N = b$ and we define the *mesh points* $x_n = x_0 + nh$ $(n = 0, 1,..., N)$. The corresponding values of y, f, g, and q are denoted by $y_n = y(x_0 + nh)$, etc. The next step is to replace each derivative appearing in Eq. 23 by an appropriate finite difference approximation. We use central difference approximations defined by

$$y'(x_n) \approx \frac{y(x_{n+1}) - y(x_{n-1})}{2h} = \frac{y_{n+1} - y_{n-1}}{2h},$$

$$y''(x_n) \approx \frac{y(x_{n+1}) - 2y(x_n) + y(x_{n-1})}{h^2}$$

$$= \frac{y_{n+1} - 2y_n + y_{n-1}}{h^2}$$

Substituting these into Eq. 23 leads to the finite difference equation

$$\frac{y_{n-1} - 2y_n + y_{n+1}}{h^2} + f_n \frac{(y_{n+1} - y_{n-1})}{2h} + g_n y_n = q_n.$$

Multiplying by h^2 and grouping terms we obtain

$$\left(1 - \frac{h}{2}f_n\right)y_{n-1} + (-2 + h^2 g_n)y_n$$

$$+ \left(1 + \frac{h}{2}f_n\right)y_{n+1} = h^2 q_n. \qquad (25)$$

When Eq. 25 is written out for $n = 1, 2,..., N - 1$, we will obtain a linear system of $N - 1$ equations for the $N - 1$ unknown values $y_1, y_2..., y_{N-1}$. Of course, y_0 and y_N are specified by the conditions of Eq. 24. More explicitly, we obtain the system

$$(-2 + h^2 g_1)y_1 + \left(1 + \frac{h}{2}f_1\right)y_2 = h^2 q_1 - \left(1 - \frac{h}{2}f_1\right)a,$$

$$\left(1 - \frac{h}{2}f_2\right)y_1 + (-2 + h^2g_2)y_2 + \left(1 + \frac{h}{2}f_2\right)y_3 = h^2q_2;$$

$$\cdots\cdots\cdots\cdots\cdots\cdots$$

$$\left(1 - \frac{h}{2}f_{N-2}\right)y_{N-3} + (-2 + h^2g_{N-2})y_{N-2} +$$

$$\left(1 + \frac{h}{2}f_{N-2}\right)y_{N-1} = h^2q_{N-2},$$

$$\left(1 - \frac{h}{2}f_{N-1}\right)y_{N-2} + (-2 + h^2g_{N-1})y_{N-1}$$

$$= h^2q_{N-1} - \left(1 + \frac{h}{2}f_{N-1}\right)\beta. \qquad (26)$$

This linear system of equations can be solved readily by standard methods, some of which are described in the article on MATRIX COMPUTATIONS. Actually, because the matrix of coefficients of the system shown (Eq. 26) is *tri-diagonal*, a computer solution can be found very efficiently. The solution of this system will be the values $y_1,\ldots, y_{N-1}$ which approximates the solution function $y(x)$ at the mesh points. The accuracy of these approximations will depend upon how fine a mesh is chosen; i.e. on the value of h or N.

The method of finite differences works quite well on linear differential equations of any order. However, if the differential equation is nonlinear, this method becomes more complicated, and in such cases the shooting or collocation methods may be more appropriate.

Conclusion In a short article on numerical analysis, one can hope to present to the reader only a synopsis of the work of the numerical analyst. We have discussed only a small number of algorithms. These algorithms work well on some classes of functions, but no algorithm is uniformly best for all classes of functions. The numerical analyst must be constantly alert to indications that an algorithm is not functioning properly. We have tried to stress those qualities of good algorithms that are important for computational purposes. These qualities are speed, efficiency, and automatic error analysis and control. There are many good books on numerical analysis at various levels for the reader interested in pursuing this subject, among which are Atkinson (1989), Ralston and Rabinowitz (1978), and Hamming (1973).

References

1960. Wilkinson, J. H. "Error Analysis of Floating Point Computations," *Num. Math.,* **2**: 319–340.
1970. Ortega, J. M. and Rheinboldt, W. C. *Iterative Solution of Nonlinear Equations in Several Variables.* New York: Academic Press.
1971. Gear, C. W. *Numerical Initial Value Problems in Ordinary Differential Equations.* Englewood Cliffs, N.J.: Prentice-Hall.
1972. Conte, S. D. and deBoor, Carl J. *Elementary Numerical Analysis: An Algorithmic Approach.* New York: McGraw-Hill.
1973. Hamming, R. W. *Numerical Methods for Scientists and Engineers,* 2nd Ed. New York: McGraw-Hill.
1975. Shampine, L. and Gordon, M. *Computer Solution of Ordinary Differential Equations: The Initial Value Problem.* San Francisco: Freeman.
1975. Shampine, L., Watts, H., and Davenport, S. *Solving Non-Stiff Ordinary Differential Equations—The State of the Art,* SAND 75-01812. Albuquerque, NM: Sandia Corp.
1978. Ralston, A. and Rabinowitz, P. *A First Course in Numerical Analysis,* 2nd Ed. New York: McGraw-Hill.
1979. Dongarra, J. J., Moler, C. B., Bunch, J. R., and Stewart, G. W. *LINPACK Users' Guide.* Philadelphia: SIAM.
1980. Hindmarsh, H. "LSODE and LSODEI, Two Initial Value Ordinary Differential Equation Solvers," *ACM SIGNUM Newsletter,* **15**, 10–11.
1983. Golub, G. H. and Van Loan, C.F. *Matrix Computations.* Baltimore: The Johns Hopkins University Press.
1983. Piessens, R., de Doncker, E., Uberhuber, C., and Kahaner, D. QUADPACK: A Subroutine Package for Automatic Integration. Berlin: Springer-Verlag.
1983. Weaver, H. J. *Applications of Discrete and Continuous Fourier Analysis.* New York: John Wiley.
1984. Davis, P. and Rabinowitz, P. *Methods in Numerical Integration* 2nd Ed. New York: Academic Press.
1985. Aiken, R. *Stiff Computation.* Oxford: Oxford University Press.
1989. Atkinson, K. E. *An Introduction to Numerical Analysis,* 2nd Ed. New York: John Wiley.
1989. Kahaner, D., Moler, C., and Nash, S. *Numerical Methods and Software.* Englewood Cliffs, NJ: Prentice-Hall.

SAM D. CONTE AND DAVID K. KAHANER

OBJECT-ORIENTED PROGRAMMING

For articles on related subjects *see* ABSTRACT DATA TYPE; CLASS; ENCAPSULATION; INFORMATION HIDING; PACKAGE; SOFTWARE ENGINEERING; and STRUCTURED PROGRAMMING.

Introduction A programming language is said to be *object-based* if it supports objects as a language feature, and is said to be *object-oriented* if, additionally, objects are required to belong to classes that can be incrementally modified through inheritance. Among the object-based languages are Simula, Smalltalk, C++, Eiffel, and Ada, but not Fortran or Pascal. Ada (*q.v.*) is object-based, supporting the functionality of objects, but is not object-oriented, since it does not support the management of objects through classes and inheritance.

Before defining the key notions of objects, classes, and inheritance, we will indicate some general features of the object-oriented paradigm. The essence of object-oriented programming is the hiding or *encapsulation* (*q.v.*) of the "inner" state of entities and the specification of interactive properties of entities by an interface of operations (the events in which they may participate). This separates the inner functioning of entities like banks, airplanes, or people from their external behavior in interacting with other entities. This separation is realized by partitioning the state into chunks associated with objects so that each chunk is responsible for its own protection against access by unauthorized operations. In a concurrent environment, objects protect themselves against asynchronous access, removing the synchronization burden from processes that access the object's data.

Early programmers thought of programs as instruction sequences. Procedure-oriented languages (*q.v.*) introduced procedural abstractions that encapsulate sequences of actions into procedures. Object-oriented languages encapsulate data as well as sequences of actions, providing a stronger encapsulation mechanism

than procedures and, consequently, a more powerful modeling tool. Both procedures and objects are server modules that may be called by clients to determine a stimulus/response behavior in interacting with their environment. The role of procedures is to transform input data specified by parameters into values, while the role of objects is to serve as a repository of data (the current system state) and to respond in a manner determined by the current system state. For example, the response of a bank to a withdrawal request depends on the value of the current balance. Object-oriented programming is a modeling paradigm that models objects of the real world by collections of interacting objects of a programming system.

The procedure-oriented paradigm has strong organizing principles for managing actions and algorithms, but has weak organizing principles for managing shared data, while object-oriented systems organize data by restricting applicable operations to those associated with a specific object or class. Inheritance provides a second layer of structure by structuring classes into hierarchies. We can think of classes as a mechanism for classifying objects into categories with similar interface behavior, and inheritance as a mechanism for classifying classes by factoring out properties common to several subclasses into a superclass.

Objects *Objects* in programming languages are collections of operations that share a state. The operations determine the messages (calls) to which the object can respond, while the shared state is hidden from the outside world and is accessible only to the object's operations (see Fig. 1). Variables representing the internal state of an object are called *instance variables* and its operations are called *methods*. The collection of methods of an object determines its *interface* and its *behavior*:

name:object
  local instance variables (shared state)
   operations or methods (interface of message
    patterns to which the object may respond)

959

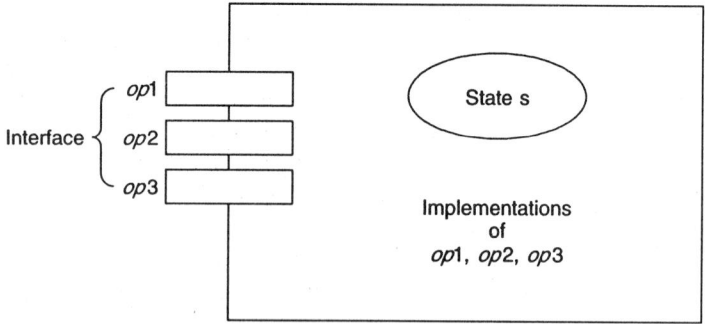

FIG. 1. Object modules.

An object named *point* with instance variables *x, y* and methods for reading and changing them may be defined as follows:

point:object
  x := 0; y := 0;
  read-x: ↑*x; —return value of x*
  read-y: ↑*y; —return value of y*
  change-x(dx):x:=x + dx;
  change-y(dy):y:=y + dy;

The object *point* protects its instance variables x,y against arbitrary access, allowing access only through messages to *read* and *change* operations. The object's behavior is entirely determined by its responses to acceptable messages and is independent of the data representation of its instance variables. Moreover, the object's knowledge of its callers is entirely determined by its messages. Object-oriented message passing facilitates two-way abstraction: senders have an abstract view of receivers and receivers have an abstract view of senders.

An object's interface of operations (methods) can be represented by a record:

untyped object interface: (op1,op2,...,opN)

Objects whose operations *opi* have type *Ti* have an interface that is a typed record. Typed record interfaces are called *signatures*.

Typed Object Interface (Signature): (op1:T1,op2:T2, ..., opN:TN)

The *point* object has the following signature:

*point-interface = (read-x:***Real***, read-y:* **Real***,*
  *change-x:***Real** → **Real***, change-y:***Real** → **Real***)*

The parameterless operations *read-x* and *read-y* both return a **Real** number as their value, while *change-x* and *change-y* expect a **Real** number as their argument and return a **Real** result.

The operations of an object share its state so that state changes by one operation may be seen by subsequently executed operations. Operations access the state by references to the object's instance variables. For example, *read-x* and *change-x* share the instance variable *x*, which is non-local to these operations, although local to the object.

Non-local references in functions and procedures are generally considered harmful, but they are essential for operations within objects, since they are the only mechanism by which an object's operations can access its internal state. Sharing unprotected data within an object is combined with strong protection (encapsulation) against external access. The strong encapsulation at the object interface is realized at the expense of modularity (and reusability) of component operations. This captures the distinction within any organization or organism between closely integrated internal subsystems and contractually specified interfaces to the outside world.

Classes We distinguish between object-based languages that support objects as a language primitive and object-oriented languages that additionally support the management of objects through classes (*q.v.*) and inheritance. In object-oriented languages, the behavior of objects is specified by classes, which are like types of traditional languages, but serve additionally to classify objects into hierarchies through the inheritance mechanism.

Classes serve as templates from which objects can be created. The class *point* has precisely the same instance variables and operations as the object *point*, but their interpretation is different. Whereas the instance variables of a *point* object represent *actual* variables, class instance variables are *potential*, being instantiated only when an object is created:

point:class
  local instance variables (private copy for each object of the class)
  operations or methods (shared by all objects of the class)

Instances of a class can be created by a *make-instance* operation, which creates a copy of the class instance variables that may be acted on by the class operations:

p := make-instance point;   *—create a new instance of the class point, call it p*

Instance variables in class definitions may be initialized as part of object creation:

p1 := make-instance point (0,0); —create point initialized to (0,0), call it p1 p2 := make-instance point (1,1); —create point initialized to (1,1), call it p2

The two points *p1, p2* each have private copies of the class instance variables and share the operations specified in the class definition. When an object receives a message to execute a method, it looks for the method in its class definition. We may think of a class as specifying a behavior common to all objects of the class. The instance variables specify a structure (data structure) for realizing the behavior. The public operations of a class determine its behavior, while the private instance variables determine its structure.

Inheritance   *Inheritance* is a mechanism for sharing code and behavior. It allows us to reuse the behavior of a class in the definition of new classes. Subclasses of a class inherit the operations of their parent class and may add new operations and new instance variables.

Fig. 2 describes mammals by an inheritance hierarchy of classes (representing behaviors). The class of mammals has persons and elephants as its subclasses. The class of persons has mammals as its superclass and students and females as its subclasses. The instances John, Joan, Bill, Mary, and Dumbo each have a unique base class. Membership of an instance in more than one base class, such as Joan being both a student and a female, cannot be expressed.

Why does inheritance play such an important role in object-oriented programming? Inheritance can express relations among behaviors such as classification, specialization, generalization, approximation, and evolution. Thus, in Fig. 2 we classify mammals into persons and elephants. Elephants specialize the properties of mammals, and conversely mammals generalize the properties of elephants. The properties of mammals approximate those of elephants. Moreover, elephants evolved from early species of mammals.

Inheritance classifies classes in much the same way that classes classify values. The ability to classify classes provides greater classification power and conceptual modeling power. Classification of classes may be referred to as second-order classification. Inheritance provides second-order sharing, management, and manipulation of behavior that complements first-order management of objects by classes.

Virtual classes are incomplete behavior specifications that require subclasses to complete their behavior specification before they can be instantiated. The class of mammals in Fig. 2 is a virtual class. It specifies behavioral attributes common to all mammals and must be supplemented by behavioral attributes of specific mammals (persons or elephants) before instances like Joan and Dumbo can be created. Summarizing:

virtual class: incomplete behavior specification, cannot be directly instantiated (mammals)

subclass: completes virtual behavior specification (persons or elephants)

Incomplete behaviors are natural building blocks in constructing composite behavior specifications. Composition of incomplete behaviors during program development may be contrasted with modification of already complete behaviors during maintenance and enhancement.

Tree structure is a general mechanism for sharing of the properties of ancestors by descendants. Just as block structure facilitates the sharing of data declared in ancestor blocks by descendant blocks, inheritance hierarchies facilitate the sharing of code and behavior of superclasses by subclasses. Multiple inheritance facilitates a descendant sharing of the behavior of several ancestors.

Implementation of Inheritance   Consider a class A with instance a and a subclass B with instance b, as in Fig. 3. Both A and B define behavior by operations shared by their instances, and have instance variables that cause a private copy to be created for each instance of the class or subclass. The instance a of A has a copy of A's instance variables and a pointer to its base class. The instance b of B has a copy of the instance variables of both B and its superclass A and a pointer to the base class of B. The class representation of B has a pointer to its superclass A, while A has no superclass pointer, since it is assumed to have no superclass.

When b receives a message to execute a method, it looks first in the methods of B. If found, the method is executed using the instance variables of b as data. Otherwise, the pointer to its superclass is followed. If it finds the method in A, it executes it on the data of b. Otherwise, it searches A's superclass if there is one. If A has no superclass and the method has not been found, it reports failure. This search algorithm may be defined by the following procedure:

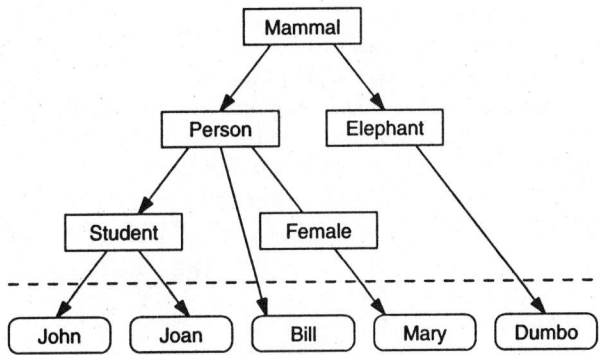

FIG. 2.   Example of an inheritance hierarchy.

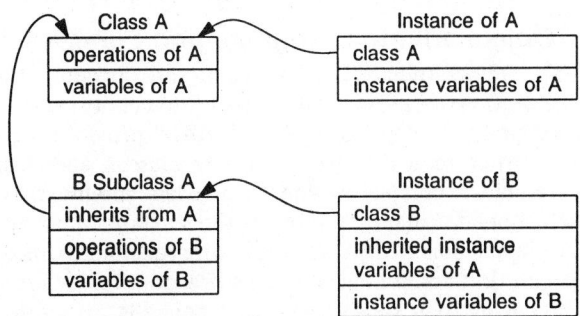

FIG. 3.   Implementation of inheritance.

procedure search (name, class)if (name = localname)
 then do localaction
else if (inherited-module = nil) then undefinedname
 else search (name, inherited-module)

The restriction that instances have precisely one base class may be understood in terms of implementation considerations. Instances must know where to start looking for methods when they receive a message to be executed. Having pointers to more than one base class would make method lookup complex and possibly ambiguous. Allowing Joan to be both a student and a female in Fig. 2 would considerably complicate object-oriented semantics.

Evolution of Object-Oriented Programming

Simula 67 (Dahl et al., 1968) was the first object-oriented language. Its language primitives included objects, classes, and inheritance, and it was used extensively for simulation and other applications, primarily in Europe. Smalltalk (Goldberg and Robson, 1983), developed by the software concepts group at Xerox PARC in the 1970s and embodied in a stable implementation in Smalltalk 80, caught the public imagination because of its implementation on personal computers and its interactive graphical interface that permitted browsing and the display of objects in multiple windows. Smalltalk implementations were initially too slow to be commercially viable, but in the 1990s are becoming increasingly competitive with traditional languages.

The Department of Defense language Ada (*q.v.*) included the notion of packages, which are like objects, but did not have a notion of classes or inheritance. Starting in the mid-1980s, object-oriented programming became a popular term, and object-oriented dialects of existing programming languages began to appear, like object-Pascal, objective C, and C++. C++ has proven to be a popular object-oriented language because of its connection with C and its support by AT&T Bell Labs. The language Eiffel (Meyer, 1988) is backed up by an excellent textbook and has many esthetically pleasing features.

Object-oriented technology is being adopted by the software engineering community. Two recent books on object-oriented software design serve to consolidate software design methodology (Booch, 1991 and Rambaugh et al, 1991). There is much work on computer-aided software engineering (CASE - *q.v.*) tools for object-oriented programming.

Is Object-oriented Programming Fundamental?

Object-oriented programming has become the buzzword of the 1980s, rivaling the fashionability of structured programming (*q.v.*) in the 1970s. It provides high-level structure at the level of objects, classes, and class hierarchies, complementing structured programming techniques for microstructure at the level of statements and expressions. Object-oriented programming is more specific and comprehensive in its prescription for problem solving than structured programming is. Structured programming is concerned with "structure" in general,

while object-oriented programming focuses on a specific form of structure: that associated with objects.

Modeling entities by their behavior (their response to messages) is a central principle of scientific method in many disciplines: behaviorism in psychology, operationalism in physics, and Platonic ideals in philosophy. Objects are a canonical form of description for any discipline or domain of discourse. Its universality as a representation, modeling, and abstraction technique supports the view that the object-oriented paradigm is conceptually and computationally fundamental.

References

1968. Dahl, O. J., Myrhaag, B., and Nygaard, K. *Simula 67 Common Base Language*. Norwegian Computing Center. Revised in 1970, 1972, and 1984.

1983. *Reference Manual for Ada Programming Language*. U. S. Dept of Defense.

1983. Goldberg A., and Robson D., *Smalltalk 80: The Language and its Implementation*. Reading, MA: Addison-Wesley.

1988. Meyer B., *Object-Oriented Software Construction*. Englewood Cliffs, NJ: Prentice Hall International.

1990. Wegner P., *Concepts and Paradigms of Object-Oriented Programming*, OOPS Messenger, **1**, *1* (August).

1991. Booch, G., *Object-Oriented Design with Applications*. Menlo Park, CA: Benjamin Cummings.

1991. Rumbaugh, J., Blaha, M., Premerlani, W., Eddy, F., and Lorensen W., *Object-Oriented Modeling and Design*. Englewood Cliffs, NJ: Prentice Hall.

PETER WEGNER

OBJECT PROGRAM

For articles on related subjects *see* LANGUAGE PROCESSORS; LINKER; LOADER; PROCEDURE-ORIENTED LANGUAGES; and SOURCE PROGRAM.

An *object program* is the output of a translating program, such as an assembler or a compiler, which converts a *source program* written in one language into another language, such as machine language, capable of being executed on a given computer.

This output may be in one of several forms: It may be in an intermediate language, needing further translating; it may be *relocatable*, in which data and program references are still expressed relative to a base address; or it may be *absolute*, in which all linkages between program elements have been made and absolute address assignments established so that the program is ready to be loaded and executed. Usage varies as to which of these may be called the *object program*. In some sense, any output of a translating program is the object of that step, and hence is an object program, but the term is most often used to denote a binary file that, after *linking* to other binary files, is ready for direct execution (*see* LINKER).

CHARLES H. DAVIDSON

OCR.   *See* OPTICAL CHARACTER READERS.

OEM. *See* ORIGINAL EQUIPMENT MANUFACTURER.

OFFICE AUTOMATION. *See* ELECTRONIC OFFICE.

ONE-LEVEL MEMORY

For articles on related subjects *see* ADDRESSING; CACHE MEMORY; MEMORY; STORAGE HIERARCHY; and VIRTUAL MEMORY.

A *one-level memory* is a computer memory in which all stored items are accessed by a uniform mechanism. In computer systems that possess such a memory, the programmer is relieved from considerations of data residence and does not have to be concerned with I/O manipulations to access data that is stored on auxiliary memory devices. This is in contrast to the more common situation in which the programmer has to distinguish between data resident in main memory and auxiliary memory and has to monitor in the program all the changes of residence for each data item and program module.

One-level memories and the mechanisms provided to implement them are related to *virtual memories*. However, virtual memories are introduced only to provide a user with an apparently larger main memory space. Thus, in using a virtual memory, the programmer is not relieved of the need to be cognizant of auxiliary devices for the reading and writing of files. Another major difference between a virtual memory and a one-level memory is in the protection mechanisms, as will be explained below.

One-level memories and the access mechanisms associated with them can be implemented in various ways. The hardware support for the implementation is usually a memory hierarchy in which physical memories built of different technologies and possessing different access and storage characteristics are connected together. The choice of sizes and technologies usually reflects the price/performance criteria chosen by the implementor, and typically constitutes a range starting from a small but very high speed memory (e.g. a cache) through larger fast memory (e.g. main memory) and through still larger medium-speed memories (e.g. extended memories) into high-volume pseudo-random access devices (e.g. disks), and in some cases into a very large but slow archival device. To construct a one-level memory from such a hierarchy requires the addition of hardware, firmware (*q.v.*), and software, which then allows the user to access the entire memory hierarchy in a uniform manner.

Since a one-level memory access mechanism replaces regular I/O to peripheral devices, it has to include in it those protection mechanisms that are available in file access systems. Therefore, one-level addressing is more complex as well as more powerful than regular memory addressing. It typically relies on the division of the whole addressing space into *segments*, each of which possesses its own protection and access characteristics. In particular, one-level memory is well suited to *capability*-type addressing, in which the access rights of each process are matched with the execution and access characteristics of other processes, data items, or devices. One-level memories are thus ideal candidates for accessing data in a highly secure operating system.

Reference

1972. Organick, E. I. *The Multics System: An Examination of its Structure,* Cambridge, MA: M.I.T. Press.

GIDEON FRIEDER

OPEN AND CLOSE A FILE

For articles on related subjects *see* BLOCK AND BLOCKING FACTOR; FILE; INPUT-OUTPUT CONTROL SYSTEM; LOGICAL AND PHYSICAL UNITS; and SCRATCH FILE.

A file is considered *open* when it may be accessed for reading, writing, or possibly both. It is considered *closed* when it cannot be so accessed. An open routine changes the state of a file from closed to open; a close routine does the opposite.

The open and close routines are the primary mechanisms by which various parameters in the logical device tables and physical device tables are initialized, or stored, and the associations between logical and physical device tables are maintained. The open and close routines also handle the initialization and update of tape and file labels. After the open routines have been executed, all data needed for further processing is available in the appropriate table. When a file has been closed, the file is in a state suitable for subsequent reopening.

When a program opens a data file, it often declares a number of attributes that the file will have. It is the responsibility of the open routines to initialize the proper table entries to reflect the declared attributes. For example, a file typically may be opened for reading only, writing only, or in some cases for both reading and writing (update). As another example, most systems allow a programmer to create a *scratch file* for temporary storage of data. In such cases, the temporary file will be destroyed at the end of the job or interactive session.

Upon receipt of a request to open an existing permanent file, the open routines must first find the file, which usually involves the accessing of the system directories. In MS/DOS, for example, the device name (A:, B:, C: etc) must often be supplied to resolve ambiguity. With indexed sequential files where the index is to be kept in main storage, the open routines will locate the index and read it into an internal buffer. If the file has been declared as temporary, then the open routines will interact with the secondary storage allocation routines to reserve space for the data that will be saved.

The next task is one of label verification and initialization of logical and physical device tables with parameters that are carried in the file description block. These parameters will be copied to the proper fields in the logical and physical device tables.

The open routines will also set the read/write/update status so that subsequent requests can be checked for validity. If the file is to be written, then a fresh directory entry must be created, giving the date written, the edition number (multiple copies of files with the same name are updated by editions, much like newspapers), and other pertinent data.

File directory information is stored with the file and gives information concerning blocking factors, storage allocation, and storage organization. The storage organization information will often be complex. For example, the strategy to be used when storing new records that might not fit in a given storage area (*overflow policies*) would be part of the file control information for some files stored on a disk.

The routines to close a file have a number of tasks to perform before the file is ready for subsequent reopening. First, some of the data that has been logically "written" may still reside in a buffer because the buffer was not full and no physical "write" had yet been generated. The close routines will cause actual transfer of data to the recording medium. For this reason, closing a file that was open for writing—and doing so prior to the end of program execution—is much more important than closing a file that was merely opened for reading. If the file resides on tape, an end-of-file marker and perhaps also an end-of-file label will then be written. Alternatively, if the file is on a direct-access device, the close routine will restore indices and file directory information, updating such parameters as the size of the file in bytes. Closing a temporary file usually results in the release of the allotted file space.

When the file is on tape, the closing routines may or may not rewind the file; often the programmer specifies which option is desired. If the file is rewound, then subsequent reopening causes the first record of the previously closed file to be processed. If not, the next file on the tape will be processed on the subsequent opening.

Closing a file also results in the logical device table for the appropriate logical device being restored to a state that indicates that there is no file currently attached to this device. This allows subsequent requests on the logical device to be invalidated.

ROBERT W. TAYLOR

OPEN ARCHITECTURE

For articles on related subjects *see* BIOS; BUS; DIGITAL COMPUTERS: HISTORY: IBM-PC AND PC-COMPATIBLES; MOTHERBOARD; and PERSONAL COMPUTING.

A peripheral device made by one computer vendor can always be attached to a computer made by another through use of cabling whose terminal connections are compatible with the host computer. Such plug-to-plug compatible peripherals have been marketed since the 1960s and, at the mainframe level, once provided a major component of the revenues of the Control Data Corporation (*q.v.*). The term *open architecture*, in contrast, is of more recent vintage and pertains primarily to personal computers. An open architecture is one that allows insertion of additional logic cards to the interior of the computer chassis beyond those used with the most primitive configuration of the system. This is done by inserting the cards into *slots* in the computer's *motherboard*, the main logic board that holds its central processing unit (CPU - *q.v.*) and memory chips. A computer vendor who adopts such a design knows full well that, since the electronic characteristics of the motherboard slots will be public knowledge, other vendors who wish to do so can design and market customized logic cards. The rationale is that the greater variety of cards marketed, the greater will be sales of the host computer itself. The logic cards provide a host of services, such as one form of hard disk (*q.v.*), greater degrees of color graphics resolution, supplemental memory, and enhanced floating-point processing power through use of *coprocessor* boards.

Interestingly, a reversal of position with regard to the merits of an open architecture has played a significant role in the commercial history of Apple Computer (*q.v.*). Its initial, highly successful products, the Apple I and II (particularly the latter) used an open architecture, whereas its Macintosh line uses a closed architecture. Just as significantly, at just about the time of introduction of the Macintosh, IBM brought out its PC, which was based on an open architecture. The combination of open architecture and a bus and BIOS system that were easy to reverse-engineer led to the marketing of a plethora of IBM-PC compatibles that, perhaps more than any other factor, led to the rapid growth of personal computing. The Macintosh, which is very difficult to clone, has also enjoyed sales success, but not to the same degree as the aggregate of PC-compatible products. Those who are watching to see what kind of computer will emerge from the joint IBM-Apple Taligent venture announced in 1991 are hopeful that the product will capitalize on Apple's expertise with graphical user interfaces (GUIs) while maintaining IBM's commitment to an open architecture.

EDWIN D. REILLY

OPEN SYSTEMS INTERCONNECTION (OSI)

For articles on related subjects *see* COMMUNICATIONS AND COMPUTERS; DATA COMMUNICATIONS; NETWORK PROTOCOLS; and PROTOCOL.

Two computer systems can communicate successfully only if they are prepared to use the same set of communication *protocols* (*q.v.*). If machines from different manufacturers each use a set of communication protocols designed by their manufacturer, they will not generally be able to communicate. Each machine could, in principle, be provided with facilities for translating foreign protocols, but if the range of systems involved is large, this becomes a burdensome task.

The alternative is for all machines to use the same set of protocols so that no translation is needed. The objec-

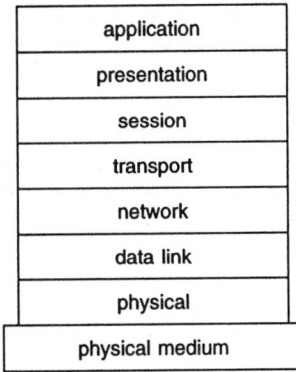

application
presentation
session
transport
network
data link
physical
physical medium

FIG. 1. The seven OSI protocol layers.

tive of the *open systems interconnection* (OSI) is to create such a single set of standard protocols, drawing on the best features of existing practice. Use of the OSI protocols thus opens the possibility of communication between any two computer systems, regardless of their origin.

The term "open" is used here in the sense of freedom from technical barriers to communication. The decision as to what information should be communicated and when communication should take place must be taken by the owner of each system, and the OSI standards include the facilities to provide the security mechanisms that may be necessary.

The OSI standards define only the protocols between systems. They do not constrain the internal structure of the systems that use them, because to do so would limit the freedom of the vendors to improve their designs. Thus, the same protocol may be used to convey information between systems with totally different internal structures and user interfaces. In testing that a system conforms to the published standard, only the data that flows between them is considered.

The work to create the set of OSI standards was begun by the International Standards Organization in 1978. The first step was the creation of the OSI Reference Model, the communication architecture that provides a framework for the various component standards making up the OSI family of protocols. This was followed by a series of standards for the individual members of the family, which were published one by one throughout the 1980s.

The OSI Reference Model divides the process of communication into a number of functional layers, splitting it up into pieces that are small enough to handle and specify separately. The layers build up from the underlying electrical signals transmitted to a much more abstract description of the user activity that exploits the communication. Two types of standards are defined for each layer. The first is a service definition, which states what the layer does on behalf of the layers above, so that higher layers are shielded from lower layer detail. The second is the protocol specification, which sets out how the layer performs its function, and achieves the service by defining the messages actually exchanged and the actions taken in consequence.

The OSI Reference Model defines seven layers of protocol (Fig. 1). Starting from the most abstract, these provide the following functions:

Level 7 The *application layer* performs the functions that are the reason for the communication. They are determined or selected by the enterprise using the network. Only some of these can be standardized.

Level 6 The *presentation layer* manages the problems of format and encoding between the two systems, providing a typed data channel.

Level 5 The *session layer* provides tools for the structuring of the dialogue between the two application entities.

Level 4 The *transport layer* handles problems of end-to-end reliability and quality of service.

Level 3 The *network layer* allows networks to be used in combination and handles problems of routing and switching.

Level 2 The *data link layer* provides an orderly error-free path between adjacent systems.

Level 1 The *physical layer* is concerned with electrical compatibility (or its equivalent in optical or radio transmission systems).

Reference

1988. Henshall, J. and Shaw, S. OSI Explained: End-to-End Computer Communication Standards. New York: Ellis Horwood.

PETER F. LININGTON

OPERAND

For articles on related subjects *see* ADDRESSING; ARGUMENT; COMPUTERS, MULTIPLE ADDRESS; EXPRESSION; and POLISH NOTATION.

An *operand* is an entity on which operations are performed. In a typical computer, an instruction will specify an operation such as FETCH, ADD, MOVE, MULTIPLY, EDIT, etc. It will also usually specify one or more operands (see Fig. 1). The operands are the data items that will be fetched, added, moved, multiplied, edited, etc.

In some special cases the operand itself may be contained in the instruction, in which case it is usually called *immediate*. Usually, the instruction contains a memory address, or a number of fields from which a memory address can be calculated. That memory address is then a pointer (*q.v.*) that points to the operand and that permits the operand to be retrieved.

Many computers provide single-precision arithmetic operations in which the operands are numbers stored in single computer words. Some provide double-precision or multiple-precision operations in which operands may occupy two, three, or more words each.

In many non-arithmetic operations (and even in some arithmetic ones), the operands are strings of characters (or bytes). The operand address points to the beginning of the string. The extent of the string may be specified in

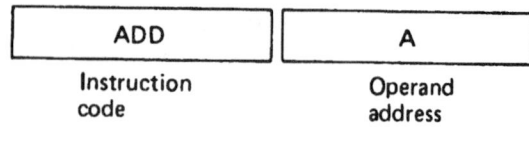

(Add the operand at address A to the accumulator.)

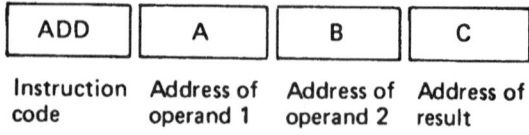

(Add the operand at A to the
operand at B and store the result at C.)

FIG. 1. Typical single operand and multiple operand computer instructions.

the instruction, but in many cases it is determined by a count field or by a termination code in the operand itself.

SAUL ROSEN

OPERATING SYSTEMS

For articles on related subjects *see* ACCOUNTING SYSTEM, COMPUTER; BOOT AND REBOOT; CACHE MEMORY; COMMAND AND JOB CONTROL LANGUAGE; CONCURRENT PROGRAMMING; DIRECTORY; DISTRIBUTED SYSTEMS; FILE SERVER; INTERRUPT; KERNEL; LOGIN FILE; MEMORY MANAGEMENT; MEMORY PROTECTION; MULTIPLEXING; MULTIPROCESSING; MULTIPROGRAMMING; MULTITASKING; PARALLEL PROCESSING; POLLING; PRIVILEGED INSTRUCTION; QUEUEING THEORY; SCHEDULING ALGORITHM; SHELL; SUPERVISOR CALL; SWAPPING; THRASHING; THROUGHPUT; TIME SHARING; UNIX OPERATING SYSTEM; USER INTERFACE; VIRTUAL MEMORY; WINDOW ENVIRONMENTS; and WORKING SET.

GENERAL PRINCIPLES

Introduction Early operating systems were control programs a few thousand bytes long that scheduled jobs, drove peripheral devices, and billed users. Modern operating systems are much larger, ranging from tens of thousands of bytes for personal computers (e.g. MS-DOS, Xenix) to tens of millions of bytes for mainframes (e.g. DEC's VMS, Honeywell's Multics, IBM's MVS, AT&T's Unix). Besides managing the hardware resources, such as processors, memory, and dozens of input/output devices, modern operating systems also provide numerous services, such as inter-process communication, file and directory systems, data transfer over networks, and a command language for invoking and controlling programs. Operating systems also hide the primitive facilities of the base computer, such as interrupts, status registers, and device interfaces, from the user. The operating system builds its high-level services by wrapping the low-level hardware facilities in layers of software, resulting in

a powerful virtual machine that is much easier to use than the bare hardware. Thus, an *operating system* can be defined as "a set of software extensions of primitive hardware, culminating in a virtual machine that serves as a high-level programming environment and manages the flow of work within a network of computers."

The virtual machine visible to the user is only the outermost of a series of software layers refining the base hardware. The principle behind the layered architecture is called *information hiding (q.v.)*—confining the details of managing a class of "objects" to within a module that has a good interface with its users. With information hiding, designers can protect themselves from extensive reprogramming if the hardware or some part of the software changes: the change affects only the small portion of the software interfacing directly with that system component. By nesting these modules, we create a hierarchy of levels of abstraction so that at any level we can ignore the details of what is going on at all lower levels. At the highest level are system users who, ideally, are insulated from everything except what they want to accomplish. Operating systems structured in this way can support diverse environments: programming, text processing, real-time processing, office automation, database, and hobbyist. We will use the idea of virtual machine layering and information hiding when discussing the design of operating systems.

Current Operating Systems Most operating systems for large mainframes are direct descendants of third-generation systems, such as Honeywell Multics, IBM VMS and VM/370, and CDC Scope. These systems introduced important concepts, such as time sharing, multiprogramming, virtual memory, sequential processes cooperating via semaphores, hierarchical file systems, and device-independent I/O (Denning 1971, 1976).

During the 1960s, many projects were established to construct time-sharing systems and test several new operating systems concepts. These included M.I.T.'s Compatible Time Sharing System (CTSS), the University of Cambridge Multiple Access System, IBM TSS/360, and the operating systems for the Manchester University Atlas and the RCA Spectra/70. The most ambitious project of all was Multics (short for Multiplexed Information and Computing Service) for the General Electric 645 processor (later renamed the Honeywell 6180) (Organick, 1972). Multics simultaneously tested new concepts of processes, interprocess communication, segmented virtual memory, and page replacement, linking new segments to a computation on demand, automatic multiprogrammed load control, access control, protection rings, hierarchical file system, device independence, I/O redirection, and a high-level language *shell*.

Perhaps the most influential current operating system is Unix, a complete re-engineering of Multics, originally developed at AT&T Bell Laboratories for the DEC PDP computers. Although an order of magnitude smaller than Multics, Unix retains most of its predecessor's useful characteristics, such as processes, hierarchical file system, device independence, I/O redirection, and a high-level language shell. Unix dispensed with virtual memory (though it was later added) and the detailed protection system. It introduced the *pipe*. It offered a large library of utility programs that were well integrated with the command language. Most of Unix is written in the high-level language C (*q.v.*), allowing it to be transported to a wide variety of processors from mainframes to personal computers (Ritchie and Thompson, 1974; Kernighan and Pike, 1984).

In systems with multiple Unix machines connected by a high-speed local network, it is desirable to hide the locations of files, users, and devices from those who do not wish to deal with those details. Locus, an IBM-owned distributed version of Unix, satisfies this need through a directory hierarchy that spans the entire network (Popek *et al.*, 1981).

In the 1980s, a large family of operating systems were developed for personal computers, including MS-DOS, PC-DOS, Apple-DOS, CP/M, Coherent, and Xenix. All these systems were of limited function, being initially designed for 8- and 16-bit microprocessor chips with small memories. In many respects, the growth pattern of personal computers repeated that of mainframes in the early 1960s—e.g. multiprocessor operating systems for microcomputers appeared only late in the 1980s, mostly as Unix variants. Processor speeds and memories of personal computers are now sufficient to support full-fledged operating systems.

With multiprocessors and computer networks in the early 1980s, operating systems began to manage the resources of multiple computers at once. An early example is StarOS, an operating system for the CM* (pronounced "CM star") machine, a multicomputer consisting of several dozen individual computers linked by a special network; StarOS supports the "task force," a group of processes cooperating in a distributed computation (Jones *et al.*, 1979). Medusa, another operating system for CM*, is composed of several "utilities," each of which implements a particular abstraction, such as a file system; there is no central control (Ousterhout *et al.*, 1980).

Xerox's Grapevine, a distributed database and message delivery system, contains special *nameservers* that can locate users, groups, and other services when given their symbolic names. Because Grapevine has no central control, it can survive failures of the nameserver machines (Bitrell *et al.*, 1982). Because it does not provide a high-level programming environment, it is not a true operating system.

Established, single-machine operating systems, such as Unix and DEC's VMS evolved to accommodate networks of computers. Such operating systems typically support standards for accessing files on remote servers from any machine in a network. Sun's Network File System (NFS) was one of the first widely available Unix-based file systems that provided a single filename space on top of a network of servers and workstations (Sandberg *et al.*, 1985). Carnegie-Mellon's Andrew system provides a Unix-based network file system that spans more than 5,000 computers around the campus; it allows users to access files without having to know their locations, and it improves performance by caching whole files at individual nodes in the network (Howard *et al.*, 1986). The Mach operating system, also developed at Carnegie-Mellon University, handles a variety of distributed system operations, including a uniform file name space, a virtual shared computational memory, and multiprocessing; it is compatible with Unix (Accetta *et al.*, 1986; Rashid *et al.*, 1988). Many of these systems rely on a remote procedure call facility within the operating system to support operations distributed among many machines.

With massively parallel computers containing thousands and more processors, new challenges arise. Operating systems for these machines must support extremely fast synchronization and communication among thousands of processes. Each processor may have its own devices attached, and hence the operating system must control thousands of I/O channels at once. The concepts of virtual memory and time-sharing must be extended to accommodate massive parallelism. Perhaps the most important challenge is that the programming environment should permit parallel programs to be written with only modest effort beyond that required for sequential ones (Denning and Tichy, 1990). Current operating systems research addresses these problems.

A Model Operating System

Overview In the hierarchical structure of a model operating system, functions are separated according to their characteristic time scales and their levels of abstraction.

Table 1 shows an organization spanning 14 levels. It is not a model of any particular operating system, but rather exhibits the relationships among the functions present in most operating systems.

Each level is the manager of a set of objects, either hardware or software, the nature of which varies greatly from level to level. Each level also defines operations that can be carried out on those objects, obeying two general rules:

Hierarchy—Each level adds new operations to the machine and hides selected operations at lower levels. The operations visible at a given level form the instruction set of an abstract machine. Hence, a program written at a given level can invoke visible operations at all lower levels, but not operations on higher levels.

Information hiding—The details of how an object is represented or where it is stored are hidden within the level responsible for that type. Hence, no part of an object can be changed, except by applying an authorized operation to it.

The principle of data abstraction embodied in the levels model traces back to Dennis and Van Horn's 1966 paper, which emphasized a simple interface between users and the kernel. The first instance of a working operating system with a kernel spanning several levels was reported by Dijkstra in 1968. The idea has been extended to generate families of operating systems for related machines (Habermann *et al.*, 1976) and to increase the portability of an operating system kernel (Cheriton,

TABLE 1. An Operating System Design Hierarchy

Level	Name	Objects	Example Operations
14	Shell	User programming environment, data structures	Statements in shell language
13	Directories	Directories	Create, destroy, attach, detach, search, get
12	User processes	User process	Fork, suspend, resume, kill
11	Stream I/O	Streams	Open, close, read, write
10	Devices	External devices, including printers, displays, keyboards	Create, destroy, open, close, read, write
9	File system	Files	Create, destroy, open, close, read, write
8	Communications	Pipes	Create, destroy, open, close, read, write
7	Virtual memory	Addresses, segments	Create, destroy, map
6	Local secondary	Blocks of data, devices	Read, write, allocate, free store
5	Primitive processes	Primitive process, semaphores, ready list	Fork, suspend, resume, wait, signal, kill
4	Interrupts	Interrupt vectors, fault-handler programs	Invoke, mask, unmask, retry
3	Procedures	Procedure segments, call stacks, displays	Mark stack, call, return
2	Instruction set	Evaluation stacks, memory arrays	Load, store, index, unary and binary operators, etc.
1	Electronic circuits	Registers, gates, busses, etc.	Clear, transfer, complement, etc.

1982). The Provably Secure Operating System (PSOS) is the first complete level-structured system reported and formally proved correct in the open literature (Neumann *et al.*, 1982).

Single-machine Levels: 1–7 Levels 1 through 7 are called "single-machine levels" because their operations are well understood from single-machine operating systems and require little modification for multi-machine operating systems. A single machine may contain one or several processors that share a common memory. A multi-machine consists of several, physically separate computer systems, each of which has its own processor(s) and private memory. There is no shared memory among the separate computers in a multi-machine; instead, they are connected by a communications network.

The lowest levels include the hardware and firmware of the system. Level 1 is the electronic circuitry, where objects are registers, gates, memory cells, and the like, and operations are clearing registers, reading memory cells, and the like. Level 2 adds the instruction set, which can deal with somewhat more abstract entities, such as evaluation stacks and arrays of memory locations. Level 3 adds the procedure and the operations for call and return. Level 4 introduces interrupts and a mechanism for invoking special procedures when the processor receives an interrupt signal.

The first four levels correspond roughly to the basic machine as it is received from the manufacturer, although there is some interaction with the operating system. For example, interrupts are generated by hardware, but the interrupt-handler routines are part of the operating system.

Level 5 adds primitive *processes*, which are simply single programs in the course of execution. The information required to specify a primitive process is its *stateword*, a data structure that can hold the values of the registers in a processor. This level provides a context switch operation, which transfers a processor's attention from one process to another by saving the stateword of the first and loading the stateword of the second. A scheduler in this level selects, from a "ready list" of available processes, the next process to run after a process is switched off its processor. This level also provides *semaphores*, the special variables used to cause one process to stop and wait until another process has signalled the completion of a task. Primitive processes are analogous to "system processes" in PSOS, "lightweight processes" in Locus, and "threads" in Mach.

Level 6 handles the access to the secondary storage devices of a particular machine. The programs at this level are responsible for operations such as positioning the head of a disk drive and transferring blocks of data. Software at a higher level determines the address of the data on the disk and places requests for it in the device's queue of pending work; the requesting process then waits at a semaphore until the transfer has been completed.

Level 7 implements a virtual memory, a scheme that gives the programmer the illusion of having a main memory space large enough to hold the program and all its data even if the available memory is much smaller (Denning, 1970). Software at this level handles the interrupts generated by the hardware when a block of data is addressed that is not in the main memory; this software locates the missing block in the secondary store, frees space for it in the main store, and requests level 6 to read in the missing block.

Multi-machine Levels: 8–14 Through level 7, the operating system deals exclusively with the resources of a single machine. At the next level, however, the operating system begins to encompass a larger world, including peripheral devices such as terminals and printers, as well as other computers attached to the network. In this world, pipes, files, devices, user processes, and directories can be shared among all the machines.

Level 8 is concerned with communication between processes, which can be arranged through a single mechanism called a pipe. A *pipe* is a one-way channel: Data streams in one end and out the other. A request to read items is delayed until items are actually in the pipe. A pipe can connect two processes of the same machine or on different machines equally well. A set of pipes linking levels in all the machines can serve as a broadcast facility, which is useful for finding resources anywhere in the network. Pipes are implemented in Unix (Ritchie and Thompson, 1974) and have since been copied to other systems.

Level 9 provides for long-term storage of files. While level 6 deals with disk storage in terms of tracks and sectors—the physical units of the hardware—level 9 deals with more abstract entities of variable length. Indeed, a file may be scattered over many noncontiguous tracks and sectors. To be examined or updated, a file's contents must be copied between virtual memory and the secondary storage system. If a file is kept on a different machine, level 9 software can create a pipe to level 9 on the file's home machine to accomplish the transfer.

Level 10 provides access to external input and output devices, such as printers, plotters, and the keyboards and display screens of terminals. There is a standard interface with all these devices, and a pipe can be used to gain access to a device attached to another machine.

Level 11 provides a means of attaching user processes interchangeably to pipes, files, or I/O devices. The idea is to make each fundamental operation of levels 8, 9, and 10 (OPEN, CLOSE, READ, and WRITE) look the same so that the author of a program need not be concerned with the difference in these objects. This strategy has two parts. First, the information contained in pipes, files, and devices is regarded as streams of bytes; requests for reading or writing move segments of data between streams and user processes. Second, a user process is programmed to request all input and output via *ports* (*q.v.*), attached by the OPEN operation at run-time to specific pipes, files, or devices.

Level 12 implements user processes, which are virtual machines executing programs. It is important to distinguish the user process from the primitive process at level 5. All information required to define a primitive process can be expressed in a stateword that records the contents of the registers in a processor. A *user process* is a significant extension. It includes one or more primitive processes, a virtual memory containing the program and its workspace, a list of arguments supplied as parameters when the process was started, a list of objects with which the process can communicate, and certain other information about the context in which the process operates. A user process is called a "task" in Mach and a "process" in Unix.

Level 13 manages a hierarchy of directories that catalogs the hardware and software objects to which access must be controlled throughout the network: pipes, files, devices, user processes, and the directories themselves. The central concept of a directory is a table that matches external names of objects to internal names. An external name is a string of characters having some meaning to users; an internal name is a binary code used by the system to locate the object. The user controls mapping from external to internal names by directories. A hierarchy arises because a directory can include among its entries the names of subordinate directories.

The directory level is responsible only for recording the associations between the external and internal names; other levels manage the objects themselves. Thus, when a directory of devices is searched for the string "laser," the result returned is merely an internal name for the laser printer. The internal name must be passed to a program at level 10 which handles the actual transmission to that printer.

Level 14 is the *shell*, so called because it is the level that separates the user from the rest of the operating system. The shell interprets a high-level command language through which the user gives instructions to the system. Incorporating a listener program that responds to a terminal's keyboard, it parses each line of input to identify program names and parameters, creates and invokes a user process for each program, and connects those as needed to pipes, files, and devices. Many shells incorporate window managers that allow users to refer to objects by manipulating icons denoting those objects on the display screen and that allow objects to send and receive data from different regions of the display.

General Comments on Operating System Architecture

Level Structure The level structure is a hierarchy of functional specifications designed to impose a high degree of modularity and enable incremental software verification, installation, and testing.

In a functional hierarchy, a program at one level may directly call any visible operation of a lower level, with no information flows through any intermediate level. The level structure can be completely enforced by a compiler, which inserts procedure calls or expands functions in-line (Habermann *et al.*, 1976). A well-documented example of its use is XINU (Unix backwards), a distributed operating system for microcomputers (Comer, 1984).

It is important to distinguish the level structure discussed here from the layer structure of the International Standards Organization model of long-haul network protocols (Tanenbaum, 1981). In the ISO model, information is passed down through all the layers on the sending machine and back up through all the layers on the receiving machine (*see* OPEN SYSTEMS INTERCONNECTION). Since each layer adds delay to a data transmission whether or not that delay is required, long-haul network protocols may not be efficient in a local network (Popek *et al.*, 1981). A significant advantage of functional levels over information-transferring layers is efficiency: a program that does not use a given function will experience no overhead from that function's presence in the system.

Internal Names The external names of sharable objects are character strings of arbitrary length that have meaning to users. Because these strings are difficult to manipulate efficiently, the operating system provides internal names for quick access to objects. Whenever a program requests creation of an object, such as a user process, pipe, or file, the operating system returns an internal name for that object. The internal name is used to identify the object in subsequent calls. In its simplest form, an internal name is a pointer to the object or an index into a table of objects managed by a particular level. Internal names are usually called *handles*; we will use this term henceforth for brevity.

Handles can be implemented as pointers or indices on a single machine with shared memory. On a multi-machine with objects shared across a network, two extensions are necessary. First, handles are extended by adding extra bits to hold the identifier of the creating machine; this makes handles unique throughout the network.

Second, there must be search rules to locate objects, which may be moved to machines other than the ones on which they were created. Object managers must poll other machines during searches for objects. To speed up multiple accesses to the same object, an object manager can maintain a cache that notes the locations of recently requested objects. Policies of moving or replicating objects to requesting machines and updating caches were explored in the Purdue Ibis (Ruan and Tichy, 1987) and Carnegie-Mellon Andrew (Howard *et al.*, 1988) file systems, as well as in the Xerox Grapevine system (Birrell, 1982).

A further extension of handles leads to the capability concept. A capability is a handle, together with type and access codes. The additional codes prevent a process from applying invalid operations to an object with a known handle. Hardware protection of the codes allows capabilities to be passed to other processes while still controlling the access rights to the associated objects. Capabilities were explored, among others, in the Carnegie-Mellon Hydra system (Wulf *et al.*, 1981), the Cambridge CAP system (Wilkes and Needham, 1979), and the Intel iMax system (Organick, 1983). An operating system design incorporating a single level for managing distributed capabilities appears in Brown *et al.*, 1984. Capability-based operating systems are not common because none of the prototypes yielded sufficiently efficient designs.

Heterogenous Systems The systems discussed above deal with many computers on a network by running the same operating system on each machine, an approach often called *homogeneous distributed computing*. Since all the operating systems deal with similar structures and objects, sharing information and moving objects among them is straightforward.

The open system philosophy, now practiced by many manufacturers of hardware and software, aims for networks whose components can be supplied by different vendors and that will work together anyway because those vendors follow basic standards (*see* OPEN ARCHITECTURE and OPEN SYSTEMS INTERCONNECTION). These are often called *heterogenous distributed computing systems* because they may not have the same operating system or internal understanding of formats and structures.

It is very important, therefore, to have a firm understanding of the functions that must be provided by a network of cooperating computers. These functions are enumerated in the levels introduced in Table 1 and will be discussed in more detail below. All machines on the network will need to implement at least a standard level 5 so that they can communicate effectively. They may require translating filters to convert formats and structures as they are sent between machines with different operating systems.

Primitive Processes: Level 5 In this and the following subsections, we give some details about the operation and assumptions of the major levels of an operating system. We omit further discussion of levels 1–4 because they are well covered in other articles.

A primitive process is described by its stateword or statevector, (i.e. the contents of the processor registers). The set of registers includes not only the general-purpose registers holding intermediate results, but also the program counter plus any other registers such as condition codes and stack pointers that influence the execution of a program. The stateword must be loaded into a processor's registers to run the process.

A primitive process is in one of three states: running, ready, or suspended. In the running state, a process's stateword has been loaded into a processor's registers, and the processor executes the sequence of instructions addressed by the program counter. In the ready state, a process is waiting for a free processor. In the suspended state, the process is blocked waiting for a condition to arise before being able to proceed; an example of such a condition is the completion of an I/O operation.

Operation P_FORK (see Table 2) creates a primitive process with a default stateword whose instruction pointer is set from the parameter passed to P_FORK. A primitive process is created in the suspended state. With P_RESUME, it is placed in the readylist, a data structure containing all primitive processes awaiting their turns for execution on a processor. The ready list is commonly organized as a priority queue, allowing fast lookup of the ready process with highest priority. When the currently running process has to wait for a condition, or a new process is added to the ready list with higher priority than the currently running one, then the operating system performs a context switch: it switches the running process off its processor by first unloading the processor registers, and then loads the stateword of the process with highest priority into the processor registers. A context switch changes the states of two processes.

The frequency of context switches and the setting of priorities are important parameters for the performance

TABLE 2. Specification of Primitive Process Level Interface (Level 5)

Form of Call	Effect
pproc_handle : = P_FORK(adr)	Creates a suspended, primitive process by allocating a stateword for it. Sets its program counter to adr and returns a handle to the process.
P_SUSPEND(pproc_handle)	Takes the given primitive process off the list of ready processes or off the processor and marks it as suspended; reschedules remaining processes. (Fails if the process is already suspended.)
P_RESUME(pproc_handle)	Adds the given primitive process to the list of ready processes and marks it as ready; reschedules processes if necessary. (Fails if the process is not suspended.)
P_KILL(pproc_handle)	Destroys the given primitive process (Undoes P_FORK).
sem_handle : = CREATE_SEM(val)	Creates a semaphore with val as initial counter value and an empty waiting list.
WAIT(sem_handle)	Decrements the counter of the given semaphore. If the counter is now negative, WAIT suspends the invoking process, enqueues it on the semaphore's waiting list, and reschedules remaining processes.
SIGNAL(sem_handle)	Increments the counter of the given semaphore, removes a process from the semaphore's waiting list (if not empty) and resumes that process.
DESTROY_SEM(sem_handle)	Destroys the given semaphore (undoes CREATE_SEM).

of an operating system: The former specifies how often other processes are given a chance to run and the second determines which ones are selected most often.

Process priorities are partly set by the operating system and partly by the users. Processes that must react to time-critical situations, such as interrupts from high-speed I/O devices, have highest priority. The lowest priority of all is assigned to the idle process. The idle process consists of an infinite loop of no-ops (empty instructions) and enters the running state only if there is no other ready process. The idle process is needed because processors cannot normally be turned on and off quickly. The priorities of other processes are set between these two extremes. Processes that involve a great deal of user interaction, as in a time-sharing system, obtain a relatively high priority, while background or compute-intensive jobs are assigned a lower priority.

In order to prevent any one process from monopolizing the processor, most operating systems implement *time slicing*, a policy of limiting the maximum period during which a process may run continuously. When a process begins a period of execution, a timer in the processor is set to a standard value. When it reaches zero, the timer generates an interrupt. The interrupt handler performs a context switch to another ready process.

Requests for I/O are the most common events generated by processes. A typical I/O request has a simple form: The process specifies the I/O operation with a memory address, a device address, and a size, and it sends a start signal to the device; the device performs a data transfer of the given size between the memory and device addresses; and the device sends a completion signal to the process. The usual mechanism to implement the wait for the completion signal is a *semaphore* (*see* CONCURRENT PROGRAMMING). In the case of an I/O operation, a sema-

phore is a data structure that consists of a waiting bit plus a location to hold the name of a waiting process. The job of the interrupt handler that receives the device completion signal is to reset the waiting bit to zero and place the waiting process's name in the ready list.

There are many instances of process coordination that allow more than one process to be waiting for an event—e.g. several processes can be stopped while a shared file is locked during an update. To deal with these cases, as well as I/O, a more general semaphore is used: It contains a counter (rather than a waiting bit) and a queue (rather than the name of a single waiting process). A semaphore acts like a barrier that lets only a certain number of processes pass. If its counter is positive, one process may pass, reducing the count by one; when the count is zero or less, further processes will be stopped and their names added to the queue. The operation WAIT implements the testing of the counter and the queueing, while the operation SIGNAL increases the counter and lets waiting processes pass (see Table 2 for exact specifications).

Semaphores are a practical way to avoid *busy waiting*, in which a process enters a loop testing a lock until the lock is reset by another process. By avoiding busy waiting, the operating system assures that most processor cycles are devoted to useful work.

A simple application of SIGNAL and WAIT is the implementation of a critical region or critical section. A *critical region* is a segment of instructions accessing data that must be executed by only one process at a time. Were two or more processes allowed access at once, they could produce results that depend on their relative speeds. For example, if two teller machines try to add deposits to the same account at once, one of the deposits will be lost and the balance will depend on which deposit was entered

TABLE 3. Specification of Local Secondary Store (Level 6)

Form of Call	Effect
(B,L) : = ALLOC(size)	Return the base and length of a free segment of memory of the given size (L = size).
FREE((B,L))	Return the segment (B,L) to the pool of free space in memory.
dev_handle : = CREATE_DEV(spec)	Add the specification of a new device to the device table.
DESTROY_DEV(dev_handle)	Free up the entry occupied by the given device in the device table.
READ_SEG((B,L), dev_handle, dev_addr, size)	Copy min (L,size) bytes from the device, starting at address dev_addr, to the segment of memory starting at base B.
WRITE_SEG((B,L), dev_handle, dev_addr, size)	Copy min(L,size) bytes from the segment of memory at base B to the device starting at address dev_addr.

last. The critical region implements exclusive access thus:

```
WAIT(mutex)
    access to shared data
SIGNAL(mutex)
```

In order to limit the number of processes accessing the shared data to at most one, the counter of the semaphore mutex must be initialized to 1.

Local Secondary Store: Level 6 This level deals with simple transfers of blocks of information between devices and the main store. The segment of main store acting as one end of the transmission is specified by a two-part descriptor (B,L), giving the base address and length. As shown in Table 3, the operations ALLOC and FREE create and remove memory segments.

Each device has a detailed specification giving its hardware address, speed and bandwidth parameters, error parameters, etc. The set of all device specifications are stored in a *device table* in a segment of memory. The operations CREATE_DEV and DESTROY_DEV are used to add and remove entries from this table.

A device-to-memory transfer is initiated by a READ_SEG operation. It copies a number of bytes given by a size parameter from the device to a segment of memory. Simi-larly, a WRITE_SEG operation carries out a memory-to-device transfer by copying a specified number of bytes from a memory segment to the device.

Virtual Memory: Level 7 *Virtual memory* is a simulation of an address space that is fully resident in the main store. To accomplish this simulation, the operating system must provide means to map virtual addresses to main memory addresses. A mapping failure generates an interrupt that causes the operating system to locate a missing block in the secondary store, transfer it into the main store, and update the mapping table so that the map operation will succeed when retried. The principal operations are shown in Table 4.

Communications: Level 8 The communications level provides a single mechanism, the pipe, for moving information from a writer process to a reader process on the same or different machines. The most important property of a pipe is that a reader must stop and wait until a writer has put enough data into the pipe to fill the request. Level 8 gives the higher levels the ability to move objects among the nodes of the network.

Specifications for six pipe operations are outlined in Table 5. There are commands to create and delete pipes.

TABLE 4. Specification of Virtual Memory (Level 7)

Form of Call	Effect
vm_handle : = CREATE_VM(size, dev_addr, dev_handle)	Create a new virtual memory of given size, initialized to the contents of the given secondary storage device at the given device address.
DESTROY_VM(vm_handle)	Delete the given virtual memory and free up space it occupied in the secondary storage system.
A : = MAP (V, vm_handle)	Translate the virtual address V generated by a processor into an address A in the main store, using the mapping table of the given virtual memory. If the mapping table says that the block containing V is not present, generate a mapping fault (the fault handler will move the missing block into memory, update the table, and retry the MAP operation).

TABLE 5. *Specification of Communications Level Interface (Level 8)*

Form of Call	Effect
pipe_handle : = CREATE_PIPE( )	Creates a new empty pipe and returns a handle for it. (If the caller is a user process, it can store the handle in a directory entry and make the pipe available throughout the system.)
opipe_handle : = OPEN_PIPE(pipe_handle, rw)	Opens the given pipe by allocating buffer storage and performing setup operations. Initially, the pipe is empty. If rw = write (rw can be read or write), the pipe is enabled for writing, otherwise, for reading. The operation returns immediately; it fails if the pipe has already been opened with the same rw parameter. If both sender and receiver are on the same machine, shared memory may be used for the pipe; otherwise, a network protocol must be used.
READ_PIPE(opipe_handle, buf, n)	Waits until there are at least n bytes in the open pipe, then moves them from the pipe into segment buf. (Fails if the open pipe does not permit reading.) May awaken waiting writer.
WRITE_PIPE(opipe_handle, buf, n)	Causes the first n bytes of segment buf to be transmitted over the given open pipe. (Fails if the open pipe does not permit writing.) May awaken waiting reader.
CLOSE_PIPE(opipe_handle)	Undoes OPEN_PIPE. If pipe contains a waiting reader, returns to that reader the remaining segment in the pipe.
DESTROY_PIPE(pipe_handle)	Destroys the given pipe (undoes the corresponding CREATE_PIPE).

A pipe handle can be passed to another machine (over an existing open pipe) for later use by a companion process on that machine; a pipe handle can also be listed in the directory hierarchy, whereupon the pipe becomes accessible throughout the system. There are commands to open and close pipes: the sender and receiver must each open the pipe; at most, one sender and one receiver are allowed. And there are read and write commands for moving a segment of information across the pipe.

When two communicating processes are on the same machine, a pipe between them can be stored in shared memory, and the READ_PIPE and WRITE_PIPE operations are implemented in the same way as SEND and RECEIVE operations for message queues (Brinch Hansen, 1973). When the two processes are on different machines, the communications level must implement the network protocols required to move information reliably between machines (Fig. 1). These protocols are much simpler than long-haul protocols, because congestion and routing protocols are not needed, packets cannot be received out of order, fewer error types are possible, and errors are less common. (Popek *et al.*, 1981).

The semantics of READ and WRITE operations must be defined even if one end of the pipe is not connected. Should a writer be blocked from entering information until the reader opens its end? What happens if either the reader or writer breaks its connection? Questions like these are answered by a *connection protocol*. A simple connection protocol, called *rendezvous* on open and close, has the following properties:

- The open-for-reading and the open-for-writing request may be called at different times, but both returns are immediate.

- The CLOSE operation, executed by the reader, shuts both ends of the pipe; when executed by the writer, the operation is deferred until the reader empties the pipe.

A network protocol must be used when two processes connected by a pipe are on different machines. The WRITE_PIPE requests that the sender append segments to a stream awaiting transmission. The sender process transmits the stream as a sequence of packets, which are converted back into a stream and placed in the receiving buffer. Each READ_PIPE request of the receiver waits until

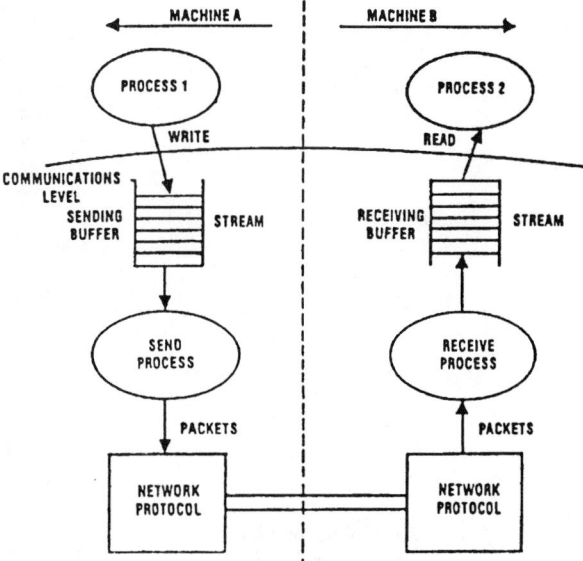

FIG. 1.   Two processes connected by a pipe.

the requested amount of data is in the buffer, and then returns it.

Files: Level 9

Level 9 implements a long-term store for files, named strings of bytes of known but arbitrary length that are accessible from all machines in the network. Table 6 summarizes file operations.

To establish a connection with a file, a process must present a file handle to the OPEN_FILE operation, which will find the file in secondary storage and allocate buffers for transmissions between the file and the caller. The transmissions themselves are requested by READ_FILE and WRITE_FILE operations. Each READ_FILE operation copies a segment of information from the file to the caller's virtual memory and advances a read pointer by the length of the segment. Each WRITE_FILE operation copies a segment from the caller's virtual memory into the file, beginning with the position indicated by the file's write pointer. OPEN_FILE initializes the read pointer to the beginning and the write pointer to the end of the file. The SEEK_FILE operation can change the read and write pointers to allow for random (non-sequential) file access.

In a multi-machine system, the file level must deal with the problems of non-local files. When a process on one machine requests to open a file stored on another machine, there are two feasible alternatives:

- Remote Open—Open a pair of pipes to level 9 on the file's home machine; READ_FILE and WRITE_FILE requests are relayed via the forward pipe for remote execution; results are passed back over the reverse pipe. The open-file handle returned by the command OPEN_FILE must point to a descriptor block that indicates that READ_FILE and WRITE_FILE operations must interact with a surrogate process on another machine. Examples are the Berkeley Cocanet System (Rowe and Bitman, 1982) and the Network Filesystem (NFS) (Sandberg *et al.*, 1985).

- File Migration/Replication—Move or replicate the file from its current machine to the machine on which the file is being opened; all READ_FILE and WRITE_FILE operations are local thereafter. In case of write operations, the file level also has to send messages to outdate replicates. Examples are Purdue's Ibis (Ruan and Tichy, 1987) and CMU's Andrew (Howard *et al.*, 1988).

One important improvement to the basic file system is to allow multiple readers and writers by building into READ_FILE and WRITE_FILE operations a solution to the "readers and writers" problem (Holt, 1978). Another is to use a version control system to retain automatically different versions of a file; the file system can then provide access to the older versions when needed (Tichy, 1985).

Devices: Level 10

The devices level implements a common interface to a wide range of external I/O devices, including terminal displays and keyboards, printers, plotters, time-of-day clock, and optical readers. The interface attempts to hide differences in devices by making input devices appear as sources of data streams and output devices as sinks. Obviously, the differences cannot be completely hidden—cursor-positioning commands must be embedded in the data stream sent to a graphic display, for example—but a substantial degree of uniformity is possible.

TABLE 6.   Specification of Files Level Interface (Level 9)

Form of Call	Effect
file_handle : = CREATE_FILE( )	Creates an empty file and returns a handle for it. (If the caller is a user process, it can store the handle in a directory entry and make the file available throughout the system.)
ofile_handle: = OPEN_FILE(file_handle, rw)	Opens the given file by allocating buffer storage and performing setup operations. The file is enabled for reading, writing, or both, depending on the value of rw. The read pointer r is set to zero, and the write pointer w to l (file length). (Fails if the file is already open).
READ_FILE(ofile_handle, buf, n)	Sets $m : = \min(l - r, n)$. Copies m bytes from the given file, starting with position r, into segment buf. Updates l to $l + m$. (Fails if reading is not enabled.)
WRITE_FILE(ofile_handle, buf, n)	Copies the first n bytes of segment buf into the given file, starting with position w. Sets $l : = \max(l, w + n)$; $w : = w + n$: (Fails if writing is not enabled.)
SEEK_FILE(ofile_handle, pos, rw)	Stores the value of pos into the read pointer n, the write pointer w, or both, depending on the value of rw. (Fails if pos is larger than file length l.)
ERASE_FILE(ofile_handle)	Sets file length, read and write pointers to zero; releases secondary storage blocks occupied by the file. (Fails if writing not enabled.)
CLOSE_FILE(ofile_handle)	Undoes OPEN_FILE.
DESTROY_FILE(file_handle)	Destroys the given file (undoes the corresponding CREATE_FILE).

Corresponding to each device is a device driver program that translates commands at the interface into instructions for operating that device. A considerable amount of effort may be required to construct a reliable, robust device driver. When a new device is attached to the system, its physical address is stored in a special file accessible to device drivers.

Table 7 summarizes the interface for external devices. It is similar to the interface for files and pipes, except that SEEK and ERASE operations are unavailable.

Stream I/O: Level 11 An important principle adopted in many operating systems is I/O independence. At levels 8, 9, and 10, the same fundamental operations (namely OPEN, CLOSE, READ, and WRITE) are defined for pipes, files, and devices. Although writing a block of data to disk requires a sequence of events quite different from that needed to supply the same data to a printer or to the input of another program, the author of a program does not need to be concerned with these differences. All READ and WRITE statements in a program can refer to I/O ports, which are attached to particular files, pipes, or devices only when the program is executed.

This strategy, an instance of delayed *binding*, can greatly increase the versatility of a program. A library program (such as the pattern-finding "grep" program in Unix) can take its input from a file or directly from a terminal and can send its output to another file, to a terminal, to a window on a screen, or to a printer. In particular, a screen window can receive the output, provided that it is managed by a process that receives data via a pipe. Without delayed binding, each program would have to be written to handle each possible combination of source and destination.

A common model of data must be used for pipes, files, and devices. The simplest possibility is the stream model in which these objects are media for holding streams of bits. Corresponding to each of these objects is a pair of pointers—r for reading and w for writing; r counts the number of bytes read thus far and w counts those written thus far. Each READ request begins at position r and advances r by the number of bytes read. Similarly, each WRITE request begins at position w and advances w by the number of bytes written.

Because the stream model has already been incorporated into the pipes, files, and devices levels, the only new mechanism involves a method of switching from a level 11 operation to its counterpart in the level for the type of object given.

For example, OPEN(handle, rw) is defined as

```
CASE typeof(handle) OF
   pipe: RETURN OPEN_PIPE(handle,rw);
   file: RETURN OPEN_FILE(handle,rw);
   dev:  RETURN OPEN_DEV(handle,rw);
   ELSE: error;
END CASE
```

All that is needed is a facility for deriving the type of a handle. The other three operations at this level—READ, WRITE, and CLOSE, are analogous.

The stream model is not used in every operating system. For example, in Multics, because segments in virtual memory are retained indefinitely until deleted explicitly, a separate concept of file is not needed (Organick, 1972). Permanent data is simply stored in segments, and the four operations above are implicit. The first time a process refers to a segment, a "missing-binding" interrupt causes the operating system to load and bind that segment to the process. The process can thereafter read or write the segment using ordinary addressing. Certain segments of the address space are permanently bound to devices, so reading or writing those segments is equivalent to reading or writing the device. The concept of a pipe is missing from Multics, but the interprocess communication mechanism allows a stream of data to be transmitted from one process to another.

User Processes: Level 12 A user process is a virtual machine containing a program in execution. It consists of one or more primitive processes, a virtual

TABLE 7. Specification of Device Level Interface (Level 10)

Form of Call	Effect
dev_handle : = CREATE_DEV(type, address)	Returns a handle for a device of the given type at the given address. (If the caller is a user process, it can store the handle in a directory entry and make the device available throughout the system.)
odev_handle : = OPEN_DEV(dev_handle,rw)	Opens the given device by allocating buffer storage and performing setup operations. The device is enabled for reading, writing, or both, depending on the value of rw and on whether the device is an input or output device or both. (Fails if the device is already open.)
READ_DEV(odev_handle, buf, n)	Reads n bytes into segment buf, as for files. (No effect for output device.)
WRITE_DEV(odev_handle, buf, n)	Sends the first n bytes of segment buf to the device, as for pipe. (No effect for input device.)
CLOSE_DEV(odev_handle)	Undoes OPEN_DEV.
DESTROY_DEV(dev_handle)	Detaches the given device from the system (undoes the corresponding CREATE_DEV).

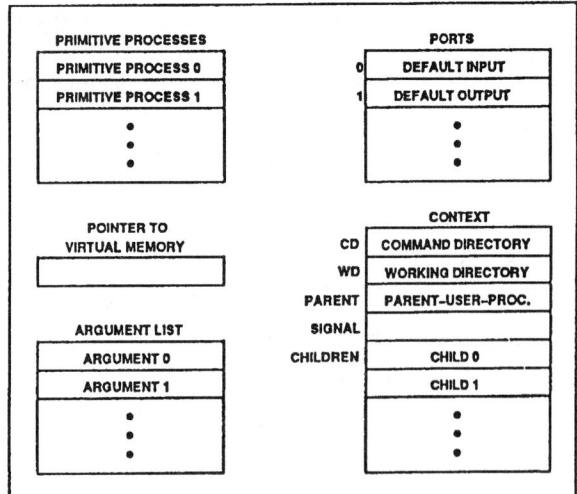

FIG. 2 Format of a user-process descriptor block. A user process is a virtual machine created to execute a given program. It contains primitive processes, a virtual memory holding the given program, a list of arguments supplied at the time of the call, a list of ports, and a set of context variables. By convention, PORTS [0] is the default input and PORTS [1] is the default output; these two ports are bound to pipes, files, or devices when the process is created. The process can open other ports as well, after it begins execution.

memory, a list of arguments passed as parameters, a list of ports, and a context. Each port represents a handle for an open pipe, file, or device. The context, a set of variables characterizing the environment in which the process operates, includes the current working directory, the command directory, and some data structures for handling subordinate user processes. Fig. 2 illustrates the format of a user-process descriptor block.

A user process can create and control new primitive processes with the facilities described in level 5. The primitive processes within the same user process form a team working on a common task; they share the same virtual memory, arguments, ports, and context. A user process can also use FORK to create additional user processes with their own independent teams of primitive processes operating in separate, virtual memories. The creator is called the "parent," and the new user process the "child." A parent can exercise control over its children by resuming, suspending, or killing them. These operations affect all primitive processes of the child. A parent can stop and wait for its children to complete their tasks by a JOIN operation, and a child can signal its completion by an EXIT operation (Table 8).

The OPEN operation that appears in Table 8 saves the handle returned by the level 11 OPEN into the PORTS table. When a user process terminates, level 12 can assure that all open objects are closed properly by invoking the level 11 CLOSE operation for each entry in the PORTS table.

TABLE 8. Specification of User-process Operations (Level 12)

Form of Call	Effect
uproc_handle : = FORK(n, file_handle, params, in, out)	Allocates a user process descriptor block. Creates n suspended, primitive processes ($n > 0$) and records their handles in the descriptor block. Creates a virtual memory and loads the executable file denoted by file_handle. Copies the parameters into the ARGS list. Verifies that in and out are handles for pipes, files, or devices; if so, opens in for reading, puts the open handle in PORTS [0], opens out for writing and puts the open handle in PORTS [1].
KILL(uproc_handle)	Terminates the given user process, but only if it is a child of the caller. This entails destroying its primitive processes and virtual memory, closing open ports, releasing the descriptor block, and removing the given process from the list of the caller's children.
EXIT( )	Terminates the caller process and increments the SIGNAL variable of the parent process.
JOIN(m)	Waits until caller's SIGNAL variable is m, then returns.
SUSPEND(uproc_handle)	Puts the primitive processes of the given user process into the suspended state, but only if the user process is a child of the caller.
RESUME(uproc_handle)	Puts the primitive processes of the given user process back into the state they had at the time of the last SUSPEND operation on the user process, but only if the given process is a child of the caller.
ohandle : = OPEN(handle, rw)	Invokes the OPEN command in level 11 with handle, stores a copy of the result in the next available position in the PORTS table, and returns the result to the caller (handle identifies a pipe, file, or device).

Directories: Level 13 Level 13 is responsible for managing a hierarchy of directories containing handles for sharable objects. In our hypothetical system, these handles are pipes, files, devices, directories, and user processes; handles for open pipes, files, and devices are not sharable and cannot appear in directories. A hierarchy arises because a directory can contain handles for subordinate directories.

A *directory* is a table that matches an external name, stored as a string of characters, with an access code and a handle. In a tree of directories (Fig. 3), the concatenated sequence of external names from the root to a given object serves as a unique, systemwide external name (pathname) for that object. Since directories are at a higher level than files, the file system can be used to store directories.

The principal operation of level 13 is a search command that locates and returns the handle corresponding to a given external name. Thus, the directory level is merely a mechanism for mapping external names to internal ones. Information about attributes of objects stored in directories, such as ownership, time of last use, and access codes is not kept in directories, but rather in the object descriptor blocks within the various object-manager levels.

Portions of the directory hierarchy, especially the lower levels, may be replicated across machines. The methods for replication in a distributed database are adequate to guarantee consistency of the replicated portions (Selinger, 1980). Other approaches have been explored by Ibis (Ruan and Tichy, 1987) and Andrew (Howard *et al.*, 1988). To control the number of update messages in a large system, the full directory database may be kept on only a small number of machines. Other nodes can encache those portions of the directory database that are accessed by users on their nodes. Operations that modify an entry in a directory must send updates to the stable-store machines (i.e. ones with permanent, non-volatile stores), which relay them to affected machines.

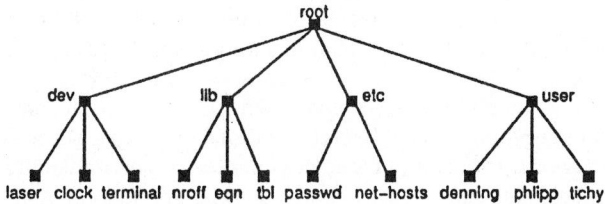

FIG. 3   A Directory Tree. Some directories of the directory tree are permanently reserved for specific purposes. For example, the "dev" directory lists all the external devices of the system. The "lib" directory lists the library of all executable programs maintained by the system's administration. A "user" directory contains subdirectories for each authorized user; that subdirectory is the root of a subtree belonging to that user. In Unix, the unique external name of an object is formed by concatenating the external names along the path from the root, separated by "/" and omitting the root. Thus, the laser printer's external name is "/dev/laser."

Specifications for the directory level's principal operations are given in Table 9. These operations allow higher-level programs to create objects and store handles for them in directories. The table is not a complete specification of a directory manager, however; for example, it contains no command to change the name and access codes of a directory entry.

The CREATE_DIR operation creates an empty, unattached directory. The access codes passed to this operation indicate which classes of processes have the right to search or modify the directory. The ATTACH operation is used to create a new entry in a directory. When a directory is attached, this directory's parent pointer must also be defined. The parent pointer is a backward link that simplifies the removal of the directory. The DETACH operation only removes entries from directories, but has no effect on the object to which a handle points. To destroy an object, the DESTROY operation of the appropriate level must be used. To minimize inadvertent deletions, the operation to destroy a directory fails if applied to a nonempty directory.

The ATTACH and DETACH operations must notify other machines so that changes become effective throughout the system. By maintaining two conditions, this process can be made simple: (1) an empty directory must first be attached to the global directory tree before entries are made in it, and (2) a directory must be empty before being detached. A more complicated notification mechanism will be needed if a process is allowed to construct a directory subtree before its root is attached to the global directory tree. The COUNT and GET operations are the primitives used by a formatting program to prepare a summary of the objects listed in a directory.

Shell: Level 14 Most system users spend a great deal of time executing existing programs, not writing new ones. When a user logs in, the operating system creates a user process containing a copy of the shell program, with its default input connected to the user's keyboard and its default output connected to the user's display. The shell is the program that listens to the user's terminal and interprets the inputs as commands to invoke existing programs in specified combinations and with specified inputs.

The shell scans each complete command line of the input to pick out the names of programs to be invoked and the values of arguments to be passed to them. For each program called in this way, the shell creates a user process. The user processes are connected according to the data flow specified in the command line.

Operations of substantial complexity can be programmed in the command language of the Unix shell. For example, the operations that format and then print a file named *text* can be set in motion by the command line:

```
tbl < text | eqn | lptroff > output
```

The first program is `tbl`, which scans the data on its input stream and replaces descriptions of tables of information with the necessary formatting commands. The "<" symbol indicates that `tbl` is to take its input from the file `text`. The output of `tbl` is directed by a pipe (the "|" symbol) to the input of `eqn`, which replaces descriptions

TABLE 9.   Specification of a Directory Manager Interface (Level 13)

Form of Call	Effect
dir_handle : = CREATE_DIR(access)	Allocates an empty directory, sets its access codes to access, and returns a handle for the directory. (This directory is not attached to the directory tree.)
DESTROY_DIR(dir_handle)	Destroys the given directory. (Fails if the directory is not empty or still attached.)
ATTACH(dir_handle, name, obj_handle)	Makes an entry called name in the directory dir_handle and stores in it the handle obj_handle. If obj_handle denotes a directory, sets its parent entry to dir_handle. Notifies the stable store of directories of the change. (Fails if name already exists in the directory dir_handle, if the directory dir_handle is not attached, or if obj_handle denotes an already-attached directory.)
DETACH(dir_handle, name)	Removes the entry of the given name from the given directory. Notifies the stable store of directories of the change. (Fails if the given name does not exist in the given directory, or if the given directory is not empty, or if the access codes of the directory prohibit changes.)
obj_handle : = SEARCH(dir_handle, name)	Finds the entry of the given name in the given directory and returns a copy of the associated handle. (Fails if the name does not exist in the given directory, or if the access codes of the directory prohibit searching.)
n : = COUNT(dir_handle)	Returns the number of entries in the given directory. (Fails if the the access codes of the directory prohibit searching.)
dir_entry : = GET(dir_handle, i)	Returns the i-th directory entry (name and handle) in the given directory. (Fails if there are fewer than i entries, or if the access codes of the directory prohibit searching.)

of equations with the necessary formatting commands. The output of eqn is then piped to lptroff, which generates the commands for the laser printer. Finally, ">" indicates the output of lptroff is to be placed in the file output. If ">" output" is replaced with "| laser," the data is instead sent directly to the laser printer.

After the components of a command line are identified, the shell obtains handles for them by a series of commands:

```
c1 := SEARCH(CD, "tbl");
c2 := SEARCH(WD, "text");
c3 := CREATE_PIPE();
c4 := SEARCH(CD, "eqn");
c5 := CREATE_PIPE();
c6 := SEARCH(CD, "lptroff");
c7 := CREATE_FILE();
ATTACH(c7, WD, "output");
```

The variable CD holds a handle for a commands directory and WD holds a handle for the current working directory. Both CD and WD are part of the shell's context (Fig. 2).

The shell then creates and resumes user processes that execute the three components of the pipeline and awaits their completion:

```
RESUME(FORK (1, c1, - , c2, c3));
RESUME(FORK (1, c4, - , c3, c5));
RESUME(FORK (1, c6, - , c5, c7));
JOIN(3);
```

After the join completes, the shell can kill these processes and acknowledge completion of the entire command to the user through a "prompt" symbol.

If the specification "< text" is omitted, the shell connects tbl to the default input, which is the same as its own, namely the terminal keyboard. In this case, the second search command is omitted and the first fork operation is

```
FORK(1, c1, - , PORTS[0], c3);
```

where PORTS [0] is the standard input for a user process. Similarly, if "> output" is omitted, the shell connects lptroff to the default output, the shell's PORTS [1].

If an elaborate command line is to be performed often, typing it can become tedious. Unix encourages users to store complicated commands in executable files called *shell scripts* that become simpler commands. A file named *format* might be created with the contents

```
tbl < $1 | eqn | lptroff > $2
```

where the names of input and output files have been replaced by variables $1 and $2. When the command format is invoked, the variables $1 and $2 are replaced by the arguments following the command name. For example, typing

```
format text output
```

would substitute `text` for $1 and `output` for $2 and so would have exactly the same effect as the original command line.

System Initialization One small but essential piece of an operating system has not been discussed—the method of starting up the system. The start-up procedure, called a *bootstrap* sequence, begins with a very short program copied into memory from a permanent read-only memory (ROM) (*see* BOOT AND REBOOT). This program loads a longer program from disk, which then takes control and loads the operating system itself. Finally, the operating system creates a special login process connected to each terminal of the system. (*See* LOGIN FILE.)

When a user correctly types an identifier and a password, the login process will create a shell process connected to the same terminal. When the user types a logout command, the shell process will exit and the login process will resume.

Conclusion We have used the levels model to describe the functions of multi-machine operating systems and how it is possible to hide systematically the physical locations of all sharable objects, yet be able to locate them quickly when given a name in the directory hierarchy.

The directory function can be generalized from its traditional role of naming files to naming arbitrary, sharable objects. No user machine has to have a full, local copy of the directory structure; it needs only to encache the view with which it is currently working. The full structure is maintained by a small group of machines implementing a reliable, dependable storage system.

The model can deal with heterogeneous systems consisting of general-purpose user machines, such as workstations (*q.v.*), and special-purpose machines, such as stable stores, file servers (*q.v.*), and supercomputers (*q.v.*). Only the user machines need a full operating system; the special-purpose machines require only a simple operating system capable of managing local tasks and of communicating on the network.

The levels model is based on the same principle found in nature to organize many scales of space and time. At each level of abstraction are well-defined rules of interaction for the objects visible at that level; the rules can be understood without detailed knowledge of the smaller objects making up those objects. The many parts of an operating system cannot be fully understood without keeping this principle in mind.

References

1966. Dennis, J. B. and Van Horn E. C. "Programming Semantics for Multi-programmed Computations," *Communications of the ACM* **9** (*3*) (March) 143–155.

1968. Dijkstra, Edsger W. "The Structure of the THE-Multiprogramming System," *Communications of the ACM* **11** (*5*) (May), 341–346.

1970. Denning, Peter J. "Virtual Memory," *Computing Surveys*, 2(3) (September), 154–216.

1971. Denning, Peter J. "Third Generation Computer Systems," *Computing Surveys* **3** (*4*) (December), 175–212.

1972. Organick, E. I. *The Multics System: An Examination of its Structure*. Cambridge, MA: The M.I.T. Press.

1973. Brinch Hansen, P. *Operating System Principles*. Englewood Cliffs, NJ: Prentice-Hall.

1974. Ritchie, D. M. and Thompson, K. L. "The UNIX Time-Sharing System," *Communications of the ACM* **17**(*7*) (July), 365–375.

1976. Denning, Peter J. "Fault-Tolerant Operating Systems," *Computing Surveys* **8** (*4*) (December), 359–389.

1976. Habermann, A. N., Flon, Lawrence, and Cooprider, Lee W. "Modularization and Hierarchy in a Family of Operating Systems," *Communications of the ACM* **19** (*5*) (May), 266–272.

1978. Holt, C. R. *Structured Concurrent Programming with Operating System Applications*. Reading, MA: Addison-Wesley.

1979. Jones, Anita K. *et al.* "StarOS, A Multiprocessor Operating System for the Support of Task Forces," *Proceedings of the Seventh Symposium on Operating Systems Principles*, (December), 117–127.

1979. Wilkes, M. V. and Needham, R. M. *The Cambridge CAP Computer and its Operating System*, New York: Elsevier/North-Holland Publishing Co.

1980. Neumann, Peter G., Boyer, Robert S., Feiertag, Richard J., Levitt, Karl N., and Robinson, Lawrence "A Provably Secure Operating System, its Applications, and Proofs," CSL-116 (2nd edition), Menlo Park, CA: SRI International.

1980. Ousterhout, John K. *et al.* "Medusa: An Experiment in Distributed Operating System Structure," *Communications of the ACM* **23** (*2*) (February), 92–105.

1980. Selinger, P. G. "Replicated Data," in *Distributed Data Bases*, F. Poole (Ed.) Cambridge, England: Cambridge University Press, 223–231.

1981. Popek, G. *et al.* "Locus: A Network Transparent, High Reliability Distributed System," *Proceedings of the Eighth Symposium on Operating Systems Principles*, (December) 169–177.

1981. Wulf, William A., Levin, Roy, and Harbison, Samuel P. HYDRA/C.mmp, An Experimental Computer System, New York: McGraw-Hill.

1982. Birrell, A. D. *et al.* "Grapevine: An Exercise in Distributed Computing," *Communications of the ACM* **25** (*4*) (April), 260–274.

1982. Cheriton, D. R. *The Thoth System: Multi-process Structuring and Portability*. New York: Elsevier Science.

1982. Rowe, L. A. and Birman, K. P. "A Local Network Based on the UNIX Operating System," *IEEE Trans. Software Engineering*, **SE-8** (*2*) (March), 137–146.

1983. Organick, E. I. *A Programmer's View of the Intel 432 System*. New York: McGraw-Hill.

1984. Brown, R. L., Denning, P. J., and Tichy, W. F. "Advanced Operating Systems," *IEEE Computer* **17** (*10*) (October), 173–190.

1984. Comer, D. *Operating System Design: The XINU Approach*. Englewood Cliffs, NJ: Prentice-Hall.

1984. Kernigham, B. W. and Pike, R. *The Unix Programming Environment*. Englewood Cliffs, N.J.: Prentice-Hall.

1985. Sandberg, Russel *et al.* "Design and Implementation of the Sun Network Filesystem," *Proceedings of USENIX 1985 Summer Conference* (June), 119–130.

1985. Tichy, W. F. "RCS—A system for Version Control," *Software-Practice & Experience*, **15** (*7*) (July), 637–654.

1986. Accetta, M. *et al.* "Mach: A New Kernel Foundation for Unix Development," *Proceedings of USENIX 1986 Summer Conference*, 93–112.

1987. Ruan, Zuwang and Tichy, Walter. "Performance Analysis of File Replication Schemes in Distributed Systems," *Performance Evaluation Review* **15** (*1*) (May), 205–215.

1987. Tanenbaum, Andrew S. *Computer Networks*, Englewood Cliffs, NJ: Prentice-Hall.

1988. Howard, J. H. *et al.* "Scale and Performance in a Distributed File System," *ACM Transactions on Computer Systems,* **6** (*1*) (February), 51–81.
1988. Rashid, R. *et al.* "Machine-Independent Virtual Memory Management for Paged Uniprocessor and Multiprocessor Architectures," *IEEE Transactions on Computers* **37** (*8*) (August), 896–908.
1990. Denning, Peter J. and Tichy, Walter F. "Highly Parallel Computation," *Science* **250** (30 November), 1217–1222.

PETER J. DENNING AND WALTER F. TICHY

CONTEMPORARY ISSUES

The Role of an Operating System

An operating system is a collection of programs that acts as an intermediary between the hardware and its user(s), providing a high-level interface to low-level hardware resources, such as the CPU, memory, and I/O devices. The operating system provides various facilities and services that make the use of the hardware convenient, efficient, and safe. Examples of these facilities and services are memory management, process management, communication facilities, a command language interpreter, and a file system. The *sharing* of resources among users and/or programs is a key goal of most operating systems.

Wide variations are encountered both in the demands that are placed upon operating systems, and in the operating system structures that are adopted in response to those demands. Real-time systems, personal computers (*q.v.*), workstations (*q.v.*), timesharing systems, and scientific supercomputers (*q.v.*) may impose significantly different demands on their operating systems. Operating system structures range from highly monolithic to highly modularized and decentralized.

An Historical Perspective

The earliest computer systems were employed by a single user at a time to run a single program at a time. By operating toggles on the front panel of the system, the user would cause a machine language program to be loaded at a specific memory address from a simple device, such as a paper tape reader. Execution of the program would be commenced manually, again using toggles to specify an address to which control should be transferred. During execution, the program might read input or produce output; low-level machine instructions to operate the I/O device(s) would be embedded in the program. Execution would terminate when the program branched to a "halt" instruction. When the lights stopped flashing, the job was finished.

Among the drawbacks to this style of operation were that every user had to know the computer system at a detailed level; even for the single active program, the operation of the system was essentially sequential—read input, compute, read more input, compute, write output, etc.; the sharing of the computer system was very inefficient; and facilities that we take entirely for granted today, such as large virtual memories and file systems, did not exist.

Some of the requirements for detailed knowledge of the computer system were ameliorated by the simple expedient of sharing partial programs: a single individual would write routines to control the I/O devices and would make these routines available (physically) to others. In some sense, these were the first operating system routines. The idea of a *resident monitor* was a further improvement: these routines would be permanently loaded in a region of memory (see Fig. 1), and user programs (loaded in the remainder of memory) would call them. The resident monitor often controlled an operator's console, providing a "soft substitute" for the physical toggles: the user could cause a program to be loaded and initiated by entering simple console commands. The existence of a resident monitor immediately raises the issue of protection: without protection, an errant program could eradicate the resident monitor, affecting not only the current user (who at least was presumably responsible for the accident) but future ones, and requiring the resident monitor to be reloaded.

The word *boot*, short for *bootstrapping*, is used to denote the initial loading of the operating system (*see* BOOT AND REBOOT). In these days of large read-only memories, it's easy to forget the relevance of this term. Imagine, though, how the user program or the resident monitor was read into the memory of an early computer. Typically, the hardware of the CPU or of the I/O device was capable of independently reading some small amount of binary data—say, several words—into a fixed memory location. In a typical bootstrap procedure, this binary data would be a very small program that was capable of commanding the I/O device to read a somewhat larger amount of data, which would be a slightly larger program that was capable of commanding the I/O device to read more data, and so forth. Into the 1970s, computer systems were bootstrapped from card decks in which successive cards had greater amounts of binary data punched into them; "hauling yourself up by your own bootstraps" is indeed an apt analogy.

The inefficiencies that resulted from the sequential nature of system operation were ameliorated by overlap-

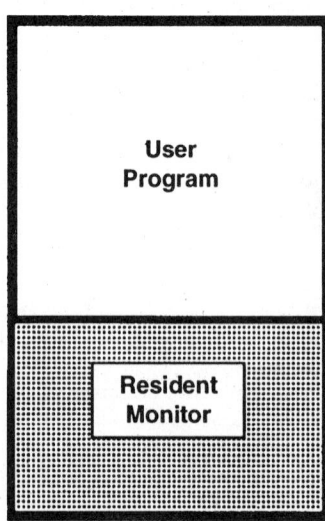

FIG. 1. Resident monitor.

ping I/O with computation within a single job. The program would initiate a physical input operation before the data was actually required; the I/O device would read the data into a buffer other than the one the program was currently accessing. Output also used multiple buffers. The obvious performance benefit was accompanied by a significant drawback: programs became more complex, particularly because concurrent activities now had to be managed. Indeed, nearly all operating systems are complex concurrent programs, but many of them suffer because of the historical precedent of handling this concurrency in an *ad hoc* manner.

I/O devices, such as paper tape readers and punches, card readers and punches, and line printers, are inherently slow. Even in a system that ran a single user program at a time, considerable efficiency could be gained by processing one job, while simultaneously transferring the next job from a slow input device to a higher-performance I/O device, such as a disk, from which it could be retrieved quickly when needed. Similarly, output would be written to disk when generated, and then asynchronously sent to the punch or printer. *Spooling*—an acronym for "simultaneous peripheral operations on-line"—was the term used to describe this.

Time-sharing (multi-user interactive computing) was possible, even on computer systems that ran a single program at a time. M.I.T.'s Compatible Time Sharing System (CTSS) was a very simple landmark time-sharing system. The memory of the computer system on which CTSS ran was only large enough to accommodate a single user. At the end of a time slice (*q.v.*), *swapping* was used to suspend temporarily the execution of one user program and allow another to execute; the former program's memory image was sent to disk, after which the latter's memory image was retrieved from disk. (Clearly, the swap image needed to contain more state information than simply the contents of memory to make it possible to resume the user program at the point where it had been suspended.)

Multiprogramming was a significant advance, for it allowed multiple users to share a computer system simultaneously, rather than sequentially. In early multiprogramming systems, the memory of the computer system was partitioned into a fixed set of regions of various sizes (see Fig. 2). The *long-term scheduling* algorithm determined which of the waiting jobs would be allocated the next available region of memory. The *short-term scheduling* algorithm determined which of the memory-resident jobs would be allocated the CPU. In a multiprogramming system, programs needed to be *relocatable*, since the address range of the program depended on the region to which it was assigned. (Hardware techniques such as *base registers* (*q.v.*) or *relocation registers* typically were employed.) It also was mandatory that the operating system be responsible for I/O activity, since the simultaneous physical sharing of I/O devices by user programs was fraught with peril. Typically, users ceased to attempt to overlap their own CPU and I/O activity; the operating system achieved overall efficiency by overlapping the I/O of one user with the computation of another.

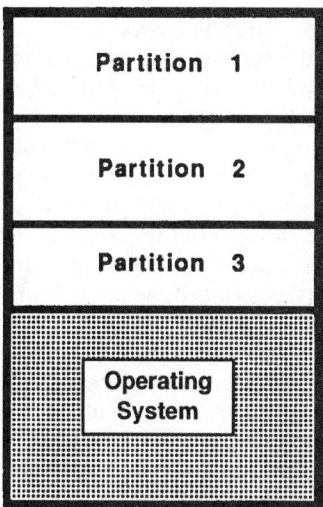

FIG. 2. Multiprogramming with a fixed number of partitions.

More sophisticated multiprogramming systems divided memory into a variable number of regions of sizes tailored to the specific requirements of jobs. *Memory fragmentation* was a problem with either fixed-partition or variable-partition multiprogramming systems: *internal* fragmentation if a program was allocated a larger region than it required; *external* fragmentation if regions went unused because of a mismatch with the actual demands of the available jobs. Swapping was sometimes used to suspend temporarily the execution of a job and allow another job to use its region of memory.

A drawback of all of the operating system designs discussed thus far is that each user program was required to be fully resident in a contiguous region of memory. *Paging* and *segmentation* are two approaches to removing the requirement for contiguity by using an indirection table. *Virtual memory* systems remove the requirement for full residency; a *page fault* occurs when a reference is made to a portion of a program's address space that is not memory-resident, and this page is fetched from secondary storage and the program resumed. These developments, and others such as file systems, will be discussed later in this article.

Concepts such as protection, asynchronous I/O, multiprogramming, virtual memory, and file systems are as important in single-user workstation systems as they are in multi-user timesharing systems. A single user may wish to continue computing while the printer is active and to run multiple programs simultaneously (e.g. an editor and a compiler). These programs may not fit in the available physical memory, may be untrustworthy and need to be protected from one another; etc. One of the most interesting phenomena of the recent past has been to see operating systems for personal computers quickly recapitulate the 30-year history of development of operating systems for mainframes.

Concurrency in Operating Systems *Concurrency* is a prevalent theme in operating systems. There is physical concurrency: multiple I/O devices simultaneously active. There is logical concurrency: multiple users sharing the system, even though only one can actually be using the CPU at a particular instant (on a uniprocessor system).

In early operating systems, this concurrency was managed using *ad hoc* techniques. A user program would *trap* to the operating system, requesting some service. The program's state would be saved as part of the trap procedure. The operating system would initiate the requested activity, typically by sending a *start I/O* command to a device. The operating system would then *resume* some other program, restoring its previously-saved state. When the I/O completed, the device would *interrupt* whatever program happened to be running at the time, saving the program's state and transferring control to an *interrupt handling routine* in the operating system. The operating system would resume the program that had been waiting for the I/O to complete (see Fig. 3). Errors were avoided by *disabling interrupts* when the operating system was active, thereby preventing the operating system from being interrupted at inopportune moments (such as when a critical shared data structure was in some intermediate state).

An operating system structured in this way is a bit like a juggler with lots of balls up in the air: as long as nothing out of the ordinary happens, things are fine, but the entire operation is somewhat fragile. There are a huge number of critical shared data structures, of which the corruption of any one could potentially wreak havoc on the system's operation. Techniques to cope with the complexities arising from concurrency were a major accomplishment of operating systems research in the 1960s.

The most important of these techniques was the idea, due to Dijkstra, of structuring the system as a collection of *cooperating sequential processes*. A *process* is the execution of a program by a (virtual) CPU. A *sequential* process does not deal with asynchronous events, although it does communicate with other processes through a well-defined synchronous interface. An individual process may be in one of three states: running (i.e. actively computing),

ready (i.e. ready to run, but not currently allocated the CPU), or blocked (awaiting some event, such as a message or an interrupt) (see Fig. 4). These multiple processes, *cooperating* through the communication interface, can be used to implement an operating system.

An extreme system design based upon these ideas would involve a small *kernel* whose main responsibilities are to support processes and interprocess communication. Most operating system functions would be performed by processes. For example, separate processes would be used to manage each I/O device, to implement spooling, to represent each user, to manage virtual memory, etc. These processes would interact by means of a mechanism such as *monitors* (*q.v.*) or *message passing*. When a user program has an I/O request, the request is communicated by the user's process, through the kernel, to the manager process for the appropriate device. The user's process is then blocked. The device manager process, which was blocked waiting for a request message, is unblocked. In response to the message, it contacts the kernel to initiate the physical I/O and then blocks again. The effect of a device interrupt is to cause the kernel to ready the appropriate device manager process, which takes whatever actions may be necessary, and eventually signals the blocked user process that it can continue by communicating with it through the kernel. The role of the kernel is to translate asynchronous interrupts into synchronous signals that awaken device manager processes, and more broadly to implement interprocess communication and process scheduling. The kernel interface, then, would support operations such as `Create` (create a new process), `Destroy` (kill a process), `Send` (send a message to a process and block awaiting a response), and `Receive` (block awaiting a message from some process); in addition, the kernel would make resource allocation decisions among processes, at least at the level of allocating the CPU. Asynchronism is an issue when programming the kernel, but not when programming the remainder of the operating system. Interrupts must be disabled only

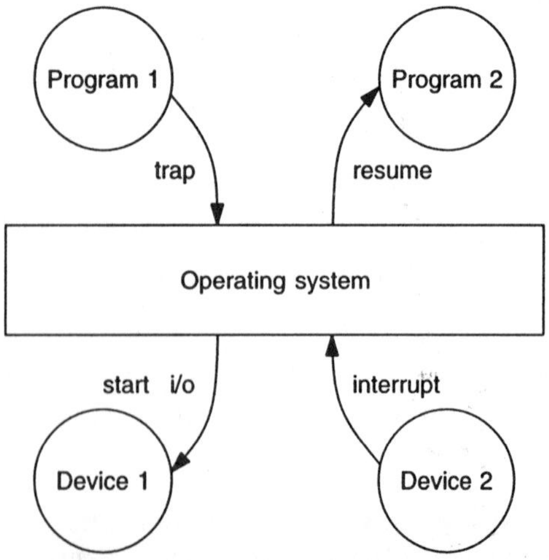

FIG. 3.   Communication with the operating system.

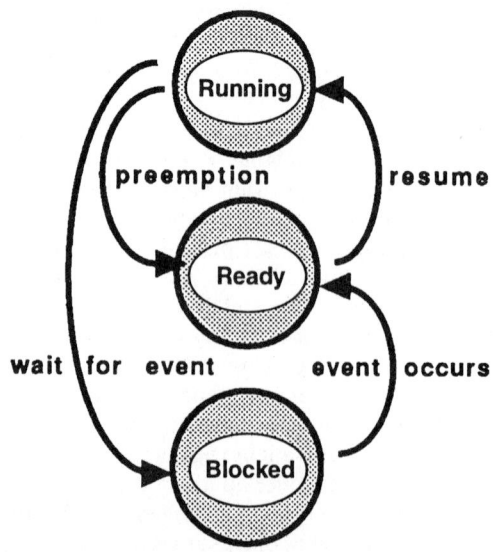

FIG. 4.   The states of a process.

during the very brief periods of time when the kernel itself is active.

Although most contemporary operating systems support the notions of processes and structured interprocess communication, few go to the extreme of delegating all traditional operating system functionality to processes, despite the obvious advantages of this sort of small-kernel structure. The first reason for this is inertia, alluded to previously. The second is performance. A small-kernel operating system places significant demands on the interprocess communication mechanism and will perform poorly if this mechanism is not efficient. Version 3.0 of the Mach operating system is one of the first commercial systems to be structured as a small-kernel operating system. Various research systems (e.g. the V system) have been structured in this manner for many years.

Concurrent Programming Using Monitors

Monitors, attributed to Hoare, are one key approach to programming operating systems. As a first example to motivate the use of monitors, consider the *critical section problem*, which arises frequently in operating systems. A *critical section* is any piece of code that must be accessed by only one process at a time. For instance, suppose that several processes are counting occurrences of some type of event, such as I/O operations at various disks. When an I/O operation takes place at the disk being managed/observed by a particular process, this process loads the value of a shared counter, adds one, and stores back the result. The code to increment the counter is a critical section, for consider the following interleaving of operations:

Time	Observer A	Observer B
1	load	
2		load
3	add 1	
4		add 1
5	store	
6		store

Two events occur, but the value of the shared counter only increases by one.

To make the problem more interesting, we introduce a different type of process, which periodically reports the number of events that have occurred in the reporting interval. It does this by reading the value of the counter, displaying it on a terminal, and zeroing the counter. (This example is due to Holt.) Consider the following interleaving of operations:

Time	Observer A	Reporter
1	load	
2		load
3	add 1	
4		display
5	store	
6		store 0

The event being tallied by Observer A is "lost."

Clearly, the observers and the reporter are cooperating sequential processes: they loop, working largely independently but interacting through the shared counter. However, some discipline must be imposed on accesses to the shared counter, or the "cooperation" leads to erroneous results. A *monitor* is one way to discipline this interaction.

A monitor includes data structures that are accessed by multiple processes (in this case, just the shared counter) and procedures that are used to access these data structures (in this case, a procedure Count, which is called by the observers, and a procedure Report, which is called by the reporter).

Thus far, monitors sound like data types. Each monitor, however, has the key property that at most one process may be executing its procedures at any time. This is implemented by calls to the kernel at the start and end of each of the monitor's procedures. The kernel call at the start, Monitor_Enter, checks a flag to see if the monitor is occupied. If not, this flag is set and the process is allowed to continue. If so, then the process is blocked and placed on a kernel queue, waiting for the monitor to be free. The kernel call at the end, Monitor_Exit, checks the queue to see if any processes are waiting for the monitor. If not, the flag indicating that the monitor is occupied is unset. If so, then one of the waiting processes is made ready. In either case, the process exiting the procedure remains ready. The kernel calls themselves (Monitor_Enter and Monitor_Exit) must be done under hardware-level mutual exclusion (e.g. by disabling interrupts) to ensure the integrity of the kernel's queues and flags.

It is easy to see that this mechanism solves the problem just posed. To motivate the remaining properties of monitors, consider the more complex example of the *bounded buffer producer-consumer problem*, which again arises in many places in an operating system. The *producer* is a process that generates something (e.g. lines of output destined for a printer). The *consumer* is a process that disposes of what the producer generates (e.g. the device manager process for the printer). The producer and the consumer interact through a set of buffers (in this case, a fixed number of one-line buffers managed as a ring). The producer and the consumer run at irregular rates. The buffers increase overall throughput by allowing some "elasticity" between these two processes. But discipline is necessary: If the consumer is operating slowly and all of the buffers are full, the producer must block; if the producer is operating slowly and all of the buffers are empty, the consumer must block.

In this case, the data within the monitor includes the ring of buffers, a counter indicating the number of buffers that are full, and pointers to the next buffer to be filled and the next buffer to be emptied. There are two access procedures: Deposit (called by the producer), and Remove (called by the consumer). Within the Deposit procedure, the producer checks to see if any empty buffers are available. If so, the producer deposits its data in the appropriate buffer, updates the counter and the pointer to the next buffer to be filled, and executes a Signal statement on a *condition variable* used to indicate that there is at least one full buffer. If not, the producer executes a `Wait` statement on a condition variable used to indicate that there is at least one empty buffer. This causes the producer to block, logically outside of the monitor, until the condition is signaled. Within the `Remove` procedure, the consumer checks to see if any full buffers are available. If so, the consumer removes the data from the appropriate buffer, updates the counter and the pointer to the next buffer to be emptied, and executes a `Signal` statement on a condition variable used to indicate that there is at least one empty buffer. If not, the consumer executes a `Wait` statement on a condition variable used to indicate that there is at least one full buffer. This causes the consumer to block, logically outside of the monitor, until the condition is signaled.

With some thought, it should be clear that monitors are an appropriate mechanism for concurrent programming within an operating system. A kernel supporting monitors would simply need to implement the procedures `Monitor_Enter`, `Monitor_Exit`, `Signal`, and `Wait`, plus the appropriate queues and flags.

Deadlock   *Deadlock* is a problem that can arise in concurrent systems when one process is waiting for a resource that is held by a second process, which in turn is waiting for a resource that is held by the first process. For example, suppose that the system's input spooler fills the disk with jobs waiting to run, with the result that there is no space in which to put the output of jobs that are trying to complete. (Things can, of course, be much more complicated than this.)

The deadlock problem was studied extensively in the early 1970s. A number of algorithms exist for preventing deadlock, offering various trade-offs between concurrency and overhead. One such algorithm is to have each process claim every resource it will need at the outset, aborting if this is not possible; this is clearly safe, but may dramatically restrict the set of jobs that can execute concurrently. A second algorithm is to number resources and require that resources always be acquired in ascending order; this algorithm is also safe (less obviously so) and is less restrictive. A third algorithm, called the *Banker's algorithm*, requires each process to state at the outset its maximum simultaneous requirement for each type of resource. Then, whenever a process requires a unit of a resource, the "banker" sees if this allocation would lead to deadlock if every process then requested its maximum claim. (Implicit in this is the fact that efficient algorithms for *detecting* deadlock also have been devised.) If not, the allocation is made; if so, the process is blocked.

An alternative to preventing deadlock is to allow it to occur (rarely, it is hoped), and then detect this occurrence and correct it, typically by terminating one of the offending processes. The cost/performance trade-offs between prevention and detection/correction are highly system- and application-dependent.

Renewed interest in the deadlock problem has arisen from the advent of transaction processing (*q.v.*) systems in which data items are locked to avoid concurrency-related errors: if process A locks data item 1 and process B locks data item 2, and then process A attempts to lock data item 2 and process B attempts to lock data item 1, a deadlock results (see Fig. 5).

Processor Scheduling   *Processor scheduling* is another aspect of process management that has been thoroughly studied and is well understood. The most important theoretical result is that *shortest remaining processing time first* (SRPT) is the optimal strategy to minimize response time when jobs' service times are deterministic and known at the instant the job arrives. Unfortunately, neither of these things is typically true in practice, but most actual schedulers attempt in some way to mimic the behavior of SRPT.

Round-robin is a practical policy that preemptively rotates the CPU among the ready jobs, giving each job some *quantum* of service before moving on to the next. Its advantage over *first-come-first-served* is that a short job cannot get "stuck" behind a long job.

Feedback policies are an enhancement of round-robin in which a job, after receiving a certain amount of round-robin service, is "demoted" to a sequence of lower-priority queues. The relationship to SRPT is clear: service times aren't known in advance, but as jobs prove themselves to be long-running, they receive progressively worse service; each newly arriving job is given the "benefit of the doubt" and begins its service in the highest priority queue. Most real systems use some variation of feedback scheduling.

Memory Management   In a traditional multiprogramming system and in many small personal computers, there is a single *address space* with a size equal to the size of physical memory. Different programs are allocated different parts of this address space, with protection typically achieved by hardware tags associated with fixed-size pieces of memory.

This organization is simple, but, as noted earlier, has several drawbacks. A program must be fully resident in a contiguous region of memory, with provision made for relocating the program once its region is determined.

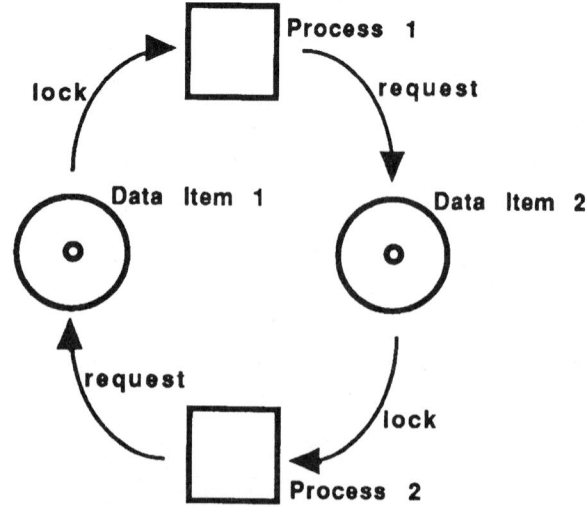

FIG. 5.   Two-process deadlock.

Most computer systems today, at least above the level of personal computers, employ some form of paged virtual memory. In a paged virtual memory system, each program has its own address space, which begins at address 0 and runs to some hardware-defined maximum. All address references in the program are within this address space. All address spaces are logically divided into *pages* of some fixed size. The physical memory is physically divided into *page frames* of the same fixed size. Any logical page can be stored in any physical page frame, which greatly simplifies memory allocation for the operating system, and eliminates external fragmentation. The mapping from program addresses (referred to as *virtual addresses*) to memory addresses (referred to as *physical addresses*) is accomplished by indirection using a *page table*—one per address space. A virtual address is considered to consist of two parts: a page number and an offset within that page. When the program issues an address, a *dynamic address translation* unit uses the page number as an index into the appropriate page table (determined from the ID of the address space that is active). The contents of the indexed page table entry is the physical memory address of the start of the *page frame* holding the correct page of data. The offset (from the virtual address) is added to this address to form the physical address, and the reference takes place. (See Fig. 6; note that there are other possible organizations for page tables.)

A key point is that a page table entry may be marked as *invalid*, meaning that the correct page of data is not resident in memory. Should a reference to such a page occur, the dynamic address translation unit generates a *page fault* interrupt. The operating system gets control, brings the desired page from secondary storage to a page frame in primary memory (retiring the page that had occupied that frame, if any, to secondary storage), updates the page table entry, and then restarts the user program. This allows a program's physical memory allocation to be less than the size of its address space—sometimes by a very large factor.

Most systems rely on *demand paging*: they do not attempt to anticipate the pages that a program will need, but rather wait for a fault to occur and then fetch the page. (Obviously, some other program is run during the I/O activity.) An exception to this rule is that, when a program is temporarily suspended and swapped out, performance may be improved by writing all of its memory-resident pages to a contiguous swap area on disk, and then reading all of these pages back in prior to restarting the program.

A variety of *page replacement algorithms* are used to determine which page frame should be allocated to a page that has been faulted in. Some variation of *least recently used* (LRU) is common in practice. A thorough discussion of this topic is beyond the scope of this article.

Most contemporary computer systems also support some rudimentary form of *segmentation*. In a fully flexible segmentation system, such as that employed by Multics, each program element is assigned to a variable-sized segment, and dynamic linking between segments is supported. More common is to have just a few segments in each address space (e.g. an operating system segment, a user code segment, and a user data or stack segment). (The VAX VMS operating system supports a scheme similar to this.)

Paging and segmentation ease a number of the problems of protection and sharing. A process or program can only generate addresses within its address space. The address space is defined by the page table. The page table is built by the operating system. As long as the operating system is correct, the potential for one user illicitly reading or destroying the data of another (or of the system, which has its own address space) is eliminated. Sharing between two processes can be accomplished by having certain page table or segment table entries for these processes that are the same.

File Systems Typical file system operations are `Create`, `Destroy`, `Open`, `Close`, `Read`, `Write`, and `Seek`. Four key issues in the design of a file system are *allocation*, *organization*, *naming*, and *protection*.

Allocation concerns the way in which a file is mapped onto the physical disk. Among the desirable properties for an allocation strategy are ease of file creation and expansion, rapid direct access (access to a specific byte of the file), rapid sequential access (access to consecutive bytes of the file), and minimization of wasted disk space. Two extreme allocation strategies are *contiguous* and *linked*. Under contiguous allocation, the file is allocated in a contiguous area on disk. This makes access rapid, but makes creation and expansion difficult and may result in considerable wasted space. Under linked allocation, the file is allocated in fixed-size blocks that are linked together. This makes creation and expansion easy and reduces wasted space, but access is slow. A compromise is *indexed* allocation: the file is allocated in fixed-size blocks that are accessed through a set of index blocks, making random access efficient (although sequential access still requires many slow disk seeks). Some cleverness is required to ensure that the index itself remains a manageable size. Unix uses an indexed allocation scheme in which each file is headed by an *i-node* containing

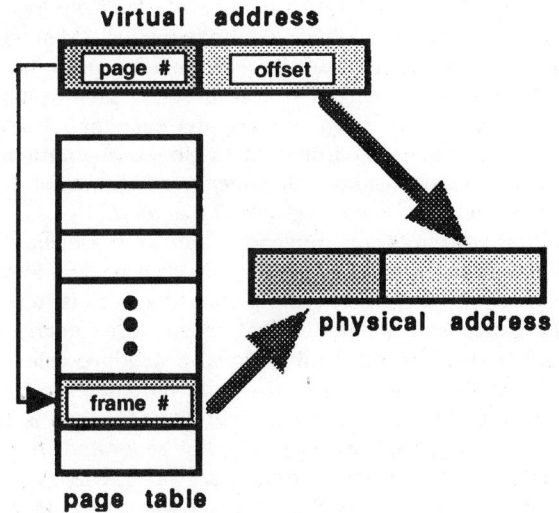

FIG. 6. Address translation.

(among other things) a small number of pointers (13 in one recent implementation), the first few of which point to 4K-byte blocks of data, but the last three of which point, respectively, to a 4K-byte block of pointers to 4K-byte blocks of data, a 4K-byte block of pointers to 4K-byte blocks of pointers to 4K-byte blocks of data, and a 4K-byte block of pointers to 4K-byte blocks of pointers to 4K-byte block of pointers to 4K-byte blocks of data (see Fig. 7). (Obviously, neither data blocks nor pointer blocks are allocated until the file expands to require them.) This scheme allows the efficient representation and access of files ranging from very small to very large. While Unix supports only this one allocation strategy, many production operating systems support several.

Organization concerns the "file model" available to the programmer. In Unix, all files adhere to a single model: files are sequential streams of bytes. This has the advantage of simplicity, and integrates well with other fundamental abstractions of Unix (e.g. pipes). Most operating systems support several file models, though (indexed, for example, in addition to sequential byte stream). The organization and the allocation strategy interact closely with one another. Certain allocation strategies are most efficient for particular organizations.

Nearly all modern operating systems employ a hierarchical directory structure for naming. A directory maps names to files; files can be either data or other directories. A hierarchical directory structure allows the user to organize files in a structured and intelligent manner.

Protection is a significant issue that transcends the file system and cannot be treated fully in this article. *Access control lists* (lists associated with each file specifying who can access the file in what ways) and *capabilities* (unforgeable entities handed to users that indicate what files they can access in what ways) are two well-studied approaches to file protection.

The scheduling of disk operations is a topic that received much attention in the 1960s and 1970s. Four common algorithms are *first-come-first-served* (FCFS), *shortest seek time first* (SSTF), *scan*, and *sweep*. In the presence of a large queue of requests, FCFS offers a fairly uniform but fairly large response time. In SSTF, service is always given to the request whose seek distance is the shortest from the current head position; SSTF offers excellent average response time but a high variance, because requests located on the inner or outer cylinders may be "starved." In scan and sweep, the head moves from one edge of the disk to the other, handling all requests it encounters. (These algorithms differ only in their details.) Scan and sweep offer good compromise performance: mean response time almost as low as that of SSTF, and variability almost as low as that of FCFS. In truth, though, on most systems (particularly those with multiple disks), the length of the disk request queue is seldom long enough to benefit appreciably from clever scheduling.

Distributed Systems The preceding material, although widely applicable, has been oriented towards centralized, multiuser, uniprocessor systems. In this and the next few sections, we briefly consider several other system structures.

Distributed systems involve multiple computer systems (*hosts*) connected by networks. The hosts often are high-performance single-user workstations. The idea of dedicating to a single user the power of a traditional multiuser computer, of coupling this computing power to a high-resolution bitmap display, and of viewing these workstations as participants in a distributed system rather than as isolated computers, was pioneered by Xerox in the 1970s and was made commercially successful by a number of vendors in the 1980s.

The basic operating system requirements for a single-user workstation differ little from those for a more traditional multiuser computer. Unix, developed in the early 1970s as a timesharing system, has become widely accepted as a workstation operating system, with the key addition of a *window system* to provide multiple logical displays on the single physical bitmap display. (Menu-oriented window systems are largely replacing more traditional command language interpreters as the user interface on a wide range of computer systems.) A number of key issues arise from distribution, though. Among these are *communication, file systems, authentication and security*, and *distributed programming support*.

In the realm of communication, *remote procedure call* (RPC) has received wide acceptance as a program-level mechanism. The goal of remote procedure call is to provide syntax and semantics that resemble as nearly as possible those of the familiar local procedure call: the synchronous transfer of control and parameters. In remote procedure call, the *client* and *server* programs are linked to *stubs* that are mechanically generated from a description of the *server interface* (see FILE SERVER). To the client, its stub looks like the server. To the server, its stub looks like the client. The stubs insulate the client and the

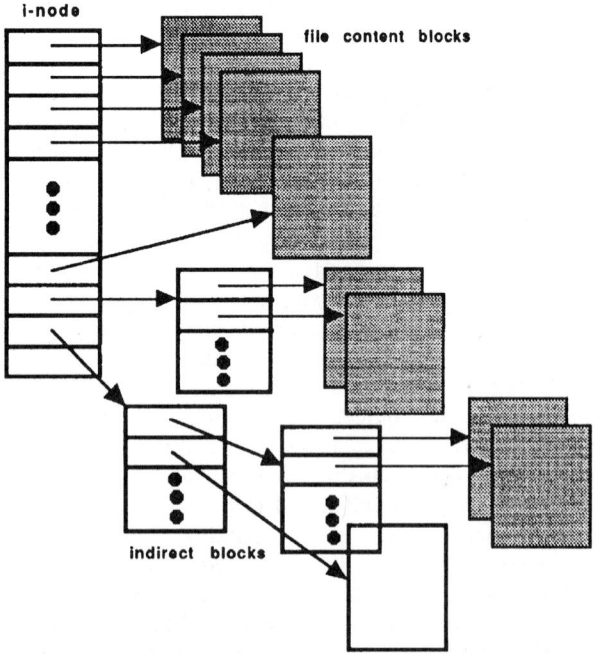

FIG. 7. Unix file allocation.

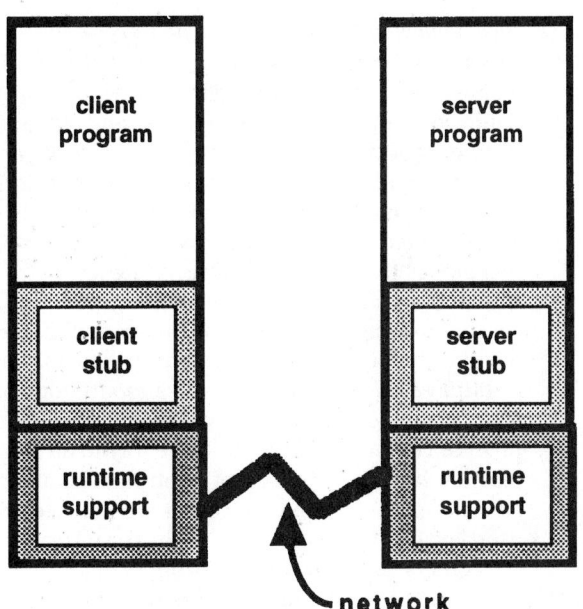

FIG. 8. Remote procedure call structure.

server from the details of network communication (see Fig. 8).

File sharing in a distributed system can be achieved by a mechanism as crude as the explicit transfer of files (using, for example, the Internet's File Transfer Protocol (FTP) or the remote copy (rcp) command of Berkeley Unix). Much greater integration, though, is provided by file systems such as the Network File System (NFS) and the Andrew File System (AFS).

NFS can be viewed as a fairly straightforward extension of the Unix file system, in which remote directory subtrees can be *mounted* so that they appear to be (and behave as if) part of the local file system. As originally designed and implemented, NFS does not provide replication or nice semantics for files actively shared by users at multiple sites. AFS also is integrated into Unix, but pays considerable attention to scalability, security, file sharing semantics, and system management. These are among the critical issues in distributed file systems.

Authentication is more difficult in a distributed system than in a centralized system because one entity cannot necessarily trust another. In a centralized system, once the user is authenticated (say, by the entry of a password), all parts of the system accept the identity of the user. Not so in a distributed system. *Kerberos* is an example of an authentication service that offers considerable promise in the distributed environment. Kerberos is a scalable system that employs a secret key cryptographic protocol for initial authentication, and then grants "tickets" of finite lifetime, enabling the use of specific services.

Security is more difficult in a distributed system than in a centralized one because there are many opportunities for eavesdropping. Both public-key and private-key cryptographic systems have been used to provide secure communication. (*See* CRYPTOGRAPHY, COMPUTERS IN.)

The issue of distributed programming support is a complex one. A distributed application differs from a centralized application in more respects than merely

communication. A distributed environment provides the potential for partial failure, which must be dealt with. At the same time, replication offers the potential for much higher overall reliability, availability, and performance than is possible with a centralized service. The critical question is which programming techniques make it easiest to realize this potential? The integration of *transactions* into distributed programming systems is one key approach, as exemplified by the Argus and Camelot systems. *Object-based systems* (e.g. Argus and Emerald) also are popular in the distributed environment.

Multiprocessor Systems Multiprocessor computer systems are becoming increasingly common because they offer the promise of significantly improved cost/performance for midrange systems, and significantly improved absolute performance for high-end systems. In this section we restrict our attention *to MIMD shared-memory multiprocessors*—systems with multiple independent processors executing out of shared memory.

It is possible, although not trivial, to take a uniprocessor operating system (e.g. Unix) and make it run on a multiprocessor. The difficulty arises because the way in which shared kernel data structures are protected from corruption in uniprocessor operating systems usually relies on the existence of only a single processor. In particular, when the kernel is active, hardware-level mutual exclusion is achieved by disabling interrupts. This doesn't work on a multiprocessor because a second processor can launch into the kernel even in the absence of interrupts. Thus, the mechanism for achieving hardware-level mutual exclusion must be changed (e.g. to one involving *busy-waiting (spin-locks)*).

Once accomplished, such a change would yield a multiprocessor operating system that worked, but likely with mediocre performance. There are two separate issues that must be addressed to improve this performance: parallelism in applications and parallelism in the operating system.

Although multiprocessors can be used to execute a conventional workload, the more interesting application domain involves parallel programs—programs that bring multiple processors to bear on a single problem. An example is matrix multiplication. In multiplying two $N \times N$ matrices A and B to yield an $N \times N$ result matrix C, each entry $[i,j]$ of C is computed as:

$$C[i,j] = \sum_{k=1}^{N} A[i,k]\, B[k,j]$$

It is clear that N^2 processors can easily be employed in computing the product of two matrices.

A key thing that a multiprocessor operating system must provide, then, is a facility for running parallel programs. The process mechanism, discussed earlier, is conceptually suitable, but such large overheads may be incurred for creating and synchronizing processes that only parallel computations with very coarse *granularity* (a word used to denote the relative size of a parallel unit of work) can be run with reasonable efficiency. (In the worst case, converting a sequential program into a parallel program may yield a *slowdown* rather than a *speedup*!) Much effort in the design of multiprocessor operating systems has been devoted to the design of *light-weight threads*—threads of control that can be created and synchronized more efficiently than traditional processes, and thus can be used in programming fine-grained applications.

It also is important to exploit parallelism in the operating system itself. Earlier, we showed how to achieve a *correct* operating system by changing the hardware-level mutual exclusion mechanism to ensure that only one processor at a time would execute in the kernel. Unfortunately, however, measurements show that computer systems often spend between 25% and 50% of the time executing operating system code as opposed to user code. If the bulk of this operating system code is single-threaded, the overall speedup of the system will be dramatically limited. *Amdahl's law* states that, if *S*% of a program is inherently sequential, the maximum attainable speedup is $1/S$. So, for example, if 25% of the time when running on a uniprocessor is spent executing inherently sequential operating system code, then, even if all user programs have unlimited parallelism and there are an unlimited number of processors, the overall system speedup will be at most 4. Thus, in order to achieve good performance from a multiprocessor operating system, it must be structured to allow the maximum possible internal physical concurrency.

There are a number of more subtle issues concerning the division of labor between the kernel and the application address spaces in multiprocessor operating systems which are beyond the scope of this article.

Personal Computer Systems As noted earlier in this article, operating systems for personal computers have quickly recapitulated the development history of operating systems for mainframes.

Early personal computers had simple resident monitor operating systems. A single application program ran at a time, fully resident in a contiguous region of physical memory. I/O was done through synchronous system service calls—the application was blocked while the I/O was in progress.

The user interface aspects of personal computers have advanced faster than other aspects of their operating systems, with many personal computer operating systems supporting menu-oriented window systems on bitmap displays. MS/DOS and the Macintosh operating system are examples of such systems: they support highly refined user interfaces and a huge suite of user-friendly applications, but otherwise are relatively primitive. OS/2, introduced around 1990, was among the first personal computer operating systems to support true multitasking—multiple address spaces and multiple processes.

The hardware capabilities of personal computers, workstations, and multi-user systems are increasingly similar, as are the demands on their operating systems.

Current Issues In this section we simply enumerate some issues of current interest in the field of operating systems:

- *High-bandwidth, low-latency networks*—For 15 years, local area network (*q.v.*) bandwidth remained at 10M bits/second. Networks with bandwidths in the 100M bits/second range are now becoming widespread, and gigabit networks are not far behind. This 100-fold increase in bandwidth presents a number of opportunities, particularly if accompanied by operating system structuring techniques that reduce the access latency.

- *High-performance parallel processing*—Multiprocessors present both the opportunity and the demand to rethink operating system structures. The traditional role of the kernel—to support address spaces, threads of control, scheduling, and interprocess communication—will give way to an organization in which threads of control, scheduling, and interprocess communication are managed at user level in the application address space, with the kernel responsible only for supporting address spaces and allocating processors to them.

- *Very large distributed systems*—Internetworks today connect hundreds of thousands of computer systems. How can file systems (organization, naming, and access), authentication, administration, etc., be designed to function effectively on a national or international scale?

- *Real-time multimedia systems*—The integration of real-time audio and video with computer workstations poses a number of exciting challenges and opportunities.

- *Integrated mobile computing*—The question here is how a user can compute "on the move" while remaining fully connected to his or her "home" environment.

- *Inexpensive, high-performance I/O*—The price/performance of CPUs has improved dramatically over the course of the past decade. Not so for disks. What innovations in operating systems and I/O subsystems will lead to cost-effective high-performance I/O?

- *Authentication and security*—Despite the progress represented by systems such as Kerberos, much work remains to be done in order to provide flexible, scalable, manageable authentication and security for large-scale systems.

References

1983. Holt, R. C. *Concurrent Euclid, the UNIX System, and TUNIS.* Reading, MA: Addison-Wesley Publishing Company.

1984. Birrell, A. D. and Nelson, B. J. "Implementing Remote Procedure Calls," *ACM Transactions on Computer Systems* **2**, *1*: 39–59 (February).

1984. Lazowska, E. D., Zahorjan, J., Graham, G. S., and Sevcik, K. C. *Quantitative System Performance: Computer System Analysis Using Queueing Network Models.* Englewood Cliffs, NJ: Prentice-Hall, Inc.

1984. Schroeder, M. D., Birrell, A. D., and Needham, R. M. "Experience with Grapevine: The Growth of a Distributed System." *ACM Transactions on Computer Systems* **2**, *1*: 3–23 (February).

1988. Shaw, A. C. (Ed.). Special Issue on Operating Systems. *Communications of the ACM* **31**, *3* (March).

1989. Leffler, S. J., McKusick, M. K., Karels, M. J., and Quarterman, J. S. *The Design and Implementaion of the 4.3BSD UNIX Operating System*. Reading, MA: Addison-Wesley Publishing Company.

1989. Satyanarayanan, M. "A Survey of Distributed File Systems." *Annual Review of Computer Science* 4: 73–104. Palo Alto, CA: Annual Reviews.

1991. Silberschatz, A., Peterson, J. L., and Galvin, P. B. *Operating System Concepts* (3rd Ed.). Reading, MA: Addison-Wesley Publishing Company.

EDWARD D. LAZOWSKA

OPERATIONS RESEARCH (OR)

For articles on related subjects *see* MATHEMATICAL PROGRAMMING; QUEUEING THEORY; SIMPLEX METHOD; and SIMULATION.

The Beginnings The modern origins of operations research (OR) are attributed by Trefethen (1954) to the British military during World War II. A group known as Blackett's Circus assisted in the employment and coordination of radar equipment at gun sites. The success of the venture stimulated others, and the term *operational research* was applied to the application of scientific techniques to military operations. Operations research (OR) became the term in vogue in the U.S. as interest grew in both industry and the military following the war. Gradually, courses emerged in universities in both England and the U.S. Mathematics, statistics, and industrial engineering provided early impetus (and often an academic home) for the discipline, which is now an integral part of the curriculum in almost all major universities. Memberships in the Operations Research Society of America exceeded 8,000 as of 1 January 1990.

In a disciplinary sense, OR emerged from applied mathematics. The early probabilistic models of telephone problems by A. K. Erlang in the period 1909–1920 and the work of T. C. Fry (1928) precede the beginnings of OR, but both are acknowledged ancestral contributions. The paper by D. C. Palm (1947), formulating the machine interference problem, is an early example of the use of queueing models in production settings. The discovery of the simplex method of linear programming by George B. Dantzig (in 1947) triggered extensive research in constrained optimization, which emerged as a major element of OR. The papers of Kendall (1951, 1954) exerted major influence on subsequent developments in queueing theory. As early books integrated optimization and probability studies within the nucleus of the modeling approach, OR assumed a more recognizable disciplinary form.

Views of Operations Research Contemporary views of operations research have tended to reflect the particular responsibilities and interests of the viewer. For several years, the research community emphasized techniques and methodologies, dwelling principally on the mathematical underpinnings. The simplex method, having assumed a focal position, was examined, tested, and extended as the research community sought to understand its necessary assumptions and to expand its applicability. Special classes of linear programming models were recognized, such as the transportation, network, and assignment problems, and algorithms were designed for efficiently solving them. (see Dantzig, 1963). Researchers in queueing theory formed their own problem classification as they refined their understanding of the relations among the factors that contribute to a waiting line situation—the arrival and service processes; the behavior of the potential and actual members of the queue; and the constraints on arrivals, service, or queue size.

Another view of OR might be characterized as the *model* view. Those adopting this vantage derived their own partitioning of OR activities, depending on the model type and the objectives of the modeler. For example, *descriptive models* furnished an understanding of an existing or planned problem situation without necessarily suggesting the means for improvement. Early queueing theory models were of this type. In contrast, *prescriptive models* offered solutions in terms of the desirability of outcomes. The determination of optimum or near-optimum conditions through a linear program exemplified this type.

The partitioning of OR along model types was supported also by the differences in the underlying assumptions and the supporting mathematical subdiscipline. Linear programming and, later, mathematical programming (including linear, nonlinear, integer, and mixed) drew heavily on the areas of analysis and topology, while random process applications emanated from probability theory. Inevitably, problems arose with characteristics based on more than one underlying area of mathematics; scheduling and inventory decisions are two prime examples.

Scheduling theory seeks to provide prescriptive models under deterministic or probabilistic conditions governing the sequencing of events, such as the order of task assignments to a single central processor. *Inventory theory* supports the development of prescriptive models of replenishment decisions possibly subject to uncertain conditions, for example, in the lead time between reorder and the arrival of the ordered stock. As significant questions forced attention to the use of both deterministic and probabilistic models within a single problem area, the size and complexity of models also increased. Consequently, the digital computer became an indispensable tool for solving the more challenging problems prompting such models.

Yet another perspective on OR might be described as the *algorithmic* view. This view, often held by those practicing the profession in industry or government, stems naturally from the roots of the discipline in problem solving within an operational context. An algorithm might be broadly applicable, or it could be developed only to treat an isolated problem. The emphasis is on an efficient solution using the simplest modeling techniques that achieve the problem-solving objective. Increasing importance is attached to heuristic approaches—that is, the use of "rules of thumb," perhaps guided by theory or knowledge of the problem domain—to obtain "good" but not necessarily optimum solutions.

A modern perspective, made possible by new computer technology, is the cognitive view. This view overlaps OR with cognitive science (*q.v.*), including elements of artificial intelligence (*q.v.*), which focuses on communication between humans and computers. To some OR practitioners and researchers, the real bottleneck is how to understand results obtained from computer-resident models designed for decision support. This embodies principles of model management and discourse at many levels, including linguistic and graphic interfaces. In this view, the emphasis is on new roles for the computer to assist in the design of a decision support system and in understanding its results.

The concern for improved (but not necessarily optimal) behavior and the increased complexity of models combined to lend emphasis to the technique of computer simulation. Computer simulation as an early problem-solving tool received the attention of von Neumann and other noted scientists during the late 1940s. While simulation had historical origins predating computers and OR, the technique became significant only when development of the digital computer established its practical feasibility. Simulation is not an optimization technique, but is the combination of a simulation model and a search routine that enables directed improvement to be realized.

Examples of the Operations Research Approach
Fundamental in the OR approach is the development of a model to describe the particular problem. The following problem scenarios serve as simple illustrations of the several classes of models described above. Each consists of a problem description, a solution description, and comments on the assumptions regarding the problem or implications of the solution technique.

A Scheduling Model for Throughput Maximization

Problem An integral part of the operation of a computer system is the *task scheduler*, the program that assigns tasks to a CPU according to some criterion. One such criterion is to maximize throughput (the number of tasks completed per unit time). The designer of an operating system for a single-processor installation might utilize an OR modeling approach to implement the scheduling decision.

Solution Assume that the order of task completions is immaterial and the completion of one task causes no change in the task completion time of a successor.

Let $t(i)$ = the completion time for the *i*th task to be completed; t^* = the arbitrary final time (with $t = 0$ at the start); and n = the number of completed tasks. The objective is to

$$\text{maximize } n \text{ such that } t(n) \leq t*.$$

That is, to find the largest number of tasks that can be completed in the interval from 0 to t^*. Following intuition, the solution is to assign to the CPU the task that requires the least processing time. This scheduling rule assures

that the maximum number of tasks are fitted into the t^* period.

Comments (1) The above rule, known as the Shortest Processing Time (SPT) rule, can be shown to be optimal for criteria other than the maximization of throughput and to problems involving more than one processor [see Conway, Maxwell, and Miller (1967) and Coffman and Denning (1973)]. (2) Note that this solution requires that, during the time t^*, the CPU is continuously busy. (3) The task completion times are assumed to be known and deterministic, which is not the usual case.

A Job Mix Resource Allocation Problem

Problem A university computing center processes two types of jobs—teaching and research. The center is heavily loaded and seeks to maintain balanced service providing the highest satisfaction level to the entire user community. The center has a single computer with 5,120 Kb-hrs (kilobyte-hours, where 1 Kb-hr is the use of 1,000 bytes of memory for one hour) of memory and 48,000 seconds of CPU time available per day. The problem is to determine the balance between teaching and research jobs that provides the highest overall satisfaction level.

Solution Working with the user community and the administration, the OR analyst estimates a "relative satisfaction return" per job of 6 to 4 for research and teaching, respectively. From a study of center records, the analyst obtains estimates of 32 Kb-hrs of memory and 200 seconds of CPU time for each teaching job. Each research job takes 40 Kb-hrs of memory and 400 seconds of CPU time. Using this data, the analyst constructs a linear programming model.

Let X_1 = the number of research jobs processed, and
X_2 = the number of teaching jobs processed.

Then, the objective (represented as the function z) is to maximize the overall satisfaction level:

$$\text{maximize } z = 6 * X_1 + 4 * X_2$$

while not exceeding the available memory and the CPU time limitation, subject to:

$$40 * X_1 + 32 * X_2 \leq 5,120$$
$$400 * X_1 + 200 * X_2 \leq 48,000$$

and noting that the number of research and teaching jobs processed must be non-negative:

$$X_1 \geq 0, X_2 \geq 0.$$

This simple linear program in two variables (X_1 and X_2) can be solved graphically, as shown in Fig. 1 (*see* MATHEMATICAL PROGRAMMING). The solution of 107 research and 26 teaching jobs per day gives an overall maximum satisfaction level of 746.

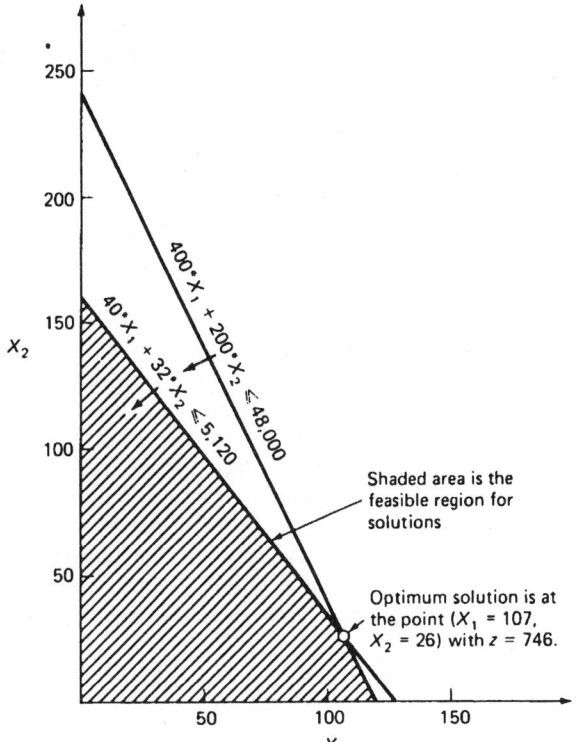

FIG. 1. Graphical solution of the job mix problem.

Comments (1) The determination of "relative satisfaction returns" is not a simple task, and another subdisciplinary area of OR—decision analysis—deals with the definition, measurement, estimation, and integration of preferences. (2) The solution was given in terms of integer values because fractional jobs are not meaningful. Non-integer solutions are to be expected using linear programming, and roundoffs to integer values do not guarantee the preservation of an optimal solution.

Disk Access: A Queueing Problem

Problem A disk is a peripheral storage device consisting of several recording surfaces, each of which resembles a phonograph record. A surface is divided concentrically into tracks and each track is divided into sectors of storage locations. The two basic types of disk design are movable head and fixed head (also known as head per track). The latter type has its read and write mechanisms—the heads—fixed in place, one pair for each track. Rotation of the disk brings the storage locations under the read/write (R/W) heads that permit the retrieval (reading) and storage (writing) of data (*see* MEMORY: AUXILIARY).

Access requests contain a sector identifier so that the search in a fixed-head disk consists of sector identification followed by address location within a sector. The access delay is made up of (1) the time to place the sector identifier (initializing address) under the R/W heads, which is called *latency* (*q.v.*), and (2) the time to locate the specific address within a sector (*location time*). Fig. 2(a) illustrates these access operations, which utilize a single-access request queue for a track.

The objective in programming the access to data stored on a fixed-head disk is to minimize the total access time (latency plus location time). The simplest approach to this problem is to program the disk access as a "first come/first served" decision. However, some alternative decision rules can be suggested, providing that certain specific data are available for implementing the solution. For example, if the sector identifiers for access requests and the current rotational position are known, then the closest sector could be accessed first. A mathematical (queueing) model offers a means for experimenting with different decision rules or alternative data organizations without incurring the expense of constructing the devices.

Solution The latency can be estimated to be one-half the time for one complete revolution (the request is equally likely to be any address on a track). However, the estimation of the seek time requires the use of probability theory beyond the scope of this article. Nevertheless, one can appreciate a suggested solution that defines a queue of disk requests for each sector and provides for service of any non-empty queue encountered by the R/W heads during the rotation of the surface. This multi-queue operation, illustrated in Fig. 2(b), significantly reduces the rotational latency.

Comments The multi-queue operation can be modeled, with the appropriate assumptions, so as to admit a solution through mathematical derivations. A more complicated model is likely to require the use of computer simulation, which could be more costly to produce but more detailed in its description.

Relationships with Computer Science

Computer science and OR are linked by the similarities in their evolutions, their mutual dependencies on mathematics, and the close proximities of their research and applications areas. A scan of the prominent overlapping technical areas reveals both similarities and contrasts in the two disciplines, especially when each is viewed in relation to the other. (A comprehensive picture of OR techniques is given in Moder and Elmaghraby, 1978.)

William Orchard-Hays (1978) provides an excellent history of the development of mathematical programming systems which documents not only the significant advances enabled by the rapid development of computing technology, but also notes the contributions to the technology stimulated by the reactions to the demands of those producing mathematical programming systems. Expanding computational capabilities has enabled the solution of larger, more complex problems. However, caution is warranted in attributing the ability to solve more extensive problems simply to more capable computer systems; actually, the expanded capabilities can be traced to one or more of the following sources.

1. The discovery of new mathematical techniques that are embodied in existing algorithms (e.g. the solution of traveling salesman problems with 200 cities in 1990 compared to only 20 cities in 1960).

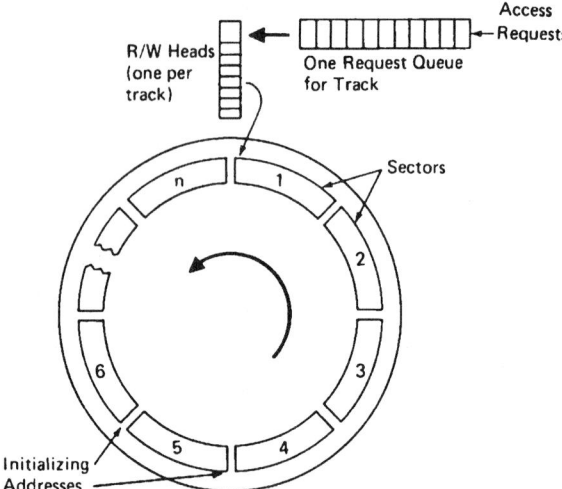

(a) Track organization and a single request queue

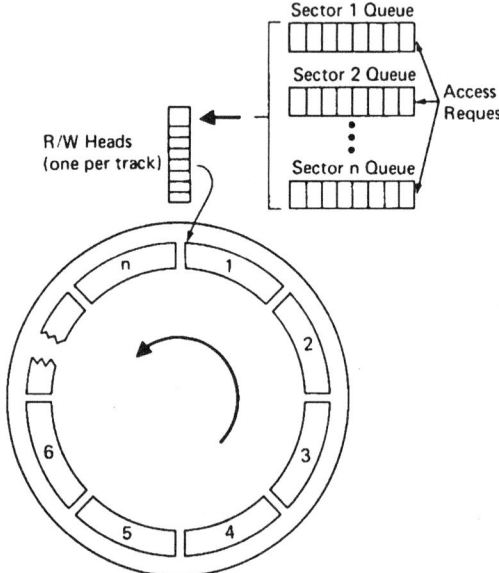

(b) A request queue for each sector

FIG. 2. Single- and multi-queue request illustrations.

2. The design or redesign of algorithms, involving both changes in data structures and revisions in the operations and control structures (e.g. enabling the solution of linear programs with 10,000 rows and 100,000 columns).

3. The revelation of the complexity inherent in classes of problems so that heuristic techniques can be employed to obtain near-optimal solutions (e.g. the general scheduling problem).

4. The increase in storage and speed provided with current computing systems.

Advances in numerical approximation techniques, predominantly through research in computer science, have extended the range of "solvable" probabilistic models. Researchers in OR, sensitive to the utility of the approximate but more informative models, have

contributed to the improvement and extension of the techniques (see Bhat, 1969). Instead of exact solutions to queueing models, given in terms of complex and abstract Laplace-Stieltjes transforms, approximate answers are now more common, both for the long-term (steady-state) and the short-term (transient) behavior of the system being studied. So important have computational approximations become in the solution of probabilistic models that an area of inquiry—computational probability—has emerged within OR (see Neuts, 1980).

Advances in the development and applicability of computer simulation have proceeded through the extensions to the methodology for statistical analysis of model output and the improved capabilities of simulation programming languages (e.g. Simula 67, Simscript II.5, GPSS V) and model development tools (e.g. the DELTA Project underway at the Norwegian Computing Center, 1977). Fundamental inquiry into the representation of simulation models and efficient experimentation represents a research area of mutual interest for computer scientists, operations researchers, and systems theorists (see Zeigler, 1976).

Perhaps the nucleus of the intersection of OR and computer science is the algorithm. The derivation and design of algorithms has dominated OR throughout its history and has been recognized as a major element of computer science since the early 1950s. More recently, the interest in algorithms has broadened for both disciplines, and the future might portend the merging of research in this fundamental area.

References

1928. Fry, T. C. *Probability and Its Engineering Uses.* New York: D. Van Nostrand.

1947. Palm, D. C. "The Distribution of Repairmen in Servicing Automatic Machines" (Swedish), *Industritidningen Norden* **75**: 75.

1951. Kendall, D. G. "Some Problems in the Theory of Queues," *Journal of the Royal Statistical Society* B13: 151.

1954. Kendall, D. G. "Stochastic Processes Occurring in the Theory of Queues and Their Analysis by the Method of the Imbedded Markov Chain," *Annals of Mathematical Statistics* 24: 338.

1954. Trefethen, F. N. "A History of Operations Research," in McCloskey, J. F. and Trefethen, F. N. (Eds.), *Operations Research for Management* 1. Baltimore: Johns Hopkins Press.

1963. Dantzig, G. B. *Linear Programming and Extensions.* Princeton: Princeton University Press.

1967. Conway, R. W., Maxwell, W. L., and Miller, L. W. *Theory of Scheduling.* Reading, MA: Addison-Wesley.

1969. Bhat, U. N. "Sixty Years of Queueing Theory," *Management Science* **15**, 6: B-280 (February).

1973. Coffman, E. G., and Denning, P. E. *Operating Systems Theory.* Englewood Cliffs, NJ: Prentice-Hall.

1976. Zeigler, B. P. *Theory of Modeling and Simulation.* New York: Wiley.

1977. Holbaek-Hanssen, E., Handlykken, P., and Nygaard, K. *System Description and the DELTA Language, Report No. 4* (Publication No. 523). Oslo: Norwegian Computing Center.

1978. Orchard-Hays, W. "History of Mathematical Programming Systems," in Greenberg, H. J. (Ed.), *Design and Implementation of Optimization Software.* Alphen aan den Rijn, The Netherlands: Sijthoff and Noordhoff.

1978. Moder, J. J. and Elmaghraby, S. E. *Handbook of Operations Research*. New York: Van Nostrand Reinhold.

1980. Neuts, M. F. *Matrix-Geometric Solutions for Stochastic Models: An Algorithmic Approach*. Baltimore: Johns Hopkins Press.

HARVEY J. GREENBERG AND RICHARD E. NANCE

OPERATOR PRECEDENCE

For articles on related subjects *see* EXPRESSION; GRAMMARS; POLISH NOTATION; and PROGRAMMING LINGUISTICS.

Operator precedence refers to the hierarchy of precedence relations that determine the order in which operators are applied to their operands in a high-level language expression.

As an example of the need for such relationships, consider the expression

$$A + B * C$$

Is this to be interpreted as $A + (B*C)$ or $(A + B)*C$? One way to solve this problem would be to enforce a strict left-to-right or (as in APL) a right-to-left order of evaluation. However, most programming languages resolve possible ambiguities by establishing precedence relations that determine the order in which operators are applied. A major purpose of such relations is to assure that as many expressions as possible have their "natural" interpretation (e.g. most people would regard $A + (B*C)$ as the natural interpretation of $A + B*C$).

The operator hierarchy includes not only arithmetic operators but also relational operators ($<, >, \leq, \geq, =, \neq$), logical operators [**and, or, not**], concatenation (*q.v.*), and other operators (such as those that apply to bit strings). Table 1 gives the arithmetic, relational, and logical operator hierarchy in Fortran, Pascal and C. It is to be interpreted as follows: In an expression containing more than one operator, the operator to be applied first is the one that is highest in the hierarchy. Thus,

Expression	Interpretation
$3 + 4 * 5 - 6$	$3 + (4 * 5) - 6 = 17$
$16/4 + 8$	$(16/4) + 8 = 12$
$3 < 4 + 5$	$3 < (4 + 5) = $ true

Note that the position of the relational operators relative to the arithmetic operators is forced if expressions containing a combination of these operators are to be meaningful. Thus, the Pascal or C expression

$$3 < 4 + 5$$

makes sense only if interpreted as

$$3 < (4 + 5).$$

When an expression contains two operators of equal precedence, the usual rule is to evaluate them from left to right (although successive exponentiations are often evaluated right to left). Thus, $A/B * C$ is to be interpreted as $(A/B*C)$. Finally, in all languages, parentheses may always be used to override the precedence rules.

ANTHONY RALSTON

OPTICAL CHARACTER READERS

For articles on related subjects *see* IMAGE PROCESSING; PATTERN RECOGNITION; PERCEPTRON; and UNIVERSAL PRODUCT CODE.

Optical character readers are automated electromechanical systems that perform optical character recognition (OCR). OCR may be defined as the process of converting images of machine printed or handwritten numerals, letters, and symbols into a computer-processable format. The long history of research in this area, commercial success, and the continuing need and ability to handle less restricted forms of text make OCR, to date, the most important application area in machine perception.

Two types of automated reading equipment, distinct from optical character readers (OCR systems), are *optical mark readers* (OMRs) and *magnetic ink character readers* (MICRs). OMRs characteristically read non-textual input, such as bar codes. Examples of OMRs are grocery store bar code readers that read the Universal Product Code (UPC) and the United States Postal Service's wide area bar code reader that reads ZIP codes encoded in the PostNet code. MICRs classify alphanumeric characters by utilizing the pattern corresponding to the magnetic field generated by character ink. One common MICR is a bank check reader that reads account numbers on the bottom of checks.

Commercial OCR predominantly pertain to machine-printed text. Although neatly printed handwriting is accepted by OCR systems, the technology for handwriting recognition is generally distinct from OCR technology. Handwriting recognition systems can be divided into two

TABLE 1. Operator Hierarchy

	Fortran	Pascal	C
High	**		
		not	!
	$-$ (unary)		$-$ (unary)
	*, /	*, /, **div, mod, and**	*, /, %
	+, $-$	+, $-$, **or**	+, $-$
	Relational ops.	Relational ops	<, <=, >, >= == , !=
	.NOT.		
	.AND.		&&
	.OR.		||
	.EQV.		
Low	.NEQV.		

**	—Exponentiation
div	—Integer quotient of integer division
mod and %	—Integer remainder of integer division
==	—Equality
!=	—Inequality

types: on-line and off-line. On-line systems allow recognition of characters and words as they are written onto a surface. The interactive nature of these systems enables recognition algorithms to use information about how characters are written. Many on-line systems allow interactive correction of misrecognized characters. Off-line systems recognize characters that have been previously written on a document. Therefore, no information is available on the writing style or the implement path used to create the character strokes.

The ensuing exposition explores commercial OCR technology with respect to its structure, technological attributes, application areas, and availability.

Basic Structure of OCR Systems As illustrated in Fig. 1, a typical off-line OCR system contains three logical components:

1. Image scanner.
2. OCR software/hardware.
3. Output interface.

The image scanner optically captures text images to be recognized. Text images are processed with OCR software and hardware by extracting individual character images and recognizing these images. Contextual processing may also be used to correct misclassifications made by the recognition algorithm. The output interface is responsible for communication of OCR system results to the outside world.

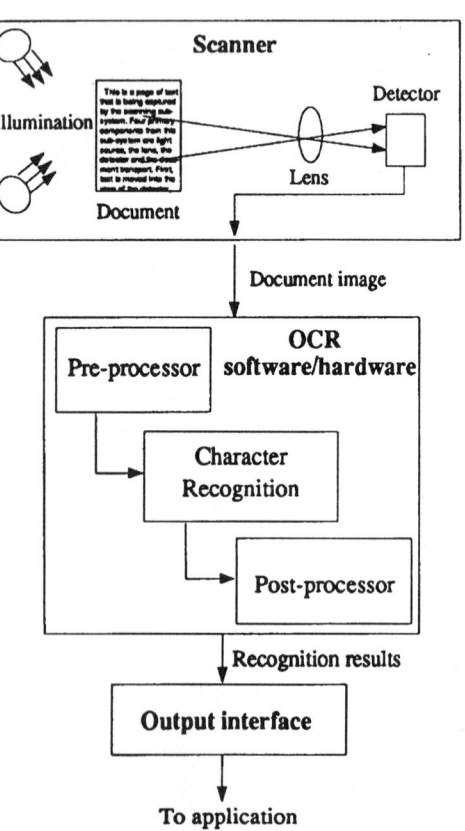

FIG. 1. General structure of an off-line OCR system.

Image Scanner Four basic building blocks form functional image scanners: a detector (and associated electronics), a light source, a scan lens, and a document transport. To capture an object's image, the document transport places the object in the scanning field, the light source illuminates the object, and the lens forms the object's image on the detector. The detector consists of an array of elements, each of which converts incident light into a charge or analog signal. These analog signals are then converted into an image. Scanning is performed by the detector and the motion of the text object, with respect to the detector. After an image is captured, the document transport removes the document from the scanning field.

The choice of the illumination source and lens depends upon detector characteristics. The document must be illuminated with enough light so that the amount reflected from the document through the lens is of sufficient intensity to allow the detector to operate with a good signal-to-noise ratio. Since non-uniform illumination over the scanned area affects the signal-to-noise ratio, compensation for negative effects should be performed in signal extraction/processing.

Three types of integrated circuits (*q.v.*) dominate the current detector market: *photodiode arrays, charge-coupled device* (CCD) *arrays*, and *charge-coupled photodiode device* (CCPD) *arrays*. They differ in how light is converted into analog signals and in how signals are transferred off-chip. Each technology can be used to capture one-dimensional or two-dimensional image sections. Both CCD and CCPD arrays are easier to integrate into scanning systems than photodiode arrays. Further, *time-delay integration* (TDI) CCDs operate under low illumination levels, since they collect photons over a larger temporal span.

The document transport defines each scanner as either a *fixed document* or *moving document* scanner. *Fixed document* scanners capture images by either moving the detector relative to the document or by using a two-dimensional detector that contains the object in its fovea. *Moving document* scanners, on the other hand, use rollers or other mechanical devices to move the document past a stationary detector.

Fixed document scanners capture images using focal-plane or platen-based methodologies. Focal-plane techniques use two-dimensional detectors. This type of imaging is similar to that used in television cameras, and the resolution is often not sharp enough for high-quality OCR system results. Platen-based systems are much like photocopiers. The document is placed on a glass surface, either flat or curved, and the image is lifted from the document as the detector traverses the document. Flat-bed scanners are platen-based. The document transport on fixed document scanners ranges from humans that place pages onto a flat-bed scanner to automatic feed mechanisms.

Moving document scanners generally use one-dimensional detectors (linear arrays) to capture images. As the document is moved past the detector, a single scan line is extracted in parallel before the document is moved to the next position. These scanners are most often used with automatic feed mechanisms that can attain very high speed. Postal OCR systems, for instance, can feed and scan letters at the rate of 120 inches per second. Moving document scanners are also used in hand-held OCR systems, such as the Saba *Handscan*. Documents must be properly aligned so that recognition rates are not reduced, and, in high-speed systems, the documents must be prevented from flying off the document transport.

OCR Software/Hardware The software/hardware system that recognizes characters from a registered image can be divided into three operational steps: image preprocessing, character recognition, and post-processing.

Image Preprocessor

The preprocessor performs operations that are necessary for preparing the scanned and registered text image for segmentation and recognition. Reliable character segmentation and recognition depend upon both original document quality and registered image quality. Processes that attempt to compensate for poor quality originals and/or poor quality scanning include image enhancement, underline removal, and noise removal. Image enhancement methods emphasize character versus non-character discrimination. Underline removal erases printed guidelines and other lines that may touch characters and interfere with character recognition, and noise removal erases portions of the image that are not part of the characters.

Prior to character recognition, it is necessary to isolate individual characters from the text image. Many OCR systems use connected components for this process. For those connected components that represent multiple or partial characters, more sophisticated algorithms are used. In low-quality or non-uniform text images, these sophisticated algorithms may not extract characters correctly, and thus recognition errors may occur. Recognition of unconstrained handwritten text can be very difficult because characters cannot be isolated reliably, especially when the text is cursive handwriting.

Character Recognition

Two essential components in a character recognition algorithm are the *feature extractor* and the *classifier*. Feature analysis determines the descriptors, or feature set, used to describe all characters. Given a character image, the feature extractor derives the features that the character possesses. The derived features are then used as input to the character classifier.

Template matching, or *matrix matching*, is one of the most common classification methods. In template matching, individual image pixels are used as features. Classification is performed by comparing an input character image with a set of templates (or prototypes) from each character class. Each comparison results in a similarity measure between the input character and the template. One measure increases the amount of similarity when a pixel in the observed character is identical to the same pixel in the template image. If the pixels differ, the measure of similarity may be decreased. After all templates

have been compared with the observed character image, the character's identity is assigned as the identity of the most similar template.

Template matching is a trainable process because template characters may be changed. In many commercial systems, PROMs store templates containing single fonts. To retrain the algorithm, the current PROMs are replaced with PROMs that contain images of a new font. Thus, if a suitable PROM exists for a font, template matching can be trained to recognize that font. The similarity measure of template matching may also be modified, but commercial OCR systems typically do not allow this. Calera *TrueScan* is an example of a commercial OCR system that uses template matching.

Structural classification methods use structural features and decision rules to classify characters. Structural features may be defined in terms of character strokes, character holes, or other character attributes, such as concavities. For instance, the letter P may be described as a vertical stroke with a hole attached on the upper right side. For a character image input, the structural features are extracted and a rule-based system is applied to classify the character. Structural methods are also trainable, but construction of a good feature set and a good rule-base can be time-consuming. The *Kurzweil Personal Reader* uses a structural approach to character recognition.

Many character recognizers are based on mathematical formalisms that minimize a measure of misclassification. These recognizers may use pixel-based or structural features. Some examples are discriminant function classifiers, Bayesian classifiers, artificial neural networks (ANNs) and template matchers. Discriminant function classifiers use hypersurfaces to separate the featural description of characters from different semantic classes and, in the process, reduce the mean-squared error. Bayesian methods seek to minimize the loss function associated with misclassification through the use of probability theory. ANNs, which are based on concepts closer to theories of human perception, employ mathematical minimization techniques. Both discriminant functions and ANNs are used in commercial OCR systems. The *Multiline Optical Character Reader B* (MLOCR-B) from ElectroCom Automation uses a linear discriminant function, and the *HNC IDEPT* uses an ANN.

Character misclassifications stem from two main sources: poor quality character images and poor discriminatory ability. Poor document quality, image scanning, and preprocessing can all degrade performance by yielding poor quality characters. On the other hand, the character recognition method may not have been trained for a proper response to the character causing the error. This type of error is difficult to overcome because the recognition method may have limitations and all possible character images cannot possibly be considered in training the classifier. Recognition rates for machine-printed characters can exceed 99%, but handwritten character recognition rates are typically lower because every person writes differently. This random nature often manifests itself by resulting in misclassifications. Fig. 2 shows several examples of machine printed and handwritten capital Os. Each

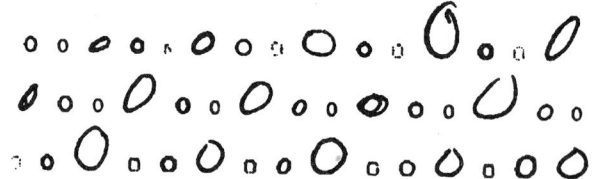

FIG. 2. Machine-printed and handwritten capital Os.

capital O can be easily confused with the numeral 0 and the number of different styles of capital O demonstrates the difficulties that recognizers must cope with.

Postprocessor

Postprocessing gives an OCR system the opportunity to correct recognition errors. One method used to postprocess character recognition results is to apply a spelling checker (q.v.) to verify word spelling. Calera offers such a capability. Similarly, other postprocessing methods use lexicons to verify word results, or recognition results may be verified interactively by the user. Additional methods to correct or prevent errors by using contextual knowledge are state-of-the-art and should appear in commercial systems shortly.

Output Interface The output interface allows character recognition results to be transferred electronically into the domain that uses them. For example, many commercial systems allow recognition results to be placed directly into spreadsheets (q.v.), databases, and word processors. Other commercial systems use recognition results directly in further automated processing, and when the processing is complete, the results are discarded.

Historical Perspective

An ideal model OCR system uses the human eye as the scanner and the human brain as the character recognizer. Accordingly, many of the early developments in OCR technology stemmed from attempts to help visually impaired people read. According to H. F. Schantz, the first steps towards OCR systems were made in 1809 when the first patents for reading devices to aid the blind were awarded. The first retinal scanner was developed by C. R. Carey in 1870 by using a mosaic of photocells to scan characters. In 1890, P. Nipkow developed a scanning disk that many consider a forerunner of modern television cameras, and in 1912, E. Goldberg converted scanned text into Morse code to be sent over a telegraph line.

Modern OCR technology is said to have been born in 1951 with M. Sheppard's invention, GISMO—A Robot Reader-Writer. In 1954, J. Rainbow developed a prototype machine that was able to read uppercase typewritten output at the "fantastic" speed of one character per minute. Several companies, including IBM, Recognition Equipment, Inc., Farrington, Control Data, and Optical Scanning Corporation, marketed OCR systems by 1967. During the late 1960s, the technology underwent many dramatic developments, but OCR systems were considered exotic and futuristic, used only by government agen-

cies or large corporations. Systems that cost 1 million dollars were not uncommon.

In the early years of OCR, many standards were developed to help guide automatic document processing. These standards included:

- Character Set for Optical Character Recognition (OCR-A). ANSI X3.17-81.
- Character Set for Optical Character Recognition (OCR-B). ANSI X3.49-75.
- Paper Used in Optical Character Recognition Systems. ANSI X3.62-87.
- Optical Character Recognition (OCR) Inks. ANSI X3.86-80.
- Optical Character Recognition (OCR) Character Position. ANSI X3.93-81.

The two ANSI standard machine-printed fonts along with the ANSI standard handwritten font are pictured in Fig. 3.

Current OCR systems are less expensive, faster, and more reliable. It is not uncommon to find PC-based OCR systems for under $8,000 capable of recognizing several hundred characters per minute. A large number of fonts can be recognized, and some systems are advertised as being *omnifont*: able to read *any* machine printed font. Less expensive electronic components and extensive research paved the way for these new systems. With continued commercial demand for OCR systems, these trends

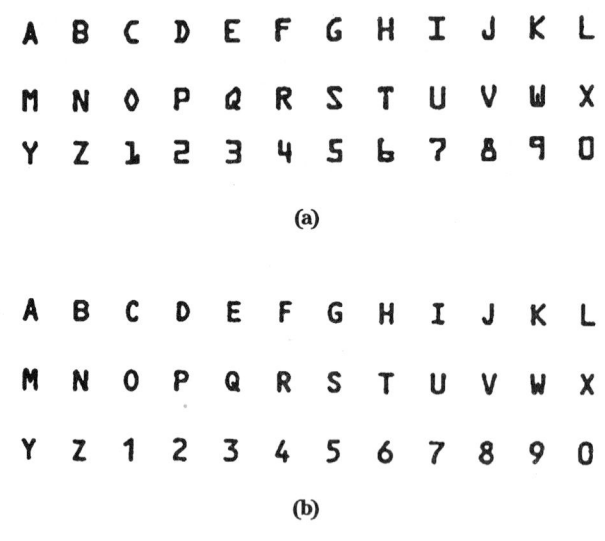

FIG. 3. Standardized fonts: (a) OCR-A font, (b) OCR-B font, and (c) Handwritten font.

will continue. Increased productivity through reduced human intervention and the ability to store text efficiently are two major selling points.

Reliable recognition of handwritten cursive script is now under intensive investigation. In addition, research is being conducted in "reading" forms (i.e. using all available information to formulate an interpretation of the document). For instance, some United States Postal Service research focuses on assigning ZIP Codes to letter images that do not contain a ZIP Code by interpreting their various address fields. The use of contextual information in both handwriting recognition and form reading is essential.

Commercial OCR Systems

Commercial OCR systems can be grouped into two categories: *task-specific readers* and *general purpose page readers*. A task-specific reader handles only specific document types. Some of the most common task-specific readers read bank check, letter mail, or credit card slips. These readers are usually based on custom-made image lift hardware that captures only a few predefined document regions. For example, a bank check reader may scan just the courtesy (numerical) amount field and a postal OCR system may scan just the address block on a mail piece. Such systems emphasize high throughput rates and low error rates. Applications such as letter mail reading have throughput rates of 12 letters per second with error rates less than 2.0%. The character recognizer in many task-specific readers is able to recognize both handwritten and machine-printed text.

General purpose page readers are designed to handle a broader range of documents, such as business letters, technical writings, and newspapers. These systems capture an image of a document page and separate the page into text regions and non-text regions. Non-text regions, such as graphics and line drawings, are often saved separately from the text and associated recognition results. Text regions are segmented into lines, words, and characters, and the characters are passed to the recognizer. Recognition results are output in a format that can be postprocessed by application software. Most of these page readers can read machine-written text, but only a few can read hand-printed alphanumerics. General purpose page readers are usually less expensive than task-specific readers.

Task-Specific Readers Task-specific readers are used primarily for high-volume applications that require high system throughput. Since high throughput rates are desired, handling only the fields of interest helps reduce time constraints. Since similar documents possess similar size and layout structure, it is straightforward for the image scanner to focus on those fields where the desired information lies. This approach can considerably reduce the image processing and text recognition time. Some application areas to which task-specific readers have been applied include:

- Verification of account numbers and courtesy amounts on bank checks;
- Assigning ZIP Codes to letter mail;
- Reading data off preprinted forms;
- Automatic accounting procedures used in processing utility bills;
- Automatic accounting of airline passenger tickets; and
- Automatic validation of passports.

Check Readers

Check readers capture check images and recognize courtesy amounts and account information on the checks. Manufacturers of check reading machines include Banctec, Inc., HNC, IBM, and TRW Financial Systems. Banctec Inc.'s *Impac System* reads check accounts optically and magnetically. An operator can correct misclassified characters by cross-validating the recognition results with the check image that appears on a system console.

The *Character Recognition Server 100* (CRS 100) from HNC reads handwritten numeric characters in the courtesy amount field on checks. The system consists of an IBM PC 386 AT or compatible computer augmented by a co-processing board. Its character recognition software uses a neural network (*q.v.*) approach. The system throughput is 1 to 2 seconds per check.

The IBM *Image Plus High Performance Transaction System* (HPTS) recognizes hand-printed numeric courtesy amounts on checks. HPTS uses a combination of the IBM 3890 reader/sorter and the Check Processing Control System (CPCS). Depending on the system configuration and hardware support, the system can read 1,100 to 2,400 checks per minute and costs between $600,000 and $1.5 million.

The image-based OCR system from TRW Financial Systems reads the value on a computer-printed remittance slip and uses the value to cross-check the hand-printed courtesy amount on the accompanying check. This system can be adapted to read a wide range of forms.

Address Readers

The address reader in a postal mail sorter locates the destination address block on a mail piece and reads the ZIP Code in this address block. If additional fields in the address block are read with high confidence, the system may generate a 9-digit ZIP Code. The resulting ZIP Code is then used to generate a bar code, which is sprayed on the envelope. Approximately 400 of these systems are used in the United States Postal Offices, and many others are used by other postal services throughout the world. By 1995, an address recognition unit (ARU) prototype will be delivered that will attain an accuracy rate of 90% for machine-written addresses and 50% for handwritten addresses. Major manufacturers of postal OCR systems are AEG, ElectroCom Automation, Elsag, NEC, Recognition Equipment, Inc., and Toshiba.

The *Automatic Letter Sorting System* from AEG incorporates several OCR address readers that, in the aggregate, can handle up to 120,000 items per hour for the German Federal Post Office. The mail pieces are presorted by the address readers and then fed into the final sorting machines, which distribute the mail pieces to 140 bins.

The *Multiline Optical Character Reader B* (MLOCR-B) from ElectroCom Automation locates the address block on a mail piece, reads the whole address, identifies the ZIP + 4™ code, generates a 9-digit bar code, and sorts the mail to the correct stacker. The character classifier recognizes up to 400 fonts, and the system can process up to 45,000 mail pieces per hour. Several hundred of these systems will be used by the United States Postal Service (USPS). The system is shown in Fig. 4.

The ELSAG postal address reading machine is realized by the SARI (Italian for Automatic Address Recognition System) implementation. This multiprocessor architecture can process up to 50,000 items per hour and is being employed in the French and Italian Postal Administrations.

Form Readers

A form reading system needs to discriminate between preprinted form instructions and filled-in data. The system is first trained with a blank form. The system registers those areas on the form where the data should be printed. During the form recognition phase, the system uses the spatial information obtained from training to scan the regions that should be filled with data. Some manufacturers of form reading systems are AEG, CompuScan, Eastman Kodak, and HNC.

The *PFL 6150* form reader from AEG can read handprinted data, as well as various machine-written text. It reads data on a form without being confused with the form instructions. The system can recognize up to 255 areas on a form, and the system throughput peaks at 1,400 forms per hour.

The *FormsReader Laser Data Entry System* from CompuScan, Inc. is a super-minicomputer-based form reading system. The system can process forms at a rate of 5,800 forms per hour. The system reads mark-sense (marks made on a multiple-choice form) and hand-printed and machine-printed alphanumerics.

The *Forms Reader Model 1* from Eastman Kodak is designed to work with an IBM PC/AT or compatible and is

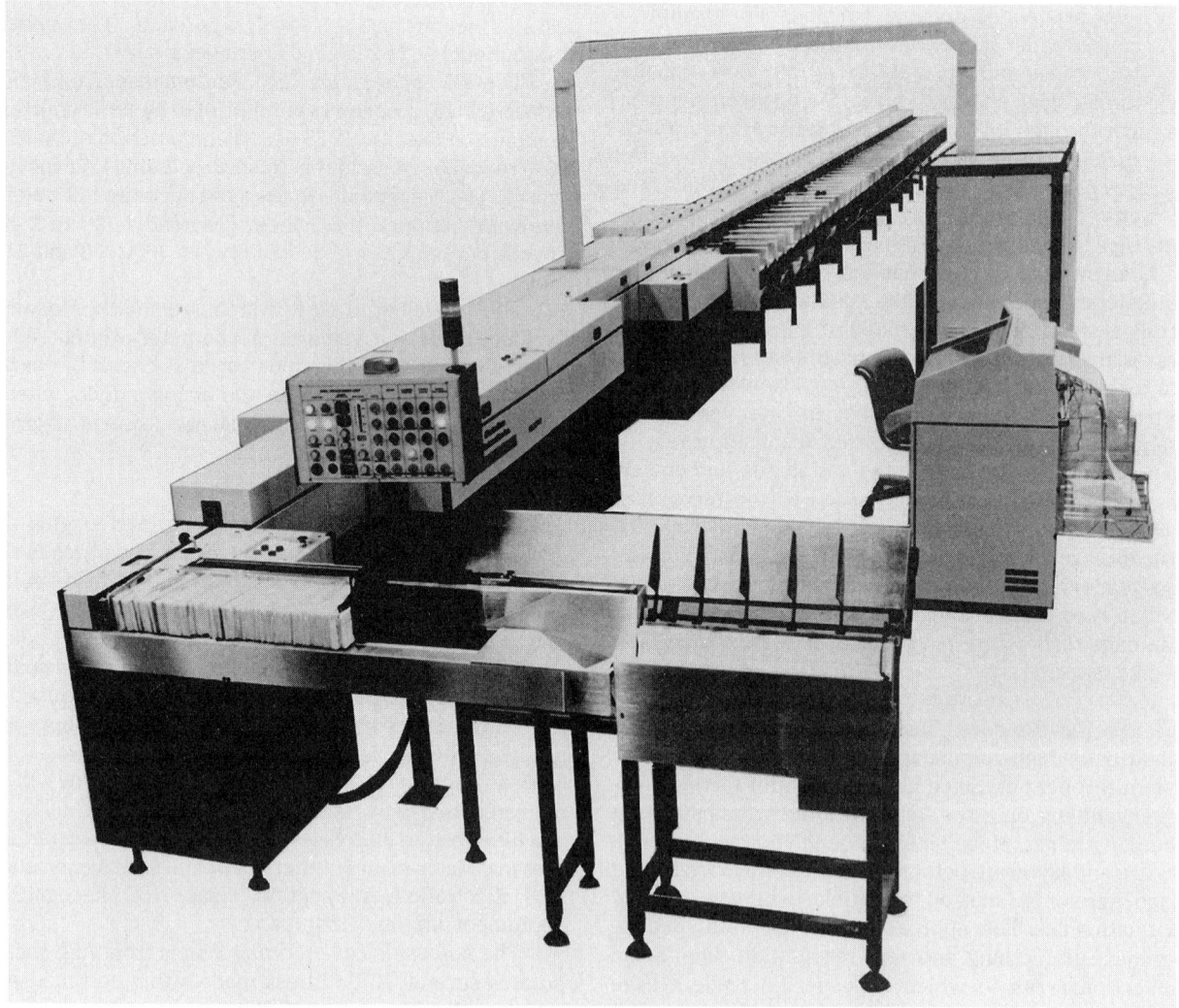

FIG. 4. An example of a mail sorter: the Multiline Optical Character Reader B employed by the United States Postal Services (courtesy Electro-Com Automation). The mail feeder, in the foreground to the left, feeds mail onto the document transport. The scanner is positioned under a cover on the left, a few feet from the feeder. The OCR hardware and software are housed in the cabinet in the right background. Mail is sorted into the 60 stackers in the background.

able to read machine-printed text. The system throughput is 750 documents per hour.

The *Image Document Entry Processing Terminal* (IDEPT) from HNC automates the form reading process by using HNC's software, OSCAR™, to read hand-printed alphanumerics, bar codes, and machine-printed text. The OSCAR software performs form reading, form layout file generation, and on-line verification.

The *IntelliForm* from Executive Technologies is a software-only form reader that works with the IBM PC or compatibles. It can analyze a blank form and register those areas where data should be placed. It is limited to reading machine-printed text.

Bill Processing Systems

In general, a bill processing system is used to read payment slips, utility bills, and inventory documents. The system focuses on document regions where certain expected information is located (e.g. account number and payment value).

The *System 4000* from Bell and Howell reads accounting information from remittance documents at a rate of 3,200 documents per hour.

An OCR transaction system from Cognitronics can read utility bills and inventory documents and can process 2,400 documents per hour.

Airline Ticket Readers

In order to claim revenue from an airline passenger ticket, an airline needs to have three records matched: reservation record, the travel agent record, and the passenger ticket. However, it is impossible to match all three records for every ticket sold. Current methods that use manual random sampling of tickets is far from accurate in claiming the maximal amount of revenue.

Northwest Airlines uses a *Passenger Revenue Accounting System* (PRA) to account accurately for passenger revenues. The PRA reads the ticket number on a passenger ticket and matches it with the one in the airline reservation database. It scans up to 260,000 tickets per day and achieves a sorting rate of 17 tickets per second.

Passport Readers

An automated *Passport Reader* from Caere Corporation is used to speed up returning American passengers through customs inspections. The Reader reads a traveler's name, date of birth, and passport number on the passport and checks these against the database records, which contain information on fugitive felons and smugglers.

General-Purpose Page Readers There are two general categories of page readers: *high-end page readers* and *low-end page readers*. High-end page readers are more advanced in recognition capability and data throughput than the low-end page readers. A high-end page reader usually costs more than $5,000, the price reflecting the speed at which the documents can be read. Many of the high-end page readers come with a built-in document scanner and hardware support to increase processing speed. On the other hand, low-end page readers cost less

than $5,000 and many are software only; recognition is done on a personal computer. A low-end page reader usually does not come with a scanner and is compatible with many flat-bed scanners.

High-End Page Readers

Some manufacturers of high-end page readers are Caere, Calera, Dest, Kurzweil Computer Products, and Recognition Equipment, Inc.

The *Parallel Reader* from Caere (cost: $11,000) has recognition speeds from 220 to 700 characters per second. The key to the reader's performance is its parallel-processor configuration, a pipeline design. The reader sends a document through a series of processor boards. This allows more than one document in the system at the same time, since a processor board is ready to process a new document after it has sent the current document to the next processor board. It reads all stylized fonts from 6 to 72 points of machine-printed text. It does not come with a scanner.

The *Compound Document Processor* (CDP) from Calera (cost: $18,000) is a reader for high-volume applications. It can recognize most typewritten and computer-printed fonts in sizes from 6 to 28 points with the recognition speed going up to 250 characters per second. It is designed to connect with an IBM PC/AT, which is used for image capturing and data post-processing.

The *Discover 7320* from Kurzweil Computer Products (cost: $9,950) comes with a sheet-fed scanner. The system connects with an IBM PC/AT as the host machine, and the character recognition is performed in the background by the system. Kurzweil 4000 is another high-end product ($35,000) from Kurzweil Computer Products. It can be trained to recognize variations in character shapes.

The *Workless Station Model 211* from Dest is a simple and easy-to-use reader that comes with a sheet-fed scanner.

Low-End Page Readers

Many of the low-end page readers are software only and require a host machine for the recognition process. However, some more expensive low-end readers come with a co-processor that allows the recognition to operate in the background and speeds up the recognition process. There are several features shared by the page readers discussed in this section:

- *Host Machine*—An IBM PC/AT or compatible with a 20MB hard disk that runs on DOS 3.0 or later versions. The PC connects with an image scanner to capture document images and performs data post-processing with application software.
- *Omnifont*—Most readers can recognize typewritten, dot-matrix, and computer-printed text.
- *Text/Graphics Separation*—The readers are able to decompose a page automatically, to ignore or save graphics separately, and to locate text blocks for recognition.
- *Text Layout Recognition*—The reader can automat-

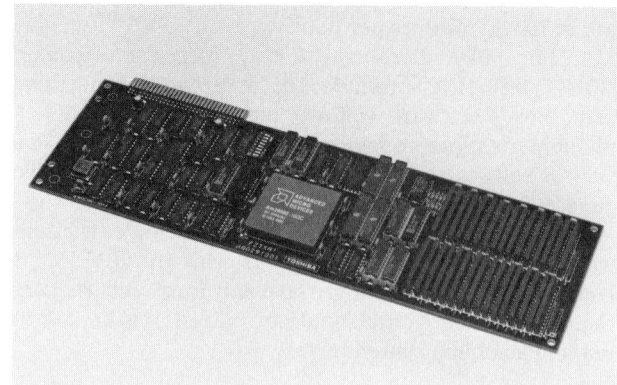

FIG. 5.   An example of a low-end page reader. (a) The reader host machine which connects with a flat-bed scanner to capture document images. (b) The OCR board which fits into an IBM PC expansion slot (courtesy Toshiba Corporation).

ically identify page orientation (landscape or portrait) and handle multiple columns.

- *Accuracy*—Accuracy is claimed to be greater than 99% with good quality documents.

Some manufacturers of low-end page readers are Caere, Calera, Cannon, OCR Systems Inc., Dest, Intelligent Optics Corp., Toshiba, and Xerox.

The *OmniPage 2.1 Model 112* from Caere (cost: $1,995) has an OCR co-processor that attains the peak speed of 115 characters per second for character sizes from 6 to 72 points.

The *TrueScan* from Calera (cost: $3,995) has an OCR card that allows recognition to perform in the background. The recognition rate is up to 100 characters per second for character sizes from 6 to 28 points.

The *ReadRight 2.01* from OCR Systems Inc. (cost: $495) is limited to analyze simple layout documents. The system is software only. Character sizes range from 4 to 24 points.

The *Express Reader* from Toshiba has a RISC-based expansion board to perform recognition at speeds up to 60 characters per second (Fig. 5).

References

1982. Schantz, H. *The History of OCR*. Manchester Center, VT: Recognition Technologies Users Association. (The history of OCR is related from its inauspicious beginnings up to its current commercial success.)

1985. Smith, J. W. and Merali, Z. *Optical Character Recognition: The Technology and its Application in Information Units and Libraries*. The British Library. (This report is intended for use by anyone who is considering OCR in an information or library context. Since minimal knowledge of OCR is assumed, general background material is abundant.)

1985. "Optical Character Readers," *PC Magazine*. July, 105–127. (This article introduces a few high-end general-purpose page readers.)

1990. "Document Imaging Sparks a New Airline Business Era," *Advanced Imaging*. June, 62–63. (This Northwest Airlines' Passenger Revenue Accounting system is described in this article.)

1990. Adams, R. *Sourcebook of Automatic Identification and Data Collection*. New York: Van Nostrand Reinhold. (This book is good general reference for OCR. It also considers a number of commercially available OCR systems. Names, addresses, and phone numbers of many OCR vendors are given.)

1990. "How Does IBM Spell Check Processing? H-P-T-S," *Intelligent Document Management Research*. 26 March 418–425. (This article describes the IBM HPTS check reading system.)

1990. "OCR Software," *PC Magazine*. October 30, 299–356. (This article surveys ten low-end general-purpose page-readers for the IBM PC. Test results for these readers are presented.)

RICHARD FENRICH, STEPHEN LAM AND SARGUR SRIHARI

OPTICAL COMPUTING

For articles on related subjects *see* FAST FOURIER TRANSFORM; and FIBER OPTICS.

Digital computing with the use of optical components was considered at least as early as the 1940s by John von Neumann (*q.v.*), a pioneer in electronic computing. If lasers were available at the time, the first digital computers may well have used optics. Historically, optical technology has found a few limited uses as an adjunct technology to electronics for analog and digital computing. In the early 1960s and throughout the 1970s and 1980s, optical technology was employed for computing Fourier transforms of military images in matched filtering operations (Feitelson, 1988). A simple lens setup realizes a Fourier transform which maps a two-dimensional image from the space domain to the frequency domain. Aerial views of isolated objects are scanned by an optical/electronic setup that identifies features of interest in the frequency domain. Synthetic aperture radar (SAR) signal processing is an optical *pattern recognition* (*q.v.*) application that matches images in stored photographic form with input images, at a very high rate. Spectrum analysis is another application that is performed with acousto-optic signal processing. These applications as well as others are performed optically when bandwidth needs exceed electronic capability. There were renewed interests in optical information processing in the late 1970s as advances were made in optical transmission and optically nonlinear materials. Limits of electronic digital circuits grew increasingly severe as the need for communication bandwidth increased, and attention returned to optical digital computing.

Even though the fastest transistors switch on the order of 5 picoseconds, the fastest computers have cycle times on the order of only 5 nanoseconds. This disparity arises from a number of problems related to conventional electronics that includes:

- Electromagnetic interference at high speed.
- Distorted edge transitions.
- Complexity of metal connections.
- Drive requirements for pins.
- Large peak power levels.
- Impedance matching effects.

Electromagnetic interference arises because the inductances of two current-carrying wires are coupled. Sharp edge transitions must be maintained for proper switching, but higher frequencies are attenuated more than lower frequencies as an electrical pulse travels through a wire, resulting in sloppy edges at high speeds. The complexity of metal connections on chips, on circuit boards, and between system components affects connection topology and introduces complex fields and unequal path lengths. This translates to signal skews that are overcome by slowing system speeds so that signals overlap sufficiently in time. Large peak power levels are needed to overcome residual capacitances, and impedance matching effects at connections require high currents, which are generated by driver circuits that increase delays between integrated circuits (ICs).

A technology based on optics offers solutions to these problems if the advantages of optics are exploited without introducing new complexities or limitations that render the use of optics ineffective. Advantages of optics include:

- High connectivity through imaging.
- No physical contact for interconnects.
- Non-interference of signals.
- High spatial and temporal bandwidth.
- No inherent feedback to the power source.
- Inherently low signal dispersion.

High connectivity is achieved by imaging a large array of light beams onto an array of optical logic devices. There is no need for physical interconnects, unless fibers or waveguides are used, so that connection complexity is simplified and drive requirements are reduced. Optical signals do not interact in free space, which means that beams can pass through each other without interference. This allows for a high density of signals in a small volume. High bandwidth is achieved in space because of the non-interference of optical signals, and high bandwidth is achieved in time because propagating wavefronts do not interact. There is no inherent feedback to the power source as there is in electronics, so there are no data-dependent loads. Finally, inherently low signal dispersion means that the shape of a pulse as it leaves its source is virtually unchanged when it reaches its destination.

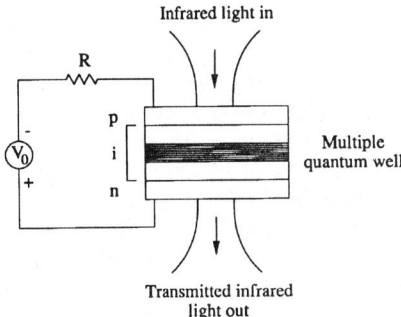

FIG. 1. Schematic of the self–electrooptic effect bistable device.

The success of digital optics depends heavily on advances in optical hardware, and a number of efforts have focused on the creation of optical logic gates, optical interconnection networks, optical power supplies, novel cooling methods, and problems related to the manufacture of optical systems. The development of suitable optical logic gates has historically been one of the most critical obstacles to achieving an all-optical digital computer and continues to pose a significant challenge. For that reason, hybrid optical/electronic approaches are gaining favor (see below). Properties expected of optical logic gates are that they support a fan-in and fan-out of at least two, comprise a logically complete set such as {AND, OR, NOT}, {NAND}, or {NOR}, support indefinite cascadability, operate at low switching powers, and switch at high rates with respect to electronics. For some configurations, it is also necessary to have signal inputs and outputs oriented normal to the surfaces of the device substrates so that free space is used for interconnection. Devices that meet these goals are typically fabricated from semiconductor materials such as GaAs and GaAlAs, although promising devices are also made from other materials. Device research is a quickly moving area and is difficult to capture in its entirety, but the underlying idea is that

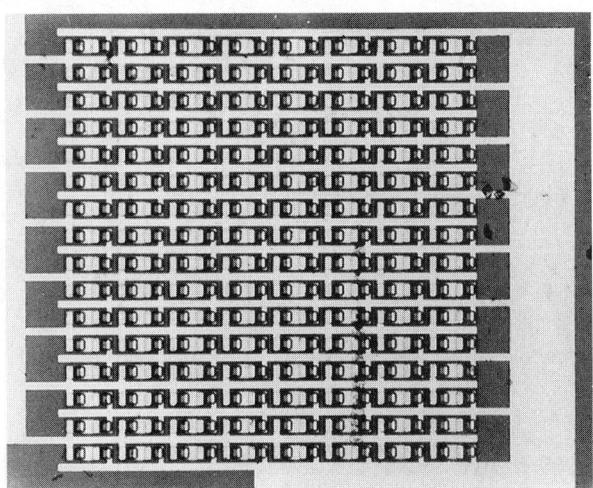

FIG. 2. Array of S-SEEDs with a 40 μm spacing between mesas.

light is used to switch light through an optically sensitive medium, such as GaAs at a wavelength of 850 nm.

There are a number of ways that optics can supplement or replace electronics in computing. Optical fibers typically transport information long distances, on the order of several tens of kilometers without a need for signal restoration (*see* FIBER OPTICS). Fibers are a preferred medium for long-haul transmission because of low losses and high information carrying capacity. Fibers are also used for distances on the order of a few tens of centimeters in connecting circuit boards, such as within AT&T's 5ESS telephone central office switch. Both of these applications address transmission problems, but optics can be used for computation as well as transmission of information.

Information in digital electronic computers is carried in binary values 0 and 1 (typically low and high voltages), and computing is done with configurations of transistors that use a small signal to control a larger signal. Similarly, in digital optical computing, information is carried by beams of light and computing is done with the optical equivalent of a transistor. The symmetric self-electro-optic effect device (S-SEED) (Lentine *et al.*, 1987) is a more recent version of the SEED (Miller *et al.*, 1985), which is used in an optical processor testbed at AT&T Bell Laboratories, which was reported in a January 1990 press release as the first all-optical digital processor to employ this technology. The SEED is based on an electrically coupled optical modulator and detector pair. The device is made up of approximately 1,200 alternating layers of GaAs and GaAlAs in an 8 μm-thick quantum well structure placed inside a PIN photodiode detector, as shown in Fig 1. When

light is applied to the detector, a current is generated that reduces the potential across the quantum well. When a strong enough current is created, the positive feedback allows the device to retain its state after the light source is removed. One of the operating modes of the device is to pass light of low intensity and to absorb light of high intensity, implementing negating logic. The electrical properties of the device make it relatively easy to use in experimental setups and, since communication is handled optically, the system speed of a computer made up of these devices is limited only by the device speed. Potential operating rates are several hundred megahertz, although, in practice, devices operate only in the tens of megahertz range due to high power requirements and the need for novel cooling methods. A fabricated array of commercially available S-SEEDs is shown in Fig. 2.

Interconnections between optical logic gates are handled in a number of ways. *Holography* provides enormous flexibility by imaging light sources onto a number of targets. Bulk optical components, such as beam-splitters, prisms, mirrors, and lenses, are more easily manufactured than holograms, but provide more limited interconnection schemes, restricting connections to well-defined patterns. Fibers can also be used in a hybrid optical/electronic approach by carrying synchronization signals between electronic components, which reduces the number of metal connections and reduces signal skews that arise from complex two-dimensional electronic layouts of integrated circuits.

A conceptual layout of an optical computer based on arrays of optical logic gates and free space optical inter-

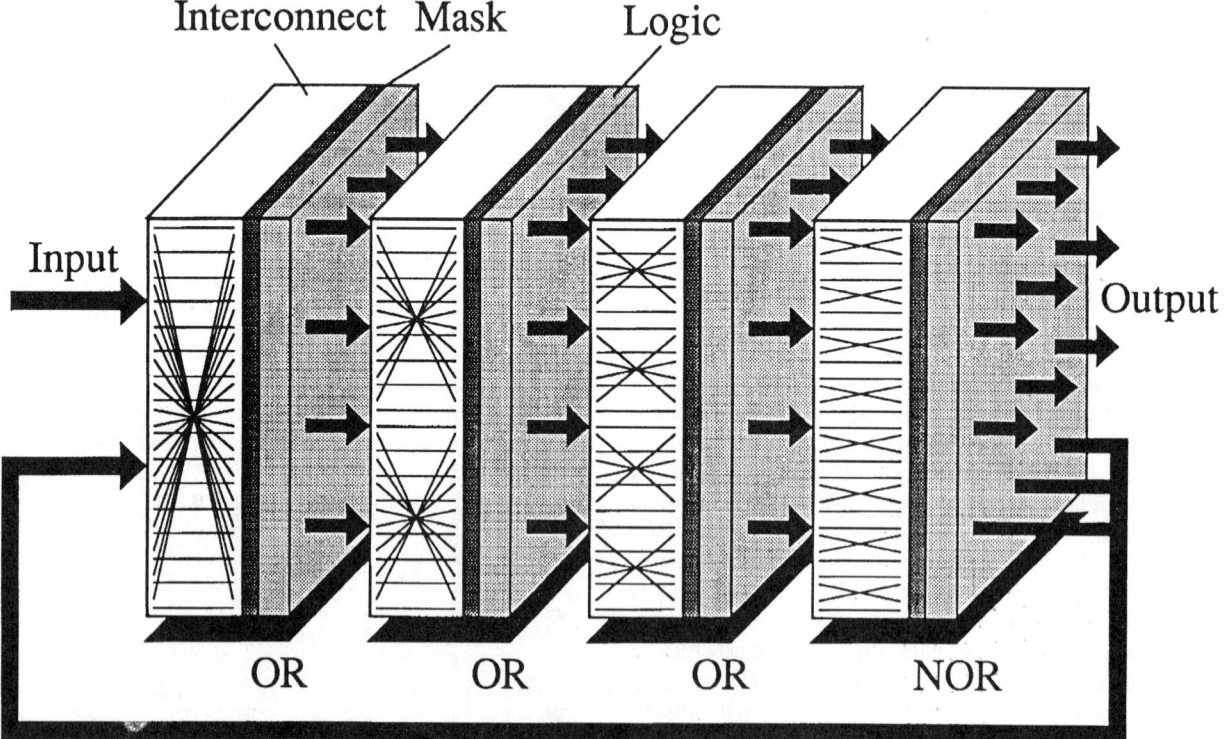

FIG. 3. Arrays of optical logic gates are interconnected holographically or with passive components made of glass or metal, such as beam-splitters, mirrors, and lenses. Masks in the image planes customize the gate-level interconnect by blocking light at selected locations.

FIG. 4. An optical implementation of the model shown in Fig. 3 is made up of four 4 × 8 arrays of S-SEED NOR gates and free-space interconnects. Size is approximately 60 cm × 60 cm × 15 cm deep. (Photograph provided by the courtesy of Nicholas Craft, AT&T Bell Laboratories.)

connects (Murdocca, 1990) is shown in Fig. 3. Optical signals travel orthogonal to the device substrates, through alternating connection and logic stages. Masks in the image planes block light at selected locations, which allows the interconnect to be customized for specific functions, such as binary addition and multiplication. The system is fed back onto itself and an input channel and an output channel are provided, allowing for a conventional model of a digital circuit. Feedback is imaged with a single-row vertical shift so that data spirals through the system, allowing a different section of each mask to be used on each pass.

A four-stage implementation of this model using free space interconnects has been constructed at AT&T Bell Laboratories (Prise, 1990), as shown in Fig. 4. The system is composed of four S-SEED arrays with an 8 × 4 matrix of NOR gates on each array. Fan-in of the logic gates is two and fan-out is two. Operating speed is 1 megahertz. The four modules occupy an area that is approximately 60 cm × 60 cm × 15 cm. Although the speed and array size of this initial setup are not impressive when compared with electronics technology, the architecture can remain virtually unchanged as device performance and optical power improve. Device performance and optical power are not trivial problems, but neither do they pose fundamental limitations.

The best electronic logic is currently faster and requires less power than optical logic used in practical systems, and for this reason hybrid optical/electronic approaches are gaining favor. The general idea is that silicon or gallium arsenide technologies are used to implement digital circuits in the conventional manner, but that connections between chips are made with on-chip optical sources and detectors. In this way, much smaller chip areas are devoted to interconnection than in conventional all-electronic approaches, and a greater number of channels can be provided between ICs since signals are brought off through the surfaces rather than through the edges.

In general, digital optical computing has the potential to achieve a greater level of performance than electronic digital computing, but this superiority has yet to be demonstrated due to the current technology limits of the optical logic devices and optical systems.

References

1985. Miller, D. A. B., Chemla, D. S., Damen, T. C., Wood, T. H., Burrus, C. A., Gossard A. C., Wiegmann, W., "The quantum well self-eletrooptic effort device: optoelectronic bistability and oscillation and self-linearized modulation," *IEEE J. Quant. Electron.*, **QE-21**, 1462.

1987. Lentine, A. L., Hinton, H. S., Miller, D. A. B., Henry, J. E., Cunningham, J. E., and Chirovsky, L. M. F., "The symmetric self electro-optic effect device," in *Conference on Lasers and Electrooptics*, Technical Digest Series, **14**, Optical Society of America, Washington, D.C., 249.

1988. Feitelson, D. G., *Optical Computing.* Cambridge, MA: The M.I.T. Press.

1990. Murdocca, Miles J. *A Digital Design Methodology for Optical Computing.* Cambridge, MA: The M.I.T. Press.

1990. Prise, M. E., Craft, N.C., LaMarche, R. E., Downs, M. M., Walker, S. J., D'Asaro, L. A., and Chirovsky, L. M. F., "Module for optical logic circuits using symmetric self-electrooptic effect devices," *Appl. Opt.*, **29**, 2164, (May 10).

MILES MURDOCCA

OPTIMIZATION METHODS

For articles on related subjects *see* LEAST-SQUARES APPROXIMATION; MATHEMATICAL PROGRAMMING; NUMERICAL ANALYSIS; OPERATIONS RESEARCH; QUEUEING THEORY; SIMPLEX METHOD; SIMULATION; and TOMOGRAPHY, COMPUTERIZED..

Mathematical optimization deals with the problem of finding (or approximating) a point that gives an *optimal* (minimal or maximal) *value* to some function (called the *objective function*), subject to some additional conditions (called *constraints*).

Many problems in various scientific and technological fields, such as physics, engineering, chemistry, economics, and operations research, as well as other fields of mathematics, can be cast as optimization problems and thereby benefit from and contribute to the reservoir of knowledge of mathematical optimization. In this field, numerical analysis, computational methods, and other branches of mathematics, as well as the study of practical applications, interact with and fertilize one another and promote our understanding and ability to solve concrete problems.

The two main branches of optimization are *dynamic optimization* and *static optimization*. The latter is more commonly called *mathematical programming*.

Dynamic optimization is particularly concerned with decision-making situations or economic growth models and mathematical formulations of problems involving moving objects in which the time variable enters naturally into the optimization problem and therefore also appears in its solution. The objective function here usually takes the form of an integral, while the constraints are described by a system of differential equations. The forerunner of this discipline was the *calculus of variations*, which, later on, upon the formulation of *Pontryagin's maximum principle*, developed into the modern theory of *optimal control* (see McShane, 1978). In between, the theory of *dynamic programming* appeared. This proved itself particularly efficient in handling multistage decision processes [see Denardo (1982)].

Static optimization is concerned with all forms of time-independent optimization. In the general formulation of the static optimization problem (*see* MATHEMATICAL PROGRAMMING), there is a function of n variables to be optimized (i.e. maximized or minimized), called the *objective function*, subject to m constraints on the variables. When the objective function and the constraints are all linear, this area is called *linear programming* and the best known method is called the *simplex method*.

Obviously, the rest of mathematical programming is called *nonlinear programming*, of which one sub-branch is *convex programming*, in which the objective function is a convex function and the *feasible set* (i.e. those points in the Euclidean n-space R^n that satisfy the constraints) is a *convex set*. Part way between linear and convex programming lies the theory and practice of *quadratic programming*, dealing with problems where the objective function is a positive definite quadratic function and the constraints are linear.

If the additional condition that some or all variables should take only integer values is imposed on the problem, *integer programming* is obtained.

Other specialized branches of mathematical programming are *stochastic programming*, *geometric programming*, *multiobjective programming*, and *large-scale programming*.

Real systems most often lead to large optimization problems which can be solved practically only by implementation of appropriate solution algorithms on a computer. Success or failure then depends strongly on computer-programming talent, acquaintance with machine specifications, and the right methodology of implementation.

Some Optimization Methods

In this section, we shall sample briefly the huge number of methods of mathematical optimization.

Solving Nonlinear Equations The general problem is that of solving a system of equations $Fx = 0$, where F is an operator mapping some domain D of the Euclidean R^n space into R^n. This problem arises frequently in numerous fields of applications so that the importance of having at hand effective methods of solution for it can hardly be exaggerated. One fruitful approach is to replace it by an equivalent optimization problem. With the aid of a real-valued function f on R^n, which has the property that its global minimum is uniquely attained at $\mathbf{x} = \mathbf{0}$, a new function g is defined by

$$g(\mathbf{x}) = f(F\mathbf{x}) \quad \text{for} \quad \mathbf{x} \in D.$$

Then the optimization problem

Minimize $g(\mathbf{x})$
such that $\mathbf{x} \in D$,

has to be solved to find $\mathbf{x}^* \in D$, which gives g its global minimum on D.

If $F\mathbf{x} = \mathbf{0}$ has a solution, then this must be $\mathbf{x}^*$. If $F\mathbf{x} = \mathbf{0}$ has no solution in D, then $\mathbf{x}^*$ is called an *f-minimal solution* of $F\mathbf{x} = \mathbf{0}$ (see Ortega and Rheinboldt, 1970). The special choice $f(\mathbf{x}) = \mathbf{x}^T\mathbf{x}$ gives rise to an *f*-minimal solution, which is called a *least-squares solution* of $F\mathbf{x} = \mathbf{0}$ (*see* LEAST-SQUARES APPROXIMATION).

The Method of Steepest Descent Also called the *gradient method*, this method for minimizing a real-valued, continuously differentiable function f, defined on R^n, consists of an iterative algorithm

$$\mathbf{x}^{k+1} = \mathbf{x}^k - \alpha_k \nabla f(\mathbf{x}^k)$$

in which $\mathbf{x}^{k+1}$ and $\mathbf{x}^k$ are the new and old iterates, respectively, $\nabla f(\mathbf{x}^k)$ is the gradient vector of f calculated at $\mathbf{x}^k$, and α_k is a nonnegative scalar minimizing $f(\mathbf{x}^k - \alpha \nabla f(\mathbf{x}^k))$. This means that from the point $\mathbf{x}^k$, a search is made along the direction of the negative gradient $-\nabla f(\mathbf{x}^k)$ to a minimum point on this line that is taken to be the next iterate [see, e.g. Luenberger (1984)].

Newton's Method Newton's method for solving a system of equations (for the case of a single equation, *see* NUMERICAL ANALYSIS) may be applied to the system

$$\nabla f(\mathbf{x}) = \mathbf{0}$$

which describes the necessary condition for a minimum of the function f. To do this, f has to be twice continuously differentiable and its Hessian $\nabla^2 f(\mathbf{x})$ (the matrix of all second order partial derivatives) must be invertible at every iteration point. The resulting Newton-type optimization method then takes the form:

$$\mathbf{x}^{k+1} = \mathbf{x} - [\nabla^2 f(\mathbf{x}^k)]^{-1} \nabla f(\mathbf{x}^k),$$

where the -1 denotes matrix inversion. Various modifications of this method have been suggested for these as well as a great variety of other optimization methods [see, e.g. Polyak (1987) and Minoux (1986)].

Applications of Optimization Methods

Examples of problems from various fields of application to which optimization methods are applied are abundant and can be found in the books cited in the references. *Optimal planning* in economics and *optimal allocation of resources* lead to optimization problems. So do many other applications in *mathematical economics, decision theory*, and *game theory*. Numerous real-world *engineering* problems in virtually every field are cast as optimization problems and are solved by optimization methods. In mathematics, one finds optimization problems in *approximation theory, numerical analysis*, and *functional analysis*. Specific models in physics, chemistry, biology, and other sciences lend themselves to treatment with optimization methods. Problems of *least-squares approximation* and *entropy optimization* occur in statistics and *data analysis.* The list of applications of optimization methods is extensive and, not surprisingly, also includes problems within computer science, such as *computer networks (q.v.)* and *image processing (q.v.).*

One such recent application of great importance is the problem of *image reconstruction* in which an image (a function of two variables) has to be recovered from experimentally available integrals of its grayness (i.e. its overall brightness) over thin strips. An important version of this problem in medicine, called *computerized tomography,* is concerned with the density distribution within the human body from X-ray projections.

In the *series expansion approach* to the image reconstruction problem [other approaches are available (see Herman, 1980)], the mathematical formulation takes the form of a system of equations

$$\mathbf{p} = M\mathbf{x} + \mathbf{e}$$

where **p** is the *m*-dimensional vector of actual measurements, **x** is the *n*-dimensional unknown vector representing the grayness levels of the image to be reconstructed, and **e** is an (also unknown) *m*-dimensional vector of the errors that are due to the inaccuracy of the physical measurements and possibly also to the *discretization* of the original problem. The $m \times n$ matrix **M** is huge (of the order of magnitude $10^5 \times 10^5$), sparse (i.e. has many zero elements), but lacks any structure in its sparsity.

By setting up various optimization criteria (i.e. objective functions), according to which a "solution" that agrees with the measurements is sought, the problem is transformed into an optimization problem. Quadratic optimization and entropy optimization have received considerable attention (see Censor and Herman, 1987, for a unified approach).

References

1970. Ortega, J. M. and Rheinboldt, W. C. *Interactive Solution of Nonlinear Equations in Several Variables.* New York: Academic Press.

1978. McShane, E. J. "The Calculus of Variations from the Beginning through Optimal Control Theory," in Schwarzkopf, A. B., Kelley, W. G., and Eliason, S. B. (Eds.). *Optimal Control and Differential Equations.* New York: Academic Press.

1980. Herman, G. T. *Image Reconstruction From Projections: The Fundamentals of Computerized Tomography.* New York: Academic Press.

1982. Denardo, E. V. *Dynamic Programming: Models and Applications.* Englewood Cliffs, N. J.: Prentice-Hall.

1984. Luenberger, D. G. *Linear and Nonlinear Programming,* 2nd Ed. Reading, MA: Addison-Wesley.

1986. Minoux, M. *Mathematical Programming: Theory and Algorithms.* Chichester, UK: John Wiley and Sons.

1987. Censor, Y. and Herman, G. T. "On Some Optimization Techniques in Image Reconstruction from Projections," *Applied Numerical Mathematics* 3: 365–391.

1987. Polyak, B. T. *Introduction to Optimization.* New York: Optimization Software, Inc.

YAIR CENSOR

ORIGINAL EQUIPMENT MANUFACTURER (OEM)

For articles on related subjects *see* INPUT-OUTPUT DEVICES; and MEMORY: AUXILIARY.

One descriptor for the originator of equipment sold by one manufacturer to another for use in the latter's products is *original equipment manufacturer (OEM),* as opposed to a manufacturer who produces equipment destined to be shipped to an *end user.* OEM equipment usually comprises complete components such as disk files and central processors, rather than circuit cards, metal parts, and the like. OEM equipment is often delivered to its purchaser without power supplies and cabinets necessary for its ultimate location on customer premises. OEM prices for computer components are generally much lower than end-user prices, the former applicable to lots of 10, 100, or more units and the latter to single purchase.

DAVID N. FREEMAN

OVERHEAD

For articles on related subjects *see* ACCOUNTING SYSTEM, COMPUTER; OPERATING SYSTEMS: GENERAL PRINCIPLES; and SCHEDULING ALGORITHM.

Overhead is the time a computer system spends doing computations that do not contribute directly to the progress of any user tasks that are being processed by its operating system.

Offhand, it might seem that, whenever an operating system program is executing (i.e. the system is running in *supervisor state*), no user task is making progress and the time so spent should be attributed directly to overhead. However, equating supervisor state time with overhead is generally incorrect. First, many important functions employed by user tasks are implemented as part of the operating system (e.g. input and output, network communications, error handling), and user programs are indeed making progress when these services are being performed by the operating system. Second, some actual overhead functions may be executed by dedicated processors, such as intelligent channels and peripheral processors, yet are not accounted for by supervisor state time. Consequently, overhead cannot be measured simply as the time the central processor spends in supervisor state; it must be measured in terms of the total system resources expended on system functions.

Thus, for example, an observation that an operating system spends 80% of its time in its supervisor state cannot be interpreted to mean that the system spends only 20% of its time doing useful work: We need to know what portion of the 80% is spent on running systems programs specifically requested by some user task. Also, an observation that a certain processor spends 90% of the time running user tasks cannot be interpreted to mean that overhead is low if there are eight or more peripheral processors concurrently carrying out systems functions.

There are at least four sources of overhead in most systems: allocation of resources, responding to exceptional conditions, providing protection and reliability, and accounting. Each will consume some system resources to provide, for example, time on central and peripheral processors to execute systems programs, or space in various memory devices to store information about the running tasks and the system state.

With respect to *resource allocation*, a portion of system capacity will be devoted to functions such as scheduling the use of resources, initiating and terminating tasks, switching processors among tasks, allocating space in primary and secondary memory, and managing information transfers among levels of memory. With respect to *exceptional conditions*, a portion of the system's capacity will be devoted to handling such errors as arithmetic contingencies, data transmission failures, addressing snags, and illegal actions by tasks. With respect to *protection and reliability*, a portion of the system's capacity will be devoted to monitoring accesses to various resources for authenticity, to periodic testing of equipment, and to periodic dumping and copying of information off line.

With respect to *accounting*, a portion of the system's capacity will be devoted to collecting information on each task's usage of resources, figuring costs and billings for users of the system, and generating statistics on resource usage and performance.

The cost of overhead is borne by the users of the system. Where possible, these costs are allocated to the tasks that caused the overhead function to be performed (e.g. initiating a task, switching a processor to a task, moving information of a task among the levels of memory). Otherwise, these costs are distributed among all users according to some pro rata formula.

Overhead detracts from system performance only to the extent that the overhead functions interfere with the processing of user tasks. But many services are provided by the system to relieve programmers from having to provide these functions themselves. As long as the system can provide these functions more efficiently than its users, the resulting increases in overhead may well be offset by better service, improved performance, and lower overall costs to the users.

PETER J. DENNING AND DOROTHY E. DENNING

PACKAGE

For articles on related subjects *see* ADA; ENCAPSULATION; INFORMATION HIDING; MODULAR PROGRAMMING; and OBJECT-ORIENTED PROGRAMMING.

A *package system* is that part of a programming language that supports multiple name spaces. Package systems were developed in part to prevent name space collisions. Name space collisions occur when different programmers accidentally use the same variable or function name when working on different parts of the same program. Package systems help prevent name space collisions and encourage the development of more modular programs. A package system requires programmers to be explicit about shared variables and functions. Variables and functions that are not explicitly shared are safely hidden in the package. Since usually only a small portion of variables and functions are shared between packages, packages help programmers manage the complexity of large software systems.

A *package* is a data structure used by a package system to maintain a mapping between names and the variables or functions referred to by those names. Given a name, a programming language uses the currently active package to look up the name and find the memory location corresponding to a variable or function. The same name may refer to different memory locations depending on which package it belongs to. Every name belongs to some package. Usually, there is a default user package to which all names belong, unless the user specifies a new package.

Perhaps the most confusing aspect of packages is understanding their relationship to files and modules. A *file* is part of the operating system. Modules and packages are part of a programming language. A *module* is a data structure that allows one or more files to be referred to as a group and loaded as a group. A *package* is a data structure that shields names in one part of a program from names in another part of a program, unless the names are explicitly shared. A file contains not only source code and data, but also contains information about which module and package the source code belongs to and depends on.

Reference

1986. Ross, D. "Classifying Ada Packages," *Ada Letters* **6**, *4*.

JAMES C. SPOHRER

PACKAGES, SOFTWARE. *See* SOFTWARE-LIBRARIES.

PACKET SWITCHING

For articles on related subjects *see* COMMUNICATIONS AND COMPUTERS; DATA COMMUNICATIONS; DISTRIBUTED SYSTEMS; and NETWORKS, COMPUTER.

Packet switching is a term used to describe the internal operations of a particular type of data communications network that usually has a fixed topology and uses software to route information in a special format through the network from source to destination. A packet-switched data communication network is composed of a number of geographically separate nodes connected by dedicated high-speed data links. The nodes are (usually) stored program computers that have internal data link connections to the other nodes and external data links connected to local terminals and computers. Fig. 1 illustrates an example of a packet-switched data communications network.

The general theory of operation is that a unit of information, called a *packet* (usually 128 bytes or less), is routed from one *packet-switching exchange* (PSE) to another via transmission lines until the packet reaches its destination. The destination address for the information is contained in the header of the packet. Each packet may,

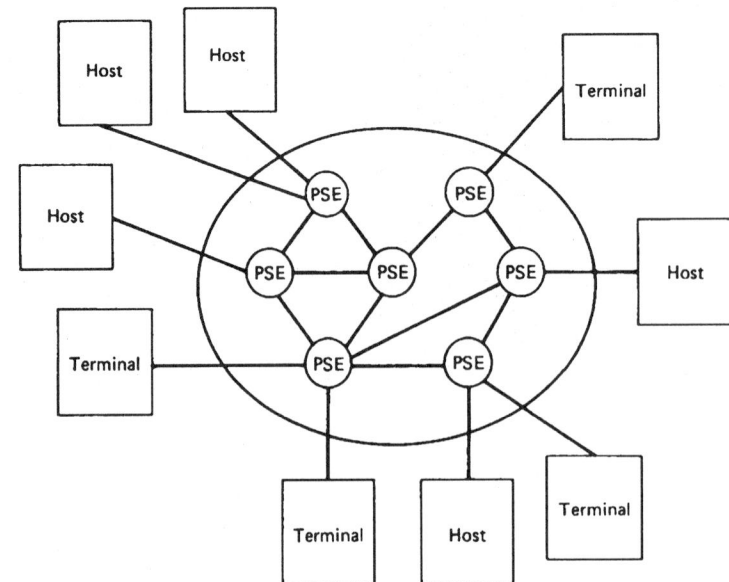

FIG. 1. Typical packet-switched network.

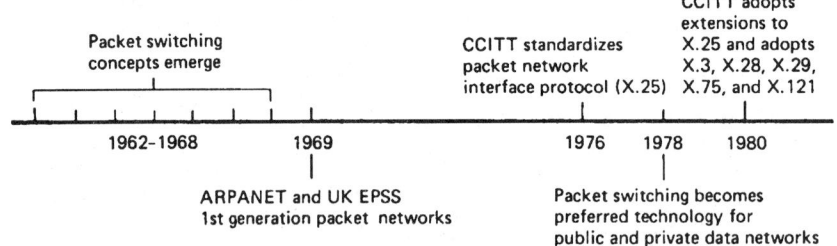

FIG. 2. Evolution of packet switching.

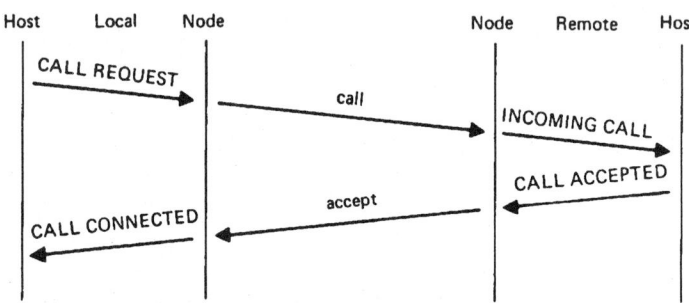

FIG. 3. Virtual circuit setup.

therefore, go to a different destination; hence the term *packet switching*.

When a packet arrives at a PSE, the exchange determines whether it is a transit node or a destination node. If the former, it chooses a transmission line to send the packet toward its destination. This type of operation is called *store-and-forward* transmission, a term created in message-switching systems. In packet-switching systems, the store-and-forward operations generally occur in tens to hundreds of milliseconds. End-to-end transmission delay (source to destination) is usually in the range of 200 milliseconds to one second.

Two alternative strategies have evolved (see Fig. 2) in the implementation of packet-switching systems—*datagrams* and *virtual circuits*. In the datagram strategy, each packet of information is totally independent of all others. They are independently routed and have the properties that they can be lost or duplicated (this phenomenon is caused by transmission errors and retransmissions) with some probability, and transmission order between packets is not preserved. Proponents of the datagram approach argue that a simpler network interface can be achieved and that transmission of datagrams can easily be routed around failed links and nodes.

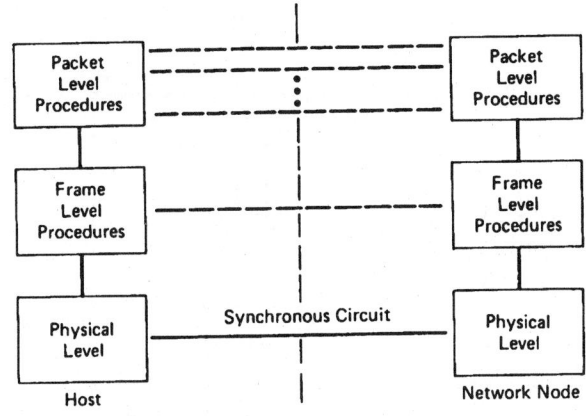

FIG. 4. X.25 Interface.

In the virtual circuit (VC) approach, a logical path is created by the network between the source and destination (see Fig. 3). The virtual circuit allows the network to maintain order, discard duplicates, and detect missing packets. The VC uses special packet types to establish and clear calls. VC proponents argue a simpler end-to-end protocol, better flow control by the network, and lower transmission and processing overhead as the VC's chief assets.

All public data networks use the VC approach, while some of the earlier packet networks, such as the ARPA network, use the datagram approach.

In 1976, the international standards body responsible for the worldwide telecommunications standards (CCITT) recommended an interface protocol for attaching terminal equipment to a packet network. This standard, called X.25 (see Fig. 4), has been adopted by public networks, many private networks, and is available in a growing number of types of data processing equipment.

The packet-switching networks (usually) provide interfaces to terminals not supporting the packet mode of operation (X.25). These terminals are supported through PADs (packet assembler-disassemblers), which convert the native protocols (such as asynchronous, binary synchronous (BSC), synchronous data link control (SDLC), etc.) into X.25 for transmission through the network (see Fig. 5).

BARRY D. WESSLER

PAGE, MEMORY. *See* VIRTUAL MEMORY.

PAPER TAPE

For articles on related subjects *see* ASCII; BAUDOT CODE; BINARY-CODED DECIMAL; CODES; and EBCDIC.

Punched *paper tape* is a storage medium used for the preparation, storage, and transmission of data in various applications. Slow-speed paper tape may be used as a control device for numerically controlled machine tool operations. At higher speeds, paper tape may be used for typesetting, telegraphic and data transmission, and automated typewriting, as well as for storing computer programs and data, and also for other data processing functions (e.g. to control the carriage movement in line printers).

The use of punched paper tape for data preparation, storage, and transmission is not a new technique. It was introduced by Sir Charles Wheatstone in 1857 for telegraphic purposes, just 21 years after the first practical demonstration of the electric telegraph. One year later, in 1858, a Morse tape reader-transmitter operated at 100 words per minute. Five-track tape keyboard punches were in common use in 1908. In 1925, five-track readers were commonly operating at four letters, or 20 bits per second. When multiplexed for transmission use, the line speed was 80 bits per second. Adoption of this technique for data processing saw a vast increase in applications of punched paper tape.

Speed requirements and therefore performance have increased manyfold, and the available number of tracks has increased from five to eight to accommodate the various alphabets required. Small sprocket holes appear

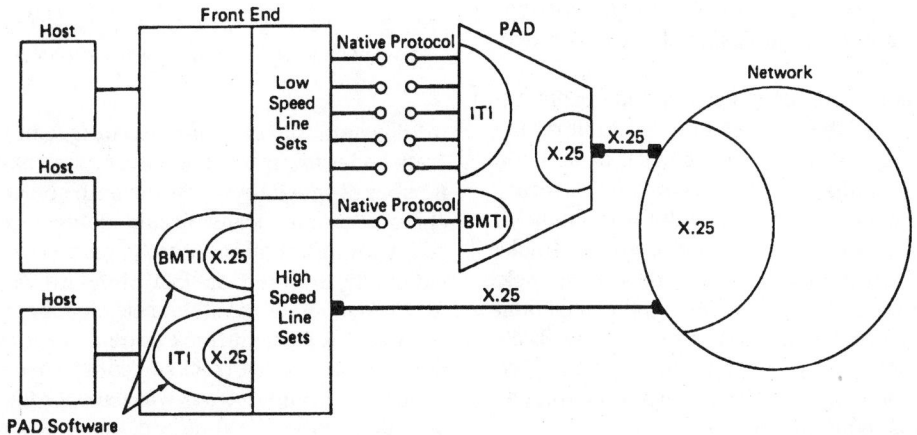

FIG. 5. Typical interfaces to hosts. (X.25 above indicates hardware and software that implements the X.25 standard.)

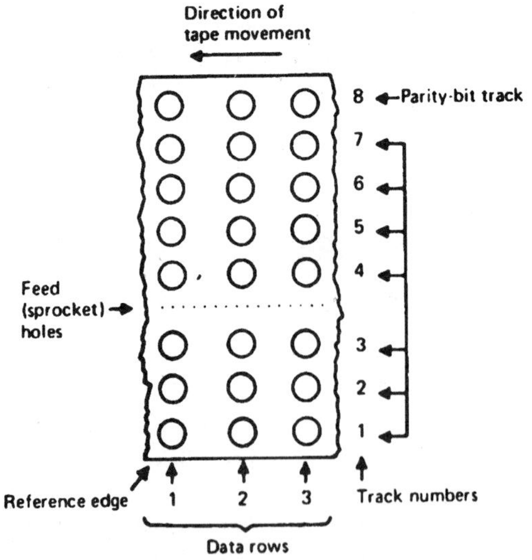

FIG. 1. Punched paper tape terminology. Note: Each data row represents one seven-bit character.

along the length of the tape and are used to feed the tape mechanically as they engage toothed wheels in slow-speed readers; in high-speed machines, these sprocket holes (or feed holes) act as a clock pulse when a tape is read by a photoelectric head (see Fig. 1). Data is recorded in the tape by punching holes in a row across the width. Each row represents one character, and the pattern of the holes punched indicates the particular character.

In the narrowest tape (with five tracks, and which is 11/16-inch wide), since a hole can be punched in any track, the number of unique hole combinations possible is 2^5, or 32. Thus, 32 characters can be represented by a five-hole code. More than 32 separate items can be identified if each code group is made to represent two or more characters, and a special character (e.g. letter or figure shift) precedes the punched data to indicate which interpretation is to be used (see Fig. 2). In certain circumstances, this arrangement can be cumbersome; hence, it has resulted in the development of tape with more information tracks so that a larger number of characters can be identified uniquely. Nevertheless, economic considerations caused many first-generation computer manufacturers (especially in the U.K.) to opt for five-track paper tape input, and many of them designed their own five-track paper tape code.

With the advent of the second generation of computers, the limitations of the five-track tape led to introduction of a sixth track, giving the possibility of 64 code combinations. To this was also added a parity track, resulting in seven-track paper tape whose width was about 7/8 in. IBM's paper tape code, however, used seven data tracks and had a single character ("new line") in the eighth track. This resulted in a tape width of 1 inch, and the maximum number of code combinations was increased to 65. IBM's eight-track paper tape has been widely adopted by office machine manufacturers because it provides enough codes for various miscellaneous commands.

The demand for further paper-tape code combinations was brought about by the larger character sets of

Letters	Figures and Symbols	Code 1	2	3	4	5 (Track number)
A	–	●	●			
B	?	●			●	●
C			●	●	●	
D	Who are you?	●			●	
E	3	●				
F		●		●	●	
G			●		●	●
H				●		●
I	8		●	●		
J	Bell	●	●		●	
K	(	●	●	●	●	
L	)		●			●
M				●	●	●
N	,			●	●	
O	9				●	●
P	0		●	●		●
Q	1	●	●	●		
R	4		●		●	
S	'	●		●		
T	5					●
U	7	●	●	●		
V	=		●	●	●	●
W	2	●	●			●
X	/	●		●	●	●
Y	6	●		●		●
Z	+	●				●
Blank						
Letters shift		●	●	●	●	●
Figures shift		●	●		●	●
Space				●		
Carriage return					●	
Line feed			●			

FIG. 2. The five-track code standarized by the International Communications Union, known as Alphabet CCITT No. 2.

third-generation computers. These computers had discrete codes for upper- and lower-case characters, a larger number of special symbols for both control and graphical characters, and transmission control codes. Seven-bit codes for information interchange were set up and internationally adopted as ISO Standard No. 646 (revised 1973). Many national standards have been based upon it, such as ASCII. Eight-track paper tape was then used so that the first seven tracks accommodated the seven-bit code and the eighth track was used for parity. Despite the adoption of the ISO standard, many other codes are still in use (e.g. the six-bit BCD code and the eight-bit EBCDIC).

Paper tape for computers is normally supplied in an

11/16-inch width (which satisfies the teleprinter tape standard now established at 11/16-inch wide by 1,000 ft long in coil form), or 7/8-inch or 1-inch widths to suit the requirements of 5-, 6-, 7-, or 8-track information. Tapes for most applications are supplied in coils with a nominal length of 1,000 feet and an outer diameter of 8 inches. The center supporting cores are available in plain and serrated plastic.

Several kinds of substances are available for paper tape manufacture, depending upon the application and the machines in which the tape is to be used. For computer applications, the most suitable substance is a low-filler paper tape, either with or without the inclusion of oil. There are also more durable tapes of the paper variety suited for long-life cyclic uses, and long-life polyester plastic tapes are used for continuous cyclic work that needs tapes of exceptional durability.

Despite the inexpensiveness of paper tape and its usefulness as a by-product (e.g. from a cash register or ticket issuing machine), its disadvantages, such as the difficulty of correcting errors and the relatively slow speeds at which it can be read, have meant its almost complete disappearance as a computer input medium and its replacement by tape cassettes or floppy disks (*q.v.*).

JIRI NECAS

PARALLEL PROCESSING

For articles on related subjects *see* COMPUTER ARCHITECTURE; DATAFLOW; MULTIPROCESSING; and SUPERCOMPUTER.

PRINCIPLES

Parallel processing is the use of concurrency in the operation of a computer system to increase throughput, increase fault-tolerance, or reduce the time needed to solve particular problems. Parallel processing is the only route to reach the highest levels of computer performance. Physical laws and manufacturing capabilities limit the switching times and integration densities of current semiconductor-based devices, putting a ceiling on the speed at which any single device can operate. For this reason, all modern computers rely upon parallelism to some extent. The fastest computers exhibit parallelism at many levels.

We begin by describing *pipelining* and *parallelism*, the two traditional methods used to increase concurrency in a computer system. We survey low-level and high-level parallel processing mechanisms that appear in hardware, and we examine some of the most popular processor interconnection topologies. The final sections discuss parallelism in software. We describe the generation and coordination of software processes and the problem of scheduling the execution of these processes on actual parallel hardware.

Pipelining and Parallelism
To reduce the time needed for a mechanism to perform a task, we must either increase the speed of the mechanism or introduce concurrency. Two traditional methods have been used to increase concurrency: pipelining and parallelism. If an operation can be divided into a number of stages, *pipelining* allows different tasks to be in different stages of completion. An automobile assembly line is an example of pipelining. *Parallelism* is the use of multiple resources to increase concurrency. A group of combines working together to harvest a wheat field is an example of parallelism.

To illustrate and contrast these two fundamental methods for increasing concurrency, we present the following pizza-baking example. Suppose a pizza requires 10 minutes to bake. An oven that holds a single pizza can yield 6 baked pizzas an hour. To increase the number of pizzas baked per hour, either the baking time must be reduced or a way must be found to have more than one pizza baking at a time. (Assume that quality control constraints prevent us from raising the oven's temperature in order to reduce the baking time.)

One way to increase production is through use of parallelism. If 5 ovens are used, the ovens yield 5 pizzas every 10 minutes and 30 pizzas an hour. Note that the 5 ovens are used most efficiently if the number of pizzas needed is a multiple of 5. For example, the ovens require the same amount of time—20 minutes—to produce 6, 7, 8, 9, or 10 pizzas.

Another way to increase production is through the use of pipelining. Imagine a conveyer belt running through a long pizza oven. A pizza placed at one end of the conveyer belt spends 10 minutes in the oven before it reaches the other end. If the conveyer belt has room for 5 pizzas, a cook can place an unbaked pizza at one end of the belt every 2 minutes. Ten minutes after the first pizza has been put into one end of the oven, it appears as a baked pizza at the other end. From that time on, another baked pizza will appear every two minutes, and the production of the oven will be 30 pizzas an hour. The pizza-baking speeds of the single-oven, parallel-oven, and pipelined-oven methods are compared in Table 1.

The speedup achieved is the ratio between the time needed for the single pizza oven to produce some number of pizzas and the time needed to produce the same number of pizzas using pipelining and/or parallelism. For ex-

TABLE 1. Contrasting the Pizza-Baking Times of a Single Oven, Five Ovens, and a Conveyor-Belt Oven.

Pizzas Baked	Single Oven	Five Ovens	Conveyer Oven
1	10 min.	10 min.	10 min.
2	20	10	12
3	30	10	14
4	40	10	16
5	50	10	18
6	60	20	20
7	70	20	22
8	80	20	24
9	90	20	26
10	100	20	28
11	110	30	30
12	120	30	32

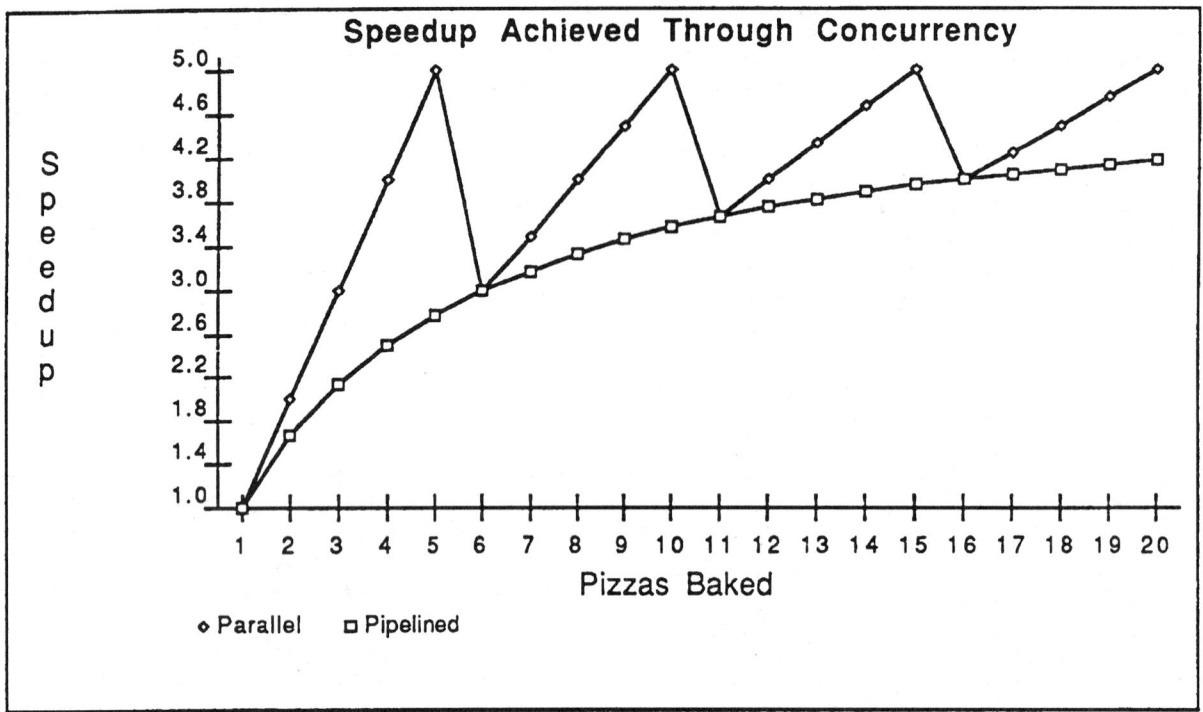

FIG. 1.   Contrasting the speedup achieved through pipelining and parallelism.

ample, producing 8 pizzas requires 80 minutes using a single pizza oven, 20 minutes using 5 pizza ovens, and 24 minutes using the conveyer belt oven. The speedup achieved using 5 pizza ovens to bake 8 pizzas is 80/20 = 4; the speedup achieved using the conveyer-belt oven to bake 8 pizzas is 80/24 = 3 1/3. Speedup can be plotted as a function of problem size. Fig. 1 illustrates the speedup achieved by the parallel and the pipelined pizza ovens as a function of the number of pizzas baked. Observe the jagged speedup plot of the parallel scheme; speedup is equal to 5, the number of ovens, only when the number of pizzas is a multiple of 5. The speedup curve of the pipelined machine is a monotonically increasing function that approaches an asymptote of 5, the concurrency of the pipeline. Because of the time needed to fill and empty the pipeline, speedup never reaches 5. However, because this filling and emptying time is constant, it becomes less and less significant as the problem size increases.

Parallelism in Hardware Virtually all modern computer systems take advantage of at least some low-level hardware parallelism in order to improve performance. We summarize the most common sources of low-level parallelism. A *bit-parallel memory* allows all the bits in a word to be accessed in parallel. A *bit-parallel arithmetic unit* performs an arithmetic operation on all bits of a pair of operands in parallel. An *I/O processor*, or *channel* (*q.v.*), receives I/O instructions from the CPU, but then works independently, freeing the CPU to resume arithmetic processing. An *interleaved memory* is a memory unit divided into a number of *memory banks* which can be accessed concurrently (*see* INTERLEAVING). Computers with *instruction look-ahead*, or *instruction buffering*, prefetch instructions from memory, which reduces the amount of

waiting done by the instruction unit. *Instruction pipelining* is the use of pipelining to allow more than one instruction to be in some stage of execution at the same time.

In the fastest contemporary computers, parallelism

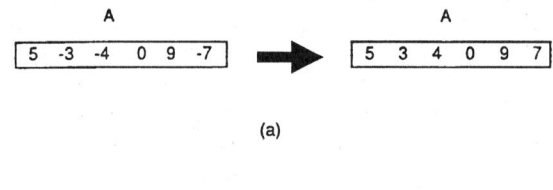

(a)

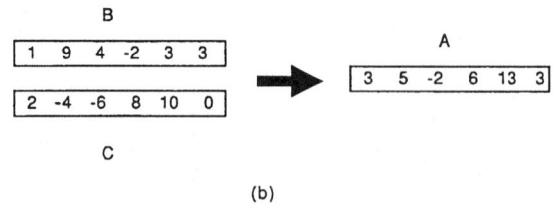

(b)

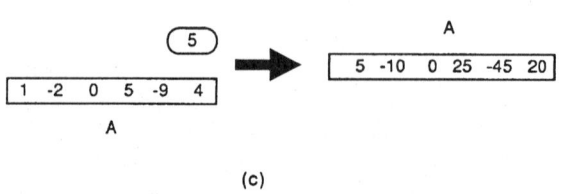

(c)

FIG. 2.   A vector is an ordered collection of values. Here are three examples of vector operations. (a) A ← |A|. (b) A ← B + C. (c) A ← 5 × A.

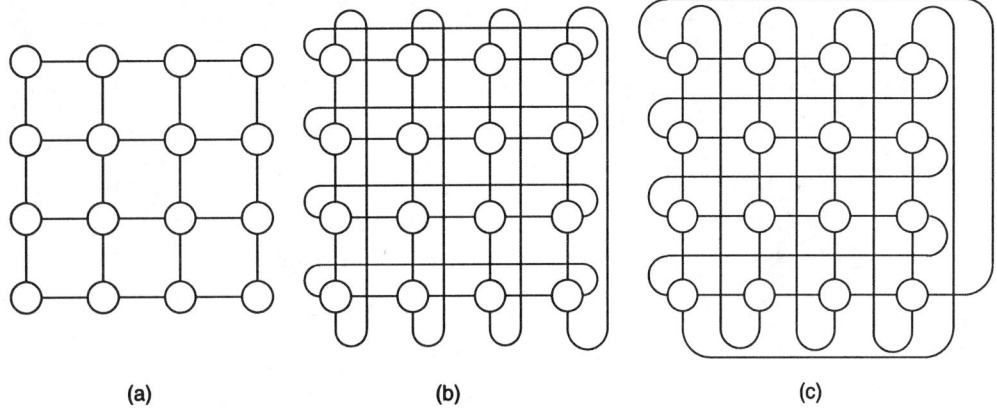

FIG. 3.   Two-dimensional mesh networks. (a) No wraparound connections. (b) Wraparound connections link nodes in same row or column. (c) Toroidal wraparound connections.

also appears at higher levels in the architecture, allowing large numbers of arithmetic-logic operations to be performed concurrently. Two important categories of high-speed computers are vector computers and multiple-CPU computers. A *vector computer* is a computer with an instruction set that contains operations on vectors as well as scalars (Fig. 2). Processor arrays and pipelined vector processors are two examples of vector computers. A *processor array* is a set of identical synchronized processing elements managed by a single control unit that is capable of simultaneously performing the same operation on different data elements in parallel. By associating each processing element with a vector element, vector operations, such as element-wise vector addition (Fig. 2(b)), can be performed in a single step. A *pipelined vector processor* pipelines the flow of data from memory through pipelined functional units and back to memory, eliminating the overhead involved in fetching, manipulating, and storing the individual scalar elements of a vector.

A *multiple-CPU computer* contains multiple CPUs, each capable of independently executing its own instruction stream. A *multiprocessor* is a multiple-CPU computer with a single address space. Every processor can read from and write to every memory location. A *multicomputer* is a multiple-CPU computer in which each CPU has its own local address space. Since a processor cannot directly access non-local memory locations, communication and synchronization between processors is accomplished solely through message passing.

Processor Organizations   Many diverse processor organizations have been proposed. We illustrate a few that are especially popular, either because they are easy

to build in hardware or because they can implement important parallel algorithms efficiently.

Mesh   In a mesh network, the nodes are arranged into a lattice with dimension one or greater. Since communication is allowed only between neighboring nodes, interior nodes in a q-dimensional mesh have $2q$ neighbors. The number of links per processor is a constant, independent of the network size. Fig. 3(a) illustrates a simple two-dimensional mesh. Some variants of the basic mesh model allow wrap-around connections between processors on the edges of the mesh. These connections may connect processors in the same row or column (Fig. (3b)), or they may be toroidal (Fig. 3(c)).

Because all links connect adjacent processors, two-dimensional meshes are relatively inexpensive to implement in hardware. The Goodyear MPP and the AMT DAP are processor arrays with a two-dimensional mesh processor organization. The Intel Touchstone Delta is a multicomputer organized as a two-dimensional mesh.

Shuffle-exchange   A shuffle-exchange network contains $n = 2^k$ nodes, numbered $0, 1,..., n - 1$, and two kinds of connections, called *shuffle* and *exchange*. The perfect shuffle connection links node i with node $2i$ modulo $n - 1$, with the exception that node $n - 1$ is connected to itself. The exchange connection links node i with the node whose number differs from i only in its least significant bit. Fig. 4 illustrates a shuffle-exchange network with eight nodes. Solid arrows denote shuffle links; dotted lines denote exchange links.

To understand the derivation of the name *perfect shuffle*, consider a deck of eight cards, numbered 0, 1, 2, 3, 4, 5, 6, 7. If the deck is divided into two exact halves and

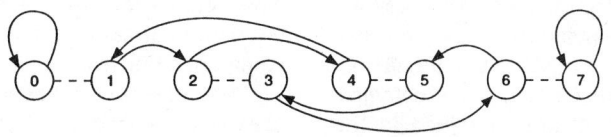

FIG. 4.   Eight-node shuffle-exchange network. Solid lines denote shuffle links. Dashed lines denote bidirectional exchange links.

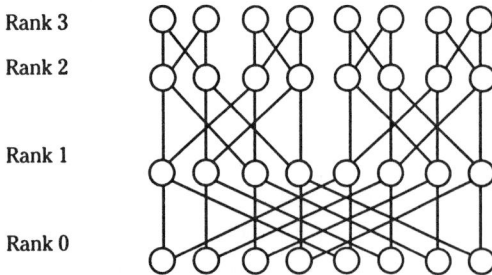

Rank 3
Rank 2
Rank 1
Rank 0

FIG. 5. A 32-node butterfly network.

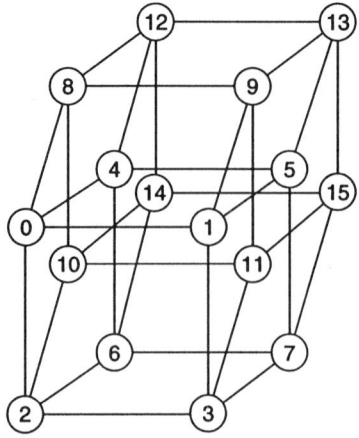

FIG. 6. A 16-node (four-dimensional) hypercube is constructed out of two 8-node (three-dimensional) hypercubes.

these halves are shuffled perfectly, the result is the following ordering of the cards: 0, 4, 1, 5, 2, 6, 3, 7. The location of card i after the perfect shuffle is determined by following the shuffle link from node i in the shuffle-exchange routing network.

The shuffle-exchange network has several nice properties. The number of links per node (two incoming, two outgoing) is a constant, independent of the size of the network. Important fundamental algorithms, such as sorting and matrix multiplication, can be done quickly on this topology.

Butterfly A butterfly network contains $(k + 1)2^k$ nodes divided into $k + 1$ rows, or ranks, each containing 2^k nodes. The ranks are labeled 0 through k, although ranks 0 are k are sometimes identical, giving each node on this rank four connections to other nodes.

Let $node(i,j)$ refer to the jth node on the ith rank. Then $node(i, j)$ on rank $i > 0$ is connected to two nodes on rank $i - 1$: $node (i - 1, j)$ and $node(i - 1, m)$, where m is the integer found by inverting the ith most significant bit in the binary representation of j. The entire network consists of "butterfly" patterns, because a connection between $node(i,j)$ and $node(i - 1,m)$ implies a connection between $node(i,m)$ and $node(i - 1,j)$. Fig. 5 illustrates a 32-node butterfly network. The BBN TC2000 is a commercial multiprocessor that uses the butterfly routing network to allow processors to access the memories of other processors.

Hypercube Informally, a *hypercube* (also called a binary n-cube) is a butterfly network with its columns collapsed into single nodes. Formally, a hypercube network contains $n = 2^k$ nodes, numbered 0, 1,..., $n - 1$. Two nodes are adjacent if their binary representations differ in exactly one bit position. Fig. 6 illustrates a 16-node (four-dimensional) hypercube.

Some theoreticians have criticized the hypercube processor organization because the number of connections per processor is not a constant: the number of links is the base-two logarithm of the number of processors. The hypercube has been a popular topology, however, because it allows fast solutions to a variety of fundamental parallel algorithms, and other important topologies, such as the ring and the mesh, are contained in the hypercube. A number of manufacturers, including Thinking Machines and CUBE Corporation, market parallel computers whose processors are organized into hypercubes.

Parallelism in Software In order to take advantage of parallel hardware to solve a particular problem more quickly, there must be some way to express parallelism in, or extract parallelism from, a user's program. In the case of a vector computer, which executes a single instruction stream containing vector as well as scalar operations, all that is needed is some mechanism to express or extract vector operations. In the case of a multiple-CPU computer, which supports the concurrent execution of multiple instruction streams, there must be some way to express or extract the generation and cooperation of parallel processes. The remainder of this section discusses process control issues for multiple-CPU computers. This aspect of parallel processing has been heavily influenced by what has been learned about managing cooperating processes for multiprogrammed operating systems. (*see* CONCURRENT PROGRAMMING and CONCURRENCY CONTROL).

Process generation may be explicit or implicit. Many different constructs have been proposed for explicitly generating processes in an imperative programming language. These include the fork/join construct of C, cobegin/coend style constructs in Algol 68 and Occam, and process declarations in Distributed Processes and SR. If process generation is implicit, as in a program written in an ordinary sequential programming language, a functional programming language, or a logic programming language, then a greater burden rests upon the compiler.

In order for processes to cooperate, they must have the ability to communicate and synchronize. Communication is achieved either through shared variables or through message passing. The underlying architecture may dictate the communication mechanism. For example, because multicomputers do not have a shared memory, communication is possible only through message passing.

Synchronization has two uses: to constrain the order of events and to control process interference. For example, consider an algorithm in which, at some point, a global sum of a list of values must be computed. Every process sums a portion of the list, and then the subtotals

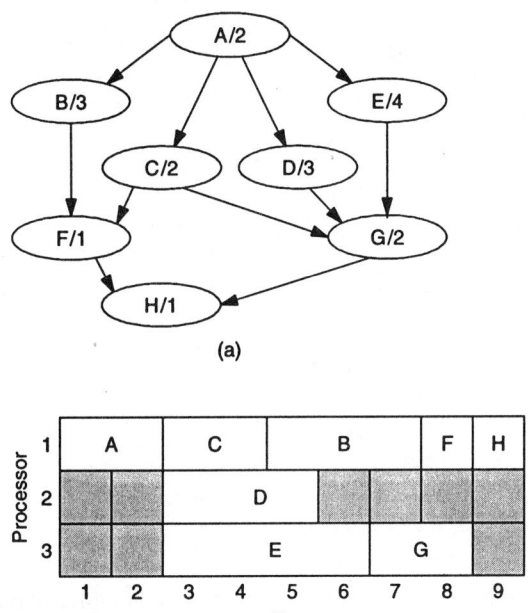

(a)

(b)

FIG. 7. Use of a Gantt chart to represent a deterministic schedule. (a) Process flow graph. (b) Gantt chart showing scheduling of processes on processors.

are combined to form the global sum. The first kind of synchronization is needed to ensure that the global sum is initialized to zero before any process adds its subtotal. The second kind of synchronization is needed to ensure that only one process at a time adds its subtotal to the current value of the global sum.

Scheduling Parallel Processes

A *schedule* is an allocation of processes to processors. Processing scheduling may be *static* (occurring before program execution) or *dynamic* (occurring during program execution). Dynamic scheduling of processes to processors is more feasible on a multiprocessor, in which all CPUs share a single global memory, than it is on a multicomputer, in which every CPU has its own private memory and where fetching code or data from another processor's memory is relatively costly.

Deterministic models are used to perform a static allocation of processes to processors. In a deterministic model, the execution time needed by each process and the precedence relations between the processes are fixed. Deterministic models are unrealistic, in that they ignore variances in the execution time of processes due to interrupts, contention for shared memory, etc., but these simplifications make process allocation more feasible.

An optimal schedule minimizes the total execution time of the parallel algorithm, given some fixed number of processors. However, since even quite simple instances of the scheduling problem are NP-hard, we must be content with polynomial-time heuristics that do a good, but not perfect, job of scheduling processes to processors.

Deterministic schedules are often illustrated with Gantt charts. A Gantt chart plots processors against time,

showing, for any time, which processes are executing on which processors. Because they also show when processors are idle, Gantt charts graphically illustrate the utilization of each processor. Fig. 7(a) contains a directed acyclic graph representing the execution of a parallel algorithm. Nodes represent computations to be performed; the number inside the node represents the execution time of the process. (e.g. process A requires two units of time). Arcs represent precedence constraints (e.g. processes B and C may execute concurrently, but both B and C must finish before process F may begin). Figure 7(b) is a Gantt chart representing one possible scheduling of the processes on three processors.

Work has also been done with nondeterministic scheduling models. In a nondeterministic model, the execution time of a task is represented by a random variable, making the scheduling problem more difficult.

References

1987. Perrott, R. H. *Parallel Programming.* Wokingham, England: Addison-Wesley.
1987. Quinn, M. J. *Designing Efficient Algorithms for Parallel Computers.* New York: McGraw Hill.
1988. Babb, R. G. II, (Ed.) *Programming Parallel Processors.* Reading, MA: Addison-Wesley.
1988. Gehani, N. and McGettrick, A.D., Eds. *Concurrent Programming.* Wokingham, England: Addison-Wesley.
1990. Denning, P. J., and Tichy, W. F. "Highly Parallel Computation," *Science* **250,** *4985* (November) 1217–1222.

MICHAEL J. QUINN

ARCHITECTURES

Introduction Serial computers have been the staple of computing since the development of stored-program computers, such as the Electronic Discrete Variable Automatic Computer (EDVAC - *q.v.*) in the early 1950s. Technological advances, such as increasing the speed of the circuitry, increasing the number of components per integrated circuit chip (IC), and performing certain low-level operations concurrently, have given rise to a roughly 10-fold increase in the speed of a serial computer every 5 years. In fact, rapid improvements in component technology led early component designers to believe that increases in speed could always be obtained by better component design. Unfortunately, the speed of light (1 foot per nanosecond) places a physical limitation on the speed at which electronic components of a given size can operate. (In the late 1970s, Seymour Cray designed his CRAY-1 supercomputer in the shape of a horseshoe instead of a straight line to overcome such physical limitations.) Since serial computers now operate within two orders of magnitude of this limit, alternative solutions must be considered for problems that require orders of magnitude more computing power than today's fastest machines (supercomputers - *q.v.*). Such problems include weather prediction, molecular modeling, and flow dynamics. A logical and feasible alternative to the familiar single processor (serial) machines is to consider machines that incorporate more than one processor, where the multiple processors have the ability to cooperate in solving individual problems.

In 1952, John von Neumann designed (with paper and pencil) a machine, which he called a "cellular structure," that consisted of a two-dimensional array of simple processors. (See CELLULAR AUTOMATON.) In the late 1950s, another parallel computer was designed by S. H. Unger, who proposed a two-dimensional array of processors targeted at problems in image processing and pattern recognition. Unger also considered arrays of different dimensions and shapes.

Eventually, such theoretical designs led to the production of what was then called "the first supercomputer," the 64-processor ILLIAC IV, which was designed in 1967 and became operational in 1975. The 64 processors were connected as an 8×8 two-dimensional grid. The ILLIAC IV, originally designed to have four 8×8 arrays of powerful processors, was targeted at applications involving matrices and partial differential equations. It consisted of a control unit that broadcast one instruction at a time to all processors. Each processor executed the instruction on the contents of its own local memory. Unfortunately, due to technological limitations and inadequate software, many of the early parallel machines were destined to fail.

However, due to recent advances in computer chip (VLSI), compiler, language, and operating system technology, as well as the realization that serial computers will not be able to provide much more computing power, parallel computers have been made commercially available and are currently being used to solve significant problems.

Terminology
The field of parallel computing is relatively new, so its terminology has not yet been standardized. However, in this section we present some fundamental terms and concepts that are fairly well accepted.

Shared Memory Versus Distributed Memory In a *shared memory* machine, there is a single global set of memory that is available to all processors, as shown in Fig. 1. The processors in a shared memory system are connected to the common global memory by a bus (*q.v.*) or switch. Memory and bus contention in such a system is a primary concern when developing algorithms. For example, care must be taken when two processors try to write to the same memory location simultaneously.

Each processor in a *distributed memory* machine has access only to its own private (local) memory, as shown in Fig. 2. Distributed memory machines avoid the memory

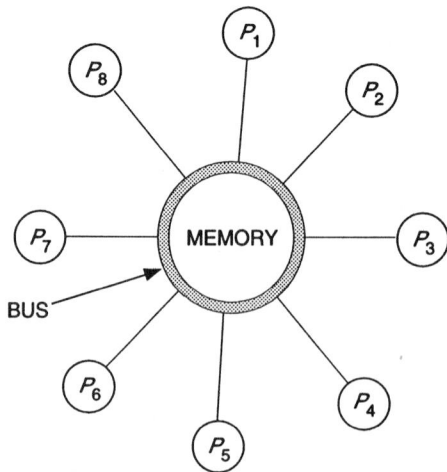

FIG. 1. A shared memory system in which the processors (P_i) are connected to a common global memory via a bus.

contention problem. However, access to non-local data in a distributed memory system is provided by passing messages between the processors through the interconnection network (defined in Section 3). In a distributed memory system, contention for message passing channels is a major concern.

Flynn's Taxonomy In 1966, Michael Flynn classified computer architectures with respect to instruction stream and data stream. He defined an *instruction stream* as a sequence of operations performed by the computer, and a *data stream* as the sequence of items operated on by the instructions. While a number of extensions, modifications, and complete overhauls to Flynn's taxonomy have been proposed, his original taxonomy is still widely used. Flynn characterizes an architecture as belonging to one of the following four classes.

- Single-instruction stream, single-data stream (SISD).
- Single-instruction stream, multiple-data stream (SIMD).
- Multiple-instruction stream, single-data stream (MISD).
- Multiple-instruction stream, multiple data stream (MIMD).

Most serial computers fall into the *single-instruction stream, single data stream (SISD)* category, in which one

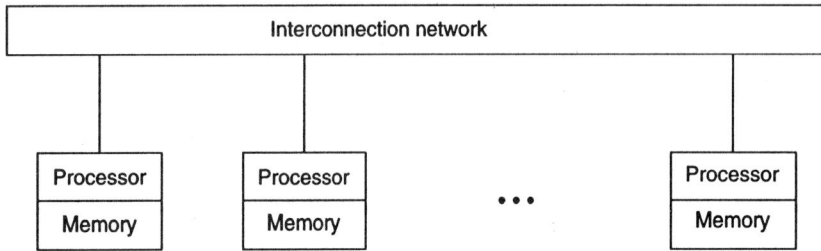

FIG. 2. A distributed memory system. Every processing element consists of a processor and memory module.

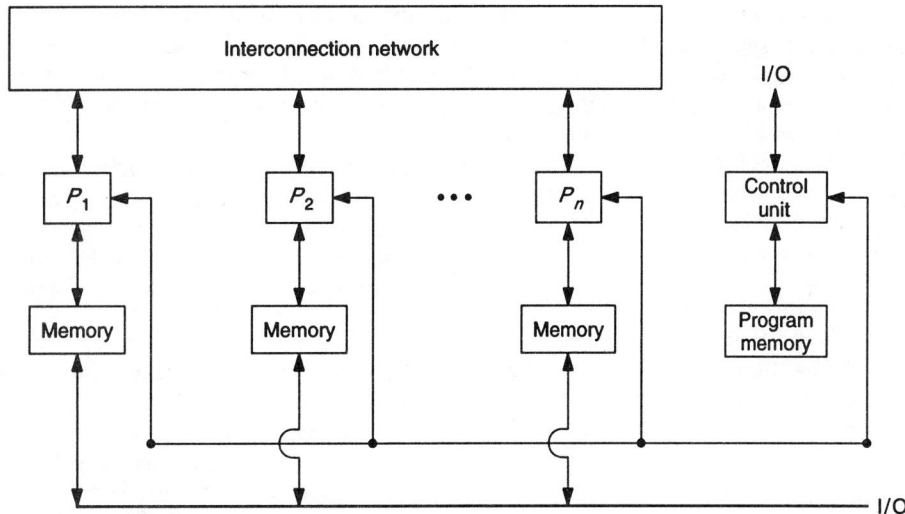

FIG. 3. A distributed memory SIMD model, in which each processor (P_i) is coupled with a memory module.

instruction is executed per unit time on its operands. This is the so-called "von Neumann" model of computing, in which the stream of instructions and stream of data can be viewed as being tightly coupled so that one instruction is executed at a time, to produce one useful result (*see* VON NEUMANN MACHINE).

A *single-instruction stream, multiple-data stream (SIMD)* machine typically consists of n processors, a control unit, and an interconnection network. The control unit stores the program and broadcasts the instructions to all processors simultaneously. Active processors execute the instruction on the contents of their own local memory. Through the use of a *mask*, processors may be in either an active or inactive state at any time during the

execution of the program. Fig. 3 shows a typical SIMD machine.

Multiple-instruction stream, single-data stream (MISD) machines consist of two or more processors that perform separate instructions on the same data. This approach is thought to be impractical, with no current machines falling in this category.

A *multiple-instruction stream, multiple-data stream (MIMD)* machine typically consists of n processors, n memory modules, and an interconnection network. In contrast to the single instruction stream model, the multiple instruction stream model allows each of the n processors to store and execute its own program. (Thus, there are multiple instruction streams, as opposed to the

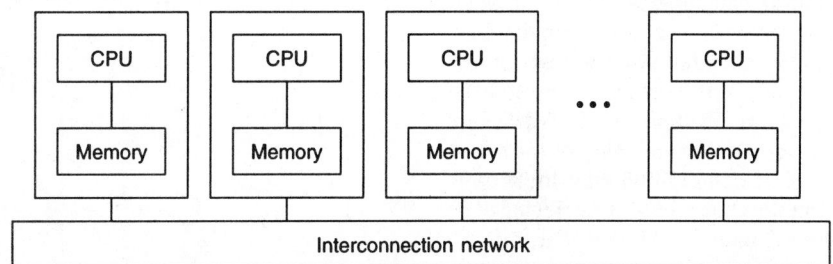

FIG. 4. A distributed memory MIMD machine, in which each processing element consists of a processor (CPU) and a memory module.

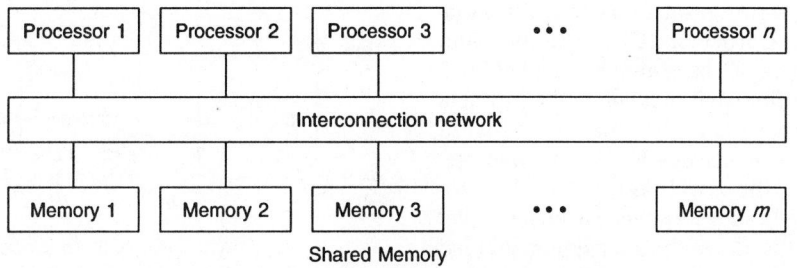

FIG. 5. A shared memory MIMD machine in which processors communicate with each other and with the memory modules through the interconnection network.

SIMD model, in which there is only a single instruction stream.) Each processor fetches its own data on which to operate. (Thus, there are multiple data streams, as in the SIMD model.) MIMD machines are organized either with the memory distributed, as in Fig. 4, or with a common global (or shared) memory, as in Fig. 5.

To see why alternatives have been proposed to Flynn's taxonomy, consider classifying a machine such as the CRAY-1. The CRAY-1 has multiple functional units that operate under the direction of a single control unit. All of the functional units can operate concurrently on the data that they have retrieved from the global memory. For this reason, some authors claim that the CRAY belongs to the SISD category, while others claim that it belongs in the SIMD category. In either case, the appropriate category is usually modified somewhat, to accommodate such a machine.

Granularity When discussing parallel architectures, the term *granularity* is often used to refer to the relative number and complexity of the processors. A *fine-grained machine* typically consists of a relatively large number of small, simple processors (in terms of local memory and computational power), while a *coarse-grained machine* typically consists of a few large, powerful processors. With respect to early 1990s technology, fine-grained machines have on the order of 10,000 simple processors, while coarse-grained machines have on the order of 10 powerful processors. *Medium-grained* machines represent a compromise in performance and size between that of fine-grained and coarse-grained machines, with on the order of 100 processors.

Fine-grained machines typically fall into the SIMD category, where all processors operate in lockstep fashion (i.e. synchronously) on the contents of their own small local memory. Coarse-grained machines typically fall into the shared memory MIMD category, where processors operate asynchronously on the large shared memory. Medium-grained machines typically fall into the distributed memory MIMD category, where the programming style is often that of *single program, multiple data (SPMD)*. In SPMD, all processors store an identical copy of the same program, which consists of computations on local data interspersed with communication steps for retrieving necessary data from nonlocal memory. Notice that, due to data dependencies, at any given time different processors could be executing very different sections of the code.

Due to technological advances, it can be expected that by the middle 1990s, fine-grained machines will have on the order of 1,000,000 processors, coarse-grained machines will have on the order of 100 processors, and medium-grained machines will have on the order of 10,000 processors. It is also anticipated that, while the physical memory might move towards a combination of shared and distributed memory, especially for coarse- and medium-grained machines, there will be a major effort towards maintaining a single address space on most parallel machines. In fact, the BBN Butterfly is a medium-grained distributed memory MIMD machine that can be used in a combination of shared and distributed memory modes—that is, the user can specify how much memory of each

processor should be considered shared memory. This shared memory is programmed as a single (global) address space, where references to remote memory naturally take longer than references to local memory.

Interconnection Networks Interconnection networks are used for processor-to-processor (in distributed memory machines) and processor-to-memory (in shared memory machines) communication. In this section, we briefly discuss a small subset of these interconnection networks.

Processor-to-Processor Interconnections In order to discuss some specific processor-to-processor interconnection networks, some terminology is in order. The *degree of a processor P* is defined to be the number of other processors that P is directly connected to via bi-directional communication links. The *degree of the network* is defined to be the maximum degree of any processor in the network. The *communication diameter* of the network is defined to be the maximum of the minimum distance between any two processors.

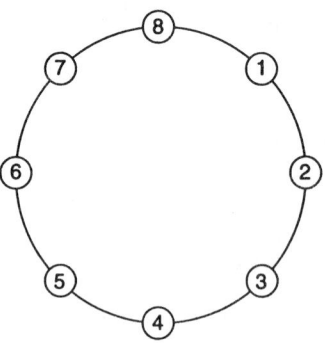

(a) A ring of size 8.

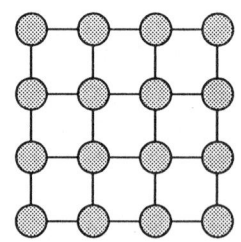

(b) A mesh of size 16.

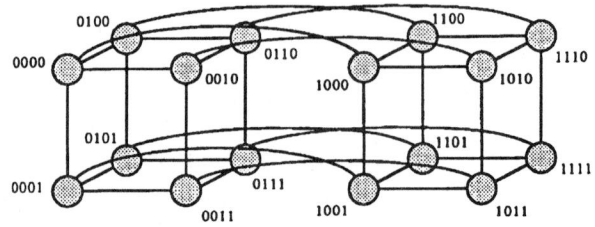

(c) A hypercube with 16 processors indexed by their binary representations.

FIG. 6. Processor-to-processor interconnection networks.

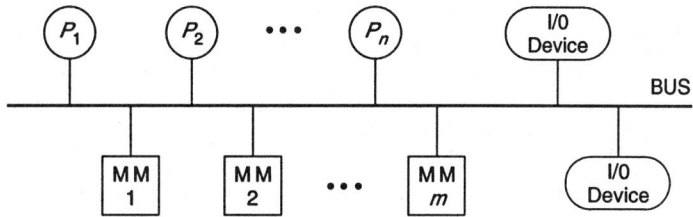

(a) A single bus-based system with *n* processors and *m* memory modules.

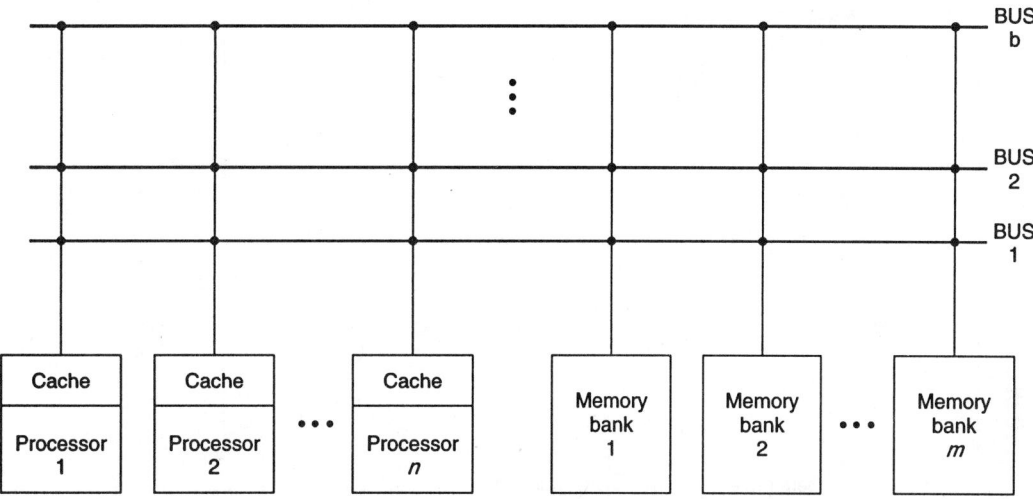

(b) A multiple bus-based system with *n* processors and *m* memory modules.

FIG. 7. Bus-based systems.

In the sections that follow, we will see that a set of *n* processors connected as a ring (Fig. 6(a)) has a degree of 2 (each processor is directly connected to two other processors) and a communication diameter of $\lceil n/2 \rceil$. We will also see that, if the processors are connected as a hypercube (Fig. 6(c)), the degree of the network is $\log_2 n$ and the communication diameter is $\log_2 n$. Naturally, one of the goals in designing processor-to-processor interconnection networks is to minimize both the degree of the network and the communication diameter, subject to physical layout constraints. Unfortunately, reducing the communication diameter of a network often requires increasing the degree of the network, and vice versa.

Ring

In a *ring* network, as shown in Fig. 6(a), the *n* processors are connected in a circular fashion so that processor P_1 is directly connected to processors P_{i-1} and P_{i+1}. While the degree of the network is only 2, the communication diameter is $\lceil n/2 \rceil$, which is quite high.

Mesh

The *n* processors of a two-dimensional square mesh network, as shown in Fig. 6(b), are typically configured so that an interior processor P_{ij} is connected to its four neighbors—processors $P_{i-1,j}$, $P_{i+1,j}$, $P_{i,j-1}$, and $P_{i,j+1}$. The four corner processors are each connected to their two neighbors, while the remaining processors that are

on the edge of the mesh are each connected to three neighbors. So, by increasing the degree of the network to 4, the communication diameter of the network is reduced to $2(n^{1/2}-1)$.

Hypercube

A hypercube with *n* processors, where *n* is an integral power of 2, has the processors indexed by the integers

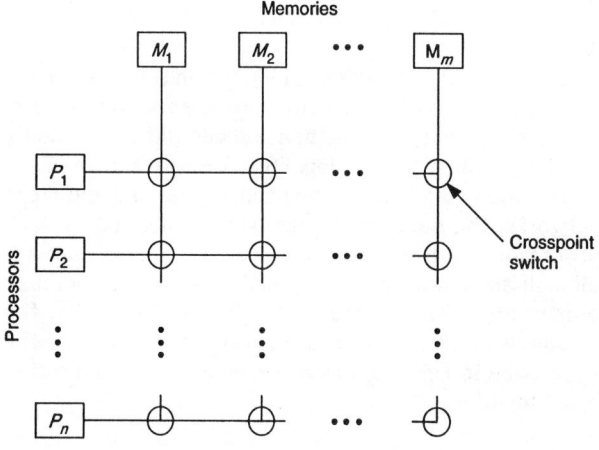

FIG. 8. A crossbar switch with *n* processors and *m* memory modules.

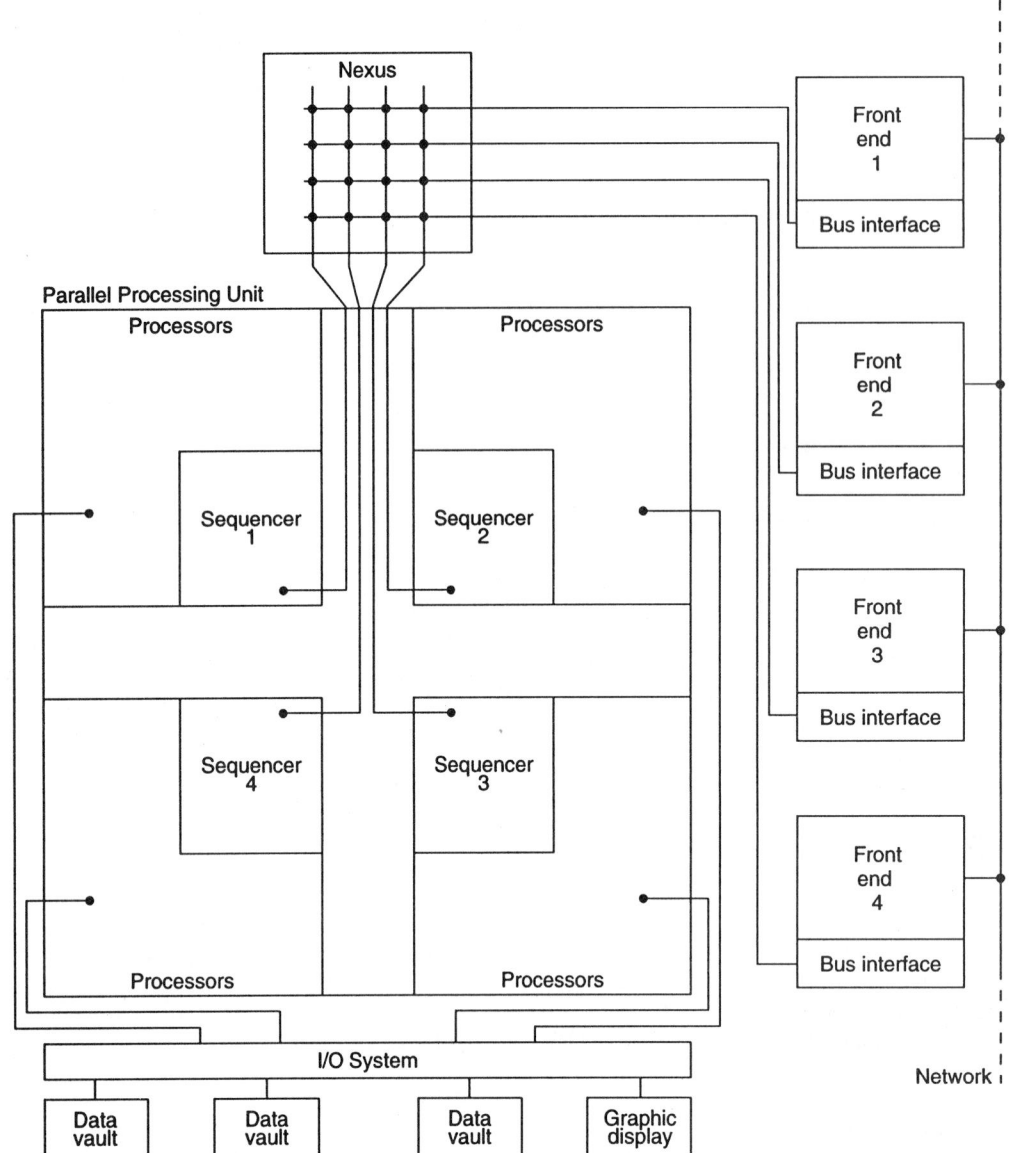

FIG. 9.   The Connection Machine.

{0, . . ., $n - 1$}. Viewing each integer in the index range as a ($\log_2 n$)-bit string, two processors are directly connected if and only if their indices differ by exactly one bit, as illustrated in Fig. 6(c). A disadvantage of the hypercube is that, unlike the fixed degree ring and mesh networks, the number of links that are needed by each processor in a hypercube grows as $\log_2 n$. This makes it difficult to manufacture reasonably generic hypercube processors. The advantage of a hypercube is that the communication diameter is only $\log_2 n$. Notice that the hypercube in Fig. 6(c) has a degree and communication diameter of 4.

Processor-to-Memory Interconnections   In this section, some common processor-to-memory interconnections are discussed.

Bus

In a *single bus-based system*, the processors, memory modules, and I/O devices are connected by a single high-speed bus. This is the least complicated interconnection network, but it has the disadvantage that only one processor can access the shared memory at a time. An alternative to using a single bus is to use *multiple buses*, where each of the processors and memory modules are connected to multiple buses, and the performance of each processor is augmented through the use of *cache memory (q.v.)* (Fig. 7).

Crossbar Switch

A *crossbar switch* provides every one of the n processors with a logical connection to each of the m memory modules. This allows every processor to communicate simul-

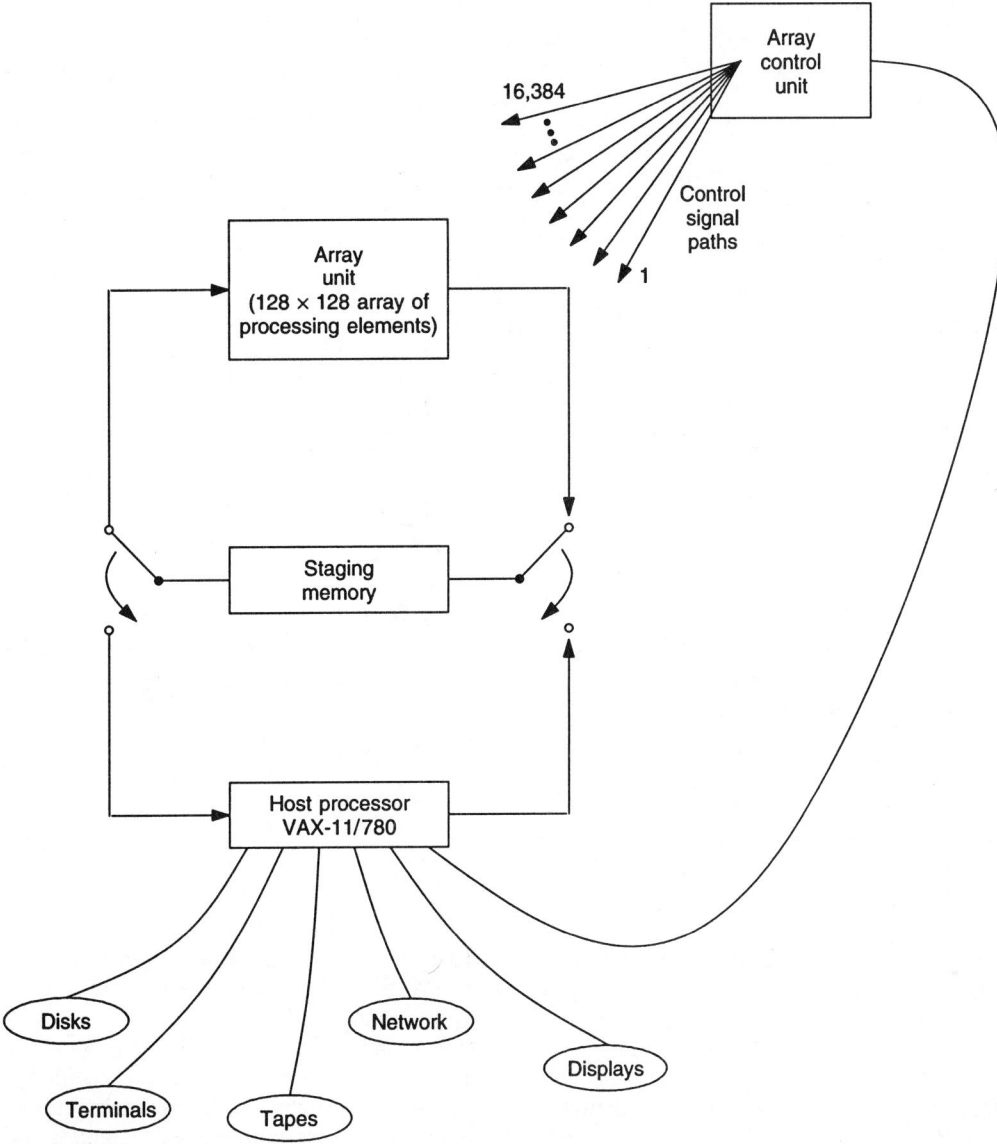

FIG. 10. An overview of the MPP.

taneously with a distinct memory module without contention, but generally requires *nm* switches, as shown in Fig. 8.

Multistage Interconnection Networks

A *multistage interconnection network (MIN)* connects processors and memory modules through a specialized switching network. These networks typically have logarithmic depth (i.e. a message must go through a logarithmic number of switches to get from the processor to the memory module). An advantage of MINs is that they permit multiple paths between processors and memory modules and require fewer components than a crossbar switch, while still allowing good connectivity between the processors and memory.

Examples This section provides examples, chosen from commercially available machines, that illustrate some of the previous concepts. These examples include fine-, coarse-, and medium-grained machines and SIMD and MIMD machines, as well as a variety of interconnection schemes.

Fine-Grained Machines The *Connection Machine* is a distributed memory SIMD family of machines manufactured by Thinking Machines Corporation. The CM-2 can be configured with a maximum of 65,536 bit serial processors, each with 8K bytes of local memory, and 2,048 Weitek floating point units. Sixteen bit serial processors reside on a chip, and every disjoint pair of chips shares a floating point unit (i.e. one floating point unit is shared by

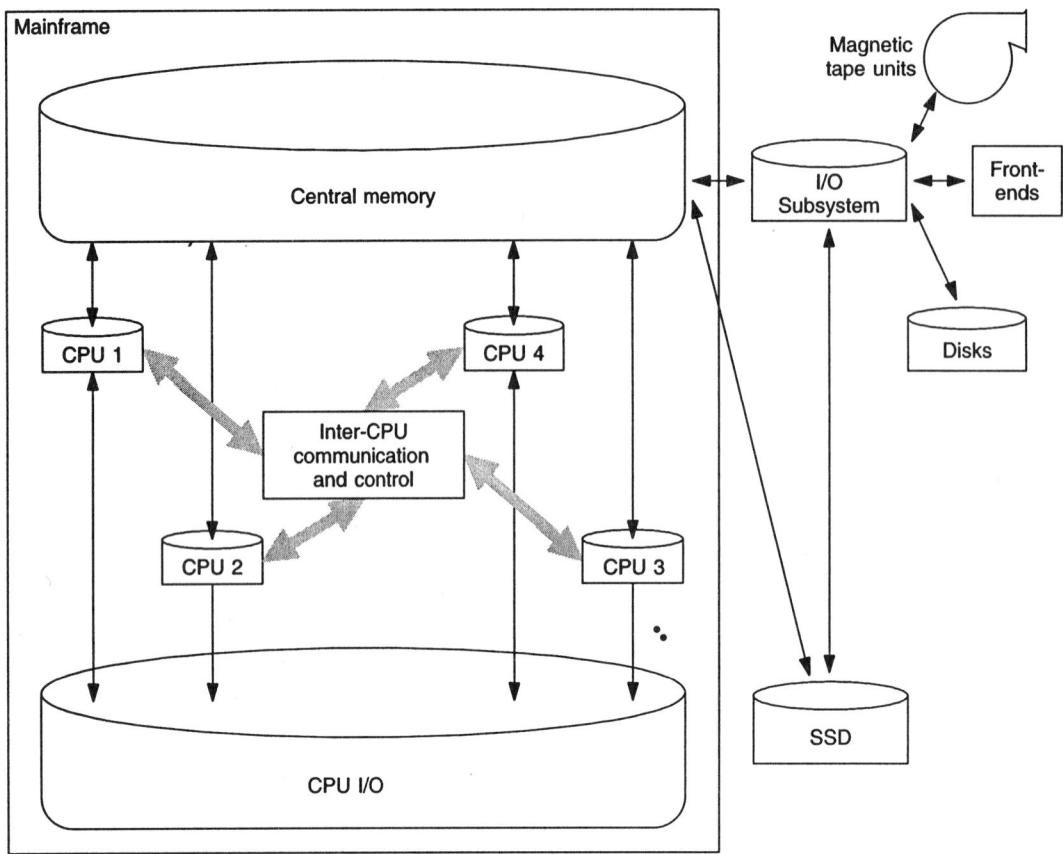

FIG. 11. CRAY X-MP system organization.

32 bit serial processors). A full machine consists of the following (Fig. 9).

- A front end (a Sun, Symbolics, or VAX).
- Four computational units, each consisting of 16,384 bit serial processors and 512 floating point units.
- An I/O system connected directly to the processors.
- A switch (called *Nexus*) that allows up to four front ends to be connected to the parallel processing unit.

The instructions issued by the front end are sent to the *sequencers*, which break down the instructions into a series of low-level operations that are broadcast to the processors. Communication between processors on a chip is achieved through a local interconnection network. General communication between the 4,096 chips is by a 12-dimensional hypercube topology, where all 16 processors on a chip share a *router*. For grid-structured communication, however, a faster NEWS (North, East, West, and South) network is provided. The CM-2 has a peak performance of 32 GFLOPS, and an observed performance for scientific applications in the 1–5 GFLOPS range.

The *Massively Parallel Processor (MPP)* is a distributed memory SIMD machine developed by the Goodyear Aerospace Corporation. It is currently controlled by the Loral Systems Group, which is a division of the Loral Corporation. The MPP consists of 16,384 bit serial processors, each with its own 1K bits of local memory. The processors are connected using a two dimensional mesh interconnection network, where each generic processor is connected to its four nearest neighbors. The processors along the edge of the array may be connected in a variety of fashions to other such processors. This allows the processors to form topologies, including a cylinder, torus, or spiral. The peak performance of the MPP is 6.5 GFLOPS. In addition to the array unit, the MPP has an *array control unit* for controlling the operations of the processors, a unique *staging memory* that buffers and permutes data, and a standard front end (Fig. 10). While the MPP was initially developed for processing images, it has been used for a wide variety of scientific applications.

Coarse-Grained Machines The CRAY series of supercomputers are coarse-grained shared memory machines in which each of the vector processors may operate independently on separate jobs or may be organized in various combinations to operate together on a single job. A *vector processor* may be defined as a processor containing special hardware to allow a sequence of identical operations to be performed faster than a sequence of non-identical operations on data arranged as

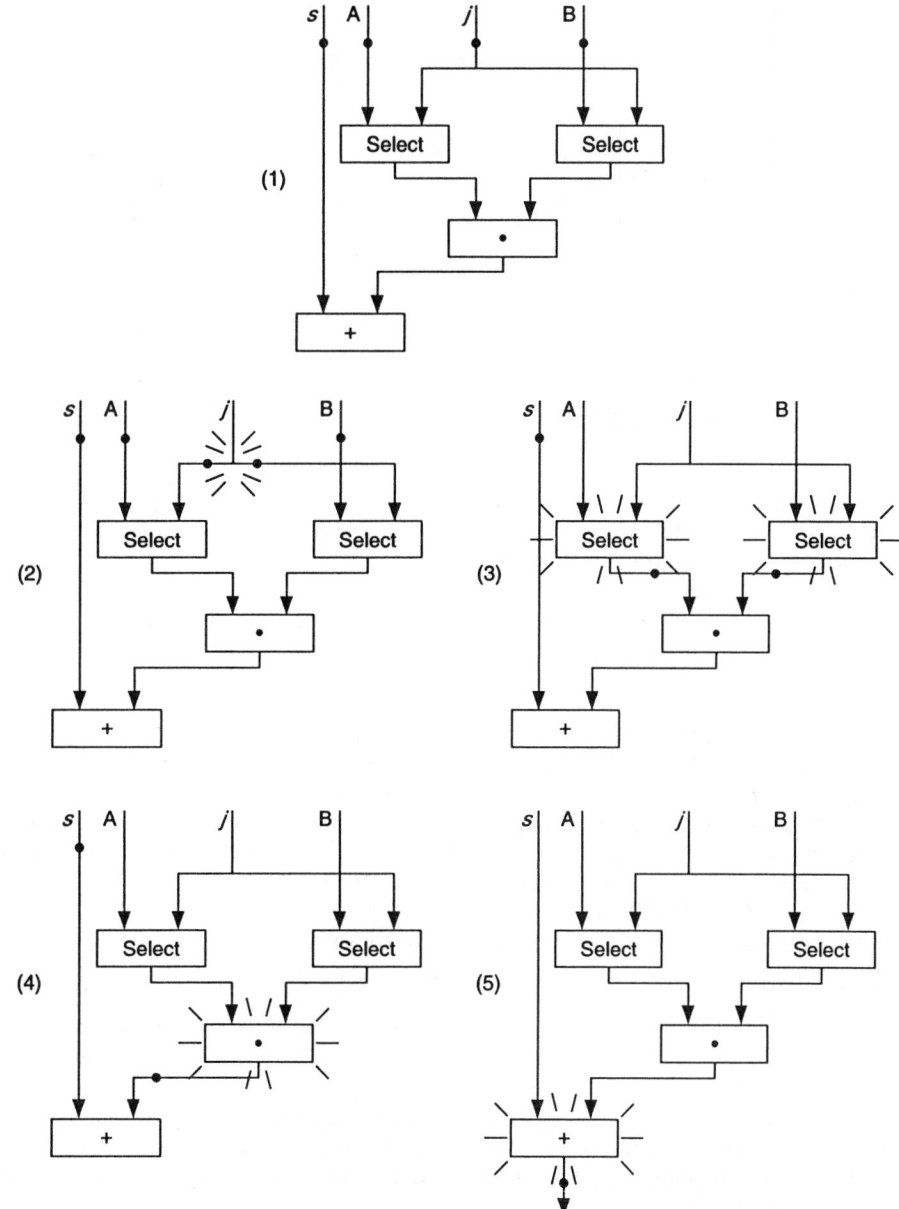

FIG. 12. A firing (activation) sequence for the simple expression " $s + A[j] \times B[j]$ " on a dataflow computer.

a regular array. The CRAY X-MP/48 system is a system with four vector processors and a total of 8 million 64-bit words. The peak performance of the system is 0.8 GFLOPS. Each processor contains 12 functional units that can operate concurrently. The CRAY I/O *subsystem (IOS)* enables fast, efficient data access and processing by the CPUs, handling I/O distribution for a variety of front-end computer systems and peripherals. The *solid-state storage* device (SSD) is a very fast random access device. Fig. 11 gives an overview of the CRAY X-MP/48 system.

While the CRAY series of machines are relatively expensive supercomputers that rely on special cooling sys-

tems, other coarse-grained machines are available that are relatively less expensive, are based on standard microcomputer chips, and do not require any special cooling. For example, the Sequent Symmetry Series is a coarse-grained shared memory machine with up to 30 80386-based processors and 240 Mbytes of shared memory. A similar shared memory machine is the Encore Multimax, which supports up to 20 NS32332-based processors and 128 Mbytes of shared memory. Both of these are bus-based machines.

Medium-Grained Machines Medium-grained machines typically have microprocessor-class processors—that is,

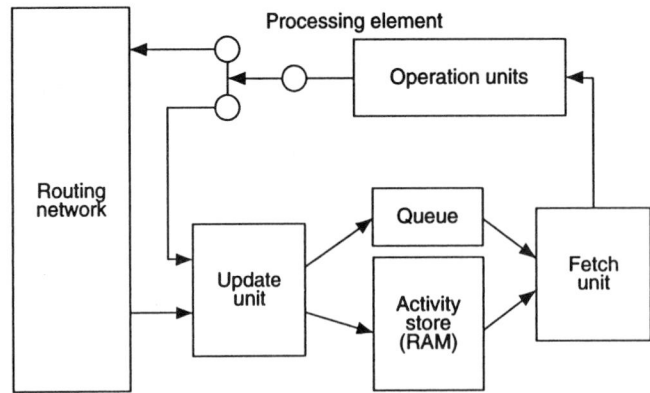

FIG. 13. A dataflow processor.

the processors of a medium-grained machine typically have computational power weaker than the processors of a coarse-grained supercomputer, but more powerful than the processors of a fine-grained machine. However, since these MIMD machines can scale to thousands of processors, they have the ability of providing supercomputer performance.

Meiko has delivered transputer-based machines with an array of 1000 processors connected as a mesh. Each T800 transputer (*q.v.*) has a peak performance of 1 MFLOPS, so the peak performance of the system is 1 GFLOPS. Each transputer in such a configuration can have 8 Mbytes of local memory.

Another large, commercially available medium-grained MIMD machine is the NCUBE 2 Model 6480. The 6480 can contain 8,192 proprietary processors connected in a hypercube topology, and has a peak performance of 27 GFLOPS.

Additional Models

Dataflow Computers Dataflow computers (*q.v.*) are similar to conventional computers in some aspects. For ex-

ample, dataflow computers execute stored programs, and machine-level programs consist of individual instructions that call for conventional operations to be performed. The difference is in the manner in which instructions are identified for execution. There is no program counter in a dataflow computer. Instead, an instruction is activated when it has received (as results from other instructions) the data it needs to operate. Fig. 12 shows an example of computing a simple result on a dataflow machine.

A dataflow computer generally consists of many *processors*, a *packet routing network* that allows any processor to send information packets to any other, and *array memory units* for holding large databases of information required by many problems.

A dataflow processor typically consists of mechanisms for reorganizing when instructions are enabled, and mechanisms for carrying out their execution (Fig. 13). The dataflow instructions assigned to a processor are held in the processor's *activity store*. A simple queue holds addresses of those instructions that are enabled. The *fetch unit* picks the address of some enabled instruction from the queue, fetches the instructions (with its operands) from the activity store, and delivers it to an *operation unit*. Execution of the instruction creates one or more result

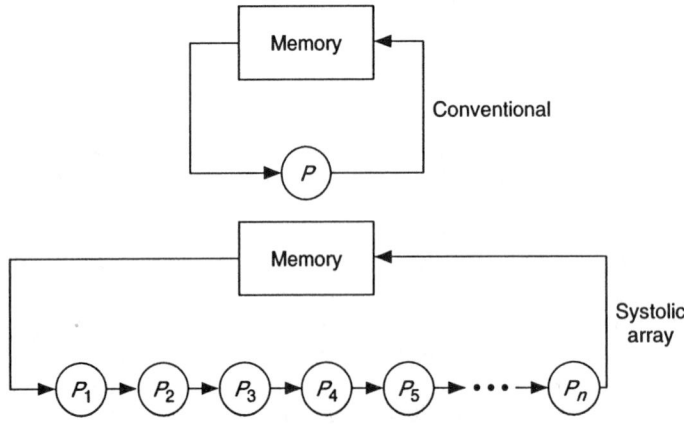

FIG. 14. Comparison of a single processor machine with a systolic array. The systolic array has data brought out of memory and "pulsed" through an array of processors before returning to memory.

packets, which are sent on to the *update unit*. The update unit places the result value in the operand field of the target instruction, and decides whether the instruction has become enabled. If the instruction is enabled, its address is entered in the queue. If the target instruction of a result packet resides in some other processor of the machine, the packet is sent off through the network. While experimental and prototype dataflow machines have been designed since the mid 1970s, the entry of such machines into the commercial market has been extremely limited.

Systolic Arrays (*q.v.*) A *systolic system* consists of a set of interconnected processors, each capable of performing some simple operation. The processors in a systolic system are typically interconnected to form a *systolic array*, where "systolic" is used to mean that pipelined (assembly line) computations take place along all dimensions of the array. Communication with the environment occurs only at the boundary processors. The basic principle of a systolic architecture is that by replacing a single processor with an array of processors, a higher computation throughput can be achieved without increased memory bandwidth. Data is typically viewed as being "pulsed" through the array of processors from the memory. Once a data item is brought out from memory, it can be used effectively at each processor it passes, while being "pumped" from processor to processor along the array (Fig. 14).

References

1984 Hwang, K. and Briggs F. A., *Computer Architecture and Parallel Processing*. New York: McGraw-Hill.

1988. Babb, R. G. *Programming Parallel Processors*. Reading, MA: Addison-Wesley Publishing Company.

1988. Quinn, M. J. *Designing Efficient Algorithms for Parallel Computers*. New York: McGraw-Hill.

1989. Miller, S. E. (Amherst Systems, Inc.), *A Survey of Parallel Computing*, 2nd Ed., RADC-TR-89-68, June. Rome Air Development Center, Air Force Systems Command, Griffiss AFB, NY.

1989. Almasi, G. S. and Gottlieb, A. *Highly Parallel Computing*. New York: Benjamin/Cummings.

RUSS MILLER

ALGORITHMS

Introduction For computationally intensive problems, such as processing data collected from satellites to predict the earth's weather, it is estimated that information must be processed at a minimum of 10^{13} operations per second, where an operation may be defined as the addition or multiplication of two values. In fact, applications such as three-dimensional image reconstruction, aircraft testing, and modeling fusion reactors require machines that can process 10^{15} operations per second. Current supercomputers process on the order of 10^8 operations per second, and physical constraints (such as the speed of light) dictate that the speed of such machines can increase by, at most, two orders of magnitude. One way to transcend these physical limitations is to consider

machines designed as a collection of processors that can cooperate to solve a given problem. There are a number of basic approaches that can be used in developing efficient parallel algorithms. One approach is to port existing serial algorithms to these new machines (either by hand or by using parallelizing compilers). However, many algorithms that run well on serial computers are not easily ported to run efficiently on parallel computers. Another approach is to design a new solution to the problem with parallelism in mind. A third approach is to adapt an existing parallel algorithm that was developed to solve a different problem to solve the new problem. Each approach has its place, and examples of the first two will be discussed.

Most of the large software packages that have been implemented on existing parallel machines rely on numerical algorithms to solve scientific problems. It is fortunate that many such algorithms can be implemented in a relatively straightforward fashion on existing parallel machines, since these operations are often critical in solving problems, including those involving air-traffic control, the design of airplanes and automobiles, and modeling various physical situations, as well as problems in biology, chemistry, physics, geology, and astronomy. The thrust of most theoretical work, however, is on developing efficient parallel algorithms to solve problems in areas such as computational geometry (*q.v.*), intermediate-level image analysis, and graph theory (*q.v.*). Examples will be given for fundamental operations such as sorting (*q.v.*) and searching (*q.v.*), matrix operations, and a fundamental problem in image analysis. In addition, general paradigms and fundamental operations are discussed that serve as building blocks for designing efficient parallel algorithms.

Examples and Discussion

Sum Suppose we need to sum n values that are initially distributed one per processor on a fine-grained machine with n processors. Consider an algorithm for a square mesh of processors. First, sum the values in each row simultaneously and independently so that the leftmost processor in each row knows the sum of its row. Then, in the first column, sum these partial sums to the topmost processor. Finally, the sum of these n values, which is stored in the top-left processor of the mesh, can be distributed to all processors by reversing the previous data movement, as follows. Send the solution from the top-left processor to all processors in the first column, and then in a similar fashion distribute the solution in parallel within each row. So, if processor $P_{i,j}$ starts with value $v_{i,j}$, the following code shows how to compute the sum of these values.

for $j := n^{1/2}$ **downto** 2 **do**
$v_{i,j-1} \leftarrow v_{i,j-1} + v_{i,j}$ (simultaneously for all rows i)

for i $:= n^{1/2}$ **downto** 2 **do**
$v_{i-1,1} \leftarrow v_{i-1,1} + v_{i,1}$

Summing n values on a serial machine takes $O(n)$ time, but this mesh algorithm requires only $O(n^{1/2})$ time. While this is asymptotically optimal for the mesh, since the communication diameter of the mesh is $O(n^{1/2})$, it is possible that other architectures can compute the sum even faster. In fact, a hypercube with n processors can compute the sum in $O(\log n)$ time.

Matrix Transpose Consider computing the transpose of a matrix on a mesh computer. Given an $n \times n$ matrix A, stored so that processor $P_{i,j}$ contains element $a_{i,j}$, it is possible to compute the transpose of A in $O(n)$ time, where the transpose of A, denoted A^T, is given by $a_{i,j}{}^T = a_{j,i}$. The algorithm consists of two complementary phases that are each completed in $O(n)$ time as follows. Denote diagonal processors $P_{i,i}$, $1 \le i \le n$, as *routers*. For all above-diagonal processors $P_{i,j}$, $i < j$, send the value of $a_{i,j}$ down to diagonal processor $P_{j,j}$ in lock-step fashion. Each value $a_{i,j}$, $i < j$ reaches diagonal processor $P_{j,j}$ in $k = j - i$ steps. As each router $P_{j,j}$ receives an $a_{i,j}$ it sends the data to the left, where it will move for $k = j - i$ steps, until it reaches below-diagonal processor $P_{j,i}$. Next, in a similar fashion, all below-diagonal processors $P_{i,j}$, $i > j$, send their data to the right, where diagonal processor $P_{i,i}$ routes the data upwards. Finally, in $O(n)$ time, every processor $P_{i,j}$ contains $a_{j,i}$. As with the previous example, this algorithm is asymptotically optimal for the mesh. However, as before, other parallel architectures can compute the transpose faster.

Matrix Multiplication We now consider matrix multiplication, a more computationally intensive problem than the previous ones. Given two $n \times n$ matrices, A and B, the matrix product $C = AB$ is given by $c_{i,j} = \sum_{k=1}^{n} a_{i,k} b_{k,j}$. The algorithm we give shows how to compute $C = AB$ in $O(n)$ time on a mesh with $4n^2$ processors. Assume that matrix A is stored in the lower-left quadrant, matrix B is stored in the upper-right quadrant, and the resultant matrix C is to be constructed in the lower-right quadrant of the mesh, as shown in Fig. 1. At time 1, in lock-step fashion, all

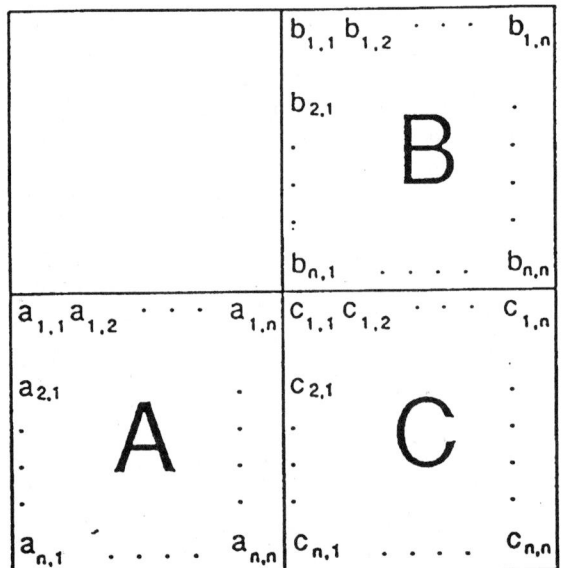

FIG. 1. Multiplying two $n \times n$ matrices on a mesh with $4n^2$ processors.

processors containing an element of the first row of A send their values to the right and all processors containing an element of the first column of B send their values down. The processor responsible for $c_{1,1}$ can now begin to compute its running sum. At time 2, row 1 of A and column 1 of B continue to move in the same direction, and row 2 of A and column 2 of B start to move right and down, respectively. In general, at time i, the ith row of A and the ith column of B start to move right and down, respectively. Each processor that simultaneously receives a piece of data from a processor to its left and from a processor above computes the product of these two values and adds it to the running sum. At time $i + 1$, every processor sends values received during time i to neighboring processors in the direction that the values were moving. So, at time k, rows $1 \ldots k$ of A and columns $1 \ldots k$ of B move right and down, respectively, where this is the first such movement for row k of A and column k of B. Therefore, row and column n of A and B start moving at time n, $c_{n,n}$ is the last value computed, and $c_{n,n}$ is fully computed at time $3n - 2$. Hence, the algorithm runs in $O(n)$ time on a mesh of size $4n^2$. Since the algorithm takes $O(n)$ time with $O(n^2)$ processors, the amount of work performed by the algorithm is $O(n^3)$, which is asymptotically optimal with respect to the number of operations required by the standard sequential matrix multiplication algorithm. Therefore, it is not possible to achieve a better running time with any other architecture unless the number of processors is increased.

Remarks In developing efficient parallel algorithms, one often relies on general paradigms, such as divide-and-conquer, which is particularly useful in a parallel setting since subproblems can be solved simultaneously. (*see* ALGORITHMS, ANALYSIS OF and ALGORITHMS, DESIGN AND CLASSIFICATION OF.) Data reduction techniques are often used to reduce an initial set of data to a smaller pertinent set of data that can be used to solve the problem efficiently. In addition to these techniques, it is becoming more common to design parallel algorithms in terms of a variety of fundamental operations. These operations include *sorting* which is frequently used to route data on parallel machines (i.e. by sorting with respect to a destination address), *parallel search* and *parallel prefix* (given a_i stored in processor P_i, and an associative binary operator $\otimes$ compute the initial prefix $a_1 \otimes a_2 \otimes \ldots \otimes a_i$ simultaneously for all P_i), which can be used to sum elements, detect a minimum value, broadcast values, and compress data. The next example will incorporate some of these techniques and operations.

Component Labeling The *component labeling problem* requires that all *figures* (i.e. maximally connected components) be uniquely labeled. We assume that an $n \times n$ digitized picture $A = \{a_{i,j}\}$ is stored one *pixel (picture element)* per processor on a machine with n^2 processors. The pixels are assumed to be in one of two states: black or white. It is helpful to think of this digitization as being a black picture on a white background. The picture is stored so that pixels that are adjacent in the picture are mapped to processors that are directly connected in the machine. Define a black pixel $a_{i,j}$ to be a *neighbor* of black pixels $a_{i+1,j}$, $a_{i-1,j}$, $a_{i,j+1}$, and $a_{i,j-1}$. (Notice that black pixels $a_{i,j}$ and $a_{i+1,j+1}$, for example, are not neighbors, though they may still be in the same figure if there is a path of neighboring black pixels between them.)

Each processor that contains a black pixel uses its unique index as the label of the pixel that it contains. When a labeling algorithm terminates, each processor that contains a black pixel will store the label of the smallest labeled black pixel that its pixel is connected to—that is, each such processor will know the label of the figure that its pixel is a member of.

A simple parallel *propagation* algorithm can be used to label the figures, as follows. Each black processor (i.e. a processor containing a black pixel) initially assumes that the label of its pixel is the component label of the figure that its pixel belongs to. During each iteration of the algorithm, each black processor sends its current component label to its (at most) four black neighbors. Each black processor then compares its current label with the (at most) four labels just received, and keeps as its new label the minimum of these labels. It is easy to see that, for each figure, the minimum label L is propagated from processor P_L (i.e. the processor with index L) to each black processor P_i in its figure in the minimum number of steps required to pass a message from P_L to P_i, under the restriction that data is passed only between neighboring black processors. Therefore, this labeling algorithm terminates in $\Theta(D)$ time, where $\Theta(D)$ is the maximum amount of time that it takes any figure to propagate its minimum label to all processors in its figure. So, given "blob-like" figures, as in Fig. 2, all processors can know the label of their figure in $O(n)$ time. However, it is easy to construct non-"blob-like" figures, such as spirals or snakes, as in Fig. 3, for which this propagation algorithm would require $\Theta(n^2)$ time.

Next, we outline a general parallel algorithm that is much more efficient, in the worst-case, than the $O(n^2)$ time propagation algorithm for labeling all figures, regardless of the number, shape, or size of the figures.

(a) A spiral is not a "blob-like" figure.

(b) A snake is not a "blob-like" figure.

FIG. 3.   Pictures consisting of non-"blob-like" figures.

The algorithm follows a recursive divide-and-conquer solution strategy that relies on efficient data reduction. The first step of the algorithm is to label recursively the four quadrants of the picture independently. After this step, the only figures that could have an incorrect global label are those figures that have a pixel on the border between the quadrants. For instance, assuming that Fig. 4 represents the labels of figures after the independent and parallel recursive labeling of the quadrants, then figures A and H are labeled correctly in a global sense, while the other figures do not necessarily have the correct final labels, since they have pixels along the border between quadrants. Two common methods for resolving conflicts are:

1. To compress $O(n)$ pieces of information representing the border pixels into a subregion of the machine where interprocessor communication is minimized, resolve the conflicts, and inform all processors of their final label; or

FIG. 2.   A picture containing "blob-like" figures.

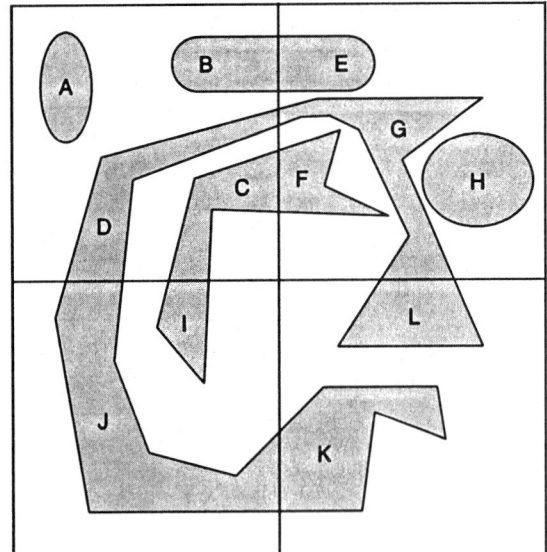

FIG. 4.   Sample labeling after recursively relabeling each quadrant.

2. Create an adjacency matrix representing the connections between border pixels, compute the transitive closure of the matrix to resolve the conflicts, and inform all processors of their final label.

Both resolution techniques exploit the fact that the pertinent data has been reduced from an amount proportional to the area of the image to an amount proportional to the perimeter of the image.

The running time of component labeling on a serial machine is linear in the number of pixels. So, for an $n \times n$ image, the running time is $O(n^2)$. On a mesh, the running time of the algorithm just described is given by $T(n^2) = T(n^2/4) + O(n)$, which is $O(n)$, while on a hypercube the running time is given by $T(n^2) = T(n^2/4) + O(\log^2 n)$ which is $O(\log^3 n)$.

Final Comments   Research in parallel algorithms considers developing efficient paradigms, algorithms, and fundamental operations for a variety of real machines and theoretical models of computation. The theoretical RAM model closely matches real serial machines, in that the observed performance of an algorithm on a real serial machine can be expected to match closely the theoretical analysis. Unfortunately, a corresponding situation does not yet exist for parallel machines. The parallel model that corresponds most closely to the RAM is the so-called *PRAM (Parallel RAM)*, which consists of a set of processors, all of which have unit-time access to a shared memory. Unfortunately, while ignoring communication costs allows one to concentrate on developing lower bounds for parallel algorithms, it does not have much effect on making decisions as to which algorithms to implement on real parallel machines. Distributed memory models, such as the mesh and hypercube, are somewhat better at modeling real parallel machines, especially fine-grained ma-

chines. However, even with the fine-grained distributed memory models, the constants that are masked in the asymptotic analysis of algorithms become critical when implementing algorithms on real machines, since existing machines are not currently large enough to consume the overhead.

References

1984. Uhr, L. *Algorithm-Structured Computer Arrays and Networks.* New York: Academic Press.

1988. Quinn, M. J. *Designing Efficient Algorithms for Parallel Computers.* New York: McGraw-Hill, Inc.

1988. Fox, G. C. "What have we learnt from using real machines to solve real problems?" Proceedings of The Third Conference on Hypercube Concurrent Computers and Applications. New York: ACM Press.

1989. Akl, S. G. *The Design and Analysis of Parallel Algorithms.* Englewood Cliffs, NJ: Prentice-Hall, Inc.

1989. Miller, R. and Stout, Q. F. *Parallel Algorithms for Regular Architectures.* Cambridge, MA: The MIT Press.

1989. Miller S. E. *A Survey of Parallel Computing,* 2nd Ed., RADC-TR-89-68, June 1989. Rome Air Development Center, Air Force Systems Command, Griffiss AFB, NY.

RUSS MILLER

LANGUAGES

Most commercial parallel computer systems make use of primitive languages that make program development and debugging much more difficult than on sequential computers. A good deal of work remains to be done to improve parallel programming environments. We will examine several of the more promising approaches.

Fundamental Approaches   Parallel programming languages can be categorized according to whether the parallelism inherent in a program must be specified explicitly by the programmer or left implicit. Languages in which potential parallelism is implicit include common imperative programming languages such as Fortran, Pascal, and C; functional programming languages such as FP and VAL; and logic programming languages (*q.v.*) such as Prolog. In order for a program written in such a language to take advantage of the power of parallel hardware, a *parallelizing compiler* must determine which operations may be executed in parallel.

Because of the huge investment in software written in conventional imperative programming languages, there has been a great deal of interest in the development of parallelizing compilers, particularly for the language Fortran. These compilers have been most successful in transforming Fortran DO loops into vector operations suitable for high-speed execution on pipelined vector processors. These compilers have been least successful transforming Fortran programs into code that executes efficiently on multicomputers; the absence of a shared memory and the resulting problem of distributing data among the local memories of many processors makes parallelization particularly difficult.

Development of parallelizing compilers for functional

and logic programming languages has continued for over a decade, with even less outstanding results.

Languages with Explicit Parallelism

We will now consider languages in which the programmer indicates explicitly those operations that may be performed in parallel. The focus is exclusively on imperative languages. It is likely that most of the parallel programs written in the near future will be in imperative languages, since that is the most familiar programming model, and because it is well understood how to compile imperative code into instruction streams that execute efficiently on contemporary processors. Languages with explicit parallel constructs can be categorized as being either low level or high level.

A typical parallel programming language with low-level constructs is little more than a conventional sequential language augmented with a few machine-specific extensions. For example, Distributed Array Processor Fortran allows the declaration of *vectors* and *matrices*. A vector is an array of size 64, and a matrix is a two-dimensional array of size 64 × 64. These particular dimensions are chosen to match the topology of the Distributed Array Processor, which is a 64 × 64 grid of bit-serial processing elements. Special operators allow vectors and matrices to be shifted up, down, left, or right, taking advantage of the machine's nearest neighbor interconnection scheme.

Program Example: Matrix Multiplication in DAP Fortran

We present a DAP Fortran program segment to multiply two 64 × 64 matrices. It makes use of functions MATC and MATR. Given a vector argument, function MATC returns a matrix whose columns are all identical to the vector. Given a vector argument, function MATR returns a matrix whose rows are all identical to the vector.

To illustrate these functions, we assume vectors have length 2 rather than 64. Given $V = (1 \ -2)$

$$\text{MATC(V)} = \begin{pmatrix} 1 & 1 \\ -2 & -2 \end{pmatrix} \text{ and MATR(V)} = \begin{pmatrix} 1 & -2 \\ 1 & -2 \end{pmatrix}$$

Now consider the following DAP Fortran code segment to multiply two matrices (Perrott, 1987):

```
INTEGER AA(,),BB(,),CC(,)
CC = 0
DO 1 K = 1,64
  CC = CC + MATC(AA(,K))*MATR(BB(K,))
1 CONTINUE
```

This program computes all 4,096 dot products in parallel. Each dot product is the sum of 64 products of two scalar values. The parallel summing occurs inside the DO loop. We illustrate this program segment assuming that vectors have length 2 rather than 64. For example, given

$$AA = \begin{pmatrix} 1 & 2 \\ 3 & 4 \end{pmatrix} \ BB = \begin{pmatrix} 5 & 6 \\ 7 & 8 \end{pmatrix} \ CC = \begin{pmatrix} 0 & 0 \\ 0 & 0 \end{pmatrix}$$

in the first iteration of the DO loop:

$$CC = CC + \frac{(1 \ 1) \times (5 \ 6)}{(3 \ 3) \times (5 \ 6)} = \begin{pmatrix} 5 & 6 \\ 15 & 18 \end{pmatrix}$$

and in the second iteration of the DO loop:

$$CC = \begin{pmatrix} 5 & 6 \\ 15 & 18 \end{pmatrix} + \frac{(2 \ 2) \times (7 \ 8)}{(4 \ 4) \times (7 \ 8)} = \begin{pmatrix} 19 & 22 \\ 43 & 50 \end{pmatrix}$$

Programs written in languages with low-level constructs based upon machine-dependent information have two notable attributes. First, they can be compiled into object code that executes efficiently on the target architecture. Second, they are not portable from one architecture to another. Hence, programming languages with low-level parallel constructs cannot be considered general purpose.

Higher-level Languages

Parallel programming languages based upon higher-level constructs are more portable than languages with low-level constructs, but at this time there is insufficient real-world experience to judge how significant the difference is. These languages are based upon abstract models of parallel computation that hide details of particular architectures from the programmer. The abstract model may be SIMD (single instruction stream, multiple data stream) or MIMD (multiple instruction stream, multiple data stream).

C* is an example of an SIMD-oriented higher-level parallel programming language. C* allows the programmer to assume an unbounded number of virtual processing elements, one per fundamental unit of data. The compiler is responsible for mapping these virtual processing elements onto the actual physical processors. Contrast this high-level approach with the approach taken in Distributed Array Processor Fortran, where vectors and matrices are constrained to size 64 and larger data sets must be explicitly mapped to physical processors by the programmer.

Occam is a higher-level programming language based upon an MIMD model and Hoare's CSP (Communicating Sequential Processes). Occam has been particularly popular in Europe, at least in part because of its strong mathematical foundation.

Some high-level parallel methodologies are designed to be grafted onto existing imperative languages, transforming a sequential programming environment into an MIMD system. A well-known example of this approach is *Linda*. Linda primitives allow multiple sequential processes to communicate and synchronize through a global data area called a *tuple space*. Processes may insert tuples into the tuple space, remove tuples from the tuple space, and copy tuples from the tuple space. A tuple may represent a piece of data or a function to be evaluated.

Prognosis

No single parallel computer architecture has achieved dominance as the best general-purpose parallel computing engine. New architectures continue to appear. Given this uncertain situation in parallel computer hardware, parallel programming languages that are portable have a clear advantage. The best prospects are for languages with these features: an imperative programming style, because that is the most familiar paradigm;

explicit parallelism, because it makes compilers easier to write; and syntax and semantics based upon a high-level model of parallel computation, because it makes programs more portable. In some sense, languages with these features represent a compromise between two extreme positions. Languages with low-level parallel constructs expect the compiler to do nothing but blindly execute the directives of the programmer. Unfortunately, given a primitive set of parallel constructs, it is easy for the programmer to make mistakes. Languages with implicit parallelism expect the compiler to do everything. The programmer cannot help the compiler by providing it with information about operations that ought to be performed in parallel. Languages with explicit parallelism expressed through high-level constructs allow a team effort between a competent programmer and a good optimizing compiler.

References

1987. Perrott, R. H. *Parallel Programming.* Wokingham, England: Addison-Wesley.

1988. Babb, R. G. II, Ed. *Programming Parallel Processors.* Reading, MA: Addison-Wesley.

1988. Gehani, N. and McGettrick, A. D., Eds. *Concurrent Programming.* Wokingham, England: Addison-Wesley.

1988. Sabot, G. W. *The Paralation Model.* Cambridge, MA: The MIT Press.

MICHAEL J. QUINN

PARAMETER PASSING

For articles on related subjects *see* ARGUMENT; CALLING SEQUENCE; EXPRESSION; SIDE EFFECT; and SUBPROGRAM.

This article is concerned with the means by which the arguments supplied to a procedure or function are transferred. There are three basic techniques:

1. Call by value.
2. Call by reference.
3. Call by name.

Call by Value   In the case of call by value, the subprogram is provided with the value of the argument, and no path leads back to the referencing program or to any of its storage elements. Call by value is illustrated in Fig. 1(a) for the argument Y*Z. The subprogram thus has no control over the referencing program. In this manner, no side effect can affect the calling program through passage of an unprotected argument.

Call by Reference   In this case, the calling routine does not provide the value of the argument to the subprogram but provides instead the address of the memory location at which that value can be found. It is then the responsibility of the subprogram to access the data through this mechanism. This is illustrated in Fig. 1(b) for the argument Y. Somewhere in the body of the procedure P is a memory location that will store the address of Y in

the calling program. Thus, with call by reference, the subprogram in effect shares memory with the calling program. (Call by reference is sometimes called Call by Location.)

For an argument that itself is an expression rather than a variable name, like Y*Z in Fig. 1(b), there is no automatically corresponding address in the calling program. Therefore, if Y*Z is called by reference, the calling program must create a location for the value of Y*Z, evaluate Y*Z, put it in this location, and then transfer the address of this location to the subprogram. Since this would then have essentially the same effect as calling by value, Pascal, in particular, does not allow expressions to be passed by reference; actual parameters passed by reference must be variable names.

But, in two other cases, calling by reference and calling by value are quite different:

1. If the calling argument is an array of, say, 1,000 elements, then calling by value would require that all 1,000 elements be transferred and that memory space be allocated in both calling program and subprogram for these 1,000 elements. But, if the call is by reference, then only the address of the first element in the array need be transferred to the subprogram (since all other array elements can be accessed relative to that address).

2. If the formal argument appears on the left-hand side of an assignment statement in the subprogram, then, if the call is by value, the value of this argument (an *input* arguement) is changed *only in the subprogram* when the assignment statement is executed. But if the call is by reference, the value *in the calling program* is changed (an *output* argument). In the case where the argument is intended to convey information back to the calling routine, this is just what is desired. In other cases, call by reference may result in undesirable side effects.

Call by Name   In the case of call by name, the actual expression itself is passed to the subprogram (so that it might better have been called *call by expression*). However, rather than passing the symbolic string that defines the expression, there is passed instead a machine language subprogram created by the compiler. Such a generated subprogram is often called a *thunk*. This is illustrated in Fig. 1(c) for the argument Y*Z. In addition to the code to be evaluated, the thunk contains the referencing environment for variables in that code, since it may be different from the referencing environment in the called subprogram. In the subprogram, each time parameter X is referenced, the thunk is executed and the current value of the argument expression is determined and used as the value of X. Such values may change during the execution of the subprogram as the result of side effects. When the argument is a simple identifier (i.e. unsubscripted) the process of call by name is equivalent to call by reference, but interesting differences can arise when a subscript and

(a) Call by value (Pascal):

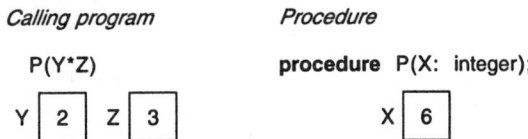

Calling program   Procedure

P(Y*Z)   **procedure** P(X: integer);

Y [2] Z [3]   X [6]

(b) Call by reference (Pascal):

Calling program   Procedure

P(Y, Z)   **procedure** P(var W, X: integer);

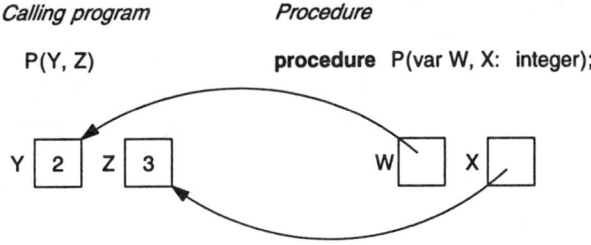

Y [2] Z [3]   W [   ] X [   ]

(c) Call by name (Algol):

Calling program   Procedure

P(Y*Z)   **procedure** P(X: integer);

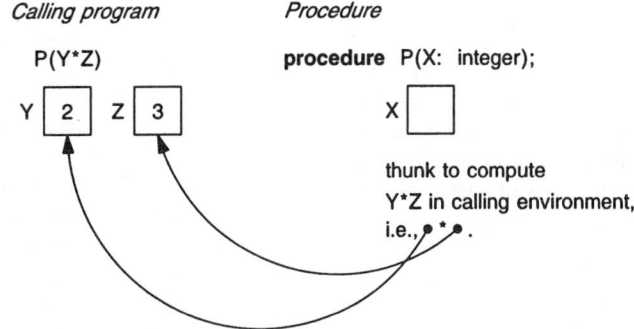

Y [2] Z [3]   X [   ]

thunk to compute
Y*Z in calling environment,
i.e., ● * ● .

FIG. 1. Passing arguments to procedures.

an array variable that depends on that subscript are both passed by name.

In Fortran, all parameters are passed by reference. In Pascal, the programmer may choose between call-by-value and call-by-reference. Call-by-value is the default, and call-by-reference is specified by preceding the formal parameter with the word **var** (for **var**iable, in the sense "able to be varied"). In C, all parameters are passed by value, but the programmer can explicitly pass a pointer to any variable, so the effect of call-by-reference can be achieved as well. In Algol, any parameter that is not explicitly stated to be passed by value is passed by name.

Whatever the language used, the programmer must always be aware of how that language implements parameter passing. Otherwise, programs may not execute as planned or may cause undesirable side effects.

References

1964. Randell, B. and Russell, L. J. *Algol 60 Implementation*. New York: Academic Press.

1971. Ralston, A. *An Introduction to Programming and Computer Science*. New York: McGraw-Hill.

1975. Pratt, T. W. *Programming Languages: Designs and Implementation*. Englewood Cliffs, NJ: Prentice-Hall.

1989. Reilly, E. D. and Federighi, F. D. *Pascalgorithms*. Boston, MA: Houghton-Mifflin.

J. A. N. Lee and Adrienne Bloss

PARITY

For articles on related subjects *see* CODES; CYCLIC REDUNDANCY CHECK; ERROR-CORRECTING CODE; and UNIVERSAL PRODUCT CODE.

Parity is a synonym for equality. Parity checking is an extensively used error-checking facility provided to insure correct recording of data, its input into a computer system, and its transfer within the system, transmission included. A *parity check* consists of adding up the bits in a unit of data, calculating the parity bit required, and comparing the calculated parity bit with that transferred with the data item. This form of check will normally be performed by hardware.

A *parity bit* is a check bit whose binary value (0 or 1) depends upon whether the sum of bits with value 1 in the unit of data being checked is odd or even. If the total number of bits with value 1, including the parity bit (or bits) is even, the unit of data is said to have even parity; if it is odd, it has odd parity. Checking methods use either even or odd parity. Each information system must use the same parity principle, even or odd throughout. An error caused by incorrect parity detected as a result of a parity check is called a *parity error.*

The unit of data to which a parity check is applied may be a character, a byte, a word, etc., the character parity check being most common. The smaller the unit of data to which the check is applied, the higher the probability that compensating errors will not occur.

Jiri Necas

PARTIAL DIFFERENTIAL EQUATIONS

For articles on related subjects *see* Finite Element Method; Matrix Computations; Numerical Analysis; and Scientific Applications.

A major scientific application of large-scale digital computers is the numerical solution of problems involving *partial differential equations.* These problems have application in such areas as weather forecasting, nuclear diffusion studies for reactor design, fluid flow, supersonic flow, and elasticity. An important class of partial differential equations is the class of *linear equations of second order* in two independent variables. The most general such equation is

$$L[u] = Au_{xx} + 2Bu_{xy} + Cu_{yy} + Du_x + Eu_y + Fu = G,$$

where A, B, C, D, E, F, and G depend on x and y. The equation is elliptic, hyperbolic, or parabolic at a point (x, y) according as the discriminant $B^2 - AC$ is negative, positive, or zero. Simple examples are Laplace's equation $u_{xx} + u_{yy} = 0$ (elliptic); the wave equation $u_{xx} - u_{yy} = 0$ (hyperbolic); and the heat or diffusion equation $u_{xx} - u_y = 0$ (parabolic).

Two important classes of problems involving partial differential equations are *initial-value problems* and *boundary-value problems.* For an initial-value problem in two variables, the desired function $u(x,y)$ is to satisfy the differential equation in an unbounded region R and to satisfy auxiliary conditions on the boundary S. Such conditions might involve prescribing the values of $u(x,y)$ on S or (as for the Cauchy problem) u and the normal derivative $\partial u/\partial n$ might be prescribed on S. For a boundary-value problem the region R is bounded, and one prescribes either u, $\partial u/\partial n$, or a linear combination of u and $\partial u/\partial n$ on S. For Laplace's equation, $u_{xx} + u_{yy} = 0$, these conditions would correspond to the Dirichlet, Neumann, and mixed problems, respectively.

Before attempting to solve a problem involving a partial differential equation, one should determine whether or not it is *well set* or *well posed.* To be well set, there should exist a unique solution that depends continuously on the boundary data. For linear equations

of second order, boundary-value problems involving hyperbolic or parabolic equations are usually not well set, nor are initial-value problems involving elliptic equations.

A basic tool in the solution of partial differential equations is the method of finite differences. Here one covers the region under consideration by a mesh, usually consisting of horizontal and vertical lines, and one seeks approximate values of the solution at the intersections, or nodes. The partial derivatives appearing in the differential equation are represented by difference quotients (e.g. u_{xx} might be represented by $h^{-2}[u(x + h,y) + u(x - h,y) - 2u(x,y)]$, where h is the spacing between the adjacent lines in the mesh. Substituting the difference quotient in the differential equation leads to a difference equation. For a boundary-value problem, one then obtains a system of linear algebraic equations, with the number of equations equal to the number of interior mesh points. It can usually be shown without difficulty that the linear system has a unique solution. Direct methods, designed to take advantage of sparseness and to minimize fill-in, are often used. Alternatively, iterative methods may be used. One such method is the *successive overrelaxation* (SOR) method. Other procedures involve the use of a basic iterative method combined with Chebyshev acceleration or conjugate gradient acceleration. Among the basic iterative methods that may be used are the Jacobi method, the symmetric SOR method, and methods based on approximate factorizations of the matrix of the system.

As an example, consider the problem of solving the Poisson differential equation $u_{xx} + u_{yy} = G(x,y)$ in the region shown in Fig. 1. The unknown function $u(x,y)$ is required to agree with a given continuous function $g(x,y)$ on the boundary. For each interior mesh point, we have

$$\frac{u(x + h,y) + u(x - h,y) - 2u(x,y)}{h^2}$$

$$+ \frac{u(x,y + h) + u(x,y - h) - 2u(x,y)}{h^2} = G(x,y).$$

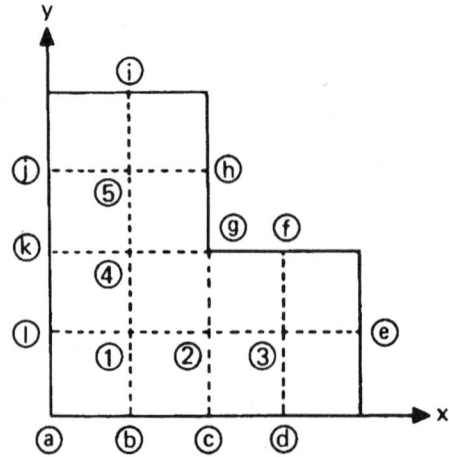

FIG. 1.

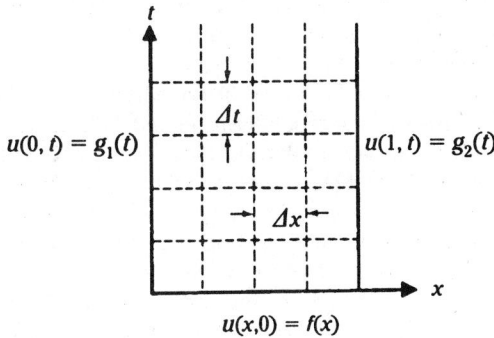

FIG. 2.

The application of the difference equation at the point labeled 1 leads (after multiplying by $-h^2$) to the linear equation

$$4\,u_1 - u_2 - u_4 - u_l - u_b = -\,h^2\,G(x_1, y_1).$$

where the subscripts refer to the points with those labels. Similar equations correspond to the other interior points ②, ③, ④, and ⑤. The values u_a, u_b,..., are equal to the known values g_a, g_b,....

Another alternative procedure for solving boundary-value problems is the *finite element method*. Here, again, one eventually obtains a linear system. However, instead of using finite differences, one generates the linear equations based on functional approximation techniques, using certain subsets of the region (elements), and based on variational procedures, Galerkin procedures, or collocation procedures.

One class of initial-value problems involves the differential equation $u_1 = L[u]$, where $L[u]$ is an elliptic operator in one or two "space" variables. Frequently, one is given $u(\vec{x}, 0)$ for all $\vec{x}$ in the region (where $\vec{x}$ represents x when there is one space variable and x, y when there are two) and $u(\vec{x}, t)$ for $\vec{x}$ on the boundary and for all $t > 0$. In the method of finite differences, one constructs a mesh in the space variables, as in the case of a boundary-value problem. In the *forward difference method*, one replaces u_1 by $[u(\vec{x}, t + \Delta t) - u(\vec{x}, t)]/(\Delta t)$ and sets it equal to $L_h[u](\vec{x}, t)$, where $L_h[u]\,\vec{x}, t)$ is a finite difference representation of $L_h[u](\vec{x}, t)$. The determination of $u(\vec{x}, \Delta t)$, $u(\vec{x}, 2\Delta t)$, etc. can be carried out explicitly. However, numerical stability considerations require that $\Delta t/h^2$, where $h = \Delta x = \Delta y$, be bounded as $h \to 0$. The work required because of the excessively small value of Δt is usually prohibitive.

A more popular method, which greatly relaxes the restriction on Δt, is the *Crank-Nicolson method*, where one replaces $L_h[u](\vec{x}, t)$ by $1/2\ [L_h[u](\vec{x}, t) + L_h[u](\vec{x}, t + \Delta t)]$. An implicit rather than an explicit procedure is thus developed. However, with one space dimension, the implicit calculation involves solving a linear system with a tridiagonal matrix. (This is relatively easy.) With two space dimensions, one must solve a boundary-value problem for each time step. However, certain iterative methods can be shown to converge much more rapidly than in the case of a pure boundary-value problem.

As an example, consider the diffusion equation $u_t =$

u_{xx} for $0 < x < 1, t > 0$, subject to the boundary conditions $u(0, t) = g_1(t)$, $u(1, t) = g_2(t)$, for $t > 0$, and the initial condition $u(x, 0) = f(x)$ (Fig. 2). Here, $g_1(t)$, $g_2(t)$, and $f(x)$ are given. The forward difference method is given by

$$\frac{u\,(x, t + \Delta t) + u\,(x, t)}{\Delta t} = \frac{u\,(x + h, t) + u\,(x - h, t) - 2u\,(x, t)}{h^2}$$

From this, the values of $u(x, t + \Delta t)$ can be calculated explicitly in terms of values of $u(x, t)$. For the Crank-Nicolson method, the right-hand side is replaced by

$$\frac{1}{2}\left\{ \frac{u\,(x + h, t) + u\,(x - h, t) - 2u\,(x, t)}{h^2} + \right.$$
$$\left. \frac{u\,(x + h, t + \Delta t) + u\,(x - h, t + \Delta t) - 2u\,(x, t + \Delta t)}{h^2} \right\}$$

Hyperbolic equations of the form $u_{tt} = L[u]$ can often be treated in a manner similar to that described above. Other hyperbolic equations, or systems of equations, are treated by the *method of characteristics*.

In recent years, several software packages have been developed for solving partial differential equations. One such package, known as ELLPACK, is designed to be a research tool for studying and comparing methods for elliptic equations (Rice and Boisvert, 1985). ELLPACK has several modules, including input, mesh generation, discretization, equation solution, and output. The ITPACK package of programs for solving large, sparse linear systems (Kincaid and Young, 1988) using iterative methods can be used for the equation solution module. Alternatively, the equations can be solved using programs of LINPACK for solving linear systems by direct methods or by using programs of the Yale Sparse Matrix Package. Some of the packages of ITPACK have been adapted for use with vector and parallel computers.

The book by Forsythe and Wasow (1960) treats the solution of hyperbolic, parabolic, and elliptic equations by finite difference methods. The solution of initial value problems by finite difference methods is treated in detail by Richtmyer and Morton (1967). Methods for solving elliptic equations, including the solution of large sparse linear systems by direct and iterative methods are discussed by Birkhoff and Lynch (1982). Finite element methods are treated by Strang and Fix (1972). Algorithms for solving large sparse systems of linear equations are described by Hageman and Young (1981).

References

1960. Forsythe, G. E. and Wasow, W. R. *Finite Difference Methods for Partial Differential Equations*, New York: John Wiley.

1967. Richtmyer, R. D. and Morton K. W. *Difference Methods for Initial-Value Problems* (2nd. Ed.). New York: Interscience.

1972. Strang, G. and Fix, G. *An Analysis of the Finite Element Method*. Englewood Cliffs, NJ: Prentice-Hall.

1981. Hageman, L. and Young, D. *Accelerated Iterative Methods*. New York: Academic Press.

1984. Birkhoff, G. and Lynch, R. E. *The Numerical Solution of Elliptic Problems*, SIAM Studies. Philadelphia: SIAM.

1985. Rice, J. R. and Boisvert R. F. *Solving Elliptic Problems Using ELLPACK.* New York: Springer-Verlag.

1988. Kincaid, D. R. and Young, D. M. "A Brief Review of the ITPACK Project." *Journal of Computational and Applied Mathematics*, **24**, 121–127.

DAVID M. YOUNG

PASCAL. See PROCEDURE-ORIENTED LANGUAGES.

PASCAL, BLAISE

For articles on related subjects *see* CALCULATING MACHINES; DIGITAL COMPUTERS: HISTORY: ORIGINS; and LEIBNIZ, GOTTFRIED WILHELM VON.

Blaise Pascal (b. Clermont, France, 1623; d. Paris, 1662) was educated by his father Etienne, and, after discovering a proof of Euclid's Proposition 32 at age 12, he became a participant in Mersenne's Circle. Four years later he presented to them his well-known theorem in projective geometry.

In 1640, he started developing a calculating machine to help in his father's tax work in Rouen. He completed the first operating model in 1642 and built 50 more during the next ten years. The machine was a small box with eight dials (resembling telephone dials), each geared to a drum that displayed the digits in a register window. Pascal's fundamental innovation was a ratchet linkage (*sautier*) between the rotating drums, which transferred rotating motion from one drum to the next higher-position drum only during carryover. This kept the digit of each drum aligned with its display window. The machine added and subtracted directly, and multiplied and divided by using

FIG. 1. Death Mask of Blaise Pascal. (Courtesy N.Y. Public Library).

repeated additions and subtractions, analogous to present-day pencil-and-paper algorithms. The machine was presented publicly in 1645.

In 1646, Pascal learned of Torricelli's experiment with the vacuum and successfully repeated it. Because of illness, he moved back to Paris in 1647, where he associated with Roberval, met Descartes, published treatises on the vacuum and on conics, and prepared the Puy-de-Dômes (barometer) experiment. Around 1651, he met the Duc de Roannez and the Chevalier de Mere and became reinvolved in research; in 1654, he produced two papers establishing the foundations of the integral calculus and of probability theory. In 1658, using the pseudonym Amos Dettonville, he challenged mathematicians to a mathematical contest and created a controversy by awarding himself the prize. No further significant research followed.

Pascal had been converted to Jansenism in 1645 and, in 1654, he had an ecstatic religious experience that drew him into the Port-Royal Jansenists' machinations with the Jesuits, resulting in his writing the *Provincial Letters*, the beginning of French classical literature. His general health, which had been poor, degenerated and he became more mystical in his interests. During his last months in 1662, he created the first public transportation system— an omnibus service in Paris.

CHARLES V. JONES

PATCH. See DEBUGGING.

PATH. See DIRECTORY.

PATTERN RECOGNITION

For articles on related subjects *see* ARTIFICIAL INTELLIGENCE; COMPUTER VISION; IMAGE PROCESSING; OPTICAL CHARACTER READERS; and PERCEPTRON.

Pattern recognition is concerned with the classification or description by computer of objects, events, or other meaningful regularities in noisy or complex environments. As an area of computer science and engineering, pattern recognition is the study of concepts, algorithms, and implementations that provide artificial systems with a perceptual capability to put abstract objects, or patterns, into categories in a simple and reliable way. As a human experience, pattern recognition refers to a perceptual process in which patterns in any sensory modality (vision, hearing, touch, taste, or smell) or patterns in conceptual or logical thought processes are analyzed and recognized (or classified) as being familiar, either in the sense of having been previously experienced or of being similar to or associated with a previous experience.

Motivation for the study of pattern recognition is threefold. First, it is a part of the broader field of *artificial intelligence*, which is concerned with techniques that en-

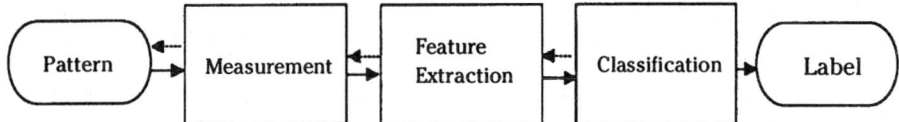

FIG. 1.   Stages in a pattern recognition system.

able computers to do things that seem intelligent when done by people. Second, it is an important aspect of applying computers to solve problems that involve analysis and classification of measurements taken from physical processes. Third, pattern recognition techniques provide a *unified framework* for the study of a variety of techniques in mathematics and computer science that are individually useful. For example, pattern recognition algorithms are based on statistical, linguistic, geometrical, and graph-theoretic concepts, and data structures for pattern representation encompass a spectrum extending from the simple concept of a vector to knotty questions concerning knowledge representation (*q.v.*).

The major applications of pattern recognition fall into three categories: (1) patterns in images (or spatial patterns); (2) patterns in time (or temporal patterns); and (3) patterns in more abstract data environments. The most important image processing applications are optical character recognition for systems ranging from bank check processing to reading machines for the blind, industrial robot vision, and unmanned planetary exploration systems; biomedical analyses, such as, automated cytology and computerized tomography (*q.v.*); and remote sensing applied to earth resources, meterology, and military applications. Signal processing applications include speech recognition (*q.v.*), radar and sonar signal analysis, seismological monitoring, and medical waveform analysis, as in electrocardiography (EKG) and electroencephalography (EEG).

Terminology   The process of a general pattern recognition system is shown in Fig. 1. In observing a pattern, measurements of an object are made that directly or indirectly reflect attributes of the object that distinguish it from other objects. *Features* are functions of the measurements intended to recover the defining attributes. The extracted features are used by a *classification procedure* to give a class assignment to the object. Since the overall process is one of reducing the pattern data in stages, pattern recognition may also be viewed as an information reducing process.

As an example, let us consider the recognition of hand-printed characters on a page. The measurement process consists of optically scanning a region of the paper where the character (i.e. pattern) is written so as to represent the pattern as a two-dimensional array whose values represent shades of gray from white to black. A second stage of the measurement process is concerned with enhancing the data prior to analysis and includes operations such as smoothing to reduce noise (irrelevant variations), sharpening to enhance edges, segmentation of the image into separate characters, and transformations to allow for variations in size, position, and orientation of the charac-

ters to be recognized. The feature extraction stage searches for features in the input, *global* features such as the number of holes in the character, the number of concavities in its outer contour, or the relative protrusion of character extremities, or *local* features such as the relative positions of line-endings, line crossovers, and corners. The final classification stage identifies each input character by considering the detected features. In practice, it is difficult to choose a set of features that reliably distinguishes handwritten characters (see for example, Fig. 2, in which the letters H and A are represented almost identically). Thus, the later phases may need to reinvoke earlier phases to re-examine ancillary (often contextual) evidence to help in the development of a particular interpretation. The *top-down* flow of control information (as opposed to the *bottom-up* flow of pattern information), necessary to utilize *context*, is represented by dotted lines in the process organization diagram of Fig. 1.

Class Definitions   A *class* is a group or set of patterns that are similar or equivalent in some sense. Class definitions are based on the intuitive notion that members of a class share some common properties or attributes. To represent a class, either a prototype (an ideal form on which all member patterns are based, the class "essence") or a set of samples must be known. A philosophical distinction may be made between *canonical*, or natural, pattern classes, such as animal species and diseases, and *conventional*, or symbolic, pattern classes, such as letters and musical notes. The feature selection process attempts to recover the pattern attributes characteristic of each class. For canonical classes, appropriate features may be inferred from an understanding of the natural phenomenon. For conventional classes, the features may be specified by the class definition, although, as in the case of hand-printed characters, they may not be explicit.

Depending on the nature of the data analysis problem, the various classes may or may not be distinguished *a priori*. In the first case, representative samples are available for each class and the problem is one of classification of subsequently observed patterns. In the second case, referred to as the *clustering problem*, the data consists of an unlabeled collection of samples and the analytic task is the detection and description of naturally occurring

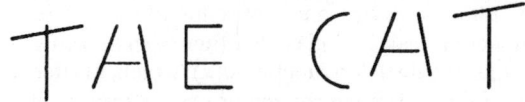

FIG. 2.   Identical patterns in different contexts have different meanings; most people read the same pattern as 'H' in the first word and 'A' in the second.

groups or clusters in the data. Additional samples may then be classified into the empirically established groups.

Approaches to Pattern Classification

Ultimately, the process of pattern recognition consists of assigning a pattern to a class. The assignment is made by a classification algorithm (or *classifier*), based on the features extracted and the relationships among the features. Since members of a class are equivalent or similar inasmuch as they share defining attributes, the measurement of similarity, either explicitly or implicitly, is central to any classifier. Depending on the features extracted—which, in turn, depend on the data environment, variability within classes, and defined attributes—classifiers are derived by using quite different approaches.

In the *statistical* approach, patterns are represented by points in a multidimensional *feature space*. Each component of the feature space is a measurement or feature value, which is a random variable reflecting the inherent variablity within and between classes. A classifier partitions the feature space into regions associated with each class, labeling an observed pattern according to the class region into which it falls. The partition is based on the multivariate probability distribution of each class, as specified by a sample set of patterns (e.g. means, covariance matrices) or, identically, the joint probability density function of the random variable features. The classification algorithm commonly employs generalized distance measures in *n*-dimensional feature space.

Although many problems are successfully dealt with by using the statistical approach, it is often more appropriate to represent patterns explicitly in terms of relationships among features other than statistical covariance. In such cases, the structure or arrangement of components or primitive elements is taken as the defining attribute of the pattern. The *structural* approach to pattern recognition represents patterns in terms of *primitives* and *relations* among primitives in order to describe pattern structure explicitly. Computer vision, where the primitives are simple objects and the relations are spatial, is an application that uses this approach. Most commonly, the concepts of formal language theory (*q.v.*) are employed to represent pattern structure in terms of rules of syntax and classes in terms of grammars and their associated languages. An observed pattern is assigned to the class whose grammar allows a successful parsing.

Statistical Pattern Recognition

In the statistical approach to pattern recognition, a pattern that is represented by a set of *m* measurements is thought of as a point **p** in an *m*-dimensional measurement space. Feature extraction is expressed as a transformation that maps **p** into a point **x** in an *n*-dimensional feature space; it may be viewed pragmatically as a process that reduces pattern space dimensionality and consequently simplifies the classification task. The classifier then assigns **x** to a class by means of a decision function d(**x**), which, in effect, is a method of partitioning the feature space into territories corresponding to different classes. The performance of the classifier is measured by objective function, which is usually the probability of error (misclassification).

An example of feature space partitioning used to classify a data set of 50 characters into five different classes {C,E,T,X,Y} is illustrated in Fig. 3. The decision functions for each class are measures of distance from the classes (see geometric classifiers, below), and the dotted lines are equidistant from the classes they separate. The positions of some characters in the feature space show that two features are not enough to separate the characters with an acceptably low misclassification probability.

If we considered the entire alphabet (i.e. all 26 characters), samples of different character classes may not be clustered equally close about class centers and features may interact with each other, producing ellipsoidal rather than spherical distributions.

We will discuss a variety of mathematical techniques that have been developed to handle such problems. The techniques themselves are conveniently grouped into three categories: feature extraction methods, classification methods, and clustering methods.

Feature Extraction On a conceptual level, feature extraction is concerned with recovering the defining attributes obscured by imperfect measurements. Ideally, the feature extraction transformation would be derived according to a minimum probability of error (or misclassification) criterion, but in most practical situations this approach is not possible. Consequently, feature extraction schemes generally attempt to choose features that minimize within-class variability; i.e. find a feature space in which the samples within each class are as close together as possible, while insuring that different class sets are well separated. Other feature selection criteria include measures of correlation between features (different features should be uncorrelated, to minimize redundancy in the representation object) and information theoretic measures relating features to classes. The mathematical transformation of the measurements obtained using such criteria generally results in features that are functions of the original measurements and that may or may not have physical interpretations. In general, if the system's performance in the resulting feature space is ultimately inadequate, additional measures and features must be sought.

Classification On the basis of their implementations, statistical pattern classifiers may be distinguished as being *probabilistic, geometric,* or *discriminant-based.* Other elaborations also exist. The first of these uses *context* in making decisions. We shall discuss this technique in greater detail in a subsequent section. The second extension is based on *sequential decision theory*, which applies to a situation in which successive features are measured only as necessary, to achieve a desired expected probability of error. Finally, the theory of *fuzzy* sets has been applied in classification problems where a non-exclusive assignment of patterns to classes is desired. If the classes do not have precisely defined criteria of membership (e.g. tall people, beautiful women, numbers much greater than one), the concept of a membership function with value between 0 and 1 is a useful characteristic. Rather than probabilistically assigning a pattern to one class or an-

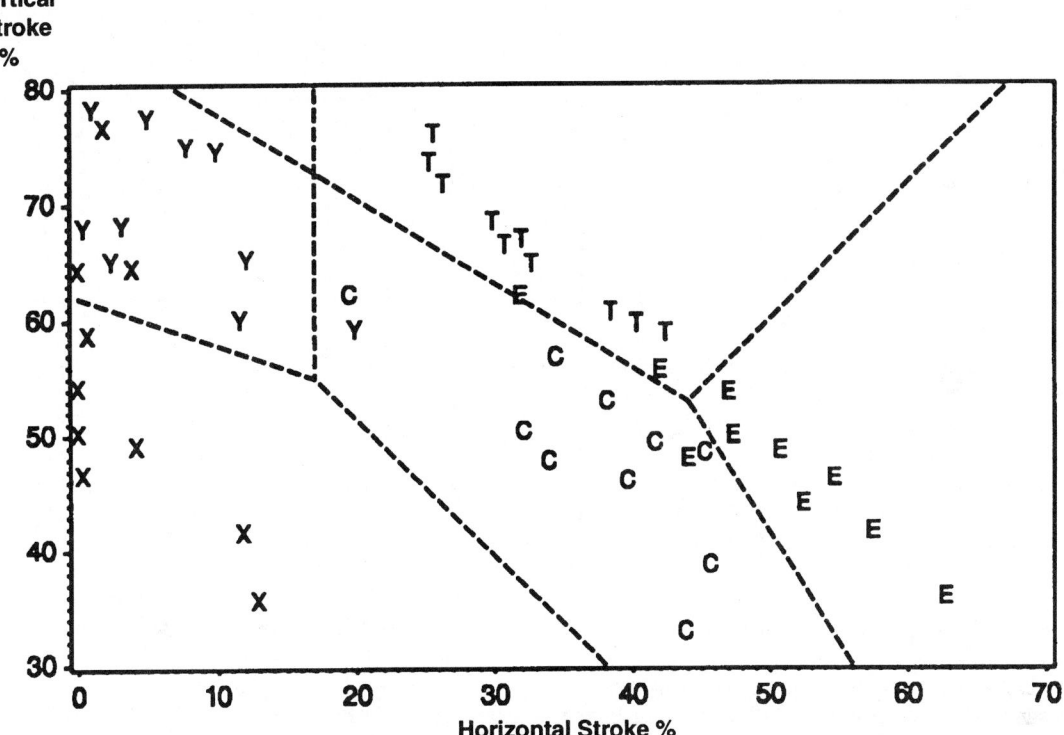

FIG. 3.   Classes are separated into categories by partitioning the feature space. The data set consists of 50 printed characters in different fonts from five different classes $\{C, E, T, X, Y\}$. The feature space represents the percentage of black pixels in the horizontal and vertical strokes.

other, but not both simultaneously, a fuzzy classifier would provide the degree of membership of a pattern to each of the classes. One can usually find mathematically equivalent algorithms by using each approach.

1. *Probabilistic classifiers* are based on the principle that a pattern should be assigned to the class that is most probable, given the observed features; *i.e.* a point **x** of feature space is assigned to the class that maximizes the *a posteriori* probability $P(C_i|\boldsymbol{x})$ over the set of classes $\{C_i\}$. From the Bayesian theory of conditional probabilities, this is mathematically equivalent to assigning **x** to the class C_i, which maximizes $p(\boldsymbol{x}|C_i)*P(C_i)$, where $p(\boldsymbol{x}|C_i)$ is called the *class-conditional probability density function* (it gives the probability that the pattern has value **x**, given that it is in class C_i) and $P(C_i)$ is the probability of class C_i before the pattern is observed (the *a priori* probability). Labeled samples representative of each class are generally used to determine the $p(\boldsymbol{x}|C_i)$ and $P(C_i)$ values necessary to implement such a classifier. In some cases, the functions $p(\boldsymbol{x}|C_i)$ may be assumed to have a particular form (normal, binomial, etc.) and samples are used to estimate their parameters (mean, covariance, etc.). More often, the forms of $p(\boldsymbol{x}|C_i)$ are unknown, in which case nonparametric estimation techniques are used that are usually based on computing the sample histogram. In either case, the estimates are used

in the classifier with a result that is optimum to the extent to which the estimates are accurate.

2. *Geometric classifiers* are based on a kind of template matching in which the observed pattern is compared to *templates* (or *prototypes*) that represent each class and are classified according to the best match (or minimum mismatch). The distance between pattern **x** and the prototype of class C_i is computed by a *metric function* $d(\boldsymbol{x}, C_i)$ and **x** is assigned to the class that minimizes this function. $d(\boldsymbol{x}, C_i) = (\boldsymbol{x} - \boldsymbol{m})^T S_i^{-1} (\boldsymbol{x} - \boldsymbol{m}_i)$, where $\boldsymbol{m}_i$ and S_i are the mean and covariance matrix of class C_i.

A metric that is useful for patterns having binary valued features is the *Hamming distance*—the number of features in which the observed pattern differs from the prototype of class C_i. A character recognition example using three prototypes and the Hamming distance measure is shown in Fig. 4.

Variations of the template matching scheme can be obtained by defining a similarity measure instead of a distance measure. For example, if n_{ij} is the number of pixels having values i and j in the template and pattern, then $\dfrac{n_{11}}{n_{11} + n_{01}}$ is the ratio of the number of correct matches of 1s to the number of 1s in the unknown target pattern. Thus, the procedure ignores matches of 0s and does not penalize incorrect matches. Measures are often

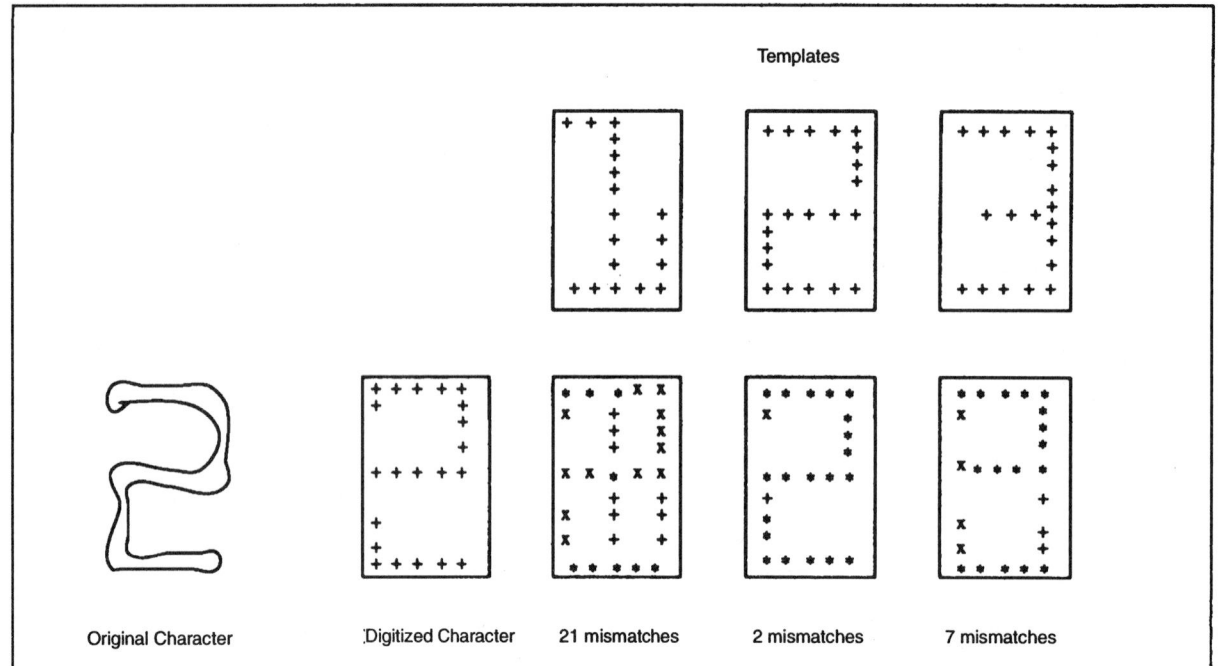

FIG. 4. Template matching using the Hamming distance. All points of the digitized character (i.e. features) are compared with corresponding points in each template. If the two are not the same (i.e. both 0 or both 1), a mismatch, or distance 1, is counted. Here, the second template is selected as a result of minimum mismatch.

constructed by weighting individual matches and mismatches according to their statistical separability. A metric that is commonly used for patterns with continuous (or real) valued features is the Euclidean distance.

In addition to specifying the metric distance, it is necessary to choose a prototype pattern for each class carefully. Using the class mean as a prototype results in a classifier that is well-suited for classes that are spherically distributed about the mean in the feature space. By using the member of C_i nearest to $\mathbf{x}$ as the prototype, the *nearest neighbor* rule tends to provide for more general (i.e. non-spherical) distributions.

3. *Discriminant function classifiers* associate a function $f_i(\mathbf{x})$ with class C_i and assign $\mathbf{x}$ to the class that has the maximum discriminant function value. In the case where the classes are *linearly separable* (i.e. there is a linear decision function that is greater than zero for all samples in one class and less than zero for all samples in the other class) in the chosen feature space, an iterative algorithm known as the *perceptron (q.v.)* finitely converges to discriminant functions, which correctly classify all given samples. For linearly non-separable classes, various criterion functions can be used in gradient descent procedures to obtain discriminant functions. As with geometric classifiers, some of the discriminant function classifiers are equivalent to probabilistic classifiers.

For instance, polynomial discriminant functions can be adopted to perform character recog-

nition. Typically, a character is represented as a feature vector $\mathbf{x}$. The binary character image is first mapped into an $n \times n$ binary array. The image is then represented by an $n^2 = N$-element column vector $\mathbf{v} = (v_1, v_2, \ldots, v_N)^t$. Using the components of $\mathbf{v}$ as linear terms and products of the components as polynomial terms, an M-element polynomial feature vector $\mathbf{x}$ is constructed by a predefined mapping $p(\mathbf{v}) = \mathbf{x}$. Generally, the components of $\mathbf{x}$ are of degree two or less, which results in a quadratic feature vector of the form,

$$\mathbf{x} = (x_1, x_2, \ldots, x_M)^t = (1, v_1, v_2, \ldots, v_N, v_1 v_2, \ldots, v_{N-1} v_N)^t$$

Not all pixel pairs are typically used, and M tends to be far fewer than $(1 + N(N + 1)/2)$.

Given K classes to be discriminated, based on the polynomial feature vector $\mathbf{x}$, a K-dimensional discriminant vector $\mathbf{d} = (d_1, \ldots, d_K)$ is formed. Each of the K discriminant functions d_i is defined to be a linear expression in the components of $\mathbf{x}$,

$$d_i = a_{i1} x_1 + \ldots + a_{iM} x_M \quad i = 1, \ldots, K$$

and thus a quadratic polynomial expression in the components of $\mathbf{v}$. The discriminant vector $\mathbf{d} = (d_1, \ldots, d_K)^t$ can therefore be written as $\mathbf{d} = A^t \mathbf{x}$, where A is an $M \times K$ matrix, whose i^{th} column, $i = 1, \ldots, K$, consists of the elements $a_{i1}, \ldots, a_i^M$.

4. *Contextual processing.* With reference to character recognition, contextual processing tech-

niques use knowledge at the word level to correct errors in character recognition. These methods use information about other characters that have been recognized in a word, as well as knowledge about the text in which the word occurs to carry out the task. Typically, the knowledge about the text takes the form of a dictionary (a list of words that occur in the text). For example, character recognition may not be able to distinguish reliably between a *u* and *v* in the second position of *qXote*. A contextual postprocessing technique would determine that *u* is correct, since it is very unlikely that *qvote* would be in the English language dictionary.

The problem of assigning a set of character images to a symbol string is known as compound decision theory. The problem is formulated as follows. The observed sequence of patterns (or vectors with feature elements) is $\mathbf{X} = x_1, ..., x_m$ Each pattern x_i is to be assigned to one symbol (character class) in the set $\mathbf{L} = \{L_1, L_2, ..., L_r\}$. Since there are r possible choices for each pattern, there are r^m possible assignments for $\mathbf{X}$. The goal is to choose that assignment $\mathbf{W}_j = w_{j1}, ..., w_{jm}, w_{ji} \varepsilon \mathbf{L}$ that has the maximum probability over all possible assignments $j = 1, ..., r^m$.

Estimating all joint probabilities in order to perform the exact probability computation is impractical. One simplifying assumption is to assume that a character icon string arises from a Markov source. Assuming a first-order Markov source, the task of determining the joint probability of a given word reduces to a product involving first-order transitional probabilities between letters and the class-conditional (or confusion) probabilities associated with each pattern. The word with the highest probability is computed efficiently by a method known as the Viterbi algorithm; it involves $(m-1) r^2$ computations instead of r^m computations.

Clustering   Both feature extraction and classification depend critically on the nature of the *a priori* information about the classes with which the system is to deal. An important class of problems deals with unlabeled data sets in which class definitions must be determined empirically. Clustering algorithms are concerned with establishing any empirical classes—sets of samples that are more similar to each other than to patterns outside the

set—that are present in the given set of unlabeled samples.

Simpler clustering algorithms establish clusters on the basis of the similarity of (distance between) individual samples, while more complex schemes employ formal criteria, such as measures of within and between cluster scatter (variability) in iterative optimization algorithms. In the first category are the hierarchical clustering algorithms, such as the *nearest neighbor algorithm*, in which clusters are merged (or split) in a hierarchical fashion according to the proximity of the nearest neighbors, and graph-theoretic algorithms relating clusters with connected subgraphs, patterns with nodes, and similarities (distances) with edges. A well-known algorithm of the second category is ISODATA (Iterative Self-Organizing Data Analysis Technique), which combines scatter criteria and user intuition in an effective interactive scheme.

Structural Pattern Recognition   Interpreting a list of characteristic attributes of a pattern as the coordinates of a point in feature space reduces the classification problem to one of partitioning the feature space. In problems such as computer vision, the patterns are quite complex and the number of features required is often very large. Thus, the idea of using the structural information that describes each pattern to simplify its representation is attractive. The basic idea of the structural approach is to describe complex patterns in terms of a composition of simpler patterns. Another approach is to extract structural features and represent them as a feature vector and use statistically determined discriminant functions.

When asked to describe an alphanumeric character, people are most likely to use structural features (Fig. 5). For example, an upper-case 'A' has two straight lines (strokes) meeting with a sharp point (end point) at the top, and a third line crossing the two at approximately their midpoint (cross points), creating a gap in the upper part (hole). The basis of any structural technique is the representation of the pattern with a set of feature primitives that are able to describe all encountered patterns and to discriminate between them.

An example of structural approaches to numeric patterns is illustrated in Fig. 6. It is based on the curvatures around the inner and outer contours of the pattern. The primitive feature set has eight features: five concave features (three simple arc-like structures of varying curvature and two endpoints) and three convex features of varying curvature. Associated with each

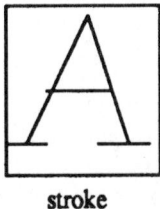 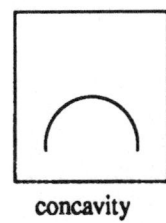 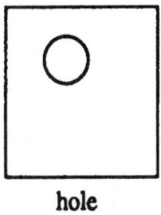 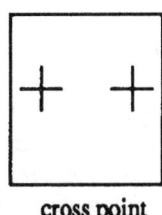 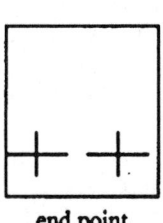

| stroke | concavity | hole | cross point | end point |

FIG. 5.   Structural features of *stroke, concavity, hole, cross points,* and *end points* can be used as the dimensions of a feature space to classify characters; the locations of these features for 'A' are illustrated.

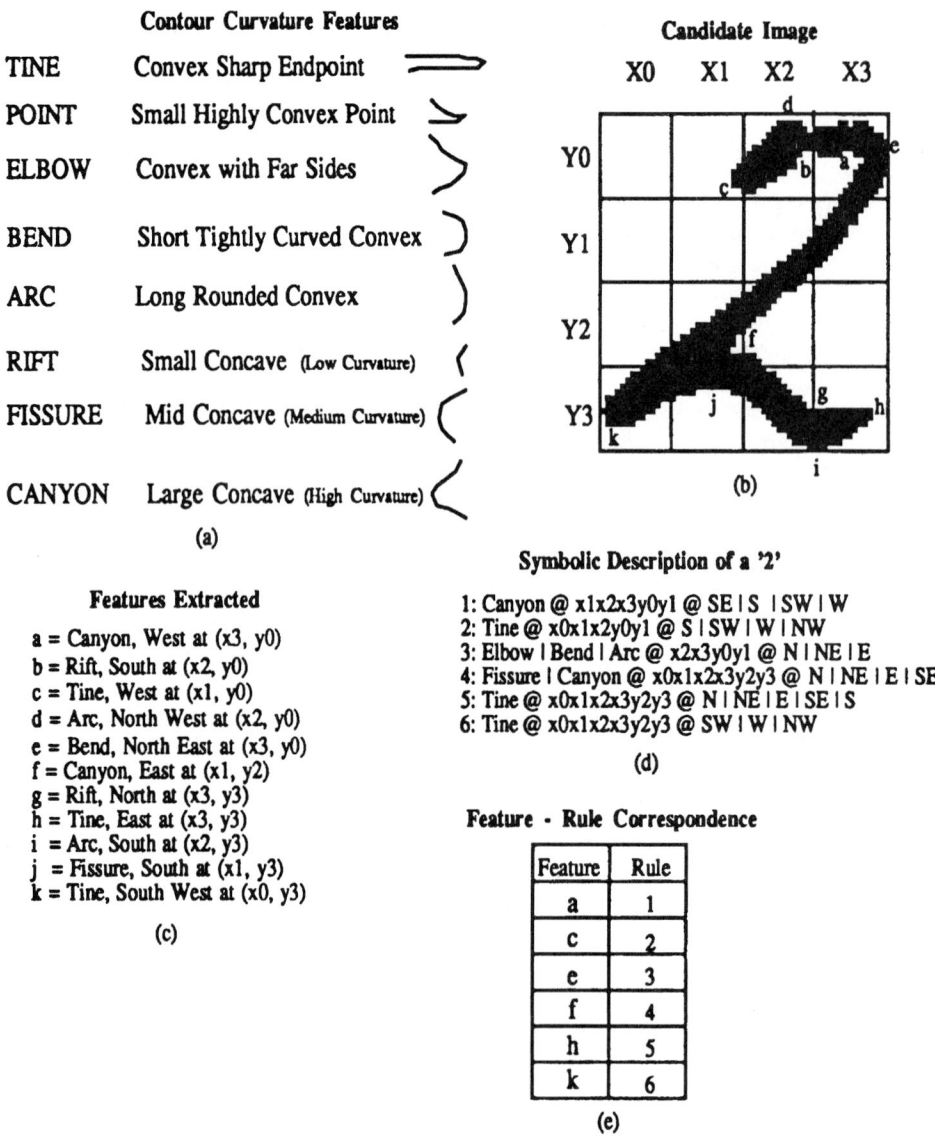

Contour Curvature Features

TINE	Convex Sharp Endpoint	
POINT	Small Highly Convex Point	
ELBOW	Convex with Far Sides	
BEND	Short Tightly Curved Convex	
ARC	Long Rounded Convex	
RIFT	Small Concave (Low Curvature)	
FISSURE	Mid Concave (Medium Curvature)	
CANYON	Large Concave (High Curvature)	

(a)

Candidate Image

(b)

Features Extracted

a = Canyon, West at (x3, y0)
b = Rift, South at (x2, y0)
c = Tine, West at (x1, y0)
d = Arc, North West at (x2, y0)
e = Bend, North East at (x3, y0)
f = Canyon, East at (x1, y2)
g = Rift, North at (x3, y3)
h = Tine, East at (x3, y3)
i = Arc, South at (x2, y3)
j = Fissure, South at (x1, y3)
k = Tine, South West at (x0, y3)

(c)

Symbolic Description of a '2'

1: Canyon @ x1x2x3y0y1 @ SE I S I SW I W
2: Tine @ x0x1x2y0y1 @ S I SW I W I NW
3: Elbow I Bend I Arc @ x2x3y0y1 @ N I NE I E
4: Fissure I Canyon @ x0x1x2x3y2y3 @ N I NE I E I SE
5: Tine @ x0x1x2x3y2y3 @ N I NE I E I SE I S
6: Tine @ x0x1x2x3y2y3 @ SW I W I NW

(d)

Feature - Rule Correspondence

Feature	Rule
a	1
c	2
e	3
f	4
h	5
k	6

(e)

FIG. 6.   Contour feature analysis: (a) contour features, (b) digitized image, (c) extracted features, (d) rules in database that need to be satisfied for a digit 2, and (e) extracted features that match the size rules.

feature is a direction quantized to eight compass points, and the location quantized to a 4×4 Cartesian grid with the origin in the upper left (Fig. 6). The contour of the figure is first represented in the form of a chain-code; the chain code is an eight-direction code following the contour such that a change of one unit in the positive direction of the chain code represents a 45° turn in the positive direction and a negative change of one unit represents a 45° turn in the other direction. The chain code contour trace is converted to a curvature trace around the figure. The relative degree of curvature for each point along the original image is calculated. Local variations and noise are filtered by looking at the preceding and following points when calculating the curvature at the current point. Points along the image contour where the degree of curvature changes are the places where the features are defined.

A rule base is used to classify the extracted feature string. The rule base is designed as a decision tree, where each successive branch narrows down the possible candidates that can match the feature string. The rules are generalized to have a one-to-many relationship. Each class can be fully covered by just a few rules (Fig. 6).

In the case where patterns consist of (one-dimensional) waveforms or (two-dimensional) images of flat objects, the structure of patterns can usually be described in a manner analogous to the syntax of languages. Patterns are specified as being hierarchically built up from sub-patterns in various ways of composition by a grammar. In this approach, also called the *syntactic approach*, the important element is the pattern description language that provides the structural description of patterns in terms of a set of pattern primitives (or *morphs*) and their composition operations defined by the grammar.

In the syntactic approach, after each primitive within a pattern is identified in the feature extraction stage, classification is accomplished by analyzing syntax (or parsing) of the sentence describing the given pattern to determine whether or not it is syntactically correct with respect to the specified grammar. Syntax analysis produces a structural description of the given pattern in the form of a tree structure. The grammar itself may be inferred from sample patterns by using *grammatical inference* techniques. The most attractive aspect of this approach is its capability to use the recursive nature of a grammar to express in a very compact way some basic structural characteristics of infinite sentences. Again, for this approach to be practical, recognition of the simple pattern primitives and their relationships, as represented by the composition operations, is essential.

References

Journals that regularly contain research papers in pattern recognition include:

IEEE Transactions on Pattern Analysis and Machine Intelligence
IEEE Transactions on Accoustics, Speech and Signal Processing
Pattern Recognition
Artificial Intelligence
Computer Graphics and Image Processing
International Journal of Pattern Recognition and Artificial Intelligence
Machine Vision and Applications

1973. Duda, R. O. and Hart, P. E. *Pattern Classification and Scene Analysis.* New York: Wiley. (A classic in the field. Discusses both statistical and structural approaches in depth up to its time of publication.)
1978. Gonzalez, R. C. and Thomson, M. G. *Syntactic Pattern Recognition.* Reading, MA: Addison-Wesley. (Describes the application of formal language and automata theory to the description of patterns.)
1980. Lea, W. A. (Ed.). *Trends in Speech Recognition.* Englewood Cliffs, NJ: Prentice-Hall. (Overviews of approaches to speech recognition taken by different research groups.)
1981. Bezdek, J. C. *Pattern Recognition with Fuzzy Objective Function Algorithms.* New York: Plenum. (Models of feature selection, clustering, and classification based on fuzzy set theory are discussed.)
1982. Fu, K. S. *Syntactic Pattern Recognition and Applications.* Englewood Cliffs, NJ: Prentice-Hall. (Syntactic methods applied to the recognition of patterns in a variety of applications.)
1982. Devijver, P. A. and Kittler, J. *Pattern Recognition: A Statistical Approach.* Englewood Cliffs, NJ: Prentice-Hall. (A collection of papers on statistical methods.)
1984. Srihari, S. N. *Computer Text Recognition and Error Correction.* Silver Spring, MD: IEEE Computer Society Press. (A tutorial, including landmark papers, in contextual character recognition.)
1986. Devijver, P. A. and Kittler, J. *Pattern Recognition Theory and Applications.* Berlin: Springer-Verlag. (A collection of papers representing major areas of research.)
1988. Simon, J. C. *From Pixels to Features.* New York: North-Holland. (A collection of papers dealing with implementation of pattern recognition systems and underlying concepts.)

S.N. SRIHARI AND V. GOVINDARAJU

PERCEPTRON

For articles on related subjects *see* NEURAL NETWORKS; and PATTERN RECOGNITION.

In 1957 the psychologist Frank Rosenblatt proposed "The Perceptron: A perceiving and recognizing automaton" as a class of artificial nerve nets, embodying aspects of the brain and receptors of biological systems. Fig. 1. shows the network of the Mark 1 Perceptron. Later, Rosenblatt protested that the term "perceptron," originally intended as a generic name for a variety of theoretical nerve nets, was actually associated with a very specific piece of hardware (Rosenblatt, 1962).

The basic building block of a perceptron is an element that accepts a number of inputs x_i, $i = 1...I$, and computes a weighted sum of these inputs where, for each input, its fixed weights ω can be only $+1$ or -1. The sum is then compared with a threshold θ, and an output y is produced that is either 0 or 1, depending on whether or not the sum exceeds the threshold. In other words,

$$y = \begin{cases} 1 & \text{if } \left(\sum_{i=1}^{1} \omega_i x_i \right) \geq \theta \\[2em] 0 & \text{if } \left(\sum_{i=1}^{1} \omega_i x_i \right) < \theta \end{cases}$$

A perceptron is a signal transmission network consisting of sensory units (S units), association units (A units), and output or response units (R units). The receptor of the perceptron is analogous to the retina of the eye and is made of an array of sensory elements (photocells). Depending on whether or not an S-unit is excited, it produces a binary output. A randomly selected set of retinal cells is connected to the next level of the network, the A units. Each A unit behaves like the basic building block discussed above, where the $+1$, -1 weights for the inputs to each A unit are randomly assigned. The threshold for all A units is the same.

The binary output of the kth A unit ($k = 1, \ldots, m$) is multiplied by a weight a_k, and a sum of all m weighted outputs is formed in a summation unit that is the same as the basic building blocks with all weights equal to $+1$. Each weight a_k is allowed to be positive, zero, or negative, and may change independently of other weights. The output of this block is again binary, depending on a threshold that is normally set at 0. The binary values of the output are used to distinguish two classes of patterns that may be presented to the retina of a perceptron. The design of a perceptron to distinguish between two given

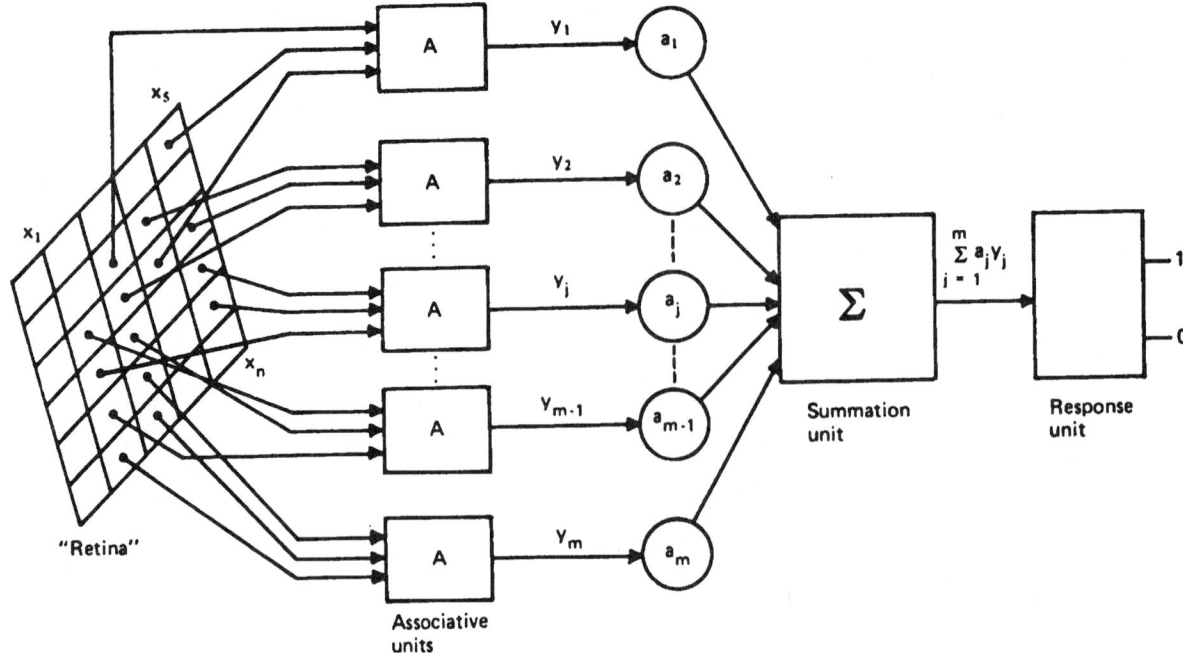

FIG. 1. Mark-1 Perceptron structure.

sets of patterns involves adjusting the weights a_k, $k = 1$, $\ldots$, m, and the threshold θ.

Rosenblatt (1962) proposed a number of variations of the following procedure for "training" perceptrons. The set of given patterns of known classification are presented sequentially to the retina, with the complete set being repeated as often as needed.

The output of the perceptron is monitored to determine whether a pattern is correctly classified. If not, the weights are adjusted according to the following "error correction" procedure: If the n-th pattern was misclassified, the new value $a_k(n + 1)$ for the k-th weight is calculated as

$$a_k (n + 1) = a_k(n) + y_k(n) \star \delta(n),$$

where $\delta(n)$ is 1 if the n-th pattern is from class 1 and $\delta(n)$ is –1 if the n-th pattern is from class 2. No adjustment to the weight is made if a pattern is correctly classified.

If there exists a set of weights such that all patterns can be correctly classified, the pattern classes are said to be linearly separable. It was conjectured by Rosenblatt that, when the pattern classes are linearly separable, the error correction "learning" procedure will converge to a set of weights that correctly classifies all the patterns. Many proofs of this perceptron convergence theorem were subsequently derived, the shortest by A. J. Novikoff. Subsequent contributions related the simple perceptron to statistical linear discriminant functions and related the error-correction learning algorithm to gradient-descent procedures and to stochastic approximation methods that were originally developed for finding the zeros and extremes of unknown regression functions (see e.g. Kanal (1962) and Sklansky and Wassel (1981).)

The simple perceptron described is a series-coupled perceptron with feed-forward connections only from S units to A units and A units to the single R unit. The weights a_k, the only adaptive elements in this network, are evaluated directly in terms of the output error. This is sometimes referred to as a *single-layer perceptron*. There is no layer of "hidden" elements—i.e. elements for which the adjustment is only indirectly related to the output error. A perceptron with one or more layers of hidden elements is termed a *multilayer perceptron*. Rosenblatt investigated *cross-coupled perceptrons* in which connections join units of the same type, and also investigated *multilayer back-coupled perceptrons*, which have feedback paths from units located near the output. For series-coupled perceptrons with multiple R units, Rosenblatt proposed a "back-propagating error correction" procedure that used error from the R units to propagate correction back to the sensory end. But neither he nor others were able to demonstrate a convergent procedure for training multilayer perceptrons.

By 1968, interest had moved away from perceptrons and learning machines to statistical and structural pattern recognition. Then Minsky and Papert (1969) proved various theorems about simple perceptrons, some of which indicated their limited pattern-classification and function approximating capabilities. For example, Minsky and Papert proved that the single layer perceptron could not implement the Exclusive OR logical function and several other such predicates. While their results did not apply to multilayer perceptrons, their work greatly dampened work on perceptrons.

The resurgence of artificial neural networks and multilayer perceptrons since 1983 is due to the development and popularization of convergent error-back propagation algorithms for training multilayer neural networks. It has been shown that multilayer feedforward networks with a sufficient number of intermediate or "hidden" units between the input and output units have a "universal approximation" property: They can approximate "virtually any function of interest to any desired degree of accuracy" (Hornik *et al.,* 1989). It has also been shown that back propagation is essentially a special case of stochastic approximation (White, 1989), and once again neural network learning procedures are being shown to be intimately related to known statistical techniques. Gallant (1990) has examined several modifications of the basic perceptron learning procedure that make perceptron learning well behaved with inseparable training data, even when the training data are noisy and not error free.

References

1962. Rosenblatt, F. *Principles of Neurodynamics.* New York: Spartan Books.

1962. Kanal, L. "Evaluation of a Class of Pattern-Recognition Networks," in *Biological Prototypes and Synthetic Systems,* E.E. Bernard and M. R. Kare (Eds.), **1,** 261–269. New York: Plenum Press.

1969. Minsky, M. and Papert, S. *Perceptrons.* Cambridge, MA: The M.I.T. Press.

1981. Sklansky, J. and Wassel, G. N. *Pattern Classifiers and Trainable Machines.* New York: Springer-Verlag.

1989. Hornik, K., Stinchcome, M., and White, H. "Multilayer Feedforward Networks are Universal Approximators," *Neural Networks,* **2,** 359–366.

1990. Gallant, S. I. "Perceptron-Based Learning Algorithms," *IEEE Trans. on Neural Networks,* **1,** *2,* June, 179–191.

1990. Hecht-Nielsen, R. *Neurocomputing.* Reading, MA: Addison-Wesley Publishing Co.

1990. Simpson, P. K. *Artificial Neural Systems—Foundations, Paradigms, Applications, and Implementations.* New York: Pergamon Press.

LAVEEN N. KANAL

PERFORMANCE EVALUATION AND REVIEW TECHNIQUE. *See* PERT/CPM.

PERFORMANCE MEASUREMENT AND EVALUATION

For articles on related subjects *see* ACCOUNTING SYSTEM, BENCHMARKS; COMPUTER; HARDWARE MONITOR; OPERATING SYSTEMS; OVERHEAD; PERFORMANCE OF COMPUTERS; SCHEDULING ALGORITHIM; SIMULATION; SOFTWARE MONITOR; THROUGHPUT; TIME SHARING; and TURNAROUND TIME.

The main purposes of the *measurement* and *evaluation* of computer systems are to:

1. Aid in the design of hardware and software.
2. Aid in the selection of a computer system.
3. Improve the performance of an existing system.

The first of these must use some type of model of the system being designed. The latter two may use actual measurements or models or some combination of the two.

Measurement and evaluation of computer system performance is difficult due to the complexity of the internal structure of computer systems and because of the difficulty of describing and predicting the workload. As shown in Fig. 1, a computer system is composed of subsystems, each of which can be viewed as a system with its own workload and performance. Total system performance is related to the performance of the subsystems, although the relationship can be complex.

Computer system and subsystem performance measures fall into three categories—*responsiveness, throughput,* and *cost.* The response time for interactive commands or the turnaround time for batch jobs are typical measures of responsiveness. *Throughput* is a measure of the computational work accomplished by the system per unit time. There is, however, no generally acceptable definition of a unit of computational work. Measures such as jobs per unit time or transactions per unit time become meaningful only when the resource requirements of these tasks are described; this is one aspect of the workload characterization problem. The cost of a computer system is the dollar amount required to buy or lease the system. Response and throughput characteristics have to be evaluated in terms of the cost of the system.

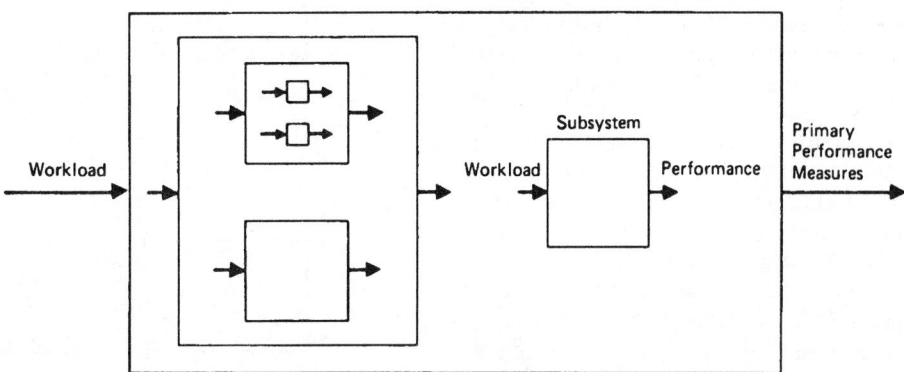

FIG. 1. Computer system and subsystems.

It is necessary to characterize the load on a system in order to make meaningful statements about its performance. One aspect of this problem is determining which characteristics of the load largely determine the performance measures of interest. Another is determining the values of the workload model parameters for a particular performance study and is particularly difficult if the system is not yet operational. But even with an operational system, the workload may vary with time, and the workload characteristics measured will depend on the measurement period chosen.

This article is concerned with the use of measurement data in computer system performance evaluation and not with the techniques for collecting the appropriate data. For details on computer system monitoring methodologies, *see* SOFTWARE MONITOR and HARDWARE MONITOR.

Purposes of Performance Measurement and Evaluation

In this section, we provide some detail about the goals and constraints of the types of performance studies listed at the beginning of the article.

Optimization Modern computer systems offer a number of options in terms of hardware and software configuration that allow wide flexibility in tailoring a given installation to the workload and the desired performance characteristics. Some examples of the options are main memory size, number, type, and interconnection of channels and I/O devices; location of files on secondary storage; selection of non-resident portions of the operating system; and parameters for resource allocation algorithms. *System tuning* refers to the optimization of software-related options, and *reconfiguration* refers to the hardware aspects.

Computer System Selection One of the considerations in the selection of a new system is the comparative cost/performance of the systems being considered. Judgments as to expected performance can be made informally based on the experience of others or the manufacturer's claims. More formal studies involve experimentation using benchmarks or system models. Prediction of the workload is an obvious problem if the system is being acquired for a new application. However, even upgrading of an existing system usually involves new functionality and features that have to be accounted for in the projected workload. Optimization is a part of the selection problem, since it is only reasonable to compare the cost/performance of systems that are tuned to the workload.

Evaluation of Design Alternatives The simulation or mathematical models used for this purpose require values for workload parameters. Measurements from currently operational systems can give some insight into the range of parameters that might be expected for the new system. Specific details of the workload can be very difficult to predict, since (1) the system may be used in many different environments and (2) the characteristics of the system can affect how it is used. However, general characteristics of program behavior have been isolated and found to be useful in system design. A good example is the characteristic of *locality of reference*—the tendency of programs to execute in phases such that, in each phase, the program references only a restricted portion of its address space (a locality) or a subset of its pages. This is the basis for most memory management policies of paged memory systems.

Models of Computer System Performance

As a practical matter, when actual measurements cannot be made, we must use models. Two kinds of models need to be considered—system models and workload models.

System Models System models are simplifications of the real system that describe the relationship between workload measures and performance measures. The major types of system models are given below.

Functional Models

These describe the operation of the system. They may be written down (e.g. as a flow-chart or as a Petri net - *q.v.*, but often they exist only in the mind of the performance analyst. This type of model is used informally to relate observed load and performance measures, or as a first step in developing a more formal model.

Simulation Models

Discrete event simulation is still the most commonly used technique in computer system modeling because of its flexibility in modeling details of the system. Its disadvantage is the cost of developing and then using a complex simulation. (*See* SIMULATION.)

Stochastic Models

The range of applicability of queueing models has greatly expanded since the early 1970s, when queueing network models of computer systems began to be explored. A queueing network is a multiple resource model in which jobs "visit" the resources in a sequence that is probabilistically defined. A special case of a queueing network, called a *central server model*, is illustrated in Fig. 2.

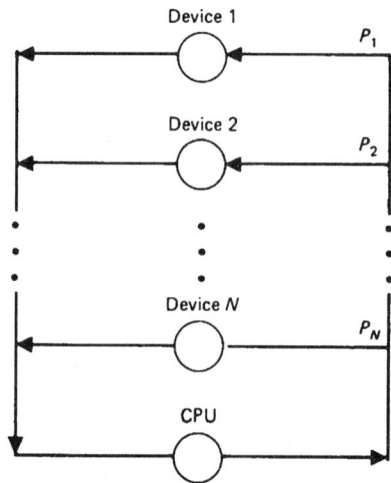

FIG. 2. Central server queueing network model.

The resources in this example are labeled to indicate the computer system resources represented. The numbers P_i on the arcs from the CPU to the I/O devices represent, for each I/O device, the probability of that device being visited by a job after receiving CPU service. The goal is to obtain closed form performance equations from which performance predictions may be easily calculated. However, there are many restrictions on the class of queueing networks for which closed form performance equations are known. For example, priority scheduling and some other common scheduling disciplines are not permitted, and no limit can be set on the number of jobs at a resource or in a subset of the network. (*See* QUEUEING THEORY.)

Hierarchical Decomposition

This term refers to a methodology in which subsystems are analyzed to obtain their performance characteristics, and these results are then used in a higher-level analysis of the system. An example is the use of a queueing network model to obtain throughput rates for the jobs currently being multiprogrammed and then use of these results in a higher-level simulation of job scheduling strategies. This significantly reduces simulation run time, since the very high-rate events (CPU dispatching and I/O requests) are not simulated. However, the assumptions that must be made to analyze subsystems can introduce serious errors and approximations into hierarchical models.

Workload Models An *executable* workload model is either a set of benchmark programs selected from the real workload or a set of synthetic programs that have been designed to exhibit certain resource utilization patterns expected in the real workload. These programs are directly executable on the system(s) being studied, and the performance of the system can be measured in actual operation. A *non-executable* workload model is a parametrization of the real workload that is to be used in conjunction with a simulation or stochastic system model.

There are two types of non-executable workload models:

1. Recorded sequences of resource demands by actual programs, which are used with trace-driven simulations.
2. Statistical descriptions of the workload distribution of (for example) CPU execution times between I/O requests or working set (*q.v.*) size distribution, which can be used as input to either simulation or mathematical models.

Use of Models The various uses of workload models and system models are illustrated in Fig. 3. Fig. 3(a) indicates measurement of an operational system. A functional model is used to diagnose a performance problem and to hypothesize a remedy. Measurements taken after implementing the remedy are used to validate the hypothesis.

Fig. 3(b) illustrates the use of a workload model that is executable on the system under study. The workload

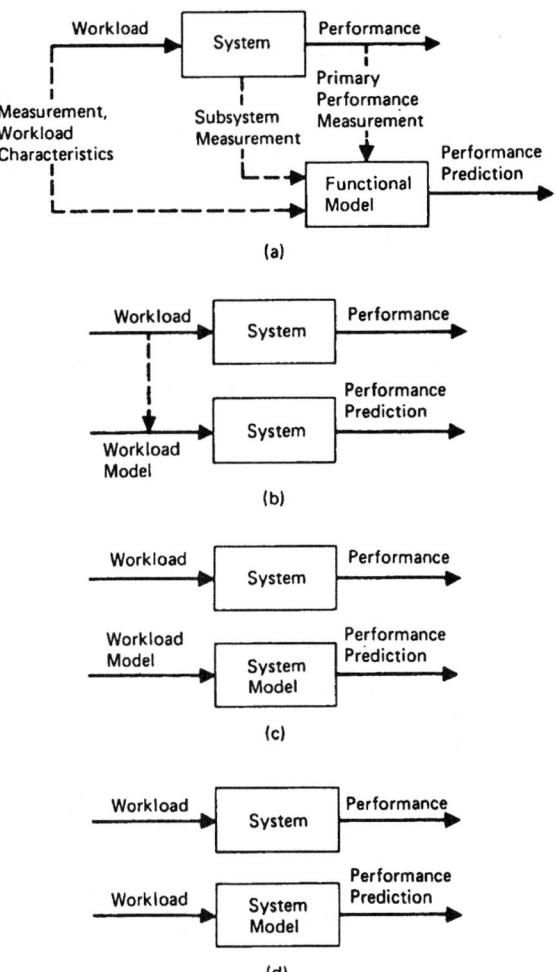

FIG. 3. Uses of workload and system models.

model in this case consists of a set of programs or "scripts" of terminal commands that are representative of the real workload (*see* BENCHMARK). This method is common in computer system selection in which the experiment is repeated for systems being considered and their performance compared. This method can also be used to experiment with changes to an operational system. The advantages are that the workload during the experiments is reproducible and that the behavior of the system under a wide range of workloads can be explored. A major disadvantage is that it requires exclusive use of the system and interrupts normal service.

In Fig. 3(c), both a workload model and a system model are used. This is the case with simulation and analytic modeling. If a model is being developed for an operational system, measurement experiments are useful for calibrating the model. The workload parameters and performance are measured for a number of measurement periods. The model can be calibrated by driving it with the workload parameters from each measurement period and comparing the model performance predictions with the observed system performance in the corresponding period: The model is corrected or refined until the performance predictions are sufficiently close to the measured variables. Performance predictions involve either a change in the workload or a change in the system. If a change in workload is to be considered, the workload parameters for the new workload must be estimated. A change in the system is reflected by a corresponding change in the system model. Clearly, the calibration of a model gives some confidence in its ability to model the real situation. Confidence in the predictions of the model after alteration is a function of the magnitude of the alteration.

Fig. 3(d) illustrates the last possibility, which is using a real workload to drive a system model. This is not feasible to do precisely, but it can be approximated. For example, a real workload might be interpretively executed on a system model. However, experiments that most closely approximate the true situation involve using a virtual machine monitor that simulates nonexistent hardware. A faster I/O device, for example, can be simulated by controlling the virtual time at which interrupts occur. One limitation is the ability to synchronize internal events with external events that occur in real time. Terminal activity by real users could reasonably be expected to be different because the system response time would be affected.

To illustrate how these techniques are actually used, we consider, first, the optimization of computer system performance, and then the prediction of system performance.

Optimization of Computer System Performance

Fig. 4 illustrates a model of major resources of a computer system and their interconnection. The resources explicitly shown are the CPU, the main memory, channels, and the secondary storage devices. The active set of tasks constitute those that have been allocated main memory and are competing for the CPU and I/O system resources. The box labeled *task queues* represents tasks that are waiting for entry into the active set. This simple model can be used to describe the notion of a *system bottleneck*.

As a first-order approximation, assume that tasks submitted to the system require known mean amounts of service at each resource. For example, the mean CPU time required per task might be 20 seconds. (This is the total CPU time required, which is received in many "visits" to the CPU.) Then the throughput of the system cannot be greater than 1/20 tasks per second (or three tasks per minute), since the CPU, even if 100% busy, cannot process tasks at a higher rate. This is the capacity of the CPU measured in tasks per unit time. Similar calculations can be made for the other resources. The throughput of the system is bounded above by the capacity of the individual resources. If one resource has a capacity that is significantly lower than that of any of the other resources, then the usual effect is that this resource has a relatively high utilization and a relatively long queue of tasks waiting for it. This resource is called a *bottleneck* or *limiting resource*, and is generally a major contributor to reduced throughput and poor responsiveness. The contrary situation, a balanced system, occurs when all resources have similar utilizations. Balanced resource utilization generally results in greater throughput, since there is greater concurrent utilization of resources (CPU and I/O).

Using the model of Fig. 4 and an appropriate workload model, *system profiles*, which are a set of measurements giving the utilization of the major system resources and the amount of overlap in CPU and I/O utilization, can be generated. These values might be simply given in table form, but are more easily interpretable if shown as a Gantt chart (Fig. 5) or in a Kiviat graph (Fig. 6). This data is useful in the exploratory phase of a performance optimization study to determine system bottlenecks, which then have to be studied in more detail. When considering the

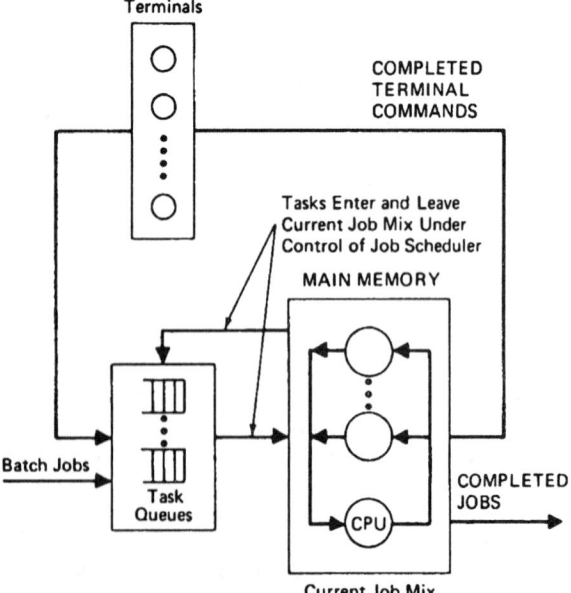

FIG. 4.   Simple computer system model.

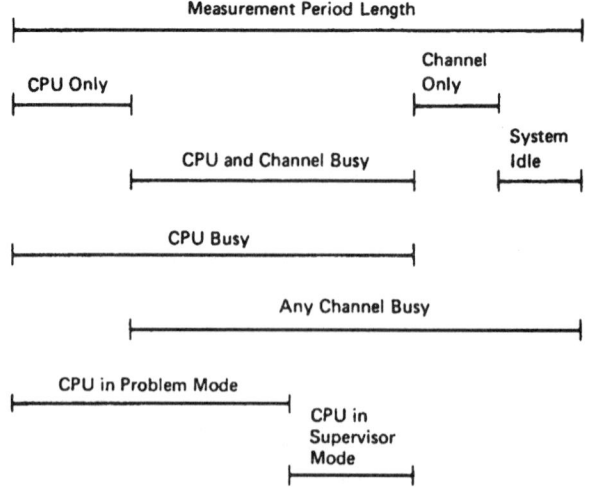

FIG. 5.   System profile shown as a Gantt chart. Each line represents a possible state of the system, and the length of each line corresponds to the total time the system was in that state during the measurement period.

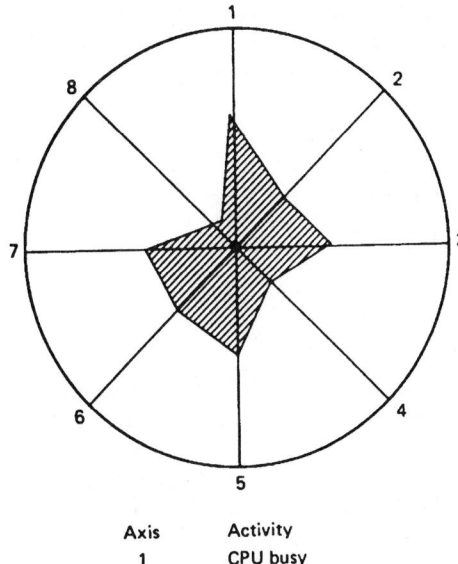

Axis	Activity
1	CPU busy
2	CPU only
3	CPU and channel busy
4	Channel only
5	Any channel busy
6	CPU idle
7	CPU in problem mode
8	CPU in supervisor mode

FIG. 6. System profile shown as Kiviat graph.

possible reasons for the observed resource utilizations, it is useful to consider the following factors:

1. System overhead.
2. The hardware characteristics of the resource.
3. Intrinsic resource requirements of the tasks.
4. The scheduling algorithm used to manage the resource.
5. Interactions among tasks; e.g. thrashing (*q.v.*) in main memory, contention on a disk.
6. Complex interactions between resources; e.g. the relationship between channel and disk utilization. Disk utilization can appear artificially high because of a bottleneck in the channel. A major portion of the disk utilization might then be due to waiting for the channel to become free.

Several examples of behavior that might be observed from a system profile and a partial list of possible explanations are given below.

Low utilization of CPU and I/O resources:

1. Insufficient workload.
2. Insufficient main memory to fit enough tasks in the active set to utilize resources.
3. Poor memory management policy that results in insufficient active set size.

High CPU utilization and low I/O device utilization:

1. Excessive CPU overhead.
2. Workload is CPU intensive.

3. Poor job mix scheduling algorithm.
4. Poor CPU scheduling algorithm; e.g. not giving priority to I/O bound jobs.

Computer System Performance Prediction

The information gathered to aid in diagnosing a performance problem often suggests a remedy for the problem. Easy and inexpensive remedies are often implemented and the effects observed. Tuning of system parameters falls into this category. But if a large number of alternatives must be examined or the changes are costly to implement, some more formal method of predicting the effect of the changes is desirable. Simulation or stochastic modeling are alternatives, particularly when the cost of model development can be amortized over many applications; e.g. when the model is to be used for tuning or capacity planning for many installations. A relatively new approach called *operational analysis* is briefly discussed next.

In operational analysis, precise definitions of measured values and minimal assumptions about the system are used to derive invariant relationships among the measured data. These relationships can be considered to be consistency requirements for the values measured in any particular measurement experiment. The following formula for the average response time for an interactive system is an example of the type of result available from operational analysis.

$$R > \frac{N}{X} - T$$

where:

R = average response time
N = number of active terminals
X = number of terminal commands completed, divided by measurement period (rate of terminal command completion)
T = average think time at terminals (think time is the time elapsed from the instant the system finishes one command until the user gives the next command).

Under very general conditions, the above relationship can be shown to be *exact* for any measured period. This is an invariant relationship between measured values and not a formula for computing the average response time. However, it can also be useful for prediction of performance under changed conditions, although the problem of estimating or bounding new values for some of the variables is still present. For example, if the effect on the rate of terminal command completion X due to a proposed system change could be estimated, then the equation yields an estimate of the new value for R as a function of N and T. Bounding X also yields some information. For example, if it can be determined that $X < X_0$, then

$$R > \frac{N}{X_0} - T.$$

A value for X_0 might be estimated by considering system bottlenecks as previously discussed.

Operational analysis has succeeded in developing relationships among performance and load measures that are analogous to many of the results available from queueing theoretic models but without the strong assumptions typically required in queueing theory (*q.v.*). However, operational analysis has limitations and is not as powerful as queueing theoretic methods for analysis.

Queueing Network Models   Queueing network models have been mentioned several times in this article (e.g. the central server model in Fig. 2 and the computer system model in Fig. 4). This class of models is very powerful and has been the basis for many succesful performance analysis and prediction tools. In general, these models have the following components: (1) the resources or queues, and (2) a specification of the customer behavior. The resources are characterized by the capacity of the server and the scheduling discipline (first-come-first-serve, etc.), while the customers are characterized by the manner in which they require the resources—both the service required per visit to a resource and the pattern of visits. The actual application of queueing network models raises many issues that have been the subject of much research over the past two decades. Some of these issues are (1) characterizing the class of models that have a closed form solution, (2) determination of model parameters from measurement data, (3) approximate analysis methods for queueing network models for which closed form solutions are not known, and (4) computational procedures for calculating performance measures from a model. This is now a fairly mature field and there are several excellent texts (Kant, 1991; Lavenberg, 1983; Lazowska, 1984). Queueing network models are also widely used in diverse application areas, such as communications and flexible manufacturing, where the representation of multiple resources and the resource access patterns are vital to accurate modeling.

References

1978. Ferrari, Domenico. *Computer Systems Performance Evaluation*. Englewood Cliffs, NJ: Prentice-Hall. (A comprehensive treatment of the issues discussed in this article.)

1983. Lavenberg, Stephen S. (Ed.). *Computer Performance Modeling Handbook*. New York: Academic Press. (An in-depth treatment of queueing models and simulation as applied to computer systems modeling.)

1984. Lazowska, Edward D., Zahorjan, John, Graham, G. Scott and Sevcik, Kenneth C. *Quantitative System Performance*. Englewood Cliffs, NJ: Prentice-Hall.

1989. Molloy, Michael K., *Fundamentals of Performance Modeling*. New York: Macmillan Publishing Company. (An accessible account of queueing and simulation with case studies.)

1990. Jain, Raj. *Techniques for Experimental Design, Measurement, Simulation and Modeling; The Art of Computer Systems Performance Analysis*. New York: Wiley-Interscience. (An introduction to measurement techniques and tools, experiment design, simulation and queueing models.)

1991. Kant, K. *Introduction to Computer System Performance Evaluation*. New York: McGraw-Hill. (Contains a good discussion of queueing network models.)

RICHARD R. MUNTZ

PERFORMANCE OF COMPUTERS

For articles on related subjects *see* BENCHMARKS; and GROSCH'S LAW

Introduction   The relationship between computer price and hardware performance has been of interest to researchers and practitioners in the field since the early 1960s. There has been a steady stream of research articles examining this relationship and how it has evolved since then. Many of the studies, especially the earlier ones, have reinforced a concept known as "Grosch's Law," which states that the power of computer systems increases as the square of their cost.

The implication for this economy of scale concept is that it offers evidence to proponents of highly centralized data processing applications. By centralizing, organizations are able to achieve work performed at less expense per unit and an overall cost savings. Recent advances in computing technology have led to trends toward greater decentralization of computing. If economies of scale, as predicted by Grosch's Law, are still attainable, the trend toward decentralization would seemingly be uneconomical and non-rational. Three possible explanations could be:

1. Economies of scale are no longer obtainable.
2. There are other benefits and/or cost economies associated with decentralized computing.
3. Some combination of 1 and 2 above.

This article has four remaining sections: a discussion of important issues in the empirical testing of economies of scale; a review of previous research; an analysis of computer performance during the 1980s; and a summary, with conclusions.

Issues Related to Empirical Testing of Computer Performance   Several problems exist regarding the data collection and empirical testing of computer performance. The first is finding a satisfactory measure of computer system power. There is often little consistency in the choice of a dependent measure, making comparisons among studies difficult. In two cases (Knight, 1966, and Solomon, 1966), the measure of power was also used as a basis for computing the average cost of computation, defined as:

$$p = c/w \quad \text{or} \quad p' = w/c \tag{1}$$

where p is the average cost (dependent variable), p' is the amount of computation per dollar, c is the system cost, and w is the system performance—the amount of work performed per unit of time. Other studies have used price/MIPS (Ein-Dor, 1985, Kang *et al.*, 1986, Mendelson, 1987), price (Cale *et al.*, 1979; Sircar, 1986), and certain performance indices (Ein-Dor *et al.*, 1987; Kang *et al.*, 1989; Kang, 1989). A performance index is a single number used to indicate the relative performance of a computer against a standard machine. This allows different machines to be compared in a hierarchical manner.

In one of the earlier studies, Knight (1966) developed an algorithm for power that served as a surrogate for benchmark measurements. Knight first determined, through a set of benchmarks, how a particular jobstream influenced various operating components of the computer. Based on this, a set of weights was generated that allowed for the development of a measure of computer processing speed for the jobstream. Knight's power measurement, in instructions per second, may be stated as:

$$power = f(\text{memory/compute time} + \text{I/O time}) \quad (2)$$

where memory is the number of bits in main storage, weighted by a constant value, as determined by a group of experts (Ein-Dor, 1985). Compute time is the time it takes for the machine to execute a certain mix of instructions (fixed-point and floating-point addition, multiply, divide, and logical compare). Input/output time is the time the computer remains idle while waiting to execute one of the above instructions. Knight developed a complex equation to derive this quantity.

Knight's approach has the advantage of providing a single measure of computer power that can be related to system cost (Cale, Gremillion, and McKenney, 1979). However, this approach is no longer considered feasible since computers have undergone considerable change in design and architecture. Specifically, Knight's formulation is no longer applicable because:

1. Power depends on *how* the users utilize the system (timesharing, database, batch, business, or scientific).
2. Recent advances now allow software to perform certain hardware functions.
3. Systems now have vast architectural differences (virtual memory (*q.v.*), cache memory (*q.v.*), tape vs. disk emphasis, etc.)

Another problem with testing computer performance empirically is distinguishing improvements in performance due to economies of scale from improvements due to changes in technology through time (Ein-Dor, 1985). This problem may be solved either by relating each system to a specific generation of technology (Cale, Gremillion, and McKenney, 1979; Ein-Dor, 1985; Knight, 1966) or by limiting the study to systems of the same generation (Solomon, 1966).

Review of Empirical Studies

Table 1 summarizes the major studies dealing with the issue of computer performance since the early 1960s. One should note that al-

though a number of studies have found empirical support for Grosch's Law, recent studies have found fault with the past research models or data. For example, Ein-Dor's study (1985) separated computers into distinct classes based on the size of the machines. Mendelson (1987) challenged Ein-Dor's conclusion that there are economies of scale within separate categories of machines. Mendelson explains that there is a selection bias, or "regression phenomenon," inherent in the formation of Ein-Dor's computer groups. This selection bias gives the appearance of economies of scale within categories of computers when the true model has constant returns to scale. In addition, Kang, Miller, and Pick (1986) re-analyzed Ein-Dor's data to allow for different slopes across computer categories. Their analysis showed that the slopes are significantly different and that Grosch's Law does not hold for minicomputers.

Results from Kang's (1989) study lend support to the notion of constant returns to scale, as found by Kang and Pick (1989) and Mendelson (1987). Kang criticizes previous work on the basis of the lack of a strong theoretical model to interpret the model parameters. Kang uses both a cost function and a production function model to cross validate and ensure the robustness of the model specifications.

Empirical Test of the Issue In order to evaluate what has happened to computer performance during the 1980s and to examine the current validity of Grosch's Law, an analysis of mainframe and super-minicomputers was performed. We decided to limit our data set to this group of computers, due to consistent data availability and comparability with previous studies. Lynch, Rao, and Lin (1990), in an examination of microcomputer performance, found items such as slots, chip, and other unique features to be of importance in the performance ratios for this class of machines. These unique features argue against their being included in the present analysis.

The technique used to examine the relationship between computing power and cost was justified by Ein-Dor in 1985. His study indicated that MIPS (millions of instructions per second) was an acceptable surrogate measure of computer CPU performance. MIPS data and related cost data are readily available in annual surveys published by *Computerworld* and are consistent over the time period 1981 to 1989. We chose to look at data for 1981, 1985, and 1989. This provides a snapshot of the technology available at the beginning, in the middle, and at the end of the decade. This allows an examination of how the technology progressed during the 1980s. All dollar values used in this study are expressed in terms of 1981 dollars. This was achieved by using the Bureau of Labor Statistics Consumer Price Index as a deflator. The variables used in comparing computing costs c and power w are expressed in the following formula:

$$p = c/w \quad (3)$$

where: $\begin{aligned} p &= \text{Average cost} \\ c &= \text{Cost in millions of dollars} \\ w &= \text{MIPS} \end{aligned}$

TABLE 1.   Summary of Research Studies (Adapted from Kang, 1989)

Authors	Dependent Variables	Independent Variables	Comments
Cale, *et al.* (1979)	Price	Main memory, DASD, Intro. Yr.	Price is a better measure of a computer's power than speed is; more hardware "power" per dollar was evident with advanced technology. Identified two distinct computer markets (large and small machines); memory size alone was a good predictor for large machines.
Ein-Dor (1985)	Price/MIPS	Computer category	Identified distinct classes of machines.
Ein-Dor, *et al.* (1987)	Performance Index	Cache, Main memory, (I/O channel/cycle time)	In favor of a multi-characteristics model.
Fedorowicz (1981)	Price	Main memory, introduction year, DASD	A theoretical piece that criticizes the model specification of Cale, *et al.*
Kang, *et al.* (1986)	Price	MIPS, Intro. Yr., computer category, IBM compatibility	Grosch's Law doesn't hold for minicomputers; supports Grosch's Law otherwise; supports Ein-Dor's [1985] analysis. All studies should allow for separate categories of computers.
Kang and Pick (1989)	Performance Index	Price, computer category, data year, IBM compatibility, vendor dummy	Criticizes Ein-Dor, *et al.* (1987), for data problems, use of stepwise regression, improper model specification. Should explicitly include machine cycle time. Grosch's law is not supported by Ein-Dor's data set, and the economies of scale suggested by Grosch's law may be much less.
Kang (1989)	Price, Lease price	Price, MIPS, computer category, main memory, channels	Grosch's Law is not supported. Used both a cost function and a production function to cross-validate results. Used both lease and purchase prices.
Knight (1966, 1968)	Rental price	Power index	Supported Grosch's Law.
Mendelson (1987)	Price	MIPS, Intro. Yr.	Grosch's Law not supported; constant scale economies were found.
Sircar, *et al.* (1986)	Price	Main memory, DASD, Benchmarks	Supports the use of benchmarking for micros.
Solomon (1966)	Lease price	Benchmarks	Grosch's Law support.

These calculations utilize the cost based on a minimally configured system cost while expressing power as a function of CPU performance.

Computer Performance During the 1980s

Regression analysis was used to determine average cost as a function of power for any year. The coefficients in the regression equation were calculated using the data on 405 computers marketed by 35 vendors during this time period. The data was used to plot the regression equation (Fig. 1) which depicts the technology available in any given year per unit of average system cost. Logarithmic scales are used for both variables. The curves in Fig. 1 present the regression results and selected examples of values for p and w for the three time periods in the study.

The results shown in Fig. 1 lead to two observations: (1) computer technology, in terms of how much computing power one may buy per dollar, has been improving since 1981 and (2) economies of scale, as predicted by Grosch's Law, are no longer obtainable for large scale computers.

The regression equation used for Fig. 1 has the form:

$$\ln(p) = a \ln(w) + k \qquad (4)$$

It may be used to test Grosch's Law for the years 1981 through 1989. We first rewrite this equation as

$$p = k * w^a \quad \text{or} \quad \text{Computations/dollar} = \frac{1}{p} = \frac{1}{k} * w^{-a}$$

Grosch's Law predicts that computing power increases as a function of cost squared so that, for twice the

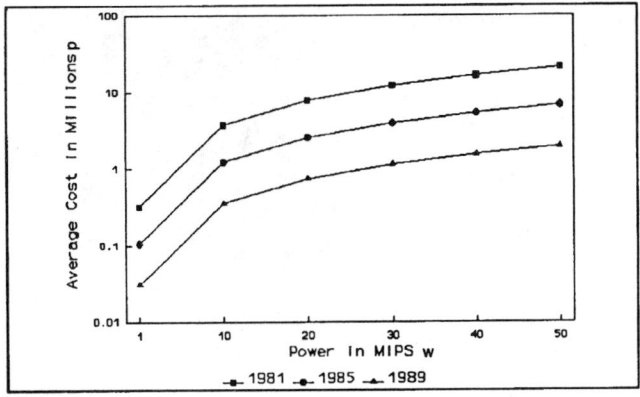

Average Cost vs Power

	Selected Regression Values			Regression Equation
	MIPS	Power		$\ln(p) = -3.493 + 0.068(\ln(w)) + 2.354(Y_{81})$
	1	0.320		$+ 1.24226(Y)_{85}$
1981	10	0.374	where:	p = average cost
	50	0.417		w = power in MIPS
	1	0.105		Y_{81} = 1 if technology year
1985	10	0.123		is 1981, 0 otherwise
	50	0.137		Y_{85} = 1 if technology year
	1	0.030		is 1985, 0 otherwise
1989	10	0.036		
	50	0.040		

FIG. 1   Regression results.

cost, one should have four times as much computing power. The actual a found from Fig. 1 is –0.07. Grosch's Law predicts $a = -0.50$, so there is no apparent agreement.

The analysis we have used continues work first developed in 1963 by Knight. While the measure of computing power used here is different from Knight's, due to changes in hardware technology, the robustness of the underlying phenomenon is evident, as all studies of the behavior of computer performance since the original Knight study have supported the rather steady progress in the technology.

References

1966. Knight, K. E. "Changes in Computer Performance," *Datamation*, **12**, *9*, (September), 40–54.

1966. Solomon, M. B. "Economies of Scale and the IBM System/360," *Communications of the ACM*, **9**, *6* (June), 435–440.

1968. Knight, K. E. "Changes in Computer Performance 1963–1967," *Datamation*, **14**, *1* (January), 31–35.

1976. Knight, K. E. and Cerveny, R. P. "Performance of Computers," *Encyclopedia of Computer Science*. New York: Petrocelli/Charter, 1065–1070.

1979. Cale, E. G., Gremillion, L. L., and McKenney, J. L. "Price/Performance Patterns of U.S. Computer Systems," *Communications of the ACM*, **22**, *4* (April), 225–232.

1979. Chow, G. C. "Techological Changes and the Demand for Computers," *American Economics Review*, **22**, *4* (April) 225–232.

1981. Fedorowicz, J. "Comments on Price/Performance Patterns of U.S. Computer Systems," *Communications of the ACM*, **24**, *9* (September), 585–586.

1981. Henkel, T. "Hardware Roundup: A look at 98 systems from 17 vendors," *Computerworld*, 19 July, 11–20.

1983. King, J. L. "Centralized versus Decentralized Computing: Organizational Considerations and Management Options," *Computing Surveys*, **15**, *4*, (December), 319–349.

1983. Cerveny, R. P. and Knight, K. E. "Performance of Computers," in Ralston, A. and Reilly, E. D. (Eds.), *Encyclopedia of Computer Science and Engineering, Second Edition*. New York: Van Nostrand Reinhold Company, 1127–1131.

1985. Ein-Dor, P. "Grosch's Law Re-Revisited: CPU Power and the Cost of Computation," *Communications of the ACM*, **28**, *2*, 142–151.

1985. Henkel, T. "Hardware Roundup: A look at 212 systems from 28 vendors," *Computerworld*, 19 August, 23–32.

1986. Kang, Y. M., Miller, R. B., and Pick, R. A. "Comments on 'Grosch's Law Re-revisited: CPU Power and the Cost of Computation'," *Communications of the ACM*, **29**, *8* (August), 779–781.

1986. Sircar, S., and Dave, D. "The Relationship Between Benchmark Tests and Microcomputer Price," *Communications of the ACM*, **29**, *3* (March), 212–217.

1986. Cole, R., Chen, Y. C., Barquin-Stolleman, J. A., Dulgerger, E., Helvacian, N., and Hodge, J. H. "Quality-adjusted Price Indexes for Computer Processors and Selected Peripheral Equipment," *Survey of Current Business*, **66**, *1*, (January), 41–50.

1987. Ein-Dor, P. and Feldmesser, J. "Attributes of the Performance of Central Processing Units: A Relative Performance Prediction Model," *Communications of the ACM,* **30,** *4* (April), 308–317.

1987. Mendelson, H. "Economies of Scale in Computing: Grosch's Law Revisited," *Communications of the ACM,* **30,** *12* (December), 1066–1072.

1989. Hamilton, R. "Hardware Roundup: Large and Medium Scale Systems," *Computerworld,* 18 September, 71–93.

1989. Kang, Y. M. and Pick, R. A. "Comments on 'Attributes of the Performance of Central Processing Units: A Relative Performance Prediction Model'," *Communications of the ACM,* **32,** *2* (February), 256–261.

1989. Kang, Y. M. "Computer Hardware Performance: Production and Cost Function Analyses," *Communications of the ACM,* **32,** *5* (May), 586–593.

1990. Lynch, B. D., Rao, R, and Lin, W. "A Cost Function Analysis of Microcomputer Hardware Characteristics," School of Management Working Paper, SUNYAB, Buffalo, New York.

1990. Hennessy, J. L., and Patterson, D. A. *Computer Architecture: A Quantitative Approach,* Chapter 2. San Mateo, CA: Morgan Kaufmann.

ROBERT P. CERVENY AND EDWARD J. GARRITY

PERIPHERAL DEVICE. *See* MEMORY: AUXILIARY.

PERLIS, ALAN J.

For articles on the related subjects *see* SOFTWARE HISTORY; and WHIRLWIND.

FIG. 1.   Alan J. Perlis

Alan J. Perlis was born in Pittsburgh on 1 April 1922 and died in New Haven, Connecticut on 7 February 1990. He was renowned as a developer of programming systems and languages and as an educator—indeed, as a founding father of computer science as a separate discipline.

Perlis received a B.S. in chemistry in 1942 from the Carnegie Institute of Technology (now Carnegie Mellon University), and did graduate work at both the California and the Massachusetts Institutes of Technology in mathematics. He received a Ph.D. from the latter in 1950, and spent the next two years developing programs for the multi-machine computing laboratory of the Ballistic Research Laboratories at Aberdeen Proving Grounds and for Whirlwind at M.I.T.

While an assistant professor at Purdue University from 1952 to 1956, he also served as head of a computing center that first had an IBM CPC (card programmed calculator) and then later a Datatron 205. Similarly, he served as associate professor of mathematics and head of its IBM 650-based computing center at Carnegie Tech from 1956 to 1960. Starting at Purdue and continuing at Carnegie Tech, he headed a group that defined the language IT (Internal Translator) and developed compilers for it. IT was quickly in wide use on 650s around the country, as were a succession of algebraic languages and assemblers that were also designed by the group that he led.

Perlis served as a professor at Carnegie Tech from 1960 to 1971. In 1965, he helped establish and became the first chairman of a graduate department of computer science. In 1971, he joined the new computer science department at Yale University as Eugene Higgins Professor of Computer Science, serving as chairman several times until his death. Many of the dozens of graduate students who received their degrees under his guidance at Carnegie-Mellon and Yale are now well-known leaders in teaching and research in the U.S. and abroad.

In 1957, ACM president John W. Carr III appointed Perlis chairman of a programming language committee and head of a subcommittee that met in Zurich with a similar subcommittee of GAMM (Gesellschaft für angewandte Mathematik und Mechanik). This group of eight persons specified Algol 58, whose report by Perlis and Klaus Samelson became the basis of a formal specification of Algol 60. During the 1960s, he developed such extensions as Formula Algol and LCC, a form of Algol adapted to interactive, incremental programming.

Perlis was the first editor-in-chief of the *Communications of ACM* (1958–1962), President of ACM (1962–1964), and, in 1966, the first recipient of ACM's Turing Award (*q.v.*). He received honorary degrees from Davis and Elkins College, Purdue, the University of Waterloo, and Sacred Heart University. He was invited to give numerous lectures abroad, including the Soviet Union, Denmark, Italy, China, Israel, Mexico, Peru, Venezuela, Scotland, and The Netherlands.

Throughout his career, Alan Perlis served on national and international committees and boards related to medical research, natural language processing and translation, and software engineering within such organizations as the National Science Foundation, the Pennsylvania Council on Science and Technology, and the National Research Council Assembly on Engineering. He was elected to the American Academy of Arts and Sciences (1973), the National Academy of Engineering (1976), and he received the AFIPS Education Award in 1984.

References

1970. Galler, B. and Perlis, A. *A View of Programming Languages.* Reading, MA: Addison-Wesley.

1972, 1975. Perlis, Alan J. *Introduction to Computer Science.* New York: Harper & Row.

1981. Perlis, Alan J. "The American Side of the Development of ALGOL," in *History of Programming Languages*, Richard L. Wexelblat (Ed.), 75–91. Reading, MA: Academic Press.

1987. Perlis, Alan J. "The Synthesis of Algorithmic Systems," and "Postscript—20 years after" in Turing Award Lectures, 5–16, Reading, MA: Addison-Wesley.

SAUL GORN

PERSONAL COMPUTING

For articles on related subjects *see* APPLE COMPUTER; BIOS; BULLETIN BOARD; CACHE MEMORY; CD-ROM; COMPUTER GAMES; DESKTOP PUBLISHING; ELECTRONIC MAIL; ENTREPRENEURS; FLOPPY DISK; HACKER; HARD DISK; IBM-PC AND PC-COMPATIBLES; INTERACTIVE INPUT DEVICES; LAPTOP COMPUTER; LOCAL AREA NETWORK; MEMORY MAPPED I/O; MODEM; MOTHERBOARD; MOUSE; OPEN ARCHITECTURE; PORT, MEMORY; POWER USER; SPELLING CHECKER; SPREADSHEET; USER INTERFACE; WAIT STATE; WINDOW ENVIRONMENTS; WIZARD; WORD PROCESSING; and WORKSTATION.

The *personal computer* has been in existence only since 1974 and did not gain widespread popularity until the 1980s. Yet in this very short time span, it has radically changed the way society does business, learns, plays, and gathers information. Bill Gates, chairman of the board of Microsoft Corporation, has said that, when he and Paul Allen, both teenagers, founded Microsoft in the mid 1970s to write software for a computer whose sales were in the low hundreds, they set as a goal for their fledgling company to have a "computer in every office and home in the country running Microsoft software." Less than 20 years later, this seemingly farfetched dream now actually appears to be achievable. Personal computing, the ability of average persons to perform computing tasks for themselves, has had a profound effect on society, an effect that was possible only through a combination of technological advancement and the introduction of a new "metaphor" or vision of what is meant by computing. The personal computer has, in a very short time, made the typewriter, slide rule, accountant's pads, teletypes, and large reference libraries close to obsolete. It has changed the way virtually every industry, from printing and publishing to legal to television and movies to military defense, does

business. It has moved society dramatically toward a democratization of information, when all sizes of businesses and all classes of people have access to legal, financial, and scientific information. It has brought with it a whole new raft of legal, ethical, and moral problems concerning the value of information, constitutional rights of electronic information publishers and "bulletin board" operators, access to computer training and use, government control over computer communications, health hazards related to long-term computer use, and threats to privacy made possible by computer technology.

History   In Albuquerque, New Mexico, in 1974, a small manufacturer named MITS developed a kit to build a microcomputer. Named the Altair by reviewer Leslie Solomon at the suggestion of his teenage daughter (after a fictitious planet on the *Star Trek* television series), the system was built around an Intel 8080 microprocessor. When Solomon's story about the kit appeared as a cover feature in the January 1975 issue of *Popular Electronics* magazine, MITS was deluged with orders and the age of personal computing began.

Soon other companies began offering add-on parts or "peripherals" for the Altair, and Gates and Allen founded Microsoft to develop a Basic interpreter, a program to allow programmers to use the Basic programming language on the Altair. Other firms began to develop commercial software for the computer, and competitive computer manufacturers began to appear. One of the earliest, Processor Technology, came quickly to market with a system, the "Sol," designed by industry pioneer Lee Felsenstein and named after the aforementioned Leslie Solomon. Computer retail stores came into existence to market the new computers and in September 1975, *Byte* magazine became the first of the half dozen periodicals that would spring up within a year to address the new market. In short, the microcomputer was upon us.

The early models mentioned above, however, had little overall impact on society. The majority were built from kits and attracted only a group of hobbyists and electronics "tinkerers" across the country. These early computer users banded together into computer clubs—places where persons could come together and exchange information about these novel new machines.

Shortly thereafter, two existing companies, Commodore and Radio Shack, entered the marketplace with their "Pet" and "TRS-80" systems (see Fig. 1). These systems differed from those that had come before in that they were pre-assembled and were intended to attract hobbyists and "end-users," persons who saw the new device as a tool to do things, rather than as an end in itself.

While the Pet and TRS-80 made personal computers available to the non-hobbyist, it was the rise of Apple Computer and the development of a software product called "VisiCalc" that caused the proliferation of personal computers throughout corporate America. Apple Computer had its genesis at the California Homebrew Computer Club where Steve Wozniak, a young Hewlett-Packard engineer, hung around and frequently brought in computers that he had designed. Another member, Steve Jobs, became convinced of the business opportunities

FIG. 1.   A Radio Shack TRS-80 Microcomputer System.

attendant to this new technology and, after much effort, persuaded Wozniak to leave Hewlett-Packard (who had exhibited no interest in Wozniak's creations) and join with him in founding Apple Computer, Inc. Although the company began operations in Jobs's garage and living room, the firm grew rapidly when Jobs was able to entice retired millionaire A. P. "Mike" Markkula to join the firm as a partner. Markkula was able to bring establishment venture capital into the firm to provide the funding necessary for Apple's development. The Apple II, built around the Mostek 6502 processor, and the Apple II floppy disk drive were extremely successful with computer enthusiasts and brought much technical praise to largely self-taught engineering genius Wozniak.

As the Apple II was gaining in popularity, a young graduate student at the Harvard School of Business, Daniel Bricklin, was groping with the "case method" system used in business school that required students to continually redo large financial workpapers or "spreadsheets" to show the effect of such normal business occurrences as interest rate changes, tax increases or decreases, inflation, etc. The process was extremely tedious and often required recalculating a large number of formulas and totals dependent in some way on the changed variable. Bricklin, a former programmer at Digital Equipment Corporation, reasoned that there must be something that could be done with these new inexpensive personal computers to reduce drastically the effort involved. He and a friend, Bob Frankston, designed what became the first electronic spreadsheet, "VisiCalc." (It is hard for most to believe that electronic spreadsheets, one of the most important uses of personal computers, did not exist as recently as 1976.)

Since each of the existing computers of that time used a different microprocessor, it was necessary for Bricklin and Frankston to decide which of the existing

microcomputers to choose as a host for VisiCalc. Because of its design and the availability of disk drives for the system, they chose the Apple II and completed the product for that system. Upon product completion, they took out a small ad in *Byte Magazine* and began to sell the product through a software publisher, Personal Software.

As part of their marketing effort, Bricklin and Frankston were able to get a copy of VisiCalc into the hands of the editor of the prestigious *Morgan Stanley Electronics Letter*, Benjamin M. Rosen. Rosen, extremely impressed with the potential of such a product and what he saw as its possible impact on Apple II sales, wrote in the newsletter "VisiCalc may be the software tail that wags the hardware dog." Rosen's prediction became reality when people went into computer stores in droves asking for VisiCalc (at that time, $100) and something to run it on (which, at that time, could only be an Apple II which cost anywhere from $3,000 to $9,000 depending on the type of printer, monitor, and disk drive attached to the computer). VisiCalc and the Apple II swept through corporate offices, often bucking the resistance of data processing managers unprepared for end users having direct access to computer power.

With the success of VisiCalc and the Apple II in large corporations, it became only natural for persons wishing to develop products for that marketplace to choose the Apple II as their platform. One, Mitchell Kapor, a graduate school student at Yale, produced a graphics and statistics program, "Tiny Troll," which he sold from his house for the price of $100. Another, John Draper, who had previously served a prison sentence for "phone-phreaking" (using telephone systems for long distance calls without paying) developed a word processing program, "EasyWriter," which allowed persons to use the Apple II to write and constantly revise material before final printing. A third, Dennis C. Hayes, developed a microprocessor, the

"Hayes Micromodem II," which allowed the Apple II to communicate over telephone lines and obtain information from the many large "databases," such as Dow Jones, CompuServe, Source, and Dialog, that were beginning to spring up. Each of these products generated additional sales for the Apple II and caused new developers to come into the market.

As the number of products grew, it became clear that the lack of integration between them caused annoyance to users. A person using both VisiCalc and Tiny Troll to analyze data had to enter it twice through the keyboard, a practice that was both time consuming and error prone. To eliminate this problem, Personal Software, now renamed "VisiCorp," contracted with Kapor, the developer of Tiny Troll, to produce a new product, "VisiTrend + VisiPlot," with improved features and the ability to exchange data with VisiCalc, using a new standard file format, "Data Interchange Format" (DIF).

Computer industry giant IBM had remained on the sidelines for most of the early rapid development in personal computers. Its desktop offerings, the 5100 series, had been overly expensive for most and had fallen far short of the Apple II in "user-friendliness." In an effort to develop a system that could properly compete in this marketplace, IBM set up a small business within IBM under the direction of IBM executive Philip D. "Don" Estridge in Boca Raton, Florida, and gave it the charter to do whatever was necessary to enter the market successfully.

Estridge and his staff embarked on a program unlike anything in IBM's history and formed alliances with strong players in the microcomputer field to develop versions of existing successful software products for the as-yet-unintroduced IBM computer. When the IBM-PC was introduced in August 1981, there were versions of VisiCalc, EasyWriter, the PeachTree Accounting System, and Microsoft Adventure ready to run on the brand new equipment. As its operating system (*q.v.*) IBM chose MS-DOS, a system adapted by Microsoft from a product developed by a small West Coast firm. They called their version PC-DOS.

From the moment of its introduction, the IBM-PC was dramatically successful. Data processing managers, weary from confrontations with accountants, analysts, engineers, portfolio managers, etc., who wanted to buy and use strange sounding computers named Apple and Pet, could now recommend a firm that they knew well and that understood mainframe data processing.

VisiCalc actually ran faster and used less memory on the Apple II than on the newer system. The Apple technical advantage was, however, short-lived. When VisiCorp asked Mitchell Kapor to create a version of VisiTrend for the IBM-PC, Kapor chose to sell his rights to the $265 product to VisiCorp for $1.5 million and go off on his own to develop a new product. Kapor took the proceeds (together with an additional $1.2 million amassed in royalties) to the recently started venture capital firm, Sevin-Rosen Management (Rosen being the same Ben Rosen who started the VisiCalc ball rolling with his Morgan Stanley Electronics Newsletter article). Sevin-Rosen raised $4 million dollars and Kapor set up Lotus Development Corp. and, with co-developer Jonathan Sachs, developed "1-2-3," a spreadsheet program that became the most successful computer program in history. When 1-2-3 was introduced at a press conference at New York City's World Trade Center, the advertising budget for the first year of the product was announced to be $6 million dollars—a far cry from a short time before when Bricklin took a small ad for VisiCalc in Byte and sent a copy of the program to Ben Rosen, hoping for publicity.

1-2-3 became the "VisiCalc" of the IBM-PC, causing sales of the new system to skyrocket. The success of the system caused other manufacturers to come into the marketplace with "compatible" computers that ran like the IBM-PC. While the Apple II contained proprietary hardware that was illegal to copy, the IBM did not, and firms of all sizes brought compatible machines to market. The most successful of these, Compaq Computer Corporation, debuted with a "transportable" system, a 22-lb. computer with a handle and built-in monitor and disk drives that could be rapidly moved from place to place. Computers made by firms that attempted, as Compaq did, to compete with IBM on the basis of power or features tended to be considered "compatibles," while products whose prime attraction was low price were usually called "clones." (Many clones were manufactured in Asia and imported to the United States and sold under innocuous American names.) Soon, the description of the machines that ran like the IBM-PC evolved from "IBM-compatible" to simply an "MS-DOS" machine (i.e. a system that ran under the Microsoft MS-DOS operating system). This slight change in nomenclature was in reality an indication that the industry's view was moving from one that saw IBM as the standard-maker to one that looks to Microsoft for that role.

While the majority of IBM's competitors in the personal computer market, such as Tandy, Zenith, Hewlett-Packard, Digital, Data General, Texas Instruments, and AT&T eventually came out with MS-DOS systems, Apple Computer chose to go in its own direction and, building on technology originally pioneered by Xerox with its Star microcomputer, developed a system, the Lisa, which made use of an operating environment in which all programs worked in generally the same fashion and which used a pointing device called a "mouse" to perform routine activities. Although the Lisa failed commercially, both because of its pricing and the lack of a wide universe of software, its graphical user interface (GUI) became the basis of Apple's highly successful Macintosh computer and, by extension, of Microsoft's "Windows" operating environment (*see* USER INTERFACE). The Commodore Amiga also uses a GUI and has earned a modest share of the personal computer market based on the offering of features similar to the Macintosh at a much lower price.

The Macintosh's GUI, its ease of operation, and its "what-you-see-is-what-you-get" (WYSIWYG) approach to text processing gained popularity, in large part, because of the development of high-quality laser printers, the introduction of a "page definition language" (PDL) called PostScript (*q.v.*), and the publication of a program known as PageMaker. This combination of operational environment, hardware, and software products spawned a new industry called "desktop publishing." The new industry provided a path for the Macintosh into small and large businesses alike and revolutionized the production of newsletters, magazines, and advertising copy.

The increased penetration of the Macintosh into businesses and the expanded exposure of the graphical user interface gave impetus to Microsoft's Windows environment, which provided for MS-DOS machines many of the same features of the Macintosh. It also resulted in the development of GUIs for the Unix operating system (*q.v.*), a system that had been developed in a highly technical environment at Bell Laboratories and had never been considered an end-user operating system. Additionally, Microsoft and IBM cooperated on the development of a new operating system, OS/2, also based on a graphical user interface. In short, the user interfaces—the way that persons interact with the computer—are converging even though the underlying computers are quite different.

While the software and operating systems were developing, the equipment or "hardware" itself was growing rapidly in speed and capacity. The Intel 8088 processor on which the IBM and other MS-DOS systems is based had many compatible relatives: the 8086, the 80286, the 80386, and the 80486, with each chip having greater speed and the ability to address more memory than its predecessor. On the Macintosh and Amiga side, the original Motorola 68000 processor soon fostered the 68020, 68030, and 68040 processors (*see* MICROCOMPUTER CHIP) (Figs. 2, 3, and 4 are pictures of recent IBM and Apple Macintosh computers and Apple co-founder Steve Jobs's NeXT computer.). Disk storage, limited on the original Apple II to 160,000 characters on a 5 1/4-inch floppy diskette is now available in sizes measured in megabytes (1 million characters) or even gigabytes (1 billion characters). Hard disk sizes of 100 megabytes characters are commonplace. Monitors now allow breathtaking color images and are available for desktop publishers in models that will display two full document pages at once. The speed at which personal computers may pass information across telephone lines has increased by 32 times since the introduction of the Hayes Micromodem II. Personal computers with considerably more power than the Apple II are now available in laptop and even notebook or "palmtop" models.

FIG. 3. The Macintosh IIfx computer. (Courtesy of Apple Computer, Inc.)

The phenomenal increase in processing power is not due solely to the rapid improvement of hardware and software. There has been tremendous progress in the ability to link computers for the purposes of gathering information, exchanging data, transmitting electronic mail ("e-mail"), and sharing resources. Computers are routinely connected in offices and classrooms through "local area networks" (LANs). Information is gathered from huge remote databases maintained on GEnie, Dialog, CompuServe, America OnLine, Dow Jones, Prodigy, Lexis, NewsNet, and others. E-mail is sent through many of the same services as well as through MCI, and a massive worldwide network known as the "Internet" that was developed through government funding and university activity. Society is close to the realization of ideas promulgated by industry pioneers Ted Nelson and Alan Kay in the 1970s who predicted the ability of users to obtain information without having to know either the location of the information or arcane computer commands to call for it.

Issues The advent of mass computing and telecommunications has brought new ethical and legal problems to society. The problem of "software piracy"—the obtaining of copies of programs by people who have not paid for

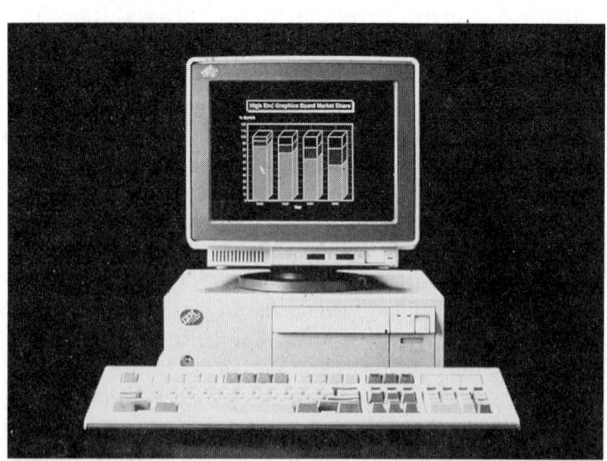

FIG. 2. An IBM PS/2 computer. (Courtesy of IBM Corporation.)

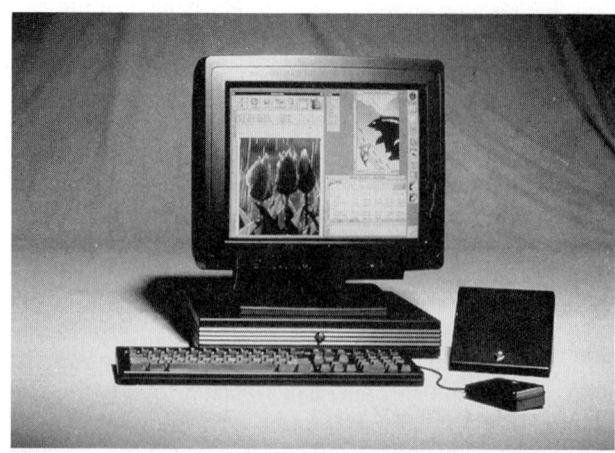

FIG. 4 The NeXT computer. (Courtesy of NeXT Corporation.)

them—has brought lawsuits, financial settlements, and debates. The ability to copy electronic documents surreptitiously without destroying the original has raised questions concerning intellectual property and the value of information. The advent of "electronic publishing"—the distribution of material to on-line subscribers—has raised constitutional questions when electronic publishers did not receive the same protection as publishers of printed material. The filing of "look and feel" lawsuits (pertaining to ownership of the way programs appear on the computer screen) by industry giants Apple Computer, Inc., Ashton-Tate, and Lotus Development Corporation raises questions of copyright law and industry practices. The proven ability of computer "hackers" to enter into computer systems to which they were not invited raises serious questions concerning security and ownership of information (global communication has even brought espionage by computer). Perhaps most important, the ability of credit, marketing, and government organizations to collect, massage, and disseminate an individual's financial, household, and employment information without the individual's prior approval has raised serious privacy issues.

These questions are complex and require careful and reasoned answers if we are to move forward technologically while retaining the freedoms and privacy to which we are accustomed. The concern for these issues is evidenced in the action of Harvard professor and constitutional law scholar Laurance H. Tribe, who, in 1991, suggested a constitutional amendment to specify the new electronic methods of communication and expression as protected rights.

Future The personal computer has become a ubiquitous device—an appliance that becomes a word processor, a communications device, a financial analysis tool, an artist's palate, etc. It has the power and capability to be all of these. The challenge of personal computing is to accommodate to the time when the computer itself begins to fade more and more into the background and lets the user accomplish the desired task without having to master or even be aware of the technology that underlies such a powerful tool.

References

Non-Fiction Books

1987. Armstrong, Jeffrey. *The Binary Bible of Saint Silicon*. Any Key Press.

1985. Bass, Thomas A. *The Eudaemonic Pie*. Boston: Houghton Mifflin.

1990. BloomBecker, Buck. *Spectacular Computer Crimes*. Homewood, IL: Dow Jones-Irwin.

1987. Brand, Stewart. *The Media Lab: Inventing the Future at M.I.T.* New York: Penguin Books.

1990. Burnham, David. *The Rise of the Computer State*. New York: Random House.

1990. Denning, Peter J. (Ed.). *Computers Under Attack: Intruders, Worms and Viruses*. Reading, MA: Addison Wesley.

1979. Dertouzos, Michael L. and Moses, Joel (Ed.). *The Computer Age: A Twenty-Year View*. Cambridge, MA: The M.I.T. Press.

1984. Ditlea, Steve, ed. *Digital Deli*. New York: Workman.

1983. Feigenbaum, Edward A. and McCorduck, Pamela. *The Fifth Generation*. Reading, MA: Addison-Wesley.

1987. Flamm, Kenneth. *Targeting the Computer: Government Support and International Competition*. Washington: Brookings Institution.

1988. Flamm, Kenneth. *Creating the Computer: Government, Industry and High Technology*. Washington: Brookings Institution.

1981. Forester, Tom Ed.. *The Microelectronics Revolution*. Cambridge, MA: The M.I.T. Press.

1985. Forester, Tom (Ed.). *The Information Technology Revolution*. Cambridge, MA: The M.I.T. Press.

1988. Forester, Tom. *High-Tech Society*. Cambridge, MA: The M.I.T. Press.

1989. Forester, Tom (Ed.). *Computers in the Human Context*. Cambridge, MA: The M.I.T. Press.

1980. Nora, Simon and Minc, Simon. *The Computerization of Society*. Cambridge, MA: The M.I.T. Press.

1984. Levy, Steven. *Hackers: Heroes of the Computer Revolution*. New York: Dell.

1984. Melvern, Linda, Hebditch, David and Anning, Nick. *Techno-Bandits*. Boston: Houghton-Mifflin Company.

1985. Johnson, Deborah G. and Snapper, John W. *Ethical Issues In The Use Of Computers*. Belmont, CA: Wadsworth Publishing.

1985. Landreth, Bill. *Out of the Inner Circle*. Tell City, IN: Tempus Press.

1985. McCorduck, Pamela. *The Universal Machine*. New York: McGraw-Hill.

1985. Traub, Joseph F. (Ed.). *Cohabiting With Computers*. Los Altos, CA: William Kaufmann, Inc.

1986. Roszak, Theodore. *The Cult Of Information*. New York: Pantheon.

1986. Tuck, Jay. *High-Tech Espionage*. New York: St. Martin's Press.

1987. Gassée, Jéan-Louis. *The Third Apple*. New York: Harcourt Brace Jovanovich.

1987. Nelson, Theodor. *Computer Lib/Dream Machine* (revised and updated edition), Tell City, IN: Tempus Press.

1987. Nelson, Theodor. *Literary Machines*. Project Xanadu; also available in hypertext version from Owl International.

1987. Sculley, John. *Odyssey*. New York: Harcourt Brace Jovanovich.

1988. Garson, Barbara. *The Electronic Sweatshop*. New York: Simon and Schuster.

1988. Halamka, John D. *Espionage In The Silicon Valley*. Alameda, CA: Sybex.

1988. Heim, Michael. *Electric Language: A Philosophical Study of Word Processing*. New Haven, CT: Yale University Press.

1989. Gilder, George. *Microcosm: The Quantum Revolution in Economics and Technology*. New York: Simon and Schuster.

1989. Kawasaki, Guy. *The Macintosh Way*. Glenview, IL: Scott, Foresman and Company.

1989. Lucky, Robert W. *Silicon Visions*. New York: St. Martin's Press.

1989. Rose, Frank. *West of Eden: The End of Innocence at Apple Computer*. New York: Viking.

1990. Forester, Tom and Morrison, Percy. *Computer Ethics*. Cambridge, MA: The M.I.T. Press.

1990. Jennings, Karla. *The Devouring Fungus: Tales of the Computer Age*. New York: W. W. Norton.

1990. LaQuey, Tracey (Ed.). *The user's Directory of Computer Networks*. Bedford, MA: Digital Press.

1990. National Research Council. *Computers at Risk: Safe Computing In the Information Age*. Washington: National Academy Press.

1990. Quarterman, John S. *The Matrix: Computer Networks and Conferencing Systems Worldwide.* Digital Press.

Fiction Books

1977. Ryan, Thomas J. *The Adolescence of P-1.* Riverdale, NY: Baen Books.
1984. Delaney, Joseph and Stielger, Marc. *Valentina: Soul In Sapphire.* Riverdale, NY: Baen Books.
1984. Gibson, William. *Neuromancer.* New York: Ace.
1984. Montelone, Thomas F. (Ed.). *Microworlds: tales of the computer age.* New York: Severn House.
1984. Varley, John. *Press Enter.* New York: Tor.
1985. Milan, Victor. *Cybernetic Samurai.* New York: Ace.
1985. Sterling, Bruce. *Schismatrix.* New York: Ace.
1986. Gibson, William. *Burning Chrome.* New York: Ace.
1986. Gibson, William. *Count Zero.* New York: Ace.
1986. Sterling, Bruce (ed.). *Mirrorshades: The Cyberpunk Anthology.* New York: Ace.
1988. Gerrold, David. *When H.A.R.L.I.E. Was One (Release 2.0),* New York: Bantam.
1988. Gibson, William. *Mona Lisa Overdrive.* New York: Ace.
1988. McLaughlin, John. *Toolmaker Koan.* Riverdale, NY: Baen Books.
1988. Sterling, Bruce. *Islands In The Net.* New York: Ace.
1989. Sterling, Bruce. *Crystal Express.* New York: Ace.
1990. Stiegler, Marc. *The Gentle Seduction.* Riverdale, NY: Baen Books.
1991. Gibson, William and Sterling, Bruce. *The Difference Engine.* New York: Bantam.
1991. Platt, Charles. *The Silicon Man.* New York: Bantam.

Magazine Articles

1986. Vinge, Vernor. "Marooned In Real Time," *Analog* (May–August).
1988. Bush, Vannevar. "As We May Think," *Atlantic Monthly* (August 1945); edited and annotated by Howard Rheingold in *Hyperage* (February–March).
1988. Nelson, Theodor. "Managing Immense Storage," *Byte Magazine* (January).
1990. Barlow, John Perry. "Crime and Puzzlement," *Whole Earth Review* (Fall).
1990. Goldstein, Emmanuel. "For Your Protection," *2600: The Hacker Quarterly* (Spring), 3.
1990. Sterling, Bruce. "The Cyberpunk Bust," *Interzone* (February), 47.
1991. Branscum, Deborah. "Ethics, electronic mail and the law," *MacWorld* (March), 63.
1991. Levy, Steven. "When The Secret Service Visited Steve Jackson Games," *MacWorld* (March), 51.

Periodicals

2600: The Hacker Quarterly
Byte Magazine
Dr. Dobbs' Journal
InfoWorld
MacUser
MacWeek
MacWorld
Mondo 2000
PC Computing
PC Magazine
PC Week
UNIX World

Computer Clubs

Among the best sources for information about personal computers are local computer clubs. They hold monthly meetings, publish newsletters, and distribute "public domain software" (programs that the authors are willing to give away) and "shareware" (programs that the authors are willing to have the user try and, if the program is useful, send a nominal payment). The following is a list of some of the larger user groups in the United States. Information on groups in other locations may be obtained by calling IBM (for MS-DOS and OS/2 users) and Apple Computer (for Macintosh Users).

ACNJ—Amateur Computer Club of New Jersey
BCS—Boston Computer Society (an umbrella organization for many smaller groups; the largest user group in the country)
BMUG—Berkeley Macintosh Users Group
Capitol PC—Washington, DC PC Users Group
HAL—Houston PC Users Group
NYACC—New York Amateur Computer Club
NYMUG—New York Macintosh User Group
NYPC—New York IBM User Group
PACS—Philadelphia Area Computer Society
Washington Apple π—Washington Apple Users Group

BARBARA E. MCMULLEN AND JOHN F. MCMULLEN

PERSONNEL IN THE COMPUTER FIELD

For articles on related subjects *see* CHIEF PROGRAMMER TEAM; PROGRAMMER; and SYSTEMS ANALYST.

Introduction During the past few years, the increase in the number of computers in use in business and industry, corporations, government, and the home has caused more jobs to be computer-based than ever before. With the advent of the personal computer, productivity of employees is greatly increased. With connectivity of personal computers, information can now be shared easily among employees. The variety of computer jobs is now expanded beyond that of the 1960s, 1970s and 1980s, causing more job specialization, more demand to keep up to date, and increased opportunity of risk due to software problems.

What Are the Computer Jobs? Many of the jobs requiring the use of computers are directly related to the computer profession, but some are more related to other professions that use the computer as a tool. The names of jobs directly related to computers and computing include:

Applications programmer
Computer engineer
Computer law specialist
Computer local area network technician

Computer local area network manager
Computer operations support personnel (librarian, scheduler, etc.)
Computer system operators
Computer operations specialist
Computer operations manager
Computer service repair technicians
Computer service representatives
Computer sales representatives
Computer programmer
Computer scientist
Computer software engineer
Computer specialist
Computer systems manager
Computer trainer
Database administrator
Data communications specialist
Data entry device operators
Data processing manager
Decision-support system specialist
Documentation specialist
Information center analyst
Management information systems specialist
Office automation analyst
Peripheral equipment operator
Programmer
Software engineer
Systems analyst
Systems designer
Systems programmer
Systems engineer
Information systems administrator
Information resources administrator
Technical support specialist
Telecommunications specialist

Jobs in many fields are requiring increased knowledge of computer usage and skill in the use of specific software for that discipline. Some of the jobs now requiring use of computers are: accountant, animator, bank teller, journalist, musician, news publisher, reporter, performing artist, theater production technician, typist, point-of-sale clerk, and video production technician.

Projections of Demand
Of those jobs directly considered "computer vocation/profession," recent data projections are:

In 1988 there were about 403,000 computer systems analysts; by the year 2000 there will be about 607,000. For computer programmers, there were about 519,000 in 1988, with about 769,000 expected in 2000. Data processing equipment repair jobs are expected to grow even more, from 71,000 in 1988 to 115,000 in 2000, about 61.2% growth. (Bureau of Labor Statistics, May 1990.)

Technological innovations continue to make equipment smaller and cheaper. New and improved applications of computers are found on a continuing basis. Re-search into high performance computing systems and advanced software technology has been proposed as a part of the Federal High Performance Computing and Communications Program (*Grand Challenges*, 1991). Although lean times have affected many corporate and government growth areas recently, it is expected that demand will remain high throughout the 1990s and into the early 2000s.

Salaries Among other scientific and engineering personnel, the salaries of computer scientists exceed those of all other science occupations regardless of experience. But new doctorates in computer science earn less, on the average, than experienced doctoral chemists and mathematicians (Vetter, 1988). The median annual salary of programmers who worked full-time in 1986 was about $27,000, while for computer systems analysts the median earned was about $32,800 (*Occupational Outlook Handbook*, 1988–89).

The College Placement Council reports average starting salary offers for 1991 baccalaureate computer science graduates of $30,696, higher than for all other traditional sciences, but lower than most engineering fields (*Manpower Comments*, October 1991, pp. 13–14).

Projections of Supply
Estimating the supply from colleges is not easy, since a variety of majors who go into the field are not classified as being in "computer and information sciences." Interest in computing as a major dropped between 1982 and 1987, according to the Cooperative Institutional Research Program (*see also* EDUCATION IN COMPUTER SCIENCE); only 2.7% of the entering freshmen expressed interest as compared to 4.8% in 1982 (*Manpower Comments*, Jan.–Feb. 1989). Estimates of the number of personnel who are going into "computer jobs" after some type of retraining is also difficult.

With the sale of desktop computers continuing to increase, there is a continuing demand for improved software and attachment devices for use in office settings. The software production process now involves increased awareness of risk and its assessment, intellectual property rights, security, human interface, and multi-media access to text and graphic records. As more students in schools learn about computers, their expectations will feed even more demand in society.

Retrained personnel are taking up the charge and are doing the job, although it has been said that many of the increased number of risk incidents can be attributed to the lack of qualified personnel. A System Security Study Committee of the National Research Council reported that many of our computing and communications systems are "vulnerable to attack" (*Computing Research News*, January 1991, p. 1). Concern for the vulnerability of computer systems has led to increased attention to security and increased discussion of the need for licensing of personnel (*see* DATA SECURITY).

Certification of Computer Professionals
In 1973, the Institute for Certification of Computer Professionals (*q.v.*) was started to carry forward the certification effort pioneered by the Data Processing Management

Association (*q.v.*). This non-profit international organization now has 11 association members, including DPMA, the Canadian Information Processing Society and the Association for Computing Machinery (ACM). Four certification programs are available:

ACP—Associate Computer Professional (entry-level computer jobs).
CCP—Certified Computer Professional (computer programmers).
CSP—Certified Systems Professional (systems analysts).
CDP—Certified Data Processor (data processing managers).

ICCP offers a voluntary certification program for computer professionals that is supported by many as a preferred alternative to licencing. ICCP examinations are given worldwide twice each year. Specialty examinations are now available in the areas of computer security and software engineering (ICCP, 1991).

Certification of software engineers is done in the U.K. by the British Computer Society (Tompsett, 1991).

Conclusion   Spawned by the development of the digital computer in the mid-1940s, jobs in the newly evolving discipline of the computer and information sciences have continued to grow and change. As the variety of computer systems and configurations increase, so do the types of responsibilities needed by personnel. Jobs tend to be in the following categories:

1. Many of the jobs are tied to the corporate record-keeping needs, grown from the methods and procedures of the early punched card era in the 1890s; these jobs are more business related. Jobs in management of computer services usually fall in this category. Usually called "information systems" jobs.

2. Many of the jobs are tied to the newer high-tech industries of today, feeding the development of computer-based control systems such as air traffic control, defense equipment, medical care, etc.; these are more scientific in nature. Usually called "high-tech computer" jobs; often called "software engineer."

3. Many of the jobs are tied to the manufacture and production of computer components and equipment systems; these are more computer engineering in nature. Usually called "hardware" jobs.

4. Many of the jobs are tied to software development to make the computer equipment easier to use (languages, operating systems, etc.) Usually called "system software" jobs, often "systems programmer."

5. Many of the jobs are related to support services, from data entry to computer operations. Usually called "computer support" jobs.

6. Many of the jobs are tied to customer service,

ranging in type from software training to installation and repair of hardware and software. Usually called "computer services" jobs.

7. Many of the jobs are tied to applications in other disciplines, such as journalism (desktop publishing, newspaper production, etc.), music and entertainment (production of special effects, music, etc.), media (tutorial delivery, computer-managed instruction, etc.). Usually called by non-computer names.

8. Many of the jobs are only indirectly related to computers, using them as a tool (bank tellers, food store check-out clerks, etc.). Usually called by non-computer names.

9. Many of the jobs relate to the research and development of new or improved methodologies for computer algorithm development and usage. Usually called "computer scientist" jobs.

10. Many of the jobs deal with devices and techniques employed for the remote or local transmission of data of any nature by any means. Usually called "computer network specialist" or "telecommunications specialist."

11. Many of the jobs deal with the education of students, whether in formal or informal settings. Usually called "computer educator" or "computer trainer."

Education and training for entering computer personnel has, in the past, ranged from none, high school, junior/community college, institutes, baccalaureate degrees, master's degrees, and doctorate degrees. Once employed, there is a strong need for computer personnel to maintain currency in knowledge and a real challenge is staying prepared for the next adaptation. Although salaries are relatively high as compared to some other fields, the work is sometimes tedious and detailed, and usually demanding; many workers enjoy the challenge offered.

References

1987. *Taxonomy of Computer Specialists*. Washington: National Science Foundation.

1989. *Manpower Comments*. Washington: Commission on Professionals in Science and Technology, January–February, 34–35.

1990. Youst, David B. and Lipsett, Laurence. "The Technical Ladder Gets Harder to Climb," *IEEE Spectrum*, **28** September, 46.

1991. *Grand Challenges: High Performance Computing and Communications, A Report by the Committee on Physical, Mathematical, and Engineering Sciences*. Washington: Federal Coordinating Council for Science, Engineering, and Technology, Office of Science and Technology Policy, U.S. Government Printing Office.

1991. *ICCP Study Guide*. Chicago: Institute for Certification of Computer Professionals.

1991. *Manpower Comments*. Washington: Commission on Professionals in Science and Technology, October, 13–14.

1991. *Computers at Risk: Safe Computing in the Information Age*. Washington: National Academy of Science.

JOYCE CURRIE LITTLE

PERT/CPM

The development of project management techniques using network methods, of which *PERT* (project evaluation and review technique) and *CPM* (critical path method) are the most widely known, was undertaken in the late 1950s by several independent groups working on different types of projects. The most widely publicized of these efforts was the use of PERT in conjunction with the design of the Polaris submarine system. It was credited with saving substantial time and cost on Polaris, which caused its use to be made mandatory on all significant development projects undertaken for and by the U. S. Department of Defense. Knowledge of this and other successful applications soon became widespread, and many variants, additional features, and computerized aids were developed and publicized. As a result, project management techniques have become the most extensively used of the quantitative tools for management, with the possible exception of linear programming.

Most uses of these techniques are in the defense and construction industries, although they are suitable for any situation where:

The *project* consists of a collection of *activities* or tasks.

The activities can be started and stopped independently of each other (in contrast to a sequential flow of processing), even if the resources employed on the various activities are not independent.

Precedence relationships exist that preclude the start of certain activities until others are complete (e.g. surfacing a road must be preceded by the laying of the road bed).

Specific and general examples of successful use include:

Space mission development and countdown procedures.

Construction projects such as a building.

Procedures for closing accounts in a bank or firm (e.g. payroll).

Ship or aircraft repair projects.

Implementation of a computer system, from ordering and site preparation through installation and checkout.

The techniques can be used in both planning and control of projects. *Planning* in this context consists of the overall layout of the project, with rough estimation of the time and resources required, and the detailed scheduling of the timing and order of activities. In short, it concerns the set of decisions made before the start of the project. By contrast, *control* takes place during the project. As actual resource use and completion times are obtained, project management techniques can be used to reallocate resources according to the revised criticality ratings of activities.

Computation of a Critical Path All variants of the project management technique compute what is

called a *critical path*. Since a project consists of an ordered set of independent activities, it can be represented as a *network* (Fig. 1), where activities are shown as branches connected at nodes to immediately preceding and immediately following activities. (Other conventions are possible, but the idea of a network remains.)

A *path* through the network is any set of successive activities that goes from the beginning to the end of the project. Associated with each activity in the network is a single number that best estimates the time that activity will consume; differences in the way this number is obtained distinguish the major variants of the technique. A *critical path*, then, is one whose sum of activity times is longer than that for any other path through the network (multiple critical paths with equal total times are, of course, possible). This path is important because, if everything goes according to schedule, its length gives the shortest possible completion time of the overall project.

In addition, a *slack time* can be associated with each activity in the project. This is the difference between the latest possible completion time of each activity that will not delay the completion of the overall project, and the earliest possible completion time, based on all predecessor activities. Activities on a critical path have zero slack time, and, conversely, activities with zero slack time are on a critical path.

The critical path and associated slack times for a project are found by simply working forward through the network, computing the earliest possible completion time for each activity, until the earliest possible completion time for the total project is found. Then, by working backward through the network, the latest completion time for each activity is found, the slack time computed, and the critical path identified.

This procedure is so straightforward that it is clearly easily programmable for a computer. For example, the complete data input, computation, and output of results can be done in fewer than 40 high-level language statements. Not surprisingly, there is a wide proliferation of programs that perform this computation, many with special features tailored to a specific industry or type of problem. Nearly every commercial time-sharing system or service bureau has such software available for use by its customers.

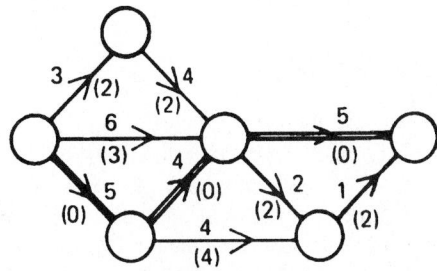

FIG. 1. Example of project network. Single-shaft arrow indicates activity with time slack (in parentheses); double-shaft arrow represents critical path.

PERT Assumptions The variant of the technique described above, which carries the name PERT, was first used in conjunction with the Polaris systems development cited earlier. Because of imperfect knowledge of the times of individual development activities, it is felt necessary to have a means to incorporate uncertainty in the estimation of such times. To do this, a three-point estimate of optimistic, pessimistic, and most likely completion times is obtained for each activity. These are used to estimate the mean and standard deviation of each activity time. The means are in turn used to find the critical path and slack times, as described in the preceding section, implying that a given activity is or is not critical. Then continuing on the assumption that activities are independent, the estimates of individual activity standard deviations are used to estimate the standard deviation of completion time for the whole project.

It seems clear that only a few additional program statements are required to convert a basic critical-path program into one that computes the results based on the foregoing assumptions. To relax the assumptions about criticality and independence requires a much more sophisticated code. To date, most practical success has been obtained by using Monte Carlo (*q.v.*) simulation to obtain the mean and variance of total project time as well as a "probability of criticality" for each activity. Research continues into the development of computational methods for relaxing these assumptions without resorting to expensive simulation.

CPM Assumptions The variant known as CPM was developed for the construction industry, where the times for each activity are assumed to be perfectly known but controllable within limits depending on the amount of additional effort to be expended. Computation typically proceeds by first assuming a nominal time for each activity, and then using this to find a critical path in the normal manner. Activities on the critical path become candidates for "crashing," i.e. for a reduction in their times by payment of a premium for early completion. By successively relaxing activities on the critical path, a curve showing total project cost versus time to completion can be obtained. These computations can be done using a simple embellishment of the basic critical-path program. If, in addition, the value of the project as a function of its completion time is known, the mix of crash and normal activity times that best balances the crash-cost premiums against the overall value of the project can be found.

Other Major Variants

Costing Methods (*e.g. PERT/COST*) The structure provided by the network representation of the project is used as a framework for collecting and allocating project cost, replacing standard functional allocation schemes. This provides a more appropriate means for aggregating the individual costs of project activities. Software that performs this costing in conjunction with a project network is available, but is more limited than the critical-path computations themselves. Such methods are used in sur-

prisingly few projects, probably because of a reluctance to abandon standard cost-accounting methods, however inappropriate.

Resource Allocation The assumption of unlimited resources available when necessary is replaced by an assumption of limited resources of various sorts (e.g. computer time, carpenters, bulldozers). The problem then becomes one not only of scheduling activities to avoid delaying the overall project, but also of insuring that the scarce resources are available when necessary. This becomes particularly interesting in the so-called *multiship, multishop* problem where several projects compete simultaneously for the same resources. Computer codes available for this purpose are usually based on heuristic methods of optimization (*see* HEURISTIC).

Reference

1969. Wiest, J. D. and Levy, F. K. *A Management Guide to PERT/CPM.* Englewood Cliffs, NJ: Prentice-Hall.

E. GERALD HURST, JR.

PETRI NET

For articles on related subjects *see* AUTOMATA THEORY; CHOMSKY HIERARCHY; CONCURRENT PROGRAMMING; DATAFLOW; FORMAL LANGUAGES; MULTIPROCESSING; and PARALLEL PROCESSING: ALGORITHMS.

Petri nets are a popular and useful model for the representation of systems with concurrency or parallelism. They are names for, and have been developed from, the work of Carl Adam Petri, currently at the Gesellschaft für Mathematik und Datenverarbeitung in Bonn, Germany. A Petri net (see Fig. 1) is a graph with two types of nodes—*places* and *transitions*. Places are drawn as circles, while transitions are drawn as bars. Directed arcs (arrows) connect places to transitions and transitions to places. For each transition, the directed arcs define its *input* places (arc from place to transition) and its *output* places (arc from transition to place).

A Petri net is *executed* by defining a *marking* and then *firing* transitions. A marking is a distribution of *tokens* to the places of the Petri net. A token is represented on a Petri net graph by a small solid dot in a place. A transition is *enabled* whenever all of its input places have one or more tokens. A transition *fires* by removing one token from each of its input places and adding one token to each of its output places.

For example, in the marked Petri net of Fig. 1, two transitions are enabled. Transition b has one input (p_2), and that place has a token, so transition b is enabled. Similarly, transition e has tokens in both of its input places (p_4 and p_7), so it is also enabled. Transition d is not enabled, since there is no token in place p_5, one of its inputs. To fire transition b, we remove the token from p_2 and put a token in p_5 and a token in p_8 (its two outputs). This would enable transition d. Firing transition e will remove a token from both p_4 and p_7 and put a token in p_{10}.

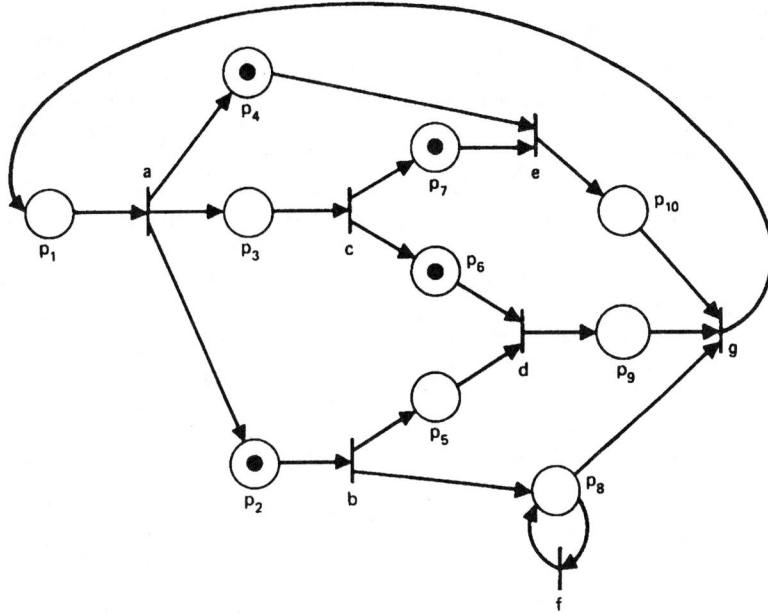

FIG. 1. An example Petri net.

If more than one transition is enabled, the firing of these transitions is generally asynchronous—they may fire simultaneously or at different times before or after each other. For example, in Fig. 1, transitions *b* and *e* are enabled and may fire completely independently. If two transitions share input places, then they are in *conflict* and only one can fire. In Fig. 1, transitions *f* and *g* are in conflict when a token is in place p_8.

Petri nets are a simple, elegant model of information flow. This makes them useful for describing and explaining systems, especially systems with concurrency and synchronization. Petri nets have been used mainly to model computer hardware (e.g. asynchronous circuits, pipelined computers, and computers with multiple functional units, such as the CDC 6600 and IBM 360/91) and computer software (e.g. sets of cooperating processes, communication protocols, and operating systems). Transitions represent *events* in the modeled system, while places represent *resources* or *conditions*. For example, Fig. 2 is a Petri net

model of a disk scheduling algorithm with two disk drives, a disk controller, and a channel (*q.v.*). The two available disk drives are represented by two tokens in the "disk drive available" place. Only one disk controller is available.

A Petri net can be associated with a nondeterministic automaton whose states correspond to the markings of the net. An execution of this automaton defines a *string* of events corresponding to a firing sequence of the Petri net. The set of all possible strings for a Petri net is its *language*. For example, if we associate the symbols (*a, b, c, d, e,*) with the transitions as shown in Fig. 2, then one possible string is *abcdebcde*; another string is *aabcdeabcdebcde*. In general, for Fig. 2, any string is made up of the substrings *a* and *bcde* such that the number of *b*s never exceeds the number of *a*s, from left to right. The *a*s can otherwise be arbitrarily interleaved with the *bcde* substrings.

The class of Petri net languages has been used as a basis for comparing the Petri net model with other models of parallel systems: If the language of a model *A* is (strictly)

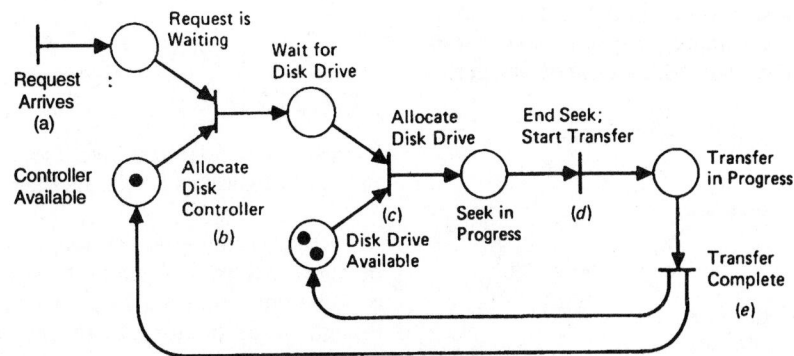

FIG. 2. A Petri net model of an algorithm for allocating a disk controller and disk drives.

contained in the language of a model B, then model A is (strictly) less powerful than model B; if the languages are equal, then the models are considered equivalent. The results of such comparisons must be judged with caution, since the representation of an execution by a linear string does not distinguish between the resolution of conflict (where only one sequence is possible) and parallelism (where many arbitrary interleavings of events are possible, but only one happens to occur). With this reservation, it can be stated that the Turing machine (*q.v.*) model is strictly more powerful than the Petri net model, while Petri nets are strictly more powerful than finite state models. All regular languages are Petri net languages, and all Petri net languages are context-sensitive (see Fig. 3).

A Petri net can be *analyzed* to determine properties of the modeled system. Analysis techniques have been developed to decide if the number of tokens in a Petri net is bounded, if tokens are conserved, if deadlocks can occur, or if mutual exclusion is violated. These correspond to important problems for concurrent systems, but more general analysis techniques would be useful. Current techniques are based on either of two approaches: (1) a matrix representation of the Petri net, or (2) representation of its state space as a tree (*q.v.*).

One typical analysis technique is the *reachability problem*: Given a Petri net with an initial marking and a desired final marking, is it possible to fire transitions and change the initial marking to the desired final marking? Researchers have shown that the reachability problem is decidable, although expensive. In the worst case, the time and memory (computational complexity - *q.v.*) needed to analyze a Petri net grows exponentially with the size of the Petri net.

Petri net execution does not include a concept of time, only the relative order of events. When performance metrics of systems are desired, the execution time of a transition must be defined. (A few models that associate time with places have been suggested, but they can be shown to be equivalent to times associated with transitions.) Two extended Petri net models are used for performance analysis: *Timed Petri nets* and *Stochastic Petri nets*. Both models have the concept of time (or a clock) associated with transition firings. For Timed Petri nets, the time value is constant; for Stochastic Petri nets, the time is a random variable (typically exponentially distributed).

The addition of a time for the firing of transitions adds significant complexity to the model. In the case of Timed Petri nets, the reachability set may be a subset of the reachability set of the underlying Petri net. When the

time is a constant time value, it has been shown that even the boundedness question becomes undecidable. In the case of stochastic Petri nets, the reachability set does not change with the introduction of time (assuming that the probability density of the random variables are non-zero on the interval 0 to ∞.

Continued work on Petri nets and their use is resulting in the development of a new research area called *general net theory*. Within this general theory, *special net theory* corresponds to the Petri net model described here.

References

1977. Peterson, J. L. "Petri Nets," *Computing Surveys* **9**, *3*: 223–252 (September).
1979. Agerwala, T. "Putting Petri Nets to Work," *Computer*, **12**, *12*: 85–94 (December).
1981. Peterson, J. L. *Petri Net Theory and the Modeling of Systems*. Englewood Cliffs, NJ: Prentice-Hall.
1982. Molloy, M. K. "Performance Modeling Using Stochastic Petri Nets," *IEEE Transactions on Computers*, **C-31**, *9*, (September) 913–917.
1985. Reisig, W. *Petri Nets*. Berlin: Springer-Verlag.
1989. Murata, T. "Petri Nets; properties, analysis, and applications," *Proc. of the IEEE*, **77**, *4* (April), 541–580.

MICHAEL K. MOLLOY and JAMES L. PETERSON

PHYSICAL UNIT. *See* LOGICAL AND PHYSICAL UNITS.

PICTURE PROCESSING. *See* IMAGE PROCESSING.

PIPELINING. *See* PARALLEL PROCESSING: PRINCIPLES; and SUPERCOMPUTERS.

PIXEL. *See* COMPUTER GRAPHICS; and IMAGE PROCESSING.

PL/I. *See* PROCEDURE-ORIENTED LANGUAGES.

POINTER

For articles on related subjects *see* ADDRESSING; DATA STRUCTURES; LIST PROCESSING; STORAGE ORGANIZATION; and TREE.

A digital computer memory contains *cells*, which may be referred to by *addresses*. The address of a memory cell is sometimes referred to as a *pointer*, since it may be thought of as pointing to the memory cell to which it refers.

Pointers may occur at the level of machine language both as direct addresses and as indirect addresses.

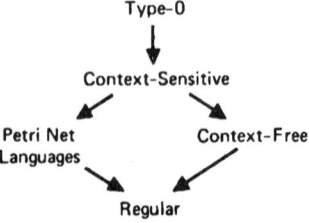

FIG. 3.   The place of Petri net languages in the Chomsky hierarchy of languages. An arrow indicates proper containment.

LOAD   100   This assembly-language instruction specifies that the content of memory cell 100 is to be loaded into the accumulator. The address 100 is a pointer to the memory cell whose address is 100.

LOAD   *100   This indirect-addressing assembly-language instruction (indicated by the *) specifies that location 100 contains the address of the quantity to be loaded into the accumulator. The address 100 is a pointer to a pointer.

In general, a pointer p_1 may point to a cell containing a pointer p_2, and the pointer p_2 may in turn contain a pointer to a cell containing a pointer p_3. A sequence of pointers $p_1, p_2, p_3...$ such that p_i points to a cell containing p_{i+1} for $i = 1, 2,...$ is called a *pointer chain*.

Pointers also occur in high-level languages such as C (*q.v.*) and Pascal. In C the declaration

    int *p

defines *p* to be of type "pointer to integer." If *A* is a variable of type integer, then the address of *A* can be assigned to *p* by writing

    p = &A

Standard Pascal has no "address of" operator but in Turbo Pascal the unary operator @ is the exact counterpart of the C operator &.

Dynamic data structures may be implemented as directed graphs in which vertices represent memory cells and directed edges represent pointers between memory cells. For example, the tree structure in Fig. 1 contains five memory cells *a, b, c, d, e*, with a pointer from *a* to *b* and pointer chains from *a* through *c* to *d* and *e*.

In general, pointers may be used to connect individual memory cells and also to point from one composite data structure to another. For example, in the diagram the pointer from *a* to *c* may be thought of not merely as a pointer from *a* to the cell *c*, but also as a pointer from *a* to the subtree having *c* as its root.

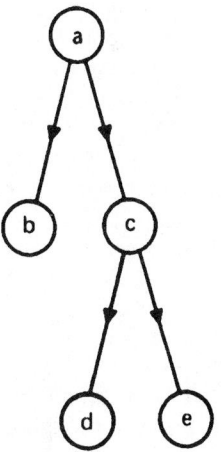

FIG. 1.

Pointers are essential in any composite data structure for linking components of the data structure. Nevertheless, they must be used with care because indiscriminate use of pointers leads to undesirable complexity in data structures in much the same way that indiscriminate use of **gotos** leads to control structure complexity.

PETER WEGNER

POINTING DEVICE.   *See* INTERACTIVE INPUT DEVICES.

POLISH NOTATION

For articles on related subjects *see* COMPILER CONSTRUCTION; EXPRESSION; LANGUAGE PROCESSORS; PARSING; PROCEDURE-ORIENTED LANGUAGES; and STACK.

In 1951, the Polish logician Jan Lukasiewicz devised a *parenthesis-free* notation for logic. This notation, extended for use in algebra and other operator-operand systems, has become known as *Polish notation*. Basically, by consistently placing operators before (or after) their operands, the need for parentheses is eliminated, provided each operator has a fixed number of operands.

Polish notation was originally developed in the *prefix* form, in which the operators precede the operands. The *postfix* or *suffix* form, also known as *reverse Polish notation* or *RPN*, which is logically equivalent to the prefix form, has been widely used in computing. Many compilers first transform an arithmetic expression from its ordinary or *infix* form into RPN, so that its evaluation can be done in a single left-to-right scan. RPN is also used as the basis of operation for some pocket calculators, such as those produced by Hewlett-Packard. However, many people find it difficult to shift their thinking from the infix notation that they have used for years to the concept of providing all of the operands before the operator, so RPN calculators have not taken over the market.

Parenthesis elimination is made possible by the fixed number of operands for each operator. Thus if "+" denotes ordinary addition, we expect two operands. Hence, "+ab" (prefix) and "ab+" (postfix) are as clearly understandable as "a + b". Similarly, if "~" denotes logical negation, exactly one operand is expected. The minus sign causes a problem, since it may be associated with one operand (negative numbers) or two (subtraction). Agreement to limit its use to defining negative numbers solves this problem at the expense of writing subtraction as "a + (− b)" rather than "a − b". Table 1 gives several examples of Polish notation.

If a prefix expression is evaluated from right to left, then whenever an operator is encountered, its operands are those that have most recently been evaluated. Hence, the operator can be immediately processed. The same is true of a postfix expression evaluated from left to right. For example, the evaluation sequence for *a+bc is c, b, +bc, a, *a+bc. Similarly, the expression +*abc (i.e. (a*b)

TABLE 1 Polish Notation

Expression	Prefix	Postfix
a + (− b)	+ a − b	ab − +
(− a) + b	+ − ab	a − b +
a* (b + c)	*a + bc	abc + *
(a * b) + c	+ * a b c	a b * c +
(p⊃q)≡(~p∨q)	≡⊃pq∨~pq	pq⊃p~q∨≡

+ c) is evaluated in the order c, b, a, *ab, +*abc. Thus, evaluated subexpressions placed on a stack are naturally "popped" from the stack in the order of their use. These two properties—ease of evaluation and unique representation of an expression without use of parentheses or other punctuation—justify Polish notation for use with computer languages and in language processors.

A variant of the prefix notation known as *Cambridge Polish notation* underlies the syntax of the programming language LISP. Cambridge Polish notation allows operators to have a variable number of operands or *scope*, but requires that the operator and all of its operands be enclosed in a pair of parentheses. The operator ADD, for example, can then be used to add together any list of numbers:

(ADD 5 7) evaluates to 12
(ADD 3 7 −2 5 9) evaluates to 22
(ADD 11) evaluates to 11

ROBERT R. KORFHAGE

POLITICAL APPLICATIONS

For articles related subjects *see* COMPUTING AND SOCIETY; and SOCIAL SCIENCE APPLICATIONS.

The political process admits definitions ranging from the very narrow, restricting the term to the campaign process, to a very broad definition that includes much of the legislative and executive activities. In this brief review of computers and politics, we adopt a relatively restrictive view. Our description of the employment of computers will be discussed under three major applications: (1) the campaign process, (2) vote projection, and (3) political reapportionment.

Campaign Process By far the major employment of computers in the political campaign takes advantage of the equipment to maintain mailing lists and generate computer-composed letters that are personalized to the extent that sentences or paragraphs reflect the previously indexed interests of the addressee. Frequently, that individual's name is embedded in the text of the letter to enhance personalization still further.

Mailing lists are maintained that specify for each person a set of personal characteristics, such as residence, degree of economic affluence, gender, religion, and prior political affiliations. In addition, the lists are indexed to reflect a history of prior campaign contributions and those political, social, and economic issues sufficiently interesting to the individual to have prompted a previous expression of opinion to a legislator or a candidate.

Although no hard statistics are available, it is estimated that 90–98% of computer applications in the campaign process relate to campaign mailings and solicitations of contributions. The small remaining balance includes more sophisticated uses of computers in the management of a campaign. Among these applications are (1) the organization and maintenance of and coping with changes in the campaign activities using PERT (*q.v.*) techniques, and (2) the development and use of models for the allocation of funds or of the candidate's time and the simulation of a campaign in different jurisdictions, where the interplay of the emphasis of different issues will have varying effects upon the voting population. Such models require a large database of voter attitudes towards issues and knowledge of the extent to which the emphasis, either in support of or in opposition to a particular issue, will sway an already committed or politically leaning voter.

The existence of a database of this type allows a final application of computers to the campaign process, the tabulation and analysis of public opinion polls wherein voter opinions on issues are related to degrees of candidate support. The results of the analyses serve as aids to campaign strategy in determining issues and areas of strength and weakness that may be defined geographically or in terms of characteristics of segments of the voting population. A candidate's campaign strategist may be able to identify issues that may influence "undecided" or "leaning" voters, without alienating those who have already decided to support the candidate.

The near universal availability of increasingly powerful personal computers that have access to many centralized dial-up databases has made the computer an essential tool used by political theorists and campaign strategists.

In 1992 for the first time an attempt is being made to have U.S. presidential candidates debate and make policy statements on computer networks and bulletin boards (*q.v.*) but it is too soon to say if this will be effective.

Vote Projection The use of computers by the television networks to project early voting returns into estimates of the final result was the first introduction of the computer and its possibilities to large parts of the U.S. population. The first broad-scale application of computers to vote projections began in the 1952 Eisenhower-Stevenson race, making use of a UNIVAC I. By the time of the 1960 election, all networks were using some form of computer assistance, and the 1964 presidential election saw the first full, large-scale, three-network competition, each network making use of its own system and its own computer to project the election results. The mathematical models that form the basis of the projection procedures for the three networks differed markedly at that time. Since then, there has been a tendency to conform to a more uniform philosophy, although considerable differences in approach and in execution still exist among the three major TV networks.

As an example, the technique used by one network makes use of an equation of the form

$$P = w_b P_b + w_p P_p + w_v P_v$$

where the ws are weights and the Ps are individual estimates of the vote for, say, the Democratic candidate obtained by considerations of the baseline (b), key precincts (p), and raw vote (v). P_b is an estimate based upon a compilation of all available pre-election information, including polls and informed opinion. P_p is an estimate based upon the change in a select sample of key precincts over a prior comparable election. The sample precincts are carefully checked to ensure that the characteristics of the voting population in each precinct have not varied significantly since the prior comparable election; e.g. that what had been a blue-collar working class precinct has not been replaced by a luxury high-rise development. The estimate provided by P_v is the actual raw vote as it is assembled at state or regional collection centers from counties and individual precincts and transmitted to the networks. The raw vote may be adjusted for reporting patterns if, for example, a larger proportion of the more Democratic urban vote typically is reported before the more Republican rural vote in a state.

Except for P_b, all quantities in the equation are constantly changing. At any time, the sum of the weighting coefficients, the ws, must be unity. They reflect the relative importance of the factors associated with them in the equation. At the beginning of the evening, $w_b = 1$ and the other two coefficients are zero, reflecting the fact that the only component of the estimate is the pre-election baseline. As the evening continues, the dominant effect is generally assumed by the second term $w_p P_p$, with its magnitude being a function both of the number of key precincts whose returns have been entered into the model and the degree of consistency they have shown. As more raw vote is received, the first two coefficients tend to zero; w_v assumes dominance and ultimately becomes 1 when all precincts have reported. In those states where absentee ballots are counted in a special way after the votes cast on election day are counted, provision is made to incorporate the effect of the absentee ballots into the model.

Operations of the networks have evolved from intense competition in reporting the largest vote returns and earliest (accurate) projections to a pooled operation that, incidentally, saves each network an estimated 9 million dollars each quadrennial election cycle. Pooling has eliminated the differentiating characteristics of the networks, except for the subjective appeal of their on-air talent and the interpretation and analysis of the vote results.

The major networks and wire services combined to form the News Election Service (NES), which was responsible for collecting the actual vote at local precinct, county, and ward levels, aggregating this vote into higher-level political jurisdictions, and sending updated totals at rapid intervals to all subscribers simultaneously. The networks agreed that the NES vote would be the only vote displayed in front of their cameras.

Beginning with the 1990 election, Cable News Network (CNN) and the other networks combined to support Voter Research and Surveys (VSR), whose nucleus was the CBS operation and its key staff. VSR was organized to provide the actual vote, exit poll data, and projections of individual races. VSR advocates claimed that, as a result, "there was no longer the fierce, and somewhat artificial, competition" that previously marked network election broadcasts. Unfortunately, however, the VSR operation failed to perform as promised in delivering results of exit polls and other data as promised to its subscribers, including several of the nation's leading newspapers. It was reported that VSR personnel were afraid a power surge would short out the computers at a critical stage of the operation, and VSR projections, absent the competition, were conservative and relatively slow. Even so, one projected race was "uncalled" for a time before being reinstated as correct.

Political Reapportionment The Supreme Court's "one person-one vote" decision in *Reynolds vs. Sims* in 1964 led to an investigation of the use of computers to aid legislators in reapportioning their electoral jurisdictions to be acceptable to the Court's dictum. Most applications have been to state legislatures, but there have also been applications to Congressional redistricting within a state and in the drawing of district lines by municipal councils.

The various models that have been developed, most of which depend upon a high-speed computer for their practicality, differ in their approach to the specification of initial conditions for the legislative reapportionment and in the criteria used to find the best allocation.

The less politically sophisticated "non-partisan" models attempt to lay a rectangular grid across a state, modifying the lines so as to obtain as nearly an equal proportion of the electorate in each of the districts as possible. Other models that reflect a greater degree of political sophistication commence with an initial allocation based upon the existing legislative boundaries and then perturbing them in such a way as to obtain population parity. To be practical, all models must recognize political boundaries, such as towns and counties, and major geographic barriers, such as bodies of water and mountain ranges.

Mathematical models and associated computer programs have been developed by various academic and commercial organizations. They differ in their degree of political sophistication, the extent to which on-line graphics are used, and in their ability to introduce degrees of partisanship, such as to give as great a representation as possible to one political party or one ethnic group.

References

1964. Moshman, Jack. "The Role of Computers in Election Night Broadcasting," *Advances in Computers V.* New York: Academic Press.

1972. Chartrand, Robert I. *Computers and Political Campaigning.* New York: Spartan Books.

1973. Moshman, Jack and Kokiko, E. M. "A Redistricting Algorithm Applied to Geographic Reorganization of Circuit Courts," *Annals of the New York Academy of Sciences* **219.**

1990. Berke, Richard L. "TV Networks Join in Voter Surveys," *New York Times,* CXL, 7 November, A1 and B6.

JACK MOSHMAN

POLLING

For articles on related subjects *see* CONTENTION; LOCAL AREA NETWORK; MULTIPLEXING; and NETWORKS, COMPUTER.

In computing, the problem often arises where a number of processes or devices compete for shared resources. *Polling* or contention techniques are used to resolve such problems and enforce discipline.

In polling, the order of accessing the shared resource is managed so that competition is avoided and each process or device can use the shared resource for a limited time only. Polling can be centralized or distributed.

Centralized polling requires a master process or device to control access by subservient devices (*slaves*) to the shared resource. The master simply addresses or polls each slave to provide access when it is needed. If access is not needed, the addressed slave sends a *negative acknowledgement*, which causes the master to poll the next slave. A polling system has the advantage that either all slaves can receive equal access, or else priority can be given by polling some slaves more often than others. Furthermore, a polling system can be arranged to function effectively over long distances since it can be adjusted to compensate for long propagation delays. For this reason, it can be used to connect a large number of widely separated slave stations to a master station or computer over a single communication line. The disadvantage is that there is a single point of failure. When the master goes down, so does the entire system. The situation is similar to a chairperson who controls a meeting by choosing the order in which to recognize those who raise their hands.

Distributed polling is usually implemented by passing a *token* in a predetermined order amongst devices connected by a bus (*q.v.*) or a ring. The owner of the token, which is a special bit pattern, has the exclusive use of the bus or ring if it has data to transfer. If not, it passes the token to the next device. The *token bus* or *token ring* systems, as they are called, provide the fairness and distance insensitivity of the polling system. However, they rely on the reliability of the nodes, and provision must be made to recover gracefully from failures that cause the token to disappear. Here, the situation is similar to a meeting where people have the opportunity to speak in a predetermined order, perhaps the order in which they sign in.

JOHN S. SOBOLEWSKI

PORTABILITY

For articles on related subjects *see* COMPATIBILITY; CROSS ASSEMBLERS AND COMPILERS; SOFTWARE; SOFTWARE FLEXIBILITY; and TRANSPARENCY.

Software is said to be *portable* if it can, with reasonable effort, be made to run on computers other than the one for which it was originally written. Portable software proves its worth when computers are replaced or when the same software is run on many different computers, whether widely dispersed or at a single site.

The simplest aid to portability is the use of standard high-level languages such as Cobol, Fortran or Pascal. Such standard languages do, however, have the following deficiencies: (1) standards change over time; (2) compilers often support non-standard language extensions; (3) standards are rarely completely precise; (4) programs sometimes require non-standard parts to interface with the local operating environment. Therefore, extra work is needed to make software properly portable. Useful methods include the use of language subsets, common to all compilers, and the use of verifier programs to ensure adherence to subsets; the use of *preprocessors* (*q.v.*) to map a source program into several alternative forms, thus catering to variations among compilers; separating out machine-dependent aspects of software; and the use of portable compilers (which themselves may use a so-called "abstract machine" as a common interface between the source language and all machine languages, thus aiding their own portability).

Several widely used programming languages owe some of their success to the availability of a portable compiler. In addition to Fortran and Cobol, these include BCPL (using the O-code abstract machine), Snobol, using the SIL abstract machine and others, UCSD Pascal (using the P-code abstract machine), and Algol-68 using Z-code. Since the late 1950s, attempts have been made to produce UNCOL (Universal Computer-Oriented Language), a universal abstract machine, to act as a common interface between all programming languages and all computers. Some computer scientists, however, fear that all such attempts are bound to fail because of their excessive generality.

It costs planning and effort to produce software that is portable. Moreover, on any one computer, a portable program will be less efficient than a specially hand-tailored one. Nevertheless, given the huge cost of rewriting non-portable software, an investment in portability is normally one that will repay handsomely.

Reference

1977. Brown, P. J. (Ed.). *Software Portability*. Cambridge University Press.

PETER J. BROWN

PORT, MEMORY

For articles on related subjects, *see* BUS; CHANNEL; INPUT-OUTPUT CONTROL SYSTEM; INPUT-OUTPUT INSTRUCTIONS; MEMORY: AUXILIARY; and POLLING.

In simple systems the main memory has a single *port* or logical connection through which data is transferred under CPU control. In more elegant systems, a single memory port is connected to a *bus* (*q.v.*) via which several CPUs and I/O devices have memory access. On still larger systems, bus traffic can become so intense that the speed

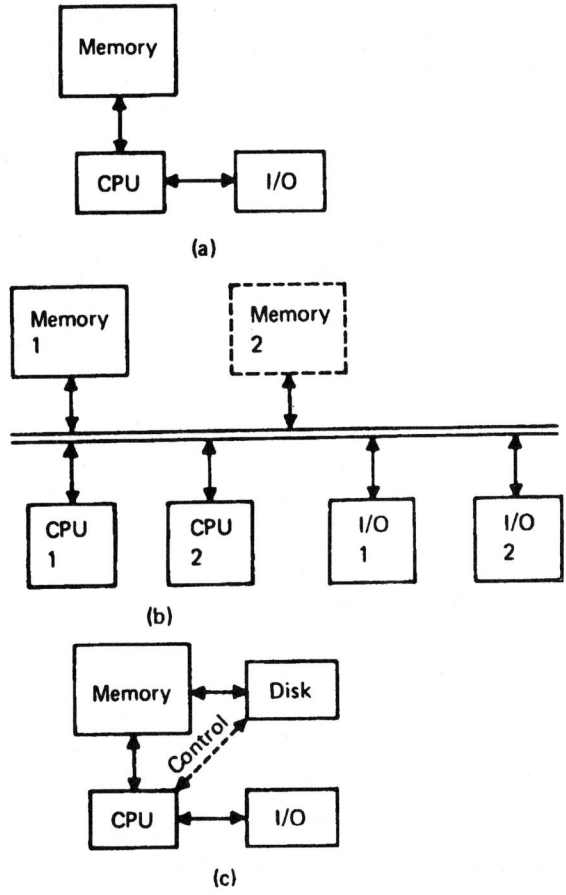

FIG. 1 Memory port connections: (a) single port, simply connected; (b) single-port, bus-connected; (c) double-port, servicing disk and CPU on separate ports.

of some important high-speed activity may be sacrificed. Because the CPU to memory path is normally high speed, a second port for the CPU may be added to the memory. Since data rates are high and over-run is possible, another port for backup store or bulk store may be provided. For example, a DEC VAX may have several ports connected typically to CPU, disk, or special high-speed I/O. In some cases, multiport memory is used to interface between autonomous buses in multiprocessor, multimemory systems; this allows, for example, the I/O and internal buses to communicate as needed through memory but to proceed normally without interference from each other's traffic.

Within a multiport memory there must, of course, be some form of interlock (*q.v.*) mechanism to arbitrate conflict between port requests. Often, a cyclic polling scheme insures access to memory by each of the ports on some priority basis with a guarantee of minimum service.

The ports on a personal computer are classified as being either serial (one bit at a time) or parallel (one byte at a time).

KENNETH C. SMITH AND ADEL S. SEDRA

POSTSCRIPT

For articles on related subject *see* DESKTOP PUBLISHING; METAFONT; PROBLEM-ORIENTED LANGUAGES; PROGRAMMING LANGUAGES; TEX; and WORD PROCESSING.

PostScript is a device-independent page description language. Page description languages are programming languages that are optimized to render document images on display devices. Display devices may be workstation (*q.v.*) screens, laser printers, film recorders, fax machines, or phototypesetters. PostScript programming is especially applicable to situations where a user knows a mathematical description of an image and wants to know what it looks like.

The PostScript Language The language specification for PostScript is in the public domain. It is derived from work that was done at Xerox Parc in the late 1970s and early 1980s. When Xerox declined to make this work the basis of a product, the Adobe Systems Corporation was formed and developed a PostScript implementation that has become the de facto standard page description language in the marketplace. Adobe Systems licensed the technology to printer manufacturers, most notably to Apple Computer for the Apple LaserWriter product which was introduced in January 1985. Steve Jobs (*see* ENTREPRENEURS) saw PostScript and the Apple LaserWriter as the missing pieces required to create a larger market for Apple Macintosh computers. PostScript is as responsible as anything else for creating the demand for desktop publishing technology that is often credited to the program Aldus PageMaker. Barely three years later, publishing products had to support PostScript output in order to be commercially viable.

PostScript source code is characterized not only by device independence, but also by an all-ASCII representation and a postfix syntax that makes it easy to generate from programs. Like Forth (*q.v.*), its stack-oriented operations are interpreted and not compiled. Dynamic binding (*q.v.*) and the postfix syntax make it possible to produce fast interpreters. PostScript supports a relatively small number of data types and a rich set of more than 200 primitives that allow specification of text, line drawings, images, and color. It supports system-defined operators, names, and dictionaries that are accessible and easily modified by expert-level programmers.

In PostScript, a page is represented as a bit map, one bit per picture element (*pixel*). When an actual page is printed, each pixel corresponding to a 1-bit is printed in black and each pixel corresponding to a 0-bit is printed in white (actually, left blank). To preserve machine independence, however, one is not allowed to read from or write to the bit map. Instead, programs include "painting" operators that set and clear bits within defined areas of the bit map.

PostScript is designed to be portable. The all-ASCII representation allows PostScript files to be transmitted across electronic networks easily and reliably. The description of objects and paths are separated from their imaging for any particular display technology or device.

```
%
% Define a procedure to print the words
% "Heather and Courtney" on the three sides
% of an imaginary box centered at the origin.
/hcprint
  {
  gsave
  90 rotate
   - 45 90 moveto (Heather) show
   - 90 rotate
   - 21 90 moveto (and) show
   - 90 rotate
   - 54 90 moveto (Courtney) show
  grestore
  }
def

% Make the current font 30 point Times
% Roman.
/Times-Roman findfont 30 scalefont setfont

% Move the coordinate system origin 3
% inches up and right.
216 216 translate

% Draw a 240 degree circular arc centered
% near the origin.
9 9 72 - 30 210 arc stroke

% Print "Heather and Courtney" 20 times at
% 20 increasingly dark gray levels, each
% time moving the origin slightly up and
% to the right.
.95 - .05 0 {setgray hcprint 1 1 translate}
for

% Print "Heather and Courtney" one more
% time in white.
1 setgray hcprint

% Produce the printed page.
showpage
```

FIG. 1.   A short PostScript program.

Objects can be stroked or filled. Stroking a path produces an image on the page consisting of a line of specified thickness. Filling a path paints areas inside the path with a specified gray level. Paths and outlines can be specified as sequences of lines, circular arcs, and Bezier cubic *splines* (*q.v.*). PostScript also supports embedded bit-map images.

PostScript's generality, power, and flexibility is a two-edged sword. Coding and debugging complex images using native PostScript can be time-consuming and difficult. Unless special care is taken, name collisions can occur between system and user operations; and applications can suffer at the hands of redefined system operators.

A typical small PostScript program is shown in Fig. 1. Lines that begin with the percent sign (%) are merely

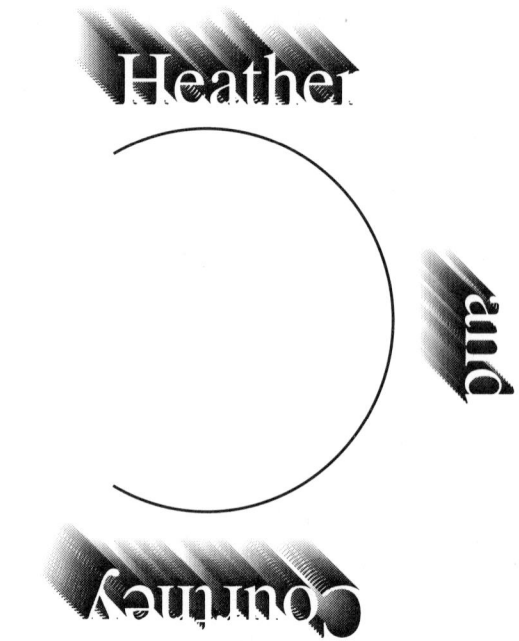

FIG. 2.   Output of PostScript program of Fig. 1.

comments. The printed output generated by the program is shown in Fig. 2.

Encapsulated PostScript   Since users often want to be able to reuse data and information, it is essential for one application to generate well-behaved PostScript code for use by another, that is, it should be easy to import and export PostScript code among different applications. For example, graphics objects or spreadsheet (*q.v.*) results often need to be incorporated into documents produced, using different desktop publishing software products.

Encapsulated PostScript provides software developers with rules and guidelines for producing PostScript code that can be easily exported. It defines a control block that contains specific information in a standard format, followed by a PostScript definition of an image and, optionally, by a hex-encoded bit-mapped representation of the image for display on raster devices that do not support a PostScript interpreter (e.g. bit-mapped screens on personal computers and workstations).

PostScript Fonts   PostScript has revolutionized the way people think about and use fonts. Characters in font families (e.g. Times Roman, Helvetica) and font style (e.g. normal, italic, bold) are largely treated as special cases of filling outlines. For this reason, characters can be scaled (e.g. 10 points, 18 points, 72 points [1 inch]), stretched, or rotated just like any other PostScript object. Outline fonts are compact, on the order of 150 bytes, and contain specially encoded "hints" to the PostScript interpreter that improve their appearance at the 300 dots/inch resolution supported by popular laser printers. By contrast, characters stored as rasters (i.e. bit-maps) do not scale well beyond about 15% of their design size and grow in storage requirements in proportion to the square of the resolution (e.g. doubling the resolution quadruples the storage requirement for a character at a particular point size). However, fonts available in raster format but not as outlines can be downloaded and processed using PostScript's support for bit-mapped images.

References

1985. Adobe Systems, Inc. *PostScript Language Tutorial and Cookbook*. Reading, MA: Addison-Wesley.
1985. Adobe Systems Inc. *PostScript Language Reference Manual*. Reading, MA: Addison-Wesley.
1987. Pelli, Denis G. "Programming in PostScript," *Byte*, **12**, *5* (May) 185–202.

DAVID L. RODGERS

POWER USER

For articles on related subjects *see* GURU; and WIZARD.

A *power user* is a person who knows and uses a particular piece of software to its maximum extent. The term is always qualified by the name of the applicable software; we speak of a Unix power user, a Wordperfect power user, a Lotus 1-2-3 power user, etc. Such a person is not usually a programmer who can modify the system, but rather one who knows its reference manual inside out and who can apply not only that knowledge, but also additional "lore" that he or she constantly gleans from trade magazines, bulletin boards (*q.v.*), conferences, user groups, and E-mail caucuses with others who share a similar desire to master use of a particular item of software.

EDWIN D. REILLY

POWERS, JAMES

For articles on related subjects *see* HOLLERITH, HERMAN; HOLLERITH'S MACHINE; PUNCHED CARD; and PUNCHED CARD MACHINERY.

James Powers, born in Odessa, Russia in 1871, was an inventor of punched card accounting machinery and founder of the Powers Accounting Machine Company. He graduated from the Technical School of Odessa and was for a time employed in a mechanical shop connected with the University of Odessa in making scientific instruments. He emigrated to the U.S. in 1889 and was employed by various engineering concerns, including Western Electric. He obtained several patents in his own name and did experimental work on office machines, including typewriters, adding machines,and cash registers, as well as early work on telephones and automatic machines of various types.

In 1907, the United States Bureau of the Census employed Powers as a mechanical expert to improve the punched card tabulating machinery developed by Herman Hollerith for the 1890 and 1900 censuses. Hollerith

FIG. 1. James Powers.

himself had broken with the Bureau in 1905 following a dispute with the director of the census. Powers introduced several major improvements to the existing census machinery, including an electrically operated card punch and a printing tabulator. In 1911, Powers left the Bureau of the Census and incorporated the Powers Accounting Machine Company to develop punched card machines for commercial applications. (In doing so, Powers followed the precedent of Herman Hollerith who, in 1896, incorporated the Tabulating Machine Company, which later became IBM.) During 1912–13, Powers and his assistant, W. W. Lasker, developed a range of machines that included the "slide" and "visible" card punches, the "double-deck" horizontal sorter, and printing and non-printing tabulating machines. The machines were actively marketed, beginning in 1913, and the first overseas operations were established shortly afterwards. Although the early Powers machines had several important advantages over those offered by Hollerith, the U.S. Powers organization never prospered as well as its competitor. The overseas operations, however, developed largely independent of the parent company, and in their territories they competed with IBM on much more nearly equal terms. In 1927, the U.S. Powers organization was acquired by Remington Rand, and Powers himself retired into obscurity and died in 1935.

MARTIN CAMPBELL-KELLY

PRAGMATICS. *See* Syntax, Semantics, and Pragmatics.

PRECEDENCE. *See* Operator Precedence.

PRECISION

For articles on related subjects *see* Arithmetic, Computer; Numbers and Number Systems; Significance Arithmetic; and Significant Digit.

For a numeric representation system that employs strings of symbols from a finite alphabet to represent numbers, the *precision attribute* of a symbol string denotes the *length* of the string, and possibly also positional information for determining a base point of the string. Those numbers representable by finite length symbol strings are termed the *finite precision numbers* of that numeric representation system.

For the fixed-point radix representation $d_m d_{m-1} \cdots d_1 d_0 \cdot d_{-1} d_{-2} \cdots d_l$, $d_m \neq 0$, the precision attribute is the triple $(m - l + 1, - l, m + 1)$; e.g. 310.25 has precision (5, 2, 3) and 0.0024 has precision (2, 4, − 2). If $l \leq 0 \leq m$, then $- l$ and $m + 1$ may be interpreted as the number of digits in the fractional and integer parts, respectively, of the $m - l + 1$ digit number. The precision triple $(m - l + 1, - l, m + 1)$ thus provides both the number of digits and base-point normalization information.

For a radix number system where computed radix representations are truncated to exhibit only significant digits, the precision attribute identifies the significant digits. In this restricted environment, precision is a measure of accuracy. For integer radix-number systems such as the "8-digit decimal integers" or the "6-digit hexadecimal integers," the precision attribute provides simply a measure of the magnitude of the representable integers.

The precision attribute is utilized for numeric formats in input, output, and internal storage allocation in high-level programming languages. In PL/I, for example, precision rules are employed to compute the precision attribute of program variables at compile time to help optimize storage utilization.

Precision, as defined here, is intimately related to the displayed representation of a number in contrast to *accuracy*, which is concerned with freedom from error. Thus, a highly precise number (i.e. one displayed with many digits) may be quite misleading regarding accuracy, since the accuracy would still be limited to the number of significant digits independent of the number of digits displayed.

Reference

1976. Matula, D. W. "Radix Arithmetic: Digital Algorithms for Computer Architecture," in Yeh, R. (Ed.), *Applied Computation Theory: Analysis, Design and Modeling.* Englewood Cliffs, N J: Prentice-Hall.

David W. Matula

PREPROCESSOR

For articles on related subjects *see* Language Processors; Macroinstruction; Object Code; and Source Code.

A *preprocessor* is a language processor that accepts as input statements written in one computer language and writes to an output file statements that are acceptable to a similar but less complete language. Suppose, for example, that we have available a standard Pascal compiler but that we would like to be able to write programs that are compatible with extended versions of Pascal that are richer in string manipulation constructs. An input file is prepared that contains source code for a particular program written in the extended language. The preprocessor must read each statement and parse it to see if its syntax pertains to string manipulation. If not, the preprocessor passes the statement along unchanged. If so, the preprocessor writes a sequence of standard Pascal statements that, when later compiled and executed as part of the artificially created (and longer) source file, produces the same effect as the desired string manipulation statement. The process is shown schematically in Fig. 1.

As the figure shows, preprocessing inevitably requires two translation passes rather than one, but on most computers the user can be given the feel of one-pass translation through creation of a library of system commands that, when invoked, runs through the multiple operations in response to a short sequence of keystrokes or one click of a picking device.

Preprocessor operation is very similar to macro expansion, but takes place at an earlier phase of language translation (*see* Macroinstruction). A macro language and assemblers that support a macro facility accept macro definitions as an integral part of language translation and then expand instances of the macro when encountered in

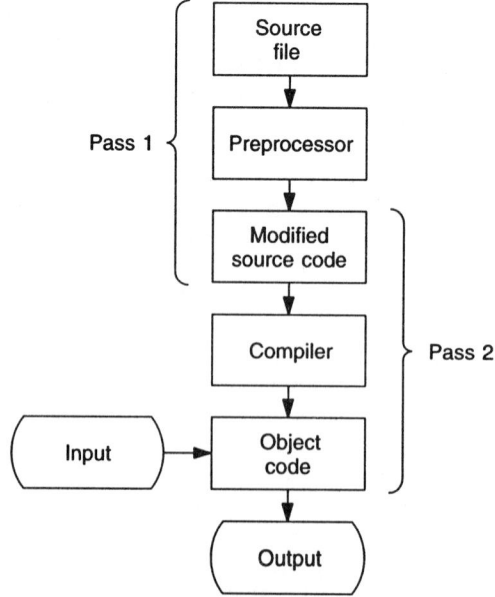

FIG. 1. Preprocessing, shown as pass 1, precedes compilation and execution, shown as pass 2.

the source code, all in one pass. To cope with a language that lacks a macro facility, we can write a preprocessor whose macro definitions are essentially embedded in its parsing logic. The definitions correspond to the syntactical constructs we wish we had in the host language but do not. The preprocessor then detects incoming statements that correspond to these constructs and expands them before the host language translator has a chance to reject them as being ungrammatical.

EDWIN D. REILLY

PRIVACY, COMPUTERS AND

For articles on related subjects *see* COMPUTER CRIME; COMPUTING AND SOCIETY; and LEGAL ASPECTS OF COMPUTING.

Privacy is a complex legal concept that covers a variety of individual rights. The rights associated with privacy stem from both statutory and case law, but essentially all of this body of law was created in the twentieth century.

Four forms of tort have been loosely grouped as invasions of privacy. These torts include intrusion on seclusion, appropriation of a person's name or likeness, unreasonable publication of private facts, and portraying a person in a false light. The latter two torts are of most concern to computer operators inasmuch as personnel-related files can contain highly personal data as well as stale or misleading information that could be negligently or even intentionally released to parties having no privilege to have such data.

Privacy refers to much more than certain forms of tort. One definition of privacy advanced by Meredith Mendez is: "Privacy is a condition in which individuals, groups, or institutions can determine for themselves, when, how, and to what extent information about themselves is communicated to others." Although this definition justifies considering the four torts mentioned earlier as invasions of privacy, it goes beyond that in suggesting that persons should be able to place limits on information that is generally available concerning themselves. Following this idea to its logical conclusion, persons should be able to control what data concerning themselves could be stored in computer files and who would have the right to access such data.

However, individuals' desires for controlling what others know about them must be balanced by the legitimate requirements that various businesses and governmental agencies and, possibly, the public as well may have for that information. Congress and state legislatures have passed legislation that allows governmental agencies to collect data, but that also imposes certain restrictions on the data and allows persons about whom data is kept to gain copies of their files. Similar laws also exist with respect to financial institutions, credit bureaus, and certain other businesses. We will review such legislation briefly later in this article.

The Mendez definition still concerns only one class of rights associated with the more general concept of privacy. The Supreme Court of the United States, in Whalen *v.* Roe, 429 U.S. 589 (1977), declared that privacy protects at least two different types of interests. "One is the individual interest in avoiding disclosure of personal matters, and another is the interest in independence in making certain kinds of important decisions." Whalen *v.* Roe involved the existence of a state database of physicians who had prescribed certain drugs. The Court found that "neither the immediate nor threatened impact...on either the reputation or the independence of patients...is sufficient to constitute an invasion of any right or liberty protected by the Fourteenth Amendment." In this, as in almost all cases in which a privacy right is alleged to exist, the court balances the needs of society against the claims of the individual.

The statutory law concerning privacy has almost exclusively concerned information about individuals. An example of such legislation is the Electronic Communications Privacy Act of 1986 (ECPA), which modifies chapters 119 and 120 of Title 18 of the United States Code. In 1985, the Office of Technology Assessment released a report that highlighted shortcomings in existing legislation concerning governmental surveillance and gave statistics on the extent to which federal agencies were involved in electronic surveillance. For example, although safeguards existed concerning tapping analog voice telephone transmissions, no such safeguards existed for digital transmissions and transmissions of data where no aural conversation was involved. The ECPA was a response to this report.

The ECPA makes it a crime to access intentionally and without authorization a facility through which electronic communication is provided or to exceed intentionally one's authorization to such access and thereby obtain, alter, or prevent authorized access to a wire or electronic communication while it is in electronic storage in such a system. The ECPA also prohibits, although without criminal penalties, unauthorized releasing of information carried, maintained, or stored on an electronic communication service.

The Right to Privacy Act of 1974, 15 USC Section 552a, primarily implemented through Office of Management and Budget Circular A-108 as amended, supposedly provides for only limited disclosure of any records that a federal agency keeps on an individual. The agency is not entitled to release a record about an individual to any agency or person unless it has first obtained either the written consent of or a written request from the individual whose record is involved. There are, however, so many exceptions to this general rule that the privacy protection accorded by this act may be minimal. Among the exceptions are: (1) the agency's own personnel can use the record to perform their duties; (2) the record can be used for a purpose compatible with that for which the record was initially compiled; and (3) federal and state law enforcement officials may obtain all or part of a record through a written request that specifies the portion of the record needed and the law enforcement activity for which it will be used.

Other federal legislation that is relevant to privacy and computing includes, but is not limited to, the Freedom of Information Act, 5 USC Sec. 552; the Fair Credit Reporting Act, 15 USC Secs. 1681–1681t; the Bank Secrecy Act, 12 USC Secs. 1829b, 1953, 31 USC Secs. 1051–1122; the Fair Credit Billing Act, 15 USC Secs. 1601, 1602, 1637, 1666–66j; the Equal Credit Opportunity Act of 1976, 15 USC Sec. 1691, 1691b–1691f; the Right to Financial Privacy Act of 1978, 12 USC Secs. 3401 et seq.; and the Privacy Protection Act of 1980, 42 USC Sec. 2000aa et seq. Most states also have legislation related to access to information in government hands and the protection of privacy.

In 1977, recommendations for legislation and other actions were transmitted to the President and Congress by a Privacy Protection Study Commission. The Commission proposed eight principles for privacy protection, none of which has yet been embodied in federal legislation. These principles are summarized as follows:

1. Personal record-keeping systems should be open as to their existence, policies, and practices.
2. Individually identifiable data should be accessible to the individual it concerns.
3. An individual should have the right to correct any error in his or her records.
4. There should be limits to the kind of data collected and the manner of its collection.
5. There should be limits on the internal use of data.
6. There should be limits of external disclosure of data.
7. Record-keeping organizations must have management policies and practices that will insure their compliance with the law.
8. A record-keeping organization shall be held accountable for its record-keeping policies, practices, and systems.

The failure of the U.S. to have more rigorous privacy policies has implications in international trade. In particular, it may mean that certain European countries that have higher privacy standards will forbid export of data stored within their borders to the U.S.

References

1985. Mendes, M. *Privacy and Computer-Based Information Services*. Cambridge, MA: Center for Information Policy Research, Harvard University.
1987. Office of Technology Assessment, *Defending Secrets, Sharing Data*. Washington: U.S. Government Printing Office.

MICHAEL GEMIGNANI

PRIVILEGED INSTRUCTION

For articles on related subjects *see* INPUT-OUTPUT INSTRUCTIONS; INSTRUCTION SET; INTERRUPT; OPERATING SYSTEMS; and SUPERVISOR CALL.

Improper use of certain instructions can easily affect system integrity in a multi-user environment. These instructions usually include storage protection setting, in-

terrupt handling, timer control, I/O, and special processor status-setting instructions.

In order to prevent accidental or intentional misuse of these instructions, many computers have a special privileged mode in which instructions of the aforementioned type, called *privileged instructions*, can be executed. In a processor that possesses such a mode, the instructions are divided into sets; each set can be executed in its own mode. The privileged mode includes *all* instructions, whereas all lower-level modes exclude some of them. The number of modes may be one (which means essentially the absence of a privileged mode), two (one user mode and one privileged mode), or more. The PDP 11/45, for example, had three modes: user, supervisor, and kernel (*q.v.*).

One way of handling the attempted execution of a privileged instruction in a non-privileged state is an illegal instruction trap, causing an interrupt (*q.v.*). Another is to ignore it completely, which is equivalent to the former if the interrupt is disabled.

Another possible approach to the division of instructions into privileged and user subsets is to structure the computing system into two or more independent processors, each dedicated to one subset. Such division was originally made, for example, in the CDC 6000 series of computers. In those machines, the central processor had no instructions that caused any system functions unless explicitly directed to do so by another processor. (This was later changed by adding one additional instruction to the central processor.)

GIDEON FRIEDER

PROBABILISTIC ALGORITHMS

For articles on related subjects *see* ALGORITHMS; ALGORITHMS, ANALYSIS OF; ALGORITHMS, THEORY OF; COMPUTATIONAL COMPLEXITY; MONTE CARLO METHOD; NP-COMPLETE PROBLEMS; PROBABILISTIC FINITE AUTOMATA; RECURSION; and TURING MACHINES.

Let $Q(x,y)$ be the two-variable polynomial $Q(x,y) = (x + y)^7 - x^7 - y^7 - 7xy(x + y)(x^2 + xy + y^2)^2$ and assume that we want to ascertain whether $Q(x,y)$ is identically equal to zero. A deterministic algorithm for this task would be to expand $Q(x,y)$ to individual terms, opening all parentheses, and then cancel out all equal terms with opposite signs. $Q(x,y)$ is identically zero if and only if all the terms cancel. A *probabilistic algorithm* for the same problem can be described as follows:

1. Choose at random integer values $\bar{x}, \bar{y}$ in the range $0 \le \bar{x}, \bar{y}, \le 49$.
2. Evaluate $Q(\bar{x}, \bar{y})$ for the chosen $\bar{x}$ and $\bar{y}$.
3. Repeat steps 1 and 2 50 times.

If and only if $Q(\bar{x}, \bar{y}) = 0$ all through the execution of the algorithm, decide that $Q(x,y)$ is identically equal to zero. The probabilistic algorithm is based on the argument described below.

One can prove that, if $Q(x,y)$ is not identically equal to zero, then only a fraction $f < 1/2$ of all the 50^2 point vectors $(\bar{x},\bar{y})$, $0 \le \bar{x},\bar{y} \le 49$ can result in $Q(\bar{x},\bar{y}) = 0$ (*see* Schwartz, 1980). We can therefore conclude that if $Q(\bar{x},\bar{y})$ is not identically equal to zero, then the probability that $Q(\bar{x},\bar{y}) = 0$ for 50 randomly and independently chosen point vectors $(\bar{x},\bar{y})$ is less than 2^{-50}. Thus, an erroneous decision is extremely improbable.

The main features of the above and similar probabilistic decision algorithms can be summarized as follows:

1. The input belongs to a given discrete domain D (e.g. the domain of all multivariate polynomials, the domain of all integers, the domain of all graphs).
2. The algorithm must decide whether the input satisfies a given property (e.g. identically equal to zero for multivariate polynomials, primality for integers, connectedness for graphs).
3. It incorporates a randomizing step (step 1 in the above algorithm) that is repeated a certain pre-assigned number of times.
4. It terminates on every input.
5. The decision it provides may be erroneous, but the probability of error can be made as small as required by increasing the number of random choices invoked in its iterative step (step 3 in the example).
6. The adequacy of the algorithm is based on the following paradigm: If D is the domain, w the element of D at input, and P the property of w to be verified by the algorithm, then the repetitive and randomized step (step 1 in the example) of the algorithm consists of a binary test t, which is "easy" to perform. The test t is applied to w several times and its result is recorded. If at any time $t(w)$ is "no," then w does not satisfy the property P. If w does not satisfy the property P, then the probability of $t(w) = $ "yes" is less than some number $\varepsilon < 1$. If t has been executed n times and the result was always "yes," then the probability of this event, given that w does not satisfy the property P, is less than ε^n, which tends to zero with n. One may, of course, also have the symmetrical situation where the implications of the "yes" and the "no" results of the test are exchanged (i.e. w satisfies P when $t(w)$ is "no").

An additional example of a probabilistic algorithm of the above type is the algorithm of Rabin (1980—one of the first probabilistic algorithms in the literature) for deciding primality: The domain D is the domain of integers, the property P is primality, and the test t is described as follows.

Given an integer w, let b be a random number $1 \le b < w$. If either $b^{w-1} \equiv 1 \bmod w$ or there is an integer i such that $(n-1)/2^i = m$ is an integer and $1 < gcd(b^m - 1, w) < w$, then $t(w) = $ "no". Otherwise $t(w) = $ "yes". It is easy to show that $t(w) = $ "no" implies that w is composite. It can be shown that if w is composite, then the probability of $t(w)$ to be "yes" is less that one half.

The randomization concept inherent in the above algorithm had been exploited even before the invention of probabilistic algorithms in Monte Carlo methods. Based on this similarity, the probabilistic algorithms described above have been termed algorithms of Monte Carlo type. Another type of probabilistic algorithm can be illustrated by the Random-Quicksort algorithm (*see* SORTING). This algorithm receives as input a list L of n numbers (or elements taken from an ordered domain) and outputs the same list in sorted order, using the following method.

1. An element of the list $s(L)$ is randomly chosen and called the *separator* (or *pivot*). (In the version of Quicksort listed in STRUCTURED PROGRAMMING, the first element of the list is used as pivot.)
2. A procedure is provided that constructs two lists L_1, containing all the elements in L smaller than $s(L)$, and L_2, containing all the elements in L larger than $s(L)$. The procedure runs in time that is proportional to the length of the list L.
3. The algorithm is applied recursively to the lists L_1 and L_2, resulting in the sorted lists S_1 and S_2 (see RECURSION).
4. Output S_1 concatenated to $s(L)$ concatenated to S_2.

The randomization introduced in step 1 has the effect that, most of the times when step 2 is applied, the lists L_1 and L_2 are almost equal in size. This implies that the number of iterations of step 2 is proportional to $\log_2 n$. As the algorithm proceeds, the number of lists to be processed at step 2 increases, but their total length is less than n (they are all disjoint sublists of the original list of n elements) and, since the time used by the procedure for any sublist is proportional to its length, the running time of each of the $\sim \log_2 n$ iterations on all the sublists produced up to that iteration is proportional to n. The running time of the algorithm is therefore proportional, on the average, to $n \log_2 n$, even though it might be proportional to n^2 in an extremely improbable worst case. As a matter of fact, the following properties of the Random-Quicksort algorithm have been proved:

1. The average running time of the Random Quicksort algorithm is proportional to $n \log_2 n$.
2. For every ε, there is n_0 such that for all $n \ge n_0$ the probability that the algorithm halts in less than $21 n \log_2 n$ steps is greater than $1 - \varepsilon$.

The main features of the Random-Quicksort and similar algorithms, termed in the literature as algorithms of the Las Vegas type, are summarized below:

1. The input belongs to an infinite and discrete domain.
2. The algorithm incorporates a randomizing step (step 1 in the example).
3. The algorithm terminates on every input.

4. The output *always* provides the correct answer.
5. The algorithm is "fast" on the average and an "acceptable" bound $B(n)$ can be proved such that the running time of the algorithm is bounded by $B(n)$ with probability approaching 1 as n grows to infinity.

Notice also that the Random-Quicksort algorithm is a computational algorithm, while the previously described algorithms are decision algorithms.

One should not confuse probabilistic algorithms with the probabilistic analysis of the running time of deterministic algorithms. In contradistinction to deterministic algorithms, probabilistic algorithms incorporate an inherent randomizing step. This randomizing step may subsequently induce probabilistic arguments in the analysis of the running time or the correctness of such algorithms.

In addition to the two types of probabilistic algorithms described above, there may be variations in several directions. For example, one may think of partial algorithms (algorithms that do not halt on every input) such that their probability of halting on any input is very high and such that, when they do halt, they either provide the correct answer or have a very small probability of being erroneous. One may also envision computational probabilistic algorithms that provide only an approximation to the required output and such that the approximation can be improved by increasing the running time of the algorithm.

Some Historical and Theoretical Comments

Randomization was first used in Monte Carlo computational methods. It was introduced in the 1960s and 1970s into theoretical models of computation (*see* PROBABILISTIC FINITE AUTOMATA and TURING MACHINES). In the 1970s and subsequently, many probabilistic algorithms were introduced for solving actual problems (primality, computational geometry, sorting, hashing, communication problems on networks, etc.—see Raghavan, 1990 for a treatise and survey). Particular emphasis has been set on probabilistic algorithms whose running time is bounded by a polynomial in the length of the input (*see* COMPUTATIONAL COMPLEXITY and ALGORITHMS, ANALYSIS OF). The class of those algorithms is denoted by RP (Random Polynomial). There are algorithms in RP such that there is no known deterministic polynomial algorithm that solves the same problems they solve. An example of such an algorithm is the primality algorithm due to Rabin (1980). (No deterministic and polynomial algorithm for deciding whether a number is prime is known.) On the other hand, it has not been proved yet that the class P (deterministic and polynomial algorithms—*see* NP–COMPLETE PROBLEMS) is properly included in the class RP, which is an intriguing and important open problem in theoretical computer science. Another open and related problem is the question of whether the class RP is properly included in the class NP. A negative answer to either of the above two problems will solve the other, and the solution of either of those two

problems will have a strong impact on the theory of computation.

Randomization and probabilistic algorithms played an important role in the development of the modern theory of cryptology (*see* CRYPTOGRAPHY, COMPUTERS IN). In particular, the concept of zero-knowledge proofs (roughly, convincing arguments that yield nothing but the validity of the assertion) depends heavily on a certain type of probabilistic algorithm.

References

1980. Rabin, M. O. "Probabilistic Algorithm for Testing Primality," *Journal of Number Theory*, **12**, 128–138.
1980. Schwartz, J. T. "Fast Probabilistic Algorithms for Verification of Polynomial Identities," *SIAM Journal on Computing*, **27**, 4, 701–717.
1990. Raghavan, P. *Lecture Notes on Randomized Algorithms*, IBM Res. Report RC 15340.

AZARIA PAZ

PROBABILISTIC AUTOMATA

For articles on related subjects *see* AUTOMATA THEORY; FORMAL LANGUAGES; and SEQUENTIAL MACHINE.

A *probabilistic* or *stochastic automaton* (pa) [probabilistic sequential machine (psm)] is a device with a finite number of internal states that scans input words over a finite alphabet, responds by successively changing its state in a probabilistic way, [and prints output words probabilistically over a finite output alphabet]. In the foregoing and on what follows, bracketed phrases refer to the psm in contrast to the pa.

Let p be a vector with entries p_i representing the probability that the automaton [machine] was in its ith state to begin with; let $A(x)$ $[A(y \mid x)]$ be a matrix with entries $a_{ij}(x)$ $[a_{ij}(y \mid x)]$ representing the probability that the automaton moved to state j from state i [the machine printed the symbol y and moved to state j from state i] upon scanning the input symbol x. Let η be a column vector with some entries equal to one, the other entries being equal to zero [with all entries equal to one]. Then,

$$p(x_1 \cdots x_k) = pA(x_1) \cdots A(x_k)\eta$$
$$[p(y_1 \cdots y_k \mid x_1 \cdots x_k) = pA(y_1 \mid x_1) \cdots A(y_k \mid x_k)\eta]$$

is a function representing the probability that the automaton entered a designated final state [the machine printed the output word $y_1 \cdots y_k$] after scanning the input word

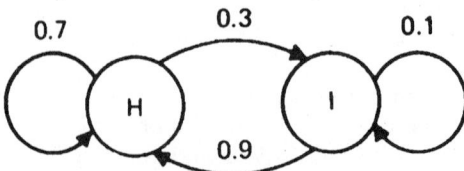

FIG. 1.   Transition characteristics

$x_1 \cdots x_k$. The function p can be used as a sorting criterion to define the probabilistic language consisting of all input words $x_1 \cdots x_k$ with $p(x_1 \cdots x_k) > \lambda$, λ being a preassigned given threshold.

The study of pa's is concerned mainly with the study of probabilistic languages, their closure properties and relation to other types of formal languages. The study of psm's is concerned with the input/output relations induced by the machines, minimization of states, and other problems connected with input/output information systems with random characteristics.

Example. Consider a physical system (or animal) assumed to be in one of two possible states (healthy or ill), with probabilities 0.2 and 0.8 correspondingly. If a sequence of stimuli (medicines) is applied to the system (animal), it undergoes probabilistically successive changes of its states. Assume that the transition characteristics of the first stimulus are as depicted in Fig. 1, which is to be interpreted as meaning that with probabilities 0.7 and 0.3, the system will stay in its first state, or will go to the second state, respectively, if the stimulus has been applied while the system was in its first state, etc. The probabilities of being in one of the two states after the application of the first stimulus (after swallowing the medicine) will then be

$$(0.2 \quad 0.8) \begin{pmatrix} 0.7 & 0.3 \\ 0.9 & 0.1 \end{pmatrix} = (0.86 \quad 0.14)$$

and the process will continue in the same way.

References

1969. Carlyle, J. W. "Stochastic Finite-State System Theory," in Zadeh, L. A. and Polak, E. (Eds.), *System Theory.* New York: McGraw-Hill, Chap. 10.

1971. Paz, A. *Introduction to Probabilistic Automata.* New York: Academic Press.

AZARIA PAZ

PROBLEM-ORIENTED LANGUAGES

For articles on related subjects *see* COMPUTER-AIDED ENGINEERING; EXPERT SYSTEMS; PROCEDURE-ORIENTED LANGUAGES; PROGRAMMING LANGUAGES; ROBOTICS; and SIMULATION: LANGUAGES.

The term *problem-oriented* languages, if taken literally, is too general to be useful in the taxonomy of programming languages. In its most general meaning, one would have to include any programming language that helps solve problems. Thus, Fortran is a problem-oriented language when one solves scientific or numeric problems. Cobol (COmmon Business-Oriented Language) is problem oriented, even in its title, for business problems. However, accepted usage in computer science literature has imposed a narrower context for problem-oriented languages than one that could encompass Fortran and Cobol. From this more restricted point of view, syn-

onyms for *problem-oriented* are *applications-oriented* or *special-purpose* or *specialized-application* or *languages for specialized application areas.*

This article discusses a number of applications-oriented and special-purpose programming languages. Some languages have been designed for very special applications, such as numerical control programming or electronic circuit analysis. Others are applications oriented, but at the same time are more general purpose. Examples of these would include simulation languages, statistical packages, and information retrieval systems. Discussion of the more general-purpose, problem-oriented languages is found in other sections of this Encyclopedia.

Numerous problem-oriented languages have been developed. It is obvious that this article can only touch upon a small part of the vast work that has been done in this field. Many of these languages have been described in Sammet (1969) and in her subsequent rosters of programming languages published in a number of journals, including the Association for Computing Machinery's *SIGPLAN Notices* (see Sammet, 1978). According to these rosters, the number of problem-oriented languages has consistently represented about half of all the high-level languages used in the U. S. The best source of technical information about a language is generally the reference manual provided by the developers or suppliers of the software.

Before looking at specific problem-oriented languages in current usage, we present an example of one of the earliest such languages and then review the characteristics of some commonly used languages in numerical control, civil engineering, electrical engineering, robotics, and expert systems. Finally, we will have a few things to say about trends in the future use and development of problem-oriented languages.

An Early Problem-Oriented Language—DYANA.
Shortly after the successful introduction of Fortran as a programming language for scientific and engineering calculations, the General Motors Research Laboratories developed a specialized language for describing vibrational and other dynamic systems. DYANA (dynamic analyzer) was developed originally for the IBM 704 in 1958 and was an extension of Fortran. See Theodoroff (1958).

DYANA provided for the definition of variables to specify the elements, excitation, and dependent and independent variables in a dynamic system. These variables have meaning in both Fortran and non-Fortran statements. The variables are constructed in such a way as to define the topology of the mechanical system. Fig. 1 illustrates a simple mechanical system. The topology of the system is contained in the variables themselves, using the letters E for element, K for spring, M for mass, F for force, etc. For example, E03K02 stands for the spring element, which is contained between the two elements 03 and 02. E03K02 is also used as the coefficient of damping for that spring element when the variable appears in Fortran arithmetic or input/output statements.

In Fig. 1, the DYANA language is first used to define

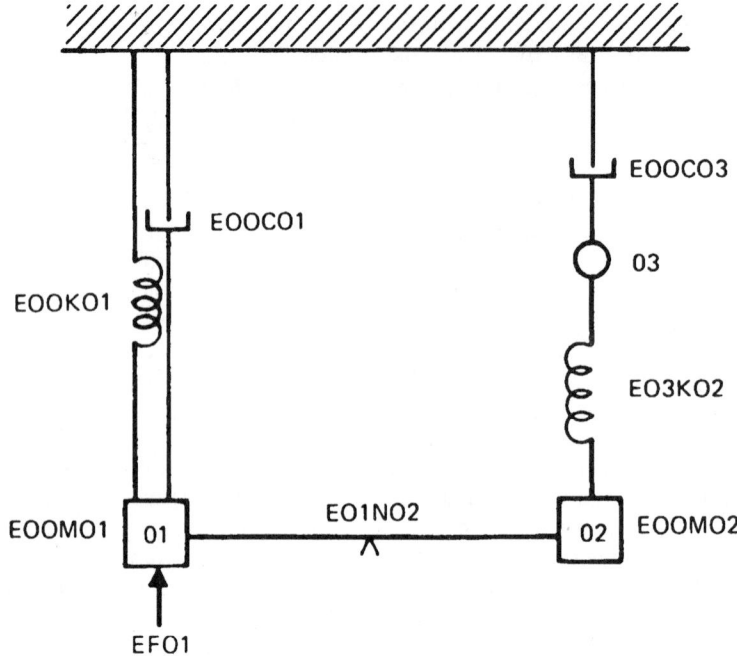

```
INPUT WITH DIAGNOSTIC COMMENTS FLAGGED BY AN X

X       SYSTEM DESCRIPTION                                              CARD 1
        E00M01, E00M02, E00K01, E00C01, E00C03                         CARD 2
        E03K02, E01N02, EF01                                           CARD 3
X       PRE-COMPUTATION                                                CARD 4
        E03K02 = 2.4 + 0.6 * E00K01                                    CARD 5
X       DAMPING RATE, E00C03(X03)                                      CARD 6
        E00C03 = A * X03 + B                                           CARD 7
X       FORCE, EF01                                                    CARD 8
        EF01 = F * SINF(W * TIME)                                      CARD 9
X       INPUT VARIABLES                                                CARD 10
        A,B,F,W                                                        CARD 11
X       PRINT PRECOMPUTATION ANSWERS                                   CARD 12
        E00M01, E00M02, E00K01, E00C01, E03K02, E01N02, A,B,F,W        CARD 13
X       PRINT TIME DEPENDENT ANSWERS                                   CARD 14
        TIME, EF01, X01, X02, X03, DX01, DX02                          CARD 15
X       TRANSLATIONAL                                                  CARD 16
X       TRANSIENT                                                      CARD 17
X       END                                                            CARD 18
```

FIG. 1.   Sample DYANA program (From J.E. Sammet, *Programming Languages: History and Fundamentals,* Prentice-Hall, 1969.)

the system description (group 1). This is done by listing all system elements, with each element name showing its relationship to each other element, and defining its type (mass, spring, force, etc.).

Next (group 2), a series of Fortran arithmetic statements specify the functional relationship of the coefficients of damping of the two spring elements, the damping rate of element E00C03 as a function of the displacement of the point 03, and the forcing function EF01. Next (group 3), parameters *A, B, F,* and *W,* and the other initial conditions are input and printed. Finally (group 4), statements are entered to begin the analysis and printout of the time-dependent answers, such as time, force, displacements, and velocities. The output from DYANA was a complete For-

tran program punched out on cards and ready to run with the requisite set of numerical data.

Using a Problem-Oriented Language - APT

The essential goal of any problem-oriented language is to provide the user, who may or may not be a computer specialist, with a relatively simple and direct way of expressing a problem for computer solution. To be maximally effective, the language must be complete enough to express the functions, algorithms, and data types that are normally used in the specific application. The value and effectiveness of a language is determined by how well this criterion is met.

To illustrate the process of using a problem-oriented

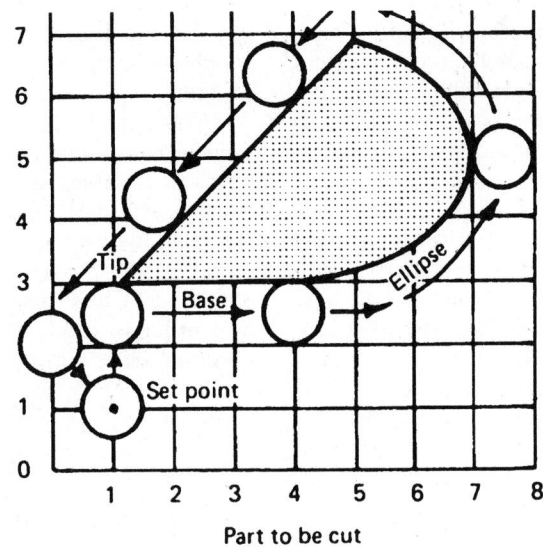

Part to be cut

Part Program	Explanation
CUTTER/1	**Use a 1 in. diameter cutter.**
TOLER/.005	Tolerance of cut is 0.005 in.
FEDRAT/80	Move tool at feed rate of 80 in./min.
HEAD/1	Use head #1.
SPINDL/2400	Turn on spindle. Set at 2,400 rpm.
COOLNT/FLOOD	Turn on coolant. Use flood setting.
PT1 = POINT/4,5	Define point PT1 as point with coordinates (4,5), used later to define ellipse.
FROM/(SETPT = POINT/1,1)	Start tool from point called SETPT, defined as point with coordinates (1,1).
INDIRP/(TIP = POINT/1,3)	Aim tool in direction of point called TIP, defined as point with coordinates (1,3).
BASE = LINE/TIP, AT ANGL, 0	Define line called BASE as line through point TIP, which makes angle of 0 deg. with horizontal.
GO/TO, BASE	Go to the line BASE.
TL RGT, GO RGT/BASE	With tool on right of part with respect to direction of motion, go right along line BASE until tangency with next surface, the ellipse, is reached.
GO FWD/(ELLIPS/CENTER, PT1,3,2,0)	Go forward along ellipse with center at PT1, semi-major axis = 3, semi-minor axis = 2, and major axis making angle of 0 deg with horizontal.
GO LFT/(LINE/2,4,1,3,), PAST, BASE	Go left along line joining points (2,4) and (1,3) past line BASE.
GOTO/SETPT	Go to point SETPT in a straight line.
COOLNT/OFF	Turn off coolant flow.
SPINDL/OFF	Turn off spindle.
END	This is end of machine control unit operation,
FINI	and the finish of part program.

FIG. 2. An APT program for the two-dimensional cam shown at top. (From J. E. Sammet, *Programming Languages: History and Fundamentals,* Prentice-Hall, 1969.)

language, we present as an example one of the most successful and widely implemented problem-oriented languages ever devised, namely, APT (IIT, 1967).

APT stands for *automatically programmed tools.* It was first developed at M.I.T. in the early 1950s to assist in the production of punched tapes for numerically controlled machine tools. The early versions of APT were restricted to two-dimensional objects, using only straight lines and circles. Later developments, which were sponsored by the Aerospace Industries Association, resulted in a system called APT II. APT II utilized a specialized language to describe geometric surfaces. In the 1960s the APT Long-

Range Program, sponsored by numerous industries and conducted by the Illinois Institute of Technology Research Institute, developed APT III, which eventually became the de facto standard for numerical control applications. Most of the currently used languages for numerical control programming are extensions, variations, or subsets of APT.

The APT System   The utilization of numerical control for machine tools is one of the most significant modern developments in manufacturing. Numerical control (N/C) has been applied to milling machines, drilling and boring machines, lathes, machining centers, automatic wiring machines, welding and flame-cutting machines, etc.

To utilize an N/C tool, one must prepare a control tape that has recorded on it a description of all motions and machine functions required to fabricate the part on the tool. In the case of continuous path-control systems, literally thousands of computations must be performed to prepare a control tape.

The APT system includes a programming language, which provides a vocabulary for describing the geometry, motions, and machine functions necessary to produce a part using N/C, and a group of computer programs, called the *part program*, which translate the APT language, perform the required calculations, and produce the control tape. The APT language provides a vocabulary to describe a large variety of two- and three-dimensional part geometry, to define tool shape, to specify tolerance, to command cutter motion, to indicate machining functions, to perform in-line computations, and to execute program logic and specify geometric transformations. These features, when used individually and in combination, offer the part programmer the possibility of producing simple or complex parts efficiently and economically.

The APT Language   We will illustrate the APT language by describing the process of writing a part program for a two-dimensional cam (Fig. 2). The APT language is used to:

1. Give names or symbols to the different geometrical elements of the part.
2. Describe the dimension and shape of the tool with which the part is to be cut.
3. Specify the computational tolerance. This tolerance is used by the computer to calculate the offset of the tool from the surfaces of the part and to determine successive cutter locations. By changing tolerances from run to run, machining can be varied from rough cuts to finer cuts.
4. Define the geometry of the part.
5. Describe the motion of the tool. Here, the part programmer acts as if sitting on the tool and driving it, like a car, around the part.
6. Specify auxiliary functions of the controller-machine tool combination.

With these elements, one obtains the part program shown in Fig. 2. The APT computer system calculates successive cutter positions to fabricate the part specified, taking into account the defined tool shape, the tolerances, the part geometry, and the tool motions contained in the part program.

This application is typical of the procedures used in a problem-oriented language. The problem is defined in terms of variables and data types (points, lines, circles, ellipses, etc, in APT), certain declarations are invoked to establish the proper environment (cutter specifications, tool positions, coordinate transformations, tolerance, etc., in APT), and then statements are executed in a specific order to produce the desired result (tool motion, program logic, arithmetic operations, input/output control, etc., in APT). These same types of expressions, declarations, and statements are found in one form or another in all languages considered here.

Civil Engineering Applications   Some of the most active development of problem-oriented languages has been for civil engineering applications. The computer was recognized very early as an invaluable tool to the civil engineer in performing the numerous calculations and in handling the complex data that are involved in the design and construction of bridges, building highways, harbors, etc.

The solution of civil engineering problems involves many disciplines. For example, in the design of a highway interchange, the engineer utilizes surveying, highway engineering, soil mechanics, structural engineering, hydraulic engineering, transportation engineering, etc. Computer aids to each of these fields have been developed over the past 30 years. Work was done to combine these separate applications into an integrated package of programs known as ICES (Integrated Civil Engineering System) which was initially developed in the mid-1960s. This section discusses some of the work that led up to the design and implementation of ICES, and then discusses ICES as an example of a unified system approach to problem-oriented languages.

Cogo   Cogo (*coordinate geometry*) is a programming language used to perform the geometric calculations required in surveying. It was developed originally by Professor C. Miller of the M.I.T. Civil Engineering Department around 1960. It is now available on most computers and has been also implemented under several time-sharing systems.

Cogo provides the civil engineer with a large number of commands and associated programs to perform plane geometry computations. Some examples of Cogo commands are given below

DIVIDE/LINE	To divide a line into a specified number of segments.
LOCATE/AZIMUTH	To define a point, given the distance and azimuth from a specified point.
AREA	To calculate the area of a triangle, given the three vertices.

Stress Structural Engineering Systems Solver (Stress) was developed (Fenves, 1964) with the objective of facilitating the use of computers in analyzing structures. The principal objective of Stress was to provide a wide variety of structural analyses with a minimum of programming effort. It can be used to analyze two- and three-dimensional structures, with either pinned or rigid joints, with prismatic or non-prismatic members, and subjected to concentrated or distributed loads, support motions, or temperature effects.

Stress was developed in the early 1960s under the direction of Professor S. J. Fenves at M.I.T. Numerous computer implementations of this language have been accomplished since this early work. It was essentially replaced later in the 1960s by STRUDL. The following statements are examples of types found in Stress.

Size Descriptors

Several statements are needed to define the size of the problem to be handled. These include:

```
NUMBER OF JOINTS
NUMBER OF SUPPORTS
NUMBER OF MEMBERS
NUMBER OF LOADINGS
```

Structural Data Descriptors

To describe completely a framed structure, it is necessary to provide information about its geometry, topology (interconnection of members and joints), mechanical properties (load-deflection relationships of the members), and the presence of local releases (such as hinges or rollers). Six types of statements are provided:

1. Geometry is specified in terms of joint coordinates by the statement

```
JOINT COORDINATES
```

followed by the X, Y, Z coordinates of each joint (or X, Y for plane structures). These statements are also used to describe the status (i.e. free or support) of the joints.

2. The presence of hinges or rollers at support joints is given as

```
JOINT RELEASES
```

followed by the joint numbers and the designation and orientation of the released (zero) force components.

3. The interconnection of the members is specified by the statement

```
MEMBER INCIDENCES
```

followed by a list giving the starting and ending joint of each member. The meaning of this statement is best illustrated by the descriptive input form, which for a typical member may be MEMBER 17 GOES FROM JOINT 10 TO JOINT 7.

4. The load-deflection properties of the members are specified as

```
MEMBER PROPERTIES
```

followed by a statement for each member, giving the type of member, and the labels and numerical values of the properties.

5. The presence of hinges in the members is given as

```
MEMBER RELEASES
```

followed by the member numbers, and the position and orientation of the released force components.

6. Constants associated with the members are specified by the

```
CONSTANTS
```

statement.

Loading Data Descriptors

The loading applied to the structure is specified in terms of loading condition descriptors, descriptors of individual loads, and descriptors of groups of loads, as follows.

The word

```
LOADING
```

followed by any identifying information, delineates groups of loads (together comprising a loading condition) and serves as a loading condition header.

Individual loads are specified by statements such as

```
JOINT LOADS
```

followed by the joint numbers and the components of applied load,

```
JOINT DISPLACEMENTS
MEMBER DISTORTIONS
MEMBER LOADS
```

followed by a statement for each load, giving the member number, the orientation, magnitude, and type of the load.

Modification Descriptors

To permit rapid evaluation of alternative designs, the following statements can be used after an initial problem has been defined.

MODIFICATION	(with information for output identification)
ADDITIONS	(interspersed with pertinent

CHANGES   statements of all the above
DELETIONS   types describing the
                modification)

Termination Statements

These statements terminate the input of portions of or all statements of a problem:

```
SOLVE
SOLVE THIS PART
FINISH
```

ICES The problem-oriented languages discussed to this point have provided the user with language capability to solve very special problems, such as producing tapes for numerically controlled machine tools, solving problems in plane geometry, and performing structural analysis. The *integrated civil engineering system* (ICES), on the other hand, was designed to function as a series of subsystems, each subsystem corresponding to an engineering discipline (Roos, 1981). Each subsystem in ICES utilizes its own data structure; nevertheless, it provides for common files of problem data. ICES also provides an engineering programming language, command-definition language, and data-definition language to create subsystems. Thus, ICES is a framework within which engineering programs can be embedded.

Subsystems under ICES in the late 1980s include BRIDGE, Cogo, DODOTRANS, LEASE, ROADS, SEPOL, STRESS, STRUDL, TOPOLOGY, TRANSET, TRAVOL, and UGH.

The engineering programming language is Icetran, which is an extension of Fortran designed to handle civil engineering programming. With Icetran, a programmer can develop problem-oriented subsystems that become part of the ICES package.

To provide for a common method of defining the language elements, the subsystem designer makes use of a command-definition language (CDL) to specify the commands needed for the necessary problem-solving capabilities, as well as the external data requirements and the internal data processing required for each command. This information is transmitted to the computer in the command-definition language. The command-definition language requests are processed by the command-definition system program (an ICES subsystem), which produces a command dictionary, a COMMON map, and command data blocks for the subsystem. The dictionary and the command data blocks are used by ICEX, the ICES executive program, which processes the engineer's problem-oriented language commands.

There are two types of commands in ICES: system commands and subsystem commands. System commands are used by an engineer to specify the name of the ICES subsystem to be used. Examples of system commands are Cogo, STRUDL (structural design language). Sepol (settlement problem-oriented language), etc. Subsystem commands refer to the engineering commands in each subsystem. The engineer specifies the appropriate system command, followed by the relevant subsystem commands. Assume, for example, that a structural engineer is working on a bridge-design problem. First the BRIDGE system command will be given, followed by BRIDGE subsystem commands. Then to design the bridge geometry, the Cogo system command will be issued, followed by the Cogo subsystem commands. After the bridge geometry has been calculated, the BRIDGE system command will be issued, which returns to the bridge subsystem.

Thus, the essence of ICES is the generation of appropriate subsystems for specific engineering applications, which are then used to solve a given class of problems. Once a new subsystem is generated, it becomes a part of the ICES package. The generation of a subsystem requires that a programmer:

1. Write a description of each subsystem command in CDL.
2. Write programs in Icetran to carry out the computations.
3. Design the load module structure.
4. Design the subsystem COMMON area.

Electrical Engineering Applications Computers are essential aids to the electrical engineer in many applications. Circuit analysis is the "bread and butter" computation for most electrical engineering applications. The two most commonly used circuit analysis programs are ECAP (Electronic Circuit Analysis Program) and SCEPTRE (respectively: Jensen and Lieberman, 1968; Bowers and Sedore, 1971). ECAP allows the electrical engineer to perform d-c, a-c, and transient analysis. Under control of ECAP, network equations are formulated and solved after the appropriate topological information and element values of the network have been provided. SCEPTRE also performs d-c and transient analysis, but was designed to provide several improvements over ECAP in transient analysis.

To illustrate the use of ECAP, a d-c analysis is illustrated (Comer, 1971). A transistor amplifier has been reduced to an equivalent circuit using the standard branches allowed in ECAP. The only branches permitted in ECAP in the d-c analysis program are independent d-c sources, dependent d-c current sources, and resistance or capacitance. Among the output quantities that can be calculated by ECAP, using the d-c program, are node voltages, element voltages, branch voltages, element currents, branch currents, and element power losses. Fig. 3(a) shows the circuit to be analyzed. Fig 3(b) shows the equivalent circuit with standard branches.

The program first specifies the type of analysis to be performed, in this case, d-c analysis followed by comment cards. Branch information is then input, starting with B1 and proceeding consecutively to the highest numbered branch in the circuit. Then nodal connectivity information for each branch specifies the two nodes which the branch connects and the direction defining positive current. Positive current flows from the first node specified to the second node. Nodal information is followed by a comma and a finite value of resistance. Independent voltage-source information follows the resistance value, and

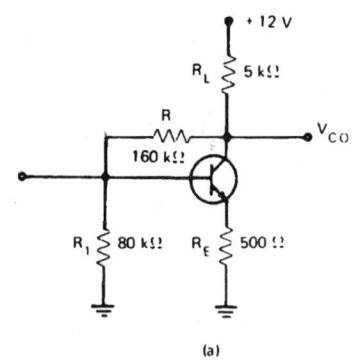

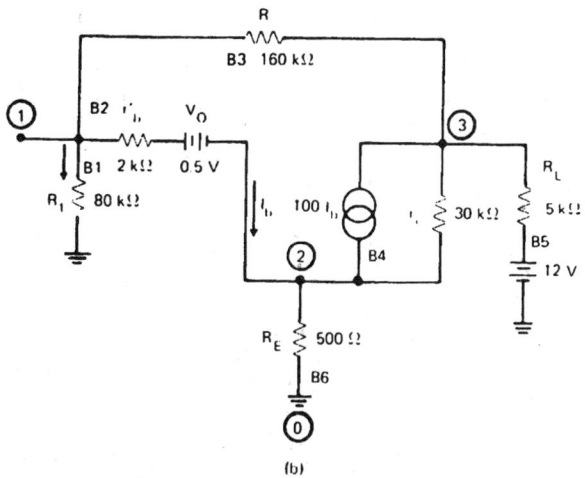

FIG. 3. Circuits on which ECAP program analyzes quiescent voltage. (a) Transistor amplifier; (b) equivalent circuit showing standard branches. (Copyright © 1971 by International Textbook Company. Reprinted from *Computer Analysis of Circuits* by David J. Comer by permission of Intext Educational Publishers, New York.)

independent source current would follow the voltage-source value if a current source appears in the branch. Commas always separate the data subgroups.

Dependent current-source cards follow the branch cards and are identified by the letter T, followed by the number of the source. The strength of the source is then specified in terms of the word BETA, which is the current gain of the source. The value of BETA can be negative, depending on the chosen directions of positive current in both the "from" branch and the "to" branch. Current-source information can also be specified in terms of a transconductance. In this case the letters GM are used instead of BETA. The current is then equal to the value of GM times the voltage appearing across the resistance of the "from" branch.

There are only four circuit elements recognized by the ECAP d-c analysis program, resistors (or conductances), independent voltage sources, independent current sources, and dependent current sources. All these elements except independent current sources are used in this example.

Robot Languages One of the more recent specialized areas is the development of languages to program robots. While some of the languages bear a striking resemblance to the numerical control languages (e.g. APT), there are fundamental differences. Various authors represent robot programming on differing levels, but the simplest way to consider the issue is to define only three conceptual levels: servo, manipulator, and task. At the servo level, a program consists of a series of endpoints, speeds, and input/output commands; the path between endpoints is generated by calculating a series of intermediate points between the endpoints. At the manipulator level, the program contains motion commands (e.g. move from Point A to Point B), some sensor capability (e.g. force specification), and branching and looping constructs (similar to what is in most programming languages). (Most robot programming languages are at this manipulator level.) At the highest (i.e. task) level, the program specifies tasks (e.g. put box A on box B) and decomposition will generate the motions necessary to perform the task; these generally will be at the manipulator level. (This is analogous to having a compiler translate a high-level language such as Fortran by generating an assembly language version of the source code.)

Unlike many of the other types of specialized languages—which tend to be "stand-alone"—there are three major approaches to developing a robot language, and only one of them is pure stand-alone. Another approach is to add commands to numerical control languages, since many of the facilities (e.g. geometry, motion) are similar, while the third approach is to add facilities to existing general languages (e.g. Pascal).

An illustration of a program to enable a robot to pick up a pin and insert it in a hole is in Fig. 4. It is written in AL, which has elements of manipulator and task levels.

Expert Systems Languages In the 1980s the concept of *knowledge-based systems* or *expert systems* (*q.v.*) became significant, with many practical applications developed. An expert system involves (1) a language, (2) an inference engine, and (3) specific rules and data for an individual application. The expert systems are specific software programs intended to operate at or close to the level of a human expert in a specific task domain (e.g. auto repair, computer configuration, medical diagnosis), although in a given case the system may be limited to a specific subset of the task domain (e.g. poor auto performance, configure minicomputers, excessive bleeding). The purpose of the rules is to specify the information and choices to be used as the system is applied. The inference engine represents the methodology used to invoke the rules, and the language expresses the computations to be performed.

The program generally consists of a declaration section and an unordered set of rules written in a language that has well-defined syntax and semantics, and generally contains facilities for data types (both scalar and aggregate), and commands for comparison, arithmetic computations, branching, and input/output. The declaration section provides information about the data (*see*

```
BEGIN "insert peg into hole"
  FRAME peg_bottom, peg_grasp, hole_bottom, hole_top;
  {The coordinates frames represent actual positions of
    object features, not hand positions}
  peg_bottom ← FRAME(nilrot, VECTOR (20,30,0)*inches);
  hole_bottom← FRAME(nilrot, VECTOR (25,35,0)*inches);
  {Grasping position relative to peg_bottom}
  peg_grasp← FRAME(ROT(xhat, 180*degrees), 3*zhat*inches);
  tries; l←2;
  grasped← FALSE;
{The top of the hole is defined to have a fixed relation to the bottom}
AFFIX hole_top to hole_bottom RIGIDLY
        AT TRANS(nilrot, 3*zhat*inches);

OPEN bhand TO peg_diameter + 1*inches;
{Initiate the motion to the peg, note the destination frame}
MOVE barm TO peg_bottom * peg_grasp;
WHILE NOT grasped AND i < tries DO
  BEGIN "Attempt grasp"
  CLOSE bhand TO 0 * inches;
  IF bhand < peg_diameter/2
    THEN BEGIN "No object in grasp"
      OPEN bhand TO peg_diameter + 1 * inches;
      MOVE barm TO ⊗ − 1 * inches; {⊗ indicates current location}
    END
  ELSE grasped← TRUE;
  i←i + 1;
  END
IF NOT grasped THEN ABORT ( "Failed to grasp the
  peg");

{Establish a fixed relation between arm and peg.}
AFFIX peg_bottom TO barm RIGIDLY;
{Note that we move the peg_bottom, not barm}
MOVE peg_bottom TO hole_top;
{Test if a hole is below us}
MOVE barm TO ⊗ − 1 * inches
ON FORCE(zhat) > 10 * ounces DO ABORT ("No Hole");
{Exert downward force, while complying to side forces}
MOVE peg_bottom to hole_bottom DIRECTLY
  WITH FORCE_FRAME = station IN WORLD
  WITH FORCE(zhat) = − 10 * ounces
  WITH FORCE(xhat) = 0 * ounces
  WITH FORCE(yhat) = 0 * ounces
  SLOWLY;
      END "insert peg in hole"
```

FIG 4. An AL program to enable a robot to pick up a pin and insert it into a
hole. (From Tomas Lozano-Perez, "Robot Programming," Proc. IEEE, **71**, No. 7,
July 1983, page 832. Reprinted by permission.)

DECLARATION). The rules are often, but not always, expressed as "IF...THEN" statements. There are generally language facilities that allow the human expert to include in the data a "certainty" or "probability" factor with regard to the effect of the input on the conclusion. Included in the coding of a specific "expert program" are questions for the user that provide the program with the necessary information in a specific case.

The inference engine executes the program by using techniques of matching, data examination, non-sequential execution, and cycling as appropriate. Some expert systems are implemented by compilers, some are purely interpretive, and some are a combination of both.

An example of the user's view of an expert program for diagnosing an automobile problem in OPS5 is shown in Fig. 5, taken from Sherman (1990). The program acts as a consultant to an auto repair business. It will ask the user pertinent questions about the condition of specific areas

AUTO CONSULTATION PROGRAM VERSION TWO

This program will analyze your car problems by asking questions about the functioning of specific areas of your automobile. Please type in one of the words that follows the three dots in each question. Any other input will produce erroneous results.

*****QUESTION 1*****
Gasoline odor is...none normal strong ?   strong

*****QUESTION 2*****
Headlights are...dim normal ?   dim

*****QUESTION 3*****
Fuel filter is...clogged not-clogged ?   not-clogged

*****QUESTION 4*****
Battery cables are...loose corroded normal ?   loose

*****QUESTION 5*****
Starter cranking is...no-crank slow-crank normal grind ? normal

*****QUESTION 6*****
Outdoor temperature is ?   45

*****QUESTION 7*****
Gas gauge reading is...empty not-empty ?   not-empty

CONCLUSIONS:
*****CF   0.000000e + 000*****
Diagnosis is that the battery is discharged.
Treatment is to charge or replace battery.

*****CF   6.000000e – 001*****
Diagnosis is that car is flooded.
Treatment is wait ten minutes then try starting
or depress accelerator to the floor while starting.

*****CF   6.000000e – 001*****
Diagnosis is that the battery cables are in disrepair.
Treatment is to clean and tighten battery cables.

FIG. 5. User view of automobile diagnostic expert system. (From Sherman, P. D. and Martin, J. C. *An OPSS Primer: Introduction to Rule-Based Expert Systems*, Prentice-Hall, 1990. Reprinted by permission.)

of the disabled auto (e.g. fuel system, electrical system, starter system, and temperature). The program will analyze the input data and make a diagnosis with recommended treatment. Fig. 5 shows what the user sees to provide input, and also what the user receives as output. The Certainty Factors (CF) indicate how sure the system is of its conclusions (0 - very unsure, 1 - certain).

Other Problem-Oriented Languages

Literally hundreds of problem-oriented languages have been developed over the past 35 years. We have looked at the areas of numerical control, civil engineering, electrical engineering, robotics and expert systems. Table 1 summarizes some other illustrative languages, by their areas of application. These, of course, are only a small percentage of the numerous languages in use today.

General Status and Future of Problem-Oriented Languages

The need for problem-oriented languages has been consistently significant since the earliest development of more general languages such as Fortran and Cobol. In particular, data collected by Sammet (1991) in the years 1971–1977 show that specialized languages consistently represented approximately 50% of all the high-level languages in use in the U. S. in a given year. (There is good reason to believe that this continues to be true, but there is no data to support that contention.) However, these specialized application languages have generally been created by the users of such languages rather than by computer scientists, who have tended to ignore this class of languages. However, computer science research in programming languages could affect the future developments in these special-purpose languages.

TABLE 1. Illustrations of Problem-Oriented Languages

Application Area	Program Name
Statistics	SPSS: Statistical Package for the Social Sciences
	SAS ®Statistical Library
	OMNITAB
Computer-assisted instruction	TUTOR
	PLANIT
	COURSEWRITER
Simulation	GPSS: General-Purpose Systems Simulator
	SIMSCRIPT
	CSSL: Continuous System Simulation Language
Systems programming	AED: Automated Engineering Design
	BLISS: Basic Language for Implementing System Software
	C
Computer design	CDL: Computer Design Language
	CSL: Computer Structure Language
	VHDL: VHSIC Hardware Description Language
Expert Systems	KRL: Knowledge Representation Language
	OPS5
Robotics	AML/2: A Manufacturing Language/2
	KAREL
	VAL: Versatile Assembly Language

One area of research is the development of techniques to permit users to define their own language requirements and have an automatic procedure for generation of the specific syntax and semantics, as well as a translator, for a language to meet those requirements. This goal has been stated for many years, but by the early 1990s had still not been achieved. The closest we have ever come to that objective in practical terms is the ICES system discussed above, which is of course limited to civil engineering applications.

The advent of personal computers (*q.v.*) has both increased and decreased the need for these special-purpose languages. It has increased the need because of the additional millions of people using personal computers. Specialists in every discipline wish to communicate with the computer in languages that are comfortable for them to use and that provide them with the greatest degree of expressiveness possible. However, this increase in the number of people using computers has been matched to some degree by the creation of an enormous number of program application *packages* that serve similar purposes but are not as general as a programming language covering the same purpose. Thus, while there could exist specific accounting languages, they are unlikely to be developed because of the existence of powerful spreadsheet (*q.v.*) programs.

As pointed out by Sammet (1969), the controversy over language structure will continue into the future. Some people advocate the use of English as a programming language. Others insist that many applications require a precision of expression that would be aided by a more formal and structured language than would be available when using natural language. Since this controversy is unlikely to subside in the near future, it seems reasonable to press for user-defined languages. In this way, the personal preference of the specific user could be satisfied. However, research in this field has been minimal in the past.

References

1958. Theodoroff, T. J. "DYANA: Dynamics Analyzer-Programmer, Part I, Description and Application," *Proc. Eastern Joint Computer Conference*, 144–147.

1964. Fenves, S. J. *et.al. STRESS: A User's Manual*. Cambridge, MA: M.I.T. Press.

1967. IIT Research Institute. *APT Part Programming*. New York: McGraw-Hill.

1968. Jensen, R. W. and Lieberman, M. D. *IBM Electronic Circuit Analysis Program—Techniques and Applications*. Englewood Cliffs, NJ: Prentice-Hall.

1969. Sammet, Jean E. *Programming Languages: History and Fundamentals*. Englewood Cliffs, NJ: Prentice-Hall.

1971. Bowers, J.C. and Sedore, S. R. *SCEPTRE: A Computer Program for Circuit and Systems Analysis*. Englewood Cliffs, NJ: Prentice-Hall.

1971. Comer, D.J. *Computer Analysis of Circuits*. Scranton, PA: International Textbook.

1978. Sammet, J.E. "Roster of Programming Languages for 1976–77," *SIGPLAN Notices* 13, 11: 56–85.

1981. Roos, Daniel (Ed.) *ICES System: General Description*. Cranston, RI: ICES Users Group (July).

1983. Lozano-Perez, Tomas. "Robot Programming," *Proc. IEEE*, 71, 7 (July) 821–841.

1986. Blahaa, James R., Lamoureux, John P, and McKee, Keith E. *Higher Order Languages for Robots*, MTIAC-SOAR-86-01, Defense Logistics Agency, Dept. of Defense.

1987. Cugini, John V. *Programming Languages for Knowledge-Based Systems*. NBS Special Publication 500-145, Gaithersburg, MD: National Bureau of Standards, Institute for Computer Sciences and Technology.

1990. Sherman, Porter D. and Martin, John C. *An OPS5 Primer: Introduction to Rule-Based Expert Systems*. Englewood Cliffs, NJ: Prentice-Hall.

1991. Sammet, Jean E. "Some Approaches to, and Illustrations of, Programming Language History," *Annals of the History of Computing*, **13**, *1*, 33–50.

BENJAMIN MITTMAN AND JEAN E. SAMMET

PROCEDURE

For articles on related subjects *see* ACTIVATION RECORD; ARGUMENT; BLOCK STRUCTURE; CALLING SEQUENCE; GLOBAL AND LOCAL VARIABLES; PARAMETER PASSING; PROCEDURE-ORIENTED LANGUAGES; RECURSION; SIDE EFFECT; and SUBPROGRAM.

A *procedure* is a portion of a high-level language program that performs a specific task necessary for that program. This term is normally used interchangeably with the terms *subprogram* (*q.v.*) and *subroutine* when referring to high-level languages, although the term *subroutine* has a wider meaning outside high-level languages. The use of procedures is so central to programming in general-purpose, high-level languages such as Fortran, Pascal, and PL/I that these languages are often known as *procedure-oriented languages* (*q.v.*).

Early in the development of programming languages, it was recognized that programs would be written in which the same process was to be executed at several different locations within the program. One example of such a process is the evaluation of mathematical functions such as logarithms and exponentials, or trigonometric functions, such as sines or cosines. To accomplish this conveniently, a facility was needed to permit the programmer to code such a procedure once and then to call that process whenever it was needed.

Procedures in high-level languages are of two types: *intrinsic* (or *built-in* or *library*) and programmer-written. Intrinsic procedures are those provided with the language so that the programmer need only cite them in a program to have them automatically *invoked*. This invocation requires only that the programmer give the *name* of the procedure and its *arguments*. (*see* CALLING SEQUENCE and PARAMETER PASSING).

Procedures may also be dichotomized as being either (unqualified) procedures, which *do* things, or *function procedures* (or just *functions*), which compute single values usable in formulas. Fortran, for example, has numerous built-in functions, a short list of which is given in Table 1. If a program contains a variable X and the programmer wishes to compute the cosine of the current value assigned to that variable, it is only necessary to embed the expression (*q.v.*) COS(X) in the desired formula. For example, if one wishes to assign to variable A the absolute value of the sum of the cosine and sine of the argument X, one may write.

```
A = ABS(COS(X) + SIN(X))
```

Similarly, to make B the maximum of the sine and exponential of the argument

```
B = AMAX1(SIN(X),EXP(X))
```

TABLE 1.   Fortran Functions

Function Name	Mathematical Definition	Fortran Name
Sine	$\sin x$	SIN
Cosine	$\cos x$	COS
Exponential	e^x	EXP
Natural logarithm	$\ln x$	ALOG[†]
Absolute value	$|x|$	ABS
Maximum	Value of maximum of $x_1, x_2, \ldots, x_n$	AMAXI[†]

[†]The A in front of these names is required because Fortran names beginning with L or M automatically have integer values as a default condition (*q.v.*).

Other high-level languages have different sets of intrinsic procedures. Pascal has a much smaller number of intrinsic procedures than Fortran, and PL/I has a much larger number. For example, PL/I and Fortran 90 have a built-in function that allows the programmer to extract a *substring* from a named string of characters that is an argument of the function.

The availability of intrinsic functions clearly suggests the need for a parallel facility to permit the programmer to define procedures and functions at the same time as the referencing or *main* program is written. Thus, the programmer could write *subprograms* in the language and then reference these in the same manner as intrinsic procedures. All general-purpose, high-level languages have such a facility, although the details of how it can be used and how it is implemented vary considerably.

In Fortran, programmer-written procedures are called *subprograms* and are of two types: FUNCTION and SUBROUTINE. The former are directly analogous to intrinsic functions in that FUNCTIONS are invoked or *called* just like intrinsic functions. Fig. 1 is an example of a programmer-written FUNCTION to calculate the sum of the products of the corresponding elements of two 100 element arrays, together with two main program statements calling this function. Note in particular that the *value* of the function is the value assigned to its name (PROD in Fig. 1).

In Fortran, SUBROUTINES differ from FUNCTIONS in the method by which they are called and in the lack of any

```
Main program
  —
  —
A = C + (D*E) /PROD(F,G)
  —
  —
Q1 = Q2*PROD(Q3,Q4)

FUNCTION PROD(X,Y)
REAL X(100), Y(100)
PROD = 0.
DO 2 I = 1,100
  PROD = PROD + X(I)*Y(I)
2 CONTINUE
RETURN
END
```

FIG. 1.   A FUNCTION in Fortran.

requirement that a specific result as such be produced. Fig. 2 is an example of a SUBROUTINE to transpose the elements of a two-dimensional square array [i.e. interchange the (I, J) and (J, I) elements]. Note that the only "result" of the subprogram is the input matrix with its elements interchanged, and that the subprogram is not invoked through an assignment statement as a function would have been but rather by a CALL statement.

Also in Fortran, as shown in Figs. 1 and 2, procedures are physically separate from the main program, but in languages that use block structure (q.v.) they are an integral part of the main program. Fig. 3 shows an example from Pascal corresponding to that in Fig. 2 for Fortran. Here the procedure is a *declaration* (q.v.) at the start of the *block* that constitutes the main Pascal program. The procedure is called by giving just its name followed by its arguments.

Pascal and C (q.v.) also have procedure facilities analogous to Fortran functions. PL/I is also a block-structured language and has procedure facilities generally similar to those in Pascal. By contrast with block-structured languages and Fortran, Cobol has a very rudimentary procedure facility that integrates subprograms into the main program in a much more restrictive context than with languages such as Pascal or PL/I.

The contrast between the physically separate procedures of Fortran and those integrated into the main program, as in block-structured languages, should be noted and understood. The former allows separate compilation of the main program and subprograms, which may be convenient during debugging (q.v.). Block-structured languages generally require recompilation of the procedure every time the program is recompiled, but the integration of procedures into the main program is an aid of great value to programming and to to thinking about programming.

J. A. N. LEE AND ANTHONY RALSTON

```
Main program
   —

   —

   —
   CALL TRANS(B,100)
   —

   —
   CALL TRANS(C,50)
   —

   —
   SUBROUTINE TRANS(A,N)
   REAL A(N,N)
   DO 2 I = , N
     DO 4 J = 1,I-1
C NOTE NEED TO SAVE A(I,J)
C BEFORE REPLACING IT BY A(J,I)
       TEMP = A(I,J)
       A(I,J) = A(J,I)
       A(J,I) = TEMP
4  CONTINUE
2  CONTINUE
   RETURN
   END
```

FIG. 2. A Fortran SUBROUTINE.

```
program test (input, output);
type matrix = array [1..100, 1..100] of real;
var B,C: matrix;

procedure TRANS (var A: matrix, N: integer;)
var I,J: integer;
    TEMP: real;
begin
    for I := 2 to N do
      for J := 1 to I - 1 do
        begin
          TEMP := A[I,J] ;
          A[I,J] := A[J,I] ;
          A[J,I] := TEMP
        end
end;
—

—

—

begin {main program}
—

—
  TRANS (B, 100);
—

—
  TRANS (C,50);
—

—
end.
```

FIG. 3. A Pascal procedure.

PROCEDURE-ORIENTED LANGUAGES

SURVEY

For articles on related subjects *see* ABSTRACT DATA TYPE; ADA; ALGOL 68; ASSEMBLER; BLOCK STRUCTURE; COMPILER CONSTRUCTION; DATA STRUCTURES; DATA TYPE; EXPRESSION; FORTH; FUNCTIONAL PROGRAMMING; LIST-PROCESSING: LANGUAGES; LOGO; MACHINE AND ASSEMBLY LANGUAGE PROGRAMMING; MODULA-2; MUMPS; NONPROCEDURAL LANGUAGES; OBJECT-ORIENTED PROGAMMING; PROCEDURE; PROGRAMMING LANGUAGES; POSTSCRIPT; RECURSION; SIDE-EFFECT; STATEMENT; and STRING PROCESSING: LANGUAGES.

Procedure-oriented languages (POLs) are artificial languages used to define, in a form understandable to humans, actions required by a computer to solve a problem. The higher-level form of a POL frees a programmer from the time-consuming and often tedious chore of expressing algorithms in lower-level languages such as assembly and machine language (*see* MACHINE AND ASSEMBLY LANGUAGE PROGRAMMING). Additionally, in a POL, actions are expressed in a machine-independent form that greatly eases the burden of moving a program from one computer to another (*see* PORTABILITY). This increases the lifetime and usefulness of the program.

The defining characteristic of a procedure-oriented language is the expression of a problem algorithm as a series of discrete statements or steps, each of which typically embodies far more logic than any one machine language instruction. Execution proceeds from one statement (*q.v.*) to the next in a sequential fashion, embodying a singular flow or thread of control. This sequential step-wise processing of the program reflects the operation of most prevailing computer hardware (but *see also* PARALLEL PROCESSING).

The solution of a problem on a computer requires its expression in a form the machine can "understand." Usually, the solution begins as an algorithm expressed in a natural language. This identifies "what" needs to be done to derive a solution. It is translated into a form that contains the steps or machine instructions executed by the computer. The latter form tells the computer "how" to get a solution. The translation process, done mentally by a machine language programmer, can be done, at least partially, by a computer using software called a *compiler*. The percentage of the translation process that can be done by the computer suggests the level of abstraction of the particular POL being used. Advancements in compiler technology allow the modern programmer to use higher-level languages that approximate the original mathematical form of the algorithm. Procedure-oriented languages belong to the higher-level category; yet they retain the "how to" flavor of machine language rather than the "what to do" flavor of mathematics or nonprocedural languages.

Procedure-oriented languages differ from machine and assembly languages in the level of data and expression abstraction available to the programmer. Data are stored in precise locations in the computer memory as sequences of binary signals. Assembler and machine language programmers use the data directly. The POL programmer accesses the data using variables that represent numbers and values with familiar types, such as real, integer, and character. Also, procedure-oriented language steps consist of expressions that operate on the variables. During execution, each expression will cause many machine-level actions to occur. The expressions and typed variables of the POL provide a higher level of abstraction that enables the programmer to develop algorithms in familiar terms.

The trend in the development of procedure-oriented languages is to increase the level of abstraction available to the programmer. A modern POL combines expressions into larger programming units called *procedures* or *subroutines*. They allow the grouping of data of homogenous type into indexed aggregates called *arrays*. They provide support such that data of intrinsic type, such as integer, real, and character, can be combined into more complex heterogeneous datatypes called *derived datatypes*, *structures*, or *records* (*q.v.*). Current levels of abstraction allow blocks that contain both *data structures* (*q.v.*) and the procedures that operate on them. Called *objects*, *modules*, or (in Ada) *packages*, the blocks separate a program into manageable, well-defined segments. The segments can be reused in other programs, or they can provide a basis for building new segments (*see* MODULAR PROGRAMMING and OBJECT-ORIENTED PROGRAMMING).

The long-term future of procedure-oriented languages is not obvious. Most commercial and scientific application programs, existing or under development, use procedure-oriented languages. This is likely to continue, with enhanced versions of existing languages evolving as advancements occur in computer science. Yet many observers believe that the magnitude of the advancements needed for future applications is not possible with these languages. Also, the sequential step-wise execution requirements of a POL may cause synchronization problems on multiprocessors. It remains to be seen whether current languages can be extended to support all forms of concurrency. A concern with multiprocessing POL extensions is the added complexity for the programmer. Nonprocedural languages can avoid the synchronization problems of stepwise execution and may be better choices for multiprocessors. On the other hand, POLs are very popular. If additional complexity can be absorbed by the compiler, they will continue to remain so.

Hundreds of procedure-oriented languages have been developed in the past 40 years. This survey discusses, in alphabetic order, the nine general-purpose procedure-oriented languages that the author perceives as having been either most popular or most significant over that time period. Information on list-processing, string-processing, and problem-oriented languages is given in articles so entitled elsewhere in the Encyclopedia.

Ada Ada, a new language of the 1980s, was the result of nearly 20 years of effort by the U.S. Department of Defense to develop a single language for all applications—commercial, scientific, and particularly *embedded computer systems* (*q.v.*). Ada is discussed in a separate article of that name.

Algol Alogol 60 was first defined by an international committee in the late 1950s and later revised so extensively that the result, Algol 68 (*q.v.*), is usually considered to be a distinct language. Algol was never commercially popular and is seldom used today, but Algol is historically important for the programming ideas it introduced. Perhaps the two most important were the introduction of block structure and the explicit declaration of variable types (*strong typing*). Block structure allows a programmer to subdivide a program into smaller units of computation. The blocks could be nested, subdividing the program into even smaller units. Explicit type declaration of variables within the blocks developed the idea of *local variables*. Local variables declared in a block structure are visible to or usable by only expressions within that block or a more deeply nested block. This reduces the potential danger of accidentally modifying variables outside the block. Block structure helps separate large programs into smaller subprograms and, when combined with explicit type declarations, helps make a program easier to read and understand (*see* STRUCTURED PROGRAMMING).

Algol also introduced recursion, whereby a procedure can call itself. Recursion allows terse and meaningful expressions that are more readable than alternative expressions. Recursive procedures, however, often compile to slower running machine code (*see* RECURSION).

Finally, Algol is important for its progeny. Pascal is derived from Algol 60, and Algol formed the basis for Ada, Algol 68, and Modula-2.

APL APL was originally developed in the 1950s by Kenneth E. Iverson as a concise mathematical notation for expressing computer science concepts. In the next decade, the notation was used by Iverson and a small group of colleagues for teaching data processing classes, writing books, and specifying hardware. During this time, it underwent refinement and improvement that was free from the constraints of hardware and from the influence of existing computer languages. The notation contains a rich set of operators based on arrays that allow the definition of complex expressions using a few very compact statements.

APL (from the initials of a 1962 book by Iverson, *A Programming Language*) differs from most modern POLs in many ways. It has no explicitly typed variables; type is determined by usage. There are no control structures such as while, if-then-else, and for. These are replaced by recursive functions, array operations, and a single transfer-of-control operator, "→," which is equivalent to the Fortran or Basic GOTO.

Instead of using keywords to designate the intrinsic operators, APL uses single non-alphanumeric characters. These differences do not detract from the usability of the language. Except for the non-standard characters used for the operators, programs written in APL are nearly identical to the mathematical notation of the original problem algorithms.

The language was first implemented on IBM mainframes in the mid-1960s, using an interpreter running in an interactive programming and execution environment. The interactive environment combines with the rich set of operators and mathematical notation to give APL a desktop calculator–style operation that is suitable for rapid prototyping. This capability makes APL popular among scientists, engineers, statisticians, and financial analysts.

Although APL has a large group of advocates, particularly in the commercial world, it has never had widespread support in the professional programming community. The factors that contribute to the lack of support are: use of non-standard characters for operators, lack of readability because of the concise style, and heavy computer resource requirements.

Basic John Kemeny and Thomas Kurtz developed Basic at Dartmouth in the late 1960s. They designed a small language that was highly portable and suitable for teaching programming to beginners. Basic was first available on time-shared computers. The major use of Basic today is in elementary and high schools. It is often the first programming language children learn.

The smallness of Basic and its lack of features prevented the use of Basic for large commercial or scientific applications. The limitations also hampered its use as a language for teaching development of large programs. Additionally, the design of Basic includes an interactive *user interface* (q.v.) that provides immediate feedback on syntax and run-time errors. While advantageous to a degree, such an interactive interface encourages a "bottom-

up" style whereby the programmer develops an application incrementally, designing the algorithm in parallel with writing the program. This bottom-up style is generally successful only with small applications. The later development of other small, more complete and more structured teaching languages, such as Pascal, reduced the popularity of Basic in colleges.

Then, in the 1980s, when computers were affordable for the hobbyist, Basic became a household word. It was the first and sometimes the only language available on many home computers. Basic remains very popular among hobbyists and many enhanced versions of Basic exist on home computers. Structured versions marketed by Microsoft and Borland have proved to be most popular. The typical Basic is now full-featured and is sometimes used for medium-scale applications. Extended versions of Basic have also been developed for control and data acquisition equipment.

C Developed in the early 1970s at Bell Laboratories as the implementation language for the Unix Operating System, C is discussed in a separate article of that name. C has become the primary language of discourse in systems programming, and an object-oriented version, C++, is rapidly increasing in popularity (*see* OBJECT-ORIENTED PROGRAMMING).

Cobol By far, the most widely used POL is Cobol (Common Business-Oriented Language). Used primarily for business data processing applications, Cobol was first specified in 1959 by the Committee on Data Systems Languages (Codasyl). It was made an ANSI standard language in 1968 and was revised in 1974. Cobol is universally available on most large computers. This is in part due to the Department of Defense requirements that restrict the purchase of new computers to those with Cobol. It is also due to the design and effectiveness of the language.

Cobol was the first language to place equal importance on data and procedures, providing separate specifications for each. Complex data structures are specified in the Data Division. Program statements that operate on elements of the data structure are specified in the Procedure Division. The emphasis on, and the separation of, data structures from the procedures that operate upon them allows a programmer to cope with complex business and financial records in a disciplined way that enforces minimum standards of documentation.

Although available on most computers, the portability (*q.v.*) of Cobol programs is surprisingly poor. This is because of differences in interpretation of the standard, the allowance of subsets by the standard, and the inclination of developers to add extensions to the language.

Fortran Fortran is in some sense both the oldest and the newest language. After IBM and several user groups developed it in the mid-1950s, it was standardized in 1966 (Fortran 66), again in 1977 (Fortran 77), and most recently in 1990 (Fortran 90). The first versions of Fortran in the late 1950s proved that a higher-level language compiler could produce efficient machine code. Before that time there was considerable doubt as to whether code produced from compiled higher-level language could be as fast and as effective as assembler or machine code.

Fortran is a general-purpose language that is most popular among mathematicians, engineers, and scientists. Most scientific software libraries are in Fortran, and users that need them must either use Fortran or use a language that provides an interface to Fortran subroutines. Because of the popularity of Fortran and of the vast libraries that exist for solving scientific programs, Fortran will continue to be an important language well into the 21st century.

From Fortran II onward, each version of Fortran added improvements in programming language technology while retaining compatibility with older versions. Fortran 90 adds many useful constructs. Perhaps the most important is the derived datatype. Derived datatypes provide the mechanism for defining complex data structures from the intrinsic types of integer, character, logical, and real. Another addition was array-valued operations that have a potential for making programs shorter and more readable. They also help identify operations that can be easily parallelized by a supercomputer or multiprocessor compiler.

Pascal Pascal was developed in the early 1970s and became an ANSI standard in 1983. It is the result of efforts by Niklaus Wirth to refine the programming ideas of Algol into a small, compact, reliable, yet full-featured language suitable for teaching the techniques of *software engineering (q.v.)*.

Pascal requires all program entities to be declared before use (*see* DECLARATION). Such strong typing provides information so that the compiler can do extensive checking for language syntax, proper data types, and consistent procedure arguments. Errors related to these concepts are the most common ones made by programmers, particularly beginners.

Pascal allows both data and procedural abstraction. It supports *records*, a derived data type that defines aggregates of the intrinsic types: integer, real, character, and Boolean (logical). This allows the definition of data structures that closely model their corresponding physical entities. The data and procedural abstractions support the stepwise refinement principles of *structured programming (q.v.)*. The higher level of abstraction and the declaration of all entities combined with the Algol-like block structure create a programming form that is easy to read and understand.

Pascal shows the usefulness of programming constructs envisioned by the designers of Algol 60 over 30 years ago. Like Algol, Pascal is important for its progeny, and forms the basis for at least four other languages: concurrent Pascal, object-oriented Pascal, Modula-2, and Ada.

PL/I PL/I was specified by IBM and several of IBM's large computer user groups in 1964. It was an attempt to extend Fortran, primarily a scientific language, for use in commercial applications and *systems programming (q.v.)*. The idea was to develop a single language that would be suitable for all programming efforts.

PL/I combines features from the first generation languages: Fortran, Algol, and Cobol. It is a large, complicated, and powerful general-purpose language that will support virtually any programming activity. It was once highly popular among users of IBM large computers and initially appeared to be very successful. But PL/I is so large and its compiler so difficult to port to smaller computers that it has never been successful on machines other than large IBM mainframes. It did not replace either Fortran or Cobol, and it is unlikely that it ever will. As PL/I declines in popularity, it is likely to be dropped from IBM's supported line of compilers.

References

1962. Iverson, K. E. *A Programming Language*. New York: John Wiley.
1974. *American National Standard Programming Language: Cobol*. New York: ANSI.
1976. *American National Standard Programming Language: PL/I*. New York: ANSI.
1978. *American National Standard Programming Language: Fortran*. New York: ANSI.
1980. Hill, I. D. and Meek, B. L. (Ed.). *Programming Language Standardization*. New York: Halsted Press (John Wiley & Sons).
1981. Wexelblat, R. L. (Ed.). *History of Programming Languages*. New York: Academic Press.
1983. Horowitz, E. *Fundamentals of Programming Languages*. Rockville, MD: Computer Science Press.
1983. Horowitz, E. *Programming Languages: A Grand Tour*. Rockville, MD: Computer Science Press.
1983. *IEEE Standard Pascal Computer Programming Language*. New York: Institute of Electrical and Electronics Engineers, Inc.

TONY L. COX

PROGRAMMING

For articles on related subjects *see* CONTROL STRUCTURE; DATA STRUCTURES; DEBUGGING; DECLARATION; DIAGNOSTIC; EXPRESSION; FUNCTIONAL PROGRAMMING; LANGUAGE PROCESSORS; LOOP; MODULAR PROGRAMMING; OBJECT-ORIENTED PROGRAMMING; OBJECT PROGRAM; OPERATOR PRECEDENCE; PROCEDURE; PROGRAMMING LANGUAGES; SOURCE PROGRAM; STATEMENT; STRUCTURED PROGRAMMING; SUBPROGRAM; and TRACE.

In contrast with the tremendous advances in computer hardware, the level at which machine and assembly languages (*q.v.*) operate has changed little over the past three decades. Instructions can be executed only if they are submitted as sequences of numerical codes. Moreover, the typical machine language instruction represents an activity that is trivial by human standards, offering no direct correspondence with our idea of a "step" in a problem solution.

Consequently, there is a gap between what the programmer wants to say and what the processor can recognize. High-level programming languages are designed to bridge this gap. It is in this context that one may examine the major conveniences provided by such languages, together with their effects on programming techniques.

Each of the hundreds of high-level programming languages is designed to meet a particular set of objectives.

Some are intended for use over a wide range of applications; others address a more limited spectrum of problem types characteristic of a specific discipline. All share a common property: The elemental vehicle for expressing the programmer's intention (i.e. the language statement) conveys a level of complexity consistent with the procedure being represented. Thus, the activity that can be described in a single "instruction" or "command" bears no direct resemblance to a single machine operation. Instead, many languages try to provide some similarity between a language *statement* (*q.v.*) and its counterpart in the notation appropriate to the application. For example, the following statement in the Fortran language,

$$H = 0.023*(C/D)*(D*V*R/U)**0.8* \\ (U*P/C)**0.4, \tag{1}$$

is easily related to the same formula in conventional algebraic form:

$$H = 0.023 \frac{C}{D} \left(\frac{DVR}{U} \right)^{0.8} \left(\frac{UP}{C} \right)^{0.4}. \tag{2}$$

This equation ultimately would require a considerable number of machine operations to produce the specified result (i.e. a value for H). Accordingly, the correspondence between the Fortran statement and the equivalent sequence of machine instructions produced by the language-translating program (the compiler) is not obvious at all.

This extensive insulation between machine and programmer has had a profound effect on the growth of computer use and the range of successful applications. Most programs are written in high-level languages, and most people who write programs are not computer specialists.

A number of fundamental programming facilities will be examined briefly. Once their functions have been defined, they will be used to synthesize programs and program segments. The discussion will center around several widely used languages whose properties typify the range of conveniences generally afforded.

Descriptions and Specifications Regardless of the language used by the programmer, the final result must be an operationally equivalent sequence of machine instructions. This consists of a numerical string in which each operation is designated by its respective code, defined for it as part of the machine's design. References to operands (data on which operations are to be performed) cannot be expressed in terms of names. Instead, such references are expressed as addresses; i.e. memory locations in which the desired data is stored.

For example, if a procedural step calls for the addition of variables X and Y, the eventual implementation in machine language has no knowledge of an X or a Y. Having previously established associations between those variables and particular storage locations, the actual instructions to be executed will be in terms of the contents of those locations. Thus, instead of saying "add Y to X," the

implied activity is to "add the contents of the location associated with variable Y to the contents of the location associated with variable X."

Similarly, when an algorithm includes a choice of processing sequences, the programmer sets up appropriate branches to different parts of the procedure, associating each destination with a particular activity. However, when this structure is represented in final form, these references are stripped of any procedural association. The destination, rather, is an address containing the instruction to be executed next.

If a machine language program is being prepared manually, then it is the programmer who must define the associations between addresses and their contents vis-à-vis their significance with respect to the procedure. The necessity of keeping track of these relationships accounted for much of the tedium required to turn out a reliable machine language program and helped motivate the development of high-level languages.

Consequently, every high-level language includes features that relieve the programmer of these bookkeeping tasks, shifting them to the software. The extent of this transfer depends on the sophistication of the language and the class of problems toward which it is oriented. In all cases, the programmer is no longer responsible for defining the direct relationships among the variables and their respective addresses. It is still necessary to make sure that ample storage is allocated to the various data items, but that process is greatly simplified. The programmer treats each variable in conventional terms, giving it a meaningful name that will apply throughout the program.

Within this general framework, the mechanism for expressing such specifications varies from one language to another. For some languages, the first stated activity involving a variable (such as the initial assignment of a value) is sufficient to trigger the automatic reservation of storage. For example, if we consider the Fortran statement shown in Eq. 1 as part of a program, and if the reference to the variable H in that statement constitutes its initial appearance in that program, the compiler automatically will allocate storage under that name for the result of the specified computations. Subsequent references to H will be processed routinely. Reliance on this type of facility tends to encourage undisciplined programming practices. Consequently, most professional programmers declare all variables explicitly, even when using languages that support implicit declarations. Certain languages (such as Pascal and Modula-2) enforce explicit *declaration* of all variables simply by designing the compiler to reject any failures to do so. Such languages are called *strongly typed* languages.

The following examples illustrate the forms for explicit reservation of storage in several languages:

(Fortran)	REAL X, Y, Z	
(C)	float x, y, z	(3)
(Pascal)	**var** x, y, z : real;	

Each of these statements reserves storage for three variables x, y, and z, each to accommodate a numerical value placed there later in the program. Since nothing further is specified, internal language rules (*default conditions - q.v.*) will determine the amount of reserved storage and the form for the numerical values.

Cobol, because of its concern with data files and records, requires a hierarchical description of the items for which storage is to be allocated. That is, unless specifically defined otherwise, each variable is considered to be a component of a larger data structure. Moreover, the storage associated with each variable must be specified in terms of the type of information to be accommodated. For example, the following specification

```
01 RENEW-INFO.
   02 R-DATE.
      03 R-MONTH PICTURE 99.        (4)
      03 R-DAY PICTURE 99.
      03 R-YR PICTURE 99.
   02 RENEW-RATE PICTURE 999V99.
```

reserves storage for a group of variables known collectively as RENEW-INFO. This structure consists of two basic components, R-DATE and RENEW-RATE. The former is a collection of three variables (R-MONTH, R-DAY, and R-YR), each of which is a two-digit integer. The second component is a single variable whose value will be expressed as a five-digit number having two decimal places.

The basic naming facility extends to the identification of statements within a program. It is possible to attach unique labels as prefixes to statements, thereby providing an unambiguous way of referring to a desired point in the processing. In most languages, statements may be associated with symbolic names such as those used for variables. In Fortran, Basic, and Pascal, the syntactic rules require numeric statement labels. The equivalent assignment statements shown below illustrate the labeling conventions for several languages:

```
17      LET C = A + Y*B      (Basic)    (5a)

24      C = A + Y*B          (Fortran)  (5b)
CALC2:  C = A + Y*B;         (C)        (5c)
CALC2.  COMPUTE C = A + Y*B  (Cobol)    (5d)
2:      c:= a + y*b          (Pascal)   (5e)
[5]     CALC2: C ← A + Y × B (APL)      (5f)
```

The label 2 in the Pascal assignment statement would not be accepted without prior definition as a label. Note the variously different assignment symbols (= , : = , and ←), and that an APL statement (that is part of a procedure definition) may have an (optional) symbolic label in addition to a naturally occurring numeric line number that doubles as a statement label.

Specification of Complex Activities in Simple Terms

The statement in Eq. 1 exemplifies the primary convenience a high-level language brings to its users—the ability to specify intricate steps with little loss in correspondence between the conventional description and its representation in a program. Syntactically, this intent is reflected in the characteristic of a language's elemental "sentence" or *statement*. Generally, the limitation on the length and complexity of a statement is designed to be sufficiently large so that it does not restrict the programmer's ability to maintain the integrity of a procedural step. Thus, it is usually the programmer, and not the computing system or the language, that determines the amount of activity to be specified in a single program "step" without serious regard to the number of actual machine steps these actions will eventually entail.

Terms, Operators, and Expressions The effect of this facility is seen perhaps more dramatically in terms of statements denoting internal manipulative operations (i.e. "computing"). In many high-level languages, the type of statement most commonly associated with such operations is the *assignment statement*. When specifying mathematical computations, the assignment statement emplified in Eq. 5 bear a superficial resemblance to equations. There is a vital difference, however; N = N + 1 makes no sense as an equation but is nonetheless a perfectly reasonable Fortran assignment statement that directs that the current value of variable N be incremented. For many languages, particularly those emphasizing mathematical capabilities, the assignment statement is some variant of the general structure

$$variable \leftarrow expression \qquad (6)$$

The ← is this construction symbolizes the operation of replacement, so that the general sense of the assignment may be represented as follows: "Evaluate the *expression* on the right-hand side of the ← by performing the indicated operations; then, let the result be the new value for *variable*, replacing its current value." In many widely used high-level languages, replacement is denoted (inaccurately) by the symbol " = ". Algol, Pascal, and Modula-2 (*q.v.*) use := and APL uses an actual ← . In (6) *variable*, the item to the left of ←, is structurally restricted to a single variable. Thus, a formulation such as

$$\frac{A+B}{C^2} = \frac{32.96\,(D+C)}{D} \qquad (7)$$

would have to be rewritten with the variable whose value is to be computed (say *B*) isolated on the left, i.e.

$$B = \frac{32.96\,C^2\,(D+C)}{D} - A. \qquad (8)$$

before the formula could be represented as a program statement.

An *expression* consists of a combination of *terms* and *operators* in which the rules of construction constitute a restricted version of those applying to ordinary algebra. The two basic restrictions given below are imposed to accommodate the computer's functional limitations and to avoid problems in compiler construction (*q.v.*).

1. Each individual arithmetic operation must be indicated explicitly; it may never be implied. (For

example, the expression $A(B + C)$, understandable in algebra, must be written as $A*(B + C)$ in a program statement.)

2. Expressions must be in linear form. For example, $(A + B)/(C - D)$ is a more awkward, but unavoidable, substitute for the conventional algebraic equivalent:

$$\frac{A + B}{C - D}.$$

The latter restriction reflects a physical limitation imposed by I/O media rather than any linguistic constraint.

Each compiler uses certain rules to evaluate expressions. Unless the user is familiar with these rules for a particular compiler, there may be constructions that appear ambiguous. For example, $A + B/C*D$ may be thought to represent

$$A + \frac{B}{CD}, \quad A + \frac{BD}{C}, \quad \text{or even} \quad \frac{A + B}{CD}.$$

Most procedure-oriented languages define an *operator precedence* (*q.v.*) or *hierarchy*, which dictates the interpretation of an expression, but different languages use different hierarchies. Most high-level languages allow the programmer to avoid ambiguity or to force the meaning intended by using parentheses to indicate the exact intent. Thus, the linear expressions $A + B/(C*D)$, $A + (B/C)*D$ and $(A + B)/(C*D)$ are the respective equivalents of the three algebraic expressions shown above.

Additional limitations are those imposed by the necessity of ensuring that there is a value associated with each variable appearing in an expression. This must be guaranteed by the programmer, since compilers generally are designed to proceed on that assumption. Once the programmer makes sure that the variables have been defined (i.e. storage has been made available for them and values have been provided), the language presents no further obstacles with regard to the length or complexity of an expression.

To illustrate, we refer again to Eq. 1, which uses the Fortran language. Assuming that values are available for each of the variables D, V, R, U, P, and C, the programmer has the prerogative of computing a value for H via a single statement, as in Eq. 2, or using several statements to produce partial results that are stored in separate variables and used subsequently:

```
V1 = D*V*R/U
V2 = U*P/C                                    (9)
H  = 0.023*(C/D)*(V1**0.8)*(V2**0.4).
```

The choice of form is governed predominantly by legibility of the resulting program.

For an increasing variety of applications, "internal manipulations" or "computation" need to be extended to include operations on strings of letters and other nonnumeric symbols. While most high-level languages accommodate such *alphanumeric* information, their facilities generally are limited to the simple movement and display of strings, treating them as labels or headings. However, capabilities for substantive processing of character strings are included in a number of languages that allow the use of nonnumeric data as constants and variables, and implement the manipulation through the general assignment statement. A fundamental operation is *concatenation* (*q.v.*), the synthesis of larger strings from smaller ones. This process is exemplified below to show the parallelism with arithmetic assignments. In each instance, we form a string consisting of the letters IDENTICAL and assign it to the variable $W3$.

Fortran:
```
CHARACTER W1*4, W2*3, W3*9
W1 = 'DENT'
W2 = 'CAL'                                   (10a)
W3 = 'I'//W1//'I'//W2
```

Turbo Pascal:
```
var w1 : string[4]; w2 : string[3]; w3 : string[9];
..........
w1 : = 'DENT';                               (10b)
w2 : = 'CAL';
w3 : = 'I' + w1 + 'I' + w2;
```

(Character strings, as such, are not uniformly supported in all Pascal implementations; several dialects, including the standard version, require strings to be constructed as arrays of individual characters.)

Built-In Functions High-level languages include features that expand considerably the range of processes expressable in a statement. The objective of these capabilities is to allow the programmer to specify as "single" operations a variety of activities, each of which actually embodies a number of steps, even by human standards. Prototypical is the extraction of the square root, a process viewed as a single mathematical operation and represented that way in conventional notation. To preserve this idea, a procedure designed to produce the square root is embedded in many high-level languages and made available to the programmer via a simple reference name (SQRT in most languages). Thus, the structure of a formulation, such as

$$C = \sqrt{A^2 + B^2} \tag{11}$$

still can be preserved in a language statement:

```
C = SQRT(A**2 + B**2)        (Fortran)  (12a)

C = SQRT(A**2 + B**2);       (PL/I)     (12b)
LET C = SQR(A↑2 + B↑2)       (Basic)    (12c)
c := sqrt(sqr(a) + sqr(b))   (Pascal)   (12d)
c = sqrt(pow(a,2) + pow(b,2)) (C)       (12e)
```

This square root facility is known as a *built-in function* or *library function*. Most high-level languages provide a library of such functions, with their exact nature being determined by the language's orientation. Accordingly, languages such as Fortran, Pascal, C, and Basic reflect their emphasis on arithmetic in terms of a substantial mathematical function library (e.g. logarithms, trigonometric functions), while those provided by Snobol and other languages directed toward nonnumeric applications offer a different spectrum of operations.

A standard collection of built-in functions represents part of a more general facility that enables a programmer to supplement the language with additional custom-designed functions. Inclusion of such functions is a relatively straightforward process independent of the complexity of the function or its intended permanency.

Decisions and Decision Structures Building on simple comparison operations available at the machine level, a high-level language generally provides the programmer with syntactic structures for expressing arbitrarily complicated tests and decision rules.

The conceptual element that forms a basis for decision statements can be represented graphically, as in Fig. 1. The nucleus is the test condition, formulated as a comparison with two possible outcomes (true or false). Accordingly, the outcome of the test will dictate which of the two alternative actions will ensue. The power of this construction can be summarized in terms of three basic properties:

1. The formulation is simple and "natural," reflecting the flowchart given in Fig. 1: "Test the specified condition. If it exists (true), perform alternative action A, ignoring B. If it is false, perform B, ignoring A. Upon completion of the action, continue that part of the processing that is independent of the test condition."
2. The test may be arbitrarily complex.
3. Either or both of the alternative actions may be arbitrarily complex, ranging from a very long sequence of program statements to no action at all.

The testing facilities in the Basic language, though rudimentary, typify the form underlying more extensive mechanisms. In general terms, the condition to be tested (in Basic) consists of a pair of arithmetic expressions con-

nected by a *relational operator* that defines the comparison. Thus, the construction

$$X*Y \ <= \ Z \tag{13}$$

specifies a comparison to determine whether the product XY is less than or equal to Z (in which case, the outcome would be "true") or not. Only one type of action is specifiable—a branch to some other place in the program, at which point the appropriate processing presumably continues; the alternative merely is to ignore the branch. Accordingly, the test and branch are combined to form a complete statement:

$$IF \ X*Y \ <= \ Z \ THEN \ 70, \tag{14}$$

as shown in Fig. 2. The "70" refers to the statement label attached to the branch's destination.

Other languages (such as Algol, PL/I, Fortran 90, Ada, C, and Pascal) provide less awkward vehicles by allowing the explicit specification of alternative actions, thereby mirroring directly the graphic representation in Fig. 1. This is seen in the following implementations of a decision rule.

C:
```
if (x*y < = z)
  then
     x = x + 7.8
  else
     x = x - 1.6 ;
t = x*y*z*(2.5 * y + w);
```
(15a)

Pascal:
```
if x*y < = z then x : = x + 7.8
                 else  x : = x - 1.6;
t : = x*y*z*(2.5*y + w);
```
(15b)

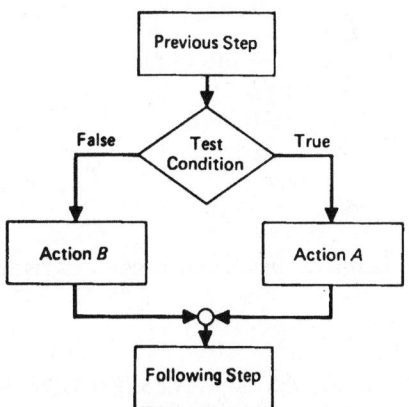

FIG. 1. Flowchart for basic high-level language decision structure.

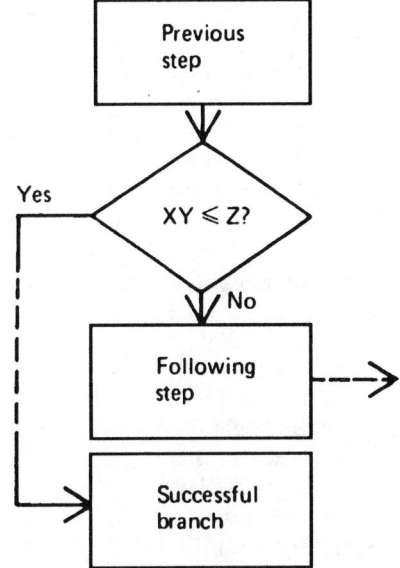

FIG. 2. Example of testing and branching in the Basic language.

Fortran 90:

```
IF (X*Y .LE. Z) THEN X = X + 7.8
                ELSE X = X - 1.6
END IF                                    (15c)
T = X*Y*Z*(2.5*Y + W)
```

The same facility is present in Cobol in a more narrative form:

```
IF X*Y < = Z ADD 7.8 TO X
    ELSE SUBTRACT 1.6 FROM X.           (15d)
    COMPUTE T = X*Y*Z*(2.5*Y + W).
```

The structural simplicity made possible by the IF...THEN...ELSE coupling is not very useful without a corresponding enlargement in the range of activities that may be attached to a decision rule. This is handled by including syntactic components wherein sequences of statements are treated as a single (conceptual) activity. To illustrate, our decision rule will be complicated: "If XY is less than or equal to Z, do the following: Add 7.8 to X, double Y, and subtract 2.2 from Z; otherwise, subtract 1.8 from X, make $Y = 0.85 \times$ its current value, and leave Z alone. In either case, compute the value $XYZ(2.5Y + W)$ and store the result in T." The appropriate program fragments are:

Fortran 90:

```
IF (X*Y .LE. Z) THEN X = X + 7.8
                Y = 2*Y
                Z = Z - 2.2            (16a)
           ELSE X = X - 1.8
                Y = 0.85*Y
END IF
T = X*Y*Z*(2.5*Y + W)
```

C:

```
    if (x*y < = z)
      then
      {x = x + 7.8;
       y = 2*y;
       z = z - 2.2; }                  (16b)
      else
      { x = x - 1.8;
        y = 0.85*y; }
      t= x*y*z*(2.5*y + w);
```

Pascal:

```
    if x*y < = z then begin
              x:= x + 7.8
              y:= 2*y;
              z:= z - 2.2
              end
          else begin                   (16c)
              x:= x - 1.8;
              y:= 0.85*y
              end
    t:= x*y*z*(2.5*y + w);
```

The delimiters **begin** and **end** play the same role as { and } in C.

Cobol uses a more casual syntax:

```
IF X*Y IS < = Z ADD 7.8 TO X
    MULTIPLY 2 BY Y SUBTRACT 2.2 FROM Z
    ELSE SUBTRACT 1.8 FROM X MULTIPLY    (16d)
    0.85 BY Y.
COMPUTE T = X*Y*Z*(2.5*Y + W).
```

Programming Loops Most high-level languages offer convenient ways to specify and control repetitive operations. In general, these enable the programmer to identify the beginning and end of a *loop* (*q.v.*), specify the number of repetitions, and define a mechanism for (automatically) keeping track of the number of cycles through the loop.

These mechanisms can be examined conveniently via an example involving arrays. An array A_1, will have its 14 elements set respectively to values of 1, 2,..., 14. A second array, A_2, also consisting of 14 elements, will receive respective values of 3, 5, 7,..., 29. The sequences in Basic, Fortran, PL/I, and Pascal are quite similar.

Basic:

```
10 DIM A1(14), A2(14)
15 FOR I = 1 TO 14
20    LET A1(I) = I
25    LET A2(I) = 2*I + 1             (17a)
30 NEXT I
```

Fortran:

```
INTEGER A1(14), A2(14)
DO 30 I = 1, 14
    A1(I) = I                         (17b)
    A2(I) = 2*I + 1
30 CONTINUE
```

C:

```
float a1[14], a2[14];
int i;
for (i = 1; i < = 14; i++)
  {
    a1[i] = i;
    a2[i] = 2*i + 1;
  }                                   (17c)
```

Pascal:

```
var a1,a2: array[1..14] of real;
      i : integer;
    begin
      for i : = 1 to 14 do
        begin                         (17d)
          a1[i]:= i;
          a2[i]:= 2*i + 1
        end
    end.
```

The mode of expression in Cobol is characteristically less formulaic:

```
01 ARRAYS.
    02 A1 OCCURS 14 TIMES PICTURE 999V99.
    02 A2 OCCURS 14 TIMES PICTURE 999V99.
```

```
77 I PICTURE 99.                              (17e)
        .
        .
        .
PERFORM BUILDUP VARYING I FROM 1 BY 1
  UNTIL I GREATER THAN 14.
BUILDUP.
    COMPUTE A1(I) = I.
    COMPUTE A2(I) = 2*I + 1.
```

These facilities may be generalized so that the programmer can implement loops in which the number of cycles and the method of cycling may vary with each use.

For some languages, the ability to specify the number of cycles is complemented by another *control structure* (*q.v.*) that is not based on a prescribed number of cycles. Instead, the programmer may construct a loop in which some arbitrarily defined criterion automatically terminates the repetitions, irrespective of the number of cycles. To see how this works, we consider the following example: X is a number, values for which are read in successively. The program is to accumulate the sum of these successive input values until that sum reaches or exceeds a value Y (said value also having been made available to the program earlier). To simplify matters, it will be assumed that Y will be reached or exceeded before all of X's values are exhausted.

Many languages include a specific mechanism to deal with such situations conveniently. Pascal serves as an appropriate example:

```
total : = 0;
while total < y do
    begin
        read (x);                              (18a)
        total : = total + x
    end;
    {further processing}
```

In the absence of this automating feature, the programmer is obliged to set up the decision mechanism manually. Accordingly, an equivalent sequence in Fortran 90 would be expressed as follows:

```
    TOTAL = 0.0
  1 IF (TOTAL .GE. Y) GO TO 30
        READ *, X
        TOTAL = TOTAL + X                       (18b)
    GO TO 1
 30 further processing
```

Although the example shown above is sufficiently simple so that there is no conspicuous difference in legibility between the two versions, use of numerous branches in more complex loops and other decision structures may lead to overly intricate, logical mazes that are extremely difficult to analyze. In such contexts, the branch may represent an operational intrusion that detracts from the resemblance between a procedural component and its implementation in a program.

As the design and analysis of programs have become more systematized, there has been a corresponding evolution of language features that facilitate the representation of complex logical situations without the use of explicit branches. This approach, known as *structured programming*, has prompted the introduction of language features that make it easy to avoid the need for such branches. For example, Pascal recognizes two distinct variations of the loop control mechanism illustrated in the previous example: One of these, the *repeat-until* construct, provides for the convenient specifications of a loop for which the programmer guarantees at least one cycle. Implementation of the previous program segment using this construct is shown below.

```
total := 0;
repeat
    read (x);                                  (18c)
    total := total + x
until total > = y
```

As the construct implies, the test (which determines whether or not to perform another cycle) occurs after the activity is completed. The alternative is the *do-while* construct, already seen. This is the most general loop control, in that it includes the possibility that the loop will not cycle at all. Accordingly, the determining test implied in this construct occurs prior to the cyclic activity.

Input/Output Operations A significant aspect of the growing variety of computer hardware technology is the widening array of available I/O devices. One of the primary duties of a high-level language is to accommodate this expanding capability without undo inconvenience to the programmer. These dual requirements of versatility and convenience often are antithetical, and language designers must seek an effective compromise.

Many languages handle I/O operations using two basic mechanisms. The first of these is to provide a unified form for specifying all data transmission. Specific circumstances pertaining to a particular operation then are defined within the statement's general structure. In Fortran, for example, these operations can be represented by the general statements:

```
READ(n, m) v1, v2, etc.
WRITE(n, m) v1, v2, etc.                        (19)
```

Access to the various peripheral devices is provided by n. Each device in a particular computing constellation is given a unique number, and a table of these designations is made available to Fortran within the supervisory software under which it operates. (These assignments are fairly standard, but they may easily be redefined at each individual installation). Accordingly, the programmer specifies the device number involved in a particular data transmission, and the appropriate association is established. The second parenthesized indicator, m, gives the number of a statement in that program in which the data format is described. For input (i.e. in a READ statement), the statement labeled m gives an item-by-item description of the appearance of the data (number of digits, location of the decimal point, number of spaces between consecutive values, etc.). Each description corresponds to a variable named in the input list $v1$, $v2$, etc. To illustrate, assume that values for three variables x, y, and z are stored on a disk, as shown in Fig. 3. Using 7 to represent the disk unit, the appropriate Fortran sequence would be

```
REAL X, Y, Z
........
READ(7, 14) X, Y, Z                 (20)
14 FORMAT (1X, F4.1,1X,F6.2,2X,F4.1)
```

The 1X indicates that the first position (column) is to be ignored. The F4.1 specifies that the next four positions are to be interpreted as a real numerical value having a single decimal place, etc. In a WRITE statement, the information in statement m describes the listed data items as they are to appear on the output medium. It is possible to define standard input and output devices. For many systems the keyboard and video display units are earmarked for such purposes. Once defined, these designations may be implied in the program. Assuming Fig. 3's data to be submitted from a standard input device, for instance, the read statement in (20) would say

```
READ(*, 14) X, Y, Z
```

Further simplification is possible when dealing with input items separated specifically by blanks. (This is the case in Fig. 3, but the 1X, 1X and 2X specifications in the previous FORMAT statement are general, causing the program to skip the indicated number of positions, irrespective of their contents.) Thus, there could have been anything at all between Fig. 3's data items without affecting the result. If the intermediate items are blanks, it is possible to exploit a special scanning mechanism available in several languages. Fig. 3's data (assumed to be from the standard device) can be read with the Fortran statement

```
READ(*,*) X, Y, Z
```

or simply

```
READ *, X, Y, Z
```

The Pascal equivalent is

```
readln (x, y, z)
```

Organization of Programs

Efforts to increase the parallels between statements in a language and steps in an algorithm have helped shape the techniques surrounding program preparation. In contrast to early approaches, in which sequences of statements were put together to produce something that "worked," increasing emphasis is being placed on facilitating the programming process through systematic exploitation of high-level language features. Some of the underlying motivations are worth noting.

On innumerable occasions, the cost of designing and perfecting a program outstrips that of using the finished product. Moreover, many programs tend to be unstable in the sense that experience, along with external events, precipitates procedural changes that ultimately must be accommodated by modifying the program. When the program's construction is haphazard to begin with, any but the most trivial changes are awkward to incorporate. In many cases, such modification is aggravated by programmers' inability to follow the tortuous path of events in their own programs after being away from them even for a short time. Under these conditions, it is understandable that a small number of such episodes often result in a decision to scrap a program and start over.

An important factor in reducing this chaos has been the use of *modular programming* (q.v.), an approach in which an explicit effort is made to construct a program from components, each representing an identifiable procedural activity. That is, instead of viewing a program as a sequence of individual statements, it is treated as a combination of modules. Most high-level languages include features that encourage and facilitate modularity.

To illustrate some aspects of this modular approach, a number of the features discussed in previous sections will be integrated to construct complete programs representing solutions to the following problem:

An array of input values X consists of 32 numbers, each in the form $YY.Y$. The array is to be divided into two component arrays, $X1$ and $X2$, such that each member of $X1$ has a value smaller than that specified by an additional input variable named CUTOFF, with the remaining elements being assigned to $X2$. The program is to print three lines of output: The first of these is to repeat the input

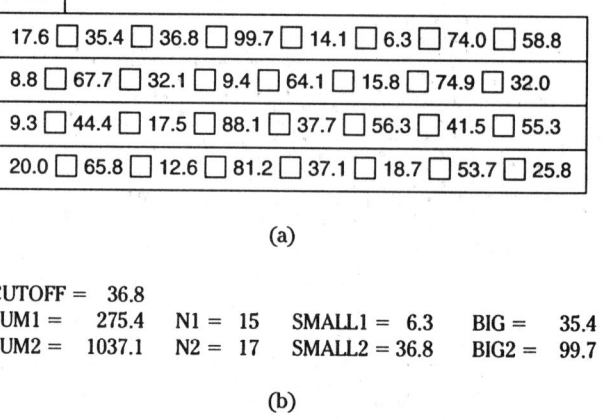

FIG. 4. (a) Input and (b) Output for programs of Figs. 5–8.

FIG. 3. Values of variables X, Y, Z for the read statement in (20). Each ☐ represents a single blank.

```
PROGRAM ARRY
   REAL X(32),SUM1,SUM2,SMALL1,SMALL2,BIG1,BIG2,CUTOFF,X1(32),X2(32)
   INTEGER N1,N2

* A 'REAL' VARIABLE IN FORTRAN IS STORED AS A FLOATING POINT NUMBER.
* THIS IS EQUIVALENT TO A DEFAULT DECLARATION IN PL/I, E.G.,
* DECLARE SUM1, SUM2; WITHOUT FURTHER QUALIFICATION
* EACH READ STATEMENT HANDLES AT LEAST ONE LINE OF INPUT DATA,
* TAKING ONLY THE INFORMATION INDICATED BY THE VARIABLE NAME(S)
* IN ACCORDANCE WITH THE FORMAT SPECIFICATIONS.

   READ *, CUTOFF

* SINCE X IS DEFINED AS CONSISTING OF 32 ELEMENTS, THE DESIGNATION
* IN THE FOLLOWING READ STATEMENT IS SUFFICIENT TO INSTIGATE THE
* READING OF 32 ITEMS.

READ *, X

* SMALL1 AND SMALL2 ARE INITIALIZED TO 10**30, THEREBY FORCING THE FIRST
* ASSIGNMENTS FROM THEIR RESPECTIVE ARRAYS, AFTER WHICH THE LOOP WILL
* PROCEED ROUTINELY. THE SAME REASONING PUTS THE LOWEST POSSIBLE
* VALUES (IF WE ASSUME NO NEGATIVES) IN THE TWO MAXIMA.

      SMALL1 = 1E30
      SMALL2 = 1E30
      BIG1 = 0.0
      BIG2 = 0.0
      N1 = 0
      N2 = 0
      SUM1 = 0.0
      SUM2 = 0.0

* SINCE THERE IS A CERTAIN AMOUNT OF BOOKKEEPING BEHIND A DO LOOP,
* IT IS MORE EFFICIENT TO MIMIMIZE THE NUMBER OF LOOPS USED.
* THUS, WE ARE SEARCHING FOR THE SMALLS AND THE BIGS WITHIN THE SAME
* LOOP, RATHER THAN DOING IT IN SEPARATE LOOPS AFTER THE ARRAYS X1
* AND X2 HAVE BEEN SEGREGATED. THIS IS A MATTER OF JUDGEMENT, BECAUSE
* OVERZEALOUS USE OF THIS PRACTICE COULD IMPAIR THE PROGRAM'S CLARITY.

      DO 20 I = 1, 32
      IF (X(I) .LT. CUTOFF)
        THEN N1 = N1 + 1
             X1(N1) = X(I)
             SUM1 = SUM1 + X(I)
             IF (X(I) .LT. SMALL1) SMALL1 = X(I)
             IF (X(I) .GT. BIG1) BIG1 = X(I)
        ELSE N2 = N2 + 1
             X2(N2) = X(I)
             SUM2 = SUM2 + X(I)
             IF (X(I) .LT. SMALL2) SMALL2 = X(I)
             IF (X(I) .GT. BIG2) BIG2 = X(I)
      END IF
 20 CONTINUE

      PRINT *, 'CUTOFF = ', CUTOFF
      PRINT *, 'SUM1 = ', SUM1, 'N1 = ', N1, 'SMALL1 = ', SMALL1, 'BIG1 = ', BIG1
      PRINT *, 'SUM2 = ', SUM2, 'N2 = ', N2, 'SMALL2 = ', SMALL2, 'BIG2 = ', BIG2

      END ARRY
```

FIG. 5.   Listing of Fortran 90 program for producing the output of Fig. 4.

value for CUTOFF; the second line is to display the sum of all the values assigned to array $X1$ (SUM1), the number of elements assigned to $X1$ (N1), the smallest element in $X1$ (SMALL1), and the largest value assigned to $X1$ (BIG1). The final line of output is to show similar values for array $X2$ (SUM2, N2, SMALL2, and BIG 2, respectively). Note that the arrays $X1$ and $X2$ are not needed to obtain the required results. Their inclusion presumes that they would be processed further in a more extensive procedure.

Fortran and Pascal solutions are shown to compare structural possibilities in the two languages. Additional explanatory material is embedded in each program by exploiting each language's ability to display supporting information that is not part of the actual program. For reference, sample input and output are shown in Fig. 4. (Standard input and output devices are assumed.)

The Fortran and Pascal programs (Figs. 5 and 6) exploit the use of compound statements to enhance structural clarity. Consequently, the implementation of the basic decision mechanism is a direct result of its narrative description.

High-level languages provide the ability to define and integrate *subprograms* (*q.v.*) easily and to make them very general. This has revolutionized programming techniques, motivating an overall approach in which frequently used procedural activities are constructed as subprograms and maintained in a library. Then, a new set of procedural requirements are fulfilled by selecting appropriate library routines and combining them by means of a relatively small main program, adding those special procedures not otherwise covered. In using this construction, each activity can be treated as a "black box" whose input requirements are known and whose results are defined, thereby enhancing the overall program's legibility. Furthermore, there may be a considerable reduction in the effort required to produce a working program, since each of the prepackaged activities is known to work and need not be redeveloped. When a new program must be constructed from the ground up because required subprograms are unavailable, careful modularization allows several people to work on the program concurrently.

This approach is seen in the reorganized Pascal program in Fig. 7. Assignment of an element from array x to another array is handled by a separate procedure that is called each time through the loop. Once all x's elements have been processed, a second subprogram is called twice, one for each of the arrays $x1$ and $x2$, to find the respective extreme values.

The perception of the aforementioned process as single conceptual activities receives additional emphasis in Pascal by defining the arrays as distinct data types. This lends further clarity to the overall process by untying it from the kinds of language restrictions that force the use of data into a small number of predefined types.

Programming in APL has a distinctly different flavor from that experienced in using any of the other POLs in this survey. Because of the richness of APL's vector-oriented functions, no explicit loops need be written to compute the values needed for Fig. 4. A vector is just APL's name for a one-dimensional array. Any vector may be *reduced* to form either a single value through use of the

```
program arry (input, output);
var
    x, x1, x2 : array [1..32] of real ;
    small1, small2, big1, big2, cutoff, sum1, sum2 : real ;
    n1, n2 : integer ;
    i : 1..32 ; {Limits values of i to integers in range 1 to 32}
begin
    readln (cutoff) ;
    small1 := 1E30 ;        small2 := 1E30 ;
    big1 := 0.0 ;           big2 := 0.0 ;
    sum1 := 0.0 ;           sum2 := 0.0 ;
    n1 := 0 ;               n2 := 0 ;
    for i := 1 to 32 do
        begin
            x1[i] := 0.0 ;    x2[i] := 0.0 ;
            read (x[i])
        end ;
    for i := 1 to 32 do
        if x[i] < cutoff then
            begin
                sum1 := sum1 + x[i] ;
                n1 := n1 + 1 ;
                xl[n1] := x[i] ;
                if x[i] < small1 then small1 := x[i] ;
                if x[i] > big1 then big1 := x[i]
            end
        else
            begin
                sum2 := sum2 + x[i] ;
                n2 := n2 + 1 ;
                if x[i] < small2 then small2 := x[i] ;
                if x[i] > big2 then big2 := x[i]
            end ;
    writeln ('CUTOFF = ',cutoff) ;
    writeln ('SUM1 = ',sum1,' N1 = ',n1,
             ' SMALL1 = ' ,small1,' BIG1 = ',big1) ;
    wiriteln ('SUM2 = ',small2,' N2 = ',n2,
             ' SMALL2 = ',small2,' BIG2 = ',big2)
end.
```

FIG. 6.   Pascal program for producing the output of Fig. 4.

reduction operator, /, in conjunction with an arithmetic or logical operator, or to form a smaller vector through reduction over a Boolean mask—a vector of 1s and 0s. For example, +/A will sum all components of vector A, and given that the size of A is 5, (1 0 1 0 0)/A will produce a new two-component vector consisting of the first and third components of A. Masks are not usually written explicitly, but rather are computed, as in

$$A \leftarrow 2\ 8\ 9\ 3\ 1\ 6$$
$$B \leftarrow (A < 5) / A$$

which produces, tentatively, (1 0 0 1 1 0) / A, so that B becomes 2 3 1.

Fig. 8 shows the APL program, complete except for the output, that is needed to compute the values shown in Fig. 4. The $\lfloor$ and $\lceil$ are APL's *min* and *max* functions,

```
program arryl (input, output);
{WE DEFINE A SPECIAL DATA TYPE NAMED ForceValues TO CONNECT
THE DATA MORE CLOSELY TO THE APPLICATION.}
type ForceValues = array [1..32] of real ;
var
    x, x1, x2 : ForceValues ;
    small1, small2, big1, big2, cutoff, sum1, sum2 : real ;
    n1, n2: integer ;
    i : 1..32 ;

    procedure augment (xval : real ; var v : ForceValues ;
                       var total : real ; var n : integer) ;
    {THE NAMES SHOWN (xval, v, etc.) DO NOT REPRESENT ACTUAL
    DATA ITEMS. THEY ARE PLACEHOLDERS TO BE MATCHED AGAINST THE
    ACTUAL ITEMS (ARGUMENTS) TO BE SUPPLIED WHEN augment IS ACTUATED.
    THE var IN FRONT OF C, total, AND n TELLS PASCAL THAT THE VALUES
    OF THE CORRESPONDING ITEMS WILL BE CHANGED BY THE SUBPROGRAM.}
    begin     {augment's PROCESSING}
              total := total + xval ;  n := n + 1 ;   v[n] :=xval
    end ;     {augment's  PROCESSING}

    procedure extremes (xval ; ForceValues ; n : integer ;
                        var small,  big ; real) ;
    var j ; 1..32 ;        {j IS USED ONLY INSIDE THIS SUBPROGRAM}
    begin {extreme's PROCESSING}
       for j := 1 to n do
          begin
             if xval[j] < small then small := xval[j] ;
             if xval[j] > big   then    big := xval[j]
          end
    end ;             {extreme's PROCESSING}

begin  {MAIN PROGRAM}
    readln (cutoff) ;
    small1 := 1e30 ;   small2 := 1e30 ; big1 := 0.0 ;  big2 := 0.0 ;
    sum1 := 0.0 ;      sum2 := 0.0 ;    n2:= 0 ;        n1 := 0 ;
    for i := 1 to 32 do
       begin
           x1[i] := 0.0 ;     x2[i] := 0.0 ;      read (x[i])
       end ;
    {THE LOOP IS THE SAME AS BEFORE, EXCEPT THAT THE ASSIGNMENT OF
    EACH ELEMENT TO THE APPROPRIATE ARRAY IS HANDLED BY THE SUB-
    PROGRAM NAMED augment. WHEN augment FINISHES ITS WORK, THE
    PROGRAM CONTINUES WHERE IT LEFT OFF. THE EFFECT IS AS IF THE
    SUBPROGRAM WERE A SINGLE STATEMENT PERFORMED OUT OF SEQUENCE.}
    for i := 1 to 32 do
       if x[i] < cutoff then augment(x[i], x1, sum1, nl)
                        else augment(x[i], x2, sum2, n2) ;
    {NOW WE USE A SEPARATE SUBPROGRAM TO FIND EACH SET OF EXTREMES}
    extremes (x1, n1, small1, big1) ;   extremes (x2, n2, small2, big2) ;
    writeln ('CUTOFF = ',cutoff) ;
    writeln ('SUM1 = ',SUM1,' N1 = ',n1,
            ' SMALL1 = ',small1,' BIG1 = ', big1) ;
    writeln ('SUM2 = ',sum2,' N2 =',n2,
            ' SMALL2 = ',small2,' BIG2 = ',big2)
end.    {MAIN PROGRAM}
```

FIG. 7. Reorganized Pascal program using procedures.

CUTOFF ← □	ᴀ	Read a cutoff value
X ← □	ᴀ	Read data to form vector X
X1 ← (X < CUTOFF)/X	ᴀ	Place values of X < cutoff into X1
X2 ← (X > CUTOFF)/X	ᴀ	Place values of X > cutoff into X2
SUM1 ← +/X1	ᴀ	Sum components of X1
SUM1 ← +/X2	ᴀ	Sum components of X2
SMALL1 ←⌊/X1	ᴀ	Find smallest value of X1
SMALL2 ←⌊/X2	ᴀ	Find smallest value of X2
BIG1 ←⌈X1	ᴀ	Find largest value of X1
BIG2 ←⌈X2	ᴀ	Find largest value of X2

FIG. 8.   APL program to compute values of Fig. 4.

respectively, so that $\lfloor/A$ returns the smallest element of A and $\lceil/A$ returns its largest value.

Aids in the Debugging Process

In the process of freeing the programmer from the minutiae of the machine, high-level languages have also removed the programmer from the vantage point of knowing what is going on inside the computer. This becomes a crucial problem when something is wrong in the program or the processing, since it may be impossible to relate an event concerning an individual machine instruction to the corresponding point in the procedure as the programmer perceives it.

To reestablish control, the software structure within which a high-level language operates is equipped with diagnostic mechanisms to provide appropriate clues that will facilitate the location, identification, and repair of difficulty. Since any software structure inherently contains rules whose violation prevents the system from operating properly, the general approach is to supplement these rules with a repetoire of diagnostic messages. Then, if a rule is broken, the appropriate message is displayed as part of the system's response. The rest of the response often is to curtail the processing at that point, but not before the programmer has been given some information.

There is continuing controversy over what is "appropriate." Users would like their high-level language implementation equipped with extensive messages that delineate the type of difficulty as well as its source. Designers, more concerned with the size and operating overhead of a software system, favor a minimal set of aids in which the difficulty is located but no attempt is made to specify its nature. The idea is that, once the user is directed to a trouble spot, presumably he or she will determine what is wrong and correct it. The direction of the inevitable compromise varies widely among languages and among implementations of the same language.

Diagnostic facilities will be examined within two basic contexts: The first deals with the compilation process during which a high-level language *source program* (*q.v.*) is analyzed to produce an equivalent machine language *object program* (*q.v.*); the second situation is concerned with events preventing a successfully compiled program from operating.

Aids During the Compilation Process

Every programming language has its syntactic rules that permit the unambiguous and repeatable analysis of a source language program by an appropriately designed compiler. As part of the same process, then, the compiler can detect and classify violations of those rules, calling the programmer's attention to them.

To become acquainted with the general nature of these responses, imagine that the illustrative program shown in Fig. 7 has been contaminated with the following errors.

1. Suppose that the closing bracket on the size specification in the **type** statement has been omitted, so that the statement (erroneously) reads

   type ForceValues = **array** [1..32 **of** real;

   (This type of oversight is surprisingly common.)
2. Suppose that storage of array *x2* has not been reserved, so that this declaration had read

   .....x, xl : ForceValues;
3. Suppose that the upper limit of the loop that reads *x*'s values had been (wrongly) set at 34, *viz.*,

   for i : = 1 **to** 34 **do**
   begin
     x1[i] : = 0.0 ; x2[i] : = 0.0 ; read(x[i])
   end ;

When processed by an interactive compiler, the program with the three deliberately embedded bugs produced the error messages shown in Fig. 9. Each of the errors was detected in a separate compilation attempt that stopped the process and produced a predefined message. The accompanying error numbers refer to entries in a separate manual containing more information about the pos-

error 93: "]" or ")" expected
error 3: Unknown Identifier
error 76: Constant out of range

FIG. 9.   Diagnostic messages produced by a compiler.

sible source of the errors, along with suggested remedies. Once the first error was corrected, the subsequent compilation attempt was thwarted by the second error, etc.

Fig. 9's messages actually are more helpful than they might seem to indicate: the programming environment is constructed so that when the compiler finds an error that prevents further processing, the offending statement is earmarked on the video screen. Thus, for instance, when the "Unknown Identifier" message appears, the accompanying display is focused on the x2[i] : = 0.0 statement, thereby calling specific attention to the perceived difficulty.

The types of diagnostic services exemplified by the example above represent but one layer of such facilities available by default (i.e. without requiring explicit requests). Many compilers include more elaborate diagnostic structures that may be activated at the programmer's option.

Diagnostic Aids During Program Execution

Successful compilation in no way guarantees subsequent successful execution of the resulting machine language program. An endless variety of anomalies and inconsistencies can appear during processing, and hardware/software systems contain features for detecting and dealing with some of these difficulties. Of course, it is impossible for the system to anticipate each particular situation. Instead, diagnostic mechanisms are sensitive to certain types of events whose occurrence can be expected to cause trouble. Typical categories include attempts to divide by zero, references to nonexistent storage addresses, or involvement of a nonnumeric data item in an arithmetic operation. Once such a situation is encountered, the resulting message usually gives the general category, together with some indication of the place in the program at which the difficulty occurred.

While there is a loose parallelism between the processes of producing a successful compilation and a successful run, the techniques associated with the latter activity are conspicuously different. Despite the extensive diagnostic aids available by default or by request during a program's execution, it often is impossible for the user to exploit them passably. Since these facilities necessarily must be general, the information they provide may be useless unless it is accompanied by more specific qualifications actively supplied by the programmer. To do this, the programmer uses a simple but effective technique: The source program must be equipped with supplementary statements designed specifically to provide helpful information for debugging. A common practice, for instance, is to print the input "as is" as soon as it is read (this is termed an *echo*), thereby providing a convenient reference point. Displays of intermediate results also may be revealing.

A frequently recurring situation is one in which execution is terminated and the regular diagnostic services report that there was an attempt to divide by zero at a point corresponding to a particular statement in the source language program. However, there are complications because that statement turns out to be part of a loop and there is no indication of the number of cycles that had

been completed before the tragedy occurred. Insertion of a statement that prints the value of the index (and, perhaps, other crucial variables) each time through the loop may be all that is required to identify the problem. Once the difficulty is found and appropriate safeguards are installed (e.g. testing potential divisors for a value of zero and specifying evasive action should this be true). Now extraneous output statements may be removed for the program's final version. Many programmers take a more conservative approach: Instead of removing the test statements, they merely surround them with the special symbols necessary to convert them to comments. In this way, they remain as physical parts of the source program and, should they ever be needed again, they can be reactivated easily. (Modern *debuggers*—*see* DEBUGGING and PROGRAMMING SUPPORT ENVIRONMENTS—automate much of this process.)

These techniques are especially helpful in dealing with the more insidious types of situations in which a program runs to completion but is procedurally wrong: Input was read properly and the program printed when it should have printed, but the output values make no sense. Correction is strictly up to the programmer, who must decide which items will be most revealing and at which time their display will be of greatest use.

Diagnostic facilities of many systems include features that facilitate this type of scrutiny. Rather than requiring the programmer to insert explicit statements at strategic points, a *trace* may be requested, during which designated variables are monitored automatically. In this mode of operation, the value of a variable is printed every time it undergoes a change, together with information regarding the point in the program at which the change occurs. Another type of trace chronicles the sequence of events during execution. This is very useful in procedures containing numerous modules and/or complex decision networks that provide a wide choice of possible actions and sequences.

Future Directions   Despite the abundance of syntactic and operational restrictions, there still is sufficient latitude to make high-level language programming a surprisingly subjective endeavor. There is no "ultimate" language (nor is its eventual definition assured), and there are no rigorous "laws" characterizing programs or the techniques pertinent to their construction. Work in structured programming and object-oriented programming and their associated design methodologies has identified valuable program properties that tend to produce clearer, more easily maintained sequences of instructions. These insights have motivated the development of high-level languages and compilers whose rules make it increasingly difficult to circumvent the use of certain structural components deemed to be desirable. The Pascal language, for example, incorporates minimal default mechanisms, compelling its users to provide explicit definitions for all data items. Many view Pascal as the beginning of a new family of high-level languages that, eventually, will shift virtually all of the subjective/creative activity to the design of the algorithm, with subsequent implementation (i.e. coding) becoming an (almost) automatic process.

Consequently, the development of high-level language programming can be described as a dynamic, spiraling process in which a continuous accumulation of experience and insight identifies linguistic deficiencies remedied by new languages or extensions to existing ones. Additional impetus is provided by newly emerging hardware and applications. Once newer languages become available, they engender new programming techniques and higher levels of algorithms that stimulate further developments, and so it goes.

An example of this process, current at this writing, is the emergence of *object-oriented programming* (*q.v.*) as a paradigm for designing and implementing software products. The fundamental idea is to define and package *objects,* where an object consists of a data structure together with the operations available for that structure. Once such objects have been defined, it is possible to build a program as a simple sequence of processes to be performed on specified instances of these objects. An integral part of object definition is the ability to create new, more elaborate objects as enhancements of those previously defined. The promise of this approach has prompted the addition of object-oriented features in existing programming languages and the creation of new languages centered around objects.

This kind of turbulence continues to characterize the development and use of programming languages. The result is an endlessly challenging arena for all people involved with computers and computing.

References

1973. Elson, M. *Programming Techniques*. Chicago: Science Research Associates.
1976. Dijkstra, E. W. *A Discipline of Programming*. Englewood Cliffs, NJ: Prentice-Hall.
1979. Pollack, S. V. and Sterling, T. D. *A Guide to PL/I*, 3rd Ed. New York: Holt, Rinehart and Winston.
1987. MacLennan, B. J. *Principles of Programming Languages*, 2nd Ed. New York: Holt, Rinehart and Winston.
1989. Reilly, E. D. and Federighi, F. D. *Pascalgorithms*. Boston: Houghton-Mifflin.

SEYMOUR V. POLLACK AND THEODOR D. STERLING

PROCEDURE, PURE. *See* REENTRANT PROGRAM.

PROCESS. *See* JOB.

PROCESSING MODES

For articles on related subjects *see* COMPUTING CENTER; DATA ACQUISITION COMPUTERS; INTERACTIVE SYSTEM; JOB; REAL-TIME BUSINESS APPLICATIONS; TELEPROCESSING SYSTEMS; THROUGHPUT; TIME SHARING; TRANSACTION PROCESSING; and TURNAROUND TIME.

Six distinct categories of computing activity can be identified:

1. Card-oriented batch processing.
2. Keyboard-oriented batch processing.
3. Interactive computing.
4. On-line inquiry and transaction processing.
5. Message switching.
6. Data acquisition and control (DAX).

The first of these is included here for historical completeness, but is now virtually obsolete.

Of these processing modes, the last four are performed on line and in real time; responses to input stimuli (or input transactions) are almost instantaneous. The batch-processing modes differ in that substantial queues of unprocessed transactions (*jobs*) are held in the computer throughout normal operation. Likewise, substantial queues of output reports are printed/punched continuously for card-oriented batch processing. (These queues are presented on request during keyboard-oriented batch processing.) Typical response times for the six modes are shown in Fig. 1.

Batch processing uses programs and data stored at all levels of a memory hierarchy:

1. Main memory.
2. Auxiliary memory.
3. Card decks, floppy disks, cassettes, etc.

Each batch installation maintains a library of systems and applications programs on fast auxiliary memory, typically drums or disks. Applications based on punched cards (or their images) required input *unit records* prepared on keypunches, key/disk key/tape systems, teletypes, or other off-line devices not connected to a computer. Input data (and specialized programs associated with the data) were submitted to the computer all at once in a high-speed stream. Little validation of data was performed during this input phase.

	10^{-2}	10^{-1}	10^0	10^1	10^2	10^3	10^4
Card-oriented batch processing						————	
Keyboard oriented batch processing					————		
Interactive computing				—			
On-line inquiry and transaction processing				—			
Message switching (per message)			————				
DAX	————						

FIG. 1. Response times to input stimuli, in seconds.

Users of keyboard-oriented batch processing prepare input data and programs much the same as for card-oriented processing. Some validation and syntax checking are performed as statements are typed directly into the computer. When accepted, images of these statements are retained temporarily/permanently on disk storage. A broad repertoire of commands is available for inserting new statements, updating existing statements, and other editing of partially developed programs.

After all input records have been read into the computer, the *job* (processing task defined by these records) is *enqueued* for execution. If small and short, it may be selected for execution a few seconds later; if large and low-priority, it may remain enqueued for hours.

When the control program selects a job for execution, its control statements are scanned for consistency and completeness. If valid, source data and programs are processed on a nonstop minimal-intervention basis. Output records are generated at this time, typically accumulated on tape or disk, rather than flowing directly to a line printer or display device.

Interactive computing is appropriate for those who wish to develop and operate programs in real time, correcting errors as soon as the latter are detected by the computer. (This contrasts with debugging in the batch-processing mode, where most errors cause immediate termination of jobs, accompanied by diagnostic printouts.) Also, programs and data may be validated as entered, syntax checked, consistency with prior program statements established, and range tests on variable values performed.

On-line inquiry and *transaction processing* use the computer to access rapidly a repository of data and to update the database or to insert new data in it. Processing time per query or transaction (e.g. making an airline reservation) is typically trivial compared with times required to enter and display information. This mode has been made feasible by development and widespread usage of large disk drives whose capacities range from 50 million to 1 billion characters per drive. Complete and up-to-date master files can be accessed by authorized clerks, management personnel, etc. using typewriter terminals or CRT (cathode ray tube) displays.

Message switching resembles on-line inquiry in that processing per input stimulus (message, query) is trivial. Whereas the inquiry mode permits retrieval and display of disk-stored records, the message-switching mode receives streams of characters (*messages*) from one site and routes them to other sites automatically, according to destination headers describing (for each message) where it is to be sent. Message switching is almost invariably used in conjunction with the public telephone network; large commercial, manufacturing, and governmental enterprises use message switching for high-speed communications among offices and for efficient usage of their telephone networks. Such systems are the forerunners of more general *electronic mail* (*q.v.*) systems.

DAX has many operational similarities to message switching—modest requirements for computational power and main memory, fast processing of incoming cassette tapes or punched paper tapes. As data are received from such instruments as voltmeters, gas chromatographs, and thermocouples, they are scaled and tested for conformance to normal operating ranges for these instruments (and associated physical processes). When the computer detects an out-of-range condition, it notifies appropriate personnel such as a plant guard, fireman, or operating engineer. Typically, the DAX-oriented computer types out a warning message, rings an alarm bell, or flashes an alarm light continuously until the out-of-range condition is corrected.

DAVID N. FREEMAN

PRODUCT CODE. *See* UNIVERSAL PRODUCT CODE.

PRODUCTION

For articles on related subjects *see* BACKUS-NAUR FORM; CHOMSKY HIERARCHY; FORMAL LANGUAGES; GRAMMARS; PROGRAMMING LINGUISTICS; and WELL-FORMED FORMULA.

A *production* is a rule, often called a *rule of inference*, in a grammar that describes how parts of a string (or word, or phrase, or construct) can be replaced by other strings. The set of productions of a grammar describe all the rules by which strings of the language can be generated by the grammar.

As an example, consider the grammar whose alphabet consists of the characters *a* and *b* and that is to generate any string consisting of any number (including zero) of *b*s followed by any number (including zero) of *a*s. A set of productions that generate this language is

$$S \to a$$
$$S \to b$$
$$S \to Sa$$
$$S \to bS$$

the first two of which read "*a* and *b* are constructs of the language" and the last two read, "If *S* is a construct of the language, then so is *S* followed by *a* or preceded by *b*." Sometimes this set of productions would be written as

$$S \to a|\ b|\ Sa|\ bS$$

where the vertical bar is to be read as "or."

Productions may be much more complex than those above. An example is the type of production found in *context-sensitive languages*,

$$S_1\, S\, S_2 \to S_1\, T\, S_2,$$

which states that, if the string *S* is found in the context (i.e. between) strings S_1 and S_2, then *S* may be replaced by the string *T*. Thus,

$$abSba \to abaSaba$$

states that, if *S* is any string surrounded by *ab* and *ba*, it may be replaced by the same string preceded and succeeded by *a*.

References

1967. Naur, P. *et al.* "Revised Report on the Algorithmic Language ALGOL 60," in Rosen, S. (Ed.), *Programming Systems and Languages.* New York: McGraw-Hill.

1975. Lewis, P. M., Rosenkrantz, D. J., and Stearns, R. E. *Compiler Design Theory.* Reading, MA: Addison-Wesley.

J.A.N. Lee and Anthony Ralston

PROGRAM

For articles on related subjects *see* Algorithm; Assembler; Literate Programming; Machine and Assembly Language Programming; Modular Programming; Object-Oriented Programming; Problem-Oriented Languages; Procedure; Procedure-Oriented Languages; Programmer; Programming Languages; Stored Program Concept; and Structured Programming.

In order to solve a computational problem, its solution must be specified in terms of a sequence of computational steps, each of which may be effectively performed by a human agent or by a digital computer. Systematic notations for the specification of such sequences of computational steps are referred to as *programming languages*. A specification of the sequence of computational steps in a particular programming language is referred to as a *program*. The task of developing programs for the solution of computational problems is referred to as *programming*. A person engaging in the activity of programming is referred to as a *programmer.*

Programming is sometimes contrasted with *coding.* Coding generally refers to the writing and debugging of programs for given program specifications, while programming includes the task of choosing an applicable algorithim as well as that of writing the program. The text of a program is sometimes referred to as *code*, and lines of program text are referred to as lines of code, especially in the case of machine-language programs. The term *coder* is used, sometimes pejoratively, to describe a person engaged exclusively in implementing detailed program specifications prepared by others.

The programs for the earliest digital computers were written in a *machine language.* Pure machine-language programming required the programmer to write out the sequences of binary or decimal digits by which each instruction was represented in the computer memory. By the mid-1950s it was realized that programmers could specify instruction codes and memory locations by symbolic mnemonics, which could be translated into the internal machine language by a translation program called an *assembler.*

In the late 1950s and in the 1960s, *procedure-oriented languages* were developed to allow programmers to specify algorithms in a notation natural to the problem being solved. Programs specified in a procedure-oriented language were translated into the internal language of a particular computer by a translation program called a *compiler.* The reader is referred to Sammet (1969) for brief descriptions of over a hundred programming languages developed in the 1950s and 1960s. (For languages of historical and current interest *see* Appendix V: Key High-Level Languages).

The flavor of programming in procedure-oriented languages can be experienced by following the logic in the Pascal function in Fig.1 which finds the maximum of a list of *n* numbers.

A problem specification is generally given in terms of a desired relation between inputs and outputs that specifies *what* is to be computed. An algorithm or program for a given problem specifies *how* the given relation between inputs and outputs is to be achieved. It is the task of the programmer to convert "static" input/output specifications of what is to be computed into dynamic specifications that specify how the computation is to be performed.

A given input/output relation may be realized by a wide variety of different algorithms, and each algorithm may in turn be realized in a variety of different programming languages. There is thus considerable freedom in developing a program for the solution of any given problem. This freedom of choice in developing programs leads to the notion that programming is as much an art as it is a science.

Although the set of all programs for realizing a given problem specification is in general infinite, there are a number of criteria other than correctness that may be

```
function max (x: list; n: integer): real;        {Result is real}

{Given that main program has defined a type list as array [1 .. n] of real; for constant n having a
particular integer value, this function returns the largest number on the list.}

var i: integer; t: real;                         {Declare two local variables}

begin
    t := x[1];                                   {Initialize t to first number, the largest seen so far}
    for i := 2 to n do                           {Test all remaining numbers}
        if x[1] > t then t := x[i];              {Update t if larger number found}
    max := t                                     {Bind the function's name to the desired result}
end {max};
```

FIG. 1   A Pascal function. Comments are delineated by braces.

used to restrict the class of acceptable programs that realize a given problem specification. A good program should economize both on computation time and on the storage space required to represent the program and data structures. It should have a modular structure in the sense that each well-defined subtask should be specified by a well-defined subprogram. Modular design of a program is important because it makes the program easier to understand, facilitates debugging, and allows modifications to be made easily. It is usually worth paying a price in computation time and memory space in order to achieve greater modularity. Modular construction is especially important in large programs, since the human mind is severely restricted in the complexity it can handle, and systematic modularity reduces the number of factors the human mind must handle at any given moment, thereby allowing the understanding of a larger system than would otherwise be possible.

Programming was regarded as an art rather than a science in the 1950s and 1960s because it was felt that the choices among different styles of implementing a given problem were creative choices based on intangible criteria of style, just as in the case of literature. However, as more experience was gained in writing large programs, the freedom of the programmer to develop a personal style became increasingly restricted by programming conventions designed to mechanize programming style. For example, it has become accepted that *goto* statements should be avoided whenever possible, and that operators that preserve modularity, such as *while* statements, should be more heavily used. (*see* STRUCTURED PROGRAMMING).

In recent years, it has been realized that maintenance of programs is more expensive than development, so reading of programs by humans is as important as writing them (*see* LITERATE PROGRAMMING). Documentation and other aids to readability are becoming increasingly important. The programs of a large system are increasingly viewed as one of several forms of system documentation and are stored in a database for manipulation by compilers and other system programming tools.

References

1968, 1969, 1973. Knuth, D. E. *The Art of Computer Programming,* Vol 1, 2, 3. Reading, MA: Addison-Wesley.

1969. Sammet, J. *Programming Languages—History and Fundamentals.* Englewood Cliffs, NJ: Prentice-Hall.

PETER WEGNER

PROGRAM CORRECTNESS. *See* PROGRAM VERIFICATION.

PROGRAM COUNTER

For articles on related subjects *see* INSTRUCTION SET; and MACHINE AND ASSEMBLY LANGUAGE PROGRAMMING.

Typically, a computer instruction is the specification of an operation to be performed, the address of operands on which the operation will be performed, the address for the location of the result, and a specification (an address) of the next instruction in the sequence. These specifications or addresses may be explicitly placed in the instruction or implicitly defined. By "implicit" is meant that the machine will assume that an operand will be in a certain place (e.g. the *accumulator*) rather than have it specified in each instruction. In the case of the specification of the next instruction location, it is common for the machine to assume that the instructions lie in sequence. That is, the next instruction is contained in the address following the location of the current instruction. This address is kept in a register called the *program counter* (or, in some systems, the *program address register* or *instruction counter*). During the execution of an instruction, the program counter is advanced by one or more address units.

If the instruction lengths are not uniform (i.e. there are several different sizes), then the algorithm to increment the program counter must take this into account. For example, in the IBM System/370, instructions are of three different sizes: 2 bytes, 4 bytes, or 6 bytes. Since addresses always refer to bytes, the program counter must be incremented by either 2, 4, or 6, depending upon the type of instruction currently being executed.

In all systems that use program counters, there must be a mechanism for initializing its value and for changing values at certain points in the program. This latter mechanism is a special instruction, usually called a *branch* or *jump*. There are two basic kinds of branch instructions—*unconditional branch* and *conditional branch*. The unconditional branch causes a new value to be placed in the program counter and hence defines the start of the location of a new sequence of instructions. The conditional branch has a similar action except that it is dependent upon the state of certain data items. Thus, whether the next instruction will be simply the next instruction in the current sequence or the beginning of a new sequence will depend upon the result (e.g. positive or negative) of a preceding instruction.

MICHAEL J. FLYNN

PROGRAM LIBRARY. *See* MATHEMATICAL SOFTWARE; and SOFTWARE LIBRARIES.

PROGRAM LOGIC ARRAY (PLA). *See* LOGIC DESIGN; and PARALLEL PROCESSING: ARCHITECTURES.

PROGRAM SPECIFICATION

For articles on related subjects *see* ABSTRACT DATA TYPE; FORMAL METHODS FOR COMPUTER SYSTEMS; INFORMATION HIDING; PROGRAM VERIFICATION; SOFTWARE MANAGEMENT; SOFTWARE PROTOTYPING; and SOFTWARE TESTING.

The term *program specification* may refer to:

1. A statement of *requirements* for a program;
2. An expression of a *design* for a program; or
3. A formal statement of conditions against which the program can be *verified*.

Properties of Specification

Whatever the kind of specification, there are several concerns:

1. *Consistency*—Is the specification logically satisfiable?
2. *Implementability*—Is the specification practically realizable?
3. *Completeness*—Does the specification capture the *full* intent of the specifier?
4. *Non-ambiguity*—Does the specification capture the *precise* intent of the specifier?

Uses of Specifications

Specifications can be used in all phases of program development. In the *requirement analysis* phase, a specification helps crystallize the customer's possibly vague ideas and reveals contradictions, ambiguities, and incompleteness in the requirements. In *program design*, a specification captures precisely the interfaces between the modules of a program. Each interface specification provides the module's client the information needed to use the module without knowledge of its implementation, and simultaneously provides the module's implementor the information needed to create the module without knowledge of its clients. In *program verification*, a specification is the statement against which a program is proved correct. Verification is the process of showing the consistency between a program and its specification. In *program validation*, a specification can be used to generate test cases for black-box testing. Together with the program, it can be used for path testing, unit testing, and integration testing. Finally, a specification serves as a kind of *program documentation*, since it is an alternative, usually more abstract description of a program's behavior.

For a more detailed discussion of formal specifications, see Wing (1990).

Example   Consider the specification of a data abstraction for a *bag* (in the sense of a sack that holds inserted items). This example is taken from Guttag *et al.* (1985). Using the Larch specification languages, we divide the specification into two parts. The first part, called a *trait*, specifies state-independent properties of data accessed by programs; the second part, called an *interface*, specifies state-dependent behavior (e.g. side effects and exceptional termination of program modules).

Fig. 1 presents a trait that is useful for describing values of multisets and is written in the style of algebraic specifications. It defines a set of function symbols and a set of equations that define the meaning of the function symbols. The equations determine an equivalence relation on terms written using the function symbols. The

```
MultiSet: trait
    introduces
        new: → MSet
        insert: MSet,E → MSet
        isEmpty: MSet → Bool
        size: C → Card
        count: MSet,E → Card
        delete: MSet,E → MSet
        numElements: MSet → Card
    constrains MSet so that
        MSet generated by [new,insert]
        MSet partitioned by [count] for all [c: MSet,e,e1,e2:E]
        isEmpty(new) = true
        isEmpty(insert(c,e)) = false

        size(new) = 0
        size(insert(c,e)) = size(c) + 1

        count(new,e1) = 0
        count(insert(c,e1),e2) = count (c,e2) + (if e1 = e2 then 1 else 0)

        numElements(new) = 0
        numElements(insert(c,e)) = numElements(c) + (if count(c,e) > 0 then 0 else 1)

        delete(new, e1) = new
        delete(insert(c,e1),e2) = if e1 = e2 then c else insert (delete(c,e2),e1)
    implies converts [isEmpty,size,count,delete,numElements]
```

FIG. 1.   Specification of multiset values.

generated by clause states that all multiset values can be represented by terms composed solely of the two function symbols, new and insert. This clause defines an inductive rule of inference and is useful for proving properties about all multiset values. The **partitioned by** clause adds more equivalences between terms. Intuitively, it states that two terms are equal if they cannot be distinguished by any of the functions listed in the clause. In the example, we could use this property to show that order of insertion of elements in a multiset does not matter (i.e. insertion is commutative). The **converts** clause is a way to state that this algebraic specification is sufficiently complete.

Fig. 2 gives a Larch/Pascal interface specification of a bag data abstraction. It introduces a type name, three procedures, and one function.

The body of each routine's specification places constraints on proper arguments for calls on the routine and defines the relevant aspects of the routine's behavior when it is properly called. It can be straightforwardly translated to a first-order predicate over two states by combining its three predicates into a single predicate of the form

requires predicate $\Rightarrow$ (**modifies** predicate & **ensures** predicate).

An omitted **requires** is interpreted as **true**.

In the body of a Larch/Pascal specification, as in Pascal, the name of a function stands for the value returned by that function. Formal parameters may appear unqualified or qualified. An unqualified formal stands for the value of that formal when the routine is called. A formal qualified by prime ('), for example b', stands for the value of that formal when the routine returns.

The values of variables on entry to and return from routines must be distinguished because Pascal is a language in which statements may alter memory. Since the function symbols in a Larch trait specification represent functions, this complication does not arise there, nor would it in an interface language for a functional programming language.

The **modifies** predicate is also related to the imperative nature of Pascal. The predicate **modifies at most** $[v_1, ..., v_n]$ asserts that the routine changes the value of no variable in the environment of the caller except possibly some subset of the variables denoted by the elements of $\{v_1, ..., v_n\}$. Notice that this predicate is really an assertion about all variables that do not appear in the list, not about those that do.

The **based on** clause associates the type Bag with the sort MSet that appears in trait MultiSet. This association means that Larch trait terms of sort MSet are used to represent Pascal values of type Bag. For example, the term "new" is used to represent the value that b is to have when bagInit returns. The **requires** clause of bagAdd states a precondition that is to be satisfied on each call. It reflects the specifier's concern with how this type can be implemented in Pascal. By putting a bound on the number of distinct elements in the Bag, the specification allows a fixed-size representation. It is quite natural for such considerations to surface in interface specifications; it would not be so natural for them to appear in traits.

The most interesting routine is probably bagChoose. Its specification says that it must set e to some value in b (if b isn't empty), but doesn't say which value. Moreover, it doesn't even require that different invocations of bagChoose with the same value produce the same result; in other words, the implementation may be non-deterministic. Our implementation is abstractly non-deterministic, even though it is a deterministic program (see Fig. 3). The value to which e is set depends on the order in which elements have been added to and removed from b, whereas this order does not affect b's abstract value.

This interface specification has recorded a number of

```
type Bag exports bagInit,bagAdd,bagRemove,bagChoose
    based on sort MSet from MultiSet with [integer for E]
    procedure bagInit(var b: Bag)
        modifies at most [b]
        ensures b' = new

    procedure bagAdd (var b: Bag; e: integer)
        requires numElements (insert(b,e)) <= 100
        modifies at most [b]
        ensures b' = insert (b,e)

    procedure bagRemove (var b: Bag; e: integer)
        modifies at most [b]
        ensures b' = delete(b,e)

    function bagChoose (b:Bag;var e:integer): boolean
        modifies at most [e]
        ensures if ~ isEmpty(b) then bagChoose & count(b,e') > 0
                else ~ bagChoose & modifies nothing
```

FIG. 2.   Interface specification of a Larch Pascal bag abstraction.

```
const MaxBagSize = 100;
type ElemVals = array [1..MaxBagSize] of integer;
     Elem Counts = array [1..MaxBagSize] of integer;
     Bag = record elems; Elem Vals; counts: Elem Counts; end;
```

{Abstraction function: the abstract bag is equivalent to the result of inserting into the empty bag each integer in elems a number of times equal to the corresponding number in counts.}

{Representation invariant: Each integer in counts is at least zero and no integer appears in elems more than once associated with a positive value in counts.}

```
procedure bagInt(var b: Bag);
    var i:1..MaxBagSize;
    begin
        for i := 1 to MaxBagSize do b.counts[i] := 0
    end {bagInit};
procedure bagAdd(var b: Bag; e: integer);
    var i,lastEmpty: 1..MaxBagSize;
    begin
        i := 1;
        while(i<MaxBagSize) and (b.elems[i] <> e) do
            begin
                if b.counts[i] = 0 then lastEmpty := i;
                i := i + 1
            end;
        if b.elems[i] = e then b.counts[i] := b.counts[i] + 1 else
            begin
                if b.counts[i] <> 0 then lastEmpty := i;
                b.elems[lastEmpty] := e:
                b.counts[lastEmpty] := 1
            end;
    end {bagAdd};
procedure bagRemove (var b: Bag; e: integer);
    var i: 1..MaxBagSize;
    begin
        i := 1;
        while (not((b.elems[i] = e) and (b.counts[i] > 0)) and i < MaxBagSize)
            do i := i + 1;
        if (b.elems[i] = e) and (b.counts[i] > 0) then
            b.counts [i] := b.counts [i] – 1
    end {bagRemove};
function bagChoose(b: Bag; var e: integer): boolean;
    var i: 1..MaxBagSize;
    begin
        i := 1;
        while (i < MaxBagSize) and (b.counts[i] = 0) do i := i + 1;
        if b.counts [i] = 0 then bagChoose := false else
                begin
                    e:= b.elems[i];
                    bagChoose: = true
                end
    end {bagChoose};
```

FIG. 3.   Pascal implementation of bag abstraction.

design decisions beyond those contained in the trait MultiSet. It says which routines must be implemented and, for each routine, it indicates both the condition that must hold at the point of call and the condition that must hold upon return. Thus, a contract that provides a "logical firewall" has been established between the implementers and the clients of type Bag. They can then proceed independently, relying only on the interface specification (*see* ABSTRACT DATA TYPE and INFORMATION HIDING).

The clients must establish the **requires** clause at each point of call. Having done that, they may presume the truth of the **ensures** clause on return, and that only variables in the **modifies at most** clause are changed. They need not be concerned with how this happens.

The implementers are entitled to presume truth of the **requires** clause on entry. Given that, they must establish the **ensures** clause on return, while respecting the **modifies at most** clause.

Because the interface specification does not specify either the representation of the type or the algorithms in routines, yet another level of design is needed. Because this level is hidden from clients of the data type, the design may be changed without affecting their correctness.

The specification of each routine in an interface can be understood without reference to the specifications of other routines—unlike traits, in which the specification constrains the operators by giving relations among them. Of course, to understand the type itself, to reason about it, or to design an efficient representation for it, the specifications of all its routines must be taken into account.

To illustrate the relation between an interface specification and an implementation, we give a Pascal implementation of type Bag in Fig. 3. Neither the data structure chosen for the representation nor the program itself is very interesting. Both the abstraction function and the representation invariant are presented informally. If we had included a formal specification of the type used in the representation, we could have presented them formally using a program annotation language. Then they could be mechanically combined with the interface specifications already given to derive a concrete specification for each routine, which could then be verified separately. Notice that the implementation of bagAdd relies on the **requires** clause of its specification.

References

1985. Guttag J. V., Horning, J. J., and Wing, J. M. "The Larch Family of Specification Languages." *IEEE Software*, **2**, *5* (September) 24–36.

1990. Wing, J. M. "A Specifier's Introduction to Formal Methods." *IEEE Computer* (September) 8–24.

JEANNETTE M. WING

PROGRAM VERIFICATION

For articles on related subjects *see* DEBUGGING; FORMAL METHODS FOR COMPUTER SYSTEMS; LOGICS OF PROGRAMS; LOOP INVARIANT; PROGRAM SPECIFICATION; SOFTWARE TESTING; and STRUCTURED PROGRAMMING.

It is important to know that a computer program meets its specifications. For example, payroll programs should issue checks to each employee for exactly the amount due, sorting programs should reorder the given elements without losing or introducing spurious elements, message-sending programs should direct the correspondence to the stated recipients and to nobody else, and compilers should produce an object program that faithfully preserves the meaning of the source program. Each of these brief informal specifications can and must be elaborated in order to ascertain whether a program satisfies precise and rigorous specifications. This determination can be done in various ways, each of which provides varying amounts of assurance.

The most common technique is known as *debugging* or *testing* a program (*see* SOFTWARE TESTING). Sample data, presumed to be representative and to cover the necessary extreme cases, are given to the program and the results are compared against known or expected answers. The major problem is to know when to stop testing—how much more assurance of meeting specifications would be gained by additional cases. Or, as E. W. Dijkstra (1972) wrote, "Program testing can be used to show the presence of bugs, but never to show their absence!"

In contrast, but often as a supplement to rather than as a distinct alternative to testing, is the technique of *program verification*. As that term is used in this article, to *verify* a program means to demonstrate, via a mathematical proof, that the program is consistent with its specifications. It may be quite useful just to prove limited properties, such as that the program terminates (and without undefined operations) or that certain variables remain unchanged. The criterion of success requires a sufficiently believable proof, as do all mathematical proofs. Failure to complete the proof may be due to a problem with either the program *or* the specifications, as well as because of insufficient information about the problem domain or even actually inability to prove a true theorem.

Basic Technique and Example The most common technique for verifying a program is known as the method of *assertions* (or *invariant assertions* or *inductive assertions*). The basic idea is to associate assertions with various points in the program. *Assertions* are propositions involving the variables of the program usually expressed in a system like the first-order predicate calculus. The intent is that each assertion be a true statement every time the execution of the program passes the point with which that assertion is associated. The proof requirement is to demonstrate that this intent is actually satisfied. Those assertions that appear at the end of a program are often called *postconditions*; assuming that the program terminates, these give the result of the program. Assertions that appear at the start of a program are called *preconditions*. Because programs do not accept arbitrary inputs, a precondition is intended to give a sufficient condition for the program to compute its result. For example, a program to compute the inverse of a matrix or the reciprocal of a number requires non-zero input and perhaps other conditions as well. The only other requirement on the association of assertions is that (the path formed by) every loop must have at least one point with an assertion. An assertion that is true for every execution of a loop is called a *loop invariant*. Such invariants can often be deduced from the program or, indeed, the loop can be constructed to preserve a previously given invariant. In either case, the loop invariant is an essential part of understanding why the program works as well as an essential ingredient of the verification.

The standard way to achieve the proof requirement is to focus on a particular assertion, say P_1, and to follow the program execution from P_1 along all possible paths, stopping on each path when another assertion, P_2, is reached (P_2 is often P_1 again if the path is a loop). One must show, for each such path, that P_1 and the effects of the statements between P_1 and P_2 imply that P_2 holds. Suppose we do this for all assertions, including the preconditions that may be assumed, and suppose that for each P_1 we can show that P_2 holds. In particular, the postconditions will be a P_2 for one or more P_1. Thus, if the postconditions are actually reached (i.e. the program halts), it will be true. This argument by mathematical induction justifies the method and motivates some of its terminology.

As a simple example, consider the program whose aim is to count the positive elements in the n-element array $A[1 \mathinner{.\,.} n]$.

```
poscount := 0; i := 1;
while i ≤ n do
  begin
    if A[i] >= 0 then poscount := poscount + 1;
    i := i + 1
  end
```

In Fig. 1 is a flowchart of this program with assertions 1, 2, and 3 added. There the notation Positive (A, j, k) informally denotes the number of positive elements of A in the range j to k inclusive. A formal recursive definition is

$$\text{Positive}(A,j,k) = \textbf{if } j > k \textbf{ then } 0$$
$$\textbf{else if } A(k) >= 0 \textbf{ then}$$
$$1 + \text{Positive}(A,j,k-1)$$
$$\textbf{else } \text{Positive}(A,j,k-1)$$

For convenience, we assume n nonnegative. The postconditions 3 express the aim of the program. A very informal proof of this program might be simply that *poscount*, initially zero, is incremented for each positive element encountered as A is inspected, element by element, by the **while** loop.

A more rigorous version of this informal proof uses the loop invariant 2 which appears just prior to the test to the **while** statement, thereby satisfying the requirement that each loop have at least one assertion point. There are four paths between assertions in this example: (a) 1 to 2, (b) 2 and $A[i] > 0$ back to 2, (c) 2 and not $A[i] \geq 0$ back to 2, and (d) 2 to 3. The four propositions to be proved follow:

a. $n \geq 0$ **and** poscount $= 0$ **and** i $= 1 \supset$
$1 \leq i \leq n + 1$ **and**
poscount $= \text{Positive}(A,1,i-1)$

b. $1 \leq i \leq n + 1$ **and** poscount $=$
Positive$(A,1\ i - 1)$ **and** i $\leq$ n **and**
$A[i] >= 0$ **and** poscount$' =$ poscount $+ 1$
and i$' = i + 1 \supset 1 \leq i' \leq n + 1$
and poscount$' = \text{Positive}(A,1,i'-1)$

The prime $(')$ has been introduced to denote the "new" value of a variable.

c. As b except poscount$' =$ poscount
and not $(A[i] > 0)$.

d. $1 \leq i \leq n + 1$ **and** poscount $=$
Positive $(A,1,i - 1)$ **and not** $(i \leq n) \supset$
poscount $= \text{Positive}(A,1,n)$

Each of these propositions can be easily proved informally, using traditional and elementary mathematical reasoning, or formally, using the techniques of, say, the

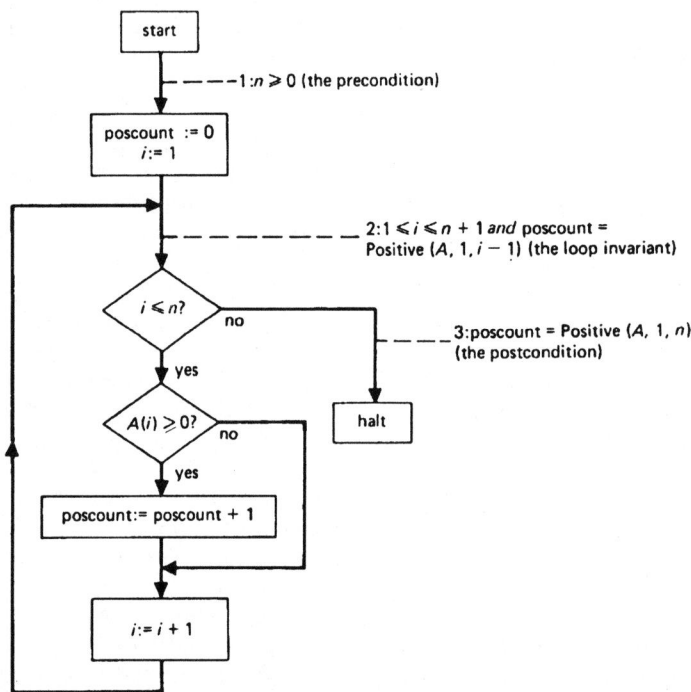

FIG. 1. Example program, including assertions, as a flowchart.

predicate calculus, which provides appropriate axioms and rules of inference for a deductive theory. Both kinds of proofs of a, b, and c use the three cases of Positive, respectively, plus substitution of equals for equals and simple inequality facts. For d, it is necessary to obtain $i = n + 1$ from $i \leq n + 1$ **and not** $(i \leq n)$. With the completion of these four proofs, the example program is verified.

The main distinctions between formal and informal proofs are the required efforts to obtain each kind, the manner of presenting the proofs, and the likelihood of having a convincing proof. Informal proofs are easier to obtain (at least for the non-clerical part), are shorter, and must be read and judged by people. Formal proofs may have to be evaluated by people, but may also be constructed and/or checked by computer programs. The large number of formal details may swamp the human reader or human constructor. Thus, we tend to have more faith in machine proofs than in human proofs, but we must always understand and question what axioms, lemmas, and other facts were simply assumed by the mechanical proof. Yet, going all the way back to first principles or giving too many details can easily obscure the essential elements of a proof. It should be noted that the example above is too simple to illustrate these distinctions.

Other methods for proving program correctness exist (e.g. Constable *et al.*, Manna and Waldinger, Morgan). Furthermore, the various methods can apply to programs consisting of (recursive) subprograms, parallelism, nondeterminism, and abstract data types (*q.v.*).

Goals and Contributions of Verification

A major aim of program verification is to provide techniques for actually verifying programs in order to eliminate the bugs in programs and to know that this has been done in particular instances, thereby significantly decreasing the incidence of unreliable program behavior. The discipline of program verification also provides an important viewpoint that affects program construction, program specification, program decomposition, and language design. How would one actually verify a program being constructed? What are appropriate invariants? What are the specifications (preconditions and postconditions) of an auxiliary procedure? Only the publicly available specifications of a program component may be used in verifying uses of the component; hidden information or hidden assumptions may not be used. If the component is later modified without changing the public specifications, then only the component itself needs to be reverified, since the verifications of the uses of the component remain valid. One measure of the modifiability of a program is how much the proof changes in response to program changes. A modular program, when modified, will cause corresponding changes to the proof, but not changes otherwise. Verification concerns can also suggest appropriate decompositions of a programming task as well as appropriate abstractions to be used.

Verification concerns have also influenced the design of several new programming languages; e.g. Euclid (Lampson *et al.*, 1977). In order that Euclid programs be semantically legal, it is necessary that conditions, known as *legality assertions* and made a part of the source language,

be true at specific points in the program. For example, a pointer must not be the nil-pointer if it is to be dereferenced. Showing that each legality assertion holds falls to the verifier unless the compiler can show it itself. Also influenced was the procedure mechanism of Euclid, which was designed to satisfy a particular style of semantic definition. Global variables are allowed, but must be stated explicitly so that any changes are directly detectable. Another decision involving procedures was to insist that distinct formal parameters must always have distinct actual parameters in a call; i.e. no *aliases* such as the two array elements $A[i]$ and $A[j]$ with $i = j$, which are both names for the same variable. This restriction removes many subtle effects in procedure calls and makes it somewhat easier to specify procedures. It should be noted that many people consider aliases harmless and a very useful feature.

In the long run, then, other aspects of program verification, besides actual proofs of specific programs, are potentially even more significant by providing tools and reasonably objective tests for developing and judging the success of new programming language designs, new language definition techniques, new programming strategies and methodologies, and new specification techniques. Because verification requires, for example, the definition of a programming language and the specifications of a programming task as integral parts of the verification effort, any inefficiencies, imprecisions, or inelegancies will soon surface. The concepts of verification have already had, and will continue to have, a deep impact on our thinking and understanding about programming and software technology.

Current Capabilities in Practice

While verification can be carried out by hand, one soon wishes to have computer assistance in this activity. Computer assistance increases the accuracy and credibility of the results and extends our abilities in achieving the requisite proofs. Various program verification systems have been implemented and have been applied to significant examples and applications. Capabilities exist to take annotated programs and produce the required propositions, to prove these propositions, to express mathematical concepts and prove consequences of those concepts, to combine proofs of parts of programs (e.g. packages - *q.v.*) or mathematical theories into proofs of programs or theories that use these parts, and to organize a database identifying the assumption basis, the progress of the development (including status of proofs), the dependencies of the parts, and reusable program components and mathematical theories.

The degree of automated support (especially with respect to automated deduction) varies from system to system. In no case can a user blindly submit a non-trivial annotated program with supporting mathematical theories and expect a quick proof with no interaction. Careful organization and decomposition of the entire programming task are required, just as these are required in programming itself. Automated deduction support varies from the level of proof checkers (which check that a presented proof satisfies the rules of a specific inference system) to highly automated provers (that can, for example, include decision procedures for various theories and heuristics (*q.v.*) that will automatically generate induction hypotheses or simplify propositions based on conditional equalities). Various verification systems are being used, though not widely, by industrial and governmental organizations. The focus of such uses is primarily that of critical systems—systems whose failure, for example, can lead to loss of life.

Examples of successful verifications by these systems include sorting (*q.v.*), searching (*q.v.*), pattern matching, implementations of abstract data types (*q.v.*), numeric calculations, simple language compilers and interpreters, functional correctness of simple chips, security properties of various fielded systems, filtering programs (e.g. variations of Unix, TR, and WC), Byzantine agreement, and properties of communication protocols. Furthermore, there have been general mathematical proofs, such as that of Gödel's theorem or model theoretic proofs of the consistency of theories described axiomatically. Though the successful application of these systems continually increases, achieving such proofs is non-trivial.

Each verification system incorporates a language for expressing mathematical theories. As a result, it is possible to use such a language to model the behavior of systems. For example, work reported by W. R. Bevier et al. (1989) describes an effort to verify the correct implementation of a (small) virtual machine in terms of an underlying (simple) real machine. The proofs were not of the form described above, but of "interpreter equivalence" between the different layers of design. The implementation of the virtual machine consisted of four layers: a Pascal-like high-level language machine, an assembler level machine, a machine code level, and a microcode gate level. The bottom level proof considered the visible registers and the internal registers and treated the microprocessor as a bit string interpreter. If such efforts can be scaled to more realistic systems, we will be able to predict with high accuracy the behavior of systems. This is a crucial concern for critical systems.

The report of the FM89 workshop (Eds. Craigen and Summerskill, 1990) includes a survey of over fifty formal methods-related projects. This survey includes brief characterizations of program verification systems, applications of the technology, and pointers to the relevant literature. Furthermore, the report discusses the use of program verification and, more generally, formal methods, in the development of computer-controlled critical systems. Gordon's book describes in detail a simple program verification system. Lindsay's article surveys various automated deduction systems.

References

1972. Dijkstra, E. W. "Notes on Structured Programming," in Dahl, O.-J., Dijkstra, E. W., and Hoare, C. A. R. (Eds.), *Structured Programming*. New York: Academic Press.

1974. Manna, Z. *Mathematical Theory of Computation*. New York: McGraw-Hill, Chapter 3.

1976. Hantler, S. L. and King, J. C. "An Introduction to Proving the Correctness of Programs," *Computing Surveys* **8**, *3* (September), 331-353.

1977. Lampson, B. W. *et al.*, "Report on the Programming Language Euclid," *SIGPLAN Notices* **12**, *2* (February).

1979. Anderson, R. B. *Proving Programs Correct*. New York: Wiley.

1985. Manna, Z. and Waldinger, R. *The Logical Basis for Computer Programming*. Reading, MA: Addison-Wesley.

1986. Constable, R. L. *et al.*, *Implementing Mathematics with the NuPRL Development System*. Englewood Cliffs, NJ: Prentice-Hall.

1986. Backhouse, R. C. *Program Construction and Verification*. Englewood Cliffs, NJ: Prentice-Hall.

1988. Gordon, M. J. C. *Programming Language Theory and its Implementation*. Englewood Cliffs, NJ: Prentice-Hall.

1988. Lindsay, P. "A Survey of Mechanical Support for Formal Reasoning," *IEE Software Engineering Journal* **3**(1), January.

1989. Bevier, W. R., Hunt, W. A., Moore, Strother, J. and Young, W. D. "An Approach to Systems Verification," *Journal of Automated Reasoning* **5**(4), November.

1990. Craigen, D. and Summerskill, K. (Eds.). *Formal Methods for Trustworthy Computer Systems* (FM89), New York: Springer-Verlag.

1990. Morgan, C. *Programming from Specifications*. Englewood Cliffs, NJ: Prentice-Hall.

RALPH L. LONDON AND DANIEL CRAIGEN

PROGRAMMABLE CALCULATOR. *See* CALCULATORS, ELECTRONIC AND PROGRAMMABLE.

PROGRAMMER

For articles on related subjects *see* APPLICATIONS PROGRAMMING; CHIEF PROGRAMMER TEAM; HACKER; HUMAN FACTORS IN COMPUTING; PERSONNEL IN THE COMPUTER FIELD; PROGRAM; SYSTEMS ANALYST; SYSTEMS PROGRAMMING, and WIZARD.

The computer *programmer* is the link between a problem or process to be computerized and its successful realization on the computer. In the fullest meaning of the term, the programmer will participate in the definition and specification of the problem itself, as well as the algorithms to be used in its solution. He or she will then design the more detailed structure of the implementation, select the most suitable programming language, write and debug the necessary programs, and provide clear and complete documentation for both the user and other programmers who may need to modify the program.

The amount of this process that is done by any one individual is highly variable. A scientist who has a small problem may do all of the above tasks personally, while in a large airline reservation system, many hundreds of people may be involved in each phase of the process. However, even in this latter case, programmers should participate in the design and documentation of at least their own portions of the overall system. It is demoralizing for most programmers to be treated as *coders*, a pejorative term reserved for those in the programming profession whose work consists of almost a direct translation of detailed flowcharts into code. One of the major attractions of programming as opposed to coding as a career is its requirement for at least some creativity on a daily basis. It is a mistake for the manager of a programming group to overspecify the team's programming tasks and thereby stifle this creativity. On the other hand, the programmer must not let ego engender bad programming practices such as the use of involved programming tricks that can only be easily understood by the programmer who used them. Good programmers write well-structured and clear programs that others can read and, if necessary, correct or modify.

Both the amateur programmer (e.g. the scientist) and the professional programmer (e.g. a member of the airline reservation team) are examples of *applications programmers*. They most frequently use high-level languages (e.g. Cobol, Fortran, Pascal) to write programs that serve particular applications. They approach the computer as a race car driver does a car—as a tool that enables a goal to be attained as efficiently as possible. As the race driver relies heavily on the mechanic, the applications programmer depends even more on the *systems programmer*, the elite member of the programming profession. The systems programmer is responsible for the compilers, assemblers, utility programs, operating systems, etc. that provide the environment for the applications programmer and is very close to the hardware. Usually, therefore, the systems programmer uses assembly language or, more frequently, the language C (*q.v.*), as this gives better access to the bits and bytes of the machine. It is hard to define what makes good systems programmers, but they are certainly a breed apart with a talent that is hard to teach. Although experience is of great importance, a good systems programmer can frequently be identified before education or experience has had a chance to have an effect. Almost any kind of background can be appropriate; once hooked, a systems programmer will find the mysteries of a full blown operating system a challenge for many years.

The distinction between applications and systems programmers is not clear cut. Applications programmers and system programmers frequently use the same language (C perhaps), and large applications such as the airline reservation system mentioned above is very much like an operating system and so would be written by many who consider themselves systems programmers.

One of the noteworthy aspects of programming is the great variation in programmer productivity, perhaps as great as a ratio of 10:1, from the best to the merely good. But for any programmer, applications or systems, there are some traits that are required if a programmer's full potential is to be realized. There is the need for creativity, of course, but it must be tempered with great patience and intense discipline if clever but unmanageable programs are to be avoided. Too many programs are written that may be a tribute to a programmer's ability to master complex logical structures but that have no place in a professional environment. The discipline of good programming practices is a severe one. *Egoless programming* is a technique that helps impose this discipline. Each member of a programming group will submit programs to the other members for criticism. The careful examination of another's program helps both the creator and the critic understand what makes a good, clearly written program. It is called "egoless" programming because, in order for it to be successful, all members must be able to submerge their own egos in the interest of good programs. The importance of good programmers cannot be overstressed because of the great variation in programmer productivity. The application of good programming techniques can do much to decrease the 10:1 ratio mentioned above.

References

1971. Weinberg, G. M. *The Psychology of Computer Programming*. New York: Van Nostrand Reinhold.
1975. Brooks, Frederick P. *The Mythical Man Month*. Reading, MA: Addison-Wesley.
1992. Yourdon, Edward. *Decline and Fall of the American Programmer*. Englewood Cliffs, NJ: Yourdon Press/Prentice-Hall.

FRANCIS D. FEDERIGHI

PROGRAMMING. *See* APPLICATIONS PROGRAMMING; FUNCTIONAL PROGRAMMING; LOGIC PROGRAMMING; MACHINE AND ASSEMBLY LANGUAGE PROGRAMMING; OBJECT-ORIENTED PROGRAMMING; STRUCTURED PROGRAMMING; and SYSTEMS PROGRAMMING.

PROGRAMMING LANGUAGE SEMANTICS

For articles on related subjects *see* FUNCTIONAL PROGRAMMING; GRAMMARS; LAMBDA CALCULUS; LOGICS OF PROGRAMS; PETRI NET; PROGRAMMING LANGUAGES; PROGRAMMING LINGUISTICS; PROCEDURE-ORIENTED LANGUAGES; PROGRAM VERIFICATION; SYNTAX, SEMANTICS, AND PRAGMATICS; and VIENNA DEFINITION LANGUAGE.

The term *semantics* is used in both linguistics and computer science to refer to the meanings of the symbol strings of a language. A program in a programming language is represented by a symbol string, but denotes a sequence of instructions to be executed by a computer. The symbol string is a *syntactic* representation of the program. Semantics associates meanings with syntactic program representations, although there are several alternative ways of doing this.

A definition of the semantics of a programming language is a finite set of rules for uniformly defining the meaning of the potentially infinite set of all programs of the language. The purpose of a semantic definition is to provide a clear, complete, and unambiguous definition of a programming language for language designers, language implementors, and language users. Unfortunately, programming language definitions appear to be inherently complex. One of the challenges in this area is to develop clear, structured definitions that allow the meaning of programming languages to be defined in a simple and intuitively natural manner.

The set of rules that constitute a definition of the semantics of a programming language may be thought of as a mapping from the set P of all programs (symbol strings) of the programming language into the set M of meanings (see Fig. 1).

However, there may, in general, be several alternative notions of meaning for programs of a programming language appropriate to alternative contexts in which the semantic definition might be used. A semantic definition appropriate to compiler writers might define the meaning of a program in the source language as the target language string generated by the compiler. The system implementor might wish to define meaning in terms of the sequence of executed instructions. The end user is not interested in the instruction sequence but only in the computational effect of the program expressed as a relation between inputs and outputs.

Semantic models may be classified by the kinds of meanings they permit. Thus, semantic models whose meanings are target language strings generated by a compiler are called *compiler models*. Semantic models whose meanings are relationships between inputs and execution sequences are called *interpreter models* or operational models. Models whose meanings are relationships between inputs and outputs are called *mathematical models*.

Compiler semantics defines the meaning of a program in a language L in terms of its translation to a second language L'. We shall be concerned with expressing the meaning of programs in terms of their execution rather than in terms of their translation, and will therefore not pursue the notion of compiler semantics.

Operational semantics defines a language L in terms of an interpreter (*abstract machine*) for executing it. The semantic definition language in which its interpreter is specified should have mechanisms for defining and manipulating program structures. The first example of an operational language definition was the definition of Lisp by an interpreter that was itself written in Lisp.

For defining operational semantics, Lisp is probably the simplest and most complete language. It has the following features: *Selectors* that allow selection of particular components of lists; *constructors* that allow construction of lists from their components; and *predicates* that allow testing whether a given structure is a list and whether two structures are equal. It has a conditional statement of the form

$$p_1 \rightarrow a_1;\ p_2 \rightarrow a_2;\ldots;\ p_n \rightarrow a_n$$

which causes the action a_i, corresponding to the first true predicate p_i to be executed. An interpreter in this context may be defined as a conditional statement in which the p_i are statement forms and a_i is the execution action associated with the statement form p_i. The Lisp interpreter (Lisp APPLY function) is, in fact, defined as a large conditional statement that takes a program in list representation and its data as arguments and produces as its value the result of applying the program to its data.

In the late 1960s, a more elaborate language for operational semantic definitions called the Vienna Definition Language (VDL) was developed by Lucas and Walk (Wegner, 1972). It was used to define PL/I (a very large language). VDL, like Lisp, has powerful facilities for manipulating structures. Programs were converted into an "abstract syntax" representation in the form of labeled trees. For example, the expression "$a + b$" could be represented in the abstract syntax by the tree structure in Fig 2.

The abstract machine for VDL starts from an abstract syntax representation of the program, just as the Lisp interpreter starts from a list representation of the program. The execution time data structure for VDL consists of a tree-structured program representation that permits nondeterministic execution of any terminal node of the program tree as the next instruction, as well as table data structures containing the relationship between symbols and their values.

A later version of VDL, using the denotational semantics of Scott (see below), was developed by Bekič, Jones, and others. From this there subsequently arose the Vienna Development Method (VDM), a systematic methodology for the development of large software systems. A survey of this is given in Bjørner and Jones (1978).

Mathematical semantic models can be classified into *denotational* models, which define the meaning of programs as denotations of an abstract algebraic domain, and *axiomatic* models, which define the meaning of primitive program constructs in terms of axioms (axiom schemes) and define the meaning of composite programs by means of theorems derivable from axioms for primitive program constructs by rules of inference for program composition.

Denotational semantic models were developed for the lambda calculus (*q.v.*) in the early 1960s but are associated with the name of Scott, who defined denotations of programs in terms of an "applicative" topological space (1976) in which every element can be interpreted both as a function and as a data element. This idea captures the fact that computer programs can be executed as functions or manipulated as bit strings. Applicative spaces occur in their purest form in the lambda calculus, where lambda expressions may

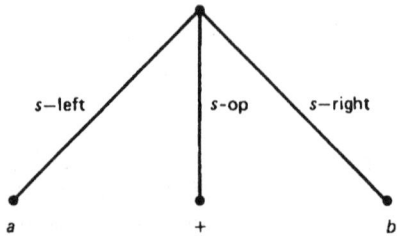

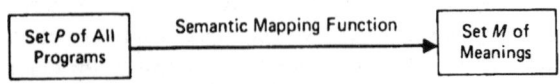

FIG. 1. Semantics as a mapping from programs to meanings.

FIG. 2. Abstract syntax in VDL.

be applied to operands or serve as operands of some other lambda expression. They serve as a basis for modeling applicative programming languages such as Lisp. Scott's denotational semantics is of mathematical interest because it provided the first mathematical model of the lambda calculus, and it is of practical interest because, by augmenting the applicative model with a model of computer memory and assignment, the semantics of real programming languages such as Algol 60, PL/I, and Ada (*q.v.*) can be defined.

Denotational models start from the notion of an underlying state set and the notion of a command as a mapping from states to states. In order to accommodate assignment, the notion of an environment as a mapping from identifiers to values is introduced, and the meaning of assignment is defined in terms of its effect on the environment. The meaning (*denotation*) of composite program structures is defined in terms of the denotation of component structures. The meaning of a recursive procedure *P* is given as the *fixed point* of a certain *functional* (or higher order function) Θ, i.e. a value *P* of *P* such that $\Theta(P) = P$.

Axiomatic semantic models define primitive statements such as assignment statements in terms of "axioms," which define their input/output (I/O) behavior (i.e. the values of variables after execution of a statement in terms of their values before execution), and define composite statements, such as **while** statements, in terms of rules of inference which allow I/O relationships for composite structures to be defined in terms of I/O relationships for their components.

The axiom for assignment was formulated by Hoare (1969) as follows.

$$\{P_E^X\}\, X := E; \{P\}.$$

In order for the predicate *P*, the *postcondition*, to be a correct assertion *after* the assignment statement *X*: = *E* is executed, then the predicate P_E^X, the *precondition*, must be true *before* the statement is executed. P_E^X is obtained from *P* by substituting *E* for all (free) occurrences of *X*.

Example

$$\{X + 1 < 10\}\, X := X + 1; \{X < 10\}.$$

If *X* < 10 is to be true after *X* := *X* + 1; has been executed, then *X* + 1 < 10 must have been true before the statement was executed.

The axiom (rule of inference) for **while** statements has the following form.

from $\{P \wedge B\}\, S\, \{P\}$ infer $\{P\}$ **while** *B* **do** $S\, \{P \wedge \neg B\}$

That is, if execution of *S* when *B* is true preserves the *invariant P* ("from $\{P \wedge B\}\, S\, \{P\}$"), then execution of "**while** *B* **do** *S*" will preserve the invariant *P*. If execution of the while statement terminates, then $P \wedge \neg B$ will be true upon termination. Meaning is essentially captured here by the invariant, which generally must be determined by human rather than automatic means. The invariant determines a constraint on execution within the **while** statement. The purpose of executing the **while** statement is to falsify *B* while not violating the constraint imposed by *P*.

Axiomatic definitions have been used to define large fragments of programming languages such as Pascal and are being extended to include language features such as procedures (*q.v.*), pointers (*q.v.*), exceptions, and tasks.

Different semantic definitions serve different purposes. Thus, compiler definitions serve the compiler-writer, operations definitions provide a model for the implementor, and axiomatic definitions are appropriate to program verification (*q.v.*). Operational semantics (at least relative to an ideal machine without restrictions of time or space) has the best claim to serving as a standard for defining meaning. However, denotational semantics, since it abstracts all details of the computation except for input and output, permits, to a large degree, sophisticated and elegant mathematical treatment. Stoy (1977) is an excellent classical reference for denotational semantics. Gordon (1979) is an exposition which avoids much of the mathematics of Scott's fixed point theory. Hennessy (1990) is a recent elementary exposition which uses operational semantics.

Recent Developments In the last decade, advances in semantics, have centered in four areas:

1. *Domain theory*—As a development of the theory of denotational models (i.e. mathematical models used in denotational semantics), the theory of *domains* has been applied. Domains can take a variety of forms, such as metric spaces, topological spaces, and lattices—in fact, any mathematical structure in which the notion of *limit* makes sense, so that *fixed point theory* for recursive procedures can be applied.

   A striking feature in this area has been the increasing applications of methods in *category theory* to domain theory. Category theory is a branch of mathematics that aims to analyze concepts found in many branches of mathematics, particularly those such as *homomorphism* and *isomorphism*, as a unified theory, and then analyze different mathematical structures in terms of these concepts.

   A recent work on the application of category theory to program semantics, and to computer science more generally, is Pierce (1991).

2. *Concurrency (q.v.)*—A great deal of work has been done recently on the semantics of concurrent systems, and this is still an area of active research. There have been two main approaches:

   a. *Interleaving semantics*—The idea here is to reduce concurrent behavior to (non-deterministic) sequential behavior by "interleaving" concurrent processes, and considering, say, the set of "traces" of all such possible interleavings corresponding a given concurrent process. The techniques of denotational semantics, and in particular domain theory, can then be applied to domains of such sets of traces. In fact, this area is the main reason for the interest in, and development of, domain theory mentioned in number 1. above. More particularly, the *theory of processes* of De Bakker and Zucker has been developed into a theory of *process algebras* by Klop, Bergstra, Baeten, and others, to model features of concurrent systems, such as interleaving. A recent book on this topic is Baeten and Weijland (1990).

    b. *True concurrency*—The approach here is to model concurrency by means of the theory of nets, arising from C. A. Petri's work in the sixties. *Petri nets* depict information flow and show *causal dependencies* explicitly. A semantic theory based on Petri nets is developed in Janicki and Lauer (1991).

        Each approach has its strong points. The first ("interleaving") permits elegant mathematical methods based on domain theory. The second ("causality"), however, seems more capable of dealing with issues such as fairness.

3. *Higher order type theory and data abstraction*—The theory of "polymorphic type systems," based on the higher order typed lambda calculus, has been developed to provide a semantics for programming languages involving *data abstraction*, such as Ada, and *functional languages* such as ML. A survey of this area is given in Cardelli and Wegner (1985).

4. *Algebraic specification semantics*—Here the semantics is based on equational specifications, which may be interpreted by "initial algebras," or implemented by *term rewriting*. The language OBJ2 was developed with such semantics in mind. A recent survey of this area is given in Bergstra, Heering and Klint (1989).

References

1969. Hoare, C. A. R. "An Axiomatic Basis for Computer Programming," *Comm. ACM*, **10**: 576-583.

1972. Wegner, P. "The Vienna Definition Language," *Computing Surveys* **4**: 5-63.

1976. Scott, D. "Data Types as Lattices," *SIAM Journal on Computing* **5**: 522-587.

1977. Stoy, J.E. *Denotational Semantics—The Scott-Strachey Approach to Programming Language Theory*. Cambridge, MA: M.I.T. Press.

1970. Bekič, H. "On the formal definition of programming languages," Proc. International Computing Symposium, Bonn. Reprinted in *Programming Languages and their Definition*. Selected papers of H. Bekič, Ed. by C.B. Jones. Lecture Notes in Computer Science, **177**. Springer-Verlag, 1984, 86–106.

1978. Bjørner, D. and Jones, C. B. (Eds.) *The Vienna Development Method: The Meta-Language*, Lecture Notes in Computer Science, **61**. New York: Springer-Verlag.

1979. Gordon, M. J. C. *The Denotational Description of Programming Languages*. New York: Springer-Verlag.

1985. Cardelli, L. and Wegner, P. "On understanding types, data abstraction, and polymorphism," *Computing Surveys* **17**: 471-522.

1989. Bergstra, J. A., Heering, J. and Klint, P. (Eds.) *Algebraic Specifications*. Reading, MA: Addison-Wesley.

1990. Baeten, J. C. M. and Weijland, W.P. *Process Algebra*, Cambridge: Cambridge University Press.

1990. Hennessy, M. *The Semantics of Programming Languages*. New York: John Wiley.

1991. Janicki, R. and Lauer, P. E. *Specification and Analysis of Concurrent Systems: The COSY Approach*. New York: Springer-Verlag.

1991. Pierce, Benjamin C. *Basic Category Theory for Computer Scientists*. Cambridge, MA: M.I.T. Press.

PETER WEGNER AND JEFFERY I. ZUCKER.

PROGRAMMING LANGUAGE STANDARDS

For articles on related subjects *see* COMPUTER GRAPHICS: STANDARDS; PORTABILITY; PROCEDURE-ORIENTED LANGUAGES; PROGRAMMING LANGUAGES; STANDARDS; and VIENNA DEFINITION LANGUAGE.

One of the earliest formal standardization activities undertaken in the field of information technology was for programming languages. This reflects the importance to users of programming languages and the benefits of language standards. There are two primary benefits of standardization (over and above the benefits of the languages themselves). These benefits relate first to the people who use the language and second to the programs written in the language. First, common education can be provided for programmers who will use a standard language, and these programmers are able to write programs for multiple computing environments that support the language. Second, the standards permit the construction of programs that are portable across these multiple environments. In neither case is the portability (*q.v.*) likely to be perfect, since language standards typically have some specifications that are environment dependent, and language compilers usually contain additional capabilities or extensions beyond those specified in the standard.

While both of these benefits are important, the early impetus came as much from people portability as from program portability. In recent years, the interest in application portability has grown, resulting in greater emphasis on reducing environment dependencies in language standards in order to decrease the amount of conversion required to move a program from one environment to another. As the standard for a language is revised, it is normally expanded in function, reducing (but not eliminating) the need for implementers to provide language extensions in their products.

There was an early belief that there would be one standard language for each major application area, e.g. Cobol for business applications or Fortran for scientific applications. This belief was dispelled by several forces tugging in different directions. First, there has been a proliferation of languages designed with specific goals in mind, with many of them gathering an enthusiastic following. As each became more popular, its proponents desired to use it to program a wider variety of applications. Second, advocates of some languages have desired the prestige and increased implementations stemming from an official standard. Third, the borderline between differing types of applications has become increasingly blurred. The result has been a growing number of language standards, with each having greater functional capability over time.

Programming language standardization under the auspices of official standardization organizations began in the early 1960s. Standardization of Algol was initially undertaken internationally, while standardization of Fortran and Cobol began in the United States. Many others have followed (see Table 1).

The development of an initial standard tends to be long and difficult. This is true even when the standards committee starts with a very good base document, and there are several reasons for this. First, the rigor of the standard tends to be greater than the way base documents are normally written. Second, it is important to make absolutely clear what conformance to the standard means, both for implementations of the language and for programs written in the language; this requires a rigorous definition of all aspects of the language. Third, the lan-

TABLE 1. LANGUAGE STANDARDS

Language	ANSI ID	ANSI Dates	ISO ID	ISO Dates
Ada	MIL-STD-1815A[1]	1983, 199x	8652	1987, 199x
Algol 60		—	1538	[2],1984
APL		199x	8485	1989
APT	X3.37	1974, 1977, 1980, 1987	3592	1978, 199y
Atlas	IEEE 416	1976[3], 1978, 1981, 1984, 1988		
C/Atlas	IEEE 716	1982, 1985, 1989		
Basic (Full)	X3.113	1987	10279	1991
Basic (Minimal)	X3.60	1978	6373	1979, 1984
C	X3.159	1989	9899	1990
C++		199x		199y
Chill			9496[4]	1989
Cobol	X3.23	1968, 1974, 1985	1989	1972, 1978, 1985
Cobol (Intrinsic Function Module)	X3.23a	1989	AM1	1991
Cobol (Corrections Addendum)	X3.23b	1992(?)		199y
DIBOL	X3.165	1988		
Forth		199x		
Fortran	X3.9	1966, 1978, R1988	1539	1972, 1980, 1991[5]
Fortran 90	X3.198	1991(?)[5]		
Fortran (Basic)	X3.10	1966 (withdrawn)	1539	1972
Lisp(Common)		199x		—
Lisp (Internat'l. Std. Lisp)		—		199y
Modula-2		199x	10514	199y
MUMPS	X11.1[1]	1977, 1984, 1990	11756	199y
PANCM	X3.94	1985		
Pascal	ANSI/IEEE770X3.97	1983, R1990	7185	1983, 1990
Pascal (Extended)	ANSI/IEEE 770X3.160	1989	10206	1991
Pilot	IEEE1154	1991		
PL/I	X3.53	1976, R1987	6160	1979, R1987
PL/I General Purpose Subset	X3.74	1981, 1987	6522	1985, 199y
Prolog		199x		199y
REXX		199x		
Scheme	ANSI/IEEE1178	1991		

[1]Existing versions of Ada and MUMPS were handled under ANSI by the canvass method.
[2]Although Algol 60 was an ISO standard for some time, it was never an ANSI standard. It was eventually withdrawn as an ISO standard and was then reinstated in 1984.
[3]The 1976 Atlas version was an IEEE standard but not an ANSI standard.
[4]Developed by CCITT.
[5]ISO 1539-1991 and ANSI/X3.198-1991(?) have identical expanded specifications. ANSI decided to retain Fortran (1978) and assign the name Fortran 90 to the new version, whereas ISO decided to replace Fortran 78 with the new specifications.

Notes

1. Use of R preceding a year means that the existing standard was reaffirmed in that year, but no changes were made.

2. Use of 199x as shown under ANSI or 199y under ISO means that the standard development work is underway (or at least contemplated), but the completion date is unknown. The use of the letters x and y throughout does *not* mean that the values will be the same in all cases nor will the ANSI and ISO dates necessarily be identical for the same standard.

3. A tentative date in the ISO column with nothing in the ANSI column means that there is an international committee at work, but no corresponding work is in progress by a group based solely in the U. S. Similarly, a tentative date in the ANSI column with nothing in the ISO column means that no work is being done internationally.

4. A question mark next to a date indicates that it is a reasonable estimate, as contrasted with the "x" or "y," which mean that the date is completely unknown.

guage committee is usually composed of members with a variety of perspectives, depending on the applications and system environments to which they are accustomed, and these differences must be reconciled or compromised. Fourth, the committee may also differ as to the scope of what functionality should even be included in the standard. Fifth, they often differ as to what constitutes an improvement from the base document. Sixth, if there is experience from numerous implementations, the differences must be resolved, and, if there are few or no implementations, there is generally large disagreement on what the standard should contain because of lack of experience.

Assuming there is agreement that a given functional capability should be part of a language standard, some believe it is helpful to have that functional capability "proven" by having been implemented and used prior to standardization. The experience of prior use can indicate those aspects that are well designed and those that should be improved, as well as indicating the general usefulness of the capability itself. On the other hand, if the standard "improves" the functional capability with desirable changes, it may cause program incompatibility problems for current users. If several vendors have implemented the functional capability differently, the experiences of these users may be helpful in discovering pitfalls, but may also cause difficulty in reaching agreement on a standard that does not place one or more group(s) of users at a significant disadvantage by making their current programs incompatible with the new standard. When actually updating an existing official standard, the problem of "improvement" versus "retaining compatibility" is one of the most difficult problems.

One issue that must be decided on early in the development of the standard is the method of documentation used. The basic question is whether to use natural language or a formal description technique for the language syntax and semantics. By now, all the syntactic definitions are formal. However, the decision on how formal the semantic definition should be may cause difficulty, since there may be disagreement as to who the primary audience for the standard is. An implementer may prefer a formal technique, since it reduces possible ambiguities. However, a formal definition of a programming language standard may be virtually unreadable to a user who may much prefer that the standard be written in a natural language such as English. This issue has been decided differently by different committees and, as a result, programming language standards vary considerably as to the documentation technique used. For example, the standards for Fortran and Cobol, while complex, are relatively easy to read and understand by a competent programmer. In contrast, the standard for PL/I is a fairly formal definition of the language and more difficult for even a professional to comprehend. One good result of the rigid PL/I definition, however, is that the PL/I committee has received only one request for interpretation or clarification since publication of the PL/I standard, whereas other language committees have typically received dozens.

In the U. S., most programming language standardization takes place in Accredited Standards Committee X3,

which has standards development committees for Fortran, Cobol, PL/I, Basic, APT, Pascal, C (*q.v.*), C++, Lisp, Prolog, DIBOL, Databus, and REXX. Other U. S. language standardization efforts are for Modula-2 (*q.v.*) in the IEEE Microprocessor Standards Committee, MUMPS (*q.v.*) in the MUMPS Development Committee (MDC), and Ada (*q.v.*) in the Department of Defense (DoD). The development and approval procedures differ substantially between X3 (an Accredited Standards Committee), IEEE (an Accredited Standards Organization), and MDC or DoD (Organizations Accredited for Canvass), but all meet the basic requirements of the American National Standards Institute (ANSI) for due process and public review before adoption. For example, the canvass process requires a proposed standard to be circulated and reviewed by a canvass group that is representative of all affected industry interests, whereas standards developed by an Accredited Standards Committee (ASC) can be approved directly by the ASC, since the ASC is itself an open, balanced committee with representation from producer, consumer, and general interest segments of the industry.

Historically, programming language standards development has tended to be concentrated in the U. S. Over the past dozen years, the development of many information technology related standards has shifted to international working groups and subcommittees. However, Subcommittee 22 (SC22) of ISO/IEC Joint Technical Committee 1 (JTC 1), which is responsible for international standardization of languages for information technology, has taken a unique approach. It is the only subcommittee of JTC 1 using the approach of "national body" development. In this mode, SC22 assigns the development of the technical specifications for a standard to a national body (normally U. S.) standards development committee, with the request that working drafts be circulated for comment at appropriate times to members of the SC22 working group from other countries and, when a stable draft document has been agreed upon, to send it to SC22 to begin the usual international balloting process for adoption as an international standard. All SC22 development is not done in this manner, but several important standards have been, notably, Cobol, Fortran, and C. This method is not without its problems, however, as there has been difficulty in synchronizing the international adoption process with the U. S. national adoption process. Improvements in synchronization continue to be made, and some form of national development is expected to continue for some language standards.

As of early 1992, JTC 1/SC22 has working groups for the following programming languages: Pascal, APL, Cobol, Fortran, Basic, Ada, Modula 2, C, Lisp, and Prolog. Also included within SC22 are working groups for VDM-SL (Vienna Development Method–Syntactic Language), FIMS (Forms Interface Management System), POSIX (Portable Operating System Interface for Computer Environments), and Internationalization.

The newest of the JTC1/SC22 working groups, Internationalization, is representative of an important direction underway in information technology standardization. Historically, standards for computers in general, and for programming languages in particular, were written in

English and were bound by interfaces provided to users in English-speaking cultures. It is now recognized that this is no longer sufficient. Significant efforts are underway to address character-handling issues, in order to allow use of natural languages with large character sets and to consider other cross-cultural issues that cause difficulty for users, e.g. date formats, currency differences, the meaning of icons. As greater understanding of these issues is attained and potential solutions are developed, Subcommittee 22 is committed to incorporate these solutions into appropriate programming language standards.

Programming language standards, no matter how comprehensive, cannot encompass all of the capability that modern users might wish. Many other standards have been adopted or are under development that are needed to work in conjunction with programming language standards. Examples are standards for databases (e.g. SQL), graphics (e.g. GKS, PHIGS), and operating system interfaces (e.g. POSIX). The interface between these functional standards and programming language standards is called a *binding*. Standards for bindings are in place or under development for all of the examples just cited. In general, these bindings have been developed by the functional standards committee (e.g. graphics) rather than the programming language committee, since the bindings are usually expressed without adding new syntax to the programming language, e.g. by specifying parameters in a CALL interface. Where new syntax is desirable, the programming language committee undertakes the assignment, as was the case with the GKS binding to Programming Language Basic.

Programming language standardization continues to grow in importance as more languages are developed to meet user application needs, and existing languages are adapted to new user and application environments. Table 1 lists the programming language standards that have been approved (or are underway) as of early 1992.

ROBERT H. FOLLETT AND JEAN E. SAMMET

PROGRAMMING LANGUAGES

For articles on related subjects *see* ADA; ALGOL 68; ASSEMBLER; AUTHORING LANGUAGES AND SYSTEMS; C; COMPILER CONSTRUCTION; FORTH; FUNCTIONAL PROGRAMMING; LANGUAGE PROCESSORS; LIST PROCESSING: LANGUAGES; MACHINE AND ASSEMBLY LANGUAGE PROGRAMMING; MODULA-2; MUMPS; NON-PROCEDURAL LANGUAGES; OBJECT-ORIENTED PROGRAMMING; PROBLEM-ORIENTED LANGUAGES; PROCEDURE-ORIENTED LANGUAGES; PROGRAMMING LINGUISTICS; SETL; and STRING PROCESSING: LANGUAGES.
See also Appendix V: Key High-Level Languages.

The definition of the term *programming language* is a controversial subject and by no means agreed to by all experts in the field. In order to lead up to the one proposed by this writer, we must consider various levels of languages used for dealing with the computer.

At the lowest level is pure binary. This is so impractical to use that humans almost never use this even

though it is actually the only language the machine "understands." A step above this is what is generally referred to as *machine code* or *symbolic machine code*. In this case the user generally writes instructions in some type of alphabetic symbols (e.g. SUB for subtract, TRA for transfer control, etc.). Machine addresses are written in normal decimal form (e.g. 1723). At the next higher level is *symbolic assembly language* in which the names of variables are written in symbols (e.g. ALPHA, TEMP, X, Y, Z) so that the location can be referred to symbolically rather than numerically. Thus a user might write

```
CLA Z  (CLA = clear accumulator and add)
ADD ALPHA
STO TEMP (STO = store)
```

meaning: "Add the variables stored in locations named Z and ALPHA and store the result in a location named TEMP." A program called an *assembler* assigns absolute storage locations to the variables and fills in the numeric values for machine addresses in the instructions. The term *assembly language* is sometimes used for what was called above (symbolic) "machine code," and is sometimes used for what was called "symbolic assembly language."

The next level of complexity involves a macro-assembler in which the user may define new "instructions" and use them in a program, with their definitions being given elsewhere in the program; for example, INCR ALPHA might represent the use of the macro INCREMENT which automatically adds 1 to the variable ALPHA. This would be shown elsewhere in the program as

```
MACRO     INCR     VAR
          CLA      VAR
          ADD      CON
          STO      VAR
          CON      1
          END
```

The previous levels bring us to what is frequently called *high-level language*. This author uses that term interchangeably with the term "programming language," although some others include the concept of assembly language in the term "programming language." The term *source program* (q.v.) means a program written in a high-level language. It is generally translated to an *object program* (q.v.), which is in a form directly understandable by the computer. The translation is usually done by a program called a *compiler*.

Definition of Programming Language* A programming language is a set of characters and rules for combining them which have the following four characteristics:

1. It requires no knowledge of machine code on the part of the user. In other words, the user need

---

*This section and the succeeding three sections are rewritten versions of material taken from Jean E. Sammet, *Programming Languages: History and Fundamentals*, © 1969, Prentice-Hall, Inc., Englewood Cliffs, N.J., pp. 9-22.

only learn the particular programming language, and can use this quite independently of (perhaps nonexistent) knowledge of any particular machine code. This does not mean that the user can completely ignore the actual computer. For example, the user may need to know how floating-point numbers are represented, or may wish to take advantage of certain known machine resources which provide more efficient programs. In particular, the user obviously cannot use input/output equipment that does not exist on a particular computer configuration. However, the fundamental point is that a knowledge of the basic machine code for the given computer is not needed.

2. A programming language must have some significant amount of machine independence. This means that there must be some high potential of having a source program run on two computers with different machine codes without completely rewriting the source program. (In the early development of programming languages this characteristic was often stated or implied as "complete machine independence." The state-of-the-art in 1992 does not provide such a capability, so the objective is to minimize the changes required to go from one computer to another.)

3. When a source program is translated into machine language, there is normally more than one machine instruction per executable unit created. For example, an executable unit in a programming language might be something of the form "A = B + C ∗ D" or "OPEN FILE ALPHA." Normally, each of these executable units would be translated into more than one machine instruction.

4. A programming language normally employs a notation that is somewhat closer to that of the specific problem being solved than is normal machine code. Thus, for example, the example "A = B + C ∗ D" might be translated into a sequence of machine instructions such as

```
CLA C
MPY D
ADD B
STO A
```

which is clearly less understandable than the programming language form.

Note that this definition of programming languages deliberately excludes menu-driven systems; they are extremely useful, but are *not* programming languages.

Advantages of Programming Languages As always, one cannot obtain something for nothing, and therefore there are both advantages and disadvantages to programming languages, where the alternative is some type of assembly language. Let us consider the advantages first.

The primary advantage of a programming language is that it is easier to learn than a machine or assembly language. It must be emphasized that there is a relative aspect involved in this advantage. An extremely powerful programming language might be harder to learn in its entirety than an assembly language on a computer which has only a dozen instructions. However, given programming and assembly languages of approximately the same complexity in their relative classes, the programming language will be easier to learn. This actually has two facets to it. The programming language may itself be extremely complex, but its ease of learning often comes because the notation is somewhat more related to the problem usage than is the machine code; furthermore, more attention can be paid to the language itself rather than to the idiosyncrasies of the physical hardware, which is necessary when one deals in machine code.

A problem written in a programming language is generally easier to debug for two major reasons. First, the program is usually shorter than its assembly language equivalent because of the expansion factor indicated as the third characteristic of a programming language. Since the number of errors tends to be roughly proportional to the length of the program, there will normally be fewer errors. A second reason for the program's being easier to debug is that the notation itself is somewhat more natural, and therefore relatively more attention can be paid to the logic of the program with relatively less attention paid to syntactic details.

A program coded in a programming language is generally easier to understand and to transfer to someone other than the originator because of the notational advantages and relative conciseness already mentioned.

Fourth, the notation of a programming language automatically provides a part of the necessary documentation because the notation is easier to understand and the logic is easier to follow.

Finally, the above advantages tend to accumulate into two general advantages, which are that the total calendar time and the total cost required for the problem solution are generally reduced significantly.

Disadvantages of Programming Languages There are disadvantages to programming languages which have varying importance in specific instances. First, the additional process of compilation obviously requires machine time, which may exceed the time saved by easier debugging.

Second, the compiler might produce very inefficient object code. This would significantly affect production runs (i.e. programs that are run repeatedly) because the machine-time requirements might be increased significantly by any inefficiencies. (The counterargument to this, of course, is that compilers today generally produce code that is at least as good as the average programmer can produce, and there are only a few really expert programmers who can write the most efficient machine code.)

Finally, the program may be much harder to debug than an assembly language program if the user does not know machine code and if the compiler does not provide the proper type of diagnostics and debugging tools. A user who must look at an unfathomable memory dump in octal is going to have more trouble than debugging an assembly language program in which what is happening is understood.

In the opinion of this author, and generally supported by common practice, the advantages of programming languages in the 1990s far outweigh the disadvantages. The normal mode for writing (at least) application programs is to use a high-level language, and the burden of justification for not doing this falls on the proponent of assembly language.

Classifications of Programming Languages

As indicated earlier, it is very difficult to define a programming language. However, it is a little easier to propose definitions for classes of programming languages, although these definitions are themselves controversial and not agreed on by everyone. The terms to be defined are the following: procedure-oriented and nonprocedural; problem-oriented, special-application and special-purpose; problem-defining; hardware, publication, and reference. Note that some of these are overlapping and that a particular language may fall into more than one of these categories. The terms *object-oriented* and *logic programming* (*q.v.*) are excluded from this classification, since those terms apply primarily to specific types of features that the languages themselves contain.

A *procedure-oriented* language is one in which the user specifies a set of executable operations that are to be performed in sequence and which specify a procedure. The key factor here is that these are definitely executable operations, and the sequencing is already specified by the user. Fortran, Cobol, and PL/I are examples. (The relation of these to domains of application is discussed later.)

The term *nonprocedural language* has been used for years without any attempt to define it. A definition is not really possible because *nonprocedural* is actually a relative term, meaning that decreasing numbers of specific sequential steps need be provided by the user as the state-of-the-art improves. The closer the user can come to stating a problem without specifying the steps for solving it, the more nonprocedural is the language. Furthermore, there can be an ordered sequence of steps, each of which is "somewhat nonprocedural," or a set of executable operations whose sequence is not specified by the user. Both cases contribute to more "nonproceduralness." Thus, before the existence of such languages as Fortran, the statement

```
Y = A + B * C - D/E
```

could be considered nonprocedural because it could not be written as one executable unit and translated by any system. In 1992, the sentences CALCULATE THE SQUARE ROOT OF THE PRIME NUMBERS FROM 7 TO 91 AND PRINT IN THREE COLUMNS and PRINT ALL THE SALARY CHECKS are nonprocedural because there is no compiler available that can accept these statements and translate them; the user must supply the specific steps required. As compilers are developed to cope with increasingly complex sentences, the nature of the term changes. Thus, what is considered nonprocedural

today may well be procedural tomorrow. The best example of a currently available nonprocedural language is Prolog; other nonprocedural systems (not really languages) are report generators (RPG) and sort generators in which the individual specifies the input and the desired output without any description of the procedures needed to obtain the output.

The term *problem-oriented* has been used in many ways by different people, but it seems that the most effective use of this term is to encompass any language that is easier for writing solutions to a particular problem than assembly language would be. Any current programming language illustrates this; thus, in this author's opinion, the term "problem-oriented" is a general catchall phrase. However, it is worth noting that many other people use the term to refer to languages for very specialized application areas.

It is a frequent misunderstanding that there is a separate category of languages called *application-oriented*. In reality, *all* languages are application-oriented, but some are for larger or smaller application areas than others. For example, Fortran is primarily useful for numerical scientific problems, whereas Cobol is best suited for business data processing. On the other hand, PL/I and Ada are useful in both those application areas, and therefore have a wider area of application. The term *general purpose* is sometimes used for PL/I or Ada (and even for Fortran), although in this author's opinion there is *no* truly general-purpose programming language. In this writer's view, the following application areas are sufficiently wide and important to justify particular consideration: numerical and nonnumerical (i.e. formal algebraic) scientific applications, business data processing, and string and list processing. Subjects other than these (or combinations of them) seem to be more specialized (e.g. graphics, simulation, machine-tool control, equipment checkout, robotics, expert systems). Languages for application areas other than those defined as fairly general should be called "special-application-oriented."

A *special-purpose* language is one designed to satisfy a single objective. The objective might involve the application area, the ease of use for a particular application, or pertain to efficiency of the compiler or the object code.

A *problem-defining*, or *specification*, language is one that literally defines the problem and may specifically define the desired input and output, but it *does not* define the method of transformation. There are significant differences among a problem (and its definition), the method (or procedure) used to solve it, and the language in which this method is stated.

A *reference* language is the definitive character set and form of a language. It usually has a unique character for each concept or character in the language, is one-dimensional, and need not be suitable as computer input. In some cases, the reference language contains English words considered as single characters; in other cases, a fixed set of symbols is provided. The concept of having a reference language, as distinguished from a publication or hardware representation language (discussed below), was introduced by the Algol committee in its first report.

The reference language need not be particularly easy to read.

A *publication* language is some well-defined variation of the reference language that is suitable for publication. It is designed to be suitable for printing and/or writing; therefore, it will have reasonable rules and characters for such things as subscripts, exponents, spaces, and Greek letters. The publication language would normally be the means of communication between people (using printed media). There can be many publication languages and they can contain different characters, but there must be a well-defined mapping between the publication and reference languages. An illustration of this is the use of an "up" arrow ↑ to denote exponentiation in the Algol reference language, but the use of a raised symbol in the publication language, e.g. A ↑ 2 becomes A^2.

A *hardware* language, sometimes called a *hardware representation*, is a mapping of the reference language into a form suitable for direct input to a computer. The number and types of characters used must be those accepted by the computer involved, and is often determined by those available on input devices. A hardware language must have a well-defined mapping between itself and the reference language; for example, ** might be a hardware representation of the ↑ in the reference language, and **begin** might be represented by 'BEGIN'.

History and Statistics A large number of higher-level languages have been developed since the first ones in the early 1950s. By 1967, there were more than 115 implemented (Fig. 1) and in use at some time just in the United States. By 1992 there were approximately 1,000 languages that had been used at one time or another, but many of them are no longer in use. Of these, roughly half were languages for specialized application areas (e.g. graphics, simulation, computer-assisted instruction, machine-tool control, equipment checkout, systems programming). The remainder are divided among the application areas cited earlier as being important and general. However, of this large number of languages developed in a 35-year time span, only a handful have been truly significant, and even fewer have been widely used.

In approximate chronological order, the languages of major significance, and the approximate dates of their earliest public documentation and/or general availability, are shown below.* In some instances, notably IPL-V and Algol 60, earlier versions of the language contributed significantly to the ones listed here.

APT (*A*utomatically *P*rogrammed *T*ools); 1957. The first language for a specialized application area.

Fortran (*FOR*mula *TRAN*slation); 1956. The first high-level language to be widely used. It opened the door to practical usage of computers by large numbers of scientific and engineering personnel.

Flow-Matic; 1958. The first language suitable for business data processing and the first to have heavy emphasis on an "English-like" syntax.

IPL-V (*I*nformation *P*rocessing *L*anguage *V*); 1958. The first—and also a major—language for doing list processing.

Comit; 1957. The first realistic string-handling and pattern-matching language; most of its features appear (although with different syntax) in any other language attempting to do string manipulation.

Cobol (*CO*mmon *B*usiness-*O*riented *L*anguage); 1960. One of the most widely used languages on an absolute basis, and the most widely used for business applications. Technical attributes include real attempts at an English-like syntax and at machine independence.

Algol 60 (*ALGO*rithmic *L*anguage); 1960. Developed for specifying algorithms, primarily numerical. Introduced many specific features in an elegant fashion and, combined with its formal syntactic definition, inspired most of the theoretical work in programming languages and much of the work on implementation techniques. More widely used in Europe than in the United States.

Lisp (*LIS*t *P*rocessing); 1960. Introduced concepts of functional programming combined with facility for doing list processing. Used by many of the people working in the field of artificial intelligence.

Jovial (*J*ules *O*wn *V*ersion of *IAL*); 1960. The first language to include adequate capability for handling scientific computations, input/output, logical manipulation of information, and data storage and han-

FIG. 1. The Tower of Babel, representing the large number of programming languages, is a concept that first appeared in the *Communications of ACM*. The form shown above was used as the jacket design for *Programming Languages: History and Fundamentals* by J. E. Sammet, © 1969, Prentice-Hall, Inc., Englewood Cliffs, N.J.

---

*This list and subsequent text are based on material excerpted with some modifications and additions from "Programming Languages: History and Future," by Jean E. Sammet, in *Communications of the ACM*, Vol. 15, No. 7 (July 1972). By permission. pp. 603-604.

dling. Most Jovial compilers were written in Jovial.

GPSS (*General-Purpose Systems Simulator*); 1961. The first language to make simulation a practical tool for people.

APL (*A Programming Language*); 1962. Provided many higher-level operators, which permitted extremely short algorithms and caused new ways of looking at some problems. Implementable version was not defined until 1967.

Joss (*JOHNNIAC Open-Shop System*); 1964. The first interactive language; it spawned a number of dialects, which collectively helped to make time sharing practical for computational problems.

Formac (*FORmula MAnipulation Compiler*); 1964. The first language to be used fairly widely on a practical basis for mathematical problems needing formal algebraic manipulation.

Pascal; 1971. Introduced some new ideas about data typing and combined numerous known constructs in a neat and elegant manner in a fairly small language.

Prolog; 1971. Developed to provide facilities for logic programming. Has been significantly used in artificial intelligence problems.

Smalltalk; 1971. This language has undergone numerous distinct versions since its earliest one, with the most widely used being that of 1980. Its most significant characteristic is the use of "objects" to permit object-oriented programming in a wide range of applications.

C; 1974. Originally created to assist in developing the Unix operating system, but subsequently became widely used and taught, primarily for systems programming, but also in other applications.

Ada; 1979. A very large, powerful language developed initially for embedded computer systems under the auspices of the Department of Defense. Has been used in multi-million line programs for non-military government applications (e.g. FAA, NASA), as well as military applications. Has also been used in numerous commercial applications in the private sector and in diverse applications such as artificial intelligence and business data processing.

Some other languages have been more widely used or more comprehensive than those on the list, specifically Basic, PL/I, Simscript, Snobol, and Icon. In many cases they have almost completely replaced some of the languages on the list (e.g. Basic for Joss and its derivatives, Snobol and then Icon for Comit). The languages just cited are omitted from the list of languages of major significance for the following reasons: Basic, although simple and economical, added no new concepts, was not the first on-line language, and was not the first to be of major practical importance. PL/I has capabilities derived from Fortran, Cobol, and Algol, but has not succeeded in one of its implicit objectives, which was to replace these languages. It was preceded by Jovial in the attempt to combine capabilities for several application areas. Simscript built on the previous discrete simulation languages. Snobol was a good but fairly obvious improvement to the

concepts introduced in Comit and then was largely superseded by Icon.

Appendix V (Key High-Level Languages) contains a list of approximately 50 languages that are deemed to be the most significant ever developed.

References

1969. Sammet, J. E. *Programming Languages: History and Fundamentals.* Englewood Cliffs, N.J.: Prentice-Hall.

1984. Pratt, T. W. *Programming Languages: Design and Implementation,* (*2nd ed.*). Englewood Cliffs, NJ: Prentice-Hall.

1986. Tucker, Allen B. *Programming Languages* (*2nd ed.*). New York: McGraw-Hill.

JEAN E. SAMMET

PROGRAMMING LINGUISTICS

For articles on related subjects *see* AUTOMATA THEORY; BACKUS-NAUR FORM; CONCATENATION; EXPRESSION; FORMAL LANGUAGES; GRAMMARS; LANGUAGE PROCESSORS; METALANGUAGE; PRODUCTION; PROGRAMMING LANGUAGE SEMANTICS; PROGRAMMING LANGUAGES; RECURSION; REGULAR EXPRESSION; STRING PROCESSING: LANGUAGES; SYNTAX, SEMANTICS, AND PRAGMATICS; VIENNA DEFINITION LANGUAGE; and WELL-FORMED FORMULA.

Languages for communication between any two systems, be they human or mechanical, can be described by three intertwining concepts: syntax, semantics, and pragmatics. This article is concerned with the methods of language description used to specify these concepts. For a discussion of the analysis of such specifications and their translation, *see* LANGUAGE PROCESSORS.

Semiotics In natural languages, the *syntax* of a language is known as its *grammar,* and it defines the valid relationships between the elements of the language. While syntax (or grammar) implies nothing about the meaning of the valid sentences (or phrases), *semantics* is the definition of meaning that is prescribed for the sentence by the originator of the sentence; i.e. by the speaker or writer. *Pragmatics,* on the other hand, is the meaning received by a listener or reader. *Semiotics,* the theory of symbols, is concerned with these three aspects of symbols.

In computer languages, the set of symbols available for the composition of sentences (or, in languages such as C (*q.v.*) or Pascal, *statements*) is highly restricted, and therefore syntactic specifications can be predicated on individual symbols rather than on words, prefixes, and suffixes. Further, since computer languages are artificial languages, it can be prescribed that there exists no difference between the semantics and the pragmatics of a language. Thus, in this article we omit any consideration of the pragmatics of computer languages, and confine our attention to those aspects of linguistics that are in use in relation to computer languages.

Initially, we review the concepts behind the use of syntactic and semantic specification with respect to programming languages and then subsequently examine the implementation of these concepts in practice.

Context-Free and Context-Sensitive Grammars

A grammar of a language is a formal system of description of the relationships among the symbols that comprise the language over the operations of symbol substitution and concatenation. A grammar is composed of four parts:

1. An alphabet of the language (character set or symbol set).
2. A set of parts of speech (known as the *component names* or *metavariables*).
3. The initial language element, such as "sentence" or "speech," from which all other sentences may be constructed.
4. A set of rules that directs the formation of instances of the language (called *productions*).

In the case of a language that may be described syntactically by rules of direct unconditional substitution and concatenation such that the substitution of a phrase for a component name is independent of the context of that component name, the language (and its grammar) is said to be *context free*. On the other hand, where such a substitution depends directly on the symbols or component names surrounding the component being replaced by substitution, the language is said to be *context sensitive*.

Language Descriptors

The terminology in which a language may be defined is a *metalanguage*, and must be uniquely distinguishable from the language being described. Thus, attempts to define a language in terms of itself can lead to paradoxes due to the indistinguishability of the metalanguage and the language. For example, we may say in the metalanguage of English that a sentence has certain qualities, such as *it is grammatically correct* or *that sentence is true*. Consider, then, the sentence: *This statement is false*. If one is not given the information as to whether this sentence is written in the language or a metalanguage, one assumes that the word *this* refers to the statement itself; then the sentence is paradoxical. However, the same utterance on the part of a scholar pointing to some other statement is clearly valid. Thus, the metalanguage for the programming language Ada (*q.v.*), for instance, must be clearly distinguishable from Ada. By these requirements, the symbolism of a metalanguage must not include the symbols used in Ada. Hence, there is a necessity to provide a distinct metalanguage that has applicability to the class of languages known as programming languages.

Symbolically, a grammar can be considered to be the definition of sets in terms of elements of other sets. For example, a member of the alphabet of Basic is a member of the set named (say) *character*; i.e.

$$character = \{A,B,C,D,E,...X,Y,Z,0,1,...8, 9, +, *, /, -,...\},$$

and, further, the class of objects named *variable* is composed of objects that are instances of the roman alphabet

($roman = \{A,B,C,...X,Y,Z\}$) or the set of single instances of roman letters concatenated with single instances of the set of digits; i.e.

$$variable = roman \cup (roman \times digit)$$

where $digit = \{0,1,2,...8,9\}$ and the operation $\times$ signifies the cross-product of the two sets.

The rules for generation of sentences in a context-free language are composed of a set of productions in which each rule has the form

$$a \rightarrow \beta_1\beta_2\beta_3 ... \beta_n \ (n \geq 1),$$

where α is a member of the set of component names and β_i is a member of the union of the set of component names and the alphabet of the language being defined. The string (or phrase) $\beta_1\beta_2\beta_3...\beta_n$ represents the concatenation of the individual elements β_i. The construct itself is taken to mean that the occurrence of α in any string may be replaced by the string $\beta_1\beta_2\beta_3...\beta_n$. The consistency of the set of production rules may be partially determined by ensuring that the following five conditions are met:

1. There shall exist only a single language component that is not derivable from other language elements. This component is known as the *root component*, or *root symbol*, and generally is given the name of the object that the grammar describes, such as *program* or *sentence*.
2. All other components shall appear on the left-hand side of at least one construct rule, thereby assuring that there are no "dead ends" in the grammar.
3. For every component in the grammar, there must exist at least one sequence of substitutions using the production rules that will lead to a string composed totally of the characters in the alphabet of the language.
4. Starting at the root symbol, there must exist for each component in the language a sequence of substitutions based on the production rules that will result in a string in which the component occurs; i.e. there are no "useless" components.
5. For every string of characters in the language, there shall exist at the most one sequence of substitutions that permits the generation of that string; i.e. the language must be *unambiguous*.

In practice, there are (at least) three forms of syntactic specification in common use: BNF (Backus-Naur Form, also occasionally known as Backus Normal Form), the Cobol language notation, and syntactic railroad charts. BNF was originally developed for the specification of the syntax of Algol 60 (Naur, 1960). This method of specification has since been widely used in the literature of computer science and has become widely accepted as a result of its ease of use and its readability.

This notation is applicable to an alphabet that is composed of the union of the alphabet of the language being described and the set of component names (names of the "parts of speech") of the language. To distinguish between the character set (alphabet) of the language and the component names, the BNF system encloses component names in angle brackets, or corner braces ($\langle$ and $\rangle$), whereas the actual alphabet symbols are free of any enclosing marks.

While the original notation used for the Algol specifications was not subject to any constraints, such as those that need to be imposed to restrict, say, the number of characters in an identifier name, BNF has been extended to include notation from regular expressions so as to provide this needed control. Table 1 defines the symbolism of BNF and compares the notation with set notation.

In the construction of the set of productions for a language, where there exists more than one possible substitution for any given component name α, two methods of description are possible: Either there exist several production rules in which α occurs on the left-hand side, or the list of alternatives is specified on the right-hand side of a single production rule, separated by the alternation symbol $|$. Thus, the definition of a language composed of the set of binary digits (0 and 1) may take either of two forms:

$$\langle binary\ digit \rangle :: = 0$$
$$\langle binary\ digit \rangle :: = 1$$

or

$$\langle binary\ digit \rangle :: = 0 \mid 1$$

As an example of a syntactic specification, consider the simple programming language (SPL) developed by Neuhold (1971) as the vehicle for the description of the Vienna Definition Language (*q.v.*). This language has two basic components, called *numbers* and *variables:*

$$\langle number \rangle \quad :: = \langle digit \rangle \mid \langle digit \rangle \langle number \rangle$$
$$\langle digit \rangle \quad :: = 0 \mid 1 \mid 2 \mid 3 \mid 4 \mid 5 \mid 6 \mid 7 \mid 8 \mid 9$$
$$\langle variable \rangle \quad :: = \langle letter \rangle \mid \langle variable \rangle \langle letter \rangle$$
$$\langle letter \rangle \quad :: = A \mid B \mid C \mid ... \mid X \mid Y \mid Z$$

In these two definitions, a recursive description system has been used which basically consists of two parts: a starter and an expander. That is, each definition contains an alternative which does not depend on the component type being formed, and an alternative which creates another instance of the component named on the left-hand side, given an instance of that component. Such recursive definitions permit the generation of unbounded strings of characters. Where an implementation restricts the length of a string (i.e. the number of characters that comprise the string), two alternative methods of description are available; either the set of permitted strings can be described individually, or a bounded repetition notation can be employed. The equivalence of these two descriptive methods is obvious. For example, let us assume that a particular implementation has restricted strings that represent *numbers* to three characters in length. Then the two representations could be

$$\langle number \rangle :: = \langle digit \rangle \mid \langle digit \rangle \langle digit \rangle$$
$$\mid \langle digit \rangle \langle digit \rangle \langle digit \rangle$$

or

$$\langle number \rangle :: = \{\langle digit \rangle\}_1^3$$

where the $\{ \}$ notation represents repeated concatenation of the object within the braces with itself, and the indices

TABLE 1.   BNF Notation vs. Set Notation

Symbol	BNF Meaning	Set Meaning, or Equivalent
$\langle X \rangle$	Component named X	An instance class of objects named X
x	Actual symbol x	The actual object x
$:: =$	...is to be replaced by...	...is a member of the set of strings...
$\mid$	"or" (the exclusive "or")	(When the separator is between two class names) set union $\cup$; (when the separator is between two elements of the alphabet) the set punctuation ','.
$\cap$	Operation of concatenation*	Product of the two sets
$\{z\}_i^j$	If z^k represents k concatenated occurrences of z, then: $\{z\}_i^j = z^i \mid z^{i+1} \mid ... \mid z^j$	$\{z^i, z^{i+1},..., z^j\}$

*Represented on the printed page by juxtaposition.

specify the upper and lower bounds of the number of repetitions.

SPL uses these elements to form programs that comprise statements that may be labeled optionally:

$$\langle label \rangle \quad ::= \langle letter \rangle \mid \langle letter \rangle \langle label \rangle$$

$$\langle statement \rangle \quad ::= \{\langle label \rangle\}_0^1 \langle statement\ body \rangle$$

$$\langle program \rangle \quad ::= \langle statement \rangle \mid \langle program \rangle;\langle statement \rangle$$

An SPL statement may take one of two forms: An arithmetic assignment statement (set statement) or a conditional branching statement (goto statement).

$$\langle statement\ body \rangle \quad ::= \langle set\ statement \rangle \mid$$
$$\langle goto\ statement \rangle$$

$$\langle set\ statement \rangle \quad ::= \text{SET } \langle variable \rangle \text{ TO}$$
$$\langle expression \rangle$$

$$\langle goto\ statement \rangle \quad ::= \text{GOTO } \langle label \rangle \text{ IF } \langle expression \rangle$$

In the latter two descriptions (productions), the uppercase characters are elements of the language being described and therefore are without the angle brackets. Finally, the description of an *expression* is required:

$$\langle expression \rangle \quad ::= \langle simple\ expression \rangle \mid$$
$$\langle simple\ expression \rangle$$
$$\langle operator \rangle\langle expression \rangle$$

$$\langle simple\ expression \rangle \quad ::= \langle number \rangle \mid \langle variable \rangle \mid$$
$$(\langle expression \rangle)$$

$$\langle operator \rangle \quad ::= + \mid -$$

This set of constructs completes the description of the syntax of the language and conforms to the five formation rules set forth previously.

As in the case of the specification of Algol 60, there existed a need in the development of Cobol for a means of syntactic specification. Whereas the Algol committee was composed of academicians and researchers, the Cobol committee was composed of a much more pragmatically-oriented group of people. Thus, the Cobol form of specification is much more oriented toward visual understanding than the (comparatively) mathematical form of BNF.

The latest version of this notation is presented in the specification of Standard Cobol (ANSI, 1985). This descriptive system uses lowercase strings to denote language components (called *generic terms* in the Cobol Standard) and uppercase strings to symbolize actual Cobol language characters. Further, uppercase strings that are underlined occur as key words in the language and must appear exactly as printed. On the other hand, uppercase characters that are not underlined are optional, and may or may not be present in the program. There are two sets of parentheses: brackets, [ ], which denote users' options and which may or may not appear in the program; and braces, { }, which denote alternatives, one of which must occur in the program. In this notation, the elements of the

brackets or braces are listed vertically. There also exists a notation that means "and so on" that is represented by the symbolism (...). According to the Cobol Standard (Chapter I, Section 5), the meaning of this becomes apparent in context.

Using this method of syntactic specification, the simple programming language (SPL) described earlier in BNF can be described as follows:

program: statement [; statement] ...

$$\text{statement: [label] } \begin{Bmatrix} \text{SET variable TO expression} \\ \text{GOTO label IF expression} \end{Bmatrix}$$

label: letter [...]
variable; letter [...]
number; digit [...]

$$\text{expression: } \begin{Bmatrix} \text{number} \\ \text{variable} \\ \text{(expression)} \end{Bmatrix} \begin{bmatrix} \begin{Bmatrix} + \\ - \end{Bmatrix} \text{expression} \end{bmatrix}$$

$$\text{letter: } \begin{Bmatrix} A \\ B \\ C \\ ... \end{Bmatrix}$$

$$\text{digit: } \begin{Bmatrix} 0 \\ 1 \\ 2 \\ ... \end{Bmatrix}$$

With the introduction of the programming language Pascal, the use of *syntax diagrams* or *railroad charts* for syntactic specification has become much more popular. Very similar in structure to the style of charts used in connection with finite state automata, these charts specify the alternative paths that may be taken in the construction of the allowable structures of a language.

Like both BNF and the Cobol notation, railroad charts can be constructed for each metavariable in the syntactic description of a language. Also like BNF, the railroad chart has been extended since its original conception to include a notation for the specification of the number of times a particular path in the chart can be traversed; this corresponds directly with the superscript and subscript notation that was added to BNF.

Using a BNF notation as a basic source of a syntactic rule, let us examine the procedures by which a railroad chart can be developed. For each BNF production, there exists a railroad chart which is named by the metavariable on the left-hand side of the BNF production.

Every occurrence of an actual language symbol (member of the language alphabet) is represented in the railroad chart by that symbol enclosed in a circle. Thus, the production

$$\langle A \rangle ::= x$$

would be represented by the chart:

$$A: \qquad \longrightarrow\!\!\!\bigcirc\!\!\!x\!\!\!\bigcirc\!\!\!\longrightarrow$$

Similarly, the occurrence of a metavariable on the right-hand side would be represented by a rectangle.

$$\langle A \rangle ::= \langle B \rangle$$

becomes

A BNF production having the form of a concatenated sequence of, say, metavariables would be represented by the sequential graph of their equivalent boxes.

$$\langle A \rangle ::= \langle B \rangle \langle C \rangle \langle D \rangle \langle E \rangle$$

is represented by:

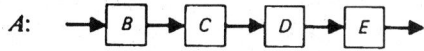

Alternatives in a production are handled very much the same as the two-dimensional scheme of the Cobol notation, wherein they are listed vertically with connecting arrows:

$$\langle A \rangle ::= \langle B \rangle \mid \langle C \rangle \mid \langle D \rangle \mid \langle E \rangle$$

Repetition or recursion is represented by a graph that loops back on itself:

where the exit from the loop is clearly identified as the alternative route out.

For the case of repetition with the possibility of zero passes through the loop, the construction

is the appropriate one.

On the following page we present the railroad chart definition for the simple programming language we have used to illustrate the prior syntactic systems.

If the restriction had been placed on the construction of, say, variables that they should not contain more than five letters, then the notation used consists of a half circle in the connecting arrow containing the number of repetitions that are permitted. The minimum number of repetitions must be represented by an explicit number of occurrences of the object being repeated. Thus, if we were to add the additional constraint on variable names that they must contain at least two letters, the chart would be constructed as follows:

Any context-free representation of syntactic description suffers from one deficiency: an inability to specify context-sensitive restriction rules. In most programming languages, there exist rules for the formation of programs that are totally independent of meaning (i.e. semantic meaning) and yet that are not adequately described in BNF. These are rules of the form, "if there exists in the program an element x, then there must also occur a declaration statement describing the attributes of the element x," or "there may only occur one element named y." Such a statement occurs in the verbal description of SPL: "(in describing the action of a GOTO statement)...To identify a target statement, the same label (mentioned in the GOTO statement) must appear exactly once as the prefix to some statement in the SPL program." While some completely formal descriptions of languages that include descriptions of both syntax and semantics include tests for multidefined program elements as part of the semantic definition portion, work has been undertaken to extend syntactic descriptive techniques to include such provisions independently of the semantic description. These include W-grammars by van Wijngaarden, Mailloux, Peck, and Koster (1969); Production Systems by Ledgard (1974); and Attribute Grammars by Lewis, Rosenkrantz, and Stearns (1976).

Syntactic Ambiguity As described in the preceding section, a grammar is considered to be ambiguous when there exists more than one sequence of substitutions that permit the generation of a single string of characters. In the English language, examples of syntactic ambiguities are common and appear most frequently in signs or titles. For example, consider the various ways in which the following three phrases can be interpreted (or formally "parsed"):

a half baked chicken
hot tiled showers
home made bake shop

Typically, an ambiguous grammar is one that contains a production rule which on its right-hand side references the same metavariable more than once, and does it in such a manner that it is impossible to discover the method of production of a string from its form. There is no known algorithmic technique to test for the existence of ambiguities in a grammar. However, examples of ambiguous grammars may help to indicate common sources of ambiguity. For example, consider the grammar

$$\langle integer \rangle ::= \langle digit \rangle \mid \langle integer \rangle \langle integer \rangle$$

$$\langle digit \rangle \quad ::= 0 \mid 1 \mid 2 \mid 3 \mid 4 \mid 5 \mid 6 \mid 7 \mid 8 \mid 9$$

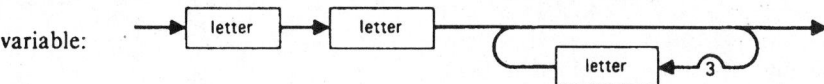

Using this syntax, there are at least two possible generation sequences to generate any string composed of three or more digits. For example, consider the string 123:

Generation sequence (1)
⟨integer⟩ → ⟨integer⟩ ⟨integer⟩ → ⟨integer⟩ ⟨digit⟩
→ ⟨integer⟩ 3 → ⟨integer⟩ ⟨integer⟩ 3
→ ⟨integer⟩ ⟨digit⟩ 3 → ⟨integer⟩ 23
→ ⟨digit⟩ 23 → 123

Generation sequence (2)
⟨integer⟩ → ⟨integer⟩ ⟨integer⟩ → ⟨digit⟩ ⟨integer⟩
→ 1 ⟨integer⟩ → 1 ⟨integer⟩ ⟨integer⟩
→ 1 ⟨digit⟩ ⟨integer⟩ → 12 ⟨integer⟩
→ 12 ⟨digit⟩ → 123

The differences between these two generation sequences can best be seen by examination of the generation trees (syntactic trees) corresponding to these sequences. In these trees, the replacement of a component by the use of a production rule is represented by a single-level tree structure, with the component being replaced at the top

and its replacement(s) below, and branch lines connecting the component and its replacement(s). Thus, sequence (1) is represented by the tree shown in Fig. 1, and sequence (2) is shown in Fig. 2. Obviously, these two trees are not equivalent, and thus we may state that this grammar appears to be ambiguous.

However, apparent ambiguity can result from a failure to be consistent in the order in which components in the partially expanded string are replaced. In fact, any rule that contains in its right-hand part more than one component is a potential source of apparent ambiguity. Thus, we insist that the order of replacement of components in a string be strictly left-to-right or right-to-left. That is, the leftmost (rightmost) component in a string is the candidate for replacement at each generation stage. Such a strict sequence of generations is known as *canonic* generation.

Returning to the definition of a digit string given above, it may be seen that a canonic generation would not alleviate the ambiguity of the grammar. However, a simple change in the grammar would solve this problem:

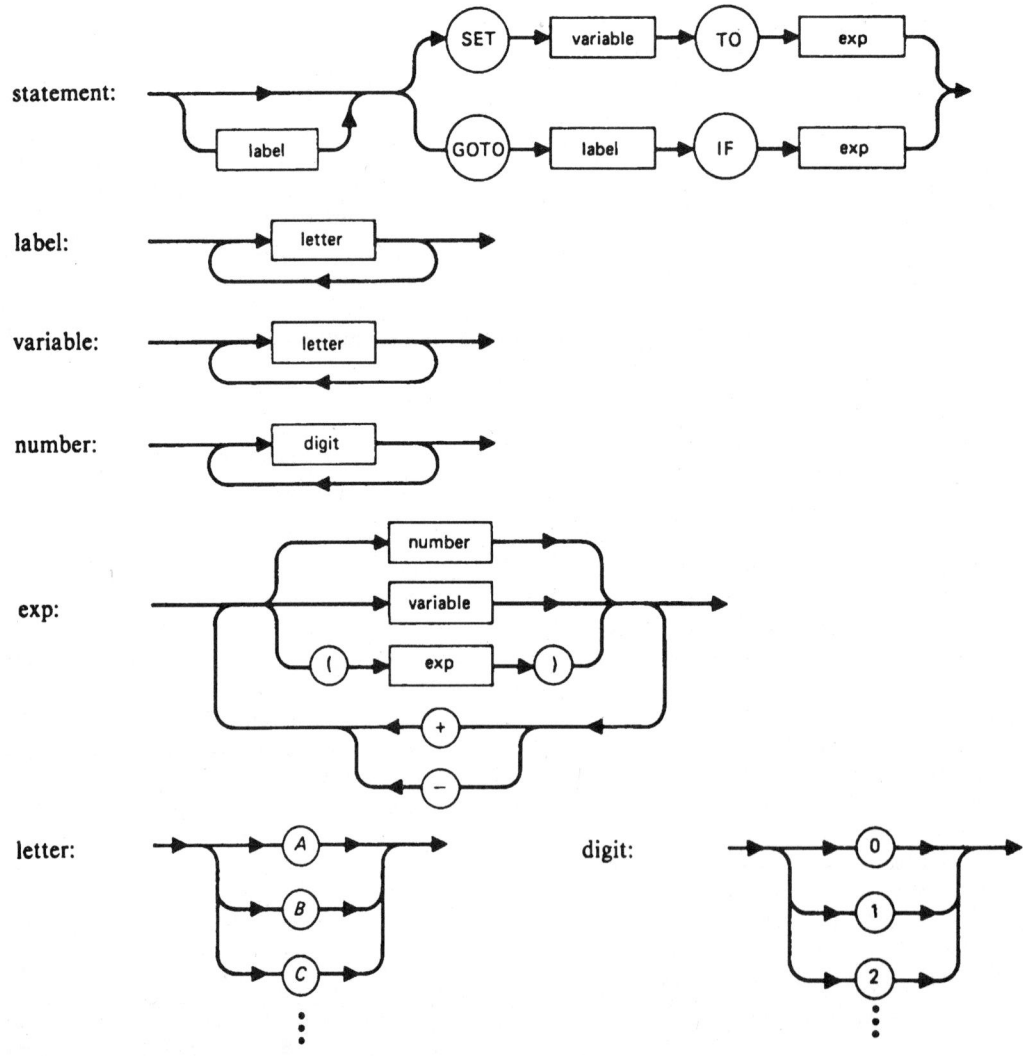

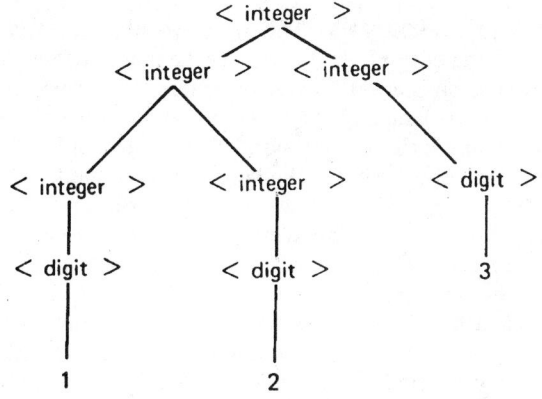

FIG. 1.   Generation sequence (1).

$$\langle integer \rangle \ ::= \langle digit \rangle \mid \langle integer \rangle \ \langle digit \rangle$$
$$\langle digit \rangle \ ::= 0 \mid 1 \mid 2 \mid 3 \mid 4 \mid 5 \mid 6 \mid 7 \mid 8 \mid 9$$

From this grammar, it would appear that there are at least two distinct ways of generating the string 123, depending on the order of application of the production rules (i.e. left or right canonic generation).

Left canonic generation sequence (3):
$$\langle integer \rangle \rightarrow \langle integer \rangle \ \langle digit \rangle$$
$$\rightarrow \langle integer \rangle \ \langle digit \rangle \ \langle digit \rangle$$
$$\rightarrow \langle digit \rangle \ \langle digit \rangle \ \langle digit \rangle$$
$$\rightarrow 1 \ \langle digit \rangle \ \langle digit \rangle \rightarrow 12 \ \langle digit \rangle \rightarrow 123$$

Right canonic generation sequence (4):
$$\langle integer \rangle \rightarrow \langle integer \rangle \ \langle digit \rangle \rightarrow \langle integer \rangle \ 3$$
$$\rightarrow \langle integer \rangle \ \langle digit \rangle \ 3 \rightarrow \langle integer \rangle \ 23$$
$$\rightarrow \langle digit \rangle \ 23 \rightarrow 123$$

While it would appear that these two generation sequences are distinct, their generation trees are in fact identical, as is shown in Fig. 3.

In general, an ambiguous grammar will be formed when two grammars are combined to define languages that have at least one element in common. For example, consider the grammar

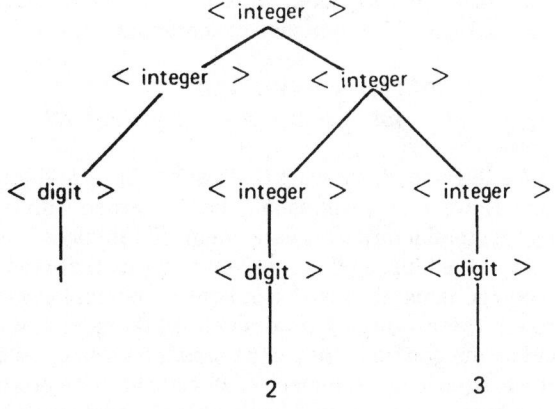

FIG. 2.   Generation sequence (2).

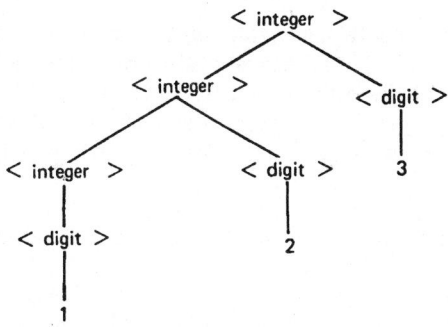

FIG. 3.   Canonic generation tree for sequences (3) and (4).

$$\langle this \rangle ::= \{A\}_1^3$$

which corresponds to the language with the sentences A, AA, and AAA. Then, if this were to be combined with the grammar

$$\langle that \rangle ::= AA$$

there would be two canonic generation sequences to develop the string AA. Thus, the grammar

$$\langle this\text{-}or\text{-}that \rangle ::= \langle this \rangle \mid \langle that \rangle$$

is ambiguous.

Although syntactic specification techniques are intended merely to provide a mechanism for describing the spatial relationships between the symbolic elements of the language, other structures inherent to the language are often introduced in order to provide guidance for compilers and other processors. The most common example is that of the arithmetic expression where the syntactic structure is organized in such a manner that it reflects the hierarchical execution (evaluation) structure of the expression. That is, if phrases within a syntactic tree are recognized in the same order in which the arithmetic factors are evaluated, then the two structures are synonomous.

Similarly, in connection with programming languages, it is important that languages be defined so that the desired meaning of a statement is unambiguous. As an example, it should be clear in defining an arithmetic expression that the implied meaning of an expression is unambiguous. Consider the simple expression

$$A - B - C$$

The interpretation (or parsing) of this string is usually considered to be equivalent to the string

$$(A - B) - C$$

and not

$$A - (B - C)$$

That is, $A - B$ is to be considered the first operand of the subtraction that contains C as its second operand. In terms of syntactic rules, this can be described by requiring that, in unparenthesized arithmetic expressions, the left (first) operand is always an *expression* and the right (second) operand is always a simple *element*, where a degenerate *expression* is an *element*. Thus, we might define

$$\langle expression \rangle ::= \langle element \rangle \mid \langle expression \rangle - \langle element \rangle$$

If we now add a semantic interpretation scheme over the syntactic form, which specifies that only *expressions* can be evaluated and *elements* are number representations, we may see that

$$9 - 7 - 2$$

can be generated only by a sequence of productions such that $9 - 7$ is an *expression* (and hence can be evaluated) that is part of the larger *expression* $\overline{9 - 7} - 2$, where the overscore identifies the left-hand operand, which must have a value (i.e. be evaluated) in order to evaluate the second subtraction term.

Context Sensitivity

In the use of syntax productions, the progression from the root symbol to the actual string of characters may be visualized as the progressive substitution of components until all components have been replaced by elements of the character set of the language. This may be further visualized as the progression through certain branches of a tree structure wherein each branch is independent of all other branches. However, this tree-like structure with no interdependence of branches exists only for *context-free* languages. If the left-hand side of a production contains more than one metavariable, then the production of the right-hand side is dependent on the occurrence of more than one metavariable, and the language is said to be *context-sensitive*. In such languages, productions of the type

$$\langle a \rangle \langle b \rangle \langle c \rangle ::= \langle a \rangle \, \pi \, \langle c \rangle$$

indicate that in the context of $\langle a \rangle$ and $\langle c \rangle$ (either but not both of which may be empty strings), the component $\langle b \rangle$ is to be replaced by the string π, where π may be any combination of characters and components. Although the majority of elements of computer languages are susceptible to description by a context-free grammar, certain features may require the use of a context-sensitive grammar, thus developing a totally context-sensitive grammar for that language. For a discussion and formal definition of context-sensitive languages, see Ginsburg (1966).

The need for context-sensitive grammars has diminished as a result of the existence of *attribute grammars* and the inability of researchers to develop syntactic analysis systems that are equivalent to those that have been developed for lexical analysis or for context-free grammars. Thus, although context-sensitive grammars are academically interesting, they are not used in any production system. The closest approach to such sensitivity is in the lookahead facilities of LR(k) grammars or LALR systems. However, such contextual checking is one-dimensional.

Syntactic Analysis

The problem of associating a given string of symbols through a grammar to a language, such that an answer to the question "does this string belong to the language?" may be determined, is known as *syntactic analysis*. It is intended that, in determining the existence of the string in the language, the syntactic tree for that string can be created. In fact, in terms of syntactic trees, the process of analysis can be thought of as the determination of the syntactic tree that was used to generate the string.

Cheatham (1967) has likened the problem of tree generation to the game of dominoes, wherein the dominoes contain the left-hand side and the right-hand side of each syntactic production. The problem, then, is to fit the dominoes together in such a manner that there exists a complete tree between the root symbol and the string in question. Such a structure is shown in Fig. 4 and is discussed later in this section.

Another means for validating the existence of a string in a language is to generate all possible strings of that language and then to investigate the existence of the string in question in the generated set. Obviously, in some languages this is impossible, since the language is infinite. However, given a string of a prescribed length (i.e. number of distinct characters in the string), it is possible to generate all sequences of that length, provided the null element is rejected from the grammar. That is, if each and every production in a given grammar either maintains or increases the length of the generated string upon application, then it is possible to discard many alternative generation sequences when the generated string is too long. In this sense, a string may consist of both characters in the language as well as components. Such strings are known as *sentential forms* of the language.

For example, given the grammar

$$
\begin{array}{ll}
(1) & \langle s \rangle ::= \langle e \rangle \\
(2) & \langle e \rangle ::= \langle e \rangle + \langle t \rangle \mid \langle t \rangle \\
(3) & \langle t \rangle ::= A \langle t \rangle \mid A
\end{array}
$$

we see that the initial symbol (root symbol) is $\langle s \rangle$ and that the character set of the language is $\{A, + \}$. The set of component names is $\{\langle s \rangle, \langle e \rangle, \langle t \rangle\}$. Given that $\langle s \rangle$ is the root symbol, then $\langle s \rangle$ is a sentential form of the language, and the replacement of any component in a sentential form by the use of one of the productions also develops a sentential form. Hence, the sequence of sentential forms

$$
\begin{aligned}
\langle s \rangle &\to \langle e \rangle \to \langle e \rangle + \langle t \rangle \to \langle t \rangle + \langle t \rangle \\
&\to A \langle t \rangle + \langle t \rangle \to AA + \langle t \rangle \to AA + A
\end{aligned}
$$

may be developed, showing that each form is *in* the language. However, we will usually be concerned with only those sentential forms that are composed totally of characters of the language; i.e. sentential forms that contain no components that are candidates for replacement through the use of any production. In the language defined by the grammar above, the *proof* that a string exists is the existence of a sequence of steps (using one production rule at each step) that leads from the root symbol to the desired string.

Such a definition of the proof of the existence of a string in a language is consistent with the definition of *proof* as related to formal systems (Mendelson, 1966):

> A proof...is a sequence A_1, A_2,...A_n of well-formed formulas such that, for each *i*, either A_i is an axiom (of the system) or A_i is a direct consequence of some preceding well-formed formula by virtue of one of the rules of inference.

In terms of syntactic forms, the existence proof may be defined as follows:

> An existence proof over a string of characters B_n in the language is a sequence B_1, B_2,..., B_n of sentential forms of the language such that, for each *i*, B_i is a sentential form that is the result of applying one of the production rules of the grammar to B_{i-1} and where B_1 is the root symbol of the language.

The means for determining this sequence is the task of a syntactic analyzer, and the sequence of productions that generates the sentential forms is known as the *parse* of the string. That is, for example, in the sequence of sentential forms that relate the root symbol $\langle s \rangle$ to the string $AA + A$ above, the parse is the sequence of rules applied. Thus, if the rules were numbered *i.j* where *i* is the rule number and *j* the alternative used, then this sequence of sentential forms is equivalent to the parse

$$1.1, 2.1, 2.2, 3.1, 3.2, 3.2$$

While we develop the parse of a string in the process of compilation, at least by implication, the most important derivative of a syntactic analysis of a string from the point of view of a compiler is the relationships between component names and the string. For example, it is comparatively easy to see in Fortran that the component name $\langle variable \rangle$ can be related to strings of characters in statements. Once this relationship has been established, then the generator of the compiler can (say) create addresses in target language instructions.

The task of analysis of a string must be initially to determine the existence of the string in the language. As noted above, one way to do this is by developing from the root component all strings of the same length as the string in question. Consider the grammar

$$\langle WFF \rangle ::= p \mid q \mid r \mid s \mid N \langle WFF \rangle \mid$$
$$\{C \mid A \mid K \mid E\}_1^1 \langle WFF \rangle \langle WFF \rangle.$$

This simple grammar (Allen, 1970) permits the production of well-formed formulas (WFF); the uppercase characters (N,C,A,K,E) represent the operators, and the lowercase characters (p,q,r,s) represent the simple operands. Fig. 4 shows Cheatham's domino game form of the generation tree of the string CNqNp. Now, obviously, since the definition of this language includes a recursive production, the language is an infinite language, and hence it will not be feasible to generate all possible strings in the language to test against any string that is believed to exist

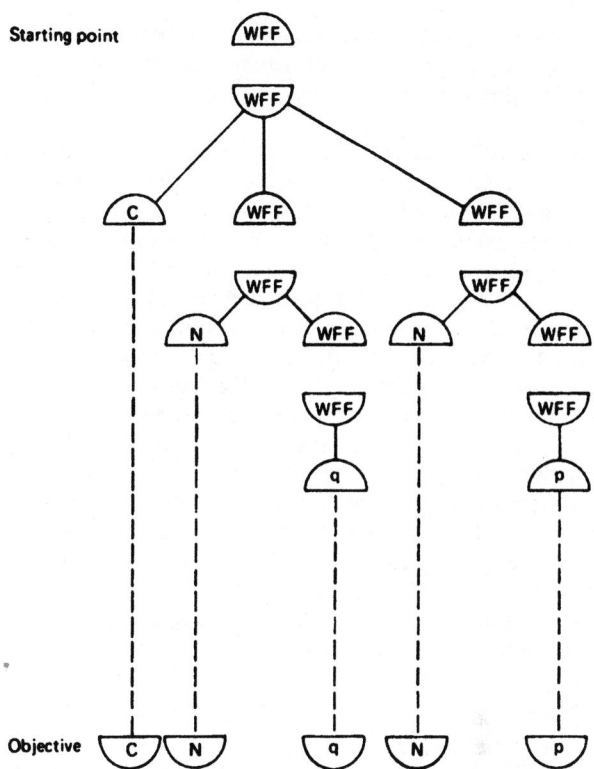

FIG. 4. Syntactic tree as a dominoes game. Given a starting point and objective as semicircles, the game is finished when all semicircles match with another containing the same character or component name.

in the language. However, it is possible to generate all strings of a certain length and then to check the existence of some string in this generated set. For example, consider again the string CNqNp. This string is composed of five characters (symbols in the language); and, by an examination of the possible substitutions that can be made, it can be seen that there are approximately 2,500 five-character strings that may be generated from this grammar! Thus, even for strings with comparatively few (5 even) characters, the number of alternatives in the algorithm for analysis is extremely large. Therefore, we must search for an alternative approach.

Syntactic analyzers can broadly be classified into two types: (1) the predictive methods, which, starting from the root symbol, attempt to predict the means by which the string was generated; and (2) the reductive methods, which attempt to reduce the string to the root symbol. These methods are loosely termed the *top-down* and *bottom-up* methods, respectively. The direction implied by these terms is related to the syntactic trees that may be generated wherein the root symbol is at the top of the page and the string at the bottom. It may then be seen that a predictive (top-down) method starts at the top of the (yet unconstructed) tree and builds down toward the string, whereas the bottom-up (*reductive*) method starts at the string and attempts to develop a tree that converges to the root symbol. It can be seen, using Cheatham's domino game, that starting from the basic game board containing only the root symbol (at the top) and the string to be analyzed (at the bottom), the two stages of analysis are well exemplified by the order in which the players fit the pieces into the puzzle.

Semantic Descriptions The formal description of the semantics of programming languages is currently in a state of active development, with several competing techniques, each emphasizing some aspect of definitional technology. There exist methods of semantic definition that are based on automata theory; these methods model processes and languages by modeling techniques. Other systems have developed abstract machines that closely resemble actual machines and that have a language of instruction that is used to describe a process or language. Although tremendous strides have been made in the methods of definition, including several examples of defining the semantics of actual languages and using those descriptions to guide the development of compilers and interpreters for those languages, there has been little practical work done in the area of formally validating those definitions. Conversely, there is a growing body of knowledge related to the proof of assertions about simple programs, which can be expected to develop to more meaningful proof techniques and systems in the future (*see* PROGRAM VERIFICATION).

Although even as early as the work on Algol 60, it was intended to accompany the syntactic specifications of languages by semantic descriptors, such a model was not available until several years later. The first large system that was described by a semantic description was the language PL/I, using the schema originally entitled *Universal Language Definer* but later dubbed the *Vienna Definition Language (q.v.)*. This method is based on a model of an abstract machine that is provided with an interpreter so that instances of the language can be executed.

This methodology has been extended and modified to the stage where there now exist three distinct methodologies for semantic definition:

1. *Operational semantics*—which is concerned with the operations of (possibly) abstract machines highly dependent on sequential activities that mirror the von Neumann style of computer architecture. This is the original technique developed as the Vienna Definition Language and used (in a slightly informal form) in the ANSI (American National Standards Institute) standard PL/I definition.
2. *Denotational semantics*—which is concerned with designing denotations for the elements of a programming language in an abstract domain (possibly the domain of data items in the language) independent of either an actual or an abstract machine system.
3. *Axiomatic semantics*—where the description of the properties of programming languages is specified in terms of the axioms to which the execution of that program must conform.

By analogy (but not necessarily in fact), these three descriptive methods correspond to the description of the interpreter for a programming language (operational semantics), the properties of the elements of the program (denotational) without regard for the end result, and the assertions that could be included in the program to show that it is correct (axiomatic definition).

References

1960. Naur, P. "Documentation Problems: Algol 60," *Comm. ACM* **3**, *5:* 299–314 (May).
1963. Floyd, R. W. "Syntactic Analysis and Operator Precedence," *Journal of the ACM* **10**: 316 (July).
1966. Ginsburg, S. *The Mathematical Theory of Context Free Languages.* New York: McGraw-Hill.
1966. Mendelson, E. *Introduction to Mathematical Logic.* New York: Van Nostrand.
1967. Cheatham, T. E. *The Theory and Construction of Compilers*, 2nd Ed. Wakefield, MA: Computer Associates.
1969. Van Wijngaarden, A., Mailloux, B. J., Peck, J. E., and Koster, C. H. A. "Report on the Algorithmic Language Algol 68," MR 101, *Mathematisch Centrum*, Amsterdam.
1969. Lucas, P. and Walk, K. "On the Formal Description of PL/I," *Annual Review in Automatic Programming, Part 3.* Oxford, UK: Pergamon Press.
1970. Allen, L. E. *Wff'n Proof.* New Haven, CT: Antotelic Instructional Materials.
1971. Branquart, P. *et al.* "The Composition of Semantics in ALGOL 68." *Comm. ACM* **14**, *11*: 697 (November).
1971. Neuhold, E. J. "The Formal Description of Programming Languages," *IBM Systems Journal* **10**, *2*: 86–112.
1972. *Proceedings of a Symposium on Proving Assertions about Programs, SIGPLAN Notices* **7**, *No. 7*, (January). New York: Association for Computing Machinery.
1974. Jensen, K. and Wirth, N. *Pascal User Manual and Report.* New York: Springer-Verlag.
1974. Ledgard, H. F. "Productions Systems: Or Can We Do Better Than BNF?" *Comm. ACM* **17**, *2*: 158–165 (February).
1976. American National Standard Programming Language PL/I, X3.53, New York: American National Standards Institute.
1976. Lewis, P. M., Rosenkrantz, D. J., and Stearns, R. E. *Compiler Design Theory.* Reading, MA: Addison-Wesley, Chapter 9.
1978. Bjorner, D. and Jones, C. B. "The Vienna Development Method," *Lecture Notes in Computer Science*, Goos, G. and Hartmanis, J. (Eds.). New York: Springer-Verlag.
1979. Gordon, M. J. C. *The Denotational Description of Programming Languages.* New York: Springer-Verlag.
1985. ANSI. *American National Standard Cobol, X3.23-1985.* New York: American National Standards Institute.
1989. Sebesta, R. W. *Concepts of Programming Languages.* Reading, MA: Addison-Wesley.

J.A.N. LEE

PROGRAMMING SUPPORT ENVIRONMENTS

For articles on related subjects *see* COMPUTER-AIDED SOFTWARE ENGINEERING; DEBUGGING; DISASSEMBLER; SOFTWARE MAINTENANCE; SOFTWARE REUSABILITY; and SOFTWARE TESTING.

Programming support environments are software tools that improve programmer productivity and enhance the usability of programming languages. All modern programming languages provide some programming support features, such as debugging tools. Advanced environments can support programmers in designing, coding, debugging, testing, maintaining, browsing, documenting, project tracking, reverse engineering, and customizing software. In addition, on-line help and embedded instructions assist programmers learning to use programming environments. Some environments support groups of programmers who work collaboratively on large software development projects. CASE (computer-aided software engineering) tools automate aspects of the software development process and encourage the use of particular programming methodologies.

The need for improved programming support environments is growing, as the development and maintenance costs of large software systems continue to increase. In the remainder of this article, a sampling of some of the features and functionality provided in programming support environments will be presented.

Design   To improve the process of designing software, programming methodologies have been developed and integrated into some support environments. For instance, tools that support authoring and viewing entity-relationship database diagrams encourage the use of that methodology. Typically, CASE systems provide a user interface (*q.v.*) for authoring models of organizations and systems, specifying complex behaviors and processes, and laying out data structures.

Coding   Libraries of subroutines and program templates allow the reuse and repurposing of software and therefore decrease the time and expense of writing new software (*see* SOFTWARE REUSABILITY). On-line help systems and menu-based programming systems improve programmer productivity by decreasing the time programmers spend searching through manuals. More sophisticated coding support techniques include programming-by-example and automatic code generation from high-level graphic or symbolic specification languages.

Debugging   Programmers use a variety of support tools during the debugging process. A *stepper* allows programmers to monitor execution of code line by line. An *inspector* is used to examine and modify data structures in memory. A *stack backtrace* facility is used to examine the stack after an error is detected. A *breakpoint* and *watchpoint* facility is used to help track down side effects (*q.v.*). A *trace* facility is used to monitor function calls and argument values.

Testing   Test case libraries are used to ensure that software meets design specifications. Tools that support developing, maintaining, and executing test cases are required. Bug tracking facilities are used to inform the development of test cases. An active area of research is concerned with automatic generation of test cases from software design specifications.

Maintenance   To perform software maintenance activities, programmers require tools that help them un-

derstand existing code that they may not have written. Tools exist to generate data flow, control flow, and calling hierarchy diagrams. If the source code is no longer available, techniques for reverse engineering the code can be applied (*see* DISASSEMBLER). Since the quality of documentation impacts maintenance programmer productivity, an active area of research is concerned with techniques for better capturing the intentions of designers, the strategies of implementors, and the reasoning of maintainers.

References

1979. Brooks, Frederick P. *The Mythical Man-Month: Essays on Software Engineering*. Reading, MA: Addison-Wesley.
1989. McClure, Carma. "The CASE Experience." *Byte*, April. Highstown, NJ: McGraw-Hill Inc.
1989. Norman, Ronald J. and Nunamaker, Jay F. *CASE Productivity Perceptions of Software Engineering Professionals*. Communications of the ACM. **32**, *9*, September.

JAMES C. SPOHRER

PROGRAMMING, MATHEMATICAL.   *See* MATHEMATICAL PROGRAMMING.

PROLOG.   *See* LOGIC PROGRAMMING.

PROOF OF PROGRAM CORRECTNESS.   *See* PROGRAM VERIFICATION.

PROPRIETARY PROGRAM.   *See* LEGAL PROTECTION OF SOFTWARE.

PROTECTION, MEMORY.   *See* MEMORY PROTECTION.

PROTOTYPING.   *See* SOFTWARE PROTOTYPING.

PROTOCOL

For articles on related subjects *see* BUS; HANDSHAKING; NETWORK PROTOCOLS; OPEN SYSTEMS INTERCONNECTION; and SYNCHRONOUS/ASYNCHRONOUS OPERATION.

A *protocol* is an agreement or set of rules that two or more communicating entities use to structure their conversation. Both hardware and software protocols are in common use.

As an example of a hardware protocol, consider a computer system with several CPUs, memories, and I/O devices on a single bus, such as a VME bus or an IBM-PC bus. When a device wants to use the bus, (e.g. to read a word from memory), it must request the bus. In most cases, a bus arbiter will examine the request and decide if it can be granted, depending on who else is using or requesting the bus. When permission is granted, the grantee can request a particular word by putting the address of that word on certain bus lines, and various control signals on other lines. In some systems, the memory is expected to respond within a fixed time (synchronous bus) or to give an explicit handshake signal when it is done (asynchronous bus). All of these rules—how the bus is requested, how it is granted, how reads and writes are requested, and how the responses are made—together form the bus protocol. Any device can be attached to the bus, provided that it obeys the bus protocol.

Software protocols are also important. Consider two machines communicating over a computer network. In order to be able to understand each other, they must agree on many things in advance—e.g. how long (in time) a bit is, how to recognize the start of data, and how to recover from errors, not to mention whether they are transmitting English text in ASCII or French text in EBCDIC. All of these rules together form the *network protocol*.

Because protocols are often highly complex, they are frequently structured in layers. The lowest layer is typically concerned with the electrical aspects (e.g. how many volts) and mechanical aspects (e.g. how many pins on the connector). The middle layers deal with grouping the bits into well-defined units (frames, packets, messages) and reliably sending them from the originator to the destination, possibly hop-by-hop over several intermediate machines. The upper layers have to do with the meaning of the information sent, such as protocols for file transfer and electronic mail (*q.v.*).

Many protocols have become either de facto or de jure standards. Standardizing a protocol makes it possible for multiple vendors to produce products that can work together. An entire industry—the making of plug-in boards for the IBM-PC and PC-compatibles (*q.v.*) is possible only because IBM has defined and published the bus protocol for its PCs. Similarly, the ethernet protocol makes it possible for workstations (*q.v.*) from multiple vendors to communicate, because they all use the agreed-upon rules for sending packets. The TCP/IP protocol makes it possible for thousands of machines over the entire world to exchange electronic mail.

As networks and applications become more complicated, new protocols are needed. The International Standards Organization has defined a complex set of protocols (ISO OSI) that are intended to cover the entire spectrum of networking applications, from the lowest layer to the highest. It is likely that these protocols will eventually become widely used, but it will take many years for this to happen due to a large existing base of non-OSI systems.

ANDREW S. TANENBAUM

PSEUDOINSTRUCTION. *See* MACHINE AND ASSEMBLY LANGUAGE PROGRAMMING.

PSEUDORANDOM NUMBER. *See* RANDOM NUMBER GENERATION.

PUNCHED CARD MACHINERY

For articles on related subjects *see* HOLLERITH, HERMAN; HOLLERITH'S MACHINE; IBM 1400 SERIES; POWERS, JAMES; PUNCHED CARDS; and WATSON, THOMAS J., SR.

Until the advent of commercially available stored-program computers in the 1950s, punched card machines represented the most technologically advanced information processing capability that was routinely available. The leading punched card machine supplier was IBM, which dominated the industry to an even greater extent than it now dominates the computer industry.

The origins of the punched card machine industry go back to Herman Hollerith who developed his census machine for the 1890 U. S. population census (*see* HOLLERITH'S MACHINE). The Hollerith system established the unit-record principle by which the data for a subject could be recorded on a punched card. Once the card had been punched, the data on it could be repeatedly tabulated and sorted entirely by machine. The Hollerith tabulating system achieved a major improvement over existing manual data processing methods in terms of economy, speed, and accuracy.

In 1896, Hollerith incorporated a small business, the Tabulating Machine Company (TMC), to exploit his system for commercial applications. By the early 1900s, the company had focused its operations on the sale of cards and the rental of tabulating machines to the accounting departments of large-scale enterprises, such as railroads, insurance companies, and engineering manufacturers. The early Hollerith equipment was based on three key machines that performed the three key data processing tasks: the *recording, tabulation,* and *sorting* of data. (These machines are shown in Fig. 1, a photograph of an early punched card office.) The simplest machine, the key punch—which was about the size of a small typewriter—was used to record original data onto a punched card. Introduced in 1901, the keypunch was to remain in use in essentially the same form for well over half a century and was a common sight in computer departments as late as the 1970s. The second machine was the tabulator. Introduced in 1906, the automatic tabulator was used to summarize and tabulate the data in a deck of cards at a speed of 150 cards per minute. The third machine, the sorter, was used to sequence a deck of cards according to some particular key field, and it operated at a speed of about 250 cards per minute. The early Hollerith sorter was known as the "vertical" model, an arrangement adopted to minimize the floor area taken up, but it soon became known as the "back breaker" because operators had to

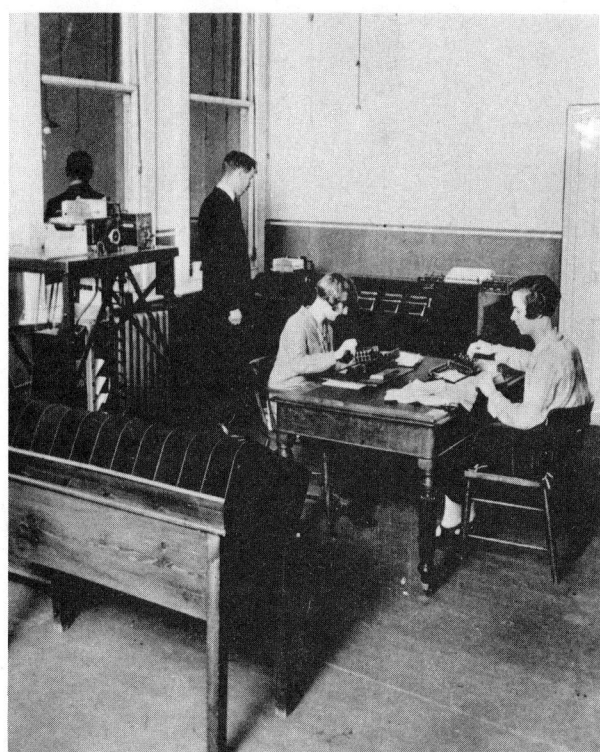

FIG. 1. A typical Hollerith installation, c.1920. The picture shows a vertical sorter (left of picture), an automatic tabulator (rear of picture), and two key punches (on the table).

stoop to remove cards from the lower receiving pockets. It was replaced by a horizontal model in 1926.

Although Hollerith's Tabulating Machine Company was successful as a small-scale enterprise, it was not until the company was merged with two other businesses to form the Computing-Tabulating-Recording Company (C-T-R) in 1911 that it became a significant force in the booming office machine industry. The same year, 1911, also saw the establishment of a rival punched card machine manufacturer, the Powers Accounting Machine Company, which introduced a highly competitive range of new machines. The Powers machines included an electrically operated card punch, a tabulator that printed its results, and a horizontal sorter. In 1924, the Powers company also introduced punched card machines for processing alphabetic data as well as numerical. From the time of the incorporation of the Powers company, rivalry between the Hollerith and Powers lines was intense, and it is a fair supposition that this competitive environment caused the machines to evolve more rapidly than otherwise would have been the case. Of the two companies, however, C-T-R—which changed its name to International Business Machines (IBM) in 1924—was much the more successful. In large part this was due to the charismatic leadership of its president, Thomas J. Watson, Sr. Although the Powers operation was fired with new vigor when it was acquired by Remington Rand in 1927, it never caught up with IBM.

Up to 1928, both Hollerith and Powers machines had used a common 45-column card format, but in that year IBM secured a major competitive advantage by introduc-ing the greater capacity 80-column card. Remington Rand responded in 1930 by introducing a 90-column card, but it was less popular than the 80-column format (*see* PUNCHED CARDS). This caused the Powers operation to be further eclipsed by IBM, which, according to contemporary accounts, sustained an 80–90% market share throughout the 1930s.

In 1931, IBM introduced the first of its 400 series accounting machines, and the following year the model 405 was announced, the first IBM tabulator to provide facilities for handling alphabetic data. The 400 series was a turning point for IBM: it marked the end of the transition from statistical machines to true accounting machines. The term "tabulator" was dropped at this time, and the machines were marketed as electric accounting machines (or EAMs). The IBM 400 series of punched card machines was to dominate the punched card scene for the next 30 years in much the same way that the IBM System/360 series was later to dominate the computer scene.

The 1930s was the heyday of the punched card machine. In the U. S., IBM benefited greatly from the increase in government bureaucracy created by the new Social Security Act. In order to satisfy the burgeoning demand for punched card data processing in public administration and private enterprise, many new "auxiliary" machines were introduced to supplement the basic punched card setup. These new machines included the multiplying punch, the interpreter, and the collator. As well as new machines, there were evolutionary improvements in the specification, speed, and reliability of the existing machines. For example, the card punch was equipped with a full typewriter-style keyboard, the tabulator was equipped with an "automatic control" that enabled several levels of sub-tabulation to be achieved, and the speed of the sorter was progressively improved, eventually reaching 600 cards per minute.

During World War II there was a hiatus in punched card machine development so that in the immediate post-war period the punched card machine companies faced three technical challenges: first, to update the existing electromechanical products; second, to introduce electronic technology which had been brought to the fore during the war; and third, to respond to the invention of the stored-program computer. While the first challenge was swiftly addressed, the initial response of the punched card machine manufacturers to electronics and computers was evolutionary. For example, IBM's first electronic product was the 603 multiplier introduced in 1946. Operating at a rate of 100 cards per minute, the 603 multiplier was the functional equivalent of the 601 multiplier introduced in the 1930s, but the incorporation of an electronic arithmetic unit produced a tenfold improvement in its speed. The model 603 was followed by several other calculating punches, the best known of which was the model 604 introduced in 1948. The 604 calculator was to become the heart of the card-programmed calculator (CPC), a scientific calculating setup, of which several hundred were sold during the early 1950s in the period before medium-priced stored-program computers became a commercial reality (Fig. 2).

FIG. 2. An IBM card-programmed calculator (CPC), c.1950. The CPC was a punched card–based computing system consisting of (left to right) a type 941 auxiliary memory unit, a type 402 electric accounting machine, and a type 604 calculating punch (two units—an arithmetic unit and a reader/punch). The CPC was a transitional product that provided a scientific computing capability until medium-priced stored-program computers became available.

The transition from punched card machines to computers, in fact, took longer and was more gradual than is often supposed. For example, throughout the 1950s, IBM continued to derive most of its revenues from its traditional punched card products; and as late as the early 1960s, Sperry Rand (the successor to Remington Rand) derived significant worldwide revenues from a transistorized calculating tabulator that was sold as the Univac 1004. It is now generally accepted that the key event that signaled the end of the punched card era and the dawn of the computer age was the launch of the IBM 1401 computer in 1959. As well as its low cost, a particular attraction of the new IBM computer was the model 1403 printer, which operated at 600 lines per minute, enabling the system to absorb the workload of several traditional tabulators. The provision of magnetic tape and disk storage enabled the system to subsume the functions of the electromechanical sorters and collators. Finally, the central processor (*q.v.*) could take over the role of auxiliary machines, such as multiplying and calculating punches. During the first half of the 1960s, some 14,000 IBM 1401 computers were sold, and sales of traditional tabulating equipment to first-time users faded away. Many existing punched card machine installations remained in operation throughout the 1960s, but by the early 1970s, the great majority of data processing departments had switched to computers.

During this changeover period, the punched card remained the most common input medium for computers, and a new generation of card readers and card punches were marketed, both by IBM and by OEM (*q.v.*) suppliers to the computer industry. The last major introduction of punched card–based equipment occurred with the launch of the IBM System/3 computer in 1969. System/3 introduced a new small 96-column card, and was equipped with optional off-line electro-mechanical sorting equipment. Active marketing of the 96-column equipment, however, was short-lived, as users turned increasingly away from card-oriented data processing methods to real-time transaction processing (*q.v.*). The use of both large and small punched cards declined steadily throughout the 1970s, and what use remains of punched cards is essentially vestigial.

References

1985. Bashe, C. J., Johnson, L. R., Palmer, J. H., and Pugh, E. W. *IBM's Early Computers: A Technical History.* Cambridge, MA: The M.I.T. Press.

1990. Norberg, A. L. "High-Technology Calculating in the Early 20th Century: Punched-Card Machinery in Business and Government." *Technology and Culture.*

1990. Campbell-Kelly, M. *ICL: A Business and Technical History.* Oxford: Oxford University Press.

MARTIN CAMPBELL-KELLY

PUNCHED CARDS

For articles on related subjects *see* HOLLERITH, HERMAN; HOLLERITH'S MACHINE; POWERS, JAMES; and PUNCHED CARD MACHINERY.

Punched card data processing was invented by Herman Hollerith in connection with the 1890 U. S. population census. In this first punched card application, a single $6 \frac{5}{8} \times 3 \frac{1}{4}$-inch card was punched for each citizen; the data recorded was essentially non-numerical (e.g. gender, marital status, nationality). Following the success of the census, Hollerith incorporated the Tabulating Machine Company in 1896 to exploit his machines for statistical and accounting applications in commerce. These applications required data to be recorded in numerical form, and for this purpose the card was redesigned with a number of vertical columns, each of which could represent a single decimal digit; a numerical value was then represented by a "field" of several adjacent columns. Early forms of the punched card had 34 and 37 columns, but eventually Hollerith standardized on a $7 \frac{3}{8} \times 3 \frac{1}{4}$-inch 45-column card with round holes (Fig. 1). The 45 columns

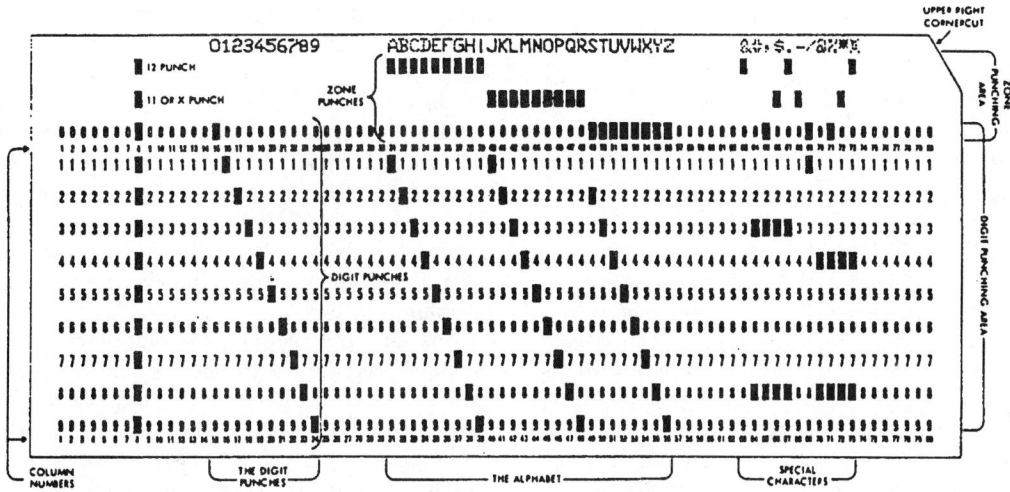

FIG. 1. Example of a 45-column card, c.1913.

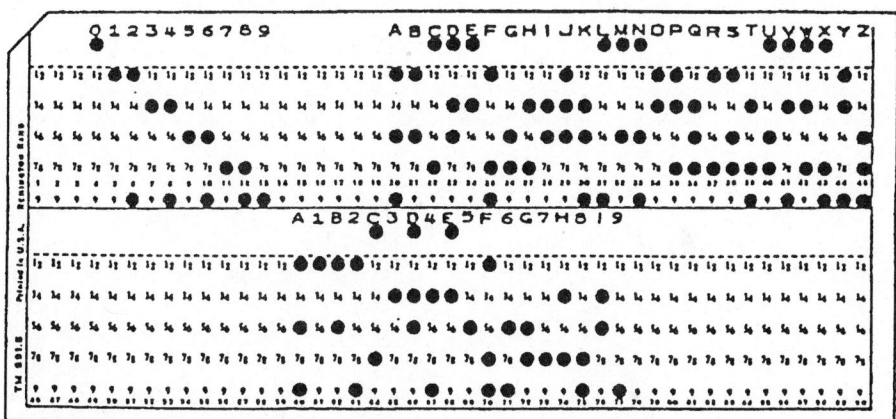

FIG. 2. IBM 80-column card, introduced 1928.

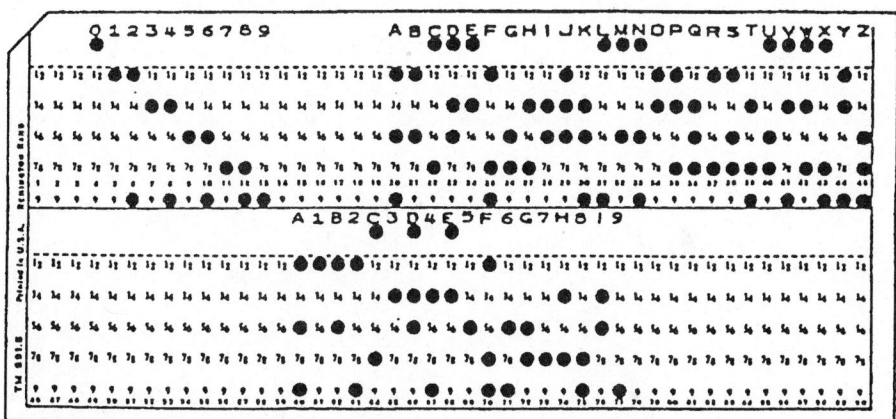

FIG. 3. Remington Rand 90-column card, introduced 1930.

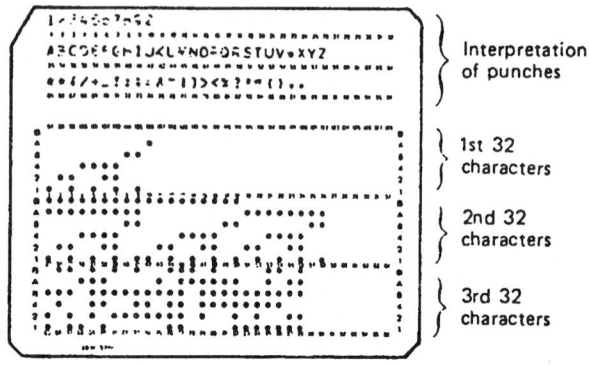

FIG. 4. IBM 96-column card, introduced 1969.

were arranged in 12 rows: the top row was known as the "12" or "Y" row; the second row was the "11" or "X" row; and the remaining rows were designated "0" through "9"; rows 0–9 were used to record the value of a digit, while the X and Y rows were used to indicate the sign of a number, or other control information. The 45-column format was also adopted by the rival Powers Accounting Machine Company, which was incorporated in 1911. (The Hollerith line subsequently became IBM, and Powers was acquired by Remington Rand in 1927.)

In 1928, IBM introduced the 80-column card using "slotted" holes. The new card enabled nearly twice as much information to be stored on the same size card. When IBM introduced alphabetic equipment in 1932, the "Hollerith Code" was introduced (Fig. 2). In the 48-character Hollerith Code, the digits 0–9 were represented by a single "digit punch" using the same code as the 45- and 80-column numerical cards. To represent the letters of the alphabet, A–Z, a single-digit punch was supplemented with one of three "zone punches." Special characters were generally coded by means of a zone punch and two-digit punches. The slotted-hole arrangement adopted by the Hollerith machines, which used electrical card-reading brushes, was not physically possible with the Powers

machines since they used mechanical sensing pins that could not be spaced sufficiently closely. In order to increase the capacity of its card, therefore, Remington Rand introduced a 90-column card, which consisted of two 45-column tiers (Fig. 3). In the 90-column card, each character was represented by a 6-hole code. This code required a relatively complicated decoding mechanism and was not compatible with the 45-column card. Because of these disadvantages—and Remington Rand's smaller market presence—the 90-column card was always much less popular than the 80-column format. Although Remington Rand and its successor, Sperry Rand, clung doggedly to the 90-column card until well into the 1960s, Sperry Rand's Univac computers generally used the 80-column format.

In the 1950s and 1960s, 80-column punched cards became the dominant input medium for computers. During this period, the old Hollerith Code was superseded by more generous character sets: These included the 64-character set of the IBM 1400 series and other second-generation computers, the 128-character ASCII code (*q.v.*), and the 256-character EBCDIC code (*q.v.*), which was introduced with the IBM System/360 computers in 1964.

In 1969, IBM introduce a new, small card with the System/3 computer. The new card, which measured 3 ¼ × 2 11/16 inches, held 96 characters arranged in three tiers of 32 characters. Each character was represented by a 6-bit code (Fig 4). By this time, however, the use of punched cards was already in decline, and the 96-column card never achieved anything like the penetration of the 80-column card.

As an input medium to computers, punched cards long out-lived the electro-mechanical machines for which they had been designed. But, from the beginning of the 1970s, the advent of key-edit equipment and interactive terminals caused a rapid falloff in punched card usage, which, for all practical purposes, ceased in the mid-1980s.

MARTIN CAMPBELL-KELLY

QUEUEING THEORY

For articles on related subjects *see* COMMUNICATIONS AND COMPUTERS; DISCRETE MATHEMATICS; FIFO/LIFO; OPERATIONS RESEARCH; SIMULATION; and STATISTICAL APPLICATIONS.

Queues are nothing more than the waiting lines that have become an accepted and often frustrating fact of modern life. Whenever demands occur in production, transportation, communication, computers, or other kinds of service systems, waiting lines are built up, resulting in a blocking of resources and in losses of time, money, patience, and good will. Efforts to control congestion are thus of vital importance, and have led to a rapid growth of research activity in *queueing theory*, which is the study of waiting-line processes through the use of mathematical and/or simulation models.

Queueing Models The basic queueing context (see Fig. 1) can be described as follows: Units from some source arrive at a service facility, wait if necessary in a queue or system of queues, receive service at a time (or times) determined by some service policy or discipline, and depart after service completion. Thus, the study of a queueing process requires the specification of each of the following elements:

1. *Source.* The source, finite or infinite, is a population or a group of populations from which the units demanding service emanate. These units may be people; paperwork, such as orders, invoices, letters, or computer programs; malfunctioning machines; or electronic signals in telecommunications systems.

2. *Arrival process.* The statistical pattern by which units arrive at the service facility is called the "arrival-time distribution." In many mathematical models, the time between successive arrivals is assumed to have the negative exponential distribution. This arrival process is also called "random arrivals" or "Poisson arrivals," since, under this assumption, the number of arrivals in a fixed period of time has the Poisson distribution.

3. *Queue structure.* The waiting line of a system may consist of a queue or a system of queues. Each queue may be constrained to a finite maximum length or be permitted to be unlimited in length. The waiting line may be conceptual rather than physical, as in the case of remote terminals waiting to be polled by a computer.

4. *Service discipline.* The rules by which units are selected from the queue structure and serviced constitute the service discipline. Service may be first-come, first-served (or FIFO, first-in, first-out), random, or according to some priority procedure. In the latter case, the priorities may be externally or internally determined, and service may be on a preemptive basis in which service on a "low" priority unit is interrupted

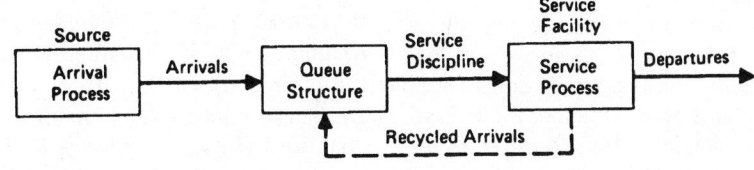

FIG. 1

(i.e. it rejoins the queue structure) whenever a "high" priority unit demands service. Whatever service discipline is to be used must be specified.

5. *Service facility.* The service facility may consist of one or more service channels in parallel; each channel may have one or more servers in series. A queueing model must specify the arrangement of the service facilities. Note that each "server" need not be a person, but may be a machine (e.g. a computer). Not all servers need be alike. (*See* FILE SERVER.)

6. *Service process.* The time required to service completely a unit at any server is referred to as that server's "service (or holding) time." A queueing model must specify the probability distribution of service times for each server (possibly for each type of unit entering the system). The service processes commonly used in mathematical models are the negative exponential and the constant service time distributions.

As an example of queueing in the computer area, consider a time-sharing system. The goal here is to provide preferential treatment (rapid response) to those jobs making small computational demands at the expense of jobs that make large demands on the CPU. Without prior information on how large a demand each arriving job makes, the feedback queueing system described essentially "tests" jobs, discovers which ones are short, and provides these with faster service. In time-sharing systems, then, the arriving units are jobs requiring computation and the server is the CPU. There is a system of queues that hold jobs awaiting service, and the service discipline is determined by a scheduling algorithm that decides which job will be serviced next and for how long. The amount of service time awarded is known as a *quantum* (or *time slice - q.v.*) and may vary. If the job being serviced is completed during this quantum, the job departs from the system. If the job is not completed, the job reenters the system of queues and awaits more service.

Simple examples of time-sharing queue structures and scheduling algorithms include the following.

Round-robin. Newly arriving jobs join the single queue which is first-come-first served. All quanta are the same size. Jobs requiring more than one quantum of service return to the end of the same queue and repeat the cycle. In the round-robin system, the response time varies directly with the computational demand made.

Foreground-background. In its simplest form, the queue structure consists of two queues. A newly arriving job joins the first queue (the foreground queue) and waits in a first-come-first-served manner for its first quantum. If the job completes, its departs the system. If not, the job joins the tail of the second queue (the background queue, which is also first-come-first-served) and waits to be awarded another quan-

tum. The second queue is serviced only at those times when the foreground queue is empty. This two-queue model is easily extended to a system having many background queues. The quanta given to a job usually get larger as a job works its way through these systems.

Problem Areas The problems associated with queueing theory may be classified as (1) analytical or theoretical and (2) operational or applications problems.

Analytical Problems. Under certain conditions, a queueing system that has been in operation for a sufficiently long time settles down to a behavior independent of time and the initial state of the system. The system is then said to be in an equilibrium (or steady-state) condition. Because the steady-state condition is less difficult to study analytically than the initial transient condition, the majority of analytical queueing results concern steady-state behavior.

A great deal of insight into the steady-state behavior of queues can be gained through the analytical results for the simplest models; consequently, a few single-source models are summarized in Table 1, which uses the following notation:

p_n = probability that the number of units in the queueing system (line length) is n.

p_0 = probability that the system is idle.

L = average line length.

Q = average queue length, where queue length is the line length minus the number of units being serviced.

W = average waiting time in the system (includes service time).

W_q = average waiting time in the queue (excludes service time).

λ_n = mean arrival rate (expected number of arrivals per unit time) of units when the line length is n.

μ_n = mean service rate (expected number of units being serviced per unit time) when the line length is n.

The first line of Table 1 gives the general results for some models in which it is assumed that the rates at which units arrive and are serviced depend only on the current line length (often called a "birth-death" process). Subsequent lines of Table 1 give results for a number of special cases.

As the table indicates, most queueing-system results depend upon the specific assumptions made; however, the following results hold under quite general conditions. Assume that $\lambda_n = \lambda$ for all n. Then $L = \lambda W$ and $Q = \lambda Wq$ (Little's result). Further, if $\mu_n = \mu$ for all n, then $W = W_q + 1/\mu$. These relationships enable us to determine all four quantities (L, Q, W, and W_q), if any one of them can be found analytically. Also, $p = \lambda/\mu$ is the utilization factor for the service facility; i.e. the expected fraction of time the server is busy.

TABLE 1. Some Sample Steady-State Queuing Results

Model Description	p_n	p_0	L	Q

1. Birth-death process
   Arrival rate = λ_n
   Service rate = μ_n
	$\left(\dfrac{\prod_{i=0}^{n-1}\lambda_i}{\prod_{i=1}^{n}\mu_i}\right)p_0 = R_n p_0$	$\dfrac{1}{1+\sum_{n=i}^{\infty}R_n}$	$\sum_{n=0}^{\infty} n p_n$	$\sum_{n=c}^{\infty}(n-c)p_n$

2. Poisson arrivals, exponential
   service times.
   Arrival rate = $\lambda_n = \lambda$ for all n.
   Service rate = $\mu_n = \mu$ for all
   $n>0$.
	$\left(\dfrac{\lambda}{\mu}\right)^n p_0 = \rho^n p_0$	$1-\rho$	$\dfrac{\lambda}{\mu-\lambda}$	$\dfrac{\lambda^2}{\mu(\mu-\lambda)}$

3. Poisson arrivals, arbitrary
   service times
   Arrival rate $\lambda_n = \lambda$.
   Service time has mean $1/\mu$ and
   variance σ^2.
		$1-\rho$	$\rho + Q$	$\dfrac{\rho^2 + \lambda^2\sigma^2}{2(1-\rho)}$

4. Poisson arrivals, constant
   service times.
   Arrival rate $\lambda_n = \lambda$ for all n
   Service time = constant
   $= 1/\mu$
		$1-\rho$	$\rho + Q$	$\dfrac{\rho^2}{2(1-\rho)}$

5. Poisson arrivals, exponential
   service time, finite maximum
   queue length M.
   Arrival rate $\lambda_n = \lambda$ for $n \le$
   M.
   Service rate $\mu_n = \mu$ for $n>0$.
	$\rho^n p_0$	$\dfrac{1-\rho}{1-\rho^{M+1}}$	$\dfrac{\rho}{1-\rho} - \dfrac{(M+1)\rho^{M+1}}{1-\rho^{M+1}}$	$L-(1-p_0)$

6. Finite source population
   (size N) exponential service
   $\lambda_n = \begin{cases}(N-n)\lambda & \text{if } n=0,1,\dots,N\\ 0 & \text{if } n\ge N\end{cases}$
   $\mu_n = \mu$ for all $n>0$
	$\dfrac{N!}{(N-n)!}\rho^n p_0 = C_n\rho^n p_0$	$\dfrac{1}{1+\sum_{n=0}^{N}C_n\rho^n}$	$N = \dfrac{\mu}{\lambda}(1-p_0)$	$N - \dfrac{\lambda+\mu}{\lambda}(1-p_0)$

Operational Problems. The study of real queueing systems is motivated by the objectives of improving their design, their control, and/or their effectiveness. The decisions that can be made usually involve the number of servers, the service rate(s) of the servers, the number of service facilities and their placement, the service discipline, and the populations to be served. All these decisions involve the general question of the appropriate level of service to provide and the appropriate trade-off to make between the costs incurred by providing the service and the costs incurred by waiting for service.

In attempting to use theoretical models for practical applications, a number of statistical problems arise, including verification of the basic assumptions of the model in order to avoid misusing mathematically derived results. In applications where the system is the least bit complex or the transient behavior of the system is of interest, many of the results of interest have not yet yielded to exact analysis. As can be seen from Table 1, even those results that can be obtained may be difficult to apply in practical situations. A relatively new branch of queueing theory deals with methods of finding simpler approximate or bounding results for queues. Computer simulation also may be used to obtain approximate results. Several higher-level computer programming languages, such as GPSS (General Purpose Systems Simulator) and Simscript, have been designed with the simulation of queueing processes in mind.

The earliest works in queueing (the classical studies by Erlang, a Danish mathematician) were concerned with highly practical problems in telephony. For many years, however, the problems studied were largely those amenable to mathematical analysis and queueing theory, as a tool for the analysis of practical problems, remained in a primitive state. More recently, the study of computer systems as queueing networks has led to many new results and applications. Queueing theory has been used to determine the effects of various quantum sizes and priority assignments on response time in time-sharing systems and to predict and evaluate the performance of different computer systems, especially networked systems. Thus, after many years in the hands of the theoreticians, queueing theory is proving to be an important application tool in the design of complex information processing systems.

References

1975, 1976. Kleinrock, Leonard. *Queueing Systems*, I and II. New York: Wiley-Interscience.

1978. *Computing Surveys* **10**, *3*. (Issue devoted to "Queueing Network Models of Computer Systems Performance.")

1981. Hillier, F. S. *et al. Queueing Tables and Graphs.* New York: North-Holland, Elsevier.

1989. Conway, A. E. and Georganas, N. D. *Queuing Networks: Exact Computational Algorithms.* Cambridge, MA: MIT Press.

1989. Gnedenko, B. and Kovalenko, I. N. *Introduction to Queuing Theory*, 2nd Ed. Cambridge, MA: Birkhauser Boston, Inc.

JOHN M. MCKINNEY

QUERY LANGUAGE. *See* DATABASE MANAGEMENT SYSTEM.

RAM. *See* MEMORY: MAIN.

RANDOM ACCESS. *See* DIRECT ACCESS.

RANDOM-ACCESS MEMORY. *See* MEM-
ORY: MAIN.

RANDOM NUMBER GENERATION

For articles on related subjects *see* MONTE CARLO METHOD;
SIMULATION; and STATISTICAL APPLICATIONS.

A *random number generator* is a computer procedure
that scrambles the bits of a current number or set of numbers to produce a new number in such a way that the result
appears to be randomly distributed among the set of possible numbers and independent of the previously generated
numbers. As experiments over the years have shown, this
appears surprisingly easy to do. A wide variety of scram-
bling methods have been proposed. Random number generators are provided for most computer systems or
software packages and they work remarkably well—at
least for limited use when only a few hundreds or thousands of numbers are required. But experience with very
fast computers doing Monte Carlo problems requiring
samples of hundreds of millions or billions has shown that
the random number generator must be carefully chosen.

The most commonly used bit-scrambling method
uses multiplication. Here is an example, using digits of the
more familiar base 10, rather than the bits for base 2 that
are used in computers: if the current "random number"
of, say, 10 digits is multiplied by a constant, then the last
10 digits of the product are taken as the new random

number. For this example, start with an initial random
number (the seed), say $x = 5362817283$, multiply by a
constant, say $a = 81734027$ to get an 18-digit product: ax
$= 435141161293554841$. Then take the last 10 digits of that
product as the new random number: $x = 1293554841$. For
the next x, form the product $ax = 105727446300274707$,
take the last 10 digits (reduce modulo 10^{10}) to get the new
$x = 6300274707$, and so on. This is called a *congruential
random number generator*. With proper choice of multiplier and modulus, such a generator produces a sequence
of numbers that are difficult to distinguish from truly
random numbers. A good congruential generator could
be used to run the casinos in Las Vegas and Atlantic City
and all the state lotteries with no one the wiser except
those in the know.

The first electronic computers of the late 1940s used
random number generators much like the one above, and
the intervening 40 years have seen many arithmetic or
algebraic schemes that seem to produce randomness,
even though the results are completely deterministic. But
modern computer speeds and exotic architectures make
possible massive Monte Carlo simulations for which standard generators may not be suitable. A summary of some
of the most common old, as well as promising new, random number generators is given below, after a description of the mathematical theory used to establish the
nature and periods of the methods.

Underlying Theory Virtually all random number
generators are based on theory that may be described as
follows: We have a finite set X and a function $f: X \rightarrow X$ that
takes elements of X into other elements of X. Given an
initial (seed) value, $x \in X$, (x might be a single computer
word or a vector of computer words), the generated
sequence is

$$x, f(x), f^2(x), f^3(x),\ldots,$$

where $f^2(x)$ means $f(f(x))$, $f^3(x)$ means $f(f^2(x)) = f(f(f(x)))$,
etc. Of key importance is the *period* of the generator, that

1145

is, how many numbers are produced until the generator produces a repeating pattern. The three most common classes of random number generators are 1) congruential, 2) shift-register and 3) lagged-Fibonacci.

For *congruential generators*, the finite set X is the set of reduced residues of some modulus m and $f(x) = ax + b$ mod m. Thus, with an initial element $x_0 \in X$, the generated sequence is

$$x_0, x_1, x_2,... \qquad \text{with } x_{n+1} = ax_n + b \text{ mod } m.$$

A wide variety of choices for a, b, and m have been described in the literature see; particularly, Marsaglia (1972) or Knuth (1981) for methods for finding periods and establishing the structure of congruential sequences. With periods around 2^{32}, congruential generators have been used successfully in Monte Carlo simulations for the past 35 years. Most of the random number generators provided by computer systems or software packages are congruential generators. But random points in higher dimensions with coordinates produced by congruential generators show a crystalline regularity that makes them unsuitable for certain applications, and that, taken with their relatively short periods, has led to the gradual adoption of longer-period generators for serious Monte Carlo studies.

For *shift-register generators*, the finite set X is the set of $1 \times k$ binary vectors $x = (b_1, b_2,..., b_k)$ and the function f is a linear transformation, $f(x) = xT$, with T a $k \times k$ binary matrix and all arithmetic mod 2. With an initial binary vector x, the sequence is

$$x, xT, xT^2, xT^3,...$$

with the matrix T chosen so that the period is long and multiplication by T is reasonably fast in computer implementation. Shift-register generators are sometimes called *Tausworthe generators*.

The use of shift-register generators is declining. Those based on standard k-bit computer words do not perform as well on tests of randomness as do congruential generators, and their periods are, like those of congruential generators, too short. Their main use is in forming part of a combination generator. The use of shift-register generators with extremely long binary vectors, $k = 607, 1279,$ or even 9689 still has some attraction, for the periods are extremely long, $2^k - 1$, and special hardware (called *shift registers* and hence the name of the general method) is easily constructed for their implementation. They are mainly used in special-purpose machines for Monte Carlo studies in physics.

For *lagged-Fibonacci generators*, the finite set X is the set of $1 \times r$ vectors $x = (x_1, x_2,..., x_r)$ *with elements* x_i in some finite set S on which there is a binary operation $\Diamond$. The function f is defined by

$$f(x_1 x_2,..., x_r) = (x_2, x_3, x_4,..., x_r, x_1 \Diamond x_{r+1-s})$$

where r and s $(1 \le s < r)$ are the two lag parameters. Informally, a lagged-Fibonacci sequence is described by means of a set of r seed values followed by the rule for generating succeeding values:

$$x_1, x_2,..., x_r, x_{r+1},... \text{ with } x_n = x_{n-r} \Diamond x_{n-s},$$

but to formally define and establish the period and structure of such sequences, they must be viewed as iterates $x, f(x), f^2(x),...$ on the set X of $1 \times r$ vectors with elements in the set S on which the binary operation $\Diamond$ is defined.

Various choices for S and $\Diamond$ lead to interesting sequences—for example, when S is the set of reduced residues of some modulus m and $\Diamond$ is addition or subtraction mod m; S is the set of reduced residues relatively prime to m and $\Diamond$ is multiplication; S is the set of $1 \times k$ binary vectors and $\Diamond$ is addition of binary vectors (exclusive-or); S is the set of floating-point computer numbers $0 \le x < 1$ having 24-bit fractions and $x \Diamond y = $ if $x > y$ then $x - y$ else $x - y + 1$}. Such generators are often designated $F(r,s,\Diamond)$ generators.

Implementations of lagged-Fibonacci generators require a table of the previous r numbers, say $L(1), L(2),..., L(r)$ and two pointers I,J pointing to the last values used in the previous $x \Diamond y$ operation. Then instructions equivalent to these are programmed:

$$K \leftarrow L[I] \Diamond L[J]$$
$$L[I] \leftarrow K$$
$$I \leftarrow I - 1: \text{ if } I = 0 \text{ then } I \leftarrow r$$
$$J \leftarrow J - 1: \text{ if } J = 0 \text{ then } J \leftarrow r$$
$$\textbf{return } K$$

While examples of generators of each of the three standard methods described above are widely used and—for most purposes—work quite well, new methods are always being developed. All standard generators (with the exception of lagged-Fibonacci using multiplication) fail one or more stringent tests of randomness, such as those described in Marsaglia (1985), and many of them have periods too short for the huge samples that current computer speeds make possible.

Combination Generators   Experience has shown, and there is theory to support, that combining two different kinds of generators, by perhaps subtraction or multiplication, produces a *combination* generator that has much longer period and performs better, or no worse than, either component in tests of randomness. The McGill Random Number Generator Super-Duper, one of the most commonly used generators of the past 20 years, combines a congruential generator with a shift-register generator. Its period is about 2^{62}. An example of a simpler high-quality combination generator is given in Table 1.

Periods and Seed Values   An ideal generator should have a period as great as the number of possible choices for seed values. Then, if the seed values are $x_1, x_2,..., x_r$ and the sequence is strictly periodic, every possible r-tuple of x's will appear in the full sequence—a desirable uniformity property. Except for trivial cases of little interest, the lagged-Fibonacci generators—until recently the record holders for long periods—do not have this property. The lagged-Fibonacci generators $F(r, s, -\text{mod } 2^{32})$ (with the binary operation subtraction mod 2^{32}), $F(r,s,*\text{mod } 2^{32})$, or $F(r,s - \text{mod } 1)$ have periods on the order of 2^{32+r}, 2^{30+r}, 2^{24+r}—far short of the ideals of 2^{32r}, 2^{30r}, or 2^{24r} that are the number of possible choices of seed values. (Nonetheless, their periods are still far longer than those for $F(r,s,\oplus)$ generators using exclusive-or, for which the period is at most 2^r, whatever the word size.)

Congruential generators satisfy the criterion that the period equals the number of choices for the seed value if a, b, and m are chosen judiciously. But that period, on the order of 2^{32}, is far too short for modern needs. The full period can be quickly exhausted, and it cannot provide the variety of possible k-tuples of numbers that probability theory says should be encountered in long streams.

There exist longer period generators for which the period equals the number of choices of seed values. One such class comes from extending the idea of a congruential generator for a prime modulus. For example, if p is the prime $2^{31} - 1$ then the sequence produced by $x_n = 1999 x_{n-1} + 4444 x_{n-2} \bmod p$ has period $p^2 - 1$ for any initial seed values x_1, x_2 not both zero, and there are $p^2 - 1$ possible choices. It is not easy, but one can find constants, c_1, c_2, c_3 so that $x_n = c_1 x_{n-1} + c_2 x_{n-2} + c_3 x_{n-3} \bmod p$ has period $p^3 - 1$ for any of the $p^3 - 1$ possible seeds x_1, x_2, x_3

not all zero, and so on: For any prime p, and any lag k, there are k constants such that the sequence $x_n = c_1 x_{n-1} \ldots + c_k x_{n-k} \bmod p$ has period $p^k - 1$ for any choice of k seed values not all zero.

Unfortunately, implementations of these maximal-period generators require, for each new x, k multiplications and additions modulo the prime p. This makes them very slow unless k is small. A recently developed method that uses only two additions or subtractions and still produces nearly maximal periods is the subtract-with-borrow method described next.

Subtract-with-Borrow Generators

These new generators, developed by Marsaglia and Zaman, produce extremely long-period sequences. They are like lagged-Fibonacci generators using subtraction: each new x is obtained by subtracting, modulo some base b, two previous x's, except that a "carry" bit is also included:

$$x_n = x_{n-s} - x_{n-r} - c \bmod b.$$

Given r seed values $x_1, \ldots, x_r$ in $0 \leq x < b$, not all zero, and an initial carry bit c, the rule for forming each new x_n and each new carry bit c is

TABLE 1. Examples of Various Kinds of Random Number Generators

Line	Seeds: Number and Type	Type and Generating Rule	Approximate Period
		Congruential	
1	1 32-bit odd integer	$x_n = 69069 x_{n-1} \bmod 2^{32}$	2.1×10^9
2	1 32-bit integer	$x_n = 69069 x_{n-1} + 1 \bmod 2^{32}$	4.3×10^9
3	1 31-bit integer $\neq 0$	$x_n = 16807 x_{n-1} \bmod 2^{31} - 1$	2.1×10^9
		Extended Congruential	
4	2 31-bit intergers	$x_n = 1999 x_{n-1} + 4444 x_{n-2} \bmod 2^{31} - 1$	4.6×10^{18}
		Lagged Fibonacci	
5	17 32-bit integers	$x_n = x_{n-17} - x_{n-5} \bmod 2^{32}$	2.8×10^{14}
6	17 32-bit odd integers	$x_n = x_{n-17} * x_{n-5} \bmod 2^{32}$	7.0×10^{13}
7	17 32-bit integers	$x_n = x_{n-17} \oplus x_{n-5} \bmod 2^{32}$	1.3×10^5
8	55 32-bit integers	$x_n = x_{n-55} - x_{n-24} \bmod 2^{32}$	7.7×10^{25}
9	55 32-bit odd integers	$x_n = x_{n-55} * x_{n-24} \bmod 2^{32}$	1.9×10^{25}
10	97 reals	$x_n = x_{n-97} - x_{n-33} \bmod 1$	1.3×10^{36}
11	607 32-bit integers	$x_n = x_{n-607} - x_{n-273} \bmod 2^{32}$	10^{192}
		Subtract-with-Borrow	
12	847 bits	$x_n = x_{n-240} - x_{n-847} - c \bmod 2$	9.4×10^{254}
13	1751 bits	$x_n = x_{n-472} - x_{n-1751} - c \bmod 2$	1.3×10^{527}
14	37 32-bit integers	$x_n = x_{n-24} - x_{n-37} - c \bmod 2^{32}$	4.1×10^{354}
15	30 64-bit integers	$x_n = x_{n-6} - x_{n-30} - c \bmod 2^{64}$	9.5×10^{577}
16	39 reals	$x_n = x_{n-25} - x_{n-39} - c \bmod 1$	8.6×10^{278}
		Combination	
17	2 32-bit x's, odd 3 y's $< 2^{30} - 35$	$x_n = x_{n-1} * x_{n-2} \bmod 2^{32}$ $y_n = y_{n-3} - y_{n-1} \bmod 2^{30} - 35$ $z_n = x_n - y_n \bmod 2^{32}$	2.3×10^{18}

Form $t = x_{n-s} - x_{n-r} - c \bmod b$.

If $t \geq 0$ then $x_n = t$ and $c = 0$,

else $x_n = t + b$ and $c = 1$.

As with lagged-Fibonacci, these generators require that the previous r values be kept in a table.

There are b^r choices for seed values, and certain choices of b, r, s will attain virtually that maximal period. For example, with b near 2^{32} and r near 30, periods on the order of 2^{960} are obtained. Several examples are given in Table 1.

Tests of Random Number Generators

A random number generator is supposed to produce a sequence of independent uniform random variables U_1, $U_2, \ldots$. Any function of the elements of such a sequence may be used to test that supposition; if the sampling distribution of the function is consistent with that called for by underlying theory, then the generator passes the test. Any number of tests are possible; many have been proposed. Probably the best test of a random number generator is to try it on a similar problem for which the answer—the probability distribution of the result—is known. A more or less standard set of tests are in Knuth (1981), but most of those are tests on the uniformity of the random numbers, not on their independence. More stringent tests on both uniformity and independence are in Marsaglia (1985).

Most of the standard generators, having periods on the order of $2^{32} \approx 4 \times 10^9$, fail one or more of the stringent tests if samples of millions or tens of millions are used. Such sample sizes are quite feasible for Monte Carlo simulations in current computers. Periods around 2^{32} are just too short to contain the variety of k-tuples of numbers that probability theory says should be encountered in large samples. However, newer generators, such as those in Table 1 having much longer periods, seem to pass stringent tests even with such large samples. Our ability to develop new generators with extremely long periods, on the order of 10^{100} to 10^{600}, far outstrips our ability to run Monte Carlo simulations for larger and larger samples. There are less than 10^{17} nanoseconds in a year, and each element of a sample is likely to require more than several hundred nanoseconds.

Some Examples

Table 1 lists examples of some of the most successful kinds of random number generators. Lines 1–3 are examples of three of the most frequently used congruential generators; line 4 is an example of an extended congruential generator with prime modulus p and period $p^2 - 1$. Lines 5–11 give examples of lagged-Fibonacci generators with increasingly long periods, except for line 7, which shows the drastic reduction of period arising from use of the exclusive-or operation rather than subtraction or multiplication.

The tremendously long periods of subtract-with-borrow generators are exemplified in lines 12–16, and line 17 gives an example of a very good generator that arises from

combining two simple generators that individually are not very promising.

References

1972. Marsaglia, George. "The Structure of Linear Congruential Sequences. *Applications of Number Theory to Numerical Analysis.* Z. K. Zaremba, Ed., New York: Academic Press.

1981. Knuth, Donald E. *The Art of Computer Programming: Volume 2: Seminumerical Algorithms*, 2nd Ed. Reading, MA: Addison-Wesley.

1985. Marsaglia, George. "A Current View of Random Number Generators," Keynote Address: *Proceedings, Computer Science and Statistics: 16th Symposium on the Interface.* New York: Elsevier.

1987. Ripley, Brian D. *Stochastic Simulation.* New York: John Wiley.

GEORGE MARSAGLIA

READ-ONLY MEMORY (ROM)

For articles on related subjects *see* CYCLE TIME; EMULATION; FIRMWARE; MEMORY: MAIN; MICROPROGRAMMING; PERSONAL COMPUTING; and STORAGE HIERARCHY.

Read-only memory (ROM) is based on a wide spectrum of storage technologies, many of which should be more accurately referred to as "slow write" storages. The basic idea behind read-only storage is that, for a number of applications, the contents of the storage are relatively fixed for a long period of time. In fact, for some applications, the contents of storage are not altered during the life of the machine. An example is the use of ROM in early microcomputers to hold an invariant copy of the processor for a high-level language, such as Basic or Pascal.

The memory cycle of read-only storage is shortened because its contents, being fixed, does not have to be regenerated. In addition, since a store operation cannot be performed by the system, the accessing mechanism usually can be designed to operate faster than otherwise. Also, in most situations, the read-only memory system

FIG. 1. A 24,000-bit read-only store chip, using field-effect transistor technology packaged in a 1-in. square metallized ceramic substrate.

will be less expensive than a read-write memory with corresponding performance.

Many technologies have been used and applied to read-only storage. These include the diode matrix, the card-capacitor approach, and magnetic or transformer type read-only storage. Modern ROM implementations frequently are actually EPROMs (erasable programmable ROMs). These are MOS (metal-oxide semiconductor) devices that are programmed by a high voltage (25–30 volts) and can be erased by exposure to ultraviolet light.

Read-only storage has been used quite extensively for microprogrammed implementations of the control function—controlling the action of an instruction execution. For this function, the read-only storage has to be as fast as the basic cycle time of the machine.

Another use of read-only storage is the area of the *bootstrap loader* (*see* BOOT AND REBOOT), which is a program that is permanently stored as part of the main memory of the system. Control is transferred to this program on machine startup so that other programs can be called in an orderly way and control can be transferred to them.

MICHAEL J. FLYNN

REAL TIME.   *See* PROCESSING MODES.

REAL-TIME BUSINESS APPLICATIONS

For articles on related subjects *see* ADMINISTRATIVE APPLICATIONS; COMMUNICATIONS AND COMPUTERS; DATABASE MANAGEMENT SYSTEM; DISTRIBUTED SYSTEMS; INFORMATION RETRIEVAL; INTERACTIVE SYSTEM; MULTIPROCESSNG; MULTIPROGRAMMING; MULTITASKING; TERMINALS; TIME SHARING; and TRANSACTION PROCESSING.

Real-time business applications have been well established in the field of computer systems for almost two decades, and, in certain areas of computer usage, have become virtually the exclusive mode of data processing. This approach to computer applications can best be described by contrasting it with batch processing, the prevailing form of computer utilization before the advent of the more sophisticated systems concepts that underlie real-time processing.

Batch Processing   In *batch processing*, transactions against a file of data are accumulated until a sufficient number are present to warrant mass updating of a master file. This processing method is particularly suitable for accounting applications, such as payroll accounting or accounts receivable, in which master files are updated with new transactions periodically and in which output is produced according to a predetermined processing cycle. The processing cycle is ordinarily defined by the frequency with which the master file must be updated.

During each processing cycle, receipts and new charges are batched for entry, as are status changes (open account, close account, change address, etc.). After entry, both classes of input go into an edit/convert run where they are validated as to correctness of account number and completeness of information. After editing, each item is written to auxiliary storage for subsequent processing. The next step is to sort these transactions into the same sequence as the master file. The master may then be updated during what is by far the most complicated and time-consuming run in the system. Outputs from this run include the updated master (which will become input to this same run during the next processing cycle) and other files, which go into output-edit runs to produce new bills and management reports.

Real-time Processing   *Real-time systems* can best be differentiated by the quality of their *responsiveness*. Conventional systems respond to their business environment by producing the requisite journals, reports, and other output according to their carefully pre-scheduled batch-processing cycles. Real-time systems, in contrast, can respond immediately at the time a transaction occurs. Thus, a bank teller using a terminal can obtain immediate information about a customer's current balance while the customer waits at the counter for completion of the transaction.

The question of how responsive a system must be before it merits designation as real-time is, of course, relative. In some situations, usually those in which the customer is awaiting a decision based upon the computer's response, the reply will be required within a few seconds; in other circumstances, a longer response time can be tolerated. Real-time systems in which there is rapid and frequent interaction between human and machine are said to operate in a *conversational* mode.

Most real-time applications require hardware and software that provide fast responses to the terminal operator. From a human factors standpoint, a system response time of 3 to 5 sec on the average is desirable. This covers the elapsed time from the dispatch of a message from a remote terminal into a central processing unit and back to the terminal in the form of a response to the user. A significant component of such response time is usually the time devoted to retrieval of one or more records to satisfy the requirements of the incoming transactions.

Besides this characteristic of responsiveness, other features of real-time systems can prove advantageous to computer users. When a transaction is processed in real time, there is no need for the laborious retranscription of source data from its original form to its processable form, which frequently must take place in preparing input for a conventional system. For example, when an airline reservation agent using an alphanumeric terminal enters each passenger's name and flight information at the time the booking is made, that is the end of it. There is no need to retranscribe these facts on paper to be sent to the "back room" for keypunching and subsequent processing. And, of course, there is no delay imposed by the real-time system if the reservation agent wishes to retrieve and modify the record just created.

In real-time applications, files are updated as new transactions occur, with results of the updating transmit-

```
*92/10 NOV-HART
```
Entry typed by agent to display record: flight, number and date, passenger's name

```
HART/JAMES MR
1. 92Y10NOV HS1 SFOBUF 845A 516P HRS SPM
```
Y: tourist class
HS1: 1 seat held
SFO: San Francisco; BUF: Buffalo;
SPM: special meal

```
TKTG TAMO 8NOV/
FONE NYC-212 555-9531-H
NYC-212 TW9-6431-H C/O CROSS
RCVD-PSGRS NIECE, MRS CROSS
AFAX CAKE WITH HAPPY BIRTHDAY UNCLE JIM
        SFO SKY CHEF
OSI PSGR IS CELEBRATING 85TH BIRTHDAY
TAM 475 FOREST ST AMHERST NY 14226
JFK 17Y10NOV HK SEAT 18D
NYC-LS 0124A/04NOV 9151CH
```
Ticket to be mailed 8 NOV.
H: home phone number
Person making reservation

AFAX: Additional facts

OSI: other supplementary information
Address to mail ticket
HK: notes seat number confirmed
LS: Agent identification
0124A: time reservation made
9151CH: disk file address of PNR-typing *9151CH will also cause display of this record

FIG. 1.   Annotated sample of terminal display of passenger name recorded (PNR) on the SABRE system.

ted back to the originator almost immediately upon receipt and processing of the transaction. Examples of this are plentiful, such as those in bank accounting systems in which the customer's balance is updated immediately after entry of a deposit or withdrawal request at a teller window equipped with a terminal connected to the bank's computer.

Classes of Real-Time Applications   The scope of real-time applications is almost as varied as the field of data processing itself. Among the pioneer systems can be found such diverse applications as:

1. The SABRE system of American Airlines, which provides instantaneous access to flight inventory information and electronic storage of passenger itinerary data. Fig. 1 shows part of the terminal display of this transaction.
2. Interactive problem-solving systems epitomized by M.I.T.'s MAC, the forerunner of today's time-sharing systems.
3. Real-time mission-control systems developed for NASA, which have supported every flight of American astronauts from the early days of Project Mercury through the Apollo moon landings and the space shuttle.

Two generic types of real-time processing can be identified.

There is, first, *transaction-oriented processing*, in which clerical personnel interact with a computer for the entry and recording of business transactions, such as airline reservations. One characteristic of such transaction processing is that the terminal operator is carefully guided through a set of input/output operations by the computer, which responds with an error message should an erroneous or unacceptable entry be submitted. For example, an airline reservation agent would be notified if an attempt was made to book a passenger on a nonexistent flight or on a flight already sold out. Similarly, a bank teller would be reminded if an inactive account number was entered or a withdrawal was requested that caused a deposit balance to become negative.

A second class of real-time processing involves interactive problem solving in a manner less highly structured than transaction processing. Here, terminal users are provided with generalized software packages such as those for information retrieval, which allow them to enter the parameters of a retrieval request and trigger a search of system files. For example, a database of personnel information might be interrogated to find out how many employees have more than ten years of service, a salary greater than $50,000, and a college degree.

Equipment Requirements for Real-Time Applications   Real-time applications of the kinds described are operational on a wide range of equipment, from minicomputers with limited storage capacity serving only a few terminals, up to the largest systems that embody multiple processing units and memory modules, billions of characters of immediate access storage, and thousands of terminals. But, regardless of size, the equipment employed in real-time systems has a number of common characteristics. Although not all real-time applications require all these features, the vast majority employ them at least to some degree. Fig 2 provides a schematic of the major equipment elements usually present in a real-time processing environment. Descriptions of these elements follow.

Terminals   Terminals for real-time applications are diverse. The terminal may be a simple numeric input device, such as a TouchTone telephone keyboard, with responses provided by computer-generated voice an-

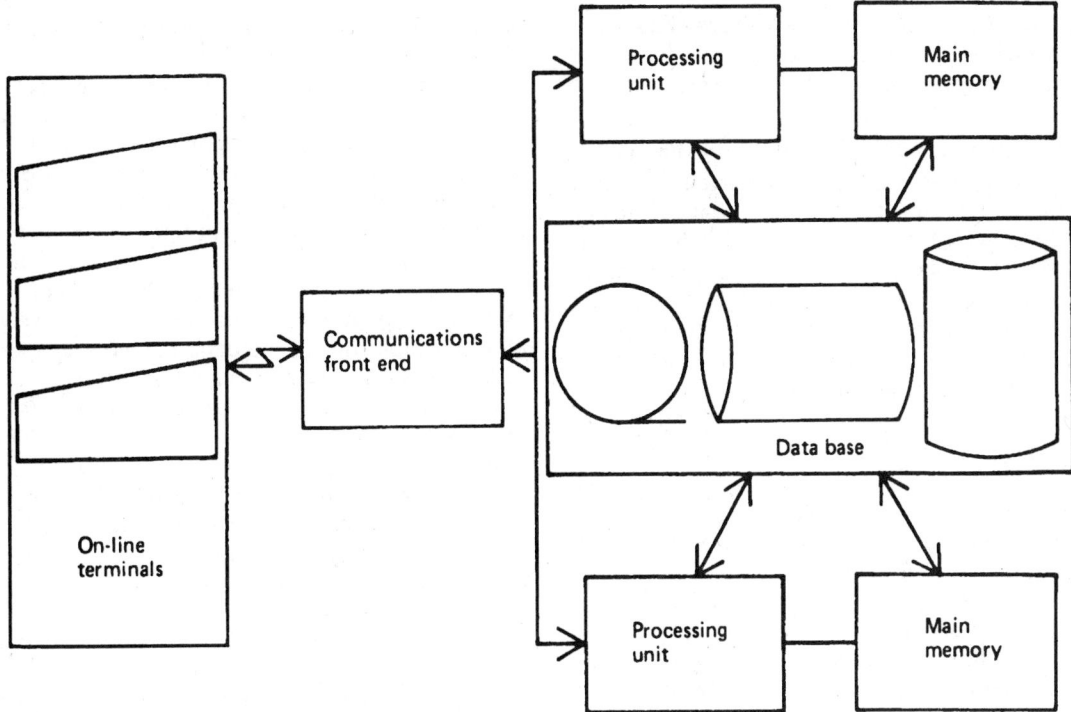

FIG. 2.   Real-time equipment configuration.

swer. At the other end of the complexity scale are *intelligent terminals*, minicomputers or microprocessors with enough storage capacity and logic to perform extensive preliminary processing before accepting a transaction for transmission to the central processing unit.

Terminals for real-time applications can also be differentiated as *special-purpose* or *general-purpose*. Special-purpose terminals are employed in such applications as stock quotations, airline reservations, and on-line banking. Such terminals may be equipped with special-purpose function keys, specialized print symbols, and templates or masks for specialized displays. However, many real-time applications, in particular those for handling relatively unstructured retrieval requests or interactive problem solving, require only a standard low-speed typewriter-like device or an input keyboard combined with a data display screen.

Communications Front End   A communications front end is necessary to interface the lines connecting remote terminals to the central processing unit. It performs such functions as assembling incoming messages, detecting transmission errors, and routing responses back to the terminal operators. In large systems, this front-end equipment may be a minicomputer and may have associated with it tapes or disks for message queueing. In smaller systems, front-end functions may be integral to the central processing unit rather than assigned to a separate processor.

Central Processing Units   Two central processing units are shown in Fig. 2 to reflect a characteristic of many real-time configurations that contain dual processing

units for greater reliability. In such systems, one processing unit may perform high-priority transaction processing, while the other performs lower-priority work, perhaps batch processing, with the second processing unit assuming the on-line processing work load if there is a malfunction in the first.

Main Memory Modules   As in the case of the central processing unit, two or more main memory modules may be configured for workload sharing and enhanced reliability.

Immediate Access Storage   Immediate access storage is found in virtually all real-time applications, and sometimes ranges into the billions of characters for storage of large databases that must be immediately accessible. In many systems, there is a hierarchy of such storage, ranging from fixed-head drums or disks with access times of a few milliseconds up to large-capacity disk files with access times averaging 100 ms or more. Removable disk storage is also present in many configurations so that files can be conveniently removed and stored once processing against them is completed. In multiprocessing configurations, each processing unit may have a channel (*q.v.*) to all immediate storage.

Other Devices   Magnetic tape drives continue to be used in real-time applications for such purposes as logging incoming transactions, maintaining duplicate copies of files and transactions for recovery purposes, and performing sorting and other batch processing for low-priority batch applications. More exotic types of storage devices are now beginning to appear as substitutes for, or augmentations of, conventional disk storage units, such as optical memory systems that provide access to billions of characters of storage within a few seconds.

Software Requirements for Real-Time Applications

The operation of real-time systems dictates the need for certain kinds of software that might not otherwise be required. Fig. 3 illustrates the major software components typically present in real-time applications. These packages may, in some cases, be housed in a single computer; in more complex systems, they may be distributed among multiple computers (e.g. communications front ends and central processors).

The Operating System All the software functions illustrated in Fig. 3 are under control of an operating system. The operating system maintains overall control of system operations by scheduling the execution of all other programs, allocating main memory, establishing job priorities, servicing interrupts, communicating with the computer operator, and performing similar housekeeping tasks. Obviously, the precise capabilities of a given operating system are dependent on the size of the computer for which it was written, as well as on the design objectives of the manufacturer in creating this all-important piece of software.

Communications Package Referring again to Fig. 3, we can identify a communications package required to control the operation of the multiple, remote terminals found in most real-time applications. In some large configurations, this front-end software may actually be lodged in a separate computer dedicated to controlling all system communications. In small systems, the communications package may simply be a subroutine of the operating system.

Besides controlling the terminals and communication lines, and interrupting the operating system when action must be taken on incoming messages, the communications package provides (or should provide) *terminal transparency* to the other programs in the system. This means that an application program need not be concerned with the *kind* of terminal from which an inquiry has been received or to which a message must be sent. Instead, these programs need concern themselves only with the substance of the data, not with its specific format. This is an important consideration in a system that employs a variety of terminal devices (e.g. teletypewriters, cathode-ray tubes, voice-response terminals, or graphics terminals). It is often necessary to change terminal types or upgrade terminal capability, as new information needs are identified or as new hardware becomes available. With terminal transparency, flexibility can be achieved by making changes only in the communications front end, *not* in the application programs themselves.

Besides communications network control, a communications package may perform such functions as input message error handling, input editing, and output report and display formatting. The communications package may also contain security provisions as well as data-logging capability and other features to facilitate recovery.

Database Management Package

At the right of Fig. 3 is shown the database management package that performs on the database a set of operations analogous to those performed at the front end of the system by the communications package. The database management package services the application programs

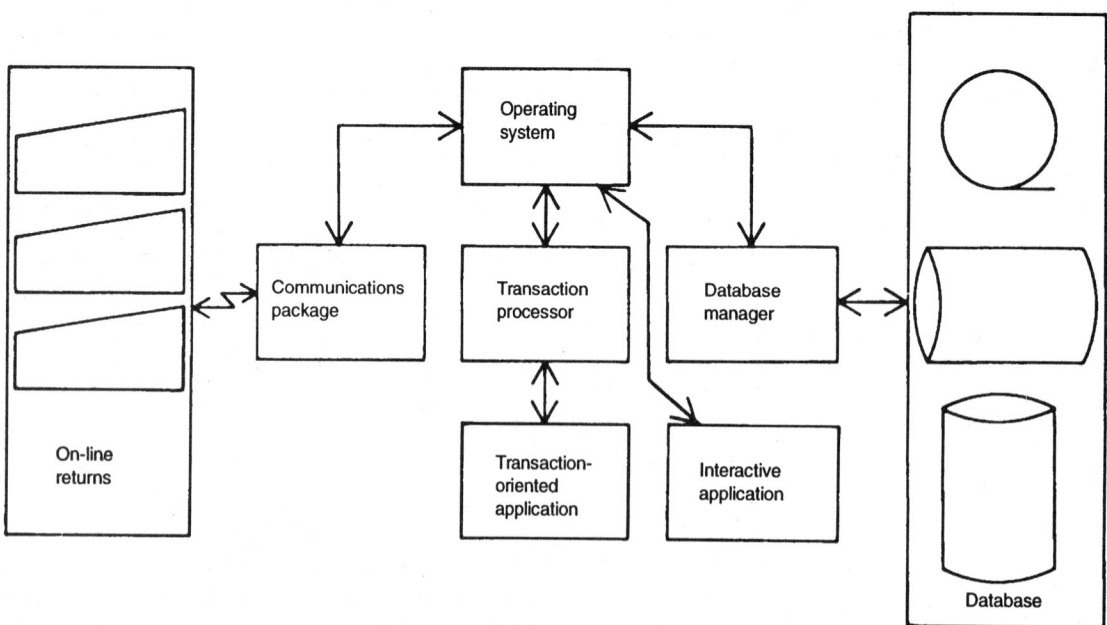

FIG. 3. Real-time software packages.

and the system users by providing retrieval and updating capability for the file records of a real-time system. Specific features of such packages vary widely, especially for functions such as *information retrieval.* Some are designed to carry out highly specialized searches in which required data elements are qualified by a series of "and/or" statements. Others permit the statistical sampling of a file or the accumulation of data from designated portions of a file. Still others allow simultaneous inquiry against mulitple files and the combination of file data into a single output, as might be required by a request for both payroll and skills inventory data for an employee.

There are numerous database management packages currently available. Not all packages are suitable for on-line usage, but may instead require the accumulation, batching, and sorting of information requests for subsequent processing against a sequentially ordered file. Further, some packages may support data retrieval only, with no provision for file updating and maintenance, in which case the package may have to be augmented by the user's own programs.

Just as the communications package aims for terminal transparency (*q.v.*), the database management package seeks to provide *program independence* by separating the application programs from the file data they operate on. This permits the database to be modified or reorganized without unduly affecting the application programs, since all requests for data are filtered through the database management package. This is in marked contrast to earlier practice, in which the application programmer was free to design files and records and embed references to these records within the program wherever convenient, unconstrained by outside standards. The objective of program independence is to permit changes to the database without requiring inordinate changes to the application programs that reference the database.

Transaction Processing Package

In early real-time systems, transaction-processing functions were performed by specially tailored software. Today, many of these functions have been sufficiently well defined that they can be generalized and packaged.

The purpose of the transaction processor is to handle large volumes of specifically defined transactions in a highly efficient manner. Examples of such transactions can be found in booking airline passenger reservations or in recording deposits to savings bank accounts. Transaction processing should be contrasted with interactive problem solving in which the nature of the processing to be performed is determined by the user during the interactive session. In transaction processing, the features and options available to the terminal operator are carefully structured in advance and are performed by specialized application programs under control of the transaction-processing software. Any deviation from the predetermined processing scenario by the operator, such as the entry of an invalid date, results in discontinuation of processing and transmission of an error response.

In a transaction-oriented real-time system, the transaction processing package is activated by the operating system upon receipt of an incoming transaction. It performs initial validation of data, establishes what application program action is required, and reacts to errors and other special conditions.

The transaction processor is responsible for maintaining control over real-time application program scheduling. Following the scheduling of an application program as the result of the arrival of a transaction, the transaction processor delivers the input transaction to the application program.

The transaction processor may initiate recovery procedures following abnormal termination of an application program. Such recovery procedures could include scheduling a special routine to repair any files damaged by the malfunctioning program; shutting the program down; releasing any facilities, such as main memory, assigned to the program; and apprising the operator of the problem. The transaction processor may also maintain statistics on such data as transaction volumes processed by type.

Real-Time Application Processing

Real-time applications require a high degree of simultaneity of processing in order to provide fast response to large numbers of system users. One approach to achieving a high level of throughput (*q.v.*) is multiprocessing, (i.e. more than one processing unit is available to handle transactions—see Fig. 2). But there is a practical limit, especially in business applications, to the amount of simultaneity that can be achieved through the addition of multiple hardware components and the distribution of incoming transactions among them.

Software techniques are commonly employed in transaction-oriented systems to enhance throughput capability. Two of the most common are multiprogramming and reentrancy.

Multiprogramming

A multiprogrammed system is defined as one in which several transactions may be in some state of process at the same time, each receiving occasional attention from a single central processing unit. This is in contrast to a sequentially programmed system, which disposes of transactions one by one, not permitting a new action to enter the processing cycle until the current one has been completely processed.

Reentrancy

In addition to multiprocessing and multiprogramming, further simultaneity of operations and hence greater throughput and responsiveness can be achieved through program reentrancy.

An application program frequently interrupts its processing of a transaction at some intermediate point prior to completion of processing; at that point, processing could begin on another transaction of the same type. But this is possible *only* if the application program is *reentrant* (*q.v.*), (i.e. written in such a manner that it is capable of starting to process the new transaction without affecting switches, variables, or working storage locations still set to handle the suspended processing of the first transaction).

Simultaneity in processing several identical transactions could, of course, also be achieved by having multiple copies of the same application program resident in main memory and assigning a single transaction to each, but the preferred method is to write these programs in such a manner that simultaneity is achieved through the ability to reenter *one* resident copy of an application program with a new transaction at any time.

System Reliability   Real-time systems must be especially reliable. Special provision must be made to compensate for equipment malfunctions or program errors in such a way that they can be isolated and corrected or bypassed without causing the entire system to "crash" and without destroying or damaging file data. This implies software and hardware that allows "graceful degradation," permitting one processor to assume the work load of another in the event of malfunction in a multiprocessing configuration. It also implies programs and procedures for recovering from errors and restoring the system and its associated files to its users in such a manner that work can proceed with minimum need for manual reentry of transactions or file data.

Real-time processing is now the normative mode for numerous applications in stock brokerage, transportation, banking, and retail merchandising.

References

1972. Head, R. V. *Manager's Guide to Management Information Systems.* Englewood Cliffs, NJ: Prentice-Hall.

1977. Tebbs, D. and Collins, G. *Real-Time Systems: Management and Design.* New York: McGraw-Hill.

1983. Glass, R. L. (Ed.). *Real-Time Systems.* Englewood Cliffs, NJ: Prentice-Hall.

ROBERT V. HEAD

REAL-TIME CLOCK.   *See* INTERVAL TIMER.

RECORD

For articles on related subjects *see* BLOCK AND BLOCKING FACTOR; DATA STRUCTURES; and FILE.

A *record* is an organized and identifiable aggregate of data transcribed on a computer storage medium. Each record comprises data values that have an underlying relationship to one another. For example, a personnel record usually contains data such as Social Security number, first name, middle initial, last name, data of birth, next of kin, and home address. All these data are *attributes* (descriptors, locators, identifiers, etc.) peculiar to this individual.

Data elements in a record may be of similar or dissimilar types: bits, numbers, character strings, etc. The contents of punched cards and printer lines were often called *unit records*, since these document lengths were pre-defined by associated electromechanical devices. Magnetic tape and disk drives usually accommodate *variable-length records* in which the amount of data per record varies according to activity, age, etc., of the individual.

Records of the same type are usually grouped into larger aggregates, called *files* or *data sets* or *databases*. When written sequentially into a file, records are collected into intermediate aggregates called *blocks*, whose lengths are efficient for transcription to tape or disk devices. In theory, a file or database could comprise a single block containing all its records. In practice, a large file or database may contain hundreds or thousands of blocks, each containing one or more records. The number of records per block, called the *blocking factor*, is an important consideration in determining the efficiency of file processing.

Several high-level languages support features that facilitate the creation of record types whose instances become the actual records to be stored in memory, usually but not necessarily external memory. The first widely used language to do so was Cobol. The corresponding PL/I entities are called *structures*. Pascal record types are defined through use of the reserved word **record**. An example record type definition and corresponding variable declaration in Pascal follows:

```
type
    payrec = record
                name: packed array[1..28] of char;
                rate: real;
                hours: array[1..7] of real;
                union: boolean
            end;
var
    r : payrec; seq : array[1..100] of payrec;
    f: file of payrec;
```

The variable *r* is now an individual instance of a *payrec*, the variable *seq* is an array of *payrecs* stored in main memory, and the variable *f* is a sequential file on an external storage medium to which *payrec* records may be written and later read with statements of the form *write(f,r)* and *read(f,r)*. On a computer whose real values occupy four bytes, each *payrec* record transmitted would consist of a sequence of 481 information bits plus any parity bits that may be added behind the scenes. Each binary record is copied as an aggregate without the programmer having to read or write record components one by one.

DAVID N. FREEMAN AND EDWIN D. REILLY

RECURSION

For articles on related subjects *see* ACTIVATION RECORD; ITERATION; LOOP; STACK; and TURING MACHINE.

Recursion refers to several related concepts in computer science and mathematics. One or more functions of an integer variable are defined by giving initial values and by giving the value for larger integers in terms of smaller ones. No single definition is generally accepted, so we will give examples of increasing complexity.

Recursion Relations

1. The Fibonacci sequence is given by the equations

$$f_0 = 1,$$
$$f_1 = 1,$$
$$f_{n+1} = f_n + f_{n-1}$$

2. When differential equations are to be solved numerically, *recursion relations* such as

$$f(x_0 + nh) = F(f(x_0 + (n-1)h), f(x_0 + (n-2)h), ..., f(x_0 + (n-k)h))$$

arise where f is, in general, a vector of real numbers.

3. When linear differential equations are solved by series, recursion relations for the coefficients of the powers of the independent variables arise.

Recursive Functions

The systematic study of recursion began in the 1920s when mathematical logic began to treat questions of definability, computability, and decidability. An important role is played by *primitive recursive functions*.

Primitive recursive functions are integer functions of integers built up from addition and multiplication of integers and previously defined primitive recursive functions by the primitive recursion scheme:

$$f(0, x_2, ..., x_k) = g(x_2, ..., x_k),$$
$$f(x_1 + 1, x_2, ..., x_k) = h(f(x_1, ..., x_k), x_1, ..., x_k).$$

Here, g and h are primitive recursive functions of $k - 1$ and $k + 1$ arguments, respectively. As an example, we define $n!$, where n is a positive integer, by $n! = f(n)$ where $f(0) = 1$ and $f(n + 1) = (n + 1) \cdot f(n)$. So, in this case, g is a function of 0 arguments, namely, the constant 1, and $h(u, v) = (v + 1) u$.

All the common functions of number theory are primitive recursive. Moreover, many important functions on countable domains other than the integers correspond to primitive recursive functions when we choose a specific enumeration for the domain.

Primitive recursive functions are included in general recursive functions. The definition of general recursive functions is like that given above for primitive recursive functions, except that the relations are replaced by an arbitrary finite collection of equations relating the values of f for different arguments, and the function is considered defined if and only if a unique value of $f(x_1, ..., x_k)$ can be deduced from the equations for each k-tuplet $(x_1, ..., x_k)$. Naturally, if someone gives you an arbitrary collection of such relations, you may not be able to determine whether $f(x_1, ..., x_k)$ is uniquely determined, so you may not know whether you have a general recursive function. This difficulty is unavoidable. There is no way to give a definition scheme that is always guaranteed to give a function but which will give all computable functions. This fact is itself expressed in the terminology of recur-

sive function theory by the statement that the set of computable functions is *recursively enumerable* but not recursive. The famous example of a general recursive function that is not primitive recursive is the *Ackermann function*, defined by the equations

$$A(0, n, p) = n + p, \quad A(1, 0, p) = 0$$
$$A(m + 2, 0, p) = 1$$

and

$$A(m + 1, n + 1, p) = A(m, A(m + 1, n, p), p).$$

An important result for computer science is that the general recursive functions coincide with the functions defined by a Turing machine, which is a simple form of computer. They also coincide with the functions of integers defined by Pascal or Fortran programs, assuming that the program can cope with whatever size integers arise.

Both programs and general recursion schemata, in general, give *partial functions* because the computation may terminate for some values of the arguments and not for others.

The study of computable functions is the domain of recursive function theory, an active branch of mathematics. The connection between current research in recursive function theory and computing practice, or even current research in computer science, is rather tenuous. This situation might change because of developments in either field.

Recursive Procedures

In programming, it is frequently convenient to have a procedure use itself as a subprocedure. If the procedure does this, it is called *recursive*. Recursive procedures are particularly natural in dealing with symbolic expressions because the structure of the programs often matches the structure of the data. As far as programming languages are concerned, recursive procedures are quite natural; it requires a special statement in the definition of the language to forbid them. However, implementing them requires that a special kind of object code be compiled, and early programming languages like Fortran do not allow them. The problem is that variables in the program correspond to locations in the machine, and when the program is called by itself, it will use these same locations, overwriting their previous contents. Therefore, recursive programs use a data structure called a *stack* to store the contents of registers that must be saved. This storage can be done by the calling routine before it enters the subroutine, or it can be done by the subroutine before it uses the registers, the latter being more common.

After the registers have been saved on the stack, the index into the stack is increased by the number of registers stored, so that subsequent saving on the stack will use fresh registers. When the subroutine exits, the contents of the saved registers are restored from the stack to their previous values, and the *stack pointer* is reduced by the amount it was previously increased. This is done by the caller or by the subroutine, according to whether the caller or subroutine did the original storing. An alternative technique is to use the stack for all temporary registers. In this case, it is unnecessary to move data around, and it is only necessary to change the stack pointer when subroutines are entered and left. However, this technique uses up the indexing capabilities of some machines that may be wanted for other purposes. Recursive programs can be written in any programming language by explicitly programming the saving and restoring.

The first languages to use recursive subroutines on a regular basis were the IPL languages of Newell, Shaw, and Simon. Lists were used for the stack and the saving and restoring was done explicitly by the programmer. The first language to provide an automatic mechanism for recursion was Lisp. Algol 60 and its successors, Modula-2 (*q.v.*), Pascal, and Ada (*q.v.*), also allow recursion, as do such other popular languages as APL, PL/I, C, and Snobol.

Many computers have special instructions for handling stacks (e.g. the PUSH and POP instructions of the Digital Equipment VAX). Other machines, such as the Burroughs B5000 and its successors, had instructions that used a hardware stack directly. These special facilities give a modest increase in the efficiency of recursive programming.

Recursive Conditional Expressions

The recursive use of conditional expressions provides an economical and elegant way of specifying the functions that are computable in terms of a collection of base functions. This technique is the basis of the Lisp prgramming language and also of the theoretical system of Dana Scott for studying the properties of computer programs. A conditional expression has the form, in Algol-like notation, of

$$\textbf{if } p \textbf{ then } a \textbf{ else } b.$$

It is evaluated by first evaluating the propositional expression p. If p is TRUE, the value of the conditional expression is that of a, and if the value of p is FALSE, the value of the conditional expression is that of b. It is important to note that only one of a or b is actually evaluated.

A simple example of the use of conditional expressions is to define the absolute value of a number by

$$|x| = \textbf{if } x < 0 \textbf{ then } -x \textbf{ else } x.$$

Conditional expressions are used to define functions recursively by writing the definition in the form

$$f(x,\ldots,z) \leftarrow E\{ x,\ldots, z, f, g,\ldots, h\},$$

where E is an expression involving the variables $x,\ldots,z$, the function f being defined, and known or previously defined functions $g,\ldots, h$. An example of such a definition is

$$n! \leftarrow \textbf{if } n = 0 \textbf{ then } 1 \textbf{ else } n \cdot (n-1)! \qquad (1)$$

The general method for evaluating recursive conditional expressions is illustrated by using the above definition to evaluate 3!. Namely, we have

$$\begin{aligned}
3! &= \textbf{if } 3 = 0 \textbf{ then } 1 \textbf{ else } 3 \cdot (3-1)! \\
&= 3 \cdot 2! = 3 \cdot (\textbf{if } 2 = 0 \textbf{ then } 1 \textbf{ else } 2 \cdot (2-1)!) \\
&= 3 \cdot 2 \cdot (\textbf{if } 1 = 0 \textbf{ then } 1 \textbf{ else } 1 \cdot (1-1)!) \\
&= 3 \cdot 2 \cdot 1 \cdot (\textbf{if } 0 = 0 \textbf{ then } 1 \textbf{ else } 0 \cdot (0-1)!) \\
&= 3 \cdot 2 \cdot 1 \cdot 1 = 6.
\end{aligned}$$

Note that the rule for evaluating conditional expressions ensures that the computer never attempts to evaluate $(-1)!$. This is necessary, since its evaluation would not terminate.

As a second example, the Ackermann function mentioned above is written as a recursive conditional expression as follows:

$$\begin{aligned}
A(m,\, n,\, p) &\leftarrow \\
&\textbf{if } m = 0 \textbf{ then } n + p \\
&\textbf{else if } n = 0 \textbf{ then } (\textbf{if } m = 1 \textbf{ then } 0 \textbf{ else } 1) \\
&\textbf{else } A(m - 1, (A(m, n - 1), p), p).
\end{aligned}$$

Several remarks are worth making:

First, in a programming language that uses recursive conditional expressions, 3! would not be evaluated by the above symbolic manipulation. Either (1) would be compiled into a recursive subroutine (i.e. a subroutine of the type explained above that calls itself and uses a stack to save intermediate results and return addresses), or a recursive interpreter would interpret a list structure version of (1).

Second, (1) can easily be replaced by another expression for the factorial that can be compiled into a non-recursive program. Namely, we write

$$n! \leftarrow \text{fact } (n, 0, 1)$$

where

$$\begin{aligned}
\text{fact}(n,m,p) &\leftarrow \textbf{if } m = n \textbf{ then } p \qquad (2)\\
&\textbf{else } \text{fact } (n, m + 1, (m + 1)\, p).
\end{aligned}$$

Now (2) can be translated into a non-recursive program because the only occurrence of "fact" on the right-hand side of the definition appears at the outer level; i.e. fact $(n, m + 1, (m + 1)\, p)$ gives the value of fact (n, m, p), in contrast to the situation in (1) where $(n - 1)!$ must be multiplied by n to give $n!$. This allows the object program to contain an ordinary jump to itself rather than a subroutine call. When this is possible, the function definition is called *iterative*. Thus, "fact" is iterative, while the definition (2) is not. Recursive definitions cannot in general be replaced by iterative definitions except by encoding the stack as a variable in the program, and, if this has to be done, there is no advantage in the replacement.

Third, there may be several occurrences of the function being defined on the right-hand side of the recursive definition, and whether the evaluation terminates may depend on which occurrence is evaluated first. The following example due to Morris shows this:

$$f(x, y) \leftarrow \text{if } x = 0 \text{ then } 0 \text{ else } f(x - 1, f(y - 2, x))$$

The reader should evaluate $f(2, 1)$ to see the problem.

It is also possible to use recursive conditional expressions to define functions that take functions as arguments or give functions as results. However, there remain unsolved problems in finding compiling algorithms that produce efficient object code and give the "right" answers in all cases.

The term *recursive* is sometimes also applied to the Backus-Naur Form (BNF - *q.v.*) used to define classes of strings of symbols.

Source Material McCarthy *et al.* (1962) has some discussion of the implementation of recursion in Lisp, and Randell and Russell (1964) discuss the implementation of recursion in Algol. Wirth (1976) discusses when to use recursion and when to use iteration. Peter (1967) has a thorough treatment of subclasses of general recursive functions. The standard reference on recursive function theory was written by Kleene (1952), who gave a more elementary treatment in a later book (1967).

Two aspects of recursion are current research topics in computer science. First, the notion of recursive program is being extended in various ways, and methods of implementing these extensions by compilers and interpreters are being studied (Bobrow and Raphael, 1973). Second, the formal properties of recursive programs are being studied as part of the mathematical theory of computation, which has as its major object the ability to prove assertions about programs and check these assertions on a computer (Manna, 1974) (*see* PROGRAM VERIFICATION).

References

1952. Kleene, S. C. *Introduction to Metamathematics*. Princeton, NJ: Van Nostrand Reinhold.

1962. McCarthy, J. *et al. Lisp 1.5 Programmer's Manual*. Cambridge, MA: The M. I. T. Press.

1964. Randell, B. and Russell, L. J. *Algol 60 Implementation: Translation and Use of Algol 60 Programs by Computers*. New York: Academic Press.

1967. Kleene, S. C. *Mathematical Logic*. New York: Wiley.

1967. Peter, R. *Recursive Functions*. New York: Academic Press.

1973. Bobrow, D. and Raphael, B. *New Programming Languages for AI Research*. Palo Alto: Xerox Research Center.

1974. Manna, Z. *Mathematical Theory of Computation*. New York: McGraw-Hill.

1976. Wirth, N. *Algorithms + Data Structures = Programs*. Englewood Cliffs, NJ: Prentice-Hall.

1989. Dewdney, A. K. *The Turing Omnibus*. Rockville, MD: Computer Science Press (Chapters 21 and 51).

JOHN McCARTHY

REDUNDANCY

For articles on related subjects *see* ERROR-CORRECTING CODE; ERRORS; FAULT-TOLERANT COMPUTING; and RELIABILITY, HARDWARE.

A system is said to be *non-redundant* or is said to have a *simplex structure* if it is designed such that only the absolute minimum amount of hardware is utilized to implement its function. If, even after using the finest components available, the desired system reliability is not achieved, or if failure tolerance is desired as a system capability, then *redundancy* as a design procedure is resorted to; i.e. more system elements are used than are absolutely necessary to realize all the system's functions. The additional system elements, referred to as the redundant elements, need not all necessarily be hardware elements, but may also be additional software (*software redundancy*), additional time (*time redundancy*—e.g. performing a computation more than once and comparing the results), and additional information (*information redundancy*—e.g. the application of error-detection and correction codes).

Naturally, redundancies are often interrelated. Additional software requires additional memory storage, and additional time is used to execute the added software. The term *protective redundancy* is often used to characterize that redundancy that has an overall beneficial effect on the system attributes, since redundancy alone without proper application may well become a liability. Protective redundancy is utilized to realize *fault-tolerant digital systems* and *self-repairing systems* by such means as triple or *N*-tuple modular redundancy (TMR, NMR), quadded redundancy, standby-replacement redundancy, hybrid redundancy, software redundancy, and the application of error-detection and correction codes.

Redundancy as a procedure for designing more reliable systems than allowed by the intrinsic reliability of the constituent components is as old as the discipline of engineering itself. An example of the use of redundancy in ancient times is provided in structures where more than the absolute minimum required number of struts were provided to support a structure. Thus, early uses of redundancy were used as insurance against (1) the lack of accurate knowledge of underlying phenomena, and (2) the lack of confidence in the available data on the materials used. Redundancy as a procedure is even more basic. This is evidenced by the testimony of evolutionary processes of life, which make abundant use of it (e.g. in the human body there are two kidneys, two lungs, two cerebral hemispheres, etc.) Also, in societal systems, protective redundancy is advocated by the truism "two heads are better than one," and conversely, the improper use of redundancy by "too many cooks spoil the broth." Among other societal systems exhibiting the principles of redundancy is the typical committee that has an odd number of members so that a tie in balloting may never occur. This is analogous to the majority voting redundancy used in some computer systems. Other examples will readily occur to the reader.

For the computer age, redundancy has been used at all levels of technology, from that of very large-scale-integrated (VLSI) devices, circuit logic, subsystem computers, and even to entire networks of digital systems.

FRANK P. MATHUR

REENTRANT PROGRAM

For articles on related subjects *see* COROUTINE; MULTIPROGRAMMING; and TIME SHARING.

In a time-sharing or multiprogramming environment, a number of user programs may be sharing a common pool of subprograms or processors. Therefore, it is necessary that the shared programs be written in such a form that each can be applied to, say, user program 1 without running to completion, then be interrupted and applied to some other user program (perhaps, or perhaps not, running to completion), and then later be *reentered* at the point of interruption of user program 1 without loss of information.

In order to allow this reentrant capability, the programs must be written so that they contain no self-modifying features and so that all data required by the reentrant program can be maintained in a separate file related to the user program rather than as part of the reentrant subprogram or processor itself. Then the execution of the reentrant program can be interrupted at any point, and—provided that the data file is stored together with the contents of the machine registers and the *program counter (q.v.)* at the point of interruption—the program can be immediately applied to another user program and can be resumed at a later time by restoring the data file and the program counter. Fig. 1 shows a schematic of a reentrant program shared by n user processes. When UPi is interrupted, perhaps before it fin-

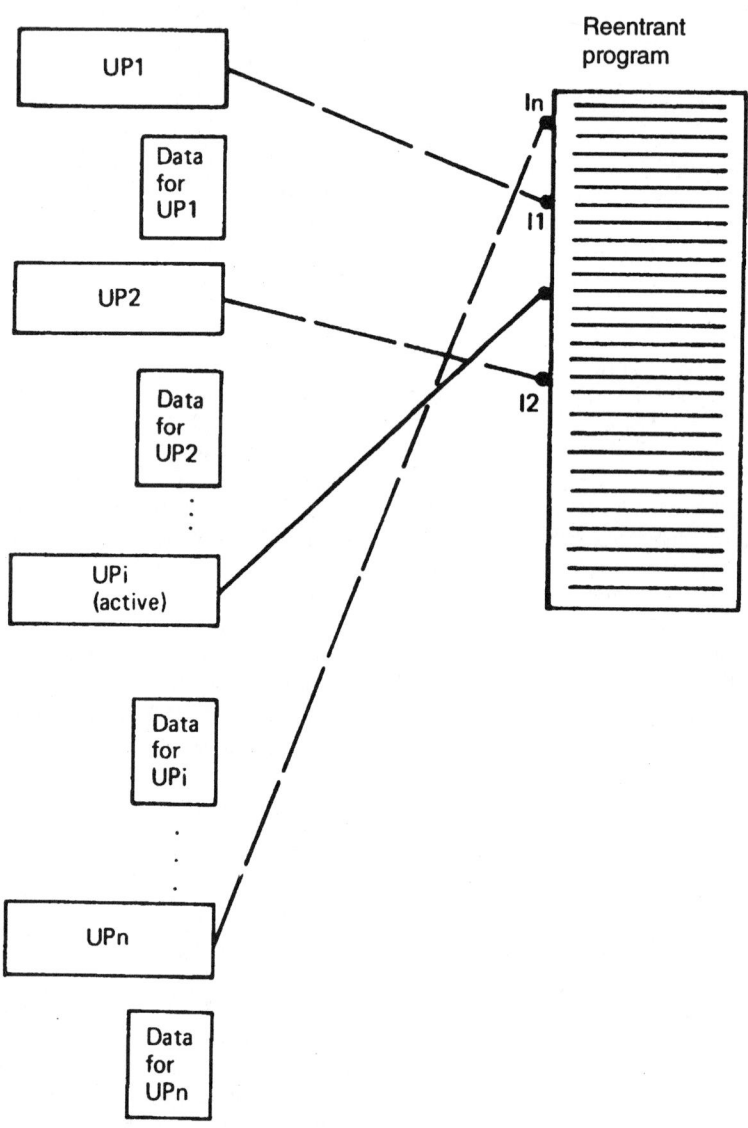

FIG. 1.   A reentrant program shared by n user processes; dotted lines indicate point in reentrant program at which user process was interrupted; solid line shows where reentrant program execution is taking place for the currently active user process.

ishes using the reentrant program, and another user process (say, UP2) gets to use the reentrant program, the reentrant program must have communicated to it the location of the data for UP2 and the place l2 where previous execution was interrupted. Reentrant programs are sometimes called *pure procedures* or *sharable code*.

J. A. N. LEE

REGISTER

For articles on related subjects *see* ARITHMETIC-LOGIC UNIT; BASE REGISTER; CENTRAL PROCESSING UNIT; GENERAL REGISTER; INDEX REGISTER; PROGRAM COUNTER; and SHIFTING.

A register is a specialized storage element of the CPU that consists of digital storage elements that respond faster than those typically used to implement main memory storage locations.

The purpose of a register is to store a string of bits (often a word) representing related information: the digits of a number, the symbols of an alphanumeric word, the bits representing the status of various parts of a computer, the bits indicating the presence of interrupt requests, etc. The bits X_i that are stored in the n-bit register X are considered to be arranged in linear order and are identified by the indices i, usually chosen in the range $0 \leq i \leq n - 1$ (Fig. 1).

All registers within a computer or other digital device are uniquely identified by names or addresses. The names (e.g. X, ACC (Accumulator), PC (Program Counter), MSW (machine status word), index register, etc. often indicate the function of a register. The addresses are a set of N consecutive integers A ($0 \leq A \leq N - 1$) which identify registers within a storage array (often called *local* memory). The number of bits that can be stored in a register is its *length*. Registers of several different lengths may be found within the same system, but the most common length is the word length of the computer.

Registers are provided with the means to *load* new words or individual bits (writing) and to *sense* the register's contents (reading). If the reading and writing operations use all bits of a register simultaneously, the register is called *parallel*, but if one bit at a time is used, the register is called *serial*. The difference affects the reaction time of the register, but not the way a programmer uses it.

Registers may be provided with other functions in addition to reading and writing. A *shift register* is a register in which all bits may be displaced by one or more positions to the left or to the right. A *counter* is a register in which the contents go through a specified sequence of states, normally those that represent consecutive binary

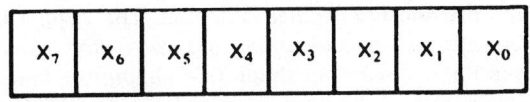

FIG. 1.   An eight-bit register X.

integers. An *accumulator* is a register to which an adder circuit adds a specified number to the prior contents of the accumulator. Shifting, counting, and accumulating are performed upon receipt of appropriate machine-language commands.

ALGIRDAS AVIŽIENIS

REGRESSION ANALYSIS

For articles on related subjects *see* LEAST SQUARES APPROXIMATION; MATHEMATICAL PROGRAMMING; MATHEMATICAL SOFTWARE; MATRIX COMPUTATIONS; NUMERICAL ANALYSIS; SIMPLEX METHOD; and STATISTICAL APPLICATIONS.

Regression methods are used to relate a *response* variable to one or more *predictor* variables. There are three main uses of regression analysis:

1. Prediction of future values of the response variable(s), given hypothetical values of the predictor variables.
2. Specification of a model by selection of a subset of the response variables.
3. Estimation of parameters in a model given by a set of response variables.

The simplest possible model has a single predictor variable and is written

$$y_i = \beta_0 + \beta_1 x_i + e_i, \quad i = 1,...,n$$

where y_i is the value of the response variable for the ith observation, x_i is the value of the predictor variable for the same observation (assumed to be fixed), β_0 and β_1 are unknown constants, and the error ϵ_i is a random variable. Typically, one assumes that the ϵ's are independent and have a Gaussian distribution with mean zero and constant variance. In this case the least-square estimates of the unknown parameters (the β's) and the maximum likelihood estimates of the unknown parameters are identical. Consequently, they have many nice statistical properties, in addition to being simple to compute. A straightforward generalization to p predictor variables is written

$$Y = X\beta + \epsilon$$

where now Y is an $n \times 1$ column vector, X is an $n \times p$ matrix of the p (fixed) predictor vectors, β is a $p \times 1$ vector of unknown parameters, and ϵ is an $n \times 1$ vector of random variables. The least squares estimates of the parameters (denoted $\hat{\beta}$) are given by the solution of the so-called *normal equations*

$$X^T X \hat{\beta} = X^T Y.$$

Standard textbooks on the subject include Draper and Smith (1981), Weisberg (1985), and Myers (1990).

The univariate Gaussian linear regression model has been generalized in many ways:

- Use of multiple response variables instead of a single response variable.
- Use of a model that is nonlinear in the unknown parameters. This implies that the normal equations will not be a linear system and will have to be solved by the Gauss-Newton method or some other iterative procedure.
- Use of a non-Gaussian error probability distribution; maximum likelihood estimation will again lead to a system of nonlinear equations for the estimates.
- Instead of assigning a particular probability distribution to the errors, one can ask for protection against gross errors in the response variable. These methods are generally referred to as *robust regression*.

Several of these generalizations can be combined in one model. Thus, one might have a multivariate robust nonlinear regression, although this particular topic is not yet well-developed.

In a univariate least squares linear regression with many predictor variables, one would often like to find the best model, where "best" refers to some specific criteria to be optimized. In the case where there are p predictor variables, there are 2^p possible regression models (considering all possible subsets of the predictors). When p is much greater than, say, 30, searching over all possible subsets becomes prohibitive; faster computers will not increase this size very much. Consequently, a variety of suboptimal search procedures have been developed to deal with larger values of p. The most commonly used procedures are known as *stepwise regression* and can be thought of as various forms of a "greedy algorithm" for doing the optimization (*see* ALGORITHMS, DESIGN AND CLASSIFICATION OF). In its simplest form, known as *forward stepwise regression*, at each step that single predictor variable that will most increase the criterion is selected to enter the equation; the procedure stops when no predictor variable provides a sufficiently large increase. An obvious variation known as *backward stepwise regression* begins with all variables entered into the equation, and removes at each step that single predictor variable that least decreases the criterion. The most popular stepwise procedure is one that allows both forward and backward stepping. It begins by entering the single variable that most increases the criterion. Then at each step it:

1. Removes the single variable that least decreases the criterion, provided the amount decreased is less than a specified threshold, if any.
2. Adds the single variable that most increases the criterion, provided the amount increased is greater than another prespecified threshold, if any.
3. Stops.

Only one of the three items is performed at each step.

Modern regression analysis focuses on the validity of the assumptions. A variety of diagnostic procedures have been developed to aid the analyst in this assessment. The diagnostic procedures usually study the predicted values $X\hat{\beta}$ and the residuals $Y - X\hat{\beta}$. One set of graphical diagnostic procedures that focuses on the response variable includes:

- Residuals versus predicted values to assess model misspecification.
- Partial regression plots to assess the contribution of a particular predictor variable.
- Partial residual plots to assess nonlinearity in a predictor variable.

Another set of procedures focuses on the predictor variables to assess their influence on the resulting regression equation.

Because many data sets are now collected automatically by computers, they are substantially larger than in the past. Data sets with thousands of potential predictor variables and millions of observations are not extremely rare. For data sets of this size, it is unreasonable to suppose that any one model holds for the entire data set. Consequently, a variety of new techniques are being developed that partition the observation space into data-dependent pieces and fit local regression models within each piece. The first widely available such method is CART (for Classification and Regression Trees) as described in Breiman *et al.* (1984).

References

1981. Draper, N. R. and Smith, H. *Applied Regression Analysis*, 2nd Ed. New York: John Wiley.
1984. Breiman, L., Friedman, J. H., Olshen, R. A., and Stone, C. J. *Classification and Regression Trees*. Belmont, CA: Wadsworth.
1985. Weisberg, S. *Applied Linear Regression*, 2nd Ed. New York: John Wiley.
1990. Myers, R. H. *Classical and Modern Regression with Applications*, 2nd Ed. Boston: PWS Kent.

WILLIAM EDDY

REGULAR EXPRESSION

For articles on related subjects *see* AUTOMATA THEORY; FORMAL LANGUAGES; PRODUCTION; and WELL-FORMED FORMULA.

The formal description for a language acceptable by a finite automaton or for the behavior of a sequential switching circuit is known as a *regular expression*. It tells how a language is built up from atomic languages, using regular operations. The atomic languages are the empty language ϕ and the singleton sets $\{a\}$, where a is a letter of some previously specified alphabet. The regular operations are *union, catenation*, and *catenation closure*. Union is the ordinary set theoretical union; the catenation (sometimes called *concatenation* - *q.v.*) XY of two languages X and Y consists of all words xy with $x \varepsilon X$

and $y \, \varepsilon \, Y$; and the catenation closure X^* of a language X consists of the empty word and of all words of the form $x_1 \cdots x_n$, where $n \geq 1$ and each $x_i \, \varepsilon \, X$. For example, $(ab \cup b)^*$ is a regular expression for the language X, obtained by catenating ab and b in an arbitrary fashion; i.e. X consists of the empty word and of all words over the alphabet $\{a,b\}$ ending with b and having no subwords aa.

A formal definition of regular expressions is now given. Assume that V and $V_1 = \{\phi, \cup, *, (,)\}$ are disjoint alphabets. A word a over the alphabet $V \cup V_1$ is a regular expression over V if and only if (1) α is a letter of V or the letter ϕ, or (2) a is of one of the forms $(\beta \cup \gamma)$, $(\beta \, \gamma)$, or β^*, where β and γ are regular expressions over V. Each regular expression a over V denotes a language $|a|$ over V according to the following conventions:

1. The language denoted by ϕ is the empty language.
2. The language denoted by $a \varepsilon V$ consists of the word a.
3. For regular expressions a and β over V,

$$|(a \cup \beta)| = |a| \cup |\beta|, \ |(a\beta)| = |a| \, |\beta|,$$
$$|a^*| = |a|^*.$$

Very different looking regular expressions may denote the same language; e.g. each of the regular expressions

$$(a \cup ab \cup ba)^*, (ba \cup a^* ab)^* a^*, a^*(ab \cup ba^* a)^*$$

denotes the same language.

The behavior of a finite automaton or a sequential switching circuit is very often better understood after a simplification of the corresponding regular expression. Especially helpful is the reduction of the star height; i.e. the maximum number of nested stars in the regular expression. A finitary axiomatization can be given to all equations among regular expressions, although rules of inference stronger than substitution are necessarily needed. Various algorithms are known for the transition from a regular expression to a finite automaton, and vice versa.

As a practical example of regular expressions, many operating systems (*q.v.*), screen editors, and word processing (*q.v.*) programs have generalized their string searching capability so that, in addition to being asked to find a particular string, they may be asked to find a string that matches a specified regular expression. Best known of these search tools is the Unix (*q.v.*) *grep* command which stands for "get regular expression."

References

1969. Salomaa, A. *Theory of Automata*. New York: Pergamon.
1991. Cohen, D. *Introduction to Computer Theory* (revised edition). New York: John Wiley.

ARTO K. SALOMAA

RELATIONAL DATABASE

For articles on related subjects *see* DATABASE COMPUTER; DATABASE MANAGEMENT SYSTEM; and DEDUCTIVE DATABASE.

A *relational database* is one that is built and operated in accordance with the *relational model of data* proposed by E. F. Codd (1970). This model has now gained wide acceptance and has engendered a great deal of additional study covering numerous aspects of database theory and practice.

Primarily, the relational model provides a simple and intuitive method for defining a database, storing and updating data in it, and submitting queries of arbitrary complexity to it. More important, it provides a firm, sound, and consistent foundation for all the other topics that database management systems must commonly embrace, such as security and authorization, database integrity, transaction management, recoverability, and distribution of data.

The relational model is founded on the mathematical disciplines of predicate calculus and set theory. All data in a relational database is organized as a set of two-dimensional arrays, or *tables*. Consider, for example, the proposition: "Brutus killed Caesar." In the context of a discussion about characters in Shakespeare's plays, we can say of this proposition whether it be *true* or *false*. If we were to construct a database of information about Shakespeare's plays, that database might well include a "record," such as (Brutus, Caesar), and that record might be one of a collection of similarly formed records, each asserting that some character killed some other character:

Brutus,   Caesar
Hamlet,   Laertes
Hamlet,   Polonius
Laertes,   Hamlet
Brutus,   Brutus
Cassius,   Caesar
.
.

Each of these records represents a proposition of the form "*x* killed *y*," where *x* and *y* are both names of Shakespearean characters. Such a record is not, per se, a proposition of that form, for the all-important word "killed" is omitted. In fact, "*x* killed *y*" is a *predicate* in two variables, and each record provides values for *x* and *y* to give one instantiation of that predicate.

The mathematical term *relation* occurs in the study of predicate logic but is most commonly used in connection with predicates in exactly two variables. See, for example, Lemmon (1965). In the relational model, a predicate in any nonnegative number, *n*, of variables is considered as an *n*-ary relation. If we want to say in which play each killing occurs, we might use the ternary (3-ary) relation "*x* killed *y* in *z*." If we want to record those characters who, like Cassius, were ambitious, we might use the unary relation "*x* was ambitious."

Here is how the binary (2-ary) relation "x killed y" might be represented according to the relational model:

KILLED	KILLER	VICTIM
	Brutus	Caesar
	Hamlet	Laertes
	Hamlet	Polonius
	Laertes	Hamlet
	Brutus	Brutus
	Cassius	Caesar

The verb of the predicate has become a *relation name*, KILLED, and the variables x and y have become *attribute names*, KILLER and VICTIM, defined in the *relation schema* of this relation. Associated with each attribute name, but not shown in the above representation, is an underlying *domain*, the set of permissible values for the attribute in question. In this case, both attributes would draw their values from the same domain, "names of Shakespearean characters."

A particular instantiation of a predicate in n variables is represented by an *n-tuple*. Thus, the 2-tuple (Brutus, Caesar), in combination with the relation schema of KILLED, represents the proposition "Brutus killed Caesar."

Arising from the visual representation of a relation are several common but informal terms:

- *Table*, for *relation*.
- *Heading* for *relation schema*.
- *Column* (name) for *attribute* (name).
- *Row* for (*n-*) *tuple*.
- *Body* (or *extension*) for the set of tuples "in" the relation.

Four important principles are illustrated in the above example:

1. At each intersection of a row and column there is exactly one value. This is the principle of *first normal form*, fundamental in the relational model. While in natural language we might say "Hamlet killed Laertes and Polonius," the relational model does not allow us to put Laertes and Polonius in the same row and so requires us to say "Hamlet killed Laertes and Hamlet killed Polonius."
2. The order in which the rows are written is unimportant. The information conveyed—the proposition formed by inserting the word "and" between the rows—is the same regardless of the order.
3. The order in which the columns are written is also unimportant. It is only important to know, for each value in a row, to which column that value pertains, and we achieve that by writing the value underneath the name of its column.
4. Writing the same row more than once is as redundant as would be writing the same proposition

twice with the word "and" in between. Such redundancy can only confuse. For instance, if we had (Brutus, Caesar) twice, we would have to be very careful how we phrase the query that asks "How many people did Brutus kill?"—the relational model expressly prohibits duplicate rows.

A *relational database* is a collection of relations. A *relational database schema* is a collection of relation schemas, along with a collection of domain definitions, with the possible addition of integrity rules, access authorizations, and so on. A relational DBMS must minimally support the definition of domains and relation schemas, the insertion, updating and deletion of tuples, and a *relational query language* for defining new relations that may be derived from the "base relations" of the database. At the time of writing, no well-known product provides this minimal support, mainly because none has correctly implemented domains.

A relational query language is one that embodies the fundamental principle that the operands *and* the result of any operator in the query language are relations. If query operations are thus closed over relations, then queries of arbitrary complexity can be expressed.

In practice, to achieve this end, relational query languages are founded on either or both of the *relational algebra* and the *relational calculus* proposed by Codd. Of these two, the algebra is considered, psychologically, to be the "lower-level" system (in the same sense as that in which programming languages are often described as "low-level" or "high-level"), but in fact the two systems have been shown to be equivalent—anything expressible in the algebra has an equivalent expression in the calculus, and vice versa.

The relational algebra draws on the notion that the body of a relation is a *set* (of tuples), and among its operators are specialized versions of the *union, difference,* and *intersection* of set theory. The algebra originally proposed by Codd included those three, two monadic operators—*project* and *restrict* (also known as *select*)—and the dyadic operator *cartesian product*. For completeness, most authorities accept three further monadic operators—*rename, extend,* and *summarize*. The nonprimitive operators *natural join* and *divide* are so useful that they are normally presented as well.

Where the relational algebra draws on set theory, the *relational calculus* draws on predicate calculus. It is characterized by its adoption of the universal and existential quantifiers ; ("for all") and ' ("there exists") of the predicate calculus.

While the calculus is in a sense "higher level" than the algebra and has more intuitive appeal to logicians and, potentially, to casual users of relational databases, it is the algebra that is more often used as a basis for theoretical discussion of many diverse aspects of database technology. Descriptions of the relational algebra and the relational calculus are given in Ullman (1982) and Date (1989).

To illustrate the completeness of the Relational Algebra and Calculus, we use our example relation, KILLED, and one other, DIED_BY, shown in the following table:

DIED_BY	VICTIM	METHOD
	Caesar	Daggers
	Hamlet	Sword
	Polonius	Sword
	Laertes	Sword
	Brutus	Sword

The predicate is "*y* died by *z*." VICTIM is the attribute name corresponding to *y*, and its domain is the same as that of VICTIM in KILLED. METHOD is the attribute name corresponding to *z*, and its domain is "methods of being killed." We assume that only one method of being killed is stated for each victim, choosing not to handle the possibility that one of Caesar's assassins used something other than a dagger.

Here, then, are some example queries against a database comprising just those two relations. Each is expressed in both the relational algebra and the tuple-oriented relational calculus, using the notation given in Date (1989), which also describes a "domain-oriented" calculus, as an alternative to the tuple calculus proposed by Codd. The result of each query is presented as a relation named ANSWER, and the attribute names are those that would arise from the algebraic solutions:

Who killed Caesar?
Algebra:

(KILLED WHERE VICTIM = 'Caesar') [KILLER]

The term WHERE signifies the relational operator known as *restriction*, the square brackets *projection*.

Calculus:

RANGE OF K IS KILLED
K.KILLER WHERE K.VICTIM = 'Caesar'

ANSWER	KILLER
	Brutus
	Cassius

Who was both a killer and a victim?
Algebra:

(KILLED[KILLER] RENAME KILLER AS KILLER_VICTIM)
INTERSECT
(KILLED [VICTIM] RENAME VICTIM AS KILLER_VICTIM)

We use *projection* and *rename* to make two unary relations, one of killers, the other of victims. The set operator *intersection* corresponds to the "both...and..." of the query.

Calculus:

RANGE OF K IS KILLED
RANGE OF V IS KILLED
K.KILLER WHERE EXISTS V (K.KILLER = V.VICTIM)

ANSWER	KILLER_VICTIM
	Brutus
	Hamlet
	Laertes

Which killers used daggers?
Algebra:

((KILLED JOIN DIED_BY) WHERE METHOD = 'Daggers')
[KILLER]

The term JOIN signifies *natural join* of KILLED and DIED_BY "over" their common attribute, VICTIM.

Calculus:

RANGE OF K IS KILLED
RANGE OF D IS DIED_BY
K.KILLER WHERE EXISTS D (K.VICTIM
        = D.VICTIM AND D.METHOD = 'Daggers')

ANSWER	KILLER
	Brutus
	Cassius

Show all cases where x killed y, and y killed z.
Algebra:

(KILLED RENAME KILLER AS KILLER1 RENAME
        VICTIM AS KILLER2)
JOIN
(KILLED RENAME KILLER AS KILLER2)

Here we join the relation KILLED to itself, using *rename* to make VICTIM, on the one hand, and KILLER, on the other, the common attribute for the join.

Calculus:

RANGE OF K IS KILLED
RANGE OF V IS KILLED
K.KILLER, V.KILLER, V.VICTIM WHERE K.VICTIM =
        V.KILLER

ANSWER	KILLER1	KILLER2	VICTIM
	Laertes	Hamlet	Polonius
	Hamlet	Laertes	Hamlet
	Laertes	Hamlet	Laertes
	Brutus	Brutus	Brutus

Which killers always used the same method? Show the method as well as the killer.

Algebra:

DIED_BY DIVIDEBY KILLED

Relational *division* is a convenient non-primitive operator for use in queries that imply universal quantification, the "for all" of the calculus. Division can be expressed using several *projections, joins,* and *differences,* and that is best left as an exercise for the keen student.

(Yes, Cassius did, like Brutus, kill himself with a sword, but we forgot to record that, so we deserve what we get!)

Note that if we divided KILLED by DIED_BY, we would be asking for (KILLER, METHOD) pairs such that KILLER killed everybody who died by METHOD.

Calculus:

RANGE OF K IS KILLED
RANGE OF D IS DIED_BY
RANGE OF V IS KILLED
RANGE OF M IS DIED_BY
K.KILLER, D.METHOD WHERE FORALL M (IF
    K.KILLER = V.KILLER AND V.VICTIM =
    M.VICTIM THEN M.METHOD = D.METHOD)

ANSWER	KILLER	METHOD
	Hamlet	Sword
	Laertes	Sword
	Cassius	Daggers

How many people killed Caesar?
Algebra:

((SUMMARIZE KILLED GROUPBY VICTIM ADD
        COUNT AS NUMBER_OF_KILLERS)
WHERE VICTIM = 'Caesar') [NUMBER_OF_KILLERS]

Alternatively, the *restriction* can be done before the *summary,* in which case the grouping could be over no attributes at all, instead of over VICTIM.

Of course, the number would be bigger if we had remembered to record Casca and all the other assassins.

Calculus:

RANGE OF K IS KILLED
COUNT (K.KILLER WHERE K.VICTIM = 'Caesar')

ANSWER	NUMBER OF KILLERS
	2

In a database containing numerical information, the result of a query might be all sorts of calculated results, including complex statistical analyses.

Relational queries have many applications, not just the obvious one of delivering answers to interesting questions. They are used to define *views,* enabling individual users to work with customized database schemas instead of all having to use the same underlying schemas. They are used to define subsets of the database, to which access can be authorized discretely for different users or user groups. And they may be used in the definitions of *integrity constraints.*

Functional Dependence, Keys, and Normalization The concept of *functional dependence* is completely orthogonal to the principles described above, but is usually included in any discussion of relational databases because of its importance in connection with database design, view updatability, query optimization, and other topics. Indeed, the relational model itself makes certain recommendations arising from it. A *functional dependency* is a truth-valued expression, written as:

$$A \rightarrow B$$

and pronounced "A determines B" or "B depends on A." If A and B are both subsets of the attributes of some relation, R, then $A \rightarrow B$ is said to hold true in R if and only if any two tuples in R that agree in value for every attribute in A also agree in value for every attribute in B. For example, suppose that a relation, R, includes an attribute, z, whose values in R are constrained to be the sum of two other attributes in R, x, and y (perhaps z is thus computed, in some query). The following functional dependencies hold true in R:

$$hx,yj \rightarrow hzj$$
$$hx,zj \rightarrow hyj$$
$$hy,zj \rightarrow hxj$$

The left operand of a functional dependency is the *determinant,* and the members of the right operand are *dependants* of that determinant.

If K is a determinant in R such that:

- All the attributes of R are dependants of K;
- There is no proper subset of K, K9, such that all the attributes of R are dependants of K9; and
- This constraint holds true over time in a changing database;

then CK is a *candidate key* of R. It follows from this definition that, if CK is a candidate key of R, no two tuples in R can have the same combined value in the attributes of CK.

The relational model requires at least one candidate key to be defined for every relation defined by a relation schema in the database schema. The functional dependency implied by such a candidate key is then treated as an integrity rule, prohibiting the insertion of a tuple, *t*, if there already exists some tuple agreeing in value with *t* for every attribute of that candidate key. When more than one candidate key is noted for the same relation, one candidate key is arbitrarily nominated as the *primary key.*

It is easy to prove that every relation has at least one candidate key, for if no proper subset of the heading is a candidate key, then the heading is the only candidate key, which is the case in our example, KILLED. The only candidate key of DIED_BY is hVICTIMj, because of our decision to state just one method for each victim.

The fundamental principle of *first normal form* of relations has already been noted. The study of database design involves further normal forms that are recommended to hold true for "base relations" (i.e. relations defined by relation schemas in the database schema) only. The most important of these is fourth normal form, also called *Boyce-Codd normal form* (BCNF). BCNF is defined as holding true in a relation, *R*, if and only if every determinant in *R* is a candidate key.

It can be shown that a base relation that is not in BCNF can involve redundancy (recording the same data more than once), giving rise to *update anomalies*, such as having to update the same data in the several different places where it occurs.

The reader is referred to Date (1989), Chapter 21, for a deeper discussion of functional dependence, keys, and normal form, where it will be found that even BCNF is not a thorough guarantee against update anomalies, and further normal forms sometimes need to be considered. One of these, called *fifth normal form*, is proved to complete the guarantee.

When a relation, *R*, includes some set of attributes, FK, such that every tuple in *R* is constrained to agree in value, for each attribute in FK, with its corresponding attribute in the primary key of a relation *S*, in some tuple of *S*, then FK is said to be a *foreign key* in *R, referencing S*. In our example database, VICTIM in the KILLED relation might be a foreign key "referencing" DIED_BY. We do not need to say which attributes of DIED_BY are involved in the reference, as the attributes of the primary key of the referenced relation are assumed. If we do declare this foreign key, we are prohibited from recording any killing without also recording its method.

Relational Databases and SQL The database language SQL (structured query language) gained such wide acceptance during the 1980s, with a multiplicity of implementations and a diversity of dialects, that we are compelled to mention it here, if only to dispel two popular misconceptions. The first misconception is that "relational means SQL." SQL is merely one of many distinct attempts to implement the principles of the relational model of data. The second and more serious misconception is that SQL is relational or, to put it more kindly, that all the principles of the relational model of data are embraced by SQL. In fact, many authorities have noted several important deficiencies in SQL, such as:

- SQL does not properly support *domains*.
- In SQL, a table is permitted to contain *duplicate rows*.
- A table that is the result of a query can contain *unnamed columns*, and columns of the same name. One consequence is that SQL does not always permit the result of a query to be input to another query, so queries of arbitrary complexity cannot be expressed.

- SQL's treatment of "missing values," using *nulls*, has been shown to be unsound and inconsistent. The relational model of the early 1970s made no provision for the treatment of missing values. Furthermore, no subsequent extension of the model in this respect—Codd (1990) for example—has yet gained general acceptance among relational scholars.

References

1965 Lemmon, E. J. *Beginning Logic*. London: Nelson.

1970. Codd, E. F. "A Relational Model of Data for Large Shared Data Banks." *Comm. ACM* **13**, 6 , 377–387.

1982. Ullman, Jeffrey D. *Principles of Database Systems,* 2nd Ed. Potomac, MD: Computer Science Press.

1989. Date, C. J. *An Introduction to Database Systems: Volume I*, 5th Ed. "Part III: The Relational Model." Reading, MA: Addison-Wesley.

1990. Codd, E. F. *The Relational Model for Database Management, Version 2*. Reading, MA: Addison-Wesley.

HUGH DARWEN

RELIABILITY. *See* HARDWARE RELIABILITY; and SOFTWARE RELIABILITY.

REMOTE JOB ENTRY. *See* PROCESSING MODES.

RESTART PROCEDURE. *See* BOOT AND REBOOT; and CHECKPOINT AND RESTART.

RING NETWORK. *See* DISTRIBUTED SYSTEMS; and LOCAL AREA NETWORK.

RISC ARCHITECTURE

For articles on related subjects *see* COMPUTER ARCHITECTURE; INSTRUCTION SET; and MICROPROGRAMMING.

Until 1975, computer architecture and consequently computer design and implementation had grown more complicated with each successive generation. Instruction sets were large, and individual instructions were complicated. Some of this complication was done to insure compatibility across a family, some was done to be a better target for compilers, and some was done for performance enhancement. The result was often an architecture and implementation that had many unused instructions because the nature of the compiler changed or because the compiler was not changed but should have been. Many more instructions were seldom used because they covered a very specific case or the implementation penalty was too large. Often, the implementation relied on a "microengine" to implement these numerous and complex instructions. The microengine had a microinstruction set. Microprograms or microcode written in these microinstructions interpreted the complex instructions.

Prior to the mid-1970s, the only computer architect whose views differed significantly from the foregoing was Seymour Cray, who, while with the Control Data Corporation (*q.v.*) in the early 1960s, designed the CDC 6600 supercomputer to have a small, simple instruction set.

In the beginning of 1975, a group was organized at IBM's T. J. Watson's Research Center that had as its goal to produce a "super" minicomputer, one in which the compiler, the operating system, and the architecture were done in concert with each other. This super mini would have a very simple data flow and instruction set. It would be implemented without the need for microcode. Many of the original ideas for the computer came from IBM Fellow John Cocke. Like many early IBM computers, a name was chosen for this computer based on the building number in which it was designed and built—building 80.

A set of principles emerged from this work that have influenced many others in this field:

1. A small instruction set consisting of simple, fixed-length, fixed-format instructions that execute in a single machine cycle;
2. Overlapped (pipelined) storage access, all storage accesses and arithmetic operations being made with respect to one or another of a large number of registers (*q.v.*);
3. Use of an optimizing compiler, where machine performance is directly dependent on the compiler's ability to manage many facilities that had previously been managed by hardware, such as storage delays.

These ideas were adapted and perfected by David Patterson at the University of California at Berkeley and John Hennessy at Stanford University (Hennessy and Patterson, 1990). It was Patterson who first used the term RISC (Reduced Instruction Set Computer) for this philosophy and contrasted it with CISC (Complex Instruction Set Computer). It was soon after this that the RISC idea took hold and many organizations began to participate.

Perhaps the best way to describe the RISC concept is through examples.

Moving a data object from one location to another in a CISC is usually done with one instruction that specifies the source address, the target address, and the length of the object. The implementation of this one instruction tests for all possible cases: source and target alignment, overlap or not, destructive or not, out of bounds or not. This one instruction spends many cycles performing these tests and then more cycles doing the actual move. In a RISC, this move operation would be done with multiple instructions: first, and only when necessary, the test for special cases, then—in a loop—a load from the source address, a store into the target

address, source address increment, target address increment, test for end of move, and a conditional branch to the loop. Obviously, the function in both CISC and RISC in the worst case is the same. The contrast, then, is between the ability of a CISC compiler to detect this situation and generate this instruction and the ability of a RISC compiler to generate specific code for actual situations in which, based on specialized knowledge, not all consistency checks need be made. This specific code might be significantly better and should not be any worse than the underlying implementation of the CISC instruction.

Another example is adding one to a counter. In a CISC, one instruction might do this whole function: fetching from storage, adding one, and storing back. In a RISC, three instructions are needed. The difference is that a CISC does not necessarily use a register (CISCs usually have a small number of registers), but in a RISC, a register is always used (RISCs have a large number of registers). Again, performance is no worse in the RISC, and when the counter value is already in a register, it need not be fetched, nor does the incremented value need to be stored to memory.

The last example is branching, particularly conditional branching. The problem with branching is knowing early enough that a branch is to be taken, so that the instructions at the branch target can be fetched without delay. A CISC might solve this problem with significant lookahead hardware (a branch history table or multiple path fetches). A typical RISC compiler, however, will rearrange the instructions leading up to and including the branch, so as to minimize disruption of the pipeline in progress (Cragon, 1991; Wayner, 1992).

The major RISC idea in these examples is to expose the underlying basic functions of the machine so that an optimizing compiler generates code for the specific case, as contrasted with a CISC that must always implement the general case. A RISC may take many more instructions to do the same programming function than a CISC. A good RISC optimizing compiler helps to lessen this increase. For equivalent levels of implementation complexity, RISC instruction execution times will be significantly faster than the corresponding CISC execution times. Thus, the product of the number of RISC instructions to do a programming function times the average execution time of these instructions will be less on a RISC than on a CISC of comparable intrinsic performance. The longer RISC programs would have been highly disadvantageous in an earlier era of small expensive main memories, but the added length is of no consequence in the current era of large inexpensive main memories.

Over time, many ideas of RISC architecture and implementation will come into CISC implementations, both the optimizing compiler and the machine implementation. However underlying differences will remain. RISC is a simpler architecture that does not have all the baggage of previous architectural generations. RISC architecture will continue to evolve, eventually acquiring its own baggage, and perhaps the architectural cycle between RISC and CISC will repeat itself.

References

1990. Hennessy, J. L and Patterson, D. A. *Computer Architecture: A Quantitative Approach.* San Mateo, CA: Morgan Kaufmann. Though *RISC* is not part of the title, this is nonetheless the definitive exposition of RISC philosophy published up through 1991.

1990. Stallings, William. *Reduced Instruction Set Computers (RISC),* 2nd Ed. Los Alamitos, CA: IEEE Computer Society Press.

1991. Cragon, H. G. *Branch Strategy Taxonomy and Performance Models.* Los Alamitos, CA: IEEE Computer Society Press.

1992. Wayner, Peter. "Processor Pipelines," *Byte,* **17,** *1*(January) 305–314. An excellent, detailed account of how optimizing compilers cope with the different pipeline strategies of two RISCs (the R400 and RISC System 6000) and a CISC (the Intel 486).

RICHARD R. OEHLER

ROBOTICS

For articles on related subjects *see* ARTIFICIAL INTELLIGENCE; AUTOMATION; COMPUTATIONAL GEOMETRY; COMPUTER-INTEGRATED MANUFACTURING; COMPUTER VISION; CONTROL THEORY; CYBERNETICS; and PATTERN RECOGNITION.

Robotics is the study of robots, programmable devices capable of executing purposeful motions. Robotics is concerned not just with the execution of motion per se, but also with sensing and reasoning processes that link sensing with action.

History The concept of automatons capable of executing motions can be traced to antiquity. In ancient Greece, a play by Aristophenes recorded the use of automated puppets operated by weights and pulleys. By the seventeenth and eighteenth centuries, elaborate mechanical devices capable of executing precise motions had been developed. An interesting example is Maillardet's programmable writing automaton that used an arrangement of cams, levers, rods, and shafts to produce written script of several texts. More applications-oriented machines began to appear in the nineteenth century, such as Joseph Jacquard's punched card programmed loom, Christopher Spencer's cam-operated lathe, and Steward Babbitt's gripper-equipped motorized crane. In the early twentieth century, the term "robot" was introduced by Karel Kapek in his 1920 play *Rossum's Universal Robots.* In this work, robot (derived from *robota,* the Czeck word for servant) referred to humanoid devices developed as servants for humans.

During the mid-twentieth century, two crucial developments proved to be direct antecedents to modern robotics: teleoperation and numerically controlled machining. The *teleoperator,* developed during World War II for handling radioactive materials, is essentially a master-slave manipulator where the end-effector (e.g. a gripper) is linked to a human operator who controls it from a distance. By the late 1940s, teleoperators had evolved to the point of joining the master and slave by an electrically powered linkage having six degrees of freedom. This allowed the slave to back-drive the master to provide force feedback. In the late 1940s, numerically controlled machining brought together servomechanisms with digital computing and digital pattern specification in response to the increasing need for precise and reproducible machined parts.

In the mid-1950s, the first true robots appeared, devices that combined the articulated linkage of a teleoperator with numerical computation and servo as exploited in numerically controlled machining. Joseph Engelberger and George Devol founded Unimation, the first robotics company, in 1954. In 1962, General Motors installed a Unimation robot, the first robot placed on a commercial production line. The early 1960s also saw important early developments in robot sensing and perception. Two key events occurred at M.I.T. Lincoln Labs. First, Ernst equipped a robot arm with tactile sensors that were used to provide feedback to the control process. Second, Roberts demonstrated that a mathematical description of a three-dimensional scene could be recovered from a corresponding digital image. The late 1960s and early 1970s yielded further demonstrations of the possibility of coupling external sensing with robot motion. The Stanford Research Institute developed a mobile robot equipped with a visual sensor, while the M.I.T. Artificial Intelligence Laboratory developed a system that could visually observe and copy an arrangement of blocks. Throughout the remainder of the 1970s, research and development focused on exploring the possibilities of sensor-based robot motion. Increased technical developments in robotics were followed by increased applications; industry further incorporated robots into manufacturing and robot arms were employed on the Viking space probes.

During the 1980s, robotics continued to make significant advances, including modeling errors, improving sensors, studying compliant motion (i.e. motion executed flexibly in response to external forces), developing fine manipulators and articulated hands, building walking machines, incorporating reasoning, exploring approaches to system integration and exploiting advances in parallel computation. With these advances, two more general issues were identified. First, the fundamentally interdisciplinary nature of robotics became apparent. Important contributions to robotics were regularly derived from mathematics, biology, computer science, control, electrical engineering, mechanical engineering, and physics. Second, heuristic methods in robotics continually gave way to approaches based on rigorous problem analyses. In robot vision, for example, techniques were increasingly founded on detailed understanding of the physics of images. Finally, the decade's relevant technical developments, such as more precise and adaptive control, allowed robots to be applied to delicate tasks such as sheep shearing and compliant assembly.

Perception Robot perception is concerned with gathering, representing, and interpreting information about a robot's world so that its actions can be based on the situation at hand. Robot perception can be conceptualized in terms of the three most common categories of robot sensors: internal state sensors, contact sensors, and noncontact sensors. Internal state sensors are con-

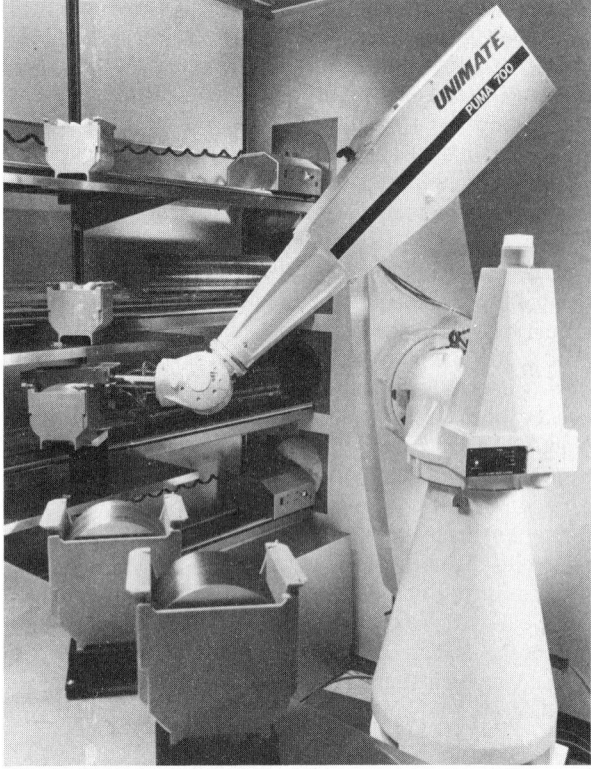

FIG. 1. Illustration of two robots. Fig. 1a shows a robot manipulator, the Unimate Puma 700 (figure courtesy of AEG Westinghouse). Fig. 1b shows a mobile robot base, the Denning MRV-3 (figure courtesy of Denning Mobile Robotics).

cerned with information about the robot's own state. The relevant representations and interpretations are defined relative to the robot itself (e.g. the relative orientation of two of the robot's components) or relative to some absolute reference frame. Numerous devices have been employed for internal state sensing, including potentiometers, odometers, tachometers, and compasses.

In contrast to internal state sensors, contact sensors are concerned with recovering information about a robot's external environment. Contact sensing comes into play when a robot is approaching or has achieved direct physical contact with a portion of its environment. In these situations, it is possible to measure directly the forces exerted between a robot and its external environment. These forces can be interpreted in terms of information about the environment's mechanical resistance, texture, shape, and temperature. Contact sensing is particularly important for guiding compliant motion, as well as for more general data acquisition when noncontact sensors are occluded. Devices employed in contact sensing include contact switches, force and proximity sensors, and VLSI tactile pads.

Like contact sensing, noncontact sensing is concerned with information about a robot's external environment. However, noncontact sensing allows a robot to gather information about its external environment without achieving direct physical contact. The interpretation and representation of information derived from noncontact sensing has dealt with quite general perceptual issues related to three-dimensional shape and position. Of the various possible approaches to noncontact sensing, vision has received more attention than all other approaches combined. This is due, at least in part, to the fact that vision is the most powerful sense in humans. Other approaches to noncontact sensing in robotics include passive audition, radar, ultrasound, and smell.

Actuation Robot actuation is concerned with the execution of motion as a robot negotiates its environment. Functionally, the range of actions considered include reaching, grasping, and locomotion. All of these activities have been realized in articulated robots. Articulated robots (e.g. jointed arms, legs, and end-effectors) can be conceptualized as a series of links that are driven by motors operating at the interlink joints. To specify adequately the behavior of articulated robots, it is necessary to consider kinematics, dynamics, and control. Kinematic equations relate the joint-based coordinate systems where motors apply their forces to the Cartesian coordinate systems in which robot motions typically are specified. For an n-joint robot, the dynamics are governed by a set of n-coupled second-order differential equations that relate joint positions, velocities, and accelerations. Efficient and numerically stable methods for solving kinematic and dynamic equations of robot motion are crucial to achieving reliable real-time robot motion. Research on these issues has yielded a number of useful solutions (e.g. recursive formulations allow for kinematic computations in time proportional to the number of joints connecting a shoulder and hand).

In addition to kinematics and dynamics, control is also a key issue in robot actuation. Much of control theory is applicable to robot control. However, standard techniques often provide only partial solutions and require further development to deal with the inherently dynamic and discontinuous nature of robot control.

Finally, not all approaches to robot locomotion involve articulated legs. Considerable research in mobile robotics has focused instead on wheeled or tracked devices. While consideration of wheeled and tracked robots simplifies certain issues in mobile actuation, legged robots are capable of negotiating a wider range of terrains.

Reasoning If robots are to function autonomously in relatively unstructured environments, then they must reason in order to coordinate information accessed from stored databases, information acquired perceptually, and their own actions. Ultimately, the reasoning a robot must exploit will encompass much of artificial intelligence. However, contemporary robotics investigates reasoning in a more limited fashion. Two areas where strides have been made in robot reasoning are path planning and task planning. A central aspect of path planning is concerned with discovering unoccupied regions of space where a robot can maneuver. Discovering free paths in cluttered environments requires careful attention to representing the geometry of potential obstacles and to developing efficient algorithms for searching the representation for unoccupied space. Task planning is concerned with automatically generating robot actions from high-level task specifications. Early results from artificial intelligence planning research (e.g. hierarchical planning techniques) remain important in robot task planning. However, simplistic assumptions used in early artificial intelligence studies must be overcome as time-critical planning, uncertainty, and dynamic world models become crucial.

Programming Robot programming must deal with most standard programming issues including user interface, database access, and more general internal symbolic and numeric calculation. However, robot programs also must have capabilities to compute and execute actions on the basis of external (perhaps sensed) events. Further, there must be an ability to deal with concurrent activities, including those of other robots. Three principal approaches have been applied to robot programming: discrete word recognition, guiding, and high-level programming. In discrete word recognition, individual (e.g. spoken) words are recognized and used to specify robot actions. This approach suffers both from the current limitations of machine word recognition as well as the expressive limitations of individual words. *Guiding* refers to programming a robot by physically moving it through the desired task while the motion is recorded for later playback. The major limitation of this approach is the difficulty in programming contingent operations, particularly those depending on sensed data. Finally, high-level programming languages have been used in robotics. In application to robotics, high-level programming languages can be thought of as either robot-oriented or task-oriented. Robot-oriented languages explicitly specify a robot's individual actions. In contrast, task-oriented languages specify a robot's actions at the level of the functional nature of the task that is to be performed. Task-oriented languages allow for powerful abstraction; however, they do not lend themselves to tight control over the specific actions that a robot executes in performing a given task.

In applying high-level programming languages to robotics, there is an interesting choice between using special-purpose robot programming languages versus using a (suitably extended) general-purpose programming language. While robot-specific languages have the advantage of exploiting the specific nature of robotics problems, they are difficult to use when robots are placed in a diverse automated environment (e.g. an integrated manufacturing environment). Programming languages developed for robotics include AML, RAPT, VAL, and WAVE. General-purpose programming languages commonly used in robotics include C (*q.v.*) and Lisp.

Current Directions Robotics is advancing rapidly. In the area of robot perception, important current research includes the design and production of better sensors, active perception strategies that adapt perceptual processing to the situation at hand, and the combination of various sources of perceptual information. Current research in actuation includes the integrated design of mechanical structures and control strategies, experimental evaluation of control strategies, and compliant motion. Focuses for the study of robot reasoning include qualitative physical modeling and the incorporation of concepts from computational geometry and topology into geometric reasoning. In robot programming, the development of task-level programming languages continues to be a major point of effort. More generally, integrated robot systems are seeing increased development. Here, the focus is not only on coordinating various capabilities in individual robots, but also on the integration of robots into larger environments. Multiprocessor architectures play an important role in integrated robot systems. Finally, as the range of capabilities of robots increase, so do their applications. In manufacturing, robots are increasingly involved in totally automated environments. In negotiating hostile situations, robots play an increasing role in deep sea and space exploration, military operations, and toxic waste management. In the slightly more distant future, robots will become important factors in home and office environments.

Current developments in robotics are reported regularly in such journals as the *International Journal of Robotics Research*; the IEEE *Journal of Robotics and Automation*; the *Journal of Robotic Systems*; *Robotica*; the IEEE *Transactions on Pattern Analysis and Machine Intelligence*; *Artificial Intelligence*; the ASME *Journal of Mechanical Design*; the *Proceedings of IEEE Conference on Robotics and Automation*; and the *Proceedings of the International Symposium on Industrial Robots*.

References

1981. Paul, R. P. *Robot Manipulators: Mathematics, Programming and Control*. Cambridge, MA: The M. I. T. Press.

1983. Brady, M. J., Hollerbach, J. M., Johnson, T. L., Lozano-Perez, T. and Mason, M. T. (Eds.). *Robot Motion: Planning and Control.* Cambridge, MA: The M. I. T. Press.

1986. Horn, B. K. P. *Robot Vision.* Cambridge, MA: The M. I. T. Press.

1987. Fu, K. S., Gonzales, R. C. and Lee, C. S. G. *Robotics: Control, Sensing, Vision, and Intelligence.* New York: McGraw-Hill.

1988. Dario, P. *Sensors and Sensory Systems for Advanced Robots.* Berlin: Springer-Verlag.

1989. Brady, M. J. (Ed.). *Robotics Science.* Cambridge, MA: The M. I. T. Press.

1989. Engelberger, J. F. *Robotics in Service.* Cambridge, MA: The M. I. T. Press.

1990. McCarthy, J. M. *Introduction to Theoretical Kinematics.* Cambridge, MA: The M. I. T. Press.

1990. Yoshikawa, T. *Foundations of Robotics.* Cambridge, MA: The M. I. T. Press.

RICHARD P. WILDES

ROM   *See* READ-ONLY MEMORY.

ROUNDOFF ERROR

For articles on related subjects *see* ERROR ANALYSIS; ERRORS; INTERVAL ARITHMETIC; and NUMERICAL ANALYSIS.

Computers typically deal with numbers of fixed length (i.e. with a fixed number of digits or bits) when performing arithmetic (although there are exceptions to this). For example, when multiplying two numbers each of which has n bits, the resulting $2n$ bit product is usually *rounded* (or, on some few computers, truncated) to n bits. The error that results from this is called *roundoff error*, or sometimes *rounding error*. With pencil and paper calculations, such roundoff is seldom significant, but with the millions or even billions of arithmetic operations performed in computer calculations, the effects of roundoff can be considerable and sometimes disastrous. In addition, even a single roundoff error can be disastrous in large problems solved on a computer (see below for an example of this). Roundoff also occurs when the data for a calculation, which may be known exactly, must be rounded to n bits when read into and stored in a computer.

As examples of how large a single roundoff error can be, we consider two cases, both assuming the use of fixed-point arithmetic on a computer using 32-bit numbers with binary point at the left end, as shown in Fig. 1.

Case 1. *Multiplication of two 31-bit numbers rounded to a 31-bit product.* Rounding to a 31-bit product means that

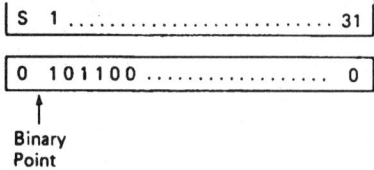

FIG. 1.   The 31-bit number shown with positive sign (0) has the value 0.1011 = 11/16.

the thirty-second bit of the product is examined. If it is 0 (i.e. bits 32–62 represent less than $\frac{1}{2} \times 2^{-31}$), then nothing is done; if it is 1 (i.e. bits 32–62 represent greater than or equal to $\frac{1}{2} \times 2^{-31}$), then 1 is added into bit position 31 of the product. The magnitude of the error in the product is therefore no greater than

$$\tfrac{1}{2} \times 2^{-31} = 2^{-32}.$$

Case 2. An exact datum is read into the computer and rounded to 31 bits. If the rounding is done as above, by looking at the thirty-second bit, then again the magnitude of the error is no greater than 2^{-32}.

The analysis of roundoff error in a long calculation is usually very difficult. Sometimes, by considering the worst possible error magnitude in each roundoff, a bound on the worst error in the result can be obtained, but this bound may be very conservative (i.e. much larger than the actual error). For example, suppose each of N numbers read into the computer, as in Case 2 above, are added. The quantity $N \cdot 2^{-32}$ is then a bound on the error in the sum, but this bound will occur only if all numbers have the maximum possible roundoff error *with the same sign.* Generally, individual roundoff errors will be less than the maximum possible and will have both positive and negative values so that there will be some cancellation of errors when they are added. Probabilistic analysis shows that, for this addition example, the *probable error*, defined as the value exceeded by the actual roundoff error one-half of the time, is given approximately by $0.2 \times \sqrt{N} \times 2^{-32}$. The *square root rule* (i.e. replacing the number of operations N by $\sqrt{N}$) is often used as a rule of thumb in making probable error estimates from maximum error bounds.

As an example of the disastrous effects that roundoff error can have, we consider the case of finding the zeros of the polynomial

$$(x - 1)(x - 2)(x - 3) \cdots (x - 20),$$

where the computer is given the coefficients A_0 to A_{19} in

$$x^{20} + A_{19} x^{19} + A_{18} x^{18} + \cdots + A_2 x^2 + A_1 x + A_0.$$

It is easily calculated that $A_{19} = -210$. Now suppose that the coefficients $A_0, A_1 \ldots A_{18}$ are all stored exactly in the computer, but that, because of a roundoff error, A_{19} is stored as $-210 - 2^{-23}$, noting that 2^{-23} is approximately one ten-millionth. This one error changes the polynomial so that—even if the computer then calculated the zeros exactly (i.e. with no further roundoff errors)—instead of $1, 2, \ldots, 20$, it would obtain (correct to three decimal places)

1.000	6.000	$10.095 \pm 0.644i$
2.000	7.000	$11.794 \pm 1.652i$
3.000	8.007	$13.992 \pm 2.519i$
4.000	8.917	$16.731 \pm 2.813i$
5.000	20.847	$19.502 \pm 1.940i$

Not only have the larger zeros become quite inaccurate, but ten of them have also changed from real to complex conjugate pairs, all because of one error in the seventh decimal place. Problems in which a single, small roundoff error in the data or in subsequent calculation results in much larger errors in the answers, are called *ill-conditioned*. Recognition of ill-condition may be difficult, although some classes of problems—such as the calculation of the zeros of high-degree polynomials—are known to be generally ill-conditioned. Unless an ill-conditioned problem can be somehow transformed to a well-conditioned form, it is usually true that the only way to overcome ill-condition is by using multiple precision arithmetic in which the individual roundoff errors will be much smaller.

References

1963. Wilkinson, J. H. *Rounding Errors in Algebraic Processes.* Englewood Cliffs, NJ: Prentice-Hall.

ANTHONY RALSTON

RUN TIME. *See* COMPILE AND RUN TIME.

SCHEDULING ALGORITHMS

For articles on related subjects *see* INTERRUPT; MEMORY MANAGEMENT; MULTIPROGRAMMING; OPERATING SYSTEMS; PROCESSING MODES; QUEUEING THEORY; SWAPPING; TIME SHARING; TIME SLICE; VIRTUAL MEMORY; and WORKING SET.

A computing system consists of a finite set of resources, such as processor cycles, memory locations, and input/output (I/O) devices which many programs or processes may need to use. The object of a *scheduling algorithm* is to allocate these resources to the programs that require them. At each decision point, a scheduling algorithm must decide which of several competing processes should next receive a given resource.

One crucial resource in any computer system is the processor itself, since every process residing in the system must have the processor allocated to it for some period of time in order for the process to complete execution and the leave the system. In this article, we will discuss processor scheduling algorithms for both single-processor and multiprocessor systems.

There are two main phases of processor scheduling activity. During the job management phase, several programs (or *jobs*) are selected for execution and are loaded into available memory. Then, during the dispatching phase, a processor is assigned to one after another of the memory resident programs. In general, the simpler dispatching algorithm is executed many times between any two executions of the more complex job management scheduling algorithm; the job management algorithm itself may be dynamically modified still more infrequently.

In describing the essential concepts of scheduling, we shall first assume a batch-oriented, single-processor computer system. While our discussion will treat the dispatching and job management aspects of scheduling separately, these two functions are often integrated in existing systems. We first discuss the simpler dispatching function.

Dispatching involves the allocation of processor cycles to active programs, those programs that are currently in memory and competing for processor time. A given active program is in one of three states. It is either *executing*, *ready* to execute, or *blocked* waiting for the occurrence of some event, such as the completion of an I/O operation. It is the task of the short-term scheduling algorithm or *dispatcher* to decide which of the ready processes is to receive processor time and for how long (the *time slice*). The usual algorithm cycles *round-robin* through the set of ready programs, allocating the processor to each program in turn. The program executes until it blocks or terminates, or until its time quantum expires (see Fig. 1). This is simple scheme is appropriate, since dispatching is done very frequently and the time involved in this type of scheduling (the *overhead*) must therefore be minimized.

The result of the dispatcher consecutively allocating processor cycles to several different memory resident processes is called *multiprogramming*. A single processor appears to be executing multiple programs concurrently. Equivalently, we can say that a single processor is made to simulate the effects of several independent virtual processors. The task of the job management algorithm then becomes the assignment of one job to each virtual processor.

The object of the short-term scheduler or dispatcher is to maintain good utilization of the processor and I/O devices. The level of multiprogramming or, equivalently, the number of virtual processors is determined primarily by how many programs (or their *working sets* in a virtual memory system) fit comfortably in the memory, and this number may vary, depending on the job mix, or may be fixed.

The object of job management scheduling, in contrast, is to carry out management objectives with respect to total system utilization. The management policy may strive to satisfy a majority of casual users at the expense of a minority of users with very high resource demands. Alternatively, the management policy may favor production runs and allow casual use only when the system is otherwise underutilized. Regardless, it is primarily the

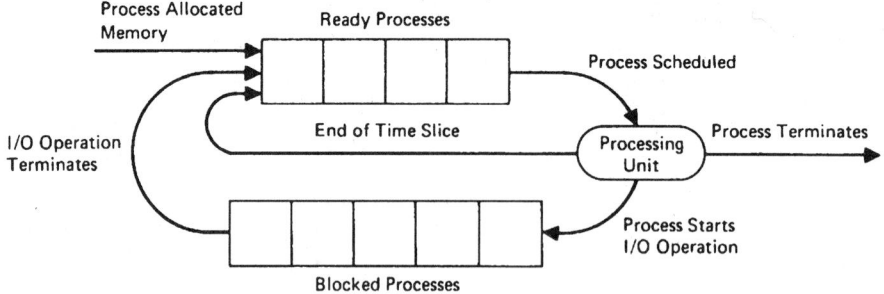

FIG. 1. Dispatching.

task of the job management scheduling algorithm to achieve the stated management objectives.

Typically, to achieve this aim, a priority function is defined and each program in the system has a priority value that is updated at fixed decision points by the scheduling algorithm. The programs having the highest priority at each decision point are then assigned virtual processors. Between these job management decision points, the programs are managed by the simpler dispatching algorithm, which typically does not involve the overhead of priority calculations.

A great deal of work has gone into the development of different job management scheduling algorithms, and many different algorithms are used on current systems. We will discuss only some general approaches rather than giving the details of any particular system.

One important factor in this level of scheduling involves the choice of decision points. One could choose to recalculate priorities only when a program enters an empty or underutilized system, or when a program terminates execution. It is more common, however, to define a preemptive scheduling algorithm where a fixed time interval is specified and the scheduling algorithm is executed at the end of each such interval. Depending upon the priority function chosen, use of this scheme can prevent a few long programs from monopolizing the processor. In general, more users are kept satisfied when shorter programs get preferential treatment.

The priority of each program may depend upon such static parameters as memory requirements, requirements for special I/O devices, or management-dictated preferential treatment; or upon such dynamic parameters as the amount of processor time already received, how long the program has been resident in the system, or recent frequency of I/O operations. The resulting set of priority values may uniquely order the waiting programs or merely group them. In the latter case, if several programs have the same highest priority, then the job management scheduling algorithm commonly cycles round-robin through these programs, giving each the opportunity to reside in memory for some time quantum.

Job management scheduling algorithms have also received much theoretical attention. The techniques of queueing theory have been used to model simple scheduling algorithms for statistically defined classes of programs, and to determine analytic system performance measures for them. While these models are necessarily somewhat simplistic, they do indicate the relative bene-

fits of such different approaches as first-in-first-out (FIFO), shortest job first (SJF), shortest remaining time first (SRTF), and round-robin (RR).

As system load characteristics change over time, the management policy may be best implemented by also changing the job management algorithm. This can be done by either switching to a totally different algorithm or by modifying parameters in the existing algorithm. To implement this adaptive control of the scheduling algorithm, a set of system descriptors such as queue lengths must be identified and updated. As the values of these descriptors vary significantly from desired norms, the job management scheduling algorithm is dynamically modified.

We now extend our discussion of single-processor, batch-oriented scheduling to describe scheduling of time-shared, real-time, and multiprocessor systems.

In a time-shared system, the processor must be allocated to each terminal user in such a way that the trivial interactive requests of the user are quickly responded to, and other requests requiring more resources have response times proportional to their resource demands. Typically, management objectives have shifted from efficient hardware usage towards satisfactory response time characteristics. In this environment, many user programs are in an inactive state waiting for the user to provide terminal input, and they need not be retained in memory. The active user programs are those that have a terminal request outstanding, and these programs must be brought into the physical memory for execution within some short time interval.

In such a time-sharing system, the scheduler may maintain two or more program queues in order to distinguish between active programs that have not received service and may therefore have just a trivial interactive request, and other active programs that have already received one or more full quanta of service, thus indicating a more substantive request. All new program requests in this multi-level treatment are serviced before the processor continues to execute any other unsatisfied requests, thus improving response characteristics. If all the active programs do not fit in memory, then response times may increase as active user programs are swapped in and out of memory to satisfy the requirement that all new active processes receive some service before others receive additional service.

Real-time systems, such as those used to control production machinery, are characterized as having certain programs whose execution must be completed within fixed time intervals. In terms of scheduling, the key parameter of the job management scheduling algorithm is the length of time remaining until the program's deadline is reached. As the time leeway diminishes, the program's priority increases. Sophisticated special-purpose algorithms have been developed to predict accurately future resource requirements and availability; to manage explicitly processor, disk, and memory aggregates to achieve real-time goals; and to shutdown selectively system functionality in such a way as to minimize external disruption.

We next consider scheduling for multiprocessors, which we characterize as consisting of several processors of similar power executing from a large common memory. The role of scheduling is the same as described before—to use the physical processors to simulate a possibly larger number of virtual processors; to allocate programs to these virtual processors; and to adapt the scheduling algorithm to changes in the workload. A key design decision for the multiprocessor concerns the choice of processor(s) to do the scheduling. The scheduling algorithms may always be executed by one processor, may float from processor to processor, or may be executed by each processor as it requires scheduling.

In a master/slave multiprocessor operating system, one processor is responsible for scheduling all work on the system. Whenever a slave processor requires service, it must request service and wait until the current program on the master processor is interrupted so that the scheduling algorithm can be executed. Although this control strategy is easy to implement, access to the scheduling processor may become a system bottleneck and any failure in the master processor stops the entire system.

In an operating system with a floating scheduler, any one processor at a time may perform the scheduling functions for the system, with either a software or hardware controller preventing two processors from scheduling simultaneously. While somewhat more difficult to implement, this form of control does have the potential for greater reliability than the master/slave organization.

In a multiprocessor operating system using distributed control, each processor is responsible for scheduling itself from a common table of scheduling information. System-wide conventions are used for processes entering into the scheduling queues and for assigning priorities; standard synchronization techniques are used to prevent two processors from accessing and changing the scheduling information at the same time. This organization, like that of the floating scheduler, has good reliability and is easily extensible to additional processors.

Over the past ten years, decreasing hardware costs and increasing chip density have led to more and more powerful single-processor computers. Increasingly, these computers are networked to each other and to specialized filing, database, printing, and communications servers. System-wide scheduling has been simplified by allocating interactive tasks to single-user workstations and other time-critical tasks to dedicated network servers. There have been few attempts to schedule more effectively the total available computing resources in distributed computing environments.

References

1984. Comer, Douglas. *Operating System Design—The XINU Approach*. Englewood Cliffs, NJ: Prentice-Hall.
1988. Finkel, Raphael A. *An Operating Systems Vade Mecum*, 2nd Ed. Englewood Cliffs, NJ: Prentice-Hall.

LESLIE JILL MILLER

SCHEMA. *See* DATABASE MANAGEMENT SYSTEM (DBMS).

SCIENTIFIC APPLICATIONS

For articles on related subjects *see* BIOCOMPUTING; COMPUTER-AIDED DESIGN/COMPUTER-AIDED MANUFACTURING; COMPUTER GRAPHICS; FAST FOURIER TRANSFORM; FINITE ELEMENT METHOD; FRACTALS; IMAGE PROCESSING; INFORMATION RETRIEVAL; MEDICAL IMAGING; MONTE CARLO METHOD; NUMERICAL ANALYSIS; PARTIAL DIFFERENTIAL EQUATIONS; PARALLEL PROCESSING; PATTERN RECOGNITION; SIMULATION: PRINCIPLES; STATISTICAL APPLICATIONS; SUPERCOMPUTERS; and TOMOGRAPHY, COMPUTERIZED.

Computation has always played a central role in the closed cycle known as the scientific method. A new theory gains acceptance or falls by the wayside in direct proportion to its success in explaining known phenomena and predicting new ones, not just qualitatively but also quantitatively. Einstein's theory of relativity predicted not just that light should be deflected in passing by a massive object such as the sun, but also the precise amount by which it should be deflected. No computer is needed for such a prediction (indeed, the first such calculation antedated electronic computers by almost a half-century), but a certain minimum amount of arithmetic computation is nonetheless required. This is typical of any new scientific discovery, since the truly fundamental physical phenomena are governed by equations that describe what happens to small particles or energy bundles as they move through space and time. In the same way in which the physicist's quest to explore particle phenomena at ever higher ranges of energy leads to the construction of ever larger (and more costly) accelerators, the attempt to solve these equations in increasing detail has led to a continual need for computers of higher speed and greater memory capacity. The initial sections of this article attempt to explain why.

The Quest for Ultra Performance   It is often of scientific interest to calculate the behavior of aggregates of particles over large regions of space or within long time intervals. Scientists facing such a task usually have a choice of two basically different approaches. One can calculate the flight of an individual particle until it is scattered by a second particle, absorbed, or leaves the region of observation. The exact history of each particle depends on a sequence of random numbers chosen and used in such a way as to constrain the particle to experience one event or another in accord with its correct probability. Tracking and accumulating statistics on thousands of such particles then enable calculation of quantities of physical interest. Such a technique is called the *Monte Carlo method* for obvious reasons, and finds application in such diverse situations as the behavior of neutrons in a reactor, light quanta in stellar atmospheres, and automobiles in heavy traffic. Monte Carlo calculations are inherently time consuming, even on very fast electronic computers, because of the necessity to follow a sufficiently large number of particles to obtain results that are accurate within statistically acceptable limits of error.

The second principal line of computational attack occurs more often—namely, when (1) the behavior of the quantity of interest is known to obey a linear or nonlinear algebraic equation, a differential equation, an integral equation, or an integro-differential equation over some region of space/time of given shape, and when (2) the desired quantity obeys specified boundary conditions in space (and initial conditions in time in time-dependent problems). Taking differential equations as an example, the simplest situations occur when the desired quantity (the dependent variable) is a function of only one independent variable, perhaps time or one-space dimension. Such differential equations are called *ordinary*. In such cases, either an analytic solution is obtainable or use of a simple difference equation approximation will allow production of desired answers in a few seconds of computer time.

When the dependent variable is a function of two or more independent variables, the appropriate differential equation is called a *partial differential equation* (PDE - *q.v.*) because it involves partial derivatives that indicate the change in the dependent variable as one or another of the independent variables change, while holding all other independent variables fixed. Except under special circumstances, the solution of such equations is computationally formidable. As an example, consider an electromagnetic wave impinging on a target of given shape and internal composition. In principle, Maxwell's system of differential equations and attendant boundary conditions completely specify the behavior of the radiation scattered from the target. When the target is either a metallic (perfectly reflecting) sphere or a penetrable sphere of homogeneous and isotropic internal electrical properties, Maxwell's partial differential equations reduce to three ordinary differential equations, one each specifying the behavior of the scattered wave along the r, θ, and ϕ directions in spherical coordinates. This has been known at least as far back as 1908, and so-called Mie calculations (after their originator), while tedious, can be programmed and normally take only a few seconds of computer time.

Imagine the target, while still spherical, to have internal electrical properties that are a function of radial position. Perhaps the core is dense and surrounded by a diffuse fringe, for example. Then Maxwell's equations still separate into three ordinary differential equations, but the radial equation, which in the homogeneous case was known to have solutions familiar to scientists (Bessel functions), must now be solved from point to point by difference methods. A digital computer is now a virtual necessity.

Now envision a progression of relaxations of symmetry conditions; each will greatly extend computer running time: Nonspherical but still axially symmetric targets will require several minutes of computer time and anisotropic targets will need a few minutes to an hour or more (depending on spatial symmetry), and so on up to completely nonsymmetric anisotropic targets, which would take several hours, even on the fastest computers presently available (*see* SUPERCOMPUTERS).

The situation described above is typical of a number of physical situations. A scientist will often know that the subject of study is governed by equations whose full complexity places exact solutions beyond the capability of the computer available. A sufficient number of approximations is then made to bring a typical calculation down to an acceptable bound, usually an hour or less, on the available computer. When the host installation increases its capability by, say, a factor of 4, the scientist will not necessarily be content to run four times as many cases in unit time, but will often remove a restriction or approximation, that will bring total running time back to an hour or so.

In reactor design, for example, it is known that neutron behavior is governed by a complex integro-differential equation known as Boltzmann's equation. This equation takes into account that, at any given spatial point, the rate of neutron flow depends on their speed and direction, and to a certain extent on their past history. The solution of such an equation everywhere throughout reactor volume for all possible neutron velocities is a task beyond presently available computers. However, what can be done, and usually is, is to make approximations that replace the Boltzmann equation with a series of coupled partial differential equations, each of which calculates neutron flux at a particular energy (speed) at a given space point. Each such equation, a so-called diffusion equation, is then calculated in either one-, two-, or three-space dimensions, whichever the symmetry of the reactor (or expediency) demands. Any horizontal plane through a reactor core can be modeled in cartesian (x,y) coordinates, but other geometric arrangements often dictate use of polar (r,θ) or cylindrical (r,z) coordinates. Any of these geometries reduces to this simple situation: Given that $p,a,c,d,$ and e are known functions of position (precalculated and stored in computer memory prior to the time-consuming calculation of neutron flux), we would like to know what values of neutron flux φ_P, φ_A, φ_C, φ_D, φ_E balance the equation

$$p\varphi_P - a\varphi_A - c\varphi_C - d\varphi_D - e\varphi_E = 0$$

at every mesh-point P, where left, right, bottom, and top neighboring points are designated A, C, D, and E, respectively. All questions of geometry, material composition, and boundary condition are buried in the calculation of the coefficients. Any one such equation has five unknowns, and hence cannot be solved uniquely, but since a similar equation must hold at every mesh point, a 10,000-point model (say) represents 10,000 equations in 10,000 unknowns. In principle, this can be solved by inverting a 10,000 × 10,000 matrix. Such an attempt would be not only foolish but unnecessary. Since most elements of such a matrix would be zero (the result of using only a nearest-neighbor numerical approximation to derivatives in the diffusion equation), the desired fluxes are best obtained iteratively. There are a variety of methods for doing this, but most process a line of points at a time, sweeping all lines a sufficient number of times to obtain the desired convergence. Here, "sweeping" means the consistent solution of just the 100 (say) points on a line by a systematic forward-elimination/backward-substitution method applicable to so-called three-term or *tridiagnonal* linear systems (matrices whose only nonzero elements are on the diagonal or next to the diagonal).

Although the preceding discussion assumed use of a two-dimensional slice taken from a full three-dimensional reactor, the technique can be extended (at great expense in computer time) to all three space dimensions, or even to four dimensions: three spatial dimensions plus time. An example from another computationally intense field, elementary particle physics, is shown in Fig. 1 (see color insert page CP-10) (Bitar and Heller, 1992). The three smaller spheres inside the larger one represent quarks that combine to form a single "hadron," such as a neutron

or a proton. The larger sphere represents a "bag" within which the quarks are forever confined, interacting in accord with the laws of quantum chromodynamics (QCD). To solve the time-dependent equations that describe these interactions, space-time is modeled by a four-dimensional grid, with force fields defined on the sites or links of the lattice. Coping with the nonlinear dynamics of the model has become one of the most demanding computational projects in physics. A typical QCD simulation on a $16^3 \times 32$ lattice (about 100,000 mesh points) requires 10^{16} floating-point operations. Fortunately, the fields at every node of the lattice are treated identically, so that such calculations are highly suitable for both vector supercomputers and for such massively parallel supercomputers as the Connection Machine 2 of Thinking Machines Corporation.

In some fields, the increasing speed and memory capacity of successive generations of digital computers have transformed the image that the computer conveys to the scientist from that of a tool—albeit a powerful one—to that of a new experimental device in its own right. Chemistry is a good example. The basic equation that governs the behavior of molecules, atoms, and (low-ve-

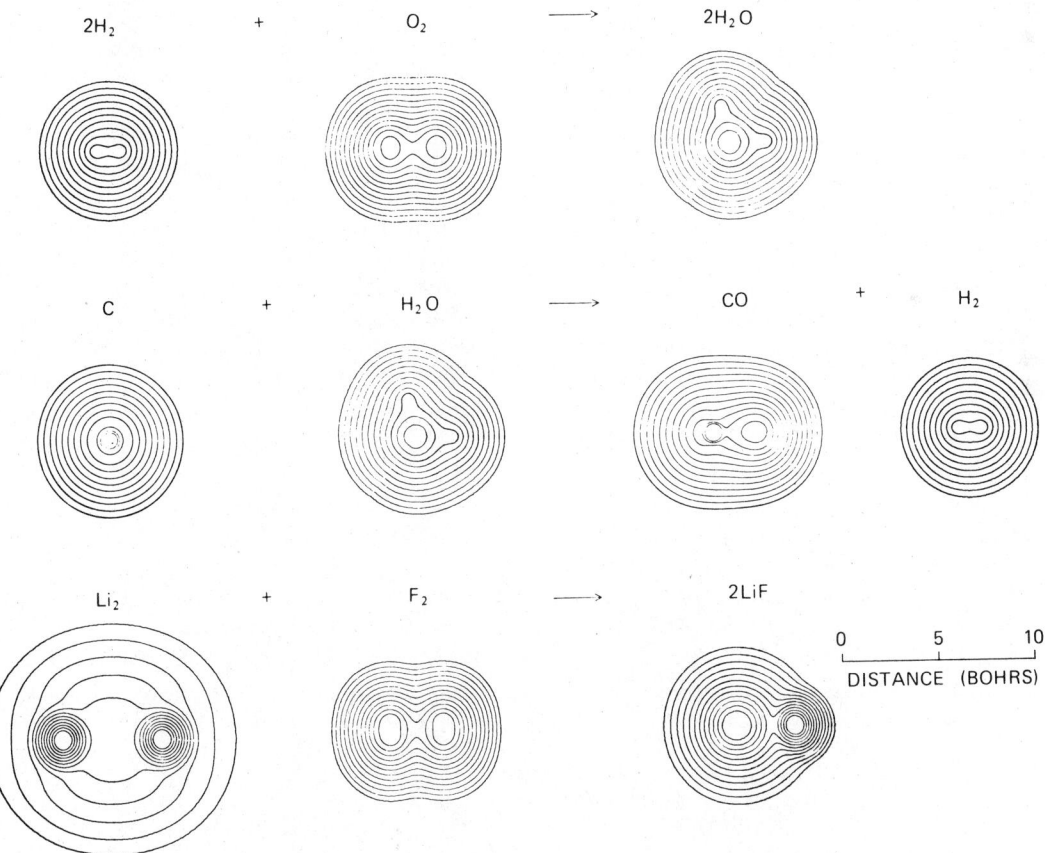

FIG. 2. Three chemical reactions portrayed in terms of changes in computer-produced electron-density diagrams. Top shows two hydrogen molecules combining with an oxygen molecule to form two water molecules. Middle shows a carbon atom and a water molecule combining to form a carbon monoxide molecule and a hydrogen molecule. Bottom shows a lithium molecule and a fluorine molecule combining to form two lithium fluoride molecules. Although these are simple reactions, it appears reasonable to expect that this general approach can be extended to much more complicated reactions. (From Arnold C. Wahl in *Scientific American*, April 1970, fig. 5.)

locity) electrons has been known for over 60 years—the Schrödinger equation. Without a computer, only simple systems consisting of two or three particles can be studied in any detail (see Fig. 2). With the latest computers, however, ions of much larger atomic number can be followed kinetically as they interact with other ions to form molecules. If the chemist is able to watch the progression of such a reaction on a TV-like display device attached to the computer, it is just as good or better (and less messy) than mixing the reagents in the laboratory. ("Better" because there are only limited means of varying the speed of an actual reaction, whereas the simulated reaction can proceed at "instant replay" slow motion on a display device through appropriate variation of program parameters.)

Inverse Calculations

All of the examples cited thus far are examples of *direct* calculational situations. We know the characteristics of a target and want to calculate its scattering properties. We know the reactor configuration and desire its lifetime behavior. We know the reagents and want to know their reactivity. As time-consuming as such calculations can be, they are routine in their demand for computer time compared to indirect or *inverse calculations,* where we have access to experimental data but no access at all to the source of the phenomena generating the data.

An example is the problem of interstellar dust particles. Astrophysicists and cosmologists would like to know the quantity, shape, and composition of these particles, since this knowledge has a bearing on theories of the origin and evolution of the universe. We cannot yet send space ships to retrieve such matter, but we can observe quantities such as the polarization and absorption of light of various wavelengths passing through it. What kinds of particles produce the scattered light: spherical? elongated? metallic? anisotropic ferrite needles? dirty ice? The question is far from settled, and the astrophysicist will need to experiment with many different

models to achieve success without being at all sure that the answer is unique.

Crystallographic calculations are another example of inverse computations. It would be straightforward to calculate the pattern of X-rays diffracted from a known spatial distribution of known atoms, but we cannot get inside crystals or molecules the way Asimov's fictional scientists traveled through the circulatory system in "Fantastic Voyage." We can observe the pattern of diffracted X-rays or neutrons impinging on a crystal of unknown structure, but in doing so, certain basic information (phase relations between atoms) is lost. Using what information is available, however, such as intensity data, suspected symmetries, and chemical formulas learned through destructive testing of portions of the same material, crystallographers are now able to use an organized trial-and-error method to deduce the structure of quite large molecules of up to 100 atoms or so, and the frontier is pushed ahead with each advance in computer technology.

As complex as they are, the structures of several proteins as well as the vitamin B_{12} have been determined by computer techniques. Some programs are so sophisticated that they produce as a final result a stereo pair (Fig. 3) of similar views of the predicted molecular structure; viewing them through an appropriate optical device brings out the spatial arrangement and vibrational characteristics of crystal constituent atoms in stunning detail.

Traditionally, biologists have not used computers intensively, but that situation is changing rapidly (*see* BIOCOMPUTING). One of the more important types of inverse calculation is that needed to ascertain DNA sequences in molecular biology. Without high-speed computers, the human genome project whose goal is to deduce the gene sequences of all human chromosomes would be impossible. For a discussion of the importance of computers in molecular biology, see Lander *et al.,* 1991.

Just as the astrophysicist and the crystallographer are barred from entering the domain of the objects of their interest, so is the geophysicist unable to examine more

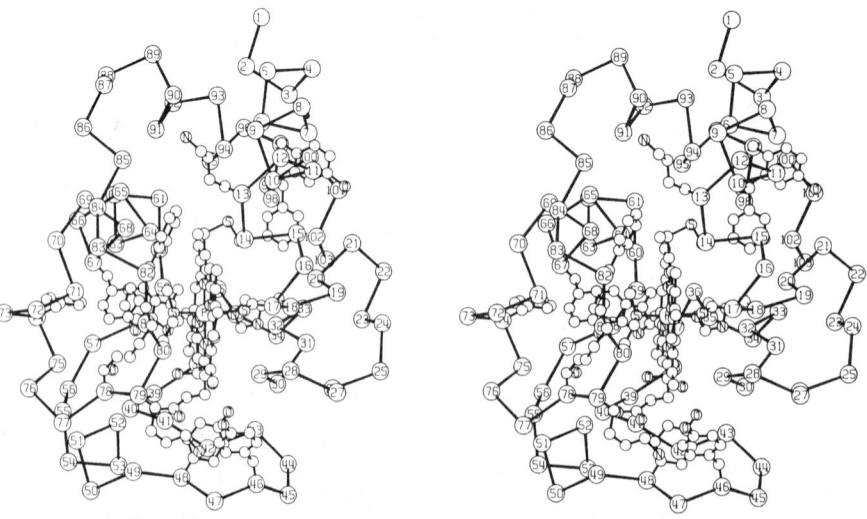

FIG. 3. Stereoscopic pair of front view of reduced cytochrome *c* molecule from a tuna. (Source: R. E. Dickerson, California Institute of Technology.)

than an infinitesimal fraction of the interior of the earth. There is data, however, that gives extremely pointed clues as to the internal composition of the earth—namely, that provided through seismological records taken during periods of earthquake, volcanic eruption, and atomic testing. The earth, like any (approximate) sphere of given internal composition, has certain characteristic modes of vibration, and allows elastic waves to propagate at certain speeds from point to point on its surface. By using digital computers to vary appropriate parameters in the equations that govern such phenomena, geophysicists have derived a profile of the earth's interior with reasonable certitude, a confidence founded on agreement between the predicted characteristics of their model and observed properties. Based on such methods, they already predict a molten liquid core, and their detailed predictions of its shape and composition are being sharpened as they make increasingly detailed comparisons with experimental data of the effects the liquid core might have on the earth's rotational and magnetic properties. Similar methods are allowing geologists to map strain energies in the earth in an attempt to understand earthquake phenomena.

Impact on Hardware Development

One obvious impact of the scientist's perceived need for ever higher performance computers to cope with the type of problems cited above is to create a market climate in which vendors are willing to design and develop supercomputers. Computers capable of 50 million floating-point operations per second (Mflops) are now rather commonplace and speeds of 500 Mflops to 1 Gflop (gigaflop) are attainable for certain problems running on massively parallel supercomputers.

Scientific users will have no difficulty absorbing the additional capacity that will be provided by ever-faster supercomputers. The four-dimensional QCD model described earlier uses 100,000 mesh points but only 16 along any one spatial dimension and 32 time-steps. Merely doubling the resolution in each dimension would require a computer 16 times faster in order to do a simulation in the same amount of running time.

A similar point has been made with regard to modeling climate (Chervin, 1990). In the early 1970s, one hour of time on a CDC 6600 was needed to simulate one day of climate evolution using a very crude oceanic general circulation model (CCM). By the early 1980s, the same computation could be done in less than two minutes on a Cray 1A supercomputer. By the early 1990s, the Cray Y-MP8/832 reached a 1-gigaflop rate that reduced running time to a few seconds, but its doing so merely enticed the modelers to refine their model. The one they had been using had a resolution of only a half degree of latitude and longitude (about 35 miles at the equator) and 20 levels of altitude. Increasing the resolution will easily tax the added power of any newer supercomputer.

An alternative approach to high performance at a price more affordable than that of a supercomputer is to attach a special-purpose floating-point array processor (FPAP) to a minicomputer. The mini handles input, output, and routine logical operations, but streams floating-point numbers to the attached processor for execution at far greater speed than could otherwise have been attained by the host computer itself. The average increase in performance is quite problem-dependent, but can often reach a factor of 10 to 50. Over a thousand FPAP devices have now been installed; their invention and proliferation is one of the major advances in scientific computation over the past ten years. Their application to high-energy physics has been described by Nash (1989).

Fittingly enough, the advance of scientific research and the development of better computing devices go hand in hand. Faster speeds depend on faster switching devices, which, in turn, depend on such scientific advances as that of the Josephson junction, an outgrowth of research in solid state physics. Computers of the future that are able to use such junctions and certain other *superconducting devices (q.v.)* will lead to still further advances in solid state physics. And so it goes.

Ancillary Roles

In addition to their obvious value for direct and inverse calculation, digital computers play a role in automating many other aspects of the scientist's personal workload. These will be discussed under the headings information retrieval, instrumentation, data reduction, comparison of theory and experiment, simulation for design, simulation for prediction, and simulation for education.

Information Retrieval The profusion of scientific papers being published makes it ever more difficult for working scientists to keep abreast of their fields, even in their own specialties. Increasing numbers of workers are subscribing to computerized information retrieval services of one kind or another, or have access to libraries that do. Principal among these would be the ability to file an interest profile with such a service center, and then be continually apprised of papers that match that profile as they are published; another service might make a specific search over past literature according to certain keywords and key concepts.

Instrumentation Many of the instruments of modern research science have themselves become so complex that it is often expedient to control their operation automatically with a small computer directly connected to the instrument. Nuclear reactors and particle accelerators are often controlled or at least monitored in this way, as are a wide range of other devices, such as radio and optical telescopes, nuclear magnetic resonance equipment, crystallographic apparatus, electron microscopes, and satellites forced to obey telemetered signals emanating from computers on the ground below.

Data Reduction, Presentation, and Pattern Recognition The data produced by an experimental instrument is seldom directly usable. It usually needs some kind of scaling, noise filtering, time integration, or other treatment that is ideally suited to computer processing. As a by-product of this data reduction, a properly equipped computer can also display the reduced data, either in hard-copy form on a graph plotter or in a transient visual form on a cathode ray tube display device. Thus, a scientist may monitor an experiment in progress and perhaps even input feedback information that alters the later course of the research.

Some of the more interesting applications of data reduction occur in a pattern recognition context. The classic example is the widespread use of devices called *bubble chambers* in high-energy physics. Particles passing through such devices leave visible tracks composed of tiny bubbles that can be photographed and scanned for the occurrence of interesting branch-like structures that indicate the presence of a collision or reaction between particles. Although humans can do this quite well, a bubble chamber can snap a new picture every few seconds and easily reach an annual production of over a million frames. Such prodigious output can be coped with only by computerized pattern-recognition techniques, and modern accelerators are serviced by large computers devoted almost exclusively to this task.

Pattern recognition, or at least computerized image processing, also plays a vital role in planetary exploration. NASA space probes that flew by Mars (and Jupiter and Saturn) in recent years transmitted pictures back to earth in digital form (Fig. 4), specifically, as a series of 40,000 six-bit data points, each representing on a scale of 0 to 63 the shade of gray that was observed at the intersection of a 200×200 grid array superimposed on the visual scene. Once read into the memory of a high-speed computer, such a digitized picture was then easily "cleaned up" by removing spurious noise and enhancing its resolution for human viewing, thus producing the sharp and often breathtaking photos presented in news magazines at the time.

In a similar vein, pattern recognition by computer has been used by scientists in other fields. Biologists have successfully identified mutant chromosomes among normal ones through such techniques. Atmospheric scientists are experimenting with attempts to identify cyclone-like disturbances in cloud-cover satellite photos.

FIG. 4.   A computer enhanced photograph of a portion of the surface of Mars. (Source: Jet Propulsion Laboratory.)

Archeologists have successfully reconstructed murals from Egyptian temples by fitting together photographs of stone fragments as if they were pieces in a gigantic jigsaw puzzle solved by computer matching of similar patterns. In a similar application, but with far fewer pieces to worry about, earth scientists have tested theories of continental drift by doing a computerized comparison of how well the east coast of North and South America fits the west coast of Europe and Africa, and found the fit to be very plausible indeed.

Comparison of Theory and Experiment   Some physical situations are insufficiently well understood to be described according to fundamental principles and therefore must be treated phenomenologically. This implies that an equation devised to cover a phenomenon contains a number of adjustable parameters whose values are not known in advance, or known only within certain bounds. An example is the scattering of nuclear particles, such as protons and electrons from atomic nuclei. In principle, the scattering properties are known (through solution of Schrödinger's equation) when the strength and shape of the force field (or *potential*) causing the scattering (i.e. the target nucleus) is known, but such characteristics of nuclei are extremely difficult to calculate quantitatively from first principles.

The solution is to characterize the potential as having a certain functional form containing several adjustable parameters, such as potential depth, nuclear radius, degree of surface diffuseness, etc., up to as many as eight or nine such parameters. It then becomes a task worthy of a modern computer to vary these parameters to achieve that degree of agreement between theory and experiment that gives the best fit, in the least squares (*q.v.*) sense. This is not a trivial task; it is something like trying to achieve the sharpest possible picture on a color TV set that has nine adjustable knobs and where adjusting one may make it necessary to readjust knobs already set by earlier trial and error. To achieve a reasonable fit, the computer must effectively search through an *n*-dimensional parameter space, recalculating the scattering at reasonably small steps in the parameters along the way. It is not unusual to consume hours of computer time in the process, but the scientist who does this considers the additional insights gained into nuclear structure well worth the effort.

Simulation for Design   The calculational problems associated with the behavior of neutrons in a reactor have been discussed previously, but the rationale for studying these problems was not considered. Initially, through the late 1940s and early 1950s, research data was reasonably fundamental, since the properties of neutron propagation in various materials under a variety of operating conditions were imperfectly understood. As in other fields, however, the widespread use of digital computers accelerated the natural progression of a given type of activity, from research to applied science to engineering. The point has now been reached where most reactor calculations are part of a design engineering process whose aim is to simulate performance of tentative reactor designs in lieu of constructing an experimental prototype. By this technique, many hundreds of design variations can be tested in theory and only the most promising results need be tested in practice.

The preceding example is typical of many applications of simulation to design practice. In the same vein, other large scientific instruments can be engineered to desired specifications through preliminary simulation of a large number of alternative designs. It would now be extremely difficult for humans using precomputer methods to design the large accelerators used in high-energy physics research or the large radio telescopes used in astronomy.

Simulation for Prediction   Another reason for simulating a complex physical system is to predict its behavior. The physical laws governing the motion of planetary bodies are intrinsically simple for two-body systems, but they are intractable analytically for the complex systems of earth, moon, multistage rockets of changing mass, satellites, etc., whose relative motions must be calculated with great precision in order to assure success of the most routine space mission. Of all the technological breakthroughs necessary to support the current space programs of the U.S. and Russia, none was more necessary than the development of reliable high-speed digital computers for design, prediction, and control.

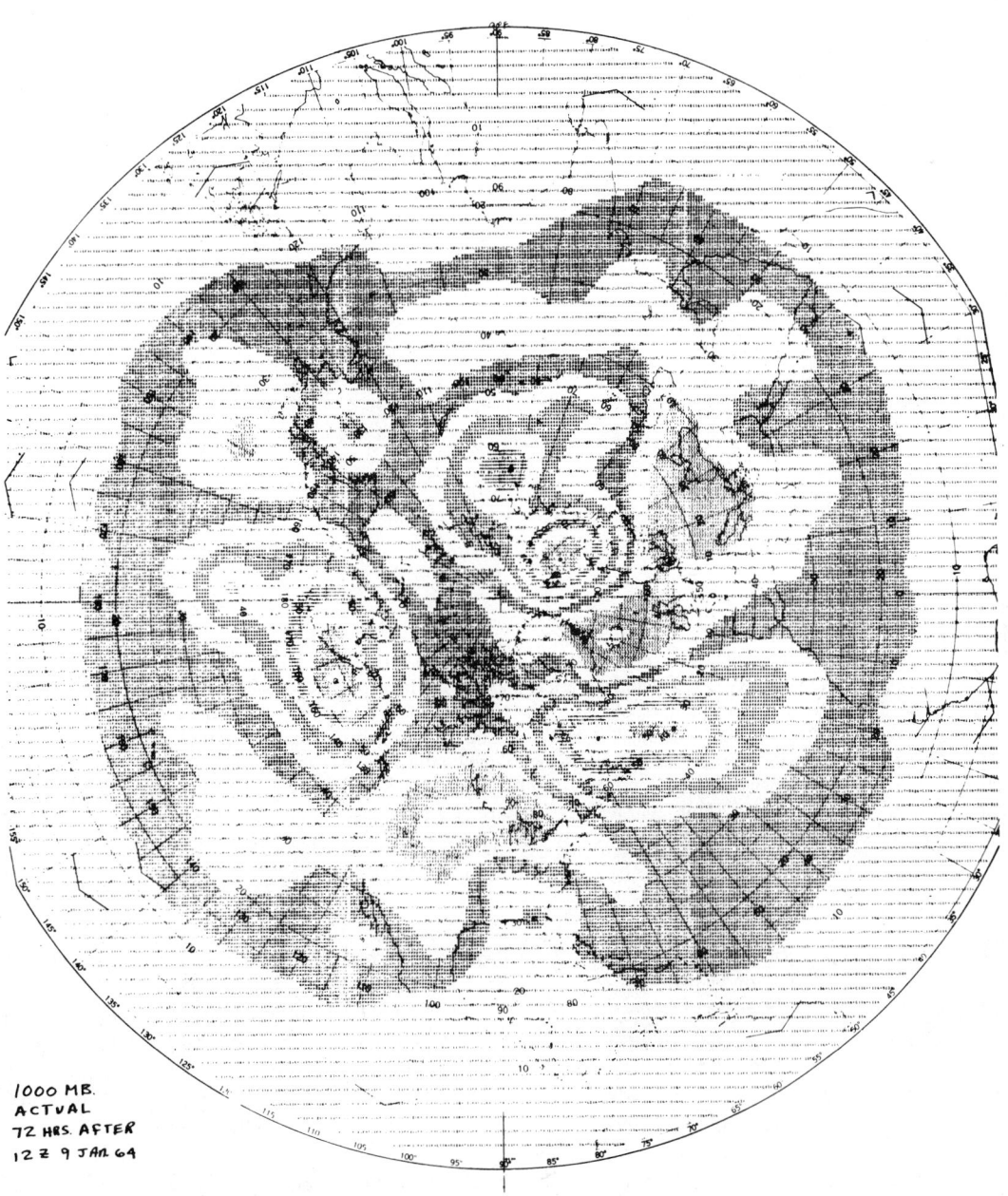

1000 MB.
ACTUAL
72 HRS. AFTER
12 Z 9 JAN 64

FIG. 5.   Computer-produced weather map of the Northern Hemisphere with geographical outlines superimposed. The four-digit numbers are observed geopotential heights of 1,000 mbar surface. The shaded swaths represent lines of constant geopotential intervals and are a rough measure of wind direction, with narrower channels indicating stronger winds.

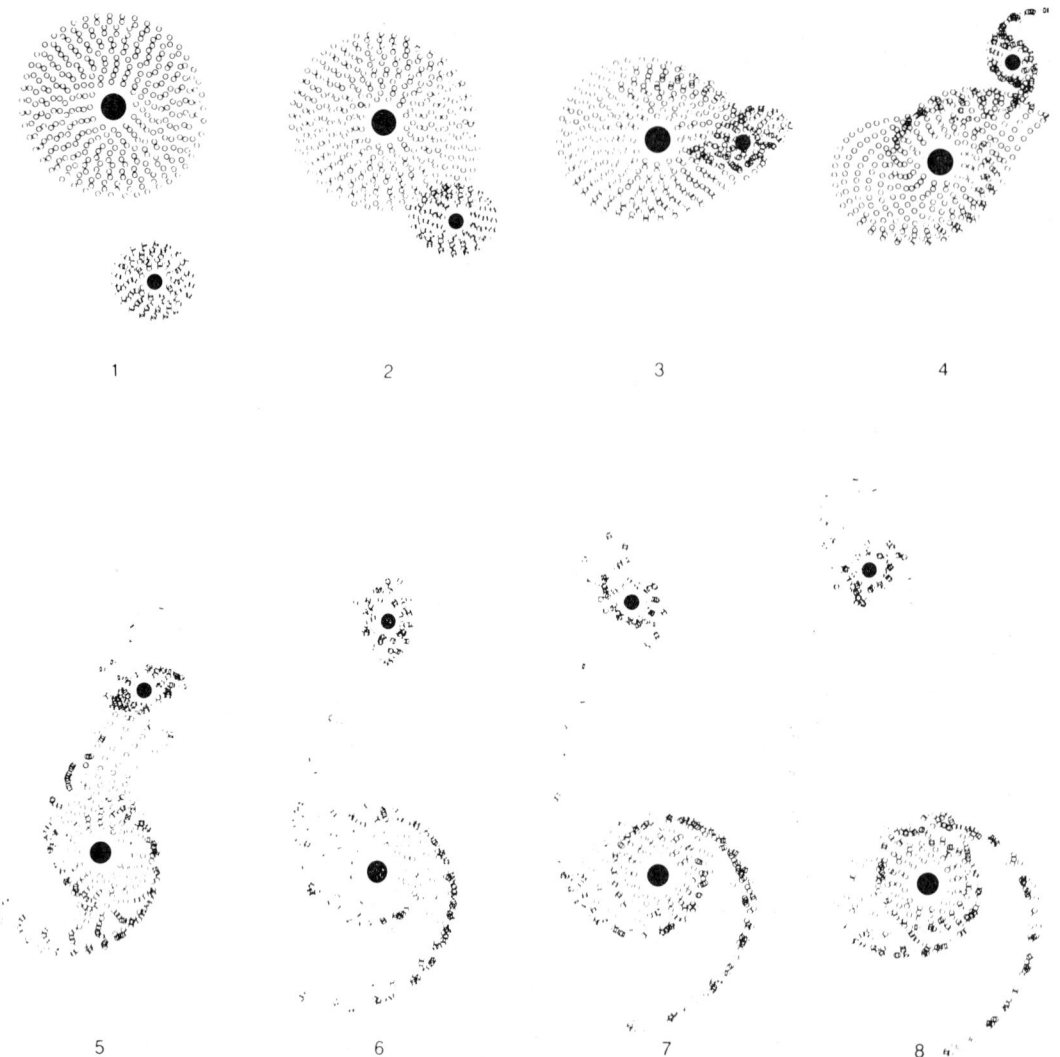

1   2   3   4

5   6   7   8

FIG. 6.   Computer simulation of flyby of small galaxy past a larger one. In time frames *1* and *2*, the barely distorted small galaxy is still rising toward the viewer. At its closest approach to the larger galaxy (*3*), it passes as much in front of it as to the right of it. The tidal effects in both disks (*4*) are distinctly two-sided. As the smaller galaxy recedes (*5–7*), the tide it raised on the side of the larger disk closer to it evolves into a narrow bridge connecting the two galaxies. The similar bulge that it caused on the far side wraps into a fine counterarm that will become sparse and eventually disappear. (From Alar and Juri Toomre, "Violent Tides between Galaxies," © December 1973 by *Scientific American, Inc.* All rights reserved. With permission.)

A second example of simulation for the purpose of prediction is the use of computers for weather forecasting. The equations governing the changes in temperature and pressure with time over even a small region of the earth's surface require large amounts of computer time. With present speeds and memory capacities, it is difficult to forecast changes in weather patterns for a period of more than a few hours, but as machines improve, longer-range forecasts of reasonable reliability may be possible (see Fig. 5).

The use of a high-speed digital computer is also essential for understanding the behavior of plasma material. This particular behavioral simulation is pursued in the hope that it will lead to fusion reactor design, although this objective is presently remote.

A beautiful example of the use of simulation for prediction in astronomy is shown in Fig. 6, where colliding galaxies produce spiral effects. A photograph of an actual galaxy, which may have been produced by exactly this process, is shown for comparison in Fig. 7.

Simulation for Education   As the sophistication and availability of computer display devices increase, computers are being used more and more for educational purposes. Rather than running actual laboratory experiments to determine behavioral characteristics of falling

FIG. 7. Photograph of the whirlpool nebula in the constellation Canis Venatici exemplifies the interior spiral pattern of the star dust and gas. The smaller, irregular galaxy appears to be a genuine companion to the larger one. (Source: Hale Observatories.)

bodies, colliding spheres, pendulums, projectiles, etc., the event to be studied can be simulated at any desired rate on a cathode ray tube display device. The student can then interact with the computer to study the effect of changing parameters, such as the mass of a pendulum bob, the angle of elevation of the initial launch of a rocket, or any one or more of other factors that affect the experiment at hand.

Using such numerical simulation and display techniques, one can even examine phenomena that are closed to easy observation in the laboratory (e.g. the tunneling of a quantum mechanical particle through a potential barrier, the slow-motion fall of water droplets into a pool, or the crashing of water waves upon a beach). These simulations are instructive to watch, and are esthetically pleasing as well. Still photographs of such sequences are often examples of computer art, just as beautiful as other designs created deliberately.

Recent Developments Over the decade that has ensued since the second edition of this encyclopedia, the principal advances in scientific computation have been the development of massively parallel supercomputers; the widespread use of graphically-oriented workstations; the increased use of computer algebra packages such as Derive, Maple, and Mathematica; and the birth of a new subfield called *scientific visualization*. Since all but the last are subjects of separate articles, only visualization will be discussed here.

By scientific visualization is meant the ability to present data in simulated three-dimensional form on a high-resolution color graphics display device, rather than as a simple two-dimensional graph or, worse, the raw form that a printed sequence of numbers would provide. The object depicted may or may not be a "real" one that a human of suitable scale could ever see, or, even when it is, "false color" may be used to bring out interrelationships that would otherwise be difficult to ascertain. An example is the computer-simulated astrophysical jet of

Fig. 8 (see color insert page CP-10). This density image reveals the basic physical features of an extragalactic radio source, including a narrow radio jet, a planar shock wave at the jet terminus, and an extended turbulent lobe, or cocoon, of gas (Burns *et al.,* 1991). But in many ways, the pattern of Fig. 9 (see color insert page CP-10) is more fascinating because the object depicted does not exist as a pattern of matter that could ever be observed by the human eye or any optical instrument (Pickett *et al.,* 1992). The "image" is that of the calculated surfaces in momentum space ("Fermi surfaces") for the charge carriers in the (relatively) high-temperature superconductor $YBa_2Cu_3O_7$. Such a beautiful "object" will never be seen directly and no artist was likely to have rendered it from imagination. Nonetheless, even those who do not benefit from the scientific information it contains can nonetheless enjoy its esthetics through the medium of scientific visualization.

As was just observed, scientific visualization often results in illustrations of such remarkable beauty that they qualify as computer art (*q.v.*). Another example is shown in Fig. 10 (see color insert page CP-11) (Duncan, 1990). The "fountain" is really a theoretical representation of the mass and energy density distribution that would result from the collision of a star with a black hole.

One of the prime applications of scientific visualization is to the study of chaotic behavior, or *chaos* (and its closely related area, the study of fractal (*q.v.*) geometry). The origin of the study of chaos as a distinct branch of scientific endeavor dates to the winter of 1961 when M.I.T. atmospheric scientist Edward Lorenz created a simulated, or "toy," weather system on a primitive computer of that era. Given a particular set of initial conditions, his model weather program would grind away and print out changing patterns of rainfall and temperature that appeared to be very realistic. Ordinarily, the program would be started from scratch each time initial conditions were changed, but one day Lorenz decided to re-enter prior output data, so as to repeat a sequence of results from an earlier run. To his surprise, however, the results obtained from the restarted run began to diverge from the original pattern after just a few time steps. After a few more, there was no resemblance whatsoever. Upon reflection, he realized that, though the program was carrying the equivalent of six decimal digits of precision throughout a run, he had re-entered data to only three. The surprise was that two sets of initial conditions that differed on the average by only one part in a thousand would cause such vastly different output. The result has had a very sobering effect on those who were once optimistic that the evolution of ever faster computers would one day allow very precise long-range weather forecasts. The phenomenon described now carries the formal name "sensitive dependence on initial conditions," but is more affectionately known as the "butterfly effect." The latter term conjures the image that the flapping of a butterfly's wings in China might somehow affect the weather in New York a week or two later.

This "chaotic behavior," as characterized by the degree of difficulty of prediction based on numerical simulation, occurs not just in meteorology but also in many other physical systems whose dynamical equations are nonlinear. With the clue that arose from his weather studies, Lorenz was soon able to show that even such seemingly simple systems as a waterwheel could exhibit chaotic behavior. He found ways of displaying this behavior that essentially anticipated the current fascination with scientific visualization.

Although known to specialists for many years, the beauty of the chaotic images and widespread public acquaintance with chaos theory in general can be dated to the appearance of James Gleick's bestseller *Chaos: Making a New Science* (Gleick, 1987). Using text and pictures that were equally colorful, Gleick introduced the public to the Lorenz Attractor and other *strange attractors,* diagrams that showed that certain chaotic systems exhibited a behavior that caused them to settle into, or oscillate around, particular loci in the diagram. The Lorenz Attractor in meteorology is the solution of a set of differential equations in three-dimensional space. Other well-studied strange attractors are the Henon attractor in astrophysics, the Yorke attractor in chemistry, and the Logistic Map in ecology.

The Lorenz Attractor has been reprinted so often (*see* FRACTALS) that we will not do so here, but an example of an even more beautiful strange attractor is shown in Fig. 11 (see color insert page CP-11). The pattern shows the behavior of a pendulum whose bob is magnetized and allowed to swing freely from a chosen initial position above an array of magnets arranged on the plane below the pendulum. To produce the diagram, each magnet is imagined to carry a different color. The pendulum will move erratically ("chaotically"), tracing an irregular, aperiodic path among the magnets, but eventually settle down in the "basin of attractiveness" of a particular magnet. Each point of the figure is then colored to correspond to the color of the magnet that captures the bob released from that point. The attractors that can be readily identified are "strange" because they are sometimes able to capture bobs that are started much closer to competing magnets.

Since physical phenomena follow laws that can be described mathematically, it is not surprising that iteration of certain mathematical equations can also produce strange attractors. Consider, for example, the very simple equation $z^4 - 1 = 0$. This equation has four obvious roots, $+1, -1, +i$, and $-i$, where i is the imaginary unit, $\sqrt{-1}$. Suppose, however, that we did not know those roots and sought to ascertain them through iteration: choose an initial guess, obtain an improved guess through use of the Newton-Raphson technique, and repeat until successive iterates pass a suitable convergence criterion. For the stated equation, the improved guess z_1 that results from a guess z_0 is $z_1 = (3 + 1/z_0^3)/4$. Now, if one were to make a guess close to an actual root, 1.1 or $-0.9i$, for example, a few iterations would show convergence to the closest root (1 and $-i$, respectively). But suppose the guess is not as good, $1/3 - i/4$, for example. In the complex plane, this guess is closest to the root at $+1$ and next closest to the root at $-i$, but its iteration actually leads to convergence to the root $+i$! So, as can readily be seen from the Fig. 12

(see color insert page CP-11), the root with the yellow basin, $+i$, is strangely able to attract initial guesses that lie in the yellow areas far from $+i$ and much closer to other roots. Furthermore, the incredible detail is fractal-like; if we were to zoom in on portions of the figure, ever smaller sections would be self-similar to patterns already seen.

Summary Digital computers are now being used in every facet of scientific work, ranging from initial library research through the preparation of copy for final journal publication on a word processing (*q.v.*) system. Wherever there occurs an element of drudgery in daily routine, there may be yet another computer application to lighten the load and leave the scientist free to concentrate on providing the human inspirational breakthroughs that cannot be automated. Although individual genius will create new systems in the future, as it has in the past, the average working scientist today cannot be competitive without access to a digital computer and reasonable proficiency in its use.

References

Journals
Computers in Physics. Woodbury, NY: American Institute of Physics.
Journal of Computational Physics. New York: Academic Press.
Journal of Scientific Computing. New York: Plenum Press.
Pixel: The Magazine of Scientific Visualization. Watsonville, CA: Pixel Communications, Inc.
SIAM Journal on Scientific and Statistical Computing

Books and Articles
1980. Rodrique, R., Giroux, E., and Pratt, M. "Perspectives on Large-Scale Scientific Computation," Computer **13**, *10* (October): 65–80.
1986. Annino, R. and Driver, R. *Scientific and Engineering Applications with Personal Computers.* New York: John Wiley.
1987. Gleick, J. *Chaos: Making a New Science.* New York: Viking.
1989. Nash, T. "The New Landscape of Parallel Computing in High-Energy Physics," *Sun Technology* **2**, *3* (Summer): 66–75.
1990. Duncan, G. C. "Visualizing the Collision of a Star with a Black Hole," *Pixel* **1**, *3* (July/August): 24–29.
1990. Wolff, R. S. "Visualization 101: A Tour Guide of Basic Concepts," *Computers in Physics* **4**, *3* (May/June): 260–265.
1990. Pickover, C. A. "The World of Chaos," *Computers in Physics,* **4**, *5* (September/October): 460–467.
1990. Chervin, R. M. "High Performance Computing and the Grand Challenge of Climate Modeling," *Computers in Physics* **4**, *3* (May/June): 234–239.
1990. Nash, S. (Ed.) *A History of Scientific Computing.* Reading, MA: ACM Press/Addison-Wesley.
1991. Lander, E. S., Langridge, R., and Saccocio, D. M. "Computing in Molecular Biology: Mapping and Interpreting Biological Information," *Computer* **24**, *11* (November): 6–13.
1991. Burns, J. O., Norman, M. L., and Clarke, D. A. "Numerical Models of Extragalactic Radio Sources," *Science* **253**, *5019* (2 August): 522–530.
1992. Pickett, W. E., Krakauer, H., Cohen, R. E., and Singh, D. J. "Fermi Surfaces, Fermi Liquids, and High-Temperature Superconductors," *Science* **255**, *5040* (3 January): 46–53.
1992. Bitar, K. M. and Heller, U. M. "Lattice Field Simulations Press the Limits of Computational Physics," *Computers in Physics,* **6**, *1* (January/February): 33–40.

EDWIN D. REILLY

SCRATCH FILE

For articles on related subjects *see* FILE; and MEMORY: AUXILIARY.

During the processing of substantial files of data, it often becomes necessary to create temporary files for later use by copying all or part of a data set to an auxiliary-memory device—tape, disk, or drum. Such a temporary file (or the associated storage device) is called a *scratch file*.

In most installations, scratch-file devices are the fastest available: drums or fixed-head disk drives; other disk drives; or high-speed magnetic tapes. In large installations, several disk drives (or tape drives, or both) are often allocated permanently for general-user scratch-file storage. In a multiprogramming environment, several users can simultaneously allocate modest amounts of scratch-file storage from this pool. This tends to economize the number of disk drives required at an installation, compared to the alternative strategy of having each user furnish private packs for scratch files.

DAVID N. FREEMAN

SCREEN EDITOR. *See* TEXT EDITING SYSTEMS.

SCS. *See* SOCIETY FOR COMPUTER SIMULATION.

SDI (SELECTIVE DISSEMINATION OF INFORMATION). *See* CURRENT AWARENESS SYSTEM.

SEAC

For articles on related subjects *see* DIGITAL COMPUTERS: HISTORY: EARLY; EDVAC; and SWAC.

In 1947, with the encouragement of the U.S. Navy, the National Bureau of Standards (NBS) established the National Applied Mathematical Laboratories under the leadership of John Curtiss. The purpose was to create a centralized national computation facility equipped with high-speed automatic computers, which would provide a computing service for other governmental agencies and play an active part in the further development of computing machinery.

The Census Bureau, the U.S. Air Force, and the U.S. Navy all supported the Laboratories, and negotiations for the acquisition of computers from Eckert and Mauchly (later acquired by Sperry Rand), from Engineering Research Associates (a supplier to the security agencies), and from Raytheon Corporation (RAYDAC), were under way in 1948. Impatient with the slow devel-

opment of computers, and feeling the need for more "hands-on" expertise, the NBS decided at a meeting in May 1948 to build its own computer; later in the same year the decision was made to build a second computer at the Institute for Numerical Analysis, an NBS field station located at the University of California at Los Angeles. These two Bureau computers became known as the SEAC and SWAC (Standards Eastern and Standards Western Automatic Computers).

The SEAC, built under the direction of Samuel Alexander, used mercury delay lines for storage. Its design was based on the EDVAC (*q.v.*) at the University of Pennsylvania. The original memory used the same type of mercury delay lines, consisting of 64 eight-word lines operating at a clock rate of 1 MHz. Initial input and output was by punched paper tape. Later, magnetic wire and magnetic tape replaced the paper tape, and a Williams' tube memory (*q.v.*) was added to the system.

Addition time (including storage access) ranged from 192 to 1,540 ms, and multiply time from 2,300 to 3,600 ms. The SEAC was the first stored-program computer to run in the U.S. It was dedicated in May 1950 and was in operation until October 1964.

References

1951. Alexander, S. N. "The National Bureau of Standards Eastern Automatic Computer (SEAC)," *IRE Eastern Joint Computer Conference,* 84–89.
1953. Shupe, P., D., Jr. and Kirsch, R. A. "SEAC—A review of Three Years of Operation," *IRE Eastern Joint Computer Conference,* 83–90.

HARRY D. HUSKEY

SEARCHING

For articles on related subjects *see* DATA STRUCTURES; LIST PROCESSING; SORTING; and TREE.

Introduction For a given *searching* problem, the particular choice of an algorithm/data structure depends on the nature of the storage medium (internal memory, magnetic tape, disk, or other), on the nature of the data being organized (does it change through insertions or deletions, is it alphabetic or numeric, are some elements more likely to occur as search objects than others etc.), and on the requirements of the search (must it be fast on average or in the worst case, how much information is available, etc.). We describe some of the most important algorithms and data structures.

We will assume that we are searching a *table* of *n* elements, in which each element has a collection of *fields* associated with it, one field for each of a number of *attributes*. One of these attributes will be the *key* that is used to refer to the element and on which the searching is based.

Lists In organizing a table as a list, we can vary only two things: the order of the elements in the list and the implementation as either an array, a linked list, or some other appropriate data structure (*q.v.*). The elements may be in no particular order, in an order based on their frequencies as search objects, or in their natural order (alphabetic or numeric).

There is a trade-off between arrays and linked lists: the ease with which we can randomly access any element in an array makes it ideal under certain conditions, while under other conditions the ease of insertion and deletion makes a linked list more appropriate. Situations also occur in which both efficient access and ease of modification are needed simultaneously, but neither arrays nor linked lists are then appropriate; instead, dynamic trees (see below) should be considered.

Linear Search *Linear search* examines each element in turn to see if it is the one sought, continuing until either the element is found or all the elements in the list have been examined. The order of the elements in the list does not affect the correctness of this algorithm, only the amount of the time it requires.

The performance of linear search is based on the number of *probes* into the list: a probe is a comparison between the search object and the key of an element in the table. We evaluate all search strategies by the number of probes required to find an object, both in the worst case and on average. The amount of work in searching for an element is not entirely in the probes, but the total work done is usually proportional to the number of probes, since only a constant number of operations are done per probe. The behavior of linear search is summarized as:

	Worst Case	Best Case	Average Case
Successful search	n probes	1 probe	$\sum_{i=1}^{n} ip_i$ probes
Unsuccessful search	n probes	n probes	n probes

where p_i is the probability that the ith item on the list is sought. If all the probabilities $p_i = 1/n$, a successful search will use an average of $\sum_{i=1}^{n} ip_i = \sum_{i=1}^{n} i/n = (n+1)/2$ probes; i.e. we expect to search half the list.

When the probabilities are not all equal, we can improve linear search by arranging the list so that the value $\sum_{i=1}^{n} ip_i$ is minimized. The minimum value occurs when the items are in decreasing order by frequency (i.e. when $p_1 \geq p_2 \geq \cdots \geq p_n$), but it is seldom possible to determine the access probabilities a priori. Even empirical observation may not give an accurate picture of the probabilities if they fluctuate in time. We can still take advantage of non-uniform access probabilities, however, by allowing the order of the elements in the table to change dynamically so that those accessed frequently gradually move to the front of the table. Such a list is called *self-organizing*.

The idea is that when an element is accessed, it is moved to a position closer to the beginning of the table. The amount of work to do this movement must be reasonable, and so the possibilities are limited. If the table is an array, we can use the *move-ahead-one strategy* or the *interchange-to-the-front strategy*. If the table is a linked list, we can, in addition, use the *move-to-the-front strategy*.

The move-ahead-one strategy, applicable to either linked lists or arrays, works well to keep the table well arranged if the table order is not too far from the desired order. However, initially it will take quite a while for the popular elements to propagate to the beginning of the list, since they move so slowly. On the other hand, the move-to-the-front strategy, applicable only to linked lists, works well to order the elements quickly when they are far out of order, but it causes erratic behavior in a table that is nearly in order; the interchange-to-the-front strategy is even worse in this regard. Thus, it is most reasonable to apply to the move-to-front strategy initially until the table order settles down, and continue thereafter with the move-ahead-one strategy.

Ordered Lists If it is possible to maintain the list in some natural order (such as numeric or alphabetic), it is almost always advantageous to do so. Linear search can then be speeded up somewhat for unsuccessful searches because in an ordered table the search can stop when it discovers the first element beyond what it is seeking, rather than go all the way to the end of the list.

The improvement for unsuccessful search times in tables in the natural order is minor in contrast to the fact that a single probe into the table can now get a good deal more information than when the table is in some other order: By comparing the item sought to the key of the middle element of the table, we can determine which half of the table is of further interest. Continuing this idea recursively yields *binary search* (see Figure 1), whose behavior is summarized in Table 1.

```
procedure BinarySearch(
    var x: ArrayType; { array to be searched }
    l: integer; { the low end of the subrange to be
                  searched }
    h: integer; { the high end of the subrange to be
                  searched }
    z: ElementType; { the object of the search }
    var loc: integer); { the location of z in x, if it was found;
                  loc = − ∞ if it was not found. }
var m: integer;
begin { BinarySearch }
    loc : = − ∞; { assume it won't be found}
    if l ≤ h then begin
    m : = (l + h) div 2;
    if z < x[m] then { search left half recursively }
        BinarySearch (x, l, m − 1, z, loc)
    else if z > x [m] then { search right half recursively }
        BinarySearch (x, m + 1, h, z, loc)
    else { found it }
    loc : = m
    end { if l ≤ h }
end; { BinarySearch }
```

FIG. 1. A Pascal implementation of the binary search procedure.

TABLE 1.

	Worst Case	Best Case	Average Case
Successful search	$\lceil \lg(n + 1) \rceil$ probes	1 probe	$(1 + \frac{1}{n}) \lg \lg(n + 1) + o(1)$ probes
Unsuccessful search	$\lceil \lg(n + 1) \rceil$ probes	$\lfloor \lg(n + 1) \rfloor$ probes	$\lg(n + 1) + o(1)$ probes

The function "lg" is the base-two logarithm, (i.e. $\log_2$) .

The values given for the number of probes in the average successful and unsuccessful searches are based on the assumption that for successful searches each of the n elements is equally probable as the place for the search to end. This assumption is rarely justified in practice, but is the only reasonable one to make in the absence of any information. When the access probabilities are known, it is possible to use the optimal search trees discussed below.

There may be useful statistical properties of the table that can aid the search. For example, in looking up the name "Smith" in a phone book, we would be unlikely to probe first at the midpoint and then at the three-quarters point, etc., as in binary search. Instead, we would assume that under normal conditions the name "Smith" would be found near the end of the listings, and we would begin our search nearer to the expected location of the search object. This idea leads to *interpolation search*.

For simplicity, assume we are dealing with numeric values $x_1 < x_2 < \cdots < x_n$, uniformly distributed in the range (x_0, x_{n+1}). If we are searching such a table for z, $x_0 < z < x_{n+1}$, the uniform distribution suggests that we interpolate linearly to determine the expected location of z. That expected location is $n(z - x_0)/(x_{n+1} - x_0)$, and this is where we should probe first. In general, if we know that $x_l < z < x_h$, then we should probe at location

$$l + \frac{z - x_l}{x_h - x_l} (h - l - 1).$$

The number of probes used in interpolation search is:

	Worst Case	Best Case	Average Case
Successful search	n probes	1 probe	lglg n probes
Unsuccessful search	n probes	2 probes	lglg n probes

The average behavior of interpolation search is a much different "average" than was considered for either linear search or binary search. In those cases, the table of elements was fixed and the average was over the occurrences of the various elements as search objects; in this case, the average is over search objects *and* tables whose elements follow a certain statistical pattern. If a particular table does not follow that pattern, the average search in that table will be poorer than expected. Furthermore, the greatly increased cost per probe in interpolation search means that interpolation search is inferior to binary search, unless the tables are much larger than most tables occurring in practice.

Binary Search Trees   A *binary search tree* is a binary tree of the table elements in which every element x has the lexicographic property that the elements in the left subtree of x are before the key of x in the natural order and the elements in the right subtree of x are after the key of x in the natural order. This property of the tree makes it easy to search for an element z: Compare z to the key of the root element; if the keys are equal, the search ends successfully, and if they are not, search the left or right right subtree according to whether z is less than or greater than the key of the root element, respectively. Fig. 2 shows a binary search tree of 16 common English words.

Static Trees   The application of binary search trees to static tables is concerned entirely with choosing the tree that minimizes search time; we assume that the table is constructed once and that its contents never change or change so infrequently that the entire table will be reconstructed to make the change. If we want to minimize the worst-case search time, we simply use the tree corresponding to binary search, and we do not need an explicit tree at all. The more difficult problem is to minimize the average search time, given some frequency distribution of how the search will end. If the table consists of elements $x_1 < x_2 < \cdots < x_n$, then the search can end successfully at any of the x_i (internal nodes) and unsuccessfully in any of the $n + 1$ intervals (leaves) specified by the x_i and the endpoints. If we are given the relative frequencies with which the search ends in these $2n + 1$ ways, we can use dynamic programming to determine the optimal shape of the tree that minimizes the average search time.

The dynamic programming algorithm can be implemented in quadratic time, but it may not be worth

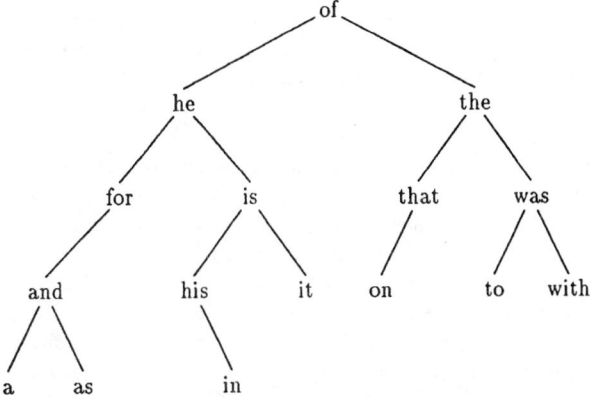

FIG. 2.   A binary search tree of 16 common English words.

spending so much time to construct the optimal tree if we have only inaccurate values for the relative frequencies. Instead, we should use a heuristic to construct a "near-optimal tree" rapidly.

The *balancing heuristic* chooses the root so as to equalize (as much as possible) the frequencies with which a search will end in the left and right subtrees. The cost of the resulting tree is always extremely close to the cost of the optimal tree. That the balancing rule does so well is even more remarkable, since it can be implemented in time linear in the number of elements in the table.

Dynamic Trees Binary search trees can be used for dynamic tables—tables whose contents change because of insertions and deletions. There is a conflict between efficient search algorithms and efficient modification: Fast search requires a rigid structure, while fast modification needs a flexible structure; *balanced trees* provide a compromise between the two requirements.

Logarithmic search times can be achieved by keeping the tree perfectly balanced at all times (as is implicit in binary search). Unfortunately, when the tree is thus constrained, it is quite costly to insert or delete an element. Instead, we allow a limited flexibility in the shape of the tree so that insertions and deletions will not be so expensive, yet search times will remain logarithmic. Such techniques keep the trees "balanced" so that they cannot become too skewed (and hence degenerate to linear search times). The height of such trees of n elements will be $O(\log n)$ so that search times are logarithmic. Insertions and deletions will require only local changes along a single path from the root to a leaf, thus requiring only time proportional to the height of the tree, which is logarithmic.

There are several strategies for keeping binary trees balanced as they undergo insertions and deletions. A binary tree is *height-balanced* (or *AVL*) if, at any node in the tree, the two subtrees of that node differ in height by at most one. A height-balanced binary tree of n elements will have height at most about $1.44\lg(n + 1)$, so, if a search tree is kept height-balanced, the worst-case search time will be logarithmic. A two-bit *condition code* is stored at each node; the condition code specifies whether the two subtrees have equal height, the left subtree is taller by one, or the right subtree is taller by one.

A binary tree is *weight-balanced* if, at any node in the tree, neither of the two subtrees contains more than a specified fraction f, $0 < f < 1/2$, of the nodes. A weight-balanced binary tree of n elements will have height at most about $\dfrac{\lg(n+1)}{-\lg(1-f)}$, so, if a search tree is kept weight-balanced, the worst-case search time will be logarithmic. The choice of f allows an explicit trade-off between search times and rebalancing times. If $2/11 \le f \le 1 - \sqrt{2}/2$, insertions and deletions can be accommodated so that a weight-balanced tree remains weight-balanced afterward. The size of the subtree is stored at each node.

Binary trees can also be kept balanced by a simple scheme in which the edges connecting nodes of the tree are colored either red or black. The balancing rule is that all paths from the root of the tree to a leaf contain the

same number of black edges and that there are never two red edges in a row along such a path; the height of such a tree with n elements will be at most $2\lg(n + 1)$. The trees are implemented by using a single bit at each node, specifying the color of the incoming edge.

In the balanced trees discussed above, some explicit balance information is maintained in each node and the trees are rebalanced on the basis of that information. Instead of maintaining such information, *splay trees* adjust the tree at each access, as well as upon an insertion or deletion. The adjustment is made along the access path, and its effect is to bring the accessed item to the root of the tree. This is similar to the move-to-the-front strategy in self-organizing lists. The resulting trees are not guaranteed to have logarithmic height, so some accesses, insertions, and deletions will be relatively costly, but the *amortized behavior* of these trees is logarithmic: The total time required by any sequence of m tree operations starting with an initially empty tree is $O(m \log n)$, where n is the number of insertion operations. Even more remarkably, splay trees are, to within a constant factor, as efficient in the amortized sense as optimal binary search trees.

Digital Search Trees We can use trees to organize tables based on the representation of the elements, rather than on the ordering of the elements, as in the previous section. If the alphabet contains c characters, each node in the tree would be a c-way branch—one branch for each possible character. The structure thus obtained, is called a *digital search tree* or *trie* (taken from the middle letters of the word "retrieval," but pronounced "try"). This concept is illustrated in Fig. 3, which shows eight mathematical constants.

To explain Fig. 3, we describe how to search it. Suppose we are given the number 1.414 as the object of the search. We consider each of the digits 1, 4, 1, and 4 in turn, starting at the root of the tree and proceeding as follows. Follow the branch labeled 1 out of the root; at the next node follow the branch labeled 4, then the branch labeled 1, and finally the branch labeled 4. At that point we are at the bottom of the tree and the letters of the search object

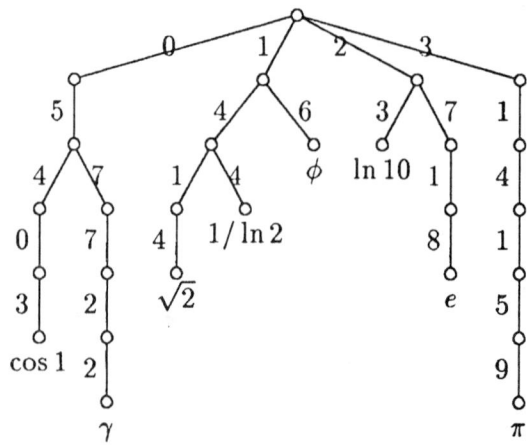

FIG. 3. A trie of eight mathematical constants.

are exhausted, so we have successfully found 1.414 in the tree. If the search object had been 1.413, we would have followed down branches in the tree corresponding to 1, 4, and 1, but then there would be no branch labeled 3, indicating that 1.413 is not in the tree.

The advantage of a digital search tree is that in many circumstances the multiway branch required at every node of the tree will require little or no more time than a binary decision.

Hashing

In *hashing*, an element is stored in a location computed directly from the key of the element. Suppose that we have an array of m table locations $T[0..m-1]$ and are given an element z to be inserted; we transform z to a location $h(z)$, $0 \le h(z) < m$, where h is called a *hash function* and $h(z)$ is called the *hash address*. We then examine $T[h(z)]$ to see if it is empty. If it is empty, we store z there, and we are done. If $T[h(z)]$ is not empty, a *collision* has occurred, and we must resolve it somehow. Taken together, the hash function and the collision resolution method are referred to as *hashing* or *scatter storage* schemes.

Under the proper conditions, hashing is unsurpassed in its efficiency as a table organization because the average times for a search or an insertion are generally *independent of the size of the table*. Some important caveats are in order, however. First, in the worst case, collisions occur every time and hashing degenerates into linear search. Second, while it is easy to make insertions into a hash table, the full size of the table must be specified a priori, because it is usually closely connected to the hash function used; this makes it extremely expensive to change dynamically. Third, deletions from the table are not easily accommodated in most schemes. Finally, the order of the elements in the table is unrelated to any natural order among the elements, and so an unsuccessful search tells us only that the element sought is not in the table; we obtain no information about how it relates to the elements that are in the table.

Hash Function

The hash function takes an element to be stored in a table and transforms it into a location in the table. If this transformation makes certain table locations more likely to occur than others, it is said to exhibit *primary clustering*. This increases the chance of collisions and decreases the efficiency of searches and insertions. The ideal hash function spreads the elements uniformly throughout the table without primary clustering.

There are four basic techniques used for constructing hash functions. While there are no absolute rules, there are several important principles. A hash function should depend on *all* the bits of the element, not just some of them. A hash function should break up naturally occurring clusters of elements. A hash function should be quick and easy to compute. The properties of any particular hash function are hard to determine because they depend so heavily on the set of elements that will be encountered in practice.

The simplest hash functions merely extract a few scattered bits from an element, putting those bits together to form an address. Such *extraction hash functions* are generally a poor way to do hashing except in *ad hoc* situations where the table contents are completely known in advance and the bits to be extracted can be carefully chosen to prevent primary clustering. The weakness of extraction is that the resulting location depends on only a small subset of the bits of an element.

A simple way to get a location from an element in such a way that every bit of the element participates is to compress the bits of the element into the number required for an address. For example, one could break a bit string to be hashed into fixed-length segments and then add them as binary numbers or take their exclusive-or. One weakness of such a method of compression is that the operations of addition and exclusive-or are commutative, so that permutations of the segments yield the same hash value. It is better to shift different segments circularly by different amounts. *Compression hash functions* are most useful for converting multi-word elements into a single word, making it easy to apply either the division- or multiplication-based hash functions that we now describe.

Given a table $T[0..m-1]$, we can take $h(z) = z \bmod m$; i.e. $h(z)$ is the remainder when z is divided by m. In using such a *division hash function*, one must choose the value of m carefully to insure that the hash location depends on all the bits of the element and that naturally occurring clusters are broken up. It generally works out best if m is prime. Furthermore, it is undesirable for $r^k \equiv \pm a \pmod{m}$, for "small" values of a and k, where r is the radix of the objects being hashed (bytes, digits, characters, or whatever).

Given a real number θ, $0 < \theta, 1$, we can construct a hash function $h(z) = \lfloor m \times (z\theta \bmod 1) \rfloor$; i.e. compute the fractional part of the product $z\theta$, multiply it by m, and take the greatest integer in the product. Unlike division hash functions, with *multiplication hash functions* we need not be concerned with the table size m, but we do need some guidelines in choosing θ. θ should not be too close to 0 or 1, nor should $r^k\theta \bmod 1$ be close to 1 for small values of k, where r is the radix of the objects being hashed. Values of θ approximately $i/(r^k - 1)$ are also problematic in terms of clustering.

Collision Resolution

A *collision* occurs when the location $T[h(z)]$ is already filled at the time we try to insert z. A *collision-resolution scheme* specifies a list of table locations then to be considered for z; these locations are inspected (in order) until an empty one is found. There are two choices: to store pointers describing the sequence explicitly (chaining), or to specify the sequence implicitly by a fixed relationship with z (linear probing).

In *chaining*, a sequence of pointers is built from the hash location $h(z)$ to the location in which z is ultimately stored. In *separate chaining*, each table location $T[i]$ points to a linked list of those elements z with $h(z) = i$. These lists can be kept in order or not, as appropriate. Separate chaining is most efficient in cases where dynamic allocation can be used. If dynamic allocation is unavailable or undesirable, we can use *coalesced chaining*, in which the record for each table location $T[i]$ contains a field NEXT. When $T[h(z)]$ is found to contain another element on an attempted insertion of z, we follow the NEXT fields until we reach one that is null; then we take an arbitrary empty table location, set that last null NEXT field to point to it, and store z there.

Assuming that we use a hash function devoid of primary clustering and that collisions are resolved by coalesced chaining, the average number of probes in a successful search in a table of m locations containing n elements is $S(\lambda) \approx 1 + \frac{1}{8\lambda}(e^{2\lambda} - 1 - 2\lambda) + \frac{1}{4}\lambda$, where $\lambda = n/m$ is called the *load factor* of the table. The behavior of a collision-resolution scheme is expressed in terms of λ because the behavior of the algorithms is governed by the fullness of the table in relative rather than absolute terms. In an unsuccessful search the average number of probes is $U(\lambda) \approx 1 + \frac{1}{4}(e^{2\lambda} - 1 - 2\lambda)$. For separate chaining, the corresponding formulas are $S(\lambda) \approx 1 + \frac{1}{2}\lambda$ and $U(\lambda) \approx e^{-\lambda}\lambda$ λ for unordered lists, and $U(\lambda) \approx 1 + \frac{1}{2}\lambda - \frac{1}{\lambda}(1 - e^{-\lambda}) + e^{-\lambda}$ for ordered lists.

The simplest alternative to chaining that does not require the storage of NEXT fields is to resolve collisions by probing sequentially, one location at a time, starting from the hash address, until an empty location is found. This is called *open addressing with linear probing*, or simply *linear probing*. Again assuming we use a hash function devoid of primary clustering, when collisions are resolved by linear probing, the average number of probes in a successful search in a table of m locations containing n elements is $S(\lambda) \approx \frac{1}{2}\left(1 + \frac{1}{1 - \lambda}\right)$ and in an unsuccessful search $U(\lambda) \approx \frac{1}{2}\left[1 + \frac{1}{1 - \lambda^2}\right]$.

Linear probing exhibits *secondary clustering*: the tendency of two elements that have collided to follow the same sequence of locations in the resolution of the collision. Such a tendency will aggravate the unavoidable fact that long lists are more likely to grow than short lists. To avoid secondary clustering we want the sequence of locations followed in resolving a collision of z to be a function of z. This can be accomplished by only a minor change to linear probing—instead of probing sequentially for an empty location, increment by an amount that is a function of z. To insure that every location in the table will be probed on a collision, the increment and m must be relatively prime. If m is a prime, we can use another hash function $\delta(z)$, $1 \leq \delta(z)$, m as the increment. This method is called *double hashing*.

Assume that we use a hash function devoid of primary clustering and further that our increment function $\delta(z)$ is ideal in the sense that all $m!$ probe sequences are equally likely in resolving the collision. Then, when collisions are resolved by double hashing, the average number of probes in a successful search in a table of m locations containing n elements is $S(\lambda) \approx \frac{1}{\lambda}\ln\frac{1}{1-\lambda}$ and in an unsuccessful search $U(\lambda) \approx \frac{1}{1-\lambda}$.

There may be a natural order of the elements that can be used to speed up unsuccessful searches in hash tables. Such an order is utilized by having an element that is being inserted "bump" a smaller element already in the table from its place during an insertion; the insertion then continues with the bumped element being inserted. The bumping makes the table appear as though its contents were inserted in decreasing order, which has the effect of reducing unsuccessful search times, just as in the case of linear search. For double hashing, the average cost of an unsuccessful search is reduced to $U(\lambda) \approx \frac{1}{\lambda}\ln\frac{1}{1-\lambda}$.

Deletion and Rehashing Except in separate chaining, deletion of an element from a hash table poses special problems. We cannot simply remove an element from the table, because such a removal will disrupt the probe sequence for elements that collided with the one to be deleted. We can mark the table location as containing an element that has been deleted. Such a location acts like an empty location with respect to insertions, but like a full location with respect to searches. This means that search times will not change for the better after a deletion; for example, if we fill a table to 90% of its capacity and then delete half the elements, the table still behaves like a table 90% full as far as searching is concerned.

The only solution to the problem of degraded search times is the ultimate reconstruction of the table by a process called *rehashing*, in which each table location is scanned in turn and its contents, if any, are relocated as necessary. Such a rehashing process is expensive, since it requires time proportional to the table size.

Table Look-up Suppose that all items z to be stored in table $T[0..m-1]$ have associated with them a unique key k such that $0 \leq k < m$. Then the simplest conceivable hash function h is $h(k) = k$, i.e. k itself is usable as a naturally occurring index into the table. In such a case, hashing is collision-free and degenerates to simple *table look-up*. If, for example, each of the 51 geographic units that comprise the U.S. is numbered 0 to 50 and their respective populations are stored in $T[0..50]$, then we can "look up" the population of the kth state by accessing $T[k]$.

Tables in External Storage The methods of table organization that have been presented so far are geared to internal memory—memory that can be accessed randomly at speeds matching the speed of the computer itself. For small or medium-sized temporary tables, internal memory is fine, but for large or long-term tables we must rely on relatively slow external memory devices such as magnetic tapes, disks, or drums.

Magnetic Tapes Magnetic tape is a sequential storage medium, so that, to examine the ith record on the tape, it is necessary to have examined or moved past the first $i-1$ records. Essentially, then, organizing a table on magnetic tape is the same as using a linked list. Such a table must be searched in a linear fashion, and the only possible refinement is to order the records on the tape so as to minimize search time. The two relevant orders are (1) the natural order of the records (alphabetical or numerical) or (2) so that $p_1/L_1 \le p_2/L_2 \le \cdots \le p_n/L_n$ where p_i is the probability that the ith record is the search object and L_i is its length—the cost of reading it into memory. In general, magnetic tapes are a poor choice for storing frequently accessed information unless that information will always be scanned in a linear fashion.

Disks and Drums Disks and drums allow random access to all records stored, but the time required for such an access is great compared to internal memory speeds. There is a high overhead in time to initiate an *access*—i.e. a transfer of records from the disk or drum to internal memory. Efficient organization of tables on disks and drums thus requires minimizing the number of times such an access is initiated and transferring large numbers of records on each access.

Since accesses are costly compared to probes, it is preferable to make many probes for each disk access. Thus, to adapt search trees to disks or drums we use m-way branches instead of two-way (binary) branches. Typically, m will be several hundred; the best choice for m depends on the precise physical characteristics of the storage device (access and transfer times), the size of the elements in the table, and the amount of internal memory available to store elements. As with binary search trees, it is quite time-consuming to keep the tree perfectly balanced while inserting and deleting: We only insist that all paths from the root to a leaf node are of equal length and that each node except the root has at least $\lceil m/2 \rceil$ subtrees. Such a tree is called a *balanced multiway tree* or *B-tree*. Search times remain logarithmic and insertions and deletions can be accommodated. In the worst case, B-trees waste about 50% of their space, but on average the storage utilization will be about 69%.

We can adapt hashing schemes to disks by having the address computed by the hash function be a disk address. To minimize the number of disk accesses needed on a search, we should enlarge the basic table component from a single element to a group of b elements called a *bucket*; a hash address would specify the disk address of a bucket, and a disk access would retrieve all the elements of the bucket. The elements in a bucket would then be searched. We should also spend much more time in computing the hash function so as to minimize collisions. Because we are hashing to buckets rather than individual table locations, we expect collisions to be no problem and can use a relatively simple-minded scheme to resolve them.

Some schemes for hashing allow the table size to be extended dynamically. These schemes, which impose a tree-like structure on the hash table, are suitable for large hash tables on disks or drums.

References

1972. Knuth, D. E. *The Art of Computer Programming, Volume III: Sorting and Searching.* Reading, MA: Addison-Wesley Publishing Co.

1974. Amble, O. and Knuth, D. E. "Ordered Hash Tables," *Computer J.* **17**, 135–142.

1975 Knott, G. D. "Hashing Functions," *Computer J.* **18**, 265–278.

1978. Guibas, L. J. and Szemeredi, E. "The Analysis of Double Hashing," *J. Comput. Syst. Sci.* **16**, 226–274.

1979. Fagin, R., Nievergelt, J., Pippenger, N. and Strong, H. R. "Extendible Hashing—A Fast Access Method for Dynamic Files," *ACM Trans. Database Sys.* **4**, 315–344.

1980. Gonnet, G. H., Rogers, L. D. and George, J. A. "An Algorithmic and Complexity Analysis of Interpolation Search," *Acta Informatica* **13**, 39–52.

1984. Gonnet, G. H. *Handbook of Algorithms and Data Structures,* Reading MA: Addison-Wesley Publishing Co.

1985. Sleator, D. D. and Tarjan, R. E. "Self-Adjusting Binary Search Trees," *J. ACM* **32**, 652–686.

1986. Reingold, E. M. and Hansen, W. J. *Data Structures in Pascal.* Boston: Little, Brown and Company.

1988. Sedgewick, R. *Algorithms,,* 2nd Ed. Reading MA: Addison-Wesley Publishing Co.

EDWARD M. REINGOLD

SEMANTICS. *See* PROGRAMMING LANGUAGE SEMANTICS; and SYNTAX, SEMANTICS, AND PRAGMATICS.

SEMAPHORE. *See* CONCURRENT PROGRAMMING.

SEQUENTIAL MACHINE

For articles on related subjects *see* AUTOMATA THEORY; FORMAL LANGUAGES; REGULAR EXPRESSION; and SWITCHING THEORY.

Basic Concepts A *sequential machine* is a mathematical model of a certain type of simple computational structure, such as that of a sequential switching circuit. It has an input σ, which can take on any value from a finite set Σ, called the *input alphabet*, and an output δ, from a finite *output alphabet* Δ, as shown in Fig. 1. The input and output values are of interest only at certain instants of time; these instants are usually referred to as instants 1, 2, 3,....At any time t, the output $\delta(t)$ depends not only on the present input $\sigma(t)$, but also on the past input sequence...$\sigma(t-k), \sigma(t-k+1),..., \sigma(t-2), \sigma(t-1)$; hence the name *sequential machine*.

The dependence of the output on past inputs implies that a sequential machine has memory. Usually, this memory is finite and corresponds to a finite set Q, called the set of *internal states*. At time t, the machine M is in some (present) state $q(t)$. It receives an input value $\sigma(t)$, and this present input and the present internal state determine the next internal state $q(t+1)$.

An example of a sequential machine is shown in Fig. 2. The machine is represented by a directed graph, a *state*

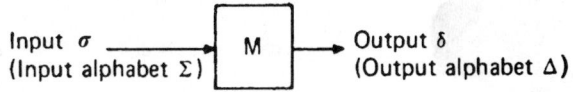

FIG. 1. Sequential machine block diagram.

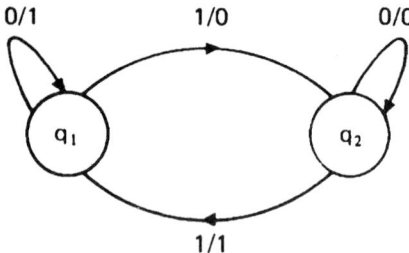

FIG. 2. Machine M_1.

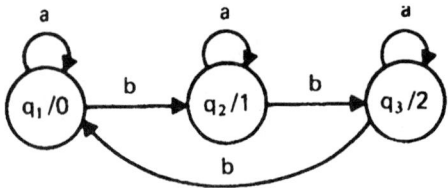

FIG. 4. Machine M_2.

graph, where the nodes correspond to internal states and the labeled edges to transitions among internal states. The labels are of the form σ/δ, where σ is the input value causing the transition and δ is the corresponding output value. For example, if M_1 of Fig. 2 is in state q_1 at time t, and if $\sigma(t) = 1$, then the transition labeled 1/0 is relevant, $\delta(t) = 0$, and at time $t + 1$ the state of M_1 will be q_2. If we are given an initial state $q(1)$—i.e. the value of q at $t = 1$—and an input sequence $\sigma(1)$, $\sigma(2)$,..., $\sigma(t)$, we can determine from the state graph the resulting state sequence $q(2)$,...,$q(t + 1)$ and the corresponding output sequence $\delta(1), \delta(2),..., \delta(t)$. A typical computation is shown in Fig. 3, where it is assumed that $q(1) = q_1$. The reader will verify that if M_1 is started in state q_1, it will produce an output of 1 at time t if and only if the number of 1's in the sequence $\sigma(1)$, $\sigma(2)$,..., $\sigma(t)$ is even.

With each sequential machine we associate two functions: the *transition function f*, which determines the next state from the present state and the present input, and an *output function g*. In the machine M_1, the present output depends on both the present state and the present input. The model in which the output depends on both the state and the input—i.e. where $\delta(t) = g(q(t), \sigma(t))$—is the *Mealy model*. In another useful model, the *Moore model*, the present output is uniquely determined by the present state, i.e. $\delta(t) = g(q(t))$.

An example of a Moore machine is shown in Fig. 4. The input and output alphabets are $\Sigma = \{a, b\}$ and $\Delta = \{0, 1, 2,\}$, respectively. Given an initial state and an input sequence, we can determine the state sequence, as in the Mealy model. Since the output is determined solely by the state, we associate it with the nodes of the state graph rather than with the edges. A typical computation for M_2 is shown in Fig. 5, assuming $q(1) = q_1$. The behavior of M_2 can be described as follows: The input value a is "ignored" by M_2, in the sense that no change of state results when

$\sigma(t) = a$. The input b advances the state of M_2 cyclically. If the machine is started in q_1, the output $\delta(t + 1)$ is congruent modulo 3 to the number of b's in the input sequence $\sigma(1)$, $\sigma(2)$,..., $\sigma(t)$.

The differences between the Moore and Mealy models are only technical. From a general point of view, these models are equivalent as far as computational power is concerned. Another model equivalent to these in the general sense is the *finite automaton* model. This is a special case of the Moore model, where $\Delta = \{0, 1\}$. If the output corresponding to an internal state is 1, that state is called *accepting*, or *final*; if the output is 0, the state is called a *rejecting* state. A single *initial state* q_0 is usually specified in the finite automaton model. A finite automaton A can be viewed as an *acceptor* of input sequences. For the input sequence $\sigma(1)$,..., $\sigma(t)$, let $q(t + 1)$ be the state reached by A, when started in q_0. If $q(t + 1)$ is a final state, the sequence is accepted; otherwise, it is rejected. An alternative point of view considers a sequential machine as a *sequence transducer*—a machine that transforms an input sequence into an output sequence, as in Figs. 3 and 5.

Realization of Sequential Machines The behavior of a sequential machine can be realized by a sequential switching circuit. We now describe an idealized model of such circuits, which we call a *sequential network*. The sequential network reflects the logical properties of the switching circuit, but not its electronic properties. Thus, it has the advantage of being independent of the actual technological implementation, while retaining many of the basic structural properties.

A block diagram of a switching network is shown in Fig. 6. As is usually the case, we assume that all signals in a sequential network are binary, with 0 and 1 as the two possible values. The network has a finite number of binary inputs $x_1,..., x_n$ and binary outputs $z_1,..., z_m$. If the output values $z_i(t)$ at time t are uniquely determined by the input values $x_j(t)$, then it has no memory. In that case, it is called a *combinational network*, and its behavior can

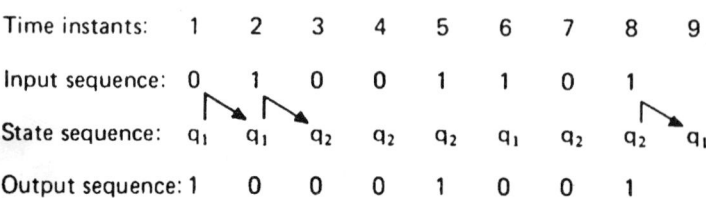

Time instants:	1	2	3	4	5	6	7	8	9
Input sequence:	0	1	0	0	1	1	0	1	
State sequence:	q_1	q_1	q_2	q_2	q_2	q_1	q_2	q_2	q_1
Output sequence:	1	0	0	0	1	0	0	1	

FIG. 3. Sequences for M_1.

Time instants:	1	2	3	4	5	6	7	8	9	10
Input sequence:	b	a	b	a	b	b	b	a	b	
State sequence:	q_1	q_2	q_2	q_3	q_3	q_1	q_2	q_3	q_3	q_1
Output sequence:	0	1	1	2	2	0	1	2	2	0

FIG. 5.   Sequences for M_2.

be described by m boolean functions, one for each output z_i. A combinational network can be implemented by a network of logic gates *without* any feedback loops.

A switching network with memory is called *sequential*. The function of memory can be performed by gate networks *with* feedback. In general, such networks have no special timing signals and are called *asynchronous*. If a special periodic input, called *clock*, is provided to control the action of the network, the network is *synchronous*. In that case, the response of the network is of interest only at certain times, once during each clock period. These times correspond to the instants 1, 2, 3,...mentioned earlier.

A synchronous sequential network can be divided into a combinational part and a memory part. The units corresponding to memory are rather complex asynchronous gate networks called *flip-flops*. For theoretical considerations, the simplest memory module is the *unit delay*, whose output y is equal to the input x delayed by one unit of time; i.e. $y(t) = x(t-1)$. The general form of a synchronous sequential network with unit delays as memory elements is shown in Fig. 7. The network can be described by two sets of equations.

1. Next-state equations:

$$
\begin{aligned}
y_i(t+1) &= Y_i(t) \\
&= f_i(x_1(t),...,x_n(t), y_1(t),...,y_s(t)), \\
i &= 1,...,s.
\end{aligned}
$$

2. Output equations:

$$
z_j(t) = g_j(x_1(t),...,x_n(t), y_1(t),...,y_s(t)),
$$
$$
j = 1,...,m,
$$

In (1) the f_i, and in (2) the g_j, are Boolean functions.

The reader will easily verify that the sequential network model of Fig. 7 is a special case of the Mealy model, where Σ is the set of all binary n-tuples (binary words of length n) and Δ is the set of all binary m-tuples.

Any abstract sequential machine can be realized by

a sequential network of the type shown in Fig. 7. This can be done by representing each element of Σ by a suitable n-tuple $x_1,...,x_n$, and Δ and Q must be coded similarly.

The unit delay is sometimes called the *D flip-flop*. Other types of flip-flops are the *T (toggle or trigger) type*, the *SR (set-reset) type*, and the *JK type*. Each type of flip-flop can be used to realize any sequential machine. In Fig. 8 we define the four types of flip-flops by *state tables*, which constitute a common way (equivalent to the state-graph representation) of representing sequential networks. The rows of the state table correspond to the internal states, and the columns to input combinations. The entries represent the next state. The most general type of flip-flop is the JK. The condition $J = 0, K = 0$ is the *remember* condition, where no change takes place. $J = 0, K = 1$ corresponds to the *reset* condition (the flip-flop is reset to 0); $J = 1, K = 0$ is the *set* condition; and $J = 1, K = 1$ is the *toggle* condition (the state changes, or *toggles*).

Behavioral Properties   Two states q and q' of a sequential machine M are *indistinguishable* if the I/O behavior of M started in q cannot be distinguished by any external experiment from that of M started in q'. In other words, any input sequence applied to M, started in q, produces the same output sequence as in the case when M is started in q'. Otherwise, q and q' are *distinguishable*. A sequential machine in which every pair of states is distinguishable is called *reduced*.

Two sequential machines M and M' are indistinguishable if for every state q of M there exists a state q' of M' such that the I/O behavior of M started in q is the same as that of M' started in q', and vice versa. For every sequen-

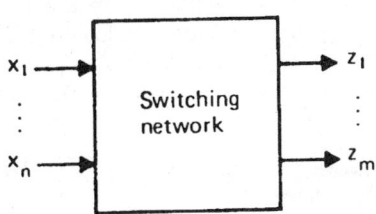

FIG. 6.   Switching network.

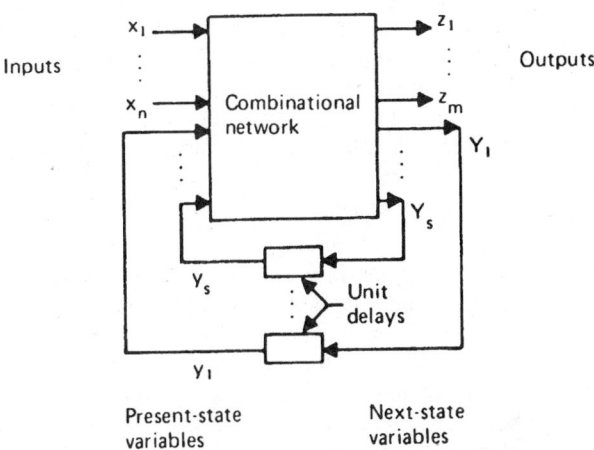

FIG. 7.   Sequential network with unit delays.

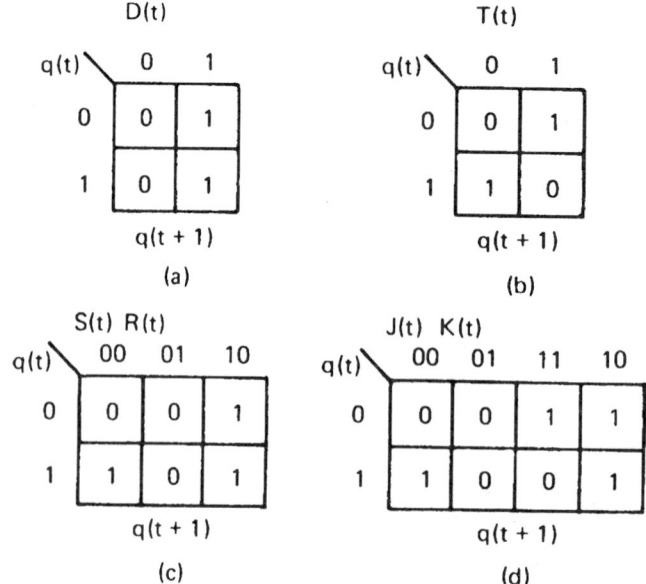

FIG. 8.   State tables. (a) D flip-flop. (b) T flip-flop. (c) SR flip-flop; note that S = R = 1 is not used. (d) JK flip-flop.

tial machine M, there exists a unique (up to isomorphism) reduced sequential machine M_0 indistinguishable from M. The machine M_0 is the minimal-state version of M.

A set of sequences over a finite alphabet is called a *language*. It is natural to associate certain languages with sequential machines. For example, in the case of a finite automaton A, we define the *language*, $L(A)$, accepted by A to be the set of all accepted sequences. Similarly, the set L_{ij} of all sequences taking a sequential machine from state q_i to state q_j, or the set L_δ, of all sequences resulting in a particular output value δ, represent useful languages. All such languages of the form $L(A)$, L_{ij}, or L_δ are *regular languages*. It can be shown that any language defined by a sequential machine in the above sense is regular, and, conversely, for every regular language there exists a sequential machine "recognizing" that language.

An important application of sequential machines is in counting. When the number of states is finite, a sequential machine can only count modulo an integer.

Another unique characterization of sequential machines is provided by the *syntactic semigroup* of the machine, defined as follows: For each input σ, the set Q of states of a reduced machine is transformed according to the transition function. The set of all transformations of states performed by all input sequences constitutes the syntactic semigroup. This representation is useful for certain structural properties.

Structural Properties   In a general network, as shown in Fig. 7, there may be feedback loops. For example, Y_1 may be a function of y_2, and Y_2 may be a function of y_1. In the special case where no such loops exist, the network is called *definite*. An example of a simple definite network is shown in Fig. 9.

The languages recognized by definite networks are particularly simple, since the behavior of such networks depends only on the last k symbols of the input sequence,

for some k. In general, feedback is required in order to realize the behavior of an arbitrary sequential machine. It can be shown, however, that every sequential machine can be realized by a sequential network having a single feedback loop.

When SR flip-flops (instead of unit delays) are used as memory elements, the class of machines realizable without feedback is considerably larger than the class of definite machines. The languages recognized by machines in this class are the so-called *noncounting* regular languages. Such machines can only "count to a threshold," in the following sense: If the threshold is the integer $k \geq 0$, then the machine may be able to determine whether a certain sequence of symbols occurs in the input sequence $0, 1,\ldots,$ or $k - 1$ times. After this, it cannot distinguish k occurrences from $k + 1$ occurrences, but can only conclude that the number of occurrences is at least k. Therefore, such machines cannot count modulo any integer greater than one, and are called *counter-free*. The languages corresponding to counter-free machines constitute a natural subclass of regular languages. They can be defined by regular expressions that use only Boolean operations and concatenation. Such expressions are called *star-free*. The syntactic semigroups corresponding to this class of machines and languages are *group-free* (i.e. only groups of order one are allowed).

Sequential machines that can be realized by networks of unit delays and exclusive-OR gates are *linear* and constitute a proper subclass of sequential machines. Linear machines have important applications in coding theory.

The problem of decomposing a sequential machine into a *cascade connection* of smaller sequential machines

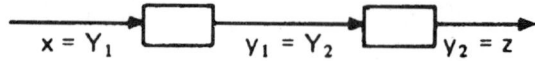

FIG. 9.   A definite network.

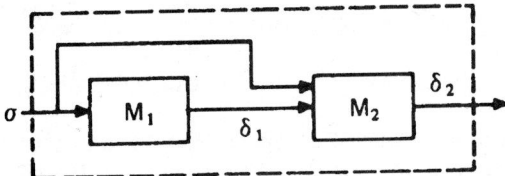

FIG. 10. Cascade connection.

has received much attention. The cascade connection of two machines is shown in Fig. 10. This connection is also known as the *series connection*. The *parallel connection* of two machines is a special case of the cascade connection, where neither machine influences the other. We have already mentioned that definite machines correspond to cascade connections of unit delays, and counter-free machines correspond to cascade connections of SR flipflops. The Krohn-Rhodes theory shows that, in general, arbitrary sequential machines correspond to cascade connections of (1) machines whose syntactic semigroups are simple groups, and (2) SR flip-flops.

Such results are of theoretical interest. For practical applications, an often-used cascade connection is a *shift register*, which is a very simple cascade connection of flip-flops. Shift registers and counters constitute basic modules in the design of sequential networks.

Related Models In practical applications, certain state-input combinations of a sequential machine may never occur. In this case, the next state and output may be irrelevant and need not be specified. The *incompletely specified* sequential machine model handles such cases.

The situation where the next state and output of a machine are not precisely predictable is modeled by *stochastic* or *probabilistic* sequential machines. The case where the transition function and the output function vary with time is modeled by *time-varying* sequential machines. Both the stochastic and the time-varying machines are more powerful than the ordinary machines in the sense that they can recognize some irregular languages.

A theoretically convenient model is the *nondeterministic* sequential machine. Here, for a given present state and input, the next state can be chosen from a set of states; i.e. it is not necessarily unique. As acceptors of languages, the nondeterministic machines are no more powerful than the deterministic machines; both types can recognize only regular languages. A nondeterministic machine can have fewer states than the corresponding reduced deterministic machine accepting the same language. Nondeterministic machines do not correspond directly to sequential circuits, since the latter do not possess any freedom of choice for the next state.

The concept of a *generalized sequential machine* (GSM) has applications in the theory of formal languages. In this model, for a given present state and input symbol, the machine can produce a sequence of output symbols, whereas the standard model permits only one output symbol. The GSM is also a more powerful model than the standard one.

In the discussion above, we have tacitly assumed that the term *sequential machine* implies that the number

of states is finite. *Infinite-state* sequential machines have also been studied. They are obviously much more powerful than the finite-state machines, and most of the results discussed above do not apply directly to the infinite-state case. Infinite-state linear sequential machines provide an example where a number of results from the finite-state case have their generalized counterparts in the infinite case.

References

1968. Ginzburg, A. *Algebraic Theory of Automata*. New York: Academic Press.

1971. McNaughton, R. and Papert, S. *Counter-Free Automata*. Cambridge: The M.I.T. Press.

1976. Eilenberg, S. *Automata, Languages, and Machines*, Vols. **A** and **B**. New York: Academic Press.

1976. Brzozowski, J. and Yoeli, M. *Digital Networks*. Englewood Cliffs, NJ: Prentice-Hall.

1978. Kohavi, Z. *Switching and Finite Automata Theory*, 2nd Ed. New York: McGraw-Hill.

1989. Dewdney, A.K. *The Turing Omnibus* (Chapter 35). Rockville, MD: *Computer Science Press*.

JANUSZ A. BRZOZOWSKI

SERVER. *See* FILE SERVER.

SETL

For articles on related subjects *see* CONTROL STRUCTURES; PROGRAMMING LANGUAGES; and PROCEDURE-ORIENTED LANGUAGES.

Very high level languages are programming languages that allow algorithms to be stated in a manner independent of detailed data structuring. *SETL* is a very high level language designed to facilitate the programming of algorithms involving sets and related structures.

SETL provides conventional control structures (**if then-else, while, case**, etc.), as well as some specifically set-oriented ones [e.g. **forall** (the members of a set)], but its data structures are very general and include arbitrary finite sets nested to any length and nested tuples with arbitrary components as objects. More specifically, SETL admits the following structures.

Tuples are arbitrary length ordered sequences of component values, which may be primitive or may themselves be tuples. Tuples correspond closely to one-dimensional vectors in familiar languages except that they have no fixed length and can be extended dynamically simply by assigning a value to a previously nonexistent element. In SETL, tuples are used to represent both ordered sequences and unordered "bags" where equal elements may occur. In the latter case, the order of the elements in the tuple is not important.

Examples of SETL tuples, which are delimited by brackets, and of the results of operations on them are as follows:

$t_1 := [0,1.3, \text{'hello'}]; \quad t_2 := [0,0, [\text{'a'},\text{'b'}]];$

$t_1(2) = 1.3, \quad t_2(3) = [\text{'a'},\text{'b'}],$

$t_2(2..3) = [0,[\text{'a'},\text{'b'}]],$

$t_1 + t_2 = [0,1.3,\text{'hello'},0,0, [\text{'a'},\text{'b'}]].$

where + represents concatenation (*q.v.*).

Sets are unordered collections of objects with the constraint that a given element cannot appear more than once. SETL provides the usual set-theoretic operations (union, intersection, etc.) and also the *arb* operator, which selects (nondeterministically) an arbitrary element from a set. Examples of sets and of the results of operations on them are the following:

$s_1 := \{0,1.3,\text{'hello'}\}; \quad s_2 \ 1.3, := \{0,[\text{'a'}, \text{'b'}]\};$

$s_1 * s_2 = \{0\}; \quad s_1 - s_2 = \{1.3,\text{'hello'}\};$

$s_1 + s_2 = \{0,1.3,\text{'hello'}, [\text{'a'}, \text{'b'}]\};$

where * represents intersection; +, union; and −, set difference.

Maps in SETL are not a separate basic type, but are simply sets of tuples of length 2 (called pairs) whose first component is a domain value and whose second component is the corresponding range value. The set of tuples in a map, therefore, defines a function. Maps may be single or multiple valued, and SETL provides functional-style constructions for evaluating maps for a given argument value, assigning new map values, etc. Since maps are sets, all set valued operators can be used with maps. An example of a map and of operations involving it are:

```
numbvowels := {['hello',2], ['goodbye',3]};

numbvowels('hello') = 2;

numbvowels('zebra') = Ω/*undefined*/.
```

The following succinct "topological sort" program illustrates the use of SETL. We read a directed graph *g*, which is assumed to be a set of ordered pairs {[*a, b*], [*c, d*],....}, each such pair representing an edge, and then attempt to arrange the nodes of *g* in a tuple in such a way that each directed edge goes from a lower to a higher numbered node (i.e. from an element of the tuple to one which follows it).

```
read(g); /* read in the graph, which is set of pairs */
set_of_nodes := {n(1) : n ∈ g} + {n(2) : n ∈ g};
                        /*all nodes of g*/
ordered_tuple : = [ ];
                /*tuple to be built up is initially empty*/
(while exists n ∈ set_of_nodes suchthat
    (forall m ∈ set_of_nodes | [m,n] ∉ g)
        /*if no [m,n] is in g, add n to end of ordered-
            tuple and remove it from set_of_nodes */
        ordered_tuple := ordered_tuple + [n];
        set_of_nodes := set_of_nodes - {n};
end while;
if set_of_nodes = { } then
                /* remaining set of nodes is not null*/
```

```
    print('topological ordering is impossible');
end if;
        /*otherwise ordered_tuple includes all nodes*/
```

The original SETL language has been implemented at New York University, and is available on the IBM 370, DEC VAX, and SUN model 3 Workstations. It has been used successfully in a number of large research projects, including the first validated Ada compiler. There are also two recent implementations of the language as well as several in progress, each having minor variations from the original.

ISETL is an interpreted, interactive implementation of SETL developed by Gary Levin at Clarkson University. It was designed specifically for teaching and learning mathematical concepts.

SETL2, developed at New York University, is targeted toward building or prototyping large applications. It features a number of extensions to SETL, including a package and library system similar to Ada's and full support of object-oriented programming (*q.v.*).

Both ISETL and SETL2 are available for a variety of Unix systems, several popular microcomputers, and DEC and IBM mainframes.

References

1975. Schwartz, J. and Kennedy, K. "An Introduction to the Set Theoretical Language SETL," in *Computers and Mathematics with Applications* 1: 97–119. New York: Pergamon Press.

1986. Schwartz, J. T., Dewar, R. B. K., Dubinsky, E., and Schonberg, E. *Programming with Sets: An Introduction to SETL*. New York: Springer-Verlag.

1989. Baxter, Nancy, Dubinsky, Ed and Levin, Gary. *Learning Discrete Mathematics with ISETL*. New York: Springer-Verlag.

1989. Snyder, W. Kirk. "The SETL2 Programming Language," Report 490. Courant Institute of Mathematical Sciences, New York University.

JACOB T. SCHWARTZ AND KIRK W. SNYDER

SHANNON, CLAUDE

For articles on related subjects *see* BUSH, VANNEVAR; CODES; DIFFERENTIAL ANALYZER; ERROR-CORRECTING CODE; INFORMATION THEORY; and SWITCHING THEORY.

Claude Elwood Shannon, a native of Gaylord, Michigan, was born 30 April, 1916. He received bachelor of science degrees in electrical engineering and in mathematics at the University of Michigan in 1936, a master's degree in electrical engineering at M.I.T. in 1940, and a Ph.D. in mathematics at M.I.T. in 1940.

At M.I.T. for these four years, he was in charge of the differential analyzer, a machine developed by Vannevar Bush for solving differential equations. In his master's thesis, Shannon showed how Boolean algebra can be used in the analysis and synthesis of switching (or computer) logical networks, a technique of enduring value. His doctoral thesis showed the application of algebraic theory to genetics. These early works presaged Shannon's many

FIG. 1. Claude Shannon.

later applications of mathematics to science and engineering.

Subsequent to receiving his Ph.D., Shannon was a National Research Fellow at the Institute for Advanced Study at Princeton. He joined Bell Laboratories in 1941. During World War II, he worked on the design of anti-aircraft gun directors and also on cryptographic problems. His publication "A Mathematical Theory of Cryptography" (published after the war) led to a deep interest in problems of communication.

In 1948, he published "A Mathematical Theory of Communication" in the *Bell System Technical Journal*. This founded what is now called *information theory*. The impact of information theory ranges from the efficient transmission systems for communication from the Voyager and Galileo spacecraft, the efficient encoding of television and speech, the analysis of radar systems, and the error-correcting encoding endemic in computers and compact discs, and on to new insights in cryptography and to many rather general applications in a host of fields.

In 1949, Shannon showed how a computer could be programmed to play chess, a goal realized years later. In 1952, he demonstrated a maze-solving mouse controlled by interconnected switching relays.

In 1958, Shannon became Donner Professor of Science at M.I.T., where he advised a number of brilliant graduate students. His later work includes various theorems on juggling.

Shannon is a member of the National Academy of Sciences, the National Academy of Engineering, the American Philosophical Society, and the American Academy of Arts and Sciences, as well as the Leopoldina Academy, the Royal Netherlands Academy of Arts and Sciences, and the Royal Irish Academy. He has received a dozen honorary degrees, and many prestigious awards, including the National Medal of Science (1966), the IEEE Medal of Honor (1966), and the Kyoto Prize in Basic Science (1985). Shannon's bold invention of information theory and subsequent work on its implications puts him among a rare few in the history of science and technology.

JOHN R. PIERCE

SHELL

For articles on related subjects *see* COMMAND AND JOB CONTROL LANGUAGE; KERNEL; OPERATING SYSTEMS; REGULAR EXPRESSION; and UNIX OPERATING SYSTEM.

A *shell* is a command interpreter through which the user gives commands to an operating system. The term reflects the principle that an operating system is constructed from a succession of layers, of which the shell is the outermost one. The shell separates the users from the rest of the operating system and provides a *virtual machine* that serves as a high-level programming environment.

Most system users spend a great deal of time executing programs, not writing new ones. When a user logs in, the operating system creates a process running a copy of the shell program. The shell listens to the user's terminal and interprets the inputs as commands to invoke existing programs in specified combinations and with specified inputs. The shell scans each command line of the input to pick out the names of programs to be invoked and the values of arguments to be passed to them. Each program called in this way is invoked as a subprogram or subprocess. The programs are connected according to the data and control flow specified in the command.

Operations of substantial complexity can be programmed in the command language of the Unix shell (Kernighan and Mashey, 1979). As a simple example, the following sequence of commands prepares a five column list of file names on the printer.

```
ls > filenames
pr -5 < filenames > columns
lpr < columns
```

The command ls lists the file names in the current directory. Instead of printing the file names on the terminal, the symbol ">" redirects the output into the file named filenames. The next line uses the multi-column capabilities of the pr command to produce output with five columns. This command obtains its input from the file filenames and writes it to the file columns. Finally, the printer spooler lpr outputs the result on the printer.

Instead of using intermediate files, the Unix *pipe* facility can take the output of one program and direct it to the input of another. The pipeline

    ls | pr −5 | lpr

has the same effect as the program above, except that no intermediate files are generated. The pipe symbol ">" connects the output of one command to the input of the next; the shell performs the necessary buffering.

If a command line is to be performed often, typing it can become tedious. Unix encourages users to store complicated commands in executable files called shell-scripts that become simpler commands. As a small example, consider searching the file /usr/lib/telnos for names and telephone numbers. The search is performed by a general-purpose pattern matcher called grep. If we do not wish to remember the details of using grep or in what file the telephone numbers are kept, we can place the line

    grep $1 /usr/lib/telnos

into a file named tel. When tel is called, $1 is replaced by the first argument. The commands tel walt, tel 3934, and tel wft all produce the output:

    walter tichy (wft) 3934

A Unix shell program is not necessarily a single line. Shell programs can be arbitrarily long and may include assignments to variables, control constructs for alternation and iteration, subroutine calls to commands in other files, and even interrupt handling. The Unix shell is a full-fledged, high-level programming language.

The shell language need not be different from a standard, interpreted programming language. In Lisp programming environments, the shell is typically a Lisp interpreter, which allows operating system commands to be invoked as if they were normal Lisp functions (Teitelman and Masinter, 1981). The shell language is used interactively and hence must be interpreted rather than compiled.

Several features in the shell interpreter simplify interactive use. One of them is an input completion facility, with which the shell completes the names of commands and files once the user has typed a unique prefix. A spelling checker (*q.v.*) can help correct typos. A dialogue history supports the reissuing of elaborate commands. The dialogue history records all commands typed in by the user, who can then select any past command on this list by pointing to it or by identifying it by typing a unique prefix. The selected command can be reissued, or first modified and then reissued. Editing and reissuing past commands is called a *redo* facility. The dialogue history can also become the basis for an *undo* facility, with which the effects of already executed commands can be removed.

References

1979. Kernighan, Brian W. and Mashey, John R. "The Unix Programming Environment," *Software Practice and Experience*, **9**, *1* (January), 1–15.

1981. Teitelman, Warren and Masinter, Larry "The Interlisp Programming Environment," *IEEE Computer*, **14**, *4* (April) 25–33.

WALTER F. TICHY

SHIFTING

For articles on related subjects *see* ARITHMETIC-LOGIC UNIT; INSTRUCTION SET; MACHINE AND ASSEMBLY LANGUAGE PROGRAMMING; MASKING; and REGISTER.

Shifting is the process of moving data that is stored in a storage device relative to the boundaries of the device (as opposed to moving it in and out of the device). The device in which the shift is performed is called a *shift register*. In order to discuss the various modes of the shift operation, we assume that the register in which the shift is to be performed is n bits wide, and number the bits from left to right, $1 \cdots n$.

A *left shift* is the operation in which the ith bit is replaced by the $(i + 1)$st one. This operation can be repeated an arbitrary number of times so that one can shift by any number of positions. The question of what replaces the nth (last) bit will be dealt with later, as will the question of what happens to bit 1.

A *right shift* is the operation in which the ith bit is replaced by the $(i - 1)$st bit. Again, this is easily generalized to a right shift by any number of positions.

There are three types of shifts: logical, circular, and arithmetic (see Fig. 1). They differ in the treatment of the first and last bits, both in the left and right shift.

In *logical shifts* the bit shifted out is lost, and the bit shifted in is zero. Note in the left shift that the bit shifted out is bit 1, and the bit shifted in occupies position n, whereas in the right shift, the bit shifted out is the nth one and the bit shifted in occupies position 1.

In *circular shifts* the bit shifted out of one end is shifted into the other end. There is, therefore, no loss of information in the circular shift.

The *arithmetic shift* is designed to take orderly advantage of the fact that shifting a bit string left multiplies the binary number represented by it by 2, whereas shifting it right divides it by 2. Multiplication and division of a positive number by 2 can therefore be accomplished by logical shifts. However, when negative numbers are present, special care must be exercised in dealing with the sign bit.

In the sign-magnitude representation of negative numbers, the sign bit should be left intact. In the 2s complement representation, it should be kept intact upon left shift and should be replicated upon right shift; i.e. in the right shift, bit 2 should be replaced by bit 1 (the sign bit) and bit 1 should be left in its previous value. In the 1s complement representation, the equivalent operation is done by circular shifts. In either of these, there are cases in which overflow can be generated.

The precise definition of an arithmetic shift depends, therefore, on the way negative numbers are represented in the computer. For 2s complement representation (Fig. 1), the definition is as follows:

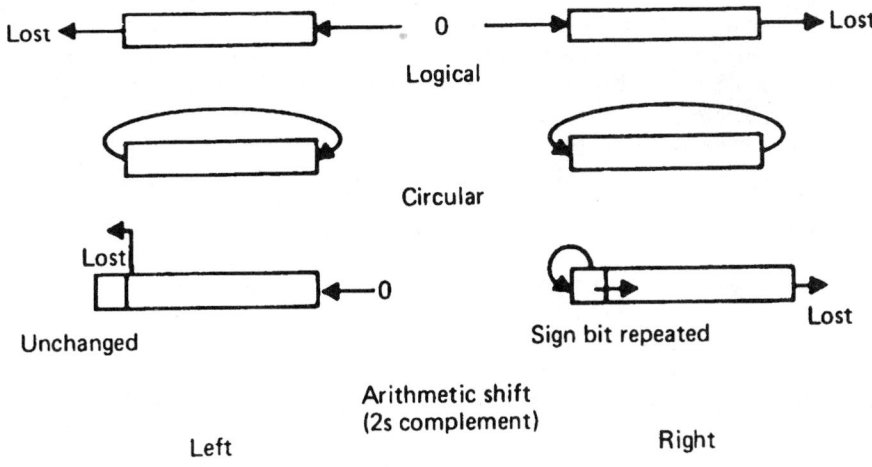

FIG. 1. Various one-bit shift operations.

In a right arithmetic shift, the nth bit is shifted out and the first bit is preserved. In a left arithmetic shift, the nth bit is filled with zero and the sign bit is replaced with former bit 2. This will usually leave the sign intact because all but very large negative numbers start with two or more 1-bits. Shifting a number that begins with 10 left one place changes a formerly negative number to a positive one and is indicative of overflow. The converse would be true for a number starting with 01. Most computers will set condition codes to indicate such overflows.

Some examples of the effect of the various shift operations on some five-bit strings are presented in Table 1.

Shift operations are usually used in field alignments, packing and unpacking of data items into storage units, and high-speed multiplication and division, especially by constants. Among the more exotic uses is that for the creation of control patterns. For example, the pattern 10110111 can be used for a switch that will do an operation once, then skip (0), then do it twice, skip again, and finally do it three times.

Many computers allow double-precision shift operations. In these shifts, two n-bit storage devices are used as one $2n$-bit device. Also, in certain computers the shift register is extended, usually by a carry indicator, so that the bit shifted out is not lost, but rather is shifted into an extra storage bit where it can be tested.

GIDEON FRIEDER

SIDE EFFECT

For articles on related subjects *see* ARGUMENT; GLOBAL AND LOCAL VARIABLES; PARAMETER PASSING; PROCEDURE-ORIENTED LANGUAGES: PROGRAMMING; SUBPROGRAM; and STRUCTURED PROGRAMMING.

A *side effect* occurs when a procedure or function changes the value of a global variable. This is one reason why the use of global variables is deplored in programming; they allow the possibility of side effects, which are usually unplanned and, therefore, undesirable. But this is not always so; sometimes, as in database systems, the database itself is global to all procedures, and modifying it is just what many of the procedures in the system are supposed to do. (*See* also STRUCTURED PROGRAMMING and Reilly and Federighi (1989) for examples of how side effects play a constructive role in the creation of gerund functions.)

Procedures or functions that cause side effects can result in nasty problems whose solution may require the programmer to know more than should be necessary about how a program is processed (e.g. compiled) by a language processor. For example, consider the expression

```
A + B*C
```

It should not matter to the programmer whether this expression is evaluated by first multiplying B times C and then adding A or by first fetching A, storing it away temporarily, multiplying B*C and then adding A although the former will usually be more efficient. But what if the expression is instead

```
FCN(A) + B*C
```

TABLE 1. 2's Complement Shift Operations

Bit String	Operation	Result	Comments
01011	Left logical	10110	
01011	Right logical	00101	Last bit lost
01011	Right circular	10101	
01011	Left circular	10110	
01011	Right arithmetic	00101	
01011	Left arithmetic	10110	Result incorrect (overflow)
11001	Left arithmetic	10010	
11001	Right arithmetic	11100	
11001	Left logical	10010	
11001	Left logical 2	00100	2-place shift

where FCN is a function with argument A? Suppose the evaluation of FCN(A) has a side effect that modifies the value of B or C or of both. Then the value of the expression is different if B*C is evaluated before FCN(A) is evaluated or afterward. A related problem can occur in the evaluation of logical expressions such as

$$I < 20 \textbf{ and } FCN(A) = 5.$$

If $I \geq 20$, then the expression must be false. Some systems will recognize this and not evaluate FCN(A) at all. Others will perform all evaluations of the arguments of **and** and then evaluate the expression. If FCN(A) modifies other variables in the program, then it is vital to know how expressions are evaluated.

To avoid problems such as these, some languages specify left-to-right evaluation of arithmetic expressions and how logical expressions are to be evaluated. The best rule is that, whether or not these matters are specified, the programmer should be careful to avoid the possibility of the kinds of side effects described above.

References

1980. Wagener, J. *Fortran 77: Principles of Programming.* New York: John Wiley.

1989. Reilly, E. D., and Federighi, F. D., *Pascalgorithms.* Boston, MA: Houghton-Mifflin.

ANTHONY RALSTON

SIGNIFICANCE ARITHMETIC

For articles on related subjects *see* ARITHMETIC, COMPUTER; INTERVAL ARITHMETIC; NUMBERS AND NUMBER SYSTEMS; PRECISION; and SIGNIFICANT DIGIT.

The significant digits of a radix approximation (from some finite precision radix-number system) to a true number implicitly convey information on the accuracy of the numerical approximation. *Significance arithmetic* is an easily applied accuracy-monitoring technique providing rules for estimating the number and positions of the significant digits of the radix approximation that results when an arithmetic operation is applied to operands in radix approximation form.

Suppose the positional digit sequence $d_m\, d_{m-1} \cdots\, d_l \cdots$ is the standard base $\beta \geq 2$ radix representation

of the real number x (i.e. $d_m\, \beta^m + d_{m-1}\, \beta^{m-1} + \ldots$ so that no radix point need be shown) with most significant digit $d_m \neq 0$. The absolute error in approximating x by the $m - l + 1$ digit real number $\tilde{x} = d_m\, d_{m-1} \cdots\, d_l$ with least significant digit d_l is less than β^l. A bound on the relative error $|(x - \tilde{x})/x|$ is given uniformly for any $x \neq 0$ by $1/\beta^{m-1}$. As a function of x, a sharper bound on the relative error is found by plotting the gap function β^l/x. This function may be interpreted as the absolute error bound divided by the true value x. The gap function then yields a bound on the relative error, which varies with x in a log periodic manner, and is best illustrated on a log-log plot (Matula, 1970).

The solid line in Fig. 1 shows the gap function for radix approximations truncated to $n = m - l + 1 = 5$ significant decimal digits; the dashed line corresponds to six significant decimal digits; and the dotted line to five significant hexadecimal digits. The decimal gap functions in Fig. 1 illustrate the rule that an additional significant digit in the base β radix approximation provides a uniformly tighter error bound on the relative error by a factor of $1/\beta$. It is also evident that an n significant digit base β radix approximation with a leading digit of unity will provide only a slightly better relative error bound than an $n - 1$ significant digit radix approximation with a leading digit of value $\beta - 1$. For example, 1.065 as a four-digit approximation to 1.065... has only a slightly smaller relative error bound than that of 0.978 as a three-digit approximation to 0.978...(this explains why four digits are as easily obtained on the left-hand side of a slide rule as are three digits on the right-hand side).

The significance arithmetic rule for radix conversion (Matula, 1970) is that an n significant digit base β radix approximation will, upon conversion to base γ, yield approximately $(n \log \beta/\log \gamma)$ significant digits in the base γ radix approximation. This estimate is inherently crude, since Fig. 1 implies that five significant digit hexadecimal radix approximations can in some regions yield more accuracy than six significant digit decimal approximations, whereas in other regions they will yield less accuracy than five significant digit decimal radix approximations (see point A in Fig. 1).

The significance arithmetic rule for addition/subtraction of radix approximations is that (if no overflow to a higher indexed most significant digit occurs) the position of the least significant digit is the higher index of the least significant digit positions of the operands, and (if overflow occurs) the least significant digit position is taken as

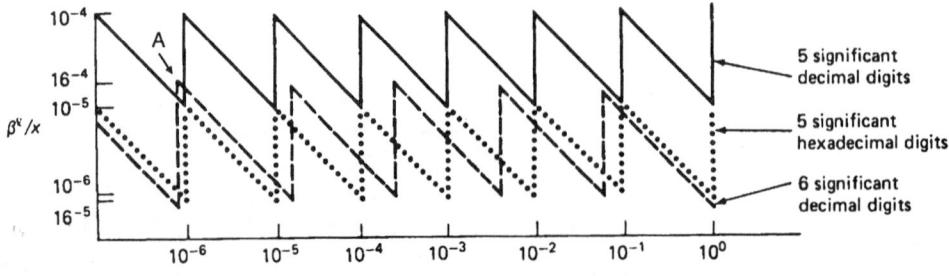

FIG. 1. Three cases of the gap function.

one unit higher. The most significant digit of the result is the highest indexed non-zero digit of the result, providing this position is at least as great as the least significant digit position. Note that subtractive cancellation can result in a severe decrease in the number of significant digits, with a possibility of leaving no resulting significant digits. In schematic radix addition form:

```
                    S S S S . S S X X
                      S S S . S X X
With no overflow:     S S S S . S X X X
With overflow:      S S S S S . X X X X
Cancellation example:  0 0 0 S . S X X X
```

where S = significant digit and X = nonsignificant digit.

The significance arithmetic rule for multiplication/division is simply that the number of significant digits in the result is the minimum of the number of significant digits in the operands.

In schematic radix multiplication form,

```
              S S . S X X
            × S . S S X
           Ⓧ X X X X X
           Ⓢ . S S S X X
          Ⓢ S . S S X X
         Ⓢ S S . S X X
           S S . S X X X X X
          S S S . X X X X X X
```

where S = significant digit and X = nonsignificant digit, Ⓢ = possible significant overflow digit, and Ⓧ = possible nonsignificant overflow digit.

In summary, significance arithmetic provides rules for estimating the significant digits of an arithmetically computed radix approximation, which in turn provides an estimate of the error of this approximation. The overall error estimate is crude but easy to compute.

References

1970. Matula, D. W. "A Formalization of Floating Point Numeric Base Conversion," *IEEE Trans. Comp.* **C-19**: 681–692.
1976. Matula, D. W. "Radix Arithmetic: Digital Algorithms for Computer Architecture," Chapter 9 in Yeh, R. (Ed.), *Applied Computation Theory.* Englewood Cliffs, NJ: Prentice-Hall.

DAVID W. MATULA.

SIGNIFICANT DIGIT

For articles on related subjects *see* ARITHMETIC, COMPUTER; INTERVAL ARITHMETIC; NUMBERS AND NUMBER SYSTEMS; PRECISION; and SIGNIFICANCE ARITHMETIC.

Let the positional digit sequence $d_m d_{m-1} \cdots d_0 \cdot d_{-1} d_{-2} d_{-3} \cdots$ with $d_m \neq 0$ be an exact radix representation for the real number x. Each digit d_i for $i \leq m$ is termed a *significant digit of the exact representation* for x, and the leading non-zero digit d_m is the *most significant digit* for x.

For example, with $x = 0.030200...$, $d_{-2} = 3$ is the most significant digit for x. Note that the leading zero digits $d_0 = 0$ and $d_{-1} = 0$ are not considered significant digits for x, even though the representation utilizes $d_{-1} = 0$ to properly position the significant digits; d_{-3} is significant because it falls after the most significant digit.

Let the positional digit sequence $d_m d_{m-1} \cdots d_0 \cdot d_{-1} d_{-2} d_{-3} \cdots$ with $d_m \neq 0$ be a radix approximation for the real number x. Suppose x is known to fall strictly between the real numbers with radix representations $d_m d_{m-1} \cdots d_{l+1}(d_l - 1)$ and $d_m d_{m-1} \cdots d_{l+1}(d_l + 1)$, where l can be positive, negative, or zero, and furthermore where the digit value d_{l-1}, such that x falls between the real numbers with radix representations $d_m d_{m-1} \cdots d_l(d_{l-1} - 1)$ and $d_m d_{m-1} \cdots d_l(d_{l-1} + 1)$, is either incorrectly chosen *or* unknown. Then each digit d_i for $l \leq i \leq m$ is a *significant digit of this radix approximation* for x, d_m is the most significant digit for x, d_l is the least *significant digit* for x, and $m - l + 1$ is *the number of significant digits* in this radix approximation for x. For example, the decimal approximations 0$\underline{3}$.0, $\underline{3.1425}$0, $\underline{3.14158}$0, and $\underline{3.141603}$, and the binary approximation 0$\underline{11.00111}$ for $\pi = 3.1415926\cdots$ have the significant digits underlined. In these cases the digit following the least significant digit is incorrect in each case. The statement that a measured value (say, 23.185), has three significant digits merely indicates that the digit value d_{-2} is not known with certitude, although $d_{-2} = 8$ might be possible (and perhaps represents a "best guess").

DAVID W. MATULA

SIMON, HERBERT A.

For articles on related subjects *see* ARTIFICIAL INTELLIGENCE; and LIST PROCESSING.

Herbert Alexander Simon (b. Milwaukee, WI, 1916) is best known in computer science for his work in artificial intelligence and cognitive psychology. As his receipt of the Nobel Prize in Economics for 1978 indicates, his intellectual base is far wider. Trained as a political scientist at the University of Chicago (Ph.D. 1943), he has made substantial and often major contributions not only to political science, but also to the study of organizations, public administration, econometrics, management science and operations research, the philosophical foundations of causality and Newtonian mechanics, and the nature of scientific discovery, as well as to psychology and computer science.

It is possible to emphasize the diversity in such a scientific career; e.g. a highly successful text on public administration (Simon, Smithburg, and Thompson, 1954), an influential research monograph on the servomechanism analysis of factory production control (Holt, Modigliani, Muth, and Simon, 1960), etc. It is preferable, and equally valid, to emphasize the common theme that runs through all this work: to understand the nature of rational behavior in humans. Simon's first book (1947) was an analysis of how the administrative human operates in

FIG. 1. Herbert A. Simon

formal organizations—a creature of institutional, informational, and computational limits who works within a frame of *bounded rationality*. This book, a core citation in the Nobel award, was central to establishing a model of economic decision making that has stood in contradistinction to the dominant model of the *homo economici*, global optimizers who know their preferences over all conceivable commodity bundles. This concern with bounded rationality—with behavior that *satisfices* rather than optimizes—also lies at the heart of his work in understanding in detail how computers and humans can behave intelligently.

Counterposed to the diversity of his intellectual career is the simplicity of his academic career. After relatively short stays at UC Berkeley and the Illinois Institute of Technology, he joined Carnegie Mellon University (then Carnegie Institute of Technology) in 1949 as a founding member of the Graduate School of Industrial Administration, which launched a revolution in graduate education in business, building it on scientific knowledge in economics, psychology, and operations research. He has been at Carnegie-Mellon University ever since, the last 20 years most closely associated with its Psychology Department (as Richard King Mellon Professor of Psychology and Computer Science).

Simon's primary contribution in computer science was his collaboration with John C. (Cliff) Shaw and Allen Newell in the development of the first heuristic programs (the *Logic Theorist*, 1956; the *General Problem Solver*, 1958) and the first list processing languages (the IPLs, 1957). This team of three, along with John McCarthy, Marvin Minsky, and Oliver Selfridge, are generally credited with having founded the area of *artificial intelligence* (McCorduck, 1979). The early programs were also taken to be models of how human thinking occurs (then usually called *simulation of thought processes*). Simon has continued to produce a stream of programs and analyses that explore how intelligent action occurs—in problem solving, memorizing, inducting, behaving in semantically rich domains, and learning. Throughout, the connection with human thinking has been explicit and often dominant. A major work on human problem solving was published in 1972 (Newell and Simon, 1972) and the range of his work can be found in Simon 1979, 1989, 1991. In 1975, Simon (jointly with Newell) was given the ACM Turing Award (*q.v.*) for his entire line of work. Simon had earlier (1969) received the Award for Distinguished Scientific Contribution of the American Psychological Association for the psychological side of this work.

Simon has received many awards and honorary degrees, and is a member of the National Academy of Sciences. He has been active in many professional societies, and in giving advice and counsel to government at all levels. His total scientific output is prodigious, even by the standards of his peers (15 books and some 600 papers). His contributions show no sign of diminishing as of the date of this writing (1990).

References

1947. Simon, H. A. *Administrative Behavior.* New York: Macmillan.

1954. Simon, H. A., Smithburg, D. W., and Thompson, V. A. *Public Administration.* New York: Knopf.

1960. Holt, C. C., Modigliani, F., Muth, J. F., and Simon, H. A. *Planning Production, Inventories, and Work Force.* Englewood Cliffs, NJ: Prentice-Hall.

1972. Newell, A. and Simon, H. A. *Human Problem Solving.* Englewood Cliffs, NJ: Prentice-Hall.

1979. McCorduck, P. *Machines Who Think.* San Francisco: Freeman.

1979. Simon, H. A. *Models of Thought.* New Haven, CT: Yale University Press.

1989. Simon, H. A., *Models of Thought,* Vol. II, New Haven, CT: Yale University Press.

1991. Simon, H. A. *Models of My Life,* New York: Basic Books.

ALLEN NEWELL

SIMPLEX METHOD

For articles on related subjects *see* MATHEMATICAL PROGRAMMING; MATRIX COMPUTATIONS; and OPTIMIZATION METHODS.

Although first developed over 40 years ago in the late 1940s by G. B. Dantzig and his associates, and although various alternative algorithms have been developed since, the *simplex algorithm* or one of its modifications remains the most common one in use today for solving the linear programming (LP) problem:

$$\text{Minimize: } f(\mathbf{x}) = \mathbf{c}^T\mathbf{x} = c_1x_1 + c_2x_2 + \ldots + c_nx_n \quad (1)$$

Subject to the constraints:

$$A\mathbf{x} = \mathbf{b} > 0, \quad (2a)$$
$$\mathbf{x} \geq \mathbf{0}, \quad (2b)$$

where A is an $m \times n$ matrix $(m < n)$, **c** and **x** are vectors of dimension n and **b** is a vector of dimension m. It is assumed that A has rank m.

If, instead of minimizing Eq. 1, we wish to maximize $\mathbf{c}^T\mathbf{x}$, we need merely minimize $-\mathbf{c}^T\mathbf{x}$, since $\max \mathbf{c}^T\mathbf{x} = -\min(-\mathbf{c}^T\mathbf{x})$.

We call a vector **x** *feasible* if it satisfies Eq. 2 and *basic* if any $n - m$ components are zero. We call an **x** that is both basic and feasible a *basic feasible solution*. If, in addition all m non-zero components are positive, the solution is called *nondegenerate*.

Suppose now that the first m columns of A are linearly independent. Let us write $A = [A_{mm}, A_{m,n-m}]$ where A_{mm} represents these first m columns. Then, if we multiplied Eq. 2a by A_{mm}^{-1}, we would obtain

$$\mathbf{x}_m = \tilde{\mathbf{b}} - \tilde{A}\mathbf{x}_{n-m} \tag{3}$$

where $\mathbf{x}_m^T = (x_1,...,x_m)$, $\tilde{\mathbf{b}} = A_{mm}^{-1}\mathbf{b}$, $\tilde{A} = A_{mm}^{-1}A_{m,n-m}$, and $\mathbf{x}_{n-m}^T = (x_{m+1},...,x_n)$. Thus, if all components of $\tilde{\mathbf{b}}$ are positive, then with $\mathbf{x}_{n-m} = \mathbf{0}$, $\mathbf{x}_m$ as given by Eq. 3 is a nondegenerate basic feasible solution (nbfs). Assume for now that we have indeed found such an nbfs.

If Eq. 3 is substituted into Eq. 1, then the *cost function* $f(\mathbf{x})$ becomes

$$f(\mathbf{x}) = z_0 + \tilde{c}_{m+1}x_{m+1} + \tilde{c}_{m+2}x_{m+2} + ... + \tilde{c}_n x_n \tag{4}$$

where $z_0 = c_1\tilde{b}_1 + c_2\tilde{b}_2 + ... + c_m\tilde{b}_m$. The $\tilde{c}_j$, $j = m+1,...,n$ are called *reduced cost coefficients*. Note that for our nbfs $f(\mathbf{x}) = z_0$. If all the reduced cost coefficients are nonnegative, any change in $x_{m+1},...,x_n$ cannot decrease $f(\mathbf{x})$. Indeed, this *local minimum* can be shown to be a *global minimum* and, thus, a solution of our LP problem.

Suppose now that some $\tilde{c}_k < 0$. Then an increase in x_k will decrease $f(\mathbf{x})$. If we choose

$$x_k = \min_{\tilde{a}_{pk} > 0} \frac{\tilde{b}_p}{\tilde{a}_{pk}} = \frac{\tilde{b}_q}{\tilde{a}_{qk}} \tag{5}$$

where $\tilde{a}_{pk}$, $p = 1,...,m$ are components of $\tilde{A}$ in Eq. 3, then it is not hard to see that x_q in Eq. 3 becomes 0 and all other x_j, $j = 1,...,m$ remain positive. Thus, we have a new nbfs with the kth component non-zero and the qth component zero. (Note that if all $\tilde{a}_{pk}$ in Eq. 5 are nonpositive, then x_k may be chosen unboundedly large, in which case $f(\mathbf{x})$ goes to $-\infty$; such a situation is almost surely indicative of a misformulation of the LP problem.)

The simplex method is essentially a mechanization of the procedure described in the previous paragraph for proceeding from one nbfs to another until all reduced cost coefficients are nonnegative. Before giving the equations to implement this mechanization, we show how to obtain an initial nbfs. Consider the LP problem:

Minimize: $g(\mathbf{y}) = y_1 + y_2 + ... + y_m$ (6)

Subject to the constraints:

$$A\mathbf{x} + I_m\mathbf{y} = \mathbf{b} > \mathbf{0}, \tag{7a}$$

$$\mathbf{x}, \mathbf{y} \geq \mathbf{0}, \tag{7b}$$

where A and **b** are as in Eq. 2 and I_m is the $m \times m$ identity matrix. An nbfs for this problem is $\mathbf{y} = \mathbf{b}$, $\mathbf{x} = \mathbf{0}$. If we apply the simplex algorithm to this problem, we end up with an nbfs for our original problem if one exists. For if such an nbfs exists for Eq. 2, then with $\mathbf{y} = \mathbf{0}$, it is also an nbfs for Eq. 7 and gives a $g(\mathbf{y}) = 0$, which is its minimum possible value. Note that solving Eqs. 6 and 7 obviates the need actually to compute A_{mm}^{-1} since the solution of Eqs. 6 and 7 automatically results in an nbfs of the form in Eq. 3 (although usually with variables other than $x_1,...x_m$ on the left).

To mechanize the simplex method we use the *tableau* shown in Fig. 1 where the coefficients are those given in Eqs. 3 and 4. $P_1,..., P_m$ are the indices of the nonzero components of the nbfs at each stage of the algorithm and $P_{m+1},...,P_n$ are the indices of the zero components. Then, assuming that $\mathbf{x}_m^T = (\tilde{b}_1,..., \tilde{b}_m)$ is an nbfs, the simplex algorithm proceeds as follows.

Step 1. Compute

$$\min_{m+1 \leq j \leq n} \tilde{a}_{0j} = \tilde{a}_{0k}$$

to find the most negative $\tilde{c}_k$. Choose the smaller index if there is a tie. If $\tilde{a}_{0k} \geq 0$, terminate the algorithm with solution $x_{p1}, x_{p2},..., x_{pm}$ (and all other components zero).

Step 2. Compute, as in Eq. 5,

$$\min_{\tilde{a}_{pk} > 0} \frac{\tilde{a}_{p0}}{\tilde{a}_{pk}} = \frac{\tilde{a}_{q0}}{\tilde{a}_{qk}}$$

If all $\tilde{a}_{pk} \leq 0$, terminate with an indication that the solution is unbounded.

Step 3. Replace P_q by P_k on the left and P_k by P_q on top in the tableau.

Step 4. Calculate the new values (indicated by primes) of $\tilde{a}_{ij}$ in the tableau:

$$\begin{aligned} \tilde{a}'_{ij} &= \tilde{a}'_{ij} - \tilde{a}'_{ik}\, \tilde{a}'_{qj}/\tilde{a}'_{qk} \quad \begin{array}{l} i = 0,...,m; i \neq q \\ j = 0,...,n; j \neq k \end{array} \\ \tilde{a}'_{ik} &= -\tilde{a}_{ik}/\tilde{a}_{qk} \quad \tilde{a}'_{qj} = \tilde{a}_{qj}/\tilde{a}_{qk} \\ \tilde{a}'_{qk} &= 1/\tilde{a}_{qk} \end{aligned} \tag{8}$$

Return to step 1.

The equations given as Eq. 8 are a consequence of substituting Eq. 5 into Eq. 3 and rearranging the equations so that x_k appears on the left side, in place of x_q.

		P_{m+1} · · · · · · · ·		P_n
	$\tilde{a}_{00} = z_0$	$\tilde{a}_{0,m+1} = \tilde{c}_{m+1}$ · · · · · · ·		$\tilde{a}_{0n} = \tilde{c}_n$
P_1	$\tilde{a}_{10} = \tilde{b}_1$	$\tilde{a}_{1,m+1}$ · · · · · · · · ·		$\tilde{a}_{1n}$
·				
·	· ·			
·				
P_m	$\tilde{a}_{m0} = \tilde{b}_m$	$\tilde{a}_{m,m+1}$ · · · · · · · · ·		$\tilde{a}_{mn}$

FIG. 1. The simplex tableau.

To begin the algorithm, we apply steps 1–4 to Eqs. 6 and 7 with the nbfs $\mathbf{y} = \mathbf{b}$, $\mathbf{x} = \mathbf{0}$. An example of the application of this algorithm may be found in Ralston and Rabinowitz (1978).

In the foregoing, we have assumed a nondegenerate bfs at each stage. Theoretically, the simplex algorithm need not converge in the presence of degeneracy, but in practice, even though degeneracy is a common phenomenon, it can be ignored, since it virtually never causes computational problems.

In addition to the form above, there are a number of variations of the simplex algorithm. The most important of these, which can be quite useful computationally, is the *dual simplex algorithm*, in which, in effect, we interchange the roles of $\mathbf{b}$ and $\mathbf{c}$ in Eqs. 1 and 2 to derive another formulation of the LP problem whose solution is easily transformed into a solution of the original problem.

In the 1980s, two new algorithms for solving LP problems were developed by Khachian and Karmarkar (see Strang, 1986). The latter, in particular, may well replace the simplex method for large problems.

References

1978. Ralston, A. and Rabinowitz, P. A *First Course in Numerical Analysis* (2nd Ed.). New York: McGraw-Hill.
1986. Strang, G. *Introduction to Applied Mathematics*. Wellesley, MA: Wellesley-Cambridge Press.

ANTHONY RALSTON

SIMULATION

For articles on related subjects *see* ANALOG COMPUTER; EMULATION; FINITE ELEMENT METHOD; HARDWARE MONITOR; MONTE CARLO METHOD; OPERATIONS RESEARCH; PERFORMANCE MEASUREMENT AND EVALUATION; QUEUEING THEORY; SCIENTIFIC APPLICATIONS; and SOFTWARE MONITOR.

PRINCIPLES

Simulation is the process of representing the dynamic behavior of one system by the behavior of another system. In computer science, simulation refers to the use of computation to implement a model of some dynamic system or phenomenon. The purpose of simulation is usually to make experimental measurements or predict behavior, thus moving the laboratory into the computer environment. Simulation thus provides a prototype system with which to answer questions of a "what if?" nature, or to use for teaching about the system being simulated.

Simulation—the process—has been one of the most consistently useful and productive applications of computer science. Simulations—the products of the process—have been used by industry, academia, and government for as long as the modern digital computer has been employed. Actually, the concept of simulation preceded the advent of digital computation through the use of analog computers, and preceded the use of analog computers through the use of physical models such as airframe models in wind tunnels and ship models in towing tanks.

This article is limited to digital simulation and emphasizes the process and applications, as well as the techniques and languages, of simulation.

Background Historically, a pioneering concept of digital simulation was proposed by John von Neumann, who conceived the application of gathering repetitive, statistical data on modeled phenomena. This was termed the *Monte Carlo method* because it imposed randomly generated parametric changes on the model. Among the earliest published applications of digital simulation were the solutions of problems related to job shops, the allocation and distribution of resources to production scheduling. Among the latest applications of digital simulation are the prediction of the performance of computers and computer networks. These applications are illustrative of one of the prime justifications for employing simulation, namely, that the economics or logistics of experimenting with the actual system may be prohibitive. Since simulation is also expensive (it is both labor-intensive and computation-intensive), economic justification for its application is of great importance.

Economically feasible simulations are those in which a model or substitute system must be used to attain predictive data. Some of these are system-design concept evaluation (the system is not physically available), system-destruction or safety experiments (too dangerous), and system-reliability or failure testing (economically unfeasible). Simulations have also been used to replace modules of systems or entire systems that are too large or cumbersome to test (e.g. spacecraft docking and maneuvering), world weather dynamics, large human/machine systems, and nuclear weapon effects. Such simulation is employed in lieu of or to enhance closed-form, mathematical means of predicting behavior. "Prediction" is an important concept. Simulation enables the mapping of the analyst's concept of the real world. Because mapping is an approximation, the results are approximate rather than precise.

One form of digital simulation—discrete event simulation—began about 1959 with the reporting of several job-shop simulators developed by large industrial corporations. In 1962 came the first general-purpose simulation languages—Simscript and GPSS. The technology has burgeoned in the intervening years, having migrated to the personal computer environment. Practitioners of simulation hold many regular national and international conferences on general applications and research, and there are periodically a number of symposia devoted to special applications (e.g. simulation of computers). Several major technical societies have simulation-oriented component organizations. The Society for Computer Simulation (SCS - *q.v.*) is devoted exclusively to simulation. Many academic institutions provide courses in simulation that are sponsored mainly in the engineering or in multidisciplinary curricula: computer science, operations research (*q.v.*), or industrial management, because simulation is, in essence, a multidisciplinary technology, comprising elements of mathematics, engineering, and management science.

Terminology

Simulation is a methodology, or process, that employs a computerized model of certain significant features of some physical or logical system. The object of the process of simulation is to provide an experimental model for the accumulation of data on the target system. The process of simulation is comprised of the steps of experiment definition, modeling, computer implementation, testing and validation, data gathering, and documentation.

Simulators are programs developed to implement and execute simulation. The term "simulator" usually implies the representation of some specific system model (job-shop simulator, computer simulator, etc.), even though the tool may be quite flexible and thus useful for many modeling adaptations. Simulators should be distinguished from *simulation languages,* which are general-purpose and contain no model bias.

The Process of Simulation

Experiment Definition The problem to be solved by simulation can be considered as the identification of the behavior of some dynamic system. "Dynamic" and "simulation" are interrelated terms. Systems that are dynamic—those whose states change with time—are customarily defined to be simulatable.

What the problem solver must determine at the outset of the simulation process is the extent and detail of the model required, and correspondingly, the scope of input and output data required.

"Extent" and "detail" are also interrelated. The extent of a system is the broadness of system function encompassed by the simulation model. The number of functions modeled is the detail or level of structure incorporated in the model. Because the host computer size and speed present a finite boundary for any application, the broader the scope of the system considered, the less detail is likely to be included. For example, the synthesis of a model of airport service might include planes landing, taking off, taxiing, and loading-unloading. Corresponding detail might be the actual runway routing and the unloading ramp services. Broader specification might include descent, ascent, flight routing, and holding. Finer structure might involve fueling, inspection, and crew assignments. In the broad extent, the incorporation of finer levels of detail would usually be irrelevant, and vice versa.

The desired output data and available input data are important ingredients in defining the simulation process. The data detail should be at a level comparable to that of the complexity of the model definition. Input data is frequently considered a simulation problem area. Hypothesized or poor-quality input data may degrade the validity of output data, but it may not diminish the viability or utility of the simulation process (see the later section, "Testing and Validation").

Modeling When the experiment has been defined, modeling can commence. Many types of simulation models exist. They are classified by the nature of the systems they represent. The most frequent classification criterion is the dynamic-change property of the system variables: continuous or discrete.

Continuous-variable models represent those systems that are describable by mathematical expressions that depict the continuous change of variables with time. Physical systems represented by differential equations, where time is the independent variable, are of this nature. Continuous-variable simulation demonstrates the behavior of the system during transient responses to perturbations and is carried out on analog, digital, or hybrid computers. It is usually conducted in the domain of engineering studies.

Discrete-variable (more commonly called *discrete-event*) models usually represent those systems in which the dynamic state changes in discrete, but not necessarily synchronous, steps.

In this case, no smooth, mathematical calculus can be found to represent system behavior. The changes are abrupt and step-like. Transients between states are not considered. Such system behavior typically results from the disruption of system status caused by the allocation and deallocation of resources within the system. Queueing is an important phenomenon in systems describable by discrete-event models. Classical queueing theory relationships can be used to represent only a limited range of model complexity and variability. To transcend this range, a simulation model involving numeric and symbolic variable representation and manipulation is employed.

Computer Implementation By *implementation* is meant the process of computerization of the model. Simulation programming may be accomplished by using various programming tools such as high-level languages or languages specifically designed to implement simulation. Computerization of the simulation model affords the benefit of automated data gathering and storage. Automation of these functions enables representation of complex dynamic processes and (optionally) the performance of Monte Carlo experiments on target systems. Monte Carlo experiments involve the perturbation of the system with randomly varying quantities and the accumulation of sufficiently large output data samples to be statistically significant.

Another benefit of computerization is the reduction of experimental data to summary reports on important system variables. Thus, the experimenter may receive deterministic or statistical output data that depicts system status and performance during and at the end of specified time intervals in individual experiments or at the conclusion of a desired statistical sample.

Continuous-variable models are implemented on the digital computer by the solution of appropriate differential equations representing the system dynamics. This methodology usually incorporates some form of numerical integration. This can be accomplished in a high-level, general-purpose language such as Fortran. There are also so-called "problem-oriented" languages that support numerical integration within the language's modular struc-

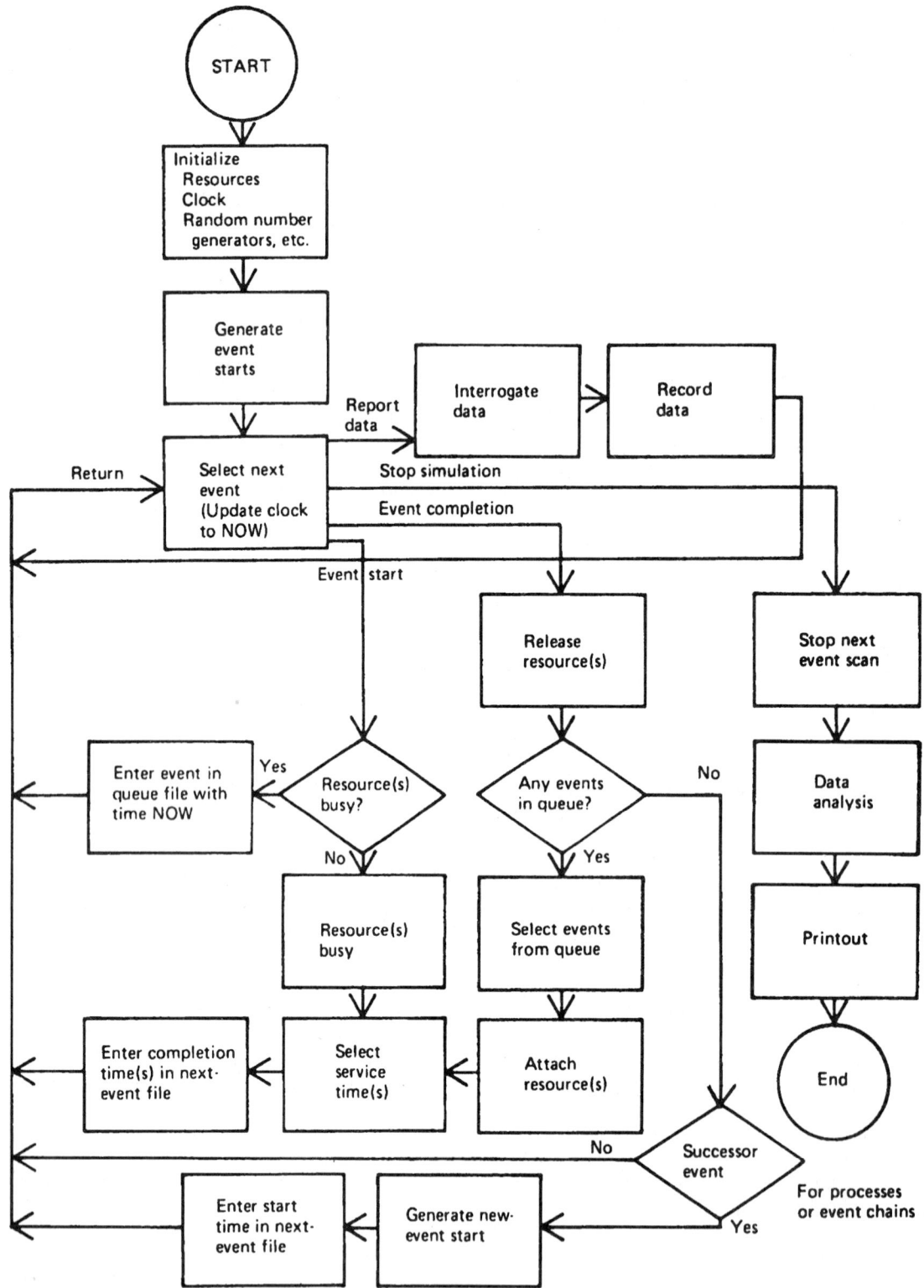

FIG. 1. Typical next-event routine for discrete-event simulation.

ture, thus enabling the programmer to represent the model as a high-level set of statements and functions (ACSL, CSMP, etc.).

Discrete-event models can also be implemented using such general-purpose, high-level languages as For-

tran. This involves the programming of such primitive constructs as data structures and queue-handling routines. As with continuous-variable applications, problem-oriented, high-level languages especially designed to enhance this implementation process are used. These are called *discrete-event simulation languages.* They can be described by various properties: dynamic orientation (transaction versus event), modeling purpose (general versus specific purpose), or coding level (statement versus database). Examples of these are GPSS and Simscript.

Testing and Validation *Testing* is the process of verifying that the computer code gives expected results within a defined range. Testing of simulation code is no different from testing of any application code. Good software engineering (*q.v.*) principles apply equally (*see* SOFTWARE TESTING).

Validation is a more perplexing aspect of simulation. There is a wide range of opinion as to the meaning, necessity, and techniques of validation. Validation, in general, refers to estimating the degree of validity of the simulation results and is a property somewhat comparable to accuracy, whereas "accuracy" has an absolute connotation; however, validity is concerned with relative accuracy. To state the validity of a result, one must impute to it an accuracy related to an understood criterion. This is important because simulation itself is an approximate process, frequently employing hypothetical or statistically varying data, constructs, and parameters. In this context, simulation results that have a specified accuracy may be valid for one purpose but invalid for another. For instance, accuracies in the simulated performance of a computer system of, say, 70% may be quite valid for configuration analysis for use in marketing, but the same results would be entirely invalid for some other purpose, such as final design tuning. The process requires the use of an understood criterion of validity.

Simulation is itself a substitute for real experimentation, and usually is conducted in the absence of a complete set of "real" data. Even when a real data comparison with some specific system state is possible, absolute accuracy of extrapolated system states is impractical, for the modeling process itself imparts assumptions, linearities, and qualified detail to the system model. In any case, establishing the final accuracy (hence, validity of the model) involves an iterative process whereby successive runs and adjustments converge and satisfy some accepted criterion.

Other means of partially validating the results of a simulation are comparison (for a limited range) with a hand-computed solution, and an estimation of relative validity. This refers to an order-of-magnitude/polarity comparison of simulated and predicted behavior sensitivities when subjecting the system to selected stresses.

Data Gathering and Output Analysis The entire subject of simulation running, data gathering, and analysis of data is not unique to simulation. This properly belongs in the category of experimental design and evaluation, which is common to technology at large. Only the nature of the data available from simulation is discussed here.

Data obtained from continuous-variable simulation can be characterized by dependent variable magnitude, rate, and acceleration time histories. These may be deterministic or show statistical variations, depending on the experiment. The main point is that continuous transient sensitivities are observed. For instance, in an airframe control simulation, some likely observables are airframe yaw, roll, and pitch histories, as the airframe responds to perturbations in some control variable or external force.

Data obtainable from discrete-event simulation fall into three primary classifications: timing, resource utilization and queueing, and historical.

Timing data include the statistics of system or event timing: average time to complete a job or process, and number of users per unit time. These are useful for gauging the dynamic performance of systems.

Resource utilization and queueing data includes the average number of requests, time utilized, waiting time, length of queue, etc., for the system resources. This is useful for determining system-flow bottlenecks and balance of resources.

Historical data usually is represented by a chronological event-by-event trace for entire or partial simulations. This is useful for debugging models and programs, and for examining transient conditions in the simulated system.

Documentation As in the case of testing, documentation for simulation programs should be guided by accepted practices for application program documentation. Since computer models comprise a special case of program documentation, a guideline on the documentation of computer models in general, produced by the National Bureau of Standards, is the current authority. The cost of thorough documentation is not insubstantial; a conservative estimate is one-third of the total project cost.

Models and Modeling Continuous and discrete models have radically different structures and approaches. There are also "combined" models that display properties of both.

Continuous-variable Models Continuous-variable models may be described rather succinctly. They are represented by the relationships of calculus and are handled by the computational processes of calculus. Dependent phenomena are expressed as equations of variables with first and higher-order linear or partial derivatives and with multiplicative and additive constants. Time is usually the continuous, independent variable.

Discrete-event Models Having no formal "calculus" as a foundation, discrete-event models are produced as an ad hoc mixture of numeric and symbolic notation, which in essence corresponds to the notation of queueing theory. Flowcharting is a useful organizing medium. Discrete-event models are primarily focused on system users who utilize system resources and expend time. Where resources are unavailable, queueing and queue-serving may occur. Models may differ in the generation of users and in method of accumulation of time and queueing statistics. However, all discrete-event models possess the basic element set: users, resources, queues, and demands.

Users

Users are the consumers of resources. They may be, for example, supermarket customers, computer applications, or factory orders. User entities may have defining attributes. For instance, supermarket customers may be differentiated by gender, number of selections, and point of origin (i.e. parking location). As another example, computer applications may be differentiated by data referenced, number of segments processed, type of origin (i.e. remote terminal, batch load, etc.). Factory orders may be differentiated by type of product ordered, number of production operations required, and shipping destination. A commonly employed attribute is *priority,* which is usually invoked to influence the competition for resources. Priority may be used for ranking or may be preemptive.

Resources

Resources may be described as single servers, pools or sets of servers, and storage entities. A *single server* is one that has uniqueness. Resources having common attributes, and considered interchangeable may be grouped in sets, called *multiservers.*

One of the main differences in expression of discrete-event models is in the approach taken to resource modeling. Resources may be passive—owned and allocated by the system as needed—or may be active—processes that have an independent life and interact with users when needed. Thus, we have the dichotomy between process/passive resource modeling and process interaction modeling. This difference may be illustrated by a supermarket model, where the users are customers who shop in the store. The carts in the store are considered as a pool of passive, interchangeable units, allocated by the store ("system") to requesting customers as needed. Store personnel, by comparison, may be considered as passive, but may also be considered as processes themselves, performing independent functions and also interacting with customer processes according to some rule of service. This is process interaction.

Queues

Queues are entities that hold and order the users waiting for resource service. A stated service discipline controls the ordering, usually by user priority and time of request. Queues may be treated as theoretically infinite or may be considered as having limited length. Examples of queues are the supermarket check-out waiting line, the computer request scheduling stack, and the job-shop subassembly storage bin. The waiting line may be effectively infinite or may be limited by floor space; the stack is necessarily limited by memory size; the storage bin has obvious physical space limitations.

Demand

Demand is the schedule of events, users, or customers to be processed through the system. Demand specification may be expressed deterministically or probabilistically. Users—sometimes termed "transactions"—may be scheduled at predetermined times or as the result of random selection from some statistical arrival-time population. An example of supermarket demand is the pattern of arrival of shoppers of various types during, say, a peak hour.

Combined Models Combined models are hybrid combinations of continuous and discrete models. A typical example is where some discrete-event process must interact with a continuous-variable process, such as the case where the flow of fluids through a tank/pipe system is stimulated and controlled by the arrival and departure of tanker vessels which are represented as discrete events.

The Tools of Computer Simulation

Continuous-Event Simulation Program Operation The construction of these models is an application of formal calculus; hence, the operation of programs that execute these models is an application of numerical integration (*see* NUMERICAL ANALYSIS). In brief, the dependent variables are initialized following which stepwise approximate integration is performed according to some solution technique. At appropriate instances in the process, measurements on the variables are taken to provide time-history information. The major differences in this process come from the method of model expression provided by the programming language, not in the execution.

Discrete-Event Simulation Program Operation Discrete-event simulation programming languages are, at the execution level, quite similar. They differ mainly in the method available to the programmer for communicating the model. Basically, programs in all simulation languages manipulate data structures that contain elements describing simulated time, event resource-and-time requirement, resource status, etc.

The main operations executed by a typical discrete-event simulation program involve *list processing (q.v.).* They primarily consist of the updating of a next-event list and the maintenance of a queue (see Fig.1).

The next-event list is an ordered list of all events to be processed. The time for activity of the event at the head of the list is used to update a "simulation clock" variable. An entry in the next-event list is made whenever the time for a future event is established. Types of events handled by this file are simulation events (such as the starting time of some process or user, the starting time of individual events, the termination time of events or processes); reporting events (start of interim or final simulation output reports); and end of the simulation.

Processing of the next-event list, and hence the clock, then becomes a continuous updating of the start and finish of various events. Obviously, all event terminations and many event starts cannot be predetermined because of blockage or delays induced by resource contention and random selection of timing and decisions.

The queue maintains a "time stamped" record of all events awaiting resource servicing and that have previously been denied resources.

LANGUAGES

Simulation languages, as distinguished from general-purpose languages, are *problem-oriented languages (q.v.).*

They are usually written in a computer-independent notation for a particular problem area, and contain statements or constructs appropriate for formulating solutions to specific types of problems. Of course, general-purpose languages, such as Fortran, C (*q.v.*), and Ada (*q.v.*), are also widely used in simulation. In continuous simulation, use of Fortran-like languages is the most prevalent. In discrete simulation, the use of problem-oriented languages is more highly favored.

These usage patterns probably reflect an established familiarity with such tools as Fortran, rather than an objective preference based on features.

Some Simulation Languages

Described below are a representative list of problem-oriented simulation languages.

Continuous-Event Languages

ACSL

Developed expressly for the purpose of modeling systems described by time-dependent, nonlinear differential equations and/or transfer functions, ACSL (Advanced Continuous Simulation Language) permits the user to develop model code from block diagrams, mathematical equations, and conventional Fortran statements. The language consists of a set of arithmetic operators, standard functions, a set of special ACSL statements, and a macro capability. The statements supplied by the user are in two distinct groups. One defines the model or structure of the system being simulated; the other exercises this model (i.e. changes parameters, starts runs, controls plotting output, etc.). ACSL is available from Mitchell and Gauthier Associates in mainframe and PC implementations.

CSMP

A CSMP (Continuous System Modeling Program) program is constructed from three general types of statements: structural statements which define the model; data statements which assign numerical values to parameters, constants, etc.; and control statements. The structural statements may be Fortran-like expressions or may be high-level functional blocks selected from a provided repertoire. CSMP is an IBM mainframe package.

Discrete-Event Languages

SIMSCRIPT II.5 A descendant of one of the original discrete-event simulation languages, Simscript II.5 permits broad expression of models, since it is a complete scientific programming language that enables discrete-event simulation. Simscript II.5 contains programming "levels," which provide a wide range of capability for use as a scientific and/or data processing language, as well as providing discrete-event–oriented simulation capability. It is a product of C.A.C.I. and is available in mainframe and PC implementations.

GPSS Developed originally by IBM, GPSS (General Purpose Simulation System) is transaction-oriented, containing a repertoire of flowchart-like blocks. It also provides a large variety of autonomously generated measurements about the simulated model. Since its original version, it has appeared in subsequent, more powerful versions: GPSS-II, -III, IV, -V, and -360. It is currently available in two versions: GPSS/H (Wolverine Software, for mainframe, workstation, and PC); and GPSS-PC (Minuteman Software). Fortran code is accessible in GPSS.

Simula An extension of ALGOL developed at the Norwegian Computing Center (NCC), Simula is process-oriented: a process (user) continues until it is prevented from execution. An operative process is considered "active"; a queued or suspended process is considered "passive." Simula allows complete user access to Algol. An advanced version, Simula 67, is a general-purpose scientific language containing simulation capability, and is available in mainframe and PC implementations through NCC.

SLAM II A language that combines a powerful "network-like" notation for discrete-event simulation with a succinct code for programming differential equations, SLAM (Simulation Language for Alternate Modeling) II supports discrete, continuous, and combined simulation. SLAM II is available from Pritsker and Associates in both mainframe and PC versions.

CONVERSIM A language that combines the transaction functionality of languages like GPSS, with an interactive menu input routine that enables the user to implement models by answering questions in English, instead of using a programmatic approach. PMR, Inc. is developing Simtalk, an advanced version of CONVERSIM, for the PC environment.

CSIM A statement language with strong C-like notation, possessing the facility for implementing C (*q.v.*) code directly. CSIM is available for Unix-environment workstations and mainframes from Microelectronics and Computer Technology.

References

1974. Schriber, T. *Simulation Using GPSS*. New York: John Wiley.
1978. Gordon, G. *System Simulation*. Englewood Cliffs, NJ: Prentice-Hall.
1983. Russell, E. *Building Simulation Models with SIMSCRIPT*, Los Angeles: C.A.C.I.
1986. Pritsker, A. *Introduction to Simulation and SLAM II*. New York: Halstead Press.
1986. Schewetman, H. *CSIM Reference Manual (Revision 9)*. Dallas, TX: Microelectronics and Computer Technology.
1987. ——*Advanced Continuous Simulation Reference Manual (ACSL)*, Concord, MA: Mitchell and Gauthier Associates.
1988. Roth, P. and Brown, R. *CONVERSIM—A Teaching Simulation Language Incorporating a Conversational Model Builder*, Proceedings of the Winter Simulation Conference, San Diego, CA.
1989. Roth, P. *Discrete, Continuous, and Combined Simulation*, Proceedings of the Winter Simulation Conference, Atlanta, GA.
1989. Hoover, S. and Perry, R. *Simulation—A Problem Solving Approach*. Reading, MA: Addison-Wesley.

PAUL F. ROTH

SLOT.   *See* MOTHERBOARD.

SMALLTALK.   *See* OBJECT-ORIENTED PROGRAMMING.

SNOBOL.   *See* STRING PROCESSING: LANGUAGES.

SOCIAL SCIENCE APPLICATIONS

For articles on related subjects *see* COMPUTING AND SOCIETY; DATABASE MANAGEMENT SYSTEM; LEGAL APPLICATIONS OF COMPUTERS; POLITICAL APPLICATIONS; SIMULATION; and STATISTICAL APPLICATIONS.

Social science research requirements have challenged the limits of computation for over a century. Several major milestones in the early history of computing were sparked by attempts to advance the social sciences. It was the United States census of 1890 that inspired Herman Hollerith. (*q.v.*), a social researcher, to design the first automated data processing machinery. Hollerith's punched card system, while not a true computer, provided the foundation for contemporary computer-based data management.

In the late 1940s, anticipating the massive tabulations needed in the 1950 census, the U.S. Bureau of the Census contracted for the building of Univac I. (*q.v.*), the first commercially produced electronic computer. The need to count, sort, and analyze the 1950 census data on this milestone computer led to the development of the first high-speed magnetic tape storage system, the first sort-merge software package, and the first statistical package, a set of matrix algebra routines.

All of the social sciences plunged into computing during the 1960s. During this period, the first book of statistical computer programs was published (Cooley and Lohnes, 1962), and that same year the first book devoted entirely to social science applications was edited by Borko (1962). Not only were social scientists writing about how to apply computers, but they were designing and developing new software. One of the most popular statistical software packages, SPSS (Nie, Bent, and Hull, 1975), was designed and developed by social science graduate students at Stanford University.

In the 20 years following what was done by these early pioneers, social science computing has evolved rapidly. Computer applications have been designed to augment or support every research task, even the more subjective ones like notetaking, interviewing, and content analysis. By the early 1990s, the processing power of desktop computers and workstations (*q.v.*) had become so compelling to social researchers that in many countries it is hard to find a social science researcher's office without one.

During the 1980s, the volume of scholarly publications in social science computing expanded enormously. Most of the current technical articles on social science applications appear in the *Social Science Computer Review*, a quarterly publication of Duke University Press. This journal publishes reviews of social science software, databases, and computer-related books, as do such journals as *Educational and Psychological Measurement*, the *Journal of Marketing Research, The American Statistician*, and *Simulation and Games*. Another source of contemporary advances in social science computing is an annual review, *Computers and the Social Sciences*, from JAI Press.

Another major development during the 1980s was the emergence of computing as subfields within the social science professional associations. The American Sociological Association (ASA) formed a Section on Microcomputing, and similar subgroups were established in the American Political Science Association, the American Psychological Association, and the American Anthropological Association. Perhaps most significant for the emerging discipline of social science computing was its first annual conference, *Advanced Computing for the Social Sciences*, held in 1990 at Williamsburg, VA. From this conference emerged a new professional association, the Social Science Computing Association. Its official journal, the *Social Science Computer Review*, is the best source of information on the activities of the association.

We begin this review by summarizing two important categories: quantitative and qualitative applications. Applications such as computer-assisted data collection that do not fit this dichotomy are discussed later.

Quantitative Computing   A large share of ongoing social data analysis, like the massive census counts, would never get done without computer technology. For example, one application of LISREL, a computer procedure that analyzes linear structural relationships by the method of maximum likelihood, would consume weeks or months without a computer.

Statistical computing offers unique views of quantitative patterns in data. Certain subtle relationships within complex patterns cannot be observed without special software tools. For example, Heise's 1988 computer program, called Ethno, gives the researcher a framework for conceptualizing, examining, and analyzing data containing event sequences. In addition, several general-purpose statistical packages offer powerful exploratory data analysis capabilities. Bi-directionality is provided through dynamic data links (Steiger and Fouladi, 1990). One type of bi-directionality puts a graph in one window and a frequency distribution in another. When the user adjusts the data in one window, it automatically changes the information in the other to conform.

The complexity of social science data challenges even the best of the available statistical and data management software. Provisions for handling missing data and a complex variety of data types are common. Complex hierarchical and non-hierarchical structures sometimes make the analysis nearly impossible. A case in point is the Survey of Income and Program Participation (SIPP), which is collected by the U. S. Bureau of the Census. SIPP contains over eight unit (entity) types (e.g. housing unit, families, married couples, persons, and income sources).

Researchers working with this data generally require months or years, not days, to complete one analysis.

Another major problem is the lack of complete documentation for social data files. To resolve this and related data access problems, many universities and research centers established data archives to bank and maintain social science data. The largest and best known is the Interuniversity Consortium for Political and Social Research (ICPSR) at the University of Michigan. The specialists in data organization who staff these data archives founded a society called the International Association for Social Science Information—Service and Technology (IASSIST). This international association meets annually and publishes the *IASSIST Quarterly*.

Simulation and Modeling Early in the history of social science computing, Coleman (1962) and McPhee and Glaser (1962) designed computer simulation models and showed how to use them to identify elusive implications of different theoretical assumptions. Other social scientists followed in their footsteps, but in the 1970s the excitement of the pioneers was lost and few simulations or formal computer models were developed. During the past decade, with the emergence of artificial intelligence (*q.v.*) and other modeling methodologies, social researchers demonstrated renewed interest in formal computer-supported models of social processes (Schrodt, 1986; Hanneman, 1988). New computer simulations for social policy analysis and instruction have emerged as well (Brent and Anderson, 1990). Neural network models combined with artificial intelligence and expert systems (*q.v.*) currently challenge several social scientists (Garson, 1990).

Qualitative Computing Historically, quantitative computing has eclipsed qualitative computing within the social sciences, but there are major signs of change. Qualitative computing in the social sciences began with computer-based content analysis (Stone, 1966). In the mid-1980s, a survey of qualitatively-oriented researchers found that three-fourths of them regularly used computers (Brent, Scott, and Spencer, 1987). Qualitative computing as it is practiced today consists of the manipulation of textual and other types of nonnumeric data for purposes of deciphering the embedded content and structure.

Several general-purpose programs for qualitative analysis of text have been widely distributed (Tesch, 1989). These tools make the analysis of large amounts of text more accurate and efficient, and potentially direct the focus of attention to analytic procedures. This methodology yields significant insight through systematic examination of comparative contrasts among diverse cases (Ragin and Becker, 1989). Recent work has extended this methodology to include the management and analysis of audio and video segments (Hesse-Biber, Dupuis, and Kinder, 1989).

The computer-based literature review is largely a qualitative problem. Whether the database is a small bibliography or a massive hypertext (*q.v.*) file with full texts, the researcher must translate a conceptual problem into a series of word searches. Social scientists pioneered computer methods for bibliographic retrieval. Now, numerous

files of references and their descriptions can be accessed from home or office using terminals or CD-ROM readers. Popular CD-ROMs include Sociofile, which contains sociological abstracts, and PsycLIT, which contains psychological abstracts. The 1990 U. S. Census and many other large tables and maps are also available on CD-ROM.

The preparation of textual documents no longer consists of simple word processing, but entails other critical research functions, such as the construction of tables, "typesetting" of mathematical equations, and the sizing and resizing of three-dimensional graphs embedded within text. Social researchers increasingly use these capabilities and are moving rapidly toward workstation environments that obscure the transition between data manipulation, data analysis, and manuscript preparation (Steiger and Fouladi, 1990).

Perhaps most profound in their impact are the trends in text processing that blur traditional distinctions between writing and publishing (Lyman, 1989). The growing body of articles and reports in an electronic medium appear to propel social science scholarship toward hypertext (Blank, McCartney, and Brent, 1989).

Computer-Assisted Data Collection Most social science research centers now use computer-assisted telephone interviewing (CATI), although its impact is not fully investigated (Groves *et al*, 1988). CATI consists of on-line questionnaires or entry screens for telephone interviewers. These systems generally, but not always, have the following characteristics: centralized facilities for monitoring individual interviewer stations, instantaneous edit checks with feedback for invalid responses, and automatic branching to different questions depending upon the respondent's answers. CATI systems run on free-standing PCs, networked PCs, or large mainframe computers.

Major variations on this mode of data collection include (1) computer-assisted personal interviewing (CAPI), face-to-face interviewing assisted with a laptop (*q.v.*) or hand-held computing device; (2) computerized self-administered questionnaires (CSAQ), on-line programs designed for direct input from respondents; and (3) data entry programs to facilitate the entry of data collected manually at a prior time.

The Questionnaire Programming Language (QPL), developed by Dooley (1989), was designed to construct on-line programs to run any of these major types of computer-assisted data collection. QPL allows the researcher to draft a questionnaire with any word processor. From embedded branching commands within the questionnaire document, the QPL software package simultaneously produces two versions of the questionnaire: one for computer administration and the other for interviewer or self-administration. An additional bonus of the program is that it automatically produces data definition commands for SPSS or SAS to use for data analysis.

Computer-Mediated Communication As electronic mail (*q.v.*) systems continue to expand, they offer social researchers opportunities for conducting studies using networks for data collection. Some investigators disseminate on-line survey instruments, using local, national, and international networks (*see* NETWORKS, COMPUTER). Methodological investigations by Kiesler and Sproull (1986) documented some of the consequences (e.g. reduced nonresponse) of this methodology. The diffusion of "computer-mediated communication" among social scientists remains concentrated within specific communities of researchers (Ploch, 1990).

Conclusion The application of computing to social research is not without problems. Errors in data and software abound. Data and software tend to be costly, and many impediments inhibit sharing of these critical resources.

Nonetheless, new breakthroughs in computer technology continue, and major new opportunities will emerge. Many of the advances in social science computing during the next few years undoubtedly will follow the lines of progress already described: hypertext networks; integrated, high-performance, graphic data analysis stations; software for computer-supported cooperative work; expert systems; and neural networks (*q.v.*) for complex models of social systems.

The challenge for the future involves a concert of these innovations directed at the problem of modeling and analyzing vast amounts of social data. One solution would incorporate three-dimensional, multicolored, dynamic graphical representations of complex social data structures. But new techniques for analyzing these data will require new models of dynamic social structures as well as parallel social processes. Computer representations of these models will require extremely fast processing, such as that found only in the supercomputers (*q.v.*) of the 1990s. Graphical workstations in concert with supercomputer systems may offer major advances in the reduction of vast amounts of demographic data, particularly if they take advantage of color shadings, graphic symbols, and user-controlled animation. The absence of these applications in the social sciences is not so much due to the lack of technology as to the underdevelopment of formal models that can be linked to represent larger social systems.

References

1962. Borko, Harold (Ed). *Computer Applications in the Behavioral Sciences*. Santa Monica, CA: System Development Corporation.

1962. Cooley, William, and Lohnes, Paul. *Multivariate Procedures for the Behavioral Sciences*. New York: John Wiley.

1962. Coleman, James S. "Analysis of Social Structures and Simulation of Social Processes with Electronic Computers," *Simulation in Social Science: Readings*, 6–69, edited by Harold Guetzkow. Englewood Cliffs, NJ: Prentice-Hall.

1962. McPhee, William N. and Glaser, William A (Eds). *Public Opinion and Congressional Elections*. New York: Free Press.

1966. Stone, Philip, *et al. The General Inquirer*. Cambridge, MA: The M.I.T. Press.

1975. Nie, Norman, Bent, Dale, and Hull, Hadley. *Statistical Package for the Social Sciences*. New York: McGraw-Hill.

1986. Kiesler, Sarah and Sproull, Lee. S. "Response Effects in the Electronic Survey," *Public Opinion Quarterly* 50: 402–413.

1986. Schrodt, Philip A. "Predicting International Events," *BYTE*, **11**,*12* (Nov), 177ff.

1987. Brent, Edward, Scott, James, and Spencer, John. "The Use of Computers by Qualitative Researchers," *Qualitative Sociology* **10** (*3*): 309–313.

1988. Groves, Robert M., Biemer, P. P., Lyberg, L. E., Massey, J. T., Nicholls, W. L., and Waksberg, J. *Telephone Survey Methodology*. New York: John Wiley and Sons.

1988. Hanneman, Robert A. *Computer-Assisted Theory Building*. Newbury Park, CA: Sage Publications.

1988. Heise, David. "Computer Analysis of Cultural Structures," *Social Science Computer Review* **6**: 183–196.

1989. Blank, Grant, McCartney, James L., and Brent, Edward (Eds.). *New Technology in Sociology: Practical Applications in Research and Work*. New Brunswick, NJ: Transaction.

1989. Dooley, Kevin. *QPL Data Collection Program*. Washington, DC: Human Resources Division, U. S. General Accounting Office.

1989. Hesse-Biber, Sharlene, Dupuis, Paul, and Kinder, Scott. "HyperResearch: A Computer Program for the Analysis of Qualitative Data Using the Macintosh," Paper presented at the 1989 annual meeting of the America Sociological Association.

1989. Lyman, Peter. "The Future of Sociological Literature in an Age of Computerized Texts," in G. Blank, J. L. McCartney, and E. Brent (Eds) *New Technology in Sociology: Practical Applications in Research and Work*, 17–32. New Brunswick, NJ: Transaction.

1989. Ragin, Charles C. and Becker, Howard S., "How the Microcomputer is Changing our Analytic Habits," in G. Blank, J. L. McCartney, and E. Brent. *New Technology in Sociology: Practical Applications in Research and Work*, 47–56. New Brunswick, NJ: Transaction.

1989. Tesch, Renata. "Computer Software and Qualitative Analysis: A Reassessment," in G. Blank, J. L. McCartney, and E. Brent (Eds) *New Technology in Sociology: Practical Applications in Research and Work*, 141–154. New Brunswick, NJ: Transaction.

1990. Brent, Edward, and Anderson, Ronald E. *Computer Applications in the Social Sciences*. New York: McGraw-Hill.

1990. Ploch, Donald R. "Computing: Communication and Control," *Social Science Computer Review* **8**, *4* (Winter), 614–626.

1990. Garson, G. David. "Expert Systems: An Overview for Social Scientists," *Social Science Computer Review*. **8**, *3* (Fall), 387–410.

1990. Steiger, James H. and Fouladi, Rachel T. "Some Key Emerging Trends in Statistical and Graphical Software for the Social Scientist," *Social Science Computer Review* **8**, *4* (Winter), 627–664.

RONALD E. ANDERSON

SOCIETY FOR COMPUTER SIMULATION (SCS)

For articles on related subjects *see* AMERICAN FEDERATION OF INFORMATION PROCESSING SOCIETIES; and SIMULATION.

Purpose The Society for Computer Simulation promotes the advancement of simulation and allied computer arts by sponsoring meetings and informal discussions, by publishing reports of these meetings and papers, and by cooperating with other technical societies and with educational and other organizations in activities that contribute to the advancement of simulation and allied arts.

How Established The Society began on the initiative of John McLeod, who called a meeting in Oxnard, CA on 7 November 1952, of people (mostly from Southern California) who were using simulation in their work. Thirty-nine people from 13 organizations attended this meeting and created "The Simulation Council," carefully excluding any reference to the type of equipment used for modeling and simulation.

McLeod was elected chairman at the organization meeting, and he and his wife Suzette immediately began putting out at their own expense a mimeographed monthly *Simulation Council Newsletter* which quickly developed national circulation and spread the Simulation Council idea across the country. In 1956, regional simulation councils elected two directors each to serve on the Board of Directors of Simulation Councils, an unincorporated association created to provide coordination and better communication among the regional councils and to advance the art of simulation.

On 3 June 1957, Dov Abramis, Dr. George Bekey, and Norman L. Irvine formed a California nonprofit membership corporation called Simulation Councils, Inc. (SCI), which is the legal name, though the Board, in 1972, adopted, and still uses, the name "The Society for Computer Simulation" as one that better describes the organization's activities. Eligibility for membership requires professional training and experience, and professional engagement in simulation or allied sciences. There were approximately 2,000 members as of 1992.

The following people have served as chairmen of the Board of Directors, an office that was retermed "President" in 1962.

Robert M. Howe, 1956–1957
B. Dov Abramis, 1958–1959
Stanley Rogers, 1959–1960
J. E. Sherman, 1960–1962
Maughan S. Mason, 1962–1964
P. J. Hermann, 1964–1966
James E. Wolle, 1966–1968
David R. Miller, 1968–1969
Francis C. Rieman, 1969–1971
Jon N. Mangnall, 1971–1972
George A. Rahe, 1972–1973
Robert D. Brennan, 1973–1975
Paul A. Berthiaume, 1975–1976
Per A. Holst, 1976–1977
Donald C. Martin, 1977–1979
Stewart I. Schlesinger, 1979–1981
Walter J. Karplus, 1982–1984
Norbert E. Pobanz, 1985–1986
Ralph C. Huntsurgh, 1987–1988
Roy E. Crosbie, 1989–1990
Carl Malstrom, 1990–

The Society was a member of the American Federation of Information Processing Societies (AFIPS).

Organization The Society is international in membership and interdisciplinary in scope. Members in 37 countries are divided geographically into 9 regional councils and one unassigned council (foreign). Councils include the U.S. and Canada, and the U.K.

International Headquarters are at 4838 Ronson Ct., Suite L., San Diego, CA 92111, (619) 277-3888.

Technical Program The Society sponsors the Summer Computer Simulation Conference and the Western and Eastern Multiconferences and co-sponsors the Winter Simulation Conference. Professional development seminars are a part of the Society's program.

The Society publishes *Simulation*, a monthly technical journal containing technical articles and information on the state-of-the-art and organization activities; *Simulation Councils Proceedings*, a semiannual series of hardbound books, each dealing with a timely topic in the field of simulation and each edited by an expert in that field; and *Transactions*, a refereed quarterly journal that examines complex issues of simulation.

ISAAC L. AUERBACH

SOCIETY FOR INDUSTRIAL AND APPLIED MATHEMATICS (SIAM)

For an article on a related subject *see* AMERICAN FEDERATION OF INFORMATION PROCESSING SOCIETIES.

The Society for Industrial and Applied Mathematics (SIAM) is a professional membership association of the U.S. established in 1952 to

- Further the application of mathematics to industry and science.
- Promote basic research in mathematics, leading to new methods and techniques useful to industry and science.
- Provide media for the exchange of information and ideas between mathematicians and other technical and scientific personnel.

To support these objectives, SIAM publishes numerous periodicals and monographs containing research and expository papers; conducts annual meetings, research conferences, and section activities; and sponsors the SIAM Institute for the Advancement of Scientific Computing.

Presidents of SIAM since its founding have been:

William E. Bradley, 1952–1953
Donald B. Houghton, 1953–1954
Harold W. Kuhn, 1954–1955
John W. Mauchly, 1955–1956
Thomas E. Southard, 1956–1958
Donald L. Thomsen, Jr., 1958–1959
Brockway McMillan, 1959–1960
F. J. Weyl, 1960–1961
Robert F. Rinehart, 1961–1962
Joseph P. LaSalle, 1962–1963
Alston S. Householder, 1963–1964
J. Barkley Rosser, 1965–1966

Garrett Birkhoff, 1967–1968
J. Wallace Givens, Jr., 1969–1970
Burton H. Colvin, 1971–1972
C. C. Lin, 1973–1974
Herbert B. Keller, 1975–1976
Werner C. Rheinboldt, 1977–1978
Richard C. DiPrima, 1979–1980
Seymour V. Parter, 1981–1982
Hirsh Cohen, 1983–1984
Gene H. Golub, 1985–1986
C. William Gear, 1987–1988
Ivar Stakgold, 1989–1990
Robert E. O'Malley, Jr. 1991–1992

SIAM publishes ten research journals, of which five are of particular interest to computer scientists:

1. *SIAM Journal on Computing*, which contains research articles in the application of mathematics to the problems of computer science and the nonnumerical aspects of computing. Topics include automata theory, analysis of algorithms, computational complexity, computational algebra, computational aspects of combinatorics and graph theory, computational geometry, computational robotics, the mathematical aspects of programming languages, artificial intelligence, information retrieval, data structures, cryptographic protocols, distributed algorithms, and computer architecture (four issues per year, first issue: March 1972).

2. *SIAM Journal on Numerical Analysis*, which contains research articles on the development and analysis of numerical methods, including their convergence, stability, and error analysis, as well as related results in functional analysis and approximation theory. Computational experiments and new types of numerical applications are also included (six issues per year, first issue: 1964).

3. *SIAM Journal on Discrete Mathematics*, which contains research articles on combinatorics and graph theory, discrete optimization and operations research, theoretical computer science, coding and communication theory, and game theory and mathematical modeling (four issues per year, first issue: February 1988).

4. SIAM *Journal on Matrix Analysis and Applications* (formerly *SIAM Journal on Algebraic and Discrete Methods*), which contains research articles on the applications of matrix analysis to areas such as Markov chains, networks, signal processing, systems and control theory, mathematical programming, economic and biological modeling, and statistics and operations research (four issues per year, first issue: January 1980).

5. *SIAM Journal on Scientific and Statistical Computing*, which contains research articles on those techniques of scientific computation concerned with the solution of continuous or statistical models (as opposed to discrete models). New

algorithms for current architectures or developing new architectures are particularly appropriate, but there should be general numerical applicability of the results. Papers should provide insight into which computational methods are suitable for which classes of problems and computer architectures (four issues per year, first issue: March 1980).

ISAAC L. AUERBACH

SOFTWARE

For articles on related subjects *see* MATHEMATICAL SOFTWARE; OPERATING SYSTEMS; PROGRAMMING LANGUAGES; SOFTWARE CONFIGURATION MANAGEMENT; SOFTWARE ENGINEERING; SOFTWARE FLEXIBILITY; SOFTWARE HISTORY; SOFTWARE LIBRARIES, NUMERICAL AND STATISTICAL; SOFTWARE MAINTENANCE; SOFTWARE MANAGEMENT; SOFTWARE METRICS; SOFTWARE MONITOR; SOFTWARE PERSONALIZATION; SOFTWARE PROTOTYPING; SOFTWARE RELIABILITY; SOFTWARE REUSABILITY; SOFTWARE TESTING; and SYSTEMS PROGRAMMING.

Very early in the development of computers, people referred to the actual physical components—the tubes and relays, the resistors and wires, and chassis—as computer *hardware*. It soon became popular within the computer industry to use the word *software* to describe the non-hardware components of the computer, in particular the programs that were needed to make the computers perform their intended tasks. The word *software* caught on rapidly, and was in quite general use by 1960. One speaks of software people, software shops (i.e. organizations that produce software), software maintenance, and, more recently, software engineering. Actually, software is a very general term that includes many areas discussed elsewhere in this Encyclopedia. The most significant are operating systems and programming languages.

Although the word *software* can be used in connection with all kinds of programs, it is usually used to denote programs whose use is not limited to one particular job or application. Thus, one speaks of systems software, of software systems, of mathematical software, of software for business applications, etc.

Early computers could run with relatively simple software systems. A loader (*q.v.*) and a library of subroutines was considered sufficient for most first-generation computers. There were some very significant and sophisticated software developments associated with UNIVAC I (*q.v.*). Grace Hopper (*q.v.*) and her colleagues designed the first, very general sorting systems, and developed the first high-level languages for business applications. Anatol Holt and William Turanski introduced many software system concepts in their GP (Generalized Programming) system, such as the *extended machine*, which refers to the *combination* of hardware and software that the user sees as the machine for which programs are written.

Still in the first generation, John Backus and his colleagues from IBM and from several IBM user installations developed the Fortran compiler for the IBM 704, perhaps the most significant piece of software ever written. Fortran became the language of discourse for scientific programmers throughout the world and throughout the computer industry, and once and for all established the importance and usefulness of high-level languages.

The separation of hardware and software, the idea that software was superimposed on hardware in order to enhance its capabilities, persisted throughout the first- and most of the second-generation computers. Even though this was already true in some earlier computers, especially those built by Univac, it is perhaps the distinguishing characteristic of third-generation systems that the hardware system is designed to operate under control of a rather sophisticated software system, and will perform very poorly or not at all in the absence of such a system. Especially in a multiprogramming (*q.v.*) and/or multiprocessor system, it is essential that there be an operating system that maintains control of the allocation of system resources and that avoids problems of conflict, blocking, interference among simultaneous users of the system. In particular, the input/output functions and the management of central and peripheral storage are software system functions that must be centralized and carefully controlled if chaos is to be avoided. These topics are discussed in detail in the article on operating systems.

The operating system provides a set of interfaces and conventions for using them that are reflected in all other major software products. A complete software system will contain, in addition to the operating system, a set of compilers for various languages, one or more system loaders, one or more database management systems (*q.v.*), sets of utility routines, special- and general-purpose debugging systems, and generalized subsystems for applications such as sorting (*q.v.*) and merging, mathematical programming, engineering design, report generation, simulation, graphics, etc. All of these must interface with the operating system and its input/output system, and in this sense they all form part of a single software system.

Up until about 1969, it was generally assumed that the purchase or rental of a computer hardware system entitled the customer to all general-purpose software produced by the manufacturer for that computer at no extra cost. The independent software industry, to the extent that it existed, was limited mostly to work on special-purpose systems and to applications programming. Software companies could attempt to produce software systems for sale that were better in some significant ways than those produced by the hardware manufacturers, but this could rarely be done on a profitable basis. The software companies argued that the manufacturers were actually selling software to their customers and including its cost in the price of the hardware. The hardware customer had to buy a bundle consisting of the hardware plus all available software. They urged the *unbundling* of software. This would presumably benefit the buyer, who would only have to pay for as much software as needed. It would also permit competitive marketing of software products.

In June 1969, IBM announced that it was introducing a new policy to implement the unbundling of computer software. With the exception of essential operating system software, all new software products would henceforth be priced separately.

The decision to unbundle software was made under pressure as a response to charges of unfair competition, but it was probably not made reluctantly. It must have been clear to IBM that software sales could become a major source of revenue to computer manufacturers. Almost all other hardware manufacturers followed the lead of IBM and unbundled their software products.

Scientific and Mathematical Software The first software systems were libraries of mathematical subroutines. In view of their very long history, it is rather surprising that major efforts in this area have continued and will continue on into the future. In fact, it was only in the early 1970s that some attempt was made to consolidate these efforts. A program supported by the National Science Foundation was initiated with the aim of taking whatever steps are necessary to make sure that high-quality scientific software is available to the whole community of scientific users of computers. Most earlier efforts in this area underestimated the magnitude of the problems, and attacked them with insufficient resources.

A number of mathematical software packages have achieved very wide distribution and very general use on computers of very diverse characteristics produced by a number of different manufacturers. One of the best known is the Bi-Med (BMDP) series of statistical programs produced at UCLA. Another is the EISPACK eigenvalue package produced at the Argonne National Laboratory.

Software Engineering Techniques of software development developed on an ad hoc basis along with the earliest computers. Application of these techniques to the production of very large software systems resulted in unexpectedly large expenditures for the relatively inefficient programs that were produced.

There has been a great deal of thought devoted to the technology of software production. In the third-generation of computers the cost of producing software seemed to be excessive, and the methods used often showed little or no advance over those used on some of the earliest systems.

Attempts have been made, with varying amounts of success, to apply to the problems of software production the engineering principles that have been reasonably successful in other disciplines. The most usual proposal is to develop sets of modules that can be used as "off the shelf" components in the development of software products. One of the factors that has limited the success of such ventures has been the continuing high rate of technological development of computer hardware. Thus, the increased use of large-scale integration and the projected development of large-scale, low-cost, fast bulk memory may produce very radical changes in software requirements and in software technology.

A more theoretical approach to the problems of program development has developed from the work of Perlis, McCarthy, Dijkstra, Wirth, Naur, Floyd, and others. This approach is based on *structured programming* (*q.v.*) and on the use of mathematical verification and proof techniques in connection with the production of programs (*see* PROGRAM VERIFICATION). The aim is to produce programs that have been proved to be correct before they are tested on a computer, and thereby to eliminate much of the program-testing activity. Proponents of this methodology claim a tremendous increase in programmer productivity at little if any cost in program-running efficiency.

References

Note: There are many books and journals devoted to the software field. Among the most important software journals are the ACM *Transactions on Programming Languages and Systems*, the IEEE *Transactions on Software Engineering*. and *Software Practice and Experience*.

1967. Rosen, S. (Ed.). *Programming Systems and Languages*. New York: McGraw-Hill. (A survey of software up to the mid-1960s.)

1987. Freeman, P. *Software Perspectives: The System is the Message*. Reading, MA: Addison-Wesley.

1987. Levy, L. S. *Software Engineering and Software Economics*. New York: Springer-Verlag.

1991. Gelernter, D. H. *Mirror Worlds, or, The Day Software Puts the Universe in a Shoebox*. New York: Oxford University Press.

SAUL ROSEN

SOFTWARE CONFIGURATION MANAGEMENT

For articles on related subjects *see* SOFTWARE ENGINEERING; SOFTWARE MAINTENANCE; and SOFTWARE MANAGEMENT.

Configuration management (CM) is the discipline of controlling changes in large and complex systems. It is intended to prevent the chaos likely to be caused by the numerous corrections, extensions, and adaptations that are applied to any large system over its lifetime. The goal of CM is to ensure a systematic and traceable development process such that a system is in a well-defined state with accurate specifications and verified quality attributes at all times.

CM was first developed in the aerospace industry in the 1950s, when production of spacecraft experienced difficulties caused by numerous and inadequately documented engineering changes. *Software configuration management* (SCM) is simply CM tailored to systems, or portions of systems, that consist predominantly of software (Bersoff *et al.*, 1980). A major difference between SCM and traditional CM is that software changes faster than hardware, and therefore needs automatic support. Fortunately, since software is normally on-line and can be manipulated automatically, SCM is susceptible to automation.

SCM Objects The primary objects of interest in SCM are software configuration items, configurations, baselines, and derived items. A *software configuration item* is any separately identifiable, machine-readable document produced during the course of a software project. It consists purely of information. Examples include require-

ments documents, design documents, specifications, interface descriptions, source program modules, machine code modules, database files, test programs, test data, test output, user profiles, user manuals, VLSI designs, digitized drawings and pictures, sound recordings, etc. A configuration item is the smallest unit of individual change: there are no practicable, smaller units contained in the item that vary independently.

By contrast, a *configuration* is an aggregate of several components, where the components are configuration items or other configurations. A configuration is changed by replacing, adding, or deleting components. An example is the configuration of hardware, software, and documentation making up an entire computer system. Each of the three main components is again a large configuration, ultimately composed of individual integrated circuits, code modules, or manual sections, for example.

A *baseline* is the description of a configuration. A baseline is essentially a parts list, stating precisely and unambiguously which components make up a given configuration. Since baselines also change, they are configuration items in their own right. More important, baselines serve as reference points in the development of a system: Once a baseline is established, all subsequent changes are described relative to it until the next baseline is recorded.

A *derived item* is generated fully automatically from other objects. Examples include compiled code, linked systems, formatted text, and test output. Derived items are special in that they can be deleted (since they can be regenerated when needed). The space/time trade-off between storage and regeneration is handled by the system building function of SCM (see below).

SCM Functions SCM allows more automation than traditional CM. The main functions of SCM that have been automated are identification, version control, configuration selection, and system building (Tichy, 1988). The traditional CM functions of change control, configuration auditing, and configuration accounting are still largely manual.

Identification assigns a unique identifier to every object. Reliable identification is crucial for effective CM. A great deal of confusion results if the same identifier is assigned to two different objects (e.g. two different versions). Therefore, a new and unique identifier is issued whenever an object is changed. A unique identifier typically consists of a descriptive name and several fields with version designators, serial numbers, or dates.

Issuing a new identifier for every change may obscure relations between objects. One may want to record, for instance, that a given configuration item is a revision of another and corrects certain errors. The *version control* function of SCM records such facts: It collects configuration items into *version groups* and manages the evolution of these groups. The items in a version group are linked by a number of relations. For instance, the relation *revision-of* records the historical development lines; the relation *variant-of* connects items that differ in some aspect of function, design, or implementation, but are the same in other respects. Fig. 1 illustrates a version group with two diverging lines of development, plus a correction that is applied to an old revision. All three lines merge eventually.

Version control performs a number of services. An important one is that it warns of overlapping changes: When developers attempt to change the same item concurrently, version control informs them of the overlap and recommends that one developer wait for the other to finish, or offers support for merging the changes after the fact. The *checkin/checkout* paradigm avoids overlapping changes: Before any actual modification is possible, the developer has to acquire exclusive change permission for the desired version by executing a checkout operation. Once the changes are completed, the checkin operation deposits the new version back into the group. Old versions are typically not deleted until it is certain that they are not used anywhere.

Version control also maintains a log stating the reasons for changes. The entries typically record time of change and the identity of the developer, plus a short commentary describing the nature of the change. The log is convenient for surveying the changes a system underwent over time. Version control must also conserve the space occupied by multiple versions. The compression technique of *delta storage*, (i.e. storing only the differences between versions rather than complete copies reduces space consumption by 90% or more). Of course, whenever a version is needed, a special program must first reconstruct it from the differences. SCCS and RCS (Rochkind, 1975, Tichy, 1985) are version control systems implemented with different delta mechanisms.

Configuration selection deals with the problem of which changes to include relative to a baseline. For instance, most developers would include their own changes plus those of others that have been tested. Another selection criterion is to choose all changes current and tested at a given point in the development history. Once the selection is defined, the configuration is handed over to *system building*. This function, also called *system generation*, produces the desired set of derived objects. It performs such tasks as compiling, linking, loading, pre- and post-processing, document formatting, installation, etc. An important issue is to avoid redundant processing steps, (e.g. compilations of objects that have already been compiled).

The MAKE system (Feldman, 1979) combines several of the functions above into one tool. It can be used to describe configurations, to select the most recent versions of all changes, to run specified building processes automatically, and even to trigger regression tests.

Change control is the process that decides which of the requested changes to implement. Since this step involves judgment, it is difficult to automate. In large software development organizations, this task is handled by a committee called the *change control board*.

Configuration auditing traces the implementation status of change requests and verifies that all steps required by quality assurance have been followed. *Configuration accounting* simply records the facts that configuration auditing found.

An important part of configuration auditing is *regression testing*. (The term derives from the fact that one wants to prevent a system from *regressing* to a worse state.) It consists of running test suites after changes and comparing the results with expected outputs. Once a test suite is defined, it is run against all future releases of a software system to make sure that old problems do not reappear. Regression testing is a mechanical task and can be automated to a high degree.

References

1975. Rochkind, Marc J. "The Source Code Control System," *IEEE Transactions on Software Engineering*, **SE-1**(*4*): 364–370 (December).

1979. Feldman, Stuart I. "Make—A Program for Maintaining Computer Programs," *Software—Practice and Experience*, **9**(*3*): 255–265 (March).

1980. Bersoff, Edward H., Henderson, Vilas D., and Siegel, Stanley G. *Software Configuration Management*. Englewood Cliffs, NJ: Prentice-Hall.

1985. Tichy, Walter F. "RCS—A System for Version Control," *Software—Practice and Experience*, **15**(*7*): 637–654 (July).

1988, Tichy, Walter F. "Tools for Software Configuration Management," in *Proceedings of the International Workshop on Software Version and Configuration Control*, 1–20. Stuttgart: Teubner Verlag.

WALTER F. TICHY

SOFTWARE ENGINEERING

For articles on related subjects *see* ABSTRACT DATA TYPE; CHIEF PROGRAMMER TEAM; COMPUTER-AIDED SOFTWARE ENGINEERING; ENCAPSULATION; INFORMATION HIDING; OBJECT-ORIENTED PROGRAMMING; PROGRAM VERIFICATION; SOFTWARE; SOFTWARE CONFIGURATION MANAGEMENT; SOFTWARE ENGINEERING INSTITUTE; SOFTWARE FLEXIBILITY; SOFTWARE HISTORY; SOFTWARE MAINTENANCE; SOFTWARE MANAGEMENT; SOFTWARE METRICS; SOFTWARE MONITOR; SOFTWARE PERSONALIZATION;

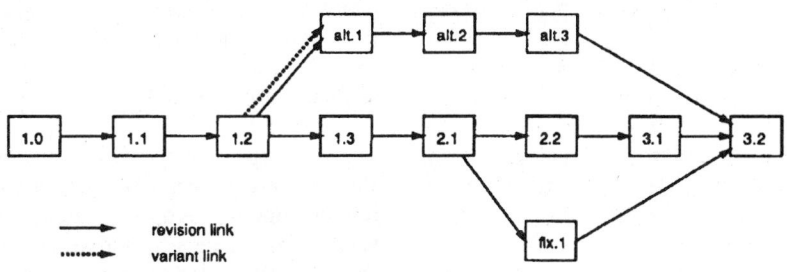

FIG. 1. Development history of a version group.

SOFTWARE PROTOTYPING; SOFTWARE RELIABILITY; SOFTWARE REUSABILITY; SOFTWARE TESTING; and STRUCTURED PROGRAMMING.

Since the earliest widespread commercial use of computers in the 1950s, dramatic improvements in hardware technology have made progressively higher performance machines available at consistently declining prices. In contrast, the volume of software required for typical system installations has steadily increased, and the costs of obtaining this software have grown even more rapidly. While there have been modest software quality and productivity improvements, the general pattern of industrial performance is one of missed schedules, cost overruns, and quality problems. With larger-scale software products, the number of development people involved has proportionately increased. Society's demand for increasingly automated systems and services has also resulted in the use of progressively larger software products in sensitive applications where defects could have severe and even life-threatening consequences. The objective of *software engineering* is to respond to these quality and productivity challenges by applying engineering disciplines to software development.

This very large subject is addressed using the general framework suggested by Ross, Goodenough, and Irvine, with some modifications, as shown in Fig. 1 (Ross, 1975). Following brief definitions and a historical summary, the goals, process, and principles of software engineering are outlined. In conclusion, a framework is described for determining the status of software development in its progression from a craft-like practice to a defined and structured engineering discipline.

History The term *software engineering* first appeared at NATO-sponsored conferences in 1968 and 1969 in Garmish, Germany, and Rome, Italy (Naur, 1976). The production of software had developed as a largely artistic practice by creative individuals, somewhat analogous to early craftsmen in the pre-industrial revolution era. Several university professors, notably Dijkstra and Perlis, recognized early the need for increasing the discipline and precision of this work and helped foster the movement to regularize, define, and automate its practice (Dijkstra, 1976). During the late 1960s and 1970s, many advances were made in both industry and academia to characterize better software products and to establish a business basis for large-scale software development. In 1982, the U. S. Deputy Under Secretary of Defense formed a joint service task force to review software problems in the U. S. Department of Defense and make recommendations. This resulted in several initiatives, including the establishment of the Software Engineering Institute at Carnegie Mellon University, the STARS (Software Technology for Adaptable Reliable Systems) Program, and the Ada (*q.v.*) Program. Examples of U. S. industrial efforts to improve software practice are the Software Productivity Consortium, which was established by a group of U.S. aerospace organizations, and the software division of the Micro-Electronics and Computer Consortium, composed primarily of computer manufacturers. Similar initiatives have been established in Europe and Japan, although largely under government sponsorship.

Definitions Software is defined as "computer programs, procedures, and possibly associated documentation and data pertaining to the operation of a computer system" (IEEE, 1988). Engineering is the systematic application of scientific knowledge in creating and building cost-effective solutions to practical problems in the service of humankind (Shaw, 1989). Software engineering is that form of engineering that applies the principles of computer science and mathematics to achieving cost-effective solutions to software problems.

Several distinctions result from these definitions. First, programming is the activity of writing computer programs. When programming uses recognized engineering standards in the production of software, it is a proper part of the discipline of software engineering. Computer science (*q.v.*) is more broadly concerned with the underlying scientific principles of information processes, structures, and procedures. It thus provides important foundation knowledge for software engineers. Computer engineering generally covers the architectural and design engineering topics required for the development and production of computing devices and systems.

The Goals of Software Engineering Much as described by Ross, *et al.*, the goals of software engineering are to produce consistently products that have the properties shown in Fig. 1. Regardless of the specific project requirements, products that meet these goals will likely withstand unusual stress and be readily adaptable to unanticipated needs.

Correctness Correctness concerns the degree to which the software product is implemented to perform its intended function properly, consistently, and predictably. While such issues as code quality and testing are part of this goal, the broader correctness issue includes recoverability, repairability, and sensitivity to failure. With larger

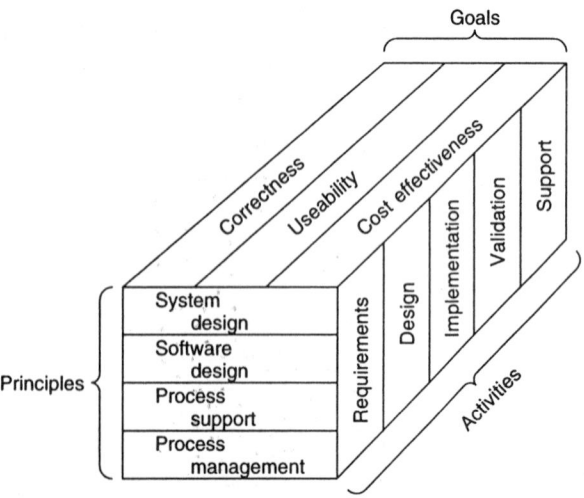

FIG. 1. Software engineering framework.

systems, these basic qualities can be achieved most practicably when care is taken from the outset to insure proper design and implementation rather than through subsequent testing and repair.

Usability Usability concerns the degree to which the basic product structure, its implementation, and its documentation are usable by the intended audience. Since software systems typically have many testers, repairers, installers, supporters, and appliers, and since each of these users has differing needs, usability is a highly challenging and often poorly satisfied goal of software engineering.

Cost Effectiveness This concerns the degree to which the total software development and operational costs meet users' needs. As computing hardware becomes less expensive, traditional system performance concerns have become less critical, and cost-effectiveness has expanded to include both operational and software maintenance and enhancement concerns. Since complex software systems cannot generally be built in one step, an incremental development strategy is frequently used to produce a basic core product and then progressively modify and enhance it to achieve the desired functionality. Overall cost effectiveness then requires that the product be readily modified and enhanced.

The Process of Software Engineering The software process concerns those steps needed to produce a finished software product that both meets its requirements and satisfies the goals of sound engineering. There are many potential models for this process, such as the waterfall model (Royce, 1970) and the spiral model (Boehm, 1988). The model selection should generally consider the particular product, as well as the needs and capabilities of the software engineering organization. Generally, however, some arrangement of the basic process evolution steps shown in Fig. 2 is needed. We will discuss that figure in more detail below.

Requirements The requirements phase involves the definition of the problem to be solved and the specification of the constraints that the resulting product must satisfy.

Design The design work is often done in two or more phases. Examples are the conceptual work to establish an overall software architecture. This might specify subsystems, components, or modules. The interfaces for each of these levels are further specified until the interfaces for each module are fully defined. A detailed design phase then produces the internal module designs from which final implementation proceeds. At each level, various studies, experiments, or prototype implementations might be performed (*see* SOFTWARE PROTOTYPING).

Implementation This phase transforms the design into a working product. This includes code production for modules and their progressive integration into larger aggregations until the product is completed. Again, various prototype experiments or tests may be performed as appropriate during this phase.

Validation Although validation should be performed throughout the entire development process, general practice typically falls far short of this standard. The requirements should be validated with both the users and designers to assure they are both implementable and likely to produce the desired results. Throughout design, implementation, and integration, further validation is needed both to identify and correct errors and to maintain conformity to likely requirements changes. A final validation step then assures that the completed product meets users' needs.

Support Following completion of development and initial use, many widely used software products require extensive continuing support, both to repair design and implementation defects and to incorporate subsequent improvements. In many cases, this support extends for many years and costs substantially more than the initial product development (*see* SOFTWARE MAINTENANCE).

The Principles of Software Engineering While it is too early in this emerging field to list its fundamental principles definitively, the following preliminary guidelines are now becoming generally accepted.

System Design Software is often part of a larger system that must be designed and partitioned into its essential elements. The relationship among software engineering, hardware engineering, and systems engineering thus often requires trade-offs and multiple requirements and design iterations. A common practice is to freeze the hardware design before the software design is completed. This frequently requires that late systems changes be implemented in the software. It is now generally recognized that effective system design requires that software design be considered from the outset and not deferred. The software-first design philosophy may be appropriate for some systems, but, where new software and hardware products are both required, a coordinated and concurrent hardware and software design effort is usually

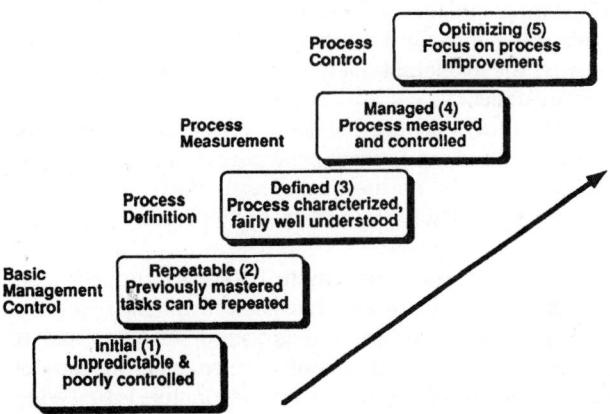

FIG. 2. Software engineering process evolution.

needed to produce a quality system that meets users' needs.

The software requirements are generally produced by the system design activity. The requirements phase is possibly the most troublesome aspect of software engineering, both because of the extraordinary detail needed in effective requirements and the importance of frequent interaction between the software developers and the ultimate system users. Since the software generally controls the user interface, its suitability thus critically depends on its precise match to the particular needs and tastes of its users. The software requirements problem is further complicated by frequent changes in the users' needs. These often occur when portions of some human activities are automated for the first time. The introduction of a new system often changes the way jobs are done, and, since such changes are difficult to anticipate, an iterative software requirements effort is thus necessary. This is further complicated when the software development personnel are not intimately familiar with the user environment, the system needs, and operational considerations. Thus, the first software engineering principle is that software engineering, as part of a larger system design process, must recognize the ill-defined and fluid nature of software requirements and take appropriate steps to insure that the resulting products faithfully meet the users' true needs.

Software Design Ross *et al.* have identified several important software engineering design considerations (Ross, 1975):

- Modularity defines how software systems should be structured.
- Abstraction and information hiding (*q.v.*) identify essential properties common to superficially different entities and make unessential information inaccessible.
- Localization highlights methods for bringing related things into physical proximity.
- Uniformity ensures consistency.
- Conformability ensures that information needed to verify correctness has been stated explicitly.

More recently, the concept of *object-oriented programming* has been introduced to foster cleaner and more modifiable designs (Booch, 1983). This concept conforms with localization by focusing on the fundamental objects with which the system or program deals and enhances modifiability by localizing the effects of change. The second software principle is, then, that sound design methods greatly facilitate the development of software, which meets the goals of software engineering.

Software Process Support Tools are as important in software engineering as they are in other fields of engineering and science. They both increase professional capability and eliminate or reduce sources of error. Software tools have evolved from small private aids supporting individual tasks to large-scale support environments providing full interactive support to entire software development teams. As the software engineering discipline continues to mature, such support systems will generally include the full software engineering life cycle from early requirements through final test and field support. These environments will increasingly support the tasks performed by the individual professionals, handle the movement of work products from task to task, and control, measure, and manage software product evolution. Such tasks include documentation, change management, and functional allocation and tracing among requirements, design, and implementation. As increasingly sophisticated software environments are introduced, they will provide extensive support to the management and planning process, including measurement, tracking, and data analysis.

Artificial intelligence (*q.v.*) also offers promise for process analysis and control. As the software process is increasingly instrumented, the high volume of process data will require automated methods for collection and analysis. Many software organizations, for example, currently have substantial amounts of test, inspection, and usage data that is not generally utilized for process management. Improved data gathering and analysis will facilitate the effective use of this material. This practice should then aid in the development of higher-quality software products and the adoption of more efficient software process methods.

It is also likely that future software environments will incorporate adaptive characteristics to support more effectively the unique abilities and preferences of individual software professionals. Each individual has substantially different habits and needs that change over time. An adaptive software support environment would thus offer the capabilities suggested by Winograd when he introduced the concept of the programmer's assistant (Winograd, 1973).

Our ability to use increasingly sophisticated software processes will also facilitate *software reusability*, the reuse of previously completed designs. Such reuse is likely to result in major productivity and quality improvements through the incorporation of large amounts of previously validated designs. Various forms of reuse have been widely practiced for many years, including macro generators, subroutine libraries, and standard product components. As the size and functionality of standardized software elements is reduced; however, progressively greater benefits can be anticipated. This trend is limited only by the availability of the needed standards and support systems.

The third software engineering principle, thus, is that the quality and economy of a software engineering project depends directly on the quality and effectiveness of the support provided to the software engineers.

Software Process Management Software process management concerns the effective use of available resources both to produce properly engineered products and to improve the organization's software engineering capability. The fourth software engineering principle is that effective software engineering can be done only when the software process is effectively managed.

Five guidelines for effective software process management are:

- The production of quality software depends on the skill, support, training, and motivation of the software professionals.
- These professionals will typically perform as effectively as they can within the limitations of their organization's process.
- Management owns the process, and only management can initiate continuing process improvement.
- Process improvement must be treated as a priority activity with dedicated resources and management priority.
- While software design is an intellectual skill, software development also involves many routine activities to which traditional management methods can be applied.

Software Process Evolution The Software Engineering Institute (SEI) at Carnegie-Mellon University has developed a framework for assessing the capability of software organizations. This framework was originally developed to provide the U. S. Department of Defense with the means to evaluate potential software vendors, but it also can be used to indicate the relative progress of the software profession from a craft-like practice to a defined and structured engineering discipline. This SEI assessment methodology is based on a five-level software process maturity framework, as shown in Fig. 2. These five levels are defined as follows (Humphrey, 1989):

1. At the initial level (level 1), organizations typically have an ad hoc, or possible chaotic, process. Much like individual craftsmen, the software professionals operate without formalized procedures, cost estimates, and project plans.
2. At the repeatable level (level 2), the organization has made an initial step toward a disciplined practice by establishing such basic project controls as project planning, management oversight, product assurance, and change control. Each project, however, generally develops its own methods and practices, since there is no mechanism for organizational learning.
3. At the defined level (level 3), the organization has laid the foundation for sound engineering practice by establishing a software engineering process group, defining the key software process activities, and introducing a family of software engineering methods and technologies.
4. The managed level (level 4) establishes those process measurements needed to control the quality and productivity parameters of each key software engineering task.
5. At the optimizing level (level 5), the organization has achieved a disciplined engineering capability: Data gathering is largely automated, and the management focus is on process control, analysis, and improvement.

Based on data from 167 projects in a large number of software organizations, the SEI has found the process maturity distribution shown in Fig. 3. (Humphrey et al, 1989). While this preliminary data is not a statistically valid sample of software engineering practice, it does indicate that approximately 85% of the projects were at maturity level 1 and a relatively modest 14% were at maturity level 2. Very few projects were represented at maturity level 3. Many organizations, however, are working to reach maturity lev-

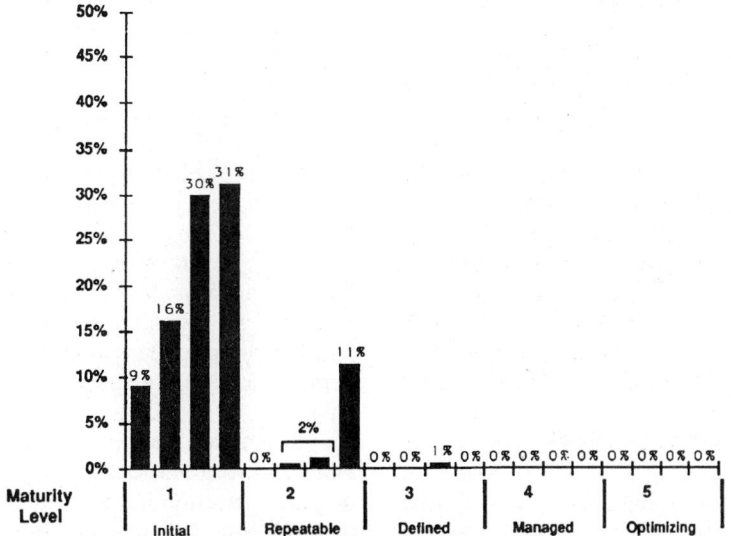

FIG. 3. Software process maturity distrubution workshop assessments. (Data from workshop assessments, as of June 1989, 167 projects.) The quantities indicate, left to right, how far the organization is from the next higher maturity level.

els 3 and 4, by establishing software engineering process groups and better defining their methods, practices, and tools.

References

1970. Royce, W. W. "Managing the Development of Large Software Systems," *Proceedings of IEEE WESCON* (August).

1973. Winograd, Terry. "Breaking the Complexity Barrier (Again)," *Proceedings of the ACM SIGPLAN-SIGIR Interface Meeting of Programming Languages—Information Retrieval*, 13–30. Gaithersburg, MD (November).

1975. Brooks, F. P. Jr. *The Mythical Man-Month: Essays on Software Engineering*. Reading, MA: Addison-Wesley.

1975. Ross, D. T., Goodenough, J. B., and Irvine, C. A. "Software Engineering: Process, Principles, and Goals," *IEEE Computer* (May).

1976. Dijkstra, Edsger W. *A Discipline of Programming*. Englewood Cliffs, NJ: Prentice-Hall.

1976. Naur, P., Randall, B., and Buxton, J. N., (Eds.). "Software Engineering: Concepts and Techniques," *Proceedings of the NATO Conferences*. New York: Petrocelli/Charter.

1983. Booch, Grady. *Software Engineering with Ada*, Redwood City, CA: Benjamin Cummings Publishing Co., Inc.

1988. Boehm, B. W. "A Spiral Model of Software Development and Enhancement," *IEEE Computer* (May).

1988. Draft IEEE Standard Glossary of Software Engineering Terminology.

1989. Humphrey, W. S. *Managing the Software Process*. Reading, MA: Addison-Wesley.

1989. Humphrey, W. S., Kitson, D. H., and Kasse, T. C. "The State of Software Engineering Practice: A Preliminary Report," SEI Technical Report CMU/SEI-89-TR-1, Pittsburgh, PA: Carnegie-Mellon University.

1989. Shaw, Mary. "Software and Some Lessons from Engineering," SEI Technical Report, Pittsburgh, PA: Carnegie-Mellon University.

WATTS S. HUMPHREY

SOFTWARE ENGINEERING INSTITUTE (SEI)

For an article on a related subject *see* SOFTWARE ENGINEERING.

The Software Engineering Institute (SEI) is a federally funded research and development center operated by Carnegie Mellon University and located in Pittsburgh, Pennsylvania. The Institute was competitively awarded to Carnegie Mellon in December 1984 by the Department of Defense (DoD). It was established because the DoD recognized the need to improve the state of software technology in order to develop higher-quality systems more economically.

The SEI has a four-part mission, stated in its charter:

- Bring the ablest professional minds and the most effective technology to bear on rapid improvement of the quality of operational software in systems that depend on software.
- Accelerate the reduction to practice of modern software engineering techniques and methods.
- Promulgate the use of modern techniques and methods throughout the mission-critical systems community.
- Establish standards of excellence for software engineering practice.

The strategy of the SEI is to promote the evolution of software engineering from an ad hoc, labor-intensive activity to a managed, technology-supported discipline.

The Institute carries out its mission and strategy through a variety of technical activities. By contract, 25% of the SEI technical efforts are devoted to research and education and to the transition of technology. There is an emphasis on technology transition for two reasons: (1) much computer software is currently being developed without the benefit of the best technology and practices available, and (2) it takes 15 to 20 years for new approaches and new technology to move from the software research community into routine practice.

Activities focus on the following aspects of software engineering:

The SEI seeks to improve software development, concentrating on how companies can produce high-quality software within the constraints of schedule and budget. A major undertaking has been to develop a model depicting maturity levels of the software development process and to create a means of assessing an organization's work within that model. The SEI provides guidance and support for organizations that are committed to improving their process.

In the area of software engineering methods, the SEI strives to accelerate the development, introduction, and reduction to practice of methods, tools, and environments that improve software productivity and enhance quality. Work has been done to define a way to select methods and tools for developing software for real-time systems. Other efforts include establishing criteria for evaluating programming support environments (*q.v.*) and developing a taxonomy for illustrating current trends and new concepts in programming environment research and development.

The SEI is working to improve the development of real-time *distributed systems* (*q.v.*) through the integration of software engineering and to reduce the risk of adopting promising new technology. The Institute is developing tools for building applications that run on networks of different types of special-purpose processors executing concurrent tasks. It is also investigating the use of Ada (*q.v.*) in real-time *embedded systems* (*q.v.*), and developing a task description language and its runtime scheduler to support building applications that use heterogeneous machines.

To increase the number of highly qualified software engineers, the SEI focuses on improving software engineering education in the academic, government, and industrial education communities. Educational activities include creating and refining curriculum recommendations for a professional Master of Software Engineering (MSE) degree and an undergraduate software engineering program, delivering MSE core courses on videotape to universities, designing and delivering continuing education courses for software practitioners, and conducting development activities and conferences for educators and trainers of software engineers.

In 1988, the SEI established the Computer Emergency Response Team Coordination Center (CERT/CC). Its responsibilities include initiating active measures to raise users' and vendors' awareness of security issues; providing a reliable, trusted, 24-hour, single point of contact for the Internet community; facilitating communications among members of that community; and maintaining an accessible, secure repository of information. The CERT/CC also conducts research targeted at improving the security of existing systems without compromising functionality, performance, or flexibility.

The SEI also addresses the problems associated with the dissemination and implementation of evolving software engineering practices and technology. It identifies needs, trends, and emerging technology in the DoD software community. Related work includes developing and testing a model of how new technology is assessed and adopted.

NORMAN E. GIBBS AND LINDA HUTZ PESANTE

SOFTWARE FLEXIBILITY

For articles on related subject *see* COMPATIBILITY; OBJECT-ORIENTED PROGRAMMING; PORTABILITY; and SOFTWARE REUSABILITY.

Software flexibility is a property of software that enables it to change easily in response to different user and system requirements. The necessary changes can be classified roughly according to their purpose:

1. To alter the user image (i.e. the "appearance" of the program to the user).
2. To adapt to different machine organizations.
3. To meet different system constraints.

These categories are not truly independent. For example, we might meet certain system constraints by changing the user image to remove expensive features. Nevertheless, the classification is a useful one because changes in different categories are normally achieved by somewhat different means.

The user image of a program is usually altered by making textual changes, principally excision of source code and selection of one of several alternatives. This implies that the body of text representing the source program incorporates the implementation of all possible user images, and is so structured that relevant changes can be made easily. Thus, some care must be taken during the implementation to modularize "by feature," avoiding if possible the use of a single procedure to provide several distinct facets of the user image. Also, wherever possible, the variations of the user image should provide a hierarchy of facilities. Changes then

consist simply of removing all routines that deal with facilities above a certain level.

To solve a particular problem on a particular computer, one must model the operations and data types (*q.v.*) required for the solution in terms of the operations and data types provided by the computer. Part of this modeling is carried out by the programmer when a program is written to solve the problem, and part is carried out when the program is translated to machine code. Adaptability for different machine organizations is enhanced when the program is written in terms of operations and data types that are more closely related to the problem than to a particular computer. Changes then involve redefinition of these operators and data types in terms appropriate to the target computer. The definition of an operator or data type should be independent of its use, so that the number of such definitions does not grow with the size of the program. Hence, a redefinition involves far less effort than would be required to recode the program.

System constraints include such items as peripheral complement, memory size, word length, and arithmetic (precision, rounding). Careful organization of the algorithm is necessary to provide flexibility in meeting these constraints, with the key point being the preservation of suitable fall-back positions. For example, the program should be structured so that sections could be overlaid to meet a memory constraint. This consideration has implications for the procedure linkage and the segmentation of data; it may affect the algorithm chosen to solve the problem.

Some form of parametrization is generally used to achieve all aspects of flexibility: Symbols are used to denote key constants such as table sizes, and conditional operations are executed during translation to select different parts of the code according to the desired user image. Assembly languages and general-purpose macroprocessors provide the most powerful facilities for parametrization; most high-level languages are deficient in this respect. The best examples of software that can be adapted through parametrization are found in the kernel (*q.v.*) of an operating system. *System generation* is the process of adapting the body of text supplied by the manufacturer to the user image desired by the installation management and to the constraints of their hardware configuration.

Flexibility is important because it increases the useful life of a piece of software and extends its range of application. This permits the development cost to be recovered over a wider market, and hence reduces the price to the user.

Reference

1973. Poole, P. C. and Waite, W. M. "Portability and Adaptability," in Bauer, F. L. (Ed.), *Advanced Course in Software Engineering*. Berlin: Springer-Verlag.

1990. Ng, P.A. and Yeh, R.T. *Modern Software Engineering*. New York: Van Nostrand Reinhold.

WILLIAM M. WAITE

SOFTWARE HISTORY

For articles on related subjects *see* DATABASE MANAGEMENT SYSTEM; DIGITAL COMPUTERS: HISTORY; OPERATING SYSTEMS; PROGRAMMING LANGUAGES; and SOFTWARE ENGINEERING.

As one looks back over the development of software since the early 1950s, one sees that the major thrusts have been in four broad areas—programming languages; operating systems; data handling; and software tools, techniques, and disciplines.

The term *programming language* involves the specific form in which the user actually writes a program for input to the computer. (This subject is emphasized in this article because it has had more direct effect on computer users than the other topics. That balance may change in the future.) The term *operating system* encompasses the general set of tools and techniques that enables both individuals and computer installations to accommodate many jobs with minimum human intervention effectively, allowing for parallel, sequential, and interactive modes. Real-time systems are also included within the framework of operating systems, even though the necessary real-time application programs are outside the operating system. The term *data handling* represents general capabilities, ranging from the early sort-merge generators to the current database management systems (*q.v.*). *Software tools, techniques,* and *disciplines* run the gamut from subroutines to debugging tools (such as program tracers), from programming library support systems to editors that facilitate program entry, modification, and neat output formatting. It is also meant to include application packages. Although the software facilities described in this section started on mainframe computers, they all became crucial in the practical usage of the personal computer, starting in the early 1980s.

The history of almost anything in the computer field is extremely controversial. The approach taken here, and the statements made, represents the personal views of the author. Further, it is possible here only to mention the highlights and give some sense of perspective. No attempt has been made to completely indicate "firsts"; rather the emphasis is on significant developments, even though earlier work may have contributed greatly.

Programming Languages

The term *programming language* as used here is considered equivalent to *high-level language*. The development of assembly language and macroassemblers is not discussed.

Language development started as far back as 1945 with the unimplemented "Plankalkül" by Konrad Zuse (*q.v.*) in Germany. Various attempts at developing a language that was closer to the problem expression than assembly language were made by numerous people and organizations, as described by Knuth and Trabb Pardo (1980) and Sammet (1969). The earliest *operational* compiler for a high-level language seems to be that developed by Laning and Zierler for mathematical computations, which was running on the M.I.T. Whirlwind (*q.v.*) in 1954. It provided capability for writing mathematical expressions (with subscripts *and* superscripts), assignment,

branching, input/output, subroutines, and some handling of differential equations. However, the first high-level language that received wide usage was Fortran, developed by John Backus and others at IBM in the mid-1950s. Its original application area was intended to be only scientific and engineering computational problems, but it has also been used for everything from payroll calculations to compiler writing. It proved the feasibility of high-level languages and thus provided a foundation for future work on languages.

In 1958, a group of Americans (representing ACM) and Europeans (representing GAMM) working together created a language for algorithmic processes known as IAL (*International Algebraic Language*); this language eventually was modified to become Algol 60 (Naur, 1960) and the earlier version was renamed Algol 58. Both Algol 58 and Algol 60 led to a major emphasis and work in the area of programming languages by universities and industry. Several languages were developed based on Algol 58 (e.g. Jovial, Mad, Neliac), and compiler techniques were developed. Algol spurred the theoretical and research effort in programming languages, whereas Fortran had far more effect on the practical side.

In parallel with these developments in scientific languages were the efforts for business data processing; the first of these was Flow-Matic, developed by Grace Hopper (*q.v.*) and her colleagues at Remington Rand Univac in the mid-1950s. Flow-Matic was the first English language-oriented language; as such, it was one of the major inputs to Cobol (Common Business-Oriented Language), which was developed by a group of computer manufacturers' representatives and users organized in 1959 under Department of Defense sponsorship. Cobol has had as large (or larger) an effect on the programming of business data processing problems as Fortran has had for scientific and engineering problems.

The two years 1958 and 1959 were probably the two most productive years in the history of programming languages. Not only were Algol 58 and Cobol developed, but Comit and Lisp were developed at M.I.T. Comit was a string processing language developed primarily by Victor Yngve for use in translating natural languages. Lisp was developed for artificial intelligence applications by John McCarthy and a number of others (primarily graduate students). Lisp continues to be heavily used by the AI community. Comit, however, has been largely supplanted by varying versions of Snobol, which was developed initially by David Farber, Ralph Griswold, and Ivan Polonsky at Bell Telephone Laboratories in the mid-1960s. Snobol has been widely used in general text manipulation applications, but has been somewhat superseded by Icon.

Because the early languages maintained the same dichotomy between scientific and data processing computations that the early computers did, it is not surprising that eventually languages began to be developed that were meant to be more general. One of the earliest of those was Jovial (an outgrowth of Algol 58), developed by Jules Schwartz and others at the System Development Corporation in 1959–1960. The first language really *intended* for both scientific calculations and business data processing, as well as systems programming, was PL/I, developed as a joint project between IBM and SHARE in 1963–1964. The next large language developed was Algol 68 (*q.v.*), which was really a new development and *not* an upward extension of Algol 60. One of its major characteristics is orthogonality, meaning that it defines a small number of basic characteristics and systematic rules for combining them so as to eliminate many arbitrary restrictions. There is also a facility to allow the programmer to define new data types and operators on them. Algol 68 was defined with a new (and difficult) definitional technique and this seems to have discouraged a number of people from seriously studying and using the language.

The next major language development was the Department of Defense effort, which started in 1975, to develop a single language suitable for embedded computer systems. (*Embedded systems* (*q.v.*) are those in which the computer is part of a system involving other equipment; e.g. air traffic control, process control, or weapons systems.) The preliminary specifications for this language, called Ada (*q.v.*) were issued in 1979, and the language specifications labeled "final" were issued in July 1980. This was the baseline for a potential standard, future development, and major implementations. Although originally intended for use on embedded computer systems, Ada has been used effectively in almost all types of applications, including artificial intelligence and business data processing.

With the advent of interactive computing systems that permitted an individual to access a computer system from a remote terminal (see below), languages were developed for effective use in an interactive environment. The earliest was Joss, developed by J. Cliff Shaw at the Rand Corporation in 1963. Starting in 1964, a simple language named Basic was developed for batch or interactive mode. Basic has been implemented on almost every computer, including many microprocessors and home computers; it was developed by John Kemeny and Thomas Kurtz at Dartmouth College in 1964.

A number of languages have been developed to do nonnumeric mathematics (i.e. formal algebraic manipulation— *see* COMPUTER ALGEBRA) on a computer. The first to receive wide usage was Formac, developed by Jean Sammet and her colleagues at IBM in 1962–1964. The most comprehensive of the current systems is Macsyma, initially developed in the early 1970s at M.I.T. by Joel Moses and others. By the early 1990s the powerful Mathematica system developed by Stephen Wolfram was in significant use.

Although the languages cited above are intended for relatively broad classes of applications, there has been a parallel development that has gone largely unnoticed or ignored by most computer scientists, namely, the development of languages for specialized application areas. The earliest of these was APT, for machine tool control, developed at M.I.T. by Douglas Ross and others starting in 1956. Other popular specialized languages include Cogo (civil engineering), Coursewriter (computer-assisted instruction), and Atlas (equipment checkout).

From 1967 to 1977, the author maintained a roster of high-level languages developed and used in the United States. The number in use in any given year ranged around 170, with roughly 25 to 30 simultaneously being added and deleted each time the annual or biannual count was made. An astounding phenomenon is that, since the tracking began, the languages for specialized application areas consistently have been about half of the total languages listed. (See, for example, Sammet, 1978.) However, the actual *usage* of these languages is much less than 50%.

As an indication of a value judgment on important languages, the ACM Special Interest Group on Programming Languages (SIGPLAN) sponsored a History of Programming Languages (HOPL) Conference in 1978. The program committee for that conference chose to discuss languages that met the following criteria: (1) they were created and in use by 1967; (2) they remained in use in 1977; and (3) they had considerable influence on the field of computing. The languages chosen were the following: Algol, APL, APT, Basic, Cobol, Fortran, GPSS, Joss, Jovial, Lisp, PL/I, Simula, and Snobol. Languages that did not meet the "ten year usage and considerable influence" criteria at that time, but did by 1990, are Ada, C, Pascal, Prolog, and Smalltalk. Papers on those languages were invited for the second ACM SIGPLAN History of Programming Languages in 1993. By the early 1980s, Pascal had become a practical base and spiritual catalyst of language development, just as Algol had been for the 1960s.

In conjunction with the actual development of individual languages, of course, has come the development of concepts which appear in, or relate to, languages. Among the important enduring language concepts are block structure (Algol); data typing, record structure, and separation in a program of the data and procedural aspects (Cobol); the class (*q.v.*) concept (Simula), which has led to modern concepts of data abstraction and object-oriented programming; and the strong data typing mechanisms (Pascal). In addition, the primary concept of a formal technique for defining language syntax came from Backus in 1959 and is known as BNF (for Backus Normal Form or Backus Naur Form— *q.v.*); aside from the Backus paper proposing the concept, it was first used in the major publication of the Algol 60 report (Naur, 1960). The metalanguage (*q.v.*) of Cobol was developed independently and has been widely used.

Along with the development of these languages have come a myriad of compiler techniques, including optimization.

Much of the early history of specific programming languages can be found in Sammet (1969); for the 13 specified languages covered by the HOPL Conference, see Wexelblat (1981). A discussion of various approaches to the history of programming languages is in Sammet (1991). See also Appendix V for a list of key high-level languages.

Operating Systems   The history of operating systems is much harder to trace than that of programming languages; for the former, the *concepts* are primary, whereas for the latter a specific *language* provides the major contribution to the field. Another major difference is that high-level languages, by definition, are *meant* to be machine-independent, whereas operating systems have normally been developed for a single computer or computer family. [Unix (*q.v.*) is an exception.]

In the earliest days of computing, each programmer tended to operate the computer alone. Before long, it became clear that it was not an efficient use of programmer's time to mount tapes, put cards in a reader, etc.; as a result, the separate function of computer operator came into being. However, it was *still* necessary for a *person* to put cards into a card reader and/or mount tapes *separately* for each job that was to be run. As computers became faster, the amount of computer time that was lost between programs became significant, and so various techniques and concepts were developed to allow efficient use of the physical computer time, which was scarce and expensive in the early days. Although computers had far greater speed and lower costs in the early 1980s than at any preceding time, the uses of computers had also grown enormously and the larger capacity was needed. Hence, operating systems continued to be needed, particularly *because* the vast speed precluded wasting time with human intervention. Even the desk-top personal computers used by a single person, which started to become significant in the early 1980s, required operating systems to enable the user to be effective and comfortable.

Around 1956, a simple operating system was developed jointly by General Motors and North American Aviation for the IBM 704. By the time Fortran became generally available, operating systems had been developed that provided facilities such as sequencing from one job to another, input/output control systems (*q.v.*), calling in components (e.g. assembler, compiler), and loading object programs along with library routines.

In the early 1960s, there were batch operating systems (e.g. IBSYS on the IBM 7090) in which programs requiring differing services (e.g. separate compilers, assemblers) were submitted to be run and printed results were received in hours (or sometimes even days if there were many users). The programmer specified what functions the operating system was to perform via some special cards known as *job control cards*. Around 1963, Burroughs released its Master Control Program (MCP) written in a high-level language and with facilities for multiprocessing and multiprogramming. OS/360, developed in the middle 1960s for the IBM System/360, typified the very large and powerful batch system, although it was actually designed for a broad range of uses (including real time). It provided facilities for handling devices and data, job management, debugging, and multiprogramming. it also provided growth, without recoding, across a family of compatible hardware and software, and often with printed results in minutes (rather than hours or days).

A third concept, which had been developed as early as the late 1950s (with SAGE) involved real-time systems, in which very rapid (and sometimes seemingly instantaneous) response from the computer is necessary. The IBM-American Airlines SABRE system of 1963 (for airline reservations) seems to be the earliest major system for transaction processing (*see* TRANSACTION PROCESSING) and was the forerunner for later facilities of that kind, as well as influencing OS/360.

A major innovation was the development of the Compatible Time-Sharing System (CTSS) at M.I.T. on the IBM 709/7090 under the direction of Fernando Corbató, starting in 1961 and becoming of significant use by 1963. This was the first significant general system with the following characteristics: (1) numerous typewriter-like terminals were connected to one computer and could be used at the same time; (2) each terminal user seemed to have available the full power and facilities of the computer hardware and software; and (3) the time required for small tasks was sufficiently small so that all users could feel the entire machine was devoted to their service. CTSS provided various language compilers, file manipulation facilities, and user-developed systems. It was used heavily at M.I.T. and proved the practicality of general interactive systems. This capability contrasts with that in a system supporting Joss, which provided (only) a single language that could be used simultaneously by many people. By the 1970s, the most powerful and flexible of the general interactive systems was Multics, for the (now called) Honeywell 645. Multics was developed in the mid-1960s as a joint effort of General Electric, M.I.T., and Bell Laboratories; it was heavily influenced by the M.I.T. experience with CTSS (*see* TIME SHARING).

Toward the late 1960s, the three operating system concepts of interactive, batch, and real time began to merge (although the similarity had been recognized earlier by some people). It became clear that the design requirement for all three concepts was resource management, and that the same basic design involving dynamic allocation of resources to independent processes could satisfy each of the "separate" problems. Included were various facilities to protect (1) the operating system against ruination from accidental or deliberate tampering by users, and (2) one user's files and programs from another user's access or tampering.

Since the early 1970s, Unix (*q.v.*) has become widely accepted as a model of a small but powerful interactive operating system. The initial version was developed by Ken Thompson of Bell Laboratories in 1969-1970 to run on the DEC PDP-7 and PDP-9 computers. Thompson and his colleague, Dennis Ritchie, developed better versions for various DEC machines, and the most widely used one runs on the VAX family. Unix and related developments— e.g. the programming language C (*q.v.*), in which Unix is written—are described in BSTJ (1978).

Along with the early development of these various methods of accessing the computer, there arose the need for capabilities by which the user could indicate what functions were desired (e.g. compilation, printout, deletion of a file, editing). From this came the concept of *job control languages*, sometimes called *command languages* (*see* COMMAND AND JOB CONTROL LANGUAGES). It is hotly debated by language experts as to whether these really are high-level languages in the same sense as those discussed earlier.

The concept of virtual memory (*q.v.*)—i.e. the facility whereby the user can write a program assuming the memory size is effectively unlimited—seems to have started in the late 1950s on the Atlas computer at Manchester University in England. A virtual memory facility was eventually put into the major operating systems of most of the computer manufacturers.

Details on some of the earlier systems mentioned above, as well as on some of the programming languages, are in Rosen (1967). A general history of operating systems is in Weizer (1981).

Data Handling The broad category of data handling refers to the tools and techniques used to manipulate large amounts of data. One of the earliest significant achievements in data handling was the 1951–1952 Sort-Merge Generator developed by Betty Holberton for the Remington Rand UNIVAC 1 (*q.v.*). Not only did this introduce the concept of a program that would be automatically tailored for a particular set of parameters, but it helped initiate the development and widespread use of many data processing tools.

One concept that has pervaded work in the data handling area is the need for *data definition* facilities. This concept involves the tools and techniques for describing both full files and individual records (down to each field) as they are represented logically, and also physically. The earliest attempt at such a facility seems to have been the COMPOOL developed at the M.I.T. Lincoln Laboratory for the SAGE Air Defense System in the early 1950s. The COMPOOL provided a way of defining the characteristics of the very large SAGE database, which was used by hundreds of programs. The COMPOOL concept was later carried over to the programming language Jovial. The early work on Flow-Matic provided this data definition facility initially in the programming language, and the first major culmination of that approach was reached in the Cobol Data Division (*see* DATA MODELS).

Research of various kinds on data definition facilities still continues, although no single technique had prevailed by 1992. However, based on concepts from IDS (mentioned later), the Codasyl (*q.v.*) Cobol committee in 1969 developed their first schema Data Definition Language for defining a total database, and a Sub-Schema Data Manipulation Language (DML) for defining various aspects of the database associated with individual languages (e.g. Fortran). This work has subsequently been updated.

By the mid- and late 1950s, various systems were available for handling large collections of files and producing reports. Report writers started as early as 1956, at the General Electric (Hanford, WA) operation. They developed a report generator called MARK I for the IBM 702. One of the first widely used report generators was the Report Program Generator (RPG) developed for the IBM 1401 in 1961. In 1962, a Report Writer module and Sort module were added to Cobol in Cobol 61 Extended, thus freeing the user from the need to have separate programs to achieve those functions. However, many users still use independent RPGs.

File handling facilities also started at GE Hanford, and the two capabilities from there were the forerunner of 9PAC, developed on the IBM 709 around 1959 by users under auspices of the SHARE users' group.

With the advent of the first Cobol specifications in 1960, the need for file manipulation facilities separate from the actual programs could be eliminated because file manipulation facilities were embedded in the support provided by Cobol. But, in most data processing environments, installations would create separate files for each set of applications; for example, an employee file was used for payroll purposes and a separate employee file was used for department assignment and transfer purposes. Eventually, it became clear that all of these separate files should be combined into a common framework, and this led to the concept now known as *database management systems* (DBMS - *q.v.*).

There have been three major technical approaches to database management systems. One is based on the Integrated Data Store (IDS), first proposed by Charles Bachman of General Electric in 1964. He proposed a network approach to storing data, and this was used as the basis for the work of the Codasyl Data Base Task Group. A second approach is the hierarchical system in which data is represented as a tree structure. The earliest manifestation of this approach seems to have been the work at North American Aviation Space Division and IBM in 1965; it is exemplified by IBM's Information Management System issued around 1969. A third approach is the relational database (*q.v.*) of E. F. Codd of IBM, first introduced around 1970. It involves the concept of linked tables of data where information is not repeated as it must be in the hierarchical systems.

Each approach has strong proponents and opponents, and tends to be useful in differing application environments, based to a large extent on the preferences of the individuals making the selections. A good technical description of these alternative approaches is given by Date (1981) and in ACM (1976). The article by Fry and Sibley (1976) provides a detailed history from which much of this section was derived.

Each approach has been implemented in one or more commercial systems. By the late 1970s, database management systems were very important from both a research viewpoint and as a major practical facility for large organizations.

Software Tools, Techniques, and Disciplines Many of the useful software tools and techniques for assisting programmers became so ingrained in the 1960s that it is hard to realize that these ideas did not exist in the early days and had to be developed. The development of disciplines is much more recent. As one example of an early technique, the crucial concepts of subroutine and subroutine libraries were promulgated as early as 1951 by Wilkes, Wheeler, and Gill (1951). As another illustration, the symbolic assembly program, which freed the programmer from worrying about absolute machine addresses, was developed by Nathaniel Rochester of IBM by 1953; it replaced the concept of regional or floating addresses implemented on the M.I.T. Whirlwind Comprehensive System.

Among the many other major software tools and techniques, only a few of the most important concepts can be mentioned. Specific early system names and dates are very difficult to identify.

Compilers are obviously a major class of tools, and the emphasis has been on developing techniques that provide rapid compilation and efficient object time code. The latter means both rapid execution and minimal use of memory. The earliest significant compiler was that for Fortran, as described by John Backus in Wexelblat (1981). The concept of a syntax-directed compiler was introduced by E. T. Irons in 1961; although this idea has inspired a great deal of research, it has not been of major practical value.

The concept of a *list* seems to have been introduced by Allen Newell, Herbert Simon, and J. C. Shaw in the mid-1950s as a useful technique in their work on developing programs that would prove theorems in the propositional calculus. Although a sequence of list processing languages (*q.v.*) was also developed (named IPL-I,...IPL-V) to do list processing, only the last became significantly used and even it eventually faded from use, while the list *concept* remains as a cornerstone of software techniques.

Debugging tools and concepts were created as part of the early development of programming. The tools ranged from very simple to quite sophisticated, and have included static and dynamic traces and cross references, simulators, measurements, and numerous features associated with compilers. In this connection, it is worth noting that, although testing is related to debugging, it was not until a conference in 1972, described by Hetzel (1973), that software testing really began to be considered seriously as a scientific subdiscipline.

Decision tables (*q.v.*) represent one specific technique (other than programming languages) for expressing problem solutions. The first decision tables appear to have been developed in 1958 by Orren Evans at Hunt Foods and Industries, Inc., and he credits the Sutherland Company of Peoria, IL with many of the ideas. Evans' work was released to the Codasyl Systems Committee in 1959 and it, as well as General Electric and IBM, then contributed to further work on this approach throughout the early and mid-1960s. The earliest implemented system seems to have been Tabsol on the GE 225 in 1959–1960.

Attempts to make software development less of an art and more of a science or engineering discipline have been under way since at least 1968, when NATO sponsored small conferences entitled "Software Engineering" (*q.v.*). There is still debate on the meaning of this term even in the early 1990s, but it is reasonably clear that the term encompasses management issues as well as specific technical concepts, and includes a concern with the full *life cycle* of software development. For example, increased emphasis on requirements and specifications and design tools has occurred in recent years. A much earlier interest in restricting the way in which programmers wrote their code in order to make the programming process more manageable led to the structured programming (*q.v.*) concepts proposed by Edsger Dijkstra in the late 1960s and early 1970s (Dahl, Dijkstra, and Hoare, 1972); these concepts were heavily promulgated by him and others, as well as being enhanced by Harlan Mills and others. By the late 1980s, educational curricula for software engineering—separate from computer science—had been developed at both the graduate and undergraduate level.

A contribution to the developing discipline of programming has been the creation of ANSI standards. The main software standards have been the programming languages that started with the first Fortran standard in 1966. Other languages that have had one or more standards, either internationally or in the United States, are Ada, Algol 60, APL, APT, ATLAS, Basic, C, Chill, Cobol, DIBOL, Mumps, PANCM, Pascal, Extended Pascal, Pilot, PL/I, and SCHEME. Standardization has been underway for various other languages. (See PROGRAMMING LANGUAGE STANDARDS for a fuller discussion of this subject.)

The relatively easy availability of interactive systems caused a large interest in text editing systems (*q.v.*) that could be used by programmers for correcting and documenting their programs. On-line editing systems then became widespread for use with ordinary text, not just programs. Major differences among the systems include the types of editing commands they use, and whether the basic unit of reference is a single line or is some unit of text controlled by a *delimiter* (*q.v.*).

One of the earliest text editors was the system running under the M.I.T. Compatible Time-Sharing System (CTSS) in 1963. A small system oriented toward text handling was the IBM Administrative Terminal System (ATS) available in the mid-1960s on the 1401. More powerful systems developed in the late 1960s include WYLBUR (Stanford University on the IBM 360/67) and TECO (M.I.T. on the DEC PDP computers). The SCRIPT system developed by IBM on the System 360/370 has evolved from earlier internal versions created in the late 1960s.

With the availability of more sophisticated terminals and display devices, there have been numerous sophisticated programs developed to provide scrolling, "pretty printing," and automatic typesetting and printing.

Under the broad heading of this section are included application packages as well as the tools for easily developing them. Although some of these existed prior to the PC, it was the advent of the latter that spurred major developments. One of the earliest major system was VISICALC for spreadsheets (*q.v.*) which was eventually replaced by programs such as LOTUS 1-2-3, EXCEL, QUATTRO, and SUPERCALC.

References

1951. Wilkes, M. V., Wheeler, D. J., and Gill, S. *The Preparation of Programs for an Electronic Digital Computer*. Reading, MA: Addison-Wesley.

1960. Naur, P. (Ed.). "Report on the Algorithmic Language ALGOL 60," *Comm. ACM 3, 5*: 299–314 (May).

1967. Rosen, S. (Ed.). *Programming Systems and Languages*. New York: McGraw-Hill.

1969. Sammet, J. E. *Programming Languages: History and Fundamentals*. Englewood Cliffs, NJ: Prentice-Hall.

1972. Dahl, O.-J., Dijkstra, E. W., and Hoare, C. A. R. *Structured Programming*. New York: Academic Press.

1973. Hetzel, W. (Ed.). *Program Test Methods*. Englewood Cliffs, NJ: Prentice-Hall.

1976. *ACM Computing Surveys, (Special Issue: Data-Base Management Systems)* **8,** *1* (March).

1976. Fry, J. P. and Sibley, E. H. "Evolution of Data-Base Management Systems," *Computing Surveys* 8, 1: 7-42 (March).

1978. *Bell System Technical Journal (UNIX Time-Sharing System)* **57,** *6, Part 2* (July–August).

1978. Sammet, J. E. "Roster of Programming Languages for 1976–77," *ACM SIGPLAN Notices* **13,** *11:* 56-85 (November).

1980. Knuth, D. E. and Trabb Pardo, L. "The Early Development of Programming Languages," in Metropolis, N., Howlett, J., and Rota, G.-C. (Eds.), *A History of Computing in the Twentieth Century*, 197–273.

1981. Weizer, N. "A History of Operating Systems," *Datamation* **27**, *1:* 119–126(January).

1981. Wexelblat, R. (Ed.). *History of Programming Languages*. ACM Monograph Series. New York: Academic Press.

1981. Date, C. J. *An Introduction to Database Systems*, 5th Ed., The Systems Programming Series. Reading, MA: Addison-Wesley.

1990. Sammet, J. E. "Some Approaches to, and Illustrations of, Programming Language History," *Annals of the History of Computing*, **13**, *1:* 33–50.

1991. Sammet J. E. "Some Approaches to, and Illustrations of, Programming Language History," *Annals of the History of Computing*, **13**, 1: 33–50.

JEAN E. SAMMET

SOFTWARE LIBRARIES, NUMERICAL AND STATISTICAL

For articles on related subjects *see* COMPATIBILITY; COMPUTING CENTER; DOCUMENTATION; MATHEMATICAL SOFTWARE; PORTABILITY; and SUBPROGRAM.

A *software library* (or program library) is a collection of computer programs for a particular application. To be characterized as a library, such a collection should contain a substantial number of computer program modules designed to solve a wide range of problems in the given area. In addition, the programs in a library are coherent, both in their external appearance and their internal design. In particular, they:

- Present a similar user interface;
- Have a fixed documentation format;
- Are designed to be used easily in combination;
- Are built upon a common set of low-level utilities; and
- Share coding and portability standards.

This article surveys software libraries for general-purpose numerical computation and statistical analysis. This includes, for example, the evaluation of the special functions of applied mathematics, the numerical solution of differential equations, regression, and analysis of variance. Most scientific computing installations make libraries of this type available to their users. Such computer sites often have additional program libraries concentrating on specific applications of local interest, structural analysis or graphics, for example. These, being site-dependent, will not be discussed here.

Program Library Development The first program libraries for numerical computation were written in machine or assembly language for a particular computer at a given site. Probably the earliest of these was a library written for the EDSAC (*q.v.*) in England by Wilkes, Wheeler, and Gill in 1951. By the early 1960s, computer manufacturers, to help their customers and to stimulate sales, were working on program libraries and, in 1961, IBM developed the SSP (Scientific Subroutine Package) library and provided it free with a computer rental or sale.

At the same time, many groups in universities, government laboratories, and private industry began to feel the need to consolidate programming effort into useful libraries. For example, statisticians in the biomedical group at the University of California put together a group of statistical routines, the first edition appearing in 1961. The library has been widely used since then, the current version being known as BMDP (Biomedical Computer Programs P-Series). Other statistical libraries originating in the early 1960s were SPSS (Statistical Package for the Social Sciences), originally written at Stanford University and further developed by the National Opinion Research Center at the University of Chicago, and SAS (Statistical Analysis System), developed at North Carolina State. Each of these systems is now supported commercially. Also during the early 1960s, the National Bureau of Standards developed a general-purpose, interpretive, and portable program called OMNITAB for statistical and numerical data analyses. A modern version of this program is still in use, and was the basis for the commercially successful MINITAB system. By the late 1960s, software library development was also occurring in the private sector, e.g. at Boeing and Monsanto, although the resulting libraries were primarily for internal use.

Libraries for numerical computation were also being built in England during this period. One was developed in 1963 for the IBM Stretch (*q.v.*) computer at the Harwell Atomic Energy Research Establishment; in 1967, the library was converted to the IBM 360; its successor remains available today. In 1970, six British computing centers began an effort to develop a library for their ICL 1906A/S computers, and in 1971, Mark 1 of the NAG (Nottingham Algorithms Group) library was released. Implementation for other computer systems followed, and, by 1976, a non-profit company, Numerical Algorithms Group Ltd., had been formed to continue development and distribution. The NAG effort continues to be characterized by close collaboration between a full-time coordination staff and a large number of specialists in numerical and statistical analysis in university and government research institutions worldwide. The NAG Fortran library is currently available in 68 implementations, of which several thousand subscriptions are held. NAG also markets general-purpose numerical libraries in Ada, (*q.v.*), Pascal, and C (*q.v.*), as well as several specialized topic libraries.

Probably the first commercial venture formed exclusively to market a general-purpose mathematical subroutine library was IMSL (International Mathematical and Statistical Libraries), which was incorporated in 1970. The next year they released a library for the IBM 360-370 class of computers and sold seven copies. By 1976, when the company showed its first profit, they had 430 customers using their library on seven different computer systems. Today IMSL maintains approximately 60 implementations of their Fortran library products; some 12,000 subscriptions are currently held in 65 countries.

In the early 1970s, the NATS (National Activity to Test Software) group was established at Argonne Laboratory under government and university sponsorship to produce quality software for specific areas of numerical computation. Two packages were produced by this project, EISPACK for eigenvalue-eigenvector computation (1972) and FUNPACK for special function evaluation (1975). The software produced by the NATS effort was very well received, and the EISPACK package, in particular, is still among the best available. The high standards for performance, transportability, testing, certification, documentation, and dissemination set by these projects have become a paradigm for subsequent numerical software collections; see Table 1 for a partial list.

Excellent public-domain packages such as these have greatly influenced program library development, and many of them have found their way into larger, more widely-distributed libraries. Their availability, in fact, was one of the prime motivations for the development of the SLATEC (Sandia National Laboratory Albuquerque–Los Alamos National Laboratory–Air Force Weapons Laboratory Technical Exchange Committee) library. These groups wished to integrate this software into a new highly portable common math library that would be (a) free of licensing restrictions for use within the laboratories, (b) supported jointly, thus reducing local library maintenance costs, (c) immediately available on newly acquired supercomputer systems, and (d) an aid to the interchange of application software among the labs. The project began in 1977, and membership in the SLATEC Common Math Library Subcommittee now also includes Sandia National Laboratory, Lawrence Livermore National Laboratory, the National Institute of Standards and Technology, and the Oak Ridge National Laboratory. The subcommittee solicits software for inclusion in the library and develops and enforces standards for portability, documentation, and testing.

Issues We next describe some of the issues that must be addressed in the development and maintenance of large numerical program libraries.

Portability The costliness of the effort to adapt libraries to ever-changing computer hardware has led to a concern for portability. Although most of the libraries under discussion here are written in Fortran, not all can be moved easily from one computer to another; instead, libraries are often provided in a different version for each brand of computer. Two things stand in the way of portability: first, the dialect of Fortran in use on each computer and, second, the arithmetic differences, both in static hardware and dynamic behavior, between computers.

Considerable progress has been made in overcoming these problems. Libraries are now usually programmed in standard Fortran, and their adherence to the standard can be verified mechanically. To cope with arithmetic differences between computers, machine-dependent code fragments are often flagged to be set by a preprocessor (q.v.) before compilation. An alternative technique is to have only one source code, with machine-dependent quantities obtained at run-time using standardized function calls. The PORT library, developed by AT&T Bell Laboratories in 1974, pioneered this technique. In PORT, machine-dependent constants are obtained from three Fortran functions—R1MACH, D1MACH, and I1MACH. These routines are freely available (from *netlib*, for example, see below) and have become the basis of portability for a number of other libraries such as SLATEC and STARPAC.

Error Handling In order to protect users from program failure and from their own programming errors, the best quality program libraries do careful error checking. Both the legality of the input parameters to a subprogram and the validity of the computation process must be scrutinized. Some errors must be signaled as *fatal*, whereas others can be designated as less serious. Unfortunately, no standard has been adopted for error handling, and procedures vary from one library to another. Within a given library, however, errors are most often reported through a fixed error-handler. Users can often control the behavior of the handler as a function of the error severity. In some cases it is reasonable to print a fatal error and abort the program, while in other cases users need the flexibility to regain control of execution with an error flag set so that they can take appropriate action. Good error handlers provide both of these mechanisms.

Storage Allocation Most library routines require workspace for scratch storage whose size is a function of problem parameters. To relieve users of the burden of supplying this through the calling sequence (q.v.), it is useful to have some sort of automatic storage allocation for internal library use. In dynamic storage allocation,

TABLE 1. Some Packages for Numerical Computation

Name	Year[1]	Size[2]	Purpose
FISHPAK	1975	19	Separable elliptic partial differential equations
BLAS	1979	42	Basic linear algebra subroutines
LINPACK	1979	164	Matrix factorizations, linear systems, determinants, inverses
FNLIB	1979	204	Elementary and special functions
MINPACK-1	1980	10	Nonlinear systems and nonlinear least squares problems
FFTPACK	1982	18	Fast Fourier and related transforms
QUADPACK	1983	68	Numerical evaluation of one-dimensional integrals
BLAS 2	1988	27	Basic matrix-vector operations
BLAS 3	1990	48	Basic matrix-matrix operations

[1]Date of first release.
[2]Number of user-callable subprograms in current release.

space is obtained from and returned to a large pool of available memory space. In general, the mechanism is system-dependent and not available with Fortran programs. However, it is possible in Fortran to set aside a sizable array in a COMMON region for use as a dynamic stack, and to provide a set of subprograms for allocation and deallocation of stack space. The PORT library pioneered this technique, which is now also used by IMSL and STARPAC.

Documentation   A program library is of no use unless it is supported by documentation that explains how to use each program. The purpose of the program, its input and output parameters, and possible error situations must be clearly described. Most libraries have detailed manuals that provide this information, as well as extensive background on the problems addressed.

Increasingly, local documentation for a library is being kept on-line, permitting users to access the information interactively. In some cases, as with the SLATEC library, documentation is provided only in machine-readable form. Because of this, the SLATEC library has established rigid documentation standards for subprograms accepted into its library. The SLATEC *Prologue*, which is included in each subprogram, includes sections on purpose, problem classification, precision, keywords, authors, description, related routines, references, routines called, and revision history. Such standards, when available, greatly ease the integration of on-line documentation into local systems.

Several libraries (IMSL, NAG, and SLATEC, for example) provide separate interactive on-line documentation systems that employ keyword search, problem classifica-

tions, and decision trees to help users locate appropriate software. The National Institute of Standards and Technology (NIST) Guide to Available Mathematical Software (GAMS) problem classification system is in widespread use for this purpose. At NIST, an on-line software advisory system that integrates information about software in 40 different libraries has been developed.

The Future   Many challenges remain in the development of numerical and statistical program libraries. Expansion of libraries into new problem areas as well as the incorporation of improved algorithms will continue indefinitely. Library developers have begun to address the problem of revising algorithms and interfaces to achieve improved performance on parallel and vector computers. Initial successes in the area of linear algebra software have been quite encouraging. Library developers will have to cope with increasing user pressure for support for other languages, principally C; IMSL and NAG have recently released libraries in this language. Finally, efforts will continue to improve the ability of software advisory systems to provide expert advice to users.

Program Library Availability   Table 2 lists a few of the program libraries currently available and tells where the libraries can be obtained. Seven of these are collections of Fortran subroutines. The remainder, all statistical software, have high-level user interfaces. The libraries classified in Table 2 as mathematical generally include evaluation of special functions, linear algebra, interpolation and approximation, solution of nonlinear algebraic equations, optimization, quadrature, solution of differen-

TABLE 2.   Some Libraries for Numerical and Statistical Computation

Name	Version	Size[1]	Area	Distributor
BCSLIB	1987	285	Mathematics	Boeing Computer Services, Mathematical Software Products, P.O. Box 24346, Mail Stop 7W-05, Seattle, WA 98124-0346
BMDP	1987	40	Statistics	BMDP Statistical Software, Inc., 1964 Westwood Blvd., Suite 202, Los Angeles, CA 90025
DATAPLOT	1989	215	Statistics	NTIS, U.S. Dept. of Commerce, 5285 Port Royal Rd., Springfield, VA 22161
HARWELL	1988	640	Mathematics	Computer Science and Systems Division, AERE Harwell, Oxfordshire, OX11 ORA, England
IMSL[2]	2.0	960	Mathematics, statistics	IMSL Inc., 2500 ParkWest Tower One, 2500 CityWest Blvd., Houston, TX 77042
MINITAB	1982.1	150	Statistics	Minitab, 3081 Enterprise Drive, State College, PA 16801
NAG	Mark 15	1045	Mathematics, statistics	Numerical Algorithms Group Ltd., 1101 31st St., Suite 100, Downers Grove, IL 60515
OMNITAB	7	N/A	Statistics	NTIS, U.S. Dept. of Commerce, 5285 Port Royal Rd., Springfield, VA 22161
PORT	3	373	Mathematics	AT&T Technology Licensing, Guilford Center, P.O. Box 25000, Greensboro, NC 27420
SAS	5.18	43	Statistics	SAS Institute Inc., Box 8000, Cary, NC 27511-8000
SLATEC	3.2	707	Mathematics	National Energy Software Center, Argonne National Laboratory, 9700 South Cass Ave., Argonne, IL 60439
SPSS	2.1	28	Statistics	SPSS Inc., 444 N. Michigan Avenue, Chicago, IL 60611
STARPAC	2.07	145	Statistics[3]	J. R. Rogers, NIST, Mail Stop 719, 325 Broadway, Boulder, CO 80303-3328

[1]Approximate number of user-callable program modules.
[2]Separate libraries for mathematics, statistics, and special functions.
[3]Primarily time series and regression analysis.

tial equations, integral transforms, and sorting (*q.v.*). The libraries classified as primarily statistical generally include data summarization, data manipulation, elementary data analysis, statistical function evaluation, random number generation, analysis of variance, regression, categorical data analysis, time series analysis, and cluster analysis.

Of course, there are many libraries and sources of programs not represented here. This has become especially true in recent years as new commercial ventures seek to exploit the growing market of personal computers and workstations. Journals in several scientific fields regularly publish algorithms and programs. For example, the Association for Computing Machinery began publishing algorithms in their *Communications* in 1960, and the *Collected Algorithms of the ACM* contains algorithms published since that time. In 1975, publication of algorithms was transferred to the *ACM Transactions on Mathematical Software (TOMS)*. Recently, numerical and statistical packages have become available for automated distribution on computer networks. For example, each of the packages listed in Table 1, as well as much additional public-domain software, can be obtained from the *netlib* service of AT&T Bell Laboratories and Oak Ridge National Laboratory. For a description of this service, send an electronic mail message with the text `send index` to either `netlib@ornl.gov` or `netlib@research.att.com`. A similar collection of statistical software is maintained at Carnegie-Mellon University using the address `statlib@stat.cmu.edu`.

References

1951. Wilkes, M. V., Wheeler, D. J., and Gill, S. *The Preparation of Programs for an Electronic Digital Computer.* Reading, MA: Addison-Wesley.

1971. Rice, J. R. (Ed.) *Mathematical Software.* New York: Academic Press.

1977. Rice, J. R. (Ed.) *Mathematical Software III.* New York: Academic Press.

1978. Fox, P. A., Hall, A. D., and Schryer, N. L. "Framework for a Portable Library," *ACM Transactions on Mathematical Software,* **4**, 177–188.

1984. Cowell, W. R. (Ed.) *Sources and Development of Mathematical Software.* Englewood Cliffs, NJ: Prentice-Hall.

1985. Boisvert, R. F., Howe, S. E., and Kahaner, D. K. "A Framework for the Management of Scientific Software," *ACM Transactions on Mathematical Software,* **11**, 313–355.

1987. Dongarra, J. J. and Grosse, E. "Distribution of Mathematical Software via Electronic Mail," *Communications of the ACM,* **30**, 403–407.

RONALD F. BOISVERT

SOFTWARE MAINTENANCE

For articles on related subjects *see* COMPATIBILITY; DEBUGGING; ERRORS; OBJECT-ORIENTED PROGRAMMING; SOFTWARE; SOFTWARE ENGINEERING; and STRUCTURED PROGRAMMING.

Because of the complexity of large software systems, there are almost always errors (bugs) and inadequacies in running them. *Software maintenance* is the activity that

addresses the correction of software errors and to remedying the inadequacies that may exist.

Computer manufacturers and other producers of software products have large software maintenance groups whose tasks vary from simple correction of typographical errors to major changes and extensions to existing software programs. These groups usually provide a formal mechanism whereby users can submit evidence of errors of inadequate performance. Corrections are then usually distributed to all users.

After a number of changes have been made, it is inconvenient to make additional changes, especially if new changes affect the results of earlier changes. Also, in some cases, very extensive changes require major revisions in the documentation of the software product. In such cases it is usual to release a new version of the software product that contains all changes to date and that serves as a new base for future changes.

In order to ease the impact on the users, the manufacturer usually continues to maintain several earlier software releases for some time after a new version is released. Ultimately, however, the older versions are declared to be obsolete and are taken off maintenance. When this happens, even reluctant users usually convert to the newer versions.

New versions of software products often have subtle effects on a user's applications systems, and large users usually have their own software maintenance personnel, not only for maintenance of the application systems, but also to install new versions of supplied software and make modifications that may be necessary to move their application programs from one version to another.

As software development and software maintenance have grown into major activities involving very large numbers of people and very large amounts of money, there has been considerable effort devoted to improving the efficiency and productivity of the whole software process.

Some software projects have claimed spectacular results through the use of a programming discipline that has come to be known as *structured programming* (Dahl *et al.*, 1972). *Top-down programming* and the use of a *chief programmer team* (*q.v.*) are related concepts (Baker, 1972). More recently, emphasis on *object-oriented programming* (*q.v.*) has improved both software development and maintenance.

References

1972. Baker, F. T. "Chief Programmer Team Management of Production Planning," *IBM Systems Journal* **11**, *1*.

1972. Dahl, O. J., Dijkstra, E. W., and Hoare, C. A. R. *Structured Programming.* New York: Academic Press.

SAUL ROSEN

SOFTWARE MANAGEMENT

For articles on related subjects *see* SOFTWARE CONFIGURATION MANAGEMENT; SOFTWARE ENGINEERING; and SOFTWARE MAINTENANCE.

Software management is concerned with managing the resources and work activities required to develop and modify software-intensive systems. The primary success criteria for software managers are delivery of systems that satisfy the stated needs and requirements, on time and within budget. Goals for software managers include better quality, increased productivity, and improved predictability of software development efforts.

A large amount of software effort is concerned with modifying existing systems to provide additional functionality, to improve performance, to adapt the software to changing hardware environments, and to fix problems in the software. For the purposes of this article, we use the term *software development* to mean initial development of a system or significant modifications to an existing system.

The major activities of software management include planning, monitoring and controlling, and leading the software development effort. Effective planning requires detailed understanding of the needs, requirements, and design constraints for the system. Because requirements and plans tend to evolve together, they should be developed iteratively.

Planning Factors to be considered in planning for software development include the products to be delivered, the resources available, and the time allocated to system development. Other essential factors include organization of the development effort, the managerial processes to be used, and the technical processes to be employed.

Organizational factors include the process model to be used, the organizational structure, organizational boundaries and interfaces, and delegation of development responsibilities. A process model specifies the procedures, methods, and interactions among work activities for a software development effort. Current process models include the waterfall model, the incremental development model, evolutionary prototyping, and the spiral model.

There are two types of issues concerning organizational structure for software development: the structure of the development organization and the structure of the development team. Organizational structures for software development include the project format, the functional format, and the matrix structure. Techniques for organizing the software development team include the democratic structure, the hierarchical structure, and the chief programmer team (*q.v.*) structure.

Managerial process considerations include management objectives and priorities for the development effort, management dependencies and constraints, identification and analysis of development risks, the monitoring and controlling mechanisms to be used, and the staffing and training needs of the development effort.

Technical processes to be planned include the methods, tools, and techniques to be used, the documentation requirements, and the supporting functions, such as quality assurance, configuration management, and validation and verification (*see* SOFTWARE ENGINEERING).

These planning considerations should be documented in a software development plan which includes detailed specification of the work activities, time dependencies among the activities, the resource requirements

over time, allocation of the budget and resources to the work activities, and an overall schedule for the development effort. Planning is an on-going activity for software development. Status reviews and replanning should continue throughout the lifetime of the development process.

IEEE/ANSI Standard 1058.1 (1987) provides a structured format for a software development plan and the IEEE Tutorial on Software Engineering Project Management contains several articles on the planning process for software development (Thayer, 1988).

Monitoring and Controlling Factors to be monitored and controlled during software development include quality, productivity, schedule, budget, and progress. Quality factors include functional characteristics, such as response time, throughput (*q.v.*), memory utilization, and mean time between failure, plus non-functional characteristics, such as user friendliness, maintainability, and quality of the user's manual. Productivity is the amount of product produced per unit of resource expended. Typical measures of productivity include lines of code per programmer month, function points (i.e. module interfaces) per programmer hour, and test cases run per programmer day.

Schedule and budget are often tracked using the earned-value technique, which compares the budgeted cost of work performed to the actual cost of work performed and the budgeted cost of work scheduled. If the actual cost of the work performed is greater than the budgeted cost of the work performed, the project is over budget. If the budgeted cost of the work scheduled is greater than the budgeted cost of the work performed, the project is behind schedule.

Progress is typically measured in terms of requirements designed/implemented/tested to date. Progress is not necessarily synonomous with productivity; it is possible to be extremely productive at doing the wrong thing.

Several articles on monitoring and controlling are contained in the IEEE Tutorial on Software Engineering Project Management. In addition, the text by Boehm (1981) provides detailed information on planning, monitoring, and controlling software development efforts.

Leading Because software development is a labor-intensive (intellect-intensive) activity, issues of leadership, motivation, and team building are of paramount importance to successful software management. Leadership and management are related but distinct concepts. Management involves presiding over institutional processes, allocating resources and assigning responsibilities, and following up on work assignments. Leadership, on the other hand, is concerned with issues such as organizational politics, vision, communication skill, values, motivation, and improving the work processes and work structures.

A particularly difficult issue for many software managers is delegation of technical decisions to those best qualified to make them. Every software development effort should have a chief architect. On small projects (three to five people), it may be possible (and desirable) for the manager to also function as chief architect. On larger projects, the manager and chief architect should be different people.

Motivation is the drive to satisfy one's psychological needs. Studies of motivational factors for software developers have shown that the major motivators are autonomy, professional growth, and confidence in the technical leadership. Autonomy refers to the freedom to make decisions concerning the best way do one's job. Professional growth is the opportunity to learn and apply new skills. Confidence in technical leadership refers to the confidence that one's technical skills and energy are being used to best effect. It is the leader's responsibility to create a work environment in which software developers can fulfill their psychological work needs and thus obtain a sense of job satisfaction.

Software systems are, for the most part, developed by teams rather than by individuals. It is therefore essential that the leader/manager know how to build an effective team so that software developers can work in a cooperative manner toward shared, common goals.

Thus the tasks of a leader/manager are to communicate values, vision, and day-to-day information; to delegate technical decisions to those best qualified to make them; to provide a work environment in which individuals can satisfy their psychological needs; and to develop effective work teams. These tasks are particularly difficult for software managers who are promoted into management as a reward for their technical skills, rather than their people skills, and who may have received no training in leadership or team building.

References

1971. Weinberg, Gerald. *The Psychology of Computer Programming*. New York: Van Nostnand Reinhold.

1975. Brooks, Fred. *The Mythical Man-Month*. Reading, MA: Addison-Wesley.

1981. Boehm, Barry. *Software Engineering Economics*. Englewood Cliffs, NJ: Prentice-Hall.

1981. Metzger, Philip. *Managing A Programming Project*. New York: Prentice-Hall.

1982. DeMarco, Tom. *Controlling Software Projects*. Yourdon Press.

1985. Fairley, Richard. *Software Engineering Concepts*. New York: McGraw-Hill.

1985. Reifer, Don (Ed). *IEEE Tutorial on Software Management*. Los Alamitos, CA: Computer Society Press.

1987. ——. *IEEE/ANSI Standard for Software Project Management Plans*. Piscataway, NJ: The Institute of Electrical and Electronics Engineers, Inc.

1988. Thayer, Richard (Ed). *IEEE Tutorial on Software Engineering Project Management*. Los Alamitos, CA: Computer Society Press.

1989. DeMarco, Tom. *Peopleware*. Englewood Cliffs, NJ: Yourdon Press.

RICHARD E. FAIRLEY

SOFTWARE METRICS

For articles on related subjects *see* SOFTWARE ENGINEERING; and SOFTWARE MANAGEMENT.

Definition *Software metrics* are units of measurement of software. Software includes both the product (programs, documentation, reports) and the process by which the product is developed (the software *life cycle* phases of specification, design, implementation, testing, and maintenance). Software metrics make it possible for software to be compared, evaluated, and analyzed quantitatively. Example software metrics and related measures are program size (source lines of code), efficiency (execution time), reliability (mean time to failure), and programmer experience (years of programming in a particular language). Metrics and measures form the basis for numerous models of the software development process. Of these, perhaps the most widely known is Boehm's (1981) COCOMO model, used for estimating the development time, staffing levels, and costs of a software project.

Background Recognition of the software crisis in the 1960s brought an awareness of the need for better management capabilities in the production of software. Metrics and models provide the ability to quantify more precisely factors in the software development process so that improvements may be made, more control exercised, productivity increased, and better quality guaranteed. This led to considerable research activity in software metrics in the 1970s and 1980s. This research may be categorized into the areas of process metrics, product metrics, experimental studies, data collection, and studies of large system evolution. Publications in software metrics have been dated back to the late 1960s with an article by Rubey and Hartwick in 1968 (Cote, 1988).

Early process models were developed by Wolverton (1974), an empirical model for cost projection, and Walston and Felix (1977), a statistical model for projecting development effort. Boehm's Constructive Cost Model (COCOMO) (1981) is a process model for cost estimation and is a result of experience, empirical studies, and intuition. Development of product metrics has concentrated primarily on code metrics and is represented by the work of Halstead (1977) on software science, control structure complexity of McCabe (1979), and knots of Woodfield, Hennell, and Hedley (1979), among many others. Henry and Kafura (1981), Albrecht and Gaffney (1983), and McClure (1978) have developed models and metrics of modularity at the design and code levels. Long-term data collection over a period of 10 years by Belady and Lehman (1976) led to the formulation of laws of software systems evolution and models of software change. Models of software errors and defects have been the basis of reliability studies by Musa (1987). Curtis (1979) and Basili (1980) have published a number of papers on experimental techniques in validating models and metrics. The Rome Air Development Center has produced numerous studies on how to obtain and process data collected during the software development cycle.

Applications The need for software metrics has been compared by Cote *et al.* (1988) to the need for dials and gauges in a nuclear plant to monitor and control the underlying process. Without metrics and measures, it would be difficult, if not impossible, to understand and improve the complex process of software development and meet the goals of software engineering. In practice, software metrics are used: (1) to make projections about management concerns in the software process, such as costs, staffing levels, resource allocation, and completion estimates, (2) to provide feedback during the development process and to signal when standards and practices have been violated and when faulty products need to be corrected, (3) to evaluate the acceptability and quality of products, determining whether specifications have been met and user needs satisfied, (4) to monitor the software process, keeping track of time, staff, costs, and quality of products during the life cycle, (5) to measure the productivity of personnel and (6) to make comparisons and decisions about trade-offs.

Criticisms Software metrics have been received with a great deal of skepticism by some software practitioners. This has been due largely to poor methodology, faulty data, and a sense that much of the research is *ad hoc.* Many models and metrics proposed by individuals for specific situations and tested in limited contexts cannot be generalized readily to other situations and contexts. Even where metrics appear to have generality, such as size, measures cannot be readily transformed across environments, applications, and languages. Investigators rely largely on intuition and experience rather than more traditional disciplined approaches toward formulating new metrics and models. Experimental studies have been criticized for using faulty designs and improper statistical techniques. Much of the criticism is well-deserved; but efforts are under way to improve the situation.

Part of the problem can be attributed to the fact that there is no sound theoretical basis upon which to develop metrics. Software does not have a concrete realization except as documents or bit strings that do not convey the true nature of software (i.e. the dynamic aspects, the interaction with hardware and humans). Software does not wear out or break; its function is frequently changed from what it was originally designed to do. Thus, the very ephemeral nature of software hampers research efforts. Fairley (1985) has compared software design to architectural design in the absence of gravity. At this time it is not clear whether the necessary scientific foundation for software is analogous to that of the natural sciences or to that of large, complex forecasting systems. In the former case, there should be identification of a set of laws, invariants, or common properties to serve as the foundation of metrics and models. In the latter case, it may not be possible to describe completely software with invariant principles, but rather to describe aspects of the process and product that can be combined into a general theory analogous to weather forecasting or economic systems.

Apart from the lack of a science of software, there are also inherent difficulties for research due to the fact that software production involves large, complex systems. This makes it impossible to repeat experiments or try different approaches in order to make comparisons of various methodologies and techniques. Another major obstacle to research and experimentation has been the lack of common sources of data, both in actual developed sample software systems and in records of how the systems were produced and developed. Part of the problem has been due to the proprietary nature of the data; companies do not want to reveal details of internal practices, since it may cause embarrassment in the presence of poor practices, or it may give competitors an edge. It has been only recently that the need for such data has been recognized by industry, with attempts made to develop collection methods that are not intrusive and do not violate confidentiality. Large databases of collected data are also being built and made accessible to all interested researchers on a national basis. At the same time, experimental techniques are being refined so that validation studies have more applicability and reliability.

Example Measures The following measures are product measures and are among the more widely known and used software product measures. The first three are source code measures that are applied to program text during the implementation phase. The fourth measure is an example of a measure that can be applied earlier in the development cycle. The sample measures are used in a variety of metrics (e.g. size, complexity, productivity, reliability, testability, maintainability). Some have been used in specifications to control program quality (e.g. code modules should not exceed 50 lines or a McCabe measure of 10).

The following Pascal program segment implementing a selection sort will be used in the discussion of the measures given below:

```
type
    LISTTYPE = array [1..1000] of INTEGER;

procedure SORT (var L : LISTTYPE; N : INTEGER);
var
    I, J, TEMP, MINLOC : INTEGER;
begin
    for I := 1 to N – 1 do
        begin
            MINLOC := I;
            for J := (I + 1) to N do
                if L[J] < L[MINLOC]
                    then MINLOC : = J;
            TEMP := L[MINLOC];
            L[MINLOC] := L[I];
            L[I] := TEMP
        end
end;
```

Lines of Code Measure (LOC) Historically, this is one of the earliest program code measures. It is a simple, intuitive measure in which the source lines of code in a program are counted. There are a variety of methods of taking the measure; the most common one counts all lines of program text except blank lines and those that contain only comments. The measure originated in the days when programs were punched on cards and a source line corresponded to a card. In current usage, a source line of code is understood to be a line printed in a listing. Even for such a simple measure, there are difficulties when applying it to different programming languages. For fixed format languages like Fortran and Cobol, there is a correspondence between a line of source code and a single executable statement. For free-format languages like Pascal, C, and Ada, a line of source code may contain exactly one statement, multiple statements, or part of a statement. For example, the Pascal statement

if (A <> B) **then** A := B / 10 **else** A := A − 1;

can be written on one line, as shown, or in a variety of ways, of which the following are but two examples:

if (A <> B)
   then A := B / 10
   else A := A − 1;

if (A <> B)
   then
      A := B / 10
   else
      A := A − 1;

Lines of code (LOC) measurements could then be 1, 3, or 5, depending upon the way the statement was written. At a glance this may not seem important; however, the measure displays instability due to the fact that source code with identical content can have many measurements simply by changing its format. Given the difficulty within a single language, direct comparisons between programs in different languages are virtually impossible. Moreover, if LOC were used to measure programmer productivity, a programmer could artificially alter the rate by compacting code or spreading it out. To remove this variability, some researchers use executable statement counts (placement on lines is ignored), while others use counts of statement separators or terminators (e.g. ";" in Pascal and C). For the above SORT example, LOC is 17 if applying the common definition (exclude counts of comments or blank lines), 8 if semicolons are counted, and 5 if executable statements are counted. Lines of code has been criticized as a measure because it does not take into account the content of the code being measured (e.g. a complex logical statement is counted the same as a simple assignment statement).

Halstead's Software Science
Halstead (1977) proposed the notion that algorithms display characteristics similar to those in the natural sciences, and attempted to define a *software science*. His system models software in terms of counts of *tokens* in the program text, and, from these counts, measures of length, volume, effort, and development time are derived. Tokens are all symbols occurring in a program including punctuation and keywords. Tokens are split into two groups: operands and operators. Halstead's rules for counting tokens are language dependent and can be subject to the preferences of individuals implementing the counts. (Note again non-standard measurement across programming languages.) For Halstead measures, the following are defined:

n_1 = number of unique operators
n_2 = number of unique operands
N_1 = total occurrences of operators
N_2 = total occurrences of operands

These are used in the following formulas:

Program vocabulary:

$$n = n_1 + n_2$$

Program length:

$$N = N_1 + N_2$$

Program volume:

$$V = N \log_2 n$$

Program level:

$$L = V^* / V \quad (V^* \text{ is the size of the minimal program implementing the algorithm.})$$

Program effort:

$$E = V / L \text{ or } E = V^2 / V^*$$

Program development time:

$$T = E / S \quad (S = \text{number of mental discriminations per second or } Stroud \, number, \text{ usually } = 18)$$

Halstead hypothesized that these quantities could be estimated using only n_1 and n_2 to obtain an estimate of the length; i.e.

$$\hat{N} = n_1 \log_2 n_1 + n_2 \log_2 n_2.$$

Tests using this length estimate ranging over a large number of samples show that it is fairly accurate for most reasonable programs (it is possible to construct pathological samples as counter-examples). Thus, simply by observing token counts and frequencies, level, volume, effort, and development time can be calculated and used to predict coding time, program complexity, size of programs, etc. Experimental results show that in some cases Halstead measures are reasonably good predictors. However, there has been no acceptance of the Halstead notion of a software science, due primarily to a lack of convincing proof. The individual Halstead measures are included in many commercial metrics packages and are available for a variety of languages. For the SORT example, Halstead measurements are:

$n_1 = 20$
$n_2 = 9$
$N_1 = 52$
$N_2 = 36$
$N = 88$
$\hat{N} = 115.0$
$V = 296.322$
$L = 0.025$
$E = 11852.881$
$T = 658.493$

McCabe's Cyclomatic Complexity Measure

The McCabe cyclomatic complexity measure is a measure of the control structure complexity of a program that is obtained by counting the number of linearly independent paths through program code. The measure is based upon graph theory (*q.v.*) and the cyclomatic number of a directed graph. A flow graph (similar to a flow chart) is created from the program text of the target program, and a count is taken of the number of nodes (n) and the edges (e) from the nodes. The McCabe complexity $v(G)$ is given as $e - n + 2$. For structured programs (no gotos or backward branches), $v(G)$ is obtained by counting the number of predicates and adding 1.

$v(G)$ is used in measuring program complexity (more paths imply more complex code), and is commonly used as a basis for comparison in program complexity experiments. Like the Halstead measures, McCabe's cyclomatic complexity has shown good correlation as a predictor in certain specific cases. The McCabe measure reflects more information about a program than the source lines of code measure. However, it has omitted nesting of control structures and data from its consideration. The McCabe measure for the SORT procedure is 4 (count 1 each for the two **for** statements, one for the single **if** statement, and add 1).

The software complexity measures mentioned above are useful to detect problematic code for the testing and maintenance stages in the software development cycle. This is too late and too costly in the development process, and measures taken earlier in the design and specification phases are needed to anticipate problems. Efforts are currently under way to look for such measures. One such measure, commonly used in data processing environments, is the *function point* measure.

Function Points *Functions points* are a measure of the interfaces between modules or subsystems in programs and large systems. The function point measure (FP) is a count of the number of external user inputs, inquiries, outputs, and master files in a subprogram or subsystem. These are then weighted by 4, 4, 5, and 10, respectively. The results are then summed to arrive at a value of FP. For the above SORT procedure, the FP measure is 13 (2 inputs: *list* and *num*; 1 output: *list*). Note that FP can be calculated without having any actual code. The weights can also be further adjusted to compensate for other factors, such as application, experience, and environment. The measure is frequently used in the development of business software and is found in metrics packages that measure commercial software. It has appeal because it anticipates problems in software development before the coding stage is reached. Intuitively, one can expect that modules with high function point measures in the specification and design phases will be more difficult to implement and require more resources. FP has not been used extensively in formal metrics research.

Current Trends While there are few metrics that are widely accepted, there is a growing awareness that metrics, even in limited cases, can be of value in understanding and controlling software products and the software development process. Increasingly, off-the-shelf metrics packages are becoming available and measures are tailored to suit each individual company's standards and practices. Management is beginning to install integrated metrics programs on a corporate basis that not only apply metrics to individual products and phases of development, but also collect, store, and analyze data taken during the entire development process. Studies are under way to determine the kinds of data, storage techniques, analysis techniques, and collection schemes that can be useful in these systematic programs. The long-range effects of these programs and the data collected should help to identify more relevant metrics and improve models of the software process.

References

1968. Rubey, R. J. and Hartwick, R. D. "Quantitative Measurement of Program Quality," *Proc. ACM National Conference*, 671–677.

1974. Wolverton, R. W. "The Cost of Developing Large-Scale Software," *IEEE TSC* **C-23**, (June) 615–636.

1976. Belady, L. A., and Lehman, M. M. "A Model of Large Program Development," *IBM Systems Journal,* **15***, 3*, 225–252.

1976. McCabe, Thomas J. "A Complexity Measure," *IEEE TSE* (December) 308–320.

1977. Halstead, Maurice, *Elements of Software Science*, New York: Elsevier North Holland.

1977. Walston, C. E., and Felix, C. P. "A Method of Programming Measurement and Estimation," *IBM Systems Journal* **16***, 1*, 54–73.

1978. McClure, Carma. "A Model for Program Complexity Analysis," *Proc. 3rd International Conference on Software Engineering,* Atlanta (May) 149–157.

1979. Curtis, Bill, Sheppard, S. and Milliman, P. "Third Time Charm: Stronger Prediction of Programmer Performance by Software Complexity Metrics," *Proc. 4th International Conference on Software Engineering*, 356–360.

1979. Woodfield, M. R., Hennell, M. A., and Hedley, D. "A Measure of Control Flow Complexity in Program Text," *IEEE TSE*, **SE-5** (January) 45–50.

1980. Basili, Victor R. *Tutorial on Models and Metrics for Software Management and Engineering.* New York: IEEE Computer Society.

1981. Boehm, V. W. *Software Engineering Economics*, Englewood Cliffs, NJ: Prentice-Hall.

1981. Henry, Sallie, and Kafura, Dennis. "Software Structure Metrics Based on Information Flow," *IEEE TSE*, **SE-7***, 5* (September) 510–518.

1981. Perlis, A. J., Sayward, F. G. and Shaw, M. *Software Metrics: An Analysis and Evaluation.* Cambridge, MA: The M.I.T. Press.

1983. Albrecht, A. J. and Gaffney, J. E., Jr. "Software Function, Source Lines of Code, and Development Effort Prediction: A Software Science Validation," *IEEE TSE*, **SE-9***, 6* (November) 639–648.

1985. Fairley, Richard E. *Software Engineering Concepts.* New York: McGraw-Hill.

1985. Kolence, K. W. *An Introduction to Software Physics.* New York: McGraw-Hill.

1986. Conte, S. D., Dunsmore, H. E., and Shen, V. Y. *Software Engineering Metrics and Models* Menlo Park, CA: Benjamin Cummings.

1986. Jones, T. G. *Programming Productivity.* New York: McGraw-Hill.

1987. Musa, J. D., Iannino, A., and Okumuto, K. *Software Reliabil-*

ity: Measurement, Prediction, Application. New York: McGraw-Hill.

1988. Cote, V. Bourque, P. Oligny, S. and Rivard, N. "Software Metrics, An Overview of Recent Results," *The Journal of Systems and Software*, **8**, 121–131.

1988. Mills, Everald E., *Software Metrics*, SEI Curriculum Module SEI-CM-12-1.1, Carnegie-Mellon University, Software Engineering Institute, Pittsburgh, PA, December.

PATRICIA B. VAN VERTH

SOFTWARE MONITOR

For articles on related subjects *see* CHECKPOINT AND RESTART; HARDWARE MONITOR; PERFORMANCE MEASUREMENT AND EVALUATION; SOFTWARE METRICS; and STRUCTURED PROGRAMMING.

A *software monitor* is, according to its most general definition, a piece of software used for performance measurement. Like other types of instruments (e.g. hardware monitors), a software monitor is capable of measuring the performance of two kinds of objects—computer systems and computer programs. A software monitor proper runs on the system or with the program whose performance it is intended to measure. A *system-oriented* monitor usually measures system performance indices (e.g. response or turnaround times, throughput rates, component utilizations), as well as system and workload variables (e.g. CPU time demands, memory space demands, paging rates, degrees of multiprogramming). A *program-oriented* monitor is usually capable of measuring such program performance indices as execution times, instruction execution counts and frequencies, total CPU times, uninterrupted CPU interval durations, numbers and types of I/O operations performed, etc.

The main functions of any monitor are event detection, data collection, data reduction, and presentation of results (see Fig. 1). A software monitor is either of the *event-driven or sampling* type. The basic type of event for an event-driven software monitor is the execution of a certain instruction within a program. This event can be detected by inserting into the program at that location a *checkpoint* or *software probe*—that is, an instruction that is executed whenever the monitored instruction is executed and that has the effect of recording the execution (e.g. by updating a counter). A wide variety of event types can be indirectly detected by this mechanism; (e.g. the use of a variable, the coincidence of the value of a variable with a given value, the updating of a register, the execution of a given arithmetic operation). System events can be expressed in terms of these program event types when the program involved is the operating system.

With a sampling software monitor, the detection is performed by an interval timer that interrupts the CPU and causes the monitor to seize control. The main advantages of a sampling monitor over an event-driven one are its much easier addition to an existing system or program and the potentially lower interference with the object being measured. The main disadvantages are its lesser accuracy when measuring certain types of indices and, in some cases, its inability to collect protected system information.

With all types of software monitors, the detection of an appropriate event causes a certain amount of data accessible to the instrument to be collected and possibly processed for reduction purposes. The types of events to be detected, the amount of collected data and the extent of their immediate reduction vary with the instrument and may often be influenced by its user. When this is not possible, the monitor is said to be *fixed*. Examples of fixed software monitors are the *meters* (checkpoints that increment a software counter whenever they are executed) and all non-modifiable checkpoints inserted into a program (e.g. those that, within an operating system, measure resource consumptions for accounting and charging purposes). The extent to which monitors reduce data at collection time varies between the extremes of *counting* (maximum immediate reduction, minimum storage requirements, maximum loss of information) and *tracing* (no immediate reduction, maximum storage requirements, minimum or no loss of information).

Depending on the time that elapses between detection/collection and reduction/presentation, a monitor can be classified as *off line* or *on line*. In an off-line monitor, the completion of data reduction and the presentation of results are deferred until a later time. In the terminology of Fig. 1, the analysis follows the extraction at a relatively long temporal distance so that, in an off-line software monitor, there is no appreciable interference between the two operations. On-line monitors are those that reduce data and present results at their full speed, which, for software monitors, is the speed of the system at which data is collected. In other words, in these monitors, analysis is performed on line with respect to extraction.

From the viewpoint of the duration of their operation, monitors can be classified as *permanent* or *temporary*. Permanent instruments are used in continuous monitoring, a fundamental aspect of performance management, and in resource usage accounting. Since they are permanently incorporated into the object being monitored, their interference (i.e. their effects on the measured quantities) is always present and can therefore be ignored, though their impact on system overhead generally cannot. Temporary monitors find their main applications in the measurement studies needed for system or program

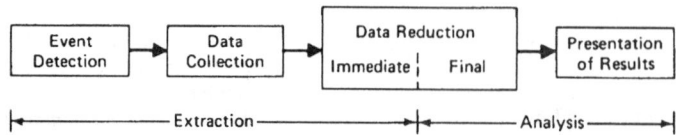

FIG. 1.

tuning, capacity planning, and benchmark design for procurement projects. Temporary event-driven software monitors consist of removable checkpoints and of appropriate measurement routines called by the checkpoints. The insertion and the removal of checkpoints can be partially automated by an interactive approach. Sampling monitors may be system or user programs that can be started and stopped by their users. On-line instruments are mostly used for fast short-term tuning, real-time detection and removal of sudden performance problems (infinite loops, deadlocks), and continuous monitoring. Any temporary instrument may be used for continuous monitoring by leaving it on without interruptions, or, more conveniently, turning it on periodically, according to a performance management plan. However, in the former case, a fixed *ad hoc* monitor normally consumes less resources than a more general type of monitor; also, in the latter case as well as in all temporary uses of a system-oriented software monitor, its interference with the measured system cannot in principle be ignored.

The amount of interference caused by a software monitor depends on the data collection rate, on the access times of the data to be collected, on the degree of immediate data reduction, on the strategies adopted for storing the data, and on the efficiency of the monitor's code.

The events a software monitor can detect and the data it can collect belong to the class of those that are accessible at the software level. Voltage pulses, control states, microinstruction delays, or contents of microregisters cannot be observed. On the other hand, variables such as the names of the jobs or transactions that have caused certain events, queue lengths, or the names of the most frequently accessed files are only, or much more easily, measured by a software monitor than by a hardware monitor. All types of software monitors are to some extent dependent on the hardware-software system on which they run. Thus, they are much less portable than hardware monitors.

Most existing event-driven software monitors have been constructed by operating system manufacturers. It is clearly much easier for the designers of a system than for outsiders to instrument it with suitable checkpoints. These monitors, like the fixed instruments also based on the checkpoint technique, were originally implemented for the exclusive use of the manufacturer, but are being distributed more and more often to the customers for their own performance monitoring or measurement needs. In some cases, the user is allowed to specify or select both the data collection operations that are to take place upon detection of the system events corresponding to the fixed checkpoints, and the subsequent data reductions; in the case of fixed monitors, such as those that collect accounting data, the user can specify the desired reduction operations; commercial software packages exist that exploit either possibility. Most of the commercial software monitors, however, as well as some of those offered by system manufacturers, are of the sampling type. The first system-oriented sampling monitor appeared on the market in 1968, and was immediately followed by the first program-oriented sampling monitor.

Several years later, the first on-line system-oriented software monitor, of the sampling type, was announced.

Three simple examples of applications of software monitors are given below:

Measurement of device utilization during a time interval of duration T. It is assumed that the operating system keeps the information about the state (busy or idle) of the device in a memory bit S.

An event-driven monitor to solve the problem consists of two checkpoints, C_1, and C_2, and two dedicated memory locations, A and B. The two checkpoints are inserted into the operating system code immediately after the instructions that update the contents of S:

$$C_1: \quad \begin{array}{l} S \leftarrow \text{busy} \\ B \leftarrow \text{clock} \end{array}$$

$$C_2: \quad \begin{array}{l} S \leftarrow \text{idle} \\ A \leftarrow A + \text{clock} - B \end{array}$$

Initialization: $A \leftarrow 0$, $B \leftarrow$ clock. Computation of the utilization (at the end of time interval T): $u = A/T$.

A sampling monitor samples the contents of S periodically (or at random times) N times during the interval: If $N_1 \leq N$ is the number of times S was found to contain "busy," then $u \cong N_1/N$.

Measurement of the mean length of a queue. It is assumed that the operating system keeps the instantaneous length of the queue in memory location Q.

An event-driven monitor uses one checkpoint C consisting of two statements, and two dedicated memory locations A and B. C is inserted into the operating system code just before the point at which an item is added to or deleted from the queue:

$$C: \quad \begin{array}{l} A \leftarrow A + q * (\text{clock} - B) \\ B \leftarrow \text{clock} \\ Q \leftarrow Q + 1 \text{ or } Q \leftarrow Q - 1 \end{array}$$

Initialization: $A \leftarrow 0$, $B \leftarrow$ clock. Computation of the mean queue length (at the end of a time interval T): $mql = A/T$.

A sampling monitor samples the contents of Q periodically (or at random times) N times during the interval and accumulates into location A the sum of the sampled queue lengths: If the initial contents of A were 0 and a is the contents of A at the end of the interval, then $mql \cong a/N$.

Measurement of the profile of a program by a sampling monitor. The monitor samples the contents of the program counter periodically and is able to determine when the program to be measured is running. (In practice, the monitor gets its data from the program status word of the process, which has just been interrupted.) A code utilization map is constructed by dividing the instruction space of the program into contiguous regions of 2^n words each, mapping each region onto one word in the map, and incrementing by 1 the contents of a map word whenever the program counter is found to point to an instruction in the corresponding region. If the map initially contains all zeroes, at the end of the measurement interval it will show the utilization profile of the program during that interval with a resolution inversely related to the value of n.

References

1976. Svobodova, L. *Computer Performance Measurement and Evaluation Methods: Analysis and Applications.* New York: Elsevier.

1978. Ferrari, D. *Computer Systems Performance Evaluation.* Englewood Cliffs, NJ: Prentice-Hall.

1983. Ferrari, D., Serazzi, G., and Zeigner, A. *Measurement and Tuning of Computer Systems.* Englewood Cliffs, NJ: Prentice-Hall.

1985. Kolence, K. W. *An Introduction to Software Physics: The Meaning of Computer Measurement.* New York: McGraw-Hill.

1988. McKerrow, P. *Performance Measurement of Computer Systems.* Reading, MA: Addison-Wesley.

DOMENICO FERRARI

SOFTWARE PERSONALIZATION

For articles on related subjects *see* HUMAN FACTORS IN COMPUTING; SHELL; SOFTWARE FLEXIBILITY; and USER INTERFACE.

Software is *personalizable* if its behavior can be altered to match a particular individual's needs. Since a good user interface makes a computer program convenient to use, it should have the means to be personalized to a user's needs. Suppose that two users are using the same application program at identical workstations, doing identical things. Depending upon personal needs and tastes, they may require different styles of user interface. For instance, if one has good eyesight but the other's is poor, the former may want text displayed in a smaller than average font to get more on the display, whereas the other may choose a large font to make the display more legible. Another example is an intelligent help system that customizes the content and presentation of material to a particular person. The importance of personalization stems from the need for mass-produced software to accommodate the individual differences typically found within a large but diverse clientele of users.

Software personalization has its roots in the operating systems of the late 1960s and 1970s that provided simple yet effective ways for programmers to customize their command-based computing environment. Users, for example, could replace oft-used but unwieldy command lines with simpler abbreviations. Similarly, preferences and options that override system defaults could be maintained by setting environment variables in a database referred to by a program at run time. But the major breakthrough in the design of personalizable operating system interfaces was to eliminate all differences between invoking a system program and a user program, as is done in Unix (*q.v.*). This allows one to tailor and extend a system to individual needs simply by writing utility programs (programs or *scripts* of command line sequences) and invoking them as needed, without having to alter the system itself in any way.

Some of these ideas have migrated to modern-day graphical computing environments that are oriented towards the non-programmer. Instead of personalizing the environment through setting syntactically baroque options or writing short programs, users are presented with a *property sheet*, a window-based form that displays items and their options as selectable and modifiable fields. For example, the Apple Macintosh provides users with a control panel that adjusts the "look and feel" of the user interface. Through it, users can choose the pattern of the background screen, adjust the repeat rate of the keyboard, tune the sensitivity of double mouse clicks, etc.

Through the concept of *user modeling*, the design of personalizable software has three important components:

1. The *modeling agent* selects and/or constructs an appropriate user model. The agent can be either a person (the user or designer) or the system itself. For example, users acts as modeling agents when they explicitly adjust preferences in a property sheet. Alternatively, the system may build a user model automatically by inferring key characteristics from the user's input.

2. The *user model* contains information about an individual user. The information represented by the model can be quite varied. One example is a simple scalar value that indicates the user's level of expertise. Other instances are *profiles*, where the user is characterized as a series of weighted parameters mapped onto weighted tasks and input traces where the model maintains a record of a user's important activities.

3. The *model use* governs how the model is to be used. Examples include predicting and anticipating user actions, adjusting the interface look and feel, etc. The method for using the model can be hard-wired into the software code or maintained explicitly as a set of independent and changeable rules within an expert system (*q.v.*).

Good examples of the application of user modeling techniques to personalizable software can be found in *intelligent tutoring systems*. These not only know what to teach, but can customize how they will present the material according to who is being taught. Based upon input from the learner, the system monitors and models the learner's knowledge, compares it with its own knowledge base, and directs tuition towards those parts that are identified as missing from the learner's understanding. Similarly, *intelligent help systems* provide users with help appropriate to their problem and level of prior knowledge. They can also expand the user's knowledge by suggesting new approaches and by correcting erroneous inputs. The user model may therefore incorporate an assessment of the user's expertise in a particular task, a model of the task in hand, and a model of the concepts known to the user.

Software personalization is still in its infancy. While it has been clearly accepted in its simpler forms, such as the ability of users to control explicitly a limited set of attributes, intelligent systems that automatically adapt their behavior to the user are rare outside research institutes. The future is promising, however, for personalizable software is a practical and economic way of allowing systems to conform to the user, rather than forcing users to conform to the system.

References

1982. Sleeman, D. and Brown, J. S. *Intelligent Tutoring Systems*. London: Academic Press.

1983. Rich, E. "Users are Individuals: Individualizing User Models." *International Journal of Man Machine Studies*, 18(3), 199–214.

1985. Greenberg, S. and Witten, I. H. "Adaptive Personalized Interfaces—A Question of Viability," *Behaviour and Information Technology*, 4(1), 31–45.

1991. Kobsa, A. (Ed.). *Journal of User Modeling and User-Adapted Interaction*. Leiden, The Netherlands, Kluwer Academic Publishers.

JANET FINLAY, SAUL GREENBERG, AND IAN H. WITTEN

SOFTWARE PIRACY. *See* LEGAL PROTECTION OF SOFTWARE.

SOFTWARE PROTOTYPING

For articles on related subjects *see* SOFTWARE ENGINEERING; SOFTWARE MANAGEMENT; SOFTWARE REUSABILITY; and SOFTWARE TESTING.

A *software prototype* is an executable model of a proposed software system that accurately reflects chosen aspects of the system, such as display formats, the values computed, or response times. *Software prototyping* is an approach to software development that uses prototypes to help both the developers and their customers visualize the proposed system and predict its properties through the iterative process shown in Fig. 1.

Prototypes are used extensively by designers and engineers working in other disciplines. For example, architects build scale models of buildings to aid visualization of three-dimensional relationships; aeronautical engineers build scale models of airplanes to measure lift and drag in wind tunnel tests; and electrical engineers build breadboard circuits to check the validity of designs based on simplified ideal models of physical components.

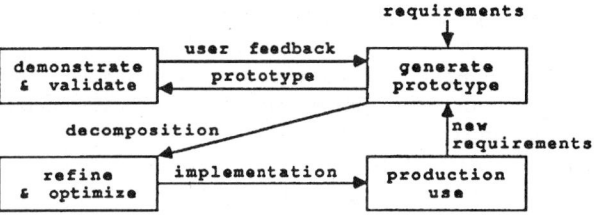

FIG. 1.

The common purpose of these prototypes is to reduce the uncertainty about the properties of a proposed design before it is implemented.

The main incentive for using prototypes is economic: scale models and prototypes are much less expensive to build than final versions. Prototypes should therefore be used to evaluate proposed systems if acceptance by the customer is in doubt. The motivation for software prototyping is essentially the same, and has become more urgent as systems being developed have grown more complex and hence more expensive and more likely to have requirements errors.

Software prototypes may not satisfy all of the constraints on the final version of the system. For example, a prototype may provide only a subset of all the required functions; it may be expressed in a more powerful or more flexible language than the final version; it may run on a machine with more resources than the proposed target architecture; it may be less efficient in both time and space than the final version; it may have limited capacity (databases may be implemented in main memory); it may not include facilities for error checking and fault tolerance; and it may not have the same degree of concurrency as the final version.

It is often not possible to put a prototype into production use, but the conceptual models and designs contained in a prototype can usually be embodied in the final version. Precise specifications for the components of a prototype and clear documentation of its design are therefore critical for effective software prototyping.

Software prototyping has gained importance in recent years because new technologies have made computer-aided prototyping feasible. These technologies have reduced the time and cost involved in producing a prototype, thus widening the gap between a software prototype and the cost of the final software system, and increasing the potential leverage of prototyping. The new technologies are based on reusable code, computer-aided design, and automatic generation of programs. The most powerful systems are designed for specific problem domains. Some problem domains for which computer-aided prototyping tools have been developed include business information processing, user interfaces, computer languages, and real-time systems.

Generators for business information systems provide graphical interfaces to databases to define database schemes, queries, and reports by graphically defining table layouts. There are many commercially available tools in this category.

Interface generation systems (Linton *et al*, 1989) generate graphical user interfaces based on a set of pre-defined components, such as windows, menus, scroll bars, and buttons. These components are placed and adapted interactively via a mouse (*q.v.*) and menu interface.

Generators for language processors are mostly based on attribute grammars. These systems can generate various tools for computer languages based on a context-free grammar for the language, augmented with equations defining computed attributes for the nodes of the parse tree (Herndon and Berzins, 1988). This technology can be used to prototype tools for computer languages, including translators, interpreters, pretty-printers, type checkers, data flow analyzers, and so forth. Applications span programming languages, specification languages, data definition languages for databases, hardware description languages (*q.v.*), and command languages for applications programs. Attribute grammar processors have been coupled to generators for syntax-directed editors (Reps and Teitlebaum, 1988) and program transformation systems (Abraido-Fandino, 1987).

Computer-aided prototyping of real-time systems is supported by the prototyping language PSDL (Lugi *et al*, 1988) and the associated prototyping system CAPS, (Lugi and Ketabchi, 1988). CAPS uses a software base of reusable components, a program generator, a static scheduler, and a dynamic scheduler to realize systems containing both functions with hard real-time constraints and non-time-critical functions. PSDL provides a simple representation of system decompositions, using dataflow diagrams augmented with non-procedural control and timing constraints (maximum response times, maximum execution times, minimum inter-stimulus periods, periods, and deadlines). The language models both periodic and data-driven tasks, and both discrete (transaction-oriented) and continuous (sampled) data streams. The CAPS system provides automated tools for generating static schedules, to guarantee hard real-time constraints as well as an execution support system that generates code for adapting, interconnecting, and controlling the execution of reusable software components.

In the future, prototyping will be integrated with final implementation. Progress will hinge on automatic procedures for optimizing implementations. Prototypes will support refinement of the prototype into the final version by supplying additional information and automatically transforming frequently used components to improve efficiency. Initially, this will be done through optional implementation advice supplied by software engineers, in analogy to the *pragmas* in the programming language Ada (*q.v.*). In the longer term, prototyping systems will have reasoning capabilities and extensive knowledge bases that may include generic models of the problem domain, common goals of customers, common system structures, and generators producing specifications and code for classes of software components. Facilities for supporting formal verification of prototype decompositions are desirable to ensure that they are viable, especially if the subcomponents are to be built by different contractors.

References

1987. Abraido-Fandino L. "An Overview of REFINE 2.0," in *Proceedings of the Second International Symposium on Knowledge Engineering*, Madrid, Spain (April) 8–10.

1988. Herndon R. and Berzins V. "The Realizable Benefits of a Language Prototyping Language," *IEEE Trans. on Software Eng.* **SE-14**, *6* (June) 803–809.

1988. Luqi, Berzins V. and Yeh R. "A Prototyping Language for Real-Time Software," *IEEE Trans. on Software Eng.* **SE-14**, *10*, (October), 1409–1423.

1988. Luqi and Ketabchi, M. "A Computer Aided Prototyping System," *IEEE Software* **5**, *2* (March), 66–72.

1988. Reps T. and Teitelbaum T. *The Synthesizer Generator: A System for Constructing Language-Based Editors*. New York: Springer-Verlag.

1989. Linton M., Vlissides J. and Calder P. "Composing User Interfaces with InterViews," *IEEE Computer* **22**, *2* (Feb), 8–22.

VALDIS BERZINS

SOFTWARE RELIABILITY

For articles on related subjects *see* DEBUGGING; PROGRAM SPECIFICATION; PROGRAM VERIFICATION; SOFTWARE MAINTENANCE; SOFTWARE MONITORS; and SOFTWARE TESTING.

It is imperative to assess the correctness of software for critical applications prior to actual use. Ideally, we would like to verify formally whether a program is correct or not. However, besides the practical difficulties encountered in applying current formal verification techniques to realistic programs, such methods cannot cope with the possibility of specification errors. An alternative approach is to use statistical methods to estimate the reliability of the software based on the result of program testing.

Software reliability is defined as the probability that a software fault that causes deviations from the required output by more than a specified tolerance, in a specified environment, does not occur during a specified exposure period. There are three distinct methods of estimating software reliability, namely, on the basis of its failure history, its behavior for a random sample of points taken from its input domain, or the number of seeded and actual faults detected by the test team. Seeded faults are those that are deliberately inserted into the program at the start of the debugging phase, the details of which are withheld from the testing team.

Software Reliability Growth Models Software reliability growth models attempt to predict the reliability of a program on the basis of its failure history. Failure history is defined to be the realization of a sequence of random variables $T_1, T_2,..., T_n$, where T_i denotes the CPU time spent in testing the program after the fault causing the $(i-1)^{th}$ failure has been removed until the ith failure is detected. These models can be further classified into *fault-counting* and *non-fault-counting* models, depending on whether they express the reliability in terms of the number of faults remaining in the program or not.

Fault-counting models assume that the failure rates of the faults remaining in the program are independent, identically distributed random variables and that the program failure rate is the sum of the individual failure rates. As an illustration, consider the General Poisson Model (GPM), which assumes that the failure rate, $r_j(t)$, after the faults causing the $(j-1)th$ failure have been removed, is proportional to the number of faults remaining in the program and a power of the elapsed CPU time; i.e.

$$r_j(t) = \varphi\,(N - M_j)\alpha\,t^{\alpha - 1}$$

where α and φ are constants, N is the number of faults originally present in the program, and $M_j = \sum_{i=1}^{j} m_i$ where m_i is the number of faults removed following the ith failure. Hence, the reliability of the program after the jth failure is given by

$$R_j(t) = e^{-\varphi (N-M_j)\,t^{\alpha}}.$$

Given $m_1, m_2, ..., m_n$ and $t_1, t_2, ..., t_n$, where t_j is the CPU time required to detect the jth failure after the faults causing the $(j-1)^{th}$ failure have been removed, the maximum likelihood estimate (MLE) of the parameters of the model (those with hats ($^$) below) can be obtained by solving the following equations:

$$\sum_{j=1}^{n} \frac{1}{\hat{N} - M_{j-1}} - \sum_{j=1}^{n} \hat{\varphi}\,t_j^{\hat{\alpha}} = 0;$$

$$\frac{n}{\hat{\alpha}} + \sum_{j=1}^{n} \log t_j - \sum_{j=1}^{n} \hat{\varphi}\,(\hat{N} - M_{j-1})t_j^{\hat{\alpha}} \log t_j = 0;$$

$$\frac{n}{\hat{\varphi}} - \sum_{j=1}^{n} (\hat{N} - M_{j-1})t_j^{\hat{\alpha}} = 0.$$

Non-fault-counting models consider the effect of a debugging action on the failure rate without concern as to the number of failures detected at a time. An example of a model in this category is the Musa-Okumoto Logarithmic model. The inputs to the model are $t_1, t_2, ..., t_n$ where t_j is the CPU *time* (not interval as in the GPM model) at which the jth failure was observed. The failure rate is given by

$$r(t) = \frac{\lambda_0}{\lambda_0 \theta t + 1}.$$

Thus, the model assumes that the failure rate decreases continuously over the testing and debugging phase, rather than at discrete points corresponding to failure detection and removal times. Further, the rate of decrease in $r(t)$ itself decreases with time, thus modeling the decrease in the number of errors detected as debugging proceeds. The reliability during the jth interval is given by

$$R_j(t) = \left\{ \frac{\lambda_0 \theta t_j + 1}{\lambda_0 \theta (t_j + t) + 1} \right\}^{1/\theta}.$$

The MLE of λ_0 and θ can be obtained by solving the following equations:

$$\frac{n}{\hat{\lambda}_0} - \hat{\theta}\sum_{j=1}^{n} \frac{t_j}{\hat{\lambda}_0 \hat{\theta} t_j + 1} - \frac{t_n}{\hat{\lambda}_0 \hat{\theta} t_n + 1} = 0;$$

$$-\hat{\lambda}_0 \sum_{j=1}^{n} \frac{t_j}{\hat{\lambda}_0 \hat{\theta} t_j + 1} + \frac{1}{\hat{\theta}^2}\log(\hat{\lambda}_0 \hat{\theta} t_n + 1) - \frac{\hat{\lambda}_0 t_n}{\hat{\theta}(\hat{\lambda}_0 \hat{\theta} t_n + 1)} = 0.$$

Sampling Models This method is similar to the sampling technique used to determine the reliability of hardware components except that, instead of selecting a random sample of components and subjecting them to operational use, the program is tested with a random sample of points from its input domain. Faults discovered in this process are not removed. If we observe n_f failures out of n runs, then the estimate of the reliability of the program for a single run is

$$\hat{R} = 1 - \frac{n_f}{n}.$$

Assuming that inputs are selected independently according to the same probability distribution used to choose the random sample, the reliability of the program over i runs is given by

$$\hat{R}(i) = (\hat{R})^i.$$

This method of estimating software reliability is the basis of the Nelson model.

While the theoretical foundations of the Nelson model are sound, it suffers from a practical drawback—namely, the need to select a very large number of random test cases in order to have a high confidence in the reliability estimate. The Ramamoorthy-Bastani input domain based model overcomes this objection to the Nelson model. It was developed for assessing the reliability of critical real-time process control programs for which no failures should be detected during the reliability estimation phase, so that the reliability estimate is one. Hence, the important metric of concern is the confidence in the reliability estimate. This model provides an estimate of the conditional probability that the program is correct for all possible inputs, given that it is correct for a given set of inputs. The basic assumption is that the outcome of each test case provides at least some stochastic information about the behavior of the program for points that are close to the test point. The main result of the model is

P{program is correct for all points in $[a, a + V]$ given that it is correct for all test cases having successive distances $x_j, j = 1, ..., n - 1$}

$$= e^{-\lambda V} \prod_{j=1}^{n-1} \left(\frac{2}{1 + e^{-\lambda x_j}} \right),$$

where λ is a parameter that is deduced from some measure of the complexity of the source code.

The above equation is derived under the assumption that the correctness of an input, given that the program works for all its neighbors, depends only on its nearest neighbor. More general assumptions, such as the influence of boundary value test cases, result in mathematically intractable derivations.

Fault Seeding *Fault Seeding* is an experimental approach to predicting the number of faults in a program. It was proposed and used by Mills and Basin. Artificial faults are inserted into the program without the knowledge of the test team. Assuming that the seeded faults have the same distribution as the original faults in the program, an approximate estimate of the number of faults remaining in the program, given that m_a actual faults and m_s seeded faults have been detected, is $\dfrac{m_a(M_s - m_s)}{m_s}$, where M_s is the total number of faults created artificially.

The problem with the fault seeding approach is that there is no way to ensure that the seeded faults have the same distribution as the original ones. Simple changes to the source code, such as deleting some statements or modifying some expressions, do not adequately reflect subtle design and requirements specification problems. An alternative approach is to use two test teams and compare the set of faults detected by each team. Suppose that the first team finds m_{a1} faults, while the second team finds m_{a2} faults, of which m_{a12} faults are the same as those found by the first team. Then an estimate for M_a, the total number of faults in the original program, is $\dfrac{m_{a1}m_{a2}}{m_{a12}}$. The number of faults remaining in the program is $M_a - m_{a1} - m_{a2} + m_{a12}$. This approach does not have to deal with the issue of selecting artificial faults. The problem here, however, is that the faults detected by the two teams are likely to be correlated, since faults with a high failure rate have a high probability of occurring in both of the sets. Finally, there is no way to make reliability statements about a program, given just the number of faults remaining in it. This number, however, may be useful in estimating the resources needed for future maintenance of the program.

System Reliability Assuming that only one component is active at a given time, then an approach proposed independently by Littlewood and Cheung can be used to assess the reliability of a software system, given the reliabilities of the models constituting the software. The system is assumed to consist of j components, among which control is switched randomly according to a semi-Markov process. Assuming that the failure process of each component is a Poisson process with the *ith* component having parameter λ_i and that no failures occur during the transition from one module to another, the overall system failure process can be approximated as a Poisson process with failure rate

$$\lambda = \frac{\sum_{t=1}^{k} \sum_{j=1}^{k} \pi_i p_{ij} \mu_{ij} \lambda_i}{\sum_{t=1}^{k} \sum_{j=1}^{k} \pi_i p_{ij} \mu_{ij}}$$

where π_i is the steady state probability that component i is active and is given by $\sum_{j=1}^{k} \pi_j p_{ji}$ subject to $\sum_{j=1}^{k} \pi_j = 1$, where p_{ij} is the transition probability from component i to component j, and μ_{ij} is the mean CPU time spent in component i before switching to component j (the *sojourn* time).

Discussion During the first decade of software reliability research, the major emphasis was on developing models based on various assumptions. This resulted in a proliferation of models, most of which were neither used nor validated. Currently, the consensus appears to be that perhaps there is no single model that can be applied to all types of projects. Hence, one area of active research is to investigate whether a set of models can be combined so as to achieve more accurate reliability estimates for various situations. Other research topics include developing methods of analyzing the confidence in the predictions of a model, and using software reliability theory to assist with the management of a project throughout its life cycle.

References

1982. Ramamoorthy, C. V. and Bastani, F. B. "Software Reliability—Status and Perspectives," *IEEE Trans. Softw. Eng.*, **SE-8**, 4, 354–371.
1985. Goel, A. L. "Software Reliability Models: Assumptions, Limitations, and Applicability," *IEEE Trans. Softw. Eng.*, **SE-11**, 12, 1411–1423.
1986. Abdel-Ghaly, A. A., Chan, P. Y., and Littlewood B., "Evaluation of Competing Software Reliability Predictions," *IEEE Trans. Softw. Eng.*, **SE-12**, 9, 950–967.
1987. Musa, J, Iannino, A, and Okumoto, K. *Software Reliability: Measurement, Prediction, Application*. New York: McGraw Hill.

FAROKH B. BASTANI AND C. V. RAMAMOORTHY

SOFTWARE REUSABILITY

For articles on related subjects *see* ABSTRACT DATA TYPE; ENCAPSULATION; INFORMATION HIDING; MACROINSTRUCTION; MODULAR PROGRAMMING; OBJECT-ORIENTED PROGRAMMING; PORTABILITY; SOFTWARE FLEXIBILITY; and SUBPROGRAM.

Software reusability is an attribute of software that facilitates its incorporation into new application programs. Reusable software shares many attributes in common with "good" software (e.g. transportability, maintainability, flexibility, understandability, usability, and reliability).

Software reuse, as a means of saving time and resources, was initially proposed by Charles Babbage as part of the Analytical Engine (*q.v.*) through a mechanism analogous to a subroutine call. The first practical implementation of software reuse, a subroutine library, was realized by Maurice Wilkes as part of the first stored-program computer, the EDSAC, at the University of Cambridge in 1951. During the early days of computer programming, the most successful examples of software reuse were subroutine libraries or system macros. The modern roots of software reuse can be traced to Doug McIlroy's 1969 paper *Mass Produced Software Components* at the NATO Conference on Software Engineering. McIlroy speculated on the viability of a Commercial-Off-The-Shelf (COTS) software parts industry furnishing the programming community with the building blocks necessary to create new software applications. Current interest in software reusability has been stimulated by advances in programming languages, such as Ada, Smalltalk, and C++, that support the adaptation of a more disciplined engineering approach to software development called object-oriented programming and design.

It is interesting to note that "reusability" is not usually a distinguishing attribute of artifacts in other engineering disciplines. That is, in areas other than programming, there is little or no differentiation between "use" and "reuse" because reuse is taken for granted. That reusability is an issue in programming is indicative of the relative immaturity of the profession as well as a common lack of discipline in the programming process.

The reusability of software is contingent upon the identification of useful software abstractions that are common to a wide number of applications within a particular application domain (vertical domain analysis) or across several application domains (horizontal domain analysis). The degree of reusability of a software module or component can be increased by providing parameters that generalize its use or by building the module so that its implementation dependencies (hardware, operating system, or database) are reduced, eliminated, or encapsulated through the use of a virtual or abstract machine interface.

There are several implementation techniques and programming technologies that enhance the reusability of software. These include:

1. Data encapsulation.
2. Information hiding.
3. Polymorphism.
4. Abstract data types.
5. Pipes and filters (such as are used with Unix and MS-DOS).
6. Inheritance (object-oriented programming).
7. Parametrization and genericity (macros and pre-processors - *q.v.*).
8. Application generators and fourth-generation languages (4GLs).
9. Virtual or abstract machine interfaces.

The Ada package (*q.v.*) in Fig. 1 exports an abstract data type called STACK as an example of a parametrized abstract data type whose implementation exhibits data encapsulation and information hiding.

This software component is reusable because it can be easily adapted it to hold any type of data (i.e. it has a broad domain of applicability). Furthermore, because the data structure is completely encapsulated, the user can manipulate the contents of the stack only through the operations exported in the interface. Thus, the abstraction (stack) is prevented from being corrupted. Finally, the user has no indication of whether a linked-list or an array was used to implement the data structure. (This information is hidden in the Ada package (*q.v.*) body, which is not shown in this example.) Conceivably, several implementations might exist that satisfy the same functionality, in which case the Ada specification serves as a virtual machine interface to a family of implementations that exhibit different time and resource attributes.

If enough well-tested, flexible, and reusable components are constructed according to these principles and placed in inventory, a new application could conceivably be implemented through assembly of selected components without a single new line of source code being written.

```
generic
    type ELEMENT is private;
package STACK is
    type STACK is limited private;
    procedure INITIALIZE (THE_STACK : in out STACK);
    procedure PUSH (THE_ELEMENT : in ELEMENT;
                    ONTO_THE_STACK : in out
                    STACK);
    procedure POP(THE_STACK : in out STACK);
    function TOP_OF (THE_STACK : in STACK)
        return ELEMENT;
    function IS_EQUAL (LEFT, RIGHT : in STACK)
        return BOOLEAN;
    function IS_EMPTY (THE_STACK : in STACK)
        return BOOLEAN;
    function LENGTH_OF (THE_STACK : in STACK)
        return POSITIVE;

    OVERFLOW : exception;
    UNDERFLOW : exception;

    private
        type DATA_STRUCTURE;
        type STACK is access DATA_STRUCTURE;

end STACK;
```

FIG. 1.   A reusable Ada package.

References

1987. Booch, G. *Software Components with Ada*. Menlo Park, CA: Benjamin/Cummings Publishing Company, Inc.

1988. Tracz, W. *Software Reuse: Emerging Technology*. Washington, DC: IEEE Computer Society Press.

1989. Biggerstaff, T. J. and Perlis, A. J. *Software Reusability: Volume I Concepts and Models, Volume II Applications and Experience.* New York: ACM Press.

WILL TRACZ

SOFTWARE TESTING

For articles on related subjects *see* DEBUGGING; PROGRAM VERIFICATION; SOFTWARE ENGINEERING; SOFTWARE MAINTENANCE; SOFTWARE MONITOR; and SOFTWARE RELIABILITY.

Overview The term *software testing* can refer to any planned, risk-reducing activity that takes place during software development, operation, or maintenance. Examples of such activities include: (1) analyzing system requirements, (2) experimentation with prototypes, (3) static reviews of designs and other intermediate engineering products, (4) static and dynamic analysis of software products, and (5) retesting software products during maintenance. As these examples show, software testing occurs at many stages of software development and operation. The article being analyzed during a test may be the actual software product, an early specification of its design, or a model of its intended use.

Two kinds of risks are addressed during a software test. The first risk is that the ultimate software product will fail to meet the needs and expectations of the end user. These expectations comprise the system *requirements*, and the process of determining the likely extent to which the eventual software product will satisfy its requirements is called *validation*. As a complex software product evolves from a set of requirements in the minds of users to a working system, intermediate engineering products are produced. These may range from high-level system designs and partially functional prototypes to nonfunctional specifications of performance and reliability, and, ultimately, to working software. The second kind of risk is that developers may introduce technical incompatibilities or inconsistencies into these engineering products. The process of comparing these products with each other to insure that they are mutually consistent is called *verification*.

The critical elements of a software test are: (1) specifications of validation or verification products to be tested, (2) goals and thresholds for the test, (3) specifications of test activities and data, and (4) evaluations. A *validation and verification product* (or V&V product) is any engineering product analyzed during the test. An example of an early V&V product is a prototype graphical interface for validating ease-of-use by end users. An intermediate V&V product is a detailed design specification that is used to verify that elaboration of high-level design has been carried out correctly. A very late V&V product is a partially integrated software system. A *goal* or *threshold* for the test is a specification of what it means to pass or fail the test. Ideally, these are quantitative specifications that correspond to direct measurements of a V&V product.

Examples of such specifications include observed failure rates, coverage criteria for correctness tests, and independent estimates of test data quality. A typical threshold requirement is that the input-output behavior of a given program unit must conform to its detailed design specification on at least k test points chosen randomly from a specified probability distribution. The *specifications of test activities and data* refer to the procedures and conditions under which the test will be carried out. The *evaluations* comprise the important results of the test. The principle question answered by the evaluation is: Does this test demonstrate that the specified goal or threshold has been achieved? These elements are frequently formalized in a series of *test plans*. The design, management and use of an effective test plan is sometimes an engineering process as complex and costly as the software product development itself. National and international standards organizations have developed and distributed standards for test plans and test documentation.

Frequently, the term "testing" is reserved for dynamic analysis (i.e. for those activities that involve running programs and observing outputs). Even in this restricted usage, however, intermediate V&V products may be involved and used for either validation or verification.

Theory of Software Tests for Correctness The aspect of software testing that has received the most attention from researchers is *testing for correctness* (i.e. the dynamic verification that a program is consistent with a detailed specification of its behavior) (*see* PROGRAM VERIFICATION). There is an extensive mathematical theory of correctness testing that revolves around test data quality, (that is, the extent to which a given test demonstrates (or fails to demonstrate) consistency of a program and its specified behavior.

Given a program P and its specification F, a test data set D is said to be *reliable* if correctness on D implies correctness on all inputs. More precisely, let $P(x)$ represent the result of running program P on input x. Let $F(x)$ represent the specified behavior for input x. Then D is reliable relative to P and F if and only if:

$$P(x) = F(x), \text{ for all } x \in D, \text{ implies } P(x) = F(x), \text{ for all } x.$$

Equivalently, if P is not correct (i.e. if $P(x) \neq F(x)$ for some input x), then P will fail to match F on some input in a reliable test for P and F. Thus, the existence of a reliable test set guarantees that "bugs" (*q.v.*) in incorrect programs will be uncovered by the test. A related concept is test data *adequacy*: a test set is adequate[1] if it distinguishes the program being tested from all nonequivalent ones. In mathematical terms, D is adequate for P if and only if for all programs Q:

$$P(x) = Q(x), \text{ for all } x \in D, \text{ implies } P(x) = Q(x), \text{ for all } x.$$

---

[1] The term *test adequacy* is also used to characterize structural coverage criteria. The two concepts are not related.

Equivalently, if $P(x) \neq Q(x)$ for some input x, then some input in D distinguishes P and Q. Thus, the existence of an adequate test set can be used as "evidence" that P is correct: If P is correct, then it is not equivalent to any incorrect program and thus D distinguishes P from all incorrect programs.

Adequate and reliable test sets are mathematical ideals. A method that is guaranteed to produce a reliable test set if the program is incorrect and an adequate test set if the program is correct would, in principle, solve the correctness testing problem. Such ideal methods are, in general, impractical (and, in some cases, impossible). In practice, a variety of other test set criteria are used to evaluate test data quality. The goal in selecting these criteria is to choose those that are most likely to result in reliable or adequate test sets in a given test environment.

Black box criteria These criteria set requirements for a test set based upon external characteristics. A typical black box criterion is correct performance on a specified number of randomly chosen data points.

White box criteria These criteria set requirements for a test based upon *coverage* of internal components or elements associated with the software. The most common white box criteria are *structural coverage* and *fault coverage*. A structural coverage criterion specifies the extent to which a given test exercises or "covers" structural components of the software (e.g. statements, branches, or dataflow chains). A fault coverage criterion specifies errors, faults, or classes of faults that are ruled out or "covered" if the given test is passed.

Major Software Testing Methodologies
Principal techniques for static analysis include reviews and inspections, measurement, reliability modeling, and other methods that have developed into subdisciplines in their own right. The following includes the major dynamic testing methodologies. There are no clear lines of demarcation between these methods, and a given set of test procedures may contain techniques drawn from several types of methods. In many cases, commercial or experimental tools have been developed to support the methodologies.

Functional testing This is a family of black box testing criteria that generate tests based on specified properties (e.g. functional properties) of the software being testing. An example of a functional testing criterion is a "special values" test that generates data points at which correctly functioning software exhibits some special behavior.

Random testing Random tests are black box tests based upon known or assumed probability distributions of inputs. Random inputs may be chosen from operational profiles, simulations, or by purely statistical means. Random testing is sometimes associated with development methodologies and can be used to predict statistical parameters of operational software systems.

Program instrumentation These white box methods are used to simply gather measurements during tests. Software monitors or *probes* are incorporated into the program text as a kind of instrumentation. These probes record or display dynamic characteristics. An important variation on instrumentation is the *executable assertion* (i.e. an embedded predicate that is evaluated during program execution).

Structural testing The simplest family of white box methods, structural testing criteria, sets coverage thresholds for program components, such as statements, decision-to-decision branches, control flow paths, and dataflow chains (i.e. program segments between successive definitions and uses of specified variables). 100% statement coverage is frequently considered to be the lowest acceptable threshold criterion for an effective software test.

Partition testing White box analysis of a program frequently leads to *partitions* of the input space to a program. For example, a typical partitioning scheme may identify all those input values that cause the program to execute the same control path. A partition testing method is used to select test data from the partitions. In one such method (domain analysis), a geometric model of the partitions is used as a guide to test data selection.

Mutation testing Mutation testing refers to a family of white box methods based upon fault coverage. The goal is to create tests that distinguish the program being tested from "mutant" programs that contain faults or bugs. A successful mutation test creates either a reliable test set if the program is incorrect or an adequate test set if the program is correct. Variations have been developed to study fault propagation (e.g. *relay* testing), early fault detection (e.g. weak mutation testing), and test case generation (error-sensitive test case analysis).

An important static analysis technique that is used in many of these dynamic methods is *symbolic execution*. With each possible control flow path in the program is associated a symbolic expression that represents the result of executing the statements along that path on symbolic inputs. Logical tools can be used to manipulate these symbolic expressions.

Organizing Tests
Industry data indicates that the cost of finding and removing faults in a software product can increase by a factor of 100 or more as the design, development, and operation process proceeds. Consequently, much of the effort in test technologies is oriented toward "front-end" activities. As the V&V products increase in size and complexity, the cost of testing increases at a disproportionate rate. Balancing the costs and benefits of testing has resulted in an identification of distinct *phases* of testing. Each phase addresses a specific type of V&V product and is used to achieve a specific set of goals. All software tests are organized around the following sequence of testing phases. In simple software systems, only programmer and regression testing may actually be used. In large and complex system development efforts, however, all of these phases are present.

Requirements analysis This may include the static analysis of software requirements (e.g. to determine their "testability") or the dynamic analysis of prototypes for requirements validation.

Development testing Development testing includes all testing associated with system design and engineering. In early development testing, models of designs may be subjected to dynamic and static analysis. In late development testing software product components are tested for correctness.

Programmer testing The least formal aspect of testing, programmer testing, consists of the testing of software components (e.g. units and modules), usually in isolation from other components. This is the testing phase in which a testing–fault isolation–fault removal cycle is the most apparent.

Integration testing All testing activities associated with the assembling of a completed software product (software system integration), replacing software drivers constructed for development or programmer testing, removing instrumentation, or integrating a completed software product with its target environment are referred to as *integration testing*.

System or function testing Since it requires a completed system, function or system testing occurs very late in the development process. This kind of testing is usually oriented toward requirements validation and may also be associated with certification or other quality activities.

Operational testing When it is conducted formally (e.g. for large systems developed under government contracts), operational testing involves the black box testing of the system in a realistic environment using typical operator personnel. Informal operational testing of commercial products may be carried out by selected, willing customers or other typical users through a program of "early" releases (*beta testing*).

In-line testing As opposed to operational testing, in which the test environment is a realistic model of the operational environment, an in-line test is carried out on the end product in its operational environment using real users. In-line testing for software is less common than for hardware, but it is an essential component of all fault-tolerant systems. Many other application domains (e.g. safety-critical applications, secure applications) use in-line probes and instrumentation and thus implement rudimentary forms of in-line testing.

Regression testing Regression tests are retests of systems after modifications have been made to enhance functionality or remove faults. A regression test can be conducted as either a black box or white box test; the critical factor in regression tests is the cost of the test, and regression tests are typically organized to minimize the amount of retesting.

Dividing the testing effort into these phases frequently facilitates hierarchical organization of the total testing process. During the earliest test phases, relatively little detailed information is available about the ultimate software product. A tester may have detailed information, for example, about overall architecture and user interface (*q.v.*) design, but may have to use "dummy" software or software stubs in place of actual system functions. A test that is organized in this way is called a *top-down* test. During later test phases—and particularly during integration testing—the situation is reversed. The tester has detailed test results about relatively low-level system structures and uses a *bottom-up* strategy to combine them systematically into a composite test of the entire system. Regression tests frequently cannot rely upon hierarchical strategies at all and therefore require more extensive tooling for analyzing global software structures.

Economics and Management of Testing

Testing frequently dominates development costs. In a large, carefully managed system development, the cost of development testing is often 45% of the total development budget. During maintenance, regression testing costs can represent 70% or more of the total maintenance effort. Integration, system, and operational tests are frequently capital-intensive, requiring special hardware platforms, simulators, and test facilities.

The goal of managing a large and complex test is to balance the cost of a test and its effectiveness. Since the costs associated with late discovery of faults are often very high, managers of successful system developments are usually willing to invest a considerable portion of their resources in early test programs.

The high costs of testing also makes managing the relationship between software testing and other quality programs more important. Control of these activities may be given to independent organizations who have overall responsibility for all quality aspects of the system.

References

1987. Howden, W. E. *Functional Program Testing and Analysis.* New York: McGraw-Hill.

1987. De Millo, R. A., Martin, R. J., McCrackena, W., and Passafiume, J., *Software Testing and Evaluation.* Redwood City, CA: Benjamin-Cummings.

RICHARD A. DEMILLO

SOFTWARE, LEGAL PROTECTION OF. *See* LEGAL PROTECTION OF SOFTWARE.

SOFTWARE, MATHEMATICAL. *See* MATHEMATICAL SOFTWARE.

SORTING

For articles on related subjects *see* ALGORITHMS, ANALYSIS OF; SEARCHING; and TREE.

INTERNAL SORTING

In computing, *sorting* is the process of rearranging an initially unordered sequence of records until they are ordered with respect to all of or that part of each record designated as its *key*. Usually, the desired result is that the records be placed in ascending order (smallest key first), but any sorting algorithm capable of placing records in ascending order can be easily modified to produce a sequence of records in descending order.

As used here, a *record* (*q.v.*) may be as small as a single bit, character, integer, or real (floating-point) number—in which case the entire record serves as a key—or it may be an arbitrarily large aggregate of data values of possibly mixed data types, in which case one or more constituent elements are designated as primary key, secondary key, tertiary key, etc. Multiple keys imply multiple sorting phases in which, for example, the goal might be to sort persons' names so that they are ordered primarily by last name and secondarily—within groups of the same last name—by first name.

The most common rationale for sorting a sequence of records is that the time to do so (once) will prove to be insignificant compared to the many times that the sequence will be searched in order to locate a particular record. When such a search is performed on an unordered sequence of n records, then, on average, $n/2$ records need to be examined during a successful search (and all n for an unsuccessful search). But an ordered sequence of n records of uniform length can be searched by examining at most $\log_2 n$ records, which, for $n = 1,024$, is 51 times faster than the average successful sequential search. Thus, the incentive to maintain sorted (ordered) record sequences is quite clear (*see* SEARCHING).

There are many algorithms for sorting unordered data. In choosing or designing one, the foremost consideration is whether all data records reside in main memory, or whether some or all are stored on an auxiliary mass storage device, such as magnetic tape or (more commonly now) magnetic disk. In the former case, one of a class of *internal sorting algorithms* may be used in which, because of the random-access property of main memory, records may be freely accessed regardless of their position in what is then essentially an indexable array of records. But when records are stored in an auxiliary mass storage memory whose latency (*q.v.*) and additional access time imposes a severe penalty on retrieval of single records, one of a class of specialized *external sorting algorithms* must be used that processes as many records as possible for each probe into auxiliary mass storage memory. Because the average size of main memory has been increasing so rapidly, this article will emphasize internal sorting algorithms, but does conclude with a brief discussion of external sorting methods.

For both internal and external sorting algorithms, an important consideration is stability. A sorting algorithm is *stable* if, during movement and possible rearrangement of records, no two records having identical keys ever have their original order reversed. For records that are "all key" or records that are to be sorted only on a primary key, stability is not a concern, but when a record sequence is to be sorted first on a secondary key and then a primary key (the logically necessary order of use of multiple keys), the desired result cannot be attained if the final sort on primary key permutes the order of records whose secondary keys differ, but whose primary keys are the same.

At least five considerations may influence the choice of an internal sorting algorithm:

1. *Running time*—How long does it take to sort n records, and by what factor does this time increase in order to sort $2n$ records?

2. *Memory space*—Do main memory limitations force choice of an algorithm that sorts "in place" (only one or two records spaces are needed beyond the space needed to hold n records), or are there an additional n record spaces available beyond the space needed to hold the data to be sorted?

3. *Initial order*—Are the records known to be already ordered with just a few exceptions? This is not the usual situation, but when it does occur, the most suitable algorithm may well be one that is not at all efficient when the initial order of the records is essentially random.

4. *Key range*—Do record keys span a very large range or possibly only a very restricted range (such as integers 0 to 999)? Certain algorithms applicable to keys of narrow range are not feasible for keys that span a large range.

5. *Programming language*—For reasons of local policy or availability, must a particular programming language be used, and if so, does that language support recursion? Many of the most efficient internal sorting algorithms are most naturally expressed recursively and hence would be awkward to encode in nonrecursive languages, such as assembly languages (other than VAX assembler), Basic, Cobol, and Fortran 90. With the increasing popularity of recursive languages such as Ada, Pascal, and C, this is less and less often an important consideration.

Unless the number of records to be sorted is very small—perhaps 100 or less—by far the most important of these five considerations is running time.

Internal sorting algorithms may be classified as being either *comparative* or *distributive*. A comparative algorithm rearranges record order by comparing record keys. A distributive algorithm moves records to or close to their final correct position based on intrinsic key characteristics.

Comparative Sorting Algorithms There is an easily derived theoretical upper limit to the rate at which records may be sorted by key comparison. There are

$n!$ different sequences of n records, only one of which (ignoring records of equal key) is the correct ascendingly (or descendingly) ordered sequence. Imagine that these $n!$ permutations form the leaves of a *binary decision tree* (a binary tree in which each node has 0 or 2 children) each of whose nodes represents a comparison of two record keys. Then the shortest path from the root of the tree (the first comparison decision made) to the particular leaf that represents the desired final ordering requires a number of decisions equal to the height of the tree (*see* TREE). But a binary decision tree of m leaves has a height of $\lceil \log_2 m \rceil$ (i.e. the smallest integer greater than or equal to $\log_2 m$). Now let $m = n!$ and note that for large n the Stirling approximation to $n!$ is proportional to $(n/e)^{n+1/2}$. Then $\log_2 n! = 1.4 \ln n! = 1.4 (n + 1/2) (\ln n - 1)$ which is $O(n \ln n)$ (i.e. approaches a constant times $n \ln n$ as $n \to \infty$) and hence is also $O(n \log_2 n)$. Thus no sorting algorithm *based on key comparisons* can have running time superior to $O(n \log n)$. Since the proof is not constructive, however, algorithms that attain this performance have to be discovered empirically. We will discuss four such sorting algorithms, but only after first examining why the four primitive algorithms of most straightforward logic fail to achieve $O(n \log n)$ performance.

Selection Sort The first sorting algorithm likely to occur to anyone is called *selection sort*: look through all n records to find the one with smallest key, then through the remaining $n - 1$ records to find the one of next smallest key, etc. By exchanging each record of successively smaller key with the appropriate record at the top of the unsorted sequence of records, the records can be sorted

in place, the length of the sorted sequence at the top growing gradually longer as the length of the unsorted sequence at the bottom shrinks to zero. Selection sort shares with the three other primitive algorithms to be discussed the undesirable property that when the number of records to be sorted is doubled, the time to do so quadruples, another way of saying that its running time is $O(n^2)$. The only desirable property of selection sort is that records of successively smaller key are identified one by one, so that output of the sorted list can proceed virtually in parallel with the sort itself.

Bubblesort A second reasonably obvious idea is based on the simplistic notion that if two adjacent records are out of order they should be exchanged. If this is done to successive (overlapped) record pairs, from the first through the record pair that starts at the $(n - 1)$st position, the original list will not necessarily yet be sorted, but one can be sure that the record of largest key (assuming an ascending order sort) will have reached the end of the list. Then, by repeating the process $n - 2$ more times, the entire list is certain to be sorted. Successive phases of the sort are called *passes* (since each requires that we reexamine (i.e. *pass through*), all remaining unsorted data). The name *bubblesort* stems from the fact that from pass to pass the records of "lighter" (smaller) key gradually rise ("bubble up") to their proper ultimate position. Because of the large number of record exchanges required, bubblesort is also known as *exchange sort*.

We will show shortly that both selection sort and bubble sort have $O(n^2)$ average and worst case running times, but because, on average, each pass of bubblesort needs more exchanges to isolate a new largest key than selection sort needs to identify a new smallest key, bubblesort runs more slowly. In fact, bubblesort runs more slowly than any other sorting algorithm one might seriously consider using, so its popularity with hobbyists can only be attributed to the ease with which its logic can be remembered.

```
procedure InsertionSort(var A: list; n : integer);
{
    Sorts the first n numbers of A, where type list =
        array [1..limit]
}
var
    i, j, k, t : integer;
begin { Make sure first number of A is the smallest: }
    for i : = 2 to n do if A [i] < A [1] then { exchange them: }
        begin t : = A[i] ; A[i] : = A[1] ; A [1] : = t end;
    for j : = 1 to n - 1 do
        begin
            t : = A[j + 1] ; { Save a copy of the next unsorted }
                            { item to be inserted }
            k : = j;
            while A[k] > t do { Move down to make room }
                            { for the new item }
                begin
                    A [k + 1] : = A[k] ;
                    k : = k - 1
                end;
            A[k + 1] : = t              { Make the insertion }
        end
end { Insertion Sort };
```

FIG. 1. A Pascal implementation of insertion sort.

```
procedure enumsort (var A : list; n : integer) ;
{
    Sorts the first n elements of A [1..lim], n < = lim
}
var
    i, j, k, t : integer ;  B, count : list;
begin
    for i : = 1 to n do count [i] : = 0;   { Initialize counts }

    for j : = 1 to n - 1 do
        for k : = 1 to n - j do
            if A [j] > A [k+j] then count [j] : = count [j] + 1
                        else count [k+j] : = count [k+j] + 1;
    for i : = 1 to n do B[count[i] + 1] : = A [i]
                            { Move keys to B array };
    A : = B                          { and then back to A }
end { enumsort };
```

FIG. 2. A Pascal implementation of enumeration sort.

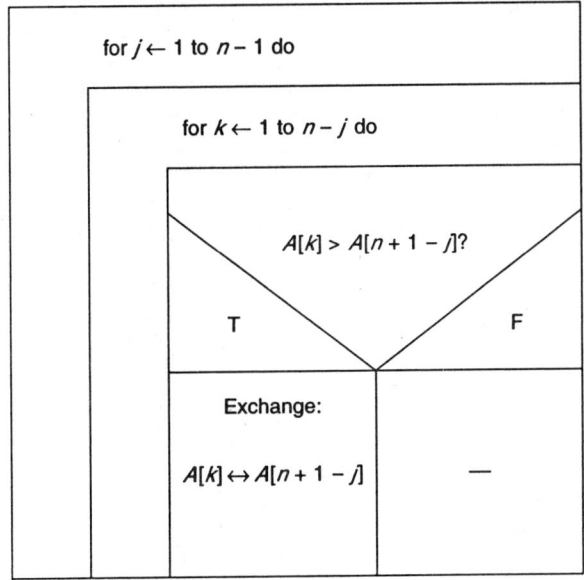

(3a) Selection sort

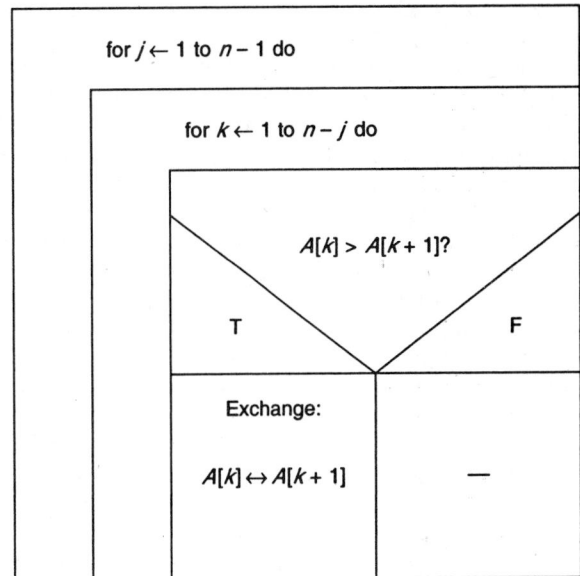

(3b) Bubble sort

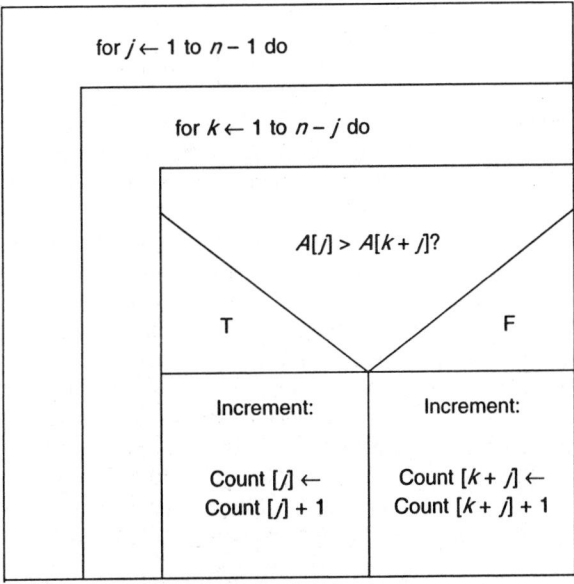

(3c) Enumeration sort

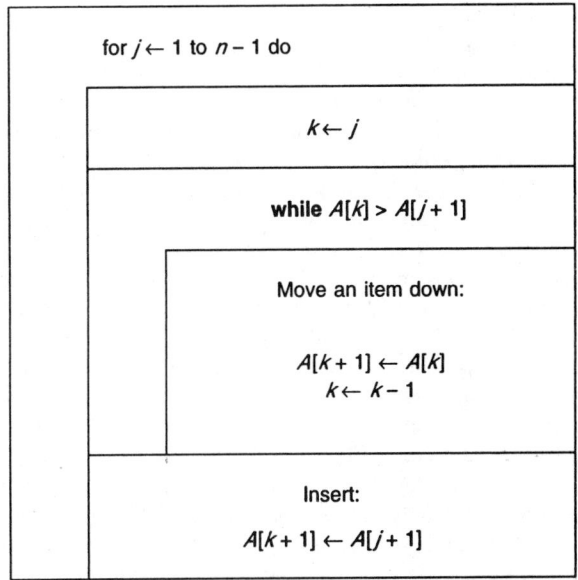

(3d) Insertion sort

FIG. 3.   Nested-loop structure of the four primitive $O(n^2)$ sorts.

The only exceptional feature of bubblesort—not enough to be a redeeming one—is that if, at the end of any pass including the first, it is noted that no exchanges were necessary, the process can be terminated and the record sequence declared to be sorted. Thus, in the best case of attempting to sort an already ordered list—a case that seldom occurs—bubblesort has $O(n)$ running time.

Insertion Sort   The *insertion sort* algorithm is likely to occur to anyone who has sorted cancelled checks or playing cards by simply holding them in the hand and inserting them one by one into the proper position in the stack or hand of already sorted items. The computer version, of course, has more difficulty making room for new insertions. Sometimes room must be made for insertion of a record at the top of the list, necessitating movement of all records in the partially ordered list down by one position. But whenever a record is encountered whose key is larger than that of the last one in the partially ordered list, it need merely be appended to the list. This implies that in the best case of an already sorted list, or even one that is almost ordered to the point where few insertions need to be made near the beginning of the list, insertion sort is $O(n)$. For the average and worst cases, however, insertion sort is $O(n^2)$.

The gradually lengthening partially ordered list need not be stored in a separate storage area from the unsorted list; since the combined number of already sorted and remaining unsorted records remains n throughout the sort, insertion sorting can be done in place by letting the partially sorted list at the top of the combined sequences gradually displace the diminishing list of unsorted records stored directly underneath. A Pascal insertion sort procedure is given in Fig.1. By making sure that the first element of the array to be sorted is smallest (by an $O(n)$ preamble), the procedure is made slightly faster. Doing so allows the inner loop to be controlled by exactly one test, while $A[k] > t$, there being no danger that the loop can run away at the top in a vain search for a number smaller than or equal to the key being inserted. The same effect could have been attained by storing the smallest negative integer, in the 0-th index position of the array to be sorted, but that would have required cooperation between the calling program and the insertion sort procedure so as to dimension the array of unsorted values $0..limit$ rather than $1..limit$ (while still placing the first meaningful unsorted data value in $A[1]$).

Enumeration Sort Selection sort, bubblesort, and insertion sort all involve movement of data records as an integral part of each pass of the sort. An alternative is to leave actual data movement to a last pass and concentrate first on key comparisons. By comparing each key to all others, we can count how many keys are smaller than any given key. If, for example, the counting phase shows that there are 17 records whose keys are smaller than the key of the first record of the unsorted list, then that record can be moved into the 18th position of the ordered list being developed. The space needed is n locations of integer length to hold counts and n locations of record length to hold the records. A Pascal implementation of enumeration sort is given in Fig. 2.

Provided that the comparisons involved are programmed carefully, all four of the primitive sorting algorithms are stable. From Figures 3a, 3b, 3c, and 3d, the $O(n^2)$ worst case running times of these four algorithms can be easily deduced from the principal portion of their highly similar structured flowcharts (Nassi-Shneiderman diagrams). Each has an inner loop that is executed an average of $n/2$ times ($n/4$ for insertion sort) for each outer loop index that ranges from 1 to $n - 1$, so that overall running time is $O(n^2)$.

Although none of the four primitive comparison sort algorithms realizes the theoretically possible $O(n \log n)$ behavior, three of the four have modifications that do. We will examine them in the same order: a modified selection sort called *heapsort*, modified exchange sorts called *quicksort* and *radix exchange sort*, and modified insertion sorts called *Shellsort*, *treesort*, and *mergesort*. We will then comment on the search for a modified enumeration sort.

Heapsort—A Better Selection Sort In 1964, John Williams realized that the principal defect of selection sort was that important information was being developed but

then discarded and lost during each pass that isolates the smallest key of the records remaining to be sorted: the value of the next smaller key. That key—almost the "winner" in the search for the smallest key—was being overwritten, perhaps at the last instant, with the smallest key. How could knowledge of that next smallest key—and the third smallest, perhaps, etc.—be preserved as the sort progresses? Williams invented an algorithm called *heapsort* based on two observations: 1) information about the relative sizes of keys could be stored in a special kind of binary tree called a *heap*, and 2) The nodes of a heap can be mapped one to one to successive cells of an *array*.

A heap (more particularly, a minheap) is a complete binary tree in which the value of every node is less than or equal to the value of either child node. (A maxheap is formed in a similar way, except that the value of every node is greater than or equal to either child node.) By "complete" is meant that there are no missing nodes except, perhaps, for one or more leaves at the right of the bottom level. Once the unsorted records are "heapified," the record at the root can be removed and made the first record of the sorted list (and issued as output, if desired, in parallel with the remainder of the sort). When the 2-tree forest that remains is reheapified, the new root will be the next record to be appended to the sorted list (or issued as output), and the process continues until the entire array of records is sorted.

The mapping of a complete binary tree of 7 nodes to successive elements of an array is shown in Fig. 4. A Pascal procedure that implements heapsort is shown in Fig. 5. For reasons of coding efficiency, the procedure forms maxheaps rather than minheaps, storing successive smaller new maximum values backward from the end of a subsidiary array. Since, unlike most $O(n \log n)$ algorithms, heapsort is iterative, the code given can be easily transliterated into Basic, Cobol, or Fortran. However complicated the record movement involved in the heapify procedure may sound, all that happens throughout is movement of a record from one indexed position in an array to another, so that heapsort might just as well have been called *array sort*. And, while the proof is omitted here, heapsort running time is $O(n \log n)$, even in the worst case, and the algorithm is stable.

Quicksort—a better Exchange Sort In 1962, C.A.R. Hoare reasoned that the principal defect of exchange sort (bubblesort) was that the records that were exchanged

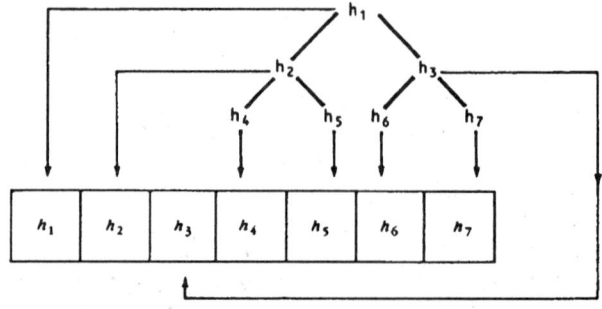

FIG. 4. Mapping a binary tree to a one-dimensional array.

```
procedure Heapsort(var a : data; n : integer);
var
    i : integer;

    procedure exchange(var a, b : integer);
    var
        t : integer;
    begin
        t : = a;  a : = b;  b : = t
    end { exchange };

    procedure rebuild(j,m : integer);
    var
        k : integer;
        sinking : Boolean;
    begin
        sinking : = true;
        k : = j + 1;
        while (k < = m) and sinking do
            begin
                if a[k] < a [k + 1] then if k < m then k := k + 1;
                                    { Find the larger child }
                    if a[j] < a[k] then  { Exchange a[j] with the
                                         larger of its children }
                begin
                    exchange(a[j],a[k]);
                    j : = k;  { Advance j to point to latest point
                              of insertion }
                    k : = 2 * k { Advance k to point to first child
                                of old k }
                end
                else sinking : = false { Change sentinel to force
                                       termination }
            end
    end { rebuild };

    procedure buildheap;
    var
        i : integer;
    begin
        for i : = n div 2 downto 1 do rebuild(i,n)
    end { buildheap };

begin { Heapsort }
    buildheap;
    for i : = n downto 2 do
        begin
            exchange(a[1] ,a[i]); { Exchange top of heap
                                  and current last element }
            rebuild(1, i – 1)              { Restore heap }
        end
end { Heapsort };
```

FIG. 5   A Pascal implementation of heapsort.

never moved very far; each exchange moved the records only one record position closer to their ultimate location, a snail's pace. What if, he pondered, records were partitioned with respect to a chosen *pivot*, a particular key taken from one of the records in the data set being parti-

tioned. All records having a key less than or equal to the pivot would be placed in a left partition; all other records would be placed in a right partition; and the pivot record would lie between them. Neither the left nor right partition would then necessarily be sorted, but the pivot record would be in its final location, never having to be moved again. Next, the left and right partitions are partitioned in the same way, etc. (recursively, in the easiest implementation to program). When all partitions have reached size 1, the sort is complete. Hoare called his algorithm *quicksort*.

A Pascal quicksort procedure is given in the article STRUCTURED PROGRAMMING. On the average—i.e. for initial sequences of records whose keys are randomly distributed—Quicksort has running time $O(n \log n)$. Running time is sensitive to the choice of pivot, however, and using the first record's key as pivot as that procedure does will yield $O(n^2)$ running time for sequences that are already in order, or are in reverse order.

For average data, experience has shown that quicksort is the fastest of all known comparison sorts. However, the conventional implementation of quicksort is unstable.

Radix Exchange Sort   Another improved version of exchange sort is the *radix exchange sort* invented in 1959 (before quicksort) by Paul Hildebrandt, Harold Isbitz, Hawley Rising, and Jules Schwartz. The basic idea is to look at the binary representation of the keys to be sorted bit by bit, a column (radix position) at a time, starting at the leftmost column that has at least one 1-bit. Then, analogously to a quicksort partition that progresses by moving a pair of pointers from the left and right sides of an array of records until they meet, pointers are moved down from the top and up from the bottom until they meet. During pointer motion, bitwise comparisons are made and, whenever a pair of keys is found such that the key having a 1-bit in the column under review lies above a key having a 0-bit in that position, the records are exchanged. When a pass is finished (complete processing of the bits in a given column), the data will have been organized into two groups—one with 0-bits in that column and (below it) one with 1-bits in that column. On the next pass, each group is examined separately with respect to bit comparisons on the next column to the right.

Suppose, for example, that there are a certain six numbers to be sorted. Begin by listing their binary representations and using variable j to label bit positions right to left:

key	j =	4	3	2	1	0
25		1	1	0	0	1
4		0	0	1	0	0
23		1	0	1	1	1
15		0	1	1	1	1
1		0	0	0	0	1
17		1	0	0	0	1

If these numbers were sorted, the "heavier" keys would be under the "lighter" keys; i.e. no number having a 1 at bit position 4 would be above a number having a 0 at that position. To proceed toward that status, we move index pointers i and k down from the top and up from the bottom, respectively, until i points to a 1 and k points to a 0; then we exchange all bits of the two numbers pointed at. If we continue moving i and k until they cross, we obtain

key	j = 4 3 2 1 0
1	0 0 0 0 1
4	0 0 1 0 0
15	0 1 1 1 1
23	1 0 1 1 1
25	1 1 0 0 1
17	1 0 0 0 1

The keys are still not in order, so the process is repeated for the group of numbers above the line at bit position j = 3, and the same is done separately for the group of keys below the line. Nothing happens to the top group (because they happen to be in order), though this is far less likely to be the case if there had been, say, 1,006 numbers to sort rather than just 6. But processing the bottom group at j = 3 will yield

key	j = 4 3 2 1 0
23	1 0 1 1 1
17	1 0 0 0 1
25	1 1 0 0 1

The next pass, at j = 2, will interchange 23 and 17 and complete the sort. Since the bookkeeping needed to keep track of the rapidly growing number of groups that need further processing is formidable, the algorithm is best implemented recursively. Also, the algorithm must be programmed in a language (such as C or Turbo Pascal) that gives the programmer some means of accessing the individual bits of a stored number. The version given in Fig. 6 exploits a Turbo Pascal feature whereby the boolean operation *and* can be applied bitwise to a pair of integer operands.

The similarity of radix exchange sort to quicksort is striking. The effect is to partition numbers according to a phantom pivot of value 2^j that is not necessarily a member of the set of record keys being examined.

Since radix exchange sort indirectly involves key comparisons, albeit bit by bit, it is subject to the proof given earlier that a comparison sort runs, at best, in $O(n \log n)$. Knuth (1973) gives an extensive analysis that this is so, but the $O(n \log n)$ behavior does not set in until very high values of n; for up to at least 16,000 items sorted, the dominant behavior appears to be that radix exchange runs in $O(pn)$ where p (for precision) is the number of bit positions to be examined. (If we think of the keys as numbers, then the more data to be sorted, the more likely it will be that keys span an ever greater range. As the range increases (ever higher large values), the more bits there are in the binary representation of these large keys.

```
procedure RadixExchangeSort (var a : data;
                                j, lo, hi : integer);
var
    i,k,mask : integer;

    procedure exchange(var a,b : integer);
    var t : integer;
    begin t : = a;  a : = b;  b : = t end;

begin
    if (j > = 0) and (lo < hi) then
    begin
        mask : = bitmask[j];
        i : = lo – 1;  k : = hi + 1;
        repeat
            repeat i : = i + 1 until (a [i] and mask > 0) or
                                (i = k) ;
            repeat k : = k – 1 until (a [k] and mask = 0) or
                                (k = i);
            if i < k then exchange(a[i] , a[k])
        until i > = k;
        RadixExchangeSort(a, j – 1,lo,i – 1);
        RadixExchangeSort(a, j – 1,i,hi)
    end
end { RadixExchangeSort };
```

FIG. 6 A Turbo Pascal implementation of the radix exchange sort.

Thus, there is a propensity that $p = \log n$, so that $O(pn)$ reduces to $O(n \log n)$ after all.)

Shellsort—An Improved Insertion Sort An interesting algorithm that improves the performance of sorting by insertion was published by Donald L. Shell in 1959. In the best case—a list already in order—insertion sort is $O(n)$ because each newly stored item can just be appended to the end of the growing output list. If the data is almost but not quite in order, performance should still be close to $O(n)$ because so few items need to be inserted far up into the output list. So, if only we could do some work taking less than $O(n^2)$, to get the list "almost" sorted prior to a final $O(n)$ insertion pass, we might be able to obtain an overall performance, which is less than $O(n^2)$. What Shell proposed was that a few earlier passes—three or four perhaps—be performed that are also insertion sorts, but of a special kind. Rather than processing all n numbers spaced one storage unit apart (as will be done on the last pass), each earlier pass divides the numbers into groups that are, say, eight index positions apart on the first pass, four apart on the second pass, two apart on the third, and then—finally—one apart on the fourth and last pass. Because of this strategy, Shellsort is also known as a *diminishing increment sort*. For a given increment i, each pass does i insertion sorts, each on a group of (approximately) n/i numbers spaced i apart. Here is how the algorithm would work for n = 13 and successive increments of 4, 2, and 1 (where the group of insertion sorts with a given increment i is called an *i-sort*):

original data	17	3	65	81	9	12	6	5	27	4	87	1	18
after the *4-sort*	9	3	6	1	17	4	65	5	18	12	87	81	27
after the *2-sort*	6	1	9	3	17	4	18	5	27	12	65	81	87
after the *1-sort*	1	3	4	5	6	9	12	17	18	27	65	81	87

Though we used increments of 4, 2, and 1 for the sake of illustration, it has been shown that if an *i-sort* is done followed by a *j-sort*, the array is still *i-sorted*. Therefore, interaction among the groups as the sequence of sorts progresses will cause the array to become more nearly sorted earlier if the increments are *not* multiples of one another. The Shell-Metzner Sort used on many microcomputers uses the sequence 31, 15, 7, 3, 1 (one less than powers of two used in reverse order). The Pascal procedure of Fig. 7 uses the seven increments 1,093, 364, 121,

40, 13, 4, 1, where each increment is one more than three times the increment to the right.

The program of Fig. 7 sorts 2,000 numbers 20 times faster than does one insertion pass ($m = 1$; $i[1] = 1$) and 60 times faster than bubblesort. Though much faster than an $O(n^2)$ sort, the behavior of Shellsort still does not attain the theoretical $O(n \log n)$ performance that we hope to attain for a comparison sort. Empirical evidence is that Shellsort runs as $O(n^{1.2})$, or perhaps $O(n \log^2 n)$. Those two functions grow at a very similar rate up through $n = 16,000$, and theory has not yet provided a guide as to which, if either, function characterizes Shellsort behavior for very large values of n.

Shellsort endures in the face of better algorithms because it is quite fast for sorting up to a few thousand items and because it is iterative rather than recursive and hence can be easily encoded in any language. However, it is unstable.

Treesort—A Still Better Insertion Sort The principal defect of insertion sort is that records occasionally need to be placed high in the list of tentatively sorted records, necessitating downward movement of a large number of records stored as a sequential list in an array. What is needed is an alternative data structure into which new records can be inserted at much less operational cost. A more suitable structure for use with a type of insertion sort is a *binary search tree*, such as is described in the article TREE. Suppose that the data to be sorted is the initial sequence of integers 9 2 7 1 4 8 7 6 10. Their corresponding search tree is shown in Fig. 8.

The first unsorted integer becomes the root of the tree. Each successive integer is then inserted recursively into the left subtree if it is strictly less than the root, and into the right subtree of it is equal to (for stability) or greater than the root. If insertions are made according to this rule, then an inorder traversal of the search tree will produce the desired sorted sequence, in this case, 1 2 4 6 7 7 8 9 10. This algorithm, known as *treesort*, was first described by David J. Wheeler in 1957 and Conway M. Berners-Lee in 1958.

With the average case of randomly distributed keys, the search tree formed will be reasonable well-balanced and treesort will perform as $O(n \log n)$. But in the worst case of already ordered (or reverse ordered) keys, the

```
procedure Shellsort(var a : data; n : integer);
{ type date = array[ – 1093..max] of integer; }
const m = 7;
var
    i : array[1..m] of integer;   { Array of diminishing
                                     increments }
    j : 1..m; k,p,s,t,inc : integer ;
begin
    i [m] : = 1;
    for j : = m – 1 downto 1 do i [j] : = 3* i [ j + 1] + 1;
                                { Calculate increments }
    for j : = 1 to m do  { j controls # of sort passes }
        begin
        inc : = i [j];
        for k : = 1 to inc do  { k controls # groups to be
                                 i[j]-sorted per pass }
            begin
            s : = inc + k ; { s marks current last item to be
                              inserted }
            while s < = n do
                begin
                p : = s;
                t : = a[p];         { Save copy of item to be
                                      inserted }
                a[1 – inc] : = t;        { Set sentinel to bound
                                      search for insertion point }
                while t < a[p – inc] do
                    begin
                    a[p] : = a[p – inc];    { Move item down
                                          one increment }
                    p : = p – inc       { Decrement position
                                          counter one inc }
                    end;
                a[p] : = t;             { Insert new item }
                s : = s + inc    { Prepare to get next item
                                  to be inserted }
                end
            end
        end
end { Shellsort };
```

FIG. 7. A Pascal version of Shellsort.

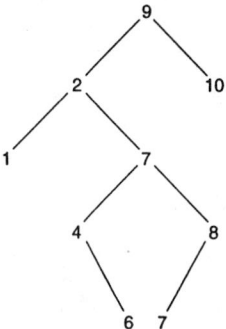

FIG. 8.

search tree will consist of one long linear right (or left) subtree and treesort will degenerate to $O(n^2)$ performance.

Mergesort An improved insertion sort algorithm based on repetitive merging was discussed as early as 1945 by John von Neumann (*q.v.*). Merging, an information processing technique similar to that of sorting, makes no sense except when applied to two (or more) lists that are already separately in order. To *merge* such lists then means to intersperse their elements to form one overall output list that is entirely in order.

Fig. 9 shows an output list C in the process of being formed through the merging of ordered sublists A and B. Four ordered numbers have already been delivered to output list C; we have no way of knowing which of lists A and B they came from. The current heads of lists A and B are 40 and 48 respectively, so the lower one, 40, gets to go next. Unlike automobiles merging from two lanes to one, where courtesy would indicate that it's now the turn of the car in lane B to go next, numbers are selected strictly by their relative size. Thus, 43, which moved up one spot when 40 left, goes ahead of 48, then 48 moves out because it is lower than 52, etc., until all numbers have been processed. When there is a tie at the heads of the lists, it is immaterial which number goes next. There is no requirement that the lists being merged have the same length.

The merging algorithm can be stated in pseudocode as:

while { still more unmerged items in either list } **do**
    begin
        if *A is empty, take the next item from B,* **else**
        if *B is empty, take the next item from A,* **else**
        take the smaller of the two items at the heads
        of lists A and *B*
    end

In the course of being merged, each number in each list is processed only once. This means that the running time needed to merge two lists of size *m* and *n* will be proportional to $m + n$: processing time increases only linearly with increasing list sizes. Thus, merging is a far more efficient process than sorting, which, using poor algorithms such as bubblesort, takes running time proportional to the square of the number of elements to be sorted.

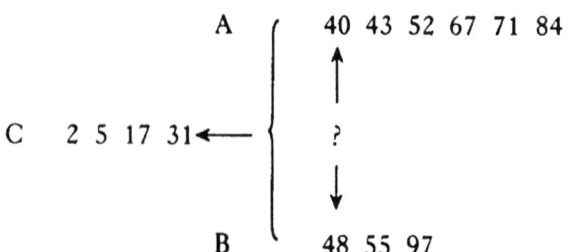

FIG. 9. A merge in progress.

As von Neumann observed, repetitive merging can be made the basis of a very efficient sort strategy. Once we are able to form some initially sorted sublists no matter how short—and that is not difficult if the sublists need only be, say, two numbers long—we can merge two lists of length two to make one of length four, two fours to make eight, etc., until we have formed one ordered list. Recursion is used in order to make the machine's memory (the stack behind the scenes) remember all currently unprocessed lists. Fig. 10 is a diagram that shows how to apply repetitive merging to effectuate sorting:

Strategy: Sort the bottom half. Sort the top half. Merge the halves.

Tactics: 1. Let the "sort" itself be a mergesort, i.e. use recursion with the termination condition being: If size < 2 do nothing. If size = 2, exchange the two items if necessary to produce the mini-sequences needed for later merging.

2. The merge procedure needed for mergesort must be slightly different than the earlier one so that merged sequences are stored back where they need to be to continue the repetitive process:

First version: Merge A & B → C
Needed now:
  a) Merge two halves of A → T
  b) A ← T

The temporary array T is needed because we can't place a partially completed merged

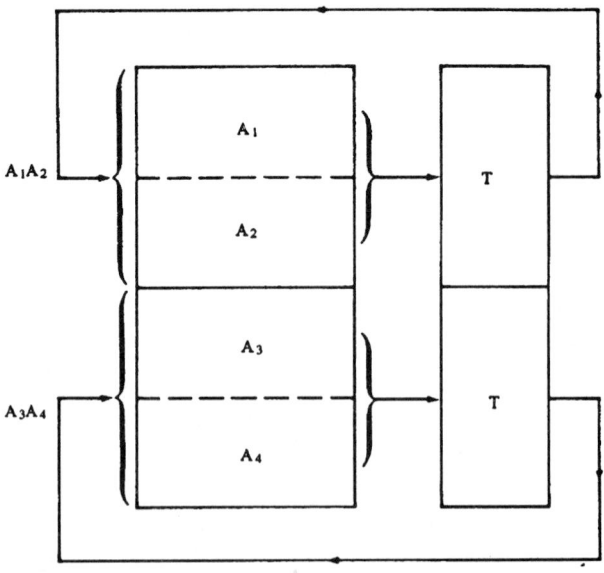

FIG. 10. Sorting by repetitive merging. Given that data segments A, A₂, A₃, and A₄ are ordered already, A₁ and A₂ can be merged into T and then stored back to A₁ A₂, and the same can be done with A₃ and A₄. Finally, a merge of A₁ A₂ and A₃ A₄ completes the sort.

list back on to top of the original lists without destroying unprocessed parts of those original lists.

A recursive Pascal version of mergesort is given in Fig. 11.

Actual time measurements on one particular computer showed that mergesort was able to sort 2,000 numbers almost 50 times faster than Bubblesort. To see why, let's make a crude analysis of how much work is involved in sorting some more manageable number of numbers,

```
procedure Mergesort (var A : list; lo,hi : integer);
{
    Sorts A [lo] through A [hi] inclusive.
}
var
    t, size : integer;

procedure merge (var A : list; lo, hi : integer);
var
    i, j,k,mid,m,n : integer ;
    T : list ;
begin
    k : = 1;  i : = 1;  j : = 1;
    lo : = lo−1;
    mid : = (lo + hi) div 2;
    m : = mid−lo;  n : = hi−mid;
    while k <= m + n do
        begin
            if i > m then begin T[k] : = A[mid + j];
                j: = j + 1   end else
            if j > n then begin T[k] : = A [lo + i];
                i : = i + 1   end else
            if A [lo + i] < = A[mid + j] then begin
                T[k] : = A[lo + i] ; i : = i + 1 end
                                      else begin
                T[k] : = A[mid + j] ;j : = j + 1  end;
            k : = k + 1
        end { while };
        for k : = 1 to m + n do A[lo + k] : = T[k]
end { merge };

begin { Mergesort }
    size : = hi−lo + 1;
    if (size = 2) and (A[hi] < A[lo]) then { exchange: }
        begin
            t : = A[hi] ;
            A[hi] : = A[lo];
            A[lo] : = t
        end
    else if size > 2 then
        begin
            Mergesort(A, lo, lo−1 + size div 2) ;
            Mergesort(A, lo + size div 2, hi) ;
            merge(A, lo,hi)
        end
end { Mergesort };
```

FIG. 11.   A Pascal implementation of mergesort.

say 64, under the simplifying assumption that pairs of lists being sorted are of equal size:

# merges		# numbers/ merge		# numbers processed
32	×	2	=	64
16	×	4	=	64
8	×	8	=	64
4	×	16	=	64
2	×	32	=	64
1	×	64	=	64
Total operations			=	64×6
or, in general				$n \times \log_2 n$

The O ($n \log n$) behavior of mergesort holds even in the worst case, and mergesort has the added advantage of being stable.

Fastcount—A Better Enumeration Sort   Since three of the four primitive $O(n^2)$ algorithms—selection sort, bubblesort, and insertion sort—have one or more modified versions that run as $O(n \log n)$, one might expect that there should be a way to modify the fourth one—enumeration sort—to run as $O(n \log n)$, but the hypothetical *fastcount* has not yet been invented. A very efficient $O(n)$ sorting algorithm based on counting will be discussed in the next section, but it is distributive rather than comparative.

Distributive Sorting Algorithms   Instead of comparing keys, a distributive sorting algorithm moves each record to or close to its final destination based on some intrinsic property of the key itself. The first such sort we will examine is the oldest, one used as the basis for the special-purpose sorting machines that were first developed in the late 1800s by Herman Hollerith (*q.v.*) for processing census data.

Radix Sort   For reasons that will become apparent momentarily, the algorithm used for sorting on physical card sorting machines is seldom used on a computer. That algorithm is called *radix sort* because it depends on multiple sort passes, one for each digit (radix) position of the maximum value number to be sorted. (On a card sorting machine, the radix is invariably 10—the digits are decimal digits—but any radix may be used from two upward.) The earliest published description of radix sort cited by Knuth (1973) is by Leslie J. Comrie in 1929.

As cards flow through the machine on any given pass, they drop into the appropriate one of ten pockets numbered 0 to 9, corresponding to the digit in the position being used as a key. Suppose we are sorting three-digit numbers 000 to 999. Though it is not the procedure followed, we can easily envision the success of a three-pass procedure that proceeds left to right, sorting cards first into piles where, say, all of the 300s drop into one pocket and all of the 700s drop into another. Separately sorting each pile on their tens digit and, later, subpiles on their units digit will complete the sort. But such a procedure involves much more card handling than is necessary. Though not obvious, passes may be made in the opposite

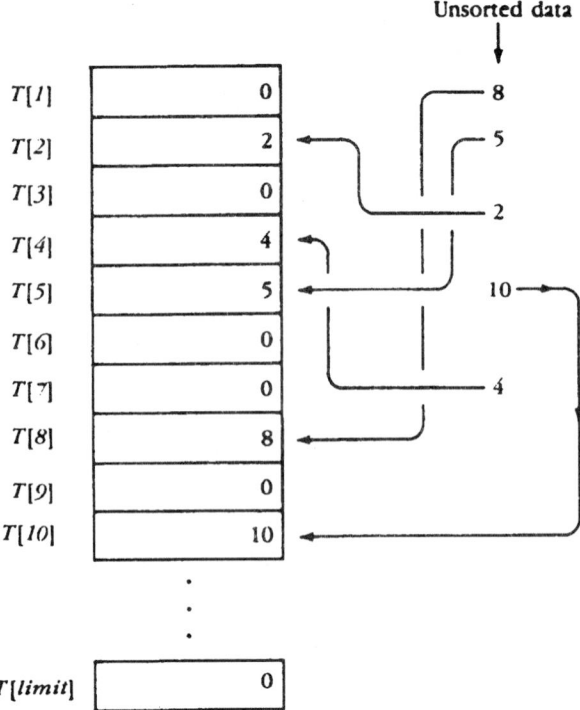

Unsorted data

FIG. 12. Sorting data by address calculation.

order, right to left from units digit to hundreds digit, provided the cards are collected and stacked properly after each pass. The entire deck participates in each pass. After all but the last pass, cards are collected by placing the 9-pocket stack on top of the 8-pocket stack, etc., picking up the 0-pocket stack last. After the last pass, collect cards in normal order, 0-pocket through the 9th. There are two problems in adapting this algorithm for use on a computer:

1. Numbers are stored internally in binary, not decimal. One might program a binary radix sort, but it is more effective to treat binary keys as if they were octal by accessing successive groups of three bits from right to left, or hexadecimal by accessing successive groups of four bits from right to left. (If all bits are accessed—the whole key—radix sort reduces to the hashsort algorithm to be described momentarily.)

2. On a physical card sorter, pockets are very deep relative to the size of the typical card deck being sorted. If pockets are simulated as arrays in a computer, each array has to be prepared to hold all n numbers being sorted (just in case they all have, say, a 7 in the same radix position). If the radix is 16 (hexadecimal), then $16n$ record locations are needed, a storage requirement that is just not competitive with the many algorithms that sort in place, or that use at most an extra n record locations. Linked lists could be used for pockets, but the resulting program is unwieldy.

Since, for a given radix r and bit precision p, the radix sort makes $\log_2 r$ passes, its running time is expected to be $O([p/\log r]n)$ in the best, average, and worst cases. Thus, for 16-bit integers and radix 16 (hexadecimal), the radix sort should run about four times more slowly than hashsort.

Sorting By Address Calculation (Perfect Hashing) An $O(n)$ distributive algorithm applicable to data of restricted range was described by Earl Isaac and Richard Singleton in 1956. Suppose that the data to be sorted are integers in the range 1 to *limit* with no duplicates. Then, if there is sufficient memory space to declare an array T of size *limit*, that array is initialized to zero (or any value outside the range 1..*limit*) and unsorted data values are directed, one by one, into the unique space reserved for each: $T[7] \leftarrow 7$; $T[19] \leftarrow 19$, etc. (see Fig. 12). After distribution to the temporary array T, the nonzero values from $T[1]$ through $T[limit]$ can be output as the sorted list, or (as in the procedure of Fig. 13) nonzero values can be moved back on top of the original array of unsorted data. When either of these operations is done properly, it takes only $O(limit)$ time, or $O(n)$ time if n is close to *limit*. Since it takes only $O(n)$ time to store the numbers and $O(n)$ time to pack them, the overall performance of the algorithm is $O(n)$. This method was called sorting by *address calculation* in the days of machine language programming—each data value being directed to an address equal to itself—but could now be called sorting by *index calculation* when implemented in a high-level language. It is also called sorting by *perfect hashing* (see SEARCHING) because, since it was postulated that the data set contained no duplicates, each value can be "hashed" to a particular destination address without danger of "collisions."

procedure *adcalcsort*(**var** A : *list*, n : *integer*)
{
    Sorts the first n numbers of list A by address calculation, where type list = array [1..limit] of integer. Assumes that all numbers to be sorted are in [1..limit] and that there are no duplicates.
}
var
    i, j : *integer*; T : *list*;
begin
        for i : = *1* **to** *limit* **do** $T[i]$: = 0; { Initialize T }
    for i : = *1* **to** n **do** $T[A[i]]$: = $A[i]$;
                { Put each $A[i]$ in its reserved slot
}

{ Now move nonzero elements of T back into A }

    j : = *1*;
    for i : = *1* **to** *limit* **do if** $T[i] <> 0$ **then**
        begin
            $A[j]$: = $T[i]$;
            j : = $j + 1$
        end { *for* }

FIG. 13. A Pascal procedure for sorting by address calculation.

```
procedure Hashsort (var a : data; n : integer);
const m = 4999; { Upper limit of hash table }
type ptr = ^node;
     node = record
               val : integer ;
               link : ptr
            end;

var
    h : array [0..m] of ptr,
    i, j, mp1 : integer ; t : ptr;
    d : integer, { Divisor to be used in the hash function }

    procedure insert (item : integer, var list : ptr) ;
    var p : ptr ;
    begin
       if list = nil then begin
                        new(p);
                        p^.val : = item;
                        p^.link : = nil;
                            list : = p
                     end
       else if item <= list^.val then begin
                        new(p);
                        p^.val : = item;
                        p^.link : = list;
                            list : = p
                     end
          else insert (item, list^.link)
    end { insert };

begin { logic of Hashsort itself }
   mpl : = m + 1;
   d : = 1 + trunc(maxnum / mp1) ;
   for i : = 0 to m do h[i] : = nil; { Empty the hash table }
   for j : = 1 to n do insert (a[j], h[ a[j] div d]); { Insert all
                                                     data }

   j : = 1; { Recover hashed items and store them back at
             array a }
   for i : = 0 to m do
     begin
        t : = h[i];
        while t <> nil do
          begin
             a[j] : = t^.val;
             j : = j + 1;
             t : = t^.link
          end
     end
   end { Hashsort };
```

FIG. 14. A Pascal hashsort procedure.

Although the procedure given for the address calculation sort applies to records that are "all key" integers, it can be easily extended to apply to records of any uniform size (memory permitting) whose keys obey the restriction cited: integers in the range 1..limit with no duplicates.

Hashsort The condition that a sequence of record keys span the range 1..limit, as was required for sorting by address calculation, occurs fairly often, but the restriction that there can be no duplicates is unrealistic. What can be done to salvage sorting by hashing under threat of collisions (two or more records hashed to the same index position)? One way is to build a linked list of collided items at each target destination (see LIST PROCESSING). A Pascal procedure called hashsort based on this idea is given in Fig. 14. (Hashsort is also called bucket sort because every record is directed into a particular receptacle, or "bucket.") All elements of a target array are initialized to nil pointers, and then all keys that hash to a given index position are entered into a linked list, even if that list never contains more than one item.

But what kind of hash function is appropriate? If no key were larger than the length of the pointer table, then no hashing would be necessary, since all keys would land inside the table and only identical keys would cause collisions. But if keys might be larger than the size of the pointer array, they must be cut down to size even though doing so will increase the frequency of collisions. If keys might be as large as, say, 9,999, and the table size is just 1,000, we could simply divide each key by 10. Then, 7,136 and 7,139 would both be mapped to index 713, but as long as the overflow list corresponding to index 713 is kept in order and its complete 4-digit components are later recovered in order, the collision will ultimately be resolved. Instead of always using 10 as a divisor, the procedure of Fig. 14 computes an optimum divisor based on the relative sizes of the maximum key and the pointer table used.

When hashsort encounters no collisions, it is clearly an $O(n)$ algorithm. At the other extreme, when the data to be sorted is so skewed that all n items hash to the same index, the sort would be only as good as the $O(n^2)$ running time needed to maintain an ordered singly linked list. But for randomly distributed keys and reasonable pointer table size, we expect collisions to be sufficiently rare so that it would be hard to detect any degradation from the $O(n)$ performance obtainable with perfect hashing. This is in fact the empirical result of experimentation with hashsort. Its high speed is attained at the cost of high storage overhead—for "all key" integer records, the table of linked lists occupies space at least three times that of the array of unsorted items. If the space is available, however, no other sorting algorithm of reasonably general applicability can come close to this performance.

Ultrasort When conditions permit, an extremely fast sorting algorithm with a worst-case performance of $O(n)$ can be based on frequency counting. Suppose that we want to sort an arbitrarily long sequence of single-digit integers. If we just count the integers, which we can do in $O(n)$ time, the counts of their relative occurrences might conceivably be

$c[0] = 147$ there are 147 0s
$c[1] = 89$ there are 89 1s
$c[2] = 463$ there are 463 2s
.
.
$c[9] = 216$ there are 216 9s

```
procedure Ultrasort (var a : data; n : integer);
var
    c : array[0..maxnum] of 0..255;
    i, j, k : integer;
begin
    for j : = 0 to maxnum do c[j] : = 0; { Initialize the
                                           counts }
    for i : = 1 to n do c[a[i]] := c[a[i]] +1 { Increment the
                              bin having the same number }
    k : = 1;
    for j : = 0 to maxnum do { Make c[j] copies of each
                                count: }
        for i : = 1 to c[j] do
            begin
                a[k] : = j;
                k : = k + 1
            end
end { Ultrasort };
```

FIG. 15. A Pascal ultrasort procedure.

Next, we overwrite the array of unsorted numbers with, consecutively, 147 zeros, 89 ones, 463 twos, etc., up through 216 nines—all in $O(n)$ time. Single-digit numbers were used only as an example, the maximum size of the integers that can be handled with this often overlooked algorithm is limited only by how large a table can be allocated to hold the frequency counts. The algorithm, first described by Harold Seward in 1954, has no standard name. It was called *mathsort* by Wallace Feurzig in 1960 and *ultrasort*, the name used here, by Reilly and Federighi (1989). A Pascal version is given in Fig. 15.

Sorting Large Records The Pascal procedures given for the internal sorting algorithms described as-

sumed that the records being sorted were "all key" integers. In most actual situations, the key that determines the collating order is just one part—a small one, perhaps—of some larger record. An example would be a nine-digit social security number that constitutes one field of a record of, say, 900 characters. The work of most sorting algorithms consists of making comparisons and moving data. When only small keys are involved, comparisons tend to dominate, but if large records are moved about, moves become very significant and can greatly distort the relative performances otherwise attainable from the various algorithms discussed herein. But large records should not be moved during sorting; only their keys and their original index positions should be shifted. Suppose, for example, that we wish to sort the array of records shown in Fig. 16, where the non-key portion of each record is quite large.

The sequence of scrambled indices represented by the $p[i]$ is in an important sense more valuable than the sorted $R[i]$ would be (which is why the APL language "grade up" function returns such indices rather than actually sorting its operand vector). Those indices (subscripts), applied in the order derived, can be used to output or move all or any part of the $R[i]$—to whatever destination is desired in precisely the order indicated by their keys.

Alternatively, we could maintain an array of pointers to the large records and, when comparison of record keys indicates an interchange, swap pointers rather than the records themselves. A pointer is a small item (a machine address); the record might be many hundreds of bytes long.

Comparative Performance of Internal Sorting Algorithms The best, average, and worst-case

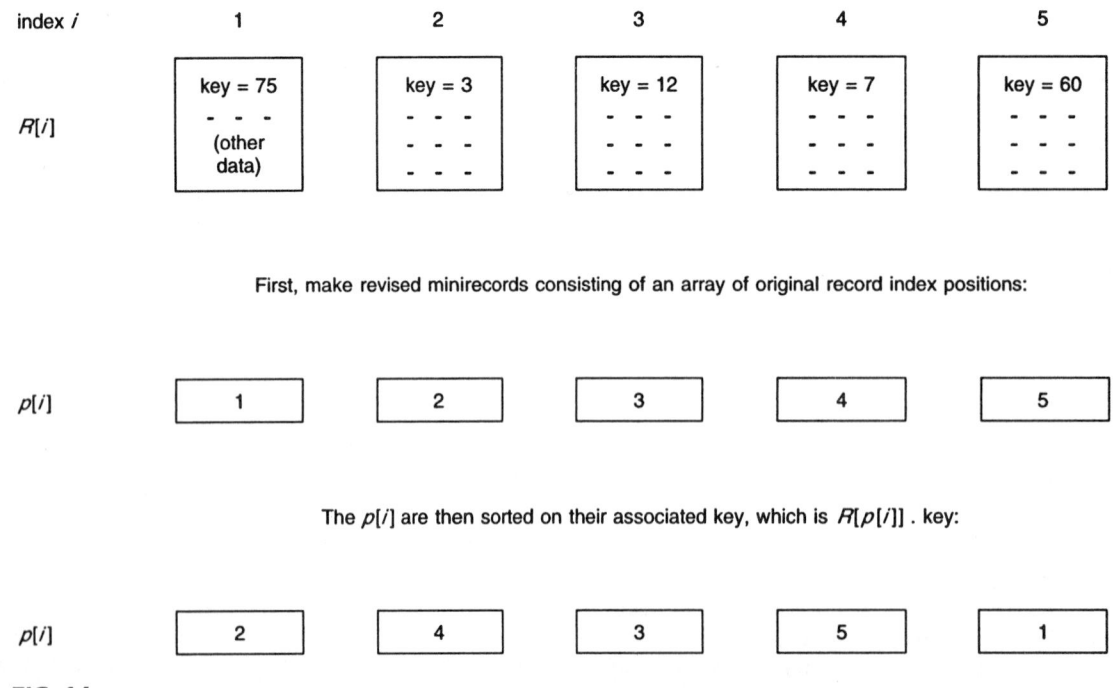

FIG. 16.

TABLE 1.   Expected Performance of Internal Sorting Algorithms

Algorithm	Best-case Performance	Average-case Performance	Worst-case Performance	Stability
Linear:				
Ultrasort	$O(n)$	$O(n)$	$O(n)$	N.A.
Hashsort	$O(n)$	$O(n)$	$O(n^2)$	Stable
Radix sort	$O([p/\log r]n)$	$O([p/\log r]n)$	$O([p/\log r]n)$	Stable
Radix exchange sort	$O(pn)$	$O(pn)$	$O(pn)$	Unstable
Logarithmic:				
Quicksort	$O(n \log n)$	$O(n \log n)$	$O(n^2)$	Unstable
Heapsort	$O(n \log n)$	$O(n \log n)$	$O(n \log n)$	Stable
Mergesort	$O(n \log n)$	$O(n \log n)$	$O(n \log n)$	Stable
Treesort	$O(n \log n)$	$O(n \log n)$	$O(n^2)$	Stable
Polynomial:				
Shellsort	$O(n)$	$O(n^{1.2})$	$O(n^2)$	Unstable
Insertion sort	$O(n)$	$O(n^2)$	$O(n^2)$	Stable
Selection sort	$O(n^2)$	$O(n^2)$	$O(n^2)$	Stable
Enumeration sort	$O(n^2)$	$O(n^2)$	$O(n^2)$	Stable
Bubblesort	$O(n)$*	$O(n^2)$	$O(n^2)$	Stable

p = precision in bits
*⟹ use of flag to abort when no exchanges made during prior pass
r = radix

TABLE 2.   Relative Running Times of 13 Internal Sorting Algorithms

Algorithm	n = 2,000	n = 4,000	n = 8,000	n = 16,000
Ultrasort	0.1 sec	0.2 sec	0.4 sec	0.8 sec
Hashsort	0.3 sec	0.6 sec	1.2 sec	2.4 sec
Radix Exchange Sort	0.7 sec	1.4 sec	2.8 sec	5.6 sec
Quicksort	0.5 sec	1.2 sec	2.6 sec	5.6 sec
Shellsort	0.9 sec	2.1 sec	4.5 sec	10.2 sec
Mergesort	1.0 sec	2.4 sec	5.1 sec	11.1 sec
Radix Sort (r = 16)	1.5 sec	3.0 sec	6.0 sec	12.0 sec
Treesort	1.2 sec	2.7 sec	6.0 sec	13.0 sec
Heapsort	1.5 sec	3.1 sec	6.6 sec	14.2 sec
Insertion Sort	0.3 min	1.2 min	4.8 min	0.3 hr
Selection Sort	0.6 min	2.5 min	10.0 min	0.7 hr
Enumeration Sort	0.7 min	2.9 min	12.0 min	0.8 hr
Bubblesort	0.9 min	3.7 min	15.0 min	1.0 hr

performance of a dozen internal sorting algorithms is given in Table 1. Actual running times for 2,000, 4,000, 8,000, and 16,000 "all key" integer records as obtained on an IBM PC/AT-class machine are given in Table 2, arranged in order of decreasing performance in sorting 16,000 integers. All times would be up to three times faster on an 80486-class PC, and considerably faster on a mainframe. The $O(n^2)$ behavior of the four primitive sorting algorithms is readily apparent, as is the linear behavior of the distributive sorting algorithms. Ultrasort was able to sort 16,000 integers almost 5,000 times faster than Bubblesort.

References

1971. Martin, William A. "Sorting," *ACM Computing Surveys* **3**, *4:* 147–174. (December).

1972. Rivest, Ronald L, and Knuth, Donald E. "Bibliography 26, Computer Sorting," *Computing Reviews* **13**, *6:* 283–289 (June).

1973. Knuth, Donald E. "Sorting and Searching," *The Art of Computer Programming* **3**. Reading, MA: Addison-Wesley.

1984. Bentley, J. "Programming Pearls: How to Sort," *Comm. Acm.* **27**, *4:* 287–291.

1989. Reilly, E. D. and Federighi, F. D., *Pascalgorithms*. Boston: Houghton-Mifflin. (Figures 4, 10 and 12 and portions of the text of this article are reprinted with permission.)

EDWIN D. REILLY

EXTERNAL SORTING

With the ever increasing size of main memory, the need for external sorting algorithms diminishes. Suppose, for example, that a file stored on a mass storage device consists of 50,000 100-character records. Such a file occupies 5 megabytes, which does not exceed the scratch main memory storage of many current PCs. To sort such a file, it is feasible to read the entire file into main memory, use an appropriate internal sorting algorithm (quicksort, perhaps, which sorts in place), and then rewrite the

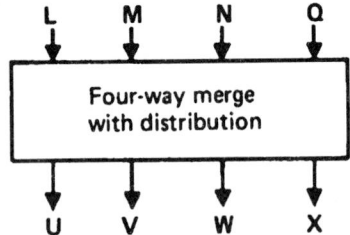

FIG. 17. Multiway merge.

sorted file back onto mass storage. But what can be done when the size of the external file does not fit in main memory?

The earliest widely used external storage medium was magnetic tape, so it is not surprising that so many external sorting algorithms were devised for sorting files stored on tape. Knuth (1973) devotes most of his discussion of external sorting to such algorithms. Since most external sorting is based on merging, we will conclude with a brief discussion of several variations on this theme.

Tape Sorts Three important tape sorts are called *Multiway Merge, Cascade Merge*, and *Polyphase Sort-Merge*. We examine each in turn.

Multiway Merge We have described merging where two lists were merged into a single list or distributed into two output lists. The number of lists that can be merged at one time is limited only by the complexity of the merge program and by the amount of main memory available in the machine. Fig. 17 shows a four-way merge, where L, M, N, and Q are input lists of ordered sublists and distribution takes place to U, V, W, and X. One sublist each from L, M, N, and Q is merged into a single sublist and distributed to the proper output list. This method is described in detail in Flores (1969, p. 109).

The advantage of the multiway merge is that it gets the job done much more quickly. The disadvantage is that it uses many I/O devices—the four-way merge uses eight devices, although this is not a serious objection if disks rather than tapes are used.

Cascade Merge To reduce the number of devices holding input or output media, more complicated merge sorts have been devised. The *cascade merge* was one of the first of these and possibly the easiest to explain. In the example of Fig. 18, we begin with four lists labeled U, V, W, and X. U is a list comprising 14 sublists. Each of these sublists was created during an internal sort. To indicate the length of each sublist, a subscript is used. A unit sublist is one whose length is the same as the sublist produced during the internal sort. V contains 11 such sublists, and W contains six. During the first phase, sublists of unit length from each list are merged by a three-way merge producing six sublists, each of which is three units long. These are placed on X. During the second phase, a two-way merge produces five sublists, each of length 2 on W.

It might seem that we are ready to do another merge. However, this sort was designed for magnetic tape. Although the tapes can be read backward, control becomes

more complicated when we try to do a merge reading U forward, and W and V backward. Hence, U is copied onto V in phase 3. Now it is possible in phase 4 to read V, W, and X, all backward, merging sublists of each into sublists of length 6. The rest of the merge is done using three- and two-way merges and copies (see Flores, 1969, p. 136).

Polyphase Sort-Merge The polyphase sort-merge provides a more advanced merge facility. It is used in most manufacturer-supplied tape sorts. It enables the user with *N* tape units to have *N* − 1 of these in use for merging most of the time. To take advantage of the sort, the tape units should be capable of reading backward and forward, and the program must be able to energize the tape units in different directions during any given phase of the sort.

The polyphase sort requires a distribution procedure that is performed during the internal sort and that is quite uneven; it is based on a complicated algorithm. The origin and principle of the algorithm is explained in Flores (1969, p. 145).

Using the notation we developed for the cascade sort, let us examine Fig. 19, which shows how the poly-

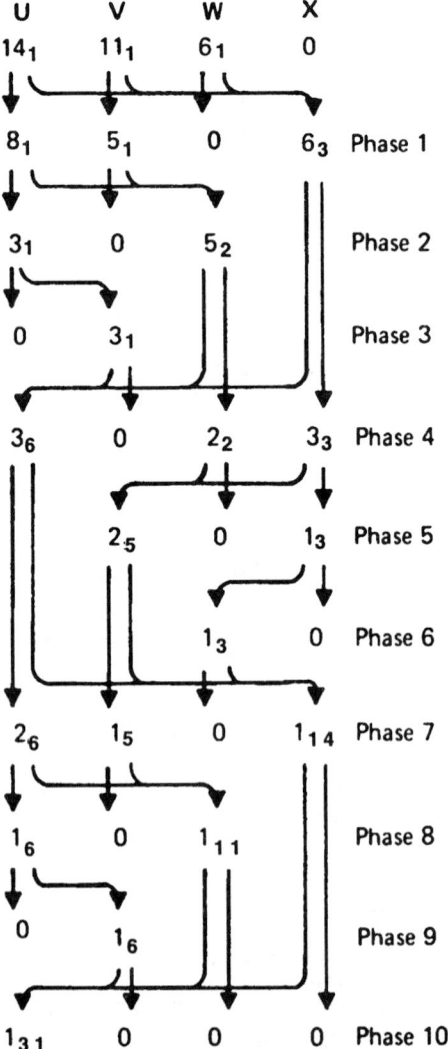

FIG. 18. Cascade merge.

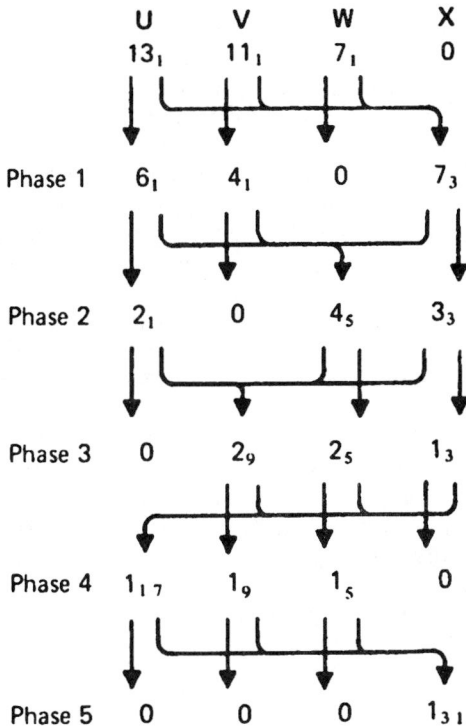

U	V	W	X
13_1	11_1	7_1	0

Phase 1 6_1 4_1 0 7_3

Phase 2 2_1 0 4_5 3_3

Phase 3   0 2_9 2_5 1_3

Phase 4 1_{17} 1_9 1_5 0

Phase 5   0   0   0 1_{31}

FIG. 19. Polyphase merge.

phase sort works. The sort displayed uses four magnetic tape units. The internal sort has produced 13 sublists of unit length on the left-hand tape unit, 11 of these on the next one, and 7 on the third unit. The fourth unit contains a working tape. Actually, this can be on the input tape unit from which the original tape was removed and a working tape mounted to secure the integrity of the original file during the sort.

During the first phase, a three-way merge produces seven sublists, each of unit length three. These go to the fourth tape unit. As the last sublist from the third unit is merged, we find that no more sublists remain on that unit. The program senses this and makes an alteration in the I/O device assignment.

During the second phase, another three-way merge occurs. The output of this merge goes on to the third tape unit. Notice during this merge that the first and second tape units continue to read forward. However, the fourth tape unit had just been written upon; to save rewinding time, it is read backward. This may cause complications as sublist lengths get large. If the allocated buffer in main memory cannot hold the whole sublist, trouble arises, since we cannot merge the end of one sublist with the beginning of another sublist. For this reason, some polyphase sorts are designed so as to rewind the destination unit after it has accepted the proper number of sublists.

At the end of phase 2, the first tape unit has two unit sublists left and is still reading forward; the second tape unit is empty; the third tape unit has just received four sublists of length 5 and is ready to read backward; the fourth tape unit has three sublists of length 3 and continues to be read backward.

From the figure it should be clear how the five phases required for this particular sort are performed. During the distribution phase, the allocation of sublists to each tape unit is very sensitive. An algorithm creates the assignment numbers, which are known as perfect numbers (not to be confused with perfect numbers in mathematics). The perfect numbers corresponding to 31 sublists are 13, 11, and 7 when four tape units are involved.

If we have only 30 sublists, we find that no perfect numbers can be generated. Several alternatives are available. The simplest of these to understand is the creation of a null sublist so that the program thinks there are 31 sublists when there really aren't. This is compensated for by counters in the program. Thus, in Fig. 19, if the first tape unit contains 12 instead of 13 sublists, then during phase 3 there will occur one three-way merge using the first, third, and fourth tape unit. A second three-way merge cannot occur during this phase; instead, a two-way merge occurs, during which the first tape unit is not activated.

Disk and Drum Sorts   Modern disk and drum sorts use an efficient internal sort coupled with a balanced multiway merge. The *balanced merge* uses an equal number of input and output lists. For sorting with magnetic tape units, each list for merging, whether input or output, requires its own device. For the disk or drum we have direct access; this means that it is easy to switch access from one list on a volume to another on the same volume, in contrast to serial access devices such as a tape unit.

The disk or drum sort designer, therefore, does not face any inherent limitation arising from the number of lists to be used. Instead, the problem is to use an optimum number of lists and space these lists in an optimum way. The crucial factor in reducing sort time is the number of seeks required by the disk mechanism. Therefore, one tries to optimize the list selection and layout with respect to minimizing the total number and length of seeks involved over the entire sort.

References

1969. Flores, Ivan. *Computer Sorting*. Englewood Cliffs, NJ.: Prentice-Hall.
1973. Knuth, Donald E. "Sorting and Searching," in *The Art of Computer Programming* 3. Reading, MA: Addison-Wesley.

IVAN FLORES

SOURCE PROGRAM

For articles on related subjects *see* LANGUAGE PROCESSORS; OBJECT PROGRAM; and PROCEDURE-ORIENTED LANGUAGES.

A *source program* is a computer program written in a language one or more steps removed from the *machine language* of a given computer. Machine language consists of the very explicit set of instructions and operation codes capable of direct execution by the hardware of the computer. It is, however, extremely tedious and error prone, for it requires that instructions be spelled out in almost microscopic detail, specifying all data and program references in terms of actual addresses within the computer memory. Accordingly, other languages have been developed to make it easier for programmers' desires to be expressed. A program written in such a language is called a source program, and must be translated by one means or another into the language of the machine before it can be executed. Fortunately, other programs can carry out this translation on the computer itself.

If the source program is in assembly (i.e. symbolic) language, the process of translating it is called *assembling*, and the result is an *object program* in machine language, ready to be executed. If the source program is in a high-level language like Pascal or C, the translating process is called *compiling*, and may involve one or more stages (e.g. a Pascal program may be first compiled into assembly language, and then that program assembled into machine language).

Source programs in high-level languages have great advantages in portability, for with only minor changes, if any, they can often be compiled to run on various machines.

CHARLES H. DAVIDSON.

SPECIFICATION, PROGRAM. *See* PROGRAM SPECIFICATION.

SPEECH RECOGNITION AND SYNTHESIS

For articles on related subjects *see* ARTIFICIAL INTELLIGENCE; COMPUTER VISION; IMAGE PROCESSING; NEURAL NETWORKS; PATTERN RECOGNITION; and PERCEPTRON.

The use of computers could be greatly expanded if human speech could be reliably utilized as an input/output medium. Such capability would allow humans to listen to synthetic speech output from a computer rather than read a display. Indeed, commercially acceptable synthetic speech can now be produced as output from a computer, even for unrestricted vocabulary and syntax. The ability of computers to recognize human speech would permit input to the computer without the use of a keyboard. Although commercial units of limited capability are available, speech recognition is a far more difficult problem than speech synthesis.

Speech Recognition In order to understand the process of speech recognition, it is useful to assume that all of the necessary information for recognizing spoken words is available in the speech signal itself. Indeed, much research and system implementation is based on this assumption. The first task is thus to represent the speech signal in a form that contains fewer bits of information, but retains those facets that are thought to be useful for recognition. Most systems base this representation on derived attributes of a model for speech production called the *source-*

filter model. The human vocal apparatus is modeled as one or two sources exciting a set of coupled resonators that intensify the sound in the neighborhood of the resonant frequencies. One source is the sequence of puffs of air that can be produced by the vibrating vocal cords, as in "voiced" sounds, such as those in the word "zen" (fricative "z", vowel "e", and nasal "n"). In addition, the vocal tract can produce turbulent air flow at any of a large number of constrictions, leading to noise-like sounds, such as the "s" in "son." Both forms of excitation can be combined, as in "z". Whatever the form of excitation, it can be considered to excite a set of resonances (called *formants*) that vary with the shape of the vocal tract. The resulting speech spectrum is thus the result of multiplying the source spectrum by the vocal tract filter spectrum. (An example is shown in Fig. 1.) Most speech recognition systems use some form of spectral representation as input to classification algorithms, since the relatively slow motion of the articulators is displayed in the formant trajectories, allowing for an insightful reduction of the input information rate. Precisely what frequency-time-amplitude features are computed is an important attribute of any speech recognition system. In many contemporary systems, all input spectra are sorted into a group of spectral equivalence classes, usually about 200 in number. This process is referred to as *vector quantization*, and allows each spectrum (usually computed at centisecond intervals) to be labeled with the name of one of the equivalence classes in the

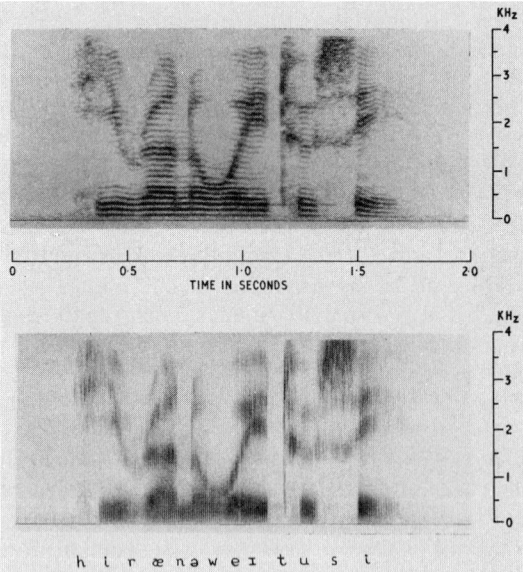

FIG. 1. Spectrogram of the sentence "He ran away to sea." The upper record is a narrow-band analysis made with a 30-Hz bandwidth filter. The fine horizontal lines are due to individual harmonics in the buzzing sound produced at the larynx. The lower record is a wide-band analysis made with a 240-Hz bandwidth filter. The fine vertical lines are due to the sound of individual pulses of air emitted by the larynx. The dark bands, or formants, are due to resonance peaks in the acoustic response of the vocal tract. Below the bottom figure the spoken phrase is written in phonetic symbols of the International Phonetic Association. Each "letter" represents a single sound.

vector quantization code book, or *library*. All further processing uses only the class label designation, and no further reference is made to specific attributes of input spectra. On the other hand, some systems attempt to extract features from the input spectra, and use the set of such feature designations distributed over the input utterance as the reduced input representation. This approach seeks to represent directly those phonetic attributes thought to be significant to human speech perception or machine speech recognition, but such early feature detection must be marked as tentative, since it is impossible to recognize these features reliably.

Following parametric (either spectral- or feature-based) representation of the speech, endpoints of the utterance are detected, and normalization may be performed to compensate for spectral warping due to variation in vocal tract length. Matching against stored templates is then performed, often using abstract mathematical formalisms and sophisticated search procedures to obtain the best match. Many systems use a procedure called *dynamic programming* to warp the time dimension of the input to secure the best match, as computed by a variety of scoring methods. Many investigators feel that the use of optimal time warping is more important than the choice of spectral representation. Fig. 2 shows how these techniques are combined to perform the speech recognition task. Several commercial systems are available that provide speech recognition based on these procedures. These pattern matching approaches are based on the assumption that only the information in the speech waveform is necessary for correct recognition. It is always desirable to use the best possible acoustic-phonetic analysis of the speech signal, but other constraints of the language being spoken are also useful in recognition of the utterance. These constraints cover the allowable consonant clusters, syllable structure, morpheme sequences, phase- and clause-level syntax, semantics, and discourse structure derivable from the nature of the specific task being performed. The representation of these *knowledge sources*, their access, and means to combine their constraining effects on the output decision are reflected in a control structure that guides the searching and decision binding tasks.

During the 1980s, great emphasis was placed on the use of hidden Markov models for speech recognition. These models provide a way of representing the constraints on spectral template sequences presented by phonemes and their distribution in syllables, as well as the constraints of word sequence represented by syntax, but summarized in statistical form. In this way, the pronunciation of individual words can be represented as a network of arcs connecting states. Using the hidden Markov model formalism, it is possible to train these networks so that the probability of traversing a given arc from one state to another can be automatically derived from many training utterances and thus characterize a statistical picture of the sequence of states in the model corresponding to a particular speaker's (or group of speakers) vocal articulations. Syntactic constraints are usually represented by "N-gram" statistics, which provide crude indications of syntagmatic word order constraints. Three-grams are often used, and it is remarkable how much improvement in performance is provided by their use. These "language models" are also trained automatically, so that word sequence constraints also become a part of the overall hidden Markov model representation. It can also be shown that dynamic time warping techniques, which had previously been shown to provide substantial increases in performance, can be formally subsumed by the hidden Markov model mechanism. During the 1980s, a great deal of research was devoted towards refinements in the use of hidden Markov models, and word error rates of 4–6 percent have been achieved over large (20,000-word) vocabularies trained for a single speaker. Research continues to develop techniques for automatic multispeaker recognition in large vocabularies, as well as low error rates of 2–3 percent in medium vocabularies of one or two thousand words. Hidden Markov modeling techniques have also been used for very small vocabularies, including the alphabet and numerals, leading to very compact and inexpensive systems of commercially acceptable performance. While hidden Markov models have been devised that can represent timing variations in speech, the representation within this framework of pitch contours is still under study. In addition, ways in which phonetic features can be incorporated within this abstract formalism are being used in experimental systems.

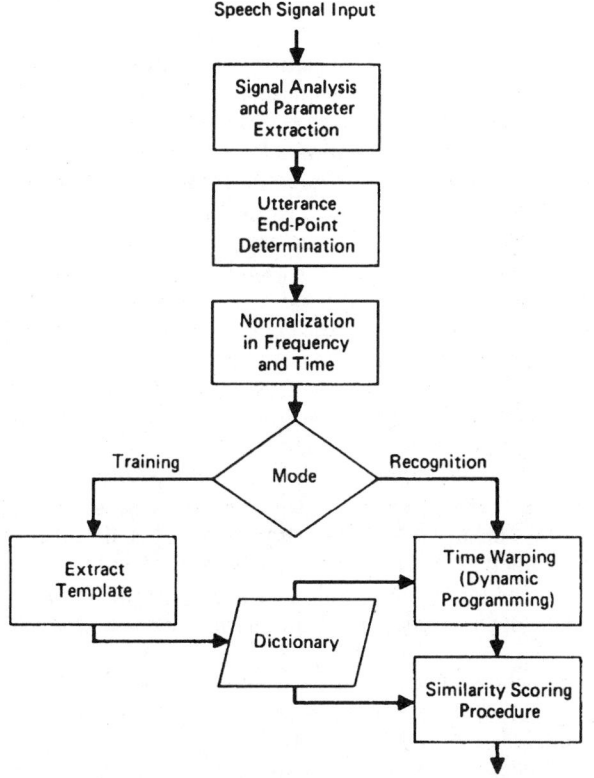

FIG. 2. Pattern-matching speech recognizer. The pattern produced from the speech signal is normalized and compared with a set of patterns derived from words of known identity. The input word is assumed to be the same as that word whose stored pattern has the highest similarity score.

Recently, neural network classifiers have been proposed for use in speech recognition. These techniques, based on massive parallelism, are also automatically trained and can provide impressive performance in discrimination between classes, such as vowels. Such static classifiers can be useful in many applications, but it is more difficult to use these techniques for sequential constraints and time-varying behavior. Nevertheless, this approach has received far less study than hidden Markov modeling, and new neural network techniques can be expected in the near future. In addition, ways in which neural networks can be incorporated within the hidden Markov model formalism are being explored in order to exploit the complementary virtues of the two approaches.

The complexity of speech recognition systems is substantial, and large vocabulary systems require at least 100 MIPS of computing power to provide real-time performance. The use of custom VLSI search engines, digital signal processing chips, and modern technology has provided this capability, and, indeed, implementation technology is not the limitation on current speech recognition systems. While speech recognition is currently useful for several applications, particularly those in which the hands and/or eyes are occupied with other tasks, the goal of building a comprehensive system that can recognize speech from multiple speakers using unrestricted vocabulary and syntax is still elusive.

Speech Synthesis The inverse of speech recognition is speech generation (synthesis). Toys and robots that "speak" have been familiar objects for quite some time. There is also an increasing interest in interactive human-computer dialogue. In these applications, the human speaks to the computer, but the computer must respond using some form of synthetic speech. When the vocabulary is small, recorded or coded speech can readily provide the required voice.

Frequently, however, large vocabularies and unrestricted syntax is needed, or the vocabulary, while possibly small, is changing rapidly enough that recording is impractical. Text-to-speech capability has been developed for these needs and is available commercially. The quality of this speech is intelligible, but somewhat unnatural. For many applications, however, these systems are acceptable and are finding increasing use as their cost and size are reduced while the speech quality continues to improve.

Speech synthesis and speech recognition share common concerns, but there are also distinctive differences. Recognition implies the use of a sophisticated search strategy, techniques for representation of partial knowledge, and means of considering alternative pronunciations, whereas speech synthesis utilizes a rich lexicon, complex and interactive rule systems, and processes for contextual smoothing and realistic articulation. Research in each of these fields is mutually constructive. Speech synthesis, while commercially useful, still faces many difficult research questions similar to those pursued in speech recognition. Thus, the multiple ways in which speech sounds are produced in synthesis is of direct utility to speech recognition, and the extensive characterization of pronunciation patterns for use in speech recognition is of equal importance to speech synthesis. Consequently, there is an important need to view these two applications in one unifying context. The benefits of such a view can be expected to improve both synthesis and recognition in future language-based systems.

References

1989. Lee, K.-F. *Automatic Speech Recognition: The Development of the SPHINX System.* Norwell, MA: Kluwer Academic Publishers.

1989. Lippmann, R. P. *Review of Neural Networks for Speech Recognition.* Neural Computation **1**, 1–38.

1991. Furui, S., and Sondhi, M. (eds.) *Recent Progress in Speech Signal Processing.* New York: Marcel Dekker.

1991. Kitano, Hiroaki. "ΦDM-Dialog—An Experimental Speech-to-Speech Dialog Translation System", Computer (IEEE) **24**, 6 (June), 36–50.

JONATHAN ALLEN

SPEED, COMPUTER. *See* PERFORMANCE OF COMPUTERS.

SPELLING CHECKER

For articles on related subjects *see* DICTIONARIES, COMPUTERIZED; NATURAL LANGUAGE PROCESSING; and WORD PROCESSING.

Computers are very useful for word processing. They are used to input, store, edit, format, and print text files ranging in size from short notes to multi-volume books. In addition to these conventional forms of word processing, computer programs can provide more advanced word processing assistance, such as *spelling checking, spelling correction,* and *grammar checking.*

The general operation of a spelling checker is simple: it checks each word in a document or file for correct spelling. Allegedly incorrect spellings are reported to the human user, who can then correct the errors. A spelling corrector checks each word (just like a spelling checker) and, in addition, will try to suggest the correct spelling for each misspelled word that is found.

Note that spelling checkers guarantee only that each word is *some* correctly spelled word, not necessarily the one you meant. If "or" is mistyped as "of" or if "affect" is misspelled as "effect," a spelling checker will not report an error. Detecting these kinds of errors would require a much more complicated program called a *grammar checker.*

Spelling checkers are used in a number of different ways. Possibly the simplest is the standalone *batch* program. A batch program reads the (input) document and produces an (output) list of any possible spelling errors. The user must find and correct these errors in the document. An *interactive* spelling checker reads a document and presents each spelling error to the user as it is found. The user can see each alleged error in context and either change it immediately or leave it alone. A word processing system may incorporate spelling checking (or correction) directly into its processing, either in response to a menu option or continually as text is entered.

How does a spelling checker know if a word is correctly spelled? Most checkers use a *word list* to define the set of correctly spelled words. The word list may be the list of all words in a dictionary (without the definitions) or may be accumulated from existing documents. Despite having no definitions, most spelling programs call their word lists "dictionaries." The list of words is generally stored in a file. A word is considered to be correctly spelled if and only if it is found in the speller's word list. The main technical problem, particularly for an interactive program, is to search the list as quickly as possible.

Differing search and data structure techniques are used for differing environments. A batch checker, for example, may form an alphabetically sorted list of all words in an input document and then make one pass over a similarly sorted word list to check for misspelled words. A speller with large amounts of main memory can keep the entire word list in that fast memory in the form of a hash table and use standard hash table search algorithms (*see* SEARCHING). A system with a fast disk might keep its word lists on disk with an in-core index and a cache of the most frequently referenced disk blocks.

The correctness of a spelling checker is determined by its word list. As long as its word list has no incorrectly spelled words, a checker will never "miss" an incorrectly spelled word that is not, coincidentally, some other legal word. On the other hand, spellers often report correctly spelled words as possible spelling errors. These may be proper names, technical terms, or uncommon words that are not in the system word list. Most systems allow a user to augment its main word list with local auxiliary word lists for special subjects, authors, or documents. Doctors and lawyers, for example, generally use extensive auxiliary word lists designed for the specialized vocabularies of their fields.

Some systems, upon flagging a suspect word, allow the user several options, including: (1) correct the word, (2) add the word to the main word list, (3) add the word to an auxiliary word list, or (4) add the word to a transient word list that endures only for the duration of the document being checked.

A very large word list might seem desirable to avoid having a spelling checker incorrectly report correctly spelled words as possible errors. However, a very large word list tends to include unusual and infrequently used words. This increases the chance that a word will be misspelled as some other word and not be caught by the checker. The appearance of "dhow" in text might indicate that the author is writing about an Arab boat, but more likely signals a typographical error for "show." In general, word lists should be kept reasonably small, in the range of 20,000 to 100,000 words, even though there are over a half-million English words (counting inflections).

One approach to keeping the word list short is to notice that many words are derived from a base word by the addition of common suffixes and prefixes. Some checkers keep only the base words in their word lists. If a suspect word is not in the word list, an attempt is made to remove suffixes and prefixes to find the base word. If the base word is in the word list, the suspect word is accepted as correctly spelled. Note that this approach may allow incorrect spellings to escape detection, such as if "design" is misspelled "desing" (which can be processed as "*de* + *s* + *ing*").

A spelling corrector is invoked when an incorrectly spelled word is found. Its problem is to produce a list of possible correct spellings for the error. For correction, the set of correctly spelled words is thought of as a set of points in a multidimensional space. The corrector tries to find the nearest neighbor or neighbors of the spelling error in that space. If an error produces one candidate correction that is much closer to the error than other possible corrections, the speller may suggest an automatic correction.

The success of a spelling corrector depends largely upon the source of the spelling errors and the methods used to find nearest neighbors. For example, many systems assume that spelling errors occur because of one of the following four types of errors:

1. One extra letter in the word (*"feeel"*).
2. One missing letter in the word (*"fel"*).
3. One wrong letter in the word (*"feal"*).
4. Two adjacent letters are transposed (*"fele"*).

These types of errors may account for 80% to 90% of the typing errors in a document.

Another source of spelling errors is the difference between spelling and pronunciation—a word like "tough" may be spelled "tuff." The most common approach for correcting these types of errors is to map the error onto a sound-based encoding. Each word in the word list is also mapped, and candidate corrections with the same sound as the error are generated. The proper use of appropriate data structures and search algorithms to provide adequate performance is particularly important in this case.

Another common typing error is to repeat an entire word, commonly at the end of one line and the beginning of the next line, creating such obvious errors as "a a" and "the the." Some checkers check for duplicate adjacent words, but would then report spurious errors in those sentences with repeated words, such as "I knew that that boy had had the measles."

Note that this type of error is not a spelling error, since each word is individually a correct word. In addition to spelling and typing errors, there are errors of grammar. Grammatical errors are defined by incorrect groups of words, not individual words. Grammar checkers try to find errors in sentences or phrases rather than separate words. While it is possible to look for certain simple errors (such as two identical words in a row, incorrect use of "a" or "an", capitalization errors, or use of any of a list of incorrect word combinations), the general problem of detecting true errors of grammar is still a research problem. We do not yet have computer programs that "understand" the structure of sentences. Understanding the structure of sentences would allow the detection of errors, such as a sentence with no verb or a plural subject with a singular verb ("they is").

Reference

1980. Peterson, James L. " Computer Programs for Detecting and Correcting Spelling Errors," *Communications of the ACM*, **23**, *12*, (December), 676–687.

JAMES L. PETERSON

SPLINE

For articles on related subjects *see* APPROXIMATION THEORY; CHEBYSHEV APPROXIMATION; LEAST SQUARES APPROXIMATION; and NUMERICAL ANALYSIS.

Polynomials are the approximating functions of choice when a smooth function is to be approximated locally. For example, the truncated Taylor series $\Sigma_{j=0}^{n} D^j$ $f(a)(x - a)^j/j!$ provides a satisfactory approximation for $f(x)$ if f is sufficiently smooth and x is sufficiently close to a. But if a function is to be approximated on a larger interval, the degree of the approximating polynominal may have to be chosen unacceptably large. The alternative is to subdivide the interval $[a,b]$ of approximation into sufficiently small intervals $[\xi_j, \xi_{j+1}]$ (with $a = \xi_1 < ... < \xi_{l+1} = b$) so that, on each such interval, a polynominal p_j of "low" degree can provide a good approximation to f. This can even be done in such a way that the polynominal pieces blend smoothly, i.e. so that the resulting patched function $s(x) := p_j(x)$ for $\xi_j \leq x \leq \xi_{j+1}$, all j, has several continuous derivatives. Any such smooth *pp* (piecewise polynominal) function is called a *spline*, the name given by I. J. Schoenberg, since a twice continuously differentiable cubic spline (with sufficiently small first derivative) approximates the shape of a draftsman's spline.

While the *pp-form* of a spline, (i.e. the description of a spline in terms of its *breakpoints* $\xi_1, ..., \xi_{l+1}$ and the *local polynominal coefficients* c_{ij} of its pieces $p_j(x)$ $= \Sigma_{i=0}^{*} c_{ij} (x - \xi_j)^j/j!$, is convenient for the evaluation and other uses of a spline, the *B-form* has become the standard way to represent a spline during its construction, since the B-form makes it easy to enforce matching of derivatives across breakpoints. The B-form describes a spline as a linear combination $\Sigma_{j=0}^{n} a_j B_{j,k}$ of B-splines, with $B_{j,k} = B(\cdot|t_j, ..., t_{j+k})$ the jth *B-spline* of *order k* for the *knot sequence* $t_1 \leq t_2 \leq \cdots \leq t_{n+k}$. In particular, $B_{j,k}$ is pp of degree $< k$, with breakpoints $t_j, ..., t_{j+k}$, is nonnegative, is zero outside the interval (t_j, t_{j+k}), and is so normalized that $\Sigma_j B_{j,k}(x) = 1$. The *multiplicity* of the knots governs the smoothness: If the number z occurs exactly r times in the sequence $t_j, ..., t_{j+k}$, then the $B_{j,k}$ and its first $k - r - 1$ derivatives are continuous across the breakpoint z, while the $(k - r)$th derivative has a jump at z. Since each B-spline has only small support, the linear system for the B-spline coefficients of the spline to be determined, by interpolation or best approximation or as the approximate solution of some

differential equation, is *banded*, hence easily solvable. Also, many theoretical facts concerning splines are most easily stated and/or proved in terms of B-splines; e.g. it is possible to match arbitrary data at points $x_1 <...< x_n$ uniquely by a spline of order k with knot sequence $t_1, ..., t_{n+k}$ if and only if $B_{j,k}(x_j) \neq 0$ for all j (Schoenberg-Whitney Theorem). Computations with B-splines are facilitated by stable *recurrence relations*.

$$B_{j,k}(x) = \frac{x-t_j}{t_{j+k-1}-t_j} B_{j,k-1}(x) + \frac{t_{j+k}-x}{t_{j+k}-t_{j+1}} B_{j+1,k-1}(x)$$

(with $B_{j,1}(x) = 1$ for $t_j \leq x < t_{j+1}$ and 0 otherwise), which are also of help in the conversion from B-form to pp-form. The *dual functional*

$$a_j(s) = \sum_{i<k} (-D)^{k-i-1} \psi_j(\tau) D^i s(\tau)$$

provides a useful expression for the jth B-spline coefficient of the spline s in terms of its value and derivatives at an arbitrary point $\tau \in (t_j, t_{j+k})$ (and with $\psi_j(t) = (t_{j+1} - t)$ $\cdots (t_{j+k-1}-t)/(k-1)!)$. This can be used to show that $a_j(s)$ is closely related to s on the interval $[t_j, t_{j+k}]$

If the coefficients a_j in the B-form $\Sigma_j a_j B_{j,k}$ are points in 2-space or 3-space instead of scalars, a spline *curve* results. More flexible parametric pp curves are available that are smooth (as curves) even though their parameterization is not. The simplest *bivarate* spline is obtained as the *tensor product* $\Sigma_{i,j} a_{ij} B_{i,h}(x) B_{j,k}(y)$ of (univariate) splines. More general bi- or multi-variable pp functions usually have to be dealt with polynominal piece by polynominal piece, since multivariate B-splines (such as *box splines*) are available only for very special partitions.

The above *constructive* approach is not the only avenue to splines. In the *variational* approach, a spline is obtained as a "best interpolant" (e.g. as the function with smallest kth derivative among all those matching prescribed function values at certain points). Among the many such splines available, only those that are piecewise polynominal (or, perhaps, piecewise exponential) functions have found much use. Of particular practical interest is the *cubic smoothing spline* $s = s_\lambda$, which, for given data (x_i, y_i) with $x_i \in [a, b]$, all i, and given corresponding positive weights w_i, and for given *smoothing parameter* λ minimizes

$$\sum_i w_i(y_i - f(x_i))^2 + \lambda \int_a^b f''(t))^2 dt$$

over all functions f with two derivatives. The smoothing spline s is a cubic spline with a breakpoint at every data point. The art of using the smoothing spline consists in choosing λ so that s contains as much of the information, and as little of the supposed noise, in the data as possible.

References

1978. Boor, C. de, "A Practical Guide to Splines", *Applied Mathematical Sciences* 27, New York. Springer-Verlag.

1981. Schumaker, L. L. *Spline Functions: Basic Theory.* New York. John Wiley & Sons.
1988. Chiyokura, H. *Solid Modeling.* Reading, MA: Addison-Wesley.

CARL deBOOR

SPREADSHEET

For articles on related subjects *see* ADMINISTRATIVE APPLICA-TIONS; DATABASE MANAGEMENT SYSTEMS; NONPROCEDURAL LAN-GUAGES; and STATISTICAL APPLICATIONS.

Introduction An electronic *spreadsheet* is a program devised to facilitate financial and business modeling, primarily on microcomputers. First constructed in 1979, spreadsheets rapidly developed into one of the most widely used software products during the 1980s. Their design, in the form of an accountant's spreadsheet of rows and columns, provides a programming environment that has proved to be accessible to managers, accountants, and a vast variety of other end users, as well as to computer professionals. Even people with no programming experience generally have found spreadsheets to be intuitive, natural, and useable tools for financial analysis, business and mathematical modeling, decision making, simulation, and problem solving. Originally regarded simply as applications programs, they are in fact effectual instruments for nonprocedural programming in general.

When first introduced, spreadsheets were used primarily with small models for low-level decision making, often by single individuals. Within a decade, however, spreadsheets had become a primary management tool, and now are used extensively as a medium for implementing increasingly larger models and for doing analysis in significant, high-level business decisions.

Spreadsheets have contributed to the popularity of personal computers. In many ways, the rapid growth of the use of spreadsheets helped drive many of the microcomputer hardware developments during the 1980s. As larger and more sophisticated models were designed for spreadsheet implementation, the need for increased memory capacity and more sophisticated spreadsheet capabilities created a corresponding need for advances in the development of computer hardware.

Spreadsheets have found extensive use in a diverse range of disciplines. Many professionals in mathematics, engineering, science, and education find the spreadsheet to be a natural tool for modeling, implementing and analyzing algorithms, constructing laboratory reports, producing graphics, and even modeling natural phenomena governed by two-dimensional partial differential equations.

Brief History The first spreadsheet program, Visi-Calc, was developed in 1979 by Bob Frankston and Dan Bricklin. The program idea emanated from creating an effective way to use the computers to solve business school problems, with the spreadsheet concept patterned after a traditional blackboard production planning layout. Originally written in assembly language for a 32K-byte Apple II, VisiCalc was a small spreadsheet with a terse single-line menu. However, its popularity and usefulness led to the rapid development of numerous other spreadsheets.

In 1981, SuperCalc was developed for the Osborne computer, and became the primary spreadsheet for 8-bit CP/M computers. In 1983 Lotus 1-2-3 was created for 16-bit MS-DOS computers. It contained many innovations and advanced features, including on-line help, sophisticated menus, graphic and database management capabilities, and macros. It immediately became the best-selling software product and set standards for competitive spreadsheet products that followed. Most spreadsheet notation and conventions are based on Lotus 1-2-3. As the number of spreadsheet users increased, the desire for additional features escalated. This led to the development of add-on programs whose features subsequently have been incorporated into newer spreadsheets. Recent years have seen the development of more powerful spreadsheets, and upgrades of old ones, with advanced features and presentation-quality graphics, often requiring computers with hard disks (*q.v.*) and at least a megabyte of memory. Leading spreadsheets include Excel, Quattro Pro, Lotus 1-2-3, and SuperCalc. These programs are written in combinations of assembler and high-level languages.

Basic Operation The spreadsheet format consists of a large rectangular array, a portion of which is shown on the screen. Spreadsheet columns are identified by letters, and rows by positive integers. Individual locations, or cells, are referenced by row and column. For example, C2 refers to the cell in column C of row 2.

One cell is highlighted on the screen by a cursor. The cursor can be moved to other cells by using either arrow keys or a mouse. After positioning the cursor on a cell, a user can then enter into that location a label (or string), a number, or a formula that references other spreadsheet cells. The program calculates the value of a formula in a cell by using the values of the cells that it references and displays the result on the screen. Generally, the calculation of a spreadsheet is performed in an order that first evaluates any of the cells referenced in another cell, although other orders are available.

One of the popular attributes of a spreadsheet is its "What if...?" capability. If the value of any cell is changed, a spreadsheet's formulas are recalculated and the display is updated. This allows a user to interrogate a model by changing its parameters or data and observing the resulting effects. Thus, in financial models it is possible to examine the compound effects of changes of such interrelated components as projected sales, prices, interest rates, and profit. Newer spreadsheets frequently have a minimal recalculation feature in which only those cells affected by the change in a given cell are recalculated.

Fig. 1 gives the output and formulas of a simple tax model. Income is taxed at a rate of 10% on the first $20,000 of income and 20% on amounts in excess of $20,000. The parameters and data of the model are entered into cells B1 through B6. A library function, @SUM, computes the

```
     A          B              A          B
 -|----------|------|       -|----------|-----------|
 1| Tax Break  20000       1| Tax Break  20000
 2| Lo Rate      10%       2| Lo Rate      0.1
 3| Hi Rate      20%       3| Hi Rate      0.2
 4| Income 1   23000       4| Income 1   23000
 5| Income 2   10000       5| Income 2   10000
 6| Income 3   12000       6| Income 3   12000
 7|           ======       7|           "======
 8| Income     45000       8| Income     @SUM(B4..B6)
 9| Tax         7000       9| Tax        (below)
10| Net        38000      10| Net        +B8-B9
```
Note: B9: @IF(B8<B1,B2*B8,B2*B1+B3*(B8-B1))

FIG. 1. Taxation spreadsheet model.

sum of the incomes in cells B4 through B6. The library function @IF in formula in cell B8 reads "IF income (B8) is less than the breakpoint (B1), THEN multiply income (B8) by the low rate (B2), ELSE add the tax on the amount below the break (B2*B1) to the tax on the amount above the break (B3*(B8−B1))". Cell B10 finds the difference between Income and Tax.

Once constructed, a model like Fig. 1 can be used repeatedly simply by changing the parameters (break point, tax rates) or the data. Such a model, or template, is often created for multiple users. In a template, data and parameter cells are initially blank, to be changed by the user, while cells containing the model's formulas can be protected by a command that prevents changes to those cells.

Spreadsheet Commands

Spreadsheet commands provide additional ways for a user to interact with a model. These commands may be selected from a series of menus through the use of either keystrokes or a mouse. Among options are commands to load and save files, format output, set column width, create graphic displays, and print. Other commands allow a model to be modified by inserting or deleting rows and columns, or by moving and copying blocks of cells, with the program automatically adjusting all formula references throughout the spreadsheet.

The Copy command is particularly useful in creating models that repeatedly perform the same computations, eliminating the need to enter many formulas individually. Fig. 2's model projects the future values of a group of investments. Current investment values are in Column C, with annual interest rates in Column A. The model assumes that a flat management fee (cell C1) is deducted from each investment at the end of a year.

A principal p at an annual rate r increases in one year to a value of $p + rp = (1 + r)p$, less the annual fee. The formula $(1 + \$A3) * C3 - \$C\$1$ is entered into cell D3, and then copied into all of the cells of rows 3–5 of columns E,F,G,...the $ symbol determines how a location identifier is interpreted by the Copy command. An identifier without the $ is treated as a relative location. Thus, in copying the formula in cell D3, giving the previous year's value, C3, is copied as a relative location, or as "the cell to the left." Identifiers preceded by the $ are treated as constants. Thus, the fee C1 is unchanged in copying, while the interest rate $A3 varies from row to row, but always comes from column A. The formulas in cells D2, C6, and D7 can be copied across their rows as well, with all locations relative.

Graphics commands allow the creation of a wide variety of graphs to display aspects of a model visually. In the some spreadsheets, graphs and output can be displayed simultaneously. Fig. 3 is a graph from the previous example produced using Quattro Pro.

While spreadsheet notation is relatively easy to learn and use, the logic of a spreadsheet model, with its many interrelated cells, can be arduous to follow, making it difficult to modify and debug a model. More structured models can result from the adoption of standardized layouts in which data, parameters, and formulas are located in separate areas, and from the use of range names, macros, and multiple files or pages.

The Name command allows ranges of cells to be named, making formulas more meaningful. For example, in Fig. 2, cells A3, A4, A5 can be named as RATEA, RATEB, RATEC, with cell C1 as FEE, and the range C3..C5 as INI-

```
     A       B         C         D         E         F
 -|------|---------|---------|---------|---------|-------|
 1| Annual fee =      100
 2| Rate   Item      1991      1992      1993      1994
 3| 5.0%   ABC Inc  1400.00   1370.00   1338.50   1305.43
 4| 5.0%   Beta Co  3000.00   3050.00   3102.50   3157.63
 5|10.0%   CST Ltd  3500.00   3750.00   4025.00   4327.50
 6|        Total     $7,900    $8,170    $8,466    $8,791
 7| Annual growth rate          3.4%      3.6%      3.8%
```

```
     A     B    C         D                 E                 F
 -|-----|----|----|----------------|----------------|-------------|
 1| Ann fee = 100
 2| Rate Item 1991 1+C2             1+D2             1+E2
 3| 0.05 ABC  1400 (1+$A3)*C3-$C$1  (1+$A3)*D3-$C$1  (1+$A3)*E3-$C$1
 4| 0.05 Beta 3000 (1+$A4)*C4-$C$1  (1+$A4)*D4-$C$1  (1+$A4)*E4-$C$1
 5| 0.1  CST  3500 (1+$A5)*C5-$C$1  (1+$A5)*D5-$C$1  (1+$A5)*E5-$C$1
 6|      Total (C6) @SUM(D3..D5)    @SUM(E3..E5)     @SUM(F3..F5)
 7|      Ann rate   +D6/C6-1        +E6/D6-1         +F6/E6-1
```
Note: C6: @SUM(C3..C5)

FIG. 2. Use of the copy command.

INVESTMENT PROJECTIONS

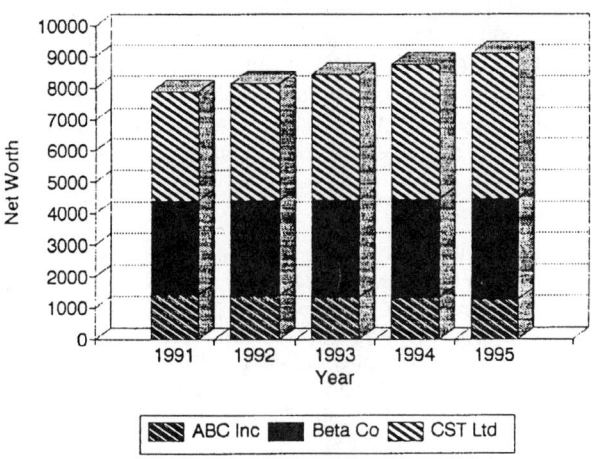

FIG. 3. Sample graphical output from Quattro Pro.

TIAL. The formulas in cells D3 and C7 are then $(1 + RATEA) * C3 - \$FEE$ and @SUM(INITIAL).

A *macro* is a user-defined series of keystrokes and commands stored in a named area of the spreadsheet. Special symbols are used to represent certain keystrokes, such as ~ for Enter and {DOWN} for the down arrow. Macros are executed by invoking the macro name. In many spreadsheets, macros can be stored in a library file accessible by any spreadsheet file.

Macros can be used to simplify the process of carrying out a complex or often-repeated series of commands. If the Lotus 1-2-3 keyboard macro /WGFC2~ is entered into a cell named \C (the letters are command menu selections), then when⟨Alt⟩-C is pressed, the macro sets the global format to the currency mode. Macros can also be used as programming tools and to implement procedures that are not easily performed in a spreadsheet. In many spreadsheets, macros can include the use of logic statements, loops, branching, and subroutines. Fig. 4 illustrates a macro that doubles those values in the range A1..A5 that are less than 50.

In the earliest spreadsheet programs, each model had to be created in a separate file. Usually, these files could not access each other. Powerful spreadsheets now allow for multipage spreadsheet files or for several spreadsheet files to be linked by formulas that reference the other files. These permit the construction of modular and multidimensional models. For example, inventory data for each of a firm's several warehouses could be stored on distinct pages or files, with a master file used to summarize the data. Fig. 5 is a Quattro Pro example using multiple files. As inventory data is updated in a warehouse, first the main file and then the supporting files are updated.

Spreadsheets contain many additional features. The screen display can be split into windows to show different sections of a spreadsheet or other files. Spreadsheets include numerical, string, table, and logic library functions from mathematics, finance, statistics, and computing. Some contain functions and commands for more advanced mathematics, including linear or multiple regression, matrix operations, and linear programming. Most can read external files composed in other spreadsheets, especially Lotus 1-2-3, or database programs. Spreadsheets incorporate database elements and allow for a number of database operations. Also, many integrated packages have been created to couple spreadsheets, database, word processing (*q.v.*), and other components. Like many other user packages, spreadsheets have built-in help libraries that can be used as on-line manuals or invoked while entering a command to supply help on the specific command.

Because spreadsheets are used increasingly for the analysis of significant and critical financial decisions, it has become crucial to ensure the correctness of spreadsheet models. To aid in this, most new spreadsheets have auditing features that can be used to locate logic errors. Auditing commands display interconnections between cells, provide lists of ranges and functions, display cells of a given data type, and step through macros. They also find, highlight, and display sources of possible errors, such as formulas that reference empty or text cells, cells not referenced, and circular references.

Additional Applications Mathematical algorithms that are iterative or recursive usually can be implemented on a spreadsheet through the use of recurrence relations. The model in Fig. 6 finds binomial probabilities. If an experiment (e.g. flip a coin) has only two outcomes, succeed and fail, and the probability, *p*, of a success does not change when the experiment is

```
     A     B          C              D              E
 _|-----|---|------------------------|-|--------------------------|
 1|  20  | \A  {GOTO}A1~               |  Go To Cell A1
 2| 100  |     {FOR D1,1,5,1,\B}        |  For D1 = 1 To 5 Step 1
 3|  50  |
 4|   4  | \B  /RNCX~~                  |  Name Cursor Cell as X
 5|   8  |     {IF X<50}{LET X,2*X}     |  If X<50 Then Double X
 6|      |     /RNDX~                   |  Delete Name For X
 7|      |     {DOWN}~                  |  Move Cursor Down
```

FIG. 4. Sample macro program.

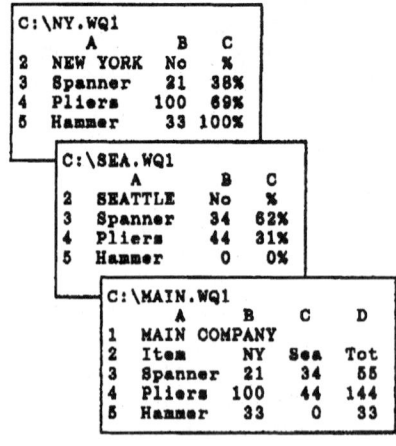

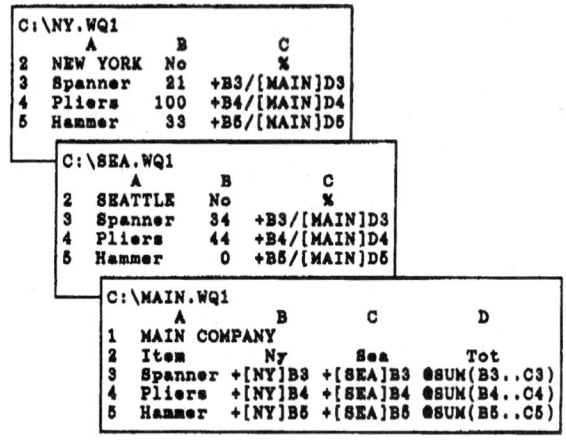

FIG. 5. A multiple-file Quattro Pro display.

repeated, then the probability $P(n,k)$ of obtaining exactly k successes in n repetitions can be found by the recurrence relation

$$P(0,0) = 1$$
$$P(n,k) = pP(n-1, k-1) - (1-p)P(n-1, k) \text{ for } n > 0.$$

This formula is based on the fact that, to have k successes after n repetitions, after $n-1$ repetitions either there were $(a)k-1$ successes followed by a success (probability $pP(n-1, k-1)$) or (b) k successes followed by a failure (probability $(1-p)P(n-1, k)$). As the result is also valid for $k = 0$ and spreadsheets treat references to blank cells as 0, a single formula can be copied throughout the table. In the example, $p = 0.6$.

References

1987. Grauer, Robert T. and Sugrue, Paul K.; *Microcomputer Applications*. New York: MCGraw-Hill.

1989. Lammers, Susan. *Programmers at Work*. Microsoft.

1989. Licklider, Tracy Robnett. "Ten Years of Rows and Columns," *BYTE*, **14**, *13*, (December) 324–331.

1989. Ronen, Boaz, Palley, Michael A. and Lucas, Henry, Jr. "Spreadsheet Analysis and Design," *Communications of the ACM*, **32**, *1*, (January) 84–93.

DEANE ARGANBRIGHT

STACK

For articles on related subjects *see* ACTIVATION RECORD; DATA STRUCTURES; FIFO/LIFO; LIST PROCESSING; POLISH NOTATION; RECURSION; SUBPROGRAM; and TREE.

A *stack* is a linear list for which all insertions and deletions, and usually all accesses, are made at one end of the list. The properties of a simple stack may be illustrated by a railroad switching network having a track into which railroad cars may be inserted and removed from only one end, as in Fig. 1. At any given time, only the most recently entered railroad car may be removed from the track. Railroad cars are said to enter and leave the track in a *last-in-first-out* (LIFO) order.

Alternatively, a stack may be defined as a linear list whose elements may be created and deleted only in a last-in-first-out order. Stacks arise in computational pro-

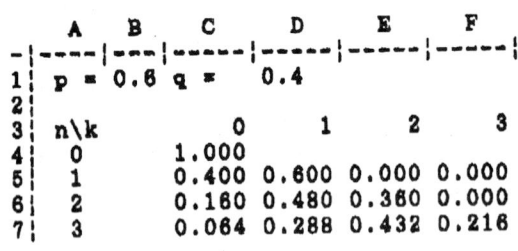

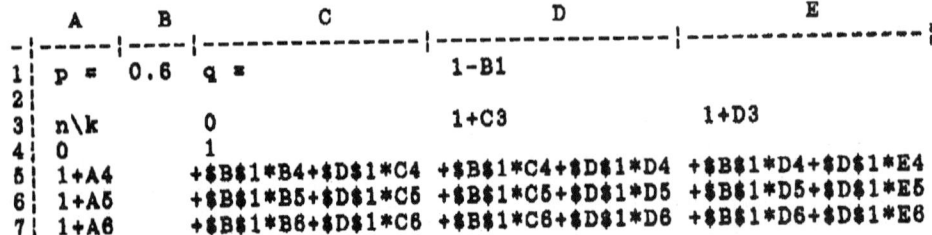

FIG. 6. Binomial probability model

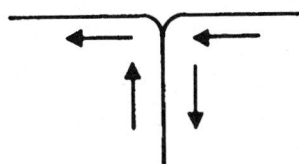

FIG. 1.

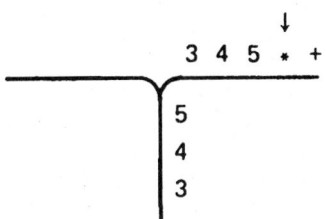

3 4 5 ∗ +

5
4
3

FIG. 2.

cesses dealing with structures whose components are nested, as in the following example.

Example from Arithmetic Expression Evaluation. The expression (3 + (4∗5)) has a subexpression (4∗5), which is nested within the complete expression and is conveniently evaluated by first converting it to the parentheses-free postfix notation 345∗+ (in which the operator ∗ immediately follows its operands 4, 5 and the operator + immediately follows its operands 3 and 45∗), and then using an operand stack for evaluation. The evaluation of the expression 345∗+, using a stack, is illustrated in Fig. 2, and is defined in detail below.

Evaluation Rule for Postfix Expressions Scan the constituents (operators and operands) of the expression from left to right. If the constituent is an operand, copy it into the operand stack. If the constituent is an operator, apply it to the two top elements of the operand stack and

replace these two elements by the result of applying the operator to its operands.

The elements 3, 4, 5 in Fig. 2 have been placed in the operand stack and the operator "∗" is about to be scanned. According to the evaluation rules, ∗ is applied to the two top elements (5 and 4) of the operand stack, which causes the elements 5 and 4 to be replaced by the value 20. The operator + is now applied to the two top elements (20 and 3) of the operand stack, which causes these elements to be replaced by the value 23.

Arithmetic expression evaluation is conveniently implemented by stacks because expressions may contain subexpressions nested inside them to an arbitrary level. A further example of nested program structure arises in the case of subroutines (procedures).

Subroutine calls have the property that a called subroutine must be completely executed before returning to the higher-level subroutine that called it. Thus, subroutines are executed in a last-in-first-out order (relative to the order in which they are called), and are conveniently implemented by a stack mechanism that creates and deletes information about subroutine parameters and the return address in a last-in-first-out order.

Nested structures may be represented by parentheses, embedding, or tree structures, as illustrated in Fig. 3.

There are many applications in which the elements of a nested structure (tree structure) must be "visited" in an order that requires the path by which the element was reached to be remembered. For example, if a tree is traversed by first visiting the root and then traversing the subtrees in a left-to-right order, then it is convenient to remember the path from the root to the current vertex on a stack, since successor subtrees of vertices along the path from the root to the current vertex must be examined in a last-in-first-out order if they are to complete the traversal of all vertices of the tree.

Reference

1973. Knuth, D. E. *The Art of Computer Programming* **1** (2nd Ed.). Reading, MA: Addison-Wesley.

PETER WEGNER

A(B,C(D,E))

1 A
　　2 B
　　2 C
　　　　3 D
　　　　3 E

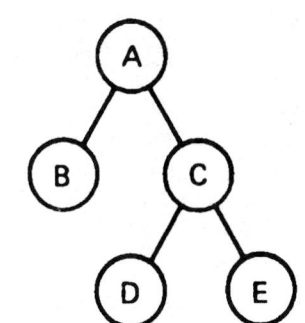

FIG. 3.

STAMPS, COMPUTING ON

For articles on related subjects *see* CALCULATING MACHINES; and DIGITAL COMPUTERS: HISTORY.

There are a large number of postage stamps featuring computers and related topics. Many of these stamps relate to the history of calculation and computation; others are more concerned with the present-day uses of computers in society. In this article we present a small selection of stamps, chosen to be as representative as possible.

From earliest times, men and women have needed to carry out computations of various kinds. Early methods of counting and calculating included *counting on the fingers* (Iran, 1966), the use in Peru of the *quipu*, a knotted cord employed for accounting and census purposes (Peru, 1972), and various forms of the *abacus* (Colombia, 1977*).

A major advance occurred in the seventeenth century with the invention of logarithms by John Napier and Henry Briggs. This simplified calculations enormously, and quickly led to such practical calculating devices as the *slide rule* (Romania, 1957). Around the same time, the first mechanical calculating machine was described by *Wilhelm Schickard* (West Germany, 1973*). Other early calculating machines, several of which still exist today, were constructed by *Blaise Pascal* (Monaco, 1973) and *Gottfried Wilhelm von Leibniz* (West Germany, 1980).

The central figure of the nineteenth century was *Charles Babbage* (Great Britain, 1991*), who may be said to have pioneered the modern computer age with his difference engine and analytical engine, even though the technology of the time was insufficiently advanced for efficient working versions to be constructed.

The modern computer age started about 50 years ago. The machines of the 1940s were large and cumbersome, and for several years were run using *punched cards* (*q.v.*) (Norway, 1969*), *punched tape* (Switzerland, 1970*; Poland, 1971*), or *magnetic tape* (Canada 1971*). Advances in electronic technology quickly led to the development of the *integrated circuit* (Japan, 1980*) and the *microchip* (Great Britain, 1989*).

Computers themselves came to be used for a wide variety of purposes, ranging from large-scale machines (Ivory Coast, 1972*; East Germany, 1966*) to conventional small-scale office equipment (Denmark, 1965). Recent technological developments have enabled computers to become increasingly compact, and desk computers in homes and offices are now commonplace (India, 1985; Austria, 1987).

Finally, computers have been used increasingly in the design of stamps. An interesting example is the set of five computer-designed stamps produced on the Eindhoven computer (Netherlands, 1970).

---

*See color insert page CP-12 for these stamps.

References

For several years, the quarterly Springer-Verlag publication *Mathematical Intelligencer* has featured a "Stamp Corner" written by the author of this article. The stamps depicted feature mathematicians and mathematical topics, many of which relate to the history of computation.

Philamath, A Journal of Mathematical Philately, is published by the Mathematical Study Unit of the American Topical Association. For information, contact Secretary-Treasurer Estelle A. Buccino, 135 Witherspoon Court, Athens, GA 30606.

ROBIN J. WILSON

STANDARDS

For articles on related subjects *see* COMPUTER GRAPHICS: STANDARDS; DATA COMMUNICATIONS STANDARDS; KEYBOARD STANDARDS; and PROGRAMMING LANGUAGE STANDARDS.

Overview *Standards* are one of the hallmarks of an industrial society. As a society becomes increasingly complex and its industrial base begins to emerge, it becomes necessary for the products, processes, and procedures of the society to fit together and to interoperate. This interoperation provides the basis for greater integration of the elements of the society, which in turn causes increased social interdependency and complexity.

There are three basic types of standards used in industry in the U. S. *de jure, de facto,* and *regulatory. De jure* standards are created by a body empowered to "create" standards, normally called a Standards Developing Organization (SDO). The SDO operates under a set of rules that encourages participation and consensus in creation of standards, and tends to standardize a product, process, service, or technology. (The use of very precise rules on participation, consensus, and operation frees the participants from prosecution under anti-trust statutes in the U. S.) Examples of SDOs are Accredited Standards Committee (ASC) X3 for information processing systems, ASC T1 for telecommunications, Accredited Organization (AO) IEEE for electrical engineering standards, and ASC Z39 for library and information science. According to the International Organization for Standardization (ISO) and the International Electrotechnical Commission (IEC), a standard is formally defined as being a "document, established by consensus and approved by a recognized body that provides for common and repeated use, rules, guidelines, or characteristics for activities or their results aimed at an achievement of the optimum degree of order in a given context. *Note:* Standards should be based upon the consolidated results of science, technology, and experience and aimed at the promotion of optimum community benefits." (*ISO/IEC Guide 2.*) *De facto* standards, on the other hand, are those products that have gained market acceptance and are recognized as the product against which others will be compared. A good example of a *de facto* standard is the AT&T operating system called Unix (*q.v.*), which, while not a formal standard, is accepted by the industry as an open operating system and an effective

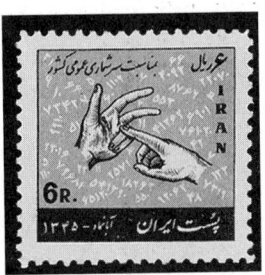

Iran

Peru

Romania

Monaco

West Germany

Denmark

India

Austria

Netherlands

Netherlands

Netherlands

Netherlands

Netherlands

industry standard. On occasion, consortia attempt to create de facto standards if they cannot find a comparable de jure standard to implement. Finally, regulatory standards are standards (usually, but not always, de jure) that have been accepted by a government and have legal force behind them and governmental ability to force acceptance and use. Most safety and environmental standards fall into this category.

The importance of standardization to the U. S. economy is significant, but it is one of the more overlooked areas of economic activity in the U. S., with less than 15 institutions of higher learning offering any coursework on the subject. The cost of industrial standardization (i.e. the creation and implementation of standards by industrial users) to the U.S. has been estimated at between $17 billion and $30 billion each year.

The rules and activities governing standardization in the U.S. are different from those in much of the rest of the world. The U.S. maintains an economy in which there is no dominant participant in the standards environment, including the government. In most of the rest of the world, however, standards and standardization are seen as methods of deliberate economic control, a situation that has been recently (1991) exacerbated by the growing tendency for governments to use standards in a regulatory fashion for trade reasons. This is an area that will form the basis of much contention in the 1990s, and is currently a subject of the Uruguay GATT talks.

Information Technology Standardization

Information technology (IT) standardization is one of the largest standardization arenas in the world. Over a quarter of all international standards published are in the IT arena, and the percentage is growing. Because IT technologies are complex, applicable standards take time to develop, while the products that are developed from the standards have an increasingly short life span.

Within the IT industry, the shortening of the product life cycle has led to the creation of "anticipatory standards," (i.e. standards developed in advance of the general implementation of technology in products). Standards bodies have become forums where viable technology is standardized to allow widespread implementation. This has caused unforeseen problems in product creation and testing, but has also created multi-billion dollar markets for products crafted from these standards.

Anticipatory standards have another important role within the industry as well. They act as "change agents" for the IT industry, driving the direction of the industry by their very existence. As an example, the concept of the Open Systems Interconnection (OSI - q.v.) was based upon a known technology—that of using a layered protocol for message transmission. The concept of a layered protocol is based upon the idea that separate elements of a communications system can be discretely described. While not an exact parallel, the idea of a telephone system with telephones, telephone wires, switching systems, electrical converters, and other equipment that can be isolated for improvement or repair without destroying the system is a good analogy. The standardization of OSI began long before there were OSI products on the market. As OSI

progressed, it was made into product sets and the market for these OSI products began to develop. Standards bodies created both the technical response to the market need and the specification to develop products, and in so doing, they changed the way that the IT industry looked at communication protocols.

Standards development can be seen to have a five-stage life cycle:

Stage 1: *External to the formal process*
Preconceptualization (or market verification of need)

Stages 2, 3, and 4: *Within the formal standards process*
Conceptualization (where technical capability is verified and assignment to an SDO is made)
Discussion (where the committee understands its mission and defines the task at hand, as well as a methodology for succeeding)
Writing (in which complex mathematical algorithms are turned into unambiguous native language statements)

Stage 5: *External to the formal process*
Implementation (where the standard is actually put into practice)

Each of the stages of the life cycle has a great deal more complexity than indicated in the preceding list. The first and last stages—outside of the formal process—are poorly understood, and it is from these areas that most of the current contention over IT standards is derived.

There is a growing tendency within the IT standardization arena to use vendor consortia to define and implement standards. For the most part, however, vendor consortia have become quickly bogged down in areas of marketing and countermarketing claims and have wasted their advantage, which is that of a closed group able to make the compromises necessary to allow quicker implementation of standardized solutions. While these consortia originally proposed to act more quickly than SDOs in these areas because they did not have to follow formal rules to reach consensus, they have found that formal rules provided structure and forced groups to work for a solution. At this writing (1992), no vendor consortium has managed to achieve the purposes for which it was originally chartered.

There is one final issue that will become critical within the U. S. over the next several years—the specter of de jure standards being used as regulatory standards. This concern is especially high during the creation of the unified Europe that is exemplified by the European initiative to harmonize the economic requirements of the European Community by 1992 (EC 92). Much of the potential of EC 92 for Europe is predicated upon the successful implementation of standards, and this implementation, in some cases, can or will be mandated. The method that will probably be chosen for implementing this course of action will be by mandating successful completion of conformance tests supplied by either the government or a governmental agency. In this case, the conformance test suite subsumes the function of the full standard, since vendors of products, goods, and services will create products to satisfy the test suite rather than the standard itself. Tests and the creation of conformance tests and test methodology will then replace the standard.

Standardization Organizations

There are various types and kinds of standardization organizations, from international SDOs to academic consortia, each having a distinct place in the standards development hierarchy. This examination will look at SDOs (from an international, national, and governmental point of view), and then examine consortia and similar organizations, including regional quasi-SDO organizations.

Standards Developing Organizations (SDOs) The premier standards organization is the International Organization for Standardization (ISO), located in Geneva, Switzerland, The ISO, which covers nearly every aspect of standardization (from machine screws to ornamental garden rocks), was born in the post–World War II era of common international cooperative efforts. It was intended to unify standardization activities throughout the world, both to improve cooperation and to lessen national trade barriers. It is recognized today as being the international body for standards in most major areas, with electrotechnical devices (International Electrotechnical Commission [IEC]) and telecommunications/telegraphy (International Telecommunication Union [ITU]) being excepted from the ISO's purview. Voting in all of these organizations is by nation (i.e. the U.S. has one vote, as do Ghana, Switzerland, and Japan). The voting member of the ISO and the IEC for the U. S. is the American National Standards Institute (ANSI), which is recognized by the ISO as being the most representative standards body in the U.S.

Until the late 1980s, both the IEC and ISO had committees devoted to looking at information technology standardization. However, with the growth of systems standards in the 1980s, the various IT-focused standardization committees of these two organizations began to expand their various scopes, leading to "turf wars" within the standards community. After several years of negotiations, the first joint ISO/IEC committee was created to deal with matters of information technology. This is ISO/IEC Joint Technical Committee 1 (JTC 1), the only joint ISO/IEC committee and the only internationally recognized committee that deals exclusively with IT standards and standardization. JTC 1 is also the largest and most prolific standards committee in existence. It currently has 22 Primary (or voting) members and 19 Observer (non-voting but contributing) members. The Secretariat for JTC 1 is held by ANSI. The Secretariat is the administrative arm of the standards organization. Because the SDO is normally composed of unpaid volunteers who cannot devote their full time to the SDO, a core paid staff (the Secretariat) is needed to administer the day-to-day affairs of the Technical Committee. It is an expensive honor; the JTC 1 Secretariat costs several million dollars a year to maintain. The JTC 1 Secretariat is responsible for scheduling meetings, maintaining documents and document registers, insuring that members receive mailings, and all of the other tasks associated with

keeping track of 2,500 documents and 3,500 volunteers in 41 nations every year.

JTC 1 is composed of Subcommittees (SCs) that deal with specific areas of IT. Because of the heavy workload associated with SCs, each SC also has a Secretariat, all of whom report to the JTC 1 Secretariat at ANSI. JTC 1 currently has 18 SCs, with the following areas of interest and national Secretariats:

SC 1:	Vocabulary	France
SC 2:	Character Sets and Information Coding	France
SC 6:	Data Communications	U.S.
SC 7:	Design and Documentation	Canada
SC 11:	Flexible Magnetic Media	U.S.
SC 14:	Representation of Data Elements	Sweden
SC 15:	Labeling and File Structure	Switzerland
SC 17:	Identification and Credit Cards	Switzerland
SC 18:	Text and Office Systems	U.S.
SC 21:	Open Systems Support Services	U.S.
SC 22:	Languages	Canada
SC 23:	Optical Digital Data Disks	Japan
SC 24:	Graphics	Germany
SC 25:	Interconnection and Information Technology	Germany
SC 26:	Microprocessor Systems	Japan
SC 27:	Security Techniques	Germany
SC 28:	Office Machinery and Stand Alone Printers	Japan
SC 29:	Coded Representation for Hypermedia	France

These subcommittees (and their subordinate Working Groups [WGs]) are the standards-creating organizations of JTC 1. The entire ISO standards process revolves around these committees. This is where the need for a standard is reviewed and accepted, where a draft is written and circulated, and where the technical accuracy of the standard is assured (as much as possible.) Upon the completion of the Working Draft (WD), a vote within the WG is taken to determine if the WD should be made into a Committee Draft (CD). If the ballot is positive, the CD is forwarded for further ballot by the Subcommittee for acceptance as a Draft International Standard (DIS). Again a balloting process occurs, and, if successful, the document becomes an International Standard after review, discussion, and approval by the JTC 1. These steps can take between 2 and 8 years to complete, with the variance in time resulting from technical complexity, political and national infighting, and any of a host of other reasons, including random intransigence. All of the participants are volunteers who participate from a belief in the intrinsic merit of what they are doing.

National Standards Bodies Most nations have a single SDO that oversees creation of national standards. In Germany, the organization is the Deutsches Institut für Normung e.V. (DIN); in Canada, the Canadian Standards Association; and so on. However, in the U. S., there is an umbrella organization—The American National Standards Institute (ANSI). It keeps the rules by which standards are written and accredits organizations that write standards by the rules that ANSI publishes. The rules have a twofold aim: allowing free and open participation to any concerned party, and the achievement of consensus in the creation of a standard. Consensus can best be defined as a state achieved when all parties reach a substantial agreement. This definition indicates more than majority approval, but does not imply unanimity. Rather, it indicates that all arguments have been heard, addressed, and dealt with in a constructive fashion.

ANSI usually accredits any organization to write standards that will agree to follow its rules. In theory, there are eight Standards Boards charged with insuring that there is no overlap between organizations accredited to write standards. In truth, the boards, which meet for 4 hours four times a year, cannot manage the complexities within their own disciplines, let alone between board areas. As an example of the potential confusion, the standardization activities necessary for a robotics (*q.v.*) assembly plant fall—if considered separately—among many of these groups (metallurgy, testing, IT, manufacturing, quality). However, the group that looks at the manufacturing standardization activities may permit the creation of a group to do floor-level local area network (LAN - *q.v.*), protocols, since these are intrinsic to the creation of a robotics activity. In the best of all worlds, this standardization activity would belong to the IT board, as part of a general standardization of LAN protocols which might not be what is needed by the manufacturing industries. Similarly, the quality arena may establish its right to determine how to create quality software, although software creation is definitely within the purview of the IT arena. This has led to accreditation of over 230 separate SDOs in the U.S., usually with poorly defined charters and overlapping responsibilities.

ANSI's position in the U.S. standards hierarchy is derived from its authority in two areas—the sole right to publish American National Standards (ANS) and all that this implies, and its position as the sole U.S. representative to ISO. In the first instance, it will succeed only as long as the appellation "ANS" has meaning to the U.S. industry and government. In the second case, it will be effective only as long as it retains a perceived leadership of the U.S. involvement in international standardization efforts.

ANSI accredits three types of organizations to write standards. The first is a canvass organization, which is highly informal and focused upon a single issue. It works by gathering consensus in what might be viewed as a single pass. Because it is a single committee of the whole, it has little chance of creating a standard from technology; normally it concentrates upon standardizing an existing process or product.

The Accredited Organization (AO) is an organization or professional society that has been organized to do something (usually continuing member education in a discipline) that also wants to create standards around that discipline. The Institute for Electrical and Electronic Engineering (IEEE) is one such organization, as is the American Association for Quality Control (ASQC), both of which are labeled as AOs when it comes to writing standards.

The Accredited Standards Committee (ASC) is an organization of professionals whose only function is to create standards. ASC X3 is the ASC for IT standards, ASC Z1 the organization for Quality Control standards, and so on. As noted above, the AO IEEE and ASC X3 overlap, as do AO ASQC and ASC Z1.

National input to ISO (and hence to JTC 1) is through ANSI, which votes the U. S. national position. However, because ANSI does not have the technical competence to create an opinion, it uses an organization called a Technical Advisory Group (TAG). The TAG that advises ANSI on JTC 1 matters is called the JTC 1 TAG, and is composed of all impacted U. S. SDOs. (This includes ASC X3, AO IEEE, ASC T1, and AO EIA.)

All of these committees operate under the concept of review and consensus, and all are bound by their charters to follow ANSI rules in the creation of standards. Of the over 200 SDOs accredited by ANSI, the most important in IT standardization is the ASC X3. X3 produces approximately 90% of the IT standards in the U. S. and contributes to approximately 90% of the worldwide IT standards. AO IEEE produces the bulk of the remainder of the IT standards in the U. S., but has little impact on the course of international standardization.

ASC X3 was created in 1960, and has as its Secretariat the Computer and Business Equipment Manufacturer's Association (CBEMA). As Secretariat, CBEMA guarantees to meet the financial, legal, and administrative needs of X3; it has no further control or management functions. (Because ASC X3 is a legal fiction, CBEMA stands as the organization that represents a legal reality for action for and against the activities of X3.) ASC X3 consists of a general committee of the whole that meets approximately three times a year, three management committees, and seven general Technical Committees. Additionally, X3 members are part of the JTC 1 by virtue of being part of X3.

X3, as a committee of the whole, attempts to maintain a balance in its membership of producers, users, and general interest groups to insure that the process is not skewed in favor of any singular interest. Membership is open to any interested organization and requires payment of nominal dues. Voting is by organization (i.e. no company can flood a committee and gain a disproportionate advantage in standards creation). ASC X3 sets broad policy, general direction, and votes on each proposed standard that comes to it for action from the Technical Committees.

The three Management Committees of X3 are the Standards Planning and Requirements Committee (SPARC), the Strategic Planning Committee (SPC), and the Secretariat Management Committee (SMC). SPARC focuses on the day-to-day management of the technical committees, reviewing the standards project proposals and insuring that the technical committees produce required standards in a timely manner. SPC is responsible for the long-range view of standards and standardization (i.e. what will be happening several years later in the industry, where the technical and managerial trends are going, and where X3 should be moving). Finally, SMC is responsible for the administration of the Secretariat's business and leadership activities, including officer appointment, financial activities, operating procedures, and finances.

The Technical Committees (TCs) of X3 are divided into eight major areas, with Technical Management Committees overseeing the TCs. These areas are:

X3A   Recognition
    X3A1   OCR and MICR

X3B   Media
    X3B5   Digital Magnetic Media
    X3B6   Instrumentation Tape
    X3B7   Magnetic Disks
    X3B8   Flexible Disk Cartridges
    X3B9   Paper Forms/Layouts
    X3B10   Credit/ID Cards
    X3B11   Optical Digital Data Disks

X3H&J   Languages
    X3H2   Database
    X3H3   Computer Graphics
    X3H4   Information Resource and Dictionary (IRDS)
    X3H5   Parallel Processing Constructs for High Level Programming Languages
    X3H6   Case Tools
    X3H7   Object Oriented Languages
    X3J1   PL/1
    X3J2   Basic
    X3J3   Fortran
    X3J4   Cobol
    X3J7   APT
    X3J9   Pascal
    X3J10   APL
    X3J11   C Language
    X3J12   DIBOL
    X3J13   Common Lisp
    X3J14   Forth
    X3J15   Databus
    X3J16   C++
    X3J17   Prolog
    X3J18   Rexx

X3K   Documentation
    X3K1   Computer Documentation
    X3K5   Vocabulary for Information Processing Standards

X3L   Data Representation
    X3L2   Codes and Character Sets
    X3L3   Audio/Picture Coding
    X3L5   Labels and File Structures
    X3L8   Data Representation

X3S   Communication
    X3S3   Data Communication

X3T&V   Systems Technology
    X3T1   Data Encryption
    X3T2   Data Interchange
    X3T3   Open Distributed Processing
    X3T4   Security Techniques
    X3T5   Open Systems Interconnection (OSI)
    X3T6   Non-Contact Information Systems Interfaces
    X3T7   Internationalization
    X3T9   I/O Interface
    X3V1   Text and Office Publishing Systems

X3W1   Office Machines

While many of these committees are simple to explain (e.g. the Cobol committee is concerned with Cobol), it is important to understand that each of these committees retains liaison with most of the of the other committees that will impact its activities. This means that the Cobol committee must be aware of changes in the way that languages are used, and it must be able and willing to respond to these changes as they impact Cobol. If "object orientation" or "network management" is seen as necessary in environments in which Cobol is specified, then the Cobol committee must understand these activities and merge them into the next iteration of the Cobol standard. This form of activity accounts for much of the work of the older committees. As the technology changes, the standards must change to be able to take advantage of the newer technology.

The work of X3T5 (Open Systems Interconnection - *q.v.*) is also worth examining. This committee is in the process of creating (in conjunction with ISO/IEC SC 21) the national and international standards for OSI—an undertaking that has already consumed nearly 10 years and produced over 300 standards describing how to implement various technical aspects of OSI. However, before these standards could be written, the model for interconnection had to be established and agreed to, as did the reason for the model, the application of the concept (what it could and couldn't do), and what the precise scope of each standard would be. Some of this was planned, and some of it was evolutionary. Once this was completed, the writing of the standards could begin. The standards had to be independent of any specific hardware technology, since the standards had to work across disparate vendors' hardware over the next 20 years. Further, the standards had to interrelate even though they were created independently by multiple committees, both national and international. Finally, all compromises in any one of the standards (for political or national reasons) had to be able to be handled in all of the other standards activities. To complicate matters even further, the lower four layers of the OSI model are the province of X3S3, data communications, and ISO/IEC JTC 1 SC 6, which must also be involved in the work that X3T5 does.

As a final example, the X3T9 committee (I/O interfaces) is dealing with new and difficult approaches to systems integration of computers. Originally begun to create disk interface standards, the committee now is creating local area network standards in the high-speed arena (greater than 70 megabits per second), since low-speed LANS are the province of the IEEE 802 committee. However, the creation of high-speed LANS and high-speed disk interconnects is not substantially different, except that there is a distance factor and usage factor involved.

If it was merely the matter of transferring data, the methodology would be simple. However, there are also the problems of distance (a LAN is local; a metropolitan area network (*q.v.*) can stretch for miles), usage (internal or external to a building), source of information (network or similar or disparate devices), timing and redundancy requirements, and applications, all of which vary tremendously. X3T9 is currently working on lower-level interfaces (the Small Computer Systems Interconnect [SCSI] found on most personal computers is a product of this committee), device level interfaces (that permit greater innovation in the peripheral industry), and the Fiber Distributed Data Interface (FDDI), which uses optical fibers for data transmission. The FDDI is probing new technologies in both the concept and the application, which makes the creation of this standard not only difficult, but where there is a need to be extremely cautious.

The AO IEEE is the second IT SDO in the U.S. Although it has international participation, it is a U. S. SDO and, as such, works through the JTC 1 TAG and ANSI to present its views to ISO. The IEEE is primarily an organization devoted to education and continued professional training of electrical engineers, but publishes standards as a sideline. The IEEE has multiple societies representing multiple disciplines. The society that is most significant in IT standardization is the IEEE Computer Society (*q.v.*). It operates in much the same way as ASC X3, since it adheres to ANSI rules on consensus. It has its own structure for creating standards, and produces primarily non-systems standards. Its two best known standards activities are the IEEE 802 series of LANs and the language POSIX, a portable set of calls to operating systems that provides some measure of application portability.

Standardization Consortia Standardization consortia are a relatively recent addition to the world of standardization. They do not produce standards *per se*, rather they provide input to SDOs and testing and implementation specifications for completed standards. Because most software and systems standards contain options, there needs to be a group—usually outside the standards process—that selects implementable subsets of the options contained in the standard. As an example of a successful consortia, the SQL Access Group (SAG) has taken the SQL standard and provided implementation guidelines for the standard, indicating what options work together to accomplish a task at hand. Additionally, some consortia provide testing and conformance validation, find holes or oversights in standards, and also find problems and bugs with the standard. They normally work in close conjunction with the SDOs and are useful adjuncts to the work of SDOs.

Governmental Agencies The National Institute for Standards and Technology (NIST) replaced the old National Bureau of Standards (NBS) in 1989. The Computer Systems Laboratory (CSL) is the federal government's primary player in the standardization arena. Although a formally chartered SDO in its own right, NIST rarely creates standards, preferring to rely upon the private process. The most important role of NIST is the maintenance of the Federal Information Processing Standards (FIPS), which are those standards that the government will use in its procurement efforts. By adopting a standard as a FIPS, NIST can cause the market to move to that standard for federal procurement. In this way, NIST has significant clout in the economic policies of standardization.

References

1984. Cerni, Dorothy M. *Standards in Process: Foundations and Profiles of ISDN and OSI Studies.* Washington, D.C.: NTIA Report 84-170.
1984. Toth, R. B. (Ed.). *The Economics of Standardization.* Minneapolis, MN: Standards Engineering Society.
1989. Cargill, Carl F. *Information Technology Standardization; Theory, Process, and Organizations,* Rockport, MA: Digital Press.
1990. U.S. Congress, Office of Technology Assessment, (Linda Garcia, Project Director). *Critical Connections: Communication for the Future* (OTA-CIT-407). Washington, DC: U.S. GAO.
1990. Berg, J. L. and Schumny, H. (Ed.) *An Analysis of the Information Technology Standardization Process.* Amsterdam: Elsevier Science Publisher B. V.

CARL F. CARGILL

STAR NETWORK. *See* DISTRIBUTED SYSTEMS; and LOCAL AREA NETWORK.

STATEMENT

For articles on related subjects *see* CONTROL STRUCTURES; DECLARATION; DEFAULT CONDITION; DELIMITER; EXECUTABLE STATEMENT; EXPRESSION; PROCEDURE-ORIENTED LANGUAGES; PROGRAMMING LANGUAGES; and STRUCTURED PROGRAMMING.

In much the same way that a sentence is the structural unit of expression in a stream of natural language discourse, the *statement* may be viewed as the elemental organizational component of a high-level language program. As such, it embodies a unit of activity in terms of the algorithm being implemented. This is quite different from, and bears no direct correspondence with, processor activity. Although many types of statements are *executable* in that they instigate the high-level language compiler to produce operationally equivalent sequences of machine language instructions, this relationship is arbitrary: A given type of statement may be expanded or contracted to designate a wide range of activities, all within the syntax of that statement. For example, the following two statements:

```
A = 7.82
B = (22.4 + (X/Y)**3) * (X*Y - Z)
```

are both syntactically legitimate assignment statements in the Fortran language, but there is clearly a considerable difference in the amount of computation each one specifies. This is completely consistent with the underlying idea that the user, rather than the processor, be the determining factor with regard to the amount of processing expressed in a high-level language statement.

Not all high-level language statements can be related to instructions in the machine language program ultimately produced. Many languages include statement types whose primary purpose is not to convey the intent of an algorithm, but rather to provide supportive information for compilation and other processes auxiliary to the actual execution of the program. These statements, which pertain to matters such as the allocation of storage and description of variables, correspond to a range of activities that do not generally show up as equivalent sequences of machine instructions. Accordingly, they are *nonexecutable*, and usually are treated as a distinct syntactic set of statements called *declarations*.

It is not always possible to provide the programmer with unlimited scope for expression in a single statement. Yet such capability is needed if the linkage between the statement and a meaningful activity is to be preserved. There are innumerable occasions in which a sequence of associated events, while clearly identifiable as a single procedural activity, contains arbitrarily diverse machine processes whose specification in a single statement would be linguistically impractical. Most high-level languages accommodate this necessity by allowing some type of compound construction. In some cases the construction is formed as a single statement with multiple clauses; in others, the idea of the *compound* statement is implemented as a group of single statements enclosed in special organizational statements or special words that serve as *delimiters* (*see* STRUCTURED PROGRAMMING).

Executable Statements Since these statement types are characterized by their ultimate relationship to explicit processing action in the object program, their general form tends to resemble the imperative sentence in many natural languages. Accordingly, it often is true that the language elements used for specifying activities are verbs. For example, an input activity in Pascal is expressed in the form

```
read(filename, list)
```

where *filename* and *list* specify the source and destination of the input, respectively. The same construction prevails when data are to be transmitted from the central processor to the outside world, with the verb `write` indicating the direction. When similarity to natural language is a primary design objective, the correspondence may be more pronounced, as in the following Cobol statement:

```
ADD a TO b GIVING c.
```

The narrative construction persists in an alternative, more formulaic form:

```
COMPUTE c = a + b.
```

The Basic language designates the same operations in a similar manner:

```
LET c = a + b.
```

The words `COMPUTE` and `LET` are included in the fixed vocabularies of their respective languages specifically to enhance the parallels with "real" sentences; the language

translators clearly can operate properly without them, as they do in such languages as Fortran, Pascal, and C (*q.v.*). It should be noted, however, that the absence of such verbs does not change the inherently imperative syntax: though now more implicit, it still remains. Thus, the Pascal statement equivalent to the previous examples, namely,

$$c := a + b;$$

can be read as a highly implicit form of this sentence: "The value in *c* is to be replaced by the result of the indicated operation on *a* and *b*."

The same construction generally carries over to compound statements. Though high-level languages vary in the type and extent of compounding their syntaxes allow, there is one category of compound activity sufficiently basic to all computing work to compel its representation across the entire spectrum of high-level languages. This is the fundamental decision mechanism in which a comparison is specified in conjunction with procedural alternatives based on the outcome of that comparison. In programmers' argot, this is termed the IF-THEN-ELSE construct. A "natural" way to articulate such a construction would be with some form of conditional sentence: "If a particular condition exists, take the action specified here; if it does not exist, ignore that action and perform this alternative action." This construction is followed closely in many languages.

To illustrate this, consider the situation in which two variables, X and Y, are to be compared. If X is less than Y, the X value is to be doubled; otherwise, X is to be decreased by 8.2. In either case, a variable Z is to be computed as the product XY. The appropriate compound statements for several languages are:

```
(Cobol)        IF X IS LESS THAN Y
               MULTIPLY X BY 2
                       ELSE SUBTRACT 8.2
               FROM X.
               COMPUTE Z = X*Y.

(Fortran 90)   IF (X .LT. Y) THEN
                   X = 2.0*X
                               ELSE
                   X = X - 8.2
               END IF
               Z = X*Y

(Pascal)       if X < Y then X := 2*X
                       else X := X - 8.2 ;
               Z := X*Y;
```

These languages provide a variety of structural features that enable such decision mechanisms to be extended. One such extension, for example, allows either or both alternative actions at the ends of an **if** statement to be **if** statements themselves.

The ability to treat arbitrarily long sequences as single procedural activities receives formal emphasis in languages such as Pascal, whose vocabulary includes special organizational statements to indicate the bounds of such sequences. This is intended to encourage a modular approach to program design wherein the implementation of an algorithm is treated as a synthesis of related but logically (and structually) distinct activities. Languages so oriented are often termed *block structured* languages (*q.v.*). In Pascal, for example, decision alternatives may be extended arbitrarily by bracketing them with **begin** and **end** *delimiters*. C uses { and } for this purpose.

On a somewhat larger scale, this method is used to enclose subprograms and other major program components (e.g. SUBROUTINE and END delimiters in Fortran, and **repeat** and **until** in Pascal).

Concurrent Statements

Technological advances have broadened interests in concurrent processes beyond their traditional association with the design and implementation of supervisory software. Feasible applications have emerged in which it is desirable to specify parallel computing activities (generally, parts of larger processes); i.e. a collection of activities whose overall outcome is to be independent of the sequence in which the activities are begun or performed.

Accordingly, facilities for specifying such processes, originally confined to low-level languages, have been incorporated into some high-level languages. One of the first languages to address this problem is concurrent Pascal, a derivative of Pascal developed by Per Brinch Hansen. Compound statements, subprograms, and programs are organized as in any block-structured sequential language. However, processing components, despite their resemblance to "main programs" in the traditional sense, will not execute until triggered by another program that establishes their concurrency and actually gets them started. The structure shown below, for example, specifies a complex of three procedures, any or all of which could be executing in parallel. Depending on the physical configuration available, these procedures may actually be running simultaneously, or, in an environment with a single processor, any or all may be started but not yet complete.

type P1 = *process* (list of pertinent components)	
var Declarations for P1	P1's
begin Activities for P1	Definition
end.	

type P2 = *process* (list of pertinent components)	
var Declarations for P2	P2's
begin Activities for P2	Definition
end.	

type P3 = *process* (list of pertinent components)	
var Declarations for P3	P3's
begin Activities for P3	Definition
end.	

var pname1:P1; pname2:P2; pname3:P3;	Activation of Concurrent Processes
begin init pname1, pname2, pname3;	pname1, pname2, pname3.
end.	(pname1 is an instance of a P1 type process, etc.)

Nonexecutable Statements

Completion of a high-level language program usually requires the inclusion of declarative statements (*declarations*) that do not correspond directly to steps in the algorithm being implemented. Rather, they provide the compiler with essential information from which it may determine the allocation of storage and other organizational characteristics of the final program. The command structure in these nonexecutable statements bears a less consistent resemblance to the imperative sentence than is found in other statement types.

A primary type of information transmitted by such statements concerns the definition and description of variables to be used in a program. For example, each of the following statements:

(Fortran)	`REAL X, Y` `    INTEGER Z`
(Pascal)	**var** x, y : real; z : integer;

associates the names *x* and *y* with certain amounts of storage, indicating further that the contents of these locations are to be treated as numerical vlaues in floating-point form. In addition, the name *z* is associated with storage whose contents represent an integer value. Note that the expandability inherent in other statement types is available here, too, since it is possible to combine an arbitrary number of different declarations in a single statement.

Definition of entire arrays is no more complicated, since the same basic descriptive structure is used, augmented by information about the array's extent and organization. For instance, the following declarations:

(Fortran)	`REAL X, Y` `    INTEGER Z(18)`
(Pascal)	**var** x, y : real; z: **array** [1.18] **of** integer;

define variables *x, y,* and *z* as they did above, except that *z* now is an array of 18 elements, each of whose contents accommodates (and expects) an integer value.

References

1967. Higman, B. *A Comparative Study of Programming Languages.* New York: Elsevier.

1969. Sammet, J. *Programming Languages—History and Fundamentals.* Englewood Cliffs, NJ: Prentice-Hall.

1978. Brinch Hansen, P. *The Architecture of Concurrent Programs.* Englewood Cliffs, NJ: Prentice-Hall.

1988. Wilson, L.B. and Clark, R.G. *Comparative Programming Languages.* Reading, MA: Addison-Wesley.

SEYMOUR V. POLLACK AND THEODOR D. STERLING

STATISTICAL APPLICATIONS

For articles on related subjects *see* LEAST SQUARES APPROX-
IMATION; MATHEMATICAL PROGRAMMING; MATHEMATICAL SOFT-
WARE; MATRIX COMPUTATIONS; NUMERICAL ANALYSIS; REGRESSION
ANALYSIS; and SIMPLEX METHOD.

At the beginning of the 1980s, there were fewer than
20 commercial statistical software "packages." At the beginning of the 1990s, there were about 500 packages, and
the annual revenue to the producers of those packages
approaches one-half billion dollars. This explosion in the
availability of software to perform statistical calculations
has caused a corresponding increase in both the available
methodology and in the diversity of applications.

There is an extensive literature on computational
techniques for the application of statistical methods.
Standard graduate-level textbooks include Kennedy and
Gentle (1980), Maindonald (1984), and Thisted (1988).
There are a number of journals publishing current re-
search in the area. Among these are *The Journal of Com-
putational and Graphical Statistics, Computing and
Statistics*, and *Computational Statistics and Data Analysis*.

Not every package includes every statistical method,
but several standard methods are included in most general-purpose packages and there are many special-purpose packages that include one or more of the less
common statistical methods.

Methods   The standard methods include regression
analysis, analysis of variance, discrete data analysis, cluster analysis, and time series analysis.

Regression analysis is used for exploring relationships
between continuous variables. In its simplest form,
a response variable is assumed to be a linear function of various predictor variables, and the coefficients of the predictor variables are estimated by
the method of least squares. More complex forms of
this method involve nonlinear relationships between the response and the predictors, multivariate responses, and robust methods for estimating
the coefficients. An introduction to the method can
be found in Weisberg (1985).

Analysis of variance is used for exploring relationships
between a continuous response variable and categorical predictor variables. Such data often arises
from designed experiments. In its simplest form,
the response variable is assumed to be a linear
function of the predictor variables, and the analysis
assigns a portion of the squared variation in the
response to each of the predictors. More complex
forms of this method involve intentionally complex
patterns in the predictor variables (fractional
designs), continuous predictor variables (covari-
ates), nonlinear relationships (response surface
methods), and multivariate responses. An introduction to the method can be found in Box, Hunter,
and Hunter (1978).

Discrete data analysis is used for exploring relationships between a categorical response variable and

categorical predictor variables. In its simplest form
the natural logarithm of the number of responses
in a category is assumed to be a linear function
of the predictor variables. This method is also
called the method of *loglinear models*. More complex forms of this method involve hierarchical and
other relationships among the predictor variables,
continuous predictor variables, nonlinear relationships, and multivariate responses. An introduction
to the method can be found in Santner and Duffy
(1989).

Time series analysis is used for exploring the relationship between a continuous response variable
and time (or some other single-ordered variable,
such as distance). The methods of analysis fall
naturally into two categories: time-domain methods and frequency-domain methods. The time-domain methods are similar in many respects to
regression analysis, with previous values of the
single response variable serving as predictor variables. The frequency-domain methods are also
similar in many respects to regression analysis; in
this case, phase-shifted cosine functions of various
frequencies serve as the predictor variables. An
introduction to the method can be found in Kendall
and Ord (1990).

Cluster analysis, sometimes called *numerical taxonomy*,
is used for grouping similar objects. When the number and identification of the groups is assumed
known, the method is often called *classification*.
Cluster analysis is distinguished from other statistical methods by the fact that each cluster analytic
method is specified by the algorithm used to calculate the results rather than by the model used to
describe the data. An introduction to the method
can be found in Hartigan (1976).

Applications   The applications listed below give
some indication of the breadth of application of statistical
methods:

Epidemiology—A major risk to public health in the U.S.
appeared during the 1980s and reached epidemic
proportions by 1990: Acquired Immune Deficiency
Syndrome (AIDS) and its etiologic agent, the human
immunodeficiency virus (HIV). The first cases of
AIDS were reported in 1981. By 1990, the cumulative
number of cases exceeded 150,000. Statistical methods were used in the earliest studies of the etiology
of AIDS. Evidence for sexual transmission of the
disease first came from controlled clinical trials
among gay men. Unusual clusters of cases were
found among sex partners and between blood
transfusion recipients and donors.

Space—On 27 January 1986, the space shuttle Challenger exploded shortly after lift-off. The Presidential Commission on the Space Ship Challenger
Accident (the Rogers Commission) subsequently
determined that the cause of the explosion was a
combustion gas leak through a joint in one of the
two booster rockets, which was sealed by an O-ring.

A subsequent statistical analysis of O-ring data from 23 of the 24 pre-Challenger flights by the Shuttle Criticality Review Hazard Analysis Audit Committee of the National Research Council (a review recommended by the Rogers Commission) strongly supports the conclusion that O-rings do not seal properly at low temperature. Furthermore, that analysis showed that (based on the pre-accident data) the probability of catastrophic O-ring failure at a temperature of 31° Farenheit (the actual temperature at lift-off) was 16%.

Physics—In 1986, the Committee on Data for Science and Technology (CODATA) of the International Council of Scientific Unions released new estimates of the fundamental physical constants. These constants include the speed of light, the gravitational constant, the mass of the proton, Avogadro's constant, and other, more esoteric, constants. The constants are of fundamental importance in the analysis and interpretation of large numbers of experiments in many scientific disciplines. The method by which the constants are estimated is entirely statistical using experimental data. In fact, the estimates are reported together with a relative uncertainty of one standard deviation. The full CODATA report gives the covariance matrix of the estimates, recognizing that not only are the estimates uncertain, but they are dependent on each other.

Forensics—DNA fingerprinting is a biochemical technique for transforming DNA (the genetic material of living cells) into a visible pattern of bands similar to the UPC bar code that appears on grocery items (*see* UNIVERSAL PRODUCT CODE). It is believed that, except for random variation, these DNA fingerprints are unique to each individual; identical twins have identical DNA, although the prints of their fingertips are not identical. Unfortunately, there is considerable random variation in the process, both in the chemical process used to produce the bands and in the assignment of the bands to various categories. It is essential, therefore, to use statistical methods in the determination of whether two DNA fingerprints match or not.

Testing—The General Aptitude Test Battery (GATB) is a series of 12 tests, taking about 2 1/2 hours to complete, that measure a range of aptitudes. It was originally developed as a distillation of some 100 occupation-specific tests used by government employment services. Beginning in 1981, the United States Employment Service (USES) adopted a plan by which all applicants would be encouraged to take the GATB and all employers would be encouraged to require the GATB. Statistical methods were the basis of the original combination of tests, and statistical methods were behind the 1981 decision. On the basis of unadjusted test scores, relatively few minorities would be referred to jobs. Consequently, the USES adjusts the test scores by a statistical method. This practice has been called into question as reverse discrimination, and in 1990 the

USES began a two-year study to find ways to improve the test.

Demography—The U.S. Decennial Census consists of an Enumeration Phase (EP), in which forms are mailed to every housing unit in the U.S. Those housing units whose occupants do not return completed forms are visited by a census enumerator. After the EP, there is a Post Enumeration Survey (PES) of 150,000 households across the nation; the purpose of the PES is to assess the validity of the data collected in the EP. Some statisticians believe that more accurate estimates of the true population could be made by adjusting the EP numbers based on the PES and other data. Their rationale is that, despite extensive efforts to enumerate everyone, there is a significant undercount and that undercount is allegedly larger for the poor and for minorities. At this writing, Judge Joseph M. McLaughlin is presiding over a federal lawsuit by New York City concerning the legality of adjustment. The judge has held that the U.S. Constitution "is not a bar to statistical adjustment" and that the "concept of statistical adjustment is wholly valid and may very well be long overdue."

References

1976. Hartigan, J. A. *Clustering Algorithms*. New York: John Wiley.

1978. Box, G. E. P., Hunter, W. G., and Hunter, J. S. *Statistics for Experimenters*. New York: John Wiley.

1980. Kennedy, W. J. and Gentle, J. E. *Statistical Computing*. New York: Marcel Dekker.

1984. Maindonald, J. H. *Statistical Computation*. New York: John Wiley.

1985. Weisberg, S. *Applied Linear Regression* (2nd Ed.). New York: John Wiley.

1988. Thisted, R. A. *Elements of Statistical Computing*. New York: Chapman and Hall.

1989. Santner. T. J. and Duffy, D. *The Statistical Analysis of Discrete Data*. New York: Springer-Verlag.

1990. Kendall, M. and Ord, J. K. *Time Series* (3rd Ed.). New York: Oxford University Press.

WILLIAM EDDY

STIBITZ, GEORGE ROBERT

For an article on a related subject *see* BELL LABS RELAY COMPUTERS.

George Robert Stibitz was born in York, Pennsylvania, on 30 April 1904. He grew up in Dayton, Ohio where his father taught ancient languages at a theological seminary of the German Reformed Church. In the seventh grade, he entered the Moraine Park School, an experimental school newly founded by Charles Kettering and Col. Edward Deeds. Its flexible curriculum and small classes provided an excellent environment for intellectual investigation and exploration.

Stibitz developed an interest in mathematics and physics while in high school, and after graduating in 1922 he received a scholarship to Denison University. Upon

FIG. 1. George Stibitz.

graduation from Denison in 1926 with a major in mathematics, Stibitz enrolled in the graduate program at Union College, where he received his M.S. degree in physics in 1927. He then took a year off and went to work for the General Electric Company in Schenectady, N.Y. In 1928, Stibitz enrolled in the Ph. D program at Cornell University. Under the tutelage of his mathematics professor, Wallie Hurwitz, he generalized his interest in the vibrations of the telephone diaphram into his Ph. D study of the differential geometry of a non-planar membrane.

In the summer of 1929, he met his future wife, Dorothea Lamson, and they were married in September 1930, after he had completed his Ph.D and had accepted a position as a "mathematical engineer" with Bell Laboratories, then located on West Street in New York City.

One weekend at home in 1937, observing the similarity between the two-state positions of telephone relays and the binary notation for integers, Stibitz decided to experiment. He fastened two relays from the Bell Labs scrap pile to a piece of plywood, cut strips from a tobacco can, bought two dry cell batteries and some flashlight bulbs, and, with some electrical wire constructed a one-digit binary adder. His colleagues were amused when he showed it to them in the lab the next day. This simple exercise might have ended there except for Stibitz's penchant for generalizing. Further evenings at home were spent sketching circuits for the arithmetic operations. When he presented his ideas to Thornton Fry, the head of the mathematical section at the Laboratory, Fry indicated a curiosity as to whether these little relay calculators could do complex arithmetic, which then involved a fair number of human computers in the Lab. With this target, Stibitz began to draw up relay circuits for the calculation of complex numbers. In February 1938 they were completed, and Stibitz began to work in earnest with Sam Williams, a switching engineer. In 1939, the Complex Calculator was completed and put into use at the Laboratories. The machine was capable of performing all four arithmetic operations. The calculator was operated by remote access from either of three teletype machines located in different parts of the Laboratory. The first public demonstration of the Complex Calculator (and perhaps first remote control of a computer) occurred at a meeting of the American Mathematical Society at Dartmouth College in September 1940. Stibilz presented a paper describing the machine, followed by Dr. Fry showing how a problem could be introduced on a teletypewriter, transmitted to New York, and the answer then received on the teletypewriter. Attendees, among them Norbert Wiener and John Mauchly, were then able to participate in using the Complex Calculator.

In 1940, Stibitz proposed that the Laboratory construct a general-purpose automatic computational device. He had developed circuit drawings to provide for interchangeable taped programs, and assembly language, an error-delection code, and a design for floating-point arithmetic. At this time the lab management showed no interest in the development of a general-purpose computational device. The onset of World War II provided the necessity for the design and contruction of automatic computing machines. The first of a series of relay devices, the Relay Interpolator, was installed on West Street in September 1943. Late in the war it was moved to the Naval Research Laboratory, where it remained until 1961. The Relay Ballistic Computer (two copies, 1943–44) was a general-purpose device, as was its successor, the Error Detector Mark 22. This sequence of relay calculators was later renamed Models 1, 2, 3, and 4. Models 5 (two copies) and 6, the most ambitious of the relay devices, were completed in 1946, 1947, and 1950, respectively. Model 3 (and its successors) contained error detection, halting trouble diagnosis, and an assembly language. Model 5 was the first to implement floating-point arithmetic. Each copy of the Model 5 incorporated a system of two arithmetic units and four problem positions. Problems were loaded into any positions that were idle, and upon the completion of one problem, the computer automatically picked up another. When the models were redesignated, Mrs. Stibitz suggested that the original one-digit binary adder be called Model K for the kitchen table on which it was constructed.

During World War II, Stibitz took a leave of absence from Bell Labs and joined Division 7 (Fire Control) of the NDRC (later OSRD), as a Technical Aide. The Dynamic Tester, a device developed by Division 7 to test and guide the design of newly developed anti-aircraft gun control directors, made great demands on the computers. Model 2 reduced the number of fundamental calculations for the early Dynamic Testers by a factor of about 10, and later models of the relay series further increased the speed and reliability of the calculations, thereby making enormous savings in human labor possible.

Stibitz did not return to the Labs at the end of the war. Instead, he established himself as a private consultant to government and business (1945–1964). One of his projects during this period grew out of his wartime association with Duncan Stewart, later President of the Barber-Coleman Company. Beginning in 1946, Stibitz began the design of a desk size electronic digital computer for use in the business world. Two working prototypes of the Barber-Coleman computer were completed, but in 1954 the project was abandoned for financial reasons.

In 1964, George was invited to join Dartmouth Medical School's Department of Physiology as a Research Associate. In this newest career, Stibitz did significant pioneering work in a field that is now referred to as biomedicine. Over the past quarter century, he has worked on a variety of biophysical problems, including the modeling of renal exchange processes, the computer display of brain cell anatomy, and a mathematical model of capillary transport phenomena. Although he retired as Professor Emeritus in 1974, Stibitz still remains active as a consultant to the medical school.

George Stibitz's honors include the AFIPS Harry Goode Award (1965), IEEE's Emanuel Piore Award (1977), IEEE's Computer Pioneer Award (1982), election to the National Academy of Engineering (1981), and election to the National Inventor's Hall of Fame (1985). He has also received honorary degrees from Denison University (1976), Keene State College (1978), and Dartmouth College (1986).

References

1964. Stibitz, G. R. "Curriculum Vitae" Dartmouth Medical School, Department of Physiology. 8pp. Includes chronological lists of publications and projects.
1967. Stibitz, G. R. "The Relay Computers at Bell Labs," *Datamation* (April) 35–44 (May) 45–49.

HENRY S. TROPP

STORAGE. *See also* articles under MEMORY.

STORAGE ALLOCATION

For articles on related subjects *see* ADDRESSING; ASSOCIATIVE MEMORY; BLOCK STUCTURE; CACHE MEMORY; DATABASE MANAGEMENT SYSTEM; GARBAGE COLLECTION; MEMORY: MAIN; MEMORY MANAGEMENT; STORAGE HIERARCHY; TIME SHARING; and VIRTUAL MEMORY.

Storage in a digital computer system must be allocated to programs and data that are being executed, just as for any other resource in the system. While the cost of hardware used for storage continues to decrease the demands for storage generated by increasingly sophisticated software systems and application programs are quickly diluting the benefits from the availability of cheaper, larger storage.

A computer system will normally have several levels of storage, usually referred to as "main" (or primary) storage, "secondary" (or auxiliary) storage, etc. Main storage is implemented using fast but relatively expensive components. Secondary storage is slower and less expensive. A typical system will have more of secondary than of main storage. The lower levels of storage are intended for storing large amounts of information for relatively long periods of time. When some part of the information is to be referenced during a computation, it is usually transferred to main storage first; i.e. it is *loaded* into main storage.

Sound resource management dictates that programs and data should be allocated only the minimum amount of main storage that is necessary, but additional amounts are often acquired and are released dynamically. Thus, a program may be allocated an initial amount of *static* main storage when it is loaded from secondary storage, which it will use until its execution is completed. During the computation, there may be requests to a supervisory system for additional dynamically allocated main storage which will receive temporary values for subsequent computation or communication to other *processes*, and which may then be released back to the supervisory system when it is no longer required.

Another use for dynamically acquired storage (as well as the initially acquired storage) is for the introduction of additional segments of programs and/or data, while parts of the program or data that were used and are no longer needed are released or overwritten. When the same storage is used and reused in this way, it is called an *overlay* process. It should be noted that dynamic acquisition of space is not just an alternative to explicit overlay management; for certain types of programs, such as recursive programs, one cannot anticipate in advance the amount of storage that will be necessary. Depending on the depth of the recursion, one might need a very long chain of temporary storage acquisitions, each to be released on return to the next higher level of recursion. String and list processing (*q.v.*) programs also require dynamic storage allocation.

A considerable amount of program and data management is involved in an explicit overlay process. It has been estimated that as much as 50% of a program development effort may be concerned with design and implementation of overlay procedures. For this reason, various software and hardware systems have included features that help to alleviate the overlay burden. For example, the PL/I language provides for the allocation of *static* storage to variables, and also for two modes of dynamic allocation, one of which acquires storage for variables declared at the time of entry to a block (with automatic release of the storage back to the supervisory system on exit from the block), and the other of which gives complete control to the program to request space at any time, with subsequent responsibility for its explicit release.

One concept introduced at least partly because of the overlay problem is *virtual memory (q.v.)*. Here, program and data are assigned addresses independent of the amount of physical storage actually available and independent of the location from which the program will actually be executed. Thus, one might use 32 bits to represent an address (thus addressing about four billion items), while the available physical (main) storage might accommodate about a quarter-million items (needing only 18 bits for the representation of a particular address). This large ratio of total virtual storage to total physical storage implies a potentially massive overlay problem, although only occasionally will a program or its data be expected to occupy a very large fraction of the virtual storage.

Given that the program and data are allocated enough addresses in virtual storage to enable them to be accommodated there without any worry about overlay, but also given the expectation that the physical storage will be shared with other programs and data in a typical time-sharing or multiprogramming system, it is quite commonly necessary for the system to invoke an automatic overlay procedure. This is typically accomplished in a virtual storage system by bringing into physical storage from secondary storage only those parts of virtual storage that have been referenced (or can reasonably be expected to be referenced shortly). By recording in a table the mapping (i.e. the correspondence between parts of virtual storage and physical storage established when pieces of virtual storage are brought into main memory), addresses may be translated dynamically. Those references to virtual addresses that are not already mapped into physical storage can be intercepted by special hardware, and that part of virtual storage now needed, called a *page*, can then be brought into main memory. Pages are usually of a fixed size and therefore may be deposited into physical storage wherever a space of that size can be found.

Because the current location is entered into a mapping table whenever a page is introduced into physical storage, dynamic address translation can provide up-to-date interpretation of addresses (see below). This allows the effect of dynamic relocation without the overhead of actually modifying the addresses within instructions. The determination of which pages are to be removed from physical storage to make room for the needed incoming pages has itself been the object of research. Also, the question of pages of variable size is being studied, since

a fixed size inevitably leads to some wasted space whenever a block of programs or data does not fill exactly a multiple of the page size.

Although it is possible to implement in software the mapping described above, the overhead is considerable, and computers that incorporate virtual storage concepts generally provide a hardware implementation for dynamic address translation. In addition, several computers have introduced an additional concept, *segmentation*. Here, one views virtual storage as having identifiable regions, called *segments*, each containing enough addresses so that programs or data stored in them will not try to assign the same addresses more than once, even if they expand during execution by means of dynamic allocation of additional virtual storage. Segments are thus different from pages in that page boundaries assume a predetermined relationship to blocks of physical storage, whereas segments are viewed as functional subdivisions of virtual storage (and usually contain a number of virtual pages).

An important motivation behind the use of segments is the facility for sharing programs and data. In physical storage systems, one often finds programs written so that all addresses are given as displacements from a *base address,* and this is implemented by maintaining the base address in a hardware register. In this way, different copies of the program (or data) can be placed into storage in different locations while executing. Similarly, by establishing a *convention* that programs and data be *address-free* (i.e. that all addresses be represented as displacements from the expected contents of a base register) and by arranging for base addresses of segments to be maintained in registers during execution, relocation within virtual storage can be accomplished. This is illustrated in Fig. 1. Now individual users of the system may load programs or data into different areas of virtual storage (i.e. into different segments), and can arrange to share the copies that are actually loaded into physical storage through the paging mechanism. Fig. 2 illustrates this sharing.

Various hardware devices are included in systems to facilitate the implementation of paging, and—to a lesser extent—segmentation. One example of a hardware implementation of the dynamic address translation described above is give in Fig. 3. The virtual address is separated into three parts. The first, called the *segment number,* can be viewed (with an appropriate number of trailing zeroes) as the base address of a segment of virtual storage. In the implementation as shown in Fig. 3, however, it is used as an index into a *segment table* maintained

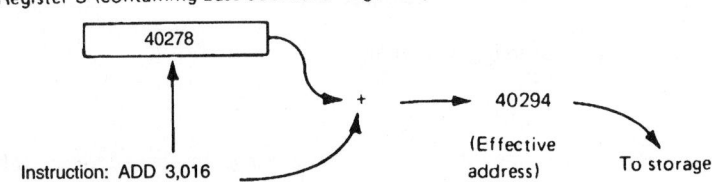

Register 3 (containing base address of segment)

40278

Instruction: ADD 3,016

40294
(Effective address)

To storage

FIG. 1.   Relocation within virtual storage.

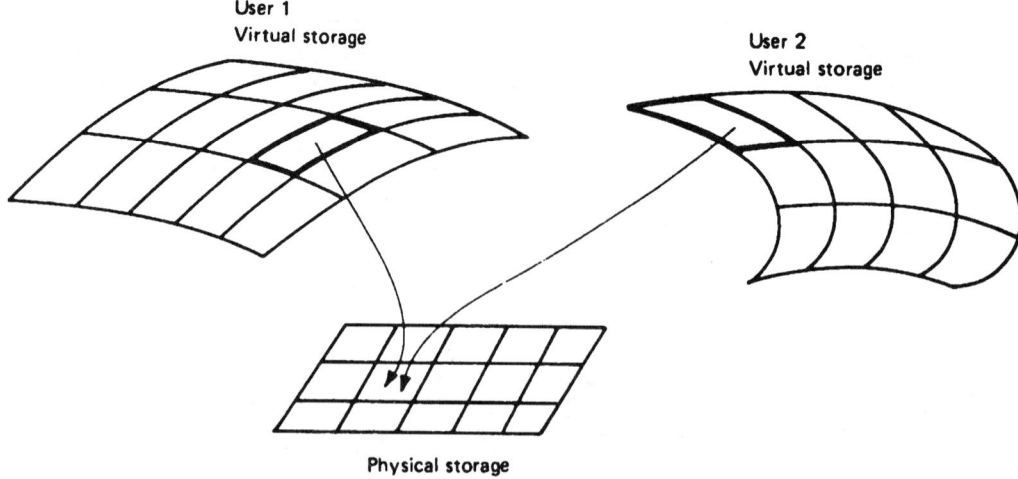

FIG. 2. Sharing in physical storage.

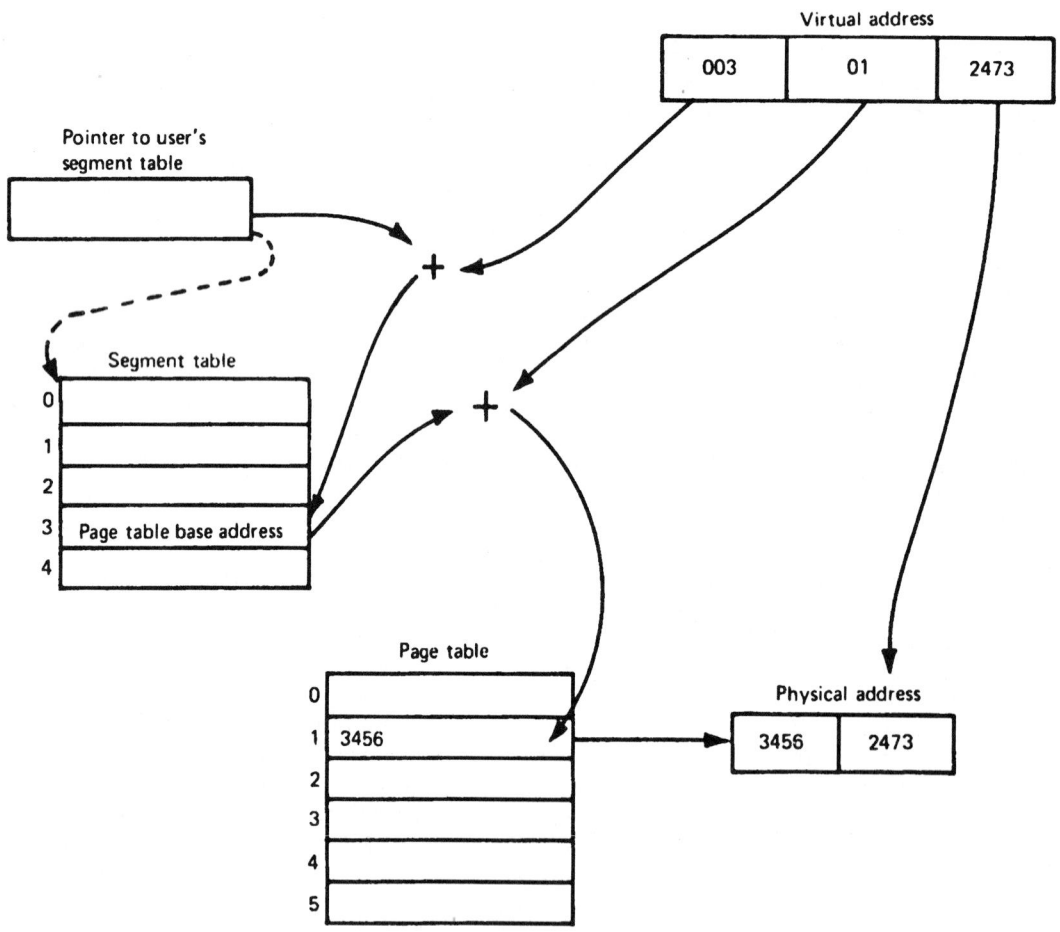

FIG. 3. Mapping from virtual address to physical address.

for that user to retrieve the appropriate page table; i.e. a table showing the virtual-to-physical mapping for those pages of the referenced segment for which the mapping exists. Once the page-table base address has been re-

trieved from the segment table, the page number obtained as the second part of the original virtual address is used as an index into the page table to retrieve the physical address corresponding to the base of that page in virtual storage. The third part of the original virtual address is then added (in fact, appended, since trailing zeroes are not included in the page table), and the result—generated in this manner by the hardware—is the desired physical address.

If the virtual page containing the reference address is not present in physical storage—and only a few will be, depending on the number of other users of the system and the amount of physical storage available—an *interrupt (q.v.)* will be generated, causing a delay in the execution of that program while the desired page is found and loaded into physical storage. (This system service is the substitute for the cumbersome overlay process described earlier.) Of course, all tables mentioned above must be protected by the supervisory system from access by programs that are not authorized to do so.

Accessing segment and page tables, as in Fig. 3, does imply additional storage references, thus potentially implying a large overhead. Several hardware systems include provisions for some *associative memory*, which retains several of the most recent mapping results. Thus, around a dozen entries will be maintained, each consisting of a segment and page number pair, together with the corresponding physical-page/base-address. A subsequent search with the same segment-page pair will quickly produce the physical-page/base-address without the need for accessing the segment and page tables. This is illustrated in Fig. 4, where the segment table and page table would not be accessed once a match is found in associative storage.

Another interesting application of virtual storage is the implementation of the *virtual machine*. Here a program is written as if it had a segment of virtual storage as its physical storage, and most (nonprivileged) instructions are executed on the hardware at full speed. When interrupts are thus generated because of missing virtual pages or the execution of privileged instructions, the intended system services are provided by means more conducive to an environment in which several users are actually sharing the hardware. In addition, because paging services are provided for the bulk of virtual storage, large storage can be simulated for each virtual storage machine at a fraction of the overhead incurred in the planning and implementation of overlay processing. To the users of such a system, it appears as if each one has a different physical (or software) system on which to run a program.

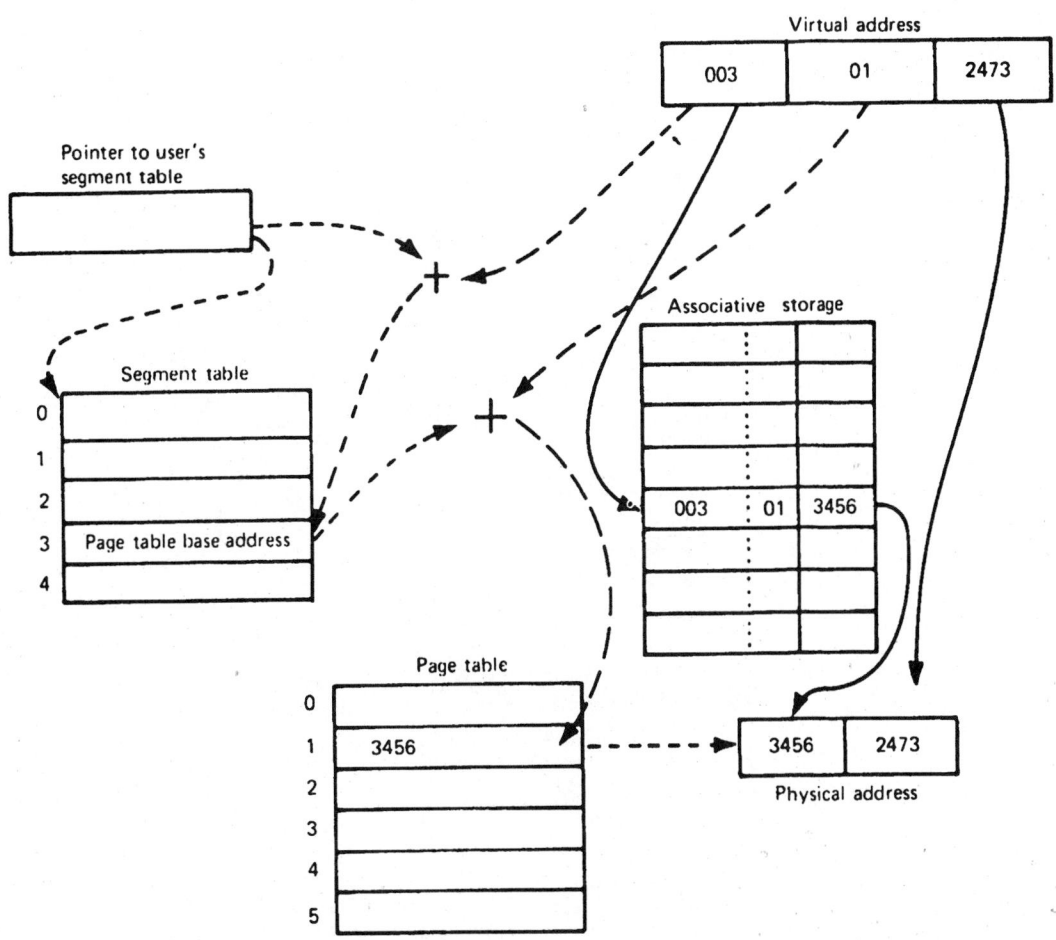

FIG. 4.   Mapping from virtual address to physical address, showing the use of associative storage.

References

1969. Rosin, Robert F. "Supervisory and Monitor Systems," *Computing Surveys* **1**, 1: 37–54 (March).

1970. Denning, Peter J. "Virtual Memory," *Computing Surveys* **2**, 3:153–190 (September).

1987. Tanenbaum, Andrew S. *Operating Systems: Design and Implementation.* Englewood Cliffs, NJ; Prentice-Hall.

BERNARD A. GALLER

STORAGE HIERARCHIES

For articles on related subjects *see* ASSOCIATIVE MEMORY; BUFFER; CACHE MEMORY; MEMORY; VIRTUAL MEMORY; and WORKING SET.

A *storage hierarchy* comprises a series of memory levels between a processor (small and relatively fast) and a central database (large and, therefore, relatively slow). Functionally, it provides two services. First, it allows multiple processors to share a common (*coherent*) view of the centrally maintained database. Second, it provides an access time (*q.v.*) commensurate with the processor speed for most accesses made to a relatively slow, large memory.

Coherency is a factor that defines the degree of *coupling* between processors in a multiprocessor system. In a tightly-coupled multiprocessor, all processors must observe identical contents of main storage. In a loosely-coupled multiprocessor, coherency definitions are relaxed, and software effects common views of shared data. (In a distributed system, storage itself may be distributed, and the notion of a "central database" is a logical notion that is effected by software.)

Performance thresholds must be met to enable general application of a hierarchical memory system. The access times of the highest and lowest elements of a storage hierarchy may differ by several orders of magnitude. Most applications would be rendered impractical if limited by the access time of the highest (large, slow) level, and rendered impossible if the storage capacity were limited by the size of the lowest (small, fast) level.

Technology Considerations—The Need for a Hierarchy Fig. 1 is taken from Pence and Krusius (1987), and shows projections of the delay limitations of various technologies as a function of physical size. Of course, the speed of light is a generally accepted limitation, and this asymptote is shown explicitly.

For the logic technologies that are used to construct the smallest, fastest elements of storage hierarchies, switching delays are in the 1 to 100 picosecond range (one picosecond = 10^{-12} sec). If the lowest level of a storage hierarchy is kept small enough so that the speed of light does not dominate the system-level access time, these access times can be in the 10 to 1,000 picosecond range.

For *bulk-storage* devices, such as disks, tapes, optical media, and other magnetic media, the physical packaging requires a machine-room sized setup for a large database. That is, even if the individual bulk-storage devices were very fast, there is still a speed of light limitation over 10 to 1,000 meters. Thus, accesses made to the largest level in the storage hierarchy are inherently longer than a microsecond, perhaps longer than a millisecond.

The difference in access times between the largest and smallest levels in the hierarchy is inherently several orders of magnitude. (While it is true that the densities of bulk-storage devices have improved dramatically and will continue to do so, it is also true that the sizes of typical databases have increased dramatically and will continue to do so. The one thing that has remained constant is the size of a typical machine room; this is likely to remain constant. The aggregate capacity of a bulk-storage system

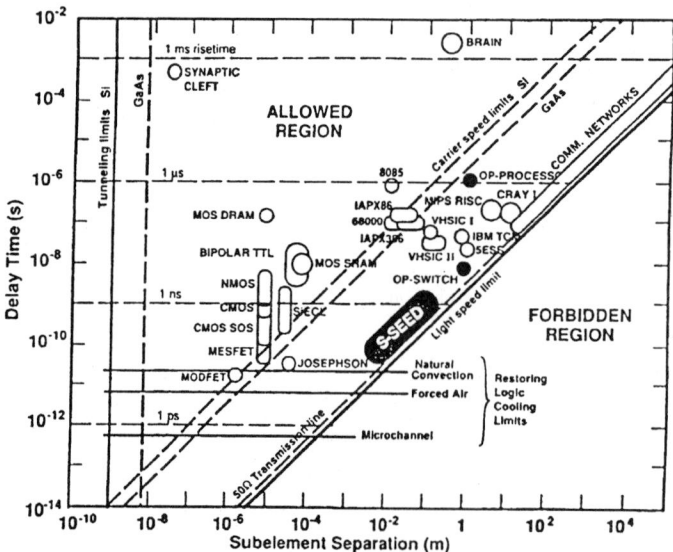

FIG. 1. Fundamental limits for logic technology, from Pence and Krusius (1982).

then tends to be "whatever fits into a machine room," and the speed of light limitation over 10 to 1,000 meters remains.)

In modern large systems, there are at least three, and as many as seven, levels in a hierarchy. The three levels always present are called L1, L3, and L5, by convention. The four optional levels are called L0, L2, L4, and L6. The lowest level (L0), is the smallest, fastest level; it is merely addressable buffer space. Each successive level is slower and larger. Levels L0 to L3 are generally byte-addressable, and levels L4 to L6 are paging levels—i.e. data cannot be addressed at a finer grain than the page size. (Usually, a page is 4K bytes.)

From the viewpoint of any particular level L_i in the hierarchy, the next lowest level, L_{i-1}, is considered to be a *cache* (*see* CACHE MEMORY). Thus, a memory hierarchy can be treated as a succession of cache levels. Very roughly, the capacity of a cache and the overhead associated with managing it justifies its existence (i.e. makes it a good engineering choice) if there is an order-of-magnitude disparity in access times between the levels. A seven-level hierarchy roughly covers the six orders-of-magnitude represented in Fig. 1.

Fig. 2 shows an example of a memory hierarchy in the context of a multiprocessor system (*see* MULTIPROCESSING). In this figure, each box that is labeled "P" represents a processor. Each processor is connected to its own (private) L1 cache. There are two L2 caches in the system—each L1 in the system is connected to exactly one of the L2s, both L2s are connected to the L3.

By convention, L3 is usually called "main memory." In this figure, L3 is connected to L5; there is no L4. By convention, the distinction between L4 and L5 is that L4 usually implies random access (semiconductor) memory, and L5 usually implies sequential access (magnetic or optical) memory. There is no L6 in the figure. By convention, L6 is usually archival storage (e.g. a tape library).

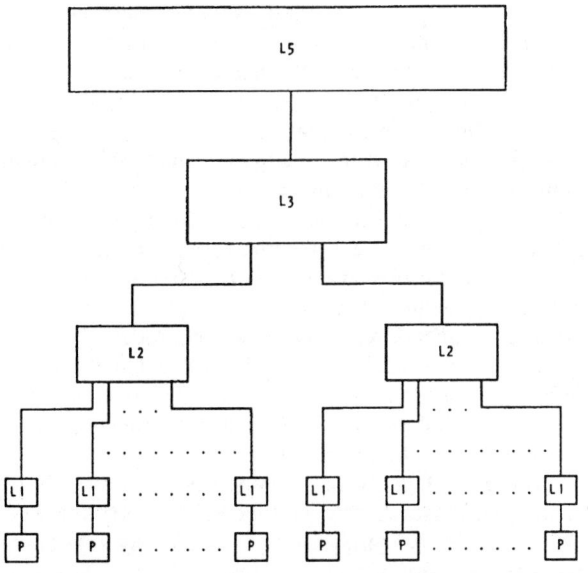

FIG. 2. Example of a memory hierarchy in a multiprocessor system.

Levels L4 and above are typically page-addressable levels, and levels L3 and below are byte addressable. In addition, levels up to the smallest private level (in this case, L1 only) usually operate on the basis of *virtual addresses*, while levels above this operate on *real addresses* (*see* VIRTUAL MEMORY). The following section distinguishes these two forms of addressing.

Virtual Addressing and Dynamic Address Translation

Main memory is a facility that contains data and instructions for active processes that are being run on a system. An item in main memory is accessed by specifying the location that contains the item; the name of the location is called the *real address* of the item. As a facility, main memory must be able to accommodate the operating system (*q.v.*), system utilities, applications, and workspaces for whatever number of users are being served by the machine.

Since main memory cannot physically accommodate everything that will ever be required by all users, and since it has no need to do so at any given instant (i.e. everything cannot be active simultaneously), the operating system attempts to allocate pieces of main memory to those address-spaces that are most current. Thus, the contents of main memory change over time as a function of usage, and hence there is no permanent binding of real addresses to data items or to instructions.

Since a program cannot reliably reference an item with a real address if the real address changes as a function of time, programs reference items with *virtual addresses*. Within a program, virtual addresses are logically bound to items that are referenced by the program independently of where the items physically reside in main memory. Thus, as the real address of an item changes, there is no confusion on the part of a program that references the item with a virtual address, given that a method exists for translating virtual addresses to real addresses dynamically. *Dynamic address translation* is such a method.

A *dynamic address translation mechanism* is a table-driven mechanism; a virtual address is used to index an entry in a table whose contents specify the corresponding real address. When an address space is active, the table itself must be contained in main memory since, before a virtual address is translated, it must be interpreted as a real index into the table. Thus, main memory must contain the virtual-to-real address translations of all items that are currently bound to real addresses, as well as items themselves.

To keep the amount of space required by the translation mechanism small, it is desirable to allocate memory in very large "chunks"—i.e. if the chunks are large, fewer of them fit into real storage, and consequently, less storage is required to hold the translations. However, if there are only a small number of chunks that can be allocated, the usefulness of the machine is severely limited (i.e. only a small number of users or applications can be serviced at any one time).

Thus, it is desirable to have a small number of large chunks so that the storage required for translation is small, and, on the contrary, it is desirable to have a large number of small chunks so that they can be allocated to a large number of users or applications. Both of these opposing objectives are satisfied via a multilevel address-translation process.

In most commercial architectures, there are two levels of translation. An address space is considered to be partitioned into large chunks called *segments*, and these segments are considered to be partitioned into smaller chunks called *pages*. Real storage is allocated at the page level. For example, in IBM System 370 and upward-compatible architectures, a page is 4 kilobytes.

As shown in Fig. 3, a virtual address is considered to be broken into three fields. These are the segment index, the page index, and the byte displacement. Note that the byte displacement of a virtual address is the same as the byte displacement of the corresponding real address; the virtual-to-real translation process is then the process of translating the virtual segment index and virtual page index into a real page address.

An address space is initiated by the operating system; the segment table origin (STO) for the space is obtained from an address-space control block, and is loaded into a control register (STOR). The STO points to the beginning of the segment table that is used for the address space in question. For each active segment in the space, the segment table contains a page table origin that points to the beginning of the page table that is used by that segment. The page table contains the real page addresses of all active pages in the segment.

For a successful translation, the segment index portion of the virtual address is used as an offset into the segment table; this first lookup provides the page table origin. The page index portion of the virtual address is then used as an offset into the selected page table; this lookup provides the real page address, which is the dynamic translation of the segment index and the page index. The item that is logically bound to the virtual

address can then be referenced via its current dynamically-bound real address.

Thus, the translation process logically requires two memory accesses—i.e. every memory access request that is made with a virtual address requires two memory accesses to perform the virtual-to-real translation, as well as one additional access that is made with the translated address to actually satisfy the memory access request. Since in a high-performance machine it is undesirable to perform three physical accesses on behalf of every access that is logically made by a program, machines shortcut the translation process via a mechanism called a *directory lookaside table* (DLAT).

A DLAT is a cache that contains past virtual-to-real page translations. When an access is made with a virtual address, the segment index, the page index, and the STO are used in conjunction to access the DLAT. A *DLAT hit* is the event in which an entry is found in the DLAT that corresponds to these three fields; this entry contains the real page address of the associated virtual address that was used to access the DLAT.

In the event of a DLAT hit, the real page address is immediately concatenated with the byte displacement to form a real address, and the physical translation process described above is by-passed. A *DLAT miss* is the event in which the desired entry is not found in the DLAT. In the event of a DLAT miss, the physical translation process described above is performed, and the resulting translation is stored in the DLAT for future use.

The Cache Mechanism and Behavior   For the ensuing discussion, the term "cache" will be used to mean "Level i-1 in the hierarchy," and "main memory" will mean "Level i in the hierarchy." A fairly comprehensive survey and an exhaustive bibliography of cache and related memory hierarchy issues is contained in Smith (1982) and in Smith (1986), respectively.

A *cache* is a memory that is packaged as an integral component of a processing unit in a computer system. As such, it is much smaller than the *main memory* of the system; its purpose is to emulate the main memory of the system, but with a much faster access time. Since a cache is smaller than the main memory, it can contain only a subset of the contents of main memory. Thus, a directory is required in a cache for identifying which parts of main memory are resident in the cache.

Although there is a wealth of formal theory about the operation of the cache, the entire foundation for the theory is empirical observation. Two heuristically observable phenomena drive the behavior of the cache: *temporal locality of reference* (the observation that a referenced item is likely to be rereferenced within some temporal window), and *spatial locality of reference* (the observation that items close (by address) to a referenced item are likely to be referenced).

Temporal locality of reference is the rationale for keeping the most recently referenced items in the cache—e.g. the cache is managed such that newly referenced items replace items that are least recently referenced. Spatial locality of reference is the rationale for storing contiguous chunks of data (called *cache lines*) in the

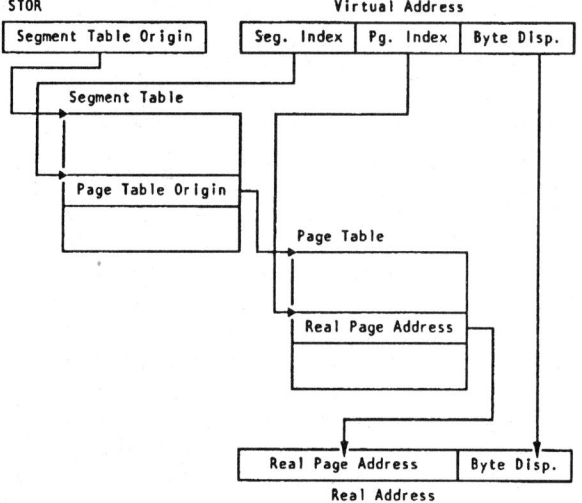

FIG. 3.   Example of a two-level virtual-to-real address mapping.

cache, rather than merely the specific items that have actually been referenced. For example, a *cache miss* is a reference made to an item that is not in the cache; a cache miss causes an entire line to be transferred from main memory to the cache.

Therefore, the most important parameters in a cache design (for a cache of fixed capacity) are the cache management strategy (which lines to keep) and the line size. The cache management strategy comprises a *replacement algorithm* (which lines to replace—this is invariably some form of LRU (least recently used)) and, for multiprocessor systems only, algorithms that determine "ownership" of lines such that the various processors in the system share some coherent view of storage. The line size is selected based on numerous factors—choosing the "best" line size is typically much more difficult than determining appropriate cache management algorithms.

Set Associativity

The degree of *set associativity* of a cache determines (and is equal to) the number of places that a line with a given address can be located in the cache. A subfield of the address specifies the *congruence class* into which the line is mapped, and when the line is brought into the cache, it is placed into any one of the *sets* within this congruence class. The particular set into which the line is placed depends on the replacement algorithm used—i.e. it is replaces the line that is selected by the algorithm.

Since the capacity of the cache (in number of lines) is given by the product of the number of congruence classes and the degree of set associativity, these two factors are inversely related for a fixed cache size and line size. If the number of lines in the cache is equal to the degree of set associativity, a line can be placed anywhere in the cache; such a cache is said to be *fully associative*. At the other extreme, if the number of lines in the cache is equal to the number of congruence classes, then a line can be placed into exactly one location; such a cache is said to be *direct mapped*.

From the perspective of miss rate, it is desirable to have as large a degree of set associativity as possible; this can be easily understood in terms of the replacement algorithm. When a new line is brought into the cache, the replacement algorithm attempts to select the line that is least likely to be referenced in the future, and to replace this line with the new line. Since the new line must be placed into a specific congruence class, the replacement algorithm must select a line in this congruence class.

If the cache is not fully associative, the line that is selected by the replacement algorithm is not necessarily the best choice of all lines in the cache; it is merely the best choice for a specific congruence class. In a fully associative cache, the replacement algorithm can choose any line in the cache for replacement; in a direct mapped cache, there is no choice whatsoever.

Thus, from the perspective of miss rate, the degree of set associativity is merely a parameter that limits the global effectiveness of the replacement algorithm. Practical considerations limit the degree of set associativity in terms of hardware and cycle time for any real implementation.

Virtual Placement and Real Placement—The Access Path

The virtual-to-real address translation process is required in any virtual memory machine; the requirement of this translation process is independent of the presence or absence of levels of cache in the machine. A cache is a buffer that holds items that were most recently referenced by the processor so that, if these items are referenced again, they can be obtained locally. As such, references that are serviced by the cache must logically produce the same results that would have been obtained had the references been serviced by the main memory. Since the cache must logically emulate main memory, items in the cache must be referenced via real addresses.

The real address of an item is a dynamic binding of the item to an actual storage location in the main memory, but this binding does not determine the location of the item in the cache (i.e. the set within congruence class). Thus, a mechanism is required that dynamically binds the real address of an item to a physical location (set) in the cache. The *cache directory* performs this function.

The directory is a buffer of entries, where each entry corresponds to a line that is resident in the cache. The directory is also organized by congruence class, and it may be set associative, but it need not have the same associativity as the cache. For each set within a congruence class, a directory entry identifies the real line address, and the set within the cache arrays that contains the line associated with that real address. Thus, in order to determine the set in which a line is stored in the cache arrays, it is necessary to find the entry for the line (based on the real line address) in the directory.

Therefore, a cache access is logically a three-step process. First, the virtual address of the item that is being referenced must be translated into a real address via the DLAT. Next, the real address of the item must be translated into a cache address for the item via the directory. Finally, the item is referenced in the cache using the cache address of the item. A cache that performs these three steps in sequence is said to use *real placement*, since the data is physically placed in the cache according to its real address.

Thus, even with a DLAT that eliminates the two references that are logically required to do a virtual-to-real address translation, a cache access logically requires three separate accesses. These are the DLAT lookup, the directory lookup, and the actual access of the cache arrays. Further, since the first two accesses represent successive translations that are required to determine the location of the item in the cache, it would appear that the three references must be done sequentially. In practice, these three accesses can be done in parallel if the data is placed in the cache according to its virtual address. Caches that use virtual placement are called *virtual caches*.

Fig. 4 is a simplified sketch of a possible cache access path that effects all lookups simultaneously. In this figure, the access is made on a doubleword (8-byte) basis. (This sketch makes some assumptions about the cache size and organization, so it does not readily generalize.) The

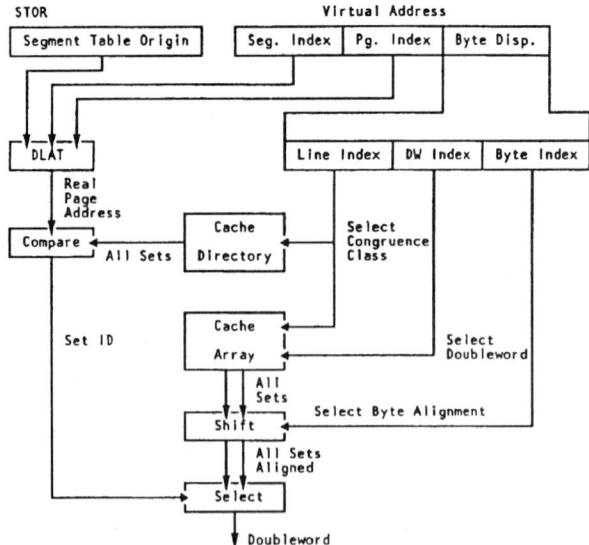

FIG. 4. Example of a virtual cache.

figure shows a DLAT, a directory, and the cache arrays; each is set associative, but the degree of set associativity may be different for each of them. In the figure, the virtual segment index, the virtual page index, and the STO are used collectively to access the DLAT; this produces the real page address. Since, for this particular cache, the line index is independent of the real page address (which is not true in general), the directory and the cache arrays can be accessed in parallel with the DLAT.

The directory access produces the real line address of each line that is stored in the cache arrays for each set in the directory. With the real line address, each directory entry also contains the set identification of the line in the cache arrays. The real line address from each set in the directory is compared to the real page address as translated by the DLAT; if a match is found, the corresponding set identification is used to select the appropriate set from the cache arrays.

In parallel with the directory access, the line index is used to select a congruence class in the cache arrays; the doubleword index selects the appropriate doubleword (or quadword in some caches) from each set in the congruence class. Since the doubleword must be aligned on a byte boundary, the byte index is used to shift all selected doublewords. The shifting is usually done prior to the final select, since the comparison (at the directory) may still be in progress.

A Caveat for Virtual Placement—Synonyms

If the size of a virtual cache is larger than the product of the page size and the degree of set associativity of the cache, *synonyms* can exist in the cache. For example, if the page size is 4 kilobytes, a 4-way set associative cache can have synonyms if it is larger than 16 kilobytes.

Two distinct virtual addresses are said to be *synonyms* if they both map to the same real address—i.e. if their real translations are identical. Synonyms pose a problem in large virtual caches because the congruence

class must be selected by untranslated address bits. If, in Fig. 4, the cache size is greater than the product of the page size and the degree of set associativity, the byte displacement portion of the virtual address (which is the same as the byte displacement portion of the real address) does not contain enough bits to select the congruence class.

Thus, if the cache array access is done in parallel with the address translation, additional bits need to be fabricated to select the cache array congruence class. Since, in any given application environment, an item with a given real address that has multiple virtual synonyms is likely to be referenced repeatedly using only one of the virtual names, these additional bits are usually taken from the virtual page index (as a guess only). The number of such bits that are used is the log of the number of congruence classes in which an item with a given real address can reside. This set of congruence classes is called a *synonym class*.

In order for a cache to be self-coherent, it must search all possible congruence classes to detect synonyms when certain operations are performed (e.g. store operations). This can be done either by sequentially attempting to reference the item in every congruence class in the appropriate synonym class or by making the degree of set associativity of the directory large enough such that the directory is synonym-free. In the latter case, the directory lookup reveals the congruence class as well as the set for any specific line. If the directory lookup reveals that the array access was made to the wrong congruence class, the correct congruence class can be accessed on the next cycle.

Line Size Trade-offs
Among the difficulties in the choice of line size is that a large line (which exploits spatial locality) implies a smaller number of lines for a fixed cache capacity. Consequently, the temporal window (for the smaller number of lines) is shorter and temporal locality is sacrificed.

In general, lines that contain instructions exhibit more spatial locality than lines that contain data. Therefore, it is desirable to have a large line size to capitalize on the spatial locality of instructions, and conversely, it is desirable to have small lines so that a larger number of lines can be used to capitalize on temporal locality. In practice, a compromise must be made. Two other relevant factors that work in opposition are that large lines incur a larger penalty for a cache miss, but they allow the cache to be managed by a smaller directory.

A *cache miss* occurs when the processor references an item that is not in the cache. In this event, the line that contains the referenced item is transferred from the main memory to the cache, where it replaces a line that is selected by the replacement algorithm. The number of processor cycles required to recognize that a miss has occurred and to complete the transfer is called the *miss penalty*.

If a line is wider than the bus (*q.v.*) that is used to perform the transfer, the transfer of the line is performed as a sequence of transfers of packets, where the size of a packet is limited by the bus width. In machines that transfer a line starting with the packet containing the item that was actually referenced, the part of the miss penalty attributed to the actual reference is independent of the line size. This part of the miss penalty is called the *leading edge* of the miss.

Since the arrivals of subsequent packets in the line causes the cache to be busy (unavailable for other references while it is storing these packets), the remaining portion of the miss penalty is directly proportional to the line size. This part of the miss penalty is called the *trailing edge* of the miss. (Another component of trailing edge arises from accesses to later portions of the line made subsequent to the initial miss, but prior to the time that the later portions of the line arrive at the cache.) Therefore, it is a poor choice to make the line size larger than the spatial locality that is likely to be captured since (among other reasons) the trailing edge is needlessly increased.

In the other extreme, the line size can be chosen to be a single packet (e.g. the bus width) so that no part of the miss penalty is superfluous. However, if the line fails to capture readily available spatial locality, this is also a poor choice, since more misses are needlessly incurred to capture the remainder of the locality. Further, a cache directory is required so that the identities of the lines resident in the cache are known. Since the directory must have one entry per physical cache line, a small line size may require that the directory be prohibitively large.

To Study Locality, First Consider Reuse A large line size most benefits applications in which spatial locality of reference is prevalent over temporal locality of reference (i.e. large lines capture more spatial context). However, if the prevalence of these phenomena is reversed, increasing the number of lines is more beneficial than increasing the line size (i.e. if an application has little spatial locality, large lines contain much "dead space" that could otherwise be used to hold more temporal context). To the extent that either of these phenomena can be exploited for a given cache size, there is some specific line size that is optimal.

A critical aspect of cache performance that clarifies the relative importance of these two phenomena subject to a given cache size is the aspect of *reuse*. Reuse is a measure of the probability that a specific item (e.g. a word), once referenced, will be referenced again before it ages out of the cache. Reuse is a direct indicator of temporal locality that is not clouded by the specific line size in a cache.

If reuse is negligible, the cache hit ratio is determined by spatial locality of reference—i.e. it can be approximated by the *utility* of the line. The utility of a line is the average number of items in the line that are actually referenced during a period of residency. For example, if the average utility is 5 items per line and there is negligible reuse, the hit ratio of the cache is roughly 80% (i.e. 1 miss per 5 references).

Since the average period of residency of a line is gauged by the capacity of the cache in number of lines (i.e. with fewer lines, it is more likely that any specific line is replaced quickly), the likelihood of reuse is better in a cache with a large number of small lines than in a cache with a small number of large lines. However, the number of items that are referenced in a line is directly related to the line size (i.e. a large line contains more items than a small line, so it is likely to satisfy more references). Thus, large lines have a higher utility. Therefore, to the extent that line size (and hence utility) can be increased without greatly reducing reuse (as related to the number of lines), it is advantageous to implement large lines.

Note that for extremely small caches, reuse may be negligible for any line size. If this is the case, there is no real leverage in increasing the number of lines; hence, spatial locality of reference is the dominant factor. Further, if the specific spatial reference pattern is sequential in nature (as is typically the case for instruction lines), there is no real need for a cache. This is because the only beneficial aspect of a cache in such a case is that the unit of fetch is a line; the cache can be replaced with a simple mechanism that continuously prefetches next-sequential items.

In extremely large caches, the situation is entirely different. Once a cache is large enough so that the average residency of a line is extremely long (i.e. the temporal "window" is large), then information within the spatial context of an item is likely to be temporal as well. Thus, temporal locality and spatial locality are less distinct in a large cache.

For a medium sized cache, the spatial and temporal aspects of locality remain fairly distinct, and there is a significant aspect of reuse. The relative importance of each of these qualities can be estimated fairly well with simple models. This analysis is done in the next two sections.

Matching Line Size to the Leading Edge An appropriate line size is chosen based on the degree to which increasing the line size reduces the miss rate of a fixed-capacity cache. Let $C(N,L)$ denote a cache with N lines, each of size L, and let $M(N,L)$ be the miss rate of $C(N,L)$. In this analysis, the miss rates of caches $C(2N, L)$ and $C(N,2L)$ are compared. Note that both caches have the same capacity, $2NL$.

Heuristically, and in many independent studies by different researchers, it has been found that, for a fixed line size, the miss rate decreases in an exponential form as the number of cache lines is increased. Specifically, $M(ZN,L) \simeq Z^{-1/y}M(N,L)$. Of course, this holds over limited ranges of Z, and should not be extrapolated wildly. Different values of y have been observed; y is characteristic of the workload.

Let p be the *occupancy* of $C(N,2L)$. Simply, p is the probability that both halves of a line of length $2L$ are referenced during its residency in $C(N,2L)$. (Note that the occupancy is independent of N.) Then the cache $C(N,2L)$ has as much useful contents as the cache $C((1 + p)N,L)$. But to maintain that same useful contents, $C((1 + p)N,L)$ must take $1 + p$ misses for every miss made by $C(N,2L)$—i.e. $M(N,2L) \simeq (1 + p)^{-1} M((1 + p)N,L)$.

From the previous heuristic rule with $Z = 1 + p$, $M((1 + p)N,L) \simeq (1 + p)^{-1/y} M(N,L)$. Therefore, $M(N,2L) \simeq (1 + p)^{-(y+1)/y} M(N,L)$. Since $M(2N,L) \simeq 2^{-1/y} M(N,L)$, then $M(2N,L) \simeq M(N,2L)$ if and only if $2^{-1/y} = (1 + p)^{(y+1)/y}$—i.e.

if $p \geq 2^{1/(y+1)} - 1$, then $C(N,2L)$ has a lower miss rate than $C(2N,L)$.

For several common workloads, $y \simeq 2$ has been observed (but should not be used as a general value). Then, for these workloads, if $p \geq 0.25$ for the particular line size L being studied, the miss rate can be reduced by doubling the line size. This analysis ignores trailing-edge effects.

Accounting for Trailing-Edge Effects

Let A be the leading-edge portion of the miss penalty. A good approximation is that the leading edge of a miss is independent of line size, and the trailing edge of a miss is directly proportional to the line size. Let a be the constant of proportionality. Then a miss for $C(2N,L)$ costs $A + aL$ cycles, and a miss for $C(N,2L)$ costs $A + 2aL$ cycles.

The total penalty incurred for a fixed number of instructions is the product of the miss penalty and the miss rate. The relevant comparison is then $M(2N,L) \times (A + aL)$ with $M(N,2L) \times (A + 2aL)$. The same analysis as is used above yields equality in the two cache systems if the ratio $(A + aL)/(A + 2aL)$ is equal to $2^{1/y} (1 + p)^{-(1+y)/y}$.

Note that the break-even point for p is not directly expressed in terms of a. Instead, a determines the significance of the trailing edge with respect to the leading edge. Let a new parameter, γ, define this significance directly: $\gamma = aL/A$.

As before, with $y = 2$, the break-even point is determined by $(1 + \gamma)/(1 + 2\gamma) = \sqrt{2} (1 + p)^{-3/2}$. A reasonable design-point for a cache system is $\gamma = 1/2$—i.e. doubling the line size would cause the miss penalty to be shared evenly between the leading and trailing edges. For such a system, the occupancy must be $p \geq 0.526$ to justify doubling the line size—more than twice the value $p \geq 0.25$ that was obtained in the analysis above when the trailing edge was ignored. This shows the dramatic effect that the trailing edge can have.

Mitigating Trailing-Edge Via Sectoring

The first commercial processor that had a cache was the IBM 360 Model 85, described by Liptay (1968). In this machine, the directory was constrained to be very small (for engineering reasons), which necessarily caused the line size to be extremely large, so that superfluous miss penalty seemed inevitable. To circumvent this problem, the notion of *cache sectoring* was introduced.

In this scheme, a cache line is considered to be composed of *sectors* (where a sector can be composed of *packets*). On a cache miss, enough space is reserved in the cache to hold the entire line, but only the sector that contains the referenced item is transferred to the cache. Therefore, the directory is kept small (one entry per very large line), but the miss penalty is related to the sector size (smaller than the line size).

The only change to the directory that is required to implement a sectored cache is that each entry (an entry represents a line) contains one "residence" bit per sector in the line; these bits indicate which of the sectors in the line are resident in the cache. In the Model 85, the motivation for sectoring was to keep the number of entries in the directory small without incurring large miss penalties.

Sectoring can also be motivated in an environment where there are two classes of lines: one with a large spatial locality (e.g. instruction lines), and another with a smaller spatial locality (e.g. data lines). In such an environment, a miss to an instruction line can cause the transfer of the entire line (thereby avoiding superfluous misses in the future), and a miss to a data line can cause the transfer of only the relevant sector (thereby avoiding superfluous miss penalty). This motivation and the motivation used in the Model 85 are uniprocessor motivations—i.e. they are valid motivations in any system.

Cache Coherency in Multiprocessor Systems

Cache algorithms are required in a multiprocessor for determining the "ownership" of lines so that the various processors in the system share some *coherent* view of storage. A general discussion of *cache coherency* is more esoteric than is warranted here, and can be found in a comprehensive work by Collier (1992). The definition of coherency is integral to (and specific to) the definition of a processor's architecture. Such a definition specifies the order in which fetches and stores done by the processor are observed to occur by other processors or channel programs.

The crux of any such definition is that the results of a store operation done to a memory location must eventually be observed by fetch operations done to that same memory location. Specifically, there must be a means for determining when cached data in a given processor becomes obsolete as a result of store operations performed by another processor. In many machines, this is accomplished with *exclusive bits*. Each entry in the cache directory contains an *exclusive bit*. If this bit is set in a given processor's cache directory, no other processor has the corresponding line in its cache; otherwise, other processors may have copies of the corresponding line.

Some terminology is necessary for the ensuing discussion. A line is said to be *held exclusive* if the directory entry for the line has the exclusive bit set; if this bit is not set for a resident line, then the line is said to be *held read-only*. When a line that is held exclusive by a cache is written back to main memory, it is said to be *castout*. (The word "castout" is also used to refer to the particular line that is castout, as well as to the event in which the line is castout.) A *cross invalidate* (denoted XI) is the act of invalidating (marking "not-resident") a line in a remote processor's cache. Note that an XI performed to a line that is held exclusive must also cause the line to be castout. A *change exclusive to read-only* (denoted CERO) is the act of forcing a remote processor to change the status of a line from exclusive to read-only. Note that when a CERO is performed, the line must also be castout. A possible operation of exclusive bits that implements a common form of coherency is as follows:

1. Fetch operations are permitted to all resident lines.
2. Store operations are permitted only to resident lines that are held exclusive.

3. A fetch operation that generates a miss eventually results in the line being held read-only. If the line is held exclusive by a remote processor at the time of the miss, a CERO is issued to that processor (and a castout is generated) prior to sending a copy of the line to the processor that generated the miss. (Note that this ensures that the processor that missed receives a "current" copy of the line.)

4. A store operation that generates a miss eventually results in the line being held exclusive. If the line is held exclusive by a remote processor at the time of the miss, a CERO is issued to that processor (and a castout is generated) prior to sending a copy of the line to the processor that generated the miss. If the line is held read-only by any remote processors at the time of the miss, XIs are issued to all such processors prior to sending a copy of the line to the processor that generated the miss. (This ensures that no other processor can fetch from this line without missing.)

5. A store operation that is attempted to a resident line that is held read-only will first cause the actions in the previous rule to be implemented. Following these actions, the line will be held exclusive, and the store is performed as in the second rule. Note that since the line is resident to begin with, it is not possible that another processor holds the line exclusive. Thus, implementing the previous rule to obtain the line exclusive will generate XIs only to other read-only copies. In this particular context, the act of obtaining the line exclusive is said to be a *fetch no data* (denoted FND).

This set of rules merely exemplifies one possible cache management algorithm for implementing one specific kind of coherency. In general, cache management algorithms can be much more complex and subtle. For example, it may be possible to reduce the frequency of FNDs by gaining exclusive status more aggressively (e.g. requesting the line exclusively by certain kinds of load misses). If FNDs are reduced in this way, it is not always the case that an exclusively held line has been modified locally; thus, it may be possible to reduce castouts by recording local change information.

The act of storing to a line will (somehow) cause copies of that line to be invalidated in remote caches, and, if a remote processor subsequently attempts to store into the same line, it will generate a miss and cause the current copy of the line to be invalidated.

Implementing a coherency scheme, although necessary, will cause more misses in a multiprocessor system than in a uniprocessor. This is a portion of the multiprocessor degradation factor. In accordance with the rules above, shared data will "ping-pong" between caches when it is updated. Even when data is not logically shared, the fact that data is managed on the basis of lines causes additional misses since:

1. Lines comprise a plurality of spatially close words.

2. Two or more processors may be operating (loading and storing) on different words in the same line, although the operations are logically disjoint (i.e. no two processors operate on the same words).

3. The line is forced to "ping-pong" between the caches via misses and XIs only because the (disjoint sets of) words happen to reside in the same line.

Store-In Management and Store-Through Management The coherency algorithm cited has implicitly described operation for a *store-in cache*. For the purpose of illustrating coherency, this choice was arbitrary. It is appropriate to generalize the discussion to include various *store-through caches*.

A *store-in cache* is so called because stores cannot be done to lines that are not resident in the cache. That is, if a store request is made to a non-resident line, a miss is generated, and the line is brought into the cache (made resident) before the store is permitted to occur. Further, that store and other stores done to that line during its period of residency are not reflected in main memory until the line is castout.

Since the castout is a single event, the order in which stores were done to the line that is castout cannot be reconstructed at the time of the castout—i.e. all stores that occurred during the period of residency appear (to the system) to be done simultaneously at the time of the castout. Thus, to guarantee coherency (observable order of fetches and stores) in a store-in cache, exclusive control (use of exclusive bits) is mandatory.

Precisely, exclusive control guarantees the following: while a processor is storing (changing the state of the system), it is not possible for any other processor to observe these changes (hence, not possible to observe the changes in a haphazard order). If another processor attempts to observe a change (via a CERO request that will force a castout), it is guaranteed to observe *all* changes that have logically taken place. (Since it observes all changes simultaneously, it cannot observe a state that is inconsistent with the logical order in which the changes were made). Thus, exclusive control is implicit to any discussion of store-in caches.

On the other hand, a *store-through cache* need not have exclusive control. A store-through cache is so called because all stores that are issued by a processor are "stored through" the cache, such that main memory is updated on a "per store" basis. Note that there is no such thing as a castout in a store-through cache, since main memory is made consistent as the stores occur.

There are three basic types of store-through caches denoted: WTWAX (for "Write-Through, Write-Allocate with Exclusive management"), WTWA (for "Write-Through, Write-Allocate" (without exclusive management)), and WTNWA (for "Write-Through, No Write-Allocate" (without exclusive management)).

For all intents and purposes, a WTWAX cache operates exactly like a store-in cache, except that the stores are stored-through to the main memory at the time that they are issued, and consequently there are no castouts. Since each store is issued to main memory as a separate event, the memory controller is required to honor the stores from a given processor in the order that they are issued (no ordering of stores from different processors is required). Note that in a store-in cache, the memory controller need not concern itself with this, since the ordering between the individual stores is inherently handled by the castout.

A WTWA cache operates like a WTWAX cache, with the exception that there is no exclusive management. Without such management, a processor must follow more stringent rules to ensure coherency between caches. The central concept in any meaningful discussion of coherency is the notion of "when" a store completes. A simple statement that essentially captures this notion is: "a store *completes* when the results of the store become observable." For caches with exclusive management, the store completes when it is issued by the processor, since any other processor that attempts to load from the stored location can only observe the new contents of that location (the process that implements this is the CERO).

For caches without exclusive management, the store completes only when it can be guaranteed (through other means) that all other processors will observe the new value in the stored location. The sequence of events that guarantee this without exclusive management is as follows:

1. A processor issues a store.
2. This store request is transmitted to the memory controller.
3. The memory controller checks its global directory to determine if the line to which the store was issued resides in other caches, and if so:
   a. The memory controller broadcasts invalidate signals to those caches;
   b. Those caches invalidate their copies of the line, and send acknowledgement signals back to the memory controller; and
   c. The memory controller receives the acknowledgement signals.
4. The memory controller stores the new data in main memory.
5. The memory controller sends a "store completion" signal back to the initiating processor.
6. The initiating processor receives this signal, and only at this time is it sure that store completion has occurred.

Until store completion has occurred, further fetching by the initiating processor is restricted as follows: if a fetch is issued to a location to which a store has been issued and store completion has not occurred, no subsequent fetching is permitted until the store completes.

Thus, it is feasible to operate a store-through cache without exclusive management, and the choice is only conditioned on performance and complexity considera-

tions. If exclusive management is not to be used, a further option is whether to allocate lines on stores. The WTWA cache (as just described) does the allocation, but the WTNWA cache does not. That is, the difference between WTNWA and WTWA is that stores done to non-resident lines do not generate misses in a WTNWA cache, but they do generate misses (and cause the relevant lines to become resident) in a WTWA cache.

Shared-Bus Systems and Directory-Based Systems

In this final section, the differences between shared-bus systems and directory-based systems are discussed. Logically, the two systems are identical. A directory-based system is merely a centralized implementation of the distributed directories that comprise a bus-based system. The reason for centralizing the directories of a shared-bus system to create a directory-based system is electrical. In very high-performance systems, timing constraints force this choice.

Much of the discussion about coherency centered on the operation of the global memory controller, the principle functions of which are: 1) to honor requests (misses, stores, FNDs) from each specific processor in the order that they are made, and 2) to issue XIs and CEROs to caches in the system pursuant to implementing these requests. In the following discussion, the implementation of a memory controller in a high-performance system is motivated. High-performance systems tend to be *directory-based*; systems that emphasize low cost/performance are more likely to be *shared-bus* systems.

First, consider a system composed of "low-end" processors. For the purposes of this discussion, the essential properties of a low-end processor are: 1) a slow clock cycle time, 2) a diminutive size (physical volume), and 3) a relatively large average number of cycles required to execute an instruction.

The implication of properties 1 and 2 is that it is electrically possible to transmit a signal that will propagate throughout the system in a small number of cycles (perhaps only 1). The implication of property 3 is that the need to transmit signals (such as XIs and CEROs) is relatively infrequent. These two implications in conjunction suggest a *shared-bus* system, structure—i.e. they suggest a system comprising a single bus, with main memory and all processors connected to the bus.

The shared-bus structure is natural since no single transmission occupies the bus for more than one cycle (or a small number of cycles), and since the frequency of such transmissions from any single processor is low enough so that a single bus can support the bandwidth requirements of a number of processors. (Note that the number of cycles in the leading edge is small, so the line size in such systems tends to be small, keeping the trailing edge commensurate with the leading edge.)

Further, since all processors are connected to the bus, each processor is able to observe all of the traffic in the system. Therefore, there is no need for a global memory-control function in such a system. Rather, the memory control function is distributed among the processors, and comprises the shared bus and all cache directories that are connected to the bus.

Caches in such a system are sometimes called *snooping caches* (or even "snoopy caches") since they are able to observe ("snoop on") all transmissions in the system. A snooping cache must search its directory for every transmission that appears on the bus, since some of these transmissions will be XIs or CEROs that must be acted on. However, from the perspective of any specific processor in the system, the vast majority of the transmissions are irrelevant (i.e. do not contain information that is relevant to that specific processor).

Thus, with no special provisions made in the design, a snooping cache devotes many of its cycles (cycles during which the cache is unavailable for use by the local processor) doing searches on behalf of system messages that are irrelevant. This represents an unnecessary performance loss that practical designs avoid. In practice, a snooping cache has two directories (identical copies with identical information): one directory is available for constant use by the local processor, and the other copy monitors the bus and serves as a "message filter." The message filter directory only disrupts the other directory when a relevant message (XI or CERO) is encountered.

Now, consider a system composed of high-performance processors. For the purposes of this discussion, the essential properties of a high-performance processor are: 1) a fast clock cycle time (order of magnitude or faster than a low-end processor), 2) a large physical size (order of magnitude or more larger than in the low-end), and 3) a relatively small average number of cycles required to execute an instruction (several times smaller than in the low-end).

The implication of properties 1 and 2 is that it requires many cycles to electrically propagate a signal throughout the system. The implication of property 3 is that the need to transmit signals (such as XIs and CEROs) is frequent. These two implications in conjunction suggest that a shared-bus system structure is not feasible—that is, a single message would require many cycles for its transmission on a shared bus, and the number of such transmissions is larger than can be supported by a single bus.

In high-performance systems, the memory control function comprises a single global directory, hence the term *directory-based* system. Each processor in a directory-based system has (at least) one dedicated bus for communicating with the global directory. The memory controller maintains this directory for all lines that are cached anywhere in the system. Philosophically, this directory is the "message filter" for the entire system; in principle, the directory of a high-end memory control function comprises the collection of "snooping filter" directories that compose the (analogous) low-end memory control function.

The global directory may be implemented as a collection of individual directories, or it may be implemented as a unified directory. In order for a unified directory to function as a filter, each entry in the directory must contain information that identifies those particular caches that hold copies of the associated line. A line that is held exclusive can reside in only one cache, but a line that is held read-only may arbitrarily reside in many caches.

In a system of n processors, this information may be represented with $n+1$ bits: 1 bit to indicate exclusive status, and n bits to indicate residence in each of the n processors. If the exclusive bit is set, exactly one of the remaining n bits must be set; otherwise (for shared read-only lines), any or all of the n bits can be set.

References

1968. Liptay, J. S. "Structural Aspects of the System/360 Model 85—Part II, The Cache," IBM *Systems Journal*, **7**, *1*, 15–21.

1982. Smith, A. J. "Cache Memories," *ACM Computing Surveys*, **14**, *3*, September, 473–530.

1986. Smith, A. J. "Bibliography and Readings on CPU Cache Memories and Related Topics," *Computer Architecture News*, **14**, *1*, January, 22–42.

1987. Pence, W. E., and Krusius, J. P "The Fundamental Limits for Electronic Packaging and Systems," IEEE *Transactions on Components, Hybrids, and Manufacturing Technology*, **CHMT-10**, *2*, June, 176–183.

1992. Collier, W. W. *Reasoning About Parallel Architectures*, Englewood Cliffs, NJ: Prentice-Hall.

PHILIP EMMA

STORE (n.). *See* MEMORY.

STORED PROGRAM CONCEPT

For articles on related subjects *see* ADDRESSING; ANALYTICAL ENGINE; ASSEMBLER; DIGITAL COMPUTERS; BABBAGE, CHARLES; MACHINE AND ASSEMBLY LANGUAGE PROGRAMMING; MARK I; PROGRAM COUNTER; VON NEUMANN, JOHN; and VON NEUMANN MACHINE.

The key design feature of modern computers, which allows the instructions to be held in the internal store while they are awaiting execution, is known as the *stored program concept*. Many computers, beginning with the Analytical Engine of Charles Babbage, and including the Automatic Sequence Controlled Calculator (Harvard Mark I), were designed to perform discrete operations, each specified by a concisely coded instruction. Prior to the use of electronics, however, these instructions were taken by the control unit from a special input device that read a tape or belt. Program loops required a loop of tape to be mounted (and the Harvard Mark I had three readers) with provision for control to be passed from one to another, to allow some flexibility in the logical structure of the program.

Electronics forced a departure from this arrangement because no tape reader could scan instructions fast enough to keep up with the internal speed of the computer. The first electronic computer, ENIAC (*q.v.*), went back to plugboard programming (as used on punched card machines), but this proved extremely clumsy. The stored program concept emerged as an alternative solution from discussions that took place at the Moore School of Electrical Engineering, where ENIAC was under construction in 1944. Participants in these discussions included J. Presper Eckert (*q.v.*), J. W. Mauchly (*q.v.*), John von Neumann, and H. H. Goldstine, and the concept was first documented in a Moore School report drafted by von Neumann (1945).

Besides solving the speed problem, the concept had two important long-term effects. First, program jumps could be used liberally without incurring the time penalty required to hunt along the program tape. (Some early machines, especially those based on drum stores, had some residual timing penalties affecting the arrangement of jumps, but these were comparatively unimportant.) Therefore, much more complex program structures could be contemplated. Secondly, and more significantly, the instructions held in the internal store were accessible to be operated upon the same way as the data during the execution of the program.

Both these possibilities were quickly exploited when the first stored-program computers, EDSAC (*q.v.*) and BINAC, came into service in 1949. Alteration of programs during execution enormously increased the scope of automatic computing, and was heavily used in the early days. Since then, its use has diminished considerably, for several reasons, the main ones being the introduction of *index registers* (these achieved more economically the effect of address modification, which had been the commonest purpose of program alteration) and the trend toward time-sharing systems and run-time diagnostic systems (which required programs to be *pure procedures*, i.e. unaltered and unalterable during execution, all variations being embodied in sets of parameters held in a working store segment).

Another development, which demanded the abandonment of program alteration during execution, was the use of read-only memories for programs needed very frequently. This approach is now rather widely used in microcomputers.

The potentialities of program-processing were much more fully exploited later in the preprocessing of programs by assemblers and compilers before execution, and, although the stored-program concept was not essential to this development, it certainly encouraged it strongly. In fact, the load-and-go compiler (*q.v.*), now very commonly used in some kinds of installations, depends on the ability to store the program.

From the beginning it was inherent in the stored program concept that the instructions be made to fit (perhaps in groups) into the same word length as the data so that the same store could be used interchangeably for both with reasonable efficiency. Indeed, the ability of the machine to modify its program depended on having the program accessible in the same way as the data. However, the Harvard Mark IV was remarkable in having separate stores for the instructions and the data.

A. M. Turing had touched on the stored program concept in a paper on mathematical logic in 1936 (which led to the term *Turing machine* (*q.v.*)), though not in a form that showed its potential practicality. The first electronic stored-program machine to obey instructions was that built by Williams and Kilburn in Manchester, England, and the first to carry out practical calculations was the EDSAC, built by Wilkes at Cambridge, England, which was operating in May 1949. Both EDSAC and EDVAC, designed at the Moore School by Eckert and Mauchly, embodied many of the ideas incorporated in von Neumann's report (1945), but EDVAC did not become operational until 1951.

In the years that have followed these early implementations, the stored program concept has been elaborated in many ways. Programming techniques and languages of many kinds have been developed, as well as operating systems and all the various components of modern software. Perhaps the most fundamental variation from the original idea has been the introduction of program interrupts (*q.v.*), which means that the sequence of execution of the instructions is no longer uniquely determined by the program and its data, but can be affected by external events occurring during the execution.

These, however, are all auxiliary to the stored program concept itself, an essentially simple, but profoundly important, concept that has characterized the main stream of digital computer development since 1945. This concept, together with the practical development of electronics, has made possible the computer revolution as we now know it.

Reference

1945. von Neumann, John. "First Draft of a Report on the EDVAC," Contract No. W-670-ORD-4926, U.S. Army Ordnance Department and University of Pennsylvania, Moore School of Electrical Engineering, University of Pennsylvania, Philadelphia, PA. (30 June).

STANLEY GILL

STRACHEY, CHRISTOPHER

For articles on related subjects *see* FUNCTIONAL PROGRAMMING; and TIME SHARING.

Christopher Strachey (1916-1975) was Professor of Computer Science at Oxford University from 1971 until his death. He was born into the well-known Strachey family, associated with the English artistic circle, the "Bloomsbury Group." He showed a scientific bent, however, and graduated in physics from Cambridge University in 1939. During World War II he served in an electronics development laboratory at Standard Telephones and Cables, where he gained some computing experience using a differential analyzer (*q.v.*). Strachey was a gifted teacher, and in 1944 he became a schoolmaster. While teaching at Harrow School in 1951, he began in his spare time to program the Pilot ACE computer at the National Physical Laboratory and the Mark I computer at Manchester University. As a result of this early involvement with computers, in 1952 he became a technical officer with the National Research Development Corporation (NRDC)—a quasi-government organization created for the commercial exploitation of British technological innovations. While with the NRDC, he played a leading part in the

FIG. 1.   Christopher Strachey.

calculations for the St. Lawrence Seaway in Canada, and undertook the logical design of the Ferranti Pegasus computer. Each achievement was considered a *tour-de-force*. In the late 1950s, Strachey was one of the first proselytizers of time sharing (*q.v.*) in computers. From 1959-65, he was a private consultant, and in 1962 he joined the University Mathematical Laboratory, Cambridge, on a half-time basis. At Cambridge he led the development of the CPL programming language. Although CPL was never satisfactorily implemented, the design of the language and the people associated with the project subsequently made their mark on programming language development. During this period he also developed the General Purpose Macrogenerator. In 1965, Strachey wound up his consultancy in favor of the academic life—first spending a year at M.I.T., and in 1966 founding the Programming Research Group at Oxford University. He was appointed to a personal chair in 1971. During his last years, Strachey collaborated with the American logician Dana Scott, with whom he laid the foundations of denotational semantics. Although Strachey had a notorious reluctance to publish throughout his life, the few papers he did produce show the literary elegance and wit characteristic of his family.

Reference

1985. Campbell-Kelly, M. "Christopher Strachey, 1916-1975: A Biographical Note," *Annals of the History of Computing* **7**: 19–42.

MARTIN CAMPBELL-KELLY

STRETCH

For articles on related subjects *see* DIGITAL COMPUTERS: EARLY; LIVERMORE AUTOMATIC RESEARCH COMPUTER; and SUPERCOMPUTERS.

The *Stretch* computer (formally the IBM 7030) was the outcome of a research and development project started in 1955 and aimed at an advance in performance of about two orders of magnitude over the then existing computer technology and organization. It was a joint project between the IBM Corporation and the Los Alamos Scientific Laboratory of the U.S. Atomic Energy Commission.

The first computer (Fig. 1) was delivered to Los Alamos in 1961. Although the machine did not "stretch" quite as far as the ambitious performance goal originally set, at that time it was still the most powerful computer in existence. After ten years of service, the Los Alamos machine was dismantled in 1971. Seven other Stretch machines were built.

Stretch was the first major solid-state computer developed by IBM, and its transistor, core, and disk storage technologies were applied extensively to other computers of the 7000 series. Its sophisticated internal organization (Buchholz, 1962) departed substantially from that of previous computers. An instruction lookahead unit, for example, permitted up to six instructions at one time to be in various stages of execution; thus, Stretch became the first pipelined computer. While the sophistication contributed to the high speed of Stretch, the resulting complexity of implementation, in retrospect, also kept the speed somewhat short of the objective.

Other than speed, perhaps the most significant feature was the provision in one computer system of both the parallel floating-point arithmetic then associated with "scientific" computers, and the serial, variable-length, fixed-point arithmetic and character processing functions then found only in "commercial" computers.

The computer had been planned as the largest of a single line of general-purpose compatible machines. However, this concept did not materialize until the later IBM 360/370/390 (*q.v.*), which also adopted several other basic concepts of Stretch. Some of the terminology from the Stretch project (computer architecture, byte) has since entered general use.

FIG. 1.   The first Stretch computer being tested just prior to its installation at the Los Alamos Scientific Laboratory.

A major non-arithmetical extension to Stretch, referred to as *Harvest*, provided very powerful data streaming and table look-up operations on a byte-by-byte basis (Buchholz, 1962, chap. 17). Only one Harvest machine was built.

Reference

1962. Buchholz, W. (Ed.). *Planning a Computer System (Project Stretch)*. New York: McGraw-Hill.

WERNER BUCHHOLZ

STRING PROCESSING

For articles on related subjects *see* CONCATENATION; LIST PROCESSING; MUMPS; PROGRAMMING LANGUAGES; and PROGRAMMING LINGUISTICS.

PRINCIPLES

In programming contexts, the term *string* usually refers to a sequence of characters. For example, ABC is a string of three characters. Strings are more prevalent in computing than is generally realized. In most cases, computer input is in the form of strings (e.g. commands entered at a terminal). Similarly, computer output is in the form of strings since printed lines are simply strings of characters.

Strings and String Processing The facilities of the most widely used programming languages are concentrated on numerical and business data processing. However, a substantial amount of string processing is performed. For example, compilers accept strings as input, analyze them, and produce either bit or character strings as output. Command interpreters analyze command strings and perform appropriate actions. These kinds of programs are used heavily, so they must be extremely efficient. For this reason, they are usually written in systems programming languages such as C (*q.v.*) rather than in higher-level string processing languages. Nevertheless, higher-level string processing languages offer many advantages for solving complex problems. Examples of such problems are language translation (*q.v.*), computational linguistics, computer algebra (*q.v.*), text editing (*q.v.*), and document formatting (*see* DESKTOP PUBLISHING).

While mathematical notation for numerical computation has developed over centuries, string processing is a new area. There is no general agreement on what operations should be performed in string processing, nor is there a standard notation. The developers of string processing languages started largely without conventions. As a result, notation, program structure, and approach to problem formulation are often radically different from those of more conventional programming languages.

Operations on Strings Four string processing operations have achieved reasonably general acceptance: concatenation, identification of substrings, pattern matching, and transformation of strings to replace identified substrings by other strings.

Concatenation (sometimes called "catenation") is the process of appending one string to another to produce a longer string. Thus, the result of concatenating the strings AB and CDE is the string ABCDE. This operation is a natural extension of the concept of a string as a sequence of characters. A *substring* is a string wholly contained within another string. For example, BC and CDE are substrings of ABCDE.

The most important string operation is *pattern matching*, examining a string to locate substrings or to determine if a string has certain properties. Examples are the presence of a specific substring, substrings in certain positions, substrings in a specified relationship to each other, etc. *Transformation* of strings is typically accomplished in conjunction with pattern matching, using the results of pattern matching to effect a replacement of substrings.

The language descriptions below emphasize approaches to string processing and the major facilities that deal with strings. No attempt has been made to describe these languages completely; details can be found in the references.

LANGUAGES

Comit Comit (Yngve, 1963), designed in 1957–58, was the first string processing language. It was motivated by the need for a tool for mechanical language translation. Comit strongly reflects these origins and is oriented toward the representation of natural languages.

Basic Concepts In Comit, unlike most other string processing languages, a string is composed of *constituents* which may consist of more than one character. Thus, a word composed of many characters may be a single constituent in a string. A string is written as a series of constituents separated by + signs—e.g.

```
FOURSCORE + AND + SEVEN + YEARS + AGO
```

The character – represents a space (blank). Thus, to include spaces between words, the string above becomes

```
FOURSCORE + - + AND - + SEVEN + - YEARS
+ - AGO
```

All characters other than letters have syntactic meaning. A star (asterisk) in front of a character other than a letter indicates that the character is to be taken literally rather than for its syntactic meaning. For example,

```
33 ARE IN THE TOP 1/2.
```

is written

```
*3*3 + - + ARE + - + IN + - + THE + - +
TOP + - + *1*/*2*.
```

Attention focuses on a *workspace*, which contains the string currently being processed. There are 128 *shelves*, any of which may be exchanged with the workspace to change the focus of attention. Thus, there may be at most 129 distinct strings in a program at any one time.

Comit programs are a sequence of rules, each of which has five parts:

name left-half = right-half / / routing goto

The *name* identifies the rule. The *left-half* is a pattern applied to the workspace, and the *right-half* specifies processing to be performed on the portion of the workspace matched by the *left-half*. The *routing* performs operations other than pattern matching. If a rule has no routing field, the slashes are not required. The *goto* controls program flow.

Pattern Matching The left-half may specify full constituents as written in a string, a specific number of constituents of unspecified value, an indefinite number of constituents, an earlier constituent referenced by its position in the left-half, etc. A full constituent is written as it is in a string. Other left-half constituents are represented by special notations. For example: n matches n consecutive constituents, regardless of their value; $ matches any number of constituents. The integer n matches the same string that the nth constituent of the left-half matched. For example, the left-half

```
THE + $1 + $ + 2
```

has four constituents: the characters THE, followed by any single constituent, followed by any number of constituents until one is encountered that is the same as the one matched by the second constituent, namely, $1. Pattern matching is left to right. Left-half constituents must match consecutive constituents in the workspace.

If the workspace contains

```
THE + FIRST
|___| |___|
  1     2

 + PERSON + IN + LINE + IS + SERVED + FIRST
|_____| |____|
              3                       4
```

the match for each of the constituents is as shown. Note that the fourth constituent of the left-half matches the same constituents as the second constituent of the left-half. The third constituent of the left-half consequently matches the intervening five constituents. When a match occurs, workspace constituents are associated with the left-half constituents they matched and are subsequently referenced by the number of the corresponding left-half constituent.

The right-half may contain full constituents and integers that correspond to the constituents of the left-half. The matched portion of the workspace is replaced by

constituents specified in the right-half. Continuing the example above, the rule

```
THE + $1 + $ + 2 = 1 + SECOND + 3 + 4
```

transforms the workspace into

```
THE + SECOND + PERSON + IN + LINE + IS
+ SERVED + FIRST
```

Other Facilities The routing part of a rule permits operations that cannot be performed in the right-half. Examples are exchange of the workspace with a shelf, movement of constituents between the workspace and shelves, printing the workspace, reading data into the workspace, etc.

The goto part of a rule controls program flow. Control may be transferred to a named rule, back to the same statement for execution again, to the next statement, etc.

Loops may be programmed in a number of ways. One conditional operation is left-half matching, which may fail. For example, the left-half $10 would fail to match the workspace given above because the workspace does not contain ten constituents. When a left-half fails to match, the remainder of the rule is not performed and control passes to the next rule in line. Special notations are used for names and gotos in writing loops. A * may be used for the name of a rule that needs no other specific identification. A * in the goto indicates that control is to be transferred to the next rule in line. A / in the goto indicates that control is to be returned to the present rule if it is executed successfully. Thus,

```
* THE = /
```

which has a blank right-half and a / in the goto, removes all occurrences of THE from the workspace. When the left-half finally fails to match, execution continues with the next rule in line.

Status The current version of Comit is Comit II, which has been implemented on the IBM 360/370/390. Because of its early origin, Comit lacks a number of features that are available in more recently developed languages.

SNOBOL and SNOBOL3 The first SNOBOL (string-oriented symbolic language) language was designed and implemented in 1962–63. Its major motivation was the need for a general-purpose language for string processing. Manipulation of symbolic mathematical expressions was also an important consideration.

Basic Concepts In SNOBOL, unlike Comit, a string is simply a sequence of characters. Enclosing quotation marks delimit the string, but are not part of the string. An example is

```
'FOURSCORE AND SEVEN YEARS AGO'
```

Such a string is said to be specified *literally*. Strings may be assigned to names for subsequent reference, e.g.

```
FIRST = 'MORGAN'
```

assigns the string MORGAN to the name FIRST. There is no limit to the number of distinct strings. Storage management is automatic; there are no declarations. Concatenation is denoted by the juxtaposition of strings. Such strings can be given literally or as the value of names, e.g.

```
FULLNAME = FIRST 'ᵤSMITH'
```

assigns the string MORGANᵤSMITH to the name FULLNAME. The blank, shown here as ᵤ for clarity, is simply a character like any other.

A SNOBOL program consists of a sequence of statements. There are three kinds of statements: Assignment, pattern-matching, and replacement. The respective forms are

label	*subject = object*	*goto*
label	*subject pattern*	*goto*
label	*subject pattern = object*	*goto*

An optional *label* identifies the statement. The *subject* provides the focus for the statement and is the name on which operations are performed. The *goto* controls program flow and is optional. An assignment statement assigns a value to a name. A pattern-matching statement examines the value of a name for a *pattern,* and a replacement statement modifies that part of the subject matched by the pattern.

Pattern Matching   Patterns in SNOBOL consist of a sequence of components. There are two types of components: specific strings and *string variables*. A specific string may be given literally or referred to by name. A string variable is indicated by delimiting asterisks, which bracket a name. There are several types of string variables. An *arbitrary string variable* can match any string. It is similar to the Comit $ notation, except that whatever the string variable matches is assigned to the name between the asterisks. Pattern matching is left to right, and components of the pattern must match consecutive substrings of the subject. For example, in

```
Z 'T' *FILL* 'N'
```

the value of Z is matched for any string that begins with a T and ends with an N. The substring between the T and N is assigned to the name FILL. If the value of Z is TEEN, the value assigned to FILL is EE.

A *balanced string variable* matches a string that is properly balanced with respect to parentheses like an ordinary mathematical expression. A *fixed-length string variable* matches any string of a specific length and is indicated by a / and a quoted number following the name. For example,

```
TEXT ',' *C/"1/*
```

examines the value of TEXT for a comma and assigns the character following the comma to C.

Replacement is a combination of pattern-matching and assignment in which the matched substring is replaced by the object. The statement

```
FULLNAME 'SMITH' = 'JONES'
```

replaces the substring SMITH by JONES and consequently changes the value of FULLNAME to MORGANᵤJONES.

Indirect Referencing   A string may be computed and then used as a name. A $ placed in front of a string uses the value of that string as a name. For example, the statements

```
X = 'NUM'
N = '3'
HOLIDAY = X N
$HOLIDAY = 'EASTER'
```

first assign the value NUM3 to HOLIDAY and then assign the value EASTER to NUM3. The indirect referencing operator, similar in concept to indirect addressing in assembly language, provides a way of constructing names of data during execution.

Other Facilities   Input and output take place using specially designated names as subjects. Arithmetic facilities are rudimentary (e.g. integer arithmetic on strings of digits).

The goto part of a statement controls program flow. Gotos can be unconditional to a labeled statement, or conditional on the success or failure of pattern matching. Loops are programmed using the conditional nature of pattern matching.

Status   SNOBOL was superseded by SNOBOL3 in 1965. SNOBOL3 is similar to SNOBOL, but has several additional features, including a number of built-in functions and a facility for programmer-defined recursive functions. SNOBOL3 was in turn superseded by SNOBOL4 in 1967.

SNOBOL4   (Griswold *et al.,* 1971) is a natural descendant of earlier SNOBOL languages and is based on many of the same ideas and approaches to string processing. SNOBOL4, however, introduced a number of new concepts. The most important are those dealing with pattern matching.

Patterns   In Comit and the earlier SNOBOL languages, different types of patterns are indicated by specific notations. In SNOBOL4, patterns are data objects that are constructed by functions and operations. Consequently, quite complicated patterns can be built piecemeal.

There are two basic pattern-construction operations: alternation and concatenation. The alternation of two patterns is a pattern that will match anything that either of its two components will match. The concatenation of two patterns is a pattern that will match anything that its two components will match consecutively. Alternation is represented by a vertical bar and concatenation by a blank; e.g.

```
PET = 'CAT' | 'DOG'
PETKIND = PET '-LIKE'
```

The pattern PET matches either of the strings CAT or DOG, and PETKIND matches anything PET matches followed by the string -LIKE (i.e. CAT-LIKE or DOG-LIKE).

Pattern-valued functions generalize the concept of patterns and avoid special notations for each type. For example, the value returned by LEN(n) is a pattern that matches n characters, and the pattern returned by TAB(n) matches a substring through the nth character of the subject string. For example,

```
OPER = TAB(6) 'X'
```

creates a pattern that will match any string containing an X as its seventh character. Other pattern-valued functions create patterns that match any one of a number of specific characters, search for specific characters, etc. Examples are SPAN('0123456789'), which matches a substring consisting only of digits, and BREAK(';,'), which matches the substring beginning at the current position up to the next comma or semicolon.

As in SNOBOL, pattern matching is left to right, and components must match consecutive substrings of the subject string. When a component fails to match, alternative matches are attempted. If no alternative is specified, the pattern-matching process backs up to earlier, successfully matched components, seeking other ways in which the entire pattern match can succeed. Conceptually, the pattern-matching process manipulates a cursor, which is an imaginary marker in the subject string indicating the current position of the match. Movement of the cursor is implicit, not under direct control of the programmer, although in some patterns there is a direct correlation. Thus, LEN(3) moves the cursor to the right three characters. The cursor cannot be moved to the left by a successful match.

Names may be attached to components of patterns so that when the component matches a substring, that substring is assigned to the name. Attachment is indicated by the binary $ operator, e.g.

```
HEAD = LEN(7) $ LABEL
```

constructs a pattern that matches seven characters. The seven characters, when matched, are assigned to LABEL, so

```
CARD HEAD
```

assigns the first seven characters of the value of CARD to LABEL. If the match fails (as it would because CARD is less than seven characters long), no assignment is made to LABEL.

Another aspect of pattern matching is the ability to modify the pattern during matching depending on substrings matched by earlier components. Evaluation of an expression in a pattern may be deferred by prefacing the expression with *. The expression is then left unevaluated until it is encountered in pattern matching. An example of the power of this facility is given by

```
LIT = ('"' | '"') $ C BREAK(*C).STRING LEN(1)
```

When LIT is used in pattern matching, the argument of BREAK is not evaluated until after the first part of the pattern has matched. The pattern matches a single or double quote and assigns it to C. The remainder of the pattern matches everything up to the next occurrence of character just assigned to C, assigns that substring to STRING, and then LEN(1) matches the second quote. Thus, LIT matches literal string constants as used in many programming languages.

Other Facilities Other string processing facilities include alphabetical comparison of strings, mappings from one set of characters to another, and deletion of trailing blanks. Earlier SNOBOL languages were purely string processing languages; SNOBOL4 includes many types of data. In addition to types such as integer and real, SNOBOL4 includes arrays as data objects, tables that provide associative look-up features, and a facility for defining record types during execution. In many cases it is possible to perform data-type conversions between various types of data. It is possible to convert a string into program statements during program execution, and hence to modify or extend the program while it is running. SNOBOL4 is actually a general-purpose language that strongly emphasizes string processing and contains a number of exotic features.

Status SNOBOL4 is a widely used and generally available string-processing language. It and a number of dialects have been implemented on a wide range of machines, from personal computers to mainframes.

Icon The major emphasis in pattern matching in the SNOBOL languages, as in other string-processing languages, is on the *specification* of patterns that analyze strings. There is little facility for indicating *how* the matching is accomplished or for describing the synthesis of new strings from the results of pattern-matching.

In many cases, this bias toward pattern specification is useful; it frees the programmer from the necessity of spelling out too much detail concerning the actual matching. This is especially the case in SNOBOL4, in which the process of matching embodies a powerful search and backtrack algorithm that is particularly complex and obscure.

In other cases, however, programming tasks may fall outside the capabilities of the pattern matching facility. Faced with this dilemma, programmers resort to inefficient or obscure techniques that are typically unrepresentative of the capabilities of the language as a whole. This situation is due largely to the inextensibility of the pattern-matching facility. In SNOBOL4, for example, the pattern matching facility is not as extensible as is the rest of the language. While there is a facility for programmer-defined functions and datatypes, there is no facility for programmer-defined *matching* procedures (i.e. procedures, which are invoked during matching, that describe how a particular pattern is to be matched). This deficiency can be better understood by considering the pattern assigned to HEAD above:

```
HEAD = LEN(7) $ LABEL
```

LEN(7) constructs and returns a pattern that, when applied, attempts to advance the cursor by 7 characters. LEN itself plays no role in the matching—it merely constructs a data object that contains an indication of the action to be taken during pattern-matching. It is this latter component of the pattern that corresponds to the matching procedure and that cannot be defined by the programmer.

SNOBOL4 and its variants suffer a common problem: They are each, in reality, composed of two languages—a basic language and a pattern matching language (Griswald and Hanson, 1980). In each language, the programmer is burdened with the construction of pattern-matching "programs." This corresponds to construction of a pattern, which is subsequently applied, or to the construction of the set of procedures, which eventually cooperate during pattern-matching. This two-step process—pattern construction and pattern application—is due largely to the central role of patterns as distinguished objects in string processing languages. It is the elimination of patterns, but not of pattern-matching, that differentiates the newest string processing language, Icon, from its predecessors.

Icon (Griswold and Griswold, 1990), developed in late 1970s, has a number of relatively low-level lexical primitives, some of which are related to patterns in SNOBOL4. Icon also has control structures and a goal-directed evaluation mechanism that make pattern-matching—called *string scanning* in Icon—an integral part of the language. The central feature of Icon is this evaluation mechanism, which embodies a search and backtrack algorithm similar, but simpler, than that used in SNOBOL4 pattern matching. An important aspect of this mechanism is that it pervades the entire language, instead of being restricted to a component of the language. The combination of the lexical primitives and the evaluation mechanism yields string scanning capabilities comparable to those of SNOBOL4.

String scanning in Icon is accomplished in a manner that appears similar to SNOBOL4 but does not involve anything like pattern construction. The expression *s* ? *e* establishes *s* as the subject to which string processing operations in *e* apply. The expression *e* typically includes string analysis operations, but may include *any* Icon operation. A *scanning environment* is characterized by a pair of implicit variables {subject,pos}; subject is the string to which scanning operations apply, and pos is a location with the subject and usually changes as the subject is analyzed. The expression *s* ?*e* establishes a new scanning environment {*s*,1}, and then evaluates *e*. After evaluating *e*, the previous scanning environment is restored.

Some of the scanning operations in Icon operate on the position in the absence of other specifications. An example is move(*n*), which attempts to advance the position by *n* characters. If the advancement is successful, move returns the *n*-character substring between the initial and final positions. For example,

```
line ? write("[", move(7), "]")
```

writes the first seven characters of line enclosed in brackets to the output. The equivalent SNOBOL4 program

```
HEAD = LEN(7) $ LABEL
LINE HEAD
OUTPUT = "[" LABEL "]"
```

first constructs the necessary pattern and assigns it to HEAD, then applies this pattern to LINE, which causes the first seven characters to be assigned to LABEL, and finally writes the desired result.

This simple example illustrates an important aspect of string scanning in Icon: move does not construct a pattern, but simply carries out the analysis in the current scanning environment. The SNOBOL4 equivalent involves construction of a pattern, followed by its application, and finally the output of the desired result.

Another important advantage resulting from the integration of string processing with the rest of Icon is that any language operation can be performed during string scanning. An example is

```
line ? while t := t || move(1) || "."
```

which produces a string t containing the characters of line separated by periods. The || operator denotes string concatenation, and while repeatedly evaluates

```
t := t || move(1) || "."
```

until it fails, which occurs when move(1) is invoked at the end of the subject string. Note the use of a standard control structure, while, within the ? expression. To accomplish the same thing in SNOBOL4 requires the separation of the analysis of the subject and the synthesis of the result, since there is no provision for using arbitrary constructs within a pattern. Thus, the SNOBOL4 equivalent requires two statements:

```
LOOP TEXT LEN(1) $ C =     :F(DONE)
     T = T C "."           :(LOOP)
DONE
```

If the pattern in the first line fails to match, control is transferred to the line labeled DONE; otherwise, the matched character and a period are appended to T, and control is returned to the line labeled LOOP.

String *synthesis* often accompanies string scanning. In the example above, t is synthesized during scanning, and it is t that is the result of interest. In some cases, the result of interest can be returned as the value of the scanning expression. The result of *s* ?*e* is the result of *e*, so both of the expressions

```
line ? write("[", move(7), "]")
write("[", line ? move(7), "]")
```

produce the same output.

The function move(*n*) is called a *matching function* because it returns the substring of the subject that is "matched" as a result of changing the position. Another matching function is tab(*i*), which moves to position *i* in the subject and returns the substring between the old and new positions. For both move and tab, the new position can be to the left of the old position.

Lexical functions return positions in the subject instead of substrings in the subject. For example, find(*s*) returns the position of the string *s* in the subject following the current position, so the output of

```
"Icon is a programming language" ?
    write(find("program"))
```

is 11. Likewise, upto(*s*) returns the position of any of the characters in string *s*, and many(*s*) returns the position following the longest possible substring containing only characters in *s* starting at the current position.

It is important to note that functions like many return positions, but the specific values of those positions are rarely important. Positions are used most often as arguments to matching functions like tab. For example,

```
line ? while tab(upto(&letters)) do
    write(tab(many(&letters)))
```

writes the "words" in line. The value of the keyword &letters is a string containing all of the upper- and lower-case letters. The expression tab(upto(&letters)) advances the position up to the next letter, and tab(many(&letters)) matches and returns the word, which is passed to write. The while loop terminates when tab(upto(&letters)) fails because there are no more words in line.

Most changes to the scanning environment (e.g. changing the position) are made implicitly by matching functions. Explicit reference to the scanning environment can be made through the keywords &subject and &pos; e.g.

```
&pos := 1
```

sets the scanning position to 1. This assignment is equivalent to tab(1). Likewise,

```
&subject := read()
```

changes the subject to the next line of input. Assignments to &subject cause &pos to be set to 1. It is usually undesirable to access or change the subject and position explicitly. However, doing so is necessary when writing matching procedures to augment the built-in repertoire of matching functions (see Griswold, 1990).

Icon has an alternation expression that resembles alternation in SNOBOL4: $e_1 \mid e_2$. The important difference is that, while the SNOBOL4 alternation operator constructs a pattern, alternation in Icon simply carries out the operation directly. The operation is similar to that performed during pattern matching in SNOBOL4 when the pattern constructed by P1 | P2 is applied.

In the Icon expression, $e_1 \mid e_2$, e_1 is evaluated first and, if that evaluation succeeds, the value of e_1 is the result of the entire expression. If, however, evaluation of e_1 fails, the result is the result of evaluating e_2. Another way in which e_2 can be evaluated is if the entire expression is used in a context where the value of e_1 is unacceptable. An example is

```
move(10 | 5)
```

The expression 10 | 5 has two literal subexpressions, and the first, 10, succeeds. Suppose, however, that the subject is only six characters long. In this case, move(10) fails. This causes the re-evaluation of 10 | 5, which yields the value 5. This time, move(5) succeeds. Note that

```
move(10 | 5)
```

is equivalent to

```
move(10) | move(5)
```

which corresponds to the SNOBOL4 pattern

```
LEN(10) | LEN(5)
```

Note, however, that SNOBOL4 has no direct counterpart to move(10 | 5). Alternation in SNOBOL4 is restricted to specific contexts; alternation in Icon may be used anywhere that an expression may be used.

In Icon, operations that have the capacity for producing alternative values that are required by the context in which they appear are called *generators*. In addition to alternation, many of the low-level lexical primitives are generators whose behavior when used in string scanning is designed to facilitate string processing. For example, find(*s*) is capable of generating all of the positions at which *s* appears in the subject. If only one value is needed, only one is generated, so the output of

```
"a fish is a fish is a fish" ?
    write(find("fish"))
```

is 3. Additional values are generated as demanded by the context in which find is used; for example, in

```
"a fish is a fish is a fish" ?
    write(find("fish") > 20)
```

the first value produced by find is 3, which is less than 20. The comparison (>) fails, which causes find to be resumed. It produces 13 and the comparison again fails. Finally, find produces 23 and the comparison succeeds. A successful comparison returns its right operand, so the output is 20.

Icon's procedure mechanism allows the construction of programmer-defined generators. This capability corresponds to the definition of programmer-defined matching procedures in SNOBOL4. Generators are not limited to the string processing aspects of Icon, but are meaningful for many operations. Generators allow a more natural expression of some constructions than is possible in most other programming languages. It is often possible to express constructions more concisely and closer to the way that programmers think in mathematical and natural languages. For further information about this aspect of Icon, see Griswold *et al.*, 1981. Griswold and Griswold, 1986, describes an implementation of Icon in detail.

Status Icon has been implemented on a wide range of computers from PCs to large-scale mainframes. It is the most widely used and generally available high-level string processing language.

Other String Processing Languages Ambit (Wolfberg, 1972), developed in 1964, is a string processing language oriented toward algebraic manipulation. Ambit is similar in many respects to Comit and the SNOBOL languages. However, its strings are parenthesized expressions that correspond to tree structures, and they are implemented as fully linked trees. In Ambit, unlike most other string processing languages, two strings having the same sequence of non-blank characters are considered equivalent even if they differ in the position and number of blanks they contain. A *basic replacement* rule consists of a *citation,* specifying a pattern, and a *replacement,* which effects a transformation on the string under consideration. The citation may match only one way; the replacement rule must be unambiguous. An important aspect of Ambit pattern-matching is the explicit reference to pointers, which identify specific positions in strings. There are three variants of Ambit: Ambit/S for manipulating strings, Ambit/G for manipulating general data structures, and Ambit/L for list processing.

Convert (Guzman and McIntosh, 1966) is an extension of Lisp incorporating pattern-matching and transformation operations. There are a number of fundamental patterns and facilities for constructing more complicated ones. The function RESEMBLE applies patterns to strings, and REPLACE performs transformations using skeletons that specify the structure of the replacement. A rule consists of a pattern and a skeleton. Convert applies the pattern to a string. If a "resemblance" is found, values of relevant parts are identified and substituted into the skeleton to effect the conversion.

Axle (Cohen and Wegstein, 1965), like Comit, has a workspace that is the focus of attention for pattern-matching and replacement. Axle has *assertion tables,* which specify patterns. These specifications may be recursive. *Imperative tables* specify patterns to be matched and corresponding replacements. A pattern-matching procedure determines which imperative is applicable. Axle has *markers,* which may be positioned in the work space. These markers may be used to avoid reprocessing previously transformed parts of the workspace.

Panon (Fotino, 1968) is based on generalized Markov algorithms and includes a number of pattern-matching facilities and rules for transforming strings. A Panon program is itself a string, and hence susceptible to self–modification.

References

1963. Yngve, Victor H. *Computer Programming with COMIT II.* Cambridge, MA: The M.I.T. Press.
1965. Cohen, Kenneth and Wegstein, J. H. "AXLE: An Axiomatic Language for String Transformations." *Communications of the ACM,* **8**(*11*): 657–661 (November).
1966. Guzman, Adolfo and McIntosh, Harold V. "Convert," *Communications of the ACM,* **9**(*8*): 604–615 (August).
1968. Forino, A. Caracciolo. "String Processing Languages and Generalized Markov Algorithms." In *Proceedings of the IFIP Working Conference on Symbol Manipulation Languages,* 141–206, Amsterdam: North-Holland.
1971. Griswold, Ralph E., Poage, James F. and Polonsky, Ivan P. *The SNOBOL4 Programming Language* (2nd Ed.). Englewood Cliffs, NJ: Prentice-Hall.
1972. Wolfberg, Michael S. "Fundamentals of the Ambit/L List-processing Language," *SIGPLAN Notices,* **7**(10): 66–75 (October).
1980. Griswold, Ralph E. and Hanson, David R. "An Alternative to the Use of Patterns in String Processing," *ACM Transactions on Programming Languages and Systems,* **2**(*2*): 153–172 (April).
1981. Griswold, Ralph E., Hanson, David R., and Korb, John T. "Generators in Icon," *ACM Transactions on Programming Languages and Systems,* **3**(*2*):144–161 (April).
1986. Griswold, Ralph E. and Griswold, Madge T., *The Implementation of the Icon Programming Language.* Princeton, NJ: Princeton University Press.
1990. Griswold, Ralph E., "String Scanning in the Icon Programming Language," *The Computer Journal,* **33**(2): 98–107 (April).
1990. Griswold, Ralph E. and Griswold, Madge T. *The Icon Programming Language* (2nd Ed.). Englewood Cliffs, NJ: Prentice-Hall.

RALPH E. GRISWOLD AND DAVID R. HANSON

STRUCTURED PROGRAMMING

For articles on related subjects *see* ADA; ALGOL 68; C; CONTROL STRUCTURES; LOOP INVARIANT; MODULA-2; MODULAR PROGRAMMING; PROCEDURE-ORIENTED LANGUAGES: PROGRAMMING; PROGRAM; and PROGRAM VERIFICATION.

Structured programming (SP) may be defined as a methodological style whereby a computer program is constructed by concatenating or coherently nesting logical subunits that either are themselves structured programs or else are of the form of one or another of a small number of particularly well-understood *control structures.* Such a definition is inherently and deliberately recursive. Though the idea is of uncertain and undoubtedly multiple parentage, an explosion of interest in the concept followed the publication of a letter to the editor in *Communications of the ACM* in March 1968 by Edsger Dijkstra. In this letter, entitled "Go to Statement Considered Harmful" (by the editors of *CACM,* not the author), Dijkstra reported his observation that the ease of reading and understanding program listings was inversely proportional to the number of unconditional transfers of control ("**goto**") that they contained. This rule of thumb is quite plausible since, when a programmer suddenly writes **goto**, what he or she is essentially saying to the reader is "However hard you were concentrating on the logical flow of my program, stop and find the continuation of this logic at another (possibly remote) physical point. That new point is presumably marked by a label of some sort (numeric in Fortran or Pascal, or alphanumeric in Algol or APL, etc.), which may not even be on the same page that contained the **goto**. The front page of any daily newspaper is full of **goto** (e.g. "cont'd on p. 6") for the obvious reason that the editors want to draw attention to a large number of unrelated stories of approximately co-equal importance. At least some magazines are more considerate, however, and always finish one thought (article) before beginning another. Why can't programmers? Their ability to do so is at the heart of structured programming.

Control Structures for Structured Programming

One possible barrier to writing structured programs is lack of a sufficiently flexible grammar. Consider the Fortran IV segment:

```
IF (A .GT. B) K = K + 1
J = 3*K
L = 7
```

Such a segment scans well because the possible detour consists of the single statement K = K + 1. But, when either branch requires two or more statements, the programmer is forced to write something like the following:

```
        IF (A .GT. B) GOTO 20
10        J = 3*K
          L = 7
        GOTO 30
20        K = K + 1
          M = 2
        GOTO 10
30      _____
```

Following the flow of control in even this simple example is not trivial; if, instead of two statements each at labels 10 and 20, there were 30 or 50 or more, readability would suffer greatly. At least as early as the development of Algol in the late 1950s, it was noted that use of a compound statement, two or more statements separated by a special character (say ";") and delimited by others, typically "**begin**" and "**end**", could have a very beneficial effect. In Algol or Pascal, the last example can be rendered:

if A > B **then begin** K := K + 1 ; M := 2 **end**;
J := 3*K; L := 7; .....

In this example, the sequence starting with J : = 3*K is to be executed regardless of whether the consequent of the **then** is executed or not. When different and mutually exclusive actions are desired, the Algol or Pascal programmer can write:

if A > B **then begin** K := K + 1; M := 2 **end**
        else begin K := K − 1; M := 7 **end**

This **if-then-else** structure, which allows the selection of compound statement alternatives, turns out to be one of the essential control structures for structured programming. Interestingly enough, Cobol, which is seldom thought of as a structured language, has such a decision construct, whereas the more "scientific" language Fortran (in dialects up through IV) did not.

What else is needed? The answer was given in 1964 in a seminal paper by Bohm and Jacopini, who proved that every "flowchart" (program), however complicated, could be rewritten in an equivalent way using only repeated or nested subunits of no more than three different kinds—a *sequence* of executable statements, a *decision* clause of the **if-then-else** type described above, and an *iteration* construct, which repeats a sequence of statements **while** (or **until**) some condition is satisfied. Using conventional flowchart notation, these so-called *canoni-*

cal forms are typically rendered as in Fig. 1. Note that each of these control structures has a single entry point and a single exit, a key to their intelligible interconnectibility.

The two forms of iteration differ in this regard: The **repeat-until** variation of iteration does something first and asks a question later (as to whether a termination condition has yet become true), whereas the **do-while** variation of iteration cautiously asks a question first, since, if the condition tested is false, the loop under consideration is not executed at all. The Fortran DO statement and the Basic FOR statement are essentially weak forms of **repeat-until**; e.g. the Fortran segment:

```
DO 17 I 5 1,L
       .
       .
       .
17 CONTINUE
```

will iterate until I > L becomes true.

Using most compilers for Fortran dialects up through IV, the loop will run once even if L < 1 (and hence I > L) to start with. This can be avoided in Algol through use of the construction:

I := 0;
for I := I + 1 **while** I < L **do**
(a single, possibly compound, statement);

which does not iterate at all if L < 1.

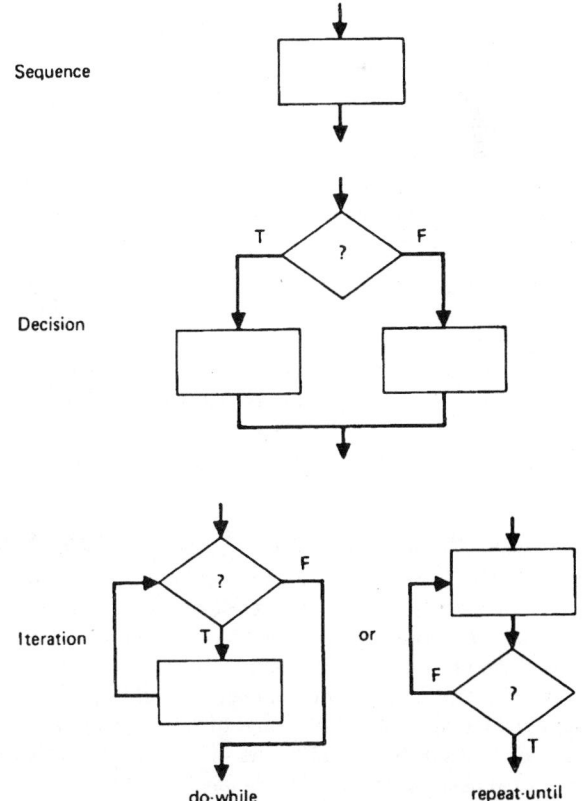

FIG. 1. SP canonical forms.

Do we need both iteration variants? The Bohm-Jacopini theorem says "no," but that theorem addresses only constructibility and not convenience. For this reason, programmers like to have both variants, as they do in Pascal. For similar reasons of convenience, three other constructs—**case, exit,** and **return**—have proved to be desirable adjuncts to the canonical forms since each eliminates the need for an unconditional branch to a label under some circumstances. The utility of **case** is discussed in the article CONTROL STRUCTURES; **exit** (from a loop) and **return** (from a procedure) are closely related in that it is often contingently desirable to terminate a logic segment abruptly. Consider the following fragment of code in the language C:

```
true = 1; false = 0;
found = false;
for(i = 1; i <= 100; i = i + 1)
 if (a[i] = gold) {found = true;  exit}
/* if executed, exit sends control here */.
```

Such a loop runs at most 100 times, but terminates sooner if the search is successful. Without the **exit** construct, the only way to avoid a structure-destroying **goto** is (with the same true/false values):

```
found = false;
i = 1;
while (i < = 100) && (found = false)
if(a[i] = gold) found = true else i = i + 1;
```

Note that the **while** loop will terminate if *found* becomes true before *i* reaches 100, but the price paid for such structure is three decisions versus the original two (counting the implied test for $i < = 100$). Most SP advocates would consider the price too high and say, "If your language doesn't support **exit** then, by all means, use a **goto** to break a loop when necessary."

The occasional need for **return** from a procedure or function is quite similar. The foregoing logic embodied in a C function called "found" would be:

```
    found (a,gold)
    int a[], gold;
    { int i;
      found = false;
      for (i = 1); i <= 100; i = i + 1)
        if a[i] = gold return (true);
      return(false);
    } /* end definition of found */.
```

Input/Output Aspects of Structured Programming

None of the canonical control structures were specifically designed to handle input/output; yet the way such statements are treated can have a significant impact on program structure and intelligibility. As a minimum, embedded program comments should describe the significance and expected range of each quantity to be read or written. When valid data or results are available for transmission, read/write statements are merely particular examples of *sequence*. The principal problem that impacts program structure arises when an abnormal or other special case occurs, such as, for example, the perennial problem of how best to handle the end-of-file condition. From the SP standpoint, one of the poorer ways is the PL/I (and typical microcomputer Basic) method of allowing the programmer to place a statement such as "On endfile do something" or "ON ERROR GOTO 5000" anywhere in the program—possibly far removed from the I/O statement it may affect. To the unwary reader of such a program, the logic being followed is subject to a "disembodied goto," i.e. something could occur during execution that could snatch control away from a presumably imperative statement that is actually a conditional one.

Even Fortran IV provides a better answer by means of such a statement as

```
READ (5, 12, END = 100) A,B,C
```

The Fortran-knowledgeable reader is now able to see the conditional nature of the READ statement explicitly; it is saying, "If possible, read three numbers from input unit 5 according to the FORMAT specified at statement 12. But if an end-of-file condition is detected prior to receipt of three valid numbers, goto statement 100." Though the implied **goto** (and associated label) is annoying, the meaning is quite clear.

Somewhat better is the Pascal (and C) solution:

> **while** not eof **do**
> **begin**
>   read (a,b,c);
>   {process this data set}
> **end;**

Finally, the preferred solution would be the ability to write:

> **while** reading(a,b,c) **do**
> {process data set}.

where "reading" is what Federighi calls a *gerund function*, one that returns a Boolean value **true** (when valid input is available) and **false** (upon encountering end-of-file) and whose *side effect* (something usually undesirable, but not so here) is the principal action desired, namely, the reading of data. An end-of-file, of course, terminates the **while** loop in a way analogous to the **exit** construct discussed earlier. This is the only solution that both preserves structure and directly associates the end-of-file with its proximate cause.

Structured Programs

While a fully structured program has no **gotos** (and hence needs no labels), rewriting a program merely to eliminate **gotos** does not necessarily result in a structured program; more is needed.

While still further evolution of SP is to be expected, most experts agree that the term connotes certain basic principles:

1. *Control structures*—Use of only those canonical control structures of Fig. 1 supported by the host language being used unless deviation therefrom removes a gross inefficiency or (most unlikely) enhances readability.

2. *Modular composition*—Subdivision of a program into modules, where a *module* is a program segment that embodies a complete logical thought in about one page of code. Depending on their relative sizes, a module may be larger or smaller than a procedure, but the two should be kept commensurate; i.e. either one module consists of one or more small procedures, or else a large procedure is divided into several page-size modules. A program is divided into procedures both for the sake of processing efficiency and for ease of construction. It is divided into modules partially for ease of construction, but mostly for the sake of the human reader. Significant computer programs usually have only one or, at most, a few authors, but they may have many readers.

3. *Program format*—Careful organization of each such page into clearly recognizable paragraphs based on appropriate indentation of iteration, decision, and nested structures.

4. *Comments*—Judicious use of embedded comments that describe the function of each variable and the purpose of each module and procedure. A program whose every statement is annotated is often harder to read and understand than one that is devoid of comment; the right density is about one comment for every few lines of code that express a coherent logical action.

5. *Readability versus efficiency*— A preference for straightforward, easily readable code over slightly more efficient but obtuse code.

6. *Stepwise refinement*—Creation of the final program through an evolutionary process of *stepwise refinement (top-down design)* whereby the overall logic is first sketched in using a generous admixture of English, which is then gradually replaced in subsequent versions by more detailed logic syntactically acceptable to the intended compiler or interpreter.

7. *Program verification*—The ability to make assertions about key segments of a structured program so as to "prove" that the program is correct (*see* PROGRAM VERIFICATION).

Before discussing further the prospective benefits of adhering to these rules, we make two observations. First, note that nothing in all of the foregoing referred to the concepts of *algorithm* or *data structure*. The selection of an appropriate algorithm and associated data structure is a strategic concept; the application of SP techniques is a tactical methodology. Neither a structured program that implements an inferior algorithm nor an unstructured program that implements an excellent one is as desirable as the constructive use of good strategy *and* good tactics. To paraphrase the title of Niklaus Wirth's book: "Algorithms + Data Structures = (possibly unstructured) Programs," but "(Good) Algorithms + (associated) Data Structures + SP Techniques = An Efficient Structured Program."

Second, a purported structured program can be examined by a reader who can form value judgments as to whether characteristics one through five have been met, but unless the author chooses to display intermediate versions, it is impossible to tell (nor need we care) whether the final result was attained using stepwise refinement. This is not to denigrate rule six; there is now sufficient professional experience to support its continued advocacy.

Benefits of SP An increasing number of advocates claim at least the following benefits for SP:

1. Structured programs are more readable and hence more intelligible than unstructured ones.
2. This greater readability makes it easier to maintain and modify structured programs, especially by programmers other than the original author.
3. Structured programs are more likely to be correct in the first instance and are more easily "proved" correct by systematic program verification.
4. The greater likelihood of correctness cited above lessens elapsed time to create a new program because there are fewer bugs to find and fix. Instead of the routine expectation that a program will not run properly the first time, the goal of the structured programmer is "zero defects"; reasonably complex structured programs have indeed been known to run perfectly on the first attempt.

Though the foregoing claims are difficult to substantiate quantitatively, there is no question but that the majority of professionals who teach programming and language design have moved heavily toward the SP philosophy. This movement is reflected in at least four identifiable recent developments: (1) the widespread use of Pascal or Modula-2 as the language of choice for teaching introductory computer science courses in universities, (2) the U.S. government's decision to choose a structured format for its new command and control language Ada, (3) the concession of the Fortran community that it was time to introduce some structure through the medium of Fortran 77 (and later, Fortran 90), and (4) the fact that all recently developed versions of Basic are structured.

Structured Flowcharts Since SP has caused a significant change in programming, or at least in the way we think about programming, it should not be surprising that other related tools that once served us well need reformulation. One of these is the time-honored *flowchart (q.v.)*, which so often contains a spaghetti-like maze of transfers from box to box, just the antithesis of SP. An interesting and useful remedy has been proposed by Nassi and Shneiderman, who recommend use of certain new diagrams for each principal SP control structure. Among these are a rectangular box for a declarative sequence (or process), "L" or inverted "L" structures for iteration, and other distinctive diagrams

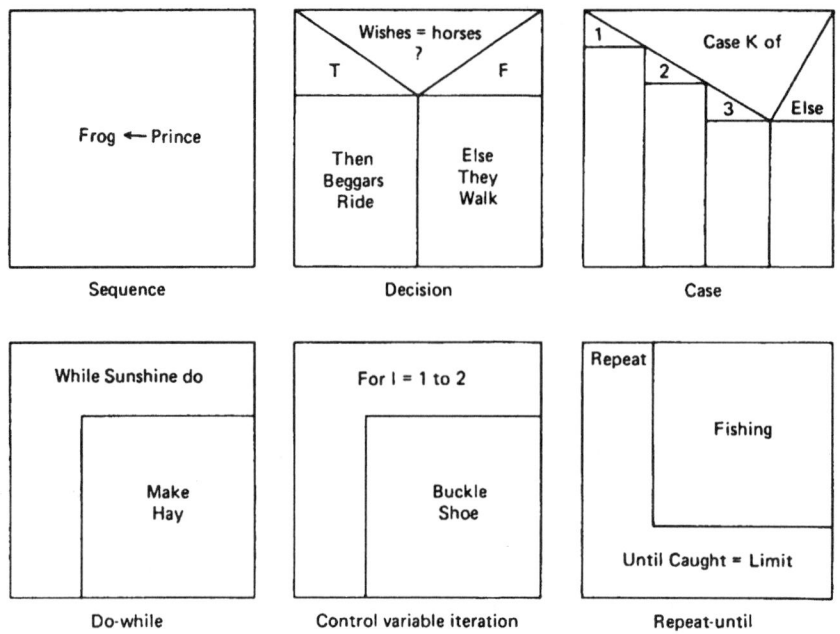

FIG. 2. Structured flowchart building blocks.

for binary (if-then-else) or multiple (case) decisions (Fig. 2). Since each diagram's outer outline is a rectangle and since the subdivision of any structure always leaves rectangles that may be further subdivided, a set of such diagrams can always be sequenced or nested within an outermost rectangle in a manner that models faithfully the recursive definition of a structured program given in the first sentence of this article. Examples of diagram intercombination are given in Figs. 3 and 4, which represent, respectively, procedures for calculating the factorial of N and the product of two N × N matrices. Such *structured flowcharts* are also called *iteration diagrams* or, after their inventors, *Nassi-Shneiderman diagrams*.

Apart from their virtues in providing clear and concise documentation, teachers of computer science have noted that the great psychological difficulty that some students encounter in trying to write structured code (especially those who learned an early dialect of Basic or Fortran as a first language) is often dissipated by forcing them to prepare an iteration diagram first.

Still another significant feature of iteration diagrams is that the clarity with which nested logic is displayed often facilitates algorithm analysis; note in particular the three nested loops in Fig. 4, which so vividly emphasize that conventional matrix multiplication of N × N matrices takes running time proportional to N^3.

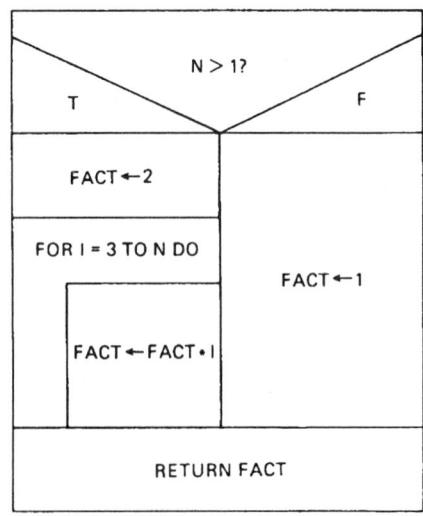

FIG. 3. Factorial.

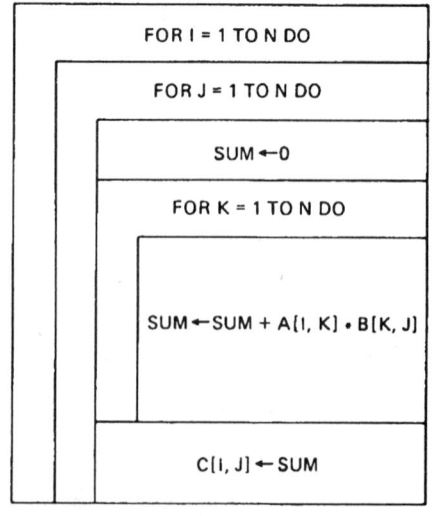

FIG. 4. Matrix multiplication.

An Example As an example of SP, consider the classic *Quicksort* algorithm for sorting an initially unordered one-dimensional array of (say) integers. One step of this algorithm will partition the array into three parts—a single interior element called the *pivot*, which is guaranteed to have gravitated to its correct final position; a left partition, all of whose elements are less than or equal to the pivot; and a right partition, all of whose elements are greater than the pivot. Repetitive (i.e. recursive) application of this process to the left and right partitions and to their subpartitions (until all such subpartitions are reduced to size one) will complete the sort.

The program logic is illustrated progressively in four forms, stepwise-refined stages in Figs. 5 and 6, a structured flowchart in Fig. 7, and, finally, in Fig. 8, the completed structured program and an example of its operation on a specific data set.

Not only does the program shown work correctly for the data set shown, we can prove that the basic partitioning algorithm works for *any* data set if, according to the precepts of program verification, we can identify two relations, say p and c, such that the combined truth of p and $\neg c$ (not c) guarantees a correct partitioning. The relation c is the loop control relation $I <= J$; i.e. an inspec-

Procedure Quicksort (L, R : integer);
{sorts global array A[L..R] where A[R + 1] >
$\qquad$ any A[L..R]}

Choose pivot arbitrarily to be element at left end of array A.

[Set pointers to mark positions such that all elements to left of left pointer I are less than or equal to the pivot and all elements to right of right pointer J are greater than the pivot, leaving $J - I + 1$ elements between I and J (inclusive to be examined.]

{The initial choices of I and J that satisfy the above are $I = L + 1$ and $J = R$.}

Move left pointer to right and right pointer to left until either

$\qquad$ a) the bracketed condition above is temporarily violated, in which case we exchange elements addressed by the pointers in order to restore that condition, and then continue moving the pointers, or
$\qquad$ b) the pointers cross.

Replace the first element with element addressed by right pointer and then replace that right element with the pivot in order to achieve the desired partition.

Now operate similarly on left and right partitions until all subpartitions are of size one.

FIG. 5. First version of Quicksort written primarily in English.

procedure Quicksort (L, R : integer);
{sorts global array A[L..R] where the main program has set A[R + 1] to "infinity"; i.e., a number guaranteed to be larger than any A[L..R]}

if L < R **then**
begin
by initializing a left pointer I : = L + 1, which
$\qquad$ shall move to the right, and a right pointer J : = R,
$\qquad\qquad$ which shall move to the left.

$\qquad$ As an arbitrary pivot element, select PIV : = A[L],
$\qquad$ the first element. Now

repeat
$\qquad$ -edly move pointers toward each other in such a way
$\qquad$ that

while A[I] <= PIV we increment the left pointer,
$\qquad$ and then
while A[J] > PIV we decrement the right pointer.

$\qquad$ After this movement, if I still < J, then pointers
$\qquad$ haven't crossed so

$\qquad$ Exchange A[I] and A[J].
$\qquad$ After this exchange, keep moving pointers

until I > J.

$\qquad$ Now that pointers have crossed, copy A[J] to first
$\qquad$ position, A[L], and replace A[J] with the pivot
$\qquad$ element. This completes a partition. Finally,
$\qquad$ complete the work by recursively sorting the left
$\qquad$ partition via:

$\qquad\qquad$ Quicksort (L, J − 1)

and the right partition via:

$\qquad\qquad$ Quicksort (I, R)

End logic performed only when L < R.
end procedure Quicksort.

FIG. 6. Second version of Quicksort using English embedded in Pascal-like control structures.

tion of the program shows that the principal loop runs until $\neg c$ ($I > J$) is true. A more careful inspection of the program reveals that c switches from true to false in such a way that $\neg c$ is equivalent to the truth of $J = I - 1$. The other relation, p, is the so-called *invariant relation* of the loop, one that was true before the loop began and whose truth is preserved throughout the running of the loop (*see* LOOP INVARIANT). There may be many candidate relations for p, most of them irrelevant—we seek the particular one such that p and $\neg c$ proves the desired "theorem." That particular p has been right before us all along; it is precisely the statement in square brackets in Fig. 5. When

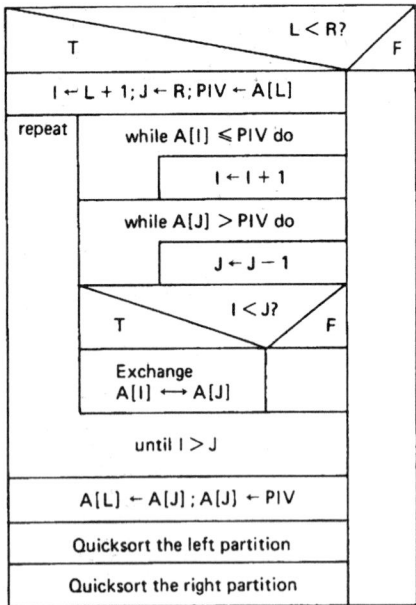

FIG.7. Procedure Quicksort (L, R).

that invariant relation is written with the substitution $J = I - 1$, we obtain:

> "Set pointers to mark positions such that all elements to the left of the left pointer I are less than or equal to the pivot and all elements to the right of the right pointer J are greater than the pivot, leaving 0 elements between I and J to be examined,"

which "proves" our theorem to the degree of conviction we achieve that our chosen "invariant" relation really is an invariant; i.e. no program step destroys the validity it had prior to execution of the primary loop to which it pertains.

Structured Programming Languages

Earlier it was mentioned that Cobol has the equivalent of an if-then-else control structure even though Cobol is not usually considered to be a structured language. Why not? We shall adopt the criterion that a structured language must have, as a minimum, an **if-then-else** compound statement-oriented decision statement, and at least one form of iteration based on a boolean decision; i.e. either **do-while** or **repeat-until**. The statements **case, exit,** and **return** are luxuries. Note that, although classical iteration based on a control variable is not cited as being necessary despite its obvious utility, most SP languages retain such a form in addition to **do-while** and/or **repeat-until**.

Table 1 summarizes the SP features of eight particular high-level languages. *Sequence* has not been tabulated because all of them have such a construct. Recursion, on the other hand, has been included because many procedures are much more intelligible (though, of course, not more efficient) when written in recursive form (as in our

```
program QuickDriver (input, output);
const max = 10001;
var
    A: array [1..max] of integer;
    i: integer;                    { Control variable }
    n: integer;          { Number of integers to be sorted }

procedure Quicksort (L, R : integer);
{sorts global array A[L..R] where A[R + 1] >
                                    any A[L..R]}
var I, J, PIV, T : integer;
begin
  if L < R then
    begin
      I : = L + 1; J : = R; PIV : = A[L];
      repeat {move pointers I and J inwards as far
                                    as possible}
          while A[I] <= PIV do I : = I + 1;
          while A[J] > PIV do J : = J − 1;
          if I {still} < J then {exchange items pointed
                                    to by I and J}
            begin T : = A[I]; A[I] : = A[J]; A[J] := T
            end
      until I > J;
      {now two final replacements finish a partition}
      A[L] := A[J]; A[J] := PIV;
      {finish by recursively sorting the left and right
                                    partitions}
      Quicksort (L, J − 1); Quicksort (I, R)
  end {logic performed only when L < R}
end {procedure Quicksort};

begin
    write ('Enter number of integers to be sorted: ');
    readln (n);
    for i := 1 to n do read (A [i]);      { Read integer data }
    A[n+1] := maxint;          { Set "infinite" right guard }
    Quicksort (1,n);
    for i := 1 to n do write (A[i]:5);
                                    { Write sorted numbers }
    writeln;
end { qs driver }.
```

Example

I	J									
2	8	8	6	12	20	2	5	47	14	Initial array;
3	6	8	6	5	20	2	12	47	14	pivot = 8
4	5	8	6	5	2	20	12	47	14	
5	4	2	6	5	[8]	20	12	47	14	Final result of one partitioning

Left partition   Right partition

To be further processed recursively
(by 3rd-last line of the procedure)
until partitions of size one result
in completely ordered (sorted) data.

FIG. 8. Final structured version of Quicksort implemented as a Pascal procedure and embedded in a sample driver together with an example of how a particular data set would appear after a single partitioning.

TABLE 1.   Language Features that Facilitate SP.

	Algol 60	Pascal	Ada	Algol 68	PL/I	C	Fortran 77	Modula-2
If-then-else decision	√	√	√	√	√	√	√	√
Control varible iteration	√	√	√	√	√	√	√	√
do-while	√	√	√	√	√	√	—[a]	√
repeat-until	—	√	—	—	—	√[c]	—	√
case	—	√	√	√	√[c]	—[b]	—	√
exit	—	—	√	—	—	√	—	√
return	—	—	√	—	√	√	√	√
recursion	√	√	√	√	√	√	—	√
Flexibility of comments	Fair	Exc.	Good	Exc.	Good	Good	Poor	Good

[a]*Not in the standard but present in many actual implementations.*
[b]*The structure that C calls case does not have a common single exit and hence is more properly classified as a form of Fortran-like computed goto.*
[c]*Uses different terminology.*

Quicksort example) than they are when written out non-recursively. Also, since embedded comments play an important role in readability, each language has been characterized in this regard as being *poor* if comments must be confined to separate lines, *fair* if they may be placed at certain restricted points internal to a statement, *good* if they may be placed within or at least to the right of statements, and *excellent* (exc.) if such comments are delimited by single characters [such as {..} in Pascal] rather than the surprisingly jarring double-character delimiters/* and */ that PL/I and C use and the (*..*) that Modula-2 uses.

The influence of the SP philosophy has now become quite pervasive, and deservedly so, even in environments where, for one reason or another, programs are still written in a traditional unstructured language. This is manifesting itself in several ways:(1) the creation of compilers for structured versions of languages such as Basic, Cobol, Lisp, and Snobol (i.e. versions in which, typically, options for **if-then-else** and **do-while** control structures are superimposed on the original language); (2) the creation of preprocessors (software translators), which change structured syntax into conventional statements acceptable to existing compilers; and, as a last resort, (3) hand translation of structured flowcharts or hypothetical structured code into transliterated conventional equivalents.

The major contributions of the SP approach have been twofold—the elevation of programming technique to something less of an art and more of a science, and also the demonstration that carefully structured programs can be creative works of sufficient literary merit to deserve being read by humans and not just by computers.

References

1964. Bohm, C. and Jacopini, G. "Flow Diagrams, Turing Machines, and Languages With Only Two Formation Rules," *Comm. ACM* **9**, 5.
1968. Dijkstra, E. "Go to Statement Considered Harmful," *Comm. ACM* **11**, 3.
1972. Dahl OJ Dijkstra, E., and Hoare, C. A. R. *Structured Programming.* New York: Academic Press.
1973. Wirth, N. *Systematic Programming: An Introduction.* Englewood Cliffs, NJ: Prentice-Hall.
1975. McGowan, C. and Kelly, J. *Top-Down Structured Programming Techniques.* New York: Petrocelli/Charter.
1976. Dijkstra, E. *A Discipline of Programming.* Englewood Cliffs, NJ: Prentice-Hall.
1977. Yeh, R. (Ed.). *Current Trends in Programming Methodology. Vol. 1: Software Specification and Design.* Englewood Cliffs, NJ: Prentice-Hall.
1979. Linger, R., Mills, H., and Witt, B. *Structured Programming, Theory and Practice.* Reading, MA: Addison-Wesley.

EDWIN D. REILLY

SUBPROGRAM

For articles on related subjects *see* ACTIVATION RECORD; ARGUMENT; BLOCK STRUCTURE; CALLING SEQUENCE; COROUTINE; GLOBAL AND LOCAL VARIABLES; PARAMETER PASSING; PROCEDURE-ORIENTED LANGUAGES; RECURSION; and SIDE EFFECT.

A *subprogram* is a portion of a high-level language program that performs a specific task necessary for that program. This term is often used interchangeably with the term *subroutine* when referring to high-level languages, although the term *subroutine* is more usual in the context of machine language programs.

Early in the development of programming languages, it was recognized that programs would be written in which the same process was to be executed at several different locations within the program. One example of such a process is the evaluation of mathematical functions such as logarithms and exponentials, or trigonometric functions such as sine or cosine. Another example is the printing of output in a particular format, or the updating of a central table with newly computed information. To accomplish these tasks conveniently, a facility was needed to permit the programmer to write the appropriate code once, and then call that code whenever it was needed.

There are two basic kinds of subprograms: procedures and functions. A *procedure* is a collection of code that performs an action but returns no value. For example, a procedure might print a value or update a data structure (*q.v.*). A procedure call is therefore a statement, as statements perform actions. A *function* is a sequence of code that returns a single value, as do mathematical functions. A pure function does not perform an action that affects memory of concern to its calling program; a function that performs such an action in addition to returning a value is said to have a *side effect*. Since it returns a value, a function call is an expression (*q.v.*). Both functions and procedures are widely used in general-purpose, high-level programming languages, such as Fortran and Pascal. However, since procedure calls are statements, and the fundamental element of these languages is the statement, these languages are said to be *procedure-oriented languages*. Languages that rely solely on function calls, and in which the fundamental element is the expression, are said to be *functional*. (See FUNCTIONAL PROGRAMMING).

Subprograms in high-level languages may be *instrinsic* (or *built-in* or *library*) or programmer-written. Intrinsic subprograms are those provided with the language so that the programmer need only cite them in a program to have them automatically invoked. This invocation requires only that the programmer give the name of the subprogram and its *arguments*. Pascal, for example, has numerous built-in functions, a short list of which is given in Table 1. If a program contains a variable X and the programmer wishes to computer the cosine of the current value assigned to that variable, it is only necessary to write cos(X) as the right-hand side of an assignment statement [such as B:= cos(X)] or to embed cos(X) in an appropriate expression. If, for example, the programmer wishes to assign to variable A the absolute value of the sum of the cosine and sine of the argument, he or she may write.

```
A := abs(cos(X) + sin(X))
```

Other high-level languages have different sets of intrinsic functions. Both Fortran and PL/I have a much larger number of intrinsic functions than Pascal. For example, PL/1 and Fortran 77 have a built-in function that allows the programmer to extract a *substring* from a named string of characters, and another that returns the maximum of two integers.

TABLE 1. Pascal functions

Name of function	Mathematical Definition	Pascal Name
Sine	$\sin x$	sin
Cosine	$\cos x$	cos
Natural logarithm	$\ln x$	ln
Absolute value	$|x|$	abs
Square root	$\sqrt{x}$	sqrt

In addition to built-in functions, Pascal offers the built-in procedures *read* and *write*. Thus, the following Pascal code would read in a value, store it in X, add 1 to X, and print out the result:

```
read(X)
X := X + 1;
write(X);
```

The availability of intrinsic subprograms clearly suggests the need for a parallel facility to permit programmers to define their own subprograms that can be referenced in the same manner as intrinsic subprograms. All general-purpose, high-level languages have such a facility, although the details of how it can be used and how it is implemented vary considerably.

Fig. 1 is an example of a programmer-written Pascal function to calculate the sum of the products of the corresponding elements of two 100-element arrays. Also shown are two main program statements calling this function. Note that the value returned by the function is the value assigned to its name, and that the type of the return value is specified after the types of the parameters. Also

```
program TEST(input, output);
type array100 = array[1..100] of real;
var A, B, C, D: real;
    Q1, Q2, F, G: array100;

function PROD(X,Y: array100):real;
var I: integer;
    SUM: real;
begin {PROD}
    SUM := 0;
    for I := 1 to 100 do
        SUM := SUM + X[I] * Y[I];
    PROD := SUM
end; {PROD}

begin {TEST}
    ...
    C := A + (B*D)/PROD(F,G);
    ...
    A := B * PROD(Q1,Q2);
    ...
end. {TEST}
```

FIG. 1 A Pascal function.

```
program TEST2(input, output);
type matrix = array[1..50, 1..50] of real;
var A,B: matrix;

procedure TRANS(var A: matrix; N: integer);
var I,J: integer;
        TEMP: real;
begin {TRANS}
        for I := 2 to N do
                for J := 1 to I−1 do
                begin
                        TEMP := A[I,J];
                        A[I, J] := A[J, I];
                        A[J, I] := TEMP
                end
end {TRANS}

begin {MAIN}.
        ...
        TRANS(A,50); {Transpose the full 50 x 50 matrix A}.
        ...
        TRANS(B,10); {Transpose the 10 x 10
                        {matrix in upper left corner of B}
        ...
end. {MAIN}
```

FIG. 2   A Pascal procedure.

note that the function is a *declaration* (*q.v.*) at the beginning of the *block* that is the Pascal program.

Pascal procedures are defined in a manner similar to Pascal functions. A procedure, however, returns no value and is expected to perform an action to modify something in its environment, something passed as a parameter, or the input or output stream. Fig. 2 shows a Pascal procedure that transposes the elements of a two-dimensional square array (i.e. interchanges the (i,j) and (j,i) elements). Note that the action performed by this procedure is to modify the matrix whose name is passed as a parameter. The parameter is specified as a **var** (*var*iable) parameter to allow the actual parameter to be modified when the formal parameter is (see PARAMETER PASSING).

Fortran has FUNCTION and SUBROUTINE facilities analogous to Pascal's **function** and **procedure** facilities, respectively. An important difference in Fortran is that subprograms are physically separate from the main program, as opposed to being embedded in it as in block-structures languages such as Pascal. This facilitates separate compilation of the main program and subprograms, and may be convenient during debugging. Block-structured languages may require recompilation of the subprogram every time the program is recompiled, but the integration of procedures into the main program is an aid of great value to programming and to thinking about programming. Some block-structured languages, such as Modula-2 (*q.v.*), Ada (*q.v.*), and VAX Pascal allow creation of modules that allow separate compilation of subprograms.

C has only functions, but any function may be called as a statement, in which case its return value is thrown away. Thus, C functions can double as procedures. Furthermore, a C function may have return type VOID, in which case it is an error to call it in an expression, since it can return no useful value.

J. A. N. LEE AND ADRIENNE BLOSS

SUBPROGRAM, CALLING A. *See* CALLING SEQUENCE; and PARAMETER PASSING.

SUBROUTINE. *See* PROCEDURE; and SUBPROGRAM.

SUPERCOMPUTERS

For articles on related subjects *see* COMPUTER- AIDED ENGINEERING; DATAFLOW; MULTIPROCESSING; PARALLEL PROCESSING; SCIENTIFIC APPLICATIONS; SUPERCOMPUTING CENTERS; and SYSTOLIC ARRAY.

The term *supercomputer* is usually applied to the largest and fastest computers available at a given time. Most often, supercomputers have been used to simulate physical phenomena by executing numerically intensive programs. Computer simulation is accepted today as a third mode of scientific research that complements experimentation and theoretical analysis by making possible the exploration of some phenomena that cannot be handled otherwise, and by providing intuition to guide experimental and theoretical work. Also, computer simulation is an important engineering tool that provides fast feedback on the quality and feasibility of new designs. Because of the large number of operations involved in many problems of science and engineering, supercomputers are an enabling technology, making possible advances that cannot be achieved by any other known approach.

Supercomputers have been used successfully in many disciplines, including weather forecasting, materials analysis, high-energy physics, oil exploration, circuit design, and aircraft design. However, even though the supercomputers of today are capable of executing hundreds of millions of operations per second, computer power is often a limiting factor on the accuracy of a simulation, and it is commonly accepted that machines that are several orders of magnitude faster than current computers are necessary to produce important breakthroughs in scientific simulation.

High-performance computers have also been used for non-numerical and semi-numerical problems, although much less frequently than for numerically intensive computations. For example, to help us understand the molecular basis of disease, researchers need very fast algorithms to compare normal and pathological genetic sequences. Supercomputers have also been used to decompose large numbers into prime factors, a semi-numerical problem with applications to code breaking (*see*

FACTORING INTEGERS, NUMBER THEORETIC CALCULATIONS; and CRYPTOGRAPHY, COMPUTERS IN).

Machine Organization Supercomputers use different strategies to achieve their characteristic high speed. Some machines use the fastest electronic components available, while others use conventional components. However, all past and present supercomputers have in common a parallel organization based on either one of or a combination of the following four approaches:

1. *Multiprocessing*—Each processor in a multiprocessor computer is capable of executing instructions independently of the others. Parallelism is achieved by decomposing programs into components that can be executed simultaneously on separate processors. Clearly, the parallel execution of a program requires that the processors coordinate their work and share their information. There are two main multiprocessor organizations: shared memory and distributed memory. In the *shared-memory* multiprocessor, some or all of the memory requests go through an interconnection network to a collection of memory modules accessible to all processors (Fig. 1). In this way, data stored in the shared memory modules can be fetched and modified by all processors. Coordination between the processors is achieved by the execution of synchronization instructions that operate on the shared-memory modules or on some special hardware device. Under certain circumstances it is possible to synchronize using just load and store operations. However, most machines include special synchronization instructions, such as test-and-set and compare-and-swap. A special device of the Alliant FX/80, the concurrency control bus, can execute some restricted class of synchronization operations without accessing the memory. Also, the Cray X-MP and Y-MP (see Fig. 2) include a collection of registers for interprocessor communication and synchronization.

Shared-memory multiprocessors have existed since the early 1960s when the first Burroughs

FIG. 2. (a) The Cray Y-MP8I Supercomputer. (b) The Cray Y-MP8E Supercomputer.

B5000 and D-825 were delivered. However, multiprocessing was most often used to increase the reliability of the system and to overlap I/O with computation. Since the introduction of the Cray X-MP in 1984, there has been a growing interest in the use of multiprocessing to increase computation speed. In fact, the most powerful machines produced today by many supercomputer manufacturers are shared-memory multiprocessors.

In the *distributed-memory* organization, each processor has exclusive access to its own memory module. Coordination and information sharing is achieved via messages that travel through an interconnection network (Fig. 3). The processors send messages and wait for them under explicit program control. Some researchers believe that this need for explicit communication

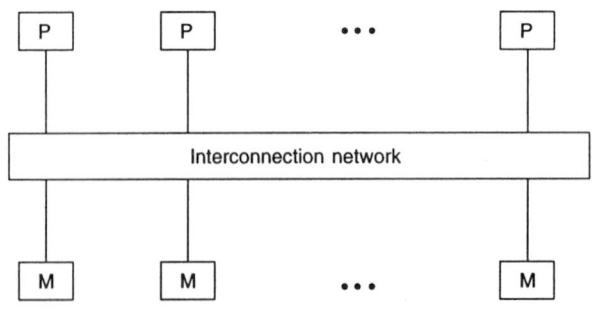

P: Processor
M: Memory Module

FIG. 1. Schematic of a shared-memory multiprocessor.

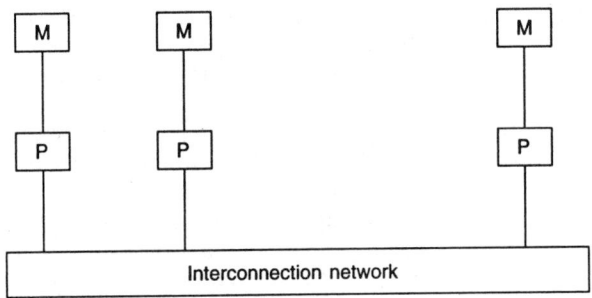

P: Processor
M: Local Memory

FIG. 3. Schematic of a distributed-memory multiprocessor.

makes programming distributed-memory machines more difficult than programming their shared-memory counterparts. However, since the introduction of Caltech's Cosmic Cube in the early 1980s, there has been much activity in the design and use of distributed-memory machines. This interest is motivated, at least in part, by the large number of processors that can easily be connected by following this approach. Clearly, distributed-memory machines are ideal for those problems that can be easily decomposed into many uniform modules that do not require frequent interactions, but the question of how easy it is to use this type of machine for a wide range of applications is still the subject of debate.

Processors with quite different organizations sometimes coexist in a single multiprocessor. These machines, called *heterogeneous multiprocessors,* can be useful in the execution of programs whose components have different computational requirements. Both distributed-memory and shared-memory machines have used heterogeneous processors. For example, the Intel iPSC/860, a distributed-memory machine, can use two types of microprocessors: the i860, to support numerical computations, and the 80386, which is more convenient for symbolic computing. The FPS 500 system, a shared-memory multiprocessor, accepts three types of processors, as discussed below. Heterogeneous computing can also be achieved by *multicomputing,* in which several machines, connected through a local area network (LAN) (*q.v.*) cooperate in the execution of a single program. Multicomputer networks are logically similar in their organization and programming to distributed-memory machines.

2. *Multifunction Processors*—In multifunction processors, the set of all arithmetic and boolean operations is divided into subsets, and one or more functional units are assigned to each subset. For example, one functional unit could be devoted to floating-point multiplication and division and another to boolean operations. Parallelism is achieved by operating these functional units in parallel with each other. Fig. 4 (and Fig. 8

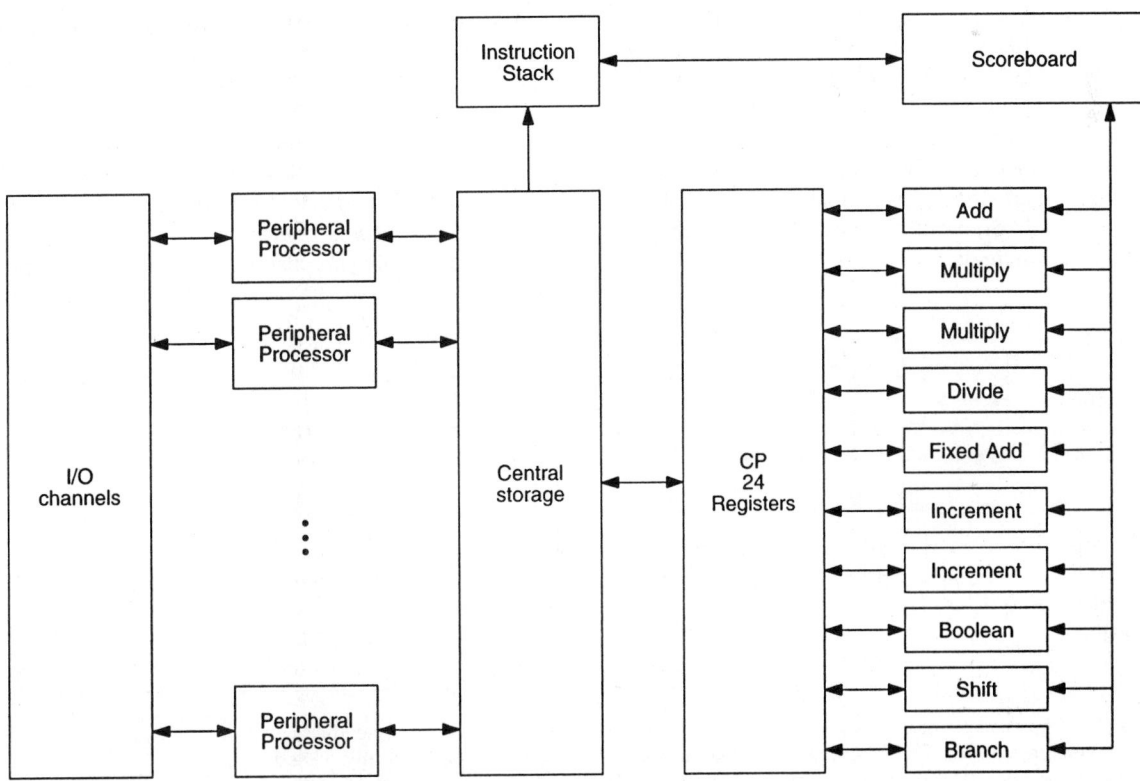

FIG. 4. Schematic of the CDC 6600 showing 10 functional units.

below) present examples of processors organized into several functional units.

There are two strategies to control multifunction parallelism. In the first approach, parallelism is exploited at run-time by a complex control unit that, under certain circumstances, can issue an instruction before preceding ones have been completed. An instruction will have to wait only when the functional unit it needs is busy or when it collides with an executing instruction. Two instructions are said to *collide* if both access the same memory location or register and at least one of these accesses is a write. In this first approach, some of the parallelism present in sequential programs (or sequential components of parallel programs) can be exploited automatically by dynamic run-time analysis without the need for human intervention or compiler transformations. However, code reorganization, done manually or automatically, can increase its performance. The Bull Gamma 60, designed in the 1950s, is one of the earliest examples of a run-time-controlled multifunction processor. However, it was the introduction of the CDC 6600 (Fig. 4) in the early 1960s that made this a popular approach.

In the second strategy, used by the *very-long-instruction-word (VLIW)* processors, the instructions contain several operation fields that indicate explicitly which functional units are to be put to work (Fig. 5). Programming this type of machine is cumbersome because of the need to schedule manually the arithmetic operations and the loads and stores. For this reason, the extraction of parallelism is usually left to the compiler. During the late 1980s, several companies, including Cydrome and Multiflow Computer, marketed VLIW processors. However, by 1990, both were out of business. The Intel i860 microprocessor, mentioned above, uses a limited form of this approach. Some of its instructions include two operation fields.

3. *Pipelined processors*—In this approach, an operation is separated into several stages, each accomplishing a fraction of the work required by the operation. For example, a floating-point multiplication can be divided into several stages, each performing one sub-operation, such as adding the exponents, multiplying the mantissas, rounding, and normalizing the result. The stages are connected in a linear sequence or *pipe*. An operation enters through an end of the sequence and proceeds from one stage to the next until, finally, the result exits at the other end of the pipe. Parallelism is achieved by operating the pipe like an assembly line; i.e. in such a way that several operations, each at a different stage, could be underway at any given time. Usually, pipes are synchronous and, at periodic intervals, the operations on all the stages move simultaneously to the next, and the first stage accepts a new operation. The length of time between such moves is called the *cycle time* of the processor. To see how much speed improvement can be derived from the pipelined approach, consider a pipe with s stages that is to perform a sequence of m operations. The pipe will take s cycles to be filled, and after that, one result will come out of the pipe at the end of every cycle. If the cycle time is T, the total time to complete the m operations will be $(s + m)T$. On the other hand, if pipelining were not used, the total time required to complete the m operations using the same s stages would be smT. For large m, pipelining is then approximately s times faster than the non-pipelined version. The maximum performance of a pipelined unit is $1/T$ operations per second if it includes only one pipe. In some machines, several identical pipes are used, which allows several operations to be processed simultaneously at each stage. A functional unit with n identical pipes has a maximum performance of n/T operations per second.

Pipelining has also been used in the processor's

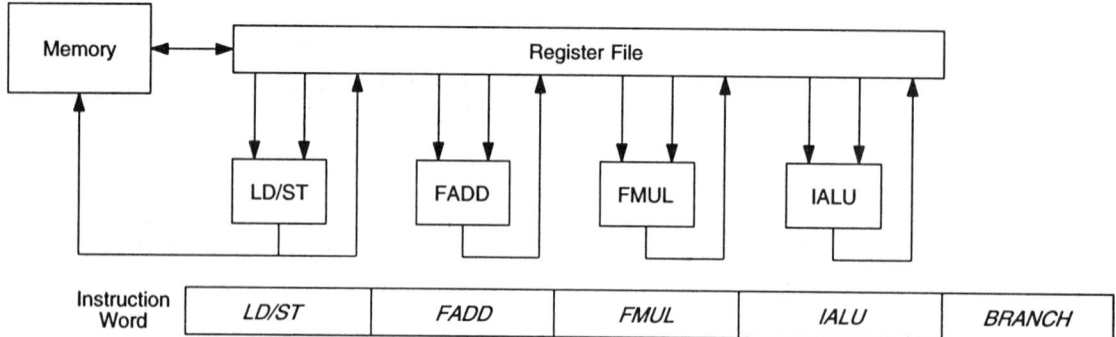

FIG. 5.   An example of a VLIW Processor and its instruction. In this simple example, the instruction includes a load or store operation, a floating point add, a floating point multiply, a fixed point operation (IALU), and a conditional branch. The functional units (except for the load/store unit) operate only on registers.

control unit. In this case, each stage could perform, for example, the instruction fetch, the instruction decode, the fetching of the operands, or the execution of the operation. Use of this technique is now widespread, and today the control unit of most processors, including microprocessors, is pipelined.

In multifunction processors, pipelining can be used as a second and complementary form of parallelism to process operations from different scalar instructions. An operation can be issued to a pipelined functional unit whenever the first stage of the functional unit is idle. This can be accomplished either dynamically by the control unit or statically in a VLIW processor. Dynamically controlled pipelining of scalar operations was used in the CDC 7600 and the IBM 360/91 in the late 1960s, and is also used today in several supercomputers. Also, Multiflow's TRACE, a VLIW machine, pipelined some of the scalar operations.

Pipelining is also usually used to execute vector instructions. Vector instructions that could handle vectors of any size were built into the Texas Instruments Advanced Scientific Computer (TI-ASC), first delivered in 1972, in the form of memory-to-memory vector instructions. Today, vector instructions are used in practically all pipelined supercomputers.

The major limitation of pipelining is that most functions can only be broken into a relatively small number of stages. For example, in the Cray Y-MP, pipes have from 2 to 15 stages. This small number of stages limits the amount of parallelism that can be exploited and therefore also limits the potential of pipelining to achieve high computing speeds independently.

4. *Array processors*—An array processor consists of a number of identical arithmetic-logical units (ALUs - *q.v.*) usually called processing elements (PEs). The processor control unit broadcasts the commands corresponding to each instruction to all the PEs (Fig. 6). In this way, vector instructions can be executed by applying the same operation simultaneously to different (pairs of) array elements. Each PE can be temporarily dis-

abled independently of the others, and, as a consequence, array processors can operate on vectors with fewer elements than the number of PEs and can also perform operations on a subset of the array elements. Memory is usually divided in such a way that each slice can be accessed by only one PE. In addition, the PEs are usually connected through a network whose purpose is to align the data before the execution of an array operation. This alignment is achieved by a command from the control unit requesting that the PEs interchange data through the network. An alternative, used in the Burroughs Scientific Computer (BSP), is to place the alignment network between the PEs and the memory modules and perform the alignment of the operands while the data travels between the memory and the processors.

ILLIAC IV, a machine designed at the University of Illinois by Daniel Slotnik, is an early example of an array processor. Completed in 1972, it was designed to include four quadrants of 64 PEs each. The quadrants could be configured to work synchronously under a single control unit or configured as four independent processors. Although it had only one quadrant, the final machine was the world's faster computer until 1981, when it was shut down. Another historically important machine is the just-mentioned BSP, which was completed in 1976. However, the project was cancelled before a machine had been delivered.

Array processing does not suffer from the limited scalability of pipelining. Parallelism can be increased just by increasing the number of PEs. As discussed below, there are today array machines with up to 2,048 floating-point processors, and even larger machines are expected to be produced in the near future.

Pipelined and multifunction processors have been used as multiprocessor components, and, at least in theory, multiprocessors could include several array processors. However, array processing is often considered an alternative to multiprocessing. When we compare these two approaches, we find that each approach has ad-

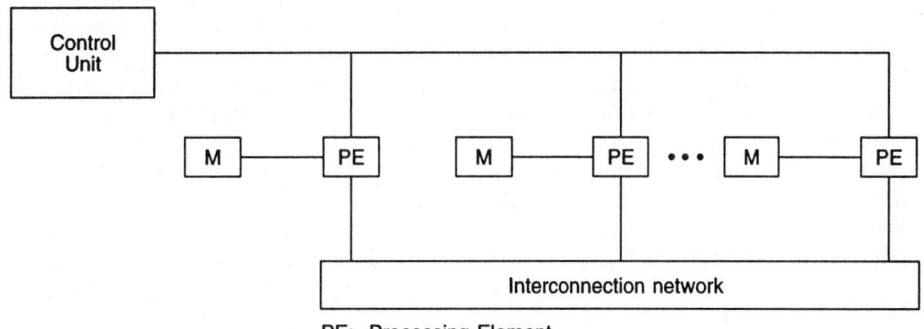

PE: Processing Element

FIG. 6. Schematic of an array processor.

vantages and disadvantages. For example, there is no need for synchronization instructions to coordinate the execution of parallel operations in array processors. Also, array processor programs use parallelism only in array operations and therefore can be considered as sequential programs, which means that the array processor programs do not suffer from the danger of the race conditions that make some multiprocessor programs difficult to debug. However, such advantages do not come without a price. Array processors are less flexible, and the independent program streams in multiprocessors allow them to perform better on a wide range of applications.

Machines   During the decade of the 1980s, there was an unprecedented proliferation in the number of supercomputers, as well as a corresponding increase in the number of supercomputer manufacturers. Also, Japan emerged during this decade as an important center of supercomputer design and manufacture.

Some important characteristics of several supercomputers that were developed mostly during the 1980s are presented below. For this discussion, the machines are grouped into three categories: shared-memory multiprocessors, distributed memory multiprocessors, and array computers. A frequently used measurement is *theoretical peak performance,* the maximum number of floating-point operations that a machine can execute per second, assuming that all the floating-point units are continuously busy. This peak performance is never achieved in the execution of real-life programs, which usually are unable to utilize fully all the computational resources available in the machine. Despite all this, the theoretical peak performance can give some idea of the computational resources in the machine, especially when used in conjunction with the cycle time. The units used to measure the theoretical peak performance are megaflops (millions of floating-point operations per second - Mflops) and gigaflops (billions of floating-point operations per second - Gflops).

1. *Shared Memory Multiprocessors*—During the 1980s, several manufacturers, including Cray Research in the United States and Fujitsu, NEC, and Hitachi in Japan, designed and built powerful uniprocessor computers. All these machines were similar to the Cray-1, which was introduced in 1976, and perhaps one of the most influential machines ever built. The Cray-1 and the early Fujitsu and NEC machines were uniprocessors. However, by 1990 these machines had evolved into shared-memory multiprocessors. Cray Research was again a pioneer by introducing the first multiprocessor supercomputer, the Cray X-MP, in 1984, years before the other manufacturers. By the end of 1990 Hitachi was the only member of this group that had not announced a multiprocessor, but it is expected to do it soon.

In the Cray-1 and in all the supercomputers later built by Cray, Fujitsu, NEC, and Hitachi, the processors use multifunction parallelism and pipelining. In addition, their instruction set includes vector instructions, and both scalar and vector operations can be pipelined. However, there are some differences, for example, in the number and size of scalar and vector registers and in the type and number of functional units. Another important distinction is that, on the Cray machines, some functional units can be used to pipeline both scalar and vector operations, whereas in the Fujitsu and NEC machines, all functional units are devoted to one or the other type of operands.

An important factor influencing the performance of these machines is the use of sophisticated technology in electronics, packaging, and cooling. For example, the Fujitsu 2000 series uses silicon emitter-coupled-logic with an 80 picosecond propagation delay, and the Cray-3 prototype is built from gallium arsenide logic components. An example of sophisticated cooling is provided by the Cray-2, whose boards are immersed in fluorocarbon fluid. When maintenance is required, the liquid is rapidly pumped into a reservoir.

Another important characteristic of these machines is the presence of a large main memory with a high bandwidth, achieved by the use of hundreds of memory banks. The large bandwidth is necessary to balance the data streaming ability of the memory with the computational power of the processors. Table 1 presents some important characteristics of some of the most recent shared-memory supercomputers. The Cray-1 is included in this table for comparison purposes. In Table 1 we can see how the processor cycle time has been reduced by a factor of more than six during the 14-year period from 1976 to 1990. The peak performance of the machines has also increased noticeably, in part because of the shorter cycle time, but also and to a greater extent because of the increase in the number of processors. For comparison purposes, Table 2 lists some of the machines produced between 1976, when the Cray-1 appeared, and 1990. A block diagram and picture of a shared-memory multiprocessor, the NEC SX-3, is presented in Fig. 7.

A related group of shared memory multiprocessors called *minisupercomputers* were introduced in the 1980s. These machines have lower performance than the machines discussed above, but also have a lower cost (about $1.5 million dollars for a complete configuration in 1990 vs. around $5 million for a single-processor Cray Y-MP). In their latest machines, Alliant and Convex, two minisupercomputer manufacturers, have taken different approaches in technology. Alliant uses microprocessors for the main computational engines, and Convex uses custom-made processors built from ECL components. Table 3 presents

TABLE 1. Characteristics of Some Shared-Memory Multiprocessors

System	Year	Maximum No. of Processors	Cycle Time (Nanoseconds)	Theoretical Peak Performance (Gigaflops)	Maximum Memory Size (Megabytes)	Maximum Number of Memory Banks
Cray-1	*1976*	*1*	*12.5*	*0.16*	*32*	*16*
Cray Research C-90	1992	16	4	16	4,096	1,024
Cray Computer Cray-3	(1)	16	2	16	4,096	512
NEC SX-3	1991	4	2.9	22	2,048	1,024
Fujitsu VP2400/40	1992	4(2 vector units)	3.2	5	2,048	512

(1) In early 1992 Cray cancelled its plan to manufacture a 16-processor machine. Only 2-processor machines are planned for the near future even though the design allows 16 processors.

some of the characteristics of Alliant and Convex machines.

An interesting shared-memory multiprocessor that can also be classified as a minisupercomputer is the FPS System 500. This machine allows three different types of processors: scalar microprocessors, and vector and matrix coprocessors. The peak performance of the machine is 167 Mflops without the matrix coprocessor, which by itself has 6.7 Gflops of peak performance. Fig. 8 presents a block diagram of the FPS System 500.

2. *Distributed-Memory Multiprocessors*—This group of machines includes some early designs, such as the Intel iPSC/860 and the nCube 2, and recently-designed machines such as the Intel Paragon XP/S, the Fujitsu AP1000 and the CM-5 from Thinking Machines, Inc. of Cambridge, MA. Furthermore, Convex, Cray, IBM, and NEC are all working on machines of this class.

All these machines consist of a large number (128–8,192) of nodes, each containing a microprocessor, a memory unit, and a routing controller to manage the messages traveling through the network. The type of network used by the Intel iPSC/860 and nCube 2 is the *n*-dimensional cube. This type of interconnection has the advantage that the number of steps required to move data between the furthest processors in the system is only the logarithm of the total number of proces-

sors. However, in the Paragon XP/S machine, a two-dimensional mesh is used, owing in part to its simplicity and scalability. The routing strategy is called *wormhole routing*; it works by first creating a path in the network and then pipelining the different parts of the message through the path. Table 4 presents some characteristics of four machines in this class. Fig. 9 is the block diagram of the AP1000, which has an organization quite similar to that of the Paragon XP/S.

3. *Array Machines*—Several array machines have been built since the time of the ILLIAC IV. However, only recently has there been an increasing commercial interest. Several array processors were designed during the late 1970s whose PEs were bit-serial. Two of these machines were the Distributed Array Processor (DAP), designed in the United Kingdom by ICL, and the Massively Parallel Processor, designed at Goodyear by K. Batcher. The MPP was designed primarily to process satellite image data, but it has also been used in several numerical applications. In both of these machines, each PE is connected to its nearest neighbors.

A design of the 1980s is the Connection Machine, built by Thinking Machines. There are two versions—CM-1, first delivered in 1986, and CM-2, delivered in 1987. The Connection Machine (see Fig. 10) is similar to the MPP and DAP, in that

TABLE 2. Characteristics of Some Supercomputers of the 1980s

System	Year	Maximum No. of Processors	Cycle Time (Nanoseconds)	Theoretical Peak Performance (Megaflops)
Cyber 205	1981	1	20	400
Cray X-MP	1986	4	8.5	940
Cray Y-MP	1988	8	6	2,667
Cray-2	1985	4	4.1	1,952
Fujitsu VP-400	1986	1	7.5	1,142
NEC SX-2	1986	1	6	1,300
Hitachi S-820/80	1988	1	4	3,000

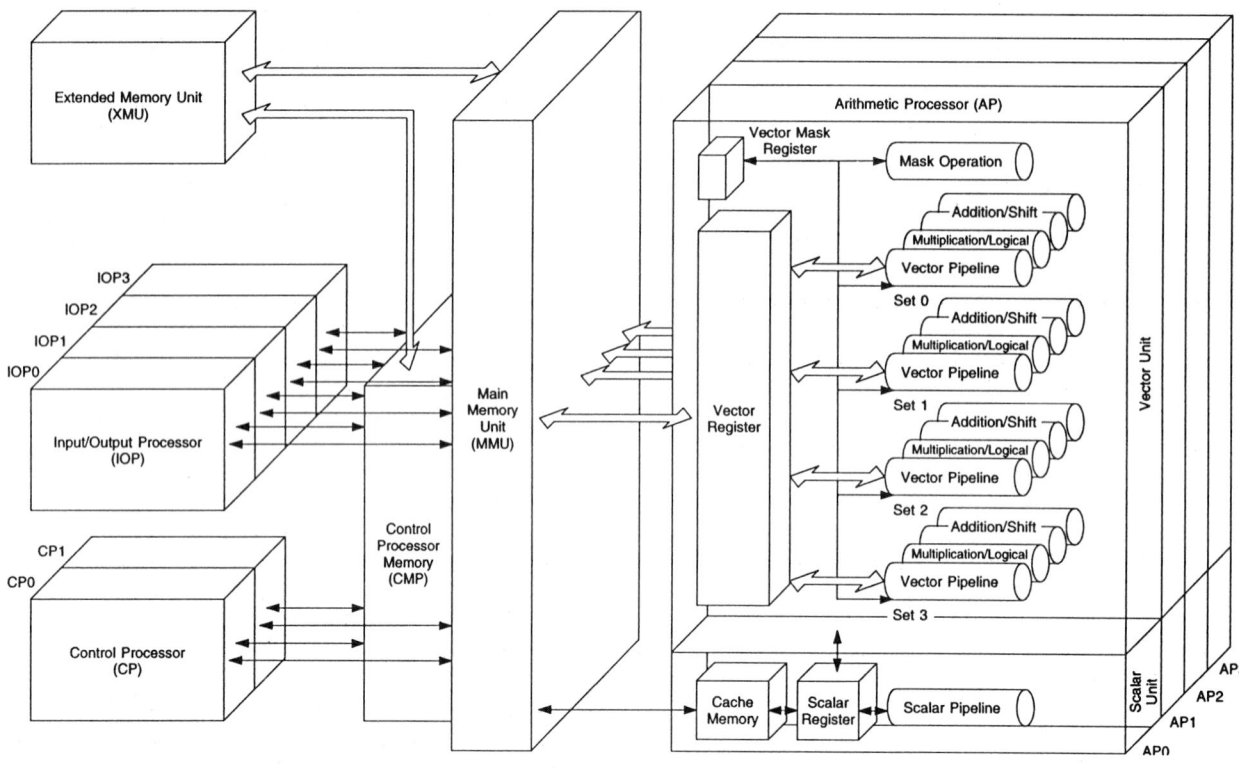

FIG. 7. (a) Schematic of the NEC SX-3 multiprocessor. The processor includes four floating point functional units each with four identical pipes. (b) The NEC Supercomputer SX-3, Model 44.

TABLE 3.   Characteristics of Some Minisupercomputers

System	Year	Maximum No. of Processors	Cycle Time (Nanoseconds)	Theoretical Peak Performance (Megaflops)	Maximum Memory Size (Megabytes)
Alliant FX/8	1985	8	170	94	80
Alliant 2800	1990	14	25	560	1,024
Convex C-1	1984	1	100	20	128
Convex C-2	1988	4	80	200	2,048
Cray Y-MP EL	1991	4	30	532	1,024
Convex C3880	1992	8	16.67	960	4,096

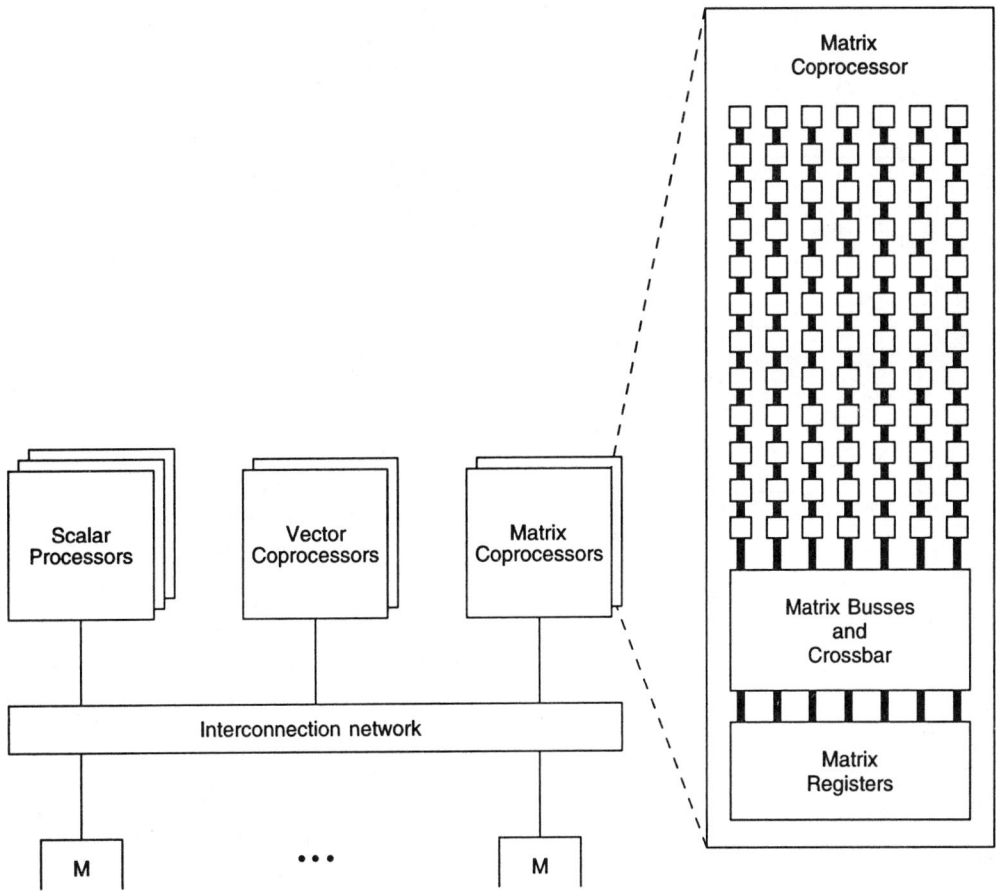

FIG. 8. Schematic of the FPS system 500. The matrix co-processor can accept up to 84 processing elements.

its processors are bit-serial and in the use of the nearest neighbor interconnection between the PEs. But there are also some differences. One difference is the presence of an *n*-dimensional cube interconnection that makes global routing possible. The second difference, present only in CM-2, is the availability of a floating-point accelerator associated with groups of 32 PEs.

Table 5 presents characteristics of several array machines, including the GF-11 and the MasPar 1200. The GF-11, developed by the IBM Research Laboratories, has quantum chromodynamics as its main intended application. The MasPar machine is similar to the Connection Machine; it includes connections to the nearest neighbor and a shuffle-exchange global interconnection network. The processors are four-bit-wide microprocessors capable of performing floating-point operations.

Programming Languages and Compilers

Two complementary approaches have been followed to program the machines discussed above. The first is to use explicitly parallel languages (i.e. languages with parallel constructs, such as vector operations or parallel do-loops). Since the days of ILLIAC IV, most of the parallel languages developed have been Fortran extensions, a consequence of the predominance of numerical applica-

TABLE 4. Characteristics of Some Distributed-Memory Multiprocessors

System	Maximum No. of Processors	Processor	Theoretical Peak Performance (Gigaflops)	Inter-connection Network	Memory size per Processor (Megabytes)	Interprocessor Channel Bandwidth (Megabytes per Second)
nCube 2	8,192	Custom	27	N-D Cube	4	2.22
iPSC/860	128	Intel i860 or 80386	7.6	N-D Cube	16	2.8
AP1000	1,024	Sun's SPARC	12.8	2-D Mesh	16	25
Paragon XP/S	1,024 (nodes)	Intel i860XP	300	2-D Mesh	128	200

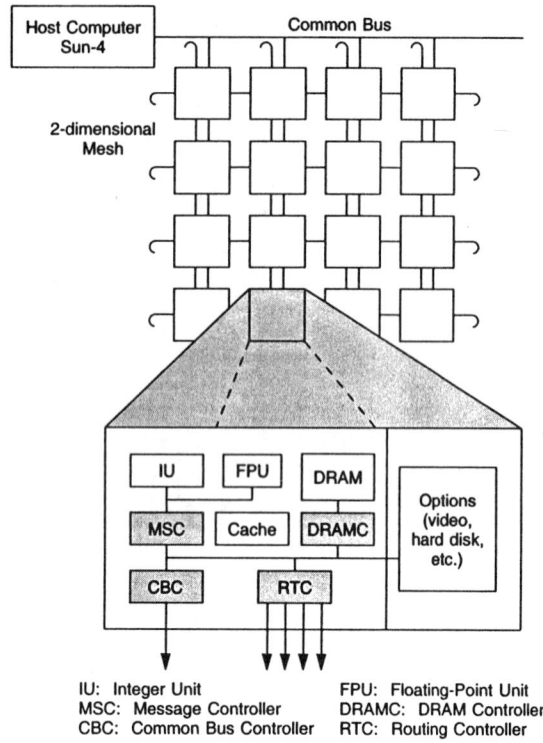

IU: Integer Unit
MSC: Message Controller
CBC: Common Bus Controller

FPU: Floating-Point Unit
DRAMC: DRAM Controller
RTC: Routing Controller

FIG. 9. Schematic of the AP1000.

FIG. 10. The Connection Machine.

tions in supercomputers. Recently, however, there has been some activity in the design of extensions to other sequential languages, such as Lisp and C (*q.v.*).

Vector Fortran extensions were developed during the 1970s for the ILLIAC IV and the TI-ASC. Another vector Fortran extension of the 1970s was VECTRAN, developed by researchers from IBM and heavily influenced by APL, a vector language developed in the early 1960s by Kenneth Iverson. VECTRAN in turn influenced Fortran 90, the next ANSI Fortran standard, which includes vector operations and vector intrinsic functions (as well as many other new constructs). Compilers for vector Fortran dialects, inspired by early drafts of the Fortran 90 standard, have already been developed for the Alliant machines, CM-2, and the MasPar array computer.

There are also Fortran extensions for programming shared-memory multiprocessors. An early example is the Fortran dialect developed as part of a study conducted during the 1970s by Burroughs Corporation. Parallel dialects were also developed by the Cedar project at the University of Illinois in 1985 and by IBM in 1988. In 1989, an ANSI committee was created to develop a standard multiprocessor Fortran extension. Unfortunately, because of the long debate on Fortran 90, this ANSI committee decided to base their work on Fortran 77 and not on Fortran 90. This leaves us with two different standards, one for vector operations and another for multiprocessors. Clearly, a unified standard is needed.

The second alternative for programming supercomputers, used by almost all of the shared-memory multiprocessors and pipelined uniprocessors, is to use *parallelizing* compilers, which automatically translate sequential Fortran 77 programs into parallel form. The use of sequential Fortran simplifies portability across different parallel machines and also permits the use of programs written for sequential machines. Parallelizing compilers can also be traced back to the ILLIAC IV and the TI-ASC machines. Since those days, much progress has been made on compiler algorithms. However, much still remains to be done, especially in the development of translation algorithms for distributed-memory machines.

As mentioned, automatic parallelization and explicit parallel programming are complementary approaches. A programmer should have access to both strategies, possibly in the form of a parallelizing compiler for a parallel

TABLE 5. **Characteristics of Some Array Processors**

System	Year	Maximum No. of PEs	Interconnection Network (Gigaflops)	Theoretical Peak Performance
ILLIAC IV	1972	64	Nearest Neighbor	0.128
GF-11	1989	586	Benes Network	11
CM-2	1989	65,536	Nearest Neighbor & N-D Cube	>10
MasPar 1200	1990	16,384	Nearest Neighbor and Shuffle-Exchange Network	1.3

TABLE 6. Linpack and Perfect Benchmark Performance of Some Supercomputers (The Perfect Benchmark figures reflect only the performance of nine of the thirteen codes.)

System	Theoretical Peak Performance (Gigaflops)	Perfect (Harmonic Mean)	Linpack
Cray X-MP	940	12.4	178
Cray Y-MP	2,667	16.6	275
Cray-2	1,952	10.7	101
Hitachi S-820/80	3,000	15.5	107
NEC SX-2	1,300	13.6	941

programming language, such as the IBM Parallel Fortran compiler. In this way, many error-prone optimizing transformations can be left to the compiler, and the programmer can concentrate on the development of clean programs and, when needed, concentrate on those sections of code where the compiler does not produce code with the expected performance.

Performance To evaluate the performance of supercomputers, several collections of programs or subroutines have been used. Two of the most popular are the Perfect Benchmarks, a collection of 13 programs representing supercomputer applications, and the LINPACK Benchmark, a collection of linear algebra subroutines. Table 6 presents the performance of several supercomputers as measured by each benchmark.

From Table 6, two interesting facts can be observed. First, the performance of all the machines for these codes is only a small fraction (sometimes less than 1%) of the theoretical peak performance. Second, higher peak performance does not mean higher performance on real programs.

The poor performance shown in Table 6 results from the nature of the programs and the limitations of the compilers and machine organizations. Unfortunately, the exact nature of the difficulties is not well understood. Improving understanding of the performance of supercomputers and using this information to design better machines, compilers, and parallel programs is among the most important challenges computer scientists face today.

References

1981. Kogge, P. M. *The Architecture of Pipelined Computers.* New York: McGraw-Hill Book Company.

1986. Padua, D. A., and Wolfe, M. J. "Advanced Compiler Optimizations for Supercomputers." *Communications of the ACM.* **29**, *12*, 1184–1201.

1989. Almasi, G. S., and Gottlieb, A. *Highly Parallel Computing.* Redwood City, CA: The Benjamin/Cummings Publishing Company, Inc.

1990. Guzzi, M. D., Padua, D. A., Hoeflinger, J. and Lawrie, D. H. "Cedar Fortran and Other Vector and Parallel Fortran Dialects," *The Journal of Supercomputing,* **3**, 37–62.

1990. Stone, H. S. *High-Performance Computer Architecture.* Reading, MA: Addison-Wesley Publishing Company.

DAVID A. PADUA

SUPERCOMPUTING CENTERS

For articles on related subjects *see* PARALLEL PROCESSING: ARCHITECTURE; and SUPERCOMPUTERS.

The National Science Foundation (NSF) *supercomputing centers* began as a partnership between academic, industrial, and government communities to further research in computational science. Congress established the NSF centers in response to studies done in the early 1980s that indicated that there was an insufficient number of advanced computational resources to serve the scientific community. It was predicted that unless support was given to the development of computational science and the researchers who use it, research would suffer.

The goal of the NSF centers is to allow researchers to produce results on a supercomputer that simulate phenomena that cannot be investigated in a laboratory. Since the centers were formed in the mid-1980s, there has been an increased demand for faster and more powerful computers. In the course of their brief history, the supercomputing centers have continually expanded and upgraded their equipment and other resources to meet the needs of researchers.

There are four supercomputing centers in the U. S.: the Cornell Theory Center at Cornell University, the National Center for Supercomputing Applications at the University of Illinois at Urbana-Champaign, the Pittsburgh Supercomputing Center at Carnegie-Mellon University, and the San Diego Supercomputer Center at the University of California, San Diego. The centers are joined through Internet, a global system of interconnecting networks. NSFNET is a part of this network and is used by researchers at the centers to send electronic mail, access remote resources, and transport data. There are plans to develop an even more far-reaching network called the National Research and Education Network (NREN). This network will allow for transmissions at gigabyte speeds.

Cornell Theory Center The Cornell Theory Center was established in 1984 and is supported by the National Science Foundation, New York State, IBM Corporation, and other members of the Center's Corporate Research Institute. The Cornell National Supercomputer Facility (CNSF), a division of the Theory Center, supports the national research community through a variety of education, training, and technical support programs. The Theory Center has special programs to support industry, through its Corporate Research Institute. Research into large-scale parallelism is furthered through the Advanced Computing Research Institute.

The Theory Center has two coupled IBM ES/3090 600J supercomputers, each with six vector facilities, giving a total peak throughput of more than 1.65 Gflops and providing the potential for 12-way parallelism. Each machine has 512 Mbytes of real memory and 2 Gbytes of expanded storage. The total disk storage capacity is 196 Gbytes. The Theory Center's partnership with Syracuse University's Northeast Parallel Architecture Center (NPAC) brings to the Center the resources of two 32K processor Connection Machines, the Alliant FX/80, the Encore 520 Multimax, and the Encore 320 Multimax.

The Cornell supercomputers use a VM/XA SP2 operating system that runs both CMS and AIX. The language used for scalar, vector, and parallel modes of computing is Fortran. IBM Corporation and the Theory Center have recently developed Clustered Fortran, which can be adapted to two or more supercomputers, to speed up large-scale computations.

More than 2,000 researchers in many disciplines all over the U. S. use the Theory Center's supercomputers for their work. A few of the more than 500 current projects include a study of earth vibrations and seismic imaging, a model of equilibrium and economic competition, an investigation into the nature of the heartbeat, the complication of simple mathematical algorithms, and the origin of black holes.

Through various programs, groups of researchers make use of the Theory Center's supercomputer: the Computational Science and Engineering Research Group consists of scientists, researchers, and post-doctoral fellows doing advanced research in the computational sciences; the Smart Node program provides on-site support for researchers at more than 60 participating institutions; and each year teams of high school students spend three weeks at Cornell working on projects involving the supercomputer as part of the SuperQuest program.

National Center for Supercomputing Applications

The National Center for Supercomputing Applications (NCSA) at the University of Illinois was established in February 1985 and opened a year later with the help of a grant from the National Science Foundation. NCSA has more than 2,500 users.

NCSA operates three supercomputers: a Cray X-MP/48, a Cray-2S/4-128, and a Connection Machine Model 2 (CM-2). NCSA will soon replace the X-MP with a 4-processor, 64-megaword Y-MP system. The Cray supercomputers run the Unicos operating system. A mass storage system, which runs on an Amdahl 5860, houses much of the collected data. An extensive array of workstations provide a strong peripheral environment for NCSA's supercomputing operations.

NCSA has pioneered state-of-the-art visualization software suitable for a variety of workstations and scientific applications. This equipment is useful for media production specialists, animators, artists, and scientists interested in producing complex three-dimensional simulations of scientific phenomena. Using NCSA's Scientific Visualization Suite, researchers can produce animated images from datasets. Software programs enable users to share and transfer files from various machines, workstations, and operating systems.

NCSA offers a number of programs for the advancement of computational science. The Industrial Program includes researchers from a select group of corporations. NCSA also provides infrastructural support to over 100 universities and other institutions, including technical assistance and consulting services.

Pittsburgh Supercomputing Center

The Pittsburgh Supercomputing Center (PSC), funded by a grant from the National Science Foundation and supplemented by the Commonwealth of Pennsylvania, was established in 1986 as a joint project of Carnegie-Mellon University, the University of Pittsburgh, and Westinghouse Electric Corporation. To date, over 2,400 researchers at 270 universities and research centers in 48 states have used the Center's facilities to advance their projects.

PSC operates an 8-processor CRAY Y-MP/832. The "Y" is supported by a solid-state Storage Device (SSD), which holds 128 million words, and an IBM 4381-P21 with 30 Gbytes of storage. The most recent addition to PSC's computing environment is a 32,768-processor Connection Machine (CM-2). The CM-2, a data-parallel computing system, will be used to interact directly with the Y-MP through a high-speed network operating at 800 megabits per second, thus providing the center with more overall computing power.

PSC supports a variety of graphics packages, including NCAR-GKS, DI3000, SMDLIB, DISSPLA, and DRAWCGM. These packages can be used to display two-dimensional arrays of data and to produce video animations. A P3D software system is available for developing images from three-dimensional models.

Research at PSC spans a diverse range—air quality studies, the microeconomics of Wall Street, bone-tissue healing, protein structure, and galaxy evolution—and has resulted in the publication of over 600 papers in science and engineering journals.

San Diego Supercomputer Center

The San Diego Supercomputer Center (SDSC) began in 1985. SDSC is supported by a grant from the National Science Foundation and a consortium of academic and research institutions that reviews research applications and provides guidance to SDSC staff. Nearly 3,500 researchers at 150 institutions use SDSC resources.

Supercomputing at SDSC is done on a CRAY Y-MP8/864. The Y-MP has 8 CPUs and contains 64 million words of memory. Short-term file storage is provided on high-speed disk drives with a total storage capacity of 65 Gbytes. The supercomputer has a Unicos operating system, which is the Cray version of Unix. Long-term storage is provided by an IBM-based system and Data Tree applications software. SDSC has compilers for Fortran, C, and Pascal.

Like other supercomputing centers, SDSC serves users with a wide range of interdisciplinary projects. Some of the projects that have used the SDSC computing environment include studies of aromaticity and ring strain, DNA and carcinogens, carbon dioxide and climate, probes of the earth's interior, accelerating particles with density waves, and lattice gauge theory.

Ann Redelfs

SUPERCONDUCTING DEVICES

For articles on related subjects *see* COMPUTER CIRCUITRY; INTEGRATED CIRCUITRY; and MICROCOMPUTER CHIP.

The Josephson tunnel junction, whose operation is based on an effect predicted by Brian Josephson in 1962, typically consists of a thin insulating layer (~30Å = 3 × 10^{-9}m, or about 10 atomic layers thick) sandwiched between two superconducting (zero resistance) films. When placed in a suitable cryogenic environment (such as liquid helium at 4.2·K = −269·C), these junctions form the basis of ultra-fast switching circuits with transitions times of picoseconds (ps) and power dissipations of less than two microwatts. Such high-speed and low-power dissipation make Josephson junction devices a strong contender for use in high-performance computers.

The Josephson tunnel junction is characterized by two states, one of zero resistance and the other of non-zero resistance. When the junction is in the zero resistance state, an externally applied current is transported through the insulating layer, or tunnel barrier, by superconducting electrons (paired electrons) which, via a quantum mechanical tunneling mechanism, cross the barrier without resistance. If the junction is in the non-

zero-resistance state, an externally applied current passes through the barrier as a normal electron tunneling current with an associated voltage drop. A current biased (~1 mA) junction in the zero-resistance state can be switched to a non-zero voltage (~3mV) by increasing the bias current above a particular value (the critical current), or by applying a magnetic field generated by a current in an overlying control line. The magnitudes of the current and the voltage lead to power dissipation measured in microwatts. The switching speed of ~1 ps is set primarily by the time required to charge the junction capacitance (measured in picofarads for devices with LSI dimensions). Josephson switching devices frequently consist of two or more junctions incorporated in a superconducting loop to form a Superconducting Quantum Interference Device (SQUID—see Fig. 1). In logic applications, current diverted from one SQUID as it makes a transition to non-zero voltage state can be used to induce switching in another SQUID. Complete SQUID logic families have been successfully designed and tested.

Memory cells have also been constructed with Josephson devices. The cells rely on the phenomenon of "magnetic flux trapping," whereby a persistent circulating current can flow in a SQUID loop indefinitely with no loss of energy. Such a current can be initiated or

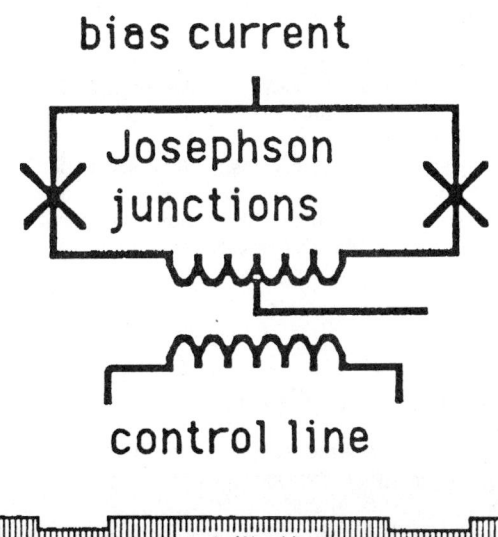

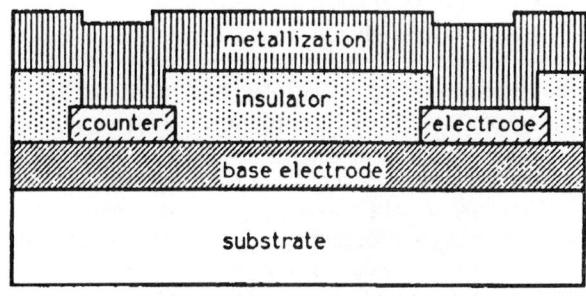

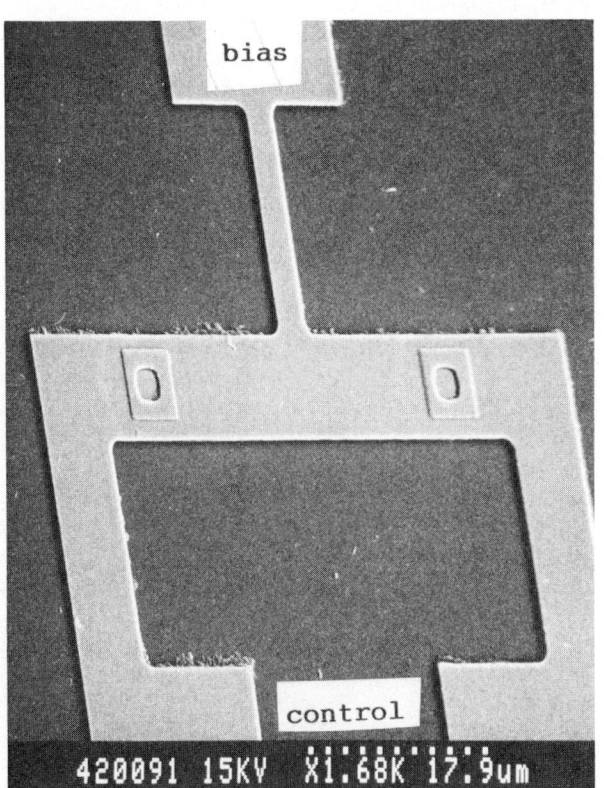

FIG. 1.   (a) Circuit diagram, (b) schematic cross-section, and (c) scanning electron micrograph of a two-junction Superconducting Quantum Interference Device (SQUID). The SQUID is normally biased in the zero-resistance state with bias current less than the critical current of the SQUID. When a current passes through the control line, it generates a magnetic field that interacts with the device and causes the SQUID to switch to a non-zero voltage. (Courtesy of HYPRES, Inc., Elmsford, NY).

terminated, and its presence or absence can be detected by the use of Josephson junctions and SQUIDS. Again, the advantages of high-speed and low-power dissipation are significant.

The fabrication process for Josephson junction devices and circuits is similar in complexity to that of LSI semiconducting devices. Josephson structures are formed by multiple vacuum depositions on silicon substrate rather than by diffusion and induced crystal growth (epitaxy) as is common with semiconductor devices. The vertical structure typically consists of a niobium groundplane, followed by approximately ten layers of various metals (primarily niobium superconductors) interleaved with insulating layers (primarily silicon oxide). The most sensitive step in the fabrication process is tunnel barrier formation. A decrease of 1 Å in thickness of the barrier (nominally ~ 20 Å) leads to a typical critical current increase on the order of 300 percent. The niobium used for junction electrodes is also used to make lossless transmission lines. Such lines used with matched resistive terminations serve to transport signals without loss or degradation, both on circuit chips and within the package in which the circuit chips are embedded. Such chips have been fabricated and integrated into commercial systems such as sampling oscilloscopes.

The primary advantages of Josephson technology arise from extremely fast switching speeds and low power dissipation. Chips cooled by natural convection in liquid helium can be packed tightly together in a three-dimensional package with lossless superconducting transmission lines for communication. A Josephson

junction-based 8-bit digital signal processor has been designed and tested (Fig.2). It exhibits 1 giga-operations per second with only 12mW of power dissipation at 4.2K. For a large-scale Josephson computer based on Josephson technology, the cost of providing and maintaining the cryogenic environment will amount to a small fraction of the total cost of the machine.

For ultra-high-performance machines, it appears that the cost of manufacturing and maintaining a Josephson computer will be similar to that for a semiconductor computer of comparable complexity. One of the major factors in determining the future of Josephson technology is memory technology. Even though significant progress has been made in recent years in this area, improvements in the design as well as fabrication process are necessary. The state-of-the-art in memory technology has exhibited a 1 K bit ROM with access time of better than 400 ps and at 1.6mW. Although much work remains to be done, the future for Josephson technology looks promising.

References

1987. Yu, L. S. *et al.* "An All-Niobium Eight Level Process for Small and Medium Scale Application," *IEEE Trans. on Mag.* **MAG-23,** 1476.

1988. Whiteley, S. R. *et al.* "Technologies for a Superconducting Sampling Oscilloscope/Time Domain Reflectometer," Proceedings of SPIE Symposium on Advances in Semiconducting and Superconductors: Physics and Device Applications (Interconnection of High Speed and High Frequency Devices and Systems), Newport Beach, CA, March.

1990. Kotani, S. *et al.* "A 1 GOPS 8-bit Josephson Digital Signal Processor," Proceedings of IEEE International Solid-State Circuits Conference, February.

1990. Aoyagi, M. *et al.* "A Josephson 10-bit Instruction 128-Word ROM Unit," *IEEE Journal of Solid-State Circuits,* **25,** 971.

1992. Hasuo, S. "Toward the Realization of a Josephson Computer," *Science,* **255,** *3,* 301–305.

MASOUD RADPARVAR

SUPERVISOR CALL

For articles on related subjects *see* INTERRUPT; MULTIPROGRAMMING; OPERATING SYSTEMS; and PRIVILEGED INSTRUCTION.

A typical operating system has a set of system programs collectively known as the *supervisor,* whose function is to provide services for and to supervise the running of a number of user programs. Control goes to the supervisor every time the normal flow of processing is interrupted by a change of state in the system.

The purpose of a *supervisor call* is to provide a mechanism whereby a program can interrupt the normal flow of processing and ask the supervisor to perform a function for the program that the program either cannot or is not permitted to perform for itself.

The most typical supervisor calls have to do with input and output. In a multiprogramming system, it is essential to have system control of I/O devices, especially those devices shared by a number of programs.

FIG. 2. Photograph of a digital signal processor fabricated and tested. The die includes more than 23,000 Josephson junctions using 1.5 μm all-niobium technology. The chip has a similar architecture as a silicon-based processor and contains ALU, Multiplier, RAM, ROM, and Registers. (Courtesy of Fujitsu Limited, Atsugi, Japan.)

Most computers that were designed for multiprogramming systems have a supervisory mode of operation and hardware *interlocks* (*q.v.*) that prevent certain supervisory operations from taking place except when the computer is operating in supervisory mode. This may be handled by means of special *privileged instructions* that can be executed only in supervisory mode, or only in some other way.

In the IBM 360/370/390 systems, for example, a supervisor call is made through the execution of an instruction whose effect is to create an *interrupt* (*q.v.*). The instruction is two bytes long. The first byte is the supervisor-call instruction code, and the second byte describes the nature of the supervisor call. This second byte goes into a special register that is used in connection with all interrupts to transmit information to the system as to the status of that particular interrupt.

The interrupt now proceeds like any other interrupt. It stores the status of the computer (the old program status word) and loads a new status that gives control to a resident supervisory routine, which operates in supervisor mode and whose function is the handling of supervisor calls. This routine then analyzes the second byte of the supervisor-call instruction and determines the nature of the call.

It is, of course, possible—and usually essential—that additional information is passed to the supervisory routine as a result of the supervisor call. This information may be in a *general register* (*q.v.*) or in an area of memory pointed to by a special register.

The supervisor may have resident routines for handling certain classes of supervisor calls, and may have available areas of central memory (transient areas) into which overlays can be loaded for the handling of less frequent supervisor calls. Fast response to supervisor calls is usually an important factor in system performance, and systems that have large amounts of central memory can often improve their responsiveness by increasing the number of resident supervisor-call routines.

SAUL ROSEN

SWAC

For articles on related subjects *see* DIGITAL COMPUTERS: EARLY; and SEAC.

SWAC [(National Bureau of) Standards Western Automatic Computer] was dedicated in August 1950, and at that time was the fastest computer in existence. It was begun in January 1949 at the National Bureau of Standard's field station, the Institute for Numerical Analysis at the University of California at Los Angeles, and was designed and constructed under the direction of the author. Originally named the ZEPHYR, it was later renamed the SWAC because of its modest sized budget and staff, as contrasted with much larger projects being carried on elsewhere.

The SWAC was a parallel computer using a Williams tube (cathode-ray tube) memory (*q.v.*). The memory cycle

FIG. 1. The SWAC.

was 16 μs consisting of an 8 μs action cycle and an 8 μs restore cycle (where some other memory location was restored). An addition of two 37-bit operands occurred in 64 μs, and multiplication occurred in 384 μs. Due to technical difficulties with Williams' tube storage, the memory was never increased beyond 256 words. A 4,096-word magnetic drum was added to the system with coordinated addressing so that block transfers of 32 words between the two memories occurred with no latency (*q.v.*).

Initial input and output was by typewriter and punched paper tape. These were soon replaced by a card reader (240 cards per minute) and a card punch (80 cards per minute). The SWAC used a four-address command structure. A floating-point interpretive system named SWACPEC was developed, which made it much easier for users to write programs.

In 1953, the SWAC was producing about 53 hours of useful computing time per week. SWAC was used in a research computing environment, and therefore many of the problems tended to be quite large. Solution times from 177 to 453 hours are reported by Huskey *et al.* (1953). Some of the early problems included the search for Mersenne primes, the Fourier synthesis of X-ray diffraction patterns of crystals, the solution of systems of linear equations, and problems in differential equations.

When the National Bureau of Standards ceased to support the Institute for Numerical Analysis, the SWAC was transferred to the University and moved to the Engineering Building at UCLA. There it continued in useful operation until December 1967. Parts of the SWAC are now on exhibit in the Museum of Science and Industry in Los Angeles.

References

1951. Huskey, H. D. "Semiautomatic Instruction on the Zephyr," *Proceedings of a Second Symposium on Large-Scale Digital*

Computing Machinery. Cambridge, MA: Harvard University Press, 83–90.

1953. Huskey, H. D., Thorensen, R., Ambrosio, B. F., and Yowell, E. C. "The SWAC—Design Features and Operating Experience," *Proceedings of the I.R.E.* **41**, *10*: 1294–1299 (October).

1978. National Computer Conference Pioneer Day. (Edited transcript available from Charles Babbage Institute, Madison, WI.)

1980. Huskey, Harry D. "The National Bureau of Standards Western Automatic Computer (SWAC)," *Annals of the History of Computing*, **2**, *2* (April), 111–121.

HARRY D. HUSKEY

SWAPPING

For articles on related subjects *see* MEMORY: AUXILIARY; SCHEDULING ALOGORITHM; TIME SHARING; TIME SLICE; VIRTUAL MEMORY: and WORKING SET.

Swapping is a name for the information transfer that occurs when a program is temporarily unloaded from main to secondary storage and later reloaded to continue processing. The term originated in the time-sharing systems of the early 1960s. Because there was no memory protection hardware to isolate multiple programs, these early systems permitted only one user program at a time to reside and execute in the main memory. When a program reached the end of a *time slice* or stopped for I/O, the operating system exchanged it for another waiting program.

Most modern operating systems use multiprogrammed *virtual memory*. In these systems, there are two kinds of information transfer between main and secondary memory:

1. Loading a program at the start of an execution period, and unloading it at the end of that period.
2. Fetching new pages or segments on demand during the execution period.

Swapping is often used to name the first type of information transfer, and *demand fetching* (or *demand paging*) the second type. The term *roll-in* is sometimes used to name the process of loading a program, and *roll-out* the process of unloading.

Both types of transfer need not be used in the same system. CDC Cyber series computers, for example, load a complete program for execution; these machines employ swapping but no form of demand fetching. On the other hand, paged virtual memory systems, such as the VAX VMS operating system, are capable of starting a program with no initial loading; in this case, demand paging also serves to load the program after the start of execution. This is not an effective use of demand paging. It is much more efficient to load and unload full *working sets* (*q.v.*) at the starts and ends of execution periods; demand fetching should be used to add pages to the working set during the execution period.

Early time-sharing systems had to control the overhead of swapping. In CTSS, for example, the CPU would be idle during a swap because the user memory was uniprogrammed. The CTSS multilevel scheduler started programs at priority levels whose quanta were at least as long as the swap time; this limited CPU idle time due to swapping to 50% (*see* Corbato, 1962). Schedulers in modern multiprogramming systems do not pay as much attention to this because the swapping of one program occurs in parallel with the execution of another.

Reference

1962. Corbato, F. J., Merwin-Daggett, M., and Daley, R. C. "An Experimental Time-Sharing System," *Proceedings of the Spring Joint Computer Conference 21*. (In Rosen (Ed.), *Programming Languages and Systems*. New York: McGraw-Hill (1967), 335–344.)

PETER J. DENNING

SWITCHING THEORY

For articles on related subjects *see* ARITHMETIC-LOGIC UNIT; BOOLEAN ALGEBRA; CODES; COMPUTER ARCHITECTURE; COMPUTER CIRCUITRY; INTEGRATED CIRCUITRY; LOGIC DESIGN; and SEQUENTIAL MACHINES.

Switching theory is the abstract, mathematical formalization used in logic design of digital networks. It is so called because when it was first developed by Claude Shannon (*q.v.*) in 1938, most logic networks were implemented using switches and electromechanical devices such as relays. Modern logic networks are usually constructed using electronic integrated circuits comprising networks of logical elements such as Inverters, AND Gates, OR Gates, etc. These elements operate on binary signals; they are constrained to take on only two different voltage values (such as 0 or 5 volts). Switching theory uses a two-valued Boolean Algebra (sometimes called *switching algebra*) as a notation to represent the operation of such logic networks. The two algebraic values are most often represented as "0" and "1", although "T" and "F" are also used to emphasize the relation to propositional logic. The correspondence between the algebraic symbol used to represent a signal and the voltage present is arbitrary, although the *positive logic convention* in which the algebraic 1 represents the more positive voltage signal is now most common. Each input or output signal of a logic network is represented by a Boolean variable. Boolean algebra has three basic operations: inversion, logical addition, and logical multiplication; these operations are implemented directly by logic gates called Inverters, OR Gates, and AND Gates.

There are two classes of logic networks: *combinational networks* for which the output at any time depends only on the inputs present at the same time, and *sequential networks*, for which the output depends on past as well as present inputs.

Combinational Networks A combinational network implements a Boolean function. Such a function can be represented by a Table of Combinations, (or *truth table*) that lists all possible combinations of input values and the corresponding output values, as in Table 1a, or by

TABLE 1. An Example of a Boolean Function—The 2-bit Multiplexer Function (a) Table of Combinations (b) Algebraic Expressions

(a)

x	y	z	f(x, y, z)
0	0	0	0
0	0	1	1
0	1	0	0
0	1	1	0
1	0	0	0
1	0	1	1
1	1	0	1
1	1	1	1

(b)
$$f(x,y,z) = xy + y'z = (x + y')(y + z)$$

an algebraic expression, as in Table 1b. This function is called the 2-bit multiplexer function. Two logic networks that each implement this function are shown in Fig. 1.

Analysis Switching theory was developed to solve the two major issues of analysis and synthesis. In analysis, the Boolean function realized by a network is determined and compared with the specified function. Like many of the issues that arise in switching theory, this problem is very simple conceptually. It can be easily solved for functions of a small number of variables (up to 10) by comparing the Tables of Combinations for the network and the specification. The difficulty is that many important combinational designs have far more than ten

inputs and the time required to compare a design and its specification grows exponentially with the number of inputs. All that can be done is to invent techniques that require less computation for some of the possible Boolean functions.

Since the size of the Table of Combinations doubles for each additional input variable, other representations are needed. The most promising approach uses a binary tree called a binary decision diagram (BDD). In this tree, each level corresponds to one of the variables and the leaf nodes correspond to function values (0 or 1). The binary decision diagram for the 2-bit multiplexer function is shown in Fig. 2.

Synthesis In synthesis, the problem is to find a network (preferably an optimum one) that realizes a given specification. There is no challenge to find a network. An algebraic expression, called the *canonical sum* or *disjunctive normal form*, is easily found for any function: this expression is a sum-of-products in which each product term (called a *fundamental product* or *minterm*) corresponds to a row of the Table of Combinations for which the function is to equal 1. The canonical sum for the 2-bit multiplexer function of Table 1 is: $f(x,y,z) = x'y'z + xy'z + xyz' + xyz$. The first product, $x'y'z$, corresponds to row 1 of the Table of Combinations. The variables x and y are primed because the entries in this row for x and y are 0; z is unprimed since it corresponds to a 1 entry. When the input variables have the values given in row 1 of the table, the first product will equal 1 and all other products will be 0. A network is easily drawn from the canonical sum:

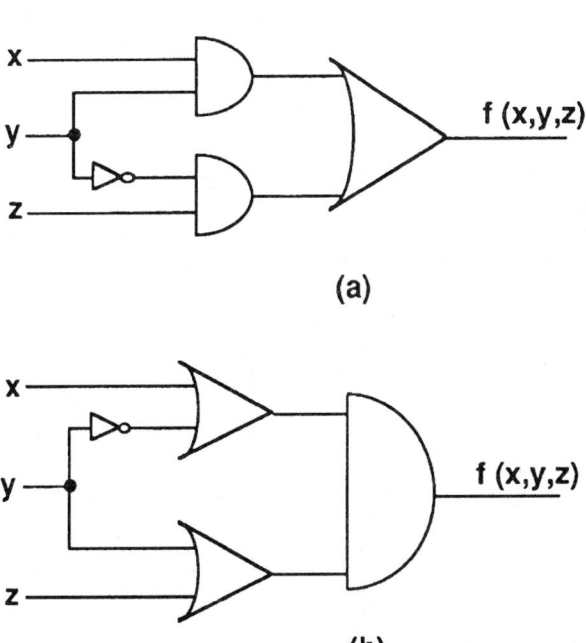

(a)

(b)

FIG. 1. Logic Networks that Implement the Function of Table 1. (a) $f(x,y,z) = xy + y'z$. (b) $f(x,y,z) = (x + y')(y + z)$.

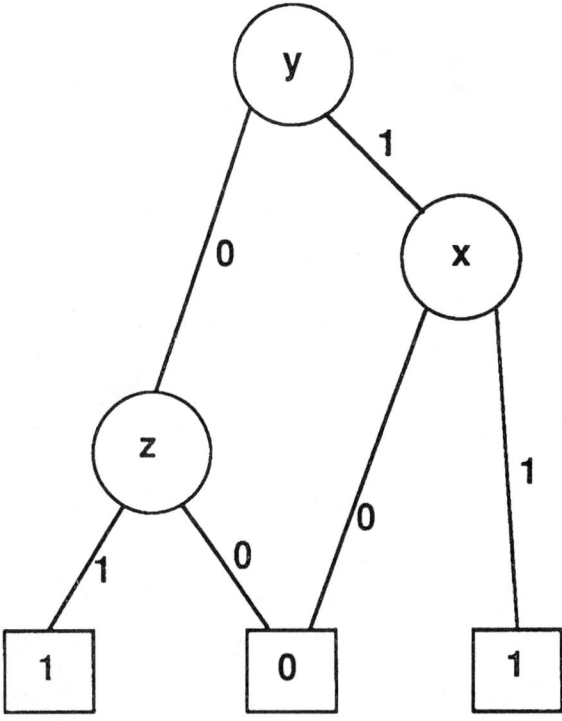

FIG. 2. Binary decision diagram for the 2-bit multiplexer function.

each product term is represented by an AND Gate whose output is connected to an OR Gate; the OR Gate output is the network output, Fig. 3. Networks such as that in Fig. 3 in which there are (at most) two gates between an input signal and the output are called *two-stage networks*. Each network input is a signal representing either an input variable (such as x) or the complement of an input variable (such as x').

Although the canonical sum network is easily designed, it is often a very inefficient implementation—compare the networks of Figs. 1 and 3. The historical objective of switching theory is to develop techniques for synthesizing optimum networks. The first issue that arises is deciding which network characteristics to optimize. Cost usually comes first, although performance and testability are also very important. Silicon area is typically the major cost factor; it depends on which gates are required and how difficult it is to implement the required interconnections. A precise cost cannot be determined from an algebraic expression or logic network, but the total number of required gate inputs is usually a good approximation to relative cost. Most synthesis techniques attempt to minimize the gate-input count. This is done by finding an expression having the fewest possible literals (variables or complemented variables) present. Performance can be taken into account by limiting the maximum number of gates in any path from an input to an output. Testability is a more complex issue. Combinational synthesis tries to enhance testability by ensuring that there are no untestable (redundant) elements in the synthesized networks.

A canonical sum can be transformed into another expression by using the Boolean Algebra theorems: $W + W = W$ and $WU + WU' = W$, in which W and U stand for arbitrary Boolean expressions. For example, in the canonical sum for the 2-bit multiplexer function

$$f(x,y,z) = x'y'z + xy'z + xyz' + xyz$$

the last two terms differ only in z, so they can be combined: $xyz' + xyz = xy$. A similar operation on the first two terms allows them to be replaced with the single product $y'z$. These operations result in a simpler expression for the 2-bit multiplexer function:

$$f(x,y,z)) = y'z + xy.$$

This expression corresponds to the Fig. 1a network. Of all the possible sum-of-products expressions for this function, it is the one having the fewest literals. Such an expression is called a *minimal sum*. In the example just given, the theorem $W + W = W$ was not used; but for most functions this theorem is needed to find a minimal sum.

The minimal sum is a very important expression for synthesis: it corresponds directly to an efficient design for a PLA (programmable logic array) and is the starting point for many of the methods used to synthesize multistage gate networks. A minimal sum has two basic properties:

1. None of the product terms are redundant in the sense that they could be removed from the expression without changing the function represented, and
2. None of the product terms can have a literal removed without changing the function represented.

Product terms with property 2 are called *prime implicants*.

The Quine-McCluskey algorithm is a well-known procedure for finding a minimal sum for any arbitrary Boolean function. There are two parts to this algorithm: First, the two theorems just mentioned are used to find all possible prime implicants. Then, some of the prime implicants are chosen for use in forming the minimal sum. While this algorithm is straightforward, it is impractical for functions with many input variables. There are storage

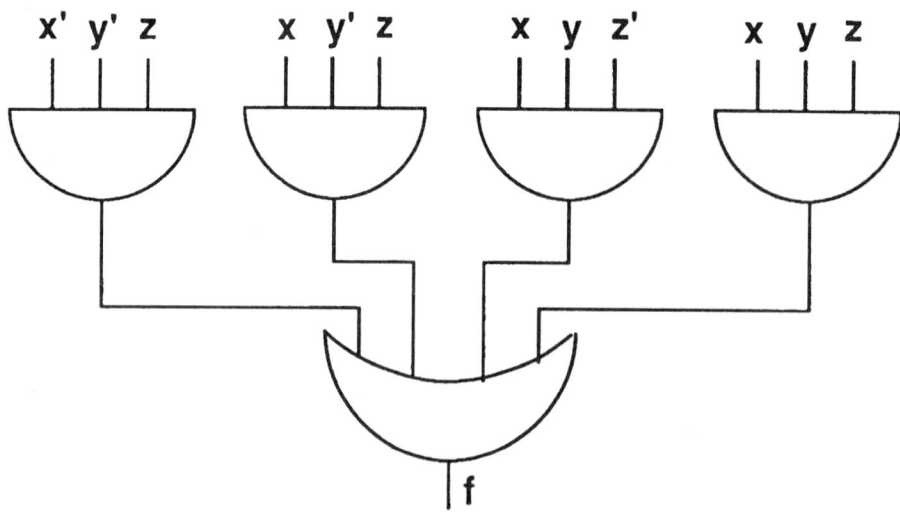

FIG. 3. Network for the 2-bit multiplexer function derived from its canonical sum.

problems, since there can be as many as $3^n/n$ prime implicants for an n-variable function. This means that if $n = 15$, the number of prime implicants can be almost 1 million, and for $n = 20$, almost 175 million. The second step of choosing those prime implicants with which to form the minimal sum requires solving a minimum covering problem. This problem is NP-complete (*q.v.*). No algorithm is known for solving such problems faster than a running time that grows exponentially in the number of variables. This means that, for functions with more than 15 variables, it isn't possible to guarantee finding a minimal sum in a reasonable time. Two approaches have been taken to handle such functions: one is to develop a procedure that either will produce a minimal sum or will not get any output in a reasonable time; and the other is to use a procedure that will always produce an output even though that output is not always a true minimal sum.

For very simple functions such as the 2-bit multiplexer function and for PLA implementations, the minimal sum produces the best design. For other technologies, such as gate networks or more complex functions, *multilevel networks*—those with more than two gates between input and output—are often more efficient. The Carry Function, $f(a,b,c) = ab + ac + bc$ is a very simple example of this situation. This sum-of-products expression corresponds to a two-stage network with 9 gate inputs (Fig. 4a). This expression can be factored using the Boolean algebra theorem, $WU + WV = W(U + V)$, to form the factored expression $a(b + c) + bc$. The multi-stage network of Fig. 4b, with 8 gate-inputs, results from this expression.

Another approach to finding efficient networks seeks to decompose the network into interconnections of subnetworks. The simple disjoint decomposition, illustrated in Fig. 5, is the most important such decomposition. Subnetwork N_1 implements the subfunction $G(x_1, x_2,...,x_s)$, and subnetwork N_2 implements the subfunction $F(G, x_{s+1},..., x_n)$, which is equal to $f(x_1, x_2,..., x_n)$. Not all functions can be decomposed in this fashion. Tests have been developed to check whether a given function can be realized by a network of this structure. It has been proved that most Boolean functions cannot be realized this way, but the functions used in computers are not typical and many of these functions can be decomposed effectively.

Sequential Networks The output of a sequential network depends on past as well as present inputs. Thus, the network must have some internal memory, which is typically implemented with latches or flip-flops. These elements contain feedback loops that store signals. The stored signals constitute the *state* of the network. The most common form of sequential network is the *finite state machine* that has one input (usually called the clock), on which pulse signals occur while the remaining inputs have level signals. When a clock pulse occurs, the state of the machine may change to another state that is determined by the present state and the values of the remaining inputs. The network output is based on the state and the inputs.

The simplest finite state machine is the D flip-flop, which has two inputs: CK is the clock input and D is the level input (Fig. 6a). When a clock pulse occurs, the out-

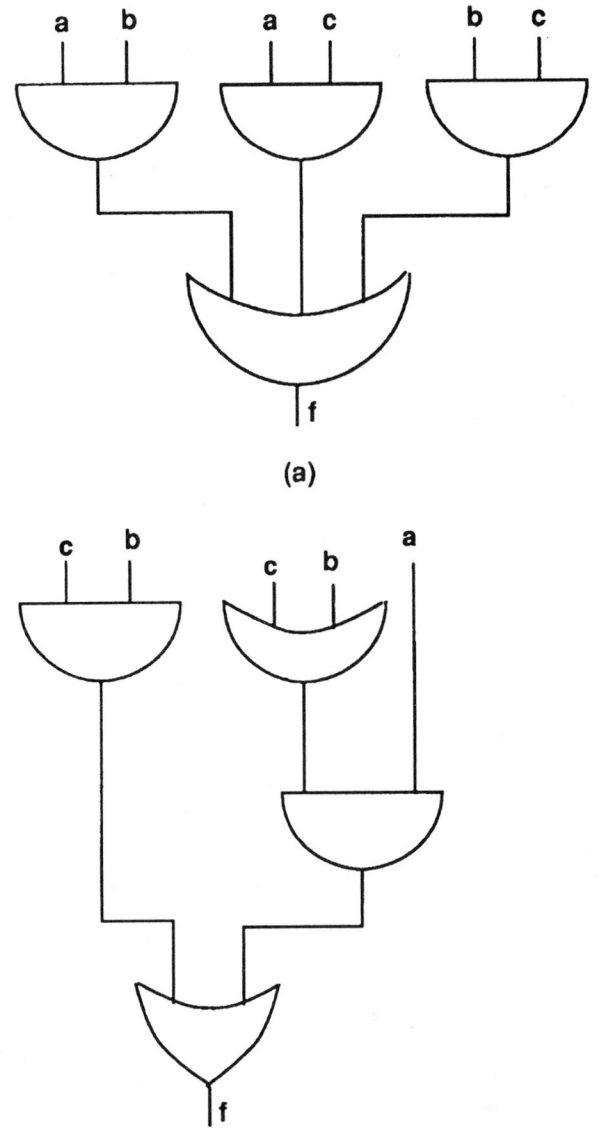

FIG. 4. Two networks for the carry function. (a) two-stage, (b)

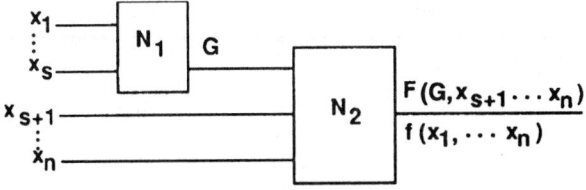

FIG. 5. Simple disjoint decomposition.

put Q becomes equal to the value at D and remains equal to this value until the next clock pulse. Clearly, there must be two states to "remember" the last D value between successive clock pulses. The operation of a finite state machine is usually described by means of a *state diagram*, a graph that has one node for each state and an edge for each transition between states. The state diagram for the D flip-flop is shown in Fig. 6b.

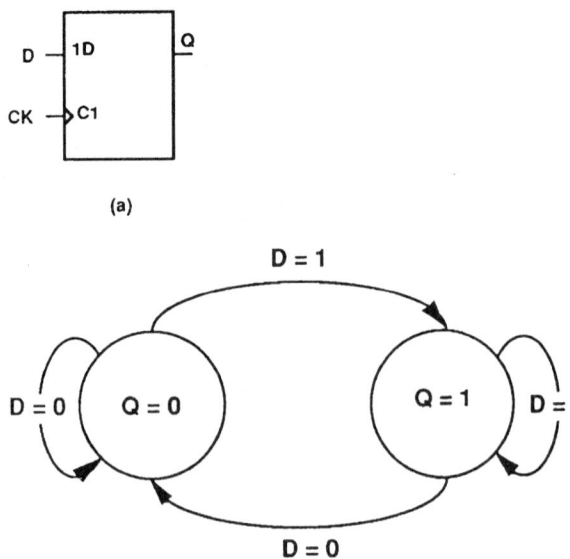

FIG. 6. D Flip-flop. (a) symbol, (b) state diagram.

Synthesis of a finite state machine starts with a state diagram specification of the desired behavior. There are algorithms for checking to determine whether fewer states can be used (state minimization). After a minimum-state diagram is found, a binary encoding of the states must be chosen. The complexity of the final design depends on this encoding, but there are only heuristic procedures to choose a good encoding. Once the state encoding is fixed, the remaining steps to complete the design are mainly combinational design problems.

With the increased power of modern design workstations, it is now possible to use switching theory synthesis techniques to carry out a major portion of the design of new computer systems.

References

1970. Kohavi, S. *Switching and Finite Automata Theory.* New York: McGraw-Hill.
1984. Brayton, R. K., et al. *Logic Minimization Algorithms for VLSI Synthesis,* Norwell, MA: Kluwer Academic Publishers.
1986. McCluskey, E. J. *Logic Design Principles.* Englewood Cliffs, NJ: Prentice-Hall.

EDWARD J. McCLUSKY

SYMBOL MANIPULATION

For articles on related subjects *see* ADDRESSING; AUTOMATA THEORY; COMPUTER ALGEBRA; INFORMATION PROCESSING; LANGUAGE PROCESSORS; LANGUAGE TRANSLATION; LIST PROCESSING; STORED PROGRAM CONCEPT; and STRING PROCESSING.

The power of a modern computer derives from its being more than an arithmetic calculator. It is, in fact, a general-purpose symbol-manipulating system. A symbol *token* is a pattern that can be compared by an information

processing system with some other symbol token and judged equal with it or different from it. The basic test for equality of tokens incorporated in an information processing system determines the fundamental alphabet of symbols it is prepared to recognize and distinguish. A symbol, then, is a class of equal tokens with respect to this basic test.

The key characteristic of symbols for an information processing system is their ability to *designate*, i.e. to have referents. This means that an information process can take a symbol token as input and use it to gain access to a referenced object in order to affect it or be affected by it in some way: to read it, modify it, build a new structure with it, and so on. Hence, three concepts are central to understanding symbol manipulation: an information processing system, symbol structure, and designation.

Information Processing Systems An information processing system (IPS) is a system (Fig. 1) consisting of a memory containing symbol structures, a processor, effectors, and receptors. Leaving out of account the effectors and receptors, we can summarize the characteristics of an IPS in this way:

1. There is a set of elements, called *symbols*.
2. Symbols may be formed into symbol structures by means of a set of *relations*.
3. There is a *memory*, capable of storing and retaining symbol structures.
4. There is a set of *information processes* that take symbol structures as inputs and produce symbol structure outputs.
5. The IPS has a component, the *processor*, that consists of (a) an ability to execute a set of *elementary information processes* (EIP); (b) *short-term memory* (STM) that holds the input and output symbol structures of the EIPs; and (c) an *interpreter* that determines the sequence of EIPs to be executed by the IPS as a function of the symbol structures in STM.

Symbol Structures We say that a symbol structure *designates* (or *references*, or *points to*) an object if there exist information processes that admit the symbol structure as input, and either: (1) affect the object; or (2) produce, as output, symbol structures that are affected by the object.

A symbol structure serves as a *program* if the object it designates is an information process, and the interpreter, if given the program, can execute the designated process.

A symbol is *primitive* if its designation is fixed by the elementary information processes or by the external environment of the IPS.

The "objects" that symbols designate may include symbol structures stored in the IPS memories (data structures and programs), processes that the IPS is capable of executing, or objects in an external environment of sensible (readable) stimuli. To *read* is to create in memory internal symbol structures (representations) that designate external stimuli; to *write* is to create responses in the

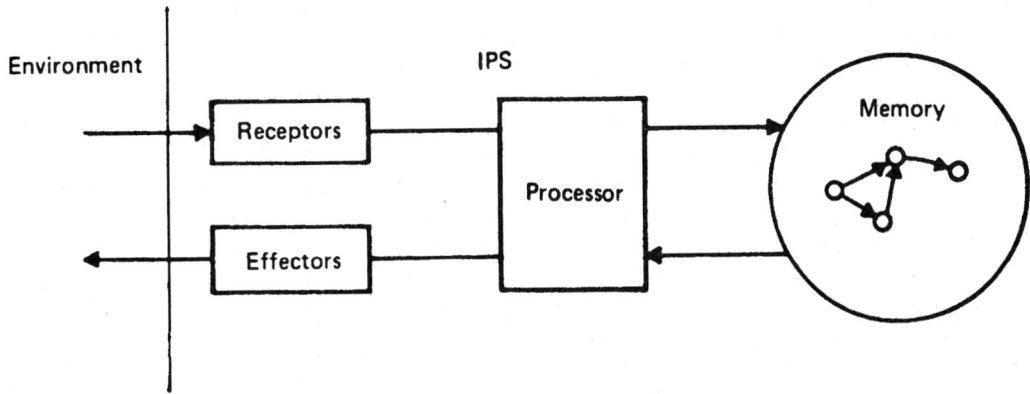

FIG. 1.   General structure of an information processing system. (From *Human Problem Solving*, Allen Newell and Herbert A. Simon. Englewood Cliffs, N. J.: Prentice-Hall, 1972.)

external environment that are designated by internal symbol structures.

The relation between a designating symbol and its object may have any degree of directness or indirectness. A structure can point to a structure that points to a structure that points to....

Example.   The meaning of these concepts can be illustrated by an example. An IPS for receiving Morse Code will have to be able to perceive the basic external stimuli: dots, dashes, letter spaces, and word spaces. These stimuli could be represented internally by two different primitive symbol types, say "·" and "–", together with conventions for representing letters as lists of primitive symbols, and words as lists of letters. Sequences of stimuli could be represented by ordered sets (*lists*) of primitive tokens. Thus, if the external stimulus were a sequence of three dashes followed by a letter space, the read processes might store the symbol structure (–,–,–), the ")" representing the letter space.

In turn, each of these simple symbol structures would be assigned a *name*—i.e. a designating symbol. The structure (–,–,–), for example, might be designated by S. Then, larger structures could be built up as lists of such naming symbols [e.g. (W,A,S)], and so on indefinitely.

There would exist an elementary information process to find the member of a list next to a given member. Thus, given the token A and the list (W,A,S), this process would find the symbol token S. Another elementary process would test pairs of symbols for identity, to determine the equality, for example, of the second symbols of the lists (W,A,S) and (H,A,S), respectively.

The elementary processes would also have symbolic names, which could then be combined into composite processes, designated by lists of such names, thus allowing an arbitrarily complex subroutine structure. For example, the process for testing symbol identity could be combined with the process for finding the next symbol on a list, to test whether two lists are identical.

To execute composite processes, the IPS could use an interpretive process. (*See* LANGUAGE PROCESSORS). A symbol structure (the program) would designate the se-

quence of elementary processes to be executed. The interpreter would keep track of the current elementary process being executed, and after execution would find the next process to be executed.

Finally, additional information could be associated with the symbol structures. With the list (W,A,S) might be associated the descriptors—part of speech (verb) and tense (past)—the two pairs constituting a description of the list. There would then be additional elementary processes to obtain the descriptions, given the list.

These postulates for an IPS are entirely abstract, making no assertions about how the structures and processes are realized, whether physically or biologically. Digital computers are physical systems that fit this abstraction; some psychologists, though not all, believe that the human cognitive system is also an information processing system in the sense of these postulates. Whether or not this view is correct cannot be settled conclusively on the basis of the evidence now available. Some success has been achieved, however, in modeling a range of human cognitive capabilities by means of appropriately defined information processing systems.

Designation   It would be more correct to say that symbol *structures* designate than to say that *symbols* designate. For example, if an information process takes as input the symbol structure (color, houseA) and produces the symbol "white," then the symbol structure (color, houseA) designates *white*, and hence indirectly designates the color of the house in question.

In discussing linguistic matters, one normally takes as prototypical of designation the relation between a proper name and the object named—e.g. "George Washington" and a particular man who was once President of the United States. One then attempts to pass from that relation to the others more difficult to envision: e.g. the relation between "house" and any of a certain class of sheltering structures, and so on to "truth," "beauty," and "justice."

Any discussion of the basic characteristics of symbols and symbol structures always assumes the existence of information processes for acting on those symbols and structures. Each of the components, as is typical in abstract systems, remains essentially undefined, except when taken in conjunction with the other parts. Thus, the concept of *list* is inextricably mingled with the concept of a process for finding the *next* item on a list—i.e. for responding to the ordering relation that defines the list (*see* LIST PROCESSING).

Some symbols have their meaning fixed by the existence of elementary information processes that treat them in fixed ways. The most important examples are:

1. Symbols that designate specific external events or structures (e.g. internal representations of real characters).
2. Symbols that designate elementary information processes, so that these EIPs can be executed when these symbols call for the execution.

What collection of symbols is primitive for a specific IPS will vary with the particular application. For example, for purposes of visual *pattern recognition* (*q.v.*), the primitive symbols might be set up to correspond, more or less approximately, to the elementary discriminations of which the retina is capable, and it is usual in such applications to describe the sensory input as a two-dimensional array of intensities. Similarly, an information processing theory of *speech recognition* (*q.v.*) might take as primitive symbols the elementary features that are postulated to define phonemes. In applications where sensory discrimination is not the central concern, it may be more convenient to omit pattern recognition at this elementary level and to take encodings of familiar configurations of sensory objects as the alphabet of primitive symbols. Thus, for particular applications, letters of the alphabet, or even whole words, might be taken as primitive symbols. An important consequence of taking letters as primitive symbols is that we cannot then speak of one pair of letters as more closely resembling each other than another pair. There is no notion of degree of difference or similarity among them.

Representation   A simple example has already shown how primitive symbols can be combined into lists and descriptions. A couple of additional examples will illustrate the wide range of representations that can be accommodated by these means. In storing chess information, the pieces can be designated by symbols that have descriptions—defining each piece's type (King, Queen, Rook, etc.), color, and position on the board. Squares can also be represented as described symbols, whose descriptions include information about the geometry of the board, i.e. which squares adjoin them. A position, in this representation, is a symbol structure that associates with each square the symbol or the piece occupying that square, if any, and which identifies the adjacent squares in various directions.

A somewhat different representation might be suitable for expressions from symbolic logic; e.g. $(P \vee Q) \cdot (Q \supset R)$. This expression can be represented by just this list of symbols, including parentheses. The expression can also be represented in prefix rather than infix form by a list structure, whose main list is $(\cdot, A, B)$, where A is the

symbol that designates the list $(\vee, P, Q)$, and B the symbol that designates the list $(\supset, Q, R)$. Alternatively, making use of the relations of left (for left subexpression) and right (for right subexpression), the same logic expression could be represented as a tree structure (Fig. 2). Yet another representation of the expression uses descriptions. Take as attributes *term, connective, left,* and *right,* and as symbols a number of nodes, $x1, x2....$ Then the logic expression could be represented as the following set of descriptions:

connective($x1$) = $\cdot$ left($x1$) = $x2$ right($x1$) = $x3$
connective($x2$) = $\vee$ left($x2$) = $x4$ right($x2$) = $x5$
connective($x3$) = $\supset$ left($x3$) = $x6$ right($x3$) = $x7$
term($x4$) = P
term($x5$) = Q
term($x6$) = Q
term($x7$) = R

These associations can be represented pictorially, as in Fig. 3. All of these representations are very closely related, as can be observed. That there are many ways of representing something should not be surprising. We could give still others, e.g. prefix notation. All that is needed for a representation is some scheme of associations (relations) together with a set of information about connections. It is not usually possible to tell from its output exactly what internal representation is being used by an IPS, especially when alternative representations are as isomorphic as those presented here. However, in other cases, particularly in representing problems, the choice of representation can have striking observable consequences for external behavior.

If too limited a repertory of symbol structures and designations is provided by an IPS, the encoding of complex information can become an exercise in virtuosity that yields little benefit of any other kind. It appears that the structures essential to provide appropriate direct representation of a very wide range of stimuli are list structures and descriptions, the two types of structures we have used extensively in our examples. Other types of structures may be needed occasionally, but these two types are the core of the representational capability used in most information processing systems.

Elementary Information Processes   There must be a sufficiently general and powerful collection of ele-

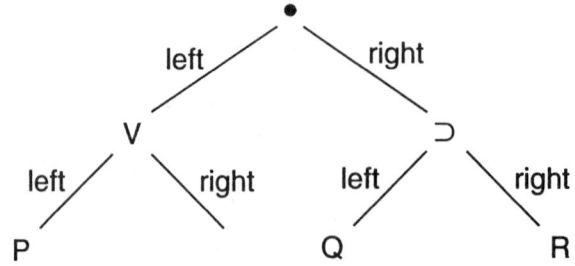

FIG. 2.   Tree structure for $P \vee Q) \cdot (Q \supset R)$. (From *Human Problem Solving,* Allen Newell and Herbert A. Simon. Englewood Cliffs, N. J.: Prentice-Hall, 1972.)

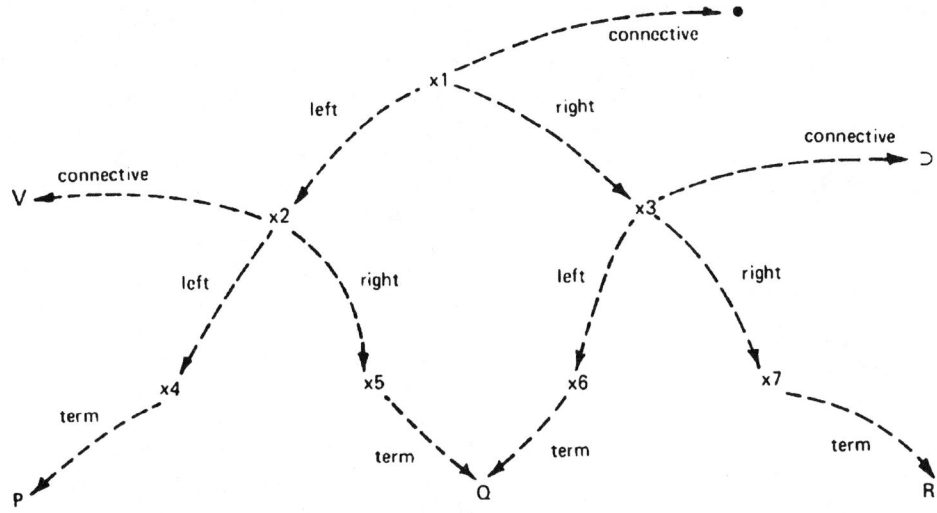

FIG. 3. Association structure for $(P \lor Q) \cdot (Q \supset R)$. (From *Human Problem Solving*, Allen Newell and Herbert A. Simon. Englewood Cliffs, N.J.: Prentice-Hall, 1972.)

mentary information processes to extract from them all the macroscopic performances of the IPS. Furthermore, it is essential that these elementary processes be well defined so that they are realizable by known mechanisms. It is one of the major foundation stones of computer science that a relatively small set of elementary processes suffices to produce the full generality of information processing. On the other hand, there is no *unique* basis. However, all alternative schemes do incorporate certain fundamental types of EIPs that constitute a sufficient basic set. (Proof of their sufficiency is somewhat more involved.) Among these types are the following:

Discrimination—It must be possible for the system to behave in alternative ways, depending on what symbol structures are in its STM. Furthermore, the behavior needs to be *arbitrarily* alterable; i.e. transfer of control to an independent program must be possible.

Tests and comparisons—It must be possible to determine that two symbol tokens do or do not belong to the same symbol type. Comparisons are often directly coupled with conditional behavior, but they may equally well lead to the production of a conventional symbol (e.g. *true* or *false*) that can later be discriminated.

Symbol creation—It must be possible to create new symbols and set them to designate specified symbol structures. Again, this process must be performable arbitrarily; i.e. whenever a new symbol is desired, it can be created, but it should carry no meaning other than its designation of the specified symbol structure. Whether the system must also be able to destroy symbols depends primarily on whether memory capacity is limited.

Writing symbol structures—It must be possible to create a new symbol structure, copy an existing symbol structure, and modify an existing symbol structure, either by changing or deleting symbol tokens belonging to the structure or by appending new tokens with specified relations to the structure.

Reading and writing externally—It must be possible to designate stimuli received from the external environment by means of internal symbols or symbol structures, and to produce external responses as a function of internal symbol structures that designate these responses.

Designating symbol structures—It must be possible to designate various parts of any given symbol structure, and to obtain designations of other parts, as a function of given parts and relations. Again, this may be achieved in many ways, but there must not be any parts of symbol structures that are in principle inaccessible.

Storing symbol structures—It must be possible to remember a symbol structure for later use, by storing it in the memory and retrieving it at any arbitrary time via a symbol structure that designates it. How much memory is available, of course, conditions strongly how complex the totality of stored structures may be. The memory must be highly reliable over time.

Even the earliest stored-program computers essentially met these requirements for an information processing system. The abstract characterization of a system such as that outlined here was developed in close relation with the invention and application of list processing and string manipulation languages, particularly in the domains of artificial intelligence, computer simulation of human cognitive processes, machine translation of language, and compiler construction (*q.v.*). These applications make little use of the computer as a rapid arithmetic calculator, and depend basically upon its generality as a system for manipulating symbols.

Source Information This article is drawn in large part from pages 20 to 30 of Newell and Simon (1972). For a formal approach to symbol manipulation *see* Chapter 2 of Knuth (1968). Description of a widely used list-processing language illustrating many of the concepts discussed in this article will be found in Siklossy (1970). A recent discussion can be found in Newell, Rosenbloom, and Laird (1989).

References

1970. Siklossy, L. *Let's Talk Lisp.* Englewood Cliffs, NJ: Prentice-Hall.
1972. Newell, Allen and Simon, H. A. *Human Problem Solving.* Englewood Cliffs, NJ: Prentice-Hall.
1973. Knuth, Donald E. *The Art of Computer Programming* **1** (2nd Ed.). Reading, MA: Addison-Wesley.
1989 Newell, A., Rosenbloom, P. S. and Laird, J. E. "Symbolic architectures for cognition," in Posner, M. (Ed.) *Foundations of Cognitive Science*, Cambridge, MA: MIT Press.

ALLEN NEWELL and HERBERT A. SIMON

SYMBOL TABLE. *See* ASSEMBLER; and COMPILER CONSTRUCTION.

SYMBOLIC MATHEMATICAL SYSTEMS. *See* COMPUTER ALGEBRA.

SYNCHRONOUS/ASYNCHRONOUS OPERATION

For articles on related subjects *see* CONCURRENCY CONTROL; CONCURRENT PROGRAMMING; CYCLE STEALING; CYCLE TIME; HANDSHAKING; MULTIPLEXING; and PETRI NET.

The flow of information within a digital network may be said to be either *synchronous* or *asynchronous*. In the case of synchronous operation, a transfer of data from one point to another is assumed to occur within a fixed time interval known to both the sending and receiving devices. The sender and receiver are synchronized by a signal called the *clock*, which may be supplied externally to both, or generated by the sender with the data, and occasionally incorporated within it, but often sent on a separate signal line. In the case of asynchronous operation, the sending device or circuit need have no knowledge of the time scale on which the receiver (and intervening connection) operates, but rather transmits its data with a "data ready" signal and then awaits a reply to the signal sent. Upon receipt of the reply by the sender, it removes its original data and status signal from the line, often (but not necessarily) waiting for the removal of the reply by the sender before proceeding with a second transfer.

The distinction between synchronous and asynchronous operation extends over an extremely broad range of digital design. It can apply to the logic gate and flip-flop level, to the logic unit interconnect level, to the bus trans-

fer level, to the I/O device transfer level, and even to the level of communication with remote systems.

At the logic design level, the synchronous design technique is most straightforward and, accordingly, the most common. It is characterized by a cascade of alternating levels of combinatorial logic gates and synchronizing flip-flops driven by a common system clock. The system remains synchronized provided that the total worst-case propagation delay through the combinatorial logic, from one flip-flop level to the next, is less than the interval between consecutive clock events. Accordingly, in synchronous logic designs, it is usual practice to "capture" the state of the external environment by incorporating clocked flip-flops at the inputs, where, by means of the clock, a snapshot of the input is taken for processing. While the input sampling rate and internal clock rate are the same, the resulting process is essentially the one called *pipelining* in the context of large systems designs. In smaller-scale applications, the input sampling rate is usually at a small fraction of the clock rate of the internal logic, since the limited amount of hardware must be used in a succession of tasks between each input sample.

It is usual that the external inputs to a logic device are not inherently synchronized and thus may be said (causally) to be asynchronous. For example, the time at which an operator presses a button to signal a modified operation is quite random. As indicated previously, one approach is to synchronize such inputs by sampling them under control of the logic clock. However, it is possible to deal with them directly using logic operating in an asynchronous mode.

In asynchronous operation, the flip-flops used are of the simple unclocked reset-set (RS) kind, which wait in readiness for a gating event. Often, the event is directly applied. For example, the RS flip-flop used with mechanical single-pole, single-throw (SPST) input pushbuttons and switches to *debounce* them (i.e. to mask the intermittent connection provided by switch contact for a short time after its operation) is operating asynchronously; there is no clock; the flip-flop simply changes state upon the first transient contact of the bouncing switch element with its ultimate resting place.

Generally, in asynchronous logic design, a large network of race-free combinatorial logic, in which the possibility of a transiently incorrect output (*glitch*) has been eliminated through care in the design of signal paths, may precede each RS storage element. A signal change at the input of this network is propagated to the flip-flop as fast as is possible at the actual speed of propagation of the intervening gates. While for this part of the operation, no detailed knowledge is needed of the actual timing characteristics of the gates, it is quite difficult to know that gating is complete. Clearly, an estimate can be made from the specified worst-case propagation delays of all intervening gates.

On the larger systems level, synchronous and asynchronous operation are well illustrated by the signaling protocols that characterize both internal and external bus communications. Interestingly, one finds a synchronous protocol for links that are either very, very short or very, very long. The former choice is made when the environment is well-controlled and the maximum delay assumptions underlying synchronism can be made. The latter choice applies when the cost of waiting in an asynchronous exchange is thought to be too great.

Fig. 1 illustrates the synchronous exchange of data between two devices, the sender acting as master (M) and the receiver acting as slave (S). The letters M and S at the right edge of the waveforms in Figs. 1 and 2 indicate the association device to be either master or slave.) The bus clock is common to both. At t_1, the master transmits the address of the slave, I/O mode information for control of the slave, and data (if any). The clock falling at t_2 signals the slave(s) to look at the bus and accept data (if sent) or send data (if required). The interval t_1 to t_2 allows for the time of signal propagation in the drivers, the line, and the receivers, as well as its variability (*skew*). At t_3, data, if requested by the master and sent by the slave, is gated into the master. The interval from t_2 to the following t_1 ensures settling of the bus prior to the next cycle.

When a bus is very long and serves many devices of different characteristics, the time required to handle a given device may be highly variable. However, if the synchronous protocol is used, all must go as slow as the slowest. This problem is avoided with asynchronous operation, as indicated in Fig. 2. Here, one device, the master (M) initiates the process at t_1 (having checked that the bus is not busy by noting that Ready and Accept lines are low), sending address, mode and data (if any) to the slave (S). Later, to allow for bus skew (the propagation time difference between signals on two lines), the master raises Ready at t_2, which signal propagates to all slaves. One, recognizing its address (indicated to be valid by Ready) at t_3, takes in (*strobes*) the data (if sent) or sends data (if requested) and raises the signal Accept. Subsequently, at t_4, having noted Accept and allowed for bus skew, the master strobes data from the slave (if requested) and lowers Ready. However, to ensure correct operation of the slave while Ready is high in the presence of bus skew, the Master waits until t_5 to remove the Address and Control information. Meanwhile, the slave, having sensed the fall of Ready, removes Accept and Data (if any) at t_6, preparing the bus for a new cycle. In systems in which the role of master is not fixed, another control line, called Busy, is used to prevent the use of the bus by another (third) device connected to

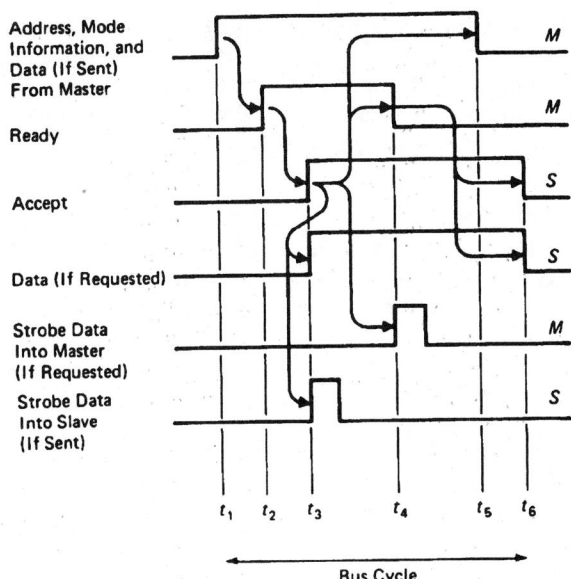

FIG. 2.   Timing of data exchange between master and slave on an asynchronous bus with handshake control.

it. In simple systems, such conflict cannot occur, since slave devices do not "speak unless spoken to."

For links of greater length, particularly between major components of a machine (such as CPU and memory, or CPU and Disk) or between two machines (CPU and CPU), asynchronous operation tends to dominate, since the Ready-Accept exchange can compensate for both transmission uncertainties as well as for busy states, etc., of one of the participating machines. However, as links lengthen, transmission time looms larger. Accordingly, for transmission at a distance, the message enlarges from a byte or two to a great many bytes. Within the message, the operation is synchronous, although the initiation and completion of the message as a whole remains asynchronous in nature. In the limit, for large distances, the asynchronous element virtually disappears. The situation may be likened to that of sending a Telex. A message is sent with the assumption of availability of the recipient. If the receiver gets a garbled message, a repeat is requested. If no response at all is received by the sender, the message is sent again. These messages, while illustrating synchronism within themselves (i.e. locally), are embedded in a system that is asynchronous overall (i.e. globally).

Another important example of a combination of synchronous and asynchronous techniques occurs in the start-stop codes used by teletypewriters and other terminals, both in their connection to processing units and to each other. This connection often consists of a current loop connecting two or more devices through which loop current normally flows when the system is in the idle (rest) state. Transmission commences with the sender opening the line for a one-bit interval to signal the start bit, following which the sender opens and closes the loop corresponding to the 0 and 1 digits, respectively, of a serial code. When the desired bit string is complete (at the end of eight data bits for seven-bit ASCII), the loop is closed for a time corresponding to at least two bit inter-

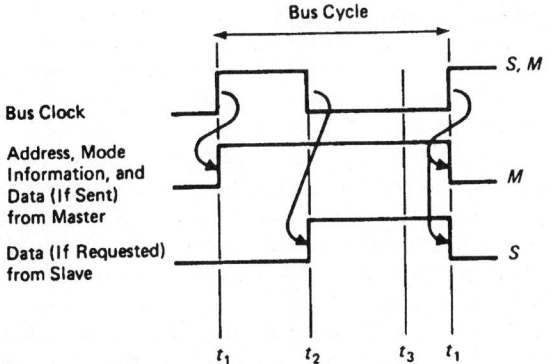

FIG. 1.   Timing of data exchange between master and slave on a synchronous bus under common clock control.

vals. These trailing "1" bits are called *stop bits* and signal to the receiver that a complete character has been sent, while preparing the line for the next transmission. A new character may be signaled by any device in the loop at any time following the last stop bit.

Reference

1978. Hamacher, V. C., Vranesic, Z. G., and Zaky, S. G. *Computer Organization.* New York: McGraw-Hill.

KENNETH C. SMITH

SYNTAX-DIRECTED COMPILER. *See*
COMPILER CONSTRUCTION.

SYNTAX, SEMANTICS, AND PRAGMATICS

For articles on related subjects *see* BACKUS-NAUR FORM; FORMAL LANGUAGES; GRAMMARS; LANGUAGE PROCESSORS; PROGRAMMING LANGUAGES; PROGRAMMING LANGUAGE SEMANTICS; and PROGRAMMING LINGUISTICS.

Every language of communication possesses two identifiable properties—the form of the language and the meaning associated with the form. In the case of natural languages (i.e. those languages used for human-to-human communication), the syntax of the language is generally referred to as its *grammar*. The syntax is a set of rules specifying which forms of the language are grammatically acceptable. For example, if a simple English sentence is specified to have the grammar

noun phrase verb phrase

and a *noun phrase* is composed of an *article* followed by a *noun*, while a verb phrase is defined to be a *verb* followed by a *noun phrase*, we may see that the sentence

"The cat drank the milk"

is a syntactically correct English sentence, provided the word "the" is in the class of *articles*, "cat" and "milk" are *nouns*, and "drank" is a *verb*. However, by the same reasoning, the sentence

"The milk drank the cat"

is equally valid syntactically even though it has no valid meaning.

The *meaning* associated with syntactically correct instances of a language can be viewed from two points of view—the meaning intended by the originator of the sentence and the meaning retrieved by a receiver. It is not always the case that these two meanings are identical. The former is called the *semantics* of the language, and the latter the *pragmatic* meaning. Much of modern humor is based on the skillful interplay between these two aspects

of meaning, particularly with respect to the pun and the riddle.

Linguistic ambiguity may be caused by syntactic inadequacies or by a confusion between semantic and pragmatic meanings. An example of the former is the sign on a jet airplane:

NO SMOKING AREA
IN REAR CABIN

Does this imply there is a place in the rear cabin where smoking is not allowed (a NO-SMOKING AREA) or that there is no place in the rear cabin where smoking is allowed (NO SMOKING-AREA)? On the other hand, the sentence

"I did not say that he stole the money"

can have a multitude of meanings in the spoken language, depending on such factors as emphasis, articulation, and tone. Each pair of the different meanings is a candidate for ambiguity between its semantic and pragmatic meaning.

In the case of programming languages, the distinctions above also apply, but in addition, there are some relatively subtle differences that have developed between computer languages and their associated formal language theory. When used by a computer linguist, grammar is usually applied to the rules governing the generation of strings in a language, while syntax is usually concerned with the recognition by the computer as to whether or not a given string is a legal string in the language. There is, therefore, a complementary relationship between the productions (*q.v.*) of a grammar and the rules of syntax used by a computer language processor to recognize strings in the language.

The implementation of a computer language on a particular computer automatically removes any syntactic ambiguity that may have been present in the language definition by giving one and only one meaning to any language construct. Semantic and pragmatic ambiguities are still possible; they cause much confusion between what the programmer intended and what the computer interprets as the meaning of what the programmer wrote.

J.A.N. LEE

SYSTEMS ANALYST

For articles on related subjects *see* ADMINISTRATIVE APPLICATIONS; PERSONNEL IN THE COMPUTER FIELD; and PROGRAMMER.

The title *systems analyst* is most often applied to the people who investigate, analyze, design, install, and evaluate information systems. Systems analysts first appeared in significant numbers in the 1940s, when the organization now called the Association for Systems Management (ASM) was formed.

Currently, systems analysts are usually located in or near the computer function in an organization. It is most common to find them in a project development department that reports to the Director of Information Systems.

Less commonly, systems analysis and design is decentralized into the functional areas (e.g. marketing or finance) that process information.

The systems analyst needs to be competent as a communicator, a technician, and a business generalist. Communication skills needed are oral, written, and interpersonal. These include persuasive skills, the ability to be effective in leading and attending meetings, and supervisory skills. Technical skills include fact gathering, identification of information needs, feasibility analysis, equipment evaluation, and systems design. As a business generalist, the analyst needs to know the several business functional areas, the company, and the industry. Since systems analysts usually work in teams, the skill deficiencies of one team member may be compensated for by others.

The tasks performed by systems analysts and programmers are similar in that analysts program and programmers analyze. The main difference is in the frequency with which the tasks are performed. The tasks that differentiate the two occupations are shown below.

Tasks Frequently Done by Programmer/Infrequently by Systems Analyst

- Translate detailed flowcharts into programs
- Maintain program
- Debug or test
- Prepare test data
- Prepare operator instructions

Tasks Frequently Done by Systems Analyst/Infrequently by Programmer

- Define requirements
- Prepare functional specifications
- Prepare system specifications
- Prepare systems flowcharts
- Design forms and reports
- Design data items
- Define data organization
- Define systems calculations

Systems analysis is a rapidly growing occupation. A college degree in business with an information systems emphasis is the preferred education. Some firms hire systems analysts, while others promote from programming or user areas. A growing number of organizations are now requiring masters' level education.

Some organizations choose to combine the jobs of systems analyst and programmer and use the title *programmer-analyst*. Others split the systems analyst job into administrative systems analyst and computer systems analyst. These differences, plus the use of the same or a similar job title for engineers and economists, make it difficult to infer competencies from the job title alone.

References

1971. Dickmann, Robert A. *Personnel Implications for Business Data Processing.* New York: Wiley-Interscience.
1975. Willoughby, Theodore C. and Senn, James. *Business Systems.* Cleveland: Association for Systems Management.

THEODORE C. WILLOUGHBY

SYSTEMS PROGRAMMING

For articles on related subjects *see* ASSEMBLER; COMPILER CONSTRUCTION; CROSS ASSEMBLERS AND COMPILERS; DISASSEMBLER; DISTRIBUTED SYSTEMS; LINKER; LOADER; MACHINE and ASSEMBLY LANGUAGE PROGRAMMING; OBJECT PROGRAM; and OPERATING SYSTEMS.

Systems programming is concerned with the utility programs and library software needed to keep computer systems running smoothly. Unlike traditional areas of computer science, such as compilers, operating systems (*q.v.*) or data structures (*q.v.*), the topics included in systems programming are less focused and more diverse. In short, systems programming can be described as the glue that ties together a machine's hardware, its operating system, support utilities such as compilers, editors, and debuggers, and other aspects of proper day-to-day computer operation.

In traditional large computing centers, systems programming comprises three job categories. *Operators* are concerned with the nuts-and-bolts issues of keeping machines running, rebooting machines that crash, performing file system backups, running special jobs, mounting tapes, and so forth. *Systems programmers* focus on such software aspects as installing new releases of application and operating system software or porting software to a new machine, while *systems analysts* focus on planning and managing growth, finding and eliminating performance bottlenecks, and improving overall throughput (*q.v.*) and response time. With the increasing prevalence of smaller systems or networked personal computers and workstations (*q.v.*), the three tasks may fall on a single systems programmer, which we assume to be the case in the following discussion.

A *systems programmer* is a handyperson whose overall responsibility is to keep machines and software running properly so that other computer users can get their work done. Those users, whether using or writing applications software, expect their computers to function properly. Most users operate at a high level, not knowing or caring to know low-level details of the systems they use. They work on specific application development projects, or use a small set of software utilities, such as spreadsheets (*q.v.*) or text formatters on a regular basis.

In practice, keeping a computer system operating smoothly requires constant attention. New releases of software utilities and operating systems must be installed; hardware devices fail and require servicing; machines crash; errant programs consume excessive amounts of system resources, such as disk space, memory, or processing time; etc. It is the systems programmer's task to insure that the software and hardware of a computer system functions properly for its users and that systems resources are allocated fairly among users.

Historically, systems programmers tended to know one system particularly well, reflecting a time when computers were expensive and a site was likely to have only one or two machines. Today, most sites support an entire range of computers, from personal computers and workstations to mainframes (*q.v.*) and supercomputers (*q.v.*).

The principal systems programmer's responsibility is that all machines function properly, and that they can communicate with one another across networks. For example, to reduce costs through sharing, printers and disks may be concentrated on a subset of the available machines, with individual machines accessing the resources across a network (*see* FILE SERVER).

Systems programming begins with a basic understanding of the architecture of the machines in use because some software problems can be resolved only with an understanding of the underlying hardware. For example, in the 1960s, most machines had separate machine instructions for loading single-byte quantities and 4-byte longwords into machine registers. Moreover, a longword quantity could be fetched only if its memory address was on a longword boundary (e.g. a multiple of four); longword fetches from improper addresses produced hardware traps that led to program failures. During the 1970s, improved hardware eliminated that restriction, and programmers no longer needed to concern themselves with such details. More recently, however, the advent of reduced instruction set computers (RISC - *q.v.*) has reintroduced the problem. From a programmer's perspective, software that works correctly on one machine may crash on another. Although compilers can reduce the likelihood of such errors and debuggers can help pinpoint them, the recognition of such errors requires familiarity with the hardware.

Systems programming also requires basic knowledge of operating system principles, as well as specific information about the local operating system in use. The operating system *kernel* (*q.v.*) controls access to all hardware resources and defines the protection mechanism used to prevent processes created by one user from interfering with another. In addition, the operating system provides access to the file system, defining how files can be created, accessed, and destroyed; how the files of one user are protected from unauthorized access by another; or how a subset of users can share files protected from access by general users. Finally the operating system supports and controls access to many services, such as accessing network devices, accessing tape drives, and using special printers and plotters.

With the increased variety of machine configurations, many sites need to tailor the operating system kernel to match their local configuration of peripheral devices. For example, some sites have more disk drives than others, or may use those supplied by different manufacturers. In addition, the actual job mix may influence kernel parameters. If a system runs programs that require a large virtual memory (*q.v.*), additional swap space may need to be added to the system, or existing space may need to be distributed among multiple devices to reduce contention for backing store, thereby reducing latencies (access times - *q.v.*).

In addition to the operating system kernel itself, computer systems include a set of software libraries and utility programs. Some utilities help support proper system administration, such as programs that perform file system backups, read and write tapes, repair corrupted file systems, display system activity, and create or delete user accounts. Other utilities such as editors, compilers, mail processing software, and text formatters are oriented towards end users. In either case, systems programmers uses them during the course of their work, and must be able to locate, verify, and possibly fix problems related to their use.

When a user has problems with a particular utility or application, the systems programmer is often consulted for advice. The first step in locating the cause of the problem is to identify the system component causing the problem. The problem could be with the utility itself, with one of the system-supplied library routines, with the operating system, or with obtaining necessary resources (e.g. memory) to run the program. The systems programmer must be sufficiently familiar with each of these areas in order to isolate the problem. If the problem is with the program itself, a debugger would be used to obtain more information. In the early days of computing, debugging (*q.v.*) programs was an especially difficult task. Often, a dump of the program's memory contents was all that was available. More recently, interactive debuggers allow a user to set *breakpoints* at arbitrary statements in their programs. When the program reaches a breakpoint, the debugger suspends the program and allows the user to display the contents of active variables by their symbolic names. Likewise, when a program error terminates the program, the debugger allows interactive inspection of its data structures, from which the high-level cause of the problem can be ascertained.

Compilers translate high-level programs into assembly language. *Assemblers*, in turn, translate assembly language programs into object files, and a *linker* combines object files into a single executable load module. Because of their dependence on the underlying hardware and operating system, the creation and maintenance of assemblers, linkers, and loaders belong to the realm of systems programming.

The availability of low-cost workstations and personal computers has led to the development of *distributed computing*. One of the most common applications of distributed computing—electronic mail (*q.v.*)—allows a user on one machine to send mail ("E-mail") to someone having an account on another. One challenging aspect of systems programming is the configuration and maintenance of networked systems. Adding a new machine to the network requires configuring it into the local system, including the assignment of a low-level network address and a user-friendly name by which E-mail users can refer to it. In addition, support software, such as name servers and file servers (*q.v.*), may need to have the new machine registered with them so that existing machines can determine how to communicate with the new one.

A basic understanding of computer networks (*q.v.*) helps in the maintenance of systems in a distributed environment. The machines of various vendors may be unable to interoperate properly because one or the other (or both) fails to adhere to the appropriate protocol specification precisely. If each vendor blames the other, the systems programmer may be forced to locate the offender, perhaps with the aid of a network monitor and a description of the protocol specification.

In addition to networked systems, the availability and proliferation of low-cost computers has produced several interesting challenges for systems programmers. First, because users prefer consistent environments, it is often necessary to install the same version of a software program on multiple machines. With the plethora of machine architectures and operating systems, porting an application from one system to another may pose difficulties (*see* PORTABILITY). Applications may use a subtle operating system feature, or a compiler for one architecture may accept a slightly different language dialect than the compiler for another. Moreover, existing compilers are often modified to generate code for a new architecture, and some of its more advanced features, such as a code optimizer, may not generate correct code in all cases. The systems programmer must be prepared to recognize these potential pitfalls and take corresponding action.

Although most users make use of compilers, editors, and other tools, a systems programmer generally needs to have a more detailed understanding of such tools. For example, when compiling system software or new applications, it may be helpful to invoke the compiler with options that produce highly optimized code. Selecting the proper options involves knowing how the program will be used and on what machines. Some machines, for example, may not support certain floating-point operations in hardware, and the compiler may need to be directed to disable generation of such hardware instructions and, instead, generate software sequences that do the same thing (though more slowly, of course). Alternatively, some optimizations can be safely performed only if the application follows certain coding conventions, such as not being invoked from interrupt handlers. The more information systems programmers have about a system and its tools, the better they are able to improve system performance.

References

1980. Gear, C. William. *Computer Organization and Programming.* New York: McGraw Hill.

1985. Beck, Leland L. *System Software: An Introduction to Systems Programming.* Reading, MA: Addison Wesley.

THOMAS NARTEN

SYSTOLIC ARRAY

For articles on related subjects *see* PARALLEL PROCESSING; SUPERCOMPUTERS; and TRANSPUTER.

Systolic arrays are a family of parallel computer architectures capable of using a very large number of processors simultaneously for important computations in applications such as scientific computing and signal processing. This article gives a general description of systolic arrays, illustrates the idea by two simple examples, lists some applicable computations, and describes fine-grain interprocessor communication in systolic arrays.

General Description Systolic arrays are suited for processing repetitive computations. Although this kind of computation usually requires a great deal of computing power, such computations are highly regular and paral-

lelizable. The systolic array architecture exploits this regularity and parallelism to deliver the required computation speed.

In a systolic array, all processing elements, called *systolic cells*, perform computations simultaneously, while data, such as initial inputs, partial results, and final outputs, are being passed from cell to cell. When partial results are moved between cells, they are computed over these cells in a pipeline fashion. In this case, the computation of each single output is partitioned over these cells. This contrasts to other parallel architectures based on data partitioning, for which the computation of each output is computed solely on one single processor.

When a systolic array is in operation, computing at cells, communication between cells and input from and output to the outside world all take place at the same time to achieve high performance. This is analogous to the circulatory system; data are "pulsed" through all cells where they are processed.

Being able to perform many operations simultaneously is just one of the many advantages of systolic arrays. Other advantages include modular expendability of the cell array, simple and regular data and control flows, simple and uniform cells, efficient fault-tolerant schemes, and nearest-neighbor data communications. These properties are highly desirable for VLSI (Very Large Scale Integration) implementations. Indeed, the advances in VLSI technology have been a major motivation for much interest in systolic arrays.

Two Systolic Array Examples For illustration, consider first a simple systolic array for implementing a finite impulse response (FIR) filter. Given inputs x_i and weights w_i, the filtering problem is to compute outputs y_i, defined by $y_i = w_1 x_i + w_2 x_{i-1} + \ldots + w_k x_{i+k-1}$. Fig. 1 depicts a one-dimensional systolic array for a FIR filter with $k = 3$ weights, each of which is preloaded into a cell.

During computation, both partial results for y_i and inputs x_i flow from left to right, where the former move twice as fast as the latter. More precisely, each x_i stays inside every cell it passes for one additional cycle, and thus each x_i takes twice as long to march through the array as does a y_i. One can check that each y_i, initialized to zero before entering the leftmost cell, is able to accumulate all its terms while marching to the right. For example, y_1 accumulates $w_3 x_3$, $w_2 x_2$, and $w_1 x_1$ in three consecutive cycles at the leftmost, middle, and rightmost cells, respectively.

Note that, although each output y is computed using several inputs x and several weights w, and each input and each weight is used in computing several outputs, the systolic array described here uses no "global" communication. More precisely, data communication at each cycle is always between adjacent cells.

Fig. 2 illustrates another systolic array. This is a two-dimensional array capable of performing matrix multiply, $C = A \times B$ for 3×3 matrices $A = (a_{ij})$, $B = (b_{ij})$ and $C = (c_{ij})$. As indicated, entries in A and B are shifted into the array from left and top, respectively. It is easy to see that the c_{ij} at each cell can accumulate all its terms $a_{i1} b_{1j}$, $a_{i2} b_{2j}$, and $a_{i3} b_{3j}$ while A and B march across the systolic array.

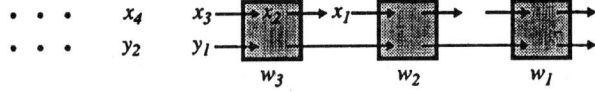

FIG. 1. One-dimensional systolic array for implementing FIR filter.

Scope of Applicable Computations

A large number of systolic array designs have been developed and used to perform a broad range of computations. In fact, recent advances in theory and software have allowed some of these systolic arrays to be derived automatically. The following is a representative list of computations for which systolic designs exist:

- *Signal and image processing*—Digital filters, convolution and correlation, discrete Fourier transform, Fast Fourier Transform (FFT - *q.v.*), encoding/decoding for compression and error-correction, etc.
- *Matrix arithmetic*—Matrix multiplication, solution of linear systems of equations, solution of Toeplitz linear systems, QR-decomposition, least squares computation, singular value decomposition, eigenvalue computation, etc.
- *Polynomial and multi-precision integer arithmetic*—Multiplication, division, greatest common divisor, etc.
- *Nonnumeric applications*—Searching (*q.v.*), sorting (*q.v.*), pattern matching, regular language recognition, dynamic programming, relational database operations such as join and intersection, data structures such as priority queues, and graph and geometric algorithms such as minimum spanning trees, convex hull calculations, etc.

Fine-Grain Communication in Systolic Arrays

In a systolic array, each cell processes a data word immediately after it arrives, and sends out a data word immediately after it is processed. Therefore, the unit of communication is a single word. This contrasts to the classic message-passing communication, where the unit of communication is an entire message, which typically consists of a large number of words. Thus, supporting this fine-grain communication, also called *systolic communication*, is a unique architectural feature of a systolic array computer.

To support systolic communication, each cell in a systolic array allows its CPU to access the input and ouput ports directly, in addition to the local memory. This differs from message-passing machines, for which each processor can only access its local memory. Fig. 2 illustrates the difference.

Summary

Systolic arrays are an effective parallel architecture for a wide range of computations that are repetitive in nature. By using fine-grain communication, the architecture can use a large number of processors simultaneously. Moreover, systolic arrays have simple and regular design, so their implementations are relatively easy. As software and hardware technologies continue to advance to allow efficient systolic designs or programs to be derived automatically and routinely, and to allow very large systolic arrays to be implemented inexpensively, widespread use of systolic arrays can be expected in solving many computationally demanding problems.

References

1990. Lang, T. and Moreno, J. H. "Matrix Computations on Systolic-type Meshes," *Computer*, **23**, *4* (April) 32–51. Begins with an excellent tutorial on systolic parallel processing.

1990. Dostie, A. J., Seidman, S. B., and Clessas, A. C. "Systolic Computing on Transputer Networks," Proceedings of North American Transputer Users Group, Durham, SC, October 1989, Amsterdam, Netherlands: IOS 123–137.

H. T. Kung

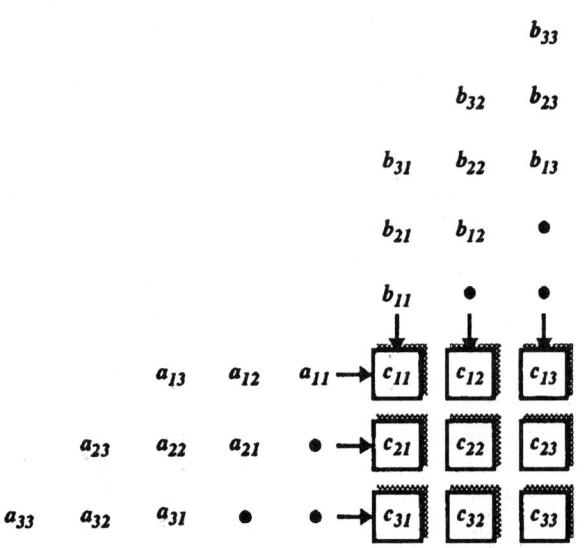

FIG. 2. Two-dimensional systolic array for matrix multiplication.

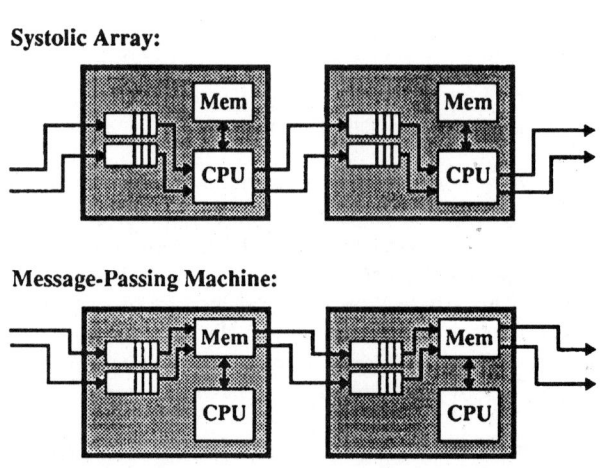

FIG. 3 Comparing systolic array with message-passing machine.

TABLE LOOK-UP. *See* SEARCHING.

TASK. *See* JOB; and MULTITASKING.

TELECOMMUNICATIONS. *See* DATA COM-
MUNICATIONS; and TELEPROCESSING SYSTEMS.

TELEPROCESSING SYSTEMS

For articles on related subjects *see* COMMUNICATION CON-
TROL UNIT; INTERACTIVE SYSTEM; REAL-TIME BUSINESS APPLICA-
TIONS, TIME SHARING; and TRANSACTION PROCESSING.

Teleprocessing systems refer to a form of on-line processing in which users at remote terminals are able to
access a central computer to store, retrieve, or process
data. Such systems can provide a variety of services to
many simultaneous users at many different locations
without the necessity of having a computer and/or unique
data at each such location. The basic types include:

1. *Inquiry and response systems*—In these systems,
   the computer is used as a mass storage facility
   that can be accessed by a large number of users
   over a communication network. The best examples of such systems include airline and hotel
   reservation, document retrieval, and inventory
   control systems. The user enters a query at a
   terminal, causing the computer to search its
   files and send the retrieved information to the
   user.
2. *Data collection systems*—In such systems, sometimes also called *data acquisition* or *data entry
   systems*, information from user terminals or

other input devices (e.g. cash registers in a
store) is entered and stored. This data may be
processed immediately or at some subsequent
time, or it may be used to update records that
will be used for inquiry and response or some
other purposes. Examples of such systems include weather recording, recording of transactions on the stock exchange or at banks, and
keeping track of inventory at stores.
3. *Data distribution systems*—These systems are the
   converse of pure data collection systems in that
   the main flow of data is in the opposite direction
   (i.e. from computer to the terminal). Distribution
   of stock quotations or airline arrival and departure times are examples of such systems. The
   updates may be continuous, batched, or provided on demand, depending on the application.
4. *Conversational systems*—These systems are designed to permit many convenient dialogues
   between a central computer and local or remote
   users. In this mode, each statement or command
   entered by a user is executed immediately, and
   a response or a prompt is sent back before the
   next command can be entered. Such systems
   are also called *time-sharing* or interactive systems, and usually allow access to a wide range
   of services, including a variety of compilers,
   program development tools, and application
   packages.
5. *Remote batch-processing systems*—Such systems
   are often called *remote job entry* (RJE) systems
   and permit submission of entire jobs from remote terminals. When received, these jobs are
   placed in the batch queue along with other jobs
   in the system. After execution, the output is usually sent back to the originating terminal. This
   may take several seconds or hours, depending
   on the size of the job. Contrast this with conversational systems where a virtually instantaneous
   response is essential.

6. *Message switching systems*—These systems may be considered as special cases of data collection and data distribution systems. Information is collected from certain terminals, stored, and then forwarded to other terminals. Consequently, they are often called *store and forward systems*, and are used extensively for file transfer and electronic mail (*q.v.*) over a large network with distributed computers.

7. *Other systems*—The systems described above serve only to summarize the general characteristics of teleprocessing systems. In practice, many variations and combination are possible, making the distinction between them difficult. *Monitoring systems*, for example, are similar to data collection systems, but the input is usually from some source other than a terminal (e.g. a transducer monitoring the temperature of a chemical process). *Process control systems* may be thought of as closed-loop monitoring systems that regulate a process (e.g. keep the temperature of a chemical process constant). Other examples include electronic funds transfer (*q.v.*) and transaction-based applications.

Characteristics of Teleprocessing Systems

Since teleprocessing systems may be required to service hundreds or even thousands of local and remote users, the hardware and software must be designed for high reliability and availability, high transaction volumes, efficient and flexible file management capabilities, and an efficient communication access method to communicate with large numbers of local and remote terminals.

JOHN S. SOBOLEWSKI

TERMINALS

For articles on related subjects *see* COMMUNICATIONS AND COMPUTERS; DATA COMMUNICATIONS; DISTRIBUTED SYSTEMS; DSU/CSU; INTERACTIVE INPUT DEVICES; INTERACTIVE SYSTEM; MODEM; NETWORKS, COMPUTER; PERSONAL COMPUTING; TELEPROCESSING SYSTEMS; and WORKSTATION.

Introduction A *terminal* is a device through which information from a remote computer is made available to an end user and that possibly accepts input from that user. This article addresses two categories of terminals: general-purpose and job-oriented. The personal computer is the embodiment of a general purpose terminal. Job-oriented terminals comprise all others which are designed to do specific tasks.

Implicit in the notion of a terminal is that it is in communication with another device, usually one of greater capability. Since communication is an essential part of this notion, a brief discussion of this topic will be presented.

Personal Computer as a Terminal General-purpose terminals commonly use as hardware a personal computer loaded with appropriate communications software. Such a system is shown in Fig. 1. The distinguishing features that make it a terminal are a communications adapter and terminal software.

A personal computer is a stored program system consisting of at least a microprocessor, memory, and input/output devices. A block diagram of a typical system is shown in Fig. 2. The microprocessor executes the programmed instructions that are stored in memory, as are the data resulting from the operation. Human interaction occurs most frequently through use of a keyboard for input and a CRT display for output, although a wide range of other devices can be attached, such as printers, scanners, voice recognition equipment, cash drawers, and beepers. In terminal applications, the stored programs are usually sent from a host computer and loaded into the personal computer memory, although local disk storage can be used for this purpose, too.

Personal computers are readily available off the shelf for most general-purpose terminal applications. Also readily available are items such as communication adapters, modems, local area network adapters, terminal programs, and network programs.

FIG. 1. A typical personal computer is comprised of a system unit, disk storage, display, keyboard and, optionally, a mouse. (Courtesy of IBM Corp.)

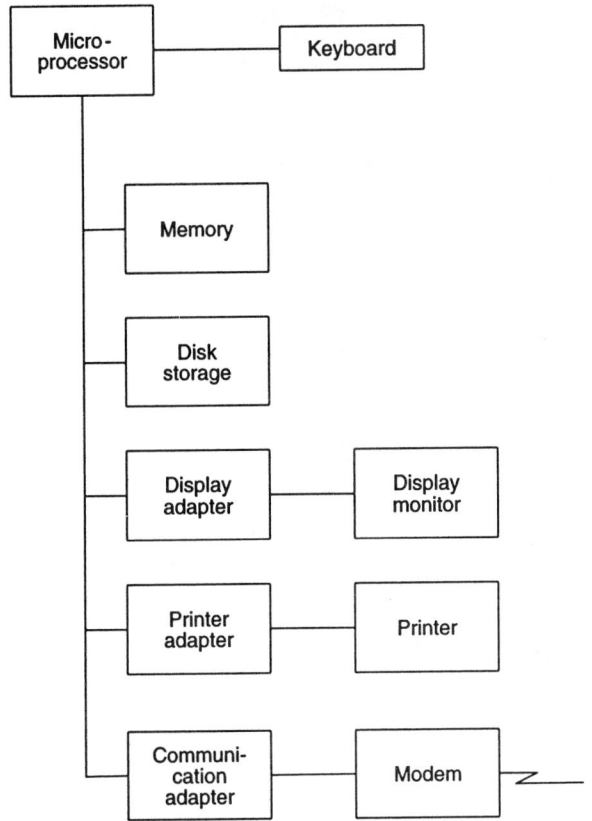

FIG. 2. Block diagram of a typical personal computer system. The communication adapter is essential for a PC to become a terminal. If the communication line is analog, then a modem is also required.

Communication Facilities
This section briefly describes the items associated with terminal operation.

Hardware The communications adapter is a group of electronic components, sometimes packaged separately on a printed circuit board, that provides the interface between the personal computer's microprocessor bus and the transmission standard being used. This is necessary because the microprocessor bus operates at a very high speed (of the order of 30 megahertz) and at low signal levels, while the communication standards are usually at slower speeds and higher signal levels. One example of such a device is an RS-232 adapter, which implements a common standard that defines connector pin assignments and signal descriptions.

A *modem (q.v.)* is a device that takes the output from a communications adapter and provides a connection directly to the transmission facility. This device changes information from digital to analog form and vice versa. The modem interfaces to the telephone transmission system, which, at most end-user locations, has a 4-kilohertz analog bandwidth. Common bit rates (sometimes called baud) are 1,200, 2,400, 4,800, and 9,600 bits per second. At the high end, sophisticated circuits are required to pass that much information through a limited bandwidth. In addition to sending and receiving digital data, the mo-

dems also perform the other functions required of a telephone, such as sending dial pulses or tones, detecting busy signals, answering a ring signal, and hanging up.

Local area network *(q.v.)* adapters are the other most common communications device used with personal computers. Their function is to interface data from the microprocessor bus to a wire (or optical fiber, or electromagnetic radiation), which connects to a host computer. The local area transmission facility is usually digital and hence does not require a modem. It generally runs at speeds much faster than those associated with analog telephone lines.

Software Terminal software consists of a program that can interpret the data in a standard form. For example, when receiving a data stream, the program knows which bytes are for the addressee, which bytes are the sender's address, which bytes convey data, which bytes are error correction codes, and which bytes tell where to direct the data. Fig. 3 shows a screen from the terminal software associated with Microsoft Windows applications. As can be noted by the messages on the bottom line, a file is being sent. At the same time, the operator is using the dialog box to convey some of the characteristics of the terminal being used so that a return message can be received. There are terminal emulation programs for standard conventions that the host system supports, including such popular terminal emulators as the TTY, IBM 3270, or the DEC VT-100. Use of the Hayes modem conventions also facilitates systems communications.

If many terminals are communicating to one or several hosts or peers, a networking program will also be needed to establish such things as which terminal is allowed to send at a particular instant, who has priority, what facilities should be used, and what are the security levels. The various functional levels are prescribed under the ISO/OSI Standard (International Standards Organization/Open System Interconnection) for network control. [*See* OPEN SYSTEMS INTERCONNECTION (OSI).]

Transmission Systems The telephone system is the most prevalent transmission system and uses either the dial-up network or leased lines. Dial-up is accessed by the terminal emitting the tones or pulses just like a person would do in making a voice call. Leased lines are usually permanently attached and ready for use. Commonly leased lines are the standard analog voice phone lines, although telephone companies also make available, particularly in commercial districts, a digital transmission service. A worldwide standard system called ISDN (Integrated Services Digital Network - *q.v.*) is currently available in many cities at a standard transmission rate of 64 kilobits per second and higher. This is a good bandwidth for PCM (pulse code modulation) voice transmission and also allows higher data rates than are usually achievable on conventional telephone lines. These higher rates often provide more throughput than required for an individual terminal; thus they can be shared among many terminals in what is called a *multipoint system*.

Within a building or campus complex, a popular transmission system is the Local Area Network (LAN),

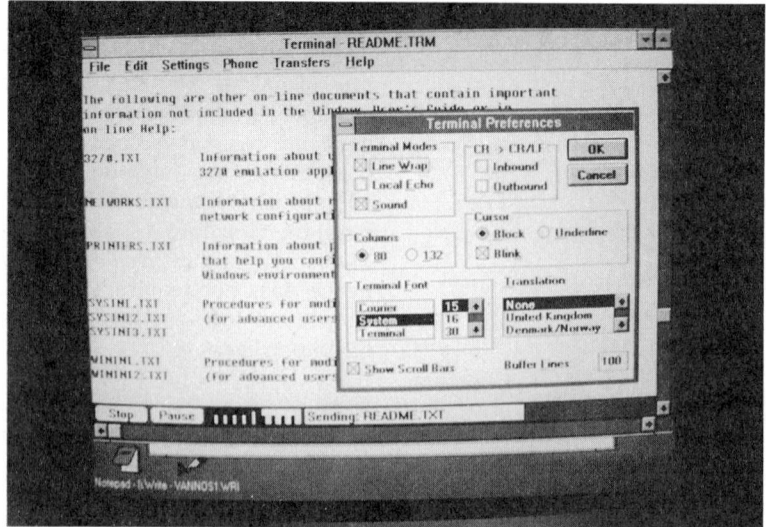

FIG. 3. A Microsoft Windows display screen showing some of the choices to be made when setting up a terminal for communication.

which is usually a private system of wires or optical fiber cables. These typically run at higher rates and are time-shared among many terminals. Certain LAN standards must also be adhered to, among which are ethernet, the IBM Token Ring, and the FDDI (Fiber Distributed Data Interface). The FDDI, using fiber optics (*q.v.*), is specified to run as high as 100 megabits per second. The LANs are digital and thus do not require a modem, but they do require an adapter that can be quite complex at the high rates used on the network (*see* DSU/CSU).

Typical General-Purpose Applications

Just a few of the general purpose applications will be discussed, to provide a feeling for the range of jobs that can be done with a personal computer terminal.

Messaging When using electronic mail (*q.v.*), the sender keys in an address plus the body of the message. Most often, these messages go to a central computer from which a connection is then made to the recipient and the message is relayed. This is called a *store and forward system* and has the advantage that the sender can forward a message without having to wait for a connection to be made to the recipient. Within a building, such systems are implemented via a LAN to a host computer, but if the addressee is off premises, then the message is sent via common carrier to another host at the recipient's site. For small business, for broad coverage connectability, or for home use, the messaging capability is available through electronic mail networks, such as Western Union's EasyLink, AT&T Mail, or the Internet available at most universities and research laboratories.

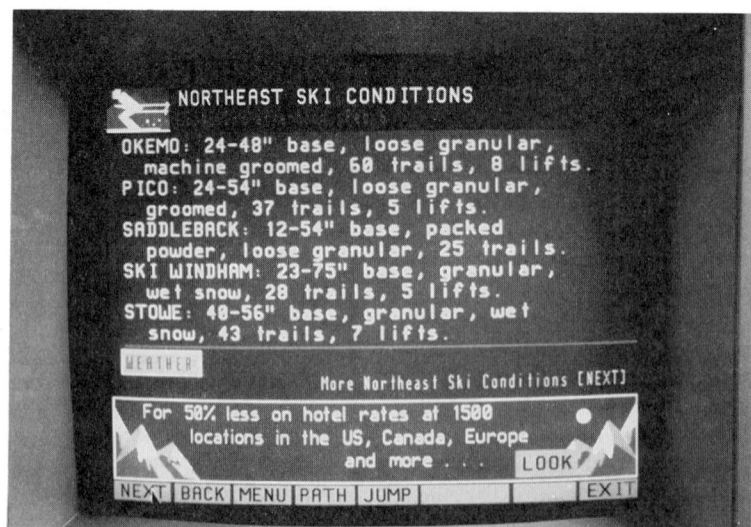

FIG. 4. A Prodigy information service screen showing ski conditions. Other typical screens would display sales advertisements, stock quotes, news, reference articles, and messages.

Information Services Electronic mail service is also offered by information service companies, such as CompuServe or Prodigy. These service corporations provide a range of general-purpose information to terminals that are almost always personal computers. Typical information includes weather, stock quotes, news, encyclopedia references, research reports, files, computer programs, and advertisements. Fig. 4 illustrates a screen from the Prodigy service showing current skiing conditions from some mountains in the Northeast.

Specialized Databases Information services are primarily general-purpose database systems that appeal to a large segment of the population. But a very large segment of terminal usage pertains to access to specialized databases. While special programs and databases are used, the applications nevertheless use personal computers as the terminal equipment. Typical, though far from inclusive of these applications, are stock brokers' terminals, real estate terminals, CAD/CAM design and manufacturing terminals, and terminals used in business accounting and publishing.

For example, the broker's terminal shown in Fig. 5 would access a host computer for the latest stock and bond quotes, provide search functions, retrieve research reports, and make transactions. The Merrill Lynch terminal, for example, uses an IBM PS/2 terminal connected via a LAN to a local data server which contains a comprehensive set of data that is transmitted to it via satellite each night. Current information is transmitted over land lines on a real time basis. The terminal is a standard personal computer; what makes it a terminal is its connection to a network and the installation of terminal and network software.

Real estate terminals, as shown in Fig. 6, are also PC-based and use both a local as well as a remote database. What is unique in this application, beyond the usual searching and recalling of data, is the potential to store and display a photograph of the house or building

FIG. 5. A broker's terminal, which is a PC that has been customized to perform the functions required at a stock brokers desk. (Courtesy of IBM Corp.)

FIG. 6. A PC in a real estate office that has been customized to perform the functions required at a real estate agent's desk. (Courtesy of IBM Corp.)

that is for sale. Image information requires that a large storage capability be a part of the PC system.

CAD/CAM applications illustrate the combination of a significant amount of local processing with occasional access to information at a host database. In these applications, design drawings and data are archived at the host and accessed or updated by the terminal. Most of the interaction is handled locally, but when a request to the host is made, it generally involves a large file transfer. In these kinds of applications, it is important to have high-speed lines that can dump a large file in a reasonable time.

Another variety of terminal configuration is typified by a publishing terminal, where news reports are received over communication lines and edited locally into a stylized publication that in turn may be sent over other communication lines to an off-site printer. Here the input is from a different location than is used for the output of the terminal. In a case like this, two or more communication ports may be used on a given terminal.

Job-Oriented Terminals With job-oriented terminals, the applicable job is so unique that something more or less than a personal computer is required. Typical applications include airline reservation terminals, automatic teller machines, credit card verification terminals, grocery store check-out terminals, fast food terminals, or terminals for hospital patient monitoring. In this class, the hardware and software are customized to fit the application.

Airline terminals provide a simple example where the customization is a stripped-down PC. Here the agent interacts with the host database to find routings, seat availability, and lowest cost fares, as well as to make reservations. The database is maintained at a central location and handles thousands of terminals on a time-shared basis with minimal delay times. In this application, fast response times, frequent interactions, and short message lengths are characteristic.

The hardware of an automatic teller machine (ATM) contains a magnetic stripe reader, a numeric keyboard, a display, an electromechanical device for cash issuing and deposits, and a receipt printer. All of these must be weather-resistant, vandalproof, and operable from a car window. Fig. 7 illustrates a typical walk-up terminal mounted on the outside wall of a bank building. These terminals connect to a local controller that continually monitors and activates the functions of the terminal. It is connected to another local business computer for account information, authorization for disbursement, and debiting the user's account. This local account computer is in turn connected to a larger network for credit and transaction processing when the user's account resides in some other bank or financial institution. These networks are so broad that users can access their accounts from most places in the U.S. as well as from many foreign countries. The terminal itself is a combination of technologies to do a specific job. The display usually is a cathode ray tube that has increased brightness capability so as to be visible in bright sunlight and glare treatment to reduce reflections, and displays large characters. The cash-issuing device consists of a stack of bills and a picker to disburse a precise number of them into a receiving tray. These devices can be adjusted to handle new bills or used ones. The plastic card readers use standard magnetic stripe technology. In some installations, it is merely a slot reader through which the user slides his or her card, but in others such as shown in the photograph, the card slot must be designed to take the card within the machine to read it. This is done so that if credit is overdrawn or there is suspicion of a stolen card, it will not be returned to the customer. A greatly scaled-down version of the ATM is the credit verification terminal where just the card reader is implemented and credit authorization is received from the user's credit card institution.

Another pervasive example is the supermarket checkout terminal where the most unusual device is the laser bar code scanner as shown in Fig. 8. The terminal

FIG. 8. A supermarket scanner terminal showing a view of the pattern that the laser beam traverses to insure that it scans the bar code no matter where it occurs on the product. (Courtesy of IBM Corp.)

reads the universal product code (q.v.), opens the cash drawer, allows for key entry of some items, and prints the receipt. These checkout terminals are usually connected via a LAN to an in-store computer which may in turn communicate in batch mode with a corporate host for inventory, reordering, and business performance processing. The in-store computer is updated on a daily basis with the latest prices. The bar code scanner consists of a laser beam that scans across the bar code, and from this sequence of variable width bars the in-store computer can translate to a product item and its price. The laser beam sweeps across the bar code at a variety of angles and is able to read the code even when the code is not directly over the aperture. This technology is easily extrapolated to other terminal applications, such as retail sales, manufacturing operations, or inventory data collection.

In applications such as fast food, the job-oriented terminal is designed for simplicity and ease of use by untrained operators. In patient monitoring, the terminal is equipped with sensors. The list of these special applications is too long to enumerate further.

Future Trends The upward trend in terminal use will continue, not only because unique job-oriented applications are continually being developed but also because personal computers are becoming ubiquitous. The driving force is economics; computer applications can either reduce the cost of doing a function, or the level of service can be increased, or both.

The most dramatic increase in terminal use is likely to come in the home. One trend will be widespread use in home education; another will be increased use in home occupations. This latter category has seen a large growth due to many factors, among which are the cost of business space, the desire to combine a career with child raising, and the low cost of terminal, communication, and host services. These terminals will be primarily personal

FIG. 7. An automatic bank teller terminal, which has a cash issuing slot, a deposit receiving slot, a credit card slot, a keyboard, and a display. (Courtesy of First National Bank, Rhinebeck, NY.)

computers, where the function is done partly on the PC and partly on the host. Computer programmers effectively use this arrangement now by working at their home terminal while accessing their corporate database as needed.

Fig. 9 shows PC-based education terminals, but in this case additional technology is required for full effectiveness: the integration of photographic quality images, both stills and moving images, with textual data. This will evolve through the merging of television technology with computer technology. This technology is in active development with several companies demonstrating laboratory experiments. The TV technology includes the use of video cassette recorders and laser videodisc (*q.v.*) players. Computers can access a particular frame from a laser disk containing thousands of images or can select a particular segment of video to be shown at the appropriate time in an educational sequence. The video database could be co-located with the personal computer, but as broadband wiring becomes pervasive, a higher level of service can be provided if the video as well as the text is delivered over a communication line. The TV medium provides the high bandwidth needed for this application, and it will be available due to the widespread existence of TV cable service. Existing cable has unused bandwidth that could be used for such customized service.

This kind of service has appeared under the name of Teletext in some European countries, where one-way transmission of single TV frames are broadcast during the vertical retrace time. Users select the frame they want to capture and hold for viewing, but no interaction is possible. Interactive TV systems will first appear in large corporations or on educational campuses, where the LAN, host computers, and TV equipment are all under one control. Later, as the worth of this approach is proven, cable companies are likely to make it available to the home.

TV technology is now moving to greater use of digital circuitry in conventional sets to implement more stable

FIG. 9. Education terminals in a library. Students can be viewing applications of their choice accessed from a central database. (Courtesy of IBM Corp.)

circuits and to provide more function. High Definition TV (HDTV) will also depend on digital signal processing, data compression (*q.v.*), and bit-mapped buffers to obtain higher resolution with minimum use of the available broadcast spectrum. Thus, the integration of computer function and video function is about to happen and the terminal will be the TV set.

References

1988. Wright, M. "Networking Software," *Electronic Design News*, **33**, *5*, 3 March.

1989. Inagaki, T. "Hologram Lenses Lead to Compact Scanners," *IEEE Spectrum*, **26**, *3*, March, 39–43.

1991. Rosenblatt, A. and Raychaudhuri, D. "Data Communications," *IEEE Spectrum*, **28**, *1*, January, 48–51.

DAVID R. BALDAUF

TESTING. *See* DEBUGGING; and SOFTWARE TESTING.

T_EX

For articles on related subjects *see* DESKTOP PUBLISHING; LITERATE PROGRAMMING; and METAFONT.

T_EX is a computer-controlled typesetting system designed by Donald E. Knuth. The name, which should be pronounced "tech" to rhyme with "blech," is the Greek root for English words such as technique and technology.

In 1977, Knuth saw phototypeset proofs for a new edition of a book in his series, *The Art of Computer Programming*. The quality of the typesetting had deteriorated seriously from the previous editions, which had been set with lead type. Knuth had just learned about "digital" devices for typesetting, in which each image on each page is made up of tiny black dots arranged on a grid. He realized that such equipment gave him the power to make his books look good again; all he had to do was write a computer program to put tiny bits of ink in the right places. So he began the T_EX project, which turned out to be a 9-year-long program of research in digital typography.

From the beginning, Knuth wanted to produce a system capable of high-quality typesetting, one that would incorporate the finest traditions of the printing industry. This meant that T_EX users would specify a bit more than was customary with ordinary typewriters. For example, the numeral "1" needs to be distinguished from the letter "l" (lowercase L); opening quotation marks are distinguished from closing quotes. Several kinds of hyphens and dashes can be used, just as in fine printing. T_EX is especially adept at mathematical typesetting (see Fig. 1), which involves embedded formulas, subscripts, superscripts, a multitude of symbols, and arrangements of tabular material in rows and columns.

Portability and stability were also important goals. The system is designed to be device-independent; T_EX now runs on hundreds of different computers, from PCs

Input to T$_E$X:

```
The names of variables in math formulas
such as $e^{x_1^2+\cdots+x_n^2}$ are
usually set in {\it italic type}.
```

Output from T$_E$X:

The names of variables in math
formulas such as $e^{x_1^2+\cdots+x_n^2}$ are
usually set in *italic type.*

FIG. 1. T$_E$X automatically chooses sizes and styles of type for mathematical material that the user has enclosed in dollar signs.

to mainframes, producing identical results on each. The finished output can be directed to many devices, including video screens, impact printers, laser printers, and phototypesetters. A T$_E$X file prepared today should be able to produce the same output 20 or more years from now, on the machines of the future.

Knuth felt strongly that T$_E$X should be in the public domain, available to everyone without payment of royalties, and that the algorithms of T$_E$X should be published as a contribution to computer science. These algorithms may be freely incorporated into other systems. But Knuth requires that the name T$_E$X be restricted to systems that are fully compatible with the program he wrote, so that anybody using a system of that name can be sure that the system conforms to a definite standard.

The metaphor of boxes and glue (see Fig. 2) is used to illustrate the way T$_E$X assembles elements on a page. Each letter or character can be thought of as a small box containing an image. These boxes are glued together; a horizontal string of characters forms a bigger box to make up a word. Words, in turn, make sentences, which combine to make paragraphs, etc. Boxes can be glued together vertically as well as horizontally.

The glue used to assemble groups of boxes has the ability to stretch or shrink. Boxes can be set right next to each other with no glue at all, or they can be spaced far apart with thick glue. The capacity to control the stretching and shrinking of the glue is an important feature of T$_E$X that allows an almost infinite variety of formats to be defined in terms of a small number of basic operations.

Another unique feature of T$_E$X is the way it decides to break the text of a paragraph into individual lines (see Fig. 3). T$_E$X looks at the paragraph as a whole, instead of examining one line at a time. Penalties of varying severity are imposed upon bad line breaks, which are charged with a number of demerits. T$_E$X finds the combination of line breaks that adds up to the fewest demerits overall. Therefore, what comes later in a paragraph can influence the

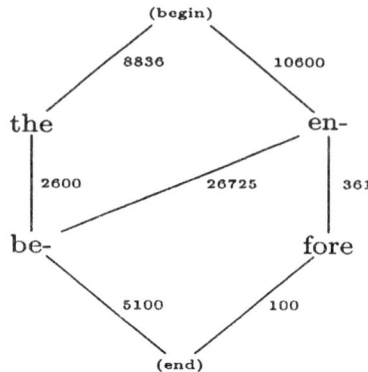

FIG. 2. T$_E$X typesets pages by constructing boxes inside of boxes inside of boxes, with flexible glue to hold them in place.

Better spacing is often possible when the entire text of a paragraph is considered before it is broken into lines.

Better spacing is often possible when the entire text of a paragraph is considered before it is broken into lines.

Better spacing is often possible when the entire text of a paragraph is considered before it is broken into lines.

FIG. 3. Three ways to break a sample paragraph into lines. If the word "entire" must be hyphenated on the first line, the word "before" must be hyphenated on the second line. T$_E$X assigns demerits of 8836 + 2600 + 5100, 10600 + 26725 + 5100, and 10600 + 361 + 100 to the respective paragraphs shown here, and chooses the third alternative because it has minimum total demerits. Optimum line breaks can be discovered by finding the least-cost path in a "demerit network," like the one shown here.

final appearance of lines in the earlier part. This aspect of T$_E$X was developed with the help of Michael Plass.

The procedure by which T$_E$X hyphenates words, developed by Frank Liang, is constructed in such a way that it can easily be adapted to different languages and to different conventions within a single language. Patterns that appear in a word are used to decide where hyphens are permissible and where they should be forbidden. For example, an English word containing the sequence "onc" normally permits a hyphen after the "n"; consider "bronchitis," "discon-certing," "incon-clusive," "non-chalant," "recon-ciled," "violon-cello."

When users of T$_E$X find that they are repeating certain groups of instructions over and over, they can create macros to remember those sequences. Collections of macros help to define the appearance of specific kinds of documents (memos, business letters, newsletters, music programs, price lists, poetry verses, computer listings, chess games, etc.). This is particularly useful when many people are typing the same sort of document and each example should have the same appearance.

Users can describe the format of their documents in terms of brief generic codes. Such code names can be invented for personal use or borrowed from other systems. Once macros have been written that convert each brief code into a series of T$_E$X instructions, the user needs only to type the codes; low-level typesetting commands rarely need to be specified directly.

Several children of T$_E$X have been born, each using its own set of macros. For example, L^{A}T$_E$X (by Leslie Lamport) encourages its users to create documents with nested structure: Chapters, sections, subsections, illustrations, equations, etc. It has automatic facilities for assigning numbers to itemized lists, and for generating indexes and tables of contents. A$_M$S-T$_E$X (by Michael Spivak) is designed for technical material that contains advanced mathematics; the American Mathematical Society uses this system to typeset all of its journals and books. P$_I$CT$_E$X (by Michael J. Wichura) specializes in the creation of pictorial images.

At the simplest level, a T$_E$X user who relies on macros created by other people needs only to observe a few typing conventions related to quotes, hyphens, and dashes, and to insert brief codes when a change in typeface or spacing is desired. At the other end of the spectrum, an expert T$_E$Xnician may fill computer files with T$_E$X instructions to create extremely complex formulas and charts.

As Knuth was writing T$_E$X, he also developed the WEB system of structured documentation. WEB encourages *literate programming*, in which a computer program is thought of as an essay to be read by human beings rather than a set of instructions to be read by computers. The program is broken into small parts and presented as a combination of informal text and formal computer language. These small parts are knit together in a "web" that can be used in two distinct ways; it can either be processed by a compiler and executed by a computer, or it can be processed by T$_E$X and printed as a document with automatic cross-indexing. The WEB system also includes macros and substitution facilities that greatly simplify the transportation of programs from one type of computer to another.

The T$_E$X Users Group, formed in 1979 and numbering about 3,000 members in 1989, publishes a quarterly journal called *TUGboat*. TUG holds annual meetings, provides publications and consulting services, organizes short courses, and sponsors an electronic newsletter available via TeXhax@cs.washington.edu.

References

1979. Knuth, Donald E. "Mathematical Typography," *Bulletin of the American Mathematical Society* (new series) **1**: 337–372.

1984. Knuth, Donald E. "Literate Programming," *The Computer Journal* **27**: 97–111.

1984. Knuth, Donald E. *The T$_E$Xbook*, Volume A of *Computers & Typesetting* Reading, MA: Addison-Wesley.

1986. Knuth, Donald E. *The Program*, Volume B of *Computers & Typesetting* Reading, MA: Addison-Wesley.

1986. Lamport, Leslie. L^{A}T$_E$X: *A Document Preparation System*. Reading, MA: Addison-Wesley.

1986. Spivak, Michael D. *The Joy of T$_E$X*. Providence, RI: American Mathematical Society.

1989. Knuth, Donald E. "The errors of T$_E$X," *Software—Practice & Experience* **19** (July).

DONALD E. AND JILL G. KNUTH

TEXT EDITING SYSTEMS

For articles on related subjects *see* DESKTOP PUBLISHING; HYPERTEXT; INTERACTIVE INPUT DEVICES; KEYBOARD STANDARDS; METAFONT; MOUSE; POSTSCRIPT; T$_E$X; USER INTERFACE; WINDOW ENVIRONMENTS, and WORD PROCESSING.

Introduction Interactive *text editing* is one of the most well-known and widely used applications of computer technology. A text editing program uses the power of the computer to create, add, delete, and modify textual material, such as letters, manuscripts, program statements, and numeric and statistical data. Computer editing systems are faster and more flexible than their manual and mechanical counterparts, and the proliferation of personal computers (*q.v.*) and word processors is due in large part to the wide appeal of computer-based text editing.

This popularity has affected the design of text editing systems. Once considered tools for programmers and others familiar with computer systems, an increasing number of text editors have been designed exclusively for non-computer–related tasks. Programmer's editors are now specialized tools, and many modern text editors have been designed with generality of use and ease of learning as their primary goals.

Today, editing systems are most frequently used by *knowledge workers* to compose, organize, study, and format computer-based textual information. For such users, the editor represents the primary interface to the computer, and its *user interface* is of crucial importance in determining how they use the system.

The Editing Process An *interactive editor* is a computer program used to create and revise a *target document*. We use the term "document" to include such targets as computer programs, text, equations, tables, diagrams, line art, and halftone or color photographs—anything that one might find on a printed page. Here we restrict our discussion to *text editors*, programs in which the primary elements being manipulated are character strings of the target text. We also examine programs that are designed to help structure text, either in a generic structure such as a tree, as in *outline processors*, or in a more free-form manner, as in *page layout systems*.

The document editing process can be seen as a user-computer dialogue in which (1) the user selects what part of the target is to be viewed and manipulated, (2) the editor determines how to format and display this section of the target, (3) the user specifies and executes operations that modify the target document, and (4) the editor updates the view to reflect the changes.

In order to select which part of the document is to be viewed and edited, the user *travels* through the document to locate the area of interest. Text editors typically provide commands that let the user travel by character, by line, by page, by screenful, or to an absolute location, such as the beginning or end of the file. Other commands may let the user travel to the location of a particular string or pattern. Once the user has issued the appropriate commands, the computer retrieves the document, extracting the relevant subset to determine which section is being viewed. *Formatting* then determines how the result of the filtering will be displayed.

In the actual *editing* phase, the target is created or altered as per a set of operations, commonly including insert, delete, cut, copy, and paste. The editing functions are often specialized to operate on elements meaningful to the type of the editor, such as characters, words, lines, and paragraphs for a word processor, or programming language keywords or statements for programmers' editors.

In a simple scenario, then, the user might *travel* to the end of a document. The appropriate screen's worth of text would then be retrieved, this subset would be *formatted*, and the view would then be displayed on the screen. The user, then, for example, could delete the first three words of this view.

The Editor: A User Viewpoint

The user of an interactive editor is presented with a *conceptual model* of the system, which is the designer's abstract framework on which the editor and the "world" in which it operates are based, and with a *user interface*, the collection of tools and techniques by which the user communicates with the editor.

The conceptual model provides an easily understood abstraction of the target document and its elements, and a set of guidelines with which to anticipate the effects of operations on these elements. Conceptual models range from those that are not very cohesive and hardly visible to the user to those that are well articulated and provide a consistent and complete framework, both for using and for implementing the system. Some of the early *line editors* simulated the world of the keypunch, allowing operations on numbered sequences of 80-character lines, like cards. More modern *screen editors* define *window environments*, a world in which the display serves as a rectangular window onto a portion of a larger document. Through a variety of commands, the users can move this window horizontally or vertically relative to the underlying document. Unlike line editors, screen editors allow operations across lines.

The user interface contains the *input devices*, the *output devices*, and the *interaction language* of the system. (Each of these is discussed below). In addition to the user interface, users are typically supplied with documentation that serves to clarify the editor's functionality through a description of the system architecture in user-level terminology, a tutorial for learning the system, and a reference manual for information on specific commands, capabilities, or techniques.

Each user forms a personal *user model* of an editing system, partly extrapolated from information provided in the documentation or passed on by "experts," and partly extrapolated from the experience of using the system. The user model may differ from the conceptual model in several ways. Since it is developed around the experience of the individual user, it will not necessarily reflect the entire scope of operations available from within the editor. However, it may be thought of as an extension to the conceptual model in cases in which the user uses the editor in ways not originally encompassed by the conceptual model. At the same time, the user model can be seen as operationally equivalent but logically different from the conceptual model. For example, rather than considering themselves to be moving a window over a stationary document, the user may consider the window to be stationary and the document to be scrollable horizontally and vertically. In short, the user model is the personalized, high-level understanding of the editor's manipulable entities and its user interface.

User Interface

Input Devices

Input devices are used for three main purposes: (1) to enter text elements, (2) to enter commands, and (3) to select elements. These devices can be divided into three categories: *text* devices, *button* devices, and *locator* devices.

The most commonly used text device is the standard alphanumeric keyboard, which is used for text entry on nearly all editing systems. These keyboards are primarily of the QWERTY variety, named after the first six letters in the second row of the keyboard. This odd key layout, first used by Christopher Latham Sholes in the 1860s, was arranged this way for purely mechanical reasons—letters most commonly used together were placed as far apart as possible so as to avoid a clash of the mechanical keys. Despite its origin, this style keyboard remains the primary means of text entry for modern editing systems.

Nevertheless, several competing devices have been developed for use with editing systems. The Dvorak Simplified Keyboard is much like a standard keyboard but with keys rearranged to reduce fatigue and increase typing speed, though it is not used very widely. On the Stanford Research Institute NLS system, a keyset consists of a pad of five long keys, similar in shape to white piano keys, and provides a method for entering small text additions or corrections. Each key corresponds to a position in a five-bit binary word called a "chord"; by depressing the proper combination of keys, the user can represent 31 different codes (Englebart and English, 1968).

As an alternative to keyboards, some recently announced personal computers, especially hand-held or portable models, offer handwriting recognition as a means of text or command entry. In these systems, the user "writes" either on a special pad or on a special display screen with an electronic stylus. The computer reads the position and ordering of the user's stylus strokes and converts the input into textual characters.

Locator devices are used to "point" to a place on the screen. With a such a device, the user can quickly move a cursor to the desired position on the screen. These devices are *x-y* analog-to-digital transducers, which convert a physical position or gesture into a digital format, which can in turn be used by the editing system. The most common locator devices are the *mouse, trackball, joystick, touch screen panel,* and *data tablet.* The first two are the most common locator devices for editing applications. The mouse (*q.v.*), is a hand-held device which when rolled over a flat surface (or, in the case of optical mice, moved over a special tablet), causes corresponding changes in the position of the cursor. A trackball is a kind of upside-down mouse—by rolling the top of an encased ball, the user can move the cursor around. Trackballs have the advantage of requiring little table space and being easily accessible from the keyboard.

Buttons or choice devices are most commonly found in the form of function keys, a set of specially labeled keys on the left or top of a keyboard or occasionally at the base of a display. As distinct from ordinary keys, these keys trigger the execution of a certain command, or interrupt the system in a specific way. One frequently used, and specially labeled, set of function keys are the cursor (or arrow) keys, used to simulate a locator device (see below). Also, *modifier keys,* such as Control or Alt, when used in combination with alphanumeric keys, are often used to trigger commands or to simulate function keys. In some modern systems, button devices are often simulated, appearing on the display as a visual button that the user can "press" via a locator device. Other systems have labelled buttons on the screen that serve to describe the keyboard function keys.

Many locator devices are coupled with button devices so that the user can designate a particular point on the screen. In this way, the user can simply point to the text which he or she would like to edit, or easily specify the beginning and end of a range of characters to be operated upon. When the cursor has been positioned over an element, the user presses a button to indicate the selection.

Still in the research stage, *voice input devices* may prove to be the input devices of the future. These systems, which may be used to translate spoken words into their textual equivalent, are already viable for command translation. However, increased speed and vocabulary will be required before they can be used for real-time voice transcription.

Output Devices

The output device serves to let the user view the elements being edited and the result of the editing operation. Output devices have evolved considerably since the days of teletypewriters and other character-printing terminals. Following these devices came the "glass teletype," which used *cathode ray tube* (CRT) technology to simulate a hard-copy terminal. Next came more advanced video terminals, which allowed for moving the cursor, inserting and deleting characters and lines, and scrolling lines and pages.

Today, editing systems run on either character-based displays or graphics (bitmap) displays. On character displays, the screen is divided into a grid of rectangles, each of which can display a single character. Typical character displays show 24 lines of 80 characters each, and some allow characters to be underlined or otherwise highlighted. In contrast, a graphics display allows control over every *pixel* (picture element) displayed on the CRT, and typically displays 480 rows of 640 pixels. These displays extend the possibilities for user interfaces, and can also support accurate imaging to produce on-screen displays that are facsimiles of typeset documents. Thus, the user can view complex documents portrayed essentially as they would look printed on paper.

To assist in the process of displaying such documents, graphic imaging software allows text editors and other applications to specify only an ideal, high-level description of the document, which is then *rendered* for the appropriate output device. In the case of Adobe's PostScript (*q.v.*) language, the same program-generated description of a document can be displayed on-screen, printed to a laser printer, or output on a high-end typesetter. Systems such as this allow the text editor to make use of sophisticated output devices while still maintaining a degree of device independence.

Interaction Language

The interaction language of a text editor defines the rules and means by which a user interacts with the program. The language may include a variety of input *tokens*: keystrokes, mouse clicks, menu commands. The interaction language of a text editor is generally one of a few common types. The oldest is the *command-oriented* interface in which the user issues commands by typing text strings both for command names and for operands. One problem with this form of command specification is that it requires the user to remember the exact form of all the commands, or at least a valid abbreviation. If the interaction syntax is complex, the user must continually refer to the manual or to an on-line "help" command in order to determine the name and form of commands.

The *function-key* interface is meant to address these deficiencies. Here, each command is associated with a marked key (or a key identified on a template) on the user's keyboard. For the common functions, usually only a single key needs to be pressed. Function-key syntax is typically coupled with cursor-key movement for specifying operands, thereby eliminating the need to type commands or operands.

For less frequently invoked commands or options in a function key editor, an optional textual syntax may be used in which commands that are not attached to a function key can be invoked by typing their names. More commonly, more keys are used to make more function keys. Modifier keys "shift" the standard function key interpretations, and alphanumeric keys are *overloaded* to simulate function keys. Generally, functions are assigned to alphanumeric keys in two ways: topologically and mnemonically. In topological layouts, keys with related functions are grouped in close proximity. For example, in WordStar, the keys that move the cursor up, down, left, and right are arranged in a diamond (Control-E, Control-X, Control-S, Control-D). In contrast, Emacs uses the mnemonic Control-P ("previous-line") and Control-N ("next-line") to move the cursor up and down.

Function-key–oriented systems also suffer from deficiencies. They either have too few keys, requiring confusing multi-keystroke commands, or have too many unique keys, resulting in an unwieldy keyboard. The *menu-oriented* system is an attempt to address these problems. A *menu* is a multiple-choice set of text strings or icons (graphical symbols that represent objects or operations) from which the user can select items to perform actions. The editor prompts the user with a menu of only those actions that may be taken, given the current state of the system. The user knows that if a command appears in a menu, it can be issued, and the typical "you-can't-do-that-in-this-mode" messages that occur with other types of interfaces are eliminated.

One problem with menu-oriented systems arises when there are many available options or when a single action requires multiple choices. Since the display area given the menu is usually limited, the user might be presented with several consecutive menus in a hierarchy before a command can be chosen. Since this can annoy and slow down a seasoned user, some menu-oriented systems allow the user to hide the menus, leaving a language or function-key–oriented editor as a base. Others have the functions that are used most on a main menu and have secondary menus to handle other functions. Still others display menus only when the user asks for it. In the case of Apple's Macintosh, users point to the menu bar on the top of the screen and hold down the mouse button to view any of the menus. The menu pops up and temporarily obscures any material that might be "under" the menu. The menu disappears as soon as the user lets go of the mouse button, and the command chosen is executed.

The Editor: A System Viewpoint Although the facilities and structure of individual editors vary considerably, most follow the general structure presented in Fig. 1.

A user interface component decodes the input from the input devices and translates the raw actions or *lexemes* (normally keystrokes and mouse clicks) into tokens that are in turn associated with the appropriate semantic routines. The semantic routines invoke the editor's functionality—traveling, editing, and displaying.

While users always specify what and where to edit, they do not always specify traveling and viewing operations—these may be invoked implicitly through other operations. Deleting a paragraph, for instance, may bring additional text into view, which is then displayed, although the user did not specifically request that this text be displayed.

In editing a document, the editor maintains two pointers of interest. The first is the *current editing pointer*, which is maintained by the *editing component* of the editor, the collection of modules dealing with editing tasks. The current editing pointer determines the location within the text buffer of certain editing operations. It can be moved explicitly, through traveling commands, or implicitly, through the side effects of other commands such as deletions. The editing component also maintains the *current selection*, or scope, for various editing operations. The editing component works with the *editing buffer*, the portion of the document that is in main memory. In documents that are structured differently from linear text files, it may be necessary for the editor to maintain multiple editing buffers, as in the case of a word processor that supports headers, footers, and footnotes.

Similarly, in viewing a document, the start of the area on display is determined by the *current viewing pointer* maintained by the viewing component of the editor. Once again, the current viewing pointer may be moved by explicit traveling commands—such as moving the cursor downward beyond the bottom of the screen—or it can be moved through other commands. When the display needs to be updated, it invokes the *viewing filter*, which creates a *viewing buffer*. This is in turn passed to the *display component* of the editor, which maps it to the display (Fig. 2).

In many modern editing systems, the user may view more than one viewing buffer at once, whether from different files or from different parts of the same file. This multi-file capability provides for easier "side-by-side" comparison between files, as well as cut-and-paste capability. In such cases the editor can provide this capability

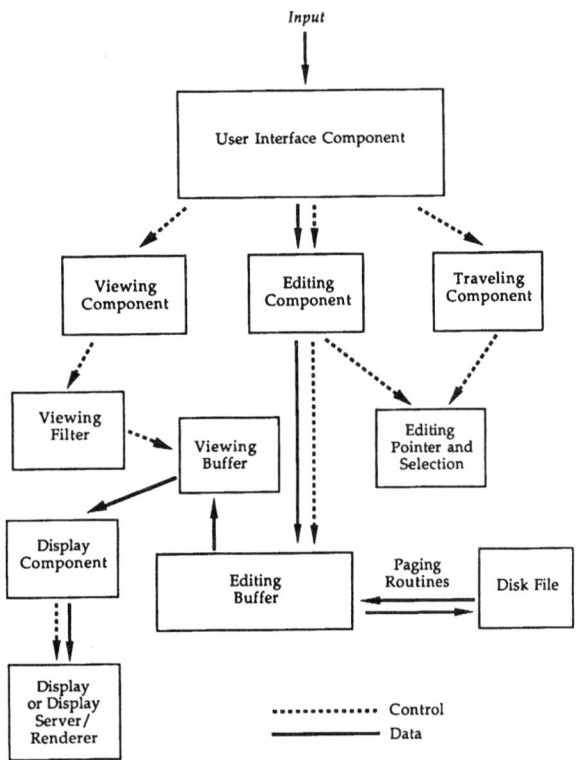

FIG. 1. The text editor: a system architecture.

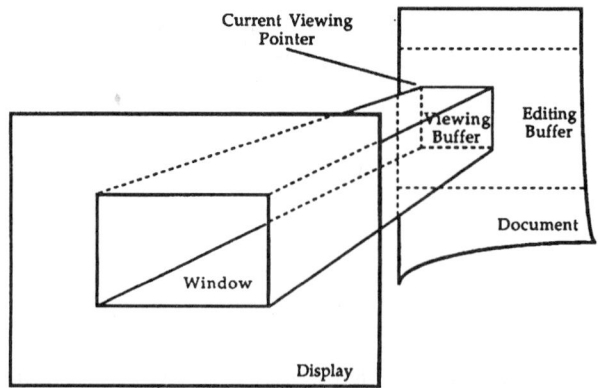

FIG. 2. This diagram illustrates the way in which the document and display are related. The section of the document that is loaded into memory at any time is called the *editing buffer*. The *viewing buffer* is that portion of the editing buffer that is visible; this is mapped into a *window* on the display, which may or may not fill the entire display.

in one of two ways. It can either make use of an underlying *window manager* or it can manage the display on its own. When a window manager is used to provide multiple windows, the editor need not be concerned with much of the display mechanism or even (in some cases) with cut and paste. When there is no windowing system, the editor may implement its own routines for dividing and managing the display. In the case of Emacs, for example, the editor itself has a subsystem for making a text-only display into a tiled multi-window display without the use of any underlying windowing system.

The viewing buffer to window mapping is accomplished using the display and viewing components. The display component examines the viewing buffer and maps it to a physical output device. The details of this process vary considerably, depending on the configuration of the system being used. On character-based terminals connected over low-speed lines, the procedures send text characters and terminal commands or escape sequences to the terminal. Optimal screen updating algorithms compare the current version of the screen with the following version, and transmit only the characters necessary to effect the desired change.

Over high-speed lines or on a personal computer, there is little need for intelligent updating because the bandwidth (*q.v.*) is so high. Some editors running on character-based personal computers write directly to the memory-mapped representation of the computer's display (*see* MEMORY-MAPPED I/O). If more portability is desired, several approaches can be taken. An editor can be written to use a *terminal control database*, which provides information on how specific features are accessed on specific terminals. This way, instead of having explicit terminal control sequences in display routines, the editors simply call terminal-independent library routines, such as "scroll down" or "read cursor position." Terminal control databases, however, function best with text-only output, and different approaches are required when the editor wants to take advantage of a graphical display. A flexible alternative is a graphical display server protocol, such as MIT's X-windows system. This system allows a graphical editor to be run on many different kinds of displays, as long as each supports the X protocol.

In addition to the traveling, editing, viewing, and displaying components, special *utility components*, such as spelling checker (*q.v.*)/correctors, grammar checkers, and word-count analyzers, may be provided to help in the document production process.

The components communicate with a user document on two levels: through main memory and through the disk file system. Loading the entire file into memory may be infeasible. In this case, the editor can rely on the operating system's virtual memory (*q.v.*) capabilities. If virtual memory is not available, the editor will use its own paging routines. These will read in one or more logical chunks of a document into the editing buffer, where they reside until another portion of the document is required by a user operation. In either case, documents in memory are often represented not as sequential strings of characters, but in an *editor data structure* that allows efficient addition, deletion, and modification of text anywhere in the file.

When stored on disk, the editor stores the file either in its own format, often a direct representation of this data structure, in text-only (straight ASCII) format, or in some well-known common format, such as Microsoft's Rich Text Format (RTF). Currently, there are a number of national efforts underway to establish common interchange formats for electronic text.

Configurations Editors function in three basic types of computing environments: *stand-alone*, *distributed*, and *time-shared*. In a stand-alone environment, a single, self-sufficient personal computer or dedicated word processor is used for processing, input, and display. Most often, a disk drive is contained within the unit, and a printer is directly connected. Such systems can be highly interactive and responsive, but often memory or disk storage space is at a premium. In a distributed computing environment, a local area network (*q.v.*) of personal computers or workstations shares disk space and printers. In this kind of environment, the editor still runs on each machine, but is not restricted to the resources of that machine, and must contend for some resources (*see* FILE SERVER).

The time-shared environment, embodied by mainframes and minicomputers, is becoming an increasingly less common environment for editing. In such a setting, the editor runs on a central processor, and users interact with the system through remote terminals. The time-sharing (*q.v.*) system must function swiftly within the context of the load on the system's processor, memory, and disk. In some time-sharing environments that use *intelligent terminals*, some of the processing is performed on the terminal rather than the central processor. These terminals have their own microprocessors and memory in which editing manipulations can be done, thus saving the time to read and write main computer memory, but inviting tricky data structure synchronization problems. In a system using an IBM 3270 series terminal, for example, the editor sends a full screen of material from the mainframe computer to the terminal. The user is free to add and delete characters and lines; when the buffer has been edited, its updated contents are transmitted back to the mainframe.

Historical Development of Editors Over the years, editing systems have evolved from simple tools meant primarily for systems programmers into polished products for use by knowledge workers in many fields. The history of this technological development is one of many complementary developments running in parallel. Editors are so numerous and their relationships so cloudy that it is very difficult to provide an accurate chronology. Rather, we overview some of the important concepts briefly, citing familiar and representative examples.

Noninteractive computerized editing began with the manipulation of "unit record" punched cards (*q.v.*). The basic unit of information was the 80-column line; the user made corrections on a line-by-line basis, retyping mispunched cards. Compared to toggling in bits at the system console, the card gave the programmer new freedom. One could store information in both human- and machine-readable form, and one could "travel" through this information, changing its order, discovering and fixing errors, recognizing color-coded groups of cards, or simply browsing through the deck.

To address the deficiencies of the punched card in the still predominantly batch environments of the 1960s, *card* or *batch editors* were created. Here the programmer's initial deck of cards was stored as a tape or disk file. Each card was referenced by a unique sequence number. Changes were made by creating an *edit deck*, composed of cards containing editing requests, and by running the deck through the batch editor program. For example, the request "in card 35, correctly spell the word 'rate'" would be made by simply typing the desired sequence number, 35, on one card, followed by a card containing the new contents of line 35, or more simply, by composing a card with a sequence number and an editing command, as in

```
35 CHANGE/RATA/RATE/
```

Batch editors removed the problems of dropped cards and of retyping (in many cases), and, in some versions, provided new operations, such as global replacement of a pattern. There were several disadvantages, however. Programmers needed to have a line-printer listing of the entire card deck before making any change. Also, some of the organizational characteristics offered by cards, such as the easy visual inspection of a properly sequenced, color-coded, and well-labeled card box, were lost.

With the advent of time-sharing in the mid-1960s, interactive *line editors* were designed that allowed the user to create and modify disk files from terminals. These editors attached either fixed or varying (sequential relative to the top of the file) line numbers to lines of limited length, initially 80 characters. Early examples of these include IBM's ATS of 1970 and VIPcom, a 1969 product of VIP Systems, Inc. Simple command languages allowed the user to make corrections within a line or even within a group of contiguous lines, using much the same syntax as did batch editors.

Another advance was the creation of the *context-driven line editor*, which allowed the user to identify the line containing the target of an operation by specifying a character context pattern for the editor to match, rather than by giving an explicit line number. One of the first examples of the context-driven line editor was the trend setting editor running on the IBM 7090 as part of Project MAC's CTSS (Crisman, 1965). Other classic examples include IBM's 1969 CMS editor and Stanford's 1973 WYLBUR. At this point in the history of editing, users were still forced to think about multiline entities such as paragraphs and program blocks as groups of integral lines, usually in card image format; no interline commands were available that would, for example, delete text spanning from the middle of one line to the middle of the next line.

The first break from the 80-column card image came in the form of *variable-length line editors*, typified by Com-Share's Quick Editor (QED) (Deutsch and Lampson, 1967)). The main element of operation was still the line, but now each line could be of "arbitrary" length. Initially, these lines were actually limited to some maximum. QED

popularized the notion of a "superline" (limited to 500 characters in length), which the on-line display process broke into viewable lines of 80 characters each, until the superline was exhausted.

Even with superline editors, three basic problems in manuscript editing remained: truncation when the line length was exceeded, inability to edit a string crossing line boundaries, and inability to search for a pattern crossing line boundaries. This last problem is an especially difficult one when transcribing editing changes from formatted hard copy, in that even a short phrase that appears on one line within the paper may be spread across two lines in the document's source file, unbeknownst to the user. Consider, for example, the familiar "the the" typo problem. If a document being edited on a line editor contained the lines

```
...The power of the
the stream editor...
```

the search command

```
locate/the the
```

would not find the pattern "the the," since it appears on two separate lines. The *stream editor* concept solved all three problems by eliminating line boundaries altogether: the entire text was considered a single stream or string that was broken into screen lines by display routines. An arbitrary string between any two characters could be defined for searching and editing.

Another way of dealing with the limitations of line/superline editors was to use the power of multiline display screens that provided cursor addressability and (possibly) local buffers, to create what are called synonymously *full-screen*, *display*, or *cursor editors*. These editors work either with variable-length lines or with streams offering the user an entire screenful of text to view and edit without regard to line boundaries. An early example of a time-shared display editor is Stanford University's TVEDIT (Tolliner, 1965). Commands, represented by control character sequences, could be interspersed with the input of "normal" text. Users were able to move the cursor to point to the text they wished to manipulate, rather than having to describe text arguments in some awkward syntax. Characters could be replaced by simply typing over them. Characters could be deleted by placing the cursor on the character and pressing the delete control character; characters to the right of the cursor moved left so that the cursor seemed to "swallow" characters. Similarly, for insertions, the characters to the right of the pointer moved to the right, "making room" for the new characters. The TVEDIT concepts and similar work by Ned Irons (1972) form the basis of many screen editors in use today.

A major new way of thinking about editing was introduced as early as 1959 by Douglas Engelbart at Stanford Research Institute. His NLS (oNLine System), implemented in the 1960s to create an environment for on-line thinking and authoring, showed the power of display terminals, multicontext viewing, flexible file viewing, and a consistent user interface (Englebart, 1963, 1968, 1973). One of the NLS project's many important contributions was the mouse, an input device that achieved broad commercial acceptance in the 1980s. NLS was the first structure editor in that it provided support for text structure and hierarchy, not just for manipulating raw strings of text: the user could manipulate documents in terms of their outline structure, not only their content. NLS and related editors are particularly important because they view the editor as an *author's tool*, an interactive means for organizing and browsing through information, rather than simply as a mundane tool for altering characters in a single file.

Hansen's 1971 EMILY extended the concept of the structure editor and developed the *syntax-directed editor*, in which the structure imposed on a program being edited was the structure of the programming language itself. Users were able to manipulate logical constructs such as do-while loops and their nested contents as single units.

In the late 1960s, general-purpose time-sharing facilities typically supported only simple interactive line-editing and batch formatting facilities for line-printer output. These "value-added" facilities were barely adequate to create and modify programs and rudimentary documentation. By the early 1970s, text processing had become sufficiently important to be the single dedicated application on both stand-alone and time-shared minicomputers. Since these minicomputers did not need to support general-purpose computing facilities, manufacturers were able to offer comprehensive editing and formatting/typesetting capabilities, as well as features oriented toward document production, such as database management, information retrieval, work-flow management, and print and job queue management, that were usually unavailable on general-purpose systems. For a time, owners of these systems often had more text-processing power than those with much more expensive and much larger general-purpose computers.

An important milestone in text editing and text processing was the early 1970s development and mid-1970s acceptance of the Unix (*q.v.*) time-sharing system, the first general-purpose computing environment in which text utilities were given as much weight as programming utilities. In Unix, a suite of utilities (the *ed* text editor, the *troff* text formatter, the *eqn* equation formatter, the *tbl* table formatter, the *refer* bibliographic database and formatter, the *spell* spelling corrector, and the *style* and *diction* text analyzers (Kernighan, 1982)) introduced and popularized an extensive set of text tools in the general-purpose computing community. At the same time the publishing industries—newspapers, magazines, wire services, the graphics arts—converted wholesale to electronic typesetting and layout of pages, borrowing ideas from traditional computer-based text processing, and also channeling ideas in typesetting and page layout back to the computing community.

In the then separate area of computer graphics (*q.v.*), picture editors were being designed to allow the user to manipulate graphical elements. Interactive drawing techniques from Sutherland's pioneering Sketchpad system (Sutherland, 1963) were later incorporated into editor interfaces. The Carnegie-Mellon tablet editor (Coleman, 1969) is an example of the use of this technology. In this experimental editor, hand-drawn proofreader's symbols were used to edit displayed text. The symbols were drawn on a data tablet and were recognized by the program by passing various characteristics for a given symbol through a decision tree. For a "delete" or "substitute" operation, for instance, the user drew a line through the text to be deleted. The system deleted this line, blinked the indicated text for verification, separated the text by opening a blank line, and inserted a cursor, enabling new text to be typed in from the keyboard. For a "transpose" operation, the user simply used the familiar transposition mark.

The major innovations of the 1970s in text handling and the user interface, specifically the Bravo editor and the Smalltalk environment, took place at Xerox's Palo Alto Research Center (Xerox PARC). These systems demonstrated the expressive power of blending text and graphics on a high-resolution, bit-mapped, raster graphics screen, using a dynamic graphical interface provided by a dedicated personal computer. Editing was done by selecting items on the screen, using the mouse as a pointing device. These systems were also the first *interactive editor/formatters*, in which the user's text was displayed on the bit-mapped screen in a facsimile of the typography and layout of the final document, as the document was being input or modified. For the first time, the user was given a notion not only of the up-to-date content, but also of the up-to-date form of the document.

Throughout the 1980s, the ideas developed at Xerox PARC spread even farther as the idea of WYSIWYG (what-you-see-is-what-you-get) influenced the creation of a whole new generation of personal computers. These new computers, exemplified by Apple's Macintosh (1984), placed a heavy emphasis on ease-of-use, user interface consistency, and WYSIWYG interactive typesetting/editing throughout their operating environment. The line that once separated text editing from text formatting and structuring had been blurred. With the proliferation of microcomputer-based word processing technology, content editing and format editing have become increasingly intertwined to the point that only a small portion of computer-assisted text processing is distinct from formatting. Text editors are no longer exclusively editors; it is now common for a single piece of software to be used for everything from word processing to typographical style selection and page placement.

There are a number of reasons for this shift. Until recently, users interested in computer-assisted document preparation used a text editor to edit unembellished ASCII text. Users entered textual formatting instructions into their text. These instructions, along with the source text, would then be processed non-interactively by a separate text formatting facility. Now it is more common for the "editor" to provide these formatting facilities itself, so that users need not "compile" their documents to see (on screen or on paper) the effects of their formatting. Most modern text editors offers at least rudimentary formatting and manuscript management facilities. In the case of the original MacWrite (Apple, 1984), the bare text editing facilities were not very sophisticated—the size of the document was limited to eight or ten pages on a standard system, but the visualization facilities included multiple fonts, multiple sizes, and an interactive graphical *ruler* for changing the margins and tabs of paragraphs. Newer systems, including a new version of MacWrite, also manage references, indices, and tables of contents dynamically, so that as a document is edited, the references to items in the index or table of contents will be automatically updated to reflect their new locations within the document.

Other recent developments in interactive text editing involve the integration of textual material with other kinds of information. Page composition software allows linked blocks of text and graphical elements to be intermixed freely within a single document. These programs are designed to assist in the composition and production of complex multi-page publications that would ordinarily require extensive manual paste-up. Systems such as Interleaf allow users to create and edit text and graphics, while other systems such as Aldus's PageMaker, while permitting text creation and editing, allow only limited creation and editing of graphic elements.

Several systems take this idea of elements farther and allow the creation of fully editable *composite documents*. In such a system, a user can create a document that contains blocks or sub-documents of various types— graphics, text, spreadsheet, etc.—each of which may be "owned" (created and edited) by a different editor. For example, a single document in such a system may contain data from a spreadsheet and a word processor. The user can use the tools of the word processor to edit the text portion of the document and the tools of the spreadsheet to edit that portion.

These systems are exemplified by Quill, an editing system developed at IBM's Almaden Research facility. The developers of this system call it "an extensible system for editing documents of mixed type." (Chamberlain, 1988). Another system with related functions is Hewlett-Packard's NewWave operating environment. In this system, which is overlaid on Microsoft Windows, users create "objects"—documents or part of documents—that can be placed in any document, regardless of their type.

Functional Capabilities
In this section we examine the functional capabilities of text editors from the perspective of the user.

Traveling User actions frequently cause the *current editing* and *viewing pointers* to be moved. Traveling ranges from simple movement, such as "arrow key" traversals, to more complex pattern searches and hypertext "jumps." Early editing systems provided only simple traveling capabilities; they were oriented toward transcription of editing changes from hard copy. Many modern systems are oriented toward on-line reading and writing. These require sophisticated browsing facilities that support studying and organizing, not just composition and revision.

Simple Movement

In display editors that operate on character-based displays, the position of the editing pointer is indicated by the position of the cursor, normally a reverse-video or flashing mark over a single character on the screen.

Graphical, mouse-based text editors typically use an *insertion point*, a flashing bar that can be positioned only between two characters. The insertion point, as first used in Xerox PARC's Gypsy editor, resolves the ambiguity of the character-sized cursor and eases the precise selection of a range of text.

When navigating about a file, some editors allow the user to move the cursor or editing pointer separately from the viewing pointer. Mouse-based graphical editors typically permit the user to scroll the document so that the cursor is not visible, and allow the user to easily jump back to the location of the cursor. Thus, these editors support two different kinds of traveling: motion that moves the viewing window and motion that alters the location of the cursor. Other editors support only cursor movement, and alter the viewing window as necessary.

Editors commonly support two kinds of *intrafile motion*: *absolute* and *relative*. An absolute specification indicates a destination independent of the current position, while a relative specification indicates the destination relative to the current position. Commands to move the cursor forward or backward by characters, words, paragraphs, or screens are examples of relative movement; beginning-of-file, end-of-file, and goto-page are examples of absolute movement. Mouse-based editors provide another means of navigation—the user can move the cursor to a given position within the file by simply "pointing" there. Most mouse-based editors require the user to press the mouse's button in order to actually move the cursor or insertion point; others track the mouse directly so that the mouse cursor and the text editing cursor are the same.

In line-oriented editors, line numbers can be *fixed* or *varying*. In editors with fixed line numbers and numeric labels provided by the user or the system, the user can easily specify an absolute goto to that number. As an example, the editor portions of Basic interpreters use fixed line numbers specified with even intervals, such as

```
10 J = 0
20 FOR I = 1 TO 10
30 J = J + I * I
40 NEXT I
```

To add a print statement after the increment statement, one could simply type

```
35 PRINT I, J
```

and the editor would put the new line between lines 30 and 40, as indicated by its numeric label.

In contrast, editors with varying line numbers keep track of a line's position internally as an offset from the top of the file. When a new line is added, the internal line numbers of all lines beneath the new line are incremented by one. Since the line numbers change dynamically, the deletion (insertion) of a line near the top of the file causes all the line numbers below it to be decremented (incremented) by one.

Many editors have *mark* or *saved-position stacks* or *rings* that record locations that the user has visited in the file. Some maintain an implicit mark ring, automatically storing the location each time that the user makes a selection for a command, and allowing the user to retrace his or her steps. Others have explicit marking facilities; Apple's Macintosh Programmer's Workshop, for example, provides for named marks that designate a range of text in a given file. Once named, the mark will appear on a menu and may be used to travel immediately to that position. These marks are saved along with the file proper.

There are also a variety of target-dependent traveling operations. In document editors, for example, simple movements are provided to bring a user to the beginning of a section or chapter. In a program editor, a traveling command might take the user to the beginning of an expression, or might match braces or parentheses by briefly traveling to the "matched" character and then returning.

Pattern Searching

The above methods of traveling are position dependent. Text editors also allow a content-dependent specification of location: *pattern searching*. A pattern searching command (usually called search, find, or locate) generally will locate and display (and sometimes select) the next occurrence of the pattern specified.

Since typing an entire pattern can be a tiresome operation, specification aids have been developed. The "..." (ellipsis) construct can sometimes be specified to abbreviate a long pattern by indicating simply a few characters of context at the beginning and end of the pattern. Thus, one might locate the text string:

```
Now is the date for some good people
```

with the command:

```
locate /Now...people
```

Regular expression (q.v.) context patterns extend the ellipsis concept to more powerful pattern-matching capabilities—for instance, matching a pattern that does or does not contain a particular set of characters, matching a pattern only if it occurs at the beginning of the line, or matching a pattern regardless of the case of the characters (known as *case-insensitive pattern matching*).

Because of the difficulty of constructing regular expression search strings, some editors offer simplified searching options, such as one that allows the user to search for whole-word occurrences only. In this case a search for the pattern "time" would not find the string "timezone."

Interfile Motion

The ability to travel between two or more files is extremely useful in on-line authoring. Often, the process of authoring involves the examination of multiple sources which are best viewed at the same time. With this capability, users can easily move text between files, compare the contents of files, etc.

At the very least, the user must be provided with commands to switch the file being edited. Ideally, the user will be provided with an integrated operating environment in which a large number of editing windows can be opened and viewed at the same time. Most editors have at least a small level of integration with the operating system, or enough to load in a new file. Some also feature directory browsing from within the editor; systems such as Emacs provide "directory editing"—file editing, renaming, and deleting.

Editors running under a windowing system have system-level support for multiple documents on display. Under Microsoft Windows, users can open documents for editing, and the corresponding editor windows will be opened automatically. Under this system, documents from multiple editors may be displayed at once in multiple windows, along with application and system windows. Even single-file editors can be loaded into multiple windows if the windowing system provides the support.

Hypertext

The above types of interfile navigation are usually employed by the user during the editing process; the paths of travel are not stored from one editing session to the next. Occasions do arise when the user wants to set up (semi-)permanent paths or links within a document or between documents. The motivation for such text links is well stated in a seminal article by Vannevar Bush, who envisioned the "memex" device for authors and readers in 1945:

> The human mind...operates by association. With one item in its grasp, it snaps instantly to the next that is suggested by the association of thoughts, in accordance with some intricate web of trails carried by the cells of the brain. It has other characteristics, of course; trails that are not frequently followed are prone to fade, items are not fully permanent, memory is transitory. Yet the speed of action, the intricacy of trails, the detail of mental pictures, is awe-inspiring beyond all else in nature....Consider a future device for individual use, which is a sort of mechanized private file and library. It needs a name, and, to coin one at random, "memex" will do. A memex is a device in which an individual stores all his books, records, and communications and which is mechanized so that it may be consulted with exceeding speed and flexibility...when numerous items have been thus joined together to form a trail, they can be reviewed in turn, rapidly or slowly, by deflecting a lever like that used for turning the pages of a book....It is exactly as though the physical items had been gathered together from widely separated sources and bound together to form a new book. It is more than this, for any item can be joined into numerous trails. (Bush, 1945, pp. 106–107)

Hypertext editing systems are the modern-day incarnation of Bush's pre-computer memex. Hypertext, a term coined by Ted Nelson, is "the combination of natural language text with the computer's capacities for interactive branching, or dynamic display...a nonlinear text ...which cannot be printed conveniently...on a conventional page" (Nelson, 1967, p. 195). Simply, hypertext is defined as nonsequential writing—writing that is written and read nonlinearly.

Some hypertext systems allow the user to forge arbitrary links from any chosen *anchor*—a point in a document or a part of a document—to any other anchor in that document or in any other document in the user's domain. These links can then be followed—a user can easily jump from one end of the link to the other, and the destination text will be quickly displayed. Other systems support linking and navigation between hypertext *nodes*, "idea-sized" chunks of text that are stored in a database. Links can have purposes other than navigation; some systems support *warm linking*, in which the contents of the source anchor can be "pushed" to replace the contents of the destination anchor.

Systems that combine linking with non-textual information are called *hypermedia* systems. In these systems, the general concept of linking has been extended to graphics, sound, animation, and video.

Viewing   To provide a basis for editing and browsing and to provide feedback as editing commands are issued, the viewing component creates an up-to-date view on the display. Two types of operations support this process: the formatting procedures, whereby the raw textual data is marked up and prepared for display, and the display procedures, which map the formatted view onto the display.

Formatting

In a text-only, straight ASCII text editor, the text is shown exactly as it is stored in the internal buffer, with the exception of the carriage return and linefeed characters which are translated into a new line on the display. Text-only editors may also perform similar special translation of the tab character, translating it into several spaces.

However, this formatting is typically sufficient only for a simple programmer's editor. Editors intended for manuscript work must provide additional formatting capabilities, or must provide an interface to a formatting system that provides these capabilities. Early text processing systems provided *formatting codes* (such as .pp for paragraph, .in 5 for indent five spaces, .ce for center) that were were typed in as literal text and subsequently compiled by a text formatter to produce formatted pages; no on-line feedback was available.

Later, *soft-copy* or *proof-copy* facilities were made available to display (but not to allow editing of) monospaced output on the alphanumeric terminal. With high-resolution graphics displays, even proportionally spaced typeset text could be previewed. The next major step in the formatting field was the creation of the interactive editor/formatter. Today, most editors, especially commercial word processors, instantly display the results of commands with local effect (such as indent, tab, embolden, and center) as they are entered or changed. Interactive editor/formatters make possible an especially useful view in which all operations on the document take place immediately on a displayed facsimile of the printed page, thus giving instant user feedback.

Since the spread of the graphical work station, users have come to demand increasing formatting and display sophistication. Proportionally spaced fonts and WYSIWYG margins are only the beginning; the latest commercial graphical word processors offer interactive editing of multiple column pages, embedded graphics, footnotes, and equations. (Many products offer limited WYSIWYG, but provide a print previewer that will display a facsimile of the printed page.) Other editors, such as Ashton-Tate's FullWrite or T/Maker's WriteNow, have more complete WYSIWYG, down to on-screen columns, page numbers, and footnotes.

The ultimate text formatters are *page composition systems*. Initially developed as specialized products for use in the publishing industry, scaled-down programs have found their way onto personal computers where they are now frequently used as adjuncts or replacements for standard text editors. These systems allow users to freely position multiple arbitrarily shaped blocks of text on pages. These blocks can be linked together so that a single file may span one or more blocks on different pages (allowing for the "jump" stories that are common in newspapers and magazines), and insertions or deletions in any block will be reflected in the others as appropriate. Graphics blocks may be intermixed on a page with text blocks; this way, it is possible to create full layouts interactively with these systems.

Formatting Commands   There are many approaches to format specification. In most word processing systems, the editor provides commands to effect the proper formatting directly. For example, it is possible in many editors to select one or more lines and then issue a "center" command which will change the on-screen representation of these lines, as well as change the internal representation of the document.

Many word processors provide a *ruler*, an on-screen simulation of a typewriter's margin and tab controls, that contains the current margin settings, fonts, tab stops, etc. The user can reformat the text by simply changing the ruler's attributes. In other editors, the formatting specifications are entered as textual formatting codes in the same manner as "normal" (literal) text. In some systems, these codes must be entered on separate lines to distinguish them from literal text; in other systems, a special character is used as a delimiter (*q.v.*) so that the codes can be imbedded in the normal text stream; two delimiters in a row then designate a literal delimiter character.

Format specifications fall into two categories: *procedural* and *declarative*. In a procedural specification, the author indicates the exact operations to be done to effect the formatting choices (e.g. put this text in 12-point Times, skip two lines). Conversely, in a declarative system, *tags* or *styles* are used to identify or mark elements of the document, such as paragraphs, items in a numbered list, chapter headings, and running heads. These sets of attributes may be named and applied to a range of text. For example, a "paragraph" style might be created with the specifications 12-point Palatino, line spacing 14 point, ragged right. These attributes could be collected under the name "paragraph" and for all standard paragraphs. Any subsequent revision of the "paragraph" definition would change the appearance of all the text that had been marked as "paragraph." Some systems provide *hierarchical styles*, in which styles are defined in terms of other styles. For example, suppose a style were created for "indented paragraph," which was based on the style for "paragraph." If the typeface of the "paragraph" style were changed, the typeface for "indented paragraph" would also change. Styles can be grouped and saved as *stylesheets*, which may be reused so that documents can be formatted with a common "look." Such facilities allow the same document to be formatted in different ways (possibly for different output devices) by simple parameterization: for instance, the user could format a *Computing Surveys* document by specifying the stylesheet "Surveys" and for *Communications of the ACM* by specifying the stylesheet "CACM." Declarative formatting can provide less complicated user specifications and often less complicated editor interfaces for on-line formatting; the user need not supply detailed formatting commands, and need use only high-level structural indicators as tags. SGML is a popular formatter-independent declarative language.

Editing

Specification of Scope

The range of a document used as an operand for an editing operation is called its *scope*. The scope is of central importance with commands that operate on blocks of text, such as move, delete, or reformat.

The user typically thinks of the scope not in terms of "raw" text, but rather in terms of logical elements that can be edited and traversed. These elements are also known as units, nouns, objects, and structures, and are often a function of the internal representation of the target data. In line editors, for example, manuscript text may be stored as sequential lines and edited and traversed on a line basis. In stream editors, the text may be stored as a one-dimensional, indefinitely long stream of characters, broken into discrete lines by formatting routines for viewing purposes.

In addition to logical elements that match the internal representation, editors provide a variety of elements corresponding to user-level abstractions, often grouped in order of increasing scope: characters, words, lines, sentences, paragraphs, and sections are typical for text. In addition to these standard system-provided elements, users can also define arbitrary *selections*, *regions*, or *blocks* that exist only for the duration of a given operation. A third class of elements may be a set of document components, such as sections, headings, titles, running headers, footers, and numbered lists.

The goal of scope specification for all these elements is to approximate within the limitations of the computer interface the ways that users would manually gesture ("delete this, move that over there"). In a mouse-based editor, this is quite simple: Users simply point to a particular screen location to establish the location. Mouse-based interfaces provide a number of ways to specify scope. Many editors provide the standard "double-click" functionality: If the user presses the button twice in a row while positioned over a word, the editor will highlight that word and make it the current selection. Some editors provide similar means for establishing a sentence or paragraph as the selection. Mouse-based editors also often provide a means for selecting the text between the insertion point and the current position of the mouse.

In editors with keyboard-based interfaces, the editor will provide at least a pair of commands to specify the scope—one to mark the beginning of the block and one to mark its end. These editors may also offer commands to extend the block by character, word, or line.

In line editors, the user establishes the current line (by specifying its line number or by traveling to it via scrolling or pattern searching) and then specifies the scope (by typing either a context pattern within that line or an integer to indicate a group of one or more discrete lines whose first line is the current one). In stream editors, of course, the pattern matching is not limited to a current line, but has potentially the entire file as its domain. Emacs provides a means of narrowing the region of the file available for display and manipulation. When the "narrow-to-region" command is issued, the part of the file outside the scope (region) disappears. It is not available for editing or viewing until the "widen" command is issued. This way, the user can focus on a few paragraphs and then restore the larger context when this text is satisfactory.

Editing Operations

Creating Text is most often inserted into a computer-based document by typing on a keyboard. The typing process is similar to typing on a typewriter, but text editors provide a number of facilities that make computer-based typing more flexible. First, the backspace or delete key can be used to erase the last character typed. Many editors also provide automatic *wordwrap* which eliminates the need for typing a carriage return at the end of each line. When the editor senses that the word currently being typed has exceeded the right margin, it breaks the line at the first blank space before the overflowing word and automatically pushes it, followed by the cursor, to the next display line.

Non–mouse-based display editors generally accept typed input in two ways: *typeover mode* or *insert mode*. In typeover mode, generally offered by editors designed for monospaced character displays, each character typed replaces the character at which the cursor is pointing. In insert mode, each time a user types a character, the character at the cursor position and all those to its right are shifted right and the typed character is inserted at the cursor position. Many editors allow the user to toggle between typeover mode and insert mode.

Mouse-based display editors typically follow the insertion point paradigm invented by Tesler and Deutsch in the Gypsy editor, popularized by the Macintosh, and now the standard for editing on Microsoft Windows, Motif, and Open Look. In this paradigm, the insertion point is always between two characters. Typing at the insertion point adds characters at the insertion point. Yet, if characters are selected (done by dragging the mouse with the mouse button down, then releasing the button), typing will replace the selected characters.

Another keyboard aid is that of *glossaries* or *abbreviations*. Editors that offer these facilities allow commonly entered words to be entered in an abbreviated form and then automatically expanded. For example, the words "time zones" could be abbreviated as "tz" and then automatically expanded upon entry. A similar creation facility is named *variables*, in which the user can establish named variables, such as "company," which may be inserted into the text at any point. If "company" is set to "General Electric," then this string will appear in all places in which the variable has been inserted. This facility is often used in mail-merge systems, in which the editor successively reads values from a *data file* and substitutes their values for the variables in the *source file*.

Other creation techniques include the capability of *embedding* files or parts of files into the document being edited, thus making it possible to recycle previously created material. The user can create *boilerplate* documents, as is often done with proposals, contracts, and specifications, by using bits and pieces from the entire domain of user files on the computer. Similarly, some editors support *stationary* or *template* files, whose contents are automatically copied into a new file when they are opened.

Deleting   The delete command requires the user to select the scope of the operation. Since deletes are obviously dangerous commands, some systems require confirmation before actually completing the operation. Other systems allow the user to *undo* commands, making the deletion operation reversible. For the delete command, as well as the copy and move operations described below, many systems provide *delete buffers*. This allows the deleted elements to be placed in "limbo" so that they can be used later as the objects of paste (also called insert or put) operations, which put the elements from the delete buffer back into the text. To move a paragraph, for instance, the user first selects it and specifies the delete or cut operation; the editor then deletes the paragraph and places it in the delete buffer. To put the paragraph back in somewhere else, the user indicates the desired destination and specifies the *yank* or *paste* operation. Often, systems provide multiple, named delete buffers for more complex manipulations. The Unix vi editor, for instance, has a *buffer stack*, which keeps track of the last nine pieces of text that have been deleted.

Changing   Many of the changes made to a document are corrections of typographical and other minor errors. The simplest change is the replacement of one letter with another. In the typeover mode of a display editor, the correction is made by simply typing the new character over the erroneous one. In the insert mode of a display editor, the correction is made by typing the new character and then deleting the old character, which has been pushed to the right by the insertion of the new character.

Similarly, changing a word in typeover mode simply involves typing over the erroneous word. However, since the replacement word may be longer or shorter than the original word, a delete or insert character function may also be needed. In insert mode, changing a word would be done entirely with the implicit insertion combined with delete-word functions. On mouse-based systems, this can be done by selecting the word to be replaced and simply typing its replacement.

In line editors, the user needs a method of specifying what character(s) to replace. These editors have a change or substitute command, as shown previously, that takes as arguments both the scope of the change and the replacement string.

Because of its speed, the computer can offer the facility of global changes—operations that take place uniformly throughout a document or throughout a specified scope. The global change command allows the user to specify a pattern to be found throughout a document and a replacement string to replace that pattern wherever it appears. In some systems, this command may do its work, but not indicate what changes have been made. In others, a count of the number of changes is given. Still others prompt the user each time the search string is found, to see if the substitution should be made.

Transpose is a convenient special-purpose change command that is notably absent from most editors. In Emacs, for example, the "transpose-character" (Ctrl-T) command will exchange the character at which the cursor points with the one directly to its left, and similarly, the "transpose-word" command will do the same for words.

Moving   One of the great advantages of electronic text processing is the ease and accuracy with which text can be rearranged. Text editors replace the scissors-and-tape editing operations of cut, copy, and paste with electronic equivalents. To move a block of text, the user specifies a source (the scope of text to be copied) and destination (the place where the text is to be pasted). In an editor in which the scope is specified by pointing, the user defines the source by selecting the beginning and end of the text to be moved, and then defines the destination by pointing to the location at which it should be placed.

Many editors use the cut/copy/paste paradigm, as popularized by the Macintosh. Under this system, the cut and copy commands act upon a selection within a document. When a copy command is issued, the selection is copied into a buffer called the *clipboard*. When a cut command is issued, the selection is placed in the clipboard and removed from the document. A paste command inserts the contents of the clipboard at the location of the insertion point. If the paste command is issued when there is a selection, the selection is replaced with the contents of the clipboard. For example, the misordered poem by Frost

Two roads diverged in a yellow wood,
And looked down one as far as I could
To where it bent in the undergrowth;
And sorry I could not travel both
And be one traveler, long I stood

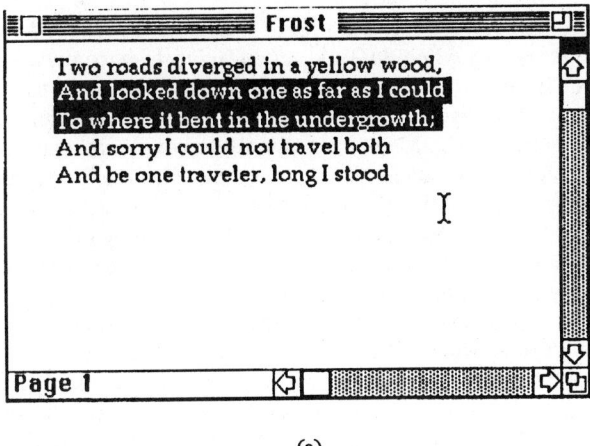

(a)

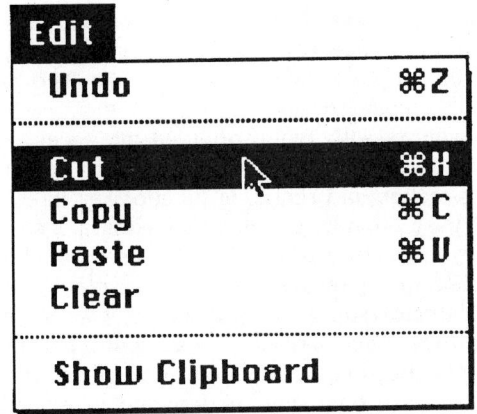
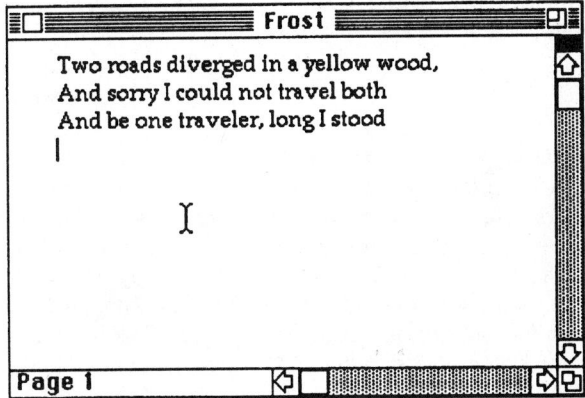

(b)

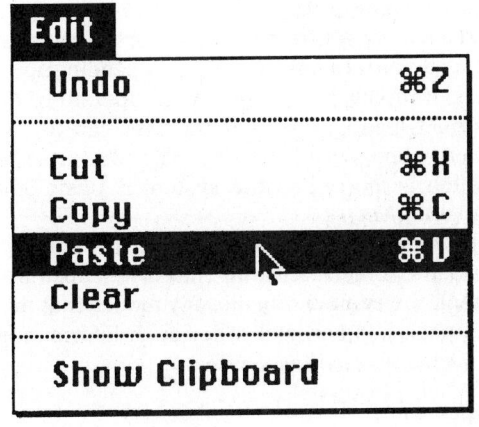
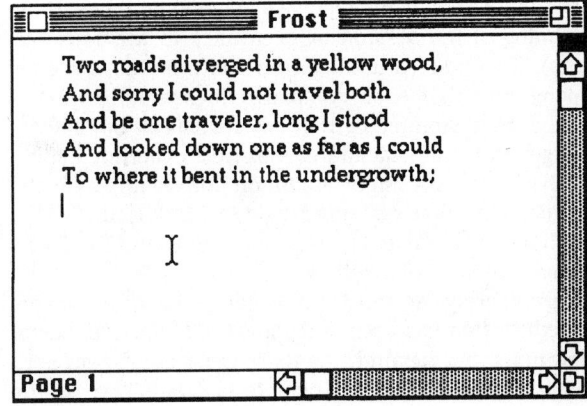

(c)

FIG. 3. The poem is reordered with a mouse-based editor using Cut and Paste. (a) The two misplaced lines are selected. This is accomplished by positioning the mouse pointer to the left of "And looked," pressing the button, moving the pointer to the right of "undergrowth," and releasing the button. (b) The "Cut" command is issued. At this point, the selected text is removed from the document and stored in the clipboard. (c) The pointer is moved to beyond the last line, the button is pressed (to position the insertion point) and the "Paste" command is issued. The editor then inserts the contents of the clipboard at the position of the insertion point.

could be ordered properly with such an editor by selecting the lines "And looked down one as far as I could/To where it bent in the undergrowth;" issuing the cut command, traveling to the beginning of the last line, and issuing the paste command, as illustrated in Fig. 3.

In a typical line editor, one might accomplish the same thing by traveling to the line "And looked down one as far as I could" and issuing a command such as "move 2 down 2." This would temporarily delete the following two lines, including the one currently being pointed to, thereby moving the current pointer to the line following the last line deleted, and then move it down two more lines and insert the temporarily deleted lines where the current pointer now points.

Miscellaneous Capabilities Commands grouped under this heading are not directly involved with manipulating text, but rather with assuring the integrity of a user's work and with making the user interface more powerful and helpful.

Reliability

Backup Capability To minimize the possibility of the accidental erasure or destruction of a document, editors often have *backup* capabilities. One strategy is to give the user copies of the files being edited to work with so that the file cannot be destroyed by a system crash. Some editors offer *autosave* or *checkpointing*, in which files are automatically saved after a certain number of keystrokes or after a specified amount of time has elapsed.

Undo Facility The undo facility is a critically important, time-saving feature. The most basic version allows the user to undo the last command entered. More useful systems have an *n-level* undo stack that allows the user to undo commands *n*-levels back (sometimes to the beginning of the session or even back to previous sessions). The undo feature frees the user from the burden of making sure that each command does exactly what is wanted, by guaranteeing that any result can be undone. The general undo facilitates risk-free experimentation, which is especially important for on-line composition and organization. Some systems provide an undo/redo facility, which allows the user to undo operations and then redo them at the push of a button.

Only rarely can editors undo every kind of command. Any editor that has undo will allow the undoing of delete operations, but beyond this there is no agreement over which kinds of commands need to be "undoable". In the case of commands that effect a complex transformation of the document text, such as global search/replace, many editors do not offer an undo capability.

User Aids

Since interactive editors are meant for frequent and extended use by a wide class of users, it is particularly important that they be designed with careful attention to human factors.

On-Line Documentation/Help Facility An on-line *help facility* is extremely important to new and occasional users, as well as dedicated users who do not use all parts of the system regularly. The help facility can provide an expanded explanation of an error message, a short summary of a command syntax, or perhaps complete access to an on-line version of the manual. Some systems create a separate help window, allowing the user to have access simultaneously to both the help information and to the document being edited, rather than forcing the user to leave the document and lose the information on which the user sought help in the first place.

Some editors provide context-sensitive help. In these systems the user can get information relevant to the current state of the editor by issuing a single command. Other systems enable the user to determine the meaning of any function key or menu item.

User Feedback Feedback is a vital part of the editing process; it is necessary for specifying operations, for specifying scopes, and for showing the results of an operation in the updated view.

In editors with typing-oriented interfaces, echoing the typed command provides immediate feedback on both operation and scope. In function-key interfaces, a button push provides no inherent feedback. If no supplementary feedback was supplied, the user would have to rely on examining the results of the operation to see if the specification was correct; by this time, it would often be too late to reverse the results. Thus, feedback techniques, such as highlighting a selection in progress (with such techniques as brightening, underlining, or reversing) in display editors, or highlighting the menu items as they are browsed through in menu-oriented interfaces, are vitally important.

Other audio and visual cues aid the user at little cost to efficiency or to implementation. Beeping to signal errors usually ensures that a user does not miss the occurrence of an error. Programmable cursors allow the cursor to take on different symbolic forms, depending upon what the user is doing. Time-consuming operations require intermittent feedback so that the user can be satisfied that the system is still working. The Macintosh uses a wristwatch cursor when the system is busy; Smalltalk uses an hourglass.

In some editors, a status line at the top or at the bottom of the screen indicating the current position in the document, the name of the file, any modes that might be set, the page number, and other such information, is a useful means of providing feedback.

Customization

Profiling A *profiling* or *preferences* facility allows the user to "tune" the editor environment. This allows important or preferred environment settings to be saved and restored automatically and removes the need for all users to accept a common default. Some editors allow the user to save relatively simple information, such as the unit of measurement to be used on the rulers. Others allow each user to reconfigure major parts of the interface. Microsoft Word, for example, allows each user to choose which commands appear on which menus.

User-Defined Commands (Macros) Editing systems often allow the user to define *macros* or *editing scripts* based upon the system operation repertoire, using an editor *macro language*. The user can thus package under one name sequences of commands that are often executed as groups. In some systems, these commands prompt for or simply accept parameters (operands) and even provide conditional execution for maximum power and flexibility. Some editors offer the less flexible *keystroke macros*; the system "captures" a set of keystrokes typed in by the user and can then repeatedly execute those keystrokes as if they were typed as one command. Some keystroke macro systems allow the user a form of parameterization, temporarily stopping the execution of the keystroke macro, allowing the user to type in the "parameter," and then finishing the execution.

Extensibility Some editors allow the user to extend the command set in the same language in which the editor is written. Thus, the user is not limited to designing macros made up of editor primitives, but can design operations using the same lowest-level primitives that the nucleus of the editor uses itself. The fact that the extension is being done in an actual programming language, rather than a special-purpose editor macro language, implies greater efficiency and ease of expression of new functions. In Emacs, for instance, the editor can be used to modify or create a function, and this function can be "linked" into the editor without ever leaving the editing environment. Of course, such a feature is not targeted to the general public, but to more advanced users or programmers who are willing to learn the internals of the editor to modify or add code.

Utilities

A number of add-on utilities can ease the more mechanical aspects of text creation and text editing. Many text editors offer spelling checkers, which check the words in the user's file against words in a dictionary file. Unrecognized words are flagged, and some spelling checkers offer suggestions, often based on phonetic similarity. Some dictionaries also contain definitions, allowing users to look up words easily from within the editor, and others contain a thesaurus, allowing users to select a word and quickly obtain a list of synonyms.

Along similar lines, some text editors offer word count facilities, beyond the usual character count and page count facilities. With word count, writers can quickly and accurately write to specifications.

System Implementations While most editors, regardless of implementation and configuration, offer a set of frequently used "standard" editing and traveling functions, there is a wide difference in formatting capabilities and a number of more specialized features, as well as in the types of user interface available. Much of this diversity is illustrated by the three editors described below: GNU Emacs, MacWrite II, and WordPerfect. Emacs is a programmer-oriented plain-text editor that offers tremendous flexibility and extensibility. MacWrite II is a mouse-based WYSIWYG interactive typesetter/formatter that emphasizes formatting flexibility and ease of use. WordPerfect is a full-featured office word processor which operates on character and graphics-based displays.

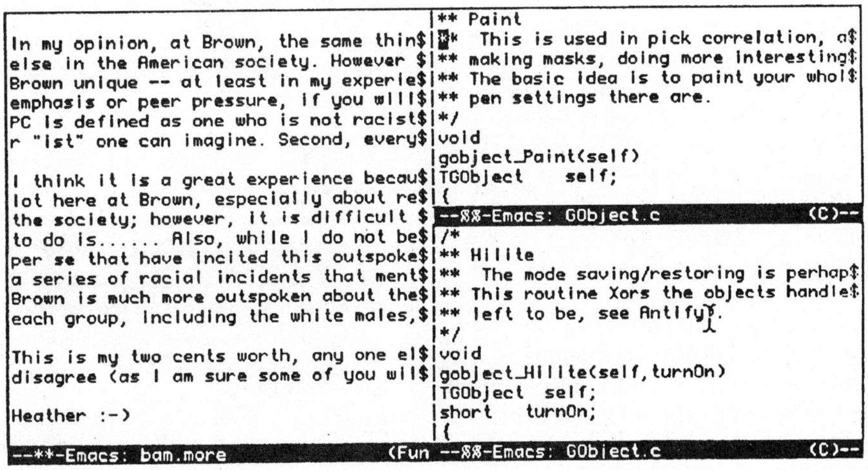

FIG. 4.   An Emacs screen. Here, the editor is running on a standard 80 × 24 character ASCII terminal; the three windows are generated by Emacs itself. On the left, a text file is being edited in "Fundamental" mode; on the right, two parts of a single C source file are being examined in C mode. The cursor is in the upper right window. To insert text, the user simply types text; it will be inserted to the left of the cursor (the inverted block in the upper-right window). Characters are deleted using various control characters.

GNU Emacs GNU Emacs, from the Free Software Foundation, is a display editor designed to be extensible, customizable, and self-documenting. It is the most recent of the Emacs family of editors which originated at M.I.T. with Richard Stallman's original version for the Tops-20 operating system. Emacs has a large and faithful following in the academic research community.

Emacs is a plain-text editor. It is designed for editing ASCII text files, especially program source code. It has multi-window editing (even on ASCII terminals) and is remarkably easy to customize (see Fig. 4). The editor loads files into buffers; buffers may be displayed in one or more windows, or they may be set aside until they need to be viewed.

The distinguishing feature of Emacs is its extensibility. Not only can users change various definitions and command keys, but they can actually extend the system's capabilities. Emacs contains its own Lisp interpreter; advanced users can add functionality to the system by writing entirely new commands in this language. Most of the editing commands are written in Lisp; those that are not are written in C for efficiency, according to Stallman (1987). Any user-written extensions may be loaded automatically at invocation time.

Of course, not all users can take advantage of these facilities, but there are other ways of tailoring the system. In Emacs, every typed character is considered to be a command. Each keypress triggers the execution of a Lisp function; the mapping of keys to functions is recorded in a table called a *keymap*. The key bindings can be altered without programming; users are also free to record keystroke sequences and play them back, using keystroke macros. This uniformity makes reconfiguring the system quite straightforward; it also makes the help system general. At any time, a user can issue the "describe-key" command, which causes Emacs to retrieve the documentation for the command that is bound to that key. Emacs also has a large documentation database called "info" that can be browsed from any context.

Because it is so extensible, the system offers innumerable facilities and functions that have been written by many different people. The editor and a variety of extensions are included with the Free Software Foundation releases, and users are invited to submit their extensions for inclusion in future releases. The extensions that are included in the release run from facilities for reading and sending Unix electronic mail or editing TEX (*q.v.*) files to a "flame" extension which will generate random insults at the user's request.

Emacs offers *major modes*, editing environments that are tailored for a particular kind of file. For example, text mode treats the hyphen as a word separator; Lisp-mode distinguished between lists and s-expressions; dired (directory editing) mode provides commands to view, delete, or save files. The major mode includes a set of key bindings designed to support its particular application, such as indentation in programming languages. There are also *minor modes*, which are options that can be used in conjunction with major modes. Minor modes include auto-fill-mode, which will fill lines with spaces to a fixed width.

Emacs has much to offer as a program development environment. Besides the C-mode features, such as indentation and parenthesis balancing, it has the capability of launching "make" from within the editor, and the "next-error" command will step through compiler errors, displaying the appropriate file at the appropriate position. The editor also provides a *tags* facility, which includes a separate program, etags. Etags builds a tags table containing the file name and position in that file in which each program function is defined. This table is then loaded into Emacs; issuing the command Meta-.*function-name* causes Emacs to load the appropriate file and travel to the appropriate function within that file.

All these features do, however, have a downside. One Emacs can be quite different from the next—for example, one user might use Control-D for "down-line," while another might use it for "delete-character." Thus, with extensibility in any editor comes the price of widespread divergence over various installations and even within a single installation. The trade-off between a large number of divergent but customized dialects and a single, standard language is unclear.

MacWrite II Claris' MacWrite II, the successor to the first Macintosh word processor, is notable for the simplicity of its user interface and the flexibility of its formatting features. In its functional capabilities, it offers only the now-standard word processing features: footnotes, form letters, and spelling checking, among others. At all times, MacWrite takes full advantage of the graphical Macintosh environment for its user interface and its display, presenting a WYSIWYG view of the document, including typeface and size, line spacing, multiple columns, and footnotes (see Fig. 5). The program's design is such that the means of completing any given task are nearly always self-

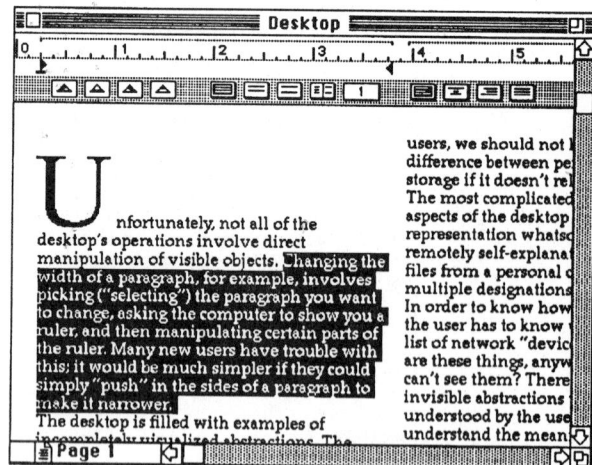

FIG. 5. A MacWrite II window. At the top of the window is the ruler, which controls tabbing, margins, and indentation. On the right and at the bottom are the scroll bars, which allow the user to travel through the document. This document demonstrates multiple columns and two different type sizes. The text that is inverted is the selection; this is the text that will be replaced if the user presses a key.

explanatory; still, it comes with a graphical hierarchical on-line help system.

Following the Macintosh conventions, all MacWrite commands can be issued through mouse actions, although some keyboard "shortcuts" may also be used. Users can scroll through documents with the scroll bars at the right and bottom of the screen. This is done by moving the mouse cursor over one of the "arrow" icons and holding the button down. While the mouse button is held down, the document will scroll in the appropriate direction, as if a piece of paper is being slid underneath the window. For more extensive traveling, MacWrite provides a graphical thumbnail, which indicates the approximate position within the document of the displayed portion. The thumbnail may be moved to any position within the file.

To move the cursor or *insertion point*, the mouse cursor is moved to the desired position and the button is then pressed. The insertion point will then appear as a blinking vertical line between two letters. Any text that is typed will be inserted at this point. When there is no selection, MacWrite II is in insert mode; text typed does not replace existing text. All text entry in MacWrite II is done within the main document window at the location.

Many commands are issued by indicating a selection or scope and then issuing a command, either via the ruler, a menu, or through a keyboard equivalent for a menu command. Text can be selected by clicking (pressing the mouse button) more than once, rapidly in the same position. Clicking twice will select the word under the cursor; additional rapid clicks will select the line, paragraph, and document. Many commands act on the current selection.

At the top of a MacWrite window is the ruler, which controls certain formatting attributes. Above the numbers, a dotted line indicates the width of the page, or the available printing width. The triangles control tabbing, the icons and numeric indicator in the center control line spacing, and the icons on the right are used to determine whether a paragraph's lines are left justified, centered, right justified, or filled. To change the format of one or more paragraphs using the ruler, this text must be selected and then the components of the ruler can be repositioned as desired to effect the proper formatting modification.

At all times, MacWrite shows page breaks in the proper positions, accounting for the size of the page, the number and height of lines on the page, and any headers, footers, or footnotes that might be present. It also takes account of any graphics that might be inserted into the document. Any text may be displayed and edited in any font which is installed in the Macintosh "System" folder. In this and many other ways, MacWrite II is a part of the Macintosh editing environment, not just a stand-alone application. It can accept graphics that are created in standard formats, while text that is cut or copied from a MacWrite II document can be easily pasted into other documents. It supports Macintosh-standard single-level undo.

MacWrite offers a facility called *stationary* to save default values and create boilerplate documents. Any document can be saved as stationary; when a stationary file is opened, its contents and settings are copied into a new file for editing, while the stationary file remains untouched. When MacWrite is started, it copies the contents and setting of the template "MacWrite II Settings" into the blank window.

WordPerfect WordPerfect, from WordPerfect Corp., is one of the leading office word processors, running in many different computer environments, but most commonly on the IBM PC and PC-compatible systems (*q.v.*). It can be used to edit everything from memos to multi-chapter books, and contains facilities to handle most mainstream document-editing needs. It is oriented toward the general user and is not particularly suited for program editing.

WordPerfect delivers its vast array of functions through a function-key–based interface. Each of the function keys has four different meanings—one when pressed by itself, and three others when pressed in combination with Shift, Control, and Alt. Since there are so many commands, the keys and their associated commands are color-coded on the plastic keyboard template that is provided with the software. As an alternative, WordPerfect also offers a mode in which commands may be chosen from pull-down menus with the keyboard or with a mouse.

The editor's greatest strength is in the breadth of its functionality. It has a serious macro and macro editing facility that includes constructs such as IF, CASE, and WHILE. It provides automated table of contents generation, outlining, mathematical calculations, and facilities for managing multi-file documents through the use of a "master document." It also comes standard with spelling checking and a thesaurus, and includes the capability of including (and to some degree editing) certain kinds of graphics generated using other software. There are also facilities for editing mathematical equations.

Since the editor operates on a character-based display, only limited formatting is visible on-screen. While the program supports multiple font sizes, it will not display them during the editing process. Similarly, line breaks on the screen will not necessarily occur in the same position when printed. It is, however, possible to enter *review mode*, in which the program will generate an uneditable on-screen representation of the printed version. From this rendition, the user can judge whether or not the document is ready to print, thus avoiding wasted paper, but still causing delay. The user can use the "Reveal codes" mode and view the document on a split screen so that on the top half of the screen the standard editable file is visible, and on the bottom half a version of the text that includes all formatting codes is displayed.

Conclusion Editing systems, as we know them, have reached a level of maturity—for the most part, most future changes will be evolutionary ones. Possible revolutionary changes in editing systems by the millennium will be threefold. First, composite document editors, in which one can edit text, graphics, spreadsheets, charts, etc., will become more prevalent. Second, the emerging technologies of lightweight portable computing and handwriting recognition will make it easier for casual users to put large amounts of textual information into a computer without typing. Finally, as speech recognition continues to be developed, it will be possible for users to input text merely by dictating.

The computer, since its appearance in the 1940s, has changed from a tool of a small scientific community to an appliance of the mass market. Text editing, starting with the punched card, has evolved steadily with interactive editors for programs, simple editors for documentation, and sophisticated editors for word processing. Now, 50 years later, we are at the point of extremely inexpensive but powerful editor/formatters that can be used to create the mixed text and graphics necessary in the highest-quality magazine pages, but are simple enough for those with no formal education to use and master.

References

1945. Bush, V. "As We May Think," *The Atlantic Monthly* **176**, *1* (July) 101-108.

1963. Engelbart, D. C. "A Conceptual Framework for the Augmentation of Man's Intellect," in *Vistas in Information Handling*, P. Howerton (Ed.). Washington, D.C.: Spartan Books. 1–29.

1963. Sutherland, I. E. "THOR: A Display Based Timesharing System," in *Proc. Spring Jt. Computer Conf.*, **23**, Baltimore, MD: Spartan. 329.

1965. Crisman, P. A. (Ed.). *The Compatible Time Sharing System: A Programmer's Guide*, 2nd Ed., Cambridge, MA: M.I.T. Press.

1965. Tolliver, B. "TVEDIT," Stanford Time-Sharing Memo. No. 32, Dep. of Computer Science, Stanford Univ., Palo Alto, CA.

1967. ——, *QED Reference Manual*. Ann Arbor, MI: Com-Share Inc.

1967. Deutsch, P. and Lampson, B. "An Online Editor," *Commun. ACM* **10**, *12* (December), 793–799, 803.

1967. McCarthy, J., Dow, B., Feldman, G., and Allen, J. "THOR—A Display Based Timesharing System," in *Proc. Spring Jt. Computer Conf.*, **30**, Arlington, VA: AFIPS Press. (Spring) 623–633.

1967. Nelson, T. H. "Getting It Out of Our System," in *Information Retrieval: A Critical Review*. G. Schecter, Ed. Washington, D.C., Thompson Book Co. 191–210.

1968. Engelbart, D. C. and English, W. K. "A Research Center for Augmenting Human Intellect," in *Proc. Fall Jt. Computer Conf.* **33**. Arlington, VA: AFIPS Press. 395–410.

1969. Coleman, M. "Text Editing on a Graphic Display Device Using Hand-drawn Proofreader's Symbols," in M. Faiman and J. Nievergelt (Eds.), *Pertinent Concepts in Computer Graphics*. Urbana, IL: University of Illinois Press. 282–290.

1969. IBM. *A Conversational, Context-directed Editor*.

1969. *VIPcom User's Guide*. Washington, D.C.: VIP Systems.

1970. IBM. *System/360 Administrative Terminal System*.

1970. Hansen, W. J. "Creation of Hierarchic Text with a Computer Display," Rep. ANL7818, Argonne National Laboratory, Argonne, IL. July.

1972. Irons, E. T. and Djorup, F. M. "A CRT Editing System," *Commun. ACM* **15**, *1* (January) 16–20.

1973. Engelbart, D. C., Watson, R. W., and Norton, J. C. "The Augmented Knowledge Workshop," in *Proc. National Computer Conf.*, **42**, Arlington, VA: AFIPS Press. 9–21.

1982. Kernighan, B. W. and Lesk, M. E., in *Document Preparation Systems*, J. Nievergelt, G. Coray, J. Nicoud, and A. Shaw (Eds.). Amsterdam and New York: North-Holland.

1987. Stallman, Richard *GNU Emacs User's Guide*. (March) 9.

1988. Chamberlain, et al. "Quill: An Extensible System for Editing Documents of Mixed Type." *Proceedings of the 21st Hawaii International Conference on System Sciences*, Kailu-Kona, Hawaii (January). 317–326.

1989. Claris Corp. *MacWrite II User's Guide*.

NORMAN MEYROWITZ AND DAVID TEMKIN

THEOREM PROVING

For articles on related subjects *see* ARTIFICIAL INTELLIGENCE; EXPERT SYSTEMS; HEURISTIC; LOGICS OF PROGRAMS; and PROGRAM VERFICIATION.

The two approaches to automated *theorem proving* are *proof finding* and *consequence finding*. A proof-finding program attempts to find a proof for a certain given theorem. A consequence-finding program is given some axioms and then tries to deduce consequences from the axioms and to select "interesting" consequences.

Purposes Some of the purposes of programming a computer to prove theorems concern artificial intelligence and deduction (Winston, 1984). Artificial intelligence researchers point out that proving a nontrivial theorem is an intellectually difficult problem. Most of the theorem-proving programs we mention in this article use mathematical logic or, to be specific, the *first-order predicate calculus*, which is also called *quantification theory* (Wos 1988). In mathematical logic, one can express fairly conveniently almost all kinds of deductive arguments. Writing a theorem-proving program that uses mathematical logic allows the researcher to study deduction in its purest form. Deduction is important because it plays a major role in solving many kinds of problems (not just in mathematics). A program that can prove theorems has what John McCarthy has called *common sense*; i.e. it has the ability to make deductions from given facts. This kind of common sense is an important part of human intelligence. Programs that use mathematical logic to find proofs have been extended to deduce answers to questions.

The other purposes of programming a computer to prove theorems concern mathematics and mathematical logic. Mathematicians point out that a program that could prove new and interesting theorems would be useful in itself. The first new and interesting theorem proved by a program was proved by the program of Guard *et al.* (1969). It would be a tremendous achievement if some program of the future could prove or disprove either the famous last theorem of Fermat or the Goldbach conjecture. Mathematical logic is well suited to computers, since logicians have striven for decades to make their inference rules "mechanical." It is an attractive idea to write a program based on mathematical logic, since this is a well-formulated and well-studied branch of mathematics. In addition, programming a computer to prove theorems is a way to study mathematical logic. For example, the programmer may develop powerful, natural, and intuitive inference rules to which heuristics can be added easily.

History We begin the history of automated theorem proving by mentioning some programs that have proved theorems in areas other than the first-order predicate calculus. A 1957 program called the "Logic Theorist," or simply LT, by Allen Newell, J. C. Shaw, and Herbert Simon (*q.v.*) proves theorems in *propositional calculus* (also called *sentential calculus*, or *boolean algebra* (*q.v.*)). It performs at approximately the level of a fair-to-good college student on the same theorems. A 1959 program mainly due to Herbert Gelernter proves geometry theorems at the level of a good high school student. A program called ADEPT proves theorems in group theory. It performs at approximately the level of an intelligent college student.

A program of R. Boyer and J. Moore (1979) proved the correctness of one of the fastest string-searching algorithms, the correctness of a simple expression parser and the prime factorization theorem, the soundness and completeness of a simple mechanical theorem prover, and the correctness of an arithmetic simplifier. As an integral part of the success of each of these proofs, the user of the theorem prover had to suggest useful intermediate theorems to prove.

P. Gilmore and Hao Wang, as well as Martin Davis and Hilary Putnam, were among the first to program a computer to find proofs in the first-order predicate calculus. (Each of these programs substitutes many constant terms for the variables and then checks to see if the theorem has been proved. If not, more constant terms are added and another check is made, etc.) After these programs had been written, J. A. Robinson developed an inference rule, which he called the *resolution principle*. Roughly speaking, the resolution principle draws the most general, possible conclusion from two given statements, where the conclusions and the two statements generally contain variables. The resolution principle is more natural, more intuitive, and easier for people to use than are the inference rules used by the previous predicate calculus programs. Furthermore, it is easier to think of heuristics to add to the resolution principle.

A procedure that uses the resolution principle for proof finding tries to show that the negation of the given theorem to be proved is unsatisfiable (contradictory, inconsistent). The resolution principle is complete for proof finding in the sense of the following theorem, first proved by J. A. Robinson: "If a finite set of clauses [statements] is unsatisfiable, a contradiction can be found in a finite number of applications of the resolution principle." This means that there is, in principle, a computer program that, for any true theorem in first-order predicate calculus, can find a proof using the resolution principle. In practice, however, limitations of computer time and memory space prevent programs from finding proofs for many theorems. However, people have written proof-finding programs embodying the resolution principle. These programs are more powerful than the previous predicate calculus programs.

The resolution principle is complete for consequence finding in the sense of the following theorem, first proved by R. Lee: "If a clause *C* is a consequence of a finite nonempty set of clauses, a clause *T* can be found in a finite number of applications of the resolution principle such that *C* is an immediate consequence of *T* alone." Lee wrote a consequence-finding program based on the resolution principle.

Several researchers have strengthened these completeness theorems by showing that certain restricted forms of the resolution principle are still complete. This is of practical importance to automated theorem proving because theoretical considerations and computer experiments indicate that restricted and complete resolution tends to be more efficient than is unrestricted resolution.

Programs using the resolution principle or its restrictions have proved theorems already known (found proofs and found consequences) (e.g. theorems in group theory and abstract algebra). To speed up the search for proofs of theorems involving the equality predicate, complete, valid, and efficient (in time) inference rules, namely, *paramodulation* and *E-resolution*, were developed for theories with equality. Each of the new rules replaces the equality axioms and is used in addition to the resolution principle. Such a program with paramodulation added (Winker and Wos, 1978) answered some open question in ternary boolean algebra.

Slagle pointed out the general advantages of building in theories and built in several such theories (e.g. partial and total ordering (Slagle and Norton, 1973, 1975)). He advocated clause compiling (replacing axioms by programs; e.g. inference rules) and narrowing (generalized replacement using equations).

A general theorem proving program called OTTER (McCune, 1989), written in C (*q.v.*), is orders of magnitude faster than previous programs. Its speed is attained by using discrimination trees. It has proved many difficult theorems, including some new and interesting ones.

References

1969. Guard, J., Oglesby, F., Bennett, J., and Settle, L. "Semi-automated Mathematics," *JACM* **16**: 49–62 (January).

1973. Slagle, J. and Norton, L. "Experiments with an Automatic Theorem Prover having Partial Ordering Inference Rules," *Comm. ACM* **16**: 682–688 (November).

1975. Slagle, J. and Norton, L. "Automated Theorem-Proving for the Theories of Partial and Total Ordering," *Computer Journal* **18**: 49–54 (February).

1978. Winker, S. and Wos, L. "Automated Generation of Models and Counter Examples and its Application to Open Questions in Ternary Boolean Algebra," *Proc. of the 8th Int. Symp. on Multiple-Valued Logic*. Rosemont, IL: IEEE.

1979. Boyer, R. and Moore, J. *A Computational Logic*. New York: Academic Press.

1984. Winston, P. *Artificial Intelligence, 2nd Edition*. Reading, MA: Addison-Wesley.

1988. Wos, L. *Automated Reasoning: 33 Basic Research Problems*. Englewood Cliffs, NJ: Prentice Hall.

1989. McCune, W. "OTTER: User's Guide," *Technical Report ANL-88-44*. Argonne, IL: Argonne National Laboratory.

JAMES R. SLAGLE

THEORY OF ALGORITHMS. *See* ALGORITHMS, THEORY OF.

THRASHING

For articles on related subjects *see* OPERATING SYSTEMS; THROUGHPUT; TIME SHARING; and WORKING SET.

Thrashing is a collapse of throughput of a system of communicating servers as the load on the system is increased. When a single server is subjected to an increasing load (backlog of unfinished work), its output rate increases towards a saturation asymptote. When many servers are connected in a network and the visit ratios depend on the load in the network, intuition based on the well-behaved single server does not carry over: the output rate of the network can rise with load, attain a peak, and then drop with further increasing load.

Thrashing was first observed in the early multiprogrammed time-sharing systems of the 1960s. Designers were surprised to discover that as the multiprogramming level (load) was increased, system throughput would suddenly drop to a very low level. Throughput would not return to its former high until the load was reduced below the load that triggered the thrashing—a form of hysteresis. The explanation was that the size of the memory partition assigned to each program decreased as the load increased, forcing an increase in demand paging that limited the system (Denning, 1968). This explanation was made more precise through the theory of queueing networks, which showed that the number of visits each task makes to the paging disk grows with load; at some load, the paging device would become the bottleneck, and its very slow output rate would become the system's output rate. At smaller loads, the central processor would be the bottleneck; its much higher output rate would be the system's output rate (Courtois, 1977).

The solution to thrashing was a load controller. The simplest form was to set a limit on how many tasks in the "active set" were allowed to hold space in main memory; any additional submitted tasks would be held in a special queue. The load controller would act as a valve controlling the flow from the submitted-tasks queue into the active set. The simplest criterion for load control was a fixed, preset value; the valve is open only when the size of the active set is less than the preset limit. The optimal criterion is to open the valve whenever the unused memory space is large enough to hold the *working set* of the next submitted task. The working-set criterion was found in experiments to be not only more efficient but more robust than the fixed-load criterion (Denning, 1980).

Thrashing has also been observed in packet-switched communications where many servers vie for slots in a common medium, such as a satellite channel or ethernet cable. Suppose each server follows the protocol: if the medium is busy, wait until it is idle; when it is idle, begin transmitting a packet and, if someone jams the medium before transmission is finished, stop transmitting and restart the protocol. As the number of contending computers (load) increases, the number of successful packet transmissions increases. Past some threshold of load, however, it becomes highly likely that two or more computers wind up cycling endlessly through the transmit-until-jammed part of their protocol loops. When this happens, few packets are transmitted successfully. These phenomena were first observed with the ALOHA satellite communication network in the late 1960s.

Again, a load controller prevents thrashing. The control affects when a computer can transmit rather than whether it is allowed to be connected to the medium. Each computer has a value called the "backoff interval" associated with it. When its transmission is jammed, the computer waits for an amount of time equal to its backoff interval before restarting the protocol. The backoff interval can be adjusted dynamically: when a computer finds the medium idle and transmits successfully, its backoff interval is decreased; when the computer is jammed, its backoff interval is increased; otherwise, its backoff interval is unchanged. Backing off reduces the frequency at which computers attempt transmissions whenever jamming is excessive. Kleinrock (1976) gives a full treatment of a variety of strategies for load control in packet-oriented communication systems.

Thrashing can occur in any network where the bottleneck shifts as the load is increased. It can be avoided by a load controller.

References

1968. Denning, P. J. "Thrashing: Its Causes and Prevention," *Proc. AFIPS Conf.* **32** (1968 FJCC), 915–922.

1976. Kleinrock, L. *Queueing Theory Vol. 2.* New York: John Wiley, 360–407.

1977. Courtois, P. J. *Decomposability.* New York: Academic Press.

1980. Denning, P. J. "Working sets past and present," *IEEE Trans. Software Engrg.* **SE-6,** *1* (January), 64–84.

PETER J. DENNING

THROUGHPUT

For articles on related subjects *see* JOB; PERFORMANCE MEASUREMENT AND EVALUATION; PERFORMANCE OF COMPUTERS; SCHEDULING ALGORITHM; and TURNAROUND TIME.

The *throughput* of a computer system during a given interval of time is the average rate at which jobs are completed by the system in that interval. If n jobs are completed in an interval of t seconds, the throughput is taken as n/t jobs per second during that interval.

Throughput is frequently used as a figure of merit for a system: the higher the throughput, the more highly regarded the system. Considered alone, however, throughput can prove to be a most deceptive measure. At least five factors affect throughput: 1) the capacity of the system, 2) the time interval over which throughput is measured, 3) the load on the system, 4) the scheduling method, and 5) the job mix.

The capacity of the system is the maximum rate at which the system can process work. It is usually stated with respect to each job class to which the system caters, a job class being the set of jobs whose resource requirements (processor, memory, devices) fall in specified intervals; for example, all jobs whose processor time requirement is between 30 and 60 sec, main memory requirement is between 5K and 10K words, and that use no I/O devices, might constitute one class.

The precise specifications of job classes in a given system will depend on the objectives of that system. The capacity of a given class is the maximum rate at which the system can complete the jobs in that class. Evidently, the throughput of jobs in a given class cannot exceed the system's capacity in that class; in fact, if the arrival rate of such jobs approaches the capacity of the system to process them, a large backlog will accumulate, making system response time to them unacceptably long. Put another way, whenever throughput is maximized in the sense that it approaches system capacity in each job class, intolerable delays to jobs will be the inevitable result, and throughput in this case clearly gives a deceptive picture of the system's performance.

The time interval over which throughput is measured is the second factor of importance. It is well known that, by giving priority to short jobs (i.e. jobs whose residence time in the system, or whose processing time, is short), the system throughput will be high. However, because little attention is being devoted thereby to the long jobs, a backlog of long jobs may accumulate. Assuming that the system management intends to get all submitted work completed eventually, there will necessarily come a time when the long jobs must be processed and the short ones are left as backlog, but during their processing, the throughput will be low. Thus, over a time interval long enough so that all jobs submitted are processed; the throughput will be proportional to $1/S$, where S is the mean service time over all job classes. However, over an interval during which short jobs are favored, the throughput can be considerably higher than $1/S$, whereas during another interval during which the backlog of long jobs is removed, the throughput can be considerably less than $1/S$. Once again, throughput can give a deceptive picture of system performance.

As suggested in the discussion of the first factor, *the load* on the system is a third factor affecting throughput. For job class i, let F_i denote the fraction of time during which such a job queue for this class is present in the system demanding processing, and let S_i denote the mean time to service each job. Then, the system

capacity in class i is proportional to $1/S_i$ (mean output rate if queue is never empty), and the throughput in class i is proportional to F_i/S_i. This is illustrated in Fig. 1. Evidently, as the load of class i jobs increases, F_i increases and approaches unity so that the throughput of class i jobs increases correspondingly. However, even as the load increases, the response time within class i may increase sharply (it is usually proportional to $1/(1 - F_i)$), so that, once again, judging performance merely by throughput can be deceptive.

The scheduling method is a fourth factor affecting throughput. It was shown above that giving preference to short jobs during an interval will produce high throughput during that interval. In more general terms, suppose the system devotes a fraction G_i of total capacity to class i jobs; the throughput in class i is then proportional to G_iF_i/S_i. Since the values of G_i for each class i are a function of the scheduling method, the throughput in each class depends on the scheduling method, and the total throughput is proportional to T, where

$$T = G_1F_1/S_1 + G_2F_2/S_2 + \ldots + G_nF_n/S_n,$$

will also depend on the scheduling method. This is illustrated in Fig. 2. (The reader should observe that there is interaction between G_i and F_i, since increasing G_i will reduce the backlog in class i and thus reduce F_i; therefore, the computation of throughput by the preceding formula cannot be carried out directly.) As noted above, T is also proportional to the constant $1/S$, where S is the mean service time over all job classes. The implication of this is: If the scheduling method increases throughput above $1/S$ for some classes, it will reduce it below $1/S$ for others. Once again, the interpretation of the throughput can be deceptive if the scheduling method is unknown.

The final factor affecting throughput is the *job mix* (i.e. the distribution of jobs among the job classes). The effect of this factor should be clear, in light of the preceding discussion.

It is apparent, therefore, that one needs to conduct a thorough analysis of a system with respect to the five factors before a useful or meaningful interpretation can be attached to throughput. But performance of a single system cannot be judged solely by its throughput, nor can two systems be compared simply by comparing their throughputs. Similarly, if one wishes to improve system throughput, consideration must be given to how this can

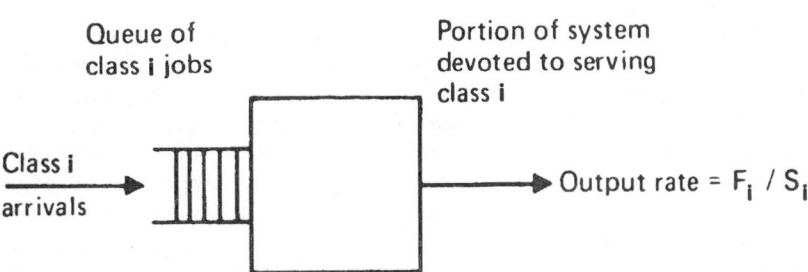

FIG. 1.   Load on the system.

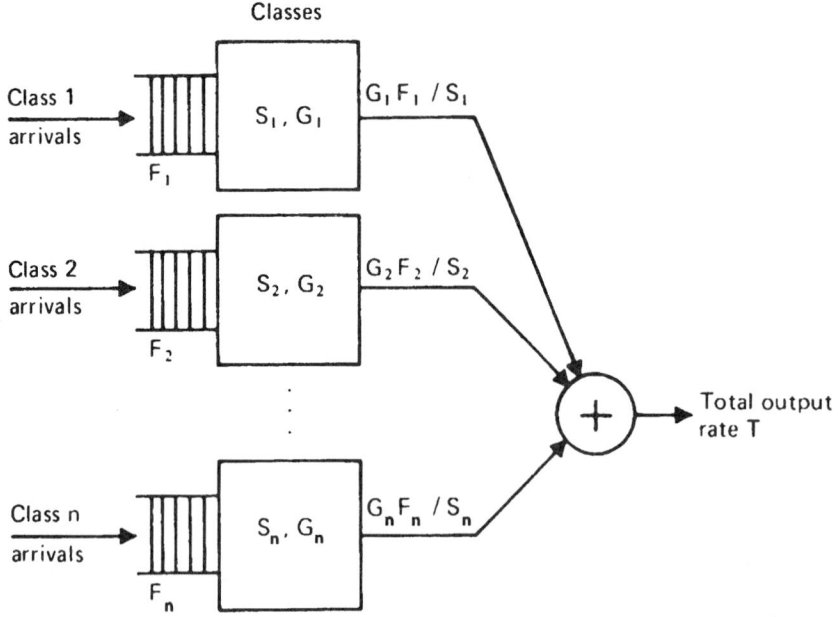

Classes

Class 1 arrivals

F_1

S_1, G_1

$G_1 F_1 / S_1$

Class 2 arrivals

F_2

S_2, G_2

$G_2 F_2 / S_2$

Class n arrivals

F_n

S_n, G_n

$G_n F_n / S_n$

Total output rate T

FIG. 2. Throughput.

be done while considering the constraints imposed by the five factors. It is not an easy problem.

PETER J. DENNING AND DOROTHY E. DENNING

TIME SHARING

For articles on related subjects *see* ACCOUNTING SYSTEM, COMPUTER; FILE SERVER; INTERACTIVE SYSTEMS; MULTIPROGRAMMING; MULTITASKING; PROCESSING MODES; SCHEDULING ALGORITHM; SWAPPING; TIME SLICE; UNIX OPERATING SYSTEM; and VIRTUAL MEMORY.

Origins *Time sharing* is a technique of organizing a computer so that several users can interact with it simultaneously. The term also refers to multi-user systems in which arbitrary general-purpose computation is performed and users operate independently of one another, often at locations remote from the computer itself. Although time sharing was initially perceived by many as a programming convenience for debugging, the perception soon was extended to include the provision of a wide variety of on-line services and the availability of a large central memory shared among the user community.

Time sharing originated in the late 1950s and early 1960s. By then, relatively reliable commercial computers had been available a few years, high-level languages were easing the task of programming applications, and ever larger programs were being constructed. At the same time, the operating staffs of most large computation centers were trying hard to make more efficient use of the still expensive equipment. Typically, programs and data for a batch of jobs would be prerecorded on magnetic tape, and then, under the supervision of a monitor program, the

jobs would run serially without interaction until they terminated or encountered an error condition. While effective in keeping the equipment utilized, batch processing made the debugging of programs increasingly difficult. Not only was the time to correct even the most trivial error a matter of hours, but the problem was aggravated as one wrote larger and more ambitious programs.

The above state-of-affairs for program debugging was particularly frustrating to users in universities and research laboratories where large programming projects were being attempted, often with computers saturated by near-continuous use. In 1959, Christopher Strachey (*q.v.*), then at the National Research Development Corporation in England, presented a paper at a UNESCO Conference describing the possibility of doing program debugging while time-sharing the computer with the normal production computing load; independently, that same year, Professor John McCarthy, in an influential but unpublished internal memorandum at M.I.T., proposed key hardware modifications to an IBM 709 computer that would allow the possibility of time-shared debugging by multiple users. Indeed, it was McCarthy's early advocacy of time sharing that inspired much of the interest in developing such systems.

In retrospect, it is not surprising that the notion of time sharing emerged, for it was in a sense a rediscovery of earlier, more experimental modes of computer use. Although not widely known, it was in the early 1940s at a mathematics conference that the Stibitz relay computer at the Bell Telephone Laboratories was operated remotely by a single user a few hundred miles away (*see* STIBITZ, GEORGE and BELL LABS RELAY COMPUTERS). Also in the early to mid-1950s, there was developed for U. S. Air Defense the massive SAGE System, which at each of several sites had multiple users, each at a terminal interacting independently with information displayed on cathode ray tubes. In addition, in the late 1950s, IBM and American Airlines had begun development of the SABRE System, an on-line airline reservation system with hundreds of terminals distributed geographically. But these early multiterminal systems were dedicated in purpose to their single applications. What was new and striking in the proposals of Strachey and McCarthy was the vision of a computer used independently by different persons for entirely different programs, each of which might still have serious mistakes or "bugs" in them. In short, the notions were planted of a *computer utility* where users would view the system as a set of services and conveniences provided to them and the primary goal was the larger one of optimizing the effectiveness of the users and equipment rather than just the equipment alone.

It was also particularly fortunate for the development of time sharing that two key technology improvements occurred when they did. These key changes were the replacement of the vacuum tube by the transistor and the availability of large-capacity rotating disk memories. Without transistors, the higher level of reliability required by on-line systems would have been economically infeasible, and, without disk memories, the critical central storage for communal programs and data would not have been possible.

By the early 1960s, work on different implementations of the computer utility vision had begun at various places. The Cambridge area was particularly active, largely due to the influence of McCarthy. Some of the first working prototypes were the following: at M.I.T., the Compatible Time Sharing System (CTSS) of F. J. Corbató, initially on an IBM 709 (1961) and, later, the IBM 7090 and 7094 (1963); also at M.I.T., the DEC PDP-1 System of J. B. Dennis; and, at the Bolt Beranek and Newman Company in Cambridge, MA, a DEC PDP-1-based time-sharing system developed by a team consisting of J. McCarthy, S. Boilen, E. Fredkin, and J. C. R. Licklider. Other early influential prototypes were the Dartmouth College Basic System of J. Kemeny and T. Kurtz, initially implemented on a GE 235; the JOSS System implemented at the Rand Corporation by C. Shaw; and, at the System Development Corporation, a time-sharing system developed by J. Schwartz for the AN/FSQ-32 military computer. The emphasis differed in each case. CTSS was oriented toward a general-purpose service offered by a central computing service; this system was to become the initial research vehicle of Project MAC, an M.I.T. research laboratory organized by R. M. Fano to explore the implications of time-sharing and human-machine interactions. The M.I.T. PDP-1 system was organized to allow each user direct control of input/output (I/O) devices in native machine language, but with protection from other users, so that each user was presented with a virtual machine capable of running arbitrary programs. The BBN PDP-1 system was oriented toward an environment for interactive program development that included the use of a high-performance graphical display. The Dartmouth System focused on introducing computing to nonprofessionals with the constrained, but easy to learn, Basic Language; the JOSS system focused on a carefully human-engineered computational programming interface; and the developers of the AN/FSQ-32 system were interested in similar objectives to those of CTSS, but in the context of developing and maintaining large programs for military applications.

The above time-sharing systems, while among the earliest and more significant, were not the only ones developed in the 1960s. Rather, they display some of the variety of objectives and directions taken. With hardware obsolescence, none of the systems has survived in original form. Most time-shared systems are now used either for specialized purposes, such as applications involving common databases or for communal sharing of a high-performance workstation (*q.v.*) among a few users. Nevertheless, the early time-sharing systems have had direct influence on almost all forms of interactive computing, frequently by the students of one system becoming the designers and implementors of the next.

Particularly important to the early growth of time sharing was J. C. R. Licklider, who, after participating in the implementation of the BBN system, joined the Department of Defense Advanced Research Projects Agency (then called ARPA, now DARPA), where he headed the Information Processing Techniques Branch. Licklider was not only an eloquent advocate of the benefits of time-sharing use, but from his ARPA office was also able to support the development of time-sharing systems at several companies and universities active in computer science research.

By the mid-1960s, time-sharing systems, especially those of M.I.T.'s Project MAC and of Dartmouth College, had attracted considerable attention among computer users, managers, and manufacturers, and the obvious impact of time-sharing systems forced these different groups to reevaluate their roles and the desired modes of computer use. Moreover, development of extensive new time-sharing systems had begun. Among the more notable plans were those for the Multics System (by M.I.T.'s Project Mac, the Bell Telephone Laboratories, and the General Electric Company) and the TSS System (by IBM for the IBM 360/67), which were especially comprehensive in their goals. Indeed, this very comprehensiveness led to underestimations of the scale of the software engineering required. The Multics System, eventually marketed by Honeywell (which had acquired the GE Computer Department), took several years longer to develop than initially anticipated. The TSS System, implemented by a much larger group, was not as delayed as Multics, but had disappointing performance and human interfaces when first delivered. But despite these warning signs of engineering complexity, by the end of the decade, dozens of time-sharing system implementations were being implemented both by ambitious users and by major manufacturers, and time sharing was well recognized as a significant mode of computer interaction.

How Time Sharing Works

The basic notion of how a time-sharing system works is straightforward. The computer can be considered to have, in its main high-speed memory, the programs for each of its users, as well as a master supervisory program (sometimes called an *executive* or *monitor*) under whose control the on-line system runs. The role of the supervisor is to commutate sequentially the central processor through the programs associated with the users, running each for a brief burst of time (often called a *quantum* or *time slice - q.v.*). One can imagine a simple form of such a system with *n* terminals and up to *n* users, each with a program area in the main computer memory which also contains the supervisor program (see Fig. 1). Of course, any program that is waiting for input from its associated user terminal does not need processor time, nor does a program that completes its immediate computation in less than a quantum need the remainder of the quantum allotted to it. In the simplest or *round robin* case, where all the user programs are cycled through in order, the programs appear to their users to proceed as if they each had the computer all alone, albeit one that appears to operate slower on extensive requests.

To carry out the above scheme effectively requires three hardware features beyond the basic von Neumann computer (*q.v.*). The first feature is a program settable "alarm" clock (sometimes called an *interval timer*), which the supervisor can use to interrupt user programs that are not finished after their quantum of time. The second feature is a privileged operation mode for the supervisor, not permitted to the user, which allows only the supervisor to execute the powerful instructions for initiating I/O operations, setting the alarm clock, etc; the effect is that any user program misbehavior, intentional or unintentional, causes program control to revert to the supervisory program. The third feature is a pair of *bounds registers*, set by the supervisor, that can be compared with each memory access attempted by the processor. As with the user mode, any attempt by a user program to reference a location outside of its area in memory automatically causes program control to revert or *trap* (*q.v.*) into the supervisor program. The important aspect of these three features is that the supervisor program can never lose control of the computer, no matter how undebugged or misprogrammed

a user program might be. Furthermore, one user program can be prevented from interfering with, or even reading, the programs or data of another user.

Consequences   There are several technical and sociological consequences and observations one can observe about the above time-sharing framework. The first is that, since users have human response times, the necessary input and output data rates may be limited. With simple text-oriented terminals, telephone lines are usually adequate for user communication, and they can be conveniently located remotely. However, this very remoteness introduces anonymity and the need for the supervisor program to authenticate user identities to prevent improper computer use or program access. Simple password schemes usually suffice to identify users at "login" time for ordinary applications, but, when sensitive data is involved, cryptographic techniques and secure communications may also be necessary. (*See* CRYPTOGRAPHY, COMPUTERS IN.)

A further consequence of users communicating with the central computers at relatively low data rates is that, for users to have significant amounts of programs and data available conveniently for processing, it is necessary to store the programs and data centrally on some storage medium, typically a disk memory. But this central storage in turn creates a requirement for great storage reliability so that users feel it is safe to leave the results of many months or years of work inside the system. To ensure such reliability, most time-sharing installations periodically record "backup" copies, typically on magnetic tape, of the centrally stored information so that, even in the event of a severe system failure or "crash" that garbles the contents of the on-line storage, it is possible to restore operation with possibly only slight loss of the most recently modified information.

Time sharing demands rapid interactive responsiveness and high overall system reliability. In general, users,

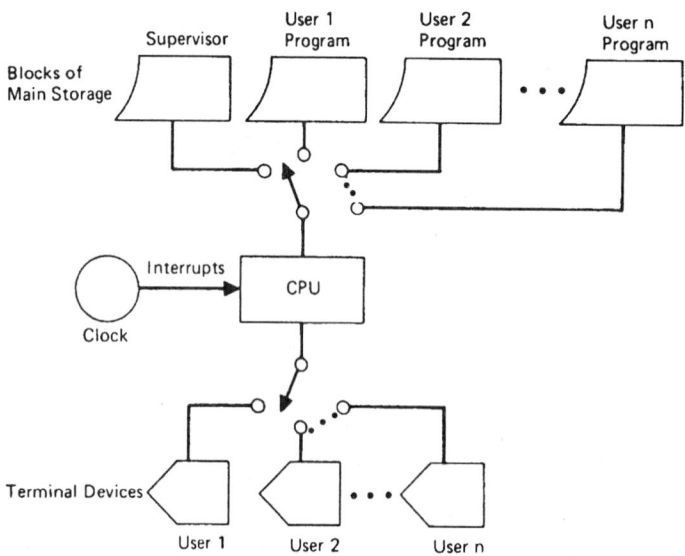

FIG. 1.   A highly simplified time-sharing system.

when devoting their attention to using the system, have no fruitful activity to perform if forced to wait too long for computer responses. Users, if required to wait, become quickly frustrated, much as if they were conversing with an exceedingly slow-speaking person. Similarly, if system outages occur with any frequency, users will experience severe frustration with the system undependability, since they will normally not have any contingency work to perform.

Properly managed, time-sharing systems are analogous to electric and telephone utilities in that they should have sufficient processing power, primary memory, and other computing resources to accommodate the peak computing load of the maximum number of users while maintaining good response times for modest requests. One of the potential advantages of time-sharing systems is that the pooling of resources required allows any individual user to have infrequent but large bursts of memory or processing demands. As a consequence, the effective allocation and management of resources is a fundamental requirement of time-sharing supervisor programs. Of course, resource management is also a requirement of any operating system, but because time-sharing systems must be responsive to human users and because allocations and de-allocations often occur in fractions of a second, the supervisor program must be particularly well designed and constructed. Moreover, the supervisor, in the case of utility-like operation, should not only be able to keep track of each user's resource usage, but also, for effective administrative control, should be able to prevent a user from exceeding individually preset resource allocations.

Supervisor Techniques

The required supervisor resource allocations extend over many devices, but most critical are those of the processor (or processors in more elaborate systems) and the primary memory. For processor management, the basic alarm or interrupt clock described earlier allows straightforward switching from user to user under the policies of a *scheduling algorithm*. However, the case of *memory management (q.v.)* is more difficult.

The simplest case of memory management occurs in the rare circumstance when the primary memory is larger than the space required by the sum of the user program sizes; then a fixed mapping of user programs to memory suffices. The next level of complication is when the sum of user program sizes exceeds the physical memory capacity, and it is necessary that user programs be "swapped" in and out of the primary memory from a secondary memory device (e.g. a disk) whenever processor service is requested. *Swapping (q.v.)* although conceptually simple, has the disadvantage that when user program sizes become large and comparable to the size of main memory, the processor often is idle while waiting for programs to be swapped in and out. It is to avoid the complications of simple swapping strategies for memory management that the most sophisticated time-sharing systems use a *virtual memory (q.v.)*.

With virtual memory, the main memory is divided into equal sized blocks, typically 512 or 1,024 words, and each user program is divided into *pages* of the same size as the blocks. The supervisor, then, when bringing a program into memory for service, has only the job of finding enough available blocks. It need not consider location or order in memory of these blocks, since the processor has special page-mapping hardware that allows it to make the program virtual address correspond to the correct physical block. The final refinement of memory management occurs with the strategy of *demand paging*, where the majority of the pages of a user program are not even brought in until the program, while executing, attempts to reference them. In this way, the unnecessary loading of never exercised program sections is avoided.

Supervisor Services

Time-sharing supervisors also need to manage secondary storage resources, such as magnetic tapes and disk packs. To the extent that storage devices are removable, the supervisor must, of course, mediate a dialogue between an operator at the central facility and a user making a request for mounting or dismounting. However, the most important service the supervisor provides is a *file system*, which maps the physical storage resources into a logical framework that users can address in their programs.

File systems at their simplest offer each user a *directory (q.v.)* into which a collection of user-named programs or data may be stored, usually without great concern for the physical location of the stored information. In the better-organized systems, users are selectively able to share *segments* of stored information with other users and have detailed control over which users (or user classes) and precisely what kinds of access (e.g. read-only, read-write, append-only) are allowed to each segment.

The most elaborate time-sharing supervisors also provide a large collection of elementary services. One such service, usually supported by special hardware, is a non-recycling calendar clock to provide users with a unique time-stamp for such purposes as branding successive generations of information, preserving event sequences, and facilitating the purging of obsolete files by age or last use. Other services typically include support for a large variety of competitive brands of terminals, including both typewriter-like units and video displays.

Interactive Software Services

Time-sharing supervisors are similar to any large operating system in that they offer extensive libraries of subroutines, and often a choice of many programming languages. But, in addition, the interactive environment allows several important new services. One such service is the ability of a user to detach and leave as a batch job an otherwise interactive program along with the anticipated input that the program will need when run automatically at a later time. Thus, in many instances, a time-sharing system combines the virtues of both interactive and batch processing.

A second class of service that becomes feasible with time sharing consists of language and debugging systems that are exclusively designed around interactive use. One of the earliest examples was the Joss system; other examples are the APL, Basic, and Lisp language systems that are in wide use today.

A third service is that of *electronic mail (q.v.)* wherein user A can send a message to user B, directly if B is present and logged in at a terminal, or, if not, indirectly by leaving the message in B's mail box (i.e. a special file in user B's directory). The service resembles a high-speed telegraph system, especially if the time-sharing computer is linked by networking with other such computers geographically distant.

A fourth service, which originated with time-sharing and today is the mainstay of word processing on personal computers, is the easy manipulation of natural language text and document preparation. Most systems have one or more *editor* programs that allow a user to type and edit a manuscript as it is written and revised. On-line editor programs often have powerful global features (e.g. change all occurrences of "which" to "that" in the entire manuscript) and with the advent of fast communications and flexible display terminals, frequently have intricate interfaces and behavior. Hand-in-hand with editors are document preparation programs that, when combined with appropriate output devices, are analogous to phototypesetting machines. Thus, by proper preparation of a manuscript file with suitable embedded instructions for the document preparation program, it is possible to produce output files that can be directly fed into laser-driven xerographic printers or other equally versatile typesetting systems (*see* DESKTOP PUBLISHING and POSTSCRIPT).

The effect of on-line editors and document preparation programs is to transform a user into a combined author, typist, proofreader, editor, layout artist, publisher, and printer. Time-sharing systems characteristically have extensive documentation and "help" files available for on-line perusal. Such files minimize or eliminate the need to reference laboriously the many volumes of conventional printed documentation.

Future Directions There were several original motivations for time sharing. They included reducing user costs, allowing interactive program use, and the possibility of users operating as a community and conveniently sharing or exchanging information, data, and programs. As the cost of both computational logic and communications technology declines, new system arrangements are developing where each time-sharing system may be a node in a large network of other computer systems all connected together with high bandwidth packet communications. Furthermore, many of these other computer systems may be workstations or personal computers being operated by a single user. Even one person may have many computing processes proceeding simultaneously—one attached to the terminal, others managing I/O equipment, and some doing background computation (*see* MULTITASKING). In the limit, one has a large network connecting nothing but one-person time-sharing systems. With a network of such personal machines, in effect, one has both distributed and replicated the functionality of the time-sharing supervisor. Perhaps the greatest advantage of such a structure is that it also partitions the engineering design of the system, allows greater heteroge-

neity of software and hardware modules, and thereby allows easier system construction and evolution. Nevertheless, such distributed forms of time-sharing systems involving personal computers, if they are to be complete, must include the same user functions and services as a centrally operated time-sharing system, and it is the magnitude of design and engineering effort required to create such systems on modest-sized hardware units that prevents rapid revolutionary changes. Furthermore, there will always remain computational tasks so intensive that, in order to produce useful and timely results, they will require a single, large computer system. Moreover, some applications such as multiple user database systems may still require time-sharing systems for adequate interactive response.

Thus, it seems likely that the inner structures of time-sharing systems will continue to evolve as the economics and engineering convenience factors dictate; but it also seems clear that the key advantages which time-sharing systems introduce—those of convenient interactive service and elaborate software functions—will survive indefinitely.

References

1962. McCarthy, J. "Time-Sharing Computer Systems," in Greenberger, Martin (Ed.), *Computers and the World of the Future* (originally published as *Management and the Computer of the Future*). Cambridge: M.I.T. Press.

1975. Wilkes, M. V. *Time Sharing Computer Systems.* 3rd Ed. New York: Elsevier.

1983. Christian, K. *The Unix Operating System.* New York: John Wiley.

1987. Tanenbaum, Andrew W. *Operating Systems: Design and Implementation.* Englewood Cliffs, NJ: Prentice-Hall.

F. J. CORBATÓ

TIME SLICE

For articles on related subjects *see* SCHEDULING ALGORITHM; SWAPPING; and TIME SHARING.

In the late 1950s and early 1960s, computer systems were envisioned that could be used simultaneously by several people, each at a typewriter-like terminal, each appearing to have exclusive use of the computer. The computer was to take advantage of the typing time of one user by turning its attention to another. If the computational tasks requested were short enough, then all users could be serviced, and the illusion of a single-user private computer is maintained. Early systems served less than a dozen people, whereas modern systems service 10 to 1,000 or more. But what if there were one or more very long computational tasks?

Time slicing provided a part of the answer. At the end of each time slice (or *quantum*) of, say, 100 ms, the operating system interrupts the current user program and turns its attention to other user requests, usually held in a FIFO queue (*q.v.*), before returning to the interrupted program for another slice of time. A variety of scheduling algorithms were developed whose purpose was to maintain high-speed response to terminal requests with reasonable computer efficiency. Multiplexing (*q.v.*) among compute-bound programs (i.e. ones that require I/O only at relatively long intervals) by time slicing uses the machine less efficiently than serial run-to-completion because a certain amount of time is required to switch from program to program. Also, longer average start-to-finish turnaround times (*q.v.*) occur: Serially run, two equal jobs finish at time *n* and 2*n* (for an average turnaround of 3*n*/2); with time slicing, both finish in somewhat more than 2*n* for an average of somewhat more than 2*n*. But the important characteristics of time sharing and time slicing are high-speed response to many short computational requests and nearly continuous access to the machine; total problem turnaround time is a secondary consideration.

Early systems, which often took care of the low-speed terminal I/O with a separate "front-end" computer (and some still do) were driven exclusively by the time-slice clock and ignored the loss of CPU time incurred by the inability to overlap it with I/O to disk file and tape. The loss became more pronounced as time-sharing system applications became more sophisticated. Explicit interrupt signals from the I/O hardware, together with the later introduction of multiple programs in memory, combined to give the new operating systems both knowledge of possible overlaps of I/O and CPU execution, and means of making use of these periods of time. Some modern systems can achieve 95% CPU use together with significant concurrent use of swapping and file I/O devices.

The event-driven systems, which required the operating system to make a scheduling decision (for each time slice, I/O, and other events) ran the risk of spending too much time deciding and not enough time doing. To solve this problem, Xerox's UTS and CP-V, and later CP-6 on Honeywell Bull computers, adopted two control quanta in addition to the primary time-slicing quantum. One of these established a minimum interval between changes from program to program, regardless of the importance of the intervening events; it thus established a lower bound on the system overhead incurred in such changes. The second provided corresponding control and minimums for swapping, allowing a program to execute for a minimum period (if needed) before swapping is permitted.

Modern workstations (*q.v.*) for individual users have much higher performance than the time-sharing systems that were so carefully shared, so the need for algorithmic care is much less. Moreover, the algorithms are being rediscovered and re-used as multitasking workstations evolve to serve the individual with multiple concurrently executing processes.

Reference

1985. Peterson, James L. and Silberschatz, Abraham. *Operating System Concepts*. Menlo Park, CA: Addison-Wesley.

G. EDWARD BRYAN

TOMOGRAPHY, COMPUTERIZED

For articles on related subjects *see* BIOCOMPUTING; COMPUTER GRAPHICS; IMAGE PROCESSING; MEDICAL APPLICATIONS; MEDICAL IMAGING; OPTIMIZATION METHODS; and PATTERN-RECOGNITION.

Tomography is defined in Webster as "a diagnostic technique using X-ray photographs in which the shadows of structures before and behind the section under scrutiny do not show." The origin of the word *tomography* is Greek, in which "tomos" means "section." *Computerized tomography* (CT) is a relatively recent development in which only the section under scrutiny is irradiated, and a computer (rather than an X-ray film) is used to produce an image of the section. (An alternative abbreviation used for the same process is CAT, for *computer-assisted tomography*, and hence the result of applying the technology is called a CAT-Scan.) CT produces images of cross-sections of the human body from measured attenuation of X-rays through the cross-section. Since the appearance of the first commercial CT scanner in 1972 (built by EMI, Ltd.), CT has revolutionized diagnostic radiology. The 1979 Nobel prize in medicine was awarded to Allan M. Cormack and Godfrey N. Hounsfield for their pioneering contributions to the development of CT.

An engineering drawing of a typical CT scanner (one built by the General Electric Company) is shown in Fig. 1. The patient lies on the table, and the table's sliding top moves into the hole of the gantry, which in turn houses the X-ray tube and collimator on one side (the collimator limits the X-ray beam to the section under scrutiny) and the data acquisition/detector unit on the other side. The detector unit contains a large number of detectors (typically about a thousand) arranged on an arc of a circle centered at the X-ray source. X-rays travel along straight lines between the source and the detectors. From the strength of the X-ray beam reaching the detector, we can estimate the total X-ray attenuation along the line between the source and the detector. Since tissues and tumors of different types attenuate X-rays differently, such measurements provide information regarding the cross-section of the body which lies in the plane of the X-ray source and the detectors.

If we keep the X-ray source and detector assembly stationary and slide the patient through the gantry, we can obtain an image similar to images obtained in traditional X-ray film radiography. Such an image is shown at the top left of Fig. 2. Intensities in this image are representative of total X-ray attenuation between source and detector. The image is built up row by row, each row corresponding to a separate incremental position of the patient through the gantry. The intensities in each row correspond to the total X-ray attenuations as measured by the array of detectors. The difficulty with such an output as a diagnostic tool is that images of bones, organs, air spaces, and any existing tumors overlap. It is often impossible to determine the exact nature, or even the presence, of a tumor.

In CT, the body is kept stationary while the gantry rotates around it. This way, we obtain an image of the type

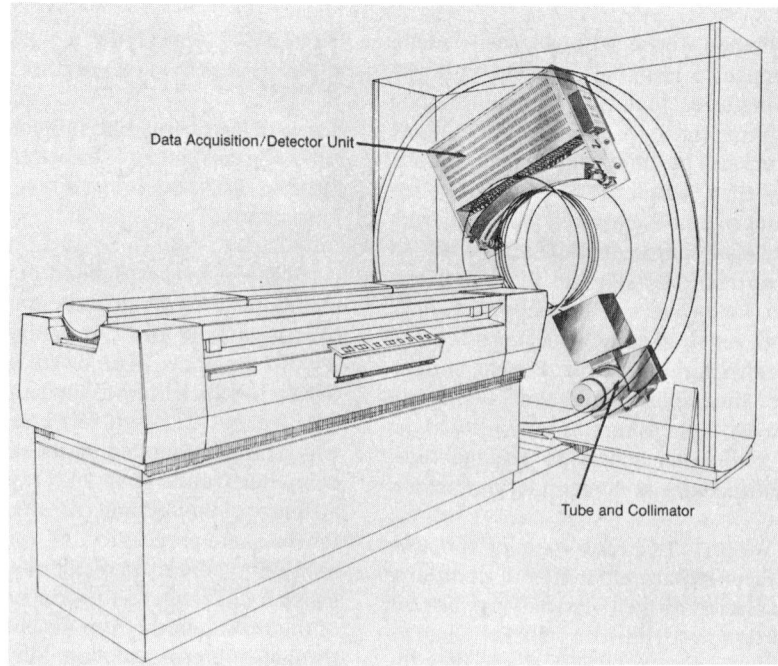

Data Acquisition/Detector Unit

Tube and Collimator

FIG. 1. Engineering drawing of a typical CT scanner. *(Courtesy General Electric Co.)*

shown at the top right of Fig. 2. This image is also built up row by row, but now each row corresponds to a separate incremental position of the gantry as it rotates around the patient. The interpretation of intensities in each row is the same as before.

The total X-ray attenuation between a source and a detector is the integral of a physical parameter called the "X-ray attenuation coefficient" along the line from the source to the detector. Since the X-ray attenuation coefficient at a point in the cross-section is indicative of the tissue (or tumor) type at that point, it is diagnostically useful to obtain a distribution of the X-ray attenuation coefficient in cross-sections of the human body. Measurements by the CT scanner (as represented by Fig. 2 top right) provide us with estimates of the integrals of this distribution along a large number of lines of known location.

A schematic representation of such a situation is shown in Fig. 3. The distribution of X-ray attenuation coefficients is indicated by a function of two polar variables $f(r,\varphi)$. The X-ray source moves in a circle around the origin 0, taking projections at M distinct locations $S_1,\ldots, S_M$. Let $L_{j,n}$ denote the line from S_j to the center of the nth (of an array of $2N + 1$ detectors. Then the measurement for the jth position of the X-ray source at the nth detector is approximately the line integral

$$\int_{L_{j,n}} f(r,\varphi)\, ds$$

where ds is the incremental distance from source to detector. Hence, we are faced with the following computational problem: Given estimates of the integrals of an unknown function of two variables along a number of lines of known

location, estimate the values of the function at a number of points of given location.

The desired clinical information mandates that we estimate the function at a large number (typically, 10^5-10^6) of closely spaced (typically, less than 1 mm in each direction) points. Accordingly, data is collected for 10^5-10^6 source/detector positions. For such a device to be useful, computational turnaround has to be rapid, and computational costs (which are eventually paid by the patients) have to be kept low. Thus, we are faced with an unusually large computational problem that has to be solved rapidly and inexpensively. Ingenious computational procedures have made the state of the art such that an image of a cross-section (such as shown at the bottom right of Fig. 2) can be produced from the data in less than a second by a minicomputer complemented by a standard array processor.

An example of a reconstruction method is the following. Mathematical analysis of the problem leads to three functions, p, q, and w, such that

$$f(r,\varphi) \simeq \sum_{j=1}^{M} w(r,\varphi, \beta_j)\left[\sum_{n=-N}^{N} q(p(r,\varphi, \beta_j)n\sigma)g_{j,n}\right],$$

where the $g_{j,n}$ form the measurement data (approximations to the line integrals defined above) and $f(r,\varphi)$ is the distribution to be reconstructed. The functions p, q, and w are chosen independently of data; the important fact is that they can be chosen so that the approximation indicated above is close for the class of functions $f(r,\varphi)$ that we desire to reconstruct.

The approximation as shown above implies that a separate double sum has to be calculated for each point

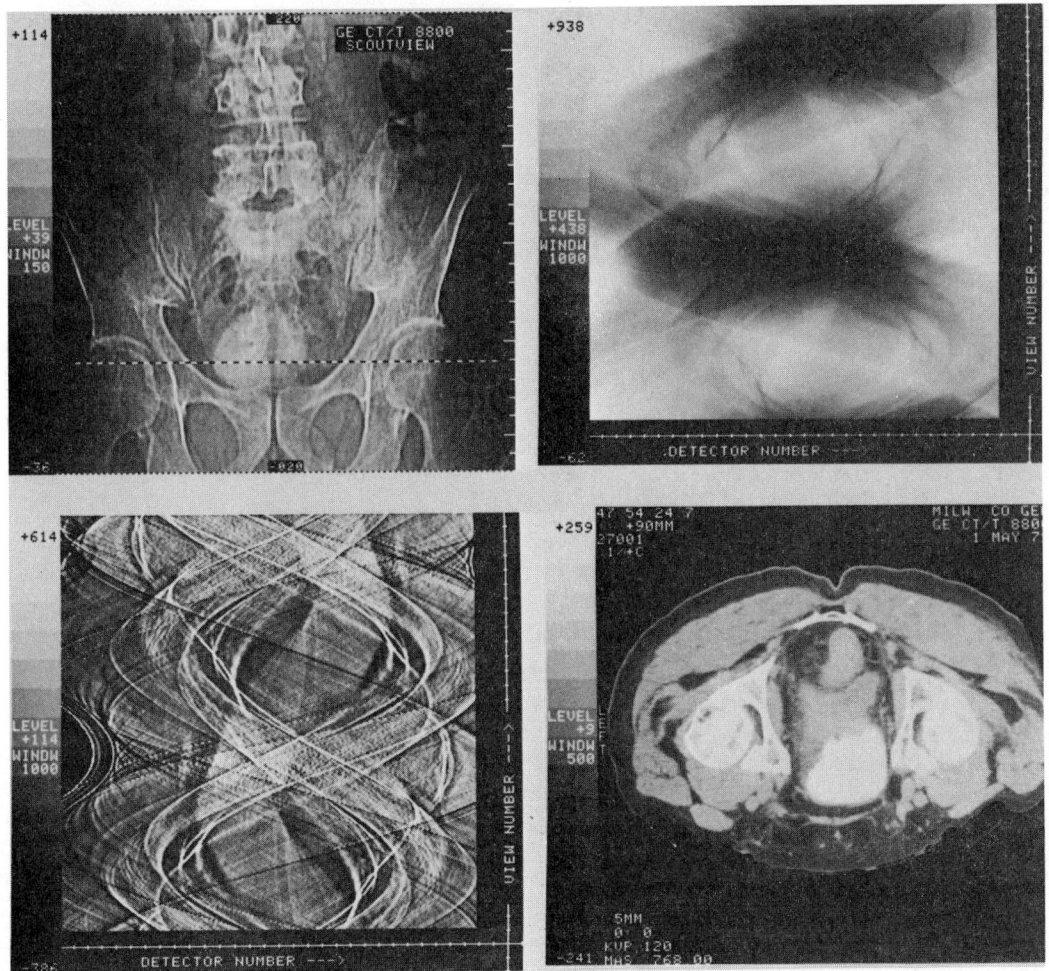

FIG. 2. *Top left:* Scout View (a General Electric Trademark) obtained by sliding a patient through the stationary gantry of a CT scanner. The cross-section of interest is marked by a broken line. *Top right:* Projection data for the cross-section indicated on the left, obtained by rotating the gantry around a stationary patient (see also Fig. 3). These data are referred to in the text as $g_{j,n'}$. *Bottom left:* The modified projection data referred to in the text as $g'_{j,n}$. *Bottom right:* The CT reconstruction of the cross-section of interest. *(Illustration provided by Dr. G. H. Glover.)*

(r,φ) at which the reconstructed value is to be obtained. Significant speed-up is obtained by the following observation: For a fixed j, the value of the inner sum is the same for all points (r,φ) that lie on the same line $L_{j,n'}$. For $1 \leq j \leq M$ and $-N \leq n' \leq N$,

$$g'_{j,n'} = \sum_{\substack{n=-N \\ (r,\varphi)\in L_{j,n'}}}^{N} q(p(r,\varphi,\beta_j),n\sigma)g_{j,n}.$$

The bottom left of Fig. 2 is a pictorial representation of g', in the same way as the top right of Fig. 2 is a pictorial representation of g. In practice, for each j, the $g'_{j,n'}$ are calculated from the $g_{j,n}$ by the formula given above. Note that this can be done independently for the different j's. Special-purpose array processors are usually used for the independent calculations of these sums. The estimation of $f(r,\varphi)$ is then done by using interpolation of the $g'_{j,n'}$ to estimate the values of the inner sum for a given j, r, and φ. These processes are usually implemented in firmware (*q.v.*).

The field of study dedicated to such computer algorithms is referred to as *image reconstruction from projections*. A book devoted to this topic was written by Herman in 1980. The usefulness of image reconstruction goes way beyond CT. Essentially the same computational procedure has been found useful in many other areas of science and medicine, such as radioastronomy, solar physics, nuclear medicine, and physiology (see Herman, 1979). There are a number of journals that are largely or wholly devoted to CT; two examples are *Computerized Tomography* and the *Journal of Computer-Assisted Tomography*.

Recent developments in CT include scanners that are fast enough (both physically and computationally) to reconstruct the beating heart inside the intact thorax and display of the appearance of organs, using computer graphics, based on a sequence of computerized tomograms. (See Udupa and Herman, 1990, for details, and Fig. 4, color insert page CP-12, for an example.) These capabilities justify describing the medical procedures with such machines as *noninvasive vivisection*.

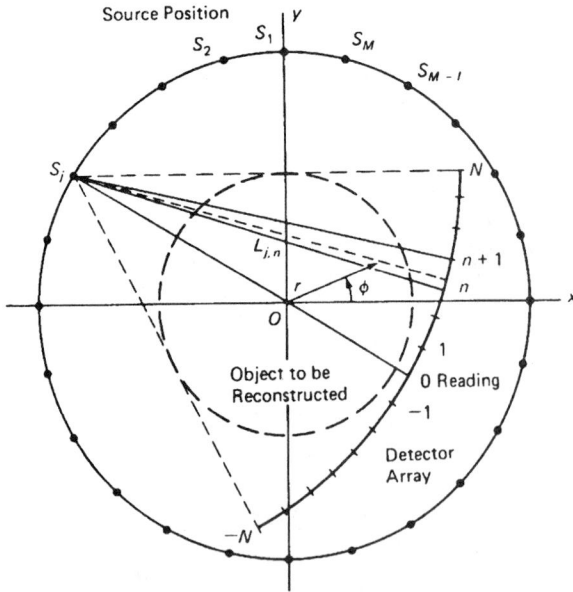

FIG. 3. A schematic drawing showing the lines along which integrals of the X-ray attenuation coefficient distribution in the cross-section are assumed to be collected. *(Reprinted with the permission of G. T. Herman and A. Naparstek, from* "Fast Image Reconstruction Based on a Radon Inversion Formula Appropriate for Rapidly Collected Data," *SIAM J. Appl. Math.* **33**: 511-533, 1977.)

References

1979. Herman, G. T. (Ed.). *Image Reconstruction from Projections. Implementation and Applications.* Berlin: Springer-Verlag.

1980. Herman, G. T. *Image Reconstruction from Projections: The Fundamentals of Computerized Tomography.* New York: Academic Press.

1990. Udupa, J. U. and Herman, G. T. *3-D Imaging in Medicine.* Boca Raton, FL: Lewis Publishers.

GABOR T. HERMAN

TOP-DOWN DESIGN. *See* STRUCTURED PROGRAMMING.

TORRES QUEVEDO, LEONARDO

Don Leonardo Torres Quevedo was born on 28 December 1852 in Santa Cruz de Inguña, Santander, northern Spain. He grew up in Bilbao, in the Spanish Basque country and was educated there up to secondary school level. He spent two years at a Catholic school in France before joining the exclusive *Escuela de Caminos*, in Madrid, organized on the model of the French École de Ponts et Chaussées. He graduated from there in 1876.

A bequest from distant relatives allowed him to develop his scientific interests without financial worries. After extensive travelling in Europe, he alternated life in Madrid and at his country home in the north with occa-

FIG. 1. Torres Quevedo

sional journeys abroad, mainly to France, where he became friendly with several leading scientists. One of them, Maurice d'Ocagne, publicized Torres Quevedo's work on calculating machines.

In the early 1890s Torres Quevedo became interested in the mechanical representation of general algebraic and transcendental expressions. By 1893, he had designed a machine based on a series of devices, called *arithmophores*, capable of handling monomial expressions. Polynomials were constructed by an original use of a mechanical analogue of Gauss' additive logarithms. A quite large range for the argument was made accessible through an ingenious use of logarithmic scales. To preserve high accuracy, all contacts between parts of his machine were geometric, i.e. dependent only on the geometry of the mechanisms.

His machine was theoretically capable of estimating the real (positive) roots of any given algebraic equation. He also showed how to proceed in the cases of complex roots and in that of special types of transcendental equations. A prototype, capable of solving trinomial equations of degree less than 10, was built in France on his orders and shown in 1895 at a meeting of the French Association for the Advancement of Science. Details of this machine were reported in the proceedings of the French Academy of Science in 1895.

The design of Torres Quevedo's early calculating machines is closely related to d'Ocagne's ideas on *nomography*, which he interpreted in mechanical terms with remarkable originality.

His designs rested on a new, more comprehensive *kinematic* definition of machines, which departed from the classical one given by A. M. Ampère and also from the more modern of R. Willis. Theoretical questions became central to Torres Quevedo's interests; in 1901, he read a paper at the Academy of Sciences, Madrid, in which he dealt with the question of the definition of algebraic machines. His paper was translated into French the following year. In 1914, at the same Academy he read his interesting *Essay on Automatics* (Randell, 1973). Like Babbage, Torres Quevedo confronted the problem of describing complicated pieces of machinery; in 1906 he proposed a system of notations and symbols to facilitate such descriptions.

In later work, Torres Quevedo moved away from geometrically modeled calculating machines, making use of electrical and electromechanical devices. In 1903, he started a series of experiments on telecontrol by radio signals with a machine he called the *Telekino*. He was able to control the movements of a small boat at sea from a distance of several kilometers. This work was related to the design of radio controlled torpedos.

By 1906, a group of leading Spanish scientists and scholars requested official support for Torres Quevedo's research work. This initiative resulted in the creation of a national Institute of Applied Mechanics, later called the Institute of Automatics, in Madrid.

In 1910, he read a paper on electromechanical calculating machines at the National Engineering Society, in Buenos Aires, Argentina, in which he stressed the importance of discussing an *abstract* automatic machine, rather than a specific practical implementation. An enlarged version of this paper was published in the proceedings of the French Academy of Science in 1920.

These ideas were later implemented in a number of mechanical and electromechanical calculating devices built at his Institute in Madrid in the 1910s and 1920s. An advanced electromechanical calculator was shown in Paris in 1920. It operated with numbers of three to five digits. Depending on the operation, the result was a number of up to seven digits. It stored numbers in electromechanical units and had an electrical device to compare the size of numbers. The latter was useful for accelerating divisions. Output and input was effected through one or several typewriters that could be at some distance from the machine. A central station controlled the sequence of operations from input to calculation and printing.

In 1912, Torres Quevedo finished a working model of his well known electromechanical chess playing machine, which he showed in Paris two years later. A more elaborate model was built with the help of his son Gonzalo in 1920. Torres Quevedo's interest in chess-playing and calculating machines was, again, influenced by his desire to show the possibilities that existed in the field of electromechanical automation.

He also did substantial work in other fields of engineering, particularly on aerial cablecars and large airships. His best known design for aerial cablecars is the one over the Whirlpool of the Niagara River in Ontario, Canada, near Niagara Falls, which was commissioned in 1916 and is still operational.

Torres Quevedo had close contact with the industrial and financial community of the Basque Country, where industry was developing fast by the turn of the century. Some of his projects were financially supported by colleagues and friends from that area. In the early years of this century, a private mechanical engineering company was formed in Bilbao to develop his inventions. Calculat-

ing machines, however, remained outside his commercial interests.

He began experiments with airships with a flexible structure in Spain, at a state institute created for him near Madrid. Later models were built in France by the company Astra under the name of Astra-Torres; they played a role in the First World War. Torres Quevedo was also interested in problems of scientific and technical documentation. As a member of the Royal Spanish Academy of Science, where he concentrated a substantial part of his scientific activities, he promoted the publication of a dictionary of new scientific and technical terms with the aim of unifying their use in the Spanish-speaking world. He died in Madrid in 1936.

References

1973. Randell, B. *The Origins of Digital Computers*. New York: Springer-Verlag.

EDUARDO L. ORITZ

TOUCHSCREEN. *See* INTERACTIVE INPUT DEVICES.

TRACE

For articles on related subjects *see* DEBUGGING; and PROCEDURE ORIENTED LANGUAGES: PROGRAMMING.

A *trace* is a debugging aid consisting of a display that chronicles the actions and results of individual steps in a program; the term is sometimes used for a control program that produces this kind of display.

The debugging process precipitates countless problems whose correction may require a detailed stepwise record of a program's execution path. A trace is designed to provide this type of information by taking the user's program and placing it under control of a special routine that monitors the progress of the program. Continuous execution of the user's program is replaced by a process whereby the trace program intercedes between steps of the user's program, displaying a variety of material before permitting execution of the next step. Of course, the type of information varies with the particular trace facility; however, the contents of most traces are characterized by such items as a copy of the instruction (or statement for high-level language programs), its location (or line number), and operand and register values before and after execution. In addition, some trace facilities are concerned with the sequence of events in a program, as well as with the history of various data items. In this case, the display will include indications as to whether certain branches have been followed, information about cyclic processes, etc.

Since these facilities are intended specifically for debugging, they are designed so that their insertion and subsequent deletion are straightforward. In many systems, a trace is superimposed by explicit specifications external to the program itself, in which case the request is communicated via the command language to the operating system under which the program functions. In other systems, the trace facilities are packaged in a separate program (a *debugger*) that, when activated, controls the execution of the program under scrutiny.

Because of its iterations, branches, and calls, the execution of even a modest-sized program may involve thousands of individual steps. Consequently, an unfettered trace routine easily can generate hundreds of screenfuls of information, most of which is of no interest. Accordingly, all trace facilities include provisions for damping their zeal. For example, the user may limit the trace to a certain section of the program, allowing the rest of it to execute normally. In addition, one may choose to examine certain variables; if so, the trace output will show only those steps in which the selected variables are affected. Moreover, the user's primary interest may be in the flow of logic, in which case the trace can be restricted to a record of branches, subroutine calls, and other sequence changes.

SEYMOUR V. POLLACK

TRACKBALL. *See* INTERACTIVE INPUT DEVICES.

TRANSACTION PROCESSING

For articles on related subjects *see* ADMINISTRATIVE APPLICATIONS; BANKING APPLICATIONS; DATABASE MANAGEMENT SYSTEM; ELECTRONIC FUNDS TRANSFER SYSTEM; PROCESSING MODES; and TELEPROCESSING SYSTEMS.

In broadest computing terms, *transaction processing* describes the activity performed by a computer upon the introduction of an external stimulus, usually data. A *transaction* consists of a collection of functionally related data elements in combination with a signal that is either explicit (often referred to as a *transaction code*) or implied through the context of the application. The transaction code requests that a particular operation be performed in regard to the associated data elements.

A *transaction process* is the action (or series of actions) performed upon an object. Similar to a sentence, a transaction process requires a noun or object (data) and a verb (action). Data without an action is just inactive or stored data. An action may not be taken unless there is an object upon which to act. A transaction process is often referred to as a *unit of work*.

Transaction processing may be roughly divided into two modes of operation—batch processing and interactive, or *real-time* processing.

Batch Processing In a batch processing mode, transactions are collected into a group, called a *batch*, and processed together in a job initiated by an operator. Batch processing is applicable where large volumes of data must be processed, the immediacy of the data is not critical,

and user interaction is not required. Batch processing of transactions is also useful where a number of relatively static reports must be produced. A classic business example of batch processing is payroll. Individual time documents, which may be reported instantly through a time-capture mechanism, daily or weekly, are collected and periodically processed in scheduled jobs to produce checks, registers, and audit reports. A personal example of batch processing is the manner in which many people collect their bills and pay them at the end of the month. Each bill or invoice (itself the result of a transaction process) is a request that an action (payment) be performed on the associated data. When an individual sits down to write the checks at the end of the month, he or she is in effect processing a batch of transactions. The check resulting from the processing of each transaction is itself a transaction request to the recipient.

On-Line, Real-Time Processing In contrast to batch transaction processing, real-time processing is event-driven. In a real-time processing mode, transactions are acted upon as soon as they are entered into the computing system, thus allowing the user and machine to operate in the same time frame. In this interactive mode of operation, errors may be detected by the system and reported back to the user, who may then take corrective action. The user may ask for help in entering the data, and the results of the transaction process may be instantly reported back to the user. In order for this process to take place, the user must have *on-line* access to the computer.

In most internal business applications, user access is accommodated through the use of a video display terminal (VDT), which utilizes a cathode ray tube (CRT) much like a television receiver. A list of actions which an operator is allowed to perform is displayed on the face of the screen in a form called a *menu*. The operator selects an action by indicating the appropriate option using an attached keyboard or mouse (*q.v.*). Depending upon the complexity of the underlying application, one or more secondary menu screens may be processed before an operator is presented with a screen into which specific data for a transaction may be displayed and/or entered. Data is then typed onto the screen and, when the enter key is depressed, the content of the screen is sent via a telecommunications link to the central computer, where it is edited for completeness and accuracy. If an error condition is detected, a screen is sent back down the telecommunications link to the user with an appropriate error message. The user then makes the required correction and sends the new data back to the central computer. This interactive process, often referred to as a *dialogue*, continues until the transaction information is complete and correct. Depending upon how the application is written, the operator may again be presented with the transaction input and asked to verify the data. After the transaction dialogue is complete, the transaction is processed and the results are presented back to the user along with a request for the user to indicate further action.

Hybrid Processing Transactions may also be processed in a hybrid mode where the dialogue portion of the transaction is processed in a real-time environment and the data entered by the user is stored in a data file for subsequent batch processing. An easily identifiable example of this type of on-line (but not real-time) process may be found with the ubiquitous automated teller machine (ATM). The user is identified to the computer as a result of identification data read from the magnetic strip on the back of the user's ATM access card. The user's legitimacy is verified by entry of a personal identification number (PIN). After the user passes the verification test, a *menu* screen showing the available options of transaction types is displayed. By indicating the desired option using the keypad of the ATM, the user may inquire about account balances, transfer funds between accounts, enter deposits, or make withdrawals. Each of these options is an implied transaction type. When the user indicates that no further transactions are required, a receipt is printed that verifies the transaction(s), money may be provided to the user, and the ATM card is returned.

In the ATM example above, the user's account balances are not normally updated during the transaction process, but rather the transaction data is written to a holding file where the activity is posted to the user's account in a subsequent batch job. This process is often referred to as a "shadow file" update. After the transactions are posted to the accounts, a new shadow file is produced against which subsequent transaction activity is recorded. This type of hybrid transaction processing mode has merit in certain types of activities in that the amount of work performed to meet the end user's needs (in our example, the dialogue verification, and perhaps provision of money) is separated from the operational requirements of the organization which need not be performed in a real-time mode (again in our example, the daily account balancing, posting of interest, audit reports, etc.). This approach allows more mainframe computing resources to be dedicated to maintaining high service levels for the on-line network and allows those functions not requiring interactive response by the end user to be performed when the demand for the on-line system is low.

On-line processing of transactions is useful in applications where the number of transactions from any one point of input at any one time is small, the timeliness of the process is important, and interaction with the user is desirable. On-line transaction processing also allows data to be captured at the source from geographically widespread areas.

Characteristics of Transactions
Transactions fall roughly into two types—inquiry and file maintenance.

Inquiry transactions, which are requests that information be displayed, are most commonly requested and serviced on-line. They may be as simple as looking up a telephone number or as complex as calculating an employee's pension benefit, which requires the examination and analysis of his or her monthly earnings for the past ten years and extensive calculation. Inquiry transactions may also produce a printed report, which may be produced in a batch environment.

File maintenance transactions generally involve modifications to a *master file* or database. The user has the ability to add data to the file, delete data from the file, or change or update data currently on file. Whether it is better to perform these transactions in a batch or real-time mode depends upon the application. For example, updating a telephone directory might best be served in a batch update, due to the large volume of transaction data and the large number of telephone directories that must be produced. Additionally, the transactions are relatively simple, little user interaction is required, and the immediacy of the update is not critical. Making an airline reservation is a good use of real-time transaction processing in that the person making the reservation has decisions to make based on available data and timeliness is critical.

Transaction Structure   An on-line transaction process consists of several different steps:

- Obtain access—This step gets the computer's attention and is normally performed once in a session in which multiple transactions may be processed. Teleprocessing applications continuously poll terminals to see if any users are out there waiting for service or, in the case of a dial-up network, a new terminal has entered the network. Obtaining access may involve dialing a telephone number, entering a card such as an ATM card, depressing the enter key on a keyboard, or any other action that starts the process.
- Verify—With on-line applications, the application must assure that the person at the terminal is authorized to have access to the information being requested. The user is asked to enter a password (such as a PIN) or some other piece of information to which only the specific user should have access. Normally, this step is performed only once, but, depending upon the complexity of the application, may be done when a user crosses major functional areas of the application.
- Dialogue—Once the user has obtained access to the system and the identity of the user has been verified, the transaction process presents a screen or series of screens to determine the type of transaction the user wishes to perform and collect the data required to perform the transaction. During the dialogue, data entered by the user is edited and, where errors are detected, the user is given an opportunity to enter corrections. Many applications also allow the user to request *help screens*, which provide additional information to aid the user in entering the transaction data.
- Process the transaction—When the data has been entered and edited and the process has been determined, the central computer performs the requested action, either processing the update or retrieving the data that is to be displayed.
- Confirmation—Once the transaction has been processed, the user is presented with the results of the transaction (as in the case of an inquiry trans-

action) or confirmation that the transaction process has been completed. The application then returns control to the dialogue portion of the process to allow additional transactions to be entered and operated upon. The user is also presented with an option that there are no further transactions to be processed in which case the application disconnects the user.

The time required for an on-line system to complete the processing of a transaction and return the results to the user on a terminal is called *response time*. While the user is entering data, the computer is idle (in relation to the transaction being entered). When the enter key is depressed and the data is sent to the computer for processing, the user is idle while the transaction is being processed. Only when one transaction is complete may the user commence work on another. By separating a transaction into smaller discrete units of work, the amount of work to be performed by the mainframe with each exchange of data over the teleprocessing link is smaller, resulting in faster response to the user. This separation of function into smaller units of work enhances transaction throughput (the number of transactions which may be processed in a given period of time).

Transaction processing is becoming increasingly available to the general public. In addition to the ATM example above, tone generating telephones may also be used as communication terminals between computers and end users. The user dials a telephone number that completes the log-on process to a computer in the same way as an ATM card is entered to permit access to the ATM network. Depending upon the sensitivity of the information requested, the user may be asked to enter an account number and perhaps even a PIN and will then be presented with an oral menu. Output to the user is in the form of voice response. Scanning devices used in grocery stores and retail outlets are also examples of on-line transaction processing. Many hotels now allow their guests to complete the room check-out process using the television screen and the remote control keypad in the room.

The current trend in business is moving away from simple display and entry type of non-programmable or *dumb* terminals, such as those discussed above, and increasingly towards the use of programmable or *intelligent* terminals. These intelligent terminals (often called programmable workstations) are actually personal computers that are connected to mainframe computers via telecommunication links. These devices allow information to be displayed using graphical images, called *icons*, and capture information using a pointing device such as a mouse or, for the more casual user, touch sensitive screens. One major advantage of using icons is that they allow applications to be written in a manner much more intuitive to users. Traditional transaction processing requires the user to perform a series of actions (such as menu selections) before an object (such as a screen) is presented, where in the real world, users are presented with an object and then determine the action to be taken.

The use of the intelligent workstation in transaction processing also permits the work performed in the processing of a transaction to be shared between a central mainframe, which must service many users at the same time, and the workstation, which is a resource dedicated to a single user at a time. Just as transaction processing as described in the ATM example has been broken down into smaller units of work, the use of intelligent workstations can break the process down to still smaller units. If the dialogue portion of the transaction process, with its requirement to gather and display data and perform a variety of edits, may be performed on a workstation rather than the mainframe, then those computing resources previously oriented towards servicing a single user by formatting displays and performing the edits, may be reallocated to more users. Where editing is performed on a workstation, the telecommunications link need not pass data back and forth to report on error conditions and receive the corrections. Transaction processing cycles performed on a workstation are also less expensive than those performed on a central mainframe.

NELSON G. RUSSELL

TRANSFER RATE. *See* MEMORY: AUXILIARY.

TRANSLATION, LANGUAGE. *See* LANGUAGE TRANSLATION.

TRANSPARENCY

For articles on related subjects *see* COMPATABILITY; and PORTABILITY.

When changes are made to a computer's hardware or software configuration that do not require any action on a user's part, the changes are said to be *transparent* to the user. The usage derives from the concept of something (such as a pane of glass) that is so clear that one can look right through it as if it weren't there. This does not mean that the user will see no effect of the change, just that no action is required by the user to experience it. If, for example, a computing center replaces its mainframe with a faster version of the same model, users will notice that their programs run faster. Similarly, a software vendor might issue a new version of a compiler or a word processor that, given exactly the same input in the same form, functions identically to the prior version. In each case, the change would be said to be "transparent to the user."

EDWIN D. REILLY

TRANSPUTER

For articles on related subjects *see* PARALLEL PROCESSING; SUPERCOMPUTERS; and SYSTOLIC ARRAY.

A *transputer* is a microcomputer that combines a processor, a random access memory, and a number of communications links in a single VLSI chip (Fig. 1).

The communication links are the most important feature of the transputer. They allow transputers to be connected together to construct multiprocessor systems. The links operate concurrently with the transputer processor, transferring data directly from the memory of the outputting transputer to the memory of the inputting transputer. The scheduling of processing operations and communications is integrated into the hardware of the transputer and is very efficient.

Transputers are used in many specialized electronic systems, such as office equipment, industrial control, communications, signal processing, and image processing (*q.v.*). They are also used in computer subsystems to implement graphics, visualization, animation, and database systems. A number of general-purpose supercomputers, some containing hundreds of transputers, have also been developed.

The concurrent processing architecture of the transputer follows the concepts embodied in the Occam programming language, introduced by Inmos in 1984. Occam is itself based on the ideas of concurrent processes and synchronized message passing developed during the 1970s, especially Hoare's CSP. In Occam, an application is expressed as a collection of concurrent processes that communicate via channels. An Occam program is executed by a collection of transputers.

The hardware process scheduler within each transputer allows it to share its time between a number of Occam processes. Communication between processes on the same transputer is performed using the local memory; communication between processes on different transputers is performed using a link between the two transputers. Consequently, an Occam program can be executed either by a single transputer or by a collection of transputers connected in a network. Three different ways of using transputers to execute the component processes of a typical Occam program are shown in Fig. 2.

Transputer systems can be programmed directly in Occam, or alternatively in an ordinary sequential programming language (such as C or Fortran) extended with

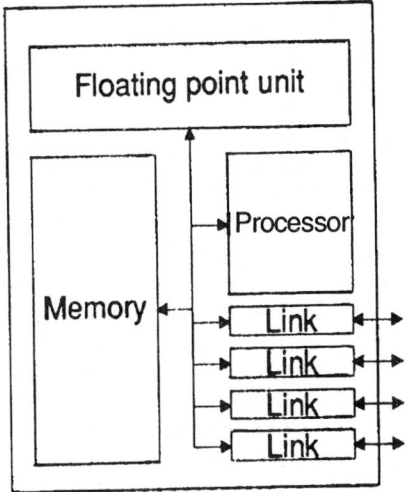

FIG. 1. T800 Transputer.

the processes and channels of Occam. In many applications, a combination of languages has been used, with Occam used to write concurrent programs in which the individual sequential processes are written in ordinary sequential languages.

Transputers were first introduced by Inmos in 1985. Initial products included a 16-bit transputer (T212) and a 32-bit transputer (T414). In 1987, a floating-point transputer (T800) was introduced. In 1991, a new transputer (T9000) and associated communications component (C104) providing hardware support for system-wide communication were introduced.

References

1989. Cosnuau, A. and Leca, P. "Scientific Parallel Computing with Transputer Networks," *J. High-Speed Computing* (Singapore), **1**, 3 (Sept.) 383–398.

1990. Graham, Ian and King, Tim. *The Transputer Handbook*. Englewood Cliffs, NJ: Prentice-Hall.

1990. Wallace, D. J. "Supercomputing with Transputers," *Supercomputer* (Netherlands), **7**, 2 (March), 120–131.

1990. Strickland, P., Naghdy, I., Hollis, J., and Billingsley, J. "Automatic Reconfigurable Transputer Networks," *Microprocessing and Microprogramming* (Netherlands), **28**, 1-5 (March), 223–228.

DAVID MAY

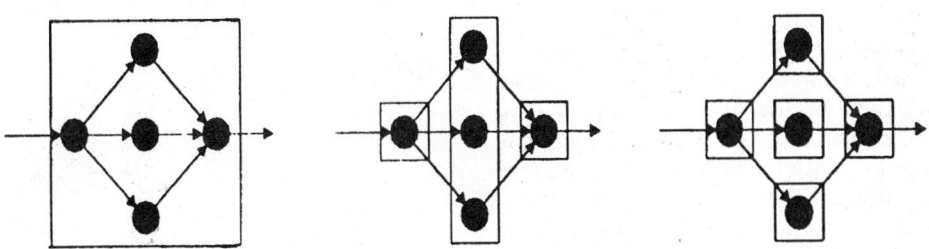

FIG. 2. Executing processes on transputers.

TRAP

For articles on related subjects *see* EXCEPTION HANDLING; and INTERRUPT.

When the occurrence of an exceptional event in a processor results in an automatic transfer to a special routine for handling that event, this transfer is called a *trap*.

Some writers consider *trap* and *interrupt* to be synonyms while others use trap in a somewhat narrower context, i.e. the range of exceptional events that occur within the central processor, in contrast to externally triggered interrupts. Whatever the categorization, the point is that when an exceptional condition (such as an attempt to divide by zero) occurs in a processor equipped with trapping facilities, the hardware automatically executes a transfer to a specific storage location that is permanently assigned for that particular contingency. That location is used to store a transfer instruction to the appropriate software handling routine.

Although an exceptional condition may produce circumstances that cannot be remedied by a programmed procedure, there are other conditions from which it is possible to recover. (For example, in some contexts it may be appropriate to set an underflow value to zero without undue harm to the process.) Accordingly, pertinent address information is preserved automatically so that a proper return can be made, once the trapping routine has been completed.

Several such locations might be reserved, depending on the types of conditions the processor is designed to recognize. Typically, separate trapping addresses would be provided for overflow, underflow, illegal address, and illegal operation, in addition to division by zero, already mentioned.

Prior to the introduction of trapping facilities (generally associated with second-generation computers), the programmer had to include explicit test instructions at each point where some exceptional condition might possibly occur. The need to do this is obviated by the trapping facility, since it can operate over an entire program. However, software trapping facilities still exist to give the programmer additional control over the program's behavior when confronted by an exceptional condition. For instance, many Pascal implementations include facilities whereby the compiler can be directed to include instructions that override the system's automatic trapping activity. In its place, the program produces a signal (*e.g.* a predefined value in a special variable) that can be detected and used as a basis for a response.

Systems equipped with trapping facilities usually include a machine instruction that allows the user to force one of several kinds of traps, thereby providing the opportunity to simulate a given type of exceptional condition. This capability has been used to considerable advantage in developing a variety of debugging aids and special features in software programs. Certain trapping facilities may also be explicitly turned off (disabled) by the programmer for all or part of a procedure, whereupon the system ignores the precipitating event and refrains from intervention.

SEYMOUR V. POLLACK AND THEODOR D. STERLING

TREE

For articles on related subjects *see* COMPUTER GAMES: TRADITIONAL; DATA STRUCTURES; and GRAPH THEORY.

A *tree* is a special form of directed graph with the following properties: (1) either it has no vertices or it has a distinguished vertex called the *root*, which has no predecessors; and (2) every vertex other than the root has a unique predecessor.

Vertices (or *nodes*) of a tree that have successors are called *nonterminal vertices*, or *parent nodes*, while vertices that have no successors are called *terminal vertices* or *leaves*. Fig. 1 illustrates a tree with root vertex *a*; two nonterminal vertices *a, c*; and three leaves *b,d,e*. Nodes *b* and *c*, since they have the same parent, are said to be *sibling nodes*, as are nodes *d* and *e*. Similarly, all nodes that have a parent (all those other than the root)—*b, c, d,* and *e* in Fig. 1.—are said to be *child nodes*.

Trees in which each nonterminal vertex has at most *n* successors are called *n-ary* trees. Trees in which each nonterminal vertex has at most two successors would then be 2-ary trees, but such structures have little or no application in computer science. But 2-ary trees with the additional restriction that only-children are either *left child nodes* or *right child nodes* are very useful; these are called *binary* trees. The tree in Fig. 1 is an example of a binary tree.

Each node of a tree determines a subtree whose root is the given node and whose vertices include all descendants of the node. In a binary tree, each nonterminal node has an associated left subtree and right subtree.

A tree is said to be *unordered* if there is no special significance to the order in which the descendants of a given node are listed, and is said to be *ordered* if the order of descendant nodes is significant.

The root of a tree is said to be at level 0, the children of the root at level 1, the grandchildren at level 2, etc. The

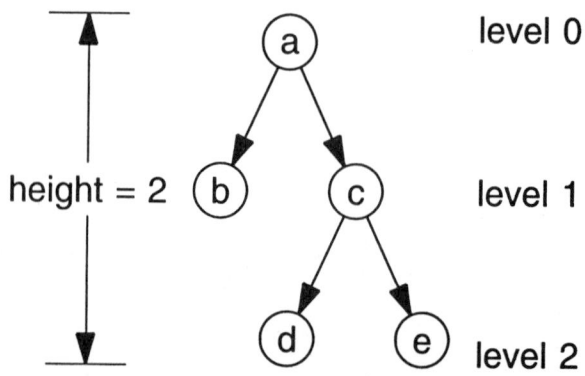

FIG. 1. A tree showing terminal and nonterminal vertices.

highest numbered level is called the *height* (or depth) of the tree (see Fig. 1).

Binary trees are a natural data structure for expressing the operator-operand structure of arithmetic expressions. The expression $x + y * z$ may be represented by the tree structure in Fig. 2, where the operators are represented by nonterminal vertices and the operands of an operator are represented by successor subtrees of the operator vertex. Thus, the operands of $+$ are x and $y*z$, and are represented by successor subtrees of the vertex $+$.

There are three fundamentally different ways to list the nodes of a binary tree. When applied to an expression tree such as that in Fig. 2, each yields a recognizable variation of the original expression.

1. *Preorder traversal*—Visit (print) the root. Traverse the left subtree (if any). Traverse the right subtree (if any). When applied recursively, this algorithm yields

$$+ \; x * yz,$$

which is the *Polish prefix* form of the original expression.

2. *Inorder (or symmetric) traversal.* Traverse the left subtree. Visit (print) the root. Traverse the right subtree. This yields

$$x + y * z,$$

which recaptures the original *infix* form of the expression.

3. *Postorder (or endorder) traversal.* Traverse the left subtree. Traverse the right subtree. Visit the root. This yields

$$x \, y \, z * +$$

which is the *reverse Polish* or *Polish postfix* form of the expression.

Given the diagram of a binary tree, its preorder, inorder, and postorder traversals can be immediately determined, but the converse is not necessarily true. No one of the three traversals alone is sufficient to allow unambiguous reconstruction of the tree that produced that traversal, nor will knowledge of just the combination of preorder and postorder traversals. Knowledge of the preorder and inorder traversals, however, or the inorder and postorder traversals, *is* sufficient to allow deduction of the corresponding binary tree.

Binary trees play an important role in computer science. Of particular importance in various applications are *height-balanced* trees, in which the height (maximum distance from the root to a leaf) of the left subtree of any node differs from that of the right subtree by, at most, one. Such trees are also called AVL trees after their inventors G. M. Adel'son-Vel'skii and E. M. Landis (1962). Keeping a tree balanced in this way provides far superior search time as compared to trees that become highly unbalanced through a preponderance of insertions into one or the other of the left or right subtrees.

The concept of height balancing can also be extended to *n*-ary trees. When data is stored in an external medium, such as a disk file, disk accesses are expensive relative to the reading of the data once an access is completed. Accordingly, it is reasonable to organize the data into a tree structure having a large number of keys per node so that the nodes have a large branching factor. Such trees were called B-trees by R. Bayer and E. McCreight (1972), who were the first to propose use of multiway balanced trees for external searching.

The 2-3 tree, invented by John Hopcroft in 1970, is a special case of a B-tree in which each node contains two keys and either two or three children (and hence is a 3-ary, or *ternary* tree). A typical node might be

Upon arrival at this node in search of a numeric key that is ≤ 7, the left branch is taken; for a key ≥ 11, the right branch; and for keys of intermediate value, the center branch. For a comprehensive survey of B-trees, see Comer (1979).

Now consider the 5-ary tree in Fig. 3. For *n*-ary trees ($n > 2$), inorder traversal has no meaning, but preorder and postorder traversals still do if the subtrees are visited left to right. The preorder traversal of this tree yields

$$a \; b \; e \; f \; g \; c \; h \; i \; d \; j \; k \; l \; m \; n$$

which coincides with the ordering obtained by the *depth first search (DFS)* algorithm. (An alternative strategy is *breadth-first search (BFS)*, in which nodes at the same level are listed from left to right, starting at the root. For the above example, BFS yields a b c d e f g h i j k l m n.)

Surprisingly, a binary tree can be used to represent an *n*-ary tree. This is done by linking all children of a given node and forming them into a left subtree of their parent in such a way that each left child in the original tree

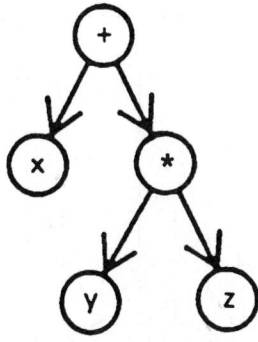

FIG. 2. A tree representing an operator-operand structure.

becomes the parent of a linear chain of its siblings. The binary tree equivalent to the 5-ary tree of Fig. 3 is given in Fig. 4.

This tree is equivalent to the original 5-ary tree in the sense that their preorder traversals are identical and the inorder traversal of the binary tree is the same as the postorder traversal of the 5-ary tree. Unlike the case of a binary tree, which in some sense contains more information than an *n*-ary tree because of the chirality ("handedness") of its subtrees, an *n*-ary tree *can* be reconstructed from knowledge of its preorder and postorder traversals. Since these traversals can be obtained from the binary tree of Fig. 4, there is just as much information in Fig. 4 as in Fig. 3, justifying the claim that every *n*-ary tree has an "equivalent" binary tree.

A special kind of n-ary tree called a *trie* (from re*trie*val, but pronounced "try") has a letter at each node, and any path from its root to a leaf represents a valid word in a given dictionary of entries. Imagine that the trie is used with a spelling checker (*q.v.*). If a "word" cannot be found in the trie, it is probably misspelled (though it may merely be missing from that particular dictionary).

A trie is a kind of search tree in which, instead of checking whole keys (words) against a target item, constituent letters are checked one by one until either a leaf is reached (success) or no further branch can be taken whose root matches the next letter of the target word (failure). Fig. 5 shows a small trie taken from Reilly and Federighi (1989) in which leaves, the ends of successful search paths, are represented by squares. The trie shown contains the words THE, THEM, THEN, THEY, THAN, THAT, THAW, TRAM, TRAP, TRAY, and TRUE. A Turbo Pascal program that searches this trie for the presence of an input word is given in Fig. 6. It is unusual in the sense that, though we usually think of control structures (*q.v.*) as distinctly different from data structures, here is a situation—the only one known to the authors—where a control structure (nested case statements) is used as a data structure, and an executable one at that.

Trees are a natural data structure for any data objects whose components stand in a hierarchical relation to each other. For example, the organization chart of a company may be represented by a tree structure, and family trees are, as their name implies, representable by a tree structure. The biblical family tree in Fig. 7 is taken from Knuth (1973).

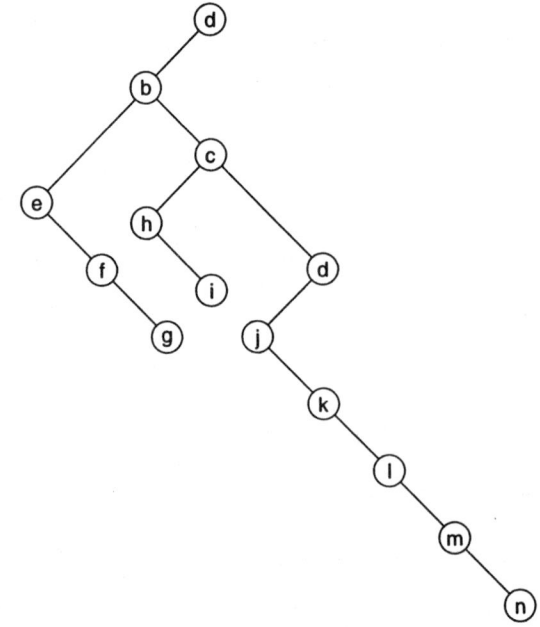

FIG. 4.   The binary tree equivalent of Fig. 3.

Tree structures may be indicated by parentheses, nesting, or indentation, as illustrated in Fig. 8, which shows alternative representations of the tree of Fig. 1.

The representation (A)(B) (C(D) (E)) may be viewed as a list structure in which the successor nodes of A are represented by the sublists (B) and (C(D) (E)). This representation is used to represent trees in languages such as Lisp.

Tree structures are convenient for storing sets of lexicographically ordered objects for purposes of alphabetically-oriented information retrieval. For example, the five words "dog," "cat," "lion," "fox," "tiger" can be stored in the tree structure shown in Fig. 9. A word in this tree structure can be found by comparing it to successive nodes, starting at the root node and taking the left successor if the word occurs earlier in a dictionary ordering or the right successor if it occurs later. Success is reported if the word matches; failure is reported if there is no successor of the

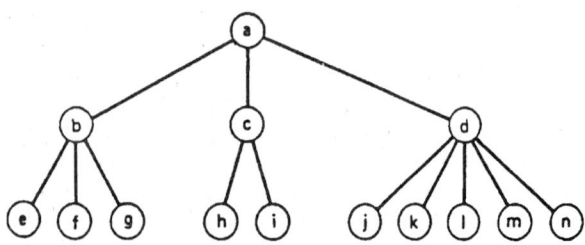

FIG. 3.   A 5-ary tree.

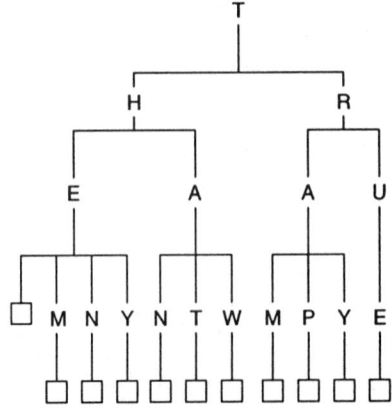

FIG. 5.   A small trie.

```
program trie;
{
    Searches a trie, encoded as nested case statements,
to see whether or not a target word of up to four
    uppercase letters is in the trie
}
const  success = ' is in the trie';
        failure = ' is not in the trie';
var W: string[4];
begin
    write('Enter a target word of up to four uppercase
letters: ');
    while not eof do
      begin
      W := '    '; { In case target word has less than
four letters }
        readln(W);
        if W[1] <> 'T' then writeln(failure) else

            case W[2] of
              'H' : case W[3] of
                      'E' : case W[4] of
                              ' ','M','N','Y' :
writeln(success)
                                                else
writeln(failure)

                            end;
                      'A'   : case W[4] of
                                'N','T','W' : writeln(success)
                                              else
writeln(failure)

                            end
                    else writeln(failure)
                    end;
              'R' : case W[3] of
                      'A' : case W[4] of
                              'M','P','Y' :
writeln(success)
                                                else
writeln(failure)

                            end;
              'U' : case W[4] of
                              'E' : writeln(success)
                                    else
writeln(failure)

                            end
                    else writeln(failure)
                    end
              else writeln(failure)
              end;
            write('Enter a target word of up to four
uppercase letters):')
        end {while not eof}
      end { trie }.
```

FIG. 6. A Turbo Pascal program for searching the trie of Fig. 5.

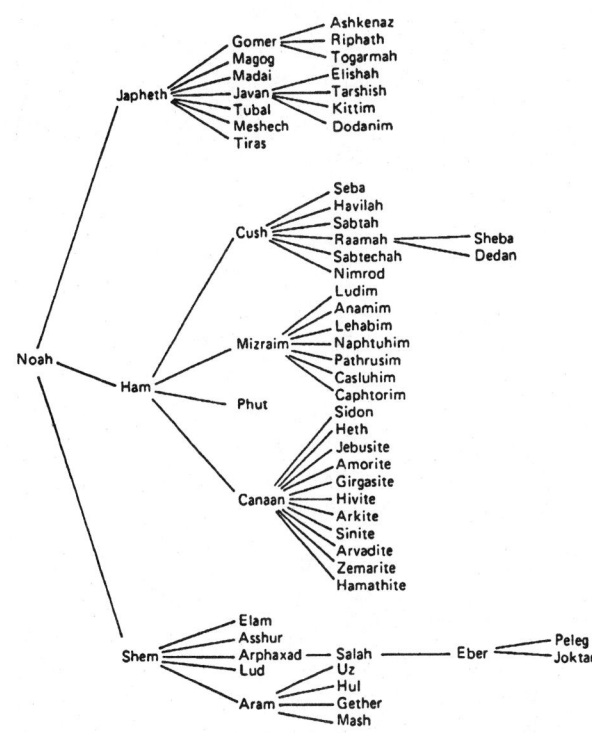

FIG. 7. Family tree.

kind required for the next step of search. The failure signal may be used to trigger a procedure for adding the new word to the tree as a new successor at the point of failure.

Example. (1) Assume that we want to determine if the word "fox" is in the tree. The word "fox" is compared with the word "dog," and since 'f' occurs later in the alphabet than 'd', the right branch is taken. Then "fox" is compared with "lion," and since 'f' occurs earlier in the alphabet than 'l', the left branch is taken. The third comparison results in a match.

(2) Determine whether the word "chicken" is in the tree; if absent, add it to the tree. First compare "chicken" with "dog" and take the left branch. Then compare "chicken" with "cat" and take the right branch. Then report failure because there is no right successor of "cat." Add "chicken" as the new right successor of "cat."

The tree structure representing a given set of sorted words depends on the order in which the words are presented during the construction of the tree. However, the tree representation of the sorted words is convenient, both because of the ease with which new words may be added to the structure and because the number of accesses in general depends on the logarithm of the number of words in the tree. An important problem in computer science is how to convert *unbalanced* sorting trees (i.e. those in which one subtree has height at least 2 greater than the other) into *balanced* (i.e. AVL) trees which can still be sorted by inorder traversal.

Trees are often used in the analysis of strategies for games such as chess and checkers (*see* COMPUTER GAMES: TRADITIONAL). In this case, the vertices of the tree represent positions in the game, and a given vertex has

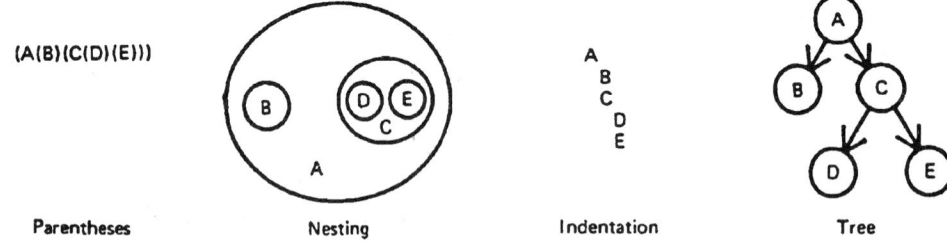

(A(B)(C(D)(E)))

Parentheses   Nesting   Indentation   Tree

FIG. 8. Alternative representations of the tree of Fig. 1.

as its successors all vertices that can be reached in one move from the given position. The set of all continuations of a game from a given position can be represented by a tree having the given position as its root vertex. The set of all games can be represented by a tree having the initial position as its root vertex. Each path through the tree from the root vertex to a terminal vertex represents a complete game.

It has been estimated that the complete game tree for checkers has about 10^{40} vertices, while the complete game tree for chess has about 10^{120} vertices. Complete game trees for most nontrivial games are much too large to be exhaustively searched or even stored in a computer. In developing strategies for playing games such as chess and checkers, *tree-pruning strategies* must be used to prune the complete game tree, creating subtrees that explore a limited number of continuations for a limited number of moves. Strategies for playing chess and checkers on a computer are effectively strategies for deciding how the complete game tree should be pruned, and for choosing a move on the basis of information in the pruned game tree.

References

1962. Adel'son-Vel'skii, G. M. and Landis, E. M. "An Algorithm for the Organization of Information," *Soviet Mathematics Doklady*, **3**: 1259–1263.

1972. Bayer, R. and McCreight, E. M. "Organization and Maintenance of Large Ordered Indexes," *Acta Informatica*, **1**(3): 173–189.

1973. Knuth, D. E. *The Art of Computer Programming 1* (2nd Ed.). Reading, MA: Addison-Wesley.

1979. Comer, D. "The Ubiquitous B-tree," *ACM Computing Surveys*, **11**(2): 121–137.

1989. Reilly, E. D. and Federighi, F. D. *Pascalgorithms*. Boston: Houghton Mifflin.

1990. Cormen, T. H., Leiserson, C. E., and Rivest, R. L. *Introduction to Algorithms*. Cambridge, MA: MIT Press, and New York: McGraw-Hill.

PETER WEGNER AND EDWIN D. REILLY

TROJAN HORSE. *See* COMPUTER VIRUS.

TURING, ALAN M.

For articles on related subjects *see* ALGORITHMS, THEORY OF; CHURCH, ALONZO; DIGITAL COMPUTERS: HISTORY: EARLY; KILBURN, THOMAS; TURING MACHINE; and WILLIAMS, SIR FREDERICK C.

Alan Mathison Turing (1912–1954) was born in London, the son of Julius Mathison Turing of the Indian Civil Service and of Ethel Sara Turing (neé Stoney). The Stoneys were a family of considerable scientific distinction, three of them having been Fellows of the Royal Society.

From an early age, Alan Turing showed an extraordinary aptitude for science and mathematics, and, in 1931, he entered Kings' College Cambridge as a Mathematical Scholar. He was clearly bored with the rather trivial first-year course, and gained only a second class in Part I of the Mathematical Tripos. At the end of the third year, however, he was a Wrangler, and gained a distinction in the advanced papers. He was elected a Fellow of King's in 1935 for a dissertation on the Central Limit Theorem of Probability. Characteristically, he rediscovered this, being quite unaware of previous work. The following year he was awarded a Smith's Prize for his thesis on the same topic.

It was in 1935 that he first became interested in mathematical logic and, in 1937, he published his now celebrated paper "On Computable Numbers with an Application to the Entscheidungsproblem," in which he in-

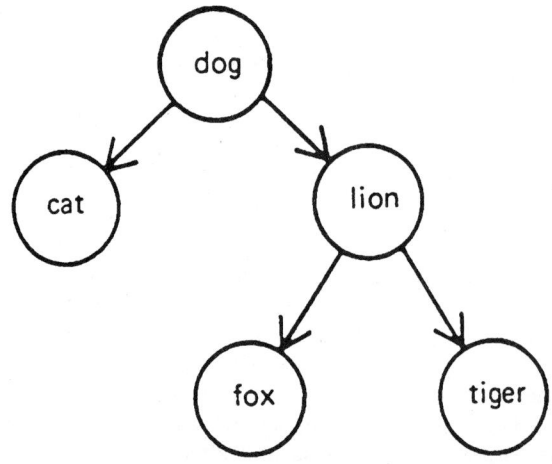

FIG. 9. Tree used for information retrieval.

FIG. 1. Alan Mathison Turing.

troduced the concept of a Turing machine. This paper attracted immediate attention and led to an invitation to Princeton, where he worked with Alonzo Church (*q.v.*). He took his Ph.D. there in 1938, the subject of his thesis being "Systems of Logic based on Ordinals." Turing contemplated staying in the U.S. and was offered a post as assistant to John von Neumann, but he decided to return to Cambridge in 1938. Until the outbreak of war, he worked on "A Method for the Calculation of the Zeta-Function," a topic to which he was to return in later years.

During World War II, Turing (being of military age) was required to work on government scientific research. He spent 1939–1945 at the British Foreign Office on work of a highly confidential nature which has not yet been declassified. For his work he was awarded the Officer Order of the British Empire (OBE). It is certain that in this period he gained a detailed knowledge of pulse techniques, and this was to have a decisive influence on his subsequent career. In 1942, he visited the U.S. on official business. During this visit he had the opportunity to see the latest work on computers and to renew old contacts at Princeton.

In 1945, he declined an offer of a Fellowship at Kings' in favor of joining the newly formed Mathematics Division at the National Physical Laboratory (NPL). His early work on computability, combined with his wartime experience in electronics, had fired him with an enthusiasm for working on the design of an electronic computer. The machine he designed, which was called the Automatic Computing Engine (ACE) in recognition of Babbage's pioneering work, was characteristically original. Although Turing knew something of the von Neumann proposals for EDVAC, he was not unduly influenced by them. The ACE, as Turing conceived it, was too ambitious a project, considering the current state of electronic techniques. Therefore, he left NPL in 1948, dissatisfied with the rate of progress.

While in the Mathematics Division of NPL, Turing became keenly interested in numerical analysis. His

paper, "Rounding-off Errors in Matrix Processes," showed that the acute anxiety about the effect of rounding errors in Gaussian elimination was largely unjustified. This paper has been overshadowed to some extent by the von Neumann and Goldstine paper on matrix inversion, but it is a brilliant piece of work and would have repaid a closer study at the time. After Turing left NPL, it was decided to build a pilot model embodying Turing's ideas (the Pilot ACE), and this was completed in 1950. It was a highly successful computer, and some 30 engineered versions of it were subsequently constructed by the English Electric Company under the name DEUCE. The original Pilot ACE is in the Science Museum in Kensington, London.

On leaving NPL, Turing was appointed to a Readership at Manchester University, where he worked in close collaboration with F. C. Williams and T. Kilburn, both pioneers in the electronic computer field. He was elected a Fellow of the Royal Society in 1951. Papers published while he was at Manchester include further work on the Riemann zeta function, a remarkable discussion on computing machinery and intelligence, and on the chemical basis of morphogenesis. The latter was his main interest at that time, and he left uncompleted another substantial paper on the same topic.

Turing died tragically in 1954 at the age of 41, a probable suicide. His publications, impressive though some of them are, give only the merest hint of his extraordinary originality and versatility. In recognition of his outstanding pioneering work, the ACM has named its most prestigious award the Turing Award (*q.v.*). It is awarded annually for contributions to computer science of a technical nature.

A definitive biography of Turing has been written by Hodges (1983). *Breaking the Code*, a play based on Hodges' book written by Hugh Whitemore, was performed in London and New York in the late 1980s.

References

1955. Newman, M. H. A. *The Biographical Memoirs of Fellows of the Royal Society* 1. London: The Royal Society, 253–263.
1959. Turing, Sarah. *A. M. Turing*. Cambridge: Heffer & Sons.
1970. Wilkinson, J. H. "Some Comments from a Numerical Analyst" (The 1970 A. M. Turing Lecture), *JACM* **18**, *2*: 137–147.
1983. Hodges, Andrew, *Alan Turing: The Enigma*. New York, Simon and Schuster.

JAMES H. WILKINSON

TURING AWARD WINNERS

For an article on a related subject *see* MCDOWELL AWARD WINNERS.

The A. M. Turing Award is made annually by the Association for Computing Machinery (ACM) "for contributions of a technical nature in the computing community." The award, which currently includes a prize of $25,000, memorializes the extraordinary genius, Alan M. Turing (*q.v.*), and recognizes his unique and original contribution to the beginning of computing with automatic machinery.

Each recipient gives a lecture that is published in an ACM periodical. The first 22 have been collected into a single volume (Ashenhurst and Graham, 1987).

ACM's almost exclusive devotion to software and computing theory is reflected in the fact that none of the awards have been for strictly hardware contributions, a field dominated by the IEEE Computer Society.

1966

Alan J. Perlis (1922–1990) (*q.v.*) for his work in programming language definition and design and programming techniques, and for his leadership in computer science education.

1967

Maurice V. Wilkes (1913–) (*q.v.*) for his leadership in the early development of stored program computers, his invention of labels, macros, and microcode, and for his co-invention of subroutines.

1968

Richard W. Hamming (1915–) for his invention of the error-detecting/correcting codes that bear his name (*see* ERROR-CORRECTING CODE), and for his famous aphorism, "The purpose of computing is insight, not numbers."

1969

Marvin M. Minsky (1927–) for his contributions to the theory of computation, programming languages, education, and the beginnings of artificial intelligence (AI - *q.v.*).

1970

James H. Wilkinson (1919–1986) (*q.v.*) for his contributions to numerical analysis, particularly in the fields of matrix computations and error analysis.

1971

John McCarthy (1927–) for his contributions to artificial intelligence, particularly the invention of Lisp.

1972

Edsger W. Dijkstra (1930–) for his style and his persuasive influence on programming, of which his memorable indictment of the GO TO statement is most famous.

1973

Charles W. Bachman (1924–) for his work in database technology, particularly the creation of both the Integrated Data Store (IDS), which is the basis of the CODASYL database systems, and a powerful method for displaying data relationships.

1974

Donald Knuth (1938–) for his contributions to the analysis of algorithms, the design of programming languages, and his series of classic texts, *The Art of Computer Programming*.

1975

Allen Newell (1927–) and Herbert A. Simon (1916–) (*q.v.*) for their basic contributions to artificial intelligence, the psychology of human cognition, and their invention of list processing (*q.v.*).

1976

Michael O. Rabin (1931–) and Dana S. Scott (1932–) for their contributions to the course of theoretical computer science which set a standard of clarity and elegance for the entire field.

1977

J. W. Backus (1924–) for leading the development of Fortran and the creation of the syntax description language Backus-Naur Form (BNF - *q.v.*).

1978

R. W. Floyd (1936–) for helping to found the theory of parsing, the semantics of programming languages, automatic *program verification* (*q.v.*), automatic program synthesis, and analysis of algorithms (*q.v.*).

1979

Kenneth E. Iverson (1920–) for his pioneering effort in programming languages and mathematical notation, resulting in the language APL (*see* FUNCTIONAL PROGRAMMING).

1980

C. A. R. Hoare (1934–) for his fundamental contributions to the definition and design of programming languages, specifically their axiomatic definitions by using axiomatic semantics; his development of ingenious algorithms and advanced data structuring techniques; and his contributions to operating systems (*q.v.*).

1981

Edgar F. Codd (1923–) for his contributions to the theory and practice of database management systems (DBMS - *q.v.*) and the creation of the relational model (*see* RELATIONAL DATABASE).

1982

Stephen A. Cook (1939–) for his contributions to the theory of computational complexity (*q.v.*), which laid the foundations for the theory of NP-completeness (*see* NP-COMPLETE PROBLEMS).

1983

Dennis M. Ritchie (1941–) and Ken L. Thompson (1943–) for their development and implementation of the Unix operating system (*q.v.*) and the language C (*q.v.*).

1984

Niklaus E. Wirth (1934–) for his development of a sequence of innovative computer languages: Euler, Algol-W, Modula-2 (*q.v.*), and Pascal, particularly the latter.

1985

Richard M. Karp (1935–) for his fundamental contributions to complexity theory, which extended the earlier work of Stephen Cook.

1986

John Hopcroft (1939–) and Robert E. Tarjan (1938–) for their fundamental achievements in the design and analysis of algorithms and data structures.

1987

John Cocke (1925–) for his contributions to the design and theory of compilers and to the architecture of high-performance computers.

1988

Ivan E. Sutherland (1938–) for his contributions to interactive computer graphics (*q.v.*), exemplified by his invention of Sketchpad, which established and defined the field.

1989

William M. Kahan (1933–) for his drive and determination to establish and have adopted the current standards for binary and radix-independent floating-point computations.

1990

Fernando J. Corbató (1926–) for formulating the concepts and leading the development of the Compatible Time-Sharing System (CTSS) and Multics (Multiplexed Information and Computer Service).

1991

A. J. R. G. Milner (1934–) for three developments: LCF, the mechanization of Scott's logic of computable functions; ML, the first language to contain polymorphic type-inference together with a type-safe exception-handling mechanism; and CCS, a general theory of concurrency.

Reference

1987. Ashenhurst, Robert L. and Graham, Susan (Eds.). *ACM Turing Award Lectures, The First Twenty Years*. New York: ACM Press.

Eric A. Weiss

TURING MACHINE

For articles on related subjects *see* Algorithms, Theory of; Automata Theory; Chomsky Hierarchy; Formal Languages; Sequential Machines; and Turing, Alan M.

A *Turing machine* is an abstract computing device invented by Alan M. Turing in 1936. A reprint of his original paper appears in Davis (1965). A Turing machine consists of (1) a *control unit*, which can assume any one of a finite number of possible states; (2) a *tape*, marked off into discrete squares, each of which can store a single symbol, taken from a finite set of possible symbols; and (3) a *read-write head*, which moves along the tape and transmits information to and from the control unit (see Fig. 1).

The Basic Model A Turing machine computes via a sequence of discrete steps. Its behavior at a given time is completely determined by the symbol currently being scanned by the read-write head, and by the internal state of the control unit. On a given step, it will write a symbol on the tape, move along the tape at most one square to the left or right, and enter a new internal state. The new symbol is permitted to be the same as the current symbol; similarly, it is permissible to stay on the same tape square on a given step and/or to reenter the same state. Certain symbol-state situations may cause the machine to halt.

For example, on a single step the machine in Fig. 1 could begin in state q_3, change the A under scan to an E, move left one square and enter state q_5. It would now be scanning a T; its next action would be uniquely determined by the new state q_5 and the fact that it was scanning a T. It would continue indefinitely in this step-by-step fashion unless it reached a state-symbol combination, causing it to halt.

The tape of a Turing machine is often depicted as infinite, and some persons view this idealization as hopelessly unrealistic. A better approach is to view the tape as finite but indefinitely extendible; i.e. new blank squares can be attached to either end of the tape at will to prevent the machine from running off the tape.

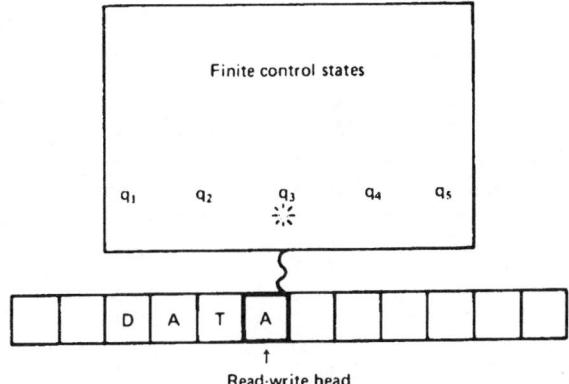

FIG. 1. Architecture of a Turing machine.

Thus, there is no uniform bound on either the time or space used by a Turing machine; both are allowed to grow indefinitely.

The *program* of a Turing machine defines its action for the various state-symbol combinations that are possible. This program can be presented in a number of different ways, (e.g. state transition diagrams, assembly-like languages). The two most common ways are a tabular form and representation as a set of quintuples. Each state-symbol combination is represented by either an entry in the table or a single quintuple in the set. In the quintuple convention, the action described above would have been due to the presence of the quintuple

$$\langle q_3, A, E, L, q_5 \rangle$$

where we abbreviate left, right, and no-shift by L, R, and N, respectively.

An example of a Turing machine in tabular form is now presented. The state set of this machine M corresponds to rows in Table 1 and the symbol set (alphabet) to columns. The blank symbol is denoted by B. M will compute the function $f(x) = 2^x$ according to the following conventions:

1. x and $f(x)$ are written as binary integers.
2. The tape initially contains x and is blank elsewhere.
3. M begins in state q_1, scanning the leftmost bit of x.
4. When it halts, $f(x)$ will be the only non-blank item on the tape.

The algorithm used is given by the flowchart in Fig. 2. Essentially, each time the string that initially represents x is changed to represent the next smaller integer, a 0 is written on the tape to the right of x. When x has been decreased to 0, a 1 is written to the left of the generated string of x zeros. The zeros to the left of the 1 are then erased, and M halts. As is often the case, the algorithm is best thought of as an exercise in symbol manipulation rather than as arithmetic.

The entries in Table 1 labeled *error* cannot occur in a normal computation. By convention, M would halt if started in such state-symbol situations.

An *instantaneous description* (total machine configuration) of a machine consists of the entire set of machine conditions at a given point in a computation (i.e. the contents of the tape, the position of the read-write head on the tape, and the internal state of the machine). A computation, then, is simply an entire history of instantaneous descriptions beginning with the start configuration and ending with a halt configuration. Table 2 gives the computation of the machine M when started in state q_1 on the input 10 (binary 2). The symbol scanned is set in boldface type. Note that, when M halts, its read-write head is not scanning the leftmost digit of the output 100; the reader is invited to add one more state to M and get it to do this.

Modified Turing Machines Turing's original model has been altered in a number of ways by a number of different authors. In each of the cases discussed below, it has been proved that the altered model and the original model can each compute the same class of functions. This is done by showing that, for every machine of a given type, there exists a standard Turing machine that can simulate its behavior, and conversely. Turing machines have also been shown capable of defining exactly the same classes of functions definable by the formal systems of Kleene, Church, (*q.v.*), Rosser, Markov and others. *Church's Thesis* and *Turing's Thesis* assert that their respective models correctly capture the mathematical notion of *effective computability*, (i.e. of explicit algorithmic processes). Since the models are equivalent in the sense given above, the two theses are equivalent.

The following list contains some of the more common variations that do not affect the classes of functions that can be computed (although the efficiency of a computation may change with the model).

1. *Post-Davis*—The machine cannot both change the symbol under scan and move along the tape on the same step (Davis, 1958).
2. *One-ended Tape*—The tape can be extended to the right, but not to the left. Thus, the read-write head could fall off the left end of the tape.
3. *Paper Tape*—A blank square can have a nonblank symbol written on it, but this symbol cannot be changed thereafter.

TABLE 1   Program for M

Present State	B is scanned write/shift/state	0 is scanned write/shift/state	1 is scanned write/shift/state	Comment
q_1	1, L, q_7	0, R, q_1	1, R, q_2	Is x 0?
q_2	B, R, q_3	0, R, q_2	1, R, q_2	$x \neq 0$
q_3	0, L, q_4	0, R, q_3	Error	Write a new 0
q_4	B, L, q_5	0, L, q_4	Error	Go back to x
q_5	Error	1, L, q_5	0, L, q_6	Decrease x
q_6	B, R, q_1	0, L, q_6	1, L, q_6	Go to starting position
q_7	Halt	B, L, q_7	Error	Clean up

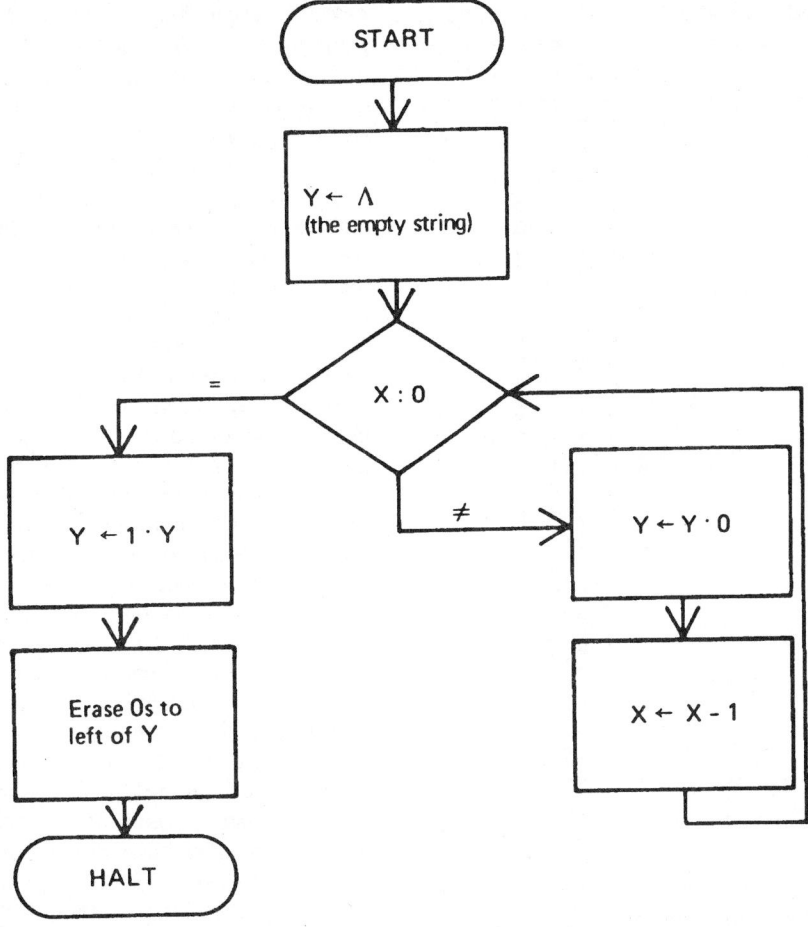

FIG. 2. Flowchart for *M*.

4. *Two-Symbol*—Only the symbols *B* (blank) and 1 are allowed, although the number of states may be large.

5. *Two-State*—Only two states are permitted, although the number of symbols may be large. The generality of this and the previous case is due to Shannon (1956).

6. *Multitape*—More than one tape is permitted, each tape having its own read-write head. In this case, the action of the machine depends upon the internal state and the symbols scanned by each of the read-write heads; i.e. for a *k*-tape machine, the action depends upon the state and an ordered *k*-tuple of symbols. The tape motions are independent; on a given step some heads could move left, some right, and some could remain in place.

7. *Multihead*—More than one head is allowed per tape. Again, the action of the machine is determined by the state and the ordered set of symbols scanned by the various read-write heads as they crawl around their shared tapes. Usually, the machine is allowed access to information concerning which heads are currently scanning the same tape square.

8. *Multidimensional*—The "tapes" are multidimensional structures. In the two-dimensional case, the plane is marked off into squares and the permissible head motions are north, south, east, west, and no move. For higher dimensions, one uses a coordinate system, and a move changes at most one of the coordinates by ± 1.

Advantages of Turing's Model The usefulness of the Turing model of computation lies in its simplicity, despite which it has all the fundamental properties that a computing system must possess: a finite program, a large data store, and a deterministic step-by-step mode of computation. In particular, one can show that any computer can be simulated (albeit rather slowly) by a Turing machine. The converse is also true, provided that provisions are made to handle larger amounts of storage as needed.

For example, it is true that a minicomputer with an accumulator and "sufficiently large" storage can do any computation with only the instructions SUBTRACT, STORE,

TABLE 2. Computation of 2^2 by M

Time	State	Nonblank Portion of Tape					
0	q_1			**1**	0		
1	q_2			1	**0**		
2	q_2			1	0	**B**	
3	q_3			1	0	B	**B**
4	q_4			1	0	**B**	0
5	q_5			1	**0**	B	0
6	q_5			**1**	1	B	0
7	q_6		**B**	0	1	B	0
8	q_1		B	**0**	1	B	0
9	q_1		B	0	**1**	B	0
10	q_2		B	0	1	**B**	0
11	q_3		B	0	1	B	**0**
12	q_3		B	0	1	B	0	**B**
13	q_4		B	0	1	**B**	0	0
14	q_4		B	0	1	**B**	0	0
15	q_5		B	0	**1**	B	0	0
16	q_6		B	0	**0**	B	0	0
17	q_6		**B**	0	0	B	0	0
18	q_1		B	**0**	0	B	0	0
19	q_1		B	0	**0**	B	0	0
20	q_1		B	0	0	**B**	0	0
21	q_7		B	0	**0**	1	0	0
22	q_7		B	**0**	B	1	0	0
23	q_7		**B**	B	B	1	0	0
24	Halted		No change					

and TRANSFER ON MINUS, if one assumes the usual conventions of a single-address von Neumann machine (*q.v.*). It is much easier to prove this by showing how to simulate a Turing machine on the minicomputer, rather than by attempting to simulate all of the instructions of a large-scale computer.

Since a Turing machine can simulate any computing device, it follows that anything that cannot be computed on a Turing machine cannot be computed at all. The fact that there are such unsolvable problems motivated Turing to devise his abstract machine. This has also given rise to the theory of algorithms.

Turing machines can also simulate each other by interpretive procedures. In particular, it is possible to program a Turing machine to accept the description of the program and input data of any other Turing machine computation, and to simulate that computation. Such a machine is called a *universal Turing machine*.

Although Turing machines have probably been studied theoretically more than other abstract computing devices, two other models deserve mention. A *random-access machine* looks much like a single-address computer and stores its data in a finite number of cells. The idealization used here is that each cell can store any integer, and hence must have an unbounded number of bits. An *iterative array* consists of a network of finite-state sequential machines. Again, an unbounded memory is needed; this is achieved by allowing the network to be expanded in the middle of a computation, if necessary. Iterative arrays are useful in studying certain kinds of parallel processes.

Time Complexity of Turing Machine Computations

A number of theoretical results have shown that studying the complexity of Turing machine computations can yield insight into the efficiency of computations on real hardware. Within a broad range of conditions, the cost of a computation on a Turing machine (e.g. the number of steps required) is within a polynomial function of the cost on any machine with a finite number of processors. If the real Turing machine has at least two tapes, the relationship to cost on a real machine will often be linear.

On the other hand, Turing machine time studies are insensitive to a constant factor—i.e. computations on a multitape Turing machine can always be sped up by a factor of 2 by increasing the symbol set so as to pack at least two symbols of the original alphabet on a tape square. (Some additional programming is required to make this work in all cases.) Doubling the speed of real machines, on the other hand, cannot be achieved without either a technological breakthrough or an increase in the cost of the hardware, and hence the cost per machine hour.

The Post-Davis, one-ended tape, and two-state variants introduced in the preceding section can be made to run as fast as ordinary (one-tape) Turing machines. The two-symbol variant will run within a constant factor of the others, but since the number of symbols is fixed, the speed-up trick may not be employed.

Although the multihead variant appears to be more powerful than the multitape model, P. Fischer, A. Meyer, and A. Rosenberg have shown that the two variants are equivalent in a very strong sense. Any multihead machine can be replaced by an equally fast equivalent multitape machine (but with perhaps a greater total number of heads).

On the other hand, one-tape Turing machines cannot always simulate multitape machines without loss of time. There exist examples for which the time on the one-tape machine must be the square of the multitape machine time. Thus, multitape (and multihead and multidimensional) machines are more efficient than ordinary Turing machines. For this reason, the multitape model is probably the most useful model for efficiency studies, although the one-tape version is better for computability-noncomputability investigations because of its greater simplicity.

The squaring of time to go from a multitape machine to a one-tape machine is never exceeded. In fact, any variant of a Turing machine with a bounded number of processors requiring time t for a computation can be simulated by an ordinary Turing machine in time at most t^2.

When considering multitape Turing machines with different numbers of tapes, some interesting questions remain unsolved. Aanderaa has shown that, for any k, certain problems can be solved faster on a k-tape machine than on a $(k - 1)$–tape machine. However, the amount of saving cannot be large, since Hennie and Stearns have shown that any multitape machine requiring time t can be simulated by a two-tape Turing machine in time at most $t(\log_2 t)$. Whether this bound can be improved is still an open question.

References

1956. Shannon, C. E., and J. McCarthy (Eds.). *Automata Studies*. Princeton, N. J.: Princeton University Press.

1958. Davis, Martin. *Computability and Unsolvability*. New York: McGraw-Hill.

1963. Trachtenbrot, B. *Algorithms and Automatic Computing Machines*. Boston: D. C. Heath.

1965. Davis, Martin (Ed.). *The Undecidable*. Hewlett, NY: Raven Press.

1978. Hartmanis, J. *Feasible Computations and Provable Complexity Properties*. Philadelphia: Society for Industrial and Applied Mathematics.

1981. Lewis, H.R. and Papadimitriou, C.H. *Elements of the Theory of Computation*. Englewood Cliffs, NJ: Prentice-Hall.

1989. Dewdney, A.K. *The Turing Omnibus*. Rockville, MD: Computer Science Press (Chapter 48).

PATRICK C. FISCHER

TURNAROUND TIME

For articles on related subjects *see* INTERACTIVE SYSTEM; JOB; THROUGHPUT; and TIME SHARING.

Turnaround time is the elapsed time from the moment a batch job is submitted to be run on a computer until the results are available. From the point of view of the input/output data control clerk, turnaround extends from the time when the job arrives for processing to the time when the job deck and report(s) are available to the user. From the machine operator's point of view, it lasts only from the time the job is started until the last line of the report has been printed. From the user's point of view, turnaround time is the period that begins when the job is submitted and ends when the output is delivered to the point where it can be picked up.

In time-sharing systems, the time elapsed between sending a trivial command and the computer response to it is a form of turnaround time called *response time*.

Typical computing center turnaround times vary from a few minutes to a few hours, while response time should be no more than a couple of seconds (unless the user has just submitted a computationally intensive request).

From a communications standpoint, turnaround time is the length of time required to reverse a communication line from the send mode to the receive mode. Since messages in some applications are very short (and must be verified through return of some signal), the turnaround time can be as long or longer than the time required to send the message or return the verification. Therefore it becomes an important consideration in investigation of line efficiency.

CHESTER L. MEEK

TURNKEY

Turnkey preparation of a facility means that a single contractor acquires and sets up all necessary premises, equipment, supplies, and operating personnel to bring a project to a state of operational readiness. All the customer needs to do is "turn the key" to begin full and effective usage of the new facility. Sometimes the contractor continues to operate the facility for the customer (usually called *facilities management*); in other cases, the customer assumes operational control.

Turnkey facilities are appropriate for customers who are unable to perform (or wish to avoid) their own subcontracting for ordering and testing components acquired from several different vendors. Recruiting, screening, and training a technical staff is also a highly specialized and sensitive task. A turnkey contractor is compensated either through surcharges on each item or service procured for the facility or by a commitment in advance to a fixed price.

DAVID N. FREEMAN

ULTRASONIC MEMORY

For articles on related subjects *see* EDSAC; EDVAC; MEM-ORY: MAIN; and UNIVAC I .

Ultrasonic memories played an important role in the early development of digital computers, but are now only of historical interest. The report on the EDVAC (*q.v.*) drafted by von Neumann in June 1945 on behalf of the group at the Moore School of Electrical Engineering, Philadelphia, clearly envisaged this type of memory, although it did not describe the physical principles on which it operated. Of the early machines, the EDSAC, SEAC (*q.v.*), Pilot ACE, EDVAC, and UNIVAC I all had ultrasonic memories.

The principle is illustrated in Fig. 1. A train of pulses representing the numbers to be stored is modulated onto a carrier and applied to a piezoelectric crystal in contact with a column of mercury. The ultrasonic pulses so generated travel along the column until they reach another crystal at the far end. This converts them back into electric signals, which are amplified and rectified. The resulting pulses are applied to a gate together with pulses from a continuously running clock pulse generator. This gating operation serves the twin purposes of regeneration and synchronization. The emerging pulses, which are exact replicas of the original pulses, are reapplied to the modulator and continue to circulate. The operations of reading, clearing, and writing can be performed by applying to the gates shown suitable waveforms accurately synchro-

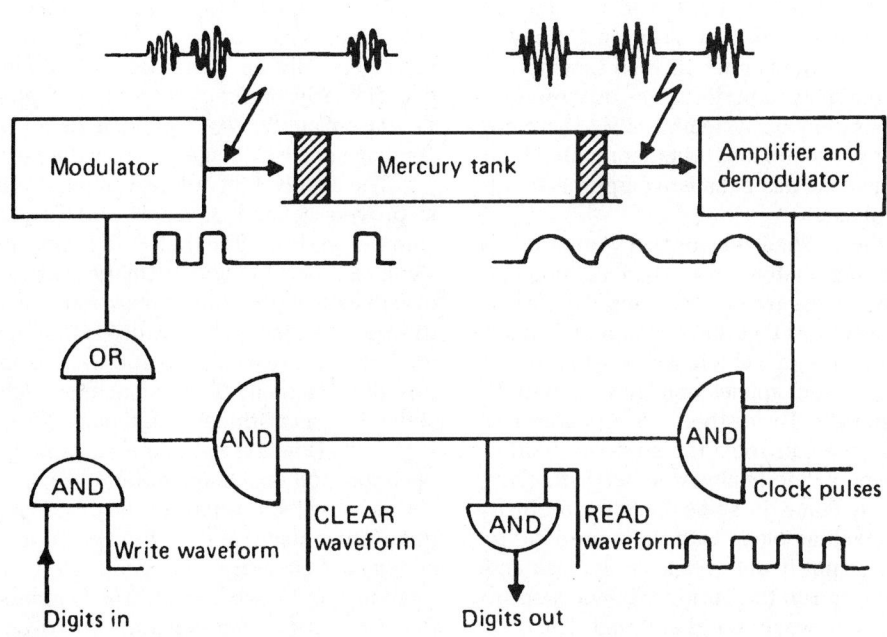

FIG. 1. Ultrasonic memory.

nized with the clock. A typical main memory consisted of a group of 32 tanks, as the columns were called, each between 0.5 and 1.5 meters long and giving a delay of between one-third and 1 ms.

In the mid-1950s, ultrasonic memories using a fine nickel wire in the form of a coil as the propagation medium appeared in some low-cost computers. The waves were excited by making use of the magnetostrictive properties of the nickel.

Reference

1956. Wilkes, M. V. *Automatic Digital Computers.* New York: John Wiley.
1985. Wilkes, M. V. *Memoirs of a Computer Pioneer.* Cambridge, MA: The M.I.T. Press.

MAURICE V. WILKES

UNDECIDABLE PROBLEMS

For articles on related subjects *see* ALGORITHMS, THEORY OF; CHURCH, ALONZO; LAMBDA CALCULUS; NP-COMPLETE PROBLEMS; TURING, ALAN; and TURING MACHINE.

One of this century's major intellectual discoveries is that there are some perfectly precise problems that can never be solved. This is a technical result, not a mystical one. There is nothing ineffable about these problems; indeed, one can give specific examples of them. Nor should this result be confused with the claim that some problems (e.g. what is the meaning of life?) are too imprecise to be solved computationally. Actually, these unsolvable problems are just as precise as the problem of computing a sum. Also, the result is not based on the fact that some problems are just too large to solve in practical terms. Rather, these problems are unsolvable even under the assumption that wholly unreasonable amounts of time and space are available for their solution. By way of contrast, it is a trivial matter under such an assumption to write a program that plays a perfect game of chess: just explore all of the possibilities systematically. (There are only a finite number of possibilities, but that number is so astronomically large that this exhaustive approach will never be of practical use.)

In the 1930s, the mathematician Alan Turing introduced a conceptual automaton, now called a *Turing machine,* to model the process by which a computer carries out a computational task. At that time, "computer" meant "one who computes" (i.e. a person who carries out a calculation), but the model applies equally well to modern electronic computers. Turing then proved rigorously that no Turing machine can solve the so-called Halting Problem, the problem of determining whether Turing machines eventually halt. Some do, some don't: the problem is, given a Turing machine along with its input data, to determine whether or not it will ever finish its task and halt. Of course, one can run the Turing machine step by step, and, if it halts, one would see that it had. The difficulty is that if it does not halt then this method will not reveal that fact; no matter how long one continues the

simulation, it is conceivable that the machine would have halted if processing had continued an additional few moments.

Turing's proof is a formalization of the following idea. Establish a *pairing* between all possible Turing machines (there are infinitely many) and all possible sets of input data (also infinitely many) in a systematic way. Now suppose there were a Turing machine H that could solve the Halting Problem. Starting from H, one could build a "perverse" machine P that acts as follows: P takes its input data x and determines (by using H as a subroutine) whether the particular machine M, which is paired off with x, would halt or run forever on input x; and P then perversely either halts or enters an infinite loop, whichever causes it to behave differently from M. Now P has succeeded in behaving differently from *every* machine; specifically, it differs from any machine M on the particular input data x that is matched with M in the pairing. But this is impossible, since P would have to differ even from itself. So H cannot exist after all.

Turing's method of proof is very general. It applies equally well to show that it is impossible to write a Pascal program, say, that can test Pascal programs for infinite loops. If this were the end of the story, Turing's result would merely establish certain limits on self-referential application, suggesting, for example, that if one wants to test programs written in a particular language then one must write the tests in a different language. But at the same time that Turing was describing his machines, Alonzo Church and various other logicians were proving that many models of computation (including Turing machines) that are superficially very different are in fact all equivalent. As a result of this work, the *Church-Turing Thesis* has become generally accepted: Any method of performing a computation that might conceivably be proposed in the future, no matter how apparently powerful, will turn out to be performable by a Turing machine. This implies that the Halting Problem is unsolvable not merely in the sense that no Turing machine can solve it, but that, more generally, no computational procedure of any type can. Similarly, one cannot test Pascal programs for termination no matter what present or future programming language one is willing to use for the task.

The unsolvability of the Halting Problem can be used to prove a celebrated result of the logician Kurt Gödel, who showed in 1931 that it is impossible to capture a significant portion of mathematics with any finite number of axioms, thus demonstrating a fundamental limitation of the axiomatic method. The idea is that by carefully encoding both Turing machines and data as integers, one can turn the statement "Turing machine i halts on input j in k steps" into an arithmetic statement $T(i,j,k)$ about i, j, and k. (By this is meant a statement involving addition, multiplication, and logical quantifiers: Working out the details of this is the tedious part of the proof.) Now suppose that this Turing machine runs forever on its input. Then the statement "There is no integer k satisfying the arithmetic relation $T(i,j,k)$" would be a true statement of arithmetic. But if enough of mathematics could be axiomatized to make all true statements of arithmetic provable from the axioms, then the futile process of observing the machine as it runs forever could be short-circuited by instead giving a finite-length proof that it never halts. Yet this cannot always be possible, since it would contradict the unsolvability of the Halting Problem.

The proof of the Gödel Incompleteness Theorem just outlined differs in some details from Gödel's original proof, which predated Turing's result, but which used the same idea of arithmetic encoding. The Gödel and Turing results are closely related. In essence, Gödel proved that any sufficiently rich axiomatic system contains undecidable but nonetheless true propositions. Turing proved that one cannot write a computer program that, fed an axiomatic system and an arbitrary proposition as input, can determine whether the proposition is undecidable (*see* Hofstadter, 1985, pp. 484–487).

The unsolvability of the Halting Problem can also be used to prove that various other problems are unsolvable. Suppose that one wants to prove that Problem X is unsolvable. If one can write a procedure for solving the Halting Problem with the assistance of a hypothetical subprocedure for solving X, one can be sure that X in fact cannot be solved (otherwise, the Halting Problem could be). This is called *reducing* the Halting Problem to Problem X. By reducing a problem known to be unsolvable to a new problem, one can prove that the new problem is also unsolvable. In this way, many problems of interest in computer science have been shown to be unsolvable, which establishes that any attempt to write a program to solve all cases of the problem is doomed to fail. Often, an appropriate response is to seek solutions for special cases.

When the solution to a problem requires a yes or no answer to each problem instance, the problem is called a *decision* problem; if it is unsolvable, it is said to be *undecidable*.

Undecidability plays an important role in many theoretical areas of computer science, such as in the study of formal languages (*q.v.*). A typical problem is the *membership* problem for a language: determine, for each given word, whether or not the word is in the language. Languages for which this problem is decidable are called *recursive* languages. As a general rule, almost all problems about regular languages are decidable, while most problems about context-sensitive languages are undecidable (one exception: they are recursive); whereas, for context-free languages, it is difficult to give any guidelines. For example, the problem of determining whether a context-free grammar generates infinitely many strings is decidable, but determining whether it generates all strings is not. (Of course, it is possible to tell whether or not certain context-free grammars generate all strings; what is impossible is to find a method that works for all context-free grammars.) Similarly, it is undecidable in general to determine whether two context-free grammars generate the same language.

As was mentioned earlier, a problem is solvable if it can be solved in principal, even though the amount of time required to compute the solution may be totally infeasible. More recent research has attempted to divide solvable problems into those that are feasibly solvable and those that are not: *see* NP-COMPLETE PROBLEMS.

References

1974. Brainerd, W. S. and Landweber, L. H., *Theory of Computation*. New York: John Wiley & Sons.

1981. Lewis, H. R. and Papadimitriou, C. H. *Elements of the Theory of Computation*. Englewood Cliffs, NJ: Prentice-Hall.

1982. Kfoury, A. J., Moll, R. N. and Arbib, M. A. *A Programming Approach to Computability*. New York: Springer-Verlag.

1984. Tourlakis, G. J. *Computability*. Reston, VA: Reston Publishing Co.

1985. Hofstadter, D. R. *Metamagical Themas*. New York: Basic Books.

JONATHAN GOLDSTINE

UNIVAC I

For articles on related subjects *see* DIGITAL COMPUTERS: EARLY; ECKERT, J. PRESPER; and MAUCHLY, JOHN W.

UNIVAC I (Universal Automatic Computer) was the first commercially available computer in the United States. Work on the prototype was begun by the Eckert-Mauchly Computer Corporation in 1948 and completed in 1951, when it was delivered to the U.S. Bureau of the Census. During this period, Eckert-Mauchly was acquired by Remington Rand Inc. (subsequently merged with The Sperry Corporation in 1955 to form the Sperry-Rand Corporation).

A total of 46 UNIVAC I computers were delivered to a wide variety of customers during the period 1951–1958. All of them have been subsequently phased out.

The UNIVAC I, a high-speed, general-purpose electronic data processing system, was different from earlier computers in that it handled both numbers and alphabetical characters equally well. One of the innovative features of this computer was that it divorced the complex problems of input and output from the actual computational facility.

The program, which was stored in mercury delay lines (*see* ULTRASONIC MEMORY), circulated within the lines in the form of acoustical pulses that could be read from the line and written into it. Information could be accessed at a speed of 40 to 400 microseconds.

FIG. 1.   UNIVAC 1.

Raw data was transcribed to magnetic tape by a key-to-tape device. Data on punched cards was transcribed to magnetic tape with a card-to-tape converter. Magnetic tape was the principal input medium and was also used for permanent storage of data. Input could also be effected from the keyboard of the control console during the processing of a program.

Output was recorded on magnetic tape. Data on output tapes was transcribed to punched cards by a tape-to-card converter or to printed copy by a printer. Alphabetical, numeric, and symbolic characters were accommodated in any combination in reading, writing, and processing operations.

Buffered storage registers permitted the central computer to continue processing while other data was being read from or recorded on magnetic tape. The system featured many automatic self-checking techniques, including duplicate circuits for all computing operations.

The operating characteristics were as follows: circuitry—chiefly serial, 2.25 MHz bit rate; Internal Operating Code—7 bits (four numeric pulses in excess-three notation, two zone pulses, and one parity pulse); word length, 12 characters including sign; block length, 60 words; program code, single address, automatic sequencing; internal storage capacity, 1,000 words or 12,000 characters.

The speed of the basic arithmetic functions were: addition or subtraction, 0.525 ms; multiplication, 2.150 ms; division, 3.890 ms; comparison, 0.365 ms.

MICHAEL M. MAYNARD

UNIVERSAL PRODUCT CODE

For articles on related subjects *see* CODES; OPTICAL CHARACTER READER; and PATTERN RECOGNITION.

Symbols such as that shown in Fig. 1 now appear on almost all retail products for use in electronic checkout procedures. The code is designed to be read by an optical scanner, and is obviously non-secret, since the numbers used are interpreted at the bottom of the figure. The five leftmost digits identify the manufacturer through a code assigned by the Uniform Grocery Product Code Council. The five rightmost digits are assigned by the manufacturer to identify various individual products; thus, the price itself is not encoded, but instead a product identification number, from which a computer (on-line to the scanner) can obtain the price by table lookup. The digit 0 appearing at the left of the pattern is called the *code symbol*; it will be 0 for grocery products, but some other digit for other types of enterprise. Since it will also participate in a *checksum* calculation to be described later, it is incorporated into the bar pattern itself (but not reprinted as an underlying digit).

Disregarding the guide bars at the left and right and the two center bars separating the two five-digit groups, all of which are longer than the bars over the interpreted digits, each digit is encoded by a sequence of four alternating light and dark bars of one of four different thicknesses. Each digit will have a unique sequence of bars, or, more precisely, a pair of such sequences, since the pattern of a digit on the right hand side is the encoded one's complement of the pattern it would have had on the left. This is done so that the program processing the scanner's input can detect whether the product was passed over the reading aperature right-to-left or left-to-right.

Using 0 and 1 to represent the thinnest light and dark stripes, respectively, and 0000 and 1111 the thickest such stripes, the code is as follows:

Digit	Left Representation	Right Representation
0	0001101	1110010
1	0011001	1100110
2	0010011	1101100
3	0111101	1000010
4	0100011	1011100
5	0110001	1001110
6	0101111	1010000
7	0111011	1000100
8	0110111	1001000
9	0001011	1110100

Thus, for example, the code for 4 on the left is, sequentially, the thinnest light bar (0), the thinnest dark bar (1), the next to thickest light bar (000), and the next to thinnest dark bar (11).

Certain patterns can be ascertained in the code assignments. First, note that all left-hand codes have *odd parity* (i.e. an odd number of 1s), so of course their right-hand complements have *even parity*. Second, the first bit of the left codes is always 0 and bit 7 is always 1, so that these code patterns always begin with a light bar and end with a dark one (and *vice versa* on the right). Of the 32 patterns that could have been assigned to the interior 5 bits, 16 (half) have the desired odd parity. But only 10 of these 16—the 10 selected—consist of exactly two light and two dark stripes. This will allow the scanner to make the further check that the pattern read contained exactly

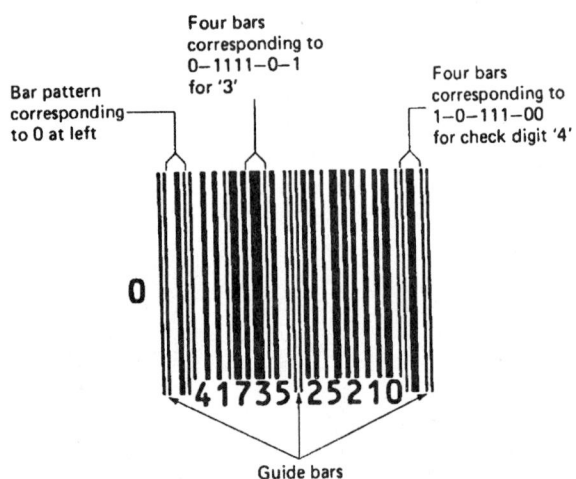

Four bars corresponding to 0–1111–0–1 for '3'

Four bars corresponding to 1–0–111–00 for check digit '4'

Bar pattern corresponding to 0 at left

0

4 1735 25210

Guide bars

FIG. 1.

30 dark and 29 light stripes, 59 in total, originating as follows:

10 interpreted digits × 4 stripes each	=40
2 uninterpreted digits × 4 stripes each	= 8
2 dark-light-dark side guides	= 6
1 light-dark-light-dark-light center guide	= 5
Total	59

Since each of the 12 digits has a 7-bit representation and each of the 11 guide stripes a 1-bit representation, these 59 stripes would correspond to a string of 95 bits. The uninterpreted check digit is positioned between the guide bars on the right and the last interpreted digit. For further accuracy, the scanner verifies that the check digit read has a value such that

3 3 [code symbol + 2nd, 4th, 6th, 8th, and 10th printed digit]
+ [1st + 3rd + 5th + 7th + 9th printed digit]
+ check digit

is a multiple of 10. Thus, if the product is a grocery item (code symbol at left = 0) whose identification number is 4173525210 (as in Fig. 1), its check digit must be 4 so that

3 3 [0 + 1 + 3 + 2 + 2 + 0]
+ [4 + 7 + 5 + 5 + 1]
+ 4 (the check digit) = 50, a multiple of 10.

Such bar codes have applications other than for retail checkout, inventory control being an obvious candidate.

References

1976. Banks, W. "Samples of Machine Readable Printed Software," *Byte* **1**, *12*: 12.
1977. Mellen, G. E. "Universal Product Code," *The Cryptogram* **42**, *1*: 1–3, 23–24.
1980. Helmers, C. "Bar Codes, Revisited...," *Byte* **5**, **4**: 6–10.
1991. Gallian, J. A. "The Mathematics of Identification Numbers," *The College Mathematics Journal*, **22**, *3*, (May) 194–202.

EDWIN D. REILLY

UNIX™ OPERATING SYSTEM

For articles on related subjects *see* C; DIRECTORY; FILE SERVER; INTERACTIVE SYSTEM; KERNEL; MULTITASKING; OPERATING SYSTEMS; REGULAR EXPRESSION; SHELL; VIRTUAL MEMORY; and WORKSTATION.

Unix* is a general-purpose time-sharing system developed in the early 1970s at Bell Laboratories by Ken Thompson and Dennis Ritchie. More than two decades later, Unix stands as one of the most influential systems in computing history, and its popularity continues to grow. It has been ported to dozens of hardware platforms,

---

*Unix is a registered trademark of AT&T Bell Laboratories.

and nearly every major vendor supports a product line based on Unix. In 1983, Thompson and Ritchie received the ACM Turing Award (*q.v.*) for their contributions to the computing field.

The roots of Unix can be found in the Multics project of the 1960s, in which Thompson and Ritchie were participants. But where Multics was a high-profile collaborative project involving several organizations, government funding, and many researchers, Unix was developed more quietly by individuals searching for a more hospitable environment in which to perform their activities. Indeed, the name Unix is a pun on Multics; where Multics attempted to explore many alternatives, Unix would concentrate on providing just one.

Unix began in 1969 with Thompson's file system experiments on a PDP-7. The first production version appeared in 1971 and ran on a PDP-9. In 1973, Unix became the first operating system to be written in a high-level language when all but a small part of the system was rewritten in C, a programming language developed specifically for Unix. The first widely available public release, version 6, was released in 1976 and ran on a PDP-11. Version 7, the first portable Unix system, came two years later and ran on several different hardware platforms, including the PDP-11, Interdata 8/32, and the VAX. The ease with which Unix could be modified led to development efforts at many universities and research laboratories. The most influential of the non-AT&T development sites was the University of California at Berkeley, which produced the Berkeley Software Distributions (BSD) versions of Unix. Berkeley ported Unix to the VAX architecture and added support for virtual memory, demand paging, and the TCP/IP network protocols. Today, many parts of Unix and the C language have been standardized by international standards committees, and Unix has become the operating system of choice for RISC architecture (*q.v.*) workstations.

Unix carefully distinguishes between the operating system *kernel* and user applications. Each user program runs as a separate *process*, making system calls into the kernel to perform such tasks as accessing files or allocating additional memory. The kernel itself was deliberately kept small; Thompson (1978) reports: "The kernel is the only Unix code that cannot be substituted by a user to his own liking. For this reason, the kernel should make as few real decisions as possible. This does not mean to allow the user a million options to do the same thing. Rather, it means to allow only one way to do one thing, but have that way be the least-common divisor of all the options that might have been provided." This design philosophy paved the way for the evolution of Unix over time. By implementing services in processes, users could easily replace an existing implementation of a service with an entirely new one by replacing the utility providing the service. As programmers experimented with new services, services evolved into superior ones.

The command interpreter, called a *shell*, processes keyboard input and performs user-requested tasks. In Unix, the shell is a regular (albeit sophisticated) program executing as its own process. Running the shell as a process has two benefits. First, users can modify the shell as easily as any other program. More than a half dozen shells, including the C shell and Korn shell, have become popular in addition to the original Bourne shell. Each subsequent shell provided new features that its predecessor lacked. The Bourne shell, for example, supports the creation of multiple simultaneous jobs, but provides limited means of controlling them once they have been started. The C shell permits users to suspend and later resume jobs, and to move jobs from foreground to background. Having shells run as regular programs also makes it possible to write *command scripts*, files containing arbitrary commands. In Unix, the shell can just as easily process commands contained in a file as those entered at the keyboard.

Unix provides a hierarchical file system in which directories hold files and other (sub)directories. The resultant file tree is shared by all users, making it straightforward to name and find files, including those belonging to other users. A file can be named by its full path name, which lists the directories on the path from the root of the tree to the file, or by its short name, in which case the file is assumed to be in the current directory.

Unix provides a single, uniform way of accessing a file's contents. The lack of different file types means that programs process all files in exactly the same manner; they need not concern themselves with record sizes or differing access methods *(q.v.)*. Programs treat the data in files as an uninterpreted byte sequence. In addition, Unix uses *device independence* to make such devices as terminals and printers appear the same as files, allowing programs to read from either a file or terminal without knowing where the data actually comes from. For example, the command *sort* reads lines from the terminal (until the user signals end of input) sending the sorted contents back to the terminal. To sort data contained in a file, the same utility is invoked, but its input is redirected from the specified file (here *input*):

$$\text{sort} < \text{input}$$

Finally, to save the sorted output in a file, output can be redirected to an arbitrary file (here *output*) as follows:

$$\text{sort} < \text{input} > \text{output}$$

Unix provides a service called *pipes*, which allows users to connect the output of one program to the input of another. For example, entering:

$$\text{who} \mid \text{sort}$$

invokes the utility *who*, which displays the names of logged in users, and pipes its output into *sort*. The result is a sorted list of users. The commands of a pipeline execute *concurrently*, with each process running just long enough to fill its output or empty its input pipe. The length of a pipeline can be arbitrarily long, and the programs used in forming pipelines are called *filter programs* (or just *filters*) because they act as data filters, transforming the data passed on to the next command in the pipeline.

Tools Unix is not just an operating system; it is an environment complete with a rich set of powerful tools. The operating system kernel itself runs on a bare machine, controlling access to such resources as memory, devices, and the CPU *(q.v.)*. Although a crucial part of the system, users interact with the kernel only indirectly. Instead, they invoke editors, compilers, text processors, and other utility programs that in turn request kernel services when accessing files. Thus, from a user's perspective, Unix refers to the tools it provides for carrying out tasks. Unix pioneered the use of many tools now taken for granted, including document formatters and spelling checkers *(q.v.)*. Several utilities in particular deserve special mention. While most of the following tools are widely available on many systems, Unix introduced many of them.

The *make* utility takes a recipe describing the exact steps needed to build a system, but rebuilds only those parts of the system that have changed since the last time the system was built. In a large system constructed from hundreds of files, for example, a change in a single important program file might require recompiling the entire system, while a change in another file might require only rebuilding one component of the system.

The *lex* and *yacc* utilities facilitate the construction of compilers and other translation tools. Programmers attach C source code "action" statements to a high-level description of the task they want to perform. The utilities generate actual C program source code that recognizes the specified condition and then arranges for the user-supplied action to be performed. These tools increase programmer productivity by eliminating the need to implement and debug every low-level function performed by a program.

The *grep* utility searches text files for lines matching a specified *regular expression (q.v.)*. *Grep* makes it possible to quickly locate all references to a particular variable or keyword in a collection of files.

The *awk* utility provides a quick way to extract or modify the information in text files. Users provide (*pattern, action*) pairs, where *pattern* is a regular expression describing the line of interest, and *action* defines what should be done to that line. For each line in the file that matches the regular expression, the corresponding action is performed. An *awk* program might perform the same action on every line (such as reversing the order of columns), or different actions for different lines (such as removing blank lines, but leaving others unchanged).

For document processing, Unix provides a set of utilities for drawing pictures and graphs, creating tables, displaying equations, managing bibliographic references, and justifying plaintext. Other utilities include spelling checkers and tools for analyzing the grammar and style of documents. The document-processing tools demonstrate the power of using pipes to create an application from a set of smaller applications. Most of the described utilities are stand-alone programs, acting as preprocessors *(q.v.)* for the main formatting program called *troff*. Each filter interprets the commands it understands, passing the remaining commands unchanged to the next filter.

Evaluation Why has Unix been so successful? First, it was the first operating system to focus entirely on interactive use. Unix was written by programmers for programmers, and interactive systems provide the most productive environment for them. By using the system as it was being developed, its positive and negative features quickly became apparent to those developing the system, who were then able to correct them before it was too late. Unix's unique ability to change and evolve in response to feedback from its user community and to exploit changes in hardware technology has been a major factor in its success. Indeed, Ritchie (1978) reports: "the success of the Unix system is largely due to the fact that it was not designed to meet any predefined objectives."

Second, Unix was made available at almost no cost to universities and other research labs, putting it into the hands of those in the best position to appreciate its features. Moreover, most of the Unix kernel and its support utilities were written in the C programming language, and source code was distributed with the system. Including source allowed users of the system to find and correct bugs on their own and expand the system to support new features. Demonstrably positive features would frequently find their way back into an official release. Thus, the system was able to evolve through the contributions of many. A noteworthy aspect of the evolutionary development of Unix is that important and useful utilities were frequently replaced by more sophisticated and extended versions. For example, one of Unix's early debuggers allowed users to execute programs one machine instruction at a time and to examine machine registers and memory locations. Although the basic idea behind the original debugger hasn't changed, newer debuggers display the contents of variables and show users the program statements being executed.

Finally, because Unix was written in the C programming language, it was the first system to run on machines of vastly differing architectures. This allowed Unix to take advantage of new hardware technologies as they came along. In the late 1970s, Unix became available on VAX machines, whose large virtual address space made the VAX/Unix combination particularly popular among computer scientists. Another boost was received in the early 1980s when Berkeley released its 4BSD versions of Unix, one of the first widely available systems to support the TCP/IP network protocols (*q.v.*). At the same time, vendors introduced local area networks (LANs - *q.v.*) such as the Ethernet, and the availability of cheap LAN hardware created a huge demand for Unix. More recently, Unix was adopted for use by workstation manufacturers, making it the first system to exploit the performance of RISC-based microprocessors.

References

1978. Ritchie D. M. and Thompson K., "The UNIX Time-Sharing System" *The Bell System Technical Journal*, **57**(6): 1905–1930, July–August. Special issue devoted to the Unix time-sharing system.

1978. Thompson, K. "UNIX Implementation". *The Bell System Technical Journal*, **57**(6): 1931–1946, July–August.

1985. Quarterman, John, Silberschatz, Abraham, and Peterson, James. 4.2bsd and 4.3bsd as Examples of the Unix System. *ACM Computing Surveys*, **17**(4): 379–418, December.

1989. Leffler, Samuel J., McKusick, Marshall K, Karels, Michael J., and Quarterman, John S. *The Design and Implementation of the 4.3BSD UNIX Operating System*. Reading, MA: Addison-Wesley.

1986. Bach, M. J. *The Design of the UNIX Operating System*. Englewood Cliff, NJ: Prentice-Hall.

THOMAS NARTEN

USER GROUPS

The brief history of the rise, maturation, and old age of computer user groups represents a sociological textbook example of any volunteer organizational entity. Computer user groups began because the manufacturers did not understand how to support the hardware they produced. A forceful, activist community arose. As a manufacturer's products mature and a support infrastructure emerges, the need for a user group diminishes. The oldest, largest user groups have developed a bad case of stagnation; the newer groups continue to grow and thrive.

History The precise origin in 1955 of the first user group, SHARE, is clear. Users of the IBM 701 in the Los Angeles area worked cooperatively on a primitive automatic programming system. While working on its successor for the soon-to-be-delivered IBM 704, the users felt the need for a united front against a proposed IBM assembler. The first formal user group meeting was held in a basement room at the RAND Corporation's headquarters in Santa Monica, California, during the week of 22 August 1955 (Armer, 1956).

Installations represented were a cross section of the scientifically-oriented computer community of that era. There was one government agency (NSA - National Security Agency), three government-sponsored research establishments (RAND, Los Alamos, and Livermore), eight aerospace organizations (Boeing, Curtis-Wright, Hughes, North American, United Aircraft, and three Lockheed divisions), three industrial giants (General Electric, General Motors, and Standard Oil of California), and IBM (Steel, 1956).

A few months after the founding of SHARE, a group of IBM users of commercial computers (the 702 and the undelivered 705) recognized the merit in the user group idea and founded GUIDE. Since 1965, when IBM's System 360 was announced, membership requirements for SHARE and GUIDE have been almost identical. GUIDE appeals to the banks, insurance companies, retailers, and other large commercial establishments, while SHARE retains the loyalties of universities, engineering organizations, and research establishments. Direct SHARE spin-offs included VIM for CDC 6600 and successors, as well as now-defunct groups that supported the GE 600 series and the Philco Transac equipment.

The user group idea has spread beyond computers. Today there are groups that support such widely diverse products and services as the Xerox 9700 copier, Pascal, C (*q.v.*), and MUMPS (*q.v.*), software systems, and several commercial spreadsheet (*q.v.*), database, and word processing (*q.v.*) products. While DECUS probably is the largest of all user groups, some of the most active groups are those supporting a single software product or one piece of hardware on a regional basis.

Purposes

Before software was sold, a major role of a user group was exchanging home-grown software. Before manufacturers supplied utilities, users had little but their own ingenuity on which to rely for routines to keep a system running. A memory dump from Phillips Petroleum, an internal sort from UCLA, and an assembly program from United Aircraft all crossed and recrossed the country, spread by word of mouth and the SHARE library, founded and operated by Ben Faden of North American Aviation Corporation.

Early on, user groups generated specifications and did most of the implementation for an entire operating system. One such was SOS, the SHARE operating system, designed for the IBM 709. The complexity of today's systems has made it virtually impossible for a loosely organized, volunteer association to implement a large project. To survive, user group purposes had to be altered. SHARE's purpose is now stated as "...to foster the development, free exchange and public dissemination of research data pertaining to SHARE companies...in the best scientific tradition." It implies that the group exists to generate a climate for the exchange of information, rather than for the creation of new data.

Despite this pretense of innovative objectives, the general view is that large user groups are underpowered lobbying forces attempting, with only marginal success, to translate user needs into product specifications. No longer the aggressive developers of the late 1950s and early 1960s, the groups now display reactive tendencies.

Membership

Membership in user groups generally is confined to installations that have installed or have on order the specific hardware, program, or service around which the group is organized. Some groups relax this requirement of eligibility to permit attendance by all who express interest in the "system." Although softening attendance rules invites extended participation, a broader membership base may lead to more emphasis on marketing than on the interests of real customers. This sales device is a perversion of the reasons that users organize.

Membership counts vary widely. DECUS claims 35,000. SHARE, the oldest, counts over 2,300 installations. Local, regional, or one-product groups may be as small as 50 members. Usually, acquiring and retaining membership requires little more than a declaration of interest and installing a particular product. However, some more formal groups require meeting attendance on at least a biennial basis.

The bona fide nature of an application for membership is an unsolved problem. A user group has almost no way to verify that the statements on the application are genuine. It is not unknown for a paper company with no resources to join a user group before its corporate certificate of incorporation was on file.

Legal Status

A greeting at some user group meetings is: "Fellow Conspirators!" The legal status of user groups is vague. While no group has framed a conspiracy to control a market, from time to time groups have been on thin ice. The exact status of user groups is questionable and likely will remain undefined. Nobody is interested in testing the matter in court.

A few user groups have incorporated to obtain the protections of corporate law for their officers. From a tax viewpoint, a user group should be a not-for-profit, tax-exempt organization of a scientific and/or educational nature. Unfortunately, the U.S. Internal Revenue Service (IRS) does not agree with this position. The point of contention is the restrictive nature of the membership rules. The IRS emphasized this in withdrawing the 50l(c)(3) tax exemption from several user groups.

Practices

Attending a first visit to a major user group meeting is equivalent to a three-ring circus—exciting, stimulating, and confusing. Activity swirls from early morning to late at night; 20 meetings may be running in parallel; social events continue into the wee hours; and small knots of people are seen huddling in corridors. Actually, what is happening are small, face-to-face technical confrontations, limited-size working parties planning implementation and specification priorities, medium to large groups listening to technical presentations with a minimum of interaction, and formal assemblies hearing sales pitches such as, "you'll love it when you get it," a phrase coined by IBM's Carl Reynolds at a SHARE meeting.

To move beyond listener status, an attendee should strive to match installation needs to the information dispensed, not always an easy matter. Meeting agendas are broad in scope and never include the most important sessions. The intimate, unlisted (but critical) meetings held at odd hours in private rooms are the most important, but only the regular delegate will know how to find these.

Accomplishments

What is actually accomplished by user groups? The record is erratic. The group effectiveness curve seems to be dipping. The vastness of today's systems, the size of the vendors, the difficulties of sustaining voluntary action, and the rising expenses involved have combined to squeeze the user group's effectiveness.

Today's user has almost no opportunity to impact the primary thrust of product developmental efforts; those lines are set by marketing requirements, competitive timings, and product life cycles. The user group can do minor cosmetic surgery on the specifications, detect and note the gross functional errors, and flag basic implementation faults after the product is released.

But user groups tend not to fade away, even when their original incentive is gone. As each grows too large or as the manufacturer with whom it is dealing becomes too rigid, new groups form to deal more specifically with a single machine or product. The manufacturers recognize the value of even superficial cooperation as a marketing tool, and both sides enjoy the social amenities.

The newer single-product groups or those that deal with smaller manufacturers carry considerable influence. There are cases of a user group demanding a pricing change and getting it. No vendor can stand still when a room packed with irate users representing 75% of annual revenue unanimously screams about a policy. In unity there is strength, at least until the manufacturer involved gets so large that there is no major penalty if a few users grumble.

Getting a change or fix done properly and on time can save thousands of dollars of machine time and hundreds of programming and debugging hours, so the justification for and investment in user groups is likely to continue.

References

1956. Armer, P. "SHARE—An Eulogy to Cooperative Effort," RAND Report P-969 (October).
1956. Steel, T.B. *SHARE Reference Manual*, pp. 0.1-01.

PHILIP H. DORN

USER INTERFACE

For articles on related subject *see* HUMAN FACTORS IN COMPUTING; MOUSE; OPERATING SYSTEMS; and WINDOW ENVIRONMENTS.

The *user interface* is that part of a computer system through which human user and computer communicate. With the increasing prevalence of interactive personal computer systems, the importance of human communication is growing steadily, and many systems now stand or fall on the quality of their interfaces. Interfaces consume a large amount of software construction and maintenance effort—estimates of the fraction of an interactive system's code devoted to the user interface vary from one-third to almost two-thirds.

User interfaces evolved from the *command and job control languages (q.v.)* available on batch computing systems that allowed users to describe to the system the requirements of their tasks. These provided facilities for users to identify themselves to the system for security and accounting purposes; inform the computer about the resources required by tasks; specify input/output devices and files needed; and determine what action the computer should take in the event of error. Interactive systems renamed their job control languages *command languages*. These environments simplified some aspects of the human/computer interface. A stream of English-like commands could be submitted and interpreted one line at a time, which allowed users to respond to evolving situations rather than forcing them to anticipate all conditions. The computer could to some extent take the initiative in the dialogue, prompting the user for whatever information it needed. In other respects, interactive environments complicated the interface, for a great many new facilities became possible and were absorbed into the command language (examples include file management, interactive editing, and social functions, like getting information about users and processing electronic mail).

User interfaces changed dramatically when interactive systems were liberated from the tyranny of the teletype—although change came slowly and, at first, uncertainly. The advent of cursor-addressable display screens allowed the temporal sequence of events, imposed on the user by a command language, to be relaxed in favor of business-form-style spatial layouts that gave users control over the sequence in which items were entered. The widespread use of bitmapped graphic displays provided opportunities to employ iconic (pictorial) rather than textual representations, multi-font typographic-style text, and other artwork. Interfaces based on this technology are called *graphical user interfaces* (GUIs). Transient pop-up menus decoupled the information that could be accessed from the physical limitations of the screen. Multiple windows transferred even more control to users' hands, allowing them to switch between tasks and visual contexts at will. Color, motion, and audio all provided more realism and a richer space of sensory cues. As these technical advances escalated, so did the programming problems of user interfaces, problems that are only now being tamed by suitable programming environments.

Meanwhile, users began to expect each application program to have its own interface, not just the operating system, as before. The prospect of interactive editing created the need for editing interfaces, first as powerful command languages for specifying text transformations (for teletype-style editing), then as fully-interactive screen editors, and eventually as on-screen typographical editors that allowed users to manipulate a typeset image—often with built-in graphical editing facilities for illustrations as well. The growing use of text editors or word processors by non-programming personnel emphasized the importance of interface design. Following editors, other programs began to acquire individual interfaces. The invention of the spreadsheet (*q.v.*) provided a great spur to interface design, for it became immediately apparent that vast power could be gained from reactive, screen-oriented interfaces.

Current User Interface Technology *Command-driven* interfaces employ an artificial, imperative linguistic medium to allow users to control the machine through incremental interactions. The system is a passive slave awaiting orders; no attempt is made to guide or help users. On receiving an order, it executes it and then awaits the next command. The Unix system interface, called a *shell (q.v.)*, is a typical example (Fig. 1). Teletype-like, it makes no use of the cursor control features provided by display screens. With the single exception of the character-erase and line-erase characters, the screen is treated like a long roll of paper. As further commands are entered, old information scrolls irretrievably off the screen.

Menu interfaces, in contrast, explicitly reveal all possible options to the user, by analogy to a restaurant that presents the diner with an explicit list of choices. There are many different ways of arranging menus, including *direct access* menus, which show all possible choices on a single display, perhaps as a panel of buttons, and *taxonomic* menus, which classify the domain hier-

```
Unix: pwd
/home/saul/encyclopedia-article
Unix: ls
figures              ians-comments      sauls-comments
working-draft
Unix: mail
No mail
Unix:
```

FIG. 1. A Unix command screen, showing user-typed commands in italics and prompts underlined. In this sequential dialogue, the user prints the current location in the file directory hierarchy, requests a listing of files, and checks for mail.

archically and allow the user to navigate through it. In many circumstances, it is not necessary for a menu to remain permanently visible on the display screen, and it can be "popped up" on the screen when required. Typically, a mouse button is depressed to display it, and the menu is painted on the screen near the cursor position (at the focus of visual attention). When the button is released, the menu disappears and the hole left by it is automatically repaired. Menu selection is achieved by pointing at the desired item with the mouse, and indicated visually by shading that menu item. The pop-up menu is a convenient way to keep frequently used commands accessible without occupying space on the screen. Several different menus can be provided by having *buttons* on the screen that, when moused, display a menu; these are called *pull-down* menus (Fig. 2). Normally they remain drawn only while the mouse button is pressed, but sometimes the user can move them with the mouse and post them elsewhere on the screen—*tear-off* menus.

Forms are a natural user interface medium, being widely used tools for structuring information in conventional offices. A form is a template that, when filled in, becomes a text document (Fig. 3). Either it can be viewed as a document in itself, or the filled slots can be regarded as a collection of entries in a database. This dual nature gives the form an important advantage over other ways of recording information.

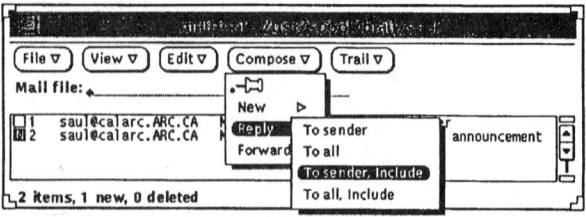

FIG. 2. Sun's XView Mailtool, showing a variety of menu styles. The buttons on the top can act as both a direct access menu to execute a function immediately and as entry points to hierarchies of pull-down and "pull-right" menus. Menus can be torn off by pinning them to the display with the pin icon. The scrollable list (middle of the display) is itself a selectable menu of old and new mail.

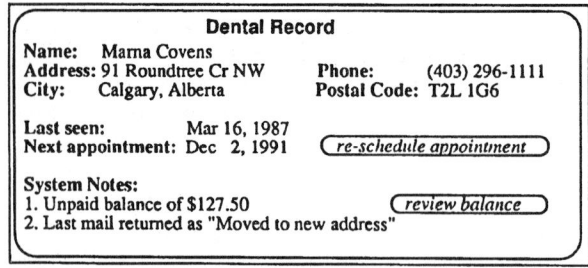

FIG. 3. A simple computerized form. Acting on a call from a dental patient, the secretary supplies the patient's name and desired appointment time. All other fields are retrieved and displayed by the system. The appointment date is automatically entered into the dentist's schedule form, checking for conflicts. Hidden parts of the form are raised by pressing the appropriate button.

A conventional paper form can:

- Display information as a structured and stereotyped document.
- Collect information, and permit its modification.
- Store and retrieve information as records in a database.
- Transfer information as messages.

Each role can be expanded within a computer forms system. First, the medium of display is not fixed. Viewed as a document, the form may be displayed, printed, typeset, even spoken over the telephone. Different text templates can be used to present different views of the same information. Only the necessary portions of the form need be disclosed to the viewer. Second, there is a similar variety of media for information collection: hand-printing on a tablet, screen interaction, speech input, and off-line data entry. Third, the relational database (*q.v.*) model is the most natural for storing form-based information—each instance of the form representing a single *tuple* of a relation. As with a spreadsheet, implicit references to other database entries allow fields to be filled automatically (e.g. to look up an address associated with a user-supplied name field) or be defined to contain the result of operations on other fields (e.g. a "total"). Fourth, mailing of forms may be expedited by transmitting only the form identification and the contents of the fields; the text template can be regenerated by the recipient from a master copy. Finally, the act of entering values may cause side effects—filling in a patient record may trigger the automatic mailing of a bill.

Natural language seems an attractive proposition for user interfaces. However, despite the existence of some sophisticated example systems, it has not achieved the maturity of the other techniques discussed here, and its future is still uncertain. It offers the potential of very high expressiveness, combined with ease of use and familiarity for all. Users feel comfortable, are practiced in its use, and need no special training. Set against this is verbosity and the difficulty many people have with typing. Although speaking natural language seems attractive, existing speech recognition systems are highly limited research projects. A serious problem with natural language interfaces is that they implement only a rather *unnatural* subset of the language. It is very easy for users to step outside their limited domain and context accidentally. There is no warning of the boundaries of the system, and the only way to learn them is by trial and error. It is very hard to constrain one's word and syntax usage according to pre-specified rules.

Direct manipulation interfaces behave as though the interaction were with a real-world object rather than an abstract system—video games provide an excellent illustration. By de-emphasizing verbs (commands) in favor of nouns (objects), communication can be made more concrete because the objects can be represented pictorially as *icons* rather than as linguistic tokens. Language syntax and symbolic references are replaced by direct manipulation of the object of interest (usually with a mouse). Direct manipulation systems map the interface structure on to some facet of the real world—a metaphor for interaction—and proceed to simulate this. A "soft machine" is an interface that employs a literal metaphor to simulate directly all features of a physical machine (such as a hand-held calculator). By choosing a metaphor familiar to the user and appropriate to the task, rich interfaces can be learned with little training. Many modern electronic office (*q.v.*) systems follow a "desktop" metaphor through simulation of document windows, in/out trays, rolodexes, folders, filing cabinets, and trashcans (Fig. 4). Abstract operations on these objects are accessed through pop-up menus. By allowing only "legal" manipulations of the object, and by altering the menu so that only appropriate abstract actions are included, errors of syntax can be avoided altogether.

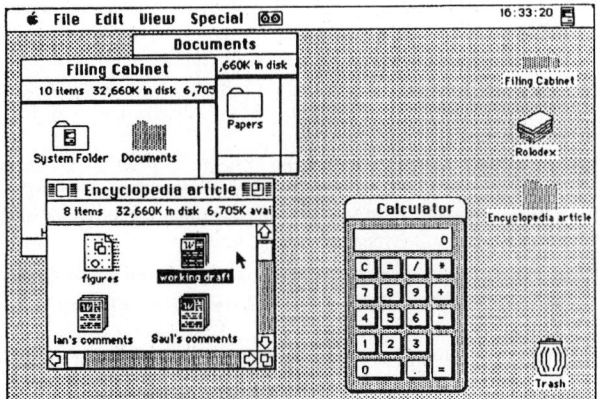

FIG. 4. The Apple Macintosh desktop. Folders and documents are visible as graphical icons. Open folders are displayed in the three overlapping windows. Also visible is a calculator (a soft machine), a Rolodex icon for accessing a phone list, and a trash can for discarding unwanted items. The bar on the top of the screen includes entry points to a pull-down menu system and status information. The "Filing Cabinet" icon actually represents the internal hard disk.

New Paradigms New paradigms for interfaces are continually being developed. Some examples follow.

Hypertext (*q.v.*) extends the notion of a document beyond sequential text by allowing complex interwoven structures to be created and manipulated by linking text fragments. The fundamental idea is simple: links can be added anywhere in the text database that, when followed, will transport the reader to another location. Associating types with links extends the power for enhancing semi-structured access to a document's contents, with instant availability of related information; rich searching and indexing facilities; selective and personal in-depth explorations; annotations comprising definitions, footnotes, and asides; and convenient opportunities for activities such as adding personal annotations and place-marking.

Hypertext becomes *hypermedia* when any media form can be used and linked into the document. An author's point may be annotated with an instantly accessible image, sound track, or video clip. Sometimes active sections may be incorporated into otherwise passive documents to permit user interaction. When this ability is added, hypermedia becomes a rich new metaphor for interacting with computers and file stores.

Multimedia interfaces transcend text and the stylized images seen on conventional systems. Color and three-dimensional graphics, animation, audio, and video can make the interface come alive. Just as sound provides enriching feedback in the natural world, so it can enhance the user interface. Moving a file icon across a desktop may be accompanied by a dragging sound that reflects the underlying surface—the harmonic fullness of the file folder, the hollow tones of the background screen, and the clanging contact with the trashcan. Similarly, animation of interface constructs can make visual objects seem to behave just as their physical counterparts do. Color, properly used, enriches the interface esthetically and supplies the user with additional information without occupying extra screen space. Inclusion of video brings a new way of importing "real-life" data and impressions into the computer.

Groupware (*q.v.*) encompasses software applications for several users working together by promoting general communication between people. Considering the collaborative nature of most of today's work, it is surprising that the vast majority of current applications support only a single person's on-line activities. Teleconferencing and videoconferencing bring geographically separated people together for real-time meetings. Electronic mail (*q.v.*), with a delivery time of minutes, has proved to be an effective means for asynchronous communication, and augments the roles more conventionally assumed by surface mail, inter-office memos, facsimile transmission, (fax), and even quick phone calls. Advanced mail systems allow people to compose multi-media messages, specify criteria for filtering mail, and enforce a specific message exchange protocol. Bulletin boards (*q.v.*) are communal mail boxes where people can post, read, and reply to messages, and connect an extended community of geographically separated people with common interests. Groupware also promotes task-specific collaboration:

multi-user applications can help groups to record brainstorming, list ideas, collaborate on documents, and even compare personal beliefs.

Cyberspace is an innovative and futuristic approach to human-computer interaction. It immerses a person's senses in a three-dimensional simulated virtual world. Seeing the world in a stereoscopic head-mounted display that has a screen for each eye, one moves through it by head and body gestures. Motion sensors pick up and translate real movements to virtual ones, and the view is adjusted accordingly. Users interact with the simulated world through a data-glove or data-suit that allows them to grasp and manipulate the virtual objects they see. They hears sounds through a 3-D audio display. The effect, although still primitive, is to exist and interact within a *virtual reality*—cyberspace.

Designing User Interfaces Designing and building a viable user interface requires creativity, knowledge of design guidelines, suitable tools, and techniques of evaluation.

Design guidelines are distilled from empirical studies and practitioners' experience. The golden rule is "know the user," which includes familiarity with the task, environment, personal capabilities and limitations, and likely reaction to the system. Other guidelines range from common sense ("provide good feedback") to quite specific rules ("do not use the color blue for critical data"). Some computer vendors even provide *style sheets* that recommend a generic "look and feel" for interfaces to follow. Guidelines and style sheets require informed interpretation, and do not constitute recipes that should be blindly adhered to. Nevertheless, they serve to indicate what might be considered, and what choices other designers have found useful.

User interface toolkits encapsulate standard interface constructs (such as windows, menus, control panels, and dialogue boxes) into a subroutine package for programmers. User interfaces are notoriously time-consuming to build, and, as their complexity increases, so must the sophistication of the tools used to develop them. Toolkits not only help the designer create interfaces rapidly, but also promote consistency in style between applications. Many vendors now endorse standard toolkits (for ease of portability across various hardware platforms), and a standard "look and feel" (for consumer acceptance). The most notable is *X-windows*, a portable window system. Consortia such as the Open Software Foundation and Unix International are promoting the Motif and Open Look toolkits, respectively, for developing applications within X-windows. In contrast, the Apple Macintosh has a high quality but proprietary user interface toolkit, and Apple has not hesitated to sue vendors who copy their "look and feel."

User interface management systems (UIMS) decouple application programs from the appearance of their interface, the two being linked by some intermediary abstract specification. The UIMS manages interface presentation and user interaction at run time. This architecture allows the interface to be changed without altering the application program. The application can be built independently, and the interface can undergo iterations of rapid software prototyping (*q.v.*) and user testing until a satisfactory design is found. Some systems even allow interactive selection and layout of the user interface building blocks through "interface builders." Examples of commercial UIMSs are *MacApp* for the Macintosh, and *Open Dialog* for the Apollo, and *Visual Basic*, *Object Vision*, *C-scape*, and *Realizer* for the IBM-PC and PC-compatibles (*q.v.*).

Interface evaluation is necessary if interfaces are to be improved by iterative design and testing. It is difficult for a designer to discover if the interface built is actually a good one. Intuition, while valuable, can seriously mislead because the designer is often quite dissimilar to the targetted user. More objective evaluation requires watching (perhaps on videotape) the intended user trying out the system, and noting where the design fails. This should happen early in the design process, possibly through prototypes, mockups, or even paper walk-throughs. More formal methods of evaluation involve collecting data on user activity, statistical testing, and protocol analysis.

References

1983. Card, S. K., Moran, T. P., and Newell, A. *The Psychology of Human-Computer Interaction*. Hillsdale, NJ: Lawrence Erlbaum Associates.

1984. Smith, S. L. and Mosier, J. N. *Design Guidelines for User-System Interface Software*. Bedford, MA: Mitre Corporation.

1986. Norman, D. A. and Draper, S. W. (Eds.). *User Centered System Design—New Perspectives on Human-Computer Interaction*. Hillsdale, NJ: Lawrence Erlbaum Associates.

1987. Baecker, R. M. and Buxton, W. A. S. (Eds.). *Readings in Human-Computer Interaction*. Los Altos, CA: Morgan Kaufmann.

1987. Carroll, J. M. (Ed.). *Interfacing Thought: Cognitive Aspects of Human-Computer Interaction*. Cambridge, MA: The M.I.T. Press.

1987. Schneiderman, B. *Designing the User Interface*. Reading, MA: Addison-Wesley.

1990. Thimbleby, H. *The User Interface Design Book*. Reading, MA: Addison-Wesley.

SAUL GREENBERG AND IAN H. WITTEN

VARIABLE.   *See* GLOBAL AND LOCAL VARIABLES.

VECTOR GRAPHICS.   *See* COMPUTER GRAPHICS.

VECTOR PROCESSOR.   *See* PARALLEL PROCESSING; SUPERCOMPUTERS.

VERIFICATION.   *See* FORMAL METHODS FOR COMPUTER SYSTEMS; HARDWARE VERIFICATION; and PROGRAM VERIFICATION.

VIDEODISC

For articles on related subjects *see* CD-ROM; COMPUTER ANIMATION; and HYPERTEXT.

Eventually, computer-based motion video will be digitally encoded, but most of today's motion video applications involve the presentation of analog video under computer control. The *videodisc* is the most common source of analog video material for interactive applications because it allows random access, and the economies of scale derived from the extensive home and entertainment market have reduced player prices. This article discusses standard recording formats, player control and computer interfaces, and applications.

Videodiscs are either 8 or 12 inches in diameter, with 12-inch discs being most common. Information is recorded by pressing microscopic pits into a polished surface. There are about 14 billion pits on one side of a 12-inch disc. In contrast to the concentric tracks used with hard or floppy disks (*q.v.*), the pits are arranged in a spiral.

Information may be recorded at either constant linear velocity (CLV) or constant angular velocity (CAV). Table 1 shows the capacities of each format. With CLV discs, drive speed varies from 600 to 1,800 RPM as a function of head position. The innermost "track" (rotation) of a 12-inch, CLV disc holds one frame, the outermost track holds three frames. With the CAV format, the disc rotates at a constant 1,800 RPM and there is always one frame per track. CAV discs are most commonly used in computer-based systems because they allow random access to any track, freeze frame, step frame, and multi-speed playback. The remainder of this article assumes CAV discs.

Audio information is recorded along with the video. There are two frequency-modulated (FM) channels with signal-to-noise ratios of 70 dB. The FM channels may be used as a single stereo soundtrack or two independent (typically bilingual) soundtracks. National Television System Committee (NTSC) discs have the capacity for an additional digital audio track with a signal-to-noise ratio of 96 dB; however, this track is not available with Phase Alternate Line (PAL) discs.

With an LD-ROM (laser-disc, read-only memory), all or a portion of the digital audio may be replaced with digital information in the CD-ROM format. This allows up to 270 megabytes of program or data to be stored on the disc along with the video and FM audio.

Videodisc players accept commands to seek a specified frame, play forward or reverse at normal or variable speed, freeze a frame, etc. It is common to speak of three

TABLE 1. Videodisc Capacities

	Time/Side (minutes)	Frames/Side
CAV, 8-inch	14	25,200
CAV, 12-inch	30	54,000
CLV, 8-inch	20	na
CLV, 12-inch	60	na

FIG. 1. The Pioneer LD-V4200 LaserDisc Player.

levels of videodisc, depending upon how these commands are issued. Level 1 refers to manual control with the user issuing commands using a remote control device or buttons on the player console. Level 2 players can display characters over the video image and store sequences of commands in an internal memory. Using the overlaid characters for multiple choice questions allows simple branching programs. The control information may be read from the disc or, more commonly, by using a bar-code reader with printed material that accompanies the disc.

In level 3, the player is connected to a computer through an RS-232 interface, and control commands are issued by the computer. The video image may either be displayed on the computer display screen or an independent monitor or television set. Both approaches have advantages and disadvantages. Displaying the image on the computer screen focuses the user's attention on one monitor, reduces the system footprint, and saves the cost of a second monitor; however, it requires a special video adapter for the computer. Displaying the video image on an independent monitor gives additional viewing area and simplifies programming. If a television set is used, it may also play the audio; otherwise, a sound system must be provided. Playing an LD-ROM disc requires a special adapter, with an SCSI interface to the computer.

Level 3 videodisc is used for applications, including industrial training, education, games, and retail sales support. The bulk of early applications were in industrial training, using IBM's InfoWindow™ system for the computer controller and development software. Development tools, and hence applications, have proliferated in recent years. In addition to authoring systems tailored to education and training, there have been videodisc control extensions to HyperCard, HyperPad, ToolBook, and other general-purpose tools for creating interactive applications on personal computers (*see* HYPERTEXT).

A developer may either produce a custom videodisc or re-use a previously existing disc. Producing a custom disc requires video production equipment and skills, a one-time mastering charge, and disc reproduction charges. While producing a custom disc requires

considerable expense and professional expertise, general users such as classroom teachers and industrial trainers can produce interactive material using pre-existing discs and the development tools mentioned earlier.

The pre-existing disc may be a movie, documentary, "how-to" disc produced for the home and entertainment market, or a disc produced specifically for use in interactive computer applications. According to Emerging Technology Consultants (1990), the number of education and training video disc titles has grown from fewer than 200 in 1985 to over 1,200 in 1990. As of 1990, they estimate over 40% annual growth in new titles.

Reference

1990.— *The Videodisc Compendium.* Saint Paul, MN: Emerging Technology Consultants.

LAURENCE PRESS

VIDEOTEX

For articles on related subjects *see* BULLETIN BOARD; COMMUNICATIONS AND COMPUTERS; DATA COMMUNICATIONS; GATEWAY; and PACKET SWITCHING.

Introduction *Videotex* is a generic term that refers to systems allowing end users to access information and services located in remote computers and databases through the public switched telephone network (PSTN) or television broadcasting (whether via radio waves or cable).

The use of the telephone versus a TV-based network results in two basic types of videotex systems: *interactive videotex,* permitting two-way communications between the end user and a remote computer, and *broadcast videotex,* or *teletext,* which is a one-way system that uses portions of the bandwidth of a TV or cable television (CATV) signal.

In the literature, *interactive videotex* (named "viewdata" by its original developers in the United Kingdom) is often simply called *videotex,* while *broadcast videotex* is referred to as *teletext.* This terminology will be used in the remainder of this article.

Teletext and videotex were first developed in the United Kingdom in the early and mid-70s, respectively. The French and the Canadians were also experimenting with similar systems at about the same time, but were using different technologies (Gecsei, 1983). Videotex and teletext systems exist today in a number of countries, primarily in Europe, North America, and Japan. It is the French, however, that have implemented the largest videotex service in the world (called Télétel), with more than 5 million households having access to over 12,000 services through a simple videotex terminal called the *Minitel.*

System Architecture In an interactive videotex system (Fig. 1), users typically access services through simple, low-cost videotex terminals or through micro-

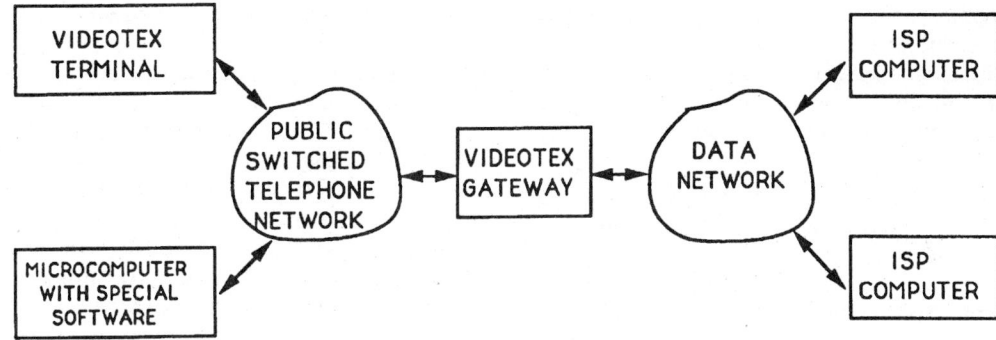

FIG. 1. Typical interactive videotex system.

computers equipped with special emulation software. The end user connects to a videotex *gateway* (*q.v.*) through the public switched telephone network (PSTN). The gateway acts as an intermediary between users and information and service providers (ISPs). It generally provides a directory of services, connects the end user to the selected ISP computer in a simple manner, and handles billing functions on behalf of ISPs. ISP computers are linked to the videotex gateway via a data network, usually a packet-switched data network. In some systems, however, ISPs must have their data stored in central computers managed by the videotex network operator.

In a teletext system (Fig. 2), data is continuously and cyclically transmitted to all receivers—typically TV sets equipped with specialized decoders. ISPs have their data transmitted and stored in a centralized Teletext Center that broadcasts the data cyclically on unused portions of the TV or CATV bandwidths. The user selects the required information via a keypad, and the decoder captures and stores locally the portion of data of interest to the user. While teletext is actually a one-way broadcast system, the user nevertheless has the impression of interacting with the system.

Because of the cyclic nature of teletext, the amount of data available to end users is limited, and true interactivity, such as in teleshopping and telebanking, is better achieved through interactive videotex.

Applications The application programs offered by ISPs fall under four main categories:

- Information-retrieval applications, which allow end users to query general or specialized databases and to obtain up-to-date reports on such information as airline schedules, stock quotations, and driving conditions.
- Transactional applications, which enable subscribers to purchase tickets, pay bills, order goods, etc.
- Messaging applications, which allow for the exchange of messages with a single person or a group

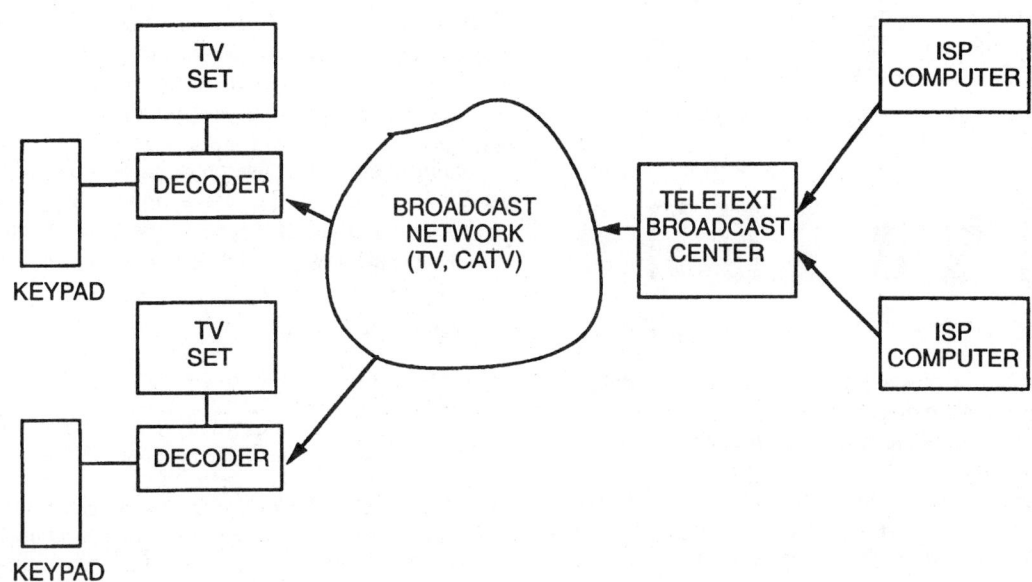

FIG. 2. Typical teletext system.

of people, through electronic mail (*q.v.*), bulletin boards, and chat lines.

- Recreational applications, intended for entertainment and consisting of single- and multiplayer games such as chess and quizzes.

Information-retrieval and recreational applications are present in both videotex and teletext systems, while transactional and messaging applications are generally available in interactive videotex systems only. In practice, most ISP services offer a combination of applications; it is not uncommon to find information-retrieval and transactional applications incorporated within a single videotex service.

Presentation Standards While a videotex/teletext service may present textual information only, using the ASCII standard, it is often desirable to display graphics and pictorial information in addition to basic text. This is particularly true with residential users, where the services offered should be pleasant and user-friendly.

There are three major presentation standards that support graphics: CEPT (Council of European Postal and Telecommunications Authorities), which has been endorsed by a consortium of European nations, NAPLPS (North American Presentation Level Protocol Syntax), which has jointly been adopted by the American National Standards Institute (ANSI) and the Canadian Standards Association (CSA), and CAPTAIN (Character and Pattern Telephone Access Information Network), the standard chosen by the Japanese Ministry of Posts and Telecommunications. These standards have been adopted internationally by the CCITT (International Telegraph and Telephone Consultative Committee) and are referred to in the T-series recommendations (CCITT, 1988).

The main difference between these standards is the presentation coding scheme. CEPT uses alphamosaic coding, NAPLPS alphageometric coding, and CAPTAIN alphaphotographic coding. The alphamosaic coding mode makes it possible to compose simple graphics out of block mosaic characters. Each character is composed of a set of sub-blocks (two across by three down), as illustrated below:

These block mosaic characters can be combined to form a rudimentary picture or graphic design.

In the alphageometric mode, graphics are not defined character by character, but rather by a series of basic geometric shapes (dots, lines, rectangles, arcs, and polygons). Commands, called "picture description instructions" (PDIs), are used to draw the geometric shapes. The drawing operation performed by each of these commands is very simple, but, when they are combined, sophisticated drawings can be generated using relatively few bytes of data.

These standards support the representation of the alphanumeric characters contained in the ASCII character set (*q.v.*). The CEPT standard incorporates four profiles to satisfy slight variations required by national requirements in Great Britain (Prestel), France (Télétel), Germany (Bildschirmtext), and Sweden (Datavision).

The presentation scheme used in the Japanese CAPTAIN system is the alphaphotographic mode, in which graphics are drawn dot by dot, as in the facsimile (fax) process. It permits the transmission of stationary images with a high degree of precision, but requires high transmission speeds to be efficient. The CAPTAIN standard incorporates the Japanese characters.

Worldwide Videotex Service Offerings In North America, videotex services are offered by a number of Bell operating companies (BOCs). Some BOCs offer ASCII-only services, while others support multi-standard (ASCII, Télétel, and NAPLPS) videotex services. Prodigy, a joint venture of IBM and Sears, offers a videotex service that is NAPLPS-based. Many ASCII-based electronic services are provided by organizations such as CompuServe and GE Information Services (GEnie). In Canada, Bell Canada offers the ALEX interactive videotex service, which supports the NAPLPS standard (Chammas, 1990).

In Europe, the telecommunications administrations of many countries (Austria, Belgium, Denmark, Finland, France, Germany, Great Britain, Greece, Ireland, Italy, Luxembourg, Portugal, Spain, Sweden, Switzerland, and the Netherlands) offer videotex services using the French Télétel, British Prestel, German Bildschirmtext, Swedish Datavision, or ASCII presentation scheme, or a combination thereof.

Videotex services also exist in Japan and Australia, and are being introduced in many other countries across the world.

Conclusion The use of videotex is growing rapidly worldwide. For videotex to be a success, however, a larger subscriber base is required to attain the critical-mass that will make it profitable to operate and maintain. This will be achieved only if the services offered are easy to use and appealing to computer-literate and non–computer-literate users alike, and if they provide the capability to perform tasks faster and/or at a lower cost than through other media such as television, newspapers, and the telephone.

References

1983. Gecsei, J. *The Architecture of Videotex Systems*. Englewood Cliffs, NJ: Prentice-Hall.

1988. CCITT (The International Telegraph and Telephone Consultative Committee), Recommendations F.300 and T.101, Geneva.

1990. Chammas, J. "The ALEX Service—A Technical Overview," ICC (International Conference on Communications) Proceedings, Atlanta, GA.

JOSEPH CHAMMAS

VIENNA DEFINITION LANGUAGE

For articles on related subjects *see* Backus-Naur Form; Metalanguage; Programming Linguistics; and Syntax, Semantics, and Pragmatics.

The *Vienna Definition Language* (VDL) is a language for defining the syntax and semantics of programming languages. It consists of a *syntactic metalanguage* for defining the syntax of program and data structures and a *semantic metalanguage* that specifies programming language semantics "operationally" in terms of the computations to which programs give rise during execution.

Syntactic structures in VDL may be graphically represented by means of unordered trees whose edges are labeled by selectors. For example, the expression $a + b$ might be represented in VDL by any one of a set of equivalent unordered trees such as those in Fig. 1.

These tree (t) structures may in turn be represented in linear notation as

$$t = (\langle s_1 : a \rangle \langle s_2 : b \rangle, \langle s-\text{op}: + \rangle)$$

or

$$t = (\langle s_1 : a \rangle, \langle s-\text{op}: + \rangle, \langle s_2 : b \rangle)$$

Selectors in a VDL syntactic structure serve the same role as pointers in a list structure and may be used to select components of the syntactic structure by "applying" the selector to the syntactic structure. In the preceding example, $s_1(t)$, $s_2(t)$, $s-\text{op}(t)$ yield the respective components $a, b, +$.

Syntactic objects may be either *elementary (atomic) objects* with no components (such as the objects $a, b, 1$ above) or *composite objects* (such as the tree t above) whose components may be selected by selectors.

The syntactic metalanguage of VDL is illustrated by the following definition of a simple class of arithmetic expressions:

$$\text{expr} = \text{const} \vee \text{var} \vee \text{binary}$$
$$\text{binary} = (\langle s_1 : \text{expr} \rangle, \langle s_2 : \text{expr} \rangle, \langle s-\text{op}: \text{op} \rangle)$$
$$\text{op} = \{ +, * \}$$

This definition specifies that an expression can be a *constant* (const), a *variable* (var), or a *binary*, where constants and variables are elementary objects with no components, and a binary is a composite object with two components of the type "expr" selectable by the selectors s_1, s_2, and a third component of the type "op" selectable by $s-\text{op}$. The expression $a + b * c$ may be represented in terms of the preceding syntax by a tree structure whose edges are labeled by selectors as shown in Fig. 2.

If the tree structure in Fig. 2 is denoted by t, then $s_1(t) = a$, $s_2(t) = b * c$, $s-\text{op}(t) = 1$, $s_1 \cdot s_2(t) = b$, $s_2 \cdot s_2(t) = c$, and $s-\text{op} \cdot s_2(t) = *$.

The example illustrates that syntactic objects in VDL are represented by trees whose edges are labeled by selectors, and that components of a tree-structured syntactic object may be selected by specifying the sequence of selectors along the path from the root to the selected subtree.

It is instructive to contrast syntactic specification in VDL with syntactic specification of a corresponding class of expressions in BNF (Backus-Naur form). The previously given class of arithmetic expressions could be specified in BNF as follows:

$$\langle \text{expr} \rangle ::= \langle \text{const} \rangle \mid \langle \text{var} \rangle \mid \langle \text{binary} \rangle$$
$$\langle \text{binary} \rangle ::= \langle \text{expr} \rangle \langle \text{op} \rangle \langle \text{expr} \rangle$$
$$\langle \text{op} \rangle ::= + \mid *$$

The difference between the BNF and VDL syntactic metalanguages is brought out by comparing the two specifications of binary. In BNF a binary is a string consisting of an expression followed by an operator followed by a second expression. In VDL a binary is a structure with three components selectable by the selectors s_1, s_2, and $s-\text{op}$. If the representation for expressions were changed from infix to prefix notation, so that $a + b * c$ were written as $+a * bc$, then the BNF specification would have to be modified to reflect this change in order, but the VDL representation could remain the same. Because VDL specifies structure independently of the order in which components appear in a specific representation, a VDL syntactic specification is sometimes referred to as an *abstract syntax*.

The *semantics* of a programming language is defined in VDL in terms of the sequences of information-structure transformations to which programs give rise during execution. Every computation starts with an initial configuration ξ_0, which contains a syntactic representation of both the program structure and the data structure on which the program is to operate. Terminating computations consist of a finite sequence of configurations $\xi_0 \rightarrow \xi_1 \rightarrow \ldots \rightarrow \xi_n$, where ξ_{j11} is obtained from ξ_j by the execution of an instruction. The configurations ξ_j are referred to as

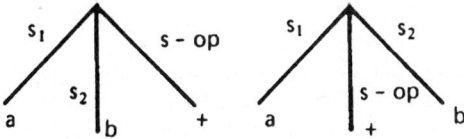

FIG. 1.

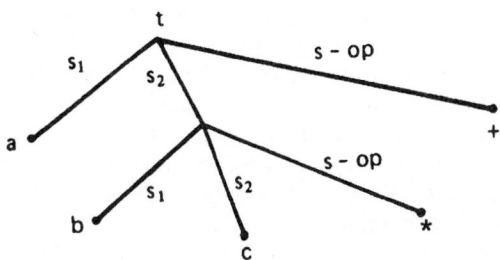

FIG. 2.

instantaneous descriptions, snapshots, or *states.* The instructions form the heart of the semantic specification of a programming language and have the following general form of definition:

$$\text{instruction-name } (x_1, x_2,..., x_n) = \begin{array}{l} p_1 \to a_1 \\ p_2 \to a_2 \\ \cdots \\ p_m \to a_m \end{array}$$

where $p_1, p_2,..., p_m$ are a sequence of predicates, $a_1, a_2,..., a_m$ are a sequence of actions to be performed, and $x_1, x_2,..., x_n$ are a sequence of formal parameters that may appear in the predicate specifications p_i and action specifications a_i.

Example

$$\begin{array}{l} \text{abs(x)} = x > 0 \to x \\ \quad\quad\quad x = 0 \to 0 \\ \quad\quad\quad x < 0 \to -x \end{array}$$

When an instruction of this form is executed with given actual parameters, the current configuration is tested to see whether it satisfies successive predicates p_i for $i = 1, 2,..., n$. The action a_i corresponding to the first true predicate p_i is then executed. Actions a_i specify transformations of the current configuration ξ_j into the next configuration ξ_{j+1}.

The VDL instruction execution cycle differs from that of conventional computers. At any moment of execution, there is a tree of executable instructions called a *control tree*, and the next executable instruction may be *any* terminal vertex of the control tree. This leads to a certain amount of non-determinacy in the instruction execution process, which allows VDL to model non-determinacy in specifying (for example) the order of execution for certain expressions in PL/I, and also to model non-determinacy of execution in certain kinds of multitasking (*q.v.*).

There are two kinds of instructions in VDL:

1. Self-replacing instructions, which, when they are executed, replace the terminal vertex of the control tree at which they occur by a subtree of instructions.
2. Value-returning instructions, which return a computed value to predecessor vertices of the control tree and delete the executed instruction from the control tree.

A computation in VDL generally starts with a control tree consisting of a single vertex containing an instruction such as interpret-program(*t*), where *t* is the syntactic specification of the program to be executed. The first few executed instructions are generally self-replacing instructions that generate successively larger control trees (determined by the abstract syntax of *t*) until terminal vertices corresponding to value-returning instructions are generated. Execution terminates when an empty control tree is generated.

The Vienna definition language was developed by Peter Lucas, Kurt Walk, and others at the IBM Vienna Laboratory. It has been applied to the definition of PL/I

(Lucas and Walk, 1969), Basic (Lee, 1972), and a number of other programming languages. A more detailed introduction to the basic concepts of VDL may be found in Wegner (1972).

References

1969. Lucas, P. and Walk, K. "On the Formal Description of PL/I," *Annual Review of Automatic Programming* **6**, 9.
1972. Lee, J. A. N. *Computer Semantics.* New York: Van Nostrand Reinhold.
1972. Wegner, P. "The Vienna Definition Language," *Computing Surveys* **4**: 5–63.

PETER WEGNER

VIRTUAL MEMORY

For articles on related subjects *see* ASSOCIATIVE MEMORY; CACHE MEMORY; DISTRIBUTED SYSTEMS; MEMORY MANAGEMENT; MEMORY PROTECTION; MULTIPROGRAMMING; OPERATING SYSTEMS; SCHEDULING ALGORITHM; and WORKING SET.

The term *virtual memory* (or virtual storage) denotes the simulation of a uniformly addressable computational memory large enough to accommodate all instantiations of a program on all configurations of the computing machine. Virtual memory originated in the 1950s as a way to simplify programming in machines with memory hierarchies: with it, programmers no longer had to include commands to move blocks of information among the levels of the hierarchy or to recompile their programs when the size of any level of the hierarchy changed. It is just as useful in the computers of the 1990s, which also have memory hierarchies whose levels include caches on the microprocessor chip, RAM on separate chips, and disk storage. Virtual memory hides multilevel memory.

Virtual memory is gradually being incorporated into highly parallel multicomputers that consist of thousands of computers—each with processor and local RAM—hooked together by an interconnection network. Its uniform addressing scheme allows any processor to refer to any data element in any of the component computers' memories; the one algorithm scales across many sizes of machine. Virtual memory hides distributed memory.

Uniform Addressing The key to virtual memory is a uniform address format and addressing protocol that is independent of the sizes of the memory levels and the number of computing elements. A random access memory (RAM) is an example of a uniformly addressable memory. Because RAM is only a component of the hardware in the simulation, virtual memory does not guarantee the same access time for every item; in fact, it tends to give the lowest access times for items that have been referred to most recently.

The set of addresses that a processor can generate as it executes a program is called the *address space* (or name space) *A* of the program; each of these addresses denotes a byte (or word) with which a value can be associated. *A* contains 2^a bytes (or words) on a machine whose processors generate *a*-bit addresses. The name space *A* is frequently referred to as the "virtual address space," or the "virtual memory," within which the processor operates.

The set of addresses recognized by the hardware of a RAM is called the *memory space M* of the machine. *M* contains 2^b bytes (or words) on a machine with *b*-bit RAM addresses.

The virtual address space does not have to be the same size as the memory space. If it is smaller, RAM can hold several address spaces and the virtual memory system implements multiprogramming. If it is larger, the virtual memory system will automatically move information into RAM as it is needed, to simulate the appearance that the whole address space is in RAM. Even if it is larger, the same RAM can be partitioned among several address spaces, again implementing multiprogramming.

The mapping *f* from processor-generated addresses (in *A*) to memory-recognizable addresses (in *M*) is carried out by a dynamic address translator (DAT) interposed between a processor and the memory system. The idea is that when the processor generates a request (*read,x*), the DAT presents (*read,f(x)*) to the memory system, and passes back the value *v* read to the processor. Similarly, when the process generates a request (*write,v,x*), the DAT presents (*write,v,f(x)*) to the memory system. This design makes address translation transparent to the programmer. Addressing invariance with respect to changes in the machine's configuration or the distribution of data among memory elements is achieved by allowing the operating system to change the mapping tables during a program's execution, thereby reflecting the system state dynamically in *f*, rather than in the program itself.

Distributed-memory multicomputers were introduced in the mid 1980s with the Intel iPSC hypercube, which had 128 component computers and were quickly expanded to large scales with the Connection Machine, which had 65,536 component computers (*see* PARALLEL PROCESSING). These machines provide automatic address translation to assist processors in referring to items stored in the memories of other processors. This first generation of multicomputers did not, however, automate the movement of information among the levels of the memory hierarchy; a program had to be fully loaded into the multicomputer before its execution could begin. Some of the machines did allow a multicomputer to be partitioned among several programs, a form of multiprogramming. The initial concerns of designers were focused on whether these machines could be programmed to keep most of their processors busy most of the time. Now that this question has been answered affirmatively, we can expect future multicomputers to include virtual memory implementations of multiprogramming and memory hierarchy management.

Implementation Although the address translator described above is simple in concept, its practical implementation is complicated by requirements:

Fast update. The mapping function *f* is time dependent. When the operating system moves a block of infor-

mation to a new location in memory, it must update the tables for *f* quickly.

Fast context switching. The mapping function *f* is program dependent. When a processor switches context from one program to another, the mapping function of the new program must take effect quickly.

Fast mapping. The mapping function must be so simple to compute that the increase of memory access time due to mapping is negligible.

Efficient memory hierarchy management. Portions of the address space may not be loaded into RAM. Requests for those portions must be intercepted and held up until the operating system can load them into RAM (see Wilkes, 1975).

The elements of virtual memory for a multilevel hierarchy are depicted in Figure 1 and are discussed in the paragraphs following.

The map from *A* to *M* is usually stored in a direct lookup table for fast retrieval and update. Both *A* and *M* are divided into blocks. The map records the correspondence between blocks only, and blocks are the unit of transfer between levels of the memory hierarchy. Because the mapping tables can be large, the requirement for fast context-switching can be met only by placing the mapping tables permanently in the RAM. The context-switch operation merely changes the mapping table pointer register in the processor to the base address of the mapping table of the current program.

There are two important block-oriented mapping schemes. One is called *paging*. The blocks of the address space are called *pages*, and the blocks of the memory space are called *page frames*. All the blocks are the same size, a power of 2. Any page can be stored in any page frame. The mapping table specifies the page frame in which each page is stored. An address *x* generated by the processor is partitioned into the high-order bits *h* and the low-order bits *w*: *x=(h,w)*. The high-order bits are treated as a page number and the low-order bits as a byte (or word) offset within the page. Address translation is nothing more than the substitution of the page frame number for the page number:

$$(h,w) \rightarrow (f(h),w) \qquad (1)$$

An example will help clarify the relationships among these elements. Suppose that virtual addresses are 32 bits, real addresses are 24 bits, and the page size is $256=2^8$ bytes. The address space contains 2^{24} (about 16.8 million) pages and the memory space contains 2^{16} (about 65 thousand) page frames. The page table *f* contains 2^{24} entries, each of which is a 16-bit word. During address translation, the 24 high-order bits of the virtual address are replaced with the corresponding 16 bits from the page table. (We will see shortly that the page table requires more bits per entry than those specifying page frames.)

The other block-oriented mapping scheme is called *segmentation* (see Fig. 1). A segmented name space is partitioned into blocks of various sizes (segments), usually corresponding to logical regions. In the Burroughs

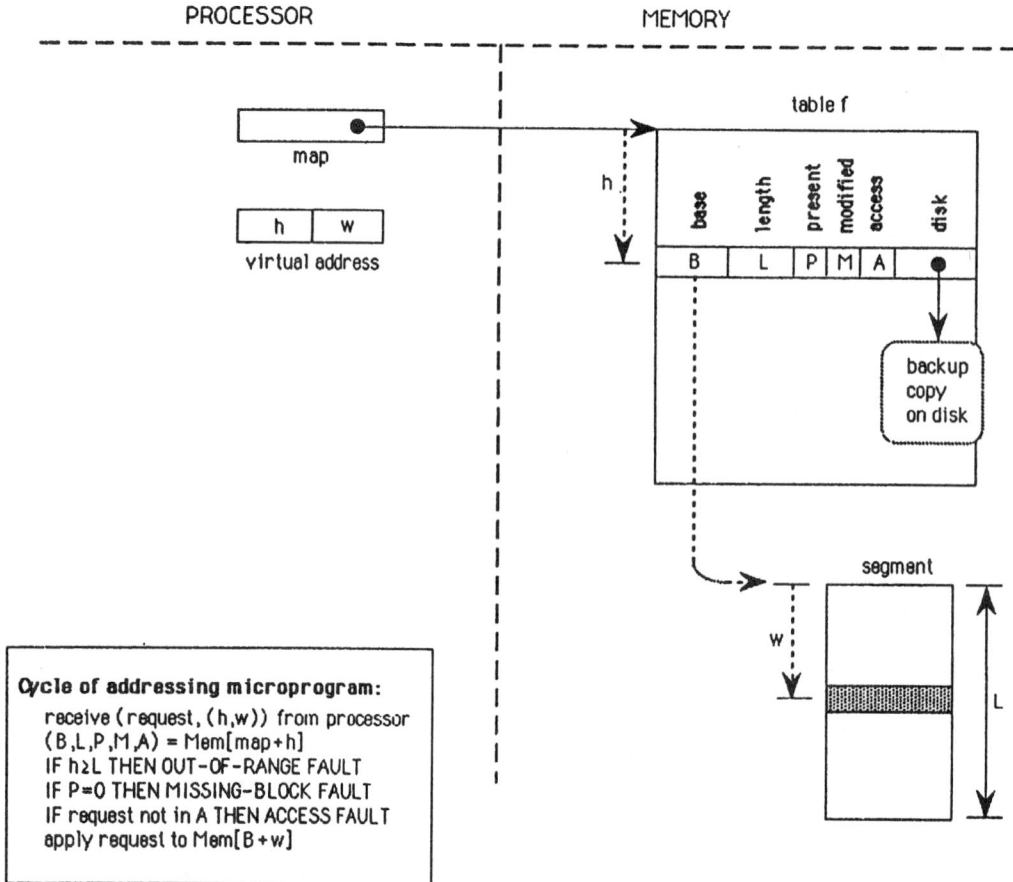

FIG. 1

B5000 and later series, for example, the Algol compiler created segments corresponding to the block structure of the language and the organization of the data (Organick, 1973). The Honeywell 6180 (which implemented a segmented name space under Multics) required the programmer to define the segments and refer to operands by symbolic two-part addresses of the form (segment-name, offset-name) (Organick, 1972). In either case, all virtual addresses are compiled in the form of pairs (h,w). The size of each block must be explicitly recorded in the mapping table, since offsets w that are larger than the block size are illegal. The mapping is the same as in Eq. (1), except that an out-of-range fault signal is generated if w exceeds the size of block h.

Under either paging or segmentation, the basic translation step of Eq. (1) can be completed as fast as the bits $f(h)$ can be retrieved from the mapping table. Since the mapping tables are stored in RAM, it would appear that retrieving the bits $f(h)$ costs one memory cycle time; if this were so, every virtual address reference would cost two memory references. An ingenious solution has been found. A small associative memory called a *translation lookaside buffer* (TLB), is included inside the translator mechanism. If the TLB is on the same chip as the processor, its access time will be quite small compared to the access time of the RAM. Each TLB cell contains an entry

of the form $(z, f(z))$. To perform the basic step of Eq. (1), the translator first interrogates the TLB using the block number h as the key. If there is an entry $(h, f(h))$, it can complete the translation step rapidly. If not, it must access RAM to look up $f(h)$ and the new entry $(h, f(h))$ replaces the least recently used entry in the TLB. Experience has shown that modest sized TLBs (e.g. on the order of 64 cells) will keep the mean translation time in the range of 1% to 3% of the RAM access time.

Thus, a block-oriented mapping scheme coupled with a TLB will satisfy the design requirement for fast mapping. It should be noted that these principles apply to a variety of implementations, including cache/RAM and RAM/disk hierarchies.

To satisfy the fourth design requirement, we must extend the mechanism to allow for the possibility that a given block is not present in RAM when the translation of Eq. (1) is attempted. This can be accomplished by including in $f(h)$ a "presence bit" that tells whether block h is present in RAM. If it is present, the translation can be completed as described above. If it is not present, the translation must be aborted and a "missing-block fault signal" sent to the operating system, which will suspend the faulting program until the missing block can be retrieved from the secondary storage system. When this is accomplished, the base address of the block in RAM can be entered in the mapping table and the presence bit turned on; then the suspended program can be restarted and the failed instruction retried.

It is important to understand that a full copy of all the blocks of the address space must be kept in the secondary store and that only a subset of those blocks will be in RAM. The blocks in RAM must be copies of those in the secondary store. To enforce this, the mapping table entries also contain a "modified bit" turned on automatically during any write request to the block. The operating system must detect modified blocks and write them back into the secondary store before they can be deleted from RAM.

It is now obvious that the policy that determines which blocks are in RAM can be an important determinant of the performance of a virtual memory system. Since most systems load new blocks only on demand (when a missing-block fault occurs), the policy in question amounts to a rule for determining which blocks to replace when additional RAM space is needed for an incoming block. Most such replacement policies tend to keep the most recently referenced blocks in RAM. The most sophisticated policies dynamically adjust the amount of RAM allocated to a program to minimize the memory space-time product of a program, for this will maximize the throughput of the system. A good heuristic for accomplishing this is to detect and preserve in RAM the dynamic locality set of a program in execution (Denning, 1980).

Although it is true that most virtual memory systems present the programmer with a large uniform name space and handle the memory management, it is not true that the virtual memory behaves as a random access store. The locality-seeking characteristic of the memory management policies causes the access time to an object in the virtual memory to be short when the object or a neighbor has been referenced recently, and long otherwise. The programmer, therefore, can be confident of highly efficient operation of a program in a virtual memory only if the algorithm and data are organized to cluster references to small groups of objects for extended intervals.

Relocation and Protection Virtual memory solves the relocation problem because it permits program pieces to be moved around in memory without altering their virtual addresses. It solves the memory protection problem because each program piece can have its own access mode (read, write, or execute) that can be validated by the address translator; for example, a request to read from a block would be allowed only if the block's read-bit (stored in the mapping table) is on. Moreover, a process can refer only to the blocks listed in its mapping table, meaning that blocks of different address spaces are completely inaccessible. Virtual memory thus provides a good deal of flexibility in allocating program blocks in RAM, while maintaining isolation between processes with disjoint address spaces.

History and Prospects Virtual memories have been used to meet one or more of five needs:

1. *Solving the overlay problem* that arises when a program exceeds the size of the computational store available to it. Paging on the Atlas machine at the University of Manchester (1959) was the first example. (*See* MANCHESTER UNIVERSITY COMPUTERS.)

2. *Storing variable-size program objects* off the run-time stack. The size of local arrays in Algol, for example, may not be known at compile time; storing them in segments elsewhere, with fixed-size descriptors on the stack, permits the compilation of addresses. Segmentation on the Burroughs B5500 (1963) was the first example.

3. *Long-term storage* of files and segments forces the programming of information transfers between the file system and the virtual memory. The Multics virtual memory (1968) eliminated this by merging the two storage systems. Users could declare their own segments and keep them in the address space indefinitely.

4. *Memory protection* requires that references to segments be in range and conform to enabled access modes (read, write, or execute). These constraints are easily checked by the hardware in parallel with the main computation. Several experimental machines have been designed explicitly to study descriptor-based addressing as a means of memory protection and improved software reliability (Myers, 1978). These architectural principles are likely to be used in future, highly efficient implementations of object-oriented programming (*q.v.*).

5. *Scalable algorithms* that can be configured at run-time for any number of processors are essential to mastery of highly parallel computations on multicomputers. Virtual memory gives a means of joining the memories of a multicomputer into a single address space that allows compilers to translate source-code object references into fixed-format addresses (Denning and Tichy, 1990).

It is sometimes argued that advancing memory technology will soon permit us to have all the RAM we could possibly want and, hence, we will soon be able to dispense with virtual memory. Users' ambitions for new ways of using resources have, however, continually defied this assumption. It is unlikely that today's predictions of the passing of the overlay problem will prove to be any more reliable than similar predictions made in 1960, 1965, 1970, 1975, 1980, 1985, and 1990. Moreover, the new generations of multicomputers are providing new motivations to provide uniform addressing structures that will scale across machines of many sizes.

References

1970. Denning, P. J. "Virtual Memory," *Computing Surveys* **2**, 3 (September), 153–189.

1972. Organick, E. I. *The Multics System: An Examination of Its Structure.* Cambridge, MA: The M.I.T. Press.

1973. Organick, E. I. *Computer System Organization: The B5700/B6700 System.* New York: Academic Press.

1975. Wilkes, M. V. *Time Sharing Computer Systems* (3rd Ed.). Amsterdam: Elsevier/North-Holland.

1976. Denning, P. J. "Fault Tolerant Operating Systems," *Computing Surveys* **8**, *3* (December).

1978. Myers, G. J. *Advances in Computer Architecture*. New York: John Wiley.

1980. Denning, P. J. *IEEE Transactions on Software Engineering* **SE-6**, 1 (January), 64–84.

1990. Denning, P. J. and Tichy, W. F. "Highly parallel computation," *Science* **250** (30 Nov), 1217–1222.

PETER J. DENNING

VIRTUAL REALITY. *See* COMPUTER ART.

VISION, COMPUTER. *See* COMPUTER VISION.

VISUALIZATION. *See* SCIENTIFIC APPLICATIONS.

VLSI. *See* INTEGRATED CIRCUITRY.

VOICE RECOGNITION AND SYNTHESIS. *See* SPEECH RECOGNITION AND SYNTHESIS.

VOLUME

For articles on related subjects *see* FILE; and RECORD.

A volume is a physical unit of a storage medium (e.g. tape reel, drum, disk pack). Just as there are single and multivolume books, there are also single and multivolume physical files, or databases. Volumes consist of *extents*: each extent contains one or more *pages* (also called *blocks*). The size of a physical page is generally a function of the physical characteristics of the storage medium, of the computer main store architecture, and of the amount and structure of data.

Corresponding to the title page of a book, the first data element encountered on a volume, called the *data set label*, should—and almost always does—identify the database that (partially or in its entirety) resides on it, the volume number, page size, number of pages, "author," plus whatever additional information (such as read/write authority, available space, etc.) is appropriate to the intelligent perusal of the data contained in the volume.

SUSAN C. BREWER

VON NEUMANN, JOHN

For articles on related subjects *see* DIGITAL COMPUTERS: Early; EDVAC; ENIAC; STORED PROGRAM CONCEPT; and VON NEUMANN MACHINE.

John von Neumann (b. 28 December 1903, Budapest, Hungary; d. 8 February 1957, Washington, D.C.) has become one of the legendary figures of twentieth century mathematics. The stories of his quickness of mind, power of absolute recall, linguistic range, and sense of humor abound in the literature and among his former associates. During his career he made significant contributions to logic, to quantum physics, to the theory of high-speed computing machines, and to economics through the mathematical theory of games and strategy. His work in any one of the fields would have secured him a distinguished position in present-day science.

Von Neumann received his early education at the Lutheran gymnasium in Budapest from 1911 through 1921. Toward the end of this period he was also privately tutored by M. Fekete, later to become another well-known Hungarian mathematician, with whom von Neumann published his first paper before he reached the age of 18.

There is a story that von Neumann's father opposed his desire to study mathematics. So, although he enrolled in the University of Budapest, he studied chemistry in Berlin (1921-1923) and Zurich (1923-1925), where he received his diploma in chemical engineering. In 1926, however, he received a Budapest Ph.D. in mathematics with a dissertation concerning the axiomatization of set theory.

FIG. 1. John von Neumann (From the Institute for Advanced Study, Princeton, N.J.)

During the late 1920s, he was Privatdozent at Berlin and Hamburg. He quickly established a reputation with publications in set theory, algebra, and quantum mechanics in this period. In 1928, he proved the minimax theorem of game theory. This was later elaborated and applied in his work (with Oskar Morganstern), *The Theory of Games and Economic Behavior* (1944).

In 1930, he was invited to be a visiting lecturer at Princeton University. When the Institute for Advanced Study was founded in 1933, he was appointed one of the original professors of its School of Mathematics. He kept this position for the rest of his life.

Von Neumann's work in the 1930s firmly established his already highly regarded reputation as a mathematician. In 1931, he published a book on the mathematical foundation of quantum mechanics, and in that same decade he formulated and proved the mean ergodic theorem for unitary operators. He published a series of papers (some with F. J. Murray) in the latter half of the 1930s, on what he called "rings of operators" (now known as von Neumann algebras), which led him to work in what he called "continuous" geometry.

World War II was a watershed mark in von Neumann's career. Prior to 1940, his work fell primarily into the area of theoretical mathematics and physics, but for the remainder of his career he appeared as an applied mathematician. The citation on his honorary D.Sc. from Princeton (1947) identified him as a mathematician, but the encomium described him in terms of his impact as a physicist, engineer, and patriot. His papers from 1940 were mainly on statistics, hydrodynamics, ballistics, problems of detonation, meteorology, the applicability of game theory, and the theory and design of computers.

Although von Neumann had the ability to perform incredible mental calculations, his research led him to examine the possibility for machine assistance. His work on the hydrogen bomb in 1944 and the problem of implosion led him to make use of the computational ability of Howard Aiken's Automatic Sequence Control Calculator (Mark I - *q.v.*) at Harvard. During the late summer of 1944, a chance encounter with Herman Goldstine made him aware of the world's first electronic computer being built under the direction of John Mauchly and J. Presper Eckert at the Moore School of Electrical Engineering of the University of Pennsylvania. His first visit to the ENIAC project occurred in August of that year, and this marked the beginning of his role in the theory of electronic computers and automata.

Von Neumann's role in the next level of conception and implementation is difficult to assess. There is evidence that Eckert and Mauchly were involved in discussions that included the development of a mercury delay-line memory with the ability to store both numbers and instructions. Shortly before von Neumann's first visit in 1944, the group had already committed itself to the construction of a successor to ENIAC as soon as time permitted. While von Neumann's authorship of the first EDVAC proposal in mid-1945 may not entitle his admirers to claim for him stored program conceptual priority, it is indicative of the great impact of his presence as a consultant to the group, his probing questions, and his ability to synthesize critical ideas. With the EDVAC paper, the modern era of electronic computers took a major stride forward.

By late 1945, von Neumann had decided to build a high-speed, general-purpose electronic computer at the Institute for Advanced Study. His documents of the period clearly articulate his vision on the ability of the proposed computer to "...revolutionize the purely mathematical approach to the theory of nonlinear differential equations...extend quantum theory to systems of more particles and more degrees of freedom...render a computational approach...to the phenomenon of turbulence...remove many bottlenecks in the computing approach to ordinary and electron optics...Such a machine if intelligently used will completely revolutionize...the field of approximation mathematics." (Memorandum on the Program of the High Speed Computer, 8 November 1945.) The impact of the IAS computer and its progeny (such as Illiac, Maniac, Johnniac, etc.) is well known. The whole family is still generally referred to as *von Neumann machines*.

Von Neumann's clarity and precision of thought had a profound impact in many areas from which we will continue to benefit in the decades ahead. He was clearly one of the major scientific figures of this century.

References

1958. Bochner, Salomon. "John von Neumann," in National Academy of Sciences *Biographical Memoirs* **32**: 438–457.

1972. Goldstine, Herman H. *The Computer from Pascal to von Neumann*. Princeton: Princeton University Press, 167–183.

1973. Halmos, Paul R. "The Legend of John von Neumann," *American Mathematical Monthly* (April), 382–394.

1980. Heims, Steve J. *John von Neumann and Norbert Wiener: From Mathematics to the Technologies of Life and Death*. Cambridge, MA: The M.I.T. Press.

1990. Heppenheimer, T. A. "How von Neumann Showed the Way," *American Heritage of Invention & Technology*, **6**, 2, 8–16.

1992. Macrae, Norman. *John von Neumann*, Pantheon Books.

HENRY S. TROPP

VON NEUMANN MACHINE

For articles on related subjects *see* PROGRAM COUNTER; STORED PROGRAM CONCEPT; and VON NEUMANN, JOHN.

The most influential paper in the history of computer science, whether or not anyone else expressed similar ideas earlier, was written in 1946 by John von Neumann, then on the staff of the Institute for Advanced Study at Princeton University, in collaboration with Arthur W. Burks and Herman H. Goldstine. Its title is "Preliminary Discussion of the Logical Design of an Electronic Computing Instrument," and the ideas it contains, collectively known as *the von Neumann machine,* have provided the foundation for essentially all computer system development since that date.

Central to the von Neumann machine is the concept of the stored program—the principle that instructions and data are to be stored together in a single, uniform storage medium rather than separately, as was previously the case. Not only can computations proceed at electronic speeds, but instructions as well as data can be read and written under program control. From this basic idea it follows that an element in storage has an ambiguous quality with respect to its interpretation; this ambiguity is resolved only temporarily when it is fetched and either executed as an instruction or operated on as data. One exploitation of this ambiguity results in the technique of instruction modification in which a datum, created as the result of some operations in the arithmetic-logic unit (*q.v.*) of the computer, is placed in storage as would be any other datum, but is then fetched and executed as an instruction. Iteration is realized by refetching the instruction as a datum, modifying it by operating on its address field, and then storing it and refetching and reexecuting it as an instruction. Contemporary programming practice, particularly in a multiprogramming environment, precludes the physical modification of instructions in storage. However, the basic idea of logical instruction modification is still central in computer science, but it is supported by more recent developments such as index registers, base registers, and indirect addressing, which provide similar effects but leave instructions unchanged.

Another concept central to the von Neumann machine is the *program counter*, a register that is used to indicate the location of the next instruction to be executed and that is automatically incremented by each instruction fetch. With the rare exception of machines that use rotating memory devices for main storage, essentially all computers use this technique, since it clearly reduces the storage space that would otherwise be necessary if each instruction contained a field to indicate the address of its successor. The idea of branching, which is often very difficult for a beginning machine language programmer to understand, can in this context become obvious in that it is effected merely by the replacement of the contents of the location counter from some other source, often but not always a field in the current instruction.

Since no short article can do justice to these and the many other ideas expressed so clearly by von Neumann and his colleagues in 1946, every computer scientist should read the original report, (see, for example, Taub, 1963).

References

1963. Taub, A. H. (Ed) *The Collected Works of John von Neumann* **5**. New York: Macmillan, 34–79.

1971. Bell, C. G. and Newell, A. *Computer Structures*. New York: McGraw-Hill, 92–119.

ROBERT F. ROSIN

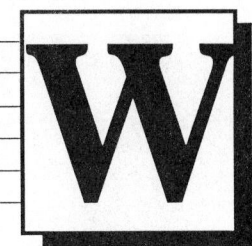

WAIT STATE

For articles on related subjects *see* ACCESS TIME; CACHE MEMORY; CENTRAL PROCESSING UNIT; and INTERLEAVING.

The suspension of a microprocessor's CPU activity for one or more clock cycles while memory access catches up is called a *wait state*. The central processing unit (CPU) depends upon an internal clock for the critical timing needed to optimize performance. This clock typically operates at millions of cycles per second. One million cycles per second is called a *megahertz* (MHz). A typical 80286 chip operating at 10 MHz would have a window of 100 nanoseconds between ticks of the clock during which a memory access could be effectuated. Seemingly, then, RAM chips with access times of 100 ns or less should be fast enough to do the job, but actuality is more complicated.

RAM memory is usually composed of chips that store information in tiny capacitors. As with any capacitor, the ability to hold a charge for a period of time depends upon the quality of the insulator that separates the two charged surfaces. In a typical RAM chip, the charge breaks down after a few milliseconds and must be electrically refreshed. Since the information must be maintained dynamically, these chips are called *dynamic random access memory chips* (DRAMs). While it may take only 100 nanoseconds to access a DRAM chip under optimum circumstances, this can occur only if the capacitors have been refreshed recently. The actual access time is a combination of the refresh cycle time and the access cycle time. If these two times exceed the CPU clock cycle window between clock ticks, the CPU must wait another clock cycle for the information or instruction to be retrieved from memory. We then say that a wait state has been introduced. If two CPU clock cycles are needed, then the computer is a two-wait-state machine.

The introduction of wait states can severely reduce the performance of even the fastest CPU chips. Designers try to reduce wait states to zero. There are several ways to do this. One way is to use faster RAM chips. DRAM chips faster than 80 nanoseconds are currently very expensive and raise the cost of a machine considerably. Static RAM chips called SRAM do not need to be refreshed because capacitors are not used for storage. These chips use latches or flip-flops and therefore can be accessed during their rated cycle times, but these too are very expensive. Manufacturers usually use sophisticated memory management techniques to reduce wait states. Schemes such as memory caching where only a small piece of memory is made up of very fast chips are used (*see* CACHE MEMORY). Another strategy is to break the memory up into pages that operate as small caches. This is called Page-Mode RAM. Yet another strategy is to interleave or bank the memory and store sequential information in alternate banks. While one bank is being accessed, the other is being refreshed (*see* INTERLEAVING).

Memory is not the only component for which wait states may have to be introduced, but it is the most critical to system performance. The power and efficiency of a machine can be reduced as much as 50% by the use of wait states. A typical 80286 running at 8 MHz with zero wait states will almost always outperform a machine running the same 80286 at 10 MHz with one wait state.

STEPHEN J. ROGOWSKI

WATSON, THOMAS J., SR.

For articles on related subjects *see* DIGITAL COMPUTERS: HISTORY: EARLY; ENTREPRENEURS; and HOLLERITH, HERMAN.

Thomas John Watson was born in East Campbell, Steuben County, New York, on 17 February 1874, of Scots-Irish descent. The son of Thomas and Jane White Watson, he was educated at the Addison Academy and the School of Commerce in Elmira, New York.

He started work in May 1892 as a bookkeeper in Painted Post, New York, at a salary of $6.00 a week. Fol-

FIG. 1.   Thomas John Watson.

lowing this first job, he sold sewing machines and musical instruments in the same village before joining the National Cash Register Company in Buffalo, New York, as a salesman. Four years later, National Cash Register promoted him to manager in Rochester. Promotion to special representative followed, and four and a half years later he was appointed the company's general sales manager.

It was at this time that Watson, bent on inspiring a dispirited NCR sales force, introduced the motto "THINK." He is quoted (THINK, 1956) as having told a meeting of salesmen that the phrase "I didn't think" had cost the world millions of dollars. Overnight, framed placards with the single word "THINK" sprouted throughout the offices of the company. Later, when he took the helm at IBM, he reintroduced this motto.

Watson resigned from NCR in 1913, a few months after his marriage to Jeannette M. Kittridge, to assume the presidency of the ailing Computing-Tabulating-Recording Company, a 1911 merger of the Computing Scale Company of America, the Tabulating Machine Company, and the International Time Recording Company.

From 1913 until his death 43 years later, Thomas J. Watson built the C-T-R Company, which became the International Business Machines Corporation in 1924, into the leading manufacturer first of automatically operated electromechanical business machines and then of electronic computers and business machines. It became one of the largest, most successful corporations in the world. During this time he always placed heavy emphasis on education, research, and engineering in order to insure the growth of the company. Under his leadership, IBM's history was a succession of technical innovations and inventions that included new applications of punched cards to business, government, and education, the introduction of the first commercially successful electric typewriter in 1934, opening the electronic computer era commercially in 1948 with the marketing of the 604 programmable electronic calculator, and the top position in the electronic computing and data processing field in the 1950s.

A great deal of Watson's success was due to his un-

derstanding of customer's needs, which resulted in steady improvements in IBM's product lines.

One of Watson's lifelong interests was in education, and he sought to put his business acumen at the service of the universities and their faculties, giving equipment for the Columbia University Statistical Bureau (1928) and the Astronomical Computing Bureau at Columbia (1934); designing and building as a gift the first large-scale computer, the IBM Automatic Sequence Controlled Calculator (the Mark I - *q.v.*) for Harvard (1944); and dedicating the Selective Sequence Electronic Calculator to "assist the scientist in institutions of higher learning, in government, and in industry to explore the consequences of man's thought to the outermost reaches of time, space, and physical conditions" (1948). In the early 1930s he began serving as a trustee of various universities, including Lafayette College, which always remained a sentimental favorite, partly because it was there that he received the first of over 30 honorary degrees he would accumulate before his death. He also served for many years as a trustee of Columbia University.

A month before he died on 19 June 1956, Watson turned over the post of chief executive officer of IBM to his eldest son, Thomas Watson, Jr., who in 1952 had succeeded his father as president of the corporation.

References

1956. Anon. THINK (July-August-September), 4–48.
1962. Belden, T. and Belden, M. *The Lengthening Shadow.* Boston: Little, Brown.
1969. Rodgers, W. THINK— *A Biography of the Watsons and IBM.* New York: Stein and Day.
1990. Watson, Thomas J. Jr, and Petre, Peter. *Father, Son, and Company: My Life at IBM.* New York: Bantam.

JOHN C. MCPHERSON

WELL-FORMED FORMULA (WFF)

For articles on related subjects *see* FORMAL LANGUAGES; GRAMMARS; PRODUCTION; PROGRAMMING LINGUISTICS; and REGULAR EXPRESSION.

A *well-formed formula* (WFF) over a set G of grammatical or syntactical rules is a finite sequence or string of symbols that is grammatically or syntactically correct; i.e. it belongs to the set of all sequences of symbols that can be constructed or formed by using the rules in G.

For instance, if $G = \{S \rightarrow aSb, S \rightarrow ab\}$ is the set of grammatical rules in a generative grammar, then a string x is well formed if and only if it is of the form $a^n b^n$ for $n \geq 1$. Other examples of well-formed formulas are arithmetic expressions, well-formed parentheses expressions (Dyck sets)—where each left parenthesis has to be properly matched by a right parenthesis—well-formed formulas in propositional calculus, and *regular expressions*.

Given an arbitrary grammar G, the question whether an arbitrary string is well formed with respect to G is equivalent to the question of whether it belongs to the language generated by *G*. This question is decidable for many important classes of languages or sets; i.e. there exists an algorithm that determines after finitely many steps whether a given string is well formed. Examples of such languages include WFFs in the propositional calculus, syntactically correct Pascal statements, etc.

PATRICK C. FISCHER

WHIRLWIND

For an article on a related subject *see* DIGITAL COMPUTERS: HISTORY: EARLY.

Project Whirlwind was sponsored at the Massachusetts Institute of Technology by the Special Devices Division of the Office of Research and Inventions, U.S. Navy. It was originally started in 1944 to investigate the solution of aircraft stability and control problems associated with flight simulation by analog methods. By 1946, it had become apparent that the use of an analog computer (*q.v.*) would lead to excessive complexity, and therefore other computing techniques should be studied. Thus, in 1946, a proposal was made for a 16-bit binary general-purpose computer using electrostatic storage and a 1 MHz pulse rate. Although initially proposed as serial, the requirement for 20,000 multiplications per second led eventually to a parallel machine.

Whirlwind was constructed under the leadership of J. W. Forrester. When first put in service during the third quarter of 1949, the computer had 3,300 tubes and 8,900 crystal diodes (germanium point-contact diodes). By June of 1950, one hour of error-free operation with 256 words of electrostatic storage had been achieved. In March of 1951, it was operational on a routine basis on a 35-hour per week schedule. During 1953, a magnetic tape system and a magnetic drum system were installed, and electrostatic storage was replaced by two banks of core memory consisting of 1,024 words of 16 bits each. By December 1954, the computer had grown to 12,500 vacuum tubes and 23,800 crystal diodes.

Whirlwind occupied a two-story building. The CPU, control console, and CRT displays occupied the second floor. One bit of the arithmetic-logic unit was a bay of equipment 2 ft wide and 12 ft high. The drum storage system and data communications interface occupied the ground floor. The basement was filled with power supplies, and the roof of the building was covered with air-conditioning equipment to remove the heat generated by a power consumption on the order of 150 KW.

Whirlwind was a 16-bit parallel, single-address, binary computer. Instructions as well as data occupied 16-bit memory words. The operation code had 5 bits and the address had 11 bits. Eventually, all 32 possible operation codes were utilized. Multiplication and division were included in the operation codes. The initial program-load problem was solved by the use of a bank of 32 registers of toggle switches. In routine operation, various bootstrap programs were stored in the toggle-switch memory (*see* BOOT AND REBOOT).

Automatic marginal checking was initiated during the fourth quarter of 1949. The computer had the ability to select any section of itself, vary the voltages to that section, and test for failure. By comparing the results from day to day, it was possible to determine if trends toward failure were developing in the components.

Whirlwind used magnetic tape and magnetic drum for auxiliary memory. Input/output equipment included large cathode-ray tubes, photoelectric tape readers, Flexowriters, and, in connection with the Air Force semi-automatic ground-environment air defense system (SAGE), data communication links were established with a number of radar sets and with other computers. One of the cathode-ray tubes had a microfilm camera attached so that large-volume output could be displayed on a CRT and microfilmed. This was a common method of obtaining memory dumps. Prints of the microfilm were available the next morning. With electrostatic storage, the computer was capable of approximately 20,000 operations per second, which increased to 40,000 per second when a magnetic-core memory system was installed.

On the software side, there were pioneering efforts in the development of a symbolic assembler, a comprehensive interpretive system that provided a comprehensive mathematical package, including floating-point operations, a batch operating system, and an off-line printout system that permitted recording the results at high speed on magnetic tape and later printing the results off line without the use of the computer.

Despite its physical size, Whirlwind was, in modern terms, a 16-bit minicomputer (*q.v.*). It was, however, a most important project in the development of parallel, binary computers. The Whirlwind project itself and those it spawned (the Memory Test Computer, the TX-0 and TX-2 computers at the Lincoln Laboratory of M.I.T., and the AN/FSQ-7 manufactured by IBM for the SAGE system) led to many hardware and software developments, most notably magnetic-core memories and the first operating systems (*q.v.*). Whirlwind influenced the early IBM 700 series computers and the computers developed by the Digital Equipment Corporation, much of whose initial staff came from the Lincoln Laboratory.

Whirlwind operated until 1959. Parts of it are now in the Smithsonian Institution in Washington, D.C. and the Digital Computer Museum in Boston.

References

1980. Redmond, K. C. and Smith, T. A. *Project Whirlwind: The History of a Pioneer Computer*. Bedford, MA: Digital Press.

JOHN N. ACKLEY

WIENER, NORBERT

For articles on related subjects *see* CYBERNETICS; and DIGITAL COMPUTERS: HISTORY: EARLY.

Norbert Wiener (b. Columbia, Missouri, 26 November 1894; d. Stockholm, Sweden, 18 March 1964) was one of America's most important mathematicians, and a contro-

FIG. 1. Norbert Wiener.

versial scientist who left a rich heritage of accomplishments, not only through his more than one hundred publications, but also through his personal contacts with scientists throughout the world.

Of his boyhood, Wiener said: "I got my classical education from my father, who was professor of Slavic languages at Harvard. My scientific education I got for myself." (*Current Biography*, 1950.)

Wiener received his A.B. degree from Tufts College in 1909 and his Ph.D. from Harvard in 1913 with a thesis in mathematical logic. The years 1913 to 1915 were significant ones. Traveling under Harvard's Sheldon Fellowship, he worked under Alfred North Whitehead, Bertrand Russell, G. H. Hardy, and J. E. Littlewood in Cambridge, and David Hilbert and Edmund Landau at Göttingen.

After America's entry into World War I, Wiener joined the facility at Aberdeen Proving Ground, where he worked on designing artillery range tables. In 1919, with the help of Harvard Professor W. F. Osgood, he secured an appointment as an instructor at M.I.T., an association he maintained until his retirement in 1960.

He was a Guggenheim Fellow at Copenhagen and Göttingen in 1926, and he was also a visiting lecturer at Cambridge (1931–1932) and at Tsing Hua University in Peiping, China (1935–1936). Many significant influences occurred during this pre-war era. At Cambridge, Bertrand Russell encouraged him to read Rutherford's work on the theory of the electron and the nature of matter. At M.I.T. he formed a close friendship with Harold Hazen, and was early exposed to the theory of feedback and servomechanisms. It was also during this period that he met Arturo Rosenblueth, who was engaged in neurophysiological research.

Wiener's direct contributions to the early development of electronic digital computers are difficult to determine. His wartime work on prediction theory and the research in radar and fire control were all to have a major impact by the end of the 1940s. By then, however, his name was synonomous with cybernetics (Wiener, 1948). In his writings on cybernetics, Wiener laid the foundation for the philosophical relations between mechanistic and mathematical scientific theories. This work may not have directly contributed to the actual machine developments, but it did much to stimulate research in automata and in attempts to simulate human thought processes. Wiener was also very conscious of the long-range impact of the computer on man and society. In "The Human Use of Human Beings" (Wiener, 1950), he warned of the dangers that could be caused by selfish exploitation of the computer's potential.

Norbert Wiener was active in professional societies both in the United States and abroad. He also received many honors, such as the Bôcher Prize of the American Mathematical Society (1933). His major publications, in addition to the above, include works on the Fourier integral and its application, Brownian motion, time series, relativity and quantum theory, mathematical foundations, postulational theory, vector and differential spaces, and potential theory.

References

1948. Wiener, Norbert. *Cybernetics, or Control and Communication in the Animal and Machine.* Cambridge, MA: M.I.T. Press.

1950. Anon. *Current Biography*, pp. 615–617.

1950. Wiener, Norbert. *The Human Use of Human Beings; Cybernetics and Society.* Boston: Houghton Mifflin.

1953. Wiener, Norbert. *Ex-Prodigy.* Cambridge, MA: M.I.T. Press.

1956. Wiener, Norbert. *I Am A Mathematician.* Cambridge, MA: M.I.T. Press.

1980. Heims, Steve J. *John von Neumann and Norbert Wiener: From Mathematics to the Technologies of Life and Death.* Cambridge, MA: The M.I.T. Press.

HENRY S. TROPP

WILKES, MAURICE V.

For articles on related subjects *see* DIGITAL COMPUTERS: EARLY; EDSAC; and MICROPROGRAMMING.

Maurice Vincent Wilkes (b. 1913) studied mathematics and physics at Cambridge and conducted research on the ionosphere. He worked on radar during World War II, and then directed the Mathematical Laboratory (now the Computer Laboratory) of the University of Cambridge from 1945 onward throughout the whole development of stored program computers. It was here that the first of these to go into service, the Electronic Delay Storage Automatic Calculator (EDSAC), built by Wilkes and his team, began operating in May 1949. He became a Fellow of the Royal Society in 1956, was the first president of the British Computer Society 1957–1960, and the first United Kingdom member of the Council of IFIP 1960–1963. He was the ACM Turing Lecturer in 1967 and received the Harry Goode Award from AFIPS in 1968. In 1974, he was elected a foreign Honorary Member of the American Academy of Arts and Sciences. In 1977, he became a foreign Associate of the U.S. National Academy of Engineering, and in 1980 of the U.S. National Academy of Sciences.

In 1980, he retired from Cambridge as Emeritus Professor of Computer Technology and became Senior Consulting Engineer at Digital Equipment Corporation. He received the Eckert-Mauchly Award of the Association for Computing Machinery and IEEE Computer Society in

FIG. 1.   Maurice Vincent Wilkes.

1980, and the IEEE Computer Society's McDowell Award and the IEEE Faraday medal in 1981. In 1982, he received the Pender Award of the University of Pennsylvania and in 1988 the C&C Prize (Tokyo). From 1981–1985, he was an Adjunct Professor of Electrical Engineering and Computer Science at M.I.T.; in 1986, he returned to the U.K. and became Member for Research Strategy of the Olivetti Research Board.

Wilkes led the first practical development of programming for stored program machines, including the first program library. He originated labels (which he called "floating addresses"), an early form of macros (which he called "synthetic orders"), and microprogramming (which was used in the design of the second Cambridge machine, EDSAC II). He later became interested in machine-independent computing, and in this connection developed a simple list-processing language known as Wisp. He was an early advocate of data transmission. He contributed to the development of time-sharing systems, both as a visiting member of Project MAC at M.I.T. and through the system developed in his own laboratory during 1965–1970. In particular, he and his colleagues introduced many ideas relating to facilities for filing and editing for the ordinary user.

In addition to numerous papers and articles, he has written the following books: *Oscillations of the Earth's Atmosphere* (1949), *Preparation of Programs for an Electronic Digital Computer* (joint author; 1951, 2d ed. 1958), *Automatic Digital Computers* (1956), *A Short Introduction to Numerical Analysis* (1966), *Time-Sharing Computer Systems* (1966, 2d ed. 1972), and *The Cambridge CAP Computer and its Operating System* (joint author, 1979).

Reference

1985. Wilkes, M. V. *Memoirs of a Computer Pioneer*. Cambridge, MA: M.I.T. Press.

STANLEY GILL

WILKINSON, JAMES H.

For articles on related subjects *see* DIGITAL COMPUTERS: HISTORY; ERROR ANALYSIS; and TURING ALAN M.

James Hardy Wilkinson was born in Strood in Kent, England on 27 September 1919, and died at his home in Teddington, England on 5 October 1986. At school, he quickly exhibited an exceptional ability in mathematics and, at the age of only 16, won a Trinity Major Scholarship, thus enabling him to enter Cambridge University. He graduated with Distinction, gaining a First Class Honours degree in 1939 when he was still only 19. In common with many mathematicians during World War II, Wilkinson was then drafted into military work, where his interest in computational mathematics started. It was during this period that he met his future wife Heather Nora Ware, herself a mathematician with a First Class Honours degree. They married in 1945 and Heather remained an important source of support and encouragement throughout his life.

In 1946, Wilkinson joined the Mathematics Division of the National Physical Laboratory (NPL) in Teddington,

FIG. 1.   James Hardy Wilkinson.

working half his time for the Desk Computing Section and the other half for the famous Alan M. Turing on the design of an electronic computer, the Automatic Computing Engine (ACE, later called Pilot ACE). When Turing left, Wilkinson was largely responsible for seeing the project through to fruition. Pilot ACE first operated in May 1950 and continued to do much useful computing over the next 5 years. Wilkinson remained at the NPL until his formal retirement in 1980. By this time he had become a Special Merit Chief Scientific Officer, a very rare distinction in the U. K. Civil Service and a position that allowed him to continue his research unhindered by administrative duties. Despite retirement, Wilkinson remained actively involved in numerical analysis until his untimely death.

Wilkinson's understanding of hardware and software issues through his intimate knowledge of Pilot ACE, his earlier involvement with the Desk Computing Section, his enthusiasm for numerical work, and his knowledge of mathematics were unique at that time and he soon began to produce papers that were to have an important influence on numerical analysis, particularly in the area of numerical linear algebra. In the first of three papers cited in the references, Wilkinson developed a fundamental theory called *backward error analysis* that increased understanding of the behavior of many numerical algorithms. The second has become the classic reference for algorithms for the algebraic eigenvalue problem and related topics, and the third, co-edited with Christian Reinsch and commonly referred to simply as "The Handbook," presented the algorithms as properly documented quality software. Both through his publications and his personal interest, Wilkinson influenced a number of software projects, such as the Numerical Algorithms Group Library in the U. K. and EISPACK in the U. S.

Wilkinson was a frequent visitor to the U. S. and over the years held a number of visiting positions at institutions such as the University of Michigan, Argonne National Laboratory, and Stanford University. Although he never held a full-time academic post, it was through such visits and through many invited lectures that he influenced and encouraged a great number of students and fellow researchers who bear witness to the quality of his lectures and the generosity with which he gave his time.

Wilkinson received many awards in recognition of his outstanding contributions, including a Doctor of Science from Cambridge in 1963; Fellowship of the Royal Society in 1969; both the Turing award (*q.v.*) of the Association for Computing Machinery and the von Neumann award of the Society for Industrial and Aplied Mathematics (SIAM) in 1970; Honorary Fellowship of the Institute of Mathematics and its Applications in 1977; and the Chauvenet Prize of the Mathematical Association of America in 1987.

His memory is honored through a Fellowship at Argonne National Laboratory and two prizes, one sponsored by SIAM for numerical analysis and scientific computing and the other jointly sponsored by Argonne, NPL, and NAG for numerical software. Aside from his scientific contribution, Wilkinson will long be remembered for his warmth, kindness, and sense of humor.

References

1964. Wilkinson, J. H. *Rounding Errors in Algebraic Processes*. New York: Prentice-Hall.
1965. Wilkinson, J. H. *The Algebraic Eigenvalue Problem*. Oxford: Clarendon Press.
1971. Wilkinson, J. H. and Reinsch, C. *Handbook for Automatic Computation, Vol.2, Linear Algebra*. Berlin: Springer-Verlag.
1971. Fox, L. *James Hardy Wilkinson—Biographical Memoirs of Fellows of the Royal Society*, **33**, 671–708. Cambridge, England: Cambridge University Press.
1985. Nash, John C. "The Birth of a Computer: An interview with James H. Wilkinson on the building of a computer designed by Alan Turing" *Byte*, **10**, *2*, 177–194.

SVEN HAMMARLING

WILLIAMS, SIR FREDERIC C.

For articles on related subjects *see* KILBURN, THOMAS; MANCHESTER UNIVERSITY COMPUTERS; WILKES, MAURICE; and WILLIAMS TUBE MEMORY.

Frederic Calland Williams, the inventor of the Williams tube, was born on 26 June 1911 at Romiley, near Stockport, England and died at Manchester on 11 August 1977. He was educated at Manchester University, graduating with first class honors in engineering in 1932. He received a doctorate in 1936 at Oxford University before

FIG. 1. Sir Frederic Calland Williams.

returning to Manchester as an assistant lecturer. During the Second World War, Williams conducted important work on radar at the Telecommunications Research Establishment (TRE) at Great Malvern, where he also became interested in the problem of electronic storage for computers. In December 1946, Williams was appointed to the Chair of Electro-technics at Manchester University. Here, his work on cathode ray tube storage, which he had begun at the TRE, was brought to a successful conclusion with his invention of the Williams tube. This was the first successful electrostatic random access memory, and it was used by Williams and his collaborator, Tom Kilburn, to build a small, working machine. This device, which became operable on 21 June, 1948, was the world's first stored-program computer.

Financial support from the government and the technical resources of Ferranti Ltd. resulted in a commercial version of this machine, the Manchester Mark I, which was delivered in February 1951—another world first. In addition to the CRT store, the machine pioneered the use of index registers and the magnetic drum back-up store. Although the patents were controlled by the National Development Research Corporation, the Williams tube was used under license by IBM in the 701 computer and by the Princeton University team in the Institute of Advanced Study (IAS) computer. By the end of 1956, the Williams-Kilburn partnership and their collaborators had generated 81 computer patents.

After 1952, Williams handed over supervision of the Manchester University computer projects to his colleague, Tom Kilburn. Henceforth, he pursued other aspects of electrical engineering, particularly linear induction motor design.

F. C. Williams was a member of numerous technical societies and committees. Among his many honors and awards were election as Fellow of the Royal Society in 1950, the John Scott Award of the City of Philadelphia in 1960, and a knighthood in 1976.

References

———. Papers of F. C. Williams, National Archive for the History of Computing, Manchester University.

1975. Lavington, Simon H. *A History of Manchester Computers.* Manchester: National Computer Centre.

1978. Kilburn, Tom and Piggott, L. S. "Frederic Calland Williams 1911–1977," *Biographical Memoirs of Fellows of the Royal Society* **24** (November).

GEOFFREY TWEEDALE

WILLIAMS TUBE MEMORY

For articles on related subjects *see* MEMORY: MAIN; ULTRASONIC MEMORY; and WILLIAMS, SIR FREDERIC C.

The first stored-program computers were based on two kinds of memory—ultrasonic delay lines and a cathode-ray tube (CRT) system named after F. C. Williams of Manchester University. Experimentation with both schemes was being carried on in 1947 in England and in the U.S., and by 1949–1950 computers of both types were operational. By 1954, magnetic-core memories had superseded both delay line and Williams' tube memories.

Storage of information at a spot on the inside of the face of the CRT was determined by the relative charge level. The secondary emission ratio for phosphors (and for glass) is greater than 1. Thus, if the face is bombarded with a primary electron beam (1,000–2,000-volt acceleration), then the spot becomes positively charged because more low-energy secondary electrons are emitted by the surface than arrive in the primary electron beam. Equilibrium is reached when the relatively positive charge of the spot attracts enough electrons to balance the flow. If a spot is charged, then the nearby area is "discharged" by the secondary electrons from the primary spot.

Williams used the CRTs in a bit-serial mode. To write information on the tube, the electron beam is deflected along a horizontal line, and at each point where the beam is turned off, a residual positive charge remains (Fig. 1). To read the information from the CRT, an electrode is placed on the outside of the face of the CRT (Fig. 2). As the beam again sweeps over a line, the change of potential on the inside face is capacitively picked up by the electrode. Since the spots of positive charge occur just before the turn-off points, the resulting signal occurs in time to turn off the beam again at the same place. (Williams called this an "anticipation" pulse.) As the beam sweeps a horizontal line, the induced potential on the electrode is amplified, and via the gating circuits and the control grid of the CRT (Fig. 2), the beam is turned off in a pattern identical to that of the previous sweep. Thus, the line being read is not destroyed by the reading process. However, since reading a given line tended to discharge the neighboring lines, it was necessary to regenerate the whole array systematically. A typical scheme was to regenerate during odd-word times and to access information during even-word times.

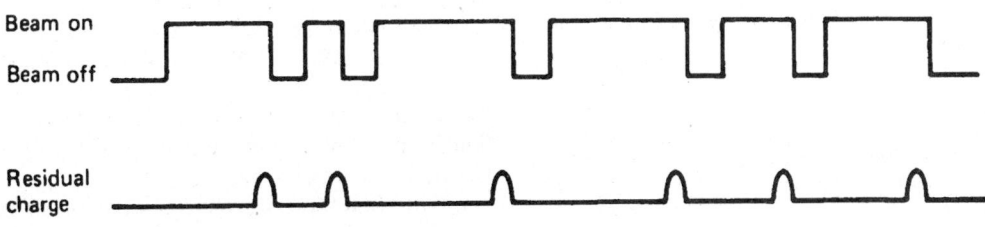

FIG. 1. Williams' charge storage pattern.

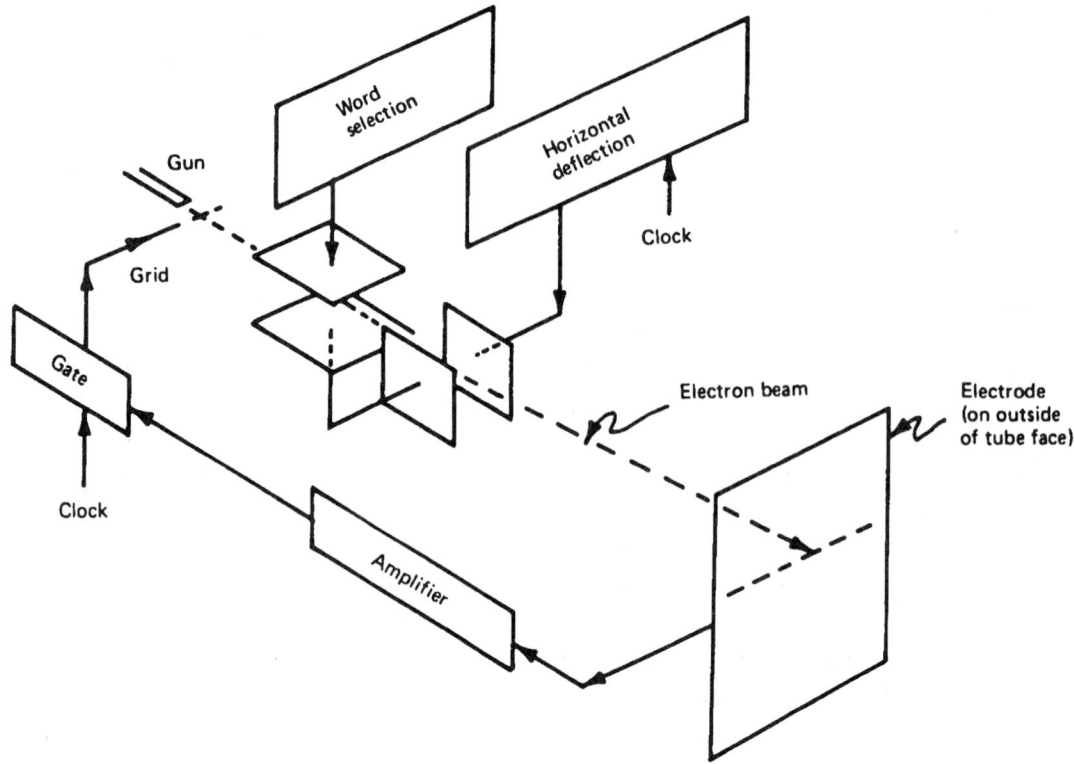

FIG. 2. Williams' CRT information storage system.

The beam, being on or off at a given position (or clock time), can represent the zeros or ones of a binary number. Alternative storage schemes involved using focus/defocused spots, or dots and dashes, at grid points on the face of the cathode-ray tube. By changing the vertical or word deflection (Fig. 2), several different numbers can be stored on one CRT. (Williams stored thirty-two 32-bit numbers.)

The SWAC at the Institute for Numerical Analysis used the Williams tube in a parallel mode with the kth bit of the memory words stored in the kth CRT. Williams tubes in the parallel mode were also used in the computer at the Institute for Advanced Study. Parallel systems stored 256 to 1,024 bits per tube.

Other memory systems (e.g. Whirlwind - *q.v.*) used special tubes with a second "flooding gun" to maintain the storage. Jan Rajchman (RCA) designed a special memory tube called the "Selectron," which was originally intended to be used in the computer at the Institute for Advanced Study.

Commercially, Ferranti (England) marketed the Williams serial scheme, and IBM used the parallel mode in its 701 computers (1953).

References

1949. Williams, F. C. and Kilburn, T. "A Storage System for Use with Binary Digital Computing Machines," *J. Inst. Elect. Engrs.* **96**, *Part III:* 81–100.

HARRY D. HUSKEY

WINCHESTER DRIVE. *See* HARD DISK; and MEMORY: AUXILIARY.

WINDOW ENVIRONMENTS

For articles on related topics *see* DESKTOP PUBLISHING; and USER INTERFACE.

A *window environment* is a software system that manages interactions between a user and an application through a graphics screen. A window system manages the use of devices like a screen, a keyboard, and a mouse (see Fig. 1).

Typically, the screen is managed following the *desktop metaphor*, where the screen is thought of as being the surface of an electronic desk, and applications are represented as electronic sheets of paper displayed in rectangular areas of the screen called *windows*. Fig. 2 shows a snapshot of a typical desktop.

Each of the large regions on the desktop is a window onto an application. The application presents information to the user by drawing some image, graphics, or text on the window. The user passes information to the application by pointing at objects with a mouse-driven cursor and typing on the keyboard.

Windows typically have a number of decorations around their borders (see Fig. 3). Features like the close box, buttons, and scroll bar represent devices that the

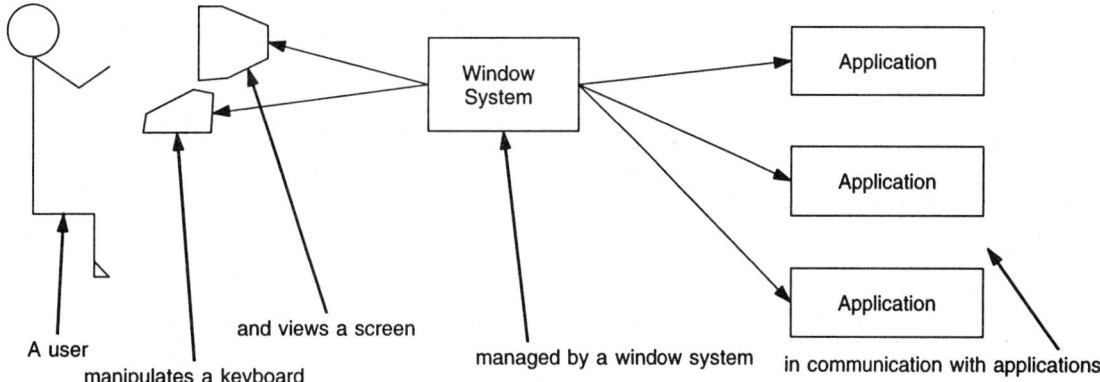

FIG. 1. Schematic organization of a window environment.

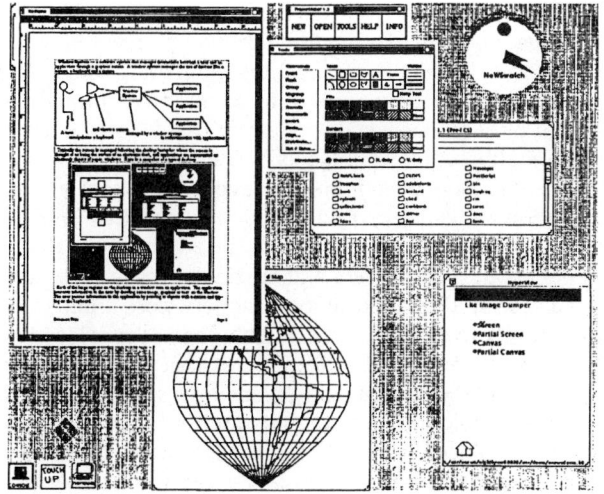

FIG. 2. Snapshot of a desktop with several open windows.

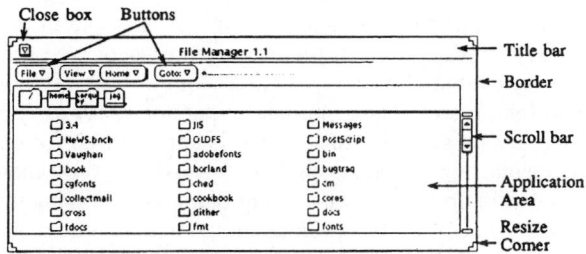

FIG. 3. Window control features.

similar to the ISO multi-layer model of network architecture.

Application
User Interface Toolkit
Window Manager
Base Window System
Graphics Library
Hardware

The term "window system" refers to all of the components in these intermediate layers.

At the bottom is the hardware that supports it all. Besides the basic computer, this consists of some sort of display device, a keyboard, and usually a pointing device like a mouse. Above that is the graphics library, which is primarily the device-dependent software that drives the display. The base window system is built on top of this and is concerned with resource allocation, inter-application communication, and multiplexing the access of higher layers to the underlying components. Then comes the window manager, which handles the user interface to the basic window operations and the decorations around the border of each window. The final part of the window system is the *user interface* toolkit. It provides the higher-level facilities that implement the buttons, sliders, and such that applications use to build up their user interface.

Window systems like one in the Macintosh and the Presentation Manager (OS/2) have all of these layers, but they are pretty much mixed together. In the Unix (*q.v.*) window systems, NeWS and X11, these layers are much more distinct.

References

1991. Mendelson, E. "Making the Most of Windows 3.0," *PC Magazine* **10**, *4* (26 Feb.) 105–107.

1991. Simone, Luisa. "Presentation Graphics," *PC Magazine* **10**, *9* (14 May) 107–123.

JAMES GOSLING

user can point at with a mouse and manipulate. The application will be informed, via the window system, that the button (or whatever) has been pressed.

There are many window systems, each with their own particular software architecture. These architectures can be classified using a multi-layer model that is

WIZARD

For articles on related subjects *see* HACKER; GURU; and POWER USER.

As used in computing, a *wizard* is a programmer who knows a particular piece of software—a compiler, operating system, or text editor, perhaps—so well that he or she can modify or enhance its code on short notice to accomplish an important objective. The wizard is now accorded the admiration and respect that the *hacker* once enjoyed, but unlike the latter term, which has taken on mixed connotations, *wizard* has no pejorative overtone. Wizards are generally quiet competent people who operate with surgical precision in a restricted local environment. Wizards seldom aspire to the world stage of the *guru*. Gurus know things; wizards do things.

EDWIN D. REILLY

WOMEN AND COMPUTING

For articles on related subjects *see* COMPUTER SCIENCE, ACADEMIC; COMPUTERS IN SOCIETY; EDUCATION IN COMPUTER SCIENCE; EDUCATION IN COMPUTER ENGINEERING; and PERSONNEL IN THE COMPUTER FIELD.

Despite the success of women such as the late Rear Admiral Grace Murray Hopper (*q.v.*), women are severely underrepresented in computer science and engineering. As Table 1 shows, in the most recent years for which data is available, women received 36% of the bachelor's degrees awarded in computer science, 30% of the master's degrees, and 13% of the doctoral degrees. While women's participation increased in the 1970s and early 1980s, it appears to

TABLE 1   Percentage of Computer Science Degrees Awarded to Women

Year	Bachelor's	Master's	Ph.D.s
1976	19.8	14.5	5.7
1977	23.9	16.7	6.7
1978	25.8	18.7	8.5
1979	28.1	18.8	9.7
1980	30.3	20.9	12.2
1981	32.5	23.0	11.1
1982	34.8	26.5	11.1
1983	36.4	28.3	12.1
1984	37.2	29.3	10.6
1985	36.9	28.7	9.8
1986	35.8	29.9	12.1
1987			10.9
1988			10.4
1989			13.9
1990			13.2
1991			13.1

Sources: NSF (1990) and Gries (1992). Bachelor's and master's degree data later than 1986 is not available.

have leveled off in recent years and may even be declining (Leveson, 1991). In Ph.D.-granting computer science departments, women comprise 10% of assistant and associate professors and 4% of full professors. In Ph.D.-granting computer engineering departments, women comprise 7% of assistant professors, 4% of associate professors, and 2% of full professors (Gries and Marsh, 1992). 29% of Ph.D.-granting computer science and computer engineering departments have no female professors, 34% have one, and the remaining 36% have two or more (Frenkel, 1990).[1]

Among computer specialists with doctorates working full-time in the U.S., women on average earn 78% of what men earn, the greatest gap in any scientific field. For recent graduates however, computer science is more equitable than many other fields. At the bachelor's degree level, women earn 98% as much as men, and at the master's degree level, 92.5% (NSF, 1990).

Of course, a scarcity of female computer scientists and engineers or lower salaries does not necessarily imply that discrimination exists. Research has consistently shown, however, that females face bias that discourages them from scientific pursuits at every stage of their lives. While conscious discrimination does still occur, girls and women more frequently face biased behavior by someone who is not aware that he or she treats females differently from males. For example, teachers of both sexes have been found to devote significantly more attention and energy to male students (WCCRW, 1992).

Sexual stereotypes influence the advice given to students about their careers and curricula. When given artificial case studies, high school teachers were found to be more likely to advise male students than otherwise-identical female students to take classes that would prepare them for college. Additionally, many high school guidance counselors intentionally steer high school girls away from advanced placement science courses, with such motives as not wanting the girl to have to work too hard or preventing her from eventually taking jobs away from "men who need them" (Spertus, 1991).

In what is thought to be a consequence of years of subtle bias, females have consistently been found to have lower self-esteem than equally qualified males. This can cause females to be less ambitious. An example of this was reported by a math professor who discovered that her department's honors calculus course had been all male for several years. She made a major effort to convince female students to take the exam required for entrance into the course, even though most said they knew they would not pass it. As a result of her encouraging the women to take the test, half of the people who qualified that year were female (Spertus, 1991). Unfortunately, such encouragement is usually not given.

Negative bias occurs in the evaluation of girls' and women's performance. Numerous studies have found that an article attributed to a female author is rated lower than when the same article is said to have been written by a male author. This bias is strongest in traditionally male

[1]In this paragraph and Table 1, all numbers are for both Canada and the U.S., except for bachelor's and master's degree production, which are for the U.S., only.

fields. In one study, department chairs were asked to make hypothetical hiring decisions on the basis of curricula vitae. For vitae with male names, chairs recommended the rank of associate professor, while the identical vita with a female name received a recommendation of assistant professor (Spertus, 1991). Additionally, the SAT has been found to be biased in that it underpredicts women's college grades and overpredicts men's (WCCRW, 1992).

All of the problems so far described are equally applicable to other scientific and engineering fields. Some problems exclusive to computer science described by Pearl *et al.* (1990) and Spertus (1991) are:

- Computer games and educational software are geared to the preferences and interests of boys, such as war and sports.
- Parents appear to be more willing to send their sons than daughters to expensive computer camps. According to one camp director, "Mothers bring their boys to the classes. Girls have to beg to enroll."
- Some women find the overwhelmingly male hacker (*q.v.*) culture offensive or intimidating.

Female undergraduates and graduate students face additional problems due to being a minority in computer science and engineering departments. It can be difficult for women to find mentors, because the overwhelming majority of professors are male, many of whom are more comfortable interacting with male students. Additionally, when members of departments or research groups informally interact by going drinking together or playing sports, the rare female student may feel uncomfortable or unwelcome and not participate. This problem continues in the workplace.

Sexual harassment is also a major problem. A survey of Harvard students and faculty revealed that 32% of the tenured female professors, 49% of those without tenure, 41% of the female graduate students, and 34% of the female undergraduates reported having been sexually harassed by a person in authority at least once during their time at Harvard. 15% of the graduate students and 12% of the undergraduates reporting harassment consequently changed their academic plans because of it. Other surveys have yielded similar results (Spertus, 1992).

A factor that discourages doctoral women from becoming professors is that the model for academic careers developed during a time when faculty positions were overwhelmingly held by men who had wives to tend their needs and the needs of their home and family. Because an enormous amount of work is required to obtain tenure, which typically is not granted until the mid-30s, women often have to choose between having and caring for children or being a professor (Pearl *et al.*, 1990).

Still, there are reasons for optimism. In recent years, there has been a growing awareness of sexual bias and an interest in eliminating it. Recently, the Association for Computing Machinery (*q.v.*) and the Computing Research Association (*q.v.*) have created committees on the status of women in the profession. Additionally, many programs have been implemented to encourage girls and women in computer science (Leveson, 1989). These include:

- Summer science programs for high school girls.
- Mentoring activities to provide female students and junior faculty members with advisors and role models.
- Reentry programs to encourage women to return to school for computer science education.
- An electronic mailing list for women in computer science to reduce their isolation and to allow them to share advice on how to deal with the problems they face (Frenkel, 1990).

Still, with the low level of women in the computer education pipeline, there is no reason to expect large increases in the number of female computer scientists in the near future.

References

1990. Frenkel, K. "Women and Computing," *Communications of the ACM* **33**, *11*: 34–46.

1992. Gries, D. and Marsh, D. "The 1990-91 Taulbee Survey," *Computing Research News*, January.

1989. Leveson, N. "Women in Computer Science: A Report for the NSF CISE Cross-Disciplinary Activities Advisory Committee." Washington, DC: National Science Foundation.

1990. National Science Foundation (NSF). *Women and Minorities in Science and Engineering.* Washington, DC: National Science Foundation.

1990. Pearl, A., Pollack, M. E., Riskin, E., Thomas B., Wolf, E., and Wu. "Becoming a Computer Scientist," *Communications of the ACM* **33**, *11*: 47–57.

1991. Spertus, E. "Why Are There So Few Female Computer Scientists?," Technical Report 1315. M.I.T. Artificial Intelligence Laboratory, 545 Technology Square, Cambridge, MA 02139.

1992. Wellesley Council Center for Research on Women (WCCRW). "How Schools Shortchange Girls." American Association for University Women Educational Foundation, 1111 Sixteenth Street, N.W., Washington, DC 20036.

ELLEN SPERTUS

WORD PROCESSING

For articles on related subjects *see* DESKTOP PUBLISHING; METAFONT; TEXT EDITING SYSTEMS; SPELLING CHECKER; T$_E$X; USER INTERFACE; and WINDOW ENVIRONMENTS.

The term *word processing* was invented by IBM as a way to market a new product, a Selectric typewriter that could record words on magnetic tape. Characters, punctuation, and some limited formatting instructions, such as tabs, margins, underline, double space, etc., could be saved on tape as the typist typed them, and then typed out automatically. The recording capability meant that corrections and revisions could be made in the recorded text by re-recording over the original error. It also meant that unlimited copies of the original could be produced, to all appearances personalized and hand-typed, without manually retyping the document.

IBM marketed word processors to business customers as dedicated, single-purpose (or stand-alone) devices for the creation (through a keyboard), revision, storage, and output of text documents. Word processors offered the benefit of speeding the document production process and increasing the productivity of office typists. Although IBM originally expected only limited success for these products, by the mid-1970s an enthusiastic customer response led to a burgeoning industry. New vendors of word processors, such as Wang Laboratories and others, soon surpassed inventor IBM in sales and product innovation.

Vendors enlarged and improved their word processing system's storage media from magnetic tape to magnetic cards to magnetic diskettes. Cathode ray tube (CRT) display screens were added that allowed documents to be viewed, revised, and corrected on screen before final hard copy versions were printed. For the sake of economy and efficiency, vendors developed clustered systems, in which, by employing minicomputer technology, several word processors were linked in centralized groups, sharing a central processor and periherals such as printers.

Although it did not restrain their popularity, the dedicated word processors of this period were far from cheap. A stand-alone fully functioned display word processor with diskette storage and a printer would range in price from about $8,000 to about $15,000, including training and vendor support. The cost to install a multi-user dedicated word processing system would range from about $8,000 to about $15,000 per workstation, and between $2,000 and $6,000 to add an additional workstation.

To help cost-justify expensive word processing equipment and accommodate its capabilities, a large organization's clerical staff would frequently be reorganized into specialized functions: those who typed, using centralized word processing equipment, and those who were employed in non-typing administrative support tasks. Thus, *word processor* became a term frequently used as a job description, as well as a reference to computer-based typing equipment.

Although the intention was to relieve secretaries of time-consuming typing tasks and generally to improve the productivity of office workers, this reorganization became in many cases the source of conflict. A traditional office staff tended to view the word processing function with disdain, as little different from a typing pool. Among word processing operators, the possible health risks imposed by long-term, daily use of CRT display screens became a concern, leading to some scattered litigation regarding their use (limiting operators' hours between work breaks, for example), as well as to some, largely unsuccessful, attempts to organize clerical workers. Nevertheless, word processing was established as a familiar and valuable office tool.

Word processing gained further acceptance in the office environment through another route. Investigations conducted by universities and the research centers of some large data processing vendors, such as Xerox and IBM, suggested that the productivity of highly paid managerial and professional personnel could be improved if supported by computer technology, by sharing applica-

tions, storage and processing power residing on a centralized computer via linked desktop terminals.

As a result, minicomputer-based "Office Automation" systems were introduced and marketed by such minicomputer builders as Digital Equipment Corporation, Data General, Wang, and IBM. Word processing as a software application was included on these systems as an essential function. Indeed, in the view of many users, the comparable worth of these systems could be judged by the functionality and ease of use of their word processing features, where their other functions (typically, file and records sharing, electronic mail (*q.v.*), appointment calendars, financial forecasting tools, etc.) were largely equal.

The IBM-PC personal computer (PC), introduced in 1981, changed the identity of word processing. Once the PC became a widely accepted office tool, virtually all word processing products have been software applications for personal computers rather than cumbersome stand-alone word processors.

Microprocessor-based personal computer products were commercially available before the introduction of the IBM-PC, but were regarded as chiefly of interest to very small businesses with little need of computer processing power, or to hobbyists. Early microcomputers lacked storage capacity, normally included an inept, data processing-oriented keyboard design, offered small screen size with poor resolution, could not be linked in clusters, and were almost exclusively based on limited eight-bit central processor technology. Furthermore, except for the reasonably successful Scripsit program marketed by Radio Shack (now Tandy), they were typically manufactured and marketed by obscure start-up companies, not the major mainframe or minicomputer vendors in whom business customers had built confidence over years of contact.

The IBM-PC, however, was based on a 16-bit processor and on the MS-DOS operating system, which provided software developers with a powerful and flexible platform on which to write software applications. The PC could run word processing as well as other programs, and, as it became the popular standard among personal computer products in a growing business market, developers were encouraged to write an increasing number of applications for it.

In addition to the inducement of a growing wealth of software applications, the PC, at the time of its introduction, was one-half or less the cost of a stand-alone dedicated word processing product. Furthermore, PCs did not require the commitment to a single vendor or the expense of installation that a mini-based system required. Finally, the IBM name established the credibility of the PC in the skeptical mainstream business community, particularly since most business computer users were already IBM customers. Consequently, as the PC market boomed, the dedicated word processor quickly became obsolete.

Since the introduction of the PC and the many subsequent compatibles that also use MS-DOS, most word processing application packages for personal computers have been written and marketed by independent software vendors (ISVs). Although these organizations are independent of the hardware vendors, the applications are written specifically for certain personal computer platforms. Each advance in hardware has been followed by improved and enhanced software products that take advantage of the new hardware capabilities.

Unlike some other kinds of personal computer applications, spreadsheets (*q.v.*) or databases for example, the word processing market has never been dominated for very long by a single vendor's product. A new hardware platform or technological innovation has meant a new market, and the "lead" among word processing products, in terms of market share, has changed many times. As of 1991, the most popular PC word processing programs were Microsoft Word, Wordperfect, Wordstar, Multimate, and Volkswriter. Although ISVs may convert a popular product, or "port" it, to a new platform, it is equally likely that a brand new product may capture the market.

The success of current word processing products depends upon the set of useful features it includes and the ease with which it can be learned and used. Clearly, certain features will appeal to certain users for certain tasks, and ISVs may aim a product specifically at users with special needs. In a business environment, success also favors a product that employees are able to learn quickly, minimizing training and support costs. Price, naturally, will also play a role in a product's acceptance. Most fully featured word processing packages currently cost about $300 to $500. Products offering fewer features typically cost less.

Current word processing products can be expected to provide a feature set far beyond the standard document creation and error correction of the early systems. Few features that could be useful to a document author have been overlooked. They will search for certain words or phrases; merge letters with lists of names and addresses; move blocks of text; display italic, boldface, and underlining; display page breaks; allow text to be arranged in multiple columns; display multiple pages on screen at one time; combine text and graphic images; offer shortcuts for keyboard commands; count characters, words, and paragraphs; provide automatic hyphenation and justification; create footnotes, tables of contents, and indexes; correct spelling errors; provide a thesaurus; and, in a few cases, correct grammar and evaluate the readability of a document according to the reading level of the intended document recipients. The foregoing is a random, partial list; not all word processors offer all of these features.

While word processing products based on the MS-DOS operating system have improved greatly since the early programs for the first PCs, they have remained relatively difficult to learn and to use. The difficulty lies in the MS-DOS character-based *user interface*—i.e. the interaction (commands and responses) between user and computer. In a character-based interface, the commands (or instructions) given by the user to the computer to perform certain functions are made via the keyboard by specific keys or key combinations. Normally, the user of a character-based system must know these commands or refer to a manual to find them. As the character commands may differ from product to product, each new word processing package must be learned.

This difficulty has been overcome by the development of the graphical user interface (GUI), invented by the Xerox Corporation but popularized by Apple Computer's Macintosh personal computer, introduced in 1984. Unlike the many PC compatibles, the Macintosh is an entirely different platform; it is not based on the MS-DOS operating system, and runs only its own software. Nevertheless, the ease with which it can be learned and used, thanks largely to the GUI, has made it a serious rival to MS-DOS personal computer products.

In a GUI-based system, "pop-up" or "pull-down" menus listing command selections are available to an operator at all times, regardless of what else may be displayed on the screen. There is no need, for example, to close a document and return to a main menu screen in order to select functions and issue commands. Menus can be activated and functions selected by pointing to them with a cursor controlled by a hand-operated *mouse (q.v.)* rather than through striking keys on the keyboard. Thus, training—beyond identifying proper commands and basic eye-hand mouse operation—is minimal. Moreover, training remains minimal from one GUI-based application to the next, as all follow the same basic approach.

Another advantage of a GUI is the so-called WYSIWYG (What-You-See-Is-What-You-Get) display. In most traditional MS-DOS word processors, the characters displayed on screen are monospaced—i.e. each character, space, or punctuation mark is assigned to an equal space, one in a matrix of 2,000, on a single screen, regardless of typeface or type size. A WYSIWYG display shows the user proportional typefaces, in different fonts and type sizes, nearly exactly as they will appear when printed on paper, provided the printer will support the application. A GUI and WYSIWYG display also allows graphic images to be created, positioned, and incorporated with text in compound documents on screen as they will look when printed.

GUI-based systems also simplify the creation of style sheets (prerecorded formats for text and graphics), including charts and tables, that appear consistently in certain documents. An operator can create a new document by using the recorded margins, tabs, centering, justification, graphics position, etc., and entering only new or altered text. In a character-based system, the creation of style sheet formatting is an operation that can be accomplished only with great difficulty, by employing obscure operating system commands and menus.

The powerful advantages offered by the GUI, ease of use, WYSIWYG display, and graphics capability have exerted a strong influence on the way software developers will design future products. A few currently available high-end, fully featured word processing products already reflect this influence. As of 1992, the leading Macintosh products were Macwrite, Microsoft Word, Fullwrite Professional, Wordperfect, Wordfinder, and Omnipage. On the IBM PC and compatibles (*q.v.*), there are now versions of Microsoft Word which run under the Microsoft Windows 3.1 GUI.

The GUI influence can be seen in two current developments. The first is in the features increasingly found in word processing products that until recently were found almost exclusively in desktop publishing (DTP) systems (*q.v.*).

DTP, also pioneered by the Apple Macintosh, is only possible with the GUI. DTP applications typically include many of the text entry features of word processors, but add highly sophisticated typesetting and layout functions, such as variable text and display fonts, type styles and sizes, graphics capabilities, and page layout and design features. Where the purpose of word processors is the flexible creation of standard business documents, DTP is intended for the commercial quality design and production of newsletters, brochures, and books.

Although word processing and DTP products are currently distinctly different applications—under normal circumstances, neither application could be substituted for the other—GUI word processors can and do include DTP functions, such as the integration of graphic images with text, and columnar page design. Although DTP features may be unnecessary for many word processing users and may be added by vendors chiefly to expand a product's feature set as a marketing advantage, this trend can be expected to continue. As a result, the distinction between word processing and DTP will become less clear, and word processors will increasingly play both roles.

The influence of the GUI advantage can also be seen in the introduction of graphical operating environments, such as the Microsoft Windows product mentioned above. These are additional software programs that, among other things, provide GUI control to character-based products.

Running under an operating environment of this kind, a user can have the advantages of a GUI and protect his or her investment in character-based applications at the same time. Furthermore, an operating environment offers the same GUI advantage to other MS-DOS applications. The user of a supported word processing program will be presented with the same user interface on a supported spreadsheet or database application.

In addition, the environment allows the exchange of information between applications, or Dynamic Data Exchange (DDE). With DDE, not only can a section of a spreadsheet, for example, be copied, moved, and incorporated into a word processing document, but if the data contained in the original spreadsheet is changed, the change will automatically appear in the section included in the document.

Although these operating environments greatly expand the functionality of MS-DOS word processing programs, further advances will come with the introduction of new operating systems. For example, IBM's OS/2, the successor to MS-DOS as the IBM personal computer operating system, promises true multitasking (*q.v.*)—running two separate applications at once—of which DDE is a foretaste. Apple Computer's System 7, the new Macintosh operating system, also promises future innovation in features and functions.

A future challenge for word processing and a direction it is likely to take is the support of multiple users working on the same documents simultaneously. Traditionally, personal computer word processing packages have been designed for and sold to single users. An individual user of an individual computer uses an individual package to produce his or her own documents. Changes or corrections are rekeyed by the same user on the same system.

Sharing a document in editable, electronic form between personal computer users has been possible in two ways. Another user, with the same software package and the same or fully compatible computer, can borrow the storage media containing the document. Or, with extra hardware, files can be communicated via telephone lines to another user's computer, provided the remote user has the same software and compatible hardware. But, in either case, the data is processed on different computers by users at different times.

In recent years, the trend in office computing has been toward networking, typically in local area networks (*LANS - q.v.*). In a LAN, the personal computers within a department or workgroup are linked so that, typically, they are able to communicate electronic messages and share applications and data files. The applications and shared files are stored on a *file server* (*q.v.*) dedicated to this purpose. Unlike the earlier Office Automation model, however, the processing power resides in the users' personal computers, not in a shared minicomputer. The result is many of the advantages offered by the mini-based system but with more flexibility (in adding or subtracting users, for example) and without the high cost of the minicomputer.

In keeping with the trend toward networking, ISVs now normally offer network versions of their word processing programs. Network versions can be shared by LAN users and, although they are more expensive than single-user versions of the same software, are more economical than purchasing individual packages for each user.

Along with the conveniences of networking, however, come limitations. First, users of LAN word processing are limited to the application that is stored on the network, which may not be their preference. Second, shared data files and documents typically can be accessed and worked on only by one user at one time. To see document changes or to make copies of the document for their personal use, other network users must access the file individually. In a workgroup situation where a document may be the product of several authors, it would be more efficient for several users, working separately or simultaneously, to have access to shared applications and documents. It seems probable that the future of word processing will include an environment in which multiple users with multiple platforms will jointly prepare documents, each using his or her own preferred hardware and software.

References

1988. McWilliams, Peter A. *The Word Processing Book*. Los Angeles: Prelude Press (Random House).

1990. Ruhl, Janet. *The Writer's Toolbox: Buying and Using a Computer for the Literary Life*. Englewood Cliffs, NJ: Prentice-Hall.

AMY WOHL

WORKING SET

For articles on related subjects *see* MEMORY MANAGEMENT;
MEMORY PROTECTION; MULTIPROGRAMMING; OPERATING SYS-
TEMS; PROCESSING MODES; SCHEDULING ALGORITHMS; THRASHING;
and VIRTUAL MEMORY.

Computer systems have memory hierarchies that
consists of at least two levels: a high-speed primary level
that is directly accessible to the processor and a low-
speed secondary level for large files. The primary level is
usually random-access memory (RAM) and the secondary level disks. Blocks of information are moved between
the disks and RAM on request by processors. The designers of the early electronic computers (1940s) called the
primary level the *working store*, and they called its contents the set of working information, or *working set* for
short.

Multiprogramming was introduced (late 1950s) to
share RAM among several active programs and to increase system throughput (*q.v.*) by maintaining a reserve
of ready-to-execute programs. The space allocated to a
particular program was called its *partition* of the RAM. An
important question was how to determine what subset of
a program to store in that program's partition. The term
"working set" was abstracted so that it did not depend on
the RAM and could be used to designate that subset. By
the middle 1960s, working set had come to mean the
smallest subset of a program's address space that needed
to be present in RAM to keep the work of moving information between RAM and disk under control. Within this
understanding, the size as well as the content of the
working set varies over time.

A 1968 proposal defined the working set precisely as
the set of blocks read or written by the program during a
timing window of size T looking backward from the current time (Denning, 1968). Here, time is understood as
"virtual time," measured as the number of operations
performed by the program since starting.

This definition has many useful mathematical properties that permit efficient calculation of the demand that
a given program will place on the secondary memory
system (Denning, 1980). The demand is often presented
as a "lifetime function," giving the mean time between
requests for blocks to be moved from disk to RAM as a
function of the size of the partition allocated to it. The
lifetime function can be computed in a single pass over a
program's address trace, a recording of the block addresses it generates during execution. The lifetime function is useful in the performance evaluation of a given
computer system, using multiprogramming or virtual
memory.

This definition also offered a means of controlling
thrashing (*q.v.*), a problem that afflicted many early multiprogrammed computer systems (Rosell and Dupuy,
1973). As the multiprogramming level was increased, the
partition size decreased, and the demand for disk-to-RAM
block transfers rose. Up to a certain level, system
throughput would nonetheless increase with multiprogramming level. But after a critical value of the multiprogramming level, the demand for block transfers would
swamp the system, producing a sharp drop in throughput. Because the window-based working set gave a measure of a program's intrinsic memory demand, it was easy
to enforce a rule that programs would be loaded only if
their working sets fit into RAM, implying a limit on the
multiprogramming level. This rule caused the multiprogramming level to rise and fall with the variations in
working set sizes without swamping the secondary storage system. With proper adjustment of the window size,
the multiprogramming level could be controlled to stay
near the system's optimum throughput possible.

By 1980, a considerable number of analytic and empirical studies had been reported in the literature about
the relationships between partition size, load control, and
throughput in multiprogrammed systems. These studies
indicated that a properly adjusted working set policy
would maintain a system's throughput close to its optimal
level. The adjustment consisted of nothing more than
selecting a single window size that would be used for all
programs in the system.

In practice, the moving-window definition of working
set is expensive to implement. This definition, therefore,
is most useful to define the analytic tools for calculating
system throughput and response time under various configurations and program loads. A variety of alternatives
have been devised to use a single usage bit associated
with each block stored in RAM to measure an approximation of the working set. One of the simplest has been
called the "clock" strategy, so-called because it can be
visualized with the aid of a clock face. Imagine that the
names of all the blocks in RAM are noted around the
circumference of a clock, and that the clock's hand is
pointing to one of them. When a running program generates a request to move a new block into RAM, the clock
hand begins scanning for a block whose usage bit is off; it
turns off the usage bits of those it passes over. The block
thus selected is removed from RAM to make way for the
incoming block. This scheme can be implemented easily
as part of the linked-list structure that keeps track of
block allocations in RAM. A limit must be placed on the
multiprogramming level because this scheme does not
prevent an overload.

In some systems, working sets can be deduced from
a program's structure rather than by measurement of
usage bits. For example, on machines using block-structured programming languages such as Ada (*q.v.*) or Pascal, the working set can be defined as the current
procedure segment, the stack, and all arrays accessible
from activated procedures.

The success of working set policies derives from the
dynamic property called *locality of reference*. In each
phase of virtual time, a program will refer to only a subset
of the blocks in its address space. This is a direct consequence of software design: programmers usually organize
algorithms to work with subsets or regions of their data
space during specific algorithmic phases. It is plain that
the working set estimates the set of blocks used by the
program during the current phase. When most virtual
time is covered by phases that are long compared to the
secondary memory access time, and when there is a
substantial overlap of blocks between successive phases

(the usual case), the working set is an excellent predictor of memory demand in the immediate future.

In paging systems it is sometimes advantageous to "restructure" a program by clustering small, logical segments of the same locality on large pages. By preserving in the page references the locality originally present in the segment references, this strategy can yield the smallest possible working sets and efficient performance in systems with large page size. It is less important in modern systems, which tend to use page sizes that are comparable to or smaller than the block sizes that appear in the program's address space.

References

1968. Denning, P. J. "The Working Set Model for Program Behavior," *Comm. ACM* **11**, 5 (May) 323–333.

1973. Rodriguez-Rosell, J., and Dupuy, J. P. "The Design Implementation, and Evaluation of a Working Set Dispatcher," *Comm. ACM* **16**, 4 (April).

1980. Denning, P. J. "Working Sets Past and Present," *IEEE Trans. Softw. Engrg.* **SE-6**, 1 (January), 64–84.

PETER J. DENNING

WORM (WRITE ONCE, READ MANY). *See* MEMORY: AUXILIARY.

WORKSTATION

For articles on related subjects *see* DISTRIBUTED SYSTEMS; FILE SERVER; LOCAL AREA NETWORK; PERSONAL COMPUTING; USER INTERFACE; and WINDOW ENVIRONMENTS.

A *workstation* is characterized by several important features. First, the conventional character-oriented terminal has been replaced by a graphics-oriented bit-mapped display device, and the keyboard is supplemented by a mouse (*see* MOUSE; and INTERACTIVE INPUT DEVICES). Second, workstations connect to local area networks (LANs - *q.v.*) and run sophisticated software that provides access to a wide array of network services provided by machines residing elsewhere on the network. In particular, they usually run versions of the Unix operating system (*q.v.*), which supports execution of multiple, concurrent processes. Used initially by scientists and engineers, workstations are rapidly becoming commonplace in educational and business settings as they become cost-competitive with personal computers.

Output displayed on a graphics-oriented, bit-mapped display allows applications to show pictures, graphics, program output, and text containing arbitrary fonts. A special *window-manager* utility divides the display screen into multiple independent windows, with individual applications controlling one or more windows (*see* WINDOW ENVIRONMENTS). The window manager allows a user to control the size and location of windows in a uniform way, while the application focuses on updating a window's contents rather than its location. Higher-end workstations provide color graphics with hardware support for computationally intensive operations, such as rotating images, while lower-end models support a monochrome screen.

Input is supplemented by a pointing device called a *mouse* (*q.v.*). As the user moves the mouse, an on-screen pointer tracks its motion. The pointer is used to move the focus of attention to a particular window (so that keystrokes are delivered to the appropriate application) or to move or resize existing windows. In addition, the mouse includes one or more buttons that trigger screen events when pressed. For example, pressing one button may cause a help menu to be displayed, while another might pop up a menu of applications.

Workstations are designed to connect to local area networks, and special software allows them to access files located on remote *file servers* as easily as if the files resided on a disk attached to the local workstation. Network access is facilitated by the use of an operating system (usually Unix), which hides the details of accessing remote files from user programs. In addition, network software based on the TCP/IP or similar protocols provides easy access to services provided by machines attached to the network. Users send electronic mail (*q.v.*) to persons on remote machines, establish interactive login sessions with remote machines, and send and retrieve files.

The idea of a personal workstation originated at Xerox Parc during the 1960s. It was not until the development of microprocessor technology, however, that workstations became commonly available. Current workstations are equipped with 32-bit microprocessors, virtual memory (*q.v.*), and a large physical store. Workstations have become the primary beneficiaries of reduced instruction set computing (RISC - *q.v.*) technology, a technique in which the instruction set of the central processor is stripped down to its bare essentials. Although the raw processing power of high-end workstations approaches that of mainframes, their reduced input/output capacity limits their ability to compete with mainframes directly. Physically, they require space comparable to that of a terminal, easily fitting on a desk. Workstations will continue to become cheaper and faster through improved hardware technology and economy of scale in manufacturing.

Despite their power, workstations are designed primarily for use by a single user. Although hardware speed is important, a workstation's power derives from its software. Workstation users can develop sophisticated documents such as books, newsletters, and papers, inspecting the final output before ever sending it to a printer.

References

1988. Tanenbaum, Andrew. *Computer Networks*, 2nd Ed. Englewood Cliffs, NJ: Prentice Hall.

1990. Comer, Douglas E. *Internetworking with TCP/IP: Principles, Protocols, and Architecture*, 2nd Ed. Engelwood Cliffs, NJ: Prentice Hall.

THOMAS NARTEN

ZUSE COMPUTERS

For articles on related subjects *see* DIGITAL COMPUTERS: HISTORY; and ZUSE, KONRAD.

Konrad Zuse and the computer company he headed designed and built a number of computers between 1938 and 1969. The first four, which he called Z1 through Z4, have a special place in the history of computing.

Because World War II isolated him from the Anglo-American computing mainstream, Zuse's early machines embody genuinely different design alternatives to those produced in that mainstream. Thus, study of the Zuse designs raises the historical question of the extent to which the nature of modern computer architecture reflects "laws" of computer science that are independent of social and cultural forces.

The Z1, begun in 1936 and completed in 1938, used an arrangement of slotted metal plates through which pins passed to store, read, and write binary digits. Calculation was effected by similar mechanical interlocks that provided the fundamental Boolean operations. Zuse knew of binary arithmetic before he turned to building computers and then independently discovered its relation to Boolean logic while working on the arithmetic unit of the Z1. This computer never worked properly, however, due to difficulties he had in joining its arithmetic and memory units.

The failure of Z1 led Zuse to use surplus telephone relays instead of mechanical devices to perform arithmetic for his second machine, the Z2. The Z2, completed in 1939, was built in a workshop at Zuse's parents' Berlin apartment and was succesfully demonstrated before the German Aerodynamics Research Institute (AVA) that same year.

With funds from the German military, Zuse built the Z3, the first of his machines to work reliably in all respects. The Z3 used 1,800 telephone relays for memory, 600 for calculation, and 200 for sequence control. Sequences were encoded in 8-bit code by manually punching holes onto strips of discarded 35mm movie film. The computer exe-cuted linear sequences with no provision for conditional jumps. Operations included ordinary arithmetic, square root, store and recall from memory, and binary-decimal conversion. The Z3 had a memory of 64 22-bit floating-point numbers consisting of 7 bits for the base-2 exponent, 1 bit for the sign, and 14 for the mantissa. Clock speed was about 4 to 5 Hz, with one multiplication taking about 3 to 5 seconds. The Z3 was completed in early December 1941, and essentially ran only test programs until its destruction in a bombing raid on Berlin in 1944.

In 1945, Zuse built the Z4, a much more capable machine and one that stands with the Harvard Mark I and the Bell Labs' relay computers (*q.v.*) as a mature and sophisticated digital computer. For the Z4, Zuse returned to the mechanical memory of his first two computers.

When the Z4 was finally completed in 1949, it had a memory of 512 32-bit words and a very sophisticated instruction set (Fig. 1). Although it did not store its programs internally, it nonetheless served as the inspiration for much theoretical work in programming and programming languages, by Zuse himself as well as by Heinz

FIG. 1. The Zuse Z4 Computer.

Rutishauser and a number of other continental European researchers. This was at a time when operational digital computers were rare or inaccessible, especially for those not based in England or the United States.

Zuse's computers were characterized by electromechanical technology, binary floating-point arithmetic, and a simple and clean logical structure. Their existence supports the argument that binary logic and a separation of memory and processing units are fundamental to computer science, regardless of cultural heritage.

PAUL E. CERUZZI

ZUSE, KONRAD

For articles on related subjects *see* DIGITAL COMPUTERS: HISTORY: ORIGINS, and EARLY; and ZUSE COMPUTERS.

Konrad Zuse (b. 1910 in Berlin) studied construction engineering at the Technische Hochschule Berlin-Charlottenburg and received the degree Dipl. Ing. in 1935. In 1934, he had already started development work on program-controlled computing machines with electro-mechanical and mechanical elements. He felt that the tiresome calculations required in this field should be done by a machine. In 1938, he had completed his first model (Z1). In 1941, his first fully working machine (Z3) was operational; it used the binary number system with floating-point arithmetic. Zuse invented a relay adder in which four relays produced the sum of two binary places and

FIG. 1. Konrad Zuse.

that, in an *n*-place binary adder, yields the *n*-place sum in one switching step.

During the next four years, Zuse built a number of special machines and the all-purpose relay computer Z4. The Z3 was destroyed by bombs (it was reconstructed in the 1960s), but the Z4 was saved, and in 1949 it was installed at the Eidgenössische Technische Hochschule in Zürich. In 1954, it was transferred to a research institute in St. Louis near Basle, where it was operated for five years. Around 1945, when facilities for circuit development were not available to Zuse, he turned to programming and designing an algorithmic language, which he called Plankalkül (Bauer and Wössner, 1972). Its notation was in a kind of matrix form, and it could be used for both numerical and non-numerical problems (Zuse used it to describe a full chess program).

In 1949, Zuse formed his own company ZUSE KG, and went into manufacturing. His first successful product was Z11, a relay computer for geodetical and optical applications. His second product was Z22, a vacuum-tube computer (later replaced by its transistorized version Z23); it had an extremely flexible instruction code, achieved by a set of functional bits, an early form of microprogramming (*q.v.*). The Z22 was delivered first in 1958, and more than 50 were made. In 1958, Zuse published one of his ideas that was ahead of his time. This was the field computer, a parallel processor especially suited for differential equations. In the same year, he designed a computer-controlled plotter called Z64, or Graphomat.

After a number of financial difficulties, Zuse left ZUSE KG, which was absorbed by Siemens AG in 1969. Three years before he had become a professor at the University of Göttingen.

In 1957, Zuse received the honorary degree of Dr.techn. in Berlin; in 1964, he received the Werner von Siemens-Ring; in 1965, the Harry Goode Medal from AFIPS; in 1969, the German Diesel Medal; in the same year, the Austrian Exner Medal; and, in 1975, on his 65th birthday, appointment as an Honorary Citizen of Huenfeld. Zuse has received four honorary doctoral degrees (Berlin 1956, Hamburg 1979, Dresden 1981, and Reykjavik 1986) and he is an Honorary Professor at the Göttengen University. The IEEE Pioneers Award was presented to him in 1982.

Zuse received four high German distinctions: two federal, one of Berlin, and one Bavarian. He is an Honorary Member of the Academia Leopoldina in Halle, a Foreign Associate of the U.S. National Academy of Engineering and an Honorary Member of the German Society for Informatics (GI).

The achievements of Dr. Zuse can be properly evaluated only if his isolation is taken into account. His background was construction engineering, and he knew practically nothing about other computer developments (in Germany or abroad, in his time or earlier) until a very late stage. During all his life, Dr. Zuse received too little understanding and support. The German military had no interest in his work, and while the German Research Council after the war did its best to support him, their efforts were not enough to keep his company alive.

Two ZUSE medals are awarded every year, one by the German Building Industry and one by the Gesellschaft für

Informatik. Since 1970, Zuse has been famous as a painter, and he could now make his living from painting.

References

1972. Bauer, F. L. and Wössner, H. "The Plankalkül of Konrad Zuse: A Forerunner of Today's Programming Languages," *Comm ACM.* **15**, 678–685.

1978. *Proceedings of the SEAS Anniversary Meeting in West Berlin: "General Considerations of the Evolution of Computers."*

1983. Ceruzzi, Paul: *Reckoners*, Chapter "Computers in Germany," 10–42. Westport, CO: Greenwood Press.

1986. Zuse, K: *Memoirs (Der Computer—mein Lebenswerk)*, 2nd Ed. Berlin: Springer Verlag.

HEINZ ZEMANEK

APPENDIX I

ABBREVIATIONS AND ACRONYMS

Judging by the rate at which they are coined, computing people seem to love abbreviations and acronyms. The list that follows contains all of the abbreviations and acronyms used in this Encyclopedia other than those invented by authors strictly for local use in their articles.

It also contains additional entries that are in common use in computer magazines and more formal computing literature, but it does not contain all of the language-related acronyms in Appendix V nor does it include abbreviations for the units of measurement that follow the list.

A/D	Analog-to-Digital
AAAI	American Association of Artificial Intelligence
ABC	Atanasoff-Berry Computer
ABET	Accreditation Board for Engineering and Technology
ABI	Applications Binary Interface
AC (or ACC)	Accumulator
ACE	Automatic Computing Engine
ACH	Association for Computing in the Humanities
ACK	Acknowledgement
ACL	Association for Computational Linguistics
ACM	Association for Computing Machinery
ACTRAN	Analog Computer Translator
ADAPSO	Association of Data Processing Service Organizations
ADB	Apple Desktop Bus
ADI	American Documentation Institute
ADP	Automatic Data Processing
ADT	Abstract Data Type
AED	Automated Engineering Design
AEDS	Association for Educational Data Systems
AESC	American Engineering Standards Committee
AFCET	Association Française pour la Cybernetique Economique et Technique
AFIPS	American Federation of Information Processing Societies
AHPL	A Hardware Programming Language
AI	Artificial Intelligence
AIAA	American Institute of Aeronautics and Astronautics
AIEE	American Institute of Electrical Engineers
AL	Assembly Language
ALGOL	ALGOrithmic Language
ALLC	Association for Literary and Linguistic Computing
ALPAC	Automatic Language Processing Advisory Committee
ALU	Arithmetic-Logic Unit
AM	Amplitude Modulation

AMP	Access Module Processor
AMS	American Mathematical Society
ANSI	American National Standards Institute
ANSVIP	American National Standards Vocabulary for Information Processing
APEC	Automated Procedures for Engineering Consultants
API	Applications Programming Interface
APL	A Programming Language
APPC	Advanced Program to Program Communication
APS	American Physical Society
APSE	Ada Program Support Environment
APT	Automatic Programmed Tool
ARIES	Automated Reliability Estimation Program
ARPA	Advanced Research Projects Agency
ARPANET	Advanced Research Projects Agency Network
ASA	American Standards Association
ASA	American Statistical Association
ASC	Advanced Scientific Computer
ASC	Accredited Standards Committee
ASCII	American Standard Code for Information Interchange
ASIS	American Society for Information Science
ASL	Available Space List
ASM	Association for Systems Management
ASTM	American Society for Testing Materials
ATDM	Asynchronous Time-Division Multiplexing
ATM	Automated Teller Machine
ATM	Asynchronous Transfer Mode
ATS	Administrative Terminal System
ATSU	Association of Time-Sharing Users
AUUA	America's Univac Users Association
AVL	Adel'son-Vel'skii and Landis (tree)
AWC	Association for Women in Computing
BASIC	Beginners All-Purpose Symbolic Instruction Code
BBN	Bolt Beranek and Newman
BBS	Bulletin Board Systems
BCD	Binary-Coded Decimal
BCPL	Basic Combined Programming Language
BCS	British Computer Society
BCTIC	Biomedical Computing Technology Information Center
BDAM	Basic Direct Access Method
BDP	Business Data Processing
BEMA	Business Equipment Manufacturers Association
BFS	Breadth First Search
BOC	Bell Operating Company
BINAC	Binary Northrop Automatic Computer
BIOS	Basic Input-Output System
BISAM	Basic Indexed Sequential Access Method
BISYNC	Binary Synchronous Communications Protocol
BITNET	Because It's Time NET
BJT	Bipolar Junction Transistor
BLISS	Basic Language for the Implementation of System Software
BMD	Biomedical (Computer Programs)
BMDP	Biomedical (Computer Programs—P Series)
BNF	Backus-Naur Form
BOCA	Borland Object Component Architecture
BSAM	Basic Sequential Access Method
BSD	Berkeley Systems Division (Unix version)
BSP	Burroughs Scientific Processor
BTAM	Basic Telecommunications Access Method
C.mmp	Carnegie Multi-Mini Processor
CACM	Communications of the Association for Computing Machinery
CAD	Computer-Aided Design

CAD/CAM	Computer-Aided Design/Computer-Aided Manufacturing
CADD	Computer-Aided Design and Drafting
CAE	Computer-Aided Education
CAE	Computer-Aided Engineering
CAI	Computer-Aided Instruction
CAI	Computer-Assisted Instruction
CAL	Computer-Aided Learning
CALS	Computer-aided Acquisition in Logistic Support
CAM	Computer-Aided Manufacturing
CAN	Computer Architecture News
CAPP	Computer-Aided Process Planning
CAPTAIN	Character And Pattern Telephone Access Information Network
CARE	Computer-Aided Reliability Estimation
CAS	Communicating Applications Specification
CASE	Computer-Aided Software Engineering
CAT	Computer-Assisted Tomography
CATV	Cable TeleVision
CAUSE	College And University System Exchange
CBCT	Customer-Bank Communication Terminal
CBE	Computer-Based Education
CBEMA	Computer and Business Equipment Manufacturers Association
CBF	Charles Babbage Foundation
CBI	Charles Babbage Institute
CBT	Computer-Based Training
CC	Compiler-Compiler
CC	Computer Conferencing
CCD	Charge-Coupled Device
CCITT	Comité Consultatif Internationale Télégraphique et Téléphonique
CCS	Common Channel Signaling
CD	Compact Disc
CDC	Control Data Corporation
CDL	Computer Description Language
CDL	Computer Design Language
CDP	Certificate in Data Processing
CD-ROM	Compact Disc—Read Only Memory
CEPA	Civil Engineering Programming Applications
CEPTA	Council of European Postal Telecommunications Authorities
CG	Computer Graphics
CGA	Color Graphics Adapter
CGI	Computer Graphics Interface
CGM	Computer Graphics Metafile
CHIPS	ClearingHouse Interbank Payments System
CICS	Customer Information Control Systems
CIE	Computer-Integrated Enterprise
CII	Compagnie Internationale pour Informatique
CIM	Computer Input from Microfiche
CIM	Computer-Integrated Manufacturing
CIPS	Canadian Information Processing Society
CISC	Complex Instruction Set Computer
CISI	Compagnie Internationale de Services et Informatique
CLSR	Computer Law Service Reporter
CMCS	Computer-Mediated Communications System
CMI	Computer-Managed Instruction
CMOS	Complementary Metal-Oxide Semiconductor
CMS	Conversational Monitor System
CNC	Computerized Numerical Control
COBOL	COmmon Business-Oriented Language
CODASYL	COnference on Data Systems Languages
COM	Computer Output on Microfilm
CONTU	Commission On New Technological Uses of copyrights
COP	Communications Processor

COSATI	Committee On Scientific And Technical Information
COSMIC	Computer Software Management and Information Center
CPC	Card Programmed Calculator
CP/M	Control Program for Microcomputers
CPM	Critical Path Method
CPSR	Computer Professionals for Social Responsibility
CPU	Central Processing Unit
CRAM	Card Random Access Memory
CRC	Cyclic Redundancy Check
CRT	Cathode Ray Tube
CSA	Canadian Standards Association
CSE	Computer Science and Engineering
CSMA/CD	Carrier-Sense Multiple Access with Collision Detect
CT	Computerized Tomography
CTSS	Compatible Time-Sharing System
CUA	Common User Access
CUMREC	College and University Machine RECords conference
D/A	Digital-to-Analog
DAA	Data Access Arrangement
DAG	Directed Acyclic Graph
DAM	Direct Access Method
DAP	Distributed Array Processor
DARPA	Defense Advanced Research Projects Agency
DASD	Direct Access Storage Device
DAX	Data Acquisition and Control
DBA	DataBase Administrator
DBM	DataBase Management
DBMS	DataBase Management System
DBTG	DataBase Task Group
DCA	Digital Computer Association
DCS	Distributed Control System
DDE	Dynamic Data Exchange
DDL	Data Definition Language
DDP	Distributed Data Processor
DDS	Dataphone Digital Service
DEC	Digital Equipment Corporation
DECUS	Digital Equipment Corporation Users Society
DES	Data Encryption Standard
DEQUE	Double-Ended QUEue
DETAB	Decision Table (Language)
DFS	Depth First Search
DFT	Discrete Fourier Transform
DFT	Distributed Function Terminal
DIF	Data Interchange Format
DIP	Dual-In-line Package
DLAT	Directory Look-Aside Table
DLCL	Doubly-Linked Circular List
DLL	Dynamic Link Library
DLLL	Doubly-Linked Linear List
DMA	Direct Memory Access
DML	Data Manipulation Language
DNA	Digital Network Architecture
DOS	Disk Operating System
DPMA	Data Processing Management Association
DRAM	Dynamic Random Access Memory
DRO	Destructive Read Out
DSDD	Double-Sided Double Density (diskette)
DSP	Digital Signal Processing
DSS	Decision Support System
DSU	Disk Storage Unit
DTL	Diode-Transistor Logic

DTP	DeskTop Publishing
DVA	Distributed Voting Algorithm
DVST	Direct View Storage Tube
DVI	Digital Video Interactive
DYANA	Dynamic Analyzer
EAI	Electronic Associates, Inc.
EARN	European Academic Research Network
EBCDIC	Extended Binary-Coded Decimal Interchange Code
EBNF	Extended Backus Naur Form
ECL	Emitter-Coupled Logic
ECMA	European Computer Manufacturers Association
ECR	Electronic Cash Register
ECS	Extended Core Storage
EDI	Electronic Data Interchange
EDP	Electronic Data Processing
EDS	Electronic Data Systems
EDSAC	Electronic Delay Storage Automatic Calculator
EDUCOM	Education Communications (Interuniversity Communications Council)
EDVAC	Electronic Discrete Variable Automatic Computer
EEPROM	Electronically Erasable Programmable Read-Only Memory
EFT	Electronic Funds Transfer
EGA	Enhanced Graphics Advisor
EIA	Electronic Industries Association
EISA	Extended International Standard Architecture
ELI	Extensible Language I
EMS	Expanded Memory Specification
ENIAC	Electronic Numerical Integrator and Computer
EOF	End-Of-File
EOL	End-Of-Line
EPP	Enhanced Parallel Port
EPROM	Erasable Programmable Read-Only Memory
EPS	Encapsulated PostScript (file)
EPSS	Experimental Packet Switching System
ERA	Engineering Research Associates
ESDI	Enhanced System Device Interface
FAP	Fortran Assembly Program
FAT	File Allocation Table
FAX	Facsimile
FDDI	Fiber Distributed Data Interface
FDM	Frequency Division Multiplexing
FED	Field Emission Display
FEM	Finite Element Method
FET	Field-Effect Transistor
FF	Flip-Flop
FFT	Fast Fourier Transform
FIACC	Five International Associations Coordinating Committee
FIFO	First-In-First-Out
FIMS	Forms Interface Management System
FIPS	Federal Information Processing Standards
FLOPS	Floating-Point Operations per Second
FM	Frequency Modulation
FMS	Fortran Monitor System
FOPC	First Order Predicate Calculus
FORTRAN	FORmula TRANslator
FOSDIC	Film Optical Sensing Device for Input to Computer
FPAP	Floating Point Array Processor
FPS	Floating Point System
FPU	Floating Point Unit
FSA	Finite State Automaton
FSM	Finite State Machine
FTMP	Fault Tolerant Multiprocessor System

FTP	File Transfer Protocol
FTSC	Fault Tolerant Spaceborne Computer
GASP	General Activity Simulation Program
GEM	Graphical Environment Manager
GENESYS	General Engineering System
GIGO	Garbage-In-Garbage-Out
GIPSY	General Information Processing System
GIS	Geographical Information System
GIS	Graphical Information System
GKS	Graphical Kernel System
GPF	General Protection Fault
GPM	General Purpose Macrogenerator
GRIPHOS	General Retrieval and Information Processing for Humanities-Oriented Studies
GSAM	Generalized Sequential Access Method
GSM	Generalized Sequential Machine
GUI	Graphical User Interface
GUIDE	Guidance of Users of Integrated Data Processing Equipment
HB	Honeywell-Bull
HDAM	Hierarchical Direct Access Method
HDL	Hardware Description Language
HDLC	High-level Data Link Control
HDTV	High-Definition TeleVision
HEP	Heterogeneous Element Processor
HGA	Hercules Graphics Adapter
HIPAC	Hitachi Parametron Automatic Computer
HIPO	Hierarchy plus Input-Process-Output
HIS	Honeywell Information Systems
HIS	Hospital Information System
HLL	High-Level Language
HP	Hewlett-Packard
HPPA	High-Performance Precision Architecture
HWIM	Hear What I Mean
I/O	Input-Output
IAC	International Apple Core
IAG	International Applications Group (of IFIP)
IAL	International Algebraic Language
IAPR	International Association for Pattern Recognition
IASC	International Association for Statistical Computing
IBM	International Business Machines
IC	Instruction Counter
IC	Integrated Circuit
ICCA	International Computer Chess Association
ICCCM	Inter-Client Communications Conventions Manual
ICL	International Computers Ltd.
ICP	International Computer Programs
ICSU	International Council of Scientific Unions
ICT	International Computers and Tabulators
IDC	International Data Corporation
IDE	Integrated Development Environment
IDFT	Inverse Discrete Fourier Transform
IDS	Integrated Data Store
IDT	Interrupt Descriptor Table
IDU	Instruction Decoding Unit
IEEE	Institute of Electrical and Electronics Engineers
IEEE-CS	Institute of Electrical and Electronics Engineers—Computer Society
IFAC	International Federation of Automatic Control
IFIP	International Federation of Information Processing
IFORS	International Federation of Operations Research Societies
IFP	InterFace Processor
IGES	Initial Graphical Exchange Specification
ILLIAC	Illinois Automatic Computer

IMACS	International Association for Mathematics and Computing in Simulation
IMIA	International Medical Informatics Association
IMP	Interface Message Processor
IMS	Information Management System
IMSL	International Mathematical and Statistical Libraries
IOCS	Input-Output Control System
IOP	Input-Output Processor
IP	Instruction Processor
IP	Internet Protocol
IPC	Interprocess Communication
IPS	Information Processing System
IR	Information Retrieval
IR	Instruction Register
IRE	Institute of Radio Engineers
IRG	Inter-Record Gap
IRIA	Institut de Recherche d'Informatique et d'Automatique
ISA	Industry Standard Architecture
ISA	Instrument Society of America
ISAM	Indexed Sequential Access Method
ISDN	Integrated Systems Digital Network
ISO	International Standards Organization
ISODATA	Interactive Self-Organizing DATA analysis technique
ISP	Instruction Set Processor
ISP	Information and Service Provider
ISPS	Instruction Set Processor Specifications
ISSMB	Information Systems Standards Management Board
ISTE	International Society for Technology in Education
ITC	International Typeface Corporation
JACM	Journal of the Association for Computing Machinery
JCL	Job Control Language
JOD	Journal of Development
JUG	Joint Users Group
KSR	Keyboard Send-Receive
KWIC	Keyword-In-Context
KWOC	Keyword-Out-of-Context
LALR	Lookahead Left-to-Right
LAN	Local Area Network
LARC	Livermore Automatic Research Computer
LAT	Local Area Transport
LBA	Linear Bounded Automaton
LCD	Liquid Crystal Display
LEC	Local Exchange Carrier
LED	Light-Emitting Diode
LIFO	Last-In-First-Out
LINC	Laboratory Instrument Computer
LISP	LISt Processor
LIU	Line Interface Unit
LP	Linear Programming
LPC	Linear Predictive Coding
LRC	Longitudinal Redundancy Check
LRU	Least Recently Used
LS	Least Squares
LSB	Least Significant Bit (or Byte)
LSI	Large Scale Integration
LSTTL	Low-Power Schottky Transistor-Transistor Logic
LT	Logic Theorist
LTM	Long-Term Memory
MAA	Mathematical Association of America
MAC	Machine-Aided Cognition (or Man And Computer) (MIT Project MAC)
MACSYMA	MAC SYmbol MAnipulation
MAP	Manufacturing Automation Protocol

MAR	Memory Address Register
MARC	Machine-Readable Cataloging
MBQ	Modified Biquinary Code
MCA	Micro Channel Architecture
MCGA	Multi-Color Graphics Array
MCP	Master Control Program
MDI	Multiple Document Interface
MEDIX	MEdical Data Interchange
MEDLARS	MEDical Literature Analysis and Retrieval System
MEDLINE	MEDlars on-LINE System
MFM	Modified Frequency Modulation
MFT	Multiprogramming with a Fixed Number of Tasks
MICR	Magnetic Ink Character Recognition
MIDAC	Michigan Digital Automatic Computer
MIDI	Musical Instrument Digital Interface
MIMD	Multiple-Instruction Stream, Multiple-Data Stream
MIMR	Magnetic Ink Mark Recognition
MIS	Management Information System
MISD	Multiple-Instruction Stream, Single-Data Stream
MLA	Modern Language Association
MMU	Memory Management Unit
MODEM	MOdulator-DEModulator
MOS	Metal-Oxide Semiconductor
MPP	Massively Parallel Processor
MOSFET	Metal-Oxide Semiconductor Field Effect Transistor
MPU	Microprocessing Unit
MPW	Macintosh Programmer's Workshop
MRP	Manufacturing Resource Planning
MSM	Message Switching Multiplexing
MQ	Multiplier-Quotient
MSB	Most Significant Bit (or Byte)
MSI	Medium Scale Integration
MSS	Mass Storage System
MSUDC	Michigan State University Discrete Computer
MT	Machine Translation
MTBF	Mean Time Between Failures
MTS	Michigan Terminal System
MTTF	Mean Time To Failure
MTTR	Mean Time To Repair
MULTICS	Multiplexed Information and Computer Service
MVS	Multiprogramming with Virtual Storage
MVT	Multiprogramming with a Variable Number of Tasks
NACHA	National Automated Clearing House Association
NAG	Numerical (formerly Nottingham) Algorithms Group
NAK	Negative AcKnowledgement
NAN	Not A Number
NAP	Network Access Protocol
NAPLPS	North American Presentation Level Protocol Syntax
NAND	Not AND
NATS	National Activity to Test Software
NC	Numerical Control
NCC	National Computer Conference
NCEFT	National Commission on Electronic Funds Transfers
NCLIS	National Commission on Libraries and Information Science
NCR	National Cash Register
NDRO	Non-Destructive Read-Out
NEC	Nippon Electric Corporation
NeWS	Network/extensible Window System
NFF	Negation as Finite Failure
NFS	Network File System
NLP	Nonlinear Programming

NLP	Natural Language Processing
NLQ	Near Letter Quality
NMA	National Micrographics Association
NMOS	Negative Metal-Oxide Semiconductor
NOR	Not OR
NORC	Naval Ordnance Research Computer
NP	Nondeterministic Polynomial (-time or -space)
NREN	National Research and Education Network
NVRAM	Non-Volatile Random Access Memory
OBR	Optical Bar Code
OCR	Optical Character Recognition
ODE	Ordinary Differential Equation
ODS	Open Distributed System
OECD	Organization for Economic Cooperation and Development
OEM	Original Equipment Manufacturer
OLCP	On-Line Complex Processing
OLE	Object Linking and Embedding
OMR	Optical Mark Reading
ONA	Open Network Architecture
ONC	Open Network Computing
OOPS	Object-Oriented Programming System
ORDVAC	Ordnance Variable Automatic Computer
OS	Operating System
OS/MFT	Operating System/Multiprogramming with a Fixed Number of Tasks
OS/MVS	Operating System/Multiprogramming with Virtual Storage
OS/MVT	Operating System/Multiprogramming with a Variable Number of Tasks
OSI	Open Systems Interconnection
OWL	Object Windows Library
PACS	Picture Archiving and Communications System
PARC	Palo Alto Research Center (Xerox)
PBX	Private Branch Exchange
PC	Personal Computer
PC	Program Counter
PCB	Printed Circuit Board
PCI	Peripheral Controller Interface
PCM	Plug Compatible Mainframe
PDA	Personal Digital Assistant
PDE	Partial Differential Equation
PDES	Product Data Exchange Specification
PDL	Page Description Language
PDP	Programmed Data Processor
PE	Processing Element
PERT	Program Evaluation and Review Technique
PF	Page Fault
PHIGS	Programmer's Hierarchical Interactive Graphics System
PID	Proportional-Integral-Derivative (control system)
PIM	Personal Information Manager
PIN	Personal Identification Number
PIN	Positive-Instrinsic-Negative (diode)
PKC	Public Key Cryptosystem
PLA	Programmable Logic Array
PLATO	Programmed Logic for Automatic Teaching Operation
PLC	Programmable Logic Controller
PM	Phase Modulation
PM	Presentation Manager
PMOS	Positive Metal-Oxide Semiconductor
PMS	Processor-Memory-Switch
POL	Procedure-Oriented Language (or Problem-Oriented Language)
POS	Point-of-Scale
PP	Peripheral Processor
PPL	Polymorphic Programming Language

PRAM	Parallel Random-Access Machine
PROM	Programmable Read-Only Memory
PSA	Pushdown Stack Automaton
PSL/PSA	Problem Statement Language/Problem Specification Analyzer
PSS	Packet Switching Service
PSTN	Public Switched Telephone Network
PSW	Program Status Word
PTT	Postal-Telephone-Telegraph
PUFFT	Purdue University Fast Fortran Compiler
QBE	Query By Example
QISAM	Queued Indexed Sequential Access Method
QSAM	Queued Sequential Access Method
QTAM	Queued Telecommunications Access Method
R-S	Reset-Set (Flip-Flop)
RAM	Random Access Memory
RAMAC	Random Access Method for Accounting and Control
RAMDAC	Random Access Memory Digital to Analog Converter
RDA	Remote Database Access
RDBMS	Relational DataBase Management System
RGB	Red-Green-Blue
RIP	Raster Image Processor
RISC	Reduced Instruction Set Computer
RJE	Remote Job Entry
RLIN	Research Libraries Information Network
RLL	Run-Length Limited (recording)
RMM	Read Mostly Memory
ROM	Read-Only Memory
RPC	Remote Procedural Call
RPG	Report Program Generator
RPS	Rotational Position Sensing
RSA	Rivest-Adleman-Shamir (encryption algorithm)
RSL	Requirements Specification Language
RT	Register Transfer
RTL	Register-Transistor Logic
RTL	Register Transfer Language
RTM	Register Transfer Module
R/W	Read/Write
SAA	Systems Application Architecture
SAM	Sequential Access Method
SAP	Symbolic Assembly Program
SCI	Simulation Councils, Incorporated
SCS	Society for Computer Simulation
SCSI	Small Computer Systems Interface
SDC	System Development Corporation
SDI	Selective Dissemination of Information
SDK	Software Development Kit
SDLC	Synchronous Data Link Control protocol
SDS	Scientific Data Systems
SEAC	Standards Eastern Automatic Computer
SIAM	Society for Industrial and Applied Mathematics
SID	Society for Information Display
SIFT	Software-Implemented Fault Tolerance
SIG	Special Interest Group
SIMD	Single-Instruction Stream, Multiple-Data Stream
SIMM	Single In-Line Memory Module
SISD	Single-Instruction Stream, Single-Data Stream
SJF	Shortest Job First
SLAM	Simulation Language for Alternative Modeling
SLCL	Singly-Linked Circular List
SLLL	Singly-Linked Linear List
SLR	Simple Left-to-Right (parsing)

SLT	Solid Logic Technology
SMIS	Society for Management Information Systems
SMTP	Simple Mail Transfer Protocol
SNA	System Network Architecture
SNOBOL	StriNg-Oriented symBOlic Language
SOAP	Symbolic Optimizer and Assembly Program
SONET	Synchronous Optical NETwork
SOR	Successive Overrelaxation
SOS	Share Operating System
SP	Structured Programming
SPAP	Special Purpose Array Processor
SPARC	Standard Planning and Requirements Committee
SPC	Statistical Process Control
SPL	Simple Programming Language
SPMD	Single Program, Multiple Data
SPOOL	Simultaneous Peripheral Operations On Line
SPSS	Statistical Programs for the Social Sciences
SQA	Software Quality Assurance
SQC	Statistical Quality Control
SQL	Structured Query Language
SQUID	Superconducting Quantum Interference Device
S-R	Set-Reset (Flip-Flop)
SRAM	Static Random Access Memory
SRTF	Shortest Remaining Time First
SSEC	Selective Sequence Electronic Calculator
SSI	Small-Scale Integration
SSP	Scientific Subroutine Package
STAR	Self Testing and Repair (Computer)
STDM	Synchronous Time-Division Multiplexing
STEP	STandard for Exchange of Product (Model Data)
STM	Short-Term Memory
STRESS	Structural Engineering Systems Solver
STRUDL	Structural Design Language
SVGA	Super VGA (*see* VGA)
SVID	System V Interface Definition (Unix)
SWAC	Standards Western Automatic Computer
SWIFT	Society for Worldwide Interbank Financial Telecommunications
TAXIR	Taxonomic Information Retrieval
TBM	Terabit Memory
TCOS	Technical Committee on Operating Systems (IEEE)
TCP/IP	Transmission Control Protocol/Internet Protocol
TDM	Time-Division Multiplexing
TEI	Text Encoding Initiative
TERC	Technology Education Research Center
TI	Texas Instruments
TICCIT	Time-Shared Interactive Computer-Controlled Informational Television
TIES	Total Integrated Engineering System
TIFF	Tagged Image File Format
TIP	Terminal Interface (message) Processor
TLB	Translation Lookaside Buffer
TMR	Triple Modular Redundancy
TODS	Transactions on Database Systems (ACM)
TOCS	Transactions on Computer Systems (ACM)
TOG	Transactions on Graphics (ACM)
TOIS	Transactions on Information Systems (ACM)
TOMS	Transactions on Mathematical Software (ACM)
TOPLAS	Transactions on Programming Languages and Systems (ACM)
TOPS	Transcendental Operating System
TP	Transaction Processing
TSS	Time-Shared System
TTL	Transistor-Transistor Logic

TTY	Teletype
UAE	Unrecoverable Applications Error
UART	Universal Asychnronous Receiver Transceiver
UHF	Ultra-High Frequency
ULSI	Ultra Large Scale Integration
UNI	User Network Interface
UNIVAC	Universal Automatic Computer
UPC	Universal Product Code
UPS	Uninterruptible Power Supply
USASCII	USA Standard Code for Information Interchange
USASI	United States of America Standards Institute
USE	Univac Scientific Exchange
UUA	Univac Users Association
VAL	Vicarm Arm Language
VAN	Value-Added Network
VAR	Value-Added Reseller
VB	Visual Basic
VC	Virtual Circuit
VDL	Vienna Definition Language
VDT	Video (Visual) Display Terminal
VDU	Video (Visual) Display Unit
VESA	Video Electronics Standards Association
VGA	Video Graphics Adapter
VHF	Very High Frequency
VIM	VI (Roman 6) M (Roman 1000) (CDC users' association)
VLIW	Very Long Instruction Word
VLSI	Very Large-Scale Integration
VM	Virtual Memory
VM	Virtual Machine
VMEbus	VersaModule Eurocard bus
VMS	Virtual Memory System (DEC VAX operating system)
VRAM	Video Random Access Memory
VRC	Vertical Redundancy Check
VSAM	Virtual Storage Access Method
VTAM	Virtual Telecommunications Access Method
VTP	Virtual Terminal Protocol
VUP	VAX Unit of Processing
WAN	Wide Area Network
WATFOR	WATerloo FORtran
WATS	Wide Area Telephone Service
WCS	Writable Control Store
WELL	Whole Earth 'Lectronic Link
WFF	Well-Formed Formula
WORM	Write-Once Read-Many
WYSIWYG	What You See Is What You Get
XDR	eXternal Data Representation
XMS	eXtended Memory Specification
XNS	Xerox Network System (architecture)
XOR	eXclusive OR
YACC	Yet Another Compiler-Compiler

Mathematical Notation

Symbol   *Meaning*

GENERAL

$\sum$

$$\text{Summation} \left(\sum_{i=1}^{n} a_i = a_1 + a_2 + \ldots + a_n \right)$$

$\int$	Integral
$\|\ \|$	Absolute value ($\|a\|=a$ *if* $a \geq 0$, $= -a$ *if* $a < 0$)
$\lfloor\ \rfloor$	Floor function (greatest integer less than or equal to: $\lfloor 2.4 \rfloor = 2$, $\lfloor -2.4 \rfloor = -3$)
$\lceil\ \rceil$	Ceiling function (least integer greater than or equal to: $\lceil 2.4 \rceil = 3$, $\lceil -2.4 \rceil = -2$)
$[\ ]$	Closed interval ($[a,b]$ includes all x such that $a \leq x \leq b$)
$(\ )$	Open interval $[(a,b)$ includes all x such that $a < x < $ b$]$
$[\ ),(\ ]$	Half-open (half-closed) interval $[[a,b)$ includes all x such that $a \leq x < b]$
$\approx, \simeq, \cong, \doteq$	Approximately equal
$\sim$	Asymptotic to
$\times$	Set product $[A \times B$ consists of all pairs (a,b) where $a \in A, b \in B]$
modulo (or mod)	Remainder ($x \bmod y$ is remainder when x is divided by y; thus, 8 mod 3 is 2)
$\circ$	Binary operation (i.e., denotes any operation like $+$ which requires two operands)
fl	Floating point ($\mathrm{fl}(x + y)$ denotes the floating-point sum of x and y)
iff	If and only if
$\lg(x)$	$\log_2 (x)$
$\ln(x)$	$\log_\in (x)$
wrt	With respect to

LOGIC

$\vee$	Or
$\wedge$	And
$\sim, \neg$	Not
$\supset$	Implication
$\equiv$	Equivalence
$\not\equiv$	Inequivalence

Notes

1. For a description of the notation used in describing computer language constructs, *see* BACKUS-NAUR FORM.
2. For symbols used in logical circuitry, *see* COMPUTER CIRCUITRY.

Asymptotic Growth Notation Used in Analysis of Algorithms

Notation	*Meaning*
$f(n) = O(g(n))$	The rate of growth of $f(n)$ does not exceed that of $g(n)$
$f(n) = \Omega(g(n))$	The rate of growth of $f(n)$ is at least as great as that of $g(n)$
$f(n) = \Theta(g(n))$	The rate of growth of $f(n)$ is essentially the same as that of $g(n)$
$f(n) = o(g(n))$	The rate of growth of $f(n)$ is strictly less than that of $g(n)$
$f(n) = \omega(g(n))$	The rate of growth of $f(n)$ is strictly greater than that of $g(n)$

Units of Measure

This list contains abbreviations of units of measure used in the Encyclopedia; these usually appear in their abbreviated form.

General

K	1,000 or 1024 ($= 2^{10}$); the latter refers mainly to measures of computer storage capacity
M	1,000,000 or 1,048,576 ($= 2^{20}$)
G	2^{30} (approximately 1 U.S. billion)

Time

ms, msec	millisecond (10^{-3} sec)
μs, μsec	microsecond (10^{-6} sec)
ns, nsec	nanosecond (10^{-9} sec)
ps, psec	picosecond (10^{-12} sec)
fs, fsec	femtosecond (10^{-15} sec)
as, asec	attasecond (10^{-18} sec)

Speed

Megaflop or Mflop	Million floating-point operations per second
Gigaflop or Gflop	Billion floating-point operations per second
MIPS	Million instructions processed per second

Electricity

Hz	Hertz (cycles/sec)
KHz	Kilohertz (10^3 cycles/sec)
MHz	Megahertz (10^6 cycles/sec)
Kc	Kilocycle (10^3 cycles)
Mc	Megacycle (10^6 cycles; sometimes, 10^6 cycles/sec = 1 MHz)
μW	Microwatt (10^{-6} watts)
mW	Milliwatt (10^{-3} watts)
KW	Kilowatt (10^3 watts)
mV	Millivolt (10^{-3} volt)
mA	Milliamp (10^{-3} amp)
μF	Microfarad (10^{-6} farad)
nF	Nanofarad (10^{-9} farad)
pF	Picofarad (10^{-12} farad)
fF	Femtofarad (10^{-15} farad)
aF	Attafarad (10^{-18} farad)

Storage

Kb	Kilobit (10^3 bits)
Mb	Megabit (10^6 bits)
Gb	Gigabit (10^9 bits)
Tb	Terabit (10^{12} bits)
Pb	Petabit (10^{15} bits)
Eb	Exabit (10^{18} bits)
KB	Kilobyte (10^3 bytes)
MB	Megabyte (10^6 bytes)
GB	Gigabyte (10^9 bytes)
TB	Terabyte (10^{12} bytes)
PB	Petabyte (10^{15} bytes)
EB	Exabyte (10^{18} bytes)
L(x)	Location of x (in main memory)
C(A)	Contents of location A (in main memory)

I/O

bps	Bits per second
bpi	Bits per inch
chps	Characters per second
chpi	Characters per inch
lpm	Lines per minute
rpm	Revolutions per minute
KB/sec or Kbytes/sec	Kilobytes per second
MB/sec or Mbytes/sec	Megabytes per second
GB/sec or Gbytes/sec	Gigabytes per second

Miscellaneous

μ	Micron (10^{-6} meter)
mbar	Millibar (10^{-3} [cgs unit of pressure])

APPENDIX II

NUMERICAL TABLES

POWERS OF TWO TABLE

2^n	n	2^{-n}
2	1	0.5
4	2	0.25
8	3	0.125
16	4	0.625×10^{-1}
32	5	$0.312\ 5 \times 10^{-1}$
64	6	$0.156\ 25 \times 10^{-1}$
128	7	$0.781\ 25 \times 10^{-2}$
256	8	$0.390\ 625 \times 10^{-2}$
512	9	$0.195\ 312\ 5 \times 10^{-2}$
1 024	10	$0.976\ 562\ 5 \times 10^{-3}$
2 048	11	$0.488\ 281\ 25 \times 10^{-3}$
4 096	12	$0.244\ 140\ 625 \times 10^{-3}$
8 192	13	$0.122\ 070\ 312\ 5 \times 10^{-3}$
16 384	14	$0.610\ 351\ 562\ 5 \times 10^{-4}$
32 768	15	$0.305\ 175\ 781\ 25 \times 10^{-4}$
65 536	16	$0.152\ 587\ 890\ 625 \times 10^{-4}$
131 072	17	$0.762\ 939\ 453\ 125 \times 10^{-5}$
262 144	18	$0.381\ 469\ 726\ 562\ 5 \times 10^{-5}$
524 288	19	$0.190\ 734\ 863\ 281\ 25 \times 10^{-5}$
1 048 576	20	$0.953\ 674\ 316\ 406\ 25 \times 10^{-6}$
2 097 152	21	$0.476\ 837\ 158\ 203\ 125 \times 10^{-6}$
4 194 304	22	$0.238\ 418\ 579\ 101\ 562\ 5 \times 10^{-6}$
8 388 608	23	$0.119\ 209\ 289\ 550\ 781\ 25 \times 10^{-6}$

POWERS OF TWO TABLE (Continued)

2^n	n	2^{-n}
16 777 216	24	0.596 046 447 753 906 25 $\times 10^{-7}$
33 554 432	25	0.298 023 223 876 953 125 $\times 10^{-7}$
67 108 864	26	0.149 011 611 938 476 562 5 $\times 10^{-7}$
134 217 728	27	0.745 058 059 692 382 812 5 $\times 10^{-8}$
268 435 456	28	0.372 529 029 846 191 406 25 $\times 10^{-8}$
536 870 912	29	0.186 264 514 923 095 703 125 $\times 10^{-8}$
1 073 741 824	30	0.931 322 574 615 478 515 625 $\times 10^{-9}$
2 147 483 648	31	0.465 661 287 307 739 257 812 5 $\times 10^{-9}$
4 294 967 296	32	0.232 830 643 653 869 628 906 25 $\times 10^{-9}$
8 589 934 592	33	0.116 415 321 826 934 814 453 125 $\times 10^{-9}$
17 179 869 184	34	0.582 076 609 134 674 072 265 625 $\times 10^{-10}$
34 359 738 368	35	0.291 038 304 567 337 036 132 812 5 $\times 10^{-10}$
68 719 476 736	36	0.145 519 152 283 668 518 066 406 25 $\times 10^{-10}$
137 438 953 472	37	0.727 595 761 418 342 590 332 031 25 $\times 10^{-11}$
274 877 906 944	38	0.363 797 880 709 171 295 166 015 625 $\times 10^{-11}$
549 755 813 888	39	0.181 898 940 354 585 647 583 007 812 5 $\times 10^{-11}$
1 099 511 627 776	40	0.909 494 701 772 928 237 915 039 062 5 $\times 10^{-12}$
2 199 023 255 552	41	0.454 747 350 886 464 118 957 519 531 25 $\times 10^{-12}$
4 398 046 511 104	42	0.227 373 675 443 232 059 478 759 765 625 $\times 10^{-12}$
8 796 093 022 208	43	0.113 686 837 721 616 029 739 379 882 812 5 $\times 10^{-12}$
17 592 186 044 416	44	0.568 434 188 608 080 148 696 899 414 062 5 $\times 10^{-13}$
35 184 372 088 832	45	0.284 217 094 304 040 074 348 449 707 031 25 $\times 10^{-13}$
70 368 744 177 664	46	0.142 108 547 152 020 037 174 224 853 515 625 $\times 10^{-13}$
140 737 488 355 328	47	0.710 542 735 760 100 185 871 124 267 578 125 $\times 10^{-14}$
281 474 976 710 656	48	0.355 271 367 880 050 092 935 562 133 789 062 5 $\times 10^{-14}$
562 949 953 421 312	49	0.177 635 683 940 025 046 467 781 066 894 531 25 $\times 10^{-14}$
1 125 899 906 842 624	50	0.888 178 419 700 125 232 338 905 334 472 656 25 $\times 10^{-15}$
2 251 799 813 685 248	51	0.444 089 209 850 062 616 169 452 667 236 328 125 $\times 10^{-15}$
4 503 599 627 370 496	52	0.222 044 604 925 031 308 084 726 333 618 164 062 5 $\times 10^{-15}$
9 007 199 254 740 992	53	0.111 022 302 462 515 654 042 363 166 809 082 031 25 $\times 10^{-15}$
18 014 398 509 481 984	54	0.555 111 512 312 578 270 211 815 834 045 410 156 25 $\times 10^{-16}$
36 028 797 018 963 968	55	0.277 555 756 156 289 135 105 907 917 022 705 076 125 $\times 10^{-16}$
72 057 594 037 927 936	56	0.138 777 878 078 144 567 552 953 958 511 352 539 062 5 $\times 10^{-16}$
144 115 188 075 855 872	57	0.693 889 390 390 722 837 764 769 792 556 762 695 312 5 $\times 10^{-17}$
288 230 376 151 711 744	58	0.346 944 695 195 361 418 882 384 896 273 381 347 656 25 $\times 10^{-17}$
576 460 752 303 423 488	59	0.173 472 347 597 680 709 441 192 448 139 190 673 828 125 $\times 10^{-17}$

TABLE OF IMPORTANT NUMERICAL CONSTANTS

	Decimal (Rounded)					Hexadecimal (Truncated)				
$1/10$	0.10000	00000	00000	00000	00000	0.1999	9999	9999	9999	9999
$\sqrt{2}$	1.41421	35623	73095	04880	16887	1.6A09	E667	F3BC	C908	B2FB
$\sqrt{3}$	1.73205	08075	68877	29352	74463	1.BB67	AE85	84CA	A73B	2574
$\sqrt{5}$	2.23606	79774	99789	69640	91737	2.3C6E	F372	FE94	F82B	E739
$\sqrt{10}$	3.16227	76601	68379	33199	88935	3.298B	075B	4B6A	5240	9457
$\sqrt[3]{2}$	1.25992	10498	94873	16476	72106	1.428A	2F98	D728	AE22	3DDA
$\ln 2$	0.69314	71805	59945	30941	72321	0.B172	17F7	D1CF	79AB	C9E3
$\ln 10$	2.30258	50929	94045	68401	79915	2.4D76	3776	AAA2	B05B	A95B
$\log_{10}2$	0.30102	99956	63981	19521	37389	0.4D10	4D42	7DE7	FBCC	47C4
$\log_{2}10 = 1/\log_{10}2$	3.32192	80948	87362	34787	03194	3.5269	E12F	346E	2BF9	24AF
$\log_{2}e = 1/\ln 2$	1.44269	50408	88963	40735	99247	1.7154	7652	B82F	E177	7D10
$\log_{10}e = 1/\ln 10$	0.43429	44819	03251	82765	11289	0.6F2D	EC54	9B94	38CA	9AAD
$1^{\circ} = \pi/180$	0.01745	32925	19943	29576	92369	0.0477	D1A8	94A7	4E45	7076
π	3.14159	26535	89793	23846	26434	3.243F	6A88	85A3	08D3	1319
$1/\pi$	0.31830	98861	83790	67153	77675	0.517C	C1B7	2722	0A94	FE13
π^{2}	9.86960	44010	89358	61883	44910	9.DE9E	64DF	22EF	2D25	6E26
$\sqrt{\pi}$	1.77245	38509	05516	02729	81675	1.C5BF	891B	4EF6	AA79	C3B0
e	2.71828	18284	59045	23536	02875	2.B7E1	5162	8AED	2A6A	BF71
$1/e$	0.36787	94411	71442	32159	55238	0.5E2D	58D8	B3BC	DF1A	BADE
e^{2}	7.38905	60989	30650	22723	04275	7.6399	2E35	376B	730C	E8EE
$\sqrt{e}$	1.64872	12707	00128	14684	86508	1.A612	98E1	E069	BC97	2DFE
γ (Euler's constant)	0.57721	56649	01532	86060	65121	0.93C4	67E3	7DB0	C7A4	D1BE
$\varphi = (1 + \sqrt{5})/2$ (Golden Ratio)	1.61803	39887	49894	84820	45868	1.9E37	79B9	7F4A	7C15	F39C

APPENDIX III

Computer Science and Engineering Research Journals

The list of journals that follows includes most of the major research journals devoted entirely to computer science and engineering, as well as a few that publish articles of significant technical interest, although they are not necessarily research journals. In addition, we list first journals devoted to reviews and abstracts of the computer science and technology literature:

Computing Reviews, published monthly by the Association for Computing Machinery.

Computer Abstracts, published monthly by the Technical Information Company in Great Britain.
Computer and Control Abstracts, published monthly by the Institution of Electrical Engineers, UK.
Computer and Information Systems Abstract Journal, published monthly by Cambridge Scientific Abstracts of Riverdale, Maryland and Oxford, England.

The full addresses of all journals listed below can be found periodically in *Computing Reviews* (e.g. November 1991).

Journal	*Publisher*
Acta Informatica	Springer-Verlag
Annals of the History of Computing	IEEE
Artificial Intelligence	Elsevier
Australian Computer Journal	Australian Computer Society
Bit (Nordisk Tidskrift for Informationsbehandling)	Swedish Institute for Informationsbehandling
Byte	McGraw-Hill
Communications of the ACM	ACM
Computer	IEEE
Computer Bulletin	British Computer Society
Computer Graphics	ACM
Computer Journal	British Computer Society
Computer Languages	Pergamon Press
Computer Networks and ISDN Systems	Elsevier
Computers and Graphics	Pergamon Press
Computers and the Humanities	Pergamon Press
Computing	Springer-Verlag
Computing Surveys	ACM
Discrete Applied Mathematics	Elsevier

Journal	*Publisher*
Expert Systems with Applications	Pergamon Press
IBM Systems Journal	IBM
Information Processing Letters	Elsevier
Information Sciences	Elsevier
Information Processing and Management	Pergamon Press
International Journal of Supercomputer Applications	MIT Press
Journal of Algorithms	Academic Press
Journal of Computer and System Sciences	Academic Press
Journal of Information Processing	Information Processing Society of Japan
Journal of Information Science	Elsevier
Journal of Intelligent and Robotic Systems	John Wiley
Journal of Logic Programming	Elsevier
Journal of Parallel and Distributed Computing	Academic Press
Journal of Symbolic Computation	Academic Press
Journal of Systems and Software	Elsevier
Journal of the ACM	ACM
Machine Vision and Applications	Springer-Verlag
Mathematics of Computation	American Mathematical Society
Numerische Mathematik	Springer-Verlag
Pattern Recognition	Pergamon Press
SIAM Journal on Computing	SIAM
SIAM Journal on Discrete Mathematics	SIAM
SIAM Journal on Numerical Analysis	SIAM
SIAM Journal on Scientific and Statistical Computing	SIAM
Simulation	Society for Computer Simulation
Software Engineering Journal	Institution of Electrical Engineers
Software—Practice and Experience	John Wiley
Theoretical Computer Science	Elsevier
Transactions on Computers	IEEE
Transactions on Computer Systems	ACM
Transactions on Database Systems	ACM
Transactions on Graphics	ACM
Transactions on Information Systems	ACM
Transactions on Mathematical Software	ACM
Transactions on Modeling and Computer Simulation	ACM
Transactions on Pattern Analysis and Machine Intelligence	IEEE
Transactions on Programming Languages & Systems	ACM
Transactions on Software Engineering	IEEE
Transactions on Software Engineering and Methodology	ACM

Note: See the article *Literature of Computing* for a survey of all types of computer science and engineering literature.

APPENDIX IV

Universities Offering the Ph.D. Degree in Computer Science and/or Computer Engineering

The list that follows includes departments at universities in the United States and Canada that offer a Ph.D. in computer science (CS) or computer engineering (CE) or both. Almost all offer the master's degree and have undergraduate major programs in computer science and/or computer engineering. In addition to the programs listed here, some departments of mathematics and electrical engineering also offer doctorates in computer science or computer engineering or with an option in one or the other.

The data in this list comes from the "Forsythe List" which is named after George Forsythe who was one of the founders of academic computer science while on the faculty at Stanford University. The list is compiled and maintained by the Computer Research Association (*q.v.*).

University	Name of Department or Program with Degree Designation	Telephone Number
Alabama, Birmingham, University of	Computer and Information Science (CS)	205-934-2213
Alberta, University of	Computer Science (CS)	403-492-4589
Arizona, University of	Computer Science (CS)	602-621-4239
Arizona State University	Computer Science (CS)	602-965-3190
Auburn University	Computer Science (CE/CS)	205-844-4330
Boston University	Computer Science (CS)	617-353-8919
Brandeis University	Computer Science (CS)	617-736-2700
British Columbia, University of	Computer Science (CS)	604-228-3061
Brown University	Computer Science (CS)	401-863-7600
Calgary, University of	Computer Science (CS)	403-220-5454
California Institute of Technology	Computer Science (CS)	818-356-6840
California at Berkeley, University of	Computer Science (CS)	415-642-0930
California at Davis, University of	Computer Science and Engineering (CS)	916-752-7004
California at Irvine, University of	Information and Computer Science (CS)	714-856-7405
California at Los Angeles, University of	Computer Science (CS)	213-825-8878
California at San Diego, University of	Computer Science and Engineering (CS)	619-534-1246
California at Santa Barbara, University of	Electrical and Computer Engineering (CE)	805-893-3821
California at Santa Cruz, University of	Computer Engineering (CE)	408-459-2565
	Computer Science (CS)	408-459-2565
Carnegie-Mellon University	Electrical and Computer Engineering (CE)	412-268-2537
	Computer Science (CS)	412-268-2592

1467

University	Name of Department or Program with Degree Designation	Telephone Number
Case Western Reserve University	Computer Engineering (CE)	216-368-2802
Central Florida, University of	Computer Engineering (CE)	407-281-5840
	Computer Science (CS)	407-275-2341
Chicago, University of	Computer Science (CS)	312-702-6011
Cincinnati, University of	Electrical and Computer Engineering (CE)	513-556-4769
City University of New York	Computer Science (CS)	212-642-2201
Clemson University	Electrical and Computer Engineering (CE)	803-656-5249
	Computer Science (CS)	803-656-3444
College of William and Mary	Computer Science (CS)	804-221-3453
Colorado at Boulder, University of	Computer Science (CS)	303-492-7554
Colorado State University	Computer Science (CS)	303-491-5792
Columbia University	Computer Science (CS)	212-854-2736
Concordia University	Computer Science (CS)	514-848-3003
Connecticut, University of	Computer Science and and Engineering (CS)	203-486-3719
Cornell University	Computer Science (CS)	607-255-7416
Dartmouth College	Computer Science (CS)	603-646-3385
Delaware, University of	Computer and Information Sciences (CS)	302-451-2712
Drexel University	Electrical and Computer Engineering (CE)	215-895-2359
Duke University	Computer Science (CS)	919-684-3048
Florida, University of	Computer and Information Science (CS)	904-392-1200
Florida Atlantic University	Computer Science (CS/CE)	407-367-3180
Florida Institute of Technology	Electrical and Computer Engineering (CE)	407-768-8000 X-7331
	Computer Science (CS)	407-768-8000 X-7315
Florida International University	Computer Science (CS)	305-348-2744
Florida State University	Computer Science (CS)	904-644-2296
George Mason University	Computer Science (CS)	703-323-2713
George Washington University	Electrical Engineering and Computer Science (CS)	202-994-6083
Georgia Institute of Technology	Computing (CS)	404-894-3186
Harvard University	Applied Sciences (CS)	617-495-5829
Houston, University of	Electrical Engineering (CE)	713-749-2511
	Computer Science (CS)	713-749-4791
Illinois at Chicago, University of	Electrical Engineering and Computer Science (CE)	312-996-3422
Illinois at Urbana, University of	Electrical and Computer Engineering (CE)	217-333-2300
	Computer Science (CS)	217-333-3373
Illinois Institute of Technology	Computer Science (CS)	312-567-5150
Indiana University	Computer Science (CS)	812-855-6486
Iowa, University of	Electrical and Computer Engineering (CS)	319-335-5197
	Computer Science (CS)	
Iowa State University	Electrical and Computer Engineering (CE)	515-294-7709
	Computer Science (CS)	515-294-4377
Johns Hopkins University	Electrical and Computer Engineering (CE)	301-338-7031
	Computer Science (CS)	301-338-8775
Kansas, University of	Electrical and Computer Engineering (CE)	913-864-4620
	Computer Science (CS)	913-864-4482
Kansas State University	Computing and Information Sciences (CS)	913-532-6350
Kent State University	Mathematical Sciences (CS)	216-672-2209
Kentucky, University of	Computer Science (CS)	606-257-3961
Lehigh University	Computer Science and Electrical Engineering (CE/CS)	215-758-4070
Louisiana State University	Computer Science (CS)	504-388-1495
Louisville, University of	Computer Science and Engineering (CE/CS)	502-588-6304
Manitoba, University of	Computer Science (CS)	204-474-8313
Marquette University	Electrical and Computer Engineering (CE)	414-288-6820
Maryland, University of	Computer Science (CS)	301-405-2661
Maryland at Baltimore County, University of	Computer Science (CS)	301-455-3000
Massachusetts at Amherst, University of	Electrical and Computer Engineering (CE)	413-545-0962
	Computer Science (CS)	413-545-2742
Massachusetts Institute of Technology	Electrical and Computer Engineering (CS)	617-253-2506
McGill University	Computer Science (CS)	514-398-7072
Michigan, University of	Electrical Engineering and Computer Science (CS)	313-764-3317
Michigan State University	Computer Science (CS)	517-353-6484
Minnesota, University of	Computer Science (CS)	612-625-4002
Mississippi State University	Computer Science (CS)	601-325-2756
Missouri at Rolla, University of	Computer Science (CS)	314-341-4492

University	Name of Department or Program with Degree Designation	Telephone Number
Montreal, University of	Information et Recherche Operation (CS)	514-343-7090
Naval Postgraduate School	Computer Science (CS)	408-646-2449
Nebraska at Lincoln, University of	Computer Science and Engineering (CS)	402-472-3200
New Mexico, University of	Electrical and Computer Engineering (CE)	505-277-2600
	Computer Science (CS)	505-277-3112
New Mexico State University	Computer Science (CS)	505-646-3723
New Mexico Tech	Computer Science (CS)	505-835-5126
New York University	Computer Science (CS)	212-998-3103
North Carolina at Chapel Hill, University of	Computer Science (CS)	919-962-1777
North Carolina State University	Electrical and Computer Engineering (CE)	919-737-2336
	Computer Science (CS)	919-737-7775
North Dakota State University	Computer Science (CS)	701-237-8171
North Texas, University of	Computer Science (CS)	817-656-2767
Northeastern University	Electrical and Computer Engineering (CE)	617-437-4159
	Computer Science (CS)	617-437-3539
Northwestern University	Electrical Engineering (CS)	708-491-3641
Notre Dame, University of	Electrical and Computer Engineering (CE)	219-239-5483
Ohio State University	Computer and Information Science (CS)	614-292-5973
Ohio University	Computer Science (CS)	614-593-1242
Oklahoma, University of	Electrical Engineering and Computer Science (CS)	405-325-4721
Oklahoma State University	Electrical and Computer Engineering (CE)	405-744-5151
	Computer Science (CS)	405-744-5668
Old Dominion University	Computer Science (CS)	804-683-4817
Oregon, University of	Computer and Information Science (CS)	503-346-4408
Oregon Graduate Institute	Computer Science and Engineering (CS)	503-690-1151
Oregon State University	Electrical and Computer Engineering (CE)	503-737-3617
	Computer Science (CS)	503-737-3273
Pennsylvania, University of	Computer and Information Science (CS)	215-898-0051
Pennsylvania State University	Computer Science (CS)	814-865-9505
Pittsburgh, University of	Computer Science (CS)	412-624-8493
Polytechnic University	Computer Science (CS)	718-260-3003
Princeton University	Computer Science (CS)	609-258-5030
Purdue University	Electrical Engineering (CE)	317-494-3536
	Computer Science (CS)	317-494-6003
Rensselaer Polytechnic Institute	Electrical, Computer, and Systems Engineering (CE)	518-276-6316
	Computer Science (CS)	518-276-8326
Rice University	Electrical and Computer Engineering (CE)	713-527-4020
	Computer Science (CS)	713-527-4834
Rochester, University of	Computer Science (CS)	716-275-5288
Rutgers University	Computer Science (CS)	201-932-3546
Santa Clara University	Electrical Engineering and Computer Science (CE)	408-554-4483
Saskatchewan, University of	Computational Science (CS)	306-966-4886
Simon Fraser University	Computing Science (CS)	604-291-3128
South Carolina, University of	Electrical and Computer Engineering (CE)	803-777-7548
	Computer Science (CS)	803-777-2840
South Florida, University of	Computer Science and Engineering (CS)	813-974-3652
Southern California, University of	Electrical and Computer Engineering Systems (CE)	213-740-4579
	Computer Science (CS)	213-743-5512
Southern Methodist University	Computer Science and Engineering (CE/CS)	214-692-3083
Southwestern Louisiana, University of	Advanced Computer Studies (CE/CS)	318-231-6147
Stanford University	Computer Science (CS)	415-723-9745
Stevens Institute of Technology	Electrical Engineering and Computer Science (CS)	201-420-5622
SUNY at Albany	Computer Science (CS)	518-442-4270
SUNY at Binghamton	Computer Science (CS)	607-777-6204
SUNY at Buffalo	Electrical and Computer Engineering (CE)	716-636-2426
	Computer Science (CS)	716-636-3182
SUNY at Stony Brook	Computer Science (CS)	516-632-8462
Syracuse University	Electrical and Computer Engineering (CE)	315-443-2652
	Computer and Information Science (CS)	315-443-2368
Temple University	Computer and Information Science (CS)	215-787-8199
Tennessee at Knoxville, University of	Electrical and Computer Engineering (CE)	615-974-5465
	Computer Science (CS)	615-974-5067
Texas A&M University	Computer Science (CS)	409-845-5534
Texas at Arlington, University of	Computer Science and Engineering (CE/CS)	817-273-3783

University	Name of Department or Program with Degree Designation	Telephone Number
Texas at Austin, University of	Electrical and Computer Engineering (CE)	512-471-6179
	Computer Science (CS)	512-471-7316
Texas at Dallas, University of	Computer Science (CS)	214-690-2184
Texas Tech University	Computer Science (CS)	806-742-3527
Toronto, University of	Computer Science (CS)	416-978-8954
Tulane University	Computer Science (CS)	504-865-5840
Tulsa, University of	Mathematics and Computer Sciences (CS)	918-631-2228
Utah, University of	Computer Science (CS)	801-581-7026
Vanderbilt University	Computer Science (CS)	615-322-2796
Virginia, University of	Computer Science (CS)	804-982-2225
Virginia Polytechnic Institute	Computer Science (CS)	703-231-6931
Washington State University	Electrical Engineering and Computer Engineering (CE)	509-335-8148
	Computer Science (CS)	509-335-8148
Washington, University of	Computer Science (CS)	206-543-1695
Washington University	Computer Science (CS)	314-889-6132
Waterloo, University of	Computer Science (CS)	519-885-1211
Wayne State University	Electrical and Computer Engineering (CE)	313-577-3920
	Computer Science (CS)	313-577-2478
Western Ontario, University of	Computer Science (CS)	519-661-3563
Wisconsin at Madison, University of	Computer Science (CS)	608-262-1204
Wisconsin at Milwaukee, University of	Electrical Engineering and Computer Science (CS)	414-229-5357
Worcester Polytechnic Institute	Computer Science (CS)	508-831-5357
Wright State University	Computer Science (CS)	513-873-2292
Wyoming, University of	Computer Science (CS)	307-766-5190
Yale University	Computer Science (CS)	203-432-1200

APPENDIX V

KEY HIGH-LEVEL LANGUAGES

Introduction

The following list of languages represents the author's personal view of the (approximately 50) high-level languages that are deemed most significant (in 1991) from among the over 1,000 high-level implemented languages (not counting dialects) that have been defined since work in computing started. The defined characteristics of a high-level language are given in this author's article on Programming Languages in this encyclopedia. The languages selected had to satisfy (in the author's personal judgment) one or more of these criteria: significant usage, influence on language design, overall impact on the computing environment, novelty (first of its kind), uniqueness, and existing or potential standard. Changes from the list in the 1983 article were made to bring it up-to-date and also to keep the total number under 50. The languages added are C++, Icon, Mathematica, Prolog, Smalltalk, and VHDL. The languages PL/M and TRAC were deleted.

The languages have been grouped into two major categories: (1) those not really in significant use in 1991 (although perhaps a few hardy souls may continue to use them) and (2) those believed to be in significant use, where "significant" is judged relative to the size of the expected user community for that type of language. Within the second group, the languages have been listed by name under the *primary* application areas for which they are intended. This is because of the author's firm belief that the *most important characteristic* of any programming language is the application area for which it is intended to be used. Of the application areas, the first five

(i.e. numerical scientific, business data processing, string and list processing, formula manipulation, and multipurpose) are relatively common or well-known. The remainder are narrow, specialized areas. Following this list, each language is listed in alphabetical order, with the following entries:

> Name
> Meaning of the acronym (when there is one)
> Date of first publication (described below)
> Reference(s) (described below)
> Computers on which the language has been implemented
> The primary application area
> A comment to indicate very briefly something about the language and/or why it is on the list.

For the date of first publication, this means the earliest dissemination of the following (although sometimes labeled "draft" or "preliminary"): published paper, official technical report, language manual, etc. In many cases, the date refers to a much earlier version of the current language. Thus, the 1956 publication on Fortran has little resemblance to the 1978 ANSI standard or to the 1991 ISO/IEC standard. Where a question mark is used, it means the author is not certain of the date. In a few cases, a specific date has been omitted entirely because of lack of knowledge.

Specific references are not listed (aside from the standard numbers, if they exist). For older references and information on most of these languages, there are four main sources, and they are referred to with the indicated abbreviations in the listings:

Roster: "Roster of Programming Languages for 1976–77," J. E. Sammet, *ACM SIGPLAN Notices* **13**, *No. 11.*

HOPL: *History of Programming Languages*, R. L. Wexelblat (Ed.). New York: Academic Press, 1981.

PL: *Programming Languages: History and Fundamentals*, J. E. Sammet. Englewood Cliffs, NJ: Prentice-Hall, 1969.

ANSI, ISO: For any language that is an ANSI or ISO standard, the appropriate number has been shown. Where both standards exist, the initial or primary location is used wherever possible. In those cases where standardization is underway, the organization is shown without any number. Further details on programming language standards are in the article PROGRAMMING LANGUAGE STANDARDS, which contains a complete list of standards including languages which are not on the list below.

For any language contained in more than one of the above sources, all relevant references have been given. The reader should note that there may be more current references for some of these languages (including, but not limited to, articles in this encyclopedia). In a very few cases, these have been included.

The computers are described either as a specific family, or as "many" or "most" where there are too many to list. More implementations may exist but are not known to the author. Implementations include mainframes, minicomputers, and personal computers, and an entry of "many computers" can apply to any or all of these categories. An entry of "most computers" applies to all sizes. An entry of "some" means that there is more than one implementation, but it is not practical to provide a specific list.

The list of computers on which the language has been implemented, and, to a lesser extent, the comment and the implicit value judgment in including the language at all, stem primarily from the author's old language roster, mentioned above, and some updating of that information based on more recent research. However, time has not permitted a thorough updating of implementation and/or usage details.

JEAN E. SAMMET

LIST OF LANGUAGES BY APPLICATION AREA

Historically Important But NOT In SIGNIFICANT Current Use

Algol 60
Algol 68
Comit [II]
Flow-Matic
Formac
IPL-V
IT
Joss
Jovial
Mad
Neliac
Simula 67

Current Usage—Broad Application Areas

Numerical Scientific
Basic
Fortran
Speakeasy

Business Data Processing
Cobol

String and List Processing
Icon
Lisp
Snobol4

Formula Manipulation
Macsyma
Mathematica
Reduce

Multipurpose
Ada
APL
C++
Mumps
Pascal
PL/I
Prolog
Smalltalk

Social Science and/or Statistics
OMNITAB II
SPSS

Systems Programming (including debugging aids)
Bliss
C

Current Languages For Specialized Application Areas

Computer-Assisted Instruction
Coursewriter III
PILOT
TUTOR

Circuit Design
ECAP II
SCEPTRE

Civil, Mechanical, Structural Engineering
COGO
ICES

Computer Hardware Design (including simulation)
ISPL
VHDL

Equipment Checkout
ATLAS

Machine Tool Control
APT

Mathematical/Linear Programming
MPSX
PDS/MaGen

Simulation (continuous)
CSMP
CSSL
DYNAMO III

Simulation (discrete)
GPSS
SIMSCRIPT II.5 ®

DESCRIPTION OF LANGUAGES

Ada
1979
ANSI 1815A-1983.
Many computers.
Multipurpose.
Very powerful language developed over many years with much public commentary. Sponsored by U. S. Department of Defense, but designed by French language team. Used primarily in embedded computer systems (e.g. military, FAA, NASA), but also in numerous commercial applications.

Algol 60
ALGOrithmic Language 1960
May 1960
Roster, HOPL, PL.
Many computers.
Numerical scientific.
Suitable for problems involving numeric computation and/or logical processes. Its predecessor (Algol 58) had several significant languages based on it (e.g. Jovial, Mad, Neliac).

Algol 68
ALGOrithmic Language 1968
1968
Roster.
Many computers.
Multipurpose.
Very powerful language but not upward-compatible from Algol 60.

APL
A Programming Language
1962
Roster, HOPL, PL, ISO 8485-1989.
Many computers.
Multipurpose.
Has unusual character set and cryptic syntax, but has very powerful, concise primitive array operations.

APT
Automatically Programmed Tools
1957
Roster, HOPL, PL, ANSI X3.37-1987.
Most computers.
Machine tool control.
Language for programming numerically controlled machine tools. Was first language developed for a specialized application area.

ATLAS
Abbreviated Test Language for "All" Systems
1968
Roster, ANSI/IEEE Standard 416-1988.
Most computers in differing versions.
Equipment checkout.
For test engineers to control automatic test equipment.

Basic
Beginner's All Purpose Symbolic Instruction Code
1964
Roster, HOPL, PL, ANSI X3.60-1987.
Almost all computers.
Numerical scientific.
Very simple language but with some advanced features. Available on many micro- and personal computers for uses beyond just numerical scientific.

Bliss
Basic Language for Implementation of System Software
1970
Roster.
Several computers.
Systems programming.
For writing compilers and operating systems.

C
1975
Roster, ANSI X3.159-1989.
Many computers.
Systems programming.
Used to write the Unix operating system and most of its application software.

C++
1982(?)
ANSI
Many computers.
Multipurpose.
An extension of C with facilities for object-oriented programming.

Cobol
COmmon Business-Oriented Language
1960

Roster, HOPL, PL, ANSI X3.23-1985.
Most computers.
Business data processing.
English-like in style, developed and maintained by committee of users and manufacturers under Codasyl. One of the most widely used languages.

COGO
*CO*ordinate *GeO*metry
1963 (?)
Roster, PL.
Several computers.
Civil engineering.
Useful for solving coordinate geometry problems in civil engineering.

COMIT [II]
1957
Roster, PL.
IBM System/360.
String processing.
First major language for string handling and pattern matching.

Coursewriter III
1966 (?)
Roster.
IBM System/360.
Computer-assisted instruction.
Simple language for preparing computer-assisted instruction courses.

CSMP
*C*ontinuous *S*ystem *M*odeling *P*rogram
1968
Roster.
Several computers.
Simulation (continuous).
General term for two languages (statement- and block-oriented) used to simulate the dynamics of continuous systems describable by ordinary differential equations.

CSSL
*C*ontinuous *S*ystems *S*imulation *L*anguage
1967
Roster.
CDC 6400 and XDS Sigma 7.
Simulation (continuous).
Statement-oriented language to simulate dynamics of continuous systems describable by ordinary differential equations. Many varying versions with different names are implemented.

DYNAMO III
1959 (?)
Roster.
Most large and medium-sized computers.
Simulation (continuous).
Used to construct large models of economic and social systems.

ECAP II
*E*lectronic *C*ircuit *A*nalysis *P*rogram *II*
1966
Roster.
Several computers.
Circuit design.
Simple language for analyzing electrical networks.

Flow-Matic
1958
PL.
UNIVAC I, II.
Business data processing.
Was first English-like language for business data processing and was a major input to design of Cobol.

Formac
*FOR*mula *MA*nipulation *C*ompiler
1964
Roster, PL.
IBM System/360, 370.
Formula manipulation.
First language to be widely used for formal algebraic manipulation.

Fortran
*FOR*mula *TRAN*slation
1956
Roster, HOPL, PL, ANSI X3.9-1978, ISO/IEC 1539: 1991.
Almost all computers.
Numerical scientific.
First language to be widely used and remains in wide use.

GPSS
*G*eneral *P*urpose *S*ystems *S*imulator
1961
Roster, HOPL, PL.
Several computers.
Simulation (discrete).
Based on block-diagram approach, with statements used for computer input.

ICES
*I*ntegrated *C*ivil *E*ngineering *S*ystem
1967 (?)
Roster.
Several computers.
Civil engineering.
General system for engineering which has internal languages for subsystem development and includes languages such as COGO and STRUDL.

Icon
1978
Many computers.
String processing.
Based on concepts from SNOBOL for string processsng, but is broader and has different syntax.

IPL-V
*I*nformation *P*rocessing *L*anguage *V*

1958
PL.
Many second-generation computers.
List processing.
Was used heavily in the 1960s for list processing applications. Had close notational resemblance to an assembly language.

ISPL
*I*nstruction *S*et *P*rocessor *L*anguage
1971
Roster.
DEC PDP-10.
Computer hardware design.
Used to describe general register transfer systems and digital computer architecture.

IT
*I*nternal *T*ranslator
1957
PL.
IBM 650.
Numerical scientific.
First language implemented on small computer; inspired much compiler research.

Joss
*J*OHNNIAC *O*pen *S*hop *S*ystem
1964
Roster, HOPL, PL.
Many computers in different versions.
Numerical scientific.
First language designed for on-line use. Is very simple. Had many dialects under differing names.

Jovial
*J*ules *O*wn *V*ersion of *I*nternational *A*lgebraic *L*anguage
1960
Roster, HOPL, PL.
Many computers in many versions.
Multipurpose.
Based on Algol 58 (originally called International Algebraic Language) and had many versions. Newest version is Jovial J73. Many early Jovial compilers were written in some version of Jovial.

Lisp
*LIS*t *P*rocessing
1960
Roster, HOPL, PL, ANSI.
Many computers.
List processing.
Sophisticated and theoretically oriented with several dialects. Used for much artificial intelligence research.

Macsyma
Project *MAC*'s *SY*mbol *MA*nipulation
1972
Roster.
DEC PDP-10 and HIS 6180.
Formula manipulation.

Very powerful language for doing formal algebraic manipulation.

Mad
*M*ichigan *A*lgorithm *D*ecoder
1960
Roster, PL.
Several computers.
Systems programming.
Original version was based on Algol 58 and designed for numerical computation. Later version was extended significantly.

Mathematica
1986
Formula manipulation.
Several computers.
Powerful language for doing formal algebraic manipulation that contains many mathematical built-in functions and powerful graphics facilities.

MPSX
*M*athematical *P*rogramming *S*ystem E*X*tended
1966
Roster.
IBM System/360, 370.
Mathematical programming.
Controls solution strategy for mathematical programming problems. Other similar languages run on different computers.

Mumps
*M*assachusetts General Hospital *U*tility *M*ulti-*P*rogramming *S*ystem
1969
Roster, ANSI X11.1-1990.
Several computers.
Multipurpose.
Fairly general language with emphasis on string handling and complex file handling. Used heavily in medical areas, but also in commercial applications.

Neliac
*N*avy *E*lectronics *L*aboratory *I*nternational *A*lgol Compiler
1960
PL.
Many second-generation computers.
Numerical scientific.
Was based on Algol 58 and was used to write its own compilers.

OMNITAB II
1966
Roster.
Most large computers.
Statistics.
Primarily for non-programmers, using desk-calculator-type operations, but also containing powerful mathematical facilities (e.g. regression, matrix inversion).

Pascal
1971
Roster, ANSI X3.97-1990.
Most computers.
Multipurpose.
Small but elegant language with many significant features. Used heavily for teaching programming. Many Pascal compilers are written in Pascal.

PDS/MaGen
*P*roblem *D*escriptor *S*ystem
1973 (?)
Roster.
Many computers.
Mathematical programming.
Facilitates generation of matrices and reports for mathematical programming systems.

PILOT
1969 (?)
Roster.
Many computers.
Computer-assisted instruction.
Simple language that has been written in Basic, APL\360, Algol, Fortran, and PL/I.

PL/I
(Not an acronym, although often erroneously thought to stand for *P*rogramming *L*anguage *I*.)
1964
Roster, HOPL, PL, ANSI X3.53-1976.
Several computers.
Multipurpose.
First of the very large, powerful languages, combining many features and concepts from Algol, Cobol, Fortran, and other languages.

Prolog
1971
ANSI and ISO.
Many computers.
Multipurpose.
For use in logic programming, which can itself be applied to many specific applications. Has a major use in artificial intelligence.

Reduce
1967
Roster.
Many computers.
Formula manipulation.
Algol-like language written in itself and using Lisp as an intermediate language.

SCEPTRE
1960s (?)
Roster.
Several computers.
Circuit design.
Used for designing and analyzing circuits.

SIMSCRIPT II.5®
1963 (?)
Roster.
Many computers.
Simulation (discrete).
Advanced language for large discrete simulation problems. Several previous numbered versions exist. (® Trademark and Service Mark of C.A.C.I., Inc.)

Simula 67
*SIMU*lation *L*anguage, 1967
1967
Roster, HOPL, PL.
Many computers.
Multipurpose.
An extension of Algol 60 and quite distinct from its predecessor (Simula I), which was primarily a simulation language. Introduced the important concept of classes.

Smalltalk
1971
Many computers.
Multipurpose.
Design allows object-oriented programming, and is first language with that facility to be significantly used. Has developed as several distinct versions (1971, 1972, 1976, 1980).

Snobol4
*StriN*g-*O*riented *SymBO*lic *L*anguage
1963
Roster, HOPL.
Most large computers.
String processing.
Emphasizes string processing and pattern matching.

Speakeasy
1968
Roster.
Several computers.
Numerical scientific.
Easily learned but powerful array processing language with built-in matrix algebra and powerful library-oriented system.

SPSS
*S*tatistical *P*rograms for the *S*ocial *S*ciences
1975 (?)
Roster.
Most computers.
Statistics.
Is really a language (albeit simple) and is implemented in batch and interactive versions.

TUTOR
1971 (?)
Roster.
CDC 6500, Cyber series.
Computer-assisted instruction.
Runs under PLATO.

VHDL
*V*HISIC *H*ardware *D*escription *L*anguage
1983
IEEE Standard #1076 (1987)
Several computers.

Computer hardware design.
International standard used to describe input/output transformations and interconnections of components for a digital electronic system.

APPENDIX VI

GLOSSARY OF MAJOR TERMS IN FIVE LANGUAGES

English	French	German	Spanish	Russian
Access Time	Temps d'Accès	Zugriffszeit	Tiempo de Acceso	Время Выборки, Время Обращения
Accumulator	Accumulateur	Akkumulator	Acumulador	Накопитель
Adder	Additionneur, Addeur	Addierer, Addierwerk	Sumador	Сумматор
Address	Adresse	Adresse	Dirección	Адрес
Algorithm	Algorithme	Algorithmus	Algoritmo	Алгоритм
Alphanumeric	Alphanumérique	Alphanumerisch	Alfanumérico	Алфавитно-Цифровой
Analog Computer	Calculateur Analogique	Analogrechner	Computador Analógico	Аналоговая Вычислѧтельная Машина, Аналоговый Компьютер
Architecture (computer)	Architecture (de système informatique)	Architektur (Rechnerarchitektur)	Arquitectura (De Computadores)	Структура
Argument	Argument	Argument, Parameter, Aktualparameter	Argumento	Переменная, Аргумент
Array	Tableau	Feld	Arreglo	Массив
Artificial Intelligence	Intelligence Artificielle	Künstliche Intelligenz	Inteligencia Artificial	Йскусственный Разум, Йскусственный Интеллект
Assembler	Assembleur	Assemblierer, Assembler	Ensamblador	Ассемблер
Associative Memory	Mémoire Associative	Assoziativspeicher	Memoria Asociativa	Ассоциативная Память
Automation	Automatisation	Automation, Automatisierung	Automatización	Автоматизация
Automaton	Automate	Automat		Автомат
Bandwidth	Largeur de Bande	Bandbreite	Ancho de Banda	Диапазон Частот
Base Register	Registre de Base	Basisregister, Basis-addressregister	Registro Base	Регистр Базы, Базовый Регистр
Benchmark	Banc d'Essai	Benchmark	Banco de Pruebas	Эталон, Начало Отсчета
Binary	Binaire	Binär	Binario	Двойчный
Bit	Bit	Bit	Bit, Dígito Binario	Бит
Block	Bloc	Block, physischer Satz	Bloque	Блок
Branch Instruction	Branchement	Verzweigungsbefehl, Sprungbefehl	Instrucción de Bifurcación	Команда Перехода (Передачи Управления)
Buffer	(Mémoire) Tampon	Puffer, Zwischenspeicher	Memoria Intermedia	Буфер
Bug	Erreur, Défaut, Panne	Fehler, Programmfehler	Error	Ощибка
Bulletin Board	Les News	Schwarzes Brett	Cartel de Anuncios	Информационный Листок

English	French	German	Spanish	Russian
Bus	Bus	Bus, Übertragunsleitung	Barra, Enlace Común	Щина
Byte	8 Bit Byte 5 Octet 6 Bit Byte 5 Sextet	Byte	Octeto	Байт
Cache Memory	Mémoire à Cache	Pufferspeicher, schneller Pufferspeicher	Memoria de Cache	Память
Calculator	Calculatrice	Taschenrechner	Calculador	Ќалькулятор
Calling Sequence	Séquence d'Appel	Aufruffolge (eines Unterprogrammes)	Sequencia de Llamada	Вызывающая Последовательность
Card	Carte	Karte, Lochkarte	Tarjeta, Ficha	Карта
Central Processing Unit	Unité Centrale	Zentrale Recheneinheit, Prozessor	Unidad Central de Proceso	Ценеральный Процессор
Channel	Canal	Kanal	Canal	Канал
Character	Caractère	Zeichen, Schriftzeichen	Carácter, Símbolo	Символ
Code	Code	Code	Código	Код
Compiler	Compilateur	Kompilierer, Compiler, Übersetzer	Compilador	Компилятор
Complement	Complément	Komplement	Complemento	Дополнение
Computability	Calculabilité	Berechenbarkeit	Computabilidad	Вычисликость
Computation	Calcul-Traitement	Berechnung	Computación, Cálculo	Вычисление
Computer	Ordinateur	Rechner, Datenverarbeitung-sanlage, Computer	Computador	Вычислительная Мащина, Компьютер
Computer Graphics	Informtique Graphique	Computergrafik	Gráficos de Computador	Мащинная Графика
Computer Science	Informatique	Informatik	Informática, Ciencia de la Computación	Вычислительная Математика и Вычислительная Техника
Concatenation	Concaténation	Verkettung	Concatenación	Сцепление
Constant	Constante	Konstante	Constante	Постоянная, Константа
Control Unit	Unité de Contrôle	Steureinheit, Steurewerk, Leitwerk, Kommandowerk,	Unidad de Control	Блок (Устройство Управления)
Core Memory	Mémoire à Tores	Kernspeicher	Memoria de Núcleos	Оперативная Память
Cybernetics	Cybernétique	Kybernetik	Cibernética	Кибернетика
Cycle Time	Cycle de Base	Zykluszeit	Tiempo de Ciclo	Время Цикла, Время Выборки
Data	Donnée	Daten	Datos	Данные
Data Bank	Banque de Données	Datenbank	Banco de Datos	Банк Данных
Data Communications	Transmission de Données	Datenübermittlung	Communicación de Datos	Перелача Данных
Data Encryption	Codage	Datenverschlüsselung	Codificación de Datos	Кодирование Данных
Data Processing	Traitement de l'Infor-mation, Informatique	Datenverarbeitung	Proceso de Datos	Обработка Данных
Data Structure	Structure de Données	Datenstruktur	Estructura de Datos	Структура Данных
Database	Base de Données	Datenbasis, Datenbank	Banco de Datos	База Данных
Deadlock	Bloquage	Verklemmung, System-verklemmung, Deadlock	Punto Muerto, Bloquero	Стоп, Полная Остановка, Тупиковая Ситуация
Debugging	Mise au Point (d'un programme), Dépannage (d'une machine)	Fehlerbeseitgung, Fehlerkorrektur, Programm-debugging	Depuración, Corrección	Отлалка
Delimiter	Borne	Begrenzer, Begrenzungs-symbol, Trennzeichen	Delimitar	Ограничитель
Desktop Publishing	Publication Asssistee par Ordinateur	Desktop Publishing	Editora de Escritoro	Подготовка публикаций с использованием настольных редакционно-издательских средств
Diagnostic	Diagnostic	Diagnoseprogramm	Diagnóstico	Диагностический
Disk Memory	Mémoire à Disque	Plattenspeicher	Memoria de Disco	Дисковая Память
Diskette	Disquette	Diskette	Disqueta	Дискета, Диск, Гибкий Диск
Drum Memory	Mémoire à Tambour	Magnettrommel, Trommel-speicher	Memoria de Tambor	Память на Барабане
Dump	"Dump"-Cliché	Speicherabzug, Speicherauszug	Vaciado de Memoria	Копировать Память на Внещее Запомина-ющее Устройство
Electronic Mail	Courrier Électronique	Elektronische Post	Correo Electrónico	Злектронная Почта
Expert System	Systeme Expért	Expertensystem	Sistema Experto	Зкспертная Система
Exponent	Exposant	Exponent	Exponente	Показатель Степени
Expression	Expression	Ausdruck	Expesión	Выражение
Extensible Language	Langage Extensible	Erweiterbare Sprache	Lenguage Extensible	Свободная Грамматика
Field	Champ (for an instruction field), Domaine (for a field of interest)	Feld	Campo	Поле

English	French	German	Spanish	Russian
File	Fichier	Datei	Archivo	Файл, Массив
Fixed Point	Virgule Fixe	Festpunkt(zahl)	Punto Fijo	Фиксированная Запятая
Flag	Drapeau	Kennzeichen, Marke	Señalador, Indicador	Флаг, Признак
Flip-flop	Flipflop	Flipflop, bistabiles Kippglied	Circuito Biestable, Circuito Basculante	Триггер
Floating Point	Virgule Flottante	Gleitpunkt(zahl)	Punto Flotante	Плавающая Запятая
Floppy Disk	Disquette	Diskette	Disco Flexible	Гибкий Диск
Flowchart	Organigramme, Ordinogramme	Flussdiagram, Datenfluss- plan, Programmablaufplan	Carta De Flujo	Блок-Схема
Fractal	Fractal	Fraktale	Fractal	Фракталь
Function	Fonction	Funktion	Función	Функция
Gate	Porte	Gatter, Verknupfungsglied	Puerta	Злектронный Переключатель, Логический Злемент
Global Variable	Variable Globale	Globale Variable	Variable Global	Глобальная Переменная
Grammar	Grammaire	Grammatik	Gramática	Грамматика
Hard Disk	Disque dur	Festplatte	Disco rígido	Жесткий Диск
Hardware	Matériel	Hardware, Maschinen- ausrüstung, Apparatur	Equipo Físico, Compo- nentes Fisicos	Аппаратура
Hashing	Hashing, Hash Code	Streuspeicher verfahnen, Hashing		Контрольное Суммирование, Поиск
Heuristic	Heuristique	Heuristisch, Heuristisches Verfahren, Heuristik	Método Heurísico	Звристический
Hexadecimal	Hexadécimal	Sedezimal, Hexadezimal (coll)	Hexadecimal	Щестнаддатиричный
Hybrid Computer	Calculateur Hybride	Hybridrechner	Computadora Híbrida	Гибридный Компьютер
Identifier	Identificateur	Identifikator, Identifizierer, Bezeichner, Name	Identificador	Идентификатор
Image Processing	Traitement d'Images	Bildverarbeitung	Procesamento de Imágenes	Обработка Изображений
Index Register	Registre d'Index	Indexregister	Registro de Indice	Индексный Регистр
Indirect Address	Adresse Indirecte	Indirekte Adresse	Dirección Indirecta	Косвенный Алрес
Information Processing	Informatique, Traitement de l'Information	Datenverarbeitung, Infor- mationsverarbeitung	Procesamiento de la Información	Обработка Информации
Information Science	Informatique	Informationswissenschaft	Ciencia de la Información	Теория Информации
Information Theory	Théorie de l'Information	Informationstheorie	Teoría de la Información	Теория Информации
Input	Entrée	Eingabe, Eingang, eingeben (v), einlesen (v)	Entrada	Ввод, Входные Данные
Instruction	Instruction	Befehl, Instruktion	Instrucción	Команда
Integrated Circuit	Circuit Intégré	Integrierter Schaltkreis, Integrierte Schaltung	Circuito Integrado	Интеградьная Схема
Interpreter	Intrepréteur	Interpretierer, Interpretier programm, Interpreter	Interpretador	Интерпретирующая Программа
Interrupt	Interruption	Unterbrechung, Interrupt	Interrupción	Прерываеь
Iteration	Itération	Iteration	Iteración	Итерация
Job	Tâche, Travail	Job, Auftrag	Trabajo	Задание
Key	Clé	Schlüssel, Kennbegriff, Taste	Llave, Clave	Ключ, Кдавища
Keyboard	Clavier	Tastatur	Teclado	Кдавиатура
Knowledge Representation	Représentation de Connaissances	Wissensrepräsentation	Representatión del Conocimiento	Представление Знаний
Label	Etiquette	Marke, Label, Etikett, Kennsatz	Etiqueta	Метка
Language Processor	Compilateur	Sprachprozessor, Sprachübersetzer, Übersetzer	Procesador de Lenguage, Compilador	Транслятор Языка
Laptop Computer	Ordinateur Portable	Tragbarer Rechner	Computador Portátil	Лаптоп
Latency	Latence	Wartezeit, Latenzzeit	Latencia	Время Задержки (Часть Времени Выборки)
Linker	Editeur de Liens	Binder	Linker	Редактор Связей, Линкер
List Processing	Traitement de Liste	Listenverabeitung	Procesamiento de Listas	Обработка Списков
Loader	Chargeur	Lader, Ladeprogramm, Programmlader	Cargador	Загрузчик
Local Area Network	Réseau Local	Lokales Netzwerk	Red de Area Local	Локальная Сеть
Loop	Boucle	Schleife	Ciclo Iterativo	Пикл
Machine Language	Language Machine	Maschinensprache	Lenguage de Máquina	Мащинный Язык
Macroinstruction	Macroinstruction	Makroinstruktion, Makro- befehl, Makro (coll)	Macroinstrucción	Макрокоманда
Magnetic Core	Tore Magnétique	Magnetkern	Toroide Magnético, Núcleo Magnético	Магнитная Память
Magnetic Tape	Bande Magnétique	Magnetband	Cinta Magnética	Магнитная Лента
Mantissa	Mantisse	Mantisse	Mantisa	Мантисса
Memory	Mémoire	Speicher, Gedächtnis	Memoria	Память
Memory Protection	Protection de Mémoire	Speicherschutz, Speicher- Schreibsperre	Protetión de Memoria	Защита Памяти
Microprocessor	Microprocesseur	Mikroprozessor	Microprocesador	Микропроцессор

English	French	German	Spanish	Russian
Microprogramming	Microprogrammation	Mikroprogrammierung	Microprogrammación	Микропрограммирование
Microcomputer	Micro-Ordinateur	Mikrocomputer, Mikro (coll)	Microcomputador	Микрокомпьютер
Microsecond	Microseconde	Mikrosekunde	Microsegundo	Микросекунда
Millisecond	Milliseconde	Millisekunde	Milisegundo	Миллисекунда
Minicomputer	Mini-Ordinateur	Kleinrechner, Mini-computer, Mini (coll)	Minicomputador	Миникомпьютер
Modem	Modem	Modem, Signalumsetzer	Modulador-Demodulador, Modem	Модем (Модулятор-Демодулятор)
Monitor	Moniteur	Monitor, Überwachungs-programm, überwachen (v)	Monitor	Монитор
Multiplexer	Multiplexeur	Multiplexer (Communications multiplexor: Datenübertragungs-Steuereinheit)	Multiplexor	Мультиплексор
Multiprocessor	Multiprocesseur	Mehrprozessorsystem	Procesador Múltiple	Мультипроцессор
Multiprogramming	Multiprogrammation	Mehrprogrammbetrieb, Multiprogrammierung	Multiprogramación	Мультипрограммирование
Nanosecond	Nanoseconde	Nanosekunde	Nanosegundo	Наносекунда
Network	Réseau	Netzwerk, Rechnernetz	Red (De Computadores)	Сеть
Object Program	Programme Objet	Objektprogramm, Maschinencode-Programm, Zeilprogramm	Programa Objeto	Рабочая Программа (Объектна Программа, Программа на Мащинном Языке)
Object-Oriented Programming	Programmation Orientée Objet	Objektorientierte Programmierung	Programmación Orientada por Objetos	Объектно-ориентированное Программирование
Octal	Octal	Oktal	Octal	Восьмеричный
Operand	Opérande	Operand	Operando	Операнд
Operating System	Système d'Exploitation	Betriebssystem	Sistema Operativo	Операционная Система
Output	Sortie	Ausgabe, ausgeben (v)	Salida	Выход, Выходные Данные, Выдача Результатов
Overflow	Dépassement de Capacité	Überlauf	Sobrecarga, Desborda-miento de Carga	Переполнение
Paper Tape	Bande Perforée	Lochstreifen, Papierstreifen	Cinta de Papel	Перфолента
Parallel Processing	Traitement Parallèle	Parallelverarbeitung, Simultanverarbeitung	Procesamiento en Paralelo	Параллельная Обработка
Parameter	Paramètre	Parameter	Parámetro	Параметр
Parity	Parité	Parität, Parigkeit	Paridad	Уетность
Parsing	Analyse Grammaticale	Syntaktische Analyse, Parsing, Zerteilung	Análisis Gramatical	Анализ Команды
Pattern Recognition	Reconnaissance de Formes	Mustererkennung	Reconocimiento de Formas	Распознавание Образов
Peripheral	Périphérique	Peripher	Equipo Periférico	Периферический
Personal Computer	Ordinateur Personnel	PC	Computador Personal	Персональная Вычислительная Мащина (Компьютер)
Plotter	Traceur	Kurvenschreiber, Kurven-zeichner, Plotter, Zeichengerät	Graficador	Графопостроитель
Pointer	Pointeur	Zeiger	Puntero	Указатель
Portability	Portabilité	Übertragbarkeit, Portabilitat	Portabilidad	Портатиность
Printer	Imprimante	Drucker	Impresora	Печатающее Устройство
Precision	Précision	Genauigkeit, Stellenzahl	Precisión	Точность
Procedure	Procédure	Prozedur	Procedimiento	Процедура
Processor	Processeur	Prozessor, Zentrale Recheneinheit, verarbeitende Funktionseinheit in Hardware oder Software	Procesador	Продессор
Program	Programme	Programm, programmieren (v)	Programa	Программа
Program Counter	Compteur Ordinal	Programmzähler	Contador de Programa	Счетчик Команд
Programmer	Programmeur	Programmierer	Programador	Программист
Queue	File d'Attente	Warteschlange	Cola	Очередь
Random Access	Accès Direct	Direktzugriff, direkter Zugriff, Wahlfreier Zugriff	Acceso Directo	Произвольный Доступ, Прямой Доступ
Random Number	Nombre Aléatoire	Zufallszahl	Número Aleatorio	Случайное Число
Record	Enregistrement	Datensatz, Satz, Aufzeichnung	Registro	Запсь
Recursion	Récurrence	Rekursion	Recursión	Рекурсия
Register	Registre	Register	Registro	Регистр
Regular Expression	Expression Régulière	Regulärer Ausdruck	Expresión Regular	Правильное Выражение
Relational Database	Base de Données Relationelle	Relationale Datenbank	Banco de Datos Relacionales	Реляционная База Данных
Response Time	Temps de Réponse	Antwortzeit (Ansprechzeit, Analaufzeit)	Tiempo de Respuesta	Время Ответа

English	French	German	Spanish	Russian
Robotics	Robotique	Robotik	Robótica	Робототехника
Roundoff Error	Erreur d'Arrondi	Rundungsfehler	Error de Redondeo	Ошибка Округления
Run Time	Temps d'Execution	Laufzeit, Durchlaufzeit	Tiempo de Ejecución	Время Выполнения
Scanner	Balayage	Abtaster, Abtastvorrichtung, Scanner	Explorador	Сканнирующее Устройство
Scheduler	Régulateur, Planificateur	Scheduler	Regulador, Planificador	Планировщик
Semantics	Sémantique	Semantik	Semántica	Семантика
Shifting	Décalage	Verschieben, Schieben, Stellenversetzen, Schiften (coll)	Desplazamiento	Сдвиг
Side Effect	Effet Secondaire, Effet de Bord	Nebenwirkung, Seiteneffekt	Efecto Secundario	Побочный Эффект
Simulation	Simulation	Simulation, Nachbildung	Simulación	Моделирование
Software	Logiciel	Software, Programmausrüstung	Software, Componentes Lógicos	Программное Обеспечение
Software Engineering	Ingénérie du Logiciel	Software-Engineering, Software-Technologie	Ingenieria de Software	Разработка Программого Обеспечения
Sorting	Tri	Sortieren, Sortierung	Ordenar, Clasificar	Сортировка
Source Program	Programme Source	Quellprogramm, Quellenprogramm, Primärprogramm, Quelle, Sourceprogramm	Programa Fuente	Исходная Программа
Spelling Checker	Vérificateur orthographique	Rechtschreibhilfe	Verificador de ortografía	Корректор
Spreadsheet	Tableur	Tabellenkalkulation	Planilla electrónica	Электронная Таблица
Stack	Pile	Keller, Kellespeicher, Stapelspeicher	Pila	Набор, Пакет, Буфер
Statement	Instruction	Anweisung	Sentencia, Instrucción	Команда, Утверждение, Оператор
Storage	Mémoire	Speicher, Speicherung	Almacén, Memoria	Запоминающее Устройство, Память
String	Chaîne	Zeichenreihe, Zeichenfolge, Kette, Folge, String	Cadena, Serie, Tira	Строка
Structured Programming	Programmation Structurée	Strukturierte Programmierung	Programación Estructurada	Структурное Программирование
Subroutine	Sous-Programme	Unterprogramm, Subroutine	Subrutina	Подпрограмма
Subscript	Indice	Index, indizieren (v)	Subindice	Индекс
Switching Theory	Theorie de la commutation	Theorie der Scheltwerke	Teoría de circuitos	Теория Переключательных Схем
Symbol	Symbole	Symbol	Simbolo	Символ
Symbol Manipulation	Manipulation de Symboles	Symbolverarbeitung, Symbolmanipulation	Manipulación de Simbolos	Обработка Символов
Syntax	Syntaxe	Syntax	Sintaxis	Синтаксис
Systems Analysis	Analyse Fonctionnelle	Systemanalyse	Análisis de Sistemas	Системный Анализ
Systems Programming	Programmation Système	Systemprogrammierung	Programacion de Sistemas	Системное Программирование
Task	Tâche	Task, Aufgabe	Tarea	Задание, Задача
Teleprocessing	Télétraitement	Datenfernverarbeitung	Teleprocesamiento	Телеобработка, Дистанционная Обработка
Terminal	Terminal	Terminal, Endgerät, Datensichtgerät	Terminal	Терминал, Устройство Ввода/Вывода
Time Sharing	Temps Partagé	Teilnehmerbetrieb, Zeitmultiplex verarbeitung, zeitlich verzahne Verarbeitung	Tiempo Compartido	Система с Разделением Времени
Trace	Trace, Historique	Protokoll, Ablaufprotokoll, Ablaufverfolgung, Ausführungsprotokoll, Trace	Rastreo	След
Tree	Arborescence	Baum	Arbol	Дерево
User Interface	Interface Utilisateur	Benutzerschnittstelle	Interface del Usuario	Пользовательский Интерфейс
Variable	Variable	Variable	Variable	Переменная
Virtual Memory	Mémoire Virtuelle	Virtueller Speicher	Memoria Virtual	Виртуальная Память
Word	Mot	Wort	Palabra	Слово
Word Processing	Traitement de Texte	Textverarbeitung	Procesamento de Texto	Редактор

PHILIPPE L. DREYFUS
PHILIPPE JORRAND

HORST HÜNKE
THOMAS STROTHOTTE

ENRIQUE I. OVIEDO

VICTOR YA. PAN
BORIS YAMROM

APPENDIX VII

TIMELINE OF SIGNIFICANT COMPUTING MILESTONES

The basic idea of this timeline is that those who have seen close to four decades of computing evolve will enjoy the nostalgia of seeing certain developments pass before their eyes as they read. The mathematics milestones are there because those discoveries or events are significant antecedents to the development of a science of computing. The cipher machines are mentioned because cryptography provided so much of the driving force that inspired creation of ever-better computing machines. The entries were compiled from a number of secondary sources and certainly should not be used to settle questions of priority. Boldface phrases indicate the names (or portions thereof) of articles that appear in this encyclopedia. The editors are grateful to Martin Campbell-Kelly of the University of Warwick for a critical reading of a draft of this timeline and for providing a copy of a similar one compiled by David Singmaster of the Polytechnic of the South Bank in London. Readers who suspect errors of commission or omission are encouraged to write the editors so that appropriate corrections can be made in the fourth edition.

15 billion B.C.	Universal computer boots up with a Big Bang.
5 billion B.C.	First full-scale **analog computer** computes planetary orbits.
500 million B.C.	First cell, address unknown.
200 million B.C.	Cells assembled into first **memory** and attached to a rudimentary **central processing unit.**
50,000 B.C.	Earliest evidence of counting.
2400 B.C.	Babylonians use abacus and approximate pi as 3 1/8.
1900 B.C.	Stonehenge erected.
800 B.C.	I-Ching exhibits binary properties; concept and symbol for zero used.
600 B.C.	Abacus used in Greece.
300 B.C.	Euclid's *Elements*.
230 B.C.	*Sieve of Eratosthenes*, an early **algorithm.**
140 B.C.	Trigonometry invented.

150	Ptolemy's *Almagest.*
250	Diophantus' *Arithmetica.*
850	Al Khowarizmi's *Algebra* transmits Hindu art of reckoning to the Arabs and thus to Europe.
1050	Chinese scholars arrange the 64 I-Ching hexagrams in a 6-bit binary order called the Fu Hsi arrangement.
1202	Raymond Lull's logic machine; Fibonacci sequence.
1303	Chu Shi-kie anticipates **"Pascal's"** triangle.
1409	Use of plus and minus signs by Widmann.
1430	Baptista Alberti's cipher machine.
1435	Jamshid ben Mas'ud ben Mahmud Ghiath ed-Din al-Kashi invents several special-purpose astronomical calculators, calculates pi to 16 places, and is first to express a fraction as a positional decimal.
1492	Pellos invents decimal point. Columbus, all at sea, doesn't notice.
1527	Apian publishes **"Pascal's"** triangle.
1580	Francois Vieta causes a sensation by using letters to stand for numerical parameters, thus inventing the concept of a variable; Rabbi Judah ben Loew's automaton.
1614	**John Napier's** Canon of Logarithms.
1617	Napier's *Rabdologia* describes "Napier's bones."
1623	Wilhelm Schickard's calculator does automatic addition and subtraction and semiautomatic multiplication and division.
1630	William Oughtred and Richard Delamain invent circular slide rule.
1637	Descartes' *Discours de la Methode* describes analytic geometry, which is indispensable for modern work in **computer graphics.**
1643	**Blaise Pascal's** calculator, which he names "Pascaline."
1665	Newton invents calculus but does not publish his discovery.
1666	**Gottfried Wilhelm von Leibniz's** *De Arte Combinatorica.*
1672	Samuel Morland's *The Description and Use of Two Arithmetic Instruments.*
1673	Rene Grillet's adding machine; **Leibniz** invents calculus independently of Newton and, in his spare time, develops the Leibniz "wheel," a calculator that can add, subtract, multiply, and divide, all automatically. He believes that he has invented binary numbers, but is later stunned when he learns of the 11th century Fu Hsi arrangement of the I-Ching.
1687	Newton's *Principia.*
1706	Use of the symbol π by William Jones; John Machin computes pi to 100 decimal places.
1715	Brook Taylor shows that most basic mathematical functions can be expanded into an infinite series of terms that require only arithmetic for their computation.
1730	Stirling's formula for n!, which is now indispensable for the **analysis of algorithms.**
1736	Vaucanson's automata; Euler generalizes and solves the *Seven Bridges of Konigsberg* problem, thereby inaugurating modern **graph theory.**
1777	Buffon's Needle Problem is first **Monte Carlo** simulation; Earl of Stanhope's "Logic Demonstator" is first mechanical logic machine.

1786	J. H. Muller's automatic difference engine; Gripenstierna's cipher machine.
1801	Gauss's *Disquisitiones Arithmeticae;* Jacquard's **punched-card** controlled loom.
1814	J. H. Hermann's planimeter.
1820	Charles Xavier Thomas (Thomas de Colmar) Arithmometer.
1822	**Charles Babbage's** design and partial construction of a **difference engine.**
1832	**Babbage** designs his **analytical engine;** Menabrea advocates use of **parallel processing.**
1843	Menabrea's memoir with commentary by Ada Augusta, the **Countess of Lovelace**; Hamilton's quaternions.
1850	Amedee Mannheim designs the logarithmic slide rule, which would dominate mechanical calculation for the next 100 years.
1853	Pehr Georg and Edvard Scheutz's tabulating machine.
1854	**George Boole's** *Laws of Thought.*
1855	James Clerk Maxwell's improved planimeter; Richter computes pi to 500 decimal places.
1860	**Boole's** "Finite Differences" is first text on subject.
1867	Wheatstone's cipher machine.
1876	Lord Kelvin's harmonic analyzer and tide predictor devices.
1878	Thomas Edison, in a letter to a friend, uses **"bug"** in its modern context 65 years before the legendary moth invades a Harvard **Mark I** relay circuit.
1880	Baudot's punched paper tape telegraph code, **Baudot Code**.
1883	*Towers of Hanoi* problem invented by Edouard Lucas.
1884	**W. S. Burroughs'** first adding machine.
1885	Dorr Felt invents the comptometer, though he calls it a "Macaroni Box."
1890	Punched-card machines patented by John Shaw Billings and implemented by **Herman Hollerith; Leonardo Torres Quevedo** builds an electromechanical machine for solving certain end-game problems in chess.
1893	Chess-playing machine envisioned by Ambrose Bierce in his short story "Moxon's Master."
1894	Variable-toothed gear invented by Ohdner and Baldwin and becomes basis for the Monroe calculator.
1896	**Hollerith** founds Tabulating Machine Company which later became Computing, Tabulating, and Recording Co. (CTR) in 1911 and IBM in 1924; proof of the prime number theorem.
1899	Founding of Burroughs Adding Machine Company.
1904	Diode vacuum tube invented by J. A. Fleming.
1906	Triode vacuum tube invented by Lee De Forest.
1908	Percy Ludgate's analytical engine.
1910	H. P. Babbage assembles mill of his father's design and builds a printer to go with it; **James Powers** develops mechanical **punched-card machinery** for use with 1910 census and later forms Powers Accounting Machine Company; Russell and Whitehead's *Principia Mathematica*.

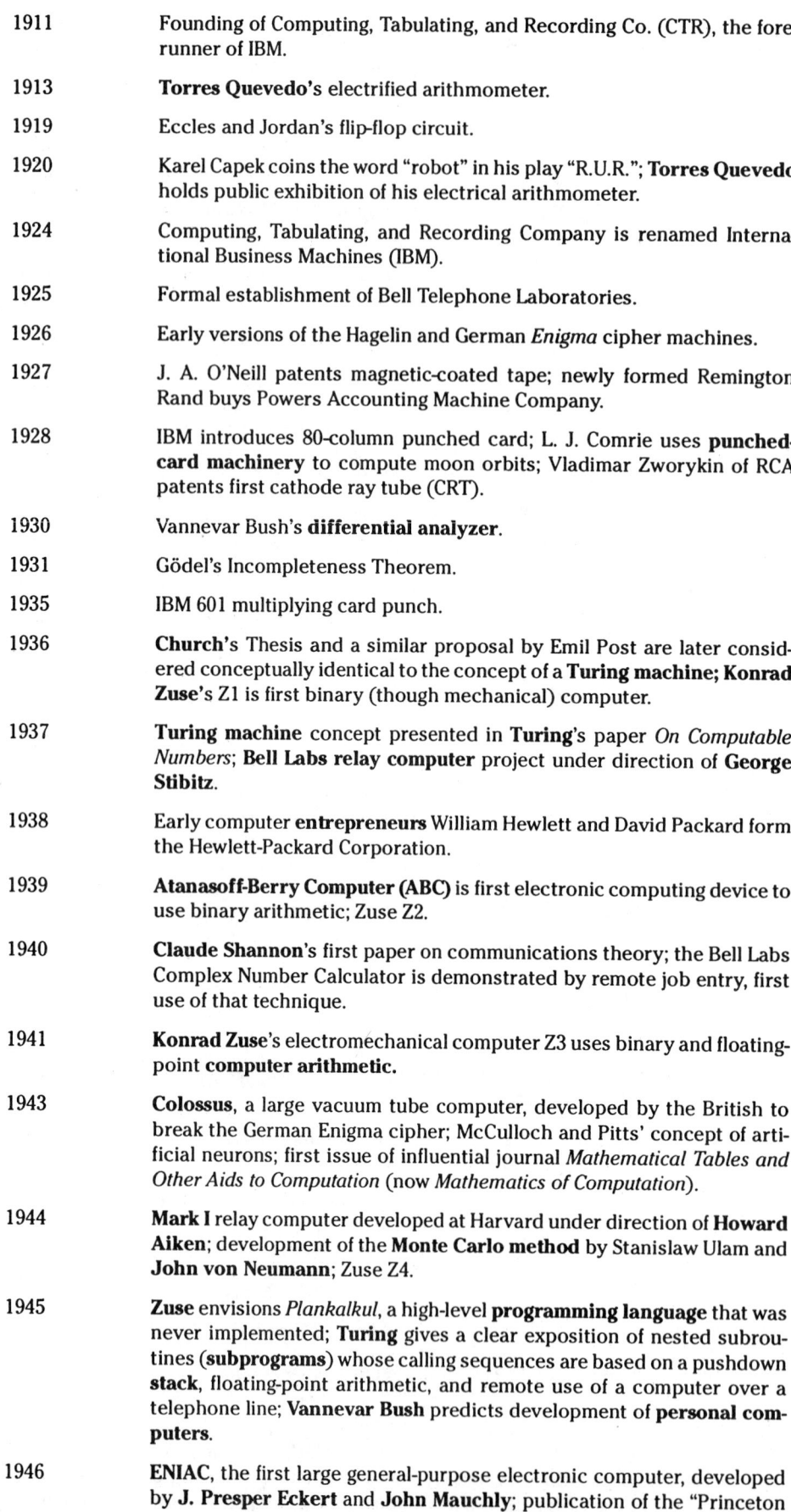

1911   Founding of Computing, Tabulating, and Recording Co. (CTR), the fore-runner of IBM.

1913   **Torres Quevedo's** electrified arithmometer.

1919   Eccles and Jordan's flip-flop circuit.

1920   Karel Capek coins the word "robot" in his play "R.U.R."; **Torres Quevedo** holds public exhibition of his electrical arithmometer.

1924   Computing, Tabulating, and Recording Company is renamed International Business Machines (IBM).

1925   Formal establishment of Bell Telephone Laboratories.

1926   Early versions of the Hagelin and German *Enigma* cipher machines.

1927   J. A. O'Neill patents magnetic-coated tape; newly formed Remington Rand buys Powers Accounting Machine Company.

1928   IBM introduces 80-column punched card; L. J. Comrie uses **punched-card machinery** to compute moon orbits; Vladimar Zworykin of RCA patents first cathode ray tube (CRT).

1930   Vannevar Bush's **differential analyzer**.

1931   Gödel's Incompleteness Theorem.

1935   IBM 601 multiplying card punch.

1936   **Church's** Thesis and a similar proposal by Emil Post are later considered conceptually identical to the concept of a **Turing machine; Konrad Zuse's** Z1 is first binary (though mechanical) computer.

1937   **Turing machine** concept presented in **Turing's** paper *On Computable Numbers*; **Bell Labs relay computer** project under direction of **George Stibitz.**

1938   Early computer **entrepreneurs** William Hewlett and David Packard form the Hewlett-Packard Corporation.

1939   **Atanasoff-Berry Computer (ABC)** is first electronic computing device to use binary arithmetic; Zuse Z2.

1940   **Claude Shannon's** first paper on communications theory; the Bell Labs Complex Number Calculator is demonstrated by remote job entry, first use of that technique.

1941   **Konrad Zuse's** electromechanical computer Z3 uses binary and floating-point **computer arithmetic.**

1943   **Colossus**, a large vacuum tube computer, developed by the British to break the German Enigma cipher; McCulloch and Pitts' concept of artificial neurons; first issue of influential journal *Mathematical Tables and Other Aids to Computation* (now *Mathematics of Computation*).

1944   **Mark I** relay computer developed at Harvard under direction of **Howard Aiken**; development of the **Monte Carlo method** by Stanislaw Ulam and **John von Neumann**; Zuse Z4.

1945   **Zuse** envisions *Plankalkul*, a high-level **programming language** that was never implemented; **Turing** gives a clear exposition of nested subroutines **(subprograms)** whose calling sequences are based on a pushdown **stack**, floating-point arithmetic, and remote use of a computer over a telephone line; **Vannevar Bush** predicts development of **personal computers.**

1946   **ENIAC**, the first large general-purpose electronic computer, developed by **J. Presper Eckert** and **John Mauchly**; publication of the "Princeton Reports" by Burks, Goldstine, and **von Neumann** defines **stored-pro-**

gram concept and uses "flow diagrams" **(flowcharts)**; **F. C. Williams** applies for patent on what is now called a **Williams Tube Memory; Chomsky hierarchy;** Warren Weaver and Andrew Booth propose natural **language translation** by machine; founding of Engineering Research Associates (ERA); Harvard Mark II; IBM 603 Calculating Punch.

1947	Founding of the **Association for Computing Machinery (ACM)**; Dantzig's Simplex Method; Hamming invents **error-correcting codes**; Harvard Mark II.
1948	The **Manchester University** "baby" machine, a prototype of its later Mark I, is built by **F. C. Williams** and **Tom Kilburn** using **Williams Tube Memory** and becomes first electronic stored program computer to run a complete program; **index register** (B-box) invented by Newman and **Kilburn**; transistor invented at Bell Labs by Bardeen, Brattain, and Shockley; **Norbert Wiener's** *Cybernetics*; IBM's Selective Sequence Electronic Calculator (SSEC); **Shannon** founds **Information Theory**.
1949	**EDSAC**, first practical stored-program computer, becomes operational at Cambridge and uses a "relocating **loader**"; work begins on LEO, a copy of **EDSAC**; Harvard Mark III; BINAC, first stored-program computer built in U.S.; Zipf's Law; **Grosch's Law**; An Wang and Jay Forrester independently invent magnetic core memory; **ENIAC** is converted to a stored-program computer by Richard Clippinger and used to compute pi to 2,037 decimal places.
1950	Pilot Ace computer; **Wilkes**, Wheeler, and Gill develop concepts of subroutines and subroutine libraries for **EDSAC**; **SEAC; Whirlwind; Turing's** test for machine intelligence; Asimov's "Three Rules of **Robotics**"; Harry Huskey builds **SWAC** for NBS at UCLA; ERA 1101; M.I.T. Lincoln Laboratory founded to develop SAGE; Edmund Berkeley's *Giant Brains*.
1951	Ferranti Mark I and **Univac I**, first commercial computers; Holberton's sort-merge generator; Lukasiewicz's parenthesis-free **Polish notation**; founding of the Computer Group of the Institute of Radio Engineers (renamed the **IEEE Computer Society** in 1972); **Grace Hopper** proposes use of word "compiler" for her A-O programming system.
1952	Autocode, the first working high-level language, is developed by Alick Glennie; MANIAC at Los Alamos under direction of Nicholas Metropolis; ORDVAC at Aberdeen Proving Grounds; IAS under leadership of Julian Bigelow at Institute for Advanced Study at Princeton; RAYDAC at NBS; ABNER at NSA; Svoboda's SAPO in Czechoslovakia is first **fault-tolerant** computer; ILLIAC I at University of Illinois; first flexible disks; Harvard Mark IV; core memory installed on **Whirlwind** and **ENIAC**; Sidney Fernbach heads computer group at Lawrence Livermore National Laboratory that uses a **Univac I** to predict Eisenhower's election based on early returns; Arthur Samuel begins development of a program to play checkers; Huffman encoding.
1953	Nathaniel Rochester's symbolic **assembler; von Neumann** demonstrates the possibility of a self-reproducing automaton; IBM 701; ERA 1103, first commercial computer to use **interrupts**; BESM1 and STRELA in Russia; JOHNNIAC at Rand Corporation; **Maurice Wilkes** recommends use of **microprogramming**; a firm founded in 1896 is renamed Burroughs; B.V. Bowden's *Faster than Thought*.
1954	Eiichi Goto's Parametron; DYSEAC, first computer to use **interrupts** for I/O; **NORC**; DEUCE; Laning and Zierler implement first operational compiler for **Whirlwind**.
1955	Alwac III-E, an early **minicomputer**, time-shares four remote terminals; **Grace Murray Hopper's** Flow-matic is first business-oriented high-level language; **index registers** added to EDSAC; IBM 650; first **optical char-**

acter reader (OCR); IBM Sage is first computer to use direct memory access (DMA); Sperry Gyroscope absorbs Remington Rand to form Sperry Rand.

1956
IBM 704 and Univac 1103 are first commercial computers to use magnetic core storage; Ferranti Pegasus is first computer to use **general** (purpose) **registers**; first **operating system** is developed for the IBM 704 through cooperative effort of General Motors and North American Aviation; TAC (Tokyo Automatic Computer) under direction of Hideo Yamashita; Logic Theorist of Newell, Shaw, and **Simon** is the first **heuristic** program and first to exploit linked lists; John McCarthy coins **"artificial intelligence"**; work on ATLAS begins at **Manchester University** under direction of **Tom Kilburn**; A.I. Dumey publishes first paper on **hashing**; Kruskal's minimum spanning-**tree** algorithm; Doug Ross's APT language for numerical control of machine tools becomes an early successful **problem-oriented language**.

1957
Fortran developed under leadership of John Backus; Harlan Herrick names its unconditional transfer a GOTO; Roy Nutt introduces FORMAT statement into the language; Herb Bright is first Fortran user to receive an error message; Yngve's Comit is first **string-processing** language; Bill Norris leaves Sperry to form **Control Data Corporation (CDC)**; Fairchild Semiconductor formed by a group led by Gordon Moore and Robert Noyce; IBM 305 is first commercial computer to use disk drives; Lejaren Hiller creates first **computer music** composition, the "ILLIAC Suite."

1958
Digital Equipment Corporation (DEC) founded by Ken Olsen; first **decision table** system developed by Orren Evans at Hunt Foods; Bernstein's chess-playing program; Philco Transac S-2000 forms base for first family of upward-compatible computers; Jack Kilby's **microcomputer chip**; I/O **interrupt** reinvented by Morton Astrahan of IBM; Daniel McCracken authors first Fortran textbook.

1959
IBM 1400, 7070, and 7090; DEC PDP-1; **University of Manchester's ATLAS** is first computer to use a paged **virtual memory**; RPG; McCarthy's Lisp **list processing** language based on the **lambda calculus** of **Alonzo Church**; oblivious of antecedents, John McCarthy and **Christopher Strachey** independently propose **"time-sharing"**; Herb Gelernter's program that proves high-school geometry theorems; Donald Shell's *Shellsort* algorithm.

1960
Algol 60 language popularizes concepts of **recursion** and **block structure**; Algol 60 Report introduces notation initially called Backus Normal Form (BNF) in honor of John Backus, but later renamed **Backus-Naur Form** to give equal credit to Peter Naur; Cobol; IBM 1620; first **integrated circuit** patent applied for by Robert N. Noyce of Fairchild; Soviet KIEV computer; E.H. Fredkin's trie data structure; M.D. McIlroy describes high-level language **macro** expansion.

1961
MIT's Compatible Time Sharing System (CTSS) under direction of Fernando Corbató; Licklider's DEC **time-sharing** system; E.T. Irons' syntax-directed compiler; Newell's IPL V is the first **list-processing** language; first **"supercomputers"** are IBM's **Stretch**, the first pipelined computer, and Univac's **LARC**; Rosenblatt's self-organizing **Perceptron**, an early **neural network** used for **pattern recognition**; Samuel's checker-playing program attains master's rank and is routinely able to defeat its inventor; **AFIPS** founded; C.A.R. Hoare publishes *Quicksort* algorithm that he invented while a visiting British student at Moscow State University; Shanks and Wrench use IBM 7090 to compute pi to 100,000 decimal places.

1962
University of Manchester's ATLAS computer is first to use **Tom Kilburn's** idea of a two-level memory; Stanford and Purdue establish first departments of **computer science**; Green's question-answering program, Baseball, anticipates modern **database** queries; Univac 1100 se-

ries begun; Steve Russell's Space War for the PDP-1 is the first interactive video game; Iverson's *A Programming Language*; Werner Buchholz's *Planning a Computer System*; Adel'son-Vel'skii and Landis (AVL) **tree.**

1963
Burroughs B-5000, specified by Ted Glaser and designed by Bob Barton; Snobol; **Forth**; Weizenbaum's Eliza; SABRE, American Airlines reservation system; Ivan Sutherland's Sketchpad, first interactive graphics system; Cliff Shaw's JOSS **interactive system** at RAND.

1964
IBM 360, the first byte-addressable machine; in conjunction with its description, IBM is first to use term "**computer architecture**." CDC 6600, essentially the first **RISC** computer, 16 years prior to coinage of the acronym; Kemeny and Kurtz develop Dartmouth **time-sharing** system and Basic programming language; DEC PDP-8; RCA Spectra series; Honeywell 200 series; Bohm and Jacopini's paper on the sufficiency of canonical **control structures** is basis for **structured programming**; development of FORMAC, first **computer algebra** program, by an IBM team led by Jean Sammet; DENDRAL is first diagnostic **expert system** program; Robert Floyd and John Williams invent *Heapsort* **sorting** algorithm.

1965
Wilkes proposes use of a **cache memory** and attributes idea to G. Scarott; PL/I; SPSS; Dijkstra's semaphores advance state of the art of **concurrent programming**; K.C. Knowlton's *buddy system* for **multiprogramming** storage management; Bachman's Integrated Data Store is forerunner of **database management systems (DBMS)**; Project MAC at M.I.T.; Englebart invents **mouse** at SRI; IBM develops **floppy disks** for use with 370 series; Cooley and Tukey's **Fast Fourier Transform (FFT)** algorithm.

1966
Iverson and Falkoff's APL language incorporates elastic **data structures** and absence of levels of **operator precedence**; Flynn's classification scheme for **computer architectures**; **Stretch** is used to compute pi to 250,000 decimal places.

1967
LOGO; Greenblatt's chess-playing program, Mac Hack VI, is made an honorary member of the U.S. Chess Federation; S.G. Tucker coins term **emulation** to mean hardware-assisted **simulation**; IBM 360/85 is first commercial computer to use a **cache memory**.

1968
Dijkstra's letter "Goto considered harmful"; ARPA network; **Algol 68**; ACM Curriculum 68; NCR Century series; Denning's **Working Set** model; Arthur C. Clarke's HAL in *2001* alerts world to the possibility of highly intelligent machines; Multics **operating system** on the GE (later Honeywell) 645 at M.I.T.; Volume 1 of Knuth's *Art of Computer Programming*.

1969
Unix; Seymour Papert and Marvin Minsky solidify computational limits of the Rosenblatt **perceptron.**

1970
IBM 370; DEC PDP-11 uses Unibus, first multivendor **bus**; Conway's Game of Life, a popular **cellular automaton**; Codd's first paper on **relational database** systems; Hoare invents the "case" statement; Gene Amdahl leaves IBM to form corporation bearing his name.

1971
Wirth defines Pascal language; Intel 4004 chip inaugurates era of **very large scale integration (VLSI)**; CDC Cyber 70; appearance of electronic hand-held **calculators**; Harlan Mills advocates use of the **chief programmer team**; Cook's concept of **NP-complete problems**; Weinberg's *The Psychology of Computer Programming*.

1972
Founding of Cray Research; Joel Moses's MACSYMA; B-tree invented by Bayer and McCreight; first vector computers, the CDC STAR-100, and the Texas Instruments Advanced Scientific Computer (TI ASC); Ken Thomp-

son of Bell Labs invents a language called B; Dennis Ritchie extends it to form C.

1973   Alan Kay's Smalltalk inaugurates **object-oriented programming** systems (OOPS), but idea doesn't catch fire for 13 more years; first international **computer chess** tournament; Gary Kildall forms Digital Research Corporation in order to market CP/M microcomputer **operating system**.

1974   Hewlett-Packard's programmable **calculator**; Texas Instrument's SR-50 and SR-51 **calculators**; Alto **workstation** at Xerox PARC; July issue of *Radio Electronics* describes first home computer, Jonathan Titus' Mark 8, which uses an 8008 chip.

1975   Altair MITS, first **personal computer** kit; ILLIAC IV; Rubik's Cube; Fred Brooks' classic *The Mythical Man-Month*.

1976   Introduction of the CRAY-1; First Edition of *Encyclopedia of Computer Science*; Appel and Haken's computer-aided proof of the four-color theorem; Ethernet **local area network** (LAN) **protocol**; Diffie and Hellman's Public Key Cryptosystem.

1977   IEEE Curriculum in Computer Science and Engineering; Mandelbrot's **Fractals**; DEC VAX-11/780; IBM 303x series; Erwin Tomash founds the **Charles Babbage Institute**; Data Encryption Standard (DES); Knuth-Morris-Pratt string pattern matching algorithm.

1978   Apple II and Radio Shack TRS-80 achieve wide sales and inaugurate the **personal computer** era; DEC VAX-11; VISICALC **spreadsheet** program; Rivest-Shamir-Adleman (RSA) trapdoor function for use with public key cryptosystem.

1979   IBM 4300 series; ACM Curriculum 78; Allan M. Cormack and Godfrey N. Hounsfield receive Nobel Prize in Medicine for work in **computerized tomography**; Boston Computer Museum founded by C. Gordon Bell and Gwen Bell; Knuth's T$_E$X and **Metafont**.

1980   **Ada** (language); Patterson and Ditzel coin term **Reduced Instruction Set Computer (RISC)** and advocate this approach.

1981   **IBM PC**; CDC Cyber-205; Japan announces Fifth Generation.

1982   AT&T antitrust suit is settled; Osborne is first luggable computer; Turbo Pascal for the **IBM PC and compatibles**.

1983   Cray X-MP; Fujitsu VP100 and VP200; Second Edition of the *Encyclopedia of Computer Science and Engineering*; first CD ROM storage; pi is computed to 16 million decimal places

1984   Introduction of **Apple Computer**'s Macintosh popularizes use of a **mouse**-driven graphical **user interface** (GUI), as inspired by earlier research at XEROX PARC.

1986   Commodore Amiga; Burroughs and Sperry merge to form Unisys; Apple Macintosh generates increasing interest in **desktop publishing**.

1987   C++ language stimulates growth of **object-oriented programming**; pi is computed to 134 million decimal places by Yasumasa Kanada of the University of Tokyo using a Nippon Electric SX-2 supercomputer.

1988   Foundation of SPEC, the System Performance Evaluation Cooperative; widespread use of **workstation** networks popularizes use of client/server architecture in general and **file servers** in particular.

1989   Stardent corporation begins to ship computers that combine **RISC architecture** with vector processing.

1990   **Window environments**, long popular on the Apple Macintosh, begin to take hold on the **IBM PC and compatibles**.

1991   IBM and **Apple Computer** announce Taligent joint venture; NCR, Tandy and Apple market "clipboard" (pen) computers that allow input of handwritten printed characters; working version of the original Babbage **difference engine** is displayed at the Science Museum in London; brothers David and Gregory Chudnovsky, mathematicians at Columbia University, use a formula of their discovery and a low-budget supercomputer of their design and construction to compute pi to 2.1 billion decimals.

1992   Increasing popularity of lightweight notebook and pen-based computers; widespread use of **data compression** software to double effective capacity of microcomputer **hard disks**; Michelangelo **virus** causes media frenzy, but does little actual damage; discovery of 32nd Mersenne prime by Slowinski and Gage; Third Edition of the *Encyclopedia of Computer Science*.

NAME INDEX

This index contains the names of those cited in the text other than authors and those merely listed in References. Certain historical figures (Ampère, Celsius, Volta, etc.) are present only through the units named for them. The editors would appreciate comments on errors and omissions, information regarding missing first names or initials, and dates for persons who have died.

GENERAL INDEX

Subjects of biographical articles are included in this index. Names of contributors begin on page vii. For other persons cited, see the preceding Name Index.

A citation such as CP-3 refers to Color Plate 3. A parenthesized item such as (catalog) indicates an approximate synonym of the indexed term to which it is affixed. A bracketed term such as [Lisp] or [graph] indicates the context in which the indexed term appears.

1's complement, 212, 1198
10's complement, 211
2's complement, 211, 212, 1198
2–3 tree, 1391
2–D graphics, 304
2–out-of-5 code, 182
2001: A Space Odyssey, 513, 626, 766, 1491
2DOF keyboard, 342
3–D graphics, 304, 331, 838, 842, 873
3M Corporation, 259
4GL (4th-Generation Language), 580, 938, 1244
4th Dimension (4D), 518
5/10 code, 398
7421 and 742–1 codes, 181
8421 code, 181, 776
9's complement, 211

A posteriori error bounds, 530, 711
A Programming Language, 1491
A-0 [compiler], 615, 1489
A-2 [compiler], 615
AARON, 258
Abacus, 162, 435, 1274, 1485, CP-12
Abbott-Northwestern Hospital, 126
Abelian group, 236
Aberdeen Proving Ground, 504, 512, 513, 834, 1052, 1430, 1489
ABNER, 1489
Absolute address, 17, 18, 731, 7683, 962
Absolute error, 1200
Absolute value, 210, 1087
Abstract algebra, 475
ABSTRACT DATA TYPE, 1–2, 10, 11, 178, 187, 409, 511, 542, 658, 754, 898
Abstract machine, 1068, 1116, 1134
Abstract syntax, 1419
Abstraction, 1, 180, 1089

ABSYS, 778
Abyss, The, 243, 515, 516
Academic American Encyclopedia, 165
Academic computer science. *See* **COMPUTER SCIENCE, ACADEMIC.**
Accepting state, 106, 1192
Access code, 977
Access control 404
ACCESS METHODS, 2–5, 553, 1408
    BDAM, 4, 5
    BSAM, 4
    BTAM, 5
    DAM, 4
    ISAM, 4, 5
    SAM, 3
    QSAM, 4, 5
    VSAM, 5
    VTAM, 5
ACCESS TIME, 5–7, 248, 436, 553, 849, 1290, 1344
Accolade Corporation, 287
Accounting system, business, 22
ACCOUNTING SYSTEM, COMPUTER, 7–9, 193, 1006
Accreditation Board for Engineering and Technology (ABET), 493
Accredited Standards Committee (ASC), 1120
Accumulator, 14, 78, 144, 246, 333, 334, 433, 437, 441, 442, 445, 450, 512, 640, 878, 882, 890, 891, 1159, 1399
Accuracy, 29, 433, 710, 1072, 1200, 1207
ACE, 1395
ACH. *See* Association for Computers and the Humanities.
ACIUS, Inc., 518, 519
ACK, 207
Ackermann function, 1155, 1156
Acknowledgment, communications, 389
ACM. *See* **ASSOCIATION FOR COMPUTING MACHINERY.**
ACM Curriculum 68 and 78, 1491–1492